Proceedings

33rd Annual Symposium on Foundations of Computer Science

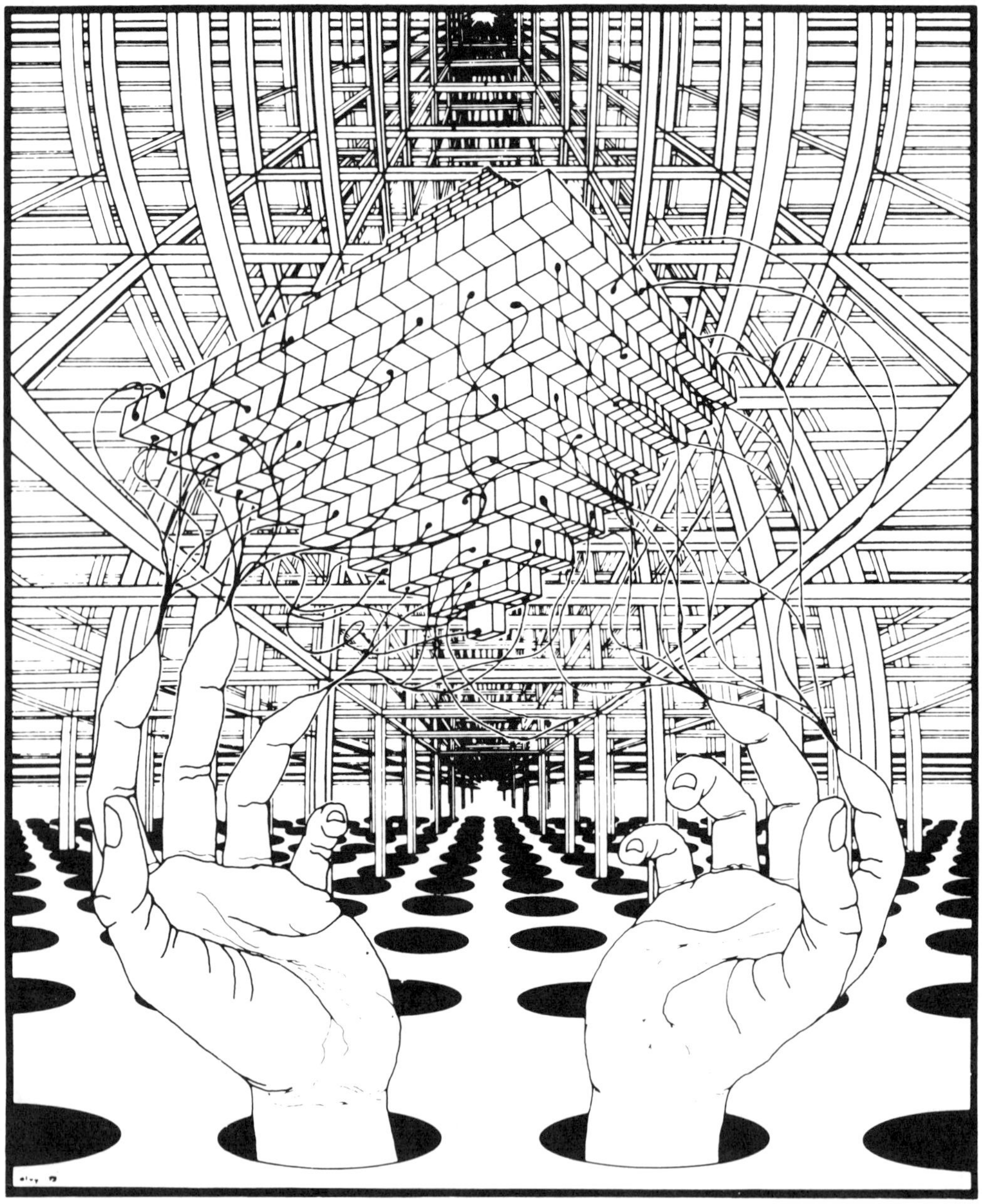

Proceedings

33rd Annual Symposium on Foundations of Computer Science

October 24–27, 1992 • Pittsburgh, Pennsylvania

Sponsored by

IEEE Computer Society Technical Committee on Mathemathical Foundations of Computing

IEEE Computer Society Press
Los Alamitos, California

Washington • Brussels • Tokyo

Published by the
IEEE Computer Society Press
10662 Los Vaqueros Circle
PO Box 3014
Los Alamitos, CA 90720-1264

IEEE Computer Society Press Order Number 2900
Library of Congress Number 80-646634
IEEE Catalog Number 92CH3188-0
ISBN 0-8186-2900-2 (paper)
ISBN 0-8186-2901-0 (microfiche)
ISSN 0272-5428

Additional copies can be ordered from

IEEE Computer Society Press
Customer Service Center
10662 Los Vaqueros Circle
PO Box 3014
Los Alamitos, CA 90720-1264

IEEE Service Center
445 Hoes Lane
PO Box 1331
Piscataway, NJ 08855-1331

IEEE Computer Society
13, avenue de l'Aquilon
B-1200 Brussels
BELGIUM

IEEE Computer Society
Ooshima Building
2-19-1 Minami-Aoyama
Minato-ku, Tokyo 107
JAPAN

Production Editor: Catherine Harris
Cover: Alvy Ray Smith
Printed in the United States of America by Braun-Brumfield, Inc.

THE INSTITUTE OF ELECTRICAL AND ELECTRONICS ENGINEERS, INC.

FOREWORD

The papers in this volume were presented at the 33rd Annual Symposium on Foundations of Computer Science, held October 25–27, 1992, in Pittsburgh, Pennsylvania. The symposium was sponsored by the IEEE Computer Society Technical Committee on Mathematical Foundations of Computing.

The program committee met June 26–28 of this year to select 77 papers from approximately 230 abstracts submitted in response to the Call for Papers. The selection was based on originality, quality, and relevance to theoretical computer science. The submissions were not refereed, and many of them represent reports of continuing research. It is anticipated that most of these papers will appear in a more polished and complete form in scientific journals.

The program committee wishes to thank all who submitted papers for consideration.

Paul Beame
Allan Borodin
Anne Condon
Cynthia Dwork
Harold Gabow
Russell Impagliazzo
Ravi Kannan
Nati Linial
Michael Luby, *Chair*
Milena Mihail
Gary Miller
David Peleg
Ron Rivest
Micha Sharir
Moshe Vardi

Conference Organization

Conference Chair
Manuel Blum, *University of California at Berkeley*

Program Chair
Michael Luby, *International Computer Science Institute; University of California at Berkeley*

Local Arrangements Chair
Gary Miller, *Carnegie Mellon University*

Publicity Chair
Michael Berman, *Glassboro State College*

Site Coordinator
Alok Aggarwal, *IBM Yorktown Heights*

Machtey Award

"A Subexponential Algorithm for Abstract Optimization Problems"
Bernd Gärtner, *Freie University, Berlin*
is the winner of the 1992 Machtey Award for the most outstanding paper written by a student or students, as judged by the program committee.

Industrial Sponsors

AT&T Bell Laboratories
IBM Corporation, Almaden Research Center
IBM Corporation, Thomas J. Watson Research Center
Instituto di Analisi dei Sistemi Ed Informatica (Rome, Italy)
Xerox Palo Alto Research Center

Contents

Tuesday, October 27, 1992

Session IA

Session IB

Session IIA

Session IIB

Session IIIA

Session IIIB

Session IVA

Session IVB

Sunday

October 25, 1992

Probabilistic Checking of Proofs; A New Characterization of NP

(draft)

Sanjeev Arora
U. C. Berkeley *

Shmuel Safra
Stanford U. & IBM Almaden

Abstract

We give a new characterization of **NP**: the class **NP** contains exactly those languages L for which membership proofs (a proof that an input x is in L) can be verified probabilistically in polynomial time using *logarithmic* number of random bits and *sub-logarithmic* number of queries to the proof.

This is a non-relativizing characterization of **NP**.

We discuss implications of this characterization; specifically, we can show that approximating Clique (or Independent Set) is **NP**-hard.

1 Introduction

1.1 Context of This Work

Cook ([Coo71]) and independently Levin ([Lev73]) characterized the class **NP** as all problems that can be solved in non-deterministic polynomial-time. They posed the question whether all such problems are tractable (i.e. can be solved in deterministic polynomial time) — now known as the **P** vs **NP** question. They also showed that deciding whether a Boolean formula has a satisfying assignment (SAT) is an **NP**-complete problem. A langauge L is **NP**-complete if $L \in \mathbf{NP}$ and L is **NP**-hard, i.e., any **NP** problem is reducible to L in polynomial-time; hence, if $L \in \mathbf{P}$ then $\mathbf{NP} = \mathbf{P}$.

The notion of **NP**-completeness was greatly strengthened by Karp ([Kar72]) who showed that many basic combinatorial problems are **NP**-hard, and thus unlikely to have efficient algorithms.

Classifying computational problems as tractable (i.e. in **P**) or **NP**-hard has since been a basic project in computer science. The main source of problems for which we still know neither a polynomial-time algorithm nor an **NP**-hardness result is *approximation* problems.

Approximation Problems

Take your favorite **NP**-hard function $e(x)$ (e.g. computing the chromatic number of a graph) and consider the complexity of an algorithm that approximates it. Formally, we say that function $f(x)$ *approximates* $g(x)$ within a factor $h(n)$ ($n = |x|$) if $\frac{1}{h(n)} < \frac{f(x)}{g(x)} < h(n)$. For a given factor of approximation $h(n)$, what is the complexity of approximating $e(x)$ within $h(n)$? Is there a polynomial-time algorithm for it, or is it essentially as hard as computing the exact value?

Interactive Proofs

The model of *interactive proofs* was introduced by Goldwasser, Micali and Rackoff ([GMR89]) for cryptographic applications, and by Babai ([Bab85]) as a game-theoretic extension of **NP**. The model consists of a probabilistic polynomial-time verifier V communicating with a prover P who tries to convince V that the input x is in a language L. A language L is in **IP** (for interactive proofs) if there exists a verifier V that is always convinced when $x \in L$, but if $x \notin L$ then any prover P has only a small probability of convincing V to the contrary.

The model of *multi-prover interactive proofs* was introduced by Ben-Or, Goldwasser, Kilian, and Wigderson ([BGKW88]). The model consists of a random polynomial-time verifier V communicating with two infinitely powerful provers who cannot communicate with each other during the protocol. The provers try to convince the verifier that the input x is in a language L. A language L is in the class **MIP** (for multi-prover interactive proofs) if there exists a V that is always convinced when $x \in L$ and, when $x \notin L$, the provers have only a small probability of convincing V to the contrary.

Proof Verification

An equivalent formulation of the **MIP** class was suggested by Fortnow, Rompel and Sipser ([FRS88]); in this model a random polynomial-time Turing machine M is interacting with an oracle O_x which is trying to convince M that $x \in L$. As in the multi-prover model, when $x \in L$, there is an oracle that convinces the verifier always, and when $x \notin L$ any oracle has only a small probability of convincing the verifier to the contrary.

Since the oracle's replies (unlike a prover's) are fixed in advance, we can think of the oracle as a string of bits

*Supported under NSF PYI Grant CCR 8896202.

0-8186-2900-2/92 $3.00 © 1992 IEEE

to which the verifier has random access. This string is expected to represent a proof that $x \in L$ (i.e. a *membership proof*). Hence, **MIP** can be characterized as all languages L for which a membership proof can be verified probabilistically in polynomial-time.

The Unexpected Power of Interaction

The class **IP** was thought by many to be slightly larger than **NP**. In fact, it was shown ([FS87, FRS88]) that there is an oracle O such that **co-NP**, given access to O, is not contained in the class **IP** (or **MIP**), given access to O. Consequently, this was believed to be true for the actual classes, without the presence of an oracle, as well.

In a surprising twist, influenced by techniques developed for program checking ([BK89, BLR90, Lip89]), it was shown ([LFKN90, Sha90]) that **IP** = **PSPACE**. (The class **PSPACE** is believed to be quite larger than **NP**.) Shortly after, it was shown ([BFL90]) that **MIP** = **NEXPTIME**.

Scaling Down MIP = NEXPTIME

Since **NEXPTIME** can be characterized as all languages that have exponential sized membership proofs, the result that **MIP** = **NEXPTIME** ([BFL90]) combined with the oracle formulation of **MIP**, shows that any exponentially long proof can be transformed into a proof that can be checked in random polynomial-time

There were two independent efforts to "scale down" the above result (i.e., to show more efficient verification procedures for subexponential proofs). It is clear that for **NP** languages the verifier must run for more than polylogarithmic-time, simply in order to read the entire input.

It was noticed however ([BFLS91]) that if the model of computation is changed and the input is given using a certain error-correcting code, then membership proofs for any $L \in$ **NP** can be verified in polylogarithmic time. This scheme, in which the input is given using an error-correcting code ([BFLS91]), enables the verifier to randomly sample only a small number of bits of the input and be convinced that the proof is correct for that input.

However, if we choose not to change the model of computation, we can still get a scale-down result. It was observed ([FGLSS91]) that the fact that, going from **NEXPTIME** to **NP**, while the proof size becomes smaller, the input size remains the same, prohibits only the *running time* of the verifier from being scaled down. The number of *random* bits and *query* bits (number of bits looked at in the proof) can be reduced to polylogarithmic.

MIP and Hardness of Approximation

The **MIP** = **NEXPTIME** result ([BFL90]) received a much deserved renewal of interest due to the surprizing implications of this result to the seemingly unrelated question — of twenty years and a few sections ago — of the hardness of approximation problems ([FGLSS91]).

A *clique* of size k in a graph G is a subset of k vertices that constitutes a complete subgraph. Computing the size of the largest clique in a graph is one of the first problems shown **NP**-hard by Karp ([Kar72]). Let $\omega(G)$ denote the size of the largest clique in a graph G.

The above mentioned paper ([FGLSS91]) showed a twofold hardness result for the problem of approximating $\omega(G)$. The authors first show that if there is a polynomial-time approximation procedure that approximates $\omega(G)$ even to within a factor of $2^{\log^{1-\epsilon} n}$, then any **NP** problem can be solved deterministically in quasi-polynomial($= n^{\log^{O(1)} n}$) time. This discourages attempts to design efficient algorithms that learn even that small amount of information on $\omega(G)$ (unless one believes that **NP** has almost polynomial time deterministic complexity). On the other hand, in an effort to get as close as possible to **NP**-completeness, it was shown that if $\omega(G)$ can be approximated to within a constant factor in polynomial time, then any **NP** problem can be solved deterministically in $n^{O(\log\log n)}$ time.

As an immediate corollary of our results and the reduction to Clique approximation ([FGLSS91]), we show that:

Theorem: If there is a polynomial time procedure that approximates $\omega(G)$ to within a factor $2^{O(\sqrt{\log n})}$, then **NP** = **P**. □

The techniques we develop for that purpose enable further extensions of the work of [FGLSS91] (see Discussion).

1.2 Probabilistic Checking of Proofs

The notion of efficient verification of membership proofs for a language, and especially the distinction between the verifier's running time, number of random bits and number of queries to the proof seems to be of basic importance. Consequently, one can generalize this notion and define a hierarchy of complexity classes **PCP** (for probabilistically checkable proofs), as follows:

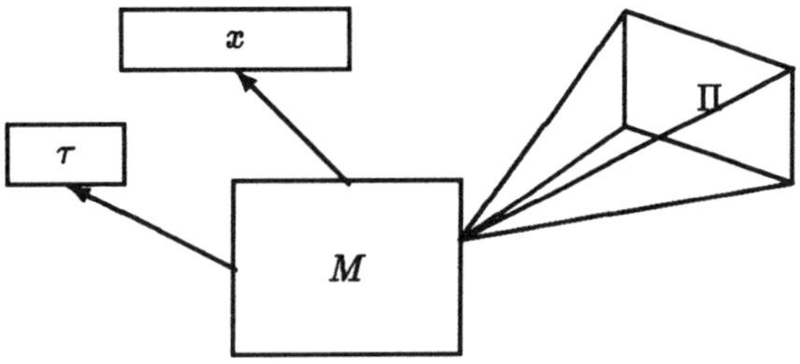

A **PCP** proof system

A *verifier* M is a random polynomial-time Turing machine with random access to a string Π representing a membership proof; M can *query* any bit of Π. Call M an $(r(n), q(n))$*-restricted* verifier if, on an input of size n, it is allowed to use at most $O(r(n))$ random bits for its computation, and query at most $O(q(n))$ bits of the proof. Define $M^{\Pi}(x, \tau)$ to be 1 if M accepts x, with access to the proof Π, using a random string τ, and 0 otherwise.

Definition 1 *A language L is in* $\mathbf{PCP}(r(n), q(n))$ *if there exists an $(r(n), q(n))$-restricted verifier M such that for every input x:*

1. *If $x \in L$, there is a proof Π_x which causes M to accept for every random string (i.e. with probability 1).*

2. *If $x \notin L$ then for all proofs Π,*

$$\Pr_{\tau \in \{0,1\}^{r(n)}} [M^{\Pi}(x, \tau) = 1] < \frac{1}{2}.$$

This generalizes **NP**, the class of languages for which membership proofs are checkable in deterministic polynomial-time, since $\mathbf{NP} = \mathbf{PCP}(0, poly(n))$.

One would like to characterize **NP** as low as possible in the **PCP** hierarchy (i.e., use the fewest possible random and query bits in verifying membership proofs for **NP** languages). The above mentioned paper ([FGLSS91]) came close to an exact characterization of **NP** in terms of **PCP**. Using the shorthand $\mathbf{PCP}(c(n))$ for $\mathbf{PCP}(c(n), c(n))$, the authors show that $\mathbf{NP} \subseteq \mathbf{PCP}(\log n \cdot \log\log n)$.

A New Characterization of NP

It is easy to see that $\mathbf{PCP}(\log n, n^{O(1)}) \subseteq \mathbf{NP}$, (since a $(\log n)$-restricted verifier can only access proofs of size $n^{O(1)}$) and so it remained an open question what the exact characterization of **NP** is in terms of **PCP**. We are able to settle this question by showing the following:

Theorem 1 (Main) $\mathbf{NP} = \mathbf{PCP}(O(\log n), O(\log n))$.

This result is probably optimal, since if $\mathbf{NP} \subseteq \mathbf{PCP}(o(\log n))$ then $\mathbf{NP} = \mathbf{P}$ (since, in the spirit of [FGLSS91], the problem of membership in a language $L \in \mathbf{PCP}(o(\log n))$ can be reduced to a sublinear instance of an **NP**-problem; this reduction can then be applied repeatedly untill the size of the problem is small enough to solve deterministically). Somewhat surprisingly, we are able to give a slightly better characterization of **NP** as

$$\mathbf{NP} = \mathbf{PCP}(\log n, \sqrt{\log n})$$

i.e.,

$$\mathbf{PCP}(\log n, \log n) = \mathbf{PCP}(\log n, \sqrt{\log n}).$$

In other words, by increasing the number of random bits by a constant factor the number of queries can be made sub-logarithmic. It is an interesting open question how low the number of queries can be made, and what is the tradeoff between the number of random bits and the number of queries.

Note that in order to achive this new characterization of **NP** we use techniques that do not relativized. Furthermore, this chracterization is non-relativizing, i.e., there exists an oracle that separates it from the Cook-Levin characterization of **NP** ([For]). We discuss some possible implication of this in the discussion section.

1.3 Other Related Works

A somewhat different characterization of **NP** was given by Fagin ([Fag74]) in terms of spectra of second order formulae. This characterization was used by Papadimitriou and Yannakakis ([PY88]) to define some retriced subclasses of **NP**, and show relations between the approximation versions of these problems.

More recent work in program checking and interactive proof systems has resulted in other characterizations of **NP**. For instance, Lipton ([Lip89]) showed that membership proofs for **NP** can be checked by probabilistic logspace verifiers that have one-way access to the proof and use $O(\log n)$ random bits. It is easily seen that this is another exact characterization of **NP**. Lipton's work has recently been extended by Condon and Ladner ([CL89]) to give a somewhat stronger result. In these characterizations, the verifier, though very restricted, at least receives a polynomial number of bits of information about the proof.

Condon ([Con91]) already pointed out that the bounded-away probability in such characterizations of **NP** can be used to show that approximating the Max-Word problem is **NP**-hard.

The main difference between the above probabilistic characterizations of **NP** and our characterization is that they restrict the computational power of the verifier while we restrict the number of random bits and the number of bits extracted from the nondeterministic guess.

2 Overview of Our Proof

Our starting point is the protocol of [BFL90] in its scaled-down form ([BFLS91, FGLSS91]). Our key new idea is to make the proof structure (and the proof-verification procedure) recursive.

Let $L \in \mathbf{NP}$. As shown in ([BFLS91]), a ($\log^c n$)-verifier can check proofs for the statement "$x \in L$." Furthermore, if the input x is provided in a suitably encoded form $\sigma(x)$, then the running time of the verifier is $\log^c x$ (now the verifier must also check that the input is encoded correctly). This probabilistically checkable proof, Π, has a simple structure: it is a table of $poly(n)$ entries; each entry a string of logarithmic size. Assume for now that that the verifier's action consists only of randomly choosing an entry y from the table, and accepting iff it satisfies a polynomial time predicate P (the verifier in [BFLS91] does something similar). Then we claim that a more efficient verifier exists. It stipulates that each table entry y in Π should be present in its encoded form $\sigma(y)$, alongwith a probabilistically checkable proof, π, showing that $P(y) = 1$. The verifier can verify π by querying of $poly(\log|y|) = poly(\log\log|x|)$ bits in total from π and the encoded string $\sigma(y)$, and end up being convinced that this table entry satisfies P! (of course, the verification of π is only probabilistic, but then so was the overall process. Just the overall error probability must be kept below $\frac{1}{4}$).

Actually the recursion technique is more complicated, because the verifier in ([BFLS91]) is somewhat more complicated than the one described above. It uses randomness to select some k addresses in the table to query. Subsequently it reads the strings $y_1, y_2, \ldots, y_k$ from these adresses and accepts iff their concatenation $y_1 \circ y_2 \cdots y_k$ satisfies predicate P. It is not immediately clear how the recursion described above could be applied to this situation. In section 5 we show that the encoding σ has the convenient property that if $\sigma(y_1), \ldots, \sigma(y_k)$ are provided separately, then a proof for the statement "$P(y_1 \circ \cdots y_k) = 1$" can still be checked very efficiently while looking at very few bits of the encoded strings $\sigma(y_1), \ldots, \sigma(y_k)$.

More concretely, given an input x of length n, let $\mathcal{C}(n)$ be the number of query bits that the verifier needs to check a membership proof for x, when the number of random bits it is allowed is $O(\log n)$. Our idea yields the following recurrence for $\mathcal{C}(n)$.

Theorem 2 *Let h, m be such that $h = \Omega(\log n)$ and $(h+1)^m = n^{\Theta(1)}$. Then*

$$(i).\ \ \mathcal{C}(n) = O(\log^2 n).$$

$$(ii).\ \ \mathcal{C}(n) \leq O(m \log\log(h)) + 2 \cdot \mathcal{C}(poly(mh)).$$

□

Substituting $h = 2^{\sqrt[4]{\log n}}$ and $m = \sqrt[4]{\log^3 n}$ gives $\mathcal{C}(n) = O(\log^{\frac{3}{4}} n)$. $\mathcal{C}(n)$ can be reduced further by being more careful; details are omitted.

2.1 Small Degree Extension

We will refer to a *multivariate polynomial* as just "polynomial." By its *degree* we will mean the maximum degree in any variable.

Let $x \in \{0,1\}^n$ be a string, and let m be such that $(h+1)^m \geq n$ (thus $m = \frac{\log n}{\log h}$). Then each bit-position in x can be labelled by an integer having m digits in its base $h+1$ representation, which makes x a function from $[0..h]^m$ to $\{0,1\}$. Assume that $\mathcal{F}$ is a field containing $[0..h]$.

Definition 2 *For f: $[0..h]^l \to \mathcal{F}$, the* degree-h extension *of f over $\mathcal{F}$, denoted $\widehat{f}$, is a polynomial in l variables $y_1, \ldots, y_l$ that has degree h in each variable, and which satisfies:*

$$\forall \vec{y} \in [0..h]^l : \widehat{f}(\vec{y}) = f(\vec{y})$$

Lemma 3 *Any function f: $[0..h]^l \to \mathcal{F}$ has a unique degree-h extension over $\mathcal{F}$.*

Proof: For $u \in [0..h]$ denote by $L_u(y)$ the univariate polynomial of degree h which is 1 at u and 0 at all $y \in [0..h] \setminus \{u\}$. Then $\widehat{f}$ is the polynomial defined as:

$$\widehat{f}(y_1, \ldots, y_l) = \sum_{(a_1,\ldots,a_l)\in[0..h]^l} f(a_1, \ldots, a_l) \cdot \prod_{i=1}^{l} L_{a_i}(y_i).$$

Clearly it has degree h and coincides with f over $[0..h]^l$. Uniqueness follows easily. □

A function can be close to being a polynomial, in the following sense.

Definition 3 *A function f: $\mathcal{F}^l \to \mathcal{F}$ is δ-close if there exists a degree-h polynomial g such that f and g agree on at least $1 - \delta$ fraction of the points in $\mathcal{F}^l$ ($\delta > 0$).*

(Note: If $|\mathcal{F}|$ is large, then there is at most one polynomial within δ of f; see Section 7.)

Following the above-mentioned papers, we assume that a membership proof for NP contains the degree-h extension, $\widehat{A}$, of a satisfying assignment to a $3SAT$ formula. How can the verifier be convinced of the existence of a satisfying assignment even though it reads only a few bits of the representation of $\widehat{A}$? Assume "magically" for now that the provided $\widehat{A}$ does represent some degree-h polynomial. Then there exists a probabilistic test (see section 6) to verify that $\widehat{A}$ represents a satisfying assignment, while evaluating $\widehat{A}$ in only one random point. The fact that it uses only one random value of $\widehat{A}$ allows the test to perform just as well even if $\hat{A}$ is not "magically" guaranteed to be a degree-h polynomial but only guaranteed to be δ-close. δ-closeness can be tested for by a simple test, the *small-degree test* (see Section 7) which examines $\widehat{A}$ at $O(1)$ random points. Thus very few values of $\widehat{A}$ need to be read.

The main point of this observation is that it lets us blur the distinction between functions that're degree-h polynomials and those that're δ-close, since they behave roughly the same in a probabilitic test that probes them at only $O(1)$ random points.

3 Organization of the Paper

Section 4 gives a brief overview of a generic proof-verification procedure along the lines of [BFLS91, FGLSS91]. Section 5 applies the recursion idea to reduce the number of queries used by the procedure in Section 4 (specifically, we prove Theorem 2). The later sections 6 and 7 give details of two sub-procedures of the proof-verification process, the sum-check and the small-degree-test, respectively. Understanding them isn't crucial to following the overall picture in Sections 4 and 5. Our small-degree-test is an improvement upon small-degree-tests known to us, and was crucial to obtaining our result.

4 The Verification Procedure

For completeness we briefly describe the generic proof verification procedure of previous papers. The following is an observation from [LFKN90, Sha90, BFL90]. Let ϕ be a $3SAT$ fromula, and h, m be such that $(h+1)^m$ is greater than the number of variables and clauses in ϕ.

Lemma 4 (Algebraic View of $3SAT$**)** *Given the degree-h extension of an assignment,* $\widehat{A}: \mathcal{F}^m \to \mathcal{F}$*, there is a polynomial* $\varphi^A: \mathcal{F}^{4m} \to \mathcal{F}$ *of degree* $6h$ *such that:*

1. *the value of* φ^A *at any point depends on the value of* $\widehat{A}$ *at 3 distinct points.*
2. $\widehat{A}$ *is the extension of a satisfying assignment iff* φ^A *is zero everywhere on* $[0..h]^{4m}$.

Proof: For $j = 1, 2, 3$, let $\chi_j(c, v)$ be the function from $[0..h]^m \times [0..h]^m$ to $\{0,1\}$ such that $\chi_j(c, v) = 1$ if v is the jth variable in clause c and 0 otherwise. Similarly let $s_j(c)$ be a function from $[0..h]^m$ to $\{0,1\}$ such that $s_j(c) = 1$ if the jth variable of clause c is unnegated and 0 otherwise.

Thus assignment A satisfies ϕ if and only if for every clause c and every triple of variables v_1, v_2, v_3,

$$\prod_{j=1}^{3} \chi_j(c, v_j) \cdot (s_j(c) - A(v_j)) = 0.$$

Contructing the degree-h extensions $\widehat{\chi_j}(\vec{c}, \vec{v})$ and $\widehat{s_j}(\vec{c})$ of χ_j and s_j respectively, we get the expression

$$\varphi^A(\vec{c}, \vec{v}_1, \vec{v}_2, \vec{v}_3) = \prod_{j=1}^{3} \widehat{\chi_j}(\vec{c}, \vec{v}_j) \cdot \left(\widehat{s_j}(\vec{c}) - \widehat{A}(\vec{v}_j)\right)$$

Then φ^A is a polynomial in $4m$ variables of degree at most $6h$ (note: $\vec{c}$ and $\vec{v}$ are not single variables but vectors of m variables each). Further, A is a satisfying assignment iff $\varphi^A(\vec{y}) = 0 \quad \forall \vec{y} \in [0..h]^{4m}$ □

Now we describe the verification. Assume $|x| = n$, $(h+1)^m = n^{\Theta(1)}$ and $h = \Omega(\log n)$. $\mathcal{F}$ is a field of size h^3m^2. Unless otherwise stated, all sub-procedures quoted in Theorem 5 run in *poly*(mh) time.

Theorem 5 . (i) *The membership proof can be provided as a table of poly*(n) *entries, each entry of* $O(h \log h)$ *bits. A verifier can check the proof by using* $O(\log n)$ *random bits to select* $O(m)$ *of the entries to read* (ii) *If the input is provided as its degree-h extension, the running time is poly*(mh)*.*

Proof: ¿From the proof of the Cook-Levin Theorem ([Coo71],[Lev73]) it follows that for every n, there is a 3-CNF formula, $\phi_n(z_1, \ldots, z_n, y_1, \ldots, y_{n^c})$, such that $x (= x_1 \cdot x_2 \cdots x_n) \in L$ iff $\exists y_1 y_2 \cdots y_{n^c}$ such that $\phi_n(x_1, \ldots, x_n, y_1, \ldots y_{n^c}) = 1$. Thus it suffices to provide the verifier with an assignment $A: [1, n + n^c] \to \{0,1\}$ such that

1. A satisfies ϕ_n. Using Theorem 4, this is equivalent to
$$\varphi^A(\vec{c}) = 0 \quad \forall \vec{c} \in [0..h]^{4m}.$$
2. $A(i) = x_i$ for $i = 1, 2, \ldots, n$. We assume w.l.o.g. that there is some k, such that this is equivalent to the condition
$$\widehat{A}(\vec{i}) - \widehat{x}(\vec{i}) = 0 \quad \forall \vec{i} \in [0..h]^k$$
where $\widehat{x}$ is the degree-h extension of x that the verifier can construct in *poly*(n) time.

Abstractly, checking these conditions involves checking that some small-degree polynomial vanishes over a range of the form $[0..h]^l$. As was shown in [FGLSS91, BFLS91]), a little randomness can be used to reduce such $(h+1)^l$ conditions to a single condition.

Lemma 6 *There exists a family of* $h^{O(l)}$ *polynomials* $\{R_1, R_2, \ldots\}$*, each a degree-h polynomial in l variables, such that if* $f: [0..h]^l \to \mathcal{F}$ *is any function not identically 0, then*

$$Prob[\sum_{y \in [0..h]^l} R(y) f(y) = 0] \leq \frac{1}{100},$$

if R is chosen randomly from this family. This family is constructible in $h^{O(l)}$ *time.*

□

The proof has to contain some information for each polynomial R of this family showing:

$$\sum_{\vec{y}\in[0..h]^l} R(\vec{y}) \cdot \varphi^A(\vec{y}) = 0. \quad (1)$$

The verifier needs only $O(\log n)$ random bits to choose one polynomial from the family and check the information corresponding to it. A similar check is done for the condition about $\widehat{x}$.

Previous papers [LFKN90, Sha90, BFL90], use the following procedure to check a proof for Equation 1 (details in Section 6).
Sum-Check: Given the table of values of a degree-d polynomial $f: \mathcal{F}^m \to \mathcal{F}$, checks a proof for the statement

$$\sum_{\vec{y}\in[0..d]^l} f(\vec{y}) = 0$$

while evaluating f at only one random point in $\mathcal{F}^l$.

Thus φ^A is evaluated at only one random point, and so $\widehat{A}$ at only 3 random points. By the observation in subsection 2.1 the sum-check works sufficiently well if $\widehat{A}$ is δ-close, for δ small enough. δ-closeness can be tested for easily (details in Section 7) by sampling $\widehat{A}$ at only $O(1)$ random points.

Examining the complexity of the Sum-Check and the Small-Degree Tests, Part (i) follows. □

4.1 When the Input is Encoded

It was pointed out in [BFLS91] that the input is used during the verification only to construct its small degree extension $\widehat{x}$. $\widehat{x}$ is then used in a sum-check to verify that the first n bits of the assignment are consistent with x, which examines $\widehat{x}$ at one random point. So if $\widehat{x}$ is provided (instead of the bit-string x) then the verifier can use it after checking that it is δ-close. Then the running time is essentially the time to do a Sum-check and a Small-degree Test, which is $poly(mh)$ (we omit details of how to construct in $poly(mh)$ time a value each of ϕ^A and of R_i of Lemma 6; refer to the cited papers). This proves part (ii) of Theorem 5
Most importantly, the verifier has to read only $O(1)$ values of $\widehat{x}$ in all, which will be crucial now.

5 Recursive Proof Checking

Now we give details of the recursion idea introduced in Section 2. More specifically, we use the verifier of Theorem 5 to prove Theorem 2
Proof:(*Theorem* 2) We assume w.l.o.g. (see section 4.1) that the input is provided as its small degree extension.

Consider V_0, the verifier of Theorem 5. In a proof for the statement "$x \in L$" it expects a table with $poly(n)$ entries. It uses $O(\log n)$ random bits to select some $O(m)$ entries from the tables, and $O(1)$ values of $\widehat{x}$. It accepts iff the concatenation of these $O(m)$ strings, say $y_1 \circ y_2 \circ \cdots y_{O(m)}$ satisfies a certain polynomial time predicate P (note:the length of $y_1 \circ y_2 \cdots y_{O(m)}$ is $poly(mh)$).

Substituting $h = \log n$ achieves $\mathcal{C}(n) = O(\log^2 n)$. We show a more efficient verifier that uses V_0 as a subprocedure.
Proof Structure: The verifier stipulates that (i) the table-entries in the proof should be encoded in the form of their small-degree extensions. (ii) for each choice of V_0's random string, say τ, the proof should contain a sub-proof, π_τ showing that V_0 would have accepted the original proof using τ.In other words π_τ shows that that $P(y) = 1$, where y is the concatenation of the table-entries chosen with τ. (note: π_τ has exactly the same structure as the larger proof, except that the field-sizes, degrees, etc. are scaled down according to the size of y.)

Clearly the verifier can verify π_τ with a recursive call to itself, provided it is given a table for $\widehat{y}$, the encoding of the input y. However, the proof contains only the encodings $\widehat{y_i}$. We show that the encoding $x \to \widehat{x}$ allows the following to be done efficiently:

- Check that each $\widehat{y_i}$ is an encoding of some bit-string.
- Construct any value of $\widehat{y}$.

We first show how to construct $\widehat{y}$, assuming $\widehat{y_i}$'s are actually encodings of strings. Assume field $\mathcal{Q}$ contains $[0..d]$.

Lemma 7 *Let $y_1, y_2, \ldots, y_m$ ($m = (d+1)^k$) be bits strings of length $(d+1)^l$ each. Then every value of the degree-d extension of $y_1 \circ \cdots \circ y_r$ can be interpolated from one value each of the degree-d extensions of $y_1, .. y_r$ (the extensions are over a field $\mathcal{Q}$ containing $[0..d]$).*

Proof: Let $\widehat{y}$ be the degree-d extension of $y_1 \circ \cdots \circ y_r$. and $\widehat{y_i}$ the degree-d extension of y_i (note that $\widehat{y}$ is a polynomial in $k + l$ variables though each y_i is a polynomial in l variables). The value of $\widehat{y}$ at the point $(\vec{u}, \vec{v}) \in \mathcal{Q}^{l+k}$ is clearly

$$\widehat{y}(\vec{u}, \vec{v}) = \sum_{i\in[0..d]^k} L_i(\vec{u}) \cdot \widehat{y_i}(\vec{v})$$

where $L_i(\vec{u})$ is the unique degree-d polynomial in k variables that is 1 if $\vec{u} = i$ and 0 if $\vec{u} \in [0..d]^k \setminus \{i\}$. The verifier can construct L_i easily. □

Since the $\widehat{y_i}$'s provided may be arbitrary functions, we give a test to verify that all the $\widehat{y_i}$ are δ-close: Just test that the $\widehat{y}$ constructed using Lemma 7 is δ-close. *Note:* This only requires constructing $O(1)$ values of $\widehat{y}$ (and thus, by the lemma, only $O(m)$ values of the $\widehat{y_i}$'s).

Lemma 8 *In Lemma 7, if $\widehat{y_i}$ is given as a table $\mathcal{Q}^l \to \mathcal{Q}$, and the $\widehat{y}$ constructed from them is δ-close to a degree-d polynomial, then each $\widehat{y_i}$ is δ+$o(1)$-close. Furthermore,*

$\widehat{y}$ encodes the concatenation of the strings encoded by the $\widehat{y_i}$'s.

Proof: Needs concepts defined later; see appendix. □

Lets see why the verifier's efficiency is as claimed by Theorem 2. Given a proof Π of size $n^{O(1)}$ that has the recursive structure described above, V_1 can probabilistically reduce the correctness of Π to the correctness of a sub-proof of size $poly(mh)$. The subproof shows that "$P(y) = 1$" where $y = y_1 \circ \cdots \circ y_{O(m)}$. To verify it, V_1 needs $O(m)$ values of the $\widehat{y_i}$'s, each value an element of a field Q of size $polylog(mh)$.

Note that an error could occur in the procedure from two sources. Either V_0's cointosses were such that it would have accepted incorrectly (and therefore the recursive call also accepts). Or else an erroneous sub-proof is accepted during the recursion, causing acceptance even though V_0 would have rejected. The probability of either of these happening is at most $\frac{1}{4}$, by definition of "Proof Checking." To make the overall probability $\frac{1}{4}$ again, we just repeat the whole procedure twice, thus obtaining

$$C(n) = O(m \log\log(mh)) + 2 \cdot C(poly(mh)).$$

□

6 Sum Check

We describe [LFKN90, Sha90, BFL90] an efficient verification procedure that, given a degree-h polynomial $f: \mathcal{F}^l \to \mathcal{F}$ verifies a proof for the statement

$$\sum_{\vec{y} \in [0..h]^l} f(\vec{y}) = c \qquad (*).$$

The procedure satisfies the following:

1. It runs in $poly(lh)$ time, and uses $h \log |\mathcal{F}|$ random bits.
2. In the proof it expects a table of $\mathcal{F}^l$ entries, each a bit string of length $O(h \log |\mathcal{F}|)$.
3. It reads l entries of the table and examines f at only one random point.

For any i, $1 \le i \le l$, and $a_1, ..., a_{i-1} \in \mathcal{F}$, let $g_{a_1,...,a_{i-1}}$ be the degree-h univariate polynomial such that:

$$g_{a_1,..,a_{i-1}}(y_i) = \sum_{y_{i+1},..,y_l \in H} \tilde{f}(a_1, .., a_{i-1}, \; y_i, \; y_{i+1}, .., y_l).$$

(We denote the single polynomial, where $i = 1$, by g_ϵ). The proof has a table containing, supposedly, all the $g_{a_1,..a_i}$'s. We call these provided polynomials as $g'_{a_1,..a_i}$.

Sum Check:

> Π contains f and $g'_{a_1,...,a_i}$ for every $0 \le i < l$ and $a_1, ..., a_i \in \mathcal{F}$

Choose random $a_1, ..., a_l \in_R \mathcal{F}$ and check that:

1. $c = \sum_{y_1 \in H} g'_\epsilon(y_1)$
2. For each i, $1 \le i < l$,
$$g'_{a_1,..,a_{i-1}}(a_i) = \sum_{y_{i+1} \in H} g'_{a_1,..,a_i}(y_{i+1})$$
3. $g'_{a_1,...,a_{l-1}}(a_l) = f(a_1, ..., a_l)$.

Clearly, if $(*)$ is true, then there is a proof that succeeds in all tests, simply by making $g' = g$ everywhere. On the other hand, if $(*)$ is false, then a simple induction (using the fact that a univariate polynomial of degree h has at most h roots) shows that the test accepts the proof with probability at most $\frac{hl}{|\mathcal{F}|}$. Refer to referenced papers for details.

Complexity of the Test: The test clearly requires $O(l \log |\mathcal{F}|)$ random bits. It performs $O(l)$ tests of the form:

$$g'[a_1, ..., a_{i-1}](a_i) = \sum_{y_{i+1} \in H} g'[a_1, ..., a_i](y_{i+1}).$$

Notice that the whole test is therefore a polynomial time procedure on the input $\{(a_i, g'[a_1, ..., a_{i-1}], g'[a_1, ..., a_i]) : i = 1, 2, \ldots, l\}$, which is a bit string of length $O(lh \log |\mathcal{F}|)$.

7 Small Degree Test

In this section we show a procedure that, given $B: \mathcal{F}^l \to \mathcal{F}$, efficiently checks a proof for the statement "B is a degree-h polynomial." (It rejects with high probability if B is not δ-close, and requires $|\mathcal{F}| = \Omega(l^2 h^3)$). We use new ideas from algebra and coding theory (as opposed to the counting arguments used previously) to prove its efficiency; previous tests implicit in [BFL90], [FGLSS91] need to probe far too many places in the proof.

The proof has to consist of a table of $|\mathcal{F}|^l$ entries, each a bit-string of size $O(h \log |\mathcal{F}|)$. The test uses $O(l \log |\mathcal{F}|)$ random bits and runs in $poly(hl)$ time. It reads only $O(1)$ values of f and $O(l)$ entries of the table.

First some facts and definitions about polynomials.

Definition 4 *The distance between two functions $f, g: \mathcal{F}^l \to \mathcal{F}$, denoted $\Delta(f, g)$ is the fraction of points on which they differ. Denote by $\Delta_h(f)$ the distance of f to the nearest degree-h polynomial.*

Clearly, Δ is a metric. Also, a lemma due to Schwarz says that for two degree-h polynomials f and g, $\Delta(f,g) \geq 1 - \frac{lh}{|\mathcal{F}|}$. Since $\frac{lh}{|\mathcal{F}|} = o(1)$, the triangle inequality implies that an arbitrary function f can be within 0.2 (say) of at most one degree-h polynomial.

Definition 5 *If $\Delta_h(f) \leq 0.2$ then denote by $\tilde{f}$ the unique degree-h polynomial closest to f.*

Definition 6 *For $f: \mathcal{F}^l \to \mathcal{F}$, denote by $f_{x_i=a}$ the restriction of f on the space $x_i = a$.*

Now we describe the verification procedure. For a tuple $(a_1, \ldots, a_{i-1}, a_{i+1}, \ldots, a_l) \in \mathcal{F}^{l-1}$, call the set of points $\{(a_1, \ldots, a_{i-1}, x, a_{i+1}, \ldots, a_l): x \in \mathcal{F}\}$ as a *line* in dimension i. Note that $B: \mathcal{F}^l \to \mathcal{F}$ is a polynomial of degree h iff its restriction on all the lines in $\mathcal{F}^l$ is a univariate polynomial of degree h.

The proof is required to contain, for every line $(a_1, \ldots, a_{i-1}, *, a_{i+1}, a_l)$, a degree-$h$ univariate polynomial in y_i that supposedly describes B on that line. Denote this polynomial as $g[a_1, ..., a_{i-1}, *, a_{i+1}, ..., a_l]$ By *decomposition* of B, we mean the set of all such polynomials where $1 \leq i \leq l$ and $(a_1, \ldots, a_{i-1}, a_{i+1}, \ldots, a_l) \in \mathcal{F}^{l-1}$.

Note that $\forall i \in [1, l-1]$ and $\forall(a_1, \ldots, a_l) \in \mathcal{F}^l$, the decomposition ought to satisfy:

$$\begin{aligned} B(a_1, \ldots, a_l) &= g[a_1, ..., a_{i-1}, *, a_{i+1}, ..., a_l](a_i) \\ &= g[a_1, ..., a_i, *, a_{i+2}, ..., a_l](a_{i+1}) \end{aligned}$$

Definition 7 *A* checkpoint *is an element of the set $\{\langle i, a_1, ..., a_l\rangle \mid 1 \leq i < l$ and $a_1, ..., a_l \in \mathcal{F}\}$. The decomposition is* inconsistent *at a checkpoint $\langle i, a_1, ..., a_l\rangle$ if*

$$g[a_1, .., a_{i-1}, *, a_{i+1}, .., a_l](a_i) \neq g[a_1, .., a_i, *, a_{i+2}, .., a_l](a_{i+1}).$$

Small Degree Test:

Π contains B and $g[a_1, ..., a_{i-1}, *, a_{i+1}, ..., a_l]$ for every $1 \leq i \leq l$ and $a_1, ..., a_{i-1}, a_{i+1}, ..., a_l \in \mathcal{F}$

1. Repeat $\frac{8}{\delta}$ times:
   Choose random $a_1, ..., a_l \in_R \mathcal{F}$ and check that
   $$B(a_1, ..., a_l) = g[*, a_2, ..., a_l](a_1).$$
2. Choose randomly $O(l)$ check points and for each of them, $\langle i, a_1, ..., a_l\rangle$, verify that the decompostion is consistent at them.

Clearly, if B is a polynomial of degree h and the proof contains the decomposition that correctly describes f, this test accepts it with probability 1. We show that if B is not δ-close, then the test rejects with probability $\geq \frac{3}{4}$. Define a function $f: \mathcal{F}^l \to \mathcal{F}$ as

$$f(y_1, .., y_l) = g[*, y_2, .., y_l](y_1).$$

Note that test 1 compares B with f on a constant number of points in $\mathcal{F}^l$.

If $\Delta(B, f) > \frac{\delta}{2}$, then with probability at least $\frac{3}{4}$, test 1 would fail. We show below that if $\Delta_h(f) > \frac{\delta}{2}$, then test 2 rejects the decompostion with probability at least $\frac{3}{4}$. Combining the two, if $\Delta_h(B) > \delta$, then, either $\Delta(B, f) > \frac{\delta}{2}$ or $\Delta_h(f) > \frac{\delta}{2}$, and so the test would reject with probability at least $\frac{3}{4}$.

Complexity: We actually prove that if $\Delta_h(f) > \frac{\delta}{2}$ then the fraction of checkpoints on which the decompostion is inconsistent is at least $\frac{\delta}{4l}$. Hence by sampling in a pairwise independent fashion, the verifier can choose a set of $O(l)$ check points such that with probability $\frac{3}{4}$, at least one of them is inconsistent. This sampling uses only $O(l \log(|\mathcal{F}|))$ random bits. That the running time is $poly(lh)$ is clear.

To finish the proof of correctness we need to prove that if $\Delta_h(f) > \frac{\delta}{2}$, the fraction of inconsistent check points in the decomposition is $\geq \frac{\delta}{4l}$.Let $\Upsilon(l, \varepsilon)$ be the fraction of inconsistent check points.

Lemma 9 *If $\Delta_h(f) = \varepsilon$, then*

$$\Upsilon(l, \varepsilon) \geq \frac{\gamma^{2l}}{l} \cdot \min\{\delta, \varepsilon\},$$

where $\gamma = 1 - \sqrt{\frac{h}{|\mathcal{F}|}}$.

Proof: The proof is by induction on l, the number of variables, details are deferred to the final version. The only new idea we use over existing techniques is the following lemma which shows how to infer a strong global property about f from fairly weak local properties.

Recall that the restriction of f on a 1st dimension line is (by defn. of f) a degree-h univariate polynomial.

Lemma 10 *If there exist points $\{b_1, \ldots, b_{2h}\}$ such that $\Delta_h(f_{y_1=b_j}) < 0.1$ for $i = 1, ..., 2h$, then there exists a degree-h polynomial ϕ in l variables which agrees with f on 0.8 of the points in $\mathcal{F}^l$.*

□

Proof: View the values of f as lying in a matrix with $|\mathcal{F}|$ columns and $|\mathcal{F}|^{l-1}$ rows. (For $\vec{a} \in \mathcal{F}^{l-1}$ and $b \in \mathcal{F}$, $f(b, \vec{a})$ is at the intersection of the column given by b and the row given by $\vec{a}$). According to the hypothesis:

1. All $|\mathcal{F}|$ values in a row lie on a univariate degree-h polynomial.
2. $2h$ of the columns, given by $b_1, b_2, \ldots, b_{2h}$ are within 0.1 (over $\mathcal{F}^{l-1}$) of a degree-h polynomial in $l-1$ variables. From now on, $\tilde{f}_i$ denotes the unique degree-h polynomial which fits the column b_i closely.

The polynomial ϕ claimed by the lemma is the plausible candidate, namely

$$\phi(x_1,\ldots,x_l)=\sum_{i=1}^{h+1}L_{b_i}(x_1)\widetilde{f}_i(x_2,\ldots,x_l).$$

Here $L_{b_i}(x_1)$ is the degree-h univariate polynomial which is 1 if $x_1=b_i$ and 0 if $x_1\in\{b_1,\ldots,b_{h+1}\}\setminus\{b_i\}$. Thus ϕ, which fits the whole matrix, is just the extrapolation of the polynomials which fit the first $h+1$ columns.

For a row $\vec{a}\in\mathcal{F}^{l-1}$ and column $i\in\{1,2,\ldots,2h\}$, call $(b_i,\vec{a})$ an *error-point* if f and $\widetilde{f_{x_1=b_i}}$ do not agree on it. Notice that if a row has no error-points in the first $h+1$ columns, then f and ϕ coincide everywhere on that row (this is because the restriction of both f and ϕ on that row is a univariate degree-h polynomial, and two such distinct polynomials cannot agree on $h+1$ points). The claim is that 0.8 of the rows are of this type.

Notice that this claim follows easily if for each i, $\Delta_h(f_i)=\frac{0.1}{h+1}$ instead of 0.1. Then an averaging argument shows that at most 0.1 of the rows have any error-points at all. The averaging argument fails if $\Delta_h(f_i)=0.1$. So we give an algebraic argument will show the result.

The averaging argument does show that $\frac{1}{2}$ of the rows have fewer than $0.4h$ error-points (since the fraction of error-points in each of the $2h$ columns is at most 0.1). Let's denote this set of rows by B, that is

$$B=\left\{\vec{a}\in\mathcal{F}^{l-1}:\text{the row }\vec{a}\text{ has}\le 0.4h\text{ error-points}\right\}.$$

For $\vec{a}\in\mathcal{F}^{l-1}$, we denote by $c_{\vec{a}}(x_1)$ the univariate polynomial in x_1 that describes f in the row. If $\vec{a}\in B$, then for all but $0.4h$ values of i,

$$\widetilde{f}_i(\vec{a})=c_{\vec{a}}(b_i).\quad(*)$$

Therefore there exists a univariate polynomial of degree $0.4h$, which we call $e_{\vec{a}}(x_1)$, such that

$$\widetilde{f}_i(\vec{a})\cdot e_{\vec{a}}(b_i)=c_{\vec{a}}(b_i)\cdot e_{\vec{a}}(b_i)\quad\forall i\in\{1,2,\ldots 2h\}$$

This polynomial e absorbs all the errors by becoming 0 on them, and is similar to *error-locating* polynomials used often in coding theory.

Now we analyze the algebraic structure of $e_{\vec{a}}(x_1)$ to claim that for almost every $\vec{a}\in B$, row $\vec{a}$ contains no error-points (as opposed to the $\le 0.4h$ error-points guaranteed by the averaging argument). Firstly, note that $c_{\vec{a}}(x_1)\cdot e_{\vec{a}}(x_1)$ is a univariate polynomial of degree $1.4h$. Let's denote it by $d_{\vec{a}}(x_1)$. Furthermore, for $\vec{a}\in B$, the coefficients of $e_{\vec{a}}$ and $d_{\vec{a}}$ (there are $1.8h+2$ such coefficients in all) must satisfy the system of $2h$ equations given as

$$\widetilde{f}_i(\vec{a})\cdot e_{\vec{a}}(b_i)=d_{\vec{a}}(b_i)\quad\forall\, i\in\{1,2,\ldots 2h\}.$$

Then the results of Berlekamp and Welch ([BW]; see also [GS91]) imply that the solution to such a system for $\vec{a}\in B$ is unique as far as the ratio $\frac{d_{\vec{a}}(x_1)}{e_{\vec{a}}(x_1)}$ is concerned. Therefore $\frac{d_{\vec{a}}(x_1)}{e_{\vec{a}}(x_1)}=c_{\vec{a}}(x_1)$ for $\vec{a}\in B$. Thus if $e_{\vec{a}}(b_i)\neq 0$ for $\vec{a}\in B$ then $(b_i,\vec{a})$ is not an error point.

But lemma 11 implies that the coefficients of $e_{\vec{a}}$ and $d_{\vec{a}}$ are within $O(\frac{h^2 l}{|\mathcal{F}|})$ (over $\mathcal{F}^{l-1}$) of degree-$1.8h^2$ polynomials. Therefore for any fixed u, $e_{\vec{a}}(b_u)$ is close (over $\mathcal{F}^l$) to a polynomial of degree $O(h^l)$, and so can be 0 for at most a fraction $O(\frac{h^2 l}{|\mathcal{F}|})$ of the points in $\mathcal{F}^{l-1}$. As noticed before, $(b_i,\vec{a})$ is an error-point only if $e_{\vec{a}}(b_i)=0$, and so at most a fraction $O(\frac{h^3 l}{|\mathcal{F}|})=o(1)$ of the rows in B have any error-points at all, thus proving the claim.

Note that this means ϕ coincides with f on $0.5-o(1)$ of the rows. Since each column b_i is within 0.1 of the polynomial $\widetilde{f}_i$, it follows that the restriction of ϕ on this column, $\phi_{x_1=b_i}$, is within $0.6-o(1)$ of $\widetilde{f}_i$. Using the "large-distance" property of degree-h polynomials pointed out before, we conclude that $\phi_{x_1=b_i}=\widetilde{f}_i$ for $i\in[1..2h]$.

Finally, note that this implies (using the fact that a univariate polynomial of degree h has at most h roots) that a row with any error-points must have at least h error points. Therefore an averaging argument shows that the number of rows with any error-points at all is less than 0.2.

To complete the proof we state and prove the lemma used above. It is a generalization of the simple fact from linear algebra that a system of equation $C\cdot\vec{x}=\vec{0}$ has a non-trivial solution iff $rank(C)$ is less than the number of variables.

Lemma 11 *Let A be an $l\times n$ matrix whose entries are degree d polynomials (taking values in $\mathcal{F}^m$). If $rank(A)<n$ at more than $\frac{nmd}{|\mathcal{F}|}$ of the points in $\mathcal{F}^m$, then there exist functions $x_1,x_2,..x_n:\mathcal{F}^l\to\mathcal{F}$, such that $A\cdot\vec{x}=\vec{0}$, where $\vec{x}=(x_1,..,x_n)^T$ and $\vec{0}$ is the zero function. Furthermore, each x_i is within $\frac{md}{\mathcal{F}}$ of some degree-nd polynomial.*

Proof:(*Sketch:*) Notice that the determinant of a $k\times k$ submatrix of A is a polynomial of degree kd. If it is not identically zero, it is non-zero at at least $1-\frac{kdm}{|\mathcal{F}|}$ of the points.

The statement of the lemma implies that every $n\times n$ submatrix has zero determinant at $\frac{nmd}{|\mathcal{F}|}$ of the points in $\mathcal{F}^m$. It follows that these determinants are identically 0, so $rank(A)<n$ everywhere. Furthermore, if $rank(A)=k$ at any point in $\mathcal{F}^m$, then some $k\times k$ submatrix has non-zero determinant, and this determinant is non-zero almost everywhere. The x_i's are obtained by Cramer's Rule on this submatrix. It is easily seen that a solution thus obtained is close to a degree-kd polynomial. □

□ □

8 Discussion

As mentioned above, our chracterization of **NP** in terms of **PCP** is non-relativizing. This opens up the tantalizing possibility of seperating the class **NP** from other classes (e.g., **EXPTIME**) *using relativizing techniques (e.g., diagonalization).* This can be done by seperating the class $\mathbf{PCP}(\log n)$ from the other class (a feat that perhaps may be done using relativizing techniques).

Alternatively, it would be interesting to show that even this new characterization of **NP** cannot be seperated from **EXPTIME** by relativizing techniques, say by showing an oracle that makes this chracterization equal **EXPTIME**. However, the oracle that makes the usual characterization of **NP** equal **EXPTIME** ([Lis86]) seems to be inherently non-generelaziable to the **PCP** characterization of **NP**. This suggests the following conjecture, which strengthen the conjecture that $\mathbf{NP} \neq \mathbf{EXPTIME}$:

Conjecture 1 *There is no oracle O such that* $\mathbf{PCP}^O(\log n, \log n) = \mathbf{EXPTIME}^O$.

With the current definition of **PCP**, one cannot use relativizing techniques in order to separate **NP** from **PSPACE**, since even the lowest **PCP** classes contain **P**, which is known to be equal to **PSPACE** under some oracle.

However, the only reason the **PCP** verifier runs in polynomial time, instead of polylogarithmic time, is in order to compute the small-degree extension of the input. Therefore, one can redefine **PCP** so that the verifier is very weak except for that specific computation. Then, it may be possible, using relativizing techniques and this **PCP** characterization of **NP**, to seperate **NP** from **PSPACE** — this would imply that $\mathbf{P} \neq \mathbf{PSPACE}$ — or from the polynomial-time hierarchy — this would imply that $\mathbf{P} \neq \mathbf{NP}$.

The initial motivation for our work was to show an **NP**-hardness result for the Clique approximation problem, thereby solving an open problem of [FGLSS91] (how to get rid of the "almost"). Indeed, by showing that $\mathbf{NP} = \mathbf{PCP}(\log n, \log n)$ and applying the reduction to Clique approximation ([FGLSS91]), we get that approximating Clique to within a constant factor is **NP**-hard.

We were surprised to find out that our technique enables us to show an even better chracterization of **NP** in terms of **PCP**, with a sub-logarithmic number of queries. This left us with no natural lower-bound to the number of queries required for **NP**, and we left it as an open problem to figure out how low can the number of queries be made.

The smaller number of queries enabled us to show **NP**-hardness result for Clique approximation with even a larger factor. Furthermore, the small number of queries turned out to be important in order to achieve hardness result for approximating problems other than Clique.

Papadimitriou and Yannakakis ([PY88]) introduced the class MAX-SNP and showed approximation preserving reductions among the problems in this class. A reduction from **PCP** to a MAX-SNP problem (MAX-3SAT) was observed independently by Mario Szegedy and Madhu Sudan. The reduction shows hardness for a factor of approximation that depends on the *number of queries* used in the verification procedure, and such that when the number of queries is constant, the factor of approximations shown to be **NP**-hard is constant.

This connection between the number of queries and the hardness of approximating MAX-SNP problems encouraged attempts to improve upon our method. Indeed, shortly after the first circulation of our paper, the number of queries was decreased to $(\log \log n)^{O(1)}$, yielding an **NP**-hardness result for approximating any MAX-SNP problem to within a factor of $1 - \frac{1}{(\log \log n)^{O(1)}}$ as reported in [AMSSS92].

A short while after that it was shown ([ALMSS92]) that $\mathbf{NP} = \mathbf{PCP}(\log n, O(1))$, giving an optimal, up to a constant factor, characterization of **NP** in terms of **PCP**.

The proof of [ALMSS92] follows the same structure as our proof, while decreasing the number of pieces of information required for the recursion to a constant. This is achieved using techniques of Feige and Lovasz ([FL92]) and Gemmell et al. ([GLRSW91, RS92]), while making an essential use of our main technical lemma (lemma 10). In addition, they show how to stop the recursion once the proof size is small enough, using a procedure which is inefficient in the number of random bits it uses (polynomialy many), however uses only a constant number of queries.

A while after that, a simpler proof that $\mathbf{NP} = \mathbf{PCP}(\log n, 1)$ was given ([PS92]), thereby improving the constant (by some orders of magnitude), yielding hardness results for factors of approximation that are within a single order of magnitude from what is known to be achievable in polynomial time.

In another recent interesting development in this line of work, Lund and Yannakakis ([LY92]) obtained **NP**-hardness results for approximating several other problems, including Chromatic-Number and Set-Cover.

Independently of these works, other hardness results for varaity of approximation problems where obtain by Bellare ([Bel92]), Bellare and Rogaway ([BR92]) and Zuckerman ([Zuc92]).

Acknowledgment

We thank Mike Luby for many discussions in the early stages of this work; specifically, his lower bound on the complexity of the protocol as presented in [FGLSS91] is what started this work. We also thank Ron Fagin, Oded Goldreich, Noam Nisan, Madhu Sudan, Steven Phillips,

Mario Szegedy and Moshe Vardi for many insightful discussions. Yuval Shahar's comments contributed a lot to the clarity of the presentation.

References

[AMSSS92] S. Arora, R. Motwani, S. Safra, M. Sudan and M. Szegedy. PCP and the hardness of approximation problems. Unpublished note, February 1992.

[ALMSS92] S. Arora, C. Lund, R. Motwani, M. Sudan and M. Szegedy. Proof verification and intractability of approximation problems. March 1992.

[Bab85] L. Babai. Trading group theory for randomness. In *Proc. 17th ACM Symp. on Theory of Computing*, pages 421–429, 1985.

[BFL90] L. Babai, L. Fortnow, and C. Lund. Non-deterministic exponential time has two-prover interactive protocols. In *Proc. 31th IEEE Symp. on Foundations of Computer Science*, pages 16–25, 1990.

[BFLS91] L. Babai, L. Fortnow, L. Levin, and M. Szegedy. Checking computations in polylogarithmic time. In *Proc. 23rd ACM Symp. on Theory of Computing*, 1991.

[Bel92] M. Bellare. Interactive Proofs and Approximation. IBM Research Report RC 17969 (May 1992).

[BR92] M. Bellare and P. Rogaway. The Complexity of Approximating a NonLinear Program. IBM Research Report RC 17831 (March 1992).

[BGKW88] M. Ben-or, S. Goldwasser, J. Kilian, and A. Wigderson. Multi prover interactive proofs: How to remove intractability. In *Proc. 20th ACM Symp. on Theory of Computing*, pages 113–131, 1988.

[BW] E. Berlekamp and L. Welch. Error correction of algebraic block codes. US Patent Number 4,633,470.

[BK89] M. Blum and S. Kannan. Designing programs that check their work. In *Proc. 21th ACM Symp. on Theory of Computing*, pages 86–97, 1989.

[BLR90] M. Blum, M. Luby, and R. Rubinfeld. Self-testing/correcting with applications to numerical problems. In *Proc. 22nd ACM Symp. on Theory of Computing*, pages 73–83, 1990.

[CL89] A. Condon and R. Ladner. On the complexity of space bounded interactive proofs. In *Proc. 30th IEEE Symp. on Foundations of Computer Science*, pages 462–467, 1989.

[Con91] A. Condon. The complexity of the max word problem. In *8th STACS*, 1991.

[Coo71] S. A. Cook. The complexity of theorem-proving procedures. In *Proc. 3rd ACM Symp. on Theory of Computing*, pages 151–158, 1971.

[Fag74] R. Fagin. Generalized first-order spectra and polynomial-time recognizable sets. In Richard Karp, editor, *Complexity of Computer Computations*. AMS, 1974.

[FGLSS91] U. Feige, S. Goldwasser, L. Lovász, S. Safra, and M. Szegedy. Approximating clique is almost NP-complete. In *Proc. 32nd IEEE Symp. on Foundations of Computer Science*, pages 2–12, 1991.

[FL92] U. Feige and L. Lovasz. Two-Prover One-Round Proof Systems: Their Power and Their Problems. In *Proc. of 24th ACM Symp. on Theory of Computing*, 1992.

[For] Lance Fortnow. Personal Communication.

[FRS88] L. Fortnow, J. Rompel, and M. Sipser. On the power of multi-prover interactive protocols. In *Proc. 3rd STRUCTURES*, pages 156–161, 1988.

[FS87] L. Fortnow, M. Sipser Are there interactive protocols for co-NP Languages? In *Information Processing Letters* 28, North-Holland, 1988, pages 249-251.

[GJ79] Michael R. Garey and David S. Johnson. *Computers and Intractability: A Guide to the Theory of NP-Completeness*. W. H. Freeman, 1979.

[GS91] P. Gemmell and M. Sudan. Highly resilient correctors for polynomials. Technical Report 91/662, U.C. Berkeley, 1991.

[GLRSW91] P. Gemmell, R. Lipton, R. Rubinfeld, M. Sudan, and A. Wigderson. Self-Testing/Correcting for Polynomials and for Approximate Functions. In *Proc. 23th ACM Symp. on Theory of Computing*, pages 32–42, 1991.

[GMR89] S. Goldwasser, S. Micali, and C. Rackoff. The knowledge complexity of interactive proofs. *SIAM J. of Computation*, 18:186–208, 1989.

[IZ89] R. Impagliazzo and D. Zuckerman. How to recycle random bits. In *Proc. 30th IEEE Symp. on Foundations of Computer Science*, pages 248–253, 89.

[Kar72] Richard M. Karp. Reducibility among combinatorial problems. In Raymond E. Miller and James W. Thatcher, editors, *Complexity of Computer Computations*, pages 85–103. Plenum Press, 1972.

[Lev73] L. Levin. Universal'nyĭe perebornyĭe zadachi (universal search problems : in russian). *Problemy Peredachi Informatsii*, 9(3):265–266, 1973.

[Lip89] R. Lipton. Efficient Checking of Computations In *6th STACS* 1989.

[Lis86] G. Lischke. Relationships Between Relativizations of **P**, **NP**, EL, NEL, EP and NEP. *Zeitschrift fur Mathematische Logik und Grundlagen der Mathematik*, 1986 (2) pages 257 –270.

[Lub] Mike Luby. Personal Communication.

[LFKN90] C. Lund, L. Fortnow, H. Karloff, and N. Nisan. Algebraic methods for interactive proof systems. In *STOC90*, pages 2–10, 1990.

[LY92] C. Lund, M. Yannakakis. On the Hardness of Minimization Problems. Manuscript, July 1992.

[PY88] C. Papadimitriou and M Yannakakis. Optimization, approximation and complexity classes. In *Proc. 20th ACM Symp. on Theory of Computing*, pages 229–234, 1988.

[PA] Steven Phillips and Yossi Azar. Personal Communication.

[PS92] S. Phillips and S. Safra. PCP and tighter bounds for approximating MAX-SNP. April 1992.

[RS92] R. Rubinfeld, and M. Sudan. Testing Polynomial Functions Efficiently and over Rational Domains. In *Proc. 3rd Annual ACM-SIAM Symp. on Discrete Algorithms*, pages 23-32, 1992.

[Sha90] A. Shamir. IP=PSPACE. In *Proc. 22nd ACM Symp. on Theory of Computing*, pages 11–15, 1990.

[Zuc91] D. Zuckerman. Simulating BPP using a general weak random source. In *Proc. 32nd IEEE Symp. on Foundations of Computer Science*, pages 79–89, 1991.

[Zuc92] D. Zuckerman. Manuscript.

Appendix

Proof:(*Lemma* 8) Since $\widehat{y}$ is δ-close, there is a unique degree-d polynomial nearest to it. Call it $\widetilde{y}$. Consider the set

$$V = \left\{\vec{v} \in \mathcal{Q}^l | \exists \vec{u} \in \mathcal{Q}^k s.t. \widehat{y}(\vec{u}, \vec{v}) \neq \widetilde{y}(\vec{u}, \vec{v})\right\}.$$

We claim that $\frac{|V|}{|\mathcal{Q}^l|} \leq \delta + o(1)$.

For $\vec{a} \in \mathcal{Q}^l$ consider the functions $\widehat{y}_{\vec{v}=\vec{a}}$ and $\widetilde{y}_{\vec{v}=\vec{a}}$ (as defined in Definition 6). They are both degree-d polynomials (taking values in $\mathcal{Q}^k$). If $\vec{a} \in V$ they must be distinct and thus agree in $o(1)$ of the points. For $\vec{a} \notin V$ they are identical. Hence the number of points $\widehat{y}$ and $\widetilde{y}$ differ in is at least $|V| \left|\mathcal{Q}^k\right| \cdot (1 - o(1))$, and (by hypothesis) is at most $\delta \cdot |\mathcal{Q}|^{l+k}$. The claim follows.

Since $\widehat{y}_{\vec{u}=i}$ is (by definition) $\widehat{y}_i$, and $\Delta(\widehat{y}_{\vec{u}=i}, \widetilde{y}_{\vec{u}=i}) \leq \frac{|V|}{\mathcal{Q}^l}$, the lemma is proved. □

Proof Verification and Hardness of Approximation Problems

Sanjeev Arora[*] *Carsten Lund*[†] *Rajeev Motwani*[‡] *Madhu Sudan*[§] *Mario Szegedy*[¶]

Abstract

The class PCP($f(n), g(n)$) consists of all languages L for which there exists a polynomial-time probabilistic oracle machine that uses $O(f(n))$ random bits, queries $O(g(n))$ bits of its oracle and behaves as follows: If $x \in L$ then there exists an oracle y such that the machine accepts for all random choices but if $x \notin L$ then for every oracle y the machine rejects with high probability. Arora and Safra very recently characterized NP as PCP($\log n, (\log\log n)^{O(1)}$). We improve on their result by showing that $NP = PCP(\log n, 1)$. Our result has the following consequences:

1. *MAXSNP-hard problems (e.g., metric TSP, MAX-SAT, MAX-CUT) do not have polynomial time approximation schemes unless P=NP.*

2. *For some $\epsilon > 0$ the size of the maximal clique in a graph cannot be approximated within a factor of n^ϵ unless P=NP.*

1 Introduction

The notion of NP-completeness [Coo71, Kar72, Lev73] has been used since the early seventies to show the hardness of finding optimum solutions for a large variety of combinatorial optimization problems. The apparent intractability of these problems motivated the search for approximate solutions to these hard optimization problems. For some problems this effort gave good approximation algorithms, but for others it seemed hard even to find near optimal solutions.

The task of proving hardness of the approximation versions of such problems met with limited success. For the traveling salesman problem without triangle inequality Sahni and Gonzalez [SG76] showed that finding a solution within any constant factor of optimal is also NP-hard. Garey and Johnson [GJ76] studied MAX-CLIQUE: the problem of finding the largest clique in a graph. They showed that if a polynomial time algorithm computes MAX-CLIQUE within a constant multiplicative factor then MAX-CLIQUE has a polynomial-time approximation scheme (PTAS) [GJ78], i.e., for any $c > 1$ there exists a polynomial-time algorithm that approximates MAX-CLIQUE within a factor of c. They used graph products to construct "gap increasing reductions" that mapped an instance of the clique problem into another instance in order to enlarge the relative gap of the clique sizes. Berman and Schnitger [BS92] used the ideas of increasing gaps to show that if the clique size of graphs with bounded co-degree (degree of the complement) does not have a randomized PTAS then there is an $\epsilon > 0$ such that MAX-CLIQUE cannot be approximated within a factor of n^ϵ in randomized polynomial-time.

Yet for the most part, not much could be said for a wide variety of problems until very recently. A connection between two seemingly unrelated areas within theoretical computer science, established by Feige et al. [FGLSS91], led to surprisingly strong hardness results for approximating optimization problems. Feige et al. exploited a recent characterization of multi-prover interactive proof systems by Babai, Fortnow and Lund [BFL91] to obtain intractability results for approximating MAX-CLIQUE under the assumption that $NP \not\subseteq DTIME(n^{O(\log\log n)})$.

Recently Arora and Safra [AS92] improved on this by showing that it is NP-hard to approximate MAX-CLIQUE within any constant factor (and even within a factor of $2^{\log n/(\log\log n)^{O(1)}}$). Their solution builds on and further develops the techniques of Feige et al. and yields an elegant new characterization of the class NP in terms of probabilistically checkable proofs.

Relying on their work we further develop these techniques and show that there is no PTAS for a large number of combinatorial optimization problems unless P=NP. These problems, like traveling salesman problem with triangle inequality, minimal steiner tree, maximum directed cut, shortest superstring, etc. be-

*Computer Science Division, U. C. Berkeley, Berkeley, CA 94720. Supported by NSF PYI Grant CCR 8896202.

†AT&T Bell Labs, Murray Hill, NJ 07974.

‡Department of Computer Science, Stanford University, Stanford, CA 94305. Supported by NSF Grant CCR-9010517, and grants from Mitsubishi and OTL.

§Computer Science Division, U. C. Berkeley, Berkeley, CA 94720. Supported by NSF PYI Grant CCR 8896202.

¶AT&T Bell Labs, Murray Hill, NJ 07974.

0-8186-2900-2/92 $3.00 © 1992 IEEE

long to the class of MAXSNP-hard problems, defined by Papadimitriou and Yannakakis [PY91] in terms of logic and reductions that preserves approximability.

Our result also improves the parameters for the MAX-CLIQUE result of Arora and Safra. We show, that there is an $\epsilon > 0$ such that approximating MAX-CLIQUE within a factor of n^ϵ in NP-hard.

In the next section we elaborate on the definition of the class MAXSNP and then move on to give background on probabilistically checkable proofs and formulate our main lemma, which is a characterization of NP that improves on the one in [AS92]. Then we relate this characterization to the non-approximability of MAXSNP. The rest of the paper will be devoted to the proof of the main lemma.

1.1 The class MAXSNP

Given a maximization problem, formulated as $opt_F(x) = \max_y F(x, y)$, an approximation algorithm A is said to achieve worst-case performance ratio $\alpha(n)$ if for every input $x : F(x, A(x)) \geq \alpha(n)^{-1} opt_F(x)$, where n is the size of x.

In 1988 Papadimitriou and Yannakakis [PY91] using Fagin's definition of NP [Fag74] observed that there is an approximation algorithm which has constant performance ratio for any maximization problem that is defined by a quantifier free first order formula φ as

$$opt_\varphi(X) = \max_S : |\{z|\varphi(S, X, z)\}|, \qquad (1)$$

where z is a vector of constant number of first order variables.

Definition 1.1 (Papadimitriou-Yannakakis) *An optimization problem $opt(x)$ belongs to MAXSNP if there is a polynomial-time algorithm that encodes input x into X in (1) such that $opt(x)$ becomes $opt_\varphi(X)$.*

They further considered the following type of "constant gap preserving" reductions:

Definition 1.2 (Papadimitriou-Yannakakis) *Let opt and opt′ be two optimization problems defined by functions F and F'. We say that opt L-reduces to opt′ if there exist two polynomial time algorithms f and g and constants $\alpha, \beta > 0$ such that for each instance x of opt:*

1. *Algorithm f produces an instance x' of opt′ such that $opt'(x') \leq \alpha opt(x)$.*

2. *For any y' algorithm g outputs a y with the property:*

$$|F(x, y) - opt(x)| \leq \beta |F'(x', y') - opt(x')|.$$

A problem *opt* is MAXSNP-hard (complete) if every problem in MAXSNP L-reduces to it (and $opt \in MAXSNP$). Papadimitriou and Yannakakis showed that if any of the MAXSNP-hard problems have a PTAS then every problem in MAXSNP has a PTAS.

MAX-3SAT is a typical MAXSNP-complete problem: Given a conjunction φ of clauses, each a disjunction of 3 variables or their negation, maximize the the number of satisfied clauses over all possible assignments to the variables of φ.

The following problems are also MAXSNP-complete or hard: MAX-SAT; MAX-2SAT; INDEPENDENT SET-B; NODE COVER-B; MAX-CUT; MAX-DIRECTED CUT; METRIC TSP; STEINER TREE; SHORTEST SUPERSTRING; MULTIWAY CUTS; THREE DIMENSIONAL MATCHING. The exact definitions can be found in [PY91, PY92, BP89, BJLTY91, DJPSY92, Kan91].

1.2 Probabilistically checkable proofs

The notion of probabilistically checkable proofs (*PCP*) was introduced by Arora and Safra [AS92], as a slight variation of the notions of *randomized oracle machines* due to Fortnow, Rompel and Sipser [FRS88] and *transparent proofs* due to Babai, Fortnow, Levin and Szegedy [BFLS91]. All these models are in turn variations of interactive proof systems [Bab85, GMR89] and multiprover interactive proof systems [BGKW88].

Definition 1.3 (Arora-Safra [AS92]) *A language L is in PCP$(f(n), g(n))$ if there is polynomial-time randomized oracle machine $M^y(r, x)$ which works as follows:*

1. *It takes input x and a (random) string r of length $O(f(n))$, where $n = |x|$.*

2. *Generates a query set $Q(r, x) = \{q_1, \ldots, q_m\}$ of size $m = O(g(n))$.*

3. *Reads the bits $y_{q_1}, \ldots, y_{q_m}$.*

4. *Makes a polynomial-time computation using the data r, x and $y_{q_1}, \ldots, y_{q_m}$ and outputs $M^y(r, x) \in \{0, 1\}$.*

Moreover the following acceptance conditions hold for some $\delta > 0$ and for all x:

1. *If $x \in L$ then there exists a y such that for every r we have $M^y(r, x) = 1$.*

2. *If $x \notin L$ then for every y we have $Prob_r(M^y(r, x)) = 0) \geq \delta$.*

Observe that the definition does not say anything about the length of y, but it is easy to see that we can assume without loss of generality that $|y| = 2^{O(f(n))}g(n)$. This definition is a generalization of NP since it is clear that $NP = PCP(0, n^{O(1)})$.

Theorem 1 (Arora-Safra [AS92]) $NP = PCP(\log n, (\log\log n)^{O(1)})$.

We improve on the second parameter:

Theorem 2 $NP = PCP(\log n, 1)$.

Much of the paper will be devoted to the proof of this theorem. The connection to clique approximations, of Feige et al., shows that if $NP = PCP(\log n, g(n))$, then the clique size cannot be approximated within a factor of $2^{\Omega(\log n/g(n))}$ unless P=NP. Thus Theorem 2 has the corollary:

Corollary 3 *There is an $\epsilon > 0$ such that to approximate MAX-CLIQUE within a factor of n^ϵ is NP-hard.*

1.3 Related Areas

The results in this paper borrow significantly from results in the area of self-testing/self-correcting of programs (see [BLR90], [Rub90]). The areas of self-testing/correcting are closely connected to the areas of error-detection/correction in coding theory. In particular, we observe that results from the former area can be interpreted as yielding very efficient randomized error-detecting and error-correcting schemes for some well known codes. In Section 4 we use the "linearity tester" of Blum, Luby and Rubinfeld [BLR90] as an efficient error-detection scheme for the Hadamard Codes and this plays a crucial role in our proof. Later in Section 7 we use the "low-degree test" of Rubinfeld and Sudan [RS92], with its improved efficiency due to a technical lemma from [AS92], as an efficient mechanism to test Reed Solomon Codes.

Other ingredients in our proof borrow from work done in "parallelizing" the MIP=NEXPTIME protocol [LS91],[FL92]. The result described in Section 7 uses ideas from their work.

2 PCP and MAXSNP

The methods of [FGLSS91] and [AS92] have been applied so far only to the clique approximation problem. Here we show that the whole class of optimization problems can be handled in the same vein. The results of this section are due to independent observations of Mario Szegedy and Madhu Sudan and appear in [AMSS92].

Proof checking itself is a maximization problem from the point of view of the prover: the task is to maximize the chance of acceptance of the verifier. More formally, let $M^y(x, r)$ be a probabilistic oracle machine and let R be the set of all possible values of r for a given parameter n. The prover's intention is to solve the following optimization problem:

$$\mathbf{opt}(x) = max_y |\{r \in R|\ M^y(x, r) = 1\}|. \quad (2)$$

In this paper we prefer to use the following reformulation of this problem:

$$opt(x) = \max_y Prob_r M^y(x, r). \quad (3)$$

For fixed values of r and x the value of $M^y(x, r)$ can be computed by a circuit, which takes as many input bits from y as the size of the query set. Let us denote this circuit by $C_{x,r}$. Equation 3 can now be rewritten as

$$opt(x) = \max_y Prob_r(C_{x,r}(y) = 1) \quad (4)$$

If M is a $PCP(f(n), g(n))$ machine for a language L then there exists a δ such that $opt(x)$ is 1 if $x \in L$ and $opt(x) \leq 1 - \delta$ if $x \notin L$.

Conversely, if $C_{x,r}(y)$ is a family of circuits such that

1. $|r| = O(f(n))$;
2. given x and r, the circuit $C_{x,r}$ can be built in polynomial size;
3. $C_{x,r}(y)$ feeds from at most $g(n)$ bits of y;
4. for every x the maximization problem corresponding to Equation 4 either has solution 1 or it has solution less than $1 - \delta$ for some fixed δ,

then a probabilistic oracle machine can be built that recognizes the language $x : opt(x) = 1$.

Definition 2.1 *We say that an optimization problem opt is well behaved if there is a δ such that for every x either $opt(x) = 1$ or $opt(x) \leq 1 - \delta$.*

Our observation above can be stated so that there is a one to one correspondence between well behaved optimization problems, where the underlying family of circuits (parameterized by x and r; $|r| = f(|x|)$) is polynomially constructible and the problems in the class $PCP(f(n), g(n))$, where $g(n)$ is determined by the upper bound imposed upon the input size of circuits $C_{x,r}$ where $|x| = n$.

Let $M^y(x, r)$ be a machine PCP machine with constant size query sets that recognizes a language L. Then the size of the members of the the corresponding family of circuits $\{C_{x,r}|x, r\}$ is bounded, since their input size is bounded. To maximize the number of satisfiable constant size circuits each feeding from the same input is in MAX SNP. This can be seen or by reducing the problem to MAX-3SAT or directly (due to Yannakakis):

The input structure consists of a $(k+1)$-ary relation A and 2^k unary relations B_v indexed by the bit-vectors v of length k. A tuple $(r, i_1, ..., i_k)$ is in A if and only if $C_{x,r}$ inputs bits $i_1, ..., i_k$ on this choice (thus, A contains one tuple for each choice). A relation B_v contains a random choice r if and only if the bit vector v satisfies $C_{x,r}$.

The problem is to maximize over all unary relations (sets) S (these are the sets of 1 bits in y) the number of tuples $(r, y_1, ..., y_k)$ that make the following formula true:

$$A(r, y_1, ..., y_k) \wedge \{[B_1 1..1(r) \wedge S(y_1) \ldots \wedge S(y_k)] \vee \ldots$$

$$\vee[B_0..0(r) \wedge \neg S(y_1) ... \wedge \neg S(y_k)]\}$$

When $|r| = f(n)$, the size of the instance $\{C_{x,r}|r\}$ is $2^{|r|} = 2^{O(f(n))}$. Taking the advantage of the gap δ between the optimal value $opt(x)$ for those instances x that are in L versus those that are not in L, an algorithm could solve the membership problem for L, which approximates the $opt(x)$ close enough to 1. Thus we conclude:

Theorem 4 *If MAX SNP complete problems have PTAS, then $PCP(f(n), 1)$ is in $DTIME(2^{O(f(n))})$.*

3 Outline of the Proof of the Main Theorem

Feige et al [FGLSS91] elaborated on the techniques of Babai, Fortnow and Lund [BFL91] to show $NP \subset PCP(\log n \log\log n, \log n \log\log n)$. The $\log n \log\log n$ barrier stood in the way of a full characterization of *NP* by *PCP*. Arora and Safra [AS92] introduced a new technique – recursive proof checking – that enabled them to characterize *NP* as $PCP(\log n, \log\log n)$ [AS92]. In this section we translate this technique into our optimization problem scenario. Among the technicalities we build on data encoding stands out, and it is also a major motif in [BFL91, BFLS91, AS92].

Our proof of Theorem 2 is arrived at by the following basic steps. We observe that the recursion idea of [AS92] can be generalized to apply to any arbitrary proof system provided it satisfies certain restrictions. We shall consider a restricted type of the optimization problems discussed in Section 2.

Definition 3.1 *A well behaved optimization problem $opt(x) = \max_y Prob_{r \in_U \{0,1\}^{f(n)}}(C_{x,r}(y) = 1)$ is restricted with parameters $(f(n), g(n))$ if*

1. *We can partition y into a disjoint union of segments y_i, where each segment has size $O(g(n))$ and that each circuit $C_{x,r}$ depends only on a constant number of such segments.*
2. *Each circuit $C_{x,r}$ has size $(g(n))^{O(1)}$.*

The class of languages recognized by such optimization problems we call $OPT(f(n), g(n))$.

We remark that $PCP(f(n), g(n)) \supseteq OPT(f(n), g(n))$ is straightforward, but the other direction is true but not so straightforward.

In Sections 4 and 7, we work towards the development of such restricted proof systems. The results of these sections show that $NP \subset OPT(\text{poly}(n), 1)$ (Theorem 5) and $NP \subset OPT(\log n, \text{polylog}\, n)$ (Theorem 8). Theorems 9 and 10 show that the recursion idea applies to these proof systems, and in particular shows the following:

1. $OPT(f(n), g(n)) \subset OPT(f(n) + O(\log g(n)), (\log g(n))^{O(1)})$ and
2. $OPT(f(n), g(n)) \subset OPT(f(n) + (g(n))^{O(1)}, 1)$.

This allows us to conclude that $NP \subset OPT(\log n, \text{polyloglog}\, n)$ (by composing two $OPT(\log n, \text{polylog}\, n)$ proof systems) and then by composing this system with the $OPT(\text{poly}(n), 1)$ proof system we obtain $OPT(\log n, 1)$ proof system for *NP*.

4 A PCP machine for NP with constant number of queries

In this section we prove:

Theorem 5 $NP \subseteq PCP(poly(n), 1)$.

When contrasted with $PCP(\log n, 1) = NP$ the lemma may appear weak, nevertheless a slight variation of the construction is an essential ingredient of our proof of Theorem 2.

We construct for 3SAT a $M^y(r, x)$ as in Definition 1.3. For every x let us turn the 3-CNF formula represented by x into an arithmetic circuit C_x over $GF(2)$ with $l = O(|x|)$ gates. Look at x as a Boolean formula and use DeMorgan's laws to eliminate the OR gates and add gates such that the fanin for every gate is at most 2. Thereafter replace every AND gate by a multiplication gate and every negation gate with a gate that computes the function $x \mapsto 1 - x$.

If C_x is satisfiable, the successful setting of the input as well as the values of the gates for this input setting will be encoded by the prover into an exponential size table. The table will also facilitate the lookup of any quadratic expression of these values. If the table errs in more than 1% of the cases, the checking will reveal it with fixed positive probability. Lookups will be error corrected by random reduction. Looking at an appropriate random quadratic expression will reveal if the circuit makes a computational error. The checks are performed simultaneously. Only constantly many bits of the table will be checked.

Introduce variables $g_1, \ldots, g_l$ corresponding to the gates of C_x. We assume that g_l corresponds to the output gate. We define:

$$\mathcal{P}_1 = \{\sum_{i=1}^{l} c_i g_i \mid c_i \in GF(2) \text{ for } 1 \leq i \leq l\};$$

$$\mathcal{P}_2 = \{c_0 + \sum_{i=1}^{l} c_i g_i + \sum_{1 \leq i < j \leq l} c_{ij} g_i g_j \mid c_i,\, c_{ij} \in GF(2)\}.$$

We identify the index set of y with $\mathcal{P}_2$ i.e., y will have lenght $l^2 + l$ and for any $P \in \mathcal{P}_2$ we have a bit y_P in y.

We construct a probability distribution $\mathcal{D}$ over $\mathcal{P}_2$ that depends on C_x (thus on x). For every $1 \leq i \leq l$ let P_i be the polynomial that is 0 if and only if the gate g_i functions properly. That is, if g_i is supposed to compute the product of g_j and g_k, then $P_i = g_i - g_j g_k$. Similarly, for gates that compute addition, $P_i = g_i - (g_j + g_k)$, and for negation gates $P_i = g_i - g_j + 1$. If g_i is one of the input gates then $P_i = 0$. We also introduce a polynomial P_{l+1}, which is 0 if and only if the output gate is 1: $P_{l+1} = g_l - 1$.

Define

$$P_\lambda = \sum_{i=1}^{l+1} \lambda_i P_i,$$

where λ_i are independent uniformly distributed random variables over $GF(2)$; $\lambda = (\lambda_1, \ldots, \lambda_l)$. Clearly $P_\lambda \in \mathcal{P}_2$. Distribution $\mathcal{D}$ is defined by the way a random instance is generated: we take a random seed λ and compute P_λ.

$M^y(x, r)$ is the value of the predicate $I_1 \wedge I_2 \wedge I_3 \wedge I_4$, where

$I_1 : y_P + y_Q = y_{P+Q}$

$I_2 : y_Z + y_{Z+1} - 1 = 0$

$I_3 : (y_R + y_{R+L_1})(y_S + y_{S+L_2}) = (y_T + y_{T+L_1L_2})$

$I_4 : y_U + y_{U+V} = 0$

$P, Q, R, S, T, U, Z \in_{\mathcal{U}} \mathcal{P}_2$; $L_1, L_2 \in_{\mathcal{U}} \mathcal{P}_1$; $V \in_{\mathcal{D}} \mathcal{P}_2$, where $\in_{\mathcal{U}}$ means "chosen according to the uniform distribution" and $\in_{\mathcal{D}}$ means "chosen according to the distribution $\mathcal{D}$." P,Q,R,S,T,U,Z,L_1,L_2 are generated in an obvious manner; V is generated from a random seed λ. Altogether $6(1 + l + \binom{l}{2}) + 2l + (l + 1)$ random bits are used. All the computations can be done in polynomial time. The number of query bits is 13: $q_1 = P; \ldots; q_{13} = U + V$. We are yet to prove that the acceptance conditions hold.

If $x \in L$ then there is an assignment A to the variables of x that $x(A) = 1$. Evaluate C_x on A. We define γ_i as the value of the gate g_i under this evaluation. Clearly $P_i(\gamma) = 0$ for $1 \leq i \leq l$, and $P_{l+1}(\gamma) = 0$, where $\gamma = (\gamma_1, \gamma_2, \ldots, \gamma_l)$. The latter because $C_x(A) = x(A) = 1$.

Define y by $y_P = P(\gamma)$ for $P \in \mathcal{P}_2$.

I_4 holds for every r, since

$$y_U + y_{U+V} = U(\gamma) + (U + V)(\gamma) =$$

$$V(\gamma) = \sum_{i=1}^{l+1} \lambda_i P_i(\gamma).$$

The latter sum evaluates to 0 since γ was defined so that each $P_i(\gamma)$ is 0. To show that I_1, I_2 and I_3 hold is even more obvious.

We prove now that if $x \notin L$ then the test fails with probability at least 0.01 for every y. Assume the opposite, that is that $I_1 \wedge I_2 \wedge I_3 \wedge I_4$ holds with probability at least 0.99 for some y.

First we show that there is a linear function $\mathbf{L}$ from $\mathcal{P}_2$ to $GF(2)$ such that

$$Prob_{P \in_{\mathcal{U}} \mathcal{P}_2}(y_P = \mathbf{L}(P)) \geq 0.98. \qquad (5)$$

Since I_1 holds with probability at least 0.99 we have that $Prob(y_P + y_Q = y_{P+Q}) \geq 0.99$.

The existence of $\mathbf{L}$ now follows directly from the following lemma, due to Blum, Luby and Rubinfeld [BLR90]. The bound we state here appears in Rubinfeld [Rub90] and Gemmel et al. [GLRSW91].

Lemma 6 *Let g be a function such that*

$$Prob_{x,y}(g(x) + g(y) \neq g(x + y)) \leq \delta/2$$

then there exists a linear function $\mathbf{L}$ *such that* $Prob(g(x) \neq \mathbf{L}(x)) \leq \delta$.

Whereas y_P is not always $\mathbf{L}(P)$, Equation 5 gives that for every $P \in \mathcal{P}_2$:

$$Prob_{R \in \mathcal{P}_2}(\mathbf{L}(R) = y_{R+P} + y_P) \geq 0.96. \qquad (6)$$

This fact is referred to as "random reduction." Three instances of random reduction occur in the predicate I_3 and one instance in predicates I_2 and I_4. Our indirect assumption and Inequality 6 allow us to write:

$$Prob_{L_1, L_2 \in_{\mathcal{U}} \mathcal{P}_1}(\mathbf{L}(L_1)\mathbf{L}(L_2) = \mathbf{L}(L_1 L_2)) \geq 0.87, \qquad (7)$$

$$\mathbf{L}(1) = 1, \tag{8}$$

$$Prob_{V \in_{\mathcal{D}} \mathcal{P}_2}(\mathbf{L}(V) = 0) \geq 0.95. \tag{9}$$

We claim that $\mathbf{L}(g_i)\mathbf{L}(g_j) = \mathbf{L}(g_i g_j)$ for all $1 \leq i, j \leq l$. Consider the matrices Y and Z defined by $Y(i,j) = \mathbf{L}(g_i)\mathbf{L}(g_j)$ and $Z(i,j) = \mathbf{L}(g_i g_j)$. Let the vector $v = v(L_1)$ be the vector of the coefficients of the linear function L_1. Similarly $w = w(L_2)$ is the vector of the coefficients of L_2. $\mathbf{L}(L_1)\mathbf{L}(L_2) = v^T Y w$ and $\mathbf{L}(L_1 L_2) = v^T Z w$. If the linear forms L_1 and L_2 are drawn randomly and independently from $\mathcal{P}_1$ then the vectors v and w are drawn randomly and independently from $GF(2)^l$.

We now use the argument of Freivald [Fre79] to show that $Y = Z$. It is easily verified that if $Y \neq Z$ then with probability at least 0.5, $v^T Y \neq v^T Z$. Moreover, for vectors $\alpha, \beta \in \mathcal{Z}_2^n$ and $w \in_R \mathcal{Z}_2^n$, if $\alpha \neq \beta$ then with probability at least 0.5, $\alpha^T w \neq \beta^T w$. It follows that for random v and w, if $Y \neq Z$ then with probability at least 0.25, $v^T Y w \neq v^T Z w$. Thus from Inequality 7 we get that $Y = Z$. This in turn vindicates our claim.

The values $\mathbf{L}(g_i)$ for $i = 1, \ldots, l$ and $\mathbf{L}(g_i g_j) = \mathbf{L}(g_i)\mathbf{L}(g_j)$ determine the value of $\mathbf{L}(P)$ for any $P \in \mathcal{P}_2$ by linearity. Let us denote $\mathbf{L}(g_i)$ by γ_i. Then $\mathbf{L}(P)$ is expressed as $P(\gamma)$ (note that we here use that $\mathbf{L}(1) = 1$).

Now, since x is not satisfiable, $\mathbf{L}(P_i) = P_i(\gamma) \neq 0$ for at least one of $1 \leq i \leq l+1$. But then

$$Prob_{V \in_{\mathcal{D}} \mathcal{P}_2}(\mathbf{L}(V) = 0) =$$

$$Prob_{V \in_{\mathcal{D}} \mathcal{P}_2}(V(\gamma) = 0) =$$

$$Prob_{\lambda \in_U GF(2)^l}(\sum_{i=1}^{l+1} \lambda_i P_i(\gamma) = 0) = 0.5,$$

which contradicts Inequality 9. □

Later we need the following interpretation of the theorem:

Theorem 7 *Let $C(y)$ be a circuit, where $|y| = n$. We can construct a family $\mathcal{F}_c = \{C_r(y') | r \in R\}$ of circuits each of size at most $O(1)$ where y' is identified with $\mathcal{P}_2$ such that*

1. $|R| = 2^{O(2^n)}$;
2. *If $C(y) = 1$ then there is a setting of y' such that*
   - *(a) $Prob_r(C_r(y') = 1) = 1$*
   - *(b) $Prob_{Q \in \mathcal{P}_2}(y_Q + y_{Q+g_i} = g_i(y_i)) = 1$, where $g(y)$ is the value of gate g for input y.*
3. *If $Prob_r(C_r(y') = 1) \geq 1 - \delta$ then there is a y such that $C(y) = 1$ and for every gate g_i of C $Prob_{Q \in \mathcal{P}_2}(y_Q + y_{Q+g_i} = g_i(y_i)) \geq 1 - 4\delta$.*

5 Reducing the number of query bits

In this section we reduce the size of the circuits that define well behaved optimalization problem. We will heavily use ideas in [BFLS91, AS92].

5.1 Encoding schemes

An encoding scheme $E = \{E_n\}$ is a polynomial time computable sequence of functions $E_n : \{0,1\}^n \rightarrow \{0,1\}^{p(n)}$, where $p(n)$ is a function that is polynomial in n. Moreover there is a $\delta > 0$ such that for every n if x and x' are two different strings of length n then the hamming distance $dist(x, x')$ between $E(x)$ and $E(x')$ is at least δn. An encoding scheme can be constructed using the Reed-Solomon codes [MS81]. For an encoding scheme we define the decoding $E^{-1}(z)$ as the x that minimizes $dist(E(x), z)$.

5.2 Circuit verification

The theorem of proof verification in [BFLS91] we turn into circuit verification.

Theorem 8 *Let $C(y)$ be an arbitrary circuit. Then a polynomial size family of circuits $C_r(y', y'')$ can be computed in polynomial-time from C and r with the properties:*

1. *Each circuit has size $(\log n)^{O(1)}$ and each of them depends only on a constant number of input bits from y'.*
2. *If $C_x(y) = 1$, then there exists a y'' such that $Prob_r(C_r(E(y), y'') = 1) = 1$.*
3. *If $Prob_r(C_r(y', y'') = 1) \geq 1 - \delta$ then $C(E^{-1}(y')) = 1$.*

The theorem can be generalized to circuits with constant number of inputs $y_1, y_2, \ldots, y_c$:

Theorem 9 *Let $C(y_1, y_2, \ldots, y_c)$ be an arbitrary circuit. Then a polynomial size family of circuits $C_r(y'_1, \ldots, y'_c, y'')$ can be computed in polynomial-time from C and r with the properties:*

1. *Each circuit has size $(\log n)^{O(1)}$ and each of them depends only on a constant number of input bits from y'_i for all $i = 1, 2, \ldots, c$.*
2. *If $C_x(y) = 1$, then there exists a y'' such that $Prob_r(C_r(E(y_1), \ldots, E(y_c), y'') = 1) = 1$.*
3. *If $Prob_r(C_r(y', y'') = 1) \geq 1 - \delta$ then $C(E^{-1}(y'_1), \ldots, E^{-1}(y_c)) = 1$.*

Theorem 10 *In Theorem 9 we can also assume that y'' in segmented in such a way that the corresponding family of circuits meets the the segmentation requirement in Definition 3.1.*

The proof of this theorem is the topic of Section 7.

5.3 The reduction step

We show that we can take a well behaved optimization problem and use the circuit verification results from the previous section and obtain another well behaved optimization problem that recognizes the same language but where the circuits are much smaller. The basic idea is to use the circuit verification to verify that the circuits describing the optimization problem is satisfied.

Theorem 11 $OPT(f(n), g(n)) \subset OPT(f(n) + O(\log g(n)), (\log g(n))^{O(1)})$.

Proof: Let $opt(x) = \max_y Prob_r(C_{x,r}(y) = 1)$ be a well behaved and restricted optimization problem that recognizes a language in $OPT(f(n), g(n))$. We construct another opt' as follows. Fix x and r. Without loss of generality for notational simplicity we assume that the circuit $C_{x,r}(y', y'')$ relies only on segments $y_1, \ldots, y_c$. Consider the family of circuits $\mathcal{F}_{x,r} = \{C_{x,r,r'}(y'_1, \ldots, y'_c, y''_r)|r')\}$ given by Theorem 10.

The set of circuits $\bigcup_r \mathcal{F}_{x,r}$ is such that

1. each circuit can be computed from x, r and r' in polynomial time;
2. each circuit has size $\log^{O(1)} g(n)$;
3. the new input set $y' = \bigcup_i y'_i \cup \bigcup_r y_r$ can be segmented in the following way: each y_r is segmented as required in Theorem 10 and the segment size is $\log^{O(1)} g(n)$. Let us decompose the first union (each y'_i) into segments of size 1. As it is required in Theorem 10, each $C_{x,r,r'}$ takes only a constant number of bits from $\bigcup_i y'_i$ and a constant number of segments from $\bigcup_r y_r$.

We have to argue now that the optimization problem

$$opt'(x) = \max_y Prob_{r,r'}(C_{x,r,r'}(y') = 1) \qquad (10)$$

is well behaved and the underlying language is the same as for opt.

Assume $opt(x) = 1$. then if we set each y'_i to $E(y_i)$ for $(1 \le i \le l)$, where y_i $(1 \le i \le l)$ is a solution of $opt(x)$, then by Theorem 7 for every r there exists a y''_r such that under this setting α of y' all the circuits $C_{x,r,r'}$ output 1. Thus $Prob_r(C_{x,r,r'}(\alpha) = 1) = 1$.

Assume now that $opt(x) \le 1 - \delta$. Let us denote the set of all possible random strings r by R. Let y' be arbitrary. Let $y_i = E^{-1}(y'_i)$ $(1 \le i \le l)$. Let us denote by B the set of those r's for which $C_{r,x}(y_1, y_2, \ldots, y_c) = 0$. By our assumption $|B|/|R| \le 1 - \delta'$. We have

$$Prob_{r,r'}(C_{x,r,r'}(y') = 1) =$$

$$\sum_{r \in R} \frac{Prob_{r'}(C_{x,r,r'}(y') = 1)}{|R|} \le$$

$$\frac{|B|(1-\delta) + (|R| - |B|)}{|R|} \le 1 - \delta\delta'. \square$$

6 The final verification

Theorem 12 *Let E be an arbitrary encoding scheme with parameter $p(n)$. Let $C(y_1, y_2, \ldots, y_c)$ be an arbitrary circuit of size n. Then there is a family $\mathcal{F} = \{C_r | r \in R\}$ of circuits on inputs $y'_1, \ldots, y'_c, y''$, $\delta > 0$ such that:*

1. *$|R| = 2^{n^{O(1)}}$.*
2. *Each circuit has size $O(1)$ and can be constructed in polynomial time given x and r.*
3. *If $C(y) = 1$, then there exists a y'' such that $Prob_r(C_r(E(y_1), \ldots, E(y_c), y'') = 1) = 1$.*
4. *If $Prob_r(C_r(y'_1, \ldots, y'_c, y'') = 1) \ge 1 - \delta$ then $C(E^{-1}(y'_1), \ldots, E^{-1}(y_c)) = 1$, where $\delta > 0$ is some constant depending only on c.*

Proof Let $C'(y_1, y_2, \ldots, y_c)$ be such a circuit that we obtain from C by adding extra gates to it to compute all the bits of each $E(y_i)$ for $i = 1 \ldots c$. We denote by $g_{i,j}$ the gate that computes the jth bit of $E(i)$ $(E(i,j))$. Build a circuit verification scheme for C' as in Theorem 7. We identify y'' with the bits of this verification scheme. Let each y'_i have length $p(|y_i|)$. Now flip a coin.

1. If tail, then by further coin flips choose a circuit from the verification scheme for C'.
2. If head, then pick randomly a number between 1 and c, and compare a randomly chosen bit $y'_i[j]$ of y'_i with the value that the scheme y'' gives for $E(i,j)$. To compute this bit we have to look at y_Q and $y_{g_{i,j}+Q}$, where Q is a random element of $\mathcal{P}_2$. The check $y_Q + y_{g_{i,j}+Q} = y'_i[j]$ can be computed by a constant size circuit $C_{i,j,Q}$.

Family $\mathcal{F}$ is a union of $\{C_{i,j,Q} | 1 \leq i \leq c; 1 \leq j \leq p(|y'_i|); Q \in \mathcal{P}_2\}$ and the circuits of the circuit verification scheme for C'. The multiplicity of each circuit in the family is proportional to the probability with which it occurs in the above checking procedure. We leave the easy proof to the reader that the scheme satisfies the conditions of the theorem. □

Using the recursion idea (Theorem 11) and the above circuit verification procedure we obtain:

Theorem 13 $OPT(f(n), g(n)) \subset OPT(f(n) + (g(n))^{O(1)}, 1)$.

7 Segmentation

The major obstacle is that the proof y can not be segmented in such a way that the verifier only accesses a constant number of segments. We overcome this by showing that we can transform an unsegmented proof into a segmented proof where the verifier only accesses a constant number of segments.

Lemma 14 *For any polynomial-time computable collection (the old query set)*

$$\{Q_r \subset \{1, 2, \ldots, n\} | r \in \{0,1\}^t\}$$

then there exist a polynomial-time computable family of circuits $D_{r,r'}$ and a $\delta > 0$ such that for every string y such that $|y| = n$ there exists a string $\tilde{y}$ such that:

1. *We can partition $\tilde{y}$ into segments $\tilde{y}_1, \tilde{y}_2, \ldots, \tilde{y}_{\tilde{m}}$ all of length $l = O(k \log^2 n)$, where $k = \max_r |Q_r|$.*
2. *Each circuit has size $l^{O(1)}$ and has inputs from only a constant number of segments. The circuit $D_{r,r'}$ outputs either reject or a string of length $|Q_r|$. Furthermore r' has length $O(\log n + \frac{\log k \log n}{\log \log n})$.*
3. *For all r, r' we have that $D_{r,r'}(\tilde{y}) = y[Q_r]$, where $y[Q_r]$ is the substring of y indexed by Q_r.*
4. *For all $z \in \{0,1\}^{\tilde{m}}$ if there exists an r_0 such that*

   $$Prob_{r'}(D_{r_0,r'}(z) = reject) \leq \delta$$

   then there exists a y such that for all r:

   $$Prob_{r'}(D_{r,r'}(z) \notin \{reject, y[Q_r]\}) \leq 3\delta$$

Proof: The proof relies on the low degree code E [BFL91, BFLS91] and a technical lemma about checking E [RS92].

$E(y)$ is a function $E(y) : GF(p)^d \rightarrow GF(p)$, where $d = \lceil \log n / \log \log n \rceil$ and p is a prime in $[(k \log n)^c, 2(k \log n)^c]$ for some constant c. Let $I = \{1, 2, \ldots \lceil \log n \rceil\} \subset GF(p)$. Since $|I^d| \geq n$ we can use I^d as indexes of the bits of y. Thus we can look at y as a function from I^d to $\{0,1\}$. Given a function $y : I^d \rightarrow \{0,1\}$ there exists a unique multivariate polynomial $E(y)$ over $GF(p)$ that for all $\alpha \in I^d$ agrees with y and the degree of any variable is bounded by $|I| - 1$. Note that the "total" degree of $E(y)$ is at most $d|I|$.

The new string $\tilde{y}$ contains three tables:

- A table Y indexed by $GF(p)^d$, where segment α contains $E(y)(\alpha)$.
- A table Y_{lines} that is indexed by $(GF(p)^l)^2$, where segment (α, β) contains the polynomial $E(y)(t\alpha + (1-t)\beta)$.
- A table T that is indexed by $\{0,1\}^t \times GF(p)^d$. Let $Q_r = \{q_1, q_2, \ldots, q_k\}$. The segment (r, α) contains a polynomial $p_{r,\alpha}$ of degree at most $k(|I|-1)d$ such that $p_{r,\alpha}(0) = E(y)(\alpha), p_{r,\alpha}(1) = E(y)(q_1), \ldots, p_{r,\alpha}(k) = E(y)(q_k)$.

  The $p_{r,\alpha}$ exists, since it is possible to construct, by interpolation, a parameterized curve $C_{r,\alpha} : F_p \rightarrow F_p^l$ such that $C_{r,\alpha}(0) = r, C_{r,\alpha}(1) = q_1, \ldots, C_{r,\alpha}(k) = q_k$ and such that each coordinate function of $C_{r,\alpha}$ is a polynomial of degree k. Now $p_{r,\alpha}(t) = E(Y)(C_{r,\alpha}(t))$.

Let $r' = (\alpha, \beta, t, t')$ where $\alpha, \beta, \in GF(p)^d$ and $t, t' \in \{k+1, \ldots, p-1\}$. The circuit $D_{r,r'}$ checks that $Y[t\alpha + (1-t)\beta] = Y_{\text{lines}}[\alpha, \beta](t)$, $T[(r, \alpha)](t') = Y[C_{r,\alpha}(t')]$. If any of the checks fail then $D_{r,r'}$ rejects otherwise it's ith output for $i = 1, \ldots, k$ will be the least significant bit of $T[(r, \alpha)](i)$.

Note that given these definition it follows that

$$\forall r, r' : D_{r,r'}(\tilde{y}) = y[Q_r].$$

Thus we only need to prove the 4th claim, hence assume $z = (Y, Y_{\text{lines}}, T)$ is a string and for some r_0 we have that

$$Prob_{r'}(D_{r_0,r'}(z) \neq \text{reject}) \geq 1 - \delta.$$

This implies that

$$Prob_{(\alpha,\beta,t)}(Y[t\alpha + (1-t)\beta] \neq Y_{\text{lines}}[\alpha, \beta](t)) < \delta.$$

As in Section 4 we need a code checking lemma. This one is due to Rubinfeld and Sudan [RS92].

Lemma 15 (Rubinfeld-Sudan [RS92]) *Let* $g : GF(p)^d \mapsto GF(p)$ *be a function and let* g_{lines} *be a function that given* $\alpha, \beta \in GF(p)^d$ *determines a polynomial* $p_{\alpha,\beta}$ *of degree at most* k *such that* $p = O((kd)^c)$, *where* c *is some universal constant, and*

$$Prob_{\alpha,\beta,t}(g(t\alpha + (1-t)\beta) \neq g_{lines}(\alpha,\beta)(t)) \leq \delta$$

then there exists a multivariate polynomial f *of degree at most* k *such that* $Prob_\alpha(g(\alpha) \neq f(\alpha)) \leq 2\delta$.

Thus we can conclude that there exists a polynomial g such that

$$Prob_\alpha(Y[\alpha] \neq g(\alpha)) < 2\delta. \qquad (11)$$

Let y_i be the least significant bit of $g(i)$, where $i \in I^d$ (remember that we index the bits in a n bit string by I^d).

Let r be an arbitrary random string. If $T[(r,\alpha)] \neq g(C_{r,\alpha})$ then for at most $k(|I|-1)d$ values of t we have that $T[(r,\alpha)](t) = g(C_{r,\alpha}(t))$. Note that $C_{r,\alpha}(t)$ is uniformly distributed over $GF(p)^d$ when $\alpha, t \in_{\mathcal{U}} GF(p) \times \{k+1, \ldots, p-1\}$. Thus

$$\begin{aligned} & Prob_{r'}(D_{r,r'}(z) \notin \{\text{reject}, y[Q_r]\}) \\ = \; & Prob_{r'}(T[(r,\alpha)] \neq g(C_{r,\alpha}) \text{ and} \\ & \quad T[(r,\alpha)](t) = Y[C_{r,\alpha}(t)]) \\ \leq \; & Prob_{r'}(T[(r,\alpha)] \neq g(C_{r,\alpha}) \text{ and} \\ & \quad T[(r,\alpha)](t) = g[C_{r,\alpha}(t)]) + 2\delta \\ \leq \; & \frac{k(|I|-1)d}{p-k-1} + 2\delta < 3\delta \; \square \end{aligned}$$

8 Further Work

Several questions remain open. There is a big gap between the (negligible) constants in the hardness results and the approximation ratio currently achievable for the MAXSNP problems. For example, MAX SAT can only be approximated to a ratio of 4/3 [Yan92], while MAX CUT and vertex cover can only be approximated to a ratio of 2 [GJ79, Mot92].

The recent results of Lund and Yannakakis [LY92] showed that the chromatic number is as hard to approximate as the clique and thus solce a long-standing open problem. They also show that the logarithmic ratio achievable for the set cover problem is essentially the best possible. Can the former result be extended to the case of 3-colorable graphs?

Another open problem is that of approximating the longest path in a graph. Based on our results, Karger, Motwani and Ramkumar and Azar [KMR92, Azar92] show that unless $P = NP$ there is no constant ratio approximation algorithm for longest paths. It is conjectured that this problem is as hard to approximate as clique or chromatic number.

Acknowledgments

We acknowledge the contribution of Muli Safra. Furthermore we would like to thank the contributions of Yossi Azar, Manuel Blum, Tomas Feder, Joan Feigenbaum, Lance Fortnow, Magnus Halldorsson, David Karger, Moni Naor, Steven Phillips, Umesh Vazirani and Mihalis Yannakakis.

References

[AMSS92] S. Arora, R. Motwani, S. Safra and M. Sudan. PCP and Approximation Problems. Unpublished note, 1992.

[AS92] S. Arora and S. Safra. Probabilistic Checking of Proofs: A New Characterization of NP. In *Proc. 33rd IEEE Symp. on Foundations of Computer Science*, 1992.

[Azar92] Y. Azar. Personal Communication. 1992.

[Bab85] L. Babai. Trading group theory for randomness. In *Proc. 17th ACM Symp. on Theory of Computing*, pages 421–420, 1985.

[BFL91] L. Babai, L. Fortnow, and C. Lund. Non-deterministic Exponential Time has Two-Prover Interactive Protocols. *Computational Complexity*, vol. 1, pages 3–40, 1991.

[BFLS91] L. Babai, L. Fortnow, L. Levin, and M. Szegedy. Checking Computations in Polylogarithmic Time. In *Proc. 23rd ACM Symp. of Theory of Computing*, pages 21–31, 1991.

[BGKW88] M. Ben-Or, S. Goldwasser, J. Kilian and A. Wigderson. Multi-prover interactive proofs: How to remove intractability. In *Proc. 20th ACM Symp. on Theory of Computing*, pages 113–131, 1988.

[BJLTY91] A. Blum, T. Jiang, M. Li, J. Tromp and M. Yannakakis. Linear Approximation of Shortest Superstrings. In *Proc. 23rd ACM Symp. on Theory of Computing* pages 328–336, 1991.

[BLR90] M. Blum, M. Luby, R. Rubinfeld. Self-Testing/Correcting with Applications to Numerical Problems. In *Proc. 22th ACM Symp. on Theory of Computing*, pages 73–83, 1990.

[BP89] M. Bern and P. Plassmann. The Steiner problem with edge lengths 1 and 2. *Information Processing Letters*, vol. 32, pages 171–176, 1989.

[BS92] P. Berman and G. Schnitger. On the Complexity of Approximating the Independent Set Problem. *Information and Computation*, vol. 96, pages 77–94, 1992.

[Coo71] S. A. Cook. The complexity of theorem-proving procedures. In *Proc. 3rd ACM Symp. on Theory of Computing*, pages 151–158, 1971.

[DJPSY92] E. Dahlhaus, D. S. Johnson, C. H. Papaditriou, P. D. Seymour and M. Yannakakis. The complexity of multiway cuts. In *Proc. 24th ACM Symp. on Theory of Computing*, pages 241–451, 1992.

[Fag74] R. Fagin. Generalized First-Order Spectra and Polynomial-time Recognizable Sets. In Richard Karp (ed.), *Complexity of Computer Computations*, AMS, 1974.

[Fre79] R. Freivalds. Fast Probabilistic Algorithms. In *Mathematical Foundations of Computer Science*. Springer-Verlag Lecture Notes in Computer Science, No. 74, pages 57–69, 1979.

[FGLSS91] U. Feige, S. Goldwasser, L. Lovász, S. Safra, and M. Szegedy. Approximating clique is almost NP-complete. In *Proc. 32nd IEEE Symp. on Foundations of Computer Science*, pages 2–12, 1991.

[FL92] U. Feige and L. Lovasz. Two-Prover One-Round Proof Systems: Their Power and Their Problems. In *Proc. of 24th ACM Symp. on Theory of Computing*, pages 733–744, 1992.

[FRS88] L. Fortnow, J. Rompel and M. Sipser. On the power of multi-prover interactive protocols. In *Proc. 3rd IEEE Symp. on Structure in Complexity Theory*, pages 156–161, 1988.

[GJ76] Michael R. Garey and David S. Johnson. The complexity of near-optimal graph coloring. *J. of the ACM*, vol 23, pages 43-49, 1976.

[GJ78] Michael R. Garey and David S. Johnson. "Strong" NP-completeness results: motivation, examples and Implications. *J. of the ACM*, vol 25, pages 499-508, 1978.

[GJ79] Michael R. Garey and David S. Johnson. *Computers and Intractability: A Guide to the Theory of NP-Completeness*. W. H. Freeman, 1979.

[GLRSW91] P. Gemmell, R. Lipton, R. Rubinfeld, M. Sudan, and A. Wigderson. Self-Testing/Correcting for Polynomials and for Approximate Functions. In *Proc. 23th ACM Symp. on Theory of Computing*, pages 32–42, 1991.

[GMR89] S. Goldwasser, S. Micali and C. Rackoff. The Knowledge Complexity of Interactive Proof Systems. *SIAM Journal on Computing*, vol. 18, pages 186–208, 1989.

[Kan91] V. Kann. Maximum bounded 3-dimensional matching is MAXSNP-complete. *Information Processing Letters*, vol. 37, pages 27-35, 1991.

[Kar72] R.M. Karp. Reducibility among combinatorial problems. In Raymond E. Miller and James W. Thatcher, editors, *Complexity of Computer Computations*, pages 85–103. Plenum Press, 1972.

[KMR92] D. Karger, R. Motwani and G. D. S. Ramkumar. On Approximating the Longest Path in a Graph. Manuscript, 1992.

[Lev73] L. Levin. Universal'nyĭe perebornyĭe zadachi (Universal search problems, in Russian), In *Problemy Peredachi Informatsii*, vol. 9, pages 265–266, 1973. A corrected English translation appears in an appendix to Trakhtenbrot [Tra84]

[LFKN90] C. Lund, L. Fortnow, H. Karloff, and N. Nisan. Algebraic methods for interactive proof systems. In *Proc. 22nd ACM Symp. on Theory of Computing*, pages 2–10, 1990.

[LS91] D. Lapidot and A. Shamir. Fully Parallelized Multi Prover Protocols for NEXP-time. In *Proc. 32nd IEEE Symp. on Foundations of Computer Science*, pages 13–18, 1991.

[LY92] C. Lund and M. Yannakakis. On the Hardness of Approximating Minimization Problems. Manuscript, 1992.

[MS81] F. MacWilliams and N. Sloane. *The Theory of Error-Correcting Codes*. North-Holland, 1981.

[Mot92] R. Motwani. Lecture Notes on Approximation Algorithms. Technical Report, Dept. of Computer Science, Stanford University (1992).

[PY91] C. H. Papadimitriou and M. Yannakakis. Optimization, Approximation, and Complexity Classes. *Journal of Computer and System Sciences*, vol. 43, pages 425–440, 1991.

[PY92] C. H. Papadimitriou and M. Yannakakis. The traveling salesman problem with distances one and two, *Mathematics of Operations Research*, to appear.

[Rub90] R. Rubinfeld. A Mathematical Theory of Self-Checking, Self-Testing and Self-Correcting Programs. Ph.D. Thesis, Computer Science Department, U.C. Berkeley, 1990.

[RS92] R. Rubinfeld, and M. Sudan. Testing Polynomial Functions Efficiently and over Rational Domains. In *Proc. 3rd Annual ACM-SIAM Symp. on Discrete Algorithms*, pages 23–32, 1992.

[Sha90] A. Shamir. IP=PSPACE. In *Proc. 22nd ACM Symp. on Theory of Computing*, pages 11–15, 1990.

[SG76] S. Sahni and T. Gonzalez. P-complete approximation problems. *JACM*, vol. 23, pages 555–565, 1976.

[Tra84] B. A. Trakhtenbrot. A survey of Russian approaches to *Perebor* (brute-force search) algorithms. In *Annals of the History of Computing* vol. 6, pages 384–400, 1984.

[Yan92] M. Yannakakis. On the Approximation of Maximum Satisfiability. In *Proc. 3rd Annual ACM-SIAM Symp. on Discrete Algorithms*, pages 1–9, 1992.

Undirected Connectivity in $O(\log^{1.5} n)$ Space*

Noam Nisan
CS Department
Hebrew University
Jerusalem, Israel

Endre Szemeredi
Department of Mathematics
Rutgers University
New Brunswick, N.J

Avi Wigderson
CS Department
Hebrew University
Jerusalem, Israel
and
Princeton University
Princeton, N.J.

Abstract

We present a deterministic algorithm for the connectivity problem on undirected graphs that runs in $O(\log^{1.5} n)$ space. Thus, the recursive doubling technique of Savich which requires $\Theta(\log^2 n)$ space is not optimal for this problem.

1 Introduction

The *st*-connectivity problem is one of the most basic graph problems, and has received much attention. Given a directed graph G and two vertices in it s and t, the problem is to determine whether there exists a directed path from s to t in G. Several linear time algorithms are known for this problem; they all require linear space. The best space complexity known for this problem is $O(\log^2 n)$, which is achieved by Savitch's algorithm [Sav70]. It is a long standing open problem to find a smaller space algorithm for connectivity. As connectivity is complete for the complexity class NL, such an algorithm would imply improved deterministic simulation of nondeterministic space. It has thus been conjectured that such algorithms cannot be found and that Savitch's algorithm is indeed optimal.

A special case of the connectivity problem which is of special interest is "undirected connectivity", i.e. the case where G is undirected. For this case a *randomized* Logspace algorithm was given in [AKL*79] (with a zero-error version in [BCD*89]). No *deterministic* algorithm that improved upon Savitch's space requirement was known, although improved time-space tradeoffs were given in [BR91, Nis91]. It has also been a long standing open problem to improve upon Savitch's algorithm even for undirected graphs.

In this paper we present such an algorithm. Our algorithm solves the connectivity problem on undirected graphs and uses only $O(\log^{1.5} n)$ space. The algorithm uses the universal sequences obtained from the pseudorandom generators of [Nis90], as well as pair-wise independent sampling. It is also possible to give a variant of our algorithm that does not rely on any pseudorandom generators and still beats Savitch's algorithm by requiring only $O(\log^2 n/ \log\log n)$ space.

An immediate application is a EREW parallel algorithm for undirected connectivity that runs in $O(\log^{1.5} n)$ time and uses a polynomial number of processors. The same time bound was achieved in [JM91] in the weaker CREW model using only a linear number of processors. Recently, [KNP92] show how a variant of our algorithm can be implemented on an EREW PRAM using a linear number of processors.

2 The Algorithm

2.1 Top Level

The input to our algorithm is an undirected graph G over N vertices. It outputs whether or not vertex 1 is connected to vertex 2 in the graph.

The main procedure we will use is procedure *shrink*. This procedure accepts as input a graph G over n vertices and a parameter n'. Its output can take two forms. It may either output an answer whether vertex 1 is connected to vertex 2 in G or else it may output a graph G' over n' vertices with the property that vertex 1 is connected to vertex 2 in G' if and only if vertex 1 is connected to vertex 2 in G. Procedure shrink requires $O(\log n + (\log(n/n'))^2)$ space.

*The first and last authors were partially supported by the Wolfson Research Awards

0-8186-2900-2/92 $3.00 © 1992 IEEE

Let us now see how we solve the connectivity problem on a graph G with N vertices using procedure shrink. We can view procedure shrink as answering queries of the form $(u, v) \in E(G')$?, where its input is given by queries of the form $(u, v) \in E(G)$?. We will thus use procedure shrink recursively. For $i = 0 \ldots \sqrt{\log N}$ define $n_i = 2^{i\sqrt{\log N}}$. The i'th recursion level of procedure shrink will work on a graph G_i over n_i vertices, and its output will be the graph G_{i-1} over n_{i-1} vertices. It will answer queries of the $(i-1)$'st recursion level regarding G_{i-1} by running procedure shrink on the graph G_i (using queries which are, in turn, answered by the $i+1$'st recursion level etc.). The base of the recursion is the $\sqrt{\log N}$'th level where we have the original graph G.

Notice that (1) G_0 is trivial so the first recursion level tells us whether vertex 1 is connected to vertex 2; (2) The recursion depth is only $\sqrt{\log N}$; (3) Each recursion level requires $O(\log N)$ space (since $\log(n_i/n_{i-1}) = \sqrt{\log N}$).

2.2 Procedure Shrink: Overview

Procedure shrink accepts a graph G over n vertices, and must output a graph G' which is smaller than G by a factor of $f = n/n'$ and still captures the connectivity of G. The Outline of the algorithm is as follows:

1. For each vertex v we find a set $N(v)$ of vertices that are connected to v in G. This set is of size polynomial in f. (Unless v's connected component is smaller than that – these cases are immediately discarded).

2. A subset R of the vertices of G is chosen. R is of size $n' = n/f$ and it satisfies the condition that for every vertex v it intersects $N(v)$. R will be the vertex set of G'.

3. For each vertex v we choose a representative vertex $rep(v) \in R \cap N(v)$. The edges of G' are now all the edges of the form $(rep(u), rep(v))$ where (u, v) is an edge of G.

The first stage is implemented by walking in G, starting form v, along a universal sequence for graphs of size $poly(f)$. We use the universal sequences of Nisan [Nis90] which can be generated in space $O(\log^2 f)$.

The second stage is implemented by using pair-wise independence, where each vertex decides at random to be in R with probability $O(1/f)$. This takes care of intersecting almost all $N(v)$'s, and we have to add only a small number of extra vertices from the unsatisfied $N(v)$'s. Again by trying all possibilities from the pair-wise independent space this stage is done deterministically.

Remark: as is usual when working in sub-linear space we cannot store any of the intermediate results (such as $N(v)$ or R) in our limited working storage. One should thus view this outline as describing procedures, each one implemented using calls to the previous one.

2.3 Details of Procedure Shrink

2.3.1 Computing $N(v)$

$N(v)$ is computed by walking along a universal sequence. We will use universal sequences for 3-regular graphs as defined in [AKL*79].

Definition 1 *A 3-regular graph G is called labeled if the three edges adjacent to each vertex are numbered by some permutation of $1, 2, 3$. For a vertex v in G and a string $\sigma \in \{1, 2, 3\}^*$, a walk on G starting from v and following the directions of σ is naturally defined.*

We say that σ is an m-universal traversal sequence if for every connected 3-regular m-vertex graph G, every labeling of it and every vertex v, the walk on G starting from v following σ visits all vertices of G.

In [AKL*79] it is shown that polynomial length universal sequences exist. The best explicit construction known is due to [Nis90]:

Theorem 1 *For every m there exists an m-universal sequence σ of length $m^{O(\log m)}$. Each entry σ_i of these sequences can be computed in $O(\log^2 m)$ space.*

Let $\sigma \in \{1, 2, 3\}^*$. We wish to walk on a non-regular graph G according to σ. To do this we imagine each vertex of degree $d > 3$ as composed of d pseudo-vertices connected to each other by a cycle. Each of these pseudo-vertices has degree 3: two edges being part of the cycle, and one edge going outward, being one of the edges of the original vertex. We can now naturally use σ to perform a walk on the 3-regular graph composed of these pseudo-vertices.

Remark: One can easily extend the definition and constructions of universal sequences to non-regular graphs. If this is done then this slight complication of "converting" a non-regular graph to a 3-regular one can be eliminated.

Fix $m = 6^4 f^4$, and let $\sigma \in \{1, 2, 3\}^*$ be an m-universal sequence. For every vertex v we will walk on G, starting from v, according to σ. Define $N(v)$ to be the set of vertices encountered in this walk, as well as their immediate neighbours.

For the computation of each step of the walk we need only remember the current pseudo-vertex and generate one entry from the sequence. Thus each step and hence enumerating $N(v)$ can be done in space $O(\log n + \log^2 f)$.

It is clear that $N(v)$ is a subset of the connected component of v. We will show that $N(v)$ is also rather large, unless it equals to the whole connected componnet of v (denoted $Comp(v)$).

Lemma 1 *If σ is an m-universal sequence, then either $N(v) = Comp(v)$ or $|N(v)| \geq \sqrt{m}$.*

Using our choice of m we get that for every vertex v, $|N(v)| \geq 36f^2$.

2.3.2 Representatives

We first choose a subset L of the vertices to be possible representatives. L will be chosen from a pairwise independent distribution, as to satisfy a certain condition given below. Vertices 1 and 2 will then be added to it. L will be represented succintly using $O(\log n)$ bits by its index in the probability space. Once L is chosen we define $rep_L(v)$ for every vertex v as follows:

1. If $N(v) = Comp(v)$ then $rep_L(v) = 0$. (No representative needed if component is too small.)
2. Else, if $N(v) \cap L = \emptyset$ then $rep_L(v) = v$.
3. Else (the "usual" case), $rep_L(v)$ is the smallest labeled vertex in $N(v) \cap L$.

The final set of representatives will be $R_L = \{rep_L(v)\}$ where v ranges over all vertices of G. I.e. R_L will contain some vertices from L as well as those vertices v that have no L-member in $N(v)$ even though $N(v) \neq Comp(v)$.

The condition that L must satisfy is that $|R_L| \leq n' = n/f$. The fact that such a set can be found in a pairwise independent distribution space is ensured by the following lemma.

Lemma 2 *If L is chosen at random such that every vertex is in L with probability $1/(6f)$ and the choices are pair-wise independent, then $Pr[|R_L| \leq n'] > 0$.*

Let us briefly discuss the algorithmic aspects. Let us first see that $rep_L(v)$ can be computed form v and L in space $O(\log n + \log^2 f)$. Cases 2 and 3 are easy as we need only enumerate the vertices of $N(v)$. Checking whether $N(v) = Comp(v)$ is done by going over all vertices $u \in N(v)$; for each u we check that for all its neighbours w it is also true that $w \in N(v)$.

Choosing L is done as follows. We use a space of polynomial (in n) size satisfying the conditions of the lemma, and such that computing for a vertex v whether $v \in L$ is easy given the $O(\log n)$ bits which are the index of L in the space. (Such spaces are well known, e.g., take a field F_q of size poly(n); each L is defined by two elements $a, b \in F_q$; and $v \in L_{a,b}$ if $av + b \in \{1 \dots q/(6f)\}$.) We go over all possibilities of L in the space (in a fixed order). For each we construct R_L, and check whether its size is small enough. If so we stick with this (first encountered) L.

2.3.3 The Algorithm

1. If $N(1) = Comp(1)$ or $N(2) = Comp(2)$ Then
   (a) If $2 \in N(1)$ Then Output("Connected") and Halt.
   (b) Else Output("Not Connected") and Halt.
2. Choose L as described in the previous subsection.
3. If $rep_L(2) = 1$ Then Output("Connected") and Halt.
4. The vertex set of G' is R_L.
5. An edge (u, v) is an edge of G' if there exists an edge (u', v') of G such that $rep_L(u') = u$ and $rep_L(v') = v$.

Remark: Formally one should rename the vertices of R_L to have the names $1 \dots n'$. This is easily done by renaming v to be its rank in R_L.

It is clear that in those cases that this algorithm actually gives an answer it is correct. Correctness when a graph G' is produced is ensured by:

Lemma 3 *If the previous algorithm outputs a graph G' then Vertex 1 is connected to vertex 2 in G if and only if vertex 1 is connected to vertex 2 in G'.*

3 Proofs of correctness

3.1 Proof of lemma 1

Assume that $N(v)$ does not satisfy the lemma. Let $N'(v)$ be the subset of vertices actually visited by the walk. ($N(v)$, by definition, includes also the neighbours of vertices in $N'(v)$).

As $N(v)$ is contained in $Comp(v)$, but is not equal to all of it, there must be a vertex $u \in Comp(v) - N(v)$

which is adjacent to a vertex $w \in N(v)$. It is clear that $w \notin N'(v)$. Now consider the induced graph on $N(v)$, and consider the graph of pseudo-vertices composing the vertices of this graph. This is a connected 3-regular graph. Its size is at most m since $|N(v)| \leq \sqrt{m}$ and each vertex is composed of at most $\sqrt{m}$ pseudo-vertices. However, a walk from v according to σ on this graph will behave exactly as the walk from v performed in G, and thus will not visit w. This contradicts σ being a universal sequence for 3-regular m-vertex graphs.

3.2 Proof of lemma 2

R_L is composed of two types of vertices: those in L and those vertices v such that satisfy both $N(v) \cap L = \emptyset$ and $|N(v)| \geq 36f^2$. Call the second set of vertices B. We will show that (w.h.p.) these two subsets are small.

Claim 1: With probability of at least 2/3, $|L| \leq n'/2$.

Claim 2: With probability of at lest 2/3, $|B| \leq n'/2$.

It follows that with probability of at least 1/3 the size of both sets combined is at most n'.

Proof of Claim 1: The expected size of L is $n/(6f) = n'/6$. Using the Markov inequality, the probability that $|L|$ is at least 3 times its expected value is at most 1/3.

Proof of Claim 2: Fix a vertex v such that $|N(v)| \geq 36f^2$. We assume w.l.o.g. that actually $|N(v)| = 36f^2$. We will first show that

$$Pr_L[v \in B] = Pr_L[N(v) \cap L = \emptyset] \leq 1/(6f)$$

For each vertex $u \in N(v)$ we define a random variable X_u which is 1 if $u \in L$ and 0 otherwise. The variables X_u are pairwise independent. We also define a random variable $X = \sum_{u \in N(v)} X_u$. We have that $v \in B$ iff $X = 0$. We bound the probability that $X = 0$ using the Chebyshev inequality. The expected value of X is $E(X) = |N(v)|/(6f) = 6f$. The variance of X may be computed as if the X_u's were truly independent, and is $Var(X) = |N(v)| \cdot 1/(6f) \cdot (1 - 1/(6f)) \leq 6f$. Using the Chebyshev inequality,

$$Pr[X = 0] \leq Pr[|X - E(X)| \geq 6f] \leq$$

$$\leq (6f)^{-2} Var(X) \leq 1/(6f)$$

It follows that the expected size of B is at most $n/(6f) = n'/6$. Finally, using the Markov inequality, the probability that $|B|$ is more than 3 times its expected value is at most 1/3.

3.3 Proof of lemma 3

First note that $rep(1) = 1$ and $rep(2) = 2$ since we always put vertices 1 and 2 in L and we always take the smallest numbered vertex in $N(v) \cap L$ as $rep(v)$. (The algorithm has specifically ruled out the possibilities that $rep(1) = 0$ or $rep(2) = 0$ or $rep(2) = 1$.)

Assume that vertex 1 is connected to vertex 2 in G'. Notice that if u is a neighbour of v in G' then there is a path from u to v in G. The reason is that there exists an edge (u', v') in G such that $rep(u') = u$ and $rep(v') = v$. Since, in G, u' is connected to $u = rep(u')$ and v' is connected to $v = rep(v')$, we get that u is connected to v in G. It follows that if vertex 1 is connected to vertex 2 in G' they are also connected in G.

Conversely, assume that 1 is connected to 2 in G say thru the path $v_1, v_2, ..., v_k$. In this case we claim that 1 will be connected to 2 in G' thru the path $rep(v_1), rep(v_2), ..., rep(v_k)$. Indeed, notice that if v and u are neighbours in G then either $rep(u) = rep(v)$, or else $rep(u)$ is a neighbour of $rep(v)$ in G'.

4 Variants and Remarks

Small modifications of this algorithm, as well as using some of its ideas can give several other results. In particulr the following remarks should be made.

- It is possible to obatin an $O(\log^2 n / \log\log n)$ algorithm for connectivity without using any pseudorandom generators. This gives an elementary algorithm beating Savitch's bound. By taking, starting from a vertex v, all possible walks specified by $O(\log n)$ bits, one can ensure seeing at least $\log n / \log\log n$ vertices. This is so since it is sufficient to keep track of which outgoing edge was taken from each encountered vertex in the DFS, and untill a vertex of degree higher than $\log n$ is encountered (in which case we can stop), only $\log\log n$ bits are needed per vertex. Doing this enables one to get sets $N(v)$ of size $\log n / \log\log n$ (instead of size $2^{\sqrt{\log n}}$ using universal sequences). Procedure shrink can then be used to shrink the graph by a factor of $(\log n)^{\Theta(1)}$, getting a recursion depth of only $\log n / \log\log n$.
- It has been suggested by [KNP92] and by [RT92] that the usage of pair-wise independence can be eliminated. The following mechanism can be used to choose the set of representatives R instead: a vertex v is in R if $N(v)$ does not intersect $N(w)$

for all vertices w of lower rank (in a fixed ordering). As the chosen v's have pairwise disjoint $N(v)$'s, we have $|R| \leq n/f$ as long as $|N(v)| \geq f$ for every vertex v. Choosing a representative $rep(v)$ for every vertex v is now slightly more complicated as is is not always true that R intersects $N(v)$. However, the following simple loop easily finds a representative $rep(v) \in R$:

1. $u \leftarrow v$
2. while $u \notin R$ do
   - $u \leftarrow min(w)$ such that $N(u) \cap N(w) \neq \emptyset$.
3. $rep(v) \leftarrow u$

- For various specific families of graphs one can get an $O(\log n)$ space algorithm. For example, let $t(n)$ be the largest size of a graph for which we can test connectivity in $O(\log n)$ space (we have $t(n) \geq exp((\log n)^{2/3})$). It is possible to test connectivity on graphs of minimum degree $n/t(n)$ in Logspace. Simply we let $N(v)$ be the neighbour set of v, and one application of procedure shrink can reduce the graph size to $t(n)$.

- One can find neighbour sets $N(v)$ of size n^ϵ quite easily using BFS or DFS. This allows procedure shrink to shrink the graph by a factor of n^ϵ and achieve only a constant recursion depth. This yields a polynomial-time $O(n^\epsilon)$-space algorithm for connectivity. In fact this algorithm resembles that of [BR91].

- It is well known (see e.g. [KR90]) that LOGSPACE can be simulated by an EREW PRAM running in logarithmic time and polynomial number of processors. Thus it is not difficult to convert our algorithm to a parallel one that requires $O(\log^{3/2} n)$ time on an EREW PRAM, and uses a polynomial number of processors. This matches the time bound of the recent algorithm of [JM91], which works on the stronger CREW PRAM. We note, however, that they need only a linear number of processors, while in our algorithm the polynomial is quite hugh. In [KNP92] a linear-procesor variant of our EREW algorithm is obtained.

- All the algorithms above can be easily converted so as to produce the connected components of the input graph, as well as a path between every connected pair of vertices.

- Any improved construction of universal sequences may be plugged into our algorithm to obatin an improved algorithm for connectivity. In fact our algorithm may be seen to convert a wide variaty of algorithms for connectivity (e.g. some JAG algorithms [CR80]) to faster ones. This is done by using such an algorithm to find the sets $N(v)$.

References

[AKL*79] R. Aleliunas, R.M. Karp, R.J. Lipton, L. Lovasz, and C. Rackoff. Random walks, universal sequences and the complexity of maze problems. In 20th *Annual Symposium on Foundations of Computer Science, San Juan, Puerto Rico*, 1979.

[BR91] G. Barnes, and W.L. Ruzzo. Deterministic algorithms for undirected $s-t$ connectivity using polynomial time and sublinear space. In *Proceedings of the* 23st *Annual ACM Symposium on Theory of Computing*, 1991.

[BCD*89] A. Borodin, S.A. Cook, P.W. Dymond, W.L. Ruzzo, and M. Tompa. Two applications of inductive counting for complementation problems. *SIAM J. Comput.*, 18(3):559–578, 1989.

[BNS90] L. Babai, N. Nisan, and M. Szegedy. Multiparty Protocols and Logspace-hard pseudorandom sequences. In *Proceedings of the* 22nd *Annual ACM Symposium on Theory of Computing*, 1990.

[CR80] S. Cook and C. Rackoff. Space Lower Bounds for Maze Threadability on Restricted Machines. In *SIAM J. Comput.*, 9(3): 636–652, 1980.

[JM91] D.B. Johnson, and P. Metaxas. Connected Components in $O(\log^{3/2}|V|)$ parallel time for the CREW PRAM. *Proceedings of the* 32nd *Annual Symposium on Foundations of Computer Science, San Juan, Puerto Rico*, 1991.

[KNP92] D. Karger, N. Nisan, and M. Parnas. Fast Connected Components Algorithms for the EREW PRAM. To appear in *SPAA*, 1992.

[KR90] R. M. Karp and V. Ramachandran. Parallel Algorithms for Shared-Memory Machines.

In *Handbook of Theoretical Computer Science*, Vol A, J. van Leeuwen Ed., 869–932, 1990.

[Nis90] N. Nisan. Pseudorandom generators for space-bounded computation. In *Proceedings of the 22st Annual ACM Symposium on Theory of Computing*, 1990.

[Nis91] N. Nisan. $RL \subseteq SC$. *Proceedings of the 24th Annual ACM Symposium on Theory of Computing*, 1992.

[RT92] V. Rakesh and M. Tompa. Private communication.

[Sav70] W.J. Savitch. Relationships between nondeterministic and deterministic space complexities. *J. Comp. and Syst. Sci.*, 4(2):177-192, 1970.

The Isomorphism Conjecture Holds Relative to an Oracle*

Stephen Fenner† Lance Fortnow‡ Stuart A. Kurtz§

Abstract

Is it possible to define a notion of genericity such that all **NP**-*complete sets are p-isomorphic?* Judy Goldsmith and Deborah Joseph [GJ86]

We introduce symmetric perfect generic sets. These sets vary from the usual generic sets by allowing limited infinite encoding into the oracle. We then show that the Berman-Hartmanis isomorphism conjecture [BH77] holds relative to any sp-generic oracle, i.e., for any symmetric perfect generic set A, all $\mathbf{NP}^A$-complete sets are polynomial-time isomorphic relative to A. Prior to this work there were no known oracles relative to which the isomorphism conjecture held.

As part of our proof that the isomorphism conjecture holds relative to symmetric perfect generic sets we also show that $\mathbf{P}^A = \mathbf{FewP}^A$ for any symmetric perfect generic A.

1 Introduction

We construct an oracle relative to which the Berman-Hartmanis Isomorphism Conjecture [BH76, BH77] is true. This conjecture holds that any two **NP**-complete sets are isomorphic to one another by a polynomial time computable and invertible one-one reduction. The Isomorphism Conjecture has been the subject of considerable research. We recommend the surveys by Joseph and Young [JY90] and Kurtz, Mahaney and Royer [KMR90].

The attempt to construct oracles relative to which the isomorphism conjecture either succeeded or failed began soon after the conjecture was made in 1976.

Success was first obtained in finding oracles relative to which the conjecture fails. In 1983, Kurtz (in an unpublished manuscript) constructed an oracle relative to which the conjecture failed. Hartmanis and Hemachandra [HH91] later combined Kurtz's construction with Rackoff's construction of an oracle relative to which **P** = **UP**. In 1989, Kurtz, Mahaney and Royer [KMR89] showed that the conjecture fails relative to a random oracle; and Kurtz [Kur88] gave an improved version of his original construction that showed that the conjecture fails relative to a generic oracle.

The attempt to construct an oracle relative to which the conjecture succeeds has proven much more difficult. Even partial successes have been viewed as important advances. In 1986, Goldsmith and Joseph [GJ86] constructed an oracle relative to which a partially relativized version of the isomorphism conjecture holds, specifically, there is an oracle A such that all of the p-complete sets for $\mathbf{NP}^A$ are p^A-isomorphic. In 1987, Kurtz, Mahaney and Royer [KMR87] gave a relativized version of their collapsing degree

*A full version of this paper is available from the second author.

†University of Southern Maine, 96 Falmouth St., Portland, ME 04103. Email: fenner@usm.maine.edu. Partially supported by NSF grant CCR 92-09833.

‡University of Chicago, Department of Computer Science, 1100 E. 58th St., Chicago, IL 60637. Email: fortnow@cs.uchicago.edu. Partially supported by NSF grants CCR 90-09936 and RCD 92-53582.

§University of Chicago, Department of Computer Science, 1100 E. 58th St., Chicago, IL 60637. Email: stuart@cs.uchicago.edu.

0-8186-2900-2/92 $3.00 © 1992 IEEE

construction, and showed that there is an oracle A relative to which *some* **NP** m-degree collapsed. Finally, in 1989, Homer and Selman [HS89, HS92] gave an oracle relative to which the complete degree for Σ_2^{P} collapsed.

We introduce a new notion of genericity, and define the *symmetric, perfect generic sets* (a.k.a. the *sp-generic sets*), and show

Theorem 1.1 *Relative to any symmetric perfect generic set A, all* **NP***-complete sets are polynomial-time isomorphic.*

After describing the mathematical background needed for this paper, in Section 3 we will describe sp-generic sets and give some of their properties. In Section 4 we will give some intuition for the proof of the isomorphism conjecture followed by the detailed proof.

2 Mathematical Preliminaries

The natural numbers are denoted by $\mathbf{N}$. The cardinality of a set X is denoted by $\|X\|$. Let $\Sigma = \{0, 1\}$.

We will use lower case Greek letters for partial functions from $\Sigma^* \rightarrow \{0, 1\}$. We say τ *extends* σ to mean that τ is equal to σ everywhere that σ is defined. We often identify a language $A \subseteq \Sigma^*$ as its characteristic function. The everywhere undefined function is denoted by $\emptyset$. Two functions are *compatible* if they agree everywhere both are defined. For compatible σ and τ, the smallest partial function extending both is denoted $\sigma \cup \tau$. We use dom(τ) and range(τ) to represent the domain and range of τ respectively.

We will sometimes need a machine to know the domain of τ as well as the values of τ on its domain. For these machines we will define the total function $\bar{\tau} : \Sigma^* \times \{0, 1\} \rightarrow \{0, 1\}$ as follows:

$$\bar{\tau}(x, i) = \begin{cases} 1 & \text{if } x \in \mathrm{dom}(\tau) \ \&\ \tau(x) = i \\ 0 & \text{otherwise} \end{cases}$$

By abuse of terminology we will on occasion use the expression "$f^A(x)$" to refer to one of: (i) the value $f^A(x)$, (ii) the function $x \mapsto f^A(x)$, or (iii) the computation of a particular machine computing f on input x using oracle A. We will try to make clear which interpretation of "$f^A(x)$" we mean when it cannot easily be inferred from context.

A 1-1 polynomial-time function f^A is *invertible relative to A* if there exists a polynomial-time function g^A such that for all $x \in \Sigma^*$, $g^A(f^A(x)) = x$.

For a function f and an oracle A, let $f^{A(-1)}(z)$ be the set of strings x such that $f^A(x) = z$.

Let CNF^A be the set of closed relativized conjunctive normal formulae (see [GJ86]) allowing only "$\exists$" as a quantifier. We consider the formulae in a closed form, e.g., instead of a formula looking like $(x \vee y)$ it will look like $\exists x \exists y(x \vee y)$. This will allow us to talk about "true" and "false" formulae and make it easier to combine formulae with other expressions. SAT^A consists of the CNF^A formulae that are true relative to the oracle A.

We assume that for all oracles A, the following properties of CNF^A and SAT^A hold:

1. For every nondeterministic oracle Turing machine M that runs in time $O(n^i)$ there exists a polynomial-time unrelativized function f such that
   (a) f reduces $L(M^A)$ to SAT^A, and
   (b) for all x, $|f(x)| = O(|x|^{2i})$.
2. Every formula $\varphi \in \mathrm{CNF}^A$ has a representation as a binary string. Every binary string represents a formula in CNF^A.
3. Every formula represented by a binary string of n bits can only depend on A on strings of length shorter than n.
4. There is an unrelativized padding function p such that for all formulae φ and strings z,
   (a) $p(\varphi, z)$ is true if and only if φ is true,
   (b) $|p(\varphi, z)| > \max(|\varphi|, |z|)$, and
   (c) from $p(\varphi, z)$ we can in polynomial time recover φ and z.

Berman and Hartmanis [BH77] observed that for any languages B and L such that B is $\mathbf{NP}^A$-complete and has such a padding function and L

in $\mathbf{NP}^A$, there is a one-to-one length-increasing invertible reduction from L to B.

Let $i = \langle i_0, i_1 \rangle$ using the standard pairing function. Let $f_0, \ldots$ be an enumeration of functions where f_i simulates the deterministic oracle Turing machine with code i_0 running in time n^i. Let $M_0, \ldots$ be an enumeration of nondeterministic oracle machines where M_i simulates the Turing machine with code i_1 running in time n^i.

We use **FP** to represent the class of polynomial-time computable functions.

3 sp-Generic Sets

Definition 3.1 *A sequence $\langle a_i \rangle_{i \in \mathbf{N}}$ of integers form an* iterated-polynomial sequence *if there exists a polynomial p such that $p(n) \geq n^2$ for all n, $a_0 \geq 2$ and $a_{i+1} = p(a_i)$ for all i.*

Definition 3.2 *A partial characteristic function $\tau : \Sigma^* \to \{0, 1\}$ is a* symmetric perfect forcing condition *if there is an iterated-polynomial sequence $\langle a_i \rangle_{i \in \mathbf{N}}$ such that*

$$\left(\bigcup_{i \in \mathbf{N}} \Sigma^{a_i}\right) \cap \mathrm{dom}(\tau) = \emptyset$$

In other words $\tau(x)$ is undefined for all x such that $|x| = a_i$ for some $i \in \mathbf{N}$. Note that $\tau(x)$ may be undefined on other x as well.

We generally refer to symmetric perfect forcing conditions as *sp-conditions.* As opposed to conventional forcing conditions, sp-conditions cannot necessarily be coded into finite objects.

Definition 3.3 *A set S of symmetric perfect forcing conditions is* dense *if every sp-condition τ is extended by an sp-condition σ in S.*

Definition 3.4 *A language A is* symmetric perfect generic *(sp-generic) if for every definable dense set S of sp-conditions, there is a $\sigma \in S$ extended by A.*

By *definable* we mean Π_1^1-definable.

The following theorem is a simple adaptation of the Baire Category Theorem.

Theorem 3.1 *Every sp-condition τ is extended by an sp-generic language A.*

Proof: Let $D_1, \ldots$ be an enumeration of the definable dense sets. Let $\sigma_0 = \tau$. For every $i > 0$, let $\sigma_i = \sigma$ for some $\sigma \in D_i$ such that σ extends σ_{i-1}. For all $x \in \Sigma^*$, let $A(x) = \lim_{i \to \infty} \bar{\sigma}_i(x, 1)$. □

Definition 3.5 *A proposition $P(A)$ is said to be* forced *by an sp-condition τ if $P(A)$ is true for all oracles A extending τ.*

Note that this definition is simpler but different from the usual definition of forcing on generic sets.

We can already see the power of sp-generic sets by the following lemma:

Lemma 3.2 *Given any sp-condition τ and any language X there is an sp-condition σ extending τ such that σ forces $X \in \mathrm{P}^A$.*

Proof: Let $\langle a_i \rangle_{i \in \mathbf{N}}$ be the iterated-polynomial sequence such that τ is undefined on strings of length $\langle a_i \rangle_{i \in \mathbf{N}}$. For each i, let $b_i = a_{2i}$ and $d_i = a_{2i+1}$. Let $f(x) = x01^j$ where j is the smallest value such that $|x01^j| = d_i$ for some i. Clearly j is bounded by a polynomial in $|x|$, f is 1-1 and $\mathrm{range}(f) \cap \mathrm{dom}(\tau) = \emptyset$. Define $\sigma(y)$ as

$$\sigma(y) = \begin{cases} \tau(y) & \text{if } y \in \mathrm{dom}(\tau) \\ 1 & \text{if } y = f(x) \ \& \ x \in X \\ 0 & \text{if } y = f(x) \ \& \ x \notin X \\ \text{undefined} & \text{otherwise} \end{cases}$$

Thus for any A extending σ, $x \in X$ if and only if $f(x) \in A$. The partial function σ is undefined on strings of length $\langle b_i \rangle_{i \in \mathbf{N}}$ so σ is an sp-condition. □

Theorem 3.3 *If A is an sp-generic oracle then $\mathbf{P}^A = \mathbf{FewP}^A$.*

The idea of the proof is as follows: Given a (usual) generic set G and an arbitrary $\mathbf{UP}^G$ machine M^G, an algorithm is constructed in [BI87] (using techniques from [HH91]) to compute $L(M^G)$ in polynomial time using G and SAT as oracles. We generalize this algorithm to compute $L(M^G)$ for an arbitrary $\mathbf{FewP}^G$ machine M, again using G and SAT as oracles. Now if G is sp-generic, the same algorithm works, but we can now encode SAT directly into G by Lemma 3.2, thus we can compute $L(M^G)$ using G alone. This puts $L(M^G)$ into $\mathbf{P}^G$. A crucial ingredient in the [BI87] algorithm was that the generic oracle forced M to behave like a **UP** machine *for all oracles.* The same forcing occurs with sp-generics.

Immediate corollary:

Corollary 3.4 *For any sp-generic oracle A, $\mathbf{P}^A = \mathbf{UP}^A$.*

4 Isomorphism Conjecture

In this section we give some of the ideas of the proof that the isomorphism conjecture holds relative to sp-generic oracles. A detailed presentation begins in Section 4.1.

We first consider how researchers created oracles for which the isomorphism conjecture fails. Typically, they would create a hard function f^A and an oracle A such that $f^A(\mathrm{SAT}^A)$ is **NP**-complete, but not isomorphic to SAT^A. One approach is to have f^A scramble SAT in a way that no reduction to $f^A(\mathrm{SAT}^A)$ could be invertible. Kurtz, Mahaney and Royer used this approach to show that the isomorphism conjecture fails to a random oracle [KMR89]. However since we know that $\mathbf{P}^A = \mathbf{UP}^A$ for sp-generic oracles A (Corollary 3.4), any purported scrambling function can be unscrambled.

When Kurtz showed that the isomorphism conjecture fails for regular generic oracles [Kur88] and Hartmanis and Hemachandra created an oracle A relative to which the isomorphism conjecture fails while $\mathbf{P}^A = \mathbf{UP}^A \neq \mathbf{NP}^A$ [HH91] they had to use a different approach. They created functions f^A that work as follows: $f^A(\varphi)$ using A will try to find a witness to φ. If a witness is found then f^A will map to some small fixed true formula, otherwise f^A will output φ. Note for any oracle A and this kind of f^A, $f^A(\mathrm{SAT}^A)$ is $\mathbf{NP}^A$-complete. Using an A that encodes solutions to SAT^A and an f^A that knows how to find those solutions, Kurtz and Hartmanis and Hemachandra show that $f^A(\mathrm{SAT}^A)$ contains large gaps and cannot be isomorphic to SAT^A on density issues alone.

We will need a notion of "goodness" for the computation of $f^A(\varphi)$. In order to motivate the notion of "goodness" of a computation that we will eventually use, we will consider for the next few paragraphs a reduction $\tilde{f}^A$ which has the property of those used by Kurtz and Hartmanis and Hemachandra, i.e., $\tilde{f}^A(\varphi)$ will either find an assignment to φ and map to a small fixed true formula or $\tilde{f}^A(\varphi)$ will map to φ.

Kurtz and Hartmanis and Hemachandra design an oracle A and such a function $\tilde{f}^A(\varphi)$ that prevent isomorphisms to SAT^A work by having $\tilde{f}^A(\varphi)$ use A to find an assignment to φ. Since we are trying to create an oracle A such that the isomorphism conjecture holds, we will call $\tilde{f}^A(\varphi)$ *bad* if $\tilde{f}^A(\varphi)$ finds an assignment to φ and all other computations $\tilde{f}^A(\varphi)$ we will call *good.* Note that if $\tilde{f}^A(\varphi)$ is good then $\tilde{f}^A(\varphi) = \varphi$. Whether $\tilde{f}^A(\varphi)$ is good may depend on A.

We will show that for any sp-generic A and any such $\tilde{f}^A$, $\tilde{f}^A(\mathrm{SAT}^A)$ is isomorphic to SAT^A.

Berman and Hartmanis [BH77] show that in order to have SAT^A isomorphic to $\tilde{f}^A(\mathrm{SAT}^A)$ we need only find a polynomial-time 1-1 length-increasing invertible function g^A that reduces SAT^A to $\tilde{f}^A(\mathrm{SAT}^A)$. Our $g^A(\varphi)$ will work as follows: Find a ψ such that

1. $|\psi| > |\varphi|$
2. ψ is true relative to A iff φ is true relative to A
3. $\tilde{f}^A(\psi)$ is good.

Then $g^A(\varphi) = \tilde{f}^A(\psi) = \psi$ is our reduction. The trick is for $g^A(\varphi)$ to find such a ψ.

We use a straight-forward combinatorial argument to show that there exists an invertible polynomial-time function $h(\varphi, w)$ such that

1. For all w, $|h(\varphi, w)| > |\varphi|$
2. For all w and sp-generic A, $h(\varphi, w)$ is true relative to A iff φ is true relative to A

3. For all sp-generic A there exists a w such that $\tilde{f}^A(h(\varphi, w))$ is good.

We will often use φ_w to represent $h(\varphi, w)$. Now all g^A has to do is find a w such that $\tilde{f}^A(\varphi_w)$ is good. We will use $\tilde{f}^A$ to help g^A in this task.

Let $s(\varphi)$ be the formula that encodes the **NP** statement: "φ is true and there exists a w such that $\tilde{f}^A(\varphi_w)$ is good." Clearly for all sp-generic A, $|s(\varphi)| > |\varphi|$ and $s(\varphi)$ is true iff φ is true because there always is a w such that $\tilde{f}^A(\varphi_w)$ is good.

We now create $g^A(\varphi)$ as follows: Look at the computation of $\tilde{f}^A(s(\varphi))$. If $\tilde{f}^A(s(\varphi))$ is good then output $\tilde{f}^A(s(\varphi)) = s(\varphi)$. Otherwise $\tilde{f}^A(s(\varphi))$ found an assignment to $s(\varphi)$ and thus a w such that $\tilde{f}^A(\varphi_w)$ is good. The function g^A then outputs $\tilde{f}^A(\varphi_w) = \varphi_w$ for that w. Notice that g^A is not only length-increasing but also 1-1 and invertible.

Of course there is no reason that a general f^A has to act like $\tilde{f}^A$. We will however force f^A to look similar to a $\tilde{f}^A$ or not be a reduction.

Suppose f^A reduces SAT^A to $L(M^A)$ where f^A is an arbitrary deterministic function running in time n^i and M^A is a nondeterministic Turing machine also running in time n^i. Let us define φ_w as a formula that encodes the following:

$$(\varphi \wedge \exists y \langle \varphi, w, y, 1\rangle \in A) \vee \exists y \langle \varphi, y, 0\rangle \in A$$

where the y's are quantified over strings of length $|\varphi|^i$. If we put in at least one string of the form $\langle \varphi, w, y, 1\rangle$ in A and no strings of the form $\langle \varphi, y, 0\rangle$ then φ is true if and only if φ_w is true.

We now need a notion of goodness for $f^A(\varphi_w)$ for arbitrary f^A. We would like to call $f^A(\varphi_w)$ good if $f^A(\varphi_w)$ fails to find an assignment to φ_w. However such a thing could be hard to verify. We could, however, determine which queries to A are made by $f^A(\varphi_w)$. Thus we call $f^A(\varphi_w)$ good if $f^A(\varphi_w)$ does not query any string $\langle \varphi, w, y, 1\rangle$ when $\langle \varphi, w, y, 1\rangle \in A$, i.e., $f^A(\varphi_w)$ does not find this part of an assignment to φ_w. If $f^A(\varphi_w)$ is good then we can alter the truth value of φ_w without affecting the value $f^A(\varphi_w)$.

Roughly, if $f^A(\varphi_w)$ is good then $f^A(\varphi_w)$ must map to something similar to φ_w. If $f^A(\varphi_w)$ maps to a string no longer than φ, or if $f^A(\psi_{w_1}) = f^A(\theta_{w_2})$ for $\psi \neq \theta$, then an sp-generic oracle will prevent f^A from being a reduction as described below.

Suppose $f^A(\varphi_w)$ is good and $q = |f^A(\varphi_w)| \leq |\varphi|$. Then $M^A(q)$ cannot ask questions of the form $\langle \varphi, w, y, 1\rangle$ or $\langle \varphi, y, 0\rangle$ because they are too long. We can prevent f^A from being a reduction by setting the truth value of φ_w to true if $M^A(q)$ rejects or setting the truth value of φ_w to false if $M^A(q)$ accepts.

Suppose $f^A(\psi_{w_1}) = f^A(\theta_{w_2})$ and neither machine asks questions about whether $\langle \psi, w_1, y, 1\rangle$, $\langle \psi, y, 0\rangle$, $\langle \theta, w_2, y, 1\rangle$ or $\langle \theta, y, 0\rangle$ are in A. Then we can prevent f^A from being a reduction by setting the truth value of ψ_{w_1} to true and the truth value of θ_{w_2} to false.

We can combine the above techniques under the auspices of sp-generics to produce a reduction g that is length-increasing and almost 1-1. Using the fact that $\mathbf{P}^A = \mathbf{FewP}^A$ for sp-generic A and applying this construction twice we can produce a 1-1 length-increasing reduction g. Grollmann and Selman [GS88] show that we get g invertible for free since $\mathbf{P}^A = \mathbf{UP}^A$ for sp-generic A.

4.1 Proof of the Relativized Isomorphism Conjecture

In order to formally prove Theorem 1.1, we need the following technical lemma.

Lemma 4.1 *For any sp-generic set A: If a polynomial-time function f^A reduces SAT^A to $L(M^A)$ where M^A is a nondeterministic polynomial-time machine then there is a polynomial-time function g^A and a polynomial $p(n)$ such that*

1. *g^A reduces SAT^A to $L(M^A)$*
2. *g^A is length increasing*
3. *For all $q \in \Sigma^*$, if $\|g^{A(-1)}(q)\| > 1$ then*
   (a) $\|f^{A(-1)}(q)\| > 1$
   (b) *q is in $L(M^A)$*
   (c) $\|g^{A(-1)}(q)\| \leq p(|q|)$

We sketch a proof of Lemma 4.1 in Section 4.2.

Using this lemma, we can now show that the isomorphism conjecture holds relative to an sp-generic oracle A:

Let L be $\mathbf{NP}^A$-complete. There must exist an nondeterministic polynomial-time machine M and a polynomial-time function f such that $L = L(M^A)$ and f^A reduces SAT^A to L. Apply Lemma 4.1 and let g^A be the function that fulfills the properties of this lemma.

Let $T = \{q \mid \|g^{A(-1)}(q)\| > 1\}$. Note that T is in $\mathbf{FewP}^A$ because of 2 and 3(c) and thus T is in $\mathbf{P}^A$ since $\mathbf{P}^A = \mathbf{FewP}^A$ relative to sp-generic oracles (Theorem 3.3).

Let θ be a fixed tautology such as $(\exists x)x \vee \bar{x}$. Define $\hat{f}^A(\varphi)$ as follows:

$$\hat{f}^A(\varphi) = \begin{cases} g^A(\theta) & \text{if } g^A(\varphi) \in T \\ g^A(\varphi) & \text{otherwise} \end{cases}$$

Note that $\hat{f}^A$ is a reduction from SAT^A to L because of 3(b).

Apply Lemma 4.1 this time to $\hat{f}^A$ and let $\hat{g}^A$ be the resulting function. Note that the only possible q such that $\|\hat{g}^{A(-1)}(q)\| > 1$ is $q = g^A(\theta)$ because of 3(a).

Let $G^A(\varphi) = \hat{g}^A(p(\varphi, q))$ where p is the padding function for SAT^A. Berman and Hartmanis [BH77] show that Lemma 4.2 below immediately implies that SAT^A is p^A-isomorphic to L.

Lemma 4.2 *The function G^A is a 1-1 length increasing reduction from SAT^A to L whose inverse is computable in* $\mathbf{FP}^A$.

Proof: Clearly G^A is a reduction. Since $\hat{g}^A$ and p are length increasing then G^A is length increasing. Also G^A is 1-1: Suppose $G^A(\varphi) = G^A(\psi)$ then $\hat{g}^A(p(\varphi, q)) = \hat{g}^A(p(\psi, q)) = q$ but this contradicts the fact that $\hat{g}^A$ is length increasing.

By Corollary 3.4, we know that $\mathbf{P}^A = \mathbf{UP}^A$. Grollmann and Selman [GS88] show that $\mathbf{P}^A = \mathbf{UP}^A$ implies that all 1-1 length-increasing polynomial-time functions relative to A are invertible relative to A. □

4.2 Proof Sketch of Lemma 4.1

We define requirement R_i as follows: Lemma 4.1 holds for $f^A = f_i^A$ and $M^A = M_i^A$. Note that by the definitions of f_i and M_i in Section 2, all pairs of reductions and machines will be covered by some R_i.

We will show that for each i, the set of sp-conditions that force R_i is dense. Then any sp-generic A will extend a τ such that τ forces R_i. We will show these sets are dense by showing how to extend any sp-condition τ to another condition σ such that σ forces R_i.

Fix i and let τ be an sp-condition and $\langle a_j \rangle_{j \in \mathbf{N}}$ be the corresponding iterated-polynomial sequence. We will create an sp-condition σ with corresponding sequence $\langle b_j \rangle_{j \in \mathbf{N}}$ that forces R_i. Let $f = f_i$ and $M = M_i$.

Suppose τ does not force "f^A reduces SAT^A to $L(M^A)$." For some A extending τ and some φ, we will have that either φ is true and $f^A(\varphi) \notin L(M^A)$ or φ is false and $f^A(\varphi) \in L(M^A)$. Let $m = \max(|\varphi|^i, |f^A(\varphi)|^i)$. Let $\sigma = \tau \cup (A$ restricted to strings of length at most $m)$. Clearly σ extends τ and forces "f^A does not reduce SAT^A to $L(M^A)$" and thus forces R_i. To see that σ is an sp-condition pick a c such that $a_c > m$ and let $b_j = a_{c+j}$ for all $j \in \mathbf{N}$.

For the remainder of this proof we will assume that τ forces "f^A reduces SAT^A to $L(M^A)$."

Pick an e such that $a_{j+e} > a_j^{3i}$ for all j. Since $p(n) \geq n^2$ for all n by Definition 3.1, any $e > \log_2(3i)$ will suffice. Pick a c such that a_c is sufficiently large to avoid all the degenerate cases in this proof. For all j, let $b_j = a_{c+2ej}$ and $d_j = a_{c+2ej+e}$. This proof will never do any encoding on strings of length b_j, guaranteeing that σ is an sp-condition. In fact all of the interesting coding for σ will occur for strings of length d_j. Initially, set $\sigma = \tau$ and also define $\sigma(x) = 0$ for every $x \notin \mathrm{dom}(\tau)$ such that x does not have length b_j or d_j for some j.

Let φ be an arbitrary CNF^A formula. Pick the smallest j such that $d_j > 4|\varphi|^i$. We define special tupling functions $\langle \varphi, y, 0 \rangle$, $\langle \varphi, w, y, 1 \rangle$ and $\langle \varphi, w, y, 2 \rangle$ such that they all have disjoint ranges over the strings of length exactly d_j and y and w will always range over strings of length $\lfloor d_j/4 \rfloor$. The details of such a tupling function are straightforward and will not be given here.

Let $\varphi_w = h(\varphi, w)$ be the formula that encodes:

$$(\varphi \wedge \exists y \langle \varphi, w, y, 1\rangle \in A) \vee \exists y \langle \varphi, y, 0\rangle \in A$$

In other words, create a nondeterministic oracle Turing Machine M such that M^A accepts if this expression is true and apply the reduction mentioned in Section 2. We will have $|\varphi_w| = O(d_j^2)$.

Define $\mathbf{f}^A(\varphi_w)$ as follows: Simulate $f^A(\varphi_w)$. Whenever $f^A(\varphi_w)$ queries a string of the form $\langle \varphi', w', z, 1\rangle$, $\mathbf{f}^A$ will query $\langle \varphi', w', z, 2\rangle$.

We say the computation $\mathbf{f}^A(\varphi_w)$ is *good* if, for all z, if $\mathbf{f}^A(\varphi_w)$ queries $\langle \varphi, w, z, 2\rangle$ then $\langle \varphi, w, z, 2\rangle \notin A$. Note that whether $\mathbf{f}^A(\varphi_w)$ is good does not depend on whether any string of the form $\langle \varphi', w', z, 1\rangle$ is in A.

Let $r(\varphi)$ be the formula that encodes:

$$\exists w[(\exists y \langle \varphi, w, y, 1\rangle \in A) \text{ and } \mathbf{f}^A(\varphi_w) \text{ is good}].$$

Let $s(\varphi)$ be the formula that encodes:

$$(\varphi \wedge r(\varphi)) \vee \exists y \langle \varphi, y, 0\rangle \in A$$

We can assume that we have constructed s and h such that each is 1-1 and range$(h) \cap$ range$(s) = \emptyset$. Note that h, r and s can be computed in unrelativized polynomial time.

Lemma 4.3 *There is a way to set σ on the strings of length $\langle d_j \rangle_{j \in \mathbf{N}}$ such that*

1. *σ forces "For every formula φ, $r(\varphi)$ is true."*
2. *For every φ and w there is exactly one y such that $\sigma(\langle \varphi, w, y, 1\rangle) = 1$.*
3. *For all φ and y, $\sigma(\langle \varphi, y, 0\rangle) = 0$.*
4. *for all φ, y and w, $\sigma(\langle \varphi, w, y, 1\rangle) = \sigma(\langle \varphi, w, y, 2\rangle)$*

This is a combinatorial lemma that follows mainly because there are many more ways to set σ then there are extensions to σ that $\mathbf{f}^A(\varphi_w)$ could query. We will give a complete proof of Lemma 4.3 in Section 4.3.

Note that $\mathbf{f}^A(\varphi_w) = f^A(\varphi_w)$ for all w and A where A extends σ. Also note that σ forces "For every φ and w, φ is true if and only if φ_w is true if and only if $s(\varphi)$ is true".

We now create our function $g^A(\varphi)$:

1. Simulate $f^A(s(\varphi))$ and let S be the set of w such that $f^A(s(\varphi))$ queried a string of the form $\langle \varphi, w, y, 1\rangle$.
2. If for some $w \in S$, $\mathbf{f}^A(\varphi_w)$ is good then output $\mathbf{f}^A(\varphi_w)$ for the first such w.
3. Otherwise output $f^A(s(\varphi))$.

Lemma 4.4 *For any A extending σ, the function g^A is a reduction from SAT^A to $L(M^A)$.*

Proof: The fact that g^A is a reduction now follows from the construction of g^A and the fact that τ forces f^A to be a reduction. □

We now show that σ forces g^A to fulfill the conclusions of Lemma 4.1. We will show that if g^A fails to fulfill these conclusions for some A extending σ then there will be an oracle B extending τ such that f^B does not reduce SAT^B to $L(M^B)$. This contradicts the assumption that τ forces f^B to be such a reduction.

We will create a B that disagrees with A only on strings longer than the formulae we will be dealing with. This will guarantee that the truth values of these formulae will remain unchanged.

Lemma 4.5 *The sp-condition σ forces that g^A is length-increasing.*

Proof: Suppose by way of contradiction that $|g^A(\varphi)| \leq |\varphi|$. Let $q = g^A(\varphi)$. Note that $M^A(q)$ cannot look at any string of the form $\langle \varphi, y, 0\rangle$, $\langle \varphi, w, y, 1\rangle$ or $\langle \varphi, w, y, 2\rangle$ because they are too long.

We have two cases each with two subcases:

1. $q = \mathbf{f}^A(\varphi_w)$ output by $g^A(\varphi)$ in step 2:
   (a) $M^A(q)$ rejects: There must be some y such that $f^A(\varphi_w)$ did not query $\langle \varphi, y, 0\rangle$. If we let $B = A \cup \{\langle \varphi, y, 0\rangle\}$ then f^B would not be a reduction.
   (b) $M^A(q)$ accepts: By the definition of g^A, $\mathbf{f}^A$ and parts 3 and 4 of Lemma 4.3 we have that $f^A(\varphi_w)$ queries $\langle \varphi, w, z, 1\rangle$ only if $\langle \varphi, w, z, 1\rangle \notin A$. Thus if we let $B = A$ removing all strings of the form $\langle \varphi, w, z, 1\rangle$ then f^B will not be a reduction.

2. $q = f^A(s(\varphi))$ output by $g^A(\varphi)$ in step 3:

   (a) $M^A(q)$ rejects: There must be some y such that $f^A(s(\varphi))$ did not query $\langle\varphi, y, 0\rangle$. If we let $B = A \cup \{\langle\varphi, y, 0\rangle\}$ then f^B would not be a reduction.

   (b) $M^A(q)$ accepts: Let S be the set from the definition of g^A. Let $B = A$ removing all strings of the form $\langle\varphi, w, z, 1\rangle$ for $w \notin S$. If $r(\varphi)$ is false relative to B then f^B is no longer a reduction since $f^B(s(\varphi)) = f^A(s(\varphi)) = q$, $s(\varphi)$ is false relative to B and $q \in L(M^B)$.

   Suppose $r(\varphi)$ is true relative to B. By the definition of $r(\varphi)$ we have that for some $w \in S$, $\mathbf{f}^B(\varphi_w)$ is good. Note that the computation of $\mathbf{f}^B(\varphi_w)$ is identical to the computation of $\mathbf{f}^A(\varphi_w)$. Since $\mathbf{f}^B(\varphi_w)$ is good then $\mathbf{f}^A(\varphi_w)$ also is good, and so g^A would have output $\mathbf{f}^A(\varphi_w)$ in step 2.

Thus g^A is length-increasing. □

We use similar techniques to show that g^A fulfills the other conditions of Lemma 4.1.

4.3 Proof Sketch of Lemma 4.3

We will use relativized Kolmogorov complexity for this proof. For an introduction to Kolmogorov complexity see the excellent survey by Li and Vitányi [LV90].

Fix a j and let ℓ and u be such that ℓ is the least integer such that $d_{j-1} \leq 4\ell^i$ and u is the greatest integer such that $d_j > 4u^i$. For $j = 0$ let $\ell = 0$. The values ℓ and u bound the lengths of formulae φ such that $\langle\varphi, y, 0\rangle$, $\langle\varphi, w, y, 1\rangle$ and $\langle\varphi, w, y, 2\rangle$ all have length d_j.

Let $z = |w| = |y| = \lfloor d_j/4 \rfloor$. Let $m = z2^z \sum_{\ell \leq e \leq u} 2^e$. Let x be a string of length m such that $K^{\bar{\tau}}(x) \geq m$, i.e., x is a Kolmogorov random string relative to $\bar{\tau}$.

View x as a concatenation of strings $x_{\varphi,w}$ of length z where φ ranges over all formulae of length between ℓ and u, and w ranges over all strings of length z. Set $\sigma(\langle\varphi, w, x_{\varphi,w}, 1\rangle) = \sigma(\langle\varphi, w, x_{\varphi,w}, 2\rangle) = 1$ for all φ and w, and set σ to zero for all other strings of length d_j.

Clearly this σ fulfills conditions 2, 3 and 4 of Lemma 4.3. Now if there is some A extending σ such that for some some formula φ, $\mathbf{f}(\varphi_w)$ queries $\langle\varphi, w, x_{\varphi,w}, 2\rangle$ for all w, then we can use the $\mathbf{f}(\varphi_w)$ computations to provide a shorter description for x by carefully specifying which of their queries are of the form $\langle\varphi, w, x_{\varphi,w}, 2\rangle$. □

5 Other Properties

We can also show that relative to sp-generics that the isomorphism conjecture holds for a host of other complete degrees. Also relative to sp-generics, **P** = **BPP** = **NP** ∩ co-**NP** = **SPP** but the polynomial-time hierarchy is proper.

In a future paper we will look at sp-generics in greater detail including showing these results. We will also contrast sp-generics with the usual generic sets as well as alternative definitions of sp-genericity.

6 Open Questions

We have shown that relative to sp-generic oracles the isomorphism conjecture holds. Several obvious open questions remain:

- Does the isomorphism conjecture hold in the unrelativized world? Despite Theorem 1.1, the authors believe the evidence supports the position that the conjecture does not hold. However such a result would likely be very difficult to prove.

- How complicated must an oracle A be such that the isomorphism conjecture holds relative to A? By Lemma 3.2 we can easily see that there are no sp-generic oracles in the arithmetic hierarchy. However we can fulfill just the requirements necessary for the isomorphism conjecture with a set recursive in the halting problem.

  Is there a recursive oracle A? One could wonder whether we could recursively fulfill all the necessary requirements. We could use time-bounded Kolmogorov complexity in Section 4.3 but determining whether τ forces f to be a reduction is not decidable.

However, we believe that a careful finite injury argument could lead to a recursive oracle.

- Is there an oracle relative to which the isomorphism conjecture is true and $\mathbf{P} \neq \mathbf{UP}$, i.e., there exist one-way functions?

- Is there an oracle relative to which the isomorphism conjecture is true and the polynomial-time hierarchy collapses? A related question is whether there exists an oracle A such that $\mathbf{P}^A = \mathbf{UP}^A$ and $\mathbf{NP}^A = \mathbf{EXP}^A$. This oracle A also would imply that the isomorphism conjecture holds relative to an oracle (see [HS92]).

Acknowledgments

This paper grew from discussions at the Dagstuhl workshop on structural complexity theory with many people especially Ted Slaman, Bill Gasarch, Steve Homer and Alan Selman.

We would like to thank other people for helpful discussions on the isomorphism conjecture over time: Steve Mahaney, Jim Royer and Mike Sipser.

We also thank Richard Beigel, Bill Gasarch, Steve Homer and Jim Royer for their comments on earlier drafts of this paper.

And, of course, we would like to acknowledge Juris Hartmanis for bringing this challenging problem to the world.

References

[BH76] L. Berman and J. Hartmanis. On isomorphism and density of NP and other complete sets. In *Proceedings of the 8th ACM Symposium on the Theory of Computing*, pages 30–40. ACM, New York, 1976.

[BH77] L. Berman and J. Hartmanis. On isomorphism and density of NP and other complete sets. *SIAM Journal on Computing*, 1:305–322, 1977.

[BI87] M. Blum and R. Impagliazzo. Generic oracles and oracle classes. In *Proceedings of the 28th IEEE Symposium on Foundations of Computer Science*, pages 118–126. IEEE, New York, 1987.

[GJ86] J. Goldsmith and D. Joseph. Three results on the polynomial isomorphism of complete sets. In *Proceedings of the 27th IEEE Symposium on Foundations of Computer Science*, pages 390–397. IEEE, New York, 1986.

[GS88] J. Grollmann and A Selman. Complexity measures for public-key cryptosystems. *SIAM Journal on Computing*, 17:309–355, 1988.

[HH91] J. Hartmanis and L. Hemachandra. One-way functions and the nonisomorphism of NP-complete sets. *Theoretical Computer Science*, 81(1):155–163, 1991.

[HS89] S. Homer and A. Selman. Oracles for structural properties: The isomorphism problem and public-key cryptography. In *Proceedings of the 4th IEEE Structure in Complexity Theory Conference*, pages 3–14. IEEE, New York, 1989.

[HS92] S. Homer and A. Selman. Oracles for structural properties: The isomorphism problem and public-key cryptography. *Journal of Computer and System Sciences*, 44(2):287–301, 1992.

[JY90] D. Joseph and P. Young. Self-reducibility: Effects of internal structure on computational complexity. In A. Selman, editor, *Complexity Theory Retrospective*, pages 82–107. Springer, 1990.

[KMR87] S. Kurtz, S. Mahaney, and J. Royer. Progress on collapsing degrees. In *Proceedings of the 2nd IEEE Structure in Complexity Theory Conference*, pages 126–131. IEEE, New York, 1987.

[KMR89] S. Kurtz, S. Mahaney, and J. Royer. The isomorphism conjecture fails to a random oracle. In *Proceedings of the 21st ACM Symposium on the Theory of Computing*, pages 157–166. ACM, New York, 1989.

[KMR90] S. Kurtz, S. Mahaney, and J. Royer. The structure of complete degrees. In A. Selman, editor, *Complexity Theory Retrospective*, pages 82–107. Springer, 1990.

[Kur88] S. Kurtz. The isomorphism conjecture fails relative to a generic oracle. Technical Report 88-018, Department of Computer Science, University of Chicago, 1988. Accepted for publication to TCS.

[LV90] M. Li and P. Vitányi. Applications of Kolmogorov complexity in the theory of computation. In A. Selman, editor, *Complexity Theory Retrospective*, pages 147–203. Springer, 1990.

Data Structural Bootstrapping, Linear Path Compression, and Catenable Heap Ordered Double Ended Queues

Adam L. Buchsbaum[1,4,5,6] Rajamani Sundar[1,2,6] Robert E. Tarjan[1,3,5,6,7]

1 Introduction

A *deque with heap order* is a linear list of elements with real-valued keys which allows insertions and deletions of elements at both ends of the list. It also allows the *findmin* (or *findmax*) operation, which returns the element of least (greatest) key, but it does not allow a general *deletemin* (*deletemax*) operation. Such a data structure is also called a *mindeque* (*maxdeque*). The restricted access and lack of deletemin distinguish mindeques from general heaps and allow faster operation times than do heaps. Gajewska and Tarjan [10] show how to implement mindeques with constant time (amortized or worst-case) per operation; they leave open the problem of how to catenate mindeques.

This paper provides an efficient implementation of catenable mindeques. The important algorithmic technique employed is an idea of Driscoll et al [7], which is best described as *data structural bootstrapping*: The mindeques of Gajewska and Tarjan are abstracted so that their elements represent other mindeques, effecting catenation while preserving heap order. To prove that the resulting data structure achieves constant amortized time per operation, we consider *order preserving path compression*. This is a generalization of special cases of path compression originally introduced by Hart and Sharir [11] and subsequently analyzed by Loebl and Nešetřil [15, 16, 17] and Lucas [18]. We prove a linear bound on *deque ordered spine-only path compression*, a case of order preserving path compression employed by our data structure.

Our result is important in the following respects. It shows how the bootstrapping technique of Driscoll et al, originally developed to create confluently persistent catenable lists, is in fact a generally useful tool in the design of efficient data structures. Additionally, we not only unify the special cases of path compression considered by Loebl and Nešetřil and by Lucas, but we extend their results to a more general case. Furthermore, we provide what we believe is the first practical application of this type of result.

Sections 2 and 3 of this paper describe our data structure for catenable mindeques, using the bootstrapping technique of Driscoll et al. Sections 4 and 5 define and analyze deque ordered spine-only path compression, proving the linearity of this special case of path compression. These latter sections are the more technically difficult of the paper. Finally, we conclude and offer some open problems in Section 6.

[1]Dept. of Computer Science, Princeton University.
[2]DIMACS, Rutgers University, Piscataway, NJ.
[3]NEC Research Institute, Princeton, NJ.
[4]Supported by the Fannie and John Hertz Foundation.
[5]Supported by NSF Grant No. CCR-8920505.
[6]Supported by DIMACS under NSF-STC88-09648.
[7]Supported by ONR Contract No. N00014-91-J-1463.

2 Lists, Heap Order, and Catenation

Consider the following operations, to be performed on a linear list d of elements:

push(x, d) Insert x as the new first element of d; the previous ith element becomes the $(i+1)$st.

pop(d) Remove and return the first element of d (or $\emptyset$ if d is empty); the previous ith element, for $i \geq 2$, becomes the $(i-1)$st.

inject(x, d) Insert x as the new last element of d.

eject(d) Remove and return the last element of d (or $\emptyset$ if d is empty).

We assume the existence of a *makelist* operation that returns an initially empty list. If only push and pop (or inject and eject) are allowed, d is a *stack* (formally a *list of type stack*). If only push and eject (or inject and pop) are allowed, d is a *queue*. If all the operations are allowed, d is a *double ended queue*, or *deque*. If both insertion operations but only one of the deletion operations are allowed, d is an *output restricted deque*. Such data structures can easily be implemented by doubly-linked (in some cases singly-linked) lists yielding $O(1)$ worst case times for each of the allowed operations [21].

0-8186-2900-2/92 $3.00 © 1992 IEEE

If each element in d has a real-valued key, we may also want to consider the following operation:

findmin(d) Find and return an element of minimum key in d (or $\emptyset$ if d is empty).

Findmin does not modify the list. If d is a deque, then d together with findmin is a *heap ordered deque* or *mindeque*. Analogous data structures are obtained by adding findmin to stacks, queues, and output-restricted queues. A related data structure is the *priority queue with attrition* [20]. We can also consider the *findmax* operation but will restrict ourselves without loss of generality to findmin.

Finally, if d_1 and d_2 are lists of the same type and of size (number of elements) s_1 and s_2 respectively, then we define the following operation:

catenate(d_1, d_2) Add the elements of d_2 to the back of d_1; i.e., let the $(s_1 + i)$th element of d_1 be the ith element of d_2 for $1 \leq i \leq s_2$. The first s_1 elements of d_1 are unchanged. This operation destroys d_2.

Catenating lists in $O(1)$ time is straightforward; catenating heap ordered lists is more problematic. This paper demonstrates how to implement *catenable heap ordered deques* (or *catenable mindeques*) efficiently. Our data structure performs n insertions (pushes and injects), m deletions (pops and ejects), and q catenations, all intermixed on $q + 1$ catenable mindeques, in total time $O(n+m+q)$, such that findmin always takes $O(1)$ worst case time. Further, if q is fixed, each operation requires $O(1)$ worst case time.

An equivalent formulation of the problem is to have the makelist operation take an element as an argument and return a list of one element. Then, push and inject can be treated as special cases of catenation. We choose the former suite of operations in order to distinguish catenation as a special operation which complicates the implementation of mindeques.

2.1 Related Work and Applications

Queues with heap order (or *minqueues*) are useful in pagination [6, 12, 14, 19] and VLSI river routing [5]. Booth and Westbrook [3] use catenable minqueues in the sensitivity analysis of various network problems. Larmore and Hirschberg [14] and Cole and Siegal [5] independently showed how to implement minqueues in $O(1)$ amortized time per operation [22]. Gajewska and Tarjan [10] modified their techniques to produce mindeques with $O(1)$ time per operation; they give both amortized and worst case solutions. Applications of mindeques include computing all pairs shortest path information [9] and external farthest neighbors for simple polygons [1]. Whereas a simple extension of the previous minqueue techniques yields efficiently catenable minqueues (again $O(1)$ amortized time per operation), Gajewska and Tarjan left as an open problem how to construct efficiently catenable mindeques.

2.2 Reviewing Heap Ordered Queues and Deques

For completeness, we begin by reviewing how to implement minqueues and mindeques. Identify the head of a list (where the first element sits) as the left end of the list and the tail as the right. A *minimum element* of a list is an element of minimum key. To implement a minqueue d, maintain a secondary list d' of *rightward minima*. This list has as its first element the minimum element x of d; the second element is the minimum element of d to the right of x, and so on; see Figure 1a.

To pop an element from d, if the element is minimum, the new minimum element of d becomes the element's successor in d' (and that element becomes the new head of d'—i.e. d' is also popped). Otherwise, no change to d' takes place. To inject an element e of key k into d, consider the rightmost element x of d'. If $key(x) > k$, eject x from d' and continue the search with the new rightmost element of d'. Once the rightmost element of d' is of lessor value than k, inject k into d'; note that k might be the only element of d' after this procedure. The findmin operation on d is now implemented by returning the head of d'. This is one possible implementation of the technique of [5, 14], yielding $O(1)$ amortized time bounds for all the queue operations. We note that the technique also extends to implement heap ordered stacks, which will be used to create mindeques, as well as heap ordered output restricted deques. Further, it is simple to add catenation to heap ordered queues, stacks, and output restricted deques using the same idea.

Gajewska and Tarjan [10] implement mindeques by representing them as two heap ordered stacks, as in Figure 1b. When one stack is emptied, the mindeque is rebuilt such that the two stacks differ in size by no more than one. The findmin operation returns the minimum of the minimum elements in the left and right stacks. By gradually rebuilding the stacks concurrently with the deque operations, they achieve $O(1)$ worst case time per operation. Using two stacks, how-

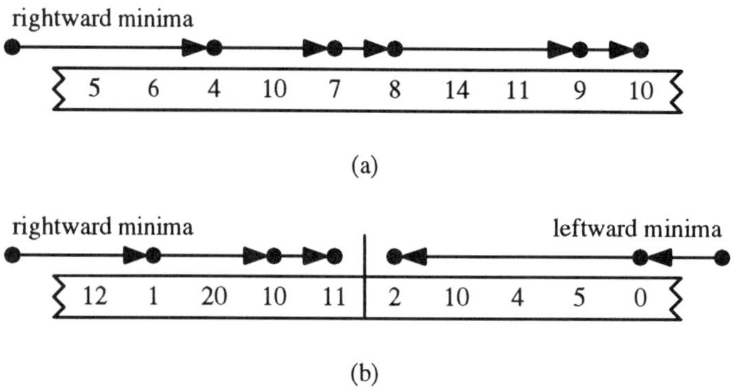

Figure 1: (a) A minqueue with minimum key 4. (b) A mindeque with minimum key 0; the center line is the break point between the two stacks.

ever, does not allow the easy implementation of catenation that is possible with minqueues.

3 Data Structural Bootstrapping and Catenable Mindeques

We employ a technique of Driscoll et al [7] to bootstrap the mindeques and allow their efficient catenation. We wish to implement a catenable mindeque d; call the elements of d *basic elements*. We freely interchange the notion of elements and their keys (e.g. $x > y$ for two elements x and y implies that the key of x is greater than the key of y).

Our data structure D is itself a mindeque. Each element of D consists of a basic element of d combined with a pointer. For an element x of D, let e be x's basic element and p x's pointer. If $p = \emptyset$, then e is a basic element of d; in this case we call x a *d-element* of D. Otherwise, e is the minimum basic element of a mindeque to which p points. This other mindeque has the same type of elements as does D, and the structure is recursive; the minimum element of D thus contains the minimum basic element in all the mindeques which D subtends. The d-elements of D occur in a natural *left-to-right* order that can be enumerated by recursively visiting each element from head to tail in D, listing d-elements as they are encountered. The resulting ordered list of d-elements corresponds to the basic elements in order in the catenable mindeque d we are implementing.

In this fashion, there is a one-to-one correspondence between the elements of D and the nodes of a heap ordered tree; see Figures 2a and 2b. In the tree, the leaves represent d-elements of D and hence basic elements of d, and we maintain a *heap invariant* on the tree: The non-leaf (or internal) nodes contain the lowest values among their children. The internal nodes are precisely those elements of D and its subtended mindeques which are not d-elements. The leaves in the tree also have a natural left-to-right order, corresponding to that on the d-elements of D.

The concept of representing a heap ordered linear list of items by exploiting the induced left-to-right order of the leaves in a normal heap ordered tree arises in the pagodas of Françon et al [8]. Similar data structures are the Cartesian tree [25] and the treap [2]. These maintain one tree under both symmetric and heap orders (on two distinct keys per node). If the symmetrically ordered key represents the position of the node in a linear list, the data structure supports heap ordered list access operations. The idea of bootstrapping mindeques to implement catenable mindeques in the above recursive fashion generalizes the technique of Kosaraju [13], by which he designs catenable deques (not heap ordered) by decomposing the deques into contiguous pieces and storing those pieces in a stack. His data structure can be extended to maintain heap order, but it only accommodates a fixed number of deques. Driscoll et al [7] bootstrap fully persistent lists to implement confluently persistent catenable (output restricted) lists.

3.1 The *Pull* Operation

We now define a *left pull* operation on the heap ordered tree T similar to the *pull* operation of [7]. If the leftmost child x of the root of T is a leaf, a *left pull on* T does nothing. Otherwise, a left pull on T removes the leftmost child x' from x and makes x' the new leftmost child of T; if x is now a leaf, it is deleted. See Figure 2c for an example. The heap invariant of the tree is maintained by making each internal node

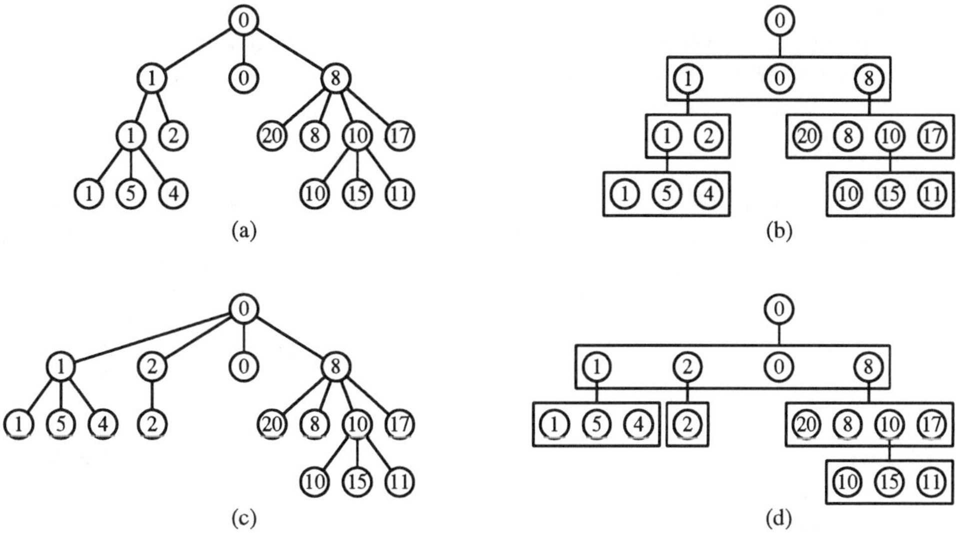

Figure 2: (a) A heap ordered tree. (b) The corresponding catenable mindeque; boxes surround mindeques, the minimum values of which are elements in the parent mindeque. (c) The tree of (a) after a left pull. (d) The corresponding catenable mindeque.

contain the lowest key of its children. We define a *right pull on* T symmetrically. Both pull operations preserve the left-to-right order of the leaves of T.

A left pull is now extended to the data structure D as follows: If the first element x of D is a d-element (has a $\emptyset$ pointer), a left pull on D does nothing. Otherwise, pop D, returning x. Denote by $d(x)$ the mindeque to which x's pointer points. Pop $d(x)$, returning x'. If $d(x)$ is still non-empty, push x back onto D; x's pointer still points to $d(x)$, but popping $d(x)$ may change x's basic element (the minimum basic element of $d(x)$). Then push x' onto D. A right pull on D is defined symmetrically. Since we use only mindeque operations to implement pulls on D, the minimum values of all the mindeques, in particular that of D, are maintained correctly. The popping and repushing of x is executed precisely to maintain the correct minimum values; i.e. if x' is the minimum element of x, then popping x' from x and pushing it onto D necessitates changing the minima lists of D, which is effected by the popping and pushing of x before the pushing of x'. Figure 2d shows the result of a left pull on D. Again, the pull operations preserve the left-to-right order of the d-elements of D.

It is now straightforward to implement the catenable mindeque operations on d as follows. We assume that the makelist operation returns an empty D.

push(x, d) — Create element $\tilde{x}$ composed of basic element x and pointer $\emptyset$. Push $\tilde{x}$ onto D.

pop(d) — Repeatedly left pull D until its head element is a d-element. Then pop D; this returns an element $\tilde{x}$. Return the basic element x of $\tilde{x}$.

inject(x, d) — Symmetric to push.

eject(d) — Symmetric to pop.

findmin(d) — Return the basic element in the minimum element of D.

catenate(d_1, d_2) — For $i \in \{1, 2\}$, let $\tilde{D_i}$ be an element containing the basic element in the minimum element of D_i and a pointer to D_i. Push $\tilde{D_1}$ onto D_2; equivalently, we could inject $\tilde{D_2}$ into D_1.

That D correctly simulates d is easily provable by induction on the number of operations.

3.2 Time Analysis

We now state:

Theorem 3.1 *An intermixed set of n insertions, m deletions, and q catenations on $q+1$ catenable mindeques takes total time $O(n+m+q)$ such that findmin always takes $O(1)$ worst case time.*

PROOF: (SKETCH) Each operation requires some constant amount of overhead to process an element and performs some number of "real" mindeque operations. Each real mindeque operation takes $O(1)$ (amortized or worst-case) time, using the Gajewska-Tarjan mindeques [10]. The mindeque operations correspond to an instance of disjoint set union [23] with leaf deletions; i.e., a sequence of pulls effects a path compression. Further, the compressions are all *spine compressions*, a notion to be defined in Section 4. Theorem 5.4 will prove the linearity of these path compressions. We note that it is unnecessary to maintain the heap-ordered trees in a balanced fashion. □

Note that if $q = O(1)$, that is if there is only a constant number of mindeques to be catenated, our data structure implements all the operations in $O(1)$ time each. Thus our structure unifies the general problem with this special case mentioned in [10], which was solved by using the techniques of Kosaraju [13].

Corollary 3.2 *An intermixed sequence of insertions, catenations, deletions, and findmins can be performed on a fixed number of catenable mindeques in $O(1)$ worst case time per operation.*

PROOF: If $q = O(1)$ each sequence of pulls is of constant length. □

4 Path Compression

In this section, we introduce some definitions necessary to the analysis of our special case of path compression. Initially, we have a tree T with n nodes (and $n-1$ edges). An edge (u, v) connects node u with its *parent* v in the tree; we say that $p(u) = v$ *in* T. Each node except for the root of T has precisely one edge joining it to its parent. The parent pointers define a *path* from x to the root of T in the natural way. A node x is a *descendant* of a node y if y lies on the path from x to the root of the tree; symmetrically, y is an *ancestor* of x. Note that x is both an ancestor and a descendant of itself. A *proper ancestor (descendant)* of x is an ancestor (descendant) y of x such that $y \neq x$.

A *path compression from* x_0 on a tree T is a sequence of nodes $C = (x_0, \ldots, x_l)$ such that $l > 0$ and $p(x_i) = x_{i+1}$ in T for $0 \leq i < l$. Its effect is to update the parents of the nodes along the path, making them all point to x_l, the *root of the compression*:

- $p(x_i) \leftarrow x_l,\ 0 \leq i < l.$

We say that the compression C *roots at* x_l; further, x_i for $0 \leq i < l$ is a *non-root node* of the path compression. The *cost* of C is $|C| = l$.

If $C = (x_0)$ and x_0 is a *leaf node*, i.e. a node with no children, then C is a *leaf deletion*; the effect of C is to remove x from T. In this case the cost of C is $|C| = 1$. A *sequence of path compressions on* $T = T_0$ is a sequence $(C_1, \ldots, C_m)$ such that C_i is a path compression or a leaf deletion on T_{i-1} and the result of C_i applied to T_{i-1} is T_i. The *cost* of a sequence of path compressions on T is $\sum_{i=1}^{t} |C_i|$.

We now define the *Rising Roots Condition* [18], which will link the notion of path compressions above with the well known union and find operations used in the disjoint set union problem (see, e.g., [23]).

Definition 4.1 (Rising Roots Condition) *A sequence of path compressions $(C_1, \ldots, C_m)$ satisfies the* Rising Roots Condition *if and only if for every node x, if x appears as a non-root node in any compression C_i, then for every $j > i$, x appears as a non-root node in C_j if C_j is a compression from y and y is a descendant of x in T_{j-1}.*

The Rising Roots Condition tells us precisely when a sequence of path compressions on some initial tree corresponds to an intermixed sequence of unions, finds, and leaf deletions:

Lemma 4.2 *A sequence of path compressions (on an initial tree) satisfying the Rising Roots Condition corresponds to some sequence of intermixed union, find, and leaf deletion operations. Conversely, a sequence of intermixed union, find, and leaf deletion operations corresponds to some sequence of path compressions satisfying the Rising Roots Condition.*

PROOF: See [18, Lemma 1]. □

The correspondence above is straightforward. The roots of the compressions in the path compression sequence are the roots of the finds in the union-find instance, and vice-versa. This correspondence can be used to simplify the analysis of disjoint set union instances by assuming that all the unions are done before the first find. Any result for a class of path compressions satisfying the Rising Roots Condition maps to a result for a class of disjoint set union problems.

We now introduce the notion of order to restrict the path compression sequences we shall consider. Given a tree T, embed T in the plane, yielding a left-to-right order on the children of each node. The *nearest common ancestor* of two nodes x and y ($nca(x, y)$) is the deepest node z in T such that z is an ancestor of both x and y. For x a proper descendant of z, let $c_x(z)$ be the child of z that is an ancestor of x; note that $c_x(z)$ might equal x. We define a partial order on T as follows: For any pair of nodes x and y, if $z = nca(x, y)$ and $z \notin \{x, y\}$, then $x < y$ if $c_x(z)$ is to the left of $c_y(z)$.

Definition 4.3 *A path compression on a tree T which yields a tree T' is* order preserving *if $x < y$ in $T \Longrightarrow x < y$ in T'. A leaf deletion is always taken to be* order preserving. *A sequence $(C_1, \ldots, C_m)$ of path compressions on T_0 is* order preserving *if C_i is order preserving for $1 \le i \le m$.*

Note that as there is in general more than one way to effect a path compression (in terms of the left-to-right order of the newly acquired children of the root of the compression), Definition 4.3 depends upon the actual implementation of the path compressions involved. We assume for simplicity that a compression is effected in an order preserving way if it can be. We now describe exactly when a path compression (sequence) is order preserving.

Lemma 4.4 *A path compression $(x_0, \ldots, x_l)$ is order preserving if and only if x_i is the leftmost or rightmost child of x_{i+1} for $0 \le i < l - 1$.*

PROOF: (SKETCH) See Figure 3. Note that the last non-root node in the compression need not be a leftmost or rightmost child of its parent; only the nodes whose parents change need be. □

Note that an only child, i.e. a node with no siblings, qualifies as both a leftmost and a rightmost child of its parent. Now consider a postorder (preorder) assigned to the nodes of a tree. In this paper we consider a restricted case of order preserving path compression:

Definition 4.5 *A path compression $(x_0, \ldots, x_l)$ is a* left-spine compression (right-spine compression) *if x_i is the leftmost (rightmost) child of x_{i+1} for $0 \le i < l - 1$ and the compression preserves the postorder (preorder) of the tree. A sequence of path compressions is a sequence of* spine-only *path compressions if each path compression in the sequence is a left-spine compression or a right-spine compression.*

Clearly left- and right-spine compressions are order preserving. Lucas [18] proves that a sequence of left-spine path compressions *done in postorder* and satisfying the Rising Roots Condition requires linear time; i.e., given an initially postordered tree, each node, in postorder, is the subject of one left-spine path compression and is then deleted. Loebl and Nešetřil [15, 16, 17] prove the linearity of a more general problem: that of a sequence of left-spine path compressions satisfying the Rising Roots Condition; they refer to this as a *local postorder*. These works derive from an open problem of Hart and Sharir [11]: What is the complexity of a sequence of path compressions done in postorder? I.e., the Hart-Sharir open problem does not require the Rising Roots Condition. Both the Lucas and the Loebl-Nešetřil problems are special cases of this problem.

We now introduce a more general order of the path compressions than that of either Lucas or Loebl and Nešetřil. Let $T^{(v)}$ be the subtree rooted at v just before the first path compression which changes $p(v)$, and let $T_x^{(v)}$ be the subtree of $T^{(v)}$ rooted at x for some child x of v in $T^{(v)}$.

Definition 4.6 *An order preserving sequence of path compressions is a* deque ordered sequence *if and only if for any v with two children x and y in $T^{(v)}$ such that $x < y$ the following is true: If the first path compression C' that orders v and y results in $y < v$, then all path compressions from nodes in $T_x^{(v)}$ precede C'; otherwise, if the first path compression C'' that orders v and x results in $v < x$, then all path compressions from nodes in $T_y^{(v)}$ precede C''.*

It is important to note that Definition 4.6 refers to nodes in a tree, e.g. $T_x^{(v)}$, with respect to $T^{(v)}$. I.e., the actual compressions may take place from nodes which at that time are no longer descendants of x (or v).

In the next section we prove our main result, namely that a deque ordered sequence of spine-only path compressions that satisfies the Rising Roots Condition requires at most linear time.

5 Linearity of Deque Ordered Spine-Only Compression

We unfortunately find it necessary to divide the following definitions into two separate cases to handle differently what happens to the left and to the right of various nodes. Let $p_i(v)$ be the parent of v in T_i. For some path compression sequence $(C_1, \ldots, C_m)$ on T_0 and a node v, we call C_i a *left compression with respect to* v if

1. C_i starts from a node x which is a descendant of v in T_0;

2. C_i is a left-spine compression.

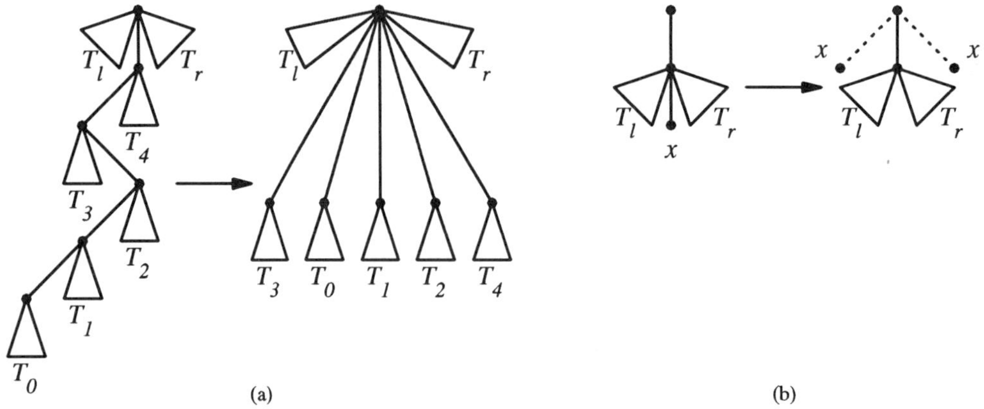

Figure 3: (a) An order preserving path compression; triangles denote subtrees. (b) A path compression which cannot be order preserving; x must become either left of T_l or right of T_r.

We define a *right compression with respect to* v symmetrically by replacing (2) above with (2) C_i is a right-spine compression. Note that x may not be a descendant of v at the time the path compression occurs. Let $high_L(v)$ be the shallowest node w which is a proper ancestor of v in T_0 and which is the root of a left compression with respect to v; if there is no such path compression, then $high_L(v) = \emptyset$. Symmetrically, let $high_R(v)$ be the shallowest node w which is a proper ancestor of v in T_0 and which is the root of a right compression with respect to v; $high_R(v) = \emptyset$ if no such compression exists. Again, it is critical to realize that the compression may not be from a descendant of v at the time.

Letting $level_L(\emptyset) = level_R(\emptyset) = -1$, we now define:

$$\begin{aligned} level_L(v) &= level_L(high_L(v)) + 1 \\ last_L(v) &= \min\{\, i \mid v \text{ is not a proper descendant of } high_L(v) \text{ in } T_i \,\} \\ level_R(v) &= level_R(high_R(v)) + 1 \\ last_R(v) &= \min\{\, i \mid v \text{ is not a proper descendant of } high_R(v) \text{ in } T_i \,\} \end{aligned}$$

To make $last_L$ and $last_R$ well-defined, we say that v is never a descendant of $\emptyset$. The definition of $level_L$ and $level_R$ is static; they are defined purely with respect to the initial tree and the sequence of path compressions. A *left level defining descendant* of v is a descendant (if one exists) x of v in T_0 such that a left compression with respect to v from x roots at $high_L(v)$; we call the actual compression a *left level defining compression* of v. Symmetrically define a *right level defining descendant* and *right level defining compression* of v.

We now prove a set of technical lemmas that localize the compressions affecting a vertex to one or two left levels and one or two right levels adjacent to those of the vertex. Again we let $p(v)$ ($p_i(v)$) be the parent of v (in T_i) (for v not the root), and $c_x(v)$ be the child of v which is an ancestor of x if x is a proper descendant of v.

Lemma 5.1 *In a path compression sequence* $(C_1, \ldots, C_m)$ *on* T_0*, for any node* v*:*

1. $0 \le i < last_L(v) \Longrightarrow level_L(v) \ge level_L(p_i(v))$*;*

2. $0 \le i < last_R(v) \Longrightarrow level_R(v) \ge level_R(p_i(v))$*.*

PROOF: We prove the lemma for (1); the proof for (2) is symmetric. In T_0, consider any root-to-leaf path partitioned by nodes of $level_L$ 0. We use induction on the length of each partitioned subpath. The base case is the head r of the path; $level_L(r) = 0$. Note that $level_L(r) = 0 \Leftrightarrow high_L(r) = \emptyset \Leftrightarrow last_L(r) = 0$; the claim for the base case is thus vacuous.

For a node v such that $level_L(v) > 0$ and r is the nearest ancestor of v such that $level_L(r) = 0$, let x be a left level defining descendant of v. Any left compression with respect to v from x is also a left compression with respect to $p_0(v)$ from x. Thus, if $high_L(v) = r$ then $high_L(y) = r$ for every y such that y is an ancestor of v and a proper descendant of r in T_0. (No left compression with respect to r may root at a proper ancestor of r, since $level_L(r) = 0$.) By the definition of $level_L$ and the induction hypothesis $level_L(v) \ge level_L(p_0(v))$. On the other hand, if $high_L(v) \ne r$ then $high_L(v)$ is a descendant of $high_L(p_0(v))$ in T_0. Both $high_L(v)$ and $high_L(p_0(v))$ are descendants of r in T_0. So again, by the definition of $level_L$ and the induction hypothesis $level_L(v) \ge level_L(p_0(v))$.

For a node v in T_i such that $0 < i < last_L(v)$, by definition v is a proper descendant of $high_L(v)$ in T_i.

By the above proof of monotonicity, it is still the case that $level_L(v) \geq level_L(p_i(v))$.

Leaf deletions clearly preserve the property. □

Lemma 5.2 *In a path compression sequence $(C_1, \ldots, C_m)$ on T_0, for any node v not the root of T_0:*

1. *$level_L(p(v))$ changes at most once during compressions C_1 through $C_{last_L(v)-1}$;*
2. *$level_R(p(v))$ changes at most once during compressions C_1 through $C_{last_R(v)-1}$.*

Proof: Again we prove the Lemma for (1); the proof for (2) is symmetric. Let $level_L(v) = l$. Via the path compression sequence, v becomes a child of higher and higher nodes on the initial path from v to the root of T_0. By Lemma 5.1, $level_L(p(v))$ never increases during path compressions C_1 through $C_{last_L(v)-1}$. However, by definition the highest node that becomes $p(v)$ during these compressions is of $level_L$ not less than $l-1$. Assuming $last_L(v) > 0$, Lemma 5.1 states that $level_L(p_0(v)) \leq level_L(v)$, and therefore $level_L(p(v))$ can change only once, from l to $l-1$, during compressions C_1 through $C_{last_L(v)-1}$. □

Note that Lemmas 5.1 and 5.2 are completely general; they apply to any sequence of path compressions. We have not yet used the Rising Roots Condition, spine-only compression, or deque order. The following lemma is critical to the counting argument used in the proof of Theorem 5.4, and it is here that we rely upon these conditions. We use the notation $T^{(v)}$ and $T_x^{(v)}$ as in Definition 4.6.

Lemma 5.3 *In a deque ordered sequence $(C_1, \ldots, C_m)$ of spine-only path compressions satisfying the Rising Roots Condition, any node v can be in at most one compression of each of the following two types:*

1. (a) *The compression is a left-spine compression from a proper descendant x of v;*
   (b) *$level_L(c_x(v)) = level_L(v) = level_L(p(v))$ before the compression; and*
   (c) *$p(v)$ changes during the compression, but $level_L(p(v))$ does not.*
2. (a) *The compression is a right-spine compression from a proper descendant x of v;*
   (b) *$level_R(c_x(v)) = level_R(v) = level_R(p(v))$ before the compression; and*
   (c) *$p(v)$ changes during the compression, but $level_R(p(v))$ does not.*

Proof: Again we prove the Lemma for (1); the proof for (2) is symmetric. Let $l = level_L(v)$. Consider the children of v in $T^{(v)}$; by the Rising Roots Condition v can acquire no more children. Further, each compression as specified in the lemma removes a child from v. Now, if v has more than one child of $level_L$ l just before the first such compression, consider any two such children x and y such that $x < y$. Let x' be a left level defining descendant of x. Note that x' is a node in $T^{(v)}$; by order preservation, $c_{x'}(v) < y$ in $T^{(v)}$.

Consider the first compression C_i that orders y and v. If C_i makes $y < v$ (i.e., is a left-spine compression), then by Definition 4.6 all the compressions from nodes in $T^{(v)}_{c_{x'}(v)}$ must precede C_i. In particular, the left level defining compression from x', rooting at a $level_L$ $l-1$ node, must occur before C_i. By the Rising Roots Condition, C_i must therefore root at a node of $level_L$ no greater than $l-1$, and thus $level_L(p(v))$ changes during C_i. From that point until compression $C_{last_L(v)}$, $level_L(v) \neq level_L(p(v))$, completing the proof. Note that $i < last_L(v)$. □

We can now prove our main result:

Theorem 5.4 *Any deque ordered sequence of m spine-only path compressions (and intermixed leaf deletions) satisfying the Rising Roots Condition on an initial tree of n nodes incurs cost at most $3m + 4n$.*

Proof: Consider any left-spine path compression $C = (x_0, \ldots, x_k)$. Using the definition of $level_L$ from before, the definition together with Lemma 5.1 shows that there is some b and l such that $level_L(x_i) = l$ for $0 \leq i \leq b$, and $level_L(x_i) = l-1$ for $b < i \leq k$. If all the nodes on the path compression are of the same $level_L$, we say that $b = -1$. See Figure 4a.

Whereas before the compression, $p(x_i) = x_{i+1}$ for $0 \leq i < k$, after the compression $p(x_i) = x_k$ for $0 \leq i < k$. Each node x_i for $0 \leq i < b$ has the $level_L$ of its parent change, which by Lemma 5.2 can happen only once per node; we therefore charge each of these pointer changes to the nodes themselves. Further, for all nodes x_i for $b+1 < i < k-1$, x_i is involved in the one type (1) compression allowed by Lemma 5.3. Again, the related charges are incurred against the nodes themselves. Symmetric charges can be made against the nodes for a right-spine compression. The remaining charges, those for nodes x_b (if it exists), x_{b+1}, and x_{k-1}, are incurred against the compression itself. See Figure 4b. Since leaf deletions take unit time, the bound follows. □

It is not hard to see that the data structure of Section 3 employs a deque ordered sequence of spine-only

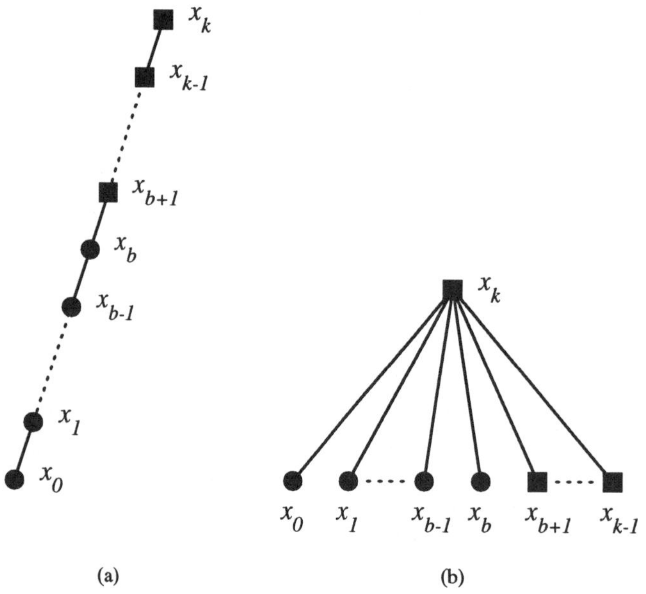

Figure 4: (a) A left-spine (incident subtrees not shown); circles are nodes of $level_L$ l, and squares are nodes of $level_L$ $l-1$. (b) After compressing the path of (a).

path compressions satisfying the Rising Roots Condition. Thus, Theorem 5.4 completes the proof of Theorem 3.1. We again mention that the initial tree T_0 need not be balanced.

6 Conclusion and Open Problems

We have described how to implement catenable heap ordered double ended queues in constant amortized time per operation (worst case for a fixed number of queues). The important pieces of our work are the use of the bootstrapping technique of Driscoll et al [7] in designing the data structure and the analysis of deque ordered spine-only path compression in proving its efficiency. Our path compression result generalizes the work of Loebl and Nešetřil [15, 16, 17] and of Lucas [18] and provides what we believe is the first application for such results.

We leave the following open problems. First, is there an implementation of catenable mindeques that achieves constant worst case time per operation (for an arbitrary number of deques)? Also, is there a linear time implementation of catenable mindeques that does not involve the bootstrapping technique and path compression?

Data structural bootstrapping holds promise as a general tool for designing data structures with some sort of *join* operation together with a property secondary to the original data structure. Driscoll et al [7] use it to effect persistence in catenable lists, and Buchsbaum and Tarjan [4] have recently used two types of it to effect persistence in catenable deques; we employ bootstrapping to effect heap order in catenable deques. Work on formalizing this method and finding further applications seems worthwhile.

The Hart-Sharir [11] open problem of postorder path compression without the Rising Roots Condition remains tantalizingly open. However, we do have a construction proving that a sequence of n general order preserving path compressions satisfying the Rising Roots Condition on an initial tree of $O(n)$ nodes can require $\Omega(n \log n)$ time. Space precludes us from showing the details, but they involve repeatedly compressing the longest path of a binomial-like tree [24], yielding a similar structure each time. We note, though, that this construction does not involve any order on the compressions themselves. Further, our construction yields an unbalanced initial tree. Thus, one can still formulate intermediate open problems incorporating different notions of order as well as the absence or presence of Rising Roots and balance that might be easier to solve than the Hart-Sharir problem.

Acknowledgements

Jeff Westbrook initially brought the problem of catenable mindeques to our attention. Milena Mihail and Peter Winkler provided thoughtful criticism of an earlier draft of Sections 2 and 3. Greg Frederickson pointed us to [3].

References

[1] P. K. Agarwal, A. Aggarwal, B. Aronov, S. R. Kosaraju, B. Schieber, and S. Suri. Computing external farthest neighbors for a simple polygon. *Disc. Appl. Math.*, 31(2):97–111, 1991.

[2] C. R. Aragon and R. G. Seidel. Randomized search trees. In *Proc. 30th IEEE FOCS*, pages 540–5, 1989.

[3] H. Booth and J. Westbrook. Linear algorithms for analysis of minimum spanning and shortest path trees in planar graphs. Technical Report YALEU/DCS/TR-763, Yale U. Dept. of Comp. Sci., February 1990. To appear in *Algorithmica*.

[4] A. L. Buchsbaum and R. E. Tarjan. Confluently persistent deques via data structural bootstrapping. Manuscript; submitted, 1992.

[5] R. Cole and A. Siegel. River routing every which way, but loose. In *Proc. 25th IEEE FOCS*, pages 65–73, 1984.

[6] G. Diehr and B. Faaland. Optimal pagination of B-trees with variable-length items. *C. ACM*, 27(3):241–7, 1984.

[7] J. R. Driscoll, D. D. K. Sleator, and R. E. Tarjan. Fully persistent lists with catenation. In *Proc. 2nd ACM-SIAM SODA*, pages 89–99, 1991.

[8] J. Françon, G. Viennot, and J. Vuillemin. Description and analysis of an efficient priority queue representation. In *Proc. 19th IEEE FOCS*, pages 1–7, 1978.

[9] G. N. Frederickson. Planar graph decomposition and all pairs shortest paths. *J. ACM*, 38(1):162–204, 1991.

[10] H. Gajewska and R. E. Tarjan. Deques with heap order. *IPL*, 22(4):197–200, April 1986.

[11] S. Hart and M. Sharir. Nonlinearity of Davenport-Schinzel sequences and of generalized path compression schemes. *Combinatorica*, 6(2):151–77, 1986.

[12] D. S. Hirschberg and L. L. Larmore. New applications of failure functions. *J. ACM*, 34(3):616–25, 1987.

[13] S. R. Kosaraju. Real-time simulation of concatenable double-ended queues by double-ended queues. In *Proc. 11th ACM STOC*, pages 346–51, 1979.

[14] L. L. Larmore and D. S. Hirschberg. Efficient optimal pagination of scrolls. *C. ACM*, 28(8):854–6, 1985.

[15] M. Loebl and J. Nešetřil. Linearity and unprovability of set union problem strategies. In *Proc. 20th ACM STOC*, pages 360–6, 1988.

[16] M. Loebl and J. Nešetřil. Postorder hierarchy for path compressions and set union. In *Proc. 5th Int'l. Mtg. of Young Computer Scientists*, volume 381 of *LNCS*, pages 146–51. Springer-Verlag, 1988.

[17] M. Loebl and J. Nešetřil. Linearity and unprovability of set union problem strategies I. Linearity of on line postorder. Technical Report 89-04, U. Chicago Dept. of Comp. Sci., April 1989.

[18] J. M. Lucas. Postorder disjoint set union is linear. *SIAM J. Comp.*, 19(5):868–82, October 1990.

[19] E. M. McCreight. Pagination of B^*-trees with variable-length records. *C. ACM*, 20(9):670–4, 1977.

[20] R. Sundar. Worst-case data structures for the priority queue with attrition. *IPL*, 31(2):69–75, 1989.

[21] R. E. Tarjan. *Data Structures and Network Algorithms.* SIAM, Philadelphia, PA, 1983.

[22] R. E. Tarjan. Amortized computational complexity. *SIAM J. Alg. Disc. Meth.*, 6(2):306–18, 1985.

[23] R. E. Tarjan and J. van Leeuwen. Worst-case analysis of set union algorithms. *J. ACM*, 31(2):245–81, 1984.

[24] J. Vuillemin. A data structure for manipulating priority queues. *C. ACM*, 21(4):309–15, 1978.

[25] J. Vuillemin. A unifying look at data structures. *C. ACM*, 23(4):229–39, 1980.

Fully Dynamic Biconnectivity in Graphs

Monika Rauch*
Department of Computer Science
Princeton University
Princeton, NJ 08544

Abstract

We present an algorithm for maintaining the biconnected components of a graph during a sequence of edge insertions and deletions. It requires linear storage and preprocessing time. The amortized running time for insertions and for deletions is $O(m^{2/3})$, where m is the number of edges in the graph. Each query of the form "Are the vertices u and v biconnected?" can be answered in time $O(1)$. This is the first sublinear algorithm for this problem.

If the input is a planar embedded graph, the amortized running time for insertions and deletions drops to $O(\sqrt{n \log n})$ and the worst case query time is $O((\log n)^2)$, where n is the number of vertices in the graph. The best previously known solution takes time $O(n^{2/3})$ per update or query.

1 Introduction

An undirected graph $G = (V, E)$ is *biconnected* if there are at least two vertex–disjoint paths from each vertex to every other vertex. It is well known [1] that a graph G is not biconnected if and only if there is a vertex whose removal disconnects G. Such a vertex is called an *articulation point* of G. A graph that is not biconnected is naturally partitioned into *biconnected components*. Two vertices are *biconnected* if they are in a common biconnected component. Similarly a graph is *2-edge-connected* it there are at least two edge–disjoint paths from each vertex to every other vertex. An edge whose removal disconnects G is called a *bridge*.

Tarjan [10] gave a linear time algorithm for computing the biconnected components and the 2-edge-connected components of a graph. Westbrook and Tarjan [11] solved the problem of maintaining biconnected components under a sequence of edge insertions. The running time of m insertions intermixed with queries of the form: "Are the vertices u and v biconnected?" is $O(m\alpha(m, n))$, where n is the number of vertices in the graph. They achieved the same running time for maintaining 2-edge-connected components under insertions.

The fully dynamic version of the problem allows both insertions and deletions of edges. It is significantly harder than the versions that allow only insertions or only deletions. Frederickson [5] gave an algorithm for maintaining 2-edge-connected components in a graph which takes $O(\sqrt{m})$ time per update, where m is the number of edges in the graph. This result was recently improved by Eppstein et al. [3] to $O(\sqrt{n}\log(m/n))$. The running time for maintaining 2-edge-connected components in a planar embedded graph drops to $O((\log n)^2)$ [8].

Maintaining blocks adds complications, since, unlike 2-edge-connectivity, biconnectivity is not an equivalence relation on the vertices of a graph. Additionally, standard techniques to transform G into a bounded degree graph, which are used by all the previous fully dynamic connectivity algorithms, preserve connectivity and 2-edge-connectivity, but destroy the biconnectivity properties of G. Thus it is not yet known whether biconnected components can be maintained in the same running time as 2-edge-connected components during the following sequence of operations:

Insert(u, v): Insert an edge between the two vertices u and v.
Delete(u, v): Delete the edge (u, v).
Query(u, v): Return *true* if vertices u and v are in the same biconnected component and an articulation point separating u and v otherwise.

We give an algorithm for general graphs with $O(m^{2/3})$ amortized update time and $O(1)$ query time. Independently Eppstein et al. [3] developed an algorithm for this problem whose running time per update operation is $O(n\log(m/n))$ and whose running time per query is $O(1)$.

*This research was supported by the German Fellowship Foundation, Studienstiftung des deutschen Volkes.

0-8186-2900-2/92 $3.00 © 1992 IEEE

For an embedded planar graph, we achieve $O(\sqrt{n \log n})$ time per update and $O((\log n)^2)$ time per query operation. The best previously known solution requires time $O(n^{2/3})$ per update or query operation [6].

Our algorithm uses linear space and preprocessing time. The new techniques for fully dynamic graph algorithms introduced in this paper involve precomputation and "lazy" updating. We split the graph into connected subgraphs and build a data structure for each subgraph which allows us to efficiently answer queries in the subgraph. If an edge is inserted or deleted, the data structures of the subgraphs maintaining its end points are updated. To avoid reconfiguring the entire data structure at each update we adopt a lazy strategy which spreads the reconfiguration costs over time. With this approach we are able to show that during l insertions and deletions only l data structures have to be updated. We also create a new data structure to handle the problems created by the transformation of G into a bounded degree graph.

In the next section we introduce our terminology and explain the partition of the graph. Section 3 and 4 present the data structure. Section 5 and 6 describe updates and queries, respectively.

2 Partitioning the graph

Let $G = (V, E)$ be an undirected graph with $n = |V|$ vertices and $m = |E|$ edges. For expository convenience we assume that G is always connected. Let T be a spanning tree of G. We denote by $\pi_G(u, v)$ the spanning tree path from u to v in G. If G is understood, we use $\pi(u, v)$. We call two adjacent tree edges (w, x) and (x, y) *covered* if there exists a path from w to y that does not contain x. Otherwise, the two tree edges are called *uncovered*. Obviously, if (w, x) and (x, y) are uncovered, then x is an articulation point separating w from y. We use this property of edges to test whether two vertices are biconnected.

Lemma 2.1 *Two vertices u and v of G are biconnected if and only if every pair of adjacent edges on $\pi(u, v)$ is covered.*

To split the graph into small connected subgraphs, we need a graph of bounded degree. Therefore we apply a well known transformation [7] to transform G into a graph G', whose vertices have degree no greater than 3. For each vertex x of G of degree $d \geq 4$ with $y_1, \ldots, y_d$ the vertices adjacent to x (in the clockwise order of the embedding in the planar case) we replace x with new vertices $x_1, \ldots, x_d$ and replace the edge (x, y_i) with a *solid* edge (x_i, y_i), $1 \leq i \leq d$. Furthermore, we add new *dashed* edges (x_i, x_{i+1}), $1 \leq i \leq d-1$. These dashed edges *belong* to x. If the graph is embedded, we add the dashed edges such that $(x_i, x_{i-1}), (x_i, y_i), (x_i, x_{i+1})$ is the clockwise order of the edges at x_i. Thus each vertex in G' is incident to at most two dashed edges and each edge in G corresponds to a unique solid edge in G'. The number of vertices and edges of G' is $O(m + n)$. If G is a planar embedded graph, then this transformation gives a planar embedding for G'. Note that every node is incident to at most two dashed edges.

To *contract* a dashed edge (x, y), we remove (x, y) and identify x with y. We need dashed edges for partitioning the graph. For answering a *query*(u, v) operation, however, we have to contract the dashed edges, since two vertices u and v that are not biconnected in G can be biconnected in G'.

Lemma 2.2 *If all dashed edges of every vertex on $\pi_{G'}(u, v)$ are contracted, then u and v are biconnected in G if and only if they are biconnected in G'.*

We give each solid edge of G' cost 2 and each dashed edge cost 1. This guarantees that all the dashed edges are contained in any minimum spanning tree of G'. G' can be generated in time $O(m + n)$ and a minimum spanning tree T of G' can be determined in time $O(m + n)$ by computing a spanning forest of all edges of cost 1 and then connecting the spanning forest into a spanning tree with cost 2 edges.

A *cluster* with respect to T is a set of vertices such that the subgraph of T induced on the cluster is connected. The *tree degree* of a cluster is the number of tree edges with precisely one endpoint in the cluster. A *restricted partition of order k* [5] with respect to T is a partition of the set of vertices of T such that

1. Each set in the partition is a vertex cluster of tree degree at most 3 .
2. Each cluster of tree degree 3 is of cardinality 1.
3. Each cluster of tree degree less than 3 is of cardinality at most k.
4. No two adjacent clusters can be combined and still satisfy the above.

Figure 2.1(a) depicts a restricted partition of order 4. The number of clusters in a restricted partition of order k is $\Theta(m/k)$ and a partition can be found in time $O(m + n)$ [5].

We extend this definition slightly: An edge with exactly one endpoint in a cluster C is called *incident* to C. We require that all dashed edges incident to a cluster belong to the same vertex of G. Note that each cluster is incident to at most two dashed edges. Thus, if the dashed edges of a cluster C belong to two different vertices of G, we split C into two clusters, each incident to one dashed edge. This increases the time to find a partition and the number of clusters in the partition only by a constant factor.

The restricted partition defines the *high-level graph* H of G'. Its vertices are the clusters. If G is a general graph, there is an edge between two vertices C and C' of H if and only if there exists an edge from a vertex in the cluster C to a vertex in the cluster C' (see Figure 2.1(b)).

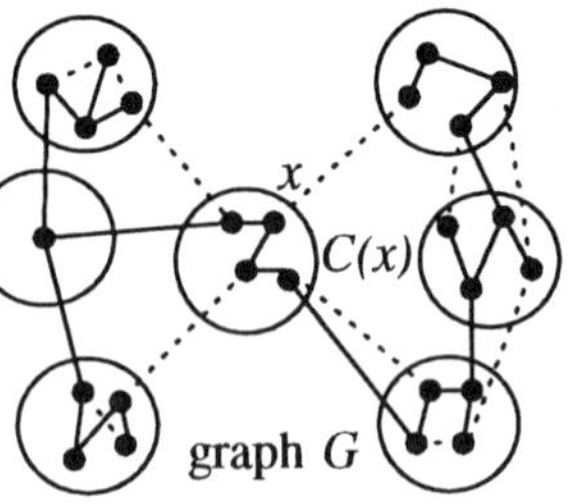

Non-tree edges are dotted.

Figure 2.1(a)

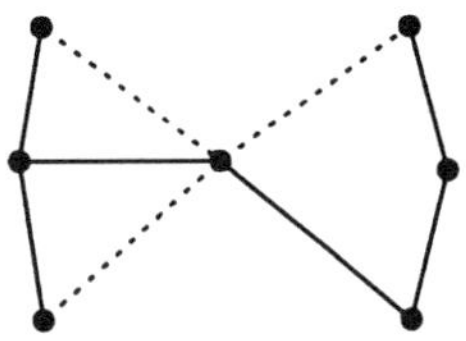

High-level graph of G.
Non-tree edges are dotted.

Figure 2.1(b)

If G is a planar embedded graph, the edges incident to C are embedded in a fixed order at C. We say two edges e_1 and e_2 which are connecting the same clusters are *equivalent*, if $e_1 = e_2$ or e_1 is a neighbor of e_2 in the given order at each cluster containing their endpoints or there exists an edge e_3 which is equivalent to e_1 and to e_2. An *edge bundle* is an equivalence class on the set of all edges according to this equivalence relation. As shown in [8] there are at most 3 edge bundles between two clusters. If G is a planar embedded graph, H contains as edges the edge bundles of G. Thus H is an embedded planar graph with $O(m/k)$ edges.

The cluster which contains the vertex u is called $C(u)$ and a pointer to it is stored at u. If (x, y) with $C(x) \neq C(y)$ is a tree edge in G, then $(C(x), C(y))$ in a general graph and the edge bundles to which (x, y) belongs in a planar embedded graph is a tree edge in H. If (x, y) is dashed, then the edge representing it in H is dashed. The tree edges define a spanning tree of H. An edge with both endpoints in C is called an *internal edge* of C. A *tree neighbor* of a cluster C is a neighbor of C in the spanning tree of H. A *non-tree neighbor* of C is a neighbor of C in H which is not connected to C by a tree edge. The *high-level degree* of a cluster is the number of edges incident to the cluster in H. For two clusters C_1 and C_2 there is a vertex $b(C_1, C_2)$ of C_1 such that the tree path from any vertex of C_1 to any vertex of C_2 goes through $b(C_1, C_2)$. Note that $b(C_1, C_2) \neq b(C_2, C_1)$.

For $d > 3$, a vertex s in G of degree d is represented in G' by a chain of $d-1$ dashed edges. If the endpoints of l, $0 < l < d$, of these dashed edges are in different clusters, then s is *shared* by these $l+1$ clusters and thus we call s a *shared vertex* of G. There are $O(m/k)$ shared vertices in G. Since all the dashed edges incident to a cluster belong to the same shared vertex, a cluster contains at most one shared vertex. We call a *tree neighboring cluster of a shared vertex* s a cluster that does not share s, but that is a tree neighbor of a cluster sharing s. We further call a cluster that is connected to clusters sharing s only by non-tree edges, but that does not share s a *non-tree neighboring cluster of* s.

To maintain a graph whose vertices have at most degree 3 during the insertion of an edge (u, v), we may have to add a constant number of vertices to G'. In a general graph this increases the number of vertices in a cluster. In a planar embedded graph the new vertices have to be added consistently with the embedding. Thus, either the number of vertices in a cluster or the number of clusters increases by a constant. During a deletion these numbers are not increased, except if the cluster is split into a constant number of clusters. *We want to keep as an invariant that each cluster has at most* $2k$ *vertices and that there are* $O(m/k)$ *clusters.* Thus we rebuild the complete data structure every $\min\{k, m/k\}$ insertions and every m/k deletions. As we show later, the cost of a complete rebuild is $O(m)$. Thus the rebuilds add an amortized cost of $O(k)$ to each of the deletions and an amortized cost of $O(m/k + k)$ to each of the insertions.

3 The internal data structure

The data structure described in this section is used to test in constant time whether two vertices which are in a cluster C or which are adjacent by tree edges to C are biconnected in G. Since a cluster with tree degree 3 consists of only one vertex which is incident to three tree edges, it follows that we can answer the above question in constant time provided we know the blocks of H. Thus we can assume in the following section that every cluster for which we build an internal data structure is incident to at most two tree edges in H.

We maintain a data structure at each cluster C, called the *internal data structure* of C. It contains a graph $G(C)$ for C which consists of all the vertices and internal edges of C. The internal dashed edges of C are contracted in $G(C)$. Additionally $G(C)$ contains a *big vertex* for every cluster which is adjacent to C. There are no edges between big vertices in $G(C)$. If

$u \in C$, then all edges of the form (u, v), $v \in C'$, are represented as a single edge from u to C' in $G(C)$ and stored alongside (u, C').

After a delete operation it is possible that two or more clusters adjacent to C are represented by the same big vertex in $G(C)$. Note that this data structure does not make use of the embedding in the planar case. Since we guarantee that C has at most $2k$ vertices of degree at most 3 and there are $O(m/k)$ clusters, $G(C)$ consists of $O(k)$ edges and vertices and the total size of all internal data structures is $O(m)$.

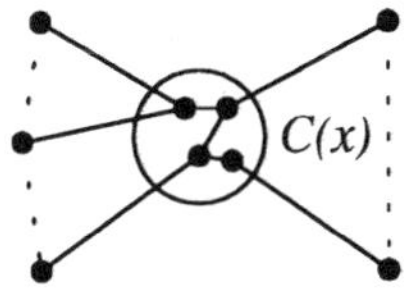

Internal data structure $G_a(C(x))$.
Artificial edges are dotted.

Figure 3.1

By adding *artificial* edges (i.e. edges which are not necessarily in G) between big vertices of $G(C)$ we create a new graph called $G_a(C)$. If C_1 is a tree neighbor of C, we add for every non–tree neighbor C_2 of C which is connected to C_1 by a tree path not containing C the artificial edge (C_1, C_2). Figure 3.1 shows $G_a(C(x))$ of the graph G in Figure 2.1. In our data structure artificial edges are not added to our representation of $G(C)$, but to a compressed version of $G_a(C)$.

For the following lemma we assume that the vertex of a tree neighbor C_1 of C in $G_a(C)$ represents the vertex $b(C_1, C)$ of G. Thus the vertices of G contained in $G_a(C)$ are all the vertices of C and the end points of tree edges incident to C.

Lemma 3.1 *If a cluster C has one tree neighbor or two tree neighbors which are not biconnected in H, then two vertices u and v of G in $G_a(C)$ are biconnected in G if and only if they are biconnected in $G_a(C)$ and the shared vertex of C is not an articulation point separating u and v.*
If C_1 and C_2 are biconnected, then two vertices u and v of G in $G_a(C)$ are biconnected in G if and only if they are biconnected in $G_a(C)$ with the additional edge (C_1, C_2) and the shared vertex of C is not an articulation point separating u and v.

Thus to test the biconnectivity of two vertices of C it is sufficient to test their biconnectivity in $G_a(C)$ and to check the shared vertex of C. We will discuss the latter in the next section.

Our next goal is to store $G(C)$ in a data structure such that $d-2$ artificial edges between d big vertices can be added (or removed) in time $O(d)$ and that queries whether two vertices are biconnected in the resulting graph can be answered in time $O(1)$. Thus we build the *block tree* of $G(C)$ [7] by making each block a round node and each vertex of $G(C)$ a square node in the block tree. There is an edge from the round node of a vertex x of $G(C)$ to the square node of every block which contains x in $G(C)$.

The compressed graph *Comp*(C) is created in the following way: We remove all edges and nodes of the block tree which are not contained on a simple path between two big vertices. If we discard a vertex x and all its blocks, then x is only biconnected in G to the vertices of its blocks. Let $x_0, x_1, \ldots, x_{l+1}$ for $l \geq 1$ be a path in the resulting block tree such that the degree of x_i for $1 \leq i \leq l$ is 2 and the degree of x_0 and x_{l+1} is not 2. We substitute the chain $x_2, \ldots, x_{l-1}$ by one vertex r and we replace $(x_1, x_2) \ldots (x_{l-1}, x_l)$ by (x_1, r) and (r, x_l). We store a pointer to r at every node x_i, $2 \leq i < l$. Then we add all artificial edges of $G_a(C)$ to *Comp*(C). (Note that every big vertex of $G(C)$ is represented by its own round node in *Comp*(C).)

The graph *Comp*(C) has size $O(d)$, where d is the high–level degree of C. Each node r of the compressed block tree represents either one vertex x of $G(C)$ or one block b of $G(C)$ or a collection of adjacent blocks and vertices of degree 2. In the first case r is the *representative* of x, in the second case r is the representative of every vertex in b which does not have its own representative, and in the third case r is the representative for every vertex which is without its own representative and which belongs to one of the blocks in the collection.

The data structure which we actually maintain for C is the graph $G(C)$ and the graph *Comp*(C). We introduced $G_a(C)$ only for ease of description. At each edge of $G(C)$ we remember its block of $G(C)$ and at each vertex its representative in *Comp*(C). We use *Comp*(C) to test whether two vertices of $G_a(C)$ are biconnected in the following way.

Lemma 3.2 *Let r_1 and r_2 with $r_1 \neq r_2$ be nodes of Comp(C) and let x_i for $i = 1, 2$ be a vertex of $G(C)$ whose representative is r_i. The nodes x_1 and x_2 are biconnected in $G_a(C)$ if and only if there is no bridge on $\pi_{Comp(C)}(r_1, r_2)$ and every articulation point separating r_1 and r_2 in Comp(C) is a node which represents a block of $G(C)$.*

To record at each edge of *Comp*(C) the block of $G_a(C)$ to which it belongs, we mark all edges of a block of *Comp*(C) as being in the same block of $G_a(C)$. Let a be an articulation point of *Comp*(C) that is the representative of a block of $G(C)$. We mark the edges of any two blocks of $Comp(C)$ which contain a and which have at least three vertices as belonging to the same block of $G_a(C)$. (A block with two vertices is a bridge.) Now we answer biconnectivity queries in $G_a(C)$ in the following way.

Lemma 3.3 *Two vertices u and v are biconnected in $G_a(C)$ if and only if*

(i) there exists a block (consisting of more than 1 edge) in $G(C)$ which contains u and v or

(ii) u and v do not have a common block in $G(C)$, but they are represented by the same node r in $Comp(C)$ and the edges (r_1, r) and (r, r_2) to the two neighbors r_1 and r_2 of r are marked as being in the same block of $G_a(C)$ or

(iii) the representatives of u and v in $Comp(C)$ are not identical, but their representatives have a common block in $G_a(C)$.

To be able to test in constant time whether there is a block in $G(C)$ which contains u and v, we root the spanning tree of $G(C)$ at a fixed tree neighbor C_1 of $G(C)$. Whenever we rebuild $G(C)$, we store at each vertex u of $G(C)$ the closest ancestor of u which is an articulation point separating u from C_1. These articulation points can be found for all vertices of $G(C)$ during one depth-first traversal of the spanning tree of $G(C)$ starting at C_1. During this traversal we also label the vertices by their preorder and postorder ranks. To test whether u and v have a common block in $G(C)$ we first determine with the help of the labels whether u is an ancestor of v or vice versa. If not, then u and v have a common block if and only if the edge from u to its parent and the edge from v to its parent are in the same block. Otherwise u and v have a common block if and only if the same articulation point is stored at them. All these tests can be answered in constant time. We proceed in the same way when we test whether two nodes of $Comp(C)$ have a common block in $G_a(C)$. Thus we can execute all tests of Lemma 3.3 in constant time. Using these articulation points we can also find an articulation point which separates u and v in constant time.

As shown in Lemma 3.1, if C has only one tree neighbor in H or two tree neighbors which are not biconnected, it is enough to test for biconnectivity in $G_a(C)$ as described in Lemma 3.3 and check the shared vertex of C as described in Section 4. If, however, C_1 and C_2 are two tree neighbors of C which are biconnected, the edge (C_1, C_2) has to be added to $G_a(C)$. We solve this problem by marking all the nodes on $\pi_{Comp(C)}(C_1, C_2)$ and checking additionally whether the representatives of the two query vertices are marked.

If a cluster C has two tree neighbors C_1 and C_2, we often have to test whether there are two vertex disjoint paths from $b(C_1, C)$ to $b(C_2, C)$. Thus we store a bit called *coverage bit* at each cluster C with two tree neighbors C_1 and C_2. It is set to 1 if C_1 and C_2 are biconnected in either $G_a(C)$ or in H. Otherwise it is 0. Since either property can be tested in constant time, the coverage bit can be computed in constant time.

Lemma 3.4 *Let $b_i = b(C_i, C)$ for $i = 1, 2$ if (C_i, C) is solid and let it be the shared vertex to which (C, C_i) belongs otherwise. The coverage bit of C is 1 if and only if b_1 and b_2 are biconnected in G.*

Lemma 3.5 *If $C_0, C_1, \ldots, C_{g+1}$ for $g \geq 1$ are all the clusters on $\pi_H(C_0, C_{g+1})$ and every tree edge between C_i and C_{i+1} is solid for $1 \geq i \geq g$, then $b(C_1, C_0)$ and $b(C_g, C_{g+1})$ are biconnected in G if and only if the coverage bits of all clusters C_i, $1 \leq i \leq g$, are 1.*

We show in the next section, how we handle dashed edges on $\pi_{G'}(u, v)$.

To insert $e = (u, v)$, we add e to $G(C(u))$ and $G(C(v))$. To delete it, we remove e from $G(C(u))$ and $G(C(v))$. In both cases the internal data structure of $C(u)$ and of $C(v)$ have to be rebuilt. During a deletion it is possible that a constant number of clusters is split into $O(1)$ new clusters. Thus a constant number of new internal data structures has to be created. All this can be accomplished in time $O(k)$. We also recompute the blocks of H. This takes time $O((m/k)^2)$ in a general graph and $O(m/k)$ in a planar graph. If the deleted edge (u, v) is a tree edge, the artificial edges along the path $\pi_H(C(u), C(v))$ in the new high-level graph have to be changed. Since the cost at a cluster is proportional to its high-level degree, this has a total cost of $O(m/k)$ in a planar graph and $O((m/k)^2)$ in a general graph. Additional rebuilds of internal data structures are required, but we can limit their amortized number per update operation to a constant.

Lemma 3.6 *During l deletions and insertions at most $6l$ internal data structures are rebuilt.*

Lemma 3.7 *The amortized cost for updating all internal data structures after an insertion or a deletion is $O(k + m/k)$ in a planar graph and $O(k + (m/k)^2)$ in a general graph. Rebuilding all internal data structures takes time $O(m)$.*

4 The connectivity data structure

For each shared vertex s of G we keep a data structure called the *connectivity data structure* or *c-structure* of s. We need this data structure to contract all dashed edges of every shared vertex s which occurs on $\pi_G(u,v)$ during a $query(u,v)$ operation. It allows to test in constant time whether s is an articulation point separating u and v. Its three parts, the local, the global, and the look–up data structure are described in the following sections.

Additionally we maintain the graph H_c created by contracting all dashed edges of H. We rebuild this graph after every insertion and deletion and compute its blocks. This adds time $O(m/k)$ to every update operation in a planar graph and $O((m/k)^2)$ in a general graph.

4.1 The local data structure

Let $C_1, \ldots, C_f$ for some positive integer f be the clusters which share s. After each rebuild of all data structures the *local data structure of s* consists of all vertices of $C_1, \ldots, C_f$ with s removed, and all edges between these vertices. It contains also for every edge incident to exactly one of these vertices an *e–vertex*. The e–vertex representing the edge (x, y) is connected to y where y is the vertex contained in some C_i. Every neighboring cluster C of a cluster C_j for $1 \leq j \leq f$ is represented by the e–vertices of all edges incident to C. These vertices are connected in the following way. If there are only two e–vertices, we connect them by one edge. Otherwise, we fix some arbitrary order of the edges at each vertex of C in a general graph and we take an order given by the embedding in a planar embedded graph. Now an Eulerian tour of the (bidirected) spanning tree of C determines an order on the edges from C to vertices of $C_1, \ldots, C_f$. We connect the e–vertices representing these edges by a cycle in this order (see Figure 4.1).

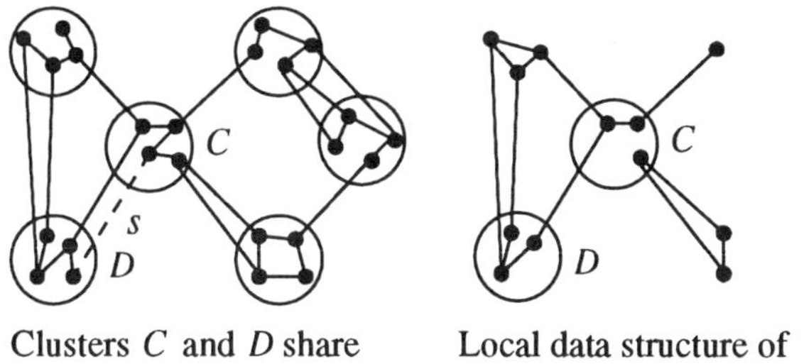

Clusters C and D share vertex s. | Local data structure of s in a general graph.

Figure 4.1

The local data structure can also contain the vertices of clusters not sharing s (because of splitting of clusters), but *we maintain as an invariant that each vertex of G is contained in at most a constant number of local data structures.* In a planar embedded graph if $A_1, \ldots, A_g$ are all the neighboring clusters of s which belong to a certain biconnected component of H_c, we connect them (resp. their cycles) by $g-1$ edges in a way that preserves the planar embedding of the local data structure. For general graphs we cannot afford to do this.

Lemma 4.1 *Let G be a planar embedded graph. Then two neighboring clusters C and C′ of s are connected in the local data structure of s if and only if s is not an articulation point separating the vertices of C from the vertices of C′.*

Lemma 4.2 *Let G be a general graph. If two neighboring cluster C and C′ of s are connected in the local data structure of s, then s is not an articulation point separating the vertices of C from the vertices of C′.*

The reverse of Lemma 4.2 is not true, however.
If G is a planar embedded graph, every local data structure is stored in the data structure of Eppstein et al. [2] for fully dynamic connectivity testing in planar embedded graphs. It maintains a planar embedded graph under a sequence of insertions and deletions of edges and queries of the form:"Are u and v connected?" in time $O(\log n)$. If G is a general graph, we store each local data structure in a data structure of Frederickson [4] which maintains a general graph under the same operations in time $O(1)$ per query and in time $O(\sqrt{m'})$ per update where m' is the number of edges in the graph.

Since each vertex in $C_1, \ldots, C_f$ has degree at most 3, there are $O(fk)$ vertices and edges in the local data structure of s and it can be built in time $O(fk)$ [2] [4]. Each vertex is contained in a constant number of them. Thus the total size of the $O(m/k)$ local structures and the time to rebuild them is $O(m)$

Now we discuss how the local data structures are updated during insertions and deletions of an edge $e = (u, v)$. If e is inserted, we add it the local data structure which contains u and v (if it exists). If it is deleted, we remove it from this data structure.

Let s be a shared vertex and let C be a neighboring cluster of s. Then an edge e' is called a *predecessor of e relative to s and C* if e' is an edge between C and a cluster sharing s, and e' is the last such edge encountered by the Eulerian tour of the spanning tree of C before the edge e is encountered. By symmetry let a *successor of e relative to s and C* be the first such edge encountered after e is encountered. There are at most two predecessors and at most two successors relative to s for every tree edge e of C, one for each direction. If e is inserted and $C(v)$ shares a vertex s which is not shared by $C(u)$, then we have to find a predecessor e_1 and a successor e_2 of e relative to s and $C(u)$ such that e_1 and e_2 are connected by an edge in the local data structure of s. In the planar case we have to choose the predecessor and the successor in accordance with the embedding. Finding these edges by an Eulerian tour takes time $O(k)$. Then we create an e-vertex for e, remove (e_1, e_2) and add (v, e), (e_1, e), and (e, e_2) to the local data structure of s. If e is deleted, we execute the inverse operation. Since each vertex is contained in a constant number of local data structures, each such insertion or deletion causes a constant number of operations in $O(1)$ local data structures. Thus their total time is $O(k + \log n)$ in a planar graph and $O(k + \sqrt{m})$ in a general graph.

If G is a planar embedded graph, the local data structure of s contain edges between neighboring clusters of s. After each insertion or deletion of an edge we remove all artificial edges, determine which new edges have to be added, and add them. This can be done in time proportional to the high-level degree of the clusters sharing s. Thus the total time for it is $O((m/k) \log n)$.

Additionally some special cases have to be considered when a cluster is split or a tree edge in a neighboring cluster of s is deleted, but they can be handled in time $O((k + m/k) \log n)$ in a planar graph and in time $O(k + m/\sqrt{k})$ in a general graph.

Lemma 4.3 *In a planar embedded graph it takes time $O(\log n)$ to answer a query in a local data structure and time $O((k + m/k) \log n)$ to update all local data structures after an insertion or a deletion. In a general graph a query can be answered in time $O(1)$ and the total time spent for updating all local data structures is $O(k + m/\sqrt{k})$. Rebuilding all local data structures takes time $O(m)$.*

4.2 The global data structure

In general graphs the local data structures do not consider that two tree neighboring clusters C and C' of s can also be connected in G through a path which is not contained in the local data structure of s. In the latter case C and C' are biconnected in H_c. Thus we build a *global data structure of s* which is a graph whose vertices are the tree neighboring clusters of s. Two clusters C and C' are connected by an edge, if C and C' are connected in the local data structure of s or C and C' are biconnected in H_c.

Lemma 4.4 *Let C and C' be tree neighboring clusters of s. Then C and C' are connected in the global data structure of s if and only if s is not an articulation point separating the vertices of C from the vertices of C' in G.*

The global data structures are completely rebuilt after each insertion or deletion of an edge. Let t be the number of vertices in the global data structure of s. To build it we test every pair of its vertices whether they are either connected in the local data structure of s or biconnected in H_c. Since every such test can be executed in constant time, it takes time $O(t^2)$ to construct the global data structure of s. Then we compute its connected components in time $O(t^2)$. Since each cluster is incident to at most three tree edges and each endpoint of a tree edge is contained in only a constant number of local data structures, each cluster is contained in a constant number of global data structures. Thus the total number of vertices in all global data structures is $O(m/k)$. Therefore all of them can be rebuilt in time $O((m/k)^2)$.

Lemma 4.5 *The time for rebuilding all global data structures is $O((m/k)^2)$. Thus all global data structures can be updated in time $O((m/k)^2)$ after an insertion or deletion. A connectivity query in a global data structure can be answered in constant time.*

4.3 The look-up data structure

Using the global data structure of s we can test in constant time whether s is an articulation point separating the vertices in one tree neighboring clusters of s from the vertices in another tree neighboring cluster of s. However, we still cannot test whether s also separates two vertices which are contained in clusters sharing s. Thus we build a third data structure, called the *look-up data structure of s*. Let $C_1, \ldots, C_f$ for some positive integer f be the clusters which share s. The look-up data structure of s is a graph whose vertices are all the vertices of $C_1, \ldots, C_f$ with s removed. Its edges are the edges between vertices of $C_1, \ldots, C_f$ in G'. Every vertex in a look-up data structure has at most degree 3.

Whenever all data structures are rebuilt, we compute the connected components of the look-up data structures. Now we form *groups* of vertices in the following way. Each connected component which consists of at most k vertices is a group. If one of the connected components contains more than k vertices, we find a spanning tree T_s for it and determine a restricted partition of order k with respect to T_s. Each cluster of the partition forms a group. The vertices of every group are connected and every group contains at most k vertices. Additionally we keep a *graph of groups* which consists of a vertex for every group and an edge between two groups g_1 and g_2 labeled l if there are l edges between g_1 and g_2. Note that every connected component of the graph of groups consists of $O(m/k)$ groups. At each vertex we store a pointer to its group. We store additionally at each group g a pointer to a neighboring cluster of s which is connected to g in the local data structure of s if such a cluster exists. We also store at each non-tree neighboring cluster C of s a pointer to a tree neighboring cluster of s which is biconnected to C in H_c. Using this information we can find in constant time for a vertex v in the look-up data structure of s a tree neighboring cluster of s which is connected to v on a path without s (if it exists). We call this cluster $L(v)$.

Lemma 4.6 *Let u and v be two vertices which are lying in clusters that are sharing s. The vertex s is an articulation point separating u and v if and only if u and v are not connected in the local data structure of s and $L(u)$ and $L(v)$ (if they exist) are not connected in the global data structure of s. Additionally s is an articulation point separating u from the vertices of a tree neighboring cluster C of s if and only if u and C are not connected in the local data structure of s and $L(u)$ (if it exists) and C are not connected in the global data structure of s.*

This shows that using the local, the global, and the look-up data structures we can test in constant time whether s is an articulation point separating u and v.

Whenever the inserted or deleted edge e has at least one endpoint in a cluster sharing s, the look-up data structure of s has to be updated. Since each vertex is contained in a constant number of look-up data structures, only a constant number of them have to be changed. In each of these look-up data structure the topological partition and all pointers have to be updated. As shown in [4] it takes time $O(k)$ to maintain a topological partition of order k, the graph of groups, and the pointers at the vertices. To update the pointers at the groups we determine for each endpoint of e the group g to which it belongs. Then we test whether g is connected in the local data structure of s to any neighboring clusters of s and update its pointer appropriately. This takes time $O(m/k)$. We store this information also at the pointers of the $O(m/k)$ groups which are in the connected component of g in the graph of groups. Since none of the other groups are connected to g, they cannot be influenced by the changes in g. Thus the graphs in the look-up data structures can be updated in time $O(k+m/k)$.

Additionally the pointers at each non-tree neighboring cluster of s have to be updated. Removing all clusters sharing s splits the tree of H into subtrees, each containing one tree neighboring cluster of s. Note that every non-tree neighboring cluster of s is biconnected in H_c with the tree-neighboring cluster in its subtree. Thus we set the cluster pointers of all clusters in a subtree to the tree neighboring cluster of this subtree. This takes time $O(m/k)$ per shared vertex and thus time $O((m/k)^2)$ for all shared vertices.

If a cluster is split, some special cases have to be considered which we omit here.

Lemma 4.7 *A connectivity query can be answered in time $O(1)$ in a look-up data structure and all look-up data structures can be updated in time $O(k+(m/k)^2)$ after an insertion or deletion. The time for rebuilding all look-up data structures is $O(m)$.*

Lemma 4.8 *In a general graph a connectivity query can be answered in time $O(1)$ and it takes time $O(k+m/\sqrt{k}+(m/k)^2)$ to update all connectivity-structures. Rebuilding all connectivity data structures takes time $O(m)$.*

5 Insertions and deletions

If an edge (u,v) is inserted, we add it to H and to the appropriate internal and connectivity data structures. Additionally we rebuild all data structures every $\min\{k,m/k\}$ insertions. Together with the time of updating all internal data structures and all c-structures (see Section 3 and 4) the amortized time of an insertion is $O((k+m/k)\log n)$ in a planar graph and $O(k+(m/k)^2+m/\sqrt{k})$ in a general graph.

If an edge $e=(u,v)$ is deleted, we test whether u and v lie in the same cluster. If they do and e is a tree edge, the spanning tree of $C(u)$ is disconnected by the deletion. Thus we look for a non-tree edge that connects the two pieces and add it to the tree. If we cannot find such an edge in $C(u)$, $C(u)$ is split into two clusters, each corresponding to a connected component. Since $C(u)$ consists of $O(k)$ edges and vertices, this can be done in time $O(k)$.

If e is a tree edge between two clusters, we test all edges in H to find a non-tree edge which connects the two disconnected subtrees of H and add it to the tree.

If during an insertion or deletion the tree degree of a cluster becomes 3 and the cluster contains more than one vertex, we split it in up five clusters, one of tree degree 3 and up to four of tree degree 2 such that every cluster shares at most one vertex. All this takes time $O(k+m/k)$ in a planar graph and $O(k+(m/k)^2)$ in a general graph. Together with the time for updating the internal data structure and the c–structures (see Section 3 and 4) and the cost of rebuilding the whole data structure every m/k deletions, the amortized running time of a delete operation is $O((k + m/k)\log n)$ in the planar case and $O(k + m/\sqrt{k} + (m/k)^2)$ in the general case.

To speed up queries we compute some information in the general case after each update operation for each pair of clusters C_1 and C_2. We maintain a bit which is 1 if and only if the coverage bits of all clusters on $\pi_H(C_1, C_2)$ (excluding C_1 and C_2) are 1 and if for each shared vertex s the query(C_3, C_4) operation in the c–structure of s returns yes, where C_3 and $C_4 \neq C_3$ are the tree neighboring clusters of s on $\pi_H(C_1, C_2)$. Otherwise, the bit is set to 0.

Lemma 5.1 *Let $b_1 = b(C_1, C_2)$ and $b_2 = b(C_2, C_1)$. Then the bit for C_1 and C_2 is 1 if and only if b_1 and b_2 are biconnected in G.*

If one of the queries in the c–structure of a shared vertex s returns no, we store s as an articulation point separating C_1 and C_2 at the bit. If the bit of a cluster C on $\pi_H(C_1, C_2)$ is zero, we store the articulation point separating the tree neighbors of C (which is stored at one of them in $Comp(C)$) as an articulation point. If C_1 and C_2 are sharing a vertex, we remember this vertex. If they have no common shared vertex, but the edge incident to C_1 on $\pi_H(C_1, C_2)$ is dashed and belongs to the shared vertex s, we store s and the tree neighboring cluster of s on $\pi_G(s, b(C_2, C_1))$ at C_1. All information stored at C_1 can be computed during one traversal of the spanning tree of H. This takes time $O(m/k)$. Thus all this information can be computed in time $O((m/k)^2)$.

This, however, is too expensive in the planar case. Thus we keep two dynamic trees, one for each of the spanning trees of G and of H. A dynamic tree [9] represents a rooted tree by solid and dashed edges and at most two edges incident to a vertex are solid. We call the dashed edges in dynamic trees *dotted* edges to avoid confusion with the dashed edges in our data structure. We use a slight variation of dynamic trees at which costs are associated with vertices rather than with edges. In a dynamic tree the operations $link(x, y)$, $cut(x)$, $root(x)$ and $mincost(x)$ can be executed in time $O(\log n)$, where n is the number of nodes in the tree. A $link(x, y)$ operation links the tree of x with the tree of y by adding the edge (x, y). A $cut(x)$ operation removes the edge from x to its parent in the tree. A $root(x)$ operation roots the tree at x and a $mincost(x)$ query computes the minimum cost stored at a vertex on the path from x to the root of the tree of x.

The first dynamic tree contains the spanning tree of H. The cost at every cluster with tree degree 2 is its coverage bit. If a cluster C has three tree neighbors C_1, C_2, and C_3 and the tree edges (C_1, C) and (C, C_2) are the current solid edges incident to C, we store the coverage bit for C_1 and C_2 at C. Note that whenever a dotted edge (C_1, C) is converted into a solid edge, we know the other solid edge (C, C_2) which is leaving C and we can change in time $O(1)$ the bit at C to be the coverage bit of C_1 and C_2. Thus the coverage bits can be updated during the operations in the dynamic tree without increasing their running time. After each update operation we update the coverage bits in the dynamic tree in time $O(\log n)$ per bit. If a tree edge of H is deleted and a non–tree edge becomes a tree edge, we execute the appropriate *cut* and *link* operations in the dynamic tree. There are $O(1)$ of these operations, at a cost of $O(\log n)$ each. Thus, the total time for updating the tree after an update operation is $O((m/k)\log n)$.

A similar idea is used to handle dashed edges between clusters. We store the spanning tree of G in the second dynamic tree. We store a 1 as cost at each shared vertex s if (a, s) and (s, b) are the current solid edges at s in the dynamic tree and the query(a, b) operation in the c–structure of s returns yes. Otherwise we store a 0 at s. As above, these bits can be updated during the operations of the dynamic tree. Computing one bit takes time $O(\log n)$. Since $O(\log n)$ bits are computed during an operation in the dynamic tree, the running time of each operation in this dynamic tree is $O((\log n)^2)$. After an insertion or deletion we execute a constant number of *cut* and *link* operations and update all the bits. This takes time $O((m/k)\log n)$.

Lemma 5.2 *Let $b_1 = b(C_1, C_2)$ and $b_2 = b(C_2, C_1)$. The vertices b_1 and b_2 are biconnected in G if and only if all bits on $\pi(b_1, b_2)$ (excluding b_1 and b_2) in the second dynamic tree are 1 and all bits on $\pi(C_1, C_2)$ (excluding C_1 and C_2) in the first dynamic tree are 1.*

Lemma 5.3 *The amortized time of an insertion or a deletion of an edge is $O((k + m/k)\log n)$ in a planar embedded graph and $O(k + m/\sqrt{k} + (m/k)^2)$ in a general graph.*

6 Queries

To test the biconnectivity of two vertices u and v of the same cluster C we check, according to Lemma 3.1, whether u and v are biconnected in $G_a(C)$ and connected in the c–structure of the shared vertex of C (if it exists). This takes constant time.

If u and v are not in the same cluster, we distinguish between two cases. In a general graph we check the information stored for the tuple $(C(u), C(v))$. Let $b(u) = b(C(u), C(v))$ and $b(v) = b(C(v), C(u))$. If $C(u)$ and $C(v)$ share a vertex s, we test in the c–structure of s whether u and v are connected. If they are, we know that s is not an articulation point on $\pi_G(u, v)$ and we have to test the biconnectivity of $b(u)$ and u and of $b(v)$ and v. (Note that they are in the same cluster.) If $C(u)$ and $C(v)$ do not share a vertex, we check the bit of the tuple $(C(u), C(v))$. If it is 0, u and v are not biconnected. If it is 1, there is no articulation point on $\pi_G(b(u), b(v))$ (according to Lemma 5.1) and we have to test whether the edge $(C(u), C)$ on $\pi_H(C(u), C(v))$ is dashed. If it belongs to the shared vertex s, we test in the c–structure of s whether u and the cluster stored at $C(u)$ for this dashed edge are connected. Afterwards and if the edge $(C(u), C)$ on $\pi_H(C(u), C(v))$ is solid, we test the biconnectivity of u and C. The edge incident to $C(v)$ is treated symmetrically. All these tests take constant time. Thus, the running time of a query is $O(1)$.

In a planar embedded graph we perform a *mincost* query in both dynamic trees. Let u_1 (resp. v_1) be the tree neighbor of u (resp. v) on $\pi_G(u, v)$. We find u_1 by rooting the second dynamic tree at v and determining the parent of u. The vertex v_1 is found similarly. Then we root the dynamic tree of the spanning tree of G at u_1 and perform a $mincost(v_1)$ query. If the answer is 1, no shared vertex is an articulation point separating u and v. Otherwise, we return one of the shared vertices on $\pi_G(u, v)$ whose cost is 0 as an articulation point separating u and v. The total time for this is $O((\log n)^2)$. Then we root the first dynamic tree of the spanning tree of H at C_1, where C_1 is the tree neighbor of $C(u)$ on $\pi_H(C(u), C(v))$. Let C_2 be the symmetric tree neighbor of $C(v)$. If the $mincost(C_2)$ query returns 1, there is no articulation point separating u and v on $\pi_G(b(u), b(v))$ (according to Lemma 5.2) and we check the biconnectivity of u and C_1 and of v and C_2. If the $mincost(C_2)$ query returns 0, the algorithm outputs the vertex stored at one of the clusters on $\pi_H(C(u), C(v))$ whose cost is 0. Each operation in this dynamic tree takes time $O(\log n)$. Thus the total time of a query in a planar embedded graph is $O((\log n)^2)$.

Theorem 6.1 *In a planar embedded graph the worst case query time is $O((\log n)^2)$ and the amortized update time is $O(\sqrt{n \log n})$. In a general graph the worst case query time is $O(1)$ and the amortized update time is $O(m^{2/3})$.*

Proof: Let m_0 be the number of edges in G' during the last rebuild. Then the current number of edges is $O(m_0)$. Setting $k = \lfloor\sqrt{m_0 \log n}\rfloor$ in the planar case and $k = \lfloor m_0^{2/3} \rfloor$ in the general case gives the desired result. ∎

Acknowledgments

I want to thank Bob Tarjan, Bernard Chazelle, Han La Poutré, and Brandon Dixon for fruitful discussions and helpful comments.

References

[1] A. V. Aho, J. E. Hopcroft, J. D. Ullman, *The Design and Analysis of Computer Algorithms,* Addison-Wesley, 1974.

[2] D. Eppstein, G. F. Italiano, R. Tamassia, R. E. Tarjan, J. Westbrook, M. Yung, "Maintenance of a Minimum Spanning Forest in a Dynamic Planar Graph" *Proc. 1st Annual Symp. on Discrete Algorithms* 1990, 1 –11.

[3] D. Eppstein, Z. Galil, G. F. Italiano, A. Nissenzweig, "Sparsification - A technique for speeding up dynamic graph algorithms" *Proc. 33nd Annual Symp. on Foundations of Computer Science,* 1992.

[4] G. N. Frederickson, "Data Structures for On-line Updating of Minimum Spanning Trees" *SIAM J. Comput.* 14 (1985), 781–798.

[5] G. N. Frederickson, "Ambivalent Data Structures for Dynamic 2-edge-connectivity and k smallest spanning trees" *Proc. 32nd Annual Symp. on Foundations of Computer Science,* 1991, 632–641.

[6] Z. Galil, G. F. Italiano, "Maintaining Biconnected Components of Dynamic Planar Graphs" *Proc. 18th ICALP,* LNCS, Springer-Verlag, 1991, 339–350.

[7] F. Harary, *Graph Theory,* Addison-Wesley, Reading, MA, 1969.

[8] J. Hershberger, M. Rauch, S. Suri. "Fully Dynamic 2–Edge-Connectivity in Planar Graphs" *Proc. 3rd Scandinavian Workshop on Algorithm Theory,* LNCS 621, Springer-Verlag, 1992, 233–244.

[9] D. D. Sleator, R. E. Tarjan. "A Data Structure for Dynamic Trees" *J. Comput. System Sci.* 24 (1983), 362–381.

[10] R. E. Tarjan, "Depth First Search and Linear Graph Algorithms" *SIAM J. Comput.* 1 (1972), 146–160.

[11] R. E. Tarjan, J. Westbrook, "Maintaining bridge-connected and biconnected components on-line" *Algorithmica* 7 (1992), 433–464.

Sparsification – A Technique for Speeding up Dynamic Graph Algorithms*
(Extended Abstract)

David Eppstein[†] Zvi Galil[§]

Giuseppe F. Italiano[‡] Amnon Nissenzweig[¶]

Abstract

We provide data structures that maintain a graph as edges are inserted and deleted, and keep track of the following properties: minimum spanning forests, best swap, graph connectivity, and graph 2-edge-connectivity, in time $O(n^{1/2}\log(m/n))$ per change; 3-edge-connectivity, in time $O(n^{2/3})$ per change; 4-edge-connectivity, in time $O(n\alpha(n))$ per change; k-edge-connectivity, in time $O(n\log n)$ per change; bipartiteness, 2-vertex-connectivity, and 3-vertex-connectivity, in time $O(n\log(m/n))$ per change; and 4-vertex-connectivity, in time $O(n\log(m/n) + n\alpha(n))$ per change. Further results speed up the insertion times to match the bounds of known partially dynamic algorithms.

Our algorithms are based on a new technique that transforms algorithms for sparse graphs into ones that work on any graph, which we call *sparsification.*

1 Introduction

Graph algorithms are fundamental in computer science, and much work has gone into the study of *dynamic* graph algorithms; that is, algorithms that maintain some property of a changing graph more efficiently than recomputation from scratch after each change. If the changes allowed include both edge insertions and deletions, the algorithm is *fully dynamic*; a *partially dynamic* algorithm only allows insertions. Among many problems that have been studied from this point of view, the minimum spanning tree [7, 8, 10, 15] is perhaps the most important. Other recent work has focused on several types of connectivity [1, 11, 16, 17, 19, 22, 23, 31].

Despite much effort in this area, no general technique for dynamizing graph problems was known up to date, and all the previous algorithms made use of *ad hoc* approaches. In contrast, the design of general methods for dynamizing static problems has been a significant development in other fields such as geometric searching [2] and data structures [26].

In this paper, we introduce a new general technique for designing dynamic graph algorithms, which we call *sparsification.* We use this technique to speed up many fully dynamic graph algorithms. Roughly speaking, when the technique is applicable it speeds up a $T(n,m)$ time bound for a graph with n vertices and m edges to $T(n,O(n))\log(m/n)$; i.e. almost to the time needed if the graph were sparse.[1]

The new result that most stands out is our $O(n^{1/2}\log(m/n))$ time bound for maintaining the minimum spanning forest of a graph. The best previous result, $O(m^{1/2})$ [10], stood for eight years without improvement. Our bound contradicts a supposed $\Omega(m/n)$ lower bound [3]; however, that result placed unreasonably small limits on preprocessing time, and does not apply to our algorithm. Perhaps the most surprising fact about our general technique, and its application to minimum spanning forests, is that it had been overlooked for so long.

The technique itself is quite simple. We partition the edges of the graph into a collection of sparse subgraphs. The information relevant for each subgraph can be summarized in an even sparser subgraph, which we call a *sparse certificate.* We merge certificates

*Work supported in part by NSF Grant CCR-9014605.

†Department of Information and Computer Science, University of California, Irvine, CA 92717.

‡IBM T.J. Watson Research Center, P.O. Box 704, Yorktown Heights, NY 10598. On leave from Università di Roma, Italy.

§Computer Science Department, Columbia University, New York, NY 10027 and Computer Science Department, Tel-Aviv University, Tel-Aviv, Israel.

¶Computer Science Department, Tel-Aviv University, Tel-Aviv, Israel.

[1] Throughout this paper $\log x$ stands for $\max(1, \log_2 x)$, so $\log(m/n)$ is never smaller than 1 even if $m < 2n$.

0-8186-2900-2/92 $3.00 © 1992 IEEE

in pairs, producing larger subgraphs which we make sparse by again applying the certificate reduction. The result is a balanced binary tree in which each node is represented by a sparse certificate. Each update involves $\log(m/n)$ graphs with $O(n)$ edges each, instead of one graph with m edges.

We develop three variants of our technique. We use the first variant in situations where no previous fully dynamic algorithm was known. We use a static algorithm to recompute a sparse certificate in each tree node affected by an edge update. If the certificates can be found in time $O(m+n)$, this variant gives time bounds of $O(n \log(m/n))$ per update.

In the second variant, we maintain certificates using a dynamic data structure. For this to work, we need a *stability* property of our certificates, to ensure that a small change in the input graph does not lead to a large change in the certificates. This variant transforms time bounds of the form $O(m^p)$ into $O(n^p \log(m/n))$. In many instances, certificates can be maintained even more efficiently than the property they certify, and the $O(\log(m/n))$ term vanishes.

In the third variant, we perform deletions as in the first variant, and insertions using a partially dynamic algorithm. This leads to insertion times often matching those of known partially dynamic algorithms, together with deletion times similar to those of the first variant.

2 New Results

We describe fully dynamic data structures for the following problems.

1. We maintain the minimum spanning forest of an edge-weighted graph in $O(n^{1/2} \log(m/n))$ time per edge insertion, deletion, or weight change, improving a longstanding $O(m^{1/2})$ bound [10]. We can instead take time $O(\log n)$ per insertion and $O(n \log(m/n))$ per deletion, strengthening known partially dynamic algorithms.

2. We give a fully persistent, fully dynamic data structure for maintaining the best swap in the minimum spanning tree of a graph, in time $O(n^{1/2} \log(m/n))$ per update. As a consequence we find the k smallest spanning trees of a graph in time $O(m \log \beta(m,n) + kn^{1/2} \log(m/n))$. The best previous times were $O(m^{1/2})$ and $O(m \log \beta(m,n) + km^{1/2})$ respectively [11].

3. We use a randomly weighted version of our minimum spanning forest algorithm to perform a certain random walk among the spanning trees of a graph in time $O(n^{1/2} \log(m/n))$ per step. Feder and Mihail [9] prove that this walk can be used to sample the space of spanning trees in time $O((n \log m + \log \epsilon^{-1}) m^{1/2} n^3)$; we improve this to $O((n \log m + \log \epsilon^{-1}) n^{7/2} \log(m/n))$.

4. We give a data structure for querying membership in the connected components of a graph, in $O(n^{1/2} \log(m/n))$ time per edge insertion or deletion, and $O(1)$ time per query. As with minimum spanning forests, the best previous bound was $O(m^{1/2})$ [10].

5. We maintain the 2-edge-connected components of a graph, in time $O(n^{1/2} \log(m/n))$ per update, and $O(\log n)$ per query, improving the previous $O(m^{1/2})$ bound per update [11].

6. We maintain the 3-edge-connected components of a graph, in $O(n^{2/3})$ time per update or query, improving the previous $O(m^{2/3})$ bound [19].

7. We maintain 4-edge-connected components of a graph in $O(n\alpha(n))$ time. No fully dynamic algorithm was known for this problem. The best static algorithm takes time $O(m+n\alpha(n))$ [18, 22].

8. For any fixed k, we maintain the k-edge-connected components in time $O(n \log n)$ per update. No dynamic algorithm for this problem was known, even for insertions only. The best known static algorithm takes time $O(m+n \log n)$ [12, 13].

9. We maintain the connected, 2- and 3-edge-connected, and 2- and 3-vertex connected components of a graph in time $O(\alpha(q,n))$ per insertion or query and time $O(n \log(m/n))$ per deletion, strengthening known partially dynamic algorithms [1, 16, 23, 31]. Rauch [27] has recently discovered a fully dynamic algorithm for 2-vertex connectivity, which takes $O(1)$ time per query and $O(m^{2/3})$ amortized time per update. No previous fully dynamic algorithm for 3-vertex connectivity was known. All the static problems can be solved in time $O(m+n)$ [21, 29].

10. We maintain the 4-vertex-connected components of a graph in $O(n \log(m/n) + n\alpha(n))$ time per update, or in time $O(\log n)$ per insertion and $O(n \log n)$ per deletion. No fully dynamic algorithm was previously known. The static problem can be solved in time $O(m + n\alpha(n))$ [22].

11. We maintain a bipartition of a graph, or determine that the graph is not bipartite, in $O(\alpha(n))$

amortized time per insertion and $O(n\log(m/n))$ time per deletion. No dynamic algorithm was previously known. The static problem can be solved in time $O(m+n)$.

3 Sparsification

We first describe an abstract version of our sparsification technique. Our technique is based on the concept of a *certificate*:

Definition 1. *For any graph property $\mathcal{P}$, and graph G, a* certificate *for G is a graph G' such that G has property $\mathcal{P}$ if and only if G' has the property.*

Cheriyan and Thurimella [4] use a similar concept, however they require G' to be a subgraph of G. We do not need this restriction. However Definition 1 allows trivial certificates: G' could be chosen from two graphs of constant complexity, one with property $\mathcal{P}$ and one without it.

Definition 2. *For any graph property $\mathcal{P}$, and graph G, a* strong certificate *for G is a graph G' on the same vertex set such that, for any H, $G\cup H$ has property $\mathcal{P}$ if and only if $G'\cup H$ has the property.*

In all our uses of this definition, G and H will have the same vertex set and disjoint edge sets. A strong certificate need not be a subgraph of G, but it must have a structure closely related to that of G. The following facts follow immediately from Definition 2.

Lemma 1. *Let G' be a strong certificate of property $\mathcal{P}$ for graph G, and let G'' be a strong certificate for G'. Then G'' is a strong certificate for G.*

Lemma 2. *Let G' and H' be strong certificates of $\mathcal{P}$ for G and H. Then $G'\cup H'$ is a strong certificate for $G\cup H$.*

A property is said to have *sparse certificates* if there is some constant c such that for every graph G on an n-vertex set, we can find a strong certificate for G with at most cn edges. Our main result is the following.

Theorem 1. *Let $\mathcal{P}$ be a property for which we can find sparse certificates in time $f(n,m)$, and such that we can construct a data structure for testing property $\mathcal{P}$ in time $g(n,m)$ which can answer queries in time $q(n,m)$. Then there is a fully dynamic data structure for testing whether a graph has property $\mathcal{P}$, for which edge insertions and deletions can be performed in time $f(n,O(n))O(\log(m/n))+g(n,O(n))$, and for which the query time is $q(n,O(n))$.*

Proof: We maintain a partition of the edges of the graph into $\lceil m/n\rceil$ groups, all but one of which contain exactly n edges. The remaining group, which we call the *small group*, may contain between 1 and n edges. When we insert an edge, it is placed in the small group. When we delete an edge, we move another edge from the small group into the group from which we deleted the edge, to maintain the group size invariant. If we delete the small group's last edge, we remove the group, and if we insert an edge when there are n edges in the small group, we start a new small group.

We form a complete binary tree with $\lceil m/n\rceil$ leaves corresponding to the $\lceil m/n\rceil$ groups. Each node in this *sparsification tree* corresponds to a subgraph formed by the edges in the groups at the leaves of the tree that are descendants of the given node. For each such subgraph, we maintain a sparse certificate of $\mathcal{P}$. The certificate at a given node is found by forming the union of the certificates at the two child nodes, and running the sparse certificate algorithm on this union. By Lemmas 1 and 2 this gives a sparse certificate for the subgraph at the node. Each certificate can be computed in time $f(n,2cn)$. Each change in the number of groups will cause a single leaf of the tree to split, or two leaves to merge. Since we only allow edge insertions and deletions, the number of edges per group will never change.

When an edge is inserted or deleted, we change $O(1)$ groups. For each of these groups, and for their $\log(m/n)$ ancestors in the sparsification tree, we recompute a new sparse certificate. This results in a sparse certificate for the whole graph at the root of the tree. We update the data structure for property $\mathcal{P}$, on the graph formed by the sparse certificate at the root of the tree, in time $g(n,cn)$. The total time per update is thus $f(n,cn)\log(m/n)+g(n,cn)$. □

This technique is very effective at producing dynamic graph data structures for a multitude of problems, in which the update time is $O(n\log^{O(1)}n)$ instead of the static time bounds of $O(m+n\log^{O(1)}n)$. To achieve sublinear update times, we further refine our sparsification idea.

Definition 3. *Let A be a function mapping graphs to strong certificates. Then A is* stable *if it has the following two properties: (1) For any graphs G and H, $A(G\cup H)=A(A(G)\cup H)$. (2) For any graph G and edge e in G, $A(G-e)$ differs from $A(G)$ by $O(1)$ edges.*

Informally, we refer to a certificate as stable if it is the certificate produced by a stable mapping. The certificate consisting of the whole graph is stable, but not sparse.

Theorem 2. *Let $\mathcal{P}$ be a property for which stable sparse certificates can be maintained in time $f(n, m)$ per update, and for which there is a data structure for property $\mathcal{P}$ with update time $g(n, m)$ and query time $q(n, m)$. Then $\mathcal{P}$ can be maintained in time $f(n, O(n))O(\log(m/n)) + g(n, O(n))$ per update, with query time $q(n, O(n))$.*

Proof: As before, we group the edges into $\lceil m/n \rceil$ groups of n edges each, arranged in a complete binary tree. We propagate changes up the tree, using the data structure for maintaining certificates, and update the data structure for property $\mathcal{P}$, defined on the graph formed by the sparse certificate at the tree root.

At each node of the tree, we maintain a stable certificate on the graph formed as the union of the two certificates in the two child nodes. The equality in the first part of the definition of stability implies that this certificate will be the same as the stable certificate that would have been selected by the mapping A on the subgraph of all edges in groups descending from the node. The second part of the definition of stability bounds the number of changes in the certificate by some constant s, since the subgraph is changing only by a single edge. Thus at each level of the sparsification tree there is a constant amount of change.

When we perform an update, we find these s changes at each successive level of the sparsification tree, using the data structure for stable certificates. We perform at most s data structure operations, one for each change in the certificate at the next lower level. Each operation produces at most s changes to be made to the certificate at the present level, so we would expect a total of s^2 changes. However, many of these changes will cancel out, since as argued above the net effect of the update will be at most s changes in the certificate.

In order to prevent the number of data structure operations from blowing up, we perform this cancellation before passing the changes in the certificate up to the next level of the sparsification tree. Cancellation can be detected by leaving a marker on each edge, to keep track of whether it is in or out of the certificate. Only after all s^2 changes have been processed do we pass the at most s uncancelled changes up to the next level. Each change takes time $f(n, O(n))$, and the total bound follows as in Theorem 1. □

Theorem 1 can be used to dynamize static algorithms, while Theorem 2 can be used to speed up existing fully dynamic algorithms. In order to apply effectively Theorem 1 we only need to *compute* efficiently *sparse* certificates, while for Theorem 2 we need to *maintain* efficiently *stable sparse* certificates.

4 Bipartiteness

As a simple example of sparsification, let property $\mathcal{P}$ be bipartiteness. If graph G is not bipartite, it contains an odd cycle, and that cycle is a sparse strong certificate of non-bipartiteness. For a smaller certificate, take the edges of a triangle (which need not be a subgraph of G). If G is bipartite, any spanning forest of G is a strong certificate, since for any path connecting two vertices in G there will be one of the same parity in the spanning forest. In either case the certificate can be found in linear time. Thus Theorem 1 proves the following result.

Theorem 3. *We can perform edge insertions or deletions in a graph, and compute whether the graph is bipartite after each update, in time $O(n \log(m/n))$ per update.*

5 Minimum Spanning Trees and Connectivity

Given an undirected graph with non-negative edge weights, the *minimum spanning forest* is the subgraph of minimum total weight that has the same connected components as the original graph. This subgraph will always be a forest, hence the name. A minimum spanning forest is not a graph property, since it is a subgraph rather than a Boolean function. However sparsification still applies to this problem. Alternately, our data structure maintains any property defined on the minimum spanning trees of graphs. This data structure will also be an important subroutine in some of our later results.

In the static case, it was well known that a minimum spanning forest can be computed by either of two dual algorithms:

- **Blue rule.** Add edges one at a time to the spanning forest until it spans the graph. At each step, find a cut in the graph that contains no edges of the current forest, and add the edge with lowest weight crossing the cut.

- **Red rule.** Remove edges one at a time from the graph until only a forest is left. At each step, find a cycle in the remaining graph and remove the edge with the highest weight in the cycle.

Most efficient minimum spanning tree algorithms use the blue rule. The best such static algorithm takes time $O(m \log \beta(m,n))$ [14]. The best fully dynamic algorithm takes time $O(m^{1/2})$ per update [10]. For eight years no improvement had been made to this algorithm. For insertions only, a minimum spanning tree can be maintained in $O(\log n)$ time per insertion by the dynamic tree data structure of Sleator and Tarjan [28]; this was the only known efficient minimum spanning tree algorithm based only on the red rule. An $O(\log n)$ time per update offline algorithm using a combination of the red and blue rules was described by Eppstein [7]. For planar graphs, $O(\log n)$ time fully dynamic algorithms are known [8, 15]; these exploit planar duality and hence also combine red and blue rules.

Our sparsification technique can be interpreted as a red rule algorithm, and together with the insertion-only algorithm provides evidence that the red rule is more suited than the blue rule as a basis for dynamic algorithms. We will need the following analogue of strong certificates for minimum spanning trees:

Lemma 3. *Let T be a minimum spanning forest of graph G. Then for any H there is some minimum spanning forest of $G \cup H$ which does not use any edges in $G - T$.*

Proof: If we use the red rule on graph $G \cup H$, we can eliminate any cycles in G (removing all edges in $G - T$) before dealing with cycles involving edges in H. □

Thus we can take the strong certificate of any minimum spanning forest property to be the minimum spanning forest itself. Minimum spanning forests also have a well-known property which, together with Lemma 3, proves that they satisfy our definition of stability:

Lemma 4. *Let T be a minimum spanning forest of graph G, and let e be an edge of T. Then either $T - e$ is a minimum spanning forest of $G - e$, or there is a minimum spanning forest of the form $T - e + f$ for some edge f.*

If we modify the weights of the edges, by combining them with the numbers of the vertices involved taken in lexicographic order, we do not change the total weight of the resulting minimum spanning forests, but we can then guarantee that there will be exactly one minimum spanning forest. The mapping from graphs to unique minimum spanning forests is stable, since part (1) of the definition of stability follows from Lemma 3, and part (2) follows from Lemma 4.

We base our algorithm on the result of Frederickson [10], that minimum spanning trees can be maintained in time $O(m^{1/2})$. We improve this bound by combining Frederickson's algorithm with our sparsification technique.

Theorem 4. *The minimum spanning forest of an undirected graph can be maintained in time $O(n^{1/2} \log(m/n))$ per update.*

Proof: Apply the stable sparsification technique of Theorem 2, with $f(n,m) = g(n,m) = O(m^{1/2})$ by Frederickson's algorithm. □

Most minimum spanning forest properties can be maintained in these bounds by the dynamic tree data structure of Sleator and Tarjan [28], with a query time of $O(\log n)$. One such property, namely testing whether vertices are in the same tree of the forest (which is well-known to be equivalent to testing connected components of the graph) can be maintained even with an $O(1)$ query time.

Corollary 1. *The connected components of an undirected graph can be maintained in $O(n^{1/2} \log(m/n))$ time per update, and $O(1)$ time per query.*

Proof: Again, use Theorem 2 with Frederickson's algorithm. As noted by Frederickson [11], connectivity queries in his data structure can be performed in constant time. □

As a more complicated application, we consider a random walk used by Feder and Mihail [9] to randomly sample spanning trees of a graph G. The state at each point in the walk consists of a set of edges, which is either spanning tree of G, or a forest with $n - 2$ edges (i.e. a spanning tree with an edge removed). At each step we stay with the current edge set with probability 1/2. If we do not stay with the current step, we either remove a randomly chosen edge from the edge set if it is already a spanning tree, or we add an edge chosen randomly among those edges which augment the set to become a spanning tree. Thus whenever the edge set changes, it alternates between being a spanning tree and a separated forest.

We can implement this random walk if we can perform the following *combined step* efficiently: given a spanning tree of the graph, remove a randomly chosen edge, and then augment the resulting forest to be a spanning tree again by choosing another edge randomly among the edges which cross the cut spanned by the removed edge.

We do this as follows. At each point in time, the edges in the current spanning tree are given weight zero. The edges outside the tree are given weights corresponding to their positions in a permutation chosen uniformly at random among all possible permutations of these edges. When we remove an edge from the spanning tree, we add it to this random permutation by choosing a position at random among the $m - n$ possibilities. We then use our data structure to find a new minimum spanning tree with the weights described above; this will select an edge spanning the cut uniformly at random among the possible such edges. We remove this edge from the random permutation and give it weight zero. The removal of this edge will not bias the distribution of permutations of the remaining edges, so the overall permutation will continue to be chosen uniformly at random.

To implement this, we need to compute minimum spanning trees in a graph with weights that may change as edges are inserted to and deleted from the random permutation. Our minimum spanning tree algorithm, and Frederickson's algorithm on which ours is based, do not perform arithmetic on edge weights; they can operate in the given time bounds if they can merely compare any two weights in constant time. These comparisons can be performed using a data structure of Dietz and Sleator [5] to find which of the two edges occurs earlier in the permutation. We have proved the following:

Theorem 5. *We can implement the random walk of Feder and Mihail [9] on the spanning forests of a given graph, in time $O(n^{1/2}\log(m/n))$ per step.*

Feder and Mihail show that this walk converges to the uniform distribution in $O((n\log m+\epsilon^{-1})n^3)$ steps; thus we can select a spanning tree from the uniform distribution in time $O((n\log m+\epsilon^{-1})n^{7/2}\log(m/n))$.

6 Best Swaps and Persistence

In any graph, the minimum spanning tree (in short *MST*) differs from the spanning tree with the second smallest weight by the addition of an edge not already in the MST, and the removal of an MST edge. Frederickson [11] described a ***fully persistent*** algorithm for maintaining this ***best swap***: each update operation is performed in one of a number of ***versions*** of the data structure, and creates a new such version. Frederickson uses two operations: (1) perform the best swap, and delete the removed MST edge from the graph; and (2) change to $-\infty$ the weight of the MST edge that would be removed. He uses these operations to find the k minimum weight spanning trees of a graph in time $O(m\log\beta(m,n) + k\min(k,m)^{1/2})$.

Theorem 2 is easily modified to support full persistence: each version of a node of the sparsification tree points to a version of a persistent data structure for maintaining the certificate at that node, and to the versions of its two child nodes. When we perform an update, we find the appropriate leaf by following pointers from the appropriate version of the root, and make new versions of the nodes along that path.

Frederickson's data structure can support edge insertions and deletions in $O(m^{1/2})$ time, and the two update types listed above may be simulated using $O(1)$ insertions and deletions. The MST and best swap edge do not form a strong certificate for the best swap, but they are a subgraph of another graph, the union of the MST T_1 of G and the MST T_2 of $G-T_1$, which forms a stable certificate for the best swap problem. These two MST's can be maintained by Frederickson's MST algorithm, which can easily be made persistent using the same techniques as Frederickson's best swap data structure. Thus we achieve the following results.

Theorem 6. *The best swap of an undirected graph can be maintained in time $O(n^{1/2}\log(m/n))$ per update, with full persistence.*

Theorem 7. *We can find the k minimum weight spanning trees of a graph in time $O(m\log\beta(m,n) + k\min(n,k)^{1/2}\log(\min(m,k)/n))$.*

Proof: As Frederickson [11] shows, this problem can be solved using $O(k)$ operations in the persistent best swap data structure. The data structure can be constructed in time $O(m\log\log^* n)$, the bottleneck being constructing a minimum spanning tree in each node of the sparsification tree. This can be improved to $O(m\log\beta(m,n))$ by allowing the leaf nodes of the sparsification tree to contain $O(n\log(m/n))$ edges. A technique of the first author [6] replaces n by $\min(n,k)$ and m by $\min(m,k)$ in the time bounds. □

7 Edge Connectivity

The best previous data structure for 2-edge-connectivity is due to Frederickson [11], who improved a previous $O(m^{2/3})$ time algorithm [16] to $O(m^{1/2})$.

Galil and Italiano [16] and La Poutré [23] gave algorithms for maintaining 3-edge-connectivity with insertions only, in amortized time $O(\alpha(q, n))$ per insertion. Galil and Italiano recently discovered a fully dynamic algorithm for 3-edge-connectivity, with an $O(m^{2/3})$ time bound [19]. No nontrivial dynamic algorithm was known for any higher order of connectivity.

If a graph is k-edge-connected, we could use a minimal k-edge-connected subgraph as a sparse certificate. However, it has only been recently that algorithms were developed for finding such subgraphs in linear time, even for 2-edge-connectivity [20]. Further, no sublinear time algorithms are known for maintaining such graphs, let alone with any sort of stability properties.

Instead we use the following technique, which produces certificates guaranteed to be both sparse and stable. Given a graph G, let $T_1 = U_1$ be a spanning forest of G. Let T_2 be a spanning forest of $G - U_1$, and let $U_2 = U_1 \cup T_2$. In general, let T_i be a spanning forest of $G - U_{i-1}$, and let U_i be $U_{i-1} \cup T_i$. Thurimella [30] and Nagamochi and Ibaraki [25] note that U_k is a certificate of k-edge-connectivity for G. More generally, U_k and G have the same set of $(k-1)$-cuts, and the same set of k-edge-connected components. We need the following stronger result:

Lemma 5. *U_k is a strong certificate of k-edge-connectivity for G.*

Proof: Consider any k-edge-connected graph $G \cup H$, and build a certificate in the following way. Start with T_1, and augment it with edges of H to be a spanning forest for $G \cup H$. Then start with T_2, and augment it with some of the remaining edges of H to be a spanning forest for $G \cup H$. In this way we obtain a collection of forests, which is a certificate for $G \cup H$, and which is a subgraph of $U_k \cup H$. Therefore if $G \cup H$ is k-edge-connected, so is $U_k \cup H$. On the other hand, if $G \cup H$ is not k-edge-connected, then neither can be its subgraph $U_k \cup H$. So U_k is a strong certificate for G. □

For any fixed k we can maintain a graph U_k in time $O(km^{1/2})$ per update, using k copies of Frederickson's dynamic minimum spanning forest algorithm. The resulting certificate is stable, since each update involves at most a single edge flip in each of k minimum spanning trees.

We are now ready to state our results for edge connectivity.

Theorem 8. *The 2-edge-connected components of an undirected graph can be maintained in time $O(n^{1/2} \log(m/n))$ per update. Queries asking whether two vertices are in the same component can be answered in $O(\log n)$ time.*

Proof: We use Frederickson's minimum spanning tree algorithm [10] to maintain the stable strong certificate U_2, giving $f(n, m) = O(m^{1/2})$. Each update to the graph translates to $O(1)$ changes to U_2. The 2-edge-connected components of U_2 can be maintained in time $g(n, m) = O(m^{1/2})$, with queries whether two vertices are in the same component answered in time $q(n, m) = O(\log n)$ [11]. Applying Theorem 2 gives our result. □

Theorem 9. *The 3-edge-connected components of an undirected graph can be maintained in $O(n^{2/3})$ time per update and $O(n^{2/3})$ per query.*

Proof: We maintain the 3-edge-connected components in U_3 with the $O(m^{2/3})$ time algorithm of Galil and Italiano [19]. $f(n, m) = O(m^{1/2})$ as before, and $g(n, m) = q(n, m) = O(m^{2/3})$, so the total time is $O(n^{1/2} \log(m/n) + n^{2/3}) = O(n^{2/3})$. □

Theorem 10. *The 4-edge-connected components of an undirected graph can be maintained in $O(n\alpha(n))$ time per update.*

Proof: Transform the problem into testing 4-vertex-connectivity by replacing every vertex of the root certificate by a 2-hub wheel [18], and then use the $O(m + n\alpha(n))$-time 4-vertex-connectivity algorithm of Kanevsky et al. [22]. □

Theorem 11. *For any fixed constant k, the k-edge-connected components of an undirected graph can be maintained in time $O(n \log n)$ per update.*

Proof: Maintain the stable strong certificate U_k using our dynamic minimum spanning tree techniques, and recompute the k-edge-connected components of U_k after each update using Gabow's $O(m + n \log n)$-time algorithm [13]. □

8 Vertex Connectivity

Vertex connectivity seems to be harder in general than edge connectivity. The best static connectivity testing algorithms are significantly faster for edge connectivity than for vertex connectivity. While fully dynamic algorithms were known for 2- and 3-edge-connectivity, no similar results were known for vertex connectivity, except for special cases such as planar graphs [17]. The only partially dynamic algorithms known were for 2-, 3- and 4-vertex connectivity [1, 22, 31]. This relative hardness was made explicit by Galil and Italiano [18], who reduced computations of edge connectivity to vertex connectivity; no reduction in the reverse direction is known.

Sparsification provides the first nontrivial fully dynamic algorithms for vertex connectivity. We first define our certificates as a restricted form of the certificates U_k used for edge connectivity. Given a graph G, let $B_1 = C_1$ be a breadth first spanning forest of G; i.e., start from any vertex and perform a breadth first search until all edges are exhausted, then continue by restarting at any unvisited node until all connected components of the graph are covered. Let B_2 be a breadth first forest of $G - C_1$, and let $C_2 = C_1 \cup B_2$. In general, let B_i be a breadth first forest of $G - C_{i-1}$, and let $C_i = C_{i-1} \cup B_i$. Cheriyan and Thurimella [4] prove that C_k is a certificate for the k-vertex-connectedness of G. As before, we need a stronger result.

Lemma 6. *C_k is a strong certificate of k-vertex-connectivity for G.*

Proof: Consider a $(k-1)$-vertex cut S in any graph $C_k \cup H$, partitioning the remaining vertices into two components A and B. Obviously H can contain no edges from A to B. Let x be the vertex of S first visited by the breadth first search defining forest B_1. Suppose x was visited from a vertex in A. Then all the edges from x to B in G will be visited before any edge from another vertex of S to B. So all such edges will be in B_1 instead of $C_k - B_1$, and $S - x$ forms a $(k-2)$-vertex cut in $C_k - B_1$. Continuing in the same way, we see that each breadth first search eliminates a vertex, and so B_k must be disconnected. But this can only happen if S is also a cutset in G, and hence in $G \cup H$. Thus we see that any cut in $C_k \cup H$ is also a cut in $G \cup H$. The converse follows immediately from the fact that C_k is a subgraph of G. Hence C_k is a strong certificate. □

Each certificate C_k can be found in time $f(n,m) = O(km)$. At the root of the sparsification tree, we can identify 2- or 3-vertex-connected components in linear time [21, 29]. 4-vertex-connected components can be found in time $O(m + n\alpha(n))$ [22]. The basic sparsification technique of Theorem 1 leads to the following results:

Theorem 12. *The 2- and 3-vertex-connected components of an undirected graph can be maintained in time $O(n \log(m/n))$ per update.*

Theorem 13. *The 4-vertex-connected components of an undirected graph can be maintained in time $O(n \log(m/n) + n\alpha(n))$ per update.*

9 Faster Insertions

In some applications we may perform more insertions than deletions, so it might be appropriate to speed up insertion time at some expense in deletion time. One way of doing this would be to use a partially dynamic data structure for insertions, and rebuild the data structure from scratch after each deletion. Sparsification can provide an improvement in this situation as well.

Theorem 14. *Let $\mathcal{P}$ be a property for which we can find sparse certificates in time $f(n,m)$, and such that we can construct a partially dynamic data structure for testing property $\mathcal{P}$ in time $g(n,m)$ which can handle edge insertions in time $p(n,m)$ and answer queries in time $q(n,m)$. Then there is a fully dynamic data structure for testing whether a graph has property $\mathcal{P}$, for which edge insertions can be performed in time $O(f(n,O(n)))/n + g(n,O(n))/n + p(n,O(n))$, edge deletions can be performed in time $f(n,O(n))O(\log(m/n)) + g(n,O(n))$, and for which the query time is $q(n,O(n))$.*

This version of sparsification is stronger than Theorem 1, since there is no $O(\log(m/n))$ term in the insertion times even if insertions also rebuild a static data structure.

We saw earlier that the property of bipartiteness can be maintained in time $O(n \log(m/n))$ per update. Using Theorem 14 we can improve this result by combining sparsification with a partially dynamic algorithm for the same problem:

Lemma 7. *In linear time we can construct a data structure such that edges can be added, and the bipartiteness of the resulting graph tested, in amortized time $O(\alpha(n))$ per insertion.*

Proof: We modify the well-known union-find data structure. We represent each vertex by a set element, and each connected component of the graph by a set. Sets in the union-find data structure are represented by trees; we augment the data structure so that each tree edge stores a bit of information, denoting the parity of the paths between the two elements it connects. All operations can be performed in the same time as the basic union-find algorithm, which is well-known to have an $O(\alpha(n))$ amortized time bound. □

Theorem 15. *We can construct a data structure for testing bipartiteness for which insertions and deletions can be performed in time $O(\alpha(n))$ and $O(n \log(m/n))$ respectively.*

We next apply this technique to the spanning tree and connectivity problems we solved using the other versions of sparsification.

Theorem 16. *The minimum spanning forest of a graph can be maintained in time $O(\log n)$ per insertion and $O(n \log(m/n))$ per deletion.*

Proof: We apply Theorem 14, using a partially dynamic algorithm based on the dynamic tree data structure of Sleator and Tarjan [28]. □

Theorem 17. *The connected, 2-edge-connected, 3-edge-connected, 2-vertex-connected, and 3-vertex-connected components of a graph can be maintained in amortized time $O(\alpha(q, n))$ per insertion or query and $O(n \log(m/n))$ per deletion, where q is the total number of queries made.*

Proof: For connected components, we use the well known union-find algorithm as our partially dynamic data structure. For 2-connected components, we use the partially dynamic algorithms of Westbrook and Tarjan [31], while for 3-connected components, we use the algorithms of La Poutré [23, 24]. □

Theorem 18. *The 4-vertex-connected components of a graph can be maintained in time $O(\log n)$ per insertion and $O(n \log n)$ per deletion.*

Proof: Apply Theorem 14 using the partially dynamic data structure of Kanevsky et al. [22], for which $p(n, m) = O(1)$ and $g(n, m) = O(m + n \log n)$. □

10 Conclusions

We have presented a new technique, called sparsification, that proves to be very useful in the design of fully dynamic graph algorithms. As an application, we have presented new improved algorithms for dynamic minimum spanning forests, and for several types of dynamic edge- and vertex-connectivity. Sparsification can also be applied to static problems such as computing the k smallest spanning trees of a graph. The technique is quite general and uses previous algorithms as subroutines. Any future improvement in those algorithms might in itself provide better bounds in our running times.

For minimum spanning forests, connectivity, 2- and 3-edge connectivity, we achieve sublinear update times. Can these results be extended to the other problems we considered? We believe that bipartiteness can be maintained $O(n^{1/2} \log(m/n))$ time by using sparsification together with Frederickson's technique of ***ambivalent data structures*** [11], with certificates consisting of a minimum spanning tree and a single additional edge. If we are to use sparsification for sublinear vertex connectivity we would need a different way of producing strong certificates, since the ones we use now are not stable. Do such certificates exist?

Acknowledgments

We are grateful to Tom Spencer for useful comments.

References

[1] G. Di Battista and R. Tamassia. On-line graph algorithms with SPQR-trees. 17th Int. Coll. Automata, Languages, and Programming (1990) 598–611.

[2] J.L. Bentley and J.B. Saxe. Decomposable searching problems I: static-to-dynamic transformation. *J. Algorithms* 1 (1980) 301–358.

[3] A.M. Berman, M.C. Paull, and B.G. Ryder. Proving relative lower bounds for incremental algorithms. *Acta Informatica* 27 (1990) 665–683.

[4] J. Cheriyan and R. Thurimella. Algorithms for parallel k-vertex connectivity and sparse certificates. 23rd ACM Symp. Theory of Computing (1991) 391–401.

[5] P.F. Dietz and D.D. Sleator. Two algorithms for maintaining order in a list. 19th ACM Symp. Theory of Computing (1987) 365–372.

[6] D. Eppstein. Finding the k smallest spanning trees. 2nd Scand. Worksh. Algorithm Theory (1990) 38–47. *BIT* 32 (1992) 237–248.

[7] D. Eppstein. Offline algorithms for dynamic minimum spanning tree problems. 2nd Worksh. Algorithms and Data Structures (1991) 392–399.

[8] D. Eppstein, G.F. Italiano, R. Tamassia, R.E. Tarjan, J. Westbrook, and M. Yung. Maintenance of a minimum spanning forest in a dynamic plane graph. *J. Algorithms* 13 (1992) 33–54.

[9] T. Feder and M. Mihail. Balanced matroids. 24th ACM Symp. Theory of Computing (1992) 26–38.

[10] G.N. Frederickson. Data structures for on-line updating of minimum spanning trees, with applications. *SIAM J. Comput.* 14 (1985) 781–798.

[11] G.N. Frederickson. Ambivalent data structures for dynamic 2-edge-connectivity and k smallest spanning trees. 32nd IEEE Symp. Foundations of Computer Science (1991) 632–641.

[12] H. Gabow. A matroid approach to finding edge connectivity and packing arborescences. 23rd ACM Symp. Theory of Computing (1991) 112–122.

[13] H. Gabow. Applications of a poset representation to edge connectivity and graph rigidity. 32nd IEEE Symp. Foundations of Computer Science (1991) 812–821.

[14] H.N. Gabow, Z. Galil, T.H. Spencer, and R.E. Tarjan. Efficient algorithms for minimum spanning trees on directed and undirected graphs. *Combinatorica* 6 (1986) 109–122.

[15] H.N. Gabow and M. Stallman. Efficient algorithms for graphic matroid intersection and parity. 12th Int. Coll. Automata, Languages, and Programming (1985) 210–220.

[16] Z. Galil and G.F. Italiano. Fully dynamic algorithms for edge-connectivity problems. 23rd ACM Symp. Theory of Computing (1991) 317–327.

[17] Z. Galil and G.F. Italiano. Maintaining biconnected components of dynamic planar graphs. 18th Int. Coll. Automata, Languages, and Programming (1991) 339–350.

[18] Z. Galil and G.F. Italiano. Reducing edge connectivity to vertex connectivity. SIGACT News 22(1) (1991) 57–61.

[19] Z. Galil and G.F. Italiano. Fully dynamic algorithms for 3-edge connectivity. Manuscript, 1992.

[20] X. Han, P. Kelsen, V. Ramachandran, and R.E. Tarjan. Computing minimal spanning subgraphs in linear time. 3rd ACM/SIAM Symp. Discrete Algorithms (1992) 146–156.

[21] J. Hopcroft and R.E. Tarjan. Dividing a graph into triconnected components. *SIAM J. Comput.* 2 (1973) 135–158.

[22] A. Kanevsky, R. Tamassia, G. Di Battista, and J. Chen. On-line maintenance of the four-connected components of a graph. 32nd IEEE Symp. Foundations of Computer Science (1991) 793–801.

[23] J. A. La Poutré. Dynamic graph algorithms and data structures. Ph.D. Thesis, Utrecht University, September 1991.

[24] J. A. La Poutré. Maintenance of triconnected components of graphs. 19th Int. Coll. Automata, Languages, and Programming (1992) 354–365.

[25] H. Nagamochi and T. Ibaraki. Linear time algorithms for finding a sparse k-connected spanning subgraph of a k-connected graph. *Algorithmica* 7 (1992) 583–596.

[26] M. Overmars. The design of dynamic data structures. *Lecture Notes in Computer Science* 156 (1983).

[27] M. Rauch. Fully dynamic biconnectivity in graphs. 33rd IEEE Symp. Foundations of Computer Science (1992), these proceedings.

[28] D. Sleator and R.E. Tarjan. A data structure for dynamic trees. *J. Comput. Sys. Sci.* 26 (1983) 362–391.

[29] R.E. Tarjan. Depth-first search and linear graph algorithms. *SIAM J. Comput.* 1 (1972) 146–160.

[30] R. Thurimella. Techniques for the design of parallel graph algorithms. Ph.D. Thesis, Univ. Texas, Austin, 1989.

[31] J. Westbrook and R.E. Tarjan. Maintaining bridge-connected and biconnected components on-line. *Algorithmica* 7 (1992) 433–464.

On Four-Connecting a Triconnected Graph† (Extended Abstract)

Tsan-sheng Hsu
Department of Computer Sciences
University of Texas at Austin
Austin, Texas 78712-1188
tshsu@cs.utexas.edu

Abstract

We consider the problem of finding a smallest set of edges whose addition four-connects a triconnected graph. This is a fundamental graph-theoretic problem that has applications in designing reliable networks.

We present an $O(n\alpha(m,n)+m)$ time sequential algorithm for four-connecting an undirected graph G that is triconnected by adding the smallest number of edges, where n and m are the number of vertices and edges in G, respectively, and $\alpha(m,n)$ is the inverse Ackermann's function.

In deriving our algorithm, we present a new lower bound for the number of edges needed to four-connect a triconnected graph. The form of this lower bound is different from the form of the lower bound known for biconnectivity augmentation and triconnectivity augmentation. Our new lower bound applies for arbitrary k, and gives a tighter lower bound than the one known earlier for the number of edges needed to k-connect a $(k-1)$-connected graph. For $k = 4$, we show that this lower bound is tight by giving an efficient algorithm for finding a set of edges with the required size whose addition four-connects a triconnected graph.

1 Introduction

The problem of augmenting a graph to reach a certain connectivity requirement by adding edges has important applications in network reliability [6, 14, 28] and fault-tolerant computing. One version of the augmentation problem is to augment the input graph to reach a given connectivity requirement by adding a smallest set of edges. We refer to this problem as the *smallest augmentation* problem.

†This work was supported in part by NSF Grant CCR-90-23059.

Vertex-Connectivity Augmentations
The following results are known for solving the smallest augmentation problem on an undirected graph to satisfy a vertex-connectivity requirement.

For finding a smallest biconnectivity augmentation, Eswaran & Tarjan [3] gave a lower bound on the smallest number of edges for biconnectivity augmentation and proved that the lower bound can be achieved. Rosenthal & Goldner [26] developed a linear time sequential algorithm for finding a smallest augmentation to biconnect a graph; however, the algorithm in [26] contains an error. Hsu & Ramachandran [11] gave a corrected linear time sequential algorithm. An $O(\log^2 n)$ time parallel algorithm on an EREW PRAM using a linear number of processors for finding a smallest augmentation to biconnect an undirected graph was also given in Hsu & Ramachandran [11], where n is the number of vertices in the input graph. (For more on the PRAM model and PRAM algorithms, see [21].)

For finding a smallest triconnectivity augmentation, Watanabe & Nakamura [33, 35] gave an $O(n(n+m)^2)$ time sequential algorithm for a graph with n vertices and m edges. Hsu & Ramachandran [10, 12] developed a linear time algorithm and an $O(\log^2 n)$ time EREW parallel algorithm using a linear number of processors for this problem. We have been informed that independently, Jordan [15] gave a linear time algorithm for optimally triconnecting a biconnected graph.

For finding a smallest k-connectivity augmentation, for an arbitrary k, there is no polynomial time algorithm known for finding a smallest augmentation to k-connect a graph, for $k > 3$. There is also no efficient parallel algorithm known for finding a smallest augmentation to k-connect any nontrivial graph, for $k > 3$.

The above results are for augmenting undirected graphs. For augmenting directed graphs, Masuzawa, Hagihara & Tokura [23] gave an optimal-time sequential algorithm for finding a smallest augmentation to k-connect a rooted directed tree, for an arbitrary k. We are unaware of any results for finding a smallest augmentation to k-connect any nontrivial directed graph other than a rooted directed tree, for $k > 1$.

Other related results on finding smallest vertex-connectivity augmentations are stated in [4, 19].

Edge-Connectivity Augmentations
For the problem of finding a smallest augmentation for a graph to reach a given edge connectivity property, several polynomial time algorithms and efficient parallel algorithms are known. These results can be found in [1, 3, 4, 5, 8, 9, 13, 16, 19, 24, 27, 30, 31, 34, 37].

Augmenting a Weighted Graph
Another version of the problem is to augment a graph, with a weight assigned to each edge, to meet a connectivity requirement using a set of edges with a minimum total cost. Several related problems have been proved to be **NP**-complete. These results can be found in [3, 5, 7, 20, 22, 32, 33, 36].

Our Result
In this paper, we describe a sequential algorithm for optimally four-connecting a triconnected graph. We first present a lower bound for the number of edges that must be added in order to reach four-connectivity. Note that lower bounds different from the one we give here are known for the number of edges needed to biconnect a connected graph [3] and to triconnect a biconnected graph [10]. It turns out that in both these cases, we can always augment the graph using exactly the number of edges specified in this above lower bound [3, 10]. However, an extension of this type of lower bound for four-connecting a triconnected graph does not always give us the exact number of edges needed [15, 17]. (For details and examples, see Section 3.)

We present a new type of lower bound that equals the exact number of edges needed to four-connect a triconnected graph. By using our new lower bound, we derive an $O(n\alpha(m,n)+m)$ time sequential algorithm for finding a smallest set of edges whose addition four-connects a triconnected graph with n vertices and m edges, where $\alpha(m,n)$ is the inverse Ackermann's function. Our new lower bound applies for arbitrary k, and gives a tighter lower bound than the one known earlier for the number of edges needed to k-connect a $(k-1)$-connected graph. The new lower bound and the algorithm described here may lead to a better understanding of the problem of optimally k-connecting a $(k-1)$-connected graph, for an arbitrary k.

2 Definitions

We give definitions used in this paper.

Vertex-Connectivity
A graph[‡] G with at least $k+1$ vertices is *k-connected*, $k \geq 2$, if and only if G is a complete graph with $k+1$ vertices or the removal of any set of vertices of cardinality less than k does not disconnect G. The *vertex-connectivity* of G is k if G is k-connected, but not $(k+1)$-connected. Let $\mathcal{U}$ be a minimal set of vertices such that the resulting graph obtained from G by removing $\mathcal{U}$ is not connected. The set of vertices $\mathcal{U}$ is a *separating k-set*. If $|\mathcal{U}| = 3$, it is a *separating triplet*. The *degree* of a separating k-set $\mathcal{S}$, $d(\mathcal{S})$, in a k-connected graph G is the number of connected components in the graph obtained from G by removing $\mathcal{S}$. Note that the degree of any separating k-set is ≥ 2.

Wheel and Flower
A set of separating triplets with one common vertex c is called a *wheel* in [18]. A wheel can be represented by the set of vertices $\{c\} \cup \{s_0, s_1, \ldots, s_{q-1}\}$ which satisfies the following conditions: (*i*) $q > 2$; (*ii*) $\forall i \neq j$, $\{c, s_i, s_j\}$ is a separating triplet except in the case that $j = ((i+1) \bmod q)$ and (s_i, s_j) is an edge in G; (*iii*) c is adjacent to a vertex in each of the connected components created by removing any of the separating triplets in the wheel; (*iv*) $\forall j \neq (i+1) \bmod q$, $\{c, s_i, s_j\}$ is a degree-2 separating triplet. The vertex c is the *center* of the wheel [18]. For more details, see [18].

The *degree* of a wheel $W = \{c\} \cup \{s_0, s_1, \ldots, s_{q-1}\}$, $d(W)$, is the number of connected components in $G - \{c, s_0, \ldots, s_{q-1}\}$ plus the number of degree-3 vertices in $\{s_0, s_1, \ldots, s_{q-1}\}$ that are adjacent to c. The degree of a wheel must be at least 3. Note that the number of degree-3 vertices in $\{s_0, s_1, \ldots, s_{q-1}\}$ that are adjacent to c is equal to the number of separating triplets in $\{(c, s_i, s_{(i+2) \bmod q}) \mid 0 \leq i < q$, such that $s_{(i+1) \bmod q}$ is degree 3 in $G\}$. An example is shown in Figure 1.

A separating triplet with degree > 2 or not in a wheel is called a *flower* in [18]. Note that it is possible that two flowers of degree-2 $f_1 = \{a_{1,i} \mid 1 \leq i \leq 3\}$ and $f_2 = \{a_{2,i} \mid 1 \leq i \leq 3\}$ have the property that $\forall i$, $1 \leq i \leq 3$, either $a_{1,i} = a_{2,i}$ or $(a_{1,i}, a_{2,i})$ is an edge in G. We denote $f_1 \mathcal{R} f_2$ if f_1 and f_2 satisfy the above

‡Graphs refer to undirected graphs throughout this paper unless specified otherwise.

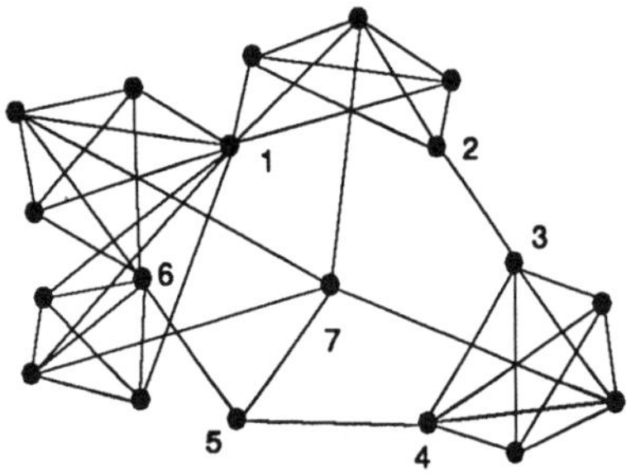

Figure 1: Illustrating a wheel $\{7\} \cup \{1,2,3,4,5,6\}$. The degree of this wheel is 5, i.e. the number of components we got after removing the wheel is 4 and there is one vertex (vertex 5) in the wheel with degree 3.

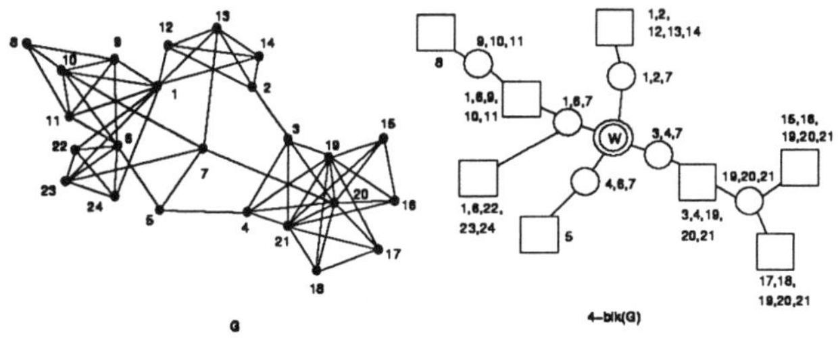

Figure 2: Illustrating a triconnected graph and its 4-$blk(G)$. We use rectangles, circles and two concentric circles to represent R-vertices, F-vertices and W-vertices, respectively. The vertex-numbers beside each vertex in 4-$blk(G)$ represent the set of vertices corresponding to this vertex.

condition. For each flower f, the *flower cluster* $\mathcal{F}_f$ for f is the set of flowers $\{f_1, \ldots, f_x\}$ (including f) such that $f\mathcal{R}f_i$, $\forall i$, $1 \leq i \leq x$.

Each of the separating triplets in a triconnected graph G is either represented by a flower or is in a wheel. We can construct an $O(n)$-space representation for all separating triplets (i.e. flowers and wheels) in a triconnected graph with n vertices and m edges in $O(n\alpha(m,n)+m)$ time [18].

K-Block

Let $G = (V, E)$ be a graph with vertex-connectivity $k-1$. A *k-block* in G is either (i) a minimal set of vertices $\mathcal{B}$ in a separating $(k-1)$-set with exactly $k-1$ neighbors in $V \setminus \mathcal{B}$ (these are *special k-blocks*) or (ii) a maximal set of vertices $\mathcal{B}$ such that there are at least k vertex-disjoint paths in G between any two vertices in $\mathcal{B}$ (these are *non-special k-blocks*). Note that a set consisting of a single vertex of degree $k-1$ in G is a k-block. A *k-block leaf* in G is a k-block $\mathcal{B}_l$ with exactly $k-1$ neighbors in $V \setminus \mathcal{B}_l$. Note also that every special k-block is a k-block leaf. If there is any special 4-block in a separating triplet $\mathcal{S}$, $d(\mathcal{S}) \leq 3$. Given a non-special k-block $\mathcal{B}$ leaf, the vertices in $\mathcal{B}$ that are not in the flower cluster that separates $\mathcal{B}$ are *demanding vertices*. We let every vertex in a special 4-block leaf be a demanding vertex.

Claim 1 *Every non-special k-block leaf contains at least one demanding vertex.* □

Using procedures in [18], we can find all of the 4-block leaves in a triconnected graph with n vertices and m edges in $O(n\alpha(m,n)+m)$ time.

Four-Block Tree

From [18] we know that we can decompose vertices in a triconnected graph into the following 3 types: (i) 4-blocks; (ii) wheels; (iii) separating triplets that are not in a wheel. We modify the decomposition tree in [18] to derive the *four-block tree* 4-$blk(G)$ for a triconnected graph G as follows. We create an R-vertex for each 4-block that is not special (i.e. not in a separating set or in the center of a wheel), an F-vertex for each separating triplet that is not in a wheel, and a W-vertex for each wheel. For each wheel $W = \{c\} \cup \{s_0, s_1, \ldots, s_{q-1}\}$, we also create the following vertices. An F-vertex is created for each separating triplet of the form $\{c, s_i, s_{(i+1) \bmod q}\}$ in W. An R-vertex is created for every degree-3 vertex s in $\{s_0, s_1, \ldots, s_{q-1}\}$ that is adjacent to c and an F-vertex is created for the three vertices that are adjacent to s. There is an edge between an F-vertex f and an R-vertex r if each vertex in the separating triplet corresponding to f is either in the 4-block H_r corresponding to r or adjacent to a vertex in H_r. There is an edge between an F-vertex f and a W-vertex w if the the wheel corresponding to w contains the separating triplet corresponding to f. A *dummy R-vertex* is created and adjacent to each pair of flowers f_1 and f_2 with the properties that f_1 and f_2 are not already connected and either $f_1 \in \mathcal{F}_{f_2}$, $f_2 \in \mathcal{F}_{f_1}$ (i.e. their flower clusters contain each other) or their corresponding separating triplets are overlapped. An example of a 4-block tree is shown in Figure 2.

Note that a degree-1 R-vertex in 4-$blk(G)$ corresponds to a 4-block leaf, but the reverse is not necessarily true, since we do not represent some special 4-block leaves and all degree-3 vertices that are centers of wheels in 4-$blk(G)$. A special 4-block leaf $\{v\}$, where v is a vertex, is represented by an R-vertex in 4-$blk(G)$ if v is not the center of a wheel w and it is in one of separating triplets of w. The degree of a flower F in G is the degree of its corresponding vertex in 4-$blk(G)$. Note also that the degree of a wheel W in

G is equal to the number of components in 4-*blk*(G) by removing its corresponding W-vertex w and all F-vertices that are adjacent to w. A wheel W in G is a ***star wheel*** if $d(W)$ equals the number of leaves in 4-*blk*(G) and every special 4-block leaf in W is either adjacent to or equal to the center. A star wheel W with the center c has the property that every 4-block leaf in G (not including $\{c\}$ if it is a 4-block leaf) can be separated from G by a separating triplet containing the center c. If G contains a star wheel W, then W is the only wheel in G. Note also that the degree of a wheel is less than or equal to the degree of its center in G.

K-connectivity Augmentation Number
The ***k-connectivity augmentation number*** for a graph G is the smallest number of edges that must be added to G in order to k-connect G.

3 A Lower Bound for the Four-Connectivity Augmentation Number

In this section, we first give a simple lower bound for the four-connectivity augmentation number that is similar to the ones for biconnectivity augmentation [3] and triconnectivity augmentation [10]. We show that this above lower bound is not always equal to the four-connectivity augmentation number [15, 17]. We then give a modified lower bound. This new lower bound turns out to be the exact number of edges that we must add to reach four-connectivity (see proofs in Section 4). Finally, we show relations between the two lower bounds.

3.1 A Simple Lower Bound

Given a graph G with vertex-connectivity $k-1$, it is well known that $\max\{\lceil \frac{l_k}{2} \rceil, d-1\}$ is a lower bound for the k-connectivity augmentation number where l_k is the number of k-block leaves in G and d is the maximum degree among all separating $(k-1)$-sets in G [3]. It is also well known that for $k=2$ and 3, this lower bound equals the k-connectivity augmentation number [3, 10]. For $k=4$, however, several researchers [15, 17] have observed that this value is not always equal to the four-connectivity augmentation number. Examples are given in Figure 3. Figure 3.(1) is from [15] and Figure 3.(2) is from [17]. Note that if we apply the above lower bound in each of the three graphs in Figure 3, the values we obtain for Figures 3.(1),

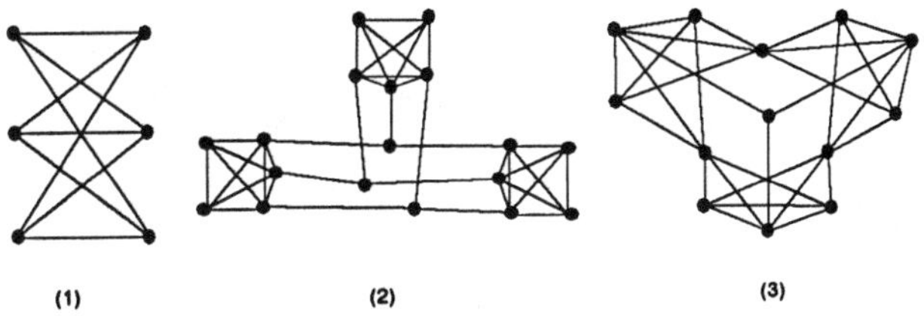

Figure 3: Illustrating three graphs where in each case the value derived by applying a simple lower bound does not equal its four-connectivity augmentation number.

3.(2) and 3.(3) are 3, 3 and 2, respectively, while we need one more edge in each graph to four-connect it.

3.2 A Better Lower Bound

Notice that in the previous lower bound, for every separating triplet $\mathcal{S}$ in the triconnected graph $G = \{V, E\}$, we must add at least $d(\mathcal{S})-1$ edges between vertices in $V \setminus \mathcal{S}$ to four-connect G, where $d(\mathcal{S})$ is the degree of $\mathcal{S}$ (i.e. the number of connected components in $G-\mathcal{S}$); otherwise, $\mathcal{S}$ remains a separating triplet. Let the set of edges added be $\mathcal{A}_{1,\mathcal{S}}$. We also notice that we must add at least one edge into every 4-block leaf $\mathcal{B}$ to four-connect G; otherwise, $\mathcal{B}$ remains a 4-block leaf. Since it is possible that $\mathcal{S}$ contains some 4-block leaves, we need to know the minimum number of edges needed to eliminate all 4-block leaves inside $\mathcal{S}$. Let the set of edges added be $\mathcal{A}_{2,\mathcal{S}}$. We know that $\mathcal{A}_{1,\mathcal{S}} \cap \mathcal{A}_{2,\mathcal{S}} = \emptyset$. The previous lower bound gives a bound on the cardinality of $\mathcal{A}_{1,\mathcal{S}}$, but not that of $\mathcal{A}_{2,\mathcal{S}}$. In the following paragraph, we define a quantity to measure the cardinality of $\mathcal{A}_{2,\mathcal{S}}$.

Let $\mathcal{Q}_\mathcal{S}$ be the set of special 4-block leaves that are in the separating triplet $\mathcal{S}$ of a triconnected graph G. Two 4-block leaves $\mathcal{B}_1$ and $\mathcal{B}_2$ are *adjacent* if there is an edge in G between every demanding vertex in $\mathcal{B}_1$ and every demanding vertex in $\mathcal{B}_2$. We create an ***augmenting graph for*** $\mathcal{S}$, $\mathcal{G}(\mathcal{S})$, as follows. For each special 4-block leaf in $\mathcal{Q}_\mathcal{S}$, we create a vertex in $\mathcal{G}(\mathcal{S})$. There is an edge between two vertices v_1 and v_2 in $\mathcal{G}(\mathcal{S})$ if their corresponding 4-blocks are adjacent. Let $\overline{\mathcal{G}(\mathcal{S})}$ be the complement graph of $\mathcal{G}(\mathcal{S})$. The seven types of augmenting graphs and their complement graphs are illustrated in Figure 4.

Definition 1 *The* **augmenting number** $a(\mathcal{S})$ *for a separating triplet* $\mathcal{S}$ *in a triconnected graph is the number of edges in a maximum matching* $\mathcal{M}$ *of* $\overline{\mathcal{G}(\mathcal{S})}$ *plus the number of vertices that have no edges in* $\mathcal{M}$ *incident on them.*

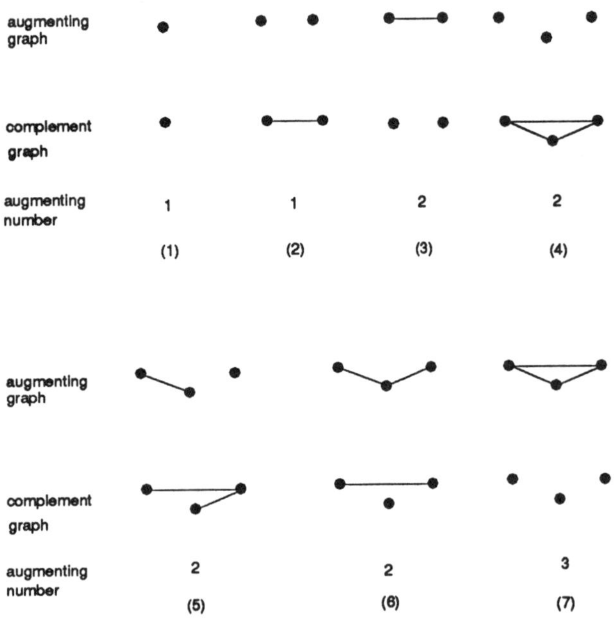

Figure 4: Illustrating the seven types of augmenting graphs, their complement graphs and augmenting numbers that one can get for a separating triplet in a triconnected graph.

The augmenting numbers for the seven types of augmenting graphs are shown in Figure 4. Note that in a triconnected graph, each special 4-block leaf must receive at least one new incoming edge in order to four-connect the input graph. The augmenting number $a(\mathcal{S})$ is exactly the minimum number of edges needed in the separating triplet $\mathcal{S}$ in order to four-connect the input graph. The augmenting number of a separating set that does not contain any special 4-block leaf is 0. Note also that we can define the *augmenting number* $a(\mathcal{C})$ for a set $\mathcal{C}$ that consists of the center of a wheel using a similar approach. Note that $a(\mathcal{C}) \leq 1$.

We need the following definition.

Definition 2 *Let G be a triconnected graph with l 4-block leaves. The* **leaf constraint** *of G, $lc(G)$, is $\lceil \frac{l}{2} \rceil$. The* **degree constraint** *of a separating triplet S in G, $dc(\mathcal{S})$, is $d(\mathcal{S}) - 1 + a(\mathcal{S})$, where $d(\mathcal{S})$ is the degree of $\mathcal{S}$ and $a(\mathcal{S})$ is the augmenting number of $\mathcal{S}$. The degree constraint of G, $dc(G)$, is the maximum degree constraint among all separating triplets in G. The* **wheel constraint** *of a star wheel W with center c in G, $wc(W)$, is $\lceil \frac{d(W)}{2} \rceil + a(\{c\})$, where $d(W)$ is the degree of W and $a(\{c\})$ is the augmenting number of $\{c\}$. The wheel constraint of G, $wc(G)$, is 0 if there is no star wheel in G; otherwise it is the wheel constraint of the star wheel in G.*

We now give a better lower bound on the 4-connectivity augmentation number for a triconnected graph.

Lemma 1 *We need at least* $\max\{lc(G), dc(G), wc(G)\}$ *edges to four-connect a triconnected graph G.*

<u>**Proof:**</u> Let $\mathcal{A}$ be a set of edges such that $G' = G \cup \mathcal{A}$ is four-connected. For each 4-block leaf B in G, we need one new incoming edge to a vertex in B; otherwise B is still a 4-block leaf in G'. This gives the first component of the lower bound.

For each separating triplet $\mathcal{S}$ in G, $G - \mathcal{S}$ contains $d(\mathcal{S})$ connected components. We need to add at least $d(\mathcal{S}) - 1$ edges between vertices in $G - \mathcal{S}$, otherwise $\mathcal{S}$ is still a separating triplet in G'. In addition to that, we need to add at least $a(\mathcal{S})$ edges such that at least one of the two end points of each new edge is in $\mathcal{S}$; otherwise $\mathcal{S}$ contains a special 4-block leaf. This gives the second term of the lower bound.

Given the star wheel W with the center c, 4-$blk(G)$ contains exactly $d(W)$ degree-1 R-vertices. Thus we need to add at least $\lceil \frac{d(W)}{2} \rceil$ edges between vertices in $G - \{c\}$; otherwise, G' contains some 4-block leaves. In addition to that, we need to add $a(\{c\})$ non-self-loop edges such that at least one of the two end points of each new edge is in $\{c\}$; otherwise $\{c\}$ is still a special 4-block leaf. This gives the third term of the lower bound. □

3.3 A Comparison of the Two Lower Bounds

We first observe the following relation between the wheel constraint and the leaf constraint. Note that if there exists a star wheel W with degree $d(W)$, there are exactly $d(W)$ 4-block leaves in G if the center is not degree-3. If the center of the star wheel is degree-3, then there are exactly $d(W) + 1$ 4-block leaves in G. Thus the wheel constraint is greater than the leaf constraint if and only if the star wheel has a degree-3 center. We know that the degree of any wheel is less than or equal to the degree of its center. Thus the value of the above lower bound equals 3.

We state the following claims for the relations between the degree constraint of a separating triplet and the leaf constraint.

Claim 2 *Let $\mathcal{S}$ be a separating triplet with degree $d(\mathcal{S})$ and h special 4-block leaves. Then there are at least $h + d(\mathcal{S})$ 4-block leaves in G.* □

Claim 3 *Let $\{a_1, a_2, a_3\}$ be a separating triplet in a triconnected graph G. Then a_i, $1 \leq i \leq 3$, is incident on a vertex in every connected component in $G - \{a_1, a_2, a_3\}$.* □

Corollary 1 *The degree of a separating triplet $\mathcal{S}$ is no more than the largest degree among all vertices in $\mathcal{S}$.* □

From Corollary 1, we know that it is not possible that a triconnected graph has type (6) or type (7) of the augmenting graphs as shown in Figure 4, since the degree of their underling separating triplet is 1. We also know that the degree of a separating triplet with a special 4-block leaf is at most 3 and at least 2. Thus $dc(\mathcal{S})$ is greater than $d(\mathcal{S}) - 1$ if $dc(\mathcal{S})$ equals either 3 or 4. Thus we have the following lemma.

Lemma 2 *Let $low_1(G)$ be the lower bound given in Section 3.1 for a triconnected graph G and let $low_2(G)$ be the lower bound given in Lemma 1 in Section 3.2. (i) $low_1(G) = low_2(G)$ if $low_2(G) \notin \{3,4\}$. (ii) $low_2(G) - low_1(G) \in \{0,1\}$.* □

Thus the simple lower bound extended from biconnectivity and triconnectivity is in fact a good approximation for the four-connectivity augmentation number.

4 Finding a Smallest Four-Connectivity Augmentation for a Triconnected Graph

We first explore properties of the 4-block tree that we will use in this section to develop an algorithm for finding a smallest 4-connectivity augmentation. Then we describe our algorithm. Graphs discussed in this section are triconnected unless specified otherwise.

4.1 Properties of the Four-Block Tree

Massive Vertex, Critical Vertex and Balanced Graph

A separating triplet $\mathcal{S}$ in a graph G is *massive* if $dc(\mathcal{S}) > lc(G)$. A separating triplet $\mathcal{S}$ in a graph G is *critical* if $dc(\mathcal{S}) = lc(G)$. A graph G is *balanced* if there is no massive separating triplet in G. If G is balanced, then its $4\text{-}blk(G)$ is also *balanced*. The following lemma and corollary state the number of massive and critical vertices in $4\text{-}blk(G)$.

Lemma 3 *Let $\mathcal{S}_1$, $\mathcal{S}_2$ and $\mathcal{S}_3$ be any three separating triplets in G such that there is no special 4-block in $\mathcal{S}_i \cap \mathcal{S}_j$, $1 \le i < j \le 3$. $\sum_{i=1}^{3} dc(\mathcal{S}_i) \le l+1$, where l is the number of 4-block leaves in G.*

<u>Proof:</u> G is triconnected. We can modify $4\text{-}blk(G)$ in the following way such that the number of leaves in the resulting tree equals l and the degree of an F-node f equals its degree constraint plus 1 if f corresponds to $\mathcal{S}_i$, $1 \le i \le 3$. For each W-vertex w with a degree-3 center c, we create an R-vertex r_c for c, an F-vertex f_c for the three vertices that are adjacent to c in G. We add edges (w,f_c) and (f_c,r_c). Thus r_c is a leaf. For each F-vertex whose corresponding separating triplet $\mathcal{S}$ contains h special 4-block leaves, we attach $a(\mathcal{S})$ subtrees with a total number of h leaves with the constraint that any special 4-block that is in more than one separating triplet will be added only once (to the F-node corresponding to $\mathcal{S}_i$, $1 \le i \le 3$, if possible). From Figure 4 we know that the number of special 4-block leaves in any separating triplet is greater than or equal to its augmenting number. Thus the above addition of subtrees can be done. Let $4\text{-}blk(G)'$ be the resulting graph. Thus the number of leaves in $4\text{-}blk(G)'$ is l. Let f be an F-node in $4\text{-}blk(G)'$ whose corresponding separating triplet is $\mathcal{S}$. We know that the degree of f equals $dc(\mathcal{S})+1$ if $\mathcal{S} \in \{\mathcal{S}_i \mid 1 \le i \le 3\}$. It is easy to verify that the sum of degrees of any three internal vertices in a tree is less than or equal to 4 plus the number of leaves in a tree. □

Corollary 2 *Let G be a graph with more than two non-special 4-block leaves. (i) There is at most one massive F-vertex in $4\text{-}blk(G)$. (ii) If there is a massive F-vertex, there is no critical F-vertex. (iii) There are at most two critical F-vertices in $4\text{-}blk(G)$.* □

Updating the Four-Block Tree

Let v_i be a demanding vertex or a vertex in a special 4-block leaf, $i \in \{1,2\}$. Let $\mathcal{B}_i$ be the 4-block leaf that contains v_i, $i \in \{1,2\}$. Let b_i, $i \in \{1,2\}$, be the vertex in $4\text{-}blk(G)$ such that if v_i is a demanding vertex, then b_i is an R-vertex whose corresponding 4-block contains v_i; if v_i is in a special 4-block leaf in a flower, then b_i is the F-vertex whose corresponding separating triplet contains v_i; if v_i is the center of a wheel w, b_i is the F-vertex that is closet to $b_{(i \bmod 2)+1}$ and is adjacent to w. The vertex b_i is the *implied vertex* for $\mathcal{B}_i$, $i \in \{1,2\}$. The *implied path P between $\mathcal{B}_1$ and $\mathcal{B}_2$* is the path in $4\text{-}blk(G)$ between b_1 and b_2. Given $4\text{-}blk(G)$ and an edge (v_1,v_2) not in G, we can obtain $4\text{-}blk(G \cup \{(v_1,v_2)\})$ by performing local updating operations on P. For details, see [18].

In summary, all 4-blocks corresponding to R-vertices in P are collapsed into a single 4-block. Edges in P are deleted. F-vertices in P are connected to the new R-vertex created. We *crack* wheels in a way that is similar to the cracking of a polygon for updating 3-block graphs (see [2, 10] for details). We say that P is *non-adjacent* on a wheel W, if the cracking of W creates two new wheels. Note that it is possible that a separating triplet $\mathcal{S}$ in the original graph is no longer a separating triplet in the resulting graph by adding an edge. Thus some special leaves in the original graph are no longer special, in which case they must be added to 4-$blk(G)$.

Reducing the Degree Constraint of a Separating Triplet

We know that the degree constraint of a separating triplet can be reduced by at most 1 by adding a new edge. From results in [18], we know that we can reduce the degree constraint of a separating triplet $\mathcal{S}$ by adding an edge between two non-special 4-block leaves $\mathcal{B}_1$ and $\mathcal{B}_2$ such that the path in 4-$blk(G)$ between the two vertices corresponding to $\mathcal{B}_1$ and $\mathcal{B}_2$ passes through the vertex corresponding to $\mathcal{S}$. We also notice the following corollary from the definitions of 4-$blk(G)$ and the degree constraint.

Corollary 3 *Let $\mathcal{S}$ be a separating triplet that contains a special 4-block leaf. (i) We can reduce $dc(\mathcal{S})$ by 1 by adding an edge between two special 4-block leaves $\mathcal{B}_1$ and $\mathcal{B}_2$ in $\mathcal{S}$ such that $\mathcal{B}_1$ and $\mathcal{B}_2$ are not adjacent. (ii) If we add an edge between a special 4-block leaf in $\mathcal{S}$ and a 4-block leaf $\mathcal{B}$ not in $\mathcal{S}$, the degree constraint of every separating triplet corresponding to an internal vertex in the path of 4-$blk(G)$ between vertices corresponding to $\mathcal{S}$ and $\mathcal{B}$ is reduced by 1.* □

Reducing the Number of Four-Block Leaves

We now consider the conditions under which the adding of an edge reduces the leaf constraint $lc(G)$ by 1. Let *real degree* of an F-node in 4-$blk(G)$ be 1 plus the degree constraint of its corresponding separating triplet. The real degree of a W-node with a degree-3 center in G is 1 plus its degree in 4-$blk(G)$. The real degree of any other node is equal to its degree in 4-$blk(G)$.

Definition 3 (The Leaf-Connecting Condition) *Let $\mathcal{B}_1$ and $\mathcal{B}_2$ be two non-adjacent 4-block leaves in G. Let P be the implied path between $\mathcal{B}_1$ and $\mathcal{B}_2$ in 4-$blk(G)$. Two 4-block leaves $\mathcal{B}_1$ and $\mathcal{B}_2$ satisfy the* **leaf-connecting condition** *if at least one of the following conditions is true. (i) There are at least two vertices of real degree at least 3 in P. (ii) There is at least one R-vertex of degree at least 4 in P. (iii) The path P is non-adjacent on a W-vertex in P. (iv) There is an internal vertex of real degree at least 3 in P and at least one of the 4-block leaves in $\{\mathcal{B}_1, \mathcal{B}_2\}$ is special. (v) $\mathcal{B}_1$ and $\mathcal{B}_2$ are both special and they do not share the same set of neighbors.*

Lemma 4 *Let $\mathcal{B}_1$ and $\mathcal{B}_2$ be two 4-block leaves in G that satisfy the leaf-connecting condition. We can find vertices v_i in $\mathcal{B}_i$, $i \in \{1,2\}$, such that $lc(G \cup \{(v_1, v_2)\}) = lc(G) - 1$, if $lc(G) \geq 2$.* □

4.2 The Algorithm

We now describe an algorithm for finding a smallest augmentation to four-connect a triconnected graph. Let $\delta = dc(G) - lc(G)$. The algorithm first adds 2δ edges to the graph such that the resulting graph is balanced and the lower bound is reduced by 2δ. If $lc(G) \neq 2$ or $wc(G) \neq 3$, there is no star wheel with a degree-3 center. We add an edge such that the degree constraint $dc(G)$ is reduced by 1 and the number of 4-block leaves is reduced by 2. Since there is no star wheel with a degree-3 center, $wc(G)$ is also reduced by 1 if $wc(G) = lc(G)$. The resulting graph stays balanced each time we add an edge and the lower bound given in Lemma 1 is reduced by 1. If $lc(G) = 2$ and $wc(G) = 3$, then there exists a star wheel with a degree-3 center. We reduce $wc(G)$ by 1 by adding an edge between the degree-3 center and a demanding vertex of a 4-block leaf. Since $lc(G) = 2$ and $wc(G) = 3$, $dc(G)$ is at most 2. Thus the lower bound can be reduced by 1 by adding an edge. We keep adding an edge at a time such that the lower bound given in Lemma 1 is reduced by 1. Thus we can find a smallest augmentation to four-connect a triconnected graph. We now describe our algorithm.

The Input Graph is not Balanced

We use an approach that is similar to the one used in biconnectivity and triconnectivity augmentations to balance the input graph [10, 11, 26]. Given a tree T and a vertex v in T, a *v-chain* [26] is a component in $T - \{v\}$ without any vertex of degree more than 2. The leaf of T in each v-chain is a *v-chain leaf* [26]. Let $\delta = dc(G) - lc(G)$ for a unbalanced graph G and let 4-$blk(G)'$ be the modified 4-block tree given in the proof of Lemma 3. Let f be a massive F-vertex. We can show that either there are at least $2\delta + 2$ f-chains in 4-$blk(G)'$ (i.e. f is the only massive F-vertex) or we can eliminate all massive F-vertices by adding an edge. Let λ_i be a demanding vertex in the ith f-chain leaf. We add the set of edges $\{(\lambda_i, \lambda_{i+1}) \mid 1 \leq i \leq 2\delta\}$. It is also easy to show that the lower bound given in Lemma 1 is reduced by 2δ and the graph is balanced.

The Input Graph is Balanced

We first describe the algorithm. Then we give its proof of correctness. In the description, we need the following definition. Let $\mathcal{B}$ be a 4-block leaf whose implied vertex in 4-$blk(G)$ is b and let $\mathcal{B}'$ be a 4-block leaf whose implied vertex in 4-$blk(G)$ is b'. $\mathcal{B}'$ is a *nearest* 4-block leaf of $\mathcal{B}$ if there is no other 4-block leaf whose implied vertex has a distance to b that is shorter than the distance between b and b'.

```
{* G is triconnected with ≥ 5 vertices; the algorithm finds
a smallest four-connectivity augmentation. *}
graph function aug3to4(graph G);
{* The algorithmic notation used is from Tarjan [29]. *}
  T := 4-blk(G); root T at an arbitrary vertex;
  let l̃ be the number of degree-1 R-vertices in T;
  do ∃ a 4-block leaf in G →
    if ∃ a degree-3 center c →
1.    if lc(G) = 2 and wc(G) = 3 →
        {* Vertex c is the center of the star wheel w. *}
        u1 := the 4-block leaf {c};
        let u2 be a a non-special 4-block leaf
      | ∃ another degree-3 center c' non-adjacent to c →
        let u2 be the 4-block leaf {c'}
      | ∃ a special 4-block leaf b non-adjacent to u1 →
        let u2 := b
      | ∄ (degree-3 center or special 4-block leaf)
      non-adjacent to u1 →
        let u2 be a a 4-block leaf such that ∃ an internal
        vertex with real degree ≥ 3 in their implies path
      fi
    | lc(G) ≠ 2 or wc(G) ≠ 3 →
      if l̃ > 2 and ∃ 2 critical F-vertices f1 and f2 →
2.      find two non-special 4-block leaves u1 and u2 such
        that the implied path between them passes through
        f1 and f2
      | l > 2 and ∃ only one critical F-vertex f1 →
        if ∃ two non-adjacent special 4-block leaves in the
        separating triplet S1 corresponding to f1 →
3.        let u1 and u2 be two non-adjacent 4-block leaves
          in S1
        | ∄ two non-adjacent special 4-block leaves in the
        separating triplet S1 corresponding to f1 →
4.        let v be a vertex with the largest real degree
          among all vertices in T besides f1;
          if real degree of v in T ≥ 3 →
            find two non-special 4-block leaves u1 and u2
            such that the implied path between them
            passes through f1 and v
          fi
          {* The case when the degree of v in T < 3 will
          be handled in step 8. *}
        fi
      | ∃ two vertices v1 and v2 with real degree ≥ 3 →
5.      find two non-special 4-block leaves u1 and u2 such
        that the implied path between them passes
        through v1 and v2
      | ∃ an R-vertex v of degree ≥ 4 →
6.      find two non-special 4-block leaves u1 and u2 such
        that the implied path between them passes
        through v
      | ∃ a W-vertex v of degree ≥ 4 →
7.      let u1 and u2 be two non-special 4-block leaves such
        that the implied path between them is
        non-adjacent on v
      | ∃ only one vertex v in T with real degree ≥ 3 →
        {* T is a star with the center v. *}
8.      find a nearest vertex w of v that contains a 4-block
        leaf v1;
        let w' be a nearest vertex of w containing a 4-block
        leaf non-adjacent to v1;
        find two 4-block leaves u1 and u2 whose implied
        path passes through w, w' and v
        {* The above step can always be done, since T is a
        star. *}
      {* Note that T is path for all the cases below. *}
      | ∃ two non-adjacent special 4-block leaves in one
      separating triplet S →
9.      let u1 and u2 be two non-adjacent special 4-block
        leaves in S
      | ∃ a special 4-block leaf u1 →
10.     find a nearest non-adjacent 4-block leaf u2
      | l̃ = 2 →
        let u1 and u2 be the two 4-block leaves
        corresponding to the two degree-1 R-vertices in T
      fi
    fi;
    let yi, i ∈ {1,2}, be a demanding vertex in ui such that
    (y1,y2) is not an edge in the current G;
    G := G ∪ {(y1, y2)};
    update T, l̃, lc(G), wc(G) and dc(G)
  od;
  return G
end aug3to4;
```

Before we show the correctness of algorithm aug3to4, we need the following claim and corollaries.

Claim 4 *[26] If 4-blk(G) contains two critical vertices f_1 and f_2, then every leaf is either in an f_1-chain or in an f_2-chain and the degree of any other vertex in 4-blk(G) is at most 2.* □

Corollary 4 *If 4-blk(G) contains two critical vertices f_1 and f_2 and the corresponding separating triplet $\mathcal{S}_i$, $i \in \{1,2\}$, of f_i contains a special 4-block leaf, then its augmenting number equals the number of special 4-block leaves in it.* □

Corollary 5 *Let f_1 and f_2 be two critical F-vertices in 4-blk(G). If the number of degree-1 R-vertices in 4-blk(G) > 2 and the corresponding separating triplet of f_i, $i \in \{1,2\}$, contains a 4-block leaf $\mathcal{B}_i$, we can add an edge between a vertex in $\mathcal{B}_1$ and a vertex in $\mathcal{B}_2$ to reduce the lower bound given in Lemma 1 by 1.* □

Theorem 1 *Algorithm aug3to4 adds the smallest number of edges to four-connect a triconnected graph.* □

We now describe an efficient way of implementing algorithm aug3to4. The 4-block tree can be computed in $O(n\alpha(m,n)+m)$ time for a graph with n vertices and m edges [18]. We know that the leaf constraint, the degree constraint of any separating triplet and the wheel constraint of any wheel in G can only be decreased by adding an edge. We also know that $lc(G)$, the sum of degree constraints of all separating triplets and the sum of wheel constraints of all wheels are all $O(n)$. Thus we can use the technique in [26] to maintain the current leaf constraint, the degree constraint for any separating triplet and the wheel constraint for any wheel in $O(n)$ time for the entire execution of the algorithm. We also visit each vertex and each edge in the 4-block tree a constant number of times before deciding to collapse them. There are $O(n)$ 4-block leaves and $O(n)$ vertices and edges in $4\text{-}blk(G)$. In each vertex, we need to use a set-union-find algorithm to maintain the identities of vertices after collapsing. Hence the overall time for updating the 4-block tree is $O(n\alpha(n,n))$. We have the following claim.

Claim 5 *Algorithm aug3to4 can be implemented in* $O(n\alpha(m,n)+m)$ *time where* n *and* m *are the number of vertices and edges in the input graph, respectively and* $\alpha(m,n)$ *is the inverse Ackermann's function.* □

5 Conclusion

We have given a sequential algorithm for finding a smallest set of edges whose addition four-connects a triconnected graph. The algorithm runs in $O(n\alpha(m,n)+m)$ time using $O(n+m)$ space. The following approach was used in developing our algorithm. We first gave a 4-block tree data structure for a triconnected graph that is similar to the one given in [18]. We then described a lower bound on the smallest number of edges that must be added based on the 4-block tree of the input graph. We further showed that it is possible to decrease this lower bound by 1 by adding an appropriate edge.

The lower bound that we gave here is different from the ones that we have for biconnecting a connected graph [3] and for triconnecting a biconnected graph [10]. We also showed relations between these two lower bounds. This new lower bound applies for arbitrary k, and gives a tighter lower bound than the one known earlier for the number of edges needed to k-connect a $(k-1)$-connected graph. It is likely that techniques presented in this paper may be used in finding the k-connectivity augmentation number of a $(k-1)$-connected graph, for an arbitrary k.

Acknowledgment

We would like to thank Vijaya Ramachandran for helpful discussions and comments. We also thank Tibor Jordan, Arkady Kanevsky and Roberto Tamassia for useful information.

References

[1] G.-R. Cai and Y.-G. Sun. The minimum augmentation of any graph to a k-edge-connected graph. *Networks*, 19:151–172, 1989.

[2] G. Di Battista and R. Tamassia. On-line graph algorithms with spqr-trees. In *Proc. 17th Int'l Conf. on Automata, Language and Programming*, volume LNCS # 443, pages 598–611. Springer-Verlag, 1990.

[3] K. P. Eswaran and R. E. Tarjan. Augmentation problems. *SIAM J. Comput.*, 5(4):653–665, 1976.

[4] D. Fernández-Baca and M. A. Williams. Augmentation problems on hierarchically defined graphs. In *1989 Workshop on Algorithms and Data Structures*, volume LNCS # 382, pages 563–576. Springer-Verlag, 1989.

[5] A. Frank. Augmenting graphs to meet edge-connectivity requirements. In *Proc. 31th Annual IEEE Symp. on Foundations of Comp. Sci.*, pages 708–718, 1990.

[6] H. Frank and W. Chou. Connectivity considerations in the design of survivable networks. *IEEE Trans. on Circuit Theory*, CT-17(4):486–490, December 1970.

[7] G. N. Frederickson and J. Ja'Ja'. Approximation algorithms for several graph augmentation problems. *SIAM J. Comput.*, 10(2):270–283, May 1981.

[8] H. N. Gabow. Applications of a poset representation to edge connectivity and graph rigidity. In *Proc. 32th Annual IEEE Symp. on Foundations of Comp. Sci.*, pages 812–821, 1991.

[9] D. Gusfield. Optimal mixed graph augmentation. *SIAM J. Comput.*, 16(4):599–612, August 1987.

[10] T.-s. Hsu and V. Ramachandran. A linear time algorithm for triconnectivity augmentation. In *Proc. 32th Annual IEEE Symp. on Foundations of Comp. Sci.*, pages 548–559, 1991.

[11] T.-s. Hsu and V. Ramachandran. On finding a smallest augmentation to biconnect a graph. In *Proceedings of the Second Annual Int'l Symp. on Algorithms*, volume LNCS #557, pages 326–335. Springer-Verlag, 1991. *SIAM J. Comput.*, to appear.

[12] T.-s. Hsu and V. Ramachandran. An efficient parallel algorithm for triconnectivity augmentation. Manuscript, 1992.

[13] T.-s. Hsu and V. Ramachandran. Three-edge connectivity augmentations. Manuscript, 1992.

[14] S. P. Jain and K. Gopal. On network augmentation. *IEEE Trans. on Reliability*, R-35(5):541–543, 1986.

[15] T. Jordan, February 1992. Private communications.

[16] Y. Kajitani and S. Ueno. The minimum augmentation of a directed tree to a k-edge-connected directed graph. *Networks*, 16:181–197, 1986.

[17] A. Kanevsky and R. Tamassia, October 1991. Private communications.

[18] A. Kanevsky, R. Tamassia, G. Di Battista, and J. Chen. On-line maintenance of the four-connected components of a graph. In *Proc. 32th Annual IEEE Symp. on Foundations of Comp. Sci.*, pages 793–801, 1991.

[19] G. Kant. Linear planar augmentation algorithms for outerplanar graphs. Tech. Rep. RUU-CS-91-47, Dept. of Computer Science, Utrecht University, the Netherlands, 1991.

[20] G. Kant and H. L. Bodlaender. Planar graph augmentation problems. In *Proc. 2nd Workshop on Data Structures and Algorithms*, volume LNCS #519, pages 286–298. Springer-Verlag, 1991.

[21] R. M. Karp and V. Ramachandran. Parallel algorithms for shared-memory machines. In J. van Leeuwen, editor, *Handbook of Theoretical Computer Science*, pages 869–941. North Holland, 1990.

[22] S. Khuller and R. Thurimella. Approximation algorithms for graph augmentation. In *Proc. 19th Int'l Conf. on Automata, Language and Programming*, 1992, to appear.

[23] T. Masuzawa, K. Hagihara, and N. Tokura. An optimal time algorithm for the k-vertex-connectivity unweighted augmentation problem for rooted directed trees. *Discrete Applied Mathematics*, pages 67–105, 1987.

[24] D. Naor, D. Gusfield, and C. Martel. A fast algorithm for optimally increasing the edge-connectivity. In *Proc. 31th Annual IEEE Symp. on Foundations of Comp. Sci.*, pages 698–707, 1990.

[25] V. Ramachandran. Parallel open ear decomposition with applications to graph biconnectivity and triconnectivity. In J. H. Reif, editor, *Synthesis of Parallel Algorithms*. Morgan-Kaufmann, 1992, to appear.

[26] A. Rosenthal and A. Goldner. Smallest augmentations to biconnect a graph. *SIAM J. Comput.*, 6(1):55–66, March 1977.

[27] D. Soroker. Fast parallel strong orientation of mixed graphs and related augmentation problems. *Journal of Algorithms*, 9:205–223, 1988.

[28] K. Steiglitz, P. Weiner, and D. J. Kleitman. The design of minimum-cost survivable networks. *IEEE Trans. on Circuit Theory*, CT-16(4):455–460, 1969.

[29] R. E. Tarjan. *Data Structures and Network Algorithms*. SIAM Press, Philadelphia, PA, 1983.

[30] S. Ueno, Y. Kajitani, and H. Wada. Minimum augmentation of a tree to a k-edge-connected graph. *Networks*, 18:19–25, 1988.

[31] T. Watanabe. An efficient way for edge-connectivity augmentation. Tech. Rep. ACT-76-UILU-ENG-87-2221, Coordinated Science lab., University of Illinois, Urbana, IL, 1987.

[32] T. Watanabe, Y. Higashi, and A. Nakamura. Graph augmentation problems for a specified set of vertices. In *Proceedings of the first Annual Int'l Symp. on Algorithms*, volume LNCS #450, pages 378–387. Springer-Verlag, 1990. Earlier version in Proc. 1990 Int'l Symp. on Circuits and Systems, pages 2861–2864.

[33] T. Watanabe and A. Nakamura. On a smallest augmentation to triconnect a graph. Tech. Rep. C-18, Department of Applied Mathematics, faculty of Engineering, Hiroshima University, Higashi-Hiroshima, 724, Japan, 1983. revised 1987.

[34] T. Watanabe and A. Nakamura. Edge-connectivity augmentation problems. *J. Comp. System Sci.*, 35:96–144, 1987.

[35] T. Watanabe and A. Nakamura. 3-connectivity augmentation problems. In *Proc. of 1988 IEEE Int'l Symp. on Circuits and Systems*, pages 1847–1850, 1988.

[36] T. Watanabe, T. Narita, and A. Nakamura. 3-edge-connectivity augmentation problems. In *Proc. of 1989 IEEE Int'l Symp. on Circuits and Systems*, pages 335–338, 1989.

[37] T. Watanabe, M. Yamakado, and K. Onaga. A linear time augmenting algorithm for 3-edge-connectivity augmentation problems. In *Proc. of 1991 IEEE Int'l Symp. on Circuits and Systems*, pages 1168–1171, 1991.

Dynamic Half-Space Reporting, Geometric Optimization, and Minimum Spanning Trees

Pankaj K. Agarwal* David Eppstein† Jiří Matoušek‡

Abstract

We describe dynamic data structures for half-space range reporting and for maintaining the minima of a decomposable function. Using these data structures, we obtain efficient dynamic algorithms for a number of geometric problems, including closest/farthest neighbor searching, fixed dimension linear programming, bi-chromatic closest pair, diameter, and Euclidean minimum spanning tree.

1 Introduction

Dynamic data structures involve updating the solution to a problem (either explicitly or implicitly, depending on the problem) as the set of input objects changes dynamically. The study of dynamic algorithms has been motivated by applications in several applied areas including optimization, computer graphics, and VLSI. Also, solutions to several static problems require efficient dynamic algorithms either for a similar problem in lower dimensions (e.g. point-location [31, 30] or computing the area of rectangles [29]), or for a different problem (e.g., convex layers [6] or hidden surface removal [4]). As a result, a lot of attention has been paid to studying dynamic geometric algorithms. For some examples see [3, 4, 16, 18, 20, 23, 28, 32, 33, 34], or see [11] for an excellent survey on this subject. Researchers have also studied the special cases when objects are only allowed to be inserted (deletions are not allowed), or when the sequence of insertions and deletions is known in advance. If the problem is decomposable (i.e., the solutions in subsets of the input can be efficiently combined to determine the overall solution) then one can obtain fast dynamic algorithms for these special cases [5, 17]. Recently Dobkin and Suri extended these techniques to a *semi-online* model in which insertions are completely arbitrary, but when an object is inserted we are told its deletion time [16]. However, these techniques do not seem to extend to the general case where deletions are also arbitrary.

In this paper we present efficient solutions to two dynamic geometric problems: halfspace range reporting and finding the minima of a decomposable function. Using these results, we develop new algorithms for a wide variety of fully dynamic geometric optimization problems, including maintenance of a minimum spanning tree of a point set. Our algorithms are either the first known solutions to these problems, or they are significantly faster than previously known algorithms. The following list describes the problems considered here and Table 1 summarizes the results presented in this abstract.

Half-space range reporting: The first result of this paper is a dynamic data structure for half-space range reporting, which can be formally defined as follows: Store a set S of points in $\mathbb{R}^d$ into a data structure, so that all k points of S lying in a query half-space can be reported quickly.[1] In several applications it suffices to determine whether the query half-space contains any point of S. We will refer to this restricted version as the *empty half-space problem*. Half-space range reporting is a special case of the general simplex range searching problem in which one wants to report all points of S lying in a query simplex. Using an algorithm due to Clarkson, one can store S in a data structure of size $O(n^{\lfloor d/2 \rfloor+\varepsilon})$ so that a half-space query can be answered in time $O(\log n + k)$ [12]. Recently Matoušek showed that a half-space query can be answered in time $O(n^{1-1/\lfloor d/2 \rfloor} \log^{O(1)} n + k)$ using $O(n \log n)$ preprocessing time and $O(n \log\log n)$ space [24]. Combining these two approaches, for a

*Computer Science Department, Duke University, Durham, NC 27706. Work supported by National Science Foundation Grant CCR-91-06514.

†Department of Information and Computer Science, University of California, Irvine, CA 92717.

‡Department of Applied Mathematics, Charles University, Prague, and Freie Universität Berlin.

[1] Throughout this paper we assume d to be some fixed positive integer and ε to be an arbitrarily small positive constant. The constants in the time complexity of the algorithms depend on d and ε.

0-8186-2900-2/92 $3.00 © 1992 IEEE

given parameter m, $n \le m \le n^{\lfloor d/2 \rfloor}$, one can answer a half-space query in time $O(\frac{n}{m^{1/\lfloor d/2 \rfloor}} \log n + k)$ using $O(m^{1+\epsilon})$ space and preprocessing.

Known simplex range searching data structures can be dynamized easily. In the plane, dynamic half-space range searching can be performed using the dynamic convex hull structure of Overmars and van Leeuwen [28]. But no efficient algorithm was known for higher dimensional half-space searching. We present a data structure that can answer a half-space range reporting query in time $O(\frac{n}{m^{1/\lfloor d/2 \rfloor}} \log n + k)$, and can insert or delete a point in amortized time $O(m^{1+\epsilon}/n)$. It can also answer an empty half-space query in time $O(\frac{n}{m^{1/\lfloor d/2 \rfloor}} \log n)$ (cf. Section 2).

Minima of decomposable functions: Our second result is an algorithm for maintaining the minima of a decomposable function over a set of points in $\mathbb{R}^d$. Let R be a set of red points and let B be a set of blue points. For a given distance function $\delta(.,.)$, we define $\delta(R, B) = \min_{p \in R, q \in B} \delta(p, q)$. The goal is to maintain $\delta(R, B)$ as points are inserted to or deleted from $R \cup B$. This problem can also be viewed as computing a shortest edge in the complete weighted bipartite graph $R \times B$. One can also compute maxima with the same algorithm by negating function $\delta(.,.)$.

This problem in its full generality was first studied by Dobkin and Suri [16]. They showed that the minima can be maintained efficiently in the semi-online model. But no fully dynamic algorithm was known for this problem. We show that if we have a dynamic data structure that can compute a nearest neighbor for a query point with respect to $\delta(.,.)$, then $\delta(R, B)$ can be maintained in amortized time $O(T(n) \log^2 n)$, where $n = |R| + |B|$ and $T(n)$ is the query/update time of the nearest neighbor searching structure (cf. Section 3).

In [2] several geometric problems have been reduced to answering empty half-space queries, and in [16] a number of problems have been reduced to computing the minima (or maxima) of a decomposable function. Our algorithms yield efficient dynamic solutions to these problems too. We mention some of them here.

Ray shooting in a convex polyhedron: Given a convex polyhedron P in $\mathbb{R}^d$ defined as the intersection of n half-spaces, preprocess it, so that the first intersection point of P and a query ray can be computed quickly. Agarwal and Matoušek [2] showed that such a query can be answered using a data structure for the empty half-space queries (satisfying certain mild requirements, which are satisfied by the data structure we construct), with some polylogarithmic overhead in query time. Hence, the above query can be answered in time $O((n \log^3 n)/m^{\lfloor d/2 \rfloor})$ and a half-space can be inserted or deleted in time $O(m^{1+\epsilon}/n)$. They also showed that dynamic ray shooting procedure can be used to compute convex layers and higher order Voronoi diagrams. Combining these reductions with our results, we can compute the convex layers of n points in $\mathbb{R}^3$ in time $O(n^{1+\epsilon})$, and we can compute the kth-order Voronoi diagram of n points in the plane in time $O(n^{1+\epsilon} k)$.

Closest/farthest neighbor queries: Given a set S of n points in $\mathbb{R}^d$, maintain a data structure so that the closest (or farthest) neighbor of a query point in S can be computed efficiently. Although there are efficient dynamic algorithms for maintaining the closest distance in S, no such procedure was known for computing the closest neighbor of a query point in S. It is shown in [2] that this problem can be reduced to answering a ray shooting query in a convex polyhedron in $\mathbb{R}^{d+1}$ defined by n half-spaces, which implies that the closest/farthest neighbor queries can be answered in time $O((n \log^3 n)/m^{1/\lceil d/2 \rceil})$ and a point can be inserted to or deleted from S in amortized time $O(m^{1+\epsilon}/n)$. In particular, closest/farthest neighbor queries in $\mathbb{R}^2$ can be answered in time $O(\log^3 n)$, and a point can be inserted to or deleted from S in amortized time $O(n^\epsilon)$. The previously best known algorithm took time $O(\sqrt{n \log n})$ per update or query.

Bi-chromatic closest pair and diameter: Given a set R red points and a set B of blue points, determine the closest or farthest red-blue pair. The best known algorithm for computing the bi-chromatic closest pair, due to Agarwal et al. [1], has time complexity $O(n^{2(1-1/(\lceil d/2 \rceil+1))+\epsilon})$. Recently Chazelle et al. [7] showed that a bi-chromatic farthest pair can be computed in time $O(n^{2(1-1/(\lfloor d/2 \rfloor+1))+\epsilon})$. The diameter can be computed using this algorithm by setting $R = B = S$.

Dobkin and Suri [16] gave efficient solutions to these problems in the semi-online model. Vaidya [34] described an algorithm for closest pairs which allows insertions and deletions to R, but only allows insertions in B. Supowit [33] showed that if we allow only deletions, then the diameter of a planar point set can be maintained in $O(\sqrt{n} \log n)$ amortized time. But even in two dimensions, no fully dynamic algorithm was known for these problems. Using our algorithms for nearest neighbors and for minima of decomposable functions, we present a data structure that can maintain the bi-chromatic closest or farthest pair, or the diameter, in time $O(n^{1-2/(\lceil d/2 \rceil+1)+\epsilon})$ per update. In particular, this is $O(n^\epsilon)$ for planar point sets.

Linear Programming: Store a set of linear con-

Problem	Query time	Update time
Empty half-space	$O(\frac{n \log n}{m^{1/\lfloor d/2 \rfloor}})$	$O(\frac{m^{1+\epsilon}}{n})$
Half-space reporting	$O(\frac{n \log n}{m^{1/\lfloor d/2 \rfloor}} + k)$	$O(\frac{m^{1+\epsilon}}{n})$
Ray shooting in convex polyhedron	$O(\frac{n \log^3 n}{m^{1/\lfloor d/2 \rfloor}})$	$O(\frac{m^{1+\epsilon}}{n})$
Closest/farthest neighbor	$O(\frac{n \log^3 n}{m^{1/\lceil d/2 \rceil}})$	$O(\frac{m^{1+\epsilon}}{n})$
Linear programming	$O(\frac{n \log^{O(1)} n}{m^{1/\lceil d/2 \rceil}})$	$O(\frac{m^{1+\epsilon}}{n})$
Bi-chromatic closest/farthest pair		$O(n^{1-2/(\lceil d/2 \rceil+1)+\epsilon})$
Diameter		$O(n^{1-2/(\lceil d/2 \rceil+1)+\epsilon})$
MST, L_1 or L_∞ metric		$O(\sqrt{n} \log^d n)$
EMST, $d \leq 4$		$O(\sqrt{n} \log^d n)$
EMST, $d > 4$		$O(n^{1-2/(\lceil d/2 \rceil+1)+\epsilon})$

Table 1: Summary of results

straints (half-spaces) in $\mathbb{R}^d$ into a data structure, so that one can find a point that minimizes a query linear objective function. This problem had been previously been solved in $O(\log^2 n)$ time per operation in two dimensions [28] and $O(\sqrt{n} \log n)$ randomized expected time in three dimensions [19]. If we use Megiddo's parametric search, the problem can be solved using a suitable data structure empty for half-space queries [25], which implies that we can answer queries in time $O((n \log^{O(1)} n)/m^{1/\lfloor d/2 \rfloor})$, and can insert or delete a constraint in $O(m^{1+\epsilon}/n)$ amortized time.

Smallest enclosing disk maintenance. A corollary of the previous result is that a smallest enclosing disk for an n point set in $\mathbb{R}^d$ can be maintained in amortized $O(n^{1-\frac{1}{\lceil d/2 \rceil+1}+\epsilon})$ time per insertion or deletion of a point of S [26].

Euclidean minimum spanning tree: Given a set S of n points in $\mathbb{R}^d$, compute a Euclidean minimum spanning tree of S. For $d = 2$, an optimal $O(n \log n)$ static algorithm has long been known. For $d \geq 3$ the best known algorithm, due to Agarwal et al. [1], has time complexity $O(n^{2(1-1/(\lceil d/2 \rceil+1))+\epsilon})$. Point insertions are not difficult to handle, and an offline algorithm for the planar EMST with insertions and deletions is described in [18]. But no fully dynamic algorithm was known. We use a reduction to the bichromatic closest pair problem due to Agarwal et al. together with a modification of the new dynamic graph MST algorithm of Eppstein et al. [21] to show that the EMST of S can be maintained in $O(\sqrt{n} \log^d n)$ amortized time for $d \leq 4$ and in amortized time $O(n^{1-2/(\lceil d/2 \rceil+1)+\epsilon})$ for $d > 4$ (cf. Section 4).

2 Half-Space Range Reporting

In this section we describe an algorithm for dynamic half-space range reporting. The main result of this section is

Theorem 2.1 *Given a set S of n points in $\mathbb{R}^d$ ($d \geq 3$), the half-space range reporting problem can be solved with the following performance:*

(i) *$O(n \log n)$ space and preprocessing time, $O(n^{1-1/\lfloor d/2 \rfloor+\epsilon}+k)$ time per query, and $O(\log^2 n)$ amortized update time*

(ii) *$O(n^{\lfloor d/2 \rfloor+\epsilon})$ space and preprocessing, $O(\log n+k)$ query time and $O(n^{\lfloor d/2 \rfloor-1+\epsilon})$ amortized update time, and*

(iii) *For a parameter m between n and $n^{\lfloor d/2 \rfloor}$, $O(\frac{n}{m^{1/\lfloor d/2 \rfloor}} \log n)$ query time, $O(m^{1+\epsilon})$ space and preprocessing time, and $O(m^{1+\epsilon}/n)$ amortized update time.*

Due to lack of space, we will prove only the second (most difficult) part of the above theorem. We will follow an approach similar to that of Chazelle et al. [10]. Essentially, we will dynamize Clarkson's data structure, and we will use a technique borrowed from Chazelle et al. [10] to overcome an obstacle preventing a completely straightforward dynamization. Since the half-space range reporting problem is decomposable, i.e., the answers for two disjoint point sets S_1 and S_2 can be combined into an answer for $S_1 \cup S_2$ in constant time, it suffices to describe a data structure that supports only delete operations. Such a data structure can be modified to handle insertions as well; e.g., see [27].

We first describe a data structure for the empty half-space problem (i.e., given a query half-space determine whether it contains any point of S), and then extend it to the half-space reporting problem. Let H be the set of n hyperplanes dual to the points in S. Answering an empty half-space query for S reduces to determining whether a query point p lies above all hyperplanes of H; we refer to the dual problem as the *upper envelope problem* for H. We describe our data structure in this dual formulation.

We need the following results of [24]. The $(\leq k)$-level of H is the set of points $p \in \mathbb{R}^d$ such that at most k hyperplanes of H lie (strictly) above p. For a parameter $r \leq n$, we define a $(1/r)$-cutting of $(\leq k)$-level of H to be a set Ξ of pairwise disjoint simplices such that Ξ covers the $(\leq k)$-level of H and that each simplex of Ξ intersects at most n/r hyperplanes of H. We say that a hyperplane h is *relevant* for a simplex $\triangle$ if h lies above $\triangle$ or intersects $\triangle$. Let $H_\triangle \subseteq H$ denote the set of hyperplanes relevant for a simplex $\triangle \in \Xi$. If $|H_\triangle| > k+n/r$, then $\triangle$ cannot contain any point of $(\leq k)$-level of H, so we can drop $\triangle$ from Ξ. Henceforth we assume that $|H_\triangle| \leq k + n/r$.

Theorem 2.2 (Matoušek [24]) *Let H, k, and r be as above, with $k = O(n/r)$. Then there exists a $(1/r)$-cutting Ξ for the $(\leq k)$-level of H, consisting of $s(r) = O(r^{\lfloor d/2 \rfloor})$ simplices. For $r \leq n^\alpha$ (where $\alpha > 0$ is a constant depending on d), such a cutting can be computed in $O(n \log r)$ time.*

2.1 The data structure

Let δ be a small positive constant fixed throughout the construction (the ε in the resulting performance bounds as well as the constants hidden in the asymptotic notation will depend on δ). The data structure will be periodically rebuilt from scratch after deleting some of the hyperplanes present at the moment of the previous global reconstruction. We use m to denote the number of hyperplanes in H when the data structure was constructed last time, and n to denote the number of hyperplanes in the current H. We set $r = m^\delta$; this setting remains valid between global reconstructions.

We reconstruct the data structure from scratch after deleting $m/2r$ hyperplanes from H. Thus $n \geq m(1 - 1/2r)$. Let $P(m)$ denote the time spent in preprocessing H. The time spent for these global reconstructions can be amortized by charging $2rP(m - \frac{m}{2r})/m \leq 2rP(n)/n$ time to each delete operation. As we will see, this contribution to the amortized deletion time will not affect the asymptotic performance of the structure.

The data structure for H is a recursively defined tree, denoted by $\Psi(H)$. The substructures of $\Psi(H)$ will be periodically reconstructed during the deletions, but this reconstruction will not change the value of r. Let us describe how a subtree for a subset $G \subseteq H$, denoted by $\Psi(G)$, is constructed: If $\nu = |G| \leq r$, then $\Psi(G)$ is a leaf node. We preprocess G in time $O(r^{\lfloor d/2 \rfloor + \varepsilon})$ for the upper envelope problem using Clarkson's static data structure. Thus, for a leaf node, the upper envelope problem for G can be solved in $O(\log r)$ time.

Let us now assume $\nu > r$. The root of the tree $\Psi(G)$ will store the following items:

- A partition of G into disjoint subsets $G_1, G_2, \ldots, G_t$.
- For every $i = 1, 2, \ldots, t$, a cutting Ξ_i and a point location structure for Ξ_i; see below for details.
- For every $i = 1, 2, \ldots, t$ and every simplex $\triangle \in \Xi_i$, a pointer to a subtree of the form $\Psi(G_{i,\triangle})$, where $G_{i,\triangle}$ is the subset of hyperplanes of G_i relevant for $\triangle$.
- For each hyperplane $h \in G_i$, the list L_h of simplices $\triangle \in \Xi_i$ for which h is relevant.
- A counter *dcount* (used for the deletion algorithm).

After the construction of $\Psi(G)$ (before any deletions takes place), these objects will have the following properties:

1. The counter *dcount* is set to $\nu/2r$.
2. For every i, the simplices of Ξ_i cover all points of level at most ν/r with respect to G.
3. For every i and $\triangle \in \Xi_i$, $|G_{i,\triangle}| \leq 2\nu/r$.
4. For every hyperplane $h \in G_i$, h intersects at most

   $$\kappa = c_1 \cdot r^{\lfloor d/2 \rfloor - 1 + \delta}$$

   simplices of Ξ_i, where c_1 is some constant.

Property 3 implies that the depth of $\Psi(G)$ is $O(\log_r \nu) = O(1/\delta)$.

The construction of these objects proceeds by induction. Suppose that the collections $G_1, G_2, \ldots, G_{i-1} \subseteq G$ have already been constructed. Let $\bar{G}_i = G \backslash (G_1 \cup \ldots \cup G_{i-1})$, $\nu_i = |\bar{G}_i|$.

Let $r_i = r\nu_i/\nu$ and $k = \nu/r = \nu_i/r_i$. We compute a $(1/r_i)$-cutting Ξ_i of size $O(r_i^{\lfloor d/2 \rfloor})$ for the $(\leq k)$-level of $\bar{G}_i$, as mentioned in Theorem 2.2, and preprocess Ξ_i for point location queries as follows. We extend the simplices of Ξ to hyperplanes and preprocess the set of resulting hyperplanes using the algorithm of Clarkson [14]. The space and preprocessing required by this structure is $r^{O(1)}$ and the query time is $O(\log r)$.

For every $\Delta \in \Xi_i$, let $\bar{G}_{i,\Delta}$ denote the collection of hyperplanes of $\bar{G}_i$ relevant for Δ (recall that a hyperplane is relevant for Δ if its passes above or through Δ). As explained above, we assume

$$|\bar{G}_{i,\Delta}| \leq \frac{\nu_i}{r_i} + k = \frac{2\nu_i}{r_i} = \frac{2\nu}{r}.$$

A hyperplane $h \in \bar{G}_i$ is called *good* if it is relevant for at most κ hyperplanes of $\bar{G}_i$, and *bad* otherwise. Since

$$\sum_{\Delta \in \Xi_i} |\bar{G}_{i,\Delta}| \leq O(r_i^{\lfloor d/2 \rfloor}) \cdot \frac{2\nu_i}{r_i} = c_1 \nu_i \left(\frac{\nu_i r}{\nu}\right)^{\lfloor d/2 \rfloor - 1}$$

(c_1 is a constant appearing in the bound on the size of Ξ_i), the number of 'bad' hyperplanes in $\bar{G}_i$ is at most

$$\left(\sum_{\Delta \in \Xi_i} |\bar{G}_{i,\Delta}|\right) / \kappa \leq \frac{\nu_i}{r^\delta} \cdot \left(\frac{\nu_i}{\nu}\right)^{\lfloor d/2 \rfloor - 1} \leq \frac{\nu_i}{r^\delta}.$$

Let G_i be the set of good hyperplanes in $\bar{G}_i$ and $\bar{G}_{i+1} = \bar{G}_i - G_i$.

If $|\bar{G}_{i+1}| > \nu/r$, we continue the above described construction inductively for $i+1$. Otherwise Ξ_{i+1} consists of a sufficiently large simplex and $G_{i+1} = \bar{G}_{i+1}$. This finishes the construction of the objects stored at the root of $\Psi(G)$. The appropriate subtrees $\Psi(G_{i,\Delta})$ are constructed recursively. The above construction guarantees $\nu_i/\nu_{i+1} \geq r^\delta$, and it finishes when $\nu_i \leq \nu/r$, therefore $t \leq 1/\delta$. It can be shown that the properties 1–4 are guaranteed by the construction.

Let us estimate the space $S(\nu)$ needed for $\Psi(G)$. If $\nu \leq r$, then the space required is $O(r^{\lfloor d/2 \rfloor + \varepsilon})$. Otherwise, we need $O(tr^c)$ space to store the point location structures for $\Xi_1, \ldots, \Xi_t$ and $O(t\nu r^{\lfloor d/2 \rfloor - 1})$ space to store the lists L_h for each $h \in G$. Since $|G_{i,\Delta}| \leq 2\nu/r$, we get the following recurrence:

$$S(\nu) = \begin{cases} O(r^{\lfloor d/2 \rfloor + \varepsilon}) & \nu \leq r \\ O(\nu r^{\lfloor d/2 \rfloor - 1} + r^c) + \sum_{i \leq t,\, \Delta \in \Xi_i} S(\frac{2\nu}{r}) & \nu > r\,. \end{cases}$$

Since each Ξ_i consists of $O(r^{\lfloor d/2 \rfloor})$ simplices and t is bounded by a constant, the solution of the above recurrence is $S(\nu) = O((r\nu)^{\lfloor d/2 \rfloor + \varepsilon})$. By a similar computation, we get $P(\nu) = O((r\nu)^{\lfloor d/2 \rfloor + \varepsilon})$ for the time required for building $\Psi(G)$.

2.2 Answering a query

We answer an upper envelope query for a query point p recursively. Suppose we are at the root v of a subtree $\Psi(G)$. If v is a leaf node, we answer a query in $O(\log r)$ time using Clarkson's structure stored at v. Otherwise, p lies in the upper envelope of G if and only if for each $i = 1, 2, \ldots, t$ it lies in the upper envelope of G_i. To test this, first determine the simplex $\Delta \in \Xi_i$ that contains p. If there is no such simplex, p does not lie in the upper envelope of G_i. Otherwise, recursively answer the query in $\Psi(G_{i,\Delta})$.

The depth of the overall tree $\Psi(H)$ is $O(1/\delta)$ and the branching degree in this query answering process is always at most $t = O(1)$, which implies that only $O(1)$ nodes are visited. Since we spend $O(\log r)$ time at each node, the total query time is $O(\log n)$.

2.3 Deleting a hyperplane

Let us describe the algorithm for deleting a hyperplane h from H. We visit $\Psi(H)$ in a top-down fashion, and at the root v of each subtree $\Psi(G)$ visited, we do the following: If v is a leaf, we rebuild the structure stored at v. If v is not a leaf, we first decrement the counter *dcount* stored at v by one. If *dcount* becomes zero, we rebuild $\Psi(G)$ (for the current G). Otherwise, we find the i with $h \in G_i$. We delete h from G_i, and then recursively delete h from all subtrees of the form $\Psi(G_{i,\Delta})$ with $\Delta \in L_h$. By construction, $|L_h| \leq \kappa$.

The deletion algorithm guarantees that the properties 3 and 4 always hold, and 2 is replaced by a weaker one:

> 2′. For each i, the simplices of Ξ_i cover all points of level at most $\nu/2r$ with respect to the current set G.

The correctness of the query answering algorithm follows immediately from 2′ (actually even a weaker version of 2′, where all points of level 0 are covered, would suffice; this stronger form anticipates the extension to half-space range reporting) and the above discussion.

In order to finish the proof of Theorem 2.1(ii), it suffices to estimate the amortized deletion time. To this end, let $D(\nu, k)$ denote the maximum time needed for deleting k hyperplanes from the data structure $\Psi(G)$ with $|G| = \nu$, starting at the moment $\Psi(G)$ was built anew. As noted above, a deletion of one hyperplane from G propagates into at most κ children of the root of $\Psi(G)$, thus before the next complete reconstruction of $\Psi(G)$, there are at most $(\nu/2r)\kappa$ deletions in the children. We thus get the following recurrences:

$$D(\nu,k) \le \begin{cases} O(kr^{\lfloor d/2\rfloor+\varepsilon}) & \text{for } \nu \le r \\ D(\nu,\frac{\nu}{2r}) + D(\nu-\frac{\nu}{2r}, k-\frac{\nu}{2r}) + \\ P(\nu-\frac{\nu}{2r}), & \text{for } \nu > r,\ k > \nu/2r \\ \max\{\sum_j D(\frac{2\nu}{r}, k_j) \mid \sum_j k_j \le k\kappa\} + \\ O(k\log\nu) & \text{for } \nu > r,\ k \le \nu/2r \end{cases}$$

The solution of the above recurrence is

$$D(\nu,k) \le C^{\log_r \nu} k \nu^{\lfloor d/2\rfloor-1+\delta} r^{\lfloor d/2\rfloor+\varepsilon},$$

for some large enough constant C. In particular, we get $D(m,m) = O(m^{\lfloor d/2\rfloor+c_2\delta})$, where the constant c_2 is independent of δ.

Hence we obtain a data structure that, using $O(n^{\lfloor d/2\rfloor+\varepsilon})$ space and preprocessing, can answer an empty half-space query in time $O(\log n)$ and can delete a point in $O(n^{\lfloor d/2\rfloor-1+\varepsilon})$ amortized time. In view of the discussion in the beginning, we obtain

Theorem 2.3 *Given a set S of n points in $\mathbb{R}^d$, we can preprocess it in $O(n^{\lfloor d/2\rfloor+\varepsilon})$ time and space, so that an empty half-space query can be answered in $O(\log n)$ time, and a point can be inserted to or deleted from S in amortized time $O(n^{\lfloor d/2\rfloor-1+\varepsilon})$.*

2.4 Half-space reporting

We will now briefly describe how to modify the above procedure for half-space reporting (actually its dual version — reporting hyperplanes of H lying above a query point). Let v be a node in the above described data structure for empty half-space queries, and let G be the corresponding set of hyperplanes. We preprocess G for half-space reporting using Clarkson's static data structure (using space and preprocessing time $O(m^{\lfloor d/2\rfloor+\varepsilon})$) and store this secondary structure at v.

When we reconstruct $\Psi(G)$, we also reconstruct the secondary structure with the current G. But when we delete a hyperplane h we just update the primary structure as described earlier. The time spent in deleting a hyperplane obviously remains the same. Notice that we are updating the secondary structure only when we reconstruct $\Psi(G)$, so the secondary structure will store $\tilde{G}$, the set of hyperplanes in G when $\Psi(G)$ was constructed last time.

As for answering a query, if v is a leaf, we report, in time $O(\log\nu + k_v) = O(\log r + k_v)$, all k_v hyperplanes of G lying above p using the structure stored at v. If v is not a leaf, we determine in time $O(\log r)$ the simplex $\Delta_i \in \Xi_i$ $(i \le t)$ that contains p. If Δ_i is defined for all $i \le t$, then we recursively search in $\Psi(G_{i,\Delta_i})$ with p. Otherwise there is some i such that p does not lie in any simplex of Ξ_i, which, by condition $2'$, implies that there are at least $\nu/2r$ (current) hyperplanes above p. In this case, we query the secondary structure stored at v and compute in time $O(\log\nu + \tilde{k}_v)$ all $\tilde{k}_v$ hyperplanes of $\tilde{G}$ that lie above p. We then report the subset of these hyperplanes that have not been deleted. Since $\tilde{k}_v \le k_v + \nu/2r$ and $k_v \ge \nu/2r$, we have $_v \le 2k_v$ and the overall query time is thus $O(\log n + k)$. This finishes the proof of Theorem 2.1 (ii).

An immediate corollary of Theorem 2.1 is

Corollary 2.4 *Given a set S of n points in $\mathbb{R}^d$ and a parameter $n \le m \le n^{\lceil d/2\rceil}$, we can preprocess it in $O(m^{1+\varepsilon})$ time and space, so that a closest neighbor of a query point in S can be computed in $O((n\log^3 n)/m^{1/\lceil d/2\rceil})$ time, and a point can be inserted to or deleted from S in amortized time $O(m^{1+\varepsilon}/n)$.*

3 Minima of Decomposable Functions

We now describe a data structure for maintaining minima of a decomposable function defined over a set of points. Let R be a set of m red points and B a set of n blue points, and let $\delta(.,.)$ be a distance function. (Note that δ need not satisfy the triangle inequality, so it may not be a metric.) We define $\delta(R,B) = \min\delta(p,q)$, where p varies over all points of R and q varies over all points of B. The goal is to maintain $\delta(R,B)$ as points are inserted to or deleted from $S = R\cup B$. One can maintain maxima instead of minima by negating δ. We first introduce the notion of ordered nearest neighbors and then describe our algorithm.

3.1 Ordered nearest neighbors

Let $x_1, x_2, \ldots, x_n$ be a sequence of points, each of which is colored red or blue. We define the *bi-chromatic ordered nearest neighbor* of a red (resp. blue) point x_i to be a blue (resp. red) point x such that $\delta(x, x_i)$ is minimized over all blue (resp. red) points in the set $\{x_j : j > i\}$. If all $x_i, \ldots, x_n$ have the same color, then their ordered bi-chromatic closest neighbors are not defined. The *ordered bi-chromatic nearest neighbor graph* is a directed graph in which each point has an edge directed to its bi-chromatic ordered nearest neighbor. Suppose we have a dynamic data structure for answering nearest neighbor queries with respect to $\delta(.,.)$, with preprocessing time $P(n)$ and query and update time $T(n)$.

Lemma 3.1 *Let S be any bi-chromatic point set with m red points and $n > m$ blue points. Then the points of S can be ordered into a sequence, in time $O(P(n) + mT(n))$, such that the ordered bi-chromatic nearest neighbor graph forms a simple path.*

Proof: Choose x_1 arbitrarily. Assume inductively that we have chosen x_1 through x_i so the nearest neighbor of each point x_j $(1 \leq j < i)$, among points later in the sequence or not yet chosen, is x_{j+1}. To extend this sequence by one more point, choose x_{i+1} to be the nearest neighbor to x_i among the unchosen points. The resulting path will have length at most $2m$, after which we can place the remaining $n - 2m$ points in any order. We maintain a nearest neighbor searching structure for computing a nearest neighbor among the unchosen points. When we choose a point we remove it from the structure. There are at most $2m$ queries and a similar number of deletions, so the total time is $O(P(n) + mT(n))$. □

The $O(P(n))$ term is a one time start up cost for building the nearest neighbor searching data structure. Once we have computed the ordered bi-chromatic nearest neighbor graph, we can add back the deleted points in time $O(mT(n))$, matching the time for constructing the graph. Then we can remember the data structure and re-use it in later computations, avoiding the start-up cost. If a point is inserted to or deleted from S, the nearest neighbor searching structure can be updated in time $O(T(n))$.

3.2 The data structure

We partition the point set S into *levels* numbered from 0 to $O(\log n)$. The points at each level may be of either color. Let S_i be the set of points at level i; S_i will contain at most 2^i points. For each S_i we maintain a graph G_i.

As we will show below, one of these graphs will contain an edge (p, q) such that $\delta(p, q) = \delta(R, B)$, and it can be found by storing all edges of these graphs in a priority queue. We store the edges of each G_i in a separate priority queue Q_i, and determine the overall minimum length edge by examining the $O(\log n)$ minima from the different queues.

G_i is initially constructed as follows. Let $R_i = S_i \cap R$ and $B_i = S_i \cap B$. G_i consists of two ordered nearest neighbor paths, one for $R_i \cup B$ and one for $B_i \cup R$. G_i can be constructed in time $O(|S_i|T(n))$ by Lemma 3.1 and the discussion following it. As the algorithm progresses we delete edges from G_i and periodically reconstruct it from scratch. We will also periodically reconstruct the overall data structure.

If there were m points in S when it was last reconstructed, we reconstruct it after performing $m/2$ update operations. This ensures that, n, the number of points in S is always between $m/2$ and $3m/2$. The amortized time spent in a global reconstruction is $O(T(n))$ per update, which can be charged to each update operation without affecting the asymptotic running time. The amortized time incurred by this reconstruction can be made worst case per operation by a standard trick of keeping two copies of the data structure, one of which is gradually reconstructed while the other is in use.

3.3 Inserting and deleting points

Whenever we insert a point p into S, we place p in level 0. Then, as long as p is in a level i containing more than 2^i points, we move all points of level i to level $i + 1$, making level i empty. Once p enters a level i in which there are at most 2^i points, we remove all graphs G_j for $j < i$, and reconstruct graph G_i as described above. We also discard all priority queues Q_j, for $j < i$, and reconstruct Q_i storing the edges of new G_i.

Next, we delete a point q from S as follows. We delete all the edges incident to q from each G_i. If $q \in S_i$, then there are at most four edges incident to q, otherwise there are at most two such edges. If we deleted a directed edge of the form (p, q), then we also delete p from its present level, and add p to level 0 as if it were newly inserted. However we do not delete any other edges incident to p. Since there are most two edges of the above form in each G_i, only $O(\log n)$ points are moved to level 0. As in the insertion procedure, we then move these points as a group through successive levels until the level they are in is large enough to hold them, and then reconstruct the graph for the level they end up in.

3.4 Correctness

In order to prove the correctness of the algorithm, we need the following simple lemma.

Lemma 3.2 *Let i be some level. Then the level of all points, which are inserted to S or moved to level 0 after the most recent construction of G_i, is less than i.*

The correctness of the algorithm now follows from the following lemma.

Lemma 3.3 *There is an edge (p,q) in one of the graphs G_i such that $\delta(p,q) = \delta(R,B)$.*

Proof: Let (p,q) be a bi-chromatic closest pair in S. Suppose that $p \in R_i$ and $q \in B_j$, and that $j \geq i$. It follows from Lemma 3.2 that $q \in S$ when G_i was constructed the last time. First assume that $q < p$ in the ordering for which we have defined the ordered nearest neighbor graph for $R_i \cup B$. Let (q,r) be the edge in G_i when it was constructed the last time. By definition of the ordered nearest neighbor graph, $\delta(q,r) \leq \delta(q,p)$ since $q < p$. If the edge (q,r) still exists, then the lemma is obviously true, so assume that (q,r) has been deleted. The only way (q,r) could be deleted from G_i was that r was deleted from S. In that case, q would have been moved to level 0, which, by Lemma 3.2, implies that $j < i$, a contradiction. A similar contradiction can be obtained if $p < q$. Hence, the lemma is true. □

Thus $\delta(R,B)$ can be found by maintaing the edges of each G_i in a priority queue.

3.5 Time analysis

We define a potential function of a point $p \in S_i$ to be

$$\Phi(p) = cT(n)(k-i),$$

where $k = O(\log n)$ is the maximum number of levels and c is some appropriate constant. We define the overall potential function $\Phi(S) = \sum_{p \in S} \Phi(p)$. First, let us analyze the time spent in reconstructing G_i. The actual time spent in constructing G_i is $O(2^i T(n))$. We also spend an additional $O(2^i)$ time to reconstruct the priority queue Q_i [15]. But observe that G_i is constructed only when the the points from S_{i-1} are moved to S_i. Since the points are moved from S_{i-1} to S_i only if $|S_{i-1}| > 2^{i-1}$, $\Phi(S)$ decreases by at least $c2^{i-1}T(n)$. The amortized time in reconstructing G_i and updating the structure is thus zero if c is chosen sufficiently large.

When we insert a new point, we add it to S_0, which increases $\Phi(S)$ by $cT(n)$. Since the actual time spent in adding a point is $O(\log n)$ plus the time spent in reconstructing the appropriate graphs, the amortized running time of an insert operation is $O(T(n)\log n)$.

Deleting a point involves removing at most four edges from each G_i and Q_i, moving $O(\log n)$ points to S_0, and reconstructing appropriate graphs. The total time spent in deleting the edges from G_i and Q_i is $O(\log^2 n)$, and moving the points to S_0 increases the total potential $\Phi(S)$ by $O(\log n) \cdot ckT(n) = O(T(n)\log^2 n)$. Since the amortized time spent in reconstructing the graphs is zero, the total amortized time spent in deleting a point is $O(T(n)\log^2 n)$.

Theorem 3.4 *Let $\delta(.,.)$ be a distance function for which we can perform point queries, and insert and delete points, in time $O(T(n))$ per operation. Then we can maintain $\delta(R,B)$ in amortized time $O(T(n)\log n)$ per point insertion, and $O(T(n)\log^2 n)$ per deletion.*

The above theorem and Corollary 2.4 imply that

Corollary 3.5 *A Euclidean bi-chromatic closest pair or farthest pair of a set of n points in $\mathbb{R}^d$, as well as the diameter of such a set, can be maintained in amortized time $O(n^{1-2/(\lceil d/2 \rceil+1)+\epsilon})$ per update.*

These techniques also yield efficient fully dynamic algorithms for maintaining the minimum separation among rectangles or higher-dimensional orthogonal boxes, the minimum or maximum distance between points and hyperplanes, and the minimum or maximum box defined by a set of points.

4 Euclidean Minimum Spanning Trees

We have seen how to use the nearest neighbor searching problem to maintain the bi-chromatic closest pair of a point set, as points are inserted and deleted. We now apply these results in an algorithm for maintaining the Euclidean minimum spanning tree of a point set. The connection between bi-chromatic closest pairs and minimum spanning trees can be seen from the following lemma.

Lemma 4.1 (Agarwal et al. [1]) *Given a set of n points in $\mathbb{R}^d$, we can form a hierarchical collection of $O(n\log^{d-1} n)$ bi-chromatic closest pair problems, so that each point is involved in $O(i^{d-1})$ problems of size $O(n/2^i)$ ($1 \leq i \leq \log n$) and so that each MST edge is the solution to one of the closest pair problems.*

Lemma 4.1 reduces the geometric MST problem to computing a MST in a graph whose vertices are the points of S and whose edges are $O(n\log^{d-1} n)$ bi-chromatic closest pairs. Insertion or deletion of a point changes $O(\log^d n)$ edges of the graph. Hence, we can maintain the geometric MST by performing $O(\log^d n)$ updates in an algorithm to maintain the MST in a dynamic graph. The following recent result strengthens an $O(\sqrt{m})$ time dynamic graph MST algorithm of Frederickson [22].

Lemma 4.2 (Eppstein et al. [21]) *Given a graph subject to edge insertions and deletions, having at most n vertices and m edges at any one time, the minimum spanning tree can be maintained in time $O(\sqrt{n}\log(m/n))$ per update.*

If we combine these two results, we get an $O(\sqrt{n}\log^d n \log\log n)$ time algorithm for maintaining the MST, once we know the corresponding BCP information. We can save a further factor of $O(\log\log n)$ by maintaining MSTs of subproblems defined by the hierarchical structure of Lemma 4.1, in a similar fashion to the way Eppstein et al. prove Lemma 4.2 using a hierarchical partition of the graph. The time for solving the BCP problems reduces to a geometric series which is bounded by the time for a single problem. The hierarchical structure of Lemma 4.1 can be periodically rebalanced in a similar amortized time bound. Thus we have

Theorem 4.3 *A Euclidean minimum spanning tree of a set of points in $\mathbb{R}^d$ can be maintained in amortized time $O(\sqrt{n}\log^d n)$ per update for $d \leq 4$ and in time $O(n^{1-2/(\lceil d/2\rceil+1)+\epsilon})$ for $d > 4$.*

We note that for rectilinear (L_1 and L_∞) metrics, orthogonal range query data structures can be used to answer dynamic bi-chromatic closest pair queries in $O(\log^d n)$ time per update [34].

Theorem 4.4 *The rectilinear MST of a set of n points in $\mathbb{R}^d$ can be maintained in time $O(\sqrt{n}\log^d n)$ per update.*

References

[1] P.K. Agarwal, H. Edelsbrunner, O. Schwarzkopf, and E. Welzl. Euclidean minimum spanning trees and bichromatic closest pairs. *Proc. 6th ACM Symp. Comput. Geom.* (1990) 203–210. *SIAM J. Comput.*, to appear.

[2] P.K. Agarwal and J. Matoušek. Ray shooting and parametric search. *Proc. 24th ACM Symp. Theory of Computing* (1992) 517–526.

[3] P.K. Agarwal and M. Sharir. Planar geometric location problems and maintaining the width of a planar set. *Proc. 2nd ACM/SIAM Symp. Discrete Algorithms* (1991) 449–458.

[4] P.K. Agarwal and M. Sharir. Applications of a new partitioning scheme. *Discrete Comput. Geom.* to appear.

[5] J. Bentley and J. Saxe. Decomposable searching problems I: Static-to-dynamic transformation. *J. Algorithms* 1 (1980) 301–358.

[6] B. Chazelle. An optimal algorithm for computing convex layers. *IEEE Trans. Information Theory* IT–31 (1985) 509–517.

[7] B. Chazelle, L. Guibas, H. Edelsbrunner, and M. Sharir. Diameter, width, closest line pair, and parametric searching. *Proc. 8th ACM Symp. Computational Geometry* (1992) 120–129.

[8] B. Chazelle, L. Guibas, and D. T. Lee. The power of geometric duality. *BIT* 25 (1985) 76–90.

[9] B. Chazelle and F. P. Preparata. Halfspace range searching: An algorithmic application of k-sets. *Discrete Comput. Geom.* 1 (1986) 83–93.

[10] B. Chazelle, M. Sharir, and E. Welzl. Quasi-optimal upper bounds for simplex range searching and new zone theorems. *Proc. 6th ACM Symp. Computational Geometry* (1990) 23–33.

[11] Yi Chiang and R. Tamassia. Dynamic algorithms in computational geometry. Tech. Rept. CS-91-24, Dept. Computer Science, Brown University, 1991.

[12] K. L. Clarkson. New applications of random sampling in computational geometry. *Discrete Comput. Geom.* 2 (1987) 195–222.

[13] K. L. Clarkson. A randomized algorithm for closest-point queries. *SIAM J. Comput.* 17 (1988) 830–847.

[14] K. L. Clarkson and P. Shor. New applications of random sampling in computational geometry II. *Discrete Comput. Geom.* 4 (1989) 387–421.

[15] T. Coreman, C. Leiserson and R. Rivest. *Introduction to Algorithms*, The MIT Press, Cambridge, MA, 1990.

[16] D. Dobkin and S. Suri. Dynamically computing the maxima of decomposable functions, with applications. *J. ACM* 38 (1991) 275–298.

[17] H. Edelsbrunner and M. Overmars. Batched dynamic solutions to decomposable searching problems. *J. Algorithms* 6 (1985) 515–542.

[18] D. Eppstein. Offline algorithms for dynamic minimum spanning tree problems. *Proc. 2nd Worksh. Algorithms and Data Structures*, Springer-Verlag LNCS 519 (1991) 392–399.

[19] D. Eppstein. Dynamic three-dimensional linear programming. *Proc. 32nd IEEE Symp. Found. Computer Science* (1991) 488–494. *ORSA J. Comput.*, to appear.

[20] D. Eppstein and J. Erickson. Iterated nearest neighbors and finding minimal polytopes. Manuscript, 1992.

[21] D. Eppstein, Z. Galil, G.F. Italiano, and A. Nissentzweig. Sparsification — A technique for speeding up dynamic graph algorithms. *Proc. 32nd IEEE Symp. Found. Computer Science* (1992), this proceedings.

[22] G.N. Frederickson. Data structures for on-line updating of minimum spanning trees, with applications. *SIAM J. Comput.* 14 (1985) 781–798.

[23] J. Hershberger and S. Suri. Offline maintenance of planar configurations. *Proc. 2nd ACM/SIAM Symp. Discrete Algorithms* (1991) 32–41.

[24] J. Matoušek. Reporting points in halfspaces. *Proc. 32nd IEEE Symp. Found. Computer Science* (1991) 207–215.

[25] J. Matoušek and O. Schwarzkopf. Linear optimization queries. *Proc. 8th ACM Symp. Computational Geometry* (1992) 16–25.

[26] N. Megiddo. Linear-time algorithms for linear programming in $\mathbb{R}^3$ and related problems. *SIAM J. Computing* 12 (1983) 720–732.

[27] K. Mehlhorn. *Multi-dimensional Searching and Computational Geometry.* Springer-Verlag, Belin–Heidelberg–New York, 1985.

[28] M. Overmars and H. van Leeuwen. Maintenance of configurations in the plane. *J. Comput. Sys. Sci.* 23 (1981), 166–204.

[29] F. Preparata and M. Shamos. *Computational Geometry: An Introduction*, Springer-Verlag, New York, 1985.

[30] F. Preparata and R. Tamassia. Efficient point location in a spatial cell complex. *SIAM J. Comput.* 21 (1992) 267–280.

[31] N. Sarnak and R. Tarjan. Planar point location using persistent search trees, *Commun. ACM* 29 (1986) 669–679.

[32] M. Smid. Maintaining the minimal distance of a point set in polylogarithmic time. *Proc. 2nd ACM/SIAM Symp. Discrete Algorithms* (1991) 1–6.

[33] K.J. Supowit. New techniques for some dynamic closest-point and farthest-point problems. *Proc. 1st ACM/SIAM Symp. Discrete Algorithms* (1990) 84–90.

[34] P.M. Vaidya. Geometry helps in matching. *SIAM J. Comput.* 18 (1989) 1201–1225.

Randomized geometric algorithms and pseudo-random generators

(Extended abstract)

Ketan Mulmuley *
The University of Chicago

1 Introduction

Recently a lot of effort has been invested in reducing the number of random bits required by various randomized geometric algorithms. This is justified by the fact that random bits constitute a valuable computational resource and hence should be used judiciously. In this vein, Karloff and Raghavan [6] have recently shown that the number of random bits used by Quicksort can be reduced to $O(\log n)$ without affecting its expected running time. There scheme works as follows. Consider the iterative version of Quicksort which proceeds by considering a sequence of partitioning items one at a time. If this sequence were a truly random permutation of the list of given items (which can be thought of as points on a line) then the expected running time of this algorithm is $O(n \log n)$. [6] shows that this expected running time remains $O(n \log n)$ even if the sequence of partitioning items is not chosen in a truly random fashion but using some simple pseudo random generator, which uses only $O(\log n)$ bits.

The so called randomized incremental algorithms in computational geometry (for example, see [4, 9]) can be thought of as a generalization of Quicksort to higher dimensional geometric problems. They all construct the geomtric complex in the given problem, such as a Voronoi diagram or a convex polytope, by adding the objects in the input set, one at a time, in a random order. We show that the expected running times of most of the randomized incremental algorithms in computational geometry do not change (up to a constant factor), when the sequence of additions is not truly random but is instead generated using only $O(\log n)$ random bits. The pseudo-random generator that we use is a generalization of the well known linear congruential generator. It generates a random polynomial $f(x)$ of a fixed degree by choosing its coefficients at random from the set $\{0, \cdots, n-1\}$, where n is a large enough prime number.

A sequence of random variables is then generated by letting x take all values from 1 to n and evaluating $f(x)$ modulo n. We shall call this Bounded Degree Congruential Generator (BDCG). The same generator was used in [6]. Our pseudo-randomization scheme is described in Section 4. When N is a set of points on the line, the scheme specializes to the one in [6].

We actually prove some general results and then apply them in a uniform way to various applications. A crucial tool in our technique is a certain combinatorial series, called θ-series. It was defined earlier in some special cases [10, 11] with different motivation. Here it unexpectedly becomes a crucial tool of analysis in a pseudo-random setting.

We state below some of the randomized incremental algorithms whose expected running times do not change by more than a constant factor when they are pseudo-randomized using BDCG. The degree of a random polynomial used by BDCG is assumed to be a large enough constant. Its exact value depends on the problem under consideration.

Trapezoidal decompositions: Computing intersections among a given set of segments in the plane has received a considerable attention in computational geometry; see eg. [2, 4, 9]. The algorithms in [4, 9] are randomized and incremental. Their expected running time is $O(k + n \log n)$, where k is the number of intersections among the given segments. This is clearly optimal. Given the simplicity of the algorithm in [9], it is naturally interesting to know how it performs if the sequence of additions is generated using a pseudo-random generator, such as the one we described above. In this paper, we show that the expected running time of the algorithm is not affected by more than a constant factor, when it is pseudo-randomized using BDCG.

Convex hulls and Voronoi diagrams Convex hulls have had long history. Clarkson and Shor [4] gave a simple randomized incremental algorithm for constructing convex hulls with optimal expected running time. This algorithm can be made online either through linear programming or by remembering history of the computation [12, 15]. In this paper we show that the ex-

*Supported by Packard Fellowship

0-8186-2900-2/92 $3.00 © 1992 IEEE

pected running times of these algorithms do not change by more than a constant factor when they are pseudo-randomized using BDCG. By the connection between convex hulls and Voronoi diagrams we get similar results for Voronoi diagrams.

Linear programming [7] gave a linear programming algorithm that has $O(n)$ time provided the dimension d is constant. The constant factor within the big-oh notation is very big, of the order of 2^{d^2}. This was improved subsequently; e.g. see [3, 15]. The algorithm in [15] is randomized and incremental. Its expected running time is $O(d!n)$. We show that the expected running time of this algorithm is $O(d^{O(d)} n \log^{d-1} n)$, when it is pseudo-randomized using BDCG. It is open if the expected running time of the pseudo-randomized algorithm remains linear.

Hidden surface removal: [10] gives a simple randomized incremental algorithm for the hidden surface removal problem in computer graphics. This algorithm is quasi-output-sensitive. We show that its running time does not change by more than a constant factor when it is pseudo-randomized using BDCG.

Our results can also be applied to several other randomized incremental algorithms. These will be considered in the full version; the basic idea in these other applications is the same.

The above randomized algorithms can also be made online by remembering history of computation [1, 5, 12, 14, 16]. This history can be used for answering certain forms of queries, such as point location queries. The queries are answered by searching through the history of computation. The cost of a query depends on the length of the search path in the history. One can also show that the expected length of this search path remains logarithmic in a pseudo-random setting as well (this is omitted in this abstract).

Two notable exceptions where our results do not seem to apply are the following. [11] gives a randomized incremental algorithm for constructing higher order Voronoi diagrams in arbitrary dimension with optimal expected running time. We could not show that its expected running time does not change by more than a constant factor in a pseudo-random setting. Our techniques also do not apply to the randomized incremental algorithm for triangulating simple polygons [16].

We should remark here that only one of our general results (Lemma 1) depends on the actual nature of pseudo-randomization. The remaining results have nothing to do with pseudo-randomization. If one wishes to use a pseudo-random generator different from the one used in this paper, only Lemma 1 needs to be reproved. The rest remains the same.

The rest of this paper is organized as follows. In Section 2 we state randomized incremental algorithms in an abstract general form. In Section 3 and Section 4 we state our pseudo-randomization scheme. It consists in replacing a random sequence of additions used in the algorithm with a suitable pseudo-random sequence of additions. Section 5 discusses quicksort to motivate the later treatment. In Section 6 we prove general results that are basic to all applications in this paper. Section 7, Section 8 give some applications of these results; applications to linear programming and hidden surface removal mentioned above are omitted in this abstract.

Notations: We use $| \ |$ denote the size. Thus if X is a set, $|X|$ denotes its cardinality. If $H(N)$ is a geometric partition, $|H(N)|$ denotes its size, i.e., the total number of faces in it of all dimensions. If I is a random varible, we denote its expected value by $E[I]$.

We implicitly assume throughout the paper that all objects in the given set N are in general position. This assumption can be removed by standard perturbation techniques.

2 Randomized incremental algorithms

The so called randomized incremental algorithms in computational geometry can be thought of as a generalization of quick sort to higher dimensional geometric problems. These algorithms have the following abstract form. Let us say we are interested in constructing a certain geometric partition $H(N)$ induced by a set N of "objects". The objects depend upon the problem under consideration. For example, N can be a set of sites in R^d and $H(N)$ can be its Voronoi diagram. A randomized incremental algorithm for constructing $H(N)$ has the following general form:

1. Construct a random sequence (permutation) $S_1, S_2, \cdots, S_n$ of the objects in N.
2. Add the objects in N one at a time according to this sequence. Let N^i denote the set of the first i added objects. At the i-th stage, the algorithm maintains the partition $H(N^i)$ formed by the set N^i and other necessary data structures. All these structures need to be updated efficiently during the addition of a new object.

There are several subtleties that we have skipped in the above formulation of randomized incremental algorithms. In particular, it turns out that the partition $H(N)$ needs to be well behaved for the above incremental construction to work. What this roughly means is that each face of $H(N)$, at least of the dimension that matters, should be "defined" by a bounded number of objects. If this is not true, one has to work with some suitable refinement (triangulation) of $H(N)$ instead. Why this restriction is needed will become clear in Section 6.

The simplest example of a randomized incremental algorithm is quick sort. Let us see why this is so. Let N denote a set of points in R. Let $H(N)$ denote the partition of R formed by the points in N. Sorting the set N is equivalent to building the partition $H(N)$, i.e. determining the intervals in $H(N)$ and adjacencies among them.

In the randomized incremental version of quick sort, the points in N are added, one at a time, in a random order. In other words, we choose a random permutation of N and then add the points in N, one a time, according to that permutation. Let N^i denote the set of the first i added points. At the i-th stage, the algorithm maintains the partition $H(N^i)$ formed by N^i. Let us say that a point in $N \setminus N^i$ is in conflict with an interval $I \in H(N^i)$ if I contains that point. With each interval $I \in H(N^i)$, we maintain the (unordered) conflict list of the points in $N \setminus N^i$ that it contains. Conversely, with each point in $N \setminus N^i$ we associate a pointer to the conflicting interval in $H(N^i)$. The addition of the $(i+1)$-st point $S = S_{i+1}$ is carried out by trivially splitting the conflicting interval in $H(N^i)$ and its conflict list.

It is well known that the expected running time of the algorithm is $O(n \log n)$, if the order of additions of the the points in N is random,

3 A pseudo-random generator

In this section we describe the pseudo-random generator that we shall be using in this paper. It is a generalization of the well known linear congruential generator. We shall call it Bounded Degree Congruential Generator (BCDG). The same generator was used in [6].

A set of $X_0, X_1, \cdots, X_{n-1}$ of random variables is called t-wise independent, if every t-tuple of distinct variables in the set is independent, but the knowledge of any t may determine all the others. In this section, each random variable X_i is assumed to a take value from the set of integers $< n >= \{0, \cdots, n-1\}$. For every fixed constant t, our goal is to generate a t-wise independent sequence of random variables X_i using only a few random bits – $t\lceil \log n \rceil$ random bits will suffice [1].

We choose t numbers, also called *seeds*, $a_0, \cdots, a_{t-1}$ independently from a uniform distribution on $< n >$. Assume that n is prime. For each $i \in < n >$, let $X_i = a_0 + a_1 i + a_2 i^2 + \cdots + a_{t-1} i^{t-1} (mod n)$.

Proposition 1 *[6] For each i, X_i is uniform on $< n >$ and $X_0, \cdots, X_{n_1}$ is t-wise independent. Given $z \in < n >$, conditioning on $X_i = z$, each X_j, $j \neq i$, is still uniform on $< n >$ and $X_0, \cdots, X_{n-1}$ is still $(t-1)$-wise independent.*

[1] All logarithms in this paper are to the base two.

4 Pseudo-randomization

Our scheme for making randomized incremental algorithms pseudo-random is simple. As already noted in Section 1, every randomized incremental algorithm has the same abstract form. It constructs the geometric partition induced by a given set N of objects by adding the objects in N one at a time in a random order. A pseudo-randomized algorithm differs from the truly randomized algorithm in that the sequence of additions will be pseudo-random. The rest of the algorithm remains the same.

A pseudo random sequence of additions is generated as follows. Let N be the set of n objects as before. We assume that the set N is given to us in the form of an array of length n, where each entry contains the description of an object. For $0 \leq i \leq n-1$, we let $N[i]$ denote the object contained in the i-th entry of this array.

Without loss of generality assume that n is prime; otherwise pad the set N with dummy objects so that its size equals a prime number not much larger than n. We first construct a t-wise independent sequence $X_0, \cdots, X_{n-1}$ of numbers using the scheme in Section 3. The constant t will depend on the problem under consideration.

A pseudo-random sequence of additions is generated as follows:

For $i = 0$ to $n-1$ **do**:
  Add $N(X_i)$, if it is not already added.

It is possible that at the end of the above *main phase* of additions, some objects in N are still not added. This is because the n variables X_i need not take distinct values. In the last *clean up phase*, we add the remaining objects in N in *any* order.

5 Quick sort

We remark that when we pseudo-randomize Quick sort using the scheme in the previous section with five seeds, we get exactly the algorithm in [6]. We elaborate on this specialization a bit more, because Quicksort is the simplest randomized incremental algorithm.

Let N denote a set of points in R. Recall the randomized incremental version of quick sort in Section 2. In a pseudo-randomized version of quick sort, we add the points in N, one at time, in a pseudo-random order generated as in Section 4. We let t, the number of seeds, be sufficiently large. For quick sort five seeds suffice. Let N^i denote the set of first i added points. At the i-th stage, the algorithm maintains the partition $H(N^i)$ formed by N^i, and the unordered conflict list of each interval in $H(N^i)$. The addition of the $(i+1)$-st point $S = S_{i+1}$ is carried out by trivially splitting the conflicting interval in $H(N^i)$ and its conflict list.

In [6] it is proven that the expected running time of the above pseudo-randomized quick sort remains $O(n \log n)$. Here we reformulate the analysis in a somewhat different way so as to pave the way for our later higher dimensional generalization.

Observe that the cost of adding the $(i+1)$-st point $S = S_{i+1}$ is proportional to the total conflict size of the newly created intervals in $H(N^{i+1})$, ignoring an additive $O(1)$ term. The newly created intervals in $H(N^{i+1})$ are the ones that are adjacent to S_{i+1}.

Let $\Pi \subseteq N \times N$ denote the subset of all pairs of distint points. For a fixed pair $(p,q) \in \Pi$, let us define the set $L(p,q)$ as the set of points in N between P and Q. $L(p,q)$ is called the conflict list of the pair (p,q). It size $l(p,q)$ is called the *conflict size* of the pair (p,q). The elements of $L(p,q)$ are also called *stoppers* associated with (p,q). Finally, we define the set $D(p,q)$ as simply $\{p,q\}$. The elements of $D(p,q)$ are called *triggers* associated with (p,q).

Let $\bar{u}$ denote the sequence of additions of points in the algorithm. Let us say that the pair (p,q) is *created* during $\bar{u}$ iff (p,q) occurs as an interval in $H(N^i)$, for some i. This happens iff p and q are added in $\bar{u}$ before any point in $L(p,q)$. In other words, all triggers associated with (p,q) are added before the stoppers associated with (p,q). Let us define a 0-1 indicator function $i(p,q)$ by: $i(p,q) = 1$ iff the pair (p,q) is created during $\bar{u}$. It is then clear that the cost of the whole algorithm is proportional to

$$\sum_{(p,q)\in\Pi} i(p,q)(1 + l(p,q)). \qquad (1)$$

It follows that the expected running time of the algorithm is proportional to

$$\sum_{(p,q)\in\Pi} (1 + l(p,q)).\text{Prob}\{i(p,q) = 1\}. \qquad (2)$$

If the sequence $\bar{u}$ were purely random, then

$$\text{Prob}\{i(p,q) = 1\} = 1 / \binom{2 + l(p,q)}{2}.$$

This follows because every pair of elements in $L(p,q) \cup D(p,q)$ is equally likely to be added first.

But it can be shown that

$$\text{Prob}\{i(p,q) = 1\} = O(1/1 + l(p,q)^2), \qquad (3)$$

even if the sequence $\bar{u}$ is pseudo random as in this case. This can be shown using the results in [6]. Alternately, this also follows from the more general result to be proved later in this paper (Main Lemma).

From eq.(3) it now follows that the expected running time of pseudo-randomized quick sort is proportional to

$$\sum_{(p,q)\in\Pi} \frac{1}{l(p,q)+1} = \sum_{p\in N}\sum_{q\in N} \frac{1}{1 + l(p,q)}.$$

The inner sum can be broken in two parts, corresponding to the points on the left and right side of p. Both these parts are bounded by $\sum_{i=1}^{n} 1/i = O(\log n)$. Hence, the whole expression is $O(\log n)$.

Thus it follows that the expected running time of pseudo-randomized quick sort is $O(n \log n)$.

6 Basic results

The goal of this paper is to generalize the one dimensional analysis in Section 5 to the other higher dimensional randomized incremental algorithms in computational geometry. This will be done by proving some general results in the setting of abstract configuration spaces [4, 12]. In particular, a combinatorial series called a θ-series [10, 11, 12] that can be associated with these configuration spaces will play a crucial role.

Let us first recall the notion of a configuration space [4, 12]. Let us assume that we are given an abstract universe N of elements (objects). A configuration σ over N is a pair (D, L), where D and L are disjoint subsets of N. We say that the elements in D, called *triggers*, *define* σ and that the elements in L, called *stoppers*, *conflict* with σ. Let $d(\sigma)$, the degree of σ, be defined as the cardinality of $D(\sigma)$. Let $l(\sigma)$, the conflict size (or the level) of σ, be defined as the cardinality of $L(\sigma)$. We shall always assume that $d(\sigma)$ is bounded.

We say that the configuration σ is active over a subset $M \subseteq N$ if M contains the trigger set $D(\sigma)$ but no stopper in $L(\sigma)$.

By a configuration space $\Pi(N)$ over N we shall mean any set of configurations over N with bounded degree. We also assume that the number of configurations in Π with the same trigger set is bounded.

Example 1: (Points on the line)

Let N be a set of points on the real line. Let Π be the configurations space of all pairs (p,q) of the points in N. This is the configuration space that we used in the analysis of Quick sort in Section 5. The stopper set $L(p,q)$ of a configuration (p,q) is the set of all points in N that lie between P and Q. The trigger set $D(p,q) = \{P, Q\}$.

Given a subset $M \subseteq N$, the configuration (p,q) is active over M iff (p,q) occurs as an interval in the partition of the line formed by M.

Example 2: (Segments in the plane)

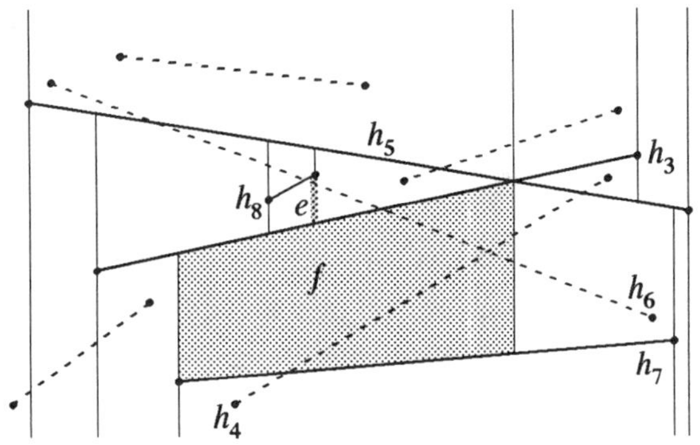

Figure 1: A trapezoidal decomposition

Let N be a set of segments in the plane. These segments decompose the plane into several regions. Unfortunately, the regions in the resulting decomposition can have complicated shapes. Hence, it is convenient to refine this partition further by passing a vertical attachment through every endpoint or point of intersection. Each vertical attachment extends upwards (and downwards) until it hits another segment, and if no such segment exists then it extends to infinity. This yields a *trapezoidal decomposition* $H(N)$ of the plane (eg. see fig. 1; ignore the dotted segments). The regions in $H(N)$ are called trapezoids, even though they can be triangles, really speaking. Triangles are considered degenerate forms of trapezoids. The trapezoidal decompositions are heavily investigated in computational geometry. In Section 7 we shall investigate a randomized incremental algorithm for constructing trapezoidal decompositions. Here we only give an example of a configuration space that will arise in in its analysis.

Let us call a trapezoid f in the plane *feasible* with respect to N, if f occurs in some trapezoidal decomposition $H(M)$, where $M \subseteq N$. We let $D(f)$, the triggers associated with f, be the set of segments in N that "define" f, i.e., the segments that are adjacent to f. We define the stopper set $L(f)$ to be the set of remaining segments in N that intersect f. For example, in fig. 1 the trigger set of f is $\{h_3, h_5, h_7\}$ and the stoper set is $\{h_4, h_6\}$.

Similarly, define a racquet in a trapezoidal decomposition $H(M)$ as a pair $\sigma = (f, e)$, where f is a trapezoid in $H(M)$ and e is a vertical attachment that is adjacent to f (fig. 1). We say that f is the face of the racquet. It could possibly be unbounded. The attachment e is called the handle.

Now let N be the given set of segments in R^2. Define a *feasible racquet* σ over N as a racquet that occurs in a trapezoidal decomposition $H(M)$, for some $M \subseteq N$. We define the trigger set $D(\sigma)$ to be the set of segments in N that define σ, i.e., the segments in N that are adjacent to the face or the handle of σ. We define the stopper set $L(\sigma)$ to be the set of remaining segments in N that intersect this racquet. Thus in fig. 1 the trigger set of the raquet (f, e) is $\{h_3, h_5, h_7, h_8\}$ and the stopper set is $\{h_4, h_6\}$.

The degree of any racquet is clearly bounded. The number of racquets with the same trigger set is also bounded.

In this fashion, given a set of segments N, we get a configuration space $\Sigma(N)$ of feasible trapezoids or racquets over N. This configuration space will be used in the analysis of a pseudo-randomized incremental algorithm for trapezoidal decompositions.

Given a subset $M \subseteq N$, a feasible trapezoid or a racquet in $\Sigma(N)$ is active over M iff it occurs in the trapezoidal decomposition $H(M)$.

Example 3: (Trivial configuration space)
We say that a configuration space $\Pi(N)$, over a given object set N is *trivial*, if for every subset $M \subseteq N$, the number of configurations in $\Pi(N)$ active over M is $O(1)$. We give a simple example of a trivial configuration space. Let $\Sigma(N)$ be the configuration space in Example 2. For a fixed point $p \in R^2$, let $\Sigma_p(N)$ be the subspace of all feasible trapezoids in Σ that contain p. It is clear that Σ_p is trivial. This is because, for any $M \subseteq N$, exactly one trapezoid in $H(M)$ can contain p.

Let us get back to the abstract situation. Let $\Pi = \Pi(N)$ be any configuration space over a given object set N. Consider any sequence $\bar{u}$ of additions of the objects in N. Let N^i denote the first i added objects in this sequence. Let σ be a fixed configuration in Π. We say that σ is active at time i during $\bar{u}$, if it is active over the set N^i. We say that σ is *created* during $\bar{u}$, if it is active at some time $i \leq n$. If i is the least such integer, then we say that σ is created during $\bar{u}$ at time i. We say that σ gets killed (or destroyed) at time j, if σ is active over N^{j-1} but not over N^j. Note that a created configuration during $\bar{u}$ can be destroyed only once.

Proposition 2 *If the sequence $\bar{u}$ of additions is a truly random permutation of N, then the probability that σ is created during $\bar{u}$ is* $1/\binom{l(\sigma)+d(\sigma)}{d(\sigma)}$.

Proof. Observe that σ is created during $\bar{u}$ iff the first $d(\sigma)$ elements that are added from the set $L(\sigma) \cup D(\sigma)$ are all in $D(\sigma)$. Because $\bar{u}$ is truly random, each subset of $d(\sigma)$ elements in $L(\sigma) \cup D(\sigma)$ is equally likely to be added during $\bar{u}$ before the remaining elements in $L(\sigma) \cup D(\sigma)$. ▯

What happens when $\bar{u}$ is pseudo-random sequence of additions, as generated by the scheme in Section 4? We prove that the following generalization of the above proposition still holds.

Lemma 1 *(Main Lemma) Let $\bar{u}$ be a pseudo-random sequence of additions generated as in Section 4 with t seeds. If $t \geq 3d(\sigma)+2$, the probability that σ is created during $\bar{u}$ is $O(1/\binom{l(\sigma)+d(\sigma)}{d(\sigma)})$.*

Proof. See the appendix. $\Box$

Notice that the crucial eq.(3) in the analysis of Quick sort immediately follows by applying the above lemma to the configuration space in Example 1.

Now let $\Pi = \Pi(N)$ be any configuration space. Let $\bar{u}$ be any sequence of additions of the objects in N. Define, $\beta(\Pi, \bar{u})$, the total *structural change* during $\bar{u}$, to be the number of configurations in Π that get created during $\bar{u}$. More precisely, for each configuration $\sigma \in \Pi$, let us define a 0-1 indicator function by: $i(\sigma, \bar{u})$=1, if σ is created during $\bar{u}$. It is zero otherwise. Then

$$\beta(\Pi, \bar{u}) = \sum_{\sigma \in \Pi} i(\sigma, \bar{u}). \tag{4}$$

Note that $\beta(\Pi, \bar{u})$ also bounds the number of configurations that are destroyed during $\bar{u}$ since a created configuration can be destroyed only once.

More generally, given $a \geq 0$, we define a-th order conflict change during $\bar{u}$ as

$$\beta_a(\Pi, \bar{u}) = \sum_{\sigma \in \Pi} (1 + l(\sigma))^a i(\sigma, \bar{u}). \tag{5}$$

Thus the 0-th order conflict change is simply the structural change as defined before. As each created configuration is destroyed only once, $\beta_a(\Pi, \bar{u})$ also bounds the sum of the a-th powers of the conflict sizes of the destroyed configurations.

We omit $\bar{u}$ from the notation if it is understood from the context. Thus $\beta_a(\Pi, \bar{u})$ and $\beta(\Pi, \bar{u})$ are simply denoted as $\beta_a(\Pi)$ and $\beta(\Pi)$ respectively.

Let $d = d_{max}(\Pi) = \max\{d(\sigma) \mid \sigma \in \Pi\}$. Let $\bar{u}$ be a pseudo-random sequence of additions that is generated by the scheme in Section 4 using at least $3d+2$ seeds. Then it follows from the Main Lemma that $E[\beta_a(\Pi)]$, the expected value of $\beta_a(\Pi)$, is proportional to

$$\sum_{\sigma \in \Pi} \frac{(1 + l(\sigma))^a}{\binom{l(\sigma)+d(\sigma)}{d(\sigma)}} \approx \sum_{\sigma \in \Pi} \frac{1}{(l(\sigma) + d(\sigma))^{d(\sigma)-a}}.$$

Here, as well as in what follows, $\approx$ denotes asymptotic equality with constant factors ignored. The above expression naturally leads us to associate the following combinatorial series with Π, which we shall call its Θ-series. Let $d_{min}(\Pi) = \min\{d(\sigma) | \sigma \in \Pi\}$. We shall define the θ-series for Π by:

$$\Theta(\Pi, s) = \sum_{\sigma \in \Pi} \frac{1}{l(\sigma)^{d(\sigma)-s}}, \text{ for } 0 \leq s \leq d_{min}(\Pi).$$

As a convention, $0^0 = 1$. This means $l(\sigma)^{d(\sigma)-s}$ is 1 if $l(\sigma) = 0$. This generalizes the previous definition of θ-series [10, 11] to abstract configuration spaces.

All uses of the Θ-series in this paper are based on the following theorem which immediately follows from Proposition 2 and Main Lemma 1.

Theorem 1 *(Main Theorem) Let Π be any configuration space over an abstract set N. Let $\bar{u}$ be a truly random sequence of additions or a pseudo-random sequence of additions for which Main Lemma holds. In particular, this happens if one uses the scheme in Section 4 using at least $3d_{max}(\Pi)+2$ seeds. Then, for each $a \geq 0$, the expected value of the a-th order conflict change $\beta_a(\Pi)$ is $O(\Theta(\Pi, a))$. If $\bar{u}$ is a truly random sequence of additions then this expected value is also $\Omega(\Theta(\Pi, a))$.*

As an example, let Σ be the configuration space of feasible trapezoids and racquets over a set of segments N (Example 2). By the above theorem, the expected value of the a-th order conflict change $\beta_a(\Sigma)$ is $O(\Theta(\Sigma, a))$, as long as the pseudo-random sequence of additions is generated using $3d_{max}(\Sigma)+2) = 20$ seeds. The quantity $\Theta(\Sigma, a)$ might look complicated at first. However, it follows from a result to be proved soon that, if k denotes the number intersections among the segments in N, then

$$\begin{aligned} \Theta(\Sigma, a) &= O(k+n), && \text{if } a < 1, \\ &= O(k + n \log n), && \text{if } a = 1. \end{aligned}$$

So let us get back to the abstract setting again.

Let Π and Σ be any two configuration spaces over the same set of objects N. For any subset $R \subseteq N$, define $n(\Sigma, R)$ to be the number configurations in Σ that are active over R. We define $n(\Pi, R)$ similarly. We define the *index* $\Sigma : \Pi$ as:

$$\Sigma : \Pi = \max\{n(\Sigma, R)/n(\Pi, R) | R \subseteq N\}.$$

Theorem 2 *(Index Theorem) Let Σ and Π be two configuration spaces over N such that that the index $\Sigma : \Pi$ is bounded. Let n be the number of elements in N. For any fixed s:*

1. $\Theta(\Sigma, s) = O(\Theta(\Pi, s))$, *if s is less than $d_{min}(\Sigma)$ and $d_{min}(\Pi)$.*
2. $\Theta(\Sigma, s) = O(\Theta(\Pi', s) + |\Pi''| \log n)$, *if $s = d_{min}(\Pi) < d_{min}(\Sigma)$.*

Here $\Pi' \subseteq \Pi$ is the subspace of configurations of degree greater than s and $\Pi'' \subseteq \Pi$ is the subspace of configurations of degree equal to s. $|\Pi''|$ denotes the cardinality of Π''.

Let us see how the Index Theorem can be applied to the configuration space Σ of feasible trapezoids and racquets over a set of segments N (Example 2). Let $\Pi = \Pi(N)$ be the configuration space that consists of all endpoints of the segments in N and all intersections among the segments in N. If v is an endpoint of a segment $S \in N$, we let the trigger set$D(v) = \{S\}$. If v is the intersection of two segments $S, S' \in N$, then we let the trigger set $D(v) = \{S, S'\}$. The stopper set $L(v)$ is defined to be empty, for every v. It is easy to see that the index $\Sigma : \Pi$ is $O(1)$. This follows because the total number of racquets in the planar partition $H(R)$, $R \subseteq N$, is proportional to the size of R plus the total number of intersections among the segments in R. Let k denote the number of intersections among the segments in N. Since $d_{min}(\Sigma) = 1$, the Index Theorem implies that

$$\begin{aligned} \Theta(\Sigma, a) &= O(\Theta(\Pi, a)) = O(k+n), \text{ if } a < 1, \\ &= O(k + n \log n), \text{ if } a = 1. \end{aligned} \tag{6}$$

We also note the following immediate corollary of the Index Theorem.

Corollary 1 *If Π is trivial configuration space over a set N of objects, then $\Theta(\Pi, 0) = O(\log n)$.*

Let us now turn to the proof of the Index Theorem. We shall prove it using a probabilistic method. We must emphasize here that the randomness that is used in the proof has nothing to do with the randomness or pseudo-randomness used in the algorithm. Our proof depends on the following crucial probabilistic lemma.

Lemma 2 *Let Γ be a system of configurations over N. Let $m(\Gamma, r)$ denote the expected number of configuration in Γ that are active over a truly random subset of N of size r. If $0 \le s < d_{min}(\Gamma)$ ·*

$$\sum_{r=s+1}^{n} m(\Gamma, r) \frac{[n]_s}{[r]_{s+1}} \approx \Theta(\Gamma, s).$$

If $s = d_{min}(\Gamma)$

$$\sum_{r=s+1}^{n} m(\Gamma, r) \frac{[n]_s}{[r]_{s+1}} \approx \Theta(\Gamma', s) + |\Gamma''| \log n.$$

Here $\Gamma'' \subseteq \Gamma$ is the subspace of configurations of degree $d_{min}(\Gamma)$ and $|\Gamma''|$ denotes its cardinality. $\Gamma' \subseteq \Gamma$ is the subspace of configurations of degree greater than $d_{min}(\Gamma)$

Let us see how Lemma 2 can be used to prove the Index Theorem.

Because $\Sigma : \Pi$ is $O(1)$, it follows that $m(\Sigma, r) = O(m(\Pi, r))$, for any $r \le n$. Applying Lemma 2 to the system Σ and noting that $s < d_{min}(\Sigma)$, we get

$$\Theta(\Sigma, s) \approx \sum_{r=s+1}^{n} m(\Sigma, r) \frac{[n]_s}{[r]_{s+1}} = \sum_{r=s+1}^{n} O(m(\Pi, r)) \frac{[n]_s}{[r]_{s+1}}$$

If $s < d_{min}(\Pi)$, the right hand side is again seen to proportional to be $\Theta(\Pi, s)$, by applying Lemma 2 again.

If $s = d_{min}(\Pi)$, the right hand side is proportional to $O(\Theta(\Pi', s) + |\Pi''| \log n)$.

This proves the Index Theorem, assuming Lemma 2.

Proof of Lemma 2:

When $s = 0$, the result was known [12, 14] and can be proved easily by backward analysis [16]. We recall the proof for the sake of completeness. Let $\bar{u}$ be an imaginary truly random sequence of additions of the objects in N. By Main Theorem, $\Theta(\Gamma, 0)$ is essentially the expected structural change during $\bar{u}$. Hence it suffices to show that the expected number of configurations in Γ that are created during $\bar{u}$ is of the order of

$$\sum_{r=1}^{n} m(\Gamma, r)/r.$$

Fix $r \le n$. Also fix N^r, the set of first r added objects. Let $M(\Gamma, N^r)$ denote the set of configurations in Γ that are active at time r, i.e., they are active over the set N^r. The newly created configurations at time r are precisely the ones in $M(\Gamma, N^r)$ whose trigger set contains S_r, the object added at time r. Let $M(\Gamma, N^r; S_r)$ denote the set of these configurations. Because the sequence $\bar{u}$ is truly random, each object in N_r is equally likely to be S_r. Hence, conditional on a fixed N^r, the expected number of newly created configurations at time r is

$$\frac{1}{r} \sum_{S_r \in N_r} |M(\Gamma, N^r; S_r)| = \frac{1}{r} O(|M(\Gamma, N^r)|).$$

The last equality follows because the trigger set of each configuration is bounded. Because N^r is a random subset of N of size r, the expected value of $|M(\Gamma, N^r)|$ is $m(\Gamma, r)$. Hence, it follows that the expected number of newly created configurations at time r is $O(m(\Gamma, r)/r)$. This proves the lemma for $s = 0$.

The general proof follows a different method.

Let σ be any configuration over N. Let $\Theta(\sigma, s) = \frac{1}{l(\sigma)^{d(\sigma)-s}}$. $\Theta(\sigma, s)$ denotes Θ-series of the trivial configuration space containing only one configuration σ. let $p(\sigma, r)$ denote the probability that σ will be active over a (truly) random subset of N of size r. Let $[x]_s$ denote the generalized factorial $x(x-1)\dots(x-s+1)$.

Because

$$\Theta(\Gamma, s) = \sum_{\sigma \in \Gamma} \Theta(\sigma, s),$$

Lemma 2 follows from the following lemma.

Lemma 3

$$\begin{aligned} \sum_{r=s+1}^{n} p(\sigma, r) \frac{[n]_s}{[r]_{s+1}} &\approx \Theta(\sigma, s) \quad \textit{for } 0 \le s < d(\sigma) \\ &= O(\log n) \quad \textit{for } 0 \le s = d(\sigma). \end{aligned}$$

Here n is the number of elements in N and $\approx$ denotes equality with constant factors ignored.

Proof. The configuration σ is active over a set R of r elements iff $D(\sigma) \subseteq R$ and $L(\sigma) \cap R = \emptyset$. Letting $d = d(\sigma)$ and $l = L(\sigma)$, it follows that $p(\sigma, r) = \binom{n-l-d}{r-d} / \binom{n}{r}$. Hence, for $0 \leq s < d(\sigma)$,

$$\sum_{r=s+1}^{n} p(\sigma, r) \frac{[n]_s}{[r]_{s+1}} = \sum_{r=s+1}^{n} \frac{\binom{n-l-d}{r-d}}{\binom{n}{r}} \frac{[n]_s}{[r]_{s+1}}$$

$$= \frac{l!(d-s-1)!}{\binom{n-s}{l+d-s}(l+d-s)!} \sum_{r=s+1}^{n} \binom{n-r}{l} \binom{r-s-1}{d-s-1}$$

$$= \frac{l!(d-s-1)!}{(l+d-s)!\binom{n-s}{l+d-s}} \binom{n-s}{l+d-s},$$

using Van-der-Mond equality for binomial coefficients,

$$= \frac{l!(d-s-1)!}{(l+d-s)!} = \frac{1}{(t-s)\binom{l+d-s}{d-s}} \approx \Theta(\sigma, s).$$

When $s = d = d(\sigma)$, we have:

$$\sum_{r=d+1}^{n} p(\sigma, r) \frac{[n]_d}{[r]_{d+1}} = \sum_{r=d+1}^{n} \frac{1}{r-d} \cdot \frac{[n-l-d]_{r-d}}{[n-d]_{r-d}},$$

which is bounded by $\sum_{r=d+1}^{n} \frac{1}{r-d} = O(\log n)$.
□

7 Trapezoidal decompositions

Let N be a given set of segments in the plane. Let $H(N)$ denote the resulting *trapezoidal decomposition* as defined before. The trapezoidal decompositions are heavily investigated in computational geometry. They arise in several applications, notably in computer graphics.

In this section, we want to pseudo-randomize the randomized incremental algorithm in [9] using the scheme in Section 4. We show that its expected running time remains $O(k + n \log n)$, where k is the number of intersections among the segments in N. This is clearly optimal.

First we briefly recall the algorithm in [9]. The algorithm adds the segments in N, one at a time, in a random order. At the i-th stage it maintains the partition $H(N^i)$ formed by the set N^i of the first i added segments. We assume that $H(N^i)$ is represented as an obvious planar graph. [2] It also associates with each trapezoid in $H(N^i)$ a *conflict list* of the endpoints of the (unadded) segments in $N \setminus N^i$ that lie within that trapezoid. Conversely, with each endpoint of an unadded segment, there is an associated pointer to the trapezoid containing it.

Addition of a segment $S \in N \setminus N^i$ is done as follows. We locate an endpoint of S in $H(N^i)$ by using a conflict pointer associated with it. After this we travel along S in $H(N^i)$, from its one endpoint to the other, and update the the partition concurrently. This is done by contracting the vertical attachments intersected by S and adding new vertical attachments through the endpoints of S and the intersection points on S. The conflict information is also concurrently updated. See [9] for the details.

It is easy to see that the addition of S can be accomplished in time proportional to

$$\sum_{f} \text{facelength}(f) + \text{conflict-size}(f) \qquad (7)$$

where f ranges over all trapezoids in $H(N^i)$ intersecting S. Here facelength(f) denotes the total number of vertices of $H(N^i)$ lying on the border of f and conflict-size(f) denotes the size of the conflict list associated with f.

A pseudo-random version of the above algorithm is obtained by adding the segments in N, one at a time, in a pseudo-random order generated by the scheme in Section 4. We assume that t, the number of seeds, is large enough – $t = 20$ will do. The rest of the algorithm remains the same.

Let us turn to the analysis. When the sequence of additions is truly random, it was shown in [9] that the expected running time of the algorithm is $O(k+n \log n)$. This was done using certain probabilistic games. [4] analyses another randomized incremental algorithm using a different method. Later [16] gave a very simple backward analysis of the randomized incremental algorithm in [9]. Here we reanalyze the the above algorithm in such way that its analysis remains valid in the pseudo-random setting as well.

Let us ignore for a while the cost of updating the conflict information. Consider the cost of adding a segment S to N^i. Referring to eq.(7) notice that the face-length of f is essentially the number of racquets in $H(N^i)$ with face f (for the definition of racquet refer to Example 2 in Section 6 and fig. 1). All these racquets are destroyed at the end of the addition of S. Thus the cost of adding S is proportional to the number of racquets in $H(N^i)$ that are destroyed during the addition of S.

Thus the total cost of the algorithm, ignoring conflicts, is proportional to the total number racquets that are destroyed in the algorithm. This is bounded by the total number of racquets created in the whole algorithm, since a created racquet can be destroyed only once. The total number of created racquets is equal to $\beta(\Sigma)$, where Σ is the configuration space of feasible racquets (Example 2 in Section 6). By Main Theorem the expected

[2] [9] uses a different representation for the purpose of space efficiency. Our results hold for that representation too.

value of $\beta(\Sigma)$ is $O(\Theta(\Sigma, 0))$. We have already seen (eq. 6, Section 6) that $\Theta(\Sigma, 0)$ is $O(k+n)$, where k is the number of intersections among the segments in N. Thus the expected total cost of the algorithm, ignoring conflicts is $O(k+n)$.

Let us turn to the cost of updating conflicts. We can amortize this cost during the addition of S by charging $O(1)$ cost to each point that occurs in the conflict list of a destroyed trapezoid. Thus, for a fixed endpoint v of a segment in N, the total cost charged to v in the whole algorithm is proportional to the total number of trapezoids containing v that got destroyed in the course of the algorithm. Let Σ_v be the configuration space of feasible trapezoids over N containing v (Example 3 in Section 6). By the above observation, the total cost charged to v is $O(\beta(\Sigma_v))$. By Corollary 1, the expected value of this cost is $O(\log n)$.

This proves:

Theorem 3 *Let N be a set of segments in the plane. The expected running time of the pseudo-randomized incremental algorithm for constructing the resulting trapezoidal decomposition is $O(k + n \log n)$. Here k is the number of intersections among the segments in N.*

8 Convex polytopes

In this section we consider the construction of a convex polytope, i.e., its facial lattice. Let N be a set of half spaces in R^d. We assume that the half spaces are in general position. Let $H(N)$ be the convex polytope formed by intersecting these half spaces.

$H(N)$ can be built in a randomized incremental fashion [4] by adding the half spaces in N, one at a time, in a random order. Let N^i be the set of the first i added half spaces. Without loss of generality, we can assume that, for each i, $H(N^i)$ is bounded; otherwise we add right in the beginning the half spaces bounding a large cube approaching infinity.

At the i-stage, we maintain the polytope $H(N^i)$. We also maintain for each vertex $v \in H(N^i)$ the set of conflicting half spaces in $N \setminus N^i$. We say that a half space in $N \setminus N^i$ conflicts with v if its complement contains v. The number of such half spaces is called the conflict size of v, which will be denoted by conflict(v). Similarly, with each half space in $N \setminus N^i$ we maintain the list of all conflicting vertices in $H(N^i)$. (Actually it suffices to maintain a pointer to just one vertex conflicting with that half space.)

Addition of the $(i+1)$-st half space $S = S_{i+1}$ to $H(N^i)$ is achieved as follows. Let $\bar{S}$ denote the complement of S. The idea is to remove $\bar{S} \cap H(N^i)$ from $H(N^i)$. The conflict information tells us one vertex in $H(N^i) \cap \bar{S}$. (If there is no such vertex, S contains $H(N^i)$ and hence can be ignored.) After this $H(N^i)$, together with the associated conflict information, can be updated [4] in time proportional to the total structural and conflict change

$$\sum_v 1 + \text{conflict}(v). \qquad (8)$$

Here v ranges over all destroyed vertices in $H(N^i)$ and all newly created vertices in $H(N^{i+1})$.

In a pseudo-random version, we add the half spaces in the order generated by the scheme in Section 4, using $3d+2$ seeds.

In [4] it was shown that the expected running time of the genuinely randomized version is $O(n^{\lfloor d/2 \rfloor})$, for $d > 3$, and $O(n \log n)$, for $d = 3$.

Here we reanalyze the algorithm so that the analysis remains valid even in the pseudo-random setting. Our analysis here is influenced by [11].

Let $A(N)$ denote the arrangement formed by the hyperplanes bounding the half spaces in N. Let Σ denote the configuration space of the vertices in $A(N)$. For any vertex $v \in A(N)$, the trigger set is defined to be the half spaces in N whose bounding hyperplanes contain v. The stopper set is defined to be the half space in N whose complements contain v.

It follows from eq.(8) that the total running time of the algorithm is $O(\beta_1(\Sigma))$. By Main Theorem, the expected running time is $O(\Theta(\Sigma, 1))$. It was shown in [11] that $\Theta(\Sigma, 1) = O(n^{\lfloor d/2 \rfloor})$, for $d > 3$ and $O(n \log n)$, for $d = 2, 3$. This can also be seen from Lemma 2 as follows. By the well known upper bound theorem for convex polytopes, the number of faces of a convex polytope formed by intersecting r half spaces is $O(r^{\lfloor d/2 \rfloor})$. We apply Lemma 2 to the configuration space Σ. By the upper bound theorem, the quantity $m(\Sigma, r)$, as defined in the lemma, is $O(r^{\lfloor d/2 \rfloor})$. Hence, it follows that $\Theta(\Sigma, 1) = O(n^{\lfloor d/2 \rfloor})$, for $d > 3$ and $O(n \log n)$, for $d = 2, 3$.

Thus the expected running time of the pseudo-randomized algorithm is $O(\Theta(\Sigma, 1)) = O(n^{\lfloor d/2 \rfloor})$, for $d > 3$ and $O(n \log n)$, for $d = 2, 3$.

The above algorithm is not online because it makes use of the conflict information which depends on the unadded half spaces. However, it is possible to make the algorithm online by remembering the history of computation. The vertex of $H(N^i)$ in conflict with a newly added half space can then be determined by a conflict search through the history (for example, see [12] for the details). This does not increase the running time by more than a constant factor. Hence, the expected running time of the resulting online algorithm is also $O(\Theta(\Sigma, 1)) = O(n^{\lfloor d/2 \rfloor})$, for $d > 3$, and $O(n \log n)$, for $d = 3$.

Note that $\Theta(\Sigma, 0)$ is the lower bound on the expected running time of any online algorithm on a random sequence of additions (Main Theorem). Hence, it is an interesting open question if there is an online algorithm for convex polytopes whose expected running time is close to $O(\Theta(\Sigma, 0))$. [15] gives a related online algorithm for convex polytopes, which makes use linear programming to determine a conflicting vertex. This algorithm can also be pseudo-randmoized using the scheme in this paper. The expected running time of this algorithm can be shown to be $O(\Theta(\Sigma, 0) + n^2)$. It is illuminating to compare this with the $O(\Theta(\Sigma, 1))$ bound for th earlier algorithm: $\Theta(\Sigma, 0)$ can be much smaller than $\Theta(\Sigma, 1)$. On the other hand, the quadratic overhead in the second algorithm can be bad.

Acknowledgements: I shall like to thank Sundar Vishwanathan for several illuminating discussions.

References

[1] Boissonnat J., Teillaud M., On the randomized construction of the Delauney tree, Technical Report 1140, INRIA (France), 1989.

[2] Chazelle B., Edelsbrunner H., An optimal algorithm for intersecting line segments in the plane, *Proceedings of the FOCS, 88.*

[3] K. Clarkson, A Las Vegas algorithm for linear programming when the dimension is small, *FOCS 88.*

[4] K. Clarkson, P. Shor, Applications of random sampling in computational geometry, II, *Disc. and Comp. Geo. 4:387-421 (1989).*

[5] L. Guibas, D. Knuth, M. Sharir, Randomized incremental construction of Delauney and Voronoi diagrams, *Springer LNCS (1990), pp. 414-431.*

[6] H. Karloff, P. Raghavan, Randomized algorithms and pseudorandom numbers, *STOC 88.*

[7] N. Megiddo, Linear programming in linear time when the dimension is fixed, *J. ACM 34, 1981, 114-127.*

[8] K. Mehlhorn, S. Meiser, C. O'Dunlaing, On the construction of abstract Voronoi diagrams, *Disc. Comp. Geom., 6:211-224, 1991.*

[9] K. Mulmuley, A fast planar partition algorithm, I, *Proc. of the 29th FOCS, 1988, pp.580-589.*

[10] K. Mulmuley, "An efficient algorithm for hidden surface removal", *Proceedings of the ACM SIGGRAPH, Computer Graphics, Vol.23, Number 3, 1989.*

[11] K. Mulmuley, "On levels in arrangements and Voronoi diagrams", *Disc. and Comp. Geom., vol. 6, number 4, 1991.*

[12] K. Mulmuley, Randomized Multidimensional Search trees: lazy balancing and dynamic shuffling, *FOCS 1991.*

[13] J. Reif, S.Sen, Optimal parallel randomized algorithms for 3-D convex hulls and related problems, *manuscript, preliminary version appears as "Polling: a new randomized sampling technique for computational geometry", STOC 89.*

[14] Schwarzkopf O. Dynamic maintenance of geometric structures made easy, *FOCS, 1991.*

[15] Seidel R., Linear programming and convex hulls made easy, *Sixth Ann. ACM Symp. Computational Geometry, pages 211-215, 1990.*

[16] Seidel R., A simple and fast incremental randomized algorithm for computing trapezoidal decompositions and for triangulating polygons. *Technical Report B 90-07, Freie Universität Berlin, October 1990.*

Appendix

Here we sketch the proof of the main lemma. We begin with the following result which follows from the standard Chebychev's technique.

Lemma 4 *[13] Let $I = \sum_j I_j$ be the sum of $2k$-wise independent, identical Bernoulli random variables, each of which has a success probability $p > 0$. Let $\mu = E(I) = mp$. Then, for a fixed k,* $\text{Prob}\{|I - \mu| \geq \mu\} = O(\frac{1}{\mu^k})$.

Let us turn to the Main lemma. Let N be any set of objects. Let σ be a configuration over N. Let D and L denote the disjoint trigger and stopper sets of the configuration σ. Let $d = |D|$ and $l = |L|$. We assume that d is a constant.

Let $Z_i, \ldots, Z_d$ be the elements of D in any order. Let $X_0, X_1, \ldots, X_{n-1}$ be the t-wise independent sequence of random variables generated as in Section 3. Here each X_i is uniformly distributed over $< n >$.

Lemma 5 *Assume that the sequence of random variables $X_0, \ldots, X_n$ is t-wise independent, where $t \geq 3d + 2$. Then, for any $i_1, \ldots, i_d > 0$, and $i_1 + \cdots + i_d \leq i \leq n$, the probability that*

$$N[X_j] \notin L, \text{ for any } j \leq i,$$

conditional on

$$N[X_{i_1}] = Z_1, N[X_{i_1+i_2}] = Z_2, \ldots, N[X_{i_1+\cdots+i_d}] = Z_d,$$

is $O\left((\frac{n}{l(i-d)})^{\lfloor \frac{t-d}{2} \rfloor} \right)$.

Proof: For each $j \notin \{i_1, i_1 + i_2, \ldots, i_1 + \cdots + i_d\}$, let us define a conditional random variable Y_j as follows. Y_j is equal to X_j, conditional on

$$N[X_{i_1}] = Z_1, N[X_{i_1+i_2}] = Z_2, \ldots, N[X_{i_1+\cdots+i_d}] = Z_d.$$

By Proposition 1, the sequence of random variables Y_j is $(t-d)$-wise independent. Moreover, each Y_j is uniformly distributed on $< n >$.

For each $j \notin \{i_1, i_1 + i_2, \ldots, i_1 + \cdots + i_d\}$, let us define the indicator function I_j by

$$\begin{aligned} I_j &= 1 \quad \text{if } N(Y_j) \in L, \\ &= 0 \quad \text{otherwise.} \end{aligned}$$

It follows that the sequence of random variables I_j is also $(t-d)$-wise independent. Because Y_j is uniformly distributed on $< n >$, it follows that

$$p = \text{Prob}\{I_j = 1\} = \tfrac{l}{n}, \quad \text{for each } j.$$

Let $I = \sum_{j \leq i} I_j$, where $j \notin \{i_1, i_1+i_2, \ldots, i_1+\cdots+i_d\}$. It follows that the expected value of I is given by $\mu = (i-d)\frac{l}{n}$.

Observe that $N[X_j] \notin L$, for any j, iff I is zero, which trivially implies that $\mu - I \geq \mu$. Hence, the proof can be completed by applying Lemma 4. □

Corollary 2 *If $X_0, \ldots, X_n$ is a t-wise independent sequence, then for any subset $L \subseteq N$, with $l = |L| > 0$, the probability that*

$$N[X_j] \notin L, \text{ for any } j \leq n$$

is $O\left((\frac{1}{l})^{\lfloor \frac{t}{2} \rfloor}\right)$.

Proof: Put $i = n$ in for the Lemma 5, and let D be the empty set. □

Now fix L and D as before, where $d = |D|$ is assumed to be constant.

Corollary 3 *Under the same conditions as in Lemma 5, the probability that $N[X_j] \notin L$, for any $j \leq i$, and*

$$N[X_{i_1}] = Z_1, N[X_{i_1+i_2}] = Z_2, \ldots, N[X_{i_1+\cdots+i_d}] = Z_d$$

is

$$\begin{aligned} &= O(\tfrac{1}{n^d} \cdot (\tfrac{n}{l(i-d)})^{\lfloor \frac{t-d}{2} \rfloor}), && \text{if } i-d > \tfrac{n}{l} \\ &= O(\tfrac{1}{n^d}) && \text{if } i-d \leq n/l. \end{aligned}$$

Proof: The probability that

$$N[X_{i_1}] = Z_1, N[X_{i_1+i_2}] = Z_2, \ldots, N[X_{i_1+\cdots+i_d}] = Z_d \quad (9)$$

is $1/n^d$ since the random variables X_j are uniformly distributed and t-wise independent, where $t \geq 3d+2 > d$.

By Lemma 5, the probability that $N[X_j] \notin L$, for each $j \leq i$, under the condition in Eq. (9), is

$$\begin{aligned} &= O\left((\tfrac{n}{l(i-d)})^{\lfloor \frac{t-d}{2} \rfloor}\right), && \text{if } i-d > n/l \\ &\leq 1, && \text{otherwise (trivially).} \end{aligned}$$

Hence, the corollary follows. □

Now we turn to the proof of Main Lemma. Let σ be the configuration as in that lemma. Let D and L be its trigger and stopper sets, with $l = |L|$ and $d = |D|$. Let $\bar{\sigma}$ be a pseudo-random sequence of additions generated using the scheme in Section 4 with at least $3d+2$ seeds. We only need to estimate the probability that σ gets activated during the main phase of additions in $\bar{u}$. This is because σ can get active in the clean up phase only if no stopper in L is added during the main phase of additions. By Corollary 2, the probability of the latter event is $O(\frac{1}{l+d}^{3d+2}) = O(\frac{1}{l+d}^{d})$.

So we only need to worry about the main phase of additions. For $l = 0$, Main Lemma holds trivially since d is constant. For $l > 0$, Main Lemma follows from the following.

Lemma 6 *Assume that the sequence of random variables $X_0, \ldots, X_n$ is $(3d+2)$-wise independent. The probability that the first d elements chosen from $L \cup D$ all belong to D is $O(\frac{1}{l^d})$, for $l > 0$.*

Proof: Label the elements in D as $Z_1, \ldots, Z_d$ in any fashion. The number of different ways of labeling is clearly $d! = O(1)$, since d is a constant. We shall show that, for each fixed labelling, the probability that, for each $k \leq d$, the k-th element chosen from $L \cup D$ is Z_k, is $O(\frac{1}{l^d})$.

Fix the labelling $Z_1, \ldots, Z_d$ of the elements in D. For any $i_1, \ldots, i_d > 0$, and $i = i_1 + \cdots + i_d$, let $\text{pr}(i_1, \ldots, i_d)$ denote the probability that $N[X_j] \notin L$, for anyj $\leq i$, and

$$N[X_{i_1}] = Z_1, \ldots, N[X_{i_1+\cdots+i_d}] = N[X_i] = Z_d.$$

By Corollary 3,

$$\begin{aligned} \text{pr}(i_1, \ldots, i_d) &= O\left(\tfrac{1}{n^d}\left[\tfrac{n}{l(i-d)}\right]^{d+1}\right), && \text{if } i > n/l + d \\ &= O(\tfrac{1}{n^d}), && \text{if } i \leq n/l + d \end{aligned}$$

Thus the probability that the first d elements chosen from $L \cup D$ are $Z_1, \ldots, Z_d$ in that order is

$$\sum_{i_1, i_2, \ldots, i_d} \text{pr}(i_1, \ldots i_d)$$

which is bounded by (ignoring a constant factor)

$$\sum_{\substack{i_1, i_2, \ldots, i_d : \\ i_1 + \cdots + i_d \leq n/l+d}} \frac{1}{n^d} + \sum_{\substack{i_1, i_2, \ldots, i_d : \\ i_1 + \cdots + i_d \geq n/l+d}} \frac{n}{l^{d+1}(i_1 + \cdots + i_d - d)^{d+1}}$$

The first sum contains $\binom{n/l+d}{d}$ terms, and hence is bounded by

$$\binom{n/l+d}{d} \frac{1}{n^d} = O(\frac{1}{l^d})$$

The second term is also $O(1/l^d)$. This follows from the following lemma. In the lemma we let $j_k = i_k - 1 \geq 0$, for each $k \leq d$, $x = n/l + d$, and $y = 0$. □

Lemma 7 *For each $c > d$, and $x, y \geq 0$,*

$$\sum_{\substack{j_1, \ldots, j_d \geq 0 \\ j_1 + \cdots + j_d \geq x}} \frac{1}{(j_1 + \cdots + j_d + y)^c} = O(\frac{1}{(x+y)^{c-d}}).$$

Proof: Omitted. ▯

Drawing Planar Graphs Using the *lmc*-ordering

(Extended Abstract)*

Goos Kant
Utrecht University
the Netherlands
goos@cs.ruu.nl

Abstract

We introduce a new method to optimize the required area, minimum angle and number of bends of planar drawings of graphs on a grid. The main tool is a new type of ordering on the vertices and faces of triconnected planar graphs. With this method linear time and space algorithms can be designed for many graph drawing problems. We show that every triconnected planar graph G can be drawn convexly with straight lines on an $(2n-4)\times(n-2)$ *grid. If G has maximum degree four (three), then G can be drawn orthogonal with at most* $\lfloor\frac{3n}{2}\rfloor+3$ *(at most* $\lfloor\frac{n}{2}\rfloor+1$*) bends on an* $n\times n$ *grid (*$\lceil\frac{n}{2}\rceil\times\lceil\frac{n}{2}\rceil$ *grid, respectively). If G has maximum degree d, then G can be drawn planar on an* $(2n-6)\times(3n-6)$ *grid with minimum angle larger than* $\frac{1}{d-2}$ *radians and at most* $5n-15$ *bends. These results give in some cases considerable improvements over previous results, and give new bounds in other cases. Several other results, e.g. concerning visibility representations, are included.*

1 Introduction

The problem of "nicely" drawing a graph in the plane has received increasing attention due to the large number of applications [5, 25]. Examples include VLSI layout, algorithm animation, visual languages and CASE tools. Several criteria to obtain a high aesthetic quality have been established. Typically, vertices are represented by distinct points in a plane, and are sometimes restricted to be grid points. (Alternatively, vertices are sometimes represented by line segments [12, 19, 21].) Edges are often constrained to be drawn as straight lines [9, 7, 21, 22] or as a contiguous set of line segments [23, 24, 26, 27] (e.g., when bends are allowed). The objective is to find a layout for a graph that optimizes some cost function, such as area, minimum angle, number of bends, or satisfies some other constraint.

It is well-known ([7]) that every planar graph can be drawn planar with straight lines, and by recent algorithms ([4, 9, 10, 22]), this can be done in linear time and space on a grid of size $O(n)\times O(n)$ (m and n denote the number of edges and vertices of the graph, respectively.) Planar drawings require $\Omega(n^2)$ area in the worst-case [9]. However, a drawback of all these drawing algorithms is that the minimum angle between lines can be very small, which makes the drawing unattractive. In [18] it was shown that every d-planar graph G can be drawn planar such that the minimum angle is at least α^d radians, where $0<\alpha<1$ is a constant (a d-planar graph is a planar graph of degree at most d). However, the proof is non-constructive, and the minimum angle is still quite small. On the other hand, G can be drawn non-planar with straight lines such that the minimum angle is at least $\Omega(\frac{1}{d})$ [8].

In [29], Tutte showed that every triconnected planar graph can be drawn with straight lines such that every interior face is convex (a so-called *convex drawing*). This criterion is quite essential for the readability of this class of planar graphs, and has therefore gained a lot of interest [2, 28, 29, 30]. Thomassen [28] characterized the class of planar graphs with admit a convex drawing, and Chiba et al. [2] presented a linear drawing algorithm for it. However, the coordinates of the vertices can be reals.

A lot of work has been done for the case that all angles are multiples of $\pi/2$ [8, 23, 24, 26, 27]. These so-called *orthogonal drawings* have numerous important applications in the field of VLSI-design and graphics [23] (see also figures 4 and 5). Storer presented three heuristic algorithms for minimizing the bends of orthogonal drawings of 4-planar graphs [23]. Tamassia & Tollis presented linear implementations for this problem [26]. The results are that every biconnected 4-planar (3-planar) graph can be drawn orthogonal and planar on a grid of size at most

*This work was supported by the ESPRIT Basic Research Actions program of the EC under contract No. 4171 (project ALCOM II). Author's address: Dept. of Computer Science, Utrecht University, Padualaan 14, 3584 CH Utrecht, the Netherlands.

max. degree	tric.	grid	angle	bends
d (new)	no	$2n \times 3n$	$1/(d-2)$	$5n-15$
4	yes	$n \times n$	$\pi/2$	$\lfloor \frac{3n}{2} \rfloor + 3$
previous:	no	$n \times n$	$\pi/2$	$2n+4$
3	no	$\lceil \frac{n}{2} \rceil \times \lceil \frac{n}{2} \rceil$	$\pi/2$	$\lfloor \frac{n}{2} \rfloor + 1$
previous:	no	$n \times n$	$\pi/2$	$n+2$

Figure 1: Summary of results with bends.

be drawn orthogonal and planar on a grid of size at most $n \times n$ such that there are at most $2n+4$ (at most $n+2$) bends [23, 26]. (Biconnectivity (triconnectivity) means that deleting any vertex (two vertices) preserves the connectivity.) This bound is tight for biconnected 4-planar graphs [27]. Tamassia also presented an $O(n^2 \log n)$ exact algorithm to draw every *embedded* 4-planar graph on an $n \times n$ grid with a minimum number of bends [24]. An embedding means that the edges around each vertex are given in clockwise order with respect to a planar drawing.

In this paper we introduce a new ordering on the vertices and faces of a triconnected planar graph. We call this ordering the *leftmost canonical ordering*, or the lmc-ordering. It generalizes the orderings in [9, 14, 16]. Every lmc-ordering is also an st-ordering [5, 21, 26] and has direct consequences for the lmc-ordering of the dual graph. Using special techniques an lmc-ordering can be obtained in linear time and space. This leads to a general framework for drawing triconnected planar graphs G on a grid, and implies several further results.

The planar straight-line grid drawing algorithm of De Fraysseix, Pach & Pollack [9] can be implemented in linear time. (In [4] an alternative linear implementation is described, where the planar graph has to be triangulated.) For our algorithm, it is sufficient that the input graph is triconnected instead of triangulated. In particular we show that, using the lmc-ordering, all interior faces can be made convex. This result outperforms the algorithms of [2, 30] and is not only of theoretical interest, but also leads to more pleasing pictures (see figure 3). This also gives a new and rather simple proof that every triconnected planar graph admits a convex planar drawing.

If G is triconnected and 4-planar, then G can be drawn orthogonal with at most $\lfloor \frac{3}{2}n \rfloor + 3$ bends on an $n \times n$ grid (see figure 4). This improves the best known bound of $2n+4$ considerably in the triconnected case. For any 3-planar graph G we show that G can be drawn orthogonal with at most $\lfloor \frac{n}{2} \rfloor + 1$ bends on an $\lceil \frac{n}{2} \rceil \times \lceil \frac{n}{2} \rceil$ grid (see figure 5). A nice characteristic is that G has a spanning tree of straight-line edges, and all non-tree edges have at most 1 bend. These bounds improve all previous bounds and match the lower bounds [23, 26].

We also show that every triconnected d-planar graph G can be drawn planar with at most $5n-15$ bends on an $(2n-6) \times (3n-6)$ grid with minimum angle $> \frac{1}{d-2}$ radians, with vertices and bends placed on grid points. Every edge has at most 3 bends and length $O(n)$. This seems to be the first practical drawing algorithm, having good bounds on the grid size, number of bends, and on the minimum angle for general planar graphs. On the negative side, we prove the following theorem:

Theorem 1.1 *Deciding whether a biconnected planar graph can be drawn planar with with straight lines with minimum angle $\geq K$ is NP-hard.*

For clarity, figure 1 summarizes all results.

We can also use the lmc-ordering to construct a *visibility representation* of a d-planar graph G on a grid of size at most $(2n-4) \times n$, which drawings seems to be more compact than the existing algorithms [12, 19, 21] (see figure 7). All algorithms mentioned above can be implemented to run in linear time and space.

The paper is organized as follows: in section 2 we introduce the lmc-ordering, the general framework and some definitions. In section 3 we show how to draw a triconnected planar graph convex on a grid. In section 4 we inspect the orthogonal drawings of triconnected 4-planar graphs. In section 5 we present the results of orthogonal drawings of 3-planar graphs. In section 6 we present extensions, combinatorial aspects and optimizations. Section 7 contains some final remarks and open questions. Omitted proofs can be found in the full paper.

2 The general framework

In this section we introduce the *leftmost canonical* ($lmc-$) *ordering* for triconnected planar graphs, which will be used in various ways to get better planar drawing algorithms. Let an *embedding* of a triconnected planar graph G be given. (Such an embedding is unique for triconnected planar graphs, and can be constructed in linear time [1].) We first introduce the canonical ordering for G. This ordering generalizes the orderings, described in [9, 14, 16]. Let G_k be the induced subgraph on the vertices $v_1, \ldots, v_k$.

Theorem 2.1 *The vertices of a triconnected planar graph G can be ordered in a sequence $v_1, \ldots, v_n$ such that v_2 and v_n are neighbors of v_1 and share a common face, and for every k, $k > 3$:*

1. *either v_k is in the exterior face of G_k and has at least two neighbors in G_{k-1}, which are on the outerface of G_{k-1}. v_k has at least one neighbor in $G - G_k$. The subgraph G_k of G is biconnected,*

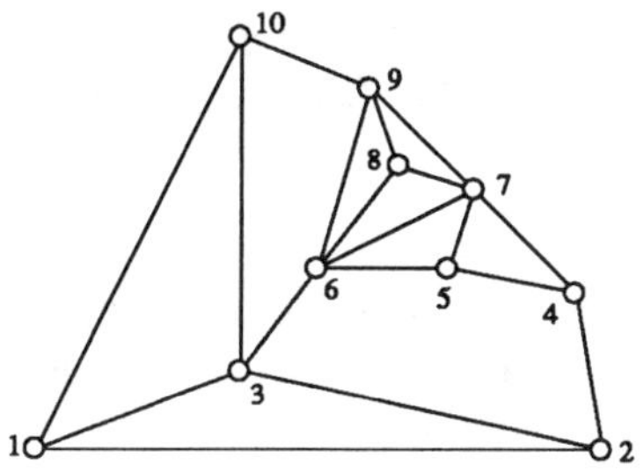

Figure 2: The *lmc*-ordering.

2. *or there exists an $l \geq 1$ such that $v_k, \ldots, v_{k+l}$ is a chain in the exterior face of G_{k+l} and has exactly two neighbors in G_{k-1}, which are on the outerface of G_{k-1}. The subgraph G_{k+l} of G is biconnected, and the vertices $v_k, \ldots, v_{k+l}$ have degree 2 in G_{k+l}.*

This means that starting with an edge (v_1, v_2) one can add in every step either a vertex v_k or a face (which is implied by the chain $v_k, \ldots, v_{k+l}$ and the involved vertices of G_{k-1}). We call this added face F_k.

Theorem 2.2 *The canonical ordering can be computed in linear time and space.*

Proof: (Sketch) Let an embedding of the triconnected planar graph G be given. We store for each vertex and face an edge-list, which is a circular list of edges in clockwise order of visiting them around each vertex or face. We store for each vertex and face a variable *interval*, denoting the number of intervals of visited edges in the edge-list of this vertex or face (see also section 4 of [9] for this idea). Starting with v_n, we compute the canonical ordering in reverse order. A face F or a vertex v (having no more than 2 neighbors on the outerface) with *interval*-value 1 can be the next one in the ordering. We delete the corresponding vertex (or vertices). We visit their neighbors and the edges, which become part of the outerface now. Every edge will be visited twice, and updating the variables can be done in constant time. □

Let there be K steps total, in which we add either a vertex v_k or a face F_k, implied by the added vertices $w_1, \ldots, w_p$. In step 1 and 2 we add vertex v_1 and v_2 and in step K vertex v_n is added. The added vertices of step k are called *new*, and all vertices $\in G_{k-1}$ are called *old*. Let $C_{k-1} : v_1 = c_1, c_2, c_3, \ldots, c_r = v_2$ be the outerface of G_{k-1}, and assume w.l.o.g. that v_1 is drawn leftmost and v_2 is drawn rightmost. When adding a face F_k or vertex v_k, let c_i and c_j be two adjacent vertices of v_k (F_k) on G_{k-1}, with i and j as small and as big as possible, respectively. We call c_i the *leftpoint* and c_j the *rightpoint* of v_k or F_k. The other adjacent vertices c_l ($i < l < j$) of v_k on C_{k-1} are called *internal* vertices. All these edges to v_k are called *incoming* edges of v_k, the other edges of v_k are called the *outgoing* edges of v_k. Every vertex has at most one internal outgoing edge.

The general idea now is to place the vertices in such a way on the grid that for a vertex v_k, the direction for the incoming edges of v_k is horizontal or downwards. To maintain this, we have to know the coordinates of the old neighbors, when adding v_k or F_k. Moreover, $x(c_1) \leq x(c_2) \leq \cdots \leq x(c_r)$ must hold in every step, hence when adding v_k (F_k), maybe $c_j, \ldots, c_r$ must be "shifted to the right" to maintain this invariant. Of course, also some vertices, not on the outerface, must be shifted to the right, but updating all these distances in every step will take too much time. Hereto we use *lazy evaluation*: we compute the exact coordinates of a vertex only when we need them. This means that only the exact coordinates of the vertices on the outerface are essential during the insertions. As a first step, we refine the canonical ordering to the *leftmost* canonical ordering, which we will call the *lmc*-ordering from now on:

Definition 2.1 *A canonical ordering is a leftmost canonical ordering if at any step k, if v_i (or face F_i) has rightpoint c_α and v_j (or face F_j) has leftpoint c_β ($c_\alpha, c_\beta \in C_k$), with $\beta \geq \alpha$, then $k \leq i < j$ (or if $v_i, \ldots, v_{i+a}$ and $v_j, \ldots v_{j+b}$ are the new vertices of F_i and F_j, resp., then $k < i + a < j$).*

This means that at any step k during the canonical ordering, when we can add both v_i (or F_i) and v_j (or F_j), then we take this vertex or face, for which the rightpoint c_l is minimal with respect to l.

Theorem 2.3 *The lmc-ordering can be computed in linear time.*

In figure 2 an example of the *lmc*-ordering is given, which will serve as an example for all drawing algorithms in this paper.

In the drawing algorithms, we distinguish the insertcoordinates of v_k (when we insert v_k by the *lmc*-ordering), and the endcoordinates of v_k (in the complete drawing). We introduce a boolean variable *correct*(v), denoting whether $x(v)$, with $v \in C_k$, is recalculated. *shift*(c_j) denotes the value, which must be added to all $x(c_k)$, $j \leq k \leq r$. When we insert v, we set *correct*(v) to *false* and *shift*(v) to zero. When adding a vertex v or face F, we walk on the outerface towards c_1 until we find the first *true* marked *correct*(c_α). Let c_j be the rightpoint of v or F. We walk from c_α to c_j. When visiting

c_β ($\alpha < \beta < j$), we add $\sum_{\alpha<k\leq\beta}$ *shift*(c_k) to $x(c_k)$ and set *correct*(c_β) to *true*, since $x(c_\beta)$ is recalculated. We add $\sum_{\alpha<k<j}$ *shift*(c_k) to *shift*(c_j), and set *correct*(c_j) to *false*. This approach is correct due to the following two lemma's:

Lemma 2.4 *For all vertices c_β with $\alpha < \beta \leq r$, correct(c_β) is false. $\alpha < j \leq r$ holds for rightpoint c_j.*

Lemma 2.5 *The total time for visiting the false marked vertices and updating shift(v), $x(v)$ and correct(v) for all vertices is $O(n)$.*

These two lemmas show that one can compute the *new* coordinates of the vertices on the outerface correctly, when we insert a vertex v_k or face F_k. Let $P(v) = (x_{\text{insert}}(v), y_{\text{insert}}(v))$ be the coordinates of v at the time of insertion of v. Computing the final coordinates can be done as follows: we visit all vertices and faces in *reverse lmc*-order, and set initially *shift*(v) = 0, for every vertex v. When visiting vertex v then (depending on the algorithms in the next sections) we add *shift*(v) to the shift of all its internal vertices and add at least *shift*(v) to its rightpoint. Then we add *shift*(v) to $x_{\text{insert}}(v)$, leading to the final coordinates of v. All this work can be done in linear time totally. We call this method the *shift-method*. It is the general framework for several planar graph drawing algorithms, described in the next sections. (This idea of shifting vertices is widely used, e.g. in the algorithm of [4].)

3 Convex drawings

The *lmc*-ordering is a generalization of the canonical ordering of De Fraysseix et al. [9]. We can apply the *lmc*-ordering and the shift-method to get a linear implementation of the straight-line drawing algorithm of triangulated planar graphs on a grid [9]. Moreover, we will show that we can modify this algorithm such that we can draw every triconnected planar graph with convex faces on a grid. (In [4] another linear implementation of [9] is described, in which the input graph has to be triangulated.)

The algorithm maintains a straight-line embedding during every step k of the *lmc*-ordering such that

1. v_1 is at $(0, 0)$, v_2 is at $(2k - 4, 0)$.
2. If $v_1 = c_1, c_2, \ldots, c_r = v_2$ is the outerface of G_k in step k, then $x(c_1) < x(c_2) < \cdots < x(c_r)$.
3. The edges (c_i, c_{i+1}) have slope $+1$ or -1.

Assume first that G is triangulated, in which case we can add a vertex v_k in every step k of the *lmc*-ordering [9]. Every planar graph can be triangulated in linear time and space [16]. Let $L(v)$ be a set of vertices. The idea of the algorithm is the following: when we add vertex v_k, then all vertices $c_{i+1}, \ldots, c_{j-1}$ are shifted 1 to the right, and the vertices $c_j, \ldots, c_r$ are shifted 2 to the right (and of course, several internal vertices of G_{k-1} must be shifted 1 or 2 to the right as well). The crossing point of the line with slope $+1$ from c_i and the line with slope -1 from c_j denotes the place for vertex v_k. All vertices $c_i, \ldots, c_j$ are visible from this point. The exact algorithm is as follows:

{ In each step k, let $c_1, \ldots, c_r$ be the outerface
  and c_i and c_j the left- and rightpoint of v_k, resp.}
$\mu((x_1, y_1), (x_2, y_2)) :=$
    $\frac{1}{2}(x_1 - y_1 + x_2 + y_2, -x_1 + y_1 + x_2 + y_2)$;
$P(v_1) := (0, 0); L(v_1) := \{v_1\}$;
$P(v_2) := (2, 0); L(v_2) := \{v_2\}$;
$P(v_3) := (1, 1); L(v_3) := \{v_3\}$;
for $k := 4$ **to** n **do**
    for $v \in \bigcup_{l=j}^{r} L(c_l)$ **do** $x(v) := x(v) + 2$;
    for $v \in \bigcup_{l=i+1}^{j-1} L(c_l)$ **do** $x(v) := x(v) + 1$;
    $P(v_k) := \mu((x(c_i), y(c_i)), (x(c_j), y(c_j)))$;
    $L(v_k) := \{v_k\} \cup \bigcup_{l=i+1}^{j-1} L(c_l)$;
rof

The correctness of this algorithm is described in [9]. There are shifts of 1 and 2 in the algorithm, and therefore we introduce 2 shift-variables. The complete algorithm can now be implemented to run in linear time as follows:

$P(v_1) := P(v_2) := (0, 0)$;
for $k := 3$ **to** n **do**
    update $x(c_i)$ and *shift*(c_j); *shift*(c_j) := *shift*(c_j) + 2;
    $P(v_k) := \mu((x(c_i), y(c_i)), (x(c_j) + \textit{shift}(c_j), y(c_j)))$;
rof;
shift(v) := *rshift*(v) := 0 for all $v \in V$;
for $k := n$ **downto** 2 **do**
    for all internal vertices v_i of v_k **do**
        shift(v_i) := *shift*(v_k) + *rshift*(v_k) + 1;
    rshift(c_j) := *rshift*(c_j) + *rshift*(v_i) + 2;
    $x(v_k) := x_{\text{insert}}(v_k)$ + *shift*(v_k) + *rshift*(v_k);
rof

Moreover, using the *lmc*-ordering, it is already sufficient that the planar graph is triconnected, because when we add a face F_k with vertices $w_1, \ldots, w_p$, we can draw $w_1, \ldots, w_p$ on a horizontal line with distance 2 inbetween. The edge (c_i, w_1) has slope $+1$, the edges $(w_1, w_2), \ldots, (w_{p-1}, w_p)$ have slope 0, and the edge (w_p, c_j) has slope -1. All edges on C_{k-1} get now slope $+1, 0$ or -1 in every step k. It is easy to see that this still gives a correct straight-line drawing on an

$(2n-4) \times (n-2)$ grid. We will now modify this algorithm a little, such that all interior faces are convex.

Assume we add a vertex v_k, and let c_p and c_q two adjacent vertices on C_{k-1}, such that there is no neighbor c_l of v_k, with $p < l < q$. Let F' be the face, containing c_p, c_q and v_k.

Lemma 3.1 *All edges* (c_a, c_{a+1}), $p \leq a < \alpha$, *have slope* -1; *all edges* (c_{b-1}, c_b), $\alpha \leq \beta < b \leq q$, *have slope* $+1$. $\beta = \alpha$ *or* $\alpha + 1$, *and if* $\beta = \alpha + 1$, *then* (c_α, c_β) *has slope 0.*

To achieve a convex face F', we add edges from c_q to $c_\beta, c_{\beta+1}, \dots, c_{q-1}$. This does not destroy the planarity in the embedding, and it means in the algorithm of [9] that if we shift c_q, then we also shift $c_{\beta+1}, \dots, c_{q-1}$ to the right when adding vertex v_k. Notice that when c_q is the rightpoint or c_p is the leftpoint of v_k, then c_q is shifted 1 more to the right than c_p. But then $c_{\beta+1}, \dots, c_q$ are shifted one more to the right than $c_p, \dots, c_\beta$. (If $\beta = q$, then no internal vertex is shifted to the right.) We now have the following slopes after adding v_k, and applying the shifts.

- The slopes of (c_p, v_k) and (c_q, v_k) are in the range $(-\infty, -1] \cup [+1, \infty)$.
- The edges $(c_p, c_{p+1}), \dots, (c_{\alpha-1}, c_\alpha)$ have slope -1.
- The edge (c_α, c_β) (if $\beta > \alpha$) has slope 0,
- The edges $(c_{\beta+1}, c_{\beta+2}), \dots, (c_{q-1}, c_q)$ have slope $+1$.
- If $\beta < q$ then the slope of edge $(c_\beta, c_{\beta+1})$ is in the range $(0, +1]$, else the slope of the edge $(c_{\beta-1}, c_\beta)$ is in the range $(-1, 0]$.

This implies that the face F' is convex when inserting v_k in step k. The same values follow when we add a complete chain $w_1, \dots, w_p$ instead of one vertex v_k, because in this case $w_1, \dots, w_p$ are placed on a horizontal line.

Lemma 3.2 *The faces remain convex during the algorithm.*

Theorem 3.3 *There is a linear algorithm to draw a triconnected planar graph convex with straight lines on a grid of size at most* $(2n-4) \times (n-2)$.

Our algorithm not only outperforms the algorithms of [30, 2], it is also much easier to implement than the algorithm of [2]. Since the vertices are placed on grid points, the resulting drawings seem to be more pleasant than in [2]. This is also the first proof that every triconnected planar graph can be drawn convex on a small grid. It is also a new proof that every triconnected planar graph admits a planar drawing, in which every interior face is

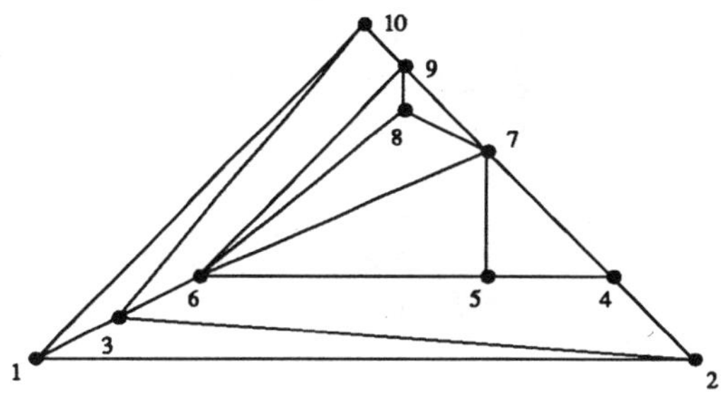

Figure 3: Convex drawing of the graph of figure 2.

convex. The outerface is a triangle. With respect to the tightness of the grid size we note that every strictly convex drawing of a cycle with n vertices requires an $\Theta(n^3)$ grid [17]. In figure 3, the straight-line convex drawing of the graph in figure 2 is given.

4 Orthogonal drawings of 4-planar graphs

In this section we consider the problem of drawing a triconnected 4-planar graph G on a rectilinear grid with orthogonal lines, i.e., the edges are polygonal chains of horizontal and vertical segments. Using a variant of theorem 2 of [27], we can obtain the following lowerbound of about $\frac{4}{3}n$ bends:

Theorem 4.1 *There are triconnected 4-planar graphs* G_n *with* $3n+1$ *vertices and* $6n+1$ *edges, for which any orthogonal drawing requires at least* $4n+2$ *bends.*

Let an *lmc*-ordering of G be given. $deg(v) \leq 4$, thus every vertex v has at most 2 outgoing edges. If vertex v_k is the rightpoint of 2 vertices, or if v_k is the rightpoint of a vertex and has an internal outgoing edge, then we set *mark*(v_k) = *left*, otherwise we set *mark*(v_k) = *right*. These marks will be important when we add v_k to G_{k-1}. There are 4 directions to connect an edge at v_k, viz., *left*, *right*, *up* and *down* of v_k, denoted by $l(v_k), r(v_k), u(v_k)$ and $d(v_k)$, respectively. A direction is called *free* if there is no edge connected in that direction of v_k yet. Let c_i and c_j be the left- and rightpoint of v_k. We connect (c_i, v_k) at $r(c_i)$, if $r(c_i)$ is free, otherwise at $u(c_i)$, if $u(c_i)$ is free, otherwise at $l(c_i)$. The opposite direction is followed for c_j. We want to add v_k such that when *mark*(v_k) = *left*, $l(v_k)$ and $u(v_k)$ are both free after addition, since this implies only a few bends. When *mark*(v_k) = *right*, then want to have $u(v_k)$ and $r(v_k)$ both free after addition of v_k. In all cases, after adding v_k to G_{k-1}, $d(v_k)$ is not free anymore. The algorithm, which tries to achieve this as much as possible, can be described as follows:

edge (v_1, v_2) via $d(v_1)$ and $d(v_2)$;
for $k := 2$ **to** $K-1$ **do**
  if we add v_k with $inc(v_k) = \{c_i, c_l, c_j\}$ **then**
    $(c_i, v_k), (c_l, v_k), (c_j, v_k)$ via $l(v_k), d(v_k), r(v_k)$;
  if we add v_k with $inc(v_k) = \{c_i, c_j\}$ **then**
    if *mark*(v_k) = *left* or
        ($l(c_j)$ free **and** $r(c_i)$ not free) **then**
      (v_k, c_i) and (v_k, c_j) via $d(v_k)$ and $r(v_k)$
    else via $l(v_k)$ and $d(v_k)$;
  if we add F_k with $w_1, \ldots, w_p$ from c_i to c_j **then**
    if $r(c_i)$ is free **then**
      (w_1, c_i) via $l(w_1)$ **else** via $d(w_1)$;
    for $l := 2$ **to** p **do**
      if $d(w_{l-1})$ is free **then**
        (w_{l-1}, w_l) via $d(w_{l-1})$ **else** via $r(w_{l-1})$;
      if *mark*(w_l) is *left* **then**
        (w_{l-1}, w_l) via $d(w_l)$ **else** via $l(w_l)$;
    if $l(c_j)$ is free **then**
      (w_{p-1}, w_p) and (w_p, c_j) via $d(w_p)$ and $r(w_p)$
    else via $l(w_p)$ and $d(w_p)$
rof;
edges from $c_i, c_\alpha, c_\beta, c_j$ to v_n via
    $u(v_n), l(v_n), d(v_n)$ and $r(v_n)$;

From these connections we have to come to a correct planar drawing, such that if (v_i, v_j) goes via $r(v_i)$ and $l(v_j)$, then (v_i, v_j) is a straight line, i.e., $x(v_j) > x(v_i)$ and $y(v_j) = y(v_i)$. When (v_i, v_j) goes via $u(v_i)$ and $l(v_j)$, then one bend b must be introduced at place $P(b) = (x(v_i), y(v_j))$ and $x(b) < x(v_j)$ and $y(b) > y(v_i)$ must hold. (Similar when (v_i, v_j) goes via $u(v_i)$ and $r(v_j)$.) Finally, when (v_i, v_j) goes via $d(v_i)$ and $d(v_j)$, then 2 bends b_1 and b_2 are introduced. (Similar when (v_i, v_j) goes via $r(v_i)$ and $r(v_j)$ or via $l(v_i)$ and $l(v_j)$.)

To calculate the coordinates of the vertices and the bends we use instead of the *shift*-method (which may also lead to a linear implementation) a new approach: We define 2 directed graphs X and Y. Every time we add a vertex v_k or face F_k, we add all new vertices and new bends as a node to both X and Y. A directed edge (v_i, v_j) in X (Y) means that $x(v_i) < x(v_j)$ ($y(v_i) < y(v_j)$) must hold. If (v_i, v_j) and (v_j, v_i) are both present in X (Y), then $x(v_i) = x(v_j)$ ($y(v_i) = y(v_j)$) must hold. Some extra edges in X and Y are introduced to ensure that the edges in G with two bends will not cross other edges. X and Y are constructed during the *lmc*-ordering, and have $O(n)$ edges. Afterwards we construct from X and Y two new directed acyclic graphs X' and Y'. Every node V' in X' (Y') corresponds with a set of nodes $\{v_a, \ldots, v_b\}$ of X (Y), which must have the same x-coordinate (y-coordinate). We now compute a topological ordering for the vertices of both X' and Y'. Let V_i' and V_j'' denote the topological ordering of the vertices of X' and Y', then vertex $v_a \in V_i'$ and $v_a \in V_j''$ has coordinates $P(v_a) = (i, j)$.

Lemma 4.2 *The topological ordering of X' and Y' corresponds with a planar orthogonal drawing of G.*

Lemma 4.3 *The number of bends is at most $\lfloor \frac{3}{2}n \rfloor + 3$.*

Proof: (Sketch) When we insert vertex v_i with *mark*(v_i) = *right* (*left*) and after the insertion, $r(v)$ ($l(v)$) is not free, then we assign the cost of the extra required bend to the insertion step of v_i. Doing this leads to the following number of bends in step $3, 4, \ldots, K-1$ (starting with (v_1, v_2) implies 4 bends, and adding v_n implies 4 bends):

step	# vertices	# edges	# bends
v_k, $inc(v_k) = 2$	1	2	1
v_k, $inc(v_k) = 3$	1	3	2
face F_k	p	$p+1$	p

Notice that every vertex v has $deg(v) \leq 4$, hence adding a vertex v_k with $inc(v_k) = 3$ occurs at most $\lceil \frac{1}{2}n \rceil - 2$ times, leading to a total of $n + \lfloor \frac{m-n}{2} \rfloor + 3 \leq \lfloor \frac{3}{2}n \rfloor + 3$ bends. □

Theorem 4.4 *There is a linear time and space algorithm to draw every triconnected 4-planar graph G orthogonal on an $n \times n$ grid with at most $\lfloor \frac{3}{2}n \rfloor + 3$ bends. Every edge has at most 3 bends and length $O(n)$.*

In figure 4 an example is given of the graph G of figure 2, minus the edge (6,7).

5 Orthogonal drawings of 3-planar graphs

In this section we inspect the problem of drawing a 3-planar graph on a grid. In [23], Storer inspected the problem of embedding a 3-planar graph in the rectilinear grid, and obtained the following negative result:

Theorem 5.1 *There are 3-planar graphs that require at least an $\frac{n}{2} \times \frac{n}{2}$ grid; there are 3-planar graphs that require at least $\frac{n}{2} + 1$ bends, in any orthogonal drawing.*

On the positive side he presented several polynomial-time heuristics to draw a 3-planar graph with at most n bends. In [26], Tamassia & Tollis presented a linear algorithm to draw every 3-planar graph with at most $n+2$ bends on an $n \times n$ grid. In this section we present a linear time and space algorithm to draw every 3-planar graph with at most $\lfloor \frac{n}{2} \rfloor + 1$ bends on a $\lceil \frac{n}{2} \rceil \times \lceil \frac{n}{2} \rceil$ grid. This improves all previous bounds and matches the worst-case

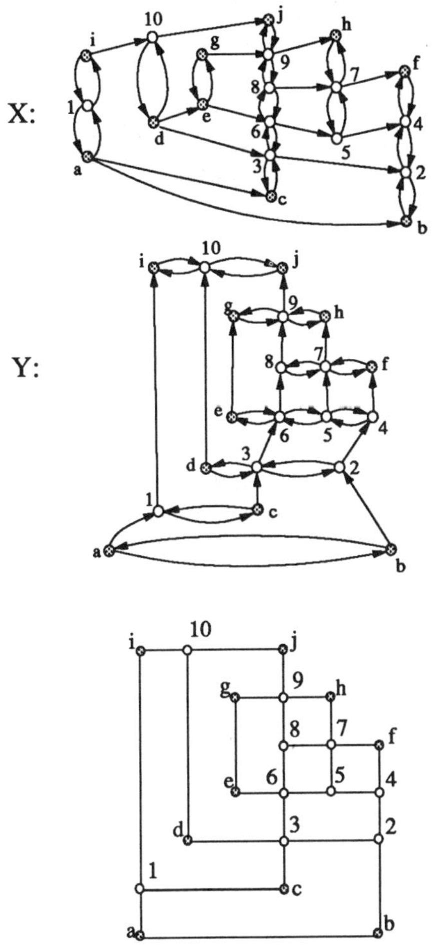

Figure 4: Orthogonal drawing of a 4-planar graph.

lower bounds and, hence, is best possible. An interesting side-effect is that there is a spanning tree of only $n-1$ straight-line edges, and all $m-n+1$ non-tree edges have at most one bend.

Assume first that G is triconnected. By Euler's formulae, n is even, $m = \frac{3}{2}n$ and $f = \frac{n}{2}+2$. Let an lmc-ordering of G be given. Similar as in section 4 there are four directions to connect an edge at v, viz., *left*, *right*, *up* and *down* of v, denoted by $l(v), r(v), u(v)$ and $d(v)$, respectively. Every vertex v (except v_1, v_2 and v_n) has one outgoing edge, and we connect this edge via $u(v)$ at v. We start with placing v_1 and v_2 at $(0,1)$ and $(1,1)$. edge (v_1, v_2) goes via $d(v_1)$ and $d(v_2)$, hence via $(0,0)$ and $(1,0)$. We place the first face on the horizontal line between v_1 and v_2, via $r(v_1)$ and $l(v_2)$. When we add a face F_k with vertices $w_1, \ldots, w_p$ from leftpoint c_i to rightpoint c_j, then we place these vertices on the horizontal line on height $1 + \max\{y(c_i), y(c_j)\}$, with $x(w_1) = x(c_i)$, and if $p > 1$, we shift c_j such that $x(w_p) = x(c_j) + shift(c_j)$. The connections inbetween go via $d(w_1), r(w_1), l(w_2), r(w_2), \ldots, l(w_p), d(w_p)$. The complete (and simple) algorithm can now be described as follows:

$P(v_1) := (0,1); P(v_2) := (1,1);$
for $k := 3$ **to** $K-1$ **do**
  assume we add F_k with $w_1, \ldots, w_p$ from c_i to c_j;
  $y(w_1) := \cdots := y(w_p) := 1 + \max\{y(c_i), y(c_j)\};$
  update $x(c_i)$ and $shift(c_j)$; $x(w_1) := x(c_i)$;
  if $p > 1$ **then**
    $x(w_p) := \max\{x(w_1) + p - 1, x(c_j) + shift(c_j)\};$
  for $l := 2$ **to** $p-1$ **do** $x(w_l) := x(w_1) + l - 1;$
  $shift(c_j) := \max\{shift(c_j), p - 1 + x(c_i) - x(c_j)\}$
rof;
let $inc(v_n) = \{c_i, c_l, c_j\}$;
$P(v_n) := (x(c_l), 1 + \max\{y(c_i), y(c_l), y(c_j)\});$
for $k := K$ **downto** 2 **do**
  assume we added $w_1, \ldots, w_p$ from c_i to c_j;
  if $p = 1$ **then** $shift(c_j) := shift(w_1)$ **else**
    $shift(c_j) := x_{\text{insert}}(w_p) + shift(w_p) - x_{\text{insert}}(c_j);$
  $x(w_i) := x_{\text{insert}}(w_i) + shift(w_i); (1 \leq i \leq p)$
rof

Lemma 5.2 *The number of bends is at most* $\frac{n}{2}+2$.

Proof: Since $m = \frac{3}{2}n$, we add at most $\frac{n}{2} - 2$ times a vertex v with $inc(v) = 2$, each one introduces 1 bend. The edge (v_1, v_2) introduces 2 bends, as well as adding v_n. □

Lemma 5.3 *The gridsize is at most* $\frac{n}{2} \times \frac{n}{2}$.

In figure 5, an example is given of a triconnected 3-planar graph from [14].

Using the technique of applying the *2-subgraph tree*, described in [14], we can generalize this result to arbitrary 3-planar graphs. Moreover, using the special variant of the lmc-ordering, described in theorem 4.1 of [14], the following theorem can be proved.

Theorem 5.4 *There is a linear time and space algorithm to draw a 3-planar graph orthogonal on an* $\lceil \frac{n}{2} \rceil \times \lceil \frac{n}{2} \rceil$ *grid with at most* $\lfloor \frac{n}{2} \rfloor + 1$ *bends. In this orthogonal drawing, there is a spanning tree of* $n-1$ *straight-line edges, all* $m-n+1$ *non-tree edges have at most 1 bend* ($n > 4$).

6 Extensions, duality aspects and optimizations

Instead of drawing triconnected d-planar graphs G with straight lines, as described in section 3, we can draw them

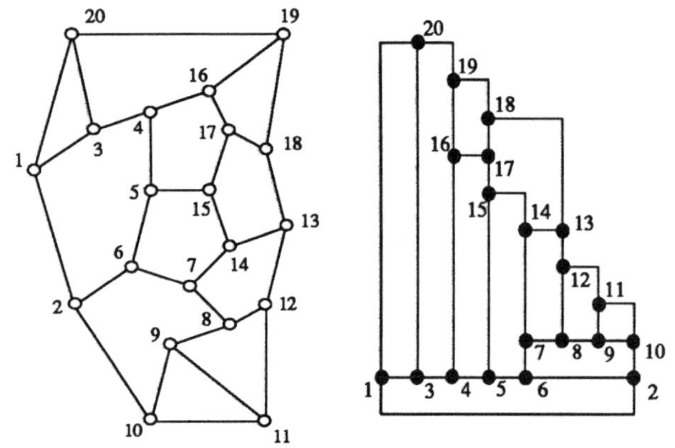

Figure 5: Orthogonal drawing of a 3-planar graph.

with bends, while increasing the minimum angle. The idea for drawing G is as follows: let an *lmc*-ordering be given. Let $out(v) = deg(v) - inc(v) = p$ be the number of outgoing edges of v, then we place these edges through the points $(x(v) - \lfloor \frac{p-1}{2} \rfloor + i - 1, y(v) + \lceil \frac{p-1}{2} \rceil), 1 \leq i \leq p$ (in this order from left to right). Similar when $inc(v) = p$, with $p \geq 3$, then the incoming edges to v, say from $w_1, \ldots, w_p$ (in this order from left to right), will go through the points $(x(v) - \lfloor \frac{p-3}{2} \rfloor, y(v) - i + 1)$, if $1 \leq i < \lceil \frac{p}{2} \rceil$, through $(x(v) + \lceil \frac{p-3}{2} \rceil, y(v) - p + i)$, $\lceil \frac{p}{2} \rceil < i \leq p$, and the edge to $w_{\lceil \frac{p}{2} \rceil}$ goes through $(x(v), y(v) - \lceil \frac{p-3}{2} \rceil)$. Let us call these points the *out-point* and *inc-point* of an edge, respectively. Every edge has one *out-point* and one *inc-point*, which can be connected by a vertical and horizontal line (which gives one extra bend, hence at most 3 bends in every edge).

In every step we add either a vertex or a face, and we have to shift the vertices on the outerface such that there is no pair of crossing edges by the involved inc- and out-points. After computing the shift-values and counting the number of bends the following theorem can be proved:

Theorem 6.1 *There is a linear time and space grid drawing algorithm to draw a triconnected d-planar graph on an* $(2n - 6) \times (3n - 6)$ *grid with at most* $5n - 15$ *bends and minimum angle* $> \frac{1}{d-2}$. *Every edge has at most 3 bends and length* $O(n)$.

In figure 6 the drawing of the graph of figure 2 is given.

In [14], the *lmc*-ordering is used to draw 3-planar graphs on a triangled grid, with in at most one edge bends. This is obtained by inspecting the dual graph H of the triconnected planar graph G: every vertex v_F in H corresponds with a face F in G. There is an edge $(v_{F'}, v_{F''})$ in H, if F' and F'' share a common edge in G. H is

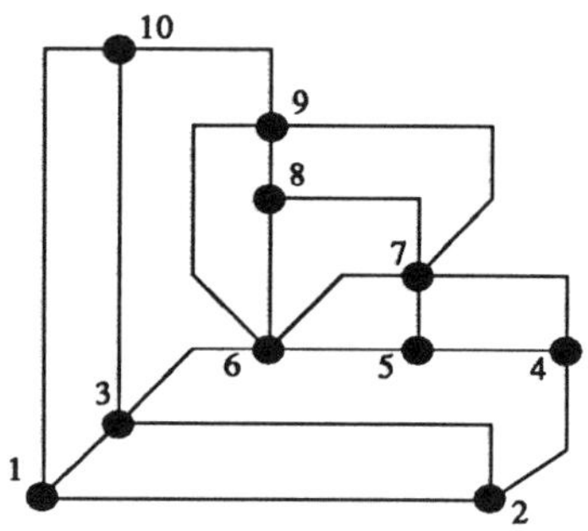

Figure 6: Drawing the graph of figure 2 with bends.

triconnected and planar as well. If G is d-planar, then every face in H has at most d edges. By Euler's formulae, $m - n - f + 2 = 0$, hence $n_H = m_G - n_G + 2$. Let an *lmc*-ordering of G be given. We construct a labeling of the faces of G as follows: when k is the smallest integer such that all vertices of face F belong to G_k in the *lmc*-ordering, then we set $label(F) = K + 3 - k$. Let $(v_1, v_n) \in F', F''$, and let also $v_2 \in F'$ (the outerface). Then we set $label(F') = 1$ and $label(F'') = 2$. Now we obtain the following interesting result:

Theorem 6.2 *The numbering of the vertices of the dual graph H of G corresponds with an lmc-ordering.*

Notice that in [21] a similar result is obtained for the st-ordering. Hence it seems that the *lmc*-ordering is a powerful generalization of the st-ordering in the triconnected case.

Theorem 6.2 is crucial in our analysis of drawing triconnected planar graphs G of degree 4 with minimum angle $\geq \pi/4$ on a grid. Let H be the dual graph of G, then H is a *maximal bipartite* planar graph. Using a related numbering for maximal bipartite planar graphs, we can obtain the following result:

Theorem 6.3 *Every triconnected planar graph of degree 4 can be drawn planar on a grid with at most* $\lceil \frac{n}{2} \rceil + 3$ *bends and minimum angle* $\geq \pi/4$. *There is a spanning tree of the vertices with* $\lfloor \frac{n}{2} \rfloor$ *straight-line horizontal and* $\lceil \frac{n}{2} \rceil - 1$ *straight-line vertical edges.*

Since every *lmc*-ordering is also an st-ordering, we can use the *lmc*-ordering in various drawing applications, e.g., in constructing *visibility representations* [21]. A visibility representation maps vertices into horizontal segments and edges into vertical segments that intersects only the two corresponding vertex segments. All endpoints are on grid points. Assume we have an *lmc*-ordering in which we add a vertex in each step. This is possible by the ordering of [9] for triangulated planar graphs. (In [13] an alternative linear time algorithm is given for constructing visibility representations of triangulated planar graphs, using De Fraysseix' canonical ordering.) When we add a vertex v_k, then the horizontal segment, representing v_k is added. Hereto we have to know the y-coordinates of the endpoints of the incoming edges of v_k, and we have to know the x-coordinates of the edges (c_i, v_k) and (v_k, c_j). In this case we give every vertex only an y-coordinate, and every edge e receives an x-coordinate and a *shift*-variable. The horizontal segment, representing v, goes from $(x((v_k, c_i)), y(v_k))$ to $(x((v_k, c_j)), y(v_k))$. In every step we add a vertex, and we place all outgoing edges of v_k on distance 1 from each other on this segment. We update *shift*$((v_k, c_j))$ accordingly. The exact algorithm is omitted from this extended abstract.

Since $inc(v) \geq 2$ for every vertex v, this means that adding v_k increases the Y-direction by 1 and the X-direction by $\max\{0, out(v_k) - 2\}$. If for every vertex $v_i, out(v_i) \geq 2$ holds, then this leads to a visibility representation on a grid of size at most $(n-2)\times(n-1)$. Several compressing and optimization techniques are possible, often leading to more compact layouts than the algorithms in [19, 21, 12]. Especially, when we add a face, then we can do it such that we increase the Y-direction by at most 2. Moreover, compared with [21], we do not have to compute the dual graph.

Theorem 6.4 *There is an alternative linear time algorithm to construct a visibility representation of a planar graph on a grid of size at most* $(2n-4) \times (n-1)$.

In figure 7 a visibility representation of the graph in figure 2 is given.

Optimizations are possible in almost all drawing algorithms, presented in the previous sections. For example, in section 4 we can set *mark*(v) left or right when $deg(v) = 3$, according to the smallest number of bends. In section 5 we originally always go upwards from c_i and c_j, even when there is no reason to. For example, if $l(c_j)$ is free and $y(c_j) > y(c_i)$, then we can place the new vertices on height $y(c_j)$. In the same way we can improve the drawings of sections 3 and 6.

If the d-planar graph G is not triconnected, then we can use the algorithm of [15] to augment the graph by adding only a few edges such that it becomes triconnected and still planar. In [16] a linear algorithm is described to triangulate a planar graph (which is triconnected), for which the maximum degree is at most $\frac{3}{2}d + O(1)$. This bound matches the worst-case lowerbound up to a constant. Using this algorithm, we can draw all planar graphs on an $(2n-6) \times (3n-6)$ grid with at most $5n - 15$ bends and minimum angle $> \frac{2}{3d} + O(1)$.

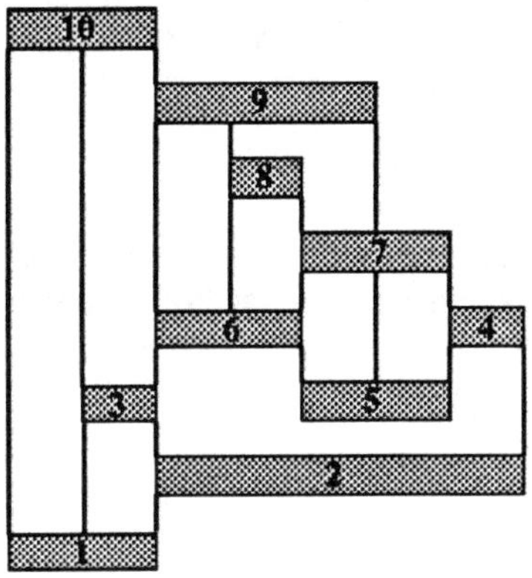

Figure 7: Visibility representation of the graph of figure 2. The vertices have been given positive thickness for clarity.

7 Final remarks and open problems

In this paper, a new ordering of the vertices and faces of a triconnected planar graph is introduced. This ordering leads to various algorithms to draw a planar graph on a grid. In some cases considerable improvements on existing results are obtained, in other cases new bounds are achieved. All algorithms can be implemented by straightforward techniques to run in linear time and space. Also the resulting pictures seems to be readable, if one compares them with the existing drawing algorithms (see the enclosed figures).

However, there are some open problems. We mention here:

- Decrease some of the bounds with respect to the grid size, number of bends or minimum angle, given in this paper.
- Is it possible to use the *lmc*-ordering in other algorithms as well, to obtain better results in planar graph drawings on a grid?
- Inspect the more combinatorial aspects of the *lmc*-ordering. Very recently, the *st*-ordering of biconnected planar graphs lead to a new characterization of planar graphs [20]. We believe that also for the *lmc*-ordering, more combinatorial observations can be made than those, given in this paper.
- Can an arbitrary planar graph be drawn planar with straight lines such that the minimum angle is $> \frac{1}{d}$ in general (see also [18] for this question)?
- Devise a dynamic algorithms for the sequential algorithms of this paper. Very recently, in [3] a dynamic framework for graph drawing problems is described,

but this approach seems not to work here. Also the parallel implementation is an interesting subject for further study.

Acknowledgements

The author wishes to thank Hans Bodlaender for the proof of theorem 1.1. The author wishes to thank Hans Bodlaender and Jan van Leeuwen for reading earlier drafts.

References

[1] Chiba, N., T. Nishizeki, S. Abe and T. Ozawa, A linear algorithm for embedding planar graphs using PQ-trees, *J. of Comp. and System Sciences*, Vol. 30 (1985), pp. 54–76.

[2] Chiba, N., T. Yamanouchi, and T. Nishizeki, Linear algorithms for convex drawings of planar graphs, in: *Progress in Graph Theory*, J.A. Bondy and U.S.R. Murty (Eds.), Academic Press, 1984, pp. 153–173.

[3] Cohen, R.F., G. Di Battista, R. Tamassia, I.G. Tollis and P. Bertolazzi, A Framework for dynamic graph drawing, in: *Proc. 8th Annual ACM Symp. on Computational Geometry*, Berlin, 1992, pp. 261–270.

[4] Chrobak, M., and T.H. Payne, *A Linear Time Algorithm for Drawing Planar Graphs on the Grid*, Tech. Rep. UCR-CS-90-2, Dept. of Math. and Comp. Science, University of California at Riverside, 1990.

[5] Eades, P., and R. Tamassia, *Algorithms for Automatic Graph Drawing: An Annotated Bibliography*, Dept. of Comp. Science, Brown Univ., Tech. Rep. CS-89-09, 1989.

[6] Even, S., and R.E. Tarjan, Computing an *st*-numbering, *Theoret. Comp. Science* 2 (1976), pp. 436–441.

[7] Fáry, I., On straight lines representations of planar graphs, *Acta Sci. Math. Szeged*, 11 (1948), pp. 229–233.

[8] Formann, M., T. Hagerup, J. Haralambides, M. Kaufmann, F.T. Leighton, A. Simvonis, E. Welzl and G. Woeginger, Drawing graphs in the plane with high resolution, *Proc. 31th Ann. IEEE Symp. on Found. of Comp. Science*, St. Louis, 1990, pp. 86–95.

[9] Fraysseix, H. de, J. Pach and R. Pollack, How to draw a planar graph on a grid, *Combinatorica* 10 (1990), pp. 41–51.

[10] Haandel, F. van, *Straight Line Embeddings on the Grid*, Dept. of Comp. Science, M.Sc. Thesis, no. INF/SCR-91-19, Utrecht University, 1991.

[11] Hopcroft, J., and R.E. Tarjan, Dividing a graph into triconnected components, *SIAM J. Comput.* 2 (1973), pp. 135–158.

[12] Jayakumar, R., K. Thulasiraman, and M.N.S. Swamy, Planar embedding: linear-time algorithms for vertex placement and edge ordering, *IEEE Trans. on Circuits and Systems* 35 (1988), pp. 334–344.

[13] Nummenmaa, J., Constructing compact rectilinear planar layouts using canonical representation of planar graphs, *Theoret. Comp. Science* 99 (1992), pp. 213–230.

[14] Kant, G., Hexagonal Grid Drawings, in: *Proc. 18th Intern. Workshop on Graph-Theoretic Concepts in Comp. Science WG'92*, Lecture Notes in Comp. Science, Springer-Verlag, 1992 (to appear).

[15] Kant, G., and H.L. Bodlaender, Planar graph augmentation problems, Extended Abstract in: F. Dehne, J.-R. Sack and N. Santoro (Eds.), *Proc. 2nd Workshop on Data Structures and Algorithms*, Lecture Notes in Comp. Science 519, Springer-Verlag, 1991, pp. 286–298.

[16] Kant, G., and H.L. Bodlaender, Triangulating planar graphs while minimizing the maximum degree, in: O. Nurmi and E. Ukkonen (Eds.), *Proc. 3rd Scand. Workshop on Algorithm Theory*, Lecture Notes in Comp. Science 621, Springer-Verlag, 1992, pp. 258–271.

[17] Lin, Y.-L., and S.S. Skiena, *Complexity Aspects of Visibility Graphs*, Manuscript, Dept. of Comp. Science, State Univ. of New York, Stony Brook, 1992.

[18] Malitz, S., and A. Papakostas, On the Angular Resolution of Planar Graphs, in: *Proc. 24th Annual ACM Symp. Theory of Computing*, Victoria, 1992.

[19] Otten, R.H.J.M., and J.G. van Wijk, Graph representation in interactive layout design, in *Proc. IEEE Int. Symp. on Circuits and Systems*, 1978, pp. 914–918.

[20] Rosenstiehl, P., H. de Fraysseix, and P. de Mendez, personal communication, 1992.

[21] Rosenstiehl, P., and R.E. Tarjan, Rectilinear planar layouts and bipolar orientations of planar graphs, *Discr. and Comp. Geometry* 1 (1986), pp. 343–353.

[22] Schnyder, W., Embedding planar graphs on the grid, in: *Proc. 1st Annual ACM-SIAM Symp. on Discr. Alg.*, San Francisco, 1990, pp. 138–147.

[23] Storer, J.A.,On minimal node-cost planar embeddings, *Networks* 14 (1984), pp. 181–212.

[24] Tamassia, R., On embedding a graph in the grid with the minimum number of bends, *SIAM J. Comput.* 16 (1987), pp. 421-444.

[25] Tamassia, R., G. Di Battista and C. Batini, Automatic graph drawing and readability of diagrams, *IEEE Trans. on Systems, Man and Cybernetics* 18 (1988), pp. 61–79.

[26] Tamassia, R., and I.G. Tollis, Efficient embedding of planar graphs in linear time, *Proc. IEEE Int. Symp. on Circuits and Systems*, Philadelphia, pp. 495–498, 1987.

[27] Tamassia, R., I.G. Tollis and J.S. Vitter, Lower bounds for planar orthogonal drawings of graphs, *Inf. Proc. Letters* 39 (1991), pp. 35–40.

[28] Thomassen, C., Planarity and duality of finite and infinite planar graphs, *J. Comb. Theory Series B*, Vol. 29 (1980), pp. 244-271.

[29] Tutte, W.T., Convex representations of graphs, *Proc. London Math. Soc.* 10 (1960), pp. 302–320.

[30] Tutte, W.T., How to draw a graph, *Proc. London Math. Soc.* 13 (1963), pp. 743–768.

Computing in Solvable Matrix Groups

Eugene M. Luks*
Computer and Information Science
University of Oregon
Eugene, OR 97403

Abstract

We announce methods for efficient management of solvable matrix groups over finite fields. We show that solvability and nilpotence can be tested in polynomial-time. Such efficiency seems unlikely for membership-testing, which subsumes the discrete-log problem. However, assuming that the primes in $|G|$ (other than the field characteristic) are polynomially-bounded, membership-testing and many other computational problems are in polynomial time. These problems include finding stabilizers of vectors and of subspaces and finding centralizers and intersections of subgroups. An application to solvable permutation groups puts the problem of finding normalizers of subgroups into polynomial time. Some of the results carry over directly to finite matrix groups over algebraic number fields; thus, testing solvability is in polynomial time, as is testing membership and finding Sylow subgroups.

1 Introduction

Over the past 30 years, Computational Group Theory has matured into a fertile and valuable discipline (see [Le], [Ca], [At], [Sc]). Within it, the most developed subdomain has been that of permutation groups, the apparent reason being that a small set of generating permutations can designate a very large group. However, that observation would be useless without methods for dealing effectively with the groups that one can specify.

Such methods exist. Fundamental is a technique first proposed by Sims in the 1960's (see, e.g., [Si]). Suppose $G \leq \mathrm{Sym}(\Omega)$, the group of all permutations of $\Omega = \{\omega_1, \dots, \omega_n\}$. For $1 \leq i \leq n$, let $G^{(i)}$ be the subgroup of G that fixes each of $\omega_1, \dots, \omega_{i-1}$ ($G^{(1)} = G$). Then $\{\omega_1, \dots, \omega_m\}$ is called a *base* for G if $G^{(m+1)} = 1$. The tower of subgroups

$$G = G^{(1)} \geq G^{(2)} \geq \cdots \geq G^{(m+1)} = 1$$

underlies almost all practical algorithms. However, to make use of it, one needs to obtain generators for every $G^{(i)}$. Fortunately, there is a classical method of Schreier (see [Ha]) that constructs generators for the subgroup $G^{(i+1)} \leq G^{(i)}$ given generators for $G^{(i)}$ together with a complete set, T_i, of right coset representatives for $G^{(i+1)}$ in $G^{(i)}$.

To appreciate the effectiveness of the tower, note, for example, that testing membership in $G = G^{(1)}$ of a permutation s reduces to testing membership in $G^{(2)}$ of st^{-1}, where $t \in T_1$ is uniquely determined by $\omega_1^t = \omega_1^s$.

Critical to the implementations of this, and the myriad practical procedures that utilize the tower, is that the indices $|G^{(i)} : G^{(i+1)}|$ are "small" ($|G^{(i)} : G^{(i+1)}| \leq n$); for example, Schreier generation demands consideration of the full T_i. This is also essential for *polynomial-time* computation in permutation groups. In fact, in 1980, Furst, Hopcroft and Luks [FHL] showed that a variant of Sims's method runs in polynomial time. That result inaugurated the now-substantial polynomial-time library for permutation groups (see [KL] for a summary).

In stark contrast to the permutation-group progress is the underdeveloped status of computation for matrix groups over finite fields. The matrix setting could be more desirable and more natural for representing and applying finite groups. Unfortunately, there have been almost no provably-efficient methods for managing matrix groups. Indeed, there are signs that even elementary problems may not have uniformly efficient procedures in this domain. Consider the basic problem of testing membership. Even for 1×1 matrices, this involves the discrete-log problem in finite fields, which seems unlikely to have a polynomial-time solution (see, e.g., [Bac]).

But, as we shall make clear, this discouraging observation does not close the door on all important instances of membership-testing. In any case, it does not fully account for the inefficiency of commonly implemented algorithms. A major bottleneck in the "standard" procedure for matrix-group membership is its direct utilization of Sims's algorithm ([Bu], [Ca]), in effect dealing with the full matrix group $GL(n, F)$ as a subgroup of the permutation group $\mathrm{Sym}(F^n)$. To be

*Research supported by NSF grant CCR-9013410

sure, one does not need to *list* this exponential-sized permutation domain, and there is still a base of reasonable size (a vector-space basis of F^n is a base for any subgroup of $GL(n, F)$). Nevertheless, there is an intrinsic blowup in the application of Sims's methods, for the indices $|G^{(i)} : G^{(i+1)}|$ can be exponential. This can happen even for elementary-abelian 2-groups represented over the 2-element field $GF(2)$. E.g., consider the subgroup $G < GL(n, 2)$ that fixes every vector in a subspace of dimension $n-1$; assuming ω_1 is any vector that is moved by G, we see that $|G^{(1)} : G^{(2)}| = 2^{n-1}$. This bottleneck is clearly unrelated to the discrete log obstruction, for the only prime in $|G|$ is 2.

We also demonstrate that not every important problem demands membership-testing. To be sure, membership-testing is so efficient in the permutation-group setting that one does not hesitate to call it. A case in point: polynomial-time testing of permutation-group solvability was touted in [FHL] as an immediate consequence of Sims's methods (membership-testing enables normal closures, therefore derived series). Nevertheless, we now show that solvability and nilpotence are polynomial-time testable for finite matrix groups (by which we mean something more than matrix groups over finite fields - see below). By comparison, previous methods for finite matrix groups put testing solvability and nilpotence in NP $\cap$ co-NP ([BS]) or in random (Monte-Carlo) polynomial-time ([BCFLS]).

For issues that must involve membership-testing, one can strive for a reduction to discrete logs, and we could state some of our main results in that fashion. However, for the sake of ready exposition of the new techniques, it is more convenient to introduce an additional parameter into the timing. To wit, we develop a large library of solvable-matrix-group problems which can be solved in time that is polynomial in $(n + \log |F| + \mu(G))$, where $\mu(G)$ is the largest prime in $|G|$ other than the characteristic of F. This includes: membership-testing; finding $|G|$; finding the subgroup that stabilizes a vector or a subspace; finding subgroup intersections; finding centralizers; in fact, finding the structural "building blocks" of $|G|$.

Lest the reader be concerned about the non-input parameter $\mu(G)$ in the timing, we emphasize that these results are new even for groups in which $\mu(G)$ is absolutely bounded, in fact, even for p-groups where p is fixed. Furthermore, we indicate some natural and important applications in which $\mu(G)$ is guaranteed to be small.

For example, $\mu(G)$ is small in various applications to permutation group problems. Most notably, we now find normalizers of subgroups of solvable permutation groups in polynomial time. A previous polynomial-time method extended only to nilpotent permutation groups [KL]. Implemented procedures for permutation groups (e.g., in the group-theory systems Cayley [Ca] and GAP [Sc]) use backtracking methods that require exponential time in the worst case.

There are also applications to permutation groups that give new perspectives on problems that were previously known to be in polynomial time, but required much deeper methods. An example is finding the intersection of subgroups of a solvable quotient G/K of permutation groups (note, only G/K is hypothesized to be solvable, G need not be). It was announced in [KL] that this can be done in polynomial time. However, the method required Kantor's algorithms for Sylow subgroups ([Ka1], [Ka2]) which make essential use of consequences of the classification of finite simple groups (so they have a 15000 page proof). We can now offer a self-contained, elementary approach to this and other previously classification-dependent problems.

Another application is to finite groups $G < GL(n, F)$, where F is an algebraic number field. Babai, Beals and Rockmore [BBR] have shown how to embed such G in $GL(n, \mathbb{Z})$. But then the natural homomorphism $\mathbb{Z} \rightarrow \mathbb{Z}_p$, for any $p > 2$, faithfully embeds G in $GL(n, p)$ and $\mu(G) \leq n + 1$. Consequently, membership-testing is in polynomial time for finite solvable matrix groups over algebraic number fields. By earlier remarks, testing whether a finite matrix group is solvable or nilpotent is also shown to be in polynomial time; indeed, much deeper structural information is available (including composition series and Sylow subgroups).

Our approach to membership-testing involves a top-down decomposition of the group (quite unlike Sims's method, wherein almost no deep knowledge of the group, other than its order, is immediately needed or revealed). This is reminiscent of methods used for NC computation in permutation groups ([LM], [Lu2], [BLS]). The common approach assumes we already have a presentation $\langle X | \mathcal{R} \rangle$ of some quotient G/H of G, and the immediate goal is to get enough information about H to produce some non-trivial presentation of a quotient H/K, which, by standard means, then yields a presentation of G/K, etc. Using the Schreier method to get generators of H is out of the question for $|G : H|$ can be exponential. However, "sifting" the relations $\mathcal{R}$ produces "normal generators" of H, i.e., generators of a subgroup whose normal closure in G is H. One then needs to construct a manageable representation domain for some H/K, an operation that may have to bootstrap from the group structure itself.

In order to maintain determinism, we do not pass to irreducible actions, as finding these presently requires Las Vegas methods when F is large [Ró]. On the other hand, our procedures do exploit invariant subspaces when these are available. In fact, we offer a divide-and-conquer paradigm for finding important subgroups, such as subspace-stabilizers, which relies on both invariant subspaces and imprimitivity systems. However, unlike their analogues in permutation-group computation (orbits and imprimitivity blocks [Lu1]), these are not easy to locate.

We summarize some of the main results in §3, with samples of the methods in §§4-6. We propose issues for further research in §7.

Finally, we emphasize that our goal is polynomial-time computation. We leave for later investigation low-level complexity issues and practical implementation, worthy projects in which we invite participation.

2 Notation and Preliminaries

We refer to standard references (e.g., [Ha]) for terminology not recalled here. G always denotes a *finite* group.

We write $H \leq G$ if H is a subgroup of G and $H \trianglelefteq G$ if H is a normal subgroup, $H < G$ and $H \triangleleft G$ indicating strict inclusion. The *index* of H in G is $|G|/|H|$ and is denoted $|G:H|$. For $A \subseteq G$, $\langle A \rangle$ is the subgroup *generated by* A, i.e., the smallest subgroup containing A. The *order of* $g \in G$ is $|\langle g \rangle|$ and denoted $o(g)$.

For $g, h \in G$, $g^{-1}hg$ is the *conjugate of* h *by* g and is denoted h^g. If $A \subset G$, the *centralizer of* A *in* G is $C_G(A) = \{g \in G \mid \forall a \in A, a^g = a\}$; $C_G(G)$ is also called the *center* of G and is denoted $Z(G)$. The *normal closure* of H in G is the smallest normal subgroup of G that contains H and is denoted H^G. The *normalizer* of H in G is the largest subgroup of G in which H is normal, i.e. $\{g \in G \mid g^{-1}Hg = G\}$.

If $g, h \in G$, $[g, h] = g^{-1}h^{-1}gh$ (the *commutator* of g and h). If $S, T \subseteq G$, $[S, T]$ denotes the subgroup $\langle \{[s, t] \mid s \in S, t \in T\} \rangle$. The *derived* subgroup of G is $G' = [G, G]$ and the *derived series* is $G \geq G' \geq (G')' \geq \cdots$; G is said to be *solvable* if the derived series terminates with 1. The *lower central series* of G is defined recursively by: $L_1(G) = G$ and $L_{i+1}(G) = [G, L_i(G)]$; G is said to be *nilpotent* if the lower central series terminates with 1; it is *nilpotent of class* i if $L_i(G) > L_{i+1}(G) = 1$. Abelian groups are nilpotent and nilpotent groups are solvable; neither converse holds.

For a prime p, G is a *p-group* if $|G|$ is a power of p and G is a *p'-group* if $\gcd(|G|, p) = 1$. A group is nilpotent iff it is a direct product of p-groups. A *Sylow p-subgroup* of G is a p-subgroup of maximal order; a group is nilpotent iff it has a unique Sylow p-subgroup for each p.

A group is called *simple* if it has no proper normal subgroups. A composition series of G is a tower $G = H_1 \triangleright H_1 \triangleright \cdots \triangleright H_m = 1$ such that each quotient H_i/H_{i+1} is simple. Then G is solvable if the simple groups in some (hence all) composition series are cyclic.

The group of all permutations of the set Ω is denoted by $\mathrm{Sym}(\Omega)$. One says that G *acts on* Ω if there is a homomorphism $G \to \mathrm{Sym}(\Omega)$. If G acts on Ω, one writes ω^g, respectively, Δ^g, for the image of $\omega \in \Omega$, respectively, the image of $\Delta \subseteq \Omega$, under $g \in G$; then G is said to be *transitive* if $\Omega = \{\omega^g \mid g \in G\}$ for some (therefore, all) $\omega \in \Omega$. A subset $\Delta \subseteq \Omega$ is said to be *G-invariant* and G is said to *stabilize* Δ if $\Delta^g = \Delta$ for all $g \in G$. If G stabilizes Δ, we denote by G^Δ the image of G in $\mathrm{Sym}(\Delta)$. For any $\Delta \subset \Omega$, the *pointwise stabilizer of* Δ *in* G is $C_G(\Delta) = \{g \in G \mid \delta^g = \delta, \forall \delta \in \Delta\}$; note that this is consistent with the centralizer notation $C_G(H)$, with G acting via conjugacy. For $G < \mathrm{Sym}(\Omega)$, the set of *fixed points of* G is $\mathrm{Fix}(G) = \{\omega \in \Omega \mid \omega^g = \omega, \forall g \in G\}$.

The standard vector space of n-tuples over a field F is denoted F^n. In any vector space, $\mathrm{Span}(A)$ is the linear span of the set A. For vector spaces V, W over F, $\mathrm{Hom}(V, W)$ is the space of linear transformations from V to W. The group of nonsingular linear transformations of V is denoted $GL(V)$. Note that $GL(V) < \mathrm{Sym}(V)$ and so the notation of the preceding paragraph applies to subgroups of $GL(V)$. A group $G < GL(V)$ is said to be *reducible* if there exists a proper G-invariant subspace of V. An *imprimitivity system* for $G < GL(V)$ is a collection, $\{W_1, \ldots, W_m\}$, of subspaces of V such that $V = W_1 \oplus \cdots \oplus W_m$ and G permutes the summands, acting transitively on that m-element collection (thus. $\dim(W_i) = \dim(V)/m$). The group of $n \times n$ matrices over the q-element field $GF(q)$ is denoted $GL(n, q)$. It is often convenient to indicate that $G < GL(V) = GL(n, q)$, where V is an n-dimensional vector space, so that we have all parameters available for the discussion.

A matrix is called *unipotent* if its only eigenvalue is 1; a matrix group is called *unipotent* if it consists of unipotent matrices. A matrix group is unipotent iff it is simultaneously triangulable with all main diagonals comprised of 1's. If the characteristic of F is p then a subgroup of $GL(n, F)$ is unipotent iff it is a p-group.

We call an abelian matrix group $A < GL(V)$ *uniform* if, for every integer m, $\mathrm{Fix}(A^m) = \{0\}$ or V, where $A^m = \{a^m \mid a \in A\}$.

Implicit to timing analyses is the fact that strictly decreasing sequences of subspaces (of F^n) or subgroups (of $GL(n, q)$) have polynomial length (bounded by n or $\log_2 |GL(n, q)| < n^2 \log_2 q$, respectively).

3 Main Results

Subgroups $G \leq GL(n,F)$ are input and output via sets of generators. Furthermore, we make the overall assumption that the input-generating-sets are not unreasonably large (e.g, for finite F, it is warranted to suppose that these are no larger than $\log|GL(n,F)| = O(n^2 \log|F|))$ so that we need not bother to incorporate their size in the asymptotic timings. We also assume reasonable encodings of finite F so that "polynomial-time," by itself, means polynomial in $(n + \log|F|)$.

Theorem 3.1 *Given $G \leq GL(n,F)$, where F is a finite field, one can test in polynomial time whether G is solvable and, if so, whether G is nilpotent.*

If G is solvable one can also find, for each prime $p \leq n^{\text{constant}}$, the p-part of $|G|$. If G is nilpotent, one can find its (unique!) Sylow p-subgroup for each such prime.

Theorem 3.2 *Given a solvable $G \leq GL(n,F)$, where F is a finite field, let μ denote the largest prime dividing $|G|$ other than the characteristic of F. The following problems can be solved in time that is polynomial in $(n + \log|F| + \mu)$.*

(1) *Find $|G|$.*

(2) *Given $x \in GL(n,F)$, test whether $x \in G$.*

(3) *Find a generator-relator presentation for G.*

(4) *Find a composition series in G.*

(5) *Given any vector $v \in F^n$, find the subgroup of G that fixes v.*

(6) *More generally, given any set A of vectors, find the subgroup of G that stabilizes the set A (assuming $|A|$ is not large, otherwise we can express the timing as a polynomial in $n + \log|F| + \mu + |A|$).*

(7) *Given any subspace $W \leq F^n$ (via a spanning set), find the subgroup of G that stabilizes W.*

(8) *Given any $x \in GL(n,F)$, find $C_G(x)$, the centralizer of x in G. Thus, given any (not necessarily solvable) $H \leq GL(n,F)$, find $C_G(H)$.*

(9) *Given $H, K \leq GL(n,F)$, find $H \cap K$.*

(10) *For any prime p, find a Sylow p-subgroup of G.*

An application of (7) leads to

Corollary 3.3 *Given permutation groups H, G, with $H \leq G$ and G solvable, one can find the normalizer of H in G in polynomial time.*

More generally, the normalizer of H in G can be found if $H/K \leq G/K$, where $K \trianglelefteq G$, assuming only that G/K is solvable.

Other applications to quotients of permutation groups include finding $C_A(B)$ and $A \cap B$ when $A, B < G/K$, with G/K solvable. These two are not new results for polynomial-time but previous methods [KL] (which are still more generally applicable) used consequences of the classification of finite simple groups.

Corollary 3.4 *Given $G < GL(n,F)$, where F is an algebraic number field, one can test whether G is a finite solvable or nilpotent group in polynomial time and, if so, test membership in G.*

One can also then find $|G|$, normalizers and centralizers of subgroups, intersections of subgroups, composition series and Sylow subgroups.

4 Membership-Testing and Basics

Throughout this section, we assume that we are dealing with solvable groups $G = \langle S \rangle < GL(n,q) = GL(V)$ for which $\mu(G)$ is bounded by a fixed polynomial in the size of the input. Alternately, the results can be rephrased, replacing "polynomial-time" by "polynomial in $|S| + n + \log q + \mu(G)$."

Assuming some reasonable encoding of the finite field F (e.g., as $GF(q)[x]/(f(x))$ for some irreducible f), it is elementary to convert our setting to matrix groups over the prime field $GF(q)$ (blowing up matrix sizes by a factor of degree(f)). Thus, we assume that $G \leq GL(n,q)$, where q is prime.

4.1 Overall Procedure

We construct, in a top-down fashion, a tower of normal (in G) subgroups

$$G = H_1 \triangleright H_2 \triangleright \cdots \triangleright H_m = 1$$

together with manageable representations $\phi_i : H_i \rightarrow M_i$ with $H_{i+1} = \text{kernel}(\phi_i)$.

By "manageable" we mean essentially that M_i is a type of group for which suitable machinery (testing membership, finding presentations) has already been developed. For example, if $M_i = \text{Sym}(\Omega)$ then we can appeal to standard permutation group machinery. The idea is further exploited by resolving all critical issues first with abelian groups (§4.4), after which M_i may be an abelian matrix group. With such representations, membership-testing, for example, becomes a *sifting* process (cf. [FHL]) through the tower: map a candidate x for membership in H_i by π_i to M_i (membership-failure could be reported in the call to the function π_i which may not be defined on x); find an $h \in H_i$ such that $\pi_i(h) = \pi_i(x)$; test membership of xh^{-1} in H_{i+1}.

"Top-down" in the tower construction has an algebraic as well as an algorithmic connotation. That is, the group that we shall have constructed at any stage is G/H_i. We shall not actually have generators for any H_i until the entire procedure has run. Furthermore, though we have indicated that we construct domains in which to study the quotients H_i/H_{i+1}, we do not necessarily have faithful representations (e.g., as permutation groups or matrix groups) of the full quotients G/H_i. However, there is a concrete way in which we do have G/H_i in hand, namely via a generator-relator presentation $\langle X_i|\mathcal{R}_i\rangle$ (the computational aspect of this is formalized in §4.2).

One particular advantage of the representation of quotient groups via presentations is that the relations provide, in a natural manner, precisely the needed elements of H_i with which to carry on. Corresponding to the relations R_i is a set $T_i \subset H_i$ such that $H_i = \langle T_i\rangle^G$ and the constructive nature of the presentation (§4.2) gives access to T_i.

The core of the method then is, using only T_i, which still may not fully generate H_i, to construct the map $\pi_i : H_i \to M_i$. More precisely, π_i is a function that would be defined on any elements of H_i as they are later encountered. The group M_i will also be acted on by G and the map π_i will be a G-map, that is $\pi_i(h^g) = (\pi_i(h))^g$ for all $h \in H_i$. Thus, in M_i, full generators for, and a presentation of $\langle \pi_i(T_i)\rangle^G$ can be constructed. All of this can be pulled back to $H_i/\text{kernel}(\pi_i)$.

Since π_i is a G-map, $\text{kernel}(\pi_i) \trianglelefteq G$. We let $H_{i+1} = \text{kernel}(\pi_i)$ and use the presentations of G/H_i and H_i/H_{i+1} to form a presentation of G/H_{i+1}, thus stepping down the tower.

When the tower is exhausted, we have in hand a data structure for membership-testing. But the procedure has other important corollaries. An easy example is that of finding $|G|$. Assuming that, for the "manageable" M_i, finding orders of subgroups is in polynomial-time (this will be the case) then $|G| = \prod_i |\pi(H_i)|$. Having access to effective presentations in a class of groups has other applications, including finding the center of a group (§4.6). In fact, we need centers in p-groups within the procedure for solvable groups. Thus, we first deal with nilpotent groups in §4.5.

4.2 Presentations

Our algorithmic formulation of presentations $\langle X|\mathcal{R}\rangle$ for quotients G/H must allow the passage back and forth between words in the free group $\mathcal{F}(X)$ and elements of G/H, which are viewed as liftings in G. Given that ability and generators for G, one can construct $T \subseteq H$ such that $H = \langle T\rangle^G$. One can also build a presentation for G/K given presentations for G/H and H/K. We formalize these notions in this subsection.

For a set X, $\mathcal{F}(X)$ denotes the free group on X. Thus, given any may $\phi : X \to G$, there is a unique homomorphism $\hat{\phi} : \mathcal{F}(X) \to G$ extending ϕ.

Let $H \trianglelefteq G$. A *constructive presentation of G mod H* (or, if $H = 1$, a *constructive presentation of* G) is a 4-tuple $\Pi = (X, \phi, \psi, \mathcal{R})$ in which

X is a set; $\phi : X \to G$; $\psi : G \to \mathcal{F}(X)$; $\mathcal{R} \subset \mathcal{F}(X)$ such that

$g(\hat{\phi}\psi(g))^{-1} \in H$ for all $g \in G$;

$\hat{\phi}^{-1}(H) = \langle\mathcal{R}\rangle^{\mathcal{F}(X)}$.

For computational purposes, it is assumed that $\Pi = (X, \phi, \psi, \mathcal{R})$ is input or output by

(i) Specifying $\phi(X)$ and $\mathcal{R}$.

(ii) Giving a procedure for determining $\psi(g)$, for any $g \in G$.

Remarks. (1) At the point of construction of ψ we do not necessarily have complete knowledge of the group G, perhaps not even a full generating set. It is only assumed that one can determine the images under $\hat{\phi}, \psi$ given elements of the respective domains.

(2) The procedure in (ii) does not need to output the full word. It would suffice to indicate a straight-line program (each step designating a product or inverse of predecessors) from X. Similarly, the words in $\mathcal{R}$ can be given by straight-line programs.

Lemma 4.1 *Given $\Pi = (X, \phi, \psi, \mathcal{R})$ as above, $\langle X|\mathcal{R}\rangle$ is a generator-relator presentation of the group G/H, with mutually-inverse isomorphisms $F(X)/\langle\mathcal{R}\rangle^{F(X)} \rightleftarrows G/H$ naturally induced by $\hat{\phi}, \psi$.*

For $g \in G$, we set $\text{Sift}_\Pi(g) = g(\hat{\phi}\psi(g))^{-1}$.

Lemma 4.2 *If $G = \langle\phi(X)\rangle$ then $H = \langle\hat{\phi}(\mathcal{R})\rangle^G$. More generally, if $G = \langle S\rangle$, then $H = \langle\hat{\phi}(\mathcal{R}) \cup \text{Sift}_\Pi(S)\rangle^G$.*

The following lemma recalls, in our setting, a recipe for gluing together presentations for G/H, H/K.

Lemma 4.3 *Suppose that $\Pi = (X, \phi, \psi, \mathcal{R})$ is a constructive presentation of G mod H and $\Pi' = (X', \phi', \psi', \mathcal{R}')$ is a constructive presentation of H mod K where $K \trianglelefteq G$. Then $\Pi'' = (X'', \phi'', \psi'', \mathcal{R}'')$ is a constructive presentation of G mod K where*

$X'' = X\dot{\cup}X'$ *(disjoint union);*

$$\phi''(x) = \begin{cases} \phi(x), & \text{for } x \in X \\ \phi'(x'), & \text{for } x' \in X'; \end{cases}$$

$\psi''(g) = \psi'(\text{Sift}_\Pi(g))\psi(g)$ *for* $g \in G$;

$$\mathcal{R}'' = \{r(\psi'\hat{\phi}(r))^{-1} \mid r \in \mathcal{R}\} \cup \mathcal{R}' \cup \{((x')^x)^{-1}\psi'(\phi'(x')^{\phi(x)}) \mid x \in X, x' \in X'\}.$$

If $G = \langle\phi(X)\rangle$ then $G = \langle\phi''(X'')\rangle$. Thus, if we start the tower method with a constructive presentation of

G mod G for which $G = \langle \phi(X) \rangle$, the condition persists through each G mod H_i.

4.3 Use of Invariant Subspaces

We assume that we have $H = \langle T \rangle^G$, with $H \neq 1$ (iff $T \not\subseteq \{1\}$) and that we seek some tractable representation $\pi : H \to M$. At various points in our procedures, we come into possession of a proper G-invariant subspace $W < V$. We can use that either to find π directly or to recurse to a "smaller" problem.

We have induced actions $\rho_1 : G \to GL(W)$, $\rho_2 : G \to GL(V/W)$. If, in either of these actions, H does not act trivially then we can recursively consider the problem for $\rho_i(G), \rho_i(T)$, which returns a representation $\pi' : \rho_i(H) \to M$, whereupon we set $\pi := \pi' \circ \rho_i$.

Suppose then that the actions of H on W and V/W are both trivial. There is then a natural nontrivial homomorphism π from H to (the additive group of) $\mathrm{Hom}(V, W)$ wherein $\pi(h)(v) = v^h - v$ for $v \in V$ and $h \in H$. There is also a natural action of G on $\mathrm{Hom}(V, W)$ such that $f^g(v) = \left(f(v^{g^{-1}})\right)^g$ for $f \in \mathrm{Hom}(V, W), v \in V, g \in G$. With this action π is then a G-map.

To determine $\pi(H) = \langle \pi(T) \rangle^G$ we need only observe that this is the smallest subspace of $\mathrm{Hom}(V, W)$ containing $\pi(T)$ and closed under the action of S. (Since q is prime, $\pi(H)$ is a vector space over q.)

It is an easy matter to write a constructive presentation for $\pi(H)$. Membership-testing in $\pi(H)$ is done via linear algebra.

Remark. Here, as in other uses of homomorphisms, the presence of a constructive membership test in $\pi(H)$ enables us to lift elements of $\pi(H)$ back to H. This is needed, for example, to lift the presentation of $\pi(H)$ to a presentation for H mod kernel(π).

We point out one useful source of invariant subspaces. For any $U \subseteq V$, $W = \mathrm{Fix}(\langle U \rangle^G)$ is G-invariant. Furthermore, given $G = \langle S \rangle$, we can find W as follows: $W := \mathrm{Fix}(U)$; **while** $\exists s \in S : W^s \neq W$ **do** $W := W \cap W^s$.

One application arises when $\langle U \rangle^G$ is unipotent, for a unipotent group has a nonzero fixed point.

We are also able to apply the idea to U for which $A = \langle U \rangle^G$ is abelian but not uniform. In such case, we can find m such that $0 < \mathrm{Fix}(A^m) < V$.

4.4 Abelian Groups

We consider the case of abelian $G = \langle S \rangle < GL(V)$.

The hypothesis on $\mu(G)$ enables us to determine $o(g)$ for any $g \in G$. (Besides q the primes that can occur in $|G|$ are less than $\mu(G)$; and we have an upper bound on the power to which they can occur, e.g., $\log_2 |GL(n, q)| < n^2 \log_2 q$). Hence, by forming suitable powers, we can express $g \in G$ as a product of elements of prime-power order. Doing this for each element of S and gathering the factors corresponding to each prime p dividing $|G|$, we get generators for the Sylow subgroups of G. Since G is the direct product of these, it suffices to show how to manage abelian p-groups. (For membership-testing, one first factors the candidate element.)

If G is q-group then it is unipotent and the reduction of §4.3 handles everything.

We assume then that G is a p-group, with $p \neq q$.

Recall that, at a generic step in the tower, we have $H = \langle T \rangle^G$. But, as G is abelian, this implies $H = \langle T \rangle$.

It suffices to give a procedure that constructs either a proper G-invariant subspace (thus leading into §4.3) or proof that $H = \langle h \rangle$, together with a method for expressing any $k \in H$ as a power of h. (A constructive presentation $\Pi = (\{x\}, \phi, \psi, \mathcal{R})$ could satisfy $\phi(x) = h$, $\psi(h) = x$, $\mathcal{R} = \{x^{o(h)}\}$.)

Lemma 4.4 *Let $G = \langle S \rangle < GL(V)$ be an abelian p-group with $p \neq q$ and $H = \langle T \rangle \leq Z(G)$. Then, in polynomial time, one can locate either a proper G-invariant subspace or prove that H is cyclic and locate a generator.*

Proof: It suffices to describe a polynomial-time procedure which, given $h, k \in H$, produces either a proper G-invariant subspace or else $z \in H$ such that $\langle h, k \rangle = \langle z \rangle$.

Without loss of generality $o(h) \geq o(k) \geq p$. Let $h_1 = h^{o(h)/p}, k_1 = k^{o(k)/p}$. If $\mathrm{Fix}(h_1) \neq 0$ then it is a proper G-invariant subspace. Else, recall that the abelian group $\langle h_1, k_1 \rangle$ necessarily acts as a cyclic group on an $\langle h_1, k_1 \rangle$-irreducible subspace V_0, and so k_1 necessarily acts on V_0 as h_1^r for some $0 \leq r < p$. Find r such that $\mathrm{Fix}(h_1^{-r} k_1) \neq 0$. If $\mathrm{Fix}(h_1^{-r} k_1) < V$ then it is a proper G-invariant subspace, else $k_1 = h_1^r$, in which case set $k' = h^{-r o(h)/o(k)} k$. Recurse for (h, k') (observing that $\langle h, k \rangle = \langle h, k' \rangle$ but $o(k') \leq o(k)/p$). ∎

If $H = \langle h \rangle$ the procedure in the above proof can be used to express any $k \in H$ as a power of h.

4.5 Nilpotent Groups

Knowing now that abelian groups are manageable, we turn to the case of nilpotent groups.

So, we assume we have nilpotent $G = \langle S \rangle < GL(V)$ and $H = \langle T \rangle^G$.

We first observe that we can test whether H is abelian (it is not sufficient for the elements of T to commute). One method involves the established membership-test of §4.4: since H is abelian, we can find generators for it (test whether $\langle T \rangle$ is closed under conjugacy by elements of S and, if not, find some new conjugate to add that increases $\langle T \rangle$). However, we offer a more generally-applicable test of commutativity of H.

In the following theorem, we do not assume either solvability of G or restrictions on $\mu(G)$.

Theorem 4.5 *Given* $G = \langle S \rangle < GL(V)$ *and* $T \subset GL(V)$. *Let* $H = \langle T \rangle^G$. *In polynomial-time, one can find (a basis of)* Span(H), *in fact, a basis consisting of elements of* H.

Proof: Span(H) is the smallest subspace of Hom(V, V) that contains T and is closed under multiplication and under conjugation by elements of S. In performing these closures by multiplying and conjugating basis elements from each stage, it is easy to keep basis elements at all stages in H. ∎

Observe that $H = \langle T \rangle^G$ is abelian iff Span(H) is commutative iff a basis of Span(H) commutes. Hence this is polynomial-time testable. Furthermore, if H is not abelian, we find witnesses to the fact, namely, $h_1, h_2 \in H$ such that $[h_1, h_2] \neq 1$.

Thus, if H is not abelian, we can find $h_0 \in H \setminus Z(H)$. As each round puts us in a smaller term of the lower central series of G, the following procedure runs in polynomial-time: start with $h_0 \in H \setminus Z(H)$; **while** $\exists s \in S : [h_0, s] \notin Z(H)$ **do** replace h_0 by such $[h_0, s]$. Note that we test whether $[h_0, s]$ is in $Z(H)$ by seeing whether it commutes with Span(H).

When we exit from the above while-loop we have $h_0 \in H \setminus Z(H)$ but $[h_0, S] \subseteq Z(H)$ and the latter implies $[h_0, G] \subseteq Z(H)$.

These conditions on h_0 imply that the map $\pi : H \to Z(H)$ such that $\pi(h) = [h_0, h]$ is nontrivial homomorphism and a G-map. As the image group is of a manageable class (abelian), we take one step down the tower.

4.6 Finding Kernels, Centers

Before proceeding to the more general class of solvable groups, we indicate an application of the procedure.

Assume that we have a class $\mathcal{C}$ of groups such that for matrix groups G in $\mathcal{C}$, the problems of membership-testing and finding-constructive-presentations are in polynomial-time. We assume that the $\mathcal{C}$ is closed under taking of subgroups and homomorphic images.

Given $G = \langle S \rangle < GL(V) = GL(n, q)$ with $G \in \mathcal{C}$ and $T \subset GL(V)$, we can test whether $T \leq G$ and, if so, we can find $\langle T \rangle^G$ (adding conjugates until the subgroup is normal). Normal closures have numerous applications but we are particularly interested in the following.

Suppose we are also given a representation $\phi : G \to GL(W)$ (say by specifying $\phi(S)$), where W is a vector space over $GF(q)$. Then we can determine a constructive presentation for $\phi(G)$ and therefore for G mod kernel(ϕ). Using Lemma 4.2, we derive $T \subset G$ such that kernel$(\phi) = \langle T \rangle^G$, whence we find generators for the normal closure kernel(ϕ).

We can then apply this result to obtain $C_G(H)$ for $H = \langle T \rangle \trianglelefteq G$ since $C_G(H)$ is the kernel of the induced action (by conjugacy) of G on Span(H).

In particular, finding $Z(G)$ is in polynomial time.

Remark. We shall ultimately be able to find $C_G(T)$ for solvable $G < GL(V)$ (with polynomially bounded $\mu(G)$) and *arbitrary* $T \subset GL(V)$ (see §6.4)

4.7 Solvable Groups

We turn finally to solvable groups. Again, we have $G = \langle S \rangle$ and $H = \langle T \rangle^G$. Note that, if H is abelian, we are done by §4.4.

There is one problem reduction that is worth singling out first. Suppose that $1 < A < GL(V)$ with A abelian and normalized by G. Then, if q divides $|A|$, A has a unipotent part whose fixed points yield a proper G-invariant subspace. If, on the other hand, A is a q'-group then dim(Span$(A)) \leq n$ (since A would be diagonalizable over an algebraic extension of $GF(q)$). Thus, if we also had $1 < C_H(A) < H$, we could recursively consider the naturally-induced representations, via conjugacy, of G, H on Span(A) (a "smaller" problem as the image of H is isomorphic to $H/C_H(A)$).

It is easy to find abelian $A < H$ with $A^G = A$: let $1 \neq h \in H$; **while** $\langle h \rangle^G$ is nonabelian **do** replace h by a nontrivial element of $[\langle h \rangle^G, \langle h \rangle^G]$. The number of loop iterations is bounded by the length of the derived series of H, so that we emerge with an abelian $A = \langle h \rangle^G$. Unfortunately, this may not suffice for a problem reduction as above, for it could be that A is a q'-group and is centralized by H ($C_H(A) = H$).

Consider, instead, the induced conjugacy-action of G on Span(H) and find $U \subset H$ such that $A = \langle U \rangle^G$ *acts as a nontrivial abelian group on* Span(H). Thus, $A \not\leq Z(H)$ but $[A, A] \leq Z(H)$.

If A is itself abelian, then it serves the aforementioned purpose as it is not centralized by H. If A is nonabelian then it is class-2 nilpotent, for $[A, A] \leq Z(A)$, so we can find full generators. Then, for some prime p, the Sylow p-subgroup, B, of A is a class-2 nilpotent p-group. (We can find B by extracting the p-parts of the generators of A.) We may assume $p \neq q$, else Fix(B) is a proper G-invariant subspace. As B is nilpotent, we may assume that we have a full set of generators. As an invariant of a loop to follow, we extract the following relevant data:

(∗) B is a class-2 nilpotent p-group, normalized by G, and $1 < C_H(B) < H$.

Before proceeding with the algorithm, we make some observations about uniform (abelian) groups.

Lemma 4.6 *Suppose $Z < GL(V)$ is uniform. Let $\{W_i\}_{i\in I}$ be the maximal Z-invariant subspaces on which Z acts as a cyclic group. Then $V = \bigoplus_{i\in I} W_i$.*

To find these unique W_i when Z is a p-group: by repeated application of Lemma 4.4, find W for which Z^W is cyclic; find $K = C_Z(W)$ (§4.6) and set $W_1 = \mathrm{Fix}(K)$; decompose $V = W_1 \oplus V'$ with a Z-invariant V' (since Z is a q'-group such decomposition exists - finding it is linear algebra); recursively decompose V.

Lemma 4.7 *Suppose $B < GL(V)$ is class-2 nilpotent and $Z(B)$ is cyclic and uniform. Then $|B : Z(B)| \le n^2$.*

In fact, one shows that distinct coset representatives are linearly independent.

(LOOP) We pick up with B satisfying (*).

We may assume $[H, Z(B)] = 1$, else we can utilize the induced actions of G, H on $\mathrm{Span}(Z(B))$ ($Z(B)$ is computable, §4.6).

We may assume $Z(B)$ is uniform, else $\mathrm{Fix}(Z(B)^{p^r})$ is a proper G-invariant subspace for some r.

With $Z = Z(B)$, decompose $V = W_1 \oplus \cdots \oplus W_r$ as in Lemma 4.6 (so $Z(B)^{W_i}$ is cyclic). Since $W_i = \mathrm{Fix}(C_{Z(B)}(W_i))$ and $[H, C_{Z(B)}(W_i)] = 1$, W_i is H-invariant.

If, for any i, the inclusion $Z(B)^{W_i} \le Z(B^{W_i})$ is strict: replace B by the strictly larger $B^{W_1} \times \cdots \times B^{W_r}$ acting naturally on $W_1 \oplus \cdots \oplus W_r$ and goto (LOOP) (noting that (*) still holds as $C_H(\text{new } B) = C_H(\text{old } B)$).

Thus, we may assume that all $Z(B^{W_i})$ are cyclic and uniform, so that $|B^{W_i} : Z(B^{W_i})| \le \dim(W_i)^2$. Set $\Omega = B^{W_1}/Z(B^{W_1}) \dot\cup \cdots \dot\cup B^{W_r}/Z(B^{W_r})$ (disjoint union), so $|\Omega| \le n^2$. There is a natural action $\pi : G \to \mathrm{Sym}(\Omega)$. If $\pi(H) \ne 1$, then we have our nontrivial representation in which to test membership and find a presentation.

Otherwise H acts trivially on Ω which implies $[H, B] \subset Z(B)$ and so H acts on B as an abelian p-group. Consider the induced conjugacy-action $\pi : G \to GL(\mathrm{Span}(B))$. Then $\pi(H)$ is a nontrivial (since $C_H(B) < H$) abelian p-group and we appeal to §4.4.

5 Testing solvability and nilpotence

We focus on the limited task of testing nilpotence and solvability, for which we can discard the §4 restrictions on $\mu(G)$. However, the developments of §4 remain relevant.

As before, we may assume q is prime.

Testing nilpotence is almost immediate. The critical observation is that, for $q \ne p > n$, the Sylow p-subgroups of $GL(n, q)$ are necessarily abelian. Let Δ be the set of primes $\le n$ together with q. Then we can express $|GL(n, q)| = ab$ where a only involves primes in Δ and b involves no primes in Δ.

Given a nilpotence candidate $G = \langle S \rangle$, let $S_a = \{s^b \mid s \in S\}$, $S_b = \{s^a \mid s \in S\}$. Then G is nilpotent iff: $\langle S_a \rangle$ is nilpotent and $[S, S_b] = 1$. Furthermore, if $\langle S_a \rangle$ is nilpotent then it involves only primes in Δ so that $\mu(\langle S_a \rangle) \le n$.

For general solvability, we show, if G is solvable, that we are still able to "construct" a normal tower

$$G = H_1 \rhd H_2 \rhd \cdots \rhd H_m$$

together with manageable representations $\pi_i : H_i \to M_i$, with M_i known solvable, for $i < m$. But, in general, we shall not have $H_m = 1$. Nevertheless, H_m will be of a special form for which solvability is readily testable. In a sense the groups in the tower will not be completely constructed since we may never have full generators, though we shall have generators for H_i/H_m.

Suppose the tower is constructed down to H, i.e., we have a presentation for G/H, which is known to be solvable, and we can express $H = \langle T \rangle^G$.

We consider a class of groups H for which solvability is directly testable, i.e., without finding presentations, etc. We say H is *$\overline{q}$-triangulable* if the transformations in H can be simultaneously triangulated over the algebraic closure of $GF(q)$. Clearly $\overline{q}$-triangulable groups are solvable. Given T we can test whether $H = \langle T \rangle^G$ is $\overline{q}$-triangulable as follows: if H is abelian then output "yes" else find $1 \ne u \in [H, H]$; if $U = \langle u \rangle^G$ is not a q-group (unipotent) then output "no" else let $W := \mathrm{Fix}(U)$; recursively test the action of H on W and V/W; if both calls respond "yes" then output "yes" else output "no".

Thus, with each new H, we perform the above test. If the answer is "yes", we announce G is solvable. Else we follow the procedure of §4.7. If we arrive at an invariant subspace W, we recurse on W if the action of H on W is not $\overline{q}$-triangulable else we recurse on V/W.

We must observe also that if the procedure goes through without finding an invariant subspace, then this round will succeed just as before for no "large" primes will appear in the induced representations. Indeed, we note that: in a representation $\pi : G \to GL(\mathrm{Span}(A))$ for an abelian q'-group A, $\mu(\pi(G)) \le n$; and the p corresponding to the class-2 nilpotent p-group B cannot exceed n.

6 Other Computational Problems

We have space herein to make only cursory comments about methods for the remaining problems in Theorem 3.2. Again we hypothesize that $\mu(G)$ is polynomially bounded.

6.1 An Algorithmic Paradigm

We indicate a divide-and-conquer paradigm for dealing with solvable matrix groups. Critical to this is

Theorem 6.1 *Given $G = \langle S \rangle \subset GL(n,q) = GL(V)$, with G solvable. In polynomial-time one can find at least one of the following.*

1. *A proper G-invariant subspace $W < V$.*
2. *$H \le G$ and an imprimitivity system $V = W_1 \oplus \cdots \oplus W_m$ for H with $|G:H| < m^{c_0}$ (c_0 is an easily computable constant).*
3. *$A \le G$ such that A is abelian and $|G:A| \le \max(12, n)$.*

The proof involves some deeper (than §4) use of the structure of solvable matrix groups and will appear in a full version of this paper.

Theorem 6.1 offers an analogue to the divide-and-conquer (orbits, imprimitivity blocks) for solvable permutation groups that solves such problems as finding-set-stabilizers, finding-intersections and finding-centralizers ([Lu1]). It also incorporates the permutation-group machinery (in case 2).

The typical situation to which it applies involves a problem that requires computing a subcoset of G. In particular, the problem should have the following characteristics.

(i) Given a G-invariant subspace $W < V$, the problem can be solved in a polynomial number of steps together with recursive calls to induced problems on W and on V/W.

(ii) The problem is in polynomial time for abelian groups.

The general procedure in cases 2 and 3 involves writing G as union of cosets of the respective subgroups, splitting into subproblems accordingly. The case 2 situation works much like the method of [Lu1,§3], finding a minimal block system in the action on $\{W_1, \ldots, W_m\}$ then splitting the group into cosets of the stabilizer of the blocks. The polynomial timing ultimately depends on the polynomial bound on the size of primitive solvable permutation groups [Pá]. (The constant c_0 is related to that same bound.)

In the next two subsections we indicate two applications of this paradigm.

6.2 Vector Stabilizer

We address Theorem 3.2(5). To accommodate recursive calls to subspaces and decomposition into cosets, we consider a generalization.

A function $f : G \to V$ is called a *crossed homomorphism* if $f(xy) = f(x)^y + f(y)$ for $x, y \in G$. It is assumed that a procedure is given for computing f. (Although, given a constructive membership-test in G, it suffices to define f on the generators. We can also verify that such a specification defines a crossed homomorphism but that is not essential to the present application.) Consider the problem:

Given: f as above and $v \in V$.
Find: $\{g \in G \mid f(g) = v\}$.

In particular, $C_G(v)$ is the solution to $v^g - v = 0$ and $g \mapsto v^g - v$ is a crossed homomorphism.

Observe that the solution to $f(g) = v$ is either $\emptyset$ or a right coset of the subgroup $\{g \in G \mid f(g) = 0\}$.

Suppose that $W < V$ is G-invariant. Then, recursively working in V/W (i.e., modulo W) we solve $\overline{f(g)} = \overline{v}$. If nonempty the solution is Hy. Since $f(H) \subseteq W$ and $f(hy) = v$ iff $f(h) = (v - f(y))^{y^{-1}}$, we recursively solve the resulting problem in W. (When solving the "local" problem in some W, we make sure, in the resulting coset Hz, that H contains $C_G(W)$, the kernel of the action).

Suppose G is abelian. We first verify that $v \in W = \mathrm{Span}(f(G)) = (\mathrm{Span}(f(S))^G$, while computing a basis of W consisting of elements of the form $f(x)$, with $x \in G$. Since G is abelian, $f(g) = v$ implies $f(x)^g = f(x) + v^x - v$ for all $x \in G$. It is a constructive membership to find such a g (if one exists) and then the set of all solutions to the latter equation is Hg where $H = C_G(W)$. Finally, for $h \in H$, $f(hg) = v$ iff $f(h) = v - f(g)$, and solving this is linear algebra (as H acts trivially on W).

6.3 Subspace Stabilizer

The algorithm for Theorem 3.2(7) also uses the paradigm. For example, we point out how invariant subspaces can be utilized. First of all we need the following generalization of the problem:

Given: Subspaces $W_1, W_2 < V$.
Find: $\{g \in G \mid W_1^g = W_2\}$.

Suppose that $W < V$ is G-invariant. Recursively let $Hy = \{g \in G \mid (W_1 \cap W)^g = (W_2 \cap W)\}$ (unless the subanswer is $\emptyset$). Then H stabilizes $W_1 \cap W$. We seek $\{h \in H \mid W_1^h = W_3\}$ where $W_3 = W_2^{y^{-1}}$. Recursively working in V/W (i.e., modulo W) we solve $\overline{W_1}^h = \overline{W_3}$ for Jz (unless $\emptyset$). We still seek $\{j \in J \mid W_1^j = W_4\}$ where $W_4 = W_3^{z^{-1}}$, but we know that J stabilizes both $A = W_1 + W = W_4 + W$ and $B = W_1 \cap W = W_4 \cap W$. For $i = 1, 4$, let $E_i \in \mathrm{Hom}(A/B, A/B)$ be the projection map onto W_i/B ($A/B = W_i/B \oplus W/B$). Then for $j \in J$, $W_1^j = W_4$ iff $E_1^j = E_4$. The latter is solved in §6.2 (viewing the J action on the space $\mathrm{Hom}(A/B, A/B)$).

We omit the solution in the abelian G case (it can be reduced to dealing with idempotents as in the end of last paragraph).

6.4 Miscellany

We briefly comment on some other problems in §3.

It is easy to keep track of a composition series (Theorem 3.2(4)) in running the basic algorithm of §4.

The method for Theorem 3.2(6) goes beyond the paradigm of §6.1 as an additional divide-and-conquer is used on the set. It is analogous to Miller's generalization [Mil] of set-stabilizer to hypergraph stabilizer.

For Theorem 3.2(8), $C_G(x)$ is the stabilizer of the "vector" x in $\mathrm{Hom}(V, V)$.

To find $H \cap K$ (Theorem 3.2(9)), observe that, in the action of $H \times K$ on $V \oplus V$, the centralizer of the linear transformation mapping $(v, w) \mapsto (w, v)$ is $\{(h, h) \mid h \in H \cap K\}$.

Finding Sylow subgroups (Theorem 3.2(10)) follows the basic methods of Kantor [Ka1] (see also [Ma]), given the machinery developed in §4.

Corollary 3.3 involves reduction to subspace stabilizer problems and constructive Frattini arguments ([KL], [Ma]).

7 Open Questions

The ideas of §4 can be reorganized around reductions to finding-irreducible-subspaces and finding-discrete-logs (i.e., solving $\alpha^x = \beta$ in finite fields). We ask whether such a reduction can be made for other classes of matrix groups. For arbitrary matrix groups?

From another point of view, we ask whether membership-testing in matrix groups is polynomial in input+$\mu(G)$. Considering the result of [BBR], this would put membership-testing for finite matrix groups over algebraic number fields into polynomial time. (Finiteness of G is essential. Babai [Bab] has observed that, as a consequence of a result of Mihailova [Mih], testing membership in 4×4 integral matrix groups is undecidable.)

Acknowledgements

The author is indebted to W.M. Kantor and C.R.B. Wright for helpful discussions on these topics.

References

[At] M.D. Atkinson, ed., Computational Group Theory, Academic Press, 1984.

[Bab] L. Babai, *Trading group theory for randomness,* Proc. 17th ACM STOC, 1985, 421–429.

[Bac] E. Bach, *Number-theoretic algorithms,* in Annual Review of Computer Science, v.4 1989-1990, Annual Reviews Inc., 119–172.

[BBR] L. Babai, R. Beals, and D. Rockmore *Deciding finiteness of matrix groups in deterministic polynomial time,* Tech Rep, U. Chicago, 1992.

[BCFSL] L. Babai, G. Cooperman, L. Finkelstein, E. Luks and Á. Seress *Fast Monte Carlo algorithms for permutation groups,* 23rd ACM STOC, 1991, 90–100.

[BLS] L. Babai, E.M. Luks and Á. Seress, *Permutation groups in NC,* Proc. 19th ACM STOC, 1987, 409–420.

[BS] L. Babai and E. Szemerédi, *On the complexity of matrix group problems,* Proc. 24th IEEE FOCS, 1984, 229–240.

[Bu] G. Butler, *The Schreier algorithm for matrix groups,* in Proc. 1976 ACM Symp. on Symbolic and Algebraic Comp., 167–170.

[Ca] J.J. Cannon, *An introduction to the group theory language Cayley,* in Computational Group Theory (ed. M.D. Atkinson), Academic Press 1984, 145–183.

[FHL] M.L. Furst, J. Hopcroft and E.M. Luks, *Polynomial time algorithms for permutation groups,* Proc. 21th IEEE FOCS, 1980, 36–41.

[Ha] M. Hall, Jr., The Theory of Groups, Macmillan, New York 1959.

[Ka1] W.M. Kantor, *Sylow's theorem in polynomial time,* J. Comp. Syst. Sci. 30 (1985) 359-394.

[Ka2] W.M. Kantor, *Finding Sylow normalizers in polynomial time* J. Algorithms 11 (1990), 523–563.

[KL] W.M. Kantor and E.M. Luks, *Computing in quotient groups,* 22nd ACM STOC, 1990, 524–534.

[Le] J. Leech, ed., Computational Problems in Abstract Algebra, Pergamon, NY, 1970.

[Lu1] E.M. Luks, *Isomorphism of graphs of bounded valence can be tested in polynomial time,* J. Comp. Syst. Sci. 25 (1982), 42–65.

[Lu2] E.M. Luks, *Parallel algorithms for permutation groups and graph isomorphism,* Proc. 27th IEEE FOCS 1986, 292–302.

[LM] E.M. Luks and P. McKenzie, *Parallel algorithms for solvable permutation groups,* J. Comp. Syst. Sci. 37 (1988), 39–62.

[Ma] P.D. Mark, *Sylow's theorem and parallel computation,* Doctoral dissertation, CIS, U.Oregon,1992.

[Mih] K.A. Mihailova, *The occurrence problem for direct products of group,* Mat. Sb. (N.S.) 70(112) (1966), 241–251.

[Mil] G.L. Miller, *Isomorphism of graphs which are pairwise k-separable,* Inform. and Control 56 (1983), 21–33.

[Pá] P. Pálfy, *A polynomial bound on the orders of primitive solvable groups,* J. Algebra, 78 (1982), 127–137.

[Ró] L. Rónyai, *Computing the structure of finite algebras,* J. Symbolic Computation 9 (1990), 355–373.

[Sc] M. Schönert et al, GAP: Groups, Algorithms and Programming, Aachen, 1992.

[Si] C.C. Sims, *Some group-theoretic algorithms,* Springer Lect. Notes in Math. 697 (1978), 108–124.

[Su] D.A. Suprunenko, Matrix Groups, AMS, 1976.

Fast Algorithms For Matrix Normal Forms

Mark Giesbrecht
Department of Computer Science
University of Toronto
Toronto, Canada, M5S 1A4
email: mwg@cs.utoronto.ca

Abstract

A Las Vegas type probabilistic algorithm is presented for computing the Frobenius normal form of an $n \times n$ matrix T over any field K. The algorithm requires $O\tilde{~}(\mathrm{MM}(n)) = \mathrm{MM}(n) \cdot (\log n)^{O(1)}$ operations in K, where $O(\mathrm{MM}(n))$ operations in K are sufficient to multiply two $n \times n$ matrices over K. This nearly matches the lower bound of $\Omega(\mathrm{MM}(n))$ operations in K for this problem, and improves on the $O(n^4)$ operations in K required by the previously best known algorithm. We apply our algorithm to evaluate a polynomial $g \in \mathsf{K}[x]$ at T with $O\tilde{~}(\mathrm{MM}(n))$ operations in K when $\deg g \leq n^2$. This nearly matches our lower bound of $\Omega(\mathrm{MM}(n))$ operations in K when $\deg g \geq 2$. Other applications include algorithms for computing the minimal polynomial of a matrix, the rational Jordan form of a matrix, for testing whether two matrices are similar, and for matrix powering, which are substantially faster than those previously known.

1 Introduction

Computing a canonical or normal form of an $n \times n$ matrix T over a field K is a classical mathematical problem with many practical applications. It is well known that any $T \in \mathsf{K}^{n \times n}$ is similar to a unique

$$S = \begin{pmatrix} C_{f_1} & & & 0 \\ & C_{f_2} & & \\ & & \ddots & \\ 0 & & & C_{f_k} \end{pmatrix} \in \mathsf{K}^{n \times n}, \qquad (1.1)$$

in block diagonal form, where each C_{f_i} is the companion matrix of some monic $f_i \in \mathsf{K}[x]$ for $1 \leq i \leq k$, and $f_i \mid f_{i-1}$ for $2 \leq i \leq k$. That is, there exists an invertible $U \in \mathsf{K}^{n \times n}$ such that $S = U^{-1}TU$. Recall that the companion matrix C_g of a monic $g = \sum_{0 \leq j \leq r} b_i x^i \in \mathsf{K}[x]$ has the form

$$C_g = \begin{pmatrix} 0 & & & -b_0 \\ 1 & \ddots & 0 & -b_1 \\ & \ddots & 0 & \vdots \\ 0 & & 1 & -b_{r-1} \end{pmatrix} \in \mathsf{K}^{r \times r}.$$

A matrix S with the above properties, called the *Frobenius form* of T, always exists and is unique and *rational*, i.e., it remains unique even if the entries of T are allowed to lie in an algebraic closure of K. The polynomials $f_1, \ldots, f_k \in \mathsf{K}[x]$ are the *invariant factors* of T, and the first of these, f_1, is T's minimal polynomial. We sometimes write $\mathrm{diag}(C_{f_1}, \ldots, C_{f_k})$ to denote the block diagonal matrix with companion blocks $C_{f_1}, \ldots, C_{f_k}$ along the diagonal.

Before discussing the complexity of our algorithms, we introduce some notation. Over any field E, we assume that $O(\mathrm{MM}(n))$ operations in E are sufficient to multiply two $n \times n$ matrices with entries in E. Using the standard matrix multiplication algorithm gives $\mathrm{MM}(n) = n^3$, while the current asymptotically best method, due to Coppersmith & Winograd (1990), yields $\mathrm{MM}(n) = n^{2.376}$. For convenience we assume throughout this paper that $\mathrm{MM}(n) = \Omega(n^{2+\epsilon})$ for some $\epsilon > 0$. We assume also that $O(\mathrm{M}(n))$ operations in E are sufficient to multiply two polynomials in $\mathsf{E}[x]$ of degree at most n. The usual polynomial multiplication algorithm gives $\mathrm{M}(n) = n^2$, but we can let $\mathrm{M}(n) = n \log n \log\log n$ with the algorithms of Schönhage & Strassen (1971) and Schönhage (1977). In summarizing results, we occasionally use "soft-O" notation: for $f, g: \mathbb{R}_{>0} \to \mathbb{R}_{>0}$, $f = O\tilde{~}(g)$ if and only if there exists a constant $k \geq 0$ such that $f = O(g \cdot (\log g)^k)$.

0-8186-2900-2/92 $3.00 © 1992 IEEE

In Sections 2 through 5 we develop a probabilistic algorithm which requires $O(\mathrm{MM}(n)\log n + n\mathrm{M}(n))$ or $O\tilde{~}(\mathrm{MM}(n))$ operations in K to compute $S, U \in \mathsf{K}^{n\times n}$ as above. This algorithm is of the Las Vegas type — with probability at least 1/4 it returns the correct answer, otherwise it reports failure. An incorrect answer is *never* returned. Also, it only works as stated when $\#\mathsf{K} \geq n^2$. When $q = \#\mathsf{K} < n^2$ we embed K in a field F, of algebraic degree $O(\log n)$ over K, which does possess n^2 elements. In this case, the Frobenius form of T still lies in $\mathsf{K}^{n\times n}$ because it is rational, but $U \in \mathsf{F}^{n\times n}$ may have entries in $\mathsf{F}\backslash\mathsf{K}$. The running time of our algorithms are multiplied by a small power of $\log_q n$ when $q < n^2$. Ozello's (1987) algorithm, which requires $O(n^4)$ operations in K to find the Frobenius form S of any $T \in \mathsf{K}^{n\times n}$, is the fastest previously known algorithm for finding the Frobenius form of a matrix (see also Howell (1973), Kannan & Bachem (1979), Lüneburg (1987), and Kaltofen *et al.* (1986, 1987)). Our algorithm is nearly optimal in that finding the Frobenius form of a matrix is at least as hard as multiplying matrices. Specifically, if we can find the Frobenius form of T, then we can find the characteristic polynomial $f \in \mathsf{K}[x]$ of T with $O(n^2)$ additional operations in K (f is the product of T's invariant factors). The determinant of T is the constant coefficient of f, and is shown by Baur & Strassen (1982) to require $\Omega(\mathrm{MM}(n))$ operations in F to compute, whence computing the Frobenius form of T requires $\Omega(\mathrm{MM}(n))$ operations in F.

The Frobenius form is of great help when evaluating a polynomial $g \in \mathsf{K}[x]$ at a matrix $T \in \mathsf{K}^{n\times n}$, allowing us to take advantage of faster polynomial, as opposed to matrix, arithmetic. In Section 6 we give a Las Vegas algorithm which, for any $g \in \mathsf{K}[x]$ of degree at most n, evaluates $g(T) \in \mathsf{K}^{n\times n}$ with $O(\mathrm{MM}(n)\log n + n\mathrm{M}(n))$ operations in K. Using fast polynomial multiplication algorithms, $g(T)$ can be computed with $O\tilde{~}(\mathrm{MM}(n))$ operations in K. The best previously known method of Paterson & Stockmeyer (1973) requires $O(n^3 + \mathrm{MM}(n)\sqrt{n})$ operations in K. Our result nearly matches a lower bound of $\Omega(\mathrm{MM}(n))$ operations in K (for non-linear g) which we also prove in Section 6. More generally, we show how to evaluate a polynomial of degree r at a matrix in $\mathsf{K}^{n\times n}$ with $O(\mathrm{MM}(n)\log n + n\mathrm{M}(n) + \mathrm{M}(r))$ operations in K. Using asymptotically slower but very practical "school" algorithms for matrix and polynomial arithmetic, our technique affords an algorithm requiring only $O(n^3 + r^2)$ operations in K to evaluate a polynomial of degree r in $\mathsf{K}[x]$ at any $n \times n$ matrix over K. Computing T^ℓ for any $\ell \geq 0$ can also be done more efficiently using the Frobenius form, and requires $O(\mathrm{MM}(n)\log n + (n + \log \ell)\cdot \mathrm{M}(n))$ or $O\tilde{~}(\mathrm{MM}(n) + n\log \ell)$ operations in K.

Other applications of finding the Frobenius form $S \in \mathsf{K}^{n\times n}$ of $T \in \mathsf{K}^{n\times n}$ include finding the minimal polynomial of a matrix and testing matrix similarity. Given S we can immediately determine the minimal polynomial of T and, indeed, all invariant factors of T with $O\tilde{~}(\mathrm{MM}(n))$ operations in K. Our Las Vegas algorithm improves on the Monte Carlo probabilistic algorithm of Wiedemann (1986), which needs $O(n^3)$ operations in K. Frobenius forms also provide a quick way of testing matrix similarity using the fact that two matrices are similar if and only if they have the same Frobenius form. Thus, we can test similarity with $O\tilde{~}(\mathrm{MM}(n))$ operations in K (Las Vegas) using our Frobenius form algorithm. This problem is also considered by Lüneburg (1987), where an algorithm requiring $O(n^4)$ operations in K is presented, and by Kaltofen *et al.* (1986), where an algorithm in the probabilistic, parallel complexity class RNC^2 is given.

In Section 7 we present an algorithm to find the rational Jordan form of a matrix $T \in \mathsf{K}^{n\times n}$. This canonical form is a generalization of the usual Jordan canonical form. Whereas a Jordan form of T exists only if K contains all eigenvalues of T, the rational Jordan form always exists and lies in $\mathsf{K}^{n\times n}$. The eigenvalues of T, found along the diagonal of the usual Jordan form, are replaced in the rational Jordan form by the companion matrices of their minimal polynomials in $\mathsf{K}[x]$. We present a reduction from the problem of finding the rational Jordan form $Q \in \mathsf{K}^{n\times n}$ of T to that of factoring completely a single polynomial in $\mathsf{K}[x]$ of degree at most n; specifically, we must factor the minimal polynomial $f_1 \in \mathsf{K}[x]$ of T, which is determined from the Frobenius form of T. Our reduction requires $O\tilde{~}(\mathrm{MM}(n))$ operations in K. Using Berlekamp's (1970) polynomial factoring algorithm to factor f_1 when K is a finite field of size q yields a Las Vegas algorithm to find the rational Jordan form of any $T \in \mathsf{K}^{n\times n}$ with $O\tilde{~}(\mathrm{MM}(n) + n\log q)$ operations in K.

2 Modular Cyclic Decompositions

The Frobenius normal form of the matrix $T \in \mathsf{K}^{n\times n}$ corresponds to a decomposition of the vector space $V = \mathsf{K}^{n\times 1}$, called the *cyclic decomposition* of V with respect to T. This is best described by viewing V as a $\mathsf{K}[x]$-module as follows. Any $g = \sum_{0\leq i\leq r} b_i x^i \in \mathsf{K}[x]$ acts on V as the linear map $\sum_{0\leq i\leq r} b_i T^i \in \mathsf{K}^{n\times n}$.

This action defines the $\mathsf{K}[x]$-module structure, and if $v \in V$, we write $f \circ v = f(T)v \in V$. An important rôle is played in this theory by polynomials which annihilate (i.e., map to $0 \in V$) vectors and subspaces of V. For any $v \in V$, define the *annihilator* $\mathrm{Ann}(T;v) \subseteq \mathsf{K}[x]$ of V as the ideal in $\mathsf{K}[x]$ of all $f \in \mathsf{K}[x]$ such that $f \circ v = 0$. Since $\mathsf{K}[x]$ is a principal ideal domain, $\mathrm{Ann}(T;v)$ is generated by a unique monic polynomial in $\mathsf{K}[x]$, the *minimal polynomial* $\min(T;v) \in \mathsf{K}[x]$ of the vector $v \in V$. The subspace $\mathrm{Orb}(T;v) \subseteq V$ spanned by $v, Tv, T^2v, \ldots \in V$ is the *cyclic subspace* of V generated by v. $\mathrm{Orb}(T;v)$ is T-invariant, that is, $Tw \in \mathrm{Orb}(T;v)$ for all $w \in \mathrm{Orb}(T;v)$, and $\dim \mathrm{Orb}(T;w) = \deg(\min(T;v))$. For any subspace $W \subseteq V$, the set of polynomials $\mathrm{Ann}(T;W) \subseteq \mathsf{K}[x]$ which annihilate *every* vector in W is also an ideal in $\mathsf{K}[x]$, called the *annihilator* of W. As an ideal, it too is generated by a unique monic polynomial, the *minimal polynomial* $\min(T;W) \in \mathsf{K}[x]$ of T on W.

The *Cyclic Decomposition Theorem* (see Hoffman & Kunze (1971), Section 7.2, Theorem 3) states that there exist vectors $v_1, v_2, \ldots, v_k \in V$ such that

$$V = \mathrm{Orb}(T;v_1) \oplus \mathrm{Orb}(T;v_2) \oplus \cdots \oplus \mathrm{Orb}(T;v_k),$$

where $\min(T;v_i) = f_i$ is the ith invariant factor of T, for $1 \le i \le k$. This is a decomposition of V as a direct sum of cyclic T-invariant subspaces. If $\deg f_i = d_i$ for $1 \le i \le k$, then the matrix

$$U = \left[v_1 \,\middle|\, Tv_1 \,\middle|\, \cdots \,\middle|\, T^{d_1-1}v_1 \,\middle|\, \cdots \,\middle|\, v_k \,\middle|\, \cdots \,\middle|\, T^{d_k-1}v_k \right] \in \mathsf{K}^{n\times n} \tag{2.2}$$

has the property that $S = U^{-1}TU$ is in Frobenius normal form. See Gantmacher (1990), Section 7.5, for a proof of this.

Our algorithm for finding the Frobenius normal form S of a matrix $T \in \mathsf{K}^{n\times n}$ proceeds by constructing the matrix U as in (2.2), and then computing $S = U^{-1}TU$. To do this we must somehow find the invariant factors $f_1, \ldots, f_k \in \mathsf{K}[x]$ and an associated set of vectors $v_1, \ldots, v_k \in V$ generating the cyclic components. Unfortunately, such vectors are very rare, and the approach of choosing them randomly fails miserably. Howell (1973), Ozello (1987), and Lüneburg (1987) construct them deterministically, but using more time than we allow ourselves. Our approach is to first choose randomly a list of vectors $w_1, \ldots, w_k \in V$. With high probability these generate a "modular cyclic decomposition" of V, from which the invariant factors and the Frobenius form S of T can be determined. The vectors $w_1, \ldots, w_k$ are then "purified" to obtain vectors $v_1, \ldots, v_k$ generating the components of the cyclic decomposition. Our construction follows approximately the geometric proof of the Cyclic Decomposition Theorem by Gantmacher (1935). See also Hoffman & Kunze (1971), Section 7.2, and Gantmacher (1990), Chapter 7.

A weaker form of the cyclic decomposition theorem can be stated in terms of modular T-invariant vector spaces. If W is a T-invariant subspace of V then the space V/W, or V modulo W, is a K-vector space of dimension $\dim V - \dim W$. For $w_1, w_2 \in V$ we denote by $w_1 + W$ and $w_2 + W$ the images of w_1 and w_2 in V/W respectively, and say $w_1 \equiv w_2 \bmod W$ when $w_1 - w_2 \in W$. Since W is T-invariant, V/W has a $\mathsf{K}[x]$-module structure induced by the action of $\mathsf{K}[x]$ on V. Let $T_W: V/W \to V/W$ be T reduced modulo W, carrying $v + W$ to $Tv + W$ for any $v \in V$. Then V/W is a $\mathsf{K}[x]$-module, where $f \in \mathsf{K}[x]$ acts as $f(T_W): V/W \to V/W$, and we write $f \circ (v + W) = f(T_W)(v + W) = f(T)v + W$. Thus, $\min(T_W; v + W) \in \mathsf{K}[x]$ is the minimal polynomial of $v+W \in V/W$ in $\mathsf{K}[x]$, that is, the monic $f \in \mathsf{K}[x]\setminus\{0\}$ of minimal degree such that $f \circ (v + W) \equiv 0 \bmod W$. For the next fact see Gantmacher (1990), Section 7.4.

Fact 2.1 (Modular Cyclic Decomposition). *For $i \ge 1$ let $w_i \in V$ and define $V_i = \mathrm{Orb}(T;w_1) + \cdots + \mathrm{Orb}(T;w_i)$ and $T_i: V/V_i \to V/V_i$ as T reduced modulo V_i (with $V_0 = \{0\}$ and $T_0 = T$). Assume that k is the smallest integer such that $V_k = V$, and that for $1 \le i \le k$ we have $\min(T_{i-1}; w_i + V_{i-1}) = \min(T_{i-1}; V/V_{i-1})$. Then $\min(T_{i-1}; w_i + V_{i-1}) = f_i$, the ith invariant factor of T on V, for $1 \le i \le k$.*

If $w_1, \ldots, w_k$ are as in the above fact, then we say that they generate a *modular cyclic basis*

$$w_1, Tw_1, \ldots, T^{d_1-1}w_1, \ldots, w_k, Tw_k, \ldots, T^{d_k-1}w_k$$

for V. Of course the summation $V = \mathrm{Orb}(T;w_1) + \cdots + \mathrm{Orb}(T;w_k)$ in Fact 2.1 is not direct, and once we have found $w_1, \ldots, w_k$, we must "purify" them to get a direct sum. This is accomplished in Section 4.

Our approach to finding $w_1, \ldots, w_k \in V$ is to choose them randomly. This only works when $\#\mathsf{K} \ge n^2$. When $\#\mathsf{K} < n^2$, we construct an algebraic extension field F of K containing n^2 elements. This is discussed in Section 5. For the remainder of this section, assume that $\#\mathsf{K} \ge n^2$.

Lemma 2.2. *Let W be any vector space of dimension $m \le n$ over K with basis $u_1, \ldots, u_m \in W$ and $T: W \to W$ a K-linear map. Let L be a subset of K containing* *at least n^2 elements. Then*

$$\operatorname*{Prob}_{(a_1,\ldots,a_m)\in L^m}\left\{\min(T;\sum_{1\le i\le m} a_i u_i) = \min(T;W)\right\}$$
$$\ge 1 - \frac{1}{n}.$$

Proof. Suppose $y_1, \ldots, y_\ell \in W$ are such that

$$W = \mathrm{Orb}(T;y_1) \oplus \mathrm{Orb}(T;y_2) \oplus \cdots \oplus \mathrm{Orb}(T;y_\ell)$$

is the cyclic decomposition of W with respect to T, where T has ℓ invariant factors on W, $g_i = \min(T;y_i) \in \mathsf{K}[x]$ is the ith invariant factor, and $g_i \mid g_{i-1}$ for $2 \le i \le \ell$. Only the component of the randomly chosen vector $\Lambda = \sum_{1\le i\le m} a_i u_i$ in $\mathrm{Orb}(T;y_1)$ need be considered. In particular, if the projection of each basis element u_i (for $1 \le i \le m$) into $\mathrm{Orb}(T;y_1)$ is $h_i \circ y_1$ for some $h_i \in \mathsf{K}[x]$, then the projection of Λ into $\mathrm{Orb}(T;y_1)$ is $\Lambda_1 = \sum_{1\le i\le m} a_i h_i \circ y_1$. Let $T_1 \colon \mathrm{Orb}(T;y_1) \to \mathrm{Orb}(T;y_1)$ be the restriction of T to $\mathrm{Orb}(T;y_1)$. Certainly $\min(T;\Lambda) = g_1$ when $\min(T_1;\Lambda_1) = g_1$. When is $\min(T_1;\Lambda_1) = g_1$? If $h = \sum_{1\le i\le m} a_i h_i$, so that $\Lambda_1 = h \circ y_1$, then $g_1 \circ \Lambda_1 = (g_1 h) \circ y_1 = 0$, and g_1 is the minimal polynomial of Λ_1 if only if $\gcd(g_1, h) = 1$.

To bound the probability that, for randomly chosen $a_1, \ldots, a_m \in L$, we have $\gcd(\sum_{1\le i\le m} a_i h_i, g_1) = 1$, consider the polynomial $\rho = \sum_{1\le i\le m} x_i h_i \in \mathsf{K}[x_1, \ldots, x_m][x]$, in the indeterminates $x_1, \ldots, x_m, x$. To prove the theorem it is sufficient to show that

$$\operatorname*{Prob}_{(a_1,\ldots,a_m)\in L^m}\left\{\gcd(\rho(a_1,\ldots,a_m)(x), g_1(x)) = 1\right\}$$
$$\ge 1 - \frac{1}{n}.$$

This is accomplished with the aid of resultants (see van der Waerden (1970), Section 5.8). The resultant of ρ and g_1, considered as polynomials in x with coefficients in the integral domain $\mathsf{K}[x_1, \ldots, x_m]$ is a polynomial $R \in \mathsf{K}[x_1, \ldots, x_m]$ of degree at most m. Moreover, $\gcd(\rho(a_1, \ldots, a_m)(x), g_1(x)) = 1$ if and only if $R(a_1, \ldots, a_m) \ne 0$. The polynomial R is non-zero, since the projection of y_1 into $\mathrm{Orb}(T;y_1)$ is y_1 itself, and hence has minimal polynomial g_1. This follows since, if $y_1 = \sum_{1\le j\le m} b_j u_j$ for some $b_1, \ldots, b_m \in \mathsf{K}$, then $\sum_{1\le j\le m} b_j h_j = 1$, and $R(b_1, \ldots, b_m) \ne 0$. Using Corollary 1 of Schwartz (1980), we find that

$$\operatorname*{Prob}_{(a_1,\ldots,a_m)\in L^m}\left\{R(a_1,\ldots,a_m) \ne 0\right\} \ge 1 - \frac{m}{\#L}$$
$$\ge 1 - \frac{1}{n}.$$

□

A modular cyclic decomposition is now constructed by simply choosing the generating vectors "randomly" from V. Actually, since we do not know the number k of invariant factors beforehand, we choose $w_1, \ldots, w_n \in V$ and consider the probability that the first k of these generate V in the desired manner.

Theorem 2.3. *Let L be a subset of K containing at least n^2 elements. For $1 \le i \le n$, randomly choose $w_i \in L^{n\times 1} \subseteq V$ and define $V_i = \mathrm{Orb}(T;w_1) + \cdots + \mathrm{Orb}(T;w_i)$ and $T_i \colon V/V_i \to V/V_i$ as T reduced modulo V_i (with $V_0 = \{0\}$ and $T_0 = T$). With probability at least $1/4$, for all $1 \le i \le k$ (where k is the number of invariant factors of T) the ith invariant factor f_i of T satisfies $f_i = \min(T_{i-1}; w_i + V_{i-1}) = \min(T_i; V/V_{i-1})$.*

Proof. At each stage i, the probability that $\min(T_{i-1}; w_i + V_{i-1}) = \min(T_{i-1}; V/V_{i-1})$ is at least $1 - 1/n$ by Lemma 2.2, since $\dim V/V_{i-1} \le n$. The number of components k in the cyclic decomposition is certainly at most n, whence

$$\prod_{1\le i\le k} \operatorname*{Prob}_{w_i\in L^n}\left\{\min(T_{i-1}; w_i + V_{i-1}) = \min(T_{i-1}; V/V_{i-1})\right\}$$
$$\ge \left(1 - \frac{1}{n}\right)^n \ge \frac{1}{4}.$$

If all the w_i are chosen correctly we know from Fact 2.1 that $f_i = \min(T_{i-1}; w_i + V_{i-1})$ for $1 \le i \le k$. □

3 Computing the Invariant Factors

Assume now that we are given $w_1, \ldots, w_n \in V$, the first k of which generate a modular cyclic basis for V, and let V_i, T_i be as in Fact 2.1 for $0 \le i \le k$. How do we find k and the invariant factors $f_1, \ldots, f_k$? We adapt an algorithm of Keller-Gehrig (1985) to accomplish this with $O(\mathrm{MM}(n)\log n)$ operations in K.

Fact 3.1 (Keller-Gehrig 1985). *Let $T \in \mathsf{K}^{n\times n}$ and $u_1, \ldots, u_n \in V$. Matrices $H_i \in \mathsf{K}^{n\times d_i}$ for $1 \le i \le n$ with the following properties can be computed with $O(\mathrm{MM}(n)\log n)$ operations in K:*

(i) $\sum_{1\le i\le n} d_i = n$, where $d_i \in \mathbb{N}$ may equal 0 for notational convenience;

(ii) for $1 \le i \le n$, $H_i = [u_i | T u_i | \cdots | T^{d_i - 1} u_i]$ if $d_i > 0$;

(iii) the columns of $H_1, \ldots, H_i$ form a basis of the $\mathsf{K}[x]$-module generated by $u_1, \ldots, u_i$, for $1 \le i \le n$ (that is, for $\mathrm{Orb}(T;u_1) + \cdots + \mathrm{Orb}(T;u_i)$).

Applying Fact 3.1 to the vectors $w_1, \ldots, w_n$ yields k, bases for $V_1, \ldots, V_k$, and the degrees of the invariant factors $f_1, \ldots, f_k$. That is, the columns of $H_1, \ldots, H_i$ form a basis for $V_i = \mathrm{Orb}(T; w_1) + \cdots + \mathrm{Orb}(T; w_i)$ and $\deg f_i = d_i$ for $1 \le i \le k$. We know $d_i = 0$ for $k < i \le n$ since $w_1, \ldots, w_k$ are assumed to generate V as a $\mathsf{K}[x]$-module.

Let $H = [H_1 | H_2 | \cdots | H_k] \in \mathsf{K}^{n \times n}$, which we call a *modular cyclic transition matrix* for T. Combining Fact 3.1 with Theorem 2.3 gives a probabilistic algorithm to find a modular cyclic transition matrix, which is correct with probability at least 1/4.

Theorem 3.2. *Let $\#\mathsf{K} \ge n^2$. Given $T \in \mathsf{K}^{n\times n}$, we can find $w_1, \ldots, w_k \in V$ and matrices $H_i \in \mathsf{K}^{n \times d_i}$ for $1 \le i \le k$ defined as follows:*

(i) $\sum_{1 \le i \le k} d_i = n$ *with* $d_i > 0$ *for* $1 \le i \le k$,

(ii) $H_i = [w_i | \cdots | T^{d_i - 1} w_i]$ *for* $1 \le i \le k$,

(iii) The columns of $H_1, \ldots, H_i$ *form a basis for* $V_i = \mathrm{Orb}(T; w_1) + \cdots + \mathrm{Orb}(T; w_i)$,

(iv) $f_i = \min(T \bmod V_{i-1}; w_i + V_{i-1}) = \min(T \bmod V_{i-1}; V/V_{i-1})$ *for* $1 \le i \le k$.

The algorithm is probabilistic, and returns the correct answer with probability at least 1/4 (it may produce an incorrect answer). It requires $O(\mathrm{MM}(n) \log n)$ operations in K.

If $w_1, \ldots, w_k$ are chosen correctly the columns of H are a modular cyclic basis for V, and H determines a change of basis on V (to this modular cyclic basis), under which T has the form

$G = H^{-1} T H =$

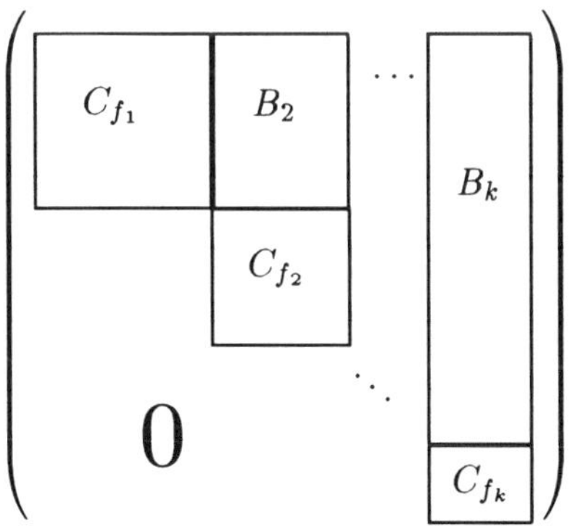

where $C_{f_i} \in \mathsf{K}^{d_i \times d_i}$ is the companion matrix of f_i, the ith invariant factor of T, for $1 \le i \le k$ (see Keller-Gehrig (1985), Section 5). Each matrix $B_i \in \mathsf{K}^{t_i \times d_i}$, where $t_i = \sum_{1 \le j < i} d_j$, is zero except for its last column; suppose this last column is

$$\vec{b}_i = (b_{i,1,0}, \ldots, b_{i,1,d_1-1}, \ldots, b_{i,i-1,0}, \ldots, b_{i,i-1,d_{i-1}-1})^{\mathrm{T}} \in \mathsf{K}^{n\times 1},$$

where $b_{ij\ell} \in \mathsf{K}$ for $2 \le i \le k$, $1 \le j < i$, and $0 \le \ell < d_j$. Under the change of basis induced by H, the vector $e_{t_i+j+1} \in \mathsf{K}^{n\times 1}$ (the column vector of all zeros except for a one in the $(t_i + j + 1)$'st row) in the basis given by the columns of H is the image of $T^j w_i$ in the standard basis for V.

The column $\vec{b}_i$ in B_i and the last column $(-a_{i,0}, \ldots, -a_{i,d_i-1})^{\mathrm{T}} \in \mathsf{K}^{d_i \times 1}$ of C_{f_i} give the dependency of $T^{d_i} w_i$ on $T^\ell w_j$ for $1 \le j \le i$ and $0 \le \ell < d_i$:

$$\begin{aligned} G e_{t_i + d_i} &= H^{-1} T^{d_i} w_i \\ &= H^{-1} \sum_{0 \le \ell < d_i} (-a_{i\ell}) T^\ell w_i \\ &\quad + H^{-1} \sum_{1 \le j < i} \sum_{0 \le \ell < d_j} c_{ij\ell} T^\ell w_j. \end{aligned}$$

whence

$$f_i \circ w_i = \sum_{1 \le j < i} g_{ij} \circ w_j,$$

where $f_i = \sum_{0 \le \ell < d_i} a_{i\ell} x^\ell$, and $g_{ij} = \sum_{0 \le \ell < d_j} c_{ij\ell} x^\ell$ with $a_{i\ell}, c_{ij\ell} \in \mathsf{K}$ for $1 \le j < i$ and $1 \le i \le k$. Thus $f_i \circ w_i \in V_{i-1}$, and since it has minimal degree, is the ith invariant factor of T on V. Note that by construction, $\sum_{1 \le j < i} \deg g_{ij} \le n$ for all $1 \le i \le k$, a fact which is required in the next section.

Theorem 3.3. *Let $w_1, \ldots, w_n \in V$ be a basis for V such that $w_1, \ldots, w_k$ generate a modular cyclic basis for V, with $f_i = \min(T_{i-1}; w_i + V_{i-1})$ the ith invariant factor of T, for $1 \le i \le k$ and V_i, T_i as in Fact 2.1. Suppose also that we have computed a modular cyclic transition matrix for T. Then we can determine $k \in \mathbb{N}$, $f_1, \ldots, f_k \in \mathsf{K}[x]$, and $g_{ij} \in \mathsf{K}[x]$ for $1 \le j < i \le k$ such that $f_i \circ w_i = \sum_{1 \le j < i} g_{ij} \circ w_j$, with $O(\mathrm{MM}(n))$ operations in K. Furthermore, $\sum_{1 \le j < i} \deg g_{ij} \le n$ for all $1 \le i \le k$.*

Combining this theorem with Theorem 3.2 gives a Monte Carlo type probabilistic algorithm for computing the Frobenius form of T (a Monte Carlo type probabilistic algorithm is one which produces the correct answer with constant positive probability, but may produce an incorrect answer). Simply apply Theorem 3.2 to find a modular cyclic transition matrix. With probability at least 1/4 we get the invariant factors $f_1, \ldots, f_k \in \mathsf{K}[x]$ of T, from which we can construct the Frobenius form S of T. Of course, with positive probability we get an erroneous Frobenius form, and since we do not get an invertible matrix $U \in \mathsf{K}^{n\times n}$ such that $S = U^{-1} T U$ from this procedure, we have no way of verifying that S is correct. This problem is addressed in the next section.

4 Purifying a Modular Decomposition

Once again, let $w_1, \ldots, w_k \in V$ generate a modular cyclic basis for V, where V_i and T_i are as in Fact 2.1 for $0 \le i \le n$, and $f_i = \min(T_{i-1}; w_i + V_{i-1})$ is the ith invariant factor of T on V for $1 \le i \le k$. Furthermore, assume that $f_i \circ w_i = \sum_{1 \le j < i} g_{ij} \circ w_j$ for some $g_{ij} \in \mathsf{K}[x]$ for all $1 \le j < i \le k$. This information can all be computed with the algorithm of the previous section (see Theorem 3.3), along with the matrix H defined there whose columns give a modular decomposition basis for V. In this section vectors $v_1, \ldots, v_k \in V$ are constructed such that

$$V = \mathrm{Orb}(T; v_1) \oplus \mathrm{Orb}(T; v_2) \oplus \cdots \oplus \mathrm{Orb}(T; v_k),$$

and $f_i = \min(T; v_i)$, for $1 \le i \le k$. The key fact required is from Hoffman & Kunze (1971), Section 7.2, Theorem 3, Step 2:

Fact 4.1. *If $w_i \in V$, and $f_i, g_{ij} \in \mathsf{K}[x]$ are as above, then $f_i \,|\, g_{ij}$ for $1 \le j < i \le k$.*

Applying Fact 4.1, assume that $g_{ij} = f_i h_{ij}$ for some $h_{ij} \in \mathsf{K}[x]$, for all $1 \le j < i \le k$. We claim that the vectors $v_i = w_i - \sum_{1 \le j < i} h_{ij} \circ w_j \in V$, for $1 \le i \le k$ are the ones desired.

Theorem 4.2. *Let $w_1, \ldots, w_k \in V$ and $V_i = \mathrm{Orb}(T; w_1) + \cdots + \mathrm{Orb}(T; w_i)$ such that $V_k = V$ and $V_{k-1} \ne V$. Also, let $f_i = \min(T_{i-1}; w_i + V_{i-1})$ such that $f_i \circ w_i = \sum_{1 \le j < i} g_{ij} \circ w_j$ and $g_{ij} = f_i h_{ij}$ for $g_{ij}, h_{ij} \in \mathsf{K}[x]$ with $1 \le j < i \le k$. If $v_i = w_i - \sum_{0 \le j < i} h_{ij} \circ w_j$, then for $1 \le i \le k$,*

(i) $f_i = \min(T; v_i)$,

(ii) $V_i = \mathrm{Orb}(T; v_1) \oplus \mathrm{Orb}(T; v_2) \oplus \cdots \oplus \mathrm{Orb}(T; v_i)$.

Proof. To show (i), note that for any i with $1 \le i \le k$ we have

$$\begin{aligned} f_i \circ v_i &= f_i \circ w_i - f_i \circ \left(\sum_{1 \le j < i} h_{ij} \circ w_j \right) \\ &= f_i \circ w_i - \sum_{1 \le j < i} g_{ij} \circ w_j = 0. \end{aligned}$$

Furthermore, since f_i is the polynomial of least degree such that $f_i \circ w_i \in V_{i-1}$, it follows that $f_i = \min(T; v_i)$.

To show (ii), we must show that $V_{i-1} \cap \mathrm{Orb}(T; v_i) = \{0\}$, or equivalently that if $g \circ v_i \in V_{i-1}$ then $g \circ v_i = 0$ for any $g \in \mathsf{K}[x]$. Suppose $g \circ v_i \in V_{i-1}$ for some polynomial $g \in \mathsf{K}[x]$. This is true only if $g \circ w_i \in V_{i-1}$, since $v_i \equiv w_i \bmod V_{i-1}$. But $f_i = \min(T_{i-1}; w_i + V_{i-1})$, so $f_i \,|\, g$, and thus $g \circ v_i = 0$. Therefore $V_{i-1} \cap \mathrm{Orb}(T; v_i) = \{0\}$ and $V_i = V_{i-1} \oplus \mathrm{Orb}(T; v_i)$. □

Note that this theorem does not assume that $w_1, \ldots, w_k$ generate a modular cyclic basis for V, only that they generate V as a $\mathsf{K}[x]$-module.

To compute $v_1, \ldots, v_k$, first compute $h_{ij} = g_{ij}/f_i \in \mathsf{K}[x]$ for all $1 \le j < i \le k$. For each $1 \le i \le k$ we note that $\sum_{1 \le j < i} \deg g_{ij} \le n$, so we can compute all g_{ij} for $1 \le j < i$ with $O(\mathsf{M}(n))$ operations in K. The number k of invariant factors is at most n, so all the g_{ij}'s can be found with $O(n\mathsf{M}(n))$ operations in K.

Computing the h_{ij}'s gives a representation of the v_i's in the modular decomposition basis for V given by the columns of H, not in the original (standard) basis for V. To find v_i in the standard basis, recall

$$v_i = w_i - \sum_{1 \le j < i} h_{ij} \circ w_j = w_i - \sum_{1 \le j < i} \sum_{0 \le \ell < d_j} c_{ij\ell} T^\ell w_j.$$

We compute v_i by the matrix-vector product $v_i = H \bar{v}_i \in V$, where

$$\begin{aligned} \bar{v}_i = (\; & -c_{i,1,1}, \ldots, -c_{i,1,d_2-1}, \ldots, \\ & -c_{i,i-1,1}, \ldots, -c_{i,i-1,d_{i-1}}, 1, 0, \ldots, 0)^{\mathrm{T}} \in \mathsf{K}^{n \times 1}. \end{aligned}$$

All of $v_1, \ldots, v_k$ can now be computed by a single matrix product

$$H \cdot [\bar{v}_1 | \cdots | \bar{v}_k] = [v_1 | \cdots | v_k],$$

with $O(\mathsf{MM}(n))$ operations in K.

Theorem 4.3. *Given $w_i \in V$ and $f_i, g_{ij} \in \mathsf{K}[x]$ for $1 \le i \le k$ and $1 \le j < i$ as above, we can compute $v_1, \ldots v_k \in V$ such that*

$$V = \mathrm{Orb}(T; v_1) \oplus \cdots \oplus \mathrm{Orb}(T; v_k)$$

and $f_i = \min(T; v_i)$ with $O(\mathsf{MM}(n) + n\mathsf{M}(n))$ operations in K.

5 Computing the Frobenius Form

The complete algorithm for computing the Frobenius normal form of any $T \in \mathsf{K}^{n \times n}$, where $\#\mathsf{K} \ge n^2$, can now be stated. A modification which works over smaller fields is presented in the sequel.

Algorithm: `FrobeniusForm`

Input: $T \in \mathsf{K}^{n \times n}$, where $\#\mathsf{K} \ge n^2$;

Output: – The Frobenius form $S \in \mathsf{K}^{n \times n}$ of T,
– an invertible $U \in \mathsf{K}^{n \times n}$ such that $S = U^{-1} T U$;

(1) Compute a modular cyclic transition matrix $H = [H_1 | \cdots | H_k] \in \mathsf{K}^{n \times n}$, where $H_i =$

$[w_i|Tw_i|\cdots|T^{d_i-1}w_i] \in \mathsf{K}^{n\times d_i}$ for $1 \le i \le k$, $d_i \in \mathbb{N}$, and the columns of $H_1,\ldots,H_i$ span the $\mathsf{K}[x]$-module generated by the vectors $w_1,\ldots,w_i$ for $1 \le i \le k$; H need not be correct — an erroneous computation is detected in step (2) or (4).

(2) If H is singular then quit, returning "failure";

(3) Compute $f_i, g_{ij} \in \mathsf{K}[x]$ from $G = H^{-1}TH$ such that $f_1 \circ w_1 = 0$ and $f_i \circ w_i = \sum_{1\le j<i} g_{ij} \circ w_j$ for $2 \le i \le k$ and $1 \le j < i$;

(4) If $f_i \nmid f_{i-1}$ for some $2 \le i \le k$, or $f_i \nmid g_{ij}$ for some $1 \le j < i$ and $1 \le i \le k$, then return "failure" and quit;

(5) Compute $h_{ij} = g_{ij}/f_i$ for $1 \le j < i$ and $1 \le i \le k$;

(6) Compute $v_i = w_i - \sum_{1\le j<i} h_{ij} \circ w_j$ for $1 \le i \le k$;

(7) Compute the matrix $U \in \mathsf{K}^{n\times n}$ as in (2.2);

(8) Output $S = \operatorname{diag}(C_{f_1},\ldots,C_{f_k})$, the Frobenius form of T and the transition matrix $U \in \mathsf{K}^{n\times n}$, where C_{f_i} is the companion matrix of f_i for $1 \le i \le k$.

Theorem 5.1. *Let $T \in \mathsf{K}^{n\times n}$ over a field K with at least n^2 elements. With probability at least 1/4,* `FrobeniusForm` *finds the Frobenius form S of T and an invertible $U \in \mathsf{K}^{n\times n}$ with $S = U^{-1}TU$. Otherwise the algorithm reports "failure". In either case $O(\mathrm{MM}(n)\log n + n\mathrm{M}(n))$ operations in K are sufficient.*

Proof. First we prove the correctness of the output. We use Theorem 3.2 to compute a modular cyclic transition matrix H, which is correct with probability at least 1/4. Assume for now that H is computed correctly. By Fact 4.1 we know $f_i \mid g_{ij}$ for $1 \le j < i$ and $1 \le i \le k$, and certainly $f_i \mid f_{i-1}$ for $2 \le i \le k$. Once the tests in step (3) are passed, Theorem 4.2 guarantees that $v_1,\ldots,v_k$ generate the cyclic composition factors of V. Gantmacher (1990), Section 7.5.2, shows that $S = U^{-1}TU$ is in Frobenius normal form.

If H is incorrectly computed, the algorithm reports failure in step (2) or (4). Certainly if H is singular then it is incorrect, and this is detected in step (2). Otherwise, assume that the tests in step (4) are passed, but $w_1,\ldots,w_k$ do not generate a modular cyclic basis. By Theorem 4.2, $V = \mathrm{Orb}(T;v_1) \oplus \cdots \oplus \mathrm{Orb}(T;v_k)$. Let $\ell \ge 1$ be the smallest integer such that $f_\ell \ne \bar{f}_\ell$, where $\bar{f}_\ell$ is the the actual ℓth invariant factor of T on V. In the vector space

$$\bar{V}_\ell = \mathrm{Orb}(T;v_\ell) \oplus \cdots \oplus \mathrm{Orb}(T;v_k) \cong V/V_{\ell-1}$$

there exists a vector $w \in \bar{V}$ with $\min(T_{\ell-1}; w+V_{\ell-1}) = \bar{f}_\ell$ (where $T_{\ell-1}\colon V/V_{\ell-1} \to V/V_{\ell-1}$ is T reduced modulo $V_{\ell-1}$). Since $f_j \mid f_\ell$ for $\ell \le j \le k$, we know $f_\ell = \min(T_{\ell-1}; \bar{V}_\ell) = \bar{f}_\ell$, a contradiction.

By Theorem 3.2, step (1) requires $O(\mathrm{MM}(n)\log n)$ operations in K, while Theorem 3.3 implies steps (2)-(4) require $O(\mathrm{MM}(n))$ operations in K. By Theorem 4.3 steps (5)-(6) require $O(\mathrm{MM}(n))$ operations in K. The matrix U in step (7) can be found using Fact 3.1 with $O(\mathrm{MM}(n)\log n)$ operations in K. □

The algorithm `FrobeniusForm` requires that the field K contain at least n^2 elements. If this is not the case, and $q = \#\mathsf{K} < n^2$, the chances of choosing $w_1,\ldots,w_k$ correctly may be very low. To remedy this we construct an algebraic field extension F of K containing n^2 elements. We then run the algorithm `FrobeniusForm` on $T \in \mathsf{F}^{n\times n}$. By Theorem 5.1 this correctly returns the Frobenius form $S \in \mathsf{F}^{n\times n}$ and an invertible $U \in \mathsf{F}^{n\times n}$ such that $S = U^{-1}TU$, with probability at least 1/4. The Frobenius form of T is a unique rational invariant of T, regardless of the field in which the entries of T are embedded, so $S \in \mathsf{K}^{n\times n}$. The only drawback to this technique, aside from the slightly increased cost of operations in F, is that U may not be in $\mathsf{K}^{n\times n}$

The field F is represented as $\mathsf{K}[x]$ modulo some monic irreducible $\psi \in \mathsf{K}[x]$ of degree $\lceil 2\log_q n\rceil$, which can be found within the allowed time (Shoup, 1990). Elements of K are constant polynomials in this representation, giving a trivial embedding of K into F. Additions and subtractions in F require $O(\log_q n)$ operations in K, while multiplications in F require $O(\mathrm{M}(\log_q n))$ operations in K and divisions in F require $O(\mathrm{M}(\log_q n)\log\log_q n)$ operations in K.

Theorem 5.2. *Let $T \in \mathsf{K}^{n\times n}$, where $q = \#\mathsf{K} < n^2$. There is a Las Vegas type algorithm which computes the Frobenius form $S \in \mathsf{K}^{n\times n}$ of T, and an invertible matrix $U \in \mathsf{F}^{n\times n}$ such that $S = U^{-1}TU$. The field $\mathsf{F} = \mathsf{K}[x]/(\psi)$ is an extension of K, given by an irreducible monic $\psi \in \mathsf{K}[x]$ of degree $\lceil 2\log_q n\rceil$. The algorithm succeeds with probability at least 1/4, and requires $O((\mathrm{MM}(n)\log n + n\mathrm{M}(n))\cdot \mathrm{M}(\log_q n)\log\log_q n)$ or $O\tilde{~}(\mathrm{MM}(n))$ operations in K.*

6 Evaluating polynomials at matrices

Computing the Frobenius form $S \in \mathsf{K}^{n\times n}$ of a matrix $T \in \mathsf{K}^{n\times n}$ allows quick evaluation of $g(T) \in \mathsf{K}^{n\times n}$ for any polynomial $g \in \mathsf{K}[x]$. Informally, it allows us to transform the problem into that of polynomial multiplication, for which faster algorithms are known. The problem of evaluating polynomials at matrices is certainly not new. Paterson & Stockmeyer (1973) give an algorithm to evaluate a polynomial $g \in \mathsf{K}[x]$ at any point in a ring extension $\mathfrak{R}$ of K, which requires $O(\sqrt{r})$ non-scalar multiplications in $\mathfrak{R}$, where $r = \deg g$. They apply their algorithm to evaluate $g(T)$ at any $T \in \mathsf{K}^{n\times n}$ with $O(\mathrm{MM}(n)\sqrt{r} + n^2 r)$ operations in K.

When $\deg g \geq n$, Paterson & Stockmeyer's algorithm can be improved considerably by reducing g modulo a multiple $f \in \mathsf{K}[x]$ of the minimal polynomial of T. For example if $g = Qf + h$ for some $Q, h \in \mathsf{K}[x]$ and $\deg h < \deg g$, then $g(T) = h(T)$ because $f(T) = 0$. Keller-Gehrig (1985) shows how to (deterministically) compute the characteristic polynomial of T with $O(\mathrm{MM}(n)\log n)$ operations in K, making it a natural candidate for our multiple f of the minimal polynomial. This yields a deterministic algorithm for evaluating $g(T)$ with $O(\mathrm{MM}(n)\sqrt{n}+n^3+\mathrm{M}(r))$ operations in K, where $\mathrm{M}(r)$ operations in K are required to reduce g modulo the characteristic polynomial of T.

Our next theorem gives a substantial improvement, especially when r is large, allowing evaluation of $g(T)$ with $O\tilde{~}(\mathrm{MM}(n) + r)$ operations in K. The simple but key observation is that if $S = U^{-1}TU$ is the Frobenius form of T (for some invertible $U \in \mathsf{K}^{n\times n}$), and $S = \mathrm{diag}(C_{f_1}, \ldots, C_{f_k})$ as in (1.1), then

$$g(T) = U\cdot g(S)\cdot U^{-1} = U\cdot \mathrm{diag}(g(C_{f_1}), \ldots, g(C_{f_k}))\cdot U^{-1}.$$

Furthermore, each $g(C_{f_i})$ can be evaluated quickly once $g \bmod f_i$ has been computed, and $g(S)$ can be computed with $O(n^2)$ operations in K when $\deg g \leq n$. The proof of this last fact is left to the reader.

For most of this section, we assume that K is any field with at least n^2 elements. For fields K with fewer than n^2 elements similar results hold with running times multiplied by a small power of $\log_q n$. These results for smaller fields are summarized in Theorem 6.3 below.

Theorem 6.1. *Given $g \in \mathsf{K}[x]$ of degree r and $T \in \mathsf{K}^{n\times n}$, we can compute $g(T) \in \mathsf{K}^{n\times n}$ with a Las Vegas type probabilistic algorithm requiring $O(\mathrm{MM}(n)\log n + n\mathrm{M}(n) + \mathrm{M}(r))$ or $O\tilde{~}(\mathrm{MM}(n) + r)$ operations in K, where $\#\mathsf{K} \geq n^2$.*

Proof. First compute the Frobenius form $S \in \mathsf{K}^{n\times n}$ of T, and an invertible $U \in \mathsf{F}^{n\times n}$ such that $U^{-1}TU = S$. For each invariant factor $f_i \in \mathsf{K}[x]$ of T, determine $g_i \equiv g \bmod f_i$, where $\deg g_i < \deg f_i$, for $1 \leq i \leq k$. This can be done with $O(\mathrm{M}(r) + n\mathrm{M}(n))$ operations in K by first reducing g modulo f_1, since all the other invariant factors divide f_1. Next compute the matrices $g_i(C_{f_i}) = g(C_{f_i})$ for $1 \leq i \leq k$. Now $g(S) = \mathrm{diag}(g(C_{f_1}), \ldots, g(C_{f_k}))$ and $g(T) = Ug(S)U^{-1}$. □

For some applications, such as cryptography, high powers of matrices must be computed. The following theorem gives an efficient method for doing this.

Theorem 6.2. *Given $\ell \geq 0$ and $T \in \mathsf{K}^{n\times n}$, we can compute $T^\ell \in \mathsf{K}^{n\times n}$ with a Las Vegas type probabilistic algorithm requiring $O(\mathrm{MM}(n)\log n + n\mathrm{M}(n) + \mathrm{M}(n)\log \ell)$ or $O\tilde{~}(\mathrm{MM}(n) + n\log \ell)$ operations in K, where K is any field with at least n^2 elements.*

Proof. Compute $g \in \mathsf{K}[x]$ such that $g \equiv x^\ell \bmod f_1$ and $\deg g < \deg f_1 \leq n$ by repeated squaring. Then $g(T) = T^\ell$, and can be evaluated using Theorem 6.1 in the desired time. □

We summarize the corresponding results for small fields below. As in Theorem 5.2 these results are obtained by working in a field extension of K with at least n^2 elements.

Theorem 6.3. *Let K be any field with $q < n^2$ elements, $T, A \in \mathsf{K}^{n\times n}$, and F the smallest extension field of K containing n^2 elements. Las Vegas type probabilistic algorithms exist as follows:*

(i) given $g \in \mathsf{K}[x]$ of degree r we can evaluate $g(T) \in \mathsf{K}^{n\times n}$ with $O((\mathrm{MM}(n)\log n + n\mathrm{M}(n)) \cdot \mathrm{M}(\log_q n)\log\log_q n + \mathrm{M}(r))$ or $O\tilde{~}(\mathrm{MM}(n) + r)$ operations in K;

(ii) given $\ell > 0$, we can find $T^\ell \in \mathsf{K}^{n\times n}$ with $O((\mathrm{MM}(n)\log n + n\mathrm{M}(n)) \cdot \mathrm{M}(\log_q n)\log\log_q n + \mathrm{M}(n)\log \ell)$ or $O\tilde{~}(\mathrm{MM}(n) + n\log \ell)$ operations in K;

A Lower Bound on Evaluating Polynomials at Matrices

The problem of evaluating a non-linear polynomial at a matrix is at least as hard as matrix multiplication. Specifically, if for a fixed $g \in \mathsf{K}[x]$ of degree $r \geq 2$ we can evaluate $g(T)$ at any $T \in \mathsf{K}^{n\times n}$ with $O(t(n))$ operations in K, then we can multiply two $n \times n$ matrices over K with $O(t(n))$ operations in K. We make a technical assumption about the cost function $t\colon \mathbb{R}_{>0} \to \mathbb{R}_{>0}$:

$$\forall \alpha \in \mathbb{R}_{>0}\ \ \forall \beta \in \mathbb{R}_{\geq 1} \qquad \beta^2 t(\alpha) \leq t(\alpha\beta) \leq \beta^{3.5} t(\alpha).$$

This assumption is quite reasonable since the problem of evaluating a polynomial at a matrix has a trivial lower bound of $\Omega(n^2)$ operations in K and, as discussed above, a deterministic upper bound of $O(n^{3.5})$ operations in K.

We begin with the case when $\#\mathsf{K} \geq r - 1$. This is later generalized to all fields. Let $A, B \in \mathsf{K}^{n\times n}$. We show how to use an algorithm for evaluating g at a matrix to multiply A and B. Consider the matrix

$$T = \begin{pmatrix} I_n & A & 0_n \\ 0_n & cI_n & B \\ 0_n & 0_n & I_n \end{pmatrix} \in \mathsf{K}^{3n \times 3n},$$

where $c \in \mathsf{K}$ and $0_n, I_n \in \mathsf{K}^{n \times n}$ are the zero and identity matrices respectively.

The next lemma is easily shown by induction.

Lemma 6.4. *For $j \geq 1$,*

$$T^j = \begin{pmatrix} I_n & \nu_j(c) \cdot A & \eta_j(c) \cdot AB \\ 0_n & c^j \cdot I_n & \nu_j(c) \cdot B \\ 0_n & 0_n & I_n \end{pmatrix} \in \mathsf{K}^{3n \times 3n},$$

where $\nu_j(c) = \sum_{0 \leq i \leq j-1} c^i$ and $\eta_j(c) = \sum_{0 \leq i \leq j-2} (j - i - 1)c^i$.

Let $C \in \mathsf{K}^{n \times n}$ be the top right $n \times n$ block of $g(T)$. If $g = \sum_{0 \leq i \leq r} b_i x^i$, then

$$C = \sum_{0 \leq i \leq r} b_i \eta_j(c) \cdot AB = h(c) \cdot AB,$$

where $h = \sum_{0 \leq i \leq r-2} z^i (\sum_{i+2 \leq j \leq r} (j - i - 1) b_j) \in \mathsf{K}[z]$ and z is an indeterminate. Since the coefficient of z^{r-2} in h is $b_r \neq 0$, we know $\deg h = r - 2$. Now, we have assumed that $\#\mathsf{K} > r - 2$, so there exists a $c \in \mathsf{K}$ such that $h(c) \neq 0$ because h has at most $r - 2$ roots. Such a c can be found by evaluating h at $r - 1$ distinct points in K, and using fast multipoint evaluation (see Aho *et al.* (1974), Section 8.5), can be found with $O(\mathrm{M}(r) \log r)$ operations in K. Now $AB = h(c)^{-1} C$, which can be found with an additional $O(n^2)$ operations in K.

If $q = \#\mathsf{K} \leq r - 2$ things are somewhat trickier. It may be the case that there does not exist a $c \in \mathsf{K}$ such that $h(c) \neq 0$. To overcome this problem we work in an algebraic extension F of K of degree $\mu = \log_q \lceil r - 1 \rceil$ over K, which clearly does contain $r - 1$ distinct elements. We are only given an algorithm which evaluates g at matrices over K, so we use the companion matrix representation of F as $\mu \times \mu$ matrices over K, where $\mathsf{F} = \mathsf{K}[\Gamma] \subseteq \mathsf{K}^{\mu \times \mu}$ and Γ is the companion matrix of a monic irreducible polynomial in $\mathsf{K}[x]$ of degree μ. If we can evaluate g at any $n \times n$ matrix over K with $O(t(n))$ operations in K, we can evaluate g at an $n \times n$ matrix over F with $O(t(n\mu))$ or $O(t(n) \log_q^{3.5} r)$ operations in K. F has at least $m - 1$ elements so the above reduction from multiplying matrices to evaluating g at a matrix applies, with some extra cost for operations in F rather than K.

Theorem 6.5. *Let $g \in \mathsf{K}[x]$ have degree $r \geq 2$. Suppose we can evaluate $g(T)$ for any matrix $T \in \mathsf{K}^{n \times n}$ with $O(t(n))$ operations in K. If $\#\mathsf{K} \geq m - 1$ we can multiply two $n \times n$ matrices with $O(t(n))$ operations in K. An additional cost of $O(\mathrm{M}(r) \log r)$ operations in K is required for each matrix order $n \in \mathbb{N}$ used. If $q = \#\mathsf{K} < m - 1$ we can multiply two $n \times n$ matrices with $O(t(n) \log_q^{3.5} r)$ operations in K. An additional cost of $O(\mathrm{M}(r) \cdot \mathrm{M}(\log r) \log r)$ operations in K is required for each matrix order $n \in \mathbb{N}$ used.*

7 The Rational Jordan Form

The rational Jordan form of a matrix in $\mathsf{K}^{n \times n}$ is a generalization of the usual Jordan form. Whereas a Jordan form of $T \in \mathsf{K}^{n \times n}$ exists only if K contains all eigenvalues of T, the rational Jordan form always exists and is a matrix in $\mathsf{K}^{n \times n}$. The eigenvalues of T, which may generate an algebraic extension of K of exponential degree over K, are replaced on the diagonal of the rational Jordan form by the companion matrices of their minimal polynomials in $\mathsf{K}[x]$. For any monic irreducible $g \in \mathsf{K}[x]$ of degree r, and any $e > 0$, define the *rational Jordan block* $J_g^{(e)} \in \mathsf{K}^{er \times er}$ as

$$J_g^{(e)} = \begin{pmatrix} C_g & I_r & & & 0 \\ & \ddots & \ddots & & \\ & & \ddots & \ddots & \\ & & & & I_r \\ 0 & & & & C_g \end{pmatrix},$$

where I_r is the $r \times r$ identity matrix, and $C_g \in \mathsf{K}^{r \times r}$ is the companion matrix of g. Any $T \in \mathsf{K}^{n \times n}$ is similar to its *rational Jordan form*, a matrix $Q = \mathrm{diag}(Q_1, \ldots, Q_\ell) \in \mathsf{K}^{n \times n}$ where $Q_1, \ldots, Q_\ell$ are rational Jordan blocks. Notice that when all eigenvalues of T lie in K, Q is the usual Jordan form of T. The rational Jordan form is unique up to the order of the (rational) Jordan blocks, as is the usual Jordan form.

To compute the rational Jordan form, we observe that once we know the Frobenius form of T and the complete factorization of its minimal polynomial f_1, then we can immediately determine the rational Jordan form of T. A transition matrix from T to its rational Jordan form can be calculated by computing a transition matrix from the rational Jordan form of T to the Frobenius form of T using `FrobeniusForm`.

Theorem 7.1. *Given $T \in \mathsf{K}^{n\times n}$, there is a Las Vegas reduction from the problem of finding the rational Jordan form $Q \in \mathsf{K}^{n\times n}$ of T, and an invertible $P \in \mathsf{K}^{n\times n}$ such that $Q = P^{-1}TP$, to factoring a polynomial in $\mathsf{K}[x]$ of degree at most n (namely the minimal polynomial $f_1 \in \mathsf{K}[x]$ of T). $O\tilde{~}(\mathrm{MM}(n))$ operations in K are sufficient for this reduction.*

Using the Las Vegas algorithm of Berlekamp (1970) for factoring polynomials over finite fields we get the following corollary.

Corollary 7.2. *Let K be a finite field and $T \in \mathsf{K}^{n\times n}$. The rational Jordan form of T can be computed by a Las Vegas algorithm with $O\tilde{~}(\mathrm{MM}(n) + n\log q)$ operations in K.*

This factorization in $\mathsf{K}[x]$ is necessary since the rational Jordan form of the companion matrix of any $g \in \mathsf{K}[x]$ yields the complete factorization of g in $\mathsf{K}[x]$.

Acknowledgement

The author would like to thank Erich Kaltofen for suggesting this problem, Wayne Eberly for his help with Theorem 6.5, and Joachim von zur Gathen and Victor Shoup for many useful discussions.

References

A. V. Aho, J. E. Hopcroft, and J. D. Ullman. *The Design and Analysis of Computer Algorithms.* Addison-Wesley (Reading MA), 1974.

W. Baur and V. Strassen. The complexity of partial derivatives. *Theor. Comp. Science* **22**, pp. 317–330, 1982.

E. R. Berlekamp. Factoring polynomials over large finite fields. *Math. Comp.* **24**, pp. 713–735, 1970.

D. Coppersmith and S. Winograd. Matrix multiplication via arithmetic progressions. *J. Symb. Comp.* **9**, pp. 251–280, 1990.

F. R. Gantmacher. Geometric theory of elementary divisors after Krull. *Trudy Odessa Gos. Univ. Mat.* **1**, pp. 89–108, 1935.

F. R. Gantmacher. *The Theory of Matrices, Vol. I.* Chelsea Publishing Co. (New York NY), 1990.

K. Hoffman and R. Kunze. *Linear Algebra.* Prentice-Hall (Englewood Cliffs, N.J.), 1971.

J. Howell. An algorithm for the exact reduction of a matrix to Frobenius form using modular arithmetic, I + II. *Math. Comp* **27**, pp. 887–920, 1973.

E. Kaltofen, M. Krishnamoorthy, and B. D. Saunders. Fast parallel algorithms for similarity of matrices. In *Proc. ACM Symp. Symbolic and Algebraic Computation*, pp. 65–70, Waterloo, Ontario, 1986.

E. Kaltofen, M. S. Krishnamoorthy, and B. D. Saunders. Fast parallel computation of Hermite and Smith forms of polynomial matrices. *SIAM J. Algebraic and Discrete Methods* **8**, pp. 683–690, 1987.

R. Kannan and A. Bachem. Polynomial algorithms for computing the Smith and Hermite normal forms of an integer matrix. *SIAM J. Comp.* **8**, pp. 499–507, 1979.

W. Keller-Gehrig. Fast algorithms for the characteristic polynomial. *Theor. Computer Science* **36**, pp. 309–317, 1985.

H. Lüneburg. *On Rational Normal Form of Endomorphisms: a Primer to Constructive Algebra.* Wissenschaftsverlag (Mannheim), 1987.

P. Ozello. *Calcul Exact Des Formes De Jordan et de Frobenius D'une Matrice.* PhD thesis, Technologique et Medicale de Grenoble, 1987.

M. S. Paterson and L. Stockmeyer. On the number of nonscalar multiplications necessary to evaluate polynomials. *SIAM J. Comput.* **2**, pp. 60–66, 1973.

A. Schönhage. Schnelle Multiplikation von Polynomen über Körpern der Charakteristik 2. *Acta Informatica* **7**, pp. 395–398, 1977.

A. Schönhage and V. Strassen. Schnelle Multiplikation großer Zahlen. *Computing* **7**, pp. 281–292, 1971.

J. T. Schwartz. Fast probabilistic algorithms for verification of polynomial identities. *J. Assoc. Computing Machinery* **27**, pp. 701–717, 1980.

V. Shoup. New algorithms for finding irreducible polynomials in finite fields. *Math. Comp.* **54**(189), pp. 435–447, January 1990.

B. L. van der Waerden. *Algebra*, vol. 1. Frederick Ungar Publishing Co. (New York), 7th edition, 1970.

D. Wiedemann. Solving sparse linear equations over finite fields. *IEEE Transactions on Information Theory* **IT-32**, pp. 54–62, 1986.

Improved Parallel Polynomial Division and Its Extensions

Dario Bini

Department of Mathematics
University of Pisa
56100 Pisa, Italy

Victor Pan

Department of Math. & Computer Sci.
Lehman College, CUNY
Bronx, NY 10468

Abstract

We compute the first N coefficients of the reciprocal $r(x)$ of a given polynomial $p(x)$, ($r(x)p(x) = 1 \bmod x^N$, $p(0) \neq 0$), by using, under the PRAM arithmetic models, $O(h \log N)$ time-steps and $O((N/h)(1 + 2^{-h} \log^{(h)} N))$ processors, for any h, $h = 1, 2, \ldots, \log^* N$, provided that $O(\log m)$ steps and m processors suffice to perform DFT on m points and that $\log^{(0)} N = N$, $\log^{(h)} N = \log_2 \log^{(h-1)} N$, $h = 1, \ldots, \log^* N$, $\log^* N = \max\{h : \log^{(h)} N > 0\}$. The same complexity estimates apply to some other computations, such as the division with a remainder of two polynomials of degrees $O(N)$ and the inversion of an $N \times N$ triangular Toeplitz matrix. This improves the known estimates of Reif-Tate and Georgiev. We also show how to extend our techniques to parallel implementation of other recursive processes, such as the evaluation modulo x^N of the m-th root, $p(x)^{1/m}$, of $p(x)$ (for any fixed natural m), for which we need $O(\log N \log\log N)$ time-steps and $O(N/\log\log N)$ processors. The paper demonstrates some new techniques of supereffective slowdown of parallel algebraic computations, which we combine with a technique of stream contraction.

1 Introduction

In this paper we will improve the known upper estimates for the parallel arithmetic complexity of computing the reciprocal of a polynomial and, consequently, of the equivalent computations, such as polynomial and power series division and triangular Toeplitz matrix inversion (compare [2], [3] and the appendix). This improvement relies on the new techniques that, in particular, decrease by q times the processor bound for a large class of parallel algebraic computations in the result of their slowdown by $s = o(q)$ times. We call such a slowdown *supereffective* since a variant of Brent's scheduling principle only implies an effective decrease of the processor bound by $O(s)$ times in this case (see [6], [8]). We demonstrate these techniques for polynomial division (sections 2–5) and for computing (modulo x^N) the $(\frac{1}{m})$-th power (or the m-th root), $p(x)^{1/m}$, of a polynomial $p(x)$ (section 6), but they can be immediately extended to some other polynomial computations based on recursive processes, such as Newton's iteration. An outline of this general approach is given in the beginning of section 6.

We will state our estimates in the form $O_A(t, P)$, which means that our computations can be performed by using $O(st)$ time-steps and $O(P/s)$ processors (for any fixed s, $1 \leq s \leq P$), under the PRAM arithmetic models of computing (see [6]). We will assume the bound $O_A(\log m, m)$ on the cost of performing (forward and inverse) discrete Fourier transforms on the m-th roots of 1 [hereafter referred to as $DFT(m)$]. This bound holds, in particular, over the complex field of constants. Over any ring (with unity), the bound $O_A(\log m, m \log\log m)$ holds [4], so that all our estimates apply if their processor bounds are increased by the factor of $\log\log N$ provided that the ring supports Bluestein's generalized FFT ([7]). In section 5 we will comment on the latter assumption. Hereafter, log stands for $\log_2$ (all logarithms are binary).

Given a natural N and the coefficients of a polynomial $p(x)$, $p(0) \neq 0$, we will compute the first N

coefficients of the reciprocal power series,

$$r(x) = \sum_{i=0}^{\infty} r_i x^i \ , \ r(x)\,p(x) = 1 \ , \ r_0 = \frac{1}{p(0)} \ , \qquad (1.1)$$

yielding the complexity estimates

$$c_N = O_A(h \log N, \tfrac{N}{h}(1 + 2^{-h} \log^{(h)} N)) \ , \quad \text{for} \quad h = 1, 2, \ldots, \log^* N \ . \qquad (1.2)$$

Here,

$$\log^{(0)} N = N \ , \ \log^{(h)} N = \log_2 \log^{(h-1)} N \ , \quad h = 1, \ldots, \log^* N \ ,$$

$$\log^* N = \max\{h : \log^{(h)} N > 0\} \ .$$

In particular, for $h = \log^* N$, (1.2) turns into

$$c_N = O_A(\log^* N \log N \ , \ N/\log^* N) \ . \qquad (1.3)$$

This improves the previous record bounds of [5],

$$c_N = O_A(\log N \ , \ N \log^2 N) \ ,$$

and of [11],

$$c_N = O_A(\log N \log\log N \ , \ N/\log\log N) \ .$$

We refer the reader to [2] and [3] on other previous works, in particular, on Reif's results of [10], including the bound $c_N = O_A(\log N, N^2)$, and Bini's results of [1], where $c_N = O_A(\log N, N)$ is proven for any precision approximation to the reciprocal of a polynomial modulo x^N.

2 Stream of Newton's Steps and Its Contraction

It is well known that, given a polynomial $p(x)$, $p(0) \neq 0$, the first m coefficients of the reciprocal power series $r(x)$ of (1.1) can be computed by performing $\lceil \log m \rceil$ steps of Newton's iteration,

$$z_0(x) = 1/p(0) \ , \quad z_{i+1}(x) = z_i(x)\,(2 - p(x) z_i(x)) \ , \quad i = 1, \ldots, \lceil \log m \rceil \ . \qquad (2.1)$$

In fact, since

$$r(x) - z_{i+1}(x) = \left(r(x) - z_i(x)\right)^2 p(x) \ , \qquad (2.2)$$

the number of coefficients shared by $r(x)$ and $z_i(x)$ is doubled in each iteration step i, so that, for all i,

$$z_i(x) = r(x) \bmod x^{2^i} \ . \qquad (2.3)$$

The algorithm of Sieveking-Kung is based on this scheme, where, however, both polynomials $p(x)$ and $z_i(x)$ of (2.1) are reduced modulo x^{2^i}. In this case step i of Newton's process outputs a polynomial of degree at most $3(2^i - 1)$, whose coefficients can be computed at the cost $O_A(i, 2^i)$, by means of forward and inverse DFT's on $m(i)$ points, $m(i) > 3(2^i - 1)$. This implies the bound $O_A(\log^2 n, n/\log n)$ on the overall cost of computing the coefficients of $r(x) \bmod x^n$, which turns into the bound

$$c_{n,k} = O_A(\log n \log(\frac{n}{k}) \ , \ n/\log(\frac{n}{k})) \qquad (2.4)$$

if we initially know the k coefficients of $r(x) \bmod x^k$.

In [5] it is pointed out that the relation (2.3) still holds even if $p(x)$ in (2.1) is replaced by $p(x) \bmod x^{2^{i+1}}$. Then the degrees of the polynomials $z_i(x)$ are bounded by $i2^i$, $i = 0, 1, \ldots,$ and thus, the coefficients of $z_d(x)$, for $d = \lceil \log n \rceil$, can be computed by means of a single inverse DFT on $O(n \log n)$ points (roots of 1) once the values of $z_d(x)$ on these points have been computed. To evaluate $z_d(x)$ on a set of points, we compute the values of $p_i(x) = p(x) \bmod x^{2^{i+1}}$ on this set and then, for each point, recursively apply the equation (2.1) for $i = 0, 1, \ldots, d-1$, thus avoiding the application of DFT until we compute the values of $z_d(x)$. This way, we *contract the stream* of recursive steps, by cutting-off their slowest parts (that is, DFT's) and thus accelerating the transition to each new step (compare another example of stream contraction in [9]). As a result, the n coefficients of $r(x) \bmod x^n$ are computed at the cost bounded by $O_A(\log n, n \log^2 n)$, ([5]).

3 A Basis Algorithm for New Improvements and Its Recursive Restarting

In this and in the next two sections, we will combine the two ways of applying Newton's iteration (2.1), that is, the coefficientwise way (Sieveking-Kung) and the pointwise way ([5]), in order to decrease the overall parallel computational cost. Moreover, we will *recursively stop and restart* the pointwise iteration process so as to bound the number of processors involved. It turns out that relatively few restarts suffice to compute a considerable part of all the output coefficients. Indeed, we will consider Newton's iteration that starts with

$$y_0(x) = r(x) \bmod x^k, \qquad (3.1)$$

for any fixed natural k (not necessarily for $k = 1$), and that continues as follows:

$$p_i(x) = p(x) \bmod x^{k2^{i+1}} , \quad (3.2)$$

$$y_{i+1}(x) = y_i(x)\,(2 - p_i(x)\,y_i(x)) , \quad (3.3)$$

$i = 0, 1, \ldots$. Then (2.2) immediately implies that

$$y_i(x) = r(x) \bmod x^{k2^i} , \quad (3.4)$$

and we verify by induction on i that

$$\deg y_i(x) \le (i+1)k\,2^i - 2^{i+1} + 1 . \quad (3.5)$$

(3.4) and (3.5) immediately imply the correctness of our basis algorithm below.

With no loss of generality, we assume that n is large enough, say, $n \ge 16$, so that $\log^* n \ge 3$. Furthermore, for convenience, let s denote an integer, $4 \le s \le n$, and let $\log\log s$ and $\log n$ be integers.

Basis algorithm.

Input: integers n and s and the coefficients of $p(x)$ and $r(x) \bmod x^{n/s}$.

Output: the coefficients of $r(x) \bmod x^{n/\log s}$.

Initialize: set $k = n/s$, $j = \log s - 2\log\log s$, $q = n/\log s$, $y_0(x) = r(x) \bmod x^k$.

Computation:

1. $j+1$ times apply DFT on q points, to evaluate the polynomials $y_0(x)$ of (3.1) and $p_i(x)$ of (3.2), for $i = 0, \ldots, j-1$, on the q-th roots of 1.
2. Use the equations (3.3), for $i = 0, \ldots, j-1$, in order to evaluate $y_{i+1}(x)$ on the q-th roots of 1.
3. Apply the inverse DFT on q points in order to evaluate the coefficients of $y_j(x)$. [$\deg y_j(x) \le (j+1)k\,2^j - 2^{j+1} + 1$; $y_j(x) = r(x) \bmod x^{k2^j}$, due to (3.4), and $k2^j = n/\log^2 s$.]
4. Update the initialized parameters by first setting $y_0(x) = y_j(x) \bmod x^{k2^j}$, $k_1 = k2^j$, $q = n(1+\log\log s)/\log s$, and then $k = k_1 \ge n/\log^2 s$, $j = \log\log s$; then redefine $p_{i-1}(x)$ and $y_i(x)$, for $i = 1, \ldots, j$, by using the equations (3.2) and (3.3); then again apply steps 1-3 to compute and to output the coefficients of the polynomial $y_j(x)$ (which equals $r(x) \bmod x^{k2^j}$, where $k2^j = n/\log s$ for the updated k and j).

The cost of the computation by the basis algorithm is clearly bounded by $O_A(\log n, n)$, and we will recursively apply this algorithm for a fixed n and for s successively taking the values

$$s_0 = n , \; s_1 = \log n , \; s_2 = \log\log n , \; \ldots, \quad s_{h-2} = \log^{(h-2)} n , \quad (3.6)$$

for $2 \le h \le \log^* n$ (for simplicity, let $\log^{(g)} n$ be integers for $g = 1, \ldots, h$). This way, we will compute the first $m(h,n) = n/\log^{(h-1)} n$ coefficients of $r(x)$ at the cost bounded by $O_A(h\log n, n)$. For $h \le \log^* n - 2$, we will extend this process to $s_{h-1} = \log^{(h-1)} n$.

Note that already the basis algorithm uses two successive recursive loops, and we are now taking advantage of recursive restarting of this algorithm. Indeed, if we applied the basis algorithm only once, by setting $s = n$, $N = n/\log s$, then the resulting cost bound $O_A(\log n, n) = O_A(\log N, N\log N)$ would have assumed too many processors.

4 Final Refinement of the Algorithm

Let $N = n2^h$. In particular, this choice of N ensures that the above cost bound $O_A(h\log n, n)$ is not greater than the desired bound (1.2). We still need, however, to compute the coefficients of $r(x) \bmod x^N$ that still remain unknown after the recursive application of the basis algorithm. We will first extend the computation to the evaluation of $r(x) \bmod x^n$ [note that $m(h,n) < n$]. Set

$$\begin{aligned} y_0(x) &= r(x) \bmod x^{m(h,n)} , \\ k &= m(h,n) , \; j = \log^{(h-1)} n , \end{aligned} \quad (4.1)$$

$$q = (j+1)k2^j - 2^{j+1} + 1 , \quad (4.2)$$

[so that $k2^j = n$, $q \le (1 + \log^{(h)} n)n$], and again apply steps 1-3 of the basis algorithm. The complexity of these steps is bounded from above by $O_A(\log n, n(\log^{(h)} n)^2)$, which we may replace by the weaker bound $O_A(h\log n, \frac{n}{h}(\log^{(h)} n)^2)$. The overall cost of computing the coefficients of $r(x) \bmod x^n$ is thus bounded by $O_A(h\log n \; , \; n(1 + \frac{(\log^{(h)} n)^2}{h}))$. For $N = n2^h$ and for $h = \log^* n - O(1)$, in particular, for $h > \log^* n - 2$, this turns into the bound

$$c^*_{N,h} = O_A(h\log N \; , \; N\,2^{-h}(1 + \frac{\log^{(h)} N}{h})) , \quad (4.3)$$

not exceeding the desired bound (1.2).

If $h \le \log^* n - 2$, we proceed similarly, but extend the computation of $r(x) \bmod x^{n/s_i}$ for $s_0, s_1, \ldots$ of (3.6) to $s_{h-1} = \log^{(h-1)} n$. This way we will compute all the coefficients of $r(x) \bmod x^n$, at the cost bounded by $O_A(h\log n, n(1 + (\log^{(h+1)} n)^2)/h)$. We replace this bound by the weaker bound

$O_A(h \log n, n(1+\frac{\log^{(h)} n}{h}))$ on the overall cost of computing all the coefficients of $r(x) \bmod x^n$. Now substitute $N = n2^h$ and arrive at (4.3) also for $h \leq \log^* n - 2$.

Finally, we will compute the remaining coefficients of $r(x) \bmod x^N$, by applying h steps of the Sieveking-Kung algorithm; the cost of this stage is bounded by $O_A(h \log N, N/h)$ [see (2.4)]. This cost bound implies the bound (1.2), for $h \leq \log^* n$. Surely, $\log^* N \leq 1 + \log^* n$ as $N \to \infty$, so that we extend (1.2) to all $h \leq \log^* N$ and then also deduce (1.3).

To relax the assumption about the integrality of $\log \log s$ and $\log^{(g)} n$ for $g = 1, \ldots, h$, we just need to replace the values of k in the basis algorithm (chosen at the initialization step and at step 4) and in (4.1), as well as the values of n/s_i [for $i = 1, \ldots, h$ and for $s_1, s_2, \ldots, s_h$ of (3.6)] and of $m(h, n)$, by their ceilings, $\lceil\ \rceil$, that is, by the minimum integers not exceeded by these values; to define q by (4.2) and to let j denote the minimum integer such that $k2^j$ is not less than the number of the coefficients or $r(x)$ that should be computed in the current stage, that is, $\lceil n/\log^2 n \rceil$ in step 3 of the basis algorithm, $\lceil n/\log s \rceil$ in its step 4, and n in the final refinement stage. It is easy to verify that such a replacement preserves (4.3).

5 Application over Abstract Rings

Our algorithms can be applied over any ring $\mathbf{R}$ of constants that contains unity and an element g such that $g^{-1} \in \mathbf{R}$ and $1, g, g^2, \ldots, g^{N-1}$ are distinct in $\mathbf{R}$. In this case we may replace FFT by its Bluestein's extension (where g replaces the principal root of 1), [7]. Such an extended FFT is performed at the cost $O_A(\log N, N \log \log N)$ over any ring $\mathbf{R}$ ([4]).

Furthermore, there exists a desired element g in $\mathbf{R}$ if the number $|\mathbf{R}|$ of distinct elements that belong to $\mathbf{R}$ together with their reciprocals exceeds $N-1$. Otherwise, there must exist such an element g in the extension $\mathbf{E}$ formed by all polynomials over $\mathbf{R}$ modulo an irreducible polynomial of degree d if $d \geq \log N / \log |\mathbf{R}|$. In the latter case, each univariate polynomial of degree at most K in $\mathbf{E}$ turns into a bivariate polynomial in $\mathbf{R}$ of degrees at most K and $d-1$ in its two variables, respectively. Multiplication of two such polynomials has computational cost $O_A(\log(Kd), Kd \log\log(Kd))$, ([4]). This implies that the transition from application of our algorithms in $\mathbf{E}$ (where they are supported by Bluestein's extension of FFT) to their application in the original ring $\mathbf{R}$ will only require increasing the resulting processor bound by the factor of d, and we may assume that $d = O(\log N / \log |\mathbf{R}|)$. As an alternative, we may compute $p^{-1}(x) \bmod x^{\lceil N/d \rceil}$ by using our algorithms and then make transition to $p^{-1}(x) \bmod x^N$ by means of the Sieveking-Kung algorithm, at the overall cost $O_A(\log N \log\log N, N)$ over any ring of constants (compare [11]).

The same comments apply to our algorithm for the evaluation modulo x^N of $p^{1/2}(x)$, to be presented next.

6 Extensions

We will demonstrate two ways of extension of the results of this paper.

1) At first we will consider application of the techniques of the previous sections to the recursive computations of the form

$$v_{i+1}(x) = h(v_i(x), x) \bmod x^N \qquad (6.1)$$

where $h(v, x)$ is a polynomial in v and x; $\deg_v h$ is small, $v(x) \bmod x^N$ is the output polynomial, and $v_i(x) = v(x) \bmod x^{m(i)}$, for a rapidly growing sequence $m(i), i = 0, 1, \ldots$. Assume that such a recursive computation is represented by a parallel algorithm which is processor efficient but relatively slow (as in the case of the Sieveking–Kung algorithm). We first contract the stream of its recursive steps (as in section 2), to arrive at a faster (although processor inefficient) algorithm. We may, however, proceed as in section 3 and apply this algorithm in a limited way, computing only a small fraction of the desired output coefficients of $v(x)$, to keep the number of processors within the desired bounds. Following the patterns of section 3, we will then apply this algorithm again, to compute more coefficients of $v(x)$, and will recursively repeat this process until we compute a considerable fraction of all the output coefficients. Then we will shift to the original algorithm, which will easily complete the evaluation of the remaining coefficients of $v(x)$, (compare section 4).

The next example once again demonstrates the efficacy of such an approach for parallelization of a large class of recursive computations. Indeed, suppose that we need to compute modulo x^N the square root, $v(x) = p(x)^{1/2} \bmod x^N$, of a polynomial $p(x)$, where $p(0) = 1$. Since $f(v, x) = v^{-2}(x)\, p(x) - 1 = 0$, we apply Newton's iteration with $v_0(x) = 1$ and recursively compute

$$\begin{aligned} v_{i+1}(x) &= v_i(x) - f(v_i, x) \,/\, f'_v(v_i, x) \\ &= 0.5\, v_i(x)(3 - p^{-1}(x) v_i^2(x)), \qquad (6.2) \\ &\quad i = 0, 1, \ldots \end{aligned}$$

We observe that

$$\begin{aligned}
&v_{i+1}(x) - p^{1/2}(x) \\
&= 0.5\, v_i(x)\left(3 - p^{-1}(x) v_i^2(x)\right) - p^{1/2}(x) \\
&= v_i(x) - p^{1/2}(x) + 0.5 v_i(x) p^{-1}(x)(p(x) - v_i^2(x)) \\
&= (v_i(x) - p^{1/2}(x))\left(1 - 0.5 v_i(x)\, p^{-1}(x)\right. \\
&\quad \left.(p^{1/2}(x) + v_i(x))\right) \\
&= (v_i(x) - p^{1/2}(x))\left[(1 - v_i(x)\, p^{-1/2}(x))\right. \\
&\quad \left. -0.5 v_i(x)\, p^{-1}(x)(v_i(x) - p^{1/2}(x))\right] \\
&= -(v_i(x) - p^{1/2}(x))^2 \left(p^{-1/2}(x) + 0.5 v_i(x)\, p^{-1}(x)\right) \\
&= O(v_i(x) - p^{1/2}(x))^2 ,
\end{aligned}$$

and therefore,

$$v_j(x) - p^{1/2}(x) = 0 \bmod x^J , \quad J = 2^j , \quad j = 0, 1, \ldots$$

As in the Sieveking-Kung algorithm, substitute $v_j(x) \bmod x^J$, $J = 2^j$, for $v_j(x)$, $j = i, i+1$, in (6.2), substitute $p^{-1}(x) \bmod x^{2^i}$ for $p^{-1}(x)$ in (6.2) and arrive at the complexity bound $O_A(\log^2 N\ ,\ N/\log N)$ for this computational problem.

Similarly to the algorithm of [5], contract the stream of Newton's steps by replacing $p^{-1}(x)$ by $p_i^{-1}(x) = p^{-1}(x) \bmod x^{2^{i+1}}$ in (6.2). Observe that in this case the degrees of the polynomials $v_i(x)$ are bounded by $\sum_{g=1}^{i} (2/3)^g 3^i < 3^{i+1}$ and deduce the bound $O_A(\log k\ ,\ k^d \log k)$, $d = \log 3 = 1.5849\ldots$, $1/d = 0.6309\ldots$, on the complexity of the evaluation of $p^{1/2}(x) \bmod x^k$.

We apply the latter result for $k = n^{0.63}$, where we will specify $n \le N$ later on [see (6.6)]. Then $k^d \log k = o(n^{0.999})$, and we obtain the k first coefficients of $p^{1/2}(x)$ at the cost bounded by $O_A(\log n, n^{0.999})$.

Next, extend the basis algorithm of section 3, by using the equations

$$p_i^{-1}(x) = p^{-1}(x) \bmod x^{k\, 2^{i+1}} ,$$

$$\begin{aligned}
y_0(x) &= v(x) \bmod x^k , \\
y_{i+1}(x) &= 0.5\, y_i(x)(3 - p_i^{-1}(x)\, y_i^2(x)) , \\
& \quad i = 0, 1, \ldots, j ,
\end{aligned}$$

instead of (3.1)-(3.3). Observe that the degrees of the polynomials $y_i(x)$ are bounded by $k 3^i \sum_{g=0}^{i} (2/3)^g < k 3^{i+1}$, so that the transition from $y_0(x) = p^{1/2}(x) \bmod x^k$ to $y_i(x) = p^{1/2}(x) \bmod x^{k 2^i}$ costs

$$\begin{aligned}
&O_A(\log(k\, 2^i), k 2^{id}(i + \log k)) \\
&= O_A(\log n,\ k(m/k)^d \log m) ,
\end{aligned} \tag{6.3}$$

for $d = \log 3$, $m = m(i, k) = k 2^i \le n$.

Let us now define recursive restarting of the algorithm. First choose an integer g and an increasing sequence of integers $k_0 = 1$, $k_1 = \lceil n^{0.63} \rceil$, $k_2, \ldots, k_g$, $k_j = \lceil n^{1-0.37^j} \rceil$, $j = 0, 1, \ldots, g$, and then recursively apply the above transition from $y_0(x)$ to $y_i(x)$, for $k = k_j \ge n^{1-0.37^j}$, $m = k_{j+1}$, $j = 0, 1, \ldots, g-1$. Denote $b_j = \log k_j / \log n \ge 1 - 0.37^j$, so that $1 - b_g \ge 1/\log n$ for

$$g = \lceil \log\log n / \log(1/0.37) \rceil . \tag{6.4}$$

In g recursive transitions we will arrive at $p^{1/2}(x) \bmod x^{k_g}$ where

$$k_g \ge n^{1 - 1/\log n} = n/2 .$$

Due to (6.3) and (6.4), the overall cost of this computation is bounded by

$$O_A(\log n \log\log n, n \log n) . \tag{6.5}$$

Now, as the final refinement, let

$$n = \lceil N/(\log N \log\log N) \rceil , \tag{6.6}$$

apply $1 + \lceil \log(\log n \log\log n) \rceil$ Newton's steps of the Sieveking-Kung type and arrive at $p^{1/2}(x) \bmod x^N$ at the additional cost

$$O_A(\log N \log\log N\ ,\ N/\log\log N) \tag{6.7}$$

where we may assume that $p^{1/2}(x) \bmod x^{k_g}$ is known for $k_g \ge n/2$. (6.7) also bounds the overall cost of computing $p^{1/2}(x) \bmod x^N$ since (6.5) turns into (6.7) for n of (6.6).

The complexity estimates (6.7) for computing the square root of a polynomial modulo x^N can be immediately extended to computing its m-th root modulo N for any fixed positive integer m. Moreover, the techniques applied above enable us to extend (6.7) as follows:

Theorem 6.1. *Suppose that for $c > 1$ and for a pair of integers k and m, $1 \le k < m$, we are given the first k components of a vector and we need to compute the next $m - k$ components. Suppose that two alternate "black box" parallel algorithms, 6.1 and 6.2, are available, which solve this problem at the cost bounded by $O_A(\log m \log(m/k), m/\log(m/k))$, and $O_A(\log m, k(m/k)^c)$, respectively. Then recursive application of Algorithm 6.2, for an appropriate recursive choice of the pairs $k = k_i, m = m_i$, for $i = 0, 1, \ldots$, such that $k_{i+1} = m_i$, for all i, followed by a single application of Algorithm 6.1, supports the solution of the problem of size N, for $k = 1$ and $m = N$, at the cost bounded by (6.7).*

For a more narrow class of computational problems, exemplified by polynomial division, we may improve (6.7) to (1.2). Somewhat similar techniques yield supereffective slowdown of some fundamental computations in linear algebra and in path algebras, where we recursively apply fast but processor inefficient algorithms to decrease the size of the problem (see [8]).

2) The complexity estimates (1.2), (1.3) and (6.7) can be extended to the computational problems readily reducible to computing the reciprocal of a polynomial $p(x)$ and its m-th root, respectively. For demonstration, let us recall the well-known reduction of polynomial division with a remainder to computing the reciprocal of a polynomial (and to polynomial multiplication).

Indeed, given the coefficients of two polynomials $s(x) = \sum_{i=0}^{m} s_i x^i$ and $t(x) = \sum_{i=0}^{n} t_i x^i$, $t_n \neq 0$,we seek the quotient $q(x) = \sum_{i=0}^{m-n} q_i x^i$ and the remainder $r(x) = \sum_{i=0}^{n-1} r_i x^i$ such that

$$s(x) = t(x)q(x) + r(x) \ . \qquad (6.8)$$

Having computed $q(x)$ we immediately obtain $r(x)$ from (6.8). To compute $q(x)$, we define

$$\begin{aligned} S(z) &= z^m s(1/z) = \textstyle\sum_{i=0}^{m} s_{m-i} z^i \ , \\ T(z) &= z^n t(1/z) = \textstyle\sum_{i=0}^{n} t_{n-i} z^i \ , \\ Q(z) &= z^{m-n}\, q(1/z) = \textstyle\sum_{i=0}^{m-n} q_{m-n-i} z^i \ , \end{aligned}$$

observe that

$$S(z) = T(z)\,Q(z) \bmod z^{m-n+1} \ , \qquad (6.9)$$

and apply the algorithms of this paper to compute the reciprocal,

$$V(z) = \sum_{i=0}^{K-1} v_i z^i = T^{-1}(z) \bmod z^K \ , \quad K = m-n+1 \ .$$

It immediately follows from (6.9) that $Q(z) = V(z)\,S(z) \bmod z^K$, so that the coefficients of $q(x)$ are the leading coefficients of the polynomial product $V(z)\sum_{i=n}^{m} s_i z^{i-n}$.

Acknowledgments. Dario Bini was supported by NSF Grants CCR 8805782 and CCR 9020690, and by MPI (40% funds). Victor Pan was supported by NSF grants CCR 8805782, CCR 9020690 and by PSC CUNY Awards #661340, #668541, #669210 and #662478.

References

[1] D. Bini, "Parallel Solution of Certain Toeplitz Linear Systems," *SIAM J. on Computing,* 13(2), (1984) 268–276.

[2] D. Bini and V. Pan, "Polynomial Division and its Computational Complexity," *Jour. Complexity,* 2 (1986) 179–203.

[3] D. Bini and V. Pan, *Numerical and Algebraic Computations with Matrices and Polynomials,* Vols. 1 and 2, Birkhauser, Boston (1992, to appear).

[4] G. Cantor and Kaltofen, E., "On Fast Multiplication of Polynomials over Arbitrary Algebras," *Acta Inf.*, 28 (1991) 693–701.

[5] R. E. Georgiev, "Inversion of Triangular Toeplitz Matrices by Using the Fast Fourier Transform," *J. New Gener. Comput. Sys.* 2(3) (1989) 247–256.

[6] R. M. Karp and V. Ramachandran, "A Survey of Parallel Algorithms for Shared Memory Machines," in *Handbook of Theor. Comp. Science,* North-Holland (1990) 869–941.

[7] D. E. Knuth, *The Art of Computer Programming: Seminumerical Algorithms,* v. 2, Addison-Wesley, Mass., 1981.

[8] V. Y. Pan and F. P. Preparata, "Supereffective Slowdown of Parallel computations," *Proc. 4th Annual ACM Symp. on Parallel Algrithms and Architectures* (1992), 402–409.

[9] V. Y. Pan and J. H. Reif, "The Parallel Computation of the Minimum Cost Paths in Graph by Stream Contraction," *Information Processing Letters,* 40 (1991) 79–83.

[10] J. H. Reif, "Logarithmic Depth Circuits for the Algebraic Problems," *SIAM J. on Computing,* 15 (1986) 231–242.

[11] J. H. Reif and S. H. Tate, "Optimal Size Division Circuits," *Proc. 21-th Ann. ACM Symp. on Theory of Computing,* (1989) 264–270 and *SIAM J. on Computing,* 19(5) (1990) 264–270.

Randomized Consensus in Expected $O(n \log^2 n)$ Operations Per Processor

James Aspnes*
IBM Almaden Research Center
aspnes@almaden.ibm.com

Orli Waarts†
Stanford University
orli@cs.stanford.edu

Abstract

This paper presents a new randomized algorithm for achieving consensus among asynchronous processors that communicate by reading and writing shared registers. The fastest previously known algorithm requires a processor to perform an expected $O(n^2 \log n)$ read and write operations in the worst case. In our algorithm, each processor executes at most an expected $O(n \log^2 n)$ read and write operations, which is close to the trivial lower bound of $\Omega(n)$.

All previously known polynomial-time consensus algorithms were structured around a *shared coin* protocol [AH90] in which each processor repeatedly adds random ± 1 votes to a common pool. Consequently, in all of these protocols, the worst case expected bound on the number of read and write operations done by a single processor is asymptotically no better than the bound on the total number of read and write operations done by all of the processors together. We succeed in breaking this tradition by allowing the processors to cast votes of increasing weights. This grants the adversary greater control since he can choose from up to n different weights (one for each processor) when determining the weight of the next vote to be cast. We prove that our shared coin protocol is correct nevertheless using martingale arguments.

1 Introduction

In the **consensus** problem, each of n asynchronous processors starts with an input value 0 or 1 not known to the others and runs until it chooses a *decision value* and halts. The protocol must be **consistent**: no two processors choose different decision values; **valid**: the decision value is some processor's input value; and **wait-free**: each processor decides after a finite expected number of its *own* steps regardless of other processors' halting failures or relative speeds.

We consider the consensus problem in the standard model of asynchronous shared memory systems. The processors communicate via a set of single-writer, multi-reader atomic registers. Each such register can be written only by one processor, its owner, but all processors can read it. Reads and writes to such register can be viewed as occurring at a single instant of time.

Consensus is fundamental to synchronization without mutual exclusion and hence lies at the heart of the more general problem of constructing highly concurrent data structures [Her91]. It can be used to obtain wait-free implementations of arbitrary abstract data types with atomic operations [Her91, Plo89]. Consensus is also **complete** for **distributed decision tasks** [CM89] in the sense that it can be used to solve all such tasks that have a wait-free solution.

Consensus is often viewed as a game played between a set of processors and an adversary scheduler. Using the standard wait-free model of an asynchronous shared-memory system, each processor can execute as an atomic step either a single read or write operation, or a flip of a local fair coin not visible to the other processors. The sequencing of the processors' actions is controlled by a **scheduler**, defined as a function that at each step selects a processor to run based on the entire prior history of the system, including the internal states of the processors. Remarkably, it has been shown that the ability of the scheduler to stop even a single processor is sufficient to prevent consensus from being solved by a deterministic algorithm [CIL87, DDS87, FLP85, Her91, LAA87]. Nevertheless, it can be solved by *randomized* protocols in which each processor is guaranteed to decide after a finite *expected* number of steps.

Chor, Israeli, and Li [CIL87] provided the first solution to the problem, but their solution deviated from

*Supported in part by an IBM Graduate Fellowship.

†Supported by an IBM Graduate Fellowship, U.S. Army Research Office Grant DAAL-03-91-G-0102, and NSF grant CCR-8814921.

the standard model by assuming that the processor can flip a coin and write the result in a single atomic step. Abrahamson [Abr88] demonstrated that consensus is possible even for the standard model, but his protocol required an exponential expected number of steps. Since then a number of polynomial-work consensus protocols have been proposed. Protocols that use unbounded registers have been proposed by Aspnes and Herlihy [AH90] (the first polynomial-time algorithm), by Saks, Shavit, and Woll [SSW91] (optimized for the case where processors run in lock step), and by Bracha and Rachman [BR91] (running time $O(n^2 \log n)$). Protocols that use bounded registers have been proposed by Attiya, Dolev, and Shavit [ADS89] (running time $O(n^3)$), by Aspnes [Asp90] (running time $O(n^2(p^2+n))$, where p is the number of active processors), by Bracha and Rachman [BR90] (running time $O(n(p^2+n))$), and by Dwork, Herlihy, Plotkin and Waarts [DHPW92] (immediate application of what they call time-lapse snapshots and with the same running time as [BR90]).

The main goal of a wait-free algorithm is usually to minimize the worst case expected bound on the work done by a single processor. Still, for all of the known polynomial-work wait-free consensus protocols, the worst case expected bound on the work done by a single processor is asymptotically no better than the bound on the total work done by all of the processors together.

Therefore, one of the main contributions of this paper is in showing that wait-free consensus can be solved without requiring the fast processors to perform much more than their fair share of the worst case total amount of work executed by all processors together. At the same time, we improve significantly on the complexity of all currently known wait-free consensus protocols, obtaining a protocol in which a processor executes at most an expected $O(n \log^2 n)$ read and write operations, which is close to the trivial lower bound of $\Omega(n)$. To do this we introduce a new *weak shared coin* protocol [AH90] that is based on a combination of the shared coin protocol described by Bracha and Rachman [BR91] and a new technique called *weighted voting*, where votes of faster processors carry more weight.[1] We believe that our weighted voting technique will find applications in other wait-free shared memory problems such as approximated consensus and resource allocation.

The rest of the paper is organized as follows. The next section describes the intuition behind our solution while emphasizing the main difference between our solution and that in [Asp90, AH90, ADS89, BR90, BR91, DHPW92, SSW91]. Section 3 describes our shared coin protocol. Section 4 reviews martingales and derives some of their properties. Section 5 sketches the proof of correctness of our shared coin protocol. A discussion of the results appears in Section 6.

[1]The consensus protocol can be constructed around our shared coin protocol using the established techniques of Aspnes and Herlihy [AH90].

2 Intuition and relation to previous results

All of the known polynomial-work consensus protocols are based on the same primitive, the **weak shared coin**. A weak shared coin returns a single bit to each processor; for each possible value $b \in \{0,1\}$ the probability that all processors see b must be at least a constant δ (the **agreement parameter** of the coin), regardless of scheduler behavior. Aspnes and Herlihy [AH90] showed that given a weak shared coin with constant agreement parameter it is possible to construct a consensus protocol by executing the coin repeatedly within a rounds-based framework which detects agreement. The number of operations executed by each processor in this construction is $O\left(\left(n+T\left(n\right)\right)/\delta\right)$, where $T(n)$ is the expected work per processor for the weak shared coin protocol. For constant δ, and under the reasonable assumption that $T(n)$ dominates n, the work per processor to achieve consensus becomes simply $O\left(T\left(n\right)\right)$.

So to construct a fast consensus protocol one need only construct a fast weak shared coin. The underlying technique for building a weak shared coin has not changed substantially since the protocol described in [AH90]; each processor repeatedly adds random ± 1 votes to a common pool until either the total vote is far from the origin [Asp90, AH90, ADS89, BR90, DHPW92] or until a predetermined number of votes have been cast [BR91, SSW91]. Any processor that sees a nonnegative total vote decides 1, and those that see a negative total vote decide 0. (The differences between the protocols are largely in how termination is detected and how the counter for the vote is implemented.)

There are many advantages to this approach. The processors effectively act as anonymous conduits of a stream of unpredictable random increments. If the scheduler stops a particular processor, at worst all it does is keep one vote from being written out to the common pool— the next local coin flip executed by some other processor is no more or less likely to give the value the scheduler wants than the next one executed by the processor it has just stopped. Intuitively, the scheduler's power over the outcome of the shared coin is limited to filtering out up to $n-1$ local coin flips from this stream of independent random variables. But the effect of this filtering is at worst equivalent to adjusting the final tally of votes by up to $n-1$. If a constant multiple of n^2 votes are cast, the total variance will be $\Omega(n^2)$, and using a normal approximation the protocol can guarantee that with constant probability the total vote is more than n away from the origin, rendering the scheduler's adjustment ineffective.

Alas, the very anonymity of the processors that is the strength of the voting technique is also its greatest weakness. To overcome the scheduler's power to withhold votes, it is necessary that a total of $\Omega(n^2)$ votes are cast— but the scheduler might also choose to stop all but one of the processors, leaving that lone processor to generate all $\Omega(n^2)$ votes by itself. Consequently, for all of the polynomial-work wait-free consensus protocols currently known, the worst-case expected bound on the work done by a single processor is asymptotically no better than the bound on the total work done by all of the processors together.

We overcome this problem by modifying the $O(n^2 \log n)$ protocol of Bracha and Rachman [BR91] to allow the processor to cast votes of increasing weight. Thus a fast processor or a processor running in isolation can quickly generate votes of sufficient total variance to finish the protocol, at the cost of giving the scheduler greater control by allowing it both to withhold votes with larger impact and to choose among up to n different weights (one for each processor) when determining the weight of the next vote to be cast.

There are two main difficulties that this approach entails; the first is that careful adjustment of the weight function and other parameters of the protocol is necessary to make sure that it performs correctly. More importantly, correctness proofs for previous shared coins based on random walks or voting [Asp90, AH90, ADS89, BR90, BR91, DHPW92, SSW91] considered only equally weighted votes, and have therefore been able to treat the sequence of votes as a sequence of independent random variables using a substitution argument. Because our protocol allows the weight of the i-th vote to depend on which processor the scheduler chooses to run, which may depend on the outcomes of previous votes, we cannot assume independence.

However, the *sign* of each vote is determined by a fair coin flip that the scheduler cannot predict in advance, and so despite all the scheduler's powers, the expected value of each vote before it is cast is always 0. This is the primary requirement of a **martingale process** [Bil86, Fel71, Kop84]. Under the right

```
procedure shared_coin()
begin
    my_reg(variance, vote) ← (0, 0)
    t ← 1
    repeat
        for i = 1 to c do
            vote ← local_flip() × w(t)
            my_reg ← (my_reg.variance +
                w(t)^2, my_reg.vote + vote)
            t ← t + 1
        end
        read all the registers, summing the
            variance fields into the local variable
            total_variance
    until total_variance > K
    read all the registers, summing the vote
        fields into the local variable total_vote
    if total_vote > 0
    then output 1
    else output 0
end
```

Figure 1: Shared coin protocol.

conditions, martingales have many similarities to sequences of sums of independent random variables. In particular, martingale analogues of the Central Limit Theorem and Chernoff bounds will be used in the proof of correctness.

3 The Shared Coin Protocol

Figure 1 gives pseudocode for each processor's behavior during the shared coin protocol. Each processor repeatedly flips a local coin that returns the values $+1$ and -1 with equal probability. The weighted value of each flip is $w(t)$ or $-w(t)$ respectively, where t is the number of coins flipped by the processor up to and including its current flip. Each weighted flip represents a vote for either the output value 1 (if positive) or 0 (if non-positive). After each flip, the processor updates its register to hold the sum of the weighted flips it has performed, and the sum of the squares of their values. After every c flips, the processor reads the registers of all the other processors, and computes the sum of all the weighted flips (the total vote) and the sum of the squares of their values (the total variance). If the total variance is greater than the quorum K, it stops, and outputs 1 if the total vote is positive, and 0 otherwise. Alternatively, if the total variance has not yet reached the quorum K, it continues to flip its local coin.

The function *local_flip* returns the values 1 and -1 randomly with equal probability. The values K and c are parameters of the protocol which will be set depending on the number of processors n to give the desired bounds on the agreement parameter and running time. The weight function $w(t)$ is used to make later local coin flips have more effect than earlier ones, so that a processor running in isolation will be able to achieve the quorum K quickly. The weight function will be assumed to be of the form $w(t) = t^a$ where a is a nonnegative parameter depending on n; though other weight functions are possible, this choice simplifies the analysis.

We will demonstrate that for suitable choice of K, c and a all processors return 1 with constant probability; the case of all processors returning 0 will follow by symmetry. The structure of the argument follows the proof of correctness of the less sophisticated protocol of Bracha and Rachman [BR91], which corresponds to Figure 1 when $w(t)$ is the constant 1, $K = \Theta(n^2)$, and $c = \Theta(n/\log n)$. Votes cast before the quorum K is reached will form a pool of **common votes** that all processors see.[2] We will show that with constant probability (i) the total of the common votes is far from the origin and (ii) the sum of the **extra votes** cast between the time the quorum is reached and the time some processor does its final read in line 13 is small, so that the total vote read by each processor will have the same sign as the total common vote.

This simple overview of the proof hides many tricky details. To simplify the analysis we will concentrate not on the votes actually written to the registers but on the votes whose values have been **decided** by the processors' execution of the local coin flip in line 7; conversion back to the values actually in the registers will be done by showing a bound on the difference between the total decided vote and the total of the register values. In effect, we are treating a vote as having been "cast" the moment that its value is determined, instead of when it becomes visible to the other processors.

Some care is also needed to correctly model the sequence of votes. Most importantly, as pointed out above, allowing the weight of the i-th vote to depend on which processor the scheduler chooses to run means the votes are not independent. So the straightforward proof techniques used for protocols based on a stream of identically-distributed random votes no longer apply, and it is necessary to bring in the theory of martingales to describe the execution of the protocol.

[2]The definitions of the common and extra votes we will use differ slightly from those used in [BR91]; the formal definitions appear in Section 5.

4 Martingales

A **martingale** is a sequence of random variables $S_1, S_2, \ldots$, which informally may be thought of as representing the changes in the fortune of a gambler playing in a fair casino. Because the gambler can choose how much to bet or which game to play at each instant, each random variable S_i may depend on all previous events. But because the casino is fair and the gambler cannot predict the future, the expected change in the gambler's fortune at any play is always 0.

We will need to use a very general definition of a martingale [Bil86, Fel71, Kop84]. The simplest definition of a martingale says that the expected value of S_{i+1} given $S_1, S_2, \ldots, S_i$ is just S_i. To use a gambling analogy, this definition says that a gambler who knows only the previous values of her fortune cannot predict its expected future value any better than by simply using its current value. But what if the gambler knows more information than just the changing size of her bankroll? For example, imagine that she is placing bets on a fair version of roulette, and always bets on either red or black. Knowing that her fortune increased after betting red will tell her only that one of eighteen red numbers came up; but a real gambler will see precisely *which* of the eighteen numbers it was. Still, we would like to claim that this additional knowledge does not affect her ability to predict the future. To do so, the definition of a martingale must be extended to allow additional information to be represented explicitly.

The tool used to represent the information known at any point in time will be a concept from measure theory, a **σ-algebra**.[3] The description given here is informal; more complete definitions can be found in [Fel71, Sections IV.3, IV.4, and V.11] or [Bil86].

4.1 Knowledge, σ-algebras, and measurability

Recall that any probabilistic statement is always made in the context of some (possibly implicit) **sample space**. The elements of the sample space (called **sample points**) represent all possible results of some set of experiments, such as flipping a sequence of coins or choosing a point at random from the unit interval. Intuitively, all randomness is reduced to selecting a single point from the sample space. An **event**, such as a particular coin-flip coming up heads or a random variable taking on the value 0, is simply a subset of the sample space that "occurs" if one of the sample points it contains is selected.

[3]Sometimes called a σ-field.

If we are omniscient, we can see which sample point is chosen and thus can tell for each event whether it occurs or not. However, if we have only partial information, we will not be able to determine whether some events occurred or not. We can represent the extent of our knowledge by making a list of all events we do know about. This list will have to satisfy certain closure properties; for example, if we know whether or not A occurred, and whether or not B occurred, then we should know whether or not the event "A or B" occurred.

We will require that the set of known events be a **σ-algebra**. A σ-algebra $\mathcal{F}$ is a family of subsets of a sample space Ω that (i) contains the empty set; (ii) is closed under complement: if $\mathcal{F}$ contains A, it contains $\Omega \setminus A$ (the **complement** of A); and (iii) is closed under countable union: if $\mathcal{F}$ contains all of $A_1, A_2, \ldots$, it contains $\bigcup_{i=1}^{\infty} A_i$.[4] An event A is said to be **$\mathcal{F}$-measurable** if it is contained in $\mathcal{F}$. In our context, the term "measurable," which comes from the original measure-theoretic use of σ-algebras to represent families of sets on which a probability distribution is well-defined, simply means "known."

We "know" about an event if we can determine whether or not it occurred. What about random variables? A random variable X is defined to be **$\mathcal{F}$-measurable** if every event of the form $X \leq c$ is $\mathcal{F}$-measurable. (The closure properties of $\mathcal{F}$ then imply that such events as $a \leq X < b$, $X = d$, and so forth are also $\mathcal{F}$-measurable.) Looking at the situation in reverse, given random variables $X_1, X_2, \ldots$ we can consider the minimum σ-algebra $\mathcal{F}$ for which each of the random variables is $\mathcal{F}$-measurable; this σ-algebra, written $\langle X_i \rangle$, is called the σ-algebra **generated** by $X_1, X_2, \ldots$, and represents all information that can be inferred from knowing the values of the generators.

A σ-algebra gives us a rigorous way to define "knowledge" in a probabilistic context. Measurability and generated σ-algebras give us a way to move back and forth between the abstract concept of a σ-algebra and concrete statements about which random variables are completely known. To analyze random variables that are only *partially* known, we need one more definition. We need to extend conditional expectations so that the condition can be a σ-algebra rather than just a collection of random variables.

For each event A let I_A be the indicator variable that is 1 if A occurs and 0 otherwise. Let $U = \mathrm{E}[X \mid \mathcal{F}]$ be a random variable such that (i) U is $\mathcal{F}$-measurable and (ii) $\mathrm{E}[UI_A] = \mathrm{E}[XI_A]$ for all A in $\mathcal{F}$. The random variable $\mathrm{E}[X \mid \mathcal{F}]$ is called the **conditional expectation** of X with respect to $\mathcal{F}$ [Fel71, Section V.11]. Intuitively, the first condition on $\mathrm{E}[X \mid \mathcal{F}]$ says that it reveals no information not already found in $\mathcal{F}$. The second condition says that just knowing that some event in $\mathcal{F}$ occurred does not allow one to distinguish between X and $\mathrm{E}[X \mid \mathcal{F}]$; this fact ultimately implies that $\mathrm{E}[X \mid \mathcal{F}]$ uses all information that is found in $\mathcal{F}$ and is relevant to X.

If $\mathcal{F}$ is generated by random variables $X_1, X_2, \ldots$, the conditional expectation $\mathrm{E}[X \mid \mathcal{F}]$ reduces to the simpler version $\mathrm{E}[X \mid X_1, X_2, \ldots]$. Some other facts about conditional expectation that we will use (but not prove): if X is $\mathcal{F}$-measurable, then $\mathrm{E}[XY \mid \mathcal{F}] = X\mathrm{E}[Y \mid \mathcal{F}]$ (which implies $\mathrm{E}[X \mid \mathcal{F}] = X$); and if $\mathcal{F}' \subseteq \mathcal{F}$, then $\mathrm{E}[\mathrm{E}[X \mid \mathcal{F}] \mid \mathcal{F}'] = \mathrm{E}[X \mid \mathcal{F}']$. See [Fel71, Section V.11].

4.2 Definition of a martingale

We now have the tools to define a martingale when the information available at each point in time is not limited to just the values of earlier random variables. A **martingale** $\{S_i, \mathcal{F}_i\}, 1 \leq i \leq n$, is a stochastic process where each S_i is a random variable representing the state of the process at time i and $\mathcal{F}_i$ is a σ-algebra representing the knowledge of the underlying probability distribution available at time i. Martingales are required to satisfy three axioms, for all i:

1. $\mathcal{F}_i \subseteq \mathcal{F}_{i+1}$. (The past is never forgotten.)
2. S_i is $\mathcal{F}_i$-measurable. (The present is always known.)
3. $\mathrm{E}[S_{i+1} \mid \mathcal{F}_i] = S_i$. (The future cannot be foreseen.)

Often $\mathcal{F}_i$ will simply be the σ-algebra $\langle S_1, \ldots S_i \rangle$ generated by the variables S_1 through S_i; in this case axioms 1 and 2 will hold automatically.

To avoid special cases let $\mathcal{F}_0$ denote the trivial σ-algebra consisting of the empty set and the entire probability space. The **difference sequence** of a martingale is the sequence $X_1, X_2, \ldots X_n$ where $X_1 = S_1$ and $X_i = S_i - S_{i-1}$ for $i > 1$. A **zero-mean martingale** is a martingale for which $\mathrm{E}[S_i] = 0$.

4.3 Gambling systems

A remarkably useful theorem, which has its origins in the study of gambling systems, is due to Halmos [Hal39]. We restate his theorem below in modern notation:

[4] Additional properties, such as being closed under finite union or intersection, follow immediately from this definition.

Theorem 1 *Let $\{S_i, \mathcal{F}_i\}, 1 \le i \le n$ be a martingale with difference sequence $\{X_i\}$. Let $\{\zeta_i\}, 1 \le i \le n$ be random variables taking on the values 0 and 1 such that each ζ_i is $\mathcal{F}_{i-1}$-measurable. Then the sequence of random variables $S'_i = \sum_{j=1}^{i} \zeta_j X_j$ is a martingale relative to $\mathcal{F}_i$. (That is, $\{S'_i, \mathcal{F}_i\}$ is a martingale.)*

Proof: The first two properties are easily verified. Because ζ_i is $\mathcal{F}_{i-1}$-measurable, $\mathrm{E}[\zeta_i X_i \mid \mathcal{F}_{i-1}] = \zeta_i \mathrm{E}[X_i \mid \mathcal{F}_{i-1}] = 0$, and the third property also follows. ∎

4.4 Limit theorems

Many results that hold for sums of independent random variables carry over in modified form to martingales. For example, the following theorem of Hall and Heyde [HH80, Theorem 3.9] is a martingale version of the classical Central Limit Theorem:

Theorem 2 ([HH80]) *Let $\{S_i, \mathcal{F}_i\}$ be a zero-mean martingale. Let $V_n^2 = \sum_{i=1}^{n} \mathrm{E}[X_i^2 \mid \mathcal{F}_{i-1}]$ and let $0 < \delta \le 1$. Define $L_n = \sum_{i=1}^{n} \mathrm{E}[|X_i|^{2+2\delta}] + \mathrm{E}[|V_n^2 - 1|^{1+\delta}]$. Then there exists a constant C depending only on δ such that whenever $L_n \le 1$,*

$$|\Pr[S_n \le x] - \Phi(x)| \le C L_n^{1/(3+2\delta)} \left[\frac{1}{1 + |x|^{4(1+\delta)^2/(3+2\delta)}}\right], \tag{1}$$

where Φ is the standard unit normal distribution with mean 0 and variance 1.

If we are interested only in the tails of the distribution of S_n, we can get a tighter bound using Azuma's inequality, a martingale analogue of the standard Chernoff bound [Che52] for sums of independent random variables. The usual form of this bound (see [AS92, Spe87]) assumes that the difference variables X_i satisfy $|X_i| \le 1$. This restriction is too severe for our purposes, so below we state a generalization of the inequality (proved in the full paper).

Theorem 3 *Let $\{S_i, \mathcal{F}_i\}, 1 \le i \le n$ be a zero-mean martingale with difference sequence $\{X_i\}$. If there exists a sequence of random variables $w_1, w_2, \dots w_n$, and a constant W, such that*

1. *Each w_i is $\mathcal{F}_{i-1}$-measurable.*
2. *For all i, $|X_i| \le w_i$ with probability 1, and*
3. *$\sum_{i=1}^{n} w_i^2 \le W$ with probability 1,*

then for any $\lambda > 0$,

$$\Pr[S_n \ge \lambda] \le e^{-\lambda^2/2W}. \tag{2}$$

Symmetry immediately gives us:

Corollary 4 *For any martingale $\{S_i, \mathcal{F}_i\}$ satisfying the premises of Theorem 3, and any $\lambda > 0$*

$$\Pr[S_n \le -\lambda] \le e^{-\lambda^2/2W}. \tag{3}$$

5 Proof of correctness

This section sketches the proof of correctness of the shared coin protocol described in Section 3. The full proof of correctness appears in the full paper.

For this section we will fix a particular scheduler. We may assume without loss of generality that the scheduler is deterministic, because any random inputs the scheduler might use cannot depend on the history of the execution and therefore may also be fixed in advance.

Consider the sequence of random variables $X_1, X_2, \dots$ where X_i represents the i-th vote that is decided by some processor executing line 7, or 0 if fewer than i local coin flips occur. For each i let $\mathcal{F}_i$ be $\langle X_1 \dots X_i \rangle$, the σ-algebra generated by X_1 through X_i. Because the scheduler is deterministic, all of the random events in the system preceding the i-th vote are captured in the variables X_1 through X_{i-1}, and the σ-algebra $\mathcal{F}_{i-1}$ thus determines the entire history of the system up to but not including the i-th vote. Furthermore, since the scheduler's behavior depends only on the history of the system, $\mathcal{F}_{i-1}$ in fact determines the scheduler's choice of which processor will cast the i-th vote. Thus conditioned on $\mathcal{F}_{i-1}$, X_i is just a random variable which takes on the values $\pm w$ with equal probability for some weight w determined by the scheduler's choice of which processor to run. Hence $\mathrm{E}[X_i \mid \mathcal{F}_{i-1}] = 0$, and the sequence of partial sums $S_i = \sum_{j=1}^{i} X_i$ is a martingale relative to $\{\mathcal{F}_i\}$.

We are not going to analyze $\{S_i, \mathcal{F}_i\}$ directly. Instead, it will be used as a base on which other martingales will be built using Theorem 1.

Let $\kappa_i = 1$ if $\sum_{j=1}^{i} X_j^2 \le K$ and 0 otherwise. Votes for which $\kappa_i = 1$ will be called **common votes**. For each processor P let $\zeta_{Pi} = 1$ if the vote X_i occurs before P reads, during its final read in line 13, the register of the processor deciding X_i, and let $\zeta_{Pi} = 0$ otherwise. In effect, ζ_{Pi} is the indicator variable for whether P would see X_i if it were written out immediately. Observe that for a fixed scheduler the values of both κ_i and ζ_{Pi} can be determined by examining the history of the system up to but not including the time when the vote X_i is cast, and thus both κ_i and ζ_{Pi} are $\mathcal{F}_{i-1}$-measurable. Consequently the sequences $\left\{\sum_{j=1}^{i} \kappa_j X_j\right\}$ and $\left\{\sum_{j=1}^{i} \zeta_{Pj} X_j\right\}$ are martingales relative to $\{\mathcal{F}_i\}$ by Theorem 1. Votes for which $\zeta_{Pi} = 1$ but $\kappa_i = 0$ will be referred to as the **extra votes** for processor P. (Observe that $\zeta_{Pi} \geq \kappa_i$ since P could not have started its final read until the total variance was at least K.) The sequence $\left\{\sum_{j=1}^{i}(\zeta_{Pi} - \kappa_i)X_i\right\}$ of the partial sums of these extra votes is a difference of martingales and is thus also a martingale relative to $\{\mathcal{F}_i\}$.

The structure of the proof of correctness is as follows. First, we show that the distribution of the total common vote, $\sum \kappa_i X_i$, is close to a normal distribution with mean 0 and variance K for suitable choices of a and K; in particular, for n sufficiently large, the probability that $\sum \kappa_i X_i > x\sqrt{K}$ will be at least a constant for any fixed x. Next, we complete the proof by showing that if the total common vote is far from the origin the chances that any processor will read a total vote whose sign differs from the common vote is small. This fact is itself shown in two steps. First, it is shown that, for suitable choice of c, the total of the extra votes for a processor P, $\sum(\zeta_{Pi} - \kappa_i)X_i$, will be small with high probability. Second, a bound Δ is derived on the difference between $\sum \zeta_{Pi} X_i$ and the total vote actually read by P.

It will be necessary to select values for a, K, and c that give the correct bounds on the probabilities. However, we will be in a better position to justify our choice for these parameters after we have developed more of the analysis, so the choice of parameters will be deferred until Section 5.5.

5.1 Phases of the protocol

We begin by defining the phases of the protocol more carefully. Let t_i be the value of the i-th processor's internal variable t at any given step of the protocol. Let U_i be the random variable representing the maximum value of t_i during the entire execution of the protocol. Let T_i be the random variable representing the maximum value of t_i during the part of the execution of the protocol where $\kappa_i = 1$.

In the proof of correctness we will encounter many quantities of the form $\sum_{i=1}^{n} \chi(T_i)$ or $\sum_{i=1}^{n} \chi(U_i)$ for various functions χ. We will want to get bounds on these quantities without having to look too closely at the particular values of each T_i or U_i. This section proves several very general inequalities about quantities of this form, all of which are ultimately based on the following constraint:

$$K \geq \sum_i \sum_{j=1}^{T_i} j^{2a} \geq \sum_i \int_0^{T_i} j^{2a}\, dj = \sum_i \frac{T_i^{2a+1}}{2a+1}. \quad (4)$$

The constant $2a+1$ will reappear often; for convenience we will write it as A. As noted above, $a \geq 0$, and hence $A \geq 1$.

Define $T_K = \left(\frac{AK}{n}\right)^{1/A}$, so that $K = \frac{nT_K^A}{A}$. The constant T_K represents the maximum value of each T_i if they are set to be equal while satisfying inequality (4). Note that T_K need not be integral. Now we can show:

Lemma 5 *Let $\psi(x) = x^A/A$ and let χ be any strictly increasing function such that $\chi\psi^{-1}$ is concave. Then for any non-negative $\{x_i\}$, if $\sum_{i=1}^{n} \psi(x_i) \leq K$, then $\sum_{i=1}^{n} \chi(x_i) \leq n\chi(T_K)$.*

Letting χ be the identity function we have $\chi\psi^{-1}(x) = (Ax)^{1/A}$, which is concave for $A \geq 1$. Hence:

Corollary 6

$$\sum_{i=1}^{n} T_i \leq nT_K. \quad (5)$$

In the case where $\chi\psi^{-1}$ is convex, the following lemma applies instead:

Lemma 7 *Let $\psi(x) = x^A/A$ and let χ be any strictly increasing function such that $\chi\psi^{-1}$ is convex. Then for any non-negative $\{x_i\}$, if $\sum_{i=1}^{n} \psi(x_i) \leq K$, then $\sum_{i=1}^{n} \chi(x_i) \leq (n-1)\chi(0) + \chi(n^{1/A}T_K)$.*

The quantity $n^{1/A}T_K$ is the maximum value that any x_i can take on without violating the constraint on $\sum x_i$. So what Lemma 7 says is that if $\chi\psi^{-1}$ is convex, $\sum \chi(x_i)$ is maximized by maximizing one of the x_i while setting the rest to zero.

For the variables U_i we can show:

Lemma 8 *Let $\psi(x) = x^A/A$ and let χ be any strictly increasing function such that $\chi(\psi^{-1}(x) + c + 1)$ is concave in x. Then,*

$$\sum_{i=1}^{n} \chi(U_i) \leq n\chi(T_K + c + 1) \quad (6)$$

Setting $\chi(x)$ to x gives

Corollary 9

$$\sum_{i=1}^{n} U_i \leq n(T_K + c + 1) \quad (7)$$

Define $g = 1 + \frac{c+3}{T_K}$; then $gT_K = T_K + c + 3$ will be an upper bound for $T_K + c + 1$ as well as a number of closely related constants involving c that will appear later.

5.2 Common votes

The purpose of this section is to show that for n sufficiently large, the total common vote is far from the origin with constant probability. We do so by using Theorem 2 to show that under the right conditions the total common vote will be nearly normally distributed.

Let $S_{Ki} = \sum_{j=1}^{i} \kappa_j X_j$. As pointed out above, $\left\{S_{Ki} = \sum_{j=1}^{i} \kappa_j X_j, \mathcal{F}_i\right\}$ is a martingale. Let $N = \lceil nT_K \rceil$. It follows from Corollary 6 that $\kappa_i = 0$ for $i > N$ and thus $S_{KN} = \lim_{i\to\infty} S_{Ki}$ is the sum of all the common votes. The distribution of S_{KN} is characterized in the following lemma.

Lemma 10 *If*

$$\frac{6A^2}{n^{1/A}T_K} \leq 1, \tag{8}$$

then for any x,

$$\left|\Pr\left[S_{KN} \leq x\sqrt{K}\right] - \Phi(x)\right| \leq C_1 \left(\frac{A}{n^{1/A}T_K}\right)^{1/5} \tag{9}$$

where C_1 is an absolute constant.

5.3 Extra votes

In this section we examine the extra votes from the point of view of a particular processor P.

Recall that ζ_{Pi} is defined to be 1 if the vote X_i is cast by some processor Q before P's final read of Q's register and 0 otherwise. Clearly, $\zeta_{Pi} \geq \kappa_i$ since P could not have started its final read until the total variance exceeded K. As discussed above, both ζ_{Pi} and κ_i are $\mathcal{F}_{i-1}$-measurable. Thus $\xi_i = \zeta_{Pi} - \kappa_i$ is a $0-1$ random variable that is $\mathcal{F}_{i-1}$-measurable, and $\left\{S_{Pi} = \sum_{j=1}^{i} \xi_j X_j, \mathcal{F}_i\right\}$ is a martingale by Theorem 1.

Define $\Delta = n(gT_K)^a$. The following lemma uses Corollary 4 to show a bound on the tails of $\sum \xi_i X_i$.

Lemma 11 *For any $x > 0$, if*

$$g^a \leq d\sqrt{\frac{T_K}{nA}} \tag{10}$$

holds for some positive $d < x$, and

$$g^A \leq 1 + \frac{(x-d)^2}{2\log(n/p)} \tag{11}$$

holds for some positive $p < n$, then for each processor P,

$$\Pr\left[\sum(\zeta_{Pi} - \kappa_i)X_i \leq \Delta - x\sqrt{K}\right] \leq p/n. \tag{12}$$

5.4 Written votes vs. decided votes

In this section we show that the difference between $\sum \zeta_{Pi} X_i$ and the total vote actually read by P is bounded by $\Delta = n(gT_K)^a$.

Lemma 12 *Let R_P be the sum of the votes read during P's final read. Then*

$$\left|\sum \zeta_{Pi} X_i - R_P\right| \leq n(T_k + c + 1)^a \leq n(gT_K)^a = \Delta \tag{13}$$

Proof: Suppose $\zeta_{Pi} = 1$, and suppose X_i is decided by processor P_j. If the vote X_i is not included in the value read by P, it must have been decided before P's read of P_j's register but written afterwards. Because each vote is written out before the next vote is decided there can be at most one vote from P_j which is included in $\sum \zeta_{Pi} X_i$ but is not actually read by P. This vote has weight at most U_j^a. So we have $|\sum \zeta_{Pi} X_i - R_P| \leq \sum_{i=1}^{n} U_i^a$.

Now let $\chi(x) = x^a$. Then $\chi\left(\psi^{-1}(y) + c + 1\right) = \left((Ay)^{1/A} + c + 1\right)^a = \sum_{k=0}^{a} \binom{a}{k} (Ay)^{k/A} (c+1)^{a-k}$, which is concave since the second derivative of each term of the sum is non-positive. The rest follows from Lemma 8. ∎

5.5 Choice of parameters

Let us summarize the proof of correctness in a single theorem:

Theorem 13 *Define*

$$\begin{aligned} A &= 2a + 1 \\ T_K &= \left(\frac{AK}{n}\right)^{1/A} \\ g &= 1 + \frac{c+3}{T_K} \end{aligned}$$

and suppose there exist $d > 0$, $x > d$ and positive $p < n$ such that all of the following hold:

$$g^a \leq d\sqrt{\frac{T_K}{nA}} \tag{14}$$

$$g^A \leq 1 + \frac{(x-d)^2}{2\log(n/p)} \tag{15}$$

$$\frac{6A^2}{n^{1/A}T_K} \leq 1 \tag{16}$$

Then the protocol implements a shared coin with agreement parameter at least

$$1 - \left[\Phi(x) + C_1 \left(\frac{A^2}{n^{1/A}T_K}\right)^{1/5} + p\right] \tag{17}$$

where C_1 is the constant from Lemma 10.

Proof: To show that the agreement parameter is at least (17) we must show that for each $z \in \{0,1\}$ the probability that all processors decide z is at least (17). Without loss of generality let us consider only the probability that all processors decide 1; the case of all processors deciding 0 follows by symmetry.

Recall the definition $\Delta = n(gT_K)^a$. Suppose that $\sum \kappa_i X_i > x\sqrt{K}$, and that for each processor P, $\sum(\zeta_{Pi} - \kappa_i)X_i > \Delta - x\sqrt{K}$. Then for each P we have $\sum \zeta_{Pi} X_i > \Delta$ and by Lemma 12 P reads a value greater than 0 during its final read and thus decides 1.

Now for this event *not* to occur, we must either have $\sum \kappa_i X_i \leq x\sqrt{K}$ or $\sum(\zeta_{Pi} - \kappa_i)X_i \leq \Delta - x\sqrt{K}$ for some P. But as the probability of a union of events never exceeds the sum of the probabilities of the events, the probability of failing in any of these ways is at most

$$\begin{aligned} &\Pr\left[\sum \kappa_i X_i \leq x\sqrt{K}\right] + \\ &\qquad \sum_P \Pr\left[\sum(\zeta_{Pi} - \kappa_i)X_i \leq \Delta - x\sqrt{K}\right] \\ \leq &\quad \left[\Phi(x) + C_1\left(\frac{A^2}{n^{1/A}T_K}\right)^{1/5}\right] + n(p/n) \quad (18) \end{aligned}$$

by Lemmas 10 and 11. So the probability that some processor decides 0 is at most (18), and thus the probability that all processors decide 1 is at least 1 minus (18). ∎

The running time of the protocol is more easily shown:

Theorem 14 *No processor executes more than* $(AK)^{1/A}(2+n/c)+2c+2n$ *register operations during an execution of the shared coin protocol.*

Proof: First consider the maximum number of votes a processor can cast. After $(AK)^{1/A}$ votes the total variance of the processor's votes will be

$$\sum_{x=1}^{(AK)^{1/A}} x^{2a} > \int_0^{(AK)^{1/A}} x^{2a}\, dx = \frac{\left((AK)^{1/A}\right)^A}{A} = K,$$

so after at most an additional c votes the processor will execute line 11 of Figure 1 and see a total variance greater than K. Thus each processor casts at most $(AK)^{1/A} + c$ votes. But each vote costs 1 write operation in line 8, and every c votes costs n reads in line 11, to which must be added a one-time cost of n reads in line 13. The total number of operations is thus at most $((AK)^{1/A} + c)\,(1 + \lceil n/c \rceil) + n \leq ((AK)^{1/A} + c)(2 + n/c) + n = (AK)^{1/A}(2 + n/c) + 2c + 2n$. ∎

It remains only to find values for a, K, and c which give both a constant agreement parameter and a reasonable running time.

Theorem 15 *If* $a = (\log n - 1)/2$, $K = (16n \log n)^{\log n}(n/\log n)$, *and* $c = n/logn - 3$, *then for n sufficiently large the protocol implements a shared coin with constant agreement parameter in which each processor executes at most* $O(n \log^2 n)$ *operations.*

6 Discussion

This paper presents the first randomized consensus algorithm which achieves a nearly optimal worst-case bound on the expected number of operations a processor needs to execute. To achieve this we construct a weak shared coin protocol based on random voting where the weight of votes cast by a processor increases with the number of votes it has already cast. The consensus protocol can then be constructed around it using the established techniques of Aspnes and Herlihy [AH90] with only a constant-factor increase in the number of operations done by each processor.

This work leads to several interesting questions. First, our voting scheme implicitly gives higher priority to operations done by processors that have already performed many operations. Such implicit priority granting may yield faster algorithms for other shared memory problems, such as approximate agreement or randomized resource allocation.

Also, although our solution improves significantly on the worst-case expected bound on the number of operations a single processor is required to perform in order to achieve consensus, the total number of operations done by all of the processors together is slightly larger (by a factor of $\log n$) than in the unweighted-voting protocol of Bracha and Rachman [BR91]. It is of theoretical interest whether there is an inherent trade-off here. This question can be generalized to other wait-free problems as well, such as performing an atomic snapshot scan.

7 Acknowledgments

We would like to thank Serge Plotkin and David Applegate for their many useful suggestions.

References

[Abr88] Karl Abrahamson. On achieving consensus using a shared memory. In *Proceedings of the Seventh ACM SIGACT-SIGOPS Symposium on Principles of Distributed Computing*, pages 291–302, August 1988.

[ADS89] Hagit Attiya, Danny Dolev, and Nir Shavit. Bounded polynomial randomized consensus. In *Proceedings of the Eighth ACM Symposium on Principles of Distributed Computing*, pages 281–294, August 1989.

[AH90] James Aspnes and Maurice Herlihy. Fast randomized consensus using shared memory. *Journal of Algorithms*, 11(3):441–461, September 1990.

[AS92] Noga Alon and Joel H. Spencer. *The Probabilistic Method.* John Wiley and Sons, 1992.

[Asp90] James Aspnes. Time- and space-efficient randomized consensus. In *Proceedings of the Ninth ACM SIGACT-SIGOPS Symposium on Principles of Distributed Computing*, pages 325–331, August 1990. To appear, Journal of Algorithms.

[Bil86] Patrick Billingsley. *Probability and Measure.* John Wiley and Sons, second edition, 1986.

[BR90] Gabi Bracha and Ophir Rachman. Approximated counters and randomized consensus. Technical Report 662, Technion, 1990.

[BR91] Gabi Bracha and Ophir Rachman. Randomized consensus in expected $O(n^2 \log n)$ operations. In *Proceedings of the Fifth International Workshop on Distributed Algorithms.* Springer-Verlag, 1991.

[Che52] H. Chernoff. A measure of asymptotic efficiency for tests of a hypothesis based on the sum of observations. *Annals of Mathematical Statistics*, 23(4):493–407, December 1952.

[CIL87] Benny Chor, Amos Israeli, and Ming Li. On processor coordination using asynchronous hardware. In *Proceedings of the Sixth ACM Symposium on Principles of Distributed Computing*, pages 86–97, 1987.

[CM89] Benny Chor and Lior Moscovici. Solvability in asynchronous environments. In *30th Annual Symposium on Foundations of Computer Science*, pages 422–427, October 1989.

[DDS87] Danny Dolev, Cynthia Dwork, and Larry Stockmeyer. On the minimal synchronism needed for distributed consensus. *Journal of the ACM*, 34(1):77–97, January 1987.

[DHPW92] Cynthia Dwork, Maurice Herlihy, Serge Plotkin, and Orli Waarts. Time-lapse snapshots. In *Proceedings of Israel Symposium on the Theory of Computing and Systems*, 1992.

[Fel71] William Feller. *An Introduction to Probability Theory and Its Applications*, volume 2. John Wiley and Sons, second edition, 1971.

[FLP85] Michael J. Fischer, Nancy Ann Lynch, and Michael S. Paterson. Impossibility of distributed commit with one faulty process. *Journal of the ACM*, 32(2):374–382, April 1985.

[Hal39] Paul R. Halmos. Invariants of certain stochastic transformations: The mathematical theory of gambling systems. *Duke Mathematical Journal*, 5(2):461–478, June 1939.

[Her91] Maurice Herlihy. Wait-free synchronization. *ACM Transactions on Programming Languages and Systems*, 13(1):124–149, January 1991.

[HH80] P. Hall and C.C. Heyde. *Martingale Limit Theory and Its Application.* Academic Press, 1980.

[Kop84] P.E. Kopp. *Martingales and Stochastic Integrals.* Cambridge University Press, 1984.

[LAA87] Michael C. Loui and Hosame H. Abu-Amara. Memory requirements for agreement among unreliable asynchronous processes. In Franco P. Preparata, editor, *Advances in Computing Research*, volume 4. JAI Press, 1987.

[Plo89] Serge A. Plotkin. Sticky bits and universality of consensus. In *Proceedings of the Eighth ACM Symposium on Principles of Distributed Computing*, pages 159–176, August 1989.

[Spe87] Joel Spencer. *Ten Lectures on the Probabilistic Method.* Society for Industrial and Applied Mathematics, 1987.

[SSW91] Michael Saks, Nir Shavit, and Heather Woll. Optimal time randomized consensus — making resilient algorithms fast in practice. In *Proceedings of the Second Annual ACM-SIAM Symposium on Discrete Algorithms*, pages 351–362, 1991.

Clock Construction in Fully Asynchronous Parallel Systems and PRAM simulation
(Extended Abstract)

Yonatan Aumann* Michael O. Rabin†

Abstract

In this paper we return to the question of simulating synchronous computations on asynchronous systems. We consider an asynchronous system with very weak, or altogether lacking any, atomicity assumptions.

The first contribution of this paper is a novel *clock* for asynchronous systems. The clock is a basic tool for synchronization in the asynchronous environment. It is a very robust construction and can operate in a system with no atomicity assumptions, and in the presence of a *dynamic scheduler*. The behavior of the clock is obtained with *overwhelming probability* ($1 - 2^{-\alpha n}$, $\alpha > 0$).

We then show how to harness this clock to drive a PRAM simulation on an asynchronous system. The resulting simulation scheme is more efficient then existing ones, while actually relaxing the assumptions on the underlying asynchronous system.

1 Introduction

Parallel algorithms and programs are most commonly designed and described for systems of tightly coupled processors working in almost complete synchrony. A typical example of such a system is the PRAM, in which all processors work step by step in complete synchrony. In less extreme models (e.g. the BSP model [Val90]), synchronization is not assumed to exist at each and every step, but is still an indispensable ingredient of the overall structure. Synchronization assumptions are convenient from the program development point of view as they free the programmer from the need to consider actual processor and network timings and let him or her focus on the major task of parallelization. These assumptions do not however correspond to the way actual parallel systems operate. Typically, processors working on separate parts of the same program may do so asynchronously and at considerably different speeds, for a multitude of reasons: interrupts, context switches, network congestion, page faults, etc..

Handling asynchrony has thus attracted much research activity and is the topic of a large body of work. One important issue is how to simulate the execution of a PRAM program on an asynchronous parallel system, but even implementing particular algorithms in an asynchronous setting is a challenging task. In this paper we focus on asynchronous systems with shared memory. Previous work regarding this setting typically assumes some sort of atomicity in carrying out basic instructions. A minimalistic assumption would be that single reads and writes are atomic, and more frequently it is assumed that some compound instruction of the form "read & write" (e.g. *test & set, fetch & add, compare & swap*) is atomic. Bootstrapping on such atoms, consensus protocols and synchronization mechanisms are then developed. Carrying out the more complex computations, such as PRAM simulations, generally required the stronger primitives. In fact, Herlihy [Her88] describes a full hierarchy of atomicity assumptions, and proves that atoms of a higher class cannot be implemented by those of a lower class, in a wait-free fashion in the deterministic setting. In particular, complex computations require the most powerful atoms such as *compare & swap* (see also [Her91]). Recently, Palem, Kedem, Rabin and Raghunatan [KPRR92] gave for the first time a PRAM simulation scheme on an asynchronous PRAM for which only individual reads and writes are assumed to be atomic.

In this paper we describe new and improved results

*Institute of Mathematics and Computer Science, The Hebrew University of Jerusalem, Israel; aumann@cs.huji.ac.il

†Aiken Computation Laboratory, Harvard University, Cambridge, MA 02138, USA, and The Institute of Mathematics and Computer Science, The Hebrew University of Jerusalem, Israel; rabin@das.harvard.edu, rabin@cs.huji.ac.il. The research of this author was supported in part by ONR contract number N0001491-J-1981, and NSF grant number CCR-90-07677, at Harvard University.

0-8186-2900-2/92 $3.00 © 1992 IEEE

for asynchronous settings with weak, or altogether lacking, atomicity assumptions. Our first contribution is clock construction for shared memory asynchronous systems. The clock is a basic tool to keep track of the overall amount of work performed by the system. Thus, if we have an estimate of the amount of work between synchronization barriers, then the clock can function as a synchronization mechanism (the notion of "work" is formally defined later). This enables to perform the synchronization on a purely computational basis without reference to actual time (which is ill-defined in asynchronous systems).

The clock is a general construction for asynchronous systems and can function in the most extreme asynchronous setting, in which even individual reads and write (even of a single bit) are not assumed to be atomic. Individual read and write operations are viewed as occupying physical time intervals of varying lengths, and the intervals of different processors may overlap without coinciding. A formal description of this Fully Asynchronous Parallel system (FAPS) is given in Section 2. The clock is a very robust construction and works, even in this extreme form of asynchrony, with *overwhelmingly high probability* $(1 - 2^{-\theta(n)})$.

In the second part of the paper we show one possible application of the clock. Using the clock as a synchronization mechanism, we show how to efficiently simulate a synchronous PRAM on an asynchronous system. The asynchronous system we assume for the PRAM simulation is not the full asynchronous model, as we assume atomic reads and writes. No further atomicity (e.g. *read & write*) is assumed. For a synchronous PRAM with n processors we obtain the simulation on a n processor asynchronous system with an $O(\log^2 n)$ work overhead, and an $O(\log n)$ work overhead if the asynchronous systems contains $n/\log n$ actual processors. This is a $\log n$ factor improvement over the previous results ([KPRR92]). We also relax the assumption regarding the concurrency allowed by the system. Our scheme requires $O(\log n)$ concurrent memory accesses (instead of $O(n)$ in the previous works).

1.1 Previous and Related Work

Several studies, over the past years, have addressed the issue of incorporating asynchrony into the shared memory and PRAM models, and designing methods for handling the difficulties it introduces ([MSP90,CZ89,Gib89,Nis90,Her88] and others). Among these studies, there is a great diversity both in the formulation of the model and the complexity measures, and in the "target" algorithms to be implemented on the asynchronous system (e.g. PRAM simulation, FFT, graph connectivity). For a detailed overview the reader is referred to the introduction in [KPRR92] (notice there especially the important distinction between our notion of *progressive* computation and that of *wait-free* computation of [Her88,Her91]).

Martel, Subramonian and Park [MSP90] give an $O(Tn)$ work simulation scheme for a T step n processor PRAM program, on an $n/\log n \log^* n$ processor actual asynchronous system, which is work-optimal. With n processors in the actual system, the scheme gives an $O(\log n \log^* n)$ work overhead. This was later improved to eliminate the $\log^* n$ factor in [MS]. Reads and writes are assumed to be atomic. In addition there is a "loose atomicity" assumption which states that no more than $O(n)$ work units are completed in the system between specified read and write instructions. (this prevents tardy processors from clobbering correct results).

Kedem, Palem, Rabin and Raghunathan [KPRR92], give a scheme for the simulation of an EREW PRAM on an asynchronous system, assuming only atomic reads and writes. For an n processor PRAM program and an n processor system, the scheme gives an $O(\log^3 n)$ work overhead. If the actual system consists of $n/\log n$ actual processors then the overhead reduces to $O(\log^2 n)$.

Both of the above schemes assume that the simulating asynchronous system allows up to $O(n)$ concurrent reads, even for an EREW program. Both schemes are randomized and work w.h.p. in the presence of an oblivious adversary.

For the PRAM simulation scheme in this paper we assume a system with atomic reads and writes (no further atomicity assumptions) and $O(\log n)$ concurrency. We obtain the simulation with $O(\log^2 n)$ work overhead for the n processor system, and $O(\log n)$ overhead for the $n/\log n$ processor system. We note, however, that our scheme is Monte-Carlo, while the previous ones are Las-Vegas.

The idea of keeping several copies of each program variable used in this work, was introduced in the simulation context in [KPRR92]. The latter paper also has a clock. Our clock is, however, rather different, both in structure and in usage, from that of [KPRR92]. We use the clock to *drive* the computation, rather than for performing lateness tests. The possibility of doing so is unique to our new clock.

A very particular form of asynchrony is the fail-stop behavior. PRAM simulation on fail-stop PRAM is dealt in [KS91,KPRS91,KPS90] and others. Clearly our results hold for this restricted model as well.

L. Lamport in [Lam86] dealt extensively with the delicate issue of atomicity of reads and writes, or the lack thereof. In the first part of [Lam86], a general definition of asynchronous systems is described. Our FAPS model is similar to the "global time model" described there.

1.2 Outline and Terminology

This paper is organized as follows. In Section 2 we give a formal description of the Fully Asynchronous Parallel System, which is the general model for the clock. In Section 3 we give the description of the clock and prove its strong properties. In Section 4 we give the application of the clock in the PRAM simulation scheme.

We, loosely, say that an event E occurs *with high probability (w.h.p.)* if for all $\alpha > 0$ there exists a proper choice of the relevant parameters such that $\Pr(E) \geq (1 - n^{-\alpha})$. We say that the event occurs *with overwhelming probability* if for α as above $\Pr(E) \geq (1 - 2^{-\alpha n})$.

2 The Fully Asynchronous Parallel System

In the definition of the asynchronous system we want to formulate the idea that each processor can have a completely non-correlated idea of "time"; non-correlated to that of other processors, and non- correlated to actual (physical) time. It is important to emphasize that not only can different processors disagree on the question "what time is it?" but also on how "fast" time passes by. In order to formulate this we express each processor's internal, subjective, view of time with regards to the actual (physical) continuous time axis. Note, however, that actual time does not exist for the processors; it is only for our convenience in formulation and analysis that it is introduced.

The asynchronous parallel computer model we assume is the following:

- The system consists of n independent parallel processors, $\{P_i\}_{i=1}^{n}$, and shared memory. Processors may also have private memory.
- Processors act by reading from and writing to shared memory, and by performing internal computations. We postulate a set of *basic actions* which include: reading or writing a single memory cell, or performing one of a predefined set of internal computations.
- Processors have an *internal* view of time. Internal time is discrete, ranging over the natural numbers, $\mathcal{N}$. At each internal time point, $\tau \in \mathcal{N}$, a processor performs exactly one of the above basic actions.
- To each processor P_i there corresponds a *schedule* T_i mapping discrete internal time into actual continuous-time intervals. Formally: let $\text{Int} = \{[a,b) | 0 \leq a < b \leq \infty\}$, the function $T_i : \mathcal{N} \rightarrow \text{Int} \cup \{\text{Failure}\}$ is a mapping with the following properties:

  1. Non overlapping: For $\tau, \sigma \in \mathcal{N}, \tau \neq \sigma$, if $T_i(\tau) \in \text{Int}$ and $T_i(\sigma) \in \text{Int}$ then $T_i(\tau) \cap T_i(\sigma) = \phi$.
  2. Order preserving: for $\tau < \sigma$ if $T_i(\tau) = [a,b)$ and $T_i(\sigma) = [c,d)$ then $b \leq c$. And if $T_i(\tau) = \text{Failure}$ then $T_i(\sigma) = \text{Failure}$.

  The mapping T_i is called the *schedule* of processor P_i, and the sequence $T = (T_1, T_2, \ldots, T_n)$ is the *total schedule.*
- An interval, $T_i(\tau)$, in the range of T_i is called an *action interval.* The action interval $T_i(\tau)$ is the actual time interval required by processor P_i to perform the basic action taking place at its internal time point τ. Throughout this interval, and nowhere else, the internal time for P_i is τ.

  This formulation implies:

  - There can be arbitrary long actual time gaps between actions of any given processor. This allows the n processors to behave in complex forms of interleaving and overlapping actions.
  - The actual time it takes to perform any action, including the basic actions of reading and writing shared memory cells, may vary from one processor to another, as well as for the same processor from action to action.
  - The model does not assume atomicity of any sort, not even of the basic actions of reading or writing single memory cells. Even a single read or write action of a processor to a single cell is spread over a time interval (rather then occupying an idealized discrete time point), and during this interval the state of the memory cell is not determined. Moreover, two processors may access the same cell during action intervals that overlap, but do not coincide.
- Concurrent memory accesses produce non-deterministic results. If two processors perform a read or write action involving the same memory cell and their action intervals overlap then

the outcome is non deterministic, and can produce any value (or no value at all). Later we refer to such overlapping accesses as *interfering* with each other (Definition 3.1).

An internal computation by a processor, however, never interferes with any other action, and cannot be interfered with, even if the physical time intervals overlap.

- The total schedule is determined by an adversary. We consider two types of adversary:
  1. Dynamic adversary: At any actual time instance the dynamic adversary may view the entire state of the computation and determine the continuation of the schedule. The adversary cannot, however, prescribe what actions processors choose to perform in the action intervals granted to them.
  2. Oblivious adversary: The oblivious adversary determines the entire schedule before the parallel computation starts. The adversary has full knowledge of the computation to be executed, but cannot make schedule changes during the course of the actual computation.
- The only time-based relations available to the system are: before, after and concurrent. In particular this means that the system is insensitive to strictly monotonic transformations of the time axis onto itself.

We call a system thus described a *Fully Asynchronous Parallel System* (FAPS).

Definition 2.1 *A FAPS, M, is a triplet $M = (n, A, T)$, where n is the number of processors, A the set of basic actions and T the total schedule.*

Complexity and efficiency in the FAPS clearly cannot be assessed by the standard measures of time or number of steps. For a FAPS it is natural to measure work in number of action intervals. Hence the following definition:

Definition 2.2 *Let M be a FAPS and $I = [t_0, t_1]$ a physical time interval. We say that I contains k work units if, summed up over all processors, there are k complete action intervals in I; i.e. $k = \sum_{i=1}^{n} |\{\tau | T_i(\tau) \subseteq I\}|$ (where $|S|$ is the cardinality of the set S).*

3 The Clock

Our first goal is to construct a robust clock which functions in this highly asynchronous environment. Clearly such a clock cannot measure actual time in the physical sense, rather it will give a good measure of the amount of work performed. For a system with n asynchronous physical processors the clock advances from π to $\pi + 1$ after $\Theta(n \log n)$ work units. In subsequent sections this clock will be harnessed to drive the entire parallel asynchronous computation. The clock can function in the *dynamic adversary* setting, with *arbitrary outcomes* for interfered actions (for reads as well as for writes).

The clock is composed of three arrays, of $k = cn \log n$ locations each (c to be determined later), $\text{Clock}^l = (C_1^l, C_2^l, \ldots, C_k^l)$, $l = 0, 1, 2$, which drive each other in a circular fashion. Before going into the technical details let us first outline the general behavior of the clock. Later on we give exact meaning to the somewhat "fuzzy" notions first used.

Locations of Clock^l hold values π such that $\pi \equiv l \bmod 3$. Initially, the value 0 is written in all locations of Clock^0, 1 in all locations of Clock^1 and 2 in those of Clock^2. Now the value 2 in Clock^2 will start driving the value of Clock^0 to 3, which in turn drives the value of Clock^1 to 4, and so forth in a circular fashion (for simplicity, in the following all operations in clock superscripts are taken $\bmod 3$, i.e. $2 + 1 = 0$ etc.). We insure that Clock^{l+1} does not start driving Clock^{l+2} from $\pi - 1$ to $\pi + 2$ until Clock^{l+1} itself has the value $\pi + 1$ "firmly" written in it. And by the time Clock^{l+2} starts driving Clock^l from π to $\pi + 3$, the value $\pi + 1$ is written in Clock^{l+1} in an extremely robust form, durable in face of any number "clobbers" by tardy processors. The actual clock value is obtained by taking the value of Clock^0 and dividing it by 3. Since the clock is of size $\Theta(n \log n)$, obtaining the value of the clock is actually achieved by sampling the clock arrays.

We now give an exact formulation of the above outline. Let X be a set of memory locations (e.g. $X = \text{Clock}^l$). A *d-sample*, S, of X is a reading of d randomly chosen locations of X. For a sample S and a value π, denote by $\text{Count}(S, \pi)$ the *fraction* of the locations in the sample S which gave the reading π. The protocol for a processor participating in updating the clock is:

Protocol 1: Clock Update

1. Choose $l \in \{0, 1, 2\}$ at random.
2. d-sample Clock^l, let S be the sample. If for all values π, $\text{Count}(S, \pi) < .7$ then exit.
3. Let π be such that $\text{Count}(S, \pi) \geq .7$ (π is unique). Choose one location of Clock^{l+1} at random and write $\pi + 1$ in it.

We prove that, with overwhelming probability, once the arrays are initialized as above, the values appearing in the vast majority of the cells of the three clock arrays advance monotonically in a circular fashion, in FAPS phases consisting of $\Theta(n \log n)$ work units.

Before we analize the overall dynamic behavior of the clock we must address the impact of concurrent memory accesses, i.e. overlapping read or write actions interfering with each other. We prove that these have a negligible effect on the overall behavior.

Denote by $A_i(\tau)$ the basic action performed by P_i in internal time point τ (i.e. occurring during actual time interval $T_i(\tau)$).

Definition 3.1 *Say that actions $A_i(\tau)$ and $A_j(\sigma)$ ($i \neq j$)* interfere *with each other, if they both access (read or write) the same shared memory cell and the corresponding action intervals overlap ($T_i(\tau) \cap T_j(\sigma) \neq \phi$). When $A_i(\tau)$ and $A_j(\sigma)$ interfere with each other we also say that $A_j(\sigma)$ interferes with $A_i(\tau)$, and vise versa.*

Lemma 3.1 *Let M be a FAPS, and $I = [t_0, t_1]$ a physical time interval containing $b \cdot n \log n$ action intervals. Assume M is running Protocol 1. Then, with overwhelming probability, no more than $O(n)$ actions are interfered with in I.*

Proof: Consider the following ordering of actions: for $A_i(\tau)$ and $A_j(\sigma)$ with $T_i(\tau) = [a, b)$ and $T_j(\sigma) = [c, d)$, $A_i(\tau) \prec A_j(\sigma)$ iff $a < c$, or $a = c$ and $i < j$. This is a complete ordering of the actions. Say that $A_j(\sigma)$ *injures* $A_i(\tau)$ if:

1. $A_j(\sigma)$ interferes with $A_i(\tau)$.
2. $A_i(\tau) \prec A_j(\sigma)$.
3. For all $A_k(\lambda)$, $A_i(\tau) \prec A_k(\lambda) \prec A_j(\sigma)$, $A_k(\lambda)$ does not interfere with $A_i(\tau)$.

The idea behind the injuring relation is that while an action can interfere with several actions, it can injure at most one. Also, every action which is interfered by a later action, is also injured by some action.

We now count the number of injuries in I. Let A^i be the *i-th* action in I, according to the above ordering. Let X_i be a Bernoulli random variable getting the value 1 if A^i injures another action in I, and 0 otherwise. Let t_i be the beginning time of action A^i. Let L_i be the set of cells in the clock arrays which are accessed at t_i by some action previous to A^i (according to the defined ordering). At any given physical time instance there are at most n read or write actions in progress, thus $|L_i| \leq n$. Each clock array contains $cn \log n$ cells and the processors randomly choose which cell to access. Thus $\Pr(X_i = 1) \leq 1/c \log n$. The X_i's, however, are not independent. We define another set of Bernoulli random variables, Y_i's, as follows. For all L_i choose a set $\bar{L}_i$ of cells of the clock, such that $L_i \subseteq \bar{L}_i$ and $|\bar{L}_i| = n$. Let Y_i be a random variable such that $Y_i = 1$ iff action A^i chooses to access a cell $\bar{L}_i$. Now, the Y_i's are independent and $\Pr(Y_i = 1) = 1/c \log n$. Thus in a total of $bn \log n$ actions occurring during the interval I, with overwhelming probability $\sum Y_i \geq 2bn/c$. Clearly $\sum X_i \leq \sum Y_i$. Thus, with overwhelming probability, there are no more then $2bn/c$ injuries in I. It remains only to notice that number of actions interfered with in I is at most double the number of injuries. Thus the total number of interfered actions is at most $2 \cdot 2bn/c = O(n)$. ∎

Denote by $\text{Count}(\text{Clock}^l, \pi)$ the fraction of location of Clock^l which hold the value π. Say that a sample, S, of Clock^l is *ϵ-distorted* if there exists a π such that throughout the physical time interval in which the sample was taken $\text{Count}(\text{Clock}^l, \pi) \geq .3$ and $|\text{Count}(S, \pi) - \text{Count}(\text{Clock}^l, \pi)| \geq \epsilon$. A sample is *interfered* if at least one of the reading actions involved in it is interfered. The following fact is proved by standard statistical arguments:

Fact 3.2 *For any $p < 1, \epsilon < 1$, there exists a d such that the probability that a non-interfered d-sample is ϵ-distorted is $\leq p$.*

Definition 3.2 *Let I be a real time interval. An execution of Protocol 1 is said to* transcend *I if the execution partially, but not fully, overlaps I.*

Fact 3.3 *For any physical time interval I there are at most $2n$ protocol executions transcending it.*

An execution of a protocol is *interfered* if the sample or the write action are interfered.

Using the above definitions and lemmas we can now prove the following *main lemma*.

Lemma 3.4 *There exist constants $c > 1, 0 < \epsilon < 1, 1 < d_1 < d_2$, such that if at some time instance, t_0, the state of the clock is the following:*

- $\text{Count}(\text{Clock}^j, \pi) > .5$,
- $\text{Count}(\text{Clock}^{(j+1)}, \pi + 1) > .7 + \epsilon$
- $\text{Count}(\text{Clock}^{(j+2)}, \pi + 2) > .7 + \epsilon$,

then, with overwhelming probability, after a time interval I containing w work units, with $d_1 n \log n < w < d_2 n \log n$, the following state will be reached:

- $\text{Count}(\text{Clock}^j, \pi + 3) > .7 + \epsilon$,
- $\text{Count}(\text{Clock}^{(j+1)}, \pi + 1) > .5$
- $\text{Count}(\text{Clock}^{(j+2)}, \pi + 2) > .7 + \epsilon$.

Proof: W.l.o.g. assume $j = 0$. Let us first concentrate on non-interfered protocol executions originating after t_0. The progress of the clock will take place in two stages. Initially, protocol executions for which the sample is at most ϵ-distorted have the following outcomes, depending on the choice of l is stage 1 of the protocol:

- $l = 0$: Write $\pi + 1$ in Clock^1 or exit.
- $l = 1$: Write $\pi + 2$ in a random location of Clock^2 (either overwriting a previous value or rewriting $\pi + 2$).
- $l = 2$: Write $\pi + 3$ in a random location of Clock^0.

By fact 3.2 at most a p fraction of the total amount of executions are with distorted samples, and will produce other values. Thus, for p small enough, with overwhelming probability, $\text{Count}(\text{Clock}^2, \pi + 1)$ and $\text{Count}(\text{Clock}^3, \pi + 2)$ will not decrease, while $\text{Count}(\text{Clock}^0, \pi + 3)$ will be constantly growing. This state of affairs continues at least until $\text{Count}(\text{Clock}^0, \pi + 3) \approx .7 - \epsilon$. Which means a change of at least 20% of the locations of Clock^0. Thus, this stage should take roughly no less than $3(.2dcn \log n)$ work units and no more than $d'n \log n$, for some d'.

Once $\text{Count}(\text{Clock}^0, \pi + 3) \geq .7 - \epsilon$ then Clock^0 can start driving Clock^1 to $\pi + 4$. At this point, for non-interfered and at most ϵ-distorted samples, the different choices of l have the following outcomes:

- $l = 0$: Write $\pi + 4$ in a random location of Clock^1, or exit.
- $l = 1$: Write $\pi + 2$ in a random location of Clock^2, or exit.
- $l = 2$: Write $\pi + 3$ in a random location of Clock^0, thus driving up $\text{Count}(\text{Clock}^0, \pi + 3)$.

As above, only a p fraction of the samples are ϵ-distorted. Thus, with overwhelming probability, $\text{Count}(\text{Clock}^3, \pi + 2)$ will not decrease, and $\text{Count}(\text{Clock}^0, \pi + 3)$ will continue growing. This state of affairs will continue at least as long as $\text{Count}(\text{Clock}^1, \pi + 2) > .5$. Initially we had $\text{Count}(\text{Clock}^1, \pi + 2) > .7$, thus, for it to fall under .5 will require at least $0.2dcn \log n$ work units. Due to the randomization roughly the same amount of work is performed with the choice $l = 2$. For a proper choice of ϵ this will be sufficient to drive $\text{Count}(\text{Clock}^0, \pi + 4)$ to at least $.7 + \epsilon$.

Interfered protocol executions, and protocol execution transcending from before t_0 may result in outcomes other than those presumed above. However, by Lemma 3.1 and Fact 3.3 there are only $O(n)$ such writes, and thus they have a negligible effect on a $cn \log n$ size clock. ∎

At any time instance t let the value of the clock be:

$$\text{Clock}(t) = \begin{cases} \pi/3 & \text{if } \text{Count}(\text{Clock}^0, \pi) \geq .6 \\ \text{undefined} & \text{otherwise} \end{cases}$$

Since the initial state of the clock obeys the conditions of the lemma we get by induction the following as a simple corollary:

Theorem 1 *Let M be a FAPS with a dynamic adversary. For all α, $m = 2^{\alpha n \log n}$ and $s > 0$ there exist constants d, c, such that if M is operating by Protocol 1, then with probability $\geq 1 - 2^{-sn \log n}$ the following holds:*

- *The value of the clock propagates monotonically through all integer values $\{1, 2, \ldots, m\}$.*
- *There exist constants d_1, d_2, d_3, d_4 such that for each integer value π the value of the clock is π for w work units, with $d_1 n \log n \leq w \leq d_2 n \log n$, and between the time the value is π and the time the value is $\pi + 1$ there are w' work units, $d_3 n \log n \leq w' \leq d_4 n \log n$.*

Thus the clock gives us a good measure of the amount of work performed on it.

Reading the clock is performed by $d \log n$-sampling Clock^0. Let S be such a sample. The value of the clock is taken to be π if $\text{Count}(S, 3\pi) \geq .7$, and undefined if this does not hold for any π. Theorem 1 tells us that this form of reading gives us a "clock-like" behavior.

4 PRAM Simulation

In this section we show how to use the clock to obtain an efficient PRAM simulation scheme. In the simulation, however, we cannot cope with full asynchrony and must introduce some minimal atomicity assumptions. We assume an Asynchronous Parallel System (APS) with an oblivious adversary, for which only single reads and writes are guaranteed to be atomic. In addition we assume the system allows up to $O(\log n)$ concurrent reads and writes to the same memory location (with some arbitration policy for conflicting writes). A formal description of a similar model with $O(n)$ concurrency may be found in [MSP90,KPRR92].

4.1 PRAM Computation and Simulation

Our overall objective is to enable execution of computations programmed for a synchronous PRAM (without failures) on an asynchronous system. This is achieved by means of *program transformation.* We give a uniform method for transforming any given

PRAM program into a APS program, which yields the same results (under an appropriate interpretation). The PRAM model we consider is the EREW (Exclusive Read Exclusive Write) PRAM. For the sake of completeness let us state the characteristics of a EREW PRAM program:

- The program is written in parallel *steps.* In every step each PRAM processor is to perform one instruction of the form $x \leftarrow f(y, z)$. It is postulated that each of the variables x, y, z, occupies a single shared memory cell.
- All instructions in a step are assumed to be performed concurrently and completed together. In particular no processor has to await the output, in the same step, of any other processor.
- It is assumed that all reads in the parallel step occur before all writes. Thus if a processor reads a variable it will obtain the value last written in it *before the current step.*
- The program is written is such a way so as to guarantee that during no one parallel step more than one processor attempts to access (read or write) the same memory cell.

Each PRAM step is translated into a *phase* in the operation of the APS, consisting of $\Theta(n \log^2 n)$ atomic actions. The transformation guarantees that, w.h.p., the computation is:

1. Correct: produces the same results (under suitable interpretation) as the original PRAM program.
2. Progressive: If $\Theta(n \log^2 n)$ work units are devoted to a phase then the corresponding PRAM step is completed.

A single step would take the synchronous PRAM $\Theta(n)$ work units. Thus, the complexity overhead is $\Theta(\log^2 n)$.

4.2 Program Transformation

In each PRAM parallel step each PRAM processor, V_i, is to perform an instruction of the form $x \leftarrow f(y, z)$. Focusing on one such step, we designate the instruction that a specific processor V_i is to perform by $x_i \leftarrow f_i(y_i, z_i)$. Following [KPRS91] we split each parallel step into two sub-steps. First V_i reads the values of y_i, z_i,, computes $f_i(y_i, z_i)$ and writes the value in the *i-th* location of a special temporary array: $\text{tmp}_i \leftarrow f_i(x_i, y_i)$. Then the new value is copied back from the temporary array into its location in memory, $x_i \leftarrow \text{tmp}_i$. This two sub-step operation mode, known as TIES, is also enforced when dealing with control variables, such as the individual processor's program counters etc.. Having split each instruction this way, each sub-step becomes *idempotent,* that is: performing it several times has the same effect as performing it once. For the exact formulation and a full description of TIES the reader is referred to [KPRS91].

To avoid confusion we refer to the work to be performed by the PRAM processors as computation *threads.* Thus, there are n computation threads $\text{Thread}_1, \ldots, \text{Thread}_n$, corresponding to the n PRAM processors to be simulated.

In an asynchronous machine processors may "go to sleep" for long periods of time and then "wake up" in a later stage without knowing it. If the processor was about to write some variable before falling asleep then when waking up it might overwrite a new value by an obsolete one. In order to avoid losing the correct values, following [KPRR92], for each memory variable we keep μ actual copies, $\mu = \Theta(\log n)$. We shall see to it that w.h.p. at all times at least 3/4 of the copies of each variable hold the correct value. The temporary array variables also have μ copies. For a variable (or temporary variable) v, we denote the by $v^{(j)}$ the *j-th* copy of v.

Processors divide their effort between working on the actual program and advancing the clock, by randomly chosing between the two. Since we have definite bounds on the amount of work it takes to advance the clock, this will also give an accurate measure of the amount of work devoted to the program. We see to it that this amount is sufficient to guarantee that w.h.p. by the time the clock advances from one value to the next, the current program sub-step has been completed.

When a processor chooses to work on the program it could either be in a computing sub-step or in a copying back sub-step. There are separate protocols for each of these. Recall that reading the clock is performed by $d \log n$-sampling Clock^0, and dividing by 3 (Section 3). The overall protocol is thus ($0 < q < 1$ to be determined later):

Protocol 2: General Step

1. Choose $r \in \{0, 1\}$ at random, with $\Pr(r = 0) = q$, $\Pr(r = 1) = 1 - q$.
2. If $r = 0$ then perform clock update protocol (Protocol 1).
3. If $r = 1$ then read clock. If clock value is undefined then abort, else let π be the value.
4. If π is odd then perform computing sub-step protocol, else perform copying back sub-step protocol.

Definition 4.1 *The π-th* phase *is the actual time interval in which the clock value is π.*

Later we will see that the individual computing and copying back protocols consist of $O(\log n)$ basic actions each. Call the work performed on the clock *clock work* and that on the program (i.e. computing and copying protocols) *program work*. Recall that processors randomly choose if to perform program work or clock work using a $(q, 1-q)$ biased coin.

Fact 4.1 *For all b there exists a q such that with overwhelming probability in each phase the number of work units devoted to program work is w, with $w \geq bn\log^2 n$, $w = O(n\log^2 n)$.*

We now turn to describing the protocols for computing and copying back, starting with the former.

At each step there are n computation threads to be simulated. Corresponding to each thread Thread_i there is a value $f_i(y_i, z_i)$ to be computed and stored in the temporary array. Each such value must be written in $\mu = \beta\log n$ copies in the temporary array. Thus there are all in all $\beta n\log n$ tasks to be performed. Each time a processor is in a computing sub-step protocol it chooses one of these tasks at random and performs it. Obtaining the value of a variable is achieved by reading all the copies of the variable and taking the value that appears in most of them.

Protocol 3: Computing Sub-Step

Let π be the clock reading obtained in the general step protocol.

1. Choose $i \in \{1, \cdots, n\}$ and $j \in \{1, \ldots, \mu\}$ at random.
2. Read *i-th* thread program counter. Let $f_i(y_i, z_i)$ be the value to be computed by Thread_i at this step.
3. Read y_i and z_i.
4. Read clock. If value other than π then exit.
5. Write value of program counter $\text{PC}(i)$ in $\text{tmpPC}(i)^{(j)}$.
6. Compute $f_i(y_i, z_i)$ and write the value $\text{tmp}_i^{(j)}$.

The protocol for the copying back substep is analogous. Both protocols consists of $\Theta(\log n)$ action each.

We now give a brief analysis and prove the correctness of the scheme.

Definition 4.2 *An execution of a protocol is said to be* in sync *if its entire execution is within one phase. The execution is* out of sync *if it spans more than one phase.*

Lemma 4.2 *For all b' there exists a b such that if at least $bn\log^2 n$ work units are devoted to program work during each phase then w.h.p. each phase contains at least $b'n\log n$ complete in-sync protocol executions of program work.*

Proof: Assume each protocol takes at most $s\log n$ work units. By Fact 3.3 there are at most $2n$ out of sync protocol executions transcending the phase. At most $2ns$ work units are devoted to these out of sync executions. Thus there are at least $(bn\log^2 n - 2sn\log n)/s\log n$ in sync protocol executions in the phase. ∎

Thus, combining this with Fact 4.1, we can see to it that each phase contain "sufficient" amount of complete protocol executions.

Say that protocol execution *successfully terminated* if it is completed (does not exit in step 4). Note that only successfully terminating protocol execution perform write actions. For a successfully terminating protocol execution, say it is a *π-th phase* execution if it works with a clock reading of π. Recall that reading the clock is performed by a $d\log n$-sample.

Fact 4.3 *With high probability, all clock reads are correct.*

Corollary 4.4 *Let E be a π-th phase successfully terminating protocol execution. W.h.p. all the readings of all variables in E where performed within the π-th phase.*

Proof: The clock is read before and after reading the variables. By Fact 4.3 w.h.p. the clock readings are correct. The value of the clock must be identical in these two readings for the execution to successfully terminate. ∎

Next we examine the write actions and the values they produce in the copies of the variables.

Definition 4.3 *Let I be a time interval. A variable v is said to be λ-*correct *in I if there exist at least a λ fraction of the copies of v that contain the correct (current) value throughout I. The entire memory is λ-correct in I if all variables which are not to be updated in I (according to the PRAM program) are λ-correct in I.*

We prove that at all times the entire memory is at least $3/4$-correct, which has the following implication:

Fact 4.5 *Assume that the memory is $3/4$-correct during the π-th phase. Then all copies written by a π-th phase protocol executions are in fact written with correct values according to the π-th PRAM step.*

Thus a copy updated by an in sync protocol executions holds the correct value (if that value was not overwritten later). There are two possible reasons why a copy does not hold the correct value.

- Old copy: the copy was not updated during the most recent update phase.
- Clobbered Copy: the copy was correctly updated, but was later overwritten by a protocol execution originating in a previous phase.

The following simple lemma bounds the probability of a copy to be old.

Lemma 4.6 *Assume that the memory is 3/4-correct during the π-th phase. Let v be a variable to be updated during this phase. For all $p < 1$ and β there exists a b' such that if there are at least $b'n \log n$ in sync protocol executions during the π-th phase then the probability that by the end of the π-th phase a specific copy of v, $v^{(j)}$, is not updated is $\leq p$.*

The next lemma bounds the probability of a copy to be clobbered.

Lemma 4.7 *The probability that a copy is clobbered is $\leq 1/\beta \log n$.*

Proof: Let $v^{(j)}$ be a copy of a variable and let π be the most recent phase that v was to be updated. The copy $v^{(j)}$ can only be clobbered by protocol executions originating before the π-*th* phase and terminating during or after it. There are at most n such protocol executions. Let us focus on one such execution. The PRAM step this execution is simulating is $\sigma < \pi$. If variable v was not to be written at the σ-*th* step then this protocol cannot cause a clobber in v. If variable v was to be written in the σ-*th* step then the probability that this specific execution chooses to update $v^{(j)}$ is $\leq 1/\beta n \log n$ (the scheduler is oblivious). Thus the total probability is $\leq n/\beta n \log n$. ∎

Each variable has $\mu = \beta \log n$ copies. Thus we obtain:

Lemma 4.8 *Let π be the most recent phase that a variable v was to be updated. For all ϵ there exist β and b', such that if v has $\beta \log n$ copies and at least $b'n \log n$ in sync protocol execution were completed in the π-th phase, w.h.p., following the π-th phase at most an ϵ fraction of the copies of v are old or clobbered.*

Thus we have:

Lemma 4.9 *Assume that the memory is 3/4-correct during the π-th phase, then w.h.p. the memory is 3/4-correct during the phase $\pi + 1$.*

Since initially the memory is completely correct we obtain the correctness of the entire simulation by simple induction. Finally we address the issue of concurrency.

Lemma 4.10 *W.h.p. no cell is accessed concurrently by more than $O(\log n)$ processors.*

Proof: The variables accessed by different threads are distinct. There are n processors and n threads. The processors randomly choose which thread to simulate. ∎

Putting this all together we obtain:

Theorem 2 *Let M be an n processor asynchronous system with atomic reads and writes, allowing up to $O(\log n)$ concurrency in memory access. Let $\mathcal{P}$ be an $m = poly(n)$ step EREW PRAM program. The above protocols are a transformation of $\mathcal{P}$ into a program for M, such that with overwhelming probability each step takes $\Theta(n \log^2 n)$ work units, and with high probability for each PRAM variable at all times at least 3/4 of the μ copies representing it hold the correct (current) value.*

For a system with $n/\log n$ actual processors we can reduce the complexity overhead to $O(\log n)$. However, the protocols and the analysis are somewhat more complex in this case, and we cannot give the details here. This is planned for the final version.

Finally, if we want to have some indication of the termination of the computation, then, w.l.o.g. the PRAM program can be augmented so as to include a control variable which will hold the value "Done", iff all the program counters, for the n PRAM processors reached "halt". Thus, by examining the copies of this variable, one can can determine that the simulation is completed. The output/results of the simulated PRAM computation can be then acquired by reading most copies of the relevant program variables.

5 Final Remarks

- The Clock described here is composed of three sub-arrays. It is also possible to construct such a clock with only two sub-array. (clearly, properly modifying the update protocols). We found the present construction to be the simplest to describe, and preferred presentation clarity over technical efficiency.
- The Phase Clock described here has size $\Theta(n \log n)$. We proved it works with probability $\geq 1 - 2^{-\alpha n}$. Actually we can prove a probability $\geq 1 - n^{-\alpha n}$. A similar construction with an $\Theta(n)$

size clock (each array with cn locations), gives a probability $\geq 1 - 2^{-\alpha n}$.

- In the present construction of the clock, we made no assumptions regarding the actual or relative speeds of the processors. The clock would work perfectly well even with the schedule in which only one processor is doing all of the work, or any other schedule chosen by the adversary. This is due to the full randomization implemented by the processors. If we substitute this adversary scheduling by a stochastic timing model, then we can do away with some of the randomization. In particular, if the clock is composed of elements with fixed connection wires, but for which the timing is determined by a proper stochastic process, then a behavior similar to the one of the present clock should be expected. Thus, this clock may be significant and applicable in other domains as well, both within the world of asynchronous and distributed computing and elsewhere. This is the topic of a current study.

References

[CZ89] R. Cole and O. Zajicek. The APRAM: Incorporating asynchrony into the PRAM model. In *Proc. of the 1st ACM Symposium on Parallel Architectures and Algorithms*, pages 169–178, 1989.

[Gib89] P. B. Gibbons. A more practical PRAM model. In *Proc. of the 1st ACM Symposium on Parallel Architectures and Algorithms*, pages 158–168, 1989.

[Her88] M. Herlihy. Impossibility and universality results for wait-free synchronization. In *Proceedings of the 7th Annual ACM Symposium on the Principles of Distributed Computing*, pages 276–290, 1988.

[Her91] M. Herlihy. Impossibility results for asynchronous PRAM. In *Proc. of the 3rd ACM Symposium on Parallel Architectures and Algorithms*, pages 327–336, 1991.

[KPRR92] Z. M. Kedem, K. V. Palem, M. O. Rabin, and A. Raghunathan. Efficient program transformation for resilient parallel computation via randomization. In *Proceedings of the 24th Annual ACM Symposium on the Theory of Computing*, 1992.

[KPRS91] Z.M. Kedem, K.V. Palem, A. Raghunathan, and P.G. Spirakis. Combining tentative and definite executions for very fast dependable parallel computing. In *Proceedings of the 23rd Annual ACM Symposium on Theory of Computing*, pages 381–390, 1991.

[KPS90] Z.M. Kedem, K.V. Palem, and P.G. Spirakis. Efficient robust parallel computations. In *Proceedings of the 22rd Annual ACM Symposium on Theory of Computing*, pages 138–148, 1990.

[KS91] P Kanellakis and A. Shvartsman. Effecient parallel algorothms on restartable fail-stop processors. In *Proceedings of the 10th Annual ACM Symposium on the Principles of Distributed Computing*, pages 23–36, 1991.

[Lam86] L. Lamport. On interprocess communication. Part i: Basic formalism, and Part ii: Algorithms. *Distributed Computing*, 1(12):77–101, 1986.

[MSP90] C. Martel, R. Subramonian and A. Park. Asynchronous PRAMs are (almost) as good as synchronous PRAMs. In *Proceedings of the 31st Annual Symposium on the Foundations of Computer Science*, pages 590–599, 1990.

[MS] C. Martel and R. Subramonian. On the complexity of certified write-all algorithms. Unpublished Manuscript.

[Nis90] M. Nishimura. Asynchronous shared memory parallel computations. In *Proc. of the 2nd ACM Symposium on Parallel Architectures and Algorithms*, pages 76–84, 1990.

[Val90] L. G. Valiant. A bridging model for parallel computation. *Communications of the ACM*, 33(8):103–111, August 1990.

Fault-tolerant Wait-free Shared Objects*

Prasad Jayanti Tushar Deepak Chandra† Sam Toueg

{prasad, chandra, sam}@cs.cornell.edu
Cornell University

1 Introduction

1.1 Background and motivation

A *concurrent system* consists of processes communicating via shared objects. Examples of shared object types include data structures such as read/write `register`, `queue`, and `set`, and synchronization primitives such as `test&set`, `fetch&add`, and `compare&swap`. Even though different processes may concurrently access a shared object, the object must behave as if all these accesses occur in some sequential order. More precisely, the behavior of a shared object must be *linearizable* [5]. One way to ensure linearizability is to implement shared objects using critical sections [2]. This approach, however, is not fault-tolerant: The crash of a process while in the critical section of a shared object can permanently prevent the rest of the processes from accessing that object. This lack of fault-tolerance led to the concept of *wait-free implementations* of shared objects. Informally, a shared object is wait-free if every operation invocation on that object by every process is guaranteed a response in finite time irrespective of the speed of the other processes, even if some or all other processes in the system crash.

Thus, a concurrent system in which all shared objects are wait-free is resilient to *process* crashes. However, such a system is not resilient to the failures of the *shared objects* themselves.[1] For example, the "crash" of a single shared object stops all the processes that need to access that object. Motivated by this observation, we study the problem of implementing wait-free shared objects that are also *fault-tolerant*. With such objects, the system is guaranteed to make progress despite process crashes *and* the failures of some underlying objects. (To simplify notation, hereafter "object" denotes a "shared object".)

1.2 Object failures

We classify object failures into two broad categories: *Responsive* and *non-responsive*. We require that wait-free objects subject to responsive failures continue to respond (in finite time) to operation invocations. The responses may be incorrect. In contrast, wait-free objects subject to non-responsive failures are exempt from responding to operation invocations. Such objects may "hang" on the invoking process.

We divide responsive failures into three models: *R-crash*, *R-omission*, and *R-arbitrary*. An object subject to R-crash failure behaves correctly until it fails, and once it fails, it returns a distinguished response $\perp$ to every invocation. As with R-crash, an object subject to R-omission failures may return a correct response or a $\perp$. However, even if it responds $\perp$ to a process p, a subsequent operation invocation by a different process q may get a correct response. This behavior models an object $\mathcal{O}$ made of several components, some of which failed. The operation by p "ran into" a failed component of $\mathcal{O}$, while the later one by q only encountered correct components of $\mathcal{O}$. Finally, objects subject to R-arbitrary failures may "lie", *i.e.*, return arbitrary responses to operation invocations.

Similarly, we divide non-responsive failures into *crash*, *omission*, and *arbitrary*. An object subject to crash failure behaves correctly until it fails, and once it fails, it never responds to operation invocations. An object subject to omission failures may fail to respond to the invocations of an arbitrary subset of processes, but continue to respond to the invocations of the remaining processes (forever). The behavior of an object subject to an arbitrary failure is completely unrestricted: it may not respond to an invocation, and even if it does, the response may be arbitrary.

*Research supported by NSF grants CCR-8901780 and CCR-9102231, DARPA/NASA Ames grant NAG-2-593, grants from the IBM Endicott Programming Laboratory.

†Also supported by an IBM graduate fellowship.

[1] Even "software" objects have underlying hardware components. The software and/or the hardware could be faulty.

0-8186-2900-2/92 $3.00 © 1992 IEEE

1.3 Fault-tolerant objects

Let T be an object type and $\mathcal{L} = (T_1, T_2, \ldots, T_n)$ be a list of object types (T_i's are not necessarily distinct). A *wait-free implementation* of T from $\mathcal{L}$ is a function $\mathcal{I}$ such that given any distinct wait-free objects $O_1, O_2, \ldots, O_n$ of type $T_1, T_2, \ldots, T_n$, respectively, $\mathcal{O} = \mathcal{I}(O_1, O_2, \ldots, O_n)$ is a wait-free object of type T. We say $\mathcal{O}$ is a *derived object* of the implementation $\mathcal{I}$, and $O_1, O_2, \ldots, O_n$ are the *base objects* of $\mathcal{O}$. The *resource complexity* of $\mathcal{I}$ is n, the number of base objects required by $\mathcal{I}$ to implement a derived object. Such a wait-free implementation $\mathcal{I}$ is *t-tolerant for failure model $\mathcal{M}$* if every derived object $\mathcal{O}$ of $\mathcal{I}$ behaves correctly (*i.e.*, is wait-free and of type T) even if up to t base objects of $\mathcal{O}$ fail according to $\mathcal{M}$. In this Introduction, we write "implementation" as a shorthand for "wait-free implementation".

The implementation $\mathcal{I}$ is a *self-implementation* if $T_1 = T_2 = \ldots = T_n = T$. In other words, in a self-implementation the base objects are of the same type as the derived object. For example, consider the object type 2-process `queue` (i.e., a queue that can be accessed by at most two processes). In Section 5.3, we show that (for every t) there is a t-tolerant self-implementation of 2-process `queue` for R-arbitrary failures. Intuitively, this means that using a set of wait-free 2-process queues, at most t of which are subject to R-arbitrary failures, we can implement a *failure-free* wait-free 2-process queue. Thus in a self-implementation fault-tolerance is achieved through replication.

1.4 Results

To study whether a general object type has a t-tolerant implementation, we focus on two particular object types: `consensus`[2] and `register`. Herlihy [4] and Plotkin [11] showed that one can implement a wait-free object of *any* type (for which a sequential implementation exists) using only consensus and register objects. Thus, if `consensus` and `register` have t-tolerant implementations, then every object type has a t-tolerant implementation.

We first study the problem of tolerating responsive failures. We give t-tolerant *self*-implementations of `consensus` for R-crash, R-omission, and R-arbitrary failures. For R-crash and R-omission failures, our self-implementation is optimal requiring only $t + 1$ base consensus objects. For R-arbitrary failures, our self-implementation is efficient requiring $O(t \log t)$ base consensus objects. We also give t-tolerant self-implementations of `register` for R-crash, R-omission, and R-arbitrary failures. Combining the above results with [4, 11], we conclude that *every* object type T has a t-tolerant implementation (from `consensus` and `register`) for *all* responsive models of failures. Moreover, if T implements `consensus` and `register`, then T has a t-tolerant *self*-implementation. This implies that familiar object types such as (2-process) `queue`, `stack`, `test&set`, `fetch&add`, and (N-process) `compare&swap` have t-tolerant self-implementations even for R-arbitrary failures!

What about tolerating non-responsive failures? Unfortunately, the results are mostly negative. We show that there is no 1-tolerant implementation of `consensus` even for crash failures, the most benign of the non-responsive models of failures.[3] This immediately implies that any object type T that implements `consensus` (such as `queue, stack, test&set, swap, compare&swap`, etc.) has no 1-tolerant implementations for crash failures. In contrast, we show that `register` has a t-tolerant *self*-implementation even for arbitrary failures. Since randomized implementations of `consensus` from `register` are well known (for example, see [1]), the above result implies that every object type has a *randomized* t-tolerant implementation from `register` even for arbitrary failures. In addition to these universality and impossibility results, this paper contains the following results.

Consider a t-tolerant implementation for failure model $\mathcal{M}$. By definition, a derived object of this implementation is guaranteed to behave correctly even if up to t base objects fail according to $\mathcal{M}$. But what happens if more than t base objects fail? In general, the derived object may experience a more severe failure than $\mathcal{M}$. In other words, implementations may "amplify" failures: derived objects may fail more severely than base objects. This undesirable behavior is prevented by implementations that are "gracefully degrading". An implementation is *gracefully degrading* for failure model $\mathcal{M}$ if it has the following property: if base objects only fail according to $\mathcal{M}$, then derived objects are only subject to failures of type $\mathcal{M}$.

From a 1-tolerant gracefully degrading self-implementation of any object type T for a failure

[2] A consensus object supports two operations *propose 0* and *propose 1*, and has the following sequential specification: If the first operation on the object is *propse v* ($v \in \{0,1\}$), then every operation is returned the response v.

[3] The impossibility of implementing a fault-tolerant consensus *object* from any finite list of base *objects*, one of which may crash, is shown using the impossibility of solving the consensus *problem* among a finite number of *processes*, one of which may crash [3, 8].

model $\mathcal{M}$, we show how to recursively construct a t-tolerant gracefully degrading self-implementation of T for $\mathcal{M}$. Thus, graceful degradation provides a method for automatically increasing the fault-tolerance of an implementation.

Requiring graceful degradation may increase the cost of an implementation. For instance, consider t-tolerant implementations of consensus for R-omission failures. We present two such implementations. One uses only $t+1$ base objects, but is not gracefully degrading. The other is gracefully degrading, but requires $2t+1$ base objects. In fact, we show that graceful degradation for R-omission failures requires at least $2t+1$ base objects (irrespective of the type of the object being implemented).

In some cases, graceful degradation cannot be even achieved. In particular, we show that there is a large class of object types that have no gracefully degrading implementations for R-crash. Intuitively, this means that whatever the implementation, the failure of the implemented object will be more severe than R-crash, even if all its base objects can only fail by R-crash. In other words, with R-crash, implementations necessarily amplify failures. In contrast, we prove the following strong possibility result for R-omission: it is possible to obtain a t-tolerant gracefully degrading implementation of any object type from consensus and register for R-omission.

We study the problem of *translating* severe failures into more benign failures [10]. In particular we show that given $3t+1$ (base) consensus objects, at most t of which are subject to R-arbitrary failures, we can implement a consensus object that can only fail by R-omission. We prove that this translation from R-arbitrary to R-omission is resource optimal.

We also show that arbitrary failures can be viewed as having two orthogonal components: omission and R-arbitrary. Specifically, for any object type T, given any t-tolerant self-implementations $\mathcal{I}'$ and $\mathcal{I}''$ of T for omission failures and R-arbitrary failures respectively, we show how to construct a t-tolerant self-implementation of T for arbitrary failures. This decomposition simplifies the problem of tolerating arbitrary failures.

We believe that the issue addressed in this paper, characterizing object failures and coping with them, is novel. Due to space constraints, our model and definitions are informal, and the proofs are omitted. They can be found in [6].

2 Preliminaries

A *concurrent system* consists of processes and shared objects. Each (shared) object O supports a set of operations and a set of *access procedures* $\texttt{Apply}(P, op, O)$ for each process P and operation op. A process P *invokes* an operation op on an object O by calling the access procedure $\texttt{Apply}(P, op, O)$, and *executes* the operation by executing this procedure. The operation *completes* when the access procedure terminates. The *response* for an operation is the value returned by the procedure.

The behavior of an object is characterized by its type. An *object type* T is a tuple (N, OP, RES, G), where N is an integer, OP, RES are sets of operations and responses respectively, and $G{=}(V, E)$ is a directed finite or infinite graph in which each edge has a label of the form (op, res) $(op \in OP, res \in RES)$. One vertex of G is distinguished as a starting vertex. Intuitively, if O is an object of type T, then O supports the operations in $OP(T)$ and may be shared by $N(T)$ processes. $G(T)$ specifies the behavior of such an object in the absence of concurrent operation executions. We refer to the vertices of $G(T)$ as the *states of* T. A sequence $S = (op_1, res_1), (op_2, res_2), \ldots, (op_l, res_l)$ is *consistent from a state s of an object type T* if there is a path labeled S in $G(T)$ from the state s. S is *consistent with respect to T* if it is consistent from the starting state of T.

An object type T is an *n-process type* if $N(T){=}\,n$. An object type T is *deterministic* if for every state s of T and every operation $op \in OP(T)$, there is at most one response $res{\in}RES(T)$ such that (op, res) is an edge from s. T is *non-deterministic* otherwise. T is a *finite object type* if $G(T)$ is finite. T is an *infinite object type* otherwise.

In a concurrent system, operations from different processes may overlap on an object. The sequential specification is therefore not sufficient to understand the behavior of an object. We use *linearizability* defined by Herlihy and Wing [5] as the criterion for the correctness of an object. Roughly speaking, linearizability requires every operation execution to appear to take effect instantaneously at some point in time between its invocation and response. We make it more precise below.

Let $\mathcal{O}$ be an object shared by processes P_i, $i = 1, N$. Let E_t be an execution of the concurrent system $(P_1, P_2, \ldots, P_N, \mathcal{O})$ up to time t. Define $\mathcal{H}(E_t)$, the *history of the object* $\mathcal{O}$ *in execution* E_t, as follows: $(P_i, op, v, t_s, t_e) \in \mathcal{H}(E_t)$ iff process P_i invokes operation op in E_t at time t_s, and that operation completes at time t_e returning the response v. Further,

$(P_i, op, *, t_s, \infty) \in \mathcal{H}(E_t)$ iff process P_i invokes operation op in E_t at time t_s, and that operation does not complete by time t. We define a *precedes* relation on $\mathcal{H}(E_t)$ as follows: (P_i, op, v, t_s, t_e) precedes $(P_j, op', v', t'_s, t'_e)$ if $t_e < t'_s$. The history $\mathcal{H}(E_t)$ is *linearizable with respect to type* T if and only if there exists an assignment of a value to each $*$ in the incomplete operations of $\mathcal{H}(E_t)$, and a sequencing $\mathcal{S}$ of the tuples in $\mathcal{H}(E_t)$ (after this assignment) such that $\mathcal{S}$ respects the *precedes* relation and $\mathcal{S}$ is consistent with T. An *object is of type* T if every history of the object, when shared by as many as $N(T)$ processes, is linearizable with respect to type T.

Processes are *asynchronous*: *i.e.*, there are no bounds on the relative speeds of the processes. Furthermore, a process may *crash*: *i.e.*, a process may stop at an arbitrary point in its execution and never take any steps thereafter. Wait-free shared objects were introduced to cope with such processes (for example, see [4]). An *object* O *is wait-free* if every $\texttt{Apply}(P, op, O)$ returns a response in a finite time, provided that P does not crash. Thus, if P invokes op on O and continues to make progress in executing the procedure $\texttt{Apply}(P, op, O)$, it will get eventually get a response even if all of the remaining processes crash. procedure will eventually terminate, returning a response. Objects, like processes, may fail. But we defer the treatment of object failures to next section. For the remainder of this section, "object" always refers to a "correct object".

Let T be an object type and $\mathcal{L}$ be a list of object types. We define the terms *wait-free implementation* of T from $\mathcal{L}$, *wait-free self-implementation* of T, *base* and *derived* objects, and *resource complexity* as in Section 1.3. Our interest lies not just in wait-free implementations, but in wait-free implementations that also tolerate the failures of some base objects. Thus, we also need to define a *fault-tolerant* wait-free implementation. We present such a definition in Section 4, after defining the failure models for objects in Section 3.

3 Models of failure

Object failures lead to undesirable system behavior. Therefore, it is important to implement derived objects that behave correctly even if some of the base objects of the implementation fail. The cost and the complexity of such a fault-tolerant implementation depends on the *failure model*, *i.e.*, the manner in which a failed base object departs from correct behavior. In this paper, we define a spectrum of failure models that fall into two broad classes: *Responsive* and *non-responsive*.

3.1 Responsive models of failure

A wait-free object subject to responsive failures responds to every operation invocation. The response is possibly incorrect, but the object never fails to respond. In other words, the object remains wait-free even after it fails. We describe below three increasingly severe models of responsive failures.

3.1.1 R-crash

R-crash is the most benign model of object failure. This model is based on the premise that an object detects when it becomes faulty. Informally, an object subject to R-crash behaves correctly until it fails, and once it fails, it returns a distinguished response $\perp$ to every operation invocation. More precisely, a wait-free object $\mathcal{O}$ of type T subject to R-crash failure satisfies the following three properties[4].

1. $\mathcal{O}$ is wait-free.
2. If $(p, op, \perp, t_s, t_e)$ precedes $(p', op', v', t'_s, t'_e)$ in $\mathcal{H}(E_t)$, then $v' = \perp$.
3. Let $\mathcal{H}'(E_t) = \mathcal{H}(E_t) - \{(p, op, \perp, t_s, t_e) \in \mathcal{H}(E_t)\}$. Then $\mathcal{H}'(E_t)$ is linearizable with respect to T.

3.1.2 R-omission

We now informally argue that an object $\mathcal{O}$ may exhibit a more severe failure than R-crash, even if one of its "hardware components", say f, fails by R-crash. If a process p invokes an operation op on $\mathcal{O}$ that accesses f, f returns $\perp$ to p, causing p to return $\perp$ for op. Suppose a different process q later invokes some operation op' on $\mathcal{O}$ and op' does not require q to access f. Process q does not "notice" the failure of f, and thus completes op' returning a correct non-$\perp$ response. This violates the "once $\perp$, everafter $\perp$" property of R-crash. Our definition of the R-omission model, formalized below, captures this type of failure.

A wait-free object $\mathcal{O}$ of type T subject to R-omission failures satisfies the following properties.

1. $\mathcal{O}$ is wait-free.

[4]In this section, we will let E_t denote *any* execution of the concurrent system $(P_1, P_2, \ldots, P_{N(T)}, \mathcal{O})$ up to an *arbitrary* point t in time, and $\mathcal{H}(E_t)$ denote the corresponding history, as defined before.

2. Let E_t be an execution in which a process that gets $\perp$ as a response from $\mathcal{O}$ never subsequently invokes an operation on $\mathcal{O}$. Defining $\mathcal{H}(E_t)$ as before, obtain $\mathcal{H}'(E_t)$ by replacing every tuple of the form $(p, op, \perp, t_s, t_e)$ by $(p, op, *, t_s, \infty)$. $\mathcal{H}'(E_t)$ is linearizable with respect to T. Note that each operation in $\mathcal{H}(E_t)$ that gets $\perp$ as the response is treated as an incomplete operation in $\mathcal{H}'(E_t)$.

3.1.3 R-arbitrary

A wait-free object subject to R-arbitrary failures is free to return arbitrary responses to operation invocations. The only property we require from such an object is that it be wait-free.

3.2 Non-responsive models of failure

Each responsive model of failure has its non-responsive counter-part. The difference lies in the fact that a wait-free object subject to a non-responsive failure model may also fail to respond to operation invocations. In other words, after failure, an object is no longer wait-free.

3.2.1 Crash

Crash is the most benign of all non-responsive models of failure. Informally, an object subject to a crash failure behaves correctly until it fails, and once it fails, it never responds to any operation invocations. More precisely, a wait-free object $\mathcal{O}$ of type T subject to crash failure satisfies the following properties.

1. If in a (temporally) infinite execution, $\mathcal{O}$ never responds to an invocation of some process p, then the total number of responses from $\mathcal{O}$ in that execution is finite.

2. $\mathcal{H}(E_t)$ is linearizable with respect to T.

3.2.2 Omission

Omission failures are more severe than crash. A wait-free object subject to omission failures satisfies only property 2 of the crash model.

3.2.3 Arbitrary

A wait-free object subject to arbitrary failures is not required to satisfy any properties at all. Thus the behavior of such an object is completely unrestricted. In particular, the object may choose not to respond to an invocation. Even if it does, the response can be arbitrary.

4 Definition of fault-tolerant implementations

As stated in Section 1, a wait-free implementation $\mathcal{I}$ of type T is *t-tolerant for failure model* $\mathcal{M}$ if every derived object $\mathcal{O}$ of $\mathcal{I}$ is wait-free and of type T even if up to t base objects of $\mathcal{O}$ fail according to $\mathcal{M}$.

A wait-free implementation $\mathcal{I}$ is *gracefully degrading for failure model* $\mathcal{M}$ if it has the following property: if base objects only fail according to $\mathcal{M}$, then derived objects of $\mathcal{I}$ are only subject to failures of type $\mathcal{M}$.

Let $\mathcal{O}$ be a derived object of a wait-free implementation which is both t-tolerant and gracefully degrading for failure model $\mathcal{M}$. The above definitions imply that: (i) if at most t base objects of $\mathcal{O}$ fail, and they fail according to $\mathcal{M}$, then $\mathcal{O}$ does not fail, and (ii) if more than t base objects of $\mathcal{O}$ fail, and they fail according to $\mathcal{M}$, then $\mathcal{O}$ may fail, but it does not experience a more severe failure than $\mathcal{M}$. Property (i) is guaranteed by t-tolerance, and property (ii) by graceful degradation.

Gracefully degrading self-implementations have the desirable property that they can be composed recursively to realize any extent of fault-tolerance. This is formalized in the following lemma.

Lemma 4.1 (Booster Lemma) *If a type T has a 1-tolerant gracefully degrading wait-free self-implementation of resource complexity k for a failure model $\mathcal{M}$, then T has a t-tolerant gracefully degrading wait-free self-implementation of resource complexity $O(t^{\log k})$ for $\mathcal{M}$.*

Hereafter we write "object" and "implementation" as a shorthand for "wait-free object" and "wait-free implementation".

5 Tolerating responsive failures

Herlihy [4] and Plotkin [11] showed that one can implement a wait-free object of any type using only consensus and register objects. Therefore, if `consensus` and `register` have t-tolerant implementations, then every object type has a t-tolerant implementation. Hence our primary focus in this section will be on fault-tolerant implementations of `consensus` and `register`.

5.1 Fault-tolerant implementation of consensus

5.1.1 The object type N-consensus

`N-consensus` is an N-process object type that supports two operations, *propose 0* and *propose 1*, and has the following sequential specification. If the first operation invoked is *propose v*, then every invocation (including the first) is returned the response v.

The propositions below will be useful in proving the correctness of the implementations given in the subsequent sections.

Proposition 5.1 *An N-consensus object satisfies validity, agreement, and integrity (defined below) when shared by as many as N processes. Conversely, an object that satisfies validity, agreement, and integrity when shared by as many as N processes is an N-consensus object.*

- Validity*: $\mathcal{O}$ returns a response $v \in \{0,1\}$ only if there is a prior invocation of* propose v *on $\mathcal{O}$ from some process.*
- Agreement*: If $\mathcal{O}$ returns v_1, v_2 to two invocations, and $v_1, v_2 \in \{0,1\}$, then $v_1 = v_2$.*
- Integrity*: The response returned to an invocation by $\mathcal{O}$ is either 0 or 1.*

A consensus object satisfies *weak integrity* if every response returned by the object is in $\{0, 1, \perp\}$.

Proposition 5.2 *Any N-consensus object that fails by R-omission satisfies validity, agreement, and weak integrity. Conversely, if a failed N-consensus object satisfies validity, agreement, and weak integrity, then the failure is R-omission.*

In describing our implementations, we write *loc* := Propose(p, v, $\mathcal{O}$) to denote that process p invokes *propose v* on $\mathcal{O}$ and stores the response in its local variable *loc*.

5.1.2 Tolerating R-crash and R-omission failures

Theorem 5.1 *Figure 1 gives a t-tolerant self-implementation of* `N-consensus` *for R-omission failures. The resource complexity of the implementation is $t+1$ and is optimal.*

```
O_1, O_2, ..., O_{t+1} : N-consensus objects

Procedure Propose(p, v_p, O)          /* v_p ∈ {0,1} */
    estimate_p, w, k : integer local to p
begin
    estimate_p := v_p
    for k := 1 to t + 1 do
        w := propose(p, estimate_p, O_k)
        if w ≠ ⊥ then estimate_p := w
    return(estimate_p)
end
```

Figure 1: t-tolerant self-implementation of `N-consensus` for R-omission

Since R-omission failures are strictly more severe than R-crash, the above self-implementation also works for R-crash. However, it is *not* gracefully degrading either for R-crash or for R-omission. To see this, suppose that $v_p = 0$ and $v_q = 1$, and the $t+1$ base objects fail by R-crash initially. It is clear that $\mathcal{O}$ returns 0 to p and 1 to q. Thus $\mathcal{O}$ does not satisfy agreement, and by Proposition 5.2, the failure of $\mathcal{O}$ is more severe than R-omission, and therefore more severe than R-crash also. In fact, we will see in Section 7 that `N-consensus` has no t-tolerant gracefully degrading implementation for R-crash. For R-omission, however, we now present a t-tolerant gracefully degrading self-implementation of resource complexity $2t+1$. We also prove that $2t+1$ is a lower bound on the resource complexity. In fact, this lower bound applies to every "non-trivial" object type (defined below), not just to `N-consensus`.

Theorem 5.2 *Figure 2 gives a t-tolerant gracefully degrading self-implementation of* `N-consensus` *for R-omission.*

An object type T is *trivial* if it admits the following implementation: there is a function f such that every `Apply`(P, op, O) blindly returns $f(op)$.

Theorem 5.3 *The resource complexity of any t-tolerant gracefully degrading implementation of a non-trivial object type for R-omission is at least $2t+1$.*

5.1.3 Translation from R-arbitrary to R-omission

A *t-tolerant translation from a failure model $\mathcal{M}$ to a* (less severe) *failure model $\mathcal{M}'$ for object type T*

```
O_1, O_2, ..., O_{2t+1} : N-consensus objects

Procedure Propose(p, v_p, 𝒪)      /* v_p ∈ {0,1} */
    V_p[1..2t+1], estimate_p, w, k: integer local to p
begin
    estimate_p := v_p
    for k := 1 to 2t+1 do
        w := propose(p, estimate_p, O_k)
        V_p[k] := w
        if (w ≠ ⊥)∧(w ≠ estimate_p) then
            estimate_p := w
            V_p[1...(k−1)] := (⊥, ⊥, ..., ⊥)
    if V_p has more than t ⊥'s then
        return(⊥)
    else return(estimate_p)
end
```

Figure 2: t-tolerant *gracefully degrading* self-implementation of N-consensus for R-omission

is a self-implementation $\mathcal{I}$ of T such that $\mathcal{O} = \mathcal{I}(O_1, O_2, \ldots, O_n)$ is only subject to failure according to $\mathcal{M}'$ if a maximum of t base objects of $\mathcal{O}$ fail, and they fail according to $\mathcal{M}$. Note that if no base objects fail, by definition of an implementation, $\mathcal{O}$ does not fail either.

In this section, we present a t-tolerant translation from R-arbitrary to R-omission for N-consensus. It is easy to see that this translation can be used along with the t-tolerant self-implementation for R-omission to obtain a t-tolerant self-implementation of N-consensus for R-arbitrary failures. This is the principal motivation for studying such a translation. We will also show that the resource complexity, $3t+1$, of our translation is optimal.

Since a consensus object that suffers an R-arbitrary failure may return a non-binary response, we always "filter" the responses to get a binary response: procedure f-propose(p,v,O) returns propose(p,v,O) if it is 0 or 1, and returns 0 otherwise.

Theorem 5.4 *Figure 3 presents a t-tolerant translation from R-arbitrary failures to R-omission failures for* N-consensus*. The resource complexity of the translation is* $3t+1$.

Theorem 5.5 *The resource complexity of any translation* $\mathcal{I}$ *from R-arbitrary to R-omission for* N-consensus *is at least* $3t+1$.

```
A[1...2t+1], B[1...t] : N-consensus objects

Procedure Propose(p, v_p, 𝒪)
    count_p[0..1], w, i, belief_p : integer local to p
begin
    count_p[0..1] := (0,0)
    for i := 1 to 2t+1 do
        w := f-propose(p, v_p, A[i])
        count_p[w] := count_p[w] + 1
    Choose belief_p such that
        count_p[belief_p] > count_p[¬belief_p].
    for i := 1 to t do
        if belief_p ≠ f-propose(p, belief_p, B[i])
            return(⊥)
            exit Propose
    return(belief_p)
end
```

Figure 3: t-tolerant translation from R-arbitrary to R-omission for N-consensus

5.1.4 Tolerating R-arbitrary failures

Since N-consensus has a t-tolerant self-implementation for R-omission failures (of resource complexity $t+1$), and has a t-tolerant translation from R-arbitrary to R-omission failures (of resource complexity $3t+1$), N-consensus has a t-tolerant self-implementation for R-arbitrary failures. However the resulting self-implementation is expensive, requiring $(3t+1)(t+1)$ base objects. In this section, we present a t-tolerant self-implementation for R-arbitrary failures whose resource complexity is only $O(t \log t)$. This self-implementation employs the divide-and-conquer strategy. For the base step ($t = 1$), we can obtain a 1-tolerant self-implementation that requires 8 base consensus objects using the above translation approach.[5] We now show how to obtain a t-tolerant self-implementation from a $t/2$-tolerant self-implementation (Figure 4).

Theorem 5.6 *Figure 4 gives a t-tolerant (gracefully degrading) self-implementation of* N-consensus *for R-arbitrary failures of resource complexity* $O(t \log t)$.

[5] We have a 1-tolerant self-implementation that requires only 6 base consensus objects [6].

$A_0[1\ldots 3t+1]$, $A_1[1\ldots 3t+1]$,
$B[1\ldots 4t+1]$: `N-consensus objects`
O_1 : $\lceil \frac{t-1}{2} \rceil$-tolerant `N-consensus` object
O_2 : $\lfloor \frac{t-1}{2} \rfloor$-tolerant `N-consensus` object

Procedure `Propose`$(p, v_p, \mathcal{O})$
$count_p[0..1]$, $WitnessCount_p[0..1]$, $belief_p$,
$ans1_p$, $ans2_p$, v'_p, i, w : `integer` local to p

begin
$count_p[0..1]$, $WitnessCount_p[0..1]$:= (0,0,0,0)

Phase 1:
for $i := 1$ to $3t+1$ do
$w :=$ `f-propose`$(p, v_p, A_{v_p}[i])$
if $w = v_p$ then $count_p[v_p] := count_p[v_p]+1$

Phase 2:
$ans1_p :=$ `f-propose`(p, v_p, O_1)

Phase 3:
for $i := 1$ to $4t+1$ do
$w :=$ `f-propose`$(p, ans1_p, B[i])$
$WitnessCount_p[w] := WitnessCount_p[w]+1$

Phase 4:
for $i := 1$ to $3t+1$ do
$w :=$ `f-propose`$(p, v_p, A_{\overline{v_p}}[i])$
if $w = \overline{v_p}$ then $count_p[\overline{v_p}] := count_p[\overline{v_p}]+1$

Phase 5:
Choose $belief_p$ such that
$WitnessCount_p[belief_p] > WitnessCount_p[\overline{belief_p}]$
if $WitnessCount_p[belief_p] \geq 3t+1$ and
$count_p[belief_p] \geq 2t+1$
then return($belief_p$); exit `Propose`
if $WitnessCount_p[belief_p] \geq 2t+1$ and
$count_p[belief_p] \geq t+1$
then $v'_p := belief_p$
else $v'_p := v_p$
$ans2_p :=$ `propose`(p, v'_p, O_2)
return($ans2_p$)

end

Figure 4: t-tolerant self-implementation of `N-consensus` for R-arbitrary failures

5.2 Fault-tolerant implementation of register

The `register` type supports two operations, *read* and *write v*. The sequential specification is simple: *read* returns the most recent value written.[6] Lamport defined a weaker (non-linearizable) object known as a *safe register* [9]. In the following, we first show how to build a fault-tolerant safe register from safe registers, some of which may suffer R-arbitrary failures. We then resort to the register construction results in the literature to show that `register` has a self-implementation for R-arbitrary failures.

Lemma 5.1 *Using $2t+1$ 1-reader, 1-writer safe registers, at most t of which may suffer R-arbitrary failures, we can implement a failure-free 1-reader, 1-writer, safe register.*

Since one can implement a multi-reader, multi-writer (atomic) register using 1-reader, 1-writer, safe registers, we have:

Theorem 5.7 `register` *has a t-tolerant self-implementation for R-arbitrary failures.*

5.3 Universality results

We now describe how to implement fault-tolerant wait-free shared objects of a generic type. Let `N-consensus with reset` be an N-process object type informally defined as follows: An object O of this type behaves exactly like an object of type `N-consensus` with the difference that O supports an extra operation called *reset*. Applying "reset" to O will initialize O and make it available for a fresh round of consensus. The operation "reset" is required to work only in the absence of concurrent operations.

Herlihy showed that every finite object type has an implementation from (`N-consensus with reset`, `unbounded register`) [4]. The use of unbounded registers can be replaced by boolean registers [7, 11]. Using this result, together with Theorems 5.6 and 5.7, we obtain the following corollary.

Corollary 5.1

- *Every finite object type has a t-tolerant implementation from* (`N-consensus with reset`, `boolean register`) *for R-arbitrary failures.*

[6]Recall from Section 2 that an object is of type T only if every history of the object is linearizable with respect to type T. Thus, a register (*i.e.*, an object of type `register`) refers to an "atomic" register.

- *Every finite object type that implements* `N-consensus with reset` *and* `boolean register` *has a t-tolerant self-implementation for R-arbitrary failures.*

Herlihy's construction can be easily modified to yield a universal implementation from (`N-consensus with reset, unbounded register`) even for *infinite* object types. Thus Corollary 5.1 holds even if T is an infinite object type, provided that `boolean register` is replaced by `unbounded register` in the statement of the corollary.

Herlihy showed that `queue`, `stack`, `test&set`, `fetch&add` *etc.* implement `2-consensus`, and `compare&swap` implements `N-consensus` [4]. It is easy to show that `test&set`, `compare&swap` implement `boolean register`; and `queue`, `stack`, `fetch&add` implement `unbounded register`. Thus,

Corollary 5.2 *The following object types have t-tolerant self-implementations for R-arbitrary failures: (2-process)* `queue`, `stack`, `test&set`, `fetch&add`, *and (N-process)* `compare&swap`.

6 Tolerating non-responsive failures

Unlike responsive failures, non-responsive failures are almost always impossible to cope with.

Theorem 6.1 *There is no 1-tolerant implementation of* `2-consensus` *for crash failures.*

This impossibility result is obtained by reducing the consensus *problem* among a finite number of *processes*, one of which may crash, to our problem, namely, implementing a consensus *object* from any finite list of base *objects*, one of which may crash. The former problem is known to be unsolvable [3, 8].

We can strengthen the above result as follows. Suppose that *at most one* base object may fail, and it can only do so by being "unfair" (by not responding) to *at most one* process. Furthermore, suppose, the identity of this process is a priori "common knowledge" among all the processes. Even with this extremely weak model of object failure, called *1-unfairness to a known process*, we can prove the following:

Theorem 6.2 *There is no 1-tolerant implementation of* `2-consensus` *for 1-unfairness to a known process.*

From the above two theorems we have

Corollary 6.1 *Let C be the class of all object types that can implement* `2-consensus`. *For all $T \in C$, there is no 1-tolerant implementation of T for crash or 1-unfairness to a known process.*

From [4] and this corollary, we conclude that `queue`, `stack`, `test&set`, `fetch&add`, `compare&swap`, and several other common types do not have a 1-tolerant implementation for crash or 1-unfairness to a known process. In contrast to the above impossibility results we show

Theorem 6.3 `register` *has a t-tolerant self-implementation for arbitrary failures.*

This follows from

Lemma 6.1 *Using $5t+1$ 1-reader, 1-writer safe registers, at most t of which may suffer arbitrary failures, we can implement a failure-free 1-reader, 1-writer, safe register.*

Randomized implementations of `N-consensus` from `register` are well known (*e.g.*, [1]). Together with Theorem 6.3, this implies that randomized t-tolerant implementations of `N-consensus` from `register` exist for arbitrary failures. Combining this with Theorem 6.3 and the universality results of [4, 11], we have

Theorem 6.4 *Every object type has a randomized t-tolerant implementation from* `register` *for arbitrary failures.*

Our next result states that the problem of tolerating arbitrary failures can be reduced to two strictly simpler problems: tolerating R-arbitrary failures and tolerating omission failures.

Lemma 6.2 (Decomposability of arbitrary failures) *A type T has a t-tolerant self-implementation for arbitrary failures if and only if T has a t-tolerant self-implementation for R-arbitrary failures and a t-tolerant self-implementation for omission failures.*

7 Graceful degradation for benign failure models

We have seen that every object type has a t-tolerant implementation for R-crash and R-omission failures. But what if we additionally require the implementation to be gracefully degrading? The results are mostly negative for R-crash, but not so for R-omission.

An object type T is *order-sensitive* if it is a deterministic N-process type ($N \geq 2$) and the following holds: there exist state S of T, operations op, op' (not necessarily distinct) in $OP(T)$, and responses u, v, u', v' such that each of (op, u),(op', u') and (op', v'),(op, v) is consistent from the state S of T, and $u \neq v$ and $u' \neq v'$. `queue` is an example of an order-sensitive object type. To see this, let S be the state in which there are two elements 5 and 10 in the queue (5 in the front), and let both op and op' be deq. Now we have $u = 5$, $u' = 10$, $v' = 5$, and $v = 10$. Thus $u \neq v$ and $u' \neq v'$, as required. `stack`, `test&set`, `compare&swap` are some other examples of order-sensitive object types.

Theorem 7.1 *There is no 1-tolerant gracefully degrading implementation of any order-sensitive object type for R-crash.*

The above theorem has the following intuitive meaning. Given any set of objects that are guaranteed to fail only by R-crash, one cannot implement any order-sensitive object that is 1-tolerant *and* is guaranteed to only fail by R-crash. In other words, any 1-tolerant implementation of such an object necessarily amplifies the R-crash failure of its base components. Surprisingly, in many cases, this amplification of the R-crash failures of base objects cannot be avoided even if we do not require implementations to tolerate failures. This is explained below.

An object type is *non order-sensitive* if it is deterministic and not order-sensitive. Examples include `sticky bit`, `move`, and `swap`. Together with `register` (which is also non order-sensitive), each of these object types can implement *any* object type [4, 11]. We prove

Theorem 7.2 *There is no gracefully degrading implementation of any order-sensitive object type from any list of non order-sensitive object types for R-crash.*

In contrast to R-crash, there are t-tolerant gracefully degrading self-implementations of `N-consensus` and `register` for R-omission (we saw one for `N-consensus` in Section 5.1.2). These implementations can be combined with the universal constructions in [4, 11] to obtain the following result for R-omission.

A list $\mathcal{L}$ of object types is *N-universal* if every N-process object type has an implementation from $\mathcal{L}$. An example of a N-universal list is (`N-consensus with reset`, `register`).

Theorem 7.3 *Every N-process object type has a t-tolerant gracefully degrading implementation from any N-universal list of object types for R-omission.*

Acknowledgement

We thank Vassos Hadzilacos for his detailed comments on an early draft of this paper.

References

[1] J. Aspnes, Time and space efficient randomized consensus, *Proceedings of the 9th Annual Symposium on Principles of Distributed Computing*, 1990.

[2] P.J. Courtois, F. Heymans, and D.L. Parnas, Concurrent control with readers and writers, *Communications of the ACM*, Vol. 14, no. 10, 1971.

[3] M.J. Fischer, N. Lynch, and M. Paterson, Impossibility of Distributed Consensus with One Faulty Process, *Journal of the ACM*, Vol. 32, no. 2, 1985.

[4] M.P. Herlihy, Wait-free synchronization, *ACM TOPLAS*, Vol. 13, no. 1, 1991.

[5] M.P. Herlihy and J.M. Wing, Linearizability: A correctness condition for concurrent objects, *ACM TOPLAS*, Vol. 12, no. 3, 1990.

[6] P. Jayanti, T.D. Chandra, and S. Toueg, Fault-tolerant wait-free shared objects, *TR 92-1281*, Department of Computer Science, Cornell University, April 1992.

[7] P. Jayanti and S. Toueg, Some results on the impossibility, universality, and decidability of consensus, *Proceedings of the 6th Workshop on Distributed Algorithms*, Haifa, Israel, 1992.

[8] M.C. Loui and Abu-Amara, Memory requirements for agreement among unreliable asynchronous processes, *Advances in computing research*, Vol. 4, 1987.

[9] L. Lamport, On interprocess communication, Parts I and II, *Distributed Computing*, Vol. 1, 1986.

[10] G. Neiger and S. Toueg, Automatically increasing the fault-tolerance of distributed algorithms, *Journal of Algorithms*, Vol. 11, no. 3, 1990.

[11] S. Plotkin, Sticky bits and universality of consensus, *Proceedings of the 8th ACM Symposium on Principles of Distributed Computing*, 1989.

Hierarchies in Transitive Closure Logic, Stratified Datalog and Infinitary Logic

Erich Grädel*

Gregory L. McColm†

Abstract

We establish a general hierarchy theorem for quantifier classes in the infinitary logic $L^{\omega}_{\infty\omega}$ on finite structures. In particular, it is shown that no infinitary formula with bounded number of universal quantifiers can express the negation of a transitive closure.

This implies the solution of several open problems in finite model theory: On finite structures, positive transitive closure logic is not closed under negation. More generally the hierarchy defined by interleaving negation and transitive closure operators is strict. This proves a conjecture of Immerman.

We also separate the expressive power of several extensions of Datalog, giving new insight in the fine structure of stratified Datalog.

1 Introduction

It is well-known that the expressive power of first order logic (FO) is limited by the lack of a recursion mechanism. One of the simplest and most fundamental queries that are not first-order expressible is the *transitive closure*, denoted TC. It assigns to a given binary relation E on universe U its reflexive transitive closure, i.e. the set of all pairs $(x, y) \in U \times U$ such that there exist $z_0, \ldots, z_r \in U$ with $z_0 = x$, $z_r = y$ and Ez_iz_{i+1} for all $i < r$. It was shown by Fagin [7], that TC is not expressible in FO (in fact not even in monadic-Σ^1_1).

On the other side, almost every logic or database query language with recursive constructs is strong enough to define transitive closures. In fact, when logics like fixpoint logic or database query languages like datalog are introduced, the example usually given is a formula (or a program) that defines TC.

It is therefore natural to define a logic that extends FO precisely by the ability to define transitive closures. This logic, called *transitive closure logic* and denoted (FO + TC), was introduced by Immerman [15]. It increases the expressive power of first-order logic by a TC-operator which, applied to a formula $\varphi(\bar{x}, \bar{y})$ with two k-tuples of free variables, defines the transitive closure of the binary relation on k-tuples, which is defined by φ.

Another important motivation for transitive closure logic comes from the fundamental discovery in complexity theory that many of the basic complexity classes can be characterized in terms of logic — or more precisely, finite model theory — as natural extensions of first order logic, provided that an ordering of the underlying structures is available. The first discovery of this sort was made by Fagin [6], who proved that the queries in NP are precisely the Σ^1_1-definable queries. Later, Immerman [14] and Vardi [24] independently identified PTIME with least fixed point logic (FO + LFP). Immerman [15] then proved that the queries (always on ordered structures) definable by transitive closure logic coincide with the queries that are computable in NLOGSPACE and that LOGSPACE is captured by a deterministic analogue of (FO + TC), denoted (FO + DTC).

An important fragment of transitive closure logic is (FO + pos TC), which only allows *positive applications* of TC operators. In fact, Immerman's original result in [15] only identified (FO + pos TC) with NLOGSPACE. At that time most people believed that NLOGSPACE would not be closed under complementation, and therefore (FO + pos TC) not be equivalent to (FO + TC). However, the closure of of NSPACE complexity classes under complementation [16, 23] implied that *on ordered structures*, transitive closure logic collapses to its positive fragment.

It has been one of the more notable open problems in finite model theory (posed in [15]) whether this is also true in the absence of order, i.e. whether (FO + pos TC) coincides with (FO + TC) on arbitrary finite structures. Immerman also formulated the more general problem of whether the hierarchy formed by interleaving TC-operators and negations collapses. Generally it has been suspected that this is not the case,

*Mathematisches Institut, Universität Basel, Rheinsprung 21, CH-4051 Basel, Switzerland, graedel@urz.unibas.ch

†Department of Mathematics, University of south Florida, Tampa, FL 33620, mccolm@math.usf.edu

0-8186-2900-2/92 $3.00 © 1992 IEEE

i.e., that (FO + pos TC) is strictly weaker than (FO + TC) on finite structures and that the TC/negation-hierarchy is infinite.

These conjectures have motivated our investigation, and they will be proved in this paper. But we will treat these questions in a more general context: Transitive closure logic can be embedded into the infinitary logic with bounded variables, denoted $L^{\omega}_{\infty\omega}$. We will develop a theory of quantifier classes in $L^{\omega}_{\infty\omega}$ — a variation of the usual prefix classes in first order logic. In particular, we will consider quantifier classes that are defined by words over the alphabet $\{\exists, \forall, \exists^*, \forall^*\}$ (where, say, $\exists^*$ represents unbounded blocks of existential quantifiers), corresponding to quantifier classes in (FO + TC), defined by words over the alphabet $\{\exists, \forall, T, N\}$ (where, say, T represents an application of the TC operator). It turns out that (for $\exists^*$ corresponding to T and $\forall^*$ to N) for all words $p \in \{\exists, \forall, T, N\}^*$, the queries definable in the quantifier class TC(p) in (FO + TC) are also definable in the quantifier class $L^{\omega}_{\infty\omega}(p)$ in infinitary logic. Our main result is a strong hierarchy theorem for these quantifier classes. It essentially says that if a word q cannot be embedded into a word p, then the quantifier class TC(q) is not contained in $L^{\omega}_{\infty\omega}(p)$.

The embedding of logics and database query languages into infinitary logic is not new. Inexpressibility results for fixpoint logic and for Datalog using game theoretic arguments that actually apply to infinitary logic have been used by several authors since the original work in [1] and [13]. Kolaitis and Vardi showed that certain queries cannot be defined in the existential negation-free fragment of $L^{\omega}_{\infty\omega}$ and are therefore not computable by Datalog programs [20]. Our more general treatment of quantifier classes in $L^{\omega}_{\infty\omega}$ yields structural results on certain extensions of Datalog, extending those in [22] and thus gives insight on the relationship between the fine structure of (FO + TC) and the fine structure of Stratified Datalog.

Here are the contents of this paper: In section 2 we recall the basic definitions on infinitary logic and introduce *quantifier classes* in $L^{\omega}_{\infty\omega}$. In section 3 we present the necessary background on transitive closure logic, discuss quantifier classes in this logic and relate them to $L^{\omega}_{\infty\omega}$. In section 4 we show how the Ehrenfeucht-Fraïssé games technique can be adapted to the quantifier classes in $L^{\omega}_{\infty\omega}$. In section 5 we use this game to prove the general hierarchy theorem on quantifier classes in infinitary logic; in particular we show that non-reachability is not in (FO + pos TC). There are several implications of our main result: First, Immerman's question about the negation/TC-hierarchy is answered. Second, it gives a new proof of our earlier result that (FO + DTC) is weaker than (FO + TC) [10]. Third, it implies a hierarchy theorem for narrow Henkin quantifiers, via results of Blass and Gurevich [2]. Finally, it extends our earlier results in [9] (on a non-collapsing hierarchy inside (FO + pos TC), formed by interleaving TC-operators and universal quantifiers). In the last section we discuss the fine structure of stratified Datalog.

2 Quantifier classes in infinitary logic

The infinitary logic with bounded number of variables, $L^{\omega}_{\infty\omega}$, extends first-order logic by allowing infinite disjunctions and conjunctions, but requires that every formula contains only a finite number of variables.

Definition 1 Let σ be a finite vocabulary of relational and constant symbols[1]. The class $L^{k}_{\infty\omega}$ over σ is the smallest set of formulae that includes the first-order formulae over σ that contain only variables among $x_1, \ldots, x_k$, and that is closed under negation, existential and universal quantification, as well as under disjunctions and conjunctions over arbitrary sets of formulae. Finally, let $L^{\omega}_{\infty\omega} := \bigcup_{k\in} L^{k}_{\infty\omega}$.

Example. It is well-known that the transitive closure can be expressed in $L^{3}_{\infty\omega}$: Let

$$\begin{aligned}\varphi_0(x,y) &\equiv (x = y)\\ \varphi_{n+1}(x,y) &\equiv (\exists z)(Exz \wedge (\exists x)(x = z \wedge \varphi_n(x,y))\end{aligned}$$

Then the formula $\psi(x,y) \equiv \bigvee_{n\in} \varphi_n(x,y)$ expresses that there is a path from x to y.

With every formula $\psi \in L^{\omega}_{\infty\omega}$, we can associate its *quantifier structure* which is a *set* of words over the alphabet $\{\exists, \forall\}$. Intuitively the quantifier structure $P(\psi)$ of a formula $\psi \in L^{\omega}_{\infty\omega}$ is constructed as follows: Consider the formula as a tree; push all negation symbols through to the leaves (the atomic formulae) using de Morgan's laws. Then a word $p \in \{\exists, \forall\}^*$ belongs to $P(\psi)$ if and only if it is a sequence of quantifiers, that occurs on a path through ψ from the root to a leaf.

More formally, if $P, Q \subseteq \{\exists, \forall\}^*$, then let $PQ = \{pq \mid p \in P, q \in Q\}$; if Q is a singleton $\{q\}$, we will write Pq rather that $P\{q\}$. We write $p \leq q$ if p is a subword of q, i.e. if p can be obtained by deleting some symbols from q; write $P \leq Q$ if, for all $p \in P$, there

[1] All vocabularies in this paper are finite and contain only relational and constant symbols (no function symbols)

exists a $q \in Q$ with $p \leq q$. Finally for $p \in \{\exists, \forall\}^*$, let $\overline{p}$ be the dual word obtained from p by replacing all $\exists$ by $\forall$ and vice versa.

Definition 2 With every formula $\psi \in L^\omega_{\infty\omega}$ we associate its *quantifier structure* $P(\psi) \subseteq \{\exists, \forall\}^*$ as follows:

- if ψ is quantifier-free than $P(\psi) = \{\epsilon\}$ where ϵ is the empty word;
- if $\psi \equiv \neg(\varphi)$, then $P(\psi) = \{\overline{p} \mid p \in P(\varphi)\}$;
- if $\psi \equiv (\exists x_i)\varphi$, then $P(\psi) = \exists P(\varphi)$; similarly, if $\psi \equiv (\forall x_i)\varphi$, then $P(\psi) = \forall P(\varphi)$;
- if $\psi \equiv \bigvee \Phi$ or $\psi \equiv \bigwedge \Phi$, then $P(\psi) = \bigcup_{\varphi\in\Phi} P(\varphi)$.

Definition 3 A set $P \subseteq \{\exists, \forall\}^*$ defines in $L^k_{\infty\omega}$ the *quantifier class*

$$L^k_{\infty\omega}(P) := \{\psi \in L^k_{\infty\omega} \mid P(\psi) \leq P\}.$$

Similarly, $L^\omega_{\infty\omega}(P) = \bigcup_{k\in} L^k_{\infty\omega}(P)$.

We are especially interested in quantifier classes defined by strings over the alphabet $\{\exists, \forall, \exists^*, \forall^*\}$.

Definition 4 Let S be the monoid generated by $\{\exists, \forall, \exists^*, \forall^*\}$, with the relations $\exists\exists^* = \exists^*\exists = \exists^*\exists^* = \exists^*$ and $\forall\forall^* = \forall^*\forall = \forall^*\forall^* = \forall^*$. A word $p \in S$ defines a *set* of words over $\{\exists, \forall\}$, when $\exists^*$ and $\forall^*$ are identified with the sets $\{\exists^k \mid k \in \}$ and $\{\forall^k \mid k \in \}$, respectively. E.g., the word $\exists^*\forall\exists\forall^*$ denotes the set $\{\exists^k\forall\exists\forall^m \mid k, m \in \}$.

Well-known examples of such classes are Σ_k and Π_k which are defined as follows: Let $\Sigma_0 = \Pi_0 = \{\epsilon\}$, and, for $k > 0$, $\Sigma_k = \exists^*\Pi_{k-1}$ and $\Pi_k = \forall^*\Sigma_{k-1}$.

Example. Connectivity is expressible in $L^3_{\infty\omega}(\forall\forall\exists^*)$.

The words in S are partially (but not linearly!) ordered: We write $p \leq q$ if the set defined by p is a subset of the set defined by q. Our main result will show that every quantifier class $L^\omega_{\infty\omega}(q)$ contains a formula ψ_q which is equivalent to a formula in $L^\omega_{\infty\omega}(p)$ if and only if $q \leq p$.

Often, we are interested in coarser formula classes, e.g., $\bigcup_{p\in Q} L^\omega_{\infty\omega}(p)$ where $Q \subseteq S$. The most interesting examples are $\bigcup_{k\in} L^\omega_{\infty\omega}(\Sigma_k)$, containing those formulae with *bounded quantifier alternations*, and the the class $L^\omega_{\infty\omega}(\mathrm{BU})$ of infinitary formulae with bounded universal depth, which is defined as follows:

Definition 5 Let $U_0 := \exists^*$, and $U_{n+1} := U_n\forall\exists^*$. The set of *infinitary formulae with bounded number of universal quantifiers* is

$$L^\omega_{\infty\omega}(\mathrm{BU}) = \bigcup_{n\in} L^\omega_{\infty\omega}(U_n).$$

Equivalently, we can say that $L^\omega_{\infty\omega}(\mathrm{BU})$ consists of those formulae in $L^\omega_{\infty\omega}$ whose quantifier structure is dominated by a word over the alphabet $\{\exists^*, \forall\}$.

3 Transitive closure logic

The logic that originally motivated this research is transitive closure logic, introduced by Immerman [15].

Definition 6 *Transitive closure logic*, denoted (FO + TC), is obtained by augmenting the syntax of first order logic by the following rule for building formulae:

Let $\varphi(\bar{x}, \bar{y})$ be a formula with (at least) the $2k$ free variables $\bar{x} = x_1, \ldots, x_k$ and $\bar{y} = y_1, \ldots, y_k$, and let $\bar{u}$ and $\bar{v}$ be two k-tuples of terms. Then

$$\psi \equiv [\mathrm{TC}_{\bar{x},\bar{y}}\, \varphi(\bar{x}, \bar{y})](\bar{u}, \bar{v})$$

is a formula, which says that the pair $(\bar{u}, \bar{v})$ is contained in the reflexive, transitive closure of the binary relation on k-tuples that is defined by φ.

Immerman was interested in this logic because of its significance for his long term project to provide logical descriptions of complexity classes (see [11, 17] for surveys on this topic). He proved that on ordered structures, transitive closure logic can express precisely the queries that are computable with nondeterministic logarithmic space [15]. More precisely: Let $\mathcal{O}$ denote the class of structures that are ordered by a successor relation S and two constants 0 and e, interpreted by the first and the last element of S.

Theorem 1 (Immerman) *Let $L \subseteq \mathcal{O}$ be a class of σ-structures for some vocabulary σ. The following are equivalent*

(i) $L \in$ NLOGSPACE;

(ii) there is a formula $\psi \in$ (FO + TC) such that L is the set of finite models of ψ;

(iii) there is a quantifier-free formula $\varphi(\bar{x}, \bar{y})$ such that L is the set of finite models of

$$[\mathrm{TC}_{\bar{x},\bar{y}}\, \varphi(\bar{x}, \bar{y})](\bar{0}, \bar{e}).$$

Theorem 1 strongly depends on the presence of the successor relation. Without successor, only the (trivial) implications $(i) \Longleftarrow (ii) \Longleftarrow (iii)$ survive wheras the reverse directions fail. It should be noted, that Immerman's original result was weaker; it said that NLOGSPACE is captured by the logic (FO + pos TC), the restriction of (FO + TC) where the operator TC can occur only positively. However, the closure of NLOGSPACE under complementation [16, 23] implies the equivalence of (FO + pos TC) with (FO + TC). See [17] for a direct proof of this fact.

In this paper we show that this is not the case on arbitrary finite structures.

Quantifier classes in transitive closure logic. Note, that the TC-operator in a formula $\psi \equiv [\mathrm{TC}_{\bar{x},\bar{y}}\ \varphi(\bar{x},\bar{y})](\bar{u},\bar{v})$ where $\bar{x}$ and $\bar{y}$ are k-tuples, can be considered as a generalized quantifier that binds $2k$ variables. So we define $\mathrm{depth}(\psi) := 2k + \mathrm{depth}(\varphi)$.

We define quantifier classes in (FO + TC) in a very similar way as in $L^{\omega}_{\infty\omega}$. The symbol T stands for a TC-operator, and N stands for a negated TC-operator.

Definition 7 For every word p over the alphabet $\{\exists, \forall, T, N\}$ with we define a *quantifier class* $\mathrm{TC}(p)$ in (FO + TC) inductively as follows:

- $\mathrm{TC}(\epsilon)$ contains the quantifier-free formulae.
- For a quantifier $Q \in \{\exists, \forall\}$, the class $\mathrm{TC}(Qp)$ is the closure under conjunctions and disjunctions of the class $\mathrm{TC}(p) \cup \{(Qx_i)\varphi \mid \varphi \in \mathrm{TC}(p)\}$.
- $\mathrm{TC}(Tp)$ is the closure under conjunctions and disjunctions of the class of all formulae of the form $[\mathrm{TC}_{\bar{x},\bar{y}}\ \varphi(\bar{x},\bar{y})](\bar{u},\bar{v})$ where $\varphi \in \mathrm{TC}(p)$;
- $\mathrm{TC}(Np)$ is the closure under conjunction and disjunction of the class of all formulae of the form $\neg[\mathrm{TC}_{\bar{x},\bar{y}}\ \neg\varphi(\bar{x},\bar{y})](\bar{u},\bar{v})$ where $\varphi \in \mathrm{TC}(p)$.

Obviously, (FO + TC) $= \bigcup_p \mathrm{TC}(p)$, and (FO + pos TC) is the union over those classes $\mathrm{TC}(p)$ where p does not contain the symbol N.

If two distinct constants are available, then quantifier classes can often be simplified: Let P be the monoid that is generated by $\{\exists, \forall, T, N\}$ with the relations $\exists T = T\exists = TT = T$ and $\forall N = N\forall = NN = N$; a maximal-reduced word via these relations is called *regular*.

Proposition 2 *Let σ be a signature that contains at least two constants a, b. Then, on the class of all σ-structures that satisfy $a \neq b$, every formula in* (FO + TC) *of signature σ is equivalent to a formula in some* $\mathrm{TC}(p)$ *where $p \in P \cap \{T, N\}^*$; moreover, every σ-formula in* (FO + pos TC) *is equivalent to a formula in* $\mathrm{TC}(p)$ *for some $p \in P \cap \{\forall, T\}^*$.*

Transitive closure logic and infinitary logic. The quantifier classes $\mathrm{TC}(p)$ in transitive closure logic can be embedded in the quantifier classes in $L^{\omega}_{\infty\omega}$:

Proposition 3 *Let* $\mathrm{TC}(p)$ *be defined by a word $p \in \{\exists, \forall, T, N\}^*$, and let $\tilde{p}$ be the word obtained from p by replacing T by $\exists^*$ and N by $\forall^*$. Then*

$$\mathrm{TC}(p) \subseteq L^{\omega}_{\infty\omega}(\tilde{p}).$$

In particular, (FO + pos TC) $\subseteq L^{\omega}_{\infty\omega}(\mathrm{BU})$.

The words $p \in P$ can be partially ordered. We say that $p \leq q$ if p can be embedded into q, possibly by replacing some occurrences of $\exists^*$ or $\forall^*$ by T or N respectively. Note that this produces an infinite, nonlinear partial order with no infinite antichains. It is obvious that $q \leq p$ implies $\mathrm{TC}(q) \subseteq \mathrm{TC}(p)$. Our aim is to show that the converse is also true: There exist formulae in $\mathrm{TC}(q)$ which are not equivalent (on finite structures) to any formula in $\bigcup_{q \not\leq p} \mathrm{TC}(p)$. In fact our main result will show that

$$\mathrm{TC}(q) \not\subseteq \bigcup_{q \not\leq p} L^{\omega}_{\infty\omega}(\tilde{p}).$$

4 The Ehrenfeucht-Fraïssé game for $L^{k}_{\infty\omega}(P)$

Ehrenfeucht-Fraïssé-games [8, 5] provide a powerful tool for proving inexpressibility results for various logics. In their classical form they give a criterion for the indistinguishability of two (classes of) structures by means of first order formulae. They were modified by Barwise [1] and Immerman [13] to deal with other logics, especially infinitary logic and fixpoint logic. Using these games, Kolaitis and Vardi [20] have established e.g. the 0-1 law for infinitary logic.

Definition 8 Suppose we have two structures $\mathfrak{A}$ and $\mathfrak{B}$ of the same vocabulary σ. Let $c_1, \ldots, c_s$ and $d_1, \ldots, d_s$ be the interpretations of the constants of σ in $\mathfrak{A}$ and $\mathfrak{B}$, respectively. The *(infinitary) k-pebble game* on the pair $(\mathfrak{A}, \mathfrak{B})$ is played by Players I and II[2] as follows: There are k pairs $(u_1, v_1), \ldots, (u_k, v_k)$ of pebbles. Each round of the game consists of either an $\exists$-move or an $\forall$-move:

The $\exists$-move. Player I picks a pebble u_i and places it on an element of $\mathfrak{A}$. Player II answers by putting the corresponding pebble v_i on $\mathfrak{B}$.

The $\forall$-move. Similarly but with 'reversed board': Player I places v_i on $\mathfrak{B}$; Player II responds with u_i on $\mathfrak{A}$.

[2] As usual we denote Player I by male and Player II by female pronouns.

After each move, Player I wins if the pebbles do not determine a *partial isomorphism* from $\mathfrak{A}$ to $\mathfrak{B}$. More precisely: Let $a_1, \ldots, a_k$ and $b_1, \ldots, b_k$ be the elements carrying the pebbles $u_1, \ldots, u_k$ and $v_1, \ldots, v_k$, respectively. If the mapping f: $a_i \mapsto b_i$, $c_j \mapsto d_j$ is not a partial isomorphism from $\mathfrak{A}$ to $\mathfrak{B}$, then Player I wins; otherwise the game goes on. Player II wins if Player I never does.

In the classical game, Player I is free to choose between $\exists$-moves and $\forall$-moves.The crucial result, relating expressibility and pebble games is:

Theorem 4 *Let $\mathfrak{A}$ and $\mathfrak{B}$ be two structures over the same vocabulary and let $k \in \mathbb{N}$. Then the following two statements are equivalent:*

(i) For all $\varphi \in L^k_{\infty\omega}$: $\mathfrak{A} \models \varphi \implies \mathfrak{B} \models \varphi$.

(ii) Player II has a winning strategy for the k-pebble game on $(\mathfrak{A}, \mathfrak{B})$.

This result is implicit in a paper by Barwise [1], although pebble games are not explicitely mentioned there. In more explicit form it is proved by Immerman in [13], but only the first-order fragment of $L^k_{\infty\omega}$ is mentioned. The most accessible proof of Theorem 4 is probably the one given by Kolaitis and Vardi in [21].

By imposing restrictions on the admissible sequences of $\exists$- and $\forall$-moves one defines games that characterize the expressive power of quantifier classes in $L^k_{\infty\omega}$: Let $P \subseteq \{\exists, \forall\}^*$ be closed under subwords. The $L^k_{\infty\omega}(P)$-game on $(\mathfrak{A}, \mathfrak{B})$ is the k-pebble game on $(\mathfrak{A}, \mathfrak{B})$ where Player I must play in such a way that the sequence of his moves defines a word P.

Remark. For sets that are defined by a word $p \in \{\exists, \forall, \exists^*, \forall^*\}$ it is convenient to consider also $\exists^*$ and $\forall^*$-moves:

The $\exists^*$-move. Player I may make an arbitrary number of $\exists$-moves, each answered at once by Player II. This continues until until Player I wants to stop.

The $\forall^*$-move. This is similar, except that Player I makes $\forall$-moves until he gets bored.

Thus, to play the p-game, where $p = Qq$, the players make the Q-move, and then, from there, play a q-game, until they reach ϵ, when they stop (notice that if, during an $\forall^*$-move or $\exists^*$-move, partial isomorphism is broken, then Player I can stop and win at once).

Our modified games characterize the classes $L^k_{\infty\omega}(P)$.

Theorem 5 *Let $\mathfrak{A}$ and $\mathfrak{B}$ be two structures over the same vocabulary, let $P \subseteq \{\exists, \forall\}^*$ and let $k \in \mathbb{N}$. Then the following two statements are equivalent:*

(i) For all $\varphi \in L^k_{\infty\omega}(P)$: $\mathfrak{A} \models \varphi \implies \mathfrak{B} \models \varphi$.

(ii) Player II has a winning strategy for the $L^k_{\infty\omega}(P)$-game on $(\mathfrak{A}, \mathfrak{B})$.

This theorem will be our major tool for proving the main theorem.

5 The Hierarchy Theorem

In this section, we will present our main results.

Definition 9 For all $i \geq 0$, let Σ^{TC}_i denote the set of formulae in (FO + TC) where $i-1$ alternations of TC operators and negations are allowed, starting with TC. More formally, let $\Sigma^{\mathrm{TC}}_0 = \Pi^{\mathrm{TC}}_0 = \mathrm{FO}$, let Π^{TC}_i be the set of negations of Σ^{TC}_i-formulae and let $\Sigma^{\mathrm{TC}}_{i+1}$ be the closure of Π^{TC}_i under conjunction, disjunction, existential and universal quantification, and under (positive applications of) the TC-operator.

Immerman conjectured that for each i, $\Sigma^{\mathrm{TC}}_i \subsetneq \Sigma^{\mathrm{TC}}_{i+1}$. We prove a much more general hierarchy theorem for infinitary logic that implies this conjecture:

Take any quantifier class $\mathrm{TC}(q) \in (\mathrm{FO} + \mathrm{TC})$ where $q \in P$, i.e. q is a reduced word over $\{\exists, \forall, T, N\}$. Further, recall that S is the set of reduced words over $\{\exists, \forall, \exists^*, \forall^*\}$. As observed in section 2, $\mathrm{TC}(q)$ can be embedded into the quantifier class $L^\omega_{\infty\omega}(\tilde{q})$ where $\tilde{q}$ is obtained by replacing T by $\exists^*$ and N by $\forall^*$.

Theorem 6 (Hierarchy Theorem for (FO + TC) and $L^\omega_{\infty\omega}$)

1. *Non-reachability is not in $L^\omega_{\infty\omega}(\mathrm{BU})$, hence not in* (FO + pos TC).

2. *Let $q \in P$. Then the quantifier class* $\mathrm{TC}(q)$ *in* (FO + TC) *contains a formula ψ_q which is equivalent to a formula in $L^\omega_{\infty\omega}(p)$ if and only if $\tilde{q} \leq p$. Thus*
$$\mathrm{TC}(q) \not\subseteq \bigcup_{\tilde{q} \not\leq p} L^\omega_{\infty\omega}(p).$$

Proof. We will construct:

- for every $q \in P$, a formula $\psi_q(x, y) \in \mathrm{TC}(q)$;
- for every $k \in \mathbb{N}$ and $q \in P$, a pair of structures $\mathfrak{C}^k(q)$ and $\mathfrak{D}^k(q)$

such that the following conditions are satisfied:

(i) $\mathfrak{C}^k(q) \models \psi_q(a, b)$ and $\mathfrak{D}^k(q) \models \neg\psi_q(a, b)$;

(ii) If $q \not\leq p$ and $k > \mathrm{length}(p)$, then Player II wins the $L^k_{\infty\omega}(p)$-game on $\mathfrak{C}^k(q)$ and $\mathfrak{D}^k(q)$.

The Theorem then follows immediately from Theorem 5.

The formulae ψ_q and the structures $\mathfrak{C}^k(q)$ and $\mathfrak{D}^k(q)$ will have the vocabulary $\sigma_m = \{E, F_1, \ldots, F_{m-1}, a, b\}$ where $m = |q|$, where E and $F_1, \ldots, F_{m-1}$ are binary predicates and a and b are constants. We will proceed by induction on the length of q. A word q is called *existential* if it begins with $\exists$ or T, and *universal* if it begins with $\forall$ or N. For $q = \epsilon$, nothing has to be proved.

The structures $\mathfrak{C}^k(q)$ and $\mathfrak{D}^k(q)$ are defined inductively. First, the structures $\mathfrak{C}^k(\epsilon)$ consists of the nodes a and b with an E-arc from a to b, and $\mathfrak{D}^k(\epsilon)$, consists of two isolated nodes a and b. To build $\mathfrak{C}^k(q)$ and $\mathfrak{D}^k(q)$ for $q \neq \epsilon$, we use coloured digraphs I^k and J^k: Let I^k consist of source a, sink b and intermediate vertices $u_1, \ldots, u_k, v_1, \ldots, v_k$ with arcs coloured amber (A) from a to each u_i and from each v_i to b, and with arcs coloured blue (B) from a to each v_i and from each u_i to b. Let J^k be I^k with an additional vertex w and with amber arcs from a to w and from w to b.

Given $\mathfrak{A}$, a digraph whose arcs are either amber or blue, and given $\mathfrak{C}$, $\mathfrak{D}$, each with binary relations $E, F_1, \ldots, F_l$, and each with source a and sink b, let $\mathfrak{A} \otimes_{A,B} (\mathfrak{C}, \mathfrak{D})$ be the result of going through $\mathfrak{A}$ and replacing each amber arc with a copy of $\mathfrak{C}$ and each blue arc with a copy of $\mathfrak{D}$ as follows. Start with $F_{l+1} := \emptyset$. Given an blue arc (x, y), replace it with a copy of $\mathfrak{C}$, identifying x with $a^{\mathfrak{C}}$ and y with $b^{\mathfrak{C}}$, and setting $F_{l+1} := F_{l+1} \cup \{(x, y)\}$. Replace blue arcs with copies of $\mathfrak{D}$ in the same way. Incidentally, if the arcs of $\mathfrak{C}$ and $\mathfrak{D}$ are coloured, say crimson and dun, then the arcs of $\mathfrak{A} \otimes_{A,B} (\mathfrak{C}, \mathfrak{D})$ are crimson and dun.

Let $\delta(\mathfrak{A})$ be the result of taking $\mathfrak{A}$ above and eliminating the relations $F_1, \ldots$. We now construct our structures, taking q to be regular. Note: if $\bar{q}$ is the dual of q, then $\mathfrak{C}^k(\bar{q}) = \mathfrak{D}^k(q)$, so we define the structures for existential q and the rest follows. Given q, let

$$\mathfrak{C}^k(\exists q) = J^k \otimes_{A,B} (\mathfrak{C}^k(q), \mathfrak{D}^k(q))$$
$$\mathfrak{D}^k(\exists p) = I^k \otimes_{A,B} (\mathfrak{C}^k(q), \mathfrak{D}^k(q)).$$

Now, let $I_1^k = I^k$ and $J_1^k = J^k$ and

$$I_{j+1}^k = I^k \otimes_{A,B} (J_j^k, I_j^k)$$
$$J_{j+1}^k = J^k \otimes_{A,B} (J_j^k, I_j^k),$$

so that J_j^k admits an amber path from a to b (while I_j^k does not), and let

$$\mathfrak{C}^k(Tq) = \delta(J_k^k) \otimes_{A,B} (\mathfrak{C}^k(q), \mathfrak{D}^k(q))$$
$$\mathfrak{D}^k(Tq) = \delta(I_k^k) \otimes_{A,B} (\mathfrak{C}^k(q), \mathfrak{D}^k(q)).$$

The predicates F_i will be needed in the following construction to identify source-sink pairs of substructures of level i. We start with $\psi_\epsilon(x, y) \equiv Exy$; once again, if $\bar{q}$ is the dual of $q \neq \epsilon$, then $\psi_q \equiv \neg\psi_{\bar{q}}$. Suppose that we have already constructed the structures $\mathfrak{C}^k(q)$ and $\mathfrak{D}^k(q)$ for $|q| = m$. The desired formulas for existential Qq are

$$\psi_{\exists q}(x, y) \equiv (\exists u)(F_m xu \wedge F_m uy \wedge \wedge\psi_q(x, u) \wedge \psi_q(u, y)),$$
$$\psi_{Tq}(x, y) \equiv [\mathrm{TC}_{u,v}(F_m uv \wedge \psi_q(u, v))](x, y),$$

which are in TC($\exists q$) and TC(Tq) respectively.

It follows immediately from the construction that $\mathfrak{C}^k(q) \models \psi_q(a, b)$ and $\mathfrak{D}^k(q) \models \neg\psi_q(a, b)$. So we have to show that if $q \not\leq p$, and k is large enough (i.e., $k >$ length(p)), then Player II wins the $L^k_{\infty\omega}(p)$-game from $\mathfrak{C}^k(q)$ to $\mathfrak{D}^k(q)$. This is proven by induction on the length of q.

Note that this is vacuously true of $q = \epsilon$. Suppose that $q = Qq'$, and the theorem is true of q', i.e., if $q' \not\leq p'$ and $k >$ length(p'), then Player II wins the $L^k_{\infty\omega}(p')$-game from $\mathfrak{C}^k(q')$ to $\mathfrak{D}^k(q')$. We want to prove that if $q \not\leq p$ and $k >$ length(p), then Player II also wins the $L^k_{\infty\omega}(p)$-game from $\mathfrak{C}^k(q)$ to $\mathfrak{D}^k(q)$. We let the reader verify:

Lemma 7 *Choose $q' \neq \epsilon$, and suppose $q \in \{\exists, \forall, T, N\}$ and $p \in \{\exists, \forall, \exists^*, \forall^*\}$ are regular.*

1. *Suppose that $q = \exists q' \not\leq p$ and that p' is maximal with the property that $p = p''p'$ and $q' \not\leq p'$. Then $p \leq \forall^*\exists p'$. Similarly, if $q = \forall q' \not\leq p$ and that p' is maximal for $p = p''p'$ and $q' \not\leq p'$, then $p \leq \exists^*\forall p'$.*

2. *Suppose that $q = Tq' \not\leq p$ and that p' is maximal with the property that $p = p''p'$ and $q' \not\leq p'$. Then for some finite t, $p \leq (\forall^*\exists)^t p'$. Similarly, if $q = Nq' \not\leq p$ and that p' is maximal for $p = p''p'$ and $q' \not\leq p'$, then for some finite t, $p \leq (\exists^*\forall)^t p'$.*

And now for the induction. Assume that Player II wins the k-pebble q'-game from $\mathfrak{C}^k(q')$ to $\mathfrak{D}^k(q')$ for any p' such that $q' \not\leq p'$ and $k >$ length(p').

Case 1: $q = \exists q'$. If $q \not\leq p$, we can assume without loss of generality that $p = \forall^*\exists p'$ for some p' such that $q' \not\leq p'$. This means that Player I begins the game with an arbitrary number of $\forall$-moves, i.e., he places and moves around as long as he likes at most k pebbles on $\mathfrak{D}^k(q)$. Note that as J^k is an extension of I^k, there exists an isomorphic embedding g: $\mathfrak{D}^k(q) \hookrightarrow \mathfrak{C}^k(q)$. Thus, the inital $\forall$-moves can be answered by 'isomorphic' moves: if Player I pebbles $d \in \mathfrak{D}^k(q)$, Player II responds by pebbling $g(d)$. Then Player I makes a single $\exists$-move, i.e. he moves one pebble on $\mathfrak{C}^k(q)$. If he chooses c in the range of g then Player II pebbles $g^{-1}(c)$. If Player I plays outside the range of g, viz., in the "line" that connects a over w to b through two copies of $\mathfrak{C}^k(q')$, then by symmetry we can assume that he pebbles an element c inside the $\mathfrak{C}^k(q')$ copy that leads from a to w. Since there are only k pebbles, at least one "line" in $\mathfrak{D}^k(q)$ from a over some u_i to b carries no pebble. Recall that a is connected to u_i by a copy of $\mathfrak{C}^k(q')$, while the way from u_i to b goes through a copy of $\mathfrak{D}^k(q')$. Player II moves her free pebble on an element c' (corresponding to c) in the $\mathfrak{C}^k(q')$-copy from a to u_i. Now Player II wins the remaining $L^k_{\infty\omega}(p')$-game. She just has to maintain the partial isomorphism of the "line" through w in $\mathfrak{C}^k(q)$ with the line through u_i in $\mathfrak{D}^k(q)$, using her winning strategy for the $L^k_{\infty\omega}(p')$-game on $\mathfrak{C}^k(q')$ and $\mathfrak{D}^k(q')$.

Case 2: $q = \forall q'$. The argument is similar to that of Case 1.

Case 3: $q = Tq'$. If $q \not\leq p$, then for some finite t, $p \leq (\forall^*\exists)^t p'$, where $q' \not\leq p'$. So it suffices to assume that $p = (\forall^*\exists)^t p'$ for some t. We claim that Player II wins the k-pebble $(\forall^*\exists)^t p'$-game from $\mathfrak{C}^k(q)$ to $\mathfrak{D}^k(q)$. The argument is similar to that of Case 1: we start with an embedding $g\colon \mathfrak{D}^k(q) \hookrightarrow \mathfrak{C}^k(q)$, and we repeat the argument t times.

Recall that $\mathfrak{C}^k(q) = J^k_k \otimes_{A,B} (\mathfrak{C}^k(q'), \mathfrak{D}^k(q'))$ and $\mathfrak{D}^k(q) = I^k_k \otimes_{A,B} (\mathfrak{C}^k(q'), \mathfrak{D}^k(q'))$ and $t < \text{length}(p) < k$. First, by the same argument as that of Case 1, Player II wins the k-pebble $\forall^*\exists p'$-game from $J^k_{k-t+1} \otimes_{A,B} (\mathfrak{C}^k(q'), \mathfrak{D}^k(q'))$ to $I^k_{k-t+1} \otimes_{A,B} (\mathfrak{C}^k(q'), \mathfrak{D}^k(q'))$. So it suffices to prove that if $t' < t$ and Player II wins the k-pebble $(\forall^*\exists)^{t'} p'$-game from $J^k_{k-t+t'} \otimes_{A,B} (\mathfrak{C}^k(q'), \mathfrak{D}^k(q'))$ to $I^k_{k-t+t'} \otimes_{A,B} (\mathfrak{C}^k(q'), \mathfrak{D}^k(q'))$, then she also wins the k-pebble $(\forall^*\exists)^{t'+1} p'$-game from $J^k_{k-t+t'+1} \otimes_{A,B} (\mathfrak{C}^k(q'), \mathfrak{D}^k(q'))$ to $I^k_{k-t+t'+1} \otimes_{A,B} (\mathfrak{C}^k(q'), \mathfrak{D}^k(q'))$. But that also follows from the same argument as that of Case 1, and we are done.

Case 4: $q = Nq'$. The argument is similar to that of Case 3.

Note that for any k, $\mathfrak{C}^k(\forall^*) \models \neg[\text{TC}_{x,y} Exy](a, b)$ while $\mathfrak{D}^k(\forall^*) \models [\text{TC}_{x,y} Exy](a, b)$. If non-reachability could be expressed in $L^\omega_{\infty\omega}(\text{BU})$, then it could be expressed in $L^\omega_{\infty\omega}((\exists^*\forall)^k)$ for some $k \in \mathbb{N}$. But since Player II wins the k-pebble $(\exists^*\forall)^{k-1}$-game from $\mathfrak{C}^k(\forall^*)$ to $\mathfrak{D}^k(\forall^*)$, this cannot be the case, and it follows in particular that non-reachability is not in (FO + pos TC). ∎

Corollary 8 *For all* $i \geq 0$, $\Sigma^{\text{TC}}_i \subsetneq \Sigma^{\text{TC}}_{i+1}$.

PROOF. We define, by induction on i, subsets E_i and A_i of $\{\exists, \forall, \exists^*, \forall^*\}^*$: Let $E_0 = A_0 = \{\exists, \forall\}^*$, $E_{i+1} = (\exists^* E_0)^* A_i$ and $A_{i+1} = (\forall^* E_0)^* E_i$. It is easy to see that, for all i, $\Sigma^{\text{TC}}_i \subseteq \bigcup_{p \in E_i} L^\omega_{\infty\omega}(p)$. Let $q_i = TNT\cdots$ be an alternating sequence of length i of the symbols T and N, starting with T. Obviously $\text{TC}(q_i) \in \Sigma^{\text{TC}}_i$. By Theorem 6, for all $i \geq 1$

$$\text{TC}(q_i) - \bigcup_{p \in E_{i-1}} L^\omega_{\infty\omega}(p) \quad \text{is not empty.}$$

∎

We conclude this section with a list of implications that follow from our main results:

Deterministic transitive closure. Immerman [15] has introduced also a deterministic version of transitive closure logic, denoted (FO + DTC). On successor structures, (FO + DTC) captures LOGSPACE. In a previous paper [10], we showed by an entirely different method, that deterministic transitive closure logic (FO + DTC) is weaker than (FO + TC). It is easy to see that (FO + pos DTC) = (FO + DTC), so Theorem 6 also implies that (FO + DTC) $\subsetneq$ (FO + pos TC). However, it should be noted that the results in [10] prove more than the mere separation of (FO + DTC) from (FO + TC): We show that on every class of graphs that satisfies a certain criterion, called the *short path criterion*, (FO + DTC) collapses to first-order logic. The most important class satisfying the short path criterion is the class of all hypercubes.

Henkin quantifiers. Blass and Gurevich [2] have shown that transitive closure logic is equivalent to (FO + NH), the extension of first-order logic by *narrow Henkin quantifiers*. More precisely, positive occurrences of TC operators correspond to negative occurrences of narrow Henkin quantifiers, and vice versa. Thus, our results imply that (FO + pos NH) is not closed under complementation, and the hierarchy, formed by interleaving narrow Henkin quantifiers and negations, is infinite.

The structure of positive transitive closure logic. In an earlier paper [9], one of us showed that there is an infinite hierarchy inside (FO + pos TC): Consider a signature with at least two constants a and b. TC^0 is the set of formulae $[\text{TC}_{\bar{x},\bar{y}}\ \varphi(\bar{x}, \bar{y})](\bar{x}, \bar{y})$ where φ is a first-order formula. Then $\forall\text{-TC}^m$ is the universal closure of TC^m and TC^{m+1} is the set of formulae $[\text{TC}_{\bar{x},\bar{y}}\ \varphi(\bar{x}, \bar{y})](\bar{x}, \bar{y})$ where $\varphi \in \forall\text{-TC}^m$. Consequently, for all m, $\text{TC}^m \subsetneq \forall\text{-TC}^m \subsetneq \text{TC}^{m+1}$.

6 Extensions of Datalog

We conclude this paper with a discussion of some extensions of Datalog, living between (FO + TC) and $L^{\omega}_{\infty\omega}$ (for game-theoretic versions, see [22]).

Datalog is a popular database query language which, in its pure form, consists of function-free and negation-free Horn clauses. Although Datalog has nice properties and handles recursion in a nice way, it also has severe limitations. For instance, some simple first-order properties are not computable by Datalog programs, usually because of difficulties involving negation. An important extension of Datalog, called *Stratified Datalog*, solves part of this problem by partitioning the program into strata, so that negation over predicates from lower strata can be used in higher strata. Here, we examine the expressive power of different extensions of Datalog and provide insights into the fine structure of stratified Datalog.

Let's first recall the basic definitions of Datalog:

Definition 10 A *Datalog program* Π consists of a finite set of rules of the form

$$H \leftarrow B_1 \wedge \cdots \wedge B_m$$

where H is an atomic formula $S(x_1, \ldots, x_r)$, called the *head* of the rule, and $B_1 \wedge \cdots \wedge B_m$ is a conjunction of atomic formulae $R(x_1, \ldots, x_m)$ and equalities $x_i = x_j$. Every x_i is either a variable or a constant. A predicate occuring in the head of some rule is called an *intensional database predicate*, abbreviated IDB predicate; a predicate occuring only in the bodies of the rules is called an *extensional database predicate*, or EDB predicate. One of the IDB predicates is the *goal predicate* of the program. The extensional vocabulary of Π is formed by all EDB predicates and by all constants occurring in Π; a finite structure of this vocabulary is called an *extensional database* EDB for Π.

Given any extensional database $\mathfrak{B}$, the program computes intensional relations, by the usual fixpoint semantics (or, equivalently, minimum model semantics). The result of Π on $\mathfrak{B}$ is the value of the goal predicate after the computation is terminated.

Consider the following extant extensions of Datalog.

Definition 11 Datalog($\neq$) extends Datalog by allowing inequalities $x_i \neq x_j$ in the body of the rules. Datalog($\neg$) allows also negated atomic formula $\neg R(x_1, \ldots, x_r)$, provided R is an extensional predicate. Finally, *Stratified Datalog*, denoted S-Datalog, allows a limited form of negation over the IDB predicates: The IDB predicates are partitioned into strata, say $I_1, \ldots, I_m$; for simplicity, let I_0 denote the set of EDB predicates. In a rule

$$S(\bar{x}) \leftarrow B_1 \wedge \cdots \wedge B_m$$

where S is an IDB predicate from stratum I_j (with $j > 0$), the body may contain atomic formulae $R(\bar{y})$ provided that R does not belong to a higher stratum than S; and it may contain negated atomic formulae $\neg R(\bar{y})$ provided R belongs to a strictly lower stratum than S, i.e. $R \in \bigcup_{k<j} I_k$.

The semantics of Datalog readily extends to Datalog($\neq$) and Datalog($\neg$). The intensional predicates of a stratified Datalog program are computed stratum by stratum; in fact the set of rules whose head is in I_j may be considered as a Datalog($\neg$) program whose EDB predicates are $\bigcup_{k<j} I_k$.

It is known [4, 19] that Stratified Datalog is strictly weaker than fixpoint logic.

We now define two more extensions of Datalog, situated between Datalog($\neg$) and S-Datalog.

Definition 12 Datalog(FO) extends Datalog by allowing rules where the expressions in the body may be atomic formulae or arbitrary first order formulae $\varphi(\bar{x})$ over the EDB predicates. The semantics of Datalog(FO) is defined in the same way as for Datalog.

Definition 13 Datalog(FO,$\forall$) extends Datalog(FO) in the following way: Let I_0 be the EDB predicates and let the IDB predicates are partitioned into strata $I_1, \ldots, I_m$. A rule with head $S(\bar{x})$ may contain the following expressions in the body:

- first order formulae over the extensional predicates;
- atoms $R(\bar{y})$ provided R does not belong to a higher stratum than S;
- formulae $(\forall \bar{z})R(\bar{y}, \bar{z})$ provided R belongs to a strictly lower stratum than S.

Again, we have fixpoint sematics for Datalog(FO,$\forall$) by computing the the least fixpoints for lower strata before going to a higher one. Datalog(FO) was defined in [9] and is arguably the simplest extension of Datalog that includes all FO-queries. Datalog (FO,$\forall$) was introduced independently in [9] and in [22] where it was called (FO + pos EFP).

Transitive closure logic and linear Datalog programs. A program in (an extension of) Datalog is *linear* if the body of each rule contains at most one

IDB predicate. There is a very close relationship between transitive closure logic and linear programs in extensions of Datalog. First of all, if S-LinDatalog is stratified linear Datalog, then:

Theorem 9 [3] S-LinDatalog = (FO + TC).

This can be refined in terms of the subclasses of TC^m of (FO + pos TC), defined at the end of section 5.

Theorem 10 [9] *Let $m \in \mathbb{N}$. A query is expressible in TC^m if and only if it is computable by a linear* Datalog(FO,∀)*-program with $m+1$ strata. In particular:*

$$\begin{aligned} \text{LinDatalog(FO)} &= \mathrm{TC}^0 \\ \text{LinDatalog(FO},\forall) &= (\text{FO} + \text{pos TC}) \end{aligned}$$

Furthermore, not all Datalog programs are linearizable. In fact, there even exist Datalog programs that are not expressible in transitive closure logic, i.e . they are not even equivalent to any *stratified* linear Datalog program. This result is implicit already in an early paper of Immerman [12]:

Theorem 11 Datalog − (FO + TC) $\neq \emptyset$.

Datalog and infinitary logic. It is known that Datalog is included in the existential fragment of $L^{\omega}_{\infty\omega}$ — see [20] for inexpressibility results on Datalog that are based on this fact — and that stratified Datalog programs can be expressed by infinitary formulae with bounded alternations:

Proposition 12 *(i)* Datalog $\subsetneq$ Datalog(¬) $\subsetneq$ $L^{\omega}_{\infty\omega}(\exists^*)$.

(ii) (FO + TC)$\subsetneq$ S-Datalog $\subsetneq \bigcup_{k\in\mathbb{N}} L^{\omega}_{\infty\omega}(\Sigma_k)$.

The extensions Datalog(FO) and Datalog(FO,∀) can be embedded into $L^{\omega}_{\infty\omega}$. A program in Datalog(FO) can be expressed by a formula $\psi \in L^{\omega}_{\infty\omega}$ with quantifier structure $P(\psi) = \exists^* p$ for some fixed $p \in \{\exists,\forall\}^*$. The fragment of infinitary logic that extends Datalog(FO,∀) is $L^{\omega}_{\infty\omega}(\mathrm{BU})$, the set of infinitary formulae with bounded number of universal quantifiers, defined at the end of section 2.

Proposition 13 *(i)* TC^0 $\subsetneq$ Datalog(FO) $\subsetneq$ $\bigcup_{p\in\{\exists,\forall\}^*} L^{\omega}_{\infty\omega}(\exists^* p)$.

(ii) (FO + pos TC) $\subsetneq$ Datalog(FO,∀) $\subsetneq$ $L^{\omega}_{\infty\omega}(\mathrm{BU})$.

Fine structure of stratified Datalog. Our hierarchy theorem allows to separate different extensions of Datalog and extends the Main Theorem of [22] on the fine structure of fixpoint logic. In particular we can conclude:

Corollary 14 *1.* Datalog(FO) *and* Datalog(FO,∀) *are not closed under complementation. Thus* Datalog(FO,∀) $\subsetneq$ S-Datalog.

2. For all k, there exists a (linear) Datalog(FO,∀)*-program with $k+1$ strata which is not expressible in $\bigcup_{m\in\mathbb{N}} L^{\omega}_{\infty\omega}((\exists^*\forall^m)^k)$, which therefore is not equivalent to any* Datalog(FO,∀)*-program with k strata.*

These results are summarized in Figure 1.

References

[1] J. Barwise, *On Moschovakis closure ordinals*, J. Symbolic Logic **42** (1977), 292–296.

[2] A. Blass and Y. Gurevich, *Henkin quantifiers and complete problems*, Annals of Pure and Applied Logic **32** (1986), 1–16.

[3] M. Consens and A. Mendelzon, *GraphLog: a Visual Formalism for Real Life Recursion*, Proceedings of 9th ACM Symposium on Principles of Database Systems (1990), 404–416.

[4] E. Dahlhaus, *Skolem Normal Forms Concerning the Least Fixed Point*, in: "Computation Theory and Logic" (E. Börger, Ed.), Lecture Notes in Computer Science Nr. 270, Springer 1987, 101–106.

[5] A. Ehrenfeucht, *An application of games to the completeness problem for formalized theories*, Fund. Math. **49** (1961) 129–141.

[6] R. Fagin, *Generalized first-order spectra and polynomial-time recognizable sets*, in: R. Karp (Ed.), Complexity of Computations, SIAM-AMS Proceedings **7** (1974), 43–73.

[7] R. Fagin, *Monadic generalized spectra*, Zeitschrift für Math. Logik Grundlagen d. Math. **21** (1975), 89–96.

[8] R. Fraïssé, *Sur quelques classifications des systèmes de relations*, Publications Scientifique de l' Université d' Alger, Série A **1** (1954), 35–182.

[9] E. Grädel, *On transitive closure logic*, Proceedings of 5th workshop on Computer Science Logic CSL 91.

[10] E. Grädel and G. McColm, *Deterministic versus Nondeterministic Transitive Closure Logic*, Proceedings of 7th IEEE Conference on Logic in Computer Science (1992).

[11] Y. Gurevich, *Logic and the Challenge of Computer Science*, in: E. Börger (Ed), Trends in Theoretical Computer Science, Computer Science Press (1988), 1–57.

[12] N. Immerman, *Number of Quantifiers is Better than Number of Tape Cells*, J. Comp. Syst. Sciences **22** (1981), 65–72.

[13] N. Immerman, *Upper and lower bounds for first-order expressibility*, J. Comp. Syst. Sciences **25** (1982), 76–98.

[14] N. Immerman, *Relational queries computable in polynomial time*, Information & Control 68 (1986), 86-104.

[15] N. Immerman, *Languages that Capture Complexity Classes*, SIAM J. Comput. **16** (1987), 760–778.

[16] N. Immerman, *Nondeterministic space is closed under complementation*, SIAM J. Comput. **17** (1988), 935–939.

[17] N. Immerman, *Descriptive and Computational Complexity*, in: J. Hartmanis (Ed.), Computational Complexity Theory, Proc. of AMS Symposia in Appl. Math. **38** (1989), 75–91.

[18] P. Kannellakis, *Elements of Relational Database Theory*, in: J. van Leeuwen (Ed.), Handbook of Theoretical Computer Science, vol. B, North Holland, Amsterdam 1990, pp. 1073–1156.

[19] Ph. Kolaitis, *The Expressive Power of Stratified Logic Programs*, Information and Computation **90** (1991), 50–66.

[20] Ph. Kolaitis and M. Vardi, *On the Expressive Power of Datalog: Tools and a Case Study*, Proceeding of 9th ACM Symposium on Principles of Database Systems (1990), 61–71.

[21] Ph. Kolaitis and M. Vardi, *0-1 Laws for Infinitary Logics*, Information and Computation **98** (1992), 258–294.

[22] G. McColm *Pebble Games and the Fine Structure of Fixedpoint Logic*, submitted for publication.

[23] R. Szelepcsényi, *The Method of Forced Enumeration for Nondeterministic Automata*, Acta Informatica **26** (1988), 279–284.

[24] M. Vardi, *Complexity of relational query languages*, Proceedings of 14th ACM Symposium on Theory of Computing (1982), 137-146.

$$
\begin{array}{ccccccccc}
 & & & \mathit{LinDatalog} & \subset & \mathit{Datalog} & \subset & L^{\omega}_{\infty\omega}(\exists^*) \\
 & & & \cap & & \cap & & \cap \\
FO & \subset & TC(0) & = & \mathit{LinDatalog}(FO) & \subset & \mathit{Datalog}(FO) & \subset & \bigcup_{p\in\{\exists,\forall\}^*} L^{\omega}_{\infty\omega}(\exists^* p) \\
 & & \cap & & \cap & & \cap & & \cap \\
 & & \vdots & & \vdots & & \vdots & & \vdots \\
 & & \cap & & \cap & & \cap & & \cap \\
 & & (FO + pos\ TC) & = & \mathit{LinDatalog}(FO,\forall) & \subset & \mathit{Datalog}(FO,\forall) & \subset & L^{\omega}_{\infty\omega}(BU) \\
 & & \cap & & \cap & & \cap & & \cap \\
 & & (FO + TC) & = & \text{S-LinDatalog} & \subset & \text{S-Datalog} & \subset & \bigcup_k L^{\omega}_{\infty\omega}(\Sigma_k) \\
 & & & & & & \cap & & \cap \\
 & & & & & & (FO + LFP) & \subset & L^{\omega}_{\infty\omega}
\end{array}
$$

Figure 1 ($\subset$ means proper inclusion)

Back to the Future: Towards a Theory of Timed Regular Languages

Rajeev Alur
AT&T Bell Laboratories
600 Mountain Avenue
Murray Hill, NJ 07974

Thomas A. Henzinger *
Computer Science Department
Cornell University
Ithaca, NY 14853

Abstract: *Timed automata* are finite-state machines constrained by timing requirements so that they accept *timed words* — words in which every symbol is labeled with a real-valued time. These automata were designed to lead to a theory of *finite-state real-time properties* with applications to the automatic verification of real-time systems. However, both deterministic and nondeterministic versions suffer from drawbacks: several key problems, such as language inclusion, are undecidable for nondeterministic timed automata, whereas deterministic timed automata lack considerable expressive power when compared to decidable real-time logics.

This is why we introduce *two-way* timed automata — timed automata that can move back and forth while reading a timed word. Two-wayness in its unrestricted form leads, like nondeterminism, to the undecidability of language inclusion. However, if we restrict the number of times an input symbol may be revisited, then two-wayness is both harmless and desirable. We show that the resulting class of *bounded two-way deterministic timed automata* is closed under all boolean operations, has decidable (PSPACE-complete) emptiness and inclusion problems, and subsumes all decidable real-time logics we know.

We obtain a strict hierarchy of real-time properties: deterministic timed automata can accept more languages as the bound on the number of times an input symbol may be revisited is increased. This hierarchy is also enforced by the number of alternations between past and future operators in temporal logic. The combination of our results leads to a decision procedure for a real-time logic with past operators.

1 Introduction

Finite automata are instrumental for the modeling and analysis of many diverse problems within computer science. The universal acceptance of finite automata as the canonical model of finite-state computation can be attributed to the robustness of the model and the appeal of its theory. In particular, the expressions of a variety of competing formalisms — deterministic and nondeterministic finite automata, regular expressions, modal formulas of (extended) temporal logic, and second-order formulas of the monadic theory of one successor (S1S) — are pairwise convertible and their equivalence is decidable. The listed formalisms define the class of *regular languages* (or ω-regular languages, if the strings in the language are infinite), and we refer to the expressions of these formalism as *finite-state* expressions.

Much effort has been invested in obtaining optimal decision procedures for testing the language inclusion of two finite-state expressions, because these decision procedures lead to algorithms for the verification of concurrent finite-state systems [9, 12, 13, 14, 15]. In a *qualitative* trace model of concurrent computation, the behavior of a system is viewed as a sequence of states or events. Consequently, the possible behaviors of a system represent a formal language, and so do the behaviors that are permitted by the requirement specification of the system. Thus we may use two finite-state expressions A and B to describe a finite-state system and its specification, and we can verify the system by checking that the regular set denoted by A is contained in the regular set denoted by B.[1]

To capture the behavior of *real-time* systems, the qualitative model of computation needs to be augmented by a notion of time. In [2] *timed automata* were proposed as an extension of finite automata

*This research was supported by the National Science Foundation under grant CCR-9200794 and by the United States Air Force Office of Scientific Research under contract AFOSR-92-NM255.

[1] Usually, the behavior of a system is modeled as an infinite sequence, and the set of all possible behaviors forms an ω-regular language. We are mainly interested in the issues arising due to the introduction of time, and hence, we will consider only finite sequences in this paper. Most of our results can be generalized to infinite sequences in a straightforward manner.

0-8186-2900-2/92 $3.00 © 1992 IEEE

for modeling the behavior of concurrent systems over time. Timed automata provide a simple, and yet powerful, way to annotate state-transition graphs with timing constraints using finitely many real-valued variables. A timed automaton accepts *timed words* — strings in which a real-valued time of occurrence is associated with each symbol. The theory of timed automata is useful for the automatic verification of real-time requirements of finite-state systems [1, 2, 3, 11], for synthesizing schedulers from temporal specifications [7], and for solving delay problems [6]. There are, however, problems with timed automata that make us hesitate to accept them as the canonical model for finite-state real-time computation. Unlike in the untimed case, the nondeterministic variety of timed automata is strictly more expressive than the deterministic variety, and both classes have their drawbacks.

Nondeterministic timed automata are too permissive, because their language inclusion problem is undecidable [2]. Thus, for algorithmic verification, one cannot use nondeterministic timed automata for specifying correctness requirements. Also, the class of nondeterministic timed automata is not closed under complementation.

Deterministic timed automata, which have all desirable closure and decidability properties, are too restrictive. Consider, for example, the standard real-time requirement ϕ of timely response, demanding that every environment stimulus p is followed by a system response q after a delay of no less than 5 and no more than 6 time units. Since the time domain is dense, in any interval of unit length an unbounded number of p symbols may occur, and a finite timed automaton cannot "remember" the times of all these p symbols. However, in [3] we showed that it is possible to construct a timed automaton that checks the property ϕ by nondeterministically "guessing" the times of the first and last occurrences of the symbol q in the next 6 unit time intervals. Indeed, as we will show in this paper, the ability of an automaton to "guess" or "predict" the future is necessary for checking timely response: the property ϕ cannot be defined by a deterministic timed automaton.

Yet we cannot put the issue to rest by concluding that even the most basic real-time properties, such as timely response, cannot be verified automatically. On the contrary, the timely-response property ϕ is definable in a simple and decidable real-time logic, MITL [3]:

$$\Box\,(\,p \rightarrow \Diamond_{[5,6]}\, q\,).$$

Thus we must conclude, instead, that the step from deterministic to nondeterministic timed automata, with the ensuing undecidability results, is unnecessarily big. Consequently, in [5] we raised the question of finding an intermediate class of automata that

(1) is effectively closed under all boolean operations;
(2) has a decidable language inclusion problem;
(3) is "maximal," at least in the sense that it subsumes both deterministic timed automata and the real-time logic MITL.

This paper presents such a desired class of automata. We define *two-way timed automata* by allowing timed automata to move backward as well as forward "in time" (i.e., over the timed input word). While in the untimed case, the ability to move back and forth over the input word does not change the expressive power of finite automata, deterministic two-way timed automata recognize more languages than their one-way counterparts. Consider, again, the timely-response requirement ϕ that cannot be checked in a deterministic forward manner. Since all the nondeterminism required to check ϕ are some predictions about the future, timely response can be checked in a deterministic way by an automaton that can travel into the future and back. In fact, the property ϕ is particularly easy to check "backwards": go to end of the input word and while coming back, remember the times of the first and the last occurrences of the symbol q for the previous 6 unit intervals and check that the time of every occurrence of p concurs with the requirement ϕ.

Our results will be twofold. First, we study the impact of two-wayness on deterministic and nondeterministic timed automata. We show that the unrestricted ability of an automaton to move both ways makes timed automata too powerful, rendering even the emptiness problem for deterministic automata undecidable. This prompts us to look at the number of trips into the future that an automaton makes when accepting an input word. For every nonnegative integer k, a *k-bounded* timed automaton is defined to be a two-way automaton that visits each symbol of an input word at most $2k + 1$ times. We show that this bounded form of two-wayness does not add to the expressiveness of nondeterministic forward automata. In the deterministic case, however, we obtain an infinite strict hierarchy of language classes recognizable by deterministic bounded timed automata, which lies between the language classes accepted by deterministic and nondeterministic forward automata. It is the limit $\cup_k \mathbf{DTA}_k$ of this hierarchy that satisfies the desired closure and decidability properties listed above.

We give PSPACE decision procedures for the emptiness and inclusion problems of $\cup_k \mathbf{DTA}_k$ (both problems are PSPACE-hard already for deterministic forward automata).

Second, we study the relationship between the proposed hierarchy of timed automata and real-time logics, and we obtain new decision procedures and verification algorithms. We show that the models of any MITL-formula can be characterized by a deterministic 1-bounded automaton. This translation is much simpler than the translation from MITL to nondeterministic timed automata [3], and it leads to an alternative decision procedure for MITL. Then we introduce a new real-time logic MITL^P, an extension of MITL with *past* temporal operators. We show that any property specified by an MITL^P-formula can also be defined by a deterministic bounded timed automaton, and this translation is used to obtain an EXPSPACE decision procedure for the satisfiability problem of MITL^P (already MITL itself is EXPSPACE-hard). Thus we have a model-checking algorithm for verifying that a system described by a timed automaton (or by an alternative formalism such as timed transition systems [8]) satisfies the correctness requirements specified in MITL^P. Interestingly, there is a close relationship between the number of alternations of past and future temporal operators in an MITL^P-formula ψ and the bound on the two-wayness of any deterministic automaton that checks the property ψ. We show that every additional alternation between past and future operators yields a strictly more expressive real-time specification language — a phenomenon not observed in any other temporal logic.

2 Two-way Timed Automata

Timed words and timed languages

We study formal languages of timed words. Formally, a *timed word* w over an alphabet Σ is a finite sequence $(\sigma_1, \tau_1)(\sigma_2, \tau_2)\ldots(\sigma_n, \tau_n)$ of symbols $\sigma_i \in \Sigma$ paired with real numbers $\tau_i \in \mathrm{R}$ such that the sequence $\overline{\tau} = \tau_1\tau_2\ldots\tau_n$ is strictly monotonically increasing. Sometimes we will denote the timed word w by the pair $(\overline{\sigma}, \overline{\tau})$.

A *timed language* over an alphabet Σ is a set of timed words over Σ. Notice that a timed language can be viewed as a formal language over the uncountable alphabet $\Sigma \times \mathrm{R}$. However, unlike in conventional formal-language theory, the structure of the alphabet is of importance to us: we use operations such as $\leq$ and $+1$ over the reals R. All results of this paper continue to hold if we replace the time domain R by the set of rational numbers Q.

Timed automata

Timed automata were proposed in [2] as an abstract model for finite-state real-time systems. These automata are finite-state machines constrained by timing requirements so that they accept (or generate) timed words. Consequently, every timed automaton defines a timed language. Timed automata, as defined in [2], can read timed words only in the forward direction. Here we study more general timed automata, which can move in both directions and, consequently, visit a symbol of a timed word any number of times.

A timed automaton operates with finite control — a finite set of locations and a finite set of real-valued variables called *clocks*. The automaton may assign to a clock a value chosen randomly from R. The transitions of the automaton put certain constraints on the clock values: a transition may be taken only if the current values of the clocks satisfy the associated constraints. We use a special variable T to denote the time of the current symbol. A *clock constraint* is an arithmetic expression of a simple form: it is a boolean combination of atomic formulas of the form $T \leq x + c$, where x is a clock variable and c is an integer constant.

It is convenient to allow our automata to recognize the end of the input. For a timed word w over the alphabet Σ, let $w\$$ be the extension of w with the pair $(\$, 0)$, where $\$ \notin \Sigma$ is the end-marker (the choice of the time value 0 associated with the end-marker is arbitrary and has no role in any of the results). A timed word w will be presented as $w\$$ to the automaton, and thus the automaton can check for \$ to detect the right end of the input.

A *two-way timed automaton* (2NTA) $\mathcal{A}$ is a tuple $(\Sigma, \mathrm{S}, \mathrm{S_0}, \mathrm{S_F}, \mathrm{C}, \mathrm{E})$, where

- Σ is a finite alphabet,
- S is a finite set of locations,
- $\mathrm{S_0} \subseteq \mathrm{S}$ is a set of start locations,
- $\mathrm{S_F} \subseteq \mathrm{S}$ is a set of accepting locations,
- C is a finite set of clock variables, and
- E is a set of transitions.

Each transition is a tuple $(s, s', \sigma, \mathit{reset}, \mathit{cond}, \mathit{dir})$, with a source location $s \in \mathrm{S}$, a target location $s' \in \mathrm{S}$, an input symbol $\sigma \in \Sigma \cup \{\$\}$, a set $\mathit{reset} \subseteq \mathrm{C}$ of clocks to be reset, a clock constraint cond, and a direction $\mathit{dir} \in \{-, +\}$.

Suppose that the timed automaton $\mathcal{A}$ reads the input $w\$$ for the timed word $w = (\overline{\sigma}, \overline{\tau})$ of length n. While the automaton moves back and forth over the input, its configuration is always determined by the location in which the control resides, the values of all clock variables, and the position of the tape head. Consequently, a *state* of the timed automaton $\mathcal{A}$ is a triple (s, γ, ℓ) consisting of a location $s \in \mathrm{S}$, a map γ from C to R that provides an interpretation for the clocks of the automaton, and a tape position $1 \le \ell \le n+1$ that indicates the input symbol being scanned.

The automaton starts in one of its start locations scanning the first symbol (σ_1, τ_1) of the input word $w\$$. The transition relation over the states of the automaton is defined as follows. The automaton can change its state from (s, γ, ℓ) to (s', γ', ℓ') using a transition of the form $e = (s, s', \sigma_\ell, reset, cond, dir)$, written $(s, \gamma, \ell) \xrightarrow{e} (s', \gamma', \ell')$, iff

1. If $dir = +$, then $\ell \neq n+1$ and the new position ℓ' of the tape head is $\ell + 1$; otherwise, $dir = -$ and $\ell \neq 1$ and the new position of the head is $\ell - 1$.
2. For each clock x, if $x \notin reset$, the new value $\gamma'(x)$ is the same as the old value $\gamma(x)$; otherwise, the new value $\gamma'(x)$ is an arbitrary real number.
3. The clock constraint *cond* evaluates to true for the interpretation that assigns the new value $\gamma'(x)$ to each clock variable $x \in \mathrm{C}$ and the value τ_ℓ to the time variable T.

If no possible next state exists then the automaton terminates; it accepts or rejects the timed word w depending on whether or not its location upon termination belongs to the set $\mathrm{S_F}$.

The behavior of two-way timed automata is captured formally by defining runs that record the state of the automaton at all transition points. A *run* r of the 2NTA $\mathcal{A} = (\Sigma, \mathrm{S}, \mathrm{S_0}, \mathrm{S_F}, \mathrm{C}, \mathrm{E})$ over the input $w\$$, for a timed word $w = (\overline{\sigma}, \overline{\tau})$ of length n, is a finite sequence

$$(s_0, \gamma_0, \ell_0) \xrightarrow{e_0} (s_1, \gamma_1, \ell_1) \xrightarrow{e_1} \cdots (s_k, \gamma_k, \ell_k) \quad (\dagger)$$

of locations $s_i \in \mathrm{S}$, clock interpretations $\gamma_i : \mathrm{C} \to \mathrm{R}$, tape positions $1 \le \ell_i \le n+1$, and transitions $e_i \in \mathrm{E}$ that satisfy the following three conditions.

- *Initialization*: $s_0 \in \mathrm{S_0}$ and $\ell_0 = 1$.
- *Consecution*: For all $0 \le i < k$, the transition relation $(s_i, \gamma_i, \ell_i) \xrightarrow{e_i} (s_{i+1}, \gamma_{i+1}, \ell_{i+1})$ holds.
- *Termination*: For every edge $e \in \mathrm{E}$ and every state (s, γ, ℓ) of the automaton, the transition relation $(s_k, \gamma_k, \ell_k) \xrightarrow{e} (s, \gamma, \ell)$ does not hold.

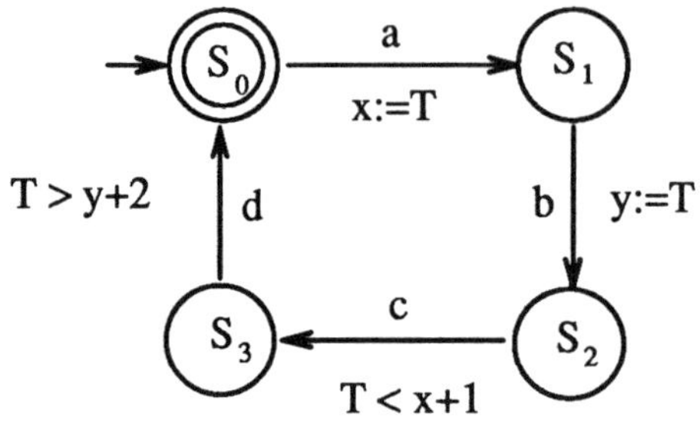

Figure 1: Timed automaton $\mathcal{A}_1$

The run r is *accepting* iff

- *Acceptance*: $s_k \in \mathrm{S_F}$.

The timed language $L(\mathcal{A})$ that is accepted by the automaton $\mathcal{A}$ consists of all timed words w such that $\mathcal{A}$ has an accepting run over the input $w\$$.

Examples

Let us consider some examples of two-way timed automata. In the figures, every transition is annotated with the associated alphabet symbol σ, clock constraint *cond*, and reset clocks *reset*. We omit σ if Σ is a singleton, omit *cond* if it equals *true* , and omit *reset* if it is empty. An annotation such as $x := T$ indicates that $x \in reset$ and $x = T$ is a conjunct of *cond*. The solid lines correspond to transitions with $dir = +$, and dotted lines represent transitions with $dir = -$.

The timed automaton $\mathcal{A}_1$ of Figure 1 uses two clocks x and y. The location s_0 is the start location, and also the only accepting location. The automaton accepts the timed language $L(\mathcal{A}_1)$ consisting of words $w = ((abcd)^*, \overline{\tau})$ such that for all $j \ge 0$,

$$\tau_{4j+3} < \tau_{4j+1} + 1 \ \wedge \ \tau_{4j+4} > \tau_{4j+2} + 2.$$

The automaton loops between the locations s_0, s_1, s_2, and s_3. Whenever $\mathcal{A}_1$ moves from s_0 to s_1 reading a, the clock x gets set to the associated time value. The clock constraint $T < x + 1$ associated with the c transition from s_2 to s_3 ensures that c is within 1 time unit of the preceding a. A similar mechanism of setting an independent clock y when reading b and checking its value when reading d, ensures that the time difference between b and the following d is always greater than 2.

The automaton $\mathcal{A}_1$ of Figure 1 always moves forward. The same language $L(\mathcal{A}_1)$ is also accepted by the automaton $\mathcal{A}_2$ of Figure 2 which reverses direction. Similar to $\mathcal{A}_1$, the automaton $\mathcal{A}_2$ sets the clock x while moving from location s_0 to s_1 reading a. But

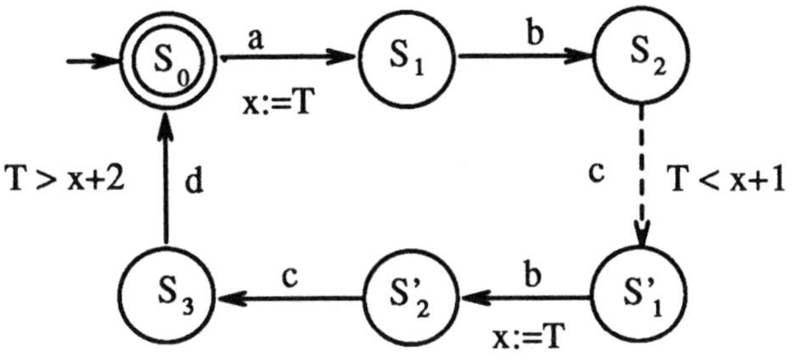

Figure 2: Timed automaton $\mathcal{A}_2$

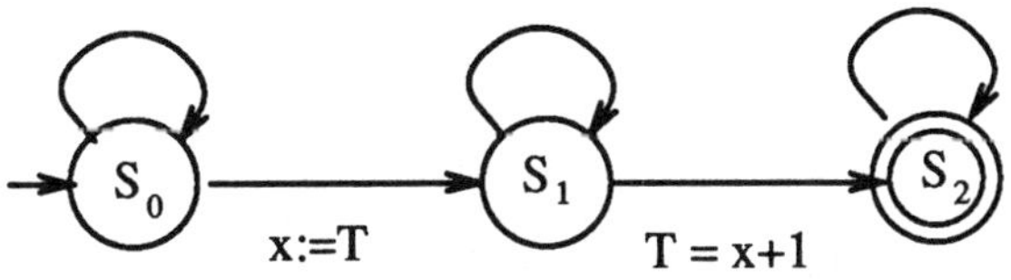

Figure 3: Timed automaton $\mathcal{A}_3$

now, it skips over the following b, and checks that the following c is within distance 1 of a. Then the automaton $\mathcal{A}_2$ moves left, back to the b symbol, and sets the clock x to the time associated with b. Subsequently it checks that the following d is at least 2 time units away from b. Thus the ability to move back and forth allows $\mathcal{A}_2$ to enforce the desired constraints using just one clock.

As another example consider the automaton $\mathcal{A}_3$ of Figure 3. The alphabet is unary and the automaton accepts a timed word iff it has two symbols whose times differ by exactly 1.

Deterministic timed automata

In the theory of finite (untimed) automata, deterministic automata form an important subclass. In the untimed case, the property of determinism requires that the input symbols labeling two different transitions with the same source location should be different. This notion was generalized for (forward) timed automata in [2]. Below we define a similar notion of determinism for two-way timed automata.

A two-way timed automaton $(\Sigma, S, S_0, C, E, S_F)$ is *deterministic*, denoted by 2DTA, iff the following conditions hold:

1. There is only one start location; that is, $|S_0| = 1$.
2. For every transition $(s, s', \sigma, reset, cond, dir) \in E$ and every reset clock $x \in reset$, the constraint $x = T$ is a conjunct of $cond$.
3. For all clock interpretations γ, all time values $t \in R$, and every pair $(s, s_1, \sigma, reset_1, cond_1, dir_1)$ and $(s, s_2, \sigma, reset_2, cond_2, dir_2)$ of transitions, if the clock interpretation that assigns $\gamma(x)$ to all clocks $x \notin reset_1$ and t to T and all clocks $x \in reset_1$, satisfies the constraint $cond_1$, then the clock interpretation that assigns $\gamma(x)$ to all clocks $x \notin reset_2$ and t to T and all clocks $x \in reset_2$, does not satisfy $cond_2$.

The first condition ensures that there is a unique way to start the automaton. The second requirement ensures that all resets are deterministic: whenever a clock is reset, there is only one possible choice for its new value, namely, the time of the symbol currently being read. The last condition ensures that the choice of the next transition is uniquely determined by the current state of the automaton. It is easy to check that a deterministic automaton has at most one run over any timed word.

In our examples, the timed automata $\mathcal{A}_1$ and $\mathcal{A}_2$ are deterministic, whereas the automaton $\mathcal{A}_3$ is nondeterministic. In fact, we will show that there is no deterministic two-way timed automaton that accepts the language $L(\mathcal{A}_3)$.

Bounded timed automata

We now proceed to define another restricted class of two-way timed automata. The number of reversals of the run r (see †), denoted by rev_r, is the smallest nonnegative integer m such that for every tape position $1 \leq i \leq n$, the run visits the i-th input symbol at most $2m+1$ times; that is, $\ell_j = i$ for at most $2m+1$ distinct values of $0 \leq j \leq k$.

A two-way timed automaton $\mathcal{A}$ is *k-bounded* iff for every timed word w and every run r of $\mathcal{A}$ over $w\$$, $rev_r \leq k$. We call a k-bounded timed automaton to be of type NTA_k. Furthermore, if it is deterministic, it is of type DTA_k.

Notice that whereas a two-way automaton may loop indefinitely while reading a timed word, the length of a run of a k-bounded automaton over an input word of length n is at most $(2k+1)(n+1)$. It is not difficult to show that the forward timed automata of [2] are of type NTA_0. In our examples, the automaton $\mathcal{A}_1$ is of type DTA_0, and $\mathcal{A}_3$ is of type NTA_0. The automaton $\mathcal{A}_2$ visits every b and c symbol twice; it is of type DTA_1.

Not all two-way timed automata need be bounded. As an example, consider the automaton $\mathcal{A}_4$ of Figure 4. Given a timed word $(a^n, \overline{\tau})$ of length $n \geq 0$, the automaton checks at every position $1 \leq i \leq n$ that either τ_j equals $\tau_i + 1$ for some $j \leq n$, or τ_n is smaller than $\tau_i + 1$. The number of visits of $\mathcal{A}_4$ to a symbol

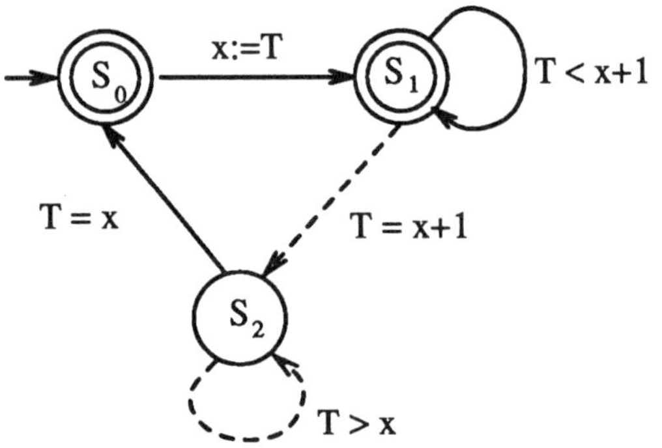

Figure 4: Timed automaton $\mathcal{A}_4$

is unbounded: to accept a word $(a^n, \overline{\tau}) \in L(\mathcal{A}_4)$ the automaton needs $k-1$ reversals, where k is the maximum number of symbols in a time interval of length 1. In fact, we will show that the language $L(\mathcal{A}_4)$ cannot be accepted by an NTA_k for any $k \geq 0$.

3 The Theory of Bounded Two-way Timed Automata

Any theory of a class of automata must (1) characterize the expressive power of the class, (2) determine under which boolean operations the class is closed, and (3) determine the complexity of the membership, emptiness, universality, and inclusion problems. In this section, we present our results on two-way timed automata with a bounded number of reversals, grouped according to these three categories. We use boldface notation for the set **A** of timed languages that can be defined by automata of type A. Our definition of forward timed automata is slightly more general than the timed automata of [2] (the reset action of [2] is always deterministic); however, all results and proofs of [2] carry over to the classes $\mathbf{DTA}_0$ and $\mathbf{NTA}_0$ in a straightforward way.

Expressiveness

In the untimed case it is well-known that all variants of finite-state machines define the class of regular languages: neither nondeterminism nor the ability to move back and forth add expressive power to finite-state machines [9]. In the timed case, nondeterminism was shown to increase the expressive power of timed automata [2]: $\mathbf{DTA}_0 \subset \mathbf{NTA}_0$. Now we show that a bounded number of reversals increases the expressive power of deterministic timed automata. In fact, each deterministic pass over the input allows the recognition of more timed languages.

Theorem 3.1 $\mathbf{DTA}_k \subset \mathbf{DTA}_{k+1}$.

Proof. It suffices to consider only timed words over the unary alphabet. For a timed word w, define a sequence of values as follows. Let $v_0(w)$ be 1. For $k > 0$, let $u_k(w)$ be the time of the last symbol in the interval $(1, 1+v_{k-1}(w))$, and let $v_k(w)$ be the time of the last symbol in the interval $(0, u_k(w)-1)$. Now we define a family of languages L_k, for $k > 0$, such that $w \in L_k$ iff w has a symbol in the interval $(1, 1+v_k(w))$. We claim that, for all $k > 0$, the language L_k belongs to $\mathbf{DTA}_k$ but not to $\mathbf{DTA}_{k-1}$.

The proof that $L_k \notin \mathbf{DTA}_{k-1}$ given in the full paper; here we outline the argument for $k = 1$. Assume, to the contrary, that the forward DTA_0 $\mathcal{A}$ with m locations defines the language L_1. Suppose that a timed word w contains more than m symbols in both the intervals $(0, v_1(w))$ and $(u_1(w)-1, 1)$. Using the fact that $\mathcal{A}$ is deterministic and has only m locations, it can be shown that after $\mathcal{A}$ reads the prefix of w up to time 1, no clock is set to the time $v_1(w)$. It follows that $\mathcal{A}$ cannot determine correctly if the interval $(1, 1+v_1(w))$ contains a symbol. For we can construct another word w' such that w' agrees with w up to time 1 but w' is in L_1 iff w is not. Since $\mathcal{A}$ either accepts or rejects both words, we arrive at a contradiction. ∎

On the other hand, any bounded number of reversals can be simulated in a single nondeterministic forward pass.

Theorem 3.2 $\cup_k \mathbf{NTA}_k = \mathbf{NTA}_0$.

Proof. Let $\mathcal{A}$ be an NTA_k. We construct a forward NTA_0 $\mathcal{A}_0$ that accepts the same language. The formal construction is given in the full paper; here we outline the construction under the simplifying assumption that the automaton $\mathcal{A}$ makes one complete forward pass over the input word followed by one complete backward pass, and then stops. The automaton $\mathcal{A}_0$ must simulate both passes of $\mathcal{A}$ in a single forward pass. For every clock x of $\mathcal{A}$, $\mathcal{A}_0$ uses two copies x_f and x_b. A location of $\mathcal{A}_0$ is of the form $(q_f, e_b, \overline{b})$, where q_f records the location of $\mathcal{A}$ on the forward pass, e_b is the transition used by $\mathcal{A}$ on the backward pass, and $\overline{b}$ contains a 3-valued bit b_x for every clock x of $\mathcal{A}$. The interpretation of these bits is as follows: while reading the i-th symbol of w, the bit b_x is 0 if $\mathcal{A}$ resets the clock x at some j-th symbol, $j > i$, on one of the two passes; otherwise, b_x is 1 if $\mathcal{A}$ resets the clock x at some j-th symbol, $j \leq i$, on the forward pass and for all $j \leq j' \leq i$, it does not reset x at the j'-th symbol on the backward pass; otherwise, b_x is 2.

A single transition of $\mathcal{A}_0$ corresponds to a forward and a backward transition of $\mathcal{A}$. If $b_x = 0$ then the clock x_f is used for checking the clock constraint of the forward transition and x_b is used for the constraint of the backward transition; if $b_x = 1$ then the clock x_b is used for both the constraints; otherwise the clock x_f is used for both. ■

This gives us the following hierarchy:

$$\mathbf{DTA}_0 \subset \mathbf{DTA}_1 \cdots \subset \cup_k \mathbf{DTA}_k \subset \mathbf{NTA}_0 = \cup_k \mathbf{NTA}_k.$$

The strictness of the last inclusion follows from the closure properties of the two classes (to be considered shortly): $\cup_k \mathbf{DTA}_k$ is closed under complementation but $\mathbf{NTA}_0$ is not.

Closure properties

Untimed finite-state machines are effectively closed under all boolean operations [9]. From the results of [2] it follows that the class $\mathbf{DTA}_0$ is closed under both intersection and complementation, but the class $\mathbf{NTA}_0$ is closed under intersection only. Now we consider these properties for bounded deterministic automata.

Theorem 3.3 *For all $k \geq 1$, the class $\mathbf{DTA}_k$ is closed under complementation, but not under intersection.*

Proof. For bounded deterministic automata, complementation corresponds essentially to complementing the accepting set. The proof of nonclosure under intersection is similar to the proof of Theorem 3.1. ■

However, the limit class $\cup_k \mathbf{DTA}_k$ has the desired closure properties.

Corollary 3.1 *$\cup_k \mathbf{DTA}_k$ is closed under all boolean operations.*

Proof. The closure under complement follows from Theorem 3.3. Given a DTA_{k_1} $\mathcal{A}_1$ and a DTA_{k_2} $\mathcal{A}_2$, the product 2DTA $\mathcal{A}_1 \times \mathcal{A}_2$ simulates first $\mathcal{A}_1$ and then A_2. The product automaton is $(k_1 + k_2 + 1)$-bounded. ■

Complexity issues

In this paper, we consider four problems of automata theory: membership, emptiness, universality, and inclusion. All four problems are decidable for untimed finite-state machines [9]. We know that the membership and emptiness problems are PSPACE-complete for $\mathbf{NTA}_0$ [2]; from our proof of Theorem 3.2, we can conclude that membership and emptiness are in PSPACE for $\mathbf{NTA}_k$ for all $k \geq 0$. The universality and inclusion problems are PSPACE-complete for $\mathbf{DTA}_0$, but undecidable for $\mathbf{NTA}_0$ [2]. Here we consider these questions for $\mathbf{DTA}_k$. The complementation of a DTA_k, its translation into an equivalent NTA_0, and the decision procedure for checking the emptiness of an NTA_0, can be combined in a straightforward manner to obtain the following result.

Theorem 3.4 *For all $k \geq 0$, the membership problem for $\mathbf{DTA}_k$ is solvable in PTIME and the emptiness, universality, and inclusion problems for $\mathbf{DTA}_k$ are PSPACE-complete.*

4 Real-time Logics

In this section we examine the relationship between timed automata and real-time logics.

Bounded-operator temporal logic

We consider the logic MITL, *Metric Interval Temporal Logic*, of [3]. MITL is an extension of the propositional linear temporal logic PTL for writing real-time requirements. It admits time-bounded temporal operators such as $\Diamond_{[2,4]}$, meaning "eventually within time 2 to 4." Formally, given a set of propositions P, the formulas ϕ of MITL are inductively built using boolean connectives and the time-bounded *until* operator:

$$\phi \ := \ p \mid \neg\phi \mid \phi_1 \wedge \phi_2 \mid \phi_1 \mathcal{U}_I \, \phi_2,$$

where $p \in \text{P}$ and I is a *nonsingular* interval of the real-line with integer end-points. The subscripting interval I may be open, half-open, or closed; bounded or unbounded. The restriction of nonsingularity, which disallows operators such as $\mathcal{U}_{[3,3]}$, is a necessary condition on the decidability of the satisfiability problem for MITL.

The formulas of MITL are interpreted over timed words over the alphabet 2^{P}.[2] Given an MITL-formula ϕ, a timed word $w = (\overline{\sigma}, \overline{\tau})$ of length n over the alphabet 2^{P}, and a position $1 \leq i \leq n$, the satisfaction relation $(w, i) \models \phi$ is defined inductively as follows:

[2] In [3], MITL-formulas are interpreted over *timed state sequences*: a timed state sequence is an infinite sequence $(\sigma_1, I_1)(\sigma_2, I_2)\ldots$ of states $\sigma_i \subseteq \text{P}$ paired with intervals I_i such that the sequence $I_1 I_2 \ldots$ of intervals forms a partition of the real line. Here, our objective is to demonstrate the connection between MITL and timed automata, and to simplify the presentation we have adopted the semantics of timed words.

$(w, i) \models p$ iff $p \in \sigma_i$;
$(w, i) \models \neg\phi$ iff $(w, i) \not\models \phi$;
$(w, i) \models \phi_1 \wedge \phi_2$ iff $(w, i) \models \phi_1$ and $(w, i) \models \phi_2$;
$(w, i) \models \phi_1 \mathcal{U}_I \phi_2$ iff $(w, j) \models \phi_2$ for some $i \leq j \leq n$ such that $\tau_j \in \tau_i + I$, and $(w, k) \models \phi_1$ for all $i \leq k < j$.

The timed word w satisfies the formula ϕ (w is a *model* of ϕ) iff $(w, 1) \models \phi$. The timed language $L(\phi)$ defined by ϕ consists of the timed words w that satisfy ϕ. Let **MITL** be the set of timed languages definable by MITL-formulas; that is, a timed language L is in **MITL** iff L equals $L(\phi)$ for some MITL-formula ϕ.

We will use some standard abbreviations for additional temporal operators. The defined operators $\Diamond_I \phi$ (time-bounded *eventually*) and $\Box_I \phi$ (time-bounded *always*) stand for *true* $\mathcal{U}_I \phi$ and $\neg\Diamond_I \neg\phi$, respectively.

From temporal logic to timed automata

In [3] we gave an EXPSPACE decision procedure for checking the satisfiability of a given MITL-formula. In particular, we showed how to construct, from a given MITL-formula ϕ, a nondeterministic forward timed automaton $\mathcal{A}_\phi$ that accepts precisely the models of ϕ; that is, $L(\mathcal{A}_\phi) = L(\phi)$. Now we show that we can construct, in fact, a DTA_1 that accepts the models of a given formula.

Consider, for example, the MITL-formula

$$\Box_{[0,1)} (p \rightarrow \Diamond_{[1,2]} q).$$

Let us try to build a deterministic timed automaton that accepts precisely the models of this formula. One possibility is that whenever the automaton reads a p symbol, it stamps a clock with the time of this state, and later checks that within 1 to 2 time units a q symbol is visited. Since the number of p symbols within the interval $[0, 1)$ is potentially unbounded, whereas an automaton has only a fixed number of clocks, this simple strategy does not work. In fact, using a proof similar to that of Theorem 3.1, we can show that the above property does not belong to $\mathbf{DTA}_0$.

The solution becomes apparent from the following observation. Let t_1 be the time of the last q symbol within the interval $[1, 2)$, and let t_2 be the time of the first q symbol within the interval $[2, 3)$. The formula $\Diamond_{[1,2]} q$ holds during the intervals $[0, t_1 - 1]$ and $[t_2 - 2, 1)$, and it does not hold during the interval $(t_1 - 1, t_2 - 2)$. Consequently, while reading the p symbols in the interval $[0, 1)$, if the automaton can "predict" t_1 and t_2 in advance, the desired property can be checked. Since a two-way timed automaton can travel back and forth on the input, it need not guess a "future" value such as t_1 nondeterministically, but it can compute t_1 deterministically. The automaton first moves forward, finds the last q symbol in the interval $[1, 2)$, and sets a clock x to the time of that symbol. Similarly, it sets a clock y to the time of the first q symbol in the interval $[2, 3)$. Then it comes back and checks that no p symbols lie in the "bad" interval $(x - 1, y - 2)$. This strategy gives us a DTA_1.

Theorem 4.1 *For every MITL-formula ϕ, there exists a* DTA_1 $\mathcal{A}_\phi$ *over the alphabet* 2^{P} *that accepts precisely the models of ϕ.*

Proof. Let ϕ be a formula of MITL and let k_{max} be the maximum of the right end-points of all the intervals appearing in ϕ. The automaton $\mathcal{A}_\phi$ has $2k_{max}$ clocks for each subformula of ϕ. To determine the truth of ϕ with respect to a timed word w at a symbol in the unit time interval $[t, t+1)$, it suffices to know (1) the truth of all subformulas of ϕ at the successor symbol, and (2) for each subformula ψ of ϕ and each interval $[t+i, t+i+1)$ with $0 \leq i \leq k_{max}$, the first and last times that ψ holds in $[t+i, t+i+1)$. The automaton $\mathcal{A}_\phi$ first moves forward to the end of the input and then backtracks. On the return pass, it remembers the finite information (1) in its location and the finite information (2) in its clocks. Thus $\mathcal{A}_\phi$ can determine the truth of every subformula of ϕ at each position on its backwards pass. The formal construction of the automaton is given in the full paper. ∎

This gives us $\mathbf{DTA}_0 \not\supseteq \mathbf{MITL} \subset \mathbf{DTA}_1$.

Temporal logic with past operators

Researchers have considered extensions of PTL with past temporal operators such as *since* [10]. These operators can be added to PTL at no extra cost, and though they do not increase its expressive power, they allow a more direct and convenient expression of many properties. We consider a similar extension of MITL.

Let MITL^P be the logic that results from MITL by adding the following clause to the inductive definition of formulas: "If ϕ_1 and ϕ_2 are formulas, then so is $\phi_1 \mathcal{S}_I \phi_2$ for a nonsingular interval I with integer end-points." The meaning of the sime-bounded *since* operator is defined as:

$(w, i) \models \phi_1 \mathcal{S}_I \phi_2$ iff $(w, j) \models \phi_2$ for some $0 \leq j \leq i$ such that $\tau_i \in \tau_j + I$, and $(w, k) \models \phi_1$ for all $j < k \leq i$.

The time-bounded versions of the other past operators such as $\diamondminus$ (*sometime in the past*) and $\boxminus$ (*always in the past*) can be defined using the *since* operator.

Now let us consider the problem of constructing a deterministic automaton that accepts the models of a formula of MITL^P. The number of reversals necessary to check the truth of a formula ϕ of MITL^P is closely related to the number of alternations between past and future operators in ϕ. For every subformula ψ of ϕ, we define *level*(ψ) inductively:

- If ψ is built from propositions using boolean connectives and the *since* operator, then *level*(ψ) is 1_F.
- If ψ is built from formulas of level k_F using boolean connectives and the *until* operator, then *level*(ψ) is k_B.
- If ψ is built from formulas of level k_B using boolean connectives and the *since* operator, then *level*(ψ) is $(k+1)_F$.

For $k \geq 0$, let MITL$_k^P$ be the fragment of MITL^P that consists of all formulas ϕ such that *level*(ϕ) is either k_B or $(k+1)_F$. Note that all formulas of MITL belong to MITL$_1^P$.

Theorem 4.2 $\mathbf{MITL}_k^P \subset \mathbf{DTA}_k$.

Proof. Given a formula ϕ, we construct a deterministic automaton $\mathcal{A}_\phi$ that checks the truth of ϕ as follows. For every level k, on the k-th forward pass the automaton determines the truth of every subformula ψ with *level*(ψ) $= k_F$. Similarly, on the k-th reverse pass the automaton determines the truth of every subformula ψ with *level*(ψ) $= k_B$. ■

The satisfiability problem for MITL is known to be EXPSPACE-complete [3]. The translation from MITL^P to bounded DTAs and the decision procedure for solving the emptiness problem for bounded DTAs can be combined to obtain a decision procedure for MITL^P.

Corollary 4.1 *The satisfiability problem for* MITL^P *is EXPSPACE-complete.*

The expressive power of MITL^P increases with the number of switches between the past and future operators. Consider, for instance, the family of languages L_k from the proof of Theorem 3.1. If we consider only those timed words all of whose symbols lie within the interval $[0, 2)$, then the language L_k is defined by the following MITL$_{k+1}^P$-formula ϕ_k:

$$\Diamond_{>1} \, (\ominus\!\!\!\Diamond_{<1} \Diamond_{>1}\,)^k \; \mathit{true}\,.$$

This shows that for all $k > 0$, $\mathbf{MITL}_{k+1}^P \not\subseteq \mathbf{DTA}_{k-1}$. It follows that the switches between the past and future operators lead to a strict hierarchy of MITL^P-formulas.

Corollary 4.2 $\mathbf{MITL}_k^P \subset \mathbf{MITL}_{k+2}^P$.

We conjecture that in general, an automaton cannot check a formula of MITL$_k^P$ with less than k reversals. If this is the case, then the previous corollary can be strengthened to $\mathbf{MITL}_k^P \subset \mathbf{MITL}_{k+1}^P$.

5 Some Results on Unbounded Two-way Timed Automata

In Section 3 we addressed expressiveness, closure, and decidability questions for two-way timed automata with a bounded number of reversals. The same questions can be asked for the unrestricted classes **2DTA** and **2NTA**. These classes are perhaps not useful for algorithmic verification, because we will see that unbounded two-wayness is so powerful as to lead to undecidability even for the emptiness problem of **2DTA**.

To get an insight into the power of 2DTAs let us consider temporal logics with punctuality constraints. Recall that the logic MITL disallows punctuality constraints such as "every p symbol is followed by a q symbol after exactly 1 time unit,"

$$\Box(p \rightarrow \Diamond_{=1}\, q). \qquad (\phi_=)$$

We showed in [4] that allowing such formulas leads to the undecidability of the satisfiability problem. Let MITL$_=$ be the extension of MITL that allows singular intervals as time bounds on the temporal operators. We show that the models of any formula of MITL$_=$ can be defined by a 2DTA. For instance, it is easy to modify the automaton $\mathcal{A}_4$ of Figure 4 so that it accepts precisely the models of the formula $\phi_=$. On the other hand, the models of $\phi_=$ cannot be recognized using a bounded number of reversals, because this property does not belong to $\mathbf{NTA}_0$ [2].

Theorem 5.1 *For every* MITL$_=$*-formula* ϕ*, there exists a* 2DTA *over the alphabet* 2^{P} *that accepts precisely the models of* ϕ.

Using the undecidability of MITL$_=$ we obtain two corollaries.

Corollary 5.1 *The emptiness problem for* **2DTA** *is undecidable.*

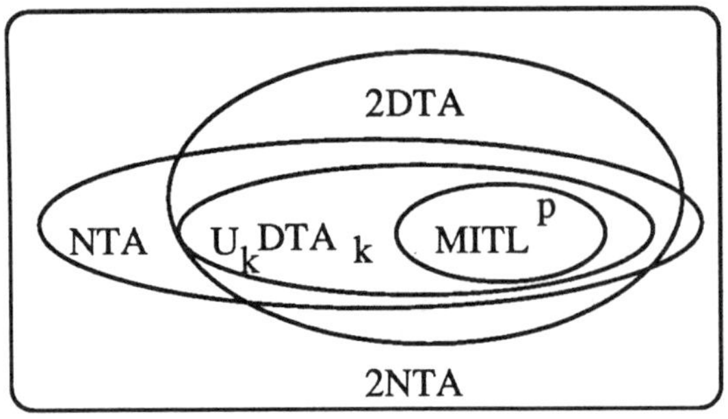

Figure 5: Relationship between various classes

Corollary 5.2 $\cup_k \mathbf{DTA}_k \subset \mathbf{2DTA} \not\subseteq \mathbf{NTA}_0$.

We conjecture that the ability to go back and forth unbounded number of times in a deterministic fashion is not powerful enough to model a nondeterministic pass:

$$\mathbf{NTA}_0 \not\subseteq \mathbf{2DTA}.$$

In particular, we believe that the following $\mathbf{NTA}_0$-language L cannot be accepted by any 2DTA. Let the timed word $(\overline{\sigma}, \overline{\tau})$ of length n over a unary alphabet be in L iff there is a sequence $1 = i_1 \leq i_2 \leq \cdots \leq i_m = n$ of positions such that for all $1 \leq k < m$, there is some $1 \leq j \leq n$ with $\tau_j = \tau_{i_k} + 1$ and either $i_{k+1} = j - 1$ or $i_{k+1} = j + 1$. If there is no 2DTA that accepts L, then nondeterminism and unrestricted two-wayness offer two proper and distinct extensions to the class $\cup_k \mathbf{DTA}_k$, which we isolated as the finite-state-verifiable real-time properties. The relationship between various classes is depicted in Figure 5.

Finally, we show that only linear space is required to simulate the behavior of a two-way timed automaton on a given input.

Theorem 5.2 *The membership problem for* **2NTA** *is solvable in PSPACE.*

Proof. Consider a 2NTA $\mathcal{A}$, and let k be the magnitude of the largest constant appearing in a clock constraint in the transitions of $\mathcal{A}$. Given a timed word $w = (\overline{\sigma}, \overline{\tau})$ of length n, define R_w to be the set comprising of $\tau_i + c$ and $(\tau_i + \tau_j + c)/2$ for $1 \leq i, j \leq n$ and $-(k+1) \leq c \leq (k+1)$. Let $\mathcal{A}^*$ be the 2NTA that behaves like $\mathcal{A}$, except that $\mathcal{A}^*$ is required to choose a value from the set R_w whenever a clock is nondeterministically reset. Then $\mathcal{A}$ accepts the timed word w iff $\mathcal{A}^*$ accepts w.

Now we can construct a nondeterministic linear-bounded Turing machine $\mathcal{A}'$ that, given a description of $\mathcal{A}$ and a timed word w, simulates the behavior of $\mathcal{A}^*$ on $w\$$. ■

References

[1] R. Alur, C. Courcoubetis, and D. Dill. Model-checking for real-time systems. In *Proc. of 5th IEEE Symp. on Logic in Computer Science*, 1990.

[2] R. Alur and D. Dill. Automata for modeling real-time systems. In *Automata, Languages, and Programming: Proc. of 17th ICALP*, LNCS 443. Springer-Verlag, 1990.

[3] R. Alur, T. Feder, and T. Henzinger. The benefits of relaxing punctuality. In *Proc. of 10th ACM Symp. on Principles of Distributed Computing*, 1991.

[4] R. Alur and T. Henzinger. A really temporal logic. In *Proc. of 30th IEEE Symp. on Foundations of Computer Science*, 1989.

[5] R. Alur and T. Henzinger. Time for logic. *SIGACT News*, 22(3), 1991.

[6] C. Courcoubetis and M. Yannakakis. Minimum and maximum delay problems in real-time systems. In *Proc. of 3rd Workshop on Computer-Aided Verification*, 1991.

[7] D. Dill and H. Wong-Toi. Synthesizing processes and schedulers from temporal specifications. In *Proc. of 2nd Workshop on Computer-Aided Verification*, 1990.

[8] T. Henzinger, Z. Manna, and A. Pnueli. Temporal proof methodologies for real-time systems. In *Proc. of 18th ACM Symp. on Principles of Programming Languages*, 1991.

[9] J. Hopcroft and J. Ullman. *Introduction to Automata Theory, Languages, and Computation.* Addison-Wesley, 1979.

[10] O. Lichtenstein, A. Pnueli, and L. Zuck. The glory of the past. In *Logics of Programs*, LNCS 193. Springer-Verlag, 1985.

[11] X. Nicollin, J. Sifakis, and S. Yovine. From ATP to timed graphs and hybrid systems. In *Proc. of REX workshop "Real-time: Theory in Practice"*, LNCS 600. Springer-Verlag, 1991.

[12] S. Safra. On the complexity of ω-automata. In *Proc. of 29th IEEE Symp. on Foundations of Computer Science*, 1988.

[13] A. P. Sistla, M. Vardi, and P. Wolper. The complementation problem for Büchi automata with applications to temporal logic. *Theoretical Computer Science*, 49, 1987.

[14] W. Thomas. Automata on infinite objects. In J. van Leeuwen, editor, *Handbook of Theoretical Computer Science*, volume B. Elsevier Science Publishers, 1990.

[15] P. Wolper, M. Vardi, and A. P. Sistla. Reasoning about infinite computation paths. In *Proc. of the 24th IEEE Symp. on Foundations of Computer Science*, 1983.

The Complexity of the Hajós Calculus

Toniann Pitassi
Computer Science Department
University of Toronto

Alasdair Urquhart
Philosophy Department
University of Toronto

Abstract

The Hajós Construction is a simple, nondeterministic procedure for generating the class of graphs that are not 3-colorable. Mansfield and Welsh have posed the problem of proving whether or not there exists a polynomial-size Hajós construction for every non-3-colorable graph. The main result of this paper is a proof that the Hajós calculus is polynomially-bounded if and only if extended Frege proof systems are polynomially bounded. This result links an open problem in graph theory to an important open problem in the complexity of propositional proof systems. In addition, we establish an exponential lower bound for a strong subsystem of the Hajós calculus. Lastly, we discuss an interesting graph-theoretical consequence of this result.

1 Introduction

The Hajós calculus (or Hajós construction) is a simple, nondeterministic procedure for generating the class of graphs that are not k-colorable [Haj]. [1] Mansfield and Welsh [MW] have posed the problem of determining the complexity of this procedure; in particular, it is an open problem whether or not there exists a polynomial-size Hajós construction for every non-3-colorable graph. Because graph 3-colorability is NP-complete, if there were polynomial-size Hajós constructions of all non-3-colorable graphs, then $NP = coNP$, so we expect that the Hajós calculus is not polynomially bounded. However, there has been very little progress toward a proof of this conjecture, despite considerable effort.

The main result of this paper is a proof that the Hajós calculus is polynomially-bounded if and only if extended Frege proof systems are polynomially bounded. This result links an open problem in graph theory to an important open problem in the complexity of propositional proof systems. It also shows that the complexity problem for the Hajós calculus is very difficult, since extended Frege systems are a very powerful class of proof systems for the propositional calculus, and no techniques currently exist which appear adequate to prove super-polynomial lower bounds for them. In addition, we study a subsystem of the Hajós calculus, which is still powerful enough to generate all non-3-colorable graphs. Our results, together with recent lower bounds for bounded-depth Frege proofs, enables us to prove an exponential lower bound for this subsystem of the Hajós calculus.

In Section 2, we introduce graph calculus terminology, and prove some facts about the Hajós calculus. In Section 3, we introduce propositional proof system terminology, and prove some lemmas about extended Frege proof systems. In Section 4, we show how to transform the rules of the Hajós calculus to obtain a propositional proof system, and analogously, how to transform the extended Frege system into a graph calculus. We then show that there are efficient simulations between these two systems. In Section 5, we prove the main theorems, and finally in Section 6, we discuss the implications of these results for the graph-theoretical complexity problem.

2 Graph calculi and the Hajós calculus

The graphs in this paper are finite, simple undirected graphs. The descriptions of the Hajós construction in the graph-theoretic literature assume that the construction operates on unlabelled graphs. However, it is more natural to think of operating on standard graphs, where the vertices are labelled. Accordingly, we define a graph G to be a pair (V, E), where V is a finite set of positive integers, and E a set of unordered pairs of elements of V; we write $e(G)$ for E, and $v(G)$ for V. Two graphs will be said to be *disjoint* if their vertex sets are disjoint. A k-coloring of a graph is

[1] This procedure was originally formulated due to its connection to the four color conjecture. In particular, when $k = 4$, proving that all graphs generated by the Hajós calculus are not planar is equivalent to proving the four color theorem.

an assignment of one of k distinct colors to each of the vertices of the graph; the coloring is *proper* if no two adjacent vertices receive the same color, otherwise *improper*.

A *graph calculus* is a collection of initial graphs, together with a finite collection of rules which allow us to derive new graphs. We shall restrict our attention to calculi for the class of non-3-colorable graphs. Let $\mathcal{C}$ be a particular graph calculus. A *construction* of a graph G in $\mathcal{C}$ is a sequence of graphs, ending with G, such that every graph in the sequence is either an initial graph, or follows from previous graphs by one of the rules of $\mathcal{C}$. $\mathcal{C}$ is *sound* if every graph constructed by $\mathcal{C}$ is non-3-colorable. $\mathcal{C}$ is *complete* if every non-3-colorable graph can be constructed in $\mathcal{C}$. The Hajós calculus is an example of a sound and complete graph calculus. Let $\Gamma = \{G_1, G_2, ..., G_k\}$ be a set of graphs, and let G be another graph, all with underlying vertex set V. Then Γ *implies* G, written $\Gamma \Rightarrow G$, if for all 3-colorings c of V, if c is an improper 3-coloring of every graph in Γ, then c is also an improper 3-coloring of G. A graph calculus $\mathcal{C}$, is said to be *implicationally complete* if for all $\Gamma = \{G_1, G_2, ..., G_k\}$, G if $\Gamma \Rightarrow G$, then there is a construction in $\mathcal{C}$ of G from the graphs in Γ. We will show in the subsequent section that the Hajós calculus is implicationally complete.

The *size* of a graph G is the number of its edges, that is, $|e(G)|$. The *size* of a graph calculus construction is the total size of all graphs in the construction. The *length* of a graph calculus construction is the number of applications of rules in it. A graph calculus $\mathcal{C}$ is *polynomially bounded* if there exists a polynomial p such that every non-3-colorable graph G can be constructed in $\mathcal{C}$ with a construction of size at most $p(|e(G)|)$.

Let $\mathcal{C}_1$ and $\mathcal{C}_2$ be two graph calculus systems. Then $\mathcal{C}_1$ *p-simulates* $\mathcal{C}_2$ if there is a polynomial-time computable function f so that for all graphs G, if s is a graph construction of G in $\mathcal{C}_2$, then $f(s)$ is a graph construction of G in $\mathcal{C}_1$. $\mathcal{C}_1$ and $\mathcal{C}_2$ are *p-equivalent* if $\mathcal{C}_1$ p-simulates $\mathcal{C}_2$, and $\mathcal{C}_2$ p-simulates $\mathcal{C}_1$.

2.1 The Hajós Calculus

In this section, we will describe the Hajós Calculus for $k = 3$; to obtain the Hajós Calculus for a different value of k, simply substitute the complete graph, K_{k+1}, for the initial graph, K_4. The set of initial graphs in the Hajós calculus contains all copies of K_4. There are three rules for generating new graphs:

(1) (Vertex/Edge Introduction) Add (any number of) vertices and edges.

(2) (Join rule) Let G_1 and G_2 be disjoint graphs, a_1 and b_1 adjacent vertices in G_1, and a_2 and b_2 adjacent vertices in G_2. Construct the graph G_3 from $G_1 \cup G_2$ as follows. First, remove edges $[a_1, b_1]$ and $[a_2, b_2]$; then add an edge $[b_1, b_2]$; lastly, contract vertices a_1 and a_2 into a single vertex.

(3) (Contraction rule) Contract two nonadjacent vertices into a single vertex, and remove any resulting duplicated edges; the single vertex can be either of the two original vertices.

Since we are using labelled rather than unlabelled graphs, it might seem necessary to include a duplication rule which allows the generation of a new copy of any graph already constructed. However, the duplication rule applied to a graph G can be simulated by repeated applications of the Contraction rule, applied to G and a collection of isolated vertices. The simulating construction which results has size $O(|v(G)|^2)$, so the systems with and without the duplication rule are p-equivalent.

It is not too hard to see that any graph constructed by means of the above Hajós calculus procedure is not 3-colorable. Moreover Hajós showed [Haj] that the Hajós calculus is complete. The proof of this completeness theorem yields an algorithm which generates a Hajós construction for any non-3-colorable graph. The length of the construction, in the worst case, is exponential in the size of the graph. Mansfield and Welsh [MW] show that for a graph with less than $n^2/3$ edges, there is a Hajós construction of the graph with length at most $2^{n^2/3-|e(G)|+1} - 1$. [2]

It will be convenient for our purposes to reformulate the Hajós calculus. The system $\mathcal{HC}$ has the same set of initial graphs, as well as rules (1) and (3) of the Hajós calculus, but now rule (2) of the Hajós calculus is replaced by the following rule:

(2) (Edge Elimination rule) Let G_1 and G_2 be two graphs with common vertex set $\{v_1, ..., v_n\}$ which are identical except that G_1 contains edges $[v_1, v_2]$ and $[v_2, v_3]$ whereas G_2 contains edges $[v_1, v_2]$ and $[v_1, v_3]$. Then from G_1 and G_2, we can construct

[2] In earlier papers on the complexity of the Hajós calculus [MW, HRT], a different definition of Hajós calculus is given. There, a Hajós construction of a graph G is defined to be a construction of a subgraph of G using only the rules (2) and (3). However, this alternative definition results in essentially the same complexity measure. (The unwritten proof of this result is due to Jason Brown.) Additionally, in earlier formulations, the size is taken to be the length rather than the size. However, the two measures are polynomially related for the formulation of the Hajós calculus employed here.

the graph G_3 which is graph G_1 with edge $[v_2, v_3]$ removed.

Claim 1 *$\mathcal{HC}$ is p-equivalent to the Hajós calculus.*

Proof. Because the only rule which differs is rule (2), it suffices to show that the join rule of the Hajós calculus can be simulated by a construction in $\mathcal{HC}$, that the Edge Elimination rule of $\mathcal{HC}$ can be simulated by a construction in the Hajós calculus, and that in each case the series of simulating steps can be constructed in polynomial time.

Let $G_1 = (V_1, E_1)$ and $G_2 = (V_2, E_2)$ be two disjoint graphs, where G_1 has a distinguished edge $[a_1, b_1]$, G_2 has a distinguished edge $[a_2, b_2]$ and G is the graph obtained from G_1 and G_2 by applying the join rule. To derive G in $\mathcal{HC}$, we first apply rules (1) and (3) to obtain a copy G_2^* of G_2 in which a_2 is replaced by a_1. Then we apply rule (1) to G_1 to obtain a new graph, G_1' with underlying vertex set $(V_1 \cup V_2) - \{a_2\}$; the edges of G_1' are the edges of G_1 and the edges of G_2^* except for the edge $[a_1, b_2]$, together with the edge $[b_1, b_2]$. Similarly, we apply (1) to G_2^* to obtain the new graph G_2' where G_2' has the same vertex set as G_1', and the edge set is the same except that edge $[a_1, b_1]$ is replaced by edge $[a_1, b_2]$. We can now apply rule (2) to G_1' and G_2' to obtain the desired graph, G.

Conversely, let G_1 and G_2 be two graphs which are identical except that G_1 contains edges $[v_1, v_2]$ and $[v_1, v_3]$ whereas G_2 contains edges $[v_1, v_2]$ and $[v_2, v_3]$. Let G be the graph obtained by applying the Edge Elimination rule. To derive G in the Hajós calculus, first apply rules (1) and (3) to generate a copy G_2^* of G_2 disjoint from G_1; if v is a vertex of G_2, then v^* is the corresponding vertex of G_2^*. Second, apply the join rule to G_1 and G_2^* to obtain a new graph, G', where vertices v_3 and v_3^* are contracted to a single vertex, and which contains the edge $[v_1, v_2^*]$, but does not contain edges $[v_2^*, v_3^*]$ or $[v_1, v_3]$. G' contains two copies of each vertex other than vertex v_3; by contracting vertices v and v^* (using rule 3), we obtain the desired graph, G. □

Definition. Let the graph system $\mathcal{HC}^-$ be the system $\mathcal{HC}$ without the Contraction rule.

In [Be, pp. 352-353], it is shown that $\mathcal{HC}$ is complete. The theorem stated below is a stronger form of completeness for $\mathcal{HC}$ than in the original proof by Hajós. The proof of this theorem follows from the more general Theorem 3 by setting V' equal to V.

Theorem 2 *$\mathcal{HC}^-$ is implicationally complete.*

Definition. Let $\Gamma = \{G_1, ..., G_q\}$, and let $G_1, ..., G_q$ and G be graphs over vertices V, $|V| = n$. For $V' \subseteq V$, let $G^{V'}$ denote the subgraph of G over the vertices in V'. The implication $\Gamma \Rightarrow G$ is *V'-local* if there exists a subset $V' \subseteq V$ such that: (1) For all $i \leq q$, the set of edges in G_i which do not lie inside V' equals the set of edges of G which do not lie inside V', (2) If c is a 3-coloring to V', and c is a proper 3-coloring of $G^{V'}$, then c is also a proper 3-coloring of $G_j^{V'}$, for some $j \leq q$. The implication will be called V'-local when the underlying vertex set is V'.

Theorem 3 *Let $\Gamma = \{G_1, ..., G_q\}$, and let $G_1, ..., G_q$ and G be graphs over vertices V, $|V| = n$. If there exists $V' \subseteq V$, $|V'| \geq 4$ such that $\Gamma \Rightarrow G$ is V'-local, then there is a $\mathcal{HC}^-$ construction of G from Γ with size at most $O(2^{|V'|}n^2)$.*

Proof. Let $G_1, G_2, ..., G_q, G$ be graphs over vertex set V and let $G_1, ..., G_q \Rightarrow G$. A *triplet* is a subgraph consisting of three vertices and a single edge between two of the three vertices. For a fixed V, $V' \subseteq V$, $|V'| \geq 4$, $G_1, ..., G_q$, we will show that if G is a graph over V such that $G_1, ..., G_q \Rightarrow G$, and the implication is V'-local, then there exists a construction (in $|V|$) of G from $G_1, ..., G_q$ of size $O(2^{|V'|}n^2)$.

The proof is by downward induction on the number of edges in $G^{V'}$. If all edges are present in $G^{V'}$, then $G^{V'}$, and hence G must contain a K_4 subgraph, and thus can be constructed from K_4 by application of rule (1). For the inductive step, assume that we have proven the theorem for all graphs, H, with underlying vertices V, such that: (1) $G_1, ..., G_q \Rightarrow H$, and the implication is V'-local; and (2) the number of edges in $H^{V'}$ is greater than m. Now fix G such that: $G_1, ..., G_q \Rightarrow G$, the implication is V'-local, and $G^{V'}$ has m edges. There are two cases to consider: either $G^{V'}$ contains a triplet, or there are no triplets in $G^{V'}$. If $G^{V'}$ does not contain any triplets, then $G^{V'}$ is a complete k-partite graph, for some k. (This follows because if there are no triplets, then the relation "is not adjacent" is an equivalence relation.) If $k > 3$, then $G^{V'}$, and hence also G, contains a K_4 subgraph and can therefore be constructed from K_4 by adding edges. Otherwise $k \leq 3$. In this case, we will show that G contains some G_i as a subgraph. Label the independent sets of $G^{V'}$ by X, Y and Z. Assume for sake of contradiction that G does not contain any of $G_1, ..., G_q$ as subgraphs. Then each G_i must contain some edge which is contained in either X, Y or Z. Now consider the 3-coloring of $G^{V'}$ which assigns all vertices of X the color red, all vertices of Y the color blue, and all vertices of Z the color green. Then this coloring properly colors $G^{V'}$, but it does not properly color any of $G_1^{V'}, ..., G_q^{V'}$. But this contradicts our assumption that $G_1, ..., G_q \Rightarrow G$ is V'-local. Thus, some G_i must be contained within G, and it follows that G can be constructed from G_i by adding edges.

The second case is when $G^{V'}$ contains at least one triplet. Consider a triplet, T, of $G^{V'}$, with vertices v_1, v_2, v_3, and edge (v_1, v_2). Let G^a be the graph G plus the additional edge (v_2, v_3), and let G^b be the graph G plus the additional edge (v_1, v_3). Because $G_1, ..., G_q \Rightarrow G$, and $G \Rightarrow G^a$, it follows that $G_1, ..., G_q \Rightarrow G^a$. By this fact, and because G^a has greater than m edges, we can apply the inductive hypothesis to obtain a construction of G^a from $G_1, ..., G_q$. Similarly, we can construct G^b from $G_1, ..., G_q$. Now, by the edge elimination rule, we can construct G from G^a and G^b.

The number of intermediate graphs constructed is $O(2^{|V'|})$, and each is of size at most $O(|V|^2)$. Thus, the total size of the construction is $O(2^{|V'|}n^2)$. □

3 Propositional Proof Systems

A *propositional proof system* is a collection of initial propositional formulas (axioms), together with a set of rules which allow us to derive new propositional formulas. The propositional proof systems we consider are systems for showing formulas to be tautologies. A propositional proof system is a *Frege system* if its axioms consists of all instances of a finite number of tautologies, and it has a finite number of inference rules which are sound (i.e. preserve truth). We shall also consider *extended Frege systems*, in which it is possible to introduce new sentence letters as abbreviations for complex formulas.

Let $\mathcal{P}$ be a fixed propositional proof system. We say that $\mathcal{P}$ is *sound* if all of its axioms are tautologies, and its rules of inference preserve truth. If $\mathcal{P}$ is sound, and $A_1, \ldots, A_n$ and B are formulas of $\mathcal{P}$, then a *proof of B from $A_1, \ldots, A_n$ in $\mathcal{P}$* is a sequence of formulas each of which is either an axiom of $\mathcal{P}$, one of the formulas $A_1, \ldots, A_n$ or derived from earlier formulas in the sequence by one of the rules of $\mathcal{P}$, and in which the last formula is B. We write $A_1, \ldots, A_n \vdash_{\mathcal{P}} B$ if there is a proof of B from $A_1, \ldots, A_n$ in $\mathcal{P}$. The *size* of a proof is defined to be the number of occurrences of symbols in it. If $\Gamma \cup \{A\}$ is a set of formulas, then we write $\Gamma \models A$ if A is a logical consequence of the set of formulas Γ. A proof system $\mathcal{P}$ is *complete* if every tautology has a proof in $\mathcal{P}$; $\mathcal{P}$ is *implicationally complete* if $\Gamma \vdash_{\mathcal{P}} B$ whenever $\Gamma \models B$.

Let $\mathcal{P}_1$ and $\mathcal{P}_2$ be two propositional proof systems which share a common language. The system $\mathcal{P}_1$ *p-simulates* $\mathcal{P}_2$ if there is a polynomial-time computable function f so that for all formulas A, if P is a proof in $\mathcal{P}_2$ of A, then $f(P)$ is a proof of A in $\mathcal{P}_1$. If $\mathcal{P}_1$ p-simulates $\mathcal{P}_2$, then there is a polynomial p so that if there is a proof of A in $\mathcal{P}_2$ of size m, then there is also a proof of A in $\mathcal{P}_1$ of size at most $p(m)$. Two proof systems are *p-equivalent* if they p-simulate each other.

Several of the proof systems we consider in this paper operate with formulas in disjunctive normal form. A *DNF formula* is a finite disjunction of a set of *terms*, each of which is a conjunction of a set of literals (variables or their negations). The complement of a literal l is written as $\bar{l}$. A term will be written in the form $\bigwedge X$, where X is a set of literals, or by juxtaposing literals, as in $l_1 l_2 \ldots l_k$. Disjunctions are written as $\bigvee X$, or in the form $l_1 \vee \ldots \vee l_k$. If X is a set of terms, and l a literal, then Xl will stand for the set of all terms Al, where A is a term in X.

If A is a formula in conjunctive normal form, then $\sim A$ is defined to be the formula in disjunctive normal form equivalent to the negation of A, that is, the formula resulting from A by replacing $\vee$ by $\wedge$, $\wedge$ by $\vee$, and literals by their complements. If l, m, n are literals, then the notation $l \leftrightarrow (m \vee n)$ will be used as an abbreviation for $(\bar{l} \vee m \vee n) \wedge (\overline{m} \vee l) \wedge (\overline{n} \vee l)$ and $(A_1, \ldots, A_k) \supset B$ as an abbreviation for $\sim A_1 \vee \ldots \vee \sim A_k \vee B$.

Let f be a DNF formula. Then the formula $f[1/p]$ denotes the formula obtained from f by removing all terms which contain $\overline{p}$, and then removing all occurrences of p. If the resulting formula contains an empty disjunction, then $f[1/p]$ is defined to be $(p \wedge \overline{p})$; if the resulting formula contains an empty conjunction, then $f[1/p]$ is defined to be $(p \vee \overline{p})$. Similarly, the formula $f[0/p]$ denotes the formula obtained from f by removing all terms which contain p, and then removing all occurrences of $\overline{p}$. If the resulting formula contains an empty disjunction, then $f[0/p]$ is defined to be $(p \wedge \overline{p})$; if the resulting formula contains an empty conjunction, then $f[0/p]$ is $(p \vee \overline{p})$. If f is a CNF formula, then $f[1/p]$, and $f[0/p]$ are defined similarly. Lastly, if Γ is a set of formulas, then $\Gamma[0/p]$ ($\Gamma[1/p]$) is the set of all formulas $A[0/p]$ ($A[1/p]$), for $A \in \Gamma$.

A depth-2 Frege system

The system $\mathcal{F}_2$ is a proof system for DNF formulas, where a term in a DNF formula will be viewed as an AND of an ordered set of literals. The proof system $\mathcal{F}_2$ has a single axiom schema, $p \vee \overline{p}$, and the following five rules. In applying the rules of $\mathcal{F}_2$ and the other systems we consider, the associative and commutative laws for disjunction will be applied tacitly. We will also assume the following generalized commutativity rule for conjunction: $(l_1 \wedge l_2 \wedge ... \wedge l_q) \vee B \Rightarrow (\pi(l_1) \wedge \pi(l_2) \wedge ... \wedge \pi(l_q)) \vee B$, where π is a bijection from $\{l_1, ..., l_q\}$ to $\{l_1, ..., l_q\}$.

$(R0)$ $A \vee A \vee B \Rightarrow A \vee B$,

$(R1)$ $A \Rightarrow A \vee B$,

$(R2)$ $AB \vee C \Rightarrow A \vee C$,

$(R3)$ $(A \vee C), (B \vee C) \Rightarrow AB \vee C$,

$(R4)$ $A \vee l, B \vee \bar{l} \Rightarrow A \vee B$,

Theorem 4 *$\mathcal{F}_2$ is implicationally complete.*

A depth-d Frege System

By adding a few more rules to the depth-2 Frege system, $\mathcal{F}_2$, we can define a more general Frege system, $\mathcal{F}$, over the basis AND, OR and NOT. We define the rules of this system to be the rules $R0 - R4$ of $\mathcal{F}_2$, plus the following rules $R5 - R9$. The symbol $\Leftrightarrow$ indicates that the rule may be applied either from left to right ($\Rightarrow$), or from right to left ($\Leftarrow$). In all rules $R0 - R9$, the formulas A, B and C are arbitrary formulas over the basis $\vee$, $\wedge$ and $\neg$, where AND and OR are unbounded-fanin boolean functions, and NOT is defined as usual.

$(R5)$ $A \wedge (B_1 \vee ... B_k) \Leftrightarrow (A \wedge B_1) \vee ... (A \wedge B_k)$,

$(R6)$ $A \vee (B_1 \wedge ... \wedge B_k) \Leftrightarrow (A \vee B_1) \wedge ... \wedge (A \vee B_k)$,

$(R7)$ $\neg(A_1 \vee ... \vee A_k) \Leftrightarrow \neg A_1 \wedge ... \wedge \neg A_k$,

$(R8)$ $\neg(A_1 \wedge ... \wedge A_k) \Leftrightarrow \neg A_1 \vee ... \vee \neg A_k$,

$(R9)$ $\neg\neg A \Leftrightarrow A$.

The *depth* of a formula is the depth of the boolean tree which represents the formula. We define a depth-d proof of a formula, A, to be a proof in the above Frege system, where each formula occuring in the proof has depth at most d. Alternatively, the *depth-d Frege system*, $\mathcal{F}_d$, is the system $\mathcal{F}$, where each formula is restricted to have depth at most d.

Proof systems with extension

Given a proof system, a natural and powerful way to extend it is to add a rule by which a complex formula can be abbreviated by a single variable.

Let $\mathcal{S}$ be any standard Frege system where no restrictions are placed on the depth of formulas (ie., the system $\mathcal{F}$). The *extended version of $\mathcal{S}$*, or $\mathcal{ES}$, is the system which results from $\mathcal{S}$ by allowing as steps in derivations lines of the form $p \leftrightarrow A$, where p is a variable that does not appear in earlier lines, in the assumptions, or the conclusion of the derivation. Such a system is an *extended Frege system*. Cook and Reckhow [CR] show that any two extended Frege systems are p-equivalent, so that the results of this paper do not depend on the formal details of a particular system.

In the case of the system $\mathcal{F}_2$, it is more convenient to introduce a form of the extension rule similar to that originally used by Tseitin [Tse] in the context of resolution systems. Let V be a set of variables, and $p_1, \ldots, p_k$ a set of new variables disjoint from those in V. Then $D_1, \ldots, D_k$ is an *extension sequence* for V if for each i, D_i is $p_i \leftrightarrow (l_1 \vee l_2 \vee ... \vee l_q)$, where $l_1, ..., l_q$ are literals which involve variables from $V \cup \{p_1, \ldots, p_{i-1}\}$. We define an $\mathcal{EF}_2$ *proof* of a DNF formula A to be a proof in $\mathcal{F}_2$ of the formula $(D_1, \ldots, D_k) \supset A$, where $D_1, \ldots, D_k$ is an extension sequence for the variables occurring in A.

Although $\mathcal{EF}_2$ only allows proofs of formulas in DNF, $\mathcal{EF}_2$ can be considered as a general proof system for propositional formulas by using the idea of extension. Let A be a propositional formula; for definiteness, let us take A to contain only the connectives $\neg$ and $\vee$. Associate a literal l_B with each subformula B of A so that: (1) the variables in A are associated with themselves; (2) if B has the associated literal l_B, then $\neg B$ has $\overline{l_B}$ as its associated literal; (3) distinct subformulas are associated with distinct literals. Then the *definitional set* for A, $Def(A)$, is the set of all formulas of the form $l_{B \vee C} \leftrightarrow (l_B \vee l_C)$, where $B \vee C$ is a subformula of A. Then we define an $\mathcal{EF}_2$ proof of the formula A to be a proof in $\mathcal{EF}_2$ of $(\bigwedge Def(A) \supset l_A)$.

Lemma 5 *The system $\mathcal{EF}_2$ p-simulates any extended Frege system.*

Proof. Let $\mathcal{ES}$ be a fixed extended Frege system, d a derivation of A in $\mathcal{ES}$, and $Def(d)$ the union of all the definitional sets $Def(B)$, where B is a line of d. It can be shown by induction on the length of d that for every line B in d, there is a derivation in $\mathcal{F}_2$ of $Def(d) \supset l_B$; hence there is a derivation d' in $\mathcal{EF}_2$ of A. The new derivation d' can be constructed in polynomial time from the old derivation d, so that $\mathcal{EF}_2$ p-simulates $\mathcal{ES}$. This proof is essentially the same as the proof by Cook and Reckhow [CR] of the corresponding result for extended resolution. □

Systems with substitution rules

Another natural and powerful rule used in many propositional proof systems is the the rule of substitution: From A derive $A[B/p]$, where p is a variable,

B any formula. This rule is unsound (except if A is required to be a tautology), so that systems including this rule no longer qualify as Frege systems. If $\mathcal{G}$ is a Frege system, then we write $\mathcal{SG}$ for the system which results from $\mathcal{G}$ by adding the rule of substitution. Such systems are called *Frege systems with substitution* by Cook and Reckhow [CR], who prove that any such system can p-simulate any extended Frege system. [3]

A weak form of the substitution rule is the rule which allows the substitution of the constants 0 and 1 for all occurrences of a propositional variable. This form of the rule we shall call the *{0,1}-substitution rule*. If $\mathcal{G}$ is a Frege system, we write $\mathcal{S}_{0,1}\mathcal{G}$ for the system which results by adding the rules: $A \Rightarrow A[0/p]$, and $A \Rightarrow A[1/p]$ to $\mathcal{G}$. If we do not have the constants 0 and 1 in our system, then $A[0/p]$ and $A[1/p]$ denote the formulas obtained from A as defined earlier. It is a result of Buss [Bu] that in the context of a Frege system this weak form of the rule is (up to a polynomial) as strong as the unrestricted form of the rule.

Lemma 6 *The system $\mathcal{S}_{0,1}\mathcal{F}_2$ p-simulates $\mathcal{EF}_2$.*

Proof. By definition, an $\mathcal{EF}_2$ proof of a formula A is a proof in $\mathcal{F}_2$ of $(D_1, \ldots, D_k) \supset A$, where $D_1, \ldots, D_k$ is an extension sequence for the set of variables in A. Thus it is sufficient to prove that if we are given a proof in $\mathcal{F}_2$ of $(D_1, \ldots, D_k) \supset A$, we can eliminate the antecedent of the conditional efficiently, using the {0,1}-substitution rule.

Let D_k be $p_k \leftrightarrow (l_1 \vee l_2 \vee \ldots \vee l_q)$. From $(D_1, \ldots, D_k) \supset A$ by substituting 1 for p_k we can derive the formula $(D_1, \ldots, D_{k-1}, (l_1 \vee \ldots \vee l_q)) \supset A$; similarly, $(D_1, \ldots, D_{k-1}, (\overline{l_1} \wedge \ldots \wedge \overline{l_q})) \supset A$. By repeated application of $R2$, $R0$ and $R4$, we can then derive $(D_1, \ldots, D_{k-1}) \supset A$. The elimination of the hypothesis D_k takes steps of total size $O(r)$, where r is the length of the formula $(D_1, \ldots, D_k) \supset A$, so that the formula A can be derived in $\mathcal{S}_{0,1}\mathcal{F}_2$ by adding extra steps of total size $O(kr)$. □

Another restricted form of the substitution rule is the renaming rule: From A derive $A[p/q]$, where p, q are propositional variables. If $\mathcal{G}$ is a Frege system, the system which results from $\mathcal{G}$ by adding the renaming rule will be denoted by $\mathcal{RG}$. It is a surprising result of Buss [Bu] that in the context of Frege systems the renaming rule is as powerful as the {0, 1}-substitution rule (up to a polynomial).

Lemma 7 *The system $\mathcal{RF}_2$ p-simulates $\mathcal{S}_{0,1}\mathcal{F}_2$.*

Proof. The proof presented here is due to Steve Cook. We show how, given a proof of A in $\mathcal{F}_2$, and p a variable in A, we can derive $A[0/p]$ in $\mathcal{RF}_2$ in a relatively efficient way. Let $p_1, \ldots, p_k$ be the variables in A, and let p_i be the variable to be eliminated. Let the length of A be r. From A we can derive $p_i \vee A[0/p_i]$ by $R0$, $R1$, and $R2$; hence by $k-1$ applications of renaming we obtain the formulas $p_1 \vee A[0/p_i]$, $p_2 \vee A[0/p_i]$, ..., $p_k \vee A[0/p_i]$. Since A is a tautology, we can derive the formula $\neg p_1 \vee \neg p_2 \vee \ldots \vee \neg p_k \vee A[0/p_i]$ by a subsidiary derivation of length $O(kr)$. Now by k applications of rule $R4$, we obtain $A[0/p_i]$, as desired. The derivation of $A[0/p_i]$ from A has size $O(r^2)$. An exactly similar process allows the derivation of the formula $A[1/p_i]$, so that the proof of simulation is complete. □

Note: In this section, we have defined all of our proof systems to be depth-2 systems for proving DNF tautologies. However, in the following sections it is more convenient to think in terms of unsatisfiable formulas in CNF. It is easy to interpret our systems as refutation systems for CNF formulas by simply replacing each AND by an OR and each OR by an AND in each rule and axiom of the system. In what follows, we will view $\mathcal{EF}_2$, $\mathcal{RF}_2$, $\mathcal{F}$ and $\mathcal{F}_2$ as refutation systems for CNF formulas.

4 Simulation Results

Using the well-known reductions between CNF unsatisfiability and graph non-3-colorability, we can translate the rules and axioms of the Hajós calculus to obtain a propositional refutation system, and similarly, we can translate the rules and axioms of $\mathcal{EF}_2$ to obtain a graph calculus.

Translation from Formulas to Graphs

We use a reduction from the theory of NP-completeness to show the similarity between graph calculus systems and propositional refutation systems. Garey, Johnson and Stockmeyer [GJS] showed that $3SAT$ is reducible to 3-Colorability, by obtaining a polynomial-time, many-one transformation from $3CNF$ formulas to graphs. Here, we slightly modify their construction so that it is a transformation from arbitrary CNF formulas to graphs. Let f be a CNF formula, $f = C_1 \wedge C_2 \wedge \ldots \wedge C_p$, with underlying variables $x_1, \ldots, x_n$. For notational convenience, let $C_i = (l_1 \vee l_2 \vee \ldots \vee l_q)$. Then $Graph(f)$ consists of the following nodes, N:

$$N = \{v1, v2, v3\} \cup \{xi, \overline{xi} \mid 1 \leq i \leq n\} \cup \{a^i_j, b^i_j, c^i_j \mid 1 \leq i \leq p, 1 \leq j \leq q-1\}.$$

[3] Somewhat surprisingly, the converse simulation also holds, a fact first proved by Dowd [Do], and later in [KP].

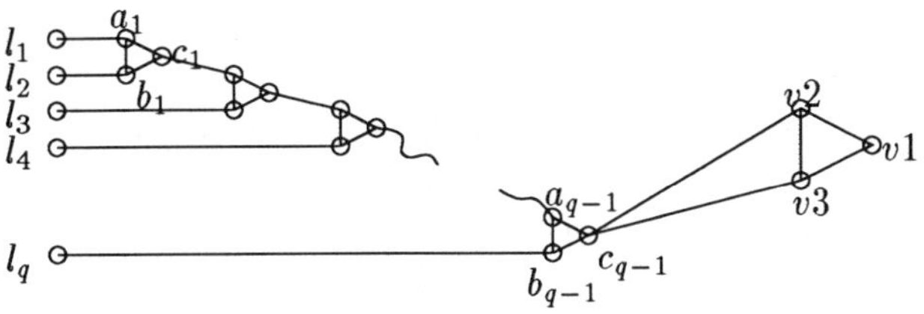

Figure 1: The subgraph G_{C_i} corresponding to C_i

The set E of edges for *Graph*(f) is given by:

$$\begin{aligned} E &= \{[v1,v2],[v2,v3],[v1,v3]\} \cup \{[xi,\overline{xi}] | 1 \le i \le n\} \\ &\cup \{[v3,xi],[v3,\overline{xi}] | 1 \le i \le n\} \\ &\cup \{G_{C_i} \mid 1 \le i \le q\}, \end{aligned}$$

where for a particular clause, $C_i = (l_1 \vee l_2 \vee ... \vee l_q)$ in f, the subgraph G_{C_i} is shown in Figure 1. When C_i is just a single literal, l, then G_{C_i} is the K_4 graph with underlying vertices $l, v1, v2, v3$.

A key property of the graph G is: for each $C_i = (l_1 \vee l_2 \vee ... \vee l_q)$, a proper 3-coloring to $l_1, ..., l_q$ can be extended to a proper 3-coloring to the underlying vertices of G_{C_i} if and only if at least one of $l_1, ..., l_q$ has the same color as $v1$. The observation leads to the following lemma, which was proven in [GJS].

Theorem 8 *f is satisfiable if and only if Graph(f) is 3-colorable.*

Translation from Graphs to Formulas

Conversely, if G is any graph, then there exists a propositional CNF formula, $Form(G)$ with the property that G is 3-colorable if and only if $Form(G)$ is satisfiable. Let $G = (V, E)$ be a graph. We define a propositional statement, $Form(G)$, with underlying variables $\{R_x, B_x, G_x \mid x \in V\}$, which expresses "G is 3-colorable" as follows:

$$\bigwedge_{x \in V} (\overline{R}_x \vee \overline{B}_x \vee \overline{G}_x)(R_x \vee B_x \vee G_x)$$
$$(R_x \vee \overline{B}_x \vee \overline{G}_x)(\overline{R}_x \vee \overline{B}_x \vee G_x)(\overline{R}_x \vee B_x \vee \overline{G}_x)$$
$$\bigwedge_{[x,y] \in E} (\overline{R}_x \vee \overline{R}_y)(\overline{G}_x \vee \overline{G}_y)(\overline{B}_x \vee \overline{B}_y).$$

Lemma 9 *G is 3-colorable if and only if $Form(G)$ is satisfiable.*

The Simulation Lemmas

By using the translations between propositional formulas and graphs described above, we can translate the Hajós calculus to obtain a new propositional refutation system. Define $Form(\mathcal{HC})$ to be the propositional refutation system obtained by translating the rules and axioms of $\mathcal{HC}$. Specifically, $Form(\mathcal{HC})$ has one axiom: $Form(K_4)$ and three rules, obtained by translating the three rules of $\mathcal{HC}$. Similarly, define $Form(\mathcal{HC}^-)$ to be the propositional refutation system obtained by translating the rules and axioms of $\mathcal{HC}^-$. Analogously, let $Graph(\mathcal{F}_2)$ and $Graph(\mathcal{EF}_2)$ be the graph calculus system obtained by translating the rules and axioms of $\mathcal{F}_2$ and $\mathcal{EF}_2$, respectively. Then we have the following simulation lemmas.

Lemma 10 *$\mathcal{F}_2$ p-simulates $Form(\mathcal{HC}^-)$.*

Proof. $Form(\mathcal{HC}^-)$ has one axiom, $Form(K_4)$, and two rules. Because all rules and axioms of $Form(\mathcal{HC}^-)$ are sound, by the implicational completeness of $\mathcal{F}_2$ (Theorem 4), there exists $\mathcal{F}_2$ proofs of: $Form(K_4)$, as well as the two rules of $Form(\mathcal{HC}^-)$. Furthermore, because each axiom and rule of $Form(\mathcal{HC}^-)$ involves only a constant number of symbols, the size of the proofs in $\mathcal{F}_2$ are polynomial in the size of of the original axiom or rule instance in $Form(\mathcal{HC}^-)$. □

Lemma 11 *$\mathcal{EF}_2$ p-simulates $Form(\mathcal{HC})$.*

Proof. We will show that $\mathcal{RF}_2$ p-simulates $Form(\mathcal{HC})$. Then because $\mathcal{EF}_2$ p-simulates $\mathcal{EF}$, and $\mathcal{EF}$ p-simulates $\mathcal{RF}_2$, it follows that $\mathcal{EF}_2$ p-simulates $Form(\mathcal{HC})$. Because $Form(\mathcal{HC}^-)$ is a subsystem of $Form(\mathcal{HC})$, and $\mathcal{F}_2$ is a subsystem of $\mathcal{RF}_2$, we only need to show how the one additional rule of $\mathcal{HC}$, rule (3), can be simulated by $\mathcal{RF}_2$. Since rule (3) is just a renaming of the variables, it can be simulated by the renaming rule. □

Lemma 12 *$\mathcal{HC}$ p-simulates $Graph(\mathcal{EF}_2)$.*

Proof. We will show that $\mathcal{HC}$ p-simulates $Graph(\mathcal{RF}_2)$. By Lemmas 6 and 7, $\mathcal{RF}_2$ p-simulates $\mathcal{EF}_2$; therefore $Graph(\mathcal{RF}_2)$ p-simulates $Graph(\mathcal{EF}_2)$, and it follows that $\mathcal{HC}$ p-simulates $Graph(\mathcal{EF}_2)$. Let P be a construction of some non-3-colorable graph, G, in $Graph(\mathcal{RF}_2)$. We will prove that there exists a polynomial-sized construction of G, by induction on the number of graphs in P. If P contains just one graph, then $P = G$, and G must be the graph $Graph(l \wedge \bar{l})$. In this case, it is easy to see that this graph contains a K_4 subgraph, and hence can be constructed easily in $\mathcal{HC}$ Otherwise, assume that we can simulate the first k lines of P, by a polynomial-sized construction in $\mathcal{HC}$. The next graph, $Graph(f')$, is either an axiom, or it follows from previous graphs by a rule. If $Graph(f')$ is an axiom, then it can be constructed in $\mathcal{HC}$ as in the base case.

Otherwise, $Graph(f')$ follows from previous graphs by a rule. If f' follows from f by Renaming, then $Graph(f')$ can be constructed from $Graph(f)$ by rule (3), the contraction rule. If $f' = A \wedge A \wedge B$ follows from $f = A \wedge B$ by $R0$, then $Graph(f')$ can be constructed from $Graph(f)$ by the contraction rule. If f' follows from a previous formula, f by $R1$, then $Graph(f')$ can be constructed from $Graph(f)$ by adding additional edges. Also, the associativity and commutativity laws for AND hold because $Graph((AB)C) = Graph(A(BC))$, and also $Graph(AB) = Graph(BA)$, up to renaming of vertices. The remaining cases, $R2$, $R3$, $R4$ and the commutativity laws for OR, are more complicated. The following definition and lemmas facilitate the proof of these cases.

Definition. Let G be a graph with underlying vertices $V \cup \{l_1, l_2, ..., l_k\} \cup \{v1, v2, v3\}$. Then we define the graph $G[l_i = 1]$ to be the graph G plus the additional edges $[l_i, v2]$, and $[l_i, v3]$. Any proper 3-coloring of $G[l_i = 1]$ must color l_i the same color as $v1$. Similarly, the graph $G[l_i = 2]$ equals G plus the edges $[l_i, v1]$, and $[l_i, v3]$; and $G[l_i = 3]$ is G plus the edges $[l_i, v1]$ and $[l_i, v2]$. More generally, the graph $G[l_1 = c_1, l_2 = c_2, ..., l_k = c_k]$ is equal to the graph $G'[l_k = c_k]$, where $G' = G[l_1 = c_1, ..., l_{k-1} = c_{k-1}]$.

Lemma 13 *Let $f = AC$ be a CNF formula, where $A = (l_1 \vee l_2 \vee ... \vee l_q)$, and let $G = Graph(f)$. Then $G[l_1 = 2, l_2 = 2, ..., l_q = 2]$ has a polynomial-sized $\mathcal{HC}$ construction.*

Proof. The lemma is obvious when $q = 1$. For $q \geq 2$, recall that the graph $G = Graph(f)$ contains a subgraph, G_C, for each clause C in G. In particular, the underlying subgraph corresponding to clause A, G_A contains a "rail" of triangle graphs, with underlying vertices $\{l_1, ..., l_q\} \cup \{v1, v2, v3\} \cup \{a_i, b_i, c_i \mid 1 \leq i \leq q-1\}$. (See Figure 1.)

Let $G' = G[l_1 = 2, l_2 = 2, ..., l_q = 2]$. First, we will generate the set of graphs: $\{G'[c_1 = 2, c_2 = 2, ..., c_{k-1} = 2, c_k = 1], G'[c_1 = 2, c_2 = 2, ..., c_{k-1} = 2, c_k = 3] \mid 1 \leq k \leq q-1\}$, and also the graph $G'[c_1 = 2, c_2 = 2, ..., c_{q-1} = 2]$. Because each of these graphs is non-3-colorable, we have $(\Rightarrow H)$, for all graphs H described above. Further, the implication is $V'-local$, where $|V'| \leq 8$. Therefore, by Theorem 3, there exists polynomial-sized constructions for each of these graphs.

Secondly, we will construct the desired graph, G' from the above graphs. We will show by downward induction on k $(1 \leq k \leq q-1)$, that we can construct the graph $G'[c_1 = 2, c_2 = 2, ..., c_k = 2]$ from the previous graphs. The base case holds because the graph $G'[c_1 = 2, ..., c_{q-1} = 2]$ is in our initial set of graphs. Now fix $k < q-1$; then we want to construct the graph $H = G'[c_1 = 2, ..., c_k = 2]$. By the inductive hypothesis, assume that we have constructed the graph $H[c_{k+1} = 2]$. Additionally, we have the graphs $H[c_{k+1} = 1]$, and $H[c_{k+1} = 3]$ in our initial set of graphs. Applying the edge elimination rule three times, we can construct H from $H[c_{k+1} = 1]$, $H[c_{k+1} = 2]$, and $H[c_{k+1} = 3]$. □

Lemma 14 *Let $f = AC$, $f' = A'C$, $A = (l_1 \vee ... \vee l_q)$, and $A' = (\pi(l_1) \vee ... \vee \pi(l_q))$, where π is a bijection from $\{l_1, ..., l_q\}$ to $\{l_1, ..., l_q\}$. Then for each k, $1 \leq k \leq q$, there exists a polynomial-sized construction of $G'[l_1 = 2, ..., l_{k-1} = 2, l_k = 1]$ from G, where $G = Graph(f)$, and $G' = Graph(f')$.*

Proof. Again, the lemma is obvious when $q = 1$. For $q \geq 2$, we first construct the graph $G[l_1 = 2, ..., l_{k-1} = 2, l_k = 1]$ from G by adding edges. Because there exists a proper 3-coloring of G_A consistent with $c(l_1) = c(v2), c(l_2) = c(v2), ..., c(l_k) = c(v1)$, we can apply the contraction rule to rename the vertices labelled a_i, b_i, c_i, $1 \leq i \leq q-1$, to either $v1$, $v2$ or $v3$ to obtain the graph $G''[l_1 = 2, ..., l_{k-1} = 2, l_k = 1]$, where $G'' = G \setminus e(G_A)$. Now by adding edges and vertices to $G''[l_1 = 2, ..., l_{k-1} = 2, l_k = 1]$, we can construct the desired graph $G'[l_1 = 2, ..., l_{k-1} = 2, l_k = 1]$. □

Lemma 15 *Let $f = AC$, where $A = (l_1 \vee l_2 \vee ... \vee l_q)$, and let $G = Graph(f)$. Then there exists a polynomial-sized $\mathcal{HC}$ construction of G from the set of graphs: $\mathcal{G} = \{G[l_1 = 1], G[l_1 = 2, l_2 = 1], ..., G[l_1 = 2, ..., l_{q-1} = 2, l_q = 1], G[l_1 = 2, ..., l_q = 2]\}$.*

Proof. Again, the lemma trivially holds when $q = 1$. We will prove by downward induction on k, $1 \leq k \leq q$, that we can construct the graph $G[l_1 = 2, ..., l_k = 2]$. The base case $(k = q)$ holds because $G[l_1 = 2, ..., l_q = 2]$ is an initial graph. Now fix $k < q$. By the inductive hypothesis, assume that we have constructed the graph $G[l_1 = 2, ..., l_k = 2, l_{k+1} = 2]$; also , $G[l_1 = 2, ..., l_k = 2, l_{k+1} = 1]$ is an initial graph. Therefore, by the edge elimination rule, the graph $G[l_1 = 2, ..., l_k = 2]$ can be constructed from the graphs $G[l_1 = 2, ..., l_k = 2, l_{k+1} = 2]$, and $G[l_1 = 2, ..., l_k = 2, l_{k+1} = 1]$. The number of intermediate graphs generated is $O(q)$; therefore the construction of G is polynomial-sized. □

The following four claims complete the proof of Lemma 12. Here we provide the proof of the first claim; the other claims are proven similarly.

Claim 16 (Commutativity) *Let* $f = AC$, $A = (l_1 \vee l_2 \vee ... \vee l_q)$, *and let* $f' = A'C$, $A' = (\pi(l_1) \vee \pi(l_2) \vee ... \vee \pi(l_q))$, *where* π *is a bijection from* $\{l_1, ..., l_q\}$ *to* $\{l_1, ..., l_q\}$. *Then there exists a polynomial-sized* $\mathcal{HC}$ *construction of* $G' = Graph(f')$ *from* $G = Graph(f)$.

Proof. We will show how to construct the graphs $\mathcal{G}' = \{G'[l_1 = 1], G'[l_1 = 2, l_2 = 1], ..., G'[l_1 = 2, ..., l_{q-1} = 2, l_q = 1], G'[l_1 = 2, ..., l_q = 2]\}$ from G. By Lemma 13, there exists a polynomial-sized construction of $G'[l_1 = 2, l_2 = 2, ..., l_q = 2]$. By Lemma 14, there exists a polynomial-sized construction of $G'[l_1 = 2, ..., l_{k-1} = 2, l_k = 1]$ for all $1 \leq k \leq q$. Therefore, by Lemma 15, there exists a polynomial-sized construction of G'. □

Claim 17 (Rule R2) *Let* $f = (A \vee B)C$, *and let* $f' = AC$. *Then there exists a polynomial-sized* $\mathcal{HC}$ *construction of* $G' = Graph(f')$ *from* $G = Graph(f)$.

Claim 18 (Rule R3) *Let* $f_1 = AC$, $f_2 = BC$, $f' = (A \vee B)C$. *Then there exists a polynomial-sized* $\mathcal{HC}$ *construction of* $G' = Graph(f')$ *from* $G_1 = Graph(f_1)$ *and* $G_2 = Graph(f_2)$.

Claim 19 (Rule R4) *Let* $f_1 = A\bar{l}$, $f_2 = Bl$, $f' = AB$. *Then there exists a polynomial-sized* $\mathcal{HC}$ *construction of* $G' = Graph(f')$ *from* $G_1 = Graph(f_1)$ *and* $G_2 = Graph(f_2)$.

5 The Main Theorem

In this section, we will prove that $\mathcal{EF}_2$ is polynomially bounded if and only if $\mathcal{HC}$ is polynomially bounded. We will first state and prove the forward direction (Theorem 20). Lemma 21 is used in the proof of Theorem 20.

Theorem 20 *If* $\mathcal{HC}$ *is polynomially-bounded, then so is* $\mathcal{EF}_2$.

Proof. Let f be an unsatisfiable CNF formula, and assume that $\mathcal{HC}$ is polynomially-bounded. Then $Graph(f)$ is a non-3-colorable graph, and therefore, $Graph(f)$ has a polynomial-size $\mathcal{HC}$ construction. Thus, there is also a short proof of $Form(Graph(f))$ in $Form(\mathcal{HC})$. By Lemma 11, this implies that there are polynomial-sized $\mathcal{EF}_2$ proofs of $Form(Graph(f))$. Because $\mathcal{EF}_2$ p-simulates $\mathcal{F}$ (by Lemma 5), it follows by Lemma 21 below that we can derive a polynomial-size refutation of f in $\mathcal{EF}_2$. □

Lemma 21 *Let* f *be a* CNF *formula. Then from* $Form(Graph(f))$, *we can derive a depth-5 refutation of* f *in* $\mathcal{F}$, *of size polynomial in the length of* f.

Corollary 22 *If* $\mathcal{HC}^-$ *is polynomially-bounded, then so is* $\mathcal{F}_5$.

Proof of Corollary. The proof of this corollary is almost identical to the proof of Theorem 20, with $\mathcal{EF}_2$ replaced by $\mathcal{F}_5$, $\mathcal{HC}$ replaced by $\mathcal{HC}^-$, and Lemma 11 replaced by Lemma 10. □

Recently, it has been shown in [B] that any depth-d proof in $\mathcal{F}$ of the propositional pigeonhole principle, PHP_n, must have size at least $2^{\Omega(n^{6^{-d}})}$. This lower bound, together with the above results gives us the following corollary.

Corollary 23 *There exists a family of non-3-colorable graphs,* $\{G_n \mid n \in N\}$ *such that for* n *sufficiently large, any* $\mathcal{HC}^-$ *construction of* G_n *has size at least* 2^{n^ϵ}, *for some* ϵ, $0 < \epsilon < 1$.

The converse to Theorem 20. is much more surprising, because $\mathcal{HC}$ is quite simple compared to the formulation of an extended Frege proof system.

Theorem 24 *If* $\mathcal{EF}_2$ *is polynomially bounded, then so is* $\mathcal{HC}$.

Proof. Let G be a non-3-colorable graph, and assume that $\mathcal{EF}_2$ is polynomially bounded. Then $Form(G)$ is an unsatisfiable formula, and therefore $Form(G)$ has a polynomial-size $\mathcal{EF}_2$ refutation. Thus there is also a short construction of $Graph(Form(G))$ in $Graph(\mathcal{EF}_2)$. By Lemma 12, this implies that there are polynomial-size constructions of $Graph(Form(G))$ in $\mathcal{HC}$. Now by the lemma below, there is a polynomial-size $\mathcal{HC}$ construction of G from $Graph(Form(G))$. □

Lemma 25 *If* G *is not 3-colorable, then there exists a polynomial-sized* $\mathcal{HC}$ *construction of* G *from the graph* $Graph(Form(G))$.

6 Graph-theoretical consequences

In this section, we explain a connection between our work relating the complexity of the Hajós calculus to the complexity of extended Frege systems, and results of Stephen Cook connecting such systems with feasibly constructive arithmetic. This connection supports the belief that proving superpolynomial lower bounds for

$\mathcal{HC}$ will be very difficult. More importantly, it should guide the search for hard examples for $\mathcal{HC}$.

Intuitively, a proof of a mathematical theorem is feasibly constructive if it involves only feasible predicates, and the logical reasoning in the proof involves only feasibly computable functions. In a seminal paper [C], Cook introduced a quantifier-free system of arithmetic, PV, and proposed to make the notion of "feasibly constructive proof" precise by identifying it with provability in PV. Cook also demonstrated a close connection between PV and $\mathcal{EF}_2$. If F is a formula of PV, then there is a family F_n of formulas in DNF, in which the nth formula F_n expresses the assertion: "The formula F is true for all numerical inputs of length n or less." The formula F_n is polynomial-time computable from n and F; secondly, F is valid if and only if all of the formulas F_n are tautologies. If in addition F is provable in PV, then even stronger consequences follow. The following basic simulation result was proved by Cook [C].

Theorem 26 *If F is provable in PV, then every F_n has a proof in $\mathcal{EF}_2$ of polynomial size.*

The above theorem has important consequences for proving lower bounds for $\mathcal{HC}$. Let us suppose that we have chosen a fixed method of encoding graphs as binary numbers. Then we can express the predicate "n encodes a graph" as a predicate $Graph(n)$ of PV. Furthermore, colorings can be encoded as numbers, and the predicate "c encodes a proper coloring of the graph coded by n" is polynomial-time computable, and hence can be expressed as a primitive predicate $Proper(c, n)$ of PV. We then have the following general result relating PV to $\mathcal{HC}$.

Theorem 27 *Let G be a primitive function symbol of PV for which the formulas $Graph(G(n))$, and $\neg Proper(c, G(n))$ are theorems of PV. Then there are polynomial-size $\mathcal{HC}$ constructions for the family of graphs G_n which are encoded by the numbers $G(n)$.*

This connection gives a very easy way to check whether or not a family of graphs is a potential candidate for proving a superpolynomial lower bound for $\mathcal{HC}$. As an example, consider the family of non-3-colorable graphs constructed by Toft which are discussed in [MW] as possible candidates for graphs which show the Hajós calculus not polynomially bounded. In fact, these graphs have short proofs by the Hajós construction, although this is not immediately obvious. However, the proof which shows all the graphs in Toft's family to be non-3-colorable is feasibly constructive, so we can infer immediately by the above result that they can be ruled out as possible hard examples. The same remark applies to other families of examples in which non-3-colorability is demonstrated by elementary constructive reasoning.

Acknowledgements.

We are grateful to Jason Brown and Stephen Cook for helpful discussions.

References

[Be] C. Berge, *Graphs.* North-Holland, 1985.

[B] P. Beame, R. Impagliazzo, J. Krajíček , T. Pitassi, P. Pudlák , W. Woods, "Exponential lower bounds for the pigeonhole principle," STOC 1992.

[Bu4] S. Buss, "Weak formal systems and connections to computational complexity," Lecture notes, 1988.

[C] S. Cook, "Feasibly constructive proofs and the propositional calculus," FOCS 1975, 83-97.

[CR] S. A. Cook, R. Reckhow, "The relative efficiency of propositional proof systems," *JSL*, 44, 1979.

[Do] M. Dowd, "Model-theoretic aspects of $P \neq NP$," manuscript, 1985.

[GJS] M.R. Garey, D.S. Johnson, L. Stockmeyer, "Some simplified NP-complete graph problems," *Theoretical Computer Science*, 1, 1976, 237-267.

[Haj] G. Hajós , "Über eine Konstruktion nicht n-färbbarer Graphen," *Wiss. Zeitschr. Martin Luther Univ. Halle-Wittenberg*, A 10, 1961.

[HRT] D. Hanson, G.C. Robinson, B. Toft, "Remarks on the graph color theorem of Hajós ," *Proceedings 17th Southeastern Conference on Combinatorics, Graph Theory and Computing*, Boca Raton, Congressus numerantium, 55 (1986).

[KP] J. Krajíček, P. Pudlák, "Propositional proof systems, the consistency of first order theories and the complexity of computations," *JSL*, 54 (1989).

[MW] A.J. Mansfield, D.J.A. Welsh, "Some coloring problems and their complexity," *Annals of Discrete Mathematics*, 13, 159-170.

[T] G.S. Tseitin, "On the complexity of derivation in the propositional calculus," *Studies in Constructive Mathematics and Mathematical Logic*, Part II, A.O. Slisenko, 1968.

A Decomposition Theorem and Bounds for Randomized Server Problems

Avrim Blum * Howard Karloff † Yuval Rabani ‡ Michael Saks §

Abstract

We prove a lower bound of $\Omega\left(\sqrt{\log k / \log\log k}\right)$ for the competitive ratio of randomized algorithms for the k-server problem against an oblivious adversary. The bound holds for arbitrary metric spaces (of at least $k+1$ points) and provides a new lower bound for the metrical task system problem as well. This improves the previous best lower bound of $\Omega(\log\log k)$ for arbitrary metric spaces [KRR], more closely approaching the conjectured lower bound of $\Omega(\log k)$. We also prove a lower bound of $\Omega\left(\frac{\log k}{\log\log k}\right)$ for the server problem on $k+1$ equally-spaced points on a line, which corresponds to some natural motion-planning problems.

Our results are deduced from a general decomposition theorem for a simpler version of both the k-server and the metrical task system problems, which we call the "pursuit-evasion game." We show that if a metric space $\mathcal{M}$ can be decomposed into two spaces $\mathcal{M}_L$ and $\mathcal{M}_R$, both very far away from each other, then the randomized competitive ratio for this game on $\mathcal{M}$ can be expressed nearly exactly in terms of the ratios on each of the two subspaces. This provides a natural way of analyzing the competitive ratio of a complex space made up of several regions in terms of the ratios of its components.

1 Introduction and Main Results

Online computation is a setting in which randomization can be shown to have a provable advantage over determinism. Many examples of this have appeared in the literature (see, e.g., [BLS, FKLMSY, MS, KMMO, Ira, Vis, BRS, FFKRRV]). One well-studied on-line problem is the k-server problem. Here an algorithm controls k servers, each of which is at some point in a metric space $\mathcal{M}$. At each time step the algorithm is given a *request*, which is a point in $\mathcal{M}$, and must serve it by moving a server to that point if none is there already. The algorithm is charged a cost equal to the total distance moved. The measure of success used is the *competitive ratio* [ST, KMRS]: roughly, this is the worst-case ratio of the cost charged to the algorithm on a request sequence, to the optimal offline cost of servicing that sequence (the optimal cost had it known the entire sequence in advance). For randomized algorithms, there are several natural notions for how requests are generated (see, e.g., [BBKTW], [RS]), and in this paper we consider requests generated by the weakest, *oblivious* adversary. This is an adversary that chooses the request sequence in advance while knowing the algorithm but not the random choices the algorithm makes. Intuitively, this can be interpreted by saying that after each successive request, the adversary "knows" only a probability distribution over states of the algorithm rather than the precise state.

It has been shown that for any metric space of at least $k+1$ points no deterministic online algorithm can achieve a competitive ratio better than k [MMS] (note that the problem is nontrivial only if there are at least $k+1$ points). The well-known k-server conjecture [MMS] says that for any metric space, there is a deterministic online algorithm that can achieve a competitive ratio of k. However, the best upper bounds known for general spaces, both for randomized and deterministic algorithms, are all exponential in k ([FRR],[Gro]).

The power of randomization in this setting was first demonstrated for the *uniform* metric space on $k+1$ points in which all pairs of distinct points are equidistant. For this space there is an $O(\log k)$-competitive algorithm, and indeed this is a lower bound. In fact, the infimum of the competitive ratios of all randomized algorithms, the *randomized competitive ratio*, is known to be exactly $1 + \frac{1}{2} + \frac{1}{3} + \cdots + \frac{1}{k} \sim \ln k$

*School of Computer Science, Carnegie Mellon University. E-mail: avrim@theory.cs.cmu.edu. Supported by an NSF Postdoctoral Fellowship.

†Department of Computer Science, University of Chicago. E-mail: howard@cs.uchicago.edu. This author was supported in part by NSF grant CCR 9107349 and by DIMACS.

‡Dept. of Computer Science, Tel-Aviv University. E-mail: rabani@math.tau.ac.il. Work partially done while visiting DIMACS.

§Dept. of Mathematics, Rutgers University and Dept. of Computer Science and Engineering, UCSD. E-mail: saks@math.rutgers.edu. This work was supported in part by NSF grant CCR89-11388 and AFOSR grants 89-0512 and 90-0008.

0-8186-2900-2/92 $3.00 © 1992 IEEE

[FKLMSY, MS, BLS]. Various people have speculated on the following conjecture:

Conjecture 1.1 *For any k and any metric space $\mathcal{M}$ on more than k points, the randomized competitive ratio of the k-server problem on $\mathcal{M}$ is $\Theta(\log k)$.*

Unlike the deterministic case where the lower bound is relatively easy and only the upper bound seems difficult, neither bound has been proved in the randomized case. For the lower bound, the previous best result is given by

Theorem 1.2 ([KRR]) *Let k be a positive integer and $\mathcal{M}$ be a metric space with at least $k+1$ points. Then the randomized competitive ratio of the k-server problem on $\mathcal{M}$ is $\Omega(\min\{\log k, \log\log|\mathcal{M}|\})$.*

If $\mathcal{M}$ is sufficiently large (exponential in k) then the lower bound in Conjecture 1.1 holds. For arbitrary spaces, however, in particular those whose size is polynomial in k, the lower bound obtained is $\Omega(\log\log k)$. One of the main results of this paper is to improve this $\Omega(\log\log k)$ bound to $\Omega\left(\sqrt{\frac{\log k}{\log\log k}}\right)$.

Theorem 1.3 *For any metric space $\mathcal{M}$ with at least $k+1$ points, the k-server problem on $\mathcal{M}$ has randomized competitive ratio $\Omega(\sqrt{\frac{\log k}{\log\log k}})$.*

The competitive ratio of the k-server problem for a space $\mathcal{M}$ is at least as large as the ratio on any subspace, as the adversary can restrict its requests to that subspace. Thus, to prove a lower bound on the competitive ratio of the k-server problem, it suffices to restrict attention to the case that the space has exactly $k+1$ points. One way to view this special case is to think of the algorithm as occupying a single point of the space (corresponding to the unique location where there is no server) and to think of the adversary as probing points of this space. When the adversary probes the point on which the algorithm stands, the algorithm must move to a different location. We call this the ***pursuit-evasion (PE) game*** and call the adversary the Pursuer and the algorithm the Evader. This paper is about the pursuit-evasion game. Using new analytic tools to study this game, we obtain lower bounds on the randomized competitive ratios of the k-server problem for *all* metric spaces, not just for those with exponentially many points. It should be noted that the pursuit-evasion game bears some resemblance to the cat-and-mouse game of [CDRS]. However, that game models the case of randomized algorithms against a more powerful adversary.

The pursuit-evasion game has applications to robotics. Imagine a robot walking down a long hallway of some width n (e.g., if $n = 3$ then the robot may walk either down the left side, the center, or the right side of the hallway). The hallway contains rectangular obstacles, and when the robot meets an obstacle, it must go left or right around it. Any algorithm at all must travel the length of the hallway, so we will not charge for that. Instead we look at the left/right motion of the robot and compare it to the least possible left/right motion by an algorithm that knew the placement of the obstacles in advance. If the hallway has width n, then this is the pursuit-evasion game for the metric space of n equally-spaced points on the real line, a metric space we call $\mathcal{L}(n)$. The above lower bound of $\Omega(\sqrt{\frac{\log(n-1)}{\log\log(n-1)}})$ applies, of course, but for this case we have a better lower bound.

Theorem 1.4 *The pursuit-evasion game on $\mathcal{L}(n)$ has randomized competitive ratio $\Omega(\frac{\log n}{\log\log n})$. Thus, if $n > k$ the k-server problem on $\mathcal{L}(n)$ has competitive ratio $\Omega(\frac{\log k}{\log\log k})$.*

This nearly matches the conjectured bounds. The best randomized algorithm known for the line $\mathcal{L}(n)$ (see [BRS]) has competitive ratio $2^{O(\sqrt{\log n \log\log n})}$.

For general spaces $\mathcal{M}$, the special case of Conjecture 1.1 with $k = |\mathcal{M}| - 1$ can be stated as:

Conjecture 1.5 *For any metric space $\mathcal{M}$ on n points, the randomized competitive ratio of the pursuit-evasion game on $\mathcal{M}$ is $\Theta(\log n)$.*

As noted, the lower bounds of Conjecture 1.5 and Conjecture 1.1 are equivalent. On the other hand, an upper bound for the pursuit-evasion game does not have immediate application to the upper bound conjecture for the general k-server problem. It is possible, however, that among all metric spaces with $k+1$ or more points, the largest randomized competitive ratios occur on those metric spaces with exactly $k+1$ points. In any case, we believe that a solution to the pursuit-evasion game would be a major step towards the solution of the more general problem and would also be interesting in its own right, particularly since there is currently no general upper bound for the randomized competitive ratio of the pursuit-evasion game that is better than the deterministic ratio of $|\mathcal{M}| - 1$.

Previously, Conjecture 1.5 was known only for the case of uniform (or nearly uniform) spaces mentioned earlier. Here, we establish Conjecture 1.5 for highly "nonuniform" spaces. If $C > 1$, a metric space is *C-unbalanced* if for any three distinct points, the ratio of the largest distance to the smallest nonzero distance is at least C. For example, the metric space consisting of 4 points in a rectangle with side lengths 1 and C is C-unbalanced.

Theorem 1.6 *There is a polynomial $p(n)$ such that for all n, the pursuit-evasion problem on any $p(n)$-unbalanced metric space with n points has randomized competitive ratio between* $\ln n$ *and* $3\ln n$.

The proof will appear in the full version of the paper.

Finally, it is worth mentioning that bounds on the competitive ratio of the pursuit-evasion game carry over to the *task system* model of [BLS]. In particular, Theorems 1.3, 1.4 and 1.6 hold if we replace "the pursuit-evasion game on $\mathcal{M}$" by "the task system on $\mathcal{M}$."

1.1 Overview of the method

Theorems 1.3, 1.4 and 1.6 are proved as a consequence of a *decomposition theorem* for the competitive ratio of the pursuit-evasion game. (Henceforth, when we say "competitive ratio" we will mean the "randomized competitive ratio.") In words this theorem says that if $\mathcal{M}$ is a metric space that can be partitioned into two parts $\mathcal{M}_L$ and $\mathcal{M}_R$ such that the distance between the two sets is sufficiently large relative to the maximum distance within the sets, then the competitive ratio of the pursuit-evasion game on $\mathcal{M}$ can be expressed almost exactly in terms of the competitive ratios of the games on $\mathcal{M}_L$ and $\mathcal{M}_R$. That one can prove almost-tight upper *and* lower bounds on the competitive ratio is perhaps surprising. The precise statement is a bit long and is given as Theorem 1.8. A simpler version, useful when $\mathcal{M}_L$ and $\mathcal{M}_R$ have nearly the same competitive ratio, can be stated more easily, as follows. Here, let $\delta(\mathcal{M})$ be the diameter of the finite space $\mathcal{M}$ and let $\lambda(\mathcal{M})$ be its competitive ratio. (We use the convention that the competitive ratio of a one point space is 0.)

Theorem 1.7 *For any $\epsilon > 0$ there exists an increasing polynomial p such that if $(\mathcal{M}_L, \mathcal{M}_R)$ is a partition of metric space $\mathcal{M}$ with $\lambda(\mathcal{M}_R), \lambda(\mathcal{M}_L) \in [\lambda_{\min}, \lambda_{\max}]$ and $\frac{\delta(\mathcal{M})}{\max\{\delta(\mathcal{M}_L),\delta(\mathcal{M}_R)\}} \geq p(\lambda_{\max})$, then*

1. $\lambda(\mathcal{M}) \leq \lambda_{\max} + 1 + \epsilon$.
2. $\lambda(\mathcal{M}) \geq \lambda_{\min} + 1 - \epsilon$.

That is, if $\mathcal{M}_R$ and $\mathcal{M}_L$ have nearly the same competitive ratio λ, then the competitive ratio of $\mathcal{M}$ is very close to $1 + \lambda$. The decomposition theorem provides a tool for estimating the competitive ratio of the pursuit-evasion game on a space by partitioning it into smaller spaces and applying induction. For example, the simpler version provided above can be used to derive Theorem 1.4 as follows (this uses a known fact that if $\mathcal{N}$ is a subspace of $\mathcal{M}$, then $\lambda(\mathcal{N}) \leq \lambda(\mathcal{M})$.) Let $\epsilon = 1/2$ and let $p()$ be the increasing polynomial whose existence is given by Theorem 1.7. Let t be the greatest integer such that $\lceil p(\log n)\rceil^t \leq n$ and let $n' = \lceil p(\log n)\rceil^t$. Note that $t = \Omega(\frac{\log n}{\log\log n})$. Let $j = n'/\lceil p(\log n)\rceil = \lceil p(\log n)\rceil^{t-1}$ and let $\mathcal{M}_L$ and $\mathcal{M}_R$ be the leftmost j points and rightmost j points of $\mathcal{M} = \mathcal{L}(n')$ respectively. By choice of j, either $\lambda(\mathcal{M}_L) > \log n$ and we are done, or else the condition on δ of Theorem 1.7 is satisfied. So, $\lambda(\mathcal{L}(n)) \geq \lambda(\mathcal{L}(n')) \geq \lambda(\mathcal{M}_L \cup \mathcal{M}_R) \geq \lambda(\mathcal{M}_L) + 1/2$. We can continue on $\mathcal{M}_L$ letting $j' = j/\lceil p(\log n)\rceil$ and so forth until after t steps we have run out of points. The competitive ratio of $\mathcal{L}(n)$ is thus at least $t/2$, which is $\Omega(\frac{\log n}{\log\log n})$.

The full decomposition theorem provides sharp bounds on $\lambda(\mathcal{M})$ even if $\mathcal{M}_L$ and $\mathcal{M}_R$ have different competitive ratios. Let $Z(x)$ be the function on $x \geq 0$ which is equal to 1 if $x = 0$, and equal to $x/(e^x - 1)$ if $x > 0$. The theorem says that the competitive ratio of $\mathcal{M}$ is well approximated by $\max\{\lambda(\mathcal{M}_L), \lambda(\mathcal{M}_R)\} + Z(|\lambda(\mathcal{M}_L) - \lambda(\mathcal{M}_R)|)$. Here is the theorem in all gory detail.

Theorem 1.8 *Let $\mathcal{M}$ be a metric space with $|\mathcal{M}| \geq 3$ and let $(\mathcal{M}_R, \mathcal{M}_L)$ be a partition. Let $\alpha_R, \alpha_L \geq 0$ with $\alpha_{\max}$ their maximum and α_{diff} their absolute difference. Let $\delta = \delta(\mathcal{M})$ and $\delta_{\max} = \max\{\delta(\mathcal{M}_L), \delta(\mathcal{M}_R)\}$. Suppose that $\alpha_{\max} \geq 1$ and $\frac{\delta}{\delta_{\max}} \geq \max\{324\alpha_{\max}, \alpha^3_{\max}\}$. Then*

1. *if $\alpha_L \geq \lambda(\mathcal{M}_L)$ and $\alpha_R \geq \lambda(\mathcal{M}_R)$, then $\lambda \leq \alpha_{\max} + Z(\alpha_{\text{diff}})(1+\zeta)$, and*
2. *if $\alpha_L \leq \lambda(\mathcal{M}_L)$ and $\alpha_R \leq \lambda(\mathcal{M}_R)$, then $\lambda \geq \alpha_{\max} + Z(\alpha_{\text{diff}})(1-\zeta)$,*

where $\zeta = 23e^{\alpha_{\text{diff}}}\sqrt{\frac{\delta_{\max}}{\delta}\alpha^3_{\max}}$.

For the proof of Theorem 1.3, the cases of the decomposition theorem needed are the case above where $\mathcal{M}_L$ and $\mathcal{M}_R$ have nearly the same competitive ratio, and the "highly unbalanced" case where $\mathcal{M}_L$ is large and $\mathcal{M}_R$ is a single point. [KRR] proved their lower bound using a Ramsey-type theorem for metric spaces: every metric space has a fairly large subspace that is highly structured, either roughly uniform or highly "superincreasing." We prove a similar type of theorem here: any metric space of n points must contain at least one of the following *three* objects: (A) a roughly uniform space of around $2^{\sqrt{\log n/\log\log n}}$ points, (B) two far-away spaces with small diameter and each having around $n/2^{\sqrt{\log n \log\log n}}$ points, or (C) one point very far from a subspace containing nearly all the rest (around $n - n/2^{\sqrt{\log n/\log\log n}}$ points).

The proof of Theorem 1.8 consists of two parts. We introduce and completely analyze a new game, called the *Walker-Jumper* game, which abstracts the essential elements of the analysis of a decomposed problem. Then we formally demonstrate that the competitive ratio of a decomposed problem can be tightly bounded by the competitive ratio of an associated Walker-Jumper game. The full proof is quite long and only part of it is given here.

In Section 3, we present an informal discussion of the proof to motivate the connection with the Walker-Jumper game. In Section 4 we define the Walker-Jumper game and state a theorem which gives its exact competitive ratio, and describe optimal strategies for each of the two players. In section 5, we give a precise statement of the lemma connecting the Walker-Jumper game to the decomposition theorem. The application of the decomposition theorem to prove Theorems 1.3 is described in Section 6.

2 Notation and Definitions

A metric space $\mathcal{M}$ consists of a set and a symmetric nonnegative distance function defined on all pairs of points, which is zero only on pairs of equal points and which satisfies the triangle inequality. We will abuse notation and use $\mathcal{M}$ to denote both the metric space and the underlying set. The underlying set is assumed to be finite unless otherwise noted. The associated metric is denoted by $d = d_{\mathcal{M}}$. The diameter of the space $\delta = \delta(\mathcal{M})$ is the maximum distance between any pair of points.

A sequence of points in a metric space is referred to as a *path* in the space. For a path $\mathbf{x}$ we define $|\mathbf{x}|$ to be the number of points in $\mathbf{x}$, and *length*($\mathbf{x}$) to be the sum of the distances between successive pairs of points in $\mathbf{x}$.

In the pursuit-evasion game there are two players, the Pursuer and the Evader, who play on some (finite) metric space $\mathcal{M}$. At the beginning of each move the Evader is at some point of the space (there is no requirement that the starting point be any particular fixed location). The Pursuer then probes some point of $\mathcal{M}$. If he picks the point the Evader occupies then the Evader must move to some other point, otherwise the Evader may stay where he is. The cost to the Evader in responding to a sequence of probes is the total distance he travels. We denote the pursuit-evasion game on $\mathcal{M}$ by PE($\mathcal{M}$).

The Pursuer is *oblivious* to the position of the Evader. Thus, a deterministic strategy for the Pursuer is just a finite probe sequence ρ from the metric space. A randomized strategy is a probability distribution $\tilde{\rho}$ over such sequences. A sequence σ is a *response path* for ρ if $|\sigma| = |\rho|$ and $\sigma_i \neq \rho_i$ for all i. We will think of a deterministic strategy for the Evader as a function A that maps probe sequences ρ to response paths $A(\rho)$ such that for any ρ and any point a, $A(\rho a)$ extends $A(\rho)$. A is called a *response algorithm*. A randomized strategy for the Evader is a distribution $\tilde{A}$ over response algorithms.

The cost function $C_A(\rho)$ is the total length of the path $A(\rho)$, and $C_{\tilde{A}}(\tilde{\rho})$ is the expectation of $C_A(\rho)$ with respect to the product distribution of $\tilde{A}$ and $\tilde{\rho}$. We define $C_{\mathrm{OPT}}(\rho)$ to be the minimum of $C_A(\rho)$ over all A, and $C_{\mathrm{OPT}}(\tilde{\rho})$ to be the expectation of $C_{\mathrm{OPT}}(\rho)$ with respect to the distribution $\tilde{\rho}$. We say that an algorithm $\tilde{A}$ is *c-competitive* if there exists a constant K such that for all ρ, $C_{\tilde{A}}(\rho) \leq c \cdot C_{\mathrm{OPT}}(\rho) + K$. The *competitive ratio* of a space $\mathcal{M}$ is the infimum over all c such that there exists a c-competitive algorithm. We denote the competitive ratio of $PE(\mathcal{M})$ by $\lambda(\mathcal{M})$. We adopt the convention that the competitive ratio of a 1-point space is 0.

Definition 2.1 *For $s > 0$, an* s-block *of $\mathcal{M}$ is a probe sequence with the property that its optimal cost is between $s - \delta$ and s, where δ denotes $\delta(\mathcal{M})$. Note that any probe sequence ρ can be parsed uniquely into subsequences $\rho_1\rho_2 \cdots \rho_k$ where each successive ρ_i is chosen to be of minimal length subject to having optimal cost at least $s - \delta$, and the last has cost no more than $s - \delta$. All blocks except possibly the last are s-blocks. We refer to this as the* s-block partition *of ρ.*

3 Overview of the Proof of the Decomposition Theorem

The decomposition theorem concerns a space $\mathcal{M}$ partitioned into two subspaces, the *left space* $\mathcal{M}_L$ and the *right space* $\mathcal{M}_R$. $\mathcal{M}$ has the property that the diameter δ of $\mathcal{M}$ is much larger than the diameters δ_L and δ_R of $\mathcal{M}_L$ and $\mathcal{M}_R$ respectively. In the present discussion, we assume that each space consists of at least two points; the degenerate case that one of the spaces consists of a single point will require some special treatment, which we omit from this abstract.

We want to express the competitive ratio λ of the big space in terms of the competitive ratios λ_L and λ_R of the two subspaces. The key idea is to abstract the behaviors of the Pursuer and the Evader so as to focus on their movements *between* the spaces, treating their movements within each space as a "black box." This idea leads to the formulation of a new game, called the Walker-Jumper game. In this section we provide an informal discussion that leads naturally to the definition of the Walker-Jumper game. Throughout the discussion we make various plausible but unjustified assumptions and approximations, which are cleaned up in the proof.

At each step, the Evader is either in $\mathcal{M}_L$ or in $\mathcal{M}_R$. While the Pursuer probes the opposite space, the Evader need do nothing. While the Pursuer probes the subspace occupied by the Evader, it seems apparent that either the Evader should follow his optimal randomized response algorithm for that space (achieving, over that interval of moves, a competitive ratio equal to that for that space) or he should move to the other space. By randomizing his choice of when to switch between spaces, he can hope to "fool" the Pursuer as to his location.

We view the probe sequence of the Pursuer as a sequence of left phases and right phases, where a left or right phase consists of probes only into the corresponding space. When the Evader uses a randomized strategy, the Pursuer only has a probability distribution on the location of the Evader. To maximize the competitive ratio, the Pursuer wants to construct a probe sequence that (i) has a good chance of catching the Evader often, and (ii) has a low offline cost. For the first goal, it would seem that he should always probe on the side with higher probability of containing the Evader, while for the second goal, it would seem that he would do well *not* to switch between spaces too often (this will make it easier for an offline algorithm to "hide" safely in one space for long intervals of moves) and thus make each phase long.

Recall that for $s > 0$, an s-block for a metric space is a probe sequence whose optimal response cost is approximately s. For some large integer D (which we will not specify at this point) we define $s = \delta/D$ and define *left blocks* and *right blocks* to be probe sequences which are s-blocks with respect to spaces $\mathcal{M}_L$ and $\mathcal{M}_R$ respectively. Note that an s-block for $\mathcal{M}_L$ or $\mathcal{M}_R$ is not an s-block with respect to the entire space. In fact, the optimal cost is 0 since an offline Evader may just stay at one location on the opposite space. Since δ is much larger than δ_L and δ_R, we may choose s so that $\lambda_L\delta_L$ and $\lambda_R\delta_R$ are much less than s, which in turn is much less than δ.

For a given probe sequence of $\mathcal{M}$, let us parse each left phase according to its s-block partition with respect to $\mathcal{M}_L$ and parse each right phase similarly. It is reasonable to expect that if s is small relative to the typical cost of a phase then we may ignore the "remainder" block of the phase and simply assume that each left (right) phase is a concatenation of left (right) blocks.

With this assumption, we view the entire probe sequence as a sequence of left and right blocks. If the Pursuer chooses to add a right block, the Pursuer can force the Evader to pay roughly $s\lambda_R$ if the Evader is on the right since λ_R is the competitive ratio of $\mathcal{M}_R$. (For this to work, we needed to bound from both above and below the additive constant in the definition of the competitive ratio. This is accomplished by Lemmas 5.2 and 5.3, and motivates the choice of s to be much larger than $\lambda_R\delta_R$ and $\lambda_L\delta_L$.) Similarly, when the Pursuer picks a left block, the Pursuer can force an Evader who stays on the left to pay roughly $s\lambda_L$.

To summarize, when the Pursuer adds a block, if the Evader is on the opposite side he pays nothing. If the Evader is on the same side, he either moves to the other side immediately, paying roughly δ, or he stays on the original side and incurs an expected cost of $s\lambda_R$ or $s\lambda_L$ depending on the side. We assume that δ is much larger than both $s\lambda_R$ and $s\lambda_L$, so that it would not pay for him to move to the opposite side at the beginning and back at the end the block. Thus, we have a good approximation to the cost of each block to the Evader, which depends on *only* (i) the side from which each block is chosen by the Pursuer and (ii) the side on which the Evader finishes responding to each block.

We'd like to get a similar estimate for the offline cost. For each probe sequence ρ, define $C_L(\rho)$ to be the minimum cost of a response sequence σ whose last point is on the left, and define $C_R(\rho)$ in the analogous way. We refer to these respectively as the left-optimal and right-optimal cost of ρ. The optimal cost of ρ is just the minimum of these. Since $C_L(\rho)$ and $C_R(\rho)$ differ by at most a constant (the diameter of $\mathcal{M}$), we may take $C_R(\rho)$ as a good estimate of $C_{\mathrm{OPT}}(\rho)$. We want to understand how C_L and C_R change when the Pursuer adds a left block or a right block. Let ρ be a sequence and consider adding a right block β to ρ. It is easy to see that $C_L(\rho\beta) = C_L(\rho)$, since the offline Evader who ends the previous block on the left can just stay where he is. On the other hand, $C_R(\rho\beta) \approx \min\{C_L(\rho)+\delta, C_R(\rho)+s\}$, since the Evader may either finish the previous block on the left and pay δ to move right at the end of β or finish the previous block on the right and respond to β on the right, paying about s. (This again uses that $s \gg \delta_L, \delta_R$ so that the optimal cost of an s-block is actually near s.)

Let us summarize this discussion by considering the evolution of the parameter $w = (C_R - C_L)/s$. Note that w is always between $-D$ and D (remember, $\delta = Ds$). Each right block increases w by (roughly) 1 subject to $w \leq D$, and similarly, each left block decreases w by 1, subject to $w \geq -D$. We can thus visualize the evolution of w as a walk on the integer points between $-D$ and D, with a right step corresponding to an increase in C_R by s and a left step corresponding to an increase in C_L by s.

Notice that if the Pursuer adds a right block that causes w to reach D, then the Pursuer may add an arbitrary number of right blocks without affecting C_L, C_R or w. Let us assume that he does this, i.e., a right step from $D-1$ to D corresponds to a huge number of right blocks. The effect of this on the Evader is clear: on such a step he must move to the left space (if he is not there already) or incur a huge cost. (Note that the Evader can compute C_R, C_L and w online and thus recognize this situation.) Similarly we may assume that a left step from $-D+1$ to $-D$ corresponds to a huge number of left blocks and the Evader must move to the right space.

We now can make the following estimates of the offline cost and the Evader's cost. The offline cost is about s times the number of steps of w to the right. The Evader's cost is 0 on any step taken by w in the direction opposite the space the Evader occupies. On a step taken in the direction of the Evader's space, the Evader's cost is $\delta = sD$ if he chooses to move to the other space and is $s\lambda_R$ or $s\lambda_L$ (depending on his space) if he doesn't move. Whenever a right (left) step is taken by w that reaches D ($-D$), the Evader must move to the left (right) space.

This idealization suggests that we can model our problem by a game between two players, the *Walker* who walks on the line (and corresponds to the Pursuer) and the *Jumper* who jumps between the left and right side (and corresponds to the Evader). In the next section we define this game precisely and analyze it.

4 Walker-Jumper games

The Walker-Jumper game $WJ[D, \alpha_R, \alpha_L]$ has parameters D (a positive integer) and nonnegative real numbers α_R and α_L. The players are referred to as the Walker (Wendy) and the Jumper (Jack). The game "board" is the set $I_D = \{-D, -D+1, \ldots, D-1, D\}$. At each integer time $t \geq 0$, Wendy is at some position $w_t \in I_D$ and Jack is at some position $j_t \in \{-D, D\}$. The initial position for Wendy is $w_0 = 0$ and Jack can choose either $j_0 = -D$ or $j_0 = D$.

At each time t, a legal move for Wendy consists of one step either to the left ($w_t = w_{t-1} - 1$) or to the right ($w_t = w_{t-1} + 1$). A deterministic strategy for Wendy is a sequence $\mathbf{w} = (w_0, w_1, \ldots)$ of such w_t's, with $w_0 = 0$.

Jack's answer to request w_t is either to stay where he is ($j_t = j_{t-1}$) or to *jump* to his other allowed position ($j_t = -j_{t-1}$), subject only to the constraint that if Wendy arrives at Jack's location ($w_t = j_{t-1}$), then Jack *must* jump ($j_t = -w_t$). Formally, a deterministic algorithm for Jack is a function A that maps each finite request sequence $\mathbf{w} = (0, w_1, \ldots, w_s)$ to a sequence $(j_0, j_1, j_2, \ldots, j_s)$ in $\{-D, D\}^{s+1}$ satisfying this constraint.

We define the sequence Δw by $(\Delta w)_i = w_i - w_{i-1}$ and refer to Δw_i as the *direction* of move i. If j_t has the same sign as $(\Delta w)_t$, i.e., Wendy's move at time t brought her closer to the location that Jack occupies after his move, then we say that Wendy *hit* Jack. It is a *left hit* or a *right hit* depending on the direction of Wendy's move.

The cost function for algorithm A on request sequence $\mathbf{w}$, $C_A(\mathbf{w})$ (representing the cost to Jack), is given as follows.

1. Each jump by Jack costs him D.

2. Each right hit by Wendy costs Jack α_R.

3. Each left hit by Wendy costs Jack α_L.

As usual, we also consider randomized strategies, i.e., probability distributions over deterministic strategies, for both players. If $\tilde{A}$ and $\tilde{\mathbf{w}}$ are randomized strategies then $C_{\tilde{A}}(\tilde{\mathbf{w}})$ is defined to be the expectation of $C_A(\mathbf{w})$ with respect to the distributions. A useful intuition in thinking about the randomized version of the game is to imagine that Jack always knows Wendy's position while Wendy knows only a probability distribution on Jack's position, which is determined by Jack's algorithm.

We are interested in the (randomized) competitive ratio $\lambda = \lambda(WJ[D, \alpha_R, \alpha_L])$ of this game with respect to a nonstandard yardstick, $C_{\mathrm{BASE}}(\mathbf{w})$, the total number of Wendy's steps to the right. That is, we say an algorithm A is c-competitive if there exists a constant K such that for all $\mathbf{w}$, $C_A(\mathbf{w}) \leq c \cdot C_{\mathrm{BASE}}(\mathbf{w}) + K$, and define λ to be the infimum over all c such that there exists a c-competitive algorithm. Note that $C_{\mathrm{BASE}}(\mathbf{w})$ is always between $(|\mathbf{w}| - D)/2$ and $(|\mathbf{w}| + D)/2$. Hence we can think of $C_{\mathrm{BASE}}(\mathbf{w})$ as roughly $|\mathbf{w}|/2$.

Let $\alpha_{\max} = \max\{\alpha_R, \alpha_L\}$. We will only be concerned with the game for $D \geq \alpha_{\max}$. To develop some intuition for this game, let us first show that $\alpha_{\max} \leq \lambda \leq \alpha_L + \alpha_R + 1$.

To see the lower bound consider the following pure strategy for Wendy (without loss of generality, assume that $\alpha_L \geq \alpha_R$). Wendy moves right D times to position D and then alternately moves between $D-1$ and D. Each time Wendy moves from D to $D-1$, Jack must start at $-D$ and pays $\alpha_{\max}$ (if he doesn't move) or D (if he does). After t steps by Wendy, Jack's cost is at least $\alpha_{\max}\frac{t-D}{2}$, which is at least $\alpha_{\max} C_{\mathrm{BASE}}(\mathbf{w}) - \alpha_{\max} D$.

To see the upper bound of $\alpha_L + \alpha_R + 1$, consider the following pure strategy for Jack: never jump unless a jump is required (because Wendy arrives at the same location). It is easy to see that if Wendy takes t steps, then Jack jumps at most $1 + t/(2D)$ times. Also, on any t-step sequence for Wendy, she takes at most $t/2 + D$ steps in each direction. So, Jack's cost can be bounded above by $(\alpha_R + \alpha_L)(t/2 + D) + t/2 + D$.

Since $C_{\mathbf{BASE}}$ is within an additive constant of $t/2$, this implies the upper bound.

As we shall see, the trivial lower bound above is much closer to the truth than the trivial upper bound. The main result of this section is an *exact* expression for the competitive ratio $\lambda(WJ[D, \alpha_R, \alpha_L])$. Define $\beta_R = 1 - \alpha_R/(2D)$ and $\beta_L = 1 - \alpha_L/(2D)$.

Theorem 4.1 *For nonnegative real numbers α_R and α_L and positive integer $D \geq max\{\alpha_L, \alpha_R\}$, the competitive ratio λ of the game $WJ(D, \alpha_R, \alpha_L)$ is given by*

$$\lambda = \begin{cases} \alpha_R + \beta_R & \text{if } \alpha_R = \alpha_L, \\ \frac{\alpha_R \beta_L^{2D} - \alpha_L \beta_R^{2D}}{\beta_L^{2D} - \beta_R^{2D}} & \text{if } \alpha_R \neq \alpha_L. \end{cases}$$

By an elementary but tedious sequence of estimates (which is omitted from this abstract) and the definition of the function $Z(x)$ from the introduction, we obtain the following corollary.

Corollary 4.2 *For nonnegative real numbers α_R and α_L, define $\alpha_{\max} = max\{\alpha_R, \alpha_L\}$ and $\alpha_{\text{diff}} = |\alpha_R - \alpha_L|$. Suppose that $\alpha_{\max} \geq 1$. Let $D \geq \alpha_{\max}^2$ be a positive integer. Then the competitive ratio λ of $WJ(D, \alpha_R, \alpha_L)$ satisfies*

$$\alpha_{\max} + Z(\alpha_{\text{diff}})(1 - \epsilon) \leq \lambda \leq \alpha_{\max} + Z(\alpha_{\text{diff}})(1 + \epsilon)$$

where $\epsilon = \frac{4\alpha_{\max}^2}{D}$.

4.1 The lower bound: a strategy for the Walker

Below is a simple randomized strategy for Wendy. The idea of the strategy is to force the expected cost to Jack to be essentially independent of what Jack does.

Walker Strategy

1. The strategy is defined in terms of two parameters σ_R and σ_L, which are real numbers between 0 and 1/2. If $w_t = D$ or $w_t = -D$ then w_{t+1} is forced. Otherwise $|w_t| < D$ and Wendy moves as follows. If move t was to the right ($w_t = w_{t-1} + 1$) then Wendy goes left at step $t+1$ with probability σ_L and to the right with probability $1 - \sigma_L$. Similarly if move t was to the left ($w_t = w_{t-1} - 1$) then Wendy goes right at step $t+1$ with probability σ_R and to the left with probability $1 - \sigma_R$.

2. The parameters σ_R and σ_L are defined by $\sigma_R = \alpha_L/(2D) = 1 - \beta_L$ and $\sigma_L = \alpha_R/(2D) = 1 - \beta_R$.

To analyze this strategy, we first state a criterion for lower bounding the competitive ratio, which follows easily from the definition. Let $\mathbf{w^t}$ denote the first t terms of $\mathbf{w}$.

Proposition 4.3 *Let $\tilde{\mathbf{w}}$ be a distribution over infinite sequences for Wendy. Suppose that b is a positive real such that for any algorithm A for Jack and any positive integer t,*

$$C_A(\tilde{\mathbf{w}}^{\mathbf{t}}) \geq t(b - g(t)),$$

where $g(t)$ tends to 0 as t tends to ∞. Then $\lambda \geq 2b$.

It is easy to show that we need consider only lazy Jumper algorithms (Jack never jumps when Wendy moves away from him), so fix a lazy deterministic strategy A for Jack and define $C(\mathbf{w}) = C_A(\mathbf{w})$. We are interested in bounding from below the expectation of $C(\mathbf{w})$ with respect to the above distribution for Wendy. It will be convenient to introduce a modified cost function, $C^*(\mathbf{w}) = C(\mathbf{w}) + \psi(\mathbf{w})$, where the correction ψ is a "potential function" that depends only on the final step: if the last step by Wendy scored a hit on Jack (precisely, $j_s = D \cdot (w_s - w_{s-1})$) then $\psi(\mathbf{w}) = D - \alpha_R$ if the hit was to the right and $D - \alpha_L$ if the hit was to the left. Otherwise $\psi(\mathbf{w}) = 0$. Thus, $C(\mathbf{w}) \geq C^*(\mathbf{w}) - D$.

The purpose of introducing this modified cost is that with respect to this cost measure, the cost to Jack of any given step does not depend on what Jack does at that step. More precisely, define Jack's *modified cost at step t* to be $(\Delta C^*)_t(\mathbf{w}) = C^*(\mathbf{w^t}) - C^*(\mathbf{w^{t-1}})$. Since we are assuming that Jack is following a lazy strategy, Jack has an option to move only if $j_{t-1} = D \cdot (\Delta w)_t$. (Otherwise, $(\Delta C^*)_t(\mathbf{w}) = 0$.) In this case, if he does not jump then his true cost increases by $\alpha_{(\Delta w)_t}$ while his modified cost increases by $\alpha_{(\Delta w)_t} + \psi(\mathbf{w^t}) - \psi(\mathbf{w^{t-1}}) = D - \psi(\mathbf{w^{t-1}})$. If he jumps at time t, then his true cost goes up by D but his modified cost goes up by $D + \psi(\mathbf{w^t}) - \psi(\mathbf{w^{t-1}}) = D - \psi(\mathbf{w^{t-1}})$, which is the same as if he did not jump. The reader can now check the following:

Lemma 4.4 *For any fixed lazy strategy A for Jack, the change in the modified cost at time t satisfies* $(\Delta C^*)_t(\mathbf{w}) =$

$$\begin{cases} \alpha_R \text{ if } ((\Delta w)_t, (\Delta w)_{t-1}, j_{t-1}) & = & (+1, +1, +D) \\ 0 & = & (+1, +1, -D) \\ \alpha_R - D & = & (-1, +1, +D) \\ D & = & (-1, +1, -D) \\ \alpha_L & = & (-1, -1, -D) \\ 0 & = & (-1, -1, +D) \\ \alpha_L - D & = & (+1, -1, -D) \\ D & = & (+1, -1, +D). \end{cases}$$

Recall that if $|w_{t-1}| = D$ then, by the rules of the game, it must be the case that $j_{t-1} = -w_{t-1}$, $(\Delta w)_{t-1} = w_{t-1}/D$, and $(\Delta w)_t = j_{t-1}/D$. In this case, $(\Delta C^*)_t(\mathbf{w}) = D$. If $|w_{t-1}| < D$ then when

Wendy moves at time t, her move can depend on $(\Delta w)_{t-1}$, the direction of her last move, but not on j_{t-1}, which she does not know. So we try a strategy for Wendy in which her probability of moving in each direction depends on the direction of her last move. This motivates condition 1 in the definition of the strategy in section 4.1. So consider a strategy satisfying this condition, with the σ_R and σ_L of the walker strategy of section 4.1 as yet unspecified. We now can write down an expression in terms of w_{t-1} and j_{t-1}, for the expectation (with respect to this randomized strategy) of the change of the modified cost at time t, for the case $|w_{t-1}| < D$. It is $(\Delta C^*)_t(\tilde{\mathbf{w}}) =$

$$\begin{cases} \alpha_R - D\sigma_L & \text{if } ((\Delta w)_{t-1}, j_{t-1}) = (+1, +D) \\ D\sigma_L & \qquad\qquad\qquad\quad = (+1, -D) \\ \alpha_L - D\sigma_R & \qquad\qquad\qquad\quad = (-1, -D) \\ D\sigma_R & \qquad\qquad\qquad\quad = (-1, +D). \end{cases}$$

By selecting σ_L and σ_R so that this expectation is independent of j_{t-1} (i.e., $\alpha_R - D\sigma_L = D\sigma_L$ and $\alpha_L - D\sigma_r = D\sigma_r$), we obtain condition 2 of the strategy.

Having motivated Wendy's strategy, we now continue with its analysis. Using $\sigma_L = \alpha_R/(2D)$ and $\sigma_R = \alpha_L/(2D)$, the change in the expected modified cost at time t can now be written as $(\Delta C^*)_t(\tilde{\mathbf{w}}) =$

$$\begin{cases} D & \text{if } |w_{t-1}| = D \\ \alpha_R/2 & \text{if } |w_{t-1}| < D \text{ and } (\Delta w)_{t-1} = +1 \\ \alpha_L/2 & \text{if } |w_{t-1}| < D \text{ and } (\Delta w)_{t-1} = -1\,. \end{cases}$$

To apply Proposition 4.3, we need to lower-bound Jack's expected cost against the sequence generated by the first j steps of Wendy's strategy. Wendy's strategy can be described by a Markov chain with state space $\{L_i : -D \le i < D\} \bigcup \{R_i : -D < i \le D\}$ where Wendy is in state L_i at time t if $w_t = i$ and $(\Delta_w)_t = -1$ (she is at point i and her last move was to the left) and Wendy is in state R_i at time t if $w_t = i$ and $(\Delta_w)_t = +1$ (she is at point i and her last move was to the right). For state U, let $N_t(U)$ denote the expected number of visits to state U during the first t steps by Wendy. Also, let $p(U)$ denote the steady state probability for state U. For large t, $N_t(U) = p(U)t(1 + o(1))$. Thus for $\tilde{\mathbf{w}}$ a sequence of t steps chosen according to Wendy's strategy,

$$\begin{aligned} C^*(\tilde{\mathbf{w}}) &= D[N_t(L_{-D}) + N_t(R_D)] + \\ &\quad \tfrac{1}{2}\textstyle\sum_{i=1-D}^{D-1}[N_t(L_i)\alpha_L + N_t(R_i)\alpha_R] \\ &= t(1+o(1)) \cdot [D(p(L_{-D}) + p(R_D)) + \\ &\quad \tfrac{1}{2}\textstyle\sum_{i=1-D}^{D-1}(p(L_i)\alpha_L + p(R_i)\alpha_R)]. \end{aligned}$$

Applying Proposition 4.3, we obtain

$$\begin{aligned} \lambda \ \ge\ & 2 \cdot [D(p(L_{-D}) + p(R_D)) + \\ & \tfrac{1}{2}\textstyle\sum_{i=1-D}^{D-1}(p(L_i)\alpha_L + p(R_i)\alpha_R)]. \end{aligned} \tag{1}$$

We proceed to determine the steady state probabilities of the Markov chain. The transition matrix of the chain yields the following equations for the steady state probabilities:

$$\begin{aligned} p(L_i) &= (1-\sigma_R)p(L_{i+1}) + \sigma_L p(R_{i+1}) \\ &\quad \text{if } -D \le i < D-1, \\ p(L_{D-1}) &= p(R_D), \\ p(R_i) &= (1-\sigma_L)p(R_{i-1}) + \sigma_R p(L_{i-1}) \\ &\quad \text{if } 1-D < i \le D, \\ p(R_{1-D}) &= p(L_{-D}). \end{aligned}$$

Solving this system and recalling that $\beta_R = 1 - \alpha_R/(2D) = 1-\sigma_L$, and $\beta_L = 1-\alpha_L/(2D) = 1-\sigma_R$, we get the following solution (which can be easily checked against the defining equations):

$$\begin{aligned} p(L_i) &= \frac{J}{4D}\left(\frac{\beta_R}{\beta_L}\right)^i, \\ p(R_i) &= \frac{J}{4D}\left(\frac{\beta_R}{\beta_L}\right)^{i-1}, \end{aligned}$$

where

$$J = \begin{cases} 1 & \text{if } \alpha_R = \alpha_L, \\ \frac{(\alpha_R-\alpha_L)(\beta_L\beta_R)^D}{\beta_L(\beta_L^{2D}-\beta_R^{2D})} & \text{if } \alpha_R \ne \alpha_L \end{cases}$$

is chosen so that the sum of the probabilities is 1. Notice that $p(L_i) = p(R_{i+1})$ for all i and therefore $\sum_i p(L_i) = \sum_i p(R_{i+1}) = 1/2$. Thus we can rewrite the lower bound on λ from equation (1) as

$$\begin{aligned} \lambda &\ge 2 \cdot [D(p(L_{-D}) + p(R_D)) + \\ &\quad (\frac{1}{2} - p(L_{-D}))\frac{\alpha_L}{2} + (\frac{1}{2} - p(R_D))\frac{\alpha_R}{2}] \\ &= 2[D(\beta_L p(L_{-D}) + \beta_R p(R_D)) + \frac{\alpha_L + \alpha_R}{4}] \\ &= \frac{1}{2}[(\frac{J \cdot (\beta_L^{2D} + \beta_R^{2D})}{(\beta_L^{D-1}\beta_R^D)} + \alpha_L + \alpha_R]. \end{aligned}$$

It can now be checked that this simplifies to the expression in Theorem 4.1. ■

4.2 The upper bound: a strategy for the Jumper

Below is an explicit description of a randomized strategy for Jack.

Jumper Strategy

1. The strategy is defined in terms of $2D+1$ parameters $0 = p_{-D} < p_{-D+1} < p_{-D+2} < \cdots < p_{D-1} < p_D = 1$ which are specified below. Initially, Jack chooses his initial position to be $-D$ with probability p_0. At round $t+1$, if Wendy

moves in the direction away from j_t, Jack does not move. If $j_t = D$ and Wendy moves rightward from $w_t = i-1$ to $w_{t+1} = i$ then Jack moves to $-D$ with probability $\frac{p_i - p_{i-1}}{1-p_{i-1}}$. If $j_t = -D$ and Wendy moves leftward from $w_t = i+1$ to $w_{t+1} = i$ then Jack moves to D with probability $\frac{p_{i+1}-p_i}{p_{i+1}}$.

2. The parameters p_i which are used are given by:

$$p_i = \begin{cases} \frac{1}{2} + \frac{i}{2D}, & \text{if } \alpha_R = \alpha_L, \\ \frac{\beta_L^i \beta_R^{2D-i} - \beta_R^{2D}}{\beta_L^{2D} - \beta_R^{2D}} & \text{if } \alpha_R \neq \alpha_L. \end{cases}$$

Due to space limitation, we only hint at the proof that this strategy guarantees the upper bound. The first part of the definition of the strategy was chosen so that the following lemma holds:

Lemma 4.5 *Each time that Wendy is at position i, Jack is at $-D$ with probability p_i.*

The particular choice of values for the p_i's was made so that the expected cost r_i to Jack for each "round trip" by Wendy from i to $i+1$ and back is independent of i. Choosing the p_i's as above, we get that for each i,

$$r_i = \begin{cases} \alpha_R + \beta_R & \text{if } \alpha_R = \alpha_L, \\ \frac{\alpha_R \beta_L^{2D} - \alpha_L \beta_R^{2D}}{\beta_L^{2D} - \beta_R^{2D}} & \text{if } \alpha_R \neq \alpha_L. \end{cases}$$

The upper bound follows from the fact that Wendy's cost is well approximated by the number of "round trips" she makes.

5 Connecting the WJ Game and the Decomposition Theorem

Recall the notation of the decomposition theorem: $\mathcal{M}$ is a metric space partitioned into subspaces $\mathcal{M}_L$ and $\mathcal{M}_R$. Their respective diameters and competitive ratios (for the pursuit-evasion game) are denoted $\delta, \delta_L, \delta_R$ and $\lambda, \lambda_L, \lambda_R$. Also, $\delta_{\max} = \max\{\delta_L, \delta_R\}$ and $\lambda_{\max} = \max\{\lambda_L, \lambda_R\}$. The overview of the proof in Section 3 developed the Walker-Jumper game as a rough model for the pursuit-evasion game on a partitioned space. We now make this connection precise.

Lemma 5.1 *Let $(\mathcal{M}_L, \mathcal{M}_R)$ be a partition of $\mathcal{M}$ such that $\frac{\delta}{\delta_{\max}}$ is at least 32. Let α_R and α_L be nonnegative numbers and $\alpha_{\max}$ be their maximum. Let D be an integer satisfying $\max\{2\lambda_{\max}+2, \sqrt{\frac{\delta}{\delta_{\max}}}\} \le D \le \frac{\delta}{4\delta_{\max}}$, and let $\eta = 6\delta_{\max}D/\delta$. Then*

1. *If $\alpha_L \ge \lambda_L$ and $\alpha_R \ge \lambda_R$, then*

$$\lambda \le \lambda(WJ[D, \alpha_R, \alpha_L])(1+\eta),$$

2. *If $\alpha_L \le \lambda_L$ and $\alpha_R \le \lambda_R$, then*

$$\lambda \ge \lambda(WJ[D, \alpha_R, \alpha_L])(1-\eta).$$

The high-level idea of Lemma 5.1 is as follows. The Walker-Jumper game was created as an idealization of the pursuit-evasion game where the adversary is required to probe in s-block "chunks" on each subspace, and the algorithm can only move between spaces in between the s-blocks. It is further an idealization in supposing that the optimal cost of an s-block is exactly s, that the on-line cost of an s-block is exactly $s\lambda_L$ or $s\lambda_R$ (so that s drops out when computing the ratio), and that the cost of moving between $\mathcal{M}_L$ and $\mathcal{M}_R$ is exactly δ. Lemma 5.1 shows that one can remove this idealization with a fudge-factor of η. The proof is surprisingly involved, however, and is omitted from this abstract. To give a flavor of what is needed we state two key lemmas, possibly of independent interest, which are used to bound the additive constants in the pursuit-evasion game.

Lemma 5.2 *Let $\mathcal{M}$ be a metric space of diameter δ and let λ denote the competitive ratio of its pursuit-evasion game. Then there exists a randomized algorithm $\tilde{A}$ such that for any probe sequence ρ,*

$$C_{\tilde{A}}(\rho) \le \lambda \cdot C_{\mathrm{OPT}}(\rho) + \delta\lambda.$$

Lemma 5.3 *Let $\mathcal{M}$ be a metric space and λ the competitive ratio of its pursuit-evasion game. For any $s > 0$ there is a distribution $\tilde{\rho}_s$ on s-blocks such that for any response algorithm A,*

$$C_A(\tilde{\rho}_s) \ge \lambda s - (2\lambda\delta).$$

6 Applications of the Decomposition Theorem

The proof of Theorem 1.4 was given in the introduction. Here we use Theorem 1.8 to prove 1.3. The proof of Theorem 1.6, which is relatively straightforward will appear in the full paper.

We need a few additional definitions. If $\mathcal{M}$ is a metric space and $\mathcal{N}$ a subspace, we say that $\mathcal{N}$ is an *ϵ-small* subspace (relative to $\mathcal{M}$) if $\delta(\mathcal{N}) \le \epsilon \cdot \delta(\mathcal{M})$. We say that $\mathcal{N}$ is *ϵ-uniform* subspace if the distance between any two distinct points in $\mathcal{N}$ is at least $\epsilon \cdot \delta(\mathcal{N})$. The following easy consequence of the fact that the competitive ratio for a uniform space is between $\ln n$ and $2 \ln n$ is left to the reader (see also [KRR]).

Lemma 6.1 *The competitive ratio of an ϵ-uniform space on n points is between $\epsilon \ln n$ and $(2/\epsilon) \ln n$.*

It will be convenient to state some special cases of Theorem 1.8. First, the special case where the lower bounds on λ_R and λ_L are the same is worth noting.

Corollary 6.2 *Let $\mathcal{M}$ be a metric space, and let $(\mathcal{M}_R, \mathcal{M}_L)$ be a partition into two subspaces each of size at least 2. Let $\beta \geq 1$ be a lower bound on both λ_R and λ_L and suppose that both spaces $\mathcal{M}_R$ and $\mathcal{M}_L$ are $(2200\beta^3)^{-1}$-small. Then $\lambda \geq \beta + 1/2$.*

We also have

Corollary 6.3 *Let $\mathcal{M}$ be a metric space of at least three points and let $\mathcal{N}$ be a subspace. Suppose that $\beta \geq 1$ is a lower bound on $\lambda(\mathcal{N})$, and $\mathcal{N}$ is $(27000e^{3\beta})^{-1}$-small. Then $\lambda(\mathcal{M}) \geq \beta + e^{-2\beta}$.*

This follows by applying the main decomposition theorem to the space $\mathcal{N}$ and the space consisting of the single point of maximum distance from $\mathcal{N}$.

Proof of Theorem 1.3:

Let Q be a positive constant to be determined and define $f(n) = \max\{1, Q\sqrt{\ln n/\ln\ln n}\}$. We prove by induction on n that the competitive ratio of the pursuit problem on any metric space $\mathcal{M}$ with n points is at least $f(n)$. The inductive argument will work for n greater than some n_0; we will then choose Q so that $Q\sqrt{\ln n_0/\ln\ln n_0} = 1$. Thus, the basis case $n \leq n_0$ will be trivial. We will also need $Q \leq 1/7$ for part of the inductive argument.

The key to the inductive step is the following structural result for metric spaces. Define the function $T(n) = e^{4f(n)}$.

Lemma 6.4 *There exists an integer n_0 so that any metric space on $n \geq n_0$ points has either:*

1. *a 1/4-uniform subspace of size at least $T(n)$,*
2. *a pair of disjoint subspaces each of size at least $j(n) = nT(n)^{-6\ln\ln n}$, such that each is $(2200 \ln^3 n)^{-1}$-small with respect to their union, or*
3. *a $(27000n^3)^{-1}$-small subspace $\mathcal{N}$ whose size is at least $n(1 - 1/T(n))$.*

Applying the lemma to $\mathcal{M}$, we can now finish the inductive step of the theorem. In the first case, we may use Lemma 6.1 to obtain a lower bound of $f(n)$ on the competitive ratio. If condition (2) holds, we apply Corollary 6.2 to the union of these two spaces. By induction, each space has competitive ratio at least

$$
\begin{aligned}
f(j(n)) &\geq Q\sqrt{\frac{\ln n - (6\ln\ln n)(4f(n))}{\ln\ln n}} \\
&\geq Q\left(\sqrt{\frac{\ln n}{\ln\ln n}} - \frac{24f(n)}{\sqrt{\frac{\ln n}{\ln\ln n}}}\right) \\
&\geq Q\sqrt{\frac{\ln n}{\ln\ln n}} - 24Q^2 \\
&\geq Q\sqrt{\frac{\ln n}{\ln\ln n}} - (1/2)
\end{aligned}
$$

where the second inequality follows from the fact that $A > B \geq 0$ implies $\sqrt{A - B} \geq \sqrt{A} - B/\sqrt{A}$, the third from the assumption that $n \geq n_0$, and the last from $Q \leq 1/7$. Taking the last quantity as β in Corollary 6.2 we obtain the required lower bound of $Q\sqrt{\frac{\ln n}{\ln\ln n}}$ for $\lambda(\mathcal{M})$.

Finally if condition (3) holds, then by induction, the subspace has competitive ratio at least

$$
\begin{aligned}
f(n(1 - 1/T(n))) &\geq Q\sqrt{\frac{\ln n + \ln(1 - 1/T(n))}{\ln\ln n}} \\
&\geq Q\sqrt{\frac{\ln n - 1/T(n)}{\ln\ln n}} \\
&\geq Q\sqrt{\frac{\ln n}{\ln\ln n}} - Q/T(n),
\end{aligned}
$$

where the last inequality follows again by using the fact that $A > B \geq 0$ implies $\sqrt{A - B} \geq \sqrt{A} - B/\sqrt{A}$. Taking the last quantity as β in Corollary 6.3 we obtain the lower bound $\lambda(\mathcal{M}) \geq f(n) - Q/T(n) + e^{-2f(n)} \geq f(n)$. ∎

So it now remains to prove Lemma 6.4. Let $\mathcal{M}$ be an arbitrary metric space on n points and assume that the first conclusion does not hold, i.e., there is no 1/4-uniform subspace of size $T(n)$.

Lemma 6.5 *Let k be a positive integer and r, s be positive real numbers. If $\mathcal{M}$ is a space that does not have a 1/4-uniform space of size at least s then there is a partition $(\mathcal{M}_0, \mathcal{M}_1, \ldots, \mathcal{M}_j)$ of the space such that $\mathcal{M}_0$ has at most r points and each of the remaining spaces is a 2^{-k} – small subspace of size at least r/s^k.*

Proof: By induction on the number of points n in $\mathcal{M}$. For $n \leq r$ the result is trivial. To prove the inductive step it will suffice to show that any space of size at least r with no 1/4-uniform subspace of size s has at least one 2^{-k}-small subspace of size at least r/s^k, as we can then remove that space and finish by induction (since if $\mathcal{N}$ is ϵ-small with respect to a subspace, then it is ϵ-small with respect to the entire space).

To prove the existence of one such space, proceed by induction on k. Since the case $k = 0$ is trivial, suppose $k > 0$. By the inductive hypothesis there is a subspace $\mathcal{N}$ of size at least r/s^{k-1} and diameter at most $\delta/2^{k-1}$. Let x_1, x_2 be two points in $\mathcal{N}$ at distance $\delta(\mathcal{N})$, and let $x_1, x_2, \ldots, x_t$ be a maximal 1/4-uniform subspace of $\mathcal{N}$ containing those two points. By hypothesis, $t < s$. Furthermore, by the maximality of the set, every point in $\mathcal{N}$ is within distance $\delta(\mathcal{N})/4$ of one of the x_i. Classify each point of $\mathcal{N}$ according to the x_i to which it is closest (breaking ties arbitrarily). Each class has diameter at most $\delta(\mathcal{N})/2$ and so is $1/2^k$-small, and the largest such class has size at least r/s^k. ■

To complete the proof of Lemma 6.4, we apply Lemma 6.5 with $k = \lfloor 6 \ln\ln n \rfloor - 2$, $s = T(n)$ and $r = n/T(n)^2$. This implies that we can partition $\mathcal{M}$ into spaces $\mathcal{M}_0, \mathcal{M}_1, \ldots \mathcal{M}_j$ where $\mathcal{M}_0$ has size at most $n/T(n)^2$ and all of the others are $2^{-\lfloor 6 \ln\ln n \rfloor + 2} \leq (4400 \ln^3 n)^{-1}$-small (this inequality holds for $n \geq n_0$, if n_0 is sufficiently large) and have size at least $\frac{n}{T(n)^{k+2}} \geq \frac{n}{T(n)^{6 \ln\ln n}}$. Now if there is a pair of spaces $\mathcal{M}_h$ and $\mathcal{M}_i$ with $i, h > 0$ whose maximum distance is at least $\delta(\mathcal{M})/2$, then they satisfy condition (2) above. So assume no such pair exists. Then the space $\mathcal{Q}_1 = \mathcal{M} - \mathcal{M}_0$ has diameter at most $\delta(\mathcal{M})/2$ and size at least $n(1 - T(n)^{-2})$. Apply the same argument to $\mathcal{Q}_1$ keeping fixed the values for k, s, and r. We obtain either a pair of spaces that are $(2200 \ln^3 n)^{-1}$-small relative to their union and have size at least $\frac{n}{T(n)^{6 \ln\ln n}}$, or a space $\mathcal{Q}_2$ of diameter at most $\delta(\mathcal{M})/4$ and size at least $n(1 - 2T(n)^{-2})$. Repeat this at most $p = \lceil \log S(n) \rceil$ times, stopping if condition (2) is satisfied. If not, we obtain a space $\mathcal{Q}_p$ of diameter at most $\delta(\mathcal{M})/S(n)$ and size at least $n(1 - \lceil \log S(n) \rceil / T(n)^2)$. Now we can choose n_0 so that for $n \geq n_0$, $\lceil \log S(n) \rceil \leq T(n)$. Then the size of $\mathcal{Q}_p$ is at least $n(1 - 1/T(n))$ and so we have condition (3). ■

References

[BBKTW] S. Ben-David, A. Borodin, R.M. Karp, G. Tardos, and A. Wigderson. On the Power of Randomization in Online Algorithms. In *Proc. of the 22nd Ann. ACM Symp. on Theory of Computing*, pages 379–386, May 1990.

[BLS] A. Borodin, N. Linial, and M. Saks. An Optimal On-Line Algorithm for Metrical Task Systems. In *Proc. of the 19th Ann. ACM Symp. on Theory of Computing*, pages 373–382, May 1987. To appear in *JACM*.

[BRS] A. Blum, P. Raghavan, and B. Schieber. Navigating in Unfamiliar Geometric Terrain. In *Proc. of the 23rd Ann. ACM Symp. on Theory of Computing*, pages 494–504, May 1991.

[CDRS] D. Coppersmith, P. Doyle, P. Raghavan, M. Snir. Random Walks on Weighted Graphs and Applications to On-line Algorithms. In *Proc. of the 22nd Ann. ACM Symp. on Theory of Computing*, pages 369–378, May 1990.

[FFKRRV] A. Fiat, D.P. Foster, H.J. Karloff, Y. Rabani, Y. Ravid, and S. Vishwanathan. Competitive Algorithms for Layered Graph Traversal. In *Proc. of the 32nd Ann. Symp. on Foundations of Comp. Sci.*, pages 288–297, October 1991.

[FKLMSY] A. Fiat, R.M. Karp, M. Luby, L.A. McGeoch, D.D. Sleator, and N.E. Young. Competitive Paging Algorithms. *Journal of Algorithms*, 12:685–699, 1991.

[FRR] A. Fiat, Y. Rabani, and Y. Ravid. Competitive k-Server Algorithms. In *Proc. of the 31st Ann. IEEE Symp. on Foundations of Computer Science*, October 1990.

[Gro] E. Grove. The Harmonic k-Server Algorithm is Competitive. In *Proc. of the 23nd Ann. ACM Symp. on Theory of Computing*, pages 260–266, May 1991.

[Ira] S. Irani. Two Results on the List Update Problem. Research report RC-15922, IBM T.J. Watson Research Center, 1990.

[KMMO] A.R. Karlin, M.S. Manasse, L.A. McGeoch, and S. Owicki. Competitive Randomized Algorithms for Non-uniform Problems. In *Proc. of the 1st Ann. ACM-SIAM Symp. on Discrete Algorithms*, pages 301–309, January 1990.

[KMRS] A.R. Karlin, M.S. Manasse, L. Rudolph, and D.D. Sleator. Competitive Snoopy Caching. *Algorithmica*, 3(1):79–119, 1988.

[KRR] H.J. Karloff, Y. Rabani, and Y. Ravid. Lower Bounds for Randomized k-Server Algorithms. In *Proc. of the 23rd Ann. ACM Symp. on Theory of Computing*, May 1991.

[MMS] M.S. Manasse, L.A. McGeoch, and D.D. Sleator. Competitive Algorithms for On-line Problems. *Journal of Algorithms*, 11:208–230, 1990.

[MS] L.A. McGeoch and D.D. Sleator. A Strongly Competitive Randomized Paging Algorithm. Submitted to *Algorithmica*.

[RS] P. Raghavan and M. Snir. Memory versus Randomization in On-Line Algorithms. In *Proc. 16th ICALP*, July 1989.

[ST] D.D. Sleator and R.E. Tarjan. Amortized Efficiency of List Update and Paging Rules. *Communication of the ACM*, 28(2): 202–208, 1985.

[Vis] S. Vishwanathan. Randomized Online Graph Coloring. In *Proc. of the 31st Ann. IEEE Symp. on Foundations of Computer Science*, pages 464–469, October 1990.

Markov Paging

(Extended Abstract)

Anna R. Karlin * Steven J. Phillips† Prabhakar Raghavan‡

Abstract

This paper considers the problem of paging under the assumption that the sequence of pages accessed is generated by a Markov chain. We use this model to study the fault-rate of paging algorithms, a quantity of interest to practitioners. We first draw on the theory of Markov decision processes to characterize the paging algorithm that achieves optimal fault-rate on any Markov chain. Next, we address the problem of efficiently devising a paging strategy with low fault-rate for a given Markov chain. We show that a number of intuitively good approaches fail. Our main result is an efficient procedure that, on any Markov chain, will give a paging algorithm with fault-rate at most a constant times optimal. Our techniques also show that some algorithms that do poorly in practice fail in the Markov setting, despite known (good) performance guarantees when the requests are generated independently from a probability distribution.

1. Introduction

This paper considers the problem of paging in a two-level store under the assumption that the sequence of pages accessed (henceforth *reference string*) is generated by a Markov chain. Each page of virtual memory is represented by a state (or node) of the Markov chain M, whose transition probabilities p_{ij} specify the probability that an access to i is immediately followed by an access to j.

Sleator and Tarjan [15] initiated the worst-case study of paging, introducing a style of worst-case analysis that has come to be known as *competitive analysis* [9]. We wish to address some shortcomings of the traditional adversarial analysis of paging [15]. Borodin *et al.* [2] provided an important step towards bridging the gap between such worst-case analysis and reality by providing a model that captured the essential aspects of locality of reference in the reference string. Here we follow their lead in assuming that the reference string is generated by a Markov chain, thereby removing the adversary's role. Indeed, this natural direction has repeatedly been suggested since the appearance of [2, 8]. A significant benefit of this approach is that it enables us to move away from competitive analysis towards a performance measure used by practitioners.

We refer to on-line paging with the reference string generated by such a Markov chain as *Markov paging.* We focus on questions such as: given a Markov chain, what is the best paging algorithm for reference strings generated by it, and how can this algorithm be computed? is there a simple algorithm that performs near-optimally on every Markov chain? can Markov paging explain why some paging algorithms perform poorly in practice?

Some salient features of our work are:

- There is recent interest in the systems

*DEC Systems Research Center, 130 Lytton Ave., Palo Alto, CA 94301.

†Computer Science Department, Stanford University, CA 94305. Supported by NSF Grant CCR-9010517, and grants from Mitsubishi and OTL. A portion of this work was done at DEC SRC.

‡IBM T.J. Watson Research Center, Yorktown Heights, NY 10598.

0-8186-2900-2/92 $3.00 © 1992 IEEE

community in designing paging algorithms that adapt to the locality characteristics of a program [3, 12]. Thus insights derived from theoretical studies may have an impact on implementations.

- Markov paging, like the access graph model in [2, 8], offers a clean theoretical abstraction for locality of reference in a program. Unlike the models in [2, 8, 9, 15], there is no adversary generating the reference string, much as in a real program. Further, certain simple properties of real programs — such as the fact that a data-dependent loop typically gets executed many times before exiting — can be modeled well.

- Practitioners study the *page-fault rate* for a program and paging algorithm, rather than competitiveness. Page-fault rate has little meaning in an adversarial model, but is eminently suited to a probabilistic model. In Markov paging, there is (as we shall see) a precise meaning to the page-fault rate of an algorithm, as well as the best page-fault rate achievable on the Markov chain. Note that if each request is drawn independently from a probability distribution, the problem of devising the paging algorithm with lowest fault-rate has an easy solution [7].

- Markov paging enables us to provide a mathematical basis for the poor performance of certain paging algorithms (such as *random replacement* and *frequency count*). For example, the *Frequency Count* algorithm is bad for Markov paging — whereas one might think that on a probabilistic input this algorithm would perform well.

- Somewhat surprisingly, we find that several plausible approaches to devising paging algorithms will fail for Markov paging. For example, all *marking algorithms*, intuitively "best" in an adversarial model, suffer from page-fault rates that are far from optimal in Markov paging. This includes probabilistic versions of the FAR algorithm of [2, 8]. We also find that natural approximations of the optimal off-line paging algorithm MIN are far from optimal in Markov paging.

- We present an on-line paging algorithm that is efficiently computable and achieves a fault-rate within a constant times the best possible, on every Markov chain.

1.1. Model

We have a memory consisting of k locations that can be accessed quickly, and some bigger number of locations whose access time is larger. An *on-line paging algorithm* is presented with a sequence of requests to items in the memory. If the item currently requested is in one of the k locations that can be accessed quickly (a *hit*), no cost is incurred. However, if the item requested is not in the k fast locations (*a fault*), it must be fetched into the fast memory at a unit cost. Further, one of the items in fast memory must be evicted to make room for it; the decision of which item in fast memory to evict must be made by the on-line paging algorithm without knowledge of future requests.

We now augment this basic model with a Markov source of references. We assume that any reasonable paging algorithm will, on a fault, evict any nodes that are in transient components of the Markov chain that are unreachable from the current state (since such a page will never be accessed again). We therefore restrict our attention to irreducible Markov chains. For an irreducible Markov chain M, and an on-line paging algorithm A, we define by $f_A(M, k)$ the *page-fault rate* of A on M using k locations of fast memory — i.e., the long-term frequency of occurrence of faults. The existence of such a quantity is established in Section 2. It also follows from Section 2 that there is an *optimal fault-rate* for every Markov chain M, which we denote by $f^*(M, k)$. We denote by k the number of locations of fast memory, and by n the total number of pages (states in M).

Note that we are not concerned here with the problem of inferring the Markov chain from the sequences we see; this problem is in the spirit of learning theory. By sampling a large enough initial prefix of the reference string, we can obtain an arbitrarily close approximation to the true transition probabilities.

1.2. Related Previous Work

The underpinnings of competitive paging were laid in The literature of computer performance modeling and analysis contains related work, both theoretical and empirical. Denning [4] (and references therein) developed the *working set* model of program behavior for capturing locality of reference. Spirn[16] gives a comprehensive survey of models for program behavior. Franaszek and Wagner [7] studied a model in which every request is drawn independently from the same probability distribution. Shedler and Tung [14] and Lewis and Shedler [11] study paging in a Markov chain whose states represent *LRU stack distances*, a model convenient for studying the *least recently used* (LRU) paging algorithm. Denning and Spirn showed empirically that in order for a first-order Markov model to reasonably approximate real program behavior, it is necessary to separate data and instruction reference streams. Borodin *et al.* [2] and Irani *et al.* [8] have studied locality of reference in paging, but with an adversarial model.

Irani, Karp, Kearns and Luby (private communication, 1991) have studied other on-line problems when requests are independently drawn from a probability distribution. Vitter and Krishnan [17] consider the problem of prefetching into a cache when the reference string is generated by a Markov source (or mth order Markov source). Under the assumption that there is always sufficient time to prefetch as many pages as wanted, Vitter and Krishnan show that data compression techniques can be used to obtain algorithms with optimal limiting page fault rates.

1.3. Guided Tour of the Abstract

Section 2 draws on the theory of Markov decision processes to characterize paging algorithms that achieve optimal fault-rate on any Markov chain. Theorem 2 shows that there is a memoryless, deterministic optimal on-line algorithm. Theorem 3 shows that there is a linear program that determines the optimal online algorithm, but this algorithm may have running time exponential in k. Section 3 shows that a number of plausible approaches for designing an efficient and provably good Markov paging algorithm will fail. Our main result, in Section 4, gives an efficiently computable paging algorithm whose fault-rate is within a constant factor of the best possible on every Markov chain.

2. Markov decision theory and optimal paging

We begin by studying the relationship between page replacement policies and Markov decision theory [5]. By re-casting the problem of optimal on-line Markov paging as a problem in Markov decision theory, we obtain two results.

A *Markov decision process* can be described as follows. Consider a discrete time Markov chain, whose state at time t is Y_t. After each observation of the system, one of a set of possible actions is taken. Say that K_i is the set of actions possible when the system is in state i. Let A_t be the action taken at time t. A (possibly randomized) policy R is a set of functions $D_a(H_{t-1}, Y_t)$, where a is an action in K_{Y_t} meaning that if H_{t-1} is the history of states and actions up to time $t-1$, and Y_t is the state at time t, then the probability action a is taken at time t is $D_a(H_{t-1}, Y_t)$. The actions can be such that they change the state of the system. We define this precisely by saying that $q_{ij}(a)$ is the probability of the system being in state j at the next instant, given that the system is in state i and action a is taken, i.e.

$$Pr(Y_{t+1} = j | H_{t-1}, Y_t = i, A_t = a) = q_{ij}(a).$$

An additional set of parameters associated with a Markov decision process are costs: when the chain is in state i and action a is taken, a known cost w_{ia} is incurred.

Let $S_{R,T}$ be the expected cost of operating a system up to time T using policy R. ($S_{R,T} = \sum_{0 \leq t \leq T} \sum_i \sum_a P_R(Y_t = j, A_t = a) w_{ja}$.)

A standard problem in Markov decision theory is to minimize the expected average cost per unit time, i.e. to find a policy R to minimize

$$lim_{T \to \infty} \frac{S_{R,T}}{T}.$$

Theorem 1: *Let M be an n state Markov chain with state space S. Suppose that states in S correspond to pages, and that the fast memory can store k pages. Then the problem of determining an on-line algorithm of optimal fault-rate is a Markov decision theory problem of the previous type.*

Proof: Define the following augmented Markov chain whose state space is S'. A state in S' has two components: r and H. r is the most recent request, and H is a subset of S of size $n-k$ representing the set of pages that are not in fast memory immediately before servicing the request r.

When the system is in the state (r, H), and $r \in H$ then there are k actions that can be taken: for each $x \in S - H$, H can be replaced by $H \setminus \{r\} \cup \{x\}$. In this case we say that the action x was taken. When the system is in state (r, H), and $r \notin H$, then no actions can be taken.

Suppose that p_{ij} are the transition probabilities of the underlying Markov chain. A policy R determines $\alpha_{(r,H),x}$, the probability that in state $(r, H), r \in H$, the action x is taken. Then for $r \in H$ and $s \in H$,

$$Pr(Y_{t+1} = (r', H') | Y_t = (r, H), A_t = x)$$

$$= p_{rr'} \alpha_{(r,H),x}$$

where $H' = H \setminus \{r\} \cup \{x\}$. If we now take $w_{(r,H),a} = 1$ if $r \in H$, then the problem of determining the page replacement strategy that minimizes the fault rate is the same as the problem of determining the policy that minimizes the expected average cost per unit time (i.e. a problem of type 2 above). Notice that this problem is equivalent to minimizing the sum of stationary probabilities for the stochastic process Y_t, i.e. minimizing $\sum_r \sum_{H | r \in H} \pi_{(r,H)}$. □

Theorem 2: *The optimal on-line page replacement policy in a Markov chain is memoryless, time-invariant and deterministic. In other words, the decision of which page to evict on a fault depends only on the current request and the k items in fast memory.*

Theorem 2 is reminiscent of the first result in Ben-David *et al.* [1], which stated that randomization added no power against the adaptive off-line adversary. Here we see that memory does not help, either.

Theorem 2 is a corollary of Theorem 1 implied by results in Markov decision theory. The following theorem also follows from Markov decision theory.

Theorem 3: *The problem of computing the optimal on-line paging strategy on Markov chain M is a linear programming problem in $n\binom{n}{k}$ variables.*

Note that this linear programming formulation gives us an algorithm for computing the optimal paging strategy on M whose running time may be exponential in k. We know of no technique to improve this upper bound, and this leads us to the study of efficiently computable strategies that approximate $f^*(M)$ well on every M. Note that when k is close to zero or to n, the linear program gives an efficient algorithm for computing the optimal on-line paging strategy. In fact, it is particularly instructive to consider the case $n = k + 1$, both for its own sake and because it has traditionally given good insights in paging [2, 6].

Theorem 4: *When $n = k+1$, for every M, there is an efficiently computable deterministic paging strategy that evicts only one of two fixed nodes ($k-1$ pages are never evicted) whose fault-rate is at most $2f^*(M,k)$.*

The proof uses the fact that the optimal paging algorithm is a *max mean cycle* [10] in the weighted digraph whose nodes are the nodes of M and each of whose edges (i,j) has weight equal to the hitting time from i to j. It follows that there is a cycle of length 2 that has page fault rate at most twice optimal. (For reversible chains, a cycle of length 2 has optimal page fault rate.)

3. Negative Results

We begin this section by establishing that two algorithms that have been proposed and found to fare poorly in practice are far from optimal in Markov paging. Following this, we begin our quest for a simple, efficiently computable paging algorithm that has page-fault rate within a constant multiple of the best possible, on every Markov chain. We show in this section that a number of intuitively "obvious" algorithms for Markov paging fail to achieve this goal, and pave the way for our optimal algorithm in Section 4. In all our negative results, $n = k+1$; however, this is for simplicity of presentation only and can be generalized.

The *Random Replacement* (RR) paging algorithm will, on a fault, evict a random item in fast memory. Although optimal in the competitive setting against an adaptive on-line adversary [13], it performs relatively poorly in practice. The *Frequency Count* (FC) algorithm maintains, for each of the n items, a count of the number of times that item has been accessed. On a fault, it evicts the the item in fast memory that has been accessed least often. When every request is drawn independently from a probability distribution, FC converges to the optimal algorithm. However, it performs poorly in practice, since it ignores locality of reference. This is reflected by the fact that it is far from optimal in Markov paging (Theorem 6).

Theorem 5: *For every $k > 2$, there is a constant c and a Markov chain M for which $f_{RR}(M,k) \geq ckf^*(M,k)$.*

Definition 1: *For positive integers a, b, the* lollipop graph *$L(a,b)$ is formed by attaching one end of a path through b nodes to a complete graph K_a on a nodes.*

Proof of Theorem 5: Let $n = k+1$, and let M be the Markov chain representing the simple random walk on $L(k-1,2)$. Then the expected time between faults incurred by RR is the average over all pairs of nodes x, y in the graph of the time to hit y on a random walk starting at x. This average is $O(k)$. On the other hand, the maximum hitting time is $\Omega(k^2)$, and thus $f^*(M,k)$ is $O(1/k^2)$. □

Theorem 6: *For every $k > 2$, there is a constant c and a Markov chain M for which $f_{FC}(M,k) \geq c(\log k)f^*(M,k)$.*

The proof uses a random walk on $L(k/2+1, k/2)$, and is omitted.

Next, we show that many algorithms that intuitively should perform well in Markov paging will in fact perform poorly on some Markov chains.

A class of on-line algorithms that one may expect to perform well are *marking algorithms.* Marking algorithms use a notion of *phases.* A *new page* is one that wasn't requested in the previous phase. A new phase begins with a request to a new page. When a page is requested, it is marked. As soon as k distinct pages are marked, the phase ends, and all pages are unmarked. A marking algorithm has the property that it never evicts a a marked page.

It has been shown in the competitive model that for the standard paging problem (arbitrary request sequences), as well as for paging with locality of reference [2], there are marking algorithms that are optimal. Therefore, one might think that the same would hold when reference strings are generated from a Markov chain. The following theorem shows that our search for a good algorithm should exclude marking algorithms.

Theorem 7: *For any $k > 2$ and any marking algorithm A, there is a Markov chain M and a constant c such that $f_A(M,k) \geq c(\log k)f^*(M,k)$.*

Proof Sketch: Let M be the Markov chain corresponding to a simple random walk on the lollipop graph $L(k/2+1, k/2)$. Let x denote the node on the clique to which the path xy is attached. A phase starts with a request at some vertex of the graph, and ends when all nodes in the graph have been requested. The important property of this Markov chain that defeats any marking algorithm is that once a node in the clique is requested, with high probability all the nodes in the clique will be requested before the node y is requested. By a standard argument, any phase that begins on y will incur $\Omega(\log k)$ faults in the clique before the phase ends. We show on average, half the phases will begin on y; thus any marking algorithm will incur $\Omega(\log k)$ faults per phase on average. On the other hand, the on-line algorithm that alternately evicts a node in the clique and y will incur an average of 1 fault per phase. □

The optimal offline algorithm for any reference string is commonly called MIN. MIN always replaces the page that will be requested furthest in the future. We now consider various on-line algorithms that mimic MIN on a Markov chain. The *maximum hitting time* (MHT) algorithm replaces, on a fault, that page in fast memory for which the *expected time* to the next request is the largest. Indeed, when the requests are drawn independently from a probability distribution, this algorithm performs well [7]; again, the locality of reference captured by Markov paging proves to be the undoing of this algorithm.

Theorem 8: *For every $k > 10$, there is a Markov chain M on $k+1$ nodes and a constant c such that $f_{MHT}(M,k) \geq ckf^*(M,k)$.*

Proof: Consider the $n = k+1$ node undirected graph G consisting of a clique on $2n/3$ nodes; attached to a node x on this clique is a simple path xy of length $n/3 - 1$; attached to y's neighbor (the penultimate node on the tail) is an additional node z. (This is a lollipop graph with a two-pronged antenna at the tip of the stick.) Suppose that the Markov chain generating the reference string is the simple random walk on G.

If MHT is run on the reference string generated by this Markov chain, eventually either y or z will be evicted. From either, the maximum hitting time is $4n^2/9$, to the other. On the other hand, the maximum hitting time from y or z to any node in the clique is $2n^2/9 + O(n)$. Thus the page not in fast memory (the "hole") will thereafter oscillate forever between y and z, so that $f_{MHT}(M,k)$ is $\Omega(1/k^2)$. The optimal algorithm will alternately evict a node in the clique and y (or z), with fault-rate $O(1/k^3)$. □

Let LAST be the algorithm that on a fault evicts the page that has the highest probability of being the last of the k pages in fast memory to be requested. An attractive variation on LAST is an algorithm we call Max Rank, (MR) defined as follows. Suppose that at the time of a fault, S is the set of pages in fast memory. Then there is some permutation on S that describes the order in which these pages will subsequently be seen. For each page $i \in S$, and $1 \leq j \leq k$, let $p_i(j)$ be the probability that page i is the jth page in S that will be seen. Define the expected rank of page i, R_i to be $\sum_j jp_i(j)$. Then MR evicts the page $p \in S$ such that R_p is maximum. We omit the proof of the following theorem.

Theorem 9: *(i) There is a constant c such that for $k > 3$, there is a Markov chain M such* *that $f_{LAST}(M,k) \geq ckf^*(M,k)$. (ii) There is a constant c such that for $k > 3$ and constant $\epsilon > 0$, there is a Markov chain M such that $f_{MR}(M,k) \geq c'k^{1-\epsilon}f^*(M,k)$*

Finally, an algorithm which is very close in spirit to our nearly optimal on-line algorithm of Section 4 is the Maximum Commute Time (MCT) Algorithm. On a fault for page v, MCT evicts the page w in fast memory that maximizes the *commute time between v and w* — i.e., the expected time for a vwv round trip. On a directed cycle of length $k+1$, the fault rate of MCT can be $\Omega(k)$ times optimal.

4. A provably good algorithm

4.1. Notation

Let $C_{a,b}$ be the commute time between a and b. For states a, b, u, v, we define the *relative distance* of the pair (a, b) to u to be

$$d[(a,b),u] = \frac{\min\{C_{a,u}, C_{b,u}\}}{C_{a,b}}.$$

Define also the relative distance of (a, b) to (u, v) to be

$$d[(a,b),(u,v)] = \min\{d[(a,b),u], d[(a,b),v]\}.$$

Let $M = \{(u_1, v_1), \ldots, (u_r, v_r)\}$ be a set of r disjoint pairs of states in a Markov chain. Let V be a subset of the states of the Markov chain and let $V_M \subset V$ be the set of vertices involved in M. We will refer to one endpoint of each pair (u_i, v_i) in M as *distinguished.* Wlog, the distinguished endpoint will always be u_i. We say that M is a *good r-matching for V* if:

1. For all i,j, $1 \leq i,j \leq r$, $i \neq j$, $d[(u_i,v_i),u_j] \leq 20$. When this condition holds, we say that "(u_i, v_i) *sees* u_j".
2. For all i, $1 \leq i \leq r$, and $a \in V \setminus V_M$, $d[(u_i,v_i),a] \leq 2$. When this condition holds, we say that "(u_i, v_i) is *close to* a."

4.2. Description of the algorithm

The Commute Algorithm (CA) [1] operates in phases. At the beginning of a new phase the set of pages, P, requested in the previous phase are resident in fast memory. Recall that a new page is one that wasn't requested in the previous phase. A new phase begins with a request to a new page, and ends when k distinct pages have been requested in this phase. The ith *subphase* of a phase begins when the ith new page, n_i, is requested. Let $V_i = P \cup \{n_1, \ldots n_i\}$.

During the ith subphase there is a set of i disjoint pairs of pages $M_i = \{(u_1,v_1)\ldots(u_i,v_i)\}$, such that for each j, $1 \leq j \leq i$, exactly one of u_j and v_j is not in fast memory. On a fault at u_j the page v_j is evicted, and vice versa.[2] We will maintain the invariant that M_i is a good i-matching for V_i (where the u's are the distinguished endpoints). Let V_{M_i} be the set of vertices involved in M_i.

The set $M_1 = (u_1, v_1)$ is the pair of states with maximum commute time in $P \cup \{n_1\}$. (The fault at n_1 is serviced by evicting either u_1 or v_1.)

M_{i+1} is constructed in two steps: The pair (a, n_{i+1}) is added where $a \in V_{i+1} \setminus V_{M_i}$ is the vertex with maximum commute time to n_{i+1}. Let $M' = \{(u_1,v_1)\ldots(u_i,v_i),(a,n_{i+1})\}$.

Case 1: If $d[(a,n_{i+1}),(u_j,v_j)] \leq 10$ for all j, then $M_{i+1} = M'$ and the fault at n_{i+1} is serviced by evicting a.

Case 2 (Flip): Otherwise, choose j so that $d[(a,n_{i+1}),(u_j,v_j)]$ is maximized and set M_{i+1} to be M' with the edges (a, n_{i+1}) and (u_j, v_j) replaced by (u_j, n_{i+1}) and (a, v_j). In this case, the fault at n_{i+1} is serviced by evicting u_j if possible, and otherwise v_j.

We may need to reverse the roles of u_ℓ and

[1] For the case $n \leq 2k$, a simpler algorithm in the same spirit can be shown to have page fault rate that is within a constant factor of optimal.

[2] Observe that CA is not a marking algorithm. However, at the end of a phase, CA makes sure that the k pages in fast memory are precisely the k distinct pages that have been requested in this phase.

v_ℓ for some ℓ in M_{i+1} in order to maintain the condition that M_{i+1} is a good matching with the u's distinguished. That this can be done will be shown below.

4.3. Analysis of the Algorithm

Theorem 10: *There is a constant c such that for any Markov chain M and any k,*

$$f_{CA}(M,k) \leq cf^*(M,k).$$

We prove the theorem using a sequence of lemmas[3]:

Observation: Commute times satisfy the triangle inequality.

Lemma 11: *M_1 is a good 1-matching for V_1.*

Lemma 12: *Suppose that M_i is a good i-matching for V_i. Then M_{i+1} is a good $i+1$-matching for V_{i+1}.*

Proof Sketch: Recall that the $(i+1)$-matching M_{i+1} is good for V_{i+1} if *every* pair (u_m, v_m) sees *every* other u_ℓ and is close to *every* $b \in V_{i+1} \setminus V_{M_{i+1}}$. We first consider the matching M'. Simple applications of the commute time triangle inequality prove that M' satisfies the following goodness conditions:

1. (a, n_{i+1}) is close to b for any $b \notin V_{M'}$.

2. For each m, $1 \leq m \leq i$, (u_m, v_m) continues to see u_ℓ, $\ell \neq m$, and continues to be close to b for any $b \notin V_{M'}$.

3. (u_m, v_m) sees a for any m.

Unfortunately, if (a, n_{i+1}) does not see some u_m, M' may not be a good $i+1$-matching. If this happens, there are two cases:

Case 1: $M_{i+1} = M'$, we didn't do a flip.

Consider an edge (u_m, v_m) not seen by (a, n_{i+1}), i.e. $d[(a, n_{i+1}), u_m] > 20$. We claim that in this case all the pairs in M' see v_m, and consequently v_m can play the former distinguished role of u_m. The intuition is that since for all j, (u_j, v_j) is close to a, and (a, n_{i+1}) is quite close to v_m ($d[(a, n_{i+1}), v_m] \leq 10$), an application of the triangle inequality implies that (u_j, v_j) sees v_m.

Case 2: We did a flip: $\exists\ j$ such that $d[(a, n_{i+1}), (u_j, v_j)] > 10$.

In this case (a, n_{i+1}) is far from both endpoints of (u_j, v_j). Consider the new edges (a, v_j) and (u_j, n_{i+1}) (chosen so that $d[(a, n_{i+1}), (u_j, v_j)]$ is maximized). Since in M_i all pairs saw u_j and were close to a, the hope would be that a and u_j can become the distinguished vertices in their new pairs, and that all other distinguished vertices remain the same. This is not necessarily so (though intuitively things are still okay since the "furthest" pair j was chosen to swap with). Since all other pairs are "closer", and see a and u_j, we can show that M_{i+1} is in fact good (with a new set of distinguished vertices). We state the following series of claims without proof.

1. For any m, (u_m, v_m) sees both a and u_j.

2. (u_j, n_{i+1}) sees a and (a, v_j) sees n_{i+1}.

3. For any $b \notin M$, (u_j, n_{i+1}) and (a, v_j) are close to b.

4. For any m, either (a, v_j) sees u_m and (u_j, n_{i+1}) sees u_m or (a, v_j) sees v_m and (u_j, n_{i+1}) sees v_m.

5. If (a, v_j) sees only n_{i+1} and not u_j, then every other edge (u_m, v_m) sees n_{i+1}, and n_{i+1} can become the distinguished vertex in the pair (u_j, n_{i+1}).

6. If (a, v_j) or (u_j, n_{i+1}) doesn't see some u_m, then every other edge (u_ℓ, v_ℓ) sees v_m, and v_m can become the distinguished vertex in the pair (u_m, v_m).

□

We omit the proof of the following lemma.

[3]The constants in this analysis can be greatly improved.

Lemma 13: *Let M be a Markov chain. Let a, b, c be three states in M. Then*

$$Pr(c \text{ visited during an } (a,b) \text{ commute}) \geq \frac{C_{ab}}{2(C_{ab}+C_{ac})}.$$

We are ready to prove the main theorem.

Proof of Theorem 10: We show that for any on-line algorithm A the expected number of faults incurred by CA in a phase is at most a constant times the number of faults incurred by A.

Consider a phase in which g new nodes are seen (i.e. there are g subphases). We refer to a commute between some u_j and v_j as a j-commute. Suppose that $m_{i,j}$ j-commutes begin during the ith subphase. (The total number of commutes started by CA and not completed during the phase is at most $2g$, since there are only $2g$ distinct commute pairs in the matchings $M_1, \ldots M_g$. Recall that there is only one swap between subphases.) Then the number of faults incurred by CA during this phase is

$$O(g + \sum_{1\leq i\leq g} \sum_{1\leq j\leq i} m_{ij}).$$

Consider any on-line algorithm A. At the beginning of the kth j-commute during the ith subphase, we associate to (u_j, v_j) a vertex $v_{i,j,k} \in V_i$. The vertices $v_{i,j,k}$ will have two properties:

- If the kth j-commute begins at time t during an ith subphase, then A has a hole on $v_{i,j,k}$ at time t. Moreover, if $v_{i,j,k}$ equals u_l or v_l, for some $l \neq j$, then at time t A has holes on *both* u_l and v_l.
- Consider a j-commute that starts at time t (with associated $v_{i,j,k}$). Then for any l-commute in progress at time t (with associated $v_{i',l,k'}$), either the vertex $v_{i,j,k}$ is different from the vertex $v_{i',l,k'}$, or A has a fault on u_l or v_l during this l-commute or the next one.

If such an assignment of vertices can be found, then the proof of the theorem can be completed as follows: Let X_{ijk} be an indicator random variable which is 1 if v_{ijk} is requested during the kth j-commute starting in subphase i and 0 otherwise. We claim that the expected number of faults incurred by A in the phase is at least

$$\Omega\left(g + \sum_{1\leq i\leq g} \sum_{1\leq j\leq i} \sum_{1\leq k\leq m_{ij}} E(X_{ijk})\right). \quad (1)$$

Indeed, if v_{ijk} is requested during this j-commute, then by condition 1 on v_{ijk}, A incurs a fault. Therefore, every j-commute completed by CA will be charged to the potential corresponding fault on v_{ijk}. Condition 2 guarantees that we don't charge more than a constant number of commutes of CA to the same fault incurred by A.

Since the pairs (u_j, v_j) are good, the properties of v_{ijk} and an application of Lemma 13 imply that

$$E(X_{ijk}) \geq \frac{1}{50}. \quad (2)$$

It is well known [6] that any algorithm (even off-line) incurs an amortized cost of $\Omega(g)$ in the phase. Hence combining equations (1) and (2), we have that the expected number of faults incurred by A in the phase is

$$\Omega(g + \sum_{1\leq i\leq g} \sum_{1\leq j\leq i} m_{ij}),$$

completing the proof of the lemma.

We have left to show that the assignment v_{ijk} satisfying conditions 1 and 2 above can be done. During the ith subphase of a phase, A must have i holes in the set V_i. We maintain a one-to-one correspondence between these holes and the pairs (u_j, v_j), $1 \leq j \leq i$, so that at the beginning of a j-commute in the ith subphase there is some A-hole associated to that commute. If at such a time, the A-hole is outside V_{M_i}, the invariants continue to hold. Otherwise, we switch the correspondence between holes and pairs (keeping it one-to-one) so that the A-hole associated to the j-commute is on some (u_m, v_m) pair that are both not in A's fast memory. The changes to this correspondence ensure that A has a hole on any pair that gets reassigned in the middle of a commute. The remaining details are omitted. □

Two comments are in order:

1. The complexity of computing the commute times in a Markov chain is polynomial in n. Therefore, with an initial preprocessing step that constructs the matrix of commute times, the complexity of running the algorithm CA is $O(k)$ per fault.

2. It is not difficult to show that the expected page fault rate of CA is at most H_k times the expected page fault rate of the optimal *off-line* algorithm (that has access to the request string output by the Markov chain, and serves it optimally). This is the best possible: for independent, uniformly distributed page reqeusts any on-line algorithm has fault rate $\Omega(H_k)$ times that of an optimal off-line algorithm [6].

References

[1] S. Ben-David, A. Borodin, R.M. Karp, G. Tardos, and A. Wigderson. On the power of randomization in on-line algorithms. In *Proc. 22nd Annual ACM Symposium on Theory of Computing*, pages 379–388, 1990.

[2] A. Borodin, S. Irani, P. Raghavan, and B. Schieber. Competitive paging with locality of reference. In *Twenty-Third Annual ACM Symposium on Theory of Computing*, pages 249–259, 1991.

[3] D. Cheriton and K. Harty. Application-controlled physical memory using external page-cache management. Technical report, Department of Computer Science, Stanford University, 1991.

[4] P.J. Denning. Working Sets Past and Present. In *IEEE Trans. Software Eng.* SE-6:64-84, 1980.

[5] C. Derman. *Finite State Markov Decision Processes.* Academic Press, New York, 1970.

[6] A. Fiat, R. Karp, M. Luby, L. McGeoch, D. Sleator, and N. Young. On competitive algorithms for paging problems. To appear in *Journal of Algorithms*, 1990.

[7] P.A. Franaszek and T.J. Wagner. Some distribution-free aspects of paging performance. *Journal of the ACM*, 21:31–39, 1974.

[8] S.S. Irani, A.R. Karlin, and S.J. Phillips. Further results on paging with locality of reference. In *Third Annual ACM-SIAM Symposium on Discrete Algorithms*, 1992.

[9] A. R. Karlin, M. S. Manasse, L. Rudolph, and D.D. Sleator. Competitive snoopy caching. *Algorithmica*, 3(1):70–119, 1988.

[10] R.M. Karp. A characterization of the minimum cycle mean in a digraph. *Discrete Mathematics*, 23:309–311, 1978.

[11] P.A.W. Lewis and G.S. Shedler. Empirically derived models for sequences of page exceptions. *IBM J. Res. and Develop.*, 17:86–100, 1973.

[12] D. McNamee and K. Armstrong. Extending the mach external pager interface to accommodate user-level page replacement policies. Technical Report 90-09-05, Department of Computer Science and Engineering, University of Washington, 1990.

[13] P. Raghavan and M. Snir. Memory versus randomization in on-line algorithms. In *16th International Colloquium on Automata, Languages, and Programming*, volume 372 of *Lecture Notes in Computer Science*, pages 687–703. Springer-Verlag, July 1989. Revised version available as IBM Research Report RC15840, June 1990.

[14] G.S. Shedler and C. Tung. Locality in page reference strings. *SIAM Journal on Computing*, 1:218–241, 1972.

[15] D.D. Sleator and R.E. Tarjan. Amortized efficiency of list update and paging rules. *Communications of the ACM*, 28:202–208, February 1985.

[16] J.R. Spirn *Program Behavior: Models and Measurements* Elsevier Computer Science Library. Elsevier, Amsterdam. 1977.

[17] J.S. Vitter and P. Krishnan. Optimal Prefetching via Data Compression In *Thirty-Second Annual IEEE Symposium on Foundations of Computer Science*, 1991.

On-line Load Balancing

(Extended abstract)

Yossi Azar * Andrei Z. Broder* Anna R. Karlin*

Abstract

The setup for our problem consists of n servers that must complete a set of tasks. Each task can be handled only by a *subset* of the servers, requires a different level of service, and once assigned can not be re-assigned. We make the natural assumption that the level of service is known at arrival time, but that the duration of service is not. The on-line load balancing problem is to assign each task to an appropriate server in such a way that the maximum load on the servers is minimized. In this paper we derive matching upper and lower bounds for the competitive ratio of the on-line greedy algorithm for this problem, namely $\frac{(3n)^{2/3}}{2}(1+o(1))$, and derive a lower bound, $\Omega(\sqrt{n})$, for any other deterministic or randomized on-line algorithm.

1 Introduction

Consider an idealized local area network that links multi-media workstations, computers, I/O devices, etc. Each device is directly connected to one or more gateways (bridges) to the net. Communication tasks arrive and disappear at arbitrary times. Upon arrival, each task requests a certain guaranteed bandwidth (e.g. low for file transfers, medium for graphic applications, high for video) and must be assigned to one of the gateways directly connected to the device, for the duration of the task. Service must begin immediately. The problem is to assign each task in such a way that no bridge is overloaded.

The above is an example of the following general problem. Consider n servers that must complete a set of tasks. Each task can be handled only by a *subset* of the servers, and requires a different level of service, called the *weight* of the task. Tasks arrive and depart one by one. Service must start as soon as the task arrives. A task once assigned can not be re-assigned. At assignment time only the weight is known, but not the duration of service. The on-line load balancing problem is to assign each task to an appropriate server in such a way that the maximum load on the servers is minimized.

As usual nowadays, we evaluate the performance of the on-line algorithm by its competitive ratio, which is the ratio between its maximum load and the maximum load of the optimal off-line algorithm for the worst case sequence of tasks.

Previous analyses (e.g. [1, 2, 3, 8]) were restricted to models where either the tasks continued forever, not a realistic assumption, or where the tasks can be delayed for arbitrarily long periods of time, thus forsaking real-time service.

If the arrival and departure times are known in advance, the servers are called machines, and the tasks are called jobs, the question becomes an instance of the well known class of static load balancing problems, studied in a myriad of variants. (See [5] and references therein.)

Azar, Naor, and Rom [1] studied this question for the case when tasks start at arbitrary times but continue forever. We call such tasks *perma-*

*DEC Systems Research Center, 130 Lytton Avenue, Palo-Alto, CA 94301.
E-mail: `azar@src.dec.com`, `broder@src.dec.com`, and `karlin@src.dec.com`.

0-8186-2900-2/92 $3.00 © 1992 IEEE

nent and the tasks that begin and end, *temporary*. Azar *et al.* showed that the competitive ratio of the greedy algorithm for permanent tasks is precisely $\log n$ and that no algorithm can do better. This is in contrast to Graham's result [4] who showed that when every (permanent) task can be assigned to any server, (we call such tasks *unrestricted*) the greedy algorithm achieves a competitive ratio of $2 - \frac{1}{n}$. (There is a very recent improvement due to Bartal *et al.* [2] to $2 - \epsilon$, using a more complicated algorithm.) In fact, it is straightforward to check that Graham's analysis of the greedy algorithm extends to temporary tasks and that the competitive ratio is still $2 - \frac{1}{n}$.

Although the analysis of [1] does not generalize to temporary tasks, it is natural to ask whether the $\log n$ competitive ratio holds for restricted temporary tasks, the way the $2 - \frac{1}{n}$ competitive ratio holds for unrestricted tasks, both permanent and temporary.

We answer this question negatively. More precisely we obtain matching upper and lower bounds that show that the competitive ratio of the greedy algorithm for restricted temporary tasks is a surprisingly high $\frac{(3n)^{2/3}}{2}(1 + o(1))$. (The function implied by $o(1)$ is different for the upper and lower, but the leading term is exactly the same!) Moreover, we show a lower bound of $\Omega(\sqrt{n})$ for any deterministic or randomized algorithm.

A variation on the model described so far is when the weight of a task can be split among its allowed servers. For this case we show that the competitive ratio for the natural, "water-level," algorithm is also $\Theta(n^{2/3})$, and for any other algorithm (deterministic or randomized) the lower bound is again $\Omega(\sqrt{n})$.

Our problems can be recast in the dynamic graph framework. Previous results on on-line algorithms for dynamic graphs (e.g. graph coloring [7, 9], on-line matching [6]) allowed only vertex additions. Our results pertain to the more challenging fully dynamic case, where arbitrarily long sequences of vertex additions and deletions are allowed. However since the tasks-on-servers framework is more natural, this is the one we adopt here.

1.1 Formal definition of the problem

Let M be a set of servers (machines) that is to run a set of tasks that arrive and depart in time. Each task j has associated to it a weight (load) $w(j) \geq 0$, an arrival time $\tau(j)$, and a set $M(j) \subset M$ of servers capable of running it.

As soon as it arrives, each task must be assigned to exactly one of the servers capable of running it, and once assigned, it can not be transferred to a different server. The assigned server starts to run the task immediately, and continues to run it until the task departs.

When task j arrives, an *assignment algorithm* must select a server $i \in M(j)$, and assign task j to it.

The *load* on server i at time t, denoted $L_i(t)$, is the sum of the weights of all the tasks running on server i at time t.

Let σ be a sequence of task arrivals and departures, and let $|\sigma|$ be the time of the last arrival. Then the cost, $C_A(\sigma)$, of an assignment algorithm A on the sequence σ, is defined as

$$C_A(\sigma) = \max_{0 \leq t \leq |\sigma|;\ i \in M} L_i(t).$$

An *on-line assignment algorithm* must assign an arriving task j at time $\tau(j)$ to a server in $M(j)$ knowing only $w(j)$, $M(j)$, the current state of the servers, and the past – the decision is made without any knowledge about future arrivals or departures. An *optimal off-line assignment algorithm*, denoted OPT, assigns arriving tasks knowing the entire sequence of task arrivals and departures and does so in a way that minimizes its cost.[1]

The competitive ratio of an on-line algorithm A is defined as the supremum over sequences σ of $C_A(\sigma)/C_{\mathrm{OPT}}(\sigma)$.

In this paper, our goal is to find on-line assignment algorithms with minimum competitive ratio.

[1]Complexity buffs know that to compute the optimal solution in the off-line case is NP-complete even when all the tasks are permanent and unrestricted

1.2 Notation

Before plunging into proofs, we summarize the notations we already used, or plan to use soon.

- M is the set of all servers (machines). $|M| = n$.
- Task (job) j has a weight $w(j)$, an arrival time $\tau(j)$, and a set $M(j) \subset M$ of servers capable of running it.
- $T_i(t)$ is the set of tasks run (by the on-line algorithm under consideration) on server i at time t, and $T(t) = \bigcup_{1 \le i \le n} T_i(t)$.
- $L_i(t)$ is the load on server i at time t, that is $L_i(t) = \sum_{j \in T_i(t)} w(j)$.
- $m(j) \in M(j)$ is the server on which OPT (the optimum off-line algorithm) runs task j. Thus, for $S \subset M$, $m^{-1}(S)$ is the set of tasks assigned by OPT to servers in S.
- $T_i^S(t)$, for $i \in M$ and $S \subset M$, is defined as $T_i(t) \setminus m^{-1}(S)$, that is $T_i^S(t)$ is the set of tasks being run on server i except for those tasks being run by OPT on servers in S.
- $L_i^S(t) = \sum_{j \in T_i^S(t)} w(j)$.

2 Upper Bounds

The greedy algorithm is formally defined as follows:

Algorithm GREEDY: Upon arrival of a task j assign it to the server in $M(j)$ with the current minimum load (ties are broken arbitrarily).

Lemma 1 *Consider an execution of the algorithm* GREEDY. *Suppose that the optimal off-line cost is l. If there is a server (without loss of generality, server 1), and a time t such that $L_1(t) = m$, then there exists a time $t_k \le t$, and a set of k servers S (without loss of generality, $S = \{1, 2, \ldots k\}$) such that*

$$\begin{aligned}
L_1^S(t_k) &\ge m - (1+k)l \\
L_2^S(t_k) &\ge m - ((1+2)+k)l \\
L_3^S(t_k) &\ge m - ((1+2+3)+k)l \\
&\vdots \\
L_k^S(t_k) &\ge m - \left(\binom{k+1}{2} + k\right) l
\end{aligned}$$

Proof: The proof is by induction on k. The base case is trivial: Take $t_1 = t$. Since $S = \{1\}$, $L_1^S(t) \ge m - l$. (The total load that may be excluded is the load that OPT has on server 1, which is at most l).

For the induction step, assume that the hypothesis holds for k. Without loss of generality assume that $S = \{1, 2, \ldots k\}$. Consider the set of tasks $T = \bigcup_{i \in S} T_i^S(t_k)$. Let $t_{k+1} = max_{j \in T}\, \tau(j)$. Let $j^* \in T$ be the task that started at time t_{k+1}. Note that the servers in S may work at time t_{k+1} on tasks that are no longer present at time t_k, but that all the tasks in T are present at time t_{k+1}.

By definition of T_i^S, the server $m(j^*) \notin S$. Without loss of generality, assume that $m(j^*) = k+1$. Therefore, at time t_{k+1}, GREEDY could have placed task j^* on server $m(j^*)$, but did not. Hence,

$$\begin{aligned}
L_{k+1}(t_{k+1}) &\ge min_{1 \le i \le k}(L_i^S(t_k)) - w(j^*) \\
&\ge m - \left(\binom{k+1}{2} + k\right) l - w(j^*) \\
&\ge m - \binom{k+2}{2} l,
\end{aligned}$$

since $w(j^*) \le l$. Similarly for any set of servers S, we have $\sum_{j \in m^{-1}(S)} w(j) \le |S| \cdot l$, thus

$$L_{k+1}^{S \cup \{k+1\}}(t_{k+1}) \ge m - \binom{k+2}{2} l - (k+1)l.$$

Finally, for $1 \le i \le k$,

$$\begin{aligned}
L_i^{S \cup \{k+1\}}(t_{k+1}) &\ge L_i^S(t_k) - l \\
&\ge m - \left(\binom{i+1}{2} + (k+1)\right) l,
\end{aligned}$$

since every task in $T_i(t_k)$ contributes to $T_i(t_{k+1})$ with the possible exception of j^*. □

Theorem 2 *For any sequence σ of task arrivals and departures the greedy on-line assignment algorithm is $\frac{(3n)^{2/3}}{2}(1+o(1))$ competitive.*

Proof: By Lemma 1, if the maximum load GREEDY ever has on some server is m and the optimal off-line algorithm reaches a maximum load of l, then there is a time when the sum of the loads on all the servers is at least

$$km - \left(k^2 + \sum_{1\le i\le k} \binom{i+1}{2}\right) l,$$

for any k such that $\left(\binom{k+1}{2}+k\right) l < m$. But by hypothesis, the sum of all loads is at most $n \cdot l$. A judicious choice for k (e.g. $k = \sqrt{2m/l} - 2$) completes the proof. □

3 Lower bounds

3.1 Lower bound for the greedy algorithm

Theorem 3 *The competitive ratio of the greedy on-line assignment algorithm is at least*

$$\frac{(3n)^{2/3}}{2}(1+o(1))$$

Proof: We assume that all tasks have integer weight one, and allow GREEDY to break ties in any deterministic way.

Let $S(t) = (S_1(t), S_2(t), \ldots, S_n(t))$ be the sorted (non-increasing) n-tuple of the loads that GREEDY has on servers at time t, and let $s_i(t)$ be the server whose load is $S_i(t)$. Write $S(t) > S(t')$ if the tuple $S(t)$ is lexicographically greater than $S(t')$.

We prove the lower bound by showing that there is a finite sequence of requests σ for which the following three conditions hold:

1. For all j such that $S_j(|\sigma|) > 0$, $S_{j-1}(|\sigma|) - S_j(|\sigma|) \ge j - 1$.

2. There are n tasks running at time $|\sigma|$.

3. The maximum off-line load at all times t, $0 \le t \le |\sigma|$, is 1.

If such a sequence σ can be found, the theorem follows, since at $|\sigma|$ GREEDY's maximum load m must satisfy

$$m + (m-1) + (m-(1+2)) + \cdots + (m-(1+2+\ldots+(q-1))) \ge n,$$

where q is the number of busy servers at time t and $\binom{q}{2} < m$. Thus,

$$m \ge \frac{(3n)^{2/3}}{2}(1+o(1)),$$

and the competitive ratio is at least $\frac{(3n)^{2/3}}{2}(1+o(1))$.

We build the sequence σ via a two step process. First we suppose that we can construct a sequence of requests ρ such that at time $|\rho|$ the following properties are satisfied:

1. The number of active tasks at time $|\rho|$, $|T(|\rho|)|$, is n.

2. At every time t, $0 \le t \le |\rho|$, every server in the optimal off-line assignment has load at most 1.

3. If at time $|\rho|$ GREEDY uses server i at all (that is, $L_i(|\rho|) > 0$) then GREEDY runs on i the task that OPT runs on i, for the simple reason that it can not be run anywhere else. (Symbolically, $M(m^{-1}(i)) = \{i\}$.)

The following sequence ρ of n requests satisfies these conditions: for each server $i \in M$, a new task v_i arrives, with $M(v_i) = \{i\}$. Clearly, both GREEDY and OPT must assign v_i to server i. Properties 1 to 3 are trivially satisfied at time $|\rho|$.

The second step is to show that any sequence ρ satisfying these three properties either has the property

P1: For all j, such that $S_j(|\rho|) > 0$,

$$S_{j-1}(|\rho|) - S_j(|\rho|) \geq j - 1,$$

or it can be extended by a subsequence ρ' such that at time $|\rho\rho'|$, properties 1 to 3 are satisfied, and $S(|\rho\rho'|) > S(|\rho|)$.

Indeed, assume that we have constructed a sequence ρ that satisfies properties 1 to 3. If it satisfies property **P1** we stop and set $\sigma = \rho$. If not, then we can extend the sequence ρ with the following subsequence ρ'.

Let $j \geq 2$ be the smallest value for which $S_j(|\rho|) > 0$ and $S_{j-1}(|\rho|) - S_j(|\rho|) = d \leq j - 2$. Let $M' = \{s_1(|\rho|), \ldots, s_j(|\rho|)\}$.

The sequence ρ' is constructed as follows:

1. For $1 \leq i \leq d$, task $m^{-1}(s_i)$ departs. This results in a decrease in the load on each of the servers $s_1, \ldots, s_d$ by 1.
2. Tasks $m^{-1}(s_j)$ and $m^{-1}(s_{j-1})$ depart.
3. For $1 \leq i \leq d$, a new task c_i with $M(c_i) = M'$ arrives. GREEDY assigns all of these tasks to s_j, since it is the least loaded of the servers in M'. The result is that $L_{j-1} = L_j$. (OPT assigns c_i to s_i.)
4. Two additional tasks c_a and c_b arrive with $M(c_a) = M(c_b) = \{s_j, s_{j-1}\}$. GREEDY assigns one of them, say c_a, to s_{j-1}, and the other to s_j. (OPT assigns c_a to s_j and c_b to s_{j-1}, that is, the opposite of GREEDY.)
5. Tasks c_i, $1 \leq i \leq d$ depart, and then arrive again renamed c'_i, this time with $M(c'_i) = \{s_i\}$, and task c_b departs and then arrives again, this time renamed c'_b with $M(c'_b) = s_{j-1}$.
6. Each task h running on server s_j departs and then arrives again, renamed h', this time with $M(h') = m(h)$.

It is straightforward to check that properties 1 to 3 hold at time $|\rho\rho'|$, and that $S(|\rho\rho'|) > S(|\rho|)$.

Finally, we note that after a finite number of extensions of the sequence, property **P1** will hold because each extension increases the lexicographic value of the state $S(|\rho|)$, which can take only a finite number of different values since it consists of n non-negative integers whose sum is n. □

Remark: The proof can be modified to handle the situation when GREEDY breaks the ties at random.

3.2 The General Lower Bound

Theorem 4 *The competitive ratio of any randomized on-line assignment algorithm is at least* $\Omega(\sqrt{n})$.

Proof: We follow the outline of the proof of Theorem 3. As before, assume that all tasks have integer weight one. Let A be any randomized on-line algorithm.

In the proof below, we will use the notion of an *adjusted load* $L'_i(t)$. The adjusted loads will always have the following properties:

- Each task j contributes to the adjusted load of exactly one server in $M(j)$, say k, and the value of j's contribution to $L'_k(t)$ is p_k, the probability that A assigns task j to server k. If $|M(j)| > 1$ the choice of $k \in M(j)$ depends on the randomized algorithm A but not on the outcome of its coin flips. Notice that if $|M(j)| = 1$, task j always contributes exactly 1 to its server.
- The sequence of requests generated by the adversary for the lower bound will ensure that task j contributes to server k's adjusted load only if $p_k \geq 1/3$. Therefore, if r tasks are running at time t, then $\sum_{i \in M} L'_i(t) \geq r/3$.

The first property implies that

- $L'_i(t)$ is a lower bound on the expected load on server i at time t, i.e. $L'_i(t) \leq E(L_i(t))$.

Let $S'(t) = (S'_1(t), S'_2(t), \ldots, S'_n(t))$ to be the sorted (non-increasing) n-tuple of adjusted loads that A has at time t. Define a partial order on

S' as follows: $S'(t) > S'(t')$ if there is a j such that for all $1 \leq i < j$, $S'_i(t) \geq S'_i(t')$, and $S'_j(t) - S'_j(t') \geq 1/3$.

We prove the lower bound by showing that there is a sequence of requests σ, and a way to define the adjusted loads L' so that the following three conditions hold:

1. For all j such that $S'_j(|\sigma|) > 0$, $S'_{j-1}(|\sigma|) - S'_j(|\sigma|) \geq 1/3$.

2. There are n tasks running at time $|\sigma|$. Therefore, $\sum_{i \in M} L'_i(|\sigma|) \geq n/3$.

3. The maximum off-line load at all times is at most 1.

If such a σ can be found, the theorem follows, since at time $|\sigma|$, A's maximum adjusted load m (and hence expected maximum load) must satisfy

$$m + (m - 1/3) + (m - 2/3) + \cdots \\ +(m - (q-1)/3) \geq \sum_{i \in M} l'_i(|\sigma|) \geq n/3,$$

where $q < 3m + 1$ is the number of non-zero adjusted loaded servers at time $|\sigma|$. Hence,

$$m \geq \frac{(2n)^{1/2}}{3}(1 + o(1))$$

and the competitive ratio is at least $\frac{(2n)^{1/2}}{3}(1 + o(1))$.

We build the sequence σ via a two step process. First we suppose that we can construct a sequence of requests ρ, and define the adjusted loads L' such that at time $|\rho|$ the following properties are satisfied:

1. The number of active tasks, $|T(|\rho|)|$, is n. Thus, $\sum_{i \in M} L'_i(|\rho|) \leq n$.

2. For any t, $0 \leq t \leq |\rho|$, every server in the optimal off-line assignment has a load of at most 1.

3. For any server i with $L'_i(|\rho|) > 0$, the algorithm A runs on i the task that OPT runs on i, for the simple reason that it can not be run anywhere else. (Symbolically, $M(m^{-1}(i)) = \{i\}$.) Therefore, this task contributes precisely 1 to i's adjusted load. We conclude that if $L'_i(|\rho|) > 0$, then $L'_i(|\rho|) \geq 1$.

The following sequence ρ of n requests satisfies these conditions: for each server $i \in M$, a new task v_i arrives, with $M(v_i) = \{i\}$. Clearly, both A and OPT must assign v_i to server i. Since we must have $L'_i(|\rho|) = 1$ for all $i \in M$, we observe that Properties 1 to 3 are trivially satisfied.

The second step is to show that any sequence ρ satisfying these three properties either has the property

P2: For all j such that $S'_j|\rho| > 0$,

$$S'_{j-1}|\rho| - S'_j|\rho| \geq 1/3,$$

or it can be extended by a subsequence ρ' such that at time $|\rho\rho'|$, properties 1 to 3 are satisfied, $S'(|\rho\rho'|) > S'(|\rho|)$.

Indeed, assume that we have constructed a sequence ρ that satisfies properties 1 to 3. If it satisfies property **P2** we stop and set $\sigma = \rho$. If not, then we can extend the sequence ρ with the following subsequence ρ'.

1. Let a and b be two distinct servers such that $1/3 > L'_a - L'_b \geq 0$ and $L'_b > 0$. Tasks $m^{-1}(a)$ and $m^{-1}(b)$ depart. By the third property, this results in a decrease in L'_a and L'_b by 1.

2. A new task j with $M(j) = \{a, b\}$ arrives. Let p_a (resp. p_b) be the probability that A assigns j to a (resp. to b). Clearly $p_a + p_b = 1$.

3. The rest of ρ' depends on the value of p_a.

   - $p_a \geq 1/3$: OPT assigns j to b. Task j contributes p_a to the adjusted load on a, and nothing to the adjusted load on b. A new task k with $M(j) = a$ arrives. All tasks T contributing to the adjusted load on b depart and then arrive again, this time with $M(v) = m(v)$ ($v \in T$).

- $p_a < 1/3$: OPT assigns j to a. Task j contributes p_b to the adjusted load on b, and nothing to the adjusted load on a. A new task k with $M(j) = b$ arrives. All tasks T contributing to the adjusted load on a depart and then arrive again, this time with $M(v) = m(v)$ $(v \in T)$.

It is straightforward to verify that properties 1 to 3 hold at time $|\rho\rho'|$.

Lastly, we show that $S'(\rho\rho') > S'(\rho)$: In case 3(a), the subsequence of adjusted loads that changed involved replacing the subsequence $(L_a(|\rho|), L_b(|\rho|), 0, 0, \ldots, 0, 0)$ by $(L_a(|\rho|) + p_a, 0, 1, 1, \ldots, 1, 1)$, where $L_a(|\rho|) \geq 1$ and $p_a \geq 1/3$. In case 3(b), the subsequence of adjusted loads that were changed involved replacing $(L_a(|\rho|), L_b(|\rho|), 0, 0, \ldots, 0, 0)$ by the subsequence $(L_b(|\rho|) + p_b, 0, 1, 1, \ldots, 1, 1)$, where $p_b \geq 2/3$ and since $(L_a(|\rho|) - (L_b(|\rho|) < 1/3$, $L_b(|\rho|) + p_b \geq L_a(|\rho|) + 1/3$. (The 0's and 1's in these vectors correspond to servers running tasks in T.)

Finally, note that after a finite number of extensions of the sequence ρ, property **P2** will hold since the number of extensions is bounded by the length of the maximum chain in the partial order on S', which is finite. □

For a general deterministic algorithm, we can simplify this proof and obtain a lower bound of $\lfloor\sqrt{2n}\rfloor$.

4 Split assignments

In this section we consider a variant of the load balancing problem where the weight of an incoming task can be split among its allowed servers. The weights can be split into arbitrary positive real portions, and once assigned can not be reassigned.

Algorithm WATER-LEVEL: Upon arrival of a task j split its weight among the servers in $M(j)$ such that $\min_{i \in M(j)} L_i$ is maximized.

The algorithm is called "water level" since it equally raises the load on the least loaded servers in $M(j)$. Azar, Naor, and Rom[1], showed that for permanent tasks its competitive ratio is $O(\log n)$ and this is tight. In the general case we show:

Theorem 5 *The competitive ratio of the* WATER-LEVEL *algorithm for the split assignment problem is* $\Theta(n^{2/3})$, *and any other deterministic or randomized on-line algorithm for this problem has competitive ratio* $\Omega(\sqrt{n})$.

Proof: Omitted. □

References

[1] Y. Azar, J. Naor and R. Rom, "The competitiveness of on-line assignment," *Proceedings of the 3rd Annual ACM-SIAM SODA*, 1992, pp. 203-210.

[2] Y. Bartal, A. Fiat, H. Karloff and R. Vohra "New algorithms for an Ancient Scheduling Problem," in *Proceedings of the 24th Annual ACM Symposium on Theory of Computing*, 1992.

[3] S. Baruah, G. Koren, B. Mishra, A. Raghunthan, L. Rosier, and D. Shasta, "Online Scheduling in the Presence of Overload," *Proceedings of the 32nd IEEE Symposium on Foundations of Computer Science*, 1991, pp. 100-110.

[4] R. L. Graham, "Bounds for certain multiprocessing anomalies," *Bell System Technical Journal* 45 (1966), pp. 1563-1581.

[5] R. L. Graham, E.L. Lawler, J.K Lenstra, and A.H.G. Rinnooy Kan, "Optimization and approximation in deterministic sequencing and scheduling: a survey," *Annals of Discrete Mathematics* 5 (1979), pp. 287-326.

[6] R. Karp, U. Vazirani, and V. Vazirani, "An optimal algorithm for on-line bipartite matching," *Proceedings of the 22nd Annual ACM Symposium on Theory of Computing, Baltimore, Maryland*, 1990, pp. 352–358.

[7] L. Lovász, M. Saks, and W. Trotter, "An on-line graph coloring algorithm with sublinear performance ratio," *Discrete Math* 75 (1989), pp. 319–325.

[8] D. Shmoys, J. Wein and D. P. Williamson, "Scheduling Parallel Machines On-line," *Proceedings of the 32nd IEEE Symposium on Foundations of Computer Science*, 1991, pp. 131-140.

[9] S. Vishwanathan, "Randomized on-line graph coloring," *Proceedings of the 31st Annual Symposium on Foundations of Computer Science*, 1990, pp. 464–469.

Improved Lower Bounds for Shellsort

C. Greg Plaxton [1,2] Bjorn Poonen [3] Torsten Suel [1,4]

Abstract

We give improved lower bounds for Shellsort based on a new and relatively simple proof idea. The lower bounds obtained are both stronger and more general than the previously known bounds. In particular, they hold for nonmonotone increment sequences and adaptive Shellsort algorithms, as well as for some recently proposed variations of Shellsort.

1 Introduction

Shellsort is a classical sorting algorithm introduced by Shell in 1959 [15]. The algorithm is based on a sequence $H = h_0, \ldots, h_{m-1}$ of positive integers called an *increment sequence.* An input file $A = A[0], \ldots, A[n-1]$ of elements is sorted by performing an h_j-sort for every increment h_j in H, starting with h_{m-1} and going down to h_0. Every h_j-sort partitions the positions of the input array into congruence classes modulo h_j, and then performs Insertion Sort on each of these classes. It is not difficult to see that at least one of the h_j's must be equal to 1 in order for the algorithm to sort all input files properly. Furthermore, once some increment equal to 1 has been processed, the file will certainly be sorted. Hence, we may assume without loss of generality that $h_0 = 1$ and $h_j > 1$ for all $j > 0$.

The running time of Shellsort varies heavily depending on the choice of the increment sequence H. Most practical Shellsort algorithms set H to the prefix of a single, monotonically increasing infinite sequence of integers, using only the increments that are less than n. Shellsort algorithms based on such increment sequences are called *uniform.* In a *nonuniform* Shellsort algorithm, H may depend on the input size n in an arbitrary fashion.

A general analysis of the running time of Shellsort is difficult because of the vast number of possible increment sequences, each of which can lead to a different running time and behavior of the resulting algorithm. Consequently, many important questions concerning general upper and lower bounds for Shellsort have remained open, in spite of a number of attempts to solve them. Apart from pure mathematical curiosity, the interest in Shellsort is motivated by the good performance of many of the known increment sequences. The algorithm is very easy to implement and outperforms most other sorting methods on small or nearly sorted input files. Moreover, Shellsort is an in-place sorting algorithm, so it is very space-efficient.

1.1 Previous Results on Shellsort

The original algorithm proposed by Shell was based on the increment sequence given by $h_{m-1} = \lfloor n/2 \rfloor$, $h_{m-2} = \lfloor n/4 \rfloor, \ldots, h_0 = 1$. However, this choice of H leads to a worst case running time of $\Theta(n^2)$ if n is a power of 2. Subsequently, several authors proposed modifications to Shell's original sequence [9, 5, 8] in the hope of obtaining a better running time. Papernov and Stasevich [10] showed that the sequence of Hibbard [5], consisting of the increments of the form $2^k - 1$, achieves a running time of $O(n^{3/2})$. A common feature of all of these sequences is that they are *nearly geometric*, meaning that they approximate a geometric sequence within an additive constant.

An exception is the sequence designed by Pratt [13], which consists of all increments of the form $2^i 3^j$. This sequence gives a running time of $O(n \lg^2 n)$, which still represents the best asymptotic bound known for any increment sequence. In practice, the sequence is not popular because it has length $\Theta(\lg^2 n)$; implementations of Shellsort tend to use $O(\lg n)$-length increment sequences because these result in better running times for files of moderate size [6]. In addition, there is no hope of getting an $O(n \lg n)$-time algorithm based on a sequence of length $\omega(\lg n)$.

Pratt [13] also showed an $\Omega(n^{3/2})$ lower bound for all nearly geometric sequences. Partly due to this result, it was conjectured for quite a while that $\Theta(n^{3/2})$ is the best worst-case running time achievable by increment sequences of length $O(\lg n)$. However, in 1982,

---

[1] Department of Computer Sciences, University of Texas at Austin.

[2] Supported by Texas Advanced Research Program (TARP) Award #003658480, and NSF Research Initiation Award CCR-9111591.

[3] Department of Mathematics, University of California at Berkeley. Supported by an ONR Fellowship.

[4] Supported by an MCD Fellowship of the University of Texas at Austin.

0-8186-2900-2/92 $3.00 © 1992 IEEE

Sedgewick [14] improved this upper bound to $O(n^{4/3})$, using an approximation of a geometric sequence that is not nearly geometric in the above sense. Subsequently, Incerpi and Sedgewick [6] designed a family of $O(\lg n)$-length increment sequences with running times $O(n^{1+\epsilon/\sqrt{\lg n}})$, for all $\epsilon > 0$. Chazelle achieves a similar running time with a class of nonuniform sequences [6]; his construction is based on a generalization of Pratt's sequence.

The sequences proposed by Incerpi and Sedgewick are all within a constant factor of a geometric sequence, that is, they satisfy $h_j = \Theta(\alpha^j)$ for some constant $\alpha > 0$. Weiss [16, 18] showed that all sequences of this type take time $\Omega(n^{1+\epsilon/\sqrt{\lg n}})$, but his proof assumed an as yet unproven conjecture on the number of inversions in the Frobenius pattern. Based on this so-called Inversion Conjecture, he also showed an $\Omega(n^{1+\epsilon/\sqrt{\lg n}})$ lower bound for the $O(\lg n)$-length increment sequences of Chazelle. The question of existence of Shellsort algorithms with running time $O(n \lg n)$ remained unresolved.

The two classes of increment sequences given by Incerpi and Sedgewick and by Chazelle are of particular interest because they not only establish an improved upper bound for sequences of length $O(\lg n)$, but also indicate an interesting trade-off between the running time and the length of an increment sequence. Specifically, using a construction described in [6], it is possible to achieve better asymptotic running times by allowing longer increment sequences.

Another goal in the study of Shellsort is the construction of sorting networks of small depth and size. The first construction of a sorting network based on Shellsort was given by Pratt [13], who describes a network of depth $\approx 0.6 \lg^2 n$ based on the increments $2^i 3^j$. Thus, his network came very close to the fastest known network at that time, due to Batcher [2], with depth $\approx 0.5 \lg^2 n$. In 1983, Ajtai, Komlós, and Szemerédi [1] designed a sorting network of depth $O(\lg n)$; however, their construction suffers from an irregular topology and a large constant hidden by the O-notation. This situation has motivated the search for $O(\lg n)$-depth sorting networks with simpler topologies or a smaller multiplicative constant. Shellsort has been considered a potential candidate for such a network due to the rich variety of possible increment sequences and the lack of nontrivial general lower bounds. The lower bounds of Pratt and Weiss also apply to network size, but they only hold for very restricted classes of increment sequences.

Cypher [3] has established an $\Omega(n \lg^2 n / \lg \lg n)$ lower bound for the size of Shellsort networks. However, his proof technique only works for *monotone* increment sequences, that is, sequences that are monotonically increasing. Though this captures a very general class of sequences, it does not rule out the possibility of an $O(\lg n)$-depth network based on some nonmonotone sequence.

1.2 Overview of the Paper

In this paper we will answer a number of open questions on worst-case lower bounds for Shellsort. In particular, we will prove a lower bound of $\Omega(n \lg^2 n/(\lg \lg n)^2)$ for the size of Shellsort networks, for arbitrary increment sequences. We also establish an identical lower bound for the running time of Shellsort algorithms, again for arbitrary increment sequences. Our lower bounds have the form of a trade-off between the running time of an algorithm and the length of the underlying increment sequence. This gives us lower bounds for increment sequences of length $O(\lg n)$ that come very close to the best known upper bounds. At the other end of the spectrum, the trade-off implies that no increment sequence can match Pratt's upper bound with significantly fewer increments. Finally, we define a class of algorithms called *Generalized Shellsort*, capturing a number of variations of Shellsort proposed in the literature, and show how to extend our results to this class.

Lower bounds very similar to those presented here were first obtained by Poonen [12]. His proof uses techniques from solid geometry and is quite intricate. More recently, Plaxton and Suel [11] independently discovered a simpler proof technique, which will be described in this paper. This new technique also leads to slight improvements in the bounds. The result by Poonen, on the other hand, is of independent interest, since it establishes a variant of the Inversion Conjecture of Weiss [18] using a new geometric approach to the Frobenius Problem. The simpler technique presented here is not based on a proof of the Inversion Conjecture. Instead, it shows how to "combine" Frobenius patterns to construct permutations with a large number of inversions. This result, together with the idea of dividing an increment sequence into "stages" (also called "intervals" in [12]), leads to the strong lower bounds of this paper.

Throughout this paper, we will limit our attention to increment sequences of length $O(\lg^2 n/(\lg \lg n)^2)$. Lower bounds for longer increment sequences are implied by the fact that Shellsort performs at least $\Omega(n)$ comparisons for every increment less than $n/2$. The results of this paper are presented in an "incremental" fashion, starting with a very basic argument for a restricted class of algorithms, and extending the lower bounds to more general classes in each of the subsequent sections.

The paper is organized as follows. Section 2 illustrates our proof technique by giving a simple and informal argument showing a lower bound for the depth of Shellsort networks. Section 3 introduces a number of definitions and simple lemmas, and then proceeds to give a formal proof of a stronger lower bound for the depth of Shellsort networks based on monotone increment sequences. We then show that this result implies a lower bound for network size, and conclude the section by extending the results to nonmonotone increment sequences. Section 4 further extends the applicability of our proof technique. First, we establish a lower bound on the running time of adaptive Shellsort algorithms based on arbitrary increment sequences. We then introduce a class of variations of Shellsort, called *Generalized Shellsort Algorithms*, and extend our lower bounds to this class. Section 5 contains a discussion of our results and a comparison with the best known upper bounds. Finally, Section 6 lists some open questions for future research.

2 The Basic Proof Idea

In this section we illustrate our proof idea by giving a very simple and informal argument showing a polylogarithmic lower bound for the depth of any Shellsort network based on a monotone increment sequence of length at most $c\lg^2 n/(\lg\lg n)^2$, for some small c. In the following sections, we will then formalize and extend this technique to obtain more general lower bounds.

Let H be a monotone increment sequence with $m \leq c\lg^2 n/(\lg\lg n)^2$ increments. We now divide the increment sequence H into a number of *stages* $S_0, \dots, S_{t-1}$. Every stage S_i is a set consisting of all increments h_j of H such that $n_i \geq h_j > n_{i+1}$, where $n_0, \dots, n_t$ are chosen appropriately. We define the n_i by $n_0 = n$ and $n_{i+1} = n_i/\lg^k n_i$, for $i \geq 0$ and some fixed integer k. In this informal argument, we will not be concerned about the integrality of the expressions obtained. Note that the n_i divide the increment sequence into at least $\frac{\lg n}{k\lg\lg n}$ disjoint stages. There are at least $s \stackrel{\text{def}}{=} \frac{\lg n}{2k\lg\lg n}$ disjoint stages consisting of increments $h_j \geq n^{1/2}$.

By averaging, one of these stages, say S_i, will contain at most $m/s \leq \frac{2ck\lg n}{\lg\lg n}$ increments. Now suppose there exists an input permutation A such that, after sorting A by all increments in stages S_0 to S_i, some element is still $\Omega(n_i)$ positions away from its final position in the sorted file. Since H is monotone, we know that from now on only comparisons over a distance of at most n_{i+1} positions will be performed. Hence, we can conclude that the element has to pass through at least $\Omega(n_i/n_{i+1}) = \Omega(\lg^k n)$ comparators in order to reach its final, correct position.

To complete the proof we have to show the existence of a permutation A such that some element is still "far out of place" after sorting A by all increments in S_0 to S_i. We will only give an informal argument at this point; a formal proof will be given in the next subsection. Consider all permutations of length n of the following form: Every element is in its correct, final position, except for the elements in a block of size n_i, ranging from some position a to position $a+n_i-1$ in the permutation. The elements in this block are allowed to be scrambled up in an arbitrary way. It is easy to see that a permutation of this form is already sorted by all increments greater than n_i, that is, all increments in stages S_0 to S_{i-1}. Hence, no exchanges will occur during these stages.

We now look at what happens in the block of size n_i during stage S_i. Note that no element outside the block will have an impact on the elements in the block. Thus, when we sort the permutation by some increment h_j with $n_i \geq h_j > n_{i+1}$, the new position of any element only depends on its previous position and on the elements in the at most $\frac{n_i}{h_j} \leq \lg^k n_i$ other positions in the block that are in its h_j-class. By our assumption, there are at most $m/s \leq \frac{2ck\lg n}{\lg\lg n}$ increments in stage S_i. Hence, the position of an element after stage S_i only depends on its position before the stage, which can be arbitrary, and on the elements in at most

$$\left(\lg^k n_i\right)^{m/s} \leq (\lg n_i)^{\frac{2ck^2\lg n}{\lg\lg n}}$$

other positions. If we choose c such that $4ck^2 < 1-\epsilon$, for some $\epsilon > 0$, then we get

$$\begin{aligned}(\lg n_i)^{\frac{2ck^2\lg n}{\lg\lg n}} &\leq 2^{2ck^2\lg n}\\ &\leq 2^{4ck^2\lg n_i}\\ &= o(n_i).\end{aligned}$$

This means that for large n, the position of an element in the block after sorting by all increments in S_i will only depend on the elements in $o(n_i)$ other positions in the block. If we assign the smallest elements in the block to these positions, then an element that is larger than these, but smaller than all other elements will end up in a position close to the largest elements after stage S_i. Hence, this element is $\Omega(n_i)$ positions away from its final position. All in all, we get the following result:

Theorem 2.1 Let H be a monotone increment sequence of length at most $c\lg^2 n/(\lg\lg n)^2$, and let k be such that $4ck^2 < 1-\epsilon$, for some $\epsilon > 0$. Then any sorting network based on H has depth $\Omega\left(\lg^k n\right)$.

The above argument is quite informal and does not make use of the full potential of our proof technique; it has mainly been given to illustrate the basic proof idea and to demonstrate its simplicity. The above result implies that we cannot hope to match the $O(\lg^2 n)$-depth upper bound of Pratt [13] with any increment sequence of fewer than $\frac{(1-\epsilon)\lg^2 n}{16(\lg\lg n)^2}$ increments, thus answering a question left open by Cypher's lower bound [3]. It also implies that we cannot achieve polylogarithmic depth with increment sequences of length $o(\lg^2 n/(\lg\lg n)^2)$.

By extending the argument we will be able to show much stronger lower bounds for shorter increment sequences. More precisely, we can get a trade-off between depth and increment sequence length by choosing appropriate values for the integers n_i that divide the increment sequence into stages. We can also extend the result to adaptive Shellsort algorithms by showing the existence of an input such that not just one, but "a large number" of elements are "far out of place" after the sparse stage S_i.

3 Lower Bounds for Networks

In this section, we will show general lower bounds for the depth and size of Shellsort sorting networks. We start off by giving a number of definitions and simple lemmas. We then show how to formalize and generalize the argument of Section 2 to obtain a trade-off between the depth of a Shellsort network and the length of the underlying increment sequence. Next, we explain how the results on network depth imply lower bounds on the size of Shellsort networks. We conclude this section by extending our results to nonmonotone increment sequences.

3.1 Definitions and Simple Lemmas

This section contains a number of basic definitions and associated lemmas. All of the lemmas are quite straightforward and so their proofs have been omitted.

We will use $\Pi(n)$ to denote the set of $n!$ permutations over $\{0,\ldots,n-1\}$. A 0-1 permutation of length n is an n-tuple over $\{0,1\}$. Thus $\{0,1\}^n$ denotes the set of 2^n 0-1 permutations.

Throughout this paper we will assume that the input files are drawn from $\Pi(n)$. We will use the letters A, B, and C to denote elements from $\Pi(n)$, and we will use X, Y, and Z to denote 0-1 permutations. We say that a file A is *h-sorted* if $A[i] \leq A[i+h]$, for $0 \leq i < n-h$. The following trivial lemma arises as a special case of the last definition.

Lemma 3.1 Every file of length n is h-sorted for any $h \geq n$.

In the following, let $H = h_0, \ldots, h_{m-1}$ be an increment sequence of length $m \geq 1$. Let $\min(H)$ denote the smallest increment in H. We say that a file is *H-sorted* if and only if it is h_i-sorted for all i such that $0 \leq i < m$.

Definition 3.1 Let *template*(H,n) denote the 0-1 permutation X obtained by setting $X[i]$ to 1 if and only if there exist nonnegative integers $a_0,\ldots,a_{m-1}$ such that

$$i = \sum_{0\leq j<m} a_j \cdot h_j.$$

Lemma 3.2 The 0-1 permutation *template*(H,n) is H-sorted.

Lemma 3.3 The number of 1's in the 0-1 permutation *template*(H,n) is at most

$$\left\lceil \frac{n}{\min(H)} \right\rceil^m.$$

Definition 3.2 For any 0-1 permutation X of length n' with $0 \leq n' \leq n$, let *pad*(X,n) denote the 0-1 permutation Y of length n obtained by setting

$$Y[i] = \begin{cases} X[i] & 0 \leq i < n', \text{ and} \\ 1 & n' \leq i < n. \end{cases}$$

Lemma 3.4 Let X be an arbitrary 0-1 permutation of length n' with $0 \leq n' \leq n$. Then X is H-sorted if and only if *pad*(X,n) is H-sorted.

Definition 3.3 For any 0-1 permutation X of length $n \geq 0$, and any integer k, let *shift*(X,k) denote the 0-1 permutation Y obtained by setting

$$Y[i] = \begin{cases} 0 & \text{if } i-k < 0, \\ X[i-k] & \text{if } 0 \leq i-k < n, \text{ and} \\ 1 & \text{if } i-k \geq n. \end{cases}$$

Lemma 3.5 For any 0-1 permutation X and any integer k, if X is H-sorted, then *shift*(X,k) is also H-sorted.

In the following definition, a Boolean expression is assumed to represent 1 if it is true, and 0 if it is false.

Definition 3.4 For any 0-1 permutation X of length $n \geq 0$, let *perm*(X) denote the permutation Y in $\Pi(n)$ obtained by setting

$$Y[i] = \sum_{0\leq j<i} (X[j] = X[i]) + \sum_{0\leq j<n} (X[j] < X[i]),$$

Lemma 3.6 Let X be an arbitrary 0-1 permutation. Then X is H-sorted if and only if *perm*(X) is H-sorted.

We say that an element $A[j]$ of a permutation A in $\Pi(n)$ is k places out of position if $|A[j] - j| \geq k$. The following lemma will be used in Section 3.2 to obtain a simple lower bound on the depth of any Shellsort sorting network.

Lemma 3.7 Let X denote any H-sorted 0-1 permutation of length n, let i denote the number of 1's in X, and let j denote the least index such that $X[j] = 1$ (if $i = 0$ then set $j = n$). Then element *perm*$(X)[j]$ is $n-i-j$ places out of position.

3.2 A More General Lower Bound

We will now generalize the proof technique presented in the previous section to obtain a trade-off between the length of an increment sequence H and the lower bound for the depth of a sorting network based on H. For the sake of simplicity, we assume H to be monotone. It will be shown later that this assumption is not really necessary.

As before, we divide the increment sequence into stages $S_0, \ldots, S_{t-1}$, such that stage S_i contains all increments h_j with $n_i \geq h_j > n_{i+1}$. We define the n_i by $n_0 = n$ and $n_{i+1} = \lfloor n_i / \lg^k n_i \rfloor$, but we now assume k to be a function of the input size n and the increment sequence length m. Note that the number of stages t is determined by our choice of k. In particular, if we choose k such that

$$\left(\lg^k n\right)^s \leq n^{1/2},$$

then we get at least s stages that contain only elements greater $n^{1/2}$. Solving this inequality we get

$$k = \left\lfloor \frac{\lg n}{2s \lg\lg n} \right\rfloor. \qquad (1)$$

as a possible choice of k. We will now formalize our earlier observation that an element can be "far out of place" after sorting by all increments up to stage S_i, provided that S_i contains "few" increments.

Lemma 3.8 Let H be an increment sequence for permutations of length n, and suppose that for some integers ν, ν' with $0 < \nu' < \nu \leq n$ there are at most μ increments h_j with $\nu' < h_j \leq \nu$ in H. If $\lceil \frac{\nu}{\nu'} \rceil^\mu = o(\nu)$, then there exists an input file A such that: (i) A is sorted by all $h_j > \nu'$, and (ii) there exists an element in A that is $\Omega(\nu)$ places away from its final position.

Proof: Let H' denote the subsequence of H consisting of all increments h_j such that $h_j > \nu'$, let H'' denote the subsequence of H' consisting of all increments h_j such that $h_j \leq \nu$, and let $X = \mathit{template}(H'', \nu)$. We know that X is H''-sorted by Lemma 3.2. Lemma 3.1 then implies that X is also H'-sorted. Note that $|H''| \leq \mu$ and $\min(H'') > \nu'$. Hence, by Lemma 3.3, the number of 1's in X is at most

$$\left\lceil \frac{\nu}{\nu'} \right\rceil^\mu = o(\nu).$$

Now let $Y = \mathit{pad}(X, n)$. By Lemma 3.4, the 0-1 permutation Y is H'-sorted. Furthermore, since the number of 1's in Y is exactly $n - \nu$ greater than the number of 1's in X, and $X[0] = Y[0] = 1$, Lemma 3.6 implies that the permutation $A \stackrel{\text{def}}{=} \mathit{perm}(Y)$ is H'-sorted, and by Lemma 3.7 some element of A is $\Omega(\nu)$ places out of position. □

Note that, in the preceding argument, we could have defined Y as $\mathit{shift}(\mathit{pad}(X, n), j)$ for any integer j with $0 \leq j \leq n - \nu$. We will make use of this observation to establish Corollary 3.1.1 below.

Theorem 3.1 Any Shellsort sorting network based on a monotone increment sequence of length m has depth

$$\Omega\left(2^{\frac{\lg n}{(2+\epsilon)\sqrt{m}}}\right),$$

for all $\epsilon > 0$.

Proof: We will partition the increment sequence H into at least $s = (1 + \epsilon_0)\sqrt{m}$ disjoint stages consisting of increments h_j with $h_j \geq n^{1/2}$, for some $\epsilon_0 > 0$. By averaging, one of these stages, say S_i, will contain at most

$$\mu \stackrel{\text{def}}{=} \left\lfloor \frac{m}{s} \right\rfloor = \left\lfloor \frac{\sqrt{m}}{1 + \epsilon_0} \right\rfloor$$

increments. Using Equation 1 we determine k as:

$$k = \left\lfloor \frac{\lg n}{2(1 + \epsilon_0)\sqrt{m} \lg\lg n} \right\rfloor$$

Define $\nu = n_i$ and $\nu' = n_{i+1}$. We now have

$$\begin{aligned}
\left\lceil \frac{\nu}{\nu'} \right\rceil^\mu &\leq \left\lceil \lg^k \nu \right\rceil^{\frac{\sqrt{m}}{1+\epsilon_0}} \\
&\leq (\lg n)^{\frac{\lg n}{2(1+\epsilon_0)^2 \lg\lg n}} \\
&= 2^{\frac{\lg n}{2(1+\epsilon_0)^2}} \\
&\leq 2^{\frac{\lg \nu}{(1+\epsilon_0)^2}} \\
&= o(\nu).
\end{aligned}$$

Thus, we can apply Lemma 3.8. According to the lemma, there exists a permutation such that an element is $\Omega(n_i)$ positions away from its final position after stage S_i. Since all subsequent increments are less than or equal to n_{i+1}, this element must pass through at least $\Omega(n_i/n_{i+1})$ comparators. We have

$$\begin{aligned}
\frac{n_i}{n_{i+1}} &\geq \lg^k n_i \\
&= (\lg n_i)^{\left\lfloor \frac{\lg n}{2(1+\epsilon_0)\sqrt{m} \lg\lg n} \right\rfloor} \\
&\geq (\lg n_i)^{\frac{\lg n}{2(1+\epsilon_0)(1+\epsilon_1)\sqrt{m} \lg\lg n}} \\
&\geq \left(2^{\frac{\lg\lg n_i}{\lg\lg n}}\right)^{\frac{\lg n}{2(1+\epsilon_0)(1+\epsilon_1)\sqrt{m}}} \\
&\geq \left(2^{\frac{1}{1+\epsilon_2}}\right)^{\frac{\lg n}{2(1+\epsilon_0)(1+\epsilon_1)\sqrt{m}}} \\
&= 2^{\frac{\lg n}{(2+\epsilon)\sqrt{m}}},
\end{aligned}$$

where ϵ is chosen to satisfy the inequality $(2 + \epsilon) \geq 2(1 + \epsilon_0)(1 + \epsilon_1)(1 + \epsilon_2)$. □

3.3 A Lower Bound for Network Size

The depth lower bound of Theorem 3.1 also implies a lower bound on the size of any Shellsort network based on a monotone increment sequence. We will not give a formal proof of this result, since it arises as a special case of the lower bound for the running time of adaptive Shellsort established in the next section. Instead, we will briefly describe the main idea.

Lemma 3.8 shows how to construct an input file A that is sorted under all increments in stages S_0 to S_i of an increment sequence H such that one element $A[z]$ in A is "far out of place". In fact, as discussed immediately after the proof of Lemma 3.8, we can use the method of the lemma to construct a set of $n - n_i$ "shifted" versions of such an input file A. In particular, let A_j, $0 \leq j < n - n_i$, denote the input file obtained by setting Y to $shift(pad(X, n), j)$ instead of $pad(X, n)$. Note that $A_0 = A$. Let $A_0[z]$ be the element proven to be far out of place in A_0. By construction, the element $A_j[z + j]$ is far out of place in A_j. Due to the common structure of the input files, element $A_j[z + j]$ in file A_j will never pass through the same comparator as element $A_k[z + k]$ in A_k, for any $j \neq k$. Instead, the two elements will always be exactly $k - j$ positions apart at each level of the sorting network. This implies the result.

Corollary 3.1.1 Any sorting network based on a monotone increment sequence of length m has size

$$\Omega\left(n \cdot 2^{\frac{\lg n}{(2+\epsilon)\sqrt{m}}}\right),$$

for all $\epsilon > 0$.

We can now compare our result to the lower bound of $\Omega(n \lg^2 n / \lg\lg n)$ for network size given by Cypher [3]. The main difference between the two results is that Cypher gets a lower bound that is independent of the length of the increment sequence, while we get a trade-off between network size and increment sequence length. This makes our lower bound much stronger for short increment sequences. Our method also implies a lower bound of $\Omega(n \lg^2 n / (\lg\lg n)^2)$ for increment sequences of arbitrary length, since every increment increases the size of a Shellsort network by at least n. This is slightly weaker than Cypher's lower bound. However, Cypher's bound only applies to monotone increment sequences, while our result also holds for nonmonotone sequences, as will be shown in the next subsection. Another strength of our method is its simplicity and flexibility, which will makes it possible to extend our lower bound to adaptive Shellsort algorithms and certain variations of Shellsort.

3.4 Nonmonotone Increment Sequences

So far, we have restricted our attention to monotone increment sequences. We will now show that this restriction is really unnecessary, and that the same lower bounds also apply to nonmonotone sequences. Recall that we obtained the depth lower bound by showing the existence of an input permutation such that an element is "far out of place" after the "sparse" stage S_i. More precisely, Lemma 3.8 showed the existence of a permutation A that is already sorted by all increments in stages S_0 through S_i and that contains such an element. Thus, no exchanges are performed by the increments in stages S_0 through S_i on input A, and the lower bound follows. We will make use of the following well-known lemma (see, for example, [13]) in order to extend this argument to nonmonotonic increment sequences.

Lemma 3.9 For any two increments h, h', if we h'-sort an h-sorted file, it stays h-sorted.

Now suppose we have a nonmonotone increment sequence H. We can divide H into stages $S_0, \ldots, S_{t-1}$ as before, with stage S_i containing all increments h_j with $n_i \geq h_j > n_{i+1}$. Again, there exists a "sparse" stage S_i with few increments, and a permutation sorted by all increments in $S \stackrel{\text{def}}{=} S_0 \cup \cdots \cup S_i$ such that some element is "far out of place". If we take A as the input permutation, then by Lemma 3.9 A will stay sorted by all increments in S throughout the network. Hence, no exchanges will take place during the applications of Insertion Sort corresponding to increments in S. This implies that all of the exchanges needed to move the "out-of-place" element to its final position are performed by increments $h_j \leq n_{i+1}$, and the lower bound follows. The same reasoning also applies to the lower bound for network size, and to the results obtained in the next section. This gives us the following result:

Corollary 3.1.2 Any sorting network based on an increment sequence of length m has size

$$\Omega\left(n \cdot 2^{\frac{\lg n}{(2+\epsilon)\sqrt{m}}}\right),$$

for all $\epsilon > 0$.

4 Extensions of the Lower Bound

In this section we extend our results to more general classes of Shellsort algorithms. First, we establish a lower bound for the running time of adaptive Shellsort algorithms based on arbitrary increment sequences. We then define a new class of algorithms called *Generalized Shellsort Algorithms*, and show a lower bound for this class.

4.1 Adaptive Shellsort Algorithms

The results obtained so far all rely on the fact, established in Lemma 3.8, that we can construct an input file such that one element is "far away" from its final position in the sorted file. We were able to extend the lower bounds to network size due to the nonadaptive nature of sorting networks. However, the results for network size do not imply a lower bound for the running time of Shellsort algorithms that are adaptive.

In this subsection, we will establish such a lower bound. The high-level structure of the proof is the same as that of the depth lower bound in the last section; we only have to substitute Lemma 3.8 by a stronger lemma showing that there exists an input file A such that not just one, but "a large number" of the elements in A are "far away" from their final position. This result is formalized in the following lemma, which we will prove later in this subsection.

Lemma 4.1 Let H be an increment sequence applied to input files of length n, and suppose that for some integers ν, ν' with $4 \leq \nu' < \nu \leq n$ there are at most μ increments h_j with $\nu' < h_j \leq \nu$ in H. If $\lceil \frac{\nu}{\nu'} \rceil^{\mu} \leq \nu / \lg^3 \nu$, then there exists an input file A such that: (i) A is sorted by all $h_j > \nu'$, and (ii) there exist $\Omega(n/\lg^3 \nu)$ elements in A that are $\Omega(\nu/\lg^2 \nu)$ places away from their final position.

Given an increment sequence H, we can establish the lower bound for adaptive Shellsort algorithms by dividing H into stages in the same way as in the proof of Theorem 3.1, and then applying the above Lemma 4.1 instead of Lemma 3.8. The lower bound obtained is slightly weaker than the one for network size, since Lemma 4.1 only shows that a polylog fraction of the elements are a polylog fraction of n_{i-1} out of place. This gives the following theorem:

Theorem 4.1 Any Shellsort algorithm based on an increment sequence of length m has running time

$$\Omega\left(\frac{n}{\lg^5 n} \cdot 2^{\frac{\lg n}{(2+\epsilon)\sqrt{m}}}\right),$$

for all $\epsilon > 0$.

We remark that the exponent "5" in the preceding theorem is not the best possible. It results from summing the exponents "3" and "2" appearing in the statement of Lemma 4.1, which can be improved to "2" and "1", respectively. We have chosen to weaken these constants in order to simplify the proof of Lemma 4.1.

Comparing the bound of Theorem 4.1 to previous results we note that the lower bounds of Pratt [13] and Weiss [16] only hold for increment sequences approximating a geometric sequence, while the lower bound of Theorem 4.1 applies to all increment sequences. Also, the bound given by Weiss, which holds for a more general class than Pratt's bound, is based on an unproven conjecture about the number of inversions in certain input files.

The remainder of this subsection contains the proof of Lemma 4.1. To establish the result, we will need a few technical lemmas. The first two lemmas are straightforward and their proofs will be omitted. In particular, Lemma 4.2 is a straightforward generalization of Lemma 3.7.

Lemma 4.2 Let X denote any H-sorted 0-1 permutation of length n, let i denote the number of 1's in X, let n' be such that $0 \leq n' < n - 2i$, and let $j = \sum_{0 \leq k < n'} X[k]$. Then at least j elements of $perm(X)$ are $n - n' - i$ places out of position.

Definition 4.1 For any 0-1 permutation X of length n' such that $0 \leq n' \leq n$, let $perm^*(X, n)$ denote the permutation Y in $\Pi(n)$ obtained from $Z \stackrel{\text{def}}{=} perm(X)$ by setting

$$Y[i] = Z[i \bmod n'] + \left\lfloor \frac{i}{n'} \right\rfloor \cdot n'.$$

Lemma 4.3 Let X be any 0-1 permutation of length n' such that $0 \leq n' \leq n$. Then X is H-sorted if and only if $perm^*(X, n)$ is H-sorted. If i elements of $perm(X)$ are j places out of position, then at least $i \cdot \lfloor n/n' \rfloor$ elements of $perm^*(X, n)$ are j places out of position.

In the following, let H be an arbitrary increment sequence. Let ν be any integer with $\nu \geq 4$, and define $\alpha \stackrel{\text{def}}{=} \nu - 2\nu/\lg^2 \nu$ and $\beta \stackrel{\text{def}}{=} \nu - \nu/\lg^2 \nu$.

Lemma 4.4 Let X denote a 0-1 permutation of length $\nu \geq 4$ with $X[0] = 1$ and $\sum_{0 \leq i < \nu} X[i] \leq \nu / \lg^3 \nu$. Then there exists an integer k, $0 \leq k \leq (\nu - \alpha) \lfloor \lg \nu \rfloor$, such that the 0-1 permutation $Y \stackrel{\text{def}}{=} shift(X, k)$ satisfies

$$\sum_{0 \leq i < \alpha} Y[i] \geq \sum_{\alpha \leq i < \nu} Y[i].$$

Proof: Suppose, for the sake of contradiction, that

$$\sum_{0 \leq i < \alpha} shift(X,k)[i] < \sum_{\alpha \leq i < \nu} shift(X,k)[i]$$

holds for all k with $0 \leq k \leq (\nu - \alpha) \lfloor \lg \nu \rfloor$. This implies that $\sum_{0 \leq i < \alpha - k} X[i] < \sum_{\alpha - k \leq i < \nu - k} X[i]$. Using $R_k \stackrel{\text{def}}{=} \sum_{0 \leq i < \alpha - k} X[i]$, this can be rewritten as $R_k < R_{k-(\nu-\alpha)} - R_k$, or $R_k < \frac{1}{2} R_{k-(\nu-\alpha)}$. Hence,

$$R_{(\nu-\alpha)\lfloor \lg \nu \rfloor} < 2^{-\lfloor \lg \nu \rfloor} R_0,$$

and from $R_0 \le \sum_{0\le i<\nu} X[i] \le \nu/\lg^3\nu$ we get

$$R_{(\nu-\alpha)\lfloor\lg\nu\rfloor} < \frac{2}{\lg^3\nu} < 1.$$

This is clearly a contradiction, since $X[0]=1$ implies $R_{(\nu-\alpha)\lfloor\lg\nu\rfloor} \ge 1$. □

In the next lemma, given 0-1 permutations X and Y, we will use $or(X,Y)$ to denote the 0-1 permutation Z obtained by setting bit $Z[i]$ to the logical OR of bits $X[i]$ and $Y[i]$, $0 \le i < n$. Clearly, if X and Y are H-sorted, then $or(X,Y)$ is also H-sorted.

Lemma 4.5 Let X be an H-sorted 0-1 permutation of length ν with $x \stackrel{\text{def}}{=} \sum_{0\le i<\nu} X[i] \le \nu/\lg^3\nu$. Let $x' \stackrel{\text{def}}{=} \sum_{0\le i<\alpha+k} X[i]$ where $(x\lg\nu)/2 \le k \le \nu/(2\lg^2\nu)$. Then there exists an H-sorted 0-1 permutation Y of length ν with $\sum_{0\le i<\nu} Y[i] \le 2x$ and

$$\sum_{0\le i<\alpha+2k} Y[i] \ge 2\left(1-\frac{1}{\lg\nu}\right)x'.$$

Proof: We will set Y to $Y_j \stackrel{\text{def}}{=} or(X, \mathit{shift}(X,j))$ for some appropriately chosen integer j, $1 \le j \le k$. Note that by Lemma 3.5, any such 0-1 permutation Y_j is H-sorted, and it is easy to see that $\sum_{0\le i<\nu} Y_j[i] \le 2x$ holds. Let $y'_j = \sum_{0\le i<\alpha+2k} Y_j[i]$. It remains to show the existence of an integer j_0, $1 \le j_0 \le k$, such that $y'_{j_0} \ge 2(1-1/\lg\nu)x'$. We will accomplish this by means of an averaging argument. We have

$$\sum_{1\le j\le k} y'_j \ge 2kx' - \binom{x'}{2}.$$

Hence, there exists a j_0, $1 \le j_0 \le k$, such that

$$\begin{aligned} y'_{j_0} &\ge \frac{2kx' - \binom{x'}{2}}{k} \\ &\ge 2x' - \frac{x'-1}{\lg\nu} \\ &\ge 2\left(1-\frac{1}{\lg\nu}\right)x'. \end{aligned}$$

Now choose $Y = Y_{j_0}$. □

Lemma 4.6 Let Y be an H-sorted 0-1 permutation of length ν with $\sum_{0\le i<\nu} Y[i] \le \nu/\lg^3\nu$ and

$$\sum_{0\le i<\alpha} Y[i] \ge \sum_{\alpha\le i<\nu} Y[i].$$

Then there exists an H-sorted 0-1 permutation Z of length ν such that $\sum_{0\le i<\nu} Z[i] \le \nu/\lg^3\nu$ and

$$\sum_{0\le i<\beta} Z[i] = \Omega(\nu/\lg^3\nu).$$

Proof: We will "transform" the given 0-1 permutation Y into a 0-1 permutation of the desired form by a sequence of applications of Lemma 4.5. Let $Y_0 \stackrel{\text{def}}{=} Y$. The jth application of Lemma 4.5 will be used to obtain Y_j from Y_{j-1}, $j \ge 1$. Let $y_j = \sum_{0\le i<\nu} Y_j[i]$, and let $y'_j = \sum_{0\le i<\alpha+2^j y_0\lg\nu} Y_j[i]$. Note that $y'_0 \ge \sum_{0\le i<\alpha} Y[i] \ge y_0/2$. Then Lemma 4.5 implies that $y_j \le 2^j y_0$, and

$$y'_j \ge \left[2\left(1-\frac{1}{\lg\nu}\right)\right]^j y'_0$$

for $j \le \lg\nu - \lg y_0 - 3\lg\lg\nu$ (the latter inequality ensures that $\alpha + 2^j y_0 \lg\nu \le \beta$). Setting j_0 to $\lfloor \lg\nu - \lg y_0 - 3\lg\lg\nu \rfloor$, and making use of the inequality $y'_0 \ge y_0/2$, we find that $y_{j_0} \le \nu/\lg^3\nu$ and

$$y'_{j_0} = \Omega(y_{j_0}) = \Omega(\nu/\lg^3\nu).$$

Hence, we can choose $Z = Y_{j_0}$. □

Given the above lemmas, we are now ready to proceed with the proof of Lemma 4.1.

Proof: Let H' denote the subsequence of H consisting of exactly those increments h_j such that $h_j > \nu'$, let H'' denote the subsequence of H' consisting of exactly those increments h_j such that $h_j \le \nu$, and let $X = \mathit{template}(H'', \nu)$. We know that X is H''-sorted by Lemma 3.2. Note that $|H''| \le \mu$ and $\min(H'') > \nu'$. Hence, by Lemma 3.3, we have

$$\sum_{0\le i<\nu} X[i] \le \left\lceil \frac{\nu}{\nu'} \right\rceil^\mu \le \frac{\nu}{\lg^3\nu}.$$

By Lemmas 3.5 and 4.4, the existence of X implies the existence of a 0-1 permutation Y of length ν such that Y is H''-sorted and

$$\sum_{0\le i<\alpha} Y[i] \ge \sum_{\alpha\le i<\nu} Y[i].$$

The existence of Y then establishes, via Lemma 4.6, the existence of a 0-1 permutation Z of length ν such that:

- Z is H''-sorted,
- $\sum_{0\le i<\nu} Z[i] \le \nu/\lg^3\nu$, and
- $\sum_{0\le i<\beta} Z[i] = \Omega(\nu/\lg^3\nu)$.

By Lemma 3.1 and Lemma 3.6 we know that $B = \mathit{perm}(Z)$ is H'-sorted, and Lemma 4.2 implies that B contains $\Omega(\nu/\lg^3\nu)$ elements that are $\Omega(\nu/\lg^2\nu)$ places out of position. Let $A = \mathit{perm}^*(Z,n)$. By Lemma 4.3, A is H'-sorted and contains $\Omega(n/\lg^3\nu)$ elements that are $\Omega(\nu/\lg^2\nu)$ places out of position. □

4.2 Variations of Shellsort

Incerpi and Sedgewick [7] consider a number of variations of Shellsort in the hope of obtaining an $O(n \lg n)$ algorithm. They introduce a sorting algorithm called *Shaker Sort* based on the *Cocktail Shaker Sort* algorithm described by Knuth [8]. *Cocktail Shaker Sort* is similar to Bubble Sort, but instead of performing sweeps over the array in only one direction, it performs *shakes* consisting of one sweep in each direction. *Shaker Sort* works essentially in the same way as Shellsort, but instead of Insertion Sort it uses the above Cocktail Shaker Sort to perform the h_i-sorts. In addition, Shaker Sort only performs a bounded number of shakes for every increment. Thus, after an h_i-sort the input may not be completely h_i-sorted. After all increments in the sequence have been processed, the algorithm uses Insertion Sort to sort the file completely.

Incerpi and Sedgewick considered several variants of this algorithm and obtained very encouraging empirical results, even when only one shake per increment is performed. Weiss [16] exhibited permutations on which Shaker Sort does not perform well, and conjectured that Shaker Sort cannot give better asymptotic running times than Shellsort. We will show that Shaker Sort belongs to a very general class of "Shellsort-like" algorithms covered by our proof technique.

In the following, we will say that a comparison-based sorting algorithm is *compatible* if all comparisons take place between adjacent positions in the input file, and any permutation that is already sorted stays sorted during the entire run of the algorithm. Note that Insertion Sort, Bubble Sort and Cocktail Shaker Sort are all *compatible* sorting algorithms (an example of a non-compatible algorithm is Shellsort itself). We now define the class of *Generalized Shellsort Algorithms.*

Definition 4.2 A *Generalized Shellsort Algorithm* $\mathcal{G}$ on inputs of size n is given by an increment sequence $H = h_0, \ldots, h_{m-1}$ and a sequence of tuples $(\mathcal{C}_i, f_i)$, $0 \leq i < m$, where

- every $\mathcal{C}_i$ is a compatible sorting algorithm, and
- every f_i is a function from $\Pi(n)$ to the set of non-negative integers.

Algorithm $\mathcal{G}$ sorts an input A of size n by performing an h_i-sort for $j = h_{m-1}, \ldots, h_0$. The h_i-sorts are implemented with the compatible sorting algorithm $\mathcal{C}_i$, but only the first $f_i(A)$ comparisons of $\mathcal{C}_i$ are executed.

Note that we do not require the functions f_i to be computable in any efficient way. We can then easily see that Shellsort is a Generalized Shellsort Algorithm, where Insertion Sort is the compatible algorithm $\mathcal{C}_i$ and $f_i(A)$ is defined as the number of comparisons required to perform the h_i-sort, for $0 \leq i < m$. If we choose Cocktail Shaker Sort for the $\mathcal{C}_i$ and define the f_i as the number of comparisons needed in a single shake on a congruence class modulo h_i, then we obtain Shaker Sort. Two other examples of algorithms in this class have been proposed by Knuth [8] and Dobosiewicz [4].

As before, we will only be interested in increment sequences of length $O(\lg^2 n/(\lg \lg n)^2)$. For longer increment sequences, we cannot hope to get any interesting general lower bounds, since every sorting network can be modeled as a Generalized Shellsort Algorithm. As an example, the AKS network [1] can be described by an increment sequence of length $\Theta(n \lg n)$. In the case of Shaker Sort, we can get lower bounds for longer increment sequences by observing that at least $\Omega(n)$ comparisons are performed for every increment less than $n/2$.

It is not difficult to see that the proof of Theorem 4.1 also goes through for the class of Generalized Shellsort Algorithms based on monotone increment sequences: Substituting any other compatible sorting algorithm for Insertion Sort does not pose a problem since the only fact about Insertion Sort that we use in our argument is that comparisons are performed over a distance of 1 in the congruence classes modulo h_i. This implies that comparisons are only performed over a distance of h_i in the input permutation. The second condition in the definition of a compatible algorithm ensures the existence of an input permutation such that a large number of elements will be out of place whenever the h_i-sort is aborted due to the function f_i. We get the following theorem:

Theorem 4.2 Any Generalized Shellsort Algorithm based on a monotone increment sequence of length m has running time

$$\Omega\left(\frac{n}{\lg^5 n} \cdot 2^{\frac{\lg n}{(2+\epsilon)\sqrt{m}}}\right),$$

for all $\epsilon > 0$.

To prove the result for nonmonotone increment sequences, however, we need an analogue to Lemma 3.9 in Section 3.4. Thus, if a Generalized Shellsort Algorithm has the property that, for any two increments h, h', an h-sorted file is still h-sorted after increment h' has been processed, then the above lower bound applies. It has been shown in [12] that Shaker Sort satisfies this property.

5 Discussion

In this paper, we have established a lower bound of $\Omega(n \lg^2 n/(\lg \lg n)^2)$ on the size of any Shellsort network, thus ruling out the existence of a network of size $O(n \lg n)$ based on a nonmonotone increment sequence.

By extending our argument to the case of adaptive Shellsort algorithms, we have also established the first lower bound for Shellsort that holds for arbitrary increment sequences.

In addition, our result establishes a lower bound trade-off between the running time of a Shellsort algorithm and the length of the underlying increment sequence. We will now compare this trade-off with the best known upper bound trade-off given by the nonuniform increment sequences of Chazelle (see Theorem 3 of [6]). Expressing the running time as a function of the increment sequence length m we obtain the following terms:

Lower Bound	$\frac{n}{\lg^5 n} \cdot n^{\frac{1}{(2+\epsilon)\sqrt{m}}}$
Upper Bound	$mn \cdot n^{\frac{(2+\epsilon)}{\sqrt{m}}}$

Note that both the factor $1/\lg^5 n$ in the lower bound and the factor m in the upper bound are only significant for increment sequences of length $\Omega(\lg^2 n/(\lg\lg n)^2)$. In every other case, the upper and lower bounds differ only by a factor of $4+\epsilon$ in the exponent.

We can also express the length of the increment sequence as a function of the running time. In this case, for $m = o(\lg^2 n/(\lg\lg n)^2)$, the lower and upper bounds are only a constant factor apart. This means that, for a given T, the length of the increment sequence of Chazelle that achieves running time T is only a factor of $16+\epsilon$ larger than the minimum length possible under our lower bound trade-off. In other words, one cannot hope to match the running time of Chazelle's sequences with significantly shorter increment sequences.

6 Open Questions

The primary remaining challenge in the study of Shellsort seems to be the virtual nonexistence of both upper and lower bounds for average case complexity. A result for a particular increment sequence is given by Knuth [8], who determines an average case running time of $\Omega(n^{3/2})$ for Shell's original sequence. Increment sequences of the form $(h, 1)$ and $(h, k, 1)$ were investigated by Knuth [8] and Yao [19], respectively. Weiss [17] conducted an extensive empirical study and conjectured that Shellsort will on average not perform significantly better than in the worst case. Any general upper and lower bound for the average case would certainly be very interesting.

It would be nice to close the remaining gap between the upper and lower bounds. Our lower bound trade-off comes quite close to the known upper bounds, but there is certainly still room for improvement.

Finally, one might try to find interesting "Shellsort-like" algorithms, not contained in the class of Generalized Shellsort Algorithms, that lead to improved running times. In this context, it might also be promising to use ideas from Shellsort in the design of small-depth sorting networks.

Acknowledgement

We thank Mark Weiss for helpful comments.

References

[1] M. Ajtai, J. Komlós, and E. Szemerédi. An $O(n \log n)$ sorting network. *Combinatorica*, 3:1–19, 1983.

[2] K. E. Batcher. Sorting networks and their applications. In *Proceedings of the AFIPS Spring Joint Computer Conference*, vol. 32, pages 307–314, 1968.

[3] R. E. Cypher. A lower bound on the size of Shellsort sorting networks. In *Proceedings of the 1st Annual ACM Symposium on Parallel Algorithms and Architectures*, pages 58–63, June 1989.

[4] W. Dobosiewicz. An efficient variation of Bubble Sort. *Information Processing Letters*, 11:5–6, 1980.

[5] T. N. Hibbard. An empirical study of minimal storage sorting. *Communications of the ACM*, 6:206–213, 1963.

[6] J. Incerpi and R. Sedgewick. Improved upper bounds on Shellsort. *Journal of Computer and System Sciences*, 31:210–224, 1985.

[7] J. Incerpi and R. Sedgewick. Practical variations of Shellsort. *Information Processing Letters*, 26:37–43, 1987.

[8] D. E. Knuth. *The Art of Computer Programming*, volume 3. Addison-Wesley, Reading, MA, 1973.

[9] R. Lazarus and R. Frank. A high-speed sorting procedure. *Communications of the ACM*, 3:20–22, 1960.

[10] A. Papernov and G. Stasevich. A method for information sorting in computer memories. *Problems of Information Transmission*, 1:63–75, 1965.

[11] C. G. Plaxton and T. Suel. Improved lower bounds for Shellsort, April 1992. Unpublished manuscript.

[12] B. Poonen. The worst case in Shellsort and related algorithms, December 1989. Unpublished manuscript.

[13] V. R. Pratt. *Shellsort and Sorting Networks*. PhD thesis, Stanford University, Department of Computer Science, December 1971. Also published by Garland, New York, 1979.

[14] R. Sedgewick. A new upper bound for Shellsort. *Journal of Algorithms*, 7:159–173, 1986.

[15] D. L. Shell. A high-speed sorting procedure. *Communications of the ACM*, 2:30–32, 1959.

[16] M. A. Weiss. *Lower Bounds for Shellsort*. PhD thesis, Princeton University, Department of Computer Science, June 1987.

[17] M. A. Weiss. Empirical study of the expected running time of Shellsort. *The Computer Journal*, 34:88–91, 1991.

[18] M. A. Weiss and R. Sedgewick. Tight lower bounds for Shellsort. *Journal of Algorithms*, 11:242–251, 1990.

[19] A. C. C. Yao. An analysis of $(h, k, 1)$-Shellsort. *Journal of Algorithms*, 1:14–50, 1980.

The Asymptotic Complexity of Merging Networks *

Peter Bro Miltersen
pbmiltersen@daimi.aau.dk

Mike Paterson
msp@dcs.warwick.ac.uk

Jun Tarui
jun@dcs.warwick.ac.uk

Computer Science Department
Aarhus University
Ny Munkegade, 8000 Aarhus C
Denmark

Department of Computer Science
University of Warwick
Coventry, CV4 7AL
United Kingdom

Abstract

Let $M(m,n)$ be the minimum number of comparators needed in a comparator network that merges m elements $x_1 \leq x_2 \leq \ldots \leq x_m$ and n elements $y_1 \leq y_2 \ldots \leq y_n$, where $n \geq m$. Batcher's odd-even merge yields the following upper bound:

$$M(m,n) \leq \tfrac{1}{2}\,(m+n)\log_2(m+1) + O(n);$$

in particular,

$$M(n,n) \leq n\log_2 n + O(n).$$

We prove the following lower bound that matches the upper bound above asymptotically as $n \geq m \rightarrow \infty$:

$$M(m,n) \geq \tfrac{1}{2}\,(m+n)\log_2(m+1) - O(m);$$

in particular,

$$M(n,n) \geq n\log_2 n - O(n).$$

Our proof technique extends to give similarly tight lower bounds for the size of monotone Boolean circuits for merging, and for the size of switching networks capable of realizing the set of permutations that arise from merging.

1 Introduction and Overview

A *comparator network*, which consists of *comparators*, is a general model of comparison-based computations in which (sequential or parallel) comparisons are made in an input-oblivious way. A comparator is a 2-input 2-output gate, where one output computes the minimum of the two inputs and the other output computes the maximum. A comparator network that merges (sorts) its inputs is called a merging (sorting) network (see Figures 1 and 2). Merging networks, which are the subject of this paper, and sorting networks are particularly important and have been studied extensively. For more precise definitions and a comprehensive account of comparator networks, see [Knu73, pp. 220–246].

An (m,n)*-merging network* is a comparator network that merges two input sequences $x_1 \leq x_2 \leq \ldots \leq x_m$ and $y_1 \leq y_2 \leq \ldots \leq y_n$ into the sequence $z_1 \leq z_2 \leq \ldots \leq z_{m+n}$. Let $M(m,n)$ denote the minimum number of comparators needed in an (m,n)-merging network. The (m,n)-merging network based on Batcher's odd-even merge [Knu73, pp. 224–226] provides the best known upper bound for $M(m,n)$ for *all* values of m, $n \geq 1$. Throughout the paper we assume $n \geq m$, and all logarithms are to the base 2. Let $C(m,n)$ denote the number of comparators in Batcher's (m,n)-merging network. Then,

$$M(m,n) \leq C(m,n) = \frac{1}{2}(m+n)\log m + O(n),$$

and in particular,

$$M(n,n) \leq n\log n + O(n).$$

The previous best lower bounds for $M(n,n)$ and $M(m,n)$ are due to Floyd [Knu73, pp. 230–232] and to Yao and Yao [YY76] who proved, respectively,

$$M(n,n) \geq \frac{1}{2}n\log n + O(n);$$
$$M(m,n) \geq \frac{1}{2}n\log(m+1).$$

We close this long-standing factor-of-two gap between the previous best lower and upper bounds for $M(n,n)$ and show that the asymptotic value of $M(n,n)$ is $n\log n$, by proving the following lower bound for $M(m,n)$.

$$M(m,n) > \frac{1}{2}(m+n)\log(m+1) - 0.73m.$$

*This work was partially supported by the ESPRIT II BRA Programme of the EC under contract # 7141 (ALCOM II).

0-8186-2900-2/92 $3.00 © 1992 IEEE

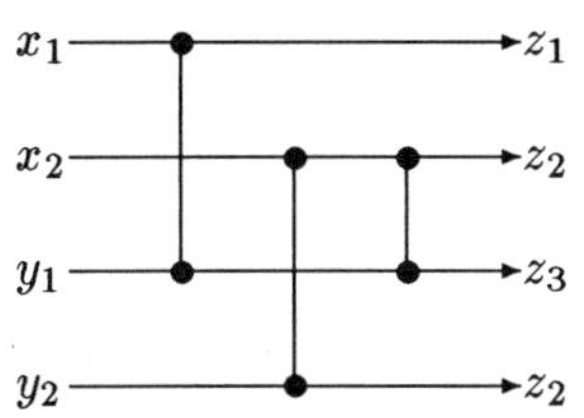

Figure 1: Batcher's odd-even $(2,2)$-merging network. A comparator is represented by a vertical line segment.

For the case $m = n$, we also prove the following lower bound, which is asymptotically better than the one obtained by setting $m = n$ in the bound above, because of the improved coefficient of the linear term.

$$M(n,n) > n \log n - 0.66n - O(\log n).$$

We obtain our lower bounds as corollaries of more general results. Let Merge(m,n) be the set of all possible input-output connections that arise from merging. We show that any graph with in-degree two that can *realize* Merge(m,n), i.e., contains vertex-disjoint paths for every connection in Merge(m,n), must have many vertices. Such a graph will be called an (m,n)-merging graph. Thus our lower bound for merging networks also holds for the number of switches in a switching network that can realize all the permutations that arise from merging.

We also obtain a tight lower bound for the size of monotone Boolean circuits for Boolean merging, improving the best previous lower bound essentially by a factor of two, in the same way that our lower bound for $M(n,n)$ improves Floyd's lower bound.

1.1 Overview of Proof

In this subsection we informally describe the main ideas involved in the proof of Theorem 1, which says that a graph capable of realizing Merge(m,n) must have many vertices. For simplicity, we explain our arguments in terms of merging networks.

Assume that two input sequences $x_1 < x_2 < \ldots < x_m$ and $y_1 < y_2 < \ldots < y_n$ are given and that $x_i \neq y_j$ for all i and j. Imagine the x_i's and y_j's actually moving through a merging network to their destination z_k's. Let Merge(m,n) be the set of $\binom{m+n}{m}$ possible merging patterns. Given $\pi \in$ Merge(m,n), the *total path length* is the sum of the lengths of the paths traversed by the x_i's and y_j's. Actually, for a merging network, the total path length is simply the number of its edges since every edge is traversed exactly once by some unique x_i or y_j, and hence it is a constant that does not depend on π. But for an (m,n)-merging graph, it may depend on π. Keep this point in mind and be flexible in interpreting the arguments below accordingly.

Let a probability distribution Ψ on Merge(m,n) be given. For each z_k, Ψ induces a probability distribution on the set of x_i's and y_j's that may arrive at z_k, and the *expected length* of the path reaching z_k is at least the *entropy* of this distribution. We construct a distribution Ψ such that the *total entropy*, the sum of the entropies of the z_k's, is large. It follows that the expected total path length is large, since it equals the sum over the z_k's of the expected length of the path reaching z_k, and hence there exists a merging pattern under which the total path length is large. Since only two inputs go through each comparator, there must be many comparators.

To construct this Ψ, we proceed as follows. For $m, n \geq 1$, define the *(m,n)-grid* to be the directed two-dimensional integer rectangular grid with lower-left corner at $(0,0)$ and upper-right corner at (m,n), in which the edges are directed upwards or to the right. There is a natural bijection from Merge(m,n) onto the set of paths from $(0,0)$ to (m,n) in the (m,n)-grid (see Figure 3). Under this bijection a probability distribution on Merge(m,n) gives rise to a *unit flow* from $(0,0)$ to (m,n) on the (m,n)-grid, and conversely, such a unit flow can be converted to a probability distribution on Merge(m,n) by considering a random walk on the grid according to the flow. Which x_i or y_j reaches z_k is determined by which edge is traversed at the diagonal corresponding to z_k.

We can finish the proof if we can construct a unit flow F on the (m,n)-grid with respect to which the total entropy, $H(F)$, is large. For Theorem 1, we use the *uniform* flow U that maintains a uniform distribution on the vertices along each diagonal.

For each (m,n)-grid, there is a unique *optimal* flow, $Z_{m,n}$, that attains the *maximum* total entropy $H(Z_{m,n})$. For the case $m = n$, we determine $H(Z_{n,n})$ fairly accurately, and using the optimal flow instead of the uniform flow we obtain Theorem 2, which provides a better bound for the case $m = n$.

1.2 Outline of Paper

In Section 2 we state Theorems 1 and 2 and explain how our lower bounds follow as their corollaries. In Sections 3 and 4 we prove Theorems 1 and 2 respectively. Finally in Section 5 we discuss some open

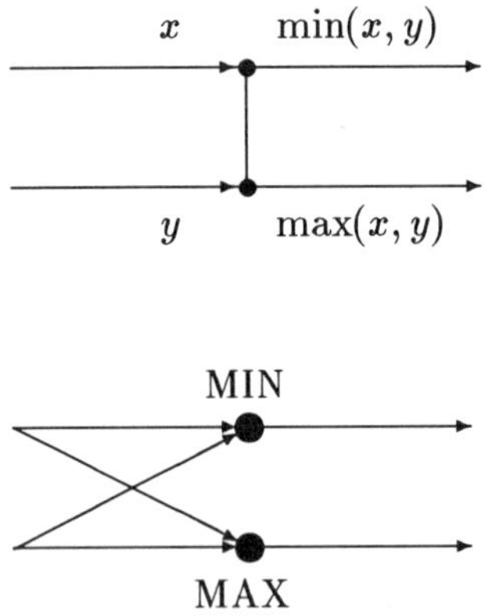

Figure 2: A comparator and an equivalent pair of MIN/MAX gates. A comparator is represented by a vertical line segment.

problems related to this work.

2 Results

Our theorems are in terms of the following general framework considered by Pippenger and Valiant [PV76].

Let $G = (V, E)$ be a directed graph and let $S = \{s_1, \ldots, s_k\}$ and $T = \{t_1, \ldots, t_k\}$ be disjoint sets of vertices. We say that G *realizes* a set M of bijections *from* T *onto* S if for each $\pi \in M$ there are k vertex-disjoint paths $p_1, \ldots, p_k$ in G, where p_i is *from* $\pi(t_i)$ *to* t_i $(1 \leq i \leq k)$.

Let $S = \{x_1, \ldots, x_m, y_1, \ldots, y_n\}$ and $T = \{z_1, \ldots, z_{m+n}\}$. There are $\binom{m+n}{m}$ ways to assign numbers from $\{1, \ldots, m+n\}$ to the x_i's and y_j's in a one-one way satisfying $x_1 < \cdots < x_m$ and $y_1 < \cdots < y_n$. Each possible assignment induces a distinct bijection π from T onto S, where $\pi(z_k)$ is defined to be the unique x_i or y_j that is assigned k. Let Merge(m, n) be the set of $\binom{m+n}{m}$ such bijections.

A graph G together with $S, T \subseteq V$, where $S \cup T = \emptyset$ and $|S| = |T| = m + n$, is an *(m, n)-merging graph* if it realizes Merge(m, n).

We can now state our theorems.

Theorem 1. *If $G = (V, E)$ together with S, $T \subseteq V$ is an (m, n)-merging graph with in-degree at most two, then*

$$|V - S| \geq (m+n)\log_2(m+1) - (\log_2 e)m > (m+n)\log_2(m+1) - 1.45m.$$

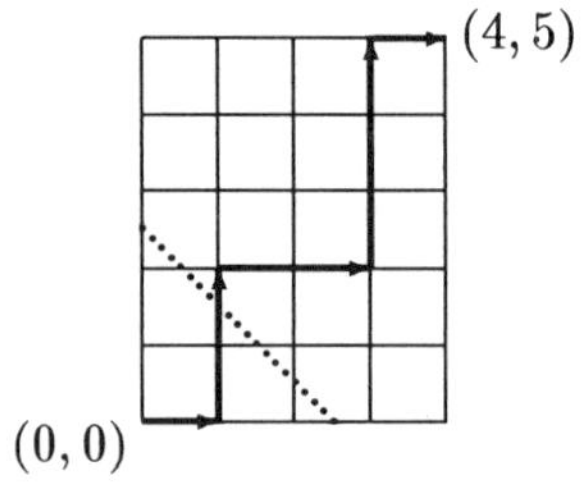

Figure 3: Path for the merge $x_1 < y_1 < y_2 < x_2 < x_3 < y_3 < y_4 < y_5 < x_4$. Which of the six edges that cross the diagonal is traversed determines z_3.

Theorem 2. *If $G = (V, E)$ together with S, $T \subseteq V$ is an (n, n)-merging graph with in-degree at most two, then*

$$|V - S| \geq 2n \log_2 n - 1.31n - O(\log n).$$

To apply our theorems we consider min-max circuits. A *min-max circuit* is a combinatorial circuit with gates of fan-in two and of unbounded fan-out, where each gate is either a MIN gate or a MAX gate that computes the minimum or the maximum of two inputs respectively. A min-max circuit with inputs $x_1, \ldots, x_m$ and $y_1, \ldots, y_n$ and outputs $z_1, \ldots, z_{m+n}$ is said to *(m, n)-merge* if it computes the merge of the x_i's and the y_j's at the z_k's.

The following observations are easy.

Fact 1. *An (m, n)-merging network N can be converted to an (m, n)-merging min-max circuit C by replacing each comparator by a MIN and a MAX gate (see Figure 2). The number of gates in C is twice the number of comparators in N.*

Fact 2. *If a min-max circuit (m, n)-merges, then its underlying graph is an (m, n)-merging graph with in-degree at most 2.*

From Facts 1 and 2, we get our two lower bounds for merging networks as corollaries of Theorems 1 and 2.

Corollary 1.

$$M(m, n) > \frac{1}{2}(m+n)\log(m+1) - 0.73m.$$

Corollary 2.

$$M(n, n) > n \log n - 0.66n - O(\log n).$$

The same bounds hold even when we allow outgoing edges of comparators to branch, since there is no constraint on out-degree in the conditions for the theorems.

2.1 Monotone Circuit Complexity

Consider a monotone Boolean circuit with $m+n$ inputs and $m+n$ outputs that merges two sorted Boolean sequences of length m and n. The following two observations yield a lower bound on the number of AND and OR gates needed.

Fact 3. *If C is a monotone Boolean circuit for Boolean (m,n)-merging, we can transform C to a min-max circuit of the same size that (m,n)-merges Boolean inputs, by replacing each AND or OR gate with a MIN or MAX gate respectively.*

The next fact is the '0-1 principle' for merging in terms of min-max circuits. (See [Knu73, p. 224] for a proof of a similar fact.)

Fact 4. *If a min-max circuit merges every pair of Boolean sequences of length m and n, then it is an (m,n)-merging min-max circuit.*

Using Facts 2, 3, and 4, we obtain the following as a corollary of Theorem 1. We omit the slightly improved bound for the case $m=n$ that can be obtained from Theorem 2 as for merging networks.

Corollary 3. *Any monotone Boolean circuit that merges two sorted Boolean sequences of length m and n must have more than $(m+n)\log(m+1)-1.45m$ gates.*

The previous best lower bounds are due to Lamagna [Lam79] and, independently, to Pippenger and Valiant [PV76]. Their bounds are essentially half our bounds when $m=n$, as in the case of merging networks.

3 Proof of Theorem 1

3.1 Entropies

Suppose that $G=(V,E)$ with $S=\{x_1,\ldots,x_m, y_1,\ldots,y_n\}$ and $T=\{z_1,\ldots,z_{m+n}\}$ is an (m,n)-merging graph, and let $M=\mathrm{Merge}(m,n)$. For each $\pi\in M$, fix a sequence $\langle P_i^\pi : i=1,\ldots,m+n\rangle$ of $m+n$ vertex-disjoint paths in G, where P_i^π is a path from $\pi(z_i)$ to z_i. For each vertex of in-degree two in G, fix arbitrarily which incoming edge is 'left' and which is 'right.' For each $\pi\in M$ and each $i\in\{1,\ldots,m+n\}$, encode the path P_i^π by following it in the reverse direction from z_i to $\pi(z_i)$ and using, say, 0 for left and 1 for right. Let C_i^π be the binary code obtained in this way. For each $i\in\{1,\ldots,m+n\}$, the set $\{C_i^\pi : \pi\in M\}$ is an instantaneous decipherable binary coding for the set $\{\pi(z_i) : \pi\in M\}$. (There may be more than one code for some x_j or y_k.)

Let a probability distribution on M be given and consider $\pi(z_i)$ and P_i^π as random variables accordingly. For a random variable X, $H(X)$ denotes the entropy of X measured in bits, and for a real random variable Y, $E[Y]$ denotes its expectation. For a path P in a graph and a binary code C, $|P|$ and $|C|$ denote their lengths.

We have

$$\begin{aligned}\sum_{i=1}^{m+n} H(\pi(z_i)) \;&\le\; \sum_{i=1}^{m+n} E[|C_i^\pi|] \;\le\; \sum_{i=1}^{m+n} E[|P_i^\pi|]\\ &=\; E[\sum_{i=1}^{m+n}|P_i^\pi|] \le \max_{\pi\in M}\sum_{i=1}^{m+n}|P_i^\pi|\\ &\le\; |V-S|,\end{aligned}$$

where the first inequality is by the well-known theorem of Shannon (for a noiseless channel and discrete memoryless source), and the equality is by the linearity of expectations. (For Shannon's Theorem, see a textbook on information theory.)

We obtain our lower bound for $|V-S|$ by defining a distribution on M and evaluating $\sum_{i=1}^{m+n} H(\pi(z_i))$ with respect to it.

3.2 Unit Flow on a Grid

Let M' be the set of directed paths in the (m,n)-grid from $(0,0)$ to (m,n). The natural bijection from M onto M' is illustrated in Figure 3.

Under this bijection a distribution Ψ on M induces a distribution Ψ' on M'. Define $\alpha_{i,j}$, for $1\le i\le m$, $0\le j\le n$, to be the probability, under Ψ', that a random path p includes the edge from $(i-1,j)$ to (i,j), and similarly define $\beta_{i,j}$, for $0\le i\le m$, $1\le j\le n$, to be the probability that p includes the edge from $(i,j-1)$ to (i,j). (See Figure 4.) For convenience, we define $\alpha_{i,j}=0$ for $i=0,m+1$ and $0\le j\le n$, and $\beta_{i,j}=0$ for $j=0,n+1$ and $0\le i\le m$. Jointly, $\alpha_{i,j}$ and $\beta_{i,j}$ define a *unit flow* from $(0,0)$ to (m,n), that is, the following equations are satisfied:

$$\alpha_{1,0}+\beta_{0,1}=1;\quad \alpha_{m,n}+\beta_{m,n}=1;$$

$$\alpha_{i,j}+\beta_{i,j}=\alpha_{i+1,j}+\beta_{i,j+1}\quad \text{for } (i,j)\ne(0,0),(m,n).$$

The equations above express the fact that one unit goes out of the source $(0,0)$, one unit goes into the sink (m,n), and at the other vertices, the amount that comes in equals the amount that goes out.

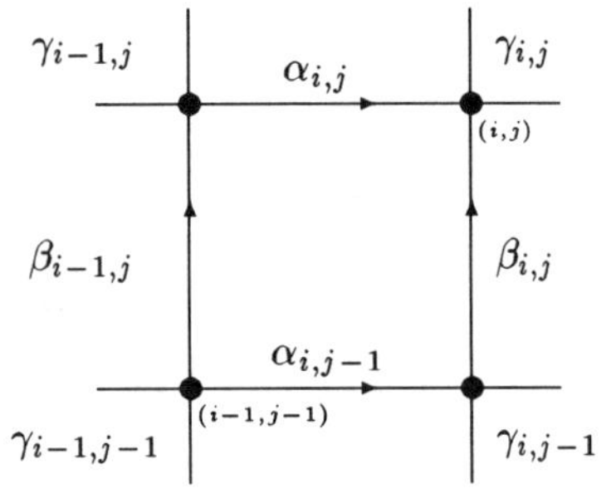

Figure 4: Names of edge- and vertex-flows

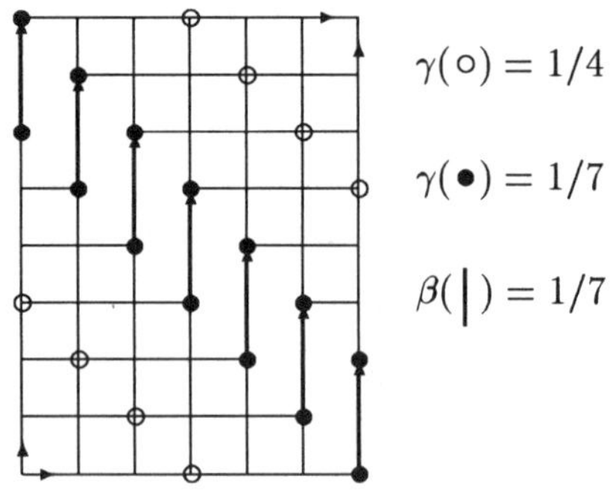

Figure 5: The flow U on the $(6,8)$-grid.

We define $\gamma_{i,j}$, the flow through vertex (i,j), as follows:

$$\gamma_{i,j} = \alpha_{i,j} + \beta_{i,j} \quad \text{for } (i,j) \neq (0,0); \qquad \gamma_{0,0} = 1.$$

Note that:

$$\begin{aligned}
\alpha_{i,j} &= \text{Prob}[\pi(z_{i+j}) = x_i]; \\
\beta_{i,j} &= \text{Prob}[\pi(z_{i+j}) = y_j]; \\
\gamma_{i,j} &= \text{Prob}\big[\{\pi(z_k) : 1 \leq k \leq i+j\} \\
&\qquad = \{x_1, \ldots, x_i, y_1, \ldots, y_j\}\big].
\end{aligned}$$

From these equations we get:

$$\begin{aligned}
&\sum_{k=1}^{m+n} H(\pi(z_k)) \\
&= -\sum_{k=1}^{m+n} \sum_{i+j=k} \alpha_{i,j} \log \alpha_{i,j} + \beta_{i,j} \log \beta_{i,j} \\
&= -\sum_{i=1}^{m}\sum_{j=0}^{n} \alpha_{i,j} \log \alpha_{i,j} - \sum_{i=0}^{m}\sum_{j=1}^{n} \beta_{i,j} \log \beta_{i,j}.
\end{aligned}$$

When $x = 0$, we take $x \log x$ to be $0 = \lim_{x \to 0} x \log x$. For a unit flow $F = (\alpha, \beta)$ from $(0,0)$ to (m,n), define the *entropy*, $H(F)$, to be the quantity expressed above.

We have described a map Γ from the set of distributions on the paths of a grid to the set of unit flows. We claim that this map Γ is surjective. To see this, let $F = (\alpha, \beta)$ be a unit flow. Consider a random walk from $(0,0)$ to (m,n) that behaves as follows: at vertex (i,j), visited with probability $\gamma_{i,j}$, move right with probability $q = \alpha_{i+1,j}/(\alpha_{i+1,j} + \beta_{i,j+1})$ and move upward with probability $1-q$. It is easy to see that the distribution on paths defined by this random walk gets mapped by Γ to the original flow F.

Thus, for any unit flow F, $H(F)$ is a lower bound for $|V - S|$. In fact, there exists a unique *optimal* flow Z such that $H(Z) = \sup\{H(F) : F \text{ unit flow}\}$. We complete the proof of Theorem 1 by constructing a natural *near*-optimal flow U and evaluating $H(U)$. In Section 4, we analyze an optimal flow, determine its entropy fairly accurately for the case $m = n$, and use it to obtain a slightly better lower bound for $M(n,n)$ in Theorem 2. Asymptotically, $H(U)$ and $H(Z)$ differ only in terms of the coefficients of the linear terms.

3.3 Uniform Flow

Consider the following flow $U = (\alpha, \beta)$ (see Figure 5). From $(0,0)$, U maintains a uniform distribution on the diagonals $i + j = 1, 2, \ldots$, that is, $\alpha_{i,j} + \beta_{i,j} = \gamma_{i,j} = 1/(i+j+1)$, until the diagonal $i + j = m$. Then U maintains the flow of $1/(m+1)$ along each vertical line until the diagonal $i + j = n$, and then U 'converges' to (m,n) from this diagonal in the same way that U 'diverges' from $(0,0)$ to the diagonal $i + j = m$.

More precisely, U can be expressed as follows.

$$\begin{aligned}
\alpha_{i,j} &= \beta_{j,i} = \alpha_{m+1-i,n-j} = \beta_{m-j,n+1-i} \\
&= \frac{i}{(i+j)(i+j+1)} \quad \text{for } 1 \leq i+j \leq m;
\end{aligned}$$

$$\alpha_{i,j} = 0, \quad \beta_{i,j} = 1/(m+1), \quad \text{for } m < i+j \leq n.$$

It is easy to verify that these equations do indeed define a unit flow.

By symmetry,

$$\begin{aligned}
&H(U) \\
&= 4\sum_{d=1}^{m}\sum_{i=1}^{d}(-\beta_{i,d-i} \log \beta_{i,d-i})
\end{aligned}$$

$$-(n-m)(m+1)\frac{1}{m+1}\log\frac{1}{m+1}$$

$$= 4\sum_{d=1}^{m}\sum_{i=1}^{d}\frac{-i}{d(d+1)}\log\frac{i}{d(d+1)} +(n-m)\log(m+1)$$

$$= 2\sum_{d=1}^{m}(\log d+\log(d+1)) -4\sum_{d=1}^{m}\frac{1}{d^2+d}\sum_{i=1}^{d} i\log i+(n-m)\log(m+1)$$

$$= 4\log(m+1)!+(n-m-2)\log(m+1) -4\sum_{d=1}^{m}\frac{1}{d^2+d}\sum_{i=1}^{d} i\log i.$$

To bound the last summation, we note

$$\sum_{i=1}^{d} i\log i \leq \sum_{i=1}^{d}\left(\frac{(i+1)i}{2}\log\frac{i+1}{\sqrt{e}}-\frac{i(i-1)}{2}\log\frac{i}{\sqrt{e}}\right) = \frac{d^2+d}{2}\log\frac{d+1}{\sqrt{e}}.$$

So, using Stirling's formula, we bound $H(U)$ as follows:

$$\begin{aligned} H(U) &\geq 4\log(m+1)!+(n-m-2)\log(m+1) -\sum_{d=1}^{m}(2\log(d+1)-\log e)\\ &= 2\log(m+1)!+(n-m-2)\log(m+1) +m\log e\\ &\geq 2(m+1)(\log(m+1)-\log e) +\log(2\pi(m+1)) +(n-m-2)\log(m+1)+m\log e\\ &\geq (m+n)\log(m+1)-m\log e \qquad \text{for } m\geq 1. \end{aligned}$$

The proof of Theorem 1 is now complete. ∎

Remark. Recall that $C(m,n)$ denotes the number of comparators in Batcher's (m,n)-merging network. Yao and Yao [YY76] have shown that for a fixed m the limit $r_m=\lim_{n\to\infty} M(m,n)/n$ exists and that

$$\begin{aligned} r_m &\geq \log(m+1);\\ r_m &\leq \frac{\lceil\log m\rceil}{2}+\frac{m}{2^{\lceil\log m\rceil}}\\ &= \lim_{n\to\infty}\frac{C(m,n)}{n}. \end{aligned}$$

See [Knu73, p. 226] for a proof of the last equality.

Let $\overline{H}(n)$ be the 'discrete entropy' function, i.e., the minimum average length of a binary code that encodes an alphabet of size n under the uniform distribution. As explained, e.g., in [Knu73, p. 374], if $\theta=\lceil\log n\rceil-\log n$, then

$$\overline{H}(n)=\log n+(1+\theta-2^{\theta});$$

and $1+\theta-2^{\theta}$ oscillates between 0 and about 0.086. We can use $\overline{H}$ instead of H in the proof of Theorem 1, and by using $\overline{H}$ we can obtain a lower bound for r_m that is slightly better than the one given by Yao and Yao:

$$\begin{aligned} r_m &\geq \overline{H}(m+1)\\ &= \log(m+1)+(1+\theta-2^{\theta}), \end{aligned}$$

where $\theta=\lceil\log(m+1)\rceil-\log(m+1)$.

4 Optimal Flow and Proof of Theorem 2

In this section we consider an optimal flow. In Section 4.1 we establish some properties of an optimal flow, and show that there is a natural 'potential' function associated with an optimal flow. In Section 4.2 we determine the entropy of the optimal flow on the (n,n)-grid fairly accurately, and obtain Theorem 2.

For a flow F and and an edge e, $F(e)$ denotes the flow along e. A flow F on a grid G is *nonzero everywhere* if $F(e)>0$ for every edge e of G.

4.1 Optimal Flow and Potential Function

Proposition 1. *For each $m,n\geq 1$, there is a unique optimal flow $Z_{m,n}$ on the (m,n)-grid. The optimal flow $Z_{m,n}$ is nonzero everywhere and it is the unique flow $F=(\alpha,\beta)$ that satisfies the following local conditions: For $1\leq i\leq m$, $1\leq j\leq n$,*

$$\alpha_{i,j-1}\beta_{i,j}=\beta_{i-1,j}\alpha_{i,j}.$$

Proof. If k is the number of edges of a grid, we can express a unit flow by k real variables such that each one ranges over $[0,1]$ and that they jointly satisfy a set of linear equations expressing the conditions of a unit flow. These constraints define a bounded and closed set in $\mathbf{R}^k$, and since the entropy is a continuous function, an optimal flow, exists.

To see that an optimal flow is nonzero everywhere, let F be a unit flow such that $F(e_1)=0$ for some edge e_1 and let p_1 be any path from $(0,0)$ to (m,n) that contains e_1. It is easy to see that there exists some path p_2 such that for each edge e in p_2, $F(e) > 0$. Let $F(t)$ be the flow obtained from F by subtracting t from each edge of p_2 and adding t to each edge of p_1. $F(t)$ is indeed a flow, and is defined for $t \in [0, \min_{e \in p_2} F(e)]$. Since the derivative of $-x \log x$ at $x = 0$ is $+\infty$, the derivative $dH(F(t))/dt$ at $t = 0$ is $+\infty$, and hence F cannot be optimal.

Now we show that any optimal flow $F = (\alpha, \beta)$ satisfies the local conditions above. Suppose that $1 \le i_0 \le m$ and $1 \le j_0 \le n$, and let $F(t) = (\alpha(t), \beta(t))$ be the flow defined as follows: $\alpha_{i,j}(t) = \alpha_{i,j}$ and $\beta_{i,j}(t) = \beta_{i,j}$ for all (i,j) except the following four points, where

$$\alpha_{i_0,j_0}(t) = \alpha_{i_0,j_0} - t; \qquad \alpha_{i_0,j_0-1}(t) = \alpha_{i_0,j_0-1} + t;$$
$$\beta_{i_0,j_0}(t) = \beta_{i_0,j_0} + t; \qquad \beta_{i_0-1,j_0}(t) = \beta_{i_0-1,j_0} - t.$$

$F(t)$ is defined for $|t| \le \min\{\alpha_{i_0,j_0}, \beta_{i_0,j_0}, \alpha_{i_0,j_0-1}, \beta_{i_0-1,j_0}\}$, and corresponds to a *local change* by t of the flow around the *cell* with (i_0, j_0) at its upper-right corner (see Figure 4).

Since F is optimal, the derivative $dH(F(t))/dt$ at $t = 0$ must be 0. But

$$\frac{dH(F)}{dt}(0) = -\log \alpha_{i_0,j_0-1} - \log \beta_{i_0,j_0} + \log \beta_{i_0-1,j_0} + \log \alpha_{i_0,j_0},$$

and so

$$\alpha_{i_0,j_0-1}\beta_{i_0,j_0} = \beta_{i_0-1,j_0}\alpha_{i_0,j_0}.$$

Finally, we show that a flow satisfying the local conditions is unique.

First, we claim that such a flow must be nonzero everywhere. To see this, assume that a flow F satisfies the local conditions but $F(e) = 0$ for some edge e in a cell c. By 'propagating' these conditions starting from c, we can obtain a set K of edges such that $F(e) = 0$ for every $e \in K$, and that K is a cut, i.e., removing K disconnects $(0,0)$ and (m,n). This is a contradiction.

Now assume that F_1 and F_2 are distinct nonzero flows satisfying the local conditions. Define the linear interpolation between F_1 and F_2 by:

$$F(t) = F_1 + t(F_2 - F_1).$$

The difference of two flows, $F_2 - F_1$, is a *circulation* and can be expressed as a linear combination σ of *local* circulations, i.e., circulations around single cells. Note that adding a local circulation corresponds to a local change. The derivative $dH(F(t))/dt$ at $t = 0$ is the same linear combination σ of the partial derivatives δ_c of H with respect to each cell c. But $\delta_c = 0$ for every cell c since F_1 satisfies the local conditions. Thus $dH(F(t))/dt$ at $t = 0$ is zero, and it is similarly zero at $t = 1$ since F_2 satisfies the local conditions. But the second derivative of $H(F(t))$ is negative for $t \in [0, 1]$, since the second derivative of $-x \log x$ is negative for $x > 0$ and there is at least one edge e_0 such that $F_1(e_0) \ne F_2(e_0)$. This gives a contradiction. ∎

If an edge e is a part of a path p, we express this by writing $e \in p$.

Let $m, n \ge 1$. Let (i,j) be a vertex of the (m,n)-grid and let p be a path from $(0,0)$ to (i,j). With respect to the optimal flow $Z = Z_{m,n}$, define $V_{i,j}^{(p)}$ by:

$$V_{i,j}^{(p)} = \sum_{e \in p} - \log Z(e).$$

Since Z satisfies the local conditions in Proposition 1, $V_{i,j}^{(p)}$ is independent of p, and thus the *potential* $V_{i,j}$ is well-defined. We may think of Z as a unit electric current flowing from $(0,0)$ to (m,n). For an edge $e = \langle (i,j), (i+1,j) \rangle$, the potential difference along e is $-\log Z(e) = V_{i+1,j} - V_{i,j}$ and $-Z(e)\log Z(e)$ is the 'work done' by $Z(e)$. Call the potential $V_{m,n}$ at the sink (m,n) the *potential of flow* Z and denote it by $V(Z)$.

In the interpretation above, the entropy $H(Z)$, which is the sum of $-Z(e)\log Z(e)$ over all edges e, is the total work done by a unit current, and thus the following is intuitively clear. A proof is not hard and is omitted.

Proposition 2.

$$H(Z_{m,n}) = V(Z_{m,n}).$$

For an *arbitrary* unit flow F on the (m,n)-grid and a path p from $(0,0)$ to (m,n), define $V^{(p)}$, which in general depends on p, similarly as above:

$$V^{(p)}(F) = \sum_{e \in p} - \log F(e)$$

(if $F(e) = 0$ for some $e \in p$ then $V^{(p)}(F) = +\infty$), and define 'max potential' $V_{\max}$ and 'min potential' $V_{\min}$ as follows, where the maximum and the minimum are over paths p from $(0,0)$ to (m,n).

$$V_{\max}(F) = \max_p V_{m,n}^{(p)}(F);$$
$$V_{\min}(F) = \min_p V_{m,n}^{(p)}(F).$$

Proposition 3. *Among unit flows on the (m,n)-grid, the optimal flow $Z_{m,n}$ is the unique flow that minimizes $V_{\max}$ and it is also the unique flow that maximizes $V_{\min}$.*

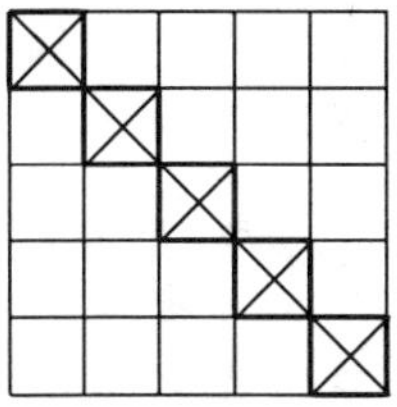

Figure 6: Cells where U does *not* satisfy the local condition on the $(5,5)$-grid.

Proof. We show that $Z_{m,n}$ uniquely minimizes $V_{\max}$. A proof for $V_{\min}$ is similar.

We can show the existence of a flow that attains the minimum in a similar way as we showed the existence of an optimal flow in the proof of Proposition 1. Thus it suffices to show that for any nonoptimal flow F, $V_{\max}(F)$ is not the minimum.

Let F be a nonoptimal flow. We may assume that F is nonzero everywhere since otherwise $V_{\max}(F) = +\infty$. Say that a path from $(0,0)$ to (m,n) is *critical with respect to* F if $V^{(p)}(F) = V_{\max}(F)$. Let $P = \{p_1, \ldots, p_k\}$ be the set of critical paths with respect to F. By Proposition 1, there exists a cell c such that F does not satisfy the local condition along c, and from this it readily follows that there exists a path $\overline{p}$ that is not critical with respect to F. Clearly, $F(e) > 0$ for every edge $e \in \overline{p}$. For sufficiently small $\epsilon > 0$, if we subtract ϵ from $\overline{p}$ and add ϵ/k to each $p_i \in P$, we obtain a unit flow F' satisfying $V_{\max}(F') < V_{\max}(F)$, since $V^{(p)}(F') < V^{(p_i)}(F)$ for each i. ∎

From Propositions 2 and 3 we immediately get the following.

Corollary 4. *For an arbitrary unit flow F on the (m,n)-grid,*

$$V_{\min}(F) \leq H(Z_{m,n}) \leq V_{\max}(F).$$

4.2 Entropy of Optimal Flow

Let $Z_{m,n}$ be the unique optimal flow on the (m,n)-grid, and let $h(m,n) = H(Z_{m,n})$. Let $U_{m,n}$ be the uniform flow considered in Section 3.3. We will write Z_n for $Z_{n,n}$, U_n for $U_{n,n}$, and $h(n)$ for $h(n,n)$. Recall that $H(U_n) \approx 2n \log n - 1.45n$. The flow U_n is not optimal since it does not satisfy the local condition above for the cells on the main diagonal, where $i+j = n$ (see Figure 6). The condition *is* satisfied at all the other cells.

Our main goal will be to show, by establishing two recurrence relations for $h(m,n)$, the existence of a constant C such that $h(n)$ can be expressed as: $h(n) = 2n \log n - Cn + o(n)$. Once this is done, numerical experiments for small values of n together with Corollary 4 yield upper and lower bounds for C, and we can obtain Theorem 2.

We first state two auxiliary lemmas. The first concerns the scaling of flows.

For any flow F, if λ is a positive real number, then λF denotes the flow with flow $\lambda F(e)$ along each edge e.

Lemma 1. *For any unit flow F on the (m,n)-grid,*

$$H(\lambda F) = \lambda H(F) - (m+n)\lambda \log \lambda.$$

Proof.

$$\begin{aligned} H(\lambda F) &= -\sum_e \lambda F(e) \log(\lambda F(e)) \\ &= \lambda H(F) - \lambda \log \lambda \sum_e F(e) \\ &= \lambda H(F) - (m+n)\lambda \log \lambda. \end{aligned}$$ ∎

Lemma 2. *The function $h(m,n)$ is strictly monotone increasing in each of the variables.*

Proof. We show that $h(m+1,n) > h(m,n)$. Construct a flow F on the $(m+1,n)$-grid by extending the flow $Z_{m,n}$ by sending one unit from (m,n) to $(m+1,n)$. Then, $H(F) = H(Z_{m,n}) = h(m,n)$. But since F is zero for some edges, by Proposition 1 F is not optimal for the $(m+1,n)$-grid. Hence $h(m+1,n) > H(F) = h(m,n)$. ∎

Lemma 3. *For any integers $d, m, n \geq 1$,*

$$h(d(m+1), d(n+1)) > d\,h(m,n) + (m+n)d \log d + H(U_{d-1}).$$

Proof. Suppose we take d copies of the (m,n)-grid, 'stretch' each edge by replacing it by a chain of d edges, and superimpose the d stretched grids by embedding their origins at the points $(0,d-1), (1,d-2), \ldots, (d-1,0)$. The construction is illustrated in Figure 7. A unit flow F on the $(d(m+1)-1, d(n+1)-1)$-grid can be constructed as follows. Use the lower-left triangle from the uniform flow U_{d-1} to feed the origin of each copy with a flow of d^{-1}, collect the flow out of the top-right nodes of the copies with the upper-right triangle of U_{d-1}, and use an optimal flow within each copy. Since there are d copies and in each copy every edge

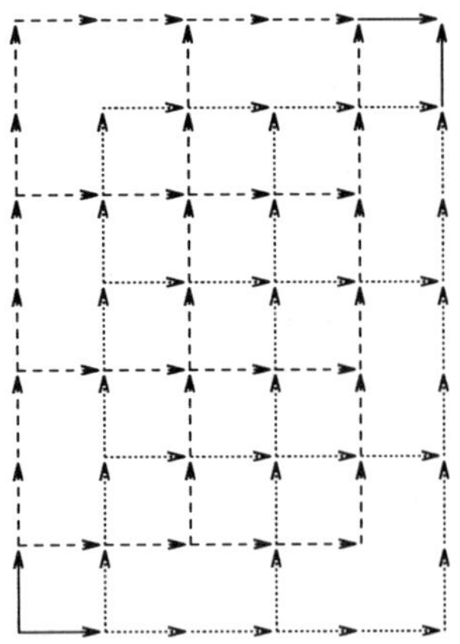

Figure 7: Illustrating Lemma 3 with the parameters $d = 2, m = 2, n = 3$.

is replicated d times, we obtain the factor of d^2 in the following expression. Using Lemma 2 for the first inequality, we get:

$$\begin{aligned} &h(d(m+1), d(n+1)) \\ &\quad > \; h(d(m+1)-1, d(n+1)-1) \\ &\quad \geq \; H(F) \\ &\quad = \; d^2\left(\frac{1}{d}h(m,n) + (m+n)\frac{1}{d}\log d\right) + H(U_{d-1}), \end{aligned}$$

where the equality is by Lemma 1 with $\lambda = d^{-1}$. ∎

The next lemma uses a decomposition into sets of parallel edges to give a complementary bound.

Lemma 4. *For any integers $d, m, n \geq 1$,*

$$h(dm, dn) \leq d\,h(m,n) + (m+n)d\log d.$$

Proof. Extend the domain of the optimal flow $Z_{dm,dn} = (\alpha, \beta)$, by defining $Z_{dm,dn}(e) = 0$ for any edge e outside the (dm, dn)-grid. We 'decompose' $Z_{dm,dn}$ into d unit flows, $(A^{(k)}, B^{(k)})$ for $k = 0, 1, \ldots, d-1$, by defining $(A^{(k)}_{i,j}, B^{(k)}_{i,j})$ as follows (see Figure 8).

For $1 \leq i \leq m, 0 \leq j \leq n$,

$$A^{(k)}_{i,j} = \sum_{t=0}^{d-1} \alpha_{di-k, dj-k+t}$$

and for convenience define $A^{(k)}_{i,j} = 0$ for $i = 0, m+1$ and $0 \leq j \leq n$. For $0 \leq i \leq m, 1 \leq j \leq n$,

$$B^{(k)}_{i,j} = \sum_{t=0}^{d-1} \beta_{di-k+t, dj-k}.$$

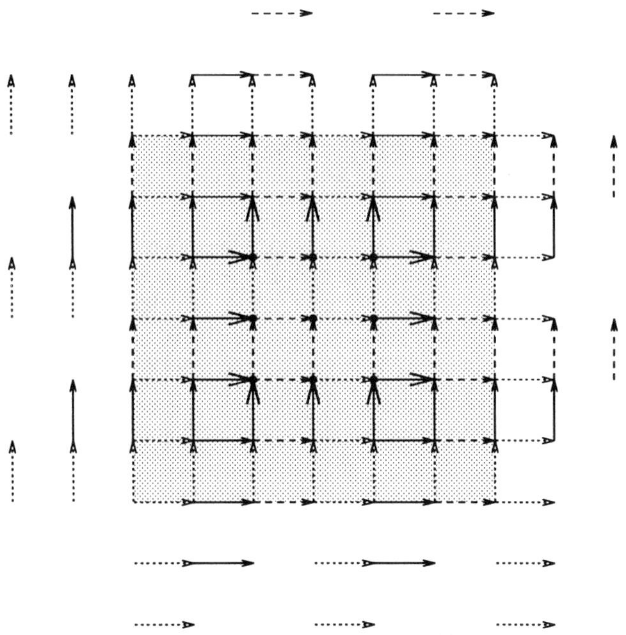

Figure 8: Illustrating Lemma 4 with the parameters $d = 3, m = 2, n = 2$. The larger arrows show the edges contributing to $A^{(1)}_{1,1}, B^{(1)}_{1,1}, A^{(1)}_{2,1}$, and $B^{(1)}_{1,2}$.

and $B^{(k)}_{i,j} = 0$ for $j = 0, n+1$ and $0 \leq i \leq m$.

Claim. *For each $0 \leq k \leq d-1$, $F^{(k)} = (A^{(k)}, B^{(k)})$ is a unit flow on the (m,n)-grid.*

Proof of Claim : For $0 \leq i \leq m, 0 \leq j \leq n$, define $\delta_{i,j}$ for the original flow (α, β) as follows:

$$\delta_{i,j} = \alpha_{i+1,j} + \beta_{i,j+1} - \alpha_{i,j} - \beta_{i,j};$$

and for $k = 0, \ldots, d-1$, define $D^{(k)}_{i,j}$ for $(A^{(k)}, B^{(k)})$ as follows:

$$D^{(k)}_{i,j} = A^{(k)}_{i+1,j} + B^{(k)}_{i,j+1} - A^{(k)}_{i,j} - B^{(k)}_{i,j}.$$

For each $i \in \{0, \ldots, m\}$, $j \in \{0, \ldots, n\}$ and $k \in \{0, \ldots, d-1\}$, the net outflow around the perimeter of the $d \times d$ array of nodes $\{\langle di-k+u, dj-k+v\rangle : 0 \leq u \leq d-1, 0 \leq j \leq d-1\}$ equals the sum of the net outflows for these nodes (see Figure 8), so we have

$$D^{(k)}_{i,j} = \sum_{u=0}^{d-1}\sum_{v=0}^{d-1} \delta_{di-k+u, dj-k+v}.$$

Since $\delta_{0,0} = +1$, $\delta_{dm,dn} = -1$, and $\delta_{i,j} = 0$ elsewhere, we have, for each $k = 0 \ldots d-1$,

$$D^{(k)}_{0,0} = +1, \; D^{(k)}_{dm,dn} = -1, \text{ and } D^{(k)}_{i,j} = 0. \qquad \blacksquare_{\text{Claim}}$$

If $X = x_1 + \ldots + x_d$, then, since the function $x \log x$ is convex, we have

$$-\sum x_i \log x_i \leq -d\frac{X}{d}\log\frac{X}{d}.$$

So if, for each k, i, j, we replace the flow on each of the d edges contributing to $A^{(k)}_{i,j}$ by $A^{(k)}_{i,j}/d$, and similarly for $B^{(k)}_{i,j}$, then the 'entropy' of the result (which is not necessarily a flow) cannot decrease. Hence,

$$\begin{aligned} h(dm, dn) &= H(Z_{dm,dn}) \\ &\leq d\sum_{k=0}^{d-1} H(d^{-1}F^{(k)}) \\ &= \sum_{k=0}^{d-1} H(F^{(k)}) + (m+n)d\log d, \end{aligned}$$

where the last equality is by Lemma 1. ∎

Lemmas 3 and 4 allow us to provide close estimates of the asymptotic behaviour of $h(n)$.

From Lemma 3 we obtain

$$\begin{aligned} h(d(n+1)) &> d\,h(n) + 2nd\log d \\ &\quad +2(d-1)\log d - (d-1)\log e, \quad (1) \end{aligned}$$

while Lemma 4 yields

$$h(nd) \leq d\,h(n) + 2nd\log d. \qquad (2)$$

Using (1) and (2), we can relate $h(p)$ and $h(q)$ for arbitrary positive integers p and q as follows.

$$\begin{aligned} h(q(p+1)) &> q\,h(p) + 2pq\log q \\ &\quad +2(q-1)\log q - (q-1)\log e; \quad (3) \\ h(q(p+1)) &\leq (p+1)h(q) \\ &\quad +2q(p+1)\log(p+1). \quad (4) \end{aligned}$$

For each $n \geq 1$, define c_n by the equation

$$h(n) = 2n\log(n+1) - c_n n.$$

By proving the following proposition, we achieve the goal stated in the beginning of Section 4.2 and finish the proof of Theorem 2.

Proposition 4. *The limit $C = \lim_{n\to\infty} c_n$ exists, $1.23 < C < 1.31$, and the following holds.*

$$C - 2\frac{\log n}{n} - O(1/n) \leq c_n < C + O(1/n).$$

Proof. From (3) and (4) and dividing by pq, we get

$$\begin{aligned} &h(p)/p + 2\log q + (1 - 1/q)(2\log q - \log e)/p \\ &\quad < (1 + 1/p)h(q)/q + 2(1+1/p)\log(p+1). \end{aligned}$$

Noting that $c_n = -h(n)/n + 2\log(n+1)$, by a simple calculation we obtain

$$c_q - c_p < O(\log p/p) + O(1/q),$$

and thus the symmetric bound,

$$|c_q - c_p| < O(\log p/p) + O(\log q/q).$$

So $\langle c_1, c_2, \ldots \rangle$ is a Cauchy sequence and the limit $C = \lim_{n\to\infty} c_n$ exists.

When we let $d \to \infty$ in (1) we obtain

$$\begin{aligned} c_n &\geq C - \frac{h(n)}{n(n+1)} + \frac{2 - \log e}{n+1} \\ &= C - 2\frac{\log n}{n} - O(1/n). \end{aligned}$$

With $d \to \infty$ in (2), we obtain a complementary bound

$$c_n \leq C + 2\log(1 + 1/n) = C + O(1/n).$$

We have computed numerical approximations to optimal flows for values of n up to 256. Using them, we directly get *lower* bounds for $h(n)$, and thus *upper* bounds for c_n. By evaluating $V_{\max}$ for approximations and using Corollary 4, we also get upper bounds for $h(n)$ and thus lower bounds for c_n.

From these upper and lower bounds for c_n together with the two inequalities for C above, we obtain the claimed bounds for C. ∎

5 Conclusion and Open Problems

We have shown that Batcher's (m, n)-merging networks are asymptotically optimal as $n \geq m \to \infty$. At present, there is no pair (m, n) for which an (m, n)-merging network with less than $C(m, n)$ comparators is known to exist, and the problem of proving or disproving:

$$M(m, n) = C(m, n) \text{ for all } m, n \geq 1,$$

which was stated as an open problem in [Knu73, p. 243, Exercise 45], remains open.

For the case $m = 2$, Yao and Yao [YY76] have shown that $M(2, n) = C(2, n) = \lceil \frac{3}{2}n \rceil$. For $n \leq 5$,

Floyd [Knu73, p. 237, Exercise 9] has shown that $M(n,n) = C(n,n)$. Thus for these cases Batcher's networks are *exactly* optimal.

Improving the lower bounds shown in this paper would be a natural step towards determining $M(m,n)$. We note that the positive lower bound for C in Proposition 4 means that the method used in this paper can only yield a lower bound of the form $n \log n - O(n)$.

We have determined $h(n)$ fairly accurately. To similarly determine $h(m,n)$ remains an open problem. Also, a description of the optimal flow $Z_{m,n}$ *itself* remains an open problem, even for the case $m = n$. As $m, n \to \infty$, the equations defining the optimal flow converge to a partial differential equation defining a continuous two-dimensional flow $(\alpha(x,y), \beta(x,y))$. The local optimality condition becomes:

$$\frac{\partial \log \beta}{\partial x} = \frac{\partial \log \alpha}{\partial y},$$

and there is a 'potential' function V such that

$$-\log \alpha = \frac{\partial V}{\partial x} \text{ and } -\log \beta = \frac{\partial V}{\partial y}.$$

The flow condition imposes the following differential equation for the potential function:

$$\left(\frac{\partial}{\partial x} e^{\frac{\partial}{\partial x}} + \frac{\partial}{\partial y} e^{\frac{\partial}{\partial y}} \right) V = 0.$$

We have found one nontrivial solution to this equation, corresponding to a uniform flow like U, but extending over the infinite quadrant. We can solve the equation numerically for the unit square, but we have no explicit solution.

References

[Knu73] D. Knuth, *The Art of Computer Programming*, Volume 3: Sorting and Searching, Addison-Wesley, 1973.

[Lam79] E. Lamagna, "The complexity of monotone networks for certain bilinear forms, routing problems, sorting and merging," *IEEE Trans. on Comp.*, 28(1979), 773–782.

[PV76] N. Pippenger and L. Valiant, "Shifting graphs and their applications," *J. Assoc. Comput. Mach.*, 23(1976), 423–432.

[YY76] A. Yao and F. Yao, "Lower bounds on merging networks," *J. Assoc. Comput. Mach.*, 23(1976), 566–571.

Truly Alphabet-Independent Two-Dimensional Pattern Matching

Zvi Galil†
Department of Computer Science
Columbia University and
Tel-Aviv University

Kunsoo Park‡
Department of Computing
King's College London
Strand, London WC2R 2LS

Abstract

Amir, Benson and Farach recently gave an algorithm for two-dimensional pattern matching (ABF for short) whose text processing is independent of the alphabet and takes $O(n^2)$ time, but whose pattern processing is dependent on the alphabet and takes $O(m^2 \log |\Sigma|)$ time. We present an algorithm that is truly independent of the alphabet and takes linear $O(m^2 + n^2)$ time. As in the Knuth-Morris-Pratt algorithm, the only operation on the alphabet is the equality test of two symbols.

All previous algorithms except the ABF algorithm reduce the two-dimensional problem into one-dimensional string matching, and use known techniques in string matching. The ABF algorithm uses two-dimensional periodicity for text processing, but their pattern processing resorts to one-dimensional techniques. We present a two-dimensional technique for both pattern processing and text processing.

1. Introduction

The two-dimensional pattern matching problem is: Given pattern $P[0..m-1, 0..m-1]$ and text $T[0..n-1, 0..n-1]$, find all occurrences of P in T. The pattern and the text contain symbols from an alphabet Σ. Let $\sigma = \min(|\Sigma|, m^2)$.

Baker [5] and Bird [6] independently gave an $O((m^2 + n^2)\log\sigma)$ time algorithm (BB for short) for two-dimensional pattern matching which uses the Knuth-Morris-Pratt algorithm [9] (KMP for short) and the Aho-Corasick algorithm [1] for one-dimensional string matching. Since the Aho-Corasick algorithm requires a totally ordered alphabet and its time depends on the alphabet size, so does the BB algorithm. For an unbounded alphabet, the BB algorithm takes $O((m^2 + n^2)\log m)$ time. Using suffix trees, Amir, Landau and Vishkin [4] also gave an algorithm whose time complexity is the same as that of the BB algorithm. Zhu and Takaoka [12] developed a randomized algorithm that uses the KMP algorithm and the Karp-Rabin algorithm [8]. Recently, Amir, Benson and Farach [3] gave an algorithm (ABF for short) whose text processing is independent of the alphabet and takes $O(n^2)$ time, but whose pattern processing is still dependent on the alphabet and takes $O(m^2 \log\sigma)$ time. We present an algorithm for two-dimensional pattern matching that is truly independent of the alphabet and takes linear $O(m^2 + n^2)$ time. As in the KMP algorithm, the only operation on the alphabet is the equality test of two symbols. Our algorithm can be easily generalized to rectangular arrays.

All previous algorithms except the ABF algorithm reduce the two-dimensional problem into one-dimensional string matching, and use known techniques in string matching. The ABF algorithm uses two-dimensional periodicity for text processing, but their pattern processing resorts to one-dimensional techniques. We present a two-dimensional technique for both pattern processing and text processing.

Amir and Benson [2] studied two-dimensional periodicity and classified two-dimensional arrays into four categories: non-periodic, lattice-periodic, line-periodic, and radiant-periodic. They also gave an $O(m^2 \log\sigma)$ time algorithm for classifying an array, which was used in the pattern processing of the ABF algorithm. We adopt the four categories, and characterize the positions of an array where another copy of the array overlaps without a mismatch in each category (especially in the cases of line-periodicity and radiant-periodicity, which was not done in [2]). Our pattern processing classifies an array into one of the four categories in $O(m^2)$ time, which also improves the pattern processing of two-dimensional run-length compressed matching [2].

2. Two-Dimensional Periodicity

Let A be an $m \times m$ square array with rows $0, \ldots, m-1$ and columns $0, \ldots, m-1$. An *element* of A is $A[i, j]$

† Work supported in part by NSF Grant CCR-9014605
‡ Work supported in part by MRC Grant G 9115730

0-8186-2900-2/92 $3.00 © 1992 IEEE

for some $0 \leq i < m$ and $0 \leq j < m$. Each element of A contains a symbol from an alphabet Σ. A *point* of A is a pair of integers (i, j) for a row coordinate i and a column coordinate j. Note the difference in the definition of points from the x, y coordinates of the plane. We use (i, j) to represent either a point or a vector. When $u = (i, j)$, $A[i, j]$ is also denoted by $A[u]$.

We divide A into four quadrants, labeled counterclockwise from upper-left: quadrants I, II, III, and IV. Let C_I (C_{II}) be the upper-left quadrant of quadrant I (lower-left quadrant of quadrant II). A vector (i, j) is a *quad-I vector* if $i \geq 0$ and $j > 0$. Similarly, (i, j) is a *quad-II vector* if $i < 0$ and $j \geq 0$. The *length* $|v|$ of a vector v is the maximum of the absolute values of its coordinates. Among quad-I (quad-II) vectors of the same length, ***the shortest*** quad-I (quad-II) vector is the smallest one in the lexicographic order of the [row,column] ([column,row]) pair. We define partial orders on points: $(i, j) \prec_I (k, l)$ if $i \leq k$ and $j < l$; $(i, j) \prec_{II} (k, l)$ if $i > k$ and $j \leq l$. A sequence of points $u_1, \ldots, u_p$ in A is called a *monotone line* if $u_i \prec_I u_{i+1}$ ($u_i \prec_{II} u_{i+1}$ in quad-II) for $1 \leq i \leq p - 1$.

Suppose we have two copies of A, one on top of the other with some overlapping elements. The two copies are said to be *in register* if the overlapping areas of the two copies are the same.

1. If the two copies are in register when $A[0, 0]$ overlaps $A[r, c]$ for $r \geq 0$ and $c > 0$, we say that A is *quad-I symmetric*, and that (r, c) is a *quad-I symmetry vector* of A.
2. If the two copies are in register when $A[m-1, 0]$ overlaps $A[m-1+r, c]$ for $r < 0$ and $c \geq 0$, we say that A is *quad-II symmetric*, and that (r, c) is a *quad-II symmetry vector* of A.

Quad-III and quad-IV symmetries are defined similarly. A symmetry vector v is *periodic* if $|v| < m/4$. A periodic quad-I (quad-II) symmetry vector will be called a quad-I (quad-II) *source*. If A has a quad-I (quad-II) symmetry vector $v = (r, c)$, we define the *regular area* of v in A to be $\{u \in A | u + v \in A \text{ or } u - v \in A\}$ (i.e., the union of $A[0..m-1-r, 0..m-1-c]$ and $A[r..m-1, c..m-1]$ ($A[-r..m-1, 0..m-1-c]$ and $A[0..m-1+r, c..m-1]$)). We will work only with quad-I and quad-II symmetries because quad-I (quad-II) symmetry implies quad-III (quad-IV) symmetry and vice versa.

We classify square arrays into the following four categories by the existence of sources.

1. Non-periodic: there are no sources.
2. Lattice-periodic: there exist a quad-I source and a quad-II source.
3. Line-periodic: one quadrant has only one independent (vector independence) source, and the other quadrant has no source.
4. Radiant-periodic: one quadrant has at least two independent sources, and the other has no source.

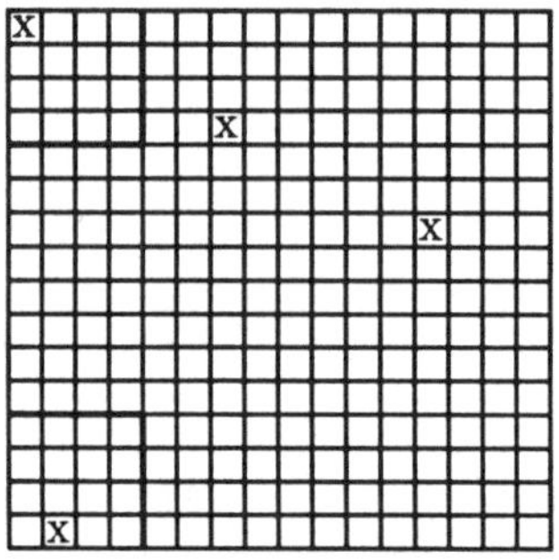

Fig. 1. Non-periodic. The upper-left corner is $(0, 0)$.

In the following we will characterize all quad-I and quad-II sources in each category. Let $v_I = (r_1, c_1)$ and $v_{II} = (r_2, c_2)$ be the shortest quad-I and quad-II symmetry vectors of A, respectively. If A is non-periodic (i.e., $|v_I|, |v_{II}| \geq m/4$), there are no quad-I and quad-II sources (see Fig. 1). In all the examples of arrays, $\Sigma = \{\text{x}, \text{o}, b\}$, where b is the blank symbol.

Lattice-periodicity

Lemma 1. [2] If $v_1 = (r_1, c_1)$ and $v_2 = (r_2, c_2)$ are quad-I (quad-II) symmetry vectors such that $|r_1| + |r_2| < m$ and $c_1 + c_2 < m$, then $v = v_1 + v_2$ is also a quad-I (quad-II) symmetry vector.

Lemma 2. [2] If $v_1 = (r_1, c_1)$ and $v_2 = (r_2, c_2)$ are quad-I and quad-II symmetry vectors, respectively, such that $r_1 + |r_2| < m$ and $c_1 + c_2 < m$, then $v = v_1 + v_2$ is either a quad-I symmetry vector (if $r_1 \geq |r_2|$) or a quad-II symmetry vector (if $r_1 < |r_2|$).

Lemma 3. [2] If $v_1 = (r_1, c_1)$ and $v_2 = (r_2, c_2)$ are quad-I and quad-II symmetry vectors, respectively, such that $r_1 + |r_2| < m$ and $c_1 + c_2 < m$, then all $iv_1 + jv_2$ for integers i, j are symmetry vectors of A.

If an array A has v_1 and v_2 that satisfy the condition of Lemma 3, the whole array A can be generated by a parallelogram defined by $(0, 0), v_1, v_2, v_1 + v_2$, which will be referred to as the *unit lattice*. We call such an array *lattice-generative*. Thus if A is lattice-periodic (i.e., $|v_I|, |v_{II}| < m/4$), the unit lattice defined by v_I and v_{II} generates the whole array A (lattice-generative).

Theorem 1. Let $v_1 = (r_1, c_1)$ and $v_2 = (r_2, c_2)$ are quad-I and quad-II symmetry vectors, respectively, such that $r_1, |r_2| < m/2$ and $c_1, c_2 < m/2$. Then (k, l) for $0 \leq k < m/2$ and $0 < l < m/2$ (for $-m/2 < k < 0$ and $0 \leq l < m/2$) is a quad-I (quad-II) symmetry vector if and only if $(k, l) = iv_1 + jv_2$ for some integers i, j.

As a corollary of Theorem 1, (k, l) for $0 \leq k < m/4$ and $0 < l < m/4$ (for $-m/4 < k < 0$ and $0 \leq l < m/4$) is a quad-I source (quad-II source) if and only if $(k, l) = iv_I + jv_{II}$ for some integers i, j. In the lattice-periodic case, v_I and v_{II} are called the ***basis vectors*** of A, and $iv_I + jv_{II}$ for integers i, j is called a ***lattice point***.

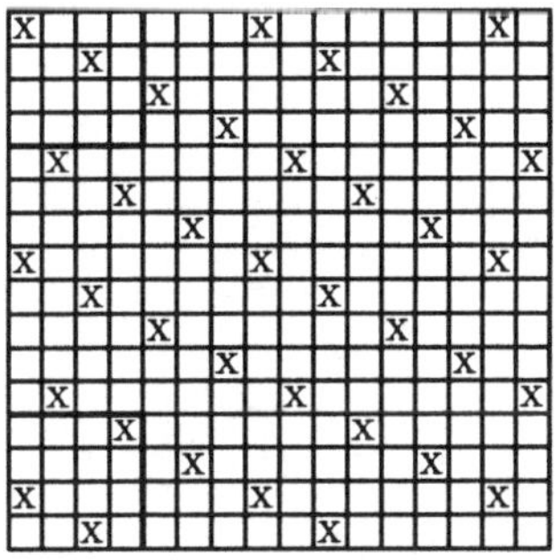

Fig. 2. Lattice-periodic: $v_I = (1, 2), v_{II} = (-3, 1)$.

Line-periodicity

If A is line-periodic or radiant-periodic, one of v_I and v_{II} is periodic and the other is not. Wlog, assume that v_I is periodic and v_{II} is not. When A is line-periodic, there is no source which is independent of v_I. There may be more than one quad-I sources, but all quad-I sources are on one line. We show that the distances between quad-I sources are nonincreasing.

Theorem 2. Let $s_1, \ldots, s_p$ be the quad-I sources of A from shortest to longest. Then $s_i = a_i s_1$ for $2 \leq i \leq p$ (a_i is not necessarily an integer), and $|s_i - s_{i-1}| \geq |s_{i+1} - s_i|$ for $1 \leq i \leq p-1$, where $s_0 = (0, 0)$.

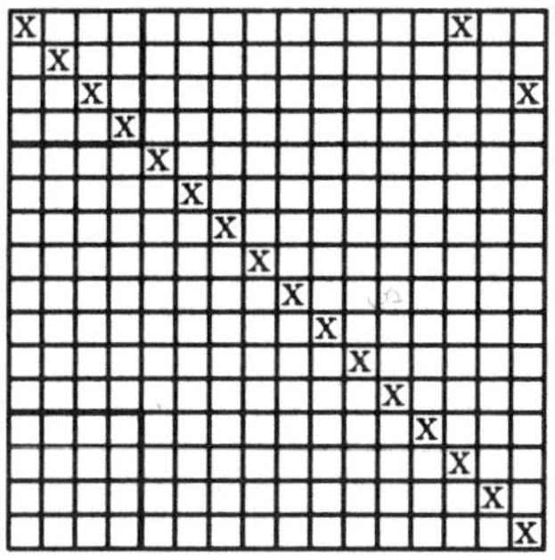

Fig. 3. Line-periodic: quad-I sources $(2, 2), (3, 3)$.

Radiant-periodicity

When A is radiant-periodic in quad-I, there is at least one quad-I source v'_I that is independent of v_I.

Lemma 4. If A is radiant-periodic in quad-I, quadrants I and III of A are lattice-generative. Furthermore, the shortest quad-I and quad-II symmetry vectors b_1 and b_2, respectively, of quadrant I (also III) satisfy $|b_1|, |b_2| < m/4$.

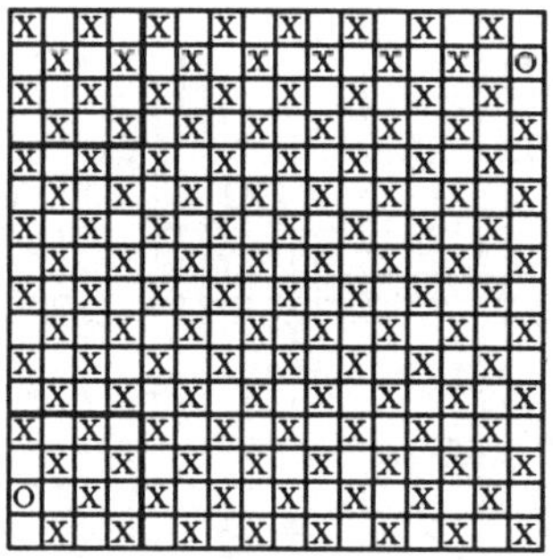

Fig. 4. Radiant-periodic (case (i)): $b_1 = (1, 1), b_2 = (-1, 1)$. Quad-I sources are $(2, 2)$, $(3, 1)$, and $(3, 3)$.

In quadrant II or IV there is at least one mismatch with the lattice of quadrant I (also III) defined by b_1 and b_2—otherwise, A would be lattice-periodic. Suppose quadrant II has at least one mismatch. We say that a symmetry vector v is *affected* by a mismatch if the mismatch is in the regular area of v. A symmetry vector v is affected by a set of mismatches if it is affected by at least one of them.

Lemma 5. Let N be a set of mismatches in quadrant II, and x (y) be the smallest row (largest column) that has a mismatch in N. Then a vector (i, j) for $0 \leq i, j < m/4$ is not affected by N if and only if $i \geq m - x$ and $j > y$.

Similarly, let N' be a set of mismatches in quadrant IV, and x' (y') be the largest row (smallest column) that has a mismatch in N'. A vector (i, j) for $0 \leq i, j < m/4$ is not affected by N' if and only if $i > x'$ and $j \geq m - y'$. Let x_2 (y_2) be the smallest row (largest column) that has a mismatch in quadrant II, and x_4 (y_4) be the largest row (smallest column) that has a mismatch in quadrant IV, if any. Now let $D = A[\max(m-x_2, x_4+1)..m-1, \max(y_2+1, m-y_4)..m-1]$, and D_{C_I} be the intersection of D and C_I.

Theorem 3. A point (k,l) in D_{C_I} is a quad-I source if and only if $(k,l) = ib_1 + jb_2$ for some integers i, j.
(i) If $v_I \in D_{C_I}$, there is no quad-I source outside D_{C_I}.
(ii) If $v_I \notin D_{C_I}$, let $s_1, \ldots, s_p$ be the quad-I sources from shortest to longest which are outside D_{C_I}. Then each s_i for $1 \le i \le p$ is a linear combination of b_1 and b_2, the sources form a monotone line, and $|s_i - s_{i-1}| \ge |s_{i+1} - s_i|$ for $1 \le i \le p-1$, where $s_0 = (0,0)$.

Even when quadrants I and III of A are lattice-generative, A may be line-periodic if the quad-I sources form a line.

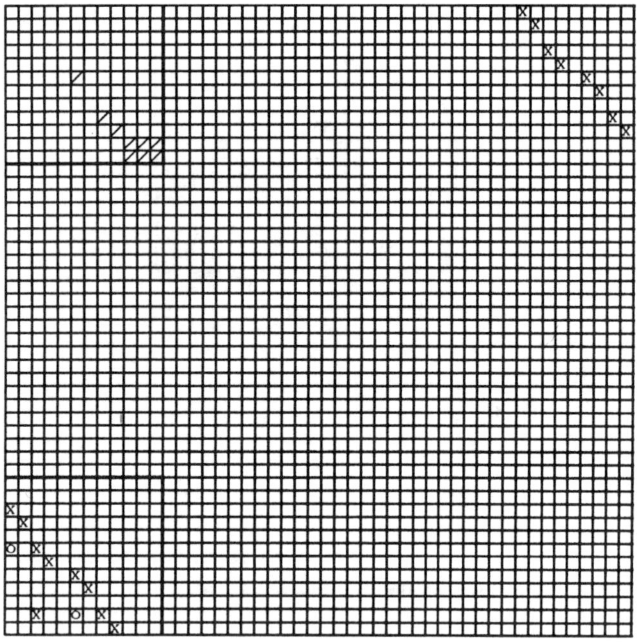

Fig. 5. Radiant-periodic (case (ii)): $b_1 = (0,1), b_2 = (-1,0)$. Quad-I sources are marked with slashes.

3. The Text Processing

Our algorithm for two-dimensional pattern matching consists of pattern processing and text processing. The pattern processing computes witnesses [11,7], which are used in the text processing. The output of the pattern processing is:

(1) QI-WITNESS$[0..m/4-1, 1..m/4-1]$ (which is denoted by QI-WITNESS(C_I)): QI-WITNESS$[i,j] = (m,m)$ if (i,j) is a quad-I source of P. Otherwise, QI-WITNESS$[i,j] = (r,c)$ such that $P[r,c] \ne P[r-i, c-j]$. The point (r,c) is called a *witness* of P against the symmetry vector (i,j), or simply a witness against (i,j).
(2) QII-WITNESS$[-(m/4-1)..-1, 0..m/4-1]$ (denoted by QII-WITNESS(C_{II})): QII-WITNESS$[i,j] = (m,m)$ if (i,j) is a quad-II source of P. Otherwise, QII-WITNESS$[i,j] = (r,c)$ such that $P[r,c] \ne P[r-i, c-j]$. Again (r,c) is a witness against (i,j).

For a point (i,j) in T, we define the *region* of (i,j) to be $T[i..i+m-1, j..j+m-1]$. We say that a text point (i,j) is a *candidate* if its region is a possible occurrence of the pattern. Initially, (i,j) for all $0 \le i \le n-m$ and $0 \le j \le n-m$ are candidates. We say that two candidates (i,j) and (k,l) for $0 \le k-i < m/4$ and $0 < l-j < m/4$ are *consistent* if QI-WITNESS$[k-i, l-j] = (m,m)$ (they expect the same text symbols in their region of overlap). Similarly, (i,j) and (k,l) for $-m/4 < k-i < 0$ and $0 \le l-j < m/4$ are consistent if QII-WITNESS$[k-i, l-j] = (m,m)$.

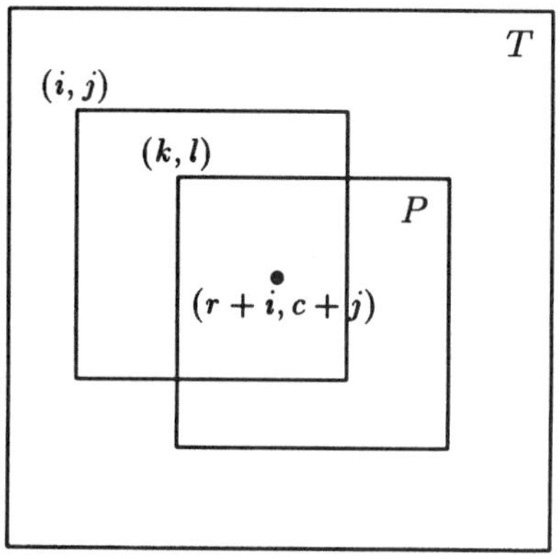

Fig. 6. Duel in text processing.

Duels: Consider two candidates (i,j) and (k,l) such that $0 \le k-i < m/4$ and $0 < l-j < m/4$. If QI-WITNESS$[k-i, l-j] \ne (m,m)$ (they are inconsistent), we can remove one or both of the candidates. Let QI-WITNESS$[k-i, l-j] = (r,c)$.

(a) If $T[r+i, c+j] \ne P[r,c]$, remove (i,j).
(b) If $T[r+i, c+j] \ne P[r-k+i, c-l+j]$, remove (k,l).

Consider two candidates (i,j) and (k,l) such that $-m/4 < k-i < 0$ and $0 \le l-j < m/4$. Let QII-WITNESS$[k-i, l-j] = (r,c)$, which is not (m,m). We can again remove one or both of the candidates with the same tests (a) and (b) above.

We define a *t-square* to be a $2^t \times 2^t$ square whose upper-left corner is (i,j) such that both i and j are multiples of 2^t. Note that each t-square consists of four $(t-1)$-squares. When we combine the four $(t-1)$-squares into one t-square, we first combine the upper-left and lower-left $(t-1)$-squares into one, the upper-right and lower-right $(t-1)$-squares into one, and then we combine the two rectangles into the t-square. In the following, a *block* will denote either a $(t-1)$-square or a rectangle that consists of two $(t-1)$-squares.

The text processing consists of consistency checking and occurrence checking. In consistency checking we remove candidates by duels until all remaining candidates in each $(\log m - 2)$-square are pairwise consistent. In occurrence checking we check if the remaining candidates are actual occurrences of the pattern.

3.1. Consistency checking

In consistency checking we use duels in each $(\log m-2)$-square to produce a set of candidates in the $(\log m - 2)$-square which are pairwise consistent. Consistency checking depends on the category of the pattern P. In each category, it consists of $\log m - 1$ stages from $t = 0$ to $\log m - 2$. At the end of stage t, we maintain the following invariants. Let S_{C_I} and $S_{C_{II}}$ be the set of quad-I sources and quad-II sources of the pattern P, respectively, including $s_0 = (0, 0)$.

(i) P is non-periodic: there remains at most one candidate in each t-square.

(ii) P is lattice-periodic: all the surviving candidates in each t-square are pairwise consistent, and they form a subset of S_{C_I}, shifted to a point in the text.

(iii) P is line-periodic: all the candidates in each t-square are pairwise consistent, and they form a line which is a subset of S_{C_I} ($S_{C_{II}}$), shifted to a point in the text, such that the distance between two neighboring candidates is at least $|v_I|$ ($|v_{II}|$).

(iv) P is radiant-periodic: all the candidates in each t-square are pairwise consistent, and they form a monotone line which is a subset of S_{C_I} ($S_{C_{II}}$), shifted to a point in the text, such that the distance between two neighboring candidates is at least $|v_I|$ ($|v_{II}|$).

All the candidates in a t-square are maintained by a doubly linked list CLIST (in the order of appearance on the line from left to right in Cases (iii) and (iv)).

When $t = 0$, Invariants (i)–(iv) hold trivially because there is only one candidate in each 0-square. Suppose that the invariants hold at the end of stage $t - 1$. Stage $t \geq 1$ is as follows.

1. P is non-periodic: Since there is at most one candidate in each $(t - 1)$-square, a t-square has at most four candidates. Perform at most three duels in each t-square in the process of combining four $(t - 1)$-squares into one t-square; we will be left with at most one candidate in each t-square.
2. P is lattice-periodic: When two blocks are combined, take one candidate (first one in CLIST) from each block. Let u and v be the two candidates. Check the consistency of u and v.
    2.1. If u and v are consistent, all candidates in the two blocks are consistent. Combine the two CLISTs into one.
    2.2. Otherwise, the two sets of candidates from the two blocks are incompatible. Thus one of them must be removed. Perform duels between candidates from the two blocks until there is no candidate in one of the two blocks.
3. P is line-periodic: When two blocks are combined,
    3.1. if the candidates in the two blocks are on two different lines, perform duels until one of the two lines is removed.
    3.2. if the candidates are on a single line, check consistency of the two candidates in the border. If they are inconsistent, have duels (and remove the losers) until the two border candidates are consistent.
4. P is radiant-periodic: When two blocks are combined, let M_1 and M_2 be the two monotone lines such that M_1 is either on top of M_2 or to the left of M_2. We have duels starting from the rightmost candidate of M_1 and the leftmost one of M_2 until the two (border) candidates are consistent.

Steps 1–4 maintain Invariants (i)–(iv). Thus at the end of stage $\log m - 2$, all remaining candidates in each $(\log m - 2)$-square are pairwise consistent.

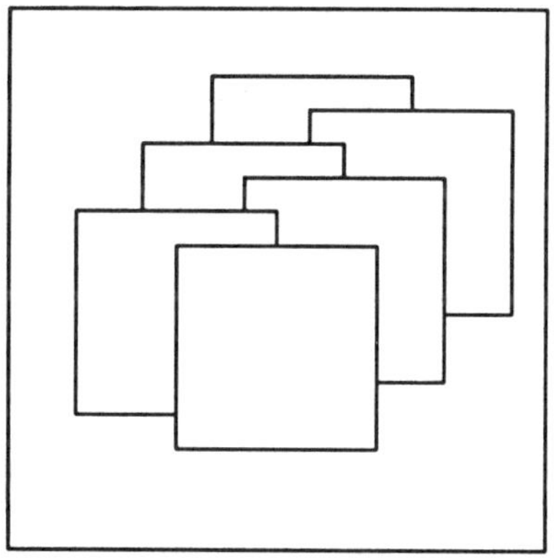

Fig. 7. The domains of candidates

3.2. Occurrence checking

Now we check if the remaining candidates are actual occurrences of the pattern. When two candidates (i, j) and (k, l) have overlap in their regions, an element in the overlap *belongs to* (k, l) if and only if $i < k$, or $i = k$ and $j < l$. We define the *domain* of a candidate (i, j) to be the subset of its region $T[i..i+m-1, j..j+m-1]$ that belongs to (i, j) (see Fig. 7). We first compute the domains of the candidates in each $(\log m - 2)$-square as follows.

1. Scan CLIST and mark candidate positions in a $(\log m - 2)$-square
2. Compute the domains from top to bottom (left to right in a row).

In each domain we compare the text elements with the corresponding pattern elements. If there is a mismatch at (i, j), it kills all candidates in $T[i-m+1..i, j-m+1..j]$. Thus removing candidates is the reverse of computing domains (now mismatches play the role of candidates):

3. Mark mismatches.
4. Remove candidates from bottom to top (right to left in a row).

All the surviving candidates represent pattern occurrences.

Theorem 4. The text processing finds all occurrences of the pattern P in the text T in $O(n^2)$ time.

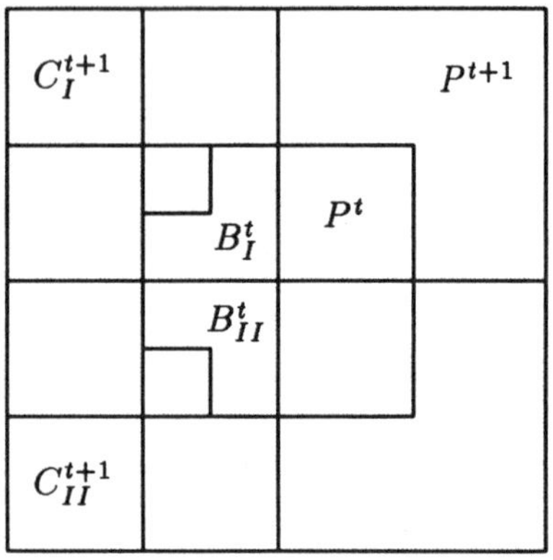

Fig. 8. Stage t in pattern processing.

4. The Pattern Processing

The pattern processing produces two arrays: QI-WITNESS$[0..m/4-1, 1..m/4-1]$ (QI-WITNESS(C_I)) and QII-WITNESS$[-(m/4-1)..-1, 0..m/4-1]$ (QII-WITNESS(C_{II})). In a one-dimensional string, witnesses can be computed from left to right [11,7]. In a two-dimensional pattern, computing QI-WITNESS from the upper-left corner (QII-WITNESS from the lower-left corner) does not work because they do not help each other in performing duels (QI-WITNESS is out of boundary for a duel in quadrant II and vice versa). We compute QI-WITNESS and QII-WITNESS from the center of the pattern towards outside (we may also start from $(m/2, 0)$).

Assume that m is a power of 2. Let B_I^t be the t-square whose lower-right corner is $(m/2-1, m/2-1)$, and B_{II}^t be the t-square whose upper-right corner is $(m/2, m/2-1)$. Let P^t be the square that consists of B_I^t, B_{II}^t, and two t-squares to the right of B_I^t and B_{II}^t. Note that $P^{\log m - 1} = P$. Let C_I^{t+1} be the upper-left t-square of B_I^{t+1}, and C_{II}^{t+1} be the lower-left t-square of B_{II}^{t+1}. See Fig. 8.

The pattern processing has $\log m - 2$ stages from $t = 1$ to $\log m - 2$. At stage t,

- consider P^{t+1} as an entire pattern (row and column indices are $0, \ldots, 4 \cdot 2^t - 1$), and
- compute QI-WITNESS$[0..2^t-1, 1..2^t-1]$ (denoted by QI-WITNESS(C_I^{t+1})) and QII-WITNESS$[-(2^t-1)..-1, 0..2^t-1]$ (denoted by QII-WITNESS(C_{II}^{t+1})).

Initially ($t = 1$), QI-WITNESS(C_I^2) and QII-WITNESS (C_{II}^2) are computed by symbol comparisons in constant time. At stage $t \geq 2$, we compute QI-WITNESS(C_I^{t+1}) and QII-WITNESS(C_{II}^{t+1}), given QI-WITNESS(C_I^t) and QII-WITNESS(C_{II}^t). At the end of stage t, therefore, QI-WITNESS$[i, j] = (m, m)$ (QII-WITNESS$[i, j] = (m, m)$) if (i, j) is a quad-I (quad-II) source of P^{t+1}; otherwise, QI-WITNESS$[i, j]$ (QII-WITNESS$[i, j]$) contains a witness $w \in P^{t+1}$ against (i, j).

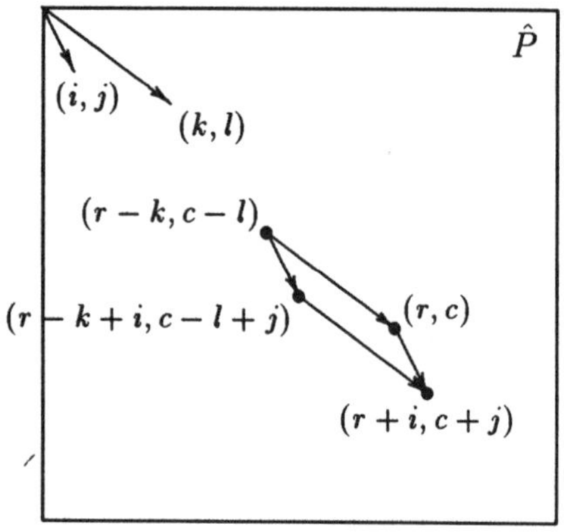

Fig. 9. Duels of type 1 and type 2.

At stage t we say that (i, j) is a *candidate* if it can still be a source of P^{t+1}. Let $\hat{m} = 4 \cdot 2^t$, which is the number of rows (columns) in P^{t+1}. Let $\hat{P}$ be another version of P^{t+1} whose row and column indices run from $-(\hat{m}/4 - 1)$ to $3\hat{m}/4$ (i.e., $\hat{P}$ and P^t have the same indices for their common points). When we perform duels in B_I^t and B_{II}^t, we will use the indices of $\hat{P}$. We use two types of duels: Consider two candidates (i, j) and (k, l) such that $0 \leq k - i < \hat{m}/8$ and $0 < l - j < \hat{m}/8$ (i.e., $(k-i, l-j)$ is in C_I^t). Let QI-WITNESS$[k-i, l-j] = (r, c)$.

1. Duel of type 1

   1a. If $\hat{P}[r+i, c+j] \neq \hat{P}[r, c]$, $(r+i, c+j)$ is a witness against (i, j).

1b. If $\hat{P}[r+i, c+j] \neq \hat{P}[r-k+i, c-l+j]$, $(r+i, c+j)$ is a witness against (k, l).

2. Duel of type 2

2a. If $\hat{P}[r-k, c-l] \neq \hat{P}[r, c]$, (r, c) is a witness against (k, l).

2b. If $\hat{P}[r-k, c-l] \neq \hat{P}[r-k+i, c-l+j]$, $(r-k+i, c-l+j)$ is a witness against (i, j).

Consider two candidates (i, j) and (k, l) such that $-\hat{m}/8 < k-i < 0$ and $0 < l-j < \hat{m}/8$. Let QII-WITNESS$[k-i, l-j] = (r, c)$. We can find witnesses against one or both of the candidates with the same tests above. The point $(r+i, c+j)$ (point $(r-k, c-l)$) will be called the *witness of the duel of type 1* (*type 2*).

Stage t has two major ingredients:

(a) Perform duels in B_I^t and B_{II}^t, using QI-WITNESS (C_I^t) and QII-WITNESS(C_{II}^t). See (a') below.

(b) Move witnesses against points of B_I^t into QI-WITNESS(C_I^{t+1}) (witnesses against points of B_{II}^t into QII-WITNESS(C_{II}^{t+1})). See (b') below.

Following are two crucial observations for our technique.

(a') When we perform duels of type 1 in B_I^t and B_{II}^t at stage t, all witnesses are in $\hat{P}$: Consider a duel between (i, j) and (k, l) such that $(k-i, l-j) \in C_I^t$ and $(i, j), (k, l) \in B_I^t$. Let QI-WITNESS$[k-i, l-j] = (r, c)$. Since (r, c) is in P^t, we have $0 \leq r+i < 3\hat{m}/4$ and $0 < c+j < 3\hat{m}/4$. Thus $(r+i, c+j)$ is in $\hat{P}$. Consider a duel between (i, j) and (k, l) such that $(k-i, l-j) \in C_I^t$ and $(i+\hat{m}/2-1, j), (k+\hat{m}/2-1, l) \in B_{II}^t$. Let QII-WITNESS$[k-i, l-j] = (r, c)$. Since $-\hat{m}/4 < i < 0$, we have $-\hat{m}/4 < r+i < \hat{m}/2$, so $(r+i, c+j)$ is in $\hat{P}$. Similarly for QII-WITNESS.

(b') Although the upper-left corners of $P^2, \ldots, P^{\log m-1}$ are all different, QI-WITNESS arrays (also QII-WITNESS) can be carried on through the stages. That is, if QI-WITNESS$[i, j] = (r, c) \in P^t$, then QI-WITNESS$[i, j] = (r+\hat{m}/4, c+\hat{m}/4) \in P^{t+1}$. Note that $(r, c) \in P^t$ and $(r+\hat{m}/4, c+\hat{m}/4) \in P^{t+1}$ refer to the same point in P. This process will be referred to as *translation* of QI-WITNESS.

Stage $t \geq 2$, which depends on the category of P^t, is as follows.

P^t is non-periodic

In this case, all of QI-WITNESS(C_I^t) and QII-WITNESS(C_{II}^t) have witnesses. Perform duels of type 1 in each of the three $(t-1)$-squares of B_I^t except C_I^t. In a $(t-1)$-square we can take any order in performing duels. At most one candidate will survive in each $(t-1)$-square, thus at most three candidates in B_I^t. Translate the witnesses into QI-WITNESS(C_I^{t+1}). Check for each surviving candidate if it is a quad-I source of P^{t+1} by symbol comparisons. Similarly for quad-II. P^{t+1} can be any of the four categories.

P^t is lattice-periodic

Let v_I and v_{II} be the basis vectors of P^t. We first compute witnesses against non-lattice points, using the witnesses against non-lattice points in the unit lattice of P^t. We need to check if lattice points in C_I^{t+1} are quad-I sources of P^{t+1}. Compare each element of P^{t+1} with the lattice of P^t. If there is no mismatch, P^{t+1} is lattice-periodic, and all lattice points in C_I^{t+1} (all lattice points in C_{II}^{t+1}) are quad-I sources (quad-II sources) of P^{t+1}.

If there are mismatches, we first find all of them. Let u be the nearest mismatch to the center of P^{t+1}. If u is in quadrant II or IV of P^{t+1} (say in II), there is no quad-II source except possibly vertical quad-II sources: Since u is a mismatch and $u+v$ is not for a non-vertical vector v, u provides a witness against v. This may not work for a vertical vector v if $u+v$ is also a mismatch (which is in quadrant I). Similarly, if u is in quadrant I or III, there is no quad-I source except possibly horizontal sources. The vertical and horizontal vectors are checked by an $O(\hat{m}^2)$ time algorithm LINE(v): Given a vector v, LINE considers all vectors of the form av, and produces sources of P^{t+1} among them. LINE also computes witnesses against non-sources av. LINE(v) divides P^{t+1} into lines parallel to v. For each line L of length p (indices are $0, \ldots, p-1$), it computes $LP[1..p-1]$ in linear time, where $LP[i]$ is the length of the longest substring which starts at position i and is also a prefix of L, by Algorithm 1 in Main and Lorentz [10] (which is a variation of the KMP algorithm). If $LP[i] < p-i$, the point corresponding to $i+LP[i]$ is a witness against the vector corresponding to position i, since $LP[i] \neq i+LP[i]$. The remaining vectors, if any, are sources of P^{t+1}.

Wlog, assume that the nearest mismatch u is in quadrant II or IV. If there is no mismatch in quadrants I and III, there is no quad-II source, but there can still be quad-I sources. We will find all quad-I sources of P^{t+1} and compute witnesses against other vectors in C_I^{t+1}.

Consider the mismatches in quadrant II. We define *layers* as if we peel an onion: Let g be the smallest row that has a mismatch in quadrant II. For each row $g \leq i < \hat{m}$, let d_i be the largest number such that (i, d_i) is a mismatch ($d_i = -1$ if row i does not have a mismatch). Also $d_i = -1$ for $0 \leq i < g$. The first layer L_1 is $\{(g, d_g), \ldots, (\hat{m}-1, d_{\hat{m}-1})\}$. For the next layer we remove the points of L_1 (peel off the layer), and consider the remaining mismatches in quadrant II. If there is no remaining mismatch, we are done. Otherwise, let $\tilde{g}$ be the smallest row that has a mismatch. The next layer is $\{(\tilde{g}, d_{\tilde{g}}), \ldots, (\hat{m}-1, d_{\hat{m}-1})\}$ constructed as above. For example, there are three layers in quadrant II of Fig. 5. Similarly, we define the layers of quadrant IV: Let g' be the smallest column that has a mismatch in quadrant IV. For each column $g' \le j < \hat{m}$, let d_j be the largest number such that (d_j, j) is a mismatch ($d_j = -1$ if column j does not have a mismatch). The first layer of quadrant IV is $\{(d_{g'}, g'), \ldots, (d_{\hat{m}-1}, \hat{m}-1)\}$. The subsequent layers are constructed similarly. A quad-I vector v is *compatible* with layer L_q if for each u in L_q,

(a) if $u+v$ is in P^{t+1}, then $u+v$ is in L_q and $P^{t+1}[u] = P^{t+1}[u+v]$, and
(b) if $u-v$ is in P^{t+1}, then $u-v$ is in L_q and $P^{t+1}[u] = P^{t+1}[u-v]$.

Lemma 6. A quad-I vector v for $|v| < \hat{m}/4$ is a source of P^{t+1} if and only if v is a lattice point and it is compatible with all layers of quadrant II and all layers of quadrant IV.

All lattice points that are not affected by the mismatches of quadrant II or IV are obviously compatible with all layers, and we find them in $O(\hat{m}^2)$ time (constant time for each lattice point by Lemma 5). We now describe how to find sources which are affected by the mismatches of quadrant II or IV and how to compute witnesses against other vectors. We will describe below a linear-time algorithm TEST(L_q, V): Given a layer L_q and a set of vectors V, TEST(L_q, V) produces the set of vectors in V which are compatible with L_q. In our case this set will always have at most $\hat{m}$ elements. TEST also computes witnesses against the vectors of V incompatible with L_q. For quadrant II, V is initially the set of lattice points v such that v is affected by the mismatches of quadrant II and $|v| < \hat{m}/4$. Note that by Lemma 5 and by the way layers are defined the vectors unaffected by the mismatches of quadrant II are the same as the vectors unaffected by L_1. We apply TEST to all layers and V: $V_2 = \text{TEST}(L_1, V)$, $V_3 = \text{TEST}(L_2, V_2)$, etc. Let V_{II} be the final set of vectors returned by TEST (those affected by the mismatches of quadrant II, and compatible with all layers of quadrant II). The first call to TEST takes $O(\hat{m}^2)$ time, and all subsequent calls take $O(\hat{m})$ time each, since TEST produces an $O(\hat{m})$ set. Thus the total time for all calls to TEST is $O(\hat{m}^2)$. Similarly, we find the set of vectors V_{IV} that are affected by the mismatches of quadrant IV, and that are compatible with all layers of quadrant IV. A vector v is a source of P^{t+1} affected by the mismatches of quadrant II or IV if either v is in both V_{II} and V_{IV}, or v is in one of them and is not affected by the mismatches of the other quadrant. In the course of this computation, the witnesses against other vectors will be computed by TEST.

TEST(L_q, V): Let $L_q = \{u_h, \ldots, u_{\hat{m}}\}$, where $u_i = (i, d_i)$ for $h \le i < \hat{m}$, and h' be the largest column that has a mismatch in L_q. Among all vectors of V affected by L_q (i.e., (r,c) for $r < \hat{m}-h$ or $c \le h'$), we can find witnesses against vectors except $u_i - u_h$ for $h < i < \hat{m}$ as follows. Consider a vector (r,c) for $r < \hat{m}-h$.

1. If $u_h + (r,c) = (i,j)$ for $j > d_i$, then (i,j) is a witness against (r,c).
2. If $u_h + (r,c) = (i,j')$ for $j' < d_i$, then (i,d_i) is a witness against (r,c).

Consider a lattice point (r,c) for $r \ge \hat{m}-h$ and $c \le h'$. A point $u' \in L_q$ which is in column h' is a witness against (r,c).

Let $p = \hat{m}-h$. For $0 \le i < p$, $v_i = u_{h+i} - u_h$ if $d_{h+i} \ne -1$; v_i is undefined otherwise. We construct a string S of length p: $S[i] = P^{t+1}[u_{h+i}]$ if $d_{h+i} \ne -1$; $S[i] = *$ otherwise, for $0 \le i < p$. By convention, $S[i] = *$ for $i < 0$. For the first layer in quadrant II of Fig. 5, $S = xx*xxxx*xx$. We define a relation: $i \sim_v j$ for $i < j$ and a quad-I vector $v = (x,y)$ if

(i) $S[i] = S[j] = *$, or
(ii) $S[i] = *$ and $S[j] \ne *$ and $d_{h+j} < y$, or
(iii) $S[i] = S[j] \ne *$ and $u_{h+j} - u_{h+i} = v$.

If v is not a quad-I vector (undefined or a quad-II vector), $i \not\sim_v j$. By convention $i \not\sim_v p$ for any i and v. Note that $\sim$ is non-commutative. However, the relation $\sim$ is transitive.

Lemma 7. If $i \sim_{v_a} j$ and $j \sim_{v_b} k$ for $i < j < k$ and quad-I vectors v_a, v_b, then $i \sim_{v_a+v_b} k$. Also, if $i \not\sim_{v_a} j$ and $j \sim_{v_b} k$ for $i < j < k$ and quad-I vectors v_a, v_b, then $i \not\sim_{v_a+v_b} k$.

We extend the relation $\sim_v$ to intervals: $[i..i+l] \sim_v [j..j+l]$ if $i+k \sim_v j+k$ for $0 \le k \le l$. A vector v_i is compatible with L_q if $[-i..p-1-i] \sim_{v_i} [0..p-1]$. Note that if $j-i \not\sim_{v_i} j$ for some j, then u_{h+j} is a witness against v_i. We divide the compatibility checking into two: $[0..p-1-i] \sim_{v_i} [i..p-1]$ (positive part) and $[-i..-1] \sim_{v_i} [0..i-1]$ (negative part). First we basically check the positive part, but at the same time we remove vectors as soon as we find a violation in the negative part. That is, we compute $lp[1..p-1]$ that satisfies the following properties:

(a) If $lp[i] \ge 0$ for $1 \le i < p$, $lp[i]$ is the largest j such that $[0..j-1] \sim_{v_i} [i..i+j-1]$.
(b) If $lp[i] = -1$, v_i is undefined or $j-i \not\sim_{v_i} j$ for some $j < i$.

Note that if $lp[i] = -1$, then v_i cannot be compatible with L_q, and thus it is not important to find if v_i is compatible in the positive part. A vector v_i is compatible in the positive part if $lp[i] = p - i$.

We compute $lp[1..p-1]$ by Procedure LPREFIX in Fig. 10, which is a modification of Algorithm 1 in [10], by replacing the equality with the appropriate $\sim$ relation. Since the $\sim$ relation can be checked in constant time, LPREFIX computes $lp[1..p-1]$ in $O(p)$ time.

```
procedure LPREFIX
  if v_1 is a quad-I vector then
    j ← 0;
    while j ~_{v_1} j+1 do j ← j+1 end do
    lp[1] ← j;
  else lp[1] ← -1 end if
  k ← 1;
  for i ← 2 to p-1 do
    if v_i is a quad-I vector then
      len ← k + lp[k] - i;
      if lp[i-k] < len then lp[i] ← lp[i-k];
      else
        j ← max(len, 0);
        while j ~_{v_i} j+i do j ← j+1 end do
        lp[i] ← j;
        k ← i;
      end if
    else lp[i] ← -1 end if
  end do
end
```

Fig. 10. Procedure LPREFIX.

Lemma 8. Let $\hat{V}$ be the set of vectors v_i such that $lp[i] = p - i$. The vectors in $\hat{V}$ form a monotone line.

Secondly, we need to check the compatibility in the negative part for each vector v_i in $\hat{V}$: $j - i \sim_{v_i} j$ for $0 \leq j < i$. If $j - i \sim_{v_i} j$ in this checking, the relation $\sim_{v_i}$ is satisfied by Condition (i) or (ii) because $S[j-i] = *$.

Lemma 9. Let $v_i, v_{i'}$ be two vectors in $\hat{V}$ such that $i < i'$. If $j - i \sim_{v_i} j$ for $j < i$, then $j - i' \sim_{v_{i'}} j$.

We can do the checking in the negative part in $O(p)$ time for all vectors in $\hat{V}$ as follows. Let v_i be the shortest vector in $\hat{V}$. We check $k - i \sim_{v_i} k$ from $k = 0$ to $i-1$ until $\not\sim_{v_i}$ is found. We remove v_i from $\hat{V}$ if there is a violation ($\not\sim_{v_i}$). Let j be the smallest integer such that $j - i \not\sim_{v_i} j$ ($j = i$ if there is no such integer). Then $[-i'..j-1-i'] \sim_{v_{i'}} [0..j-1]$ for the next shortest vector $v_{i'}$ by Lemma 9. We check $k - i' \sim_{v_{i'}} k$ from $k = j$ to $i' - 1$ until $\not\sim_{v_{i'}}$ is found, etc. The final $\hat{V}$ is the set of vectors that are affected by L_q and are compatible with L_q. The output of TEST(L_q, V) is the set of vectors $v \in V$ such that either v is in $\hat{V}$, or v is not affected by L_q. Note that the output of TEST(L_1, V) is $\hat{V}$, since the vectors unaffected by L_1 have already been handled and are not part of V. Thus the call to TEST(L_q, V) takes linear time, and produces at most $p < \hat{m}$ vectors.

If there is a mismatch in quadrant I or III in addition to one in quadrant II, then P^{t+1} is either non-periodic or line-periodic by Lemma 4. To find line-periodicity, we apply TEST twice as follows. Let V be the set of lattice points in C_I^{t+1}.

(i) Let L_1 be the first layer of quadrant II constructed as before; i.e., $L_1 = \{(g, d_g), \ldots, (\hat{m}-1, d_{\hat{m}-1})\}$. Call $U = \text{TEST}(L_1, V)$.
(ii) Let $\hat{g}$ be the largest column that has a mismatch in quadrant II. L_1' is another first layer of quadrant II constructed as follows. Let d_j be the smallest number such that (d_j, j) is a mismatch in quadrant II. $L_1' = \{(d_{\hat{g}}, \hat{g}), (d_{\hat{g}-1}, \hat{g}-1), \ldots, (d_0, 0)\}$. Let TEST' be a modification of TEST where only $(d_{\hat{g}}, \hat{g}) - (d_j, j)$ for $0 \leq j < \hat{g}$ can be compatible vectors with L_1'. Call $U' = \text{TEST'}(L_1', V)$.

Notice that if there is line-periodicity in quadrant II extending to quadrant I (III), U (U') will contain vectors of the form av for some v, but U' (U) may be empty because the line-periodicity is cut by the boundary between quadrant II and I (III). Now we find the periodicity of P^{t+1}:

1. If both U and U' are empty, P^{t+1} is non-periodic, and all witnesses have been found by TEST and TEST'.
2. If either U or U' (or both) is a set of vectors of the form av for some v, we check if the vectors av are sources of P^{t+1} by the algorithm LINE(v).
3. If either U or U' contains two independent vectors, one can show that the nearest mismatch in quadrant I or III to the center provides witnesses against the vectors in U and U'.

P^t is line-periodic (quad-I)

When P^t is line-periodic in quad-I (i.e., $|v_I| < \hat{m}/8$), it may have a quad-II symmetry vector v such that $\hat{m}/8 \leq |v| < \hat{m}/4$. First we check if P^t has such a quad-II vector as follows. Perform duels of type 1 in B_{II}^t using QI-WITNESS(C_I^t) and QII-WITNESS(C_{II}^t); the surviving candidates will form at most three lines, one for each quadrant of B_{II}^t except C_{II}^t. For each line L in B_{II}^t, choose the shortest quad-II vector v, and check if it is a symmetry vector of P^t by symbol comparisons. One can show that any mismatch kills all quad-II vectors in the line L by the line-periodicity of P^t.

1. If there is a quad-II symmetry vector of P^t (i.e., P^t is lattice-generative, though it is not lattice-periodic), finding the periodicity of P^{t+1} is the same as in the lattice-periodic case.
2. Otherwise, there are witnesses against all points of B^t_{II}. Translate them to QII-WITNESS(C^{t+1}_{II}). In order to compute QI-WITNESS(C^{t+1}_I), we will have two stages of duels: Procedure D1 and Procedure D2.

Procedure D1 performs duels of type 1 in B^t_I, using QI-WITNESS(C^t_I) and QII-WITNESS(C^{t+1}_{II}). The losers of the duels get witnesses against themselves. The surviving candidates form a monotone line M because of QII-WITNESS(C^{t+1}_{II}).

Procedure D2 performs duels among the points in the monotone line M. Here we use duels of both type 1 and type 2. In Procedure D2 we may use new witnesses obtained in Procedure D2. Thus if we rely only on duels of type 1, witnesses may not be in $\hat{P}$.

Let $v_1, \ldots, v_p$ be the candidates in M from shortest to longest. Procedure D2 considers the candidates one by one from shortest to longest. Let v_i be the current candidate. $\hat{V}$ is a subset of $\{v_1, \ldots, v_{i-1}\}$ such that if v' is the first vector in $\hat{V}$, then for each vector $\hat{v} \in \hat{V}$, $\hat{v} = av'$ for some a (a not necessarily integer). In other words, all vectors in $\hat{V}$ are on one line L passing through $(0,0)$. If v is on the line L, we put v into $\hat{V}$. Otherwise, $v - \hat{v}$ for any vector $\hat{v} \in \hat{V}$ has a witness, because $v - \hat{v}$ is shorter than v and it is not on the line L. We perform duels between v and the vectors in $\hat{V}$ (in any order among the vectors in $\hat{V}$) until either v or all vectors in $\hat{V}$ are removed. The losers of the duels get witnesses. For a duel between $\hat{v} = (i,j)$ and $v = (k,l)$ ($\hat{v} \prec_I v$), let (r,c) be the witness against $(k-i, l-j)$. We choose the type of the duel whose witness is closer to the diagonal line $x + y = \hat{m}/2 - 1$ in $\hat{P}$: type 1 if $|r + i + c + j - (\hat{m}/2 - 1)| \leq |r - k + c - l - (\hat{m}/2 - 1)|$, type 2 otherwise. One can show that in each case the needed witness is available. Procedure D2 returns $\hat{V}$ after considering all candidates (thus the remaining vectors are on one line passing through $(0,0)$). We check if the vectors in $\hat{V}$ are quad-I sources of $\hat{P}$ by LINE.

P^t is radiant-periodic (quad-I)

Lemma 10. If P^t is radiant-periodic in quad-I (i.e., $|v_I| < \hat{m}/8$), there is no quad-II symmetry vector v of P^t such that $\hat{m}/8 \leq |v| < \hat{m}/4$.

We find witnesses against all points of B^t_{II} as follows. Perform duels of type 1 in B^t_{II} using QI-WITNESS(C^t_I) and QII-WITNESS(C^t_{II}); the surviving candidates will form at most three monotone lines, one for each quadrant of B^t_{II} except C^t_{II}. For each monotone line M in B^t_{II}, choose a quad-II vector v, and find a witness of P^t against v by symbol comparisons (there exists a witness by Lemma 10). One can show that the witness kills all quad-II vectors in the monotone line M by the radiant-periodicity of P^t. Thus there are witnesses against all points of B^t_{II}. Translate them to QII-WITNESS(C^{t+1}_{II}). We now compute QI-WITNESS(C^{t+1}_I) by Procedures D1, D2, and LINE as in the line-periodic case. Thus if P^t is radiant-periodic, P^{t+1} can be either line-periodic or non-periodic.

Theorem 5. The pattern processing computes QI-WITNESS(C_I) and QII-WITNESS(C_{II}) of the pattern P in $O(m^2)$ time.

References

[1] A.V. Aho and M.J. Corasick, Efficient string matching: An aid to bibliographic search, *CACM* **18** (1975), 333–340.

[2] A. Amir and G. Benson, Two-dimensional periodicity and its applications, *Proc. 3rd SODA*, 1992, 440–452.

[3] A. Amir, G. Benson and M. Farach, Alphabet independent two dimensional matching, *Proc. 24th STOC*, 1992, 59–68.

[4] A. Amir, G. Landau and U. Vishkin, Efficient pattern matching with scaling, *Proc. 1st SODA*, 1990, 344–357.

[5] T.J. Baker, A technique for extending rapid exact-match string matching to arrays of more than one dimension, *SIAM J. on Comput.* **7** (1978), 533–541.

[6] R.S. Bird, Two dimensional pattern matching, *Inform. Process. Lett.* **6** (1977), 168–170.

[7] D. Breslauer and Z. Galil, An optimal $O(\log \log n)$ time parallel string matching algorithm, *SIAM J. on Comput.* **19** (1990), 1051–1058.

[8] R.M. Karp and M.O. Rabin, Efficient randomized pattern-matching algorithms, *IBM J. Res. and Dev.* (1987), 249–260.

[9] D.E. Knuth, J.H. Morris, and V.B. Pratt, Fast pattern matching in strings, *SIAM J. on Comput.* **6** (1977), 323–350.

[10] M.G. Main and R.J. Lorentz, An $O(n \log n)$ algorithm for finding all repetitions in a string, *J. Algorithms* **5** (1984), 422–432.

[11] U. Vishkin, Optimal parallel pattern matching in strings, *Inform. and Control* **67** (1985), 91–113.

[12] R.F. Zhu and T. Takaoka, A technique for two-dimensional pattern matching, *CACM* **32** (1989), 1110–1120.

Monday

October 26, 1992

Amplification and Percolation

Moshe Dubiner *

Dept. of Applied Math.
Tel Aviv university
Tel Aviv 69978, Israel

Uri Zwick *

Dept. of Computer Science
Tel Aviv university
Tel Aviv 69978, Israel

Abstract

Moore and Shannon had shown that relays with arbitrarily high reliability can be built from relays with arbitrarily poor reliability. Valiant used similar methods to construct monotone read-once formulae of size $O(n^{\alpha+2})$ (where $\alpha = \log_{\sqrt{5}-1} 2 \simeq 3.27$) that amplify $(\psi - \frac{1}{n}, \psi + \frac{1}{n})$ (where $\psi = \frac{\sqrt{5}-1}{2} \simeq 0.62$) to $(2^{-n}, 1 - 2^{-n})$ and deduced as a consequence the existence of monotone formulae of the same size that compute the majority of n bits.

Boppana had shown that any monotone read-once formula that amplifies $(p - \frac{1}{n}, p + \frac{1}{n})$ to $(\frac{1}{4}, \frac{3}{4})$ (where $0 < p < 1$ is constant) has size of at least $\Omega(n^\alpha)$ and that any monotone, not necessarily read-once, contact network (and in particular any monotone formula) that amplifies $(\frac{1}{4}, \frac{3}{4})$ to $(2^{-n}, 1 - 2^{-n})$ has size of at least $\Omega(n^2)$.

We extend Boppana's results in two ways. We first show that his two lower bounds hold for general read-once formulae, not necessarily monotone, that may even include exclusive-or gates. We are then able to join his two lower bounds together and show that any read-once, not necessarily monotone, formula that amplifies $(p-\frac{1}{n}, p+\frac{1}{n})$ to $(2^{-n}, 1-2^{-n})$ has size of at least $\Omega(n^{\alpha+2})$. This result does not follow from Boppana's arguments and it shows that the amount of amplification achieved by Valiant is the maximal achievable using read-once formulae.

Next, extending the results of Moore and Shannon and Valiant, we construct monotone read-once networks of size $O(n^{2.99})$ that amplify $(\frac{1}{2} - \frac{1}{n}, \frac{1}{2} + \frac{1}{n})$ to $(\frac{1}{4}, \frac{3}{4})$. This construction improves the reliability that can be obtained using a given number of relays, and shows that the first lower bound of Boppana, in contrast to his second, does not apply to contact networks, even if they are required to be both monotone and read-once.

Finally, we establish a connection between amplification and percolation and show that certain conjectures in percolation theory imply the existence of monotone read-once networks of size $O(n^{8/3+o(1)})$, and perhaps even less, that amplify $(\frac{1}{2} - \frac{1}{n}, \frac{1}{2} + \frac{1}{n})$ to $(\frac{1}{4}, \frac{3}{4})$.

1 Introduction

In a classical paper, Moore and Shannon [13] use what is now called the *amplification method* to show that relays with arbitrarily high reliability can be built from (so-called *crummy*) relays with arbitrarily poor reliability.

The amplification method was next used by several researchers to show that particular Boolean functions have small Boolean circuits and formulae. Benett and Gill [3], extending a result of Adelman [1] used it to show that every language in the complexity class BPP has polynomial-size circuits. Ajtai and Ben-Or [2] used the amplification method to show that probabilistic constant-depth circuits can be simulated by deterministic constant-depth circuits, with only a polynomial increase in size.

The main focus of attention in this paper is the elegant application of the amplification method by Valiant [19] to the construction of monotone formulae of size $O(n^{\alpha+2})$ (where $\alpha = \log_{\sqrt{5}-1} 2 \simeq 3.27$) for the majority function and its extension by Boppana [4] to the construction of $O(k^{\alpha+1} n \log n)$ size monotone formulae for the k-th threshold function of n variables.

To show the existence of $O(n^{\alpha+2})$ size monotone formulae for the majority function Valiant first con-

*Full affiliations : Departments of Applied Mathematics and Computer Science, School of Mathematical Sciences, The Raymond and Beverly Sackler Faculty of Exact Sciences, Tel Aviv university, Tel Aviv 69978, Israel.
The second author was supported in part by THE BASIC RESEARCH FOUNDATION administrated by THE ISRAEL ACADEMY OF SCIENCES AND HUMANITIES.
Contact author: Uri Zwick, e-mail: zwick@math.tau.ac.il.

0-8186-2900-2/92 $3.00 © 1992 IEEE

structs monotone read-once formulae that amplify $(\psi - \frac{1}{n}, \psi + \frac{1}{n})$ (where $\psi = \frac{\sqrt{5}-1}{2}$) to $(2^{-n}, 1-2^{-n})$. Formal definitions of all these terms will appear in the next section. The existence of monotone formulae of the same size for majority follows using a simple probabilistic argument.

Boppana [4], considered the question of whether Valiant had obtained an optimal amount of amplification in his construction and came very close to answering it positively. He observed that Valiant had actually constructed $O(n^\alpha)$ size monotone read-once formulae that amplify $(\psi - \frac{1}{n}, \psi + \frac{1}{n})$ to $(\frac{1}{4}, \frac{3}{4})$ and $O(n^2)$ size monotone read-once formulae that amplify $(\frac{1}{4}, \frac{3}{4})$ to $(2^{-n}, 1-2^{-n})$. The $O(n^{\alpha+2})$ size monotone read-once formulae that amplify $(\psi - \frac{1}{n}, \psi + \frac{1}{n})$ to $(2^{-n}, 1-2^{-n})$ are easily obtained by combining these two sub-constructions. Boppana was able to show that each one of these sub-constructions achieved an optimal amount of amplification. It does not seem to follow however from Boppana's arguments that the combined construction is also optimal.

We are able to join together the two lower bounds of Boppana and show that any monotone read-once formula that amplifies $(p - \frac{1}{n}, p + \frac{1}{n})$ to $(2^{-n}, 1-2^{-n})$ (where $0 < p < 1$ is fixed) does indeed have to be of size $\Omega(n^{\alpha+2})$. This gives a complete positive answer to the question of whether Valiant's construction obtains an optimal amount of amplification.

We are also able to strengthen Boppana's results in another respect. We show that the combined $\Omega(n^{\alpha+2})$ lower bound applies even if the read-once formulae are allowed to use negations and exclusive-or (XOR) gates (as well as the monotone AND and OR gates). To that end we show that for every formula with XOR gates there exists a probabilistic formula without XOR gates of the same size that achieves the same amount of amplification.

Boppana had used two different (we are tempted to say incompatible) methods to get his two lower bounds for the two amplification stages. To obtain the combined lower bound we have to slightly strengthen his first lower bound and exhibit an alternative proof for his second. In particular, we obtain a slightly stronger version of, what we call, Boppana's inequality (see next section). We present an analytical proof of this strengthened inequality (Boppana had resorted to numerical experimentation in the proof of his inequality). We also generalize Boppana's bound on the derivatives of univariate amplification functions to bounds on the partial derivatives of multivariate amplification functions.

As mentioned, Boppana's second lower bound applies to general monotone networks. Using a result of Lupanov [12], it can be shown that it does not apply to non-monotone contact networks. Thus, in the contact networks model negations do help amplify. We do not elaborate on it in this abstract. We also note that negations and XOR gates seem to help in the construction of formulae for the majority function. In [14],[15], non-monotone formulae of size $O(n^{4.57})$, without XOR gates, and of size $O(n^{3.13})$, with XOR gates were constructed.

Next, we construct monotone read-once undirected contact networks of size $O(n^{2.99})$ that amplify $(\frac{1}{2} - \frac{1}{n}, \frac{1}{2} + \frac{1}{n})$ to $(\frac{1}{4}, \frac{3}{4})$. This improves the results of Moore and Shannon [13] and those of Valiant [19] and shows that Boppana's first lower bound does not apply to contact networks, even if they are required to be undirected, monotone and read-once. It also implies the existence of *undirected* monotone contact networks of size $O(n^{4.99})$ that compute the majority of n bits. Smaller *directed* monotone networks for majority had been recently constructed by Radhakrishnan and Subrahmanyam [17].

Finally, we exhibit a connection between amplification and percolation. We show that certain conjectures in percolation theory imply the existence of monotone read-once (undirected) networks of size $O(n^{8/3+o(1)})$, and perhaps even less, that amplify $(\frac{1}{2} - \frac{1}{n}, \frac{1}{2} + \frac{1}{n})$ to $(\frac{1}{4}, \frac{3}{4})$ and consequently the existence of monotone (undirected) networks of size $O(n^{14/3+o(1)})$ that compute the majority function of n bits.

Other works relevant to the subjects considered in this paper are [7],[8],[9] and [16].

2 Preliminaries

Following Moore and Shannon [13] and Boppana [4] we introduce the following two definitions

Definition 2.1 (Amplification Functions) Given a Boolean function $f : \{0,1\}^n \to \{0,1\}$, we define its *multivariate amplification function* $f : [0,1]^n \to [0,1]$ as follows: $f(p_1, p_2, \ldots, p_n) = \Pr[f(\mathbf{x}_1, \mathbf{x}_2, \ldots, \mathbf{x}_n) = 1]$, where $\mathbf{x}_1, \mathbf{x}_2, \ldots, \mathbf{x}_n$ are independent random variables, $\mathbf{x}_i$ assumes the value 1 with probability p_i and the value 0 with probability $1 - p_i$. We define the *univariate amplification function* of f to be $f(p) = f(p, p, \ldots, p)$. As the (multivariate) amplification function is an extension of the original Boolean function, we use the same notation for both.

Definition 2.2 (Amplification from/to) A Boolean function function $f : \{0,1\}^n \rightarrow \{0,1\}$ *amplifies* (p,q) to (p',q') if $f(p) = p'$ and $f(q) = q'$. It amplifies (p,q) to *at least* (p',q') if $f(p) \leq p'$ and $f(q) \geq q'$.

The main computational models studied in this work are formulae and contact networks.

Definition 2.3 (Formulae) A *formula* of n variables is defined recursively as follows: (i) for $1 \leq i \leq n$, the variables x_i and their negations $\overline{x_i}$ are formulae; (ii) if f and g are formulae then so are $(\neg f)$, $(f \wedge g)$, $(f \vee g)$ and $(f \oplus g)$. A formula in which no XOR gates are used is called *unate* or *de Morgan*. A unate formula in which no negations are used is called *monotone*. Formulae define Boolean functions in the obvious way. The *size* of a formula f, denoted by *size*(f), is the number of occurrences of variables in it.

Definition 2.4 (Probabilistic Formulae) A *probabilistic* (monotone, unate) formula is simply a discrete probability distribution over conventional deterministic (monotone, unate) formulae. The size of a probabilistic formula F is defined to be the maximum size of a formula f whose probability according to the distribution induced by F is positive. The amplification function $F(p_1,\ldots,p_n)$ of a probabilistic formula F is simply $F(p_1,\ldots,p_n) = E_{f\in F} f(p_1,\ldots,p_n)$ where E denotes expectation relative to the distribution induced by F.

Definition 2.5 (Contact Networks) A *contact network* of n variables is an undirected graph with two distinguished vertices s (the source) and t (the sink) in which each edge is labeled by a variable x_i (where $1 \leq i \leq n$) or its negation. The network defines a function in the following way; for any given assignment of Boolean values to the variables $x_1,\ldots,x_n$ we check whether there is a path from s to t in which all the edges are labeled by 1. If there is such a path then the value of the function for this assignment is defined to be 1, otherwise 0. The *size* of a network is defined to be the number of edges in it. A network is said to be *monotone* if no edges in it are labeled by negations of variables.

It is easy to see that monotone and unate formulae correspond to monotone and non-monotone *series-parallel* contact networks. For more details the reader is referred to [4].

Most of the formulae and networks encountered in this work will be read-once.

Definition 2.6 (Read-Once) A formula or a network are said to be *read-once* if every variable appears in them at most once.

Definition 2.7 (Amplification Complexity) If $0 < p_0, q_0, p_1, q_1 < 1$, we denote by $N(p_1, q_1|p_0, q_0)$ the minimum size of a unate read-once formula that amplifies (p_0,q_0) to (p_1,q_1). We denote by $N_\oplus(p_1,q_1|p_0,q_0)$ the corresponding measure for general read-once formulae.

In the sequel we refer to the following inequalities

Theorem 2.8 (Hölder's inequality) *If* $\alpha,\beta > 1$ *and* $\frac{1}{\alpha}+\frac{1}{\beta} = 1$ *then for any two real vectors* x *and* y *we have*

$$\sum_{i=1}^{n} |x_i y_i| \leq \|x\|_\alpha \cdot \|y\|_\beta$$

where $\|x\|_\alpha = \left(\sum_{i=1}^n |x_i|^\alpha\right)^{1/\alpha}$.

Theorem 2.9 (Boppana's inequality) *Let* $H(x) = -x\log_2 x - (1-x)\log_2(1-x)$ *be the usual binary entropy function and let* $\beta = \log_{\frac{\sqrt{5}-1}{2}} 2 \simeq 1.44$. *Then, for every* $0 < x, y \leq 1$ *we have*

$$\left(\frac{H(x)}{x}\right)^\beta + \left(\frac{H(y)}{y}\right)^\beta \leq \left(\frac{H(xy)}{xy}\right)^\beta .$$

In the sequel we would say that a function I satisfies Boppana's inequality iff $I(x) = I(1-x) \geq 0$ for every $0 \leq x \leq 1$ and if I satisfies the inequality in the above lemma.

3 Strengthening Boppana's inequality

Boppana's inequality, stated in the previous section forms the basis of his lower bound for the first amplification stage. To get some of our extended lower bounds we need a slightly stronger version of his inequality. This version is obtained by replacing the entropy function $H(x)$ by a function $G(x)$ with the tightest asymptotic behaviour near $x = 0$ and $x = 1$. To prove his inequality Boppana had to make many numerical checks involving functions of two variables (in one point of the argument, for example, he has to estimate the third derivatives of the function $\widetilde{H}(x,y) = (H(xy)/xy)^\beta - (H(x)/x)^\beta - (H(y)/y)^\beta$ and show that the Hessian matrix of $\widetilde{H}$ is positive definite on the entire region $[0.55, 0.65] \times [0.55, 0.65]$). We are able to exhibit a much simpler proof to our strengthened inequality. We show that it follows from some relatively simple one variable inequalities.

Our new function $G(x)$ is defined as follows

$$G(x) = \begin{cases} x\left(\ln \frac{\gamma}{x}\right)^{1/\beta} & \text{if } 0 \le x \le \frac{1}{2} \\ (1-x)\left(\ln \frac{\gamma}{1-x}\right)^{1/\beta} & \text{if } \frac{1}{2} \le x \le 1 \end{cases}$$

where

$$\ln \gamma = \frac{2 - \psi - \ln 4}{\beta} \simeq -0.003005 \quad .$$

The constant γ was chosen so that $\widehat{G}(\psi) = \widehat{G}(1-\psi)$ where $\widehat{G}(x) = x \cdot \frac{d}{dx}\left(\frac{G(x)}{x}\right)^{\beta}$. This is a necessary condition that must be satisfied by any symmetric function wishing to satisfy Boppana's inequality. The function $G(x)$ has a small cusp at $x = \frac{1}{2}$ but this will not cause us any trouble. We now claim

Lemma 3.1 *For every* $0 < x, y \le 1$ *we have*

$$\left(\frac{G(x)}{x}\right)^{\beta} + \left(\frac{G(y)}{y}\right)^{\beta} \le \left(\frac{G(xy)}{xy}\right)^{\beta} \quad .$$

Proof : See the full version of the paper. □

4 Bounds on derivatives of amplification functions

The basic theorem from which all the results of this section follow is

Theorem 4.1 *If f is a unate read-once formula (or a read-once series-parallel contact network) that depends on n variables and if I satisfies Boppana's inequality then*

$$\left(\sum_{i=1}^{n} \left|I(x_i) \cdot \frac{\partial f}{\partial x_i}\right|^{\beta}\right)^{1/\beta} \le I(f) \quad .$$

Proof : The proof is by induction on the structure of f. If $f = x_i$ or $f = \overline{x_i}$ then the inequality is easily verified as $\left|\frac{\partial f}{\partial x_i}\right| = 1$ and $I(x_i) = I(1 - x_i) = I(f)$. If $f = \neg g$ then the inequality follows easily from the induction hypothesis as $f = 1 - g$ and therefore $\left|\frac{\partial f}{\partial x_i}\right| = \left|\frac{\partial g}{\partial x_i}\right|$ and $I(f) = I(1-f) = I(g)$. If $f = f_1 \wedge f_2$ and if $f_1(x_1, \ldots, x_n)$ and $f_2(y_1, \ldots, y_m)$ are the amplification functions of f_1 and f_2 then the amplification function of f is $f(x_1, \ldots, x_n, y_1, \ldots, y_m) = f_1(x_1, \ldots, x_n) f_2(y_1, \ldots, y_m)$. As a consequence $\frac{\partial f}{\partial x_i} = \frac{\partial f_1}{\partial x_i} \cdot f_2$ and $\frac{\partial f}{\partial y_j} = f_1 \cdot \frac{\partial f_2}{\partial y_j}$. For convenience we let $x_{n+1} = y_1, \ldots, x_{n+m} = y_m$. Using the induction hypothesis and then Boppana's inequality we therefore get

$$\begin{aligned} & \sum_{i=1}^{n+m} \left|I(x_i) \cdot \frac{\partial f}{\partial x_i}\right|^{\beta} \\ \le\ & f_2^{\beta} \cdot \sum_{i=1}^{n} \left|I(x_i) \cdot \frac{\partial f}{\partial x_i}\right|^{\beta} + f_1^{\beta} \cdot \sum_{i=n+1}^{n+m} \left|I(x_i) \cdot \frac{\partial f}{\partial x_i}\right|^{\beta} \\ \le\ & (f_2 \cdot I(f_1))^{\beta} + (f_1 \cdot I(f_2))^{\beta} \\ =\ & (f_1 f_2)^{\beta} \cdot \left[\left(\frac{I(f_1)}{f_1}\right)^{\beta} + \left(\frac{I(f_2)}{f_2}\right)^{\beta}\right] \\ \le\ & (f_1 f_2)^{\beta} \cdot \left(\frac{I(f_1 f_2)}{f_1 f_2}\right)^{\beta} = (I(f))^{\beta} \quad . \end{aligned}$$

This completes the proof as any unate gate can be obtained by combining an $\wedge$-gate with negations. □

If, in addition to satisfying Boppana's inequality, the function I also satisfies the following inequality

$$\left(\frac{I\left(\frac{1-x}{2}\right)}{x}\right)^{\beta} + \left(\frac{I\left(\frac{1-y}{2}\right)}{y}\right)^{\beta} \le \left(\frac{I\left(\frac{1-xy}{2}\right)}{xy}\right)^{\beta}$$

for every $0 < x, y \le 1$ then we can show directly that the inequality in the above lemma holds for general, not necessarily unate, read-once formulae. Both the entropy function $H(x)$ and the function $G(x)$ introduced in the previous section satisfy this inequality. We omit the details here as the same amplification bounds will follow from the more general arguments of Section 8.

We denote by $\nabla f(x)$ the *gradient* $\nabla f = \left(\frac{\partial f}{\partial x_1}, \ldots, \frac{\partial f}{\partial x_n}\right)$ of f evaluated at the point $(x, \ldots, x)$. As an immediate corollary to the previous lemma we get

Corollary 4.2 *If f is a unate read-once formula then*

$$\|\nabla f(x)\|_{\beta} \le \frac{I(f(x))}{I(x)} \quad .$$

In particular if p_c is the *critical probability* for which $f(p_c) = p_c$, we get that $\|\nabla f(p_c)\|_{\beta} \le 1$. We will encounter a similar relation in Section 9 that presents constructions of small amplifying networks.

As a second corollary to Lemma 4.1 we get the following result obtained by Boppana for monotone read-once formulae.

Corollary 4.3 *If f is a unate read-once formula that depends on n variables then*

$$|f'(x)| \le n^{1/\alpha} \cdot \frac{I(f(x))}{I(x)} \quad .$$

Proof : Applying Hölder's inequality we get

$$\begin{aligned} |f'(x)| &\le \sum_{i=1}^{n} \left| \frac{\partial f}{\partial x_i}(x) \right| \\ &\le \left(\sum_{i=1}^{n} 1 \right)^{1/\alpha} \cdot \left(\sum_{i=1}^{n} \left| \frac{\partial f}{\partial x_i}(x) \right|^{\beta} \right)^{1/\beta} \\ &= n^{1/\alpha} \cdot \|\nabla f(x)\|_\beta \le n^{1/\alpha} \cdot \frac{I(f(x))}{I(x)} \quad . \end{aligned}$$

□

Again, if I satisfies the additional inequality mentioned above, as G and H do, then the above corollary holds for general, not necessarily unate, read-once formulae. We claim that the inequality in Corollary 4.3 with $G(x)$ plugged into it is, up to constant factors, the strongest valid inequality of its kind. We do not elaborate on it here.

5 Local amplification bounds

Boppana [4] used the above corollary, together with the mean value theorem to get a lower bound on the size of formulae required to amplify (p_0, q_0) to (p_1, q_1). A stronger lower bound is obtained by integrating the upper bound obtained for $|f'(x)|$. Let

$$M(x, y) = \left| \int_x^y \frac{du}{G(u)} \right|^\alpha \quad .$$

Theorem 5.1 *Any read-once formula that amplifies (p_0, q_0) to (p_1, q_1) has size of at least*

$$N(p_1, q_1 | p_0, q_0) \ge \frac{M(p_1, q_1)}{M(p_0, q_0)} \quad .$$

Proof : Let f be a read-once formula that depends on n variables and amplifies (p_0, q_0) to (p_1, q_1). Using Corollary 4.3 and a simple change of variables we get that

$$\begin{aligned} \left| \int_{p_1}^{q_1} \frac{dx}{G(x)} \right| &\le \int_{p_0}^{q_0} \left| \frac{f'(x)dx}{G(f(x))} \right| \\ \le \left| \int_{p_0}^{q_0} \frac{n^{1/\alpha}dx}{G(x)} \right| &= n^{1/\alpha} \left| \int_{p_0}^{q_0} \frac{dx}{G(x)} \right| \quad . \end{aligned}$$ □

Since

$$\int \frac{dx}{x \left(\ln \frac{\gamma}{x} \right)^{1/\beta}} = -\alpha \left(\ln \frac{\gamma}{x} \right)^{1/\alpha} \quad ,$$

it is easily verified that

$$M(x, y) = \left| \int_x^y \frac{du}{G(u)} \right|^\alpha =$$

$$C \cdot \begin{cases} m(x, y) & \text{if } x \le y \le \frac{1}{2} \\ (m(x, \frac{1}{2})^{1/\alpha} + m(1-y, \frac{1}{2})^{1/\alpha})^\alpha & \text{if } x \le \frac{1}{2} \le y \\ m(1-y, 1-x) & \text{if } \frac{1}{2} \le x \le y \\ M(y, x) & \text{if } y < x \end{cases}$$

where $C = \alpha^\alpha$ and

$$m(x, y) = \left[\left(\ln \frac{\gamma}{x} \right)^{1/\alpha} - \left(\ln \frac{\gamma}{y} \right)^{1/\alpha} \right]^\alpha$$

Clearly $M(x, y) = M(y, x) = M(1-x, 1-y)$. In section 7, the function $M(x, y)$ will be compared with some other functions. It will be convenient to scale $M(x, y)$ before these comparisons and assume that $C = 10^6$. This of course will not affect the validity of Theorem 5.1.

As an immediate corollary of Theorem 5.1 we get

Corollary 5.2 *Any unate read-once formula that amplifies $(p - \frac{1}{n}, p + \frac{1}{n})$ to at least $(\frac{1}{4}, \frac{3}{4})$ (where $0 < p < 1$ is fixed) is of size $\Omega(n^\alpha)$ and any unate read-once formula that amplifies $(p - \frac{1}{n}, p + \frac{1}{n})$ to at least $(2^{-n}, \frac{1}{2})$ is of size $\Omega(n^{\alpha+1})$.*

Proof : Follows easily as $M((p - \frac{1}{n}, p + \frac{1}{n}) = \theta(n^{-\alpha})$ and $M(2^{-n}, \frac{1}{2}), M(\frac{1}{2}, 1 - 2^{-n}) = \theta(n)$. □

It can be checked (see [4]) that both these bounds are optimal. As $M(2^{-n}, 1 - 2^{-n})$ is still $\theta(n)$, the methods used so far imply only an $\Omega(n^{\alpha+1})$ lower bound on amplification from $(p - \frac{1}{n}, p + \frac{1}{n})$ to $(2^{-n}, 1 - 2^{-n})$. This will be improved in section 7 to a tight $\Omega(n^{\alpha+2})$ lower bound.

We note that the use of the function $G(x)$ in place of $H(x)$ is essential in obtaining the $\Omega(n^{\alpha+1})$ lower bounds of Corollary 5.2. Had we used $H(x)$, we would only have obtained $\Omega(n^\alpha \log n)$ lower bounds.

6 Global amplification bounds

The main result of this section is the following simple, yet powerful theorem

Theorem 6.1 *If $L(x,y)$ is defined on $(0,1)^2$ and satisfies the following two conditions*

$$\begin{aligned} L(x_1x_2, y_1y_2) &\leq L(x_1,y_1) + L(x_2,y_2) \\ L(x,y) &= L(1-x, 1-y) \end{aligned}$$

for every $0 < x_1, x_2, y_1, y_2, x, y < 1$ then for every $0 < p_0, p_1, q_0, q_1 < 1$ we have

$$N(p_1, q_1 | p_0, q_0) \geq \frac{L(p_1, q_1)}{L(p_0, q_0)} \quad .$$

Proof : We prove by induction on the structure of f that if f amplifies (p_0, q_0) to (p_1, q_1) then $size(f) \geq L(p_1,q_1)/L(p_0,q_0)$. The basis of the induction is easily established.

If $f = \neg g$ then g amplifies (p_0, q_0) to $(1-p_1, 1-q_1)$. As $size(f) = size(g)$ and $L(1-p_1, 1-q_1) = L(p_1, q_1)$, the required inequality follows immediately from the induction hypothesis.

If $f = f_1 \wedge f_2$ and if f_1, f_2 amplify (p_0, q_0) to (x_1, y_1) and (x_2, y_2) respectively, then $p_1 = x_1x_2$ and $q_1 = y_1y_2$. By the induction hypothesis and the first condition of L we have

$$size(f) = size(f_1) + size(f_2) \geq$$

$$\frac{L(x_1,y_1)+L(x_2,y_2)}{L(x_0,y_0)} \geq \frac{L(x_1x_2,y_1y_2)}{L(p_0,q_0)} = \frac{L(p_1,q_1)}{L(p_0,q_0)} \quad .$$

□

Note that in both Theorem 5.1 and Theorem 6.1 the lower bounds obtained were of a similar form. Both involved a quotient of some two-variable *potential* function evaluated at the pre and post amplification probabilities.

The approach of Theorem 6.1 seems to be more general than the approach of the previous section. Numerical tests seem to suggest that the function $M(x,y)$ of the previous section satisfies the condition $M(x_1x_2, y_1y_2) \leq M(x_1,y_1) + M(x_2,y_2)$ of Theorem 6.1. If this is indeed the case, then Theorem 5.1 follows immediately from Theorem 6.1.

With some additional work, the numerical tests that we had performed can probably be turned into a proof, similar in spirit to the original proof that Boppana had given to his inequality, that the function $M(x,y)$ satisfies the inequality $M(x_1x_2, y_1y_2) \leq M(x_1,y_1) + M(x_2,y_2)$. This should be tedious however, as four, and not just two, variables are involved this time. We did not carry out this extra work as the direct proof given to Theorem 5.1 seems to be more informative.

We now use Theorem 6.1 to obtain an alternative proof to the lower bounds for the second amplification stage obtained by Moore and Shannon [13] and Boppana [4]. The new proof works only for read-once formulae and not for general read-once networks. It does work however for general, not necessarily monotone, read-once formulae.

Let

$$L_1(x,y) = \ln\frac{1}{x}\cdot\ln\frac{1}{1-y} \quad , \quad L_2(x,y) = \ln\frac{1}{x}\cdot\ln\frac{\ln\frac{1}{x}}{\ln\frac{1}{y}}$$

for $x \leq y \leq 1-x$ and extend their definition using the symmetry condition $L(x,y) = L(y,x) = L(1-x, 1-y)$.

Lemma 6.2 *The functions $L_1(x,y)$ and $L_2(x,y)$ satisfy the conditions of Theorem 6.1.*

Proof : The proof for $L_1(x,y)$ is a simple exercise. For proof for $L_2(x,y)$ is given in the full version of the paper. □

Using $L_2(x,y)$ we extend Boppana's second lower bound to unate formulae.

Corollary 6.3 *Every unate read-once formula that amplifies $(\frac{1}{4}, \frac{3}{4})$ to at least $(2^{-n_1}, 1-2^{-n_2})$ is of size $\Omega(n_1n_2 + n_1\log n_1 + n_2\log n_2)$.*

7 A unified lower bound for amplification

Corollary 5.2 gives in particular an $\Omega(n^{\alpha+1})$ lower bound on the size of unate read-once formulae amplifying $(p-\frac{1}{n}, p+\frac{1}{n})$ to at least $(2^{-n}, 1-2^{-n})$ (for a fixed $0 < p < 1$). In this section we combine the proof techniques of the two preceding sections and improve this to a tight $\Omega(n^{\alpha+2})$ lower bound. We begin with the following generalization of Theorem 6.1

Theorem 7.1 *If $K(x,y)$ is defined on $(0,1)^2$ and satisfies the following three conditions*

$$\begin{aligned} K(x_1x_2, y_1y_2) &\leq \max\left\{ \begin{matrix} K(x_1,y_1) + K(x_2,y_2) \\ M(x_1x_2, y_1y_2) \end{matrix} \right\} \\ K(x,y) &\geq M(x,y) \\ K(x,y) &= K(1-x, 1-y) \end{aligned}$$

and if it is already known that

$$N(p_1, q_1 | p_0, q_0) \geq \frac{M(p_1, q_1)}{M(p_0, q_0)} \quad ,$$

for every $0 < p_0, p_1, q_0, q_1 < 1$, then we also have

$$N(p_1, q_1 | p_0, q_0) \geq \frac{K(p_1, q_1)}{K(p_0, q_0)} \quad .$$

Proof : Similar to the proof of Theorem 6.1. □

To get our unified lower bound we apply Theorem 7.1 to a function $K(x,y)$ obtained by stitching together the definitions of $M(x,y)$ from section 5 (with $C = 10^6$), that did well for the first amplification stage, and $L(x,y) = L_2(x,y)$ of section 6, that did well for the second amplification stage. The function $K(x,y)$ will equal $M(x,y)$ when x and y are very close to one another and it will equal $L(x,y)$ when they are far apart.

The function $K(x,y)$ is defined as follows

$$K(x,y) = \begin{cases} M(x,y) & \text{if } (x,y) \in \mathcal{A} \\ \max\{\, M(x,y), L(x,y)\,\} & \text{if } (x,y) \notin \mathcal{A} \end{cases}$$

where

$$\mathcal{A} = \mathcal{A}' \cup \mathcal{A}'' \quad , \quad \mathcal{A}' = \mathcal{R}'_2 \quad , \quad \mathcal{A}'' = \mathcal{R}''_2$$

and

$$\mathcal{R}'_d = \{\, (x,y) : \frac{1}{d} \le \left| \frac{\ln \frac{1}{x}}{\ln \frac{1}{y}} \right| \le d \,\} \quad ,$$

$$\mathcal{R}''_d = \{\, (x,y) : \frac{1}{d} \le \left| \frac{\ln \frac{1}{1-x}}{\ln \frac{1}{1-y}} \right| \le d \,\} \quad .$$

It is immediate that $K(x,y)$ satisfies the last two conditions of Theorem 7.1. To show that it also satisfies the first we define the following additional regions

$$\mathcal{C} = \mathcal{C}' \cup \mathcal{C}'' \quad , \quad \mathcal{C}' = \mathcal{R}'_6 \quad , \quad \mathcal{C}'' = \mathcal{R}''_6$$

Clearly $\mathcal{A} \subseteq \mathcal{C}$. Note that if $(x_1x_2, y_1y_2) \in \mathcal{A}$ then $K(x_1x_2, y_1y_2) = M(x_1x_2, y_1y_2)$. The fact that the function $K(x,y)$ satisfies the first condition of Theorem 7.1 will therefore follow from the following lemma

Lemma 7.2

$$L(x_1x_2, y_1y_2) \le$$

$$\begin{cases} K(x_1,y_1) + K(x_2,y_2) & \textit{if } (x_1x_2, y_1y_2) \notin \mathcal{C} \\ M(x_1x_2, y_1y_2) & \textit{if } (x_1x_2, y_1y_2) \in \mathcal{C} \setminus \mathcal{A} \end{cases} .$$

The proof of this lemma is very technical. It will be presented at the full version of the paper. As an immediate corollary of Theorem 7.1 and Lemma 7.2 we get

Corollary 7.3 *Any unate read-once formula that amplifies* $(p - \frac{1}{n_1}, p + \frac{1}{n_1})$ *to at least* $(2^{-n_2}, 1 - 2^{-n_3})$ *(where* $0 < p < 1$ *is fixed) is of size* $\Omega(n_1^{\alpha}(n_2n_3 + n_2\log n_2 + n_3\log n_3)$.

8 Exclusive-Or gates as convex combinations of unate gates

Theorem 8.1 *If f is a read-once formula that amplifies (p,q) to (p',q'), then there exists a probabilistic unate read-once formula F with size(F) $\le$ size(f) that also amplifies (p,q) to (p',q').*

Proof : The proof is by induction on the structure of f. If f is a variable then the result is clear. If $f = \neg f_1$ or $f = f_1 \wedge f_2$ then the result follows immediately from the induction hypothesis. The interesting case is if $f = f_1 \oplus f_2$. Assume that f_1, f_2 amplify (p,q) to (x_1,y_1) and (x_2,y_2) respectively. Let F_1, F_2 be two probabilistic unate formulae with *size*(F_1) $\le$ *size*(f_1) and *size*(F_2) $\le$ *size*(f_2) that also amplify (p,q) to (x_1,y_1) and (x_2,y_2) respectively. The existence of F_1, F_2 follows from the induction hypothesis. Using the next lemma, we obtain a unate connective $\circ$ and three constant $0 \le \alpha, \beta, \gamma$ with $\alpha + \beta + \gamma = 1$, depending on F_1 and F_2, such that the probabilistic formula

$$F = \begin{cases} 0 & \text{with prob. } \alpha \\ F_1 \circ F_2 & \text{with prob. } \beta \\ 1 & \text{with prob. } \gamma \end{cases}$$

achieves the same amplification as f. Clearly *size*(F) $\le$ *size*(F_1) + *size*(F_2) $\le$ *size*(f_1) + *size*(f_2) = *size*(f). This completes the proof of the Theorem. □

A unate connective here is one of the twelve connectives $(x^a \wedge y^b)^c$, x^a and y^b where $x^a = x \oplus a$, that may be obtained using one AND gate and some negations.

Lemma 8.2 *For every $0 \le x_1, x_2, y_1, y_2 \le 1$ there exists a unate connective $\circ$ such that $(x_1,y_1) \oplus (x_2,y_2)$ is in the convex hull of the points $(0,0), (x_1,y_1) \circ (x_2,y_2), (1,1)$.*

Proof : The proof uses case analysis and it will be given in the full version of the paper. □

It is easy to check that the lower bounds of the previous sections apply to probabilistic and not only to deterministic read-once formulae. All the lower bounds claimed for unate read-once formulae are valid therefore for general read-once formulae. We also have the following connection between probabilistic and non-probabilistic formulae

Theorem 8.3 *If F is a probabilistic formula amplifying (p,q) to (p',q') then there exists a deterministic formula f that amplifies (p,q) to (p'',q'') where $p'' \le 2p'$ and $1 - q'' \le 2(1-q')$. Furthermore, if F is read-once, unate or monotone then so is f.*

Proof : Recall that $p' = F(p) = E_{f\in F} f(p)$ where the expectation is according to the distribution that F induces on the deterministic formulae that it assumes. Since for every non-negative random variable X we have $\Pr[X > 2E(X)] < \frac{1}{2}$ we get that $\Pr[f(p) > 2p'] < \frac{1}{2}$, where again f is chosen according to the distribution induced by F. Applying a similar argument to $q' = F(q)$ we get that $\Pr[(1-f(q)) > 2(1-q')] < \frac{1}{2}$. As a consequence

$$Pr[\, f(p) > 2p' \,\vee\, (1-f(q)) > 2(1-q')\,] < 1$$

and therefore a deterministic formula chosen according to the distribution of F will satisfy the required conditions with a positive probability. □

Corollary 8.4

$$N_{\oplus}(p_1, q_1|p_0, q_0) \geq \min_{\substack{p_1' \leq 2p_1 \\ 1-q_1' \leq 2(1-q_1)}} N(p_1', q_1'|p_0, q_0) \quad .$$

9 Amplifying networks

Valiant's construction of $O(n^\alpha)$ size monotone formulae that amplify $(\psi-\frac{1}{n}, \psi+\frac{1}{n})$ to $(\frac{1}{4}, \frac{3}{4})$ uses a repeated composition of the basic series-parallel unit A shown in Fig. 1. Better amplification can be obtained using other units (e.g., units B, C, D of Fig. 1).

Theorem 9.1 *Let $f(x_1, \ldots, x_k)$ be the amplification function of a monotone read-once contact network with k edges. Let p_c be the critical probability for which $f(p_c) = p_c$. Let $\delta > 1$ be the unique number for which $\|\nabla f(p_c)\|_\delta = 1$. Then, by a repeated composition of f with composition ratios proportional to $(\nabla f(p_c))^\delta$ we get monotone read-once networks of size $O(n^\epsilon)$, where $\epsilon = \frac{\delta}{\delta-1}$ is the conjugate of δ, that amplify $(p_c - \frac{1}{n}, p_c + \frac{1}{n})$ to at least $(\frac{1}{4}, \frac{3}{4})$.*

Proof : (Sketch) Let $c_1, \ldots, c_k$ be positive constants that satisfy $\sum_{i=1}^k c_i = 1$. We define a sequence f_n of networks in the following way: $f_k = f$ and for $n > k$, f_n is obtained from f by replacing its i-th edge by a copy of the network $f_{c_i n}$. We ignore integrallity problems here. Clearly, we have the relation $f_n(p) = f(f_{c_1 n}(p), \ldots, f_{c_k n}(p))$ and therefore $f_n'(p_c) = \sum_{i=1}^n \frac{\partial f}{\partial x_i}(p_c) \cdot f_{c_i n}'(p_c)$. It is easy to check that asymptotically $f_n'(p_c) \sim a n^\gamma$ where $\gamma = \gamma(c)$ is the unique real satisfying $\sum_{i=1}^k \frac{\partial f}{\partial x_i}(p_c) \cdot c_i^\gamma = 1$ and $a > 0$ is some constant. It can be checked then that $f_{bn^{1/\gamma}}$ for some fixed $b > 0$, which is a network of size $O(n^{1/\gamma})$, performs the required amplification.

We want to find the composition ratios $c_1, \ldots, c_k$ for which $\gamma = \gamma(c)$ is maximized. By Hölder's inequality we get that if $\delta' = \frac{1}{1-\gamma}$ is the conjugate of $1/\gamma$ then $1 = \sum_{i=1}^k \frac{\partial f}{\partial x_i}(p) \cdot c_i^\gamma \leq \|\nabla f(p)\|_{\delta'}$. Thus, $\delta' \leq \delta$ and $1/\gamma = \frac{\delta'}{\delta'-1} \geq \frac{\delta}{\delta-1}$. On the other hand, if we choose $c_i \propto \left(\frac{\partial f}{\partial x_i}(p)\right)^\delta$ and $\gamma = 1 - \frac{1}{\delta}$ we get the required equality. Thus, the choice specified is indeed the optimal one. □

Plugging unit C of Fig. 1 into the above theorem we get networks for the first amplification stage of size $O(n^{3.12})$. The resulting exponents for the other basic units are specified in the figure. As we shall see in the next section further improvements are possible.

10 Amplification and percolation

Blocks B and C are simply 2×3 and 3×4 rectangular grids in which all the vertices on the leftmost and rightmost columns were glued together to form the source and the sink, respectively. Using a computer program we were able to compute (exactly) the partial derivatives the the amplification functions of such $m \times (m+1)$ rectangular grids, for $m = 4, \ldots, 10$, at their critical point (this took about 30 minutes on a Sun workstation) . As all these networks are self-dual, their critical probability is exactly $p_c = \frac{1}{2}$. Using a 10×11 grid as a basic building block we get amplifying networks of size $O(n^{2.99})$ for the first stage of amplification stage. Using larger and larger building blocks we expect to get better and better results. The exact computation of the derivatives of much larger grids seems impractical. Using Monte Carlo methods we estimate that by using a 50×51 grid as the basic building block we can get networks of size below $O(n^{2.9})$.

It follows from certain conjectures in *percolation theory* that constructions of the form described, using larger and larger two dimensional grids as basic building blocks will yield amplifying networks of size $O(n^{8/3+o(1)})$. There is no need in fact to use the composition process, $n^{4/3+o(1)} \times n^{4/3+o(1)}$ grids, as conjectured, will achieve the required amplification!

Percolation theory is the study of the connectivity properties of random subgraphs of d-dimensional grids and other regular graphs. Good references to the mathematical theory of percolation are Grimmett [6], and Kesten [10],[11]. We will briefly describe its fea-

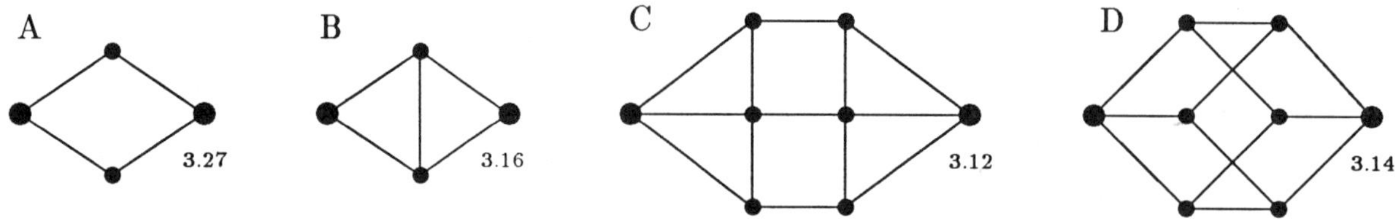

Figure 1: Basic contact networks

tures relevant to our investigation.

Consider an $m \times (m+1)$ 2-dimensional grid where each edge is independently open (i.e., present) with probability p (see Figure 2 for an example). Let $f_m(p)$ be its (univariate) amplification function and $p_c = \frac{1}{2}$ be its critical probability. Its *correlation length* $\xi(p)$ is defined for $p < p_c$ to be

$$\xi(p) = \lim_{m \to \infty} \frac{m}{\ln \frac{1}{f_m(p)}} \quad .$$

There are other definitions of $\xi(p)$ but they all agree up to a uniformly bounded factor. This quantity can be shown to exist and moreover, when p is bounded away from 0, the convergence is uniform in some sense. In particular for every $\epsilon > 0$ there exists $c > 0$ such that for each $m > \xi(p)^{1+\epsilon}, c$ we have

$$e^{-\frac{m}{\xi(p)^{1-\epsilon}}} \le f_m(p) \le e^{-\frac{m}{\xi(p)^{1+\epsilon}}} \quad .$$

The correlation length $\xi(p)$ is finite for $p < p_c$ and tends to $+\infty$ when $p \to p_c$. It is conjectured that

$$\ln \xi(p) \sim \nu \cdot \ln \frac{1}{p_c - p} \qquad \text{where} \quad \nu = \frac{4}{3} \quad .$$

The constant ν is one of the *critical exponents* encountered in percolation theory. Den Nijs [5] has given plausible but not rigorous arguments in support of this conjecture.

Assuming that this conjecture is true, we get that an $m \times (m+1)$ grid, where $m = n^{\frac{4}{3}(1+2\epsilon)}$ amplifies $(p_c - \frac{1}{n}, p_c + \frac{1}{n})$ to about $(\frac{1}{4}, \frac{3}{4})$. It is interesting to note that by taking $m = n^{\frac{7}{3}(1+2\epsilon)}$ we get networks that amplify $(p_c - \frac{1}{n}, p_c + \frac{1}{n})$ to about $(2^{-n}, 1-2^{-n})$. The bounds on $f_m(p_c - \frac{1}{n})$ follow easily from the above estimates. The bounds on $f_m(p_c + \frac{1}{n})$ follow using the same arguments for the dual grid.

An amazing consequence of the *scaling* or *renormalization* theory of percolation is the conjecture that critical exponents, such as ν, depend only on the dimension of the grid used and not on it exact structure (note that the critical probability p_c for example does depend on the exact structure). If this conjecture is true, the same asymptotic results could be obtained using triangular, hexagonal or any other regular two dimensional construct such as the ***hammock*** structure favoured by Moore and Shannon [13]. We have experimented with many small size networks and found however that of all networks with the same (small) size, rectangular grids seem to give the best results.

How about using higher dimensional grids? (note that unit D of Fig. 1 is a cube and it had quite a good behaviour). Experimental evidence (see Stauffer and Aharony [18], p. 52), gives the following approximations to the critical exponent ν in dimensions 3,4 and 5: $\nu_3 \simeq 0.88$, $\nu_4 \simeq 0.68$ and $\nu_5 \simeq 0.57$. As $3\nu_3 \simeq 2.64 < \frac{8}{3}$ it seems that we could do a bit better using 3-dimensional grids. In fact, it might be possible to use fractional dimensions between 2 and 4 to get further improvements. A d-dimensional grid is just an (infinite) graph in which each vertex has $\theta(k^d)$ neighbours at distance k.

11 Open problems

1. Do the lower bounds on amplifying formulae given in this paper apply to general, not necessarily read-once formulae? Do they apply to general monotone formulae? Do they apply, say, to read-twice formulae?

2. What is asymptotically the minimal size of a contact network that amplifies $(p - \frac{1}{n}, p + \frac{1}{n})$ (for some fixed $0 < p < 1$) to $(\frac{1}{4}, \frac{3}{4})$? Of all networks with the same number of edges, which ones have the largest derivative at their critical probability?

3. Are the optimal monotone formulae and undirected monotone contact networks for the majority obtained using the amplification method?

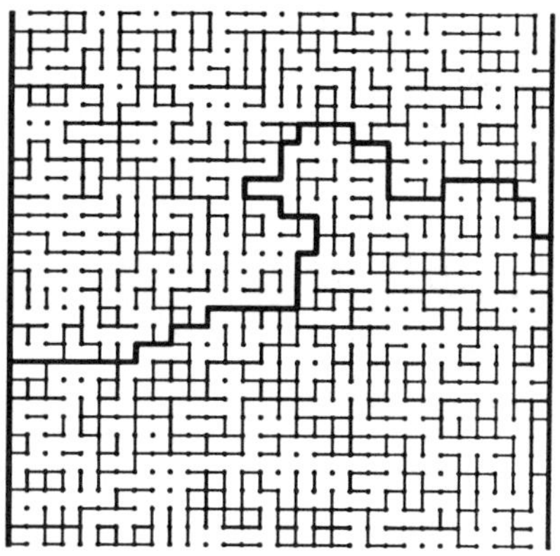

Figure 2: Percolation on a rectangular grid.

Acknowledgement

The authors would like to thank Noga Alon for many helpful discussions and to Edith Magen and Dalya Jacobsen for their continued interest and encouragement.

References

[1] L. Adelman, "Two theorems on random polynomial time", *Proceedings of the 19th IEEE Symposium on Foundations of Computer Science, 1978, pp. 75–83.*

[2] M. Ajtai and M. Ben-Or, "A theorem on probabilistic constant depth computations", *Proceedings of the 16th ACM Symposium on Theory of Computing, 1984, pp. 471–474.*

[3] C.G. Bennett and J. Gill, "Relative to a random oracle A, $P^A \neq NP^A \neq co-NP^A$ with probability 1", *SIAM Journal on Computing, Vol. 10 (1981), pp. 96–113.*

[4] R.B. Boppana, "Amplification of probabilistic Boolean formulas", in *Advances in Computer Research, Vol.5: Randomness and Computation*, JAI Press, Greenwich, Conn., 1989.

[5] M.P.M. den Nijs, "A relation between the temperature exponents of the eight-vertex and q-state Potts model", *Journal of Physics A: Mathematical and General, Vol. 12 (1979), pp. 1857-1868.*

[6] G. Grimmett, *Percolation*, Springer-Verlag, New York, 1989.

[7] Q.P., Gu and A. Maruoka, "Amplification of Bounded Depth Monotone Read-Once Boolean Formulae", *SIAM J. Computing, Vol. 20 (1991), pp. 41-55.*

[8] A. Gupta and S. Mahajan, "Using Amplification to Compute Majority with Majority", *preprint.*

[9] J. Håstad, A. Razborov and A. Yao, "On the Shrinkage Exponent for Read-Once Formulae", *preprint.*

[10] H. Kesten, *Percolation Theory for Mathematicians*, Birkhäuser, Boston, 1982.

[11] H. Kesten, "Percolation Theory and First-Passage Percolation", *Annals of Probability, Vol. 15 (1987), pp. 1231-1271.*

[12] O.B. Lupanov, "On Computing symmetric functions of the propositional calculus by switching networks" (in Russian), *Problemy Kibernet. Vol. 15 (1965), pp. 85-100.*

[13] E.F. Moore and C.E. Shannon, "Reliable circuits using less reliable relays", *Journal of the Franklin Institute Vol. 262 (1956), pp. 191-208 and pp. 281-297.*

[14] M.S. Paterson, N. Pippenger and U. Zwick, "Faster circuits and shorter formulae for multiple addition, multiplication and symmetric Boolean functions," *Proceedings of the 31st Ann. IEEE Symp. on Found. of Comp. Sci.*, St. Louis 1990, pp. 642-650.

[15] M.S. Paterson, N. Pippenger and U. Zwick, "Optimal carry save networks," *Boolean function complexity: Selected papers from the LMS symposium, Durham 1990.* To appear, Cambridge Univ. Press, 1992.

[16] M.S. Paterson, U. Zwick, "Shrinkage of de Morgan formulae under restriction", *Proceedings of 32st FOCS, San Juan, Puerto-Rico, 1991, pp. 324-333.* Journal version to appear in *Random Structures & algorithms.*

[17] J. Radhakrishnan and K.V. Subrahmanyam, *personal communication.*

[18] D. Stauffer and A. Aharony, *Introduction to Percolation Theory*, Taylor & Francis, London, 1992.

[19] L.G. Valiant, "Short monotone formulae for the majority function", *J. Algorithms 5 (1984) 363-366.*

Algebraic Decision Trees and Euler Characteristics*

Andrew Chi-Chih Yao
Department of Computer Science
Princeton University
Princeton, New Jersey 08544

Abstract

For any set $S \subseteq R^n$, let $\chi(S)$ denote its Euler characteristic. In this paper, we show that any algebraic computation tree or fixed-degree algebraic decision tree must have height $\Omega(\log|\chi(S)|)$ for deciding the membership question of a compact semi-algebraic set S. This extends a result in Björner, Lovász and Yao [BLY], where it was shown that any linear decision tree for deciding the membership question of a closed polyhedron S must have height greater than or equal to $\log_3|\chi(S)|$.

1 Introduction

Many problems in geometry and combinatorial optimization can be viewed as solving *membership* problems for sets $S \subseteq R^N$: given an input $\tilde{x} = (x_1, x_2, \cdots, x_n) \in R^n$, decide whether $\tilde{x} \in S$. For example, *Element Distinctness*, the problem of deciding whether n real numbers are all distinct, is the membership problem for $S = \{(x_1, x_2, \cdots, x_n) \mid x_i \neq x_j \,\forall i \neq j\}$; *Points Collinearity*, the problem of deciding whether any three of n given points (x_i, y_i) $(1 \leq i \leq n)$ lie on the same line, is the membership problem for S, where $S \subseteq R^{2n}$ is the set of all $(x_1, y_1, \cdots, x_n, y_n)$ satisying $x_i y_j + x_j y_k + x_k y_i - x_j y_i - x_k y_j - x_i y_k = 0$ for some $i < j < k$. Two familiar complexity models for membership problems are the fixed-degree algebraic tree model and the algebraic computation tree model (see e.g. [SY] [Be]). Let $C_d(S)$ and $C(S)$ denote the complexities in the degree-d algebraic tree and the algebraic computation tree models.

Much work has been done in the search for connections between the computational complexity of the membership problem for S and the geometric or topological properties of S, from which hopefully useful lower bounds may be derived. It is known that, when S is a convex polytope, $\Omega(\log(\phi_s(S)))$ tests are needed in the linear decision tree model, where $\phi_s(S)$ is the number of s-dimensional faces of S; the $s = 0$ case was proved in Morávek [Mo], and the general case was proved in Kalinová [Ka] and in Yao and Rivest [YR] (also see Morávek and Puklák [MP]). For any S, let $\beta_0(S)$ denote the number of connected components of S. Dobkin and Lipton [DL] showed that $\Omega(\log(\beta_0(S)))$ tests are needed in the linear decision tree model. Using the Milnor-Thom bound [Mi][T] on algebraic sets, Steele and Yao [SY] showed that $C_d(S) + n \log C_d(S) \geq \Omega(\log(\beta_0(S)))$ for any fixed d. Ben-Or [Be] improved these bounds, showing that $C_d(S)$ (for fixed d) and $C(S)$ are both at least $\Omega(\log(\beta_0(S)))$.

Recently, Björner, Lovász and Yao [BLY] found another link, proving that any linear decision tree for deciding the membership question of a closed polyhedron S must use at least $\log_3|\chi(S)|$ tests, where $\chi(S)$ is the Euler characteristic of S. This result offered an approach for proving new lower bounds to some geometric problems. For example, it was used in [BLY] to show that $\Omega(n\log(n/k))$ linear tests are needed to solve the "k-equal problem"– the problem of determining whether there are k identical elements out of n given input real numbers.

In this paper, we show that this connection be-

*This research was supported in part by the National Science Foundation under Grant CCR-8813283, and by a Guggenheim Fellowship.

0-8186-2900-2/92 $3.00 © 1992 IEEE

tween $\chi(S)$ and the computational complexity of S also exists for models much more general than linear decision trees (thus solving an open problem posed in [BLY]). We prove that any algebraic computation tree or fixed-degree algebraic decision tree must have height $\Omega(\log|\chi(S)|)$ for deciding the membership question of any compact semi-algebraic set S. Precisely, we will prove that for some constants a_d, a, the following two theorems are true.

Theorem A Let $d > 0$ be any fixed integer. Then, for any compact semi-algebraic set $S \subseteq R^n$, we have $C_d(S) \geq \Omega(\log_2|\chi(S)|) - a_d n$.

Theorem B Let $S \subseteq R^n$ be a compact semi-algebraic set. Then $C(S) \geq \Omega(\log_2|\chi(S)|) - an$.

In fact, we will derive a lower bound valid for any (compact and non-compact) semi-algebraic set S. We introduce a new quantity $\hat{\chi}(S)$, which equals $\chi(S)$ when S is compact. Theorems A and B are immediate consequences of Theorem 6 and Theorem 7 in Section 5.

We remark that there are other algebraic complexity models studied in the literature (e.g. Mansour, Schieber and Tiwari[MST], Smale [Sm], Strassen [St]), in addition to the fixed-degree algebraic trees and algebraic computation trees discussed here.

In Section 2 we review standard definitions and some needed background material. In Section 3, the "modified" Euler characteristic $\hat{\chi}(S)$ is defined. In Section 4, properties of $\hat{\chi}(S)$ are studied, which are then used in Section 5 to prove the main theorems. Section 6 discusses extensions and open problems.

2 Preliminaries

We review in this section some standard facts in topology and fix the notations. The proof of Lemma 1 will need some additional concepts not discussed here.

Throughout this paper, $n > 0$, $m, r, s \geq 0$ denote integers. For any set $S \subseteq R^n$, $\bar{S}$ is the closure of S; define the *boundary* of S by $\partial S = \bar{S} - S$. When S is considered as a topological space, it is understood that the topology is the subspace topology induced by R^n. All polynomials refer to polynomials with real coefficients.

For any topological space S and integer $i \geq 0$, let $\beta_i(S)$ denote the *i-th Betti number*, which is the rank of the i-th singular homology group. The *Euler characteristic* $\chi(S)$ is defined to be $\sum_{i\geq 0}(-1)^i\beta_i(S)$, when the Betti numbers are finite and are nonzero only for a finite number of i. It is known that, if S, T are topological spaces homeomorphic to, respectively, the unit closed ball and the unit sphere in R^n, then $\chi(S) = 1$ and $\chi(T) = 1 + (-1)^{n+1}$.

An *algebraic set* in R^n is the set of points $\tilde{x} \in R^n$ satisfying a finite set of polynomial equations. The following result is well known.

Milnor-Thom Bound [Mi] [T] Let $S = \{\tilde{x} \mid f_i(\tilde{x}) = 0,\ 1 \leq i \leq r\} \subseteq R^n$. Then all the Betti numbers of S are finite, and $\sum_{i\geq 0}\beta_i(S) \leq d(2d-1)^{n-1}$ where d is the maximum degree of any f_i.

As an immediate corollary, the above bound gives $|\chi(S)| \leq d(2d-1)^{n-1}$.

A set $S \subseteq R^n$ is a *semi-algebraic set* if S can be generated from sets of the form $\{\tilde{x} \mid f(\tilde{x}) > 0\}$ (with f being polynomials in R^n) through complementation, finite union and finite intersection. It is well known that S is semi-algebraic if and only if there exist a finite number of polynomials f_{ij}, g_{ij} on R^n such that $S = \cup_i S_i$, where S_i is the set of all $\tilde{x} \in R^n$ satisfying $f_{ij}(\tilde{x}) = 0, g_{ij}(\tilde{x}) > 0$ for all j.

Clearly, the class of semi-algebraic functions in R^n is closed under complementation, finite union, and finite intersection. It is also known that if $S \subseteq R^n$ is semi-algebraic, then $\bar{S}$ is semi-algebraic.

Let $B \subseteq R^n$ be a semi-algebraic set, and $f : B \longrightarrow R^m$ be a continuous map. We say that f is a *semi-algebraic map* if the graph $\{(\tilde{x}, f(\tilde{x})) \mid \tilde{x} \in B\}$ is a semi-algebraic set in R^{n+m}. It is known (see e.g. [H]) that the image of a semi-algebraic set under a semi-algebraic map must be semi-algebraic. In particular, the projection of a semi-algebraic set S on coordinates $i_1, i_2, \cdots, i_m$, i.e. the set $\{(x_{i_1}, x_{i_2}, \cdots, x_{i_m}) \mid (x_1, x_2, \cdots, x_n) \in S\}$, is semi-algebraic. Also, the composition of two semi-algebraic maps, when defined, is again a semi-algebraic map. Two semi-algebraic sets are *homeomorphic semi-*

algebraically if there is a homeomorphism f between them and f is a semi-algebraic map; note that this is an equivalence relation. More information about semi-algebraic sets can be found in, for example, [Br] [H].

An *open k-simplex* Δ in R^n, where $0 \leq k \leq n$, is a set of the form $\{\tilde{x} \mid \tilde{x} = \sum_{0 \leq i \leq k} t_i \tilde{p}_i, t_i > 0, \sum_{0 \leq i \leq k} t_i = 1\}$, where $\tilde{p}_i$ are $k+1$ affinely independent points in R^n; we denote this set by $[\tilde{p}_0, \tilde{p}_1, \cdots, \tilde{p}_k]$. The *dimension* of the simplex, written as $\dim(\Delta)$, is defined to be k. Let $0 \leq i_0, i_1, \cdots, i_j \leq k$ be distinct integers, where $0 \leq j \leq k$. Then the j-simplex $[\tilde{p}_{i_0}, \tilde{p}_{i_1}, \cdots, \tilde{p}_{i_j}]$ is a *face* of $[\tilde{p}_0, \tilde{p}_1, \cdots, \tilde{p}_k]$.

An *open simplicial decomposition* of a set $S \subseteq R^n$ is a finite family H of disjoint open simplices such that $S = \cup_{\Delta \in H} \Delta$, and that H contains all faces of all members of H. We list some elementary properties that will be useful later. Let H be an open simplicial decomposition of $S \subseteq R^n$. Then $\chi(S) = \sum_{\Delta \in H} (-1)^{\dim(\Delta)}$. Suppose $H' \subseteq H$, and $S' = \cup_{\Delta \in H'} \Delta$. Then S' is a closed set if and only if H' is an open simplicial decomposition of S'. See [Bj] [GH] [Mu] for more discussions on simplices and other background information in topology.

Let $S_1, S_2, \cdots, S_m$ be sets in R^n. A *triangulation* for $S_1, S_2, \cdots, S_m$ is a pair $(\mathcal{D}, h)$, where $\mathcal{D} = \{D_\alpha \mid \alpha \in A\}$ is an open simplicial decomposition of the set $E \equiv \cup_{\alpha \in A} D_\alpha \subseteq R^n$ and $h : E \rightarrow R^n$ is a homeomorphism between E and $h(E)$, such that the following is true: for any $1 \leq i \leq m$, there exists a subset $A_i \subseteq A$ satisfying $S_i = \cup_{\alpha \in A_i} h(D_\alpha)$. The existence of triangulations are known for several classes of well-behaved sets (see e.g. [LW] [Lo] [H]). We call $(\mathcal{D}, h)$ a *semi-algebraic triangulation* if h is a semi-algebraic map; it implies that $h(D_\alpha)$ is semi-algebraic for each $\alpha \in A$. We will need the following result.

The Triangulation Theorem (Hironaka [H]) Let $S_1, S_2, \cdots, S_m$ be a finite family of bounded semi-algebraic sets in R^n. Then there exists a semi-algebraic triangulation for $S_1, S_2, \cdots, S_m$.

Finally, we consider the *inverse stereographic mapping* $\varphi_n : R^n \rightarrow R^{n+1}$, given by $\varphi_n(x_1, x_2, \cdots, x_n) = (x_1(1 - y_{n+1}), x_2(1 - y_{n+1}), \cdots, x_n(1 - y_{n+1}), y_{n+1})$, where y_{n+1} is the unique solution to the system of constraints $0 < y_{n+1} < 1$ and $\sum_{1 \leq i \leq n} x_i^2 (1 - y_{n+1})^2 + (y_{n+1} - 2/3)^2 = 1/9$. Let $J_{n+1} \subseteq R^{n+1}$ denote the sphere centered at $(0, 0, \cdots, 0, 2/3)$ with radius $1/3$. Then φ_n is a homeomorphism from R^n onto $J_{n+1} - \{(0, 0, \cdots, 0, 1)\}$. Geometrically, if we identify $\tilde{x} = (x_1, x_2, \cdots, x_n)$ with the point $(x_1, x_2, \cdots, x_n, 0)$ and draw a line in R^{n+1} between it and the north pole of J_{n+1}, then $\varphi_n(\tilde{x})$ is the unique point where the line intersects J_{n+1}.

For any $S \subseteq R^n$, we call $\varphi_n(S)$ the *inverse stereographic image* of S. The mapping φ_n is clearly a semi-algebraic map. Hence, if S is a semi-algebraic set in R^n, then $\varphi_n(S)$ is a semi-algebraic set in R^{n+1}. We will write φ instead of φ_n when the dimension n is clear from the context.

3 A Modified Euler Characteristic

Let $S \subseteq R^n$ be a semi-algebraic set. We will introduce an integer-valued quantity $\hat{\chi}(S)$, which is closely related to the Euler characteristic $\chi(S)$.

We first consider the case when S is bounded. Let $(\mathcal{D}, h)$ be any semi-algebraic triangulation for S. (By the Triangulation Theorem, such triangulations exist.) Assume $\mathcal{D} = \{D_\alpha \mid \alpha \in A\}$, and $S = \cup_{\alpha \in B} h(D_\alpha)$ where $B \subseteq A$. Define $\hat{\chi}(S; \mathcal{D}, h)$ to be $\sum_{\alpha \in B} (-1)^{\dim(D_\alpha)}$. Note that $\hat{\chi}(S; \mathcal{D}, h) = 0$ if S is the empty set.

Lemma 1 Let $S \subseteq R^n$ be a bounded set, homeomorphic semi-algebraically to an open k-simplex where $0 \leq k \leq n$. Then $\hat{\chi}(S; \mathcal{D}, h) = (-1)^k$ for any semi-algebraic triangulation $(\mathcal{D}, h)$ for S.

Proof (Sketch) As mentioned in Section 2, the proof of this lemma involves additional topological concepts. See [GH] [V] for terminology and other background information.

We need to prove

$$\sum_{\alpha \in B} (-1)^{\dim(D_\alpha)} = (-1)^k. \tag{1}$$

If $k = 0$, then $|B| = 1$ and equation (1) is clearly true. If $k = 1$, then $\{D_\alpha \mid \alpha \in B\}$ consists of m open 1-

simplices and $m-1$ open 0-simplices for some $m \geq 1$. Again (1) is true.

Let $k > 1$. For each $0 \leq j \leq k$, let t_j denote the number of $\alpha \in B$ with $\dim(D_\alpha) = j$. Let Δ be some open k-simplex, and $g : S \to \Delta$ be a semi-algebraic homeomorphism. Then $\xi \equiv g \circ h$ is a semi-algebraic homeomorphism from $\cup_{\alpha \in B} D_\alpha$ to Δ. Clearly, Δ is the disjoint union of $\xi(D_\alpha)$, $\alpha \in B$.

Now, $\bar{\Delta}$ is the disjoint union of Δ and $\partial\Delta$; the latter can be regarded topologically as the union of a point and an open $(k-1)$-dimensional simplex. This suggests that we can try to construct $\bar{\Delta}$ as a spherical complex in the natural way, using t_0+1 0-dimensional cells, $t_{k-1}+1$ $(k-1)$-dimensional cells, and t_j j-dimensional cells, $j \neq 0, k-1$. For this to be possible, we need to prove that, for each $\alpha \in B$, there exists a continuous mapping from a $(j-1)$-dimensional sphere, where $j = \dim(D_\alpha)$, onto $\partial(\xi(D_\alpha))$. We leave the proof of this technical result to the complete paper.

From the theory of spherical complex, we have

$$\begin{aligned}\chi(\bar{\Delta}) &= (t_0+1) + (t_{k-1}+1)\cdot(-1)^{k-1} \\ &\quad + \sum_{j\neq 0,k-1} t_j \cdot (-1)^j \\ &= 1 + (-1)^{k-1} + \sum_{\alpha \in B} (-1)^{\dim(D_\alpha)}. \qquad (2)\end{aligned}$$

Since $\bar{\Delta}$ is homeomorphic to a k-dimensional ball, we have $\chi(\bar{\Delta}) = 1$. Thus, (1) follows from (2). □

Theorem 1 Let $S \subseteq R^n$ be a bounded semi-algebraic set. Then $\hat{\chi}(S; \mathcal{D}, h)$ is independent of the choice of $(\mathcal{D}, h)$.

Proof Clearly, we can assume that S is not empty. Let $(\mathcal{D}, h)$ and $(\mathcal{D}', h')$ be two semi-algebraic triangulations for S. Let $\mathcal{D} = \{D_\alpha \mid \alpha \in A\}$, $\mathcal{D}' = \{D_\beta \mid \beta \in A'\}$, and

$$S = \cup_{\alpha \in B} h(D_\alpha) = \cup_{\beta \in B'} h'(D'_\beta). \qquad (3)$$

We need to show that $\hat{\chi}(S; \mathcal{D}, h) = \hat{\chi}(S; \mathcal{D}', h')$, i.e.

$$\sum_{\alpha \in B} (-1)^{\dim(D_\alpha)} = \sum_{\beta \in B'} (-1)^{\dim(D'_\beta)}. \qquad (4)$$

Consider the family $\mathcal{F}$ of bounded semi-algebraic sets $\{h(D_\alpha) \mid \alpha \in A\} \cup \{h'(D_\beta) \mid \beta \in A'\}$. By the Triangulation Theorem, there exists a semi-algebraic triangulation $(\mathcal{D}'', h'')$ for $\mathcal{F}$. Let $\mathcal{D}'' = \{D''_\gamma \mid \gamma \in A''\}$. Then, for each $\alpha \in B$, there exists $A''_\alpha \subseteq A''$ such that

$$h(D_\alpha) = \cup_{\gamma \in A''_\alpha} h''(D''_\gamma). \qquad (5)$$

Also, for each $\beta \in B'$, there exists $A''_\beta \subseteq A''$ such that

$$h(D'_\beta) = \cup_{\gamma \in A''_\beta} h''(D''_\gamma). \qquad (6)$$

Let $\alpha \in B$. Applying Lemma 1 to $h(D_\alpha)$, we have $\hat{\chi}(h(D_\alpha); \mathcal{D}'', h'') = (-1)^{\dim(D_\alpha)}$. Thus, (5) gives

$$\sum_{\gamma \in A''_\alpha} (-1)^{\dim(D''_\gamma)} = (-1)^{\dim(D_\alpha)}.$$

It follows that

$$\begin{aligned}\sum_{\alpha \in B} (-1)^{\dim(D_\alpha)} &= \sum_{\alpha \in B} \sum_{\gamma \in A''_\alpha} (-1)^{\dim(D''_\gamma)} \\ &= \sum_{\gamma \in \cup_{\alpha \in B} A''_\alpha} (-1)^{\dim(D''_\gamma)}. \qquad (7)\end{aligned}$$

Similarly, we obtain from (6)

$$\sum_{\beta \in B'} (-1)^{\dim(D'_\beta)} = \sum_{\gamma \in \cup_{\beta \in B'} A''_\beta} (-1)^{\dim(D''_\gamma)}. \qquad (8)$$

Now, from (3), (5) and (6), we have $S = \cup_{\alpha \in B} \cup_{\gamma \in A''_\alpha} h''(D''_\gamma) = \cup_{\beta \in B'} \cup_{\gamma \in A''_\beta} h''(D''_\gamma)$. This implies

$$\cup_{\alpha \in B} A''_\alpha = \cup_{\beta \in B'} A''_\beta. \qquad (9)$$

From (7)-(9), we obtain (4). This proves Theorem 1.□

Definition 1 For any bounded semi-algebraic set $S \subseteq R^n$, let $\hat{\chi}(S) = \hat{\chi}(S; \mathcal{D}, h)$, where $(\mathcal{D}, h)$ is any semi-algebraic triangulation for S.

In view of Theorem 1 and the Triangulation Theorem, the above $\hat{\chi}(S)$ is well-defined. For unbounded set, we will define it to be the $\hat{\chi}$ of its inverse stereographic image.

Definition 2 For any unbounded semi-algebraic set $S \subseteq R^n$, define $\hat{\chi}(S)$ to be $\hat{\chi}(\varphi(S))$.

We note that, if S is any bounded semi-algebraic set, the equality $\hat{\chi}(S) = \hat{\chi}(\varphi(S))$ is also true. In fact, if $(\mathcal{D}, h)$ is a semi-algebraic triangulation for S, with $\mathcal{D} = \{D_\alpha \mid \alpha \in A\}$ and $S = \cup_{\alpha \in B} h(D_\alpha)$, then $(\mathcal{D}', h')$ is a semi-algebraic triangulation for $\varphi(S)$, with $\mathcal{D}' = \{D_\alpha \mid \alpha \in A\}$, $h' = \varphi \circ h$, and $\varphi(S) = \cup_{\alpha \in B} h'(D_\alpha)$; it follows that $\hat{\chi}(S) = \sum_{\alpha \in B} (-1)^{\dim(D_\alpha)} = \hat{\chi}(\varphi(S))$.

4 Properties of $\hat{\chi}$

Theorem 2 If $S_1, S_2, \cdots, S_m$ are disjoint semi-algebraic sets in R^n, then $\hat{\chi}(\cup_{1\le i\le m} S_i)$ is equal to $\sum_{1\le i\le m}\hat{\chi}(S_i)$.

Proof First we prove the theorem when all S_i are bounded. By the Triangulation Theorem, there exists a semi-algebraic triangulation $(\mathcal{D}, h)$ for $S_1, S_2, \cdots, S_m$. Let $\mathcal{D} = \{D_\alpha \mid \alpha \in A\}$ and $S_i = \cup_{\alpha\in A_i} h(D_\alpha)$, $1 \le i \le m$. By definition,

$$\hat{\chi}(S_i) = \sum_{\alpha\in A_i}(-1)^{\dim(D_\alpha)},$$

and

$$\hat{\chi}(\cup_{1\le i\le m} S_i) = \sum_{\alpha\in\cup_{1\le i\le m} A_i}(-1)^{\dim(D_\alpha)}.$$

If follows that $\hat{\chi}(\cup_{1\le i\le m} S_i) = \sum_{1\le i\le m}\hat{\chi}(S_i)$.

We now turn to the general case when some of the S_i may be unbounded. As their inverse stereographic images $\varphi(S_i)$ are disjoint bounded semi-algebraic sets, by applying the result we just derived, we obtain $\hat{\chi}(\varphi(\cup_{1\le i\le m} S_i)) = \sum_{1\le i\le m}\hat{\chi}(\varphi(S_i))$. But the $\hat{\chi}$ of any semi-algebraic set is the same as the $\hat{\chi}$ of its inverse stereographic image. This proves $\hat{\chi}(\cup_{1\le i\le m} S_i) = \sum_{1\le i\le m}\hat{\chi}(S_i)$. □

Theorem 3 If $S \subseteq R^n$ is a compact semi-algebraic set, then $\hat{\chi}(S) = \chi(S)$.

Proof By assumption, S is bounded. By the Triangulation Theorem, there exists a semi-algebraic triangulation $(\mathcal{D}, h)$ for S, with $\mathcal{D} = \{D_\alpha \mid \alpha \in A\}$ and $S = \cup_{\alpha\in B} h(D_\alpha)$. By definition, $\hat{\chi}(S) = \sum_{\alpha\in B}(-1)^{\dim(D_\alpha)}$.

Let $E = \cup_{\alpha\in B} D_\alpha$. Then $S = h(E)$. As S is compact, E is compact and thus closed, which implies that $\{D_\alpha \mid \alpha \in B\}$ must be an open simplicial decomposition of E. Hence $\chi(E) = \sum_{\alpha\in B}(-1)^{\dim(D_\alpha)}$. Since S is homeomorphic to E, this means $\chi(S) = \sum_{\alpha\in B}(-1)^{\dim(D_\alpha)}$. This proves $\hat{\chi}(S) = \chi(S)$. □

Theorem 4 Let $X \subseteq R^n$ be a semi-algebraic set, and $\psi : X \to R^s$ be a semi-algebraic map. Then $\hat{\chi}(X) = \hat{\chi}(S)$, where $S = \{(\tilde{x}, \psi(\tilde{x})) \mid \tilde{x} \in X\}$.

Proof Let $(\mathcal{D}, h)$ be a semi-algebraic triangulation for $\varphi_n(X)$, with $\mathcal{D} = \{D_\alpha \mid \alpha \in A\}$ and $\varphi_n(X) = \cup_{\alpha\in B} h(D_\alpha)$. Then

$$\hat{\chi}(X) = \sum_{\alpha\in B}(-1)^{\dim(D_\alpha)}. \tag{10}$$

Let $X_\alpha = (\varphi_n^{-1}\circ h)(D_\alpha)$. Then each X_α is a semi-algebraic set, and $\varphi_n^{-1}\circ h$ is a semi-algebraic homeomorphism between X_α and D_α. It is also clear that X is the disjoint union of X_α, $\alpha \in B$.

Let $S_\alpha = \{(\tilde{x}, \psi(\tilde{x})) \mid \tilde{x} \in X_\alpha\}$. Then each S_α is a semi-algebraic set, as S_α can be written as $S \cap \{(\tilde{x}, \tilde{y}) \mid \tilde{x} \in X_\alpha\}$. Also, S is the disjoint union of S_α, $\alpha \in B$, since X is the disjoint union of X_α, $\alpha \in B$. By Theorem 2, we have

$$\hat{\chi}(S) = \sum_{\alpha\in B}\hat{\chi}(S_\alpha).$$

However, each S_α is homeomorphic semi-algebraically to X_α and hence to D_α. Thus, the bounded semi-algebraic set $\varphi(S_\alpha)$ is homeomorphic semi-algebraically to D_α. By Lemma 1, $\hat{\chi}(\varphi(S_\alpha)) = (-1)^{\dim(D_\alpha)}$. It follows that $\hat{\chi}(S_\alpha) = (-1)^{\dim(D_\alpha)}$, and $\hat{\chi}(S) = \sum_{\alpha\in B}(-1)^{\dim(D_\alpha)}$. Comparing this equation with (10), we obtain $\hat{\chi}(X) = \hat{\chi}(S)$. □

For any set Y, let ν_Y be the *characteristic function* of Y, i.e., $\nu_Y(y) = 1$ if $y \in Y$ and 0 otherwise. We need the following lemma, which can be regarded as an extension of Theorem 2.

Lemma 2 Let $S, S_1, S_2, \cdots, S_m$ be semi-algebraic sets in R^n. If $\nu_S = \sum_{1\le i\le m} w_i\nu_{S_i}$, where w_i are real numbers, then $\hat{\chi}(S) = \sum_{1\le i\le m} w_i\hat{\chi}(S_i)$.

Proof First we prove the lemma when all S_i are bounded. By the Triangulation Theorem, there exists a semi-algebraic triangulation $(\mathcal{D}, h)$ for $S_1, S_2, \cdots, S_m$, with $\mathcal{D} = \{D_\alpha \mid \alpha \in A\}$. Let $S = \cup_{\alpha\in A} a_\alpha h(D_\alpha)$, and $S_i = \cup_{\alpha\in A} a_{i,\alpha} h(D_\alpha)$, $1 \le i \le m$, where $a_\alpha, a_{i,\alpha} \in \{0, 1\}$. Clearly, if $\tilde{x} \in h(D_\alpha)$, then $\nu_S(\tilde{x}) = a_\alpha$ and $\nu_{S_i}(\tilde{x}) = a_{i,\alpha}$. It follows from $\nu_S = \sum_{1\le i\le m} w_i\nu_{S_i}$ that $a_\alpha = \sum_{1\le i\le m} w_i a_{i,\alpha}$ for all $\alpha \in A$. This leads to

$$\begin{aligned}\hat{\chi}(S) &= \sum_{\alpha\in A} a_\alpha(-1)^{\dim(D_\alpha)} \\ &= \sum_{\alpha\in A}\sum_{1\le i\le m} w_i a_{i,\alpha}(-1)^{\dim(D_\alpha)}\end{aligned}$$

$$= \sum_{1\leq i\leq m} w_i\hat{\chi}(S_i).$$

This proves the lemma when all the $S's$ are bounded.

For the general case, one can apply the above conclusion to obtain $\hat{\chi}(\varphi(S)) = \sum_{1\leq i\leq m} w_i\hat{\chi}(\varphi(S_i))$. As $\hat{\chi}(S) = \hat{\chi}(\varphi(S))$ and $\hat{\chi}(S_i) = \hat{\chi}(\varphi(S_i))$, this implies immediately $\hat{\chi}(S) = \sum_{1\leq i\leq m} w_i\hat{\chi}(S_i)$.□

Theorem 5 Let $S = \{\tilde{x} \mid f_i(\tilde{x}) = 0, g_j(\tilde{x}) < 0, 1 \leq i \leq r, 1 \leq j \leq s\} \subseteq R^n$, where f_i, g_j are polynomials. Then $|\hat{\chi}(S)| \leq d(2d-1)^{n+s+2}$, where $d = \max_{i,j}\{\deg(f_i), \deg(g_j), 2\}$.

Proof Let $S' = \varphi(S) \subseteq R^{n+1}$. Then S' is bounded and semi-algebraic. Furthermore, $\hat{\chi}(S') = \hat{\chi}(S)$. To prove the theorem, it suffices to prove $|\hat{\chi}(S')| \leq d(2d-1)^{n+s+2}$.

We first write down the explicit constraints defining S'. For $1 \leq i \leq r$, let $F_i(\tilde{y}) = (1-y_{n+1})^d f_i(y_1/(1-y_{n+1}), y_2/(1-y_{n+1}), \cdots, y_n/(1-y_{n+1}))$, where $\tilde{y} = (y_1, y_2, \cdots, y_{n+1})$; for $1 \leq j \leq s$, let $G_j(\tilde{y}) = (1-y_{n+1})^d g_i(y_1/(1-y_{n+1}), y_2/(1-y_{n+1}), \cdots, y_n/(1-y_{n+1}))$. Let us further define $F_{r+1}(\tilde{y}) = \sum_{1\leq i\leq n} y_i^2 + (y_{n+1}-2/3)^2 - 1/9$, $G_{s+1}(\tilde{y}) = y_{n+1} - 1$, and $G_{s+2}(\tilde{y}) = -y_{n+1}$. Note that all F_i, G_j are polynomials of degrees no more than d.

From the definitions of S' and φ, it is easy to see that S' is the set of $\tilde{y} = (y_1, y_2, \cdots, y_{n+1}) \in R^{n+1}$ satisfying $F_i(\tilde{y}) = 0$, $1 \leq i \leq r+1$ and $G_j(\tilde{y}) < 0$, $1 \leq j \leq s+2$.

Let $W = \{(\tilde{y}, \tilde{u}) \mid F_i(\tilde{y}) = 0, 1 \leq i \leq r+1, G_j(\tilde{y}) + u_j^2 = 0, 1 \leq j \leq s+2\} \subseteq R^{n+s+3}$. Let $\mathcal{E} = \{1, -1\}^{s+2}$. For each $\tilde{\epsilon} = (\epsilon_1, \epsilon_2, \cdots, \epsilon_{s+2}) \in \mathcal{E}$, let $W_{\tilde{\epsilon}} = W \cap \{(\tilde{y}, \tilde{u}) \mid \forall j\, \epsilon_j u_j > 0\}$. Let $Q = W \cap \{(\tilde{y}, \tilde{u}) \mid \forall j\, u_j \neq 0\}$. Then Q is the disjoint union of all the $W_{\tilde{\epsilon}}$. Clearly, Q and $W_{\tilde{\epsilon}}$ are semi-algebraic sets. By Theorem 2, we have

$$\hat{\chi}(Q) = \sum_{\tilde{\epsilon}\in\mathcal{E}} \hat{\chi}(W_{\tilde{\epsilon}}). \tag{11}$$

We intend to utilize equation (11) to obtain the desired upper bound on $|\hat{\chi}(S')|$. The plan is to show $\hat{\chi}(S') = \hat{\chi}(W_{\tilde{\epsilon}})$ by using Theorem 4, to get an upper bound on $|\hat{\chi}(Q)|$ by using the Milnor-Thom Bound, and finally to substitute these relations into (11).

For each $\tilde{\epsilon} \in \mathcal{E}$, let $\psi_{\tilde{\epsilon}}(\tilde{x}) = (\epsilon_1(-G_1(\tilde{y}))^{1/2}, \epsilon_2(-G_2(\tilde{y}))^{1/2}, \cdots, \epsilon_{s+2}(-G_{s+2}(\tilde{y}))^{1/2})$. Clearly, $\psi_{\tilde{\epsilon}} : S' \to R^{s+2}$ is continuous over S'. Now note that $\{(\tilde{y}, \psi_{\tilde{\epsilon}}(\tilde{y})) \mid \tilde{y} \in S'\}$ is the same as $W_{\tilde{\epsilon}}$, which is by definition a semi-algebraic set. Thus $\psi_{\tilde{\epsilon}}$ is a semi-algebraic map, and we can apply Theorem 4 to obtain

$$\hat{\chi}(S') = \hat{\chi}(W_{\tilde{\epsilon}}). \tag{12}$$

We now estimate $|\hat{\chi}(Q)|$. For each subset $L \subseteq \{1, 2, \cdots, s+2\}$, let $Q_L = W \cap \{(\tilde{y}, \tilde{u}) \mid u_i = 0\ \forall i \in L\}$. In particular, $Q_\emptyset = W$. By inclusion-exclusion, we have for the characteristic funcions

$$\nu_Q = \sum_L (-1)^{|L|}\nu_{Q_L}.$$

By Lemma 2, this leads to

$$\hat{\chi}(Q) = \sum_L (-1)^{|L|}\hat{\chi}(Q_L).$$

Now as each Q_L is clearly a compact algebraic set, we have, by Theorem 3, $\hat{\chi}(Q_L) = \chi(Q_L)$. It follows that

$$\hat{\chi}(Q) = \sum_L (-1)^{|L|}\chi(Q_L). \tag{13}$$

For each L, we have from the Milnor-Thom Bound,

$$\begin{aligned} |\chi(Q_L)| &\leq \sum_{i\geq 0}\beta_i(Q_L) \\ &\leq d(2d-1)^{n+s+2}. \end{aligned} \tag{14}$$

From (13) and (14), we obtain

$$|\hat{\chi}(Q)| \leq 2^{s+2}d(2d-1)^{n+s+2}. \tag{15}$$

It follows from (11), (12) and (15) that

$$|\hat{\chi}(S')| \leq d(2d-1)^{n+s+2},$$

which completes the proof of Theorem 5.□

5 Algebraic Decision Trees

Let $S \subseteq R^n$. The *membership problem* for S is: given input $\tilde{x} = (x_1, x_2, \cdots, x_n)$, decide whether $\tilde{x} \in S$. We consider the complexity of membership problems in two familiar decision tree models (see e.g. [Be][SY]): the fixed-degree algebraic tree model and the algebraic computation tree model. In both models, an algorithm is a decision tree whose nodes perform certain algebraic tests, and each of whose leaves contains either a YES or NO answer to the membership question for the input.

In a *d-th degree algebraic tree*, $d \geq 1$, each internal node performs a test of the form $f(\tilde{x}) : 0$, where f is any polynomial of degree no more than d. In an *algebraic computation tree*, an internal node is either an *arithmetic node* or a *branching node*. Each arithmetic node v performs an arithmetic assignment $z \leftarrow z'$ op z'', where the variable z is a programming variable created at v, the operation op $\in \{+, -, *, /\}$, and z', z'' are either real constants, or the input variables x_i, or programming variables created at other arithmetic nodes along the path from the root to v. Furthermore, if the assignment operation "op" is division "/", then z'' must not take on 0 value for any input leading to v. Each branching node v performs a branching test $z' : 0$, where z' is either an input variable x_i or a programming variable created at an arithmetic node along the path from the root to v. Let $C_d(S)$, $C(S)$ be the minimum height of any d-th degree algebraic tree and that of any algebraic computation tree for solving the membership problem for S. Note that $C_d(S)$ may be infinite even for semi-algebraic S.

Let $\lambda_{1,d} = 1/(\log_2 3 + \log_2(2d-1))$, $\lambda_{2,d} = (\log_2(2d-1))/(\log_2 3 + \log_2(2d-1))$, and $\lambda_{3,d} = (\log_2 d + 2\log_2(2d-1))/(\log_2 3 + \log_2(2d-1))$.

Theorem 6 Let $S \subseteq R^n$ be a semi-algebraic set and $d \geq 1$. Then $C_d(S) \geq \lambda_{1,d} \log_2 |\hat{\chi}(S)| - \lambda_{2,d} n - \lambda_{3,d}$.

Corollary For any semi-algebraic $S, S' \subseteq R^n$, $C_d(S) \geq \lambda_{1,d} \log_2 |\hat{\chi}(S \cap S')| - \lambda_{2,d} n - \lambda_{3,d} - C_d(S')$.

Proof If S is either R^n or the empty set, the theorem is clearly true, since $\hat{\chi}(R^n) = (-1)^n$ and $\hat{\chi}(\emptyset) = 0$. We can thus assume that $S \neq R^n, \emptyset$, which implies $C_d(S) > 0$.

Let T be any d-th degree algebraic tree which solves the membership problem for S. Let m denote the height of T. We will show $m \geq \lambda_{1,d} \log_2 |\hat{\chi}(S)| - \lambda_{2,d} n - \lambda_{3,d}$.

Let $\mathcal{L}$ be the set of all YES leaves of T. Clearly, $\mathcal{L}$ is not empty. For each $\ell \in \mathcal{L}$, let V_ℓ be the set of all inputs $\tilde{x} \in R^n$ reaching ℓ. Clearly, V_ℓ are semi-algebraic sets, and S is the disjoint union of V_ℓ, $\ell \in \mathcal{L}$. By Theorem 2,

$$\hat{\chi}(S) = \sum_{\ell \in \mathcal{L}} \hat{\chi}(V_\ell). \tag{16}$$

Let $\ell \in \mathcal{L}$. Then V_ℓ can be written in the form $\{\tilde{x} \mid f_1(\tilde{x}) = 0, \cdots, f_r(\tilde{x}) = 0, g_1(\tilde{x}) < 0, \cdots, g_s(\tilde{x}) < 0\}$, where $r + s \leq m$, and f_i, g_j are polynomials of degree at most d. By Theorem 5,

$$\begin{aligned} |\hat{\chi}(V_\ell)| &\leq d(2d-1)^{n+s+2} \\ &\leq d(2d-1)^{n+m+2}. \end{aligned} \tag{17}$$

From (16) and (17), we obtain

$$d(2d-1)^{n+m+2}|\mathcal{L}| \geq |\hat{\chi}(S)|.$$

Using the fact $3^m \geq |\mathcal{L}|$, we obtain $m \geq \lambda_{1,d} \log_2 |\hat{\chi}(S)| - \lambda_{2,d} n - \lambda_{3,d}$. This proves Theorem 6. We obtain the Corollary immediately by applying the theorem to $S \cap S'$. □

Remark This generalizes Theorem 3.1 in [BLY] for linear decision trees (the case $d = 1$).

Let $c_1 = 1/(2\log_2 3)$, $c_2 = 1/2$, and $c_3 = (1 + 2\log_2 3)/(2\log_2 3)$.

Theorem 7 Let $S \subseteq R^n$ be a semi-algebraic set. Then $C(S) \geq c_1 \log_2 |\hat{\chi}(S)| - c_2 n - c_3$.

Corollary For any semi-algebraic $S, S' \subseteq R^n$, $C(S) \geq c_1 \log_2 |\hat{\chi}(S \cap S')| - c_2 n - c_3 - C(S')$.

Proof As argued in the proof of the preceding theorem, we can assume without loss of generality that $S \neq R^n, \emptyset$. Let T be any algebraic computation tree which solves the membership problem for S. Let m denote the height of T. We will show $m \geq c_1 \log_2 |\hat{\chi}(S)| - c_2 n - c_3$.

Let $\mathcal{L}$ be the set of all YES leaves of T. Clearly, $\mathcal{L}$ is not empty. For each $\ell \in \mathcal{L}$, let V_ℓ be the set of all inputs $\tilde{x} \in R^n$ reaching ℓ. As shown in [Be], V_ℓ can be expressed as the projections of algebraic sets and thus are semi-algebraic sets. Since S is the disjoint union of all V_ℓ, $\ell \in \mathcal{L}$, we have by Theorem 2,

$$\hat{\chi}(S) = \sum_{\ell \in \mathcal{L}} \hat{\chi}(V_\ell). \tag{18}$$

Let $\ell \in \mathcal{L}$. We will prove that

$$|\hat{\chi}(V_\ell)| \quad \leq \quad 2 \cdot 3^{n+m+2}. \tag{19}$$

Let $v_0 = \text{root}, , v_1, \cdots, v_s = \ell$ be the sequence of nodes along the path ξ from the root to ℓ. Clearly, $s \leq m$. Let v_i, $i \in I$, be the set of arithmetic nodes along ξ, and $I' = \{0, 1, \cdots, s-1\} - I$. Let z_i, $i \in I$, be the programming variables created at nodes v_i. For the rest of this section, we use the notation $\tilde{z}$ to denote the $|I|$-component vector $(z_i \,|\, i \in I)$.

We associate with each v_i, $0 \leq i \leq s-1$, a polynomial constraint in variables $x_1, x_2, \cdots, x_n, z_j, j \in I$. To simplify notations, let us agree that, for $j \in \{1, \cdots, n\}$, the symbol z_{-j} stands for x_j.

CASE (A): $i \in I'$. If the branch taken from v_i to v_{i+1} is labeled by z_j rel$_i$ 0, where rel$_i \in \{<, =, >\}$, then we associate with v_i the inequality $f_i(\tilde{x}, \tilde{z})$ rel$_i$ 0, where f_i is the linear polynomial z_j.

CASE (B): $i \in I$. Suppose that the arithmetic assignment performed at v_i is $z_i \leftarrow I_i$. Then I_i is one of the following: $z_j + z_k, z_j - z_k, z_j * z_k, z_j/z_k, t_i + z_k, t_i - z_k, t_i * z_k, t_i/z_k$, where $-n \leq j, k < i$ and t_i is some non-zero real constant. It is also required that, if I_i is either z_j/z_k or c_i/z_k, then z_k cannot be evaluated to 0 for any input reaching v_i. We associate with v_i the polynomial constraint $f_i(\tilde{x}, \tilde{z}) = 0$, where f_i is defined as follows:

(a) if I_i is z_j op z_k with op $\in \{+, -, *\}$, then f_i is $z_i - (z_j \text{ op } z_k)$;

(b) if I_i is z_j/z_k, then f_i is $z_i z_k - z_j$;

(c) if I_i is t_i op z_k with op $\in \{+, -, *\}$, then f_i is $z_i - (t_i \text{ op } z_k)$;

(d) if I_i is t_i/z_k, then f_i is $z_i z_k - t_i$.

Note that in all cases the degrees of f_i are at most 2.

For $i \in I$, let $a_i(\tilde{x})$ be the value assigned to z_i when the input is $\tilde{x} \in V_\ell$. Let $M \subseteq R^{n+|I|}$ be the set of all $(\tilde{x}, a_i(\tilde{x}) | i \in I)$ with $\tilde{x} \in V_\ell$.

Fact 1 M can be described as the set of all $(\tilde{x}, \tilde{z}) \in R^{n+|I|}$ satisfying $f_i(\tilde{x}, \tilde{z}) = 0$ and $f_j(\tilde{x}, \tilde{z})$ rel$_j$ 0 for $i \in I$, $j \in I'$.

Fact 2 For each $i \in I$, a_i is continous over V_ℓ.

Fact 1 is obvious from the definitions. Fact 2 can be obtained by a straightforward induction on i. (Actually, a_i are rational functions, although we do not need this fact.)

By Fact 1, M is defined by linear and quadratic constraints in $R^{n+|I|}$, with no more than $|I|'$ strict inequalities. We have from Theorem 5

$$\begin{aligned} |\hat{\chi}(M)| &\leq 2 \cdot 3^{n+|I|+|I|'+2} \\ &\leq 2 \cdot 3^{n+m+2}. \end{aligned} \tag{20}$$

Let $\psi : R^n \rightarrow R^{|I|}$ be the mapping $\psi(\tilde{x}) = (a_i(\tilde{x}) \,|\, i \in I)$. Clearly, $M = \{(\tilde{x}, \psi(\tilde{x})) \,|\, \tilde{x} \in V_\ell\}$. Now, M is semi-algebraic by Fact 1, and ψ is continuous on V_ℓ by Fact 2. Thus ψ is a semi-algebraic map, and by Theorem 4, we have

$$\hat{\chi}(V_\ell) = \hat{\chi}(M). \tag{21}$$

From (20) and (21), we obtain (19).

From (18) and (19), we obtain

$$|\hat{\chi}(S)| \leq 2 \cdot 3^{n+2m+2},$$

from which we obtain immediately $m \geq c_1 \log_2 |\hat{\chi}(S)| - c_2 n - c_3$. This proves Theorem 7. The Corollary follows immediately. □

6 Extensions and Open Problems

One can augment the algebraic computation tree model, by allowing assignments of the form $z \leftarrow z'^{1/b}$ for positive integers $b \leq \gamma$, where $\gamma > 0$ is some fixed integer, and z' are either input variables x_j or previously computed programming variables. (This augmented model was employed in [Be] as the algebraic computation tree model.) Theorem 7 remains true with constants c_i now dependent also on the value γ. The proof is an extension of the proof of Theorem 7, using $z^b - z' = 0$ as the polynomial constraints for nodes with assignments $z \leftarrow z'^{1/b}$.

One can further strengthen the above model by counting only *non-linear* operations ([St][Be][Hir]). That is, the cost of an augmented algebraic computation tree is the maximum number of nodes, counting only nodes performing branching operations, and assignments of the form $z_i \leftarrow z_j * z_k$, $z_i \leftarrow z_j/z_k$,

$z_i \leftarrow t_i/z_k$, or $z \leftarrow z'^{1/b}$ along any path from the root to a leaf in the tree. The result described in the previous paragraph remains valid. One first eliminates those nodes performing "+," "−," and constant multiplication operations by substituting appropriate linear forms for variables at other nodes of the tree, and then follows basically the same proof as before. The method of elimination and substitution is essentially the same as the one used in Ben-Or [Be] and Hirsch [Hir].

In [BLY], it was shown that the "k-equal problem" has complexity $\theta(n\log(2n/k))$ in the linear decision tree model. The theorems derived here lead immediately to a $\theta(n\log(2n/k))$ complexity in the algebraic computation tree model, and an $\Omega(n\log(n/k))$ lower bound for the fixed degree-d algebraic tree model. The determination of the exact asymptotic complexity in the fixed degree-d algebraic tree model involves additional arguments. We will discuss it in the complete paper.

Many interesting questions remain to be answered. What can be said when the inputs are restricted to be integers? (Some restrictions on S have to be added in this case.) Can one obtain nontrivial lower bounds for problems other than the "k-equal problem" by estimating the Euler characteristics? (For example, consider the following decision problem: given $n(n-1)/2$ real numbers $x_{i,j}$ where $1 \leq i < j \leq n$, decide whether there exist a size-k $V \subseteq \{1, 2, \cdots, n\}$ such that $x_{i,j}$ are identical for all $i, j \in V$.)

Acknowledgments The author wishes to thank Mike Hirsch for helpful discussions on Euler characteristics and spherical complexes.

References

[Be] M. Ben-Or, "Lower bounds for algebraic computation trees," *Proceedings of 15th Annual ACM Symposium on Theory of Computing*, May 1983, 80-86.

[Bj] A. Björner, "Topological methods," in *Handbook of Combinatorics*, edited by R. Graham, M. Grötschel, and L. Lovász, North-Holland, to appear.

[BLY] A. Björner, L. Lovász, and A. Yao, "Linear decision trees: volume estimates and topological bounds," *Proceedings of 24th Annual ACM Symposium on Theory of Computing*, May 1992, 170-177.

[Br] G. Brumfiel, *Partially Ordered Rings and Semi-Algebraic Geometry*, Lecture Note Series of the London Math. Soc., Cambridge Univ. Press, Cambridge, 1979.

[DL] D. Dobkin and R.J. Lipton, "On the complexity of computations under varying sets of primitives," in *Automata Theory and Formal Languages* (edited by H. Bradhage), Lecture Notes in Computer Science, Volume 33, Springer-Verlag (1975), 110-117.

[GH] M.J. Greenberg and J. Harper, *Algebraic Topology: A First Course*, Addison-Wesley, 1981.

[H] H. Hironaka, "Triangulation of algebraic sets," in *Proceedings of Symposia in Pure Mathematics*, Volume 29 (1975), American Mathematical Society, 165-185.

[Hir] M. Hirsch, "Lower bounds for the nonlinear complexity of algebraic computation trees with integer inputs," preprint, May 1991.

[Ka] E. Kalinová, *The localization problem in geometry and Rabin-Spira linear proofs* (Czech), M. Sci. thesis, Universitas Carolina, Prague, 1978.

[LW] S. Lefschetz and J.H.C. Whitehead, "On analytical complexes," *Trans. Amer. Math. Soc.* **35** (1933), 510-517.

[Lo] S. Lojasiewicz, "Triangulations of semianalytic sets," *Ann. Scu. Norm. di Pisa*, **18** (1964), 449-474.

[MST] Y. Mansour, B. Schieber, and P. Tiwari, "Lower bounds for integer greatest common divisor computations," *Proceedings of 29th IEEE Symposium on Foundations of Computer Science*, 1988, 54-63.

[Mi] J. Milnor, "On the Betti numbers of real varieties," *Proc. Amer. Math. Soc.* **15** (1964), 275-280.

[Mo] J. Morávek, "A localization problem in geometry and complexity of discrete programming," *Kybernetika* (Prague) **8** (1972), 498-516.

[MP] J. Morávek and P. Pudlák, "New lower bound for polyhedral membership problem with an application to linear programming," in *Mathematical Foundations of Computer Science* (edited by M.P. Chytil and V. Koubek), Lecture Notes in Computer Science, Volume 176, Springer-Verlag (1984), 416-424.

[Mu] J. Munkres, *Elements of Algebraic Topology*, Addison-Wesley, 1984.

[Sm] S. Smale, "On the topology of algorithms," Preprint, University of California, Berkeley, 1987.

[SY] M. Steele and A. Yao, "Lower bounds for algebraic decision trees," *J. Algorithms* **3** (1982), 1-8.

[St] V. Strassen, "The computational complexity of continued fractions," *SIAM J. on Computing* **12** (1983), 1-27.

[T] R. Thom, "Sur l'homologie des variétés algébriques réelles," in *Differential and Algebraic Topology*, edited by S. S. Cairns, Princeton University Press, Princeton, 1965.

[V] J.W. Vick, *Homology Theory*, Academic Press, New York, 1973.

[YR] A. Yao and R. Rivest, "On the polyhedral decision problem," *SIAM J. on Computing* **9** (1980), 343-347.

Separating the Communication Complexities of MOD m and MOD p Circuits

Vince Grolmusz

Max Planck Institute and Eötvös University

ABSTRACT:

We prove in this paper that it is much harder to evaluate depth–2, size–N circuits with MOD m gates than with MOD p gates by k–party communication protocols: we show a k–party protocol which communicates $O(1)$ bits to evaluate circuits with MOD p gates, while evaluating circuits with MOD m gates needs $\Omega(N)$ bits, where p denotes a prime, and m a composite, non-prime power number. As a corollary, for all m, we show a function, computable with a depth–2 circuit with MOD m gates, but not with any depth–2 circuit with MOD p gates.

We prove in the second part that the GIP function of [BNS] needs exponential size in n when it is computed by some depth–3 circuits, with threshold, symmetric, and MOD m gates.

1. INTRODUCTION

The connection between the circuit complexity and the communication complexity plays an important role in the recent literature of the circuit lower bound theory.

The notion of the (2–party) communication complexity was introduced by *Yao* [Y1]. Due to the algebraic characterization of the communication complexity, several strong lower bounds were proved for this model (see [L] for a survey). Many nice results appeared in the literature concerning the connection of the (2–party) communication complexity and the circuit complexity: [KW], [RW1], [RW2], [S], [Y2].

The *multi–party communication game*, defined by *Chandra, Furst* and *Lipton* [CFL], is an interesting generalization of the 2–party communication game. In this game, k players: $P_1, P_2 ..., P_k$ intend to compute the value of $g(A_1, A_2, ..., A_k)$, where $g : \{0, 1, 2, ..., m-1\}^{kn} \rightarrow \mathbf{N}$, $\mathbf{N}$ denotes the set of natural numbers, $m \in \mathbf{N}$ and $A_i \in \{0, 1, 2, ..., m-1\}^n$, for $i = 1, 2, ..., k$. Player P_i knows every variable, *except* A_i, for $i = 1, 2, ..., k$. The players have unlimited computational power, and they communicate with the help of a blackboard, viewed by all players. Only one player may write on the blackboard at a time. The goal is to compute $g(A_1, A_2, ..., A_k)$, such that at the end of the computation, every player knows this value. The cost of the computation is the number of bits written on the blackboard for the given $A = (A_1, A_2, ..., A_k)$. The cost of a multi–party protocol is the maximum number of bits communicated for any A from $\{0, 1, 2, ..., m-1\}^{nk}$. The k-party communication complexity, $C^{(k)}(g)$, of a function g, is the minimum of costs of those k-party protocols which compute g.

The theory of the 2–party communication games is well developed [L], but much less is known about the multi–party communication complexity of functions. As a general upper bound, P_1 can compute any function of A with n bits of communication: P_2 writes down the n bits of A_1 on the blackboard, P_1 reads it, and computes the value $g(A)$ at no cost. The additional cost of diffusing the result $g(A)$ to other players is the binary length of $g(A)$.

An important progress was made by *Babai, Nisan* and *Szegedy*, [BNS], proving an $\Omega(\frac{n}{4^k})$ lower bound for the k–party communication complexity of the GIP function. *Goldmann* and *Håstad* [GH] found a surprising application of the BNS–lower bound to circuit–complexity.

In this paper we use multi–party techniques to characterize some hard–to–handle circuit classes.

Smolensky [Sm] showed an exponential lower bound for the sizes of circuits with MOD p, AND and OR gates, using algebraic methods in finite fields. Deriving superpolynomial lower bounds for *non–uniform* circuits with MOD m gates remained unsuccessful, despite the widespread opinion that the powers of MOD m gates and MOD p gates do not differ considerably, where (and throughout this paper) m is a non-prime power composite number and p is a prime. Recently, for *uniform* circuits with MOD m, AND

Address: Max Planck Institute for Computer Science, Im Stadtwald, W–6600 Saarbrücken, GERMANY; email: grolmusz@mpi-sb.mpg.de

0-8186-2900-2/92 $3.00 © 1992 IEEE

and OR gates, *Allender* and *Gore* [AG] showed a subexponential lower bound for the permanent function.

On the other hand, *Kahn* and *Meshulam* [KM] showed that OR_n can be computed by a depth–2 circuit with MOD (2p) gates, while it can not be computed by any constant-depth circuits with MOD p gates.

We show a large gap between multi–party complexities of evaluating circuits with MOD p and MOD m gates, where a MOD r gate outputs 1 iff the sum of its input bits is divisible by r.

Definition 1. *Let C be a circuit, and let $k \geq 2$ be an integer. Let X denote the set of the input–variables of C, i.e. $X = \{x_1, x_2, ..., x_\ell\}$. We say that circuit C is k-evaluated with b bits of communication, if for all partitions of X into k classes $X_1, X_2, ...X_k$, there exists a k–party protocol with players $P_1, P_2, ..., P_k$, such that all the players know circuit C and partition $X_1, X_2, ...X_k$, and player P_i knows the values of all the variables, except those in X_i, for $i = 1, 2, ..., k$; and the k–party protocol computes the output of the circuit, communicating at most b bits.*

Heuristically, we can consider a circuit to be "hard" if it needs a large number of communicated bits for evaluation, otherwise it can be said "easy". The statement of the main lemma of [BNS] (whose generalization is our Lemma 12.), implies that the circuit, with a PARITY gate at the top and fan–in k AND gates at level one is hard for k–party protocols. The lower bound of [GH] uses the fact that any circuit, with a SYMMETRIC gate at the top, and arbitrary gates of fan–in at most $k-1$ at level 1 are easy for k–party protocols.

Szegedy has considered the (2–party) communication complexity of evaluating Boolean functions in [S], using the 2–party version of Definition 1. He proved that circuits with gates of bounded symmetric communication–complexity, can be simulated by circuits with MOD m, AND and OR gates of similar depth and size.

Obviously, if m and p are constants, then there is no difference between the evaluations of one MOD m or one MOD p gate. However, we shall show here, that if we consider two layers of MOD p gates versus two layers of MOD m gates, the difference is dramatic (Theorem 2 *vs.* Theorem 5), and the k–party technique becomes very important (Theorem 2 *vs.* Theorem 3).

Theorem 2. *Let p be a prime, $k \geq p$ an integer, and let C be a circuit of depth 2 and size N with a MOD p^ℓ gate on the top, for $2 \leq \ell \leq p^{\lfloor k/p \rfloor}$ and $N-1$ MOD p gates on level 1. Then C is k–evaluated with $O(k\ell)$ bits of communication.*

Note. *When p and k are constants, then the circuit is k–evaluated by a constant number of communicated bits.*

Theorem 3. *Let $q > k$, and $N \in \mathbf{N}$. Then there exists a depth–2, size–N circuit with MOD q gates, which needs $\Omega(\frac{N}{4^k})$ bits of communication, if evaluated by any k–party protocol.*

Let us note that the k–party protocols separate the powers of the circuits with MOD p gates and with MOD q gates, where $q > k \geq p$.

The next is an immediate corollary of Theorem 2:

Corollary 4. *Let $k \geq 2$, integer, and let f be a function, and suppose that the k–party communication complexity of f is non–constant. Then f cannot be computed by a depth–2 circuit of MOD p gates, for $p \leq k$.* ∎

Theorem 5. *Let m be a positive integer with at least two different prime divisors, p_1 and p_2, and let N and k be positive integers. Then there exists an explicitly constructible depth–2, size–N circuit C with MOD m gates on the first and on the second level, such that the k-evaluation of C needs $\Omega(\frac{N}{c_m^k})$ bits of communication, where constant $c_m > 0$ depends only on m.*

Obviously, the k–party communication complexity of the function, computed by C, is $\Omega(\frac{N}{c_m^k})$, so, by Corollary 4, for any $p \leq k$, this function cannot be computed by any depth–2 circuits with MOD p gates. For any m and p, choosing a $k \geq p$, this result separates the powers of depth–2 circuits with MOD m and with MOD p gates.

It is easy to see that the k'–party protocols are not weaker than the k–party protocols, for $k' > k$. Theorem 2, and, on the other hand, Theorem 3 directly imply the following hierarchy–theorem:

Theorem 6. *Let $k < k'$ two positive integers, and suppose that there is a prime p between k and k': $k < p \leq k'$. Then for all $N \in \mathbf{N}$, there exists a function of kN variable which can be computed by a k'–party protocol with a constant number of communicated bits, while any k–party protocol needs $\Omega(N)$ bits of communication to compute the function.* ∎

In the second part of this paper, using similar techniques, we investigate the circuit-complexity of the *Generalized Inner Product* (GIP) function of *Babai, Nisan* and *Szegedy* [BNS].

Given a 0–1 matrix A with n rows and k columns, then $GIP(A)$ is defined to be the number of the all–one rows of A, modulo 2.

Goldmann and Håstad [GH] - building on the results of [BNS] - gave an exponential lower bound in n for the sizes of those depth-3 threshold circuits, which compute $GIP(A)$ and have fan-in at most $k-1$ on the lowest level. The strategy of their proof is the following: it is assumed that the circuit of a given type and size M computes GIP(A). Then they show a k-party protocol, where all the players know the circuit, and which computes the output of the circuit (i.e. GIP(A)), with communicating about $O(\log M)$ bits. From Theorem 2 of [BNS], or from our Lemma 12, $O(\log M) \geq n/4^k$, which yields an exponential lower bound to M. The same proof applies to depth-3 circuits with a threshold gate at the top, arbitrary SYMMETRIC gates on the next and arbitrary gates of fan-in at most $k-1$ on the lowest level.

For the significance of this result it is worth mentioning, that no superpolynomial lower bound is known for the sizes of the depth-3 threshold circuits (without fan-in constraint), which compute a function in **NP**.

However, the $k-1$ bound on the fan-in on the lowest level is essential in the proof in [GH], with k players this facilitates the $O(\log M)$-communication protocol.

Allowing fan-in k, a very simple depth-2 circuit with $n+1$ gates computes GIP(A): the PARITY of n AND gates of fan-in k, where the k inputs of the AND gates are connected to the k variables of the corresponding rows of matrix A. Since PARITY is a SYMMETRIC gate, the result of [GH] shows that no polynomial-size circuit of one PARITY and AND gates of fan-in at most $k-1$ can compute - or even approximate - GIP(A). So the fan-in bound on the lowest level is a very sensitive parameter.

We prove an exponential lower bound for the sizes of those members of circuit-classes C', which compute $GIP(A)$, where:

- C' consists of depth-3 circuits, with a threshold-gate at the top, arbitrary symmetric gates at the next, and MOD m_i gates of fan-in k at the lowest level, where $k \equiv m_i \pmod{2m_i}$, and m_i's are odd (prime or composite) numbers.

We show, that the members of C'' cannot even compute GIP(A), where
- C'' consists of depth-3 circuits, with a threshold gate at the top, MOD p gates on the next and EXACT$_\ell$ gates of fan-in $k = p^\alpha$ on the lowest level, where $1 \leq \ell \leq k-1$.

The inputs, the entries of A with their negations, are on the bottom, in the circuits of both classes.

Our proof is based on the fact that the circuits of size M in class C' can be k-evaluated by communicating only $O(k \log M)$ bits, while circuits of size M in class C'' can be k-evaluated by communicating only a constant number of bits.

It is surprising in the proof that players can count those rows of a matrix $B \in \{0,1\}^{n\times k}$ whose sum is divisible by m, communicating only $O(k \log n)$ bits, while counting the rows with sum congruent to 1 (mod m) needs $\Omega(n/4^k)$ bits of communication (with an odd m and $k \equiv m \pmod{2m}$). Because of this phenomenon, the $k \equiv m_i \pmod{2m_i}$ assumption is important in our theorem. It is also interesting, that $\Omega(n/4^k)$ communication is needed to count the rows of B with sum in any congruence class modulo an *even* m.

2. SEPARATING CIRCUIT-CLASSES

Proof of Theorem 2. By Definition 1, we must show a k-party protocol for any k-partition $\{X_1, X_2, ..., X_k\}$ of set X which evaluates $\mathcal{C}$ with $O(k\ell)$ bits of communication. Let the partition $\{X_1, X_2, ..., X_k\}$ be fixed.

The players first compose a matrix $B \in \{0,1,2,...,p-1\}^{(N-1)\times k}$, then play a k-party protocol, using data only from this matrix. Let B_i denote column i, B^j row j of B, and B_i^j the entry in the intersection of B_i and B^j. Let $G_1, G_2, ..., G_{N-1}$ denote the MOD p gates on level 1 of $\mathcal{C}$. Gate G_j will be corresponded to row B^j as follows:

B_i^j is the sum, modulo p, of the values of those inputs of G_j which are in class X_i. The value of x_ℓ (or $\bar{x}_\ell$) should be added with multiplier c_ℓ if G_j is connected to x_ℓ (or to $\bar{x}_\ell$) with c_ℓ wires.

Let us observe that players can compose matrix B without any communication, and P_j knows every column of B, except B^j, $j = 1, 2, ..., k$.
It is easy to see that circuit $\mathcal{C}$ outputs 1 if and only if the number of those rows of B, whose sums are divisible by p, is 0 mod $p^{\lfloor k/p \rfloor}$.

Lemma 7. *Let $B \in \{0,1,2,...,p-1\}^{n\times k}$, where p is a prime and $k \geq p$ an integer. Then there exists an explicitly constructible protocol, which computes the number, modulo p^ℓ, of those rows of B, whose sums are divisible by p. Moreover, this protocol uses $O(k\ell)$ bits of communication for $1 \leq \ell \leq p^{\lfloor k/p \rfloor}$.*

Proof. Protocol "**MOD m**" will satisfy the requirements, with $m = p$:
The strategy of the players in protocol **MOD m** is the following: Player P_i ($1 \leq i \leq k$) assumes that column i of B, B_i is the all-1 vector. P_1 - using his

assumption – communicates the number of rows in each congruency– classes mod$m$:

$$\alpha = (\alpha_0, \alpha_1, ..., \alpha_{m-1}),$$

where α_i denotes the number of those rows, whose sums are believed to be $i \bmod m$. Next P_2 corrects P_1 in case of those rows which begin with 0 or 2, or 3, or ..., $m-1$, instead of the assumed 1: P_2 communicates the corrections, to be added to vector α. P_2 computes this correction, assuming that he knows the entire input. Then P_3 corrects P_1 and P_2, in case of those rows, which begins with two non–ones, and so on, until P_k comes. Then P_k corrects $P_1, P_2, ..., P_{k-1}$ in case of those rows which begins with $k-1$ non–ones. The protocol makes errors only in the case of those rows, for which *neither of the assumptions* were satisfied: the rows without 1's. Every other row will be counted correctly: since at least one player's assumption was right, he saw the row correctly, and counted it to the proper congruency–class, corrected the errors of the players with lower indices. Player P_i will not count those rows, which contain a 1 in a position lower than i.

Example. Let $m = p = 3, k = 3$, and consider row 022.
P_1 assumes this row to be 122, so he counts this row to vector α as $(0,0,1)$.
P_2 assumes this row to be 012, so he counts it as $(1,0,0)$, and P_2 assumes that P_1 saw the row to be 112, and because of this, P_1 communicated $(0,1,0)$ for this row, which should be corrected by P_2, subtracting it. In total, P_2 adds $(1,-1,0)$ to the α of P_1.
P_3 assumes the row to be 021, he adds $(1,0,0)$, and he corrects first P_1, next P_2. P_3 assumes that P_1 saw the row to be 121, and corrects him adding $(0,-1,0)$ to α. P_3 assumes that P_2 saw the row to be 011, and corrects him by adding $(0,0,-1)$. However, P_3 assumes that P_2 erroneously corrected P_1, P_3 thinks that P_2 thinks that P_1 saw the row to be 111, so P_2 is thought to correct P_1 adding $(-1,0,0)$, so P_3 corrects P_2 by adding $(1,0,0)$. So P_3 adds in total $(2,-1,-1)$. The sum of the corrections here is $(3,-2,0)$ instead of the correct value $(0,1,0)$.

Let us observe that $(3,-2,0) \equiv (0,1,0) \pmod 3$, i.e. the value computed is correct if seen modulo 3. The following lemma gives a formula for the number, computed by our protocol for rows without entry "1". We shall see that the error is 0 $(\bmod\ p^{\lfloor k/p \rfloor})$.

Notation 8. *Let* $\mathbf{N}$ *denote the set of natural numbers. We denote the elements of vector space* $\mathbf{N}^m$ *by small–case greek letters, and we index their coordinates from* 0 *through* $m-1$. *Let* $S^{n\times k}$ *denote the set of all* $n \times k$ *matrices with entries from set* S. *Let* $B \in \{0,1,...,m-1\}^{n\times k}$. *Let*

$$\delta^{(m)}(B) = (\delta_0, \delta_1, ..., \delta_{m-1})$$

denote a vector where δ_i *is the number of those rows of* B, *which are congruent to* $i \pmod m$. *Let* $v \in \{0,1,...,m-1\}^k$, *then* $CT(v,B)$ *denotes the number of those rows of* B, *which are equal to* v. *Let* $\mathbf{0} = (0,0,...,0) \in \{0,1,...,m-1\}^k$.

Lemma 9. *Protocol* **MOD m** *computes the number*

$$\delta^{(m)}(B) - \sum_{v\in\{0,2,3,...,m-1\}^k} CT(v,B)w_v,$$

where $w_v \in \mathbf{N}^m$, *and when* v *contains* d_2 2 *coordinates,* d_3 *3's, ...,* d_{m-1} $m-1$*'s, and* d_0 *0's, then*

$$w_v = \nu\Pi^{d(v)}(I - \Pi^{m-1})^{d_2}(I-\Pi^{m-2})^{d_3}...(I-\Pi)^{d_0},$$

where $\nu = (1,0,0,...,0) \in \mathbf{N}^m$, $d(v) = 2d_2 + 3d_3 + ... + (m-1)d_{m-1}$, *and* Π *is the* $m \times m$ *cyclic right–shift permutation matrix:*

$$\Pi = \begin{pmatrix} 0 & 1 & 0 & \dots & 0 & 0 \\ 0 & 0 & 1 & \dots & 0 & 0 \\ \vdots & \vdots & \vdots & \ddots & \vdots & \vdots \\ 0 & 0 & 0 & \dots & 1 & 0 \\ 0 & 0 & 0 & \dots & 0 & 1 \\ 1 & 0 & 0 & \dots & 0 & 0 \end{pmatrix}$$

Let us note that a row vector multiplied by Π is the vector with coordinates shifted with one position to right. Similarly, if a row-vector is multiplied by Π^{-1} the result is the vector, with coordinates shifted with one position to left.

Before proving Lemma 9, let us see how it implies Lemma 7. Let $m = p$. Since matrix Π commutes with its own powers, one can write w_v into the form:

$$w_v = \nu\Pi^{d(v)}(I-\Pi)^k P(\Pi),$$

where $P(\Pi)$ is a polynomial of matrix Π, since $k = d_2 + d_3 + ... + d_{m-1} + d_0$, and one can write $(I - \Pi^s) = (I-\Pi)Q(\Pi)$, where Q is also a polynomial.

By the binomial theorem:

$$(I-\Pi)^p = \binom{p}{0}I - \binom{p}{1}\Pi + ... + (-1)^p\binom{p}{p}\Pi^p \equiv$$

$$\equiv I + (-1)^p\Pi^p \equiv I + (-1)^pI \equiv 0 \pmod p,$$

so

$$((I-\Pi)^p)^{\lfloor \frac{k}{p} \rfloor} \equiv 0 \pmod{p^{\lfloor \frac{k}{p} \rfloor}}, \text{ and}$$

$$(I - \Pi)^k \equiv 0 \pmod{p^{\lfloor \frac{k}{p} \rfloor}}.$$

Hence

$$w_v \equiv 0 \pmod{p^{\lfloor \frac{k}{p} \rfloor}},$$

for all $v \in \{0, 2, 3, ..., p-1\}^k$. This means that protocol **MOD p** computes $\delta^{(m)}(B) \bmod p^{\lfloor \frac{k}{p} \rfloor}$.

However, the players are enough to communicate their α vectors only mod p^ℓ. Hence each player communicates p numbers of size $O(\ell \log p)$, and protocol **MOD p** uses $O(k\ell p \log p) = O(k\ell)$ bits of communication, which is constant if k is constant.

Proof of Lemma 9. First we prove

Sublemma 10. *The vector, computed by protocol* **MOD m** *for a row* $v \in \{0, 2, 3, ..., p-1\}^k$ *is the same for any permutation of the coordinates of* v.

Proof. It is enough to prove that our protocol computes the same vector for

$$v = (v_1, v_2, ..., v_i, v_{i+1}, ..., v_k)$$

and

$$v' = (v_1, v_2, ..., v_{i+1}, v_i, ..., v_k).$$

Obviously, P_s communicates the same vector for v and v' if $s \neq i$ or $s \neq i+1$. P_i assumes v to be v_{P_i} and v' to be v'_{P_i}:

$$v_{P_i} = (v_1, v_2, ..., 1, v_{i+1}, ..., v_k)$$

$$v'_{P_i} = (v_1, v_2, ..., 1, v_i, ..., v_k),$$

while P_{i+1} assumes v to be $v_{P_{i+1}}$ and v' to be $v'_{P_{i+1}}$:

$$v_{P_{i+1}} = (v_1, v_2, ..., v_i, 1, ..., v_k)$$

$$v'_{P_{i+1}} = (v_1, v_2, ..., v_{i+1}, 1, ..., v_k).$$

P_i sees v in the same congruency–class as P_{i+1} sees v', and P_i sees v' in the same congruency–class as P_{i+1} sees v. Moreover, P_i corrects players $P_1, P_2, ..., P_{i-1}$ for row v exactly as P_{i+1} corrects them in row v', and P_i corrects players $P_1, P_2, ..., P_{i-1}$ for row v' exactly as P_{i+1} corrects them in row v. P_{i+1} ,both in v and in v', corrects P_i assuming

$$(v_1, v_2, ..., 1, 1, ..., v_k).$$

So the sum of the vectors, communicated by P_i and P_{i+1} is the same for v and for v'. ∎

By Sublemma 10, we may assume that the first d_2 coordinates are $2's$, then d_3 3's,..., d_{m-1} $m-1$'s, and, at the end, d_0 0's. Let us note that the correct vector, to be added up for v to get $\delta^m(B)$, is $\nu \Pi^{d(v)}$. However:

P_1 assumes the first coordinate to be 1 instead of 2, so he communicates

$$\nu \Pi^{d(v)} \Pi^{-1}.$$

P_2 assumes the second coordinate to be 1, so he adds up $\nu \Pi^{d(v)} \Pi^{-1}$, too, but corrects P_1 by subtracting $\nu \Pi^{d(v)} \Pi^{-2}$, since the sum, supposed to be seen by P_1, is less by one. So P_2 communicates:

$$\nu \Pi^{d(v)} \Pi^{-1} (I - \Pi^{-1}).$$

P_i $(i \leq d_2)$ communicates the same vector as P_{i-1} communicated plus the correction for P_{i-1}. This correction is $(-\Pi^{-1})$ times the vector, communicated by P_{i-1}, so P_i communicates:

$$\nu \Pi^{d(v)} \Pi^{-1} (I - \Pi^{-1})^{i-1}.$$

The sum of the vectors communicated by $P_1, P_2, ..., P_{d_2}$ is:

$$\beta^{(2)} = \nu \Pi^{d(v)-1} [I + (I - \Pi^{-1}) + ...$$

$$... + (I - \Pi^{-1})^{d_2 - 1}] = \nu \Pi^{d(v)} \big(I - (I - \Pi^{-1})^{d_2}\big).$$

Remark: $d_2 = 0$ implies that $\beta^{(2)} = 0$.

P_{d_2+1} assumes v_{d_2+1} to be 1, instead of the correct 3. So P_{d_2+1} sees the sum of v one less than P_{d_2} has seen, this also applies to the corrections for $P_1, P_2, ..., P_{d_2-1}$. So P_{d_2} communicates $\nu \Pi^{d(v)} \Pi^{-1} (I - \Pi^{-1})^{d_2 - 1} \Pi^{-1}$ plus the correction for P_{d_2}: what is the $(-\Pi^{-2})$ times that P_{d_2} has communicated. P_{d_2} communicates:

$$\nu \Pi^{d(v)} \Pi^{-1} (I - \Pi^{-1})^{d_2 - 1} (\Pi^{-1} - \Pi^{-2}) =$$

$$= \nu \Pi^{d(v)} \Pi^{-2} (I - \Pi^{-1})^{d_2}.$$

P_{d_2+2} tells the same for the sum of v and the corrections for $P_1, P_2, ..., P_{d_2}$ as P_{d_2+1}, but he also corrects P_{d_2+1}, by subtracting Π^{-2} times the vector that P_{d_2+1} has communicated, so in total, P_{d_2+2} communicates:

$$\nu \Pi^{d(v)} \Pi^{-2} (I - \Pi^{-1})^{d_2} (I - \Pi^{-2}).$$

P_{d_2+i} $(i \leq d_3)$ communicates

$$\nu \Pi^{d(v)} \Pi^{-2} (I - \Pi^{-1})^{d_2} (I - \Pi^{-2})^{i-1}.$$

$\beta^{(3)}$, the sum of the vectors, communicated by $P_{d_2+1}, P_{d_2+2}, ..., P_{d_2+d_3}$ is

$$\beta^{(3)} = \nu \Pi^{d(v)} (I - \Pi^{-1})^{d_2} \big(I - (I - \Pi^{-2})^{d_3}\big).$$

Similarly, $\beta^{(j)}$, the sum of the vectors, communicated by $P_{d_2+...+d_{j-1}+1}$, $P_{d_2+...+d_{j-1}+2}, ..., P_{d_2+...+d_{j-1}+d_j}$, is

$$\nu\Pi^{d(v)}(I-\Pi^{-1})^{d_2}...(I-\Pi^{-j+2})^{d_{j-1}}\left(I-(I-\Pi^{-j+1})^{d_j}\right)$$

The result of the telescopic sum $\beta^{(2)}+\beta^{(3)}+...+\beta^{(m)}+\beta^{(0)}$ is:

$$\nu\Pi^{d(v)}-\nu\Pi^{d(v)}(I-\Pi^{-1})^{d_2}...(I-\Pi^{-m+1})^{d_m}.$$

So the vector w_v is equal to

$$w_v=\nu\Pi^{d(v)}(I-\Pi^{-1})^{d_2}(I-\Pi^{-2})^{d_3}...(I-\Pi^{-m+1})^{d_m}.$$

Noticing that $\Pi^m=I$, our result follows. ∎

Proof of Theorem 5. By Definition 1, we must give a circuit $\mathcal{C}$ and a k partition $X_1, X_2, ...X_k$ of X, for which every k–party protocol needs $\Omega(\frac{N}{c_m^k})$ bits for evaluation. In fact we shall prove the statement only for k's of the form $k=p_1^c$, since if for a k–partition $X_1, X_2, ..., X_k$ the k-evaluation of circuit $\mathcal{C}$ needs a bits of communication, then for $k'<k$, and for the partition $X_1'=X_1, ..., X_{k'-1}'=X_{k'-1}, X_{k'}'=\bigcup_{i=k'}^{k}X_i$, the k'–evaluation needs also at least a bits of communication. If we prove a lower bound of $\Omega(\frac{N}{4^k})$ for the least $k\geq k'$ of the form $k=p_1^c$, then it implies a lower bound $\Omega(\frac{N}{c_m^{k'}})$ with $c_m=4^{p_1}$ for the original k', and that is stated in the theorem.

Let $X=\{y_1, y_2, ..., y_m; x_{11}, x_{12}, ..., x_{1k}, x_{21}, ..., x_{2k}, ..., x_{(N-1)1}, ..., x_{(N-1)k}\}$,

The partition on X is defined as follows: $X_1=\{y_1, y_2, ..., y_m; x_{11}, x_{21}, ..., x_{(N-1)1}\}$, and $X_j=\{x_{1j}, x_{2j}, ..., x_{(N-1)j}\}$, for $j=2,3,...,k$.

Let $q_1=m/p_1$, and $q_2=m/p_2$.

Circuit $\mathcal{C}$ is defined as follows: there is a MOD m gate G on the top, and MOD m gates $G_1, G_2, ..., G_{N-1}$ on the first level; the variables of X are situated on the bottom. G is connected to variables $y_1, y_2, ..., y_m$ with one–one input wire, while to each gates $G_1, G_2, ..., G_{N-1}$ with q_1 input wires. The fan–in of G is $(N-1)q_1+m$. Gate G_i is connected to each variable from $\{x_{i1}, x_{i2}, ..., x_{ik}\}$ with q_2 input–wires, the fan–in of the MOD m gates is kq_2.

Let us remark that G_i is 1 iff $x_{i1}+x_{i2}+...+x_{ik}\equiv 0 \pmod{p_2}$. Suppose that $\sum_{i=1}^{m}y_i\equiv q_1s \pmod m$. Then G is 1 iff $q_1s+q_1(G_1+G_2+...+G_{N-1})\equiv 0 \pmod m$. Or, in other words, G is 1 iff $s+(G_1+G_2+...+G_{N-1})0 \pmod{p_1}$.

Let A denote matrix $\{x_{ij}\}$, $i=1,2,...,N-1$; $j=1,2,...,k$. Because of the definition of our partition, player j knows all the columns of this matrix, except column j. Gate G_i is 1 iff the sum of row i is divisible by p_2, and gate G is 1 iff the number of those rows of A, whose sums are divisible by p_2, is congruent to $-s \pmod{p_1}$.

Suppose now, that players $P_1, P_2, ..., P_k$ evaluates circuit $\mathcal{C}$ with communicating b bits. Then for any s and for any $A\in\{0,1,\}^{(N-1)\times k}$, they can decide, communicating b bits, whether the number of those rows of A, whose sums are divisible by p_2, is congruent to $-s$ (mod $p)_1$, or not. So the players can *compute* the number, mod p_1, of those rows of A, whose sums are divisible by p_2 with bp_1 bits of communication. The following lemma gives a lower bound to bp_1:

Lemma 11. *Let p_1 and p_2 be different primes, $k=p_1^c$, and $A\in\{0,1\}^{n\times k}$. Then any k-party protocol computing mod p_1 the number of those rows of A which are divisible by p_2, needs $\Omega(\frac{n}{4^k})$ bits of communication.*

Proof. By Lemma 9, players can compute vector

$$\delta^{(p_2)}(A)-\nu(I-\Pi)^kCT(\mathbf{0},A) \tag{1}$$

using $O(k\log n)$ bits of communication, where $\delta_i^{(p_2)}(A)$ is the number of rows of A, whose sum is $\equiv i \pmod{p_2}$, and Π is the $p_2\times p_2$ cyclic right-shift permutation matrix.

$$(I-\Pi)^k=\sum_{i=0}^{k}(-1)\binom{k}{i}\Pi^i\equiv I-\Pi^{p_1^c} \pmod{p_1},$$

since $k=p_1^c$ and p_1 divides $\binom{k}{i}$ if $0<i<k$.

Since $\nu=(1,0,0,...,0)$, $\nu(I-\Pi)^{p_1^c}=\nu(I-\Pi^{p_1^c})$ is the first row of $(I-\Pi^{p_1^c})$. The first entry in the first row of $\Pi^{p_1^c}$ is 0, since $\Pi^{p_1^c}\neq I$, because p_2 does not divide p_1^c. So the first entry of vector $\nu(I-\Pi^{p_1^c})$ is 1, thus the first coordinate of vector $\delta^{(p_2)}(A)-\nu(I-\Pi)^kCT(\mathbf{0},A)$ is

$$\delta_0^{(p_2)}(A)-CT(\mathbf{0},A) \pmod{p_1}. \tag{2}$$

From the assumption, $\delta_0^{(p_2)}(A) \bmod p_1$ is computed by the protocol, say, with z bits of communication. Then, because of (2), $CT(\mathbf{0},A) \bmod p_1$ can also be computed using $z+O(k\log n)$ bits of communication. The following generalization of ([BNS], Theorem 1) yields that $z+O(k\log n)=\Omega(\frac{n}{4^k})$.

Lemma 12. *Let p be a prime, and $A\in\{0,1,\}^{n\times k}$. Then any k-party protocol, which computes $CT(\mathbf{0},A)$ mod p, needs $\Omega(\frac{n}{4^k})$ bits of communication.*

Proof. We adopt the notation and some of the definitions of [BNS]. Let $S\subset\{0,1\}^{n\times k}$. S is called a *cylinder* if the membership of S does not depend on column i, for some $i \in \{1, 2, ..., k\}$. S is called a *cylinder–intersection* if it can be represented as the intersection of some cylinders.

It is easy to verify that for any k–party protocol, the subset $S \subset \{0,1\}^{n\times k}$, whose elements, if they are taken as inputs, lead to the same string s of communicated bits, is a cylinder intersection. Any cylinder intersection in $\{0,1\}^{n\times k}$ can be represented as the intersection of at most k cylinders.

Definition 13. *Let* $g : \{0,1\}^{n\times k} \to \{0, 1, 2, ..., p-1\}$ *be a function. The discrepancy of* g *is*

$$\Gamma(g) = \max_S \left| \sum_{i=0}^{p-1} \varepsilon^i Pr(g(A) = i, A \in S) \right|,$$

where ε *is a p-th complex root of unity, which minimizes* $|1+\varepsilon|$, *and* A *is chosen uniformly from* $\{0,1\}^{n\times k}$, *and* S *runs over all the cylinder intersections of* $\{0,1\}^{n\times k}$.

Lemma 14. *([BNS], Lemma 2.2.) For any function* g:

$$C(g) \geq \log\left(\frac{1}{\Gamma(g)}\right).$$

Proof. Let S_0 be the cylinder–intersection of the largest probability, on which g is constant. Then $\Pr(S_0) \leq \Gamma(g)$, and, on the other hand, $C(g) \geq \log\left(\frac{1}{\Pr(S_0)}\right)$. ∎

Let $g(A) = g_{n,k,p}(A) = CT(\mathbf{0}, A) \bmod p$, and let

$$f(A) = \varepsilon^{g(A)} = \varepsilon^{CT(\mathbf{0},A)}.$$

Let

$$\Delta^{(k)}(n) = \max_{\phi_1,\phi_2,...,\phi_k} |\mathop{\mathrm{E}}_A (f(A)\phi_1\phi_2...\phi_k)|,$$

where ϕ_i is a shorthand for $\phi_i(A) = \phi_i(A_1, A_2, ..., A_k)$, where A_j denotes column j of matrix A, and where the maximum is taken over all functions $\phi_i : \{0,1\}^{n\times k} \to \{0,1\}$ such that ϕ_i does not depend on A_i. E denotes the expected value on the uniformly distributed $A = (A_1, A_2, ..., A_k) \in \{0,1\}^{n\times k}$.

Let us note that $\Delta^{(k)}(n) = \Gamma(g_{n,k,p})$. Because of Lemma 14, an upper bound to $\Delta^{(k)}(n)$ yields a lower bound to $C(g)$.

Lemma 15.

$$\Delta^{(k)}(n) \leq \mu_k^n,$$

where $\mu_1 = \frac{1}{2}$, *and* $\mu_i = \sqrt{\frac{1+\mu_{i-1}}{2}}$.

Note: It is easy to show by induction that $\mu_k \leq 1 - 4^{-k}$, which is about $e^{-4^{-k}}$.

Proof. The proof is by induction. For $k = 1$,

$$\Delta^{(1)}(n) \leq 2^{-n}\left|\binom{n}{0}\varepsilon^0 + \binom{n}{1}\varepsilon^1 + ... + \binom{n}{n}\varepsilon^n\right| =$$

$$= 2^{-n}|(1+\varepsilon)^n| \leq 2^{-n} = \mu_1^n,$$

since $|(1+\varepsilon)| \leq 1$. Let $k \geq 2$. Since ϕ_k does not depend on A_k:

$$\Delta^{(k)}(n) \leq \mathop{\mathrm{E}}_{A_1,A_2,...,A_{k-1}} \left|\left(\mathop{\mathrm{E}}_{A_k}(f(A)\phi_1\phi_2...\phi_{k-1})\right)\right|.$$

We will use the following version of the Cauchy-Schwarz inequality:

Cauchy–Schwarz inequality. *For any random variable* x:

$$(E(x))^2 \leq E(x^2).$$

Using the Cauchy–Schwarz inequality with

$$x = \left|\mathop{\mathrm{E}}_{A_k}(f(A_1, A_2, ..., A_k)\phi_1\phi_2...\phi_{k-1})\right|,$$

and noticing that

$$x^2 = \left|\mathop{\mathrm{E}}_{A_k}(f(A)\phi_1\phi_2...\phi_{k-1})\right|^2 =$$

$$= \left(\mathop{\mathrm{E}}_{A_k}(f(A)\phi_1\phi_2...\phi_{k-1})\right)\left(\mathop{\mathrm{E}}_{A_k}(\bar{f}(A)\phi_1\phi_2...\phi_{k-1})\right),$$

where $\bar{f}$ denotes the complex conjugate of f, we can give an upper estimation for $\Delta^{(k)}(n)$ as follows:

$$(3)\quad \left[\mathop{\mathrm{E}}_{A_1,A_2,...,A_{k-1}} \left(\mathop{\mathrm{E}}_{A_k}(f(A)\Phi)\right)\left(\mathop{\mathrm{E}}_{A_k}(\bar{f}(A)\Phi)\right)\right]^{\frac{1}{2}} =$$

$$= \left[\mathop{\mathrm{E}}_{U,V,A_1,A_2,...,A_{k-1}} \left(f^U \bar{f}^V \Phi^U \Phi^V\right)\right]^{\frac{1}{2}}$$

where $U, V \in \{0,1\}^n$, and Φ stands for $\phi_1\phi_2...\phi_{k-1}$, f^U stands for $f(A_1, A_2, ..., A_{k-1}, U)$, $\bar{f}^V$ stands for $\bar{f}(A_1, A_2, ..., A_{k-1}, V)$,
and Φ^U stands for $\Phi(A_1, A_2, ..., A_{k-1}, U)$, Φ^V stands for $\Phi(A_1, A_2, ..., A_{k-1}, V)$.

Note: The domain of f^U, f^V and Φ^U, Φ^V is $\{0,1\}^{n\times(k-1)}$.

Let us partition the rows of matrix $A' = (A_1, A_2, ..., A_{k-1})$ into four classes: A_{00}, A_{11}, A_{01} and A_{10}, where A_{xy} contains row i of A' iff $U_i = x$, $V_i = y$, $1 \leq i \leq n$, $x, y \in \{0,1\}$. Let f_{xy}^U denote the restriction of f^U to A_{xy}: $f_{xy}^U = \varepsilon^{CT(\mathbf{0},A_{xy})}$, for $x, y \in \{0,1\}$. f^V is defined similarly.

From the definition of f:

$$f^U = f^U_{00} f^U_{01} f^U_{10} f^U_{11}, \text{ and } f^V = f^V_{00} f^V_{01} f^V_{10} f^V_{11}.$$

So

$$f^U \bar{f}^V = f^U_{00} \bar{f}^V_{00} f^U_{01} \bar{f}^V_{01} f^U_{10} \bar{f}^V_{10} f^U_{11} \bar{f}^V_{11}.$$

Let us observe that $f^U_{11} \bar{f}^V_{11} = 1$, since among those rows there are no all–0 ones, because their last coordinates are 1. $f^U_{00} = f^V_{00} = \varepsilon^{CT(\mathbf{0}, A_{00})}$, so $f^U_{00} \bar{f}^V_{00} = 1$. Moreover, $f^U_{10} = \varepsilon^0 = 1$, $\bar{f}^V_{01} = \varepsilon^0 = 1$, so we have got:

$$f^U \bar{f}^V = f^U_{01} \bar{f}^V_{10}.$$

For $i = 1, 2, ..., k-1$, let A_i be composed of two parts: B_i and C_i, where C_i corresponds to the coordinates of A_i in the rows of A_{10}, and B_i to the remaining coordinates.
Let $\xi^{U,V,B_1,B_2,...,B_{k-1}}(C_1, C_2, ..., C_{k-1}) = \Phi^U(A_1, A_2, ..., A_{k-1}) \Phi^V(A_1, A_2, ..., A_{k-1})$. Then, from (3), $\Delta^{(k)}(n)$ is less than or equal to

$$\left[\mathop{\mathrm{E}}_{U,V} \left| \mathop{\mathrm{E}}_{B_1,B_2,...,B_{k-1}} \left(f^U_{01} \mathop{\mathrm{E}}_{C_1,C_2,...,C_{k-1}} \left(\bar{f}^V_{10} \xi \right) \right) \right| \right]^{\frac{1}{2}},$$

since f^U_{01} does not depend on the C_i's.
From the induction hypothesis:

$$\left| \mathop{\mathrm{E}}_{C_1,C_2,...,C_{k-1}} \left(\bar{f}^V_{10} \xi \right) \right| \leq \mu_{k-1}^{m_{10}},$$

where m_{10} is the number of rows in A_{10}.

For $i = 1, 2, .., k-1$ let B_i be composed of two parts: D_i and F_i, where F_i corresponds to the coordinates of B_i in the rows of A_{01}, and D_i corresponds to the remaining coordinates. Then $\Delta^{(k)}(n)$ is less than or equal to

$$\left[\mathop{\mathrm{E}}_{U,V,D_1,D_2,...,D_{k-1}} \left(\mu_{k-1}^{m_{10}} \left| \mathop{\mathrm{E}}_{F_1,F_2,...,F_{k-1}} \left(f^U_{01} \right) \right| \right) \right]^{\frac{1}{2}}.$$

Again, from the induction hypothesis, choosing $\phi_1 = \phi_2 = ... = \phi_{k-1} = 1$:

$$\left| \mathop{\mathrm{E}}_{F_1,F_2,...,F_{k-1}} \left(f^U_{01} \right) \right| \leq \mu_{k-1}^{m_{01}},$$

where m_{01} is the number of the rows of A_{01}. So we have got

$$\Delta^{(k)}(n) \leq \left[\mathop{\mathrm{E}}_{U,V,D_1,D_2,...,D_{k-1}} \left(\mu_{k-1}^{m_{10}+m_{01}} \right) \right]^{\frac{1}{2}}.$$

$m_{10} + m_{01}$ is equal to the number of those coordinates i: $U_i \neq V_i$. Since U and V is distributed uniformly, the probability that $m_{10} + m_{01} = m$ is $\binom{n}{m} 2^{-n}$, so:

$$\Delta^{(k)}(n) \leq \left(\sum_{m=0}^{n} \binom{n}{m} 2^{-n} \mu_{k-1}^m \right)^{\frac{1}{2}} =$$

$$= \left(2^{-n} (1 + \mu_{k-1})^n \right)^{\frac{1}{2}} = \mu_k^n,$$

and this completes the proof of Lemma 15. ∎

Lemma 15 yields that $\Delta^{(k)}(n) \leq \mu_k^n \leq e^{-n4^{-k}}$, and from Lemma 14:

$$C(g) \geq \log \left(e^{n4^{-k}} \right) = \Omega\left(\frac{n}{4^k} \right)$$

which completes the proof of Lemma 12. ∎

We have got that $z + O(k \log n) = \Omega(\frac{n}{4^k})$, that is, $z = \Omega(\frac{n}{4^k})$, so any protocol computing $\delta_0^{(p_2)}(A)$ mod p_1 needs $\Omega(\frac{n}{4^k})$ bits of communication, and this is the statement of Lemma 11. ∎

Since $bp_2 = \Omega(\frac{n}{4^k})$, then $b = \Omega(\frac{n}{4^k})$ also holds, thus evaluating circuit $\mathcal{C}$ needs also $\Omega(\frac{n}{4^k})$ bits of communication for $k = p_1^c$, and $\Omega(\frac{n}{c_m^k})$ bits for general k. This completes the proof of Theorem 5. ∎

Proof of Theorem 3. Let p be a prime–divisor of q. Let $X = \{y_1, y_2, ..., y_q; x_{11}, x_{12}, ..., x_{1k}, x_{21}, ..., x_{2k}, ..., x_{(N-1)1}, ..., x_{(N-1)k}\}$, The partition on X is defined as follows: $X_1 = \{y_1, y_2, ..., y_q; x_{11}, x_{21}, ..., x_{(N-1)1}\}$, and $X_j = \{x_{1j}, x_{2j}, ..., x_{(N-1)j}\}$, for $j = 2, 3, ..., k$. Let $q_1 = q/p$.

Circuit $\mathcal{C}'$ is defined as follows: there is a MOD q gate G on the top, and MOD q gates $G_1, G_2, ..., G_{N-1}$ on the first level; the variables of X are situated on the bottom. G is connected to variables $y_1, y_2, ..., y_q$ with one–one input wire, while to each gates $G_1, G_2, ..., G_{N-1}$ with q_1 input wires. The fan–in of G is $(N-1)q_1 + q$. Gate G_i is connected to each variable from $\{x_{i1}, x_{i2}, ..., x_{ik}\}$ with 1 input–wire. The fan–in of the MOD q gate G_i is k, for $i = 1, 2, ..., N-1$.

Let us remark that G_i is 1 iff $x_{i1} = x_{i2} = ... = x_{ik} = 0$. Suppose that $\sum_{i=1}^q y_i \equiv q_1 s \pmod q$. Let A denote matrix $\{x_{ij}\}$, $i = 1, 2, ..., N-1$; $j = 1, 2, ..., k$. Then G is 1 iff $q_1 s + q_1 CT(\mathbf{0}, A) \pmod q$. Or, in other words, G is 1 iff $s + CT(\mathbf{0}, A) \equiv 0 \pmod p$.

Because of the definition of our partition, player j knows all the columns of matrix A, except column j. Gate G_i is 1 iff row i is the all–0 row, and gate G is 1 iff the number of the all–0 rows of A is congruent to $-s \pmod p$.

Suppose now, that players $P_1, P_2, ..., P_k$ evaluates circuit C' with communicating b bits. Then for any s and for any $A \in \{0,1,\}^{(N-1)\times k}$, they can decide, communicating b bits, whether the number of the all-0 rows of A, is congruent to $-s \pmod{p}_1$, or not. So the players can *compute* the number of the all-0 rows of A, mod p. From Lemma 12 our statement follows. ∎

3. CIRCUIT LOWER BOUNDS

The following theorems gives lower bounds for the members of circuit-classes C' and C'', defined in Chapter 1.

Theorem 16. *Suppose that the members of the circuit-family C' computes GIP(A). Then the size of $C'_{n,k} \in C'$ is exponential in n.*

Proof. We prove the statement for the members of the circuit-family C^*, where C^* is a family of depth-2 circuits $C^{(m)}_{n,k}$, where n and k are positive integers, m is odd and positive, and $k \equiv m \pmod{2m}$ is also satisfied. Moreover

- the input of $C^{(m)}_{n,k}$ is A for $A \in \{0,1\}^{n\times k}$,
- on the bottom level (level 0) situated the variables A^i_j, with their negations;
- on the top (level 2), there is a symmetric gate,
- there are MOD_m gates of fan-in k on the first level.

The original statement follows, using standard techniques from [GH] or [HMPST].

Let us consider circuit $C^{(m)}_{n,k}$, computing GIP(A), $A \in \{0,1\}^{n\times k}$, and k players, such that player i knows every column of A, except column i, for $i = 1, 2, ..., k$, and suppose that all the players know circuit $C^{(m)}_{n,k}$. On the top of the circuit there is a symmetric gate, and the output of that gate depends only on the number of MOD_m gates, evaluated to 1, on level 1.

Players will collectively compute the number of MOD_m gates, evaluated to 1. Every MOD_m gate has at most k input wires. Let us call a MOD_m gate *easy*, if it has no input from a column of A. The easy gates can be evaluated as follows [GH]: Suppose that an easy gate has no input from A_i, then P_i knows every variable of it, so he knows its output. Before the computation, the players agree in a scheme, which partitions the easy gates between the players, who know their inputs. These players simply communicate the numbers of those easy-gates in their classes, which are evaluated to 1. This can be done with $O(k \log N)$ bits of communication, where N is the size of circuit $C^{(m)}_{n,k}$.

Next, the players evaluate the non-easy gates. To do this, first they – individually, without any communication – build a matrix B. B has k columns, and each row of it corresponds to one of the non-easy MOD_m gates of the circuit; suppose that row B^i corresponds to a MOD_m gate G, and G has k input-variables, one from each column of A. Let B^i_j be equal to the input of G in A_j.

Note, that player j knows all the columns of B, except column j, B_j. Let us observe that row i, B^i is divisible by m exactly when G is evaluated to 1. Since the size of $C^{(m)}_{n,k}$ is N, B has at most N rows. From Lemma 17, protocol **MOD m** computes the number of rows B, divisible by m, with communicating $O(k \log N)$ bits. To compute the number of easy-gates, evaluated to 1, the players used $O(k \log N)$ bits, so $O(k \log N)$ bits in total. Lemma 12 (or [BNS], Theorem 2), shows that to compute GIP(A) the players should communicate

$$\Omega\left(\frac{n}{4^k}\right)$$

bits, so

$$O(k \log N) = \Omega\left(\frac{n}{4^k}\right)$$

or

$$N \geq \exp\left(c\frac{n}{4^k k}\right).$$

∎

Lemma 17. *Let m be an odd, positive integer, let $0 \leq \ell \leq m-1$, and $k \equiv m + 2\ell \pmod{2m}$. Let $A \in \{0,1\}^{n\times k}$. Then the number of those rows of A which are congruent to $\ell \pmod{m}$, can be computed by a k-party protocol, communicating $O(k \log n)$ bits.*

Proof. By Lemma 9 protocol MOD m computes

$$\delta^{(m)}(A) - CT(\mathbf{0}, A)\nu(I - \Pi)^k.$$

Using that $\Pi^m = I$, the ℓ-th coordinate of $\nu(I - \Pi)^k$ is

$$\sum_{\substack{0 \leq i \leq k \\ i \equiv \ell \pmod{m}}} (-1)^i \binom{k}{i} =$$

$$= \sum_{\substack{0 \leq i \leq k \\ i \equiv \ell \pmod{m} \\ i \text{ even}}} \binom{k}{i} - \sum_{\substack{0 \leq i \leq k \\ i \equiv \ell \pmod{m} \\ i \text{ odd}}} \binom{k}{i} =$$

$$= \sum_{\substack{0 \leq i \leq k \\ i \equiv \ell \pmod{m} \\ i \text{ even}}} \binom{k}{i} - \sum_{\substack{0 \leq i \leq k \\ i \equiv \ell \pmod{m} \\ i \text{ odd}}} \binom{k}{k-i} =$$

$$= \sum_{\substack{0\leq i\leq k \\ i\equiv \ell \pmod m \\ i \text{ even}}} \binom{k}{i} - \sum_{\substack{0\leq j\leq k \\ j\equiv \ell \pmod m \\ j \text{ even}}} \binom{k}{j} = 0,$$

since k is odd, and $k - i \equiv \ell \pmod m$.
So, there is no error in the ℓ–th coordinate, and this completes the proof. ∎

Theorem 18. *The family C'' of circuits cannot compute GIP(A).*

Proof. We prove the statement for depth–2 circuits $C_{n,k}$, where $k = p^c$ for some prime p and positive integer c. $C_{n,k}$ has a MOD p gate on the top and EXACT$_\ell$ gates of fan–in–k on the first level, where $1 \leq \ell \leq k-1$, and variables A_i^j with their negations on level 0. The original statement follows as in the previous theorem.
Let us consider circuit $C_{n,k}$, computing GIP(A), $A \in \{0,1\}^{n\times k}$, and k players, such that player i knows every column of A, except column i, for $i = 1, 2, ..., k$, and suppose that all the players know circuit $C_{n,k}$. On the top of the circuit there is a MOD p, and the output of that gate depends only on the number of the EXACT$_\ell$ gates, evaluated to 1, on level 1.

Players will compute the number of EXACT$_\ell$ gates, evaluated to 1. Every EXACT$_\ell$ gate has at most k input wires. Let us call an EXACT$_\ell$ gate *easy*, if it has no input from a column of A. The easy gates can be evaluated exactly as in the proof of Theorem 16, with $O(k \log p)$ bits of communication, since the number of the EXACT$_\ell$ gates, evaluated to 1, is needed only mod p.
Next, the players evaluate the non–easy gates. First they build a matrix B. B has k columns, and each row of it corresponds to one of the non–easy EXACT$_\ell$ gates of the circuit; suppose that row B^i corresponds to an EXACT$_\ell$ gate G, and G has k input–variables, one from each column of A. Let B_j^i be equal to the input of G in A_j. Note, that player j knows all the columns of B, except column j, B_j. Let us observe that B^i is congruent to ℓ mod k, exactly when G is evaluated to 1.

Let players play the **MOD m** protocol with $m = k = p^c$. Then for any ℓ, for $1 \leq \ell \leq k-1$, the error, made by the protocol, is 0 mod p, since from Lemma 9, the ℓth coordinate of $\nu(I-\Pi)^k$ is $(-1)^\ell\binom{p^c}{\ell} \equiv 0 \pmod p$. To compute the number of easy–gates, evaluated to 1, the players used $O(k \log p)$ bits, the **MOD m** protocol used so $O(k^2 \log p)$ bits, since it is enough to communicate every number mod p only. From [BNS], or from Lemma 12, the players should communicate $\Omega\left(\frac{n}{4^k}\right)$ bits to compute GIP, but the players can evaluate circuit with constant number of bits in n, so we have got that $C_{n,k}$ circuits cannot compute GIP(A) at all. ∎

REFERENCES

[AG] E. Allender, V. Gore: A Uniform Circuit Lower Bound for the Permanent, preprint.

[BNS] L. Babai, N. Nisan, M. Szegedy: Multiparty Protocols and Pseudorandom Sequences, Proc. 21st ACM STOC, 1989, pp. 1-11.

[CFL] A. K. Chandra, M. L. Furst, R. J. Lipton: Multi-party Protocols, Proc. 15th ACM STOC, 1983, pp. 94–99.

[G] V. Grolmusz: The BNS Lower Bound for Multi–Party Protocols is Nearly Optimal, to be appeared in "Information and Computation".

[GH] M. Goldmann, J. Håstad: On the Power of Small–Depth Threshold Circuits, 31st IEEE FOCS, 1990, pp. 610–618.

[HMPST] A. Hajnal, W. Maass, P. Pudlak, M. Szegedy, G. Turán: Threshold Circuits of Bounded Depth, Proc. 28th IEEE FOCS, 1987, pp. 99–110.

[KM] J. Kahn, R. Meshulam: On mod p Transversals, Combinatorica, 1991, (11) No. 1. pp. 17–22.

[KS] B. Kalyanosundaram, G. Snitger: The Probabilistic Communication Complexity of Set Intersection, Proc. Structure in Complexity Theory, 1987, pp. 41–49.

[KW] M. Karchmer, A. Wigderson: Monotone Circuits for Connectivity Require Super–Logarithmic Depth, Proc. 20th ACM STOC, 1988, pp.

[L] L. Lovász: Communication Complexity: A Survey, Technical Report, CS–TR–204–89, Princeton University, 1989.

[RW1] R. Raz, A. Wigderson: Probabilistic Communication Complexity of Boolean Relations. Proc. 30th IEEE FOCS, 1989, pp. 562-567

[RW2] R. Raz, A. Wigderson: Monotone Circuits for Matching Require Linear Depth. 22nd ACM STOC, pp. 287–292.

[S] M. Szegedy: Functions with Bounded Symmetric Communication Complexity and Circuits with MOD m Gates, Proc. 22nd ACM STOC, pp. 278–286.

[Sm] R. Smolensky, Algebraic Methods in the Theory of Lower Bounds for Boolean Circuit Complexity, Proc. 19th ACM FOCS, pp. 77-82, (1987).

[Y1] A.C. Yao: Some Complexity Questions Related to Distributive Computing, Proc. 11th ACM STOC, 1979, pp. 209–213.

[Y2] A.C. Yao: Circuits and Local Computation, Proc. 21st ACM STOC, 1989, pp. 186–196

Lower Bounds on the Depth of Monotone Arithmetic Computations

Extended Summary

Don Coppersmith Baruch Schieber
IBM - Research Division
T.J. Watson Research Center
P.O. Box 218
Yorktown Heights, NY 10598

Abstract

Consider an arithmetic expression of length n involving only the operations $\{+, \times\}$ and non-negative constants. We prove lower bounds on the depth of any binary computation tree over the same set of operations and constants that computes such an expression. In our main result we exhibit a family of arithmetic expressions that requires computation trees of depth at least $1.5 \log_2 n - O(1)$; thus proving a conjecture of Kosaraju [Proc. 18th STOC, 231–239]. In contrast, Kosaraju showed how to compute such expressions with computation trees of depth $2\log_2 n + O(1)$. We also consider the family of arithmetic expressions defined by alternating 5-3 trees. For this family we show a tight bound of $5/(\log_2 15)\log_2 n + O(1)$ on the depth of any computation tree. This is the best known *tight* bound for any family of arithmetic expressions.

1. Introduction

The problem of restructuring an arithmetic expression into an equivalent one of reduced depth is one of the basic problems in parallel computation ([BKM73, BM75, KM75, MP76, SS80, JS82, Kos86]). Despite long-term efforts, this problem is still unsettled, even for arithmetic expressions that seem simple to compute. To escape from some of the difficulties of the general problem researchers have considered the restricted *monotone* computation model. We follow this direction, and prove lower bounds on the depth of monotone arithmetic expressions.

Consider an arithmetic expression of length n involving only the operations $\{+, \times\}$ and non-negative constants. We wish to evaluate such an arithmetic expression by a binary computation tree over the same set of operators and constants. We exhibit a family of arithmetic expressions that requires computation trees of depth at least $1.5\log_2 n - O(1)$; the corresponding upper bound for this family is $2\log_2 n + O(1)$. We also consider the family of arithmetic expressions defined by alternating 5-3 trees. For this family we show a tight bound of $5/(\log_2 15)\log_2 n + O(1)$ on the depth of any computation tree. This is the largest known *tight* bound for any family of arithmetic expressions.

Muller and Preparata [MP76] showed that any arithmetic expression involving only the operations $\{+, \times\}$ and non-negative constants could be computed by a binary tree of depth $2.08 \log n$ (throughout, all logarithms are base 2). This is somewhat surprising, since the computation tree suggested by the form of the original expression might be quite skewed and have depth $\Theta(n)$. On the other hand, Shamir and Snir [SS80] showed a lower bound of $1.16 \log n$ for the family of arithmetic expressions defined by alternating 2-3 trees: trees in which nodes at odd levels multiply two subexpressions, and nodes at even levels add three subexpressions. (Note that these trees are not binary and hence not computation trees.) Kosaraju [Kos86] improved Muller and Preparata's upper bound to $2 \log n$. He also conjectured that expressions requiring depth at least $(1+\epsilon)\log n$ could be found among the class of arithmetic expressions where at least one operand of each addition node is a leaf. We will refer to such arithmetic expressions as *leaf-addition expressions.*

In our main result we prove Kosaraju's conjecture. Our arithmetic expressions are given by trees in which nodes at odd levels multiply two subexpressions, and nodes at even levels (including the top level) add a subexpression and a leaf. This description gives a binary computation tree of depth $2\log n + O(1)$ for an

0-8186-2900-2/92 $3.00

arithmetic expression of length n. We show that any binary computation tree computing this arithmetic expression must have depth at least $1.5\log n - O(1)$.

We also consider alternating k-ℓ trees: trees in which nodes at odd levels multiply k subexpressions, and nodes at even levels add ℓ subexpressions. A straightforward implementation of a binary tree computing the arithmetic expression given by an alternating k-ℓ tree will have depth

$$\frac{\lceil\log k\rceil + \lceil\log \ell\rceil}{\log k + \log \ell} \cdot \log n.$$

For integers $k, \ell \geq 2$, the fraction is maximized at $1.292\ldots$ when $k = \ell = 5$. So, any alternating k-ℓ tree can be implemented in depth at most $1.293\log n$. By techniques similar to Shamir and Snir [SS80], we show a matching lower bound for alternating 5-3 trees: Any binary tree computing the arithmetic expression given by an alternating 5-3 tree must have depth at least

$$\frac{\lceil\log 5\rceil + \lceil\log 3\rceil}{\log 5 + \log 3} \cdot \log n = \frac{5}{\log 15} \cdot \log n = 1.279\ldots \log n$$

and this is tight. We are unable to show the corresponding lower bound for alternating 5-5 trees.

The monotone computation model does not allow division, subtraction and negative constants, so that cancellation is not possible. This technicality enables our lower bound proofs to go through. Some arguments can be brought in favor of considering such a restrictive computation model. First, this model has absolute numerical stability ([Mil75]). Also, it generalizes to any semiring (i.e., a domain with two binary operations $+$ and $\times$, both associative and commutative, with $\times$ distributing over $+$).

Monotone *boolean* computation has been investigated extensively recently. Again, strong lower bounds in this model were proven using the restrictive nature of monotone computation (See, e.g., [Raz85, KW88, RW90].)

Most of the known lower bounds for monotone (arithmetic) computation consider only the weight (number of monomials in a polynomial) of a polynomial of a given degree computable by a tree of a given depth ([SS80, JS82, Sni91]). To get our $1.5\log_2 n - O(1)$ lower bound we need to look more closely at the specific structure of our arithmetic expression, as well as the shapes of the subtrees appearing under each multiplication node. This new technique may be found useful for proving other lower bounds.

To get our lower bound, we had to prove a slightly stronger lower bound. We actually show that given a polynomial, any polynomial with the same set of monomials, but with *arbitrary* positive coefficients, also requires depth at least $1.5\log n - O(1)$. It would be interesting if it turns that one such polynomial is indeed easier to compute than the given one.

We prove our lower bound for leaf-addition expressions. Interestingly, leaf-multiplication expressions (i.e., expressions given by trees where at least one operand of each multiplication node is a leaf) are very efficient to restructure. Kosaraju [Kos86] gave a tight bound of $\log n + \sqrt{\log n} + o(\sqrt{\log n})$ on the depth of computation trees for such arithmetic expressions. The reason for the difference is that $\times$ distributes over $+$, while $+$ does not distribute over $\times$. Notice that this is not the case in the boolean case with the operations $\vee, \wedge$. Since $\wedge$ distributes over $\vee$ and $\vee$ distributes over $\wedge$, we can get a tight bound of $\log n + \sqrt{\log n} + o(\sqrt{\log n})$ on the depth of computation trees for both leaf-addition and leaf-multiplication *boolean* expressions.

The rest of the paper is organized as follows. In Section 2 we define the family of leaf-addition expressions. In Section 3 we prove the lower bound for these expressions. In Section 4 we discuss alternating k-ℓ trees. Finally, we list some open problems.

2. Leaf-addition expressions

We define the family of arithmetic expressions for which we prove the lower bound. These arithmetic expressions are given by polynomials, each of which has a *level* k, for some non-negative integer k. The length of the polynomial of level k is $2^{k+2} - 3$, and it involves $2^{k+1} - 1$ indeterminates. We show that the evaluation of a polynomial of level k requires depth at least $1.5k$.

We describe a computation tree T_k of depth $2k$ that computes the polynomial of level k. We start from an alternating 2-2 tree of depth $2k$ (i.e., a complete binary tree of depth $2k$, in which nodes at odd levels multiply two subexpressions, and nodes at even levels add two subexpressions). Notice that the root node is an addition node. Now, for each addition node we prune its right subtree and make it a leaf. It is not difficult to see that the resulting tree T_k has $2^k + 2^k - 1 = 2^{k+1} - 1$ leaves (indeterminates) and $2^{k+1} - 2$ computation nodes.

For the lower bound proof it is more convenient to

use an alternative recursive definition of the polynomials. First, we introduce some notations.

Notation. We associate to each indeterminate a *range*: a subscript indicating a half-open interval of nonnegative integers, for example $x_{[2,4)}$. For an interval $[a, b)$, we always have that $b-a$ divides a. The polynomials are indexed by two numbers; the first is its level and the second is the "starting point" of the ranges of its indeterminates. For an index (k, a), we always have that 2^k divides a.

The polynomials we wish to compute are defined recursively:

$$P_{(0,a)} = x_{[a,a+1)} \equiv x_a$$

For all k s.t. $2^k | a$:

$$P_{(k,a)} = P_{(k-1,a)} \times P_{(k-1,a+2^{k-1})} + x_{[a,a+2^k)}$$

Thus for example

$$\begin{aligned} P_{(3,0)} = & \left[\left(x_0x_1 + x_{[0,2)}\right)\left(x_2x_3 + x_{[2,4)}\right) + x_{[0,4)}\right] \\ & \times \left[\left(x_4x_5 + x_{[4,6)}\right)\left(x_6x_7 + x_{[6,8)}\right) + x_{[4,8)}\right] \\ & + x_{[0,8)} \end{aligned}$$

To see that this recursive definition defines the same polynomials as the trees T_k, associate the indeterminates $x_{[j,j+1)}$, for $j = 0, \ldots, 2^k - 1$, to the leaves of T_k at depth $2k$, and the indeterminates $x_{[j2^i,(j+1)2^i)}$, for $i = 1, \ldots, k$ and $j = 0, \ldots, 2^{k-i} - 1$, to the leaves at depth $2k - 2i + 1$. Then, it is not difficult to check that T_k computes $P_{(k,0)}$.

We define a *pseudo-degree* of each such polynomial. The pseudo-degree of a polynomial is a set of vectors of nonnegative integers. The pseudo-degree of $x_{[a,b)}$ is the singleton set consisting of a vector of nonnegative integers, whose ith component is 1 if $a \leq i < b$, and 0 otherwise. The pseudo-degree of a sum of two polynomials is the union of the pseudo-degrees of its summands. The pseudo-degree of a product of two polynomials is the set of vectors given by $\vec{V_1} + \vec{V_2}$ (componentwise addition), for all vectors $\vec{V_1}$ in the pseudo-degree of the first multiplicand and $\vec{V_2}$ in the pseudo-degree of the second multiplicand.

The following propositions follow directly from our definition of pseudo-degree.

Proposition 2.1: *Each polynomial $P_{(k,a)}$ is homogeneous. That is, the pseudo-degree of each such polynomial consists of a singleton set.*

Proposition 2.2: *The ith component of the pseudo-degree of $P_{(k,a)}$ is 1 if $a \leq i < a + 2^k$ and 0 otherwise. Further, every monomial of this pseudo-degree in the given indeterminates is represented in $P_{(k,a)}$.*

3. The lower bound

We start with some definitions.

Definition 1: *The* weight *of a computation tree with (maximum) depth i and with a multiplication node at its root is 2^i. The weight of a computation tree with an addition node at its root is the sum of the weights of its two subtrees (the left and the right). A computation tree consisting of a single leaf has weight 1.*

Definition 2: *Let T be a computation tree with a multiplication node at its root. The two trees rooted at the children of the root are called the* major subtrees *of T, and denoted* `Left`(T) *and* `Right`(T).

Definition 3: *Define $\tilde{P}_{(k,a)}$ to be any polynomial containing the same monomials as $P_{(k,a)}$, but with arbitrary positive (nonzero) coefficients.*

Define $D(k)$ as the minimum possible weight of a tree computing $\tilde{P}_{(k,a)}$ for any a. (This weight is independent of a.)

Theorem 3.1:
If $k = 2j$ is even, then $D(k) > 2^{3j-1}$.
If $k = 2j + 1$ is odd, then $D(k) > 3 \cdot 2^{3j-1}$.

It is easy to see that the depth of a tree of weight w is at least $\log w$. Thus we have the following corollary.

Corollary 3.2: *There are polynomials P of length n involving the operations $\{+, \times\}$ and non-negative constants, such that any binary computation tree over the same set of operations and constants computing P has depth at least $1.5 \log_2 n - O(1)$.*

Proof of Theorem 3.1: The proof is by induction on k. Clearly, $D(0) = 1 > \frac{1}{2}$, and $D(1) = 3 > \frac{3}{2}$.

Suppose the first violation comes at $k = 2j$, that is, $D(2j) \leq 2^{3j-1}$ but $D(2j-1) > 3 \cdot 2^{3j-4}$. Consider a computation tree T for some $\tilde{P} \equiv \tilde{P}_{(k,0)}$ with weight at most $D \equiv 2^{3j-1}$. The proof is by contradiction: we identify three different subtrees of T each of which computes some $\tilde{P}_{(2j-1,a)}$ and show that the weight of one of them is at most $\frac{3}{8}D = 3 \cdot 2^{3j-4}$; a contradiction.

We find it useful to denote two specific indeterminates

$$\begin{aligned} L &:= x_{[0,2^{k-1})}, \\ R &= x_{[2^{k-1},2^k)}. \end{aligned}$$

Repeatedly, separate the tree if it has an addition at its root, so that we have expressed $\tilde{P}$ as a sum of polynomials, each of which is computed as a single node or as a tree with a multiplication at its root. The sum of the weights of these trees is at most D.

These trees fall into five classes:

1. N_{LR} is the class of those trees that contain both indeterminates L and R as leaves.
2. N_L is the class of those trees that contain L but not R as a leaf.
3. N_R is the class of those trees that contain R but not L as a leaf.
4. One tree of weight one consisting of the leaf $x_{[0,2^k)}$.
5. N_X is the class of those trees that do not contain any of L, R or $x_{[0,2^k)}$ as leaves.

Denote by $W(N)$ the sum of the weights of the trees in class N. We have

$$\begin{aligned} D &= 2^{3j-1} \geq \\ &\quad W(N_{LR}) + W(N_L) + W(N_R) + W(N_X) + 1 \\ D &= 2^{3j-1} > \\ &\quad W(N_{LR}) + W(N_L) + W(N_R) + W(N_X). \end{aligned}$$

In the following lemmas we prove some properties of the tree T. Without loss of generality we assume that T does not contain multiplications by zero.

Lemma 3.3: *Any polynomial computed in the tree T is a homogeneous polynomial (under our definition of pseudo-degree).*

Proof: Since cancellation is not allowed (and T does not contain multiplications by zero), an inhomogeneous polynomial multiplied by or added to another polynomial will yield an inhomogeneous polynomial. But the final $\tilde{P}$ is homogeneous. □

Since all the computed polynomials are homogeneous, we refer to their pseudo-degree as a vector (rather than a singleton set consisting of a vector).

Definition 4: *The pseudo-degree of a subtree of T is the pseudo-degree of the (homogeneous) polynomial that this subtree computes.*

Lemma 3.4: *Let P and Q be two polynomials whose pseudo-degrees have a common positive component. Then, P and Q may not be multiplied in T.*

Proof: The pseudo-degree of the resulting polynomial would have a component that is at least 2. Since (multiplicative) cancellation is not allowed the value of this component cannot be lowered in subsequent computation. However, the pseudo-degree of P has components at most 1. □

We conclude that the pseudo-degrees of all computed polynomials are zero-one vectors.

Lemma 3.5: *There is a computation tree of minimal weight that does not use constants.*

Proof: If zero is added, the zero and the addition node can be deleted. If a positive constant is added to a nonconstant polynomial, we produce an inhomogeneous intermediate result. If zero is multiplied, the whole subtree can be deleted. If a positive constant is multiplied, the constant and the multiplication node can be deleted, and only the constants in $\tilde{P}$ will be affected (but will remain positive). In any case we still compute some $\tilde{P}_{(k,0)}$ without increasing the weight. □

Henceforth we assume that our tree has no constants.

Lemma 3.6: *For each tree S in N_{LR} the root is a multiplication with one factor having the same pseudo-degree as L (i.e., a vector whose ith component is 1 for $0 \leq i < 2^{k-1}$ and 0 otherwise), and the other factor having the same degree as R.*

Proof: Without loss of generality assume that the leaf L appears in `Left`(S) (and possibly in `Right`(S) as well). This implies that the pseudo-degree of `Left`(S) is at least the pseudo-degree of L. (The partial order relation is the componentwise order.) Since the pseudo-degrees of the two major subtrees cannot have a common positive component, the pseudo-degree of `Right`(S) is at most the pseudo-degree of R. At least one major subtree contains R, and its pseudo-degree is at least the pseudo-degree of R. If the same major subtree `Left`(S) contains both L and R, then the pseudo-degree of `Left`(S) is at least the `pseudo-degree`$(L)+$ `pseudo-degree`$(R) =$ `pseudo-degree`(P), so that the pseudo-degree of $\texttt{Right}(S) = 0$, and $\texttt{Right}(S)$ computes a constant; by minimality, this does not happen. So L appears only in $\texttt{Left}(S)$, and R appears only in $\texttt{Right}(S)$. This implies that the pseudo-degrees of the two major subtrees must be exactly $\texttt{pseudo-degree}(L)$ and $\texttt{pseudo-degree}(R)$, respectively. □

Now, we identify two subtrees of T that compute $\tilde{P}_{(k-1,0)}$. The first one is given by the cofactor of R in $\tilde{P}$ (i.e., the factors that multiply R in all the monomials of $\tilde{P}$ that contain R). Note that by definition this cofactor is some $\tilde{P}_{(k-1,0)}$. The monomials of the cofactor are contained in N_R and the left major subtrees of N_{LR}. Thus we have:

$$\begin{aligned} \frac{1}{2}W(N_{LR}) + W(N_R) &\geq D(k-1) \qquad (1) \\ &> 3 \cdot 2^{3j-4} = \frac{3}{8}D. \end{aligned}$$

(The latter inequality comes from the induction hypothesis.) Similarly, the cofactor of L in $\tilde{P}$ is some $\tilde{P}_{(k-1,2^k-1)}$, which is equivalent to $\tilde{P}_{(k-1,0)}$. Thus we also have

$$\begin{aligned} \frac{1}{2}W(N_{LR}) + W(N_L) &\geq D(k-1) \qquad (2) \\ &> 3 \cdot 2^{3j-4} = \frac{3}{8}D. \end{aligned}$$

Combining with the estimate on $D(k)$, we get

$$\begin{aligned} W(N_X) &< D(k) - (W(N_{LR}) + W(N_L) + W(N_R)) \\ &< \frac{1}{4}D. \end{aligned}$$

Partition the set of trees comprising N_X into two subsets, $N_X = A_X \oplus B_X$. Each tree in N_X belongs wholly to A_X or wholly to B_X. Beyond this, the partition is *arbitrary*. Similarly, partition N_L, N_R, N_{LR}.

For a monomial M with $\texttt{pseudo-degree}(M) \geq \texttt{pseudo-degree}(L)$, let $\texttt{LFact}(M)$ be the factor of M for which $\texttt{pseudo-degree}(\texttt{LFact}(M)) = \texttt{pseudo-degree}(L)$. Similarly, for a monomial M with $\texttt{pseudo-degree}(M) \geq \texttt{pseudo-degree}(R)$, let $\texttt{RFact}(M)$ be the factor of M for which $\texttt{pseudo-degree}(\texttt{Right}(M)) = \texttt{pseudo-degree}(R)$.

To identify the third subtree that computes $\tilde{P}_{(k-1,0)}$ we need the following lemmas.

Lemma 3.7: *For each tree in N_{LR} or N_L (resp. N_R) that computes the polynomial $\sum_i \alpha_i M_i$, we can construct a tree with strictly smaller depth that computes the polynomial $\sum_i \alpha_i \texttt{LFact}(M_i)$ (resp. $\sum_i \alpha_i \texttt{RFact}(M_i)$).*

Proof: We prove only for $\sum_i \alpha_i \texttt{LFact}(M_i)$; the proof for $\sum_i \alpha_i \texttt{RFact}(M_i)$ is analogous. Consider a tree S in $N_{LR} \cup N_L$, and assume without loss of generality that the major subtree containing L is $\texttt{Left}(S)$. Clearly, the pseudo-degree of $\texttt{Left}(S)$ is at least $\texttt{pseudo-degree}(L)$, and the pseudo-degree of $\texttt{Right}(S)$ is no more than $\texttt{pseudo-degree}(R)$. Then, for each M_i, $\texttt{LFact}(M_i)$ is a factor of a monomial in the polynomial computed by $\texttt{Left}(S)$. Eliminate from $\texttt{Left}(S)$ indeterminates whose pseudo-degree is not part of $\texttt{pseudo-degree}(L)$ to achieve the desired polynomial. □

For an arbitrary partition of N_{LR}, N_L, N_R, and N_X, let

$$\begin{aligned} \mathcal{W}_A &= \tfrac{1}{2}W(A_{LR}) + \tfrac{1}{2}W(A_L) + W(A_R) + W(A_X) \\ \mathcal{W}_B &= \tfrac{1}{2}W(B_{LR}) + W(B_L) + \tfrac{1}{2}W(B_R) + W(B_X). \end{aligned}$$

Lemma 3.8: *We can construct a tree that computes some $\tilde{P}_{(k-1,0)}$ whose weight is at most $\max\{\mathcal{W}_A, \mathcal{W}_B\}$.*

Proof: Consider those monomials M such that $\texttt{pseudo-degree}(M) = \texttt{pseudo-degree}(R)$ and M is a factor of some monomial in $\tilde{P}$. The sum of those monomials is some $\tilde{P}_{(k-1,2^k-1)}$. Either all such monomials M occur as factors of monomials in the polynomials computed by the trees in $\mathcal{B} \equiv B_{LR} \oplus B_L \oplus B_R \oplus B_X$, or one such monomial M fails to appear there.

If all these monomials M appear in $\mathcal{B}$, then the right major subtrees of B_{LR} and B_R, together with the trees of B_L and B_X, compute all these monomials. (In all these trees, we eliminate all indeterminates whose pseudo-degree is less or equal to $\texttt{pseudo-degree}(L)$.) Thus, $\texttt{Right}(B_{LR})+\texttt{Right}(B_R)+B_L+B_X$, with possibly some nodes taken out, computes some $\tilde{P}_{(k-1,2^k-1)}$. The weight of this tree is $\mathcal{W}_B$.

If a monomial M fails to appear in $\mathcal{B}$ then its cofactor, which is some $\tilde{P}_{(k-1,0)}$, is computed by $\texttt{Left}(A_{LR})+\texttt{Left}(A_L)+A_R+A_X$, with possibly some nodes taken out. The weight of this tree is $\mathcal{W}_A$. □

We would like to minimize the value of $\max\{\mathcal{W}_A, \mathcal{W}_B\}$. For this we consider the weights of possible partitions of each of the tree classes. Let N be one of $\{N_X, N_L, N_R, N_{LR}\}$ and consider the partition $N = A \oplus B$. Clearly, $W(N) = W(A) + W(B)$. Recall that the weight of each tree in N is a power of two. The restriction that each tree in N must belong wholly either to A or to B, implies a restriction on the possible values of $W(A)$. In the following lemmas we bound the gaps between achievable values of $W(A)$.

Lemma 3.9: *Let w be a nonnegative integer whose binary representation is a subset of the binary representation of $W(N)$ (that is, wherever the binary representation of w has a 1, the binary representation of $W(N)$ also has a 1). Then there is a partition $N = A \oplus B$ with $W(A) = w$, $W(B) = W(N_X) - w$.*

Proof: A set of trees whose total weight is the largest power of two not exceeding $W(N)$ can be achieved by successively adding the largest trees in N until the cumulative weight is that power of two; because larger pieces are added before smaller pieces, this power of two cannot be overshot. Allocate these trees to either A or B, according to the corresponding bit in the binary representation of w. Repeat this process until A and B reach the desired weight. □

Definition 5: *Consider the achievable values of $W(A)$. Let $\texttt{Quantum}(W(N))$ be the largest gap between achievable values.*

Lemma 3.10: *If $2^{j-1} \leq W(N) < 2^j$ then $\texttt{Quantum}(W(N)) \leq 2^j - W(N)$.*

Proof: Compute i, $0 \leq i \leq j-1$, such that $2^j - 2^i \leq W(N) < 2^j - 2^{i-1}$. The binary representation of $W(N)$ has ones in positions corresponding to $2^i, 2^{i+1}, \ldots, 2^{j-1}$ (and zero in the position corresponding to 2^{i-1}). By Lemma 3.9, for each h, $0 \leq h < 2^{j-i}$, the values $h2^i$ and $h2^i + (W(N) - (2^j - 2^i))$ are achievable. The gaps between these weights are $W(N) - (2^j - 2^i)$ and $2^j - W(N)$; the latter is the larger of the two, and serves as a bound on $\texttt{Quantum}(W(N))$. □

Lemma 3.11: *For any $b_2 \leq b_1$, if $w \leq b_1$, $w + W(N) \geq b_2$, and $\texttt{Quantum}(W(N)) \leq b_1 - b_2$, then there is a partition $N = A \oplus B$ such that $b_2 \leq w + W(A) \leq b_1$.*

Proof: If $A = N$ then $w + W(A) \geq b_2$, so there is a choice of A of minimal weight such that $w + W(A) \geq b_2$. The conditions $w \leq b_1$ and $\texttt{Quantum}(W(N)) \leq b_1 - b_2$ imply that with this choice, $w + W(A) \leq b_1$. □

Using the above lemmas we give a partition that minimizes $\max\{\mathcal{W}_A, \mathcal{W}_B\}$. Assume, without loss of generality, that $W(N_L) \geq W(N_R)$. We consider two cases.

Case 1: Suppose $W(N_{LR}) + W(N_L) \geq \frac{3}{4}D$. Then, since $W(N_{LR}) + W(N_L) < D$, and D is a power of two, we know that the binary representation of $\frac{3}{4}D$ is a subset of the representation of $W(N_L) + W(N_{LR})$. By Lemma 3.9, we can choose A_{LR} and A_L, so that $W(A_{LR}) + W(A_L) = \frac{3}{4}D$. We set A_R and A_X to be the empty set, and thus $W(A_R) = W(A_X) = 0$. We get that $\mathcal{W}_A = \frac{3}{8}D$ and $\mathcal{W}_B \leq D - \frac{3}{4}D = \frac{1}{4}D$. Thus $\max\{\mathcal{W}_A, \mathcal{W}_B\} = \frac{3}{8}D$; a contradiction.

Case 2: Suppose $W(N_L) + W(N_{LR}) < \frac{3}{4}D$, so that $\frac{1}{2}W(N_L) + \frac{1}{2}W(N_{LR}) < \frac{3}{8}D$. To make the presentation clearer, we add "dummy" nodes to N_X to achieve the equality:

$$W(N_{LR}) + W(N_L) + W(N_R) + W(N_X) + 1 = D.$$

Clearly, this can be done without loss of generality. From $W(N_R) \leq W(N_L)$, we get $W(N_R) < \frac{1}{2}D$, whence $\frac{1}{2}W(N_{LR}) + \frac{1}{2}W(N_L) + W(N_X) \geq \frac{1}{2}(D - W(N_R) - 1) \geq \frac{1}{4}D$. Furthermore, since $W(N_X) < \frac{1}{4}D$, $\texttt{Quantum}(W(N_X)) \leq \frac{1}{8}D$. Thus, by Lemma 3.11, setting $w = \frac{1}{2}W(N_{LR}) + \frac{1}{2}W(N_L)$, $N = N_X$, $b_1 = \frac{3}{8}D$, and $b_2 = \frac{1}{4}D$, we can select A_X so that

$$\frac{1}{4}D \leq \frac{1}{2}W(N_{LR}) + \frac{1}{2}W(N_L) + W(A_X) \leq \frac{3}{8}D.$$

Setting $A_{LR} = N_{LR}$, $A_L = N_L$, $A_R = \emptyset$, and correspondingly $B_{LR} = B_L = \emptyset$, $B_R = N_R$, we get $\frac{1}{4}D \leq \mathcal{W}_A \leq \frac{3}{8}D$. Since $A_R = B_L = \emptyset$, we have

$$\begin{aligned} \mathcal{W}_A \quad + \quad & \mathcal{W}_B \\ = \quad & \frac{1}{2}(W(N_{LR}) + W(N_L) + W(N_R) + 2W(N_X)) \\ < \quad & \frac{1}{2}(D + W(N_X)) \\ < \quad & \frac{5}{8}D. \end{aligned}$$

Since $\mathcal{W}_A \geq \frac{1}{4}D$, $\mathcal{W}_B < \frac{3}{8}D$. Thus, $\max\{\mathcal{W}_A, \mathcal{W}_B\} \leq \frac{3}{8}D$; a contradiction.

This establishes the induction when $k = 2j$ is even.

Now, consider the case when $k = 2j+1$ is odd. Set $U \equiv 2^{3j-1}$. By the assumption $D(2j+1) \leq 3 \cdot 2^{3j-1} = 3U$. On the other hand, by inductive hypothesis we have $D(2j) > 2^{3j-1} = U$. Again, the proof is by contradiction. We consider the same three different subtrees of T that compute some $\tilde{P}_{(k-1,0)}$ as in the even case, and show that the the weight of one of them is at most $U = 2^{3j-1}$; a contradiction.

From the first two subtrees of T we get the following inequalities which correspond to Inequalities 1,2.

$$\frac{1}{2}W(N_{LR}) + W(N_R) \geq D(k-1) > U, \quad (3)$$

$$\frac{1}{2}W(N_{LR}) + W(N_L) \geq D(k-1) > U. \quad (4)$$

As in the even case the weight of the third tree is at most $\max\{\mathcal{W}_A, \mathcal{W}_B\}$; we show how to minimize this value. Assume, without loss of generality, that $W(N_L) \geq W(N_R)$. Again, we consider two cases.

Case 1: Suppose $2U \leq W(N_{LR}) + W(N_L) < 3U$. By Lemma 3.9, we can choose A_{LR} and A_L, so that $W(A_{LR}) + W(A_L) = 2U$. We set $A_R = A_X = \emptyset$. Then, as before, $\mathcal{W}_A = U$, $\mathcal{W}_B \leq 3U - 2U = U$, and $\max\{\mathcal{W}_A, \mathcal{W}_B\} = U$; a contradiction.

Case 2: Suppose $W(N_{LR}) + W(N_L) < 2U$. Let $d_1 = 2U - (W(N_{LR}) + W(N_L))$. As before, add "dummy" nodes to N_X to achieve the equality:

$$W(N_{LR}) + W(N_L) + W(N_R) + W(N_X) + 1 = 3U.$$

By Inequalities 3,4, we get $W(N_X) < U$. Let $d_2 = U - W(N_X)$, and thus $W(N_R) = d_1 + d_2 - 1$. We consider two subcases.

Case 2.1: Suppose $d_2 \geq d_1$. Then, set $A_{LR} = N_{LR}$, $A_L = N_L$, and $A_R = A_X = \emptyset$, correspondingly set $B_{LR} = B_L = \emptyset$, $B_R = N_R$, and $B_X = N_X$. We get

$$\begin{aligned} \mathcal{W}_A &= \frac{1}{2}W(N_{LR}) + \frac{1}{2}W(N_L) < U, \\ \mathcal{W}_B &= \frac{1}{2}W(N_R) + W(N_X) \\ &= U + \frac{1}{2}(d_1 - 1 - d_2) < U; \end{aligned}$$

a contradiction.

Case 2.2: Suppose $d_2 < d_1$. By Lemma 3.10, $\texttt{Quantum}(W(N_X)) \leq d_2$. Observe that $\frac{1}{2}W(N_{LR}) + \frac{1}{2}W(N_L) < U + \frac{1}{2}d_2$, and

$$\begin{aligned} \frac{1}{2}W(N_{LR}) + \frac{1}{2}W(N_L) + W(N_X) &> \\ \frac{1}{2}W(N_R) + W(N_X) &= \\ U + \frac{1}{2}(d_1 - 1 - d_2) &\geq \\ U &> U - \frac{1}{2}d_2. \end{aligned}$$

Then, by Lemma 3.11, we can select A_X so that

$$\begin{aligned} U - \frac{1}{2}d_2 &\leq \frac{1}{2}W(N_{LR}) + \frac{1}{2}W(N_L) + W(A_X) \\ &\leq U + \frac{1}{2}d_2. \end{aligned}$$

Set $A_{LR} = N_{LR}$, $A_L = N_L$, and $A_R = \emptyset$, correspondingly $B_{LR} = B_L = \emptyset$, $B_R = N_R$. We get $U - \frac{1}{2}d_2 \leq \mathcal{W}_A \leq U + \frac{1}{2}d_2$, and

$$\begin{aligned} \mathcal{W}_A \;+\; \mathcal{W}_B &= \\ &= \frac{1}{2}(W(N_{LR}) + W(N_L) + W(N_R) + 2W(N_X)) \\ &< \frac{3}{2}U + \frac{1}{2}W(N_X) \\ &= 2U - \frac{1}{2}d_2. \end{aligned}$$

This implies that $\mathcal{W}_B \leq U$. If $\mathcal{W}_A \leq U$, then we already obtain a contradiction. Suppose $U < \mathcal{W}_A \leq U + \frac{1}{2}d_2$. Let $\mathcal{A}$ be the set of trees in $\texttt{Left}(A_{LR})$, $\texttt{Left}(A_L)$, and A_X, and let $\mathcal{B}$ be the set of trees in $\texttt{Right}(B_R)$, and B_X. Since the binary representation of $W(\mathcal{A}) = \mathcal{W}_A$ contains the binary representation of U as a subset, then by Lemma 3.9 we can select a subset of the trees in $\mathcal{A}$ achieving the weight U exactly. Remove the remaining trees from $\mathcal{A}$ and add them to the set of trees in $\mathcal{B}$. Now, compute the new values of $\mathcal{W}_A$ and $\mathcal{W}_B$. Clearly, the new value of $\mathcal{W}_A$ is U. To bound the new value of $\mathcal{W}_B$, we have to estimate the effect of the trees added to $\mathcal{B}$. The effect of these trees will be at most doubled, since in the worst case a tree from A_L is moved to B_L. The total weight of the removed trees in $\mathcal{A}$ is at most $\frac{1}{2}d_2$, thus the new total value of $\mathcal{A}$ and $\mathcal{B}$ is at most $\frac{1}{2}d_2$ more than their old total value, which is $2U - \frac{1}{2}d_2$. Thus, the new total value is at most $2U$, and the new value of $\mathcal{W}_B$ is at most U; a contradiction. □

4. Alternating k-ℓ trees

Alternating k-ℓ trees are trees in which nodes at odd levels multiply k subexpressions, and nodes at even levels add ℓ subexpressions. A straightforward implementation of a binary tree computing the arithmetic expression given by an alternating k-ℓ tree will have depth

$$\frac{\lceil \log k \rceil + \lceil \log \ell \rceil}{\log k + \log \ell} \cdot \log n.$$

For integers $k, \ell \geq 2$, the fraction is maximized at $1.292\ldots$ when $k = \ell = 5$. By techniques similar to Shamir and Snir [SS80], we show a matching lower bound for alternating 5-3 trees: Any binary tree computing the arithmetic expression given by an alternating 5-3 tree must have depth at least

$$\frac{\lceil \log 5 \rceil + \lceil \log 3 \rceil}{\log 5 + \log 3} \cdot \log n = \frac{5}{\log 15} \cdot \log n = 1.279 \ldots \log n$$

and this is tight. We are unable to show the corresponding lower bound for alternating 5-5 trees.

Note that this bound is not as good as the bounds achieved in the previous section, however they are *tight* for this specific family of arithmetic expressions.

We merely summarize the results here. The reader is referred to [SS80] for notation.

Lemma 4.1 ((analogous to Lemma 9.3 of [SS80])): *Using the notation of [SS80],*

$$\begin{array}{llll}
\textit{If} & 5^r \leq k < \frac{9}{5} \cdot 5^r & \textit{then} & \\
& t(k) \geq 5r & \textit{and} & T(5r-1) \leq \frac{2}{3} W(k) \\
\textit{If} & \frac{9}{5} \cdot 5^r \leq k < 2 \cdot 5^r & \textit{then} & \\
& t(k) \geq 5r+1 & \textit{and} & T(5r) \leq \frac{2}{3} W(k) \\
\textit{If} & 2 \cdot 5^r \leq k < 3 \cdot 5^r & \textit{then} & \\
& t(k) \geq 5r+1 & \textit{and} & T(5r) \leq \frac{4}{9} W(k) \\
\textit{If} & 3 \cdot 5^r \leq k < 4 \cdot 5^r & \textit{then} & \\
& t(k) \geq 5r+2 & \textit{and} & T(5r+1) \leq \frac{4}{9} W(k) \\
\textit{If} & 4 \cdot 5^r \leq k < 5 \cdot 5^r & \textit{then} & \\
& t(k) \geq 5r+2 & \textit{and} & T(5r+1) \leq \frac{16}{81} W(k)
\end{array}$$

Corollary 4.2: *A computation tree computing an alternating 5-3 expression must have depth at least*

$$\frac{\lceil \log 5 \rceil + \lceil \log 3 \rceil}{\log 5 + \log 3} \cdot \log n = \frac{5}{\log 15} \cdot \log n = 1.279 \ldots \log n.$$

5. Open problems

It seems that the correct lower bound for the binary leaf-addition expression should be $2 \log n - O(1)$. This would close the gap with Kosaraju's upper bound. It is also possible that alternating 5-5 trees have a lower bound of $1.292 \ldots \log n$, which would settle the issue of alternating k-ℓ trees.

Acknowledgements.

We would like to thank Alok Aggarwal for introducing us to the problem, and for many fruitful discussions. We are also grateful to Uri Feige for his help.

References

[BKM73] R. Brent, D. Kuck, and K. Maruyama. Parallel evaluation of arithmetic expressions without division. *IEEE Transactions on Computers*, pages 532–534, 1973.

[BM75] A. Borodin and I. Munro, editors. *The Computational Complexity of Algebraic and Numeric Problems*. American Elsevier Publishing Co., New York, NY, 1975.

[JS82] M. Jerrum and M. Snir. Some exact complexity results for straight-line computations over semirings. *Journal of the ACM*, 29:874–897, 1982.

[KM75] D. Kuck and K. Maruyama. Time bounds on the parallel evaluation of arithmetic expressions. *SIAM Journal on Computing*, 4:147–162, 1975.

[Kos86] S.R. Kosaraju. Parallel evaluation of division free arithmetic expressions. In *Proc. of the 18th ACM Symp. on Theory of Computing*, pages 231–239, May 1986.

[KW88] M. Karchmer and A. Wigderson. Monotone circuits for connectivity require super-logarithmic depth. In *Proc. of the 20th ACM Symp. on Theory of Computing*, pages 539–550, Chicago, IL, May 1988.

[Mil75] W. Miller. Computer search for numerical instability. *Journal of the ACM*, 22(4):512–521, 1975.

[MP76] D.E. Muller and F.P. Preparata. Restructuring of arithmetic expressions for parallel evaluation. *Journal of the ACM*, 23:534–543, 1976.

[Raz85] A.A. Razborov. Lower bounds for the monotone complexity of some boolean functions. *Soviet Math. Dokl.*, 31:354–357, 1985.

[RW90] R. Raz and A. Wigderson. Monotone circuits for matching require linear depth. In *Proc. of the 22nd ACM Symp. on Theory of Computing*, pages 287–292, Baltimore, MD, May 1990.

[Sni91] M. Snir. Size depth trade-offs for monotone arithmetic circuits. *Theoretical Computer Science*, 22(1):85–93, May 1991.

[SS80] E. Shamir and M. Snir. On the depth complexity of formulas. *Math. Systems Theory*, 13:301–322, 1980.

On the Second Eigenvalue and Linear Expansion of Regular Graphs

Nabil Kahale*
MIT Laboratory for Computer Science
Cambridge, MA 02139

Abstract

We investigate the relation between the second eigenvalue and the linear expansion of regular graphs. The spectral method is the best currently known technique to prove lower bounds on the expansion. We improve this technique by showing that the expansion coefficient of linear-sized subsets of a k-regular graph G is at least $\frac{k}{2}\left(1-\sqrt{\max(0,1-\frac{4k-4}{\lambda_1(G)^2})}\right)^-$, where $\lambda_1(G)$ is the second largest eigenvalue of the graph. In particular, the linear expansion of Ramanujan graphs, which have the property that the second largest eigenvalue is at most $2\sqrt{k-1}$, is at least $(k/2)^-$. This improves upon the best previously known lower bound of $3(k-2)/8$. For any integer k such that $k-1$ is prime, we explicitly construct an infinite family of k-regular graphs G_n on n vertices whose linear expansion is $\frac{k}{2}$ and such that $\lambda_1(G_n) \leq 2\sqrt{k-1}+o(1)$. Since the graphs G_n have asymptotically optimal second eigenvalue, this essentially shows that $(k/2)$ is the best bound one can obtain using the second eigenvalue method.

1 Introduction

Given an undirected k-regular graph $G=(V,E)$ and a subset X of V, we define the expansion of X to be the ratio $\frac{|N_G(X)|}{|X|}$, where $N_G(X)=\{w \in V : \exists v \in X,\ (v,w) \in E\}$ is the set of neighbors of X. Graphs whose all subsets of size lying in a given range have large expansion are called expander graphs.

Expander graphs are widely used in Computer Science, in areas ranging from parallel computation [2, 5, 14, 19, 22] to complexity theory and cryptography [1, 6, 10, 23]. The range of the subsets whose expansion is relevant and the magnitude of the expansion needed depends on the nature of the application. For example, in the design of the AKS sorting circuit, we use expanders of constant degree such that subsets of size at most $\epsilon|V|$ have expansion at least $\frac{1-\epsilon}{\epsilon}$, where ϵ is a fixed positive constant. The depth of the resulting network is proportionnal to the degree of the expander. In other applications, like the construction of non-blocking networks in [5], we need a family of fixed degree uneven bipartite expanders where the expansion of linear-sized subsets is greater than $\frac{k}{2}$. Indeed, an expansion greater than $k/2$ guarantees that a constant fraction of any linear-sized subset have *unique neighbors*, which is crucial in the construction in [5].

It is known that random regular graphs are good expanders. For example, for any $\beta < k-1$, there exists a constant α such that, with high probability, all the subsets of a random k-regular graph of size at most αn have expansion at least β. However, the explicit contruction of expander graphs is much more difficult. The first constructions [16, 9, 11] use techniques from group representation theory and harmonic analysis to prove the desired expansion properties.

The best currently known method to calculate lower bounds on the expansion in polynomial time relies on analysing the second eigenvalue of the graph. It is known that all the eigenvalues of the adjacency matrix $A(G)$ of G are real. Let $\lambda_i(G)$ denote the i-th largest eigenvalue of G. We have $\lambda_0(G)=k$ and $\lambda(G)=\max(\lambda_1(G),|\lambda_{n-1}(G)|) \leq k$, with equality iff G is not connected or bipartite. The relation between the expansion and the spectrum of a graph was introduced by Tanner [21] who showed that, for any subset X of a k-regular graph

$$|N_G(X)| \geq \frac{k^2|X|}{\lambda^2+(k^2-\lambda^2)\frac{|X|}{n}} \qquad (1)$$

The smaller λ is, the higher expansion this bound implies. However, since $\liminf \lambda(G_n) \geq 2\sqrt{k-1}$ for any family of k-regular graphs G_n [3], the best asymptotic expansion coefficient one can get by Tanner's result is $\frac{k}{4}+o(k)$. This bound is achieved by Ramanujan graphs. By definition, a Ramanujan graph is a connected k-regular graph whose eigenvalues $\neq \pm k$ are

*Supported by the Defense Advanced Research Projects Agency under Contracts N00014-87-K-0825 and N00014-89-J-1988, the Air Force under Contract AFOSR-89-0271, and the Army under Contract DAAL-03-86-K-0171.

0-8186-2900-2/92 $3.00 © 1992 IEEE

at most $2\sqrt{k-1}$ in absolute value. Infinite families of Ramanujan graphs have been explicitly constructed in [15, 17] when $k-1$ is prime. The linear expansion of Ramanujan graphs was recently [12] improved to $3(k-2)/8$.

We define the linear expansion of a family of k-regular graphs G_n on n vertices to be the best lower bound on the expansion of subsets of size up to αn, where α is an arbitrary small positive constant. Our aim is to calculate the best linear expansion one can prove using the second eigenvalue technique. In this paper, we prove that the expansion of linear subsets of a k-regular graph G is at least $\frac{k}{2}\left(1-\sqrt{\max(0,1-\frac{4k-4}{\lambda_1(G)^2})}\right)$. In particular, linear-sized subsets of Ramanujan graphs have expansion at least $\frac{k}{2}^-$. On the other hand, for any integer k such that $k-1$ is a prime congruent to 1 modulo 4, and for any function m of n such that $m=o(n)$, we explicitly construct an infinite family of k-regular graphs G_n on n vertices such that $\lambda(G_n) \leq 2\sqrt{k-1}(1+o(1))$ and G_n contains a subset of size $2m$ with expansion $k/2$. Since such a family has asymptotically optimal second eigenvalue, this essentially shows that $k/2$ is the best bound lower bound on the linear expansion one can obtain by the second eigenvalue method. However, it is still an open question whether there exists a family of Ramanujan graphs with linear expansion $k/2$. As a biproduct of our techniques, we obtain known bounds on the number of edges in an induced subgraph of a regular graph, we give a simple proof of Tanner's inequality, and we establish a lower bound of $2\sqrt{k-1}(1+O(\log_k^{-2} n))$ on the second eigenvalue of any k-regular graph. A previous lower bound of $2\sqrt{k-1}(1+O(\log_k^{-1} n))$ was proven in [18] and improved to $2\sqrt{k-1}(1+O(\log_k^{-2} n))$ in [8]. Our results provide an efficient way to test that the expansion of linear sized subsets of random graphs is at least $\frac{k}{2}+O(k^{3/4}\log^{1/2} k)$. As an application of the improved expansion of Ramanujan graphs, we can build explicit selection networks of asymptotic size $(3+\epsilon)n\log_2 n$, for any $\epsilon>0$, improving on the bound $6n\log_2 n$ that was previously known. As defined in [19], a selection network is a network of comparators that classifies a set of n numbers, where n is even, into two subsets of $n/2$ numbers such that any element in the first set is smaller than any element in the second set.

2 Notation, definitions, and background

Throughout the paper, $G=(V,E)$ will denote an undirected connected graph on a set V of vertices. If G is regular, it is easy to see that $|N_G(X)| \geq |X|$ for any subset X. Let $L^2(V)$ denote the set of real valued functions on V and $L_0^2(V)=\{f \in L^2(V);\ \sum_{v\in V} f(v)=0\}$. As usual, we define the scalar product of two vectors f and g of $L^2(V)$ by

$$f\cdot g=\sum_{v\in V} f(v)g(v),$$

and the euclidean norm of a vector f by $||f||=\sqrt{f\cdot f}$. We denote the adjacency matrix of G by $A(G)$, or simply by A if there is no risk of confusion. $A(G)$ is the 0-1 $n\times n$ matrix whose (i,j) entry is equal to 1 iff $(i,j)\in E$. If we consider $f\in L^2(V)$ as a row vector, we have

$$(Af)(v)=\sum_{(v,w)\in E} f(w)$$

A defines a self-adjoint operator since $\forall f,g \in L^2(V)$ we have

$$(Af)\cdot g = f\cdot(Ag) = \sum_{(v,w)\in E} f(v)g(w) \qquad (2)$$

The *girth* of G, denoted by $c(G)$, is the length of the shortest cycle in G. For any subset W of V, we denote by χ_W the characteristic vector of W:

$$\chi_W(v)=\begin{cases} 1 & \text{if } v\in W \\ 0 & \text{otherwise}\end{cases}$$

For any matrix M with real eigenvalues, we denote by $\lambda_i(M)$ the i-th largest eigenvalue of M. We also denote $\lambda_i(A(G))$ by $\lambda_i(G)$. If X and Y are two subsets of a graph $G=(V,E)$, then $e(X,Y)=|\{(u,v)\in X\times Y \cap E\}|$. If $Z_0,\ldots,Z_t$ is a sequence of non-empty subsets of V, we denote by $R^{\{Z_0,Z_1,\ldots,Z_t\}}$ the set of real valued functions on $\{Z_0,Z_1,\ldots,Z_t\}$. We define $\Phi(Z_0,Z_1,\ldots,Z_t)$ to be the linear mapping in $R^{\{Z_0,Z_1,\ldots,Z_t\}}$ whose matrix in the canonical basis $(\chi_{\{Z_0\}},\ldots,\chi_{\{Z_t\}})$ is the $(t+1,t+1)$ matrix with entry (i,j) equal to $\frac{e(Z_i,Z_j)}{|Z_i|}$. $\Phi(Z_0,Z_1,\ldots,Z_t)$ can be viewed as the adjacency matrix of the weighted directed graph on $R^{\{Z_0,Z_1,\ldots,Z_t\}}$ where the weight of the edge (Z_i,Z_j) is equal to the average number of neighbors that a node in Z_i has in Z_j.

3 Lower bound on the expansion

Lemma 1 *Let $G = (V, E)$ be a graph and let $Z_0, \ldots, Z_t$ be a sequence of non-empty disjoint subsets of V. For $0 \leq i \leq t$, we have $\lambda_i(G) \geq \lambda_i(\Phi)$, where $\Phi = \Phi(Z_0, Z_1, \ldots, Z_t)$.*

Proof Define the scalar product $<,>$ on $R^{\{Z_0,\ldots,Z_t\}}$ by

$$< r, s >= \sum_{i=0}^{t} |Z_i| r(Z_i) s(Z_i).$$

Let ψ be the linear mapping from $R^{\{Z_0,\ldots,Z_t\}}$ to $L^2(V)$ that mapps $\chi_{\{Z_i\}}$ to χ_{Z_i}.

Claim 1 *For any $r, s \in R^{\{Z_0,\ldots,Z_t\}}$, we have $\psi(r) \cdot \psi(s) =< r, s >$.*

Proof Since both sides of the above equality are bilinear in r and s, it suffices to show that the equality holds when r and s are elements of the canonical basis of $R^{\{Z_0,\ldots,Z_t\}}$. But $\psi(\chi_{\{Z_i\}}) \cdot \psi(\chi_{\{Z_j\}}) = \chi_{Z_i} \cdot \chi_{Z_j} = \delta_{i,j}|Z_i| =< \chi_{\{Z_i\}}, \chi_{\{Z_j\}} >$. ■

Claim 2 *For any $r, s \in R^{\{Z_0,\ldots,Z_t\}}$, we have $\psi(r) \cdot A\psi(s) =< r, \Phi s >$.*

Proof The claim follows from bilinearity and the equalities $\psi(\chi_{\{Z_i\}}) \cdot A\psi(\chi_{\{Z_j\}}) = \chi_{Z_i} \cdot A\chi_{Z_j} = e(Z_i, Z_j) =< \chi_{\{Z_i\}}, \Phi\chi_{\{Z_j\}} >$. ■

This implies in particular that Φ defines a self-adjoint operator with respect to the product $<,>$ and so the eigenvalues of Φ are real. Using the elementary theory of quadratic forms and the injectivity of ψ, it follows that

$$\begin{aligned}
\lambda_i(\Phi) &= \max_{L} \min_{r \in L-\{0\}} \frac{< r, \Phi r >}{< r, r >} \\
&= \max_{L} \min_{f \in \psi(L)-\{0\}} \frac{f \cdot Af}{||f||^2} \\
&\leq \max_{L'} \min_{f \in L'-\{0\}} \frac{f \cdot Af}{||f||^2} \\
&= \lambda_i(G),
\end{aligned}$$

where L and L' range respectively over the subspaces of $R^{\{Z_0,\ldots,Z_t\}}$ and $L^2(V)$ of dimension $i+1$. ■

Similarly, one can prove that $\lambda_{n-1-i}(G) \leq \lambda_{t-i}(\Phi)$ for $0 \leq i \leq t$, but we will not need this inequality in the proof of Theorem 1.

Lemma 2 *Let $G = (V, E)$ be a graph and $X_{-1} = \emptyset, X_0, X_1, \ldots, X_t$ be a sequence of subsets of V such that, for $0 \leq i \leq t-1$, the degree of any element of X_i is equal to k, $N_G(X_i) \subseteq X_{i+1}$ and $|X_{i-1}| < |X_i|$. If the eigenvalues of the adjacency matrix of G are $\delta_0, \delta_1, \ldots, \delta_t$, with $|\delta_0| \geq |\delta_1| \geq \cdots \geq |\delta_t|$, then $|\delta_i|$ is greater than or equal to the i-th largest eigenvalue of the matrix $M_{t+1}(k; \rho_0, \rho_1, \ldots, \rho_{t-1})$ equal to*

$$\begin{pmatrix}
0 & k & 0 & 0 & \cdots & 0 \\
\rho_0 & 0 & k-\rho_0 & 0 & \cdots & 0 \\
0 & \rho_1 & 0 & k-\rho_1 & \ddots & \vdots \\
\vdots & \ddots & \ddots & \ddots & \ddots & 0 \\
0 & \cdots & 0 & \rho_{t-2} & 0 & k-\rho_{t-2} \\
0 & 0 & \cdots & 0 & \rho_{t-1} & 0
\end{pmatrix},$$

where $\rho_i = k\frac{|X_i|-|X_{i-1}|}{|X_{i+1}|-|X_{i-1}|}$.

Proof Note that $X_i \subseteq N^2(X_i) \subseteq X_{i+2}$. Consider the *cover graph* G_c of G defined on $V_c = V \times \{0, 1\}$ and where $((u, l), (v, m)) \in V_c \times V_c$ is an edge iff $(u, v) \in E$ and $l \neq m$. The adjacency matrix of G_c is the tensor product of $A(G)$ and $A(K_2)$, and so the eigenvalues of G_c are the pairwise products of the eigenvalues of $A(G)$ and $A(K_2)$, namely $\lambda_0, \ldots, \lambda_{n-1}$ and $-\lambda_0, \ldots, -\lambda_{n-1}$, hence $\lambda_i(G_c) = |\delta_i|$ for $0 \leq i \leq n-1$. For $0 \leq i \leq t$, let Y_i be the subset of V_c defined by $Y_i = X_i \times \{(i \bmod 2)\}$. Then, for $0 \leq i \leq t-1$, the degree of any element of Y_i is equal to k, $N_{G_c}(Y_i) \subseteq Y_{i+1}$ and $Y_{i-1} \neq Y_{i+1}$. Now, we apply lemma 1 to G_c and the subsets $Z_i = Y_i - Y_{i-2}$, for $0 \leq i \leq t$. The Z_i's are non-empty and disjoint since Y_i is a strict subset of Y_{i+2} and $Y_i \cap Y_j = \emptyset$ if $i \not\equiv j \pmod 2$. Note that $|Y_i| = |X_i|$ and $|Z_i| = |X_i| - |X_{i-2}|$. For $0 \leq i \leq t-1$, we have $e(Z_i, Z_{i+1}) = e(Y_i - Y_{i-2}, Y_{i+1} - Y_{i-1}) = e(Y_i, Y_{i+1} - Y_{i-1}) - e(Y_{i-2}, Y_{i+1} - Y_{i-1})$. But $e(Y_{i-2}, Y_{i+1} - Y_{i-1}) = 0$ since $N(Y_{i-2}) \subseteq Y_{i-1}$. So $e(Z_i, Z_{i+1}) = e(Y_i, Y_{i+1}) - e(Y_i, Y_{i-1}) = k|Y_i| - k|Y_{i-1}| = k(|X_i| - |X_{i-1}|)$. Finally, $N(Z_i) \subseteq N(Y_i) \subseteq Y_{i+1} = Z_{i+1} \cup Y_{i-1}$. On the other hand, $N(Y_{i-3}) \subseteq Y_{i-2}$ and so there are no edges between Z_i and Y_{i-3} (by convention $Y_{-2} = Y_{-3} = \emptyset$.) Hence $N(Z_i) \subseteq Z_{i+1} \cup Z_{i-1}$ and $e(Z_i, Z_j) = 0$ if $|i - j| \neq 1$. Therefore $\Phi_{G_c}(Z_0, Z_1, \ldots, Z_t) = M_{t+1}(k; \rho_0, \rho_1, \ldots, \rho_{t-1})$. This concludes the proof. ■

Lemma 3 *[12] Let W be a subset of a k-regular graph G and H the subgraph induced on W. Then $\lambda_0(H) \leq \lambda_1(G) + (k - \lambda_1(G))\frac{|W|}{n}$.*

Lemma 4 *Let $G = (V, E)$ be a k-regular connected graph and $X_0, X_1, \ldots, X_t$ a sequence of non-empty* *subsets of V such that, for $0 \le i \le t-1$, we have $N_G(X_i) \subseteq X_{i+1}$. For $l \ge 1$, $\lambda_1(G) + 4k^l \frac{|X_t|}{n}$ is greater than the largest eigenvalue of the matrix $M_{t+l}(k; \rho_0, \rho_1, \ldots, \rho_{t-1}, \underbrace{1, \ldots, 1}_{l-1 \text{ times}})$.*

Proof Since the largest eigenvalue of the matrix M_{t+l} is at most k, we can assume without loss of generality that $|X_t|k^{l-1} \le n$. We recursively construct subsets X_i of G, for $t < i \le t+l-1$, such that $N_G(X_{i-1}) \subseteq X_i$ and $\rho_{i-1} = 1$. Let $i \in \{t, \ldots, t+l-2\}$ and assume that we constructed $X_{t+1}, \ldots, X_i$ such that $\rho_j = 1$ for $t \le j < i$. The condition $\rho_j = 1$ implies that $|X_{j+1}| = k|X_j| - (k-1)|X_{j-1}| \le k|X_j|$, and so $|X_i| \le k^{i-t}|X_t| \le \frac{n}{k}$. On the other hand, $e(X_i, V - X_{i-1}) = e(X_i, V) - e(X_i, X_{i-1}) = k|X_i| - k|X_{i-1}|$ since G is k-regular and $N_G(X_{i-1}) \subseteq X_i$. Therefore, $|N_G(X_i) - X_{i-1}| \le k|X_i| - k|X_{i-1}|$. But $|V - X_{i-1}| = n - |X_{i-1}| \ge k|X_i| - k|X_{i-1}|$. Therefore, there exists a subset X_{i+1} of V containing $N_G(X_i)$ and such that $|X_{i+1} - X_{i-1}| = k|X_i| - k|X_{i-1}|$. Since G is k-regular connected and since $N_G(X_{i-1}) \subseteq X_i$ and $|X_i| < n/2$, we have $|X_{i-1}| < |X_i|$ and so ρ_i is well defined and equal to 1.

Similarly, $|X_{j-1}| < |X_j|$ for $0 \le j < t$ (we define X_{-1} to be the empty set). Now, we apply lemma 2 to the induced graph H on $W = X_{t+l-2} \cup X_{t+l-1}$ and the subsets $X_0, \ldots, X_{t+l-1}$. From the theory of matrices with non-negative entries [20], we know that $\lambda_0(H)$ is the largest eigenvalue of H in absolute value. Hence, $\lambda_0(H) \ge \lambda_0(M_{t+l}(k; \rho_0, \rho_1, \ldots, \rho_{t-1}, 1, \ldots, 1))$. By lemma 3, however, $\lambda_0(H) \le \lambda_1(G) + (k - \lambda_1(G))\frac{|W|}{n} < \lambda_1(G) + 4\frac{|X_t|k^l}{n}$ since $|\lambda_1| < k$ and $|W| \le 2k^{l-1}|X_t|$.
■

Lemma 5 *The eigenvalues of the matrix $M_{l+1}(k; \rho_0, 1, \ldots, 1)$ are $2\sqrt{k-1}\cosh\theta$, where θ ranges over the solutions (in the complex domain) to the equation*

$$((4k-4)\cosh^2\theta - k\rho_0)s_l(\theta) = 2(k-\rho_0)\cosh(\theta)s_{l-1}(\theta),$$

and $s_i(\theta)$ is the analytical extension of the function $\frac{\sinh(i\theta)}{\sinh(\theta)}$ over the domain of complex numbers. If the largest eigenvalue of $M_{l+1}(k; \rho_0, 1, \ldots, 1)$ is at most $2\sqrt{k-1}\cosh(\theta')$, with $\theta' \ge 0$, then $\rho_0 \le (1+e^{2\theta'})(1+O(\frac{1}{l}))$.

Proof For ease of notations, we assume that $\sinh(\theta) \ne 0$. The case $\sinh(\theta) = 0$ can be treated by replacing $\sinh(i\theta)$ by $s_i(\theta)$ in the proof. First, we note that any real number λ can be written as $2\sqrt{k-1}\cosh(\theta)$, where θ is a complex number. Such λ is an eigenvalue of $M_{l+1}(k; \rho_0, 1, \ldots, 1)$ with eigenvector $(r_0, \ldots, r_l)$ iff

$$\lambda r_0 = k r_1 \quad (3)$$
$$\lambda r_1 = \rho_0 r_0 + (k-\rho_0) r_2 \quad (4)$$
$$\lambda r_i = r_{i-1} + (k-1) r_{i+1} \text{ for } 2 \le i \le l-1 \quad (5)$$
$$\lambda r_l = r_{l-1} \quad (6)$$

From Eqs. 5 and 6, we see that, up to a constant factor, $r_i = (k-1)^{\frac{-i}{2}}\sinh((l+1-i)\theta)$ for $i \ge 1$. Eqs. 3 and 4 imply that $\lambda^2 r_1 = \rho_0 k r_1 + \lambda(k-\rho_0)r_2$, which reduces to the equation in the lemma.

Claim 3 *If θ is a nonnegative real and $l \ge 1$, then*

$$\frac{l-1}{l}e^{-\theta} \le \frac{\sinh((l-1)\theta)}{\sinh(l\theta)} \le e^{-\theta} \quad (7)$$

Proof To prove inequality 7, we observe that

$$\begin{aligned} e^{-\theta} - \frac{\sinh((l-1)\theta)}{\sinh(l\theta)} &= \frac{e^{-(l-1)\theta} - e^{-(l+1)\theta}}{e^{l\theta} - e^{-l\theta}} \\ &= e^{-l\theta}\frac{\sinh(\theta)}{\sinh(l\theta)} \\ &\le \frac{e^{-\theta}}{l}, \end{aligned}$$

since $\sinh(l\theta) \ge l\sinh(\theta)$. ■

By setting $h(\theta') = (\lambda'^2 - k\rho_0)\sinh(l\theta') - 2(k-\rho_0)\cosh\theta'\sinh((l-1)\theta')$, where $\lambda' = 2\sqrt{k-1}\cosh\theta'$, we see that $h(\theta')$ goes to $+\infty$ as θ' goes to $+\infty$, and so the condition in the lemma implies that $h(\theta') \ge 0$. Using Eq. 7, we get

$$\begin{aligned} (\lambda'^2 - k\rho_0) &\ge 2(k-\rho_0)\cosh(\theta')\frac{\sinh((l-1)\theta')}{\sinh(l\theta')} \\ &= 2(k-\rho_0)\cosh(\theta')e^{-\theta'}(1+O(\frac{1}{l})) \end{aligned}$$

Therefore,

$$\rho_0(k - 2e^{-\theta'}\cosh\theta') \le (\lambda'^2 - 2ke^{-\theta'}\cosh\theta')(1+O(\frac{1}{l})) \quad (8)$$

since $e^{-\theta'}\cosh\theta' \le 1$, $k \ge 3e^{-\theta'}\cosh\theta'$ and $\lambda'^2 \ge 8k/3$. By factoring $2\cosh\theta'$ in the righthand side of Eq. 8 and noting that

$$\begin{aligned} (2k-2)\cosh\theta' - ke^{-\theta'} &= k(2\cosh\theta' - e^{-\theta'}) - 2\cosh\theta' \\ &= ke^{\theta'} - 2\cosh\theta', \end{aligned}$$

we see that Eq. 8 implies $\rho_0 \le 2\cosh(\theta')e^{\theta'}(1+O(\frac{1}{l}))$.
■

Theorem 1 *If $G = (V, E)$ is k-regular and $\tilde{\lambda} = \max(\lambda_1(G), 2\sqrt{k-1})$, then for any non-empty subset X of size at most $k^{-1/\epsilon}|V|$,*

$$\frac{|N_G(X)|}{|X|} \geq \frac{k}{2}\left(1 - \sqrt{1 - \frac{4k-4}{\tilde{\lambda}^2}}\right)(1 + O(\epsilon)),$$

where the constant behind the O is a small absolute constant.

Proof Let $\tilde{\lambda} = 2\sqrt{k-1}\cosh(\theta)$, where $\theta \geq 0$. We apply lemma 4 with $t = 1$, $X_0 = X$ and $X_1 = N_G(X)$ and $l = \lfloor \frac{1}{2\epsilon} \rfloor$. Let $\lambda' = \tilde{\lambda} + 4k^l \frac{|X_t|}{n} = 2\sqrt{k-1}\cosh(\theta')$, where $\theta' \geq \theta \geq 0$. Since $|X_1| \leq k|X| \leq k^{1-\frac{1}{\epsilon}} n$, we have $|X_1| k^l \leq k^{1-\frac{1}{2\epsilon}} n$ and $\lambda' - \tilde{\lambda} \leq 4k^{1-\frac{1}{2\epsilon}} = O(\epsilon^2)$. This implies that $\lambda' = \tilde{\lambda}(1 + O(\epsilon))$ and $\cosh\theta' - \cosh\theta = O(\epsilon^2)$. Using the inequality $(x-y)^2 \leq 2(\cosh x - \cosh y)$ valid for $x \geq y \geq 0$, we see that $\theta' - \theta = O(\epsilon)$. Lemma 5 then implies

$$\rho_0 \leq (1 + e^{2\theta'})(1 + O(\epsilon)) = (1 + e^{2\theta})(1 + O(\epsilon)).$$

Hence

$$\frac{|N_G(X)|}{|X|} = \frac{k}{\rho_0} \geq \frac{k}{2e^\theta \cosh\theta}(1 + O(\epsilon)).$$

Using the equalities $e^{-\theta} = \cosh\theta - \sinh\theta = \cosh\theta - \sqrt{\cosh^2\theta - 1}$, we get

$$\frac{1}{e^\theta \cosh\theta} = 1 - \sqrt{1 - \frac{1}{\cosh^2\theta}} = 1 - \sqrt{1 - \frac{4k-4}{\tilde{\lambda}^2}}$$

This concludes the proof. ∎

Corollary 1 *If G is k-regular on n vertices, then $\lambda_1(G) \geq 2\sqrt{k-1}(1 + O(\log_k^{-2} n))$.*

Proof We apply lemma 4 with X_0 consisting of a single vertex, $t = 0$ and $l = \lfloor \frac{\log_k n}{2} \rfloor$. From the theory of non-negative matrices [20], we know that the largest eigenvalue of the matrix $M_l(k; 1, \ldots, 1)$ is no smaller than the largest eigenvalue of the same matrix where the $(1,2)$ entry is replaced by $k-1$. But a calculation similar to the one in lemma 5 shows that the largest eigenvalue of this matrix is $\cos(\frac{\pi}{l+1})$. Hence $\lambda_1(G) + 4\frac{k^l}{n} \geq 2\sqrt{k-1}\cos(\frac{\pi}{l+1})$. We conclude the proof by noting that $\frac{k^l}{n} = O(\log_k^{-2} n))$ and $\cos(\frac{\pi}{l+1}) = 1 + O(\log_k^{-2} n)$. ∎

As we mentionned in the introduction, the lower bound in Corollary 1 was independently obtained in [8].

4 A family of "almost" Ramanujan graphs with expansion $k/2$

Lemma 6 *Given $k \geq 3$, a real $\theta > 0$ and $\lambda = 2\sqrt{k-1}\cosh\theta$, let $S_l(a,b)$ be the sequence defined for $l \geq 0$ by $S_0(a,b) = a$, $S_1(a,b) = b$, $\lambda S_1(a,b) = 2S_0(a,b) + (k-2)S_2(a,b)$ and the recurrence relation*

$$\lambda S_l(a,b) = S_{l-1}(a,b) + (k-1)S_{l+1}(a,b), \text{ for } l \geq 2, \quad (9)$$

where a and b are real numbers. If $b_1 + \ldots + b_k = \lambda a$, then $\forall l \geq 1$,

$$\sum_{i=1}^{k} S_l{}^2(a, b_i) \geq (k-1)^{1-l}\cosh^2((l-1)\theta)\sum_{i=1}^{k} b_i{}^2$$

Proof First we show that, for $l \geq 0$,

$$S_{l+1}(k,\lambda) = 2(k-1)^{\frac{1-l}{2}}\left(\cosh\theta\cosh l\theta + \tfrac{k}{k-2}\sinh\theta\sinh l\theta\right) \quad (10)$$

We first notice that the two sequences $(k-1)^{-l/2}\cosh(l\theta)$ and $(k-1)^{-l/2}\sinh(l\theta)$, form a basis to the set of sequences satisfying the recurrence 9. Therefore, to prove Eq. 10, it suffices to show that the two sides are equal for $l = 0$ and $l = 1$. The case $l = 0$ is straightforward. For $l = 1$, we have

$$\begin{aligned} S_2(k,\lambda) &= \frac{\lambda S_1(k,\lambda) - 2S_0(k,\lambda)}{k-2} \\ &= \frac{\lambda^2 - 2k}{k-2} \\ &= \frac{4(k-1)\cosh^2\theta - 2k(\cosh^2\theta - \sinh^2\theta)}{k-2}, \end{aligned}$$

which is equal to the righthand side of Eq. 10.

Since $S_l(a,b)$ is a linear function of (a,b), we have $S_l(a,b) = c_l a + d_l b$, where $c_l = S_l(1,0)$ and $d_l = S_l(0,1)$. Therefore,

$$\begin{aligned} \sum_{i=1}^{k} S_l{}^2(a,b_i) &= \sum_{i=1}^{k}(c_l{}^2 a^2 + 2c_l d_l a b_i + d_l{}^2 b_i^2) \\ &= (kc_l + 2\lambda d_l)c_l a^2 + d_l{}^2\sum_{i=1}^{k} b_i^2 \end{aligned}$$

But, using the same reasoning as before, we know that $c_l = (k-1)^{1-\frac{l}{2}} c_2 \frac{\sinh(l-1)\theta}{\sinh\theta} \leq 0$ since $c_2 = \frac{-2}{k-2}$ and so $kc_l + 2\lambda d_l = 2S_l(k,\lambda) - kc_l \geq 0$. On the other hand, $k\sum_{i=1}^{k} b_i^2 \geq \lambda^2 a^2$ by Cauchy-Schwarz. Hence,

$$\sum_{i=1}^{k} S_l{}^2(a,b_i) \geq \left((kc_l + 2\lambda d_l)c_l\frac{k}{\lambda^2} + d_l{}^2\right)\sum_{i=1}^{k} b_i^2$$

But $(kc_l + 2\lambda d_l)c_l\frac{k}{\lambda^2} + {d_l}^2 = (\frac{k}{\lambda}c_l + d_l)^2 = \frac{{S_l}^2(k,\lambda)}{\lambda^2}$. We conclude by noting that $S_l(k,\lambda) \geq 2(k-1)^{1-\frac{l}{2}}\cosh\theta\cosh(l-1)\theta$. ■

Lemma 7 *If $G = (V, E)$ is k-regular on n vertices, for any $f \in L^2(V)$, we have*

$$f \cdot Af \leq \lambda_1(G)||f||^2 + \frac{k}{n}\Big(\sum_{v\in V} f(v)\Big)^2$$

Proof Let $\bar{f} = \frac{f\cdot\chi_V}{n}\chi_V$ be the orthogonal projection of f on the space spanned by the constant vector χ_V. Then $f_0 = f - \bar{f}$ is the orthogonal projection of f on $L_0^2(V)$. We have $Af = A\bar{f} + Af_0 = k\bar{f} + Af_0$, and so $f \cdot Af = k||\bar{f}||^2 + f_0 \cdot Af_0$ since $\bar{f} \cdot Af_0 = A\bar{f} \cdot f_0 = k\bar{f} \cdot f_0 = 0$. But $||\bar{f}||^2 = \frac{(f\cdot\chi_V)^2}{n^2}||\chi_V||^2 = \left(\sum_{v\in V} f(v)\right)^2/n$, and $f_0 \cdot Af_0 \leq \lambda_1(G)||f_0||^2 \leq \lambda_1(G)||f||^2$ since $||f||^2 = ||f_0||^2 + ||\bar{f}||^2$. ■

Theorem 2 *For any integer k such that $k-1$ is prime, we can explicitly construct an infinite family of k-regular graphs G_n on n vertices whose linear expansion is $\frac{k}{2}$ and such that $\lambda_1(G_n) \leq 2\sqrt{k-1}(1 + 2^{\frac{\log^2\log n}{\log_k^2 n}})$.*

Proof From [15] and [17], we know that we can explicitly construct an infinite family of bipartite Ramanujan graphs H_n on n vertices whose girth is at least $(4/3 + o(1))\log_{k-1} n$. Let $H_n = (V, E)$ be an element of the family, $u \in V$ a vertex of H_n and $t = \lfloor\frac{c(H_n)}{2}\rfloor - 2$. For $0 \leq l \leq t+1$, let V_l denote the set of nodes in H_n at distance l from v. Let $u_1, \ldots, u_k$ be the neighbors of u and let $v_1, \ldots, v_k$ be k vertices of V_2 such that $(u_i, v_i) \in E$. The subgraph of H_n induced on the subset $\bigcup_{l=0}^{t+1} V_l$ is a tree rooted at u since it is connected and contains no cycle. We will denote by T_i the subtree rooted at u_i minus the subtree rooted at v_i. Let u' and v' be two elements not belonging to V. Consider the k-regular graph $G_{n+2} = (V', E')$, where $V' = V \cup \{u', v'\}$ and $E' = E \cup \bigcup_{i=1}^k \{(u', u_i), (u_i, u'), (v', v_i), (v_i, v')\} - \bigcup_{i=1}^k \{(u_i, v_i), (v_i, u_i)\}$. Figure 1 shows the graph G_{n+2} in the neighborhood of u in the case $k = 3$. For shorthand, we denote $A(G_{n+2})$ by A' and $\lambda_1(A')$ by λ_1. Assume that $\lambda_1 > 2\sqrt{k-1}$ (otherwise we are done), and let $\lambda_1 = 2\sqrt{k-1}\cosh\theta$, with $\theta > 0$. Let $g \in L_0^2(V')$ be an eigenvector corresponding to λ_1. Since u and u' have the same neighbors in G_{n+2} and

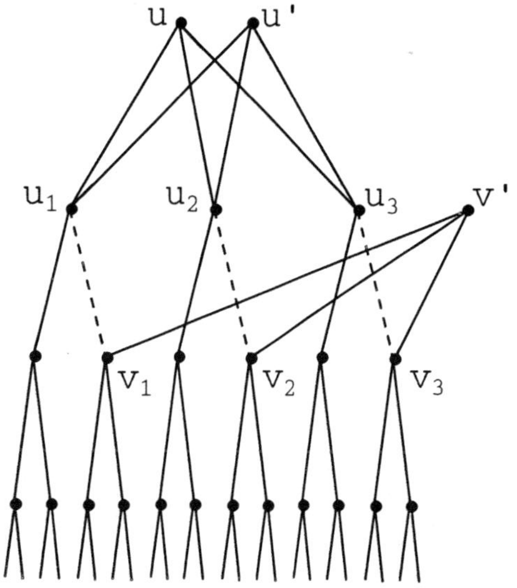

Figure 1: The graph G_{n+2} in the neighborhood of u in the case $k = 3$. The dotted edges are those belonging to $E - E'$.

$\lambda_1 \neq 0$, we have $g(u) = g(u')$. Let f be the element of $L^2(V)$ that coincides with g on V. By Eq. 2, we have

$$\begin{aligned}
\lambda_1||g||^2 &= g \cdot A'g \\
&= f \cdot A(H_n)f - 2\sum_{i=1}^k g(u_i)g(v_i) + \\
&\quad 2\sum_{i=1}^k g(u')g(u_i) + 2\sum_{i=1}^k g(v')g(v_i) \\
&\leq f \cdot A(H_n)f + \sum_{i=1}^k (g(u_i)^2 + g(v_i)^2) + \\
&\quad 2\lambda_1 g(u')^2 + 2\lambda_1 g(v')^2 \qquad (11)
\end{aligned}$$

In the third inequality, we used the equation $(A'g)(u') = \lambda_1 g(u')$ and $(A'g)(v') = \lambda_1 g(v')$. Note that $\sum_{w\in V} f(w) = -g(u') - g(v')$ since $g \in L_0^2(V')$. Using lemma 7, we get

$$\begin{aligned}
f \cdot A(H_n)f &\leq \lambda_1(H_n)||f||^2 + \frac{k}{n}(g(u') + g(v'))^2 \\
&\leq 2\sqrt{k-1}(||g||^2 - g(u')^2 - g(v')^2) + \\
&\quad \frac{2k}{n}(g(u')^2 + g(v')^2) \\
&\leq 2\sqrt{k-1}||g||^2,
\end{aligned}$$

for sufficiently large n. Combining this with Eq. 11, we obtain

$$\begin{aligned}\lambda_1||g||^2 \leq & 2\sqrt{k-1}||g||^2 + \sum_{i=1}^{k}(g(u_i)^2 + g(v_i)^2) + \\ & 2\lambda_1 g(u')^2 + 2\lambda_1 g(v')^2 \\ \leq & 2\sqrt{k-1}(||g||^2 + 2\sum_{i=1}^{k}(g(u_i)^2 + g(v_i)^2)) \quad (12)\end{aligned}$$

The second inequality follows from

$$g(u')^2 = \frac{1}{\lambda_1^2}\Big(\sum_{i=1}^{k} g(u_i)\Big)^2 \leq \frac{k}{\lambda_1^2}\sum_{i=1}^{k} g(u_i)^2$$

and a similar relation corresponding to v'. For $1 \leq i \leq k$ and $1 \leq l \leq t+1$, let $\mu_{i,0} = g(u)$ and $\mu_{i,l} = \sum_{w \in T_i \cap V_l} g(w)/|T_i \cap V_l|$. For any $w \in T_i \cap V_l$, with $l \geq 2$, we know that $\lambda_1 g(w)$ is equal to the sum of the values of g on the parent of w and on the $k-1$ children of w in T_i. By summing up these equalities, we see that $\lambda_1 \mu_{i,l} = \mu_{i,l-1} + (k-1)\mu_{i,l+1}$. Similarly, $\lambda_1 \mu_{i,1} = 2\mu_{i,0} + (k-2)\mu_{i,2}$. Hence $\mu_{i,l} = S_l(g(u), g(u_i))$, for $1 \leq l \leq t+1$, where S_l is the function defined in lemma 6. Therefore, using Cauchy-Schwarz,

$$\begin{aligned}||g||^2 &\geq \sum_{i=1}^{k}\sum_{w \in T_i \cap V_{t+1}} g(w)^2 \\ &\geq (k-2)(k-1)^{t-1}\sum_{i=1}^{k} S_{t+1}{}^2(g(u), g(u_i)) \\ &\geq \frac{1}{2}\cosh^2(t\theta)\sum_{i=1}^{k} g(u_i)^2.\end{aligned}$$

Similarly, we can prove the inequality $||g||^2 \geq \frac{1}{2}\cosh^2(t\theta)\sum_{i=1}^{k} g(v_i)^2$ by using a slightly modified version of lemma 6. Combining this with Eq. 12 yields

$$\cosh\theta \leq 1 + \frac{8}{\cosh^2 t\theta} \quad (13)$$

Using the inequalities $\cosh\theta \geq 1 + \frac{\theta^2}{2}$ and $\cosh t\theta \geq e^{t\theta}/2$, we see from Eq. 13 that $\theta = O(e^{-t\theta})$ and $\log\theta \leq -t\theta + O(1)$. Hence $\theta \leq \frac{\log t}{t}$ for sufficiently large n. Finally, $\lambda_1 = 2\sqrt{k-1}\cosh\theta = 2\sqrt{k-1}(1 + \frac{\theta^2}{2}(1+o(1))) \leq 2\sqrt{k-1}(1 + 2\frac{\log^2\log n}{\log_k^2 n})$ since $t \geq (\frac{2}{3} + o(1))\log_k n$. Theorem 1 implies that the linear expansion of the family G_n is at least $\frac{k}{2}$. Since the subset $\{u, u'\}$ has k neighbors, this bound is tight. ■

If $k-1$ is a prime congruent to 1 modulo 4, we know from [15] that there exists an infinite family of non-bipartite k-regular Ramanujan graphs with girth at least $\frac{2}{3}(1+o(1))\log_{k-1} n$. By doing the same construction as in Theorem 2, we obtain k-regular graphs whose second largest eigenvalue *in absolute value* is $2\sqrt{k-1}(1+o(1))$ and linear expansion $k/2$. Moreover, by adding nodes at regions of the graph at sufficiently large distance from each other, we can construct for any $m = m(n) = o(n)$ a family of k-regular graphs whose second largest eigenvalue in absolute value is $2\sqrt{k-1}(1+o(1))$ and containing a subset of size $2m$ with expansion $k/2$. The proof of these two statements is very similar to the proof of Theorem 2.

5 Examples and applications

1. **Number of edges in an induced subgraph.** Let $G = (V, E)$ be a k-regular graph on n vertices and Z_0 a proper subset of V. We apply lemma 1 and the remark following it with $t = 1$ and $Z_1 = V - Z_0$. Note that $\lambda_0(G) = \lambda_0(\Phi) = k$ since $\sum_{j=0}^{t} e(Z_i, Z_j) = e(Z_i, V) = k|Z_i|$. Therefore, $k + \lambda_1(\Phi) = \text{trace}(\Phi) = \frac{e(Z_0,Z_0)}{|Z_0|} + \frac{e(Z_1,Z_1)}{|Z_1|}$. But $e(Z_1, Z_1) = k|Z_1| - e(Z_1, Z_0) = k|Z_1| - k|Z_0| + e(Z_0, Z_0)$, and so $|Z_0||Z_1|(k + \lambda_1(\Phi)) = ne(Z_0, Z_0) + k|Z_1||Z_0| - k|Z_0|^2$. The inequality $|\lambda_1(\Phi)| \leq \lambda$ then becomes $|e(Z_0, Z_0) - k\frac{|Z_0|^2}{n}| \leq \lambda|Z_0|(1 - \frac{|Z_0|}{n})$. Note that this inequality is also true in the case $Z_0 = \emptyset$ or $Z_0 = V$. This result has already been established in [4].

2. **Tanner's inequality.** Again, we assume that $G = (V, E)$ is a k-regular graph on n vertices. Let X be a proper subset of V. We apply lemma 2 with $t = 3$, $X_0 = X$, $X_1 = N_G(X)$ and $X_2 = X_3 = V$. We have $\rho_0 = k\frac{|X|}{|X_1|}$, $\rho_1 = k\frac{|X_1|-|X|}{|V|-|X|}$ and $\rho_2 = k$. As before, k is an eigenvalue of $M_4(k; \rho_0, \rho_1, k)$. Since the (i, j) entry of this matrix is null if $i \equiv j \pmod 2$, the other eigenvalues of $M_4(k; \rho_0, \rho_1, k)$ are $\{\sigma, -\sigma, -k\}$, with $|\sigma| \leq \lambda(G)$. But $\det(M_4(k; \rho_0, \rho_1, k)) = k^2\rho_0(k - \rho_1) = k^2\sigma^2$, and so $\rho_0(k - \rho_1) \leq \lambda(G)^2$. A simple calculation shows that this implies Eq. 1. Note that we implicitly assumed that $N_G(X)$ is a proper subset of V. However, we can directly check that Eq. 1 holds if $N_G(X) = V$.

3. **Random regular graphs.** In [7], it was shown that, if k is even, then for "most" k-regular graphs G, we have $\lambda_1(G) \leq 2\sqrt{k-1} + O(\log k)$. Therefore, using Theorem 1, we see that for "most" regular graphs, we can prove *in polynomial time* that linear sized subsets have expan-

sion at least

$$\frac{k}{2}(1-\sqrt{1-\frac{4k-4}{(2\sqrt{k-1}+O(\log k))^2}}),$$

which is equal to $\frac{k}{2} - O(k^{3/4}\log^{1/2} k)$.

4. **Selection networks.** We can use Theorem 1 to build explicit selection networks of small size. A selection network is a network of comparators that classifies a set of n numbers, where n is even, into two subsets of $n/2$ numbers such that any element in the first set is smaller than any element in the second set. In [19], a probabilistic construction of a selection network is given using an asymptotic upper bound of $2n\log_2 n$ comparators. Also, an upper bound slightly less than $6n\log_2 n$ is shown by a deterministic construction. Using Theorem 1, we can [13] construct selection networks of asymptotic size $(3+\epsilon)n\log_2 n$, for any $\epsilon > 0$.

6 Acknowledgments

The author is indebted to Tom Leighton for many helpful discussions. He also thanks Noga Alon, Fan Chung, Persi Diaconis, Joel Friedman and Nicholas Pippenger for useful conversations.

References

[1] M. Ajtai, J. Komlós, and E. Szemerédi. Deterministic simulation in logspace. In *STOC87*.

[2] M. Ajtai, J. Komlós, and E. Szemerédi. Sorting in $c\log n$ parallel steps. *Combinatorica*, 3:1–19, 1983.

[3] N. Alon. Eigenvalues and expanders. *Combinatorica*, 6(2):83–96, 1986.

[4] N. Alon and F. R. K. Chung. Explicit construction of linear sized tolerant networks. *Discrete Mathematics*, 72:15–19, 1988.

[5] S. Arora, T. Leighton, and B. Maggs. On-line algorithms for path selection in a non-blocking network. In *STOC90*.

[6] M. Bellare, O. Goldreich, and S. Goldwasser. Randomness in interactive proofs. In *FOCS90*.

[7] J. Friedman. On the second eigenvalue and random walks in random regular graphs. *Combinatorica*, 11(4):331–362, 1991.

[8] J. Friedman. Some geometric aspects of graphs and their eigenfunctions. Technical report, Princeton University, Department of Computer science, 1991.

[9] O. Gabber and Z. Galil. Explicit constructions of linear sized superconcentrators. *J. Comput. System Sci.*, 22(3):407–420, 1981.

[10] O. Goldreich, R. Impagliazzo, L. Levin, R. Venkatesan, and D. Zuckerman. Security preserving amplification of hardness. In *FOCS90*.

[11] S. Jimbo and A. Maruoka. Expanders obtained from affine transformations. *Combinatorica*, 7(4):343–355, 1987.

[12] N. Kahale. Better expansion for Ramanujan graphs. In *FOCS91*, pages 398–404.

[13] N. Kahale and N. Pippenger. *Personal Communication.*

[14] T. Leighton and B. Maggs. Fast algorithms for routing around faults on multibutterflies. In FOCS89.

[15] A. Lubotzky, R. Phillips, and P. Sarnak. Ramanujan graphs. Combinatorica, *8(3):261–277, 1988.*

[16] G. A. Margulis. Explicit constructions of concentrators. Problemy Peredači Informacii, *9(4):71–80, 1973.*

[17] G. A. Margulis. Explicit group-theoretical constructions of combinatorial schemes and their applications to the design of expanders and concentrators. Problemy Peredači Informacii, *24(1):51–60, 1988.*

[18] A. Nilli. On the second eigenvalue of a graph. Discrete Mathematics, *91:207–210, 1991.*

[19] N. Pippenger. Selection networks. Technical Report 90-12, The University of British Columbia, Department of Computer science, 1990.

[20] E. Seneta. Non-negative matrices and markov chains. *Springer-Verlag, 1981.*

[21] R. M. Tanner. Explicit construction of concentrators from generalized n-gons. SIAM J. Algebraic Discrete Methods, *5(3):287–294, 1984.*

[22] E. Upfal. An $O(\log n)$ deterministic packet routing scheme. In STOC89.

[23] L. Valiant. Graph theoretic properties in computational complexity. J. Comput. System Sci., *13:278–285, 1976.*

Quadratic Dynamical Systems (Preliminary Version)[†]

Yuri Rabinovich[‡] Alistair Sinclair[§] Avi Wigderson[¶]

Abstract

The main purpose of this paper is to promote the study of computational aspects, primarily the convergence rate, of nonlinear dynamical systems from a combinatorial perspective.

We identify the class of symmetric quadratic systems. Such systems have been widely used to model phenomena in the natural sciences, and also provide an appropriate framework for the study of genetic algorithms in combinatorial optimisation. We prove several fundamental general properties of these systems, notably that every trajectory converges to a fixed point.

We go on to give a detailed analysis of a quadratic system defined in a natural way on probability distributions over the set of matchings in a graph. In particular, we prove that convergence to the limit requires only polynomial time when the graph is a tree. This result demonstrates that such systems, though nonlinear, are amenable to quantitative analysis.

1 Introduction

1.1 Dynamical systems

Many natural phenomena can be described by dynamical systems in Euclidean space. In such a description there is a fixed set of types, one for each dimension, and a point in the system (often called a *state* or a *population*) specifies how many elements of each type exist at a given time instant. The system evolves under a fixed map f, which attempts to capture the underlying phenomenon. We mention below a few examples; for a detailed treatment see, e.g., [5].

In Physics, the system might describe the behaviour of gas molecules in a container. Here the types correspond to, say, velocity values, and the state p specifies how many molecules of each type there are at a certain point in time. The map f includes the Newtonian laws so as to produce from each state p a new state $f(p)$ in the next time step, under some assumption about the spatial distribution of the molecules [10]. (One can also easily define a continuous-time analogue of this system). This view of dynamics is quite general and can in principle be used to describe a wide range of physical phenomena.

In Biology, the types may be the genotypes of some species (specified by the values of their genes). A population p is then simply the number of individuals of each type. The map f determines the population in the next generation according to a fixed set of rules that includes the genetic outcome of mating, the survival capacity of different types, random mutations etc. [9]. A completely different biological example describes the ecological coexistence of different species. Here the types are species, p specifies the number of creatures of each type, and f describes the outcome of their interaction: for example, one species may be the food supply of the other, or compete with it for the same resource [5].

The basic object of study in any such system is the *trajectory* of a point p in the state space, i.e., the sequence of points $p, f(p), f(f(p)), \ldots$. There are many questions one can ask about these objects, each of which has given rise to a major research area: for example, there are geometric and topological studies of the structure of the limit points or sets (attractors) of trajectories and of the initial points converging to them; ergodic and measure-theoretic questions on the recurrence of visits of trajectories to subsets of the

[†]Part of this work was done while the first and second authors were visiting DIMACS, the Center for Discrete Mathematics and Theoretical Computer Science at Princeton and Rutgers Universities

[‡]Department of Computer Science, Hebrew University, Jerusalem, Israel 91904. E-mail: yuri@cs.huji.ac.il

[§]Department of Computer Science, University of Edinburgh, Scotland. Current address: International Computer Science Institute, 1947 Center Street, Berkeley CA 94704. E-mail: sinclair@icsi.berkeley.edu

[¶]Hebrew University, Jerusalem and Princeton University. E-mail: avi@cs.huji.ac.il. Supported in part by NSF Grant CCR-8920505

0-8186-2900-2/92 $3.00 © 1992 IEEE

state space; "chaos"-type questions on the sensitivity of the trajectory and its limit to small perturbations in the initial point; and computational questions regarding the time it takes for transient behaviour to die out and the system to reach its limiting behaviour. This last type of question is of central importance both to understanding the phenomenon captured by the dynamical system and in computer simulations of the system, which are often performed as a means of realising complex limiting behaviour. Our main interest is in the last type of question, though when studying it one often needs to tackle the other questions as well.

The simplest dynamical systems arise from linear maps f. The ubiquitous example of a linear system is a Markov chain, viewed as acting on the simplex of probability distributions over types. (When f preserves the "size" of the population, it is often more convenient to take the state space to be just these probability distributions rather than all of Euclidean space; we shall adopt this view throughout.) It is well known that, if f is irreducible and aperiodic, there is a unique limit point (or stationary distribution) which attracts all initial points. Moreover, there is a beautiful spectral theory that explains how the second largest eigenvalue of the matrix representing f controls the rate of convergence of any trajectory to the limit. Although originally motivated by the study of natural phenomena, this theory has proved extremely useful in many mathematical disciplines. In particular, there has been a recent upsurge of interest in algorithmic applications of artificial Markov chains in Computer Science, spurred by the development of new tools for analysing the rate of convergence. Examples include probabilistic algorithms for approximate counting [4, 8], pseudo-random number generators [1] and "simulated annealing" type algorithms for combinatorial optimisation [7, 8, 14].

For nonlinear systems, in stark contrast, there are almost no global convergence rate bounds available (but see [2]). We now identify a class of nonlinear systems known as symmetric quadratic systems, and argue that they capture several natural and artificial phenomena for which obtaining convergence rate information is computationally important. Then we describe our results, which demonstrate that these systems are sometimes amenable to quantitative analysis.

1.2 Symmetric quadratic operators

We illustrate this class of systems by its oldest example, namely the (space homogeneous) kinetic gas model of Maxwell. Gas molecules interact by means of elastic collisions that change the distribution of their velocities. Thus the types are velocity vectors in $\mathbb{R}^3$, and when two types i, j collide they disappear and are replaced by a *random* pair k, l which preserves momentum and energy. (In classical mechanics the resulting pair would be uniquely determined, but statistical mechanics makes the outcome random by postulating a uniform distribution on all possible relative positions of the balls at collision.) Note that in this system the event that the pair i, j produces k, l has the same probability as its time reversal, in which k, l produces i, j. We call systems having this property *symmetric*. Moreover, it is clear that the map f defining this system is *quadratic*, i.e. $f(p)$ is a quadratic function of p, since outcomes depend only on pairwise collisions.

Many other physical theories assume pairwise interactions and hence define quadratic systems. Moreover, the outcomes of local interactions in physical systems are often defined in a symmetric fashion. In genetics, the feature of pairwise interaction (of parents) to produce the next generation is almost universal. Here symmetry is less common, but exists in simple genetic models where, for example, a child randomly picks each gene from either the father's or the mother's DNA (as can be seen by introducing a "complementary" child who makes the opposite choices).

The importance of understanding the evolution of natural systems of this kind, and in particular the computational issue of the rate at which they approach limiting behaviour, is well known. Further motivation for the study of these questions is provided by a family of artificial systems called genetic algorithms [6], which have recently gained acceptance as a general heuristic for solving combinatorial optimisation problems. The Appendix explains why similar questions about limit points and convergence rate arise when trying to understand these heuristics and estimate their efficiency.

1.3 Summary of results

We consider only discrete-time, finite-dimensional systems. For any symmetric quadratic system of this form, we prove that every trajectory approaches a fixed point. This is a strong property not shared by general, asymmetric systems. We go on to give a characterisation of all fixed points, and describe all the linear invariants of the system. Our main analytical tool is the fact that entropy is strictly increasing along any non-trivial trajectory. This is a discrete analogue of Boltzmann's famous H-Theorem, which he proved when studying the kinetic gas model described above. Although such results, and sometimes much more, are known for certain special cases studied in Physics, our setting is more general and focuses on the combinatorial structure of the system.

Next we define a natural quadratic system on probability distributions over the matchings in a graph, motivated both by its inherent combinatorial interest and its application to algorithms for generating matchings at random from certain probability distributions. We give a complete analysis of this system when the underlying graph is a tree. The analysis is in two parts. The first part gives an explicit closed-form formula for the limit distribution in terms of simple parameters of the initial distribution. The second, and more significant part is a proof that the system always converges to its limit in time that depends only polynomially on the size of the tree. This is a strong result in view of the fact that the number of matchings in the tree is in general exponentially large. Moreover, it appears to be the first bound of its kind for a complex nonlinear system defined on combinatorial structures.

2 Definitions and basic properties

In this section we formally define the dynamical systems of interest to us and establish some fundamental general results about their behaviour.

2.1 Symmetric quadratic operators

For convenience we shall adopt throughout terminology appropriate to the genetic applications mentioned in the Introduction, though the systems we describe have more general applicability. We consider a quadratic operator, which we shall refer to as a "mating" operator, of the following form. Let $\mathcal{N}$ be a finite set of "types", with $|\mathcal{N}| = N$. For each quadruple $(i,j,k,l) \in \mathcal{N}^4$, let β_{ijkl} denote the probability that, in a mating between the two "parent" types i and j, the two types k and l are produced as "offspring". Since any mating must have a definite outcome, we always have $\sum_{k,l\in\mathcal{N}} \beta_{ijkl} = 1$ for all $i,j \in \mathcal{N}$.

We will adopt the view that the order of parents and offspring is not significant, so that β is symmetric in i and j, and in k and l, i.e., $\beta_{ijkl} = \beta_{jikl} = \beta_{ijlk}$. We also impose the further symmetry condition that $\beta_{ijkl} = \beta_{klij}$; this means that the mating operation is locally reversible. If β satisfies all the above symmetry conditions, we call it *symmetric*. As indicated in the Introduction, the operators encountered in many applications of interest are symmetric so this does not constitute a severe restriction. Moreover, as we shall see presently, symmetric operators have much useful structure which we will be able to exploit. Finally, we call β *aperiodic* if $\beta_{ijij} > 0$ for all $i,j \in \mathcal{N}$. Aperiodicity is a technical requirement, again satisfied in most applications, that simplifies the statement of our results.

Now let $p = (p_i)$ be a probability distribution on $\mathcal{N}$, which we shall often refer to as a "population." Given a symmetric β as above, we define the population $p \times p$ by

$$(p \times p)_l = \sum_{i,j,k\in\mathcal{N}} p_i p_j \beta_{ijkl} \qquad \forall l \in \mathcal{N}. \qquad (1)$$

(In the notation of the Introduction, the map f is defined by $f(p) = p \times p$.) It should be clear that these equations describe a mating process in which two parents are selected independently at random from the population p and mated to form random offspring according to the distribution specified by β. The operator $\times$ (or, equivalently, β) defines a (deterministic) quadratic mapping from the simplex of probability distributions over $\mathcal{N}$ to itself.

By repeated application of this operator, we can define a time-dependent process (or a dynamical system) in the obvious way: denote by $p(0)$ the population at time 0, and for all $t \in \mathrm{N}$ define $p(t+1) = p(t) \times p(t)$. We shall refer to the sequence of points $p(0), p(1), p(2), \ldots$ as the *trajectory* of the point $p(0)$.

Remark: We are focusing on systems described by *pairwise* interactions, as these capture the majority of natural examples. However, it should be clear that our results can be generalised in a straightforward manner to the case of m-ary interactions (in which m parents produce m offspring) for any fixed m, provided the notion of symmetry is suitably extended. □

2.2 Attractors (limit points): existence and structure

As explained earlier, it is our main aim here to study the evolution of $p(t)$ with time. The obvious first question to ask is whether $p(t)$ tends to some limit point π as $t \to \infty$. Clearly, since β is continuous any such population π must be a fixed point, i.e., $\pi \times \pi = \pi$; we call such a population *stationary*. The fact that a limit point exists for any symmetric, aperiodic operator β and any initial population $p(0)$ is not obvious. In order to establish this and other properties of our systems, we study the *entropy* of the population. For a probability distribution p on any set S, define the entropy

$$H(p) = -\sum_{i\in S} p_i \lg p_i.$$

Theorem 1 *For a symmetric, aperiodic operator β, the entropy of any non-stationary population is strictly increased by mating; i.e., if p is not stationary then $H(p \times p) > H(p)$.*

Proof: It is helpful to work with probability distributions on the set $\mathcal{N}^2$ of ordered pairs of types. For any population p on $\mathcal{N}$, define the probability distribution $\widetilde{p}$ on $\mathcal{N}^2$ by $\widetilde{p}_{ij} = p_i p_j$. The relation between the entropies of p and $\widetilde{p}$ is easily seen to be

$$H(\widetilde{p}) = 2H(p). \tag{2}$$

We observe first that a single application of the quadratic operator β can be decomposed into two stages: a linear operation on the pair distribution $\widetilde{p}$, followed by a recomputation of the singleton probabilities. The first stage is defined by a linear operator B as follows:

$$(B\widetilde{p})_{kl} = \sum_{ij \in \mathcal{N}^2} \beta_{ijkl}\widetilde{p}_{ij} \qquad \forall\, kl \in \mathcal{N}^2.$$

In the second stage, we compute $(p \times p)_l$ for each $l \in \mathcal{N}$ by

$$(p \times p)_l = \sum_{k \in \mathcal{N}} (B\widetilde{p})_{kl}.$$

It is immediate from the definition (1) of the operator $\times$ that these two stages do indeed correctly compute $p \times p$. We now proceed to show that, if p is not stationary, each of the two stages causes the entropy of the pair distribution to increase; by (2) this will imply the theorem. I.e., we will show that

$$2H(p) = H(\widetilde{p}) < H(B\widetilde{p}) \leq H(\widetilde{p \times p}) = 2H(p \times p).$$

Consider the first stage. Note that $B = (\beta_{ij,kl})$ is the transition matrix of a Markov chain on $\mathcal{N}^2$, since $\sum_{k,l \in \mathcal{N}} \beta_{ijkl} = 1$ for all $i,j \in \mathcal{N}$. By the assumption on the symmetry and aperiodicity of β, B is symmetric and aperiodic. Now partition the state space $\mathcal{N}^2$ into classes of communicating states, i.e., equivalence classes under the equivalence relation $\sim$ defined by $ij \sim kl$ iff $B^n_{ij,kl} > 0$ for some natural number n, where B^n is the nth power of B. Each of these classes behaves under B as an independent Markov chain, which is symmetric and aperiodic and thus has the uniform distribution as its unique stationary distribution. It is well known (see, e.g., [13, Section 5.6]) that such a Markov chain causes the entropy of any non-uniform probability distribution to increase strictly on every step. This in turn implies that the entropy of the entire distribution over $\mathcal{N}^2$ increases under B, i.e., $H(B\widetilde{p}) > H(\widetilde{p})$, unless $\widetilde{p}$ is uniform on all the classes.

We turn now to the second stage. The effect of this stage on the pair distribution is to transform it from $B\widetilde{p}$ into $\widetilde{p \times p}$. Note that this operation preserves the new marginals $q_l = \sum_k (B\widetilde{p})_{kl}$ but makes the components k,l independent, i.e., $(\widetilde{p \times p})_{kl} = q_k q_l$. It is a routine matter to check that this latter distribution has maximum entropy among all distributions on $\mathcal{N}^2$ with the given marginals q_l, so $H(\widetilde{p \times p}) \geq H(B\widetilde{p})$ as claimed.

Finally, we have seen that the increase in entropy in the first stage is strict unless $\widetilde{p}$ is uniform on each communicating class. But in this case we have $B\widetilde{p} = \widetilde{p}$, which implies by the definition of the second stage that $p \times p = p$, so p is stationary. Thus we get a strict increase in entropy unless p is stationary. □

Remark: As mentioned in the Introduction, Theorem 1 is a discrete version of a classical result in statistical mechanics known as Boltzmann's H-Theorem, which asserts that the entropy of an ideal gas increases monotonically with time (see, e.g., [10]). Here the interaction probabilities β_{ijkl} have values that describe the collisions of pairs of gas molecules. The H-Theorem is generally proved for continuous time systems and assumed to hold for discrete time without rigorous justification. Theorem 1 gives a rigorous proof in the discrete-time setting and makes clear the essential combinatorial properties required of β. □

Theorem 1 is a powerful analytical tool. We use it first to prove the following fundamental result, which states that every trajectory converges to some fixed point (stationary population). To make this statement precise, for distributions p,q on a finite set S define the variation distance

$$\|p - q\| = \tfrac{1}{2}\sum_{i \in S} |p_i - q_i| = \max_{A \subseteq S} |p(A) - q(A)|.$$

We will write $p(t) \to \pi$ to denote the fact that $\|p(t) - \pi\| \to 0$ as $t \to \infty$.

Theorem 2 *For any symmetric, aperiodic operator β and any initial population $p(0)$, there exists a stationary population π such that $p(t) \to \pi$.*

Proof: Consider the trajectory $p(0), \ldots, p(t), \ldots$, and for each $l \in \mathcal{N}$ define the function $\Delta p_l(t) = p_l(t+1) - p_l(t)$. We may expand Δp_l as

$$\Delta p_l(t) = \sum_{ijk} \big(p_i(t)p_j(t) - p_k(t)p_l(t)\big)\beta_{ijkl}, \tag{3}$$

where we have used (1) to rewrite $p_l(t+1)$ and symmetry of β to rewrite $p_l(t)$.
Now define the function $h(t) = H(p(t))$. By Theorem 1, $h(t)$ increases monotonically with t, and since it is evidently bounded above (by $\lg N$) it must tend to some finite limit as $t \to \infty$. Examining the proof of Theorem 1, and in particular the definition of the Markov chain B in the first stage, one sees that the increase in entropy in going from p to $p \times p$ is bounded below by some function of the quantities $|\tilde{p}_{ij} - \tilde{p}_{kl}| = |p_i p_j - p_k p_l|$ for i,j,k,l such that ij and kl belong to the same communicating class. More precisely, for any $\epsilon > 0$ there exists a $\delta = \delta(\epsilon) > 0$ such that $\max\{|p_i p_j - p_k p_l| : \beta_{ijkl} > 0\} \geq \epsilon$ implies that $H(p \times p) - H(p) \geq \delta$. Hence the fact that $h(t)$ converges to a limit implies that $p_i(t)p_j(t) - p_k(t)p_l(t) \to 0$ as $t \to \infty$ for all such i,j,k,l. But by (3) this implies that $\Delta p_l(t) \to 0$ for all $l \in \mathcal{N}$, which ensures that $p(t)$ converges in variation distance. □

Remarks: (a) Theorem 2 is a very special property that depends crucially on the symmetry of the operator β. It is well known that asymmetric quadratic systems need not converge to a point but may exhibit more complex behaviour such as cycling [5].
(b) The proof of Theorem 2 can be used to extract crude quantitative information on the rate of convergence. The idea of using entropy to obtain global convergence rate bounds for the Boltzmann equation has recently been explored in [2].
(c) Equation (3) above indicates how to define an analogous system in continuous time: simply replace $\Delta p_l(t)$ on the left-hand side by the derivative dp_l/dt. This makes little essential difference to our results. □

A further corollary of Theorem 1 is the following elegant characterisation of the stationary populations.

Theorem 3 *For a symmetric, aperiodic operator β, a population p is stationary iff it satisfies*

$$p_i p_j = p_k p_l \qquad \forall ijkl \text{ with } \beta_{ijkl} > 0. \qquad (4)$$

Proof: The fact that (4) is a sufficient condition for p to be stationary follows immediately from equation (3) in the proof of Theorem 2. To see that (4) is also necessary, recall from the proof of Theorem 1 that p cannot be stationary unless the pair distribution $\tilde{p}_{ij} = p_i p_j$ is a stationary distribution for the Markov chain B defined in the first stage (otherwise we get a strict increase in entropy). But this happens iff $\tilde{p}$ is uniform on each communicating class, which is precisely condition (4). □

Note that the characterisation of Theorem 3 is purely structural, i.e., it depends only on which of the β_{ijkl} are non-zero and not on their numerical values.

Theorem 3 confirms that in general there will be a continuum of stationary populations, corresponding to the set of solutions of the system of equations (4). Each stationary population will have a certain domain of attraction in the simplex. The question then arises of how to determine, for a given initial population, the particular stationary population which attracts it; such a stationary population must exist by Theorem 2. The answer is to look for *invariants* of the operator β, i.e., functions ι on populations that satisfy $\iota(p \times p) = \iota(p)$ for all p.

The following family of linear invariants plays a crucial role in our systems. We say that a population p has *full support* if $p_i > 0$ for all $i \in \mathcal{N}$.

Theorem 4 *Let π be any stationary population with full support. Then the function $\iota_\pi = \sum_{l \in \mathcal{N}} (\lg \pi_l)\, p_l$ is an invariant.*

Proof: Let $\alpha_l = \lg \pi_l$, and note from Theorem 3, since π is stationary, that

$$\alpha_i + \alpha_j = \alpha_k + \alpha_l \qquad \forall ijkl \text{ with } \beta_{ijkl} > 0. \qquad (5)$$

Now using (3) we may write

$$\iota_\pi(p \times p) - \iota_\pi(p) = \sum_{ijkl} \alpha_l (p_i p_j - p_k p_l) \beta_{ijkl}$$
$$= \tfrac{1}{4} \sum_{ijkl} (\alpha_k + \alpha_l - \alpha_i - \alpha_j)(p_i p_j - p_k p_l) \beta_{ijkl},$$

where we have used the symmetry properties of β. But (5) implies that every term in this sum is zero, so ι_π is indeed invariant. □

Remark: The invariants ι_π defined above are, up to scalings, the only linear invariants of the system, in the sense that any invariant of the form $\sum_{l \in \mathcal{N}} \alpha_l p_l$ defines a family of stationary populations (with full support) of the form $\pi_i = c^{\alpha_i}/Z$, where c is a positive constant and Z a normalising factor. We omit the proof. □

The significance of the above invariants is expressed in our next theorem, which states that they completely determine the stationary population with full support to which a given initial population is attracted.

Theorem 5 *Suppose $p(t) \to p^*$ and $q(t) \to q^*$, where p^* and q^* have full support. If $\iota_\pi(p(0)) = \iota_\pi(q(0))$ for all invariants ι_π as above, then $p^* = q^*$.*

Proof: We know in particular that $\iota_{p^*}(p(0)) = \iota_{p^*}(q(0))$, and hence by continuity of the operator $\times$ that $\iota_{p^*}(p^*) = \iota_{p^*}(q^*)$. Similarly, $\iota_{q^*}(p^*) = \iota_{q^*}(q^*)$. Writing out these two equalities yields

$$\sum_l (\lg p_l^*) p_l^* = \sum_l (\lg p_l^*) q_l^*$$
$$\sum_l (\lg q_l^*) p_l^* = \sum_l (\lg q_l^*) q_l^*$$

which can be subtracted to give

$$\sum_l (\lg p_l^*/q_l^*) p_l^* = \sum_l (\lg p_l^*/q_l^*) q_l^*.$$

But by Jensen's inequality applied to the convex function $x \lg x$, the left-hand side of this equation is always positive and the right-hand side always negative. Hence both sides must in fact equal zero, which happens iff $p^* = q^*$. □

Theorem 5 gives us a finite system of equations whose *unique* solution is the limit point of the trajectory of $p(0)$. The equations consist of (4) together with a finite basis for the set of linear equations $\iota_\pi(p) = c_\pi$, where the values c_π are determined by $p(0)$, i.e., $c_\pi = \iota_\pi(p(0))$.

More can be said about the general systems described above. However, having established some key facts, we leave further development of the general setting to the full paper [11] and instead show how the above ideas may be applied to a specific example.

3 Matchings in graphs

We define below a symmetric quadratic operator that acts on probability distributions over matchings in graphs. This operator is a natural one to choose as part of an algorithm for generating a random matching in a graph from a certain probability distribution. Applications of this include approximate counting of matchings and computation of the partition function of monomer-dimer systems [8], as well as a genetic algorithm for finding a large matching. This latter application is discussed in the Appendix.

Let $G = (V, E)$ be an undirected graph and $\mathcal{M}(G)$ the set of matchings in G. Given matchings $i, j \in \mathcal{M}(G)$, construct a random pair of offspring k and l according to the following scheme. Let $G'(i,j) = (V, E')$ be the subgraph of G whose edge set E' is the symmetric difference of the edge sets of i and j. Thus each connected component of $G'(i,j)$ is a path or a cycle whose edges belong alternately to i and to j. For each such component independently, flip a fair coin; if the coin comes up heads, make k agree with i and l agree with j on the component; if it comes up tails, reverse the roles of i and j. Also, include in both k and l all edges common to both i and j, and no other edges. (Thus the unions of the edge sets of i and j and of k and l, viewed as multisets, are equal.) It is a simple matter to check that the above scheme specifies a symmetric, aperiodic operator as defined in the previous section. We shall refer to this operator as β^{match}.

First let us consider the stationary populations under β^{match}. Using Theorem 3 we can obtain a simple description of these. We call a population p on $\mathcal{M}(G)$ *normal* if it is of the form

$$p_i = \frac{1}{Z} \prod_{e \in i} \lambda_e,$$

where $\lambda_e \in \mathbb{R}^+$ for each edge e in G, and $Z = \sum_{i \in \mathcal{M}(G)} \prod_{e \in i} \lambda_e$ is a normalising factor.

Theorem 6 *Under the operator β^{match}, a population with full support is stationary iff it is normal.*

Proof: It is easy to check that any normal population is stationary. For the other direction, let p be a stationary population on $\mathcal{M}(G)$, and for each edge e of G define $\lambda_e = p_{\{e\}}/p_0$, where 0 denotes the empty matching and $\{e\}$ denotes the matching consisting of the single edge e. Since we are assuming that p has full support, each λ_e is positive and finite. Now we claim that, for each matching i, $p_i = p_0 \prod_{e \in i} \lambda_e$; note that this is enough to establish the theorem. We proceed by induction on the size of i. The claim is trivially true when the size of i is 0 or 1. Suppose $i = j \cup \{f\}$, where the edge f does not belong to matching j. Then it is easy to check that $\beta^{\text{match}}_{i0j\{f\}} > 0$, so Theorem 3 implies that $p_i p_0 = p_j p_{\{f\}} = \lambda_f p_0 p_j$. The claim now follows by applying the inductive hypothesis to j. This concludes the proof of the claim and the theorem. □

Combining Theorem 2 with Theorem 6, we see that repeated application of β^{match} to any population $p(0)$ over $\mathcal{M}(G)$ results in a normal population, provided the stationary population corresponding to $p(0)$ has full support. In this case, we say that $p(0)$ *generates* $\mathcal{M}(G)$. It can be shown that a sufficient condition for this is that $p(0)$ assigns positive weight to the empty matching in G and, for each edge e of G, to some matching containing e.

Remark: With rather more work, it is possible to derive necessary and sufficient conditions for $p(0)$ to generate $\mathcal{M}(G)$, and indeed a precise characterisation of those subsets of $\mathcal{M}(G)$ that are closed under β^{match}. These questions turn out to be intimately related to the structure of the matching polytope of G. We leave a development of these results, which we believe are of independent interest, to the full paper [11]. □

We turn now to the problem of determining the normal population to which the trajectory of a given initial population $p(0)$ converges. Following the approach of the previous section, we identify a family of invariants of β^{match}. Let e be any edge of G, and define $q_e = \sum_{i \ni e} p_i$, the probability that a matching in population p contains e. It is easy to check that, for every $e \in E$, q_e is an invariant of β^{match}. This gives us a family of polynomial equations satisfied by the parameters λ_e of our normal population. Define the matching polynomial of a graph $G = (V, E)$ over variables $\overline{x} = (x_e)_{e \in E}$ by $g(G, \overline{x}) = \sum_{m \in \mathcal{M}(G)} \prod_{e \in m} x_e$. Then we may write the system of equations as follows:

$$q_e = \frac{\lambda_e g(G/e, \overline{\lambda})}{g(G, \overline{\lambda})} \qquad \forall e \in E, \tag{6}$$

where G/e denotes the graph obtained from G by removing the endpoints of e, and the values q_e are determined by the initial population $p(0)$.

It is not hard to show that the invariants $\{q_e\}_{e \in E}$ form a basis for the family of linear invariants ι_π defined in Theorem 4. Thus, by Theorem 5, they uniquely determine the stationary population. We summarise this discussion as follows.

Theorem 7 *Let $p(0)$ be any initial population that generates $\mathcal{M}(G)$. Then the equations (6) have a unique solution $\{\lambda_e\}_{e \in E}$ which determines the normal population corresponding to $p(0)$.* □

For general graphs, the solution to these equations is not a rational function of the quantities q_e. However, as we shall see in the next section, in the case that the underlying graph G is a tree the equations do have a simple closed-form solution. More significantly, we shall also show in this case that the quadratic system defined by β^{match} converges to a normal population very rapidly, in time bounded by a low-degree polynomial in the size of the tree.

4 Matchings in trees

In this section, we present a complete analysis of the mating operator β^{match} in the case where the underlying graph G is a tree T.

4.1 The stationary population

First, we give an explicit formula for the stationary population corresponding to any initial population which generates $\mathcal{M}(T)$. This formula will be in terms of the invariants q_e and r_v, where for each vertex $v \in V$ we define $r_v = 1 - \sum_{e=(v,u)} q_e$, the probability that v is *not* covered by a matching.

Theorem 8 *Let T be a tree and $p(0)$ an initial population that generates $\mathcal{M}(T)$. Then $p(t)$ converges to the normal population π defined by*

$$\lambda_e = \frac{q_e(1 - q_e)}{r_v r_u},$$

for each edge $e = (v, u)$ of T, where the values of q_e and r_v are determined by $p(0)$. The population π satisfies

$$\pi_i = \frac{\prod_{e \in i} q_e \prod_{v \notin i} r_v}{\prod_{e \notin i}(1 - q_e)} \qquad \forall i \in \mathcal{M}(T).$$

(The notation $v \notin i$ indicates that vertex v is not covered by the matching i.) □

Theorem 8 is readily verified by considering the structure of the matching polynomial; the details are left for the full paper.

4.2 Rate of convergence

In order to analyse the rate of convergence of β^{match} on $\mathcal{M}(T)$, we split the process conceptually into a sequence of stages. Each stage is associated with a partition of $\mathcal{M}(T)$ into equivalence classes, with the partition becoming successively finer. During each stage, we analyse the time for the probability distribution over its classes to converge. The crucial observation is that this process on equivalence classes can be viewed as a *linear* system, which can then be tackled using established techniques plus some additional insight.

Let v be a leaf of T, and $e = (u, v)$ the edge adjacent to v. Let T' be the subtree obtained by removing e and v from T. Now partition the set $\mathcal{M}(T)$ into equivalence classes by placing two matchings in the same class iff they agree on T'; thus each class contains at most two matchings. Note that there is a 1-1 correspondence between equivalence classes and matchings in T'. To fix notation, let $[i]$ denote the equivalence class of matching $i \in \mathcal{M}(T')$, and if i contains two elements denote them i^+ and i^- according to whether or not they contain e. Also, for any population p on $\mathcal{M}(T)$ define the population p' on $\mathcal{M}(T')$ by $p'_i = \sum_{j \in [i]} p_j$.

Our first claim is that the operator β^{match} acting on the equivalence classes of $\mathcal{M}(T)$ induces a similar mating process on $\mathcal{M}(T')$.

Lemma 9 *For any population p on $\mathcal{M}(T)$, we have $(p \times p)' = p' \times p'$.*

Proof (sketch): Since the mating operator is bilinear, and the operation $p \mapsto p'$ is linear, it suffices to show that, for any two matchings $m_1, m_2 \in \mathcal{M}(T)$, if p_1 and p_2 are populations concentrated at m_1, m_2 respectively then $(p_1 \times p_2)' = p_1' \times p_2'$, where we have extended the definition of $\times$ in the obvious way to allow parents to be taken from different populations. This fact is straightforward to check by a simple case analysis depending on whether one, both or neither of m_1, m_2 contains e. □

In the light of Lemma 9, we can understand the evolution of the mating process on $\mathcal{M}(T)$ inductively as follows. First we view the process as working on equivalence classes: by Lemma 9, this is equivalent to a mating process on matchings in the smaller tree T', so we may argue inductively about its behaviour. Then, assuming that the process on equivalence classes has reached stationarity, we may reason about the effects of mating *within* the classes. As we shall see in a moment, this latter process is much more tractable than the original quadratic system.

Let us call a population p on $\mathcal{M}(T)$ *pseudo-stationary* if the induced population p' on $\mathcal{M}(T')$ is stationary. Our next observation is that, if we start with a pseudo-stationary population, the mating operator on $\mathcal{M}(T)$ may be viewed as a linear system. In fact, it defines a Markov chain on the space $\mathcal{M}(T)^+$ of those matchings in T that include the edge e.

Lemma 10 *Let p be any pseudo-stationary population on $\mathcal{M}(T)$. Then the probability distribution on matchings in $\mathcal{M}(T)^+$ behaves under β^{match} as a time-homogeneous Markov chain with transition probabilities*

$$\alpha_{i^+l^+} = \sum_{jk} p_j' \beta_{ijkl}' \qquad \forall i^+, l^+ \in \mathcal{M}(T)^+ \tag{7}$$

where β'_{ijkl} defines the mating operator in T'.

Proof (sketch): Let $l^+ \in \mathcal{M}(T)$. By definition of the system (and ignoring the possibility that some matching appearing in the sum may not be defined), we may write $(p \times p)_l$ as

$$\sum_{[i][j][k]} \big(p_{i^+}p_{j^+}\beta_{i^+j^+k^+l^+} + p_{i^-}p_{j^+}\beta_{i^-j^+k^-l^+} + p_{i^+}p_{j^-}\beta_{i^+j^-k^-l^+}\big) \tag{8}$$

Consider first the case where both $[i]$ and $[j]$ consist of two elements. It is not hard to check that in this case $\beta_{i^+j^+k^+l^+} = 2\beta_{i^-j^+k^-l^+} = 2\beta_{i^+j^-k^-l^+} = \beta'_{ijkl}$. Using these relationships and the fact that $p_{i^-} = p_i' - p_{i^+}$, we may write the corresponding term in the sum (8) as $\frac{1}{2}(p_i'\beta'_{ijkl})p_{j^+} + \frac{1}{2}(p_j'\beta'_{ijkl})p_{i^+}$. The case where $[i]$ consists of two elements and $[j]$ of one contributes only a single term to (8), which may be written as $p_{i^+}p_{j^-}\beta_{i^+j^-k^-l^+} = (p_j'\beta'_{ijkl})p_{i^+}$. The remaining case ($[i]$ consists of one element and $[j]$ of two) is symmetrical.
Bringing all these terms together we obtain

$$(p \times p)_{l^+} = \sum_{i^+}\Big(\sum_{jk} p_j'\beta'_{ijkl}\Big)p_{i^+} = \sum_{i^+} \alpha_{i^+l^+}p_{i^+}. \tag{9}$$

Since q_e is invariant we have $\sum_{l^+}(p \times p)_{l^+} = \sum_{i^+} p_{i^+}$, so (9), suitably normalised, does indeed define a Markov chain as claimed. □

Suppose now that p is a pseudo-stationary population on $\mathcal{M}(T)$. Then clearly $p_i' = \sum_{j \in [i]} \pi_j$, where π is the normal population corresponding to p. Now it is easy to verify the following:

Proposition 11 *The Markov chain defined in Lemma 10 is reversible and converges to the stationary distribution $\widehat{\pi}_{l^+} = \pi_{l^+}/q_e$ over $\mathcal{M}(T)^+$.* □

We now address the question of the rate of convergence of the above Markov chain. Let $\Delta(t)$ denote the variation distance of the distribution at time t from $\widehat{\pi}$ maximised over initial states, and for $\epsilon \in (0,1)$ define

$$\tau(\epsilon) = \min\{t : \Delta(t') \le \epsilon \text{ for all } t' \ge t\}. \tag{10}$$

A bound on $\tau(\epsilon)$ may be obtained by viewing the chain as a network whose vertices are the states and which has an oriented edge of capacity $C(i^+, l^+) = \widehat{\pi}_{i^+}\alpha_{i^+l^+}$ between vertices i^+ and l^+. Suppose it is possible to route $\widehat{\pi}_{a^+}\widehat{\pi}_{b^+}$ units of a commodity (a^+, b^+) from a^+ to b^+, for each pair of distinct states a^+ and b^+ simultaneously, in such a way that no oriented edge (i^+, l^+) carries more than $\rho C(i^+, l^+)$ units of flow in total and the length of any flow-carrying path is at most ℓ. Then Corollary 6′ of [16] provides the following bound (see also [3, 8]):

Theorem 12 [16] *The quantity $\tau(\epsilon)$ satisfies*

$$\tau(\epsilon) \le \rho\ell\left(\ln \widehat{\pi}_{\min}^{-1} + \ln \epsilon^{-1}\right),$$

where $\widehat{\pi}_{\min} = \min_{i^+} \widehat{\pi}_{i^+}$. □

The key to rapid convergence is the construction of a good flow in our Markov chain:

Theorem 13 *For the Markov chain of Lemma 10, there exists a flow with $\rho \leq 2q_e^{-1}$ and $\ell = 2$.* □

Proof: Note from (7) that we may view each edge (i^+, l^+) of the Markov chain as a set of parallel edges, one for each $j \in \mathcal{M}(T')$: the edge associated with j has capacity $\widehat{\pi}_{i^+} p'_j \beta'_{ijkl}$ and corresponds to mating i^+ with j^+ and producing l^+ as an offspring. We refer to this edge as the j-edge from i^+ to l^+. We will describe our flow in terms of these edges.

Let a^+, b^+ be any pair of distinct states in $\mathcal{M}(T)^+$, and consider the set $\mathcal{P}_{ab}$ of paths of length 2 from a^+ to b^+ of the following form: the first edge of the path is any b-edge leaving a^+, to c^+ say, and the second edge is the unique $\bar{c}$-edge from c^+ to b^+, where $\bar{c}$ is defined by $c \cup \bar{c} = a \cup b$ (viewed as multisets). We distribute the $\widehat{\pi}_{a^+}\widehat{\pi}_{b^+}$ units of flow from a^+ to b^+ evenly over all 2^r paths in $\mathcal{P}_{ab}$, where r is the number of non-trivial connected components in $a^+ \cup b^+$.

Now consider any j-edge e from i^+ to l^+. We may assume that the equivalence class $[j]$ contains two elements since in the above flow we have only used j-edges for which $j^+ \in \mathcal{M}(T)^+$. Let us compute the flow through e. Clearly only two flow-carrying paths use e; for if e is the first edge of a path then this path must belong to $\mathcal{P}_{ij}$, while if it is the second edge of a path then this path must belong to $\mathcal{P}_{ml}$, where m is the complement of l in the multiset $i \cup j$. Suppose e is the first edge of a path from i^+ to j^+. The flow along this path is precisely $2^{-r}\widehat{\pi}_{i^+}\widehat{\pi}_{j^+}$, where r is the number of non-trivial connected components in $i^+ \cup j^+$. Dividing this by the capacity of e we get

$$\frac{2^{-r}\widehat{\pi}_{i^+}\widehat{\pi}_{j^+}}{\widehat{\pi}_{i^+} p'_j \beta'_{ijkl}} = \frac{2^{-r}\pi_{j^+}/q_e}{(\pi_{j^+} + \pi_{j^-})2^{-r}} \leq \frac{1}{q_e},$$

where we have used the fact that $\beta'_{ijkl} = 2^{-r}$. By a symmetrical argument, the ratio of flow to capacity in the case where e is the second edge on a path can be similarly bounded. Hence $\rho \leq 2q_e^{-1}$. Evidently all flow-carrying paths have length 2 so $\ell = 2$. □

Finally, we may combine the above results to derive a bound on the rate of convergence of the original quadratic mating process. Define the quantity $\tau^{\text{match}}(\epsilon)$ in analogous fashion to $\tau(\epsilon)$ in (10) but using the variation distance of $p(t)$ from the corresponding stationary population π defined in Theorem 8.

Theorem 14 *Let T be a tree with n vertices, and $p(0)$ any population that generates $\mathcal{M}(T)$. Then $\tau^{\text{match}}(\epsilon)$ satisfies*

$$\tau^{\text{match}}(\epsilon) = O\Big((n \lg n + n \lg \pi_{\min}^{-1} + \lg \epsilon^{-1})q_{\min}^{-1}\Big),$$

where $q_{\min} = \min_e q_e$ and $\pi_{\min} = \min_{i \in \mathcal{M}(T)} \pi_i$.

Proof (sketch): By Lemma 9 we may assume inductively that, after sufficiently many steps, the population p' is close to stationarity. Lemma 10 now allows us to view the system as a Markov chain on $\mathcal{M}(T)^+$. Strictly speaking, since p' is not exactly stationary the transition probabilities appearing in (7) are not in fact constant but are perturbed by a small time-varying amount; however, this error may be effectively bounded. Now we apply Theorem 12 together with the flow bound of Theorem 13 to obtain a bound on the rate of convergence of this Markov chain. Clearly, once the Markov chain is close to its stationary distribution, near-stationarity of p' implies that the population on $\mathcal{M}(T)$ is also almost stationary. The details are left for the full paper. □

Theorem 14 is a surprisingly strong result. It says that the time required for the mating process to approach stationarity depends on the size of the tree only as a low degree polynomial, despite the fact that the number of types $|\mathcal{M}(T)|$ is in general exponentially large in n. This is apparently the first analysis of its kind for a combinatorially non-trivial problem. Moreover, although this is a somewhat simplified setting, we conjecture that the analytical tools introduced in this paper are applicable to other systems.

Acknowledgements

We thank Eric Carlen, Persi Diaconis, Jeff Kahn, Jeff Lagarias, Han La Poutré, Noam Nisan, Nick Pippenger, Dirk Vertigan and Benjamin Weiss for enlightening discussions on the ideas presented here.

References

[1] M. Ajtai, J. Komlós and E. Szemerédi. Deterministic simulation in LOGSPACE. *Proceedings of 19th ACM STOC* (1987), p. 132.

[2] E. Carlen and M. Carvalho. Strict entropy production bounds and stability of the rate of convergence to equilibrium for the Boltzmann equation. Preprint, 1992.

[3] P. Diaconis and D. Stroock. Geometric bounds for eigenvalues of Markov chains. *Annals of Applied Probability* **1** (1991), pp. 36–61.

[4] M. Dyer, A. Frieze and R. Kannan. A random polynomial time algorithm for approximating the volume of convex bodies. *Proceedings of 21st ACM STOC* (1989), pp. 375–381.

[5] M. Hirsch and S. Smale. *Differential equations, dynamical systems, and linear algebra.* Academic Press, New York, 1974.

[6] J. Holland. *Adaptation in natural and artificial systems.* MIT Press, 1992.

[7] M. Jerrum. The elusiveness of large cliques in a random graph. Report CSR-9-90, Dept. of Computer Science, University of Edinburgh, 1990.

[8] M. Jerrum and A. Sinclair. Approximating the permanent. *SIAM Journal on Computing* **18** (1989), pp. 1149–1178.

[9] H. Kesten. Quadratic transformations: a model for population growth I & II. *Advances in Applied Probability* **2** (1970), pp. 1–82 and 179–228.

[10] O. Penrose. *Foundations of statistical mechanics.* Pergamon Press, Oxford, 1970.

[11] Y. Rabinovich, A. Sinclair and A. Wigderson. Quadratic dynamical systems. Full version, in preparation.

[12] Y. Rabinovich and A. Wigderson. Analysis of a simple genetic algorithm. *Proceedings of the 4th International Conference on Genetic Algorithms* 1991, pp. 215–221.

[13] A. Rényi. *Foundations of probability.* Holden-Day, San Francisco, 1970.

[14] G. Sasaki and B. Hajek. The time complexity of maximum matching by simulated annealing. *Journal of the ACM* **35** (1988), pp. 387–403.

[15] H. Siegelmann. Personal communication.

[16] A. Sinclair. Improved bounds for mixing rates of Markov chains and multicommodity flow. Report ECS-LFCS-91-178, Dept. of Computer Science, University of Edinburgh, 1991. To appear in *Combinatorics, Probability & Computing.*

Appendix: Genetic algorithms

Genetic algorithms provide a heuristic paradigm for solving combinatorial optimisation problems based on a biological analogy. Suppose we are searching for an optimal (or near-optimal) solution amongst a set of feasible solutions; as a concrete example, consider the problem of finding a matching of maximum cardinality amongst all matchings in a graph. The algorithm starts with an initial population over simple solutions that is easily constructed; in our example, this might be the uniform distribution on all matchings that consist of a single edge. The population evolves in discrete steps under the application of two operators, called *mating* and *fitness.* Mating is designed to increase variety in the population, while fitness is designed to increase its average quality. In our example, the quality of a matching is simply its size. Usually a third operator, known as *mutation*, is added, but for the sake of simplicity we shall ignore this here.

In mating, random pairs of solutions give birth to random children; the operator β^{match} discussed in Sections 3 and 4 is a natural choice in our example. Note that the average size of a matching is an invariant of β^{match}, so mating itself does not improve the population. In fitness, solutions of low quality are discarded or their number reduced; for example, all matchings below a certain size might be removed from the population. The overall genetic algorithm repeatedly applies the mating and fitness operators alternately, in the hope that the population will quickly converge to one whose average quality is high.

Despite the apparent success of this approach in several experimental applications, few rigorous theoretical results exist to explain and motivate the experimental results or guide the design of the algorithms. One of the few such rigorous results was obtained in [12], albeit in the context of a highly artificial optimisation problem. One lesson to be learned from that work was that the interaction between the mating and fitness operators is much easier to analyse if mating is applied enough times for the system to converge to a (near-)stationary population before the fitness operator is applied; this is a reasonable strategy with mating operators which, like β^{match}, preserve or do not substantially reduce the average quality of solutions. The reason for this is clear: in general, the effect on the population of a single step of the mating operator is rather hard to quantify, but after a sufficiently long sequence of mating operations the population is close to a stationary population, which may be well understood. Interestingly, we have recently learned that this idea has led to improved performance of genetic algorithms in some experiments [15]. Given that the effect of the fitness operator is usually relatively straightforward to describe, we contend that the principal challenge in analysing the performance of genetic algorithms of the above kind lies in estimating the rate of convergence to a stationary population under the mating operator. Since the mating operator is quadratic and almost always symmetric, this is precisely the central question that is addressed in the present paper.

On the Bit Extraction Problem

Joel Friedman*
Department of Computer Science
Princeton University
Princeton, NJ 08544

Abstract

Consider a coloring of the n-dimensional Boolean cube with $c = 2^s$ colors in such a way that every k-dimensional subcube is equicolored, i.e. each color occurs the same number of times. We show that for such a coloring we necessarily have $(k-1)/n \geq \theta_c = (c/2-1)/(c-1)$. This resolves the "bit extraction" or "t-resilient functions" problem (also a special case of the "privacy amplification" problem) in many cases, such as $c-1|n$, proving that XOR type colorings are optimal, and always resolves this question to within $c/4$ in determining the optimal value of k (for any fixed n and c). We also study the problem of finding almost equicolored colorings when $(k-1)/n < \theta_c$, and of classifying all optimal colorings.

1 Introduction

The bit extraction problem of [Vaz85], aka t-resilient functions problem (see [CFG+85]), aka a special case of the privacy amplification problem (see [BBR88],[Bra89]) is equivalent to the following coloring problem. The vertices of the Boolean cube, $\mathbf{B}^n = \{-1, 1\}^n$ are to be colored with $c = 2^s$ colors such that every *k-dimensional subcube* is *equicolored*. Given n and c, what is the smallest value of k for which this possible? Here, by a k-dimensional subcube we mean a subset of $\mathbf{B}^n$ determined by fixing the values of some $n-k$ coordinates on $\mathbf{B}^n$; we denote the set of all such subcubes by $\mathcal{H}_k$. By equicolored we mean that every color appears the same number of times in the subcube, i.e. $2^k/c$ times.

To fix ideas, we refer to such a coloring as a $(c; n, k)$-coloring and write $\kappa(c, n)$ for the smallest value of k achievable for a given n and c. In this paper we are primarily interested in viewing c as small or fixed, studying κ as a function of n. We will study this problem and the problem of constructing colorings which are approximately equicolorable.

To elaborate on the context in which the problem arises, consider n boolean variables, $X = \{x_1, \ldots, x_n\}$, whose values are set by the following process. An adversary fixes some subset of the variables, $T \subset X$, to specific values, neither the values nor T being knowing to us; then the remaining variables are randomly set to boolean values, independently and uniformly. Knowing only the size of T, $t = |T|$, we wish to extract s unbiased bits from X for s as large as possible; i.e. we wish to find a function $f: \mathbf{B}^n \to \mathbf{B}^s$ such that for any setting of any t of the variables of X in the above process, our f takes on each value in $\mathbf{B}^s$ with probability $1/2^s$. For example, to extract one unbiased bit for any T of size $\leq n-1$, we can take $f = x_1 \oplus \cdots \oplus x_n$, where $\oplus$ denotes the XOR (exclusive-OR); as long as there is one bit which is not set by the adversary, this f will be unbiased. While the obvious lower bound $s \leq n-t$ is achieved in extracting $s = 1$ bit, one cannot in general attain $s = n-t$. In [CFG+85] it proven that to extract $s = 2$ bits requires $t < 2n/3$ (we assume $3|n$ for simplicity); one can achieve this taking $f = (f_1, f_2)$, with f_1 the XOR of the first $2n/3$ of the variables, and f_2 that of the last $2n/3$ of them. The bit extraction problem is equivalent to our coloring problem since constructing an f as above gives a $(2^s; n, k)$ coloring with $k = n-t$, and vice versa (and thus the name "t-resilent function").

This coloring problem also arises in a cryptographic context (as in [BBR88],[Bra89]): player A communicates to player B via a channel of n bits, $x_1, \ldots, x_n$, but there is a spy who is able to see some t of the n bits, A and B not knowing which bits the spy can see. A and B would like the spy to obtain no information about the true message, say a message of $s < n$ bits. In other words, A must takes a message of s bits, encode this to a message of n bits, using some source of randomness, send this through the channel to B, who then applies a decoding function to obtain the origi-

*The author also wishes to acknowledge the National Science Foundation for supporting this research in part under a PYI grant, CCR-8858788.

0-8186-2900-2/92 $3.00 © 1992 IEEE

nal s bit message; we require a scheme in which the spy obtains no information about the s bit message. For example, to communicate one bit, $y \in \mathbf{B}$, A can pick $x_1, \ldots, x_{n-1}$ at random and then set x_n to be the XOR of y and $x_1, \ldots, x_{n-1}$, which B will decode by computing the XOR of $x_1, \ldots, x_n$. Constructing such an encoding and decoding for general s turns out to be equivalent to the coloring problem, again with $c = 2^s$ and $k = n - t$.

Returning to the coloring problem, consider the colorings by $f: \mathbf{B}^n \rightarrow \mathbf{B}^s$, identifying $\mathbf{B}^s$ with the set of colors, for those f's formed by XOR's of the variables, i.e. $f = (f_1, \ldots, f_s)$ with each f_i being an XOR of a subset of the variables; we call such a coloring an *XOR coloring*. Let $\kappa_{\mathrm{XOR}}(c,n)$ denote the smallest value of k that an XOR coloring can achieve given c, n. It has been conjectured (e.g. [Vaz85]) that $\kappa_{\mathrm{XOR}}(c,n) = \kappa(c,n)$ for all c, n, i.e. that that XOR colorings can always achieve the optimal k; as mentioned before, this was proven for all n with $c = 4$ in [CFG+85] (and is clear for $c = 2$).

It is easy to determine $\kappa_{\mathrm{XOR}}(c,n)$ to within $O(c)$. For example, for n divisible by $c-1$, it is easy to see that $\kappa_{\mathrm{XOR}}(c,n) = n\theta_c + 1$, where $\theta_c = (c/2-1)/(c-1)$. It follows that $\kappa_{\mathrm{XOR}}(c,n)$ is always within $(c-2)/2$ of $n\theta_c + 1$.

Here we prove:

Theorem 1.1 *For any $(c;n,k)$ coloring we have $(k-1)/n \geq \theta_c$, i.e. $\kappa(c,n) \geq n\theta_c + 1$.*

Corollary 1.2 *For $c - 1|n$, $n > 0$, XOR colorings are optimal. For any n, c, XOR colorings are within $(c-2)/2$ of optimal.*

It is a non-trivial problem to determine $\kappa_{\mathrm{XOR}}(c,n)$ exactly for general n, but one can do so in certain cases to obtain other bounds as a corollary. For example, one gets:

Proposition 1.3 *For $n \geq 2$ and $\equiv -2, -1, 0, 1, c/2-1, c/2, c/2+1 \pmod{c-1}$, we have $\kappa_{\mathrm{XOR}}(c,n) = 1 + \lceil n\theta_c \rceil$ and hence $= \kappa(c,n)$. For $n > 2$ and $\equiv 2 \pmod{c-1}$ with $c \geq 8$, $\kappa_{\mathrm{XOR}}(c,n) = 2 + \lceil n\theta_c \rceil$, and hence $\kappa_{\mathrm{XOR}}(c,n)$ is at worst within 1 of $\kappa(c,n)$. For $c = 8$ the former and latter congruences hold according to whether $n \not\equiv 2 \pmod 7$ or not. For any n, c, $\kappa_{\mathrm{XOR}}(c,n)$ is within $c/4$ of $\kappa(c,n)$.*

In particular, $n \equiv 2 \pmod 7$ is the simplest case in which we don't know if XOR colorings are optimal.

We are also interested in two related problems:

Problem 1.4 *For $k < \kappa(c,n)$, how close (in various metrics involving $\mathcal{H}_k$) to equicolorable can be achieved by a c-coloring of $\mathbf{B}^n$?*

Problem 1.5 *Classify all optimal colorings, at least for $c - 1|n$. Are there optimal colorings not obtainable as XOR type colorings?*

The author knows of no optimal colorings other than XOR colorings. Of course, if one views n and k as fixed and asks for the optimal c, then there exist optimal colorings which are not XOR colorings (e.g. $k = (n/3) - 1$ with $3|n$ and n large, so that $c = 1$ is the optimal c).

In this paper we study problem 1.4 for the metric $L^2(\mathcal{H}_k)$ (defined in section 3). We give a lower bound on the distance to "equicolor" one can achieve for $k < \kappa(c,n)$. One remarkable fact is:

Theorem 1.6 *For $c - 1|n$, the optimal XOR coloring is closest to equicolorable in $L^2(\mathcal{H}_k)$ for any k.*

Both this theorem and theorem 1.1 are proven using the eigenvalues and eigenspaces of the adjacency matrix of the $\mathbf{B}^n$. Such methods can yield other inequalities expressable in terms of the distance distribution (see section 3) of a subset of $\mathbf{B}^n$. For example, the fact that the average influence of a variable on a boolean function which is 1 on half of the values is at least $1/n$ (see [KKL88]) follows immediately from the fact that the sum of the influences is just $((n-A)\chi_c, \chi_c) = 2^n \sum_{r>0} 2r\mu_r \geq 2^n \sum_{r>0} 2\mu_r = 2^n$, using the notation of section 2, where C is the subset of $\mathbf{B}^n$ where the function takes the value 1.

In general, XOR colorings are not closest to equicolor for many important metrics, such as the $\mathrm{RP}(\mathcal{H}_k)$ metric defined in section 3 (already for the case $n = c = 4$, $k = 2$). Roughly speaking, the problem is that for k one less than what can be achieved by the best XOR coloring for fixed c, n, the best XOR colorings are equicolored on almost all $H\mathcal{H}_k$, but on the other H's they avoid half the colors! It would be interesting to know about the closest to equicolor colorings for various sup-type norms, such as $\mathrm{RP}(\mathcal{H}_k)$ or $L^\infty(\mathcal{H}_k)$, and to give an explicit constructions.

In the proof that XOR colorings are optimal for $c = 4$ of [CFG+85], one produces from an optimal coloring f_1, f_2 two subsets of variables X_1, X_2 whose XOR's yield an optimal coloring (any X_1, X_2 with the Fourier coefficient of $f_1, f_2, f_1 + f_2$ non-vanishing at, respectively, $X_1, X_2, X_1 + X_2$ will do). This proof does not directly generalize because of the possibility of cancellation of Fourier coefficients in computing a convolution, and theorem 1.1 somehow precludes very bad cancellation. It would be nice to find a generalization of the method in [CFG+85], understanding precisely how much cancellation can occur in such convolutions. In our paper there is no explicit reference to Fourier coefficients of the f_i's. They occur only implicitly, in that the eigenspace of the adjacency matrix of $\mathbf{B}^n$ corresponding to the eigenvalue $n-2r$ is precisely the ($\mathbf{R}$-linear) span of the collection of all XOR's of r variables.

In section 2 we give a short proof of theorem 1.1 and prove some facts about the optimal XOR colorings, proving proposition 1.3. In section 3 study the approximate equicoloring problem for L^2. To do so we study, for a subset $C \subset \mathbf{B}^n$, its distance distribution. It seems that studying "higher-order" distance distributions may shed light on approximate equicolorings in other norms; for this and other intriguing relations between the distance distribution and the bit extraction problem, the reader is referred to the full version of the paper, [Fri91]. In section 4 we make some remarks about problem 1.5, giving a simple geometric characterization of all XOR colorings.

The author wishes to thank Kai Li, Bernard Chazelle, and Avi Wigderson for useful comments and discussions.

2 The Bit Extraction Problem

We begin by proving theorem 1.1. We do this via a somewhat stronger statement. We say that a subset $C \subset \mathbf{B}^n$ is $1/c$ dense in $\mathcal{H}_k$ if

$$\frac{|C \cap H|}{|H|} = \frac{1}{c} \qquad \forall H \in \mathcal{H}_k.$$

Theorem 2.1 *If there exists a $1/c$ dense in $\mathcal{H}_k$ subset of $\mathbf{B}^n$, then $(k-1)/n \geq \theta_c$.*

Theorem 1.1 follows by taking C to be the set of vertices of any fixed color of a $(c;n,k)$ coloring.

Proof Consider the adjacency matrix, A of the Boolean cube, and χ_C, the characteristic function of C in $\mathbf{B}^n$. Clearly $(A\chi_C, \chi_C) \geq 0$. On the other hand, the eigenvalues of A are $n-2r$ with $r = 0, 1, \ldots n$, and the corresponding eigenspaces, E_r, are just the spans of all XOR's of r variables, viewing $\mathbf{B}$ as $\{-1, +1\}$. It follows that if v_r is the projection of χ_C onto E_r, then the assumption that C is $1/c$ dense in $\mathcal{H}_k$ implies that $v_1 = \cdots = v_{n-k} = 0$ (and conversely[1]). Setting $\mu_r = |v_r|^2/|\chi_c|^2$, we have

$$\sum_{r=0}^{n} \mu_r = \frac{\sum |v_r|^2}{|\chi_C|^2} = 1$$

[1] "Conversely" follows from the invertibility of the standard $2^n \times 2^n$ Hadamard matrix. In modern lingo, all the weight 1 thru $n-k$ Fourier coefficients vanish for the function taking the value 1 on C and 0 elsewhere, as in [CFG+85], section 5.1.

and

$$(A\chi_C, \chi_C) = \sum_{r=0}^{n}(n-2r)|v_r|^2 = |\chi_C|^2 \sum_{r=0}^{n}(n-2r)\mu_r.$$

Also, E_0 corresponds to the trivial eigenvector, $(1, \ldots, 1)$, and so $\mu_0 = |C|/n = 1/c$; this and $\mu_1 = \cdots = \mu_{n-k} = 0$ give

$$0 \leq n\mu_0 + \sum_{r=n-k+1}^{n} (n-2r)\mu_r \leq$$

$$n\mu_0 + (2k-2-n) \sum_{r=n-k+1}^{n} \mu_r = n\frac{1}{c} + (2k-2-n)\frac{c-1}{c},$$

and so

$$2(k-1)\frac{c-1}{c} \geq n\frac{c-2}{c},$$

which is the desired result.

□

We will now evaluate $\kappa_{\mathrm{XOR}}(c,n)$ for some special values of n to deduce corollary 1.2 and proposition 1.3. First recall that in general $f_1, \ldots, f_s$ yield an $\mathcal{H}_k$ equicolored coloring iff all XOR's of a subsets of $\{f_1, \ldots, f_s\}$ yields a function which is half 1, half -1 on every $H \in \mathcal{H}_k$ (see, for example, [CFG+85]; this is just to say that the standard $2^s \times 2^s$ Hadamard matrix is invertible). So for a subset $T \subset S = \{1, \ldots, s\}$, consider the XOR of the f_i with $i \in T$, which we denote f_T. If the f_i are XOR's of a subsets the variables $X = \{x_1, \ldots, x_n\}$, then so is each f_T. Furthermore, an XOR of the variables is half 1, half -1 on $\mathcal{H}_k$ iff it is the XOR of at least $n-k+1$ variables. This reduces the analysis of optimal XOR colorings to a question about the possible Venn diagrams of s subsets, $X_1, \ldots, X_s$, of X, X_i being the subset of variables of which f_i is an XOR (which is equivalent to a question about error correcting codes, as in [CFG+85]).

Namely, for a non-empty $T \subset S$, consider the size of the corresponding component of the Venn diagram on the X_i's,

$$I_T = |(\cap_{i\in T} X_i) \cap (\cap_{i \notin T} \overline{X_i})|,$$

where $\overline{X_i}$ is the complement of X_i in X. The X_i's correspond to an $\mathcal{H}_k$ equicolored coloring iff for all $U \subset S$,

$$\sum_{|T \cap U| \equiv 1 \pmod 2} I_T \geq n - (k-1). \qquad (2.1)$$

Furthermore if there exist non-negative, integral I_T satisfying the above equation with $n \geq k$, then clearly there exists a $(c;n,k)$ XOR coloring.

Summing the above over all U shows that

$$\kappa_{\mathrm{XOR}}(c,n) \geq 1 + n\theta_c, \qquad (2.2)$$

and if equality holds then each of the inequalities of equation 2.1 holds with equality; the invertibiliy of the standard Hadamard matrix implies that equality holding in all the above inequalities necessitates $I_T = n/(c-1)$. So for $c-1|n$, any choice of X_i with $I_T = n/(c-1)$ for all T yields an optimal coloring, and any optimal coloring occurs in this way. For $c-1|n$ we use the term *balanced* XOR coloring for any optimal XOR coloring, to emphasise the fact that all I_T's are equal. Furthermore we have

Proposition 2.2 *For $n \geq 2$ and $\equiv -2, -1, 0, 1, c/2-1, c/2, c/2+1 \pmod{c-1}$, $\kappa_{\mathrm{XOR}}(c,n) = 1 + \lceil n\theta_c \rceil$, and thus optimal colorings can be achieved by XOR colorings in these cases.*

Proof All cases follow easily from the case $n = c/2$ and the trivial case $n = c-1$. For $n = c/2$ we take the "odd coloring," namely I_T is $= 1, 0$ according to whether or not $|T|$ is odd. It is easy to see than any U has $|T \cap U|$ odd for at least half the T with $|T|$ odd, and so $\kappa_{\mathrm{XOR}}(c, c/2) \leq c/4+1$. Rest of details omitted.

□

For general n the problem of determining $\kappa_{\mathrm{XOR}}(c,n)$ is more difficult. However, for fixed c it suffices to check the cases $n = 1, 2, \cdots, O(c^2)$ to determine $\kappa_{\mathrm{XOR}}(c,n)$ for all n. Indeed, for a fixed $r \in [0, c-2]$ let $K = K(r)$ be the smallest integer such that for all m sufficiently large there exists a $(c; (c-1)m + r, (c/2-1)m + K + 1)$ XOR coloring.

Lemma 2.3 *An XOR coloring with $I_T = 0$ for some T has $(k-1)/n \geq 1/2$. For any r there exists a unique $m_0 = m_0(r) \leq 2K(r) - r$ such that there exist $(c; (c-1)m + r, (c/2-1)m + K + 1)$ for all $m \geq m_0$.*

Proof The first statement follows from summing over all U with $|T \cap U| \equiv 1 \pmod 2$. For the second part, m_0 obviously exists, and the coloring at $n = (c-1)m_0 + r$ must have at least one I_T equal zero, or else we could subtract 1 from all the I_T's to get a coloring as above with $m = m_0 - 1$. So the first statement applies to yield $m_0 \leq 2K(r) - r$.

□

In particular, checking $\kappa_{\mathrm{XOR}}(c,n)$ for $n = 1, 2, \ldots, O(c^2)$, we can determine all $K(r)$'s, and therefore all $\kappa_{\mathrm{XOR}}(c,n)$ with $n \geq m_0(r)(c-1) + r = O(c^2)$ by the above. Another consequence of the above is:

Proposition 2.4 *$K(2) = 2$ for $c \geq 8$, and for $n > 2$ and $\equiv 2 \pmod{c-1}$ we have $\kappa_{\mathrm{XOR}}(c,n) = 2 + \lceil n\theta_c \rceil$.*

Proof $K(1) = 1$ implies that either $K(2)$ is 1 or 2. The lemma implies that to rule out $K(2)$ being 1 it suffices to check the case $m_0 = 0$, i.e. $n = 2$, where there is nothing to check (since $2^n < c$). Hence $K(2) = 2$, and then clearly $m_0(2) = 1$, i.e. for $n = c+1$ we can achieve $\kappa_{\mathrm{XOR}}(c,n) = 2 + \lceil n\theta_c \rceil$.

□

Proposition 1.3 is a consequence of the above.

3 Almost Equicolored Colorings and Profiles

For a c-coloring, $\gamma: \mathbf{B}^n \to \mathbf{B}^s$, we define its $L^p(\mathcal{H}_k)$ distance from equicolor via

$$\|\gamma\|^p_{L^p(\mathcal{H}_k)} = \sum_{v \in \mathbf{B}_s} \|\gamma^{-1}(v)\|^p_{L^p(\mathcal{H}_k)},$$

where for a $C \subset \mathbf{B}^n$ (and a fixed $c = |C|/n$ in mind) we define the summand via

$$\|C\|^p_{L^p(\mathcal{H}_k)} = \sum_{H \in \mathcal{H}_k} \Big| |C \cap H| - |H|/c \Big|^p.$$

This is one sense in which we can measure how close to being equicolored a coloring is. In this section we study the case $p = 2$. There are other important metrics suggested by the applications, and we mention

$$\|\gamma\|_{\mathrm{RP}(\mathcal{H}_k)} = \max_{H \in \mathcal{H}_k, G \subset \mathbf{B}^s, |G| = 2^{s-1}} |\gamma^{-1}(G) - 2^{k-1}| \,;$$

this measures how well the bits γ extracts work as a random source to an RP algorithm, G being interpreted as the set of witnesses.

We study $\|C\|_{L^2(\mathcal{H}_k)}$ for a $C \subset \mathbf{B}^n$ via C's *distance distribution* in the following sense:

Definition 3.1 *The* distance distribution *of a $C \subset \mathbf{B}^n$ is the collection of numbers, N_i, defined to be the number of pairs $(c_1, c_2) \in C \times C$ of points in C of distance i (i.e. in the $\mathbf{B}^n$ or Hamming distance), for $i = 0, \ldots, n$.*

The N_i is essentially the *weight enumerator* of coding theory (see [CS88] or [vL82]).

Consider, for a $C \subset \mathbf{B}^n$ with $|C| = n/c$,

$$\mathcal{E}_j(C) \equiv \sum_{H \in \mathcal{H}_j} |C \cap H|^2.$$

Since

$$\|C\|^2_{L^2(\mathcal{H}_j)} = \sum_{H\in\mathcal{H}_j} (|C\cap H|-|H|/c)^2 = \mathcal{E}_j(C)-\frac{2^{n+j}}{c^2}\binom{n}{j},$$

$\mathcal{E}_j(C)$ can be used to measure how close C is to being equicolored with respect to $\mathcal{H}_j$. Routine calculations demonstrate that one can calculate $\mathcal{E}_j$ knowing the μ_i's of section 2 (see [Fri91] for details):

Lemma 3.2

$$N_i = (q_i(A)\chi_C, \chi_C) = \sum_{r=0}^{n} q_i(n-2r)|C|\mu_r$$

where q_i is a polynomial of degree i given by $q_0 = 1$, $q_1(x) = x$, and

$$q_{i+1}(x) = \left(\frac{x}{i+1}\right) q_i(x) - \left(\frac{n-i+1}{i+1}\right) q_{i-1}(x) \quad (3.1)$$

for $i \geq 1$. Furthermore,

$$\mathcal{E}_j = \sum_{l=0}^{j} \binom{n-l}{j-l} N_l = (s_j(A)\chi_C, \chi_C) =$$

$$\sum_{r=0}^{n} s_i(n-2r)|C|\mu_r,$$

where s_j is a polynomial of degree j with leading coefficient $\big(n(n-1)\cdots(n-j+1)\big)^{-1}$, given generally as

$$s_j(x) = \sum_{l=0}^{j} \binom{n-l}{j-l} q_l(A). \quad (3.2)$$

The key point in the proof of theorem 1.6 is to understand the polynomials s_j; they are determined by the following proposition. The author admits to having discovered this proposition by example with computer-aided calculations, which once known is easy to prove (yet the author knows no direct combinatorial proof using only equations 3.2 and 3.1).

Proposition 3.3 *s_j has $-n, -n+2, \ldots, -n+2j-2$ as its j roots; i.e.*

$$s_j(x) = \frac{(x+n)(x+n-2)\cdots(x+n-2j+2)}{n(n-1)\cdots(n-j+1)} =$$

$$2^j \binom{(x+n)/2}{j}.$$

Proof It is clear from the definition of the s_j's that they are polynomials of degree j satisfying

$$(s_j(A)f, f) = \sum_{H\in\mathcal{H}_j} \left(\sum_{x\in H} f(x)\right)^2,$$

for any $f \in L^2(\mathbf{B}^n)$. The right-hand-side of the above clearly vanishes if f is the XOR of r variables with $r \geq n-j+1$. Since such an f has eigenvalue $n-2r$, we conclude that s_j has a root $n-2r$ for any $r \geq n-j+1$.

□

From this proposition we see that $s_j(x)$ restricted to $x = -n, -n+2, \ldots, n$ is a convex function, as is its restriction to $[-n+2j-2, +\infty)$, and we easily obtain the following stronger version of theorem 1.6:

Theorem 3.4 *For $c-1|n$ and $j \leq 1+\theta_c n$, the balanced XOR coloring is closest in $L^2(\mathcal{H}_j)$ to equicolor, and any coloring as close must have the same distance distribution as that of the balanced XOR coloring. In other words,*

$$\frac{\big(s_j(A)\chi_C, \chi_C\big)}{(\chi_C, \chi_C)} \geq \frac{1}{c} s_j(n) + \frac{c-1}{c} s_j\big(-n/(c-1)\big),$$

equality holding iff $c-1|n$ and all μ_i's vanish except for $\mu_0 = 1/c$ and $\mu_{n(1-\theta_c)} = (c-1)/c$. For $c-1 \not| n$, setting $-n/(c-1) = t + \alpha$ with t an integer and $\alpha \in (0,1)$, we have the sharper bound

$$\frac{\big(s_j(A)\chi_C, \chi_C\big)}{(\chi_C, \chi_C)} \geq \frac{1}{c} s_j(n) + \frac{c-1}{c}\big((1-\alpha)s_j(t) + \alpha s_j(t+1)\big),$$

with equality iff $\mu_t = (1-\alpha)(c-1)/c$, $\mu_{t+1} = \alpha(c-1)/c$.

4 Locally Symmetric Colorings and Concluding Remarks

We consider the problem of classifying for $c-1|n$ all optimal colorings, i.e. with $k = 1+n\theta_c$. We call a coloring, $\gamma: \mathbf{B}^n \to \mathbf{B}^s$ *locally symmetric* if there is an η such that for all $v \in \mathbf{B}_n$, exactly $n\eta$ of v's neighbors are colored $\gamma(v)$, and every other color occurs among v's neighbors exactly $n(1-\eta)/(c-1)$ times. In addition we say that the coloring is *sparse* if $\eta = 0$; the balanced coloring is an example.

It is easy to see that locally symmetric colorings are also symmetric in their "distance i neighborhoods" for all i, and that each color has the same distance distribution which is uniquely determined by η. In particular, a locally symmetric coloring which is optimal for $c-1|n$ must be sparse.

These considerations, and theorems such as theorem 3.4 suggest dividing problem 1.5 into two parts:

Problem 4.1 *Are all optimal colorings, i.e. with* $k = \kappa(c,n)$*, necessarily locally symmetric, at least if* $c - 1|n$*?*

Problem 4.2 *Are all locally symmetric sparse colorings necessarily XOR colorings?*

Regarding the latter question, and XOR colorings in general, one can make the following observation. Consider a general cycle of length 4 in $\mathbf{B}_n$, $(v_0, v_1, v_2, v_3, v_0)$. XOR colorings satisfy the following two conditions:

1. $\gamma(v_3)$ depends only on $\gamma(v_0), \gamma(v_1), \gamma(v_2)$, not on the particular cycle,
2. $\gamma(v_0) = \gamma(v_2)$ implies $\gamma(v_1) = \gamma(v_3)$.

Proposition 4.3 *Any locally symmetric coloring satisfying the above two conditions is an XOR coloring.*

Proof Fix any coloring, γ, of $\mathbf{B}^n$, and a vertex, $v \in \mathbf{B}_n$. We define a group law on the colors as follows. We can assume $\eta < 1$, or else there is nothing to prove. So for any $\gamma_1 \neq \gamma_2$ neither equal $\gamma(v)$, there exist neighbors v_1, v_2 of v with $\gamma(v_i) = \gamma_i$. There exists a unique v_3 making v, v_1, v_3, v_2 a simple cycle of length 4; define $\gamma_1 + \gamma_2$ to be $\gamma(v_3)$. If $\gamma_1 = \gamma_2$ define their sum to be $\gamma(v)$, and if one of γ_1, γ_2 is $\gamma(v)$ define their sum to be the other γ_i. That this defines defines a commuatative, associative group law, with identity $\gamma(v)$, and every other element of order 2, is an easy consequence of the above conditions; for example, commutativity follows from the fact that if v_0, v_1, v_2, v_3 is a simple cycle then so is v_0, v_3, v_2, v_1; associativity follows from the fact that the sum of three colors is the antipodal point to v_0 in a subcube of $\mathbf{B}^n$ isomorphic to $\mathbf{B}^3$. This sets up an isomorphism between the colors and $\mathbf{B}^s$. One can similarly show that for every cycle $(v_0, v_1, v_2, v_3, v_0)$ we have the sum of the colors vanishing (i.e. $= \gamma(v)$). Setting coordinates on $\mathbf{B}^n$ so that v is the origin, the coloring of the neighbors of v determine XOR's, $f_1, \ldots, f_s$ such that the f_i's induce the given coloring on v and its neighbors. The conditions on the coloring imply, by induction on k, that for any $w \in \mathbf{B}^n$ of distance k to v, the coloring determined by the $f_1, \ldots, f_s$ agrees with the original coloring. □

Of course, in the above proposition, one can replace the local symmetry condition by the condition that, say, each $v \in \mathbf{B}^n$ has all colors appearing among its neighbors except for, possibly, its own color. Call such a coloring *connected.* We can restate the problems as:

Problem 4.4 *Is any optimal coloring necessarily connected and does it necessarily satisfy the above two conditions?*

References

[BBR88] C.H. Bennett, G. Brassard, and J.-M. Robert. Privacy amplification by public discussion. *SIAM J. on Computing,* 17(2):210–229, 1988.

[Bra89] G. Brassard. Cryptology— Column 1. *SIGACT News,* 20(3):15–19, Summer 1989.

[CFG+85] B. Chor, J. Friedman, O. Goldreich, J. Håstad, S. Rudich, and R. Smolensky. The bit extraction problem or t-Resilient functions. In *26th Annual Symposium on Foundations of Computer Science,* pages 396–407, 1985.

[CS88] J.H. Conway and N.J.A. Sloan. *Sphere Packings, Lattices, and Groups.* Springer-Verlag, 1988.

[Fri91] J. Friedman. On the bit extraction problem. Technical report, Princeton University, December 1991.

[KKL88] J. Kahn, G. Kalai, and N. Linial. The influence of variables on boolean functions. In *29th Annual Symposium on Foundations of Computer Science,* pages 68–80, 1988.

[Vaz85] U. Vazirani. Towards a strong communication complexity theory, or generating quasi-random sequences from two communcating slightly-random sources. In *Proc. of 17th ACM Symposium on Theory of Computing,* pages 366–378, 1985.

[vL82] J.H. van Lint. *Intorduction to Coding Theory.* Springer-Verlag, 1982.

A Mildly Exponential Approximation Algorithm for the Permanent

Mark Jerrum†

Department of Computer Science, University of Edinburgh
The King's Buildings, Edinburgh EH9 3JZ, UK
mrj@dcs.ed.ac.uk

and

Umesh Vazirani‡

Department of Computer Science, University of California
Berkeley, CA 94720, USA
vazirani@cs.berkeley.edu

ABSTRACT A new approximation algorithm for the permanent of an $n \times n$ 0,1-matrix is presented. The algorithm is shown to have worst-case time complexity $\exp\left(O(n^{1/2}\log^2 n)\right)$. Asymptotically, this represents a considerable improvement over the best existing algorithm, which has worst-case time complexity of the form $e^{\Theta(n)}$.

1. Summary

The *permanent* of an $n \times n$ matrix $A = (a_{ij} : 0 \leq i,j \leq n-1)$ is defined by

$$\mathrm{per}(A) = \sum_{\pi} \prod_{i=0}^{n-1} a_{i,\pi(i)},$$

where the sum is over all permutations π of $[n] = \{0,\ldots,n-1\}$. In this paper, A will always be a 0,1-matrix, in which case the permanent of A has a simple combinatorial interpretation: namely, $\mathrm{per}(A)$ is equal to the number of perfect matchings (1-factors) in the bipartite graph $G = (V, V', E)$, where $V = V' = [n]$, and $(i, j') \in E$ iff $a_{ij} = 1$. (Primes will be used consistently to distinguish the blocks of the bipartition of G.) The permanent has been the object of extensive study, since first appearing in 1812 in the work of Cauchy and Binet. Minc [10] has provided an excellent survey of the results of these investigations.

Despite considerable effort, and in contrast with the syntactically very similar determinant, no efficient procedure for computing the permanent is known. Valiant [12] provided convincing evidence for the inherent intractability of the permanent, by demonstrating that it is complete for the class #P of enumeration problems, and thus as hard as counting the number of satisfying assignments to a CNF formula, or the number of accepting computations of a polynomial-time-bounded nondeterministic Turing machine. In the light of this result, we should not expect to find a polynomial-time algorithm for the permanent of a 0,1-matrix. Indeed, the fastest known (exact) algorithms for the permanent have time complexity $\Theta(n2^n)$; see, for example, the method of Ryser [10, p. 122].

Recently, Karmarkar, Karp, Lipton, Lovász, and Luby [6] showed that a lower time complexity can be

† Supported by SERC grant GR/F 90363; work done in part while visiting DIMACS (Center for Discrete Mathematics and Computer Science).

‡ Supported by an NSF PYI grant, with matching equipment grant from the AT&T Foundation; work done in part while visiting DIMACS.

0-8186-2900-2/92 $3.00 © 1992 IEEE

achieved, provided we are content to settle for an algorithm that provides only an *approximation* to $\mathrm{per}(A)$ within specified relative error. Their algorithm is an example of a 'randomised approximation scheme' [7]. Let f be a function from input strings to the natural numbers. A *randomised approximation scheme* for f is a probabilistic algorithm that takes as input a string x and a real number $0 < \epsilon < 1$, and produces as output a number Y (a random variable) such that Y approximates $f(x)$ within ratio $1 + \epsilon$ with high probability. (For non-negative real numbers $a, \hat{a}, \epsilon$, we say that $\hat{a}$ *approximates* a *within ratio* $1 + \epsilon$ if $a(1+\epsilon)^{-1} \leq \hat{a} \leq a(1+\epsilon)$.) For definiteness we take the phrase "with high probability" to mean with probability at least $\frac{3}{4}$. The success probability may be boosted to $1 - \delta$ for any desired $\delta > 0$ by running the algorithm $\mathrm{O}(\log \delta^{-1})$ times and taking the median of the results [5, Lemma 6.1].

The randomised approximation scheme for $\mathrm{per}(A)$ proposed by Karmarkar et al. has time complexity $\epsilon^{-2}\,\mathrm{poly}(n)\,2^{n/2}$. It is a classical Monte Carlo algorithm which performs a sequence of trials using an unbiased estimator for the permanent; this estimator is closely modelled on one given earlier by Godsil and Gutman. The worst-case time complexity of this algorithm is the lowest of any existing approximation scheme for the permanent; nevertheless it shares with the exact algorithm of Ryser the general form $\mathrm{e}^{\Theta(n)}$.

In this paper we use different techniques to design a randomised approximation scheme for $\mathrm{per}(A)$ that has time complexity $\epsilon^{-2} \exp\left(\mathrm{O}(n^{1/2} \log^2 n)\right)$. The new algorithm is easily sketched at an informal level, though the details need careful working out. The approach is one of 'divide-and-conquer', and can best be described using the graph-theoretic formulation introduced earlier. Let G be a bipartite graph, and suppose that we wish to estimate the number $N(G)$ of perfect matchings in G. The progress of the algorithm is controlled by the expansion properties of G. If G has sufficiently large expansion ratio then an existing approximation scheme of Jerrum and Sinclair [4] is used to estimate $N(G)$ directly with acceptable speed. Otherwise a set of vertices $A \subset V$ is found that has the property that A is adjacent to rather few vertices in V'. The set A foms a 'constriction' in G, which allows an economical decomposition of G into subproblems that may be solved recursively. The full description and analysis of this approximation scheme form the main body of this note.

Given our current (lack of) knowledge, it is entirely possible that there exists a randomised approximation scheme for $\mathrm{per}(A)$ that has time complexity $\mathrm{poly}(n, \epsilon^{-1})$. (Such an approximation scheme is said to be *fully polynomial.*) Thus, although the approximation scheme presented here is asymptotically much faster than any previously proposed, it may still be very far from optimal. The question of whether there exists a fully-polynomial (randomised) approximation scheme for $\mathrm{per}(A)$ presents an intriguing challenge. Optimists may take heart from the fact that such algorithms are known for some restricted classes of 0,1-matrices [4, 3]; these classes have the property that the proportion of $n \times n$ matrices lying within the class tends to 1 as n tends to infinity.

2. The algorithm and its analysis

Let G be a bipartite graph on vertex set $V + V'$ and edge set E, where $V = V' = [n] = \{0, 1, \ldots, n-1\}$. We shall use primes to distinguish vertices in V' from those in V; thus each vertex v in V has a counterpart v' in V', and each subset U of V has a counterpart $U' = \{u' \in V' : u \in U\}$ in V'. Denote by G^* the reversal of G, i.e., the graph with vertex set $V + V'$ and edge set $E^* = \left\{(u, v') \in V \times V' : (v, u') \in E\right\}$. For each subset $A \subseteq V$, let $\Gamma_G(A)$ denote the set of all vertices in V' that are adjacent to some vertex in A. Suppose α is in the range $0 < \alpha \leq 1$. We say that G is an *α-expander* if $|\Gamma_G(A)| \geq (1+\alpha)|A|$ for every $A \subseteq V$ with $|A| \leq \frac{1}{2}n$. Let $N(G)$ denote the number of perfect matchings in G and $N^-(G)$ the number of *near-perfect* matchings in G, i.e., matchings that leave precisely two vertices uncovered.

Lemma 1. If G and G^* are α-expanders then $N^-(G)/N(G) = \exp\left(\mathrm{O}(\alpha^{-1} \log^2 n)\right)$.

We postpone the proof of Lemma 1 to allow an investigation of its consequences.

Corollary 2. There is a randomised approximation

scheme MarkovSim that meets the following specification:

(i) the input to MarkovSim is a triple (G, α, ϵ), where G is a bipartite graph, α is a number which is to be interpreted as a guarantee that G and G^* are both α-expanders, and $0 < \epsilon < 1$ controls the accuracy of the result;

(ii) the output is a random variable that with probability at least $\frac{3}{4}$ approximates $N(G)$ within ratio $1 + \epsilon$;

(iii) the execution time of MarkovSim is

$$\epsilon^{-2} \exp\left(O(\alpha^{-1} \log^2 n)\right).$$

Proof. The approximation scheme in question is presented as Figure 2 of [4], which should be considered in conjunction with the discussion following Corollary 5.2, and the statement and proof of Theorem 5.3. (The quantity $q(n)$ that appears in the figure is an upper bound on the ratio $N^-(G)/N(G)$.) The algorithm works by simulating a Markov chain whose states are matchings in G; hence we dub the procedure here "MarkovSim". (The notion of basing an approximation scheme for the permanent on such a Markov chain was first proposed by Broder [1], but two years were to elapse before a correct analysis was completed [11, 4, 9].) The procedure call "$\mathcal{G}(G(c), \xi)$" which appears in MarkovSim invokes a simulation of the Markov chain; this simulation runs until the chain is near to its equilibrium distribution, at which point the current state (matching) is returned as a sample. (The parameter ξ determines how close the Markov chain must be to equilibrium before the sample is taken.) A single call to the simulation procedure has time complexity $\log(\epsilon^{-1})\,\mathrm{poly}(n, \rho)$, where ρ is an upper bound on the ratio $N^-(G)/N(G)$; and the total number of calls to the procedure is bounded by $\epsilon^{-2}\,\mathrm{poly}(n)$. Since these procedure calls dominate the time complexity of MarkovSim, the overall time complexity is bounded by $\epsilon^{-2} \log(\epsilon^{-1})\,\mathrm{poly}(n, \rho)$. Observe that there is no point in taking ϵ^{-1} to be greater than $3n!$, for this already guarantees an *exact* evaluation of $N(G)$; thus, without loss of generality, we may assume $\log \epsilon^{-1} = O(n \log n)$. Further observe that $\rho \geq N^-(G)/N(G) \geq n$. These two observations allow us to simplify the expression of the time complexity of MarkovSim to $\epsilon^{-2}\,\mathrm{poly}(\rho)$. The corollary follows from Lemma 1, setting $\rho = \exp\left(O(\alpha^{-1} \log^2 n)\right)$.

Proof of Lemma 1. Let M be any near-perfect matching in G. We demonstrate that M can be transformed to a perfect matching by augmentation along a short alternating path. It follows easily that the number of near-perfect matchings cannot exceed the number of perfect matchings by a large factor.

Define an *alternating path* (in G) to be a path that is composed of edges that are alternately elements of M and $E - M$. (The first and last edges of the path may or may not be elements of M.) Let $s \in V$ and $t' \in V'$ be the vertices left uncovered by M. We shall show that s is joined to t' via an alternating path of length at most $4k + 1$, where k is that smallest integer such that $(1 + \alpha)^k > \frac{1}{2}n$; observe that $k = O(\alpha^{-1} \log n)$. Let A_i, for $0 \leq i \leq k$, be the set of vertices in V that are reachable from s via an alternating path of length at most $2i$. The expansion property of G entails $|A_{i+1}| \geq (1 + \alpha)|A_i|$ provided $|A_i| \leq \frac{1}{2}n$. Thus $|A_k| \geq \min\{(1 + \alpha)^k, \frac{1}{2}n\} = \frac{1}{2}n$. Similarly, let B'_i, for $0 \leq i \leq k$ be the set of vertices in V' that are reachable from t' via an alternating path of length at most $2i$. The expansion property of G^* entails $|B'_k| \geq \frac{1}{2}n$. Now there must be an edge joining A_k to B'_k, and hence an alternating path from s to t' of length at most $4k + 1$. (If the edge e joining A_k to B'_k happens to be an element of M, we apparently do not obtain an alternating path; note, however, that the edge e must then occur three times in succession, and can be collapsed to a single occurrence.)

We have demonstrated that every near-perfect matching M may be associated with a perfect matching $\overline{M}$ by augmentation along an alternating path of length $O(\alpha^{-1} \log n)$. This process assigns at most $\exp\left(O(\alpha^{-1} \log^2 n)\right)$ near-perfect matchings to any given perfect matching. (To recover M from $\overline{M}$ we follow an alternating path of length at most $4k + 1$, the selection of which involves a sequence of at most $2k + 1$ choices from among at most n possibilities.) Thus $N^-(G)/N(G) = \exp\left(O(\alpha^{-1} \log^2 n)\right)$, as claimed.

Suppose the bipartite graph G contains a perfect matching, say M. It is clear that $|\Gamma_G(A)| \geq |A|$

for every set $A \subseteq V$; let us call A *tight* [8] if equality holds. Note that the collection of all tight sets in V is closed under union and intersection; in particular for each $v \in V$ there is a *smallest* tight set containing v, which we shall denote by $\Delta_G(v)$. Note that $\Delta_G(v)$ is the set of all vertices in V that can be reached by an even-length alternating path in G which starts with an edge not in M; thus the sets $\Delta_G(v)$ are easy to compute in polynomial time. The procedure TESTEXPANSION presented in Figure 1 uses the idea of tight sets to compute (approximately) the expansion ratio of the input graph G. If the expansion ratio is not too small, Corollary 2 can be applied to estimate $N(G)$ directly. Otherwise, TESTEXPANSION returns a 'constriction' in G (a set $A \subset V$ such that $|\Gamma_G(A)|/|A|$ is close to 1) which permits an efficient decomposition into subproblems which can then be solved recursively. The specification of TESTEXPANSION is made explicit in Lemma 3.

procedure TESTEXPANSION(G, α);
begin
  Let M be any perfect matching in G;
  Reorder the vertices in V' so that
    M matches each vertex v in V
    with the corresponding vertex v' in V';
  for each subset $X \subset V$ with $|X| < \frac{1}{2}\alpha n$ **do**
    Let $\widehat{G}$ be the graph obtained from G
      by removing vertices X, X',
      and all incident edges;
(1)   **if** $\exists v \in V$ with $\frac{1}{4}n < |\Delta_{\widehat{G}}(v)| \leq \frac{1}{2}n$
    then
      $A := \Delta_{\widehat{G}}(v)$
    else
      Let $v_0, v_1, \dots, v_{n-|X|-1}$ be an enumeration
        of vertices $v \in V - X$ satisfying
        $|\Delta_{\widehat{G}}(v_0)| \leq \cdots \leq |\Delta_{\widehat{G}}(v_{n-|X|-1})|$;
      $i := 0$; $A :=$;
(2)   **while** $|A \cup \Delta_{\widehat{G}}(v_i)| \leq \frac{1}{2}n$ **do**
        $A := A \cup \Delta_{\widehat{G}}(v_i)$; $i := i + 1$
(3)   **if** $|X|/|A| < 2\alpha$ **then** output A;   **halt**
(4) output "G is an α-expander"
end

FIGURE 1. *Algorithm for testing the expansion factor of a graph*

Lemma 3. On input (G, α), where G is a bipartite graph and $\alpha > 0$, the procedure TESTEXPANSION presented in Figure 1 *either*

(i) correctly identifies G as an α-expander, *or*

(ii) produces a set $A \subseteq V$ such that $|A| \leq \frac{1}{2}n$ and $|\Gamma_G(A)| < (1 + 2\alpha)|A|$.

The procedure has time complexity $\exp\big(O(\alpha n \log n)\big)$.

Proof. It is clear that the algorithm terminates, and either outputs a set $A \subseteq V$, or an assertion that G is an α-expander. In the first instance we must assure ourselves that the set A satisfies the conditions $|A| \leq \frac{1}{2}n$ and $|\Gamma_G(A)| < (1 + 2\alpha)|A|$, and in the second that the assertion is correct.

Suppose first that line (3) is reached and the condition $|X|/|A| < 2\alpha$ is true. The set A is a union of tight sets, and hence is itself tight (with respect to the graph $\widehat{G}$); equivalently, $\Gamma_{\widehat{G}}(A) = A'$. Thus $|\Gamma_G(A)| \leq |A' \cup X'| = |A \cup X| < (1 + 2\alpha)|A|$, as required.

Now suppose that the for-loop runs to completion, and line (4) is reached. We must demonstrate that the claim that G is an α-expander is correct. Suppose to the contrary that there exists a set $B \subset V$ such that $|B| \leq \frac{1}{2}n$ and $|\Gamma_G(B)| < (1 + \alpha)|B|$. Note that $\Gamma_G(B)$ can be written as a disjoint union $B' + X'$ with $|X'| < \alpha|B|$. Since $|X| < \frac{1}{2}\alpha n$, the for-loop will eventually consider the set X; observe that B is tight with respect to the graph $\widehat{G}$ obtained by removing vertices X, X', and all incident edges. We distinguish two cases and obtain a contradiction in both.

CASE 1. There exists a vertex $v \in V$ such that $\frac{1}{4}n < |\Delta_{\widehat{G}}(v)| \leq \frac{1}{2}n$. This situation is caught in line (1). Since $|A| > \frac{1}{4}n$ and $|X| < \frac{1}{2}\alpha n$, the for-loop terminates prematurely at line (3), contrary to our assumption.

CASE 2. There does not exist a vertex $v \in V$ such that $\frac{1}{4}n < |\Delta_{\widehat{G}}(v)| \leq \frac{1}{2}n$. After execution of the while-loop in line (2) we are left with a set $A \subset V$ satisfying $|A| \leq \frac{1}{2}n$ and $|A \cup \Delta_{\widehat{G}}(v_i)| > \frac{1}{2}n$. Now either $|\Delta_{\widehat{G}}(v_i)| \leq \frac{1}{4}n$ or $|\Delta_{\widehat{G}}(v_i)| > \frac{1}{2}n$. If the first inequality holds, $|A| > \frac{1}{4}n$ and we obtain a contradiction as in Case 1. If the second inequality holds then no v_j with $j \geq i$ can be a member of B, and hence $A \supseteq B$. Thus $|X|/|A| \leq |X|/|B| < \alpha$ and again the for-loop terminates prematurely at line (3).

We now have all the ingredients for the proposed approximation scheme, which is presented in Figure 2 as the function CountPM. The analysis of CountPM is the subject of Theorem 4.

function CountPM(G);
⟦Returns an approximation to the number of perfect matchings in G.⟧
begin
  if $n = 1$ **then return** 0 or 1 as appropriate;
  if G has no perfect matchings **then return** 0;
  $\alpha := n^{-1/2}$;
(1) Execute TestExpansion(G, α) and TestExpansion(G^*, α);
(2) **if** G and G^* are both confirmed as α-expanders **then**
(3)   Call MarkovSim $2t+1$ times with parameters $G, \alpha, \hat{\epsilon}$;
    ⟦The parameters t and $\hat{\epsilon}$ are initialised before top-level entry to CountPM.⟧
(4)   **return** the median of the $2t+1$ trials
  else
    Wlog, let $A \subset V$ satisfy $|A| \leq \frac{1}{2}n$ and $|\Gamma_G(A)| < (1+2\alpha)|A|$;
    sum $:= 0$;
(5)   **for** $B' \subseteq \Gamma_G(A)$ with $|B'| = |A|$ **do**
      Let G_0 be the subgraph of G induced by A and B';
      Let G_1 be the subgraph of G induced by $V - A$ and $V' - B'$;
(6)   *sum* $:=$ *sum* $+$ CountPM(G_0) $\times$ CountPM(G_1)
    return *sum*
end

FIGURE 2. *Recursive algorithm for counting perfect matchings*

Theorem 4. With appropriate choices for the parameters t and $\hat{\epsilon}$, the algorithm CountPM of Figure 2 is a randomised approximation scheme for the number of perfect matchings in G. The time complexity of CountPM is $\epsilon^{-2} \exp\left(O(n^{1/2}\log^2 n)\right)$.

Proof. Let us first deal with the correctness of CountPM, deciding on the parameters t and $\hat{\epsilon}$ as we do so. First imagine an idealised situation in which the procedure MarkovSim *always* returns the *exact* number of matchings in G. Then it is not too difficult to see that CountPM also produces the correct result. The crucial step to check is the division into sub-problems effected by the for-loop in line (5). Observe that any perfect matching M in G matches $A \subset V$ with some subset $B' \subseteq \Gamma_G(A)$ of size $|A|$, and that the set of all matchings in G can be partitioned according to the set B' so defined. The for-loop ranges over the blocks of this partition, accumulating the number of matchings in each block as it goes. To see that the body of the loop is correct, one merely needs to observe that the each perfect matching in the block defined by B' can be decomposed into a disjoint union of a perfect matching in G_0 and a perfect matching in G_1.

Next set $\hat{\epsilon} = \epsilon/2n_0$, where n_0 is the value of n at the top level of recursion, and suppose that MarkovSim always produces a result that is within ratio $1+\hat{\epsilon}$ of the correct value. (This is still an idealised situation, since the specification of MarkovSim allows large deviations with probability $\frac{1}{4}$.) Then a simple induction on n establishes that CountPM returns a result that is within ratio $(1+\hat{\epsilon})^n$ of $N(G)$ when applied to a bipartite graph G with $n+n$ vertices. In particular, the result returned from the top-level call to CountPM is within ratio $(1+\hat{\epsilon})^{n_0} = (1+\epsilon/2n_0)^{n_0} < 1+\epsilon$, as required.

Finally, suppose that MarkovSim is as specified, and produces a result that is within ratio $1+\hat{\epsilon}$ with probability at least $\frac{3}{4}$. Let us call the sequence of trials carried out in line (3) an *experiment*, and say that the experiment is a *success* if the median of the $2t+1$ trials approximates $N(G)$ within ratio $1+\hat{\epsilon}$. We shall choose t so that the probability that *every* experiment is a success is at least $\frac{3}{4}$. An easy induction on n establishes that the number of experiments is bounded by 8^n. (This is a gross overestimate, as will be apparent once we have completed the analysis of the time complexity of CountPM.) By [5, Lemma 6.1], the failure probability of a single experiment may be reduced to $8^{-(n_0+1)}$ by setting $t = 18(n_0+1) = O(n_0)$. (The point here is that t need not be very large.) With this choice of t, the probability that *every* experiment is a success is at least $\frac{3}{4}$. This completes the validation of CountPM.

Let $T(n,\epsilon)$ be the (worst-case) time complexity of CountPM as a function of the size of G and the accuracy parameter ϵ. (Technically, the time complexity depends on $\hat{\epsilon}$ and t, and hence should be a function also of n_0; however, the dependence on n_0 is cubic, and can safely be swept under the carpet in the current context.) We show, by induction on n, that $T(n,\epsilon) \le \epsilon^{-2}\exp(cn^{1/2}\ln^2 n)$, where c is a suitable constant. ¿From Figure 2,

$$T(n,\epsilon) \le \max\{T_1(n,\epsilon), T_2(n,\epsilon)\}, \qquad (1)$$

where $T_1(n,\epsilon)$ and $T_2(n,\epsilon)$ are, respectively, the time complexities conditional on whether the 'then' or 'else' part of the if-statement is selected at line (2). The time complexity T_1 is determined by the calls to TestExpansion in line (1), and the sequence of $2t+1$ trials using MarkovSim in line (3). From Corollary 2 and Lemma 3, setting $\alpha = n^{-1/2}$, we have

$$\begin{aligned} T_1(n,\epsilon) &\le \exp\left(\mathrm{O}(n^{1/2}\log n)\right) + \epsilon^{-2}\exp\left(\mathrm{O}(n^{1/2}\log^2 n)\right) \\ &\le \epsilon^{-2}\exp\left(\mathrm{O}(n^{1/2}\log^2 n)\right). \qquad (2)\end{aligned}$$

The time complexity T_2 is determined by the call to TestExpansion in line (1) and the recursive calls to CountPM in line (6). Let $S(k)$ be an upper bound on the number of subproblems generated (i.e., the number of times the for-loop is executed) when the set A returned by TestExpansion has size k. By Lemma 3,

$$\begin{aligned} T_2(n,\epsilon) &\le \exp\left(\mathrm{O}(n^{1/2}\log n)\right) \\ &\quad + \max_{1\le k\le n/2}\{S(k)[T(k)+T(n-k)]\}. \qquad (3)\end{aligned}$$

In preparation for the inductive step, we proceed to estimate each of the quantities appearing on the right hand side of (3). Suppose the set A returned by TestExpansion is of size k; then $|\Gamma_G(A)| = k+d$, where $d < 2\alpha k = 2kn^{-1/2}$, and

$$\begin{aligned} S(k) = \binom{k+d}{k} &\le n^d \le \exp(2kn^{-1/2}\ln n) \qquad (4) \\ &\le \exp(n^{1/2}\ln n). \qquad (5)\end{aligned}$$

Applying the induction hypothesis we obtain (since $k \le \frac{1}{2}n$)

$$\begin{aligned} T(k,\epsilon) &\le \epsilon^{-2}\exp(ck^{1/2}\ln^2 k) \\ &\le \epsilon^{-2}\exp(\tfrac{3}{4}cn^{1/2}\ln^2 n), \qquad (6)\end{aligned}$$

and, again,

$$\begin{aligned} T(n-k,\epsilon) &\le \epsilon^{-2}\exp\left(c(n-k)^{1/2}\ln^2(n-k)\right) \\ &\le \epsilon^{-2}\exp\left(c(1-\tfrac{1}{2}kn^{-1})n^{1/2}\ln^2 n\right) \\ &\le \epsilon^{-2}\exp\left(cn^{1/2}\ln^2 n - \tfrac{1}{2}ckn^{-1/2}\ln^2 n\right). \qquad (7)\end{aligned}$$

Now suppose $c \ge 8$. By combining inequalities (5) and (6), we have

$$S(k)T(k,\epsilon) \le \epsilon^{-2}\exp\left(\tfrac{7}{8}cn^{1/2}\ln^2 n\right), \qquad (8)$$

and by combining (4) and (7),

$$\begin{aligned} S(k)T(n-k,\epsilon) &\le \epsilon^{-2}\exp\left(cn^{1/2}\ln^2 n - \tfrac{1}{4}ckn^{-1/2}\ln^2 n\right) \\ &\le \epsilon^{-2}\exp\left(cn^{1/2}\ln^2 n - 2n^{-1/2}\right) \\ &\le (1-n^{-1/2})\epsilon^{-2}\exp\left(cn^{1/2}\ln^2 n\right). \qquad (9)\end{aligned}$$

It is immediate from (2) that

$$T_1(n,\epsilon) \le \epsilon^{-2}\exp(cn^{1/2}\ln^2 n)$$

for c sufficiently large, and it follows easily from (3), (8), and (9) that $T_2(n,\epsilon) \le \epsilon^{-2}\exp(cn^{1/2}\ln^2 n)$. Finally, from (1), $T(n,\epsilon) \le \epsilon^{-2}\exp(cn^{1/2}\ln^2 n)$, which completes the inductive step.

3. Extensions and open problems

The algorithm presented here rests on a tradeoff: a graph with a high expansion factor is amenable to direct solution using an existing approximation algorithm, while a graph with low expansion factor admits an efficient recursive decomposition into subproblems. The exponent $\frac{1}{2}$ appearing in the expression for the time complexity arises quite naturally from a consideration of the crossover point for this tradeoff, and it seems unlikely that a further improvement in asymptotic time-complexity is possible without the introduction of some new technique. The ultimate goal must surely be to construct a fully polynomial approximation scheme (or to provide convincing complexity-theoretic evidence that no such scheme exists). However, a reasonable intermediate goal might be to design an approximation algorithm with 'quasi-polynomial' time complexity, i.e., with time complexity $O(\exp(\text{poly}(\log n)))$.

Of possible generalisations of the problem considered in this note, the two most natural appear to be (1) estimating the permanent of a general non-negative integer matrix, and (2) estimating the number of perfect matchings in a general (non-bipartite) graph. Provided the entries in the matrix are small, the first of these problems can handled by reduction to the 0,1 case. Suppose A is an $n \times n$ matrix of non-negative integers whose binary expansions are uniformly bounded in length by k. It is not difficult to show that there exists an $m \times m$ matrix A' with 0,1-entries for which $\text{per}(A') = \text{per}(A)$; here $m = O(nk)$, and the matrix A' is easily constructed in polynomial time. However, if the matrix entries are very large integers (of roughly n bits) it will be seen that this reduction provides no gain in efficiency over exact computation using Ryser's algorithm. The question of whether Ryser's method can be beaten for general non-negative matrices remains open.

It seems plausible that the second generalisation (to non-bipartite graphs) can be handled by methods similar to those employed in this note. The stumbling block is Lemma 1: even if the lemma itself can be extended to non-bipartite graphs G, the proof presented here cannot.

References

[1] Andrei Z. BRODER, How hard is it to marry at random? (On the approximation of the permanent), *Proceedings of the 18th ACM Symposium on Theory of Computing*, 1986, pp. 50–58. Erratum in *Proceedings of the 20th ACM Symposium on Theory of Computing*, 1988, p. 551.

[2] C. D. GODSIL and I. GUTMAN, On the matching polynomial of a graph, *Algebraic Methods in Graph Theory, I* (L. Lovász and V. T. Sós, editors), Colloquia Mathematica Societatis János Bolyai **25**, North-Holland, 1981.

[3] Mark JERRUM, *An analysis of a Monte-Carlo algorithm for Estimating the Permanent*, Report ECS-LFCS-91-164, Department of Computer Science, University of Edinburgh, UK, June 1991.

[4] Mark JERRUM and Alistair SINCLAIR, Approximating the permanent, *SIAM Journal on Computing* **18** (1989), pp. 1149–1178.

[5] Mark R. JERRUM, Leslie G. VALIANT, and Vijay V. VAZIRANI, Random generation of combinatorial structures from a uniform distribution, *Theoretical Computer Science* **43** (1986), pp. 169–188.

[6] N. KARMARKAR, R. KARP, R. LIPTON, L. LOVÁSZ, and M. LUBY, *A Monte-Carlo Algorithm for Estimating the Permanent*, Technical Report TR-90-063, International Computer Science Institute, Berkeley CA, USA.

[7] R. M. KARP and M. LUBY, Monte-Carlo algorithms for enumeration and reliability problems, *Proceedings of the 24th IEEE Symposium on Foundations of Computer Science*, 1983, pp. 56–64.

[8] L. LOVÁSZ and M. D. PLUMMER, *Matching Theory*, North-Holland, Amsterdam, 1986.

[9] M. MIHAIL, On coupling and the approximation of the permanent, *Information Processing Letters* **30** (1989), pp. 91-95.

[10] Henryk MINC, *Permanents*, Addison Wesley, 1978.

[11] Alistair SINCLAIR, *Randomised Algorithms for Counting and Generating Combinatorial Structures*, PhD Thesis, University of Edinburgh, June 1988.

[12] L. G. VALIANT, The complexity of computing the permanent, *Theoretical Computer Science* **8** (1979), pp. 189–201.

Competitive Analysis of Financial Games

R. El-Yaniv
University of Toronto

A. Fiat
Tel-Aviv University

R. Karp *
UC Berkeley
and
ICSI

G. Turpin
University of Toronto

Abstract

In the *unidirectional conversion problem* an on-line player is given the task of converting dollars to yen over some period of time. Each day, a new exchange rate is announced, and the player must decide how many dollars to convert. His goal is to minimize the *competitive ratio*, defined as $\sup_E \frac{P_{OPT}(E)}{P_X(E)}$, where E ranges over exchange rate sequences, $P_{OPT}(E)$ is the number of yen obtained by an optimal off-line algorithm, and $P_X(E)$ is the number of yen obtained by the on-line algorithm X. We also consider a continuous version of the problem, in which the exchange rate varies over a continuous time interval. The on-line player's *a priori* information about the fluctuation of exchange rates distinguishes different variants of the problem. For three variants we show that a simple *threat-based strategy* is optimal for the on-line player and determine its competitive ratio. We also derive and analyze an optimal policy for the on-line player when he knows the probability distribution of the maximum value that the exchange rate will reach. Finally, we consider a *bidirectional conversion problem*, in which the player may trade dollars for yen or yen for dollars.

1 Introduction

Many ongoing financial activities, such as currency exchange or mortgage financing, must be carried out in an *on-line* fashion, with no secure knowledge of future events. Faced with this lack of knowledge, players of these financial games often use models based on assumptions about the future distribution of relevant quantities such as exchange rates or mortgage rates, and aim for acceptable results *on the average*.

An alternate approach in such situations - and the one we explore here - is to use *competitive analysis* (first applied to on-line algorithms by Sleator and Tarjan in [ST85]). In this approach, the performance of an on-line strategy is measured against that of an optimal off-line strategy having full knowledge of future events. For some measure of cost or of profit, we try to minimize the worst-case ratio of on-line cost to optimal cost or of optimal profit to on-line profit; if this ratio is bounded for all event sequences, we deem the on-line strategy to be *competitive* and call the supremum of this ratio the *competitive ratio* of the strategy. One advantage of this performance measure over the traditional average-case measure is that for most nontrivial financial activities it is extremely difficult to come up with an accurate probabilistic model.

In devising a competitive strategy, the on-line player will not be able to escape the necessity of making *some* assumptions, or having *some* knowledge about future events, but these need not be probabilistic in nature. For example, instead of knowledge about the distribution of future exchange rates, an on-line strategy might be based only on knowledge of the bounds on possible exchange rates over the period in question, and should work well no matter how erratically (or unfortunately) the rates vary from day to day.

Despite the obvious significance and appeal of investment problems, we have found only two previous references concerned with the competitive analysis of on-line financial decision-making. The paper [Cover91] deals with the problem of portfolio selection for investment in the stock market. Here, the (on-line) player must determine the proportion of his wealth invested in each of the stocks in the market. Cover presents a simple on-line strategy that (based on the market history) dynamically changes the distribution of its current wealth among the stocks. It is shown that this on-line strategy performs asymptotically as well as any static off-line portfolio selection strategy. Such a strategy fixes an optimal investment portfolio at the start of the game (based on a full knowledge of future events), but it is not allowed to change it thereafter. Note that the on-line portfolio selection strategy is very robust; it does not assume anything about the behavior of future events. The paper [Ragh91] analyzes the competitive performance of an on-line investment algorithm against a "statistical adversary," whose request sequence is required to satisfy certain distributional requirements. Thus, both of these papers restrict the adversary: in the first case, by limiting him to a static policy, and in the second case by restricting the request sequence.

We suspect that other potential investigators have been deterred by the belief that, in problems such as stock market investment, knowledge of the future is such an overwhelming advantage that it would be impossible for an on-line algorithm to achieve a bounded competitive ratio. Nevertheless, we shall show that, if suitable constraints are placed on the future evolution of prices or exchange rates, then finite, and indeed rather small, competitive ratios can be achieved

*Supported by NSF Grant No. CCR-9005448

0-8186-2900-2/92 $3.00 © 1992 IEEE

in fairly realistic situations.

Our main example is one-way currency conversion, which deals with converting assets from one form to another, for example, dollars to yen. For this problem, we show that a surprisingly small competitive ratio can be achieved under very moderate assumptions about the on-line player's knowledge concerning the exchange rates: only upper and lower bounds on possible exchange rates need be known. We investigate different versions of this problem, given by varying the on-line player's knowledge. We conclude with some preliminary results for two-way currency conversion, where the on-line player converts currency back and forth.

2 The Unidirectional Conversion Problem

2.1 Problem statement

In the *unidirectional conversion problem* an on-line player is given the job of converting dollars to yen over some period of time. This is unidirectional conversion since the on-line player may not convert yen already purchased back to dollars. At any given time there is an *exchange rate* giving the number of yen that can be purchased for one dollar. The problem has a *continuous version*, in which the exchange rate fluctuates during some continuous period of time and the on-line player may trade continuously, and a *discrete version*, in which a new exchange rate is announced on the morning of each trading day, and remains fixed throughout the day. At the end of the trading period the trader *must* convert the remaining dollars at the current rate. The problem is designated as *on-line* since the player must determine his transactions without knowing what the future rates will be.

Considering the discrete version first, let $E = e_1, e_2, \ldots$ be a sequence of exchange rates. Let $P_X(E)$ denote the number of yen obtained by an on-line conversion strategy X that starts with D_0 dollars (without loss of generality $D_0 = 1$) and converts the dollars to yen in accordance with E. Let OPT denote the optimal off-line strategy (i.e., the one that waits and converts all its dollars to yen when the highest exchange rate is reached). For any on-line algorithm X, the *competitive ratio* is defined as $\sup_E \frac{P_{OPT}(E)}{P_X(E)}$. A small competitive ratio implies that X can do well in comparison with OPT. The set-up for the continuous case is similar, except that the exchange rate sequence E is replaced by an exchange rate function $E(t)$ defined over some time interval $[0, T]$, and trading can take place continuously during this interval.

2.2 Assumptions about the fluctuation of the exchange rate

The on-line player's *a priori* information about the exchange rate sequence or exchange rate function defines particular variants of the game. Let

- M = upper bound on possible exchange rates,
- m = lower bound on possible exchange rates,
- a = initial exchange rate,
- $\Phi = M/m$ (call this the *fluctuation ratio*),
- n = the number of trading days (in the discrete case).

2.3 Results

In this paper we derive optimal on-line algorithms for three variants of the unidirectional conversion problem.

Variant 1 The continuous version, with M, m and a known to the on-line player;

Variant 2 The discrete version, with M, m and n known to the on-line player;

Variant 3 The discrete version, in which the on-line player knows n and Φ, but does not know either M or m.

2.4 Optimal unidirectional conversion strategy

In this section we describe a general conversion strategy that yields optimal algorithms for the three problem variants. The strategy consists of three rules. Execution of the strategy requires knowledge of r, the competitive ratio that the algorithm is trying to attain. Later we will show how the smallest attainable competitive ratio is calculated.

Rule (i) At the end of the game (on the last day in the discrete case, or at the last instant in the continuous case), spend all the remaining dollars;

Rule (ii) Except at the end of the game, purchase only when the current rate is the highest seen so far;

Rule(iii) Whenever the exchange rate reaches a new maximum convert just enough to ensure that a competitive ratio of r would be obtained if an adversary dropped the exchange rate to m and kept it there throughout the rest of the game.

For the three variants that we are considering, these rules completely determine the on-line algorithm. We refer to this algorithm as the *threat-based algorithm*, since it converts dollars to yen only when forced to by the threat that the exchange rate will drop permanently to m.

2.5 The continuous case, with m, M and a known

In this case we can formulate the threat-based algorithm in terms of two functions, $D(x)$ and $Y(x)$, giving the number of dollars and yen, respectively, that the on-line player possesses just after the exchange rate has assumed the value x for the first time. Assume that the on-line player is trying to attain the competitive ratio r. We may assume that the exchange rate is monotone increasing, since both the optimal off-line algorithm and the threat-based algorithm conduct transactions only when the exchange rate reaches a new maximum. We may also assume that the exchange rate is a continuous function, since discontinuous jumps merely enable the threat-based algorithm to exchange its dollars at more favorable rates. Suppose the exchange rate increases continuously from a to M. Then Rules (i),(ii) and (iii) imply that the functions $D(\cdot)$ and $Y(\cdot)$ satisfy the following conditions:

Condition (i) $D(x) = 1$ and $Y(x) = 0$ when $x \le rm$, since Rule (iii) does not require any exchanges until the rate reaches rm.
Condition (ii) $mD(x) + Y(x) = x/r$ for all $x \in [rm, M]$; here x is the number of yen the off-line player realizes if the maximum exchange rate is x, and $mD(x) + Y(x)$ is the amount the threat-based algorithm would realize if the rate dropped from x to m and its $D(x)$ remaining dollars were converted at rate m.
Condition (iii) For all $x \in [rm, M]$, $xD'(x) = -Y'(x)$ since each dollar exchanged at rate x yields x yen.

These conditions determine the functions $D(\cdot)$ and $Y(\cdot)$ uniquely, and thus the policy achieves its target competitive ratio r if and only if $D(M) \ge 0$; i.e., if and only if the above conditions can be satisfied without spending more than the initially available number of dollars, even when the adversary increases the exchange rate continuously from a to M.

We shall calculate the conditions under which the competitive ratio r is achievable.

Case 1: $a \le rm$. In this case $D(x) = 1$ and $Y(x) = 0$ for $x \in [a, rm]$.

For $x \in [rm, M]$ we may differentiate the equation $mD(x)+Y(x) = x/r$ to obtain $mD'(x)+Y'(x) = 1/r$. Combining this with the equation $xD'(x) = -Y'(x)$ we obtain $D'(x) = -\frac{1}{r(x-m)}$. Thus $D(M) = D(rm) + \int_{rm}^{M} D'(x)dx = 1 - \int_{rm}^{M} \frac{1}{r(x-m)}dx = 1 - \frac{1}{r}\ln\frac{M-m}{rm-m}$. It follows that the competitive ratio r is achievable if and only if $\frac{1}{r}\ln\frac{M-m}{rm-m} \le 1$. Of particular interest is the case where the initial exchange rate is unknown to the on-line algorithm, so that the pessimistic assumption $a = m$ must be made. In this case, the optimal attainable competitive ratio $r*$ is the unique root of the equation $r = \ln\frac{M-m}{rm-m}$.

Case 2: $a > rm$. In this case $mD(a)+Y(a) = a/r$ and $Y(a) = a(1-D(a))$. This gives $D(a) = \frac{a-a/r}{a-m}$ and $D(M) = \frac{a-a/r}{a-m} - \int_{a}^{M}\frac{1}{r(x-m)}dx = \frac{a-a/r}{a-m} - \frac{1}{r}\ln\frac{M-m}{a-m}$. The competitive ratio r is attainable if and only if this quantity is nonnegative.

From these results it is easy to determine the optimal attainable competitive ratio. The first step is to determine whether the competitive ratio a/m is attainable; this will be the case if and only if $1 - \frac{m}{a}\ln\frac{M-m}{a-m} \ge 0$. If this rate is not attainable then we are in Case 1 and the optimal competitive ratio is $r*$. If the rate is attainable then we are in Case 2 and the optimal competitive ratio is the unique root of $\frac{a-a/r}{a-m} - \frac{1}{r}\ln\frac{M-m}{a-m} = 0$.

We omit the proof that the threat-based algorithm achieves the best competitive ratio of any on-line algorithm. A similar theorem will be proved below, in connection with Variant 2.

Some numerical examples will indicate the slow growth of the optimal competitive ratio as a function of M/m. We consider the case $a = m$, in which the optimal competitive ratio is $r*$; larger values of a serve to decrease the competitive ratio. When $M/m = 2$, $r* = 1.28$ (rounded to two decimal places); when $M/m = 4$, $r* = 1.60$; when $M/m = 8$, $r* = 1.97$; when $M/m = 16$, $r* = 2.38$.

2.6 Variant 2: Discrete case with n, M, m known

This case is similar to Variant 1 (with $a = m$), but with the following added complication. In analyzing Variant 1 it sufficed to consider an adversary that increased the exchange rate continuously up to its maximum value and then dropped it permanently to m. Here we have to consider a more complex class of adversaries, corresponding to all the different choices of the successive exchange rate maxima $a_1 < a_2 < \ldots < a_k$ for all $k \le n$.

Without loss of generality, assume that the lower bound m on the exchange rates is 1. The upper bound M then equals the fluctuation ratio Φ. Let Y_i and D_i denote the number of yen and dollars held by the threat-based algorithm after the ith purchase (i.e. after the purchase at rate a_i). Then, by Rule (iii), $D_i + Y_i = a_i/r$. Let s_i be the amount spent on the ith purchase. Then $s_i = D_{i-1} - D_i$ and $a_i s_i = Y_i - Y_{i-1}$. Subtracting the equation $D_{i-1} + Y_{i-1} = a_{i-1}/r$ from the equation $D_i + Y_i = a_i/r$ and applying the definition of s_i we obtain: for $i > 1$, $s_i = \frac{1}{r}\frac{a_i - a_{i-1}}{a_i - 1}$. Similarly, $s_1 = \frac{1}{r}\frac{a_1 - r}{a_1 - 1}$. The competitive ratio r is achieved against the sequence of exchange rate maxima $a_1 < a_2 < \ldots < a_k$ only if $\sum_{i=1}^{k} s_i \le 1$, and the best competitive ratio that the threat-based algorithm can attain against this sequence is the unique r for which $\sum_{i=1}^{k} s_i = 1$. A brief computation yields that this r is given by

$$r = 1 + \frac{a_1 - 1}{a_1}\sum_{i=2}^{k}\frac{a_i - a_{i-1}}{a_i - 1} \qquad (1)$$

Thus, to determine the minimum competitive ratio attainable by the threat-based algorithm in an n-day game we maximize r in (1) over all choices of $k \le n$ and $a_1, \ldots, a_k$ such that $1 \le a_1$ and $a_k \le M$.

By straightforward calculus one can show that, for a fixed value of a_1, the maximum is achieved when $k = n$, $a_n = M$ and all the ratios $\frac{a_i - 1}{a_{i-1} - 1}$, $i = 2, 3, \ldots, n$, are equal. This leads to the expression $r = 1 + \frac{a_1 - 1}{a_1} \cdot (n-1) \cdot (1 - (\frac{a_1 - 1}{M - 1})^{\frac{1}{n-1}})$. Maximizing this expression as a function of a_1 we find after some manipulation that, for $n \ge 2$, r_n, the maximum value of r, is given by the implicit equation

$$r_n = n \cdot (1 - (\frac{r_n - 1}{M - 1})^{\frac{1}{n}}) \qquad (2)$$

The quantity r_n is the competitive ratio of the threat-based algorithm. We shall show in the next section that no on-line algorithm can achieve a smaller competitive ratio.

Against the optimal choice of the a_i it turns out that $s_1 = s_2 = \ldots = s_n = \frac{1}{n}$. Thus, against the optimal adversary, the threat-based algorithm obeys the conventional wisdom of investment advisers by employing a *dollar-cost averaging* strategy, in which an equal number of dollars are invested each day.

It is easy to see that r_n increases with n. If the on-line player does not know the number of days n in advance, the competitive ratio should be taken to be $r_\infty \stackrel{\text{def}}{=} \lim_{n\to\infty} r_n$. The quantity r_∞ satisfies the following implicit equation.

$$r_\infty = \ln \frac{M-1}{r_\infty - 1}. \qquad (3)$$

Not surprisingly, r_∞ is equal to the quantity r^* that arose earlier in connection with the continuous case.

2.7 Lower Bound

The threat-based algorithm is optimal for variant 2. Let S be any deterministic conversion strategy. Using a simple adversary argument, we show that, for any n, S cannot achieve a ratio smaller than r_n (as in (2)). Let the rates be the worst-case sequence $a_1, a_2, \ldots, a_n$, against which the threat-based algorithm achieves the competitive ratio r_n by spending $1/n$ dollars each day.

(a) If the first day i that S does not spend the same as our strategy it spends too little, then the adversary halts the game, forcing conversion of the remaining dollars at the lowest possible rate. The adversary acquires a_i yen and (see Rule (iii)) S acquires less than a_i/r_n yen.

(b) If the first time that S does not spend the same as our strategy it spends too much, the adversary continues the game but ends it on the first day j after that where the total T_j spent by S so far is less than or equal to our j-day total t_j. We can devise a strategy S' that spends the same total T_j by the end of the jth day, that acquires more yen than S, and still cannot achieve a ratio better than r_n. S' spends the same as our strategy on each of the first $j-1$ days (t_{j-1} in all) and $T_j - t_{j-1}$ (which is $\leq s_j$) on the jth day, and afterwards continues like S.

The generalization of this lower bound to randomized on-line conversion strategies is straightforward. Given the distributions that are used by the randomized strategy, an oblivious adversary has enough information to calculate the expected amounts that the randomized strategy will spend on each trading day.

3 Playing Against a Probability Distribution

Let y be the maximum value that the exchange rate will assume. In this section we consider the case where the on-line player knows the probability distribution of y. Let F be the cumulative distribution function for y; i.e., $F(x) = Pr[y \leq x]$. Let $F^c(x) = 1 - F(x)$. As the exchange rate varies the on-line player's estimate of y also varies; however, we assume that, if the maximum rate observed so far is s, the conditional distribution of y given the history of the exchange rate is obtained simply by excluding all values of y less than s, and maintaining the relative probabilities of values greater than or equal to s; i.e., the conditional distribution has the cumulative distribution function F_s given by: for $x < s$, $F_s(x) = 0$; for $x \geq s$, $F_s(x) = \frac{F(x)-F(s)}{1-F(s)}$.

We assume that the exchange rate varies continuously over time; discontinuous changes only work in the on-line player's favor by providing him with extra information. Let $x*$ be the value of x at which the quantity $mF(x) + xF^c(x)$ is maximized. Then the on-line player can maximize his expected return by exchanging all his dollars at rate $x*$ if the exchange rate ever reaches $x*$, and otherwise exchanging all his dollars at the rate m. His optimal expected return is thus $mF(x*) + x * F^c(x*)$. Define $r(F)$, the *return ratio against* F, as $\frac{E[y]}{mF(x*)+x*F^c(x*)}$.

Theorem 1 *Let $r(m, M, a)$ be the optimal competitive ratio attainable in the continous case, when the parameter values m, M and a are given. Then*

$$r(m, M, a) = \max_F r(F)$$

where F ranges over all probability distributions over the interval $[a, M]$.

The theorem states that the smallest competitive ratio that the on-line player can achieve is equal to the largest return ratio that the adversary can force by choosing a probability distribution for y.

Proof: Consider the two-person zero sum game where the set of pure strategies for each player is the interval $[a, M]$, and the payoff $f(x, y)$ to the first player if the first player chooses x and the second player chooses y is given by: if $x \leq y$ then $f(x, y) = y/x$ else $f(x, y) = y/m$. The interpretation is as follows. The first player is the on-line player and the second player is the adversary. The pure strategy x for the on-line player represents the decision to exchange his dollars as soon as the exchange rate reaches x, and to exchange at the rate m if the exchange rate never reaches x. The pure strategy y for the adversary corresponds to choosing y as the maximum value of the exchange rate. The payoff $f(x, y)$ is the ratio between the return to the adversary and the return to the online player when the pair (x, y) of pure strategies is played. A mixed strategy for the on-line player is a probability distribution over the values of x, giving the rate at which he will exchange dollars as the maximum observed value of the exchange rate increases continuously; if G is the cumulative distribution function for this probability distribution, then $G(x)$ represents the fraction of his dollars that the on-line player will exchange at exchange rates less than or equal to x. A mixed strategy for the adversary is a probability distribution for y, the maximum exchange rate; such a distribution can be specified by its cumulative distribution function F.

The min-max theorem of game theory implies that

$$\max_G \min_y E_G[f(x, y)] = \min_F \max_x E_F[f(x, y)] \qquad (4)$$

where $E_G[f(x,y)]$ is the expected payoff when the adversary chooses y and the on-line player plays the mixed strategy G, and $E_F[f(x,y)]$ is the expected payoff when the on-line player chooses x and the adversary plays the mixed strategy F. The common value of the two sides of equation (1) is called the *value* of the game.

Since the left-hand-side of (1) is equal to $r(m,M,a)$ and the right-hand side is equal to $\max_F r(F)$, the proof is complete. □□

Let us explicitly compute an optimal probability distribution F for the adversary in the case where $m = a$. Consider the problem of maximizing $E[y]$ subject to the constraint that $mF(x*) + x * F^c(x*) \leq z$,where z is a parameter to be specified later. The constraint is equivalent to the following condition: for all x, mF(x) + x $F^c(x) \leq z$, or, equivalently, $F^c(x) \leq \frac{z-m}{x-m}$, for $z \leq x \leq M$; also, by definition, $F^c(x) \leq 1$ for all x and $F^c(M) = 0$. Since $E(y) = m + \int_m^M F^c(x)dx$ the constraint requires that $E[y] \leq z + \int_z^M \frac{z-m}{x-m}dx = z + (z-m)\ln\frac{M-m}{z-m}$. By calculus, the ratio of $z + (z-m)\ln\frac{M-m}{z-m}$ to z is maximized when $z = m\ln\frac{M-m}{z-m}$. Let r denote $\max_F r(F)$. Then r is determined by evaluating the ratio of $z + (z-m)\ln\frac{M-m}{z-m}$ to z when $z = m\ln\frac{M-m}{z-m}$. A brief calculation shows that $r = \ln\frac{M-m}{rm-m}$. From Section 2.5 we see that this is the same implicit equation that defines the optimal competitive ratio $r* = r(m,M,m)$. This confirms that $r* = \max_F r(F)$, as Theorem 1 predicts. The probability distribution for the adversary that maximizes the return ratio is concentrated on the interval $[rm, M]$. On the half-open interval $[rm, M)$ the distribution has a cumulative distribution function given by the equation $F^c(x) = \frac{rm-m}{x-m}$. The distribution function is discontinuous at M, where the mass $\frac{rm-m}{M-m}$ is concentrated.

3.1 Some practical issues

3.1.1 Improved strategy against a clumsy adversary

The simple conversion strategy above is overly pessimistic since it fixes r at the time of the first purchase based on the assumption of a worst-case sequence of rates and does not change it thereafter. However, whenever the exchange rates deviate from the worst-case sequence, we can strictly improve the off-line to on-line ratio by recalculating the achievable r. At the start of each trading day, the on-line player has some number D of dollars and some number Y of yen. The player knows the number n' of days remaining, and is given an exchange rate a. The player acts as if the current day were the first trading day of an n'-day trading period in which the adversary starts with one dollar and the player with D dollars and Y yen. By arguments similar to those used above, an expression for r is determined and maximized over the *remaining* rates. The amount s to spend is given by

$$s = \frac{a - r\cdot(Y+D)}{r\cdot(a-1)}$$

where

$$r = \frac{a + (a-1)\cdot(n'-1)\cdot\left(1 - \left(\frac{a-1}{M-1}\right)^{\frac{1}{n'-1}}\right)}{a\cdot D + Y}.$$

3.1.2 Errors in assumptions about the exchange rate sequence

What happens if the on-line player's assumptions about the rate sequence turn out to be incorrect? Consider for example, the case in which the upper bound on possible exchange rates is underestimated. Say $M' = cM$ is the true upper bound where $c > 1$. The on-line player will play with $r = r_n$ as defined in (2). In the worst possible rate sequence, $a_{n-1} = M$ and $a_n = M'$. The on-line strategy will spend all the available dollars before the last day is reached and will acquire at least M/r_n yen. On the same sequence, OPT acquires M' yen. The attainable ratio is thus

$$M'/(M/r_n) = cr_n$$

or c times the ratio the player was aiming for.

3.2 Variant 3: only fluctuation ratio is known

In this case the player knows only Φ but not the actual bounds on possible exchange rates. A simple observation is that the estimate of the lowest possible rate changes from day to day and is given by a_i/Φ on the ith day.

The best competitive ratio for an n-day game that can be attained by thus revising the estimate of the lowest possible rate is $\Phi(1 - \frac{(\Phi-1)^n}{(\Phi^{\frac{n}{n-1}}-1)^{n-1}})$. It can be shown that as n approaches infinity this number approaches (monotonically from below) $\Phi - \frac{\Phi-1}{\Phi^{\frac{1}{\Phi-1}}} = \Theta(\ln\Phi)$.

4 The Bidirectional Conversion Problem

4.1 Problem statement

The on-line player starts with some D_0 dollars (without loss of generality we may take $D_0 = 1$) and converts back and forth between dollars and yen according to a sequence of exchange rates $E = e_1, e_2, \ldots$ which is revealed on-line. These rates (yen/dollar) must remain in the interval $[m, M]$, but otherwise may rise or fall arbitrarily. When the game ends, the money is all converted to one of the currencies at the present rate. The ratio of the amount accumulated by the optimal off-line algorithm on this sequence of exchange rates to the amount accumulated by the on-line player is the same, no matter which currency they convert to when the game ends. As in the unidirectional conversion problem, the on-line player's goal is to achieve a small *competitive ratio.*

If the number of local maxima and minima in the exchange rate sequence is unbounded, there is no competitive strategy (see lower bound argument in section 4.3). Assume there are k such maxima and minima. We show a lower bound of $(r_\infty)^{k/2}$ and an upper bound of $(r_\infty)^k$ where r_∞ is defined in (3).

4.2 Upper bound

The sequence E of exchange rates will consist of $k/2$ upward runs and $k/2$ downward runs. The optimal strategy for the off-line player is to convert all his dollars to yen at the end of each upward run, and all his yen to dollars at the end of each downward run. We describe how the on-line player can achieve a competitive ratio of r_∞^k. Suppose the first upward run consists of $e_1 \le e_2 \le \ldots \le e_i$, with $e_{i+1} < e_i$. During the first i days the on-line player plays according to our unidirectional conversion strategy, choosing r equal to r_∞. After day i he has D_i dollars and Y_i yen, where $mD_i + Y_i = \frac{e_i}{r_\infty}$. On day $i+1$ he converts all his dollars to yen. Since $e_{i+1} \ge m$ he then has at least $\frac{e_{i+1}}{r_\infty}$ yen at the beginning of the first downward run. He then proceeds similarly during the downward run beginning at day $i+1$, converting yen to dollars during the decreasing run and exchanging any remaining yen on the first day of the next increasing run. Thus, two transactions occur on the first day of any decreasing run: first, the exchange of all dollars to yen, and then the first step of the threat-based strategy with competitive ratio r_∞ for the unidirectional conversion of yen to dollars during the downward run; these conceptually distinct transactions can, of course, be combined into a single transaction. Similarly, on the first day of any increasing run after the first one, two transactions may occur. In each run the ratio between the off-line player's capital and the on-line player's capital increases by at most the factor r_∞, and thus the on-line player achieves the competitive ratio r_∞^k.

This strategy is not optimal. On any upward (downward) run the on-line player can take advantage of the knowledge that, to attain a ratio of r on the following downward (upward) run, the optimal adversary must begin that run with a particular rate. We are currently attempting to use this to get a better upper bound.

4.3 Lower bound

Let k be as described in the last section. Assume that the on-line player knows only m and M (w.l.o.g. $m = 1$ as before). For any n, it is possible for an adversary to force a competitive ratio of $(r_n)^{k/2}$ against any on-line strategy.

Our argument here follows from the lower bound proof for the unidirectional case. Suppose each player starts with one dollar. Then, regardless of what strategy the on-line player is following, the adversary can construct a sequence of n exchange rates consisting of an upward run followed by an immediate drop of the exchange rate to m, such that, at the end of the sequence, his total holdings in yen and dollars (evaluated at the exchange rate m) will exceed that of the on-line player by at least the factor r_n. Moreover, when the exchange rate drops to m, the adversary will convert all his yen to dollars, and the on-line player can do no better than to follow suit, since he will never have a more favorable conversion rate. Thus, in one upward and one downward run, the ratio of adversary currency to on-line currency can be made to increase by a factor of r_n. This yields a factor $(r_n)^{k/2}$ for the entire game. As n increases, this lower bound approaches $(r_\infty)^{k/2}$.

5 Future work

A striking feature of the unidirectional conversion problem is the conceptual simplicity of the optimal strategy. To attain a given competitive ratio r the on-line player simply defends himself against the threat of dropping the exchange rate permanently to m.

We have identified other problems in which a threat-based strategy is optimal. A typical example is the following problem of *trading on option.* A money trader starts with D_0 dollars and receives a finite sequence of option offers. Each option offer consists of a pair (e, p), where e is an *exchange rate* and $p > 0$ is an *option price.* For any $s \ge 0$ this offer enables the trader to pay ps dollars for the right to later trade s dollars for yen at the exchange rate e. The trader knows in advance that, even without purchasing options, he will always be able to exchange dollars for yen at the rate m, and that the maximum exchange rate he will ever be offered is M. As each offer (e, p) is presented, the trader chooses a corresponding value s and his stock of dollars is depleted by ps. At the end of the sequence of offers the trader converts his remaining dollars to yen by exercising some of the options he has purchased and by exchanging any remaining dollars at the rate m. The optimal off-line strategy is clear; the off-line player will choose that option (e, p) for which $\frac{e}{p+1}$ is greatest and (provided that $\frac{e}{p+1} > m$) will spend $\frac{pD_0}{p+1}$ dollars for the right to exchange his remaining $\frac{D_0}{p+1}$ dollars for yen at the exchange rate e. Under this optimal strategy the off-line player receives $\frac{eD_0}{p+1}$ yen. It can be shown that, if the trader can achieve a competitive ratio of r for this problem, then he can do so using a threat-based strategy of the following form: whenever an offer (e, p) is presented, choose the minimum value of s that will ensure that the trader can obtain $\frac{1}{r}\frac{eD_0}{p+1}$ even under the threat that no further option offers will be made.

It would be of interest to identify other financial games in which a threat-based strategy is optimal. Several problems related to inventory management, equipment replacement and investment are candidates. For example, consider the following *mortgage problem.* The on-line player initially holds a mortgage with interest rate e_0. On the ith day, where i ranges from 1 to n, the bank announces a new interest rate e_i. It is given that, for all i, $m \le e_i \le M$. Each day the on-line player must decide either to retain his current mortgage or to refinance at the new rate e_i. Each time he refinances, he incurs a transaction cost T. In addition, for each day in which he holds a mortgage at rate e, he incurs an *interest charge* of e. The player's total cost is the sum of his transaction costs and interest charges. We conjecture that the optimal on-line strategy is a threat-based strategy under which the on-line player refinances if and only if, should he fail to do so, the adversary could force a competitive ratio greater than the target value r by increasing the mortgage rate permanently to M, thus denying the on-line algorithm any further opportunity to refinance.

Acknowledgements

G. Turpin and R. El-Yaniv are very grateful to Allan Borodin for many helpful discussions and comments. R. El-Yaniv also wishes to thank Hisao Tamaki for valuable discussions.

References

[Cover91] T.M. Cover. "Universal Portfolios," *Mathematical Finance*, Vol 1, No. 1 (January 1991), 1-29.

[Ragh91] P. Raghavan. A statistical adversary for on-line algorithms. *On-Line Algorithms*, DIMACS Series in Discrete Mathematics and Theoretical Computer Science, 79-83, 1991.

[ST85] D.D. Sleator and R.E. Tarjan. Amortized efficiency of list update and paging rules. *Communication of the ACM*, 28:202–208, 1985.

Lower Bounds on the Competitive Ratio for Mobile User Tracking and Distributed Job Scheduling (Extended Abstract)

Noga Alon * Gil Kalai † Moty Ricklin ‡ Larry Stockmeyer §

Abstract

We prove a lower bound of $\Omega(\log n/\log\log n)$ on the competitive ratio of any (deterministic or randomized) distributed algorithm for solving the mobile user problem introduced by Awerbuch and Peleg [AP], on certain networks of n processors. Our lower bound holds for various networks, including the hypercube, any network with sufficiently large girth, and any highly expanding graph. A similar $\Omega(\log n/\log\log n)$ lower bound is proved for the competitive ratio of the maximum job delay of any distributed algorithm for solving the distributed scheduling problem of Awerbuch, Kutten and Peleg [AKP] on any of these networks. The proofs combine combinatorial techniques with tools from linear algebra and harmonic analysis and apply, in particular, a generalization of the vertex isoperimetric problem on the hypercube, which may be of independent interest.

1 Introduction

In this paper we establish an $\Omega(\log n/\log\log n)$ lower bound for the competitive ratio of two natural problems in distributed computing on various networks of n processors. These problems are the mobile user problem introduced in [AP], [AP1] and the distributed job scheduling problem introduced in [AKP]. For both problems there is a known polylogarithmic upper bound proved in the papers cited above, by applying the sparse partitions technique for any network with n processors. Our results thus imply that this is not far from being optimal, showing that sparse partitions yield nearly optimal bounds for these two problems. Here is a more precise formulation of the results.

1.1 Mobile users

In large communication networks, it may be desirable to allow users to move freely around the network and communicate with other users who are also free to move, an example being cellular telephone networks. Motivated by problems of this type, where the goal is to access an object which can change location in the network, Awerbuch and Peleg [AP, AP1] defined the problem of *on-line tracking of a mobile user*. We are given a data communication network, and one unique object called the *mobile user*. Initially, the mobile user is located at some node s, known to all the processors. The mobile user moves among the nodes (processors) of the network. From time to time requests are invoked at the nodes. There are two types of requests. The first is the move request, $Move(u,w)$, invoked at the current location u of the mobile user; the result of $Move(u,w)$ should be to move the user from node u to node w. The second is the find request, $Find(v)$, which can be invoked at any node v; the result should be to send a message from node v to the current location of the user. So that the "current location of the user" is well defined, we assume that requests occur in a sequential order.

We use a simple standard model for synchronous communication networks. The network is modeled as an undirected graph, where vertices represent processors and edges represent communication links. Each processor is modeled as a state machine (where the number of states can be infinite) which can receive and send messages. A processor with d incident edges has $d+1$ input channels and d output channels. d of the input and output channels are used for communicating with its neighbors. The extra input channel is

*Department of Mathematics, Raymond and Beverly Sackler Faculty of Exact Sciences, Tel-Aviv University, Tel Aviv, Israel. Research supported in part by a United States Israeli BSF grant. Email: noga@math.tau.ac.il

†Institute of Mathematics and Computer Science, Hebrew University, Jerusalem, Israel. Work performed while visiting the IBM Almaden Research Center, San Jose, CA. Email: kalai@humus.huji.ac.il

‡Computer Science Department, Raymond and Beverly Sackler Faculty of Exact Sciences, Tel-Aviv University, Tel Aviv, Israel. Email: motyr@math.tau.ac.il

§IBM Almaden Research Center, 650 Harry Road, San Jose, CA 95120-6099. Email: stock@almaden.ibm.com

0-8186-2900-2/92 $3.00 © 1992 IEEE

used for receiving input, such as *Move* and *Find* requests. The processors operate in lock step synchrony. At each step, based on its current state and the messages (if any) on its input channels, a processor may change state and send any number of messages on output channels. In the case of randomized algorithms, the choice of new state and messages can be made probabilistically. A message sent from u to a neighbor v at step t is received by v at step $t+1$.

As in [AP, AP1], we measure the cost of a distributed algorithm for the mobile user problem by its *communication cost*, the total number of messages sent. Each sending of a single message over a single link adds one to this cost. We assume no bound on the size of a "single message" when proving our lower bounds. A tracking algorithm $\mathcal{A}$ receives a sequence σ of *Move* and *Find* requests, and must execute them on-line. Let $Cost_{\mathcal{A}}(\sigma)$ be the total communication cost incurred by $\mathcal{A}$ on the request sequence σ. If $\mathcal{A}$ is randomized, then $Cost_{\mathcal{A}}(\sigma)$ is the expected value. Here we assume that a request is not invoked until all the messages of the algorithm, sent while serving the previous request, reach their destinations. This assumption only strengthens our lower bound.

Again as in [AP, AP1], the efficiency of an on-line algorithm $\mathcal{A}$ is given by its *competitive ratio*, which measures the cost of $\mathcal{A}$ relative to the *optimal cost* of a "global" algorithm which knows the entire sequence σ in advance. For the mobile user problem, the optimal cost $Cost_{opt}(\sigma)$ is easy to calculate. It is just the sum of the optimal costs of all the requests in σ, where the optimal cost of $Move(u, w)$ is the distance from u to w, and the optimal cost of $Find(v)$ is the distance from v to the current location of the user.

The algorithm $\mathcal{A}$ has *competitive ratio* c if there is a constant a such that, for every request sequence σ,

$$Cost_{\mathcal{A}}(\sigma) \leq c \cdot Cost_{opt}(\sigma) + a. \qquad (1)$$

In using this definition, we will be concerned with classes of networks of arbitrarily large size, and corresponding families of algorithms, one algorithm for each network in the class. In such cases, we let c (and sometimes a) be a function of n, the number of vertices in the network.

The competitive analysis of algorithms was introduced in [ST] and has been considered in numerous recent papers. Three representative examples that deal with problems related to the ones we consider here are [AP], [BFR] and [RB]. It should be noted that the distributed nature of the problems we consider make them different than the well-known k-server problem, and, more generally, problems which fit the framework of request-answer games [BBKTW]. In such problems, the difficulty arises because, when answering a particular request, the on-line algorithm has no knowledge of future requests, although it is usually assumed that the algorithm has perfect knowledge of all past requests. In the problems we consider, the algorithm might also have incomplete knowledge of past requests. For example, when *Find*(v) is invoked, the processor at v will not in general know the past sequence of *Move* operations which brought the user to its current location.

Awerbuch and Peleg [AP] gave a (deterministic) on-line distributed algorithm for the mobile user problem on any network with n processors, with a competitive ratio $O(\log^2 n)$. In the present paper we show that there are networks in which no algorithm can have a competitive ratio smaller than $\Omega(\log n / \log\log n)$. In proving this result, we show that a "bad" request sequence can be chosen by an *oblivious adversary* (cf. [BBKTW]) which must choose the entire sequence knowing only the algorithm. This adversary is weaker than adaptive adversaries which choose each request based on the response of the algorithm to previous requests. Of course, using a weaker adversary makes our lower bound results stronger.

Theorem 1 *There is a class of networks for which the competitive ratio of any (deterministic or randomized) on-line distributed algorithm for the mobile user problem is $\Omega(\log n / \log\log n)$ (against an oblivious adversary), where n is the number of processors in the network.*

In this result, the additive term a in (1) can be any function of n. We obtain the above lower bound for networks of three different types, described in Section 1.3. Among these networks are ones which have been considered extensively in the design of distributed networks, including the hypercube and highly expanding graphs.

1.2 Distributed job scheduling

In [AKP], Awerbuch, Kutten and Peleg define the *distributed scheduling* problem. We discuss here only a special case of the problem. We use the same synchronous network model as above. Initially, at step $t = 0$, some processors are given sets of jobs to execute. At each step, a processor can execute at most one job and can send any number of jobs and messages to neighboring processors. The algorithm continues until all the jobs are executed. More precisely, let $j_v(t)$ denote the number of jobs residing at processor v just before it executes step t. An "input" σ is an assignment of non-negative integers to $j_v(0)$ for all v.

If processor v executes k_{ex} jobs at step t, sends a total of k_{out} jobs to neighbors at step t (where $k_{ex} \leq 1$ and $k_{ex} + k_{out} \leq j_v(t)$), and receives a total of k_{in} jobs which neighbors of v send to v at step t, then $j_v(t+1) = j_v(t) + k_{in} - k_{out} - k_{ex}$. The algorithm continues until the step t_0 such that $j_v(t_0) = 0$ for all v, and this t_0 is the *cost* of the algorithm. Thus, the cost measures the maximum delay of a job. The definition of competitive ratio is the same as in (1), where $Cost_{opt}(\sigma)$ is the maximum delay of a job in an optimal schedule produced by a "global" scheduling algorithm which knows σ completely. Here, we assume that the additive term a is a constant which is independent of n. (Indeed, it is not hard to see, for this special case of the problem, that no nontrivial lower bound for the competitive ratio holds if a can depend on n.)

In [AKP], a more general problem is considered, where jobs can be initiated at any time unit, not only at time 0. The cost of an algorithm is defined as the sum of all job delays. The authors give a polylogarithmic upper bound for their measure. They also prove that their distributed on-line algorithm is competitive under a much stronger measure of competitiveness, which immediately implies a polylogarithmic upper bound under the maximum delay measure. Moreover, for the above special case where jobs are initiated only at time 0, the algorithm described in Section 4 of [AKP] has competitive ratio $O(\log n)$. We have the following lower bound for the special case.

Theorem 2 *There is a class of networks for which the competitive ratio of any (deterministic or randomized) distributed algorithm for the distributed scheduling problem, under the maximum delay measure, is* $\Omega(\log n / \log\log n)$, *even in the case that all jobs are initiated at time 0.*

As is the case with Theorem 1 we prove the above theorem for networks of all three types described in the next subsection. In addition, for the more general problem we can improve the lower bound to $\Omega(\log n)$.

1.3 The networks

The first class of networks we consider is the one we call here the *high-girth networks*. These are networks of size n whose underlying graph is d-regular and its girth, i.e., the size of the shortest cycle in it, as well as its diameter, are both $\Theta(\log n / \log d)$. It is well known that such graphs exist (see, e.g., [Bo]). For any d in the range $3 \leq d \leq (\log n)^b$, where b is any constant, we can prove the lower bounds in Theorems 1 and 2 for any such network. We note that it has been observed by several researchers, including the first author, Awerbuch, Peleg and Schäffer, that networks of high girth supply easily lower bounds on the complexity of network synchronizers [Aw] and graph spanners [PS].

The second class of networks considered is the class of hypercube networks. The *d-dimensional hypercube*, denoted $\mathbf{C}^d$, is the graph with vertices $\{0,1\}^d$ where two vertices are adjacent if the Hamming distance between them is 1, i.e., if they differ in precisely one coordinate. The number of vertices here is $n = 2^d$. Unlike the case of the high-girth networks, where the proofs are purely combinatorial, the proofs here (and especially the proof of Theorem 1) are more complicated and require some additional tools. We first apply a Harmonic Analysis technique, used previously in [KKL], to derive a certain fractional isoperimetric inequality for the cube, which may be of independent interest. In the traditional isoperimetric problem, we are given the size $|A|$ of a set A of vertices of $\mathbf{C}^d$ and an integer m. The goal is to place a lower bound on the size of any set X such that X contains all vertices that lie within distance m from some vertex in A. In this case, Harper [Ha] has shown that $|X|$ is minimized when A is as close as possible to a ball in $\mathbf{C}^d$. Given this result, a tight lower bound on $|X|$ can be calculated. We need a generalization of this problem where, for each $v \in A$, among all the vertices within distance m of v, we know only that some fraction γ of them belong to X (so the traditional problem is the case $\gamma = 1$). Although we do not have tight bounds on $|X|$ for the case $\gamma < 1$, we can prove a lower bound which is sufficient for our purposes. Roughly speaking, we show that $|X|/|A|$ must grow exponentially in m, provided that γ is not too small and $|A|$ is not too large. This lower bound is the key to proving Theorem 1. The proof that Theorem 2 holds for the cube is simpler. We also define a probabilistic generalization of the *regional matchings* defined in [AP, AP1], and give a lower bound on their complexity. This lower bound can be used to prove a lower bound on the trade-off between the *move-stretch* and the *find-stretch* of any mobile user algorithm on the cube; these are, informally, the competitive ratios restricted to the *Move* and *Find* operations, respectively, in σ.

Although the proofs for the cube are more complicated technically than the ones for the high-girth networks, the effort seems worthwhile, as the hypercube is one of the more popular architectures considered by researchers working in the design of distributed networks.

The third class of networks we consider is the class of *highly expanding graphs*. Such graphs have also been suggested to be the underlying graphs of distributed networks, as their high connectivity properties may be helpful in the implementation of various communication protocols (see, for example, [PU]). It is well known (see [Al] and its references) that there is a tight correspondence between the expansion properties of a graph and the eigenvalues of its adjacency matrix. We thus prefer to define our class of graphs in terms of their eigenvalues. Let us call a graph an (n, d, λ)-graph if it is a d-regular graph on n vertices and the absolute value of every eigenvalue of its adjacency matrix, except the largest, is at most λ. It is known ([FKS],[LPS],[Ma]) that for any n and d with nd even there are (n, d, λ)-graphs with $\lambda = O(\sqrt{d})$. We can show that Theorems 1 and 2 hold for any such graph with $d = \Theta((\log n)^b)$, for any constant $b \geq 4$. The proof here combines the Linear Algebra techniques applied commonly in the study of expanders with the basic combinatorial idea used in the proof for the hypercubes.

In the rest of the paper, Section 2 deals with the mobile user problem, and Section 3 concerns the distributed scheduling problem. Due to space limitations, many proofs are omitted or sketched. The paper [AKRS] contains full proofs of our results as well as more formal definitions of the model and the problems.

From now on we assume, whenever this is needed, that n is sufficiently large. Logarithms with no specified base are in base 2. To simplify the notation we also omit all floor and ceiling signs whenever these are not crucial. Also for simplicity, we have not tried to optimize the constants in our results.

Given a graph $G = (V, E)$ and $u, v \in V$, let $dist_G(u, v)$ denote the distance between u and v in G. Let $B_G(u, r) = \{v \mid dist_G(u, v) \leq r\}$ denote the ball of radius r centered at u. When G is clear from context, the subscript G is omitted.

2 Tracking a Mobile User

To illustrate our proof method, in Section 2.1 we prove Theorem 1 for high-girth graphs of degree $d = \log^3 n$. In Section 2.2 we outline the method used to prove Theorem 1 for the other networks, and mention how it is applied to high-girth graphs of smaller degree. Hypercubes are considered in Section 2.3. In this section we also introduce the generalization of the vertex isoperimetric problem mentioned in the Introduction, and we give a result on the complexity of regional matchings on the hypercube. The subject of Section 2.4 is highly expanding graphs.

2.1 An illustrative example

In this section we prove Theorem 1 for high-girth networks of degree $d = \log^3 n$, girth g that satisfies $g \geq \log_d n = \Omega(\log n / \log\log n)$ as well as $g \leq 2\log_d n < \log n$, and diameter $\Theta(\log n / \log\log n)$. The fact that such graphs exist for every (sufficiently large) n is well known; see, e.g., [Bo].

We first prove the result for deterministic algorithms. Fix n and let the mobile user start at vertex s of a network as above. We prove the lower bound by constructing a request sequence in phases: the cost for the on-line algorithm in each phase is $\Omega(\log^2 n / \log\log n)$; the optimal cost for each phase is $O(\log n)$; and the number of phases can be as big as we wish. The large number of phases is needed to handle a possibly large value of the additive term a (which may even depend on n) in the definition (1) of competitive ratio. Each phase ends by having the mobile user return to s, to ensure that the work done during one phase does not help during future phases.

Let us say a vertex u is *colored* at a particular time t in a particular phase if some message sent during this phase, or the mobile user itself, reached u by time t. Consider a *Find* request invoked at some vertex v. After the request, messages are sent in the network. Let *Read*(v) (also called the *read set of* v) denote the set of $g/4$ vertices which these messages visit first, assuming that no vertex other than s has been colored yet in this phase, i.e., assuming that no other operations have been invoked yet in this phase. Note that if we invoke *Find*(v) after some vertices have been colored by previous *Move* and *Find* operations in this phase, and if *Read*(v) does not contain a colored vertex, then *Find*(v) sends at least $g/4$ messages. This is true because *Find*(v) will not send a message to the current location of the mobile user unless some colored vertex receives a message.

Lemma 3 *For every phase, there exists a vertex w in the network for which no more than $\log n$ of its neighbors v choose $w \in$ Read(v).*

Proof. Fix a phase. There are at most $n \cdot g/4 \leq \frac{1}{4} n \log n$ pairs $\langle w, v\rangle$ such that $w \in$ *Read*(v). If the lemma is not correct, then there would be at least $n \log n > \frac{1}{4} n \log n$ such pairs, a contradiction. ■

Fix some w which satisfies the conclusion of Lemma 3.

Lemma 4 *There exists a sequence of vertices $\{v_i\}_{i=1}^{\log n}$ which are neighbors of w, such that the following holds:*
Consider the request sequence

$$Move(s,w), Find(v_1), \ldots, Find(v_{\log n}), Move(w,s).$$

Let W_0 be the set of vertices colored at the completion of $Move(s,w)$, and for $1 \le i \le \log n$ let W_i be the set of vertices colored at the completion of $Find(v_i)$. For $0 \le i < \log n$, if the number of vertices in W_i is smaller than $\log^2 n$, then $Read(v_{i+1})$ contains no vertex in W_i.

Proof. Let $N(w)$ denote the set of neighbors of w whose read set does not include w. By Lemma 3, $|N(w)| \ge \log^3 n - \log n$.

We construct the sequence v_j inductively. Assume we have already chosen the first i vertices in the sequence. We claim that if $i < \log n$, and the number of vertices in W_i is smaller than $\log^2 n$, then there exists a vertex $v \in N(w)$ such that $Read(v) \cap W_i = \emptyset$. To prove this claim, suppose it is false. The number of vertices in $N(w) - W_i$ is bigger than the number of vertices in W_i. Thus there is a vertex in W_i which belongs to the read set of at least two vertices in $N(w) - W_i$. However, each read set is connected and has size at most $g/4$, and hence a cycle of size at most $2(g/4) + 2 < g$ exists in the network, a contradiction. ■

The last lemma clearly implies that the total cost of the on-line algorithm, given the request sequence described in the lemma, is at least $(\log n)(g/4) = \Omega(\log^2 n / \log\log n)$. Since the optimal cost is only $O(\log n)$ this completes the proof of the theorem for deterministic algorithms.

It is not difficult to modify this proof for randomized algorithms. By the easy direction of the main result of [Ya], in order to prove a $c(n)$ lower bound for the competitive ratio of any randomized algorithm for our problem it suffices to find a probability distribution on the inputs (i.e., the request sequences) so that for every deterministic algorithm the expectation (over the request sequences) of the ratio between the cost of the on-line algorithm and the optimal cost is at least $c(n)$. The probability distribution chosen on the request sequences is the following. Let $P = P(n)$ be a fixed large number, which will be the number of phases. In each phase independently, choose a random vertex w according to a uniform distribution, and then choose randomly and independently according to a uniform distribution $\log n$ neighbors $v_1, \ldots, v_{\log n}$ of w. The request sequence for the phase is: $Move(s,w), Find(v_1), \ldots, Find(v_{\log n}), Move(w,s)$. The proof of Lemma 3 implies that at least half of the vertices w satisfy the assertion of the lemma. The proof of Lemma 4 implies that if the total cost incurred by the on-line algorithm in a phase is less than $\log^2 n$ then the probability that a randomly chosen neighbor of w will not meet the colored part in its read set is at least, say, $1/3$. Linearity of expectation now implies that the expected cost of the on-line algorithm during a phase is $\Omega((\log n)g) = \Omega(\log^2 n / \log\log n)$, whereas the optimal cost is $O(\log n)$. Thus the lower bound holds for randomized algorithms as well. ■

We note that since the diameter of our network is $\Theta(\log n / \log\log n)$, there is a simple deterministic on-line algorithm with competitive ratio $O(\log n / \log\log n)$. This algorithm is obtained by having one special vertex (say, s) be always informed of the current location of the user. Thus our bound is optimal for the specific network used.

2.2 Outline of the proof method

Let $\mathcal{G}$ be a class of graphs. The method is the following:

1. Choose appropriate functions $\delta_R(n)$, $\delta_W(n)$, $m(n)$, and choose a constant α, $0 < \alpha \le 1$. (We may write simply δ_R, δ_W, and m, when the number n of vertices is clear from context.)

2. Fix an arbitrary $G = (V, E)$ from the class $\mathcal{G}$, and let $n = |V|$. Consider a family of "read sets" $\{R(v) \mid v \in V\}$ where $v \in R(v)$ and $|R(v)| \le \delta_R$ for all v, and where each $R(v)$ induces a connected subgraph of G. Recall that $B(w,m)$ is the set of vertices within distance m from w. Say that a vertex w is *costly* if, for any set $W \subseteq V$ with $|W| \le \delta_W$, at least the fraction α of the vertices $v \in B(w,m)$ satisfy $R(v) \cap W = \emptyset$.

3. Show that, no matter how the read sets are chosen, at least the fraction α of the vertices of G are costly.

The set W corresponds to the set of "colored" vertices. Given a deterministic algorithm $\mathcal{A}$, the read sets are defined as in the previous section, using δ_R as an upper bound on the size of a read set. In the proof of the previous section, for example, we took $\delta_R = g/4$, $\delta_W = \log^2 n$, and $m = 1$.

Let $\mathcal{A}$ be a deterministic mobile user algorithm for G. Consider the probability distribution on request sequences obtained by choosing w uniformly at random from V, and choosing $v_1, \ldots, v_{\log n}$ uniformly at random from $B(w,m)$; then the sequence is $\sigma = Move(s,w), Find(v_1), \ldots, Find(v_{\log n}), Move(w,s)$. Let $D(n)$ be the maximum diameter of an n-vertex graph in $\mathcal{G}$. Then the expected cost of $\mathcal{A}$ (over the request sequences) and the optimal cost can be bounded as

$$\begin{aligned}\mathbf{E}(Cost_{\mathcal{A}}(\sigma)) &\geq \alpha \cdot \min\{\delta_W(n),\ \alpha \cdot (\log n) \cdot \delta_R(n)\},\\ Cost_{opt}(\sigma) &\leq 2D(n) + (\log n) \cdot m(n).\end{aligned}$$

If $\mathcal{A}$ is randomized, we again use [Ya] to conclude that there is a request sequence σ such that $Cost_{\mathcal{A}}(\sigma)$ is at least as large as the first bound above. As before, we repeat the construction for a large enough number of phases. In applications, we will have $\delta_W(n)$ large enough and $D(n)$ small enough that the lower bound on competitive ratio becomes simply $\Omega(\delta_R(n)/m(n))$.

To apply the method to high-girth graphs of degree d and girth $\Theta(\log n/\log d)$, where $3 \leq d \leq (\log n)^b$ for a constant b, we can again take $\delta_R = g/4$ and $\delta_W = \log^2 n$. We now take m to be a sufficiently large constant multiple of $\log_{d-1} \log n$, so that the size of $B(w,m)$ is a sufficiently large power of $\log n$. Now $B(w,m)$ in the new proof plays the role of the set of neighbors of w in the previous proof.

2.3 Hypercubes, regional matchings, and fractional neighborhoods

We outline the tools and arguments used in the proof of Theorem 1 for hypercubes and expanders. Let $G = (V, E)$ be a graph. To introduce the tools, focus for the moment on the special case of a deterministic algorithm $\mathcal{A}$ and a request sequence of the form $Move(s,w), Find(v)$, where we know an m such that $dist(v,w) \leq m$. When $\mathcal{A}$ executes $Move(s,w)$, it may write information at vertices in some set $W(w)$, called the *write set* of w. (In the language of Section 2.1, the algorithm "colors" the vertices in $W(w)$.) If $\mathcal{A}$'s communication cost when executing $Move(s,w)$ is at most C_1, then $|W(w)| \leq C_1 + 1$. Suppose that $\mathcal{A}$'s communication cost when executing $Find(v)$ is at most C_2, in the case that $dist(v,w) \leq m$. Define $R(v)$, the *read set* of v, to be the first C_2 vertices which receive messages when $\mathcal{A}$ executes $Find(v)$ in the network, assuming that $Move(s,w)$ has not yet been executed. As before, $|R(v)| \leq C_2 + 1$, and the *radius* of $R(v)$, that is, the maximum distance between v and a point of $R(v)$, is at most C_2. Correctness of the algorithm requires that

$$(\forall v \forall w)[\, dist(v,w) \leq m \Rightarrow R(v) \cap W(w) \neq \emptyset\,]. \quad (2)$$

As defined in [AP, AP1], a collection of sets $\{\, R(u), W(u) \mid u \in V \,\}$ satisfying (2) is an *m-regional matching* in G. Although [AP, AP1] used regional matchings as a tool to produce algorithms for the mobile user problem, the development above shows that they are also useful for proving lower bounds.[1] The idea is to pick a suitable m and show that, if the maximum sizes and radii of the sets $R(v)$ and $W(w)$ are too small, then the sets do not form an m-regional matching. We now outline the combinatorial argument used for this.

Let δ_R (resp., ρ_R) be the maximum, over all $v \in V$, of the size (resp., radius) of $R(v)$. Define δ_W and ρ_W similarly for the sets $W(w)$. Let $v \in V$. By definition, $R(v)$ must intersect $W(w)$ for every $w \in B(v,m)$. Since $|R(v)| \leq \delta_R$, there must be a particular $z \in R(v)$ such that $z \in W(w)$ for at least a fraction $\gamma = 1/\delta_R$ of the w's in $B(v,m)$. Define $\chi(v) = z$, and note that $dist(v, \chi(v)) \leq \rho_R$.

Now for an arbitrary z, define

$$A_z = \{\, v \mid \chi(v) = z \,\} \quad \text{and} \quad X_z = \{\, w \mid z \in W(w) \,\}.$$

It follows from definitions that, for every $v \in A_z$, the set X_z intersects $B(v,m)$ in at least the fraction γ of the points of $B(v,m)$. In general, we say that X is a *γ-fractional m-neighborhood* of A if, for every $v \in A$,

$$|\, B(v,m) \cap X \,| \geq \gamma |B(v,m)|.$$

Now suppose we knew a "multiple" M such that $|X_z| \geq M|A_z|$ for every z. Since the sets A_z partition V, an easy counting argument then shows that there exists a w with $|W(w)| \geq M$; i.e., $\delta_W \geq M$. Our problem is thus reduced to proving a result about fractional neighborhoods which yields a large enough M.

Applying a technique from harmonic analysis, we have the following for hypercubes. A discussion and proof are given in the Appendix.

Theorem 5 *There is a constant $c_1 > 0$ such that the following holds. Let $d \geq 1$, $\gamma > 0$, $1 \leq m < d/2$, and let A and X be two sets of vertices of $\mathbf{C}^d$, where $|A| \leq 2^{d/2}$. If X is a γ-fractional m-neighborhood of A, then*

$$|X| \geq \frac{c_1 2^{m/2} \gamma^2}{m} |A|.$$

Using the bound of Theorem 5 as outlined above, we can prove the following lemma. It is the key to applying the proof method of Section 2.2 to hypercubes.

Lemma 6 *There is a constant $c_2 > 0$ such that for any sufficiently large d, any m, δ_R, δ_W, ρ_R, and α, and any family of read sets $\{R(v) \mid v \in V\}$ of maximum size δ_R and maximum radius ρ_R, if $1 \leq m <$*

[1] In the proof for high-girth networks, for example, we use regional matchings implicitly.

$d/2$, $\rho_R \leq d/10$, and $\delta_W(\delta_R)^2 < c_2(1-\alpha)^6\, 2^{m/2}/m$, then at least the fraction α of the vertices of $\mathbf{C}^d$ are costly.

It is now easy to establish Theorem 1 for hypercubes. Let $\delta_R(n) = \rho_R(n) = d/10 = (\log n)/10$, $\delta_W(n) = \log^2 n$, $m(n) = 10 \log\log n$, and $\alpha = 1/2$. So all the conditions of Lemma 6 are satisfied for all sufficiently large n. The diameter of an n-vertex hypercube is $D(n) = \log n$. So this gives a lower bound on competitive ratio of $\Omega(\delta_R(n)/m(n))$.

We now return briefly to the subject of regional matchings. For any G with n vertices and any m and k, Awerbuch and Peleg [AP] construct an m-regional matching for G where all radii are at most $(2k+1)m$ and all sizes are at most $2kn^{1/k}$. We define a probabilistic generalization of regional matchings. For hypercubes, we have a lower bound on the trade-off between expected radius and expected size which has a form similar to the upper bound of [AP] for deterministic regional matchings in an arbitrary graph.

Let

$$\mathcal{R} = \{\, \mathbf{R}(x), \mathbf{W}(x) \mid x \in V \,\}$$

be a family of mutually independent random variables taking values in 2^V. $\mathcal{R}$ is a *p-probabilistic m-regional matching* for G if, for all $v, w \in V$ with $dist(v,w) \leq m$,

$$\Pr[\, \mathbf{R}(v) \cap \mathbf{W}(w) \neq \emptyset\,] \geq p.$$

Let the *expected read-size* $\overline{\delta}_R$ denote the maximum, over all $x \in V$, of the expected value of $|\mathbf{R}(x)|$. Similarly, the *expected read-radius* $\overline{\rho}_R$ is the maximum, over all x, of the expected radius of $\mathbf{R}(x)$. The *expected write-size* $\overline{\delta}_W$ and the *expected write-radius* $\overline{\rho}_W$ are defined similarly in terms of the $\mathbf{W}(w)$. (The papers [AP, AP1] define the radii normalized to m, which in our notation would be $\overline{\rho}_R/m$ and $\overline{\rho}_W/m$.)

Here is our lower bound. We state it in terms of a family $\{\mathcal{R}_d \mid d \geq 1\}$ where $\mathcal{R}_d$ is a probabilistic m-regional matching for $\mathbf{C}^d$. The various parameters are given as functions of $n = 2^d$, the number of vertices of $\mathbf{C}^d$. The proof again uses Theorem 5.

Theorem 7 *There is a constant $a_1 > 0$ such that the following holds. Fix a $p > 0$ and let $1 \leq k(n) \leq a_1 p \log n/\log\log n$. There is a function $m(n)$ such that for any family of p-probabilistic $m(n)$-regional matchings for $\mathbf{C}^d$ with $\overline{\rho}_R(n) \leq k(n)m(n)$,*

$$\overline{\delta}_W(n)\,\overline{\delta}_R(n) = n^{\Omega(1/k(n))}.$$

In [AP, AP1], the competitive ratio is broken into two parts, the *find-stretch* and the *move-stretch*, which are, informally, the competitive ratios restricted to the *Find* and *Move* operations, respectively, in the request sequence (and the additive term a is taken to be zero). For any on-line algorithm with find-stretch $\varphi(n)$ and move-stretch $\mu(n)$, we can prove a lower bound on the trade-off between them, using Theorem 7. Specifically, there is a constant $c_3 > 0$ such that, if $\varphi(n) \leq c_3 \log n/\log\log n$, then $\mu(n) = n^{\Omega(1/\varphi(n))}$.

2.4 Highly expanding graphs

As indicated in the previous section, any graph for which a sufficiently good lower bound on the size of fractional neighborhoods can be given will satisfy the assertion of Theorem 1. The next lemma gives such a lower bound for (n,d,λ)-graphs, provided λ is much smaller than d. A proof is given in the Appendix.

Lemma 8 *Let $G = (V,E)$ be an (n,d,λ)-graph, suppose $\gamma d \geq 6$, and let A and X be sets of vertices, where $|A| \leq \frac{\gamma}{2(d+1)} n$. If X is a γ-fractional 1-neighborhood of A then*

$$|X| \geq \frac{\gamma^2 d^2}{9\lambda^2}|A|.$$

Note that for $\lambda = O(\sqrt{d})$ this gives $|X| = \Omega(\gamma^2 d|A|)$. This, together with the combinatorial arguments outlined in Sections 2.2 and 2.3, gives Theorem 1 for these graphs for an appropriate choice of the parameters. We omit the details.

3 Distributed Scheduling

Recall that in the distributed scheduling problem, processors are from time to time given sets of jobs to execute. At each step, a processor can execute at most one job and can send jobs to neighboring processors. The cost measure is the maximum delay of a job, i.e., the maximum, over all jobs j, of the number of steps that j remains in the system before being executed.

In Section 3.1, we prove Theorem 2 for high-girth networks. Recall that Theorem 2 concerns the special case of the problem where all jobs are initiated at time 0. We also obtain a slightly larger lower bound for the more general problem where jobs can be initiated at any time. The proofs of Theorem 2 for hypercubes and highly expanding graphs are very similar to the proof for high-girth graphs. These proofs are sketched in Sections 3.2 and 3.3.

3.1 High-girth graphs

Proof of Theorem 2 for high-girth graphs.
For any d with $3 \leq d \leq (\log n)^b$, let G be a d-regular

high-girth graph whose girth g and diameter are both $\Theta(\log n/\log d)$.

Fix n. For every vertex v we define a scenario S_v as follows. Each vertex w in $B(v, g/4)$ receives g jobs at time 0. All other vertices do not get jobs. The subgraph of G induced by $B(v, g/2-1)$ is a tree which we denote T_v. A global algorithm can simply have each w that got jobs send its jobs, in the direction away from v in T_v, to a set of g vertices that are at distance $l = \log_{d-1} g$ from w. Since $l < g/4$ for sufficiently large n, all jobs are sent to vertices in T_v. Since T_v is a tree, each vertex receives at most one job to execute. So the optimal cost is at most $l+1$.

We prove the lower bound, again, by using the easy direction of [Ya]. Pick at random one of the scenarios S_x according to a uniform distribution on the vertices. We show that for every (deterministic) distributed algorithm, the average cost over this distribution is at least $g/16$. Indeed, assume this is false and there exists a distributed algorithm whose average cost is less than $g/16$, and let us reach a contradiction. Let U be the set of all vertices u such that the cost of the algorithm is less than $g/8$ in the scenario S_u. Clearly, $|U| \geq n/2$ since otherwise the expectation of our algorithm exceeds $g/16$. For every $u \in U$ and every vertex x, we define $charge_u(x)$ to be the number of jobs that x executes among those assigned initially to the vertex u in the scenario S_u. Define also $Charge(x) = \sum_{u \in U} charge_u(x)$.

Consider a scenario S_x. Let y be a vertex in U such that $charge_y(x) > 0$. Obviously the distance between y and x is smaller than $g/8$. The vertices x and y must behave exactly the same in the scenarios S_x and S_y at the first $g/8$ time steps, since all the vertices in $B(x, g/8)$ and in $B(y, g/8)$ receive the same number of jobs in both S_x and S_y. Thus x will execute $charge_y(x)$ jobs originated at the processor y under the scenario S_x. Moreover, it will execute them sometime during the first $g/8$ time steps. It follows that for every vertex x, $Charge(x) \leq g/8 < g/2$. Hence the total sum of $Charge(x)$ over all vertices x is strictly less than $n \cdot (g/2)$.

However, since $|U| \geq n/2$, the total number of jobs which are assigned to central vertices u of scenarios S_u with $u \in U$ is at least $(n/2) \cdot g$. Since each of these jobs contributes to $charge_u(x)$ for some u and x, the sum of $Charge(x)$ over all x must be at least $(n/2) \cdot g$, a contradiction.

The competitive ratio is $\Omega(g/\log_{d-1} g) = \Omega(\log n/\log\log n)$ since $g = \Theta(\log n/\log d)$. ■

The special case of the distributed scheduling problem can always be solved by sending all jobs to a particular processor which then distributes the jobs evenly to all the processors. For a graph of diameter D, the competitive ratio of this algorithm is $O(D)$. Therefore, for high-girth graphs of degree $d = (\log n)^b$ where $b > 0$, our lower bound is optimal to within a constant factor.

For the general scheduling problem, we have the following for high-girth graphs.

Theorem 9 *There is a class of networks for which the competitive ratio of any (deterministic or randomized) distributed algorithm for the distributed scheduling problem, under the maximum delay measure, is* $\Omega(\log n)$, *if jobs can be initiated at any time.*

Proof (sketch). Consider, for a given n, a $d = 64$-regular graph $G = (V, E)$ with n vertices and girth $g = \Omega(\log n)$.

For every vertex v we define a scenario S_v as follows. Each vertex w in $B(v, g/4)$ receives a set of $d = 64$ jobs at time $t = 2i$ for all $i \in \{0, 1, \ldots, g/64 - 1\}$. Therefore, altogether each vertex in $B(v, g/4)$ receives g jobs, and the last set of jobs is initiated at time $t = g/32-2$. All other vertices receive no jobs. It is easy to see that the optimal job delay is 2. To prove the lower bound, pick at random one of the scenarios S_x. It can be shown that for every (deterministic) distributed algorithm, the average *completion time*, i.e., time t in which all the jobs will be done, is at least $g/16$. Note that since all the jobs were initiated at times $t < g/32$, this will imply that the average value of the maximum delay of a job is at least $g/32 = \Omega(\log n)$ and hence complete the proof. The rest of the proof is almost identical to the previous one, and is omitted. ■

3.2 Hypercubes

The proof of Theorem 2 is similar to that given for high-girth graphs in Section 3.1. The scenario S_v gives $d = \log n$ jobs to each vertex within distance $d/10$ from v. The optimal scheduler can finish in time $O(\log d)$ by sending jobs "out", i.e., in the direction away from v. An argument similar to the one in Section 3.1 shows that the on-line algorithm needs time $\Omega(d)$.

3.3 Highly expanding graphs

In order to obtain Theorem 2 for highly expanding graphs it is useful to first show that every assignment of d jobs to each processor in *any* set of n/d processors in an (n, d, λ)-graph with $\lambda = O(\sqrt{d})$ can be completed (by a global algorithm) in constant time. This can be proved by combining Lemma 8 (with $\gamma = 1$)

with Hall's Marriage Theorem. The basic combinatorial idea in Section 3.1 can then be used to prove that Theorem 2 holds for such graphs with an appropriate choice of d. E.g., $d = (\log n)^b$, for any constant $b \geq 1$ will do. Simply consider, for each vertex v, the scenario S_v in which all vertices in $B(v, s)$ for, say, $s = \log_{d-1}(\sqrt{n})$, get d jobs each at time $t = 0$. Then the optimal cost is a constant, whereas it can be shown as before that the expected cost of any on-line algorithm is $\Omega(s) = \Omega(\log n / \log\log n)$.

Acknowledgement. We thank Y. Afek, B. Awerbuch, Y. Bartal, D. Dolinsky, C. Dwork, S. Kutten and A. Rosén for helpful discussions and comments.

References

[AKP] B. Awerbuch, S. Kutten and D. Peleg, *Competitive distributed job scheduling*, Proc. 24th ACM STOC (1992), 571–580.

[AKRS] N. Alon, G. Kalai, M. Ricklin and L. Stockmeyer, *Lower bounds on the competitive ratio for mobile user tracking and distributed job scheduling*, in preparation.

[Al] N. Alon, *Eigenvalues and expanders*, Combinatorica 6 (1986), 83-96.

[AP] B. Awerbuch and D. Peleg, *Sparse partitions*, Proc. 31st IEEE FOCS (1990), 503-513.

[AP1] B. Awerbuch and D. Peleg, *Online tracking of mobile users*, Technical Memo TM-410, MIT Lab. for Computer Science, Cambridge, MA, 1989.

[AS] N. Alon and J. H. Spencer, *The Probabilistic Method*, Wiley, 1991.

[Aw] B. Awerbuch, *Complexity of network synchronization*, J. ACM 32 (1985), 804–823.

[BBKTW] S. Ben-David, A. Borodin, R. Karp, G. Tardos, and A. Wigderson, *On the power of randomization in online algorithms*, Proc. 22nd ACM STOC (1990), 379–386.

[Bec] W. Beckner, *Inequalities in Fourier analysis*, Ann. of Math. 102 (1975), 159-182.

[BFR] Y. Bartal, A. Fiat and Y. Rabani, *Competitive algorithms for distributed data management*, Proc. 24th ACM STOC (1992), 39–50.

[Bo] B. Bollobás, *Extremal Graph Theory*, Academic Press, New York, 1978, pp. 107-109.

[FKS] J. Friedman, J. Kahn and E. Szemerédi, *On the second eigenvalue in random regular graphs*, Proc. 21st ACM STOC (1989), 587–598.

[Ha] L. H. Harper, *Optimal numberings and isoperimetric problems on graphs*, J. Comb. Th. 1 (1966), 385–393.

[KKL] J. Kahn, G. Kalai, and N. Linial, *The influence of variables on Boolean functions*, Proc. 29th IEEE FOCS (1988), 68–80. See also: Tech. Report No. 546, Institute for Mathematical Studies in the Social Sciences, Stanford Univ., Stanford, CA, 1989.

[LPS] A. Lubotzky, R. Phillips and P. Sarnak, *Explicit expanders and the Ramanujan conjectures*, Proc. 18th ACM STOC (1986), 240-246. See also: A. Lubotzky, R. Phillips and P. Sarnak, *Ramanujan graphs*, Combinatorica 8 (1988), 261-277.

[Ma] G. A. Margulis, *Explicit group-theoretical constructions of combinatorial schemes and their application to the design of expanders and superconcentrators*, Problemy Peredachi Informatsii 24 (1988), 51-60 (in Russian). English translation in Problems of Information Transmission 24 (1988), 39-46.

[PS] D. Peleg and A. A. Schäffer, *Graph spanners*, J. Graph Th. 13 (1989), 99–116.

[PU] D. Peleg and E. Upfal, *The token distribution problem*, SIAM J. Comput. 18 (1989), 229–243.

[RB] A. Rosén and Y. Bartal, *The distributed k-server problem – A competitive distributed translator for k-server algorithms*, Proc. 33rd IEEE FOCS (1992).

[ST] D. D. Sleator and R. E. Tarjan, *Amortized efficiency of list update and paging rules*, Comm. ACM 28 (1985), 202-208.

[Ya] A. C. C. Yao, *Probabilistic computation: Towards a unified measure of complexity*, Proc. 18th IEEE FOCS (1977), 222-227.

Appendix

Proof of Theorem 5.

First we give two definitions and state a known inequality. Let f be a real-valued function defined on $\mathbf{C}^d$. The p-norm of f is

$$\|f\|_p = \left(\frac{1}{2^d}\sum_{v\in\mathbf{C}^d}|f(v)|^p\right)^{1/p}.$$

For $0<\varepsilon<1$, let $T_\varepsilon(f)$ be the function defined on $\mathbf{C}^d$ as

$$T_\varepsilon(f)(v) = \sum_{x\in\mathbf{C}^d} f(x)\left(\frac{1+\varepsilon}{2}\right)^{d-dist(x,v)}\left(\frac{1-\varepsilon}{2}\right)^{dist(x,v)}.$$

For $X\subseteq\mathbf{C}^d$, let 1_X denote the characteristic function of X (for $v\in\mathbf{C}^d$, $1_X(v)=1$ if $v\in X$, or 0 otherwise).

The operator $f\to T_\varepsilon(f)$ was considered in [KKL]. The definition in [KKL] is given in terms of the Fourier transform of f, but it is easy to see that it coincides with our definition. Two important Lemmas of Beckner [Bec] allow us to relate the 2-norm of $T_\varepsilon(f)$ to the $(1+\varepsilon^2)$-norm of f. As shown in [KKL], Beckner's Lemmas give the following inequality:

Lemma 10 *For any real-valued function f on $\mathbf{C}^d$ and any $0<\varepsilon<1$ we have, letting $p=1+\varepsilon^2$,*

$$\|T_\varepsilon(f)\|_2 \le \|f\|_p.$$

We can now apply Lemma 10 with $f=1_X$ to prove Theorem 5. Let A, X, γ, and m be as in the statement of the theorem. Let $v\in A$. The definition of $T_\varepsilon(1_X)(v)$ involves a sum over all $x\in\mathbf{C}^d$. By taking the sum only over those $x\in B(v,m)\cap X$, and using the assumption that the size of this set is at least $\gamma|B(v,m)|$,

$$T_\varepsilon(1_X)(v)\ge\gamma\binom{d}{m}\left(\frac{1+\varepsilon}{2}\right)^{d-m}\left(\frac{1-\varepsilon}{2}\right)^{m}.$$

Therefore,

$$\|T_\varepsilon(1_X)\|_2^2\ge\frac{|A|}{2^d}\gamma^2\binom{d}{m}^2\left(\frac{1+\varepsilon}{2}\right)^{2(d-m)}\left(\frac{1-\varepsilon}{2}\right)^{2m}.$$

Letting $p=1+\varepsilon^2$,

$$\|1_X\|_p^2=(|X|/2^d)^{2/p}.$$

Substituting these bounds into the inequality of Lemma 10 and choosing $\varepsilon=1-2m/d$ gives

$$|X|\ge 2^d\left[\frac{|A|}{2^d}\gamma^2\binom{d}{m}^2\left(1-\frac{m}{d}\right)^{2(d-m)}\left(\frac{m}{d}\right)^{2m}\right]^{p/2}.$$

Since the quantity in square brackets can be at most 1, we can replace the exponent $p/2=(1+\varepsilon^2)/2$ by the larger quantity $1-m/d$. Since $2^d(2^{-d})^{1-m/d}=2^m$,

$$|X|\ge(2^m\gamma^2|A|^{1-m/d})B \qquad (3)$$

where $B=\left(\binom{d}{m}\left(1-\frac{m}{d}\right)^{d-m}\left(\frac{m}{d}\right)^m\right)^{2(1-m/d)}$.

Since $z!$ is $(z/e)^z\sqrt{z}$ to within constant factors, we have for some constant $c>0$,

$$\binom{d}{m} \ge c\sqrt{\frac{d}{m(d-m)}}\frac{(d/e)^d}{(m/e)^m((d-m)/e)^{d-m}} \ge \frac{c}{\sqrt{m}}\left(\frac{d}{m}\right)^m\left(\frac{d}{d-m}\right)^{d-m}.$$

Therefore, $B\ge(c/\sqrt{m})^{2(1-m/d)}$. So $B\ge c_1/m$ for some c_1. By assumption, $|A|\le 2^{d/2}$, so $|A|^{-m/d}\ge 2^{-m/2}$. Therefore, (3) gives the desired lower bound on $|X|$. ■

Proof of Lemma 8.

Clearly we may assume that X is minimal, i.e., any proper subset of it is not a γ-fractional 1-neighborhood of A. In this case, every member of X either is in A or is a neighbor of some vertex of A and hence $|X|\le|A|(d+1)\le\frac{\gamma}{2}n$.

Put $|X|=xn$ and observe that by the last paragraph $x\le\frac{\gamma}{2}$. For any vertex $v\in V$ let $N(v)$ denote the set of all neighbors of v. A simple Linear Algebra argument (see [AS], page 122) implies that

$$\sum_{v\in V}(|N(v)\cap X|-xd)^2\le\lambda^2x(1-x)n.$$

Therefore

$$\sum_{v\in A}(|N(v)\cap X|-xd)^2\le\lambda^2x(1-x)n. \qquad (4)$$

However, since X is a γ-fractional 1-neighborhood of A, any $v\in A$ has at least $\gamma d-1$ neighbors in X. Since $x\le\gamma/2$ and $\gamma d\ge 6$, this together with (4) implies that

$$\frac{|A|\gamma^2d^2}{9}\le\lambda^2x(1-x)n\le\lambda^2|X|,$$

implying the desired result. ■

The Distributed k-Server Problem — A Competitive Distributed Translator for k-Server Algorithms

Yair Bartal* Adi Rosén*

Abstract

We consider the k-server problem [MMS] in a distributed setting. Given a network of n processors, and k identical mobile servers, requests for service appear at the processors and a server must reach the request point. Besides modeling problems in computer networks where k identical mobile resources are shared by the processors of the network, this models a realistic situation where the transfer of information is costly and there is no central control that governs the behavior of servers that move around to satisfy requests for service.

The problem is that of devising algorithms that minimize not only the travel of the servers but also the communication cost incurred for the transmission of control messages. Thus, in addition to the traditional lack of knowledge of future requests that a global-control online algorithm has to deal with, a distributed k-server algorithm must also deal with issues of locality. As a result, the algorithm has only partial information on past requests, and even on the current configuration of all its servers.

The main contribution of this paper is a general translator to transform any deterministic global-control competitive k-server algorithm into a distributed competitive one. As consequences we get poly(k)-competitive distributed algorithms for the line, trees and the ring.

In contrast to the global-control case where there are k-server algorithms with competitive ratio that depends on k solely ([FRR, G]), we have a lower bound of $\Omega(\max\{k, \frac{1}{D} \cdot \log n / \log\log n\})$ on the competitive ratio of any distributed k-server algorithm, where D is the ratio between the cost of moving a server and of transmitting a message over the same distance.

We give a distributed version of the Harmonic randomized k-server algorithm ([RS, G]), which has the best currently proved competitive ratio. Given that the original Harmonic is c_H-competitive, the competitive ratio of the distributed version can be stated as $O(c_H \cdot (1 + \frac{1}{D} \cdot k \cdot \text{polylog}(n)))$ for the cases where the diameter of the network (i.e., the ratio between the longest and the shortest non-zero distances) is bounded by a fixed polynomial in n.

*Department of Computer Science, Tel-Aviv University, Tel-Aviv 69978, Israel. E-mail: yairb@math.tau.ac.il, adiro@math.tau.ac.il.

1 Introduction

One of the most extensively studied online problems is the k-server problem, first suggested in [MMS]. The problem is that of scheduling the motion of k identical servers that travel among the n points of a metric space as to satisfy requests for service at these points, while minimizing the total distance the servers travel. In the traditional setting communication is free, that is, there is a central algorithm that gets the requests and governs the motion of the servers, incurring no cost for the acquisition of the knowledge about all the requests and for the transmission of motion instructions to the servers.

In this paper we investigate a more realistic setting, the "costly-message" one, which represents the coordination efforts of dynamically-moving identical servers and of spread-around entities that issue requests for service, as to satisfy these requests. The transfer of information between the participating parties is costly, and an algorithm for this setting should not only minimize the total distance the servers travel but also the cost it incurs for the transmission of messages. This models real-life situations where the requests for service appear at the locations of service and not at some central control, e.g. when a set of mobile robots (AGV's) carrying tools or spare parts in a factory have to reach different work-cells upon the request of the operators of these work-cells. The problem arises in computer networks as well, when k identical mobile resources have to be scheduled between the processors of the network. The problem is also related to problems of data management [BFR, ABF], and also mentioned in [AP]. We will discuss the costly-message

0-8186-2900-2/92 $3.00 © 1992 IEEE

(*distributed*) setting in terms of networks and processors.

In either the traditional (*global-control*) or the *distributed* setting the problem is online, that is, the sequence of requests for service is not known in advance, but revealed request by request. The algorithm has, however, to satisfy each request immediately, therefore knowing only previous requests and without any knowledge about the future. Sleator and Tarjan [ST] presented the *competitive analysis* of online algorithms; the competitive ratio of an online algorithm is defined as the ratio between the cost of the online algorithm on any request sequence and the cost incurred by an optimal adversary on the same sequence. The competitive ratio is c if for all request sequences, (online cost) $\leq c \times$ (offline cost) + some additive term. An algorithm with finite competitive ratio is said to be *competitive*. If it achieves a competitive ratio of at most c, it is c-competitive. For randomized algorithms, the competitive ratio is defined as an expectation and one must make precise the power given to the adversary (see [BBKTW]). An oblivious adversary must commit to the sequence of events while not knowing the coin tosses of the online algorithm. An adaptive online adversary may decide upon the next request after seeing all previous online responses, but must react to each request immediately.

Competitive analysis of distributed algorithms was introduced in [AKP] and [BFR] in the context of job scheduling and data management; the cost of a distributed online algorithm, including the cost incurred for the transmission of messages, is compared to the cost of an optimal global-control adversary. Since in the *distributed* setting a k-server algorithm incurs some cost for the transmission of any message, such competitive algorithms cannot always inform all the processors, and even not all the servers, about every request. A distributed k-server algorithm has, therefore, to deal not only with the problems of lack of knowledge of future requests (like global-control algorithms), but also with incomplete information about previous requests. In particular, a competitive distributed algorithm cannot always know the global configuration of all its servers.

In some special cases directly deriving distributed algorithms from global-control ones is relatively easy. For the uniform metric space one can transform global-control deterministic algorithms (e.g. [KMRS, ST]) to distributed ones, by choosing a leader that will run the global-control algorithm, while ignoring requests on covered points; for the case of $k = n - 1$, one can use the algorithm of [BLS] for metrical task systems which defines a fixed traversal sequence for the single point which is uncovered at any specific time; only a single message of $O(1)$ bits has to be sent to the new uncovered point. In general, however, the behavior of known k-server algorithms depends on their entire history, making it impossible to directly transform them into distributed ones, as shipping the whole history is too costly.

In this paper we give competitive distributed k-server algorithms for all metric spaces and all k. The main contribution of the paper is a general *translator* that transforms *any* deterministic competitive *global-control* k-server algorithm for any metric space into a competitive *distributed* one. The increase in the competitive ratio is approximately the maximum between a small polynomial in k, the logarithm of the number of memory states of the global-control algorithm, and the competitive ratio of the k-server tracking mechanism (to be discussed later) which is at most $O(\mu \log n)$, where $\mu = \max\{\lceil \log n \rceil, \lceil \log \Delta \rceil\}$ and Δ is the diameter of the network, but is smaller for specific metric spaces. We get poly(k)-competitive distributed k-server algorithms for the line, trees and the ring, by applying our general result to the k-competitive global-control algorithms for the line and trees [CKPV, CL1] and the $O(k^3)$-competitive algorithm for the ring [FRRS]. Applying it to the $O(1)$-competitive algorithms for the case of $k = 2$ of [CL2, IR], gives $O(\mu \log n/D)$-competitive distributed algorithms, where D is the ratio between the cost of moving a server and of sending a message across the same distance. Applying our translator to the known k-server algorithms for general metric spaces ([FRR], and [G] via [BBKTW]) is, of course, possible; however, due to the large number of memory states of these algorithms, this yields a distributed algorithm with a competitive ratio which is greater than that of the application of an algorithm for trees to a minimum spanning tree (as suggested in [CL1]).

To build the translator we recursively divide the servers into sets according to the distances between them, and proceed in phases to apply a recursively defined distributed algorithm to these sets, while the base of the recursion is the global-control algorithm. At the end of a phase the servers are placed at the points they would occupy according to the global-control algorithm, had it served some mindfully chosen subsequence of the requests. We call this subsequence the *simulation sequence* of the phase. We also use a mechanism that we call k-server tracking in order to find a specific server when needed and to find a close server to a specific point at any time. This mechanism is a slight modification of the techniques used in [AP] for the mobile user tracking mechanism and in [BFR] for the data-tracking mechanism.

The paper also gives a new global-control algorithm for the well studied case of $k = 2$ (see e.g. [CL2, IR, MMS, RS, T]). This algorithm is easily and directly made distributed, thus also giving a simple distributed algorithm for this case. The new algorithm arises from some of the ideas behind our translator and might be of independent interest for the study of (global-control) k-server algorithms.

[MMS] proved a lower bound of k on the competitive ratio of any k-server algorithm in any metric space. In contrast to the global-control case where there are algorithms with competitive ratio that depends only on k (and not on n) for any metric space ([FRR, G]), this is not the case in the distributed setting. In fact, there is an infinite number of networks with increasing number of processors n, such that the competitive ratio against adaptive adversaries of any distributed k-server algorithm is $\Omega(\max\{k, \frac{1}{D} \cdot \log n / \log\log n\})$, thus depending also on the number of points in the metric space. We derive this lower bound by a reduction from the mobile user problem of [AP], and a result of [AKRS].

We also study the problem of devising a distributed version of the Harmonic k-server algorithm [RS]. Grove [G] proved that Harmonic is $O(k2^k)$-competitive, but it is believed that the correct competitive ratio is $O(k^2)$ (see [RS, BKT]). If the competitive ratio of Harmonic is c_H, then the Distributed-Harmonic is $O(c_H \cdot (1 + \frac{1}{D} \cdot \max\{k, \mu\} \cdot (\log \Delta) \log n))$-competitive. The Harmonic algorithm is of practical interest because of its simplicity and the fact that it is memoryless.

The rest of the paper is organized as follows: We start with the definition of the model and the problem in Section 2, while Section 3 contains the definitions of the server tracking mechanisms that we use. In Section 4 we give the general competitive distributed translator for k-server algorithms, and in Section 5 we study the distributed version of Harmonic. We conclude in Section 6 with the lower bound and the new 2-server algorithm.

2 Model and Statement of Problem

A *network topology* $\mathcal{N}$ is a weighted graph $G = (V, E)$, $|V| = n$, where the vertices represent processors and the weight of edges represent the cost or length of the link between the two adjacent processors. The weighted graph need not obey the triangle inequality, but a natural metric space can be defined where its points are the vertices and the distance between two points is equal to the length of the shortest path between the vertices in the weighted graph; we will denote by $d(a, b)$ the distance between a and b in the metric space. We use the terms network topology, weighted graph, and metric space as called for by the discussion, but they refer to the same underlying interconnection network.

We denote by Δ the diameter of the network topology, assuming the length of the shortest edge is of one unit. The cost of transmitting a $\max\{\lceil\log n\rceil, \lceil\log \Delta\rceil\}$-bit message is $\frac{1}{D}$ times the distance over which the message is sent. Henceforth let $\delta = \lceil\log \Delta\rceil$, and $\mu = \max\{\lceil\log n\rceil, \lceil\log \Delta\rceil\}$; μ is sometimes used to indicate the size of a unit-length message.

The k-server problem [MMS] is that of scheduling the motion of k identical servers in a metric space as to serve requests for service at the points of the metric space. At each request a server must be sent to the request point before the next request appears. When a server reaches a request point we say that it *serves* the request. In this setting the requests are given to some central algorithm. We call this setting the *global-control* one. The cost incurred by a global-control k-server algorithm is the total distance its servers travel.

We will use the following definition to formulate any *global-control* online k-server algorithm:

Definition. An online k-server algorithm for a specific metric space is a function $f : Q \times M \times R \rightarrow Q \times M$, where Q is the set of possible placement configurations of the servers, M is the set of possible memory states of the algorithm, and R is the set of possible requests (the set of points in the metric space).

Note that when the metric space is of n points, $|Q| \leq n^k$, and that the cardinality of M sometimes depends on the specific metric space that the algorithm is applied to, and on k. We refer to $Q \times M$ as the set of configurations of the algorithm. Any global-control online k-server algorithm whose memory size cannot grow unboundly can be formulated in this way.

The *distributed* k-server problem is that of scheduling k identical servers which reside among the processors of a network topology. At times a request for service appears at a processor and one of the servers must reach that processor. A *distributed* online k-server algorithm is a set of programs; each processor has a separate program running in it. When a request appears in a processor it is received by the program running in it. This program then sends control messages, possibly causing the transmission of messages by other processors, as to move a server to the request point. The cost of a *distributed* online k-server algorithm is the cost incurred for the travel of the servers plus the communication cost incurred for the transmission of any control messages the algorithm sends.

For competitive analysis online *distributed* algorithms are compared to the *global-control* optimal adversary; a *distributed* online k-server algorithm $\mathcal{A}$ is c_k-competitive if there exists a value a such that for any request sequence σ, $\text{Cost}_{\mathcal{A}}(\sigma) \leq c_k \cdot \text{Cost}_{\text{Adv}}(\sigma) + a$.

In this paper we do not consider the issues of concurrency and assume the requests are serialized.

3 Preliminaries

Definition. A c-competitive *k-server tracking* mechanism for tracking the k servers $s_1, s_2, \ldots, s_k$ in a network topology $\mathcal{N}$, that has an *approximation factor* λ, is a distributed algorithm that handles the following types of operations, listed with their respective costs: (1) A move of one of the servers, with an amortized cost of at most $\frac{1}{D} \cdot c$ times the distance moved. (2) The finding, by some processor p, of the location of a particular server, s_i, with an amortized cost of at most $\frac{1}{D} \cdot c$ times the distance from p to s_i. (3) The finding by some processor p, of the location of some *close* server, that is, a server whose distance from p is at most λ times the distance from p to the closest server, with an amortized cost of at most $\frac{1}{D} \cdot c$ times this distance.

The first two operations are the operations of the *mobile user* mechanism [AP], and the last one is the *data tracking* [BFR] operation. Henceforth, let $T_{\mathcal{N},k}$ be the best competitive ratio for a k-server tracking mechanism on network $\mathcal{N}$. If a processor is allowed to have $O(k\delta \log n)$ bits of memory, then it follows from the constructions of [AP, BFR] that for every $\mathcal{N}$ and k, $T_{\mathcal{N},k} = O(\mu \log n)$ and λ is $O(1)$ (note that in [BFR] the results are stated for the case that the processors have less memory). It is easy to see that for the line and the ring $T_{\mathcal{N},k} = O(1)$, and for trees $T_{\mathcal{N},k} = O(k)$ using a disjoint paths traversal [BCR].

Definition. A c-competitive *generalized k-server tracking* mechanism is a k-server tracking mechanism that also allows every processor p to find all servers at distance at most d from it, at an amortized cost of at most $c \cdot d$.

Let $\tilde{T}_{\mathcal{N},k}$ be the best competitive ratio for a generalized k-server tracking algorithm on network $\mathcal{N}$. One can use the constructions of [AP, BFR] to get this mechanism for every network $\mathcal{N}$ such that $\tilde{T}_{\mathcal{N},k} = O(\max\{k, \mu\} \cdot \log n)$.

4 A Translator to Make k-Server Algorithms Distributed

The main idea of the translator is as follows: The set of servers is recursively partitioned into two disjoint sets, in a way that in any part of the recursive partition the distance between any two servers, each pertaining to a different subset, is at least d, and one can communicate between all the servers of the part over a distance of at most the number of servers in the part times d. We call d the *separation distance* of the part.

Each request is *handled* by a close server; this is not necessarily the server that *serves* the request. Each server locally simulates the underlying global-control algorithm, starting from some initial algorithm configuration, and serving those requests it *handles*. It counts the cost incurred by the underlying global-control algorithm during this simulated run, and whenever this cost is greater than $\alpha \cdot d$, ($\alpha < 1$ to be determined later), where d is the separation distance of some part of the recursive partition, a *phase* ends. The server that thus ended the phase forces upon all the servers of this part its own simulated algorithm configuration with its associated cost. All these servers then travel to conform to this configuration. It follows that at the end of the phase all the servers are at the positions they would occupy had the *competitive* global-control algorithm been run on some mindfully chosen subsequence of the requests that we call the *simulation sequence* of the phase. In what follows we precisely define the translator.

Given a global-control k-server algorithm $\mathcal{A}$, $\mathcal{A} : Q \times M \times R \rightarrow Q \times M$, we build a distributed k-server algorithm $\text{DS}_{\mathcal{A}}$. $\text{DS}_{\mathcal{A}}$ is defined recursively and proceeds in phases; we define $\text{DS}_{\mathcal{A}}(m, S)$, where S is a set of servers, to be the algorithm that governs the behavior of the servers in the set S. The cardinality of S is m, and is added to the notation for clarity of the description; we refer to m as the *cardinality* of the algorithm. When the set of servers is obvious or irrelevant for the discussion we sometimes abuse notation and do not indicate it. Thus, the distributed k-server algorithm, based on the global-control one $\mathcal{A}$, is denoted $\text{DS}_{\mathcal{A}}(k)$.

An algorithm of cardinality m consists of recursively running two separate algorithms of lesser cardinality for two disjoint sets of the m servers until a phase of $\mathrm{DS}_{\mathcal{A}}(m)$ ends. At the end of each phase we associate with the execution of the phase a subsequence of the request sequence handled by $\mathrm{DS}_{\mathcal{A}}(m)$ during the phase; this subsequence is the *simulation sequence* of the phase. Each server participates simultaneously in a number of algorithms with decreasing cardinality. It maintains a counter for each one of the algorithms it participates in, which we denote $\bar{C}_{s,j}$, where s is the server number and j is the cardinality of the algorithm the counter is related to. These counters maintain—roughly speaking—the knowledge of the server of the cost of the simulated algorithm $\mathcal{A}$ since the start of the current phase. These counters are maintained indirectly using a parallel set of variables $\bar{P}_{s,j}$ and defining $\bar{C}_{s,j} = \sum_{i \leq j} \bar{P}_{s,i}$ (we define $\bar{P}_{s,i} = 0$ if server s does not participate in an algorithm of cardinality i). The $\bar{P}$ variables maintain—roughly speaking—the knowledge of the server of the cost of the simulated algorithm $\mathcal{A}$ since the start of the current phase and until the end of the last phase of the lower level algorithm that the server participates in. In order to simulate the underlying global-control algorithm $\mathcal{A}$, each server maintains a variable with the simulated configuration of $\mathcal{A}$. It also maintains k variables each holding an *estimated position* of another server, i.e., the position of that server when their last lowest-level common phase started.

We use a k-server tracking mechanism; when a request appears, the algorithm uses this mechanism to locate a close server, that is, a server which is at distance within a constant factor of the distance to the closest one. This server will *handle* the request (but not necessarily *serve* it). The following describes how $\mathrm{DS}_{\mathcal{A}}(m)$ handles the requests.

For $m = 1$, $\mathrm{DS}_{\mathcal{A}}(m, S)$ is the algorithm that given a request for handling, updates the simulated configuration of its single server according to the request (using the underlying algorithm $\mathcal{A}$). The cost thus incurred by $\mathcal{A}$ is added to $\bar{P}_{s,1}$. A phase starts by initializing the variable $\bar{P}_{s,1}$ to 0 and consists of handling a single request, the *simulation sequence* of the phase being this single request. At the end of a phase we update the variable associated with the higher level algorithm that the server participates in (say, of cardinality $j, j > 1$) to reflect the addition to $\bar{C}_{s,1}$ during the phase, i.e., $\bar{P}_{s,j} \leftarrow \bar{P}_{s,j} + \bar{C}_{s,1}$. The server then travels to conform to its location according to the simulated configuration.

For $m > 1$, $\mathrm{DS}_{\mathcal{A}}(m, S)$ is defined recursively as follows: Consider the minimum spanning tree (in the metric space) of the locations of the servers in S at the beginning of a phase, denote by I the maximum-length edge in this tree and denote its length by d. We divide the set S into two disjoint sets A and B ($|A| = m_A$, $|B| = m_B$, $m = m_A + m_B$), such that the edge I separates them in the minimum spanning tree; we call d the *separation distance* of the phase. It follows that for any $a \in A$ and $b \in B$, $d(a, b) \geq d$, and that the weight of the minimum spanning tree is at most $(m - 1)d$. We initialize the $\bar{P}$ variables associated with $\mathrm{DS}_{\mathcal{A}}(m)$ to 0, i.e., the $\bar{P}_{x,m} \leftarrow 0$ for every $x \in S$, and start two algorithms $\mathrm{DS}_{\mathcal{A}}(m_A, A)$ and $\mathrm{DS}_{\mathcal{A}}(m_B, B)$ which are run separately until the following occurs [1]:

In some server $s \in S$ $\bar{C}_{s,m} > \alpha \cdot d$, where α is some constant < 1 to be determined later.

At this event the current phase of $\mathrm{DS}_{\mathcal{A}}(m, S)$ terminates. We first define the *simulation sequence* of the phase: We "terminate the phase according to s". This is defined as follows: Assume w.l.g. that $s \in A$. We first force the termination of the current phase of $\mathrm{DS}_{\mathcal{A}}(m_A, A)$, i.e., we "terminate the phase of $\mathrm{DS}_{\mathcal{A}}(m_A, A)$ according s", and then define the simulation sequence to be the concatenation of the simulation sequences of all the phases of $\mathrm{DS}_{\mathcal{A}}(m_A, A)$ [2].

To end the phase we perform the following *end-of-phase procedure*: All the servers in S override their local simulated configuration with the simulated configuration of $\mathcal{A}$ as maintained by s. They also update their local variables that hold estimated positions of the servers of S. They then travel to conform to the new simulated configuration. In addition, all the counters of the servers in S are updated to reflect the cost of $\mathcal{A}$ on the simulation sequence defined above: This is done by adding to the $\bar{P}$ variables associated with the higher-level algorithm (of cardinality say, $j, j > m$) the value of $\bar{C}_{s,m}$, i.e., $\bar{P}_{x,j} \leftarrow \bar{P}_{x,j} + \bar{C}_{s,m}$ for all $x \in S$.

Note that the updates performed ensure that at the end of phases all the counters of the servers of S are equal, and all these servers have the same simulated configuration; they also agree, therefore, on the partition of the servers into disjoint sets for the next phase. Note also that the counters are at any time an upper bound to the distance of their respective servers from their positions of the beginning of the phase.

4.1 Proof of Correctness and Analysis

In the above description we do not explicitly show which server *serves* each request, and it is even not

[1] Technically, each server that handles a request checks if the condition holds, going from the upmost-level algorithm towards the lowest-level algorithm.

[2] Note that this description is for the definition of the simulation sequence only; no work is performed.

obvious that each request is served when it appears. In the following lemma we prove that $DS_{\mathcal{A}}(m, S)$ is a valid m-server algorithm.

Lemma 1 *Each request is served while handling it.*

Proof Sketch. Assume server s_1 handles a request at point r, and according to the simulation of $\mathcal{A}$ it performs, s_2 is the server that serves it. Let $DS_{\mathcal{A}}(m, S)$ be the lowest level algorithm such that $s_1 \in S$ and $s_2 \in S$, d is the separation distance of the current phase of this algorithm. We show that the current phase of $DS_{\mathcal{A}}(m, S)$ terminates while handling the request and thus s_2 will travel to r. For $i = 1, 2$ let z_i denote the position of server s_i when the request appears, and p_i its position at the beginning of the current phase of $DS_{\mathcal{A}}(m, S)$. We know that $d(p_1, p_2) \geq d$, and that $d(p_i, z_i) \leq \alpha \cdot d$ (otherwise the phase would have terminated earlier). Since s_1 is the server that handles the request, it is the server that was located by the k-server tracking mechanism, and $d(r, z_1) \leq \lambda \cdot d(r, z_2)$ (where λ is the constant approximation factor of this mechanism), therefore, by the triangle inequality $d(r, p_2) > \alpha \cdot d$ (for $\alpha < 1/(2 \cdot \lambda + 2)$); thus, when the cost incurred by $\mathcal{A}$ to serve the request at r according to the simulation is added to the counter, the phase ends. □

To prove the competitiveness of the algorithm we need several definitions: We call the server according to which the phase of $DS_{\mathcal{A}}(m)$ terminates, the *terminating server.* At any time, the server $s \in S$, such that $\bar{C}_{s,m} = \max_{x \in S}\{\bar{C}_{x,m}\}$ is called the *maximum server* of S. Note that at the time of an end of a phase the terminating server is the maximum server. We also consider an imaginary run of $\mathcal{A}$ that starts with the servers at their positions of the beginning of the phase and with the same memory state as the one that the servers of S hold at the beginning of the phase, and serves the *simulation sequence.* We call this run the *simulation run.*

Lemma 2 *For any phase of* $DS_{\mathcal{A}}(m, S)$ *the following hold:*

1. *At the end of the phase all the servers in S hold as simulated configuration the configuration of $\mathcal{A}$ at the end of the simulation run.*

2. *Let s be the* terminating server. *The cost of $\mathcal{A}$ during the* simulation run *is $\bar{C}_{s,m}$.*

Proof Sketch. We prove the lemma by induction on m. For $m = 1$ both points are obvious.
For $m > 1$ assume that the lemma holds for any $l < m$ and assume w.l.g. that the terminating server $s \in A$. Point 1 follows from the fact that the simulation sequence is defined as the concatenation of the simulation sequences of the different phases of $DS_{\mathcal{A}}(m_A, A)$, and from the induction assumption.

Using the induction assumption, the cost of $\mathcal{A}$ during the simulation run is $\sum_{i=1}^{t} C_A^i$, where t is the number of phases of $DS_{\mathcal{A}}(m_A, A)$ (including the forcibly terminated last phase), and C_A^i is the value of $\bar{C}_{s_i,m_A}$ at the end of the i'th phase, s_i being the terminating server of this phase. But this is $\bar{C}_{s,m}$ at the time of the end of the phase of $DS_{\mathcal{A}}(m, S)$, proving point 2. □

We call the messages sent during the ***end-of-phase procedure***, in order to override the simulated algorithm configuration and the counters, ***control messages of the end-of-phase procedure.***

Lemma 3 *Consider a phase of* $DS_{\mathcal{A}}(m)$ *and let s be the terminating server of the phase. The control messages of the end-of-phase procedure are sent over a total distance of at most* $2m\frac{1}{\alpha}\bar{C}_{s,m}$.

Proof. When the end-of-phase procedure starts, i.e., *before* the travel of the servers is performed, the terminating server sends the control messages to the estimated positions of the servers of S. These positions must be in the $\alpha \cdot d$-neighborhoods of the positions of the respective servers at the beginning of the phase, otherwise the phase would have terminated before. The real positions of the servers must be in the $\alpha \cdot d$-neighborhoods of the estimated ones, for the same reason. There is a tree that spans the positions of the servers at the beginning of the phase with weight at most $(m-1)d$, therefore, the total distance over which the messages are sent is at most $(m-1)d + 2m\alpha d$. Since at the end of the phase $\bar{C}_{s,m} > \alpha \cdot d$, this is $\leq 2m\frac{1}{\alpha}\bar{C}_{s,m}$ (for $\alpha < 1/2$). □

In order to know in which processor each server is, we use the k-server tracking mechanism from each server's estimated position. We discuss the cost incurred because of the use of this mechanism later.

Lemma 4 *Consider a phase of* $DS_{\mathcal{A}}(m)$. *If s is the maximum server at a certain time, then since the beginning of the phase,* $DS_{\mathcal{A}}(m)$ *has sent control messages of end-of-phase procedures over a total distance of at most* $O(m^2\bar{C}_{s,m})$.

Proof. We prove by induction on m that $DS_{\mathcal{A}}(m)$ sends such control messages over a total distance of at most $2\frac{1}{\alpha}m^2\bar{C}_{s,m}$.
For $m = 1$ no control messages of end-of-phase procedures are sent.

For $m > 1$ assume that the claim holds for any $l < m$. A phase of $\mathrm{DS}_{\mathcal{A}}(m)$, $m > 1$, consists of phases of $\mathrm{DS}_{\mathcal{A}}(m_A, A)$ and $\mathrm{DS}_{\mathcal{A}}(m_B, B)$ run separately. Assume w.l.g. that $s \in A$ and that t phases of $\mathrm{DS}_{\mathcal{A}}(m_A, A)$ have already ended. $\bar{C}_{s,m} = \bar{P}_{s,m} + \bar{C}_{s,m_A}$, but $\bar{P}_{s,m} = \sum_{i=1}^{t} C_A^i$, where C_A^i is the value of $\bar{C}_{s_i,m_A}$ at the end of the i'th terminated phase of $\mathrm{DS}_{\mathcal{A}}(m_A, A)$, s_i is the terminating server of this phase. Since at the end of each phase the terminating server is also the maximum server, by the induction assumption we know that $\mathrm{DS}_{\mathcal{A}}(m_A, A)$ has sent control messages during its i'th phase over a total distance of at most $2\frac{1}{\alpha}(m_A)^2 C_A^i$. Thus, $\mathrm{DS}_{\mathcal{A}}(m_A, A)$ has sent control messages during the current phase of $\mathrm{DS}_{\mathcal{A}}(m)$ over a total distance of at most $2\frac{1}{\alpha}(m_A)^2 \bar{C}_{s,m}$. By similar arguments applied to s', the maximum server of B, we have that $\mathrm{DS}_{\mathcal{A}}(m_B, B)$ has sent control messages over a total distance of at most $2\frac{1}{\alpha}(m_B)^2 \bar{C}_{s',m}$. But s is the maximum server of S, and this is at most $2\frac{1}{\alpha}(m_B)^2 \bar{C}_{s,m}$. $(m_A)^2 + (m_B)^2 \le (m_A + m_B)^2 = m^2$, therefore, for any time before the end of the phase of $\mathrm{DS}_{\mathcal{A}}(m)$, the claim follows from the argument that all communication done during the phase is done by lower level algorithms.

When the end-of-phase procedure is performed, the terminating server is also the maximum server, and we know by Lemma 3 that the algorithm sends messages over a distance of at most $2m\frac{1}{\alpha}\bar{C}_{s,m}$; therefore the distance over which messages have been since the beginning of the phase is at most

$$2\frac{1}{\alpha}(m_A)^2\bar{C}_{s,m} + 2\frac{1}{\alpha}(m_B)^2\bar{C}_{s,m} + 2m\frac{1}{\alpha}\bar{C}_{s,m} \le 2\frac{1}{\alpha}m^2\bar{C}_{s,m}\ . \qquad \square$$

Lemma 5 *Consider a phase of* $\mathrm{DS}_{\mathcal{A}}(m, S)$ *and let* s *be the terminating server of the phase. The total distance traveled by the servers in* S *during the end-of-phase procedure is at most* $2m\bar{C}_{s,m}$.

Proof. At the end of the phase $\mathrm{DS}_{\mathcal{A}}(m, S)$ instructs the servers in S to travel to their respective positions according to the configuration of $\mathcal{A}$ maintained by s. To do this the servers can travel back to their positions of the beginning of the phase, a distance of at most $\alpha \cdot d$, then travel to their respective new locations, a total distance of at most $\bar{C}_{s,m}$. Therefore, the total distance traveled is at most $m \cdot \alpha \cdot d + \bar{C}_{s,m}$. Since $\bar{C}_{s,m} > \alpha \cdot d$, this is at most $2m\bar{C}_{s,m}$. $\square$

Lemma 6 *Consider a phase of* $\mathrm{DS}_{\mathcal{A}}(m, S)$. *If* s *is the maximum server at a certain time, then the servers in* S *have traveled since the beginning of the phase a total distance of at most* $O(m^2\bar{C}_{s,m})$.

This lemma follows from arguments similar to those in the proof of Lemma 4, using Lemma 5 to bound the travel done during the end-of-phase procedure.

Theorem 7 *Algorithm* $\mathrm{DS}_{\mathcal{A}}(k, S)$ *is* $O(c_k \cdot k^2 \cdot (1 + \frac{1}{D} \cdot \max\{k, T_{\mathcal{N},k}, \log|M|/\mu\}))$ *-competitive if* $\mathcal{A}$ *is* c_k*-competitive.*

Proof. To analyze $\mathrm{DS}_{\mathcal{A}}(k)$ we concatenate the simulation sequences of its terminated phases and sum the values of $\bar{C}_{s_i,k}$ at the end of each phase, s_i being the terminating server of the i'th phase. We then force the termination of the last unfinished phase according to the maximum server at this time. This can be thought of as if $\mathrm{DS}_{\mathcal{A}}(k, S)$ is run as one of the two lower level algorithms of some imaginary algorithm $\mathrm{DS}_{\mathcal{A}}(k+1)$, that never ends a phase. We then terminate the phase according to the maximum server (s) at the time the algorithm halts, and consider the value of $\bar{C}_{s,k+1}$ together with the simulation sequence of this only phase of $\mathrm{DS}_{\mathcal{A}}(k+1)$.

Summing up the cost of $\mathrm{DS}_{\mathcal{A}}(k)$ we have:

- The cost incurred for the travel of servers is at most $O(k^2 \cdot \bar{C}_{s,k+1})$ by Lemma 6.
- The cost incurred for the transmission of control messages that follow the travel of servers is, therefore, at most $O(k^2 \cdot \bar{C}_{s,k+1} \cdot \frac{1}{D} \cdot (k + \log|M|/\mu))$. This is because each server maintains $O(k)$ counters of size δ bits, k simulated positions of servers having $\lceil \log n \rceil$ bits, a memory state of $\mathcal{A}$ of size $\lceil \log |M| \rceil$ bits and a tree describing the partition of the servers and their estimated positions of size $O(k \log n)$ bits.
- By Lemma 4 the communication cost incurred for the transmission of control messages of end-of-phase procedures is at most $O(k^2 \cdot \bar{C}_{s,k+1} \cdot \frac{1}{D} \cdot (k + \log|M|/\mu))$, since the size of any message sent by $\mathrm{DS}_{\mathcal{A}}(k)$ is $O(k \cdot \mu + \log|M|)$ bits.
- The cost incurred for the use of the k-server tracking mechanism is at most $O(k^2 \cdot \bar{C}_{s,k+1} \cdot T_{\mathcal{N},k} \cdot \frac{1}{D})$. This is because we use the k-server tracking mechanism to find a close server over a total distance which is at most the total distance the servers travel, and to find a specific server over a total distance which is at most the total distance over which we send control messages of end-of-phase procedures.
- An additional cost is incurred once for the transmission of the positions of all the servers when the algorithm starts; we denote this cost by a'.

We denote by σ the request sequence served by $DS_{\mathcal{A}}(k)$ and by σ' the simulation sequence of the phase of $DS_{\mathcal{A}}(k+1)$. Using Lemma 2 and since $\mathcal{A}$ is c_k-competitive,

$$\bar{C}_{s,k+1} = \mathrm{Cost}_{\mathcal{A}}(\sigma') \le c_k \cdot \mathrm{Cost}_{\mathrm{Adv}}(\sigma') + a \ .$$

The total cost of $DS_{\mathcal{A}}(k)$ on σ is

$$O(k^2 \cdot \bar{C}_{s,k+1} \cdot (1 + \frac{1}{D} \cdot \max\{k, T_{\mathcal{N},k}, \log|M|/\mu\})) + a' \ ,$$

therefore,

$$\mathrm{Cost}_{DS_{\mathcal{A}}(k)}(\sigma) \le O(k^2 \cdot (1 + \frac{1}{D} \cdot \max\{k, T_{\mathcal{N},k}, \log|M|/\mu\})) \times (c_k \cdot \mathrm{Cost}_{\mathrm{Adv}}(\sigma') + a) + a' \ .$$

Clearly $\mathrm{Cost}_{\mathrm{Adv}}(\sigma') \le \mathrm{Cost}_{\mathrm{Adv}}(\sigma)$, and $DS_{\mathcal{A}}(k)$ is $O(c_k \cdot k^2 \cdot (1 + \frac{1}{D} \cdot \max\{k, T_{\mathcal{N},k}, \log|M|/\mu\}))$ -competitive. □

4.2 Applications

We use discrete versions of the Double-Coverage algorithm of [CKPV] for the line, the algorithm for trees of [CL1], and the algorithm for the ring of [FRRS]. In these discrete versions a modified metric space is created by adding points at distance of one unit apart along the edges of the metric space, rounding their lengths upwards. Applying the algorithm to this modified metric space increases the competitive ratio by at most a factor of 2, while the servers are always located at one of the points of the modified metric space. The number of memory states of the discrete algorithms is thus at most $(n\Delta)^k$ times the number of memory states of the original algorithm. Together with the best known k-server tracking mechanisms we obtain:

Corollary 8 *There are competitive distributed k-server algorithms with competitive ratios $O(k^3 + k^4/D)$ for the line, $O(k^3 + k^4/D)$ for trees and $O(k^5 + k^6/D)$ for the ring.*

Using the results in [CL2] and [IR] for the case of 2 servers we get:

Corollary 9 *There are competitive distributed 2-server algorithms with competitive ratio $O(T_{\mathcal{N},2}/D)$.*

5 Randomized Algorithms

The Harmonic k-server algorithm, first proposed in [RS], is the algorithm that given a request at point r, chooses each server to serve the request with probability inversely proportional to its distance to r. Specifically, if the locations of the online servers are $s_1, s_2, \ldots, s_k$, and $N = \sum_{i=1}^{k} \frac{1}{d(s_i,r)}$, then server s_i is moved with probability $\frac{1}{d(s_i,r)}/N$. Grove [G] proved that Harmonic is $O(k2^k)$-competitive. It has however been conjectured ([RS, BKT]) that the correct competitive ratio is $O(k^2)$. Let c_H denote the competitive ratio of Harmonic. We present a distributed version of the Harmonic algorithm with a small increase in the competitive ratio.

The Distributed-Harmonic Algorithm (DH)
Upon a request initiated by processor r, we proceed in phases for each $1 \le i \le \delta$, where each phase occurs with some absolute probability $\tilde{p}_{i-1}$ ($\tilde{p}_0 = 1$). We use a generalized k-server tracking mechanism to find all the servers at distance at most 2^i from r. If no such server exists then we proceed to the next phase. Otherwise, let m_i be the number of servers at r's 2^i-neighborhood, and order the servers, $s_1, s_2, \ldots, s_{m_i}$ by increasing distance from r. Let $N_i = \sum_{j=1}^{m_i} \frac{1}{d(s_j,r)}$, and let $\tilde{M}_i = \frac{k-m_i}{2^i}$. Let $\tilde{p}_i = \tilde{M}_i/(N_i + \tilde{M}_i)$; note that $\tilde{p}_i$ is a function of the locations of the closest m_i servers to r, and therefore can be computed by Distributed-Harmonic in the i'th phase. With absolute probability $1 - \tilde{p}_i$ choose each server s_j, $1 \le j \le m_i$, with probability $\frac{1}{d(s_j,r)}/N_i$ to move to the request point, i.e., complete the coin tosses already made in previous phases to achieve this probability (A technical computation shows that the resulting conditional probability to move s_j, for $j \le m_{i-1}$, is: $\tilde{q}_{i,j} = \frac{1}{d(s_j,r)\tilde{p}_{i-1}}(\frac{1-\tilde{p}_i}{N_i} - \frac{1-\tilde{p}_{i-1}}{N_{i-1}})$.) With absolute probability $\tilde{p}_i$ the algorithm just proceeds with the next phase.

Analysis
The Distributed-Harmonic algorithm is defined so that it moves each server to serve the request with the same probability that the global-control Harmonic algorithm moves it. To do that, it maintains the invariant that after each phase the absolute probability that each server is moved, is a lower bound on the probability that the global-control Harmonic algorithm would have moved it. The probability that the algorithm proceeds to another phase after the i'th phase is $\tilde{p}_i = \tilde{M}_i/(N_i + \tilde{M}_i)$. Assume all k servers are found in the t'th phase. Then $\tilde{p}_t = 0$, and since $N_t = N$, the probability that s_j, $1 \le j \le k$, serves the request after the last phase, reaches that of the global-control Harmonic: $\frac{1}{d(s_j,r)}/N$. It is left to show that for each server s_j, $1 \le j \le k$, the probability that it is moved by the i'th phase, $0 \le i \le t$, is increasing.

This probability is:

$$\tilde{z}_{i,j} = (1-\tilde{p}_i)\frac{1}{d(s_j,r)}/N_i = 1/(N_i+\tilde{M}_i)\cdot\frac{1}{d(s_j,r)} .$$

For all $0 \le i \le t-1$, since for all $m_i+1 \le j \le k$, $d(s_j,r) > 2^i$, we have:

$$\begin{aligned} N_i + \tilde{M}_i &= \sum_{j=1}^{m_i}\frac{1}{d(s_j,r)} + \frac{k-m_i}{2^i} \\ &\ge \sum_{j=1}^{m_{i+1}}\frac{1}{d(s_j,r)} + \frac{k-m_{i+1}}{2^{i+1}} = N_{i+1}+\tilde{M}_{i+1} , \end{aligned}$$

and therefore $\tilde{z}_{i,j} \le \tilde{z}_{i+1,j}$.

The expected cost for the (global-control) Harmonic algorithm on the request is:

$$\mathrm{E}(\mathrm{Cost_H}) = \sum_{i=1}^{k}\frac{\frac{1}{d(s_j,r)}}{N}\cdot d(s_j,r) = \frac{k}{N} .$$

The expected cost of Distributed-Harmonic for moving the servers is the same. The messages sent by the generalized k-server tracking mechanism when the servers move add an (amortized) overhead of $\tilde{T}_{\mathcal{N},k}$ along the distance traveled by the servers (k/N) giving a total cost of $\mathrm{E}(\mathrm{Cost_{DH}}^1) = \frac{k}{N}(1+\frac{\tilde{T}_{\mathcal{N},k}}{D})$. The search messages sent to find the servers in the different phases of the algorithm give an (amortized) overhead of $\tilde{T}_{\mathcal{N},k}$ to the search distance:

$$\begin{aligned} \mathrm{E}(\mathrm{Cost_{DH}}^2) &= \frac{1}{D}\sum_{i=0}^{\delta-1}\tilde{p}_i\cdot\tilde{T}_{\mathcal{N},k}\cdot 2^{i+1} \\ &= \frac{1}{D}\sum_{i=0}^{\delta-1}\frac{\tilde{M}_i}{N_i+\tilde{M}_i}\cdot\tilde{T}_{\mathcal{N},k}\cdot 2^{i+1} . \end{aligned}$$

Since $\tilde{M}_i = \frac{k-m_i}{2^i}$ and $N_i + \tilde{M}_i \ge N_t + \tilde{M}_t = N$, we obtain:

$$\begin{aligned} \mathrm{E}(\mathrm{Cost_{DH}}) &= \mathrm{E}(\mathrm{Cost_{DH}}^1) + \mathrm{E}(\mathrm{Cost_{DH}}^2) \\ &\le \frac{k}{N}(1+\frac{\tilde{T}_{\mathcal{N},k}}{D}) + \frac{1}{D}\sum_{i=0}^{\delta-1}\frac{k}{N}\cdot\tilde{T}_{\mathcal{N},k}\cdot 2 \\ &\le (1+\frac{1}{D}\cdot 3\delta\tilde{T}_{\mathcal{N},k})\cdot\mathrm{E}(\mathrm{Cost_H}) . \end{aligned}$$

We conclude with the following theorem:

Theorem 10 *The Distributed-Harmonic k-server algorithm is $O(c_H\cdot(1+\frac{1}{D}\cdot\delta\tilde{T}_{\mathcal{N},k}))$-competitive, against adaptive online adversaries.*

From the results of [AP, BFR] we get:

Corollary 11 *The Distributed-Harmonic algorithm is $O(c_H \cdot (1+\frac{1}{D}\cdot\max\{k,\mu\}\delta\log n))$-competitive, against adaptive online adversaries, for arbitrary network topologies.*

Using similar techniques we get the following:

Theorem 12 *There is a randomized $O(k(1+\frac{\delta}{D}))$-competitive memoryless algorithm for the line against adaptive online adversaries.*

6 Additional Results

In this section we show a lower bound to the distributed k-server problem and present a new 2-server algorithm based on some of our techniques.

Lower Bound

Our lower bound is derived by a reduction from the mobile user problem [AP]. Given a network topology $\mathcal{N}$ of n points and a lower bound of $c_{\mathcal{N},k}$ achieved by using at most $n-(k-1)$ points of this network, we obtain a lower bound of $\Omega(\max\{k,\frac{1}{D}\cdot c_{\mathcal{N},k}\})$ for our problem. The details are omitted. From a lower bound of [AKRS] for the mobile user problem we get,

Theorem 13 *For all n there is a network topology of n processors, such that the competitive ratio of any distributed k-server algorithm is $\Omega(\max\{k,\frac{1}{D}\cdot(\log n/\log\log n)\})$ against adaptive online adversaries.*

A New 2-Server Algorithm

Our technique of recursively dividing the set of servers according to their distances, used for the general translator, can be extended as to simultaneously divide the points of the metric space according to each point's distance from the two sets of servers. Each set of servers thus has a "territory" in the metric space. This, together with the idea to calculate new positions for the servers with respect to their positions of the beginning of the phase, gives rise to a new global-control algorithm for the well studied case of $k=2$ that can easily be made distributed.

The Work-Count Algorithm (WC)

The algorithm proceeds in phases. Let p_1, p_2 denote the initial positions of the servers at the beginning of the phase, and let d be the distance between these positions. The metric space is divided such that the points closer to p_1 are in the "territory" of s_1, while the points closer to p_2 are in the "territory" of s_2. During a phase, requests are served by the server in whose "territory" the request point lies, and we compute the accumulated distance each server travels. We denote by f_i the first request served by s_i in the phase. A phase is ended by server s_t when one of the following occurs:

1. A request appears at a point at distance at least $2d$ from both p_1 and p_2.
2. A request served by s_t appears at distance at least $d/8$ from its first request point, f_t.
3. Server s_t reaches an accumulated cost of at least $3d$.

Let r be the request ending a phase. When the phase ends we first move the servers back to their initial positions. Then we perform the following rearrangement operation according to the 3 possible cases to end a phase:

1. We move the closest server to the request.
2. We move the servers to occupy points f_t and r.
3. We move both servers to point r.

Theorem 14 *The global-control Work-Count algorithm is $O(1)$-competitive for 2 servers.*

Proof Sketch. We use a potential function argument. The potential function is the weight of the minimum weight perfect matching between the online servers and the servers of the adversary. We analyze the change in the potential function over the phase in two stages: The change due to the adversary moves as if the online servers stay put, and the change during the reorganization procedure. □

The Work-Count algorithm can directly be made distributed using a 2-server tracking mechanism, giving an $O(T_{\mathcal{N},2}/D)$-competitive distributed algorithm.

Acknowledgments. We would like to thank B. Awerbuch, A. Fiat, D. Peleg, Y. Rabani and M. Ricklin for useful discussions. We also thank S. Ben-David, H. Karloff, Y. Mansour and M. Yung for their helpful comments as to the presentation of these results.

References

[ABF] B. Awerbuch, Y. Bartal, and A. Fiat. New Results on Competitive Distributed Data Management. Manuscript.

[AKP] B. Awerbuch, S. Kutten, and D. Peleg. Competitive Distributed Job Scheduling. In *Proc. of the 24th Ann. ACM Symp. on Theory of Computing*, pages 571–580, May 1992.

[AKRS] N. Alon, G. Kalai, M. Ricklin and L. Stockmeyer. Lower Bounds on the Competitive Ratio for Mobile User Tracking and Distributed Job Scheduling. *These Proceedings.*

[AP] B. Awerbuch and D. Peleg. Concurrent Online Tracking of Mobile Users. In *Proc. SIGCOMM.* Zurich, Sept. 1991.

[BBKTW] S. Ben-David, A. Borodin, R.M. Karp, G. Tardos, and A. Wigderson. On the Power of Randomization in Online Algorithms. In *Proc. of the 22nd Ann. ACM Symp. on Theory of Computing*, pages 379–386, May 1990.

[BCR] R.A. Baeza-Yates, J.C. Culberson, and G.J.E. Rawlins. Searching with Uncertainty. Technical report, University of Waterloo, October 1987.

[BFR] Y. Bartal, A. Fiat, and Y. Rabani. Competitive Algorithms for Distributed Data Management. In *Proc. of the 24th Ann. ACM Symp. on Theory of Computing*, pages 39–48, May 1992.

[BKT] P. Berman, H. Karloff, and G. Tardos. A Competitive 3-Server Algorithm. In *Proc. 1st ACM-SIAM Symp. on Discrete Algorithms*, pages 280–290, January 1990.

[BLS] A. Borodin, N. Linial, and M. Saks. An Optimal On-Line Algorithm for Metrical Task Systems. In *Proc. of the 19th Ann. ACM Symp on Theory of Computing*, pages 373–382, May 1987.

[CKPV] M. Chrobak, H. Karloff, T. Payne, and S. Vishwanathan. New Results on Server Problems. In *Proc. 1st ACM-SIAM Symp. on Discrete Algorithms*, pages 291–300, January 1990.

[CL1] M. Chrobak and L. Larmore. An Optimal On-Line k-Server Algorithm for Trees. *SIAM Journal of Computing*, 20:144-148, 1991.

[CL2] M. Chrobak and L. Larmore. On Fast Algorithms for Two Servers. In *Proc. Mathematical Foundations of Computer Science*, Banská Bystrica, 1990. Also, to appear in *Journal of Algorithms.*

[FRR] A. Fiat, Y. Rabani, and Y. Ravid. Competitive k-Server Algorithms. In *Proc. of the 31st Ann. IEEE Symp. on Foundations of Computer Science*, pages 454–463, October 1990. Also, to appear in *JCSS Special FOCS Issue.*

[FRRS] A. Fiat, Y. Rabani, Y. Ravid, and B. Schieber. A Deterministic $O(k^3)$-Competitive k-Server Algorithm for the Circle. Submitted to *Algorithmica.*

[G] E. Grove. The Harmonic k-Server Algorithm is Competitive. In *Proc. of the 23rd Ann. ACM Symp. on Theory of Computing*, pages 260-266, May 1991.

[IR] S. Irani and R. Rubinfeld. A Competitive 2-Server Algorithm. *Information Processing Letters*, 39:85–91, 1991.

[KMRS] A.R. Karlin, M.S. Manasse, L. Rudolph, and D.D. Sleator. Competitive Snoopy Caching. *Algorithmica*, 3(1):79-119, 1988.

[MMS] M.S. Manasse, L.A. McGeoch, and D.D. Sleator. Competitive Algorithms for On-Line Problems. In *Proc. of the 20th Ann. ACM Symp. on Theory of Computing*, pages 322-333,,May 1988.

[RS] P. Raghavan and M. Snir. Memory versus Randomization in On-Line Algorithms. In *Proc. 16th ICALP*, July 1989.

[ST] D.D. Sleator and R.E. Tarjan. Amortized Efficiency of List Update and Paging Rules. *Communication of the ACM*, 28(2) pages 202-208, 1985.

[T] G. Turpin. Recent Work on the Server Problem. Master's thesis, University of Toronto, 1989.

Undecidability of the Horn-Clause Implication Problem*

Jerzy Marcinkowski
Institute of Computer Science
University of Wrocław,
jmarcink@plwruw11.bitnet

Leszek Pacholski†
Institute of Mathematics
Polish Academy of Sciences
pacholsk@plwruw11.bitnet

Abstract

In this paper we prove that the problem "given two Horn clauses $\mathcal{H}_1 = (\alpha_1 \wedge \alpha_2 \rightarrow \beta)$ and $\mathcal{H}_2 = (\gamma_1 \wedge \ldots \wedge \gamma_k \rightarrow \delta)$, where $\alpha_i, \beta, \gamma_i, \delta$ are atomic formulas, decide if $\mathcal{H}_2$ is a consequence of $\mathcal{H}_1$" is not recursive. This solves one of the last open decidability problems concerning formulas in pure predicate logic (i.e. without equality symbol). The proof depends on a thorough analysis of derivation trees of one rule of inference with two premisses and one conclussion, and we believe, it may have further applications

1 Introduction

In this paper we prove that the problem "given two Horn clauses $\mathcal{H}_1 = (\alpha_1 \wedge \alpha_2 \rightarrow \beta)$ and $\mathcal{H}_2 = (\gamma_1 \wedge \ldots \wedge \gamma_k \rightarrow \delta)$, where $\alpha_i, \beta, \gamma_i, \delta$ are atomic formulas, decide if $\mathcal{H}_2$ is a consequence of $\mathcal{H}_1$" is not recursive, thus solving one of the last open decidability problems concerning formulas in pure predicate logic (i.e. without equality symbol). It follows from a result of M. Schmidt-Schauß ([SS]), that the problem, if a Horn clause $(\alpha \rightarrow \beta)$, with α, β atomic, implies another Horn clause, is decidable.

Problems concerning decidability of restricted classes of quantificational formulas have been studied since the thirties by many logicians including W. Ackermann, P. Bernays, J. Büchi, K. Gödel, W. Goldfarb, Y. Gurevich, L. Kalmár, M. Schönfinkel, H. Wang and many others. Accounts of the classical results in this area can be found in three books: [A], [L] and [DG] and in two papers of Y. Gurevich ([Gu1], [Gu2]). More recent results have been obtained by H.R. Lewis and W. Goldfarb ([G1], [G2], [LG]).

Several papers on the clause implication problem have been written by researchers being motivated by problems in artificial inteligence. They argue, (see e.g. [SS] and [GG]), that the deletion of implied clauses in automated deduction systems could help to avoid redundant information in the search space. This would, however, require an (efficient) algorithm that would recognize the implied clauses. In [GG],[LG],[L1], and [L2] some (very strong) sufficient criteria for decidability of clause implication have been given. But, as shown by M. Schmidt-Schauß ([SS]), the problem if an *arbitrary* clause $\mathcal{A}$ implies a clause $\mathcal{B}$ is undecidable provided $\mathcal{A}$ has at least four literals. However, the answer to the problem if the clause implication problem is decidable if $\mathcal{A}$ has at most three literals, and the answer if the implication problem is decidable for the class of Horn clauses, were, untill now, unknown.

A similar problem in logic with equality is known to be undecidable. Its unsolvability follows from the result of P. Perkins ([P]) and G. McNulty ([M1], [M2]), that the problem, if an equational theory given by a single axiom has a non-trivial model, is undecidable. However, as shown for example by the satisfiability problem for the Gödel class of first order sentences in prenex normal form, the presence or absence of equality can have a drastic impact on the decidability of the problem (see [G2]).

There has been an extensive research on the implication problem for data dependencies (see e.g. [CLM], [BV], [CV], [V]), where problems having a similar structure as the Horn clause implication problem have been studied and many undecidability results have been obtained. However, to the best of our knowledge the results in the data base theory do not follow from the undecidability of the Horn clause implication problem and conversely, we believe that our result can not be derived from the known results on implication problem for data dependencies. In some respects the language of data dependencies is stronger, which in some cases allows an application of the above mentioned results of Perkins and McNulty (and the result of R. McKenzie ([MK]) in the case of finite implication problem). On the other hand we make an extensive use of the term algebra, which is not directly possible in the pure relational language of data base dependencies.

We use standard notation and terminology. An *atomic formula* is an expression of the form $Q(t_1, \ldots, t_k)$, where Q is a relation symbol and $t_1, \ldots, t_k$ are terms. A *literal* is an atomic formula or a negation of an atomic formula. A *clause* is a disjunction of literals. A *ground* clause (term) is a clause (term) without variables. A clause with n literals is called *a n-clause,* a *unit* clause is a 1-clause. A *Horn clause* is a clause with at most one non-negated literal, or equivalently a formula of the form $\alpha_1 \wedge \alpha_2 \wedge \ldots \wedge \alpha_k \rightarrow \beta$, where $\alpha_1, \alpha_2, \ldots, \alpha_k, \beta$ are atomic formulas. The Horn clause above a *k-Horn clause.*

*This research has been supported by KBN grant 2 1197 91 01.

†Partially supported by University of Wrocław, Université de Caen and INRIA-CRIN

0-8186-2900-2/92 $3.00 © 1992 IEEE

Let $\mathcal{A}$ and $\mathcal{B}$ be two clauses. We say that $\mathcal{A}$ implies $\mathcal{B}$, if $\mathcal{A} \vdash \mathcal{B}$, or equivalently, if $(\forall x_1)...(\forall x_m)\mathcal{A} \rightarrow (\forall y_1)...(\forall y_n)\mathcal{B}$ holds, where $x_1, ..., x_m, y_1, ..., y_n$ are all variables in $\mathcal{A}$ and $\mathcal{B}$ (we can and do assume, that $\mathcal{A}$ and $\mathcal{B}$ have disjoint sets of variables). The clause implication problem is equivalent to the satisfiability problem for the set formulas consisting of the clause $\mathcal{A}$ and ground unit clauses obtained by the negation of $\mathcal{B}$.

A tree $\mathcal{T}$ is a *k-tree* if each non-leaf node of $\mathcal{T}$ has exactly k sons. We identify k-trees with sets of words over the alphabet $\{1, 2, ..., k\}$, which are closed under prefixes, i.e. if $w \in \mathcal{T}$ and v is a prefix of w, then $v \in \mathcal{T}$. Given a tree $\mathcal{T}$, we put $(\mathcal{T})_w = \{v : \exists u \in \mathcal{T}, u = wv\}$, i.e. $(\mathcal{T})_w$ is the subtree of $\mathcal{T}$ rooted at w.

It is easy to notice that to study the problem, if one Horn clause implies another, it suffices to assume that all Horn clauses under consideration are of the form

$$\mathcal{H} = (Q(\Gamma_1) \wedge Q(\Gamma_2) \wedge \ldots \wedge Q(\Gamma_k) \rightarrow Q(\Gamma)) \quad (1)$$

where $\Gamma, \Gamma_1, \Gamma_2, ..., \Gamma_k$ are n-tuples of terms, for n being the arity of Q. Again, it is easy to notice that we can furthermore assume, that the arity of Q is 1, so $\Gamma, \Gamma_1, \Gamma_2, ..., \Gamma_k$ are either variables or terms with the same main symbol.

For a given k-Horn clause $\mathcal{H}$, an *$\mathcal{H}$-derivation* is a finite labelled k-tree $\mathcal{T}$, whose each node w is labeled by a n tuple $\Delta(w)$ of constant terms (or just a constant term), and moreover, for each inner node w of $\mathcal{T}$, there exists a substitution σ, such that $\sigma\Gamma = \Delta(w)$, and $\sigma\Gamma_i = \Delta(wi)$ for each $i \leq k$.

For a set $\mathcal{G}$ of n-tuples of constant terms, an $\mathcal{H}$-derivation $\mathcal{T}$ will be called a $\mathcal{G}$-$\mathcal{H}$-derivation, if $\Delta(w) \in \mathcal{G}$, or $\Delta(w)$ is a constant, for each leaf w of $\mathcal{T}$. In other words a $\mathcal{G}$-$\mathcal{H}$-derivation for a Horn clause $\mathcal{H}$ given by (1) is an $\mathcal{H}$-derivation from the set $\{Q(t) : t \in \mathcal{G}\} \cup \{Q(c) : c$ is a constant $\}$.

In this paper we present a proof of the result mentioned in the abstract. To help the reader to get easily some idea of the proof we shall give some (almost) obvious remarks on the problem. First, let us consider an easier, and in fact decidable problem. Let $\mathcal{H}_1 = (\alpha \rightarrow \beta)$, and $\mathcal{H} = (\gamma_1 \wedge ... \wedge \gamma_k \rightarrow \delta)$, where $\alpha, \beta, \gamma_i, \delta$ are atomic formulas, with $\alpha = Q(t)$, $\beta = Q(u)$, $\gamma_i = Q(v_i)$ and $\delta = Q(w)$. To prove that $\mathcal{H}_1$ implies $\mathcal{H}$, it suffices to substitute distinct constants for variables in $\mathcal{H}$, and then to prove that $Q(\sigma(w))$ can be derived from $Q(\sigma(v_i))$, for some i, where σ denotes the above mentioned substitution, in the "logic", with the unique rule of inference:

$$\mathcal{R}_1 : \quad \frac{Q(t)}{Q(u)}.$$

It is clear that proofs using $\mathcal{R}_1$ can have length longer that 1 only if the result of application of $\mathcal{R}_1$ is unifiable with the premise. This easily leads to the conclusion that the problem above can be reduced to the problem of the existence of a sequence of substitutions $\sigma_1, \sigma_2, ..., \sigma_k$ such that $w = \sigma_1(u), \sigma_1(t) = \sigma_2(u), \sigma_2(t) = \sigma_3(u), ..., \sigma_k(t) = v_i$, for some i. Now, an analysis of the depths of the terms $\sigma_i(t)$ gives a proof of the decidability of the problem.

If, however, $\mathcal{H}_1$ is replaced by $\mathcal{H}_2 = (\alpha_1 \wedge \alpha_2 \rightarrow \beta)$, then our original problem is equivalent to the problem of derivability of one open formula without variables (ground formula) from a set of ground formulas in "logic" with just one rule of inference:

$$\mathcal{R}_2 : \quad \frac{Q(t_1) \quad Q(t_2)}{Q(u)},$$

which leads to a more difficult, and in fact undecidable problem. It is clear that the predicate symbol Q does not play any role in $\mathcal{R}_2$, and the problem reduces to an analysis of properties of (binary) trees labelled by terms in such a way, that the relationship between the label of a father and the labels of his sons agrees with the rule $\mathcal{R}_2$.

The paper is organized as follows. In the first chapter we study the notions of a semi-regular and of a regular Thue tree. We prove that the problem of existence of a semi-regular Thue tree containing a given branch is equivalent to the boundedness of the corresponding Thue system. Moreover, we establish some connection between regular and semiregular Thue trees, and between regular Thue trees and Horn derivations. Using that, we prove, in the second chapter, that for some positive integer k, and some k-Horn clause $\mathcal{H}$, the problem of existence of an $\mathcal{H}$-derivation having a given branch w in the derivation tree, is undecidable. It is, however, decidable if the Horn clause $\mathcal{H}$, defined in Chapter 2 implies another Horn clause (see the remark at the end of the chapter).

The third part reduces k to 2. It is based on the simple idea of coding k trees by binary trees, but it is slightly technical due to a more complex instance of the notion of regularity in this case. Moreover, there is a hidden idea of a postponed derivation - in some sense, a derivation according to the 2-Horn clause, coding a given k-Thue system, consists of long paths, where information stored in the term is reordered, the actual derivation taking place only at the ends of these paths. Of course, it would have been better, if we could prove a lemma that undecidability of the Horn clause implication problem implies undecidability of the problem for 2-Horn clauses. We were unable to prove such a lemma, however, the techniques of Chapter 3 can prove, that *monotonic* Horn clauses can be simulated by (monotonic) 2-Horn clauses (see the end of Chapter 2 for the notion of monotonicity).

The final, fourth part gives two last lemmas which we need to derive the main result of the paper from the result of Chapter 3. These are the steering lemma, which codes in a Horn clause $\mathcal{H}$, the information necessary to force any valid $\mathcal{H}$-derivation tree to contain a given branch, and the hiding lemma, which helps to hide a large, uncontrolable term which can appear in the root of the derivation tree, and put a small predefined term in the root of an unknown derivation.

We did not try to get the optimal value of the number of literals in the second of the Horn clauses mentioned in the abstract. Some improvement is obvious. We shall take care of this in a later version of this paper.

1 Regular Thue trees

In this chapter, for a given Thue system $\mathcal{S}$, we introduce notions of a $\mathcal{S}$-regular and of a $\mathcal{S}$-semiregular tree. For the notion of a Thue system see [PO] or [D]. To fix the terminology, by a *Thue system* $\mathcal{S}$ over an alphabeth Σ we understand a finite set of *symmetric* productions, i.e. a finite set of *unordered* pairs $< u, v >$ of words in Σ^*. We moreover require, that $\mathcal{S}$ is *closed*, i.e. if $< u, v >\in \mathcal{S}$, and $< u, w >\in \mathcal{S}$ then $< v, W >\in \mathcal{S}$. $< v, w >\in \mathcal{S}$. We write $\overset{\mathcal{S}}{\Longleftrightarrow}$ to denote that u can be obtained from v by one application of a production in $\mathcal{S}$, and $\overset{*\mathcal{S}}{\Longleftrightarrow}$ to denote that u, v are equivalent in $\mathcal{S}$.

These notions will later be used to derive the undecidability of the Horn implication problem from the undecidability of the boundedness problem for the Thue system.

Definition 1.1 *Let $\mathcal{S} = \{< u_i, v_i >: i \in I\}$ be a finite set of productions of a Thue system $\mathcal{S}$ in the alphabet $\{1, 2, ..., p\}$. We put*

$$\mathcal{T}_\mathcal{S} = \{u : u \text{ is a proper prefix of } v, \text{ for some } < v, w >\in \mathcal{S}\}.$$

For a set $\mathcal{W}$ of words over the alfabet $\{1, 2, ..., p\}$ we put

$$Thue_\mathcal{S}(\mathcal{W}) = \{u : (\exists w \in \mathcal{W})(w \overset{*\mathcal{S}}{\Longleftrightarrow} u)\}.$$

Finally, we put

$$THUE_\mathcal{S}(\mathcal{W}) = pr(Thue_\mathcal{S}(\mathcal{W})),$$

*where, for a set $\mathcal{X}$, $pr(\mathcal{X})$ denotes the set of all prefixes of $\mathcal{X}$. We call $THUE_\mathcal{S}(\mathcal{W})$, a $\mathcal{S}$-*Thue tree *of $\mathcal{W}$.*

Now, we are ready to introduce the notions of semiregularity and regularity of trees. For a Thue system $\mathcal{S}$, the semiregularity of a tree describes the fact that this tree is symmetric with respect to $\mathcal{S}$, the regularity requires, that, in addition, the tree is $\mathcal{T}_\mathcal{S}$-rich, i.e. each subtree of the tree, rooted not too close to a leaf, contains $\mathcal{T}_\mathcal{S}$. We shall usually omitt the subscript $\mathcal{S}$ and shall write $THUE(\mathcal{W})$ instead of $THUE_\mathcal{S}(\mathcal{W})$.

Definition 1.2 *(i) Let $\mathcal{T}$ be a p-tree. We call a node $w \in \mathcal{T}$, $\mathcal{S}$-*semiregular*, if $(\mathcal{T})_{wu_i} = (\mathcal{T})_{wv_i}$, for each $i \in I$. We call a node w $\mathcal{S}$-*regular* if it is $\mathcal{S}$-semiregular and if $\mathcal{T}_\mathcal{S} \subseteq (\mathcal{T})_w$.*

*(ii) A p-tree $\mathcal{T}$ is $\mathcal{S}$-*semiregular*, if every node of $\mathcal{T}$ is semiregular. Given a finite set $\mathcal{G}$ of semiregular trees, a $\mathcal{S}$-semiregular p-tree $\mathcal{T}$ is called $\mathcal{G}$-$\mathcal{S}$-*regular* if for each node w of $\mathcal{T}$, either w is $\mathcal{S}$-regular, or $(\mathcal{T})_v$ is in $\mathcal{G}$ for some, non-necessarily proper, prefix v of w.*

The following two easy lemmas establish a connection between Thue system and semiregular trees.

Lemma 1.3 *For every Thue system $\mathcal{S}$ and each set $\mathcal{W}$ of words over the alfabet $\{1, 2, ..., p\}$, $THUE(\mathcal{W})$ is a $\mathcal{S}$-semiregular p-tree.*

Proof. Let $\mathcal{T} = THUE(\mathcal{W})$ and let $r \in \mathcal{T}$. We shall prove that r is semiregular. Suppose that for some $i \in I$, $rv_i \in \mathcal{T}$ and $s \in (\mathcal{T})_{rv_i}$. Then there exists $w \in \mathcal{W}$ and a word t such that $rv_ist \overset{*\mathcal{S}}{\Longleftrightarrow} w$. Hence, also $ru_ist \overset{*\mathcal{S}}{\Longleftrightarrow} w$, and $s \in (\mathcal{T})_{ru_i}$. Therefore $(\mathcal{T})_{rv_i} \subseteq (\mathcal{T})_{ru_i}$. The inclusion $(\mathcal{T})_{ru_i} \subseteq (\mathcal{T})_{rv_i}$ follows by symmetry. ■

Lemma 1.4 *Every semiregular tree containing a node w contains all elements of the set $\{v : w \overset{*\mathcal{S}}{\Longleftrightarrow} v\}$. So, if there exists a finite semiregular tree containing w, then the set $\{v : w \overset{*\mathcal{S}}{\Longleftrightarrow} v\}$ is finite.*

Proof. It suffices to prove that for any semiregular $\mathcal{T}$, if $u \in \mathcal{T}$ and $u \overset{\mathcal{S}}{\Longleftrightarrow} v$, then $v \in \mathcal{T}$. Let $u = s_1u_is_2$ and $v = s_1v_is_2$ where $< u_i, w_i >\in \mathcal{S}$. By semiregularity of $\mathcal{T}$, the node s_1 is semiregular, so $s_2 \in (\mathcal{T})_{s_1u_i}$ implies that $s_2 \in (\mathcal{T})_{s_1v_i}$ and consequently $s_1u_is_2 \in \mathcal{T}$. ■

Definition 1.5 *We say that a closed Thue system $\mathcal{S}$ is good, if $(\mathcal{T}_\mathcal{S})_v = \emptyset$, for every $< u, v >\in \mathcal{S}$.*

In other words a Thue system is good if words that appear in productions have the prefix property: no word that appear in a production of the system, is a prefix of another such word. From now on we assume that $\mathcal{S}$ is a good Thue system.

Definition 1.6 *We denote by $\mathcal{H}_\mathcal{S}$ the Horn clause*

$$Q(\Gamma_1) \wedge Q(\Gamma_2) \wedge \ldots \wedge Q(\Gamma_p) \to Q(\Gamma),$$

where Q is an unary relation symbol, and

(i) $\Gamma = g(t_1, t_2, \dots t_p)$ *is a term built over the language containing exactly one p-ary functional symbol* g *and no constant symbols. For a word* w, Γ *has* g *in the position* w *iff* $w \in \mathcal{T}_S$. *The variables of* Γ *in positions* u *and* v *are equal iff* $< u, v > \in \mathcal{S}$.

(ii) For $i \in \{1, 2, ..., p\}$, $\Gamma_i = t_i$.

From now on, we consider terms built from variables, a function symbol g and from a constant c. So, a constant term is uniquely determined by the tree of its function symbols g, so we can, and will identify constant terms with the corresponding trees. The next lemma describes the structure of $\mathcal{G}$-$\mathcal{H}_S$-derivation and establishes a duality between terms and $\mathcal{H}_S$-derivations.

Lemma 1.7 *(i) If the root of an* $\mathcal{H}_S$*-derivation* $\mathcal{D}$ *is labeled by a constant term* Δ, *then for each node* w *of the derivation, we have* $\Delta(w) = (\Delta)_w$.

(ii) If the root of a $\mathcal{G}$-$\mathcal{H}_S$*-derivation* $\mathcal{D}$ *is labeled by a constant term* Δ, *then* Δ *is a semiregular tree.*

Proof. (i) The proof proceeds by induction on the length of w. Suppose that w and wi are nodes of $\mathcal{D}$, and the label of $\Delta(w)$ is Δ_w. Then, by the definition of $\mathcal{H}_S$, we have $\Delta(w) = g(t_1, t_2, \dots t_p)$ and $\Delta(wi) = t_i = (\Delta)_{wi}$.

(ii) Let w be a node of Δ. We shall prove that w is semiregular. Let v be the longest prefix of w such that $v \in \mathcal{D}$. If $v \neq w$, then v is a leaf of $\mathcal{D}$, and $\Delta(v) \in \mathcal{S}$. By (i) $\Delta(v) = (\Delta)_v$, so, by the assumption that $\mathcal{G}$ is a set of semiregular trees, w is a semiregular node. If $v = w$ and w is a leaf of $\mathcal{D}$, then w is clearly semiregular. If $v = w$ and w is an inner node, then $\Delta(w)$ is an instance of Γ and so, $\Delta(w)$ is semiregular. Since $(\Delta)_w = \Delta(w)$, it follows that w is a semiregular node. ∎

Lemma 1.8 *(i) If the root of a constant term* Δ *is a regular node, then there exists a substitution* σ, *such that* $\Delta_i = \sigma\Gamma_i$, *for* $i \in \{1, 2, ..., p\}$. *and*

$$\Delta = \sigma\Gamma. \tag{2}$$

(ii) If a constant term Δ *is a* $\mathcal{G}$-$\mathcal{S}$*-regular tree, then* Δ *is a label of the root of a* $\mathcal{G}$-$\mathcal{H}_S$*-derivation* $\mathcal{D}$.

Proof. (i) To prove that there exists a substitution σ, such that (2) holds, it suffices to check that

(3) if x is a variable which occur in position v in Γ, then position v exists in Δ,

and

(4) if a variable x occur in Γ in positions v and u then $\Delta_v = \Delta_u$.

To prove (3), notice that if Γ has a variable in position v, then $v = wj$ and $w \in \mathcal{T}_S$. By regularity, the term Δ has the function symbol g in position w, so it has some symbol in position wj. To prove (4) suppose that Γ has a variable x in positions v and u. Then $< v, u > \in \mathcal{S}$. By semiregularity of the root, if $u \in \Delta$, then $(\Delta)_u = (\Delta)_v$. If $u \notin \Delta$ then by (3), Δ has the constant symbol c in positions v and u. So, the existence of a substitution σ satisfying (2) is established. It immediately follows from the definition of $\mathcal{H}_S$ that $\Delta_i = \sigma\Gamma_i$, for $i \in \{1, 2, ..., p\}$.

(ii) Assume that Δ is a $\mathcal{G}$-$\mathcal{S}$-regular, and let $\mathcal{D}$ be the least full p-tree containing all regular nodes of Δ as inner nodes. Let the nodes w of $\mathcal{D}$ which are in Δ be labeled by $(\Delta)_w$, and let the other nodes be labeled by the term c. It remains to prove that such a labeling defines a valid $\mathcal{G}$-$\mathcal{H}_S$-derivation.

If w is a leaf of $\mathcal{D}$, then it is labeled by c if $w \notin \Delta$, and by $(\Delta)_w$ otherwise. By the definition of $\mathcal{D}$, w is not a regular node of Δ, so, since Δ is regular, we get $(\Delta)_w \in \mathcal{G}$. Now, let w be an inner node of $\mathcal{D}$. Then w is labeled by Δ_w, which is regular. Therefore, by (i) applied to $(\Delta)_w$, there exists a substitution σ such that $\sigma\Gamma = (\Delta)_w$. ∎

2 Existence of paths in p-clause derivations

In this chapter we shall prove, that the problem if there exists a valid $\mathcal{H}_S$-derivation containing a branch w, is undecidable. This result is a consequence of the existence of a Thue system $\mathcal{S}$, such that 1) the problem of finiteness of the set $Thue_S(w)$ is undecidable, and moreover, 2) each $\mathcal{S}$-semiregular tree can be embedded in a $\mathcal{G}$-$\mathcal{S}$-regular tree of the same depth.

Definition 2.1 *We say that a good Thue system* $\mathcal{S}$ *over* $\{1, 2, ..., p\}$ *is* very good *if it is closed, and the following conditions are satisfied:*

(i) if $< u, v >$ *is a production of* $\mathcal{S}$, *then both* u *and* v *are non-empty and have lenght at most 2. Moreover, at least one of them has length 2.*

(ii) Symbols of the alphabet are divided into two disjoint categories, called dynamic *and* static, *in such a way that:*

(a) if a symbol $i \in \{1, 2, ..., p\}$ *occurs in a production* $< i, w >$, *for* $w \in \{1, 2, ..., p\}^*$, *then it is* dynamic,

(b) if a symbol i *occurs in a production of a form* $< ji, vk >$, *where* $v \in \{1, 2, ..., p\}^*$, *and* $j, k \in \{1, 2, ..., p\}$, *and* k *is* dynamic, *then* i *is* dynamic,

(c) if a symbol i *occurs in any production of the form* $< ij, v >$ *with* v, j *as above, then* i *is* static.

(iii) The set of words w *containing exactly one dynamic symbol as the last symbol of* w *such that* $\{v : w \overset{*S}{\Longleftrightarrow} v\}$ *finite is not recursive.*

Lemma 2.2 *Assume that* $w \overset{*S}{\Longleftrightarrow} v$. *Then* w *and* v *have the same number of dynamic symbols. If* w *contains exactly one dynamic symbol as its last symbol,* *then also v contains exactly one dynamic symbol as its last symbol. If w contains no dynamic symbols then the lenght of w is equal to the lenght of v.*

Proof. A routine proof proceeds on induction on the lenght of a Thue transformation of w into v. ■

Lemma 2.3 *There exists a very good Thue process $\mathcal{S}$.*

Proof. It is not difficult to prove (compare e.g. [KTU]) that there exists a deterministic Turing Machine M, having a single tape, unbounded in one direction, for which it is undecidable, if the number of configurations that can be reached from a given initial configuration, is finite. Let A and Q denote respectively, the tape alphabet and the set of states of M. If we code configurations of M as words in $A \cup (A \times Q)$, then it is clear how to translate the transition function of M into a very good Thue system. An extra care has to be taken of the behaviour of M at the end of already visited part of the tape. To discribe that, the notion of a dynamic symbol of a Thue system is introduced.

For the rest of this section we fix $\mathcal{G} = \{g(c, c, \ldots, c)\}$. So, a tree is a $\mathcal{G}$-$\mathcal{S}$–regular iff all its nodes except the leaves are regular.

Lemma 2.4 *Let t be a word which contains at most one dynamic symbol which, moreover, can appear only as the last symbol of t, and let $\mathcal{T} = THUE(\{t\})$. If $\mathcal{T}$ is finite, then there exists a $\mathcal{G}$-$\mathcal{S}$-regular tree $\mathcal{U}$ containing $\mathcal{T}$ and having the same depth as $\mathcal{T}$.*

Proof. Let $\mathcal{T}^0 = \mathcal{T}$ and suppose that an inner node w of $\mathcal{T}$ is not regular. So there is a production $< ij, v >$ in $\mathcal{S}$ such that $wi \notin \mathcal{T}$. By Lemma 2.2 it follows that wi does not contain a dynamic symbol. Since w is regular, it is not a leaf of $\mathcal{T}$, so w is shorter than the longest word in $\mathcal{T}$. Let $\mathcal{T}^1 = THUE(\{t, wi\})$. Notice, that $\mathcal{T}^1 = THUE(\{wi\}) \cup \mathcal{T}$ and, by Lemma 2.2, $THUE(\{wi\})$ is a set of words of the same lenght as wi containing only static symbols, so dynamic symbols can appear only at leaves of $\mathcal{T}^1$. Therefore we can iterate this construction obtaining trees $\mathcal{T}^2, \mathcal{T}^3, \ldots$. Since $\mathcal{T}^i \subset \mathcal{T}^{i+1}$, $\mathcal{T}^i \neq \mathcal{T}^{i+1}$ and $\mathcal{T}^i$ has the same depth as $\mathcal{T}$, there is an integer i such that $\mathcal{T}^i$ can not be further transformed, so $\mathcal{T}^i$ is a regular tree. ■

As an immediate consequence of Lemma 1.4, Lemma 1.7, Lemma 1.8 and Lemma 2.4 we get the following corollary.

Lemma 2.5 *Let w be a word containing exacly one dynamic symbol as its last symbol. Then the set $\{v : w \overset{*\mathcal{S}}{\Longleftrightarrow} v\}$ is finite iff there exists a $\mathcal{G}$-$\mathcal{H}_\mathcal{S}$-derivation containing w as an inner node or as a leaf labeled by the term $g(c, c, \ldots c)$.* ■

As a corollary to the above lemma and Lemma 2.3 we obtain the main result of this section.

Theorem 2.6 *There exists an integer p and a p-Horn clause $\mathcal{H}_\mathcal{S}$ in a language containing one unary predicate symbol Q, a constant c and a p-ary function symbol g, such that, for $\mathcal{G} = \{c, g(c, c, ..., c)\}$, the problem whether, for a given w, there exists a $\mathcal{G}$-$\mathcal{H}_\mathcal{S}$-derivation containing w as an inner node or as a leaf labeled with the term $g(c, c, \ldots c)$ is undecidable.* ■

To conclude this chapter we would like to add an obvious remark that the Horn clause $\mathcal{H}_\mathcal{S}$ defined here is *monotonic*, in the sense, that the terms in the premisses are subterms of the term in the conclussion. From this it follows that the problem, if a set of ground unit clauses is consistent with $\mathcal{H}_\mathcal{S}$ is decidable.

3 Existence of paths in 2-clause derivations

Now, we are going to strenghten the result of Chapter 2 and prove, that a variant of Theorem 2.6 holds for $p = 2$. This will be obtained by an encoding of k-Thue trees by binary Thue trees.

Let a be a positive integer such that $p < 2^a$. For $i \in \{1, 2, ..., p\}$ we put $\mathrm{e}(i) = 110 i_1 0 i_2 0 \ldots 0 i_a 0$, where $i_1 i_2 \ldots i_a$ is the binary expansion of i as an a-digit number. Slightly abusing the notation, by e we shall also denote the extension of e to the homomorphism of $\{1, 2, ..., p\}^*$ into $\{0, 1\}^*$. This coding has the property, that in the code of a word, the begining and the end of the code of a letter can be easily distinguished.

Definition 3.1
$\mathcal{B} = \mathrm{e}(\mathcal{S}) = \{< \mathrm{e}(v), \mathrm{e}(u) >:< v, u > \in \mathcal{S}\}$.

We are going to prove that the binary representation $\mathcal{B}$ of $\mathcal{S}$ and the notions of regularity and semiregularity defined relatively to $\mathcal{B}$ retain many properties that are true for $\mathcal{S}$. Recall, that *pr* denote the closure of a set of words under prefixes.

Lemma 3.2 *If $\mathcal{W} \subseteq \{1, 2, ..., p\}^*$, then*
$pr(\mathrm{e}(THUE_\mathcal{P}(\mathcal{W}))) = THUE_\mathcal{B}(\mathrm{e}(\mathcal{W}))$. ■

Let $\mathcal{T}_\mathcal{B}$ be the small tree, and let $\mathcal{H}_\mathcal{B}$ be the Horn clause defined for $\mathcal{B}$ by Definition 1.1 and Definition 1.6, respectively.

Lemma 3.3 *$\mathcal{B}$ is good.* ■

So, the lemmas of Chapter 1 are true for $\mathcal{B}$. Let $w \in \{1, 2, ..., p\}^*$. For a set $\mathcal{F}$ of ground terms, that will be defined later, we are going to prove that $Thue(w)$ is finite iff there exists an $\mathcal{F}$-$\mathcal{H}_\mathcal{B}$-derivation containing the branch $\mathrm{e}(w)$. The *only if* implication is clear. By Lemma 1.8, to prove the other part of the claim, it suffices to prove that there exists an $\mathcal{F}$-$\mathcal{B}$-regular tree containing the node $\mathrm{e}(w)$. A natural candidate for such a tree is $pr(\mathrm{e}(\mathcal{U}))$, where $\mathcal{U}$ is the regular tree constructed in Lemma 2.4. By Lemma 1.3 and Lemma 3.2, $\mathcal{U}$ is $\mathcal{B}$-semiregular. There are, however, two reasons why it is not regular. First, it has *new* nodes, i.e. nodes which are not of the form $e(w)$, for $w \in \{1,2,...,p\}^*$. Clearly, these new nodes are not regular. Moreover, if w is an inner node of $\mathcal{U}$ such that wi is a leaf and $< ij, u >$ is a production of $\mathcal{S}$, then i is the longest proper prefix of ij, so w could be a regular node. On the other hand, $e(i)$ is not the longest proper prefix of $e(ij)$.

Recall, that we identify constant terms with trees. To be more specific let us introduce the following explicite convention.

Definition 3.4 *If $\mathcal{Q}$ is a full p-ary tree and g is a p-ary function symbol, then* $g(\mathcal{Q})$ *is the smallest term build from g and a constant symbol c, for which $\mathcal{Q}$ is the set of occurences of g.*

Before proceeding on with the technical proof, we shall give a short, very unformal description of the idea behind the proof. The proof can be described as a simulation of an (monotonic) $\mathcal{H}_{\mathcal{S}}$-derivation by an $\mathcal{H}_{\mathcal{B}}$-derivation. The basic simulation is defined locally i.e. each step of an $\mathcal{H}_{\mathcal{S}}$-derivation is replaced by a small $\mathcal{H}_{\mathcal{B}}$-derivation tree. The core of the $\mathcal{H}_{\mathcal{B}}$-derivation is the set $\mathcal{Y} = pr\{e(i) : i \in \{1,...,p\}\}$, which does not form a tree. Let $tr\mathcal{Y}$ denote the smallest binary binary tree containing $\mathcal{Y}$. The leaves of $\mathcal{Y}$ correspond to premisses of $\mathcal{H}_{\mathcal{S}}$ and are labelled by terms $t_1,...,t_p$. The information about these terms is transformed up the $\mathcal{H}_{\mathcal{B}}$-derivation tree, at branching point of $\mathcal{Y}$ it is added together and at the other points it is just transmitted up.

Now, $\mathcal{H}_{\mathcal{B}}$ has function symbols at the nodes of $\mathcal{Y}$ and (distinct) variables at the auxiliary leaves of $tr(\mathcal{Y})$. So, we are free to substitute anything for these variables. However, to make sure that the inference rule corresponding to $\mathcal{H}_{\mathcal{B}}$ will be applicable latter, we have to make sure that the premisses of that rule will have function symbols at certain positions. To do that, we add large terms at the auxiliary leaves of $tr(\mathcal{Y})$. The special form of the coding that we have choosen will secure that these new large terms will not disturb informations being transmitted up along $\mathcal{Y}$.

Now, we are ready to define our candidate for a regular tree containing the branch $e(w)$. By the choice of the coding of $\mathcal{S}$, the *new* nodes of $pr(e(\mathcal{U}))$ are $\mathcal{B}$-symmetric ($\mathcal{B}$-semiregular). In fact the notion of $\mathcal{B}$-semiregularity is void for *new* nodes. So, the only property of the new nodes to be taken care of, is the richness, which is provided by adding many short branches begining at each *new* node. Moreover, we have to make sure, that the nodes near the leaves will be regular.

Definition 3.5 *Let $\mathcal{R} = pr(e(\mathcal{U}))$. We put*

(i) $\mathcal{E} = \{w : w$ is a proper prefix of $e(i)$, for some i, $1 \le i \le p\}$, and $\Lambda = g(\mathcal{E})$.

(ii) $\mathcal{R}^1 = \mathcal{R} \cup \{wv : (\exists u \in \mathcal{U})(\exists i \in \{1,2,...,p\})$ $(ui \notin \mathcal{U},\ w = e(u), v \in \mathcal{E})\}$.

(iii) Let $\mathcal{R}^2 = \mathcal{R}^1 \cup \{wv : w$ is a new *node of $\mathcal{R}^1$ and $v \in \mathcal{T}_{\mathcal{B}}\}$.*

(iv) Let $\mathcal{F}$ consists of the empty tree, $(\mathcal{T}_{\mathcal{B}})_1$, $(\mathcal{T}_{\mathcal{B}})_1 \cup (\mathcal{T}_{\mathcal{B}})_{11}$ and $\mathcal{E}$.

Notice, that all trees in $\mathcal{F}$ are semiregular.

The fact that the only pair of consecutive 1's in $e(i)$, for $i \le p$, is the pair in the begining of the word, and that every $e(i)$ ends with 0 implies the following.

Lemma 3.6

(i) If $w \in \mathcal{R}^1$ is a new node, $j \in \{0,1\}$, and $wj \notin \mathcal{R}^1$, then $\mathcal{R}^2_{wj}$ is either the empty term, or $(\mathcal{T}_{\mathcal{B}})_1$, or $(\mathcal{T}_{\mathcal{B}})_1 \cup (\mathcal{T}_{\mathcal{B}})_{11}$.

(ii) If $w \in \mathcal{R}^1$ is a new node, then $\mathcal{R}^2_{w11} \subseteq (\mathcal{T}_{\mathcal{B}})_1 \cup (\mathcal{T}_{\mathcal{B}})_{11}$.

(iii) If w is a leaf of $\mathcal{U}$, then $\mathcal{R}^2_{e(w)} = \mathcal{E}$.

(iv) If w is a non-leaf node of $\mathcal{U}$, then $\mathcal{R}^2_{e(w)}$ is empty. ■

Lemma 3.7

(i) If $w \in \mathcal{R}^1$, then w is a $\mathcal{B}$-semiregular node of $\mathcal{R}_2$.

(ii) If $w \in \mathcal{R}^1$ is a new node, then w is a $\mathcal{B}$-regular node of $\mathcal{R}^2$.

(iii) If $w \in \mathcal{R}^2$ is an old node, then it is either a leaf of $\mathcal{R}$, or is regular in $\mathcal{R}^2$.

Proof. (i) If w is an old node of $\mathcal{R}^1$, then if $we(u_i) \in \mathcal{R}^2$, then also $we(v_i) \in \mathcal{R}$. $\mathcal{R}$ is a semiregular tree, so $\mathcal{R}^2_{we(u_i)} = \mathcal{R}^2_{we(v_i)}$. Notice, that the construction of $\mathcal{R}^2$ does not effect the equalities between the subtrees of $\mathcal{R}$.

If w is a new node of $\mathcal{R}^1$, then for every $i \in I$, $\mathcal{R}^2_{we(u_i)}$ and $\mathcal{R}^2_{we(u_i)}$ are empty.

(ii) It is just why $\mathcal{R}^2$ was constructed.

(iii) If $w \in \mathcal{R}^2$ is an old node then it is of the form $e(v)$, for a regular node v of $\mathcal{U}$. By the construction of $\mathcal{R}^2$ it follows that $\{we(i)u : i \in \{1,2,...,p\},\ u \in \mathcal{E}, vi \in \mathcal{U}\} \cup \{wu : u \in \mathcal{E}\} \subseteq \mathcal{R}^2$. Since $\mathcal{T}_{\mathcal{B}} \subseteq \{we(i)u : i \in \{1,2,...,p\},\ u \in \mathcal{E},\ vi \in \mathcal{U}\} \cup \{wu : u \in \mathcal{E}\}$, the node w is $\mathcal{B}$-regular in $\mathcal{R}^2$. ■

As a corollary we obtain:

Lemma 3.8 *Let $w \in \{1,2,...,p\}^*$ contain exactly one dynamic symbol as the last symbol. Then the set $\{v : w \overset{*\mathcal{S}}{\Longleftrightarrow} v\}$ is finite iff there exists a $\mathcal{F}$-$\mathcal{H}_{\mathcal{B}}$derivation* *containing* e(w) *as an inner node or as a leaf labeled by* Λ. ■

So, as in Chapter 2 we get the following main result.

Theorem 3.9 *There exists a 2-Horn clause* $\mathcal{H}_{\mathcal{B}}$ *such that the problem, whether for a given* w*, there exists a* $\mathcal{F}$-$\mathcal{H}_{\mathcal{B}}$*-derivation containing* e(w) *as an inner node or as a leaf labeled with term* Λ*, is undecidable.* ■

4 Two final steps

We want to prove, that it is undecidable whether for a given 2-Horn clause $\mathcal{H}$, a set $\mathcal{G}$ of (vectors) of constant terms and for a constant term t, there exists an $\mathcal{H}$-derivation with all leaves labeled with terms in $\mathcal{G}$ and with its root labeled with t. The main lemma of Section 3 asserts, that it is undecidable, if there exists an $\mathcal{H}$-derivation with leaves labeled with terms in $\mathcal{G}$, and containing the branch w in the derivation tree. However, even if such a derivation exists, we still have no control of the term in the root of it. The next two lemmas solve these problems. The first lemma gives a method to force the derivation to contain a given node w and the second hides the huge term Ω in the root of the derivation.

Definition 4.1 *Let* $\mathcal{H} = (Q(t_1) \wedge ... \wedge Q(t_p) \rightarrow Q(t))$ *be a Horn clause, let* $\mathcal{G}$ *be a set of ground unit clauses, and let* $v \in \{1, ..., p\}^l$*. By* $\mathcal{K}(\mathcal{H}, v)$ *we denote the clause*

$$Q'(t_1, f(x_1^1, ..., x_l^1)) \wedge Q'(t_2, f(x_1^2, ..., x_l^2)) \wedge ...$$
$$... \wedge Q'(t_p, f(x_1^p, ..., x_l^p)) \rightarrow Q'(t, f(x_1, ..., x_l)),$$

where $x_i = x_{i+1}^{v_i}$*, all other variables* x_i^j *are distinct and different from variables that occur in the terms* t_i*. We also put* $\mathcal{G}' = \{Q'(t, f(c, c, ..., c)) : Q(t) \in \mathcal{G}\}$.

Lemma 4.2 *Let* k *be a new constant. Then every valid* $\mathcal{K}(\mathcal{H}, v)$*-derivation of* $Q'(t, f(k, c, ...,))$ *from* $\mathcal{G}'$ *contains the branch* v*. Moreover, if there exists an* $\mathcal{H}$*-derivation of* t *from* $\mathcal{G}$*, which has the branch* v*, then there exists a* $\mathcal{K}(\mathcal{H}, v)$*-derivation of* $Q'(t, f(k, c, ...,))$ *from* $\mathcal{G}'$.

Proof. Any $\mathcal{H}$-derivation can be transformed into a $\mathcal{K}$-derivation by replacing $Q(\Delta)$ by $Q'(\Delta, f(c, ..., c))$ outside the branch v, and by $Q'(\Delta, f(c, ..., k, ..., c))$, (with k in the i-th place) in the $(i-1)$-th node along the path v. By the choice of arity of f, the constant k will not appear in leaves, so the derivation so obtained is a $\mathcal{G}'$-$\mathcal{H}$-derivation.

On the other hand replacing $Q'(\Delta, x)$ by $Q(\Delta)$ in a valid $\mathcal{G}'$-$\mathcal{K}$-derivation gives a valid $\mathcal{G}$-$\mathcal{H}$-derivation. Let $v|i$ denote the first i symbols of v. By the definition of $\mathcal{K}$, it follows that if $Q'(\Delta, x)$ is the $v|i$-th premise of the root in the $\mathcal{G}'$-$\mathcal{K}$-derivation, then $x = f(c, ..., k, ..., c)$, with k in the $(i+1)$-st place, so, since the set $\mathcal{G}'$ of formulas without variables does not contain the constant k, any valid $\mathcal{G}'$-$\mathcal{K}$-derivation contains the branch v. ■

Definition 4.3 *Let* $\mathcal{H} = (Q(\Gamma_0) \wedge Q(\Gamma_1) \rightarrow Q(\Gamma))$ *be a Horn clause and let* $\mathcal{G}$ *be a set of ground unit clauses. We put*

$$\mathcal{K} = (Q'(\Gamma_0, x, u) \wedge Q'(\Gamma_1, v, y) \rightarrow Q'(x, y, \Gamma)),$$

and $G = \{d : Q(d) \in \mathcal{G}\}$, $G' = \{d : d_0, d_1 \in G\}$. *Finally we put* $\bar{\mathcal{G}} = \{Q'(u, v, w) : u, v, w \in G\}$.

We moreover define $h : \{0,1\}^* \rightarrow \{0,1\}^*$ *as a homomorphism defined by* $h(0) = 001$ *and* $h(1) = 101$.

Let f, d *be ground terms such that* $f \in G$ *and* $d \in G'$.

Lemma 4.4 *There exists a* $\mathcal{G}$-$\mathcal{H}$*-derivation containing a branch* w *if and only if there exists a* $\bar{\mathcal{G}}$-$\mathcal{K}$*-derivation containing the branch* $0h(w)$ *and having the formula* $Q'(d, f, d)$ *in the root.*

Proof Given a triple $u = (x_1, x_2, x_3)$, and $i \leq 3$, we put $[u]_i = x_i$, and slightly abusing the notation, given a label L of an (unknown) node w of a (binary) tree and a (binary) word u, by L_u we shall denote the label of the node wu.

Assume that $\mathcal{T}'$ is a $\bar{\mathcal{G}}$-$\mathcal{K}$-derivation containing the branch $0h(w)$. Clearly, we have $[(x, y, z)_{001}]_3 = z_0$ and $[(x, y, z)_{101}]_3 = z_1$. Let $\mathcal{T}$ be the tree containing these nodes of $\mathcal{T}'$ which belong to $0\{001, 101\}^*$ labelled by the third coordinates of the corresponding nodes of $\mathcal{T}'$. Then $\mathcal{T}$ is an $\mathcal{H}$-derivation from $\mathcal{G}$ containing the branch w.

On the other hand, let $\mathcal{T}$ be a $\mathcal{G}$-$\mathcal{H}$-derivation. First, we shall prove that there exists a $\bar{\mathcal{G}}$-$\mathcal{K}$-derivation containing the branch $h(w)$ and having the formula $Q'(d_0, d, \Omega)$ in the root, where Ω is the term at the root of $\mathcal{T}$.

Each elementary part of the derivation $\mathcal{T}$, consisting of a father (labelled by z), and his two sons in $\mathcal{T}$, (labelled by z_0, and z_1), will be replaced by a binary tree $\mathcal{I}$ of depth 3, having two main branches 001 and 101, and 4 additional branches: 000, 01, 100, and 11, necessary to make a binary tree. The small tree $\mathcal{I}$ will be labelled by triples of terms. The label of the root of $\mathcal{I}$ will be the triple $(\cdot, \cdot, z_0)$ and the labels of the main leaves 001 and 101 will be $(\cdot, \cdot, z_0)$ and $(\cdot, \cdot, z_1)$, respectively. Call the terms z, z_0, z_1 the main terms. Along the main branch the position of a main term will be permuted according to $\mathcal{K}$, i.e. $(\cdot, \cdot, z)_{001} = (z_0, \cdot, \cdot)_{01} = (\cdot, z_0, \cdot)_1 = (\cdot, \cdot, z_0)$ and $(\cdot, \cdot, z)_{101} = (z_1, \cdot, \cdot)_{01} = = (\cdot, z_1, \cdot)_1 = (\cdot, \cdot, z_1)$. Going down along branches of the tree $\mathcal{I}$, other auxiliary terms, denoted above by $\cdot$, appear. At a node t, some of them will be inherited from the father of t, and some will be new. Notice, that at additional branches of $\mathcal{I}$, we have only auxiliary terms. Moreover auxiliary terms have a very short lifetime. Each such term v, or both his immediate successors v_0 and v_1, will eventually appear at the label of an additional leaf, or will appear at the end of the main branch as an auxiliary term, to be later send to additional leaves of the next small tree $\mathcal{I}'$, attached to the end of the main branch of $\mathcal{I}$. Now, to finish the construction, it suffices to choose, for each auxiliary term, a term from G or from G', depending whether the term itself, or his sons appear at leaves.

The construction descibed above gives a derivation tree having

$$\{h(u) : u \text{ is a leaf of } \mathcal{T}\} \cup$$
$$\{h(u)v : u \text{ is a node of } \mathcal{T},\ v \in \{000, 01, 100, 11\}\},$$

as the set of leaves. It is labelled by triples with main terms (i.e. the terms on the third positions at nodes belonging to $\{h(v) : v \in \mathcal{T}\}$) as in $\mathcal{T}$, and the auxiliary terms as described above.

In other words, each elementary step

$$Q(z_0) \wedge Q(z_1) \rightarrow (z)$$

of an $\mathcal{H}$-derivation, is replaced by the following set of elementary steps of a $\mathcal{K}$-derivation.

$$Q'(w_0^3, w_0^1, w^7) \wedge Q'(w_1^3, w^8, z_0) \rightarrow Q'(w_0, z_0, w^3),$$
$$Q'(w_0, z_0, w^3) \wedge Q'(w_1^1, w^4, x) \rightarrow Q'(z_0, x, w^1),$$
$$Q'(w_0^5, y_0, w_9) \wedge Q'(w_1^5, w^{10}, z_1) \rightarrow Q'(y_0, z_1, w^5),$$
$$Q'(y_0, z_1, w^5) \wedge Q'(y_1, w^6, w^2) \rightarrow Q'(z_1, w^2, y),$$
$$Q'(z_0, x, w^1) \wedge Q'(z_1, w^2, y) \rightarrow Q'(x, y, z),$$

where w^4, w^6, w^7, w^9 are in G, and $w^1, w^2, w^3, w^5, w^8, w^{10}$ are in G'.

The formulas $Q'(w_0^3, w_0^1, w^7)$, $Q'(w_1^1, w^4, x)$, $Q'(w_0^5, y_0, w_9)$, $Q'(y_1, w^6, w^2)$ are in $\mathcal{G}$, so the only unproven leaves of the above short derivations are the left $Q'(w_1^3, w^8, z_0)$, and the right $Q'(w_1^5, w^{10}, z_1)$ active grandgrandsons of $Q'(x, y, z)$ in the new derivation tree.

Now, to finish the proof we add to $\mathcal{T}'$ a new root $Q'(d, f, d)$ having $Q'(d_0, d, \Omega)$ as the left and $Q'(d_1, f, f)$ as the right son, i.e. we add the last implication $Q'(d_0, d, \Omega) \wedge Q'(d_1, f, f) \rightarrow Q'(d, f, d)$ at the root of the $\mathcal{G}$-$\mathcal{K}$-derivation that was earlier descibed. ∎

Theorem 4.5 *The problem if a Horn clause $\mathcal{H}$ is a consequence of a 2-Horn clause $\mathcal{H}_2$ is undecidable.*

Proof. Apply Theorem 3.9, then Lemma 4.4, and finally Lemma 4.2. ∎

Corollary 4.6 *The problem if a 2-Horn clause $\mathcal{H}_2$ is consistent with a finite set of unit clauses, is undecidable.* ∎

5 References

[A] W. Ackermann, Solvable Cases of the Decision Problem, Amsterdam 1954.

[BV] C. Beeri, M. Vardi, The Implication Problem for Data Dependencies, Proc. 8th ICALP, Lecture Notes in Computes Science 115, (1981), pp. 73-85.

[CLM] A. Chandra, H. Lewis, J. Makowsky, Embedded implicational dependencies and their inference problem, Proc. 13th Annual ACM Symposium on Theory of Computing, 1981, pp. 342-354.

[CV] A. Chandra, M. Vardi, The implication problem for functional and inclusion dependencies is undecidable, SIAM Journal of Computing 14 (1985), pp. 671-677.

[D] M.Davis, Unsolvable problems, in J. Barwise, ed., Handbook of Mathematical Logic, Amsterdam 1977, pp. 567-594.

[DG] B. Dreben, W. Goldfarb, The Decision Problem: Solvable Classes of Quantificational formulas, Reading 1979.

[G1] W. Goldfarb, On Decision Problems for Quantification Theory, Ph.D. Thesis, Harvard University (1974), abstract in Notices Amer. Math. Soc. 21 (4), p.280.

[G2] W. Goldfarb, The unsolvability of the Gödel class with identity, Journal of Symbolic Logic 49 (1984), pp. 1237-1252.

[GG] G. Gottlob, Subsumption and implication, Information Processing Letters 24 (1987), pp. 109-111.

[Gu1] Y. Gurevich, The decision problem for standard classes, Journal of Symbolic Logic 41 (1976), pp. 460-464.

[Gu2] Y. Gurevich, On the Classical Decision Problem, Bulletin of European Association for Theoretical Computer Science 42 (1990), pp. 140-150.

[KTU] A.J. Kfoury, J. Tiuryn, P. Urzyczyn, The undecidability of the semi-unification problem, Proc. 22-nd ACM Symposium on Theory of Computing, Baltimore 1990, pp. 468-476.

[L1] A. Leitsch, Implication algorithms for Horn clauses, Statistik, Informatik und Ökonomie, Springer Verlag 1988, pp. 172-189.

[L2] A. Leitsch, Deciding Horn clauses by hyperresolution, Proc. Computer Science Logic 89, Lecture Notes in Computer Science 440 (1989), pp. 225-241.

[L] H.R. Lewis, Unsolvable Classes of Quantificational Formulas, Reading 1979.

[LGG] A. Leitsch, G.Gottlob, Deciding Horn clause implication problems by ordered semantic resolution, Computational Inteligence II, F. Gardin and G. Mauri, ed., 1990, pp.19-26.

[LG] H.R. Lewis, W. Goldfarb, The decision problem for formulas with a small number of atomic subformulas, Journal of Symbolic Logic 38 (1973), pp. 471-480.

[MK] R. McKenzie, On spectra, and the negative solution of the decision problem for identities having a finite nontrivial model, Journal of Symbolic Logic 49 (1975), pp. 186-196

[M1] G.F. McNulty, The decision problem for equational bases of algebras, Annals of Mathematical Logic 11 (1976), pp. 193-259.

[M2] G.F. McNulty, Undecidable properties of finite sets of equations, Journal of Symbolic Logic, 41 (1976), pp. 589-604.

[P] P. Perkins, Unsolvable problems for equational theories, Notre Dame Journal of Formal Logic 8 (1967), pp. 175-185

[PO] E. Post, Recursive unsolvability of a problem of Thue, Journal of Symbolic Logic 12 (1947), pp. 1-11.

[SS] M. Schmidt-Schauß, Implication of Clauses is Undecidable, Theoretical Computer Science 59 (1988), pp. 287-296.

[V] M. Vardi, The implication and finite implication problems for typed template dependencies, Journal of Computer and System Science 28 (1984), pp.3-28..

Efficient Inference of Partial Types

Dexter Kozen
Computer Science Department
Cornell University
Ithaca, New York 14853, USA

Jens Palsberg
Computer Science Department
Aarhus University
8000 Aarhus C, Denmark

Michael I. Schwartzbach
Computer Science Department
Aarhus University
8000 Aarhus C, Denmark

Abstract

Partial types for the λ-calculus were introduced by Thatte in 1988 [5] as a means of typing objects that are not typable with simple types, such as heterogeneous lists and persistent data. In that paper he showed that type inference for partial types was semidecidable. Decidability remained open until quite recently, when O'Keefe and Wand [4] gave an exponential time algorithm for type inference.

In this paper we give an $O(n^3)$ algorithm. Our algorithm constructs a certain finite automaton that represents a canonical solution to a given set of type constraints. Moreover, the construction works equally well for recursive types; this solves an open problem stated in [4].

1 Introduction

Partial types for the pure λ-calculus were introduced by Thatte in 1988 [5] as a way to type certain λ-terms that are untypable in the simply-typed λ-calculus. They are of substantial pragmatic value, since they allow the typing of such constructs as heterogeneous lists and persistent data that would otherwise be untypable.

Formally, partial types comprise a partially ordered set $(T, \leq)$, where T is the set of well-formed terms over the constant symbol Ω and the binary type constructor $\rightarrow$, and $\leq$ is the partial order defined inductively as follows:

(i) $t \leq \Omega$ for any t;

(ii) $s \rightarrow t \leq s' \rightarrow t'$ if and only if $s' \leq s$ and $t \leq t'$.

Intuitively, the type constructor $\rightarrow$ is the usual function space constructor, and Ω is a *universal type* that includes every other type. The partial order $\leq$ can be thought of as *type inclusion* or *coercion*; that is, $s \leq t$ if it is possible to coerce type s into type t.

Clause (ii) in the definition of $\leq$ models the fact that a function with domain s and range t can be coerced to a function with domain s' and range t' provided s' can be coerced to s and t can be coerced to t'; thus the coercion order on functions is monotone in the range and antitone in the domain. That $\leq$ is antitone in the domain is considered to be the main source of difficulty in type inference algorithms.

More λ-terms are typable with partial types than with simple types. For example, the term

$$\lambda f.(fK(fI)) ,$$

where $K = \lambda x.(\lambda y.x)$ and $I = \lambda z.z$, has partial type

$$(\Omega \rightarrow (\Omega \rightarrow \Omega)) \quad \rightarrow \quad \Omega ,$$

but no simple type. The typing rules for the λ-calculus with partial types are the standard ones for subtypes [5].

As with any type discipline, the question of *type inference* is of paramount importance:

> Given a λ-term E, is E typable? If so, give a type for it.

For this particular discipline, the type inference question can be rephrased in terms of solving a finite system of *type constraints*, which are just inequalities over terms with type variables. Rephrased, the problem becomes:

0-8186-2900-2/92 $3.00

> Given a system of inequalities of the form $s \leq t$, where s and t are terms over $\rightarrow$ and variables ranging over T, does the system have a solution in $(T, \leq)$? If so, give a solution.

In his original paper [5], Thatte showed that the type inference problem for partial types is semidecidable. The problem of decidability remained unsolved until quite recently, when O'Keefe and Wand [4] presented an exponential time algorithm. Their algorithm involves iterated substitution and gives no hint of the possibility of the existence of canonical solutions; indeed, there exist satisfiable constraint systems with no $\leq$-minimal solution.

In this paper we show that the type inference problem for partial types is solvable in time $O(n^3)$, where n is the size of the λ-term. Moreover, the solutions we construct are *canonical* in the sense that they are least in the so-called *Böhm order*, a natural order different from $\leq$.

Our algorithm constructs a certain finite automaton with $O(n^2)$ states from the given system of type constraints. The canonical solution to the system is just the regular language accepted by the automaton, where we represent types as binary trees and binary trees as prefix-closed sets of strings over a two-letter alphabet. In this representation, the Böhm order is just set inclusion $\subseteq$.

The canonical solution always exists, but it may not be finite; however, since it is contained in all other solutions, we can check for the existence of a finite solution by checking whether the canonical solution is finite. Thus the typability question reduces essentially to the finiteness problem for regular sets.

Our construction works equally well for recursive types; this solves an open problem stated in [4].

The type inference problem for partial types has been shown by Henglein to be P-hard [2]; thus it is P-complete.

It can also be shown that every λ-term with a partial type is strongly normalizing [2].

Despite the fact that our polynomial-time algorithm now makes automatic type inference for partial types feasible, we feel that the more important contribution of this work is theoretical: namely, the precise mathematical characterization of the set of solutions to a system of type constraints and the identification of a canonical solution. We hope that the automata-theoretic approach developed here will be useful in dealing with other type systems.

2 From Types to Trees

In this section we rephrase the type inference problem and generalize to infinite trees. This allows us to isolate the essential combinatorial structure of the problem independent of type-theoretic syntax.

2.1 Systems of Type Constraints

Given a λ-term, the type inference question can be rephrased in terms of a system of type constraints as follows. Assume that the λ-term has been α-converted so that all bound variables are distinct. To each subterm E we assign a type variable $[\![E]\!]$. For every subterm of the form $\lambda x.E$ we generate the inequality $[\![\lambda x.E]\!] \geq [\![x]\!] \rightarrow [\![E]\!]$. For every subterm of the form EE' we generate the inequality $[\![E]\!] \leq [\![E']\!] \rightarrow [\![EE']\!]$. The solutions of this system of constraints correspond exactly to the possible types [5, 4].

2.2 Trees

Partial types are essentially binary trees. We represent binary trees as certain sets of strings over the binary alphabet $\{L, R\}$.

Definition 1 Let $\alpha, \beta, \ldots$ denote elements of $\{L, R\}^*$. The *parity* of α is the number mod 2 of L's in α. The parity of α is denoted $\pi\alpha$. A string α is said to be *even* (respectively, *odd*) if $\pi\alpha = 0$ (respectively, 1).

A *tree* is a subset $\sigma \subseteq \{L, R\}^*$ that is

- nonempty,
- closed under prefix, and
- binary, in the sense that for all α, $\alpha R \in \sigma$ iff $\alpha L \in \sigma$.

We use $\sigma, \tau, \ldots$ to denote trees. The set of all trees is denoted T.

A tree is *finite* if it is finite as a set of strings. A *path* in a tree σ is a maximal subset of σ linearly ordered by the prefix relation. By König's Lemma, a tree is finite iff it has no infinite paths.

An element $\alpha \in \sigma$ is a *leaf* of σ if it is not a proper prefix of any other element of σ. □

For $A, B \subseteq \{L, R\}^*$ and $\alpha \in \{L, R\}^*$, define

$$A \cdot B = \{\epsilon\} \cup \{L\alpha \mid \alpha \in A\} \cup \{R\beta \mid \beta \in B\}$$
$$A \downarrow \alpha = \{\beta \mid \alpha\beta \in A\} .$$

For trees σ, τ, $\sigma \cdot \tau$ is the tree with left subtree σ and right subtree τ, and $\sigma \downarrow \alpha$ is the subtree of σ at α if $\alpha \in \sigma$, $\emptyset$ if not.

The following lemma establishes some elementary properties of the operators $\cdot$ and $\downarrow$ on trees.

Lemma 2

(i) $(\sigma \cdot \tau)\downarrow L = \sigma$ *and* $(\sigma \cdot \tau)\downarrow R = \tau$

(ii) $\sigma = \sigma\downarrow L \cdot \sigma\downarrow R$

(iii) $(\sigma\downarrow \alpha)\downarrow \beta = \sigma\downarrow \alpha\beta$

(iv) α *is a leaf of* σ *iff* $\sigma\downarrow\alpha = \{\epsilon\}$.

Proof. All properties are immediate consequences of the definitions. □

The types T are in a natural one-to-one correspondence with the finite trees in $\widehat{T}$ under the embedding $e : T \rightarrow \widehat{T}$ given by

$$\begin{aligned} e(\Omega) &= \{\epsilon\} \\ e(s \rightarrow t) &= e(s) \cdot e(t) \;. \end{aligned}$$

Under this embedding, an occurrence of Ω at the fringe of a type s corresponds to a leaf of $e(s)$.

We now wish to define a partial order on $\widehat{T}$ that agrees with the order $\leq$ on T under the embedding e.

Definition 3 For $\sigma, \tau \in \widehat{T}$, define $\sigma \leq \tau$ if both of the following conditions hold for any α:

(i) if α is an even leaf of σ, then $\alpha R \notin \tau$;

(ii) if α is an odd leaf of τ, then $\alpha R \notin \sigma$.

□

Lemma 4 *The relation $\leq$ is a partial order on trees, and agrees with the order $\leq$ on types under the embedding e. In particular, for any σ, τ, σ_i, τ_i,*

(i) $\sigma \leq \{\epsilon\}$;

(ii) $\{\epsilon\} \leq \tau$ *if and only if* $\tau = \{\epsilon\}$;

(iii) $\sigma_1 \cdot \sigma_2 \leq \tau_1 \cdot \tau_2$ *if and only if* $\tau_1 \leq \sigma_1$ *and* $\sigma_2 \leq \tau_2$.

Proof. We first show that $\leq$ is a partial order. It is trivially reflexive. To show transitivity, let $\sigma \leq \tau \leq \omega$ and assume for a contradiction that α is an even leaf of σ and $\alpha R \in \omega$. Let β be the longest prefix of αR in τ. If $\beta = \alpha R$, then Definition 3(i) is violated for σ, τ. Otherwise β is a prefix of α and a leaf of τ. If β is even, then Definition 3(i) is violated for τ, ω. If β is odd, then Definition 3(ii) is violated for σ, τ. In all three cases we contradict the assumption $\sigma \leq \tau \leq \omega$. A symmetric argument under the assumption that α is an odd leaf of ω and $\alpha R \in \sigma$ likewise leads to a contradiction.

For antisymmetry, assume $\sigma \leq \tau \leq \sigma$. Let $\alpha \in \sigma$ and let β be the longest prefix of α in τ. If $\beta \neq \alpha$, then β is a leaf of τ; but then either β is even, which contradicts $\tau \leq \sigma$, or β is odd, which contradicts $\sigma \leq \tau$. Thus $\beta = \alpha$ and $\alpha \in \tau$. Since $\alpha \in \sigma$ was arbitrary, $\sigma \subseteq \tau$. A symmetric argument shows that $\tau \subseteq \sigma$.

We next establish the properties (i)–(iii) in turn.

(i) If α is an even leaf in σ, then clearly $\alpha R \notin \{\epsilon\}$. There are no odd leaves in $\{\epsilon\}$.

(ii) The *if* follows by reflexivity; *only if* follows by (i) and antisymmetry.

(iii) Let $\sigma = \sigma_1 \cdot \sigma_2$ and $\tau = \tau_1 \cdot \tau_2$. For *if*, assume that α is an even leaf in σ. We proceed by induction on the length of α. The case $\alpha = \epsilon$ is not possible. If $\alpha = L\beta$ then β is an odd leaf in σ_1, so $\beta R \notin \tau_1$, so $L\beta R \notin \tau_1 \cdot \tau_2$, so $\alpha R \notin \tau$. If $\alpha = R\beta$ then β is an even leaf in σ_2, so $\beta R \notin \tau_2$, so $R\beta R \notin \tau_1 \cdot \tau_1$, so $\alpha R \notin \tau$. Assume now that α is an odd leaf in τ. We proceed by induction on the length of α. The case $\alpha = \epsilon$ is not possible. If $\alpha = L\beta$ then β is an even leaf in τ_1, so $\beta R \notin \sigma_1$, so $L\beta R \notin \sigma_1 \cdot \sigma_2$, so $\alpha R \notin \sigma$. If $\alpha = R\beta$ then β is an odd leaf in τ_2, so $\beta R \notin \sigma_2$, so $R\beta R \notin \sigma_1 \cdot \sigma_2$, so $\alpha R \notin \sigma$.

For *only if*, assume that α is an even leaf in τ_1; then $L\alpha$ is an odd leaf in τ, so $L\alpha R \notin \sigma$, so $\alpha R \notin \sigma_1$. If α is an odd leaf in σ_1, then $L\alpha$ is an even leaf in σ, so $L\alpha R \notin \tau$, so $\alpha R \notin \tau_1$. If α is an even leaf in σ_2, then $R\alpha$ is an even leaf in σ, so $R\alpha R \notin \tau$, so $\alpha R \notin \tau_2$. If α is an odd leaf in τ_2, then $R\alpha$ is an odd leaf in τ, so $R\alpha R \notin \sigma$, so $\alpha R \notin \sigma_2$.

Finally, we show that the order on types agrees with the order on trees under the embedding e, *i.e.*, $s \leq t$ if and only if $e(s) \leq e(t)$. We proceed by induction on the structure of s and t. If $t = \Omega$ then the result follows from (i). If $s = \Omega$ then the result is immediate from (ii). If $s = s_1 \rightarrow s_2$ and $t = t_1 \rightarrow t_2$ then the induction hypothesis tells us that $t_1 \leq s_1$ if and only if $e(t_1) \leq e(s_1)$ and $s_2 \leq t_2$ if and only if $e(s_2) \leq e(t_2)$. The result now follows from (iii) and the definitions of e and $\leq$ on types. □

Amadio and Cardelli [1] give an alternative definition of a partial order on recursive types involving infinite chains of finite approximations. Definition 3 is equivalent to theirs [3].

Lemma 5 *The following properties hold for all σ, τ.*

(i) $(R \in \sigma \;\wedge\; R \in \tau \;\wedge\; \sigma \leq \tau) \;\Rightarrow\; (\sigma\downarrow L \geq \tau\downarrow L) \wedge (\sigma\downarrow R \leq \tau\downarrow R)$;

(ii) $(\sigma \leq \tau \;\wedge\; R \in \tau) \;\Rightarrow\; R \in \sigma$.

Proof. Properties (i) and (ii) follow immediately from Lemma 4(iii) and (ii), respectively. □

3 From Constraints to Graphs

Instead of systems of type constraints involving type variables, we consider a more general notion of a *constraint graph.*

Definition 6 A *constraint graph* is a directed graph $G = (S, L, R, \leq)$ consisting of a set of nodes S and three sets of directed edges $L, R, \leq$. We write $s \xrightarrow{L} t$ to indicate that the pair (s,t) is in the edge set L, and similarly $s \xrightarrow{R} t$, $s \xrightarrow{\leq} t$. A constraint graph must satisfy the properties:

- any node has at most one outgoing L edge and at most one outgoing R edge;
- a node has an outgoing L edge if and only if it has an outgoing R edge.

A *solution* for G is any map $h : S \to \widehat{T}$ such that

(i) if $u \xrightarrow{L} v$ and $u \xrightarrow{R} w$, then $h(u) = h(v) \cdot h(w)$;

(ii) if $u \xrightarrow{\leq} v$, then $h(u) \leq h(v)$.

The solution h is *finite* if $h(s)$ is a finite set for all s. □

A system of type constraints as described in §2.1 gives rise to a constraint graph by associating a unique node with every subterm, defining L and R edges from a term to its left and right subterms, and defining $\leq$ edges for the inequalities.

Definition 7 A constraint graph is *closed* if the edge relation $\leq$ is reflexive, transitive, and closed under the following two rules which say that the dashed edges exist whenever the solid ones do:

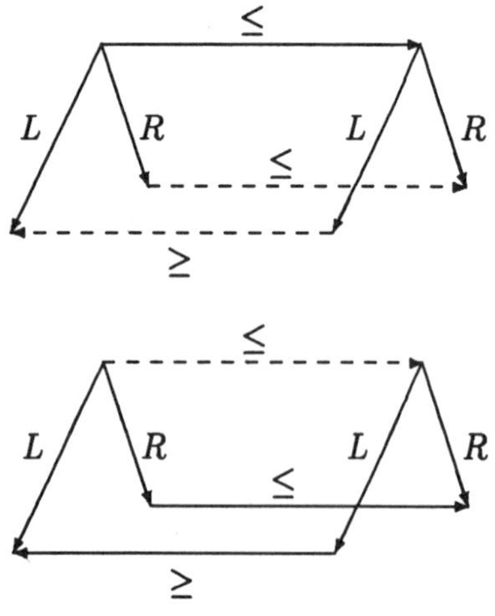

Note that these two rules resemble the two implications of Lemma 4(iii). The *closure* of a constraint graph G is the smallest closed graph containing G as a subgraph. □

Lemma 8 *A constraint graph and its closure have the same set of solutions.*

Proof. Any solution of the closure of G is also a solution of G, since G has fewer constraints. Conversely, the closure of G can be constructed from G by iterating the closure rules, and it follows inductively by Lemma 4 that any solution of G satisfies the additional constraints added by this process. □

4 From Graphs to Automata

In this section we define two automata $\mathcal{M}$ and $\mathcal{N}$ and describe their relationship. These automata will be used to characterize the canonical solution of a given constraint graph G. An intuitive account follows the formal definitions.

Definition 9 Let a closed constraint graph

$$G \;=\; (S,\ L,\ R,\ \leq)$$

be given. The automaton $\mathcal{M}$ is defined as follows. The input alphabet of $\mathcal{M}$ is $\{L, R\}$. The states of $\mathcal{M}$ are $S^2 \cup S^1 \cup S^0$. States in S^2 are written (s,t), those in S^1 are written (s), and the unique state in S^0 is written $(\,)$. The transitions are defined as follows.

$$
\begin{array}{ll}
(u,v) \xrightarrow{\epsilon} (u,v') & \text{if } v \xrightarrow{\leq} v' \text{ in } G \\
(u,v) \xrightarrow{\epsilon} (u',v) & \text{if } u' \xrightarrow{\leq} u \text{ in } G \\
(u,v) \xrightarrow{R} (u',v') & \text{if } u \xrightarrow{R} u' \text{ and } v \xrightarrow{R} v' \text{ in } G \\
(u,v) \xrightarrow{L} (v',u') & \text{if } u \xrightarrow{L} u' \text{ and } v \xrightarrow{L} v' \text{ in } G \\
(u,v) \xrightarrow{\epsilon} (v) & \text{always} \\
(v) \xrightarrow{\epsilon} (v') & \text{if } v \xrightarrow{\leq} v' \text{ in } G \\
(v) \xrightarrow{R} (v') & \text{if } v \xrightarrow{R} v' \text{ in } G \\
(v) \xrightarrow{L} (\,) & \text{if } v \xrightarrow{L} v' \text{ in } G
\end{array}
$$

If p and q are states of $\mathcal{M}$ and $\alpha \in \{L, R\}^*$, we write $p \xrightarrow{\alpha} q$ if the automaton can move from state p to state q under input α, including possible ϵ-transitions.

The automaton $\mathcal{M}_s$ is the automaton $\mathcal{M}$ with start state (s,s). All states are accept states; thus the language accepted by $\mathcal{M}_s$ is the set of strings α for which there exists a state p such that $(s,s) \xrightarrow{\alpha} p$. We denote this language by $\mathcal{L}(s)$. □

Informally, we can think of the automaton $\mathcal{M}_s$ as follows. We start with two pebbles, one green and one red, on the node s of the constraint graph G. We can move the green pebble forward along a $\leq$ edge at any time, and we can move the red pebble backward along a $\leq$ edge at any time. We can move both pebbles simultaneously along R edges leading out of the nodes they occupy. We can also move them simultaneously along outgoing L edges, but in the latter case we switch their colors. At any time, we can elect to remove the red pebble; thereafter, we can move the green pebble forward along $\leq$ or R edges as often as we like, and forward along an L edge once, at which point the pebble must be removed. The sequence of L's and R's that were seen gives a string in $\mathcal{L}(s)$, and all strings in $\mathcal{L}(s)$ are obtained in this way.

The intuition motivating the definition of $\mathcal{M}$ is that we want to identify the conditions that require a path to exist in any solution. Thus $\mathcal{L}(s)$ is the set of α that *must* be there; this intuition is made manifest in Lemma 10. It turns out that once we identify this set, we are able to show that it is a solution itself.

We now show that $\mathcal{M}$ accepts only essential strings.

Lemma 10 *If $h : S \to \widehat{T}$ is any solution and $(s,s) \xrightarrow{\alpha} p$, then $\alpha \in h(s)$. Moreover,*

(i) if $p = (u,v)$ then $h(u) \leq h(s){\downarrow}\alpha \leq h(v)$;

(ii) if $p = (v)$ then $h(s){\downarrow}\alpha \leq h(v)$.

Proof. We proceed by induction on the number of transitions. If this is zero, then $p = (s,s)$ and $\alpha = \epsilon$, and the result is immediate. Otherwise, assume that $(s,s) \xrightarrow{\alpha} p$ and the lemma holds for this sequence of transitions. We argue by cases, depending on the form of the next transition out of p.

If p if of the form (u,v), then the induction hypothesis says that $\alpha \in h(s)$ and $h(u) \leq h(s){\downarrow}\alpha \leq h(v)$.

If $(u,v) \xrightarrow{\epsilon} (u',v')$, then $u' \xrightarrow{\leq} u$ and $v \xrightarrow{\leq} v'$, so $\alpha\epsilon = \alpha \in h(s)$ and

$$h(u') \leq h(u) \leq h(s){\downarrow}\alpha \leq h(v) \leq h(v') .$$

If $(u,v) \xrightarrow{R} (u',v')$, then $u \xrightarrow{R} u'$ and $v \xrightarrow{R} v'$, so $h(u') = h(u){\downarrow}R$ and $h(v') = h(v){\downarrow}R$. Then $R \in h(v)$, so by Lemmas 2 and 5, $R \in h(s){\downarrow}\alpha$ and $\alpha R \in h(s)$, and

$$\begin{aligned} h(u') &= h(u){\downarrow}R \leq h(s){\downarrow}\alpha R \\ &\leq h(v){\downarrow}R = h(v') . \end{aligned}$$

If $(u,v) \xrightarrow{L} (v',u')$, then $u \xrightarrow{L} u'$ and $v \xrightarrow{L} v'$, so $h(u') = h(u){\downarrow}L$ and $h(v') = h(v){\downarrow}L$. Then $L \in h(v)$, so by Lemmas 2 and 5, $L \in h(s){\downarrow}\alpha$ and $\alpha L \in h(s)$, and

$$\begin{aligned} h(u') &= h(u){\downarrow}L \geq h(s){\downarrow}\alpha L \\ &\geq h(v){\downarrow}L = h(v') . \end{aligned}$$

If $(u,v) \xrightarrow{\epsilon} (v)$ then $\alpha\epsilon = \alpha \in h(s)$ and $h(s){\downarrow}\alpha \leq h(v)$.

If p if of the form (v), then the induction hypothesis says that $\alpha \in h(s)$ and $h(s){\downarrow}\alpha \leq h(v)$.

If $(v) \xrightarrow{\epsilon} (v')$, then $v \xrightarrow{\leq} v'$, so $\alpha\epsilon = \alpha \in h(s)$ and

$$h(s){\downarrow}\alpha \leq h(v) \leq h(v') .$$

If $(v) \xrightarrow{R} (v')$, then $v \xrightarrow{R} v'$, so $h(v') = h(v){\downarrow}R$. Then $R \in h(v)$, so by Lemmas 2 and 5, $R \in h(s){\downarrow}\alpha$ and $\alpha R \in h(s)$, and

$$h(s){\downarrow}\alpha R \leq h(v){\downarrow}R = h(v') .$$

Finally, if $(v) \xrightarrow{L} (\,)$, then $v \xrightarrow{L} v'$, so $h(v') = h(v){\downarrow}L$. Then $L \in h(v)$, so by Lemmas 2 and 5, $L \in h(s){\downarrow}\alpha$ and $\alpha L \in h(s)$. □

Here we give a useful alternative characterization of $\mathcal{L}(s)$ in terms of a different automaton $\mathcal{N}$.

Definition 11 Let $G = (S, L, R, \leq)$ be given as above. We define the automaton $\mathcal{N}$ over the input alphabet $\{L, R\}$ as follows. The states of $\mathcal{N}$ are $S \times \{0,1\}$; we use square brackets for states of $\mathcal{N}$ to distinguish them from states of $\mathcal{M}$. The transitions are

$$\begin{array}{ll} [s,0] \xrightarrow{\epsilon} [t,0] & \text{if } s \xrightarrow{\leq} t \text{ in } G \\ [s,1] \xrightarrow{\epsilon} [t,1] & \text{if } t \xrightarrow{\leq} s \text{ in } G \\ [s,b] \xrightarrow{R} [t,b] & \text{if } s \xrightarrow{R} t \text{ in } G \\ [s,b] \xrightarrow{L} [t,\overline{b}] & \text{if } s \xrightarrow{L} t \text{ in } G. \end{array}$$

As above, we write $[s,b] \xrightarrow{\alpha} [t,c]$ if $[s,b]$ can go to $[t,c]$ under α, including possible ϵ-transitions. □

The automaton $\mathcal{N}$ has states $[s,b]$ where b is a Boolean value. The second component is used to keep track of the parity of the scanned string. We can think of $[s,b]$ as a pebble on s; the second component gives the color of the pebble. If the pebble is green ($b = 0$), we can move it forward along $\leq$ edges. If the pebble is red ($b = 1$), we can move it backward along $\leq$ edges. We can move the pebble forward along R or L edges at any time, but if we move it along an L edge, then we switch the color.

The following lemmas relate $\mathcal{M}$ and $\mathcal{N}$.

Lemma 12

(i) $(s,s) \xrightarrow{\alpha} (u,v)$ *if and only if both*

(a) $[s,\pi\alpha] \xrightarrow{\alpha} [v,0]$

(b) $[s,\overline{\pi\alpha}] \xrightarrow{\alpha} [u,1]$.

(ii) $(s) \xrightarrow{\alpha} (t)$ *if and only if* $\alpha = R^k$ *for some* k *and* $[s,0] \xrightarrow{\alpha} [t,0]$.

(iii) $(s) \xrightarrow{\alpha} (\,)$ *if and only if* $\alpha = R^k L$ *for some* k *and* $[s,0] \xrightarrow{\alpha} [t,1]$ *for some* t.

Proof. We prove the three parts in turn. In each case we proceed by induction on α.

(i) If $\alpha = \epsilon$ then

$$\begin{aligned}(s,s) \xrightarrow{\epsilon} (u,v) &\Leftrightarrow u \xrightarrow{\leq} s \wedge s \xrightarrow{\leq} v \\ &\Leftrightarrow [s,0] \xrightarrow{\epsilon} [v,0] \wedge [s,1] \xrightarrow{\epsilon} [u,1] \\ &\Leftrightarrow [s,\pi\epsilon] \xrightarrow{\epsilon} [v,0] \wedge [s,\overline{\pi\epsilon}] \xrightarrow{\epsilon} [u,1] .\end{aligned}$$

If $\alpha = \beta L$ then

$$(s,s) \xrightarrow{\beta} (p,q) \xrightarrow{L} (q',p') \xrightarrow{\epsilon} (u,v) .$$

By the induction hypothesis, this is equivalent to

$$\begin{aligned}&[s,\pi\beta] \xrightarrow{\beta} [q,0] \wedge [s,\overline{\pi\beta}] \xrightarrow{\beta} [p,1] \wedge \\ &\quad p \xrightarrow{L} p' \wedge q \xrightarrow{L} q' \wedge u \xrightarrow{\leq} q' \wedge p' \xrightarrow{\leq} v \\ \Leftrightarrow\ &[s,\pi\beta] \xrightarrow{\beta} [q,0] \xrightarrow{L} [q',1] \xrightarrow{\epsilon} [u,1] \wedge \\ &\qquad [s,\overline{\pi\beta}] \xrightarrow{\beta} [p,1] \xrightarrow{L} [p',0] \xrightarrow{\epsilon} [v,0] \\ \Leftrightarrow\ &[s,\overline{\pi\beta}] \xrightarrow{\beta L} [v,0] \wedge [s,\pi\beta] \xrightarrow{\beta L} [u,1] \\ \Leftrightarrow\ &[s,\pi\beta L] \xrightarrow{\beta L} [v,0] \wedge [s,\overline{\pi\beta L}] \xrightarrow{\beta L} [u,1] .\end{aligned}$$

If $\alpha = \beta R$ then

$$(s,s) \xrightarrow{\beta} (p,q) \xrightarrow{R} (p',q') \xrightarrow{\epsilon} (u,v) .$$

By the induction hypothesis, this is equivalent to

$$\begin{aligned}&[s,\pi\beta] \xrightarrow{\beta} [q,0] \wedge [s,\overline{\pi\beta}] \xrightarrow{\beta} [p,1] \wedge \\ &\quad p \xrightarrow{R} p' \wedge q \xrightarrow{R} q' \wedge u \xrightarrow{\leq} p' \wedge q' \xrightarrow{\leq} v \\ \Leftrightarrow\ &[s,\pi\beta] \xrightarrow{\beta} [q,0] \xrightarrow{R} [q',0] \xrightarrow{\epsilon} [v,0] \wedge \\ &\qquad [s,\overline{\pi\beta}] \xrightarrow{\beta} [p,1] \xrightarrow{R} [p',1] \xrightarrow{\epsilon} [u,1] \\ \Leftrightarrow\ &[s,\pi\beta] \xrightarrow{\beta R} [v,0] \wedge [s,\overline{\pi\beta}] \xrightarrow{\beta R} [u,1] \\ \Leftrightarrow\ &[s,\pi\beta R] \xrightarrow{\beta R} [v,0] \wedge [s,\overline{\pi\beta R}] \xrightarrow{\beta R} [u,1] .\end{aligned}$$

(ii) If $\alpha = \epsilon$ then

$$\begin{aligned}(s) \xrightarrow{\epsilon} (t) &\Leftrightarrow s \xrightarrow{\leq} t \\ &\Leftrightarrow \epsilon = R^0 \wedge [s,0] \xrightarrow{\epsilon} [t,0] .\end{aligned}$$

If $\alpha = \beta R$ then

$$(s) \xrightarrow{\beta} (p) \xrightarrow{R} (p') \xrightarrow{\epsilon} (t) .$$

By the induction hypothesis, this is equivalent to

$$\begin{aligned}&\beta = R^k \wedge [s,0] \xrightarrow{\beta} [p,0] \wedge p \xrightarrow{R} p' \wedge p' \xrightarrow{\leq} t \\ \Leftrightarrow\ &\beta R = R^{k+1} \wedge [s,0] \xrightarrow{\beta R} [t,0] .\end{aligned}$$

The case $\alpha = \beta L$ is not possible.

(iii) The cases $\alpha = \epsilon$ and $\alpha = \beta R$ are not possible. If $\alpha = \beta L$ then

$$(s) \xrightarrow{\beta} (p) \xrightarrow{L} (\,) .$$

Using (ii), this is equivalent to

$$\begin{aligned}&\beta = R^k \wedge [s,0] \xrightarrow{\beta} [p,0] \wedge p \xrightarrow{L} t \\ \Leftrightarrow\ &\alpha = R^k L \wedge [s,0] \xrightarrow{\beta L} [t,1] .\end{aligned}$$

□

Lemma 13 *For any string* α, $\alpha \in \mathcal{L}(s)$ *if and only if there exist* β, k, u, v *such that*

(i) $\alpha = \beta R^k$ *or* $\alpha = \beta R^k L$,

(ii) $[s,\pi\beta] \xrightarrow{\alpha} [v,\pi\alpha \oplus \pi\beta]$, *and*

(iii) $[s,\overline{\pi\beta}] \xrightarrow{\beta} [u,1]$.

Here $\oplus$ *denotes addition mod 2.*

Proof. First assume $\alpha \in \mathcal{L}(s)$. Then $(s,s) \xrightarrow{\alpha} p$ for some state p. If $p = (u,v)$ then $(s,s) \xrightarrow{\alpha} (u,v)$, so by Lemma 12 we have

$$[s,\pi\alpha] \xrightarrow{\alpha} [v,0] \wedge [s,\overline{\pi\alpha}] \xrightarrow{\alpha} [u,1] .$$

But then we can choose $\alpha = \beta$ and $k = 0$. If $p = (v)$ then for some β, γ we have

$$(s,s) \xrightarrow{\beta} (u,q) \xrightarrow{\epsilon} (q) \xrightarrow{\gamma} (v)$$

so by Lemma 12 we have

$$\gamma = R^k \wedge [s,\pi\beta] \xrightarrow{\beta} [q,0] \xrightarrow{\gamma} [v,0] \wedge [s,\overline{\pi\beta}] \xrightarrow{\beta} [u,1] .$$

Since $\pi\alpha = \pi\beta$, this is equivalent to

$$\alpha = \beta R^k \wedge [s,\pi\beta] \xrightarrow{\alpha} [v,\pi\alpha \oplus \pi\beta] \wedge [s,\overline{\pi\beta}] \xrightarrow{\beta} [u,1]$$

and we are done. If $p = (\,)$ then for some β, γ we have

$$(s,s) \xrightarrow{\beta} (u,q) \xrightarrow{\epsilon} (q) \xrightarrow{\gamma} (\,)$$

so by Lemma 12 we have

$$\gamma = R^k L \wedge [s, \pi\beta] \xrightarrow{\beta} [q,0] \xrightarrow{\gamma} [v,1] \wedge [s, \overline{\pi\beta}] \xrightarrow{\beta} [u,1]\,.$$

Since $\pi\alpha \neq \pi\beta$, this is equivalent to

$$\alpha = \beta R^k L \wedge [s, \pi\beta] \xrightarrow{\alpha} [v, \pi\alpha \oplus \pi\beta] \wedge [s, \overline{\pi\beta}] \xrightarrow{\beta} [u,1]$$

and we are done.

Conversely, assume (i)–(iii). We have $\alpha = \beta\gamma$ where $\gamma = R^k$ or $R^k L$, and

$$[s, \pi\beta] \xrightarrow{\alpha} [v, \pi\gamma]$$
$$[s, \overline{\pi\beta}] \xrightarrow{\beta} [u,1]\,.$$

We must have

$$[s, \pi\beta] \xrightarrow{\beta} [p,0] \xrightarrow{\gamma} [v, \pi\gamma]$$

for some p. From Lemma 12 we have

$$(s,s) \xrightarrow{\beta} (u,p) \xrightarrow{\epsilon} (p)$$

and either $(p) \xrightarrow{\gamma} (v)$ or $(p) \xrightarrow{\gamma} (\,)$, depending on whether $\gamma = R^k$ or $R^k L$. In either case $\alpha \in \mathcal{L}(s)$. □

5 Main Result

In this section we prove the main result: that $\mathcal{L}(s)$ gives the canonical solution of G.

Theorem 14 *The sets $\mathcal{L}(s)$ are trees, and the function $\mathcal{L} : S \to \widehat{T}$ is a solution of G. Moreover, if $h : S \to \widehat{T}$ is any other solution, then $\mathcal{L}(s) \subseteq h(s)$ for any s.*

Proof. We first show that $\mathcal{L}(s) \in \widehat{T}$. It is clearly nonempty, since $(s,s) \xrightarrow{\epsilon} (s,s)$; it is prefix closed by definition; and it is binary because G always has L and R edges in pairs.

In order to show that $\mathcal{L}$ is a solution of G, we need to show

(i) if $u \xrightarrow{L} v$ and $u \xrightarrow{R} w$, then $\mathcal{L}(u) = \mathcal{L}(v) \cdot \mathcal{L}(w)$;

(ii) if $u \xrightarrow{\leq} v$, then $\mathcal{L}(u) \leq \mathcal{L}(v)$.

First, we show (i) as two inclusions. Assume that $\alpha \in \mathcal{L}(v) \cdot \mathcal{L}(w)$. We proceed by induction on α. If $\alpha = \epsilon$ then we are done, since $\epsilon \in \mathcal{L}(u)$. If $\alpha = L\beta$ then $\beta \in \mathcal{L}(v)$, so $(v,v) \xrightarrow{\beta} p$ for some p. From

$$(u,u) \xrightarrow{L} (v,v) \xrightarrow{\beta} p$$

we conclude that $L\beta \in \mathcal{L}(u)$. If $\alpha = R\beta$ then $\beta \in \mathcal{L}(w)$, so $(w,w) \xrightarrow{\beta} p$ for some p. From

$$(u,u) \xrightarrow{R} (w,w) \xrightarrow{\beta} p$$

we conclude that $R\beta \in \mathcal{L}(u)$.

Assume that $\alpha \in \mathcal{L}(u)$. We proceed by induction on α. If $\alpha = \epsilon$ then we are done, since $\epsilon \in \mathcal{L}(v) \cdot \mathcal{L}(w)$. If $\alpha = L\beta$ then from Lemma 13 there exist γ, k, p, and q such that $\beta = \gamma R^k$ or $\beta = \gamma R^k L$ and

$$[u, \pi L\gamma] \xrightarrow{\alpha} [p, \pi\alpha \oplus \pi L\gamma] \wedge [u, \overline{\pi L\gamma}] \xrightarrow{L\gamma} [q,1]$$

Since $[u, \pi L\gamma] \xrightarrow{L} [v, \pi\gamma]$, $[u, \overline{\pi L\gamma}] \xrightarrow{L} [v, \overline{\pi\gamma}]$, and $\pi\alpha \oplus \pi L\gamma = \pi\beta \oplus \pi\gamma$ it follows that

$$[v, \pi\gamma] \xrightarrow{\beta} [p, \pi\beta \oplus \pi\gamma] \wedge [v, \overline{\pi\gamma}] \xrightarrow{\gamma} [q,1]$$

so $\beta \in \mathcal{L}(v)$ and $\alpha \in \mathcal{L}(v) \cdot \mathcal{L}(w)$. If $\alpha = R\beta$ then from Lemma 13 there exist γ, k, p, and q such that $\beta = \gamma R^k$ or $\beta = \gamma R^k L$ and

$$[u, \pi R\gamma] \xrightarrow{\alpha} [p, \pi\alpha \oplus \pi R\gamma] \wedge [u, \overline{\pi R\gamma}] \xrightarrow{R\gamma} [q,1]$$

Since $[u, \pi R\gamma] \xrightarrow{R} [w, \pi\gamma]$, $[u, \overline{\pi R\gamma}] \xrightarrow{R} [w, \overline{\pi\gamma}]$, and $\pi\alpha \oplus \pi R\gamma = \pi\beta \oplus \pi\gamma$ it follows that

$$[w, \pi\gamma] \xrightarrow{\beta} [p, \pi\beta \oplus \pi\gamma] \wedge [w, \overline{\pi\gamma}] \xrightarrow{\gamma} [q,1]$$

so $\beta \in \mathcal{L}(w)$ and $\alpha \in \mathcal{L}(v) \cdot \mathcal{L}(w)$.

Second, we show (ii). We need to show that for any u, v, α,

- if $u \xrightarrow{\leq} v$, α even, $\alpha \in \mathcal{L}(u)$, and $\alpha R \in \mathcal{L}(v)$, then $\alpha R \in \mathcal{L}(u)$;
- if $u \xrightarrow{\leq} v$, α odd, $\alpha \in \mathcal{L}(v)$, and $\alpha R \in \mathcal{L}(u)$, then $\alpha R \in \mathcal{L}(v)$.

Using the characterization in terms of $\mathcal{N}$, these two cases can be rolled into one: it suffices to show for any s, t, α,

- if $[s, \pi\alpha] \xrightarrow{\epsilon} [t, \pi\alpha]$, $\alpha \in \mathcal{L}(s)$, and $\alpha R \in \mathcal{L}(t)$, then $\alpha R \in \mathcal{L}(s)$.

By Lemma 13, we have

$$[s, \pi\beta] \xrightarrow{\alpha} [u, \pi\alpha \oplus \pi\beta] \quad (1)$$

$$[s, \overline{\pi\beta}] \xrightarrow{\beta} [v, 1] \quad (2)$$

$$[t, \pi\beta'] \xrightarrow{\alpha R} [u', \pi\alpha R \oplus \pi\beta'] \quad (3)$$

$$[t, \overline{\pi\beta'}] \xrightarrow{\beta'} [v', 1] .$$

Since αR ends with R, we must have $\alpha R = \beta' R^k$ for some k and $\pi\alpha R = \pi\beta'$; thus from (3) and $[s, \pi\alpha] \xrightarrow{\epsilon} [t, \pi\alpha]$ we get

$$[s, \pi\alpha] \xrightarrow{\alpha R} [u', 0] . \quad (4)$$

If $\pi\alpha = \pi\beta$, we use (4) and (2) to get

$$[s, \pi\beta] \xrightarrow{\alpha R} [u', \pi\alpha \oplus \pi\beta]$$
$$[s, \overline{\pi\beta}] \xrightarrow{\beta} [v, 1] .$$

If $\pi\alpha \neq \pi\beta$, we use (4) and (1) to get

$$[s, \pi\alpha] \xrightarrow{\alpha R} [u', \pi\alpha R \oplus \pi\alpha]$$
$$[s, \overline{\pi\alpha}] \xrightarrow{\alpha} [u, 1] .$$

In either case we have $\alpha R \in \mathcal{L}(s)$ by Lemma 13.

To show that $\mathcal{L}$ is minimal, we need to show that for any other solution $h : S \to \widehat{T}$, $\mathcal{L}(s) \subseteq h(s)$ for all s. This follows directly from Lemma 10. □

Recursive types are just regular trees [1]. The canonical solution we have constructed, although possibly infinite, is a regular tree. Thus we have solved the type inference problem for recursive types left open in [4]. Specifically, given a λ-term, we construct the corresponding constraint graph and automaton $\mathcal{M}$. Every subterm corresponds to a node s in the constraint graph, and its Böhm-minimal type annotation is represented by the language $\mathcal{L}(s)$.

Note that the Böhm-minimal type of any typable λ-term trivially is Ω. What we compute is the unique minimal Church-style explicit type annotation. For simple types we have that types and type annotations are isomorphic. This is not so for partial types. For example, the Böhm-minimal type of $\lambda f.(fK(fI))$ is just Ω, but its Böhm-minimal type annotation, which our algorithm computes, is

$$\lambda f : (\Omega \to (\Omega \to \Omega)).(f(\lambda x : \Omega.\lambda y : \Omega.x)(f(\lambda z : \Omega.z)))$$

In the following section we give an efficient decision procedure for the existence of a *finite* type.

6 An algorithm

We have argued that the type inference problem studied in [5, 4] is equivalent to the following: given a finite constraint graph G, does G have a finite solution? Using the characterization of the previous section, we can answer this question easily.

Theorem 15 *We can decide in time $O(n^3)$ whether a constraint graph of size n has a finite solution.*

Proof. By Theorem 14, there exists a finite solution if and only if the canonical solution is finite. To determine this, we need only check whether any $\mathcal{L}(s)$ contains an infinite path. We first form the constraint graph, then close it; this gives a graph with n vertices and $O(n^2)$ edges. This can be done in time $O(n^3)$. We then form the automaton $\mathcal{M}$, which has n^2+n+1 states but only $O(n^3)$ transitions, at most $O(n)$ from each state. We then check for a cycle with at least one non-ϵ transition reachable from some (s, s). This can be done in linear time in the size of the graph using depth-first search. The entire algorithm requires time $O(n^3)$. □

A λ-term of size n yields a constraint graph with $O(n)$ nodes and $O(n)$ edges. This gives

Corollary 16 *The type inference problem for partial types is solvable in time $O(n^3)$.*

7 A Characterization of All Solutions

We have shown that any solution $h : S \to \widehat{T}$ of a constraint graph $G = (S, L, R, \leq)$ contains the canonical solution $\mathcal{L}$ in the sense that $\mathcal{L}(s) \subseteq h(s)$ for all $s \in S$. However, there certainly exist functions $h : S \to \widehat{T}$ containing $\mathcal{L}$ in this sense that are not solutions. In this section we give a precise characterization of the set of all solutions of G.

In the following, we write $\mathcal{L}_G$ for $\mathcal{L}$ to denote the dependence on G.

Theorem 17 *Let $G = (S, L, R, \leq)$ be a constraint graph. A function $h : S \to \widehat{T}$ is a solution of G if and only if there exists a (possibly infinite) constraint graph $G' = (S', L', R', \leq')$ containing G as a subgraph such that $h = \mathcal{L}_{G'}$ on S.*

Proof. First we show that if G is a subgraph of G', then $\mathcal{L}_{G'}$ gives a solution of G. Suppose $u, v, w \in S$, $u \xrightarrow{L} v$, and $u \xrightarrow{R} w$. Since G is a subgraph of G',

$u \xrightarrow{L'} v$ and $u \xrightarrow{R'} w$. By Theorem 14, $\mathcal{L}_{G'}$ is a solution of G', therefore $\mathcal{L}_{G'}(u) = \mathcal{L}_{G'}(v) \cdot \mathcal{L}_{G'}(w)$. Similarly, if $u, v \in S$ and $u \xrightarrow{\leq} v$, then $u \xrightarrow{\leq'} v$, therefore $\mathcal{L}_{G'}(u) \leq \mathcal{L}_{G'}(v)$. The two conditions of Definition 6 are met.

Conversely, let $h : S \to \widehat{T}$ be any solution of G. We construct a constraint graph G' from h containing G as a subgraph and show that h and $\mathcal{L}_{G'}$ agree on S. Define

$$\begin{aligned} S' &= S \cup \{(s,\alpha) \mid s \in S,\ \alpha \in h(s)\} \\ L' &= L \cup \{((s,\alpha),(s,\alpha L)) \mid s \in S,\ \alpha L \in h(s)\} \\ R' &= R \cup \{((s,\alpha),(s,\alpha R)) \mid s \in S,\ \alpha R \in h(s)\} \\ \leq' &= \leq \cup \{((s,\epsilon),s) \mid s \in S\} \cup \{(s,(s,\epsilon)) \mid s \in S\}\ . \end{aligned}$$

The graph $G' = (S', L', R', \leq')$ is a constraint graph, since each node has an L' successor iff it has an R' successor, and L' and R' successors are unique.

We show now that h agrees with $\mathcal{L}_{G'}$ on S. If $\alpha \in h(s)$, then $(s,\alpha) \in S'$, and there is a path from (s,ϵ) to (s,α) in G' with label α. In the automaton $\mathcal{M}'$ constructed from G', $(s,s) \xrightarrow{\alpha} ((s,\alpha),(s,\alpha))$, thus $\alpha \in \mathcal{L}_{G'}(s)$.

To show the reverse inclusion, we extend h in a natural way to a solution h' of G', and then appeal to Theorem 14 to conclude that h' contains $\mathcal{L}_{G'}$. Define

$$\begin{aligned} h'(s) &= h(s) \\ h'(s,\alpha) &= h(s) \downarrow \alpha\ . \end{aligned}$$

It remains to show that h' is a solution of G'. If $s, t, u \in S$, $s \xrightarrow{L} t$, and $s \xrightarrow{R} u$, then

$$h'(s) \;=\; h(s) \;=\; h(t) \cdot h(u) \;=\; h'(t) \cdot h'(u)\ .$$

If $\alpha L, \alpha R \in h(s)$, then by Lemma 2,

$$\begin{aligned} h'(s,\alpha) &= h(s) \downarrow \alpha \\ &= (h(s) \downarrow \alpha) \downarrow L \cdot (h(s) \downarrow \alpha) \downarrow R \\ &= h(s) \downarrow \alpha L \cdot h(s) \downarrow \alpha R \\ &= h'(s,\alpha L) \cdot h'(s,\alpha R)\ . \end{aligned}$$

Finally, if $s, t \in S$ and $s \xrightarrow{\leq} t$, then

$$h'(s) \;=\; h(s) \;\leq\; h(t) \;=\; h'(t)\ ,$$

and to satisfy the inequalities $s \leq' (s,\epsilon) \leq' s$ we have

$$h(s) \;=\; h(s) \downarrow \epsilon \;=\; h'(s,\epsilon)\ .$$

□

Acknowledgments

The first author gratefully acknowledges support from the Danish Research Academy, the National Science Foundation, the John Simon Guggenheim Foundation, and the U.S. Army Research Office through the ACSyAM branch of the Mathematical Sciences Institute of Cornell University, contract DAAL03-91-C-0027. These results were obtained while on sabbatical at Aarhus University, Denmark.

References

[1] Roberto M. Amadio and Luca Cardelli. Subtyping recursive types. In *Eighteenth Symposium on Principles of Programming Languages*. ACM Press, January 1991.

[2] Fritz Henglein. Personal communication, 1992.

[3] Dexter Kozen, Jens Palsberg, and Michael I. Schwartzbach. Efficient recursive subtyping. Technical Report DAIMI PB-405, Computer Science Department, Aarhus University, July 1992.

[4] Patrick M. O'Keefe and Mitchell Wand. Type inference for partial types is decidable. In *Proc. ESOP'92, European Symposium on Programming*. Springer-Verlag (*LNCS* 582), 1992.

[5] Satish Thatte. Type inference with partial types. In *Proc. International Colloquium on Automata, Languages, and Programming 1988*. Springer-Verlag (*LNCS* 317), 1988.

On the Completeness of Object-Creating Query Languages
(extended abstract)

Jan Van den Bussche* Dirk Van Gucht† Marc Andries‡ Marc Gyssens§

Abstract

Recently, various database query languages have been considered that have the ability to create new domain elements. These languages, however, are ***not*** complete in the sense of Abiteboul and Kanellakis [AK89]. Here, we provide a precise characterization for the class of queries that can be expressed in these languages. We call this class the *constructive queries* and motivate this term by establishing a close correspondence between object creation and the construction of hereditarily finite sets.

1 Introduction

Codd initiated database theory in a series of seminal papers [Cod70, Cod72a, Cod72b]. Some of his major contributions were the suggestions *(i)* to view a database as a relational structure; *(ii)* to view the result of a query to a database as a database itself; and *(iii)* to use first-order logic as a query language, which he called the relational calculus.

Codd also introduced a practical algebraization of first-order logic, which he called the relational algebra. The equivalence between calculus and algebra led him to qualify a query language as *complete* if its expressive power is at least that of relational calculus.

In an attempt to formulate a language-independent justification for Codd's completeness notion, Bancilhon [Ban78] and, independently, Paredaens [Par78] considered pairs of databases (I, J), and showed the following: J is the result of a relational calculus query applied to I if and only if *(i)* the domain of J is included in the domain of I; and *(ii)* every automorphism of I is also an automorphism of J.

Although the characterization of Bancilhon and Paredaens yielded the criterion a query must satisfy on the level of individual pairs of input and output databases, it did not say anything about the query as a whole. For example, while for each binary relation there is a calculus expression computing its transitive closure, there is no *single* calculus expression computing the transitive closure for *all* binary relations [AU79, GV85].

To remedy this deficiency, Chandra and Harel [CH80] lifted the conditions of Bancilhon and Paredaens from individual pairs of input and output databases to the more global level of queries as partial functions from databases to databases. The consistency criterion that resulted from this approach is that a query must commute with every permutation of the universe of possible domain values. This criterion is nowadays known as *genericity* (e.g., [AV91b]). In words, genericity requires the preservation of general database isomorphisms as opposed to merely automorphisms.

Chandra and Harel qualified a query language as *complete* if that language expresses exactly all computable (generic) queries. A first step towards a complete language is adding an iterative construct to the relational calculus or algebra. As this alone is not sufficient to get beyond PSPACE, one additional mechanism is needed to achieve completeness. Chandra and Harel themselves used unranked relation variables for that purpose.

Later, Abiteboul and Vianu [AV90, AV91a] obtained a complete language through the mechanism of *object creation*, allowing the introduction of new domain elements in a database. These new objects could only appear in intermediate computations and not in the final result, since only domain-preserving queries were under consideration.

However, recent applications of databases in object-oriented systems have made clear that the explicit appearance of new objects in query results, in conjunc-

*University of Antwerp (UIA), Dept. of Math. and Comp. Sci., B-2610 Antwerp, Belgium, e-mail: vdbuss@ccu.uia.ac.be. Research Assistant of the NFWO.

†Indiana University, Comp. Science Dept., Bloomington, IN 47405-4101, e-mail: vgucht@cs.indiana.edu.

‡Leiden University, Dept. of Comp. Science, P.O. Box 9512, NL-2300 RA Leiden, the Netherlands, e-mail: andries@rulwi.leidenuniv.nl.

§University of Limburg (LUC), Dept. WNI, B-3590 Diepenbeek, Belgium, e-mail: gyssens@ccu.uia.ac.be.

0-8186-2900-2/92 $3.00 © 1992 IEEE

tion with a more effective representation and manipulation of *set values* [HS89a], is needed to support such important concepts as object identity (e.g., [Kim89]) and updatable views (e.g., [AB91]).

To deal with these new requirements, a number of new data models and query languages were proposed. Particularly influential was the work of Abiteboul and Kanellakis [AK89]. They proposed the query language IQL, which provides the necessary mechanisms for creating new objects and manipulating set values.

In order to assess the expressiveness of IQL, Abiteboul and Kanellakis first had to extend the notions of genericity and completeness to query languages allowing new domain elements in the result. This task proved to be intricate, because the creation of new objects introduced a degree of non-determinism into the formalism. They proposed the notion of *determinate query*: a generic, non-deterministic query for which the various possible results of the query applied to a given input database are nevertheless equal *up to renaming*.

Since IQL is a natural extension of the earlier languages of Abiteboul and Vianu [AV90, AV91a], which are complete in the sense of Chandra and Harel, it was therefore expected at first that IQL would be complete for the determinate queries. Surprisingly, this is *not* the case [Abi90, AP92]. More specifically, IQL lacks the ability to eliminate certain copies from the result of a query [AK89]. The only way known to make IQL complete is adding an extra construct for copy elimination.

Still, most, if not all, queries that arise in practice can be expressed in IQL, so without copy elimination. It is therefore natural to ask for a characterization of the class of queries expressible without copy elimination. The purpose of the present paper is to provide such a characterization.

A precursor to the present study is the work by Andries and Paredaens [AP92] in the context of the GOOD query language [GPVG90a, GPVG90b], which is essentially equivalent to IQL. They showed that a database J is the result of a GOOD program applied to a database I if and only if there exists an extension homomorphism from the group of automorphisms of I to the group of automorphisms of J. Andries and Paredaens argued that this condition could be seen as the generalization of the notion of Bancilhon-Paredaens completeness from the original, domain-preserving case to the object-creating case.

We will show that simply adding to the completeness criteria of Abiteboul and Kanellakis the condition of Andries and Paredaens—although a "local" condition defined on individual pairs of input and output databases—results in the required characterization of queries expressible in IQL or, for that matter, in the GOOD query language.

It must be emphasized though that the problem stated here and the solution we propose are by no means specific to IQL or GOOD. Indeed, many other object-creating query languages have been investigated ([HY90, KV84, KW89], to name just a few), and as far as expressive power is concerned, they are all equivalent to, or even weaker than, IQL. This stems from the computational equivalence of IQL to any minimal language that can express first-order logic and is closed under unbounded looping and associating new domain elements to sets of values. It is in this setting that we will prove our results.

We will also prove that in our characterization of the expressive power of IQL-like languages, we can replace the requirement of Andries and Paredaens by another condition, relating object creation to the construction of hereditarily finite sets over the original domain elements. Hereditarily finite sets in the context of databases have been studied at length by Dahlhaus and Makowsky [DM87]. Using the alternative condition, we will point out that our characterization can also be thought of as a completeness criterion for *constructive* queries.

We will argue that Abiteboul and Kanellakis's notion of determinate query is actually an intermediate between these constructive queries on the one hand and *semi-deterministic* queries [VdBVG92] on the other hand.

Finally, our results also provide a unification between the two leading approaches to object-creation: the link we will establish between constructively creating objects and building up hereditarily finite sets indeed yields a link between "pure" object-creating approaches and "logic programming" approaches treating new objects as terms over input objects.

This abstract is organized as follows. In Section 2, we review the definition of determinate object-creating query as proposed by Abiteboul and Kanellakis, and introduce the language FO + **powerset** + **while**. In Section 3, we formally state our main result. We sketch its proof and discuss its ramifications for the notion of query. We conclude with a discussion on the conceptual implications of our results in Section 4.

2 Preliminaries

We assume the existence of an infinitely enumerable set of *relation names*. Each relation name R has an associated *arity* $\alpha(R)$. A *database scheme* is a finite set of relation names. We further assume there is an infinitely enumerable universe $\mathcal{O}$ of *objects.* A *database instance* I over a database scheme $\mathcal{S}$ assigns to each R in $\mathcal{S}$ a finite relation $R^I \subset \mathcal{O}^{\alpha(R)}$. If $\mathcal{S}$ is a scheme, then $inst(\mathcal{S})$ denotes the set of all instances over $\mathcal{S}$. If I is an instance, then $dom(I)$ denotes the active domain of I, i.e., the set of all objects appearing in R^I for some R in S. For two instances I_1 and I_2 over a common scheme $\mathcal{S}$, a bijection $f : dom(I_1) \rightarrow dom(I_2)$ is called an *isomorphism* between I_1 and I_2 if $f(I_1) = I_2$, where f is extended to instances in the natural way. If such a mapping exists, I_1 and I_2 are called *isomorphic.* An isomorphism between $I_1 = I_2 = I$ is called an *automorphism* of I. The automorphism group of I will be denoted $Aut(I)$.

We now turn to *queries.* The following definition is adapted from [AK89]:

Definition 2.1 Let $\mathcal{S}_{\text{in}} \subseteq \mathcal{S}_{\text{out}}$ be two database schemes. A *determinate query* Q from $\mathcal{S}_{\text{in}}$ to $\mathcal{S}_{\text{out}}$ is a binary relationship $Q \subset inst(\mathcal{S}_{\text{in}}) \times inst(\mathcal{S}_{\text{out}})$, such that

1. if $Q(I, J)$, then $R^I = R^J$ for all $R \in \mathcal{S}_{\text{in}}$;
2. If $Q(I, J)$, and f is a permutation of the universe $\mathcal{O}$, then also $Q(f(I), f(J))$. *(genericity)*; and
3. If $Q(I, J_1)$ and $Q(I, J_2)$, then J_1 and J_2 are isomorphic via an isomorphism that is the identity on $dom(I)$ *(determinacy).*

Item 1 of Definition 2.1 states that we view queries as *augmenting* a database with derived information. In other words, a query does not cause side-effects on the input database. Item 2 states that queries preserve database isomorphisms. By this genericity condition, object-creating queries, for which all domain elements in an output instance need not occur in the corresponding input instance, are necessarily non-deterministic. Therefore, we view queries as binary relationships rather than functions. Nonetheless, determinate queries are "nearly" deterministic: item 3 states that two different results of a determinate query applied to the same input instance I only differ in the specific choice of the new objects, not in $dom(I)$. In particular, determinate queries that do not create new objects *are* functions.

As announced in the Introduction, we will prove our main result in the context of a general query language that expresses first-order logic and is closed under unbounded looping and associating new domain elements to sets of values. The purpose of the remainder of this section is to define such a query language.

Let $\mathcal{S}$ be a scheme and let Φ be an expression of the form $\{(x_1, \ldots, x_k) \mid \varphi\}$ with φ a first-order logic formula using only relation names in $\mathcal{S}$, and having $x_1, \ldots, x_k$ as its free variables. Given an instance I over $\mathcal{S}$, Φ defines a k-ary relation $\Phi(I)$ on $dom(I)$ in the standard way. We will call Φ a k-ary *FO-expression* over $\mathcal{S}$.

Syntactically, an *FO-statement* over a scheme $\mathcal{S}$ is of the form $R \xleftarrow{+} \Phi$, in which R is a k-ary relation name, and Φ a k-ary FO-expression over $\mathcal{S}$. Given a scheme $\mathcal{S}$ for which Φ is an FO-expression over $\mathcal{S}$, the FO-statement $R \xleftarrow{+} \Phi$ defines a binary relationship $Q \subset inst(\mathcal{S}) \times inst(\mathcal{S} \cup \{R\})$ given by $Q(I, J)$ if and only if

$$\begin{aligned} S^J &= S^I, && \text{if } S \neq R; \\ R^J &= \begin{cases} R^I \cup \Phi(I), \\ \Phi(I), \end{cases} && \begin{aligned} &\text{if } R \in \mathcal{S}; \\ &\text{otherwise.} \end{aligned} \end{aligned}$$

Observe that this binary relationship satisfies items 2 and 3 of Definition 2.1, but not necessarily item 1 if R is in $\mathcal{S}$.

In order to associate new domain elements to sets of values, we introduce the *powerset* operator.

Let $\mathcal{S}$ be a scheme, and Φ a k-ary FO-expression over $\mathcal{S}$. Let I be an instance over $\mathcal{S}$, n the cardinality of the k-ary relation $\Phi(I)$, and $s_1, \ldots, s_{2^n-1}$ the non-empty subsets of $\Phi(I)$. Then **powerset** $\Phi(I)$ is defined as the set of relations $\{(s_1 \times \{o_1\}) \cup \cdots \cup (s_{2^n-1} \times \{o_{2^n-1}\}) \mid$ for all i, $1 \leq i \leq 2^n - 1$, $o_i \in \mathcal{O} - (dom(I) \cup \{o_1, \ldots, o_{i-1}\})\}$. So, for each subset of the relation defined by Φ, a unique, new object is created in a non-deterministic but nevertheless determinate way, since two possible results of a powerset operation differ only in the particular choice of the new objects.

The latter observation allows us to define *powerset-statements* in much the same way as FO-statements. A powerset-statement has the form $R \xleftarrow{+}$ **powerset** Φ, with R and Φ the same as for FO-statements. The semantics of powerset-statements is the same as for FO-statements, provided each occurrence of $\Phi(I)$ is substituted by an arbitrary relation in **powerset** $\Phi(I)$. Because of the determinacy, it is not a problem that in general **powerset** $\Phi(I)$ contains infinitely many relations; it suffices to compute one representation, as is illustrated in the following example.

Example 2.2 Let I be the instance over the scheme $\{R\}$ shown in Figure 1, left. The instance over the scheme $\{R, S\}$ shown by the whole of Figure 1 is a possible (and representative) result of $S \xleftarrow{+}$ **powerset** $\{(x, x) \mid R(x, x)\}$ applied to I.

R:	a	b
	b	b
	c	c

S:	b	b	1
	c	c	2
	b	b	3
	c	c	3

Figure 1: The result of the powerset-statement $S \stackrel{+}{\longleftarrow}$ **powerset** $\{(x,x) \mid R(x,x)\}$.

Next, we bring in iteration. A *while-statement* is any expression of the form **while** φ **do** P **od** with P a finite sequence of FO-, powerset-, and while-statements, and φ a first-order sentence. The semantics of a while-statement is obvious.

Example 2.3 If R is a binary relation name in a scheme not containing T, then

$T \stackrel{+}{\longleftarrow} R$;
while $T \circ T \not\subseteq T$ **do**
  $T \stackrel{+}{\longleftarrow} \{(x,y) \mid (\exists z) T(x,z) \wedge T(z,y)\}$
od

is a program computing the transitive closure of the R-relation in the T-relation.

Finally, a *program* over a scheme $\mathcal{S}$ is any sequence of FO-, powerset-, and while-statements in which the relation names in the left-hand sides of FO- and powerset-statements are *not* contained in $\mathcal{S}$. Hence, programs can be interpreted as binary relationships satisfying *all* items of Definition 2.1, i.e., as determinate *queries*. The language of all programs thus obtained will be denoted FO + **powerset** + **while**. It is essentially equivalent to the language IQL defined in [AK89].[1]

To conclude this section, we want to emphasize that we use powerset because it is a simple, uniform object creation mechanism. This argument of course is only of theoretical interest. In practice, other, tractable, mechanisms for object creation are used (e.g., [AV91a, GPVG90a, HY90, KW89]), of which two basic types can be distinguished. The first type creates an object for each tuple in a relation; the second type creates an object for each equivalence class of tuples grouped together according to some property. It can be shown (e.g., [VdBP91]) that replacing powerset by one operation of each type yields an equivalent language.

[1] In particular, it should be noted that, just like IQL, FO + powerset + while can create objects "from scratch" (i.e., starting from the empty input scheme) using the one-line simple program $R \stackrel{+}{\longleftarrow}$ **powerset** $\{() \mid \mathit{true}\}$, with R a unary relation name.

3 Constructive queries

As pointed out in the Introduction, the language IQL or, equivalently, the language FO + **powerset** + **while** is incomplete for the notion of determinate query. In this section, we show our main result, which is a characterization of the subclass of determinate queries that can be expressed in FO + **powerset** + **while**. We will call this subclass the class of *constructive queries*, and motivate this terminology by pointing out a close connection between the newly-created objects and hereditarily finite sets built up from original domain elements.

In order to state our characterization, we need the notion of *extension homomorphism*. Therefore, we first define:

Definition 3.1 Let Q be a determinate query and assume $Q(I,J)$. An *extension mapping* from I to J is a mapping $\psi : Aut(I) \rightarrow Aut(J)$ such that for each f, $\psi(f)$ equals f on $dom(I)$.[2]

It is not hard to see that every automorphism of I can be extended to an automorphism of J. Thereto, let $f \in Aut(I)$. Then, by genericity, we have $Q(f(I), f(J))$, and thus $Q(I, f(J))$. But then, by determinacy, there exists an isomorphism $g : f(J) \rightarrow J$ that is the identity on $dom(I)$. Hence, $\psi(f) := g \circ f$ defines the desired extension mapping.

Definition 3.2 An *extension homomorphism* is an extension mapping that is also a group homomorphism.

We observe the following property of FO + **powerset** + **while**:

Proposition 3.3 Let P be a program in FO + **powerset** + **while**, and assume $P(I,J)$. Then there is an extension homomorphism ψ from I to J.

Proof (sketch): The mapping ψ is defined inductively. Let $f \in Aut(I)$, and let $o \in \mathcal{O}$ be created by a powerset-statement in P. Then o represents a set of tuples s. By genericity, the same powerset-statement will have created an object o' representing $f(s)$. We put $\psi(f)(o) := o'$. The extension mapping ψ thus defined is a homomorphism. ∎

In the context of GOOD, Andries and Paredaens [AP92] were able to show the converse of the above proposition:

Proposition 3.4 [AP92] Let $\mathcal{S}_{\text{in}} \subseteq \mathcal{S}_{\text{out}}$ be two schemes, I an instance over $\mathcal{S}_{\text{in}}$, and J an instance

[2] Observe that $dom(I) \subseteq dom(J)$, by item 1 of Definition 2.1.

over $\mathcal{S}_{\text{out}}$, such that for each $R \in \mathcal{S}_{\text{in}}$: $R^I = R^J$ (cfr. Definition 2.1). Then there exists a program P in FO + **powerset** + **while** such that $P(I, J)$, if and only if there is an extension homomorphism from I to J.

Abiteboul [Abi90] found an example of a pair of instances I and J—shown graphically in Figure 2, left and middle, that satisfy the preamble of Proposition 3.4, but for which no extension homomorphism exists. Hence no program in FO + **powerset** + **while** can output J on input I. It should be noted though that there *does* exist a plain extension *mapping* from I to J. As a consequence, the binary relationship $Q \subset inst(\mathcal{S}_{\text{in}}) \times inst(\mathcal{S}_{\text{out}})$ defined by $Q(I', J')$ if and only if there exists a permutation f on $\mathcal{O}$ such that $I' = f(I)$ and $J' = f(J)$ is a determinate query. Thus FO + **powerset** + **while** is *not* computationally complete for the determinate queries.

Although not complete in the strict sense, FO + **powerset** + **while** is complete *up to copies* [AK89]. For example, the instance $\overline{J}$ shown in Figure 2, right, is an *instance with copies* of J. We leave it to the reader to find a program P such that $P(I, \overline{J})$. So, to achieve completeness, an additional *copy elimination* operation would be needed.

Therefore, it is natural to ask for a language-independent characterization of the subclass of queries expressible in FO + **powerset** + **while**, without having to use copy elimination. We were able to show that simply requiring the condition of Andries and Paredaens to hold for *all* individual input-output pairs of a query yields such a characterization.

Theorem 3.5 A computable query Q is expressible in FO + **powerset** + **while** if and only if for each pair of instances (I, J) such that $Q(I, J)$ there is an extension homomorphism from I to J.

In the remainder of this section we will sketch the proof of this main result, while at the same time discussing its ramifications for the notion of query.

We will first give a name to the property in Theorem 3.5:

Definition 3.6 A determinate query Q is called *constructive* if for each pair (I, J) of instances such that $Q(I, J)$ there is an extension homomorphism from I to J.

To motivate Definition 3.6, we will show that the constructive queries can be characterized as those determinate queries for which object creation can be interpreted in terms of building up hereditarily finite sets from original domain elements:

Definition 3.7 Let A be an arbitrary set. Then the set $HF(A)$ of ***hereditarily finite sets with atoms in A*** is the smallest set satisfying: *(i)* $A \subset HF(A)$; and *(ii)* every finite subset of $HF(A)$ is an element of $HF(A)$.

Definition 3.7 is a slight variation on the original definition of [Bar75], which better suits our formalism.

To link constructive object creation to hereditarily finite sets, we need the concept of *HF-query*. Thereto, we need to extend the notion of instance: an *extended instance* is defined over the extended universe $HF(\mathcal{O})$, rather than $\mathcal{O}$. Hence, if I is an extended instance, then $dom(I) \subset HF(\mathcal{O})$. The set of all extended instances over a scheme $\mathcal{S}$ will be denoted $inst^*(\mathcal{S})$. We now define HF-queries:

Definition 3.8 Let $\mathcal{S}_{\text{in}} \subseteq \mathcal{S}_{\text{out}}$ be two schemes. An *HF-query* Q from $\mathcal{S}_{\text{in}}$ to $\mathcal{S}_{\text{out}}$ is a partial function $Q : inst(\mathcal{S}_{\text{in}}) \to inst^*(\mathcal{S}_{\text{out}})$, such that

1. if $J = Q(I)$, then $R^I = R^J$ for each $R \in \mathcal{S}_{\text{in}}$;
2. if $J = Q(I)$, and f is a permutation on the universe $\mathcal{O}$, then also $\overline{f}(J) = Q(f(I))$, with $\overline{f}$ the natural extension of f to $HF(\mathcal{O})$; and
3. if $J = Q(I)$, then $dom(J) \subset HF(dom(I))$.

The notion of HF-query is not new: slightly different variations have been studied under the terms *directory queries* [DM87] and *queries for untyped sets* [HS89b].

We now establish the following characterization for constructive queries, thus motivating our terminology:

Theorem 3.9 A determinate query Q from $\mathcal{S}_{\text{in}}$ to $\mathcal{S}_{\text{out}}$ is constructive if and only if there exists an HF-query Q^{HF} from $\mathcal{S}_{\text{in}}$ to $\mathcal{S}_{\text{out}}$ such that

1. $Q^{HF}(I)$ is defined if and only if there exists a J such that $Q(I, J)$, and
2. if $Q(I, J)$, then there is an injection $\Gamma_{I,J} : dom(J) \to HF(dom(I))$ such that *(i)* for each o in $dom(I)$, $\Gamma_{I,J}(o) = o$; and *(ii)* $\Gamma_{I,J}(J) = Q^{HF}(I)$.

Proof (sketch): *From HF to constructive.* Assume $Q(I, J)$. We have to find an extension homomorphism from I to J. By item 2 of Definition 3.8, the natural extension to $HF(dom(I))$ of an automorphism f of I, $\overline{f}$, is also an automorphism on $\Gamma_{I,J}(J)$. Since the natural extension mapping $\overline{} : f \to \overline{f}$ clearly preserves composition, it is a homomorphism. Composing it with $\Gamma_{I,J}^{-1}$ hence yields the desired extension homomorphism.

From constructive to HF. In order to construct the functions $\Gamma_{I,J}$, we first associate a program $P_{I,J}$ in

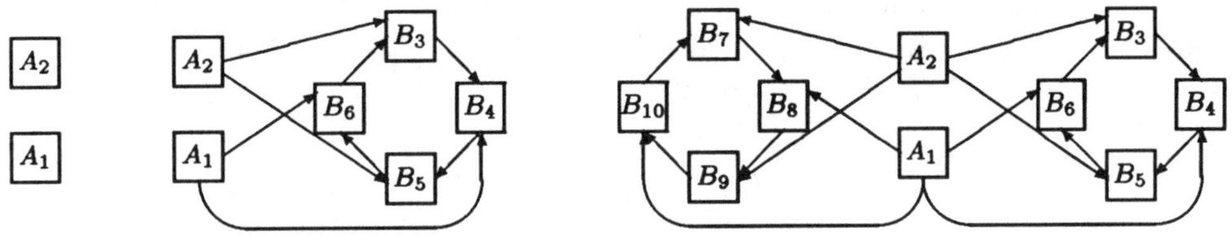

Figure 2: The instances I *(left)*, J *(middle)*, and $\overline{J}$ *(right)*.

FO + **powerset** + **while** to each pair of instances (I, J) with $Q(I, J)$ such that $P_{I,J}(I, J) = Q(I, J)$ (Proposition 3.4). By the genericity of our language, we can choose these programs in such a way that $P_{f(I),f(J)} = P_{I,J}$ for all permutations f of the universe $\mathcal{O}$.

Assume $Q(I, J)$. The mapping $\Gamma_{I,J}$ is defined inductively, as follows. On $dom(I)$, $\Gamma_{I,J}$ is the identity. Now, any new object $o \in dom(J) - dom(I)$ can be seen as having been created during the execution of $P_{I,J}$, say in the n-th invocation of a powerset-statement. As argued in the proof of Proposition 3.3, o then represents a set of tuples s. Assuming ordered pairs are interpreted as Kuratowski pairs (i.e., $(x, y) := \{\{x\}, \{x, y\}\}$), and numbers as von Neumann numerals (i.e., $0 := \emptyset$, and $i + 1 := \{0, \ldots, i\}$), we put $\Gamma_{I,J}(o) := (\Gamma_{I,J}(s), n)$.

Finally, we define Q^{HF}. Therefore, let I be any instance such that, for some J, $Q(I, J)$. Then we put $Q^{HF}(I) := \Gamma_{I,J}(J)$. It can readily be verified that Q^{HF} is well-defined and satisfies the desired properties. ■

By Theorem 3.9, a constructive query Q can be put into correspondence with an HF-query Q^{HF} over the same input and output schemes. Obviously, Q^{HF} is computable whenever Q is. From the completeness result of Dahlhaus and Makowsky [DM87], it then follows that Q^{HF} can be expressed by a program P^{HF} in (a variation of) their language DL, an extension of QL [CH80]. This program P^{HF} can be translated in a technical but straightforward manner (details omitted) into a program P expressing Q in FO + **powerset** + **while**, whence Theorem 3.5.[3]

4 Discussion

We conclude this abstract with a discussion on two issues of a more philosophical nature.

As mentioned earlier, making FO + **powerset** + **while** complete for the determinate queries requires the introduction of a copy elimination operation. However, there are some unappealing aspects to copy elimination as a query language operator; for example, all known schemes involving copy elimination are computationally intractable. Our work can be explained as an attempt to overcome that problem by proposing a more restrictive and perhaps more natural class of queries. On the other hand, one could also try to find a more natural class by relaxing the determinacy condition. We believe that the recently introduced *semi-deterministic queries* [VdBVG92] constitute such a class. From this perspective, determinate queries might be merely an intermediate between constructive queries on the one hand and semi-deterministic queries on the other hand.

But perhaps the main philosophical consequence of our results is a formal reconciliation of the two main approaches to creating new objects that have been considered in the literature. The first approach, which we call the "pure" one, recognizes created objects as new, atomic entities (e.g., [AK89, GPVG90a, KV84]). We took this approach here to define the semantics of the object-creating powerset operation. The second approach, which we call the "logic programming" approach, treats new objects in the output as terms, constructed from the objects in the input (e.g., [HY90, KW89].) Since these terms can be interpreted as hereditarily finite sets, Theorems 3.5 and 3.9 show that the two approaches can be linked together.

[3] In [HS89a], Hull and Su use a language very similar to FO + **powerset** + **while**, which they prove to be complete for plain deterministic queries. As this result can be lifted to arbitrary HF-queries [Hul92], the final argument in our proof could alternatively have been made using Hull and Su's formalism.

References

[AB91] S. Abiteboul and A. Bonner. Objects and views. In *Proc. 1991 ACM SIGMOD Int. Conf. Management of Data*, in *SIGMOD Rec.*, 20(2):238–247, 1991.

[Abi90] S. Abiteboul. Personal communications, 1990.

[AK89] S. Abiteboul and P. Kanellakis. Object identity as a query language primitive. In *Proc. 1989 ACM SIGMOD Int. Conf. Management of Data*, in *SIGMOD Rec.*, 18(2):159–173, 1989.

[AV90] S. Abiteboul and V. Vianu. Procedural languages for database queries and updates. *J. Comput. Syst. Sci.*, 41(2):181–229, 1990.

[AV91a] S. Abiteboul and V. Vianu. Datalog extensions for database queries and updates. *J. Comput. Syst. Sci.*, 43(1):62–124, 1991.

[AV91b] S. Abiteboul and V. Vianu. Generic computation and its complexity. In *Proc. 23rd ACM Symp. Theory of Computing*, 209–219. 1991.

[AU79] A.V. Aho and J.D. Ullman. Universality of data retrieval languages. In *Proc. ACM Symp. Principles of Programming Languages*, 110–120. 1979.

[AP92] M. Andries and J. Paredaens. A language for generic graph-transformations. In *Graph-Theoretic Concepts in Computer Science, Proc. Int. Workshop WG 91*, in *Lecture Notes in Computer Science*, 570, 63–74. Springer-Verlag, 1992.

[Ban78] F. Bancilhon. On the completeness of query languages for relational data bases. In *Proc. 7th Symp. on Mathematical Foundations of Computer Science*, in *Lecture Notes in Computer Science*, 64, 112–123. Springer-Verlag, 1978.

[Bar75] J. Barwise. *Admissible Sets and Structures.* Springer-Verlag, 1975.

[CH80] A. Chandra and D. Harel. Computable queries for relational database systems. *J. Comput. Syst. Sci.*, 21(2):156–178, 1980.

[Cod70] E. Codd. A relational model for large shared databanks. *Commun. ACM*, 13(6):377–387, 1970.

[Cod72a] E. Codd. Further normalization of the data base relational model. In R. Rustin, ed., *Data Base Systems*, 33–64. Prentice-Hall, 1972.

[Cod72b] E. Codd. Relational completeness of data base sublanguages. In R. Rustin, ed., *Data Base Systems*, 65–98. Prentice-Hall, 1972.

[DM87] E. Dahlhaus and J.A. Makowsky. Computable directory queries. In *Logic and Computer Science: New Trends and Applications*, Rend. Sem. Mat. Univ. Pol. Torino, 165–197, 1987. Also in *LNCS 214*.

[GV85] H. Gaifman and M.Y. Vardi. A simple proof that connectivity is not first-order definable. *Bulletin of the EATCS*, 26:43–45, 1985.

[GPVG90a] M. Gyssens, J. Paredaens, and D. Van Gucht. A graph-oriented object database model. In *Proc. 9th ACM Symp. Principles of Database Systems*, 417–424. 1990.

[GPVG90b] M. Gyssens, J. Paredaens, and D. Van Gucht. A graph-oriented object database model for database end-user interfaces. In *Proc. 1990 ACM SIGMOD Int. Conf. Management of Data*, in *SIGMOD Rec.*, 19(2):24–33. 1990.

[Hul92] R. Hull. Personal communications, 1992.

[HS89a] R. Hull and J. Su. On bulk data type constructors and manipulation primitives: a framework for analyzing expressive power and complexity. In R. Hull, R. Morrison, and D. Stemple, eds., *Proc. 2nd Int. Workshop on Database Programming Languages*, 396–410. Morgan Kaufmann, 1989.

[HS89b] R. Hull and Y. Su. Untyped sets, invention, and computable queries. In *Proc. 8th ACM Symp. Principles of Database Systems*, 347–359. 1989.

[HY90] R. Hull and M. Yoshikawa. ILOG: Declarative creation and manipulation of object identifiers. In *Proc. 16th Int. Conf. on Very Large Data Bases*, 455–468. 1990.

[Kim89] W. Kim. A model of queries for object-oriented databases. In *Proc. 15th Int. Conf. on Very Large Data Bases*, 423–432. 1989.

[KW89] M. Kifer and J. Wu. A logic for object-oriented logic programming (Maier's O-logic revisited). In *Proc. 8th ACM Symp. Principles of Database Systems*, 379–393. 1989.

[KV84] G. Kuper and M. Vardi. A new approach to database logic. In *Proc. 3rd ACM Symp. Principles of Database Systems*, 86–96. 1984.

[Par78] J. Paredaens. On the expressive power of the relational algebra. *Inf. Process. Lett.*, 7(2):107–111, 1978.

[VdBP91] J. Van den Bussche and J. Paredaens. The expressive power of structured values in pure OODB's. In *Proc. 10th ACM Symp. Principles of Database Systems*, 291–299. 1991.

[VdBVG92] J. Van den Bussche and D. Van Gucht. Semi-determinism. In *Proc. 11th ACM Symp. Principles of Database Systems*. 1992. To appear.

Enumerating the k closest pairs optimally*

Hans-Peter Lenhof Michiel Smid
Max-Planck-Institut für Informatik
W-6600 Saarbrücken, Germany

Abstract

Let S be a set of n points in D-dimensional space, where D is a constant, and let k be an integer between 1 and $\binom{n}{2}$. An algorithm is given that computes the k closest pairs in the set S in $O(n \log n + k)$ time, using $O(n + k)$ space. The algorithm fits in the algebraic decision tree model and is, therefore, optimal.

1 Introduction

There has been a lot of interest in closest pair problems. In such problems, we are given a set of n points in D-dimensional space, and we want to compute the closest pair, all k closest pairs, or just the k-th closest pair. Distances are measured in an arbitrary L_t-metric, where $1 \leq t \leq \infty$. In this metric, the distance $d_t(p, q)$ between the points $p = (p_1, \ldots, p_D)$ and $q = (q_1, \ldots, q_D)$ is defined by $d_t(p, q) := (\sum_{i=1}^{D} |p_i - q_i|^t)^{1/t}$, if $1 \leq t < \infty$, and for $t = \infty$, it is defined by $d_\infty(p, q) := \max_{1 \leq i \leq D} |p_i - q_i|$.

The problem of finding the closest pair has been solved already for a long time. Shamos and Hoey [10] and Bentley and Shamos [2] solve this problem, for the case $D = 2$ and $D \geq 2$, respectively, in $O(n \log n)$ time, which is optimal in the algebraic decision tree model. Recently, an optimal algorithm for the on-line version of this problem has been given by Schwarz et al.[12].

For the problem of computing the k-th closest pair, there are results by Agarwal et al.[1], who consider the L_t-metric for the planar case, and by Salowe [7], who shows how to select the k-th closest pair in the L_∞-metric in $O(n(\log n)^D)$ time.

For the problem of enumerating the k closest pairs, the first result was by Smid [11], who shows how to compute the $n^{2/3}$ closest pairs in $O(n \log n)$ time. This result was extended in two directions. First, for the planar case, Dickerson and Drysdale [3] compute the k closest pairs—ordered by their distances—in $O(n \log n + k \log n)$ time. Second, Salowe [8] gives an algorithm that computes the n closest pairs in $O(n \log n)$ time. The latter result holds for an arbitrary, but fixed, dimension D.

Katoh and Iwano [5] give a technique for solving related problems such as finding the k furthest pairs or the k closest bichromatic pairs. Their technique can also be applied to the k closest pairs problem. The result is an algorithm with running time $O(n \log n + k \log n \log(n^2/k))$. (See [6].)

In this paper, we prove the following

Theorem 1 *Let S be a set of n points in D-space and let $1 \leq k \leq \binom{n}{2}$. We can find the k closest pairs (w.r.t. the L_t-metric) in the set S in $O(n \log n + k)$ time, using $O(n + k)$ space, which is optimal.*

We remark that our algorithm does not enumerate the k closest pairs in sorted order; the order can be arbitrary.

The algorithm is based on the fact that once the k-th smallest L_t-distance d_k is known, we can easily enumerate the k closest pairs: Consider a grid with cells of length d_k and distribute the points over the cells. Then, compare each point with all points that are contained in one of the 3^D neighboring cells. Of course, this algorithm compares too many pairs. All pairs that are compared, however, have L_t-distance at most $2Dd_k$. (Equality can occur in the L_1-metric.) By a result of Salowe [8], see Lemma 2, the number of pairs considered is $O(k + n)$. Therefore, we find the k closest pairs in $O(n \log n + k)$ time.

Of course, the k-th smallest L_t-distance is not known at the start of the algorithm. We could approximate it by running Salowe's algorithm that finds the k-th smallest L_∞-distance. This takes, however, $O(n(\log n)^D)$ time. As we shall see, for our application, it suffices to approximate the k-th L_∞-distance.

In Section 2, we prove some combinatorial results that are needed in the analysis of the algorithm. In Section 3, we give this algorithm, which consists of

*This work was supported by the ESPRIT Basic Research Actions Program, under contract No. 7141 (project ALCOM II).

0-8186-2900-2/92 $3.00 © 1992 IEEE

two phases. First, in Subsection 3.1, we compute an L_∞-distance with rank $\Theta(k+n)$. (Here, the term n appears because of a technical reason that will become clear later.) The algorithm implicitly manipulates all possible differences $|p_i - q_i|$, where $1 \leq i \leq D$ and p and q are points of the set. It makes a binary search on these differences. (The way in which the binary search is controlled is due to Johnson and Mizoguchi [4], who use it to find the k-th element in the Cartesian sum $X+Y$.) After a presorting step, which takes $O(n \log n)$ time, we can test in $O(n)$ time, if a difference $|p_i - q_i|$ approximates the desired L_∞-distance. The approximation is found within $O(\log n)$ iterations. In Subsection 3.2, this approximation is used to find the k closest pairs w.r.t. the L_t-metric. Of course, we can use the above sketched algorithm that uses a grid. Then, however, in order to distribute the points over the cells, we need the non-algebraic floor function. Instead, we use a slightly degenerate grid that can be constructed without the floor function. We finish the paper in Section 4 with some open problems.

In Subsection 3.1, we need to compute $\lfloor (l+h)/2 \rfloor$ for integers l and h in the range from 1 to n. At the start of the algorithm, we build an array

$$F[1:2n] = [0, 1, 1, 2, 2, 3, 3, \ldots, n-1, n-1, n].$$

Clearly, F can be constructed in $O(n)$ time using only algebraic functions. Then, the value of $\lfloor (l+h)/2 \rfloor$ is stored in $F[l+h]$ and, hence, can be retrieved in $O(1)$ time, without actually using the floor-function.

2 Some combinatorial results

We recall the notion of weighted medians. Let $x_1, x_2, \ldots, x_n$ be a sequence of real numbers such that every element x_i has a weight w_i, which is a positive real number. Let $W := \sum_{j=1}^{n} w_j$. Element x_i is called a *weighted median* if

$$\sum_{j:x_j<x_i} w_j < W/2 \quad \text{and} \quad \sum_{j:x_j \leq x_i} w_j \geq W/2. \tag{1}$$

The following lemma appears already in [4]. For completeness, we give a proof.

Lemma 1 ([4]) *The weighted median of a set of n weighted real numbers can be computed in $O(n)$ time.*

Proof: The following algorithm finds the weighted median. In $O(n)$ time, compute the standard median, say x_i, and relabel the elements such that $x_j \leq x_i$ for $j \leq i$, and $x_j \geq x_i$ for $j \geq i$. Then compute the sums in (1). Using these sums we check if x_i is a weighted median. If so, we are finished. Otherwise, we know which half of the sequence contains the weighted median. We proceed recursively in this subsequence, which has length at most $n/2$. In this subsequence, we find an element with the appropriate weighted rank. ∎

We define a D-dimensional δ-cube as a hypercube of the form

$$[a_1 : a_1 + \delta) \times [a_2 : a_2 + \delta) \times \ldots \times [a_D : a_D + \delta),$$

where $a_1, a_2, \ldots, a_D$ are real numbers.

Definition 1 *Let S be a set of n points in D-space and let δ be a positive real number. A collection R of D-dimensional δ-cubes is called a* δ-covering *of S, if*

1. *the cubes are pairwise disjoint,*
2. *each cube contains at least one point of S,*
3. *each point in S is contained in one cube.*

Let R be a δ-covering of S. Label the cubes (arbitrarily) $1, 2, \ldots, r := |R|$ and define n_i to be the number of points of S that are contained in the i-th cube of R. We define

$$\Sigma(S, R) := \sum_{i=1}^{r} \binom{n_i}{2}.$$

If δ is a real number, then we denote by $r_\infty(\delta)$ the number of L_∞-distances in S that are less than δ.

Lemma 2 (Salowe [8]) *Let S be a set of n points in D-space and let δ be a positive real number. Then,*

$$r_\infty(2\delta) \leq 5^D \left(r_\infty(\delta) + n \right).$$

Remark: Salowe has a constant of 5^{2D} instead of 5^D. Lemma 2 can be proved in a similar way as Lemma 3 below, by taking for R the non-empty δ-cubes of a grid with cells of length δ, and taking for h' in (2) a 5δ-cube. Counting all pairs with L_∞-distance less than 2δ gives the bound in Lemma 2. In fact, Lemma 3 and its proof are basically the same as Salowe's proof of Lemma 2, see [8].

Lemma 3 *Let S be a set of n points in D-space, let δ be a positive real number, and let R be a δ-covering of S. Then,*

$$\Sigma(S, R) \leq r_\infty(\delta) \leq 4^D (\Sigma(S, R) + n).$$

Proof: Clearly, $\binom{n_i}{2}$ counts the number of pairs of points that are contained in the i-th cube of R. Each such pair has L_∞-distance less than δ. This proves the left inequality. To prove the other inequality, consider a cube h in R:

$$h = [a_1 : a_1 + \delta) \times \ldots \times [a_D : a_D + \delta).$$

Let h' be the 3δ-cube

$$h' = [a_1 - \delta : a_1 + 2\delta) \times \ldots \times [a_D - \delta : a_D + 2\delta), \quad (2)$$

i.e., the cube with sides of length 3δ that contains h in its center. This cube h' intersects at most 4^D cubes of R: This follows from the fact that an interval of length 3δ can intersect at most 4 intervals from a set of pairwise disjoint intervals of length δ.

We call the cubes of R that intersect h' the *neighboring cubes* of h. Let C_i denote the set of labels of the neighboring cubes of the i-th cube in R. Note that the relation "neighboring cube" is symmetric, i.e., $i \in C_j$ iff $j \in C_i$.

Now consider two points $p \neq q$ in S having L_∞-distance less than δ. Then either p and q are contained in the same cube of R, or p is contained in a cube, say $h \in R$, and q is contained in a neighboring cube of h. It follows that

$$r_\infty(\delta) \leq \frac{1}{2} \sum_{i=1}^{r} n_i \sum_{j \in C_i} n_j.$$

To prove the right inequality, it suffices to show that this double summation is bounded above by $4^D(\Sigma(S, R) + n)$. This follows from some elementary calculations:

$$\begin{aligned}
\sum_{i=1}^{r} n_i \sum_{j \in C_i} n_j &\leq \\
&\leq \sum_{i=1}^{r} \sum_{j \in C_i} (\max(n_i, n_j))^2 \\
&= \sum_{u=1}^{r} |\{v : u \in C_v, \max(n_u, n_v) = n_u\}| \times n_u^2 \\
&\leq \sum_{u=1}^{r} |\{v : u \in C_v\}| \times n_u^2 \\
&= \sum_{u=1}^{r} |\{v : v \in C_u\}| \times n_u^2 \\
&= \sum_{u=1}^{r} |C_u| \times n_u^2 \\
&\leq 4^D \sum_{u=1}^{r} n_u^2.
\end{aligned}$$

Using the fact that $n_u^2 = n_u + 2\binom{n_u}{2}$, the proof can easily be completed. ∎

We give two corollaries. The constants that appear are rather large. By a more careful analysis, however, they can be decreased, but they remain exponential in D.

Corollary 1 *Let S be a set of n points in D-space and let δ be a positive real number. Let R be any δ-covering of S, such that $k \leq \Sigma(S, R) \leq 20^D(k + 2n)$. Then,*

$$k \leq r_\infty(\delta) \leq 80^D(k + 3n).$$

Proof: This follows immediately from Lemma 3. ∎

Corollary 2 *Let S be a set of n points in D-space and let $\delta^\star$ be the $20^D(k+2n)$-th smallest L_∞-distance in S. Let R be any $\delta^\star$-covering of S. Then,*

$$k \leq \Sigma(S, R) \leq 20^D(k + 2n).$$

Proof: We know from Lemma 3 that

$$\Sigma(S, R) \leq r_\infty(\delta^\star) \leq 4^D(\Sigma(S, R) + n).$$

Since $r_\infty(\delta^\star) < 20^D(k+2n)$, it follows that $\Sigma(S, R) \leq 20^D(k + 2n)$. By Lemma 2, we know that $r_\infty(2\delta^\star) \leq 5^D(r_\infty(\delta^\star) + n)$. Since $r_\infty(2\delta^\star) \geq 20^D(k+2n)$, we get

$$20^D(k + 2n) \leq 5^D(r_\infty(\delta^\star) + n) \leq 20^D(\Sigma(S, R) + 2n). \quad (3)$$

Therefore, $\Sigma(S, R) \geq k$. ∎

Remark: In this proof, we need a lower bound on $r_\infty(\delta^\star)$. Since many L_∞-distances might be equal, the definition of $\delta^\star$ does not immediately give us such a lower bound. We derive it using $r_\infty(2\delta^\star)$.

3 The k closest pairs algorithm

Throughout this section, S is a set of n points in D-space. We assume that k is such that $20^D(k+2n) \leq \binom{n}{2}$. If this is not the case, we can find the k closest pairs, by considering all pairs of points and selecting the k that are closest. This takes $O(n^2) = O(k)$ time, which is clearly optimal.

The algorithm consists of two phases. In the first phase, we search for a real number δ for which the condition of Corollary 1 holds. (By Corollary 2, such a δ exists.) Then, in the second phase, we use this δ to enumerate all L_∞-distances that are less than $D\delta$. There are $O(k + n)$ such distances. We extract from them the k smallest L_t-distances.

3.1 The approximation phase

We want to find an L_∞-distance δ, such that $r_\infty(\delta)$ lies in between k and $80^D(k+3n)$. There are two points $p=(p_1,\ldots,p_D)$ and $q=(q_1,\ldots,q_D)$ in S, and an i, such that $|p_i-q_i|=\delta$. In order to find this δ, we do a binary search on all possible differences $|p_i-q_i|$. Of course, we maintain the candidate differences in an implicit way. (This technique appears already in [4].) Note that we do not search for the difference $|p_i-q_i|$ with a certain rank; we search for the L_∞-distance with this rank.

We maintain the following information:

1. Arrays $A_1,\ldots,A_D$ of length n, where A_i contains the points of S sorted w.r.t. their i-th coordinates. For each $1<i\leq D$, each point in A_i contains a pointer to its copy in A_{i-1}.
2. For each $1\leq i\leq D$ and $1\leq j<n$, we store with $A_i[j]$ an interval $[l_{ij}:h_{ij}]$, where l_{ij} and h_{ij} are integers, such that $j<l_{ij}\leq h_{ij}+1\leq n+1$.

We define the set of *candidate differences* as follows. Let $p=(p_1,\ldots,p_D)$ and $q=(q_1,\ldots,q_D)$ be two points in S, and let $1\leq i\leq D$. Moreover, let j and j' be such that $A_i[j]=p$ and $A_i[j']=q$. Assume w.l.o.g. that $j<j'$. Then $|q_i-p_i|$ is a candidate difference iff $l_{ij}\leq j'\leq h_{ij}$. The total number of candidate differences is equal to

$$\sum_{i=1}^{D}\sum_{j=1}^{n-1}(h_{ij}-l_{ij}+1).$$

The algorithm makes a sequence of iterations. At each iteration, this summation is decreased by a factor of at least one fourth. We maintain the following

Invariant: At each moment, the $20^D(k+2n)$-th smallest L_∞-distance $\delta^\star$ is contained in the set of candidate differences.

Initialization: At the start of the algorithm, we build the arrays $A_1,\ldots,A_D$ and add the pointers between them. Then, for each $1\leq i\leq D$ and $1\leq j<n$, we store with $A_i[j]$ the interval $[l_{ij}:h_{ij}]=[j+1:n]$.

Clearly, after the initialization, the invariant holds and the total number of candidate differences is equal to

$$\sum_{i=1}^{D}\sum_{j=1}^{n-1}(n-j)=D\binom{n}{2}.$$

Now, the algorithm starts with the

Iteration:

1. For each $1\leq i\leq D$ and $1\leq j<n$, such that $l_{ij}\leq h_{ij}$, take the pair
$$A_i[\lfloor(l_{ij}+h_{ij})/2\rfloor] \quad\text{and}\quad A_i[j]$$
and take the (positive) difference of their i-th coordinates. Give this difference *weight* $h_{ij}-l_{ij}+1$. This gives a sequence of at most $D(n-1)$ weighted differences.
2. Compute a weighted median δ of these weighted differences.
3. Construct a δ-covering R of S, and compute $\Sigma(S,R)$. There are three possible cases.
   (a) If $k\leq\Sigma(S,R)\leq 20^D(k+2n)$, then output δ and stop.
   (b) If $\Sigma(S,R)<k$, then for each pair
   $$A_i[\lfloor(l_{ij}+h_{ij})/2\rfloor] \quad\text{and}\quad A_i[j]$$
   selected in the first step such that the difference of their i-th coordinates is at most δ, set $l_{ij}:=\lfloor(l_{ij}+h_{ij})/2\rfloor+1$. Go to Step 1.
   (c) If $\Sigma(S,R)>20^D(k+2n)$, then for each pair
   $$A_i[\lfloor(l_{ij}+h_{ij})/2\rfloor] \quad\text{and}\quad A_i[j]$$
   selected in the first step such that the difference of their i-th coordinates is at least δ, set $h_{ij}:=\lfloor(l_{ij}+h_{ij})/2\rfloor-1$. Go to Step 1.

The construction of the δ-covering R will be described later. First, we prove two lemmas.

Lemma 4 *The algorithm correctly maintains the invariant.*

Proof: After the initialization, the set of candidate differences equals the set of all $D\binom{n}{2}$ differences $|p_i-q_i|$. Therefore, the invariant holds initially. Consider one iteration. First assume that case (b) applies, i.e., $\Sigma(S,R)<k$. Then, by Lemma 3, $r_\infty(\delta)\leq 4^D(\Sigma(S,R)+n)<4^D(k+n)$. We know from (3) that $r_\infty(\delta^\star)\geq 4^D(k+2n)-n>4^D(k+n)$. Therefore, $r_\infty(\delta)<r_\infty(\delta^\star)$ and, hence, $\delta<\delta^\star$. The algorithm only removes differences $|p_u-q_u|$ from the set of candidate differences that are at most equal to δ. Hence, at the end of the iteration, the invariant still holds.

If case (c) applies, then we know from Lemma 3 that $r_\infty(\delta)\geq\Sigma(S,R)>20^D(k+2n)$. Since $r_\infty(\delta^\star)<20^D(k+2n)$, we infer that $\delta>\delta^\star$. Hence, we can remove differences $|p_u-q_u|$ from the set of candidate differences that are at least equal to δ, without invalidating the invariant. ∎

Lemma 5 *The algorithm makes at most $\log_{4/3}(D n^2) = O(\log n)$ iterations.*

Proof: Let W (resp. W') be the total number of candidate differences at the start of (resp. immediately after) an iteration. Moreover, let l_{ij} and h_{ij} (resp. l'_{ij} and h'_{ij}) denote the endpoints of the intervals at the start of (resp. immediately after) this iteration.

Suppose that case (b) applies. If $l'_{ij} \neq l_{ij}$, then $l'_{ij} = \lfloor (l_{ij}+h_{ij})/2 \rfloor + 1$ and $h'_{ij} = h_{ij}$. Since l_{ij} and h_{ij} are integers, we have $l'_{ij} \geq (l_{ij}+h_{ij}+1)/2$. Therefore,

$$\begin{aligned} W &= W' + \sum_{i,j:l'_{ij}\neq l_{ij}} (l'_{ij} - l_{ij}) \\ &\geq W' + \frac{1}{2} \sum_{i,j:l'_{ij}\neq l_{ij}} (h_{ij} - l_{ij} + 1) \\ &\geq W' + \frac{1}{2}\frac{W}{2}, \end{aligned}$$

where the last inequality follows from the fact that δ is a weighted median. Hence,

$$W' \leq \frac{3}{4} W. \tag{4}$$

The same bound can be proved if case (c) applies.

The algorithm terminates as soon as it finds a real number δ such that $k \leq \Sigma(S,R) \leq 20^D(k+2n)$ holds for the corresponding δ-covering R. By the invariant and Corollary 2, such a δ is always contained in the set of candidate differences. Since this set gets smaller in each iteration, the algorithm must find such a δ. This proves that the algorithm terminates.

Let z be the number of iterations made by the algorithm. It follows from the invariant that the set of candidate differences is never empty. Hence, if we denote the number of candidate differences after z iterations by W_z, then $W_z \geq 1$. Since there are $D\binom{n}{2}$ candidate differences before the first iteration, it follows from (4) that

$$W_z \leq \left(\frac{3}{4}\right)^z D \binom{n}{2}.$$

Therefore, $z \log(4/3) \leq \log(D\binom{n}{2})$. ∎

It remains to give an algorithm that constructs a δ-covering R. Of course, we can take a D-dimensional grid of side lengths δ and distribute the points over the cells. Then, however, we must use the floor-function and, hence, the algorithm falls outside the algebraic decision tree model. We give a recursive algorithm that computes a δ-covering using only algebraic functions.

Constructing a δ-covering: The algorithm walks along the array A_1. Let $p := A_1[1]$ be the first element in this array and set a_1 to the first coordinate of p. Let $i \geq 1$, and assume that $a_1, \ldots, a_i$ have a value already.

If there is a point in S having a first coordinate lying in the half-open interval $[a_i : a_i+\delta)$, then we set $a_{i+1} := a_i + \delta$. Otherwise, we set a_{i+1} to the value of the first coordinate of the first point in A_1 that lies "to the right" of a_i. If we have reached the end of the array A_1, we set $a_{i+1} := a_i + \delta$ and the construction of the a_j's stops.

This gives a sequence of δ-intervals $[a_1 : a_1+\delta), [a_2 : a_2+\delta), \ldots, [a_l : a_l+\delta)$, for some l. During the walk along A_1, we give each point a pointer to the δ-interval to which its first coordinate belongs.

If $D = 1$, the algorithm is finished. So assume that $D > 1$. We partition S into subsets $S_1, \ldots, S_l$, as follows: Walk along the array A_2. For each point p encountered, follow the pointer to its copy in A_1, and follow the pointer stored there to the interval, say $[a_i : a_i+\delta)$, to which the first coordinate of p belongs. We add point p to subset S_i; more precisely, we store p at the end of a list representing S_i. At the end, we have l lists, where the i-th one stores the points of S_i sorted by their 2-nd coordinates.

For $i = 1, \ldots, l$, do the following. Use the same algorithm recursively to compute a δ-covering for the set S_i, where we take only the last $D-1$ coordinates into account. This gives a collection of $(D-1)$-dimensional δ-cubes of the form

$$[b_2 : b_2+\delta) \times [b_3 : b_3+\delta) \times \ldots \times [b_D : b_D+\delta),$$

together with a corresponding partition of S_i. Replace each such cube by the D-dimensional δ-cube

$$[a_i : a_i+\delta) \times [b_2 : b_2+\delta) \times [b_3 : b_3+\delta) \times \ldots \times [b_D : b_D+\delta).$$

The resulting cubes—for all i together—form the desired δ-covering R of S.

It is clear that once the δ-covering R has been constructed, we can compute $\Sigma(S,R)$ in $O(n)$ time. In fact, this value can be computed during the construction of R.

Lemma 6 *Let R be the set of hypercubes that are computed by the above algorithm. Then, R is a δ-covering of S. Moreover, the algorithm computes R and $\Sigma(S,R)$ in $O(n)$ time.*

Proof: It is clear that R is a δ-covering of S. Let $T(n,D)$ denote the running time of the algorithm.

Since at the start of a recursive call, the points are sorted already by the appropriate coordinates, we have

$$T(n,1) = O(n),$$
$$T(n,D) = O(n) + \sum_{i=1}^{l} T(n_i, D-1), \text{ if } D \geq 2,$$

for integers $n_i \geq 1$ such that $\sum_{i=1}^{l} n_i = n$. Using induction, it follows that $T(n,D) = O(n)$, because D is a constant. ∎

Theorem 2 *In $O(n \log n)$ time and using $O(n)$ space, we can compute a real number δ, such that $k \leq r_\infty(\delta) \leq 80^D(k+3n)$.*

Proof: The algorithm outputs a real number δ such that $k \leq \Sigma(S,R) \leq 20^D(k+2n)$ holds for the corresponding δ-covering R. Then, Corollary 1 implies the bounds on $r_\infty(\delta)$.

The initialization of the algorithm takes $O(n \log n)$ time. Moreover, by Lemmas 1, 5 and 6, $O(\log n)$ iterations are made, each taking $O(n)$ time. This proves that the entire algorithm has running time $O(n \log n)$. Finally, it is clear that the algorithm uses only linear space. ∎

3.2 The enumeration phase

At this moment, we have found a real number δ, such that $k \leq r_\infty(\delta) \leq 80^D(k+3n)$. That is, the number of L_∞-distances in S that are less than δ lies in between k and $80^D(k+3n)$.

In the enumeration phase, we find all L_t-distances that are less than $D\delta$. From these distances, we extract the k smallest ones. The details are as follows. (We use the notion of neighboring cube, which was defined in the proof of Lemma 3.)

1. Construct a $D\delta$-covering R of S. Note that the algorithm outputs the cubes of R in lexicographical order.

2. Build a list storing the following pairs of points of S: For each $D\delta$-cube h in R, all pairs (p,q), $p \neq q$, where $p \in h$ and q is contained in some neighboring cube of h that is (lexicographically) at least equal to h. (In this way, we get each pair only once.) These neighboring cubes can be found as follows. Let

$$h = [a_1 : a_1 + D\delta) \times \ldots \times [a_D : a_D + D\delta).$$

Search for all cubes in R that contain any of the 4^D points

$$(a_1 + \epsilon_1 D\delta, \ldots, a_D + \epsilon_D D\delta),$$

where $\epsilon_1, \ldots, \epsilon_D \in \{-1, 0, 1, 2\}$, and that are lexicographically at least equal to h.

3. Take the list of pairs that results from the previous step and find the k closest pairs w.r.t. the L_t-distance.

Lemma 7 *Given δ, the algorithm finds the k closest pairs in the set S in $O(n \log n + k)$ time, using $O(n+k)$ space.*

Proof: Let d_t^k (resp. d_∞^k) denote the k-th smallest L_t-distance (resp. L_∞-distance) in S. Since $r_\infty(\delta) \geq k$, we have $d_\infty^k < \delta$. Moreover, since $d_t(p,q) \leq D\, d_\infty(p,q)$ for $1 \leq t \leq \infty$, we have $d_t^k \leq D\, d_\infty^k$. Hence, $d_t^k < D\delta$. In Step 2, all pairs (p,q), $p \neq q$, such that $d_t(p,q) < D\delta$, are found. Hence, in Step 2, all k L_t-closest pairs are added to the list. This proves the correctness of the algorithm.

Concerning the time complexity, Step 1 takes $O(n)$ time. All pairs that are found in Step 2 have L_∞-distance less than $3D\delta$. By repeated application of Lemma 2, it follows that the number of pairs found in this step is at most

$$\begin{aligned} r_\infty(3D\delta) &\leq \\ &\leq 5^{D\lceil \log 3D \rceil}\, r_\infty(\delta) + \frac{5^{D(1+\lceil \log 3D \rceil)} - 5^D}{5^D - 1} n \\ &= O(k+n). \end{aligned}$$

Moreover, in the second step, we make at most $4^D n$ point location queries. Each query can be solved in $O(\log n)$ time by a binary search. Hence, the total time for Step 2 is bounded by $O(n \log n + r_\infty(3D\delta)) = O(n \log n + k)$.

For the third step, we use a linear time algorithm to find the k-th smallest L_t-distance d_t^k. Then, by making one scan over the list, we extract all L_t-distances that are less than or equal to d_t^k. The total time for Step 3 is bounded by the size of the list, i.e., $O(r_\infty(3D\delta)) = O(k+n)$.

The algorithm uses an amount of space that is bounded by $O(n + r_\infty(3D\delta)) = O(n+k)$. ∎

This completes the description of the algorithm and its analysis. Combining Theorem 2 and Lemma 7 proves Theorem 1.

4 Concluding remarks

We have given an optimal algorithm for the k closest pairs problem. There remain some interesting problems that need more attention. Our algorithm approximates the L_∞-distance with a certain rank r. Can it be modified to find the exact L_∞-distance with rank r? Note that Salowe [7] solves this problem in $O(n(\log n)^D)$ time. Another problem is to find the L_t-distance with rank r for other values of t.

The algorithm presented here finds the k smallest distances, but it does not output this sequence in sorted order. Of course, we can solve the "sorted k closest pairs problem" in $O((n+k)\log n)$ time. It is an open problem if the time complexity can be improved to $O(n \log n + k)$. In particular, it is an open problem if we can sort all $\binom{n}{2}$ distances in $O(n^2)$ time.

Finally, can we use the techniques of this paper to improve the time bounds in [5] for the k furthest pairs problem, or for the k closest/furthest bichromatic pairs problem? (Note that the results in [5] only hold for the planar case.)

Addendum

After we wrote the first version of this paper, Salowe's journal version of [8] appeared as [9]. There, he also proves Theorem 1. His algorithm, however, is much more complicated. Moreover, as we will show in our final paper, our algorithm can be parallelized, whereas this seems not possible for Salowe's algorithm.

Our PRAM version of the algorithm uses $n/\log n$ processors and has a time complexity of $O((\log n)^2 \log\log n + (k \log n)/n)$.

References

[1] P.K. Agarwal, B. Aronov, M. Sharir and S. Suri. *Selecting distances in the plane.* Proc. 6-th ACM Symp. on Comp. Geom., 1990, pp. 321-331.

[2] J.L. Bentley and M.I. Shamos. *Divide-and-conquer in multidimensional space.* Proc. 8-th Annual ACM Symp. on Theory of Computing, 1976, pp. 220-230.

[3] M.T. Dickerson and R.S. Drysdale. *Enumerating k distances for n points in the plane.* Proc. 7-th ACM Symp. on Comp. Geom., 1991, pp. 234-238.

[4] D.B. Johnson and T. Mizoguchi. *Selecting the Kth element in $X+Y$ and $X_1 + X_2 + \cdots + X_m$.* SIAM J. Comput. **7** (1978), pp. 147-153.

[5] N. Katoh and K. Iwano. *Finding k farthest pairs and k closest/farthest bichromatic pairs for points in the plane.* Proc. 8-th ACM Symp. on Comp. Geom., 1992, pp. 320-329.

[6] H.P. Lenhof and M. Smid. *The k closest pairs problem.* Unpublished manuscript, 1992.

[7] J.S. Salowe. *L-infinity interdistance selection by parametric search.* Inform. Proc. Lett. **30** (1989), pp. 9-14.

[8] J.S. Salowe. *Shallow interdistance selection and interdistance enumeration.* Proc. WADS'91, Lecture Notes in Computer Science, Vol. 519, Springer-Verlag, Berlin, 1991, pp. 117-128.

[9] J.S. Salowe. *Enumerating interdistances in space.* Internat. J. Comput. Geom. Appl. **2** (1992), pp. 49-59.

[10] M.I. Shamos and D. Hoey. *Closest-pair problems.* Proc. 16-th Annual IEEE Symp. on Foundations of Computer Science, 1975, pp. 151-162.

[11] M. Smid. *Maintaining the minimal distance of a point set in less than linear time.* Algorithms Review **2** (1991), pp. 33-44.

[12] C. Schwarz, M. Smid and J. Snoeyink. *An optimal algorithm for the on-line closest pair problem.* Proc. 8-th ACM Symp. on Comp. Geom., 1992, pp. 330-336.

Safe and Effective Determinant Evaluation

Kenneth L. Clarkson
AT&T Bell Laboratories
Murray Hill, New Jersey 07974
e-mail: clarkson@research.att.com

Abstract

The problem of evaluating the sign of the determinant of a small matrix arises in many geometric algorithms. Given an $n \times n$ matrix A with integer entries, whose columns are all smaller than M in Euclidean norm, the algorithm given here evaluates the sign of the determinant $\det A$ exactly. The algorithm requires an arithmetic precision of less than $1.5n+2\lg M$ bits. The number of arithmetic operations needed is $O(n^3) + O(n^2)\log \mathcal{OD}(A)/\beta$, where $\mathcal{OD}(A)|\det A|$ is the product of the lengths of the columns of A, and β is the number of "extra" bits of precision,

$$\min\{\lg(1/\mathbf{u}) - 1.1n - 2\lg n - 2, \lg N - \lg M - 1.5n - 1\},$$

where $\mathbf{u}$ is the roundoff error in approximate arithmetic, and N is the largest representable integer. Since $\mathcal{OD}(A) \leq M^n$, the algorithm requires $O(n^3 \lg M)$ time, and $O(n^3)$ time when $\beta = \Omega(\log M)$.

1 Introduction

Many geometric algorithms require the evaluations of the determinants of small matrices, and testing the signs ($\pm$) of such determinants. Such testing is fundamental to algorithms for finding convex hulls, arrangements of lines and line segments and hyperplanes, Voronoi diagrams, and many others. By such numerical tests, a combinatorial structure is defined. If the tests are incorrect, the resulting structure may be wildly different from a "sensible" result[11, 6], and programs for computing the structures may crash.

Two basic approaches to this problem have been proposed: the use of exact arithmetic, and the design of algorithms to properly use inaccurate numerical tests. While the former solution is general, it can be quite slow: naively, n-tuple precision appears to be necessary for exact computation of the determinant of an $n \times n$ matrix with integer entries. While "adaptive" precision has been proposed and used[7], the resulting code and time complexity are still substantially larger than one might hope.

The second approach is the design (or redesign) of algorithms to use limited precision arithmetic and still guarantee sensible answers. (For example, [4, 2, 13, 6, 14, 12, 11, 9, 17].) Such an approach can be quite satisfactory, when obtainable, but seems applicable only on an *ad hoc* and limited basis: results for only a fairly restricted collection of algorithms are available so far.

This paper takes the approach of exact evaluation of the sign of the determinant, or more generally, the evaluation of the determinant with low relative error. However, the algorithm requires relatively low precision: less than $3n/2$ bits, and additionally some number more bits than were used to specify the matrix entries. The algorithm is naturally "adaptive," in the sense that the running time is proportional to the logarithm of the *orthogonality defect* $\mathcal{OD}(A)$ of the matrix A, where

$$\mathcal{OD}(A) \equiv \frac{\prod_{1\leq i\leq n} \|a_i\|}{|\det A|}.$$

Here a_i is the ith column of A. (Here $\|a_i\| \equiv \sqrt{a_i^2}$ is the Euclidean norm of a_i, with $a_i^2 \equiv a_i \cdot a_i$.) In geometric problems, the orthogonality defect may be small for most matrices, so such adaptivity should be a significant advantage in running time. Note that the limited precision required by the algorithm implies that "native" machine arithmetic can be used and still allow the input precision to be reasonably high. For example, the algorithm can handle 10×10 matrices with 32-bit entries in the 53 bits available in double precision on many modern machines.

The algorithm is amenable to "rank-one updates," so $\det B$ can be evaluated quickly (in about $O(n^2)$ time) after $\det A$ is evaluated, if B is the same as A in all but one column.

0-8186-2900-2/92 $3.00 © 1992 IEEE

One limitation of the approach here is that the matrix entries are required to be integers, rather than say rational numbers. This may entail preliminary scaling and rounding of input to a geometric algorithm; this limitation can be ameliorated by allowing input expressed in homogeneous coordinates, as noted by Fortune[1]. The resulting output is plainly the output for inputs that are "near" the originals, so such an algorithm is *stable* in Fortune's sense.[2]

The new algorithm uses ideas from Lovász's basis reduction scheme [8, 10, 16], and can be viewed as a "low-rent" version of that algorithm: a result of both algorithms is a new matrix A', produced by elementary column operations, whose columns are roughly orthogonal. However, basis reduction does not allow a column of A to be replaced by an integer multiple of itself: the resulting set of matrix columns generates only a sublattice of the lattice generated by the columns of A. Since here only the determinant is needed, such a scaling of a column is acceptable since the scaling factor can be divided out of the determinant of the resulting matrix. Thus the problem solved here is easier than basis reduction, and the results are sharper with respect to running time and precision. The algorithm here yields a QR factorization of A, no matter what the condition of A, and so may be of interest in basis reduction, since Lovász's algorithm starts by finding such a factorization. In practice, that initial factorization is found as an approximation using floating-point arithmetic; if the matrix is ill-conditioned, the factorization procedure may fail.

Schnorr has given an algorithm for basis reduction requiring $O(n + \lg M)$ bits; his algorithm for this harder problem is more complicated, and his constants are not as sharp.[15]

2 The algorithm

The algorithm is an adaptation of the modified Gram-Schmidt procedure for computing an orthogonal basis for the linear subspace spanned by a set of vectors. The input is the matrix $A = [a_1\ a_2 \ldots a_n]$ with the column n-vectors a_i, $i = 1 \ldots n$. One version of the modified Gram-Schmidt procedure is shown in Figure 1. We use the operation a/b for two vectors a and b, with $a/b \equiv (a \cdot b)/b^2$, and $b^2 \equiv b \cdot b$. Note that $(a+b)/c = a/c + b/c$, and $(a - (a/c)c) \cdot c = 0$. Implemented in exact arithmetic, this procedure yields an orthogonal matrix $C = [c_1\ c_2 \ldots c_n]$, so $c_i \cdot c_j = 0$ for $i \neq j$, such that $a_k = c_k + \sum_{1 \leq j < k} R_{jk} c_j$, for some values $R_{jk} = a_k/c_j$. (In variance with some usage, in

```
matrix MGS(matrix A)
{
    for k := 1 upto n do
        c_k := a_k;
        for j := k − 1 downto 1 do c_k −= a_j(c_k/c_j);
    return C;
}
```

Figure 1: A version of the modified Gram-Schmidt procedure.

this paper orthogonal matrices have pairwise orthogonal columns: they need not have unit length. If they do, the matrix will be termed *orthonormal*.)

The vector c_k is initially a_k, and is then *reduced* by the c_j components of a_k: after step j of the inner loop, $c_k \cdot c_j = 0$. Note that even though a_j is used in the reduction, rather than c_j, the condition $c_k \cdot c_i = 0$ for $j < i < k$ is unchanged, since a_j has no c_i components for $i > j$.

Since $A = CR$ where R is unit upper triangular, $\det A = \det C$; since C is an orthogonal matrix, $|\det C| = \prod_{1 \leq j \leq n} \|c_j\|$, and it remains only to determine the sign of the determinant of a perfectly conditioned matrix.

When the same algorithm is used with floating-point arithmetic to find a matrix B approximating C, the algorithm may fail if at some stage k a column b_k of B is very small: the vector a_k is very nearly a linear combination of the vectors $\{a_1, \ldots, a_{k-1}\}$: it is close to the *linear span* of those vectors. Here the usual algorithm might simply halt and return the answer that the determinant is nearly zero. However, since b_k is small, we can multiply a_k by some large scaling factor s, reduce sa_k by its c_j components for $j < k$, and have a small resulting vector. Indeed, that vector will be small even if we reduce using rounded coefficients for a_j. With such integer coefficients, and using the columns a_j and exact arithmetic for the reduction steps, $\det A$ remains unchanged, except for being multiplied by the scaling factor s.

Thus the algorithm given here proceeds in n stages as in modified Gram-Schmidt, processing a_k at stage k. First the vector b_k is found, estimating the component of a_k orthogonal to the linear span of $\{a_1, \ldots, a_{k-1}\}$. A scaling factor s inversely proportional to $\|b_k\|$ is computed, and a_k is replaced by sa_k and then reduced using exact elementary column operations that approximate Gram-Schmidt reduction. The result is a new column $a_k = s\hat{c}_k + \sum_{1 \leq j < k} \alpha_j c_j$, where $\hat{c}_k$ is the old value of that vector, and the co-

```
float det_safe(matrix A)
{
   float denom := 1;
         S^b := 0;
   for k := 1 upto n do
      loop
         b_k := a_k;
         for j := k-1...1 b_k -= a_j(b_k/b_j);

         if a_k^2 <= 2b_k^2 then {S^b += b_k^2; exit_loop;}

         s := S^b/4(b_k^2 + 2δ_k a_k^2);
         s := min{s, (N/1.58^k - sqrt(S^b))^2/a_k^2};
         if s < 1/2 then s := 1 else s := ⌈sqrt(s)⌋;
         if s = 1 and a_k^2 <= 0.9S^b then s := 2;

         denom *= s;
         a_k *= s;
         for j := k-1...1 a_k -= a_j⌈(a_k/b_j)⌋;
         if a_k = 0 then return 0;
      end_loop;
   return det_approx(B)/denom;
}
```

Figure 2: An algorithm for estimating det A with small relative error.

efficients $\alpha_j \approx 1/2$. Hence the new a_k is "more orthogonal" to earlier vectors than the old one. The processing of a_k repeats until a_k is nearly orthogonal to the previous vectors $a_1, \ldots, a_{k-1}$, as indicated by the condition $a_k^2 \leq 2b_k^2$.

The algorithm is shown in Figure 2. All arithmetic is approximate, with unit roundoff $\mathbf{u}$, except the all-integer operations $a_k \mathrel{*}= s$ and the reduction steps for a_k (although a_k/b_j is computed approximately). The value N is no more than the largest representable integer. For a real number x, the integer $\lceil x \rceil$ is the least integer no smaller than x, and $\lceil x \rfloor$ is $\lceil x - 1/2 \rceil$.

The precision requirements of the algorithm can be reduced somewhat by "reorthogonalization," that is, simply applying the reduction step to b_k again after computing it, or just before exiting the loop for stage k. Hoffman discusses and analyzes this technique; his analysis can be sharpened in our situation.[5]

Note that the condition $a_k^2 \leq 2b_k^2$ may hold frequently or all the time; if the latter, the algorithm is very little more than Modified Gram-Schmidt, plus the procedure for finding the determinant of the very-well-conditioned matrix B.

3 Analysis

The analysis requires some elementary facts about the error in computing the dot product and Euclidean norm.

Lemma 3.1 *For n-vectors a and b and using arithmetic with roundoff* $\mathbf{u}$, $a \cdot b$ *can be estimated with error at most* $1.01n\mathbf{u}\|a\|\|b\|$, *for* $n\mathbf{u} \leq .01$. *The relative error in computing* a^2 *is therefore* $1.01n\mathbf{u}$, *under these conditions. The termination condition for stage j implies* $a_j^2 \leq 2b_j^2(1 + 2.03n\mathbf{u})$.

Proof. For a proof of the first statement, see [3], p. 35. The remaining statements are simple corollaries. □

We'll need a lemma that will help bound the error due to reductions using b_j, rather than c_j.

Lemma 3.2 *For vectors a, b, and c, let* $d \equiv b - c$, *and let* $\delta \equiv \|d\|/\|b\|$. *Then*

$$a/b - a/c \leq \|a\|\|d\|/\|c\|\|b\| = \delta\|a\|/\|c\|.$$

Note also $a/b \leq \|a\|/\|b\|$.

Proof. The Cauchy-Schwartz inequality implies the second statement, and also implies

$$a/b - a/c \leq \|a\|\|b/b^2 - c/c^2\|.$$

Using elementary manipulations

$$\frac{b}{b^2} - \frac{c}{c^2} = \frac{(dc^2 - cd \cdot c) - c(d \cdot c + d^2)}{c^2b^2}.$$

The two terms in the numerator are orthogonal, so the norm of this vector is

$$\frac{\sqrt{(dc^2 - cd \cdot c)^2 + c^2(d \cdot c + d^2)^2}}{c^2b^2} = \frac{\sqrt{c^2d^2b^2}}{c^2b^2} = \delta/\|c\|,$$

as desired. □

Lemma 3.3 *For vectors a, b and c, and d, and δ as in the previous lemma, suppose* $a^2 \leq 2b^2(1+\alpha)$, $a/c = 1$, *and* $\alpha < 1$. *Then* $\|a - b\|/\|b\| \leq 1 + 4\delta + \alpha$.

Proof. We have

$$\frac{(a-b)^2}{b^2} = \frac{a^2 - 2a \cdot b + b^2}{b^2} \leq 3 + 2\alpha - 2a \cdot b/b^2,$$

using $a^2 \leq 2b^2(1 + \alpha)$. By the assumption $a/c = 1$,

$$\frac{a \cdot b}{b^2} = \frac{a \cdot (c+d)}{b^2} = \frac{c^2 + a \cdot d}{b^2} \geq (1-\delta)^2 - \sqrt{2(1+\alpha)},$$

where the last inequality follows using the triangle and Cauchy-Schwartz inequalities and the assumption $a^2 \leq 2b^2(1+\alpha)$. Hence

$$\frac{(a-b)^2}{b^2} \leq 3+2\alpha-2((1-\delta)^2-\sqrt{2(1+\alpha)}\delta) \leq 1+2\alpha+8\delta,$$

giving $||a-b||/||b|| \leq 1+4\delta+\alpha$, as claimed. □

Notation 3.4 *Let*

$$\eta \equiv 3(n+2)\mathbf{u},$$

and for $j = 1 \ldots n$, *let*

$$\delta_j \equiv L_j\eta - \eta,$$

where

$$L_j^2 \equiv j\mu^2(\mu^2+2.04)^{j-1},$$

and

$$\mu \equiv 1.58.$$

Let

$$\phi \equiv 1+2.04/\mu^2.$$

Let

$$d_k \equiv b_k - c_k$$

for $k = 1 \ldots n$.

Theorem 3.5 *Suppose the reductions for* b_k *are performed using rounded arithmetic with unit roundoff* $\mathbf{u}$. *Assume that* $(n+2)\mathbf{u} < .01$ *and* $\delta_n < 1/32$. *(For the latter,* $\lg(1/\mathbf{u}) \geq 1.1n + 2\lg n + 7$ *suffices.) Then:*

(i) $||b_k - a_j(b_k/b_j)|| \leq 1.54||b_k||$.

(ii) *The computed value of a single reduction step for* b_k, *or* $b_k - (b_k/b_j)a_j$, *differs from the exact value by a vector of norm no more than* $\eta||b_k||$. *Before a reduction of* b_k *by* a_j, $||b_k|| \leq ||a_k||\mu^{k-1-j}$.

(ii) *After the reduction loop for* b_k, d_k *satisfies*

$$||d_k|| \leq \delta_k||a_k||/\sqrt{2},$$

and after stage k, $||d_k|| \leq \delta_k||b_k||$.

Proof. First, part (i): let

$$a_j' \equiv (a_j - b_j) - ((a_j - b_j)/b_j)b_j,$$

which is orthogonal to b_j, and express $b_k - a_j(b_k/b_j)$ as

$$\begin{aligned} &b_k - (b_k/b_j)b_j \\ &- (b_k/b_j)a_j' \\ &- (b_k/b_j)((a_j - b_j)/b_j)b_j. \end{aligned}$$

Since $b_k^2 = \alpha^2 + \beta^2 b_j^2 + \gamma^2(a_j')^2$, for some α, $\beta = b_k/b_j$, and $\gamma = b_k/a_j'$, we have

$$(b_k - (b_k/b_j)(b_j + a_j'))^2 = \alpha^2 + (\gamma-\beta)^2(a_j')^2,$$

and so

$$(b_k - (b_k/b_j)(b_j + a_j'))^2/b_k^2 \leq (\gamma-\beta)^2/(\beta^2 b_j^2/(a_j')^2+\gamma^2),$$

which has a maximum value

$$1+(a_j')^2/b_j^2 \leq 2+4\delta_j+2.03n\mathbf{u},$$

and so

$$||b_k - (b_k/b_j)(b_j + a_j')|| \leq 1.47||b_k||. \qquad (1)$$

Using part (ii) inductively and Lemmas 3.3 and 3.1, and the assumption $\delta_j \leq 1/32$,

$$\begin{aligned} &||(b_k/b_j)((a_j - b_j)/b_j)b_j|| \\ &\leq \frac{||b_k||}{b_j^2}(a_j - c_j - d_j)\cdot(c_j + d_j) \\ &= \frac{||b_k||}{b_j^2}(-c_j \cdot d_j + d_j \cdot (a_j - b_j)) \\ &\leq ||b_k||(\delta_j(1+\delta_j) + \delta_j(1+4\delta_j+2.03n\mathbf{u})) \\ &\leq ||b_k||\delta_j(2.15) \end{aligned}$$

Thus with (1),

$$||b_k - a_j(b_k/b_j)|| \leq (1.47 + 2.15/32)||b_k|| \leq 1.54||b_k||.$$

This completes part (i).

Now for part (ii). From Lemma 3.1 and Lemma 3.2, the error in computing $b_k/b_j = b_k \cdot b_j/b_j^2$ is at most

$$((1+\mathbf{u})(1+2.03n\mathbf{u})-1)||b_k||/||b_j||,$$

and $||a_j|| \leq \sqrt{2}(1+1.02n\mathbf{u})||b_j||$, and so the difference between $a_j(b_k \cdot b_j/b_j^2)$ and its computed value is a vector ϵ with norm no more than $||b_k||$ times

$$\sqrt{2}(1+1.02n\mathbf{u})((1+\mathbf{u})^2(1+2.03n\mathbf{u})-1) \qquad (2)$$
$$< 2.9002(n+1)\mathbf{u} \qquad (3)$$

A reduction step computes the nearest floating-point vector to $b_k - a_j(b_k/b_j)+\epsilon$. Hence the error is a vector $\epsilon + \epsilon'$, where

$$\begin{aligned} ||\epsilon'|| &\leq \mathbf{u}||b_k - a_j(b_k/b_j)+\epsilon|| \\ &\leq \mathbf{u}(||b_k - a_j(b_k/b_j)|| + ||\epsilon||). \end{aligned}$$

With this and (2), the computed value of b_k after the reduction step, differs from its real value by a vector that has norm no more than $||b_k||$ times

$$\begin{aligned} &2.9002(n+1)\mathbf{u}(1+\mathbf{u}) + 1.54\mathbf{u} \\ &< 3(n+2)\mathbf{u} \\ &= \eta. \end{aligned}$$

Using part (i), the norm of b_k after the reduction step is no more than $(1.54+\eta)\|b_k\| < \mu\|b_k\|$.

We turn to part (iii), using (ii) and inductively (iii) for $j < k$. (We have $d_1 = 0$ for the inductive basis.)

The vector b_k is initially a_k, which is c_k plus a vector in the linear span of $a_1 \ldots a_{k-1}$, which is the linear span of $c_1 \ldots c_{k-1}$. When b_k is reduced by a_j, it is replaced by a vector

$$b_k - (b_k/b_j)a_j + \epsilon_j, \tag{4}$$

where ϵ_j is the roundoff. Except for ϵ_j, the vector $b_k - c_k$ continues to be in the linear span of $\{c_1 \ldots c_{k-1}\}$. Hence $d_k \equiv b_k - c_k$ can be expressed as $e_k + \Upsilon$, where $e_k = \sum_{1\le j<k} \gamma_j c_j$, for some values γ_j, and Υ is no longer than the sum of the roundoff vectors, so

$$\|\Upsilon\| \le \eta\|a_k\|\mu^{k-1}/(\mu-1), \tag{5}$$

using part (ii). From the triangle inequality,

$$d_k^2 \le (\|e_k\| + \Upsilon)^2. \tag{6}$$

The quantity γ_j is

$$\begin{aligned}\frac{1}{c_j} &\cdot [b_k - (b_k/c_j)a_j + (b_k/c_j)a_j - (b_k/b_j)a_j] \\ &= b_k/c_j - b_k/b_j,\end{aligned}$$

where b_k is the value of that vector for the a_j reduction. (Note that except for roundoff, b_k/c_j does not change after the reduction by a_j.) By Lemma 3.2 and this part of Theorem 3.5 as applied to d_j,

$$|\gamma_j| \le \|b_k\|\delta_j/\|c_j\|, \tag{7}$$

Using part (ii) and (7),

$$\begin{aligned} e_k^2 &= \sum_{1\le j<k} \gamma_j^2 c_j^2 \\ &\le \sum_{1\le j<k} \delta_j^2 \mu^{2(k-1-j)} a_k^2. \end{aligned}$$

Using (5),(6), and $\delta_j < L_j\eta$,

$$\frac{d_k^2}{a_k^2} \le \mu^{2k}\frac{\eta^2}{\mu^2}\left(\frac{1}{\mu-1} + \sqrt{\sum_{1\le j<k} L_j^2/\mu^{2j}}\right)^2. \tag{8}$$

It suffices for part (iii) that

$$\delta_k \ge \mu^k\sqrt{2(1+\eta)}\frac{\eta}{\mu}\left(\frac{1}{\mu-1} + \sqrt{\sum_{1\le j<k} L_j^2/\mu^{2j}}\right),$$

where the $(1+\eta)$ term allows the statement

$$d_k^2 \le \delta_k^2 a_k^2/2(1+2.03n\mathbf{u}). \tag{9}$$

Letting $M_k = L_k/\mu^k$, we need

$$M_k \ge \frac{1}{\mu^k} + \frac{\sqrt{2(1+\eta)}}{\mu}\left(\frac{1}{\mu-1} + \sqrt{\sum_{1\le j<k} M_j^2}\right),$$

Since $L_1 = 1$ allows

$$\|d_1\| = 0 = \delta_1 = \eta - \eta,$$

$M_k = \sqrt{j(1+2(1+\eta)/\mu^2)^{k-1}}$, or $L_k^2 = k\mu^2(\mu^2 + 2.04)^{k-1}$ for $k > 1$, gives sufficiently large δ_k, using the facts

$$\sum_{1\le j<k} jx^{j-1} = \frac{kx^{k-1}}{x-1} - \frac{x^k-1}{(x-1)^2}$$

and

$$\sqrt{x-y} \le \sqrt{x} - y/2\sqrt{x}.$$

The last statement of part (iii) follows from the termination condition for stage k, which from Lemma 3.1 implies $a_k^2 \le 2b_k^2(1+2.03n\mathbf{u}) < 2b_k^2(1+\eta)$. □

Lemma 3.6 *With Notation 3.4 and the assumptions of Theorem 3.5, let $S_k^c \equiv \sum_{1\le j<k} c_j^2$ and S_k^b the computed value of $\sum_{1\le j<k} b_j^2$. Then*

$$|S_k^c - S_k^b|/S_c^k < 1/10.$$

Proof. With Theorem 3.5(iii), we have

$$b_j^2/c_j^2 \le 1/(1-\delta_j)^2,$$

implying

$$\sum_{1\le j<k} b_j^2/S_k^c \le 1/(1-\delta_j)^2.$$

Lemma 3.1 implies $S_k^b/\sum_{1\le j<k} b_j^2 \le 1 + 1.03(k+n)\mathbf{u}$, and so

$$\frac{S_k^b}{S_k^c} \le \frac{1+1.03(k+n)\mathbf{u}}{(1-\delta_j)^2},$$

implying $S_k^b - S_k^c < S_k^c/10$. A similar argument shows that $S_k^c - S_k^b < S_k^c/10$. □

For the remaining discussion we'll need even more notation:

Notation 3.7 *Let*

$$f_k \equiv a_k\%c_k \equiv a_k - (a_k/c_k)c_k,$$

so that $a_k = c_k + f_k$, c_k and f_k are perpendicular, and $a_k^2 = c_k^2 + f_k^2$. Suppose a reduction loop for a_k

is done. Let $\hat{a}_k$ denote a_k before scaling it by s, and let $\hat{c}_k$ and $\hat{f}_k$ denote the components c_k and f_k at that time. Let $a_k^{(j)}$ denote the vector a_k when reducing by a_j, so $a_k^{(k-1)}$ is a_k before the reduction loop, and $a_k^{(0)}$ is a_k after the reduction loop. We'll use z_{jk} to refer to a computed value of a_k/b_j.

Lemma 3.8 *With assumptions as in the previous theorem, before a reduction of a_k by a_j,*

$$\|a_k\| \leq s\|\hat{a}_k\|\mu^{k-1-j} + (3/4)\sum_{j<i<k} \|c_i\|\mu^{i-1-j}.$$

Proof. When reducing by a_j, $a_k = a_k^{(j)}$ is replaced by

$$a_k^{(j-1)} = a_k - z_{jk}a_j + \alpha a_j,$$

for some $|\alpha| \leq 1/2$. As in Theorem 3.5(ii), the norm of $a_k - z_{jk}a_j$ is no more than $\mu\|a_k\|$, so

$$\|a_k^{(j-1)}\| \leq \mu\|a_k^{(j)}\| + \|a_j\|/2.$$

Thus

$$\begin{aligned}\|a_k^{(j)}\| &\leq s\|\hat{a}_k\|\mu^{k-1-j} + \sum_{j<i<k} \|a_i\|\mu^{i-1-j}/2 \\ &\leq s\|\hat{a}_k\|\mu^{k-1-j} + (3/4)\sum_{j<i<k} \|c_i\|\mu^{i-1-j} \quad (10)\end{aligned}$$

where the last inequality follows from Lemma 3.1 and Theorem 3.5(ii). □

Lemma 3.9 *With the assumptions of Theorem 3.5, in a reduction loop for a_k,*

$$\hat{c}_k^2 \leq 0.55\hat{a}_k^2$$

and

$$\hat{f}_k^2 \geq 0.45\hat{a}_k^2.$$

Proof. Since the reduction loop is done, the conditional "$a_k^2 \leq 2b_k^2$" returned **false**. Therefore, using Theorem 3.5(iii) and reasoning as in Lemma 3.1,

$$\begin{aligned}\|\hat{a}_k\| &> \sqrt{2}\|b_k\|(1 - 2.03n\mathbf{u}) \\ &\geq \sqrt{2}(\|\hat{c}_k\| - \delta_k\|\hat{a}_k\|/\sqrt{2})(1 - 2.03n\mathbf{u}),\end{aligned}$$

which implies

$$\hat{c}_k^2 \leq 0.55\hat{a}_k^2, \quad (11)$$

using the assumption $\delta_k < 1/32$. The last statement of the lemma follows from $\hat{a}_k^2 = \hat{c}_k^2 + \hat{f}_k^2$. □

Theorem 3.10 *With assumptions as Theorem 3.5, after the reduction loop for a_k it satisfies*

$$a_k^2 \leq \max\{\hat{a}_k^2, 2.6S_k^c\}.$$

Also

$$S_k^c \leq M^2(3.3)^{k-2}.$$

The condition

$$\lg N \geq \lg M + 1.5n + 1$$

allows the algorithm to execute.

Proof. We begin by bounding the c_j components of a_k for $j < k$, and use these to bound $\|f_k\|$, after the reduction loop. Note that the c_j component of a_k remains fixed after the reduction of a_k by a_j. That is, using Notation 3.7,

$$a_k^{(0)}/c_j = a_k^{(j-1)}/c_j = (a_k^{(j)} - \lceil z_{jk} \rfloor a_j)/c_j.$$

Using $a_j/c_j = 1$, this implies

$$\begin{aligned}&\left|a_k^{(0)}/c_j\right| \\ &\leq \left|a_k^{(j)}/c_j - a_k^{(j)}/b_j\right| + \left|a_k^{(j)}/b_j - \lceil z_{jk} \rfloor\right| \\ &\leq \|a_k^{(j)}\|\delta_j/\|c_j\| + \left(1/2 + 2.2(n+1)\mathbf{u}\|a_k^{(j)}\|/\|c_j\|\right) \\ &< 1/2 + \|a_k^{(j)}\|(\delta_j + \eta)/\|c_j\|, \quad (12)\end{aligned}$$

where the next-to-last inequality follows from Theorem 3.5(iii) and from reasoning as for (2). Since

$$f_k^2 = \|a_k^{(0)}\|^2 - s^2\hat{c}_k^2 = \sum_{1\leq j<k} (a_k^{(0)}/c_j)^2 c_j^2,$$

and the triangle inequality implies $\|x + y\|^2 \leq (\|x\| + \|y\|)^2$, we have f_k^2 no more than

$$\begin{aligned}&\sum_{1\leq j<k} (\|c_j\|/2 + \|a_k^{(j)}\|(\delta_j + \eta))^2 \\ &\leq \left(\sqrt{S_k^c}/2 + \sqrt{\sum_{1\leq j<k} (\|a_k^{(j)}\|(\delta_j + \eta))^2}\right)^2. \quad (13)\end{aligned}$$

From the definition of δ_j and (10),

$$\begin{aligned}&\sum_{1\leq j<k} \|a_k^{(j)}\|^2(\delta_j + \eta)^2 \\ &\leq \eta^2 k \sum_{1\leq j<k} \left(s\|\hat{a}_k\|\mu^{k-j} + \frac{3}{4}\sum_{j<i<k} \|c_i\|\mu^{i-j}\right)^2 (\mu^2\phi)^j \\ &\leq \eta^2 k \left(\sqrt{\sum_{1\leq j<k} s^2\hat{a}_k^2\mu^{2k}\phi^j}\right.\end{aligned}$$

$$+\frac{3}{4}\sqrt{\sum_{1\le j<k}\Big(\sum_{j<i<k}\|c_i\|\mu^i\Big)^2\phi^j}\Bigg)^2$$

$$\le \delta_k^2(s\|\hat{a}_k\|\mu/\sqrt{2}+3\sqrt{S_k^c}/4)^2$$

With (13), f_k^2 is no more than

$$\left(\sqrt{S_k^c}/2+\delta_k(s\|\hat{a}_k\|\mu/\sqrt{2}+3\sqrt{S_k^c}/4)\right)^2$$

$$\le \left(\sqrt{S_k^c}(1/2+\delta_k)+1.2\delta_k s\|\hat{a}_k\|\right)^2. \quad (14)$$

If $s=1$, then using Lemma 3.9 and $\delta_k \le 1/32$,

$$\begin{aligned} a_k^2 = c_k^2+f_k^2 &\le 0.55\hat{a}_k^2+(\sqrt{S_k^c}(1/2+\delta_k)+1.2\delta_k\|\hat{a}_k\|)^2 \\ &\le 0.55\hat{a}_k^2+(0.54\sqrt{S_k^c}+1.2\|\hat{a}_k/32\|)^2 \\ &\le \max\{\hat{a}_k^2, S_k^c\}. \quad (15)\end{aligned}$$

If $s=2$ because the conditional "$s=1$ **and** $a_k^2 \le 0.9S^b$" returned **true**, then $\|\hat{a}_k\| \le 1.01\sqrt{S_k^c}$, and

$$\begin{aligned} a_k^2 &\le 4(0.55)\hat{a}_k^2+(\sqrt{S_k^c}(1/2+\delta_k)+2(1.2)\delta_k\|\hat{a}_k\|)^2 \quad (16)\\ &\le 2.6S_k^c. \quad (17)\end{aligned}$$

Now suppose $s>1$ and the conditional "$s=1$ **and** $a_k^2 \le 0.9S^b$" returned **false**. By Theorem 3.5(iii), $\hat{c}_k^2 \le b_k^2+2\delta_k\hat{a}_k^2$, so that when $\lceil\sqrt{s}\rfloor$ is evaluated it is no more than $\sqrt{S^b/4c_k^2}(1.03)+1/2$, where the 1.03 factor bounds the error in computing s. Thus

$$\begin{aligned} c_k^2 \le s^2\hat{c}_k^2 &\le (\sqrt{S^b/4}(1.03)+\|\hat{c}_k\|/2)^2 \\ &\le (0.55\sqrt{S_k^c}+\|\hat{c}_k\|/2)^2 \\ &\le (0.55\sqrt{S_k^c}+0.375\|\hat{a}_k\|)^2, \quad (18)\end{aligned}$$

using Lemma 3.9. When $\lceil\sqrt{s}\rfloor$ is evaluated, it is smaller than

$$1.03\sqrt{S^b/4\delta_k\hat{a}_k^2}+1/2,$$

and so

$$s\delta_k\|\hat{a}_k\| \le 0.55\sqrt{\delta_k S_k^c}+\delta_k\|\hat{a}_k\|/2.$$

With (14) and the assumption $\delta_k \le 1/32$,

$$\begin{aligned} f_k^2 &\le (\sqrt{S_k^c}(1/2+\delta_k)+0.55\sqrt{\delta_k S_k^c}+\delta_k\|\hat{a}_k\|/2)^2 \\ &\le (0.63\sqrt{S_k^c}+\delta_k\|\hat{a}_k\|/2)^2, \quad (19)\end{aligned}$$

and so with (18),

$$\begin{aligned} a_k^2 &= c_k^2+f_k^2 \\ &\le (0.55\sqrt{S_k^c}+0.375\|\hat{a}_k\|)^2+(0.63\sqrt{S_k^c}+\|\hat{a}_k\|/64)^2 \\ &\le \max\{\hat{a}_k^2, 1.4S_k^c\}. \quad (20)\end{aligned}$$

With (15), (16), and (20), we have $a_k^2 \le \max\{\hat{a}_k^2, 2.6S_k^c\}$. First we show that $c_k^2 \le \max\{\hat{c}_k^2, 2.2S_k^c\}$. It remains to bound S_k^c inductively. If $s=1$ then $c_k^2=\hat{c}_k^2$. If $s=2$ because the conditional "$s=1$ **and** $a_k^2 \le 0.9S^b$" returned **true**, then $c_k^2 \le 2.2S_k^c$. If $s>1$ and the conditional "$s=1$ **and** $a_k^2 \le 0.9S^b$" returned **false**, then with (18),

$$c_k^2 \le (0.55\sqrt{S_k^c}+\|\hat{c}_k\|/2)^2 \le \max\{\hat{c}_k^2, 2.2S_k^c\},$$

Let σ_k^c be an upper bound for S_k^c, so $\sigma_2^c = M^2$ suffices, and when stage k is finished, $\sigma_{k+1}^c = \sigma_k^c+2.2\sigma_k^c$ is large enough, so $\sigma_k^c=(3.2)^{k-2}M^2$ is an upper bound for S_k^c. □

Theorem 3.11 *Let β be the minimum of*

$$\lg(1/\mathbf{u})-1.1n-2\lg n-2$$

and

$$\lg N-\lg M-1.5n-1.$$

(The conditions of Theorems 3.5 and 3.10 are implied by $\beta>4$.) The algorithm requires $O(n^3)+O(n^2)\log\mathcal{OD}(A)/\beta$ time.

Proof. Clearly each iteration of the main loop requires $O(n^2)$ time. The idea is to show that for each stage k, the loop body is executed $O(1)$ times except for executions that reduce $\mathcal{OD}(A)$ by a large factor; such reductions may occur when a_k is multiplied by a large scale factor s, increasing $\det A$, or by reducing $\|a_k\|$ substantially when s is small.

We consider some cases, remembering that c_k^2 never decreases during stage k. The discussion below assumes that $S^b/4(b_k^2+2\delta_k a_k^2)$ evaluates to no more than $(N/1.58^k-\sqrt{S^b})^2/a_k^2$; if not, s is limited by the latter, and β is bounded to the second term in its definition.

$\mathbf{s>2, b_k^2 \ge \delta_k\hat{a}_k^2}$.

After two iterations with this condition, either $s\le 2$ or c_k^2 will be sufficiently large that $2b_k^2 \ge a_k^2$.

$\mathbf{s>2, b_k^2 \le \delta_k\hat{a}_k^2}$.

Here (19) and Lemma 3.9 show that

$$\|f_k\| \le 0.62\sqrt{S_k^c}+\delta_k\|\hat{a}_k\|/2,$$

and $s>2$ implies

$$\delta_k\|\hat{a}_k\|/2 \le \delta_k\sqrt{S^b/\delta_k}/\sqrt{4(2.5)2}/2 < 0.04\sqrt{S_k^c},$$

so $\|\hat{a}_k\| \le 0.66\sqrt{S_k^c}/\sqrt{.45} < \sqrt{S_k^c}$ during the second iteration under these conditions. Thus $s \ge 0.37/\sqrt{\delta_k}$ here for all but possibly the first iteration, while a_k^2 is bounded. Hence $\lg \mathcal{OD}(A)$ decreases by $0.5\lg(1/\delta_k)-2$ during these steps.

s $\leq$ **2**.

From (14) and Lemma 3.9,

$$\begin{aligned}||f_k|| &\leq (1/2+\delta_k)\sqrt{S_k^c} + 2.4\delta_k||\hat{f}_k||/\sqrt{.45} \\ &\leq 0.54\sqrt{S_k^c} + 4delta_k||\hat{f}_k||,\end{aligned}$$

so $y_k \equiv ||f_k||/0.54\sqrt{S_k^c}$ converges to $1/(1-4\delta_k)$.

Suppose $y_k \geq 1/(4\delta_k)^2/(1-4\delta_k)$; here $s=1$, and y_k decreases by a factor of $4\delta_k/(1-4\delta_k) \leq 4.6\delta_k$ at each reduction loop. Hence $||a_k||$ is reduced by a factor of $4.6\delta_k$, while $\det A$ remains the same. Hence $\lg \mathcal{OD}(A)$ decreases by at least $\lg(1/\delta_k)-2.3$.

Suppose $y_k < 1/(4\delta_k)^2/(1-4\delta_k)$; then in $O(1)$ (less than 7) reductions, $y_k \leq \sqrt{1.01}/(1-4\delta_k)$, so that

$$\begin{aligned}a_k^2 &\leq f_k^2/0.45 \\ &\leq 1.01(0.54)^2 S_k^c/(1-4\delta_k)^2/0.45 \\ &\leq 0.75 S_k^c,\end{aligned}$$

and so the conditional "$a_k^2 \leq 0.9S^{b}$" will return **true**. Thereafter $O(1)$ executions suffice before stage k completes, as c_k doubles in magnitude at each step. □

Here is one way to get the estimate *det_approx*(B): estimate the norms $||b_i||$, normalize each column of B to obtain a matrix $\overline{B}$ with columns $\overline{b}_j \equiv b_j/||b_j||$, for $j=1,\ldots,n$, and then return $\det \overline{B} \approx \pm 1$ times $\prod_{1\leq i\leq n} ||b_i||$. To suggest that $\det \overline{B}$ can be estimated using low-precision arithmetic, we show that indeed $|\det \overline{B}| \approx 1$ and that the condition number of $\overline{B}$ is small. In the proof, we use the matrix $\overline{C}$ whose columns are $\overline{c}_j \equiv c_j/||c_j||$, for $j=1,\ldots,n$. (Note that the truly orthonormal matrix $\overline{C}$ has $\det \overline{C} = 1$ and Euclidean condition number $\kappa_2(\overline{C}) = 1$.)

Theorem 3.12 *With assumptions as in Theorem 3.5, for any $x \in R^n$,*

$$\left| ||\overline{B}^T x||/||x|| - 1 \right| \leq 1.68\delta_n,$$

and so $|\det \overline{B}| \geq 1 - 2n\delta_n$, and $\overline{B}$ has condition number $\kappa_2(\overline{B}) \leq 1 + 3\delta_n$.

Proof. It's easy to show that for $x \in R^n$,

$$\left|\overline{b}_j \cdot x - \overline{c}_j \cdot x\right| \leq (\delta_j + \eta)||x||,$$

where the η on the right accounts for roundoff in computing $\overline{b}_j$ from b_j. Thus

$$\begin{aligned}(\overline{B}^T x - \overline{C}^T x)^2 &\leq x^2 \sum_{1\leq j\leq n} (\delta_j+\eta)^2 \\ &\leq x^2\eta^2 n \sum_{1\leq j\leq n} (\mu^2+2.04)^{j-1} \\ &\leq 2\delta_n^2 x^2.\end{aligned}$$

Since $||\overline{C}^T x|| = ||x||$,

$$\left| ||\overline{B}^T x||/||x|| - 1 \right| \leq \sqrt{2}\delta_n.$$

Recall that $\overline{B}^T$ and $\overline{B}$ have the same singular values.[3] Since the bound above holds for any x, the singular values σ_j of $\overline{B}$ satisfy $|\sigma_j - 1| \leq \delta_n$, for $j=1,\ldots,n$, and so

$$\kappa_2(\overline{B}) = \sigma_1/\sigma_n \leq \frac{1+\sqrt{2}\delta_n}{1-\sqrt{2}\delta_n} \leq 1 + 3\delta_n,$$

using $(1+x)/(1-x) = 1 + 2x/(1-x)$ and $1/(1-x)$ increasing in x. Since $|\det \overline{B}| = \sigma_1\sigma_2\cdots\sigma_n$, we have

$$|\det \overline{B}| \geq (1-\sqrt{2}\delta_n)^n \geq \exp(-1.5n\delta_n) \geq 1 - 1.5n\delta_n,$$

where we use $1 - x \geq \exp(-x\frac{\log(1-\alpha)}{-\alpha})$ for $0 < x \leq \alpha < 1$. □

With these results, it is easy to show that Gaussian elimination with partial pivoting can be used to find $\det \overline{B}$, using for example the backwards error bound that the computed factors L and U have $LU = \overline{B} + \Delta$, where Δ is a matrix with norm no more than $n^2\sqrt{n}2^{n-1}||\overline{B}||\mathbf{u}$; this implies, as above, that the singular values, and hence the determinant, of LU are close to B.

Acknowledgements

It's a pleasure to thank Steve Fortune, John Hobby, Andrew Odlyzko, and Margaret Wright for many helpful discussions.

References

[1] S. Fortune. personal communication.

[2] S. Fortune. Stable maintenance of point-set triangulations in two dimensions. In *Proc. 30th IEEE Symp. on Foundations of Computer Science*, pages 494–499, 1989.

[3] G. H. Golub and C. F. Van Loan. *Matrix Computations*. Johns Hopkins University Press, Baltimore and London, 1989.

[4] D. Greene and F. Yao. Finite-resolution computational geometry. In *Proc. 27th IEEE Symp. on Foundations of Computer Science*, pages 143–152, 1986.

[5] W. Hoffman. Iterative algorithms for Gram-Schmidt orthogonalization. *Computing*, 41:335–348, 1989.

[6] C. Hoffmann, J. Hopcroft, and M. Karasick. Robust set operations on polyhedral solids. *IEEE Comp. Graph. Appl.*, 9:50–59, 1989.

[7] M. Karasick, D. Lieber, and L. Nackman. Efficient delaunay triangulation using rational arithmetic. *ACM Transactions on Graphics*, 10:71–91, 1990.

[8] A. K. Lenstra, H. W. Lenstra, and L. Lovász. Factoring polynomials with rational coefficients. *Math. Ann.*, 261:515–534, 1982.

[9] Z. Li and V. Milenkovic. Constructing strongly convex hulls using exact or rounded arithmetic. In *Proc. Sixth ACM Symp. on Comp. Geometry*, pages 235–243, 1990.

[10] L. Lovász. *An algorithmic theory of numbers, graphs, and complexity.* SIAM, Philadelphia, 1986.

[11] V. Milenkovic. Verifiable implementations of geometric algorithms using finite precision arithmetic. *Artificial Intelligence*, 37:377–401, 1988.

[12] V. Milenkovic. *Verifiable Implementations of Geometric Algorithms using Finite Precision Arithmetic.* PhD thesis, Carnegie Mellon U., 1988.

[13] V. Milenkovic. Double precision geometry: a general technique for calculating line and segment intersections using rounded arithmetic. In *Proc. 30th IEEE Symp. on Foundations of Computer Science*, pages 500–505, 1989.

[14] D. Salesin, J. Stolfi, and L. Guibas. Epsilon geometry: building robust algorithms from imprecise calculations. In *Proc. Seventh ACM Symp. on Comp. Geometry*, pages 208–217, 1989.

[15] C. P. Schnorr. A more efficient algorithm for lattice basis reduction. *J. Algorithms*, 9:47–62, 1988.

[16] A. Schrijver. *Theory of Linear and Integer Programming.* Wiley, New York, 1986.

[17] K. Sugihara and M. Iri. Geometric algorithms in finite-precision arithmetic. Technical Report RMI 88-10, U. of Tokyo, 1988.

On Minimum and Maximum Spanning Trees of Linearly Moving Points

Naoki Katoh* Takeshi Tokuyama† Kazuo Iwano‡

Abstract

In this paper, we shall investigate the upper bounds on the numbers of transitions of minimum and maximum spanning trees (MinST and MaxST for short) for linearly moving points. Suppose that we are given a set of n points in general d-dimensional space, $S = \{p_1, p_2, \ldots, p_n\}$, and that all points move along different straight lines at different but fixed speeds, i.e., the position of p_i is a linear function of a real parameter t. We shall investigate the numbers of transitions of MinST and MaxST when t increases from $-\infty$ to $+\infty$. We assume that the dimension d is a fixed constant. Since there are $O(n^2)$ distances among n points, there are naively $O(n^4)$ transitions of MinST and MaxST. We shall improve these trivial upper bounds for L_1 and L_∞ distance metrics.

Let $c_p(n, \min)$ (resp. $c_p(n, \max)$) be the number of maximum possible transitions of MinST (resp. MaxST) in L_p metric for n linearly moving points. We shall give the following results in this paper: $c_1(n, \min) = O(n^{5/2}\alpha(n))$, $c_\infty(n, \min) = O(n^{5/2}\alpha(n))$, $c_1(n, \max) = \Theta(n^2)$ and $c_\infty(n, \max) = \Theta(n^2)$ where $\alpha(n)$ is the inverse Ackermann's function. We shall also investigate two restricted cases, i.e., the c-oriented case in which there are only c distinct velocity vectors for moving n points, and the case in which only k points move.

*Department of Management Science, Kobe University of Commerce, Gakuen-Nishimachi 8-2-1, Nishi-ku, Kobe 651-21, Japan. E-mail: naoki@kucgw.kobeuc.ac.jp

†IBM Research Division, Tokyo Research Laboratory and Thomas J. Watson Research Center, P. O. Box 218, Yorktown Heights, NY, U.S.A. 10598. E-mail: tokuyama@watson.ibm.com

‡IBM Research Division, Tokyo Research Laboratory, IBM Japan, 5-11 Sanbancho, Chiyoda-ku, Tokyo 102, Japan. E-mail: iwano@trl.vnet.ibm.com

1 Introduction

Computational geometry problems for moving objects are theoretically interesting and have important applications in motion planning of robotics. The pioneering work in this field was done by Atallah [3], who gave nontrivial upper bounds on combinatorial transitions of several fundamental geometric structures such as convex hulls for moving points. Voronoi diagrams and Delaunay triangulations for moving points have recently been investigated by Imai and Imai [7], Fu and Lee [4], and Guibas et al. [5].

Although the two-dimensional minimum spanning tree (MinST) is a sub-graph of the Delaunay triangulation, it is not even clear that the number of transitions of MinST is smaller than that of Delaunay triangulation. Recently, Monma and Suri [11] have investigated the case where only one point is allowed to move in an arbitrary manner, and gave an $O(n^{2d})$ bound (especially a $\Theta(n^2)$ tight bound in Euclidean two-dimensional space) for transitions of MinST. This bound has been recently improved to $O(n^d \log^{c(d)} n)$ by Aronov et al [2], where a constant $c(d)$ depends on d. However, to the authors' knowledge, no one has ever succeeded in improving naive bounds on the numbers of combinatorial transitions of MinST and the maximum spanning tree (MaxST) when all points move linearly.

In this paper, we shall investigate the upper bounds

0-8186-2900-2/92 $3.00 © 1992 IEEE

on the numbers of transitions of MinST and MaxST for linearly moving points. Our paper is the first to give nontrivial upper bounds for these numbers.

Let us formulate the problem: Suppose that we are given a set of n points in general d-dimensional space, $S = \{p_1, p_2, \ldots, p_n\}$, and that all points move along different straight lines at different but fixed speeds, i.e., the position of p_i is a linear function of a real parameter t. We shall investigate the numbers of transitions of MinST and MaxST when t increases from $-\infty$ to $+\infty$. We assume that the dimension d is a fixed constant.

When t is fixed, MinST and MaxST are determined only by the relative order of edge lengths. This implies that MinST (resp. MaxST) changes only if the relative order of the lengths for some pair of edges changes.

Since there are $O(n^2)$ distances among n points, there are naively $O(n^4)$ transitions of MinST and MaxST. On the other hand, it is easy to construct an example that requires $\Omega(n^2)$ transitions for each of MinST and MaxST. Therefore, there is a rather big gap between lower and upper bounds of such transitions. Note that known bounds for the number of transitions of a planar Delaunay triangulation are $O(n^3)$ and $\Omega(n^2)$ [7, 5].

Let $c_p(n, \min)$ (resp. $c_p(n, \max)$) be the number of maximum possible transitions of MinST (resp. MaxST) in L_p metric for n linearly moving points. In this paper, we shall restrict ourselves to the cases of $p = 1$ and ∞ (except in Section 3), and give improved bounds for them as follows:

$$c_1(n, \min) = O(n^{5/2}\alpha(n)), \quad c_\infty(n, \min) = O(n^{5/2}\alpha(n)),$$

$$c_1(n, \max) = \Theta(n^2), \quad c_\infty(n, \max) = \Theta(n^2),$$

where $\alpha(n)$ is the inverse Ackermann's function and is very slowly growing [1, 12]. In particular, a $\Theta(n^2)$ tight bound for MaxST is attained.

We shall then consider two restricted cases. The first is the c-oriented case in which there are only c distinct velocity vectors for moving n points. The second is the case in which only k points move, while the other points remain in their original positions. We shall improve the above upper bounds for these cases.

L_1 and L_∞ metrics are referred to as linear metrics in the subsequent discussion. The common technique we use to derive our upper bounds is the generalization of the combinatorial results obtained by Gusfield [6], and Katoh and Ibaraki [8] for the number of transitions of the minimum (or maximum) weight base in a matroid in which the weights of all elements are linear functions of a single parameter t. Note that the minimum (or maximum) weight base in a matroid is an abstract notion of MinST and MaxST for general graphs.

Since the distance between two points is piecewise linear convex in t for linear metrics, we must generalize the result of [6, 8] to the piecewise linear convex case. For this purpose, we introduce a minimum (resp. maximum) weight base problem for matroids appropriately defined on certain multigraphs such that the weights of all elements are linear in t, and the transition of the minimum (resp. maximum) weight base occurs if the transition of MinST (resp. MaxST) for the original graphs occurs.

From this, we obtain $O(m^{3/2})$ and $O(m\sqrt{n})$ nontrivial upper bounds on the numbers of transitions of MinST and MaxST, respectively, for general graphs with n vertices and m edges in which each edge length is piecewise linear convex in a single parameter t with a constant number of breakpoints. As a direct consequence of these results, we have $c_1(n, \min) = O(n^3)$ and $c_1(n, \max) = O(n^{5/2})$. These bounds are further improved to those stated above through geometric insights into the structures of the problems. In particular, we use Yao's lemma [15], with which [15] developed efficient algorithms for the Euclidean MinST.

Finally we study the problem of finding the value of t at which the total length of MaxST is minimized. For linear and L_2 metrics, we give nearly-linear time algorithms for moving points in a plane, based on the parametric search technique developed by Megiddo [9].

2 Linear metric spanning trees of moving points

We shall derive the upper bounds on the number of transitions of MinST and MaxST in L_1 and L_∞ metrics. Since the results we obtain and the techniques we use are the same for both metrics and for any d-dimensional space, we shall concentrate only on L_1 metric case and on $d = 2$. Let $p_i(t) = (x_i(t), y_i(t))$ denote the position of point p_i at t, where $x_i(t)$ and $y_i(t)$ are linear functions of t. The L_1 distance between two points in the plane is a piecewise linear convex function in t with at most two breakpoints. Here t' is said to be a *breakpoint* of a piecewise linear function if the slope of the function changes at t'. The L_p distance between points p_i and p_j is denoted by $d_p(p_i, p_j)$. Since $d_p(p_i, p_j)$ is a function of t, it should be written as $d_p(p_i(t), p_j(t))$, but for convenience we shall omit the argument t unless there is a possibility of confusion.

2.1 Number of distinct MinST's and MaxST's with piecewise linear convex weight functions

First, we introduce a theorem on the minimum weight base of a linearly weighted matroid, previously presented by Gusfield [6], and Katoh and Ibaraki [8]. Let E be a finite set and $\mathcal{B}$ a family of subsets of E. The pair $(E, \mathcal{B})$ is called a *matroid* $M(E, \mathcal{B})$, and the elements of $\mathcal{B}$ are the *bases* of $M(E, \mathcal{B})$, if the following two axioms hold [13]:

(A1) For any $B, C \subset E$ with $B \neq C$, if $B \in \mathcal{B}$ and $C \subset B$, $C \notin \mathcal{B}$.

(A2) For any $B, B' \subset \mathcal{B}$ with $B \neq B'$ and for any $e \in B - B'$, there exists $e' \in B' - B$ such that $(B - \{e\}) \cup \{e'\} \in \mathcal{B}$.

For instance, let $\mathcal{T}$ be a set of spanning trees in an undirected connected graph $G = (V, E)$; then $(E, \mathcal{T})$ forms a matroid and $\mathcal{T}$ is a set of bases [13].

The number $|B|$ of elements of a base $B \in \mathcal{B}$ is independent of the choice of B [13], and is denoted by p. Let $m = |E|$, and assume the elements of E to be indexed from 1 through m. We assume that each element i has a real-valued weight $w_i(t) = a_i t + b_i$ that is linear in the parameter t. The minimum (resp. maximum) weight base is the one in which the sum of weights of elements is minimum (resp. maximum). It is known [13] that the minimum (resp. maximum) weight base changes only if the relative order of weights of some two elements i and j changes.

Since the weight functions of two elements have at most one intersection, we have an $O(m^2)$ trivial upper bound on the number of transitions of the minimum (resp. maximum) weight base of $M(E, \mathcal{B})$. This was improved by [6, 8], as will be shown in the following theorem. The outline of its proof is given in the appendix, because the technique used is useful for deriving the results in the restricted cases discussed in Section 2.4.

Theorem 2.1 ([6, 8]) *When all $w_i(t)$ are linear in t, the number of transitions is*

$$O(m \min\{\sqrt{p}, \sqrt{m-p}\}). \tag{1}$$

Next, let us apply the above theorem to analyze the number of transitions of MinST (and MaxST) of a graph with piecewise-linear convex weights.

The weight $w_i(t)$ of an edge i of a graph $G = (V, E)$ is a piecewise linear convex function of a parameter t. Let l_i denote the number of breakpoints of $w_i(t)$, and let

$$M = \sum_{i \in E} (l_i + 1). \tag{2}$$

When t increases from $-\infty$ to $+\infty$, we want to estimate the numbers N_{min} and N_{max} of transitions of MinST and MaxST of G. Notice that MinST (resp. MaxST) changes only if the relative order between the weights for a pair of edges changes. For each pair of edges i and j, the functions $w_i(t)$ and $w_j(t)$ have at most $l_i + l_j + 1$ intersections. Therefore, the trivial upper bound for both of N_{max} and N_{min} is $O(\sum_{i \neq j} l_i + l_j + 1) = O(Mm)$

In order to improve this bound, we construct a multigraph $G' = (V, E')$ from the original graph $G = (V, E)$ in such a way that the vertex set of G' is V, the weight of each edge of G' is linear in t, and the minimum (or maximum) weight base of an appropriate matroid defined on G' changes if (not necessarily only if) the topology of MinST (or MaxST) changes. Thus, apparently the number of transition of the matroid is at least the number of transition of MinST (or MaxST).

The convex function $w_i(t)$ can be thought of as the upper envelope of l_i+1 linear functions. Let such l_i+1 linear functions be

$$z_i^k(t) = a_i^k t + b_i^k, \quad k = 1, \ldots, l_i + 1. \tag{3}$$

The edge set E' consists of $l_i + 1$ multiple edges $e_i^1, e_i^2, \ldots, e_i^{l_i+1}$ connecting two endpoints for each edge i of G. The edge e_j^k has the linear weight $z_i^k(t)$ defined by (3). $|E'| = M$ holds from the definition of M. Fig. 1 illustrates an example of graph G and its corresponding multigraph G'. As illustrated in the left side of the figure, G has three vertices and three edges indexed from 1 through 3, and the weight of each edge is piecewise linear convex with one breakpoint. The corresponding multigraph G' has six edges with linear weights as illustrated in the figure.

Lemma 2.2 *(i) Let C be a subset of E' such that at most one edge among $\{e_i^1, e_i^2, \ldots, e_i^{l_i+1}\}$ does not belong to C for each i, and the set*

$$\{i \in E \mid \text{all edges } e_i^1, e_i^2, \ldots, e_i^{l_i+1} \text{ belong to } C\} \tag{4}$$

is a spanning tree in G. Let $\mathcal{C}$ be the set of all such C's. Then $(E', \mathcal{C})$ is a matroid.

(ii) Let $\mathcal{T}$ be the set of spanning trees of the multigraph G'. Then $(E', \mathcal{T})$ is a matroid.

Proof. Since (ii) is obvious, we prove only (i). Since any $C \in \mathcal{C}$ has $M - (m - n + 1)$ edges, the axiom (A1) holds. For the axiom (A2), let us consider $C, C' \in \mathcal{C}$ with $C \neq C'$. Choose an arbitrary $e_i^k \in C - C'$. Let T and T' be two spanning trees defined by (4) for C and C' respectively. The following two cases are possible.

Case 1: $i \notin T$. There exists some $e_i^{k'} \in C' - C$, because there are exactly l_i edges with subscript i in C from $i \notin T$, and at least l_i edges with subscript i in C' from the definition of $\mathcal{C}$. Thus $(C \cup e_i^{k'}) - e_i^k$ again belongs to $\mathcal{C}$.

Case 2: $i \in T$. Since $e_i^k \notin C'$, $i \notin T'$ follows. Thus, there exists a unique path on T' connecting both endpoints of i. Choose an edge j on the path such that $j \notin T$ (such an edge always exists). Then $(T \cup \{j\}) - \{i\}$ is again a spanning tree. Since there exists a unique edge $e_j^{k'}$ such that $e_j^{k'} \in C' - C$ from $j \in T' - T$, $(C \cup e_j^{k'}) - e_i^k$ again belongs to $\mathcal{C}$. □

Theorem 2.3 *For an undirected graph $G = (V, E)$ in which the edge weights are piecewise linear convex functions of a single parameter t, (i) there exist $O(M\sqrt{m})$ transitions of MinST, and (ii) there exist $O(M\sqrt{n})$ transitions of MaxST.*

Proof. (i) Consider the matroid in Lemma 2.2(i). Given an MinST, T, at a certain value t, the set C defined by

$$C = E' - \{e_i^{k'} | i \notin T, z_i^{k'}(t) = \max_{1 \le k \le l_i+1} z_i^k(t)\}$$

is a minimum weight base in the matroid as can be easily shown. Conversely, for a minimum weight base in the matroid at a certain t, the corresponding spanning tree defined by (4) is MinST for the same t. Therefore, if MinST changes, the corresponding minimum weight base in the matroid always changes. Thus, since every base in the matroid has $M - (m - n + 1)$ elements, the theorem follows from Theorem 2.1.

(ii) Consider the matroid defined in Lemma 2.2(ii). It is clear that if MaxST changes, the corresponding maximum weight base in the matroid always changes. Thus, since every base in the matroid has $n - 1$ elements, the theorem follows from Theorem 2.1. □

2.2 Number of transitions of MinST

Based on Theorem 2.3(i), the following theorem is immediate.

Theorem 2.4 $c_1(n, \min) = O(n^3)$.

Proof. Consider a complete graph $G = (S, S \times S)$, where S is the set of n points in the plane, and the length of an edge between two points is measured in L_1 metric. Since the L_1 distance between two points is a piecewise linear convex function in t with at most two breakpoints, we have $M = 3n(n-1)/2$ from (2). Thus, the theorem follows from Theorem 2.3(i). □

This bound is further improved by using the technique developed by Yao [15]. We shall first define an L_1-version of Yao's graph introduced by Yao [15]. For a given t and a given point p_i, we divide the plane into eight regions relative to p_i. The regions are formed by four lines passing through p_i and forming angles of 0°, 45°, 90°, 135°, respectively, with the x-axis. We number the regions counterclockwise, and use $R_l(p_i)$ to denote the set of points in the l-th region (including the boundary), for $1 \leq l \leq 8$. We then have the following lemma:

Lemma 2.5 **([15])** *If p_j and p_k are points in $R_l(p_i)$ for some l, then*
$d_1(p_j, p_k) \leq \max\{d_1(p_i, p_j), d_1(p_i, p_k)\}$. □

For each $R_l(p_i)$, let p_k be the one such that $d_1(p_i, p_k) = \min\{d_1(p_i, p_j) \mid j \neq i, p_j \in R_l(p_i)\}$. The point p_k is called the *nearest neighbor to p_i in $R_l(p_i)$*. An L_1-version of Yao's graph, $G = (S, E)$, is the one such that S is the set of n points in the plane, and $(p_i, p_j) \in E$ if and only if p_j is the nearest neighbor to p_i in $R_l(p_i)$ for some l with $1 \leq l \leq 8$. $G = (S, E)$ contains at most $8n$ edges.

Lemma 2.6 **([15])** *The edge set E of $G = (S, E)$ contains an MinST in L_1-metric.* □

Since $G = (S, E)$ depends on the parameter t, we shall write it as $G(t) = (V, E(t))$. How many times does $E(t)$ change as t inceases from $-\infty$ to $+\infty$? The lemma below follows from the theory of the upper envelope of line segments [14].

Lemma 2.7 *For each p_i and each l with $1 \leq l \leq 8$, the nearest neighbor to p_i in $R_l(p_i)$ changes $O(n\alpha(n))$ times when t moves from $-\infty$ to $+\infty$, where the function $\alpha(n)$ is the inverse Ackermann's function.*

Thus, we have the following lemma:

Lemma 2.8 *The edge set $E(t)$ of $G(t) = (V, E(t))$ changes $O(n^2\alpha(n))$ times.* □

Letting $t_1, t_2, \ldots, t_r$ with $t_1 < t_2 < \cdots < t_r$ be the sequence of t's at which $E(t)$ changes, $[-\infty, +\infty]$ is divided into $O(n\alpha(n))$ disjoint intervals $I_1, I_2, \ldots, I_{n\alpha(n)}$ so that each interval contains $O(n)$ t_k's. Now let us consider the interval I_k and define

$$E_k = \{(p_i, p_j) \mid (p_i, p_j) \in E(t) \text{ for some } t \in I_k\}. \quad (5)$$

Then $|E_k| = O(n)$ follows. Consider the graph $G_k = (S, E_k)$ in which the weight of each edge (p_i, p_j) is equal to $d_1(p_i(t), p_j(t))$. Note that MinST of $G_k = (S, E_k)$ changes at some $t \in I_k$ if and only if MinST for the same point set in the plane changes. From $|E_k| = O(n)$ and Theorem 2.3(i), the number of transitions of MinST of G_k over the interval I_k is $O(n^{3/2})$. Therefore, we have the following theorem:

Theorem 2.9 $c_1(n, \min) = O(n^{5/2}\alpha(n))$. □

The Euclidean (i.e., L_2) MinST is also contained in the edge set of Yao's graph (of L_2 norm). We can easily show that the number of transitions of Yao's graph is $\lambda_4(n) = \Theta(n^2 2^{\alpha(n)})$ for L_2 norm by using the result of [1], where $\lambda_4(n)$ is the maximum length of a Davenport-Schinzel sequence of order 4. Thus, by applying the argument similar to the one given after Lemma 2.8, we immediately obtain the following:

Proposition 2.10 $c_2(n, \min) = O(n^3 2^{\alpha(n)})$.

2.3 Number of transitions of MaxST

As a direct consequence of Theorem 2.3(ii), we get $c_1(n, \max) = O(n^{5/2})$ by the same argument as in the proof of Theorem 2.4. This upper bound is further improved to $O(n^2)$. We shall also prove that $c_1(n, \max) = \Omega(n^2)$. Thus we establish the tight bound $c_1(n, \max) = \Theta(n^2)$.

Theorem 2.11 $c_1(n, \max) = \Theta(n^2)$.

Proof. The $\Omega(n^2)$ lower bound is easily given, even in the one-dimensional case (the details are omitted in this version). We show the $O(n^2)$ upper bound for the planar case. It is not difficult to generalize it for any fixed-dimensional case. As shown by [10], MaxST contains the furthest neighbor graph (FNG). The L_1 hull of S is the set of points which maximizes one of the linear form $x+y$, $x-y$, $-x+y$, and $-x-y$. From the definition, the L_1 furthest neighbor of a point of S is located on the L_1 hull. It is easy to see that the number of transitions of the L_1 hull is $O(n)$, and that the number of transitions of the FNG is $O(n^2)$.

The FNG contains at most two connected components. Let l be the longest distance between the connected components. Then, l is the distance between a point in the L_1 hull of one component and a point in the L_1 hull of the other. MaxST of S is the union of the furthest neighbor graph and l. The number of transitions of the L_1 hull of each connected component is $O(n^2)$. Since at most four points are located on the L_1 hull if the points are in general position, the edge l is changed $O(1)$ times for a fixed topology of the L_1 hulls of components. Thus, we obtain the $O(n^2)$ upper bound. □

2.4 Restricted cases

We shall consider in this section two restricted cases: the c-oriented case and the case where only k points move. We are interested in the case where c and k are small compared with n. In order to deal with the c-oriented case, we shall first give the following lemma which is a counterpart of Theorem 2.1 for the c-oriented case.

Lemma 2.12 *Let $M(E, \mathcal{B})$ be a matroid with m elements in which the weight of each element is linear in t, and suppose that there are only c' distinct slopes among all weight functions. Then the number of changes of the minimum (resp. maximum) weight base is $O((c'mp)^{1/2}+c'p)$, where p denotes the number of elements in a base.*

Sketch of the Proof. We shall consider only the case of the minimum weight base. Let $1, 2, \ldots, m$ be the indices of elements of a matroid rearranged in nonincreasing order of their slopes of $w_i(t)$ (ties are broken in an arbitrary manner). Since there are c' distinct slopes, the sequence $1, 2, \ldots, m$ is divided into c' clusters, $C_1, C_2, \ldots, C_{c'}$, each of which contains elements with weights of the same slope. We use similar notations to those used in the proof of Theorem 2.1 (see Appendix). We shall use in the analysis the fact that, when B_k is transformed into B_{k+1} by an exchange $< i, j >$, i and j belong to different clusters. We can assume that each cluster size is at least $m/2c'$, because it is possible to add dummy elements.

As in the proof of Theorem 2.1, we shall consider the case where N becomes as large as possible. This occurs when the potential increase due to each change of the minimum weight base is as small as possible. Let s_k be the size of the cluster C_k. The i-th element of C_k is denoted by $f(i; l)$ and the $(s_k - j)$-th element of C_k is denoted by $l(j; k)$.

Then, for a small $h > 0$, an exchange that increases the potential by h is the form $< l(j,k), f(h-j+1, k+1) >$. Thus, there are at most $c'h$ such exchanges for $h \leq m/2c'$. Moreover, for $h' > h$, if $< l(j,k), f(h-j+1, k+1) >$ and $< l(j,k), f(h'-j+1, k+1) >$ both appear in the sequence, there must be an exchange $< f(i,k'), l(j,k) >$ for some k' with $k' \leq k-1$ and a suitable i. This exchange increases the potential by at least $s_k - j + 1$. We charge half of the cost of $< f(i,k'), l(j,k) >$ to $< l(j,k), f(h'-j+1, k+1) >$, call this new cost the amortized cost. Then, for $h \leq m/8c'$, the number of exchanges that increase the potential by not more than h (with respect to the amortized cost) is at most $c'h$. Following the same analysis as in the proof of Theorem 2.1, we have

$$N = O((c'mp)^{1/2} + c'p). \qquad \square \qquad (6)$$

Now the number of transitions of MinST in the c-oriented case can be analyzed in the same fashion as in Section 2.2. It is easy to show that the number of transitions of Yao's graph is $O(cn^2)$ for the c-oriented case. Thus we establish the following theorem from Lemma 2.12:

Theorem 2.13 *$c_1(n, \min) = O(c^3n^2)$ holds in the c-oriented case.* □

The above bound is tight for fixed c, since it is easy to show the $\Omega(n^2)$ lower bound for the 2-oriented case.

Now let us analyze the number of transitions of MaxST in the c-oriented case. Consider the complete graph $G = (S, S \times S)$ defined in the proof of Theorem 2.4, and the corresponding multigraph G' introduced in Section 2.1. It is easy to see that there are $O(c^2)$ distinct slopes among $O(n^2)$ edge weights. Thus, from Lemma 2.12, we have the following theorem:

Theorem 2.14 *$c_1(n, \max) = O(cn^{3/2})$ holds in the c-oriented case.* □

We shall now consider the case where there are only k moving points. Other points are called *fixed.* Let S' and S'' be the sets of k moving points and $n - k$ fixed points. Let MaxST(S'') (resp. MinST(S'')) be the MaxST (resp. MinST) for the point set S''. This does not change even if t changes, since the points in S'' are fixed. MaxST (resp. MinST) for any t is contained in the set of the union of MaxST(S'') (resp. MinST(S'')) and edges connecting the points in S' and $S(= S' \cup S'')$. There are $O(kn)$ edges in this set. Furthermore, since the situation can be regarded as the $(k + 1)$-oriented case, we have the following theorems from Lemma 2.12:

Theorem 2.15 *$c_1(n, \max) = O(k^2n)$ holds when only k points linearly move.* □

Theorem 2.16 *$c_1(n, \min) = O(k^3n)$ holds when only k points linearly move.* □

3 Finding the smallest MaxST

It is an interesting problem to find the value of t when the MaxST of linearly moving points satisfies some minimality condition. In this section, we give efficient algorithms for finding the value of t when the total edge length of MaxST becomes minimum.

Theorem 3.1 *We can find the value of t when the total edge length of MaxST becomes minimum in $O(n \log^2 n)$ time and $O(n \log^4 n)$ time for L_1 and L_2 metrics, respectively.*

Proof. First, note that the total length of a given spanning tree is a convex function in t. Thus, the total length of MaxST is also convex in t, since it is an upper envelope of convex functions each of which corresponds to the total length of a spanning tree. Therefore, the optimal value t^* can be found as the supremum of t such that the slope of the function representing the total length of MaxST at t is negative. Thus, for a given t, we can tell whether $t^* < t$, $t^* > t$, or $t^* = t$ in $O(n \log n)$ time by computing the MaxST at t by using the algorithm given by [10] (for L_2 metric). The time complexity can be reduced to $O(n)$ for the L_1 case.

Next, by directly parallelizing the algorithm of [10], we obtain an $O(\log n)$ time and an $O(n)$ processor algorithm to compute the L_1 MaxST, and an $O(\log^2 n)$ time and an $O(n)$ processor algorithm to compute the L_2 MaxST. We use $O(\log^2 n)$ time and $O(n/\log n)$ processor algorithm to compute the furthest Voronoi diagram.

From the above observations, it is now an easy exercise to apply Megiddo's parametric search [9] in order to obtain the results. □

Notice that these results are valid only for $d = 2$, since no parallel algorithm with the above running time is known for the general d-dimensional case.

4 Concluding remarks

We have investigated the upper bounds on the number of transitions of dynamic MinST and MaxST of points moving linearly in a fixed-dimensional space. For linear metrics, we have obtained a tight bound

$\Theta(n^2)$ for the MaxST case. On the other hand, for the MinST case, there is still a gap of $\sqrt{n}\alpha(n)$ factor between the lower and upper bounds. We conjecture that the bound for the MinST is also $\Theta(n^2)$.

It is important to investigate the problem for the Euclidean L_2 metric. So far, we have only been able to show an $O(n^3 2^{\alpha(n)})$ bound for MinST, and a trivial $O(n^4)$ bound for MaxST. However, we believe that these bounds will significantly be improved in future.

We also investigated the problem of finding the minimum length of MaxST for moving points, and proposed an efficient algorithm with $O(n \log^4 n)$ running time for L_2 metric. The MinST version of this problem is much important in practical applications. However, the total length of MinST is neither concave nor convex in t, and it is left for future research to design subquadratic algorithms for finding the value of t minimizing the total edge length of the dynamic MinST.

Acknowledgements

The authors would like to thank Prof. Hiroshi Imai for his helpful comments.

References

[1] P. Agarwal, M. Sharir, and P. Shor, Sharp Upper and Lower Bounds on the Length of General Davenport-Schinzel Sequences, *J. Combinatorial Thoery A*, Vol **52-2** (1989), 228-274.

[2] B. Aronov, *private communication*, 1992.

[3] M.J. Atallah, Some Dynamic Computational Geometry Problems, *Computers and Mathematics with Applications*, **11** (1985), 1171-1181.

[4] J.J. Fu and R.C.T. Lee, Voronoi Diagrams of Moving Points in the Plane, *International Journal of Computational Geometry and Applications*, Vol **1-1** (1991), 23-32.

[5] L. Guibas, J. Mitchell, and T. Roos, Voronoi Diagrams of Moving Points in the Plane, *Proc. 17-th International Workshop on Graph-Theoretic Concepts in Computer Science*, LNCS 570, 1991, 113-125.

[6] D. Gusfield. Bounds for the Parametric Spanning Tree Problem. *Proc. Humbolt Conf. on Graph Theory, Combinatorics and Computing.* Utilitas Mathematica, 1979, 173-183.

[7] H. Imai and K. Imai, Voronoi Diagrams of Moving Points, Proc. Int. Computer Symposium, Taiwan, 1990, 600-606.

[8] N. Katoh and T. Ibaraki, On the Total Number of Pivots Required for Certain Parametric Combinatorial Optimization Problems, Working Paper No. 71, Institute of Economic Research, Kobe Univ. of Commerce, 1983.

[9] N. Megiddo, Applying Parallel Computation Algorithms in the Design of Serial Algorithms, *J. ACM*, **30** (1983), 852-865.

[10] C. Monma, M. Paterson, S. Suri, and F. Yao, Computing Euclidean Maximum Spanning Trees, *Proc. 4th ACM Symposium on Computational Geometry* (1988), 241-251.

[11] C. Monma and S. Suri, Transitions in Geometric Minimum Spanning Trees, *Proc. 7th ACM Symposium on Computational Geometry* (1991), 239-249.

[12] R.E. Tarjan, *Data Structures and Network Algorithms,* volume 44 of *CBMS-NSF Regional Conference Series in Applied Mathematics,* Society for Industrial and Applied Mathematics, 1983.

[13] D.J.A. Welsh, *Matroid Theory*, Academic Press, London, 1976.

[14] A. Wiernik and M. Sharir, Planar Realization of Nonlinear Davenport-Schinzel Sequences by Seg-

ments, *Discrete Comput. Geometry*, **3** (1988), 15-47.

[15] A. C. Yao, On Constructing Minimum Spanning Trees in k-Dimensional Space and Related Problems, *SIAM J. Computing*, **11** (1982), 721-736.

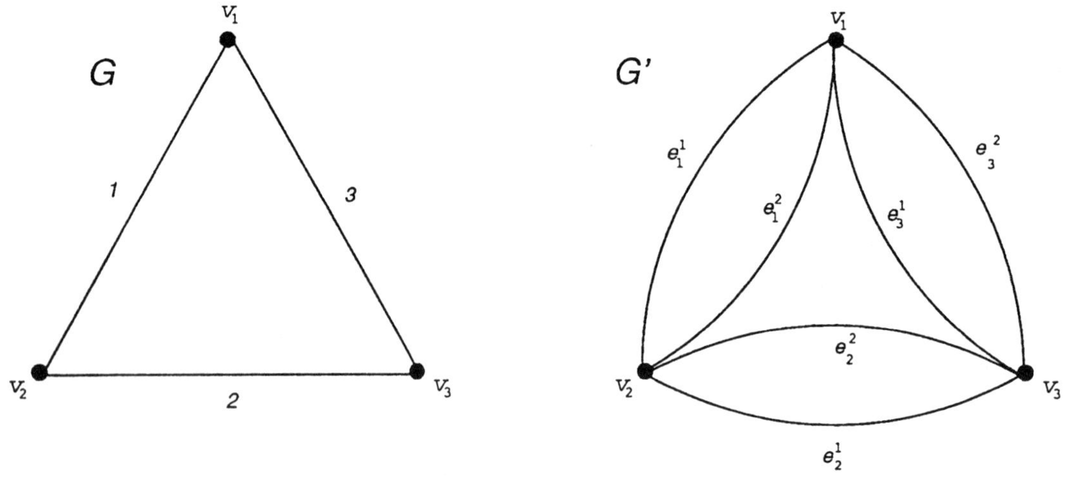

$$\begin{aligned} w_1(t) &= |t-1| \\ w_2(t) &= |2t-4| \\ w_3(t) &= |3t-5| \end{aligned} \qquad \begin{aligned} z_1^1(t) &= -t+1, & z_1^2(t) &= t-1 \\ z_2^1(t) &= -2t+4, & z_2^2(t) &= 2t-4 \\ z_3^1(t) &= -3t+5, & z_3^2(t) &= 3t-5 \end{aligned}$$

Figure 1. An example of graphs G and G'.

Appendix

We shall briefly give the proof of Theorem 2.1 which was originally given by [6] and [8].

The proof of Theorem 2.1. We shall consider only the case of the minimum weight base (the case of the maximum weight base can be treated in the same manner). For ease of exposition, we assume that all a_i's are distinct, where a_i's are coefficients of t in $w_i(t)$. We rearrange the indices 1 through m in decreasing order of a_i. Let

$$t_{ij} = \frac{b_j - b_i}{a_i - a_j},$$

which is the value of t at which the relative order of the weights of two elements i and j changes. We further assume for simplicity that all t_{ij}'s are distinct. This assumption implies that when the minimum weight base changes at t from B to B', B is transformed into B' by a single exchange, i.e., $B' = B \cup \{i\} - \{j\}$. We shall represent a base B by an m-dimensional 0-1 vector, such that the i-th element in the vector, denoted x_i, is equal to 1 if $i \in B$, and is equal to 0 otherwise. Let us define the potential of B as

$$\pi(B) = \sum_{i=1}^{m} i x_i. \tag{7}$$

Let $B_1, B_2, \ldots, B_N$ denote the minimum weight bases generated by increasing t from $-\infty$ to $+\infty$. As k increases, $\pi(B_k)$ increases. When the minimum weight base changes from B_k to B_{k+1} at t_k, it follows from the above assumption that there exist $i, j \in E$ such that $i \in B_k - B_{k+1}$, $j \in B_{k+1} - B_k$, and $B_{k+1} = (B_k \cup \{j\}) - \{i\}$. In this case, we say that B_k is transformed nto B_{k+1} by an exchange $< i, j >$. It is clear that $t_k = t_{ij}$ and $a_i > a_j$ hold, and that the change from B_k to B_{k+1} increases the potential by $j - i$. The distance of exchange $< i, j >$ is defined as $j - i$.

For any i and j with $i < j$, there exists at most one k such that B_k is transformed into B_{k+1} by an exchange $< i, j >$. Therefore, there exist at most $m - l$ k's such that the change from B_k to B_{k+1} increases the potential by l. The following inequality is clear.

$$\pi(B_N) - \pi(B_1) \leq (p-1)(m-p+1). \tag{8}$$

Therefore, the case where N becomes as large as possible, happens when the potential increase due to each change from B_k to B_{k+1} is as small as possible. More precisely, this case happens when there exist $m - 1$ exchanges with distance one, and there exist $m - 2$ exchanges with distance two and so on. From (8), the upper bound of N is obtained by first (i) computing the minimum $q = q^*$ that satisfies

$$\sum_{l=1}^{q} l(m-l) \geq (p-1)(m-p+1), \tag{9}$$

and then (ii) computing

$$\sum_{l=1}^{q^*} (m-l). \tag{10}$$

It is easy to see that $q^* = O(\min\{\sqrt{p}, \sqrt{m-p}\})$. Therefore, the term in (10) becomes $O(m \min\{\sqrt{p}, \sqrt{m-p}\})$.

Towards a Computational Theory of Statistical Tests (Extended Abstract)

Manuel Blum*
EECS Department - CS Div.
University of California
Berkeley, CA 94720, USA

Oded Goldreich†
Computer Science Department
Technion
Haifa, Israel.

Abstract

We initiate a computational theory of statistical tests. Loosely speaking, we say that an algorithm is a *statistical test* if it rejects a "negligible" fraction of strings. We say that a statistical test is *universal* for a class of algorithms if it rejects all (but finitely many) of the strings rejected by each algorithm in the class.

We consider the existence and efficiency of universal statistical tests for various classes of statistical tests. We also consider the relation between ensembles passing statistical tests of particular complexity and ensembles which are indistinguishable from uniform by algorithms of the same complexity.

Some of our results refer to relatively simple statistical tests (e.g., those implemented by counter machines). In addition to their own merit, we hope that these results will stimulate investigations directed towards results that refer to more complex statistical tests (e.g., those implemented in log-space).

1 Introduction

In the first edition of Vol. 2, Knuth lists 8 empirical statistical tests. In the second edition, 11 tests are listed. There is no apparent rhyme or reason to the test selection, and future editions may well have even more tests. A comment, at the end of Section 3.3.2 in [11], asserts that at least some of the given statistical tests are "independent of the others" in the sense that there exists a sequence that passes all but the one test. Knuth offers no clues to a theory which may govern one's decision of which test one should use.

*Research was supported in part by NSF grant No. CCR88-13632.

†Research was supported in part by grant No. 89-00312 from the United States - Israel Binational Science Foundation (BSF), Jerusalem, Israel.

It would be desirable to have *one* "universal" statistical test with the following property. If a sequence fails *any* "reasonable" statistical test, be it a test in the 1st edition, 2nd edition, or any future edition of Knuth, then the sequence will fail the universal test. The question, of course, is what is a "reasonable" statistical test.

In this work we suggest to develop a theory of statistical tests based on the computational complexity of the tests (as algorithms).

1.1 Motivation

Statistical tests are the focus of considerable attention in many scientific disciplines. The need for statistical tests arises in a context where "randomness" is required (e.g., sampling procedures, randomized algorithms, randomized constructions). In such a context, "randomness" is supplied by a *random source* and statistical tests are used to check whether the source is "good". Why should one check the source? There are several reasons and they all boil down to the possibility that the source is faulty (and the need to detect such faults). For further discussion see our technical report [1].

What is needed is a test guaranteeing that if the source output passes the test then it (i.e., the source output) can be safely used in our application. Furthermore, it would be useful to have a single fast test which accepts only bit sequences which can be safely used in any application belonging to some general "class" (of applications). Of particular interest is the class of all efficient (i.e., polynomial-time) algorithms, and the "simpler" subclass containing only log-space algorithms.

1.2 Statistical tests

Loosely speaking, a statistical test is an algorithm that accepts all but a negligible fraction of the strings. To convert this intuitive notion into a definition we need to say what is a negligible fraction. Following are three popular alternatives. A function $\mu(\cdot)$ is called *negligible* if

0-8186-2900-2/92 $3.00 © 1992 IEEE

N1) μ is smaller than any constant (i.e., for every constant $\epsilon > 0$ and all sufficiently large n it holds that $\mu(n) < \epsilon$). This interpretation is popular in statistics and other "classic" investigations.

N2) μ is smaller than any polynomial fraction (i.e., for every positive polynomial $p(\cdot)$ and all sufficiently large n it holds that $\mu(n) < \frac{1}{p(n)}$). This interpretation seems most adequate in the context of efficient computation (specifically in the context of either polynomial-time or log-space algorithms).

N3) μ is exponentially decreasing (i.e., there exists $\epsilon > 0$ so that for all sufficiently large n it holds that $\mu(n) < 2^{-\epsilon n}$). This interpretation is popular in some investigations in information theory and specifically in the area of classification theory.

The results of this paper are presented with respect to alternative (N2). Some results apply also for *some* other definitions of negligence, and in particular the other alternatives presented above. Yet *not all* results hold with respect to *all* alternatives. Remarks concerning this issue are scattered throughout the paper.

1.3 Specific classes of statistical tests

We believe that two classes of statistical tests are of special interest. The class of (deterministic) polynomial-time statistical tests, and the class of log-space statistical tests. The importance of the first class is self-evident in light of the acceptable association of efficient procedures with polynomial-time algorithms. The interest in the second class is motivated by two facts. First, many applications in which randomness is used can be modelled by log-space machines. Secondly, all the "statistical tests" used in practice, and in particular all the tests mentioned by Knuth can be implemented by log-space machines.

Many of the results in this paper relate to two subclasses of the class of log-space statistical tests: the class of finite state machines, and the class of counter machines. The investigation of these classes may be considered a first step in an attempt to understand the class of log-space statistical tests. In addition, these classes are of some interest for their own right as they contain natural variants of all the tests mentioned by Knuth. We remark that the empirical tests presented by Knuth are not fully specified in the sense that the choice of the threshold (determining whether to reject or accept a sequence) is left open. Typically, setting the threshold to be a constant causes these tests to reject a constant fraction of the sequences, whereas setting the threshold to be linear (in the length of the sequence) causes these tests to reject an exponentially small fraction of the sequences as well as to be implemented by counter machines (see below).

1.4 Universal statistical tests

Loosely speaking, a statistical test is called *universal* for a particular class of statistical tests if it accepts only bit sequences which are accepted by all tests in the class. Universal tests promise to be very useful in practice, since they provide a way of replacing an infinite class of tests by a single test. The question, of course, is whether universal statistical tests exists with respect to interesting classes of tests, and furthermore whether such universal tests can be reasonably efficient.

We shall see in the sequel that one must allow such a universal test to use (slightly) more "resources" than any test in the class. In particular, no reasonable class of statistical tests, may contain a statistical test which is universal for the class. Furthermore, for sufficiently powerful classes (e.g., any class containing all on-line log-space tests), there must exist a gap between the rejection rate of the tests in the class and the rejection rate of any recursive statistical test that is universal for the class. We believe that it suffices to make the universal test slightly more "powerful" only in these two respects (i.e., higher computational complexity and higher rejection rate). For example, we present a quasi-polynomial-time universal test for the class of on-line logspace machines with exponentially decreasing rejection rate.

The universal test just mentioned (i.e., for the class of logspace tests) is neither "natural" nor "practical". We believe that presenting such a universal test is an important research goal.

> The Lempel-Ziv algorithm [12] may seem as a plausible candidate. Unfortunately, this algorithm is not universal for the class of log-space machines (since it accepts any de-Bruijn sequence [12, Thm. 5], whereas there exists de-Bruijn sequences that can be constructed and thus recognized and rejected by a log-space machine [5]). Yet, this example should at least give an idea of what is wanted.

We believe that the ability to present reasonable universal tests for a class of statistical tests is linked to a good understanding of the structure of the tests in the class. We were able to characterize the statistical tests and present reasonable universal tests for the class of finite state machines and for the class of counter machines. We remark that the Lempel-Ziv algorithm [12] can be shown to be universal for the class of finite state tests (under alternatives (N1) and (N2)), and for the class of weak counter machines (under alternative (N2)). (The first statement is obvious whereas the second statement follows from the characterization of statistical tests which are weak counter machines.) However, the universal tests we present for these classes are much simpler.

1.5 Pseudorandomness and passing statistical tests

The ability of a probability ensemble to pass, with high probability, statistical tests of some complexity is even more useful in case such ability can be linked to pseudorandom properties of the ensemble. Loosely speaking, an ensemble is called pseudorandom with respect to some complexity class if no algorithm in the class can distinguish this ensemble from the uniform one. We stress that the distinguishing algorithm need not be a statistical test (e.g., it may reject half of the strings of each length).

We consider the relation between the set of probability ensembles that are accepted by statistical tests of a particular complexity class and the set of ensembles which are pseudorandom with respect to arbitrary algorithms (not necessarily statistical tests) with the same complexity. When putting no restrictions on the "algorithms" (i.e., allowing any function to be considered), there is a simple relation between these sets. We ask whether the same relation remains valid when restricting the class of algorithms. A positive result is presented for the class of constant-space on-line (i.e., finite state) machines, whereas a negative result is presented for the class of log-space on-line machines. Hence, much remains to be understood.

1.6 Organization

General definitions and observations are presented in sections 2 and 3, respectively. The other sections are devoted to specific classes of statistical tests. Section 4 deals with finite state machines, section 5 with (weak) counter machines, section 6 with (on-line) log-space machines, and section 7 with (probabilistic) polynomial-time machines.

Due to space limitations, this extended abstract does not contain full proofs to any of its claims. In some cases only a sketch of the proof is given and in some cases only key ideas are given. More details can be found in our technical report [1].

2 Definitions

We start with the following standard conventions. By *negligible* we call any function $\mu : \mathbb{N} \mapsto \mathbb{N}$ which satisfies, for every constant c and all sufficiently large n,

$$\mu(n) < \frac{1}{n^c}$$

By *non-negligible* we call any function $\mu : \mathbb{N} \mapsto \mathbb{N}$ which satisfies, for some constant c and all sufficiently large n,

$$\mu(n) > \frac{1}{n^c}$$

(Note that a function may be neither negligible nor non-negligible, as the notion of non-negligible is a "strong negation" of the notion of negligible.)

Remark 1 : The definition of negligence plays a pivotal role in the definition of a statistical test and in the definition of pseudorandomness. The above definition of negligence is particularly justified for the polynomial-time and/or logspace statistical tests and pseudorandomness. Nevertheless, the theory can be developed using different notions of negligence. Most of the results presented in this work hold also for other natural definitions of negligence. Yet, some of the results (specifically, those concerning counter machines) are very sensitive to the definition of negligence.

Notational Conventions: By X_n, Y_n, Z_n we denote random variables ranging over $\{0,1\}^n$. By U_n we denote the random variable uniformly distributed over $\{0,1\}^n$. An *ensemble* is a sequence of random variables $\{X_n\}_{n\in\mathbb{N}}$, such that X_n ranges over $\{0,1\}^n$.

2.1 Statistical Tests

Definition 1 (decision on individual strings): *Let A be a (probabilistic) algorithm.*

- *We say that A* accepts string *α (denoted $\overline{A}(\alpha) = \mathrm{ACC}$) if*

$$\mathrm{Prob}(A(\alpha){=}1) \geq \frac{2}{3}$$

where the probability is taken over A's internal coin tosses.

- *We say that A* rejects string *α (denoted $\overline{A}(\alpha) = \mathrm{REJ}$) if*

$$\mathrm{Prob}(A(\alpha){=}1) \leq \frac{1}{3}$$

- *In case $\frac{1}{3} < \mathrm{Prob}(A(\alpha) = 1) < \frac{2}{3}$ we say that A is* undecided *about α.*

Deterministic algorithms are never undecided (i.e. they either accept or reject each string). Also, algorithms which recognize some language with error probability which is bounded-away from one half (by some $\epsilon > 0$), can be easily modified into algorithms which are never undecided[1]. In general, it may be hard to get rid of the fact that a probabilistic algorithm is undecided on some strings without trivializing the algorithm (i.e., making it accept languages in an appropriate deterministic complexity class).

A statistical test is an algorithm which accepts all but a negligible fraction of the strings of a particular length.

[1] The latter run the original algorithm $O(1/\epsilon)$ times, and take a majority vote.

Definition 2 (statistical test): *We say that algorithm A is a* statistical test *if the function* $r(n) \stackrel{\text{def}}{=} \text{Prob}(\overline{A}(U_n) \neq \text{ACC})$ *is negligible. (Here the probability is taken over the probability space of U_n.)*

Definition 3 (acceptance/rejection of ensembles):

- *We say that an ensemble* $\{X_n\}_{n\in\mathbb{N}}$ is accepted by a statistical test T *if* $\text{Prob}(\overline{T}(X_n)\neq\text{ACC})$ *is negligible.*
- *We say that an ensemble* $\{X_n\}_{n\in\mathbb{N}}$ is rejected by a statistical test T *if* $\text{Prob}(\overline{T}(X_n)\neq\text{REJ})$ *is negligible.*

Clearly, the uniform ensemble $\{U_n\}_{n\in\mathbb{N}}$ is accepted by all statistical tests. Of course, statistical tests may neither accept nor reject specific ensembles.

A statistical test is called universal *for some class* of statistical tests if it rejects all but a finite number of the strings rejected by each test in the class. The universal test need not be itself a member of the class (and in fact no "reasonable" class has a universal test residing inside the class).

Definition 4 (universal statistical test): *A statistical test, A, is called* universal *for a class of statistical tests $\mathcal{T}$ if for every test T in $\mathcal{T}$ and all sufficiently long α, if T rejects α then so does A (i.e., the set* $\{\alpha : (\overline{T}(\alpha) = \text{REJ}) \wedge (\overline{A}(\alpha) \neq \text{REJ})\}$ *is finite).*

The definition of a universal statistical test encompasses two conflicting requirements. On one hand the universal test is *required to accept* all but a negligible fraction of the strings, whereas on the other hand it is *required to reject* all but finitely many of the strings rejected by any other test (in the class).

2.2 Pseudorandomness

Following are the two standard definitions of computational indistinguishability and pseudorandomness.

Definition 5 [6, 20]: *The ensembles* $\{X_n\}_{n\in\mathbb{N}}$ *and* $\{Y_n\}_{n\in\mathbb{N}}$ *are* computationally indistinguishable by a class of (probabilistic) algorithms $\mathcal{A}$ *if for every algorithm, $A \in \mathcal{A}$, the difference*

$$|\text{Prob}(A(X_n)=1) - \text{Prob}(A(Y_n)=1)|$$

is negligible.

Definition 6 [20]: *An ensemble is called* $\mathcal{A}$-pseudorandom *if it is computationally indistinguishable from the uniform ensemble by algorithms of the class $\mathcal{A}$.*

2.3 Domination

Definition 7 [13]: *The ensemble* $\{X_n\}_{n\in\mathbb{N}}$ *is said to* (strongly) dominate *the ensemble* $\{Y_n\}_{n\in\mathbb{N}}$ *if the function* $r(n) \stackrel{\text{def}}{=} \min_{\alpha\in\{0,1\}^n}\{\frac{\text{Prob}(X_n=\alpha)}{\text{Prob}(Y_n=\alpha)}\}$ *is non-negligible.*

A more liberal notion of domination only requires that sets assigned negligible probability by the first ensemble are also assigned negligible probability by the second.

Definition 8 : *The ensemble* $\{X_n\}_{n\in\mathbb{N}}$ *is said to* dominate *the ensemble* $\{Y_n\}_{n\in\mathbb{N}}$ *if for every sequence of sets* $\{S_n\}_{n\in\mathbb{N}}$ *if the function* $p(n) \stackrel{\text{def}}{=} \text{Prob}(X_n \in S_n)$ *is negligible so is the function* $q(n) \stackrel{\text{def}}{=} \text{Prob}(Y_n \in S_n)$.

Clearly, both notions of domination are reflexive and transitive.

3 General Investigations

In this section we present general observations and problems concerning statistical tests. To simplify the discussion, we assume without loss of generality, that all algorithms always output a Boolean value.

3.1 Pseudorandomness and Acceptance by Statistical Tests

Clearly, every pseudorandom ensemble is accepted by all statistical tests of the same complexity class. However, also ensembles which are not pseudorandom, for example ensemble $\{0U_{n-1}\}_{n\in\mathbb{N}}$, are accepted by all statistical tests. Furthermore,

Proposition 1 *Let* $\{X_n\}_{n\in\mathbb{N}}$ *be an $\mathcal{A}$-pseudorandom ensemble, for some complexity class $\mathcal{A}$, and let* $\{Y_n\}_{n\in\mathbb{N}}$ *be an ensemble which is dominated by* $\{X_n\}_{n\in\mathbb{N}}$. *Then,* $\{Y_n\}_{n\in\mathbb{N}}$ *is accepted by all statistical tests in $\mathcal{A}$.* .

proof: by contradiction. Details omitted. □

It is worthwhile noting that the ensembles satisfying the conditions of Proposition 1 may be far from pseudorandom. In particular, the ensemble $\{U_{n-1}0\}_{n\in\mathbb{N}}$ is accepted by all finite state statistical tests, but is not pseudorandom with respect to finite automata. Likewise, the ensemble $\{U_{n-\lceil\log_2 n\rceil}0^{\lceil\log_2 n\rceil}\}_{n\in\mathbb{N}}$, is accepted by all (on-line) logspace statistical tests, but is not pseudorandom with respect to (on-line) logspace machines. In general, for all natural classes of algorithms, the set of ensembles which are accepted by statistical tests is much richer than the set of pseudorandom ensembles. An intriguing problem is whether this richness is captured by Proposition 1 (i.e., whether the accepted ensembles are exactly those dominated by pseudorandom ones). An affirmative answer is obtained in case one trivializes the notion of an algorithm as done in the next observation.

Proposition 2 *Let $\mathcal{F}$ be the class of all Boolean functions* [2]*. Then, $Y \stackrel{\text{def}}{=} \{Y_n\}_{n \in \mathbf{N}}$ is accepted by all statistical tests in $\mathcal{F}$ if and only if Y is dominated by some $\mathcal{F}$-pseudorandom ensemble.*

Proof: Using Proposition 1, it remains to show that if Y is accepted by all statistical tests then it is dominated by some $\mathcal{F}$-pseudorandom distribution. We shall show that if Y is accepted by all statistical tests (in $\mathcal{F}$) then Y is dominated by the uniform ensemble. We prove this statement by proving the counter-positive. Details omitted. □

Hence, if the set of ensembles accepted by statistical tests in $\mathcal{A}$ contains more than the ensembles dominated by $\mathcal{A}$-pseudorandom ones, then this is due to intrinsic algorithmic reasons and not to pure probabilistic ones. In section 4, we show that such "algorithmic reasons" are not supplied by finite automata. Namely, the ensembles accepted by finite state statistical tests are exactly those dominated by ensembles which are pseudorandom with respect to finite automata. On the other hand, in section 6 we show that there exists ensembles which are accepted by logspace statistical tests, and yet are not dominated by (logspace-)pseudorandom one. The problem remains open for other interesting complexity classes. In particular

Open Problem 1 : Do there exist ensembles accepted by polynomial-time statistical tests which are not dominated by polynomial-time-pseudorandom ensembles?

3.2 Universal Statistical Tests

One can show that, for any natural class of statistical tests, a test universal for the class can not be itself in the class. Namely,

Theorem 1 *Let $\mathcal{A}$ be a class of algorithms satisfying the following three conditions:*

1. $\mathcal{A}$ is not trivial*: There exists $A \in \mathcal{A}$ so for every $\sigma \in \{0,1\}$ the set $\{\alpha : A(\alpha) = \sigma\}$ is infinite.*
2. $\mathcal{A}$ is closed under last bit omission*: For every $A \in \mathcal{A}$ there exists $A' \in \mathcal{A}$ so that, for every $\alpha \in \{0,1\}^*$ and $\sigma \in \{0,1\}$, it holds that $A'(\alpha\sigma) = A(\alpha)$.*
3. $\mathcal{A}$ is closed under binary operation*: For every $A_1, A_2 \in \mathcal{A}$ and every $b : \{0,1\}^2 \mapsto \{0,1\}$, there exists $A' \in \mathcal{A}$ so that for every $\alpha \in \{0,1\}^*$, it holds that $A'(\alpha) = b(A_1(\alpha), A_2(\alpha))$.*

Then $\mathcal{A}$ contains no statistical test which is universal for $\mathcal{A}$.

[2] In this case, all "pseudorandom" ensembles are statistically close to the uniform one.

proof sketch: Suppose on the contrary that $T \in \mathcal{A}$ is a statistical test which is universal for $\mathcal{A}$. Consider the algorithm T' that, on input $\alpha\sigma$, outputs 0 if either $T(\alpha\sigma)$ or $T(\alpha)$ is 0. By conditions (2) and (3), T' is also in $\mathcal{A}$. Furthermore, T' is also a statistical test, since the number of strings not accepted by T' is at most 3 times the number of strings not accepted by T. Yet, it can be shown that the universality of T implies that the fraction of strings rejected by T can be bounded below by a constant, and hence T can not be a statistical test (in contradiction to our hypothesis). Details omitted. □

In the next two subsections we present universal statistical tests for two low complexity classes. These universal tests are quite efficient, although they are not in the corresponding classes. With respect to higher complexity classes, such as logspace, there exist no universal statistical tests at all. Namely,

Theorem 2 *There exists no recursive statistical test that is universal for the class of logspace statistical tests.*

proof sketch: Assume, to the contrary, that T is a recursive statistical test that is universal for the class of logspace statistical tests. We reach a contradiction, by constructing a logspace statistical test T', which rejects much more strings than T. The test T' is constructed using traditional recursive theoretic techniques. Details omitted. □

In light of the above result we must relax the requirements of universal statistical tests for complexity classes such as logspace and higher. One possible direction is to establish a "gap" between the accepting rate of the algorithms in the class and the accepting rate required of the universal algorithm. Two approaches are possible:

1. Allow the universal algorithm to reject a *small yet non-negligible* fraction of the strings. The rejection rate of such universal algorithms can be specified. For example, one can present a universal algorithm for the class of probabilistic polynomial-time statistical tests so that this universal algorithm rejects a $\frac{1}{n^3}$ fraction of the strings of length n.
2. Investigate universal tests for subclasses of statistical tests which have a *specified* negligible rejection rate. For example, one can present a universal statistical test for the class of probabilistic polynomial-time statistical tests which accept all but an exponential fraction of all strings (i.e., the class contains algorithms which accept all but an exponential fraction, whereas the universal algorithm accept all but a negligible fraction of the strings). The universal test itself can be implemented in probabilistic quasi-polynomial-time.

We prefer the second approach.

4 Finite Automata

The simplest (and most restricted) class of algorithms we consider are finite automata. According to Definition 2, we say that a finite automaton, A, is a statistical test if the fraction of strings of length n that A rejects[3] is negligible. We start by characterizing the set of finite state statistical tests and then propose a statistical test (outside this set) which is universal for this set.

4.1 Characterization

We consider the directed graph (*digraph*), G, defined by a finite automaton A (ignoring the binary labelling of edges). Note that G may have parallel, anti-parallel and self-loop edges. We consider the strongly connected components[4] of the digraph G. Let $\{C_i : i \in I\}$ be the partition of G's vertices to strongly connected components. We consider the directed acyclic graph (*dag*), D_G, in which the C_i's are vertices and there is an edge from C_i to C_j if and only if there exists $u \in C_i$, $v \in C_j$ so that (u, v) is an edge in G. A *sink* is a strongly connected component which has outdegree zero in this dag. Using the definition of a statistical test it follows that

Proposition 3 *Let A be a finite state statistical test. Then the states appearing in its sinks must be accepting. Furthermore, there exists a finite state statistical test A' which is identical to A except (possibly) that the states of A' which are not in a sink are rejecting.*

proof sketch: We consider a random walk of length n on the digraph G (associated with the automaton A) starting in the vertex corresponding to A's initial state (this walk represents the computation of A on a random n-bit input string).

Let v be a vertex in a sink S. With constant probability (i.e., at least 2^{-q} where q is the number of states in A) this walk enters S after a constant number of steps (i.e. q). From that point on, the walk never leaves S. The "location" of the walk after $m \geq n - q$ steps is a random variable, denoted $P_s(m)$, depending on s the first vertex of S reached in the n-step walk. The behaviour of $P_s(m)$ converges to a random variable $Q(m \bmod k)$, where k, $1 \leq k \leq q$ is an integer (see [9] proof of Thm. 4.1.4 which refers to the convergence of a regular Markov Chain to the stationary distribution). The rate of convergence is exponential in $\frac{m}{k}$, and for some i $(1 \leq i \leq k)$ the probability that $Q(i)$ equals v (in which we are interested) is a positive constant depending only on A (and again being at least 2^{-q}). Hence, for $n \equiv i \pmod k$, a random walk of length n ends in v with constant probability. It follows by Definition 2 that v must be accepting.

Using an even simpler argument (cf. [9] proof of Thm. 3.1.1) it follows that the probability that a n-long random walk does not end in a sink is bounded above by $2^{-n/q}$. Hence, all non-sink vertices may be made rejecting without violating the conditions of Definition 2. □

Remark 2 : By the above proof it follows that the characterization of finite state statistical tests is not effected if the definition of negligible is changed either to "smaller than any constant" or to "exponentially small". Hence, also the results of the next two subsections remain valid also if the definition of negligence is changed to "smaller than any constant". More generally, all the results hold as long as negligible is defined as smaller than any function in a recursively enumerable set of functions which do not have a maximum element (i.e., a function in the enumeration which is greater/equal than all other functions on all but finitely many points).

4.2 A Universal Test

Following is a description of a very simple test which is universal for the class of finite state statistic tests. Let $k : \mathbb{N} \mapsto \mathbb{N}$ be any easy to compute function which is both monotonically non-decreasing, unbounded (by a constant) and bounded above by the function $\log_2 n - 3\log_2\log_2 n$. The test checks whether all $k(n)$-bit long strings appear as substrings in the n-bit long input. Namely, the test accepts the string if and only if all possible $k(n)$-bit long substrings appear in it. We call this test the `occurrence test`.

Theorem 3 *The* `occurrence test` *is universal for the class of finite state statistical tests.*

proof sketch: Let T be an arbitrary finite state statistical test. A *homing sequence* for T is any string α satisfying the following: for every state s of T an execution starting at state s and following the edges labelled by α ends in a sink of T. It is well known that every finite automaton with q states has a homing sequence of length q^2. Hence, sufficiently long strings accepted by the `occurrence test` must contain the homing sequence of T as a substring, and thus are also accepted by T. Finally, it is left to show that the `occurrence test` is indeed a statistical test. This is done by a straightforward calculation. □

Clearly, the `occurrence test` cannot be implemented by a finite automata. Furthermore, using Theorem 1, it is easy to see that no finite automata can be universal for the class of finite state statistical tests. [5] In particular, if the function k is chosen to be a constant then the resulting test (is a finite automata but) is not universal for the class.

[3] Since A is deterministic, it is never undecided.

[4] A digraph is called strongly connected if there is a directed path between every (ordered) pair of vertices. The strongly connected components of a digraph are the maximal sets of vertices inducing a strongly connected sub(di)graph.

[5] An alternative proof can be derived using Proposition 3. Details omitted.

4.3 Pseudorandomness and Acceptance by Statistical Tests

By Proposition 1, all ensembles dominated by (Finite Automata)-pseudorandom ensembles are accepted by all finite state statistical tests. We now show that these are all the ensembles which are accepted by all finite state statistical tests. Namely,

Theorem 4 *An ensemble is accepted by all finite state statistical tests if and only if it is dominated by an ensemble that is pseudorandom with respect to all finite automata.*

proof sketch: Let $X \stackrel{\text{def}}{=} \{X_n\}_{n\in\mathbb{N}}$ an ensemble which is accepted by all finite state statistical tests. We will construct an ensemble $Y \stackrel{\text{def}}{=} \{Y_n\}_{n\in\mathbb{N}}$ and show that for each i the function $g_i : \mathbb{N} \mapsto \mathbb{N}$, defined by $g_i(n) \stackrel{\text{def}}{=} |\text{Prob}(A_i(Y_n) = 1) - \text{Prob}(A_i(U_n)=1)|$ where A_i is the ith automaton (in a standard enumeration of finite automata), is negligible. The theorem will follow.

The idea behind the construction of the distributions Y_n is to rescale the distributions X_n so that they exhibit the same statistic profile as the uniform ones with respect to leading a finite automata to terminate at a particular state residing in its sink. The rescaling satisfies the domination condition and guarantees that no finite automata can distinguish Y_n from uniform. The part of the distribution which does not lead an automata to a sink remains unchanged. Using the fact that X_n is accepted by all finite state statistical tests, this later part is shown to carry a negligible probability mass. Details omitted. □

5 Counter Machines

We now consider a wider class of tests. The algorithms we consider are counter machines with on-line access to the input. (Hence, these machines are not equivalent to Turing machines.) We start by considering machines with one counter. Once a new input symbol (i.e., bit) is read, and depending on its current state and on whether the counter is empty or not, the machine may change its state and increment/decrement its counter by a fixed number of units. Allowing the counter to assume negative values does not add to the power of such machines (since the sign may be encoded by the state).

To simplify the analysis even further, we consider only *weak 1-counter machines*. In these machines, the next transition is not effected by whether the counter is empty or not. Hence, we must allow the counter to assume negative values (otherwise the power of this model is further reduced). On the other hand, the final verdict ("accept" or "reject") may depend on the sign of the counter (i.e., negative, zero, or positive). Again, as in previous section, the machines are deterministic and hence are never undecided about an input. We start by characterizing the set of weak 1-counter statistical tests, *W1CST*, and next propose a statistical test (outside W1CST) which is universal for W1CST.

5.1 Characterization of W1CST

We consider again the directed graph (*digraph*), G, defined by a finite automaton A. This time the edges are labelled by binary input symbols and by the corresponding counter modifications (which without loss of generality are 0, +1 or −1).

The characterization of weak 1-counter statistical test consists of a characterization of the accepting *configurations*. The possible configurations at the end of the computation are pairs, (s, σ), where s is a state of the finite control and $\sigma \in \{\text{P}, \text{Z}, \text{N}\}$ indicate the sign of the counter (i.e., $\sigma = \text{P}$ indicates positive counter value, $\sigma = \text{Z}$ indicates zero counter value, and $\sigma = \text{N}$ indicates negative counter value).

The characterization of configurations depends not only on the component structure of the digraph G, but also on the expected value of the counter modification in a random walk inside each sink of G. To this end we recall that a random walk in each sink defines an ergodic Markov Chain. Assume for a moment that this Markov Chain is regular (i.e., that the gcd of set of legths of all directed circuits in G is 1), and let π be the stationary distribution of this chain. Then, the *average of a sink* is defined as $\sum_e \pi(e)m(e)$, where $\pi(e)$ is the probability of passing on edge e and $m(e)$ is the counter modification on this edge. In general, the Markov Chain may be cyclic (i.e., the gcd of cycle lengths is $d > 1$) meaning that only for some $d > 1$ (but $d \leq q$) making d random steps in a row yields a regular Markov Chain. In this general case, d different "limit distributions" are defined (depending on the equivalent class of the starting vertex) and the average of the sink is defined as the average of the expected counter modifications for each of the corresponding limit distributions.

A configuration is called *reachable* if it can be reached in a computation on some input.

Proposition 4 *Let A be a weak 1-counter statistical test, and (s, σ) be an (end) configuration. Then, the configuration must be accepting if one of the following conditions hold:*

1. *s resides in a sink with positive average and $\sigma = \text{P}$.*
2. *s resides in a sink with negative average and $\sigma = \text{N}$.*
3. *s resides in a sink with zero average, and (s, σ) is a reachable configuration.*

Furthermore, there exists a weak 1-counter statistical test A' which is identical to A except (possibly) that all the configurations not mentioned in items (1-3) are rejecting.

proof sketch: As in the proof of Proposition 3 we show that for $n \equiv i \pmod{k}$, $k < q$, and every state s residing in a sink, a random walk of length n terminates at s with constant probability. The question is what is the value of the counter at termination. For states s residing in sinks in which all cycles have zero sum the value in the counter equals its value at the first time during computation in which s is visited. Hence, reachable $(s,\cdot)$ configurations, for s is such a sink, are reached with constant probability, at the end of the computation. It is also clear that configurations which are not reachable can be made rejecting without affecting the acceptance profile of the machine. It is left to deal with sinks in which not all cycles have zero sum.

Using the Central Limit Theorem for Markov Chains (cf. [9] Thm. 4.6.9) it follows that the sum of counter modifications in a random walk is unlikely to deviate linearly from the expectation (i.e., the CLT guarantees that such deviation occurs with probability tending to zero). Hence, items (1) and (2) above follow. For the justification of (the rest of) item (3) we rely on a Local Limit Theorem for Markov Chains (cf. [7] Section 20 for a general exposition and [18] for a result implying what we need). The Local Limit Theorem guarantees that the probability that the sum of counter modifications in an n-step long random walk equals its expectation, up to an additive term of q, is $\Theta(1/\sqrt{n})$. Hence, item (3) follows. To prove the "furthermore clause" referring to items (1) and (2), we need a Large Deviation Theorem for Markov Chains (cf. [4] Section 2.4). This theorem guarantees that only with exponentially small probability the sum of counter modifications in a random walk may deviate linearly from its expectation[6]. Hence, the "furthermore" clause follows and so does the entire proposition. □

Remark 3 : Unlike the situation with finite state statistical tests, the characterization does depend on the particular definition of a negligible fraction. In particular, if negligible is interpreted as "smaller than any constant" then $(\cdot, Z)$ configurations need not be accepting (and may without loss of generality be rejecting).

5.2 A Universal Test for W1CST

Following is a description of a very simple test which is universal for the class of finite state statistic tests. Let $k : \mathbb{N} \mapsto \mathbb{N}$ be any easy to compute function which is both monotonically non-decreasing, unbounded (by a constant) and bounded above by the function $\log_2 n - 5\log_2\log_2 n$. The test partitions the input string α into $\frac{|\alpha|}{k(|\alpha|)}$ blocks of length $k(\alpha|)$ each, and checks whether all $k(|\alpha|)$-bit long strings appear approximately as frequently in these blocks. More specifically, the frequency test computes, $\pi_\beta(\alpha)$ which equals $|\{i : \beta = \alpha_i\}|$, where $k \stackrel{\text{def}}{=} k(|\alpha|)$ and $\alpha = \alpha_1 \cdots \alpha_{n/k}$ with $\alpha_i \in \{0,1\}^k$. The test accepts α if and only if $|\frac{\pi_\beta(\alpha)}{n/k(n)} - \frac{1}{2^{k(n)}}| < \frac{1}{k(n)} \cdot \frac{1}{2^{k(n)}}$ for all $\beta \in \{0,1\}^{k(n)}$. We call this test the `frequency test`.

[6] Actually the quoted result can be derived using more elementary methods. Details omitted.

Theorem 5 *The* `frequency test` *is universal for the class of weak 1-counter statistical tests.*

proof sketch: Let T be an arbitrary weak 1-counter statistical test with q states. We start by proving the following

> *Claim:* For every $\epsilon > 0$ and all sufficiently long α, if α is accepted by the `frequency test` then the test T enters a sink after reading at most $\epsilon|\alpha|$ bits of its input.
>
> *proof:* omitted.

Let α be a sufficiently long string passing the `frequency test`. We consider the computation of T on input α from the moment in which T entered a sink (which by the above Claim happens after making at most ϵn steps). If all of T's sinks have average (counter modification) zero then a computation of T which enters a sink always terminates in an accepting configuration (see item (3) in the characterization). Similarly, we can discard all sinks with zero average, and concentrate on sinks with non-zero average. Let σ be the minimum deviation from zero of the average of any non-zero sink of T (i.e. of either positive or negative average). The Central Limit Theorem for Markov Chains (cf. [9] Thm. 4.6.9) guarantees that for any p and for sufficiently large K (depending only on the sink of T) the probability that a random walk of length K starting from any location in the sink yields total counter modification of less than $\frac{\sigma K}{2}$ (towards the expected direction) is at most p. Let $c \geq 1$ be the maximum counter modification in a single transition of T. Then for sufficiently large K a random walk of length K starting from any location in the sink has expected counter modification of at least $\frac{\sigma K}{2} - pcK > \frac{\sigma K}{4}$ (as p can be chosen small enough). Recall that for sufficiently large n, indeed $k(n)$ is greater than the minimal K required above. Set $\epsilon < \frac{1}{16c} \cdot \sigma$. By the above Claim, it is guaranteed that the computation of T on an n-bit string, α, accepted by the `frequency test` enters a sink of T after at most ϵn steps. If this is a zero-average sink - we are done. Otherwise, assume without loss of generality that we entered a negative-average sink. Clearly, upon entering the sink there are at most $c\epsilon n$ units in the counter. We will show next, that in the remaining $(1-\epsilon)n > \frac{n}{2}$ steps the counter is decreased so that at termination it holds a negative value. Using item (2) of the characterization it follows that T accepts the string α.

To show that in the remaining steps the counter is decreased by at least $\epsilon c n$ units, we first assume that in these steps all $k(n)$-bit long substrings appear with equal frequency. By the above, we are guaranteed that the average counter decrease per $k(n)$-bit long block is at least $\frac{\sigma k(n)}{4}$. Hence, in $(1-\epsilon)n > \frac{n}{2}$ steps of equal block frequency we get a decrease of at least $\frac{\sigma n}{8}$. However, the frequencies of occurrence of the various the $k(n)$-bit long substrings may deviate from being equal. Yet, the maximum possible deviation is bounded by $\max\{\epsilon, \frac{1}{k(n)}\}$, which for sufficiently large n yields a bound of ϵcn on the possible deviation of the sum of modifications. Hence, in the $(1-\epsilon)n$ steps we get a decrease of at least $\frac{\sigma n}{8} - \epsilon cn > \epsilon cn$ (since $\epsilon < \frac{1}{16c} \cdot \sigma$).

Finally, it is left to show that the `frequency test` is indeed a statistical test. This is done by application of Chernoff bound. The probability that a particular $k(n)$-bit string appears in t blocks, where $t \notin [(1-\frac{1}{k(n)}) \cdot \frac{n}{k(n)2^{k(n)}}, (1+\frac{1}{k(n)}) \cdot \frac{n}{k(n)2^{k(n)}}]$, is bounded above by an exponential in $-O(\frac{n}{k^3 2^k})$. The proposition follows. □

Remark 4 : The `frequency test` cannot be implemented by a weak 1-counter machine. More generally, by Theorem 1, the class of weak 1-counter machines does not have a universal test which resides in the class itself. Also, setting the function k, in the definition of the `frequency test`, to be a constant yields a test which is not universal for the class of weak 1-counter machines.

Remark 5 : Under an appropriate choice of parameters, it can be shown that a test based on the Lempel-Ziv algorithm [12] dominates the `frequency test` (i.e., rejects all the strings that are rejected by the `frequency test`). Hence, the LZ algorithm can be viewed as a universal statistical test for the class of weak 1-counter machines.

Remark 6 : Under the liberal interpretation of "negligence" (by which any non-increasing function tending to zero is negligible), the `frequency test` is not universal for weak 1-counter machines which are statistical tests. Augmenting the `frequency test` so that it is universal also under the liberal interpretation of "negligence" boils down to an algorithm that is very close to one that runs all possible statistical tests in the class. We also mention that under the liberal interpretation of "negligence" the Lempel-Ziv algorithm is not universal either. In particular the LZ algorithm accepts de-Bruijn sequences whereas such sequences can be rejected by a weak 1-counter machine which compares the number of 1's to the number of 0's (and rejects the string if their difference is zero).

5.3 Extensions

We believe that the results of the two previous subsections can be extended to weak counter machines possessing *any constant number of counters*. The difficult is *not* in the algorithmic part, but rather in our knowledge of probability theory (specifically Local Limit Theorems for Markov Chains). To be more specific, we need a Local Limit Theorem referring to a finite Markov Chain with states associated with d-dimensional vectors, and to the (vector) sum of the states visited in an n-long random walk on the chain. We believe that, under some non-degeneracy conditions, the probability that the sum over such a walk equals the expect value (which is a d-dimensional vector) is related to $\frac{1}{n^{\frac{d}{2}}}$. We refer to this conjecture as $\mathcal{LCT}(d)$. We point out that $\mathcal{LCT}(1)$ is known to hold, and this fact has been used in subsection 5.1. However, we failed in our attempts to trace such a proof of $\mathcal{LCT}(d)$, for $d > 1$. Hence, all we can say is

Theorem 6 *Suppose that for some $d > 1$, conjecture $\mathcal{LCT}(d)$ holds. Then the* `frequency test`*, presented in subsection 5.2, is universal for the class of weak d-counter statistical tests.*

We believe that the `frequency test` is universal also with respect to the class of (general) d-counter statistical tests, for every $d \geq 1$. Proving such a result, even for $d = 1$ requires a much more cumbersome characterization. Again, the difficulty is in the analysis of the behaviour Markov Chains. Further details are omitted.

6 LogSpace Machines

By a logspace machine we mean a machine which have online access to its input and work in space logarithmic in the length of its input.

6.1 Characterization of LogSpace Statistical Tests

In light of the fair amount of understanding gained in the study of logspace pseudorandomness, it is not outrageous to propose the following open problem.

Open Problem 2 : Try to find a useful characterization of logspace statistical tests.

By a useful characterization, we mean one which would lead to a "simple" and "natural" universal test for the class of logspace statistical tests which accept all but a *specified* fraction of the strings. We do not consider the universal test of the proceeding subsection as being "natural" or "simple".

6.2 Universal Tests for Subclasses of LogSpace Tests

Following is a description of a universal test for the subclass of logspace statistical tests which accept all but a *specified* negligible fraction of the strings. Unlike the tests presented in previous sections, the current universal test does not have a natural description, but rather consists of executing all relevant tests. In other words, the universal test presented below uses the "diagonalization paradigm". Namely, it enumerates all Turing Machines (up to a bound depending on the input length), and simulating the execution of each machine on the given input with a specific space-bound. The space bound is a function which also depends on the input length and has the property that it is bigger than the logarithm of the input length (to any base). The verdict of a simulated test on the given input is taken into consideration (as grounds for rejecting) only if the test is found to accept all but a *specified* negligible fraction of the strings of the given length (i.e., the length of the given input). Using the results of Nisan [16, 17], it is possible to implement the above universal test in slightly more than polynomial-time and in polylogarithmic space. Namely,

Proposition 5 *Let $f : \mathbb{N} \mapsto \mathbb{N}$ be any polynomial-time computable function which is unbounded and monotonically non-decreasing (e.g., $f(n) = \log^* n$). Then there exists a deterministic universal test for the class of logspace statistical tests which accept all but a $\frac{1}{n^{f(n)}}$ fraction of the strings of length n. Furthermore, on input of length n, the universal test runs for at most $O(n^{f(n)})$ steps and uses at most $O(f(n) \log n)$ space.*

6.3 Pseudorandomness and Acceptance by Statistical Tests

By Proposition 1, all ensembles dominated by (logspace)-pseudorandom ensembles are accepted by all logspace statistical tests. We now show that these are not all the ensembles which are accepted by logspace tests. Namely,

Proposition 6 *Let $l(n) \stackrel{\text{def}}{=} \log_2 n$, and $t(n) \stackrel{\text{def}}{=} 2n + 4 + 2\log_2 n$. Let $X = \{X_{t(n)}\}_{n \in \mathbb{N}}$ be an ensemble so that for each $\alpha \in \{0,1\}^n$ we have $\text{Prob}(X_n = 01^{l(n)}0\alpha01^{l(n)}0\alpha) = 2^{-n}$. Then the ensemble X is accepted by all logspace statistical tests and yet is not dominated by any logspace-pseudorandom ensemble.*

proof sketch: We first show that the ensemble X is indeed accepted by all logspace statistical tests. Let T be an arbitrary logspace statistical test. To show that T must accept X, we use a standard "crossing sequence" argument. Details omitted.

We now show that X cannot be dominated by any pseudorandom ensemble. Assume to the contrary that X is dominated by Y and Y is logspace pseudorandom. Even under the weak definition of dominance (i.e., Definition 8) the probability mass assigned by $Y_{t(n)}$ to strings of the form $01^{l(n)}0\alpha01^{l(n)}0\alpha$, (where $\alpha \in \{0,1\}^n$) cannot be negligible (since such strings are assigned constant probability mass by X and hence cannot be assigned negligible probability by Y). Hence for some $c > 0$ and infinitely many n's $\text{Prob}(Y_{t(n)} \in S_{t(n)}) > \frac{1}{n^c}$, where

$$S_{t(n)} \stackrel{\text{def}}{=} \{01^{l(n)}0\alpha01^{l(n)}0\alpha \;:\; \alpha \in \{0,1\}^n\}.$$

Using this fact we present a logspace algorithm, A, (which is *not* a statistical test) that distinguishes the ensemble Y from the uniform ensemble. Algorithm A tries to compare $2c\log_2 n$ positions in the prefix of the input with the corresponding positions in the suffix, and outputs 1 if and only if the bits in these positions match. Hence, on input taken from $Y_{t(n)}$ the algorithm outputs 1 with probability at least $\frac{1}{n^c}$, whereas on a uniformly chosen input the algorithm outputs 1 with probability exactly $\frac{1}{n^{2c}}$). The idea has to be slightly modified so that the algorithm can be actually implemented in lgspace. Details omitted. □

Open Problem 3 : Suppose that the ensemble X passes all logspace statistical tests. What can be said about X in terms of pseudorandomness with respect to logspace distinguishers.

7 Probabilistic Polynomial-Time Statistical Tests

It would be more natural to consider *deterministic* polynomial-time statistical tests, rather than *probabilistic* polynomial-time ones. Unfortunately, we have results only for probabilistic polynomial-time statistical tests. Our main result relates pseudorandom generators with "generators" which generate ensembles which are accepted by all probabilistic polynomial-time statistical tests. We first recall the definition of a pseudorandom generator.

Definition 9 (pseudorandom generator [2, 20]): *A (deterministic) polynomial-time algorithm G is called a* pseudorandom generator (prg) *if the following two conditions hold:*

1. *$|G(\alpha)| \geq |\alpha| + 1$, for all $\alpha \in \{0,1\}^*$.*
2. *The ensemble $\{G_n\}_{n \in \mathbb{N}}$ defined by letting $G_n = G(U_n)$ is pseudorandom (with respect to probabilistic polynomial-time algorithms).*

It is well known that if pseudorandom generators exist then for, every polynomial p, there exists pseudorandom generators G satisfying $|G(\alpha)| = p(|\alpha|)$, for all $\alpha \in \{0,1\}^*$. By a sequence of results, culminating in [8], pseudorandom generators exist if and only if one-way functions exist. Interestingly, this condition is also equivalent to the existence of *statistically-accepted generators* defined below.

Definition 10 (statistically-accepted generator): *A (deterministic) polynomial-time algorithm G is called a* statistically-accepted generator *if the following two conditions hold:*

1. *$|G(\alpha)| \geq 2 \cdot |\alpha|$, for all $\alpha \in \{0,1\}^*$.*
2. *The ensemble $\{G_n\}_{n \in \mathbb{N}}$ defined by letting $G_n = G(U_n)$ is accepted by all probabilistic polynomial-time statistical tests.*

Theorem 7 *Pseudorandom generators exist if and only if statistically-accepted generator exist.*

proof sketch: Clearly, every pseudorandom generator with sufficient expansion (i.e., with $|G(\alpha)| \geq 2|\alpha|$ for all α) is a statistically-accepted generator. The theorem follows by proving that the existence of a statistically-accepted generator implies the existence of a one-way function (and hence the existence of pseudorandom generators). To this end, we note that the construction used by Levin [14], to prove that the existence of pseudorandom generators implies the existence of one-way functions, proves in fact the stronger statement we just made. Details omitted. □

Remark 7 : The above theorem holds also if a statistically-accepted generator is only required to expand strings of length n into strings of length $n + l(n)$, where l is an arbitrary function growing faster than any logarithm in n. However, expansion of strings of length n into strings of length $n + O(\log n)$ does not suffice (since, for example, $G(\alpha) = \alpha 10^{\log_2 |\alpha|}$ generates an ensemble accepted by all probabilistic polynomial-time statistical tests and yet this does not imply the existence of one-way functions).

Remark 8 : Clearly, if statistically-accepted generators exist then for, every polynomial p, there exists statistically-accepted generators G satisfying $|G(\alpha)| = p(|\alpha|)$, for all $\alpha \in \{0,1\}^*$.

Remark 9 : We stress that the above theorem sheds no light on the open problem mentioned in Section 3. Namely, are all ensembles accepted by (probabilistic) polynomial-time tests also dominated by pseudorandom ensembles?

Acknowledgements

We would like to thank Jon Aaronson, Noga Alon, Amir Dembo, Nati Linial, and Ofer Zeitouni, for indispensable discussions and references to Large Deviation and Local Limit Theorems for finite Markov Chains. We are also grateful to Ishai Ben-Aroya for pointing out an error in an early version of this extended abstract.

References

[1] Blum, M., and Goldreich, O., "Towards a Computational Theory of Statistical Tests", TR 747, Computer Science Dept., Technion, Haifa, Israel, 1992.

[2] Blum, M., and Micali, S., "How to Generate Cryptographically Strong Sequences of Pseudo-Random Bits", *SIAM Jour. on Computing*, Vol. 13, 1984, pp. 850-864. Extended abstract in *FOCS 82*.

[3] Chaitin, G., "A Theory of Program Size Formally Identical to Information Theory", IBM Yorktown Heights Rep. RC 4805, April 1974.

[4] Dembo, A., and O. Zeitouni, *Large Deviation and Applications*, preprint, 1991.

[5] Fredricksen, H.M., "Generation of the Ford sequence of length 2^n, n large", *Journal of Combinatorial Theory*, Series A, Vol. 12 (1972), pp. 153-154.

[6] Goldwasser, S., and S. Micali, "Probabilistic Encryption", *JCSS*, Vol. 28, No. 2, 1984, pp. 270-299. Extended abstract in *STOC 82*.

[7] Gnedenko, B.V., *The Theory of Probability*, (translated from fourth Russian edition by B.D. Seckler), Chelsea Publishing Company, New York (NY), 1968.

[8] Hastad, J., R. Impagliazzo, L.A. Levin, and M.G. Luby, "Pseudorandom Generators from any One-Way Functions", preprint. Combines a work of Impagliazzo, Levin and Luby in *21st STOC* (1989) with a work of Hastad in *22nd STOC* (1990).

[9] Kemeny, J.G., and J.L. Snell, *Finite Markov Chains*, D. Van Nostrad Company, Inc., Princeton (NJ), 1960.

[10] Knuth, D.E., *The Art of Computer Programming*, Vol. 2 (*Seminumerical Algorithms*), Addison-Wesley Publishing Company, Inc., 1969 (first edition) and 1981 (second edition).

[11] Kolmogorov, A.N., "Three Approaches to the Quantitative Definition of Information", *Probl. Inform. Transmission*, Vol. 1, pp. 1-7, 1965.

[12] Lempel, A., and J. Ziv , "On the Complexity of Finite Sequences", *IEEE Trans. on Information Theory*, Vol. IT-22, No. 1, Jan. 1976, pp. 75-81.

[13] L.A. Levin, "Average Case Complete Problems", *SIAM J. of Computing*, Vol. 15, 1986, pp. 285-286.

[14] L.A. Levin, "One-way Functions and Pseudorandom Generators", *Combinatorica*, Vol. 7, No. 4, 1987, pp. 357–363.

[15] Martin-Löf, P., "The Definition of Random Sequences", *Inform. Contr.*, Vol. 9, pp. 602-619, 1966.

[16] N. Nisan, "Pseudorandom Generators for Space Bounded Machines", *22nd STOC*, 1990.

[17] N. Nisan, "RL $\subseteq$ SC", *23rd STOC*, 1991.

[18] Rousseau-Egele, W., "Un Theoreme de la Limite Locale pour une Classe de Transformations Dilatantes et Monotones par Morceaux", *Ann. Prob.*, 11 (1983), pp. 772-788.

[19] Solomonoff, R.J., "A Formal Theory of Inductive Inference", part 1 and 2, *Information and Control*, Vol. 7, 1964, pp. 1-22 ans 224-254.

[20] Yao, A.C., "Theory and Applications of Trapdoor Functions", *23rd FOCS*, 1982, pp. 80-91.

[21] Ziv. J., and A. Lempel, "A Universal Algorithm for Sequential Data Compression", *IEEE Trans. on Information Theory*, Vol. IT-23, No. 3, May 1977, pp. 337-343.

[22] Ziv, J., and N. Merhav, "A Measure of Relative Entropy between Individual Sequences with Applications to Universal Classification", preprint.

Witnesses for Boolean Matrix Multiplication and for Shortest Paths

Noga Alon*
Department of Mathematics
Tel Aviv University
Tel Aviv, 69978
ISRAEL

Zvi Galil†
Department of Computer Science
Tel Aviv University, Tel Aviv, 69978, ISRAEL
and
Columbia University, New York, NY 10027, USA

Oded Margalit
Department of Computer Science
Tel Aviv University
Tel Aviv, 69978
ISRAEL

Moni Naor
IBM Almaden Research Center
San Jose, CA 95120
USA

Abstract

The subcubic ($O(n^\omega)$ for $\omega < 3$) algorithms to multiply Boolean matrices do not provide the witnesses; namely, they compute $C = A \cdot B$ but if $C_{ij} = 1$ they do not find an index k (a witness) such that $A_{ik} = B_{kj} = 1$. We design a deterministic algorithm for computing the matrix of witnesses that runs in $\tilde{O}(n^\omega)$ time, where here $\tilde{O}(n^\omega)$ denotes $O(n^\omega(\log n)^{O(1)})$.

The subcubic methods to compute the shortest distances between all pairs of vertices also do not provide for witnesses; namely they compute the shortest distances but do not generate information for computing quickly the paths themselves. A witness for a shortest path from v_i to v_j is an index k such that v_k is the first vertex on such a path. (The last sentence is not sufficient as a definition of a witness matrix when nonpositive edges are present, see Figure 3 in page 6 for details). We describe subcubic methods to compute such witnesses for several versions of the all pairs shortest paths problem. As a result, we derive shortest paths algorithms that provide characterization of the shortest paths in addition to the shortest distances in the same time (up to a polylogarithmic factor) needed for computing the distances; namely $\tilde{O}(n^{(3+\omega)/2})$ time in the directed case and $\tilde{O}(n^\omega)$ time in the undirected case.

We also design an algorithm that computes witnesses for the transitive closure in the same time needed to compute witnesses for Boolean matrix multiplication.

*Research supported in part by a United states Israel BSF Grant.

†Work partially supported by NSF Grant CCR-9014605.

1 Introduction

Consider a Boolean matrix multiplication: $C = AB$, $C_{ij} = \bigvee_{k=1}^{n}(A_{ik} \wedge B_{kj})$. The n^3 time method that evaluates these expressions gives for every i, j for which $C_{ij} = 1$ all the k's for which $A_{ik} = B_{kj} = 1$. The subcubic methods on the other hand consider A and B as matrices of integers and do not provide any of these k's. We call a k such that $A_{ik} = B_{kj} = 1$ a *witness* (for the fact that $C_{ij} = 1$). We want to compute in addition to the matrix C a matrix of witnesses. When there is more than one witness for a given i and j we are satisfied with one such witness.

We use $O(n^\omega)$ to denote the running time of some subcubic algorithm for Boolean matrix multiplication. All our algorithms can be derived from any such algorithm yielding a corresponding time bound as a function of w. The best asymptotic bound known at present is the one with the exponent $\omega < 2.376$ and is due to Coppersmith and Winograd [3].

For two functions $f(n)$ and $g(n)$ we let the notation $g(n) = \tilde{O}(f(n))$ denote the statement that $g(n)$ is $O(f(n)(\log n)^{O(1)})$.

Several researchers, including Seidel [6], Karger (personal communication) and the first three authors, discovered a simple randomized algorithm that computes witnesses in $\tilde{O}(n^\omega)$ time. In Section 2 we describe a **deterministic** algorithm for computing the witnesses in $\tilde{O}(n^\omega)$ time. It is essentially a derandomization of a modified version of the simple randomized algorithm, and relies heavily on the known constructions of small sample spaces with almost independent random variables. We also outline an alternative approach that gives slightly worse running time but may

0-8186-2900-2/92 $3.00 © 1992 IEEE

still be useful for matrices of moderate size.

Our motivation for studying the computation of witnesses for Boolean matrix multiplication is related to our work on the all pair shortest paths problem. We use the following notation. $D = \{d_{ij}\}_{ij=1}^{n}$ is the matrix of edge lengths, $d_{ij} = +\infty$ in case there is no edge from v_i to v_j. In the positive case $d_{ij} \in \{1, 2, \ldots, M, +\infty\}$ and in the unrestricted case $d_{ij} \in \{0, \pm 1, \pm 2, \ldots, \pm M, +\infty\}$. $D^* = \{d^*_{ij}\}$ is the matrix of shortest distances.

In an earlier paper [2] the first three authors designed subcubic algorithms for computing all pair shortest distances of directed graphs with integer edge lengths whose absolute value is bounded by M. We denote the problem and its time bound by $APSD(n, M)$, where n is the number of vertices in the graph. We showed that $APSD(n, M) = O((Mn)^\nu)$, where $\nu = (3 + \omega)/2$. For $\omega < 2.376$, we have $\nu < 2.688$. In a more recent work [4] the second and third authors have improved the dependence on M and obtained better bounds for undirected graphs, in which case $APSD(n, M) = O(M^{(\omega+1)/2} n^\omega \log n)$. A simple $O(n^\omega \log n)$ algorithm for undirected $APSD(n, 1)$ was discovered independently by Seidel [6], but it does not seem to be extendable to larger edge lengths. All these algorithms do not provide any subcubic deterministic way for finding the shortest paths themselves, only the shortest distances.

One cannot have a subcubic algorithm for explicitly outputing the shortest paths between all pairs of vertices simply because in the example depicted in Figure 1 there are more than $n^3/27$ edges in all shortest paths. In fact, this holds for an exponential number of input graphs. (Replace each cycle in Figure 1 by an arbitrary connected graph of $n/3$ vertices.)

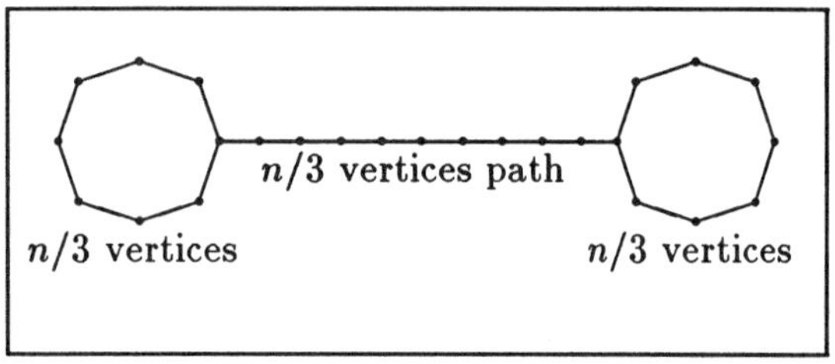

Figure 1: All shortest paths can yield a cubic output

One may use the following definition to obtain a more concise representation of all shortest paths: A *witness for a shortest path* from v_i to v_j is an index k such that v_k is the first vertex on such a path. This definition is certainly sufficient in case of positive edge lengths. A shortest path can be easily constructed from these witnesses.

This definition is insufficient in case of nonpositive cycles. If $d^*_{ij} = -\infty$ we want to be able to construct from the witnesses a simple path from v_i to v_j together with a vertex v_k on the path and a negative cycle containing v_k (i, j and k need not be distinct). This leads to the need to define witnesses for paths, not necessarily shortest paths.

Consider the transitive closure of a directed graph. One could try to define a witness for a path identically to the definition of a witness for a shortest path: A witness for a path from v_i to v_j is an index k such that v_k is the first vertex on such a path. Any method for computing witnesses for Boolean matrix multiplication can be immediately used for computing these "witnesses": compute witnesses for $A \cdot T$, where A is the incidence matrix and T the transitive closure. Unfortunately this definition is inappropriate as can be seen in Figure 2: v_k is a possible witness for the path from v_i to v_j, but it is a bad choice which leads to a cycle.

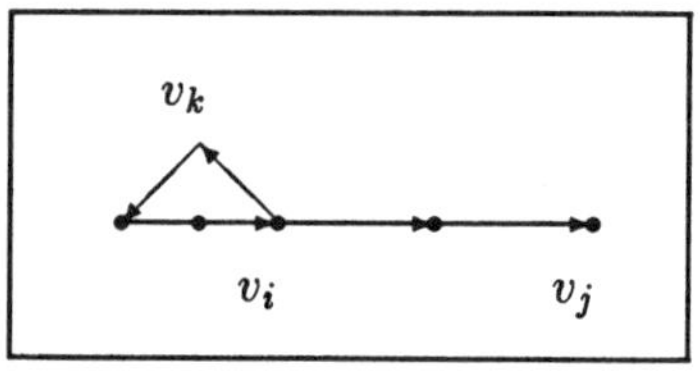

Figure 2: A naive first step is not enough for transitive closure

We require a matrix of *witnesses for the transitive closure* to satisfy the following condition: If a path from v_i to v_j exists then such a path can be constructed by following the witnesses. Namely, there is a path $v_i = v_{i_0}, .., v_{i_k} = v_j$ and for $1 \le r \le k$, i_r is the witness for the path from $v_{i_{r-1}}$ to v_j. In Section 3 we give an an $\tilde{O}(n^\omega)$ algorithm that computes witnesses for the transitive closure .

Coming back to the shortest paths problem we would like to compute in addition to the matrix D^* of shortest distances also

1. Witnesses for shortest paths.

2. A simple negative cycle for each i such that $d^*_{ii} = -\infty$.

Consequently, shortest paths of finite length can be easily obtained from 1. On the other hand, a shortest path of length $-\infty$ can be represented as a (possibly empty) path from 1 together with a negative cycle (from 2). We denote the problem of generating these witnesses for the $APSD(n, M)$ problem by $APSP(n, M)$ (All Pairs Shortest Paths).

In Section 4 we first give an algorithm for computing witnesses for shortest paths when edge lengths are positive, then when edge lengths are nonnegative. Finally we give an algorithm that generates the characterization of shortest paths in the general case. Its running time is $\tilde{O}(n^{(3+\omega)/2})$.

Summarizing, we get the following bounds for $APSP(n, 1)$: $\tilde{O}(n^{(3+\omega)/2})$ in the directed case and $\tilde{O}(n^{\omega})$ in the undirected case. Recall that the time bounds for $APSD(n, 1)$ are $O(n^{(3+\omega)/2})$ in the directed case and $O(n^{\omega} \log n)$ in the undirected case. Indeed, some of the Boolean matrix multiplications are now augmented to compute also witnesses, which explains our motivation to study the latter. (We believe that witnesses for Boolean matrix multiplication will be found useful elsewhere as well.) The fact that the bounds for $APSP$ are obtained from the bounds for $APSD$ by adding polylogarithmic factors is not immediate. This would be a simple consequence of our algorithm for matrix multiplication with witnesses if the algorithms just added witnesses to each Boolean matrix multiplication. However, this reason is not the only one needed to explain this coincidence. More details are given in Section 4.

2 Boolean matrix multiplication with witnesses

All the matrices in this section are n by n matrices, unless otherwise specified. If M is such a matrix, we let M_{ij} denote the entry in its ith row and jth column. Let A and B be two matrices with $\{0, 1\}$ entries, and let C be their product over the integers. Our objective is to find witnesses for all the positive entries of C, i.e., for each entry $C_{ij} > 0$ of C we wish to find a k such that $A_{ik} = B_{kj} = 1$. This is clearly equivalent to the problem of finding witnesses for the *Boolean* matrix multiplication $A \cdot B$. As observed by several researchers (including Seidel, Karger and the first three authors) there is a simple randomized algorithm that solves this problem in expected running time $\tilde{O}(n^{\omega})$. Here we consider *deterministic* algorithms for the problem. Our best algorithm, described in the next subsection, is, in a sense, a derandomized version of the simple randomized solution, and its running time is $\tilde{O}(n^{\omega})$. The derandomization requires several modifications in the straightforward randomized algorithm together with an interesting application of the known constructions of [5] (or [1]) of almost c-wise independent random variables in small sample spaces.

2.1 The algorithm

The first simple observation is the fact that if E and F are two matrices with $\{0, 1\}$ entries and $G = EF$ then one multiplication of matrices with entries at most n suffices for finding witnesses for all the entries of G which are precisely 1. Indeed, simply replace every 1-entry in the kth row of F by k (for all $1 \leq k \leq n$) to get a matrix F' and compute $G' = EF'$. Now observe that if $G_{ij} = 1$ and $G'_{ij} = k$ then k is a witness for G_{ij}.

Define $c = \lceil \log\log n + 9 \rceil$ and $\alpha = \frac{8}{2^c}$. For two matrices E and F with $\{0, 1\}$ entries define $G = E \wedge F$ by $G_{ij} = E_{ij} \wedge F_{ij}$.

Here is an outline of the algorithm. Besides A,B and $C = AB$ it uses two additional matrices: R and D. The way to perform steps 3c and 3d will be described later.

- While not all witnesses are known
  1. Let L denote the set of all positive entries of C for which there are no known witnesses.
  2. Let R be the all 1 matrix.
  3. Perform the following $\lceil 1 + 3 \log_{4/3} n \rceil$ times:
     (a) $D \leftarrow A \cdot (B \wedge R)$ (The matrix multiplication is over the integers)
     (b) Let L' denote the set of all entries of D in L which are at most c.
     (c) Find witnesses for all entries in L'.
     (d) $R \leftarrow$ *good* matrix (see definition of good below).

A matrix R is *good* (in step 3d above) if the following two conditions hold:

a) The total sum of the entries of $D = A \cdot (B \wedge R)$ in L is at most 3/4 of what this sum was while using the previous matrix R. (Observe that this guarantees that after $1 + 3 \log_{4/3} n$ iterations all these entries of D will vanish.)

b) The fraction of entries of D in L that go from a value bigger than c to 0 is at most α.

Lemma 1 *If $R \leftarrow R \wedge S$ in step 3d where S is a random* 0, 1 *matrix, then the new R is good with probability at least* 1/6.

The lemma follows from the following three claims:

Claim 1 *The probability that the sum of entries of D in L goes down by at least a factor of $3/4$ is at least $1/3$.*

To see this, observe that the expected sum of entries of D in L goes down by $1/2$. Thus, the claim follows from Markov's Inequality. □

Claim 2 *The probability that a fixed entry of D which is at least c drops down to 0 is at most $1/2^c$.*

This is obvious. Observe that the claim holds even if we only assume that every c entries of S are independent. □

Claim 3 *The probability that more than a fraction α of the entries of D in L drop from at least c to 0 is at most $\frac{1}{2^c}\frac{1}{\alpha} = \frac{1}{8}$.*

This follows from Claim 2 by Markov's Inequality. Since $1/3 - 1/8 > 1/6$ the lemma follows. □

Define $\epsilon = \frac{1}{2^{c+1}}$. The crucial point is to observe that the proof of the above lemma still holds, with almost no change, if the matrix S is not totally random but its entries are chosen from a c-wise ϵ-dependent distribution in the sense of [5], [1]. Recall that if m random variables whose range is $\{0, 1\}$ are *c-wise ϵ-dependent* then every subset of $i \leq c$ of them attains each of the possible 2^i configurations of 0 and 1 with probability that deviates from $1/2^i$ by at most ϵ.

Lemma 2 *If $R \leftarrow R \wedge S$ in step 3d where the entries of S are chosen as n^2 random variables that are c-wise ϵ-dependent, then the new R is good with probability at least $1/12 - 2\epsilon$.*

We note that in fact it is sufficient to choose only one column and copy it n times. The proof is by the following modified three claims, whose proof is analogous to that of the corresponding previous ones.

Claim 4 *The probability that the sum of entries of D in L goes down by at least a factor of $3/4$ is at least $1/3 - 2\epsilon$.* □

Claim 5 *The probability that a fixed entry of D which is at least c drops down to 0 is at most $1/2^c + \epsilon$.* □

Claim 6 *The probability that more than a fraction α of the entries of D in L drop from at least c to 0 is at most $(\frac{1}{2^c} + \epsilon)\frac{1}{\alpha} < \frac{2}{2^c}\frac{1}{\alpha} = 1/4$.* □

The lemma follows from the above three claims. □

As shown in [5] and in [1] there are explicit probability spaces with n^2 random variables which are c-wise ϵ-dependent, whose size is

$$\left(\log n \cdot c \cdot \frac{1}{\epsilon}\right)^{2+o(1)},$$

which is less than, e.g., $O((\log n)^5)$. Moreover, these spaces can be easily constructed in time negligible with respect to the total running time of our algorithm. Now suppose that in step 3d all the matrices S defined by such a probability space are searched, until a good one is found. Checking whether a matrix is good requires only matrix multiplication plus $O(n^2)$ operations. Therefore the inner loop (starting at step 3) takes polylog n times matrix multiplication time. It is important to note that during the performance of step 3d, while considering all possible matrices S provided by our distribution, we can accomplish step 3c as well. This is true since c-wise ϵ-dependence guarantees that every entry in L' will drop to precisely 1 for some of the matrices S and hence, by the observation in the beginning of this subsection, if we replace each matrix multiplication in the search for a good S by two matrix multiplications as described in that observation, we complete steps 3c and 3d together.

In every iteration of the inner loop 3 at most α fraction of the entries of L are "thrown" (i.e. their witness will not be found in this iteration of the outer loop). Therefore at least $(1-\alpha)^{1+3\log_{4/3} n}$ fraction of the entries of D in L will *not* be thrown during the completion of these iterations. For those entries, which are at least 1/2 of the entries in L, a witness is found. Therefore, only $O(\log n)$ iterations of the outer loop are required, implying the desired $\tilde{O}(n^\omega)$ total running time.

We have thus proved the following:

Theorem 1 *The witnesses for the Boolean multiplication of two n by n matrices can be found in deterministic $\tilde{O}(n^\omega)$ time.*

2.2 An alternative approach

The witnesses for Boolean matrix multiplication can be computed in a different manner. Although the running time obtained is slightly worse than that of our previous algorithm, it may give better performance for matrices of moderate size.

Here is a rough outline of the approach: We design a sequence of algorithms, the first algorithm ALG_0, is the naive cubic way: test all the n possible witnesses for every positive entry C_{ij}. The next algorithm ALG_1, is the following: Consider each of the two matrices A and B as an $L \times L$ block matrix where each block is of size $n/L \times n/L$. Multiply the two block matrices using the trivial L^3 time algorithm, and using fast matrix multiplication for any multiplication of two blocks. Now we know for each positive entry C_{ij}, a product of a block of A and a block of B which contains a witness. Use ALG_0 for finding witnesses inside that block. The running time is

$$O\left(L^3\left(\frac{n}{L}\right)^\omega + L^2\left(\frac{n}{L}\right)^3\right).$$

An appropriate choice of L gives an $O(n^{\frac{9-2\omega}{4-\omega}})$ time algorithm.

The sequence starting with these two algorithms can be extended, where each algorithm uses the previous one and the time complexity converges to $O(n^{\omega+O(\log^{-1/3}(n))})$. This requires several additional ideas including a generalization of the problem to that of finding witnesses for a prescribed subset of entries of the product of two rectangular matrices, given certain information on the location of these witnesses. The details are complicated and since the running time is inferior to that of our previous algorithm we do not include them. For any given problem, one can apply any of the algorithms from the sequence above. It seems that for certain possible sizes, one of the algorithms ALG_s for some small integer s may actually be faster than the algorithm in the previous subsection.

3 Computing witnesses for the transitive closure

In the introduction we explained why the immediate solution that computes witnesses for $A \cdot T$ does not work. Another simple solution is to add lengths to the edges and compute witnesses for shortest paths. However, the best time for computing only the distances in the directed case (even without the witnesses for the paths) is $O(n^{(\omega+3)/2})$.

The only reason that the immediate solution does not work are the cycles. So we first find the strongly connected components of G, then we contract them into new vertices. Now we can use the immediate algorithm to solve the new problem. Lastly, we "open" the contracted vertices and transform the solution to a solution for the original problem. More formally:

Algorithm

1. Compute the strongly connected components of the input graph $G = (V, E)$, where $V = \{v_1, \ldots, v_n\}$. Denote by $V' = \{v'_1, v'_2, \ldots, v'_m\}$ the set of strongly connected components of G, where $v'_i = \{v_{i1}, v_{i2}, \ldots, v_{ir_i}\}$. We build the contracted graph $G' = (V', E')$, where $E' = \{(v'_i, v'_j) : \exists (v_{ix}, v_{jy}) \in E\}$. Each edge $(v'_i, v'_j) \in E'$ is arbitrarily associated with one edge $(v_{ix}, v_{jy}) \in E$. This can be done in $O(n^2)$ time.

2. Solve the transitive closure problem of the graph G', denote the solution by T'. Compute witnesses for the Boolean matrix multiplication $T' \cdot A'$ by W'. This step can be done in $\tilde{O}(n^\omega)$ time.

3. For each strongly connected component we find witnesses for the transitive closure (which is a clique). Denote the witnesses matrix for that problem by $\hat{W}$; this matrix is defined only for pairs which are in the same strongly connected component. This can be done in $O(n^2)$ time, as described in Algorithm 3.1.

4. Expand the solution of the contracted problem into a solution for the whole problem. This can be done in $O(n^2)$ time as described in Algorithm 3.2.

Theorem 2 *The algorithm above computes the matrix of witnesses in time $\tilde{O}(n^\omega)$.*

3.1 Computing witnesses for a strongly connected graph

The algorithm has two stages. In the first, we perform breadth first search (BFS) from one of the vertices v_0. In the process we generate a BFS tree T. For each edge $(u, v) \in T$ and every descendant w of v we set $W(u, w) \leftarrow v$. In the second stage, we use the reverse edges and perform another BFS from v_0. We process a vertex when it is first visited. Assume we enter first u using edge (u, v). We then consider all $w \in V$ and if $W(u, w)$ is undefined we set it to v.

Obviously, each stage takes $O(n^2)$ time. Correctness follows by induction. The induction hypothesis states that for every processed vertex u, and every w, starting with u and following W we obtain a simple path from u to w. The base is true because the first stage essentially processes v_0. For the induction step, assume we process u. If $W(u, w) = z$ is defined, it was defined in the first stage and (u, z) is in the BFS tree of the first stage and following W we follow a path on the tree from u to w. If it is undefined, we set $W(u, w) \leftarrow v$, where v was processed before. The claim now follows from the induction hypothesis.

3.2 Joining solutions

Examine the solution for G'. Suppose that $W'(i, j)$-$= k$; by the definition of a witness, there exists an edge (v'_i, v'_k). Let (v_{ix}, v_{ky}) be the edge of G associated with it.

$$W(v_{ik_1}, v_{jk_2}) = \begin{cases} v_{ky} & k_1 = x \\ \hat{W}(v_{ik_1}, v_{ix}) & \text{otherwise.} \end{cases}$$

The time complexity of this algorithm is $O(n^2)$.

4 Finding paths

In this section we solve the $APSP(n, 1)$ problem. Solving the $APSP(n, M)$ problem is similar, since the treatment of 'large' edges is the same as in the $APSD$ problem. We first show what cannot be done. Then we solve the positive case (subsection 4.1). We solve the nonnegative case in subsection 4.2. The solution for the unrestricted case is complicated, and due to space limitations we omit most of the proofs for this case in subsection 4.4. In subsection 4.3 we consider the simpler special case of undirected graphs.

As explained in the introduction, one way to avoid the cubic bottleneck is to compute witnesses. For each pair (i, j) we compute an index k of a first vertex on a shortest path from v_i to v_j. This certainly works in the positive case.

4.1 Positive $APSP$

Consider the algorithm for the positive $APSD(n, 1)$ problem [2]. It uses Boolean matrix multiplications to compute short distances. Computing Boolean matrix multiplication with witnesses gives witnesses for these shortest paths.

For computing large distances, we use the separator trick: We consider in turn each vertex as a source and the layered graph obtained by single source shortest paths. We take a block of consecutive layers, choose the smallest one and use it as a separator. Each path that goes beyond the separator must go through the separator. Hence we minimize over the choice of the vertex on the separator. This part is performed naively and provides witnesses: If a shortest path from v_i to v_j goes through v_k, where v_k belongs to the separator, then the i, j witness can be taken to be the i, k witness that has already been computed.

Consequently, to obtain the time bound we can substitute $\widetilde{O}(n^{\omega})$ (the time for witnessed Boolean matrix multiplication) for $O(n^{\omega})$ in the bound for the positive $APSD(n, 1)$:

Theorem 3 *The positive $APSP(n, 1)$ problem can be solved in $\widetilde{O}(n^{(3+\omega)/2})$ time.*

4.2 Nonnegative $APSP$

Consider the nonnegative $APSD(n, 1)$ problem. One way to solve it is to eliminate the zero length edges first. We first compute Z, the transitive closure of the zero edges. It gives us all zero (shortest) distances. Let D' be obtained from D by replacing the $+\infty$ entries by zero. Compute the Boolean matrix multiplication $E \stackrel{\text{def}}{=} (Z + I)D'(Z + I)$. An edge in E corresponds to a path of length 1. Solve the $APSP$ problem for E to obtain all shortest nonzero distances.

A first attempt to obtain witnesses for shortest paths is simply to combine three sets of witnesses: the ones obtained from the solution of the positive $APSP$, the witnesses implied by the definition of E (two per entry) and the witnesses of the transitive closure Z. This approach does not give witnesses for the shortest paths as the following example shows.

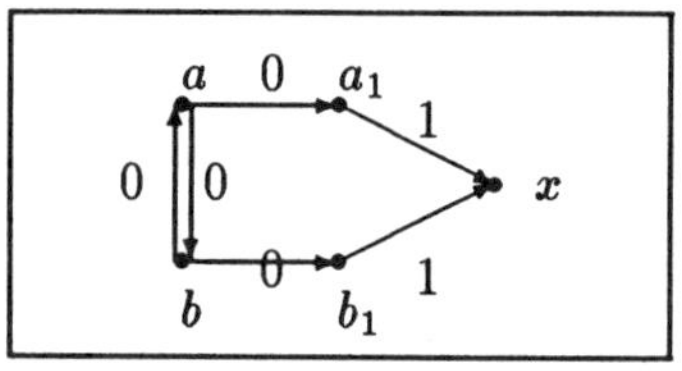

Figure 3: An example of failure of the naive solution

Consider Figure 3. E contains a direct edge of length 1 from a to x and from b to x. Suppose that the witness which was chosen in the $(Z + I)D'(Z + I)$ multiplication for the $a \rightarrow x$ pair is b_1 and for the $b \rightarrow x$ pair is a_1. Simply combining the three sets of witnesses would lead us to the infinite path $a, b, a, b, \ldots$ for the pair $a \rightarrow x$.

The difficulty above is caused by zero length cycles in G. But we overcome it as in Section 3. We find the strongly connected components of Z, compute witnesses for them and contract them in G, forming the contracted graph G'. We avoid multiple edges by always choosing a minimum length edge. We next find the witnesses for shortest paths in G' by the method described above. (In G' there are no zero length cycles.) Finally, we combine the two sets of witnesses as in Section 3 to obtain the witnesses for shortest paths of G. The full details are omitted.

Theorem 4 *The nonnegative $APSP(n,1)$ problem can be solved in $\tilde{O}(n^{(3+\omega)/2})$ time.*

4.3 Undirected $APSP$

In the undirected case, zero edges or negative edges pose no problem and can be eliminated easily. The special algorithm for the undirected $APSP$ uses essentially only Boolean matrix multiplications, which can easily be replaced by ones with witnesses. A *randomized* algorithm that solves the undirected $APSP(n,1)$ problem in (expected) time $\tilde{O}(n^{\omega})$ has been found by Seidel as well as by ourselves. Our result in Section 2 enable us to obtain a *deterministic* algorithm with the same running time.

Theorem 5 *The undirected $APSP(n,1)$ problem can be solved in $\tilde{O}(n^{\omega})$ time.*

4.4 The general case

We consider the case of $d_{ij} \in \{0, \pm 1\}$. We first solve the corresponding $APSD$ problem, so we know D^*. We reduce the unrestricted problem step by step: In Subsubsection 4.4.1 we show how to eliminate the $-\infty$ distances. In Subsubsection 4.4.2 we show how to eliminate the zero cycles. In Subsubsection 4.4.3 we solve the reduced problem where all the cycles are positive.

4.4.1 Removing the negative cycles

To handle the $-\infty$ distances, we start with the negative cycles. A *negative component* is a maximal set of vertices C such that if $v_i, v_j \in C$ then $d^*_{ij} = d^*_{ji} = -\infty$. The output for the unrestricted $APSP$ problem consists of the following parts:

1. $D^{*'}$ a matrix of distances which matches D^* in all its entries which are not $-\infty$.

2. A matrix of witnesses W: for every $1 \leq i,j \leq n$ starting from v_i and using W one obtains a simple path π_{ij} from v_i to v_j if one exists. Otherwise W_{ij} is undefined. In case d^*_{ij} is finite π_{ij} is a shortest path and in case $d^*_{ij} = -\infty$, π_{ij} passes through a negative component. Its length, in any case is $d^{*'}_{ij}$.

3. An array Neg representing a subgraph G' of G of outdegree ≤ 1. G' contains a simple negative cycle σ_C for every negative component C and a simple path from every vertex in C to σ_C.

Obviously the witnesses generate all finite length shortest paths. In case of $d^*_{ij} = -\infty$ this output can be used to generate a path from v_i to v_j of length under any specified bound: Given a bound L on the length of the path, start generating the path and update the bound. If, after reaching v_k, $D^{*'}_{kj}$ is less than the bound L, or if the Neg pointer is not defined, then follow the witnesses matrix W. Otherwise follow the Neg pointer. In any case update the bound by subtracting the length of the current edge $(v_k \rightarrow v_{k'})$.

The matrix $D^{*'}$ can be computed from the witnesses matrix W using the algorithm in Figure 4.

Set $D^{*'}_{ij} \leftarrow \begin{cases} \infty & i \neq j, \\ 0 & \text{otherwise} \end{cases}$
For all pairs i,j such that $d^*_{ij} < \infty$ do $\text{Upd}(i,j)$

$\text{Upd}(i,j)$: If $(D^{*'}_{ij} = \infty)$ $\{$ $k \leftarrow W_{ij}$; $\text{Upd}(k,j)$; $D^{*'}_{ij} \leftarrow d_{ik} + D^{*'}_{kj}$ $\}$

Figure 4: Algorithm for computing $D^{*'}$

Lemma 3 *The algorithm in Figure 4 computes $D^{*'}$ in $O(n^2)$ time.*

The computation of the array Neg is the most complicated. The reason for that is that we can not make any use of the distance matrix inside a negative component; all distances are $-\infty$. Let $P(n,m)$ be the problem of testing whether a graph with n vertices and m edges has a negative cycle and let $\widehat{P}(n,m)$ be the problem of constructing a negative cycle given the matrix D^* of shortest distances (and thus knowing that one exists).

Lemma 4 *The time complexity of P, $T(n,m)$ satisfies $T(n,m) \leq \widehat{T}(2n, m+3n-2) + O(n)$, where $\widehat{T}$ is the time complexity of $\widehat{P}$.*

The proof construcs for an input G to P a new graph $\widehat{G}$ input to $\widehat{P}$ with only constant factor more vertices and edges. Thus any subcubic algorithm will be transformed into a subcubic algorithm. (Actually the complexity in terms of number of vertices and number of edges is preserved.) Therefore, since we believe that the problem of finding whether a contains a negative cycle or not is a difficult one (no subcubic algorithm was known before), we get that the problem of explicitly finding even a single negative cycle given all the shortest distances is a difficult problem. We solve it below.

The subcubic algorithm for the unrestricted $APSP$ is a modification of the unrestricted $APSD$ of [2]. The latter is a recursive algorithm that uses Boolean matrix multiplications, transitive closure computations and the separator trick. Some recursive calls construct a new graph and then operate on it. We now show how to compute the array Neg in $\tilde{O}(n^\omega)$ time.

First we run the $APSD$ algorithm and replace the Boolean matrix multiplications by witnessed multiplications. The resulting recursive structure has logarithmic depth and each layer contains at most n edges. More precisely, we have $\log(n)$ types of edges, the zero type is an edge which appears in the input graph, and every type t edge $v_i \xrightarrow{t} v_j$ is a path $\pi^t_{ij} = \{v_{k_r}\}_{r=0}^m$ such that $k_0 = i$, $k_m = j$, $m \leq n$ and its length d^t_{ij} satisfies

$$d^t_{ij} \geq \sum_{r=0}^{m-1} d^{t-1}_{k_r k_{r+1}}. \qquad (1)$$

Call the process of replacing a type t edge with a type $t-1$ path a *refinement* of that edge.

Consider i with $d^*_{ii} = -\infty$. The APSD algorithm finds it by dicovering the existence of a triangle $(v_i, v_{k_1}, v_{k_2}, v_i)$ such that $d^t_{ik_1}, d^t_{k_2 i} \leq 0$, $d^0_{k_1 k_2} < 0$ for some $t \leq \log n$ (the recursion depth). It discovers the triangle by two Boolean matrix multiplications and computing them with witnesses yields also k_1 and k_2. We start with such a triangle and maintain a characterization of the path from v_i to v_i. We keep a linked list which specifies the refinement degree for every edge.

Repeat t times refining all the edges to edges which are one type smaller. The problem with this process is that we can end up with a path of $\Omega(n^{\log(n)})$ edges. To avoid this, in every refinement we keep the number of vertices to be no more than n by making sure that no vertex will appear more than once in the current path. To do this we also keep for every vertex v_k on the linked list a bound $dist(k)$ on the distance from v_i to v_k along the path which is being built and a unique index $num(k)$ which enables us to determine which vertex comes first on the path.

The refinement step is simple: we use the witnesses from the witnessed $APSD$ algorithm to convert a type t edge into a path of type $t-1$. Note that we always use type $t-1$ edges, it can be that some of these edges have lower type, say $t' < t-1$; e.g. in the triangles mentioned above. In this case we regard them as a type $t-1$ edge which consists of a path of one edge of type $t-2$ etc. We maintain the linked list and update the functions $dist$ and num. If while refining some edge $v_i \to v_j$ of type t, we get a vertex v_k which already was on that path, thus forming a cycle, there are two cases:

Negative cycle: We change our target: set $i \leftarrow k$ and start with the cycle between k and k which we currently have. We release the subpaths from v_i to the first occurrence of v_k and from the second occurrence of v_k to v_i (mark them as not in the current path).

Nonnegative cycle: We bypass the section between the two copies of v_k: define the successor of v_k in the list as the successor of the copy which is further in the path, and release the cycle.

It is easy to verify that while performing this algorithm we maintain a negative cycle which is refined all the time, but never has more than n vertices. So finally we will have a type zero negative cycle.

Theorem 6 *The algorithm sketched above finds a negative cycle in $O(n^2 \log n)$ time.*

After one negative cycle is build: $v_{i_0}, v_{i_1}, \ldots, v_{i_{m-1}}$, we fix Neg to follow it: $Neg(i_r) \leftarrow i_{r+1 \pmod m}$. To define Neg on the other vertices of the negative component C, remove all outgoing edges from the cycle (all edges $u \to w$ where u is in the cycle and w not). After the change there is still a path from every vertex of C to the cycle. Then run a BFS on the reverse edges from v_{i_0}. Set $Neg(v_p) = v_q$ if you reach v_p from v_q in the BFS. Clearly, Neg will not change on the cycle, and following it will lead from any vertex in C to v_{i_0}.

The time complexity of the algorithm is $O(n^2)$ per refining step (we refine no more than n edges of type t, each one of them into $O(n)$ edges of type $t-1$ and each takes $O(1)$ time), therefore the total time is $O(n^2 \log n)$. We may run this algorithm several times, once for each strongly connected component with n_i vertices. The complexity will be $\sum_i n_i^2 \log n_i$, where $\sum_i n_i = n$. From the convexity of $n^2 \log n$ we get that the time complexity is $O(n^2 \log n)$.

Now, that we have the array Neg, we remove all the $-\infty$ distances. The reduction is as follows:

1. Identify the negative components and find the Neg pointers for each one of them. All these pointers fit into a single array Neg.

2. Solve the witnessed transitive closure problem for each one of the negative components. Denote the witness matrix by T.

3. Construct a new graph $\hat{G}$ by contracting the negative components. In case of multiple edges we keep only one. In $\hat{G}$ we give edge length zero to original edges and -1 to edges incident with new vertices. Note that $\hat{G}$ does not have negative cycles. In $\hat{G}$ we compute witnesses for shortest paths (as explained in the next subsubsections). Denote the witnesses matrix by $\hat{W}$.

4. Join the last two matrices into W as follows: For every pair of vertices i and j, let $\hat{i}$ and $\hat{j}$ be the contracted negative components which contains i and j if such components exists, or the original vertices otherwise. Let $\hat{k} = \hat{W}_{\hat{i}\hat{j}}$ and let $i' \to k'$ be the edge in the original graph which was chosen to represent the contracted edge $\hat{i} \to \hat{k}$. Set

$$W^-_{ij} \leftarrow \begin{cases} T_{ij} & \hat{i} = \hat{j}, \\ k' & \hat{i} \neq \hat{j} \text{ and } i = i' \\ T_{ii'} & i \neq i'. \end{cases}$$

This completes the computation of witnesses for the $-\infty$ distances. At this point we can delete all edges which are adjacent to any vertex in a negative component, resulting in a graph $\widetilde{G}$ with no negative cycles. We solve the $APSP$ problem for $\widetilde{G}$ and merge the solution $\widetilde{W}$ with that of the $-\infty$ distances W^- by taking

$$W_{ij} = \begin{cases} \widetilde{W}_{ij} & \tilde{d}^*_{ij} \text{ finite} \\ W^-_{ij} & \text{otherwise.} \end{cases}$$

It is easy to verify that defining the witness matrix W in this way, we can follow it and get the finite distances as $\widetilde{W}$ gives them, and get for the $-\infty$ distances a simple finite path which passes though at least one negative component.

It remains to show how to compute witnesses for graphs with no negative cycles. Because of the presence of negative length edges we cannot use the simple algorithm that contracts the zero length cycles of Subsection 4.2.

4.4.2 Removing the zero cycles

We define $v_i R v_j$ if and only if $d^*_{ij} + d^*_{ji} = 0$ and refer to the equivalence classes of R as *zero components.* We then compute witnesses as follows.

1. Find witnesses inside zero components.

2. Replace each zero component with a new structure called a U–structure, so that the resulting graph has no non–trivial zero components and compute witnesses for the resulting graph.

3. Combine the two sets of witnesses.

To find witnesses inside a zero component we define a subgraph G_1 with edges (v_i, v_j) such that v_i and v_j are in the same zero component and $d_{ij} = d^*_{ij}$. Thus each edge in G_1 is a shortest path, furthermore

Lemma 5 *Each path in G_1 is a shortest path in G.*

Given a component with m vertices, its corresponding U–structure has a set of vertices containing two vertices v'_i and v''_i for each original vertex v_i and the edges are:

1. An edge from v'_i to v'_j of length -1 for every v_i and v_j such that $d^*_{ij} = -1$.

2. An edge from v''_i to v''_j of length $+1$ for every v_i and v_j such that $d^*_{ij} = +1$.

3. Zero length edges from v'_i to v'_j and from v''_i to v''_j for every pair of vertices v_i and v_j such that $d^*_{ij} = 0$ and $i < j$.

4. For every k, a zero length edge from $v'_{max(k)}$ to $v''_{min(k)}$ where $max(k) \stackrel{\text{def}}{=} \max\{\ell : d^*_{\ell k} = 0\}$ and $min(k) \stackrel{\text{def}}{=} \min\{\ell : d^*_{\ell k} = 0\}$. Note that we may count the same edge several times (there are no multiple edges).

The U–structure replaces the corresponding component by replacing any edge from v_i of some component to w_j of another component by an edge from v''_i to w'_j. An example is shown in Figure 5. In this example, all down going edges in the U–structure have length -1, all up going edges have length $+1$ and all horizontal edges have length 0. The thick edges are the edges from $v'_{\max(k)}$ to $v''_{\min(k)}$.

Lemma 6 *Let G be a graph with no negative cycles. The graph G_2 obtained from G by replacing each zero component by a U structure satisfies the following properties*

1. *Its edge lengths are in $\{-1, 0, 1\}$,*

2. *it contains no zero length cycles,*

3. *it has twice the number of vertices as G and*

4. *it contains the shortest distances structure of G.*

Every shortest path in G_2 can be translated into a shortest path in G by replacing the edges in the U-structures by paths in G (which exists from Lemma 6). Thus, we have reduced the unrestricted case to the case in which all cycles have positive lengths.

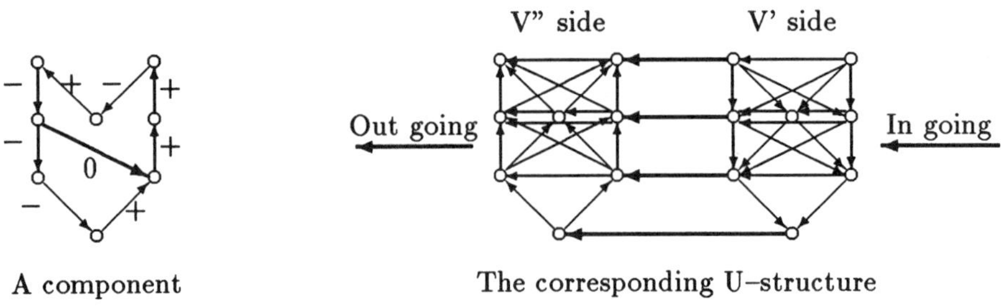

Figure 5: An example of a U–structure

4.4.3 Positive cycles only

Here, we find witnesses by unwinding the recursive *APSD* algorithm taking always the first edge.

Lemma 7 *Given a graph G with no directed nonpositive cycles, we can solve the APSP problem by replacing all the Boolean matrix multiplications in the APSD algorithm by witnessed Boolean matrix multiplications.*

Theorem 7 *The unrestricted* $APSP(n,1)$ *problem can be solved in* $\tilde{O}(n^{(3+\omega)/2})$ *time.*

Proof. Subsubsection 4.4.1 reduced the general problem into one without negative cycles. Subsubsection 4.4.2 reduced the problem even further to the case where there is no nonpositive length cycle. In this subsubsection we solved this case. □

5 Open Problems

Of course one would like to improve the time bounds for computing various types of witnesses. In particular, can we compute the witnesses for Boolean matrix multiplication in time $O(n^\omega)$? Alternatively, one would like to improve the best algorithms for $APSD(n, M)$ and $APSP(n, M)$, for directed graphs and for undirected graphs, for the nonnegative case and for the unrestricted case, by improving the exponent (in the undirected case this is not possible without improving Boolean matrix multiplication) or by improving the dependence on M.

We are also looking for other problems for which one may need the witnesses in addition to Boolean matrix multiplication or to transitive closure. It seems very plausible that these will find additional applications in the future.

Given the shortest distances, how hard is it to compute witnesses for the shortest paths? Possibly, this can be solved in $O(n^2)$ time, but all our algorithms need additional matrix multiplications.

References

[1] N. Alon, O. Goldreich, J. Hastad and R. Peralta, *Simple constructions of almost k-wise independent random variables*, Proc. 31st IEEE FOCS, St. Louis, Missouri, IEEE (1990), pp. 544-553.

[2] N. Alon, Z. Galil and O. Margalit, *On the exponent of the All Pairs Shortest Path problem*, Proc. 32th IEEE FOCS, IEEE (1991), pp. 569-575.

[3] D. Coppersmith and S. Winograd, *Matrix multiplication via arithmetic progressions*, Journal of Symbolic Computation 9(1990), pp. 251–280.

[4] Z. Galil and O. Margalit, *A faster algorithm for the all pairs shortest path problem for undirected graphs*, August 1991.

[5] J. Naor and M. Naor, *Small-bias probability spaces: efficient constructions and applications*, Proc. 22nd annual ACM STOC, ACM Press (1990), pp. 213-223.

[6] R. Seidel, *On the All-Pairs-Shortest-Path Problem*, Proc. 24th ACM STOC, ACM Press (1992), pp. 745–749.

Zero-Knowledge Proofs of Knowledge Without Interaction
(Extended Abstract)

ALFREDO DE SANTIS* GIUSEPPE PERSIANO†

Abstract

A *zero-knowledge proof system of knowledge* is a protocol between two parties called the prover and the verifier. The prover wants to convince the verifier that he "knows" the proof of a given theorem without revealing any additional information. This is different from a zero-knowledge proof system of *membership* where the prover convinces the verifier only of the veridicity of the statement.

Zero-knowledge proofs of knowledge are very useful tools in the design of secure protocols. Though, the concept of a proof of knowledge is a very subtle one and great care is needed to obtain a satisfying formalization.

In this paper, we investigate the concept of a zero-knowledge proof of knowledge in the non-interactive model of [5, 6]. Here, the prover and the verifier share a short random string and the only communication allowed is from the prover to the verifier. Although this is a simpler model than the interactive one, still formalizing zero-knowledge proofs of knowledge is a delicate task.

The main results of the paper are the following

- We present formal definitions for the concept of non-interactive zero-knowledge proofs of knowledge (NIZKPK). To reach a proper definition, it is necessary to distinguish between the cases in which the statement is given to the prover before or after the common string is presented. In the first scenario the theorem is independent from the common string, whereas in the second it might be chosen "maliciously" as a function of the common string. We also discuss a third different scenario which is the most useful for applications.
- We prove that NIZKPK's exist under complexity assumptions for all polynomial-time relations. In our construction it is sufficient for the prover to be an efficient algorithm that has a witness.
- We show that proving that one-way permutations (used as black-box functions) are sufficient for the existence of NIZKPK (where the prover is efficient) is as hard as proving $P \neq NP$.
- Finally, we demonstrate the applicability of the concept of NIZKPK to Cryptography by proving the security of a construction of public-key cryptosystems secure against chosen-ciphertext attacks based on NIZKPK.

1 Introduction

The concept of a "proof system of possession of knowledge" is one of the many contributions of [15]. It is a protocol between two parties called the prover and the verifier where the prover wants to convince the verifier that he "knows" the proof of a given theorem. This is a stronger notion of a

*Dipartimento di Informatica ed Applicazioni, Università di Salerno, 84081 Baronissi (SA), Italy. Partially supported by Italian Ministry of University and Research (M.U.R.S.T.) and by National Council for Research (C.N.R.) under grant 91.02326.CT12. E-mail: ads@udsab.dia.unisa.it

†Aiken Computation Laboratory, Harvard University, Cambridge, MA 02138, USA and Dipartimento di Informatica, Università di Salerno. Supported at Harvard by NSF Grant # NSF-CCR-90-07677. E-mail: persiano@endor.harvard.edu

proof system where the prover wants just to convince the verifier of the veridicity of the theorem in question. In the same paper, it was also proposed to formalize the concept of proof system of knowledge by using the notion of an *extractor*. The extractor is a polynomial-time algorithm that can use the prover as an oracle (for example, he can pretend to be the verifier and run the protocol and then "rewind" the prover and start again asking different questions) and produces a witness to the theorem in question. Following the suggestion of [15], [11] gave a formal definitions (other definitions have been given by [21] and [2]; see [2] also for a discussion of issues arising in defining interactive proofs of knowledge).

The relevance of zero-knowledge proofs of knowledge to the design of secure protocols has first been recognized in [13]. In their protocol for a secure oblivious transfer the receiver has to prove that he "knows" a square root of the integer he has just sent to the sender.

Encryption is a fundamental cryptographic primitive, which, by its own nature, is a non-interactive process. The construction of a cryptosystem secure against chosen-ciphertext attacks has been a long-standing open problem. In order to solve this problem, Blum, Feldman, and Micali [6] suggested that the sender proves "knowledge" (in a zero-knowledge and non-interactive fashion) of the message whose encryption he has sent. (A different construction, relying on non-interactive zero-knowledge proofs [5, 6], has been subsequently given in [19].)

However, while it is a simple exercise to show that most interactive zero-knowledge proofs (e.g., those of [16]) admit an extractor, the non-interactive case seems to present greater difficulty. Moreover, until now, no formalization of proofs of knowledge in the model of [5, 6] has been put forward.

Summary of results

Formalizing Possession of Knowledge. Following the lead of [15], we present the concept of a *Non-Interactive Zero-Knowledge Proofs of Knowledge* (NIZKPK in short). A NIZKPK is a non-interactive zero-knowledge proof system that admits an extractor. The extractor chooses a random string σ along with some auxiliary information (e.g., in our construction the factorization of the integers appearing in σ) and then feeds the prover with σ. From the proof given by the prover, the extractor using the auxiliary information relative to σ is able to compute a witness.

In our definition, we distinguish two cases depending on whether the theorem for which the prover wants to claim knowledge of a witness is chosen before the random string (and thus independently) or after the random string is presented to the prover.

Constructing NIZKPK. We show a general procedure that, under the assumption that *Dense Secure Public-Key Cryptosystems* exist, given a non-interactive zero-knowledge proof system of membership for an NP-complete theorem constructs a NIZKPK for all polynomial-time relations. A dense secure public-key cryptosystem is a particular kind of cryptosystem and it is possible to prove its existence assuming the difficulty of deciding quadratic residuosity, the security of inverting the RSA function and the security of the Diffie-Hellman secret key exchange.

One-way permutations and NIZKPK. We present strong evidence that the implication "if one-way permutations exist then NIZKPK for all polynomial-time relations exist" is not provable by standard techniques. We use the result of Impagliazzo and Rudich [17] by which proving the security of a secret-key agreement protocol that uses a one-way permutation as a black-box is as hard as proving $P \neq NP$. Our result is the first "impossibility" result about zero-knowledge proofs and suggests a separation between non-interactive and interactive settings with respect to zero-knowledge proofs.

Applications of NIZKPK. We show the applicability of NIZKPK to the design of secure protocols. In particular, we give the first proof of security for the construction of a cryptosystem secure against chosen-ciphertext attacks suggested in [6]. NIZKPK can also be used for a variety of other cryptographic applications such as memoryless secure digital signatures [3] and blind signatures which will be discussed in a forthcoming paper.

Notation. An efficient algorithm is an algorithm running in expected polynomial-time. If $A(\cdot)$ is a probabilistic algorithm, then for any input x, the notation $A(x)$ refers to the probability space that assigns to the string σ the probability that A, on input x, outputs σ.
If S is a probability space, then "$x \leftarrow S$" denotes the algorithm which assigns to x an element randomly selected according to S and $[S]$ denotes the set of strings to which S assigns positive probability. If F is a finite set, then the notation "$x \leftarrow F$" denotes the algorithm which assigns to x a randomly selected element of F. For example, the writing "$\sigma \leftarrow \{0,1\}^n$" means that σ is a randomly chosen n-bit string.
If $p(\cdot,\cdot,\cdots)$ is a predicate, the notation $\mathbf{Pr}(x \leftarrow S; y \leftarrow T; \ldots : p(x,y,\cdots))$ denotes the probability that $p(x,y,\cdots)$ will be true after the ordered execution of the algorithms $x \leftarrow S$, $y \leftarrow T, \ldots$.
By the writing $a \circ b$ we denote the string obtained concatenating the strings a and b. If a and b are binary strings of the same length, $a \oplus b$ denotes their bitwise XOR.

2 Non-Interactive Zero-Knowledge Proofs of Knowledge

Informally speaking, by a zero-knowledge proof system of knowledge we mean a protocol for two parties called the prover and the verifier where the prover convinces the verifier that he "knows" a witness to the fact that a certain input string x is in a language L without giving any additional information. For example, the prover convinces the verifier that he *knows* a legal 3-coloring of the input graph (not just prove that such a 3-coloring exists!) without giving any information on the coloring. A formalization of this notion has been given in [11] following the suggestion of [15] (see also [21] and [2] for discussion of the interactive case). Roughly speaking, according to [11] a prover gives proof of knowledge if there exists an efficient "extractor" that, using the prover as an oracle, can produce a witness to the theorem given in input. In interactive scenarios, the extractor is allowed to ask questions to the prover and then rewind the prover and ask different questions. It is not hard to see that, for example, the interactive zero-knowledge proofs of membership of [16] for NP are also proofs of knowledge.

In this work we consider the non-interactive model introduced in [6], where the prover and the verifier share a short random string and the communication is mono-directional: from the prover to the verifier only. In [5] it is proved that, under the quadratic residuosity assumption, all NP languages have zero-knowledge proofs in this non-interactive model. This has been subsequently improved in [12] that showed that trapdoor permutations are sufficient for efficient provers (see also [4]). We refer the reader to [5] for a formal definition of non-interactive zero-knowledge proof system (of membership).

Obtaining proofs of knowledge in this non-interactive setting does not seem to be as easy as in the usual interactive scenario. One of the major technical obstacle to this, is the fact that rewinding the prover does not seem to be of any help in this non-interactive settings, as the verifier (and hence the extractor) is not allowed to ask questions and therefore the extractor has to be substantially different from the ones used in the interactive case. In our model, the extractor works in two phases. First, he computes a string σ, which is given to the prover, along with some private information. In the second phase, the extractor, using the private information relative to σ, extracts a witness to the theorem from the non-interactive proof computed by the prover using σ.

In this section, we consider two different scenarios. The main difference between these scenarios is when the theorem to be proved is chosen: before, and thus independently from the common string, or after seeing the common string.

Before defining NIZKPK, we need the following two concepts.

Definition 1. A relation is a subset of $\{0,1\}^* \times \{0,1\}^*$. A *polynomial-time relation* $\mathcal{P}$ is a relation for which given an *instance* x and a *witness* w it is possible to check in time polynomial in $|x|$ whether $(x,w) \in \mathcal{P}$. For each polynomial-time relation $\mathcal{P}$ the language $L_\mathcal{P} = \{x : \exists w \text{ for which } (x,w) \in \mathcal{P}\}$ belongs to NP. Conversely, every NP language naturally defines a polynomial-time relation. Finally, if x is an instance, by W_x we denote the set of w s.t. $(x,w) \in \mathcal{P}$.

Definition 2. An extractor is a pair of probabilistic polynomial-time algorithms $(\texttt{Ext}_0, \texttt{Ext}_1)$. Algorithm $\texttt{Ext}_0$ on input 1^n outputs a pair (σ, aux), with $|\sigma| = n$.

Definition 3. Non-Interactive Zero-Knowledge Proof of Knowledge. A NIZKPK for a polynomial-time relation $\mathcal{P}$ is a non-interactive zero-knowledge proof system of membership (Prover, Verifier) for the language $L_\mathcal{P}$ such that

Validity. There exists an extractor $(\texttt{Ext}_0, \texttt{Ext}_1)$ such that for all algorithms Adversary, for all constants $a > 0$, all sufficiently large n, and all x,

$$\begin{aligned}&\mathbf{Pr}((\sigma, aux) \leftarrow \texttt{Ext}_0(1^n);\\ &\quad \Pi \leftarrow \texttt{Adversary}(\sigma, x);\\ &\quad w \leftarrow \texttt{Ext}_1(\sigma, aux, x, \Pi) :\\ &\qquad (x,w) \in \mathcal{P}) \geq p_{n,x} \cdot (1 - n^{-a}),\end{aligned}$$

where $p_{n,x}$ denotes the probability

$$\begin{aligned}&\mathbf{Pr}(\sigma \leftarrow \{0,1\}^n;\ \Pi \leftarrow \texttt{Adversary}(\sigma, x) :\\ &\qquad \texttt{Verifier}(\sigma, x, \Pi) = 1).\end{aligned}$$

Remarks. The Validity property holds with respect to any algorithm Adversary. That is, Adversary can even be an all-powerful machine and nevertheless the extractor is able to get a witness from his proof. This requires that the string σ output by $\texttt{Ext}_0$ is uniformly distributed, that is it has the same distribution of the common string, or is statistically close to it. Also notice that in the above definition the instance x is given to Adversary together with the string σ; that is, Adversary is not allowed to choose x as a function of σ.

In our definition the extractor algorithm is required to have probability of success to be no significantly smaller than $p_{n,x}$. However, as the theorem is fixed and independent from the random string, it is possible to increase the probability of extracting a witness to $1 - 2^{-n}$ in the case that $p_{n,x}$ is greater than an inverse polynomial. This can be achieved by repeating the process a polynomial number of times and each time with a different string σ.

It is easy to see that the zero-knowledge proof system for quadratic non residuosity of [5] is indeed a NIZKPK for factorization. We have thus the following theorem.

Theorem 1. There exists a NIZKPK for the relation

$$\{(x, fac) | x \in \mathit{Regular} \text{ and } \mathit{fac} \text{ is } x\text{'s factorization}\},$$

where *Regular* is the set of integers which are not perfect squares and have exactly two prime factors.

Strong NIZKPK. Let us now consider the following scenario. First, the random string σ is chosen at random. After seeing the string σ, Adversary comes up with an instance x and a Π that convinces with some probability Verifier that he knows a witness for x. The strong validity property requires that in this case the extractor, which as before works in two phases, has a no significantly smaller probability of obtaining a witness for x. We define a Strong NIZKPK to be a NIZKPK with the strong validity property. In other words, in a strong NIZKPK, even if Adversary chooses x in a malicious way after seeing the string σ and convinces Verifier, the extractor can still obtain a witness for x with a non negligible probability. This is captured by the following definition.

Definition 4. Strong NIZKPK. A *Strong* NIZKPK system for a polynomial-time relation $\mathcal{P}$ is a NIZKPK (Prover, Verifier) such that

Strong Validity. There exists an extractor $(\texttt{Ext}_0, \texttt{Ext}_1)$ such that for any algorithm Adversary, for all constants $a > 0$, and all sufficiently large n,

$$\begin{aligned}&\mathbf{Pr}((\sigma, aux) \leftarrow \texttt{Ext}_0(1^n);\\ &\quad (x, \Pi) \leftarrow \texttt{Adversary}(\sigma);\\ &\quad w \leftarrow \texttt{Ext}_1(\sigma, aux, x, \Pi) :\\ &\qquad (x,w) \in \mathcal{P}) \geq p_n \cdot (1 - n^{-a}),\end{aligned}$$

where p_n denotes the probability

$$\mathbf{Pr}(\sigma \leftarrow \{0,1\}^n; (x, \Pi) \leftarrow \texttt{Adversary}(\sigma) : \texttt{Verifier}(\sigma, x, \Pi) = 1).$$

Notice that as for Definition 3, **Adversary** is not restricted to run in polynomial time. Also, the probability of success of the extractor algorithm is bounded by the probability that the specific prover at hand convinces **Verifier**. Unlike in the interactive case or when we only consider validity, this probability cannot be pumped-up. In fact, if we try to run **Adversary** with the same random string we might obtain the same string Π which clearly would not help. On the other hand, if we feed **Adversary** with a different random string σ, then he might choose a different theorem and this, again, would not be of any help.

We now present a definition of non-interactive zero-knowledge proofs of knowledge due to Silvio Micali.

Definition 5. Non-Interactive Zero-Knowledge Proof of Witness Possession. A NIZKWP for a polynomial-time relation $\mathcal{P}$ is a non-interactive zero-knowledge proof system of membership (Prover, Verifier) for the language $L_{\mathcal{P}}$ such that the following condition holds.

There exists an extractor ($\mathbf{Ext}_0$, $\mathbf{Ext}_1$) such that for all sufficiently large n, for almost all $\sigma \in \{0,1\}^n$, for all x, and for all π if $(\sigma, aux) \in [E_0(1^n)]$ and $\texttt{Verifier}(\sigma, x, \pi) = 1$ then $E_1(\sigma, aux, x, \pi) \in W_x$.

The main difference between the concept of NIZKPK and NIZKWP consists in the fact that NIZKPK considers the set of all σ's for which the adversary can construct a convincing proof; NIZKWP is instead a string-by-string definition. We will further explore the relations between the two definitions in the final version of this paper.

3 Constructing a NIZKPK

In this section we show a general procedure that, given a non-interactive zero-knowledge proof system of membership for an NP-complete language, constructs a strong NIZKPK for all polynomial time relations, under the assumption that dense secure public-key cryptosystems exist. Informally speaking, a *d-Dense Secure Public-Key Cryptosystem*, (for d constant) is a secure cryptosystem such that

1. Each n-bit string defines an encryption algorithm.
2. If we pick an n-bit string at random, then we have probability at least n^{-d} of picking a *secure* encryption algorithm.
3. It is possible to generate uniformly distributed n-bit descriptions of encryption algorithms along with their corresponding decryption algorithms.

The assumption of the existence of dense secure public-key cryptosystems is provably no stronger than assuming the difficulty of breaking RSA, deciding quadratic residuosity and breaking the Diffie-Hellman key-exchange protocol. In fact, each of the assumptions above implies the existence of dense secure public-key cryptosystems.

We now show how dense secure cryptosystems can be constructed under the assumption of the difficulty of deciding quadratic residuosity. More precisely, the *Quadratic Residuosity Assumption* (QRA) states that there exists no efficient algorithm that decides the quadratic residuosity modulo a randomly chosen integer x product of two primes of the same length of a randomly chosen element y with Jacobi symbol $+1$ with probability significantly better than $1/2$ (see [14] for the number theoretic background). The Quadratic Residuosity Assumption has been introduced by Goldwasser and Micali [14] and has since been widely used in cryptography (see, e.g. [5]).

Theorem 2. Under the QRA, dense secure cryptosystems exist.

Proof's sketch: Our construction is based on the Goldwasser–Micali probabilistic encryption scheme [14] which we briefly discuss here.

The encryption $\texttt{GM}(x, y, b)$ of a bit b with the key (x, y) (where y has Jacobi symbol modulo x $+1$) is computed by choosing a random $r \in Z_x^*$ and setting $\alpha = y^b r^2 \bmod x$. If y is a quadratic non residue modulo x then it is possible to recover the bit b from α in polynomial-time using x's factorization. If y is a quadratic residue, instead, b cannot be recovered. If x is product of two primes of the same length and y has Jacobi symbol $+1$ then, under the QRA, no polynomial-time algorithm that does not know x's factorization can guess b with probability of success significantly better than $1/2$.

Let us now briefly sketch the construction of a dense secure cryptosystem based on the QRA. A string σ of length $n = m(m+1)$ defines an encryption algorithm in the following way. The string σ is seen as the concatenation of $m+1$ strings $x, y_1, \cdots, y_m$ of length m. A bit b is encrypted by computing $\mathtt{GM}(x, y_i, b)$, for all $1 \leq i \leq m$.

Let us now see why this constitutes a dense secure cryptosystem. First of all, with high probability, at least one of the y_i's is a quadratic non residue modulo x and thus decryption is possible. Second, from the result on the distribution of primes it follows that with probability $\Omega(n^{-2})$ a random x is product of two primes and the corresponding encryption scheme is secure. Finally, to generate pairs of encryption/decryption keys, we use the algorithm of [1] that in expected polynomial-time returns a random integer of given length in factored form. ■

The following two theorems also hold.

Theorem 3. If the RSA encryption scheme is secure then dense secure cryptosystems exist.

Theorem 4. If the Diffie-Hellman secret-key exchange protocol is secure then dense secure cryptosystems exist.

Secure public-key systems vs dense secure public-key system. A secure public-key cryptosystem (see [14, 18]) is simply an efficient algorithm that outputs the description of a secure encryption algorithm along with the corresponding decryption algorithm. The existence of dense secure public-key cryptosystems seems to be a stronger assumption than the existence of secure public-key cryptosystems. In fact by comparing the two definitions, we note that, in the definition of secure public-key cryptosystem, nothing is guaranteed about the density of secure encryption algorithms among all the descriptions of a certain size; it might be well the case that only a negligible fraction is secure. Moreover, it does not guarantee that is possible to generate the encryption algorithm by itself without the decryption algorithm. As we shall see, both of these properties are necessary for our construction.

Theorem 5. If dense secure public-key cryptosystems and non-interactive zero-knowledge proof systems of membership for an NP-complete language exist then all polynomial-time relations have a Strong NIZKPK.

Proof's sketch: Let $\mathcal{P}$ be any polynomial-time relation, L an NP-complete language, (P, V) a Non-Interactive Zero-Knowledge Proof System of Membership for L and consider the following pair $(\mathtt{Prover}, \mathtt{Verifier})$.

Suppose that `Prover` has an instance x and a witness w such that $\mathcal{P}(x, w)$ holds and wants to convince `Verifier` that he knows such a witness without giving any additional information. `Prover` proceeds as follows.

Let $\sigma = \rho \circ \tau$ be the random reference string.

1. `Prover` splits randomly the witness w into n^{d+1} pieces $w_1, \cdots, w_{n^{d+1}}$ such that $w = w_1 \oplus \cdots \oplus w_{n^{d+1}}$.
2. `Prover` considers the random string ρ as the description of n^{d+1} randomly chosen encryption algorithms $E_1, \cdots, E_{n^{d+1}}$ and computes the encryptions $\alpha_i = E_i(w_i)$, $i = 1, 2, \cdots, n^{d+1}$.
3. `Prover` runs P's algorithm on input the random string τ to prove non-interactively and in zero-knowledge that the encryptions α_i define a witness for the instance x. This is done by computing y using the known reduction and proving that $y \in L$.
   Notice that this is a proof of membership. In fact, here `Prover` needs to prove only that his construction has been performed correctly; that is, that the α_i's are encryptions of strings whose xor is a witness for the instance x.

Let us convince ourselves that the above proof system is zero-knowledge. The proof given by the `Prover` consists of the encryptions $\alpha_1, \cdots, \alpha_{n^{d+1}}$ and a zero-knowledge proof of correctness. However, as the cryptosystem is d-dense, with very high probability at least one of the encryption algorithms E_i is secure and thus at least one of the strings w_i cannot be recovered by the verifier. Therefore, as w is the xor of the w_i's, with very high probability **Verifier** cannot get any information about w from the α_i's. Moreover, the proof given at step 3 is zero-knowledge and thus does not give any information about w.

For the validity property, let us consider the following extractor $(\mathtt{Ext}_0, \mathtt{Ext}_1)$. $\mathtt{Ext}_0$ randomly generates n^{d+1} encryption algorithms $E_1, \cdots, E_{n^{d+1}}$ along with their decryption algorithms $D_1, \cdots, D_{n^{d+1}}$ and feeds the prover with the string consisting of the description of the encryption algorithms $E_1, \cdots, E_{n^{d+1}}$. Now, the prover will produce the proof of the theorem he has chosen. In particular, he will compute the encryptions α_i from which $\mathtt{Ext}_1$, by using the decryption algorithms D_i, can compute the strings w_i and thus a witness to the theorem. ∎

4 NIZKPK and One-way permutations

In this section, we present strong evidence that the implication "if one-way permutations exist then NIZKPK's for all polynomial time relations exist" is not provable by standard techniques.

Our proof uses the result of [17] by which proving the security of a secret-key agreement protocol that uses a one-way permutation as a black box is as hard as proving $P \neq NP$ and proceeds as follows. First, we show that NIZKPK and one-way permutations are sufficient for the existence of a secure public-key cryptosystem. This implies that if one-way permutations are sufficient for NIZKPK, then it is possible to construct a public-key cryptosystem, and thus a secret-key agreement proven secure based solely on one-way permutations. This is as hard as proving $P \neq NP$.

Our result is the first "impossibility" result about zero-knowledge proofs and suggests a separation between non-interactive and interactive settings with respect to zero-knowledge proofs.

In what follows, we actually show that even proving that one-way permutations are sufficient for a very weak form of NIZKPK, which we call Weak NIZKPK, is as hard as proving $P \neq NP$. In a Weak NIZKPK, the extractor $(\mathtt{Ext}_0, \mathtt{Ext}_1)$ is only required to be able to extract the witness to a theorem from the proof provided by **Prover**. That is, we have eliminated the quantification over all possible **Adversary**.

Theorem 6. One-way permutations and Weak NIZKPK for all polynomial-time relations imply secure public-key cryptosystems.

Proof's sketch: Let f be a one-way permutation and h be a hard-bit predicate for f. Each user U constructs his public file by running the algorithm $\mathtt{Ext}_0$ with input 1^n (n is the security parameter). The algorithm $\mathtt{Ext}_0$ returns a random string σ, which is placed in the public file, and some secret information aux which is kept in U's private file. To encrypt a bit b, the sender does the following. Randomly chooses a $x \in \{0,1\}^n$ such that $h(x) = b$ and sends to U the value $y = f(x)$ along with a zero-knowledge proofs of knowledge based on the string σ that he knows x such that $y = f(x)$. To decrypt, user U runs the algorithm $\mathtt{Ext}_1$ on input the proof he has just received.

Why is this a secure public-key cryptosystem? First of all, user U can decrypt. In fact, the algorithm $\mathtt{Ext}_1$ on input a zero-knowledge proof of knowledge is guaranteed to extract a witness to the theorem (in our case x, from which $b = h(x)$ can be easily computed). Moreover, the cryptosystem is secure. This can be proved from the fact that h is hard for f (thus knowing $f(x)$ does not give any information about $h(x)$) and from the fact that, being the proof zero-knowledge, it is not possible to obtain any information about the witness of the theorem being proved. ∎

5 A Cryptosystem Secure Against Chosen-Ciphertext Attacks

The problem of constructing a public-key cryptosystem secure against chosen-ciphertext attacks has been one of the most important problems in Cryptography since the introduction of the public-key model [9]. In a chosen-ciphertex attack, the adversary has access to the decryption equipment and can ask the decryption of adaptively chosen ciphertext. Then, he is challenged to decrypt a new ciphertext α.

Blum, Feldman, and Micali [6] suggested that the sender proves "knowledge" (in a zero-knowledge and non-interactive fashion) of the message whose encryption he has sent. More precisely, they proposed the following encryption scheme. The public file of a user U contains a secure encryption algorithm E and a random string σ. The encryption of a message m consists of $E(m)$ and a non-interactive zero-knowledge proof of knowledge that the sender actually knows the encrypted message. The decryption algorithm first checks the proof and, only if convinced, decrypts the message. The rationale behind this construction is that conducting a chosen-ciphertext attack the adversary can only get decryptions of ciphertexts of which he knows the cleartext. Clearly, this would not help.

Subsequently, Naor and Yung [19] gave a different construction for a cryptosystem secure against chosen-ciphertext attacks. In their scheme, the public file of a user U contains a random string σ and a pair of secure (but not against chosen-ciphertext attacks) encryption algorithms E_1 and E_2. The encryption of a message m consists of the two encryptions $E_1(m)$ and $E_2(m)$ and of a zero-knowledge proof that the same message was encrypted by using the two algorithms. The proof is a non-interactive zero-knowledge proof of membership with random string σ. Thus, the construction of Naor and Yung dispenses with the need for a zero-knowledge proof of knowledge and can be based on the no-stronger assumption of the existence of trapdoor permutations [12]. In [10], it has been presented a cryptosystem secure against the stronger attack in which the adversary knows in advance the encryption he has to break. This kind of attack has been first discussed by Rackoff and Simon (see [20]).

We now prove that a secure cryptosystem and a Strong NIZKPK can be used to build a new cryptosystem secure against chosen ciphertext attacks.

For the construction of cryptosystems secure against chosen-ciphertext attacks (and in general for any cryptographic application) we need a stronger kind of NIZKPK. The strong validity property requires the extractor algorithm to be able to extract a witness from proofs of theorems chosen after seeing the random string. In some applications, we need to be able to extract witnesses and to simulate proofs for theorems chosen by an adversary with respect to the same common string. For example, in the proof (see Lemma 1) that our proposed cryptosystem is secure against chosen-ciphertext attacks, the adversary can ask for the decryptions of theorems of his choice (which involves the ability to extract witnesses) and we need to produce a challenge for him to break (which requires the ability to simulate proofs). This calls for a blending of the validity and zero-knowledge property. More precisely, we will use three polynomial-time algorithms `Init`, `Ext`, and `Sim`. `Init`, on input 1^n prepares a string σ of length n (it is sufficient for σ to be only indistinguishable from a truly random string as for the applications we are only dealing with polynomial-time algorithms) along with some private information *aux* which will enable `Ext` to extract the witness from "real" proofs and `Sim` to simulate proofs. Such systems can be constructed using only Strong NIZKPK in the following way. Let (P, V) be a Strong NIZKPK with polynomial-time prover and an on-line simulator. An on-line simulator (see [8]) $S = (S_0, S_1)$ is a pair of efficient algorithms. S_0 receives as input 1^n and outputs σ, a string of length n, and *aux*, auxiliary information about σ. Then S_1, on input x and *aux*, produces a "proof" Π of knowledge of a witness for x s.t. the pair (σ, Π) is indistinguishable from the view of V on input x. It is possible to show that if Strong NIZKPK exist for all polynomial-time relations so do Strong NIZKPK with on-line simulator.

Let us now consider the following pair (`Prover`, `Verifier`).

Input: $(x, w) \in \mathcal{P}$ and string $\rho = \rho_0 \circ \cdots \rho_{2n}$, where $|\rho_i| = n$.

1. Randomly choose n different indices $j_1, \cdots, j_n \in \{1, \cdots, 2n\}$.
2. For $i = 1, \cdots, n$

   Run P on input ρ_{j_i}, x, w to obtain α_i, a

proof that he knows a witness for x.

3. Run P on input ρ_0 to obtain a proof that he knows $\alpha_1, \cdots, \alpha_n$ and $j_1, \cdots, j_n$ s.t., for all i, V on input $(x, \rho_{j_i}, \alpha_i)$ accepts. Let Π be P's output.
4. Send Π to `Verifier`.

Now let $(\texttt{Ext}_0, \texttt{Ext}_1)$ and (S_0, S_1) be the extractor and the simulator for (P, V). Algorithm `Init`, `Ext` and `Sim` are defined as follows.

`Init` randomly chooses a subset $\mathcal{I}$ of n indices in $\{1,\cdots,2n\}$. For each $i \in \mathcal{I}$, `Init` constructs ρ_i, and its relative information aux_i, by running S_0 on input 1^n. For indices $0 \leq i \leq 2n$ not in $\mathcal{I}$, ρ_i and aux_i are computed by running $\texttt{Ext}_0$ on input 1^n. The output of `Init` consists of $\rho = \rho_0 \circ \cdots \circ \rho_{2n}$ and $aux = aux_0 \circ \cdots \circ aux_{2n} \circ \mathcal{I}$.

Algorithm `Ext` on input an instance x and a proof Π proceeds as follows. First, it runs $\texttt{Ext}_1$ on input ρ_0, aux_0, x and Π (notice that `Init` always construct ρ_0 by running $\texttt{Ext}_0$) to obtain $\alpha_1, \cdots, \alpha_n$ and the indices $j_1, \cdots, j_n$. Let j_i be an index not in $\mathcal{I}$; if no such j_i exists `Ext` fails, but this happens with very low probability. `Ext` outputs w computed by running $\texttt{Ext}_1$ on input ρ_{j_i}, aux_{j_i}, x and α_i.

Let us now describe `Sim`. `Sim` receives as inputs ρ, aux and x and has to simulate a proof of knowledge of a witness for x. This is accomplished by running S_1 on input ρ_i, aux_i and x for all $i \in \mathcal{I}$ to obtain α_i (remember that for $i \in \mathcal{I}$, ρ_i has been "prepared" by S_0). Finally, the proof Π is computed by running P on input ρ_i, for $i \in \mathcal{I}$, and the α_i's so obtained.

Let us now describe our cryptosystem secure against chosen-ciphertext attacks. Let (`Prover`, `Verifier`) be the NIZKPK described above and $\mathcal{G}$ be a secure public-key cryptosystem.

Construction of public and private keys.
Input: security parameter 1^n.

1. Compute $(E(\cdot,\cdot), D(\cdot)) = \mathcal{G}(1^n)$.
2. Randomly choose $\sigma \in \{0,1\}^n$.

The public file of user U is $PK_U = (\sigma, E)$ and U's secret file consists of $SK_U = D$.

Encryption of a bit. To encrypt a bit b with public key (σ, E), the user performs the following computations:

1. Randomly choose a n-bit string r and compute $\alpha = E(b, r)$.
2. Run `Prover` and compute Π, a proof (based on the random string σ) that the sender "knows" b, r such that $\alpha = E(b, r)$.
3. The encryption of the bit b consists of the pair (α, Π).

To decrypt the bit received, the receiver first checks that Π is a convincing proof. If convinced, he computes $D(\alpha)$ obtaining the bit b. If not convinced, he simply outputs "?".

Lemma 1. The above cryptosystem is secure against chosen-ciphertext attacks.

Proof's sketch: Assume it is not secure against chosen-ciphertext attacks. That is, there exists an efficient algorithm *Alg* that first asks for the decryption of polynomially many (say n^c, where $c > 0$ is a constant) adaptively chosen ciphertexts. Then, *Alg*, on input a randomly chosen encryption (α, Π), guesses the bit encrypted with probability significantly greater than 1/2. We use *Alg* to construct an algorithm that breaks the encryption E.
Input: a public key E and a randomly chosen encryption α.

1. Compute $(\sigma, aux) \leftarrow \texttt{Init}(1^n)$.
2. For $i = 1, \cdots, n^c$
   Let (α_i, Π_i) be the ciphertext chosen by *Alg* on input σ, E and all decryptions previously received. If $\texttt{Verifier}(\sigma, \alpha_i, \Pi_i)$ rejects then send "?" to *Alg*. Else use `Ext` on input $(\sigma, aux, \alpha_i, \Pi_i)$ to compute b_i, r_i such that $\alpha_i = E(b_i, r_i)$. Send b_i to *Alg*.
3. Compute Π by running `Sim` on input (σ, aux, α).
4. Run *Alg* on input (σ, E, α, Π) and let b be the output of *Alg*.

Output: b, as a guess of the bit encrypted by α.

We have only assumed *Alg* to be successful when he receives "real encryptions" and when σ is truly random. To prove that the above algorithm breaks α, we need to show that at step 4, *Alg* has still probability significantly better than 1/2 of success. This is proved by using the properties of (`Prover`, `Verifier`). ∎

We have thus the following theorem.

Theorem 7. *If Strong NIZKPK with polynomial-time prover and on-line simulator exist for all polynomial-time relations then there exists a public-key cryptosystem secure against chosen-ciphertext attacks.*

Acknowledgments
We thank Silvio Micali for many stimulating discussions and for letting us include some of his ideas in this paper. We acknowledge discussions with Benny Chor, Ivan Damgård, and Phil Rogaway. We thank Oded Goldreich for his helpful comments.

The second author would like to thank Michael Rabin for his constant encouragement and support.

Literature Referenced

[1] E. Bach, *How to Generate Factored Random Numbers,* SIAM Journal of Computing, vol. 17, n. 2, April 1988.

[2] M. Bellare and O. Goldreich, *On Defining Proofs of Knowledge*, to appear in Proceedings of CRYPTO '92.

[3] M. Bellare and S. Goldwasser, *A New Paradigm for Digital Signatures and Message Authentication Based on Non-Interactive Zero-Knowledge Proofs*, in "Advances in Cryptology - CRYPTO 89", vol. 435 of "Lecture Notes in Computer Science", Springer-Verlag.

[4] M. Bellare and M. Yung, *Certifying Cryptographic Tools: The case of Trapdoor Permutations*, to appear in Proceedings of CRYPTO '92.

[5] M. Blum, A. De Santis, S. Micali, and G. Persiano, *Non-Interactive Zero Knowledge,* SIAM Journal on Computing, vol. 6, December 1991, pp. 1084–1118.

[6] M. Blum, P. Feldman, and S. Micali, *Non-Interactive Zero-Knowledge and Applications*, Proceedings of the 20th Annual ACM Symposium on Theory of Computing, 1988, pp. 103–112.

[7] A. De Santis, S. Micali, and G. Persiano, *Non-Interactive Zero-Knowledge Proof-Systems*, in "Advances in Cryptology - CRYPTO 87", vol. 293 of "Lecture Notes in Computer Science", Springer Verlag, pp. 52–72.

[8] A. De Santis and M. Yung, *Cryptographic Applications of the Non-Interactive Metaproof and Many-prover Systems,* in "Advances in Cryptology - CRYPTO 90", vol. 537 of "Lecture Notes in Computer Science", Springer-Verlag, pp. 366–377.

[9] W. Diffie and M. Hellman, *New Directions in Cryptography*, IEEE Trans. on Information Theory, vol. 22, n.6, 1976, pp. 644–654.

[10] D. Dolev, C. Dwork, and M. Naor, *Non-Malleable Cryptography*, in Proceedings of the 23rd Annual ACM Symposium on Theory of Computing, New Orleans, 1991, pp. 542–552.

[11] U. Feige, A. Fiat, and A. Shamir, *Zero-knowledge Proofs of Identity*, Journal of Cryptology, vol. 1, 1988, pp. 77–94.

[12] U. Feige, D. Lapidot, and A. Shamir, *Multiple Non-Interactive Zero-Knowledge Proofs Based on a Single Random String,* Proceedings of the 22th Annual Symposium on the Theory of Computing, 1990, pp. 308–317.

[13] M. Fischer, S. Micali, and C. Rackoff, *A Secure Protocol for the Oblivious Transfer,* Eurocrypt 1984.

[14] S. Goldwasser and S. Micali, *Probabilistic Encryption*, Journal of Computer and System Science, vol. 28, n. 2, 1984, pp. 270–299.

[15] S. Goldwasser, S. Micali, and C. Rackoff, *The Knowledge Complexity of Interactive Proof-Systems*, SIAM Journal on Computing, vol. 18, n. 1, February 1989, pp. 186–208.

[16] O. Goldreich, S. Micali, and A. Wigderson, *Proofs that Yield Nothing but their Validity, and a Methodology of Cryptographic Protocol Design,* Proceedings of the 27th IEEE Symposium on the Foundations of Computer Science, 1986, pp. 174–187.

[17] R. Impagliazzo and S. Rudich, *Limits on the Provable Consequences of One-way Permutations,* Proceedings of the 21st Annual ACM Symposium on Theory of Computing, May 1989, pp. 49–61.

[18] S. Micali, C. Rackoff, and B. Sloan, *The Notion of Security for Probabilistic Cryptosystems,* SIAM Journal on Computing, vol. 17, n. 2, April 1988.

[19] M. Naor and M. Yung, *Public-key Cryptosystems Probably Secure Against Chosen Ciphertext Attacks,* Proceedings of the 22th Annual ACM Symposium on Theory of Computing, 1990, pp. 427–437.

[20] C. Rackoff and D. R. Simon, *Non-Interactive Zero-Knowledge Proof of Knowledge and Chosen Ciphertext Attack,* in "Advances in Cryptology - CRYPTO 91", Ed. J. Feigenbaum, vol. 576 of "Lecture Notes in Computer Science", Springer-Verlag, pp. 433–444.

[21] M. Tompa and H. Woll, *Random Self-Reducibility and Zero-knowledge Interactive Proofs of Possession of Information,* Proceedings of 28rd Symposium on Foundations of Computer Science, 1987, pp. 472–482.

(Extended Abstract)

Fast Unimodular Reduction: Planar Integer Lattices

Chee K. Yap
Courant Institute, New York University
251, Mercer Street
New York, NY, 10012

Abstract

We show that a shortest basis for the 2-dimensional lattice $\Lambda(u, v)$ generated by an input pair $u, v \in \mathbb{Z}^2$ can be computed in $O(M(n) \log n)$ where n is the bit-size of the input numbers and $M(n)$ is the complexity of multiplying two n-bit integers. This generalizes Schönhage's technique for fast integer GCD to a higher dimension.

1 Introduction

Basis reduction for lattices is a key topic in the geometry of numbers and algebraic number theory. H. W. Lenstra introduced such techniques to complexity theory, leading to a polynomial-time algorithm for integer programming in fixed dimensions [13]. Later, A. K. Lenstra, H. W. Lenstra and Lovász gave the first polynomial-time algorithm for factoring integer polynomials [12]. Their basic algorithmic technique is embodied in the so-called *LLL-algorithm* for computing a *reduced basis* for lattices.

An important related problem in lattices is that of computing the *shortest vector* in a lattice. Kannan [9] has shown that this can be computed in polynomial time in fixed dimensions. A reduced basis is known to contain a vector whose length is at most $2^{n/2}$ times the length of the shortest vector in an n-dimensional lattice; for certain applications, this is "short enough". For more general references, see Kannan's survey [8] or the book of Grötschel, Lovász and Schrijver [4].

The complexity of the LLL-algorithm has been improved by Schönhage [17] and Schnorr [15]. In this paper, we introduce another method for speeding up lattice reduction, at least in the plane. One motivation comes from the fact that the shortest vector can be viewed as the higher dimensional analogue of the GCD. Thus GCD(m, n) is just the shortest vector in the 1-dimensional integer lattice

$$\Lambda(m, n) := \{sm + tn : s, t \in \mathbb{Z}\}.$$

This analogy is further reinforced by the existence of the *Gaussian algorithm* for computing shortest vectors in 2-dimensional lattices (see [8,22]). Recall that the Euclidean GCD algorithm for a pair of integers n_0, n_1 amounts to computing an *Euclidean remainder sequence*

$$n_0, n_1, n_2, \ldots, n_k, \qquad (k \geq 1)$$

where $n_{i+1} = \text{rem}(n_{i-1}, n_i)$ with the *termination condition* $0 = \text{rem}(n_{k-1}, n_k)$. Then $n_k = \text{GCD}(n_0, n_1)$. Similarly, the Gaussian algorithm for a pair u_0, u_1 of vectors in $\mathbb{R}^2$ computes a *Gaussian remainder sequence*

$$u_0, u_1, \ldots, u_k, \qquad (k \geq 1)$$

where $u_{i+1} = \text{rem}(u_{i-1}, u_i)$ with a suitable termination condition. There are several variants of this algorithm, depending on the termination condition and the definition of the remainder function (Vallee [22]). In this paper, we need to introduce yet another variant called the *coherent remainder sequence*.

Schönhage [16] has shown how the GCD of two n-bit integers can be computed in $O(M(n) \log n)$ time, where $M(n)$ is the complexity of multiplying two n-bit integers. The basic idea goes back to Lehmer but it was Knuth [10] who successfully exploited it to give the first subquadratic GCD algorithm, $O(M(n) \log^4 n)$ time to be precise. It is natural to ask if these ideas extends to higher dimensions. As stated in the abstract, our answer is in the affirmative.

1.1 Related Work

There is a fast growing literature on algorithmic applications of lattice methods to a host of related problems such as simultaneous Diophantine approximation and nearest lattice vector. See [8,4].

0-8186-2900-2/92 $3.00 © 1992 IEEE

A recent paper of Vallée and Flajolet [21] gave a probabilistic analysis of the Gaussian algorithm. They noted that, besides the intrinsic interest of the planar case, such work may shed light on the multi-dimensional problem.

Moenck extended Schönhage's method to the computation of polynomial GCD [14], but its correctness was restricted to the *normal case* where the degrees of any two successive polynomials in the underlying polynomial remainder sequence differ by one (except for the first pair). The book [1] of Aho, Hopcroft and Ullman attempted to make Moenck's algorithm work generally. Unfortunately, there was a serious error[1] that was first fixed by Brent, Gustavson and Yun [2]. The extension to polynomial GCD is important because other important related problems (e.g., Sturm sequences and subresultant sequences) yield to the same technique [19]. In [20], we gave a "unified framework" for both the integer and polynomial GCD algorithms. In particular, we gave an integer version of Half-GCD algorithm and a simple correctness proof of the polynomial case (which was lacking in [2]). The results in the present paper falls under the same unified framework.

There is a classical theory of reduction of *binary integer quadratic forms* due to Lagrange and Gauss (which incidentally is the original context of the Gaussian algorithm). Identifying a binary quadratic form $f(X,Y) = aX^2 + 2bXY + cY^2$ with the symmetric matrix $M = \begin{pmatrix} a & b \\ b & c \end{pmatrix}$, we are interested in similarity classes of such matrices. (We say M is *similar* to M' if $M = U^{-1}MU$ for some $U \in SL(2,\mathbb{Z})$, which is a subgroup of the unimodular matrices.) Certain matrices are defined to be *reduced*. The computational problem amounts to finding a reduced matrix similar to a given M. Lagarias [11] was the first to study the complexity of this problem. Recently, Schönhage [18] has solved this problem in $O(M(n)\log n)$ time. This result is evidently closely related to ours.

1.2 Significance and directions

Our result extends Schönhage's technique [16] to a higher dimension. Previous exploitation of this technique such as in polynomial GCD and subresultant sequences (see above) did not require much significant changes to the original idea.

We have added to the known techniques [17,15] for speeding up lattice reduction algorithms. The present technique may lead to a subquadratic time algorithm shortest vectors in fixed dimensions. Kannan [9] has given an $O(M(n)n)$ time algorithm for this problem.

A general setting for this work is reduction by integer unimodular matrices *i.e.*, matrices $U \in GL(n,\mathbb{Z})$ such that $\det U = \pm 1$. There is the obvious problem of generalizing the present technique to dimensions $n > 2$. But a suitable 2-dimensional technique may already lead to a speedup of the LLL-algorithm since the LLL-algorithm is ultimately based on 2-dimensional reductions: a basis $b_1, \ldots, b_n$ is "LLL-reduced" iff it is proper and each consecutive pair (b_i, b_{i+1}) forms a LLL-reduced 2-dimensional basis when projected onto the subspace spanned by $b_1, \ldots, b_{i-1}$ [7, see Definition 3.5].

There are several related reduction problems for $n = 2$. For instance, computing the GCD of a pair $u, v \in \mathbb{Z}[\sqrt{-1}]$ of Gaussian integers. The current best algorithm has $\Theta(n^2)$ complexity [3]. Although $\mathbb{Z}[\sqrt{-1}]$ is similar to the planar integer lattice, the group of reduction matrices are the Gaussian unimodular matrices. Our present techniques break down in the presence of this group, which is closely related to the *Picard groups*, $SL(n,\mathbb{Z}[\sqrt{-1}])$ or $PSL(n,\mathbb{Z}[\sqrt{-1}])$.

More generally, there is the problem of computing GCD for integers of a quadratic number field $\mathbb{Q}(\sqrt{d})$ with class number 1 (this just means we have a unique factorization domain, although the Euclidean algorithm may no longer work). The current best general algorithm has $O(n^2)$ complexity, due to Kaltofen and Rolletschek [6]. The implicit constant in the O-notation is large, depending on the determinant of the field. They also have an $O(n^3)$ algorithm for the complex case (there are only 9 such fields, by the classification theorem of Starke), by exploiting the basis reduction algorithm in 4-dimensions.

These techniques should lead to faster algorithms for integer programming in fixed dimensions.

2 Preliminary

We give the necessary terminology and some basic results in this section.

We will consider (column) 2-vectors $u, v \in \mathbb{R}^2$ ($\mathbb{R}$=reals). The *scalar product* of $u = (u_1, u_2)^T$ and $v = (v_1, v_2)^T$ is denoted $\langle u, v\rangle := u_1v_1 + u_2v_2$. The *(Euclidean) length* of u is $|u| := \sqrt{\langle u, u\rangle}$. The *unit vector along direction* u is the vector $\widehat{u} := u/|u|$. Let $\angle(u,v) = \angle(v,u)$ denote the non-reflex angle between u and v. The *double norm* of u is defined as $\|u\| := \log_2 |u|$. It will be convenient to interchangeably view $u \in \mathbb{R}^2$ as a complex number, $u \in \mathbb{C}$. Write $\mathbf{i}$ for $\sqrt{-1}$.

[1] Discounting another minor, easily-fixed error.

The *lattice generated by* u, v is the set $\Lambda(u,v) := \mathbb{Z}u + \mathbb{Z}v \subseteq \mathbb{R}^2$. The *shortest vector* in a lattice Λ is that non-zero vector of Λ with smallest length. A *shortest basis* of Λ is a pair (u, v) where u is a shortest vector of Λ and v is a shortest vector in $\Lambda \setminus \mathbb{Z}u$.

An (integer) *unimodular matrix* is a 2×2 matrix $U = \begin{pmatrix} a & b \\ c & d \end{pmatrix}$ with integer entries and determinant ± 1. If $u, v, u', v' \in \mathbb{R}^2$, it is easy to show that $\Lambda(u, v) = \Lambda(u', v')$ iff there exists an integer unimodular matrix U such that

$$\begin{pmatrix} u \\ v \end{pmatrix} = U \begin{pmatrix} u' \\ v' \end{pmatrix}. \qquad (1)$$

(Note that Equation (1) is usually written in the matrix form $[u|v] = [u'|v']U^T$ where $[u|v]$ denotes the obvious 2×2 matrix.) By analogy with a similar concept in modular groups, we define the *fundamental region* of $u \in \mathbb{R}^2$ to be the set $\mathcal{F}(u)$ comprising $v \in \mathbb{R}^2$ such that $|v| \geq |u|$ and

$$-\frac{|u|^2}{2} < \langle u, v \rangle \leq \frac{|u|^2}{2}.$$

The latter condition implies the angle $\angle(u, v)$ is between $60°$ and $120°$.

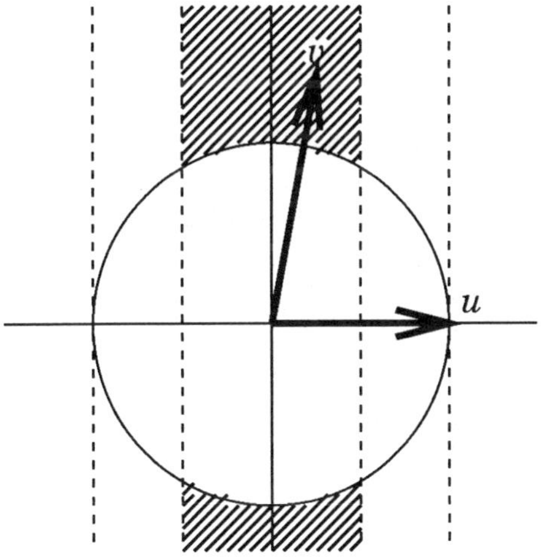

Figure 1. **Fundamental Region of u is shaded.**

Figure 1 illustrates $\mathcal{F}(u)$, and it is typical in that, when displaying the fundamental region of u, we usually rotate the axes so that u appears horizontal. The following shows the importance of the fundamental region.

Lemma 1 *If v is in the fundamental region of u then the sequence (u, v) is a shortest basis for $\Lambda(u, v)$. Moreover, this basis is unique (up to signs) unless $|u| = |v|$.*

3 Coherent Remainder Sequences

We do not use any of the variants of Gauss's algorithm discussed in Valleé [22]. Instead, we will introduce a new variant based the *coherent remainder* of two vectors. This seems necessary for our techniques to work.

Let $0 \leq \alpha \leq 1$. First, we say two vectors $u, v \in \mathbb{R}^2$ are *α-coherent* if

$$\langle \widehat{u}, \widehat{v} \rangle \geq \alpha, \quad u \neq 0, v \neq 0.$$

We say u, v are *strongly coherent* if they are α-coherent for any $\alpha > 1/2$. If u, v are 0-coherent, *i.e.*, the angle $\angle(u, v)$ is at most $90°$, we simply say "u, v are coherent". If u, v are not coherent, we say *incoherent.* The pair (u, v) is *ordered* if $|u| > |v|$; otherwise *inverted.* The pair is *α-admissible* if it is ordered and α-coherent. Again, we simply say "admissible" when $\alpha = 0$.

Definition 1 The *coherent quotient* and *remainder* of $u, v \in \mathbb{R}^2$ is given by

$$\mathrm{quo}_+(u, v) := \left\lfloor \frac{\langle u, v \rangle}{|v|} \right\rfloor,$$

and $\mathrm{rem}_+(u, v) := u - v \cdot \mathrm{quo}_+(u, v)$. The *coherent remainder sequence* (abbreviated, CRS) of u_0, u_1 is the maximal length sequence

$$\mathrm{CRS}(u_0, u_1) := (u_0, u_1, \ldots, u_k), \qquad k \geq 1$$

such that $u_{i+1} = \mathrm{rem}_+(u_{i-1}, u_i)$ and each consecutive pair (u_{i-1}, u_i) is admissible. We say each (u_{i-1}, u_i) *belongs* to the CRS of u_0, u_1. The *length* of this CRS is defined to be k.

Note that the CRS of u, v is not defined unless (u, v) is admissible. A pair (u, v) is *terminal* if $\mathrm{CRS}(u, v) = (u, v)$. This simply means that either $\mathrm{rem}_+(u, v)$ has length at least $|v|$ or is equal to 0.

Thus a CRS is the analogue of the usual Euclidean remainder sequence where remainders are taken to be non-negative. The standard Gaussian remainder sequence is based on the remainder function $\mathrm{rem}(u, v)$ which chooses $q \in \mathbb{Z}$ so that $\mathrm{rem}(u, v) = u - qv$ minimizes the length $|u - qv|$ (see [22]).

The next lemma show how one obtains the shortest vector of $\Lambda(u_0, u_1)$ from the CRS of u_0, u_1:

Lemma 2 *If (u_{k-1}, u_k) is the last pair belonging to* $\mathrm{CRS}(u_0, u_1)$ *then either u_k or $u_{k-1} - u_k$ is the shortest vector in $\Lambda(u_0, u_1)$.*

This shows that the CRS is as good as the standard Gaussian remainder sequence for shortest vectors. Once we have the shortest vector, it is easy to obtain the shortest basis.

4 Two bounds on the lengths of CRS

The two results of this section have independent interest.

4.1 Logarithmic Length of general CRS

Vallée [22] has shown that the worst case length of a standard Gaussian remainder sequence of u, v is $\Theta(\log_{1+\sqrt{2}} |u|)$. The next lemma shows that we are not giving up too much by using a CRS:

Lemma 3 *The length of the CRS of u, v is not more than $3 + \log_\phi |u|$ where $\phi = 1.618...$ is the positive root of $X^2 - X + 1$ (golden ratio).*

This proof comes from defining a sequence $\ell_0, \ell_1, \ldots, \ell_{k-1}$ such that

$$|u_0| \geq \ell_0 \geq |u_1| \geq \ell_1 \geq \cdots \geq |u_{k-1}| \geq \ell_{k-1} < |u_k|.$$

The golden ratio arises since the ℓ's satisfies the inequality $\ell_{i-1} \geq \ell_i + \ell_{i+1}$.

4.2 Bounded length of special CRS

Our second bound is interesting in that it relates the length of a CRS with a classical result on linear fractional transformations. This result will be used in our algorithm later.

Lemma 4 *For any $0 < \alpha < 1$, there is a constant $C = C(\alpha)$ such that if (u, v) is admissible but not α-coherent then the CRS of u, v has length at most C.*

Note that we impose no upper bound on $|u|$ in this lemma. This proof is obtained by a reduction to the following classical result: We will view $U \in SL(2, \mathbb{R})$ as a transformation on $\mathbb{C}$ taking $z \in \mathbb{C}$ to $Uz := \frac{az+b}{cz+d}$. We say z and z' are *equivalent* if $z' = Uz$ for some $U \in SL(2, \mathbb{Z})$. Then the classical result (see [5, p. 350]) states:

For any real $\gamma > 0$, there exists a bound $C' = C'(\gamma)$ such that for any set S of pairwise equivalent complex points where

$$\mathrm{Im}(z) \geq \gamma, \quad |\mathrm{Re}(z)| \leq \frac{1}{2}$$

holds for all $z \in S$, S has size at most C'.

5 Regular Matrices and the Half-Gaussian Algorithm

A vector $\begin{pmatrix} u \\ v \end{pmatrix}$ or pair (u, v) is said to *straddle* a real number r if $\|u\| \geq r > \|v\|$. A vector $\begin{pmatrix} u \\ v \end{pmatrix}$ is said to be *coherent, admissible*, etc, if the pair (u, v) is coherent, admissible, etc.

Define an *elementary matrix* as one with the form $\langle q \rangle := \begin{pmatrix} q & 1 \\ 1 & 0 \end{pmatrix}$ where $q \geq 1$ is a positive integer, called its *partial quotient*. A *regular matrix* is a finite product $M = \langle q_1 \rangle \langle q_2 \rangle \cdots \langle q_k \rangle$ of zero or more elementary matrices, denoted $M = \langle q_1, q_2, \ldots, q_k \rangle$. (We admit to the notational ambiguity with scalar product when $k = 2$.) We say M *transforms* a pair (u, v) to (u', v'), denoted

$$\begin{pmatrix} u \\ v \end{pmatrix} \xrightarrow{M} \begin{pmatrix} u' \\ v' \end{pmatrix}, \tag{2}$$

if $\begin{pmatrix} u \\ v \end{pmatrix} = M \begin{pmatrix} u' \\ v' \end{pmatrix}$. If, in addition, M is regular and both (u, v) and (u', v') are admissible, we call Equation (2) a *reduction*. Clearly regular matrices are unimodular and they correspond naturally to the remaindering process in the Euclidean algorithm.

The following is a key element of the "unified approach" of [20]. If (u', v') belongs to the CRS of u, v then it is clear that there is a reduction of the form (2). We prove the converse.

Lemma 5 (Reduction Lemma) *If Equation (2) represents a reduction then (u', v') belongs to the coherent remainder sequence of u, v.*

The Half-Gaussian Problem. We now specify the Half-Gaussian Problem. Recall that the Gaussian integers refers to the number ring $\mathbb{Z}[\mathbf{i}]$. Input to the Half-Gaussian Problem is a pair (u, v) of admissible Gaussian integers. The problem is to compute a regular matrix M^* such that if

$$\begin{pmatrix} u \\ v \end{pmatrix} \xrightarrow{M^*} \begin{pmatrix} u^* \\ v^* \end{pmatrix}$$

then (u^*, v^*) is admissible. Furthermore, (u^*, v^*) either is terminal with

$$\|v^*\| \geq \frac{\|u\|}{2} + c \tag{3}$$

or, (u^*, v^*) straddles $\|u\|/2 + c$:

$$\|u^*\| \geq \frac{\|u\|}{2} + c > \|v^*\|. \tag{4}$$

Here c is a sufficiently large integer constant. Although we will assume $c = 4$ in the sequel, we shall keep this constant explicit in our derivations, to show where this slack is needed. We shall call Equation (3) and Equation (4) (respectively) the *terminal case* and *straddling case* of the Half-Gaussian problem.

In contrast to the Half-Gaussian Problem, the "Full-Gaussian Problem" is to compute a regular M that takes (u, v) to the last pair in CRS(u, v). We note the well-known fact (e.g., [1,20]) that once we are in possession of a fast Half-Gaussian algorithm with a polynomial running time satisfying $T(n) = \Omega(M(n))$, we can obtain a Full-Gaussian algorithm with the same time complexity, $\Theta(T(n))$.

6 The Main Method and Issues

We sketch the big picture and then indicate the technical difficulties that arise, many of which have no 1-dimensional analogue. Although these details are worked out in Appendix A, the present roadmap may be useful.

Outline of the Algorithm Our goal is to solve the Half-Gaussian problem by exploiting the Lehmer-Knuth-Schönhage idea of using only the higher order bits of the integers involved. In this, we use the basic scheme of Schönhage's integer GCD, using two recursive calls:

(I) On input (u, v) which is admissible, the first recursive call is on u_0, v_0 which comprise roughly the higher-order half of the bits of u, v (respectively).
(II) The recursive call returns a matrix M_1 which is "fixed up" as M_1^*.
(III) We use M_1^* to reduce (u, v) to (u', v'), which is guaranteed to be a pair in CRS(u, v) which straddles roughly $3\|u\|/4$.
(IV) We do one step of the remainder process to transform (u', v') to (v', w'), with partial quotient q. This ensures both v', w' have double norms less than $3\|u\|/4$.
(V) We can again extract some higher order bits from v', w' to get (v_0', w_0') for the next recursive call. This call returns another matrix M_2 which can be "fixed up" as M_2^*.
(VI) The desired matrix M^* is then $M_1^*\langle q\rangle M_2^*$.

What can go wrong? Let us explain the "fixing up" of matrix M_i $(i = 1, 2)$ to M_i^*. Without fixing up, three main things may go wrong:

A. The matrix M_i that is returned in the recursive call may represent the terminal case of the Half-Gaussian algorithm (cf. Equation (3)). Intuitively, M_i does not reduce its input far enough. The resolution of this problem depends on Lemma 4.

B. We next focus on M_1 (since M_2 is similarly treated). We use M_1 to produce (u', v'). Consider the parallel reduction

$$\begin{pmatrix} u_0 \\ v_0 \end{pmatrix} \xrightarrow{M} \begin{pmatrix} u_0' \\ v_0' \end{pmatrix},$$
$$\begin{pmatrix} u \\ v \end{pmatrix} \xrightarrow{M} \begin{pmatrix} u' \\ v' \end{pmatrix}.$$

We know (by induction) that (u_0', v_0') is admissible. Somehow, we want this to translate into the admissibility of (u', v'). Unfortunately, this is not for free, and both conditions of admissibility can be violated:
B.1. (u', v') may be inverted, $|u'| \leq |v'|$.
B.2. (u', v') may be incoherent, $\langle u', v'\rangle < 0$.
As seen in appendix A, fixing these problems involve many subcases.

C. Finally, there is a "transfer principle" that we want to exploit. Intuitively, this principle says: *If* (u_0, v_0) *is obtained from* (u, v) *by truncating away* m *lower-order bits, then* (u_0', v_0') *straddles* $t \in \mathbb{R}$ *implies* (u', v') *straddles* $m + t$. This depends on conditions on m and t, which shows up in the proof.

The solutions to these three problems are embodied in a "fixing-up" procedure described in Appendix A.

References

[1] A. V. Aho, J. E. Hopcroft, and J. D. Ullman. *The design and analysis of computer algorithms.* Addison-Wesley, 1974.

[2] R. P. Brent, F. G. Gustavson, and D. Y. Y. Yun. Fast solution of Toeplitz systems of equations and computation of Pade approximants. *J. Algorithms*, 1:259–295, 1980.

[3] B. F. Caviness and G. E. Collins. Algorithms for Gaussian integer arithmetic. *SYMSAC 76*, pages 36–45, 1976.

[4] M. Grötschel, L. Lovász, and A. Schrijver. *Geometric Algorithms and combinatorial optimization.* Springer-Verlag, Berlin, 1988.

[5] L. K. Hua. *Introduction to Number theory.* Springer-Verlag, 1982.

[6] E. Kaltofen and H. Rolletschek. Computing greatest common divisors and factorizations in quadratic number fields. *Math. Comp.*, 52:697–720, 1989.

[7] Ravi Kannan. Lattices, basis reduction and the shortest vector problem. In L. Lovász and E. Szemerédi, editors, *Theory of Algorithms*, pages 283–312. North-Holland, Amsterdam, 1985. Colloquia Mathematica Societatis János Bolyai, 44.

[8] Ravi Kannan. Algorithmic geometry of numbers. In *Annual Review of Computer Science: Volume 2*, pages 231–267. Annual Reviews Inc., Palo Alto, California, 1987.

[9] Ravi Kannan. Minkowski's convex body theorem and integer programming. *Mathematics of Operations Research*, 12:415–440, 1987.

[10] D. E. Knuth.
The analysis of algorithms. In *Actes du Congrés International des Mathématiciens*, pages 269–274, Nice, France, 1970. Gauthier-Villars.

[11] J. C. Lagarias. Worst-case complexity bounds for algorithms in the theory of integral quadratic forms. *Journal of Algorithms*, 1:184–186, 1980.

[12] A.K. Lenstra, H.W. Lenstra, and L. Lovász. Factoring polynomials with rational coefficients. *Math. Ann.*, 261:515–534, 1982.

[13] H. W. Lenstra. Integer programming with a fixed number of variables. *Mathematics of Operations Research*, 8, 1983.

[14] R. Moenck. Fast computations of GCD's. *Proc. 5th ACM Symposium on Theory of Computation*, pages 142–171, 1973.

[15] C. P. Schnorr. A more efficient algorithm for lattice basis reduction. *Journal of Algorithms*, 9:47–62, 1988.

[16] Arnold Schönhage. Schnelle Berechnung von Kettenbruchentwicklungen. *Acta Informatica*, 1:139–144, 1971.

[17] Arnold Schönhage. Factorization of univariate integer polynomials by Diophantine approximation and an improved basis reduction algorithm. *Proc. 11th ICALP*, pages 436–447, 1984. Lecture Notes in Comp. Sci., No. 172.

[18] Arnold Schönhage. Fast reduction and composition of binary quadratic forms, 1992. preprint.

[19] Jacob T. Schwartz and Micha Sharir. On the piano movers' problem: II. General techniques for computing topological properties of real algebraic manifolds. *Advances in Appl. Math.*, 4:298–351, 1983.

[20] Klaus Thull and Chee Yap. A unified approach to fast GCD algorithms for polynomials and integers. Technical report, NYU-Courant Institute, Robotics Laboratory, 1992.

[21] B. Vallée and P. Flajolet. The lattice reduction algorithm of Gauss: an average case analysis. *IEEE Foundations of Computer Science*, 31:830–839, 1990.

[22] Brigitte Vallée. Gauss' algorithm revisited. *Journal of Algorithms*, 12:556–572, 1991.

APPENDIX A: Algorithm Development

We follow up on the outline in the main text. All proofs have been omitted.

The general setup. To capture both recursive calls in the algorithm simultaneously, we set up a slightly more general situation. Assume we are given a pair (u, v) of Gaussian integers that is admissible but non-terminal. But we are also given an integer m such that

$$8 \leq m \leq n, \qquad \text{where } n := \|u\|. \tag{5}$$

(Note: n is not assumed to be integer.) Our goal is to compute the regular matrix M^* such that

$$\begin{pmatrix} u \\ v \end{pmatrix} \xrightarrow{M^*} \begin{pmatrix} u^* \\ v^* \end{pmatrix}$$

such that (u^*, v^*) is admissible. Furthermore, (u^*, v^*) either forms a terminal pair satisfying

$$\|v^*\| \geq n - \frac{m}{2} + c \tag{6}$$

or straddles $n - (m/2) + c$:

$$\|u^*\| \geq n - \frac{m}{2} + c > \|v^*\|. \tag{7}$$

We shall call equation (7) the "straddling case" and equation (6) the "terminal case".

In order to compute such a M^*, we first break up u, v thus

$$\begin{pmatrix} u_0 & u_1 \\ v_0 & v_1 \end{pmatrix} := \begin{pmatrix} u\, \mathbf{div_c}\, 2^{n-m} & u\, \mathbf{mod_c}\, 2^{n-m} \\ v\, \mathbf{div_f}\, 2^{n-m} & v\, \mathbf{mod_f}\, 2^{n-m} \end{pmatrix}. \tag{8}$$

Note that the functions $\mathbf{mod_c}$, $\mathbf{mod_f}$ are the symmetric ceiling and floor functions defined in Appendix B. Applying some elementary bounds, we see

$$\|u_1\| < n - m + \frac{1}{2} \tag{9}$$

$$\|v_1\| < n - m + \frac{1}{2} \tag{10}$$

$$\|u_0\| = m + \delta, \quad (0 \leq \delta < \frac{1}{2}) \tag{11}$$

$$\geq \|v_0\|. \tag{12}$$

We would like to recursively call the algorithm on (u_0, v_0). But first we make sure that it is admissible.

Lemma 6 *Suppose $\|v\| \geq n - \frac{m}{2} + c$, with u, v strongly coherent. Then (u_0, v_0) is coherent.*

> *If $\|u_0\| = \|v_0\|$ or the conditions of this lemma fails, we will show that no recursive call is needed. In the subsequent development, we assume (u_0, v_0) is admissible.*

Let M be a regular matrix,

$$M = \langle q_1, \ldots, q_k \rangle, \qquad k \geq 1 \tag{13}$$

$$= \begin{pmatrix} p & q \\ r & s \end{pmatrix}. \tag{14}$$

Suppose

$$\begin{pmatrix} u_0 & u_1 \\ v_0 & v_1 \end{pmatrix} \xrightarrow{M} \begin{pmatrix} u'_0 & u'_1 \\ v'_0 & v'_1 \end{pmatrix}$$

where (u'_0, v'_0) is admissible. So this is a reduction. Moreover, (u'_0, v'_0) is either the terminal case (cf. equation (6)) with

$$\|v'_0\| \geq \|u_0\| - \frac{m}{2} + c, \tag{15}$$

or the straddling case (cf. equation (7)) with

$$\|u'_0\| \geq \|u_0\| - \frac{m}{2} + c > \|v'_0\|. \tag{16}$$

Note: M is essentially the matrix returned by a recursive call on (u_0, v_0). Since $m \leq \|u_0\| \leq m + 1$, equation (16) implies

$$\|u'_0\| \geq \frac{m}{2} + c > \|v'_0\| - 1. \tag{17}$$

Recall that p is an upper bound on the entries of M. Inverting M,

$$\begin{pmatrix} u'_0 & u'_1 \\ v'_0 & v'_1 \end{pmatrix} = \pm \begin{pmatrix} s & -q \\ -r & p \end{pmatrix} \begin{pmatrix} u_0 & u_1 \\ v_0 & v_1 \end{pmatrix} \tag{18}$$

$$= \begin{pmatrix} su_0 - qv_0 & su_1 - qv_1 \\ -ru_0 + pv_0 & -ru_1 + pv_1 \end{pmatrix} \tag{19}$$

Some Bounds on $\|p\|, \|u'_1\|, \|u'_1\|, \|u'\|, \|v'\|$.
We summarize these bounds:

a) First we bound $\|p\|$:

$$\|p\| < \frac{m}{2} - c. \tag{20}$$

b) Next we upper bound $\|u'_1\|$ and $\|v'_1\|$:

$$\|u'_1\| < n - m + \|p\| + 2 < n - \frac{m}{2} - c + 2. \tag{21}$$

$$\|v'_1\| < n - \frac{m}{2} - c + 2. \tag{22}$$

c) Now we lower bound $\|u'\|$.

$$\|u'\| > n - \frac{m}{2} + c - 0.1. \tag{23}$$

d) We upper bound $\|v'\|$ under the straddling assumption (Equations (16) and (17)).

$$\|v'\| < n - \frac{m}{2} + c + 1.1. \tag{24}$$

A. STRADDLING CASE: *First let us assume (u'_0, v'_0) is straddling $\|u_0\| - (m/2) + c$ as in equation (16). Note that $k \geq 2$ in equation (13).*

Our goal is to ensure that the pair (u', v') is admissible. We show how toggling or backing up can save the situation. If (u', v') is not admissible, it could be either inverted or incoherent. We consider these two possibilities in turn.

A.1. (u', v') is inverted, *i.e.*, **$\|u'\| \leq \|v'\|$.** Let

$$u'' := u' q_k + v'. \tag{25}$$

Hence

$$\begin{pmatrix} u \\ v \end{pmatrix} \xrightarrow{\langle q_1, \ldots, q_{k-1} \rangle} \begin{pmatrix} u'' \\ u' \end{pmatrix} \xrightarrow{\langle q_k \rangle} \begin{pmatrix} u' \\ v' \end{pmatrix}. \tag{26}$$

This is an easy case, because we simply backup one step, from (u', v') to (u'', u'). This is justified by the following lemma.

Lemma 7

i) $\|v'_0\| > \|u'_0\| - 0.2$.
ii) $\|u''_0\| > \|u'_0\| + 0.45$.
iii) (u'', u') *is coherent.*
iv)(u'', u') *is ordered.*

After stepping back to (u'', u'), we have to step forward to reach a pair that is terminal pair or straddling $n-(m/2)+c$. This is can be done with at most 3 steps since $\|u'\| \leq \|v'\| \leq n-(m/2)+c+1.1$.

A.2. (u', v') **is incoherent.** We now also assume that (u', v') is not inverted. Let

$$u'' := u' + v'. \tag{27}$$

We first note:

Lemma 8 (u'', u') *is coherent.*

SUBCASE A.2.1: $q_k > 1$. We apply the toggling transformation to M:

$$\begin{pmatrix} u \\ v \end{pmatrix} \xrightarrow{\langle q_1, \ldots, q_{k-1}, q_k - 1\rangle} \begin{pmatrix} u' \\ u'' \end{pmatrix} \xrightarrow{\langle 1\rangle} \begin{pmatrix} u'' \\ -v' \end{pmatrix}. \tag{28}$$

We consider backing up to (u', u'') or perhaps going forward again to $(u'', -v')$. There are two possibilities.
SUBCASE A.2.1.1: $\|u'\| > \|u''\|$. Hence (u', u'') is admissible and we can backup to (u', u''), in effect replacing M by

$$\langle q_1, \ldots, q_k - 1\rangle.$$

But we want to obtain a straddling admissible pair. There are two possibilities: if (u'', v') is coherent, and recalling (u', v') is incoherent, then we see that (u', u'') is already a terminal pair. [In fact, $u'' \in \mathcal{F}(v')$.] On the other hand, if (u'', v') is incoherent, we can advance from (u', u'') to $(u'', -v')$. Since $\|v'\|$ is upper bounded by $n-(m/2)+c+1.1$, in at most 3 additional remaindering steps, we obtain a pair that straddles $n-(m/2)+c$.
SUBCASE A.2.1.2: $\|u'\| \leq \|u''\|$. We get

$$\|u''\| \geq \|u'\| > \|v'\|$$

Hence we may toggle,

$$M \leftarrow MT = \langle q_1, \ldots, q_k - 1, 1\rangle$$

and thus obtain the admissible pair $(u'', -v')$. Again, in at most 3 steps, we obtain a pair to straddle $n-(m/2)+c$.

SUBCASE A.2.2: $q_k = 1$. We consider the following scenario where we backup one or two steps:

$$\begin{pmatrix} u \\ v \end{pmatrix} \xrightarrow{\langle q_1, \ldots, q_{k-2}\rangle} \begin{pmatrix} u' + q_{k-1}u'' \\ u'' \end{pmatrix} \tag{29}$$

$$\xrightarrow{q_{k-1}} \begin{pmatrix} u'' \\ u' \end{pmatrix} \xrightarrow{\langle 1\rangle} \begin{pmatrix} u' \\ v' \end{pmatrix}. \tag{30}$$

Again consider two possibilities.
SUBCASE A.2.2.1: $\|u''\| > \|u'\|$. We just backup one step to the admissible pair (u'', u'). We note that v' lies in the region (see Figure 2)

$$(I) = \{z : |z + u'| \geq |u'|, |z| \leq |u'|, \langle u', z\rangle \leq 0\}.$$

We also see that u'' lies in region (II). Hence this subcase is a terminal one (in fact, $-u' \in \mathcal{F}(v')$).

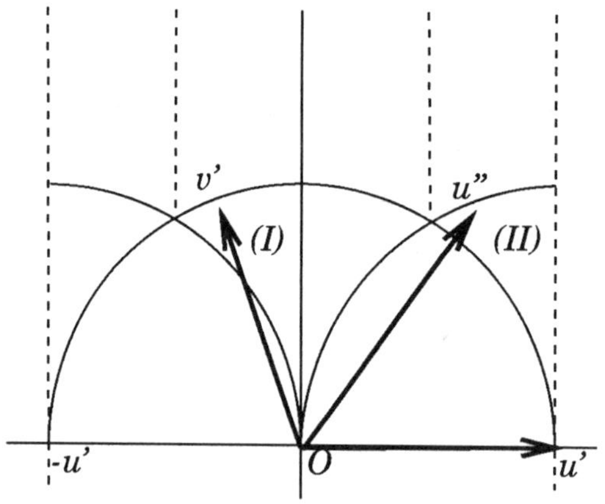

Figure 2. **Subcase 2.1:** $\|u''\| > \|u'\|$.

SUBCASE A.2.2.2: $\|u''\| \leq \|u'\|$. We backup two steps to the pair $(u' + q_{k-1}u'', u'')$. But first we must make sure that $k \geq 2$. This is immediate because if $k = 1$ then $(u'', u') = (u, v)$, contradicting our assumption that (u, v) is non-terminal. We note that $\|u' + q_{k-1}u''\| > \|u''\|$ since (u', u'') is coherent. Also $\langle u' + q_{k-1}u'', u''\rangle > 0$. Thus $(u' + q_{k-1}u'', u'')$ is admissible. Refer to Figure 3.

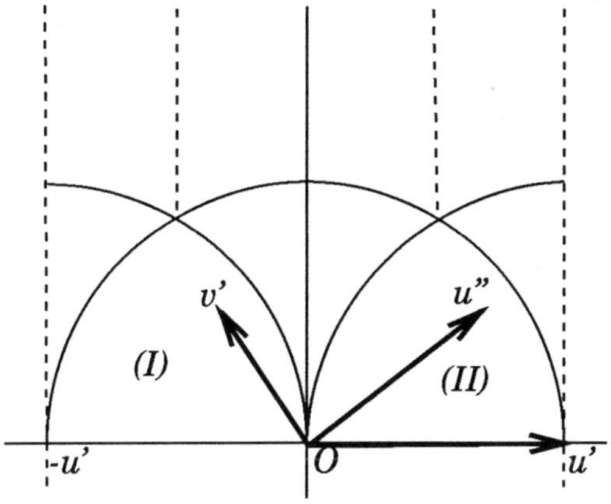

Figure 3. **Subcase 2.2:** $||u''|| \leq ||u'||$.

We now claim that the pair $(u' + q_{k-1}u'', u'')$ is terminal. This is because their coherent remainder is u' which, by the assumption of this case, causes inversion.

B. TERMINAL CASE: *Now let us assume* $||v_0'|| \geq ||u_0|| - (m/2) + c$ *as in equation (15).*

This case is settled by the following.

Lemma 9 *If* (u_0', v_0') *is terminal, then* (u', v') *is not* α*-coherent, for a suitable constant* α.

Summary. Recall

$$\begin{pmatrix} u_0 & u_1 \\ v_0 & v_1 \end{pmatrix} \xrightarrow{M} \begin{pmatrix} u_0' & u_1' \\ v_0' & v_1' \end{pmatrix}$$

where (u_0, v_0) and (u_0', v_0') are coherent. If (u_0', v_0') is terminal, then by Lemma 9, (u', v') is not α-coherent. Otherwise, it straddles $||u_0|| - (m/2) + c$ and we have two cases, depending on whether (u', v') is inverted or incoherent. In either case, in a constant number of multiplications and remaindering steps, we can produce a regular matrix M^* such that

$$\begin{pmatrix} u_0 & u_1 \\ v_0 & v_1 \end{pmatrix} \xrightarrow{M^*} \begin{pmatrix} u_0^* & u_1^* \\ v_0^* & v_1^* \end{pmatrix}$$

such that if

$$\begin{pmatrix} u^* \\ v^* \end{pmatrix} = \begin{pmatrix} u_0^* & u_1^* \\ v_0^* & v_1^* \end{pmatrix} \begin{pmatrix} 2^{n-m} \\ 1 \end{pmatrix}$$

then (u^*, v^*) is admissible. Moreover, either (u^*, v^*) is terminal with $||v^*|| \geq ||u|| - (m/2) + c$, or it straddles $||u|| - (m/2) + c$.

Note that all the multiplication and remaindering operations involve numbers of bit size at most $||u|| + O(1) = n + O(1)$. We conclude:

> *Regardless of whether* (u_0', v_0') *is straddling or not, we can produce the desired matrix* M^* *in a constant number of multiplication and remaindering steps. We call this the "fixing up" of* M *to produce* M^**. The fixing up procedure takes time* $O(M_B(n))$ *where* $M_B(n)$ *is the bit complexity of multiplying two n-bit binary integers.*

APPENDIX B: Symmetric Floor and Ceiling

We introduce a variant of the usual floor and ceiling functions and give some elementary bounds.

For a real number x, we define its *symmetric floor* as follows

$$\lfloor x \rfloor_s := \begin{cases} \lfloor x \rfloor & \text{if } x \geq 0 \\ \lceil x \rceil & \text{if } x < 0. \end{cases}$$

The definition of *symmetric ceiling* $\lceil x \rceil_s$ is similar. We extend these definitions to a complex number $x + \mathbf{i}y \in \mathbb{C}$ in a componentwise manner. Thus,

$$\lfloor x + \mathbf{i}y \rfloor_s = \lfloor x \rfloor_s + \mathbf{i}\lfloor y \rfloor_s.$$

The main advantage of these definitions is the simple inequality

$$|\lfloor u \rfloor_s| \leq |u| \leq |\lceil u \rceil_s|$$

for all $u \in \mathbb{C}$.

The infix notations for the symmetric floor and ceiling functions and the corresponding remainders are as follows. For $u, b \in \mathbb{C}$,

$$\begin{aligned} u \,\mathbf{div_f}\, b &:= \lfloor u/b \rfloor_s, \\ u \,\mathbf{div_c}\, b &:= \lceil u/b \rceil_s, \\ u \,\mathbf{mod_f}\, b &:= u - b\lfloor u/b \rfloor_s, \\ u \,\mathbf{mod_c}\, b &:= u - b\lceil u/b \rceil_s. \end{aligned}$$

We will use these functions to truncate our vectors. Some elementary bounds will be used. For instance:

Lemma 10 *Let* $u, v, a, b \in \mathbb{C}$, $k \geq 1$ *and* ϵ *denotes a suitable real value satisfying*

$$\log_2 \frac{2^k - 1}{2^k} \leq \epsilon \leq \log_2 \frac{2^k + 1}{2^k}.$$

i) $||u|| \leq ||v|| + k$ *implies* $||u + v|| = ||u|| + \epsilon$.

ii) $||a + b|| \geq ||b|| + k$ *implies* $||a|| = ||a + b|| + \epsilon$.

APPENDIX C: Half Gaussian Algorithm

We can now present the Half-Gaussian Algorithm:

PROCEDURE HALF-GAUSSIAN:

Input: (u, v) that is admissible.

Output: regular matrix M^* that reduces (u, v) to (u^*, v^*) such that (u^*, v^*) either straddles $(\|u\|/2) + c$ or is terminal with $\|v^*\| \geq (\|u\|/2) + c$.

[1] If (u, v) is not strongly coherent, then we return $M^* \leftarrow E$.

[2] Let $n \leftarrow \lceil \|u\| \rceil$ and $m \leftarrow \lceil n/2 \rceil$.

[3] FIRST RECURSION. The goal is to compute a regular M_1^* that transforms (u, v) to (u_1^*, v_1^*) that is either terminal or straddles $n - (m/2) + c$.

[3.1] If $\|v\| < n - (m/2) + c$ or $m \leq 8$, then let $M_1^* \leftarrow E$ and go to step [4].

[3.2] Set $(u_0, v_0) \leftarrow (u \, \mathbf{div_c} \, 2^m, u \, \mathbf{div_f} \, 2^m)$. If $|u_0| = |v_0|$ we can directly compute M_1^* which converts (u_0, v_0) to a terminal pair and go to step [4].

[3.3] Recursively call Half-Gaussian on (u_0, v_0) to compute M_1.

[3.4] Fixup M_1 to M_1^* using the above theory.

[4] Let (u, v) be transformed by M_1^* to (u_1^*, v_1^*).

[5] If (u_1^*, v_1^*) is terminal or straddles $(n/2) + c$, we can return M_1^*.

[6] Otherwise, compute the elementary matrix M to transform (u_1^*, v_1^*) to (v_1^*, w_1^*) which is renamed $(x, y) \leftarrow (v_1^*, w_1^*)$. Note that $\|x\| \geq (n/2) + c$. If (x, y) straddles $(n/2) + c$, we return the product $M^* M$.

[7] Let $n' \leftarrow \lceil \|x\| \rceil$ and $m' \leftarrow 2(n' - \lceil n/2 \rceil)$.

[8] SECOND RECURSION. The goal is to compute a regular M_2^* that transforms (x, y) to (x_1^*, y_1^*) that is either terminal or straddles $n' - (m'/2) + c$.

[8.1] If $\|y\| < n' - (m'/2) + c$ or $m' \leq 8$, then let $M_2^* \leftarrow E$ and go to step [9].

[8.2] Set $(x_0, y_0) \leftarrow (x \, \mathbf{div_c} \, 2^{m'}, x \, \mathbf{div_f} \, 2^{m'})$. If $|x_0| = |y_0|$ we can directly compute M_1^* which converts (x_0, y_0) to a terminal pair and go to step [9].

[8.3] Recursively call Half-Gaussian on (x_0, y_0) to compute M_2.

[8.4] Again fixup M_2 to M_2^* according to our theory.

[9] We return the matrix $M^* \leftarrow M_1^* M M_2^*$.

Correctness and Complexity. We note that M^* transforms (u, v) to (u^*, v^*) which straddles $n' - (m'/2) + c = \lceil n/2 \rceil + c$, as desired. The complexity analysis of this procedure is standard, and achieves the bound $O(M(n) \log n)$.

Implementation Details. We need to compute $\lceil \|u\| \rceil$ and make comparisons between $\|v\|$ and integers. The details are as described in [20].

How to Denest Ramanujan's Nested Radicals *

Johannes Blömer
Institut für Informatik, Fachbereich Mathematik
Freie Universität Berlin
Arnimallee 2-6, W-1000 Berlin 33, Germany

Abstract

We present a simple condition when nested radical expressions of depth two can be denested using real radicals or radicals of some bounded degree. We describe the structure of these denestings and determine an upper bound on the maximum size of a denesting. Also for depth two radicals we describe an algorithm that will find such a denesting whenever one exists. Unlike all previous denesting algorithms our algorithm does not use Galois theory. In particular, we avoid the construction of the minimal polynomial and splitting field of a nested radical expression. Thus we can obtain the first denesting algorithm whose run time is at most, and in general much less, than polynomial in description size of the minimal polynomial. The algorithm can be used to determine non-trivial denestings for expressions of depth larger than two.

1 Introduction

Throughout the last years the problem of denesting or simplifying radicals has been studied intensively by various mathematicians and computer scientists ([2],[3],[6],[7],[12]). Many of them have been attracted by equations of Ramanujan [9] such as the following:

$$\sqrt[3]{\sqrt[3]{2}-1} = \sqrt[3]{\frac{1}{9}} - \sqrt[3]{\frac{2}{9}} + \sqrt[3]{\frac{4}{9}} \quad (1)$$

$$\sqrt{\sqrt[3]{5}-\sqrt[3]{4}} = \frac{1}{3}\left(\sqrt[3]{2}+\sqrt[3]{20}-\sqrt[3]{25}\right) \quad (2)$$

$$\sqrt[6]{7\sqrt[3]{20}-19} = \sqrt[3]{\frac{5}{3}} - \sqrt[3]{\frac{2}{3}}. \quad (3)$$

These examples sufficiently explain the problem itself. Denesting a radical expression means decreasing its nesting depth over a field F. For example, the depth over $\mathbb{Q}$ of the left-hand side of Ramanujan's equations is 2 while the depth of the right-hand side is 1.

But if we are given a nested radical expression and are asked to denest it then this is at first not a meaningful question because for different values of the roots involved we may get different denestings. For example, if $\sqrt[3]{\sqrt{5}+2} - \sqrt[3]{\sqrt{5}-2}$ has to be denested in general we will assume that the two square roots have the same value and that perhaps the real third roots are meant. In this case the formula denests to 1. But if one of the square roots is positive and the other one negative the formula denests to a square root of 5, provided we still take real third roots. And for the complex third roots the denestings are again different. So the values of the roots involved in the nested radical expression have to be specified in advance and denesting a radical means finding a radical expression with the same value and of smaller depth.

In the last years a lot of progress has been made for the general problem of denesting radicals. S. Landau [6] showed how to compute a denesting for a nested radical expression that is just one off the optimal one. Horng and Huang [3] achieved a minimal denesting and also showed how to solve a polynomial by radicals of minimum nesting depth, if it is solvable by radicals at all. However, in both cases the denestings are with respect to a field containing all roots of unity. As it turns out to compute these denestings one need not consider a field containing all roots of unity which would clearly be computationally infeasible. Rather it suffices to work with a field generated by a single root of unity. Unfortunately, the order of this root is either one- (Landau) or even double-exponential (Horng, Huang) in the description size of the minimal polynomial of the expression to be denested.

These results still leave many theoretical and practical problems unanswered. For example, the denestings of Landau and Horng, Huang will always use roots of unity. On the other hand, Ramanujan's examples above use no roots of unity at all. Hence the role roots

*This research was supported by the ESPRIT II Basic Research Action of the European Community under contract No. 3075 (project ALCOM)

0-8186-2900-2/92 $3.00 © 1992 IEEE

of unity play in denesting radicals is not satisfactorily explained.

Moreover, the algorithms in [3] and [6] are inefficient. Their run time is (double-)exponential in the description size of the minimal polynomial of the nested radical expression. There is good reason to believe that this behavior is unavoidable in the approach taken in these papers. Both results use Galois theory and rely on computing the splitting field of the radical expression. But the degree of this field over $\mathbb{Q}$, say, is in general exponential in the degree of the minimal polynomial. Hence from a practical point of view it would be interesting to obtain algorithms with a better run time. Perhaps one would even be satisfied with denesting algorithms that may not achieve minimal depth but compute certain non-trivial denestings and run efficiently.

Taking a totally different approach than Landau and Horng, Huang, and especially avoiding Galois theory, in this paper we answer some open questions concerning nested radicals.

Consider for example Equation (3) given above. Multiplying the equation by $\sqrt[3]{12}$ for a real third root yields

$$\sqrt[6]{1008\sqrt[3]{20}-2736}=\sqrt[3]{20}-2.$$

And both, the right-hand side of this equation and the expression under the six root, are elements of the field generated by $\mathbb{Q}$ and $\sqrt[3]{20}$. We prove that there is a general pattern behind this behavior. To be more specific, we show the following generalization of a theorem due to Borodin et al. [2].

Let $F \subset \mathbb{R}$ be a real field and $F' = F(\sqrt[d_1]{q_1}, \sqrt[d_2]{q_2}, \ldots, \sqrt[d_k]{q_k})$, $\sqrt[d_1]{q_1}, \ldots, \sqrt[d_k]{q_k} \in F$, a radical extension of F such that any $\sqrt[d_i]{q_i}$ is real. If $\sqrt[d]{\gamma}$, $d \in \mathbb{N}$, is contained in some radical extension of F generated by real radicals of depth one over F then there exists an element $q \in F\backslash\{0\}$ with $\sqrt[Nd]{q}\sqrt[d]{\gamma} \in F'$. Here N is the degree of the extension $F' : F$.

Since F' has a basis over F consisting of depth one radicals this theorem leads to a denesting for $\sqrt[d]{\gamma}$. In particular, it applies to Ramanujan's examples and explains why no roots of unity appear in his denestings.

To some extend this result generalizes to complex radicals. In that case the base field has to contain a certain root of unity. But its degree is much smaller than the degree of the roots of unity required by the results of Landau and Horng, Huang.

These theorems explain the structure of certain denestings but in order to compute the denestings we need to determine the elements q in F with $\sqrt[Nd]{q}\sqrt[d]{\gamma} \in F'$. The main part of this paper is devoted to this problem.

In case F' is a Galois extension of F (which in general cannot be the case if F is real and F' is a radical extension) this problem has already been considered in [7],[12]. We give a much simpler characterization of the elements in F with this property that applies to arbitrary extensions.

If the field F is an algebraic number field this characterization leads to an algorithm that determines whether such an element exists, and if so, computes it. The run time of the algorithm is polynomial in the degree N of the extension $F' : F$, in d, and in the bit size of the representation of γ.

N may be as large as the product of the degree of the radicals appearing in γ but - as the basic theorem shows - the output size may also be $\Omega(N)$; so with respect to N this is the best we can hope for. Moreover, it can be shown that if γ is a linear combination of $\sqrt[d_i]{q_i}$ such that the radicals $\sqrt[d_i]{q_i}$ are linearly independent over F, then N is the degree of the minimal polynomial of γ.

We also believe that the dependence on d is best possible, i.e., no algorithm with run time polynomial in $\log d$, for example, exists. Although so far we cannot prove this, the characterizations of elements q with $\sqrt[Nd]{q}\sqrt[d]{\gamma} \in F'$ indicates that the representation of q may be of size $\Omega(d)$.

As it turns out these results already suffice to denest sums and quotients of nested radicals. In particular, it is shown that for sums of nested radicals one only needs to consider any ratio of two terms in the sum.

To prove the run time we use a general technique that may be of independent interest. We show how to compute in polynomial time the exact representation of an element β in a number field $\mathbb{Q}(\alpha)$, provided an upper bound B on the representation size of β is given and an approximation $\overline{\beta}$ to β is known such that the number of correct bits in $\overline{\beta}$ is roughly quadratic in B. The algorithm is an application of the lattice basis reduction of Lenstra et al. [8]. We believe that this algorithm will prove to be useful in many other algebraic problems.

Since the denesting algorithms of this paper work for arbitrary number fields they can be applied to radical expressions of depth larger than two in order to detect non-trivial denestings. But even if applied repeatedly the algorithms are not guaranteed to produce such general minimum depth denestings as in [6] and [3]. On the other hand, the algorithms of this paper do compute certain denestings that cannot be obtained by the algorithms of S. Landau, for example, they compute denestings like the ones found by Ramanujan.

2 The structure of radical extensions

In this section we state a few facts on radical extensions which have already been used in [1] and were originally proven by C. L. Siegel [10].

Definition 1 *Let F be a subfield of the complex numbers $\mathbb{C}$. An element $\rho \in \mathbb{C}$ is called a* **radical of order** *d over F, $d \in \mathbb{N}$, if*

$$\rho^d \in F.$$

An extension $F(\sqrt[d_1]{q_1}, \sqrt[d_2]{q_2}, \ldots, \sqrt[d_k]{q_k})$ of F generated by radicals over F is called a **radical extension**.

Observe that the order of a radical over F need not be the degree of its minimal polynomial over F. The order is not even uniquely defined rather if ρ is of order d then it is also a radical of order D for all multiples D of d.

As it turns out the following lemmata which appear in Siegel's paper as corollaries can easily be shown directly. Siegel's main result is an immediate consequence of these lemmata.

Lemma 2 *Let F be a real field and let $\sqrt[d_i]{q_i}$, $i = 1, \ldots, k$, be real radicals over F. By n_i denote the degree of the extension $F(\sqrt[d_1]{q_1}, \sqrt[d_2]{q_2}, \ldots, \sqrt[d_i]{q_i}) : F(\sqrt[d_1]{q_1}, \sqrt[d_2]{q_2}, \ldots, \sqrt[d_{i-1}]{q_{i-1}})$.*

If $\sqrt[d_k]{q_k} \in F(\sqrt[d_1]{q_1}, \sqrt[d_2]{q_2}, \ldots, \sqrt[d_{k-1}]{q_{k-1}})$ then

$$\sqrt[d_k]{q_k} = c \prod_{i=1}^{k-1} \sqrt[d_i]{q_i}^{e_i}$$

for some $c \in F$ and $e_i \in \mathbb{N}$, $0 \leq e_i < n_i$.

For complex radicals this lemma generalizes in the following way.

Lemma 3 *Let F be a field and let $\sqrt[d_i]{q_i}$, $i = 1, \ldots, k$, be arbitrary radicals over F. Furthermore assume that the field F contains primitive d_i-th roots of unity. If $\sqrt[d_k]{q_k}$ is an element of $F(\sqrt[d_1]{q_1}, \sqrt[d_2]{q_2}, \ldots, \sqrt[d_{k-1}]{q_{k-1}})$ then $\sqrt[d_k]{q_k}$ has the form*

$$\sqrt[d_k]{q_k} = c \prod_{i=1}^{k-1} \sqrt[d_i]{q_i}^{e_i}$$

for some $c \in F$ and positive integers e_i satisfying $0 \leq e_i < n_i$, where n_i is defined as above.

Throughout this paper we consider only radical extensions $F(\sqrt[d_1]{q_1}, \sqrt[d_2]{q_2}, \ldots, \sqrt[d_k]{q_k})$ such that either $F \subset \mathbb{R}$ and $\sqrt[d_i]{q_i} \in \mathbb{R}$ or such that F contains primitive d_i-th roots of unity. We refer to these cases as the *real* and *complex case*, respectively.

It will not be used in this paper but for the sake of completeness let us state Siegel's original result.

Theorem 4 (Siegel) *Let $\sqrt[d_1]{q_1}, \sqrt[d_2]{q_2}, \ldots, \sqrt[d_k]{q_k}$ be radicals over a field F. In both the real and complex case the minimal polynomial $p_i(X)$ of $\sqrt[d_i]{q_i}$ over $F(\sqrt[d_1]{q_1}, \sqrt[d_2]{q_2}, \ldots, \sqrt[d_{i-1}]{q_{i-1}})$ has the form*

$$p_i(X) = X^{n_i} - c_i \prod_{j=1}^{i-1} \sqrt[d_j]{q_j}^{e_j}$$

for some $c_i \in F$ and positive integers e_j.

3 The basic theorems

In this section we prove the basic theorems on denesting radical expressions. Basically we restrict ourselves to a single nested radical.

Given a nested radical $\sqrt[d]{\sum_{i=1}^k p_i \sqrt[d_i]{q_i}}$, say, of depth two over some field F. To describe and compute possible denestings of this radical we consider $\gamma = \sum_{i=1}^k p_i \sqrt[d_i]{q_i}$ as an element of the radical extension $F' = F(\sqrt[d_1]{q_1}, \ldots, \sqrt[d_k]{q_k})$ generated by the depth one radicals appearing in $\sum_{i=1}^k p_i \sqrt[d_i]{q_i}$. The theorems that we are going to prove in this section show that this field is in fact the right place to look for denestings.

Let us fix some notation. By $F^{(i)}$ denote the radical extension $F(\sqrt[d_1]{q_1}, \ldots, \sqrt[d_i]{q_i})$, $F^{(0)} = F$, and let n_i be the the degree of the extension $F^{(i)} : F^{(i-1)}$. Furthermore, the degree of $F' : F$ is denoted by N. Hence $N = \prod_{i=1}^k n_i$ and a basis for the field extension $F' : F$ is given by

$$B = \left\{ \prod_{j=1}^{k} \sqrt[d_j]{q_j^{e_j}},\ 0 \leq e_1 < n_1, \ldots, 0 \leq e_k < n_k \right\}.$$

B will be called the *standard basis* of $F' : F$.

The first theorem generalizes and simplifies the proof of a result due to Borodin et al. [2] who studied real nested square roots.

Theorem 5 *Let F be a real field and $F' = F(\sqrt[d_1]{q_1}, \ldots, \sqrt[d_k]{q_k})$ be a real radical extension of F whose degree is N. By $B = \{\beta_0, \ldots, \beta_{N-1}\}$ denote the standard basis of F' over F. Assume furthermore $\gamma \in F'$ and $d \in \mathbb{N}$ such that $\sqrt[d]{\gamma}$ denests over F using only real radicals, that is, $\sqrt[d]{\gamma} \in F(\sqrt[t_1]{a_1}, \ldots, \sqrt[t_m]{a_m})$ for some $t_i \in \mathbb{N}$, $a_i \in F$, $a_i > 0$. Then*

$$\sqrt[d]{q}\sqrt[d]{\beta_j}\sqrt[d]{\gamma} \in F'$$

for some $q \in F\backslash\{0\}$ and some $\beta_j \in B$.

Proof: $\sqrt[d]{\gamma} \in F(\sqrt[t_1]{a_1}, \ldots, \sqrt[t_m]{a_m})$ clearly implies $\sqrt[d]{\gamma} \in F'(\sqrt[t_1]{a_1}, \ldots, \sqrt[t_m]{a_m})$. Hence $\sqrt[d]{\gamma}$ is a radical over F' contained in $F'(\sqrt[t_1]{a_1}, \ldots, \sqrt[t_m]{a_m})$. Since F' and $F'(\sqrt[t_1]{a_1}, \ldots, \sqrt[t_m]{a_m})$ are real fields, we can apply Lemma 2, which shows

$$\sqrt[d]{\gamma} = \rho \prod_{i=1}^{m} \sqrt[t_i]{a_i}^{e_i},$$

for some $\rho \in F'$, $e_i \in \mathbb{N}$.

But $\prod_{i=1}^{m} \sqrt[t_i]{a_i}^{e_i}$ can be written as $\sqrt[t]{a}$ for some $a \in F$ and $t = \prod_{i=1}^{m} t_i$. Taking d-th powers this yields

$$\gamma/\rho^d = \sqrt[t]{a^d}.$$

$\gamma/\rho^d \in F'$ and $a^d \in F$ therefore $\sqrt[t]{a^d}$ is a radical over F that is contained in $F' \subseteq \mathbb{R}$. By Lemma 2 $\sqrt[t]{a^d} = q'\beta_h$ for $q' \in F$ and some basis element β_h.

Since $\sqrt[t]{a} = \frac{1}{\rho}\sqrt[d]{\gamma} \in \mathbb{R}$ this shows that $\sqrt[t]{a}$ can be written as a real d-th root of $q'\beta_h$. We easily deduce

$$\sqrt[d]{\frac{1}{q'}}\sqrt[d]{\frac{1}{\beta_h}}\sqrt[d]{\gamma} \in F'.$$

Finally observe that β_h^{-1} is a radical of F' over F. Hence it can be written as $q''\beta_j$ for a basis element β_j and $q'' \in F$. So q may be chosen as $\frac{q''}{q'} \neq 0$ to prove the theorem. □

Note that each basis element $\beta_j \in B$ can be written as a real N-th root of some element in F. Therefore the representation of $\sqrt[d]{q}\sqrt[d]{\beta_j}\sqrt[d]{\gamma}$ as a linear combination of elements in B will lead to a denesting of $\sqrt[d]{\gamma}$ using only real radicals and we can interpret Theorem 5 as saying that in denesting $\sqrt[d]{\gamma}$ by real radicals only radicals of order dN will help. Moreover, using the results of section 2 it is not hard to show that no denesting of $\sqrt[d]{\gamma}$ by a linear combination of real radicals of depth one can consist of fewer terms than the one described by Theorem 5. Additional results, however, are necessary to prove that if γ is a sum of linearly independent radicals that generate an extension of degree N then N is also the degree of the minimal polynomial of γ.

Next observe that, given the equation $q\beta_j\gamma = \rho^d$, $\rho \in F'$, we can apply the distinct field embeddings σ_i of F' over F to this equation. This yields $q\sigma_i(\beta_j)\sigma_i(\gamma) = \sigma_i(\rho)^d$, for all i.

Hence

$$\sqrt[d]{\sigma_i(\gamma)} = \sqrt[d]{q}^{-1}\sqrt[d]{\sigma_i(\beta_j)}^{-1}\sigma_i(\rho),$$

and by choosing an appropriate d-th root of q this is true for any d-th root of $\sigma_i(\gamma)$.

The different d-th roots of $\sigma_i(\gamma)$, $i = 0, 1, \ldots, N-1$, are the roots of the minimal polynomial of $\sqrt[d]{\gamma}$, provided $\sqrt[d]{\gamma}$ is of degree d. By Siegel's Theorem the radicals appearing in the expression for γ, β_j and ρ will be mapped by σ_i onto certain complex radicals. Hence the equation $q\beta_j\gamma = \rho^d$ leads to a denesting for all conjugates of $\sqrt[d]{\gamma}$ over F. In [3] this has been called an *exact denesting.*

For linear combinations of radicals we have the following result.

Theorem 6 *Suppose $S = \sum_{i=1}^{h} \kappa_i \sqrt[d_i]{\gamma_i}$ is a sum of real nested radicals such that $\gamma_i \in F_i$, $i = 1, \ldots, h$, $\kappa_i \in L_i$, $i = 1, \ldots, h$, and each F_i, L_i is a real radical extension of $F \subseteq \mathbb{R}$. Furthermore assume that no nested radical $\sqrt[d_i]{\gamma_i}$ denests using real radicals. Then using real radicals*

- *S can only denest to zero,*
- *If no quotient $\frac{\sqrt[d_i]{\gamma_i}}{\sqrt[d_j]{\gamma_j}}$ denests then $S = 0$ if and only if $\kappa_i = 0$ for all i.*

Proof: Omitted. □

This theorem together with Theorem 5 implies that a denesting of a linear combination of nested radicals $S = \sum_{i=1}^{h} \kappa_i \sqrt[d_i]{\gamma_i}$ consists of at most $\mathcal{O}(h \max\{m_i\} \max\{n_i^2\})$ terms, where n_i, m_i are the degrees of F_i, L_i over F. Observe that in general the minimal polynomial of S has degree $\prod_{i=1}^{h} m_i n_i d_i$, hence is exponential in h. So if we want a denesting algorithm whose run time is polynomial in the maximal output size we can not afford to compute the minimal polynomial or even the splitting field of a radical expression.

Like above it can be shown that the denestings for S using real radicals apply also to certain complex values of the roots in S.

For complex radicals we get a similar result. It partially proves a conjecture of R. Zippel [12].

Theorem 7 *Assume F contains all roots of unity. Let F' be an arbitrary radical extension of F with basis B as above. Assume $\gamma \in F'$ and $d \in \mathbb{N}$ such that $\sqrt[d]{\gamma}$ denests over F, that is, $\sqrt[d]{\gamma} \in F(\sqrt[t_1]{a_1}, \ldots, \sqrt[t_m]{a_m})$, for some $a_i \in F$. Then*

$$\sqrt[d]{q}\sqrt[d]{\beta_j}\sqrt[d]{\gamma} \in F'$$

for some $q \in F \backslash \{0\}$ and some $\beta_j \in B$.

The proof of this theorem is exactly the same as for Theorem 5 except that Lemma 2 is replaced by Lemma 3.

At first sight Theorem 7 seems to be of theoretical interest only since it is computationally infeasible to work with a field containing all roots of unity. The results of Landau [6] and Horng, Huang [3], however, show that instead of dealing with a field containing all roots of unity we can restrict ourselves to a field generated by a single root of unity. Unfortunately, so far the best bounds on the degree of this root of unity are (double-)exponential in the description size of the radical. In any case the theorem indicates that even in the general denesting problem the denestings we consider below may be the right thing to look at.

From a practical point of view the following restricted version of Theorem 7 seems to be of greater interest since it allows us to bound the maximum degree of roots of unity we want to creep into the denestings.

Theorem 8 *Assume F contains a primitive d-th root of unity. Let F' be a radical extension of F generated by radicals of order d and with basis B as above. Assume $\gamma \in F'$ such that $\sqrt[d]{\gamma}$ denests over F using radicals of order d only. Then*

$$\sqrt[d]{q}\sqrt[d]{\beta_j}\sqrt[d]{\gamma} \in F'$$

for some $q \in F\backslash\{0\}$ and some $\beta_j \in B$.

Observe that any element in B is a radical of order d so the conclusion of the theorem really leads to a denesting of $\sqrt[d]{\gamma}$ by radicals by order d radicals. It can also be shown that any denesting for $\sqrt[d]{\gamma}$ of this kind will have at least as many terms as the one in Theorem 8. Furthermore, as in the real case, if γ is a sum of linearly independent radicals generating an extension of degree N then γ is of degree N also.

Finally let us mention that Theorem 6 easily generalizes if "denest using real radicals" is replaced by "denest using radicals of order d" .

4 Denesting sets and admissible sequences

Observe that if we knew how to determine for a nested radical $\sqrt[d]{\gamma}$ in time polynomial in N one element $q \in F$ with $\sqrt[d]{q}\sqrt[d]{\gamma} \in F'$ then we could compute the denestings of Theorem 5, say, in time polynomial in N. We only had to try to compute such an element for all nested radicals $\sqrt[d]{\beta_j \gamma}$ which increases the run time of the algorithm only by a factor of N. Likewise by applying the algorithm to all ratios of nested radicals we could transform any sum S of nested radicals into a sum of nested radicals satisfying the conditions of Theorem 6. After this transformation step we easily check whether the coefficients are zero by applying results of [1].

Hence it remains to characterize and compute those elements in F with $\sqrt[d]{q}\sqrt[d]{\gamma} \in F'$.

Definition 9 *Assume $F \subset \mathbb{C}$ and let F' be an algebraic extension of F, $\gamma \in F'$, $d \in \mathbb{N}$. We say that $q \in F\backslash\{0\}$* **denests** *$\sqrt[d]{\gamma}$ or that it* **leads to a denesting** *of $\sqrt[d]{\gamma}$ if $\sqrt[d]{q}\sqrt[d]{\gamma} \in F'$ for some d-th root $\sqrt[d]{q}$ of q.*

A finite set $S \subset F$ with the property that any element denesting $\sqrt[d]{\gamma}$ differs from some element in this set only by a d-th power of some element in F is called a **denesting set** *for $\sqrt[d]{\gamma}$ over F. If no two elements in a denestings set differ from one another by a d-th power of an element in F then the denesting set is called* **irreducible**.

It is easily seen that by this definition the set of elements denesting $\sqrt[d]{\gamma}$ is independent of the specific d-th root of γ.

So far it is not clear that a radical $\sqrt[d]{\gamma}$ possesses a finite denesting set. The next lemma, that is an immediate consequence of Lemma 2 or Lemma 3, proves the existence of such a set.

Lemma 10 *Let the fields F, F', the basis B, d, and γ be either as in Theorem 5 or as in Theorem 8. If $q \in F$ denests $\sqrt[d]{\gamma}$ then any other element in F that denests $\sqrt[d]{\gamma}$ has the form*

$$p^d \beta_j^d q,$$

for some $p \in F$ and $\beta_j \in B$ such that $\beta_j^d \in F$. Likewise, any element denesting $\sqrt[d]{\gamma}$ can be written as

$$p^d \beta_j^{-d} q$$

with p, β_j as before.

For the complex case $\beta_j^d \in F$ is no restriction since any basis element is a radical of order d. The second formula has been included since it turns out to be more convenient from a computational point of view.

Although the lemma shows that a denesting set is of size N at most it is nevertheless quite restricted since it does not tell us how a single element denesting $\sqrt[d]{\gamma}$ looks like or how to compute such an element. Rather it shows how to compute a denesting set given a single element denesting $\sqrt[d]{\gamma}$. Below we give a *constructive* description of the elements denesting $\sqrt[d]{\gamma}$ which applies not only to radical extensions but to arbitrary extensions. The characterization is based on a simple lemma about the *trace* of an extension.

Definition 11 *Let F' be an algebraic extension of a field $F \subset \mathbb{C}$. Denote by $\sigma_0, \dots, \sigma_{N-1}$ the distinct field* *embeddings of F' over F. For any element $\gamma \in F$ the* **trace** *of γ over F, denoted by $\mathrm{tr}_{F':F}(\gamma)$, is the sum $\sum_{i=0}^{N-1} \sigma_i(\gamma)$ of the conjugates of γ.*

Lemma 12 *Let F' be an algebraic extension of some field $F \subset \mathbb{C}$. If $\{\beta_0, \beta_1, \ldots, \beta_{N-1}\}$ is a F-basis for F' and γ a non-zero element of E then*

$$\mathrm{tr}_{F':F}(\beta_i \gamma) \neq 0$$

for some $i \in \{0, 1, \ldots, N-1\}$.

Proof: Assume that $\mathrm{tr}_{F':F}(\beta_i\gamma) = 0$ for all i. Since the set $\{\beta_0\gamma, \beta_1\gamma, \ldots, \beta_{N-1}\gamma\}$ is also a basis of the extension this implies that the trace function is identically zero. But $\mathrm{tr}_{F':F}(1) = N \neq 0$, which proves the lemma. ◻

Lemma 13 *Let F be an arbitrary field and F' an algebraic extension of F with basis $\{\beta_0, \beta_1, \ldots, \beta_{N-1}\}$. Denote the distinct field extensions by σ_i, $i = 0, \ldots, N-1$. Assume $\gamma \in F'$, $d \in \mathbb{N}$. If there exists an element $q \in F$ with $\sqrt[d]{q}\sqrt[d]{\gamma} \in F'$ for certain d-th roots of q and γ then there exist d-th roots $\sqrt[d]{\sigma_i(\gamma)}$ of $\sigma_i(\gamma)$, $i = 0, \ldots, N-1$, such that for some basis element β_j*

$$\left(\sum_{i=0}^{N-1} \sigma_i(\beta_j) \sqrt[d]{\sigma_i(\gamma)}\right)^d \in F \backslash \{0\}.$$

Moreover, any element $q \in F$ with $\sqrt[d]{q}\sqrt[d]{\gamma} \in F'$ for certain d-th roots can be written as a product of a d-th power of an element in F and an inverse of an element in F satisfying the description above.

Proof: Assume $q \in F$ has the property $\sqrt[d]{q}\sqrt[d]{\gamma} = \rho \in F'$. Hence $q\gamma = \rho^d$ and $q\sigma_i(\gamma) = (\sigma_i(\rho))^d$. Equivalently, there exist certain d-th roots of q and $\sigma_i(\gamma)$ such that

$$\sqrt[d]{q}\sqrt[d]{\sigma_i(\gamma)} = \sigma_i(\rho),\ i = 0, \ldots, N-1.$$

We can assume that the d-th root of q is the same for all N equations since we may choose the root of $\sigma_i(\gamma)$ accordingly. Applying Lemma 12 to $\rho \in F'$ yields

$$\mathrm{tr}(\beta_j\rho) = \sum_{i=0}^{N-1} \sigma_i(\beta_j)\sigma_i(\rho) =$$

$$= \sqrt[d]{q} \sum_{i=0}^{N-1} \sigma_i(\beta_j) \sqrt[d]{\sigma_i(\gamma)} = p \in F \backslash \{0\}.$$

Therefore

$$q = \left(\frac{p}{\sum_{i=0}^{N-1} \sigma_i(\beta_j) \sqrt[d]{\sigma_i(\gamma)}}\right)^d.$$

$p \in F$ hence $\left(\sum_{i=0}^{N-1} \sigma_i(\beta_j) \sqrt[d]{\sigma_i(\gamma)}\right)^d$ is also an element of F.

Moreover, as a d-th power p^d will not help in denesting $\sqrt[d]{\gamma}$, so a d-th root of $\left(\sum_{i=0}^{N-1} \sigma_i(\beta_j) \sqrt[d]{\sigma_i(\gamma)}\right)^{-d}$ will also denest $\sqrt[d]{\gamma}$.

The claim that any number $q \in F$ denesting $\sqrt[d]{\gamma}$ can be written in the stated form follows from the fact that the process above can be applied to all these elements of the field F. ◻

This lemma generalizes results of R. Zippel [12] and S. Landau [7] who characterized elements denesting a d-th root $\sqrt[d]{\gamma}$ if F' is a Galois extension of F. Lemma 13 is correct for arbitrary extensions of a field F.

Based on this lemma an $\mathcal{O}(d)$-bound on the size of elements in a denesting set can be derived. We guess that this is also a lower bound for the size of the elements leading to a denesting although we cannot prove it. Since the algorithms we describe below will have run time polynomial in d such a bound would imply that this is the best we can hope for.

Observe that Lemma 13 almost immediately leads to an algorithm for denesting $\sqrt[d]{\gamma}$:

For all basis elements β_j and all expressions in Lemma 13 corresponding to $\sqrt[d]{\beta_j\gamma}$ check whether the expression describes an element q in F and, if so, check whether $\sqrt[d]{q\beta_j\gamma} \in F'$.

So far it is not clear how to compute the elements in F corresponding to the expressions in Lemma 13. But if we really had to check all possible expressions this could only lead to an algorithm with run time $\Omega(Nd^{N-1})$, since Nd^{N-1} is the number of different combinations of d-th roots of $\sigma_i(\beta_j\gamma)$ (the d-th root of $\beta_j\gamma$ can be fixed arbitrarily). On the other hand, considering the proof of Lemma 13 again it is obvious that we are only interested in those combinations that correspond to what we call admissible sequences.

Definition 14 *Let F be an arbitrary field and F' an extension of F. Denote the field embeddings of F' over F by σ_i, $i = 0, 1, \ldots, N-1$. Furthermore let $\sqrt[d]{\sigma_i(\gamma)}$, $i = 0, \ldots, N-1$, be fixed d-th roots of $\sigma(\gamma)$. A sequence $(1, \zeta^{(1)}, \zeta^{(2)}, \ldots, \zeta^{(N-1)})$ of d-th roots of unity is called* **admissible** *if elements $q \in F$ and $\beta \in F'$ exist such that $\zeta^{(i)}\sqrt[d]{q}\sqrt[d]{\sigma_j(\gamma)} = \sigma_j(\beta)$ for all $j = 0, 1, \ldots, N-1$, and for a fixed d-th root $\sqrt[d]{q}$ of q*

Observe that whether a sequence of d-th roots of unity is admissible or not depends on the values chosen for $\sqrt[d]{\sigma_i(\gamma)}$.

The fact that the first element in an admissible sequence is 1 corresponds to our definition of a denesting set which is independent of the specific d-th root of γ that is meant by $\sqrt[d]{\gamma}$.

As will be shown below any denesting problem for radical extensions can be reduced to several denesting problems over simple radical extensions. For these extensions we show that any admissible sequence is already determined by the triple $(\zeta^{(1)}, \zeta^{(2)}, \zeta^{(3)})$ in the real case and by $\zeta^{(1)}$ alone in the complex case.

So for the time being let F be an arbitrary field and $F' = F(\sqrt[m]{p})$ a simple radical extension of F such that $\sqrt[m]{p}$ is of degree m over F. As usual γ is an element of F'. Before we can prove the main result on admissible sequences we need one auxiliary lemmata. In the complex case $\zeta_m \in F$, equivalently, $F(\zeta_m) = F$. In the real case we have to determine the degree of $\sqrt[m]{p}$ over $F(\zeta_m)$.

Lemma 15 *Let F be a real field. Suppose $f(X) = X^m - p$, $p \in F$, $p > 0$, is irreducible in $F[X]$. Furthermore let ζ_m be a primitive m-th root of unity. Then $f(X)$ is either irreducible in $F(\zeta_m)[X]$, or $\sqrt{p} \in F(\zeta_m)$ and $f(X)$ factors as $(X^{\frac{m}{2}} - \sqrt{p})(X^{\frac{m}{2}} + \sqrt{p})$ over $F(\zeta_m)[X]$. In the latter case m must be even.*

Proof: Consider the Galois group G of $F(\zeta_m)$ over F. By Galois theory this group is isomorphic to a subgroup of the group $\mathbb{Z}_m^*$. Since $\mathbb{Z}_m^*$ is abelian the same is true for G. The fundamental theorem of Galois theory shows that all subfields between $F(\zeta_m)$ and F are Galois extensions of F.

Next consider the degree of $\sqrt[m]{p}$ over $F(\zeta_m)$. By Lemma 3, this is the smallest positive integer e such that $\sqrt[m]{p}^e \in F(\zeta_m)$. Moreover, e divides m.

If $\sqrt[m]{p}^e \in F(\zeta)$ then it generates a subfield of $F(\zeta_m)$ over F. Since $\sqrt[m]{p}$ has degree m over F the element $\sqrt[m]{p}^e$ must have degree $\frac{m}{e}$ and its minimal polynomial is $X^{\frac{m}{e}} - p$. By the observation above the field generated by $\sqrt[m]{p}^e$ must be a Galois extension of F. But if F is a real field and $\frac{m}{e} > 2$ then $\sqrt[m]{p}^e \in \mathbb{R}$ cannot generate a Galois extension since some of the roots of $X^{\frac{m}{e}} - p$ are not real. Hence $\frac{m}{e} = 2$ or $\frac{m}{e} = 1$, which proves the lemma. □

Remark 1: It follows from the proof that no field extension $F(\zeta_m) : F$ for a real field F and an m-th root of unity has subfields generated by real radicals of degree strictly larger than 2. At first sight this seems to contradict the famous Kronecker-Weber Theorem which states that any abelian extension of $\mathbb{Q}$ is contained in some cyclotomic field $\mathbb{Q}(\zeta_m)$. But although the Galois group of $\mathbb{Q}(\zeta_m, \sqrt[m]{p})$ over $\mathbb{Q}(\zeta_m)$ is abelian, for $m > 2$ this is not true for the Galois group of $\mathbb{Q}(\zeta_m, \sqrt[m]{p})$ over $\mathbb{Q}$.

Remark 2: As follows from the lemma whenever m is odd then the degrees of $\sqrt[m]{p}$ over $\mathbb{Q}$ and over $\mathbb{Q}(\zeta_m)$ are the same. The following example shows that the second situation described by the lemma can also occur. Consider the positive 10-th root of 5. Its degree over $\mathbb{Q}$ is 10. On the other we will see later that $\mathbb{Q}(\zeta_{10})$ contains the square roots of 5. Hence the degree of $\sqrt[10]{5}$ over the 10-th cyclotomic field is 5.

Lemma 16 *If F is a real field and $\sqrt[m]{p} \in \mathbb{R}$ then any two admissible sequences for $\sqrt[d]{\gamma}$ that have a common prefix $(1, \zeta^{(1)}, \zeta^{(2)}, \zeta^{(3)})$ are equal.*

If F contains a primitive m-th root of unity and $\sqrt[m]{p}$ is arbitrary then $\zeta^{(1)}$ alone determines an admissible sequence.

Proof: We prove the lemma only in the real case.

Let $(1, \zeta_1, \zeta_2, \zeta_3)$ be a common prefix of two different admissible sequences

$$\left(1, \zeta^{(1)}, \zeta^{(2)}, \zeta^{(3)}, \zeta^{(4)}, \ldots, \zeta^{(m-1)}\right)$$

and

$$\left(1, \zeta^{(1)}, \zeta^{(2)}, \zeta^{(3)}, \zeta'^{(4)}, \ldots, \zeta'^{(m-1)}\right).$$

Hence $p_j \in F$ and $\beta_j \in F'$, $j = 1, 2$, exist such that $\sqrt[d]{p_j}\sqrt[d]{\gamma} = \beta_j$, $\zeta^{(i)}\sqrt[d]{p_j}\sqrt[d]{\sigma_i(\gamma)} = \sigma_i(\beta_j)$, $i = 1, 2, 3$, $j = 1, 2$, for fixed d-th roots of p_1, p_2. This implies

$$\frac{1}{p_1}\beta_1 \left(\sigma_2(\beta_1)\right)^{d-1} = \zeta^{(2)d-1}\sqrt[d]{\gamma}\left(\sqrt[d]{\sigma_2(\gamma)}\right)^{d-1} =$$

$$= \rho \in F(\sqrt[m]{p}, \zeta_m)$$

and

$$\frac{1}{p_2}\beta_2 \left(\sigma_2(\beta_2)\right)^{d-1} = \zeta^{(2)d-1}\sqrt[d]{\gamma}\left(\sqrt[d]{\sigma_2(\gamma)}\right)^{d-1} = \rho,$$

where ζ_m is a primitive m-th root of unity.

By the previous lemma an field isomorphism τ of $F(\sqrt[m]{p}, \zeta_m)$ exists that maps ζ_m onto itself and $\sqrt[m]{p}$ onto $\zeta_m^2 \sqrt[m]{p}$. We apply τ to both equations above. As is easily checked this yields

$$\zeta^{(2)}\zeta^{(4)d-1}\sqrt[d]{\sigma_2(\gamma)}\left(\sqrt[d]{\sigma_4(\gamma)}\right)^{d-1} = \tau(\rho)$$

and

$$\zeta^{(2)}\left(\zeta'^{(4)}\right)^{d-1}\sqrt[d]{\sigma_2(\gamma)}\left(\sqrt[d]{\sigma_4(\gamma)}\right)^{d-1} = \tau(\rho).$$

One easily deduces $\zeta^{(4)} = \zeta'^{(4)}$. Moreover, $\zeta^{(2)} = \zeta'^{(2)}$ and $\zeta^{(4)} = \zeta'^{(4)}$ imply $\zeta^{(6)} = \zeta'^{(6)}$ etc.. Hence for all even indices the two sequences coincide. Starting the process above with $\zeta^{(1)}$ and $\zeta^{(3)}$ instead of $\zeta^{(0)} = 1$ and $\zeta^{(2)}$ shows that the same is true for the odd indices. $\square$

Observe that the proof of Lemma 16 more or less is an algorithm to compute a subset for the set of admissible sequences of size d^3 in the real case and of size d in the complex case.

5 The algorithms

We are now in a position to sketch the basic algorithms. We claim that the following procedure computes for a nested radical γ over an algebraic number field $F = \mathbb{Q}(\alpha)$ an element denesting it, if any such element exists.

Algorithm Denesting Element

Input

A nested radical $\sqrt[d]{\gamma} = \sqrt[d]{\sum_{i=1}^{K} \kappa_i \sqrt[d_i]{\rho_i}}$, $\rho_i \in F$, of depth two over F, where F is either real and the radicals defining γ are also real or F contains a primitive d-th root of unity and $d_i = d$ for all i.

Output

"Yes", if any element in F leads to a denesting, and witnesses $\gamma^{(0)} \in F$, $\rho \in F(\sqrt[d_1]{\rho_1}, \sqrt[d_2]{\rho_2}, \ldots, \sqrt[d_K]{\rho_K})$ such that $\sqrt[d]{\gamma^{(0)}\gamma} = \rho$; "No", otherwise.

Step 1

Determine for each i the relative degree $n_i = [F(\sqrt[d_1]{q_1}, \ldots, \sqrt[d_i]{q_i}) : F(\sqrt[d_1]{q_1}, \ldots, \sqrt[d_{i-1}]{q_{i-1}})]$. Renumber the radicals such that $n_i > 1$ for the first k indices and $n_i = 1$ for the remaining indices. Hence $F^{(K)} = F^{(k)}$ and $[F^{(k)} : F] = \prod_{i=1}^{k} n_i = N$. Also compute the set $E^{(i)}$ of those $s \in \mathbb{N}$, $s < n_i$, such that $\sqrt[d_i]{\rho_i}^{sd} \in F^{(i-1)}$.

Step 2

Set $D^{(k)} := \{\gamma\}$.

For $i = 0, 1, \ldots, k-1$ do the following:

Compute for all elements $\gamma_j^{(k-i)}$ in $D^{(k-i)}$ a superset of its set of admissible sequences. Use these sequences and the formula given in Lemma 13 to determine the inverse $\gamma^{(k-i-1)}$ of an element in $F^{(k-i-1)}$ denesting $\gamma^{(k-i)}$.

Set $D_{\gamma^{(k-i)}} = \left\{\gamma^{(k-i-1)} \sqrt[d_k]{q_{k-i}}^{sd} \mid s \in E^{(k-i)}\right\}$ and

$$D^{(k-i-1)} = \bigcup_{\gamma^{(k-i)} \in D^{(k-i)}} D_{\gamma^{(k-i)}}.$$

Step 3

Decide whether any inverse $\gamma^{(0)}$ of an element in $D^{(0)}$ has the property

$$\sqrt[d]{\gamma^{(0)}}\sqrt[d]{\gamma} = \rho \in F(\sqrt[d_1]{\rho_1}, \sqrt[d_2]{\rho_2}, \ldots, \sqrt[d_k]{\rho_k}),$$

if this is the case output $\gamma^{(0)}$ and ρ; otherwise output "No".

To prove the claim that **Algorithm Denesting Element** finds an element denesting $\sqrt[d]{\gamma}$ we use the following observation.

Assume $E \supset F$ is a proper subfield of $F^{(k)}$. We consider γ as an element of the algebraic extension F' of the field E. If $\sqrt[d]{\gamma}$ denests over F then it denests over E. Moreover, let D be a set containing the *inverses* of a denesting set for $\sqrt[d]{\gamma}$ over E. For each element in D we consider a denesting set over F of an arbitrary d-th root of this element. As mentioned these subsets of F are independent of the d-th root.

Observe that any element $q \in F$ that denests $\sqrt[d]{\gamma}$ over F also denests $\sqrt[d]{\gamma}$ over E. Hence it differs from some element $\gamma'^{-1} \in D$ by a d-th power of an element in E, i.e.,

$$q = \rho^d \frac{1}{\gamma'}, \; \rho \in E.$$

Therefore d-th roots of q and γ' exist such that $\sqrt[d]{q} = \rho\sqrt[d]{\frac{1}{\gamma'}}$, equivalently,

$$\sqrt[d]{q}\,\sqrt[d]{\gamma'} = \rho \in E.$$

By definition of a denesting set the union of the denesting sets for elements in D form a denesting set for $\sqrt[d]{\gamma}$ over F.

If we apply this result to the sets $D^{(k-i)}$, $i = 1, \ldots, k$, from the basic denesting algorithm and use Lemma 10 it easily follows by induction that $D^{(0)}$ is a denesting set for $\sqrt[d]{\gamma}$ which proves the correctness of **Algorithm Denesting Element** .

Observe that the set $D^{(k-i)}$ has at most $\prod_{j=0}^{i-1} n_{k-j}$ elements. Assume that for each element in $D^{(k-i)}$

the admissible sequences determined by the prefixes $(1, \zeta^{(1)}, \zeta^{(2)}, \zeta^{(3)})$ or $(1, \zeta^{(1)})$ can be computed efficiently. Then at each level of the algorithm we have to check for at most $d^3 \prod_{j=0}^{i} n_{k-j}$ or $d \prod_{j=0}^{i} n_{k-j}$ different complex numbers fitting into the description of Lemma 13 whether they correspond to an element in $F^{(k-i-1)}$. Hence overall this step has to be done at most

$$d^3 \sum_{i=1}^{k} \prod_{j=0}^{i} n_{k-j} =$$

$$= d^3 N \left(1 + \frac{1}{n_1} + \ldots + \frac{1}{n_1 n_2 \cdots n_{k-1}}\right) \leq 2d^3 N$$

times in the real case, and accordingly, at most $2dN$ times in the complex case.

It remains to describe how to perform the single steps of **Algorithm Denesting Element** . Taking a closer look at the algorithm shows that we basically need to solve two problems. First, we need an algorithm that determines the minimal polynomial of an algebraic number γ from an approximation to γ. Using this algorithm primitive elements and their minimal polynomials for the fields $F^{(i)}$ are computed. These informations are needed for exact arithmetic in $F^{(i)}$.

Second, we need an algorithm that computes the exact representation of an algebraic number γ as an element in some number field $\mathbb{Q}(\alpha)$, provided a good approximation to γ is given.

The first problem has been solved by Kannan et al. [5] and by Schönhage [11] using the lattice basis reduction algorithm originally invented by Lenstra et al. [8] in their break-through paper on polynomial factorization. As the following theorem shows the same technique solves the second problem.

Theorem 17 *Let $\mathbb{Q}(\alpha)$ be an algebraic number field, where α is an algebraic integer with minimal polynomial $p(X) = \sum_{i=0}^{n} p_i X^i, p_n = 1, p_i \in \mathbb{Z}$. Let $\gamma = \frac{1}{c}\sum_{i=0}^{n-1} c_i \alpha^i$, $c, c_i \in \mathbb{Z}$, be an element in $\mathbb{Q}(\alpha)$ such that $|c|, |c_i| < K$, K a positive number. Assume s and ϵ are real numbers satisfying*

$$s > 2^{2n^2} 2^{7n} n^n |p|_2^n K^{4n}, \quad \epsilon = 3s^{-1}.$$

Moreover, suppose $\overline{\gamma}, \overline{\alpha}$ are approximations to γ and α, respectively, such that the following estimates for the real and imaginary parts $\Re, \Im$ of γ, α hold

$$|\Re(\overline{\gamma}) - \Re(\gamma)| < \epsilon, \quad |\Im(\overline{\gamma}) - \Im(\gamma)| < \epsilon,$$

$$|\Re(\overline{\alpha}^i) - \Re(\alpha^i)| < \epsilon, \quad |\Im(\overline{\alpha}^i) - \Im(\alpha^i)| < \epsilon,$$

for all $i \in \{1, 2, \ldots, n-1\}$.

If $\Lambda(V)$ is generated by the columns of the following $(n+3) \times (n+1)$ matrix

$$V = \begin{bmatrix} s\Re(\overline{\gamma}) & s & s\Re(\overline{\alpha}) & s\Re(\overline{\alpha}^2) & \ldots & s\Re(\overline{\alpha}^{n-1}) \\ s\Im(\overline{\gamma}) & 0 & s\Im(\overline{\alpha}) & s\Im(\overline{\alpha}^2) & \ldots & s\Im(\overline{\alpha}^{n-1}) \\ 1 & 0 & \ldots & & & 0 \\ 0 & 1 & 0 & & \ldots & 0 \\ & & \ddots & & & \\ & & & & \ldots & \\ 0 & 0 & \ldots & & 0 & 1 \end{bmatrix},$$

then the shortest vector $\underline{g} = V(c, c_0, c_1, \ldots, c_{n-1})^T$ of a reduced basis for $\Lambda(V)$ satisfies

$$\gamma = \frac{-1}{c} \sum_{i=0}^{n-1} c_i \alpha^i.$$

Moreover, $\gcd(c, c_0, c_1, \ldots, c_{n-1}) = 1$.

If we want to use this result in **Algorithm Denesting Element** for any application of the lattice basis reduction algorithm we need to deduce an upper bound on the representation size K of the number whose exact representation we want to reconstruct. As it turns out this is no serious problem and a detailed analysis which will be given in the full paper proves the following theorems.

Theorem 18 *When applied to $d \in \mathbb{N}$ and $\gamma = \sum_{i=1}^{K} \kappa_i \sqrt[d_i]{\rho_i}$, where κ_i, ρ_i are elements of some real algebraic number field $\mathbb{Q}(\alpha)$, the number of bit operations* **Algorithm Denesting Element** *uses to determine whether an element $\gamma^{(0)}$ with*

$$\sqrt[d]{\gamma^{(0)}} \sqrt[d]{\gamma} \in F(\sqrt[d_1]{\rho_1}, \sqrt[d_2]{\rho_2}, \ldots, \sqrt[d_K]{\rho_K})$$

for real d-th roots exists, is bounded by a polynomial in the parameters n, l, L, N, d. n is the degree of the minimal polynomial p of α, 2^l is a bound on the 2-norm of p, 2^L is an upper bound on the size of the coefficients in the representation of κ_i, ρ_i as elements of $\mathbb{Q}(\alpha)$, and N is the degree of $F(\sqrt[d_1]{\rho_1}, \sqrt[d_2]{\rho_2}, \ldots, \sqrt[d_K]{\rho_K})$ over F.

An upper bound on the number of bit operations is given by

$$O(d^4 n^6 N^{12}(\log n + l + L) M(d^2 n^5 N^7(\log n + l + L))).$$

Using at most N times this number of bit operations it can decided whether $\sqrt[d]{\gamma}$ can be written as a linear combination of real depth one radicals over $\mathbb{Q}(\alpha)$.

Here $M(m)$ denotes the number of bit operations needed for multiplying two m-bit integers.

The input of **Algorithm Denesting Element** need not be of the form $\sqrt[d]{\sum_{i=1}^{K} \kappa_i \sqrt[d_i]{\rho_i}}$ rather the sum can be replaced by any rational expression in the radicals $\sqrt[d_i]{\rho_i}$ and with coefficients in $\mathbb{Q}(\alpha)$. In this case the run time gets slightly worse but is still polynomial in the parameters mentioned above.

The corresponding theorem for complex radicals is

Theorem 19 Algorithm Denesting Element *when applied to $d \in \mathbb{N}$ and $\gamma = \sum_{i=1}^{K} \kappa_i \sqrt[d]{\rho_i}$, where κ_i, ρ_i are elements of some algebraic number field $\mathbb{Q}(\alpha)$ containing a primitive d-th root of unity determines in time polynomial in n, l, L, N, d whether an element an element $\gamma^{(0)}$ with*

$$\sqrt[d]{\gamma^{(0)}}\sqrt[d]{\gamma} \in F(\sqrt[d_1]{\rho_1}, \sqrt[d_2]{\rho_2}, \ldots, \sqrt[d_K]{\rho_K})$$

for arbitrary d-th roots exists. The parameters n, l, L, N, d are as above.

An upper bound for the number of operations used is

$$\mathcal{O}(d^2 n^6 N^6 (\log n + l + L) M(d^2 n^5 N^4 (\log n + l + L))).$$

Using at most N times this number of bit operations it can be decided whether $\sqrt[d]{\gamma}$ can be written as a linear combination of radicals of depth one and of order d over $\mathbb{Q}(\alpha)$.

For sums of nested radicals we get similar results. In particular, the algorithms are polynomial in the number of terms of the sum and the maximum degree of a radical extension generated by the depth one radicals appearing in a *single* term of the sum. The generalization of these results to quotients of sums of nested radicals turns out to be straightforward.

As mentioned in the introduction the algorithms sketched above are correct for number fields and so they can be applied to nested radicals of depth larger than two. But they are not guaranteed to find a minimum depth denesting.

Acknowledgment I would like to thank Susan Landau for bringing the problem of denesting radicals to my attention.

References

[1] J. Blömer, "Computing Sums of Radicals in Polynomial Time", *Proc. 32nd Symposium on Foundations of Computer Science* 1991, pp. 670-677.

[2] A. Borodin, R. Fagin, J. E. Hopcroft, M. Tompa, "Decreasing the Nesting Depth of Expressions Involving Square Roots", *Journal of Symbolic Computation* Vol. 1, pp. 169-188, 1985.

[3] G. Horng, M. -D. Huang, "Simplifying Nested Radicals and Solving Polynomials by Radicals in Minimum Depth", *Proc. 31st Symposium on Foundations of Computer Science* 1990, pp. 847-854.

[4] N. Jacobson, *Basic Algebra I*, W. H. Freeman and Company, 1974.

[5] R. Kannan, A. K. Lenstra, L. Lovász, "Polynomial Factorization and Nonrandomness of Bits of Algebraic and Some Transcendental Numbers", *Mathematics of Computation* Vol. 50, No. 181, pp. 235-250, 1988.

[6] S. Landau, "Simplification of Nested Radicals", *SIAM Journal on Computing* Vol. 21, No. 1, pp 85-110, 1992.

[7] S. Landau, "A Note on Zippel-Denesting", *Journal of Symbolic Computation*, Vol. 13, pp. 41-46, 1992.

[8] A. K. Lenstra, H. W. Lenstra, Jr. L. Lovász, "Factoring Polynomials with Rational Coefficients", *Mathematische Annalen* Vol. 261, pp. 515-534, 1982.

[9] S. Ramanujan, *Problems and Solutions, Collected Works of S. Ramanujan*, Cambridge University Press, 1927.

[10] C. L. Siegel, "Algebraische Abhängigkeit von Wurzeln", *Acta Arithmetica*, Vol. 21, pp. 59-64, 1971.

[11] A. Schönhage, "Factorization of Univariate Integer Polynomials by Diophantine Approximation and an Improved Basis Reduction Algorithm", *Proc. 11th ICALP*, LNCS 172, pp. 437-447, 1984.

[12] R. Zippel, "Simplification of Expressions Involving Radicals", *Journal of Symbolic Computation* Vol. 1, pp. 189-210, 1985.

On Efficient Band Matrix Arithmetic

Wayne Eberly†

Department of Computer Science, University of Calgary
Calgary, Alberta, Canada T2N 1N4

e-mail: `eberly@cpsc.ucalgary.ca`

Abstract

An efficient parallel Las Vegas algorithm is presented for computation of the determinant of a nonsingular band matrix and for the solution of a system of linear equations with a band matrix as coefficient matrix. The algorithm can be implemented using time polylogarithmic in n with $O(nm^{\omega-1})$ processors, in order to process an input matrix with order n and band width m, provided that $n \times n$ matrices can be multiplied in logarithmic time with $O(n^{\omega})$ processors. If asymptotically efficient matrix multiplication is used ($\omega < 3$), then the time-processor product for the resulting algorithm is less than the number of steps used to solve these problems via Gaussian elimination.

The algorithm is more general than previous processor efficient parallel algorithms for band matrix computations, since it can be applied to invert arbitrary nonsingular band matrices over arbitrary fields.

1 Introduction

Asymptotically efficient matrix multiplication has been used as the basis for fast sequential algorithms for a variety of problems with dense matrices as input — including QR-factorization and other unitary factorizations of complex matrices ([15]), and triangular factorization and computation of the determinant and inverse of nonsingular matrices ([3]), and of the characteristic polynomial of square matrices ([12]), over arbitrary fields. More recently, Kaltofen and Pan have presented processor-efficient parallel Las Vegas algorithms for several of these problems: They show that the determinant and inverse of a nonsingular $n \times n$ matrix over an arbitrary field F can be computed in polylogarithmic time with $O(n^{\omega})$ processors, for any exponent ω such that $n \times n$ matrix multiplication can be performed in logarithmic time with $O(n^{\omega})$ processors. As well, they show that the rank and a basis for the nullspace of a singular matrix can be computed at a similar cost.

In this paper we use fast matrix multiplication to obtain efficient algorithms for sparse matrix computations. In particular, we will consider band matrices — sparse matrices with nonzero entries clustered in a small number of bands near the diagonal. If A is a nonsingular $n \times n$ band matrix with its nonzero entries in m bands near the diagonal, then a system $Ax = b$ can be solved sequentially by Gaussian elimination using $O(nm^2)$ field operations, and the determinant of A can be computed at the same cost ([8]). Faster algorithms are available for special cases. For example, the cost of these computations can be reduced to $O(n/m)$ times that of $m \times m$ matrix multiplication if A is upper triangular (by the algorithm of Chen and Kuck [4]), or if specific minors of A are nonsingular (see, for example, [2]). Processor-efficient parallel algorithms are also available in these cases (again, see [4], [2]). We will generalize these results by presenting asymptotically efficient algorithms for computation of the determinant of an arbitrary nonsingular band matrix over an arbitrary field, and for the solution of a system of linear equations with an arbitrary nonsingular banded coefficient matrix. These algorithms parallelize — they can be used to solve these problems in polylogarithmic time using $O(nm^{\omega-1})$ processors for n, m, and ω as above.

Our (parallel) algorithms can be implemented on an "algebraic PRAM" that supports field operations and the random selection of elements from a finite subset of the ground field (of polynomial size). For analysis,

† Research was supported in part by the Natural Sciences and Engineering Research Council of Canada, research grant OGP0089756.

we assume these operations have unit cost. By this measure our algorithms are efficient as defined, for example, by Karp and Ramachandran [11]: Each uses polylogarithmic time and has a time-processor product that is within a polylogarithmic factor of the number of steps used by the best known sequential algorithm for the problem being solved.

Henceforth F will denote a field. The letters $A, B, \ldots, D, G, H, \ldots, Z$ denote matrices over F, and the corresponding lower case letters denote matrix entries. For example, $a_{i,j}$ will denote the $(i,j)^{\text{th}}$ entry of the matrix $A = (a_{i,j})$. A^t denotes the *transpose* of A, with $(i,j)^{\text{th}}$ entry $a_{j,i}$. $M_{n\times m}(F)$ denotes the additive group of $n \times m$ matrices over a field F. If $n = m$ then $M_{n\times m}(F)$ is a ring (containing matrices of order n), whose additive and multiplicative identities will be denoted by 0_n and 1_n respectively.

A band matrix can now be defined as follows.

DEFINITION. A matrix $A = (a_{i,j}) \in M_{l\times n}(F)$ is a *band matrix* if there exist integers m and k such that $0 \le m \le l + n - 1$, $0 \le k \le \min(m-1, l-1)$, and such that $a_{i,j} = 0$ if $i - j > k$ or $j - i > m - k - 1$ for $1 \le i \le l$ and $1 \le j \le n$. The minimal such m and k are called the *band width* and *offset* of A, respectively.

Algorithms for the multiplication and inversion of dense matrices will be used as subroutines throughout this paper, and the cost of our algorithms will be stated in terms of the complexity of these operations. Henceforth α will denote any real number such that the product of two matrices of order n can be computed sequentially using $O(n^\alpha)$ field operations. As above, ω will denote any real number such that $n \times n$ matrix multiplication can be performed in time $O(\log n)$ using $O(n^\omega)$ processors. As discussed by Pan [13], we may assume $\omega < \alpha + \epsilon$ for arbitrary $\epsilon > 0$. For "practical" algorithms one should choose $\alpha = 3$ or perhaps use the algorithm of Strassen [17], with $\alpha = \log_2 7 \approx 2.807$. In theory one can do much better: the bound of Coppersmith and Winograd [5], $\alpha \approx 2.376$, is the best currently known. $T_{Inv}(n)$ will denote the time required to invert and compute the determinant of a nonsingular $n \times n$ matrix using $O(n^\omega)$ processors. By recent results of Kaltofen and Pan, we may assume $T_{Inv}(n) \in O(\log^2 n)$ for computations over fields of characteristic zero ([9]), and $T_{Inv}(n) \in O(\log^4 n)$ over arbitrary fields (see [10] for the general case, and for sharper estimates of $T_{Inv}(n)$ for various classes of fields).

The main result of the paper can now be stated:

THEOREM 1. *Suppose A is a nonsingular band matrix of order n and band width m over an infinite field F.*

(a) *The determinant of A and the solution of a system $Ax = b$ can be computed (from A and the vector $b \in M_{n\times 1}(F)$) using $O(nm^{\alpha-1}\log^3 n)$ field operations, by a Las Vegas algorithm that reports failure with probability at most 1/2.*

(b) *The problems described in (a) can be solved by a parallel Las Vegas algorithm that fails with probability at most 1/2, in time $O(T_{Inv}(n)\log^3 n)$ with $O(nm^{\omega-1})$ processors.*

In order to ensure that the probability of failure is at most 1/2, we assume that the ground field F contains at least $n^{\Omega(1)}$ distinct elements. We perform band matrix computations over a small finite field F by using arithmetic over a field extension of degree $O(\log_{|F|} n)$. Let

$$\gamma_F(n) = \begin{cases} 1 & \text{if } |F| \ge n, \\ (\log_{|F|} n)(1 + \log\log_{|F|} n) & \text{if } |F| > n, \end{cases}$$

so arithmetic over an extension of degree $O(\log_{|F|} n)$ over F can be performed using $O(\gamma_F(n))$ operations in the ground field.

THEOREM 2. *Suppose A is a nonsingular band matrix of order n and band width m over a finite field F.*

(a) *The determinant of A and the solution of a system $Ax = b$ can be computed (from A and the vector $b \in M_{n\times 1}(F)$) using $O(nm^{\alpha-1}\gamma_F(n)\log^3 n)$ field operations, by a Las Vegas algorithm that reports failure with probability at most 1/2.*

(b) *The problems described in (a) can be solved by a parallel Las Vegas algorithm that fails with probability at most 1/2, in time $O(T_{Inv}(n)\gamma_F(n)\log^3 n)$ with $O(nm^{\omega-1})$ processors.*

If $\Theta(nm^{\alpha-1})$ operations are necessary for the band matrix computations discussed in this paper, then our algorithms are near optimal. However, it is not known whether the complexity of solving a dense system of linear equations is as great as that of dense matrix inversion ([20]); this would certainly be implied by a lower bound of $\Omega(nm^{\alpha-1})$ nonscalar operations for the solution of a banded system of linear equations (in particular, when $m \approx n$). It is clear that the computation of the inverse of a band matrix is more expensive than the computation of its determinant, since the inverse of a band matrix is generally dense. However, the proof of Corollary 5 of Baur and Strassen [1] can be modified to show that the nonscalar complexity of computing the inner m bands of the inverse of a band matrix with odd band width m (and offset $m/2 - 1$) is at most linear in the complexity of the determinant — it suffices to consider a band matrix with indeterminates as entries rather than a dense matrix, and to apply the same argument. Since a block diagonal matrix, with n/m nonsingular dense matrices of order m on its diagonal, is a band matrix of order n and band width $2m+1$, and since the inverse of such a matrix is also banded, it follows that the complexity of the determinant of a band matrix of order n and band width $2m+1$ is at least linear in that of computing the inverses of $O(n/m)$ dense matrices of order m. Standard reductions can be used to show that this complexity is at least linear in the complexity of multiplication of $O(n/m)$ pairs of matrices, each of order m. Thus Strassen's direct sum conjecture ([18]) implies the desired lower bound for the nonscalar complexity of band matrix determinants. Unfortunately, this conjecture is at best controversial; for example, Strassen now believes that it is probably false ([19]). Thus a lower bound that does not rely on this conjecture is desirable.

In Section 2 the above band matrix problems are reduced to a row pivoting problem. This pivoting problem is solved (for problems over infinite fields) in Section 3. The time and number of processors used by parallel algorithms for these problems are analyzed here in order to prove Theorem 1(b); Theorem 1(a) follows by a similar analysis. Additional results and problems are discussed in Section 4.

2 Reduction of Inversion to a Pivoting Problem

Suppose now that $A \in M_{n\times n}$ is a nonsingular band matrix with band width m and offset k. We will assume (without loss of generality) that m divides n; let $\hat{n} \in \mathbb{Z}$ such that $n = \hat{n}m$. Since A can be inverted at the desired cost using the methods of Kaltofen and Pan if $n \leq 4m$, we will assume $\hat{n} > 4$. Let $n_1 = \lceil(\hat{n}-2)/2\rceil m$ and $n_2 = \lfloor(\hat{n}-2)/2\rfloor m$, so that $n = n_1 + n_2 + 2m$.

Consider the $n \times n_1$ matrix C_L that includes the leftmost n_1 columns of A. Since A is nonsingular C_L has full (column) rank n_1. The top $n_1 - m$ rows of C_L are linearly independent, since the top $n_1 - m$ rows of A are, and since these rows of A have no nonzero entries outside the leftmost n_1 columns. As well, the top $n_1 + m$ rows of C_L have full rank, n_1, because C_L has this rank and has no nonzero entries below these rows. It follows that there exists a set of n_1 rows of C_L, that includes the top $n_1 - m$ rows as well as m of the next $2m$ rows, that forms a nonsingular $n_1 \times n_1$ matrix. Consequently there exists a permutation matrix P_T of order $2m$ such that the principal $n_1 \times n_1$ minor of the matrix

$$\begin{bmatrix} 1_{n_1-m} & 0 & 0 \\ 0 & P_T & 0 \\ 0 & 0 & 0_{n_2+m} \end{bmatrix} A$$

is nonsingular. If P_T is chosen to preserve the relative order of the m rows it moves up, then neither the band width nor offset of this principal $n_1 \times n_1$ minor exceeds the band width or offset of A. By a similar argument there exists a permutation matrix P_B, also of order $2m$, such that if

$$P_{fix} = \begin{bmatrix} 1_{n_1-m} & 0 & 0 & 0 \\ 0 & P_T & 0 & 0 \\ 0 & 0 & P_B & 0 \\ 0 & 0 & 0 & 1_{n_2-m} \end{bmatrix}$$

then the matrix $P_{fix}A$ has nonsingular minors of orders n_1 and n_2 respectively in its top left and bottom right corners. Neither the band width nor offset of either minor exceeds that of A. Therefore,

$$P_{fix}A = \begin{bmatrix} A_1 & B_U & 0 \\ B_L & X & B_R \\ 0 & B_D & A_2 \end{bmatrix},$$

where $B_U \in M_{n_1\times 2m}(F)$, $B_D \in M_{n_2\times 2m}(F)$, $B_L \in M_{2m\times n_1}(F)$, $B_R \in M_{2m\times n_2}(F)$, $X \in M_{2m\times 2m}(F)$, $A_1 \in M_{n_1\times n_1}(F)$, $A_2 \in M_{n_2\times n_2}(F)$, and A_1 and A_2 are band matrices with band width at most m and offset at most k.

Now consider the following permutation matrices, each of which has determinant one:

$$P_L = \begin{bmatrix} 1_{n_1} & 0 & 0 \\ 0 & 0 & 1_{2m} \\ 0 & 1_{n_2} & 0 \end{bmatrix},$$

$$P_R = \begin{bmatrix} 1_{n_1} & 0 & 0 \\ 0 & 0 & 1_{n_2} \\ 0 & 1_{2m} & 0 \end{bmatrix} = P_L^{-1}.$$

Since A_1 and A_2 are both nonsingular,

$$\begin{aligned} P_{fix}A &= P_L \begin{bmatrix} A_1 & 0 & B_U \\ 0 & A_2 & B_D \\ B_L & B_R & X \end{bmatrix} P_R \\ &= P_L \begin{bmatrix} 1_{n_1} & 0 & 0 \\ 0 & 1_{n_2} & 0 \\ B_L A_1^{-1} & B_R A_2^{-1} & 1_{2m} \end{bmatrix} \begin{bmatrix} A_1 & 0 & 0 \\ 0 & A_2 & 0 \\ 0 & 0 & Y \end{bmatrix} \\ &\quad \cdot \begin{bmatrix} 1_{n_1} & 0 & A_1^{-1}B_U \\ 0 & 1_{n_2} & A_2^{-1}B_D \\ 0 & 0 & 1_{2m} \end{bmatrix} P_L^{-1} \end{aligned}$$

where $Y = X - B_L A_1^{-1} B_U - B_R A_2^{-1} B_D$. Denote by L, D, and U the second, third, and fourth matrices in the above expression respectively — so $P_{fix} A = P_L L D U P_L^{-1}$. Then, each of the matrices P_L, L, and U has determinant one, so the determinant of A is the product of the determinants of A_1, A_2, and of Y, and $Y \in M_{2m \times 2m}(F)$ is nonsingular. Consequently, $A^{-1} = P_L U^{-1} D^{-1} L^{-1} P_L^{-1} P_{fix}$, where

$$U^{-1} = \begin{bmatrix} 1_{n_1} & 0 & -A_1^{-1} B_U \\ 0 & 1_{n_2} & -A_2^{-1} B_D \\ 0 & 0 & 1_{2m} \end{bmatrix},$$

$$D^{-1} = \begin{bmatrix} A_1^{-1} & 0 & 0 \\ 0 & A_2^{-1} & 0 \\ 0 & 0 & Y^{-1} \end{bmatrix},$$

and

$$L^{-1} = \begin{bmatrix} 1_{n_1} & 0 & 0 \\ 0 & 1_{n_2} & 0 \\ -B_L A_1^{-1} & -B_R A_2^{-1} & 1_{2m} \end{bmatrix}.$$

Since A_1 and A_2 can be decomposed in the same way, both A and A^{-1} can be expressed as the product of $O(\log(n/m))$ matrices, each of which is either a permutation matrix, a sparse lower triangular matrix (resembling L, above), a sparse upper triangular matrix (resembling U), a dense nonsingular matrix of order at most $2m$, or is block diagonal with each block having one of these forms. Both the determinant and (sparse!) inverse of each of these matrices can be computed in polylogarithmic time with $O(nm^{\omega-1})$ processors.

Given this type of decomposition for A and A^{-1}, and given a matrix $b \in M_{n \times m}(F)$, the matrix $A^{-1}b$ (or $b^t A^{-1}$) can be computed in polylogarithmic time with $nm^{\alpha-1}$ processors using a sequence of $O(\log(n/m)$ multiplications of a sparse $n \times n$ matrix by an $n \times m$ matrix. Therefore a system of linear equations with a nonsingular band matrix A as coefficient matrix can be solved efficiently if decompositions of A and A^{-1} are available. In addition, if a suitable permutation P_{fix} is given along with decompositions of A_1 and A_2 (and of their inverses), then decompositions of A and A^{-1} can also be generated at this cost.

In the sequel, an algorithm is given for computation of a suitable matrix P_{fix} from the entries of A. The algorithm can be implemented using time $T_{Inv}(n) \log^2 n$ with $O(nm^{\omega-1})$ processors. Since the nonsingular minors A_1 and A_2 are band matrices with order less than $n/2$ and band width at most m, and the entries of these matrices are efficiently computed from A and P_{fix}, there is a recursive algorithm for decomposing A (and A^{-1}) in time $T(n,m)$ with $P(n,m)$ processors (which simply returns the entries of A and A^{-1} if $n \le 4m$), where

$$T(n,m) \in \begin{cases} O(T_{Inv}(n)) & \text{if } n \le 4m, \\ T(n/2, m) + O(T_{Inv}(n) \log^2 n) & \\ \qquad + O(\log^2 n) & \text{if } n > 4m; \end{cases}$$

$$P(n,m) \in \begin{cases} O(nm^{\omega-1}) = O(n^\omega) & \text{if } n \le 4m, \\ \max(2P(n/2, m), O(nm^{\omega-1})) & \\ & \text{if } n > 4m. \end{cases}$$

It is easily checked that $T(n,m) \in O(T_{Inv}(n) \log^3 n)$ and $P(n,m) \in O(nm^{\omega-1})$. Therefore A and A^{-1} can be decomposed, the determinant of A computed, and systems of linear equations with A as coefficient matrix solved, at the cost stated in Theorem 1.

3 Solution of a Pivoting Problem

It remains only to compute the matrix P_{fix}. In this section an algorithm for the computation of P_T is described; P_B (and therefore P_{fix}) can be found by a similar method.

Consider now the minor $\hat{A}$ of A that includes the top $n_1 + m$ rows and leftmost n_1 columns. Let $A_{Top} \in M_{(n_1-m)\times n_1}(F)$ and $A_{Bottom} \in M_{2m \times n_1}(F)$ be the matrices that include the top $n_1 - m$ and bottom $2m$ rows of this minor, respectively. It was established in Section 2 that the rows of A_{Top} are linearly independent, as are the columns of $\hat{A}$, so there exists a set of m rows of A_{Bottom} that can be "pivoted" up in order to produce (from $\hat{A}$) an $(n_1 + m) \times m$ matrix whose top n_1 rows are linearly independent. Computing P_T is essentially the same as finding some such set of rows of A_{Bottom}.

The following result will be useful in proving the correctness of a method for finding these rows.

LEMMA 1. *Let k and m be positive integers and let $x_1, x_2, \ldots, x_k \in M_{1\times m}(F)$ for any field F.*

(a) If $N \in M_{m\times m}(F)$ is a matrix of maximal rank such that $x_i N = 0$ for $1 \le i \le k$, and if $c_1, c_2, \ldots, c_l \in M_{1\times m}(F)$ is a basis for the vector space spanned by $x_1, x_2, \ldots, x_k$, then for any vectors $y_1, y_2, \ldots, y_s \in M_{1\times m}(F)$, the vectors $y_1 N, y_2 N, \ldots, y_s N$ are linearly independent if and only if the vectors $c_1, c_2, \ldots, c_l, y_1, y_2, \ldots, y_s$ are.

(b) Let s be a positive integer and let $R \in M_{m\times s}(F)$ be a matrix such that the vectors $x_1, x_2, \ldots, x_k \in M_{1\times m}(F)$ and the vectors $x_1 R, x_2 R, \ldots, x_k R \in M_{1\times s}(F)$ span vector spaces of the same dimension. Then, for any linearly independent subset

$x_{i_1}R, x_{i_2}R, \ldots, x_{i_t}R$ *of* $x_1R, x_2R, \ldots, x_kR$ *of maximal size,* $x_{i_1}, x_{i_2}, \ldots, x_{i_t}$ *is a maximal linearly independent subset of* $x_1, x_2, \ldots, x_k$.

Part (a) of the lemma follows from the fact that, if N is as described, then $xN = 0$ if and only if x is a linear combination of $x_1, x_2, \ldots, x_k$, for any $x \in M_{1\times m}(F)$. Part (b) is easily proved, since multiplication by R preserves the dimension of the space generated by the given vectors.

Let $\kappa \in \mathbb{Z}$ such that $\kappa \geq 4^{\omega-1}$. If $n_1 \leq (\kappa+1)m$ then an efficient algorithm for finding the desired rows of A_{Bottom} (whose correctness depends on the first half of the above lemma) is easily described: Use the methods of Kaltofen and Pan ([9], [10]) to find a matrix $N \in M_{n_1\times n_1}(F)$ of maximal rank such that $A_1N = 0$. Then, use the algorithm of Eberly [6] to choose a maximal linearly independent subset of the rows of A_2N. Since $n_1^{\omega} \in O(n_1m^{\omega-1})$ for this case, both steps can be performed efficiently — using time $O(T_{Inv}(n)\log^2 n)$ with $O(nm^{\omega-1})$ processors.

If $n_1 > (\kappa+1)m$ then there exist integers $\overline{n}_1 \leq n_1/\kappa$ and $\overline{m} \leq 4m$, and matrices $\hat{A}_{Top} \in M_{(\overline{n}_1-m)\times\overline{n}_1}(F)$ and $\hat{A}_{Bottom} \in M_{2m\times\overline{n}_1}(F)$, such that $\hat{A}_{Top}$ has full (row) rank $\overline{n}_1 - m$, the $(\overline{n}_1+m)\times\overline{n}_1$ matrix whose top rows are those of $\hat{A}_{Top}$ and whose bottom rows are those of $\hat{A}_{Bottom}$ has full (column) rank $\overline{n}_1$ and is a band matrix with band width at most $\overline{m}$, and such that any $(2m \times 2m)$ permutation matrix P_T that can be used to "pivot" rows of $\hat{A}_{Bottom}$ up in order to produce a nonsingular principal $\overline{n}_1\times\overline{n}_1$ minor can also be used to pivot up rows of A_{Bottom} as desired. Furthermore there is an algorithm (described below) for finding $\hat{A}_{Top}$ and $\hat{A}_{Bottom}$ from A_{Top} and A_{Bottom} in time $O(T_{Inv}(n)\log n)$ with $O(nm^{\omega-1})$ processors. Since $\overline{n}_1\overline{m}^{\omega-1} \leq n_1m^{\omega-1}$, this algorithm can be applied recursively (and efficiently) until the method sketched above for the case $n_1 \leq (\kappa+1)m$ is applicable: If $T(n,m)$ is the time and $P(n,m)$ the number of processors needed to find P_T by this method, then

$$T(n,m) \in \begin{cases} O(T_{Inv}(n)\log^2 n) & \text{if } n \leq (\kappa+1)m, \\ T(n/4^{\omega-1}, 4m) + O(T_{Inv}(n)\log n) & \\ & \text{if } n > (\kappa+1)m; \end{cases}$$

$$P(n,m) \in \begin{cases} O(nm^{\omega-1}) & \text{if } n \leq (\kappa+1)m, \\ \max(P(n/4^{\omega-1}, 4m), O(nm^{\omega-1})) & \\ & \text{if } n > (\kappa+1)m. \end{cases}$$

It follows that $T(n,m) \in O(T_{Inv}(n)\log^2 n)$, and $P(n,m) \in O(nm^{\omega-1})$, so P_T and P_{fix} can be computed at the cost claimed in Section 3.

Finally, it remains to show that $\hat{A}_{Top}$ and $\hat{A}_{Bottom}$ can be computed efficiently from A_{Top} and A_{Bottom}. The computation will proceed in two stages. In the first, most of the rows of A_{Top} will be eliminated. In the second, each row will be compressed in order to reduce the number of columns.

For the first stage, the rows of A_{Top} will be partitioned into two sets, R_{elim} and R_{save}. R_{elim} will include the first κm rows, R_{save} will include the next m, and thereafter R_{elim} will include sets of $(\kappa-1)m$ contiguous rows that are bordered by sets of m contiguous rows in R_{save}, possibly ending with an "incomplete" set of fewer than $(\kappa-1)m$ contiguous rows in R_{elim} — as shown in Figure 1.

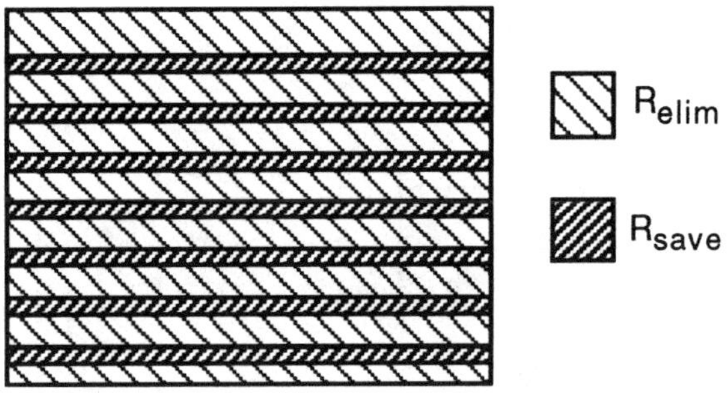

Figure 1: A_{Top}

Let $\overline{n}_1$ be m plus the number of rows in R_{save}; then, by the choice of κ and construction of R_{save}, $\overline{n}_1 \leq n_1/4^{\omega-1}$. Let $A_{elim} \in M_{(n_1-m)\times n_1}(F)$ be obtained from A_{Top} by keeping rows in R_{elim} unchanged and replacing the $\overline{n}_1 - m$ rows in R_{save} by zeroes. Then A_{elim} is block diagonal with $O(n_1/m)$ blocks, each of order at most $(\kappa+1)m$. Furthermore there exists a matrix $N_{elim} \in M_{n_1\times n_1}(F)$, of maximal rank such that $A_{elim}N_{elim} = 0$, such that N_{elim} is also block diagonal with blocks of the same sizes as in A_{elim}. This matrix can be found by considering the $O(n_1/m)$ diagonal blocks of A_{elim} independently and using the nullspace algorithm of Kaltofen and Pan $O(n/m)$ times in parallel, with each block as input. Now let $A_{save} \in M_{(\overline{n}_1-m)\times n_1}(F)$ be the matrix including the rows in R_{save} (with their relative order unchanged), let $A'_{Top} = A_{save}N_{elim} \in M_{(\overline{n}_1-m)\times n_1}(F)$, and let $A'_{Bottom} = A_{Bottom}N_{elim} \in M_{2m\times n_1}(F)$. It follows by part (a) of Lemma 1 that P_T can be found by choosing m rows of A'_{Bottom} that can be included with the rows of A'_{Top} in order to form a linearly independent set.

Let $A' \in M_{(\overline{n}_1+m)\times n_1}(F)$ be the matrix whose top rows are those of A'_{Top} and whose bottom rows are those of A'_{Bottom}. For the second stage it is sufficient (by Lemma 1 (b)) to find a matrix $R \in M_{n_1\times\overline{n}_1}(F)$ such that the ranks of $A'R$ and of A' are the same, and such that $A'R$ is a band matrix with band width at most $\overline{m}$. Then, one can set $\hat{A}_{Top} = A'_{Top}R$ and $\hat{A}_{Bottom} = A'_{Bottom}R$.

Consider the matrix A'_{Top}. It is easily verified that this is a block matrix, with blocks including between $(\kappa - 1)m$ and $(\kappa + 1)m$ columns and exactly m rows each, such that the only nonzero entries appear in blocks on and immediately above the diagonal. Similarly, A'_{Bottom} is a block matrix, with blocks having a similar number of columns and $2m$ rows each. All nonzero entries of A'_{Bottom} appear in the rightmost blocks (see Figure 2(a)).

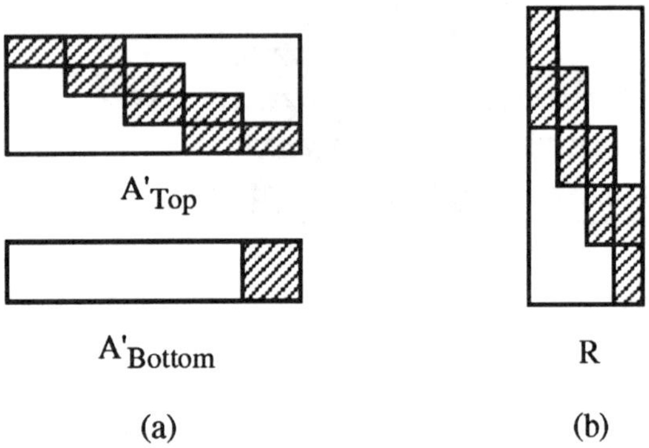

Figure 2

Lemma 2, below, indicates that a suitable matrix R can be chosen with the shape shown in Figure 2(b).

LEMMA 2. *Let matrices A', A'_{Top}, and A'_{Bottom} be as above. Then there exists a matrix $R \in M_{n_1\times\overline{n}_1}(F)$ such that*

(a) R is a block matrix, with blocks including between $(\kappa-1)m$ and $(\kappa+1)m$ rows and exactly m columns each, with nonzero entries only in blocks on and immediately below the diagonal — so that $A'_{Top}R$ has square blocks of order m, with nonzero entries only in blocks on and immediately above or below the diagonal, and $A'_{Bottom}R$ has nonzero entries only in its rightmost $2m$ columns;

(b) The matrices A' and $A'R$ have the same rank.

To prove the lemma, let r_i be the rank of the first i blocks of rows of A' for $1 \le i \le (\overline{n}_1 + m)/m$, and let c_i be the rank of the first i blocks of columns, for $1 \le i \le \overline{n}_1/m$. Then since each block of rows in A' contains only m rows, $r_{i+1} \le r_i + m$ for $0 \le i \le \overline{n}_i/m$. As well, $r_{(\overline{n}_1+m)/m} \le r_{(\overline{n}_1-m)/m} + m$, since adding the rows of A'_{Bottom} to those of A'_{Top} increases matrix rank by only m. Since A' has the shape shown above, $r_{i-1} \le c_i \le r_i$ for $1 \le i < (\overline{n}_1 - m)/m$, and $r_{(\overline{n}_1-m)/m} \le c_{\overline{n}_1/m} = r_{(\overline{n}_1+m)/m}$. It follows that a suitable matrix R can be chosen with only zeroes and ones as entries and at most a single one in any row or column (so, $A'R$ includes a subset of the columns of A'), and with the shape described in the lemma — by choosing R to select columns so that the first i blocks of columns in $A'R$ has the same rank as the first i blocks of columns in A', for $1 \le i \le \overline{n}_1/m$.

Since at least one sparse matrix R exists such that $A'R$ has the desired rank, it follows by a lemma of Schwartz [16] that with high probability $(1-O(1/n))$ a suitable matrix R can be found efficiently by selecting entries in the nonzero blocks of R randomly, from a subset of F of size polynomial in n. (This is the only place in our analysis where the assumption that F is large is needed.) With small probability this method will fail, and $A'R$ will have smaller rank than A'; this failure will be detected when the method for the case $n_1 \le (\kappa + 1)m$ is applied to try to find P_T.

Finally, it is easily checked that both stages of the process of finding $\hat{A}_{Top}$ and $\hat{A}_{Bottom}$ can be implemented using $O(nm^{\omega-1})$ processors in the time claimed.

4 Extensions and Problems

The methods described in Section 3 can be combined with the techniques described in [6] to find (and certify as correct) a maximal nonsingular minor of a singular band matrix A, such that the band width of the minor is as most twice that of the input matrix. Given such a minor, the rank of A is available immediately, and a single solution of a system $Ax = b$ can be found (for $b \in M_{n\times 1}(F)$, provided a solution exists) by solving a linear system of equations with a nonsingular banded coefficient matrix. Therefore the rank of a singular band matrix, and any one solution of a system $Ax = b$, can also be found using Las Vegas algorithms with polylogarithmic time and $O(nm^{\omega-1})$ processors.

All these band matrix problems can be solved in time $O(\log n \log m)$ using a polynomial number of processors ([7]). Unfortunately, existing "fast" methods for band matrix inversion appear to be incompatible with the methods described here, so the question of whether band matrix inversion can be performed using small time and (simultaneously) a reasonable number of processors remains open.

References

[1] W. Baur and V. Strassen, The complexity of partial derivatives, *Theoret. Comput. Sci.* **22** (1983), 317–330.

[2] R. Bevilacqua, B. Codenotti, and F. Romani, Parallel solution of block tridiagonal linear systems, *Linear Algebra Appl.* **104** (1988), 39–57.

[3] J. R. Bunch and J. E. Hopcroft, Triangular factorization and inversion by fast matrix multiplication, *Math. Comp.* **28** (1974), 231–236.

[4] S. C. Chen and D. J. Kuck, Time and parallel processor bounds for linear recurrence systems, *IEEE Trans. Comput.* **C-24** (1975), 701–717.

[5] D. Coppersmith and S. Winograd, Matrix multiplication via arithmetic progressions, *J. Symbolic Comput.* **9** (1990), 251–280.

[6] W. Eberly, Efficient parallel independent subsets and matrix factorizations, *in* "Proceedings, 3rd IEEE Symposium on Parallel and Distributed Processing" (1991), 204–211.

[7] W. Eberly, Fast parallel band matrix arithmetic. Submitted for publication.

[8] G. H. Golub and C. F. van Loan, *Matrix Computations,* Second Edition, Johns Hopkins University Press, Baltimore, 1989.

[9] E. Kaltofen and V. Pan, Processor efficient parallel solution of linear systems over an abstract field, *in* "Proceedings, 3rd ACM Symposium on Parallel Algorithms and Architectures" (1991), 180–191.

[10] E. Kaltofen and V. Pan, Professor-efficient parallel solutions of linear systems II: the positive characteristic and singular cases, *in* "Proceedings, 33rd IEEE Symposium on Foundations of Computer Science" (1992).

[11] R. Karp and V. Ramachandran, Parallel algorithms for shared-memory machines, in *Handbook of Theoretical Computer Science,* MIT/Elsevier, 1990, 869–941.

[12] W. Keller-Gehrig, Fast algorithms for the characteristic polynomial, *Theoret. Comput. Sci.* **36** (1985), 309–317.

[13] V. Pan, Complexity of parallel matrix computations, *Theoret. Comput. Sci.* **54** (1987), 65–85.

[14] V. Pan and J. Reif, Fast and efficient parallel solution of sparse linear systems, TR 88-18, Computer Science Dept., SUNY Albany, 1988.

[15] A. Schönhage, Unitäre Transformationen grosser Matrizen, *Numer. Math.* **20** (1973), 409–417.

[16] J. T. Schwartz, Fast probabilistic algorithms for verification of polynomial identities, *J. ACM* **27** (1980), 701–717.

[17] V. Strassen, Gaussian elimination is not optimal, *Numer. Math.* **13** (1969), 354–356.

[18] V. Strassen, Vermeidung von Divisionen, *J. Reine Angew. Math.* **264** (1973), 184–202.

[19] V. Strassen, Relative bilinear complexity and matrix multiplication, *J. Reine Angew. Math.* **375/376** (1987), 406–443.

[20] V. Strassen, Algebraic complexity theory, in *Handbook of Theoretical Computer Science,* MIT/Elsevier, 1990, 633–672.

A Subexponential Algorithm for Abstract Optimization Problems

BERND GÄRTNER*
Institut für Informatik, Freie Universität Berlin
Arnimallee 2-6, W 1000 Berlin 33, Germany
e-mail: gaertner@tcs.fu-berlin.de

Abstract

An Abstract Optimization Problem (AOP) is a triple $(H, <, \phi)$ *where* H *is a finite set,* $<$ *a linear order on* 2^H *and* ϕ *an oracle that, for given* $F \subseteq G \subseteq H$, *determines whether* $F = \min(2^G)$, *and if not, returns a smaller set. To solve the problem means to find* $\min(2^H)$. *We present a randomized algorithm that solves any AOP with an expected number of* $O(e^{O(\sqrt{|H|})})$ *oracle calls. In contrast, any deterministic algorithm needs to make* $2^{|H|} - 1$ *oracle calls in the worst case.*

The algorithm is applied to the problem of finding the minimum distance of two polyhedra in d-space, which gives the first subexponential bound in d for this problem. Another application is the computation of the smallest ball containing n points in d-space; the previous bounds for this problem were also exponential in d.

1 Introduction

In order to explain the idea behind the very general framework of *Abstract Optimization Problems* (AOP's) and to demonstrate its applicability, we will focus on two geometric optimization problems. In fact, these problems are the main motivation for the framework. One of them is familiar and well-studied, namely the *Linear Programming problem*:

> (LP) Given a polyhedron $\mathcal{P}$, specified by n halfspaces in d-space, and a d-vector v, find a point $p \in \mathcal{P}$ extreme in direction v.

The geometric formulation of the Linear Programming Problem is chosen in order to keep notation consistent with the second problem of *minimum separation of polyhedra*:

> (POLYSEP) Given two polyhedra $\mathcal{P}$ and $\mathcal{Q}$, specified by n points (or n halfspaces) in d-space, determine their minimum distance $\text{dist}(\mathcal{P}, \mathcal{Q}) := \min(||p - q|| \mid p \in \mathcal{P}, q \in \mathcal{Q})$.

Although looking quite different, the two problems share some combinatorial properties, which makes the algorithm of Sharir & Welzl [17] in the framework of the *LP-type problems* applicable in both cases. On the other hand, POLYSEP is not as regular as LP in a sense to be described later and is therefore not as efficiently solvable as LP by this algorithm. Our framework uses another property shared by both problems and solves POLYSEP as efficient as LP. The method also improves on the previous bounds for the *minimum spanning ball problem*:

> (MINIBALL) Given n points in d-space, determine the radius of the smallest ball containing all the points.

Basically, an AOP consists of a finite set H with a linear order on 2^H and an oracle that answers the following queries: for given $F \subseteq G \subseteq H$, does there exist a set $F' \subseteq G$ with $F' < F$? If yes, such a set is returned as a witness, otherwise the output is a special symbol $\triangleright$. To solve the problem means to find the minimum set in the linear order, and we want to bound the number of oracle queries needed to do this for any given AOP.

The algorithm we develop is *randomized*, i.e. the expected number of oracle queries is averaged over internal coin flips performed by the algorithm and is independent of the input. Moreover, randomization is crucial: if information about the linear order $<$ can only be obtained from the oracle, no deterministic algorithm can beat the trivial bound of $2^{|H|} - 1$ oracle queries in the worst case. Although this does not mean anything for a special instance of an AOP with more properties available, it gives evidence that randomized algorithms may be potentially more powerful than deterministic ones in this situation.

*Graduiertenkolleg "Algorithmische Diskrete Mathematik", supported by the Deutsche Forschungsgemeinschaft, grant We 1265/2-1

0-8186-2900-2/92 $3.00 © 1992 IEEE

The paper is organized as follows: in the rest of the introduction we give a brief survey on the history of the LP, POLYSEP and MINIBALL problem up to the state-of-the-art solutions.

In Section 2 we will see how POLYSEP and MINIBALL fit into the framework of the LP-type problems, and point out why the subexponential bound for LP established in [13] does not hold for POLYSEP and MINIBALL.

In Section 3 we formally introduce abstract optimization problems, state the main result of the paper and apply it to obtain first subexponential bounds for POLYSEP and MINIBALL.

In Section 4 we start the more technical part by presenting the algorithm in the abstract framework, followed by its analysis.

Section 5 provides a discussion and open problems.

Linear Programming. LP problems are probably the best-understood optimization problems. There exists a vast amount of literature on LP problems; the reader is referred to [15] for an introduction. There are several methods to solve LP-problems that are efficient in practice – the most successful one being the *simplex algorithm* that was introduced by Dantzig [5] in 1951.

The simplex algorithm, however, is of a heuristic nature, i.e. it behaves much better in practice than what one can prove. For a long time it was even open whether LP-problems can be solved in polynomial time (in the number d of variables and the number n of constraints). This was settled by Khachiyan [10] and Karmarkar [9], but their algorithms are not *combinatorial*, i.e. they do not only depend on d and n but also on the size of the coefficients defining the input. It is still open whether there exists a combinatorial algorithm with polynomial complexity. In particular, the simplex algorithm was shown to be exponential in d in the worst case for many pivot rules [11].

Nevertheless, there has been substantial progress on the worst case complexity of combinatorial algorithms for Linear Programming in the last years, and the most recent developments have started only a year ago. Megiddo [12] was the first to show that LP problems can be solved in time linear in the number of constraints. For improvements in the dependence on d see [6], [1], [16], [4].

The currently best randomized algorithm combines recent results of Kalai [8] or Matoušek, Sharir & Welzl [13] with an algorithm by Clarkson [2]. This gives a subexponential bound of

$$O(d^2n + e^{O(\sqrt{d \log d})}).$$

Note that the best deterministic algorithm is obtained by 'derandomizing' Clarkson's algorithm and has runtime $O(d^{O(d)}n)$, which is still exponential in d [4].

Minimum Separation of Polyhedra . Little is known about this problem. For the special case that one polyhedron is just a point, Wolfe [19] gives a simplex-like algorithm that is fast in practice, but he can not prove any nontrivial upper bound on the runtime. An algorithm for the general case was developed by Clarkson [3] and takes time $O(n^{d/2})$ (provided the polyhedra are specified by n points). Applying the algorithm in [17] this can be improved to $O(d^3 2^d n)$, but the analysis in [13] in this case fails to give a better bound (see Section 2 below). Our algorithm will bring the bound down to the subexponential term mentioned above for Linear Programming.

Minimum Spanning Ball . It was observed early that MINIBALL has a structure similar to LP and thus can also be solved in time linear in the number of points by the techniques in [12] and [6] (with the same dependence on d as in the case of LP). As observed by Welzl [18], the LP algorithm of Seidel [16] also applies to the MINIBALL problem, and the same holds for the algorithms of Clarkson and Sharir & Welzl. However, subexponential runtime could not yet be shown – the analysis fails for the same reason as in the case of POLYSEP. Application of our framework will lead to a subexponential bound.

Keep in mind that we are looking for *combinatorial* algorithms, i.e. we want to bound the number of arithmetic operations in the unit-cost model.

2 LP-type problems

In this section we shortly review the concept of the *LP-type problems* introduced in [17], where the reader can also find how LP itself fits into the framework. To motivate the concept, we consider the MINIBALL problem first. Let H be a set of n points in d-space. For $G \subseteq H$ denote by $w(G)$ the radius of the smallest ball containing the points in G. It is well known that this ball is unique and that for $e \in H$ $w(G) < w(G \cup \{e\})$ if and only if e lies outside the ball determined by G. From this it is easily seen that the following two properties hold for all $F, G \subseteq H$:

(i) if $F \subseteq G$ then $w(F) \leq w(G)$.

(ii) if $F \subseteq G$ with $w(F) = w(G)$ then $w(F) < w(F \cup \{e\}) \Leftrightarrow w(G) < w(G \cup \{e\})$, for all $e \in H$.

In general, any pair (H, w) satisfying (i) and (ii) is called an LP-type problem. A *basis* is a set $B \subseteq H$ with $w(B') < w(B)$ for all $B' \subseteq B$. A basis of $G \subseteq H$ is a basis $B \subseteq G$ such that $w(B) = w(G)$. The *combinatorial dimension* of (H, w) is the maximum cardinality of any basis. In this framework, MINIBALL has combinatorial dimension at most $d + 1$, because any minimum ball spanned by a set $G \subseteq H$ is already determined by at most $d+1$ points of G on the boundary.

POLYSEP gives rise to an LP-type problem as follows: we assume for the rest of the paper, that polyhedra $\mathcal{P}$ and $\mathcal{Q}$ are given by point sets P and Q, $P \cap Q = \emptyset$, $|P \cup Q| = n$. So $\mathcal{P}$ and $\mathcal{Q}$ are actually polytopes with $\mathcal{P} = \text{conv}(P), \mathcal{Q} = \text{conv}(Q)$ (the case where $\mathcal{P}$ and $\mathcal{Q}$ are specified by halfspaces, is quite similar).

For $P' \cup Q' \subseteq P \cup Q$, let

$$w(P' \cup Q') := \text{dist}(\text{conv}(P'), \text{conv}(Q')).$$

For P' or Q' empty, w is set to ∞. Now properties (i) and (ii) (for $w(F) = w(G) < \infty$) hold for the pair $(P \cup Q, w)$, but with '$<$' and '$\leq$' replaced by '$>$' and '$\geq$', respectively. Property (i) is obviously satisfied, and property (ii) easily follows from the following observation: assume $w(P' \cup Q') = \rho, 0 < \rho < \infty$. Then there exists a unique pair $h_{P'}, h_{Q'}$ of parallel supporting hyperplanes of distance ρ which are perpendicular to any vector $p-q$ with $p \in P', q \in Q'$ and $||p-q|| = \rho$.

Denote by $h^+_{P'}$ and $h^+_{Q'}$ the closed halfspaces containing P' and Q', respectively. For a point $e \in P - P'$ $(Q - Q')$ we have $w(P' \cup Q' \cup \{e\}) < w(P' \cup Q')$ if and only if e does not lie in $h^+_{P'}$ $(h^+_{Q'})$ (Figure 1).

The following lemma establishes the combinatorial dimension of POLYSEP:

Lemma 2.1 *Let δ be the combinatorial dimension of the LP-type problem arising from* POLYSEP *defined by polytopes $\mathcal{P}$ and $\mathcal{Q}$ in d-space. If $\mathcal{P} \cap \mathcal{Q} = \emptyset$, then $\delta \leq d + 1$, otherwise $\delta \leq d + 2$.*

Proof: omitted in this version.

We now cite the main result of [13]:

Theorem 2.2 *Let (H, w) with $|H| = n$ be an LP-type problem of combinatorial dimension δ, and denote by t_{small} the time necessary to compute a basis of G and its value $w(G)$ for $|G| = \delta + 1$. Then a basis of H and $w(H)$ can be computed in time*

$$O(t_{small}\ n e^{O(\sqrt{\delta \ln n})}).$$

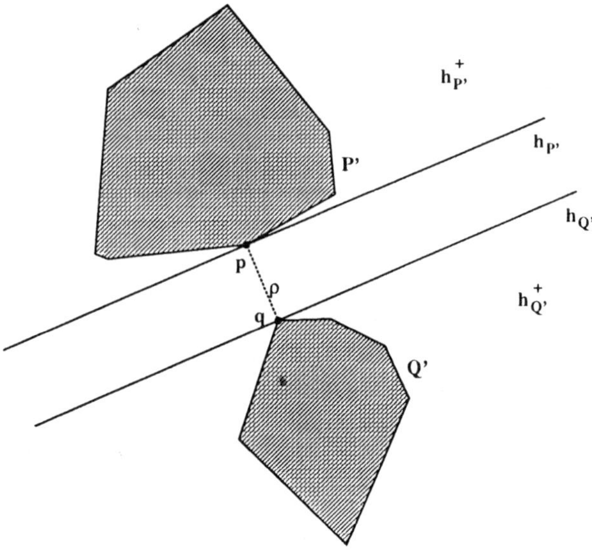

Figure 1: Minimum separation of polytopes

As this shows, the performance of the algorithm crucially depends on the complexity of the 'small' problems, and it is not clear that solving these special instances is a substantially easier task than solving the whole problem. As it turns out, the small problems are easy to solve in case of LP but are far more difficult in case of POLYSEP and MINIBALL. For d-dimensional LP, the small problem basically consists of solving a linear program with $d+1$ constraints, which can easily be done in time polynomial in d by observing that the solution is always determined by exactly d of the constraints (provided, the problem is appropriately defined), so that it suffices to test all d-subsets of the $d + 1$ constraints for optimality (for details see [13]).

In case of POLYSEP, the small problem becomes

> (SMALL_POLYSEP) Given two polyhedra $\mathcal{P}$ and $\mathcal{Q}$, specified by $d + 3$ points $P \cup Q$ in d-space, determine their minimum distance and a basis, i.e. a minimal subset $P' \cup Q'$ determining the same distance.

In contrast to LP, it is no longer true that the minimum distance is always determined by a fixed number of points; in fact, a basis of $P \cup Q$ may consist of any number of points between 2 and $d + 2$, and this also holds if $|P \cup Q| = d + 3$. Consequently, straightforward checking of every candidate basis as in the case of LP may require the examination of $\Theta(2^d)$ subsets just to solve SMALL_POLYSEP, which gives nothing better than an exponential algorithm for POLYSEP. The same difficulty arises in the MINIBALL problem: a minimum spanning ball may be determined by any number of points between 2 and $d+1$ on its boundary, so again SMALL_MINIBALL is not efficiently solvable by the trivial method.

In the next section we will succeed to solve SMALL_POLYSEP in a more efficient way and thus improve on the trivial method which was the only one known so far. As it turns out, SMALL_MINIBALL is a special case of SMALL_POLYSEP, so we will concentrate on the latter problem.

3 Abstract Optimization Problems

We repeat the definition of an AOP in a very formal way in order to have all the necessary terminology available in the next sections.

Definition 3.1 *An AOP is a triple* $(H, <, \phi)$ *where* H *is a finite set,* $<$ *is a linear order on* 2^H, *and* ϕ *is a mapping*

$$\phi : P \to H \cup \{\rhd\}, \; P := \{(F,G) \mid F \subseteq G \subseteq H\}$$

with the following property:

$$\begin{aligned} \phi(F,G) &= \rhd \Leftrightarrow F = \min(2^G), \\ G \supseteq \phi(F,G) &< F \text{ otherwise.} \end{aligned}$$

Of course, solving the AOP means to find $\min(2^H)$.

The key ingredient of the definition is the oracle function ϕ. The oracle decides for a query pair (F,G) whether F is already the minimum set among all subsets of G, and if not, returns a smaller set as a witness.

In this very general framework we achieve the following results:

Theorem 3.2 *For any* deterministic *algorithm* $\mathcal{A}$ *that solves all AOP's on a set* H, *there exists an AOP* $(H, <, \phi)$ *that can not be solved by* $\mathcal{A}$ *with less than* $2^{|H|} - 1$ *oracle queries.*

Theorem 3.3 *There exists a* randomized *algorithm that solves any AOP on a set* H *with an expected number of at most* $O(e^{(2\sqrt{2}+\epsilon)\sqrt{|H|}})$ *oracle queries, for any fixed* $\epsilon > 0$.

Note that the model of computation here allows an algorithm to gain information on $<$ only by performing oracle queries, so the linear order is only implicitly given to the algorithm.

The proofs are postponed to the technical part following this section.

Using the terminology from the previous section, we will now demonstrate how POLYSEP defined by points $P \cup Q$ fits into this framework: not surprisingly H is $P \cup Q$, and the linear order $<$ is defined according to the following rule: all the bases are ordered by their w-values with ties broken arbitrarily, and any non-basis is larger than any basis. This definition ensures that $\min(2^H)$ indeed is a basis of $H = P \cup Q$. It remains to describe the oracle ϕ. Intuitively, ϕ will test whether a given basis is already optimal for a subset of the points, and if not, 'jump' to a better basis. In the context of LP, this is exactly what the simplex algorithm does, and the abstract definition of the oracle function is motivated by this behaviour of the simplex algorithm.

The oracle for POLYSEP. First we need some terminology. For $P' \subseteq P$ (equivalently, for $Q' \subseteq Q$) we let $f(P') := \text{relint}(\text{conv}(P'))$ be the *face* defined by P', $\text{aff}(P')$ is the affine hull of P'.

Now assume $F = P' \cup Q' \subseteq G$ is a basis (the oracle will never be called on a non-basis F, so we skip this case). In addition we maintain two points $p \in f(P'), q \in f(Q')$ realizing $w(F) = \text{dist}(\text{conv}(P'), \text{conv}(Q'))$. Note that such points exist because F is minimal with value $w(F)$.

The oracle $\phi(F,G)$ now works as follows: in a first phase we check whether $w(F \cup \{e\}) < w(F)$ for some $e \in G - F$ (we have seen a criterion for this in the previous section). If no e exists with this property, we can safely return the special symbol $\rhd$, because F is already a basis of G in this case and thus can not be further improved. So assume we have found an $e \in G - F$ with $w(F \cup \{e\}) < w(F)$. Without loss $e \in P$. Obviously $F \cup \{e\}$ contains a basis B with $w(B) < w(F)$, and the goal now is to find one such basis (which not necessarily has to be a basis of $F \cup \{e\}$). The oracle will proceed by tracing some 'candidates' for this basis – starting with $F \cup \{e\}$ – and will consider a subset of the previous candidate in every step until the required basis is finally found.

In the generic step there is a candidate set $\hat{P} \cup \hat{Q}$ as well as points $\hat{p} \in f(\hat{P}), \hat{q} \in f(\hat{Q})$. Initially, $\hat{P} := P' \cup \{e\}, \hat{Q} := Q', \hat{p} := p, \hat{q} := q$. Note that by this definition the condition '$\hat{p} \in f(\hat{P})$' does not hold in the first step (where it will not be needed anyway). However, it will be satisfied in all consecutive steps.

Now do the following in the generic step:

(I) Compute points p^*, q^* that realize the minimum distance between $\text{aff}(\hat{P})$ and $\text{aff}(\hat{Q})$. If these points are not unique (i.e. $\text{aff}(\hat{P})$ and $\text{aff}(\hat{Q})$ are parallel or intersect in more than one point), choose p^* and q^* outside $\text{conv}(\hat{P})$ and $\text{conv}(\hat{Q})$.

(II) For $\lambda \geq 0$ define $\hat{p}(\lambda) := \hat{p} + \lambda(p^* - \hat{p})$, and $\hat{q}(\lambda)$ equivalently.

Let μ be the largest real such that $\hat{p}(\mu) \in \text{conv}(\hat{P})$ and $\hat{q}(\mu) \in \text{conv}(\hat{Q})$. Since $\hat{p}(0)$ and $\hat{q}(0)$ lie in the relative interior of the respective convex hulls, we have $\mu > 0$ (in the first step this follows from elementary reasoning).

(III) If $\mu > 1$, output $\hat{P} \cup \hat{Q}$. This set is a basis with p^* and q^* realizing $\text{dist}(\text{conv}(\hat{P}), \text{conv}(\hat{Q}))$. The basis-property of $\hat{P} \cup \hat{Q}$ follows from the uniqueness of p^* and q^* (for p^* and q^* not unique we can never have $\mu > 1$ by the choice of p^* and q^* in (I)!) together with the fact that $\hat{P}$ as well as $\hat{Q}$ are affinely independent (this already holds for $P' \cup \{e\}$ and Q', because $P' \cup Q'$ is a basis). We encourage the reader to work out the argument in detail.

If $\mu \leq 1$, let the new $\hat{P}$ be the minimal subset of the current $\hat{P}$ that contains $\hat{p}(\mu)$ in its convex hull, and let $\hat{p} := \hat{p}(\mu)$. In the same way update $\hat{Q}$,$\hat{q}$ and goto (I).

It is easy to see that this procedure terminates: every time it goes back to (I), $|\hat{P} \cup \hat{Q}|$ decreases by at least one. It is also true that the basis finally returned is better than the original basis F we have started with. To see this observe that by moving $\hat{p}$ and $\hat{q}$ towards p^* and q^* their distance never increases, and it decreases at least in the first step.

Lemma 3.4 *The oracle $\phi(F, G)$ can be implemented in time $O(d|G - F| + |F|^4)$.*

Proof: The $d|G - F|$-term amounts to the checking of '$w(F \cup \{e\}) < w(F)$?' for all $e \in G - F$, which can be done by computing one scalar product for every such point e. The generic step can be performed by solving a constant number of linear systems with no more than $|F|$ variables as well as doing some cheaper operations, which gives an $O(|F|^3)$-term. Now observe that the generic step is executed at most $|F|$ times. ☐

Corollary 3.5 *A* POLYSEP *problem defined by polytopes $\mathcal{P}$ and $\mathcal{Q}$ with n points in d-space can be solved in time*

$$O(d^4 n e^{O(\sqrt{d \ln n})}).$$

Proof: From the lemma and from Theorem 3.3 we get $t_{small} = O(d^4 e^{O(\sqrt{d})})$. Together with Theorem 2.2 we obtain the desired time bound. ☐

The same bound holds for polyhedra defined by n halfspaces, and also for MINIBALL:

Corollary 3.6 *A* MINIBALL *problem defined by n points in d-space can be solved in time*

$$O(d^4 n e^{O(\sqrt{d \ln n})}).$$

Proof: To get the bound we have to solve SMALL_MINIBALL as efficient as SMALL_POLYSEP. In order to do this we invoke a theorem in [14]:

> *Let $p_1, \ldots p_{d+1}$ be points in d – space (assumed to be affinely independent). The center of the smallest ball containg $p_1, \ldots p_{d+1}$ equals the point in their convex hull with minimal distance to the circumcenter of the points.*

The circumcenter can easily be computed in time $O(d^3)$, so the problem reduces to a POLYSEP problem with one polytope a single point. ☐

4 Bounds for Abstract Optimization Problems

This section contains proofs of Theorem 3.2 and Theorem 3.3. The exponential lower bound in the deterministic model is shown by using a standard adversary argument, and for the subexponential upper bound in the randomized setting we present an algorithm that works in the general framework of the AOP's. We start with the lower bound.

Proof of Theorem 3.2. Let H be a finite set and suppose we have a deterministic algorithm that solves any AOP $(H, <, \phi)$.

We start the algorithm on a problem $(H, <', \phi')$ with $<'$ and ϕ' not yet determined, and we argue that an adversary answering the oracle queries can construct $<'$ and ϕ' 'online' in such a way that the algorithm is forced to step through at least $2^{|H|} - 1$ queries. Intuitively, the adversary will pursue the strategy of hiding as much information as possible from the algorithm by modelling the AOP after the queries.

A good strategy will be the following: whenever an oracle query is performed by the algorithm, the adversary answers according to two simple rules:

(i) the answers are *consistent*, i.e. at each stage there exists an AOP such that all previous queries have been answered correctly with respect to this AOP.

(ii) $\triangleright$ is returned only if there is no other consistent answer.

It is easy to see that the adversary always has a consistent answer, so the algorithm steps through a sequence of queries with pairs (F, G) and finally stops. Suppose that less than $2^{|H|} - 1$ queries have been performed. Then there are two sets F_1 and F_2 which have never been the first component of a query pair. We show that it is consistent with all answers to assume that F_1 is the minimal set in 2^H. The same holds for F_2, so whatever the algorithm outputs, there is an AOP that is not solved correctly. Hence the adversary can force the algorithm to step through at least $2^{|H|} - 1$ queries, which means that it performs that many queries on the AOP that has implicitly been constructed by the adversary.

We are left to prove that F_1 can be chosen as $\min(2^H)$. Clearly, this choice can fail only if some answer has put a lower bound on $w(F_1)$. Since there was no query pair (F_1, G), the only remaining possibility is that some query (F, G) with $F_1 \subseteq G$ has been answered by $\rhd$, thus establishing $w(F_1) \geq w(F)$. But in the first query of this type, F_1 was not bounded from below yet, so it would have been returned instead of $\rhd$, which is a contradiction. □

Proof of Theorem 3.3. Before we give the algorithm to solve any given AOP $(H, <, \phi)$ in pseudocode, we will briefly describe its main idea which is similar to the one behind the algorithm for LP-type problems presented in [17] as well as the LP algorithm of Kalai [8].

The algorithm finally computes $\min(2^H)$, but the general step in the recursive procedure is the computation of $\min(2^G)$ for some $G \subseteq H$. Together with G, a set $F \subseteq G$ is maintained which is a 'candidate' for the minimum. The output of the algorithm does not depend on F, but its efficiency does. As we will see, the closer F is to the desired minimum, the faster will the actual minimum be obtained. Denote the function procedure computing $\min(2^G)$ in presence of candidate set $F \subseteq G$ by $\text{MIN}(F, G)$. The procedure (preliminary version) is executed as follows:

(I) if $F = \min(2^G)$ (that means, $\phi(F, G) = \rhd$) then return F.

(II) if not, choose a random element $e \in G - F$ and recursively compute $F' = \text{MIN}(F, G - \{e\})$.

(III) Let $F'' := \phi(F', G)$. If $F'' = \rhd$ then return F' else set $F := F''$ and go to (I).

Each time the procedure goes back to step (I), F gets closer to the minimum, so after at most $|2^G|$ cycles the minimum is obtained. This also holds for the recursive call in (II), so the procedure eventually terminates.

The reader might have noted that step (II) fails if $F = G$. In general, it will be undesirable to have $|G - F|$ too small – it is crucial for the performance of the algorithm to have enough elements to choose from in (II). In order to guarantee this, we fall back on a trick in [8]: if we notice that $G - F$ is too small in (II) (we will see soon what this means), we start another instance of the algorithm. However, this additional call is suspended as soon as a candidate F' occurs with an element $e \in G - F'$ which was not present in $G - F$. In addition to what was possible before, we could now recursively compute $\text{MIN}(F', G - \{e\})$ in (II), so we have one more choice. In this way we continue starting additional calls, until a sufficient number of elements e to choose from in (II) has been generated. A parameter E controls when such an additional call has to be suspended, and as the final version of our algorithm we get the function procedure

```
function MIN(F, G, E)   (* E, F ⊆ G *)
    (* returns min(2^G) or a set
       F' ⊆ G with F' ≤ F and E ⊄ F' *).
```

The implementation is given in pseudocode:

```
function MIN(F, G, E);
  if φ(F, G) = ▷ or E ⊄ F then return F
  else
    if E ⊄ φ(F, G) then return φ(F, G)
    else
      if F = G then F := φ(F, G) end;
      K := F;
      for all e ∈ G − K do F_e := F;
      while |G − K| ≤ ½|G − E| do
        F := MIN(F, G, K);
        if φ(F, G) = ▷ or E ⊄ F then return F
        else
          for all e ∈ K − F do F_e := F;
          K := K ∩ F
        end
      end;
      choose a random e ∈ G − K;
      F := MIN(F_e, G − {e}, E);
      if φ(F, G) = ▷ or E ⊄ F then return F
      else
        return MIN(φ(F, G), G, E)
      end
    end
  end
end MIN.
```

The termination and correctness of the algorithm is proved by induction on $|G - E|$ and the rank of F (the rank of F is its position in the sequence of all subsets of G sorted by $<$). The statement '**if** $E \not\subseteq$

$\phi(F,G)$...' is necessary to cover the case $F = G = E$, and setting F to $\phi(F,G)$ in case of $F = G$ ensures that $G-F$ contains at least one element. This will be convenient for the analysis. Observe that if the call $\phi(F,G)$ appears more than once with the same sets, the query is performed only once.

During the **while**-loop, the set K is the 'pool' from which new elements e may arise that broaden the choice after the loop. One might worry that storing the sets F_e during the loop needs quadratic space. To get around this is not difficult: decide immediately after a call to $\text{MIN}(F,G,K)$ whether to continue with the loop or to exit it and start the call of $\text{MIN}(F_e, G-\{e\}, F_e, E)$ after the loop with the new element e just found. The decisions can be made according to probabilities that ensure equal chances for each element as in the version presented here.

The analysis of MIN. Besides from set-operation overhead, the runtime of MIN is dominated by the number of oracle queries on the top level and in all the recursive calls. In order to bound this number, we associate two integer parameters with a triple (F,G,E). The first one is the *size*

$$r := |G-E|.$$

While r does not depend on F, the second parameter k, called the *freedom*, depends on all three parameters:

$$k := |\{e \in G-E \mid \exists\, F' \subseteq G, F' \leq F, e \notin F'\}|.$$

Here is the intuitive idea what the 'freedom' is: When a call $\text{MIN}(F,G,E)$ is executed, the algorithm traces an increasing sequence of candidates $F = F_0 > F_1 > F_2 > \ldots$ until either the minimum of 2^G is reached or some F_i fails to contain E. Let us by $\mathcal{F}$ denote the collection of all sets that may possibly show up in this sequence, so

$$\mathcal{F} := \{F' \leq F \mid F \subseteq G\}.$$

Some elements of $G-E$ lie in all members of $\mathcal{F}$. These elements have to occur in every candidate traced by the algorithm until the current call with parameters (F,G,E) terminates. In contrast, there are 'free' elements, which do not necessarily lie in every candidate $F' \leq F$ (observe that by definition, the elements in $G-F$ are free). It is quite intuitive that the less free elements there are, the faster the call will terminate. Especially, if there is no free element in $G-E$, we have $F = G$, and the call of $\text{MIN}(F,G,E)$ terminates after 1 oracle query. The freedom just counts the number of free elements in $G-E$ with respect to F.

Let $t(r,k)$ be the expected number of oracle queries in a call to $\text{MIN}(F,G,E)$, where (F,G,E) has size r and freedom k. from the previous considerations we obtain

$$t(r,0) = 1.$$

Furthermore observe that $k \leq r$ by definition. Now suppose $r,k > 0$. There are at most $2 + \lfloor r/2 \rfloor$ oracle queries necessary at the top level of the procedure – one before and one after the loop, and no more than $\lfloor r/2 \rfloor$ in the loop, since the loop is executed that many times at most.

The triples examined in the loop have size at most $\lfloor r/2 \rfloor$, so over all executions of the loop this amounts to an expected number of at most

$$\lfloor r/2 \rfloor\; t(\lfloor r/2 \rfloor, \min(\lfloor r/2 \rfloor, k))$$

oracle queries. The recursive call $\text{MIN}(F_e, G-\{e\}, E)$ has size $r-1$ and freedom at most $k-1$, so an expected number of no more than

$$t(r-1, k-1)$$

oracle queries are performed during this call. It remains to give a bound for the final call $\text{MIN}(F', G, E)$ ($F' = \phi(F,G)$). To do this we pursue an idea from [13]: consider the elements $e_1, \ldots, e_j$ that are in $G-K$ after the loop has finished, enumerated in such a way that

$$\min(2^{G-\{e_1\}}) \geq \min(2^{G-\{e_2\}}) \geq \ldots \geq \min(2^{G-\{e_j\}}).$$

Assume that for fixed $i \in \{1,\ldots,j\}$, $e = e_i$ is chosen for the call $\text{MIN}(F_e, G-\{e\}, E)$. If the subsequent call $\text{MIN}(F', G, E)$ is executed at all, then the elements $e_1, \ldots, e_i$ –which were free in (F,G,E)– are no longer free in (F', G, E), because $F' < \min(2^{G-\{e_1\}}), \ldots, \min(2^{G-\{e_i\}})$ implies $e_1, \ldots, e_i \in F''$ for all $F'' \leq F'$. This argument shows that the freedom has decreased by at least i.

Since i is equally likely to be any of the numbers $1, \ldots, j$, the expected number of oracle queries in the final recursion of the procedure is at most

$$(1/j) \sum_{i=1}^{j} t(r, k-i).$$

Observing that $\lceil r/2 \rceil \leq j \leq k$ we obtain the following recurrence which is quite similar to the one Kalai [8] obtains for Linear Programming:

$$\begin{aligned} t(r,k) &\leq 2 + \lfloor r/2 \rfloor + \lfloor r/2 \rfloor t(\lfloor r/2 \rfloor, \min(\lfloor r/2 \rfloor, k)) \\ &+ t(r-1, k-1) + \frac{1}{\lceil r/2 \rceil} \sum_{i=0}^{k-1} t(r,i). \end{aligned}$$

Theorem 4.1

$$t(r,k) = O((k+r+1)^4 e^{2\sqrt{2}\sqrt{k+r}}).$$

Proof: Precisely, we show that there exists a constant $c > 0$ such that

$$t(r,k) \leq c \prod_{i=1}^{k+r} (1 + \frac{4}{i}) e^{2\sqrt{2}\sqrt{k+r}},$$

and by observing that

$$\prod_{i=1}^{k+r} (1 + \frac{4}{i}) = \binom{k+r+4}{4},$$

the theorem follows.

We proceed by induction on $r + k$, noting that for $r + k = 0$ the bound holds with $c = 1$. For $r + k > 0$ we get
$t(r,k) \leq c' f(r,k)$, where $c' := c \prod_{i=1}^{k+r-1} (1 + \frac{4}{i})$ and $f(r,k)$ equals

$$2 + \frac{r}{2} + \frac{r}{2} e^{2\sqrt{2}\sqrt{k+r/2}} + e^{2\sqrt{2}\sqrt{k+r-2}} + \frac{2}{r} \sum_{i=0}^{k-1} e^{2\sqrt{2}\sqrt{i+r}}.$$

The last term can be estimated from above by

$$\frac{2}{r} \int_0^k e^{2\sqrt{2}\sqrt{x+r}} dx$$

and using

$$\int e^{2\sqrt{2}\sqrt{x+r}} dx = \frac{1}{\sqrt{2}} e^{2\sqrt{2}\sqrt{x+r}} (\sqrt{x+r} - \frac{1}{2\sqrt{2}})$$

we obtain

$$\frac{2}{r} \sum_{i=0}^{k-1} e^{2\sqrt{2}\sqrt{i+r}} \leq \frac{\sqrt{2}\sqrt{k+r}}{r} e^{2\sqrt{2}\sqrt{k+r}}.$$

This gives

$$\begin{aligned} f(r,k) \leq e^{2\sqrt{2}\sqrt{k+r}} (& \quad e^{\ln(2+\frac{r}{2}) - 2\sqrt{2}\sqrt{k+r}} \\ & + \frac{r}{2} e^{2\sqrt{2}(\sqrt{k+r/2} - \sqrt{k+r})} \\ & + e^{2\sqrt{2}(\sqrt{k+r-2} - \sqrt{k+r})} \\ & + \frac{\sqrt{2}\sqrt{k+r}}{r}). \end{aligned}$$

By applying the mean value theorem to the exponents of the second and third term in brackets and using $k \leq r$ we see that $f(r,k)$ is bounded by

$$e^{2\sqrt{2}\sqrt{k+r}} (e^{\ln(2+\frac{r}{2}) - 2\sqrt{2}\sqrt{r}} + \frac{r}{2} e^{-\frac{\sqrt{r}}{2}} + e^{-\frac{2}{\sqrt{r}}} + \frac{2}{\sqrt{r}}).$$

For x a real we have $e^x = 1 + x + \frac{x^2}{2} + \Theta(x^3)$, so

$$e^{-\frac{2}{\sqrt{r}}} + \frac{2}{\sqrt{r}} = 1 + \frac{2}{r} - \Theta(r^{-\frac{3}{2}}).$$

The terms $e^{\ln(2+\frac{r}{2}) - 2\sqrt{2}\sqrt{r}}$ and $\frac{r}{2} e^{-\frac{\sqrt{r}}{2}}$ tend to zero much faster than $r^{-\frac{3}{2}}$ as r goes to infinity, so there exits an integer r_0 such that for $r > r_0$ we have

$$\begin{aligned} f(r,k) & \leq e^{2\sqrt{2}\sqrt{k+r}} (1 + \frac{2}{r}) \\ & \leq e^{2\sqrt{2}\sqrt{k+r}} (1 + \frac{4}{k+r}), \end{aligned}$$

so

$$t(r,k) \leq c \prod_{i=1}^{k+r} (1 + \frac{4}{i}) e^{2\sqrt{2}\sqrt{k+r}},$$

as claimed. Finally choose c so large that the estimate also holds for $r \leq r_0$. □

This proof gives a bound of $O(|H|^4 e^{4\sqrt{|H|}})$ for the expected number of oracle queries necessary to solve an AOP $(H, <, \phi)$. The bound claimed in Theorem 3.3 is achieved as follows: recall that in the algorithm we run the **while**-loop as long as '$|G - K| \leq \frac{1}{2}|G - E|$'. The constant $\frac{1}{2}$ has no special meaning; in fact, it can be replaced by any fixed constant $\delta < 1$, and the recurrence resulting from this modification can be solved with exactly the same technique as shown above. By choosing δ arbitrarily close to 1, the exponent in the previous theorem becomes

$$(2 + \epsilon)\sqrt{k+r}$$

for any fixed $\epsilon > 0$. The polynomial factor in $k+r$ gets swallowed by the ϵ, so we finally obtain the bound of

$$O(e^{(2\sqrt{2}+\epsilon)\sqrt{|H|}})$$

for any AOP $(H, <, \phi)$ as stated in Theorem 3.3.

5 Discussion and Open Problems

We have shown that subexponential algorithms exist for the POLYSEP and MINIBALL problem by embedding their 'small' instances into the framework of abstract optimization problems. As in the case of LP, the bounds can be further improved by combining our results with the algorithm of Clarkson [2], giving an

$$O(d^2 n + e^{O(\sqrt{d \ln d})})$$

algorithm.

There is one more LP-type problem that is of interest in many areas (e.g. statistics): given n points in d-space, determine the smallest ellipsoid containing all the points. For d fixed, the problem can be solved in $O(n)$ time [7], [17]. However, all known combinatorial algorithms for this problem are exponential in d. So far we have not been able to develop an efficient oracle for the problem, so the AOP-framework does not yield a subexponential bound in this case.

An interesting open problem is to determine the (randomized) complexity of AOP's. Due to the generality and simplicity of the framework, one may come up with non-trivial lower bounds for the expected runtime of any randomized algorithm; it is even possible that this lower bound is in the range of the upper bound established by our algorithm.

Although the concept of the AOP's seems to apply to geometric problems in a natural way. there may be non-geometric applications as well. Finding applications of a more combinatorial nature may give new insights concerning 'randomized vs. deterministic complexity'.

Acknowledgement. The author would like to thank David Alberts, Jiří Matoušek and Emo Welzl for several discussions and helpful comments.

References

[1] K.L.Clarkson, *Linear Programming in $O(n3^{d^2})$*, Inform. Process. Lett. 22(1986), 21-24.

[2] K.L.Clarkson, *Las Vegas algorithms for linear programming when the dimension is small*, manuscript, 1989.

[3] K.L.Clarkson, *New Applications of Random Sampling in Computational Geometry*, Discrete and Computational Geometry 2 (1987), 195-222.

[4] B.Chazelle, J.Matoušek, *On linear-time deterministic algorithms for optimization in fixed dimension*, manuscript, 1992.

[5] G.B.Dantzig, *Maximization of a linear function of variables subject to linear inequalities*, Activity Analysis of Production and Allocation, T.C.Koopman (Ed.) Cowles Commission Monograph 13, Wiley, New York, 1951, 339–347

[6] M.E.Dyer, *On a multidimensional search technique and its application to the euclidean one-center problem*, SIAM J. Comput. 15(1986), 725-738

[7] M.E.Dyer, *A Class of Convex Programs with Applications to Computational Geometry*, Proc. 8th annual Symp. on Comp. Geom., 1992

[8] G.Kalai, *A Subexponential Randomized Simplex Algorithm*, Proc. 24th ACM Symposium on Theory of Computing, 1992

[9] N.Karmarkar, *A new polynomial-time algorithm for linear programming*, Combinatorica 4 (1984), 373–395.

[10] L.G.Khachiyan, *Polynomial algorithm in linear programming*, U.S.S.R. Comput. Math. and Math. Phys. 20 (1980), 53–72.

[11] V. Klee and G.J. Minty, *How good is the simplex algorithm*, Inequalities III, O. Shisha (ed.) Academic Press, New York (1972), 159-175,

[12] N.Megiddo, *Linear programming in linear time when the dimension is fixed*, J. Assoc. Comput. Mach. 31 (1984), 114-127.

[13] J.Matoušek, M.Sharir and E.Welzl, *A Subexponential Bound for Linear Programming*, Proc. 8th annual Symp. on Comp. Geom., 1992

[14] V.T.Rajan, *Optimality of the Delaunay Triangulation in $\mathbb{R}^d$*, Proc. 7th annual Symp. on Comp. Geom., 1991, 357–363

[15] A.Schrijver, *Theory of Linear and Integer Programming*, Wiley, New York (1986)

[16] R.Seidel, *Low-dimensional linear programming and convex hulls made easy*, Discrete Comp. Geom. 6(1991), 423-434.

[17] M.Sharir and E.Welzl, *A combinatorial bound for Linear Programming and related problems*, Proc. 1992 Symp. on Theoretical Aspects of Computer Science

[18] E.Welzl, *Smallest enclosing disks (balls and ellipsoids)*, New Results and New Trends in Computer Science, H.Maurer, Ed., 1991, Lecture Notes in Computer Science, to appear.

[19] P.Wolfe, *The simplex method for quadratic programming*, Econometrica 27, 382–398

The Algorithmic Aspects of the Regularity Lemma (Extended Abstract)

N. Alon * R. A. Duke † H. Lefmann ‡ V. Rödl § R. Yuster¶

Abstract

The Regularity Lemma of Szemerédi is a result that asserts that every graph can be partitioned in a certain regular way. This result has numerous applications, but its known proof is not algorithmic. Here we first demonstrate the computational difficulty of finding a regular partition; we show that deciding if a given partition of an input graph satisfies the properties guaranteed by the lemma is co-NP-complete. However, we also prove that despite this difficulty the lemma can be made constructive; we show how to obtain, for any input graph, a partition with the properties guaranteed by the lemma, efficiently. The desired partition, for an n-vertex graph, can be found in time $O(M(n))$, where $M(n) = O(n^{2.376})$ is the time needed to multiply two n by n matrices with $0,1$-entries over the integers. The algorithm can be parallelized and implemented in NC^1. Besides the curious phenomenon of exhibiting a natural problem in which the search for a solution is easy whereas the decision if a given instance is a solution is difficult (if P and NP differ), our constructive version of the Regularity Lemma supplies efficient sequential and parallel algorithms for many problems, some of which are naturally motivated by the study of various graph embedding and graph coloring problems.

*Department of Mathematics, Raymond and Beverly Sackler Faculty of Exact Sciences, Tel Aviv University, Tel Aviv, Israel and Bellcore, Morristown, NJ 07960. Email: noga@math.tau.ac.il. Research supported in part by a United States Israel BSF Grant

†School of Mathematics, Georgia Institute of Technology, Atlanta, GA 30332, USA. Email: duke@math.gatech.edu

‡Fakultät für Mathematik, SFB 343, Universität Bielefeld, W-4800 Bielefeld 1, Germany. Email: lefmann@math1.mathematik.uni-bielefeld.de

§Department of Mathematics and Computer Science, Emory University, Atlanta, GA 30322, USA. Email: rodl@mathcs.emory.edu

¶Department of Mathematics, Raymond and Beverly Sackler Faculty of Exact Sciences, Tel Aviv University, Tel Aviv, Israel

1 Introduction

One of the main reasons for the fast development of Combinatorics during the recent years is the widely used application of combinatorial methods in the study and the development of efficient algorithms. It is therefore surprising that many results proved by applying some of the modern combinatorial techniques merely supply existence proofs and do not yield efficient algorithms for the corresponding problems. Many examples of this type appear in [22] and in [2]. Some of these examples, like, e.g., the Lovász Local Lemma, whose algorithmic aspects have been studied recently in [6] and [3], are general techniques that have various algorithmic applications; a constructive version for such a technique immediately supplies efficient procedures for many problems.

In the present paper we consider another general technique of this form. This is the Regularity Lemma of Szemerédi [28]. This lemma has numerous applications in various areas including Combinatorial Number Theory ([27], [14]), Computational Complexity([19]) and, mainly, Extremal Graph Theory ([5], [7], [8], [9], [12], [13], [15], [16], [17], [23], [24], [25], [26]). Not all of these applications have obvious corresponding algorithmic problems, but many do. A number of these problems as well as various similar ones seem to be naturally suggested by the study of graph embedding, graph coloring and graph decomposition.

0-8186-2900-2/92 $3.00 © 1992 IEEE

The known proof of the Regularity Lemma is not algorithmic. Here we prove two main results concerning the constructive aspects of this lemma. The first result shows the computational difficulties; we show that deciding if a given partition of an input graph satisfies the properties of the partition guaranteed by the lemma is co-NP-complete. The second result shows that despite these difficulties the lemma can be made constructive; we show how to obtain, for any input graph, a partition with the properties guaranteed by the lemma, efficiently. The desired partition, for an n-vertex graph, can be found in time $O(M(n))$, where $M(n) = O(n^{2.376})$ is the time needed to multiply two n by n matrices with $0,1$-entries over the integers (see [10]). The algorithm can be parallelized and supplies efficient sequential and parallel algorithms for many problems. Some of these follow easily from the known applications of the lemma, together with our constructive version of it, and some other similar applications are new, and require several additional ideas.

In order to describe our results more precisely, we need several technical definitions, which mostly follow the ones in [28]. If $G = (V, E)$ is a graph, and A, B are two disjoint subsets of V, let $e(A, B)$ denote the number of edges of G with an endpoint in A and an endpoint in B. If A and B are non-empty, define the *density of edges* between A and B by $d(A, B) = \frac{e(A,B)}{|A||B|}$. For $\epsilon > 0$, the pair (A, B) is called *ϵ-regular* if for every $X \subset A$ and $Y \subset B$ satisfying $|X| \geq \epsilon|A|$ and $|Y| \geq \epsilon|B|$, the inequality

$$|d(A,B) - d(X,Y)| < \epsilon$$

holds.

An *equitable partition* of a set V is a partition of V into pairwise disjoint classes $C_0, C_1, \ldots, C_k$, in which all the classes C_i for $1 \leq i \leq k$ have the same cardinality. The class C_0 is called the *exceptional class* and may be empty. An equitable partition of the set of vertices V of G into the classes $C_0, C_1 \ldots, C_k$, with C_0 being the exceptional class, is called *ϵ-regular* if $|C_0| \leq \epsilon|V|$, and all but at most ϵk^2 of the pairs (C_i, C_j) for $1 \leq i < j \leq k$ are ϵ-regular.

The following lemma is proved in [28] and is usually called the Regularity Lemma.

Lemma 1.1 (The Regularity Lemma [28]) *For every $\epsilon > 0$ and every positive integer t there is an integer $T = T(\epsilon, t)$ such that every graph with $n > T$ vertices has an ϵ-regular partition into $k+1$ classes, where $t \leq k \leq T$.* □

In the present paper we first prove the following two new results.

Theorem 1.2 *The following decision problem is co-NP-complete.*
Instance: An input graph G, an integer $k \geq 1$ and a parameter $\epsilon > 0$, and a partition of the set of vertices of G into $k+1$ parts.
Problem: Decide if the given partition is ϵ-regular.

We note that the proof actually gives that the problem remains co-NP-complete even for $\epsilon = 1/2$ and for $k = 2$.

Theorem 1.3 *(**A constructive version of the Regularity Lemma.**) For every $\epsilon > 0$ and every positive integer t there is an integer $Q = Q(\epsilon, t)$ such that every graph with $n > Q$ vertices has an ϵ-regular partition into $k+1$ classes, where $t \leq k \leq Q$. For every fixed $\epsilon > 0$ and $t \geq 1$ such a partition can be found in $O(M(n))$ sequential time, where $M(n)$ is the time for multiplying two n by n matrices with $0,1$ entries over the integers. It can also be found in time $O(\log n)$ on an EREW PRAM with a polynomial number of parallel processors.*

We note that the dependence of $Q(\epsilon, t)$ (as well as that of $T(\epsilon, t)$ in the original lemma) on ϵ and t, as well as the dependence of the running time of the algorithm in the last theorem on these two parameters is rather horrible; in fact $log^* Q$ is a polynomial (of degree about 20) in $1/\epsilon$ and in t. However, in the applications ϵ will always be fixed (though small) and t will always be fixed (though large), whereas the size n of the graph considered will grow.

In most of the known applications of the Regularity Lemma, the only non-constructive part is the Regularity Lemma itself. Therefore, Theorem 1.3 supplies numerous immediate algorithmic applications. Here is a new application. Recall that a *topological copy* of a graph H is a graph obtained from H by replacing some of its edges by pairwise disjoint paths. The study of topological copies, and especially of those in which the paths that replace edges are relatively short arises in the study of various graph embedding problems. These are of interest when one tries to emulate a network of a desired topology by another one.

Proposition 1.4 *For any positive $\delta > 0$ there is a positive $c = c(\delta)$ such that for every m and for every graph H with m edges, every graph G with $n \geq cm$ vertices and with at least δn^2 edges contains a topological copy of H in which each edge is replaced by a path of length 4. Such a copy of H in G can be found in $O(M(n))$ sequential time as well as in NC.*

In some applications, the construction of the uniform partition does not yield a straightforward $O(M(n))$ algorithm for the problem, and further refinements of the partition are needed in order to obtain this bound. We present such an application, which is the algorithmic version of the main result of [23]. It supplies interesting, though maybe not so natural, information about the chromatic number of a graph that can be obtained efficiently.

Proposition 1.5 *For every fixed $\delta > 0$ and $k > 1$ there is an $O(M(n))$-time algorithm whose input is an n vertex graph G and whose output is either a short certificate that the chromatic number of G is at least k (given in the form of a subgraph of G with a constant number $c(\delta, k)$ of vertices whose chromatic number is at least k) or a subset of at most δn^2 edges of G and a proper $k-1$-coloring of the graph obtained from G by removing these edges. The algorithm can be parallelized and implemented in NC.*

The rest of this extended abstract is organized as follows. In section 2 we make a few comments on the proof of Theorem 1.2 that shows the difficulties in obtaining a constructive version of the Regularity Lemma. In Section 3 we show how to overcome these difficulties and prove Theorem 1.3. Section 4 contains various algorithmic applications. In the final Section 5 we mention a variant of the Regularity Lemma which can be used in some cases to achieve improved running times and discuss an application; an efficient (deterministic) algorithm that approximates the number of induced subgraphs of a given type in a given graph.

Due to space limitations most proofs are omitted and will appear only in the full version of the paper. The only part which is rather detailed is the algorithmic version of the Regularity Lemma, presented in Section 3.

2 The complexity of deciding if a given partition is regular

The following result implies Theorem 1.2.

Theorem 2.1 *The following problem is co-NP-complete: Given $\epsilon > 0$ and a bipartite graph G with vertex classes A, B such that $|A| = |B| = n$, determine if G is ϵ-regular. (I.e., determine if $\{\emptyset, A, B\}$ is an ϵ-regular partition of G).*

The proof of Theorem 2.1 proceeds as follows. We start from the following problem, which is known to be NP-complete [18].
The $K_{k,k}$ Problem: Given a positive integer k and a bipartite graph G with vertex classes A, B such that $|A| = |B| = n$, determine if G contains a copy of $K_{k,k}$-the complete bipartite graph with k vertices in each vertex class.

In order to deduce the co-NP-completeness of ϵ-regularity, we need a stricter version of the $K_{k,k}$ problem.

Lemma 2.2 *The following problem is NP-complete: Given a bipartite graph $G = (A \cup B, E)$ where $|A| = |B| = n$ and $|E| = \frac{n^2}{2} - 1$ decide if G contains a subgraph isomorphic to $K_{\frac{n}{2},\frac{n}{2}}$.*

This lemma can be proved by constructing, for a given bipartite graph G with m vertices in each color class and for a given k, a sequence of graphs with $n = O(m)$ vertices in each color class, each of which contains a subgraph isomorphic to $K_{\frac{n}{2},\frac{n}{2}}$ iff G contains a copy of $K_{k,k}$. It is then shown that one of the graphs in this sequence has precisly $\frac{n^2}{2} - 1$ edges, completing the proof. We omit the somewhat complicated details.

The co-NP-completeness of ϵ-regularity is a simple consequence of Lemma 2.2. A bipartite graph G with n vertices in each class and exactly $\frac{n^2}{2}-1$ edges contains a $K_{\frac{n}{2},\frac{n}{2}}$ iff it is not ϵ-regular for $\epsilon = \frac{1}{2}$.

3 Finding a regular partition efficiently

In this section we prove Theorem 1.3. We split the proof into several lemmas. Let H be a bipartite graph with equal vertex classes $|A| = |B| = n$. Let

d be the average degree of H. For two distinct vertices $y_1, y_2 \in B$ define the *neighbourhood deviation* of y_1 and y_2 by

$$\sigma(y_1, y_2) = |N(y_1) \cap N(y_2)| - \frac{d^2}{n}.$$

For a subset $Y \subset B$ denote the *deviation* of Y by

$$\sigma(Y) = \frac{\sum_{y_1, y_2 \in Y} \sigma(y_1, y_2)}{|Y|^2}.$$

Lemma 3.1 *Let H be a bipartite graph with equal classes $|A| = |B| = n$, and let d denote the average degree of H. Let $0 < \epsilon < \frac{1}{16}$. If there exists $Y \subset B$, $|Y| \geq \epsilon n$, such that $\sigma(Y) \geq \frac{\epsilon^3}{2}n$ then at least one of the following cases occurs:*

1. *$d < \epsilon^3 n$.*
2. *There exists in B a set of more than $\frac{1}{8}\epsilon^4 n$ vertices whose degrees deviate from d by at least $\epsilon^4 n$.*
3. *There are subsets $A' \subset A$, $B' \subset B$, $|A'| \geq \frac{\epsilon^4}{4}n$, $|B'| \geq \frac{\epsilon^4}{4}n$ and $|d(A', B') - d(A, B)| \geq \epsilon^4$.*

Moreover, there is an algorithm whose input is a graph H with a set $Y \subset B$ as above that outputs either
(i) The fact that 1 holds, or
(ii) The fact that 2 holds and a subset of more than $\frac{1}{8}\epsilon^4 n$ members of B demonstrating this fact, or
(iii) The fact that 3 holds and two subsets A' and B' as in 3 demonstrating this fact.
The algorithm runs in sequential time $O(M(n))$, where $M(n) = O(n^{2.376})$ is the time needed to multiply two n by n 0, 1 matrices over the integers, and can be parallelized and implemented in time $O(\log n)$ on an EREW PRAM with a polynomial number of parallel processors.

Proof We first assume that cases 1 and 2 do not hold and prove that case 3 must happen. Denote $Y' = \{y \in Y | \ |deg(y) - d| < \epsilon^4 n\}$. Note that Y' is not empty since case 2 does not hold. Choose a $y_0 \in Y'$ that maximizes $\sum_{y \in Y} \sigma(y_0, y)$. Let us estimate this quantity:

$$\sum_{y' \in Y'} \sum_{y \in Y, y \neq y'} \sigma(y', y) =$$

$$\sigma(Y)|Y|^2 - \sum_{y' \in Y \setminus Y'} \sum_{y \in Y, y \neq y'} \sigma(y', y)$$

$$\geq \frac{\epsilon^3}{2} n|Y|^2 - \frac{\epsilon^4}{8} n|Y|n.$$

Since $|Y'| \leq |Y|$ we get

$$\sum_{y \in Y} \sigma(y_0, y) \geq \frac{\epsilon^3}{2} n|Y| - \frac{\epsilon^4}{8} n^2 \geq \frac{3}{8}\epsilon^3 n|Y|. \quad (1)$$

There are at least $\frac{\epsilon^4}{4}n$ vertices $y \in Y$ whose neighbourhood deviation with y_0 is greater than $2\epsilon^4 n$. To see this we note that if there were less we would get, using the fact that the neighbourhood deviation cannot exceed n,

$$\sum_{y \in Y} \sigma(y_0, y) \leq \frac{\epsilon^4}{4} n^2 + |Y| 2\epsilon^4 n$$

$$\leq \frac{\epsilon^3}{4} n|Y| + 2\epsilon^4 n|Y| < \frac{3}{8}\epsilon^3 n|Y|$$

which contradicts (1).

Hence there is a set $B' \subset Y$, $|B'| \geq \frac{\epsilon^4}{4}n$, $y_0 \notin B'$, and for every vertex $b \in B'$ we have $|N(b) \cap N(y_0)| > \frac{d^2}{n} + 2\epsilon^4 n$. Define $|A'| = N(y_0)$. Clearly, $|A'| \geq d - \epsilon^4 n \geq \epsilon^3 n - \epsilon^4 n \geq 15\epsilon^4 n > \frac{\epsilon^4}{4}n$. We will show that $|d(A', B') - d(A, B)| \geq \epsilon^4$. Indeed,

$$e(A', B') = \sum_{b \in B'} |N(y_0) \cap N(b)| > \frac{|B'|d^2}{n} + 2\epsilon^4 n|B'|.$$

Therefore,

$$d(A', B') - d(A, B) > \frac{d^2}{n|A'|} + \frac{2\epsilon^4 n}{|A'|} - \frac{d}{n}$$

$$\geq \frac{d^2}{n(d + \epsilon^4 n)} + 2\epsilon^4 - \frac{d}{n} = 2\epsilon^4 - \frac{d\epsilon^4}{d + \epsilon^4 n} \geq \epsilon^4.$$

This completes the proof of the non-algorithmic part of the lemma.

The existence of the required sequential algorithm is simple. One can clearly check if 1 holds in time $O(n^2)$. Similarly, it is trivial to check if 2 holds in $O(n^2)$ time, and in case it holds to exhibit the required subset of B establishing this fact. If both cases above fail we continue as follows.
For each $y_0 \in B$ with $|deg(y_0) - d| < \epsilon^4 n$, we find the set of vertices $B_{y_0} = \{y \in B | \ \sigma(y_0, y) \geq 2\epsilon^4 n\}$. The last proof guarantees the existence of at least one such y_0 for which $|B_{y_0}| \geq \frac{\epsilon^4}{4}n$. The subsets $B' = B_{y_0}$ and $A' = N(y_0)$ are the required ones. Since the computation of all the quantities $\sigma(y, y')$

for $y, y' \in B$ can be done by squaring the adjacency matrix of H the claimed sequential running time follows. The parallelization is obvious. □

The basic idea in the proof of the next lemma resembles an idea used in [1].

Lemma 3.2 *Let H be a bipartite graph with equal classes $|A| = |B| = n$. Let $n^{-1/4} < \epsilon < \frac{1}{16}$. Assume that at most $\frac{1}{8}\epsilon^4 n$ vertices of B deviate from the average degree of H by at least $\epsilon^4 n$. Then, if H is not ϵ-regular there exists $Y \subset B$, $|Y| \geq \epsilon n$ such that $\sigma(Y) \geq \frac{\epsilon^3}{2} n$.*

Proof We assume that for every such Y, $\sigma(Y) \leq \frac{\epsilon^3}{2} n$, and show that H is ϵ-regular. It is not too difficult to see that the pair (A, B) is ϵ-regular if and only if for every two subsets $X \subset A$, $Y \subset B$, $|X| = \lceil \epsilon |A| \rceil$, $|Y| = \lceil \epsilon |B| \rceil$, the inequality $|d(A, B) - d(X, Y)| \leq \epsilon$ holds. We therefore fix two such subsets X and Y, and show that the inequality holds.

Claim:

$$\sum_{x \in X} (|N(x) \cap Y| - \frac{d|Y|}{n})^2 \leq$$

$$e(A, Y) + |Y|^2 \sigma(Y) + \frac{2}{5} \epsilon^5 n^3 . \qquad (2)$$

Proof Let $M = (m_{i,j})$ be the adjacency matrix of H. Then,

$$\sum_{x \in X} (|N(x) \cap Y| - \frac{d|Y|}{n})^2 \leq \sum_{x \in A} (|N(x) \cap Y| - \frac{d|Y|}{n})^2$$

$$= \sum_{x \in A} (\sum_{y \in Y} m_{x,y} - \frac{d|Y|}{n})^2$$

$$= \sum_{x \in A} (\sum_{y \in Y} {m^2}_{x,y} + \frac{d^2|Y|^2}{n^2} +$$

$$\sum_{y,y' \in Y, y \neq y'} m_{x,y} m_{x,y'} - 2\frac{d|Y|}{n} \sum_{y \in Y} m_{x,y})$$

$$= e(A, Y) + \frac{d^2|Y|^2}{n} +$$

$$\sum_{y,y' \in Y, y \neq y'} |N(y) \cap N(y')| - 2e(A, Y)\frac{d|Y|}{n}$$

$$= e(A, Y) + \frac{d^2|Y|^2}{n} +$$

$$\sum_{y,y' \in Y, y \neq y'} (\sigma(y, y') + \frac{d^2}{n}) - 2e(A, Y)\frac{d|Y|}{n}$$

$$\leq e(A, Y) + \sigma(Y)|Y|^2 + \frac{2d^2|Y|^2}{n} - 2e(A, Y)\frac{d|Y|}{n} .$$

It remains to show that

$$\frac{|Y|^2 d^2}{n} - e(A, Y)\frac{d|Y|}{n} \leq \frac{1}{5}\epsilon^5 n^3 .$$

Multiplying the last inequality by $\frac{1}{d|Y|^2}$ and rearranging the terms we must show that

$$d(A, Y) \geq \frac{d}{n} - \frac{\frac{1}{5}\epsilon^5 n^3}{d|Y|^2} .$$

Indeed,

$$d(A, Y) = \frac{e(A, Y)}{n|Y|} \geq \frac{(d - \epsilon^4 n)(|Y| - \frac{1}{8}\epsilon^4 n)}{n|Y|} =$$

$$\frac{d}{n} - \epsilon^4 - \frac{\frac{1}{8}\epsilon^4 d}{|Y|} + \frac{\frac{1}{8}\epsilon^8 n}{|Y|} \geq \frac{d}{n} - \epsilon^4 - \frac{1}{8}\epsilon^3 .$$

Using the bounds on ϵ which imply that $1 < \epsilon^4 n$ and since $|Y| \leq 1 + \epsilon n$,

$$\frac{\frac{1}{5}\epsilon^5 n^3}{d|Y|^2} \geq \frac{\frac{1}{5}\epsilon^5 n^2}{(\epsilon n + 1)^2} \geq \frac{\frac{1}{5}\epsilon^5}{(\epsilon + \epsilon^4)^2} \geq \epsilon^4 + \frac{1}{8}\epsilon^3 .$$

This completes the proof of the claim.

Returning to the proof of the lemma, we note that by the Cauchy-Schwarz Inequality

$$\sum_{x \in X} (|N(x) \cap Y| - \frac{d|Y|}{n})^2$$

$$\geq \frac{1}{|X|}((\sum_{x \in X} |N(x) \cap Y|) - \frac{d|X||Y|}{n})^2 .$$

Therefore by the previous claim we obtain

$$((\sum_{x \in X} |N(x) \cap Y|) - \frac{d|X||Y|}{n})^2$$

$$\leq |X|(e(A, Y) + |Y|^2 \sigma(Y) + \frac{2}{5}\epsilon^5 n^3) .$$

Dividing the last inequality by $|X|^2|Y|^2$ we obtain

$$|d(X, Y) - d(A, B)|^2$$

$$\leq \frac{1}{|X||Y|^2}(e(A, Y) + |Y|^2 \sigma(Y) + \frac{2}{5}\epsilon^5 n^3) .$$

Using the fact that $e(A,Y) \le (d+\epsilon^4 n)|Y| + \frac{1}{8}\epsilon^4 n^2$ and $\sigma(Y) \le \frac{\epsilon^3}{2}n$ and $\epsilon \ge n^{-1/4}$ we estimate

$$|d(X,Y) - d(A,B)|^2$$

$$\le \frac{1}{|X||Y|^2}((d+\epsilon^4 n)|Y| + \frac{1}{8}\epsilon^4 n^2 + |Y|^2 \frac{\epsilon^3}{2} n + \frac{2}{5}\epsilon^5 n^3)$$

$$\le \frac{n+\epsilon^4 n}{\epsilon^2 n^2} + \frac{\frac{1}{8}\epsilon^4 n^2}{\epsilon^3 n^3} + \frac{\epsilon^3 n}{2\epsilon n} + \frac{\frac{2}{5}\epsilon^5 n^3}{\epsilon^3 n^3}$$

$$\le \epsilon^2(1+\epsilon^4) + \frac{\epsilon^5}{8} + \frac{9}{10}\epsilon^2 \le 2\epsilon^2 < \epsilon\,.$$

Therefore, the pair (X,Y) is ϵ-regular. □

Corollary 3.3 *Let H be a bipartite graph with equal classes $|A| = |B| = n$. Let $n^{-1/4} < \epsilon < \frac{1}{16}$. There is an $O(M(n))$ algorithm that verifies that H is ϵ-regular or finds two subsets $A' \subset A$, $B' \subset B$, $|A'| \ge \frac{\epsilon^4}{16}n$, $|B'| \ge \frac{\epsilon^4}{16}n$, such that $|d(A,B) - d(A',B')| \ge \epsilon^4$. The algorithm can be parallelized and implemented in NC^1.*

Proof We begin by computing d, the average degree of H. If $d < \epsilon^3 n$, then by a trivial computation, H is ϵ-regular, and we are done.
Next, we count the number of vertices in B whose degree deviates from d by at least $\epsilon^4 n$. If there are more than $\frac{\epsilon^4}{8}n$ such vertices, then the degrees of at least half of them deviate in the same direction and if we let B' be such a set of vertices then $|B'| \ge \frac{\epsilon^4}{16}n$. A simple computation yields that $|d(B',A) - d(B,A)| \ge \epsilon^4$, and we are done.
By Lemma 3.2, it is now sufficient to show that if there exists $Y \subset B$ with $|Y| \ge \epsilon n$ and $\sigma(Y) \ge \frac{\epsilon^3 n}{2}$ then one can find in $O(M(n))$ time the required subsets A' and B'. But this follows from the assertion of Lemma 3.1. The parallelization is immediate. □

With every equitable partition P of the set of vertices of a graph into $k+1$ classes $C_0, C_1, \ldots, C_k$ we associate, following [28], a number called the *index* of P defined by

$$ind(P) = \frac{1}{k^2} \sum_{1 \le r < s \le k} d(C_r, C_s)^2.$$

The following lemma is proved in [28].

Lemma 3.4 *Fix k and γ and let $G = (V,E)$ be a graph with n vertices. Let P be an equitable partition of V into classes $C_0, C_1, \ldots, C_k$. Assume $|C_1| > 4^{2k}$ and $4^k > 600\gamma^{-5}$. Given proofs that more than γk^2 pairs (C_r, C_s) are not γ-regular (where by proofs we mean subsets $X = X(r,s) \subset C_r$, $Y = Y(r,s) \subset C_s$ that violate the condition of γ-regularity of (C_r, C_s)), then one can find in $O(n)$ time a partition P' (which is a refinement of P) into $1 + k4^k$ classes, with an exceptional class of cardinality at most*

$$|C_0| + \frac{n}{4^k}$$

and such that

$$ind(P') \ge ind(P) + \frac{\gamma^5}{20}.$$

□

Theorem 1.3 is a rather simple consequence of Lemma 3.4 and Corollary 3.3. Starting with an arbitrary equitable partition of the given input graph with appropriately chosen parameters we keep refining it, as long as it is not verified to be ϵ-regular, by applying Corollary 3.3 and Lemma 3.4. By Lemma 3.4 this process must terminate as the index keeps growing and it can never exceed 1/2. This yields the desired result. The complete details will appear in the full version of the paper.

4 Algorithmic applications

Besides Propositions 1.4 and 1.5 there are many additional algorithmic applications of Theorem 1.3 that follow from the known applications of the Regularity Lemma. Here is a list of results, whose detailed proofs are omitted. In each case the appropriate reference in which existence is proved is mentioned in brackets. The existence proof in most of these cases can be translated, with some minor additional ideas, into a sequential algorithm by Theorem 1.3. Some additional ideas, including an application of any of the many known NC algorithms for finding a maximal independent set in an appropriately defined graph (see, e.g., [20],[21], [4]) yield, in some cases, a parallel NC implementation as well.

Proposition 4.1 (Existence proved in [5]) *For every $\epsilon > 0$ and for every integer h, there exists an $n_0 = n_0(\epsilon, h)$ such that for every graph H with h vertices and chromatic number $\chi(H)$, there exists an $O(M(n))$-time algorithm that given a graph*

$G = (V, E)$ *with* $n > n_0$ *vertices and minimum degree* $d > \frac{\chi(H)-1}{\chi(H)} n$ *finds in* G *a set of* $(1-\epsilon)n/h$ *vertex disjoint copies of* H. *The algorithm can be parallelized and implemented in* NC.

Proposition 4.2 *(***Existence can be proved using the methods of [9].***) For any* $\delta > 0$ *and* $d \geq 1$ *there is a* $c = c(\delta, d)$ *such that for every bipartite graph* H *with* m *vertices and maximum degree* d, *any graph* G *with* $n \geq cm$ *vertices and with at least* δn^2 *edges contains a copy of* H. *Such a copy of* H *in* G *can be found in* $O(M(n))$*-time.*

Proposition 4.3 *(***Existence proved in [9].***) For any* $d \geq 1$ *there is a* $c = c(d)$ *such that for every graph* H *with* m *vertices and maximum degree* d, *for any graph* G *with* $n \geq cm$ *vertices either* G *or its complement contains a copy of* H. *Such a copy of* H *in* G *or in its complement can be found in* $O(M(n))$*-time.*

Proposition 4.4 *(***Existence (for a special case) proved in [17].***) For every positive integer* k *and for every* $\gamma > 0$, *there exists an* $\epsilon = \epsilon(\gamma, k)$ *such that given a graph* G *with* n *vertices and less than* ϵn^k *copies of* K_k *(the complete graph on* k *vertices), one can find in* $O(M(n))$*-time a set of at most* γn^2 *edges of* G *whose deletion will leave* G K_k*-free. The algorithm can be parallelized and implemented in* NC.

In some cases the construction of the regular partition is not enough in order to achieve an $O(M(n))$ running time, and additional refinements of the partition are needed in order to obtain this bound. Such an approach is needed in the proof of Proposition 1.5, which is more difficult than those of the other applications mentioned in this section. The proofs themselves are omitted, due to space limitations.

5 Variants of the Regularity Lemma

As mentioned in the introduction, the dependence of $Q(\epsilon, t)$, the upper bound on the number of partition classes, on the parameters ϵ and t in the algorithm in Theorem 1.3 is rather horrible. One can improve this situation in some cases by combining our basic ideas presented in Section 3 with a different type of regular partition in which the classes are sets of k-tuples of vertices from the graph. Here the number of such classes is much smaller than the bound $Q(\epsilon, t)$. A similar notion of regularity was also used in [11]. Due to space limitations we do not describe this variant and only mention an application.

Let $G = (V, E)$ be any labeled graph on n vertices and suppose that the vertex set of G, $V = \{v_1, v_2, \ldots, v_n\}$, is ordered by $v_1 < v_2 < \ldots < v_n$. Let the set $W = \{w_1, w_2, \ldots, w_k\}$, $k \leq n$, be ordered by $w_1 < w_2 < \ldots < w_k$. We say that a graph H with vertex set W is *order-isomorphic* to an induced subgraph H' of G with vertex set W' if there exists an isomorphism $\varphi: W \longrightarrow W'$ with the property that for each i and j, $1 \leq i < j \leq k$, $w_i < w_j$ implies $\varphi(w_i) < \varphi(w_j)$. Let $H_1, H_2, \ldots, H_t$, $t = 2^{\binom{k}{2}}$, be a list of all labeled graphs on the set W. We shall use $\sigma_k(G)$ to denote the t-dimensional vector $\sigma_k(G) = (h_1, h_2, \ldots, h_t)$, in which for each i, $1 \leq i \leq t$, h_i is the number of induced subgraphs of G to which H_i is order-isomorphic. Our approach enables us to approximate $\sigma_k(G)$ efficiently when k is sufficiently small relative to n. Specifically we have:

Theorem 5.1 *There is an algorithm whose input is a labeled graph* G *with* n *vertices,* n *sufficiently large, and a list* $(H_1, H_2, \ldots, H_t)$, $t = 2^{\binom{k}{2}}$, *of all labeled graphs on* k *vertices for* $k \geq 3$, $k < \left(\frac{1}{17} \cdot \log\log n\right)^{\frac{1}{2}}$, *and whose output is an approximation* $\bar{\sigma}_k(G) = (\bar{h}_1, \bar{h}_2, \ldots, \bar{h}_t)$ *to the vector* $\sigma_k(G) = (h_1, h_2, \ldots, h_t)$ *with the property that*

$$\sum_{1 \leq i \leq t} |h_i - \bar{h}_i| \leq \frac{1}{t} \sum_{1 \leq i \leq t} h_i \, .$$

This algorithm runs in $O\left(n^2 \cdot M(n)\right)$ *sequential time.*

The detailed proof is complicated and will not appear here. We note that the general approach in proving the last theorem combines our algorithmic technique and the above mentioned variant of the Regularity Lemma with methods described in [13], [24], and in a related form in [26]. Indeed an algorithm which supplies such approximations could be obtained by combining these methods with Theorem 1.3. We note, however, that due to the way in which the bound $Q(\epsilon, t)$ of that Theorem depends on $\frac{1}{\epsilon}$, an algorithm of this sort would only achieve the sort of accuracy obtained by Theorem 5.1 for subgraphs on k vertices with $k = \log^{(p)} n$, where $\log^{(p)}$ means the p-fold iterated logarithm, and p is in this case a polynomial in $\frac{1}{\epsilon}$.

References

[1] N. Alon, *Eigenvalues, geometric expanders, sorting in rounds and Ramsey Theory*, Combinatorica 6 (1986), 207-219.

[2] N. Alon, *Non-constructive proofs in combinatorics*, Proc. of the International Congress of Mathematicians, Kyoto 1990, Japan, Springer Verlag, Tokyo (1991), 1421-1429.

[3] N. Alon, *A parallel algorithmic version of the local lemma*, Random Structures and Algorithms 2 (1991), 367-378. Also: Proc. 32nd Annual FOCS, IEEE (1991), 586-593.

[4] N. Alon, L. Babai and A. Itai, *A fast and simple randomized parallel algorithm for the maximal independent set problem*, J. Algorithms 7 (1986), 567-583.

[5] N. Alon and R. Yuster, *Almost H-factors in dense graphs*, Graphs and Combinatorics, in press.

[6] J. Beck, *An algorithmic approach to the Lovász Local Lemma I*, Random Structures and Algorithms 2 (1991), 343-365.

[7] B. Bollobás, P. Erdős, M. Simonovits and E. Szemerédi, *Extremal graphs without large forbidden subgraphs*, in: Advances in Graph Theory (Cambridge Combinatorial Conference, Trinity College, 1977), Ann. Discrete Math. 3 (1978), 29-41.

[8] G. Chen and R. H. Schelp, *Graphs with linearly bounded Ramsey numbers*, J. Combinatorial Theory, Ser. B, to appear.

[9] V. Chvátal, V. Rödl, E. Szemerédi and T. Trotter, *The Ramsey Number of a graph with bounded maximum degree*, J. Combinatorial Theory Ser. B 34 (1983), 239-243.

[10] D. Coppersmith and S. Winograd, *Matrix multiplication via arithmetic progressions*, J. of Symbolic Computation 9 (1990), 251-280.

[11] N. Eaton and V. Rödl, *Ramsey numbers for sparse graphs*, preprint.

[12] P. Erdős, P. Frankl and V. Rödl, *The asymptotic number of graphs not containing a fixed subgraph and a problem for hypergraphs having no exponent*, Graphs and Combinatorics 2 (1986), 113-121.

[13] F. Franek and V. Rödl, *On Erdős conjecture for multiplicities of complete subgraphs*, Graphs and Combinatorics, to appear.

[14] P. Frankl, R. L. Graham and V. Rödl, *On subsets of Abelian groups with no 3-term arithmetic progression*, J. Combinatorial Theory Ser. A 45 (1987), 157-161.

[15] P. Frankl and Z. Füredi, *Exact solution of some Turán-type problems*, J. Combinatorial Theory Ser. A 45 (1987), 226-262.

[16] Z. Füredi, *The maximum number of edges in a minimal graph of diameter 2*, J. Graph Theory, to appear.

[17] Z. Füredi, M. Goemans and D. J. Kleitman, *On the maximum number of triangles in wheel-free graphs*, to appear.

[18] M. R. Garey and D. S. Johnson, *Computers and Intractability, A Guide to the Theory of NP-Completeness*, W. H. Freeman and Company, New York, 1979.

[19] A. Hajnal, W. Maass and G. Turán, *On the communication complexity of graph properties*, Proc. 20th ACM STOC, ACM Press (1988), 186-191.

[20] R. M. Karp and A. Wigderson, *A fast parallel algorithm for the maximal independent set problem*, Proc. 16th ACM STOC, ACM Press (1984), 266-272.

[21] M. Luby, *A simple parallel algorithm for the maximal independent set problem*, SIAM J. Computing 15 (1986), 1036-1053.

[22] C. H. Papadimitriou, *On graph theoretic lemmata and complexity classes*, Proc. 31st Annual IEEE FOCS, IEEE (1990), 794-801. See also: *On the complexity of the parity argument and other inefficient proofs of existence*, JCSS, to appear.

[23] V. Rödl and R. Duke, *On Graphs with small subgraphs of large chromatic number*, Graphs and Combinatorics 1 (1985), 91-96.

[24] V. Rödl, *On universality of graphs with uniformly distributed edges*, Discrete Mathematics 59 (1986), 125-134.

[25] R. Rödl and A. Rucinski, *Random Graphs with monochromatic triangles in every edge coloring*, submitted.

[26] M. Simonovits and V. T. Sós, *Szemerédi's partition and quasirandomness*, Random Structures and Algorithms 2 (1991), 1-10.

[27] E. Szemerédi, *On sets of integers containing no k elements in arithmetic progression*, Acta Arithmetica 27 (1975), 199-245.

[28] E. Szemerédi, *Regular partitions of graphs*, in: *Proc. Colloque Inter. CNRS* (J. -C. Bermond, J. -C. Fournier, M. Las Vergnas and D. Sotteau eds.), 1978, 399-401.

ON THE RANDOMIZED COMPLEXITY OF VOLUME AND DIAMETER

László Lovász
Eötvös Loránd University, Budapest
and
Princeton University, Princeton, NJ

Miklós Simonovits
Mathematical Research Institute
Hungarian Academy of Science, Budapest
and
Rutgers University, New Brunswick, NJ

(Extended Abstract)

Abstract. We give an $O(n^7 \log^2 n)$ randomized algorithm to approximate the volume of a convex body, and an $O(n^6 \log n)$ algorithm to sample a point from the uniform distribution over a convex body. For convex polytopes our algorithm runs in $O(n^7 \log^4 n)$ steps. Several tools are developed that may be interesting on their own. We extend results of Sinclair–Jerrum (1988) and the authors (1990) on the mixing rate of Markov chains from finite to arbitrary Markov chains. We describe an algorithm to integrate a function with respect to the stationary distribution of a general Markov chain. We also analyze the mixing rate of various random walks on convex bodies, in particular the random walk with steps from the uniform distribution over a unit ball.

In several previous positive and negative results, the problem of computing the diameter of a convex body behaved similarly as the volume problem. In contrast to this, we show that there is no polynomial randomized algorithm to compute the diameter within a factor of $n^{1/4}$.

1. Introduction

a. Survey of results.

Computing the volume of a (high-dimensional) convex body is an ancient, basic, but extremely difficult task. We in fact have negative results in this direction: Bárány–Füredi (1986), improving a result of Elekes (1986) proved that if the convex body is given by a separation oracle (a natural framework which allows the polynomial-time solution of many algorithmic problems), then any algorithm that approximates the volume within a factor of $n^{o(n)}$ necessarily takes exponential time. Dyer–Frieze (1988) and Khachiyan (1988, 1989) showed that the problem of computing the volume exactly (deterministically) is # P-hard, even for explicitely described polytopes. (A strong improvement of this is due to Brightwell and Winkler (1990), who proved that the exact determination of the number of linear extensions of a poset – which is the volume of a related polytope – is also # P-hard.) A breakthrough in the opposite direction is due to Dyer, Frieze and Kannan (1989), who designed a polynomial time *randomized* algorithm to approximate the volume of a convex body K in $\mathbf{R}^n$.

The Volume Problem

Input parameters: $\varepsilon, \delta > 0$, and a convex body $K \subseteq \mathbf{R}^n$, given by (some kind of) oracle. Compute a random variable ζ such that with probability at least $1-\delta$, the volume of K is between $(1-\varepsilon)\zeta$ and $(1+\varepsilon)\zeta$.

Several improvements of the original algorithm have been given. The following list describes these results. Our main interest is the dependence of the running time on the dimension n. The * after the O means that we suppress factors of $\log n$, as well as factors depending on the error bounds ε, δ and the "badness" of the original data.

Dyer, Frieze, Kannan [DFK]	(1989)	$O^*(n^{23})$
Lovász and Simonovits [LS1]	(1990)	$O^*(n^{16})$
Applegate and Kannan [AK]	(1990)	$O^*(n^{10})$
Lovász [L]	(1992)	$O^*(n^{10})$
Dyer and Frieze [DF]	(1991)	$O^*(n^8)$
Lovász and Simonovits [LS2]	(1991)	$O^*(n^7)$

0-8186-2900-2/92 $3.00 © 1992 IEEE

This paper is an extended abstract of [LS2], with two additions. First, a general framework for efficient integration with respect to the stationary distribution of a Markov chain is described. Second, it is shown that for the computation of other geometric quantities like diameter and width (which often behave similarly to the volume) even randomization cannot lead to a polynomial time approximation algorithm.

On the other hand, we leave out the discussion of "conductance on large sets" from [LS2] (which was already introduced in [LS1]), since it would lead only to marginal improvements.

Let us give a short survey of those ideas whose various combinations lead to the improvements in the running time of the volume algorithm.

The common feature of these algorithms are that they consist of two phases:

Sandwiching. We apply an affine transformation to K to reduce the problem to a case when K is contained in a ball (or cube) of size R and contains a ball (or a cube) of size r and R/r is small. This part is called *rounding* or *sandwiching*.

Multiphase Monte-Carlo. One cannot apply the Monte-Carlo method directly to estimate exponentially small probabilities. Therefore we split the original problem into $cn \log n$ "subproblems", "phases", in which we estimate ratios of two volumes or ratios of two integrals. These ratios are estimated by Monte-Carlo type methods, where the *sampling*, i.e. finding a random point, is done using a *random walk*.

Thus all the above algorithms are based on the fact that the random point generation is good enough. This is shown using that the *conductance*, defined below, is large. Large conductance informally means that the probability of leaving any subdomain of the convex body is sufficiently large, i.e. that its boundary is sufficiently large. Hence it is natural that all the methods use *isoperimetric inequalities.*

The improvement in [LS1] came from an improved isoperimetric inequality (conjectured in [DFK]), and from using a generalized conductance notion. [AK] suggested to use *cube-sandwiching* instead of ellipsoid-sandwiching and calculate the *integral of approximate characteristic functions*, introduced the use of log-concave functions and the use of Metropolis filtering. The improvement in [DF] comes partly from the better handling of the error-accumulation of the separate phases.

The previous papers used random walks on a grid. [L] suggested to use a continous Markov chain, by *jumping in a unit ball*, with uniform distribution.

In this paper we describe a randomized volume algorithm which requires $O^*(n^7)$ membership tests. Our algorithm builds on virtually all of the ideas mentioned above; yet we feel that the combination is very natural and leads to an algorithm which is conceptually quite simple.

To formulate the basic steps of our algorithm we need first to fix the

b. Computational model.

A convex body will be given by an *oracle*, i.e., a black box that answers certain queries about the body. We refer to Grötschel, Lovász and Schrijver (1988) for a detailed discussion of these oracles. In the first phase of our algorithms we shall use a weak separation oracle:

Definition (Weak separation oracle). For any $y \in \mathbb{Q}^n$ and error tolerance $\vartheta > 0$, the oracle returns either "YES" or "NO". The "YES" answer means that the distance of y from K is at most ϑ; the "NO" answer means that the distance of y from $\mathbf{R}^n \setminus K$ is less than δ. In this case, it also returns a "proof" of this fact, in the form a hyperplane $c^T x \leq \gamma$ through y which almost separates y from K in the sense that $\max\{c^T x : x \in K\} \leq \gamma + \vartheta|c|$. (So if y is near the boundary of K, then either answer is legal.)

In addition, we assume that we know the radius r of some ball contained in K (but we do not necessarily know the center of the ball) and the radius R of another ball, with center 0, containing K. The number of bits needed to describe both of these balls is part of the input size. This contributes $|\log R| + |\log r|$ bits to the input size.

In the main part of our algorithm we use a *weak membership oracle* (where the oracle answers "YES" or "NO" but provides no separating hyperplane.)

A statistical trick. A well-known trick [see e.g. Jerrum, Valiant and Vazirani (1986)] shows that it suffices to solve the problem with $\delta = 1/3$. Assume that we have an algorithm that computes a random variable ζ that falls in the interval $I = [(1-\varepsilon)\text{vol}(K),\ (1+\varepsilon)\text{vol}(K)]$. Let $s = 10\log(1/\delta)$, and let us compute $2s+1$ independent values of ζ, say $\zeta_1, \dots, \zeta_{2s+1}$. Let ζ_{i_0} be the median of them, i.e. the $(s+1)$st of them when ordered increasingly. Then

$$\text{Prob}(\zeta_{i_0} \in I) \geq 1 - \delta.$$

2. Results.

B denotes the euclidean unit ball, $\text{vol}(K)$ is the volume (Lebesgue measure) of the set K.

A first observation is that once we replace the volume computation by integration, the integrand need not approximate the characteristic function of the body. Let K be a convex body containing the origin in the interior and $x \in \mathbf{R}^n$. We denote by $\phi(x)=\phi_K(x)$ the least non-negative number t for which $x \in tK$. We set $F_K(x)=e^{-\phi(x)}$, then $0 < F_K(x) \leq 1$.

2.1. Lemma.

$$\mathrm{vol}(K)=\frac{1}{n!}\int_{\mathbf{R}^n} F_K(x)dx.$$

This enables us to use much smoother functions, and a large ball as the domain of integration, which eliminates most of the errors due to boundary effects.

We solve three algorithmic tasks: sandwiching, sampling (generating a random point in a convex body) and integration (which includes volume computation by Lemma 2.1). Our algorithms heavily depend on each other.

Approximate sandwiching

One benefit of using integrals is that instead of sandwiching, only "approximate sandwiching" is needed. This means that for the convex body K we shall find a ball B such that

(A1) More than 2/3 of the volume of B is contained in K.

(A2) For some parameter $m \geq 1$, more than 2/3 of the volume of K is contained in the convex body mB.

We shall call m the "rounding ratio" of K and the better "rounding ratio" can be achieved the faster our algorithms will be.

We describe deterministic and randomized algorithms to achieve (A1) and (A2) in the general case, and randomized algorithms for special classes of convex bodies.

(1) A standard application of the ellipsoid method (see [GLS]) gives that we can find an affine transformation A such that the rounding ratio of $A(K)$ is at most $n^{3/2}$; such an affine tranformation A can be computed using $O(n^4(|\log R|+|\log r|))$ operations with numbers with $O(n^2(|\log R|+|\log r|))$ digits. For polyhedra given by explicit linear inequalities, $m=O(n)$ can be achieved by the same method.

(2) As one can see from [GLS, pp. 122–124], one can find in polynomial time an affine transformation A such that the rounding ratio of $A(K)$ is at most n, provided we have an oracle that tests whether $B \subseteq A(K)$ for any affine transformation A, and returns a point in $B \setminus A(K)$ if not. Unfortunately, in most cases we have no such oracle. The following randomized algorithm can replace this oracle. Select $T=\lceil 3\log n\rceil$ independent random points in B, and test if they belong to $A(K)$. If one of them does not, we have a point in $B \setminus A(K)$. If all of them belong to $A(K)$, we conclude that at least 2/3 of the volume of B must be in $A(K)$.

This gives a randomized algorithm that achieves (A1) and (A2), with $m=O(n)$, with error probability less than 1/4. Moreover, (A2) is achieved in a much stronger sense: the ball mB in fact contains $A(K)$.

(3) In the case of centrally symmetric bodies, randomization gives the same improvement over the ratio n in [GLS], and one achieves (A1) and (strong) (A2) with $m=O(n^{1/2})$.

(4) In the special case (which is perhaps the most important) when $A(K)$ is a polytope with a polynomial number of facets, we can also improve (2). We use a "polar" form of the ellipsoid method, suggested by Lenstra (1983). In this version, we need to test whether $A(K) \subseteq mB$ (and find a point in $A(K) \setminus mB$ if not). We can do this by generating $T=\lceil \log_{3/2}(10n\log n)\rceil$ independent random points in $A(K)$ (using the Sampling Algorithm) and testing if they belong to mB. If one of them does not, we have a point in $A(K) \setminus B$. If all of them belong to mB, we conclude that at least 2/3 of the volume of $A(K)$ must be in mB. If less than 2/3 of the volume of $A(K)$ is contained in mB, then the probability that we do not find a point in the difference is less than $(2/3)^T \leq 1/(10n\log n)$.

This way we have found an affine transformation that achieves (A1) in the strong sense that B is contained in $A(K)$, and also achieves (A2). If $A(K)$ has n^c facets, then we can shrink $A(K)$ by a factor of $\Omega(\sqrt{n}/\log n)$ and still have 2/3 of the volume of B in $A(K)$. (In fact, it is well-known from geometry that each facet of $A(K)$ cuts off a fraction of less that $1/(3n^c)$ of the volume of B.) So for polytopes with a polynomial number of facets, a rounding ratio of $m=O(\sqrt{n}\log n)$ can be achieved.

(5) Similarly, if K is a centrally symmetric polytope with a polynomial number of facets, then $m=O(\log n)$ can be achieved.

In all these versions, the running time for the rounding phase exceeds the running time of the main phase by at most a factor of $\log n$.

Sampling

The following algorithm generates a random point in a convex body K. We generate a sequence $v_0 = 0, v_1, \ldots, v_t$ of points in K (where $t=O^*(n^4m^2)$) as follows. Given v_i, we flip a coin and if it is tails, we let $v_{i+1}=v_i$. Else, we generate a random point u in $v_i+(\varepsilon/100n)B$. If $u \notin K$ then $v_{i+1}=v_i$. If $u \in K$ then $v_{i+1}=u$. (We do not analyse this version, since below we will propose a better one.)

Random walks can be used to generate a random point from a given (non-uniform) distribution, by applying a *Metropolis filter*. Let $F>0$ be any integrable function on K and let Q_F denote the distribution whose density function is proportional to F, i.e.

$$Q_F(A)=\int_A F(u)\,du \Big/ \int_K F(u)\,du.$$

Consider a random walk $w_0=0,w_1,\dots,w_t$ which is defined similarly as above, but with the following modification. If $u\in K$ and $F(u)\geq F(v_i)$ then let (as before) $v_{i+1}=u$, but if $u\in K$ and $F(u)<F(v_i)$ then we choose $v_{i+1}=u$ with probability $F(u)/F(v_i)$ and $v_{i+1}=v_i$ with probability $1-F(u)/F(v_i)$ (independently of the prehistory). We call this sequence *the F-filtered random walk in K*.

Now it is not difficult to show that the distribution of v_t tends to Q_F as $t\to\infty$. It is much more difficult to estimate the rate of convergence (which may be very slow). [AK] showed that this can be done if F is (nearly) log-concave. See section 4 for our improved bounds.

It is interesting that this filtering gives a good method to generate a random point even from the uniform distribution on K.

Sampling Algorithm. Set

$$q=4mn\log(1/\varepsilon),$$
$$t=10^6nq^2(5n\log n+2\log(2/\varepsilon)).$$

We generate an F_K-filtered random walk $v_0,\dots,v_t$ of points in qB. The random point in K is

$$w=\left(1-e^{-\phi(v_t)}\right)\phi(v_t)^{-1}v_t.$$

2.2. Theorem. *For every Lebesgue measurable set $A\subseteq K$, the random point w computed by the Sampling Algorithm satisfies*

$$\left|\text{Prob}(w\in A)-\frac{\text{vol}(A)}{\text{vol}(K)}\right|<\varepsilon.$$

Moreover, the algorithm uses $O(n^3m^2\log^2\frac{1}{\varepsilon}(n\log n+\log\frac{1}{\varepsilon}))$ membership tests and $O(n^4m^2\log^2\frac{1}{\varepsilon}(n\log n+\log\frac{1}{\varepsilon}))$ arithmetic operations.

Volume computation

Let m be the rounding ratio, $\varepsilon>0$, and let F be as in Lemma 2.1. For $i=0,1,\dots,$ we define the function

$$F_i(x)=\min\{F(x),\exp(-|x|n^{1/2}2^{-i/n})\}.$$

Volume Algorithm. (a) Set

$$q=4mn\log(1/\varepsilon),$$
$$k=4n\log n,$$
$$t=2\cdot10^8nkq^2\varepsilon^{-2}.$$

(b) For $i=1,\dots,k$ we generate a sequence $(v_0^i,\dots,v_{3t}^i)$ of random points in qB. The first sequence starts with a point generated from the distribution Q_{F_0} over qB. The i-th sequence starts where the $(i-1)$-st ended, and is generated in the same way as in the Sampling Algorithm, but with F_i instead of F.

(c) We compute

$$\alpha_i=\frac{1}{t}\sum_{j=t+1}^{2t}\frac{F_{i-1}(v_j^i)}{F_i(v_j^i)}.$$

(The first t steps of each phase serve to get a point v_t^i, whose distribution is close to Q_{F_i}. So the points v_j^i ($j=t+1,\dots,2t$) will have a distribution over qB that is very close to Q_{F_i}. Also note that $F_i=F_{K_i}$, where $K_i=K\cap2^{i/n}B$. Therefore, α_i will be a good estimate on

$$\int_{qB}\frac{F_{i-1}}{F_i}\,dQ_{F_i}=\int_{qB}F_{i-1}(x)\,dx\Big/\int_{qB}F_i(x)\,dx\approx\frac{\text{vol}(K_{i-1})}{\text{vol}(K_i)}.$$

The last t steps ensure independence from the next phase.)

(d) Estimate vol(K) by $\zeta=(\alpha_1\cdots\alpha_k)^{-1}\text{vol}(B)$.

2.3. Theorem.

$$\text{Prob}((1-\varepsilon)\zeta<\text{vol}(K)<(1+\varepsilon)\zeta)\geq3/4.$$

Moreover, the algorithm uses

$$O\left(n^3m^2\varepsilon^{-2}(\log m+\log\log\frac{1}{\varepsilon})^2(n+\log\frac{1}{\varepsilon})^2\log^2(\frac{1}{\varepsilon})\right)$$

membership oracle calls and

$$O\left(n^4m^2\varepsilon^{-2}(\log m+\log\log\frac{1}{\varepsilon})^2(n+\log\frac{1}{\varepsilon})^2\log^2\frac{1}{\varepsilon}\right)$$

arithmetic operations on numbers with $O(\log n+\log\frac{1}{\varepsilon})$ bits.

(Ordinarily, a membership test takes at least n arithmetic operations (it has to look at the coordinates), so the running time will be dominated by the membership tests.)

Combining this theorem with our results on sandwiching, we obtain several corollaries. For sake of simplicity, we assume here that $\varepsilon > 2^{-n}$. We ignore the cost of sandwiching, and only give the number of oracle calls; each oracle call goes with $O(n)$ arithmetic operations on numbers with $O(\log n)$ bits.

2.4. Corollary. (a) *If K is a convex body given by a well-guaranteed separation oracle, then we can compute a random value ζ using $O(n^7\varepsilon^{-2}\log^2 n \log^2 \frac{1}{\varepsilon} \log \frac{1}{\delta})$ oracle calls such that*

$$\text{Prob}((1-\varepsilon)\zeta \leq \text{vol}(K) \leq (1+\varepsilon)\text{vol}(K)) \geq 1-\delta.$$

(b) *If K is centrally symmetric, or K is a polytope with a polynomial (in n) number of facets, then we need only $O(n^6\varepsilon^{-2}\log^4 n \log^2 \frac{1}{\varepsilon} \log \frac{1}{\delta})$ membership tests.*

(c) *If K is a centrally symmetric polytope with a polynomial (in n) number of facets, then we need only $O(n^5\varepsilon^{-2}\log^4 n \log^2 \frac{1}{\varepsilon} \log \frac{1}{\delta})$ oracle calls.*

3. Conductance of Markov chains.

a. Markov schemes and Markov chains.

We extend the theory of conductance and rapid mixing from the finite case to arbitrary Markov chains. See [LS2] for the discrete versions of some of these results.

Let $(\Omega, \mathcal{A})$ be a σ-algebra. For every $u \in \Omega$, let P_u be a probability measure on Ω, and assume that for every $A \in \mathcal{A}$, the value $P_u(A)$ is measurable as a function of u. We call the triple $\mathcal{M} = (\Omega, \mathcal{A}, \{P_u : u \in \Omega\})$ a *Markov scheme*. A Markov scheme, together with an *initial distribution* Q_0 on Ω, defines a *Markov chain*, i.e. a sequence of random variables $w_0, w_1, w_2, \dots$ with values from Ω such that w_0 is chosen from distribution Q_0 and w_{i+1} is chosen from distribution P_{w_i} (independently of the value of $w_0, \dots, w_{i-1}$).

A probability measure Q on $(\Omega, \mathcal{A})$ is a *stationary distribution* for the Markov scheme if choosing w_0 from this distribution, w_1 will have the same distribution (then, of course, so does every w_i). This is equivalent to saying that for all $A \in \mathcal{A}$, $\int_\Omega P_u(A)\, dQ(u) = Q(A)$. From now on we shall fix one stationary distribution Q. In all cases relevant for us, the existence and uniqueness of the stationary distribution follows from our results.

A Markov scheme is *time-reversible* if (roughly speaking) for any two sets $A, B \in \mathcal{A}$, it steps from A to B as often as from B to A. Formally, this means that

$$\int_B P_u(A)\, dQ(u) = \int_A P_u(B)\, dQ(u).$$

b. Laziness of Markov chains.

We call a Markov scheme *lazy* if $P_u(u) \geq 1/2$ at each point. This condition is technical; its main adventage is that (in the time-reversible case) it implies that the operator M associated with the Markov scheme is positive semidefinite.

Every Markov scheme can be made lazy by simply tossing a coin at each step and making a move only if it is tails. So (at the cost of a little slow-down) we can assume that M is positive semidefinite, which will be very convenient.

c. Conductance and rapid mixing.

Put

$$\Phi(A) = \int_A P_u(\Omega \setminus A)\, dQ(u).$$

This value is the probability of the event that choosing w_0 from the stationary distribution, we have $w_0 \in A$ but $w_1 \notin A$. One can easily show that the assumption that Q is stationary, is equivalent to that

$$\Phi(A) = \int_A P_u(\Omega \setminus A)\, dQ(u)$$

is invariant under complementation.

The *conductance* of the Markov scheme is

$$\Phi = \inf_{0 < Q(A) < 1/2} \frac{\Phi(A)}{Q(A)}.$$

We call the value $1 - P_u(u)$ the *local conductance* of the Markov scheme at element u.

Let Q_k denote the distribution of w_k, i.e., let

$$Q_k(A) = \text{Prob}(w_k \in A)$$

for $A \in \mathcal{A}$. By definition, we have the recurrence

$$Q_k(A) = \int_\Omega P_u(A)\, dQ_{k-1}(u).$$

It is well-known (and will also follow from our results below) that if $\Phi(A) > 0$ for all $A \in \mathcal{A}$ with $Q(A) > 0$, then $Q_k \to Q$ in the ℓ_1 distance. Our main point will be to give a bound on the rate of convergence.

To measure the speed of convergence, we consider all measurable functions

$$g : \Omega \to [0,1] \quad \text{with} \quad \int_\Omega g\, dQ(u) = x,$$

and define the *distance function* of Q and Q_k by

$$h_k(x) = \sup_g \int_\Omega g\, dQ_k - x = \int_\Omega g[dQ_k - dQ],$$

where the supremum is extended over all these functions. In the case of a finite Markov scheme with N atoms and with uniform stationary distribution, $h_k(j/N)$ can be obtained by adding up the j largest "errors" $Q_k(\omega)-(1/N)$. It follows easily from the definition that $h_k(x)$ is a concave function of x. Since $0\le h_k(0)\le 1$ and $h_k(1)=0$, we have $0\le h_k(x)\le 1-x$. This somewhat artificial definition will be clearer from the inequality

$$-h_k(1-x)\le Q_k(A)-Q(A)\le h_k(x).$$

where $x=Q(A)$. It is also easily seen that

$$\sup_x h_k(x)=\sup_A |Q_k(A)-Q(A)|$$

is half of the ℓ_1-distance of Q and Q_k.

3.1. Lemma. *Let $k\ge 1$. If $0\le x\le 1/2$, then*

$$h_k(x)\le\frac{1}{2}\Big(h_{k-1}(x-2\Phi x)+h_{k-1}(x+2\Phi x)\Big).$$

If $1/2\le x\le 1$, then

$$h_k(x)\le\frac{1}{2}\Big(h_{k-1}(x-2\Phi(1-x))+h_{k-1}(x+2\Phi(1-x))\Big).$$

3.2. Theorem. *Assume that c_1, c_2 are chosen so that for every $0\le x\le 1$ we have*

$$h_0(x)\le c_1+c_2\min\{\sqrt{x},\sqrt{1-x}\}.$$

Then for every $k\ge 0$ and $0\le x\le 1$ we have

$$h_k(x)\le c_1+c_2\min\{\sqrt{x},\sqrt{1-x}\}\left(1-\frac{1}{2}\Phi^2\right)^k.$$

3.3. Corollary. (a) *Let $M=\sup_A Q_0(A)/Q(A)$. Then for every $A\subseteq\Omega$,*

$$|Q_k(A)-Q(A)|\le\sqrt{M}\left(1-\frac{1}{2}\Phi^2\right)^k.$$

d. A Central Limit Theorem.

The following theorem can be proved by known spectral techniques.

3.4. Theorem. *Let $\mathcal{M}$ be a time-reversible Markov scheme with stationary distribution Q, let $w_1,w_2,\ldots$ be a Markov chain generated by $\mathcal{M}$ with initial distribution Q. Let $F\in L^2$ and $\xi=\sum_{i=0}^{T-1}F(w_i)$. Then*

$$\mathbf{D}^2(\xi)\le\frac{4T}{\Phi^2}\|F\|^2.$$

e. The Metropolis Filter.

We conclude this section with describing a version of the Metropolis algorithm (1953), which can be used to modify a given time-reversible Markov scheme so as to achieve a given stationary distribution.

Consider a time-reversible Markov scheme $\mathcal{M}$ on the σ-algebra $(\Omega,\mathcal{A})$, and let $F:\ \Omega\to\mathbf{R}$ be a nonnegative measurable function. Assume that the integral

$$\overline{F}=\int_\Omega F\,dQ$$

is finite. Recall that we denote by μ_F the measure with density function F, i.e.,

$$\mu_F(S)=\int_S F(x)dQ(x)$$

for every measurable set S. Clearly $Q_F=(1/\overline{F})\mu_F$ is a probability distribution on $(\Omega,\mathcal{A})$.

We generate a Markov chain $(w_0,w_1,\ldots)$ of elements of Ω as follows. Given w_k, we generate a random element u from the distribution P_{w_k}. If $F(u)\ge F(w_k)$, we let $w_{k+1}=u$. If $F(u)<F(w_k)$, then we "flip a biased coin" with heads probability $F(u)/F(w_k)$. If we see head, we move to $w_{k+1}=u$. Else, we let $w_{k+1}=w_k$. Note the simple but very important property of this method that we do not use the density function $F/\overline{F}$ of the desired limit distribution, but only the ratios $F(u)/F(v)$. The transition probabilities of this new Markov scheme are given, for $u\notin A$, by

$$P_u^F(A)=\int_A\min\left\{1,\frac{F(v)}{F(u)}\right\}dP_u(v)$$

(the case $u\in A$ is clearly determined by this). We call this new Markov scheme $\mathcal{M}/F$ the *filtering* of $\mathcal{M}$ by F.

3.5. Lemma. *If $\mathcal{M}$ is time-reversible, then the Markov scheme $\mathcal{M}/F$ is also time-reversible with stationary distribution Q_F.*

f. Integration

Let $\mathcal{M} = (\Omega, \mathcal{A}, \{P_u : u \in \Omega\})$ be a time-reversible Markov scheme with stationary distribution Q and conductance at least Φ. Let $F: \Omega \to \mathbf{R}_+$ be an integrable function with respect to Q. We give a general randomized algorithm to compute $I = \int F\,dQ$, and estimate its running time in terms of the conductances of $\mathcal{M}$ and some of its Metropolis filterings. We assume that we have an oracle to evaluate F at any $u \in \Omega$, and we have *a priori* numbers c_1 and c_2 such that $F \le c_1$ and $I \ge c_2$. Obviosly, $c_1 \ge c_2$. We are also given an $\varepsilon > 0$, and want to compute an estimate ξ on the integral having relative error less than ε with probability at least 3/4 (we have discussed in section 1 how this probability bound can be improved).

A natural approach is to use $\mathcal{M}$ to generate many independent points $w_i \in \Omega$ $(1 \le i \le T)$, each from a distribution very close to Q, and then use $(1/T)\sum_{i=1}^{T} F(w_i)$ as an approximation of the integral. (A slightly better algorithm (but still only auxiliary) is obtained by using our central limit theorem on Markov chains.) But T contains the factor $\frac{c_1}{c_2}$, which may be very large in quite natural problems (e.g. in Lemma 2.1). We are going to show that it can be reduced to (roughly) the logarithm of this number.

Integration Algorithm.

(a) Compute

$$m = 1 + \lceil \log(c_2/c_1) \rceil, \qquad T = \lceil \Phi^2 m^2 \varepsilon^2 \rceil,$$

and select any $w_0 \in \Omega$. Let $G = (F + c_2)^{1/m}$.

(b) For $k = 0, \dots, m-1$, run the Markov chain $\mathcal{M}/G^k$ for $2T$ steps, to get the sequence of points $w_0^{(k)} = w_0, w_1^{(k)} \dots, w_{2T}^{(k)}$.

(c) For $k = 0, \dots, m-1$, compute

$$\alpha_k = \frac{1}{T} \sum_{i=T+1}^{2T} G(w_i^{(k)}).$$

(d) Compute

$$\xi = \prod_{k=0}^{m-1} \alpha_k - c_2.$$

3.6. Theorem. *The quantity ξ computed by the Integration Algorithm satisfies*

$$\text{Prob}\left((1-\varepsilon)\xi < \int_\Omega F\,dQ < (1+\varepsilon)\xi\right) > \frac{3}{4}.$$

Remark. Our algorithm in more concrete geometric situations follows similar lines, but will make more use of the additional structure to save on running time.

4. Log-concave functions and isoperimetric inequalities

a. Log-concave functions.

We collect some known facts about convex bodies and log-concave functions.

Definition. (Log-concave function.) A function $f: \mathbf{R}^n \to \mathbf{R}_+$ is *log-concave* if it satisfies, for all $x, y \in \mathbf{R}^n$ and $0 < \lambda < 1$,

$$f(\lambda x + (1-\lambda)y) \le f(x)^\lambda f(y)^{(1-\lambda)}.$$

Equivalently, a (non-negative) function is log-concave if its support $K = \{x \in \mathbf{R}^n : f(x) > 0\}$ is convex, and $\log f$ is a concave function on K.

Every non-negative function that is concave over a convex domain is log-concave (we define its value to be 0 outside the original domain). In particular, the characteristic function of a convex body is log-concave. Log-concave functions include many density functions important in statistics, e.g. e^{-x^2} and $e^{-|x|}$.

It is obvious that the product and the minimum of two log-concave functions is log-concave (not their sum!). The following fact (Dinghas 1957, Prékopa 1971, 1973) is much less obvious:

4.1. Lemma. *The convolution $h(x) = \int_{\mathbf{R}^n} g(u) f(x-u)\,du$ of two log-concave functions (assuming that it is well-defined) is log-concave.*

If F is a non-negative integrable function on $\mathbf{R}^n$, then we denote by μ_F the measure with density function F, i.e.,

$$\mu_F(A) = \int_A F(x)\,dx.$$

Applying Lemma 4.1 with g chosen to be the characteristic function of the convex body $-K$, we obtain the following Brunn-Minkowski type theorem:

4.2. Corollary. *Let $K \subseteq \mathbf{R}^n$ be a convex body and $F: \mathbf{R}^n \to \mathbf{R}_+$ a log-concave function. Then $\mu_F(x+K)$ is a log-concave function of x.*

Specializing further, we obtain

4.3. Corollary. *Let K and K' be two convex bodies and $t>0$. If the set $\{x \in \mathbf{R}^n : \text{vol}((K'+x) \cap K) > t\}$ has an interior point, then it is a convex body. In particular, the set $K_s = \{x \in K : \text{vol}((x+K) \cap K) \ge (1-s)\text{vol}(K)\}$ is a convex body for any $0 < s < 1$.*

b. Isoperimetric inequalities for log-concave functions.

The following general lemma is a generalization of the bisection method introduced in [LS1] (a similar method was used in Payne–Weinberger 1960).

4.4. Lemma. [Localization Lemma.] *Let g and h be upper semi-continuous Lebesgue integrable functions on $\mathbf{R}^n$ such that*

$$\int_{\mathbf{R}^n} g(x)\,dx > 0 \quad \text{and} \quad \int_{\mathbf{R}^n} h(x)\,dx > 0.$$

Then there exist two points $a,b \in \mathbf{R}^n$ and a linear function $\ell\colon [0,1] \to \mathbf{R}_+$ such that

$$\int_0^1 \ell(t)^{n-1} g((1-t)a+tb)\,dt > 0$$

and

$$\int_0^1 \ell(t)^{n-1} h((1-t)a+tb)\,dt > 0.$$

(We may formulate the conclusion informally, in a more transparent way, as follows: if both g and h have positive integrals, then there exists an infinitesimally narrow truncated cone such that the restrictions of g and h to this "body" have positive integrals.)

As an application, we derive the following isoperimetric inequality, which is a slight extension of the inequality by Dyer and Frieze [DF] (which, in turn, is a slight extension of the inequality by Applegate and Kannan [AK]).

4.5. Theorem. *Let $K \subseteq \mathbf{R}^n$ be a convex body, $0<t<1$, and $K_1 \cup K_2 \cup K_3$ be a partition of K into three measurable sets such that for any two points $a,b \in K$, the distance of $K_1 \cap [a,b]$ and $K_2 \cap [a,b]$ is at least $t|a-b|$. Then for any log-concave function with support K,*

$$\mu_F(K_3) \geq \frac{2t}{1-t} \min\{\mu_F(K_1),\ \mu_F(K_2)\}.$$

4.6. Corollary. *Let $K \subseteq \mathbf{R}^n$ be a convex set, $0 < t < 1$, and $K_1 \cup K_2 \cup K_3$, a partition of K into three measurable sets such that for any two points $a,b \in K$, the distance of $K_1 \cap [a,b]$ and $K_2 \cap [a,b]$ is at least $t|a-b|$. Then*

$$\mathrm{vol}(K_3) \geq \frac{2t}{1-t} \min\{\mathrm{vol}(K_1), \mathrm{vol}(K_2)\}.$$

In particular, if (in any norm) K has diameter d and the distance of K_1 and K_2 is at least 1, then

$$\mathrm{vol}(K_3) \geq \frac{2}{d-1} \min\{\mathrm{vol}(K_1), \mathrm{vol}(K_2)\}.$$

The Localization Lemma has several applications in convex geometry; for example, it gives a simple proof of Lemma 4.1, and implies Brunn-Minkowski type results for balls and other bodies. These will be treated in detail elsewhere; here we formulate one consequence, which will be handy in our volume algorithm.

4.7. Theorem. *Let F be a log-concave function on $\mathbf{R}^n$, and let*

$$\int_{\mathbf{R}^n \setminus B} F(x)\,dx = \theta \int_{\mathbf{R}^n} F(x)\,dx.$$

Then for every $u \geq 1$,

$$\int_{\mathbf{R}^n \setminus uB} F(x)\,dx \leq \theta^{(u+1)/2} \int_{\mathbf{R}^n} F(x)\,dx.$$

As a special case we obtain

4.8. Corollary. *Let K be a convex body in $\mathbf{R}^n$ and let $\theta = \mathrm{vol}(K \setminus B)/\mathrm{vol}(K)$. Then $\mathrm{vol}(K \setminus uB) \leq \theta^{(u+1)/2}\mathrm{vol}(K)$.*

We shall also need the following related fact:

4.9. Lemma. *Let K be a convex body in $\mathbf{R}^n$ and let $\theta = \mathrm{vol}(K \setminus B)/\mathrm{vol}(K)$. Then $K \subseteq \dfrac{2n}{1-\theta}B$.*

(In fact, the bound in Corollary 4.8 could be improved to $\left(1-(1-\theta^{1/n})(u+1)/2\right)^n$ if $(1-\theta^{1/n})(u+1)/2 < 1$ and 0 otherwise, thus containing Lemma 4.9.)

5. Random walks and sampling in convex bodies

a. Random walks with B-steps.

In Section 1 we analyzed general Markov chains, i.e., random walks in abstract measure spaces. Now we turn to the special case when the underlying domain is $\mathbf{R}^n$ (or a convex body), and the step is chosen uniformly from the unit ball about the current point.

Let B be the unit ball in $\mathbf{R}^n$, with its center at the origin, and K, any convex body. We generate a Markov chain of points in K as follows. Let v_0 be drawn from some initial distribution on K. Given v_k, we flip a coin and if it is heads, we let $v_{k+1} = v_k$. Else, we generate a vector u from the uniform distribution on B, and consider $v_k + u$. If $v_k + u \in K$, we let $v_{k+1} = v_k + u$. Else, we let $v_{k+1} = v_k$. We call this the *lazy random walk in*

K with B-steps. It is straightforward to see that this is a time-reversible Markov scheme $\mathcal{M}(K,B)$ and the uniform distribution on K is stationary.

We shall analyze, more generally, a filtered version of this random walk. Let F be a non-negative log-concave function on K, and let $\overline{F}=\int_K F(x)dx$. Let μ_F denote the measure with density function F and $Q_F=(1/\overline{F})\mu_F$. Specializing the definition of the Metropolis F-filtering for this case, we have, for any measurable set A with $x \notin A$,

$$P_x(A)=\frac{1}{2\text{vol}(B)}\int_{(x+B)\cap A}\min\left\{1,\frac{F(y)}{F(x)}\right\}dy$$
$$=\frac{1}{2\text{vol}(B)}\int_{(x+B)\cap A}\min\left\{\frac{1}{F(y)},\frac{1}{F(x)}\right\}d\mu_F(y).$$

By Lemma 3.5, the measure Q_F is stationary for our Markov scheme. Also note that this Markov scheme is lazy.

Our main goal is to estimate the mixing rate of the F-filtered lazy random walk with B-steps. By the results of Section 1, it suffices to estimate its conductance. Our main result in this section asserts that the conductance of this Markov scheme is determined in a sense by its local conductance.

The main theorem of this section asserts that if the local conductance is large and the "diameter" of K is small, then the (global) conductance is large.

5.1. Theorem. *If the diameter of K is d and the local conductance of $\mathcal{M}(K,B)/F$ is at least t at each point, then its conductance is at least* $\dfrac{t^2}{15\sqrt{n}d}$

This result implies the following estimate on the conductance of the random walk used in the algorithm.

5.2. Corollary. *If K satisfies (A1) and $p\geq 10\sqrt{n}$, then the conductance of $\mathcal{M}(pB,B)/F_K$ is at least* $1/(1000p\sqrt{n})$.

6. Analysis of the volume algorithm

Now we can turn to estimating the error of the algorithm described in paragraph 2. Set

$$W_i=\int_{qB}F_i(x)\,dx.$$

(By Lemma 2.1, integrating over the whole space we would get $\text{vol}(K_i)$.) The error of our estimate ζ comes from three main sources:

I. $W_k\neq\text{vol}(K)$, $W_0\neq\text{vol}(B)$. This is taken care of by

6.1. Lemma.

$$\left(1-\frac{\varepsilon}{4}\right)\text{vol}(K)<\frac{1}{n!}\int_{qB}F(x)dx.$$

II. The **probabilistic error** of our estimate ζ has itself three possible sources:

(E1) The distribution of the points v^i_{t+1} generated in step (c) is not exactly $(1/W_i)Q_{F_i}$.

(E2) The points v^i_{t+1} are not independent.

(E3) The sum used to estimate $\frac{W_{i-1}}{W_i}$ has a standard deviation.

Corollary 3.3 can be used to handle (E1) and (E2), and Theorem 3.4, to handle (E3).

III. **Numerical errors** come from two sources: first, we can compute $\phi(x)$ only approximately and second, we have desribed the algorithm assuming that arithmetic operations with real numbers can be carried out exactly. We compute $\phi(x)$ with absolute error at most ε/n^2; this means a relative error of ε/n^2 in $F_i(x)$, and hence a relative error of ε/n^2 in α_i. Thus this adds up to a relative error of $k\varepsilon/n^2<\varepsilon/10$ in ζ.

To estimate the error coming from the fact that we calculate with finite precision, say, to $100\log n$ bits after the point, observe that the only critical point could be when at a given step we should stay at a given point and the finite precision leads to a decision that we jump, or vice versa. However, in each case, when we first make such an incorrect decision, we have to be so near to the boundary of a K_j that the probability of this is sufficiently small. The details can be found in the complete version.

The **running time** of the Volume Algorithm is clearly dominated by the time needed to carry out the random walk. This takes kt moves, where each move takes the updating of n coordinates, one test of membership in qB, the evaluation of $\phi(x)$, and a constant number of arithmetic operations (where the evaluation of e^x is considered as a single arithmetic operation; else, we need $O(\log n)$ arithmetic operations). To evaluate $\phi(x)$, we find the largest t with $tx\in K$ by binary search with error ε/n^2; this takes $O(\log n+\log(1/\varepsilon))$ membership tests. Thus the algorithm takes $O(t(\log n+\log(1/\varepsilon)))$ membership tests and $O(tn(\log n+\log(1/\varepsilon)))$ arithmetic operations. Ordinarily, a membership test takes at least n arithmetic operations (it has to look at the coordinates), so the running time will be dominated by the membership tests.

If we combine the preliminary part and the main part to a single algorithm, we face an additional difficulty: we have assumed that membership test can be carried out not only for K but also in its affine image $A(K)$ produced by the preliminary part in a single step. This is not justified if we only have an oracle for the original K, since then we have to apply each time the inverse of the affine transformation to get the point to be queried from the oracle. If the membership test takes n^2 or more operations, this is majorized by that. However, for most sensible encodings of K (say, by linear or algebraic inequalities), we can compute a new encoding for the affine image and work with this.

We may also leave K invariant and generate the random steps from an appropriate ellipsoid instead of the unit ball. This would solve the problem with the membership test but would increase the cost of generating the random step to $O(n^2)$, and hence would lead to essentially the same analysis.

7. The difficulty of the diameter

7.1. Theorem. *7.1 (a) Every randomized algorithm that computes an approximation δ of the diameter of a convex body K (given by a well-guaranteed separation oracle) such that*

$$\text{Prob}(\text{diam}(K) \leq \delta \leq n^{1/4}\text{diam}(K)) \geq \frac{2}{3}$$

holds for all $K \subseteq \mathbf{R}^n$, has to make at least $2^{n^{1/4}}$ calls on the oracle.

(b) *Every randomized algorithm that computes an approximation ω of the width of a convex body K (given by a well-guaranteed separation oracle) such that*

$$\text{Prob}(\text{width}(K) \leq \delta < n^{1/4}\text{width}(K)) \geq \frac{2}{3}$$

has to make at least $2^{n^{1/4}}$ calls on the oracle.

The proof (of (b), say) is based on a standard adversary technique, where the adversary chooses either the unit ball B, or B intersected with a random slice of width $n^{1/4}$.

The same argument gives the following. Let $K \subset B$ be a convex body, and set $M = \text{vol}_{n-1}(\partial B)/\text{vol}_{n-1}(\partial B \setminus K)$. Then any randomized polynomial-time oracle algorithm that distinguishes an isometric copy of K (given by a separation oracle) from B with probability at least $2/3$, must make at least $M/3$ calls on the oracle. On the other hand, we can generate $3M$ random points in ∂B and check if they belong to K; this distinguishes K from B with probability at least $2/3$.

References

D. Applegate and R. Kannan (1990): Sampling and integration of near log-concave functions (preprint).

I. Bárány and Z. Füredi (1986): Computing the volume is difficult, *Proc. of the 18th Annual ACM Symposium on Theory of Computing*, pp. 442-447.

G. Brightwell and P. Winkler (1990): Counting linear extensions is #P-complete (Bellcore preprint).

A. Dinghas (1957), Über eine Klasse superadditiver Mengenfunktionale von Brunn–Minkowski–Lusternik-schem Typus, *Math. Zeitschr.* **68**, 111–125.

M. Dyer and A. Frieze (1988): On the complexity of computing the volume of a polytope. *SIAM J. Comp.* **17**, 967–974.

M. Dyer and A. Frieze (1991): Computing the volume of convex bodies: a case where randomness provably helps (preprint).

M. Dyer, A. Frieze and R. Kannan (1989): A Random Polynomial Time Algorithm for Approximating the Volume of Convex Bodies, *Proc. of the 21st Annual ACM Symposium on Theory of Computing*, 375-381.

G. Elekes (1986): A geometric inequality and the complexity of computing volume, *Discrete and Computational Geometry* **1**, 289-292.

M. Grötschel, L. Lovász and A. Schrijver (1988): *Geometric Algorithms and Combinatorial Optimization*, Springer-Verlag.

M. R. Jerrum, L. G. Valiant and V. V. Vazirani (1986): Random generation of combinatorial structures from a uniform distribution, *Theoretical Computer Science* **43**, 169–188.

L. G. Khachiyan (1988): On the complexity of computing the volume of a polytope. *Izvestia Akad. Nauk SSSR, Engineering Cybernetics* **3**, 216–217.

L. G. Khachiyan (1989): The problem of computing the volume of polytopes is NP-hard. *Uspekhi Mat. Nauk 44*, 199-200.

H. W. Lenstra, Jr. (1983), Integer programming with a fixed number of variables, *Oper. Res.* **8**, 538–548.

L. Lovász (1992): How to compute the volume? *Jber. d. Dt. Math.-Verein., Jubiläumstagung 1990,* B. G. Teubner, Stuttgart, 138–151.

L. Lovász and M. Simonovits (1990): Mixing rate of Markov chains, an isoperimetric inequality, and computing the volume. *Proc. 31st Annual Symp. on Found. of Computer Science*, IEEE Computer Soc., 346–355.

L. Lovász and M. Simonovits (1991): Random walks in a convex body and an improved volume algorithm (preprint, Math. Inst. Hung. Acad. Sci. No. 1/1992).

N. Metropolis et al: Equation of state calculation by fast computing machines, *J. Chem. Physics* **21** (1953) 1087–1092.

L. E. Payne and H. F. Weinberger (1960): An optimal Poincaré inequality for convex domains, *Arch. Rat. mech. Anal.* **5**, 286–292.

A. Prékopa (1971), Logarithmic concave measures with applications to stochastic programming, *Acta Sci. Math. Szeged.* **32** 301–316.

A. Prékopa (1973), On logarithmic concave measures and functions, *Acta Sci. Math. Szeged.* **34**, 335-343.

A. Sinclair and M. Jerrum (1988): Conductance and the rapid mixing property for Markov chains: the approximation of the permanent resolved, *Proc. 20th ACM STOC*, pp. 235–244.

Tuesday

October 27, 1992

Apple Tasting and Nearly One-Sided Learning

David P. Helmbold — Computer Science, U.C. Santa Cruz, Santa Cruz, CA 95064

Nicholas Littlestone — NEC Research Institute, 4 Independence Way, Princeton, NJ 08540

Philip M. Long — IGI, Technische Universitaet Graz, Klosterwiesgasse 32/2, A-8010 Graz, Austria

Abstract

In the standard on-line model the learning algorithm tries to minimize the total number of mistakes made in a series of trials. On each trial the learner sees an instance, either accepts or rejects that instance, and then is told the appropriate response. We define a natural variant of this model ("apple tasting") where the learner gets feedback only when the instance is accepted. We use two transformations to relate the apple tasting model to an enhanced standard model where false acceptances are counted separately from false rejections. We present a strategy for trading between false acceptances and false rejections in the standard model. From one perspective this strategy is exactly optimal, including constants. We apply our results to obtain a good general purpose apple tasting algorithm as well as nearly optimal apple tasting algorithms for a variety of standard classes, such as conjunctions and disjunctions of n boolean variables. We also present and analyze a simpler transformation useful when the instances are drawn at random rather than selected by an adversary.

1 Introduction

Consider the task of learning to visually identify tasty apples. We suppose that the learner encounters apples one by one, and decides whether or not to sample each apple. (For the purpose of this paper, we suppose that a final decision about each apple must be made before the next apple is encountered.) The goal is to avoid sampling too many bad apples and to avoid missing too many good apples. Let us say that an apple that is sampled has been *accepted.* We call each acceptance of a bad apple and each rejection of a good apple a mistake and attempt to keep the number of mistakes small. This is similar to the on-line learning task that has been considered by a variety of researchers in computational learning theory [1] [4] [3] [5] [9] [10] [11] [12] [13] [14] [15]. As in that task, learning can be thought of as proceeding in a sequence of trials. In each trial, first the learner observes an object, situation, or event—we call the observation an *instance.* Next the learner makes a prediction of the correct classification of the instance. (Equivalently, in this paper, we will sometimes speak of the learner accepting or rejecting the instance.) In the standard on-line model, the learner is assumed to receive a label indicating the correct classification of the instance at the end of each trial (this label may be corrupted) [11, 12]. By contrast, here we consider a model in which the learner only receives information about the correct classification if the learner chooses the accept action. Thus in this model, unlike in the standard model, the classification information received by the learner is directly controlled by the action of the learner. If there are instances that the learner thinks, with some uncertainty, are bad, then the learner may need to accept such instances just to learn more about them. This model contains a trade-off, sometimes referred to as the exploration-exploitation trade-off, that is absent in the standard on-line model. We refer to the model that we consider here as the *apple tasting model.*

This can be formalized using the language of decision theory (c.f., [2]) as follows. We assume that at each trial the learner suffers a loss that depends on the learner's action and the category of the instance as in the following loss matrix (where $a < b < c$):

	good	bad
accept	a	c
reject	b	b

and the learner desires to achieve small loss. We assume that the learner knows the loss matrix, and that at the end of each trial the learner learns the value of the loss incurred in that trial. This provides information about the classification of the instance if the learner's action was accept, but not if it was reject.

0-8186-2900-2/92 $3.00 © 1992 IEEE

We measure the learner's total loss on a sequence of trials by simply summing the per-trial losses. The least loss that the learner can achieve on a good instance is a and on a bad instance is b. The *regret* of the learner on a particular trial is the amount by which the loss incurred exceeds the best possible. The total regret, the amount by which the total loss exceeds the best possible (for a given sequence of instances and classifications), is easily seen to be just the sum of the per-trial regrets. For the loss matrix given above, the per trial regrets are given by the following regret matrix:

	good	bad
accept	0	$c-b$
reject	$b-a$	0

Suppose that the instances are each chosen from some domain X. We assume that for any particular learning task that we consider there exists some target function $f : X \rightarrow \{0,1\}$ such that an instance x is good if and only if $f(x) = 1$. We look for algorithms that are able to do well for arbitrary target functions chosen from particular target classes and arbitrary sequences of instances from X. It will turn out that frequently the total regret will grow with the number of trials. If we fix the number of trials and a target class, then we can define an optimal algorithm to be one that minimizes the maximum total regret, where the maximum is over all sequences of instances of the chosen length, and over all target functions from the chosen class. In the terminology of decision theory, this is a *minimax regret* strategy. We will consider randomized apple tasting algorithms. For these we will look at expected regret, and attempt to minimize the maximum expected regret. In this paper, we will focus our attention on the case in which $b-a = c-b$, and we may assume that both quantities are 1 without further loss of generality. Nevertheless, our techniques appear to generalize easily to the case in which $b-a \neq c-b$.

This model represents but one of a variety of possible modifications of the standard on-line learning model that seem likely to be important in practice. The study of this model can be viewed partly as the first step of an investigation to see to what extent previous results from computational learning theory carry over to these models and to what extent new research is needed. We show that simple generally applicable transformations of existing algorithms for the standard on-line model yield bounds in the apple tasting model that are in some cases close to the best possible. However, the best apple tasting bounds that we obtain require more work. Existing research concerning the standard mistake-bound model has typically lumped the two types of mistakes (corresponding to accepting the bad and rejecting the good) together, counting them as equally costly. Because in the apple tasting model the learner does not receive immediate feedback regarding mistakes involving rejecting the good, it can help to start with algorithms (for the standard on-line model) that make a small number of mistakes of this type at the expense of a large number of mistakes of the other type. In Section 4 we consider the standard model, in which the learner is told the correct label at the end of each trial, and study the trade-off in the number of mistakes of the two types. From these we obtain upper bounds for the apple tasting model that for some target classes are nearly optimal. These results may be useful for obtaining results regarding other learning models as well.

There are many variants and extensions of this model that it would be interesting to study. One variant considered in Section 6 assumes that the sequence of instances is generated by independent random draws from some distribution on the domain. Another example (not considered here) is a common extension of this model and bandit processes. If one considers the case that the domain X is of size 1 and the classification is stochastic, then we have a kind of bandit process. (This can be thought of as modeling the case that the instances are indistinguishable to the learner, except via the loss they lead to if they are accepted, and they are presented to the learner in random order.) By extending our model to allow the classification to depend stochastically on the instance, we get a model with some of the flavor of bandit processes.

Recall that the standard model differs from the apple tasting model by giving the algorithm feedback after each prediction – even rejected instances. Another difference, convenient for proving lower bounds, is that we consider only deterministic algorithms for the standard model, while algorithms in the apple tasting model have access to a source of randomness.

Our apple tasting results are based on two simple transformations. The first transformation converts any algorithm for the standard on-line, mistake bounded model into an apple tasting algorithm. If M_+ is a bound on the number of false positives and M_- bounds the number of false negatives made by the original algorithm, then the expected number of mistakes made by the resulting apple tasting algorithm on any sequence of $T \geq M_-$ trials is at most $M_+ - M_- + 2\sqrt{TM_-}$ (see Theorem 1).

The second transformation converts any apple tasting algorithm into a (deterministic) algorithm in the standard model. This transformation is used to obtain lower bounds on problems in the apple tasting model, and is of added interest because it uses results for deterministic algorithms to bound the performance of randomized algorithms. Using the second transformation, we show that if each algorithm in the standard model can be forced to make *either* M_+ false positive mistakes *or* M_- false negative mistakes, then every algorithm in the apple tasting model expects to make at least $\frac{1}{2}\min\{M_+, M_- \left\lfloor \frac{T}{M_-+M_+-1} \right\rfloor\}$ mistakes on some sequences of T trials (Lemma 4). Further analysis gives a lower bound on the (worst case) expected number of apple tasting mistakes which is (discounting a short initial interval) $\frac{1}{2}\min\{M_+, \frac{1}{2}\sqrt{M_-T}\}$ (Theorem 5). It is worth emphasizing that these lower bounds hold for any M_+,M_- pair such that each algorithm in the standard model makes either at least M_+ false positives or at least M_- false negative mistakes on some sequence of trials.

One of the interesting features of the apple tasting model is the dependence of the bounds on T, the number of trials. In the standard model, algorithms can be forced to make all of their mistakes on the first trials [11]. The $\sqrt{T}$ factors in our bounds indicate that this is not the case in the apple tasting model. For example, for the class of all subsets of at most k elements of an n element set, the apple tasting complexity (expected number of mistakes of the best algorithm) makes phase transitions, growing linearly for short time, then roughly as $\sqrt{T}$ until it reaches its maximum value of $n - k$. In general, this maximum value is within a constant factor of the minimum number of false positive mistakes that can be made (in the standard model) by an algorithm which makes no false negative mistakes, and furthermore, the expected number of mistakes made by any apple tasting algorithm must grow at least proportionally to $\sqrt{T}$ until this maximum is reached (Theorem 6). This $\sqrt{T}$ behavior persists for at least some concept classes even when the instance sequence is drawn at random rather than being selected by an adversary (Theorem 16).

We will show in the full paper that any algorithm for learning conjunctions which never makes a false negative mistake can be forced to make exponentially many false positive mistakes. Thus, for conjunctions, the upper bound of $O(n + \sqrt{Tn})$ obtained by applying our transformation to the standard algorithms for learning conjunctions [17, 10] is somewhat comforting when T is moderately small.

For the most effective application of these transformation results, one must understand how algorithms for the standard model can trade off false negatives and false positives. We present a sequence of generic algorithms, A_0, A_1, ..., where each A_k makes at most k false negatives when learning any finite concept class $\mathcal{F}$ in the standard model. The number of false positive mistakes made by A_k is bounded by $\lfloor \psi_{k+1}^{-1}(|\mathcal{F}|) \rfloor$ where $\psi_k(n)$ is the binomial coefficient $\binom{n+k}{k}$ (Theorem 10 and Definition 7). This result can also be phrased as follows: for any finite concept class $\mathcal{F}$ and any nonnegative integers k and l such that $\binom{l+k+2}{k+1} > |\mathcal{F}|$, A_k makes at most k false negative mistakes, and at most l false positive mistakes. Note that this is symmetric in k and l, as one would expect.

These generic algorithms make the best possible false-positive to false-negative tradeoffs for some natural classes. Theorem 11 shows that any algorithm which makes at most k false negative mistakes when learning SVAR$_n$ (the set of n functions defined on $\{0,1\}^n$ by $f_i(\vec{x}) = x_i$) can be forced to make at least $\lfloor \psi_{k+1}^{-1}(n) \rfloor$ false positive mistakes. Surprisingly, this lower bound *exactly* matches the upper bound given by our generic algorithms. These results on trading off false-positives and false-negatives are of independent interest, in addition to their apple tasting application. We are currently working on generalizing these results [8].

By converting the generic algorithms, we obtain a general result showing that there is an apple tasting algorithm for any concept class $\mathcal{F}$ which, for any $\epsilon > 0$, expects to make $O\left(\min\left\{|\mathcal{F}|, \sqrt{T}\left(\frac{\ln|\mathcal{F}|}{\ln\sqrt{T}}\right)^{1/2+\epsilon}\right\}\right)$ mistakes on any sequence of T trials (Theorem 13).

We use the techniques described above to obtain upper and lower bounds on the apple tasting complexity for a variety of standard concept classes. These results are summarized in Table 1, and are often tight to within small constant factors.

2 Preliminaries

If X is a set and D is a probability distribution over X, we denote the expectation of $\phi : X \to \mathbf{R}$ with respect to D by $\mathbf{E}_{x\in D}(\phi(x))$ and we define $\mathbf{Pr}_{x\in D}$ analogously. We will assume throughout that X is finite. The results also apply to infinite domains if suitable measurability and computability assumptions are made.

Choose a set X. Let f be a function from X to $\{0,1\}$. An *example* for f is either the pair $(x, f(x))$ or just $(x, *)$, where $x \in X$ and $*$ is intended to mean that the value of the hidden function was not obtained. A sample is a finite sequence of examples. A function g is *consistent* with a sample if for each (x, ρ) in the sample for which $\rho \neq *$, $g(x) = \rho$. We denote the set of samples by $\mathcal{S}$. A *learning algorithm* A is a computable function from $\mathcal{S} \times X \times [0,1]^\infty$ to $\{0,1\}$. That is, given a sample, an element x of X and a source of numbers in $[0,1]$, A outputs an element of $\{0,1\}$, which might be interpreted as a prediction of $f(x)$. Elements of the infinite sequence that is the final argument of A will be generated one by one independently at random as needed by A. We are particularly interested in the random source R which generates numbers by sampling from the uniform distribution on $[0,1]$. We assume that R takes unit time to generate each random number. If $\sigma = \langle x_t \rangle_{t=1}^T$ is a sequence of elements of X, f is a function from X to $\{0,1\}$, A is a learning algorithm, we define $\langle \lambda_t \rangle_{t=1}^T$ and $\langle \rho_t \rangle_{t=1}^T$ inductively as follows:

- $\lambda_1 = A(\emptyset, x_1, R)$
- $\rho_1 = \begin{cases} f(x_1) & \text{if } \lambda_1 = 1 \\ * & \text{otherwise} \end{cases}$
- $\lambda_t = A(((x_1, \rho_1), ..., (x_{t-1}, \rho_{t-1})), x_t, R)$
- $\rho_t = \begin{cases} f(x_t) & \text{if } \lambda_t = 1 \\ * & \text{otherwise.} \end{cases}$

Note that the dependence of the λ_t's and the ρ_t's on σ, f and the outputs of R is not explicitly written in the notation, as their values can be understood from context throughout the paper. The apple tasting performance of A on σ and f, written as $\mathrm{AL}(A, \sigma, f)$, is defined by

$$\mathrm{AL}(A, \sigma, f) = \mathbf{E}(|\{t : \lambda_t \neq f(x_t)\}|)$$

where the expectation is over the outputs of R. We denote the worst case performance for an algorithm A learning a function from class $\mathcal{F}$ of functions from X to $\{0,1\}$ on a sequence of T inputs by

$$\mathrm{AL}(A, \mathcal{F}, T) = \sup_{f \in \mathcal{F}, \sigma \in X^T} \mathrm{AL}(A, \sigma, f).$$

Finally, we define the apple tasting learning complexity (analogous to standard learning complexity [14]) of $\mathcal{F}$ on sequences of T trials as

$$\mathrm{ALC}(\mathcal{F}, T) = \inf_A \mathrm{AL}(A, \mathcal{F}, T).$$

Note that the above definition allows a different algorithm for each T, and therefore, loosely speaking, we might view our apple tasting algorithms as "knowing" T. The need for this knowledge can be removed through application of standard doubling techniques.

We will make use of algorithms which get the value of $f(x_t)$ on each trial as subroutines for our apple tasting algorithms. We believe that results derived for our subroutine algorithms are of independent interest. Throughout, we will refer to the model in which the value of the hidden function is always received as the *standard model*. We develop here a notation for this model. If A maps $\mathcal{S} \times X$ to $\{0,1\}$ and σ is as above, define $\langle \xi_t \rangle_{t=1}^T$ as:

- $\xi_1 = A(\emptyset, x_1)$.
- $\xi_t = A(((x_1, f(x_1)), ..., (x_{t-1}, f(x_{t-1}))), x_t)$.

If $\xi_t = 1$ we say interchangeably that in trial t the algorithm: predicts 1; makes a positive prediction; or accepts the instance (the same terminology is used for λ_t). If in addition $f(x_t) = 0$, we say that the algorithm makes a false positive mistake. Analogous definitions are made for negative predictions (rejections).

Note that we require the standard model algorithm to be deterministic as it is is not given a source of random numbers. This will be useful in proving lower bounds. Continuing, let

$$\mathrm{L}_+(A, \sigma, f) = |\{t : \xi_t = 1 \text{ and } f(x_t) = 0\}|$$
$$\mathrm{L}_-(A, \sigma, f) = |\{t : \xi_t = 0 \text{ and } f(x_t) = 1\}|$$
$$\mathrm{L}_+(A, \mathcal{F}) = \sup_{\sigma, f \in \mathcal{F}} L_+(A, \sigma, f)$$
$$\mathrm{L}_-(A, \mathcal{F}) = \sup_{\sigma, f \in \mathcal{F}} L_-(A, \sigma, f)$$
$$\mathrm{L}_+^k(\mathcal{F}) = \inf_{A: L_-(A,\mathcal{F}) \leq k} L_+(A, \mathcal{F}).$$

Informally, $\mathrm{L}_+(A, \sigma, f)$ is the number of false positive mistakes made by A learning f with σ, $\mathrm{L}_-(A, \sigma, f)$ is the number of false negative mistakes, and $L_+^k(\mathcal{F})$ is the best bound on the number of false positive mistakes obtainable by an algorithm which makes at most k false negative mistakes.

3 Transformations

In this section, we show how, given an algorithm A which trades between $\mathrm{L}_+(A, \mathcal{F})$ and $\mathrm{L}_-(A, \mathcal{F})$ appropriately, we may obtain an algorithm B that is good for apple tasting. We also demonstrate how to use a good apple tasting algorithm to obtain a good learning algorithm for the standard mistake-bound model. The latter transformation is useful for proving lower bounds in the apple tasting model.

Theorem 1 *Let X be a finite set, and let $\mathcal{F}$ be a class of functions from X to $\{0,1\}$. Suppose A is a learning algorithm for which $L_+(A, \mathcal{F}) \leq M_+$ and $L_-(A, \mathcal{F}) \leq M_-$. Then there is a learning algorithm B such that for all nonnegative integers $T \geq M_-$,*

$$AL(B, \mathcal{F}, T) \leq M_+ - M_- + 2\sqrt{TM_-}.$$

Proof: We form the algorithm B as follows. On the tth trial:

- B receives x_t and passes it on to A.
- A predicts ξ_t.
- B calls R obtaining $r \in [0,1]$ and predicts

$$\lambda_t = \begin{cases} 1 & \text{if } \xi_t = 1 \text{ or } \xi_t = 0 \text{ and } r \leq \sqrt{M_-/T} \\ 0 & \text{otherwise.} \end{cases}$$

- If $\lambda_t = 0$, then, loosely speaking, A acts as if this trial never happened, i.e., A's future predictions will be functions only of the subsequence of trials in which reinforcement was received. Otherwise B receives $f(x_t)$ from the environment and passes it on to A.

Choose $T \geq M_-$, $f \in \mathcal{F}$ and a sequence $x_1, ..., x_T$ in X^T. Consider a fixed sequence of numbers generated by R and divide up the trials into classes, where the class of the tth trial depends on A's prediction ξ_t, B's prediction λ_t, and $f(x_t)$. For each $\vec{b} \in \{0,1\}^3$, let

$$S_{\vec{b}} = \{t : \xi_t = b_1, \lambda_t = b_2, f(x_t) = b_3\}.$$

Note that the $S_{\vec{b}}$'s are functions of the random numbers generated by R, which for now have been fixed. From the definition of B, $|S_{1,0,0}| = |S_{1,0,1}| = 0$. Thus,

$$\begin{aligned} \mathrm{AL}(B, \sigma, f) &= \mathbf{E}(|S_{1,1,0}| + |S_{0,1,0}| + |S_{0,0,1}|) \\ &\leq M_+ + \mathbf{E}(|S_{0,1,0}|) + \mathbf{E}(|S_{0,0,1}|) \quad (1) \end{aligned}$$

where the expectations are over the random numbers generated by R.

We can trivially bound $|S_{0,1,0}|$ by the number of times that B changes the prediction made by A, which B does with probability at most $\sqrt{M_-/T}$ on any given trial. Thus,

$$\mathbf{E}(|S_{0,1,0}|) \leq (\sqrt{M_-/T})T = \sqrt{TM_-}. \quad (2)$$

Next, by the bounds on the performance of A, we have that, for all sequences of random bits, $|S_{0,1,1}| \leq M_-$, since A receives $f(x_t)$ for these trials.

Note that $|S_{0,0,1}|$ is at most the number of failures before $|S_{0,1,1}|$ successes in independent Bernoulli trials with probability $\sqrt{M_-/T}$ of success, so (see, e.g. [6]),

$$\mathbf{E}(|S_{0,0,1}|) \leq |S_{0,1,1}|\sqrt{\frac{T}{M_-}} - |S_{0,1,1}| \leq \sqrt{TM_-} - M_-.$$

Combining this with (2) and (1) yields the desired result. □

This trivially yields the following Corollary, in which we remove the restriction that $T \geq M_-$, and record an apple tasting bound in terms of the total number of (standard) mistakes of any kind.

Corollary 2 *Let X be a finite set, and let $\mathcal{F}$ be a class of functions from X to $\{0,1\}$. Suppose A is a learning algorithm for which $L_+(A,\mathcal{F}) \leq M_+$ and $L_-(A,\mathcal{F}) \leq M_-$. Then for all nonnegative integers T the learning algorithm B described in the proof of Theorem 1 has*

$$AL(B, \mathcal{F}, T) \leq M_+ + 2\sqrt{TM_-}.$$

If A makes at most M mistakes of any kind, then the algorithm B' which behaves like B if $T > 20M$ and predicts randomly if $T \leq 20M$ has

$$AL(B', \mathcal{F}, T) \leq \sqrt{5TM} \leq 2.24\sqrt{TM}.$$

Now, we turn to the problem of using lower bounds for standard learning to obtain lower bounds for apple tasting. The following was proved [8] using techniques like those used to prove a similar theorem which doesn't differentiate between positive and negative mistakes [11].

Lemma 3 *Let X be a finite set, $\mathcal{F}$ be a class of functions from X to $\{0,1\}$, and M_-, M_+ be nonnegative integers such that for any algorithm A, either $L_-(A,\mathcal{F}) \geq M_-$ or $L_+(A,\mathcal{F}) \geq M_+$. For each A, there is a sequence σ of $M_+ + M_- - 1$ elements of X and $f \in \mathcal{F}$ such that A predicts incorrectly at every trial and either $L_-(A,\sigma,f) \geq M_-$ or $L_+(A,\sigma,f) \geq M_+$.*

A consequence of Lemma 3 is that if T is at most $\min\{M_+, M_-\}$, then $\mathrm{ALC}(\mathcal{F}, T) \geq T/2$ (the factor of $1/2$ comes in because $\mathrm{ALC}(\mathcal{F}, T)$ permits randomized algorithms where L_- and L_+ do not).

The next lemma forms the basis for our analysis of the transformation. It converts standard model lower bounds which count false positives and false negatives separately into apple tasting lower bounds.

Lemma 4 *Let X be a finite set, and $\mathcal{F}$ be a class of functions from X to $\{0,1\}$. If M_-, M_+ are nonnegative integers such that for any algorithm A, either $L_-(A,\mathcal{F}) \geq M_-$ or $L_+(A,\mathcal{F}) \geq M_+$, then for all nonnegative integers T,*

$$ALC(\mathcal{F}, T) \geq \frac{1}{2}\min\{M_+, M_-\left\lfloor\frac{T}{M_- + M_+ - 1}\right\rfloor\}.$$

Proof: Let $k = \lfloor T/(M_- + M_+ - 1)\rfloor$, $l = M_- + M_+ - 1$.

Suppose B is an apple tasting algorithm. Form a (standard, deterministic) algorithm A from B as follows: $A(((u_1, \rho_1), ..., (u_{t-1}, \rho_{t-1})), u_t)$ is 1 if the following is at least $1/2$:

> The probability (with respect to B's randomization) that if B were presented with the sequence of kt instances consisting of k copies of u_1, followed by k copies of u_2, ..., followed by k copies of u_t, where the feedback after a prediction of 1 on any copy of u_i is ρ_i, algorithm B would predict positively on at least one of the k copies of u_t.

Algorithm A predicts 0 whenever this probability is less than $1/2$.

Let $x_1, ..., x_l \in X, f \in \mathcal{F}$ be such that A either makes M_- false negative or M_+ false positive mistakes on $(x_1, f(x_1)), ..., (x_l, f(x_l))$ (the existence of such a sequence follows from Lemma 3). Form $y_1, ..., y_{kl}$ by letting $y_1, ..., y_k$ equal x_1, letting $y_{k+1}, ..., y_{2k}$ equal x_2, and so on.

Suppose A makes at least M_- false negative mistakes on the sequence $x_1, ..., x_l$. Then, by definition, B expects to make at least $(kM_-/2)$ mistakes, since for any x_t on which A predicts 0, there is probability at least 1/2 that B will never predict 1 on any of the k corresponding y_j's.

Similarly, if A makes at least M_+ false positive mistakes, B expects to make at least $M_+/2$ mistakes.

Since the length kl of the sequence of trials given to B is at most T, this completes the proof. □

Lemmas 3 and 4, together with some straightforward but tedious calculations, yield the following stronger lower bound. Its proof is omitted due to space constraints.

Theorem 5 *Let X be a finite set, $\mathcal{F}$ be a class of functions from X to $\{0,1\}$, and M_-, M_+ be nonnegative integers such that for any algorithm A, either $L_-(A,\mathcal{F}) \geq M_-$ or $L_+(A,\mathcal{F}) \geq M_+$. If $T \leq \min\{M_+, M_-\}$, $ALC(\mathcal{F},T) \geq T/2$. If $T \geq \min\{M_+, M_-\}$,*

$$ALC(\mathcal{F},T) \geq \frac{1}{2}\min\{M_+, \frac{1}{2}\sqrt{M_-T}\}.$$

The following relationship between apple tasting and one-sided learning follows immediately from Corollary 2 and Theorem 5. Recall that $L_+^0(\mathcal{F})$ is the minimum $L_+(A,\mathcal{F})$ over those algorithms A with $L_-(A,\mathcal{F}) = 0$.

Theorem 6 *Choose a finite set X, and a set $\mathcal{F}$ of $\{0,1\}$-valued functions defined on X. Then for all T,*

$$\frac{1}{2}\min\{\sqrt{T}/2, L_+^0(\mathcal{F})\} \leq ALC(\mathcal{F},T) \leq L_+^0(\mathcal{F}).$$

4 Trading optimally between mistakes

Given the results of the previous section, one would like to know how to trade optimally between positive and negative mistakes in the standard mistake bound model, where the algorithm receives the value of the hidden function regardless of its prediction. That is, what is the frontier of the set of pairs (M_-, M_+) of simultaneously obtainable bounds on the number of false negative and false positive mistakes in the standard model. An equivalent question is: for each M_- what is the smallest number M_+ of positive mistakes that can be obtained by an algorithm which makes at most M_- false negative mistakes? In this section, we describe a general-purpose method for making such tradeoffs when the concept class is finite, and describe a sense in which no general-purpose method can improve on that we describe.

We begin with the following definition.

Definition 7 *For each nonnegative integer k, define $\psi_k : \mathbf{R} \rightarrow \mathbf{R}$ by*

$$\psi_k(x) = \binom{x+k}{k} = \prod_{i=1}^{k} \frac{x+i}{i}.$$

Note that $\psi_k(x)$ is increasing when $x > 0$.

We will make use of the following approximations, which are easily verified.

Lemma 8 *For all nonnegative integers n, $k(n^{1/k}/e - 1) \leq \psi_k^{-1}(n) \leq k(n^{1/k} - 1)$.*

Choose a class $\mathcal{F}$ of functions from X to $\{0,1\}$. We will define the sequence $A_0, A_1, ...$ of algorithms where, for each k, A_k makes at most k false negative mistakes.

Suppose $f \in \mathcal{F}$ is the target and $x_1, x_2, ...$ is a sequence of elements of X. For each t, let $\mathcal{F}_t = \{g \in \mathcal{F} : \forall i < t, g(x_i) = f(x_i)\}$. Thus, $\mathcal{F}_t$ is the subset of $\mathcal{F}$ consistent with the first $t-1$ examples.

A_0 predicts 1 on trial t exactly when at least one $g \in \mathcal{F}_t$ has $g(x_t) = 1$.

For $k > 0$, A_k works recursively as follows. While A_k has made no mistakes, A_k predicts 1 exactly when at least $\psi_k(\psi_{k+1}^{-1}(|\mathcal{F}|))$ elements g of $\mathcal{F}$ have $g(x_t) = 1$. As soon as A_k makes a mistake on some trial t, it recursively uses one of the A_i's to learn the class $\mathcal{F}_{t+1}$. If the mistake was a false negative, it uses A_{k-1}; if it was a false positive, it uses A_k.

Note that if the problem of counting the number of hypotheses in $\mathcal{F}$ consistent with a given sample can be solved efficiently, then A_k can be implemented efficiently. Furthermore, if the simpler problem of determining if there exists a member of $\mathcal{F}$ consistent with a given sample can be solved efficiently, then A_0's prediction can be efficiently computed.

We'll need the following technical lemma.

Lemma 9 *For all integers $k \geq 0$ and $n \geq 1$,*

$$\psi_{k+1}^{-1}(n - \psi_k(\psi_{k+1}^{-1}(n))) = \psi_{k+1}^{-1}(n) - 1.$$

Now we are ready to bound the performance of A_k.

Theorem 10 *For all integers $k \geq 0, n \geq 1$, if $|\mathcal{F}| = n$, A_k makes at most $\lfloor \psi_{k+1}^{-1}(n) \rfloor \leq (k+1)(n^{\frac{1}{k+1}} - 1)$ false positive mistakes, and at most k false negative mistakes.*

Proof: Since A_0 never makes a false negative mistake, a trivial induction on k shows that A_k never makes more than k false negative mistakes.

Our proof that A_k makes at most $\lfloor \psi_{k+1}^{-1}(n) \rfloor$ false positive mistakes (where $n = |\mathcal{F}|$) proceeds by double induction on k and n.

If $k = 0$, trivially $1 \leq |\mathcal{F}_{t+1}| < |\mathcal{F}_t|$ on any trial t in which a mistake is made. Thus, the total number of mistakes made by A_0 is at most $n - 1$, which equals $\lfloor \psi_1^{-1}(|\mathcal{F}|) \rfloor$. Furthermore, none of the A_i's ever make a false positive mistake when learning a concept class of cardinality one.

Now, for the induction step, choose $k > 0, n > 1$. Assume as a first case that A_k's first mistake is made on the tth trial and is a false negative mistake. Then $|\mathcal{F}_{t+1}| < \psi_k(\psi_{k+1}^{-1}(n))$, and, by the IH, the number of false positive mistakes made by A_k is at most

$$\psi_k^{-1}(\psi_k(\psi_{k+1}^{-1}(n))) = \psi_{k+1}^{-1}(n).$$

Assume as a second case that A_k's first mistake is a false positive mistake. Then $|\mathcal{F}_{t+1}| \leq n - \psi_k(\psi_{k+1}^{-1}(n))$, and therefore the total number of A_k's false positive mistakes is at most

$$1 + \psi_{k+1}^{-1}(n - \psi_k(\psi_{k+1}^{-1}(n))) = \psi_{k+1}^{-1}(n),$$

by Lemma 9. This completes the proof. □

Next we show that the above general-purpose algorithm is, in a certain sense, optimal. The proof is omitted due to space constraints.

Theorem 11 *For each nonnegative integer n, there is a finite set X, and a class $\mathcal{F}$ of n functions from X to $\{0,1\}$ such that, for any learning algorithm A if $L_-(A, \mathcal{F}) \leq k$, then $L_+(A, \mathcal{F}) \geq \lfloor \psi_{k+1}^{-1}(n) \rfloor \geq (k+1)((1/e)n^{\frac{1}{k+1}} - 1) - 1$.*

We may combine Theorem 10 and Theorem 11 to obtain the following summary of this section.

Corollary 12 *Choose integers $k, l \geq 0, n \geq 1$. The following are equivalent:*

- *For any X and class $\mathcal{F}$ of n functions from X to $\{0,1\}$, there is an algorithm (in the standard model) which makes at most k false negative mistakes and l false positive mistakes,*
- $\binom{l+k+2}{k+1} > n$.

5 Applications

In this section, we give applications of the results of the previous sections to apple tasting problems.

Theorem 13 *Choose a finite set X and a class $\mathcal{F}$ of $\{0,1\}$-valued functions defined on X. Then ALC($\mathcal{F}, T$) is at most the minimum of $|\mathcal{F}| - 1$ and*

$$\left(6.36 + 3.5 \ln\left(1 + \frac{2 \ln |\mathcal{F}|}{\ln T}\right)\right) \sqrt{\frac{2T \ln |\mathcal{F}|}{\ln T}}.$$

Proof outline: The fact that ALC($\mathcal{F}, T$) $\leq |\mathcal{F}| - 1$ follows from Theorem 6. If $T \geq |\mathcal{F}|^2$ then $|\mathcal{F}|$ is less than the other term in the min. Otherwise, we apply Theorem 10. A tricky case analysis based on whether or not $T \leq ((2 \ln |\mathcal{F}|)/(\ln T))^{1+2\epsilon}$ where $\epsilon = \frac{1}{\ln(1 + \frac{2 \ln |\mathcal{F}|}{\ln T})}$ shows that ALC($\mathcal{F}, T$) is at most

$$\left(e/2 + 5 + 3.5 \ln(1 + \frac{2 \ln |\mathcal{F}|}{\ln T})\right) \sqrt{\frac{2T \ln |\mathcal{F}|}{\ln T}},$$

completing the proof. □

By applying Theorem 13, together with Theorem 6 and Theorem 5, we may obtain reasonable bounds on the difficulty of learning in the apple tasting model several natural previously studied concept classes, including:

- The class SVAR$_n$ = $\{f_i : i \leq n\}$ (single variables) of functions of n boolean variables defined by $f_i(\vec{x}) = x_i$,
- The class DIS$_n$ of disjunctions of literals defined on n boolean variables,
- The class MCON$_{k,n}$ of (monotone) conjunctions of k of n boolean variables.
- The class CON$_{k,n}$ of conjunctions of k literals defined on n boolean variables.
- The class STONS$_n$ (singletons) of all functions f from $\{1, ..., n\}$ to 1 such that $|f^{-1}(1)| = 1$,
- The class SMALL$_{k,n}$ of all functions f from $\{1, ..., n\}$ to 1 such that $|f^{-1}(1)| = k$,
- The class INSEG$_n$ of indicator functions for initial segments of $\{1, ..., n\}$, i.e., $\{\{1, ..., k\} : 1 \leq k \leq n\}$.

These results are sketched in Table 1. A variety of ad-hoc arguments can be used to establish lower bounds for these classes. Our best lower bounds are also listed in Table 1. The proofs of these upper and lower bounds will appear in the full paper.

6 Apple Tasting and Random Draws

In this section we consider the apple tasting problem where an adversary picks a distribution from which the instances are drawn rather than selecting the sequence of instances directly. We first give a simple way to convert standard algorithms into apple tasting algorithms. Instead of using mistake-bounded algorithms, this conversion uses standard algorithms having low probability of error. The resulting apple tasting algorithms have expected mistake bounds that grow with $\sqrt{T}$, as before. To get this bound, however, we use a standard algorithm which is not in

$\mathcal{F}$	Efficient Algorithm	Inefficient Algorithm	Main Lower Bound Term	$\lvert\mathcal{F}\rvert$	$L_+^0(\mathcal{F})$
SVAR_n	$(7+4\ln(1+\frac{2\ln n}{\ln T}))\sqrt{\frac{2T\ln n}{\ln T}}$	$(7+4\ln(1+\frac{2\ln n}{\ln T}))\sqrt{\frac{2T\ln n}{\ln T}}$	$\frac{1}{4}\max\{\sqrt{T\left\lfloor\frac{\ln n}{1+\ln(\sqrt{T}+1)}\right\rfloor},\sqrt{T}\}$	n	$n-1$
DIS_n	$n+1$	$n+1$	$\frac{n+1}{2}$	3^n	$n+1$
$\mathrm{MCON}_{k,n}$	$2.24\sqrt{ekT(1+\ln(n/k))}$	$\left(7+4\ln\left(1+\frac{2k\ln(en/k)}{\ln T}\right)\right)\sqrt{\frac{2kT\ln(en/k)}{\ln T}}$	$\frac{1}{4}\max\{(\sqrt{k}-\frac{1}{2})(\sqrt{T\left\lfloor\frac{\ln\lfloor n/k\rfloor}{1+\ln(\sqrt{T}+1)}\right\rfloor}),\sqrt{T}\}$	$\binom{n}{k}$	$\binom{n}{k}-1$
$\mathrm{CON}_{k,n}$	$2.24\sqrt{ekT(1+\ln(2n/k))}$	$\left(7+4\ln\left(1+\frac{2k\ln(e2n/k)}{\ln T}\right)\right)\sqrt{\frac{2kT\ln(2en/k)}{\ln T}}$	$\frac{1}{4}\max\{(\sqrt{k}-\frac{1}{2})(\sqrt{T\left\lfloor\frac{\ln\lfloor n/k\rfloor}{1+\ln(\sqrt{T}+1)}\right\rfloor}),\sqrt{T}\}$	$2^k\binom{n}{k}$	?
STONS_n	$2\sqrt{T}$	$2\sqrt{T}$	$\frac{1}{4}\sqrt{T}$	n	$n-1$
$\mathrm{SMALL}_{k,n}$	$2\sqrt{kT}$	$2\sqrt{kT}$	$\frac{1}{4}\sqrt{kT}$	$\binom{n}{k}$	$n-k$
INSEG_n	$(7+4\ln(1+\frac{2\ln n}{\ln T}))\sqrt{\frac{2T\ln n}{\ln T}}$	$(7+4\ln(1+\frac{2\ln n}{\ln T}))\sqrt{\frac{2T\ln n}{\ln T}}$	$\frac{1}{4}\max\{\sqrt{T\left\lfloor\frac{\ln n}{1+\ln(\sqrt{T}+1)}\right\rfloor},\sqrt{T}\}\}$	n	$n-1$

Table 1: **Summary of apple tasting results for specific examples of the target class $\mathcal{F}$**

The efficient algorithms all have running times bounded by a polynomial in the total length of the instances seen. For those classes above the double line, each instance has size n and for those classes below the double line, each instance has size $\log n$. The actual lower bounds are given by the formula $\min\{W, L_+^0(\mathcal{F})/2, T/2\}$ where W is the main lower bound term given in the table (for $\mathrm{CON}_{k,n}$ use $\binom{n}{k}-1$ as a lower bound on $L_+^0(\mathcal{F})$).

Similarly, the actual upper bounds that we have obtained may be obtained by replacing each algorithm's upper bound U with $\min\{U, L_+^0(\mathcal{F}), T/2\}$, except for the efficient $\mathrm{CON}_{k,n}$ and $\mathrm{MCON}_{k,n}$ algorithms. Our upper bounds for these two algorithms are $\min\{U, T/2\}$ as the only algorithms that we know for these classes that guarantee the $L_+^0(\mathcal{F})$ bound have running times exponential in k.

The algorithm used to attain a particular upper bound depends on which term of the min applies in a given situation. When the $T/2$ term is least, it suffices to predict based on random coin flips.

When the least term is the bound given in the table, a standard-model algorithm is converted as described in the proof of Theorem 1. The following standard-model algorithms are used: the bounds containing $\ln T$ come from Algorithm A_k described in Section 4. The bound independent of T (for DIS_n) comes from an algorithm making no false-negative mistakes described by Valiant [17]. The efficient algorithm used for $\mathrm{MCON}_{k,n}$ and $\mathrm{CON}_{k,n}$ is Winnow [10]. The bounds for $\mathrm{SMALL}_{k,n}$ and STONS_n come from the algorithm that predicts 1 on points known to be 1, and 0 otherwise.

When the smallest term in the min is $L_+^0(\mathcal{F})$, an algorithm is used that predicts 0 on points that must be 0, and 1 otherwise. This is straightforward except for $\mathrm{MCON}_{k,n}$ and $\mathrm{CON}_{k,n}$ for which we do not have efficient algorithms to achieve this bound.

Additional comments regarding efficient implementation for this case: For SVAR_n, the size of the class is the same as the size of each example, so efficient implementation is trivial. DIS_n is learned with the algorithm already given. For $\mathrm{SMALL}_{k,n}$ and STONS_n an appropriate search tree can be used to recall the points labeled 0 in time $O(\log n)$. For INSEG_n, it suffices to remember the smallest example known to be labeled 0.

general computationally efficient. Thus we mention other standard methods that can sometimes be used to construct efficient apple-tasting algorithms (with somewhat worse bounds).

Our simple conversion fails to take advantage of algorithms that make few false-negative mistakes relative to the number of false-positive mistakes. For some target classes this is of little or no importance—we give lower bounds indicating that the conversion is within a constant factor of optimal for several natural concept classes. Certain other concept classes can be learned in the standard model by algorithms that make no false-negative mistakes. These (standard model) algorithms determine the unique largest $f \in \mathcal{F}$ consistent with the examples and expect to make a number $O(d \ln T)$ mistakes (see [16, 9, 7]). We can easily take full advantage of this fact, obtaining algorithms with bounds that grow as $\ln T$ rather than $\sqrt{T}$. Taking full advantage of the possible trade-offs between false negatives and false positives remains an open problem. The analysis is complicated by the fact that the algorithm only sees the labels of some of the examples, and, under some obvious conversion schemes, these examples are not chosen independently.

Any of the algorithms described in previous sections can still be used under the stronger assumption that the examples are chosen independently at random. If the mistake bounds of a class for adversarially chosen examples are close to the best expected mistake bounds for random examples, then we can use the methods of the previous section to take advantage of the trade-off between false-negative and false-positive mistakes. On the other hand, finite adversarial mistakes bounds cannot be obtained for target classes such as rectangles defined over continuous domains, so the methods of the previous sections cannot be directly applied.

When the instances are drawn at random we use $\mathrm{RALC}(\mathcal{F}, T)$ instead of $\mathrm{ALC}(\mathcal{F}, T)$ to denote the expected total loss. Formally, for a set X, a class $\mathcal{F}$ of $\{0,1\}$-valued functions defined on X, and a probability distribution D on X, we define $\mathrm{RALC}(\mathcal{F}, T)$ to be

$$\inf_{A} \left(\sup_{D, f \in \mathcal{F}} \mathbf{E}_{\sigma \in D^T}(\mathrm{AL}(A, \sigma, f)) \right).$$

The VC-dimension [18] of $\mathcal{F}$ is defined to be the size of the largest set $S = \{s_1, ..., s_k\} \subseteq X$ for which $\{(f(s_1), ..., f(s_k)) : f \in \mathcal{F}\} = \{0,1\}^{|S|}$. We use d to denote the VC-dimension of the class $\mathcal{F}$ under discussion.

The conversion simply samples the first $\sqrt{dT}$ instances (by predicting 1) and uses a normal PAC algorithm to produce a hypothesis with low expected error. This hypothesis is then used to predict on the rest of the examples, ignoring any additional feedback. Standard doubling techniques can be used when T is unknown.

We will make use of the 1-inclusion graph learning strategy given by Haussler, Littlestone, and Warmuth [7]. This algorithm gives a mapping B from sequences of examples to hypotheses such that the expected error of the hypothesis is bounded as described in the following lemma.

Lemma 14 ([7]) *There is a computable mapping B from sequences of elements in $X \times \{0,1\}$ to functions from X to $\{0,1\}$ with the following property. Choose any $f \in \mathcal{F}$. For nonnegative integer T and $\sigma \in X^T$, let $h_{B,\sigma} = B((\sigma_1, f(\sigma_1)), ..., (\sigma_T, f(\sigma_T)))$, then for all probability distributions D on X,*

$$\mathbf{E}_{\sigma \in D^T}(\mathbf{Pr}_{x \in D}(h_{B,\sigma}(x) \neq f(x))) \leq d/(T-1).$$

Using the mapping of Lemma 14 as indicated above yields the following theorem.

Theorem 15 *For any concept class $\mathcal{F}$ of VC-dimension d,*

$$RALC(\mathcal{F}, T) \leq 2\sqrt{dT}.$$

To obtain lower bounds we consider k-STONS$_n$, the class of n^k functions mapping $\{1, 2, \ldots, kn\}$ to $\{0,1\}$ defined as follows. A function f is in k-STONS$_n$ iff for each $i \in \{0, 1, ..., k-1\}$, $|f^{-1}(1) \cap \{in+1, in+2, ..., in+n\}| = 1$. Thus k-STONS$_n$ consists of k copies of STONS$_n$, is a subclass of SMALL$_{k,kn}$, and has VC-dimension k when $n > 1$. The following theorem (whose proof is omitted due to space constraints) shows that there are natural classes $\mathcal{F}$ where $\mathrm{RALC}(\mathcal{F}, T)$ grows as $\sqrt{Td}$.

Theorem 16 *For $n \geq \lfloor \sqrt{T/3k} \rfloor \geq 4$,*

$$RALC(k\text{-}STONS_n, T) \geq \frac{0.15}{\sqrt{3}} \sqrt{Tk}.$$

This lower bound also applies to the class $SMALL_{k,kn}$. Furthermore, k-$STONS_n$ can be embedded in $2k$-dimensional halfspaces and k-dimensional axis-parallel rectangles, so this lower bound also applies to these natural classes.

The bounds of Theorems 16 and 15 match to within a small constant factor for the target classes to which the lower bound applies. Unfortunately, the mapping B of Lemma 14 cannot in general be computed efficiently. We briefly discuss a method for constructing efficient apple tasting algorithms that uses a consistency oracle for the concept class as described in the following lemma.

Lemma 17 **([7])** *Suppose B is a mapping from sequences of elements in $X \times \{0,1\}$ to $\mathcal{F}$ such that the function output by B is consistent with B's input sequence. Choose $f \in \mathcal{F}$. For nonnegative integer T and $\sigma \in X^T$, let $h_{B,\sigma} = B((\sigma_1, f(\sigma_1)), ..., (\sigma_T, f(\sigma_T)))$, then for all probability distributions D on X,*

$$\mathbf{E}_{\sigma \in D^T}(\mathbf{Pr}_{x \in D}(h_{B,\sigma}(x) \neq f(x))) \in O((d/(T-1)) \log(T/d)).$$

We can apply this lemma using the same conversion as above to show that if there is an algorithm which efficiently finds a function in $\mathcal{F}$ consistent with a given sample, then there is an efficient apple-tasting algorithm for $\mathcal{F}$ with an expected mistake bound of $O(\sqrt{dT \log(T/d)})$.

Certain target classes can be effectively learned in the standard on-line model by algorithms that make no false-negative mistakes [16, 9, 7]. As these algorithms are always correct when they predict 0, they can be used without modification as apple tasting algorithms. For such a target class $\mathcal{F}$, RALC($\mathcal{F}, T$) is $O(d \ln T)$. The class INSEG$_n$ (defined in Section 5) is such a class; since it has VC-dimension one, we have RALC(INSEG$_n, T$) is $O(\ln T)$. In contrast, Table 1 shows that ALC(INSEG$_n, T$) is $\Omega(\sqrt{T})$ for $T < n^2$. Thus this class has a vastly improved expected mistake bound when the instances are drawn at random.

In contrast to this case, there are cases in which learning is nearly as hard given independent random examples as it is when an adversary chooses the examples. For example, the lower bounds of Theorem 16 (for randomly drawn examples) nearly match the upper bounds on SMALL$_{k,kn}$ in Table 1 (for adversarial sequences). In particular the dependence on $\sqrt{T}$ seen in the mistake bounds for adversarial sequences also occurs for some classes when the instances are drawn at random.

Acknowledgements

David Helmbold gratefully acknowledges the support of NSF grant CCR-9102635 and Philip Long gratefully acknowledges his UC Santa Cruz Chancellor's dissertation-year fellowship. Nick Littlestone benefited from discussions of this model with Naoki Abe and Avrim Blum.

References

[1] D. Angluin. Queries and concept learning. *Machine Learning*, 2:319–342, 1988.

[2] J. Berger. *Statistical Decision Theory and Bayesian Analysis.* Springer Verlag, 1980.

[3] A. Blum. Learning boolean functions in an infinite attribute space. *Proceedings of the 22nd ACM Symposium on the Theory of Computation*, 1990.

[4] A. Blum. Separating PAC and mistake-bound learning models over the boolean domain. *Proceedings of the 31st Annual Symposium on the Foundations of Computer Science*, 1990.

[5] A. Blum, L. Hellerstein, and N. Littlestone. Learning in the presence of finitely many or infinitely many irrelevant attributes. *The 1991 Workshop on Computational Learning Theory*, 1991.

[6] W. Feller. *An Introduction to Probability and its Applications*, volume 1. John Wiley and Sons, third edition, 1968.

[7] D. Haussler, N. Littlestone, and M. Warmuth. Predicting $\{0,1\}$ functions on randomly drawn points. Technical report, University of California at Santa Cruz, 1990.

[8] D. Helmbold, N. Littlestone, and P. M. Long. On-line learning with linear loss constraints. In preparation, 1992.

[9] D. Helmbold, R. Sloan, and M. Warmuth. Learning nested differences of intersection-closed concept classes. *Machine Learning*, 5:165–196, 1990.

[10] N. Littlestone. Learning quickly when irrelevant attributes abound: a new linear-threshold algorithm. *Machine Learning*, 2:285–318, 1988.

[11] N. Littlestone. *Mistake Bounds and Logarithmic Linear-threshold Learning Algorithms.* PhD thesis, UC Santa Cruz, 1989.

[12] N. Littlestone and M. Warmuth. The weighted majority algorithm. *Proceedings of the 30th Annual Symposium on the Foundations of Computer Science*, 1989.

[13] W. Maass. On-line learning with an oblivious environment and the power of randomization. *The 1991 Workshop on Computational Learning Theory*, pages 167–175, 1991.

[14] W. Maass and G. Turan. On the complexity of learning from counterexamples. *Proceedings of the 30th Annual Symposium on the Foundations of Computer Science*, 1989.

[15] W. Maass and G. Turan. On the complexity of learning from counterexamples and membership queries. *Proceedings of the 31st Annual Symposium on the Foundations of Computer Science*, 1990.

[16] B. Natarajan. Probably approximate learning of sets and functions. *Siam J. Comput.*, 10(2):328–351, 1991.

[17] L. Valiant. A theory of the learnable. *Communications of the ACM*, 27(11):1134–1142, 1984.

[18] V. Vapnik and A. Chervonenkis. On the uniform convergence of relative frequencies of events to their probabilities. *Theory of Probability and its Applications*, 16(2):264–280, 1971.

Reconstructing Algebraic Functions from Mixed Data

Sigal Ar* Richard J. Lipton† Ronitt Rubinfeld‡ Madhu Sudan§

Abstract

We consider the task of reconstructing algebraic functions given by black boxes. Unlike traditional settings, we are interested in black boxes which represent several algebraic functions - $f_1, \ldots, f_k$, where at each input x, the box arbitrarily chooses a subset of $f_1(x), \ldots, f_k(x)$ to output. We show how to reconstruct the functions $f_1, \ldots, f_k$ from the black box. This allows us to *group* the sample points into sets, such that for each set, all outputs to points in the set are from the same algebraic function. Our methods are robust in the presence of errors in the black box. Our model and techniques can be applied in the areas of *computer vision, machine learning, curve fitting and polynomial approximation, self-correcting programs and bivariate polynomial factorization.*

1 Introduction

Suppose you are given a large set of points in the plane and you are told that an overwhelming majority of these points lie on one of k different algebraic curves of degree bound d (but you are not told anything else about the curves). Given the parameters k and d, your task is to determine or "reconstruct" these algebraic curves, or alternatively, to *group* the points into sets, each of which is on the same degree d curve. Related versions of this problem are also of interest, such as extensions to higher dimensions, and a setting where instead of the points being given in advance, one is allowed to make queries of the form "what is the value of one of the curves at point x?"[1]. This problem seems to be fundamental and its solution has a variety of applications:

*Princeton University, Supported by Dept. of Navy Grant #N00014-85-C-0456, by NSF PYI grant CCR-9057486 and a grant from MITL.

†Princeton University. Part of this research was done while at Matsushita Information Technology Labs.

‡Cornell University. Part of this research was done while at Hebrew University and Princeton University and supported by DIMACS, NSF-STC88-09648.

§U.C. Berkeley. Supported in part by NSF Grant No. CCR 88-96202.

[1]The answer to such a query will not specify which of the k curves was used to compute the value.

Computer Vision Consider a computer vision system for a robot that picks parts out of a bin. The input to the system contains an intensity map of the scene. The robot can distinguish between the parts by extracting edges from the image. Current edge detection algorithms use discretised differential operators to extract edges (e.g. [23][9]). These algorithms produce output consisting of a bit map, where for every image point (x, y), the bit value of the point, $e(x, y)$, is set to 1 if and only if this point lies on an edge. For many vision applications it is then desired to connect between neighboring points to achieve a more compact representation of the edge map. This problem, known as "the grouping problem", is complicated by the fact that the parts are cluttered, they may be nonconvex, they may contain holes, and the edges are distributed along the image creating noncontinuous sequences of curves. No polynomial time algorithm has been found for this problem.

Under the assumption that the edges of the parts are given by piecewise algebraic curves, and that the edge detection process produces results which are free of precision error, our algorithm transforms edge maps into piecewise polynomial curves in polynomial time. The second assumption is unrealistic in real computer vision applications. However, we feel that it may be possible to make a simple modification to our algorithm so that it works in a real setting.

Learning Our mechanism can be used to extend some well-known results on learning boolean functions to the setting of learning real-valued functions. Here, we present two specific instances of such situations:

- In the study of economics, the price-demand curve is often considered to be well-described by an algebraic function (e.g. $f(x) = c/x$ or $f(x) = -a \cdot x + b$). However, it is also the case that this curve may change [17]. In particular, there may be several unknown price-demand curves which apply in various situations - one may correspond to the behavior found when the country is at war, another may correspond to typical behavior on a Sunday, a third may apply after a stock market crash, and yet another behavior may be found after a change in the tax structure. Some of the factors that determine which curve applies may be obvious, however others (such as a change in behavior due

0-8186-2900-2/92 $3.00 © 1992 IEEE

to the day of the week) may occur because of more subtle reasons. The task of learning the price-demand relationship may be decomposed into the two subtasks of first determining the unknown curves, and then learning what determines the move from one curve to another. Our algorithm gives a solution for the first task.

- A *polynomial-valued decision list* given by a list of terms (conjuncts of literals), $(D_i)_{i=1}^{k}$ over boolean variables $y_1, \ldots, y_n$, and a list of univariate polynomials, $(f_i)_{i=1}^{k+1}$ in a real variable x, represents a real valued function f as follows:

  $$f(x, y_1, \ldots, y_n) = f_i(x)$$

  (where i is the least index such that $D_i(y_1, \ldots, y_n)$ is true)

  If the terms are restricted to being conjuncts of at most c literals, we call it a *polynomial-valued c-decision list*. This is an extension of the *boolean decision list* model defined by Rivest in [24], where the polynomials f_i are restricted to being the constants 0 or 1.

  In [24], Rivest shows that the class of boolean c-decision lists are learnable in polynomial time under the Valiant model of PAC learning. Using our techniques, in combination with Rivest's algorithm, we can extend this result to show that the class of polynomial-valued c-decision lists can be learned in polynomial time.

In general, our results imply that any function on input x and boolean attributes $(y_1, \ldots, y_m)$ which uses $(y_1, \ldots, y_m)$ to select f_i from a set of polynomial functions $f_1, \ldots, f_k$ and then computes and outputs $f_i(x)$, can be learned, as long as the selector function can be learned.

Independent of our work, Blum and Chalasani [6] also consider a model of learning from examples where the examples may be classified according to one of several different concepts. In their model an adversary controls the decision of which concept would be used to classify the next example. Under this model they study the task of learning boolean-valued concepts such as k-term DNF's and probabilistic decision lists.

Curve Fitting A typical curve fitting problem takes the following form: Given a set of points $\{(x_i, y_i)\}_{i=1}^{t}$ on the plane, give a simple curve that "fits" the given points. Depending on the exact specification of the "fit" the problem takes on different flavors: for instance, if the curve is to pass close to all the points, then this becomes a *uniform approximation* problem [25], while if the curve is supposed to pass through *most* of the points, then it resembles problems from coding theory. Here, we consider a problem that unifies the above two instances over *discrete domains*. For example, given a set of t points, with integral coordinates, we consider the task of finding a polynomial with integer coefficients, so that it is Δ-close to all but an ϵ fraction of the points (if such a polynomial exists), where ϵ need only be less than $1/2$.

Self-Correcting Programs One motivation for this work comes from the area of self-correcting programs introduced independently in [7][21]. For many functions, one can take programs that are known to be correct on *most* inputs and apply a simple transformation to produce a program that is correct with high probability on *each* input. But, how bad can a program be, and still allow for such a transformation? There is previous work addressing this question when the functions in question are polynomials (see for example [21],[10],[11]). The results we achieve apply to polynomials as well as to more general forms of algebraic functions, and subsume the best previously known results.

One particular situation where this is useful is in the computation of the permanent of a matrix, over a finite field. Results of Cai and Hemachandra ([8]), when used in combination with our results, imply that if there is an efficient program which computes the permanent correctly on a non-negligible fraction of the input and computes one of a small number of other algebraic functions on the rest of the inputs, then the permanent can be computed efficiently everywhere.

Factoring Bivariate Polynomials In [4] Berlekamp gave a randomized polynomial time algorithm for factoring univariate polynomials over finite fields. In [18] and [13] it is shown that the problem of bivariate factoring can also be solved in polynomial time by reduction to univariate factoring, using fairly deep methods from algebra. Our techniques give a simple method to reduce the problem of factoring bivariate polynomials to that of factoring univariate polynomials over finite fields in the special case when the bivariate polynomial splits into factors which are monic and of constant degree in one of the variables. Though the results are not new, nor as strong as existing results, the methods are much simpler than those used to obtain the previously known results.

The k-Algebraic Black Box Model

In most of the above situations, the difficulty is in *grouping* the sample points, to determine which sample points are related - i.e. come from the same algebraic function. In order to abstract this, we introduce a black box "reconstruction" problem. The problem may be stated as follows.

> Given a black box B, such that the input/output pairs (x, y) of the black box always satisfy a relationship of the form $Q(x, y) = 0$, where Q is a bivariate polynomial of total degree k, find an algebraic function[2] which describes a relationship between the input and the output on a non-trivial fraction of the points.

We call this new model of a black box a **k-algebraic black box**. This model captures situations where on any given input, the black box may output one or more of the several algebraic functions it represents. As a particular example, $Q(x, y) = \Pi_{1 \le i \le l}(y - f_i(x))$ would mean that the black box chooses to output one (or more) of l different functions $f_1(x), \ldots, f_l(x)$ at every input x (though it is not specified which ones). This is a generalization of the black box model used in [3],[15],[16],[28] and [29], where on input x, the black box outputs $f(x)$ for f polynomial or rational function. While the target we set for our analysis is that we recover at least one function f_i such that many of the y's satisfy $y = f_i(x)$, we can iterate this process, after stripping off points from f_i, to extract the remaining functions as well.

The notion naturally extends to multivariate functions, and we describe it in terms of polynomials and rational functions. In the case of multivariate functions the description of the target polynomial or rational function might be very large. In order to prevent this from requiring too much running time (to produce the output function), we instead reconstruct the function implicitly by giving a *mechanism* to compute it: we give an efficient algorithm, which is allowed to make queries to the black box. Thus our problem here is defined as follows:

> Given a black box B, such that the input $x_1, \ldots, x_n$ and the output y of the black box always satisfy a relationship of the form $Q(x_1, \ldots, x_n, y) = 0$, where Q is an $(n+1)$-variate polynomial of total degree k, find, or provide a mechanism to compute a polynomial or rational function which describes a relationship between the input and the output on a non-trivial fraction of the points.

In addition, for both the univariate and the multivariate cases, we consider extensions to noisy situations: **ϵ-noisy k-algebraic black boxes**, where the black box is allowed to output arbitrary answers on an ϵ fraction of the inputs.

In the case that *all* the l functions, $f_1, \ldots, f_l$, represented by the black box are polynomials of degree at most d, we call the black boxes **(l, d)-polynomial black boxes**, or **ϵ-noisy (l, d)-polynomial black boxes**.

Previous Work and Our Results

The setting where the black box represents a **single** polynomial or rational function, without noise, is the classic interpolation problem and is well studied. Efficient algorithms for sparse multivariate polynomial interpolation are given in [28], [16], [3] and [29], and for sparse rational functions in [15].

The case where the black box represents a single function with some noise has also been studied previously. In [5] it is shown how to reconstruct a univariate polynomial from a $(\frac{1}{2} - \delta)$-noisy 1-polynomial black box and in [10] and [11] it shown how to do the same for multivariate polynomials. Reconstructing functions from a black box representing more than one function seems to be a previously unexplored subject.

Our algorithmic results include the following: We give an efficient algorithm for explicitly reconstructing univariate polynomials and rational functions, over finite fields, $\mathcal{Z}$ and $\mathcal{Q}$, from an ϵ-noisy k-algebraic black box. The only constraint imposed on ϵ is that our algorithm is only guaranteed to find an f_i if the fraction of inputs for which the black box answers according to f_i is more than ϵ. This result is described in Theorem 2 for the case of reconstructing a polynomial, but applies essentially as it is to the case of extracting a rational function. The result can also be extended to the case of other algebraic functions (e.g. $y = \sqrt{f/g}$, with f and g polynomials), while still tolerating a non-negligible fraction of noise[3].

To reconstruct a polynomial, we first construct a bivariate polynomial $Q'(x, y)$ which is zero at **all** the sample points and then use bivariate polynomial factorization to find a factor of the form $(y - f(x))$. If it exists, $f(x)$ then becomes our candidate for output. We then show that if the number of points on f is large in the sample we see, then $y - f(x)$ has to be a factor of any Q' which all the sample points satisfy.

For the general problem of implicitly reconstructing multivariate polynomials, we show how to reconstruct multi-

[2] We use the words "algebraic function" to describe either polynomials or rational functions. Both the notion and our techniques of reconstructing extend to the more general case of algebraic relations where the (x, y) pairs satisfy an *irreducible* polynomial identity.

[3] The fraction of points from the good curve must outweigh the fraction of noise by a multiplicative factor of d where d is the maximum degree of y in the algebraic relation relating x and y - $Q(x, y)$.

variate polynomials (or rational functions) over sufficiently large finite fields, under the same restrictions on noise as in the univariate case. Our technique here is to reduce the multivariate reconstruction problem into a univariate reconstruction problem using a careful sampling technique. We then use the univariate technique described earlier to solve the new univariate problem.

A note about the specific representation of the output in the case of multivariate polynomials: The fact that we only reconstruct the output implicitly should not be considered a weakness, but rather a strength. In the particular case that the target function is a sparse multivariate polynomial, this allows for the reconstruction of a small set of explicitly represented multivariate polynomials, by the interpolation mechanisms of [16],[3],[28] or [15]. On the other hand, by using the techniques of [19] we can also continue to manipulate the black boxes as they are for whatever purposes[4].

Organization The rest of this paper is organized as follows. In Section 2, we describe our results for univariate polynomials. These results, although presented in terms of polynomials, can be applied directly to rational functions and other algebraic functions. In Section 3, we show how to extend our results to multivariate functions. Here too, the results are presented in terms of polynomials. Finally, in Section 4, we describe in more detail some of the applications of our work.

2 Univariate Black Boxes

In this section, we consider the problem of explicitly reconstructing the univariate polynomials $f_1, \ldots, f_k$, each of degree at most d, from a (k, d)-polynomial black box for them. As mentioned earlier, these results apply to rational functions and extend to algebraic functions.

2.1 An Intermediate Model

As an intermediate step towards solution, we assume that the black box outputs *all* of $f_1(x), \ldots, f_k(x)$ on any input x. These are output in arbitrary order, which is not necessarily the same for each x. We further assume that there are no errors in the output. We reduce the problem of extracting the polynomials to that of bivariate polynomial factorization.

If on x the black box outputs $\{y_1, \ldots, y_k\}$, we know that $\forall i,\ 1 \leq i \leq k,\ \exists j,\ 1 \leq j \leq k$ such that $y_i = f_j(x)$. Therefore, one relation satisfied by the input/output of the black box is:

$$\forall (x, y_1, \ldots, y_k)\ \Sigma_i \Pi_j\ (y_i - f_j(x)) = 0$$

We can construct a related polynomial which will enable us to recover the f_j's.

Consider the functions $\sigma_i : F \mapsto F,\ i \in [k]$ defined as

$$\sigma_i(x) \equiv \sum_{S \subset [k], |S|=i} \prod_{j \in S} f_j(x)$$

(these are the *primitive symmetric* functions of $f_1, \ldots, f_k$).

Observe that $\sigma_i(x)$ can be evaluated at any input x using the given (k, d)-polynomial black box (in $O(k \log k)$ time). Observe further that σ_i is a polynomial of degree at most id. Hence evaluating it at $id + 1$ points suffices to find all the coefficients of this polynomial (if the black box outputs every $f_i(x)$ for every x).

Now to find the functions f_j from the functions σ_i, we construct the following polynomial, in x and a new indeterminate y:

$$Q(x, y) = \prod_{j=1}^{k} (y + f_i(x))$$

Observe that Q can also be written as

$$Q(x, y) = y^k + \sigma_1(x) y^{k-1} + \cdots + \sigma_k(x)$$

Thus we can describe Q explicitly (in terms of its coefficients). To recover the f_j's now all we have to do is find the factors of the bivariate polynomial Q. Bivariate factorization can be done efficiently over the rationals ([13], [18], [22]), and can be done efficiently (probabilistically) over finite fields [12],[18].

We have shown the following:

Theorem 1 *Let $f_1, \ldots, f_k$ be degree d polynomials over $\mathcal{Q}$, $\mathcal{Z}$ or a finite field. Given a black box which on input x outputs $\{f_1(x), \ldots, f_k(x)\}$ in arbitrary order, we can reconstruct all the polynomials that it computes with $O(kd + 1)$ queries.*

2.2 Noisy (k, d)-Polynomial Black Boxes

We build on the methods of the previous section to reconstruct information from a (k, d)-polynomial black box

[4]The mechanism of manipulating multivariate polynomials and rational functions represented by black boxes was proposed by Kaltofen and Trager in [19]. They show that it is possible to factor and compute g.c.d.'s for polynomials given by such a representation and to separate the numerator from the denominator of rational functions given by such a representation.

which outputs the value of *one* of k univariate polynomials $f_1, \ldots, f_k$, on every input. Our method extends immediately to the case where the black box sometimes outputs a value corresponding to *none* of the f_i's, an ϵ-noisy (k, d)-polynomial black box, and we present this result directly. The technique used to achieve this also builds on a procedure of Berlekamp and Welch [5], which (in our notation) reconstructs a polynomial from a $(\frac{1}{2} - \delta)$-noisy $(1, d)$-polynomial black box, where δ can be arbitrarily small.

Given an ϵ-noisy (k, d)-polynomial black box B for the polynomials $f_1, \ldots, f_k$, each of degree at most d, over a finite field F, let p_i be defined as

$$p_i \equiv \Pr_{x \in F}[B \text{ outputs } f_i(x) \text{ on input } x].$$

We show that with high probability, we can reconstruct a polynomial f_i from the ϵ-noisy black box B, in time polynomial in k, d and $\frac{1}{p_i - \epsilon}$ provided $p_i > \epsilon$.

Theorem 2 *Let B be an ϵ-noisy (k, d)-polynomial black box representing the polynomials $f_1, \ldots, f_k$ in x over a finite field F ($|F| > O(\max\{k^2 d^2, \frac{1}{(p_1-\epsilon)^2}\})$). If $p_1 > \epsilon$ then (with high probability) a set of at most k polynomials of degree d can be reconstructed from B, such that f_1 is amongst them, with $O(\max\{k^2 d^2, \frac{1}{(p_1-\epsilon)^2}\})$ queries.*

Our problem of reconstructing $f_1, \ldots, f_k$ reduces to the following problem:

Problem 1
Given: *t pairs of points $\{(x_1, y_1), \ldots, (x_t, y_t)\}$, such that there exist polynomials $f_1, \ldots, f_k$ satisfying*
$\forall\, i\; deg(f_i) \leq d$, and for all but l values of $j \in [t]$, $\exists\, i \in [k]$ s.t. $f_i(x_j) = y_j$.
(l is the number of noise points in our sample.)

Problem: *Find $f_1, \ldots, f_k$.*

Let S_i be the subset of the indices $j \in [t]$ such that $y_j = f_i(x_j)$ and let E be the set of indices of the error points, i.e., $E = [t] \setminus (\cup_{i=1}^{k} S_i)$. (By our definition $|E| = l$.)

For every index $j \in S_i$, we have $y_j - f_i(x_j) = 0$. Thus for indices $j \notin E$ we have

$$(y_j - f_1(x_j)) * \cdots * (y_j - f_k(x_j)) = 0$$

We can construct a polynomial W, of degree at most l, such that $W \not\equiv 0$, but for all indices $j \in E$, $W(x_j) = 0$. W is simply the polynomial $W(x) = \prod_{j \in E}(x - x_j)$.

Thus we get

$$\forall j \in [t], \quad W(x_j) * (y_j - f_1(x_j)) * \cdots * (y_j - f_k(x_j)) = 0$$

Expanding the product above to represent it as a polynomial in y, we see that there are polynomials in x, $A_0, \ldots, A_k$, $deg(A_m) \leq l + m * d$, $A_0 \not\equiv 0$, s.t.

$$\forall\, j \in [t], \; A_0(x_j) * y_j^k + A_1(x_j) * y_j^{k-1} + \cdots + A_k(x_j) = 0$$

We now consider the following problem:

Problem 2
Given: *t pairs of points $\{(x_1, y_1), \ldots, (x_t, y_t)\}$, and given d, and l, such that there exist polynomials $A_0, \ldots, A_k$, $A_0 \not\equiv 0$, $deg(A_m) \leq l + m * d$, and*

$$\forall\, j \in [t], \quad \sum_{m=0}^{k} A_m(x_j) * y_j^{k-m} = 0$$

Problem: *Find $A_0, \ldots, A_k$.*

We can obtain a solution to Problem 2 by substituting unknowns for the coefficients of the A_m's and solving the linear system of equations that is obtained by the constraints of the problem statement above. If the solution to Problem 2 were known to be unique, then by factoring the bivariate polynomial $Q(x, y)$, defined as

$$Q(x, y) \equiv \sum_{m=0}^{k} A_m(x) * y^{k-m} \qquad (1)$$

we could get a solution to problem 1. (Notice that $Q(x, y)$ is effectively the same here as in Section 2.1 except that it is multiplied by a factor of $W(x)$ here.)

Unfortunately, the solution to Problem 2 might not be unique and the particular solution to Problem 2 that we may end up finding could be one that will not yield a solution to Problem 1. The following lemma guarantees that under certain constraints on the sizes of the sets $S_1, \ldots, S_k$, the solution to Problem 2 satisfies invariants which guarantee a unique solution to Problem 1.

Lemma 1 *If $|S_i| > kd + l$ then $(y - f_i(x)) \mid Q(x, y)$*

Proof: Consider the univariate polynomial $Q_i(x) \equiv Q(x, f_i(x))$.

For all indices $j \in S_i$ we have that $Q_i(x_j) = 0$. But $Q_i(x)$ is a polynomial of degree at most $kd + l$ in x and hence if it is zero at $|S_i| > kd + l$ places, then it must be identically zero, implying that $(y - f_i(x)) | Q(x, y)$ □

The lemma above guarantees that under certain circumstances, the factors of $Q(x, y)$ do give us useful information about the f_i's, leading us to the proof of the theorem:

Proof: [of Theorem 2] We sample from the black box $t = O(\max\{k^2 d^2, \frac{1}{(p_1-\epsilon)^2}\})$ times and then solve for the polynomial Q as defined in Equation 1. We find all the factors of Q that are linear and monic factors in y and output the set of polynomials $g(x)$ such that $(y - g(x)) | Q(x, y)$.

By Lemma 1 the output set will include f_1 if $|S_1| > kd + |E|$. By using Chernoff bounds we can show that, if the x_j's are picked independently and at random then

$$\Pr\left[(|S_1| < p_1 t - c\sqrt{t}) \text{ or } |E| > \epsilon t + c\sqrt{t}\right] < 2e^{-c^2/2}$$

Thus if $t = \Theta(\max\{k^2 d^2, \frac{1}{(p_1-\epsilon)^2}\})$, we have that with high probability $|S_1| > kd + |E|$ and hence our algorithm performs correctly. □

3 Multivariate Black Boxes

In this section, we extend Theorem 2 to multivariate polynomial black boxes over finite fields. Once again, we note that this extends to more general cases. The methods of Section 2 do not seem to extend directly to the general multivariate case. This is due to the possibly large *explicit* representation of the function extracted from the black box, which makes it inefficient to work with. Instead, we use techniques of pairwise independent sampling to reduce the problem to a univariate situation and then apply Theorem 2 to the new univariate problem.

Theorem 3 *Given an ϵ-noisy (k, d)-polynomial black box in n variables $x_1, \ldots, x_n$ over a sufficiently large finite field F ($|F| > \max\{4k^2d^2, \frac{1}{(p-\epsilon)^2}\}$) a black box representation of a polynomial f, which describes the output of the black box on a fraction p ($p > \epsilon$) of the input space, can be constructed in time polynomial in k, d, n and $\frac{1}{p-\epsilon}$, if such a polynomial exists.*

Proof (sketch): Fix any candidate polynomial f which describes the output of the black box on a fraction p of the input space. We show how to reconstruct a small set of polynomials which includes f.

We use the techniques of [1] and [11] to probabilistically construct a small subdomain D of F^n, parameterized by x, such that the following properties hold:

1. D contains any two given points $\hat{a}$ and $\hat{b}$. (In particular, we can ensure $D(0) = \hat{a}$ and $D(1) = \hat{b}$.)
2. Over the domain D, the polynomial $Q(x_1, \ldots, x_n, y)$ can be expressed as a bivariate polynomial in x, y i.e., the function $Q^D(x, y) = Q(D(x), y)$ is a bivariate polynomial.
3. D resembles a randomly and independently chosen sample of F^n of size $|D|$. In particular, with high probability, the fraction of points **from** D where the black box responds with $f(x_1, \ldots, x_n)$, is very close to the fraction of points **from** F^n where the black box responds with f.

D can be constructed by substituting random cubic equations in x for each variable, x_i. The construction works for large finite fields. The details of such constructions are standard and omitted here. A description of a similar construction appears for example in [11].

Claim 2 *For any two points $\hat{a}, \hat{b} \in F^n$, given a domain D containing $\hat{a}$ and $\hat{b}$ with properties (2) and (3) listed above, a set $\{(f_1(\hat{a}), f_1(\hat{b})), \ldots, (f_l(\hat{a}), f_l(\hat{b}))\}$ of values can be reconstructed efficiently such that for some i, $1 \le i \le l$, $f_i(\hat{a}) = f(\hat{a})$ and $f_i(\hat{b}) = f(\hat{b})$.*

Proof: Reconstruct l ($l \le k$) univariate polynomials $f_1^D, \ldots, f_l^D$, in x, that represent all the candidates for f restricted to the domain D. Due to Property (3) and Theorem 2, this is possible in time polynomial in k, d and $\frac{1}{p-\epsilon}$. Evaluating these l polynomials at $D(0)$ and $D(1)$ gives the desired set of values. □

We are not quite done yet because we wish to somehow select the correct value from this set so as to always output the value of the polynomial f. We would like a method to consistently order the values $\{(f_1(\hat{a}), f_1(\hat{b})), \ldots, (f_l(\hat{a}), f_l(\hat{b}))\}$ so that the ith value in the ordering always comes from f_i. In order to achieve a global ordering of this form we pick a reference point $\hat{r}$, such that $f_i(\hat{r}) \neq f_j(\hat{r})$ if $i \neq j$. The following definition and claim show that such a point exists.

DEFINITION 3.1 *For a multivariate polynomial $Q(x_1, \ldots, x_n, y)$ of degree k in y, and total degree kd, with no repeated factors, a* **reference point** *is a point $\hat{r} = < r_1, \ldots, r_n >$ such that the polynomial $f_{\hat{r}}(y)$ given by Q restricted to $\hat{x} = \hat{r}$ has no repeated factors*[5].

Claim 3 *A random point in F^n is a reference point with probability $\ge 1/2$.*

Proof (sketch): Let $\Delta(x_1, \ldots, x_n)$ be the discriminant (see [26], for instance, for a definition of discriminant) of the polynomial $Q(x_1, \ldots, x_n, y)$ when viewed as a polynomial in y with coefficients that are degree kd polynomials in $x_1, \ldots, x_n$. Observe that the discriminant satisfies the following properties:

[5]Note that if $Q(\hat{x}, y) = \Pi_{i=1}^{k}(y - f_i(x))$, this is equivalent to the condition that $f_i(\hat{r}) \neq f_j(\hat{r})$ when $i \neq j$.

- Δ is not identically zero, because Q has no repeated factors.
- Δ is a polynomial in $x_1, \ldots, x_n$ of total degree at most $2k^2d$ (since it is a polynomial in the coefficients of y of total degree at most $2k$).

Thus if $|F| \geq 4k^2d$, then

$$Pr_{\hat{r} \in_R F^n}[\Delta(\hat{r}) \neq 0] \geq \frac{1}{2}$$

But this implies that the polynomial $f_{\hat{r}}(y) = Q(\hat{r}, y)$ has a non-zero discriminant, implying $f_{\hat{r}}(y)$ has no repeated factors, and $\hat{r}$ is a reference point. □

The values of the k polynomials on $\hat{r}$, $\{s_1, \ldots, s_k\}$, can now be used to fix a "global" ordering of the candidate polynomials $f_1, \ldots, f_k$ as follows: Fix an arbitrary ordering $s_1, \ldots, s_k$ and let f_i be the (unique) polynomial that evaluates to s_i at $\hat{r}$. Now, on input $\hat{b} \in F^n$, the black box for f_i does the following:

- Construct a domain D, such that $D(0) = \hat{r}$ and $D(1) = \hat{b}$ and properties (2) and (3) hold.
- Use the univariate reconstruction technique to reconstruct the univariate polynomials $f_1^D, \ldots, f_k^D$.
- Find j such that $f_j^D(0) = s_i$.
- Output $f_j^D(1)$.

□

4 Applications

In this section, we describe the application of our techniques to some of the areas mentioned in the introduction. The other applications are more straightforward, and we will give the complete details in a later version.

4.1 (ϵ, Δ) Interpolation Problems over Discrete Domains

Consider the task of fitting a low degree polynomial on a given set of points, so that the majority of the points are "close" to the polynomial, while some fraction of the points can be very far away. We look at such computations over discrete domains. For example, over Z_p (or over the integers) the problem can be formulated as:

Problem 3
Given: *t pairs of points, $\{(x_1, y_1), \ldots, (x_t, y_t)\}$, and ϵ, such that there exists a polynomial f, of degree at most d, so that*

for all but ϵt values of j in $[t]$

$$\exists i \in [-\Delta, \Delta] \; s.t. \; y_j = f(x_j) + i$$

Problem: *Find f.*

This is exactly a $(2\Delta + 1, d)$-polynomial black box reconstruction problem and the reconstruction procedure of Section 2.2 can be used to find one of the polynomials $f_i(x) \equiv f(x) + i$ (or a small set of polynomials which includes f).

We know that there exists a bivariate polynomial $Q(x, y)$ such that $Q(x_i, y_i) = 0$ for all $i = 1, \ldots, t$. This is the polynomial: $Q(x, y) = W(x) \cdot \Pi_i (y - f_i(x))$, where f_i is the polynomial given by $f_i(x) = f(x) + i$, $i \in [-\Delta, \Delta]$, and $W(x)$ is defined by all the points where the y coordinate is more than Δ away from $f(x)$ (as in Section 2.2), so that $deg(W) \leq \epsilon t$.

From Theorem 2 we get the following claim:

Claim 4 *If there exists an i such that the fraction of points for which $y = f_i(x)$ is bigger than ϵ, then we can find f_i.*

A small set of polynomials that is guaranteed to contain f, is $\{f_i + j \; : \; j \in [-\Delta, \Delta]\}$ where the f_i's are the outputs of the reconstruction algorithm.

We want to be able to handle situations where ϵ is arbitrarily close to $1/2$. Using our mechanism directly means that the ϵ that our algorithm can handle depends on Δ. This is because there must be an $i \in [-\Delta, \Delta]$ such that more than ϵt of the points are on $f(x) + i$. An important point to note is that we can artificially decrease the influence of the *bad* points. This is due to the role of these points in defining $Q(x, y)$.

To do this, we look at the following set of points: $\{(x_j^i, y_j^i)\}_{j=1, i=0}^{t, \; 2\Delta}$, where $x_j^i = x_j$ and $y_j^i = y_j - \Delta + i$. (From each point in the original sample, we generate 2Δ additional points, by adding and subtracting up to Δ to the y coordinate of each point.)

Observe that the following conditions hold for the $(2\Delta + 1)t$ points so constructed:

- There exists a polynomial $Q(x, y)$ of degree at most $\epsilon t + (4\Delta + 1)d$ such that $Q(x, y) = 0$ for all the points. This is the polynomial: $Q(x, y) = W(x) \cdot \Pi_{i=0}^{4\Delta} (y -$

$f_i(x)$), where $W(x)$ is as before, and $f_i(x) = f(x) + i - 2\Delta$.

- At least $(1-\epsilon)t$ of the points satisfy $y = f(x)$. This is because for every point in the original (x_j, y_j) such that y_j is within Δ of $f(x_j)$ (and there were $(1-\epsilon)t$ such points), one of the new (x^i_j, y^i_j) pairs satisfies $y^i_j = f(x^i_j)$.

Claim 5 *If $\epsilon < \frac{1}{2}$ then we can find all functions f such that f is Δ-close to all but an ϵ fraction of the points, provided $t > \frac{(4\Delta+1)d}{1-2\epsilon}$.*

Proof: Find a polynomial $Q'(x,y)$ such that $Q'(x,y) = 0$ for all the points and degree of Q' is at most $\epsilon t + (4\Delta+1)d$. If $\epsilon t + (4\Delta+1)d < (1-\epsilon)t$ then by Lemma 1 we know that for every candidate function f which forms an (ϵ, Δ) fit on the given points, $(y - f(x))$ divides Q'. Thus factoring Q' will give us all the candidates. □

4.2 Reducing Bivariate Factoring to Univariate Factoring

In Section 2.1, we saw how to reduce the problem of reconstructing polynomial black boxes to the problem of factoring bivariate polynomials. In the specific case of univariate polynomial black boxes, we can also reduce the reconstruction problem to that of factoring univariate polynomials to their irreducible factors. As an interesting consequence, we find a simple way of showing that over finite fields, factoring special bivariate polynomials is reducible to factoring univariate polynomials. There are known methods to reduce factoring of bivariate polynomials to that of univariate polynomials [18], however this result is interesting in the sense that the reduction, as well as the proof of its correctness, are extremely simple and use very basic algebraic tools.

Suppose, as in Section 2.1, we want to know $f_1, \ldots, f_k$, univariate polynomials, each of degree at most d. However, all we have is a black box - B, that at any given point - x - outputs the **unordered** set $\{f_i(x)\}$. Sampling from the black box, and interpolating, we can find the polynomial $t(x) = \prod_{i=1}^{k} f_i(x)$ explicitly (in terms of its coefficients). If somehow we could guarantee that at least one of the f_i's is irreducible, we could factor t to find f_i. Such a guarantee is not available, but we simulate it via randomization.

Let $\alpha(x) \in F[x]$ be a random degree d polynomial. We can convert the given set of sample points so that on each input x we have the (still unordered) set $\{g_1(x), \ldots, g_k(x) \; : \; g_i(x) = f_i(x) + \alpha(x)\}$. Each of the polynomials g_i is a random degree d polynomial (but they are not necessarily independent). We then use the fact that random polynomials over finite fields have a reasonable chance of being irreducible.

Lemma 6 ([20], p.84) *The probability $P_q(d)$ that a random polynomial, of degree d, is irreducible over F_q, is at least $\frac{1}{d}(1 - \frac{1}{q-1})$.*

We can thus interpolate (after sampling at enough - $kd+1$ - points) and explicitly compute $t'(x) = \prod_{i=1}^{k} g_i(x)$. We factor t' into irreducible factors $r_1 \cdot \cdots \cdot r_l$. For each factor r_j of t', we verify whether or not $r_j - \alpha$ is a candidate for one of the f_i's by checking that it evaluates to one of the outputs of the black box B on all the sampled points. By Lemma 6 we know that with non-negligible probability g_i is irreducible and if this happens, we find g_i as one of the factors of t' (one of the r_j's). Subtracting α from g_i gives us f_i, which will pass the candidacy verification.

Lemma 7 *If a degree d polynomial p agrees with one of the outputs of the black box on $kd+1$ different x's, then p agrees with one of the outputs of the black box on all x's.*

Proof: If p agrees with one of the outputs of the black box on $kd+1$ different x's, then by the pigeonhole principle there is a polynomial f_i which agrees with p on at least $d+1$ different x's. Thus $p \equiv f_i$. □

Thus, no r_j which is not equal to one of the g_i's will pass the candidacy verification. By repeating this procedure enough times and outputting all the candidates, we can reconstruct all the polynomials $\{f_1, \ldots, f_k\}$. Straightforward analysis shows that the expected number of times that we need to repeat the process (choose random α) is $O(\; k/P_q(d)\;)$ to be able to reconstruct all of the f_i's. Refining the analysis, we can show that $O(\; \ln k/P_q(d)\;)$ times suffice.

From the above, we get the following algorithm for finding the monic linear factors of a bivariate polynomial $Q(x,y)$.

```
program Simple Factor
repeat O( ln k/P_q(d) ) times
    pick a random degree d polynomial
        α(x) over F
    factor Q(x, α(x))
    for every factor g(x) of Q(x, α(x))
        if (y + g(x) − α(x)) divides Q(x, y)
            output (y + g(x) − α(x))
end
```

Claim 8 *Given a bivariate polynomial $Q(x,y)$, over a finite field F, of total degree at most kd, the algorithm* **Simple Factor** *finds all the linear and monic factors of $Q(x,y)$.*

We next extend this mechanism, and apply the reconstruction mechanism of Section 2.2 to the problem of finding the factors of $Q(x, y)$ which are monic and of constant degree in y. Our mechanism tries to isolate some factor $A(x, y)$ of $Q(x, y)$ of the form

$$A(x, y) = y^c + a_1(x)y^{c-1} + \cdots + a_c(x)$$

where the a_i's are polynomials in x of degree at most d (and c is a constant).

For each $i \in [c]$ we construct a program P_i for a_i, such that the output of this program on any x is from a small set of polynomials, and is guaranteed to contain $a_i(x)$. This program can be thought of as a black box for a_i. We then use our reconstruction procedure (Theorem 2) to produce, for each $i \in [c]$, a small list of polynomials which contains a_i. This, in turn, gives a small set of polynomials in x and y which contains $A(x, y)$. $A(x, y)$ can be isolated from this set by exhaustive search.

The program P_i for a_i works as follows on input x_1:

- P_i constructs the polynomial $Q_{x_1}(y) \equiv Q(x_1, y)$ (which is a polynomial in y) and factors Q_{x_1}.
- Let S be the set of factors of Q_{x_1}. (S contains polynomials in y.)
- Let S^c be the set of polynomials of degree c obtained by taking products of polynomials in S.
- P_i picks a random polynomial f in S^c and outputs the coefficient of y^i in f.

To see that P_i computes a_i on some inputs, observe that $A_{x_1}(y) = A(x_1, y)$ divides Q_{x_1} and hence appears in the set S^c (which is the set of all degree c factors of Q_{x_1}). Thus with non-negligible probability, when P_i picks a random element of S^c, it is likely to be $A_{x_1}(y)$ and hence when P_i outputs the coefficient of y^i from this polynomial, it outputs $a_i(x_1)$ correctly.

On the remaining inputs, P_i's output is in error, but is the value of some polynomial, so that the value output in this case is obtained from an algebraic combination of elements y_i which satisfy $Q(x_1, y_i) = 0$, and this corresponds to situations for which we can solve.

Acknowledgments

We are very grateful to Avi Wigderson for asking a question that started us down this line of research and for helpful discussions. We are very grateful to Umesh Vazirani for his enthusiasm, his valuable opinion and suggestions and the time that he spent with us discussing this work. We thank Ronen Basri, Oded Goldreich and Mike Kearns for their comments on the writeup of this paper. We would like to thank Joel Friedman for technical discussions about questions related to the topics of this paper.

References

[1] D. Beaver and J. Feigenbaum. Hiding Instance in Multioracle Queries. In *STACS 1990*

[2] M. Ben-Or. Probabilistic Algorithms in Finite Fields In *Proc. 22nd IEEE Symposium on Foundations of Computer Science*, pages 394–398, 1981.

[3] M. Ben-Or and P. Tiwari. A Deterministic Algorithm for Sparse Multivariate Polynomial Interpolation. In *Proc. 20th STOC*, pages 301-309, 1988.

[4] E. Berlekamp. Factoring Polynomials over Large Finite Fields. *Mathematics of Computation*, page 713, vol. 24, no. 111, 1970.

[5] E. Berlekamp and L. Welch. Error Correction of Algebraic Block Codes. *US Patent Number 4,633,470*

[6] A. Blum and P. Chalasani. Learning Switching Concepts. In *Proc. 5th Annual Workshop on Computational Learning Theory*, pages 231–242, 1992.

[7] M. Blum, M. Luby and R. Rubinfeld. Self-Testing/Correcting with Applications to Numerical Problems. In *Proc. 22nd ACM Symposium on Theory of Computing*, 1990.

[8] J.Y. Cai and L. Hemachandra. A note on enumerative counting. Information Processing Letters 38 (1991) pp. 215-219.

[9] Canny J., 1983. Finding edges and lines in images. *M.I.T., Arificial Intelligence Laboratory Report*, AI-TR-720.

[10] P. Gemmell, R. Lipton, R. Rubinfeld, M. Sudan and A. Wigderson. Self-Testing/Correcting for Polynomials and for Approximate Functions. In *Proc. 23rd ACM Symposium on Theory of Computing*, 1991.

[11] P. Gemmell and M. Sudan. Highly resilient correctors for polynomials. To appear in *Information Processing Letters*.

[12] D. Grigoriev. Factorization of Polynomials over a Finite Field and the Solution of Systems of Algebraic Equations. Translated from Zapiski Nauchnykh Seminarov Lenningradskogo Otdeleniya Matematicheskogo Instituta im. V. A. Steklova AN SSSR, Vol. 137, pp. 20-79, 1984.

[13] D. Grigoriev and A. Chistov. Fast decomposition of polynomials into irreducible ones and the solution of systems of algebraic equations. Soviet Math. Doklady , 29 (1984) 380–383.

[14] D. Grigoriev and M. Karpinski. Algorithms for Sparse Rational Interpolation. ICSI Tech. Report, TR-91-011, January 1991.

[15] D. Grigoriev, M. Karpinski, M.F. Singer. Interpolation of Sparse Rational Functions Without Knowing Bounds on Exponents. Institut für Informatik der Universität Bonn, Report No. 8539-CS, Nov. 1989.

[16] D. Grigoriev, M. Karpinski, M.F. Singer. Fast Parallel Algorithms for Sparse Multivariate Polynomial Interpolation over Finite Fields. SIAM J. Comput., Vol. 19, No. 6, pp 1059-1063, Dec. 1990.

[17] J. Henderson and R. Quandt. **Microeconomic Theory**, McGraw Hill Book Company, 1958, 1971.

[18] E. Kaltofen. A Polynomial-Time Reduction from Bivariate to Univariate Integral Polynomial Factorization. In *23rd Annual Symposium on Foundations of Computer Science*, pages 57-64, 1982.

[19] E. Kaltofen and B. Trager. Computing with Polynomials Given by Black Boxes for Their Evaluations: Greatest Common Divisors, Factorization, Separation of Numerators and Denominators. In *29th Annual Symposium on Foundations of Computer Science*, pages 296–305, 1988.

[20] R. Lidl and H. Niederreiter. Introduction to finite fields and their applications. Cambridge University Press, 1986

[21] R. Lipton. New directions in testing. In *Distributed Computing and Cryptography*, DIMACS Series on Discrete Mathematics and Theoretical Computer Science, pages 191–202, v. 2, 1991.

[22] A. K. Lenstra, H. W. Lenstra and L. Lovasz. Factoring polynomials with rational coefficients. Math. Ann., 261 (1982), 515–534.

[23] Marr D. & Hildreth E., 1980. "Theory of Edge Detection". *Proceeding of the Royal Society London, B207*, pp. 187-217.

[24] R. Rivest. Learning Decision Lists. *Machine Learning*, 2(3), pages 229-246, 1987.

[25] T.J. Rivlin. An Introduction of the Approximation of Functions. Dover Publications, 1969.

[26] Van der Waerden. Algebra, Volume 1. Frederick Ungar Publishing Co., Inc., page 82.

[27] R. J. Walker. Algebraic Curves. Dover Publications, 1962

[28] R.E. Zippel. Probabilistic Algorithms for Sparse Polynomials. In *Proc. EUROSAM '79*, Springer Verlag LNCS, pages 216-226, v. 72, 1979.

[29] R.E. Zippel. Interpolating Polynomials from their Values. *J. Symbolic Computation* 9, pages 375-403, 1990.

On the Exact Learning of Formulas in Parallel
(Extended Abstract)

Nader H. Bshouty* Richard Cleve*
Department of Computer Science
University of Calgary
Calgary, Alberta, Canada T2N 1N4

Abstract

We investigate the parallel complexity of learning formulas from membership and equivalence queries. We consider a number of learning problems that can be solved sequentially in polynomial time. We prove some upper and lower bounds on the number of parallel steps required to solve these problems with a polynomial number of processors.

1 Summary of Results

In [AHK89], Angluin, Hellerstein and Karpinski present a polynomial-time algorithm for learning (boolean) read-once formulas from membership and equivalence queries, and they pose the question of whether it is possible to obtain significant speed-up by using parallelism. This paper addresses this question as well as the more general question of when learning problems that can be solved sequentially in polynomial-time can be solved quickly in parallel.

The model of learning that we consider is "exact" learning with membership and equivalence queries. We obtain both lower and upper bounds on the parallel complexity of several learning problems in this model.

With respect to read-once formulas, we show that boolean read-once formulas, require at least $\Omega(n/\log n)$ parallel steps to learn (assuming a polynomial number of processors). The same lower bound also applies to arithmetic read-once formulas over sufficiently small fields (specifically, fields of size n^ϵ for some constant $\epsilon < 1$, where n is the number of variables in the formula). (Bshouty, Hancock, and Hellerstein [BHH92] present polynomial-time sequential learning algorithms for arithmetic read-once formulas over any field.) In contrast to the lower bounds, we also show that, over sufficiently large fields (of size $\Omega(n^2)$), arithmetic read-once formulas are learnable in $O(\log^2 n)$ parallel steps with $O(n^4)$ processors. Moreover, only $O(n^3)$ membership queries, which can all be performed in one parallel step, and no equivalence queries are required in this case.

We also show that $\Omega(n/\log n)$ parallel steps are required for other learning problems for which sequential polynomial-time learning algorithms exist. These include the more restricted learning problems of read-once monotone formulas and read-once DNF formulas. Also, the lower bound holds for monotone DNF formulas and 2-DNF formulas (sequentially learnable in polynomial-time by Angluin [A87]).

All lower bounds hold even if the PRAM model is "information theoretic," in that it allows unlimited computational power, and the equivalence oracle accepts any boolean formula (not necessarily one in the class being learned). This latter property is significant because it implies that any of our lower bounds for a class C of formulas immediately extends to any class of functions that contains C.

For more restricted classes of boolean formulas there are simple parallel algorithms. These are read-once k-DNF formulas and monotone k-DNF formulas.

Prior work concerning learning from membership and equivalence queries in parallel addresses the problem of learning sparse polynomials with membership queries only ([BOT88], [GKS88]). Vitter and Lin [VL88] investigate the parallel complexity of learning in a quite different model: "PAC learning from examples."

Section 2 contains some preliminary definitions, Section 3 contains the lower bounds and Section 4 contains the upper bounds.

*Research supported in part by NSERC of Canada.
Author's E-mail addresses: bshouty@cpsc.ucalgary.ca and cleve@cpsc.ucalgary.ca.

0-8186-2900-2/92 $3.00 © 1992 IEEE

2 Preliminary Definitions

The learning criterion we consider is *exact identification*. There is a formula f called the *target formula*, which is a member of a class of formulas C defined over the variable set V. The goal of the learning algorithm is to halt and output a formula f from C that is logically equivalent to f.

In a *membership query*, the learning algorithm supplies an assignment a to the variables in V as input to a *membership oracle*, and receives in return the value of $f(a)$.

In an *equivalence query*, the learning algorithm supplies any formula h as input to an *equivalence oracle*, and the reply of the oracle is either "yes", signifying that h is equivalent to f, or a *counterexample*, which is an assignment b such that $h(b) \neq f(b)$.

In the learning procedures given in this paper, we assume that the algorithm has access to membership and equivalence oracles for a target formula f, and to a variable set V. We do not include these oracles, or the set V, as inputs to the procedures, but specify them when the procedures are called.

3 Lower Bounds for Parallel Learning

In this section we develop a new technique for proving lower bounds for parallel learning from membership and equivalence queries. The lower bounds are for the worst case complexity, i.e., a learner with p processors tries to learn a formula from some class C that an adversary has. The learner can ask the adversary queries and the adversary provides the learner with true answers. The adversary can change the formula during the learning process but this formula should be consistent with all the answers of the queries already asked by the learner. The adversary will change the formula so that it will be hard for the learner to learn it.

We show that k independent equivalence queries can be simulated by $k-1$ membership queries and one equivalence query. We can thus find lower bounds for the number of equivalence queries needed to learn the above classes to find lower bounds for the parallel learning.

The model of computation (of the learner) will be any PRAM model with unlimited computational power. We call this model UPRAM. All the computations computed by the UPRAM are free and the parallel learning complexity will be the number of parallel membership and equivalence queries steps. A UPRAM with p processors can ask a total number of p membership and equivalence queries in one step. The equivalence queries can be asked with any boolean function g. A UPRAM with one processor will be called URAM.

Before we give our main theorem we define some notation. Let C be a class of boolean formulas. Let $e_C(m)$ be the number of equivalence queries needed to learn the functions in C in a URAM when only m membership queries are allowed to be asked by the learner. Obviously, $e_C(m') \geq e_C(m)$ for $m' \leq m$ and for classes $C \subseteq 2^X$ where $X = \{0,1\}^n$ we have $e_C(2^n) = 0$. All the classes C in this section will be a subset of 2^X where $X = \{0,1\}^n$. The following lemma will be used later in this section.

Lemma 1: *Let C be a class of boolean formulas with n variables. Then*

$$\frac{\log|C| - m}{n} \leq e_C(m) \leq \log(|C| - m).$$

Proof: The lower bound is a trivial information theory lower bound and the upper bound is an immediate result from [A87].□

A better lower bound can be derived from [MT90].

We define $ME_C(p)$, the number of parallel steps needed to learn the formulas in C in UPRAM with p processors from membership and equivalence queries. Our main theorem is:

Theorem 2: *Let C be a class of boolean formulas. We have*

$$ME_C\left(\left\lfloor \frac{m}{e_C(m)} \right\rfloor\right) \geq e_C(m).$$

Proof: Let $\mathcal{A}$ be an algorithm (of the learner) that learns C in UPRAM with $p = \lfloor m/e_C(m) \rfloor$ processors using $e < e_C(m)$ steps. We will show how to change this algorithm to a sequential algorithm in URAM that uses $m' \leq m$ membership queries and e equivalence queries. Since $e < e_C(m) \leq e_C(m')$, we get a contradiction and the result follows.

Suppose that the first step in $\mathcal{A}$ makes r equivalence queries with distinct boolean functions $g_1, \ldots, g_r$ and s membership queries, $r + s \leq p$. In the URAM we ask the same membership queries sequentially. For the equivalence queries we define $S \leftarrow \{g_1, \ldots, g_r\}$. We now show how to change the r equivalence queries to $r-1$ membership queries and one equivalence query. At stage $j < r$ the set S will contain $r - j + 1 \geq 2$ boolean functions. We choose any two g_{i_1} and g_{i_2} functions in S and find an assignment a such that

$g_{i_1}(a) \neq g_{i_2}(a)$ (this can be done free in the URAM). We then use the membership query to find $f(a)$. Obviously, there must be $j \in \{1,2\}$ such that $f(a) \neq g_{i_j}(a)$ and then we provide algorithm $\mathcal{A}$ the counterexample a for g_{i_j} and define $S \leftarrow S \backslash \{g_{i_j}\}$. This process will stop after $r-1$ membership queries, i.e., when the set S contains one element. For this element we use the equivalence oracle. We do this for each step.

This sequential algorithm uses at most $m' = \lfloor m/e_C(m) \rfloor e \leq m$ membership queries and $e < e_C(m)$ equivalence queries.□

Lemma 1 with Theorem 2 implies:

Corollary 3: *Let C be a class of boolean formulas. Then*

$$ME_C(p) \geq e_C(\lceil p \log |C| \rceil).$$

Proof Sketch: The result follows from applying lemma 1 and Theorem 2 for $m = \lceil p \log |C| \rceil$.□

For the next result we define $x^c = x$ for $c = 1$ and $x^c = \bar{x}$ for $c = 0$.

Lemma 4: *Let C be a class of read-once DNF formulas. If $m \geq n$ then*

$$e_C(m) \geq \left\lfloor \frac{n}{2 + \lceil \log m \rceil} \right\rfloor.$$

Proof: Let $k = 2 + \lceil \log m \rceil$ and $l = \lfloor n/k \rfloor$. We will prove the lower bound for learning the class

$$C' = \{(x_1^{c_1} \wedge \cdots \wedge x_k^{c_k}) \vee \cdots \vee (x_{kl-k+1}^{c_{kl-k+1}} \wedge \cdots \wedge x_{kl}^{c_{kl}}) |$$

$$(c_1, \ldots, c_{kl}) \in \{0,1\}^{kl}\}$$

The learner will try to learn a formula hidden by the adversary. The adversary will define l sets $S_1 = S_2 = \cdots = S_l = \{0,1\}^k$. The set S_i will be the possible values of $(c_{ki-k+1}, \ldots, c_{ki})$ in the i–th term of the formula. The adversary will answer 0 for all the membership queries that the learner ask before the first equivalence query is asked. For each membership query with assignment $a = (a_1, \ldots, a_n)$ the answer 0 will eliminate the elements

$$\bigcup_{i=1}^{l} \{(x_1^{c_1} \wedge \cdots \wedge x_k^{c_k}) \vee \cdots \vee (x_{ki-k+1}^{a_{ki-k+1}} \wedge \cdots \wedge x_{ki}^{a_{ki}}) \vee \cdots$$

$$\vee (x_{kl-k+1}^{c_{kl-k+1}} \wedge \cdots \wedge x_{kl}^{c_{kl}}) | (c_1, \ldots, c_{kl}) \in \{0,1\}^{kl}\}$$

Therefore, the adversary will set

$$S_i \leftarrow S_i \backslash \{(a_{ki-k+1}, \ldots, a_{ki})\}, \quad i = 1, \ldots, l$$

for each such assignment a. Since the learner can ask only m membership queries and each membership queries eliminate at most one element from each set S_i and since the initial size of S_i is $2^k \geq 4m$, no one of the terms can be found. This implies that the learner should ask at least one equivalence query.

Let g be the boolean function that is used for the first equivalence query. If $g \not\equiv 0$ then the adversary finds an assignment $b = (b_1, \cdots, b_n)$ such that $g(b) = 1$ and then provide b as a counterexample. In this case the equivalence query eliminate only one element in each set S_i, i.e., the adversary will set $S_i \leftarrow S_i \backslash \{(b_{ki-k+1}, \ldots, b_{ki})\}$ for $i = 1, \ldots, l$. If $g \equiv 0$ then the adversary provides any counterexample $(b_1, \cdots, b_n)$ where $(b_1, \ldots, b_k) \in S_1$ and set

$$S_1 \leftarrow \{(b_1, \ldots, b_k)\}.$$

This is the case where the adversary has no other choise but to provide information about one of the terms.

After w equivalence queries the adversary assumes that the learner knows $S_1, S_2, \ldots, S_w$ (and therefore the first w terms). Suppose $S_i = \{(c_{ki-k+1}, \ldots, c_{ki})\}$ for $i = 1, \ldots, w$, i.e., $x_{ki-k+1}^{c_{ki-k+1}} \wedge \cdots \wedge x_{ki}^{c_{ki}}$ is the i-th term of the target formula for $i = 1, \ldots, w$. The adversary will act as follows. If the learner asks a membership query with $a = (a_1, \ldots, a_n)$ the adversary returns $b = (a_1^{c_1} \wedge \cdots \wedge a_k^{c_k}) \vee \cdots \vee (a_{kw-k+1}^{c_{kw-k+1}} \wedge \cdots \wedge a_{kw}^{c_{kw}})$. If $b = 0$ then this assignment will eliminate at most one element in each set S_i, $i > w$. If the learner ask an equivalence query with a function g then we have the following cases:

Case I . If

$$g(\xi_1, \ldots, \xi_{sk-k}, c_{sk-k+1}, \ldots, c_{sk}, \xi_{sk+1}, \ldots, \xi_n) = 0$$

for some ξ_i and $s \leq w$ then the adversary returns the assignment

$$(\xi_1, \ldots, \xi_{sk-k}, c_{sk-k+1}, \ldots, c_{sk}, \xi_{sk+1}, \ldots, \xi_n).$$

In this case the learner can learn nothing about the other terms in the formula.

Case II . If $g(\xi_1, \ldots, \xi_n) = 1$ and $(\xi_1^{c_1} \wedge \cdots \wedge \xi_k^{c_k}) \vee \cdots \vee (\xi_{kw-k+1}^{c_{kw-k+1}} \wedge \cdots \wedge \xi_{kw}^{c_{kw}}) = 0$ for some ξ_i then the adversary will return $(\xi_1, \ldots, \xi_n)$ as a counterexample. In this case the counterexample eliminate at most one element from each S_i, $i > w$. The sets S_i will be updated by the adversary.

Case III . If $g(x_1, \ldots, x_n) \equiv (x_1^{c_1} \wedge \cdots \wedge x_k^{c_k}) \vee \cdots \vee (x_{kw-k+1}^{c_{kw-k+1}} \wedge \cdots \wedge x_{kw}^{c_{kw}})$ then the adversary provides the counterexample $(\bar{c}_1, \ldots, \bar{c}_{kw}, b_{kw+1}, \cdots, b_n)$ where $(b_{kw+1}, \ldots, b_{kw+k}) \in S_{w+1}$ and sets

$$S_{w+1} \leftarrow \{(b_{kw+1}, \ldots, b_{kw+k})\}.$$

In this case the adversary assumes that the learner knows now the first $w+1$ terms and continues as before. This implies that l is a lower bound for the number of equivalence queries used in the program.□

Result 5: *Let C be a class of read-once DNF formulas over n variables. Then*

$$ME_C(p) = \Omega\left(\frac{n}{\log n + \log p}\right).$$

In particular, $ME_C(poly(n)) = \Omega\left(\frac{n}{\log n}\right)$.

Proof: For C' defined in lemma 4 we have $|C'| \leq 2^n$. By corollary 3 we have

$$ME_C(p) \geq e_C(\lceil p \log |C'| \rceil) \geq \Omega\left(\frac{n}{\log n + \log p}\right).\square$$

The following result is proved in a similar way.

Result 6: *Let C be a class of 2–DNF formulas over n variables. Then*

$$ME_C(p) = \Omega\left(\frac{n}{\log n + \log p}\right).$$

In particular, $ME_C(poly(n)) = \Omega\left(\frac{n}{\log n}\right)$.

Proof Sketch: We prove the result for 2-CNF. The result then follows from duality. Consider the following boolean function

$$(x_1 \equiv x_2 \equiv \cdots \equiv x_k) = (\bar{x}_1 \vee x_2) \wedge (x_1 \vee \bar{x}_2) \wedge$$

$$(\bar{x}_2 \vee x_3) \wedge (x_2 \vee \bar{x}_3) \wedge \cdots \wedge$$

$$(\bar{x}_{k-1} \vee x_k) \wedge (x_{k-1} \vee \bar{x}_k).$$

This function satisfies $(x_1 \equiv x_2 \equiv \cdots \equiv x_k) = 1$ if and only if $x_1 = x_2 = \cdots = x_k$. For a vector $\xi \in \{0,1\}^k$ we define

$$f_\xi(x_1, \ldots, x_k) = (x_{i_1} \equiv \cdots \equiv x_{i_r} \equiv 1) \wedge (x_{j_1} \equiv \cdots \equiv x_{j_s})$$

where $\{i_1, \ldots, i_r\} = \{i | \xi_i = 1\}$ and $\{j_1, \ldots, j_s\} = \{j | \xi_j = 0\}$. This formula is 2-CNF and satisfies $f_\xi(x_1, \ldots, x_k) = 1$ if and only if $x = \xi$ or $x = (1, 1, \ldots, 1)$. The adversary will define the class

$$C = \{f_{\xi_1}(x_1, \ldots, x_k) \wedge f_{\xi_2}(x_{k+1}, \ldots, x_{2k}) \wedge \cdots \wedge$$

$$f_{\xi_l}(x_{lk-k+1}, \ldots, x_{lk}) \mid \xi_1, \ldots, \xi_l \in \{0,1\}^k\}$$

where $k = \lceil \log 2m \rceil$ and $l = \lfloor n/k \rfloor$. After w equivalence queries the adversary assumes that $\xi_1, \ldots, \xi_w$ are known. The adversary also defines $S_{w+1}, \ldots, S_l$ of possible $\xi_{w+1}, \cdots, \xi_l$, respectively. It can be shown that each membership query eliminates at most one element from exactly one S_i, $i > w$ and using equivalence query the learner can learn at most one vector from $\xi_{w+1}, \ldots, \xi_l$.□

The other negative results of this paper are based on the following:

Theorem 7: *Any UPRAM algorithm with p processors that learns a class C in t steps can be changed to a UPRAM algorithm with $p(p-1)/2$ processors that learns C in $2t$ steps where in each odd step (steps $1, 3, 5, \cdots$) the algorithm asks $p(p-1)/2$ membership queries and in each even step the algorithm asks one equivalence query.*

Proof: The proof is similar to the proof of theorem 2. We have $\{g_1, \ldots, g_s\}$ the boolean functions used for the equivalence queries in some step. For every $1 \leq i < j \leq s \leq p$ we find an assignment $a^{(ij)}$ such that $g_i(a^{(ij)}) \neq g_j(a^{(ij)})$ and then use membership queries to find $f(a^{(ij)})$. It can be easily shown that this provides counterexamples for all g_i except at most one. For this one we use the equivalence query in the following step.□

The proof of this lemma is based on theorem 7.

Result 8: *Let C be a class of monotone read-once formulas over n variables. Then*

$$ME_C(p) \geq \left\lfloor \frac{n}{2 + 2\lceil \log p \rceil} \right\rfloor.$$

In particular, $ME_C(poly(n)) \geq \Omega\left(\frac{n}{\log n}\right)$.

Proof: The adversary devides the variables to vectors $v_1 = (x_1, \ldots, x_k), \cdots, v_l = (x_{lk-k+1}, \ldots, x_{lk})$ where $k = 2 + 2\lceil \log p \rceil$ and $l = \lfloor n/k \rfloor$. Define

$$f_{(\xi_1, \ldots, \xi_k)}(x_1, \ldots, x_k, y) =$$

$$\left(\bigvee_{j \in \{i \leq k | \xi_i = 0\}} x_j\right) \vee \left(\bigwedge_{j \in \{i \leq k | \xi_i = 1\}} x_j \wedge y\right)$$

This function satisfies

$$(\star) \quad f_{(\xi_1^{(0)}, \ldots, \xi_k^{(0)})}(x_1^{(0)}, \ldots, x_k^{(0)}, y) =$$

$$\begin{cases} 1 & \text{If } x_j^{(0)} = 1 \text{ for some } j \in \{i \leq k | \xi_i = 0\}. \\ 0 & \text{If } x_j^{(0)} = 0 \text{ for all } j \in \{i \leq k | \xi_i = 0\} \\ & \text{and } x_j^{(0)} = 0 \text{ for some } j \in \{i \leq k | \xi_i = 1\}. \\ y & \text{If } (x_1^{(0)}, \ldots, x_k^{(0)}) = (\xi_1^{(0)}, \ldots, \xi_k^{(0)}). \end{cases}$$

The adversary defines the set

$$C = \{f_{\xi^{(1)}}(v_1, f_{\xi^{(2)}}(v_2, \cdots f_{\xi^{(l)}}(v_l, 1) \cdots)|$$

$$\xi^{(1)}, \xi^{(2)}, \ldots, \xi^{(l)} \in \{0,1\}^k\}.$$

Obviously, C is a subset of monotone read-once formulas and learning a function in C is equivalent to learning $\xi^{(1)}, \xi^{(2)}, \ldots, \xi^{(l)}$.

We assume that the learner can ask $p(p-1)/2$ membership queries in the odd parallel steps and one equivalence query in the even parallel steps.

After $2w$ steps, the adversary assumes that the learner knows $\xi^{(1)}, \ldots, \xi^{(w)}$, two bits in $\xi^{(w+1)}$ but nothing about $\xi^{(w+2)}, \ldots, \xi^{(l)}$. In step $2w+1$ the learner asks $m = p(p-1)/2$ membership queries, $Q = \{a_1, \ldots, a_m\}$. The adversary will look at the first kw entries of each vector a_i and defines

$$G = \{a_i | (a_{i,1}, \ldots, a_{i,kw}) \neq (\xi^{(1)}, \ldots, \xi^{(w)})\} \text{ and}$$

$$E = Q \backslash G.$$

Suppose that $\xi^{(w+1)}_{j_1}$ and $\xi^{(w+1)}_{j_2}$ are the bits that are known for the learner in $\xi^{(w+1)}$. The assignments in G are the assignments that have answers independent on $\xi^{(w+1)}, \ldots, \xi^{(l)}$ (see property $(\star)$). The adversary will then look at the bits $(a_{i,kw+1}, \ldots, a_{i,kw+k})$ of each $a_i \in E$. Since at most two bits in $\xi^{(w+1)}$ are known by the learner and $2^{k-2} \geq p^2 > p(p-1)/2$ there exist $\eta \in \{0,1\}^k$ such that $\eta_{j_1} = \xi^{(w+1)}_{j_1}$, $\eta_{j_2} = \xi^{(w+1)}_{j_2}$ and for all $a_i \in E$, $(a_{i,kw+1}, \ldots, a_{i,kw+k}) \neq \eta$. The adversary then decides that $\xi^{(w+1)} = \eta$ and then for all $a_i \in E$ the value of $f(a_i)$ will depend on $\xi^{(w+1)}$ but independent on $\xi^{(w+2)}, \ldots, \xi^{(l)}$.

At step $2w+2$ the learner asks one equivalence query with some function g. We have the following cases

Case I .

$$g(x_1, \ldots, x_{lk}) \not\equiv$$

$$f_{\xi^{(1)}}(v_1, f_{\xi^{(2)}}(v_2, \cdots, f_{\xi^{(w+1)}}(v_{w+1}, h) \cdots)$$

for any $h(v_{w+1}, \ldots, v_l)$.

This case is equivalent to

$$(\forall h)(\exists v_1^{(h)}, \ldots, v_{w+1}^{(h)})$$

$$g(v_1^{(h)}, \ldots, v_{w+1}^{(h)}, x_{(w+1)k+1}, \ldots, x_{lk}) \not\equiv$$

$$f_{\xi^{(1)}}(v_1^{(h)}, f_{\xi^{(2)}}(v_2^{(h)}, \cdots, f_{\xi^{(w+1)}}(v_{w+1}^{(h)}, h) \cdots)$$

Let $h' = g(\xi^{(1)}, \ldots, \xi^{(w+1)}, x_{(w+1)k+1}, \ldots, x_{lk})$. Then for $h = h'$ we have

$$(\exists v_1^{(h')}, \ldots, v_{w+1}^{(h')})$$

$$g(v_1^{(h')}, \ldots, v_{w+1}^{(h')}, x_{(w+1)k+1}, \ldots, x_{lk}) \not\equiv$$

$$f_{\xi^{(1)}}(v_1^{(h')}, f_{\xi^{(2)}}(v_2^{(h')}, \cdots, f_{\xi^{(w+1)}}(v_{w+1}^{(h')}, h') \cdots)$$

If $v_1^{(h')}, \ldots, v_{w+1}^{(h')} = \xi^{(1)}, \ldots, \xi^{(w+1)}$ then we get a contradiction. Therefore $v_1^{(h')}, \ldots, v_{w+1}^{(h')} \neq \xi^{(1)}, \ldots, \xi^{(w+1)}$ and the above statment is equivalent to (see $(\star)$)

$$(\exists v_1^{(h')}, \ldots, v_{w+1}^{(h')})$$

$$g(v_1^{(h')}, \ldots, v_{w+1}^{(h')}, x_{(w+1)k+1}, \ldots, x_{lk}) \not\equiv \eta$$

for some $\eta \in \{0,1\}$.

The adversary chooses some vector $a = (v_1^{(h')}, \ldots, v_{w+1}^{(h')}, x^{(0)}_{(w+1)k+1}, \ldots, x^{(0)}_{lk})$ such that $g(a) \neq \eta$ and return the assignment a as a counterexample. In this case the learner can learn nothing about $\xi^{(w+2)}$.

Case II .

$$g(x_1, \ldots, x_{lk}) \equiv$$

$$f_{\xi^{(1)}}(v_1, f_{\xi^{(2)}}(v_2, \cdots, f_{\xi^{(w+1)}}(v_{w+1}, h) \cdots)$$

for some $h(v_{w+1}, \ldots, v_l)$.

Now we have the following subcases

1. $h(\eta_{(w+2)k+1}, \ldots, \eta_{lk}) = 0$ for some $(\eta_{(w+2)k+1}, \cdots, \eta_{(w+2)k+k}) \neq (0, \ldots, 0)$. Then the adversary returns

   $$a = (\xi^{(1)}, \ldots, \xi^{(w+1)}, \eta_{(w+2)k+1}, \ldots, \eta_n)$$

   as a counterexample (here $g(a) = 0$). Let $\eta_{(w+1)k+h} \neq 0$ for $h \leq k$. The adversary will also assume that $\xi^{(w+2)}_h = 0$. This bit makes sure that $f(a) = 1$.

2. $h(0, \ldots, 0, \eta_{(w+3)k+1}, \ldots, \eta_{lk}) = 1$ for some η_i. Then the adversary returns

   $$a = (\xi^{(1)}, \ldots, \xi^{(w+1)}, 0, \ldots, 0, \eta_{(w+3)k+1}, \ldots, \eta_n)$$

   as a counterexample (here $g(a) = 1$). The adversary will also assume that $\xi^{(w+2)}_1 = 1$. This bit makes sure that $f(a) = 0$.

3. If $h(x_{(w+2)k+1}, \ldots, x_{lk}) = x_{(w+2)k+1} \vee \cdots \vee x_{(w+2)k+k}$, then the adversary returns

   $$a = (\xi^{(1)}, \ldots, \xi^{(w+1)}, 1, 0, \ldots, 0)$$

   as a counterexample (here $g(a) = 1$) and define $\xi^{(w+2)}_1 = \xi^{(w+2)}_2 = 1$ to make sure that $f(a) = 0$.□

Notice that since $e_C(poly(n)) = 0$ (see [AHK89]) the above result cannot be proved using theorem 2.

Since the formula defined in result 9 is also a monoton DNF with n terms we have the following result.

Result 9: *Let C be a class of monotone DNF formulas with n-terms and n variables. Then*

$$ME_C(p) \geq \Omega\left(\frac{n}{\log p}\right).$$

In particular, $ME_C(poly(n)) \geq \Omega\left(\frac{n}{\log n}\right)$.

Result 10: *Let $\mathcal{K}$ be a finite field and $C_{\mathcal{K}} \subset \mathcal{K}[x_1, \ldots, x_n]$ be the set of arithmetic read-once formulas over $\mathcal{K}$. Then*

$$ME_{C_{\mathcal{K}}}(p) \geq \Omega\left(\frac{n}{|\mathcal{K}|\log p}\right).$$

In particular, $ME_{C_{\mathcal{K}}}(poly(n)) \geq \Omega\left(\frac{n}{|\mathcal{K}|\log n}\right)$.

The proof of Result 10 is based on the following lemma.

Lemma 11: *Let R be any finite set and $V = \{v_1, \cdots, v_m\} \subseteq R^n$. There exist $k = O(|R|\log m)$ elements $r_1, \ldots, r_k \in R$ such that*

$$(\forall 1 \leq i \leq m)(v_{i,1} = r_1 \vee \cdots \vee v_{i,k} = r_k).$$

Proof: Let $V = V_1$. There exists $d = \lceil m/|R| \rceil$ vectors $v_{i_1}, \ldots, v_{i_d}$ that have the same element r_1 in the first entry. We define $V_2 = V_1 \backslash \{v_{i_1}, \ldots, v_{i_d}\}$ and recursively apply the above for V_2. Since

$$|V_2| \leq m - \left\lceil \frac{m}{|R|} \right\rceil \leq \frac{|R|-1}{|R|} m,$$

we have that the first

$$k \leq \frac{\log m}{\log\left(\frac{|R|}{|R|-1}\right)} = O(|R|\log m)$$

entries satisfy the condition in the lemma.□

Proof Sketch of Result 10: The proof is similar to the proof of result 8. We define the function

$$f_{(r_1,\ldots,r_k),s}(x_1, \ldots, x_k, y) = (y+s)\prod_{i=1}^{m}(x_i - r_i)$$

and the class that the learner tries to learn is

$$C = \{f_{r^{(1)},s_1}(v_1, f_{r^{(2)},s_2}(v_2, \cdots f_{r^{(l)},s_l}(v_l, 0)) \cdots)\}.□$$

4 Upper Bounds for Parallel Learning

It is shown that there exists a randomized parallel algorithm that learns (with high probability) an n-variable read-once formula with $O(n^3)$ membership queries (on randomly selected inputs) in one parallel step followed by an NC^2 computation.

4.1 Definitions

An *arithmetic read-once formula* over a field $\mathcal{K}$ is a ROF over the basis of addition, subtraction, multiplication, and division of field elements whose leaves are labelled with variables or constants from $\mathcal{K}$. In this section, we refer to arithmetic read-once formulas as simply ROFs.

Following [BHH92], we consider an alternate characterization of ROFs in terms of a modified basis. The modified basis contains only two non-unary functions, addition ($+$) and multiplication ($\times$), and for each non-singular matrix $A = \begin{pmatrix} a & b \\ c & d \end{pmatrix}$, the modified basis contains the unary function f_A, where $f_A(x) = \frac{(a\times x)+b}{(c\times x)+d}$.

Between gates or leaves α and β in a ROF, the relationships *ancestor*, *descendant*, *parent*, and *child* refer to their relative position in the rooted tree. Let $\alpha \leq \beta$ denote that α is a descendant of β (or, equivalently, that β is an ancestor of α). Let $\alpha < \beta$ denote that α is a *proper* descendant of β (i.e., $\alpha \leq \beta$ but $\alpha \neq \beta$).

For any two distinct variables, x and y, let lca(x, y) denote the least common ancestor with respect to $\leq$ in the rooted tree. Also, let op(x, y) denote the operation of lca(x, y). Note that, since lca(x, y) is always a non-unary gate, op$(x, y) \in \{+, \times\}$.

Whenever two non-unary gates of the same type in a ROF are separated by only a unary gate it may be possible to collapse them together to a single non-unary gate of the same type with higher arity.

For $\star \in \{+, \times\}$, a unary operation f_A is called $\star$-*collapsible* if

$$f_A(x \star y) \star z \equiv f_B(x) \star f_C(y) \star z,$$

for some unary operations f_B and f_C. (Intuitively, the above property means that two binary $\star$ gates can be "collapsed" into a single ternary $\star$ gate with appropriate adjustments to constant gates.) In [BHH92] it is explained that a unary gate f_A is $\times$-collapsible if and only if A is of the form $\begin{pmatrix} a & 0 \\ 0 & b \end{pmatrix}$ or $\begin{pmatrix} 0 & a \\ b & 0 \end{pmatrix}$, and $+$-collapsible if and only if A is of the form $\begin{pmatrix} a & b \\ 0 & c \end{pmatrix}$. As noted in [BHH92], we may assume without loss of generality that a ROF is in the form where it contains no $\star$-collapsible unary gates ($\star \in \{+, \times\}$) whose parent and child are both of type $\star$.

For any two gates, α and β, with $\alpha < \beta$, define the *α–β path* as the sequence of gate operations along the path in the tree from α to β.

In [BHH92], a *three-way justifying assignment* is defined as an assignment of constant values to all but three variables in a ROF such that the resulting formula depends on all of the three remaining variables. A special kind of three-way justifying assignment is used in the parallel algorithm presented in Section 4.3. Define a *non-collapsing* three-way justifying assignment as a three-way justifying assignment with the following additional property. For any three distinct variables x, y, and z, if $\text{lca}(x, y) < \text{lca}(x, z)$ and all non-unary operations in the $\text{lca}(x, y)$–$\text{lca}(x, z)$ path are of the same type $\star$ (for some $\star \in \{+, \times\}$) then the function that results from the justifying assignment is of the form

$$f_E(f_C(f_A(x) \star f_B(y)) \star f_D(z)),$$

for some unary operations f_A, f_B, f_C, f_D and f_E, where f_C is not $\star$-collapsible. Intuitively, this means that, after the justifying assignment, the two gates, $\text{lca}(x, y)$ and $\text{lca}(x, z)$, cannot be collapsed—and thus the relationship $\text{lca}(x, y) < \text{lca}(x, z)$ can still be detected in the resulting function Now, define a *total* non-collapsing three-way justifying assignment as a *single* assignment of constant values to all variables in a ROF such that, *for any three variables*, if all but those three are assigned to their respective constants then the resulting assignment is non-collapsing three-way justifying.

The *skeleton* of a ROF is the ROF with all unary gates removed.

4.2 Parallel Learning Algorithm

In this section, we present a parallel algorithm for learning ROFs. Informally, the sequential algorithms in [HH91] and [BHH92] contain procedures that are either "top-down" or "bottom-up" in the following senses. The top-down procedures determine structural properties at the root gate of a ROF, and then, in a recursive manner, reapply themselves on the immediate descendants of the root, until the leaves are reached. The bottom-up procedures determine structural properties at the leaves of a ROF and then proceed upwards towards the root, one level at a time. Such procedures, even after the "obvious" parallelizations are made to them, require time at least linearly proportional to the depth of the target ROF (which can be $\Omega(n)$, for a ROF with n variables).

The algorithm has three principal components: finding a total non-collapsing three-way justifying assignment; determining the skeleton of the ROF; and, determining the unary gates of the ROF.

The basic idea is to construct a graph (called the LCAH graph) that contains information about the relative positions of the lcas of all pairs of variables. To construct this graph in $O(\log n)$ time, a stronger version of one of the primitive operations that is used in the sequential algorithm is used (this is obtained by using a total non-collapsing three-way justifying assignment). Once the LCAH graph has been constructed, the skeleton of the ROF can be constructed by discarding some of the structure of the LCAH graph (a "garbage collection" step). This is accomplished using some simple graph algorithms, as well as a parallel prefix sum computation (which is NC^1 computable [LF80]). Finally, once that skeleton is determined, the constants can be determined by a recursive tree contraction method (using results from [B74]).

4.2.1 Finding a Total Non-Collapsing Three-Way Justifying Assignment

In [BHH92], it is proven that, for any triple of variables x, y and z, by drawing random values (independently) from a sufficiently large field, and assigning them to the other variables in a ROF, a three-way justifying assignment for those variables is obtained with high probability. In the parallel algorithm, a three-way justifying assignment that is *total non-collapsing* is required. We show that the same randomized procedure also yields a total non-collapsing three-way justifying assignment with sufficiently high probability. This is a consequence of the following theorem.

Theorem 12: *Let $F(x_1, \ldots, x_n)$ be a ROF, and $x_1^{(0)}, \ldots, x_n^{(0)}$ be chosen uniformly from a set $A \subseteq \mathcal{K}$ with $|A| = m$. Then the probability that $x_1^{(0)}, \ldots, x_n^{(0)}$ is a total non-collapsing three-way justifying assignment is least $1 - \frac{4n^2}{m}$.*

We omit the proof of Theorem 12 here, but sketch a slightly weaker result: that the probability in the theorem is at least $1 - n^4/m$.

The proof of non-collapsability is based on the following fact that is straightforward to verify.

Fact 13: *If $g(y, z) = f_B(f_A(y) \star z)$, where f_A is not $\star$-collapsing then there exist at most one value $z^{(0)}$ for z such that $g(y, z^{(0)}) \equiv f_C(y)$, where f_C is $\star$-collapsing.*

Using Fact 13, we prove the following lemma, from which our desired result is an immediate consequence.

Lemma 14: *Let $F(x_1, \ldots, x_n)$ be a ROF with $lca(x_1, x_2) < lca(x_1, x_3)$ and suppose that all non-unary operations in the $lca(x_1, x_2) - lca(x_1, x_3)$ path are of the same type $\star \in \{+, \times\}$. Let $x_4^{(0)}, \ldots, x_n^{(0)}$ be independently uniformly randomly chosen from $A \subseteq \mathcal{K}$, where $|A| = m$. Then the probability that $x_4^{(0)}, \ldots, x_n^{(0)}$ is a non-collapsing three-way justifying assignment is at least $1 - (\frac{3n+1}{m})$.*

Proof: We have that $F(x_1, \ldots, x_n)$ is of the form

$$E(f_{H_k}(\cdots f_{H_1}(f_{H_0}(A(x_1)\star B(x_2))\star C_1)\cdots)\star C_k)\star D(x_3)),$$

where $A(x_1), B(x_2), C_1, \ldots, C_k, D(x_3), E(y)$ may depend on variables from $x_4, \ldots, x_n$ in addition to their marked arguments. Let $\bar{A}(x_1), \bar{B}(x_1), \bar{C}_1, \ldots, \bar{C}_k, \bar{D}(x_3), \bar{E}(y)$ denote the above formulas (respectively) with $x_4^{(0)}, \ldots, x_n^{(0)}$ substituted for the variables $x_4, \ldots, x_n$. Also, let $d_1, \ldots, d_k$ denote the degrees of $C_1, \ldots, C_k$ (respectively). Without loss of generality, f_{H_0} is not $\star$-collapsing. Therefore, by Fact 13, there exists at most one value of C_1 for which $f_{H_1}(f_{H_0}(y) \star C_1)$ is $\star$-collapsing. The probability of this occuring for $f_{H_1}(f_{H_0}(y) \star \bar{C}_1)$ is at most d_1/m by Schwartz's result in [Sch80].

Similarly, if $f_{H_1}(f_{H_0}(y)\star C_1)$ is not $\star$-collapsing then Fact 13 implies that there exists at most one value of C_2 for which $f_{H_2}(f_{H_1}(f_{H_0}(y)\star\bar{C}_1)\star C_2)$ is $\star$-collapsing, which occure with probability at most d_2/m, and so on. It follows that the probability that

$$f_{H_k}(f_{H_{k-1}}(\cdots f_{H_1}(f_{H_0}(y) \star \bar{C}_1)\cdots)\bar{C}_k)$$

is $\star$-collapsing is at most $(d_1 + \cdots + d_k)\frac{1}{m} \leq \frac{n-3}{m}$.

Now $x_4^{(0)}, \ldots, x_n^{(0)}$ is not a non-collapsing three-way justifying assignment iff $f_{H_k}(f_{H_{k-1}}(\cdots f_{H_1}(f_{H_0}(y) \star \bar{C}_1)\cdots)$ is $\star$-collapsing or $x_4^{(0)}, \ldots, x_n^{(0)}$ is not a justifying assignment. The probability of the former condition is at most $\frac{n-3}{m}$ (from above); and the probability of the latter condition is at most $\frac{2n+4}{m}$ (from [BHH92]). The result follows. □

It follows from Theorem 12 that, if t random assignments are independently drawn then the probability that at least one of them is total non-collapsing is at least $1 - (\frac{4n^2}{m})^t$. Moreover, it is straightforward to identify one of the total non-collapsing ones (assuming that at least one is total non-collapsing) in NC^1 using techniques in [BHH92].

4.2.2 Determining the Skeleton of a Read-Once Formula in Parallel

In this section, we assume that a total non-collapsing three-way justifying assignment is given and show how to construct the extended skeleton with $O(n^3)$ membership queries in one parallel step followed by an NC^1 computation.

Using a total non-collapsing three-way justifying assignments, we can implement the following primitive operation with $O(1)$ membership queries and computational work (with a single processor).

DESCENDANT$(x, y, z) =$

YES	if lca$(x, y) <$ lca(x, z) and op$(x, y) \neq$ op(x, z);
YES	if lca$(x, y) <$ lca(x, z) and all non-unary operations in the lca(x, y)–lca(x, z) path are of the same type;
YES or MAYBE	if lca$(x, y) <$ lca(x, z) (other cases);
MAYBE	otherwise.

Note that if **DESCENDANT**$(x, y, z) =$ YES then it must be that lca$(x, y) <$ lca(x, z); however, if **DESCENDANT**$(x, y, z) =$ MAYBE then it is possible that lca$(x, y) <$ lca(x, z), but op$(x, y) =$ op(x, z) and the non-unary operations on the lca(x, y)–lca(x, z) are not of the same type, or that lca$(x, y) \not<$ lca(x, z).

To construct the extended skeleton of a ROF, we first construct its least common ancestor hierarchy (LCAH) graph, which is defined as follows.

Definition: The *least common ancestor hierarchy (LCAH) graph* of a ROF with n variables consists of $\binom{n}{2}$ vertices, one corresponding to each (unordered) pair of variables. For the distinct variables, x and y, denote the corresponding vertex by xy or, equivalently, yx. Then, for distinct vertices xy and zw, the directed edge $xy \rightarrow zw$ is present in the LCAH graph if and only if lca$(x, y) \leq$ lca(z, w).

We shall prove that the following algorithm constructs the LCAH graph of a ROF.

Algorithm CONSTRUCT-LCAH-GRAPH

1. **in parallel for all distinct variables** x, y, z **do**
   if DESCENDANT$(x, y, z) =$ YES **then**
   insert edges $xy \rightarrow xz$ and $xy \rightarrow yz$
   and $xz \rightarrow yz$ and $yz \rightarrow xz$
2. **in parallel for all distinct variables** x, y, z, w **do**
   if edges $xy \rightarrow xw \rightarrow xz$ are present **then**
   insert edge $xy \rightarrow xz$

3. **in parallel for all distinct variables** x, y, z **do**
  if no edges between any of xy, xz, yz are present **then**
    insert edges in each direction between every pair of xy, xz, yz

4. **in parallel for all distinct variables** x, y, z, w **do**
  if edges $xy \rightarrow xw \rightarrow zw$ present or edges $xy \rightarrow yw \rightarrow zw$ present **then**
    insert edge $xy \rightarrow zw$

Theorem 15: *Algorithm* ***CONSTRUCT-LCAH-GRAPH*** *constructs the LCAH graph of a ROF.*

Proof: (Sketch.) The proof follows from the following sequence of observations:

(i) For all distinct variables x, y and z for which $\text{lca}(x, y) < \text{lca}(x, z) = \text{lca}(y, z)$, after executing steps 1 and 2 of the algorithm, the appropriate edges pertaining to vertices xy, xz and yz (namely, $xy \rightarrow xz$, $xy \rightarrow yz$, $xz \rightarrow yz$ and $yz \rightarrow xz$) are present.

(ii) For all distinct variables x, y and z for which $\text{lca}(x, y) = \text{lca}(x, z) = \text{lca}(y, z)$, after executing step 3 of the algorithm, the appropriate edges pertaining to vertices xy, xz and yz (namely, edges in both directions between every pair) are present.

(iii) For all distinct variables x, y, z and w, after executing step 4 of the algorithm, the edge $xy \rightarrow zw$ is present if and only if $\text{lca}(x, y) \leq \text{lca}(z, w)$.□

It is straightforward to verify that algorithm **CONSTRUCT-LCAH-GRAPH** is in AC^0. Moreover, the $O(n^3)$ membership queries can be made initially in one parallel step.

In a ROF, each non-unary gate corresponds to a biconnected component (which is a clique) of its LCAH graph. Thus, to transform the LCAH graph into the extended skeleton of the ROF, we simply "compress" each of its connected components into a single vertex and then extract the underlying tree structure of this graph (where the underlying tree structure of a graph is the tree whose transitive closure is the graph[1]).

This is accomplished using standard graph algorithm techniques, including a parallel prefix sum computation (in NC^1 by [LF80]). The detail will appear in the final version of this paper.

4.3 Determining a Read-Once Formula from its Skeleton

Once the skeleton of a ROF is determined, what remains is to determine the constants in its unary gates. We show how to do this in $O(\log^2 n)$ steps with $O(n \log n)$ processors. The main idea is to find a node that partitions the skeleton into three parts whose sizes are all bounded by half of the size of the skeleton. Then the unary gates are determined on each of the parts (in a recursive manner), and the unary gates required to "assemble" the parts are computed. This is where the "totalness" of the three-way justifying assignments are required. It insures that the justifying assignments for each subproblem are compatable.

The following lemma is an immediate consequence from a result in [B74].

Lemma 16 [B74]: *For any formula $F(x_1, \ldots, x_n)$, there exists a non-unary gate of type $\star$ that "evenly" partitions it in the following sense. With a possible relabelling of the indices of the variables,*

$$F(x_1, \ldots, x_n) \equiv G(f_A(f_B(H(x_1, \ldots, x_k)) \star f_C(I(x_{k+1}, \ldots, x_l))), x_{l+1}, \ldots, x_n),$$

and the number of variables in $G(y, x_{l+1}, \ldots, x_n)$, $H(x_1, \ldots, x_k)$ and $I(x_{k+1}, \ldots, x_l)$ are all bounded above by $\lceil \frac{n}{2} \rceil$.

A minor technicality in the above lemma is that, since the skeleton is not necessarily a binary tree, it may be necessary to "split" a non-binary gate into two smaller gates.

It is straightforward to obtain the above decomposition of a skeleton in NC^1. Once this decomposition is obtained, the recursive algorithm for computing the unary gates of the ROF follows from the following lemma.

Lemma 17: *If*

$$F(x_1, \ldots, x_n) \equiv G(f_A(f_B(H(x_1, \ldots, x_k)) \star f_C(I(x_{k+1}, \ldots, x_l))), x_{l+1}, \ldots, x_n)$$

then:
(i) Given the skeleton of $F(x_1, \ldots, x_n)$ and the subformulas $G(y, x_{l+1}, \ldots, x_n)$, $H(x_1, \ldots, x_k)$ and $I(x_{k+1}, \ldots, x_l)$, it is possible to determine A, B and C, and, thus, the entire structure of $F(x_1, \ldots, x_n)$ in $O(\log n)$ steps with $O(n \log n)$ processors.
(ii) Given the skeleton of $F(x_1, \ldots, x_n)$, the problem of determining $G(y, x_{l+1}, \ldots, x_n)$, $H(x_1, \ldots, x_k)$ and $I(x_{k+1}, \ldots, x_l)$ is reducible to the problem of determining a ROF given its skeleton.

The proof of the above lemma will appear in the final version of this paper.

[1] All edges are directed towards the root.

References

[A87] D. Angluin, Queries and concept learning. *Machine Learning*, 2, pages 319-342, 1987.

[AHK89] D. Angluin, L. Hellerstein, and M. Karpinski. Learning read-once formulas with queries. Technical report, Report No. UCB/CSD 89/528, Computer Science Division, University of California Berkeley, 1989. To appear, *J. ACM*.

[AK91] D. Angluin and M. Kharitonov. When won't membership queries help? In *Proceedings of the Twenty Third Annual ACM Symposium on Theory of Computing*, pages 444–454, 1991.

[BOT88] M. Ben-Or and P. Tiwari. A deterministic algorithm for sparse multivariate polynomial interpolation. In *Proceedings of the 20th Annual Symposium on the Theory of Computing*, pages 301–309, 1988.

[B74] R. P. Brent. The parallel evaluation of general arithmetic expressions. *J. ACM*, 21(2):201–206, 1974.

[BHH92] N. H. Bshouty, T. R. Hancock, and L. Hellerstein. Learning arithmetic read-once formulas. In *Proceedings of the 24th Annual Symposium on the Theory of Computing*, 1992.

[B2H92] N. H. Bshouty, T. R. Hancock, and L. Hellerstein. Learning boolean read-once formulas with arbitrary symmetric and constant fan-in gates. In *The 1992 Workshop on Computational Learning Theory*, 1992.

[BHHK91] N. H. Bshouty, T. R. Hancock, L. Hellerstein, and M. Karpinski. Read-once threshold formulas, justifying assignments, and transformations. Unpublished Manuscript.

[BT90] A. Borodin and P. Tiwari. On the decidability of sparse univariate polynomials. In *Proceedings of the 22nd Symposium on the Theory of Computing*, 1990.

[GKS90a] S. A. Goldman, M. J. Kearns, and R. E. Schapire. Exact identification of circuits using fixed points of amplification functions. In *Proceedings of the 31st Symposium on Foundations of Computer Science*, 1990.

[GKS88] D.Y. Grigoriev, M. Karpinski, and M.F. Singer. Fast parallel algorithms for sparse multivariate polynomial interpolation over finite fields. Technical report, Research Report No. 8523-C5, University of Bonn (1988), 1988. To appear in *SIAM J. Comp.*

[GKS90b] D.Y. Grigoriev, M. Karpinski, and M.F Singer. Interpolation of sparse rational functions without knowing bounds on the exponent. In *Proceedings of the 31st Symposium on Foundations of Computer Science*, 1990.

[Han90] T. Hancock. Identifying μ-formula decision trees with queries. In *The 1990 Workshop on Computational Learning Theory*, pages 23–37, 1990.

[HH91] T. Hancock and L. Hellerstein. Learning read-once formulas over fields and extended bases. In *The 1991 Workshop on Computational Learning Theory*, 1991.

[HS80] J. Heintz and C. P. Schnorr. Testing polynomials that are easy to compute. In *Proceedings of the 12th Annual Symposium on the Theory of Computing*, pages 262–272, 1980.

[LF80] R. E. Ladner and M. J. Fischer. Parallel prefix computation. *J. ACM* 27(4):831–838, 1980.

[MT90] W. Maass and G. Turán. On the complexity of learning from counterexamples and membership queries. In *Proceedings of the 31st Symposium on Foundations of Computer Science*, 1990.

[RB89] M. R. Roth and G. M. Benedek. Interpolation and approximation of sparse multivariate polynomials over gf(2). Manuscript (to appear in *SIAM J. Computing*), 1989.

[Sch80] J. T. Schwartz. Fast polynomial algorithms for verification of polynomial identities. *Journal of the Association for Computing Machinery*, 27(4):701–707, 1980.

[Val84] L. G. Valiant. A theory of the learnable. *Communications of the ACM*, 27:1134–1142, 1984.

[VL] J. S. Vitter and J. Lin, Learning in parallel, *The 1988 Workshop on Computational Learning Theory*, pages 106-124, 1988.

Read-Thrice DNF is Hard to Learn With Membership and Equivalence Queries (extended abstract)

Howard Aizenstein*
Computer Science Dept.
University of Illinois
1304 W. Springfield Ave.
Urbana, Illinois 61801

Lisa Hellerstein†
Dept. of EECS
Northwestern University
2145 Sheridan Rd.
Evanston, IL 60208-3118

Leonard Pitt‡
Computer Science Dept.
University of Illinois
1304 W. Springfield Ave.
Urbana, Illinois 61801

Abstract

A general technique is developed to obtain nonlearnability results in the model of exact learning from equivalence and membership queries. The technique is applied to show that, assuming NP≠co-NP, there does not exist a polynomial-time membership and equivalence query algorithm for exactly learning read-thrice DNF formulas — boolean formulas in disjunctive normal form where each variable appears at most three times. This result adds evidence to the conjecture that DNF is hard to learn in the membership and equivalence query model.

1 Introduction

We prove the following result:

Theorem 1 *Assuming NP≠co-NP, there does not exist a polynomial-time membership and equivalence query algorithm for exactly learning read-thrice DNF formulas.*

This result involves two contributions. The first is a new technique for proving nonlearnability results; the technique is applicable to the exact learning protocol in which the learner obtains information via equivalence and membership queries. This learning protocol is a standard one in which a number of interesting learning algorithms have recently been developed. The second contribution is the application of the general technique to show that the class of read-thrice DNF formulas cannot be learned according to the protocol mentioned. As will be discussed below, this class is of significant interest due to recent related positive and negative results concerning DNF with restricted "reads".

The Learning Model Let F be a class of boolean formulas, and let $f \in F$ be a hidden "target" formula to be learned. A learning algorithm L may propose as a hypothesis any formula f' *from the class* F by making an *equivalence query* to an oracle (or teacher). The response to the query is either "yes" if f' and f are logically equivalent, in which case L has successfully learned f, or else the response is "x", where x is a counterexample to the correctness of f', that is, a boolean vector x such that $f(x) \neq f'(x)$. The learner L may also make *membership queries* by choosing any vector x and asking an oracle whether or not x satisfies the target formula f. The class of formulas F is said to be exactly learnable in polynomial time if there is a learning algorithm L and polynomial p such that for any n and any $f \in F$ of n variables, L, using equivalence and membership queries for f, runs in time at most $p(n, |f|)$ (and hence makes at most as many queries) and outputs some $f' \in F$ such that f' is logically equivalent to f.

This model of exact learning with membership and equivalence queries has received much attention recently, due to a number of significant results employing interesting learning algorithms. For example, it has been shown that DFAs, monotone DNF formulas, k-term DNF formulas, conjunctions of Horn clauses, read-once boolean formulas, switch configurations, and read-once formulas over extended bases can be learned in this model [24, 5, 3, 7, 8, 23, 11, 13, 12]. This stands in contrast to the relatively few positive results that can be obtained without membership

*Supported in part by NSF Grant IRI-9014840. Author's email address: aizen@cs.uiuc.edu. Telephone: (217) 384-8119

†Author's email address:hstein@eecs.nwu.edu. Telephone: (708) 467-1242.

‡Supported in part by NSF Grant IRI-9014840. Author's email address: pitt@cs.uiuc.edu. Telephone (217) 244-6027

0-8186-2900-2/92 $3.00 © 1992 IEEE

queries.

It is known [4] that an exact learning algorithm using equivalence queries can be transformed into a "PAC" learning algorithm in the distribution-independent approximate learning model of Valiant [24]. Similarly, an exact learning algorithm with membership as well as equivalence queries can be used to obtain a PAC algorithm that also uses membership queries. The converse implications do not hold, hence a negative result for the exact model (such as the one in this paper) does not necessarily apply to the PAC model. However, quite often whenever a PAC algorithm (with or without membership queries) exists for learning a class F, a stronger exact learning algorithm may also be found. Consequently, negative results in the exact model are at least suggestive of the difficulty of PAC learning.

The Role of Representation The exact learning model discussed above is *representation dependent*, in that the hypotheses queried by the learning algorithm must be formulas from the same class F from which the target formula is known to belong. A relaxation of this model allows *extended equivalence queries*, wherein the queries made by the learner may be formulas from some larger class $H \supseteq F$, or, in the most general case, may be in the form of any polynomial-sized circuit. A representation-independent exact learning algorithm for F is one that learns F using queries chosen from any class H representable by polynomially sized circuits.

Ideally, a *positive* learning result will be representation-dependent — the algorithm will produce intermediate hypotheses, and a final hypothesis, from the class F. However there are exact learning algorithms using extended equivalence queries (and membership queries) where no representation dependent exact learning algorithm is known [18, 1, 2, 15]. Similarly, there are some classes that provably (assuming RP $\neq$ NP) cannot be learned using hypotheses from the original class (without membership queries) yet for which learning algorithms with extended equivalence queries (and no membership queries) are known [22, 10]. Thus a representation-dependent negative result such as the one shown here does not imply that the class is not learnable with extended equivalence queries.

The significance of a representation-dependent negative result rests then on the fact that we care not only about whether an unknown function can be learned, but also about the form in which the learned function may be expressed. First, in the larger context of intelligent systems, a learned rule will need to be incorporated into a knowledge base and operated on by other system components. The particular form may determine the tractability of various other operations. Second, such investigations give us insight into structural properties of the classes under consideration.

Why Read-thrice DNF? A central question in the theory of learning is deciding which subclasses of boolean formulas are learnable with respect to any of a number of reasonable learning models. Of particular interest is the learnability of disjunctive normal form formulas, which has remained open since proposed by Valiant in 1984 [24]. One way to classify the complexity of DNF formulas is based on the maximum number of occurrences (or "reads") of the variables in the formulas. It is known that read-once DNF formulas (indeed, read-once arbitrary boolean formulas) can be exactly learned with equivalence and membership queries [8]. A similar result holds for read-twice DNF (but with extended equivalence queries - which may be arbitrary DNF formulas) [1, 16]. We are interested in the limits of this approach. There is some hope that the techniques used in these algorithms can be extended to give an algorithm for learning read-thrice DNF.

The investigation of read-thrice DNF is of particular interest due to recent results concerning this class in a representation-independent version of the PAC learning model. It has been shown that if read-thrice DNF is PAC-learnable with membership queries and randomly generated examples (or exactly learnable with membership and equivalence queries) then the general class of (unrestricted read) DNF would also be PAC-learnable (using polynomially circuits as a hypothesis class) from randomly generated examples without membership queries [9].

Other Nonlearnability Results Our results may be compared with previous nonlearnability results in the PAC and exact learning models, with and without membership queries, both representation dependent and representation independent.

There are representation dependent nonlearnability results in both the PAC and exact learning models when no membership queries are allowed. These results seem to fall into one of two categories: (1) Information theoretic arguments show that DNF, DFAs, NFAs, and CFGs are not learnable with equivalence queries alone [6]. However, these arguments do not seem easily extendible to learning protocols in which membership queries are also allowed. (2) Most similar to the technique used here are arguments showing for various concept classes C that the *consistency problem* for C is NP-hard, and thus C is not learnable in the PAC (or equivalence query) learning model unless RP=NP [22, 19, 10]. These arguments also do not seem easily extendible to learning protocols in which membership queries are allowed.

Representation-independent nonlearnability results are stronger, but are achieved at the expense of perhaps stronger assumptions. Arguments based on cryptographic and number-theoretic assumptions show that boolean formulas and DFAs are not polynomially predictable (or PAC learnable) from just random labeled examples [20]. More recently, other arguments (also based on cryptographic assumptions) show that sometimes membership queries cannot help in PAC learning: boolean formulas, constant depth threshold circuits, read-thrice boolean formulas, finite unions or intersections of DFAs, 2-way DFAs, NFAs, and CFGs are not PAC learnable from random labeled examples and membership queries [9]. While these techniques are powerful, they do not seem likely to apply to classes representable by constant depth boolean circuits (and in particular, to those with small constant depth such as DNF or read-thrice DNF).

In summary then, our negative result, while representation-dependent, does not rely on the perhaps stronger cryptographic-based assumptions, and applies to an interesting class whose learnability is still open even given such ostensibly stronger assumptions. It extends the known nonlearnabilty results of the exact model (based on NP-completeness) by showing nonlearnability even when membership queries are allowed.

The remainder of this abstract is as follows. In Section 2 we develop the general technique that may be used to prove a class F is not exactly learnable with equivalence and membership queries unless NP = co-NP. Section 3 exhibits a sequence of three reductions that are used to apply the general technique to the read-thrice DNF learning problem.

2 The General Technique

Our result relies on a general theorem (Theorem 2) which shows that for many classes of formulas F, if F is polynomial-time learnable with membership and equivalence queries then the *representation problem* for F is in co-NP. Corollary 3 shows that for such a class of formulas F, if the representation problem for F is NP-hard under $\leq_m^p$ reductions (polynomial time many-one reductions) then F is not polynomial-time learnable with membership and equivalence queries unless NP=co-NP. (In the remainder of this abstract whenever we write A reduces to B we mean $A \leq_m^p B$, and when we write A is NP-hard we mean A is NP-hard under $\leq_m^p$ reductions.)

We complete this section by formally defining the representation problem, and presenting Theorem 2 and Corollary 3.

REP(F): The Representation Problem For Class F
Instance: Set $X = \{x_1, x_2, \ldots, x_n\}$ of variables and a boolean formula f over X.
Question: Is there a formula $f' \in F$ such that f' expresses the same boolean function as f?

We define a class of formulas F to be *polynomial-time recognizable* if there exists a polynomial time algorithm that decides on input of any formula f whether or not $f \in F$.

Theorem 2 *Let F be a polynomial-time recognizable class of boolean formulas such that there exists a polynomial p where for every formula $f \in F$ over n variables $|f| \leq p(n)$. If F is polynomial-time learnable with membership and equivalence queries then REP(F) $\in$co-NP.*

Proof: Let LearnF be a polynomial-time membership and equivalence query algorithm for learning F which runs in time $q(n, p(n))$ where q is a polynomial. We assume that LearnF either terminates immediately after asking an equivalence query that is answered "yes", or it terminates by outputting FAILURE (which it does only when the membership and equivalence query oracles are not oracles for an $f \in F$). These assumptions are without loss of generality because LearnF can be modified so that before outputting a formula g it always asks an equivalence query g, and so that it counts its number of steps and outputs FAILURE as soon as it exceeds $q(n, p(n))$ steps.

Consider the following non-deterministic algorithm M that accepts exactly those formulas g for which there is no equivalent formula in F. M simulates LearnF to try to learn g as follows. If LearnF asks a membership query on assignment a, then M computes $g(a)$ by evaluating g on assignment a, and gives the value $g(a)$ as the answer to the query.

If LearnF asks an equivalence query with hypothesis h, then M first verifies that $h \in F$. This can be done in polynomial-time since F is polynomial-time recognizable. By the definition of the membership and equivalence query learning protocol, the only way

LearnF could ask an equivalence query not in F would be if the oracles were not consistent with a particular $f \in F$. Thus if $h \notin F$, g cannot be representable in F, so M accepts.

Otherwise (if $h \in F$), M non-deterministically guesses an assignment a on which g and h differ, then verifies that a is indeed a counterexample by evaluating $g(a)$ and $h(a)$. M rejects if a is not a counterexample (i.e., if $g(a) = h(a)$). Otherwise, M continues the simulation of LearnF by feeding the counterexample a as a response to the equivalence query.

If g is not representable then either LearnF conjectures a hypothesis $h \notin F$ as an equivalence query and M accepts, or else LearnF always conjectures formulas in F. In the latter case, since g is not in F, for each equivalance query made by LearnF there is a counterexample. Therefore, M can run the simulation of LearnF until FAILURE is returned and then M will accept.

Conversely, if g is representable, then LearnF must only conjecture hypotheses from F, and within its polynomial time bound must output a hypothesis h equivalent to g. Since there is no counterexample to h, M does not accept. □

Corollary 3 *Let F be a polynomial-time recognizable class of boolean formulas such that there exists a polynomial p where for every formula $f \in F$ over n variables $|f| \leq p(n)$. If REP(F) is NP-hard under $\leq_m^p$ reductions, then F is not learnable with membership and equivalence queries unless NP=co-NP.*

Proof: If F is polynomial-time recognizable and F is learnable with membership and equivalence queries then, by Theorem 2, *REP(F)* $\in$ co-NP. A simple exercise shows that, since co-NP is closed under $\leq_m^p$ reductions, if some language S is NP-hard under $\leq_m^p$ reductions and in co-NP then NP = co-NP. Thus if *REP(F)* is NP-hard under $\leq_m^p$ reductions then NP = co-NP. □

3 The reductions for read-thrice DNF

Note that every read-thrice DNF formula has size at most $3n$, and clearly read-thrice DNF is polynomial-time recognizable. Thus to apply Corollary 3 to prove our main theorem (Theorem 1) it suffices to show that REP(read-3 DNF) is NP-hard. In this section we give a series of three reductions establishing this fact.

In the first reduction (Theorem 4) we use standard techniques to show that an NP-hard variant of SAT (read-3 SAT) reduces to a variant of the exact covering problem, *CFM: cover with few missing elements* — given a collection $\mathcal{C}$ of subsets of a set $\mathcal{S}$, a subset B of $\mathcal{S}$, and a positive integer k, does there exist a cover $\mathcal{C}'$ of $\mathcal{S}$ in $\mathcal{C}$ such that every element of B is missing from at most k members of $\mathcal{C}'$?

The second and third reductions are not entirely straightforward. In the second reduction (Theorem 5) we build on an old technique of Gimpel [14] to reduce the covering problem, CFM, to a DNF representation problem, *DEBVO: DNF expressibility with bounded variable occurrences* — given a collection M of all the prime implicants of a boolean function f over the set of variables X, a subset $\mathcal{B}$ of X, and a positive integer κ, does there exist a disjunctive normal form formula F expressing f such that every variable in $\mathcal{B}$ occurs at most κ times in F?

In the third reduction (Theorem 6) we complete the proof that *REP(read-3 DNF)* is NP-hard by showing that DEBVO reduces to *REP(read-3 DNF)*. Suppose $\langle X, M, \mathcal{B}, \kappa \rangle$ is an instance of DEBVO. The essential idea is to reduce the read-κ restriction on the variables in $\mathcal{B}$ in the DEBVO problem to the read-3 restriction on all the variables in the *REP(read-3 DNF)* problem.

The definitions of the problems CFM and DEBVO are not exactly as described above, as some additional technical restrictions are necessary. The formal descriptions of the two problems and the complete reductions follow after some definitions.

3.1 Definitions

A *literal* is either a variable x or its negation $\bar{x}$. An assignment a is a function $a : \{x_1, x_2, \ldots x_n, \bar{x}_1, \bar{x}_2, \ldots, \bar{x}_n\} \rightarrow \{0,1\}$ such that for each i, $\{a(x_i), a(\bar{x}_i)\} = \{0,1\}$. A term is a conjunction ($\wedge$) of literals. A DNF formula is a disjunction ($\vee$) of terms. We will use the operators $\cdot$ and $+$ to represent the operations $\wedge$ and $\vee$ respectively. Sometimes, to express relationships between literals, terms, and formulas, we will use standard set notation and treat a term as a set of literals and a DNF formula as a set of terms. Assignment a satisfies term t (also written $t(a) = 1$) iff $(\forall x \in t)\ a(x) = 1$. Assignment a satisfies DNF formula f (written $f(a) = 1$) iff $(\exists t \in f)\ t(a) = 1$. A term t is an implicant of a DNF formula f if every satisfying assignment for t is also a satisfying assignment for f. An implicant t for a DNF formula f is a *prime* implicant if no proper subset of t is also an implicant of f. An implicant σ for a DNF formula f defined over n variables is a *fundamental product* if $|\sigma| = n$. A term t is said to cover a fundamental product σ if $t \subseteq \sigma$ (i.e., if the set of satisfying assignments of t contains the unique satisfying asssignment of σ).

Let X and X' be two sets of variables such that for every variable $x \in X$ there exists a number of indexed variables $x_1, x_2, \ldots, x_J \in X'$. Suppose a is an assignment to X, then we say that a' is the extension of a to X' if for every $x_i \in X', a'(x_i) = a(x)$. Denote assignment a with literal x fixed to 0 as $a_{x \leftarrow 0}$. Similarly, denote a with the truth values of each literal in the set X fixed to 0 as $a_{X \leftarrow 0}$.

Let t_1 and t_2 be terms of a DNF formula f such that there is exactly one literal x such that x is in t_1 and $\bar{x}$ is in t_2. The *consensus* of t_1 and t_2 is the term consisting of all literals in t_1 except x, and all literals of t_2 except $\bar{x}$. For example, the consensus of xy and $\bar{x}z\bar{w}$ is $yz\bar{w}$. The consensus of two terms is only defined when there is exactly one literal that appears negated in one of the terms, and unnegated in the other. Let t_3 be the consensus of t_1 and t_2. The term t_3 is an implicant of f and thus can be added to f without changing the function computed by f. If we could form the consensus of t_3 and another term of f, this would give us yet another implicant of f that we could add to f. A repetition of this process is called *iterated consensus* of the terms of f. We will use the fact that every prime implicant of a formula f can be obtained by iterated consensus of the terms of f [21].

3.2 The first reduction

Define the combinatorial problem CFM as follows:
CFM: Cover with Few Missing elements
Instance: Collection $\mathcal{C}$ of subsets of a finite set $\mathcal{S}$ such that every element of $\mathcal{S}$ occurs in some member of $\mathcal{C}$, $|\mathcal{C}| < 2^{|\mathcal{S}|-12}$, $\forall c \in \mathcal{C}$ $|c| \leq 6$, $B \subseteq \mathcal{S}$, and a positive integer $k \leq |\mathcal{C}|$.
Question: Does $\mathcal{C}$ contain a cover $\mathcal{C}'$ of $\mathcal{S}$ (i.e., a subcollection $\mathcal{C}' \subseteq \mathcal{C}$ such that every element of $\mathcal{S}$ occurs in some member of $\mathcal{C}'$) such that for every $b \in B$, there are at most k sets $c \in \mathcal{C}'$ such that $b \notin c$?

Theorem 4 *CFM is* NP*-hard.*

Proof: Define read-3 SAT as the problem of determining the satisfiability of a CNF formula F, where every variable occurs in at most 3 clauses. Using standard reductions it is easily shown that read-3 SAT is NP-hard. We prove the theorem by showing that read-3 SAT $\leq_m^p$ CFM. Let the set of variables $U = \{u_1, u_2, \ldots, u_n\}$ and the set of clauses $C = \{c_1, c_2, \ldots, c_m\}$ be an instance of read-3 SAT. We construct the following instance of CFM:
$\mathcal{S} = \{u_i, \bar{u}_i, b_i, g_i : 1 \leq i \leq n\} \cup \{c_i : 1 \leq i \leq m\}$
$B = \{b_i : 1 \leq i \leq n\}$
$\mathcal{C} = \{\mathcal{C}_i : 1 \leq i \leq n\} \cup \{\bar{\mathcal{C}}_i : 1 \leq i \leq n\} \cup \{G_i : 1 \leq i \leq n\} \cup \{\bar{G}_i : 1 \leq i \leq n\}$, where for $1 \leq i \leq n$, $\mathcal{C}_i$, $\bar{\mathcal{C}}_i$, G_i, and $\bar{G}_i$ are defined below. For notational convenience, we define $b_0 = b_n$ and $b_{n+1} = b_1$, so that the indices of the b_i variables "wrap around".

$\mathcal{C}_i = \{u_i, b_{i-1}, b_{i+1}\} \cup \{c_j : u_i \in c_j\}$
$\bar{\mathcal{C}}_i = \{\bar{u}_i, b_{i-1}, b_{i+1}\} \cup \{c_j : \bar{u}_i \in c_j\}$
$G_i = \{u_i, b_{i-1}, b_{i+1}, g_i\}$
$\bar{G}_i = \{\bar{u}_i, b_{i-1}, b_{i+1}, g_i\}$
$k = 2n - 4$

Clearly $|\langle \mathcal{S}, \mathcal{C}, B, k\rangle|$ is polynomial in $|\langle U, C\rangle|$. To see that $\langle \mathcal{S}, \mathcal{C}, B, k\rangle$ is an instance of CFM, note first that since each variable appears in at most three clauses of C, each $\mathcal{C}_i \in \mathcal{C}$ has cardinality at most six. Further, since $|\mathcal{C}| = 4n$, $|\mathcal{S}| = 4n + m$, and $m \geq 1$, it follows that $|\mathcal{C}| < 2^{|\mathcal{S}|-12}$ whenever $n \geq 4$. To complete the proof we show that $\langle U, C\rangle \in$ read-3 SAT $\Leftrightarrow \langle \mathcal{S}, \mathcal{C}, B, k\rangle \in$ CFM.
($\Rightarrow$) Let a be a satisfying assignment for $F = \Pi_{\{c \in C\}} c$. We show that $\mathcal{C}' = \{\mathcal{C}_i : a(u_i) = 1\} \cup \{\bar{G}_i : a(u_i) = 1\}$ $\cup \{\bar{\mathcal{C}}_i : a(u_i) = 0\} \cup \{G_i : a(u_i) = 0\}$ is a CFM-k cover of $\mathcal{S}$: $\mathcal{C}'$ covers all of $\mathcal{S}$ and for every $b \in B$, there are at most $2n - 4$ sets $c \in \mathcal{C}'$ such that $b \notin c$.

First we will show that $\mathcal{C}'$ covers all of $\mathcal{S}$. Since every u_i is assigned 1 or 0, for every i, ($\mathcal{C}_i$ and $\bar{G}_i$) or ($\bar{\mathcal{C}}_i$ and G_i) will be in $\mathcal{C}'$. Thus we will cover all the u's, $\bar{u}$'s, g's, and b's. Furthermore, since a is a satisfying assignment, for each clause c_j there exists a variable $u_i \in c_j$ such that $a(u_i) = 1$ (or $\bar{u}_i \in c_j$ and $a(u_i) = 0$). Then by construction, $\mathcal{C}_i$ (respectively, $\bar{\mathcal{C}}_i$) is included in the cover, and c_j will be covered by $\mathcal{C}_i$ (respectively, $\bar{\mathcal{C}}_i$). To complete the proof of this direction we show that for every $b \in B$, there are at most $2n - 4$ sets $c \in \mathcal{C}'$ such that $b \notin c$. Since $|\mathcal{C}'| = 2n$, it suffices to show that for each i, at least four sets contain b_i. Assume that $a(u_{i-1}) = 1$ and $a(u_{i+1}) = 1$; the other three cases are analogous. Then $\mathcal{C}_{i-1}$, $\bar{G}_{i-1}$, $\mathcal{C}_{i+1}$, and $\bar{G}_{i+1}$ are all in $\mathcal{C}'$. Since each of these sets contain b_i, there are at most $2n-4$ remaining sets in $\mathcal{C}'$ which do not contain b_i.

($\Leftarrow$) Assume F is not satisfiable, and assume to the contrary that there exists a CFM-k cover $\mathcal{C}'$ in $\mathcal{C}$. Since F is not satisfiable, the only way that $\mathcal{C}'$ could cover all the c's is if for some i, $\mathcal{C}_i$ and $\bar{\mathcal{C}}_i$ are both in $\mathcal{C}'$. To include g_i, $\mathcal{C}'$ must also include G_i or $\bar{G}_i$. Suppose i does not equal 1 or n. The cases where $i = 1$ and $i = n$ are similar. For each $j < i-1$ and $j > i+1$ to include u_j, $\bar{u}_j$, and g_j, $\mathcal{C}'$ must contain ($\mathcal{C}_j$ and $\bar{G}_j$), ($\bar{\mathcal{C}}_j$ and G_j), or (G_j and $\bar{G}_j$). Since none of these sets contain

b_i we have a total of at least $3 + 2(n-3) = 2n-3$ sets in $\mathcal{C}'$ which do not contain b_i. This contradicts our assumption that $\mathcal{C}'$ is a CFM-k cover for $\mathcal{S}$. □

3.3 The second reduction

Define the combinatorial problem DEBVO as follows:

DEBVO: DNF Expressibility with Bounded Variable Occurrences

Instance: Set $X = \{x_1, x_2, \ldots, x_n\}$ of variables, $\mathcal{B} \subseteq X$, a collection M of all the prime implicants of a boolean function f over X such that $|M| < 2^{|X|-7}$, $\forall \varphi \in M$, $|\varphi| \geq |X| - 6$, and a positive integer κ.

Question: Is there a DNF formula F equivalent to the function f such that every variable in $\mathcal{B}$ occurs at most κ times in F?

Theorem 5 *DEBVO is* NP*-hard.*

Proof: We show CFM $\leq_m^p$DEBVO, and the result follows by Theorem 4.

Let $\langle \mathcal{S}, \mathcal{C}, B, k\rangle$ be an instance of CFM such that $\mathcal{S} = \{s_1, s_2, \ldots, s_n\}$ and $\mathcal{C} = \{c_1, c_2, \ldots, c_m\}$. We can assume without loss of generality that C does not contain two sets c_i and c_j such that $c_i \subset c_j$ (because if it did, and C' was a suitable cover containing c_i, then we could substitute c_j for c_i in that cover).

Using a technique similar to one used by Gimpel [14] we transform the above instance of CFM into an instance of DEBVO. First we construct two boolean formulas f_1 and f_2. f_1 will be a sum of fundamental products $\{\sigma_1, \sigma_2, \ldots \sigma_n\}$ (over the set of variables $X = \{x_1, x_2, \ldots, x_n\}$) such that each fundamental product corresponds to one of the elements of $\mathcal{S} = \{s_1, s_2, \ldots s_n\}$ to be covered. The formula f_2 will be a sum of prime implicants $\{\tau_1, \tau_2, \ldots \tau_m\}$ of f_1, corresponding to the covering sets $\mathcal{C} = \{c_1, c_2, \ldots c_m\}$. Formally, for $1 \leq i \leq n$ we define the fundamental product $\sigma_i = \{x_1, x_2, \ldots, x_{i-1}, \bar{x}_i, x_{i+1}, \ldots, x_n\}$. For $1 \leq i \leq m$ we define the prime implicant $\tau_i = \{x_j : s_j \notin c_i\}$. Note that the fundamental product σ_i is implied by the prime implicant τ_j exactly when the element s_i is in the covering set c_j. Now define $f_1 = \sum_{i=1}^{n} \sigma_i$ and $f_2 = \sum_{i=1}^{m} \tau_i$.

Each choice of a covering subset of the c_i's corresponds exactly to a choice of a subset of the prime implicants τ_i. If f_1 were equal to f_2, and the formula f_2 contained all of the prime implicants of the function described by both formulas, we would complete the proof as follows. We would argue that the sum of the prime implicants in the chosen subset is equivalent to the function expressed by $f_1 = f_2$, because each fundamental product σ_i is covered by the term τ_j for which the set c_j (which corresponds to τ_j) covers the element s_i. We would then go on to show that an appropriate choice of $\mathcal{B}$ and κ would realize the reduction, i.e., that a choice of prime implicants with "bounded variable occurrences" would correspond exactly to a choice of covering sets with "few missing elements".

Unfortunately, in general f_1 and f_2 are not equal. While it is easily argued that the set of satisfying assignments of f_2 contains the set of satisfying assignments of f_1, the converse may not hold. In the remainder of the proof, we present two new formulas, f_1' and f_2' (defined below), and use the above argument on those two formulas.

Consider all of the fundamental products of $f_2 \wedge (\neg f_1)$. We refer to this set as $D = \{d_0, d_1, \ldots\}$. Note that each of the m prime implicants of f_2 has at least $n-6$ variables (by the definition of CFM, each c has at most 6 elements), each τ_j can be replaced by at most 2^6 fundamental products; thus $|D| \leq 2^6|f_2| \leq 2^6 m$. Following Gimpel [14], we separate D into two disjoint sets D_O and D_E. $D_O = \{d : d \in D$ and d has an odd number of positive literals$\}$ and $D_E = D - D_O$. We define f_1' and f_2' over the set of variables $X \cup \{y_1, y_2\}$ as follows.

$$f_1' = \sum_{i=1}^{n} \sigma_i y_1 y_2 + \sum_{d \in D} d y_1 y_2 + \sum_{d \in D_O} d y_1 \bar{y}_2 + \sum_{d \in D_E} d \bar{y}_1 y_2$$

$$f_2' = \sum_{i=1}^{m} \tau_i y_1 y_2 + \sum_{d \in D_O} d y_1 + \sum_{d \in D_E} d y_2$$

It is easy to show that $f_1' = f_2'$. Clearly, f_1' is a sum of fundamental products. It can also be shown, using iterated consensus, that the terms in f_2' are all prime implicants of the boolean function expressed by $f_1' = f_2'$ and that there are no other prime implicants of this formula. (For example, to show that no additional prime implicant can be formed from the consensus of two terms from the second subexpression for f_2', note that if d and d' both have an odd number of positive literals, and are fundamental products (over the set of variables $\{x_1, \ldots, x_n\}$), then d cannot contain exactly one literal which is negated in d' — there must be an even number of such literals.) Furthermore, each τ_i is missing at least one variable x_j, so the terms in f_2' are all distinct.

We now construct the following instance of DEBVO, and argue that the appropriate correspondence with CFM does indeed hold. Define $X = \{x_1, x_2, \ldots, x_n, y_1, y_2\}$, $M = \{m : m$ is a term in the DNF expression f'_2}, $\mathcal{B} = \{x_i : s_i \in B\}$, and $\kappa = k + |D|$. It is easily argued that $|\langle X, M, \mathcal{B}, \kappa\rangle|$ is polynomial in $|\langle \mathcal{S}, \mathcal{C}, B, k\rangle|$ and that $\langle X, M, \mathcal{B}, \kappa\rangle$ is an instance of DEBVO. To complete the proof of this theorem we prove in Lemmas 1 and 2 that $\langle \mathcal{S}, \mathcal{C}, B, k\rangle \in$ CFM $\Leftrightarrow \langle X, M, \mathcal{B}, \kappa\rangle \in$ *DEBVO.*

Lemma 1 $\langle S, C, B, k\rangle \in$ *CFM* $\Rightarrow \langle X, M, \mathcal{B}, \kappa\rangle \in$ *DEBVO.*

Proof: Let $\mathcal{C}'$ be a CFM-k cover for $\langle S, C, B, k\rangle$. We show $F = \sum_{c_i \in \mathcal{C}'} \tau_i y_1 y_2 + \sum_{d \in D_O} dy_1 + \sum_{d \in D_E} dy_2$ is a DEBVO-κ cover for $\langle X, M, \mathcal{B}, \kappa\rangle$. First we show that $F = f'_1$. Since F only contains prime implicants from f'_2 it is clear that the set of fundamental products for f'_2 contains the set of fundamental products for F. Thus to see that $F = f'_1$ it suffices to show that all the fundamental products in f'_1 are also in F.

Observe that the second and third expressions in F cover all the fundamental products in the second, third, and fourth expressions in f'_1. Thus it remains to show that all the fundamental products in the first expression of f'_1, $\sum_{i=1}^{n} \sigma_i y_1 y_2$, are also covered by F. By assumption $\mathcal{C}'$ covers all the elements $\mathcal{S} = \{s_1, s_2, \ldots, s_n\}$ and the construction of σ_i and τ_i guarantees that if c_i covers elements $\{s_{i_1}, s_{i_2}, \ldots, s_{i_j}\}$ then τ_i will cover the corresponding fundamental products $\{\sigma_{i_1}, \sigma_{i_2}, \ldots, \sigma_{i_j}\}$. So $\tau_i y_1 y_2$ will cover the corresponding fundamental products $\{\sigma_{i_1} y_1 y_2, \sigma_{i_2} y_1 y_2, \ldots, \sigma_{i_j} y_1 y_2\}$ and $\sum_{c_i \in \mathcal{C}'} \tau_i y_1 y_2$ will cover $\sum_{i=1}^{n} \sigma_i y_1 y_2$.

To complete the proof of this lemma we will show that every variable $x_i \in B$ occurs at most $\kappa = k + |D|$ times in F. Every variable in X occurs at most a total of $|D|$ times in the second and third expressions in F; we show that every variable in B occurs at most k times in the first expression of F. Observe that $c_i \in \mathcal{C}'$ iff $\{x_j : s_j \notin c_i\} \cup \{y_1, y_2\}$ is in the first expression of F. By the definition of CFM for every $s_i \in B$ there are at most k sets in $\mathcal{C}'$ missing s_i. Thus there will be at most k terms in the first expression of F containing the variable x_i. □

Lemma 2 $\langle S, C, B, k\rangle \in$ *CFM* $\Leftarrow \langle X, M, \mathcal{B}, \kappa\rangle \in$ *DEBVO.*

Proof: Let F be a DEBVO-κ cover for $\langle X, M, \mathcal{B}, \kappa\rangle$. We will show that $\mathcal{C}' = \{c_i : \tau_i y_1 y_2 \text{ is a term in } F\}$ is a CFM-k cover for $\langle S, \mathcal{C}, B, k\rangle$.

Since f'_2 contains all the prime implicants, $F \subseteq f'_2$. Further, since $f'_1 = f'_2$, F must cover all of the fundamental products of f'_1. Recall from the definition of f'_1 that the fundamental products in the first expression of f'_1 correspond exactly to the elements in $\mathcal{S}$. Furthermore, by the definition of D, none of the prime implicants in the second or third expression of f'_2 cover any of these fundamental products. So F must cover all the fundamental products in the first expression of f'_1 with prime implicants from the first expression of f'_2. As described earlier, each of these prime implicants corresponds to a cover $c_i \in \mathcal{C}$ such that c_i covers exactly the elements of $\mathcal{S}$ corresponding to the fundamental products covered by the prime implicants. $\mathcal{C}'$ is constructed above to include exactly these c_i's. Thus $\mathcal{C}'$ will cover all the elements of $\mathcal{S}$.

To complete the proof of this claim we show that for every $s_i \in B$, there are at most k sets in $\mathcal{C}'$ which do not contain s_i. It is clear from the transformation of $\langle S, \mathcal{C}, B, k\rangle$ into $\langle X, M, \mathcal{B}, \kappa\rangle$, that if $s_i \in B$, x_i must be in $\mathcal{B}$ and $y_1, y_2 \notin \mathcal{B}$. By the definition of *DEBVO*, x_i appears at most $k + |D|$ times in F. $|D|$ occurrences of x_i can be accounted for by considering the $|D|$ prime implicants in the second and third expressions of f'_2: each one contains x_i and it can be shown that each one is necessary to cover the corresponding fundamental product in the third and fourth expressions of f'_1 (i.e., each is an essential prime implicant). Thus x_i appears at most k times in the remaining terms of F. As described above each of these terms $\tau_j y_1 y_2$ corresponds to a collection c_j in $\mathcal{C}$ such that τ_j contains the variable x_i iff c_j does not contain the element s_i. Therefore, since at most k terms contain the variable x_i, at most k of the corresponding collections in $\mathcal{C}'$ will be missing the element s_i. □

3.4 The third reduction

We prove the following theorem.

Theorem 6 *REP(read-3 DNF) is* NP-*hard.*

Proof: By Theorem 5 *DEBVO* is known to be NP-hard; thus it suffices to show that *DEBVO*$\leq^p_m$*REP(read-3 DNF)*.

Let $\langle X, \mathcal{B}, M, \kappa\rangle$ be an instance of *DEBVO* and suppose $|M| = \mu$. Note for any DNF formula F satisfying the *DEBVO* constraints for $\langle X, M, \mathcal{B}, \kappa\rangle$ every variable $b \in \mathcal{B}$ occurs at most κ times in F and every variable $x \in X - \mathcal{B}$ occurs at most μ times in F. We will construct a boolean function g over an extended variable set X' such that $\langle X, M, \mathcal{B}, \kappa\rangle \in$ *DEBVO* $\Leftrightarrow g$ is representable in read-3 DNF. The key idea is to reduce the read-κ restriction on the variables in $\mathcal{B}$ in the DEBVO problem to the read-3 restriction on all the variables in the *REP(read-3 DNF)* problem.

We define a new set of variables X' which consists of μ copies of each variable x in $X - \mathcal{B}$, and κ copies of each variable x in $\mathcal{B}$. That is, $X' = \{x_i : x \in X - \mathcal{B} \wedge 1 \le i \le \mu\} \cup \{x_i : x \in \mathcal{B} \wedge 1 \le i \le \kappa\}$. For notational convenience, we define $x_{\mu+1} = x_1$ for all $x \in X - \mathcal{B}$, and we define $x_{\kappa+1} = x_1$ for all $x \in \mathcal{B}$, so that the indices "wrap-around". For all $x \in X$, consider $x_1 \in X'$ to be the same variable as x. Thus X is a subset of X'. For each x, think of the variables x_i as synonyms for x. Now define

$$g = \alpha + \beta + \gamma,$$

where $\alpha = \sum_{m \in M} m$, $\beta = \sum_{x \in X - \mathcal{B}} \sum_{i=1}^{\mu} x_i \bar{x}_{i+1}$, and $\gamma = \sum_{x \in \mathcal{B}} \sum_{i=1}^{\kappa} x_i \bar{x}_{i+1}$. We call the terms of α the *original terms*, and the terms of β and γ the *cycle terms*. To help understand g, let's say that an assignment a to the variables of X' is *proper* if for every original variable $x \in X$, all of the copies x_i of x are assigned the same value by a. Otherwise, assignment a is said to be *improper*. Then each proper assignment a' to X' naturally corresponds to exactly one assignment a to X, and a' satisfies g exactly when a satisfies one of the terms of M — no cycle term is satisfied by a proper assignment. Further, every improper assignment must satisfy some cycle term of g. Thus g behaves as the collection of terms M does for proper assignments, and accepts any improper assignment. Note that $|g|$ is polynomial in $|\langle X, M, \mathcal{B}, \kappa\rangle|$. To complete the reduction it remains to be shown that $\langle X, B, M, k\rangle \in DEBVO \Leftrightarrow g$ is representable in read-3 DNF. This is done in Lemmas 3 and 4. □

Lemma 3 $\langle X, M, \mathcal{B}, \kappa\rangle \in DEBVO \Rightarrow g$ *is representable in read-3 DNF.*

Proof: Let F be a DNF formula satisfying the *DEBVO* constraints for $\langle X, M, \mathcal{B}, \kappa\rangle$. We will construct a read-3 DNF formula F' over X' that expresses g. Note that if we ignore the α portion of g, the remaining β and γ portions (the cycle terms) contain each variable of X' exactly twice. F' will contain these cycle terms. Further, F' will essentially contain all terms of F, except that rather than use original variables x in X, F' will use, at most one time each, the variables x_i that act as synonyms for x.

Formally, we will say that m contains the ith occurrence of variable x if in the lexicographic ordering of the prime implicants in F the ith occurrence of variable x is in the prime implicant m. Then define

$$F' = \alpha_F + \beta + \gamma,$$

where $\alpha_F = \sum_{m \in F} \{x_i : m \text{ contains the } i\text{th occurrence of } x\}$, and where β and γ are as before. For example, if $F = xy + xz + yw$ then α_F would be $x_1y_1 + x_2z_1 + y_2w_1$.

To see that F' is a read-3 DNF formula, recall that each variable of $\mathcal{B}$ occurs in F at most κ times, and each other variable occurs in F at most $|M| = \mu$ times, so there are enough copies of each type of variable to express F using synonymous variables exactly once in the α_F terms of F'. There are exactly two additional occurrences of every variable in F' in the cycle terms, thus F' is a read-3-DNF formula.

Clearly $F'(a) = g(a) = 1$ for all improper assignments a. Now any proper assignment a' has a corresponding assignment a over just the original variables of X. Then $F'(a') = 1$ iff a' satisfies some α_F term of F', which holds iff $F(a) = 1$ (because the α_F terms of F' are synonyms for terms of F, and all synonym variables are set identically since a' is proper). Further, $F(a) = 1$ iff a satisfies some term of M iff $g(a') = 1$. Thus F' and g agree on all proper assignments as well, and g is representable as a read-3-DNF. □

To prove Lemma 4, which asserts the converse of Lemma 3, we would like to argue that any representation of g as a read-3 DNF must look like the F' constructed above. One step in that direction would be to first show that any such representation must contain the cycle terms of g. However, because there are many copies of each variable, this need not be true. Instead we show that any representation of g as a read-3-DNF must contain terms that play the same role as the cycle terms of g. Similarly, a representation of g as a read-3-DNF must contain terms that play the same role as the α_F terms of F'.

Definition 1 describes variants of cycle terms and original terms, called, respectively, *pseudo-cycle* terms and *pseudo-original* terms. It is then shown (Claim 7) that these are exactly the prime implicants of g. In Claim 8 it is shown that for every variable $x \in X$ there is a negative example for α which is not *sensitive* for x (i.e., flipping the truth value assigned to x by the negative example does not cause it to become a positive example). This property is then used to show (Claim 9) that pseudo-cycle terms account for at least two occurrences of every variable in g. From this point the proof of Lemma 4 is relatively straightforward.

Definition 1 *A term t is a pseudo-cycle term if there exists a variable $x \in X$, and two integers i, j, such that $i \neq j$, $x_i, x_j \in X'$, and $t = x_i\bar{x}_j$. A term t is a pseudo-original term if there exists an original term $m \in M$ such that $|m| = |t|$ and $x \in m \Leftrightarrow$ there exists an integer i such that $x_i \in X'$ and $x_i \in t$.*

Claim 7 *t is a prime implicant of $g \Leftrightarrow t$ is either a pseudo-cycle term or a pseudo-original term.*

Proof: ($\Leftarrow$) this direction can easily be seen by a consensus argument.

($\Rightarrow$) Suppose contrary to this claim that there exists a prime implicant t which is neither a pseudo-cycle term nor a pseudo-original term. Suppose that for some variable x and positive integers i and j, t contains x_i and $\bar{x}_j$. Then t would contain a pseudo-cycle term, contradicting our assumption that t is a prime implicant and not a pseudo-cycle term. Therefore for every variable x and integers i and j, t does not contain both x_i and $\bar{x}_j$. Suppose that for some variable x and positive integers $i \neq j$, t contains x_i and x_j. Then we take the consensus of t and the pseudo-cycle term $x_i\bar{x}_j$ to obtain the implicant $t - \{x_j\}$, which is a proper subset of t, contradicting t's primality. It is similarly shown that no prime implicant t can contain both $\bar{x}_i$ and $\bar{x}_j$.

The above observations establish that for every pair of distinct variables x_i and $y_j \in t$, $x \neq y$. Now using iterated consensus on the terms in β and γ we can derive an implicant of g, t', which is equivalent to t except all the indices on the variables are removed (i.e. all have index equal to 1). We will now prove that t' is also an implicant of $\alpha = \sum_{\{m \in M\}} m$.

Assume to the contrary that t' is not an implicant of α, then there exists an assignment a to X such that $t'(a) = 1$ and $\alpha(a) = 0$. We can extend a to an assignment a' over X' such that $\alpha(a') = \beta(a') = \gamma(a') = 0$ and $t'(a') = 1$. But this contradicts our earlier observation that t' must be an implicant of g. So t' is an implicant of $\alpha = \sum_{\{m \in M\}} m$.

However, by assumption t is not a pseudo-original term, so t' is not in M; thus some proper subset of t', t'', must be a prime implicant of α, and thus must be in M. By performing consensus with terms in β and γ we can use t'' to derive an implicant of g which is a proper subset of t, thus contradicting that t is a prime implicant of g. □

Claim 8 *For every variable $x \in X$ there exists an assignment n to X such that $n(x) = 1$, $\alpha(n) = 0$, and $\alpha(n_{x \leftarrow 0}) = 0$.*

Proof: Let x be a variable in X. Consider the boolean formula α_{-x} which is the same as α except all literals of the variable x are removed. By the definition of *DEBVO* every prime implicant $m \in M$ contains at least $|X| - 6$ variables, so every term in α_{-x} contains at least $|X| - 7$ variables. We assume that $|X| > 7$, so that every term remaining in α_{-x} contains at least one variable. Notice that there exists an assignment n to X satisfying the conditions of the claim if there exists an assignment n' to $X - \{x\}$ such that $\alpha_{-x}(n') = 0$ (i.e. if α_{-x} is a non-tautology). We will now show that α_{-x} is a non-tautology.

Since every term in α_{-x} contains at least $|X| - 7$ variables, there are at most 2^7 different assignments to $X - \{x\}$ that satisfy a given term. Thus α_{-x} must be a non-tautology if it contains fewer than $2^{|X|}/2^7 = 2^{|X|-7}$ terms, and it must contain fewer than $2^{|X|-7}$ terms by the definition of *DEBVO*. □

Claim 9 *Let F' be a DNF formula equivalent to g, in which every term is a prime implicant. Then for every variable $x_i \in X'$ there exist positive integers j and k such that F' contains the (pseudo-cycle) terms $x_i\bar{x}_j$ and $\bar{x}_i x_k$.*

Proof: Let $x_i \in X'$. Let μ' denote the maximum index of the variable x in X'. By Claim 8 there exists an assignment n to X such that $n(x) = 1$, $\alpha(n) = 0$, and $\alpha(n_{x \leftarrow 0}) = 0$. Consider the assignment n' to X' produced by assigning to all $y_j \in X'$ the value $n(y)$. For j between 1 and μ', $n'(x_j) = 1$, $g(n') = 0$, $g(n'_{\{x_j : 1 \le j \le \mu'\} \leftarrow 0}) = 0$, and $g(n'_{x_i \leftarrow 0}) = 1$. Now we show that the only prime implicants satisfied by $n'_{x_i \leftarrow 0}$ are of the form $\bar{x}_i x_j$. We show this by arguing that none of the other prime implicants of g are satisfied by $n'_{x_i \leftarrow 0}$.

It is easily argued that no other pseudo-cycle term is satisfied by $n'_{x_i \leftarrow 0}$. By Lemma 7 all the other prime implicants must be pseudo-original terms and by definition if a pseudo-original term is satisfied by $n'_{x_i \leftarrow 0}$ then a term of α will be satisfied by $n'_{\{x_j : 1 \le j \le \mu'\} \leftarrow 0}$, contradicting that $g(n'_{\{x_j : 1 \le j \le \mu'\} \leftarrow 0}) = 0$. An analogous argument shows that for some k, F' contains $\bar{x}_i x_k$. □

Lemma 4 *$\langle X, M, \mathcal{B}, \kappa \rangle \in DEBVO \Leftarrow g$ is representable in REP(read-3 DNF).*

Proof: Let F' be a read-3 DNF formula representing g. Without loss of generality, assume that the terms of F' are prime implicants. We will show that there must be a DNF formula F satisfying the *DEBVO* constraints for $\langle X, M, \mathcal{B}, \kappa \rangle$. By Claims 7 and 9 we know that every prime implicant of g is either a pseudo-cycle term or a pseudo-original term, and that for every variable $x_i \in F'$ at least two occurrences of x_i in F' are accounted for by pseudo-cycle terms. Thus all the pseudo-original terms in F' can be represented as a read-once DNF formula over the variable set X'.

Now construct a DNF formula F over X by taking each pseudo-original term and replacing each indexed variable x_i with as many instances of the unindexed variable x as necessary. Formally,

$F = \sum_{\text{pseudo-original terms } m \in F'} \{x : \exists$ a positive integer i such that $x_i \in m\}$.

Since the pseudo-original terms can be represented as a read-once DNF formula, every variable $x \in X - \mathcal{B}$ occurs at most μ times, and every variable $b \in \mathcal{B}$ occurs at most κ times. To complete the proof we show that $F = \alpha$.

By the definition of a pseudo-original term each term in F must be a prime implicant in M. Thus every assignment to X which satisfies F will also satisfy α. To see the other direction, that every assignment to X which satisfies α will also satisfy F, consider an assignment a which satisfies α. Let a' be the extension of a over X' obtained by assigning the value $a(y)$ to each $y_j \in X'$. Since a satisfies α, a subset of the terms in g, a' will satisfy g, and thus will also satisfy $F' = g$. But a' does not satisfy any of the pseudo-cycle terms in F', so it must satisfy a pseudo-original term in F'. Since a' is defined so as to assign all x_i's the same value as x, a will also satisfy F. □

Acknowledgements

The simulation technique of Theorem 2 was originally applied in a less general form in [17]. We thank Manfred Warmuth for pointing out the generalization, and Nader Bshouty for pointing out the necessity of the property of polynomial-time recognizability.

References

[1] H. Aizenstein and L. Pitt. Exact learning of read-twice DNF formulas. In *Proceedings of the 32nd Annual IEEE Symposium on Foundations of Computer Science*, Washington, D.C., 1991. IEEE Computer Society Press.

[2] H. Aizenstein and L. Pitt. Exact learning of read-k disjoint DNF and not-so-disjoint DNF. In *Proceedings of the 1992 Workshop on Computational Learning Theory*, San Mateo, CA, July 1992. Morgan Kaufmann.

[3] D. Angluin. Learning k-term DNF formulas using queries and counterexamples. Technical Report YALE/DCS/RR-559, Department of Computer Science, Yale University, August 1987.

[4] D. Angluin. Learning regular sets from queries and counterexamples. *Information and Computation*, 75(2):87–106, 1987.

[5] D. Angluin. Queries and concept learning. *Machine Learning*, 2:319–342, 1988.

[6] D. Angluin. Negative results for equivalence queries. *Machine Learning*, 5(2):121–150, 1990. Special Issue on Computational Learning Theory.

[7] D. Angluin, M. Frazier, and L. Pitt. Learning conjunctions of Horn clauses. In *Proceedings of the 31st Annual IEEE Symposium on Foundations of Computer Science*, pages 186–192, Washington, D.C., October 1990. IEEE Computer Society Press. *Machine Learning, to appear.*

[8] D. Angluin, L. Hellerstein, and M. Karpinski. Learning read-once formulas with queries. Technical report, University of California at Berkeley, Report No. 89/528, 1989. (*J.ACM,* to appear. Also, International Computer Science Institute Technical Report TR-89-050.).

[9] D. Angluin and M. Kharitonov. When won't membership queries help? In *Proceedings of the 23rd Annual ACM Symposium on Theory of Computing*, New York, May 1991. ACM.

[10] A. Blum and M. Singh. Learning functions of k terms. In *Proceedings of the 1990 Workshop on Computational Learning Theory*, pages 144–153, San Mateo, CA, August 1990. Morgan Kaufmann.

[11] N. Bshouty, T. Hancock, and L. Hellerstein. Learning arithmetic read-once formulas. In *Proceedings of the 24th Annual ACM Symposium on Theory of Computing*, pages 370–381, New York, May 1992. ACM press.

[12] N. Bshouty, T. Hancock, and L. Hellerstein. Learning boolean read-once formulas with arbitrary symmetric and constant fan-in gates. In *Proceedings of the 1992 Workshop on Computational Learning Theory*, pages 1–15, San Mateo, CA, July 1992. Morgan Kaufmann.

[13] N. Bshouty, T. Hancock, L. Hellerstein, and M. Karpinski. Read-once threshold formulas, justifying assignments,and generic transformations. Technical Report TR-92-020, International Computer Science Institute (ICSI), Berkeley, 1992.

[14] J. Gimpel. A method of producing a boolean function having an arbitrarily prescribed prime implicant table. *IEEE Transactions on Electronic Computers*, 14:485–488, 1965.

[15] T. Hancock. Identifying μ-formula decision trees with queries. In *Proceedings of the 1990 Workshop on Computational Learning Theory*, pages 23–37, San Mateo, CA, August 1990. Morgan Kaufmann.

[16] T. Hancock. Learning 2μDNF formulas and $k\mu$ decision trees. In *Proceedings of the 1991 Workshop on Computational Learning Theory*, San Mateo, CA, August 1991. Morgan Kaufmann.

[17] L. Hellerstein. On characterizing and learning some classes of read-once functions. PhD Thesis, U.C. Berkeley, 1989.

[18] H. Ishizaka. Polynomial time learnability of simple deterministic languages. *Machine Learning*, 5(2):151–164, 1990.

[19] M. Jerrum. Simple translation-invariant concepts are hard to learn. Technical Report Technical Report Number CSR-12-91, Department of Computer Science, University of Edinburgh, 1991.

[20] M. Kearns and L. G. Valiant. Cryptographic limitations on learning Boolean formulae and finite automata. In *Proceedings of the 21st Annual ACM Symposium on Theory of Computing*, pages 433–444, New York, May 1989. ACM.

[21] S. Muroga. *Logic Design and Switching Theory.* Robert E. Krieger Publishing Co., Malabar Florida, 1990.

[22] L. Pitt and L. G. Valiant. Computational limitations on learning from examples. *J. ACM*, 35(4):965–984, 1988.

[23] V. Raghavan and S. Schach. Learning switch configurations. In *Proceedings of the 1990 Workshop on Computational Learning Theory*, pages 38–51, San Mateo, CA, August 1990. Morgan Kaufmann.

[24] L. G. Valiant. A theory of the learnable. *Communications of the ACM*, 27(11):1134–1142, 1984.

Efficient self-embedding of butterfly networks with random faults

Hisao Tamaki
Department of Computer Science
University of Toronto
Toronto, Ont. M5S 1A4, Canada

Abstract

We study the embedding of the butterfly network in a faulty version of itself where each node is independently faulty with some constant probability. We show that such a self-embedding of the N-node butterfly with $O(1)$ load, $O((\log\log N)^{2.6})$ dilation, and $O((\log\log N)^{8.2})$ congestion is possible with high probability, assuming sufficiently small node-failure probability. This embedding is level-preserving in the sense that each node is mapped to a node in the same level of the butterfly. We also derive a lower bound of $\log\log\log N - c$ on the dilation of a level-preserving embedding with $O(\log^{\alpha} N)$ load, for any α, $0 < \alpha < 1$, any node-failure probability $p > 0$, and some constant c depending on α and p.

1 Introduction

In this paper, we are concerned with the robustness of interconnection networks against random static faults. We assume that each node of the network is faulty with some constant probability, independently of other nodes. Faulty nodes are conceptually removed from the network together with all of its incident edges, and we ask if the remaining subnetwork can efficiently embed the fault-free version of the network. This model, which has been widely used in the literature [HLN89, KKL+90, AL91, Tam92], may be contrasted with a weaker model in which we are allowed to route through a faulty node [Ann89]. In general, an *embedding* of a network G in a network H maps each node of G to a node of H and each edge of G to a path of H consistently with the mapping of the endpoints. In our context of self-embedding, G is the fault-free network and H is the network after the removal of faulty nodes. The *load* of the embedding is the maximum number of nodes of G a single node of H receives, the *dilation* is the maximum length of the paths of H used, and the *congestion* is the maximum number of used paths that share a particular edge of H. A self-embedding with small load, dilation, and congestion implies an efficient simulation of the fault-free network by the faulty network, and thus can be considered as an evidence of the robustness of the network structure. (In fact, the slowdown of the simulation is $O(\textit{load} + \textit{dilation} + \textit{congestion})$ due to the result of Leighton, Maggs, and Rao [LMR] on off-line routing.)

Under this model, Hastad, Leighton, and Newman [HLN89] show that the hypercube is highly robust, supporting a self-embedding with $O(1)$ load, $O(1)$ dilation, and $O(1)$ congestion, with high probability. This result heavily depends on the logarithmic degree of the hypercube, and one naturally asks if a similar robustness can be achieved by bounded-degree networks. For the 2-dimensional array, this question is resolved by Kaklamanis *et al* [KKL+90], who show the upper bound of $O(1)$ load, $O(\log N)$ dilation, and $O(1)$ congestion (with high probability), together with a matching lower bound that any $O(1)$-load embedding requires $\Omega(\log N)$ dilation with high probability. Here, and throughout this paper, we use N to denote the number of nodes in the network. They also give almost tight bounds for the 3-dimensional arrays. Tamaki [Tam92] introduces a family of bounded degree networks called CCA_d, $d = 1, 2, \ldots$, and shows that the CCA_d admits $O(1)$-load self-embedding with dilation and congestion both $O(\sqrt{\log N})$ for $d = 1$, $O((\log\log N)^{\frac{3}{2}})$ for $d = 2$, approaching to $O((\log\log N)(\log\log\log N)(\log\log\log\log N)\ldots)$ as d increases. However, very little has been known about the so-called hypercubic networks, such as the butterfly, the CCC, the shuffle-exchange, and the de Bruijn networks. Annexstein [Ann89] did provide self-embedding with $O(\log\log N)$-dilation and $O(1)$-congestion for these networks, but under the weaker model mentioned above.

Very recently, Leighton, Maggs, and Sitaraman [LMS92] extensively studied worst case faults in bounded degree networks, and as one of the conse-

0-8186-2900-2/92 $3.00 © 1992 IEEE

quences, interestingly, derived a result on the butterfly with *random faults*: a faulty butterfly can simulate the complete butterfly with slowdown factor $2^{O(\log^* N)}$, which is very close to a constant. This simulation is not based on embedding, but uses the more involved scheme of replication [KLM+89].

In this paper, we give the first non-trivial upper bound for the self-embedding of a conventional hypercubic network, namely the butterfly network, with random faults.

Theorem 1.1 *For sufficiently small node-failure probability, a faulty N-node butterfly can embed the fault-free version of itself with $O(1)$ load, $O((\log\log N)^{2.6})$ dilation, and $O((\log\log N)^{8.2})$ congestion, with probability at least $1 - N^{-1}$.*

Although this upper bound is worse than those for CCA_d for $d \geq 2$, the result is important in that it applies to a conventional, widely-studied network. It is also worth noting that the maximum degree of CCA_2 is 16, and those of CCA_d, $d \geq 3$, are even larger, while the maximum degree of the butterfly is 4. In fact, our upper bound is easily transferred to the CCC network, which has degree 3, via standard embedding of the CCC on the butterfly. Thus our upper bound is achieved with the minimum possible degree.

The proof of the theorem depends on a lemma that, with very high probability, guarantees the existence of a linear-sized connected component[1] in a faulty butterfly and moreover an efficient routing capability of this connected component. We apply this lemma to small subbutterflies (roughly with $\log N$ nodes) and obtain efficient local paths for the mapping of edges. We note that the form of probability bound in the lemma is crucial, because we need *all* these subbutterflies to have, with high probability, a large enough connected component with an efficient routing capability. The proof is constructive in the sense that we can extract from it a polynomial time algorithm to find an embedding given the set of faulty nodes.

We also make an attempt to lower-bound the efficiency of a self-embedding in a faulty butterfly. Following [LMS92], we call a self-embedding of the butterfly *level-preserving* if it maps each node to a node in the same level of the butterfly. The embedding in Theorem 1.1 turns out to be level-preserving. Our lower bound is on this restricted class of embeddings.

Theorem 1.2 *For any constant α, $0 < \alpha < 1$, and any node-failure probability $p > 0$, the probability is $o(1)$ that a faulty N-node butterfly admits a level-preserving self-embedding with load $O(\log^\alpha N)$ and dilation $\log\log\log N - c$, where c is a constant which depends on α and p.*

The work of Leighton, Maggs, and Sitaraman [LMS92] includes a negative result for worst case faults: to ensure a self-embedding with $O(1)$ load and dilation, only polylogarithmic number of worst case faults can be allowed in a butterfly. Their technique does not seem to apply to random faults, nor does ours to worst case faults.

After some preparations in Section 2, we prove the main lemma in Section 3, which is the longest section. The proof of the main theorem is in Section 4, and the proof of the lower bound in Section 5. We discuss some open questions in Section 6.

2 Preliminaries

In this section, we define the butterfly network and review some of its structural properties. We also introduce some terminology for routing.

The m-stage butterfly is an undirected graph consisting of $m+1$ *levels* numbered $0, 1, \ldots, m$. Each level i consists of $M = 2^m$ nodes $< i, x >$, $x \in \{0,1\}^m$. The edges connect two consecutive levels, and fall into two categories: a *straight edge* joins node $< i, x >$ with node $< i+1, x >$ and a *cross edge* joins node $< i, x >$ with node $< i+1, x^i >$, for $0 \leq i < m$, $x \in \{0,1\}^m$, where x^i denotes x with its ith bit flipped. We say the edges between level i and level $i+1$ are in *stage i*. Note that a level refers to a set of nodes and a stage refers to a set of edges. For each $x \in \{0,1\}^m$, *row* x consists of nodes $< i, x >$, $0 \leq i \leq m$. Note that if we collapse each row x into a single node, we get an m-dimensional hypercube; a cross edge in stage i becomes an edge in dimension i and a straight edge degenerates to a self-loop.

An important structural property of the butterfly is that it contains many overlapping copies of small butterflies. If we look at k consecutive stages of the m-stage butterfly starting at level i, then the edges in these stages define 2^{m-k} disjoint copies of the k-stage butterflies. This is easy to see when we notice that collapsing these k stages and erasing other levels would produce 2^{m-k} copies of k-cubes. We call each

[1] It has been known to the author that Anna Karlin and Greg Nelson have an unpublished proof that a randomly faulty butterfly has a linear-sized connected component with high probability. Although the proof and the exact form of their result, especially the degree of "high probability", have not been available to the author and therefore the results in this paper have been independently developed, the knowledge of the existence of a proof has been greatly encouraging.

copy of these k-stage butterflies a *k-stage subbutterfly aligned at level i*.

Consider the $2m$-stage or the $(2m+1)$-stage butterfly B. We call the m-stage subbutterflies of B formed by the first m stages the *left subbutterflies* and those formed by the last m stages the *right subbutterflies*. The following observation provides the structure of induction in the proof of the main lemma.

1. If B has $2m$ stages, then each left subbutterfly intersects with each right subbutterfly at exactly one node in the middle level.

2. If B has $2m+1$ stages, then each left subbutterfly is joined with each right subbutterfly by exactly one edge in the middle stage.

Thus, we can view the global structure of a butterfly as a complete bipartite graph building on small subbutterflies.

A *routing request* on a graph G is a multiset of pairs of nodes of G. A multiset of paths of G *realizes* a routing request if it provides each pair in the request with a path connecting the pair. The *congestion* of such a realization is the maximum number of times it uses a single edge of G. A routing request is *one-to-one* if each node appears at most once in the request. Otherwise it is *many-to-many*. Finally, a routing request on a butterfly is *end-to-end*, if each pair consists of a node at level 0 and a node at the last level.

3 Connected component and end-to-end routing

This section is devoted to the proof of the main lemma, which states that a faulty butterfly for sufficiently small node-failure probability is, with high probability, "good" in the sense that

1. it has all but a small constant fraction of its nodes still connected, and

2. it sustains reasonably efficient end-to-end routing capability.

We first present the ideas of the proof, motivating a technical lemma. Then we give the precise definition of "goodness", and state and prove the main lemma more formally.

The proof is by induction on the number of stages of the butterfly. To prove a faulty butterfly is good, we split the butterfly at the middle level, and consider the left and the right subbutterflies. By the induction hypothesis, these subbutterflies are very likely to be good. To complete the induction step, we combine the connected components of these subbutterflies into one large connected component, and synthesize the routing capability of these components into a routing capability of this combined component. This step would be relatively simple if we could assume that all subbutterflies were good. However, then we would not get the high probability result needed, because the probability of this assumption failing is much larger than the probability of one subbutterfly failing to be good. Therefore, we must be prepared to lose some subbutterflies at each induction step, and thus keep losing some fractions of the network as we proceed through the induction steps. Parameters are chosen carefully so that the loss at each stage forms a geometric series, and hence the total loss will still be a small constant fraction.

We now describe how to combine the connected components of the subbutterflies. As we observed in the previous section, the connections between the left and the right subbutterflies form a complete bipartite graph; the nodes represent subbutterflies and the edges represent either shared nodes in the middle level (when the number of stages is even) or edges in the middle stage joining pairs of subbutterflies (when the number of stages is odd). The faults in the butterfly induce conceptual faults in this bipartite graph: if a subbutterfly is not good, then we kill the corresponding node; if a shared node does not belong to the connected components on both sides, or an edge in the middle stage does not span the connected components, then we kill the corresponding edge. We can expect the surviving bipartite graph to be still dense. This immediately allows us to combine the connected components of the good subbutterflies into one.

We still need to provide an efficient end-to-end routing scheme on this combined connected component. A one-to-one end-to-end routing request on this combined component induces a routing request on the bipartite graph. This induced routing request is many-to-many because each left node (right node) of the bipartite graph is responsible for all nodes in the leftmost level (rightmost level) of the corresponding subbutterfly. An efficient realization of this many-to-many routing, combined with the routing capability of each subbutterfly guaranteed by the induction hypothesis, produces an efficient realization of the original one-to-one routing on the large butterfly. Thus, the following lemma is the last major ingredient of the proof of the main lemma.

Lemma 3.1 *Let $G \subseteq X \times Y$ be a bipartite graph, such that $|X| = |Y| = n$, and such that the minimum degree* *is at least $\frac{3}{4}n$. Let Q be an arbitrary multiset of pairs from $X \times Y$ in which each node appears at most n times. Then we can route all pairs of Q in G with a multiset of paths of length 3 so that each edge is used at most 72 times.*

Proof We prove a stronger claim by induction on the size of Q: the multiset of paths described above can be chosen to have an additional property that each node appears as an internal node of at most $4n$ paths.

The base case $Q = \phi$ is trivial. Suppose Q is nonempty and the claim holds for all Q' with $|Q'| = |Q| - 1$. Removing one pair (x, y) of Q, we can route the remaining pairs of Q in G with paths Π as in the claim, by the induction hypothesis. We show that we can add a path for (x, y) to Π without violating the constraints in the claim. We say that an edge of G is *saturated* (with respect to Π) if the edge appears 72 times in Π. Similarly, a node of G is *saturated* if it appears as an internal node in $4n$ paths of Π. Because each node appears at most n times in Q, Q contains at most n^2 pairs. Therefore, the number of paths in Π which equals the number of pairs in $Q \setminus \{(x, y)\}$ is strictly less than n^2. Because each path has exactly one internal node in X, these paths in Π can saturate strictly less than $\frac{n}{4}$ nodes of X; the same holds for Y. Next consider the set of edges incident to an arbitrary node z. Because at most n paths of Π ends at z and at most $4n$ paths go through z, these edges are used at most $9n$ times in total. Therefore, at most $9n/72 = \frac{n}{8}$ edges incident to z are saturated.

Now we can choose the path for (x, y). Since x has at least $\frac{3}{4}n$ edges, of which at least $\frac{3}{4}n - \frac{n}{8} = \frac{5}{8}n$ are unsaturated, there is at least one unsaturated neighbour, say y', such that the edge (x, y') is unsaturated. We take this y' as the first intermediate node in the path. Nodes y and y' have at least $\frac{n}{2}$ common neighbours, of which at least $\frac{n}{2} - \frac{n}{8} - \frac{n}{8} = \frac{n}{4}$ are reachable from both y' and y through unsaturated edges. One of these $\frac{n}{4}$ neighbours must be unsaturated, completing a path for (x, y) free of saturated edges or nodes. It is clear that adding this path to Π preserves the conditions in the claim. ∎

We now formalize the proof ideas described above. Let δ be a constant, $0 < \delta < 1$, and λ and γ some positive values. We say a faulty m-stage butterfly is $(\delta, \lambda, \gamma)$-*good*, if it has a connected component

1. which contains at least $(1 - \delta)M$ nodes at each level of the butterfly, where $M = 2^m$, and
2. which contains a set of nodes U at level 0 and a set of nodes V at level m such that $|U| = |V| \geq (1-\delta)M$, and any one-to-one routing request from U to V can be realized by a set of paths with length at most λ and congestion at most γ. We call the nodes in U the *left terminals* and those in V the *right terminals* of the faulty butterfly.

Let B be a faulty $2m$-stage butterfly. Note that there are $M = 2^m$ left subbutterflies $L_1, \ldots, L_M$, and M right subbutterflies $R_1, \ldots, R_M$. Each of them has m stages and thus M nodes per level. Let v_{ij} denote the unique shared node of L_i and R_j. The *combining bipartite graph* of B with respect to parameters $(\delta, \lambda, \gamma)$ is defined as follows. The left (right) nodes of the bipartite graph represent the $(\delta, \lambda, \gamma)$-good left (right) subbutterflies, with l_i (r_i) denoting the node corresponding to L_i (R_i). There is an edge between l_i and r_j if and only if the shared node v_{ij} is both a right terminal of L_i and a left terminal of R_j. We call v_{ij} a *joint node* when this is the case.

The following lemma encapsulates the construction needed in the induction step for the case when the number of stages is even.

Lemma 3.2 *Let B be a faulty $2m$-stage butterfly. If the combining bipartite graph of B with respect to $(\delta, \lambda, \gamma)$ contains a subgraph $G \subseteq X \times Y$ such that $|X| = |Y| \geq (1 - \epsilon)M$, where $\epsilon \leq \frac{1}{2}$, and the degree of each node is at least $\frac{3}{4}|X|$, then B is $(\delta + \epsilon, 6\lambda, 144\gamma)$-good.*

Proof Clearly G is connected since any two nodes on the same side have at least one common neighbour. Therefore the connected components of all $(\delta, \lambda, \gamma)$-good subbutterflies corresponding to nodes of G combine into a single connected component with at least $(1 - \delta - \epsilon)M^2$ nodes at each level of B. Let U_i be the set of left terminals of L_i for $l_i \in X$, and V_j be the set of right terminals of R_j for $r_j \in Y$. We choose $U = \bigcup_{l_i \in X} U_i$ to be the set of left terminals of B and $V = \bigcup_{r_j \in Y} V_j$ to be the set of right terminals of B. (We may have to discard some number of nodes from either U or V to make there sizes equal.) It remains to established the routing capability of B between U and V. Let f be an arbitrary bijection from U to V. Then f induces a multiset Q_f of pairs from $X \times Y$ as follows: for each $u \in U_i$ such that $f(u) \in V_j$, we have a pair $q_u = (l_i, r_j)$ in Q_f. Note that each element of X or Y appears in Q_f at most $M \leq 2|X|$ times. We can split Q_f into two subsets so that each node appears in each subset at most $|X|$ times. Therefore, by Lemma 3.1, Q_f can be routed in G by a multiset of paths of length 3 with congestion at most 144.

Suppose (l_i, r_h, l_k, r_j) is the path in G to which pair q_u in Q_f is mapped. The path from u to $f(u)$ in our routing consists of four parts: a path in L_i from u to v_{ih} (recall this notation means the node shared by L_i and R_h); a path in R_h from v_{ih} to v_{kh} via some right terminal of R_h; a path in L_k from v_{kh} to v_{kj} via some left terminal of L_k; and a path in R_j from v_{kj} to $f(u)$. Now, the congestion of a particular joint node v_{ij} (counting only its use as a joint node in the above construction of paths) is exactly the congestion of the edge (l_i, r_j) in the routing of pairs Q_f in G, which is at most 144. Thus, in each subbutterfly, the total routing request contributed from all pairs of Q_f in the above path construction can be decomposed into at most 144 one-to-one end-to-end routing requests. Because all subbutterflies involved are $(\delta, \lambda, \gamma)$-good, each of these routing requests can be realized by a set of paths with length at most λ and congestion at most γ. Therefore, we have overall congestion of at most 144γ and dilation at most 6λ for the routing of f, which concludes the proof of the lemma. ∎

For a faulty butterfly with $2m+1$ stages, the combining bipartite graph is defined similarly: an edge in the middle stage induces an edge in the combining bipartite graph, if it spans a right terminal and a left terminal of good subbutterflies.

Lemma 3.3 *Let B be a faulty $(2m+1)$-stage butterfly. If the combining bipartite graph of B with respect to $(\delta, \lambda, \gamma)$ contains a subgraph $G \subseteq X \times Y$ such that $|X| = |Y| \geq (1-\epsilon)2M$, where $\epsilon \leq \frac{1}{2}$, and the degree of each node is at least $\frac{3}{4}|X|$, then B is $(\delta+\epsilon, 6\lambda+3, 144\gamma)$-good.*

The proof of this lemma is almost identical to that of the previous lemma, and is omitted.

We are now ready to complete the proof of the main lemma, which we state below.

Lemma 3.4 *Let δ be an arbitrary positive constant. Then, there exists a positive constant p_δ such that a faulty m-stage butterfly with node-failure probability p_δ is $(\delta, m^{2.6}, m^{7.2})$-good with probability at least $1 - 2^{-\sqrt{M}}$ where $M = 2^m$.*

Proof Without loss of generality we can assume that $\delta \leq 1/250$. Let m_0 be the constant $3(\lceil 3 - \log\delta \rceil)$, and define $\delta_m = \delta(1 - 2^{-\frac{m}{m_0}})$ for $m \geq m_0$ and $\delta_m = \frac{1}{2}\delta$ for $m < m_0$. In the following induction proof, the fraction of the lost nodes in the m-stage butterfly will be bounded by δ_m. Let A_m be the event that a faulty m-stage butterfly is $(\delta_m, m^{2.6}, m^{7.2})$-good. We show, for some p_δ, that A_m occurs with probability greater than $1 - 2^{-\sqrt{M}}$ for all m. The proof is by induction on m. To provide the induction basis, we choose p_δ small enough so that the probability that A_m occurs is greater than $1 - 2^{-\sqrt{M}}$ for all $m < 2m_0$.

For the induction step, we assume the claim holds for a particular $m \geq m_0$ and show that it also holds for $2m$ and $2m+1$.

We first consider a $2m$-stage faulty butterfly B. We apply Lemma 3.2 to B with ϵ, δ, λ, and γ in the lemma substituted by $\delta 2^{-(\frac{m}{m_0}+1)}$, δ_m, $m^{2.6}$, and $m^{7.2}$ respectively. Since $\delta_m + \epsilon \leq \delta_{2m}$, $6\lambda \leq (2m)^{2.6}$, and $144\gamma \leq (2m)^{7.2}$, it suffices to show that the combining bipartite graph of B satisfies the precondition of the lemma with probability at least $1 - 2^{-M}$, so that event A_{2m} occurs on B. Since the probability that A_m fails to occur on a particular left subbutterfly L_i is at most $2^{-\sqrt{M}}$ by the induction hypothesis, and since this event is independent among the left subbutterflies, we can use a Chernoff-type bound of the following form:

Proposition 3.5 *Flip M biased coins with the probability of tail being q for each coin. Then for any $\epsilon > q$, the probability that more than ϵM tails appear is less than $(\frac{eq}{\epsilon})^{\epsilon M}$.*

Applying this bound for $q = 2^{-\sqrt{M}}$, we get:

$P(A_m$ occurs on less than $(1-\epsilon)M$ left subbutterflies$)$

$$\begin{aligned} &< \left(\frac{e2^{-\sqrt{M}}}{\epsilon}\right)^{\epsilon M} \\ &= 2^{-\beta M} \end{aligned}$$

where

$$\begin{aligned} \beta &= \epsilon(\sqrt{M} + \log\epsilon - \log e) \\ &= \delta 2^{-(\frac{m}{m_0}+1)}(2^{\frac{m}{2}} + \log\delta - \frac{m}{m_0} - 1 - \log e) \\ &\geq \delta 2^{-(\frac{m}{m_0}+1)} 2^{\frac{m}{2}-1} \\ &= \delta 2^{m(\frac{1}{2}-\frac{1}{m_0})-2} \\ &> 2^{\frac{m}{3}+\log\delta-2} \\ &\geq 2, \end{aligned}$$

because $m \geq m_0 \geq 3(-\log\delta + 3)$. The same bound holds for the probability that A_m occurs on less than $(1-\epsilon)M$ right subbutterflies. Therefore, the combining bipartite graph of B has at least $(1-\epsilon)M$ left nodes and at least $(1-\epsilon)M$ right nodes with probability at least $1 - 2 \cdot 2^{-2M}$.

It remains to show that the combining bipartite graph is sufficiently dense. Let $E_L(i,j)$, for $i, j \in \{0, \ldots, M-1\}$, denote the event that A_m occurs on

L_i and node v_{ij} is a right terminal of L_i. Then,

$$\begin{aligned} &P(E_L(i,j)) \\ &= P(A_m)\cdot \\ &\quad P(v_{ij} \text{ is a right terminal of } L_i \mid A_m \text{ occurs on } L_i) \\ &\geq (1-2^{-\sqrt{M}})(1-\delta_m) \\ &> 1-\delta, \end{aligned}$$

because $2^{-\sqrt{M}} < \delta - \delta_m$ by the choice of m_0. For a fixed j, the events $E_L(i,j)$ for $i \in \{0,\ldots,M-1\}$, are independent. Therefore by the Chernoff bound, the probability that $E_L(i,j)$ occurs for less than $(\frac{3}{4}+2\delta)M$ values of i is at most:

$$\left(\frac{e\delta}{\frac{1}{4}-2\delta}\right)^{(\frac{1}{4}-2\delta)M} < 2^{-1.08M},$$

because of the assumption $\delta \leq 1/250$. Thus, with probability at least $1-2^{-1.08M}$, the left end of a particular right subbutterfly R_j contains right terminals of at least $(\frac{3}{4}+2\delta)M$ left subbutterflies. If in addition R_j is good, then the intersection of the set of these right terminals and the set of (at least $(1-\delta_m)M$) left terminals of R_j has at least $(\frac{3}{4}+\delta)M$ elements. A similar (symmetric) statement holds for each left subbutterfly L_i. Therefore with probability at least $1-2M2^{-1.08M}$, each node of the combining bipartite graph of B has degree at least $(\frac{3}{4}+\delta)M$.

To sum up the above analyses, with probability at least $1-2\cdot 2^{-2M}-2M2^{-1.08M} > 1-2^{-M}$, the combining graph has at least $(1-\epsilon)M$ nodes on both sides *and* each of its nodes has degree at least $(\frac{3}{4}+\delta)M$, and hence it contains a subgraph on sets of nodes X and Y, $|X| = |Y| \geq (1-\epsilon)M$, with minimum degree at least $\frac{3}{4}M \geq \frac{3}{4}|X|$. This establishes the precondition of Lemma 3.2 and concludes the induction step for the $2m$-stage butterfly. The analysis of the $(2m+1)$-stage butterfly is similar (using Lemma 3.3) and is omitted. ∎

Note that the allowable node-failure probability p_δ in our main lemma is not explicitly given; it must be small enough to make the statement true for all butterflies included in the induction basis of the proof, that is, butterflies with less than $2m_0$ stages. We could give an explicit value for which the statement is trivially true: choose p_δ to satisfy $p_\delta^{N_0} < 2^{-\sqrt{M_0}}$ where $M_0 = 2^{2m_0}$ and $N_0 = M_0(2m_0+1)$, so that a butterfly with less than $2m_0$ stages is completely fault-free with sufficient probability. However, the value obtained in this way is unrealistically small, and by no means indicates the best value of p_δ.

4 Efficient self-embedding

In this section we prove our main theorem that a faulty butterfly admits an efficient self-embedding with high probability, which is restated below.

Theorem 4.1 *There exists a positive constant p, such that a faulty N-node butterfly with node-failure probability p admits a level-preserving self-embedding with $O(1)$ load, $O((\log\log N)^{2.6})$ dilation, and $O((\log\log N)^{8.2})$ congestion, with probability $1-N^{-1}$.*

Proof We first prove the theorem assuming that the butterfly has wrap-around, i.e. each node $< m, x >$ in the last level is identified with node $< 0, x >$ in the first level. This allow us to use subbutterflies aligned at any level, which would be impossible for the levels close to the right end if there were no wrap-around. The modification for the butterfly without wrap-around will be given later. Let B be a faulty N-node, n-stage butterfly with wrap-around, where $N = n2^n$. Let $m = \lceil 2(\log\log N + 1)\rceil$, $M = 2^m$, and consider all m-stage subbutterflies of B. There are 2^{n-m} such subbutterflies which are aligned at each level, and hence $n2^{n-m}$ in total. By Lemma 3.4, we can choose the probability of node failure so that each particular subbutterfly is $(\frac{1}{8}, m^{2.6}, m^{7.2})$-good with probability at least $1-2^{-\sqrt{M}} \geq 1-N^{-2}$. Therefore, all of these m-stage subbutterflies are good with probability at least $1-N^{-1}$. Thus, it suffices to construct an embedding assuming that all subbutterflies are good.

Define a *block* to be the set of nodes at the leftmost level of each m-stage subbutterfly. Note that each block consists of M nodes, and all the N/M blocks form a disjoint partition of the entire nodes of B, while their corresponding subbutterflies overlap. For each block b, we denote by B_b the subbutterfly of which b is the leftmost level. In our embedding, mapping of nodes is closed within each block. Look at a typical block b. Because B_b is $(\frac{1}{8}, m^{2.6}, m^{7.2})$-good, at least $\frac{7}{8}M$ nodes of b are the left terminals of B_b. We map each node of b to a left terminal of B_b (in an arbitrary way) so that the maximum load is 2.

Having done the node mapping in all blocks, we now map edges to paths. The typical block b, at level i, is adjacent to two blocks at level $(i+1) \bmod n$, one of which we call b'. There are M edges between b and b', of which $\frac{M}{2}$ are straight edges and the rest are cross edges. We call a straight edge a *bridge* if both of its endpoints are left terminals of the respective subbutterflies. There are at least $\frac{M}{4}$ bridges between

b and b', because at most $2 \cdot \frac{M}{8}$ endpoints of those straight edges may fail to be a left terminal. We map each edge between b and b' to a path consisting of three parts: a path in B_b, a bridge, and a path in $B_{b'}$. To choose such a path for each edge (u, v), we first choose a bridge (x, y) so that the congestion of each bridge is at most 4. This can be easily done because there are at least $\frac{M}{4}$ bridges while there are M edges between b and b'. Let u' and v' denote the left terminals to which u and v are mapped respectively. Then we connect u' with x by a path of B_b via some right terminal of B_b, and connect y with v' by a similar path in $B_{b'}$. The routing requirements in B_b generated by all edges between b and b' can be decomposed into 6 end-to-end routing requests each of which is one-to-one. This is because each left terminal of B_b appears in the routing requests at most twice as node u' and at most 4 times as node x. Therefore, they can be realized by a set of paths with length at most $2m^{2.6}$ and congestion at most $6m^{7.2}$, because B_b is $(\frac{1}{8}, m^{2.6}, m^{7.2})$-good. The routing in $B_{b'}$ is done similarly. To provide paths for every adjacent pairs of blocks, we have to multiply the congestion by $4m$, because each block is adjacent to 4 blocks (to the right and to the left), and each edge belongs to m overlapping subbutterflies. We also have to add the congestion of an edge as a bridge, but this is at most 4, because an edge can be a bridge of at most one pair of blocks. Thus, the congestion of the embedding is $O(m^{8.2})$. The dilation is clearly at most $2 \cdot 2m^{2.6} + 1$. This concludes the proof for the wrap-around butterfly.

For the butterfly without wrap-around, the above embedding is still valid for the first $n - m$ stages of the butterfly. For the last m stages, we use the same embedding in which the left and the right are flipped. For example, the mapping of nodes in level m is based on the m-stage subbutterflies consisting of the last m stages of the entire butterfly. Let ψ_1 and ψ_2 denote the embeddings of the first $n-m$ stages and of the last m stages respectively. These two embeddings overlap, and conflict, at level $n - m$. To reconcile the conflict, for each node v at level $n - m$, we provide a path between $\psi_1(v)$ and $\psi_2(v)$. Let B' be the $2m$-stage subbutterfly which is centered at level $n-m$ and contains v. Since all of its left and right subbutterflies are $(\frac{1}{8}, m^{2.6}, m^{7.2})$-good, we can apply Lemma 3.2 with $\epsilon = 0$, and therefore B' is $(\frac{1}{8}, 6m^{2.6}, 144m^{7.2})$-good. Moreover, by the proof of Lemma 3.2 we can choose the left (right) terminal of B' to be the union of the left (right) terminals of the left (right) subbutterflies of B'. Let B_1 (B_2) denote the right (left) subbutterfly of B' to which v belongs. Note that B_1 defines a block associated with the embedding ψ_1 and B_2 defines one associated with ψ_2, and therefore $\psi_1(v)$ belongs to B_1 and $\psi_2(v)$ to B_2. Now the path from $\psi_1(v)$ to $\psi_2(v)$ consists of three parts: a path in B_1 from $\psi_1(v)$ to some right terminal of B_1; a path in B' from that right terminal to some left terminal of B_2; a path in B_2 from that left terminal to $\psi_2(v)$. The dilation of the combined path is clearly $O(m^{2.6})$. The routing requirements for B_1 that arise from all of its left-end nodes as v can be decomposed into 2 one-to-one end-to-end routing requests, because the load of ψ_1 is 2, and therefore the congestion thus incurred is at most $2m^{7.2}$. The same holds for B_2. Similarly, the routing requirements for B' that arise from all of its center level nodes as v incur the congestion of at most $O(m^{7.2})$. Summing up, the total congestion caused by these additional paths for the reconciliation of ψ_1 and ψ_2 is $O(m^{7.2})$. ∎

5 Lower bound for level-preserving embeddings

In this section, we prove a lower bound on the dilation of a level-preserving embedding. In fact, our lower bound is on a quantity called *drift* which in turn lower bounds the dilation. The *drift* of a level-preserving embedding is the maximum integer d such that there is an edge in, say, stage i whose image path goes through a node in either level $i-d$ or level $i+d+1$. Note that the dilation is at least twice the drift plus 1.

The proof consists of two parts: (1) an analysis of level-preserving embeddings showing that small load and drift require a large number of "good" rows in a faulty butterfly in a certain sense; (2) a probabilistic argument to show that such a large number of good rows are unlikely. We start with a definition and an elementary observation. As before, m denotes the number of stages in the butterfly, $M = 2^m$ the number of nodes in a level, and N the total number of nodes.

We say node $< i, y >$ is a d-neighbour of node $< i, x >$ if y agrees with x in all dimensions but those j in the range $i - d \leq j < i + d$. Note that a node is a d-neighbour of itself for any $d \geq 0$.

Proposition 5.1 *Assume ψ is a level-preserving embedding with drift d. Let $(v_0, v_1, \ldots, v_m)$ be an arbitrary shortest end-to-end path of the butterfly where each v_i is in level i, and let $(u_0, u_1, \ldots, u_m)$ denote the shortest path between $u_0 = \psi(v_0)$ and $u_m = \psi(v_m)$. Then for every i, $0 \leq i \leq m$, $\psi(v_i)$ is a d-neighbour of u_i.*

Proof Consider the path segment $(v_0, v_1, \ldots, v_i)$. Since ψ is level-preserving and has drift d, the image of this segment under ψ does not contain an edge in any stage $j \geq i + d$. Therefore, $\psi(v_i)$ agrees with $\psi(v_0) = u_0$, and hence with u_i, in every dimension $j \geq i + d$. Similarly considering the image of the path segment $(v_i, \ldots, v_{m-1}, v_m)$, we see that the same holds for every dimension $j < i - d$. ∎

Define a row in a faulty butterfly to be *k-good*, if it contains a contiguous segment of k nodes each having at least one non-faulty d-neighbour. The following lemma claims that small load and drift require the existence of many good rows.

Lemma 5.2 *If a faulty butterfly admits a level-preserving embedding with load at most l and drift d, then it must have at least $M/2l$ rows which are $((m+1)/2l - 2d)$-good.*

Proof Let ψ be an arbitrary level-preserving self-embedding with load at most l and drift d. We say ψ *uses* a node v, if it maps some node to v. Define, for each row x, its *span* to be $i_2 - i_1 + 1$, where i_1 (i_2) is the minimum (maximum) level such that $< i_1, x >$ ($< i_2, x >$) is used by ψ. Then, there must be at least $M/2l$ rows with span at least $(m+1)/2l$, because otherwise the number of nodes used by ψ would be less than $\frac{M}{2l}(m+1) + M \cdot \frac{m+1}{2l} = \frac{N}{l}$, forcing the load to be greater than l.

It now suffices to show that a row of span k must be $(k - 2d)$-good. Let $< i_1, x >$ and $< i_2, x >$ be the nodes that define the span of row x as above. We claim that for every level j in the range $i_1 + d \leq j \leq i_2 - d$, node $< j, x >$ has a d-neighbour used by ψ. To prove this claim, let x_1 and x_2 be such that $\psi(< i_1, x_1 >) =< i_1, x >$ and $\psi(< i_2, x_2 >) =< i_2, x >$. By Proposition 5.1 applied to the shortest path between $< 0, x_1 >$ and $< m, x_2 >$, each node on the shortest path between $\psi(< 0, x_1 >)$ and $\psi(< m, x_2 >)$ has a d-neighbour that is used by ψ. Therefore, it suffices to show that the shortest path between $\psi(< 0, x_1 >)$ and $\psi(< m, x_2 >)$ goes through the segment $< i_1 + d, x >, \ldots, < i_2 - d, x >$ of row x. Since the path from $\psi(< 0, x_1 >)$ to $< i_1, x >$ which is the image (under ψ) of the shortest path from $< 0, x_1 >$ to $< i_1, x_1 >$ does not contain an edge in any stage $j \geq i_1 + d$, the row of $\psi(< 0, x_1 >)$ agrees with x on every dimension j in that range. Similarly, the row of $\psi(< m, x_2 >)$ agree with x on every dimension $j < i_2 - d$. Therefore the rows of both $\psi(< 0, x_1 >)$ and $\psi(< m, x_2 >)$ agree with x on every dimension j in the range $i_1 + d \leq j < i_2 - d$, which implies that the shortest path between these two nodes must go through row x in that range. This proves the claim, which implies that row x is $(k - 2d)$-good where $k = i_2 - i_1 + 1$ is the span of x. ∎

Theorem 5.3 *For any node-failure probability $p > 0$, and any positive constant $\alpha < 1$, the probability is $o(1)$ that a faulty butterfly admits a level-preserving embedding with load at most m^α and drift at most $(\log\log m - c)/2$, for any $c > \log\log\frac{1}{p} - \log(1-\alpha)$.*

Proof Let $d = \lfloor(\log\log m - c)/2\rfloor$, c as above, and α' such that $c = \log\log\frac{1}{p} - \log(1 - \alpha')$. Note that $\alpha' > \alpha$. In view of Lemma 5.2, it suffices to show that the probability of at least $M/2l$ rows of a faulty butterfly being $(m/3l)$-good, where $l \leq m^\alpha$, is $o(1)$. The probability that a particular row is good can be bounded from above, for sufficiently large m, by:

$$\begin{aligned} &P(\text{a row is } (m/3l)\text{-good}) \\ &\quad\leq m(1 - p^{2^{2d}})^{m/3l} \\ &\quad\leq m(1 - p^{2^{\log\log m - c}})^{m/3l} \\ &\quad= m(1 - p^{\log m \cdot (1-\alpha')/\log\frac{1}{p}})^{m/3l} \\ &\quad\leq m(1 - m^{\alpha'-1})^{m^{1-\alpha}/3} \\ &\quad\leq me^{-m^{\alpha'-1}\cdot(m^{1-\alpha}/3)} \\ &\quad= me^{-\frac{1}{3}m^{\alpha'-\alpha}} \end{aligned}$$

Thus, the expected number of good rows is $o(M/l)$. To show that the probability that the number of good rows reaches $M/2l$ is $o(1)$, we appeal to the following lemma from the martingale theory. Note that we cannot apply a Chernoff-type bound because the events of rows being good are dependent.

Lemma 5.4 *(Azuma's inequality, see Alon and Spencer [AS92], Chapter 7, Theorem 4.2) Let A and B be finite sets, Ω the set of functions $g : B \to A$, and let L be a real valued functional $\Omega \to R$, such that it satisfies the Lipschitz condition: if g and g' agree at all but one element of B, then $|L(g) - L(g')| \leq 1$. Let X be a random variable defined by $X = L(g)$ where g is chosen randomly from Ω with the value of $g(b)$ assigned independently for each $b \in B$. Then, for any positive λ,*

$$P(X > E(X) + \lambda\sqrt{N}) < e^{-\lambda^2/2},$$

where $N = |B|$.

In our situation, B is the set of butterfly nodes, A consists of two values "faulty" and "non-faulty", thus $g \in \Omega$ represents a fault pattern, and we define $L(g) = L'(g)/2^{2d}$ where $L'(g)$ is the number of good rows under fault pattern g. Thus, $X \cdot 2^{2d}$ is the number of good rows in a butterfly with random faults. Clearly L satisfies the Lipschitz condition because the number of good rows changes by at most 2^{2d} when we flip the status of a single node. For any given $q > 0$, choose λ so that $q = e^{-\lambda^2/2}$. We have,

$$\begin{aligned} & P(\text{the number of good rows} \geq M/2l) \\ & \quad = \; P(X2^{2d} \geq M/2l) \\ & \quad < \; P(X2^{2d} > E(X2^{2d}) + 2^{2d}\lambda\sqrt{N})), \end{aligned}$$

for sufficiently large N, because

$$\begin{aligned} E(X2^{2d}) &< me^{-\frac{1}{3}m^{\alpha'-\alpha}}M \\ &= o(M/2l) \end{aligned}$$

and

$$\begin{aligned} 2^{2d}\sqrt{N} &< \log m\sqrt{M(m+1)} \\ &= o(M/2l). \end{aligned}$$

Therefore by Azuma's inequality, the probability is less than q for sufficiently large N, or in other words $o(1)$ as claimed because q is arbitrary. ∎

6 Open questions

Although our upper bound easily transfers to the CCC network, it is not clear if the result can be extended to the shuffle-exchange or the de Bruijn network. For the butterfly itself, our lower bound is restricted, and there is no reason to believe our upper bound is tight: an obvious gap to be filled in. We might also ask what is the best possible load/dilation/congestion ever achievable by any bounded-degree network.

As noted in the end of Section 3, the explicit value we can currently obtain for the allowable probability of node failure is prohibitively small. A proof with a better explicit value would be an interesting improvement.

Acknowledgements

Many thanks are due to Allan Borodin for valuable comments on this work. The author is also grateful to Jeff Edmonds and Tino Tamon for discussions and proof-reading of the manuscripts.

References

[AL91] B. Aiello and F.T. Leighton. Coding theory, hypercube embeddings, and fault tolerance. In *Proceedings of the 3rd ACM Annual Symposium on Parallel Algorithms and Architectures*, 1991.

[Ann89] F. Annexstein. Fault tolerance in hypercube-derivative networks. In *Proceedings of the 1st ACM Annual Symposium on Parallel Algorithms and Architectures*, 1989.

[AS92] N. Alon and J. H. Spencer. *The probabilistic method.* John Wiley & Sons, New York, 1992.

[HLN89] J. Hastad, F.T. Leighton, and M. Newman. Fast computation using faulty hypercubes. In *Proceedings of the 21st ACM Annual Symposium on Theory of Computing*, 1989.

[KKL+90] C. Kaklamanis, A.R. Karlin, F.T. Leighton, V. Milenkovic, P. Raghavan, S. Rao, C. Thomborson, and A. Tsantilas. Asymptotically tight bounds for computing with faulty arrays of processors. In *Proceedings of the 31st Annual Symposium on Foundations of Computer Science*. IEEE, 1990.

[KLM+89] R. Koch, T. Leighton, B. Maggs, S. Rao, and A. Rosenberg. Work-preserving emulations of fixed-connection networks. In *Proceedings of the 21st Annual ACM Symposium on Theory of Computing*, pages 227–240, 1989.

[LMR] F.T. Leighton, B.M. Maggs, and S.B. Rao. Packet routing and job-shop scheduling in O(congestion + dilation) steps. *Combinatorica*. to appear.

[LMS92] F. T. Leighton, B. Maggs, and R. Sitaraman. On the unexpected fault-tolerance of some popular bounded-degree networks. In *Proceedings of the 33d Annual Symposium on Foundations of Computer Science*. IEEE, 1992.

[Tam92] H. Tamaki. Robust bounded-degree networks with small diameters. In *Proceedings of the 4th ACM Annual Symposium on Parallel Algorithms and Architectures*, 1992.

On the Fault Tolerance of Some Popular Bounded-Degree Networks

Tom Leighton[1]

Mathematics Department, and
Laboratory for Computer Science
Massachusetts Institute of Technology
Cambridge, MA 02139
ftl@math.mit.edu

Bruce Maggs

NEC Research Institute
4 Independence Way
Princeton, NJ 08540
bruce@research.nj.nec.com

Ramesh Sitaraman[2]

Dept. of Computer Science
Princeton University
Princeton, NJ 08544
rks@cs.princeton.edu

Abstract

In this paper, we analyze the fault-tolerance properties of several bounded-degree networks that are commonly used for parallel computation. Among other things, we show that an N-node butterfly containing $N^{1-\epsilon}$ worst-case faults (for any constant $\epsilon > 0$) can emulate a fault-free butterfly of the same size with only constant slowdown. Similar results are proved for the shuffle-exchange graph. Hence, these networks become the first connected bounded-degree networks known to be able to sustain more than a constant number of worst-case faults without suffering more than a constant-factor slowdown in performance. We also show that an N-node butterfly whose nodes fail with some constant probability p can emulate a fault-free version of itself with a slowdown of $2^{O(\log^* N)}$, which is a very slowly increasing function of N. The proofs of these results combine the technique of redundant computation with new algorithms for routing packets around faults in hypercubic networks. Techniques for reconfiguring hypercubic networks around faults that do not rely on redundant computation are also presented. These techniques tolerate fewer faults but are more widely applicable since they can be used with other networks such as binary trees and meshes of trees.

1 Introduction

In this paper, we analyze the effect of faults on the computational power of bounded-degree networks such as the butterfly, shuffle-exchange network, and mesh of trees. The main objective of our work is to devise methods for circumventing faults in these networks using as little overhead as possible, and to prove lower bounds on the effectiveness of optimal methods. We consider both worst-case and random fault patterns, and we always assume that faulty components are totally disabled (e.g., a faulty node cannot be used to transport a packet of data through the network). We also assume that the faults in the network are static and detectable and that information concerning the location of faults can be used when reconfiguring the network to circumvent the faults. For simplicity, we restrict our attention to node failures since an edge fault can always be simulated by disabling the node at either end of the edge.

There are several ways to measure the effect of faults on a network. In this paper, we will be primarily concerned with the amount by which a collection of faults can slow down some computation in the network. For example, if a butterfly network is being used for packet routing, we will be concerned with how much longer it takes a faulty butterfly to deliver all of the packets than it takes a fault-free butterfly to perform the same task. More generally, we will be interested in the length of time it takes an impaired network to emulate a single step of a fault-free network of the same size and type. In particular, we define the *slowdown* caused by a set of faults in a network G to be the minimum value of S such that any computation that takes T steps on G when there are no faults can be performed in at most $S \cdot T$ steps on G when faults are present. One of our main goals will be to understand the relationship between slowdown and the number of faults for commonly-used networks. In particular, we will prove bounds on the number of faults that can be tolerated without losing more than a constant factor in speed.

We will use two methods for emulating a fault-free network G on an isomorphic faulty network H. The first approach is to embed G into H so that the nodes of G are mapped to non-faulty nodes of H, and so that the edges of G are mapped to non-faulty paths in H. The goal is to find an embedding with minimum load, congestion, and dilation. The *load* of an embedding is the maximum number of nodes of G that are mapped to any single node of H. The *congestion* of an embedding is the maximum number of paths that pass through any edge e of H. The *dilation* of an embedding is the length of the longest path. The load, congestion, and dilation of the embedding determine the time required to emulate each step of G on H. In particular, Leighton, Maggs, and Rao have shown [24] that if there is an embedding of G in H with congestion c, load l, and dilation d, then H can emulate any computation on G with slowdown $O(c + l + d)$.

In this paper, we will be most interested in embeddings for which the congestion, load, and dilation are

[1]Tom Leighton is supported in part by the Defense Advanced Research Projects Agency under Contracts N00014-87-K-825 and N00014-89-J-1988, by the Air Force under Contract OSR-89-0271, and by NEC Research Institute. [2]Ramesh Sitaraman is supported by DIMACS (Center for Discrete Mathematics and Theoretical Computer Science), a National Science Foundation Science and Technology Center - NSF-STC88-09648.

0-8186-2900-2/92 $3.00 © 1992 IEEE

all constant (independent of the size of the network). In particular, we will show in Section 2 how to embed a fault-free N-input butterfly into an N-input butterfly containing $\log^{O(1)} N$ worst-case faults using constant congestion, load, and dilation. (In other words, we will show how to reconfigure an N-input butterfly around $\log^{O(1)} N$ worst-case faults so that the resulting degradation in performance is at most an $O(1)$ factor in speed.) A similar result will also be proved for an N-node mesh of trees. Hence, these networks can tolerate $\log^{O(1)} N$ worst-case faults with constant slowdown.

Previously, no connected bounded-degree networks were known to be able to tolerate more than a constant number of worst-case faults without suffering more than a constant-factor loss in performance. Indeed, it was only known that

1. any embedding of an N-node (2 or 3-dimensional) array into an array of the same size containing more than a constant number of worst-case faults must have more than constant load or dilation [16, 19], and

2. the N-node hypercube can be reconfigured around $\log^{O(1)} N$ worst-case faults with constant load, congestion, and dilation [1].

The embeddings that we use in Section 2 are level-preserving, i.e., nodes in a particular level of the fault-free network are mapped to nodes on the same level of the faulty network. We take a significant step towards proving the limitation of embedding techniques for the emulation of these networks by showing that no level-preserving embedding strategy with constant load, congestion, and dilation can tolerate more than $\log^{O(1)} N$ worst-case faults. Whether or not there is a natural low-degree N-node network (the hypercube included) that can be reconfigured using (not necessarily level-preserving) embedding techniques around more than $\log^{O(1)} N$ faults with constant congestion, load, and dilation remains an interesting open question.

In Section 3, we shift our attention to the routing capabilities of hypercubic networks containing faults. First we prove in Section 3.1 that an N-input butterfly with f worst-case faults can support an $O(\log N)$-step randomized packet routing algorithm for the nodes in $N - O(f)$ rows of the butterfly. The ability of the butterfly to withstand faults in this context is important because butterflies are often used solely for their routing abilities. Previously, it was known that expander-based multibutterfly networks can tolerate large numbers of worst-case faults without losing their routing powers [5, 22], but no such results were known for butterflies or other hypercubic networks. A corollary of this result is that an N-input butterfly with αN worst-case faults (for some small constant α) can support an $O(\log N)$-step randomized routing algorithm for a majority of its nodes. Note that the number of faults is optimal to within a constant factor, since it is possible to partiton an N-input butterfly into components of size $O(\sqrt{N} \log N)$ with N faults. In Section 3.2 we show that butterflies with faults can also be used for circuit switching. In particular, we show that even if an N-input $O(1)$-dilated Beneš network contains $N^{1-\epsilon}$ worst-case faults (for any $\epsilon > 0$), there is still a set of $N - o(N)$ inputs I and a set of $N - o(N)$ outputs O such that for any one-to-one map $\pi : I \mapsto O$ it is possible to route edge-disjoint paths from i to $\pi(i)$ for all $i \in I$. This result substantially improves upon previous algorithms for fault-tolerant circuit switching in Beneš networks [29, 33] which dealt with a constant number of faults by adding an extra stage to the network.

In Section 4, we use the fault-tolerant routing algorithm from Section 3.2 to show that an N-input butterfly with $N^{1-\epsilon}$ worst-case faults (for any constant $\epsilon > 0$) can emulate a fault-free butterfly of the same size with only constant slowdown. A similar result is proved for the shuffle-exchange network. These results are stronger than the reconfiguration results proved in Section 2 because the number of faults tolerated is much larger. The approach used in Section 4 differs from the embedding-based approaches in Section 2 in that a single node of the fault-free butterfly will be emulated by (possibly) several nodes in the faulty butterfly. Allowing redundant computation provides greater flexibility when embedding one network in another (thereby attaining greater fault tolerance) but also adds the complication of ensuring that replicated computations stay consistent (and accurate) over time. This technique was previously used in the context of (fault-free) work-preserving emulations of one network by another [20, 32].

The techniques developed in Section 4 also have applications for hypercubes. For example, we can use the techniques to show than an N-node hypercube with $N^{1-\epsilon}$ worst-case faults can emulate any normal algorithm with constant slowdown. (The set of normal algorithms include FFT, bitonic sort, and other important ascend-descend algorithms [21].) Previously, such results were known only for hypercubes containing $\log^{O(1)} N$ faults [1, 10, 11]. Whether or not an N-node hypercube can tolerate more than $\log^{O(1)} N$ faults with constant slowdown for general computations remains an important unresolved question.

In Section 5, we show that even if each node in an N-input butterfly fails independently with probability $p = 1/\log^{(k)} N$, where $\log^{(k)}$ denotes the logarithm function iterated k times, the faulty butterfly can still emulate a fault-free N-input butterfly with slowdown $2^{O(k)}$ with high probability. For $k = O(\log^* N)$ the node failure probability is constant, and the slowdown is $2^{O(\log^* N)}$, which grows very slowly with N. Whether or not this result can be improved and whether or not there is a bounded-degree network that can sustain constant-probability random faults with only constant expected slowdown remain interesting open questions. Until very recently, no results along these lines were known for the butterfly (unless routing is allowed through faulty nodes [4], which simplifies matters substantially). Tamaki [35] has recently discovered an emulation scheme with slowdown $O((\log\log N)^{8.2})$. He has also introduced a class of bounded-degree networks called cube-connected arrays [36], and showed that an N-node network in this class with constant-probability random faults can emulate itself with expected slowdown approximately $\log\log N$. (These networks can also tolerate up to $\log^{O(1)} N$ worst-case faults with approximately $\log\log N$ slowdown.)

Several proofs and results have been omitted from this abstract due to space limitations. For a complete version of the paper, see [25].

1.1 Additional previous work

There is a substantial body of literature concerning the fault-tolerance of communication networks. We do not have the space to review all of this literature here, but we would like to cite the papers that are most relevant. In particular, [1, 4, 8, 17, 18, 19, 27, 30, 36] show how to reconfigure a network around faults so that it can emulate a fault-free network of the same size and type. References [3, 9, 12, 13] show how to design a network H that will contain G as a subnetwork even if H contains some faults. Algorithms for routing messages around faults appear in [5, 7, 18, 19, 22, 26, 28, 29, 30, 33]. The fault-tolerance of sorting networks is studied in [6, 23]. Finally, [10, 39, 40] show how to perform certain computations in hypercubes containing faults.

1.2 Network definitions

In this section, we will review the structure of some of the networks that we study in this paper. An N-input ($\log N$-dimensional) *butterfly* has $(\log N + 1)N$ nodes arranged in $\log N + 1$ levels. Each node has a distinct label (w, i), where i is the *level* of the node ($0 \le i \le \log N$) and w is a $\log N$-bit binary number that denotes the *row* of the node. All nodes of the form (w, i), $0 \le i \le \log N$, are said to belong to row w. Two nodes (w, i) and (w', i') are linked by an edge if and only if $i' = i + 1$ and either w and w' are identical (straight edge) or w and w' differ in precisely bit i' (cross edge). Sometimes the level 0 and $\log N$ nodes in each row are assumed to be the same node. Our results will hold with or without this wrap-around. For definitions of the hypercube, the shuffle-exchange network, and the mesh of trees network, see [21].

A *circuit-switching network* is used to establish edge-disjoint paths (circuits) between its inputs and outputs. Each switch in a circuit-switching network has two incoming and two outgoing edges. The incoming edges can be connected to the outgoing edges in one of two ways: either crossing or straight through. The switches at the first level of the network are called the *input switches*. The switches at the last level are called the *output switches*. The two edges into each input switch are called *input edges*, or *inputs*. The two edges out of each output switch are called *output edges*, or *outputs*. By setting the switches, each input edge can be connected to an output edge via a path through the network. A circuit-switching network with N inputs and N outputs is said to be *rearrangeable* if for any one-to-one mapping ϕ from the inputs to the outputs, it is possible to construct edge-disjoint paths in the network linking the ith input to the $\phi(i)^{th}$ output, for $1 \le i \le N$. A classical example of a rearrangeable network is the Beneš network. The Beneš network consists of back-to-back butterflies. A $\log N$-dimensional Beneš network has $2N$ inputs and $2N$ outputs. Its switches are arranged in $2\log N + 1$ levels of N switches each. The first and last $\log N + 1$ levels each form a $\log N$-dimensional butterfly. Level $\log N$ is shared by these butterflies. We will refer to the nodes (switches) in level 0, $\log N$, and, $2\log N$ as the *input nodes*, *middle nodes*, and *output nodes* respectively.

2 Emulation by Embedding

In this section, we will show how to embed a fault-free binary tree, butterfly, or mesh of trees network into a faulty version of itself with constant load, congestion and dilation. As noted in the introduction, finding a constant load, congestion, and dilation embedding is the simplest way of emulating arbitrary computations of a fault-free network on a faulty version of itself with only constant slowdown. We will first consider embedding a complete binary tree in a complete binary tree with faults only at its leaves. This result will also hold for fat-trees [15] with faults at the leaves. We use this result to find reconfigurations of butterflies and meshes of trees in which faults may occur at any node. The primary result of this section is that an N-node butterfly or mesh of trees network can tolerate $\log^{O(1)} N$ worst-case faults and still emulate itself with only constant slowdown.

2.1 The Binary Tree

Define $S(n, b)$ for $n \ge b \ge 0$ by the recurrence

$$S(n, b) = S(n-1, b) + S(n-1, b-1) + 1$$

for $n > b > 0$ with boundary conditions $S(n, 0) = 0$ and $S(n, n) = 2^n - 1$, for $n \ge 1$. The following lemma provides a useful asymptotic bound on the growth of $S(n, b)$ for large n.

Lemma 2.1 *For all $n \ge b \ge 1$, $\binom{n}{b} \le S(n, b) \le \binom{n+b}{b}$. Hence, $S(n, b) = \Theta(n^b)$ for any constant $b > 0$.*

Proof: The proof is by induction on n and follows trivially from the fact that $\binom{x}{y} = \binom{x-1}{y} + \binom{x-1}{y-1}$, for all $x > y > 0$. □

Theorem 2.2 *Given an N-leaf complete binary tree T with a set of at most $S(\log N, b) = \Theta(\log^b N)$ worst-case faults at the leaves, it is possible to embed a fault-free N-leaf complete binary tree T' in T so that*

1. *nodes on level i of T' are mapped to non-faulty nodes on level i of T, for $0 \le i \le \log N$,*
2. *the congestion and the load of the embedding are at most 2^b, and*
3. *the dilation of the embedding is 1.*

Proof: The proof is by induction on $n = \log N$ and b. For $n = 0$, the tree is a single node, and the number of faults, $S(0,0)$, is zero. Now suppose that we are given a complete binary tree T with 2^n leaves of which a set of at most $S(n,b)$ are faulty. If both 2^{n-1}-leaf subtrees of T have at most $S(n-1,b)$ faulty leaves, then we use the result inductively in both subtrees. If one 2^{n-1}-leaf subtree (say the left subtree) has $S(n-1,b)+1$ or more faults, then by definition of $S(n,b)$ the other subtree (the right subtree) has at most $S(n-1,b-1)$ faulty leaves. Hence we can use induction to embed a 2^{n-1}-leaf complete binary tree on the right subtree using dilation 1 and load and congestion 2^{b-1}. By doubling the congestion and the load, we can embed two 2^{n-1}-leaf complete binary trees in the right subtree. This means that we can embed T' in T with dilation 1 and load and congestion 2^b (using only the root and the right subtree of T in this case). □

This result can be extended to a class of binary-tree-like structures called *fat-trees*. A fat-tree of depth n is specified by a sequence of numbers $m_0, m_1, \cdots, m_n = 1$. (Typically $m_0 \ge m_1 \ge \cdots \ge m_n$.) A fat-tree of depth 0 is a single node, which is both the root node and the leaf node of the tree. A fat-tree of depth n is constructed as follows. At the root of the fat-tree there is a set of m_0 nodes. The left and right subtrees are identical and are constructed recursively. Each is a fat-tree of depth $n-1$ with number sequence $m_1, \cdots, m_n$. The root nodes of the fat-tree are connected to the root nodes of the left subtree with any number of edges in an arbitrary fashion (multiple edges are allowed). An isomorphic set of edges is used to connected the root nodes of the tree to the root nodes of the right subtree.

Corollary 2.3 *A $\log N$-depth fat-tree can be embeded in a level-preserving fashion in an isomorphic fat-tree with $S(\log N, b)$ worst-case faults at its leaves with load and congestion 2^b and dilation 1.*

Sketch of proof: The proof is essentially the same as that of Theorem 2.2. □

Corollary 2.4 *A $\log N$-dimensional butterfly can be embedded in a level-preserving fashion in an isomorphic butterfly with $S(\log N, b)$ worst-case faults at level $\log N$ with load and congestion 2^b and dilation 1.*

Proof: A $\log N$-dimensional butterfly is a fat-tree of depth $\log N$ with $m_i = 2^{\log N - i}$. The leaves of the fat-tree are the nodes in level $\log N$ of the butterfly. □

2.2 The mesh of trees and the butterfly

We can use the previous result to show that the mesh of trees and the butterfly network can tolerate $\log^{O(1)} N$ worst-case faults with constant slowdown, even when a fault can occur at *any node* of the network. The proof uses the fact that both the mesh of trees and the butterfly can be viewed as a special kind of product graph together with Theorem 2.2. We will denote the leaves of a tree and the nodes in level $\log N$ of a butterfly as *external* nodes. Given a graph G with $2^n = N$ external nodes, the *external product graph* of G (denoted PG) is defined as follows. Replicate the graph G into $2N$ copies, $G_{i,j}$, for $i = 1,2$ and $1 \le j \le N$. The external nodes of each copy are also numbered from 1 to N. Now identify the kth external node in $G_{1,j}$ with the jth external node in $G_{2,k}$, for all $1 \le j,k \le N$. (By "identify" we mean make them the same node of the product graph PG.) The resulting graph is the external product graph of G. We now show that if we can tolerate faults in the external nodes of G, then we can tolerate faults anywhere in PG.

Theorem 2.5 *If a graph G' can be embedded in a level-preserving fashion with load l, congestion c, and dilation d in an isomorphic graph G with f worst-case faults located in its external nodes, then it is possible to embed the product graph PG' in a level-preserving fashion with load l^2, congestion c^2, and dilation d in an isomorphic graph PG with $f/2$ worst-case faults located in any of its nodes.*

Proof: Let PG and PG' be made of up of graphs isomorphic to G, $G_{i,j}$ and $G'_{i,j}$, respectively, for $i = 1,2$ and $1 \le j \le N$. Let CG and CG' also be graphs isomorphic to G. The jth external node of CG is declared to be faulty iff either $G_{1,j}$ or $G_{2,j}$ contains a fault. If PG has $f/2$ faults, then CG has at most f faults (since each external node can appear in two copies of $G_{i,j}$). Let Φ be a level-preserving embedding of the fault-free graph CG' into CG with load l, congestion c, and dilation d and define ϕ so that Φ maps the jth external node of CG' to the $\phi(j)^{th}$ external node of CG. We embed PG' into PG by mapping $G'_{i,j}$ to $G_{i,\phi(j)}$ using Φ, for $i = 1,2$ and $1 \le j \le N$. It follows from the definition of faults in CG that $G_{i,\phi(j)}$ is fault-free. Therefore no nodes of PG' are mapped to faulty nodes of PG. We need to verify that every external node of PG' is mapped to a unique node of PG. The kth external node of $G'_{1,j}$ is the same as the jth external node of $G'_{2,k}$. The former is mapped to the $\phi(k)^{th}$ external node of $G_{1,\phi(j)}$ and the latter to the $\phi(j)^{th}$ external node of $G_{2,\phi(k)}$. These nodes are the same node of PG. The dilation of the mapping is d.

The number of copies $G'_{i,j}$ of PG' mapped to any particular $G_{i,\phi(j)}$ is at most l. Each copy can put l nodes on to any particular node of $G_{i,\phi(j)}$. Therefore the load is at most l^2 and the congestion is at most c^2. □

Two important networks can be expressed as external product graphs. When the graph G' is a tree the graph PG' is a mesh of trees network. If G' is a butterfly, then PG' is a butterfly with twice the dimension.

Theorem 2.6 *A $2\log N$-dimensional butterfly can be embedded in a level-preserving fashion in a $2\log N$-dimensional butterfly containing $S(\log N, b) = \Theta(\log^b N)$ worst-case faults with load and congestion 2^{2b} and dilation 1.*

Proof: The proof for follows from Corollary 2.4 and Theorem 2.5. □

Theorem 2.7 *An $N \times N$ mesh of trees can be embedded in a level-preserving fashion in an $N \times N$ mesh of trees containing $S(\log N, b) = \Theta(\log^b N)$ worst-case faults with load and congestion 2^{2b} and dilation 1.*

Proof: The proof follows from Theorems 2.2 and 2.5.□

The results of this subsection can also be formulated using the fact that the butterfly and the mesh of trees can be expressed as the Layered Cross Product [14] of two complete binary trees (or variations thereof) [2].

2.3 Limitations on level-preserving embeddings

We do not know whether or not Theorems 2.2, 2.6, and 2.7 can be improved if the level-preserving constraint is removed. However, we can show that the bounds in Theorems 2.2, 2.6, and 2.7 are tight if the embedding is forced to be level preserving. The result is stated in the next theorem.

Theorem 2.8 *For any constants, c, l, and d, there is a constant k such that there is a way of placing $\log^k N$ faults in the leaves of an N-leaf complete binary tree T such that there is no level-preserving embedding of an N-leaf fault-free complete binary tree T' in T with congestion c, load l, and dilation d. The same result holds for an N-node butterfly with faults at level $\log N$ and for an N-node mesh of trees with faults in its leaves.*

Proof: Omitted.

3 Fault-tolerant routing

In this section, we present algorithms for routing around faults in hypercubic networks. Section 3.1 presents algorithms for routing packets in butterfly networks with faulty nodes, while Section 3.2 presents algorithms for establishing edge-disjoint paths between the inputs and outputs of a Beneš network with faulty switches.

3.1 Fault-tolerant packet routing

In this section we show how to route packets in an N-input butterfly network with f worst-case faults. We show that there is some set of $N - O(f)$ rows between which it is possible to route any permutation in $O(\log N)$ steps, with high probability.

We start by describing Valiant's algorithm [37] for permutation routing in a butterfly without faults. It will be convenient for us to view the packets in this scheme as being routed on a bigger network with $4\log N + 1$ levels. Between level 0 and level $\log N$, and between levels $3\log N$ and $4\log N$, nodes are connected only by straight edges. Between levels $\log N$ and $3\log N$ the network is a pair of back-to-back butterflies isomorphic to the Beneš network. In analogy with the Beneš network the nodes in $\log N$, $2\log N$ and $3\log N$ are called input nodes, middle nodes and output nodes respectively. Note that this bigger network is easily simulated by a single butterfly. In Stage 0, a packet goes down its row to the input node in that row (say m). In Stage 1, the packet goes from m to a random middle node (say m''). In Stage 2, the packet goes from m'' to an output node m' in the row of its destination. In Stage 3, the packet goes from the row of m' to its destination. Valiant showed that these paths, which have length at most $4\log N$, also have congestion $O(\log N)$ with high probability. This is sufficient to show that the packets can be routed in $O(\log N)$ steps with high probability [24].

In a faulty butterfly, we would like to use an algorithm like Valiant's to route packets between the "good" nodes. Let F be the set of worst-case faults and $f = |F|$. Since Stages 0 and 3 require a fault-free row, any node in a row with a fault is declared to be *bad*. Furthermore, in Stage 1, every packet needs a sufficient number of random choices of middle nodes. For any input (or output) node m, let $REACH(m)$ be defined to be the set of middle nodes reachable from m using fault-free paths. If $|REACH(m)| < 4N/5$ for any input (or output) node m, then we define m and all other nodes in its row to be bad. Any node not defined as bad is the defined to be *good.* Note that there are no faults in rows containing good nodes, and every good input (output) node can reach at least $4N/5$ middle nodes via fault-free paths.

In order to route any permutation between the good nodes, we use Valiant's algorithm except that in Stage 1, we randomly select a middle node m'' from $REACH(m) \cap REACH(m')$. (This step requires us to a store at each node m a table containing information about $REACH(m) \cap REACH(m')$ for each node m'.) Since m and m' are good input and output nodes $|REACH(m) \cap REACH(m')|$ is at least $3N/5$. This is sufficient to prove that the paths selected in this manner have congestion $O(\log N)$ with high probability. This also implies that the routing will complete in $O(\log N)$ steps with high probability [24].

It now remains to show that only $O(f)$ rows contain bad nodes. This follows from the fact that only f rows can contain faults and from the fact that $|REACH(m)| \geq 4N/5$ for all but $O(f)$ input nodes m. The latter fact is proved by setting $t = N/5$ in the following lemma, which will also be used in Section 3.2.

Lemma 3.1 *In an N-input butterfly with f worst-case faults, at least $N - fN/t$ input nodes (nodes in level 0) can each reach at least $N - t$ output nodes (nodes in level $\log N$) via fault-free paths of length $\log N$, for any $t \leq N$.*

Proof: For each input node i, let n_i represent the number of output nodes in level $\log N$ that i cannot reach. If the lemma were false, then we would have

$$\sum_{i=1}^{N} n_i \geq (\frac{fN}{t} + 1)(t + 1).$$

A fault at any level of the butterfly lies on precisely N paths from input nodes to output nodes. Hence $\sum_{i=1}^{N} \leq fN$. Combining the inequalities yields $fN \geq (fN/t + 1)(t+1)$ which is a clear contradiction. Hence the lemma must be true. □

It is also possible to route on faulty butterflies without using tables. These algorithms are omitted from this abstract.

3.2 Fault-tolerant circuit-switching

In this section, we examine the ability of the Beneš network to establish disjoint paths between its inputs and outputs when some of its switches fail. We assume that no path can pass through a faulty switch. The primary result of this section is that for arbitrarily small positive constants ϵ and δ, there is a constant b such that given a b-dilated $\log N$-dimensional Beneš network with $f = N^{1-\epsilon}$ worst-case switch failures, we can identify a set of $N - 2N^{1-\delta}$ input and output nodes such that it is possible to route edge-disjoint paths in any permutation between the corresponding input and output edges. (A *b-dilated* Beneš network is one in which each edge is replaced by b parallel edges, and each 2×2 switch is replaced by a $2b \times 2b$ switch.) As an example, a 2-dilated Beneš network can tolerate up to $\sqrt{N}/4$ worst-case switch failures and still route arbitrary permutations between 75 percent of the inputs and outputs.

In a $\log N$-dimensional Beneš network, levels 1 through $2\log N - 1$ can be decomposed into two disjoint sub-Beneš networks of dimension $\log N - 1$, a top sub-Beneš network, and a bottom sub-Beneš network. Note that the two paths which originate from input edges that share an input node cannot use the same sub-Beneš network. The same is true for paths that end on output edges that share the same output node. For a full permutation, there are $2N$ input-output pairs which require paths to be routed between them. The standard algorithm for setting the switches in a Beneš network, due to Waksman [38], uses bipartite graph matching to split the set of $2N$ pairs into two sets of N pairs which are each then routed recursively in one of the smaller sub-Beneš networks.

We now present Waksman's algorithm with a twist. We will call this algorithm RANDSET (for RANDom switch SETting). The way RANDSET differs from Waksman's algorithm is that it randomly chooses which of the two sets of N pairs to route through the top (and bottom) sub-Beneš network. The input to RANDSET is a permutation ϕ represented as a $2N \times 2N$ bipartite graph. The nodes of the graph represent the $2N$ input edges and the $2N$ output edges of the network. An edge in the bipartite graph from input i to output $\phi(i)$ indicates that a path must be routed from i to $\phi(i)$ in the network. The first step is to merge pairs of nodes in the bipartite graph that correspond to input edges (or output edges) that share the same input (or output). The result is a 2-regular $N \times N$ bipartite graph. The second step is to split the edges of this graph into two perfect matchings, M_0 and M_1. Next, we pick a binary value for random variable X at random. If $X = 0$ then we recursively route the paths in matching M_0 through the top sub-Beneš network and those in M_1 through the bottom sub-Beneš network. If $X = 1$ we do the reverse. The following lemma shows that RANDSET chooses the path from i to $\phi(i)$ uniformly from among all possible paths.

Lemma 3.2 *For any i, the path chosen by algorithm RANDSET between input i and output $\phi(i)$ in a $2N$-input Beneš network passes through any of the N middle nodes (nodes in level $\log N$) with equal probability ($1/N$).*

Proof: At the first stage, the path from i to $\phi(i)$ goes to the top or the bottom sub-Beneš network with probability 1/2 depending on whether the matching that contains the edge corresponding to this input-output pair is chosen to be routed through the top or the bottom. The decisions made at the succeeding levels of the recursion are similar and independent of all other decisions. □

It is important to remember that given a permutation, the *paths themselves could be highly correlated* and determining one path gives some information about the others.

We will classify the input and output nodes of the Beneš network as either good or bad depending on whether they can reach a sufficiently large number of middle nodes. Let F be the set of faulty switches in the Beneš network. In a fault-free Beneš network, there is a path from each input (and output) node to each of the N middle nodes. The middle nodes in fact form the leaves of a complete binary tree with the input (or output) node as the root. The faults could make some of these paths unusable. We will declare an input (or output) node *bad* if the number of middle nodes that it cannot reach exceeds a certain threshold. The threshold will be chosen so that it is possible to establish edge-disjoint paths between the *good*(i.e., not bad) inputs and outputs in any permutation. (The 2 inputs coming into an input (or output) node are good or bad depending on whether the corresponding input (or output) node is good or bad).

Let $BAD(t)$ be the set of input and output nodes for which more than t middle nodes are unreachable. The first and last $\log N + 1$ levels of the Beneš network each form a $\log N$-dimensional butterfly. By using Lemma 3.1 for each of these butterflies, we know that $|BAD(t)| < fN/t$.

Theorem 3.3 *For any constants $0 < \epsilon < \delta \leq 1$, there exists a constant $b = \lceil 1 + (2-\epsilon)/(\epsilon - \delta) \rceil$ such that a b-dilated Beneš network with $N^{1-\epsilon}$ worst-case switch faults has a set of $N - 2N^{1-\delta}$ input nodes and output nodes between whose input and output edges it is possible to route any permutation using edge-disjoint paths.*

Proof: We will declare any input or output node in $BAD(N^{1+\delta-\epsilon}/2)$ to be bad. Since we need the number of good input nodes and good output nodes to be equal we may have to declare some extra input nodes or output nodes to be bad. From Lemma 3.1, we know that $BAD(N^{1+\delta-\epsilon}/2)$ is at most $2N^{1-\delta}$. Thus, the number of good input nodes (or output nodes) is at least $N - 2N^{1-\delta}$.

We now prove that we can route any permutation between the good inputs and good outputs using edge-disjoint paths. In this proof, we will simply show that for every permutation, such a set of paths *exists*, without showing how to compute these paths efficiently. Later, we give an efficient procedure for computing these paths.

Given a permutation ϕ on the good inputs and outputs, we will select paths using RANDSET in b rounds. In the first round, we route all the paths using RANDSET. Some of these paths pass through faults in the network. The number of paths that pass through faults is at most $2N^{1-\epsilon}$, since each fault can kill at most 2 paths. These paths are not permissible and have to be rerouted in the second round using RANDSET. Note that every good input node (or output node) has at most $N^{1+\delta-\epsilon}/2$ unreachable middle nodes. Thus, from Lemma 3.2, the probability that any one of the paths hits a fault in the first $\log N + 1$ levels is at most $N^{-(\epsilon-\delta)}/2$. The probability that it hits a fault in the second $\log N + 1$ levels is also at most $N^{-(\epsilon-\delta)}/2$. The net probability that the path will hit a fault is at most $N^{-(\epsilon-\delta)}$. Even though the probabilities that any two paths hit a fault is correlated, the expected number of paths that hit faults is at most $2N^{1-\epsilon}N^{-(\epsilon-\delta)}$. This implies that there is a non-zero probability that RANDSET will find paths such that at most $2N^{1-\epsilon-(\epsilon-\delta)}$ paths hit faults. Note this also means that there *exists* a way of selecting the paths so that at most $2N^{1-\epsilon-(\epsilon-\delta)}$ paths hit faults. We select paths such that this criterion is satisfied and route the paths that hit faults again using RANDSET. We continue to do the rerouting until the expected number of paths that hit faults drops below 1. At this point with non-zero probability RANDSET routes all of the paths without hitting any faults. In particular, such a set of paths exist. The expected number of paths that hit faults in the ith round is $2N^{1-\epsilon-(i-1)(\epsilon-\delta)}$. Thus, for $b = \lceil 1 + (2-\epsilon)/(\epsilon-\delta) \rceil$, the number of paths that hit faults at the end of the bth round is less than 1. Therefore all paths will be routed by the end of the bth round. Since we use at most b rounds of routing and since each edge of the Beneš network has been replaced by b edges we will obtain edge-disjoint paths for the permutation. □

In the proof of Theorem 3.3, we show the existence of edge-disjoint paths by using the fact that algorithm RANDSET will find them with non-zero probability. It is possible to construct a deterministic algorithm that always finds all of the paths using the technique due to Raghavan [31] and Spencer [34] to remove the randomness. Like Waksman's algorithm for finding the switch settings in a fault-free Beneš network with N input nodes, the algorithm runs in $O(N \log N)$ time. The details are omitted in this abstract.

4 Emulations on faulty butterflies

In this section, we show that for any constant $\epsilon > 0$, a $\log N$-dimensional butterfly with $N^{1-\epsilon}$ worst-case faults (the host H), can emulate any computation of a fault-free version of itself (the guest G) with only constant slowdown. We assume that a faulty node cannot perform computations and that packets cannot route through faulty nodes. For simplicity we assume that the butterflies wrap around, i.e., the nodes of level 0 are identified with the nodes of level $\log N$.

We model the emulation of G by H as a pebbling process. There are two kinds of pebbles. With every node v of G and every time step t, we associate a *state pebble* (s-pebble), $\langle v, t \rangle$, which contains the entire state of the computation performed at node v at time t. The s-pebble contains local memory values, registers, stacks, and anything else that is required to continue the computation at v. We will view G as a directed graph by replacing each undirected edge between nodes u and v by two directed edges: one from u to v and the other from v to u. With each directed edge e and every time step t, we associate a *communication pebble* (c-pebble), $[e, t]$, which contains the message transmitted along edge e at time step t.

The host H will emulate each step t of G by creating an s-pebble $\langle v, t \rangle$ for each node v of G and a c-pebble $[e, t]$ for each edge e of G. A node of H can create an s-pebble $\langle v, t \rangle$ only if contains s-pebble $\langle v, t-1 \rangle$ and all of the c-pebbles $[e, t-1]$, where e is an edge into

v. It can create a c-pebble $[g,t]$ for an edge g out of v only if it contains an s-pebble $\langle v,t\rangle$. A node of H can also transmit a c-pebble to a neighboring node in H in unit time. A node of H is not permitted to transmit an s-pebble since an s-pebble may contain a lot of information. Note that H can create more than one copy of an s-pebble or c-pebble. The ability of H to create redundant pebbles is crucial to our emulation schemes. In our emulations, each node of H is assigned a fixed set of nodes of G to emulate, and creates s-pebbles for them for each time step.

4.1 Assignment of nodes of G to nodes of H

We now show how to map the computation of G to the faulty butterfly H. The host H has $N^{1-\epsilon}$ arbitrarily distributed faults. We will first divide H into sub-butterflies of dimension $\epsilon \log N/2$, at levels $i\epsilon \log N/2$, for integer $i = 0$ to $2/\epsilon - 1$. (Without loss of generality, we will assume that $2/\epsilon$ and $\epsilon \log N/4$ are integers.) The butterfly contains as subgraphs $N^{1-\epsilon/2}$ sub-butterflies between each of these levels of division. There are a total of $(2/\epsilon)N^{1-\epsilon/2}$ sub-butterflies in all. The faults in the network may make some of these sub-butterflies unusable. We will identify "good" and "bad" sub-butterflies according to the following rules.

RULE 1: A sub-butterfly that contains a node that lies in a butterfly row in which there is a fault is a *bad* sub-butterfly (even if the fault lies outside of the sub-butterfly).

RULE 2: In order to apply Rule 2, we embed a Beneš network in the butterfly. The edges of the first stage of the Beneš network traverse the butterfly in increasing order of dimension and the edges of the second stage in decreasing order of dimension. The input nodes, the middle nodes as well as the output nodes of the Beneš network are embedded in level 0 of the butterfly (which is the same as level $\log N$). For $\delta = 2\epsilon/3$, identify the set of bad inputs/outputs (they are the same set here) according to the procedure outlined in the proof of Theorem 3.3 in Section 3.2. Any sub-butterfly that contains a node that has a bad input/output at the end of its butterfly row is a bad sub-butterfly.

Lemma 4.1 *For any $\epsilon > 0$, the number of rows in which there is either a fault or a bad input or output is at most $N^{1-\epsilon} + 2N^{1-2\epsilon/3}$.*

Proof: The number of rows containing a fault is at most $N^{1-\epsilon}$, since there are at most $N^{1-\epsilon}$ faults. By Theorem 3.3, for $\delta = 2\epsilon/3$, the number of bad inputs and outputs is at most $2N^{1-\delta} = 2N^{1-2\epsilon/3}$. □

Lemma 4.2 *For any $\epsilon > 0$, at least half the sub-butterflies of H are good, for sufficiently large N.*

Proof: The total number of sub-butterflies is $(2/\epsilon)N^{1-\epsilon/2}$. By Lemma 4.1, the number of rows containing either a fault or bad input or output is at most $N^{1-\epsilon} + 2N^{1-2\epsilon/3}$. Since each bad row passes through $2/\epsilon$ different sub-butterflies, the total number of sub-butterflies identified as bad by Rules 1 and 2 cannot exceed $2(N^{1-\epsilon} + 2N^{1-2\epsilon/3})/\epsilon$. Observe that $2(N^{1-\epsilon} + 2N^{1-2\epsilon/3})/\epsilon$ is at most $N^{1-\epsilon/2}/\epsilon$, for sufficiently large N. □

Now we will divide the guest G into overlapping sub-butterflies of dimension $\epsilon \log N/2$ and map them to the good sub-butterflies of H. For any node v of G, two nodes of H will receive the initial state of the computation of node v, i.e., s-pebble $\langle v, 0\rangle$. These two nodes in H will create the s-pebbles for v. The mapping proceeds as follows. Take the guest G and cut it into sub-butterflies at levels $i\epsilon \log N/2$, for integers $i = 0$ to $2/\epsilon - 1$. Map each sub-butterfly to a good sub-butterfly of H evenly such that each sub-butterfly of H gets at most two sub-butterflies of G. Now cut G again, this time at levels $(\epsilon/4 + i\epsilon/2)\log N$, for integers $i = 0$ to $2/\epsilon - 1$. Map the sub-butterflies evenly to good sub-butterflies of H as before. At most four nodes of G are mapped to each node of H.

4.2 Building constant congestion paths

We call the nodes v of G belonging to levels $i\epsilon \log N/4 - 1$ and $i\epsilon \log N/4$, for $i = 0$ to $4/\epsilon - 1$, *boundary nodes* since they lie on the boundary of some sub-butterfly that was cut out of G. Let the set of boundary nodes of G be denoted by $\mathcal{B}_{\mathcal{G}}$. Similarly we define the nodes in the levels where H was cut to form sub-butterflies, i.e., levels $i\epsilon \log N/2$, and $i\epsilon \log N/2 - 1$, for $i = 0$ to $2/\epsilon - 1$, the boundary nodes of H. Let us denote this set $\mathcal{B}_{\mathcal{H}}$.

Let ϕ be the function that maps an s-pebble, $\langle v,t\rangle$ to the node in H that creates it. The creation of $\langle v,t\rangle$ requires that node $\phi(\langle v,t\rangle)$ of H gets all the c-pebbles $[e,t]$ from some other node of H, for every edge e into v. Suppose that $\langle v,t\rangle$ is mapped to some node $m = \phi(\langle v,t\rangle)$ in the interior of a good sub-butterfly of H. Then the neighbors of m in H also contain the s-pebbles of the neighbors of v in G. Therefore m will receive the required c-pebbles from all its neighbors in H.

On the other hand, if the s-pebble for v is mapped to some node $m \in \mathcal{B}_{\mathcal{H}}$, the neighbors of m in H may not create the s-pebbles of the neighbors of v in G. However, since every node v of G is mapped to two nodes of H, there is another node m' of H which also creates an s-pebble for v. Node m' of H will send c-pebbles for *all* the edges e into v to node m. It is important to note that by the property of our mapping that *m' is necessarily a node in the center of a sub-butterfly of H*, i.e., in level $\epsilon \log N/4$ or $\epsilon \log N/4 - 1$ of the sub-butterfly.

To facilitate the transmission of c-pebbles we will establish constant congestion fault-free paths in H, using the results of Section 3.2, between all pairs of nodes m and m' of H that create the s-pebbles for the same node v in $\mathcal{B}_{\mathcal{G}}$. The number of paths originating in a row of H is simply the number of nodes mapped to sub-butterfly boundaries in that row, which is at most $4 \cdot 2/\epsilon$, i.e., a constant. Similarly the number of paths ending in any row is $8/\epsilon$. We can divide the paths into $8/\epsilon$ sets such that each set has at most one path originating in a row and one path ending in a row. Note that all paths start and end in rows which have good inputs and outputs for doing Beneš-type routing. Therefore, each set can be routed with constant congestion using the results of Section 3.2. Since there are only a constant number of such sets the total congestion is also a constant.

4.3 The emulation

We will now formally describe the emulation and prove its properties. Initially, nodes of H contain s-pebbles $\langle v, 0\rangle$ for nodes v of G. We say that H has emulated T steps of the computation of G iff for every node v, an s-pebble $\langle v, T\rangle$ has been created. The emulation algorithm is executed by every node m of H and proceeds as a sequence of macro-steps. Each macro-step consists of the following three sub steps.

1. Computation step. For each node v of G that has been assigned to m, m creates a new s-pebble $\langle v, t\rangle$, provided that m already contains s-pebble $\langle v, t-1\rangle$ and c-pebbles $[e, t-1]$ for every edge e into v.

2. Communication step. For every node v whose s-pebble was updated from $\langle v, t-1\rangle$ to $\langle v, t\rangle$ in the computation step, node m sends a c-pebble to each of its neighbors in the sub-butterfly of H that contains m. In addition, if m is a node in one of the center levels (levels $\epsilon \log N/4$ or $\epsilon \log N/4 - 1$ in the sub-butterfly), it starts four c-pebbles, one for each edge out of v, along on their way to the node m' that also creates s-pebbles for v.

3. Routing step. Node m moves every c-pebble $[e, t]$ passing through it en route to its destination, one step closer to its destination.

Lemma 4.3 *Each macro-step takes only a constant number of time steps to execute.*

Proof: There are at most 4 s-pebbles mapped to each node. Therefore the computation step takes constant time. Every s-pebble that is updated can cause at most 8 c-pebbles to be sent. Therefore the communication step takes only constant time. There can be only a constant number of c-pebbles in transit residing at any node at any time step. The reason is that there are only a constant number of paths passing through every node. Furthermore, since every c-pebble moves in every macro-step and only a constant number of c-pebbles enter a particular path at any macro-step, there can be only a constant number of c-pebbles on a particular path resident at a particular node at a particular time. Thus the routing step also takes only a constant number of time steps. □

Theorem 4.4 *Any computation on a fault-free butterfly G that takes time T can be emulated in $O(T+\log N)$ time by H.*

Proof: We will show that we require only $O(T+\log N)$ macro-steps for a T-step computation of G. The final result will then follow from Lemma 4.3.

Let ϕ be the function that maps an s-pebble, $\langle v, t\rangle$ to the node in H that creates it. The *dependency tree* of an s-pebble represents the functional dependency of this s-pebble on other s-pebbles and can be defined recursively as follows. As the base case, if $t = 0$, the dependency tree of $\langle v, t\rangle$ is a single node, $\langle v, 0\rangle$. If $t > 0$, the creation of s-pebble, $\langle v, t\rangle$, requires s-pebble $\langle v, t-1\rangle$ and c-pebbles $[e, t-1]$ such that e is an incoming edge of node v in G. These c-pebbles are sent by some other s-pebbles. There are two cases. If $\phi(\langle v, t\rangle)$ is a node in $\mathcal{B}_{\mathcal{H}}$, then s-pebble $\langle v, t\rangle$ gets all its c-pebbles from the other s-pebble for node v which we will denote by $\langle v, t-1\rangle'$. If $\phi(\langle v, t\rangle)$ is not a node in $\mathcal{B}_{\mathcal{H}}$, then it gets its c-pebbles from s-pebbles $\langle u, t-1\rangle$ such that u is a neighbor of v in G and $\phi(\langle u, t-1\rangle)$ is a neighbor of $\phi(\langle v, t\rangle)$ in H. The dependency tree of $\langle v, t\rangle$ is defined recursively as follows. The root of the tree is $\langle v, t\rangle$. The subtrees of this tree are the dependency trees of $\langle v, t-1\rangle$ and $\langle v, t-1\rangle'$ in the first case and the dependency trees of $\langle v, t-1\rangle$ and all s-pebbles $\langle u, t-1\rangle$ in the second case.

Let the emulation of T steps of G take T' macro-steps on H. Let $\langle v, T\rangle$ be an s-pebble that was updated in the last macro-step. We will now look at the dependency tree of $\langle v, T\rangle$. For every tree node s, we can associate a time (in macro-steps) $\tau(s)$ when that s-pebble was created. We choose a *critical path*, $s_T, s_{T-1}, \cdots, s_0$, of tree nodes from the root to the leaves of the tree as follows. The root of the tree, s_T, is $\langle v, T\rangle$. The creation of s_T requires the s-pebble $\langle v, T-1\rangle$ and c-pebbles $[e, T-1]$. If the s-pebble $\langle v, T-1\rangle$ was created after all the c-pebbles were received then choose s_{T-1} to be $\langle v, T-1\rangle$. Otherwise, choose the s-pebble which sent the c-pebble that arrived last at node $\phi(\langle v, T\rangle)$. After choosing s_{T-1}, we choose the rest of the sequence recursively in the subtree with s_{T-1} as the root. We will define a quantity l_i as follows. If $\phi(s_i)$ and $\phi(s_{i-1})$ are the same node or neighbors in H, then $l_i = 1$. Otherwise, l_i is the length of the path by which a c-pebble generated by s_{i-1} is sent to s_i. From the definition of our critical path and because a c-pebble moves once in every macro-step, $\tau(s_i) - \tau(s_{i-1}) = l_i$. Thus,

$$T' = \sum_{0<i\leq T} (\tau(s_i) - \tau(s_{i-1})) = \sum_{0<i\leq T} l_i.$$

Now suppose that some l_i is greater than one. This corresponds to some long path taken by some c-pebble to go from $\phi(s_{i-1})$ in the center level of a sub-butterfly of H to $\phi(s_i)$ in $\mathcal{B}_{\mathcal{H}}$. Thus l_i is the length of the constant congestion paths and is at most $4 \log N$. The key observation is that since $\phi(s_{i-1})$ is a node in the center level, working down the tree from s_{i-1} there can be no long paths until we reach an s-pebble mapped to the boundary $\mathcal{B}_{\mathcal{H}}$, i.e., $l_{i-j} = 1$ for $1 \leq j \leq \epsilon \log N/4 - 1$. Thus $T' = \sum_{0<i\leq T} l_i$ can be no more than $(16/\epsilon + 1)T + 4\log N$ which is $O(T + \log N)$. □

We can extend these results to the shuffle-exchange network using Schwabe's proof [32] that an N-node butterfly can emulate an N-node shuffle-exchange network with constant slowdown, and vice versa.

Theorem 4.5 *Any computation on a fault-free N-node shuffle-exchange network G which takes time T can be emulated in $O(T + \log N)$ time by a an N-node shuffle-exchange network H with $N^{1-\epsilon}$ worst-case faults, for any constant $\epsilon > 0$.*

Proof: Omitted.

4.4 Emulating normal algorithms on the hypercube

Many practical computations on the hypercube are structured. The class of algorithms in which every node of the hypercube uses exactly one edge for communication at every time step and further all of the edges used in a time step belong to the same dimension of the hypercube are called *leveled algorithms* (also known as *regular algorithms* [11]). A useful subclass of leveled algorithms are *normal algorithms*. A normal algorithm has the additional restriction that the dimensions used in consecutive time steps are consecutive.

Theorem 4.6 *An N-node hypercube with $N^{1-\epsilon}$ worst-case faults (for any $\epsilon > 0$) can emulate any normal algorithm on an N-node fault-free hypercube with only constant slowdown.*

Proof: Omitted.

5 Random faults

In this section we show that an N-input host butterfly H can sustain many random faults and still emulate a fault-free N-input guest butterfly G with little slowdown. In particular, we show that if each node in H fails independently with probability $p = 1/\log^{(k)} N$, where $\log^{(k)}$ denotes the logarithm function iterated k times, the slowdown of the emulation is $2^{O(k)}$, with high probability. For any constant k this slowdown is constant. Furthermore, for $k = O(\log^* N)$ the node failure probability, p, is constant, and the slowdown is $2^{O(\log^* N)}$. Previously, the most efficient self-emulation scheme known for an N-input butterfly required $\omega(\log\log N)$ slowdown [35].

The proof is omitted, but has the following outline. We begin by showing that the host, H, can emulate another N-input butterfly network B_k with constant slowdown. As in H, some of the nodes in B_k may fail at random (in which case it is not necessary for H to emulate them), but B_k is likely to contain fewer faults than H. In turn, B_k can emulate another butterfly B_{k-1} with even fewer faults. Continuing in this fashion, we arrive at B_1, which with high probability, contains so few faults that it can emulate the guest, G, with constant slowdown. There are $k+1$ emulations, and each incurs a constant factor slowdown, so the total slowdown is $2^{O(k)}$.

Theorem 5.1 *For any fixed $\gamma > 0$, with probability at least $1 - 1/2^{N^{1-\gamma}}$, an N-input butterfly in which each node fails with probability $1/\log^{(k)} N$ can emulate a fault-free N-input butterfly with slowdown $2^{O(k)}$.*

Proof: Omitted.

6 Acknowledgements

Thanks to Bob Cypher and Joel Friedman for helpful discussions. We are also grateful to Bill Aiello for suggesting that our butterfly results imply results in fault-tolerant emulations of normal algorithms. The third author wishes to thank Bob Tarjan for his support and encouragement.

References

[1] W. Aiello and T. Leighton. Coding theory, hypercube embeddings, and fault tolerance. In *Proceedings of the 3rd Annual ACM Symposium on Parallel Algorithms and Architectures*, pages 125–136, July 1991.

[2] W. A. Aiello, July 1992. Personal communication.

[3] M. Ajtai, N. Alon, J. Bruck, R. Cypher, C. T. Ho, and M. Naor. Fault tolerant graphs, perfect hash functions and disjoint paths. Unpublished manuscript.

[4] F. Annexstein. Fault tolerance in hypercube-derivative networks. In *Proceedings of the 1989 ACM Symposium on Parallel Algorithms and Architectures*, pages 179–198, June 1989.

[5] S. Arora, T. Leighton, and B. Maggs. On-line algorithms for path selection in a non-blocking network. In *Proceedings of the 22nd Annual ACM Symposium on Theory of Computing*, pages 149–158, May 1990.

[6] S. Assaf and E. Upfal. Fault-tolerant sorting network. In *Proceedings of the 31st Annual Symposium on Foundations of Computer Science*, pages 275–284, Oct. 1990.

[7] Y. Aumann and M. Ben-Or. Asymptotically optimal PRAM emulation on faulty hypercubes. In *Proceedings of the 32nd Annual Symposium on Foundations of Computer Science*, pages 440–457. IEEE Computer Society Press, Oct. 1991.

[8] S. N. Bhatt, F. R. K. Chung, F. T. Leighton, and A. L. Rosenberg. Tolerating faults in synchronization networks. Technical Report 92–14, University of Massachusetts, Amherst, MA, Apr. 1992.

[9] J. Bruck, R. Cypher, and C. T. Ho. Fault-tolerant meshes with minimal numbers of spares. In *Proceedings of the 3rd IEEE Symposium on Parallel and Distributed Processing*, pages 288–295, Dec. 1991.

[10] J. Bruck, R. Cypher, and D. Soroker. Running algorithms efficiently on faulty hypercubes. In *Proceedings*

of the 2nd Annual ACM Symposium on Parallel Algorithms and Architectures, pages 37–44, June 1990.

[11] J. Bruck, R. Cypher, and D. Soroker. Tolerating faults in hypercubes using subcube partitioning. *IEEE Transactions on Computers*, 41(5):599–605, May 1992.

[12] S. Dutt and J. P. Hayes. On designing and reconfiguring k-fault-tolerant tree architectures. *IEEE Transactions on Computers*, C–39(4):490–503, Apr. 1990.

[13] S. Dutt and J. P. Hayes. Designing fault-tolerant systems using automorphisms. *Journal of Parallel and Distributed Computing*, 12:249–268, 1991.

[14] S. Even and A. Litman. Layered Cross Product – a technique to construct interconnection networks. In *Proceedings of the 4th Annual ACM Symposium on Parallel Algorithms and Architectures*, pages 60–69, July 1992.

[15] R. I. Greenberg and C. E. Leiserson. Randomized routing on fat-trees. In S. Micali, editor, *Randomness and Computation.* Volume 5 of *Advances in Computing Research*, pages 345–374. JAI Press, Greenwich, CT, 1989.

[16] J. W. Greene and A. El Gamal. Configuration of VLSI arrays in the presence of defects. *Journal of the ACM*, 31(4):694–717, Oct. 1984.

[17] J. Hastad, T. Leighton, and M. Newman. Reconfiguring a hypercube in the presence of faults. In *Proceedings of the 19th Annual ACM Symposium on Theory of Computing*, pages 274–284, May 1987.

[18] J. Hastad, T. Leighton, and M. Newman. Fast computation using faulty hypercubes. In *Proceedings of the 21st Annual ACM Symposium on Theory of Computing*, pages 251–263, May 1989.

[19] C. Kaklamanis, A. R. Karlin, F. T. Leighton, V. Milenkovic, P. Raghavan, S. Rao, C. Thomborson, and A. Tsantilas. Asymptotically tight bounds for computing with faulty arrays of processors. In *Proceedings of the 31st Annual Symposium on Foundations of Computer Science*, pages 285–296. IEEE Computer Society Press, Oct. 1990.

[20] R. Koch, T. Leighton, B. Maggs, S. Rao, and A. Rosenberg. Work-preserving emulations of fixed-connection networks. In *Proceedings of the 21st Annual ACM Symposium on Theory of Computing*, pages 227–240, May 1989.

[21] F. T. Leighton. *Introduction to Parallel Algorithms and Architectures: Arrays • Trees • Hypercubes.* Morgan Kaufmann, San Mateo, CA, 1992.

[22] F. T. Leighton and B. M. Maggs. Fast algorithms for routing around faults in multibutterflies and randomly-wired splitter networks. *IEEE Transactions on Computers*, 41(5):578–587, May 1992.

[23] T. Leighton, Y. Ma, and C. G. Plaxton. Highly fault-tolerant sorting circuits. In *Proceedings of the 32nd Annual Symposium on Foundations of Computer Science*, pages 458–469. IEEE Computer Society Press, Oct. 1991.

[24] T. Leighton, B. Maggs, and S. Rao. Universal packet routing algorithms. In *Proceedings of the 29th Annual Symposium on Foundations of Computer Science*, pages 256–271. IEEE Computer Society Press, Oct. 1988.

[25] T. Leighton, B. Maggs, and R. Sitaraman. On the fault tolerance of some popular bounded-degree networks. Technical Report CS–TR–385–92, Department of Computer Science, Princeton University, Princeton, NJ, Sept. 1992.

[26] G. Lin. Fault tolerant planar communication networks. In *Proceedings of the 24th Annual ACM Symposium on Theory of Computing*, pages 133–139, May 1992.

[27] M. Livingston, Q. Stout, N. Graham, and F. Hararay. Subcube fault-tolerance in hypercubes. Technical Report CRL-TR-12-87, University of Michigan Computing Research Laboratory, Sept. 1987.

[28] Y. Lyuu. Fast fault-tolerant parallel communication and on-line maintenance using information dispersal. In *Proceedings of the 2nd Annual ACM Symposium on Parallel Algorithms and Architectures*, pages 378–387, July 1990.

[29] D. C. Opferman and N. T. Tsao-Wu. On a class of rearrangeable switching networks–part II: Enumeration studies and fault diagnosis. *Bell System Technical Journal*, 50(5):1601–1618, May–June 1971.

[30] M. O. Rabin. Efficient dispersal of information for security, load balancing, and fault tolerance. *Journal of the ACM*, 36(2), Apr. 1989.

[31] P. Raghavan. Probabilistic construction of deterministic algorithms: approximate packing integer programs. *Journal of Computer and System Sciences*, 37(4):130–143, Oct. 1988.

[32] E. J. Schwabe. On the computational equivalence of hypercube-derived networks. In *Proceedings of the 2nd Annual ACM Symposium on Parallel Algorithms and Architectures*, pages 388–397, July 1990.

[33] S. Sowrirajan and S. M. Reddy. A design for fault-tolerant full connection networks. In *Proceedings of the International Conference on Science and Systems*, pages 536–540, Mar. 1980.

[34] J. Spencer. *Ten Lectures on the Probabilistic Method.* SIAM, Philadelphia, PA, 1987.

[35] H. Tamaki. Efficient self-embedding of butterfly networks with random faults. In *Proceedings of the 33rd Annual Symposium on Foundations of Computer Science*, Oct. 1992. To appear.

[36] H. Tamaki. Robust bounded-degree networks with small diameters. In *Proceedings of the 4th Annual ACM Symposium on Parallel Algorithms and Architectures*, pages 247–256, July 1992.

[37] L. G. Valiant. A scheme for fast parallel communication. *SIAM Journal on Computing*, 11(2):350–361, May 1982.

[38] A. Waksman. A permutation network. *Journal of the ACM*, 15(1):159–163, Jan. 1968.

[39] A. Wang and R. Cypher. Fault-tolerant embeddings of rings, meshes and tori in hypercubes. Technical Report IBM RJ 8569, IBM Almaden Research Center, Jan. 1992.

[40] A. Wang, R. Cypher, and E. Mayr. Embedding complete binary trees in faulty hypercubes. In *Proceedings of the 3rd IEEE Symposium on Parallel and Distributed Processing*, pages 112–119. IEEE Computer Society Press, Dec. 1991.

Exact Analysis of Hot-Potato Routing

(Extended Abstract)

Uriel Feige *   Prabhakar Raghavan†

Abstract

We consider a form of packet routing known as *hot potato routing* or *deflection routing.* Its striking feature is that there are no buffers at intermediate nodes. Thus packets are always moving (possibly in the "wrong" direction), giving rise to the term "hot potato". We give a simple deterministic algorithm that on a $n \times n$ torus will route a random instance in $2n + O(\log n)$ steps with high probability. We add random delays to this algorithm so that it solves the permutation routing problem on the torus in $9n$ steps with high probability, on every instance. On a hypercube with $N = 2^n$ nodes, we give a simple deterministic algorithm that will route a random instance in $O(n)$ steps with high probability. Various other results are discussed.

1. Overview

This paper studies packet routing in a synchronous network, in which at most one packet can traverse any link in each time step. We consider a form of packet routing known as *hot potato routing* or *deflection routing* [1, 6, 7, 8, 10, 12, 15, 18]. The striking feature of this form of packet routing is that it involves no queues at intermediate nodes. A packet attempts to travel "towards" its destination. However, due to congestion, two or more packets may arrive at a node and wish to exit it on the same outgoing link. In the event of such contention, the node forwards one of the packets along the preferred edge. The other packet(s) will be "deflected" away from the preferred direction, exiting the node along other link(s). In particular, some packets may temporarily move further away from their destinations. Notice how this differs from traditional store-and-forward routing, where each packet chooses a path from its source to its destination, and proceeds along this path; if it arrives at a node and finds that the next link on its path is busy, it is placed on a queue of packets wishing to use that link. Parallel machines such as the Connection Machine [9] and the HEP multiprocessor [14], as well as high-speed communications networks [12] use deflection routing in various forms.

An important reason for favoring deflection routing is that no packets are buffered at intermediate nodes, and there are no queues as in store-and-forward packet routing. Thus packets are always moving, giving rise to the term "hot potato". This feature supports faster switching in optical networks [1, 6, 12, 15]. In order to capitalize on the potential of shorter cycle times, it is important that the routing choices a node makes are simple. In particular, the following *one pass* principle is desirable in practice: a node scans its incoming links in a fixed order. For each incoming packet, the node assigns an outgoing link not already assigned to another packet, and then continues to scan the next incoming link. All the algorithms we analyze in this paper obey this one pass principle.

The analysis of deflection routing is considerably more difficult than that of store and forward routing. There is no a-priori bound on how many links of the network a packet would traverse until it reaches its destination (if ever reached!). A packet may be deflected to unexpected regions of the network, interfering with other packets in these regions. Moreover, a packet may indirectly cause other packets to be deflected even if they actually follow disjoint paths, due to a "domino effect" in which there is a sequence of packets where each packet deflects the next packet in the sequence.

*The Weizmann Institute of Science, Rehovot, Israel. This work was done at the IBM T.J. Watson Research Center, Yorktown Heights, NY.

†IBM T.J. Watson Research Center, Yorktown Heights, NY.

1.1. Related Work

Baran [2] is widely credited with having first proposed hot-potato routing. Borodin and Hopcroft [3] proposed an algorithm for hot-potato routing on the hypercube. Numerous results on simulations of hot-potato routing on various network topologies have appeared [1, 6, 7, 10, 12, 13]. Many of these papers also include *approximate analyses*: a probabilistic analysis of simple algorithms is initiated, but various independence assumptions are made in order to make the analysis tractable. These assumptions are incorrect from a formal point of view, but in their absence virtually no analysis has been possible. Their authors refer to them as "approximate analyses", aimed at giving intuitive support for simulation results.

Very few papers contain assumption-free (exact) analyses. Hajek [8] shows that on an N-node hypercube with K packets with worst-case destinations, a natural algorithm terminates within $2K + \log N$ steps. (See also [4].) This result is important because it is deterministic and worst-case; unfortunately, the bound is large when many nodes spawn packets. Prager [13] shows that the Borodin-Hopcroft algorithm terminates in $\log N$ steps on the hypercube for a special class of permutations. Recently, Bar-Noy and Schieber (private communication) have shown that on the $n \times n$ torus, a simple deterministic algorithm routes every permutation in $O(n^{1.5})$ steps.

1.2. Model and General Observations

We model a network as a directed graph $\mathcal{N}$ whose nodes are processors and whose (directed) edges are unidirectional links between processors. Routing is performed in synchronous, discrete time steps. At the beginning of each step a node may receive upto one packet along each incoming link. At the end of the time step, the node sends each incoming packet out along one of the outgoing edges. We focus on networks in which each node has as many outgoing edges as incoming edges. Thus, any packet that enters a node at any time step is sure to have a link available along which it can leave at the end of the time step. We refer to networks that satisfy this constraint and are strongly connected as *deflection networks*. There are no buffers at any node, and packets are never stored at any node (except their source or destination). The time taken to deliver a packet is the number of steps that elapse between its generation at its source and its delivery at its destination. A subtlety: when a source wishes to inject a packet into the network, it must have a free outgoing link available at that time step, along which to send the newly generated packet. Thus the elapsed time includes any steps in which the source is unable to inject the message into the network. In the *batch routing* problem, each node is the source of one packet.

Definition 1: *Let $\mathcal{N}$ be a network with N nodes and let A be a routing algorithm. At time $t = 0$, each node holds one packet. Let $f : \mathcal{Z}_N \longrightarrow \mathcal{Z}_N$ be a function which assigns to each packet a destination node. The* batch routing time *for f using algorithm A on network $\mathcal{N}$ is the time by which the last packet reaches its destination.*

We begin with a folk theorem.

Theorem 1: *For any deflection network with E edges, there exists a deflection routing algorithm which routes any function within E steps.*

Proof: The deflection network has an Eulerian cycle. The routing algorithm can route each packet along this cycle, until it is absorbed in its destination node. □

We remark that if the network is of bounded degree, if it has a Hamiltonian cycle, or if all its links are bidirectional, then deflection routing can finish in $O(N)$ steps.

An important aspect of deflection routing algorithms is *livelock*: some algorithms will, on certain instances, route a set of packets in a manner that causes them to mutually deflect each other away from their destinations, *in an infinite loop from which they never recover.* Practitioners spend considerable effort proving their deflection routing algorithms to be livelock-free, sometimes without success [6, 7, 9].

1.3. Summary of Results

All our algorithms are livelock free and operate by the one pass principle.

For the $n \times n$ torus (two dimensional mesh with wrap around wires), $N = n^2$, we give the *three bend algorithm.* We show that for almost all destination functions, its batch routing time is at most $2\sqrt{N} + O(\log N)$. The same algorithm augmented with random delays routes any permutation in at most $9\sqrt{N}$ steps. These results are described in Section 2.

For the hypercube we give the *canonical path algorithm*, and prove that almost all destination functions are routed in $O(\log N)$ steps. These results are described in Section 3.

Additional results and open questions are mentioned in Section 4.

2. The Torus

In this section our network $\mathcal{N}$ will be an n by n two-dimensional torus (mesh with wrap around wires) with bidirectional links. Note that $N = n^2$. The rows and columns are numbered from 0 to $n-1$ (from left to right and from bottom up, starting at an arbitrary $(0,0)$ node). Address computations are done modulo n.

For clarity, we first describe our algorithm from the point of view of the motion of a packet through the network. In Section 2.2 we recast the description in terms of the actions of the nodes.

The co-ordinates of the source of a packet are denoted by (r_s, c_s) and its destination by (r_d, c_d). Along a row we say a packet travels $+R$ or $-R$ respectively to denote travel to the right or the left. Likewise, $+C$ and $-C$ denote travel up and down along a column. In the descriptions below, (r, c) denotes the current position of the packet. A packet traveling straight through a node always has priority over one wishing to make a turn there; thus as long as a packet wishes to travel straight along a row or column, it is not deflected.

Three Bend Algorithm.

1) If $c \neq c_d$, the packet travels $+R$ until $c = c_d$. When $c = c_d$ it attempts to turn to the $+C$ direction. If the $+C$ link is not free, it continues in the $+R$ direction to the first node at which the $+C$ link is free for it to turn.

2) If $r \neq r_d$, the packet travels $+C$ until $r = r_d$. When $r = r_d$, if $c \neq c_d$ it attempts to make the second turn, to $-R$. If the $-R$ link is not free, it continues in the $+C$ direction to the first node at which the $-R$ link is free.

3) When $c = c_d$, if $r \neq r_d$ it attempts to make the last turn, to the $-C$ direction. If the $-C$ link is not free, it makes full cycles (each of n steps) in the $-R$ direction until it eventually arrives at node (r, c_d) at a time step when the $-C$ link is free, so that it can make the turn.

4) The packet travels $-C$ to its destination.

5) Termination rule: In any of the phases, if the packet reaches its destination node (r_d, c_d), it is absorbed there.

Theorem 2: *For any destination function f, the batch routing time of the three bend algorithm is at most $2n^2 + 5n$ $(= 2N + 5\sqrt{N})$.*

Remark: It follows that the running time of the three bend algorithm is worst-case optimal up to a constant factor (for instance, f may map all packets to the same destination).

Proof: Consider a packet $\mathcal{P}$ that originates at (r_s, c_s) with destination (r_d, c_d). Consider the *diagonal* D_0 of nodes (r, c) such that $r + c \equiv r_s + c_s \pmod{n}$ — geometrically, this set of nodes lies on a line running northwest-to-southeast.

Only packets originating at nodes in D_0 can prevent $\mathcal{P}$ from making its first turn in the $+C$ direction. Since $\mathcal{P}$ reaches c_d in at most n steps, and is then prevented from turning on at most $n-1$ columns, it would complete Phase 1 within $2n$ steps.

Next we show that in at most $n^2 + n$ additional steps $\mathcal{P}$ completes Phase 2. Once $\mathcal{P}$ starts moving in the $+C$ direction, it takes at most n steps until it crosses its destination row. Thereafter, at every time step it attempts to turn left (to the $-R$ direction). Consider a packet $\mathcal{P}'$ which moves in the $-R$ direction and prevents $\mathcal{P}$ from turning left at time t. Then by time $t+n$ packet $\mathcal{P}'$ crosses its destination column. It either turns to the $-C$ direction, or some other packet is traveling along this column towards its destination. In any case, we can count at least one packet which is absorbed in its destination node in the following n time steps. It follows that $\mathcal{P}$ can be prevented from turning to the $-R$ direction for at most n^2 time steps.

For Phase 3, suppose that at time $t = n^2 + 3n$, packet $\mathcal{P}$ is at node r_t, c_t moving in the $-R$ direction. Consider the diagonal D_t of packets whose location at time t satisfies $r + c \equiv r_t + c_t \pmod{n}$, and which are moving in the $-R$ direction. Only the packets of D_t, and possibly one more packet moving in direction $-C$ along $\mathcal{P}$'s destination column at time t, can prevent $\mathcal{P}$ from turning to the $-C$ direction. Thus packet $\mathcal{P}$ can be prevented from entering its destination column at most n times after time t. During $n^2 + n$ time steps $\mathcal{P}$ completes $n+1$ orbits, and thus visits its destination column $n+1$ times.

Phase 4 takes at most n steps. □

The main theorem of this section shows that on average, the three bend algorithm performs within a factor of two from optimal. As an intuitive explanation for this, we think of the first two phases as bringing a packet close to its destination, and the next two phases as performing local corrections. For the first turn, we do not mind if the packet misses by a little bit, as long as it turns in a column which is approximately correct. For the next two bends, we use the fact that packets are expected to travel only very short distances along the $-R$ and $-C$ directions. Thus these directions are lightly loaded, and a packet is unlikely to miss its chance to turn.

Theorem 3: *There is a constant k such that with probability $(1 - o(1/n))$ all packets reach their destination within $2(n + k\log n)$ steps.*

Proof: The proof is by induction on t, the number of time steps that elapse after the packets are injected into the torus. The induction hypothesis will be seen to trivially hold at time $t = 0$. To make the induction step carry through from time t to time $t + 1$, we require some properties of the destination function f. It will be clear from the proof that all the desired properties simultaneously hold for all but a fraction of $o(1/n)$ of destination functions.

The inductive hypothesis consists of three inductive assumptions.

1. No packet has been deflected more than $k \log n$ times while moving in the $+R$ direction.
2. No packet has been deflected more than 3 times while moving in the $+C$ direction.
3. No packet has been deflected while moving in the $-R$ direction.

Note that if the inductive hypothesis holds, then every packet reaches its destination within $(r_d - r_s) \pmod n + (c_d - c_s) \pmod n + 2k\log n + 6$ steps.

To prove Assumption 1, consider a packet $\mathcal{P}$ originating at (r_s, c_s). Consider the diagonal D of nodes (r, c) such that $r + c \equiv r_s + c_s \pmod n$, and completely ignore all other packets on the torus. Call a column *blank* if no packet from D actually travels up the column. Observe that a necessary condition for a column to be blank is that no packet has its destination on that column. However, this is not a sufficient condition, as packets may be deflected and travel on columns other than their destination column. We shall show that within any $k \log n$ consecutive columns (for large enough k), at least one column is blank. From this it follows that any packet takes its first bend within $k \log n$ columns of its actual destination column (as otherwise too many consecutive columns are nonblank).

A set of consecutive columns is called a *slice*. The *size* of a slice is the number of columns it contains.

Lemma 4: *There exist ϵ_1, $0 < \epsilon_1 < 1$, and a positive constant k_1, such that for any slice S of size $|S|$, where $|S| > k_1 \log n$, the event "more than $(1+\epsilon_1)|S|$ packets from D have destinations within S" has probability at most n^{-4}.*

Proof: The packets of D have uniformly distributed and independent random destinations. The proof follows from the Chernoff bound. □

Call a column *dense* if more than one packet from D actually travels up the column. Clearly, there are at least as many blank columns as there are dense columns (the pigeonhole principle).

Lemma 5: *For appropriately chosen ϵ_1 in Lemma 4, there exist ϵ_2, $\epsilon_1 < \epsilon_2 < 1$, and a positive constant k_2 such that for any slice S of size $|S|$, where $|S| > k_2 \log n$, the event "at least $\epsilon_2|S|$ columns of S are dense" has probability at least $1 - n^{-4}$.*

Proof: It suffices to prove this lemma for "thin" slices (e.g., $|S| \leq \sqrt{n}$), as the bound for "fat" slices can be derived by partitioning them into thin slices. Therefore we assume that $|S|$ is at most $\sqrt{n}$.

Fix a thin slice S. Let S_1 be the slice of $n/4$ columns preceding S, and let S_2 be the slice of $n/4$ columns following S. Call a column $q \in S$ *good* if at least one packet starting in S_1 and one packet starting in S_2 have their destination in q. A Chernoff type argument shows that a constant fraction of the columns in S are good (packets from S_1 cover a constant fraction of S, and packets from S_2 cover a constant fraction of this fraction).

To complete the proof of the lemma, we show that a constant fraction of good columns are also dense. Each good column q is occupied by some packet for at least one time step t_1, where $0 < t_1 < n/4 + |S|$, and for at least one time step t_2, where $3n/4 - |S| < t_2 \leq n$. This follows from timing considerations, considering the fact that at least one packet from S_1 wants to enter q (and hence either enters q, or is deflected by some other packet which already occupies q), and similarly for S_2. We want to show that for a constant fraction of the good columns, the two packets which occupied it in t_1 and t_2 are distinct. This follows from the fact that the packet that first occupied q was bound towards a random row, and is assumed to take its second bend in the vicinity of this row (by inductive assumption 2). Hence, in approximately half the good columns the packets which first enter them evacuate them before packets that originate in slice S_2 have a chance to reach them. □

Corollary 6: *In any slice of size $k \log n$ (where $k = \max\{k_1, k_2\}$), at least one column is blank.*

Proof: By Lemma 5 at least two columns of the whole torus are dense. Then by the pigeonhole principle, at least two columns are blank. Consider S, the maximum size slice of nonblank columns, and assume that it satisfies $|S| > k \log n$. There are n^2 ways of choosing S (picking first and last column). It must satisfy three conditions: the column before first is blank, the column after last is blank, and all columns in between are nonblank. By these conditions and Lemma 4, at most $(1+\epsilon_1)|S|$ packets enter S. By Lemma 5, at least $\epsilon_2|S|$ of its columns are dense. Since $\epsilon_1 < \epsilon_2$, this contradicts our assumption that no column of S is blank. □

The above shows that Assumption 1 can be carried to time $t+1$. To prove Assumption 2, we use both Assumptions 1 and 3. They imply that any packet travels a distance of at most $k \log n$ in the $-R$ direction. Only packets that originate on diagonals either on D or in one of the $2k \log n$ diagonals just above D — i.e., at nodes (r, c) such that $r + c \equiv r_s + c_s + i \pmod{n}$, $1 \leq i \leq 2k \log n$ — might want to use the particular $-R$ link at which $\mathcal{P}$ wants to make its second turn, at exactly that time. Call the packets from these sources *dangerous*. To be deflected four times in making the second turn, there must exist some integer j such that the following holds: there are $j + 4$ packets among the $2kn \log n$ dangerous packets whose row destination is between $r_d - j$ and $r_d + 4$, and whose column destination is between c_d and $c_d + k \log n$. A simple calculation shows that this happens with probability at most n^{-3}. For large enough n, this implies that with probability $1 - o(1/n)$, Assumption 2 holds for all packets.

To prove Assumption 3, we use both Assumptions 1 and 2. If $\mathcal{P}$ were to miss its third turn, it implies that the third turn was in fact necessary for $\mathcal{P}$ — i.e., it must have failed to make its second turn (in the $-R$ direction) into the row r_d. The packet q that blocks $\mathcal{P}$'s third turn must have, at its second turn, overshot its destination row by at least two rows. By timing considerations, the packets that delayed $\mathcal{P}$'s second turn and q's second turn are distinct. Thus at least four of the $2kn \log n$ dangerous packets above had destinations within a rectangle of size at most $8k \log n$. The probability for this happening is $O((\log n/n)^4)$. □

2.1. Permutation Routing

One way of achieving permutation routing on the torus is to use a sorting algorithm for the mesh (e.g., [16]). However, this solution is not satisfactory for several reasons. It would fail if the function routed is not an exact permutation (e.g., if it is a random function). Moreover, sorting algorithms tend to be complicated and do not obey the one pass principle (since they involve comparison), defeating the requirement for simplicity. Likewise, Valiant's scheme [17] of reducing the problem of permutation routing to that of routing two random functions in succession is inappropriate, as it requires storage at intermediate nodes between the two phases of the algorithm, and this is unavailable under the hot potato paradigm.

We now give a hot potato algorithm that routes any permutation in $9n$ steps. Our algorithm is essentially the three-bend algorithm, with one important difference: every packet waits at its source for a randomly chosen, non-oblivious delay before following the rules of the three-bend algorithm.

The non-oblivious delay is chosen as follows: each source picks a random integer delay value in some appropriate range and stores it in a counter. Next, for every time step when the $+R$ link out of that source is free, it decrements this counter. When the counter reaches zero it injects its packet into the network along the $+R$ link (note that it is guaranteed to have the $+R$ link available for injection at this time, since it just decremented the counter to zero). Note that the delay is non-oblivious, because the decrementation of the counter depends on the times of passages of other packets through the source.

To simplify the analysis, we change the delay mechanism slightly, to make explicit a partitioning into "stages" (which would otherwise appear implicitly in the analysis). Each source first picks randomly one of the following three starting times: 0, $3n$, or $6n$. (This corresponds to picking one of three stages at random.) It adds to this a random integer uniform in $[0, n/2]$, to be used as a nonoblivious delay beyond the starting point.

Theorem 7: *The above algorithm completes routing any permutation in at most 9n steps (with high probability).*

Proof: We will prove that a packet will, with probability $1 - N^{-c}$ for $c > 1$, reach its destination by the end of the stage in which it was injected. It is easy to invoke the Chernoff bound to argue that with probability $1 - e^{-\Omega(n)}$, no more than $0.4n$ packets with sources or destinations in any row or column are injected in any stage. We now concentrate on a single stage.

Consider the first n steps of a phase. Since at most $0.4n$ packets in any row will be injected in this phase, there are at least $0.6n$ time steps in which any packet can be injected. The remainder of the analysis is patterned on that in the proof of Theorem 3. As before, we will establish Assumptions (1)–(3) in the proof of Theorem 3. Let us focus on a packet $\mathcal{P}$ going from r_s, c_s to r_d, c_d. Recall the notion of a diagonal from Section 2: the set of packets that can prevent $\mathcal{P}$ from making its first turn into the $+C$ direction. The diagonal D_0 for $\mathcal{P}$ is determined by the point in time it is injected. Our first question is: for any j, of the at most $0.4n(k \log n + j)$ packets with destinations anywhere in columns $c_d - j, \ldots, c_d, \ldots, c_d + k \log n$ that are injected in this stage (call these dangerous packets), how many will elect to be on the same diagonal as $\mathcal{P}$? We will argue that with high probability, fewer than $k \log n + j$ do so, so that Assumption (1) is satisfied. Assumptions (2) and (3) are proved much as in Theorem 3, with modifications similar to the proof of Assumption (1) below.

For each dangerous packet $\mathcal{P}_i$, let the indicator variable X_i be 1 if $\mathcal{P}_i$ is injected at a time step that puts it in D_0, and 0 otherwise. We wish to argue that with high probability, $\sum_i X_i \leq k \log n$. The time steps at which any packet can be injected fall into at least $0.6n$ distinct congruence classes (determined by the nonoblivious delay), of which only one will put it in D_0. Since $\mathcal{P}_i$ chooses its nonoblivious delay in the range $[0, n/2]$, we have $E[X_i] \leq 2/n$. Further, $E[X_i] \leq 2/n$ regardless of the values of the $X_j, j \neq i$. This is because the choices of the other packets can only influence the positions of the $\geq 0.6n$ time steps available for $\mathcal{P}_i$ to enter the network, but not which of them is actually chosen by $\mathcal{P}_i$ — this is determined by the random nonoblivious delay chosen by its source. It is tempting to argue that since every source chooses its random integer independently of all others, the choices of diagonals of all dangerous packets are mutually independent so that the Chernoff bound can be invoked. This is not true, since the positions of the time-steps at which $\mathcal{P}_i$ can enter are still influenced by the other packets; all we know is that $E[X_i] \leq 2/n$ whatever be the values of the X_j for $j \neq i$. We can then argue that $\sum_i X_i$ is stochastically dominated by the sum $\sum_i Y_i$, where the Y_i are independent Bernoulli trials of success probability $2/n$, and now use the Chernoff bound. □

2.2. Implementation Issues

For clarity, we have described our algorithm from the point of view of the motion of a packet rather than the actions of a node. We suggest two possible ways of implementing the three bend algorithm in terms of rules for the node. The most straightforward implementation assumes that an intermediate node can chop off a piece of the header of a passing packet. The header of a packet contains the fields (h_1, h_2, c_d, r_d). The headers h_1 and h_2 are represented by one bit each.

Consider a node v at location (r, c). It polls its incoming links in the following order. For a packet coming from above, if $r = r_d$, then v absorbs the packet. Otherwise, it is routed to $-C$. For a packet coming from the right, if $c = c_d$ and the $-C$ link is free, the packet is routed to $-C$. Otherwise, it is routed to $-R$. For a packet coming from below, if $r = r_d$, then h_2 is chopped off. Now, if h_2 is missing and the $-R$ link is free, the packet is routed to $-R$. Otherwise it is routed to $+C$. For a packet coming from the left, if $c = c_d$, then h_1 is chopped off. Now, if h_1 is missing and the $+C$ link is free, the packet is routed to $+C$. Otherwise it is routed to $+R$.

The above algorithm is very simple to implement. It requires a node to look at its incoming links in a fixed cyclic order, and requires only exact comparisons. Its drawback is the requirement to chop off parts of the header.

The second implementation does not have this drawback, but requires a packet's header to contain both its source address and destination address, and somewhat more complicated computations. The designer of the routing algorithm computes a reasonable value for $k \log n$ as in Assumption 1 of the proof of Theorem 3. A node will turn a packet coming from the left upwards only if $c \leq c_d \leq c + k \log n$. A node will turn a packet coming from below leftwards only if $r_s \leq r_d \leq r$.

The second implementation only approximates the three bend algorithm. However, the proofs of

Theorems 3 and 7 can be modified to hold for this implementation as well, though the bound in Theorem 7 has to be changed from $9n$ to $10n$.

3. The Hypercube

Consider a Hypercube with n dimensions and $N = 2^n$ nodes. Each node has a distinct n-bit label, and node v is connected to node v' iff their labels differ by exactly one coordinate. Edges (links) are bidirectional, and indexed by the coordinate on which their two end points differ. The *canonical path* between two nodes is the one in which every edge is of higher index than the one preceding it. We analyze the following deflection routing algorithm, in which a packet only travels on edges of the canonical path from its source to its destination.

The Canonical Path Algorithm.

A packet is absorbed as soon as it reaches its destination node v_d. Packet $\mathcal{P}$ is injected to the network in node v_s along link j, where j is the smallest index on which v_s and v_d differ (note that since v_s injects only one packet to the system, there can be no conflict at the time of injection). Thereafter, each node v scans its incoming links in the order $n, \ldots, 1$ in a one pass manner, assigning an outgoing link for any packet encountered before continuing the scan to the next incoming link. A packet $\mathcal{P}$ that enters v on link j is sent out along link i, where i is the smallest index on which v and v_d differ. However, in case of a conflict (link i was already assigned to another packet which entered v along link j', where $j' > j$), v sends $\mathcal{P}$ back along link j (along which it arrived).

Thus altogether, $\mathcal{P}$ visits at most n links, though each of these links may be traversed an indefinite number of times (due to deflections). Once a packet leaves a link, it never returns to it.

We now turn to the average behavior of the canonical path algorithm. It will also follow from our proof that the worst case batch routing time of the canonical path algorithm is at most $n + N - 2$ steps.

Theorem 8: *For almost all functions f, the batch routing time of the Canonical Path Algorithm is $O(n)$ $(= O(\log N))$.*

Proof: Let $t_f(\mathcal{P})$ denote the number of steps until $\mathcal{P}$ reaches its destination when f is the destination function. In what follows, all paths referred to are canonical paths. For a destination function f and packet $\mathcal{P}$, let $path_f(\mathcal{P})$ denote the set of edges along the path connecting the source and destination nodes of $\mathcal{P}$. Fix a run of the algorithm for a destination function f.

Definition 2: *For a destination function f, a* deflection chain *of packet $\mathcal{P}$ is a sequence of edges $e_1, \ldots e_k$, together with a sequence of packets $p_1 = \mathcal{P}, \ldots p_k$ and a sequence of time steps $t_1, \ldots t_k$ such that: p_k crosses e_k at time t_k, after having been on an edge different than e_k at time $t_k - 1$; for all $i \in [1, k-1]$, p_i is deflected back along e_i at time t_i by p_{i+1} which occupies e_{i+1}; for all $i \in [1, k-1]$, either $t_i = t_{i+1}$ or $t_i = t_{i+1} + 1$. The packet p_k is the* head *of the deflection chain.*

Canonical paths have the *nonrepeating property*: once two paths separate, they never rejoin. This justifies the term *tree* in the following definition:

Definition 3: *The* deflection tree *of $\mathcal{P}$ under f, denoted $D_f(\mathcal{P})$, is the union of the sets of all edges in deflection chains of $\mathcal{P}$ or on $path_f(\mathcal{P})$.*

Denote the set of packets whose path intersects $D_f(\mathcal{P})$ by $P_f(\mathcal{P})$.

Lemma 9: $t_f(\mathcal{P}) \leq |path_f(\mathcal{P})| + 2(|P_f(\mathcal{P})| - 1)$.

Proof: We prove that $\mathcal{P}$ is deflected at most $|P_f(\mathcal{P})|$ times — once for every other packet in the deflection tree. For this we develop a "charging" mechanism by which we charge each deflection of $\mathcal{P}$ to a different packet in $P_f(\mathcal{P})$.

Suppose that $\mathcal{P}$ is deflected at e at time t. Then there is a unique deflection chain that has $(\mathcal{P}, e, t)$ at its tail. Charge this deflection to the head packet p_k of the chain. Clearly, $p_k \in P_f(\mathcal{P})$. Now it remains to observe that any packet can be the head of at most one deflecting chain. This follows from the fact that $D_f(\mathcal{P})$ is a tree. Consider the first time t_k when p_k was the head of a deflection chain of $\mathcal{P}$, say at e_k Then by definition, p_k cannot again be the head of a deflection chain while still at e_k. Packet p_k cannot be the head of a deflection chain on any later edge e' on its path, as then both p_k and the packet it deflects p_{k-1} must have occupied the same edge e'' (leading into e' along the canonical path from $\mathcal{P}$'s source node) one time step earlier. □

It remains to bound $|P_f(\mathcal{P})|$ (w.h.p.). We do this by first bounding $|D_f(\mathcal{P})|$. We construct a tree $T_f(\mathcal{P})$ which contains $D_f(\mathcal{P})$. Whereas $D_f(\mathcal{P})$

contains all edges which actually participate in deflection chains, the construction of $T_f(\mathcal{P})$ will ignore timing considerations to some extent. Thus $T_f(\mathcal{P})$ will contain edges that would potentially be on some deflection chain if we could delay packets arbitrarily along their paths, even if these edges do not end up as members of deflection chains in the actual run of the algorithm. Our analysis makes use of timing considerations in only the following two ways:

1) Two packets that originate at locations differing in an odd number of coordinates will never meet. Thus without affecting any of our bounds, we restrict our attention to the packets originating at sources of even parity.

2) Packets do not overtake each other. If packet p_1 crosses edge e before packet p_2 does, then packet p_2 cannot cross edge e' before packet p_1 does.

We grow $T_f(\mathcal{P})$ incrementally. In what follows it is convenient to view the random destination function f as being constructed incrementally as well, where new parts of f are randomly constructed only at the time they are needed for the construction of $T_f(\mathcal{P})$. In this incremental random construction, we condition every new step of the construction on previously constructed portions, thus insuring that f is actually drawn from the uniform distribution.

Together with $T_f(\mathcal{P})$ we also construct $Q_f(\mathcal{P})$, the set of packets whose paths intersect $T_f(\mathcal{P})$. Each packet in $Q_f(\mathcal{P})\setminus\{\mathcal{P}\}$ is assigned to one edge, and each edge in $T_f(\mathcal{P})$ has at least one packet assigned to it. Initially $T_f(\mathcal{P})$ contains $path_f(\mathcal{P})$, and $Q_f(\mathcal{P})$ contains all packets whose paths intersect it. $\mathcal{P}$ is assigned to all edges of $path_f(\mathcal{P})$, and any other packet in $Q_f(\mathcal{P})$ is assigned to the lowest indexed edge of $path_f(\mathcal{P})$ that it traverses. Our final goal is to have a one-to-one onto mapping between packets of $Q_f(\mathcal{P}) \setminus \{\mathcal{P}\}$ and edges of $T_f(\mathcal{P}) \setminus path_f(\mathcal{P})$. In intermediate stages of the construction we do the following:
1) Select an edge e of minimal index that has more than one packet assigned to it.
2) Select a packet $p \neq \mathcal{P}$ assigned to e. The packet p corresponds to the first packet to cross e. Its choice is arbitrary, because at this stage we have not yet developed any destination bits of the packets at e beyond the edge e, so the packets are indistinguishable. Cancel the assignment of p to e.
3) Develop as many bits of the destination of p as are necessary to determine the next edge e' that p takes. (If p has already reached its destination, let e' be a "phantom" edge that no other packet crosses.)
4) If e' is already in $T_f(\mathcal{P})$, assign p to e' and start the next stage.
5) Else add e' to $T_f(\mathcal{P})$ and assign p to e'. In addition, for any packet not yet in $Q_f(\mathcal{P})$, develop as many bits as are necessary to find out if its path intersects e'. If it does, add the packet to $Q_f(\mathcal{P})$ and assign it to e'. Go to the next stage.

A stage which results in the discovery of a new edge (5 above), is termed an *effective stage.*

Lemma 10: *$T_f(\mathcal{P})$ contains all edges of $D_f(\mathcal{P})$.*

Proof: By construction, $T_f(\mathcal{P})$ contains all edges of $path_f(\mathcal{P})$ and all edges of deflection chains of $\mathcal{P}$. □

Lemma 11: *There is a constant c such that $|T_f(\mathcal{P})| < cn$, with probability at least $1 - N^{-2}$.*

Proof: For edge e_i added to $T_f(\mathcal{P})$ while following the path of p, let B_i denote the set of new packets added to $Q_f(\mathcal{P})$ as a result of adding e_i to $T_f(\mathcal{P})$. We outline the conditions under which $\mathcal{P}' \in B_i$. Edge e_i connects nodes v and v' which differ only on one bit (say the jth bit). Let $v_1v_2...v_n$ denote the bit representation of v, let $s_1s_2...s_n$ be the source address of $\mathcal{P}'$, and let $d_1d_2...d_j$ be the first j bits of the destination address of $\mathcal{P}$. The following are necessary conditions for $\mathcal{P}'$ to cross e_i:
1) For all $k > j$, $s_k = v_k$.
2) $d_j \neq s_j$.
3) For all $k < j$, $d_k = v_k$.

Since we only consider packets originating at sources of even parity, the expected number of packets crossing e_i is $1/2$. However, this is not the true expected value of $|B_i|$, since we have to condition on information we have from previous edges. This has two opposing effects:

1) Let e be the edge preceding e_i in $T_f(\mathcal{P})$. We need not consider packets whose canonical path to e_i goes through e, since they where already accounted for when considering e. We remark that with probability $1/2$, the indices of e and e_i differ by exactly 1, since the destination of the packet p that contributed e_i is chosen at random. If this is the case, not passing through e rules out one fourth of all the packets that could reach e_i.

2) For packets that cannot go through e, the information that their paths do not cross any other edge of the deflection tree may imply that they actually have a higher probability of crossing e_i. But this effect can be bounded by observing that all

nodes spanned by the deflection tree have the same value at their first coordinate, namely the value of the first bit of the destination address of $\mathcal{P}$. Thus every packet still has at least the other half of the possible destinations available to it, and hence its probability of crossing e_i can at most double.

Summing up, with probability 1/2, one fourth of the sources can be ignored. For sources that are not ignored, the probability of crossing e_i at most doubles. Thus $E[|B_i|] \leq 7/8$.

We now use the Chernoff bound: $path_f(\mathcal{P})$ can contribute at most n edges to $T_f(\mathcal{P})$. The total number of "other" edges in $T_f(\mathcal{P})$ equals the total number of effective stages. The total number of effective stages is equal to the total number of packets in $Q_f(\mathcal{P})$. When the total number of "other" edges exceeds the total number of packets, the construction of $T_f(\mathcal{P})$ stops. In each effective stage, the expected gain in number of edges relative to number of packets is 1/8. By the Chernoff bound, there exists a constant c such that in cn steps the number of edges would outnumber the number of packets with probability $1 - N^{-2}$, even if we take into acount the packets initially placed in $Q_f(\mathcal{P})$ because of the edges of $path_f(\mathcal{P})$. □

The bound on $|T_f(\mathcal{P})|$ is also a bound on $|Q_f(\mathcal{P})|$, which in turn upper bounds $|P_f(\mathcal{P})|$. Now Lemma 9 can be applied to show that $\mathcal{P}$ reaches its destination within $O(n)$ steps. By symmetry, also any other packet has probability at most N^{-2} of not reaching its destination in cn steps, implying that the probability that all packets reach their destinations in cn steps is at least $1 - 1/N$. □

4. Open Problems

Both the three bend algorithm and the canonical path algorithm were designed in a way that facilitates their analysis. They have the property that a packet may at times be deflected away from its destination even though an edge that would take it closer to its destination is free. Our analysis shows that the effect of such events is limited. However, it is a major open problem to analyze simple algorithms that do not have this disturbing property.

We have only had limited success in adapting the three bend algorithm to the three dimensional $n \times n \times n$ mesh with wrap around wires: we cannot prove a batch routing upper bound that is better than $O(n \log n)$. We have found no elegant way to adapt the three bend algorithm to the mesh (without wrap around wires) or to the Manhattan Street Network — a torus with directed edges, where rows alternate in the direction of edges, and so do columns. We know of some inelegant ways of doing so. The canonical path algorithm and its analysis can be directly applied to networks such as the Butterfly, provided that they have bidirectional wires, and that only the first layer transmits messages (to the last). Indeed, a similar analysis is used for wormhole routing on the butterfly in [5]. In this case we obtain a deterministic algorithm that routes to random destinations in $O(\log N)$ steps, with no queues at all. This should be contrasted with [11], where a similar result was proved, but with constant size queues.

For permutation routing, we suspect that the idea of random delays that we used for the torus can be replaced by taking the first bend of the three bend algorithm on a random column. We have been unable to prove this. A more challenging problem is to design simple and efficient deterministic algorithms for permutation routing on the torus (or any other network). Our canonical path algorithm can be adapted to give a randomized Valiant-like $O(\log N)$ permutation routing scheme on the 3-dilated hypercube (each edge has three copies): the first set of edges is used to route the packets to intermediate random destinations, the second set is used to route them to their final destinations. The third set of edges is used as a buffer between the two parts of the algorithm (which would be provided by storage at the intermediate destinations, if we were not dealing with the hot potato paradigm), and perhaps can be removed by careful analysis.

In *continuous* routing problems, packets are continuously generated at nodes at a rate which is determined by the throughput of the network. We have found the analysis of continuous routing problems to be more difficult than that of batch routing problems. A deceptively difficult part is to bound the number of steps that a packet remains at its source until it has a free link available on which it can be injected into the network. Our main result in this area is a deterministic algorithm that maintains optimal throughput (upto a constant factor) on the torus indefinitely, and in which each packet is expected to reach its destination in $O(\sqrt{N})$ steps. This result will be presented in a separate paper.

Acknowledgments: Special thanks to Eli Upfal for his collaboration on parts of this work. We thank Hisao Tamaki for pointing out an error in a previous version of this paper, and Baruch Schieber for many useful discussions.

References

[1] A.S. Acampora and S.I.A. Shah. Multihop lightwave networks: a comparison of store-and-forward and hot-potato routing. In *Proc. IEEE INFOCOM*, pages 10–19. IEEE Computer Society Press, 1991.

[2] P. Baran. On distributed communications networks. *IEEE Transactions on Communications*, pages 1–9, 1964.

[3] A. Borodin and J. E. Hopcroft. Routing, merging, and sorting on parallel models of computation. *Journal of Computer and System Sciences*, 30:130–145, 1985.

[4] J. T. Brassil and R. L. Cruz. Bounds on Maximum Delay in Networks with Deflection Routing In *29th Annual Allerton Conference on Communication, Control, and Computing*, pages 571–580, 1991.

[5] S. Felperin, P. Raghavan and E. Upfal. A theory of wormhole routing in parallel computers. *Proc. IEEE Symposium on Foundations of Computer Science*, 1992.

[6] A.G. Greenberg and J. Goodman. Sharp approximate models of deflection routing in mesh networks. To appear in *IEEE Trans. Communications*, 1992.

[7] A.G. Greenberg and B. Hajek. Deflection routing in hypercube networks. To appear in *IEEE Trans. Communications*, 1992.

[8] B. Hajek. Bounds on evacuation time for deflection routing. *Distributed Computing*, 5:1–6, 1991.

[9] W.D. Hillis. *The Connection Machine*. MIT Press, 1985.

[10] D.H. Lawrie and D.A. Padua. Analysis of message switching with shuffle-exchanges in multiprocessors. In *Interconnection Networks*. IEEE Computer Society Press, 1984.

[11] B. Maggs and R. Sitaraman. Simple Algorithms for Routing on Butterfly Networks with Bounded Queues. *24th ACM Annual Symposium on Theory of Computing*, pages 150–161, 1992.

[12] N.F. Maxemchuk. Comparison of deflection and store and forward techniques in the Manhattan street and shuffle exchange networks. In *Proc. IEEE INFOCOM*, pages 800–809. IEEE Computer Society Press, 1989.

[13] R. Prager. An algorithm for routing in hypercube networks. Master's thesis, University of Toronto, September 1986.

[14] B. Smith. Architecture and applications of the HEP multiprocessor computer system. In *Proc. Real Time Signal Processing IV*, pages 241–248. SPIE, 1981.

[15] T. Szymanski. An analysis of "Hot Potato" routing in a fiber optic packet switched hypercube. In *Proc. IEEE INFOCOM*, pages 918–925. IEEE Computer Society Press, 1990.

[16] C. D. Thompson and H. T. Kung. Sorting on a mesh-connected parallel computer. *Communications of the ACM*, 20:263–271, 1977.

[17] L.G. Valiant. A scheme for fast parallel communication. *SIAM Journal on Computing*, 11:350–361, 1982.

[18] Z. Zhang and A.S. Acampora. Performance analysis of multihop lightwave networks with hot potato routing and distance age priorities. In *Proc. IEEE INFOCOM*, pages 1012–1021. IEEE Computer Society Press, 1991.

A Theory of Wormhole Routing in Parallel Computers

(Extended Abstract)

Sergio Felperin* Prabhakar Raghavan † Eli Upfal ‡

Abstract

Virtually all theoretical work on message routing in parallel computers has dwelt on *packet routing:* messages are conveyed as packets, an entire packet can reside at a node of the network, and a packet is sent from the queue of one node to the queue of another node until its reaches its destination. The current trend in multicomputer architecture, however, is to use *wormhole routing.* In wormhole routing a message is transmitted as a contiguous stream of bits, physically occupying a sequence of nodes/edges in the network. Thus, a message resembles a worm burrowing through the network. In this paper we give theoretical analyses of simple wormhole routing algorithms, showing them to be nearly optimal for butterfly and mesh connected networks. Our analysis requires initial random delays in injecting messages to the network. We report simulation results suggesting that the idea of random initial delays is not only useful for theoretical analysis, but may actually improve the performance of wormhole routing algorithms.

1. Overview

Virtually all theoretical work on message routing in parallel computers has dwelt on *packet routing:* messages are conveyed as packets, an entire packet can reside at a node of the network, and a packet is sent from the queue of one node to the queue of another node until it reaches its destination [2, 15, 16, 19, 20, 21, 22]. While packet routing is very efficient asymptotically, this efficiency is often compromised by the overhead required by the packet routing mechanism; especially in maintaining queues in the intermediate nodes, and breaking long messages into small packets and then reconstructing the original messages when the pieces reach their destination (possibly out of order). Therefore, the current trend in multicomputer architecture is to use substantially simpler routing mechanisms, in particular *wormhole routing* [3, 6, 7, 8, 14, 11, 18]. A message is transmitted as a contiguous stream of bits, physically occupying a sequence of nodes/edges in the network. There are no queues in the intermediate nodes, and a node can only hold a (small) fraction of a message. The routing strategy is oblivious, keeping the overhead in the intermediate nodes minimal. When the head of a message reaches a node, the nodes reads the first few bits in the message's header, and uses them to direct the head of the message to the next node on its path. The rest of the message follows the head of the message as it moves, requiring no more intervention by the intermediate node. Thus a message resembles a worm burrowing through the network, giving rise to the name for this style of routing. In this paper we give theoretical analyses of simple wormhole routing algorithms for butterfly and mesh connected networks. The nature of wormhole routing causes messages to delay each other in ways that are very different from packet routing, and this poses the main technical challenge for us.

Parallel machines that use variants of worm-

*IBM Almaden Research Center, San Jose, CA.

†IBM T.J. Watson Research Center, Yorktown Heights, NY.

‡IBM Almaden Research Center, San Jose, CA, and the Weizmann Institute, Rehovot, Israel.

0-8186-2900-2/92 $3.00 © 1992 IEEE

hole routing include the Intel Delta-machine, Intel iPSC/2, Intel Sigma, Symult S14, MIT J-machine, MIT April, and others. Previous research on wormhole routing focuses on simulations that study the extent to which a network can be loaded (as a fraction of the available bandwidth) before it gets clogged [5, 7, 17]. Other research has addressed the issue of *deadlock*, since in wormhole routing it is possible for a set of messages to mutually block each others' path [9]. On a two-dimensional mesh, for instance, it is known that if every message first travels along its row to the column of its destination, then turns into the column (call this the *one-bend path*), there is no deadlock.

To keep implementations simple and also to avoid deadlock, practitioners have emphasized simple routing strategies (such as the one-bend path for the mesh). Practitioners find average case analyses especially useful here: they seek bounds on message latency and network loading for simple routing strategies when the message lengths and destinations are drawn from probability distributions. Such analysis supports the insights derived from their simulations. From a theoretical perspective, analyzing the delays for random destinations gives us results for Valiant's scheme for worst-case permutation routing. Given both these theoretical and practical motivations, we analyze message delays for simple schemes when messages are bound for randomly chosen destinations. This approach of probabilistic analysis gives us an additional benefit: we are able to analyze the behavior of messages in a model of continuous stochastic message generation by each node. We consider a network that is run for a "long time", in which each node generates a message at each step with some probability. We are interested in the time that elapses between the generation and the delivery of a message. Such "steady-state" results are of great value to practitioners but rare in theoretical computer science.

Leighton [12] conducts a probabilistic analysis for meshes for the related but different model of *virtual cut-through*: the buffers at each node are assumed to be large enough to hold an entire message. Thus his analysis does not pertain to true wormhole routing (see Caveat below for a detailed explanation). Indeed, Leighton [12] underscores the difficulty and practical importance of analyzing the case when buffer sizes are fixed constants independent of message lengths. A nice feature of Leighton's paper is that it deals with the *greedy algorithm*, which is of great practical interest: there are no priorities assigned to messages, and each message simply keeps moving whenever it can, along the one-bend path to its destination. Makedon and Simvonis [13] give worst-case bounds for virtual cut-through routing on the mesh, their algorithm requires buffers to be large enough to hold an entire message. Aiello *et al.* [1] give a non-oblivious algorithm for wormhole routing on a hypercube and other networks of logarithmic degree; however; their algorithm may time-multiplex a link over several worms, so that a worm does not flow contiguously across a link. When every node of an N-node hypercube has a message has length L, they guarantee delivery of all messages in time $O(L + \log N)$ with high probability, assuming that a node can handle $O(\log N)$ messages simultaneously. If this assumption is removed, their algorithm needs to inject tokens carrying co-ordinating information into the network. Thus, their algorithm attains a good bound on message delay for networks of unbounded degree, at some loss of the simplicity and obliviousness that motivates wormhole routing.

We focus instead on simple oblivious routing algorithms that are *delayed greedy algorithms*: each message waits at its source for a random initial delay before proceeding greedily on a canonical path to its destination. Our algorithms do not inject artificial tokens and are simple. In our analysis we require new techniques that differ from those used for packet routing, because in wormhole routing a message can occupy many edges and thus simultaneously delay several messages following paths that could even be disjoint. Furthermore, because we deal with the practical constraint of small buffers at each node, the techniques of

Leighton [12] do not seem to apply here. This leads us to study the sum of the sizes of almost independent branching processes.

1.1. Model

One of our goals is to develop a model that captures the essence of wormhole routing. Our model incorporates the features that make wormhole routing practically interesting (such as small buffer size), and precludes algorithms that inject co-ordinating tokens in addition to messages (as one algorithm of [1] does). By restricting ourselves to bounded-degree networks, we do not require nodes to handle an unbounded number of messages at any time step as some previous algorithms do.

We model a network by a graph; adjacent nodes are connected by two unidirectional links, one in each direction. We assume that each link has at its output a buffer that can hold one *flit* [7], or flow control unit — a message is composed of one or more flits. The length of a message is the number of flits that comprise the message. Only one flit of one message may pass through a link at any time step. Once the head of a message enters a link, all other flits of that message must pass through it before any other message can use that link. In each time step, the head of a flit may advance along the next link on its path, if that link is free. Otherwise it remains in the buffer at the output of the last link it traversed. If the head does advance, every flit in that message can advance along the next link from its current position. A message is said to be delivered when its tail arrives at its destination; we are interested in the number of steps that elapse before a message is delivered. Note that we study the most rigorous case when the buffer for each link can hold only one flit, although in practice a small constant number of flits can be accommodated.

Caveat: There is a great deal of confusion between the case we are dealing with, and the model of *virtual cut-through.* The latter resembles wormhole routing superficially, but differs in one crucial aspect: in virtual cut-through, the buffers at nodes can hold a constant number of *messages*, rather than a constant number of *flits*. Thus in virtual cut-through the buffer size at a node is proportional to the worm length. Consequently, most results for virtual cut-through follow from known results in packet routing with constant-size queues. In contrast, wormhole routing requires new analytical techniques to be developed, due to the advent of altogether new phenomena by which messages delay one another.

We study two wormhole routing scenarios: *batch* and *continuous.* In the batch case, each processor is the source of one message and we study the time taken to deliver all messages. In the continuous case, we consider the long-term behavior of the network. At each time step, each processor can independently generate a message with some probability; we study the maximum arrival rate of messages for which the network remains stable, i.e. the number of messages in the network has a limit distribution independent of time, and give bounds for the delivery time of any given message.

1.2. Results

Throughout, the phrase "with high probability" will represent "with probability $1 - N^{-c}$, where N is the number of nodes in the network, and c is any positive constant". In all cases, c can be increased arbitrarily at the expense of the constant in the asymptotic time bounds.

In Section 2 we study wormhole routing on the butterfly network with N sources; all the results in this section are for batch routing. We first analyze a simple delayed greedy algorithm when all message lengths are the same, denoted L. If the destination of each message is chosen independently at random, we show that every message is delivered in time $O(L \log N \min\{L, \log N\})$ with high probability. We then extend this result in two ways: (1) if message lengths are different and are chosen from a "well-behaved" distribution with expectation $\bar{L}$, then a message of length L_i is delivered in time $O(L_i + \log N + \bar{L} \log N \min\{\bar{L}, \log N\})$ with high probability;

(2) when message lengths are arbitrarily chosen by an adversary, we give a batching scheme that ensures that a message of length L_i is delivered in time $O(L_i \log N \min\{L_i, \log N\})$ with high probability. All the above results for random destinations can be extended to worst-case permutations using Valiant's scheme.

In the Appendix, we give detailed results of simulations for our delayed greedy algorithm. First, the simulations suggest that the random initial delays do not increase the overall completion time (for the last message to arrive). Thus the idea of random initial delays that enables us to prove Thereom 1 may have some benefits. Next, we use interpolations on a large sample of data to study how well the message latency suggested by the data fit the bound in our theorem.

Section 3 deals with a two-dimensional $\sqrt{N} \times \sqrt{N}$ mesh. We first consider batch routing with random destinations. When all messages have the same length L, we give a bound of $O(L\sqrt{N} \log N + N/\log N)$ steps on the running time of a simple delayed greedy algorithm using one-bend paths. We give a lower bound of $L\sqrt{N}$ steps, so that the above bound is good when $L \geq \sqrt{N}/\log N$. When L is smaller, we cannot prove that the one-bend algorithm is near-optimal, but do give an algorithm that uses slightly more complex paths that it is nearly optimal. This algorithm may also add oblivious delays for each message en route (rather than only at the source). We extend these results to varying message lengths and to worst-case permutations via Valiant, as for the butterfly.

We then give results for continuous routing on the mesh. We show that if each node independently generates messages (of either fixed or random lengths) at each step, we can sustain a rate of injection of flits that is nearly $\Omega(N)$, the available network bandwidth. The algorithms are similar to our routing schemes for the batch case, and the message transit times are nearly optimal.

2. The Butterfly

In this section we study wormhole routing on a butterfly for the batch case, when each message independently chooses a random destination. We first show that a simple delayed greedy algorithm is near-optimal when all messages have the same length, then extend this result to varying message lengths.

Consider a butterfly network consisting of layers numbered $0, 1 \cdots \log N$ of N nodes each. The nodes at layer 0 are *sources*, while those at layer $\log N$ are *destinations*. Each source has a message of length L, and is bound for a random destination. Let $\ell = \min\{L, \log N\}$. We consider the following algorithm: message i first chooses an integer d_i in $[0, 10\ell - 1]$. For a fixed positive constant c, the message waits $d_i \cdot cL \log N$ steps at its source before starting to travel (by the unique path in the butterfly) to its destination.

Theorem 1: There is a constant c such that at the end of $10c\ell L \log N$ steps, every message has reached its destination with high probability.

Proof: We view time as being divided into *phases* each lasting $c\ell \log N$ steps. Thus at the beginning of each phase, some of the N sources begin sending their messages. We will show that with high probability any single message reaches its destination by the end of the phase in which it was launched, and this will prove Theorem 1.

We now focus on a single message M. We say that a message A *blocks* message M at node v if the head of M is at node v and the link on which it will leave v is occupied by A. The following aspect of wormhole routing complicates the delay analysis. M can be blocked at v by A, and simultaneously A can be blocked at w by B, although the paths of M and B do not intersect. Thus M can be made to wait by messages that never intersect its path.

This distinction between the message that blocks M and the one that actually delays M is crucial to our analysis and is made precise as follows.

Definition 1: Message A *delays* message M at time t, if the following three conditions are satisfied:
1. There is a chain of messages $M = X_0, X_1, ..., X_r = A$ such that message X_i is blocking message X_{i-1};
2. Message A is moving at time t;
3. No other message in the chain $M = X_0, X_1, ..., X_r = A$ can move at this step.

Note that because the network is acyclic, if M is blocked then there is a message that delays M. In other words, if M cannot move at a given step, some other message that is delaying M moves forward.

Lemma 2: Each message can delay M no more than ℓ steps throughout the whole phase.

Proof: If message A delays M at time t, then there is a chain of messages $M = X_0, X_i, ...X_r = A$ such that message X_i is blocking message X_{i-1}, and message X_{r-1} is not blocked by the tail of message A (else whenever A moves, X_{r-1} can move). In each subsequent step in which A moves message X_{r-1} is blocked by a different flit of A. After no more than ℓ (not necessarily successive) steps in which A moves (and possibly delays M), message X_{r-1} is blocked by the tail of A. Thus if M is still blocked it is not delayed by A.

We now argue that M is never again delayed by A. Assume to the contrary that M is delayed again by A. Then there is a path from the head of M to an edge occupied by a flit of A which is not the tail of A, and the path does not cross the tail of A. But the fact that M was delayed before by A implies that there is a path from M to that flit that does cross the tail of A; but in the butterfly there cannot be two different paths to the same edge, contradicting the assumption. □

Let $\mathcal{D}_t$ denote the set of messages that delayed message M in the first t steps of the phase. Let Y_t denote the number of steps beyond time t for the head of M to reach its destination, if no message outside $\mathcal{D}_t$ were to delay it.

Clearly $Y_0 = \log N$, since M needs to traverse $\log N$ edges, and $\mathcal{D}_0$ is empty. Furthermore, the head of M reaches its destination at time τ, where τ is the smallest t for which $Y_t = 0$.

Let A be the message that would delay M at time t, if M were not delayed by messages that are not in $\mathcal{D}_t$. Let e be the next edge that A has to traverse. Let k be the number of messages not in $\mathcal{D}_{t-1}$ that traverse e in this phase. To simplify the analysis we make the following concession: all of these k messages delay M at e, one after the other, although in reality any such message could have passed too early or too late to actually delay M. We add these messages to $\mathcal{D}_{t+1}$, and add $k\ell$ to Y_{t+1} to account for the resulting delay to M. (Note that since each of these k messages will be a delaying message for ℓ steps, the delays they suffer may also add to the count Y_t, at a later time t.) This assumption eliminates all timing considerations; thus we can further simplify the analysis by assuming that only one message is moving at each step, namely the message that is delaying M.

Thus, one of the following events occurs at step t:

1. No message outside $\mathcal{D}_t$ traverses e, in which case A remains the delaying message and $Y_{t+1} = Y_t - 1$.

2. Edge e is traversed by B_t messages that are not in $\{M\} \cup \mathcal{D}_t$. We add these messages to $\mathcal{D}_{t+1}$ and set $Y_{t+1} = Y_t + \ell B_t - 1$.

Lemma 3: Let $\mathcal{E}_t(e)$ denote the event: edge e has not been traversed by messages in $\mathcal{D}_t$ in the first t steps of this phase. Conditioning on $\mathcal{E}_t(e)$, the total number of messages that traverse e in this phase is dominated by the binomial distribution with expectation no larger than $2/(10\ell)$.

Proof: Suppose that e connects a node at layer $k-1$ to a node at layer k of the butterfly. Let $x_i = 1$ if the message generated in input i traverses edge e at that phase, else $x_i = 0$. Only 2^k inputs can send a message through edge e. Each input launches a message in this phase with probability $1/10\ell$ and without the condition $\mathcal{E}_t(e)$, each launched message traverses edge e with probability 2^{-k}.

Let v be the node in layer 1 traversed by message M. To delay M a message needs to traverse an edge in the binary tree rooted in v. Since this tree spans only half of the N outputs of the butterfly, the condition that a message did not visit part of this tree can no more than double the probability that it traverses any other edge. Thus the probability that one of the 2^k messages traverse e is bounded by $2/(2^k 10\ell)$. The events for different messages are independent, and the expected number of messages that traverse e under this condition is no more than $2/10\ell$. □

Thus, we reduced the problem to that of computing τ, the first index t for which $Y_t = 0$, where $Y_0 = \log N$, $Y_{t+1} = Y_t + \ell B_t - 1$, and B_t has a binomial distribution with mean bounded by $1/5\ell$.

Let $\hat{\tau} = 30\ell \log N$. By the Chernoff bound,

$$Prob\{\sum_{i=1}^{\hat{\tau}} B_i \geq \hat{\tau} + \log N\} \leq e^{-2\log N}.$$

Thus, with probability $1/N^2$, message M reaches its destination in $30 \log^2 N$ steps, and with probability $1/N$ all messages reach their destinations in the phase in which they were injected to the system. □

A technique related to the above proof is used in an analysis of deflection routing on the hypercube [10]. We turn next to the case of varying message lengths, beginning with random message lengths and proceeding to the worst case. The former is likely to be of more interest to practitioners, while the latter holds theoretical appeal. For messages with random lengths we use the following version of the Chernoff bound [4]:

Theorem 4: Let $x_1, ..., x_n$ be independent identically distributed random variables. Assume that $\Psi(c) = E[e^{cx}] < \infty$ for some $c > 0$, and that $E[x_i] = \mu$, then for any $\alpha > 0$,

$$Prob\{\sum_{i=1}^{n} x_i > n(1+\alpha)\mu\} \leq e^{-cn(1+\alpha)\mu + n \ln \Psi(c)}.$$

Since it is reasonable to assume that in practice the length of the messages varies in some finite interval, the conditions of the above theorem hold. Thus, with high probability the total length of a set of $O(\log n)$ messages is bounded by $C\bar{L}\log n$, where $\bar{L}$ is the mean length of a message, and C is a constant. The analysis of Theorem 1 then holds for messages of various lengths, if we replace $L \log n$ by $C\bar{L}\log n$.

Theorem 5: Let L_i be the length of the message from source $i, 1 \leq i \leq N$. With high probability the message from source i is delivered in $O(L_i + \log N + \bar{L}\log N \min\{\bar{L}, \log N\})$ steps.

We now give a similar result for message lengths chosen by an adversary. Consider an instance of batch routing in which the message M_i sent by source i has length L_i. Each message is bound for a random destination as before. Let $k_i = \lceil \log_2 L_i \rceil$, and let $\ell_i = \min\{2^{k_i}, \log N\}$. We use a delayed greedy algorithm similar to the one above: M_i waits at the source for $(10\ell_i + d_i)c2^{k_i} \log N$ steps before moving greedily towards its destination, where d_i is an integer chosen uniformly from $[0, 10\ell_i - 1]$. This initial delay ensures that when M_i begins moving, messages from all sources j such that $k_j < k_i$ have already been delivered to their destinations with high probability. Then, in at most $10c2^{k_i} \log N$ additional steps, with high probability, M_i is delivered. We omit the details of:

Theorem 6: With high probability, M_i is delivered in $O(\ell_i 2^{k_i} \log N)$ steps, $\forall i$.

Observe that the delay of any message only grows with its own length, and not that of the longest (or even average) message in the instance. Noting that $2^{k_i - 1} + \log N$ is a lower bound on the number of steps needed to deliver M_i, our bound is within $O(\log^2 N)$ of the best possible when L_i exceeds $\log N$, and somewhat tighter when all messages are short.

The above result can be extended to worst-case permutations using Valiant's scheme, for the 2-dilated butterfly. Let $k = \max_i\{k_i\}$, and $\ell = \min\{2^k, \log N\}$.

Theorem 7: For every instance of permutation wormhole routing with varying message lengths, every message is delivered by the end of $20c\ell 2^k \log N$ steps using a delayed greedy algorithm for each phase of Valiant's scheme.

3. Routing on a Mesh

In this section we first give a bound on the delayed greedy algorithm using one-bend paths for the two-dimensional mesh. The bound is nearly optimal when all message lengths are at least $\sqrt{N}$; we are unable to show that the obvious extension of this scheme is near-optimal for shorter message lengths. We then give an algorithm in which the routes are slightly modified from the one-bend paths and a message may wait at an intermediate node (but obliviously), showing this new scheme to be near-optimal regardless of message length. We extend these results to varying message lengths. We then turn to the continuous routing problem, in which messages are generated continuously in time by independent stochastic processes at each node. We show that our schemes enable messages to enter the network at close to its bandwidth capacity; the network remains stable and any given message is delivered with high probability in nearly optimal transit time.

3.1. Batch Routing

Assume first that all messages are of equal length L, and each message independently chooses a random destination.

Theorem 8: For any algorithm, with high probability a random instance requires $\Omega\ (L\sqrt{N})$ parallel steps.

Proof Sketch: The proof compares the likely total bandwidth needed by random destinations to the bandwidth of $O(N)$ links that are available at each step. □

We next consider the following delayed-greedy algorithm. Source i chooses an integer d_i independently and uniformly in the range $[0, ..., \frac{2\sqrt{N}}{\log N} - 1]$. For a fixed constant b, the message M_i originating at source i then waits for $d_i(b^2 L \log^2 N + bL \log N + 2\sqrt{N})$ steps before traveling greedily by the one-bend path to its destination (traveling along its row first and then along the destination column).

Theorem 9: The above delayed greedy algorithm delivers all messages in $O(L\sqrt{N} \log N + N/\log N)$ steps with high probability.

Proof Sketch: Partition time into phases of length $b^2 L \log^2 N + bL \log N + 2\sqrt{N}$ steps. Some messages are launched at the beginning of each phase; we show that with high probability they reach their destinations by the end of that phase. □

Clearly the above bound is weak when $L \ll \sqrt{N}/\log^2 N$, because the rate at which we launch messages is too low (think of the case $L = 1$). By analogy to our approach for the butterfly, when $L < \sqrt{N}/\log^2 N$ we should only use $\tilde{O}(L)$ phases each of length $\tilde{O}(\sqrt{N})$. We are unable to prove that this works for one-bend routes, so we sketch the following alternative simple algorithm in which the paths followed by messages are not one-bend paths, for the case $L < \sqrt{N}/\log N$.

The mesh is divided into horizontal *strips* of $L \log N$ rows each. Each message randomly chooses to start traveling at the beginning of one of L phases each lasting $b\sqrt{N}\log N + 2\sqrt{N}$ steps, for some constant b. It first travels along its row until it reaches the column of its destination. It then turns *south — regardless of its destination* — until it reaches the bottom node of that column in its strip. It then turns around and goes north as far as it can while remaining within the strip, then waits until $bL\sqrt{N}\log N$ steps have elapsed since the beginning of the current phase. After that, it continues along the column to its destination as follows: if the destination is north of its position, it simply goes north on the column. If it is to the south, it goes north to the top of its strip, where it turns around and heads south.

Observing that with high probability $O(\log N)$ messages turn from any strip to any column, we prove:

Theorem 10: With high probability, the above scheme delivers every message to its destination within $L(b\sqrt{N}\log N + 2\sqrt{N})$ steps.

Proof: We bound the running time of a single phase by $(b\sqrt{N}\log N + 2\sqrt{N})$ steps, and this will prove our theorem. Let us focus on a message M traveling from row r to column c; let s denote the strip containing r. With high probability, no more than $(a\sqrt{N}\log N)/L$ messages from r are bound for c, for some constant a. Thus, the head of M will reach column c within $a\sqrt{N}\log N$ steps.

With high probability, no more than $c'\log N$ messages from s have destinations in c. These are the only messages that will delay M while it is turning into c. Thus all messages from s finish turning into c within $a\sqrt{N}\log N + c'\sqrt{N}\log N$ steps. Once they have turned into c, they "stack up" one behind the other facing north; note that the strip contains enough rows to allow this. This stacking up is complete within $b\sqrt{N}\log N$ steps, for a constant b that is no more than $a + c' + 2$. Following this, each message travels to its destination with no further delays, within $2\sqrt{N}$ steps — at most $\sqrt{N}$ steps each are required to go north in the strip if necessary (after waiting), and to turn again and go south to the destination. □

Note that the time bound in Theorem 10 is within a constant factor of the lower bound of Theorem 8, for $L \leq \sqrt{N}/\log N$; for larger L, Theorem 9 guarantees that the one-bend delayed greedy is within a logarithmic factor of optimal.

We can extend the above results using the standard methods used in Section 2 to accomodate varying message lengths, obtaining the analogues of Theorems 5 and 6 for meshes. We can also use Valiant's scheme to obtain a result for worst-case permutations.

3.2. Continuous Routing

A length L message with random destination traverses $\Omega(\sqrt{N})$ edges on the average, and each edge is occupied for at least L steps. Since a mesh has $O(N)$ edges, it can sustain no more than $\sqrt{N}/L$ new messages per step. Thus the network exceeds its maximum capacity when each processor generates a new message with probability larger than $c/L\sqrt{N}$ per step for some constant c. We call the network *stable* if the number of messages in the network has a limit distribution independent of time. We analyze two simple algorithms. The first can handle messages of arbitrary size; its sustainable generation rate and expected message delay are near optimal provided L is $\Omega(\sqrt{N})$. The second algorithm gives near optimal performance for shorter messages.

For the first algorithm we assume that all messages have length at least $2\sqrt{N}$, else the source of the message pads it to this length. When a message is generated, it first travels left on the row in which it was generated till the end of that row. Then it turns around and travels right on the row to its destination column, then turns to the column towards its destination. If a message was generated in row i, and its head it still traveling left, we say that the message is in $STORAGE(i)$, else the message is in the *critical section.* We divide time into segments of $2\sqrt{N} + L$ steps, and partition the segments into alternating odd and even segments. A message in an odd row is allowed to proceed to the critical section only during odd segments, and a message in an even row can proceed only during even segments. (This convention can be replaced by random delays.) Once a message enters the critical section it stays there until it is delivered.

Theorem 11: There is a constant $c > 0$ such that if in each step each processor generates a new message with probability $c/(L\sqrt{N} + 2N)$, then
1. The network is stable.
2. The probability that a given message spends more than $k(L + 2\sqrt{N})$ steps in the network is bounded by $2e^{-\alpha k}$ for a constant $\alpha > 0$, independent of the time the message was generated.

Acknowledgments: We thank Uri Feige for carefully reading early versions of the paper, and Nimrod Meggido and Gerald Shedler as well as Uri for many valuable discussions.

References

[1] B. Aiello, F.T. Leighton, B. Maggs, and M. Newman. Fast algorithms for bit-serial routing on a hypercube. In *Second Annual ACM Symposium on Parallel Algorithms and Architectures*, pages 55–64. ACM Press, 1990.

[2] R. Aleliunas. Randomized parallel communication. In *ACM-SIGOPS Symposium on Principles of Distributed Systems*, pages 60–72, 1982.

[3] W.C. Athas. Physically compact, high performance multicomputers. In *Sixth MIT Conference on Advanced Research in VLSI*, pages 302–313. MIT Press, 1990.

[4] H. Chernoff. A measure of asymptotic efficiency for tests of a hypothesis based on the sum of observations. *Annals of Math. Stat.*, 23:493–509, 1952.

[5] W. Dally. Performance analysis of k ary n cube interconnection networks. *IEEE Trans. Computers*, 39:775–785, 1990.

[6] W. Dally and C.L. Seitz. Deadlock free message routing in multiprocessor interconnection networks. *IEEE Trans. Computers*, 36:547–553, 1987.

[7] W.J. Dally. Fine grain message passing concurrent computers. In *Third Conference on Hypercube Concurrent Computers and Applications*, pages 2–12. ACM Press, 1988.

[8] W.J. Dally. Virtual channel flow control. In *Seventeenth Annual International Symposium on Computer Architecture*, pages 60–68. ACM Press, 1990.

[9] J. Duato. On the design of deadlock free adaptive routing algorithms for multicomputers: theoretical aspects. In *Second European Conference on Distributed Memory Computing*, pages 234–243. Springer Verlag LNCS 487, 1991.

[10] U. Feige and P. Raghavan. Exact analysis of hot potato routing. In *33rd Annual Symposium on Foundations of Computer Science*, 1992.

[11] R.J. Smith II. Experimental system kit hardware. In *Fourth Conference on Hypercube Concurrent Computers and Applications*, pages 713–725. Golden Gate Enterprises, 1989.

[12] F.T. Leighton. Average case analysis of greedy routing algorithms on arrays. In *Second Annual ACM Symposium on Parallel Algorithms and Architectures*, pages 2–10. ACM Press, 1990.

[13] F. Makedon and A. Simvonis. On bit-serial packet routing for the mesh and the torus. In *Third Symposium on Frontiers of Massively Parallel Computation*, pages 294–302. IEEE Computer Society Press, 1990.

[14] M. Noakes and W.J. Dally. System design of the j machine. In *Sixth MIT Conference on Advanced Research in VLSI*, pages 179–194. MIT Press, 1990.

[15] N. Pippenger. Parallel communication with limited buffers. In *25th Annual Symposium on Foundations of Computer Science*, pages 127–136, 1984.

[16] A. Ranade. How to emulate shared memory. In *Proceedings of the 28th Annual IEEE Symposium on Foundations of Computer Science*, pages 185–194, 1987.

[17] D.S. Reeves, E.F. Gehringer, and A. Chandiramani. Adaptive routing and deadlock recovery: a simulation study. In *Fourth Conference on Hypercube Concurrent Computers and Applications*, pages 331–337. Golden Gate Enterprises, 1989.

[18] C.L. Seitz, W.C. Athas, C.M. Flaig, A.J. Martin, J. Seizovic, C.S. Steele, and W.K. Su. The architecture and programming of the Ametek Series 2010 multicomputer. In *Third Conference on Hypercube Concurrent Computers and Applications*, pages 33–36. ACM Press, 1988.

[19] E. Upfal. Efficient schemes for parallel communication. *Journal of the ACM*, 31:507–517, 1984.

[20] Eli Upfal. An $O(\log N)$ deterministic packet routing scheme. In *21st ACM Annual Symposium on Theory of Computing*, pages 241–250, 1989.

[21] L. G. Valiant and G. J. Brebner. Universal schemes for parallel communication. In *Proceedings of the Thirteenth Annual ACM Symposium on Theory of Computing*, pages 263–277, Milwaukee, Wisconsin, May 1981.

[22] L.G. Valiant. A scheme for fast parallel communication. *SIAM Journal on Computing*, 11(2):350–361, 1982.

Appendix: Simulation results

We report simulation results for wormhole routing on butterfly networks with 256 to 16K inputs, routing messages of size 10–50 flits, with initial random delays of 0–20 steps.

In our simulator, each node has two input buffers, one for each incoming link, and two output buffers, one for each outgoing link. A buffer can store no more than two flits.

Following the general scheme of wormhole routing, a node can at each step receive one flit into each of its input buffers, move one flit from each of its input buffers to an output buffer, and send one flit from each output buffer along each of its outgoing edges. A buffer can receive a new flit only if it stores less than two other flits. Transmission of two messages cannot be multiplexed on a link.

The latency of a message is the sum of its random initial delay and the time the message spent in the network. The maximum latency is the maximum over all the messages in the network. Random delay X means that the random delay for each message was chosen uniformly at random from the range $[0, ..., X-1]$. Each point in our graphs represents an average of 30 independent experiments.

Figure 1
Maximum Latency vs # of Inputs and Message Length
Random Delay = 15

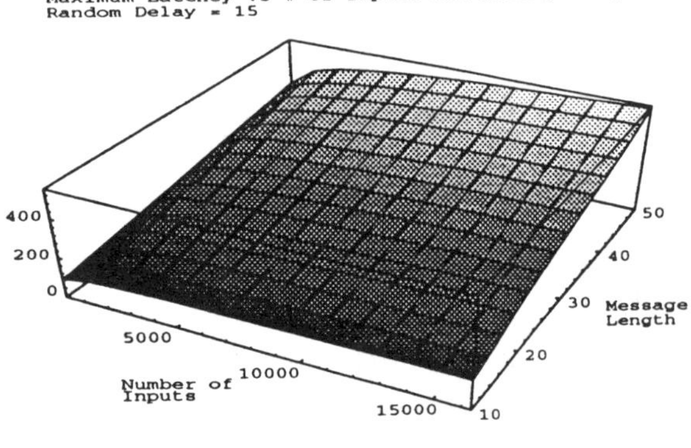

Figure 1 gives the tradeoff between network size, message size, and maximum latency. The effect of initial random delay as a function of network size is shown in figures 2 and 3. Figure 4 demonstrates the usefulness of initial random delays for messages of various sizes on a network with 4K inputs. Note that the graphs are presented as a function of the number of inputs of the network rather than the diameter.

Figure 2
Maximum Latency vs Number of Inputs
10 flits messages

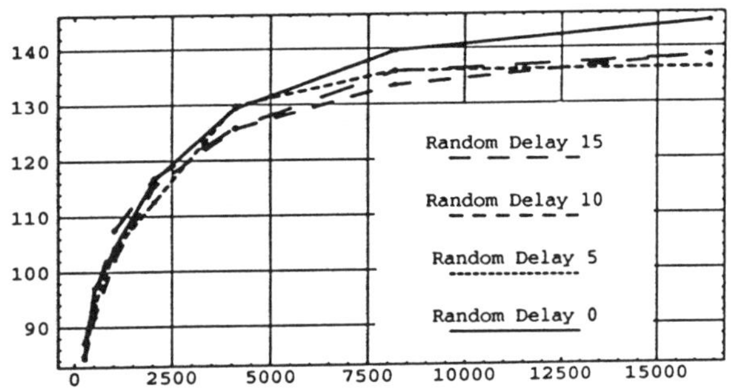

Figure 3
Maximum Latency vs Number of Inputs
30 flits messages

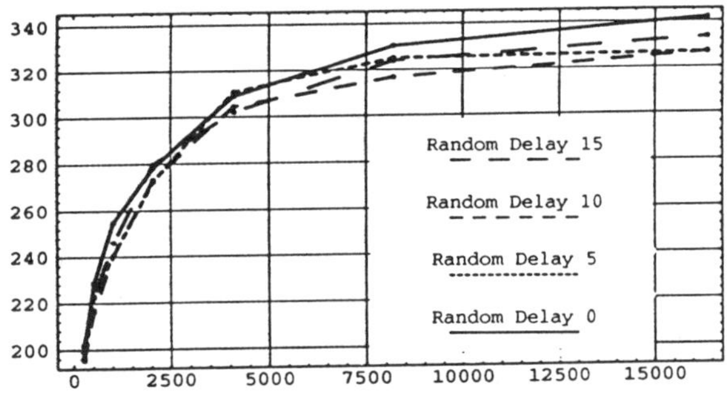

Figure 4
4K Inputs
Average Latency vs Random Delay

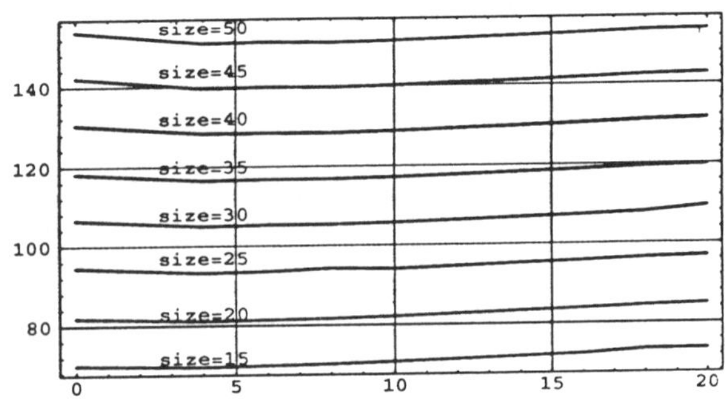

Computing a Shortest k-Link Path in a Polygon

Joseph S. B. Mitchell * Christine Piatko † Esther M. Arkin ‡

Abstract. *We consider the problem of finding a shortest polygonal path from s to t within a simple polygon P, subject to the restriction that the path have at most k links (edges). We give an algorithm to compute a k-link path with length at most $(1+\epsilon)$ times the length of a shortest k-link path, for any error tolerance $\epsilon > 0$. Our algorithm runs in time $O(n^3k^3 \log(Nk/\epsilon^{1/k}))$, where N is the largest integer coordinate among the n vertices of P.*

We also study the more general problem of approximating shortest k-link paths in polygons with holes. *In this case, we give an algorithm that returns a path with at most $2k$ links and length at most that of a shortest k-link path; the running time is $O(kE^2)$, where E is the number of edges in the visibility graph.*

Finally, we study the bicriteria path problem in which the two criteria are link length and "total turn" (the integral of $|\Delta\theta|$ along a path). Here, we obtain an exact polynomial-time algorithm for polygons with holes.

1 Introduction

There have been many algorithms in computational geometry that have addressed various notions of shortest paths. The problem of finding shortest (Euclidean length) paths among obstacles in the plane is well-studied [3, 10, 11, 14] and there has also been recent work on the problem of finding shortest paths according to other notions of "length", including L_1 and fixed orientation metrics [5, 12], *link distance* [13, 15], etc.

In this paper, we introduce a new set of results to the field of geometric shortest path algorithms: we study "bicriteria" path problems in which there are *two* objectives in the selection of a path. In particular, we examine the problem of finding a path that is "good" with respect to link distance *and* Euclidean length, and give the first algorithmic results for the problem of finding a shortest k-link path in a polygon, when there are no restrictions on the orientations of links. We also give efficient algorithms for finding a k-link path with minimum "total turn" (defined to be the integral of $|\Delta\theta|$ along the path).

The problems that we address arise due to the non-uniqueness of k-link paths; in fact, there may be an infinite number of different k-link paths joining a given pair of points in a polygon. Even for the case of k equal to the link distance between the pair of points, there is, in general, a continuum of k-link (i.e., minimum-link) paths. This phenomenon is in contrast to the situation with geodesic (Euclidean shortest) paths, where the number of shortest paths joining two points is almost surely equal to one.

One of the main technical issues we must address is the fact that shortest k-link paths (and also minimum-turn k-link paths) need not lie on a "visibility graph", or on any simple variant thereof. Shortest k-link paths may, in general, turn at points interior to the polygon whose coordinates are given by the roots of high-degree polynomials. Thus, we are unable to obtain a path that exactly minimizes the Euclidean length among all k-link paths; instead, our methods produce a *provably good* approximation of a shortest k-link path, whose length is at most $(1+\epsilon)$ times the length of an optimal path. (Note that, by expressing paths as formulas in the theory of real closed fields, one can obtain an (*exponential time*) exact solution for the decision problem: Does there exist a k-link path of length at most d?) In contrast, in the case of finding a minimum-total-turn k-link path, we obtain an exact optimal solution.

Motivation. In most applications that require one to compute an "optimal" path, there is more than one criterion by which path quality is to be measured. For example, Euclidean shortest paths among obstacles may be too "kinked", with too many links or too much total curvature, for the motion of a mobile robot through an obstacle course. On the other hand,

*Applied Math, SUNY, Stony Brook, NY 11794-3600. Partially supported by NSF grant ECSE-8857642, by Air Force Office of Scientific Research contract AFOSR-91-0328, and by a grant from Hughes Research Laboratories. email: jsbm@ams.sunysb.edu

†Computer Science, Cornell University, Ithaca, NY 14853. Partially supported by NSF Grant ECSE-8857642, Air Force Office of Scientific Research contract AFOSR-91-0328, and an NSF Graduate Fellowship. email: piatko@cs.cornell.edu

‡Applied Math, SUNY, Stony Brook, NY 11794-3600. Partially supported by NSF Grants DMC-8451984 and ECSE-8857642. email: estie@ams.sunysb.edu.

0-8186-2900-2/92 $3.00 © 1992 IEEE

a minimum-link path can be arbitrarily long (in Euclidean length) compared with a shortest length path. (Refer to Figure 2.) Thus, a naturally arising question was posed by Suri: How can one find a shortest (in Euclidean length) path that uses at most k links?

Summary of Results.

1. Using a combination of dynamic programming and a form of binary search (whose "tests" are based on tracing locally optimal shortest k-link paths), we devise an algorithm to compute a k-link path, from s to t, within a simple polygon P (without holes) whose Euclidean length is at most $(1+\epsilon)$ times the length of a shortest k-link s-t path. The algorithm runs in time $O(n^3 k^3 \log \frac{Nk}{\epsilon^{1/k}})$, where N is the largest (integer) coordinate among the n vertices of P. (Note that the dependence on ϵ is *logarithmic* in $1/\epsilon$.)

2. For the more general problem of finding short k-link paths in polygons *with* holes, we obtain an algorithm that produces a path with at most $2k$ links and a length at most that of a shortest k-link path; the time complexity is $O(kE^2)$, where E is the number of visibility graph edges. A specialized variant of this algorithm allows us to give an alternative method for simple polygons, where we can find a k-link path (not $2k$-link) with length at most $(1+\epsilon)$ times optimal, in time $O(k^3 n^2/\epsilon)$. Compared to the result mentioned above, this method has substantially inferior complexity with respect to its dependence on ϵ; but it gives an improved dependence on n, and it has no dependence on N, the size of the coordinates.

3. We study the problem of finding a k-link path from s to t in a polygon with holes, such that the *total turn* of the path is minimized. The total turn is defined as the integral of $|\Delta\theta|$ along the path, and can be thought of as the total motion of the "steering wheel" when driving a vehicle along the path. We obtain an exact algorithm, whose running time is $O(E^3 \log^2 n)$. Our algorithm is based on a method of finding minimum-link *right-turning* (or left-turning) paths among obstacles in the plane.

Related Work. In [2], we began a study of geometric bicriteria path problems, obtaining several negative results that parallel those known for graphs [7], as well as a pseudo-polynomial time algorithm for the problem of minimizing total turn and Euclidean length.

Recently, de Berg et al. [6] have studied the problem of finding a shortest rectilinear path among rectilinear obstacles, where the measure of path cost is a "combined metric" equal to the sum of the path length (L_1 distance, since they work in a rectilinear world) and a constant times the number of turns; they obtain an $O(n^2)$ algorithm. Hershberger and Snoeyink [9] have examined the special case of finding a shortest k^*-link path (where k^* denotes the number of links in a minimum-link path), for paths and obstacle boundaries required to have edges from among a given fixed set of orientations. Yang, Lee, and Wong [16] study a general class of rectilinear planar problems in which the obstacle set is rectilinear, and path costs are a function of L_1 length *and* the number of bends (rectilinear link distance); they obtain worst-case time bounds of $O(n \log^2 n)$ for the combined metric or for finding a shortest minimum-link path. All of these results on bicriteria paths in a fixed-orientation world exploit the fact that there exists a *path-preserving graph* that is guaranteed to contain the desired optimal path.

Related to our problem of optimizing the length of k-link paths is the problem of computing optimal enclosing k-gons. Aggarwal et al. [1] study the minimum *area* enclosing k-gon problem, obtaining an exact algorithm of time complexity $O(n^2 \log k \log n)$. In his thesis, Chang [4] discusses some of the local optimality properties that minimum *perimeter* enclosing k-gons must satisfy, but leaves open the problem of actually computing them for $k > 3$. It is likely that our methods discussed here will be applicable to this open problem.

Our Method. In contrast to previous work, our problem of finding shortest k-link paths *without orientation restrictions* admits no finite path-preserving graph. Instead, we perform an analysis of the local and global structure of shortest k-link paths in simple polygons. We then use global structure to decompose the problem into a set of "raceway" problems, which we then further decompose into $O(n^2)$ "elementary" problems, which ask us to find shortest i-link paths between pairs of "flush" edges (defined below). We solve these problems by a binary search whose tests consist of tracing locally optimal paths. We combine elementary problem solutions and the raceway solutions into a global solution by means of dynamic programming.

In polygons with holes, we apply a "path preserving graph" approach, constructing a special graph whose embedding has the property that it contains a $2k$-link path whose length is within factor $(1+\epsilon)$ of the length of a shortest k-link path.

2 Preliminaries

Geometric Notations. Let P be a polygon (possibly with holes) in the plane, with a total of n vertices.

We assume that the coordinates of the vertices of P are positive integers; we let N denote the largest x- or y-coordinate among the vertices.

Given two points s and t in P, a *minimum-link path* between them is a polygonal path inside P with a minimum number of edges (or, "links"). The *link distance* $d_L(s,t)$ refers to the number of links in a minimum-link path from s to t.

The visibility graph of P, denoted $VG(P)$, is the graph on the vertex set of P whose edges join mutually visible pairs of vertices. $VG(P)$ can be computed in time $O(E + n \log n)$, where E denotes the number of edges in the graph [8].

It is well-known (e.g., [10]) that, for any two points s and t in a *simple* polygon P, the (Euclidean) shortest path, also called the "geodesic" path, $\pi_G(s,t)$ is unique, lying in $VG(P)$. A minimum-link path, on the other hand, is generally not unique, even in a simple polygon. Indeed, it is precisely the non-uniqueness of k-link paths that makes the problem addressed in this paper interesting.

In a simple polygon P, we define uniquely one particular minimum-link path, which we call the *greedy* path, $\pi_L(s,t)$, from s to t. Specifically, the path $\pi_L(s,t)$ is obtained by using the "windows" (and their extensions) defined by the *window partition* of P with respect to s (as defined in [15]), where the last link is chosen to pass through the last vertex of the geodesic path $\pi_G(s,t)$.

Given a polygonal path π, an interior edge $e \in \pi$ is called an *inflection edge* if the predecessor and the successor edges of e in π lie on opposite sides of the line containing e.

Throughout this paper, the points $s,t \in P$ will remain fixed. We assume that s and t are in general position, so that $\pi_G(s,t)$ is uniquely defined. We also fix the number k to be some integer satisfying $d_L(s,t) \leq k \leq |\pi_G(s,t)|$, where $|\pi_G(s,t)|$ denotes the number of edges in the geodesic path $\pi_G(s,t)$.

3 A General Approximation Scheme

Theorem 3.1 *Let P be a polygon, possibly with holes, whose boundary consists of n edges. For any k, $d_L(s,t) \leq k \leq |\pi_G(s,t)|$, one can compute an s–t path in P that has at most $2k$ links and has length at most that of a shortest k-link s–t path, in time $O(kE^2)$, where E is the number of visibility graph edges.*

Proof Outline. We construct a discrete graph, based on an arrangement of line segments within P, that is guaranteed to contain the claimed $2k$-link path.

For each vertex v of P (and also for $v = s,t$), and for each vertex u that is visible from v, extend a segment out from v in the direction of u, stopping when we enter the exterior of P at some point u'; we say that $\overline{vu'}$ is the segment *anchored at v in the direction of u* and we say that $\overline{uu'}$ is the *extension segment associated with $\overline{vu'}$*. This yields a set S of $O(E)$ segments within P, where E is the size of the visibility graph, $VG(P)$.

We now construct a graph $\mathcal{G}$ whose nodes correspond to the segments S. We connect two nodes with an edge in $\mathcal{G}$ if the associated extension segments cross (at a point interior to P). The length of such an edge, joining nodes corresponding to segments σ_1 and σ_2 (anchored at vertices v_1 and v_2, $v_1 \neq v_2$), is defined to be the length of the path $v_1, \sigma_1 \cap \sigma_2, v_2$. We also connect node σ to node σ' with a zero-length edge, if σ and σ' are anchored at a common vertex v. We show the following claim:

Claim: (a). $\mathcal{G}$ is connected; and (b). corresponding to any shortest k-link s–t path (of length d) in P there is a path in $\mathcal{G}$ with at most $2k$ nodes, such that the corresponding segments constitute a $2k$-link s–t path with length at most d.

$\mathcal{G}$ has $O(E)$ nodes and $O(E^2)$ edges, and it is constructible in time $O(E^2)$. We can then use dynamic programming to compute a shortest $2k$-node path in time $O(kE^2)$. □

Theorem 3.2 *Let P be a simple polygon (without holes) whose boundary consists of n edges. For any k, $d_L(s,t) \leq k \leq |\pi_G(s,t)|$, one can compute, in time $O(k^3 n^2/\epsilon)$, an s–t path in P that has at most k links and has length at most $(1+\epsilon)$ times that of a shortest k-link s–t path.*

Proof Outline. We use the fact that the Euclidean metric can be approximated to accuracy ϵ by a fixed-orientation metric of $K = O(1/\sqrt{\epsilon})$ equally-spaced directions. For each of these K directions out of a vertex $v \in \pi_G(s,t)$, we extend a greedy path out for k links in the direction of t. We claim that the resulting arrangement of nkK segments is sufficiently "rich" to contain an approximating k-link s–t path. The proof involves showing that a shortest k-link path can be perturbed onto the arrangement by a sequence of "twists", in which each link is rotated slightly (by at most angle $2\pi/K$) onto a segment of the arrangement, *while maintaining the connectivity of the k links.* □

We will show that in a *simple* polygon P, the dependence on ϵ can be made *logarithmic* in $1/\epsilon$, at a cost of a factor of n and dependence on the term $\log N$. First, we need a careful analysis of the structure of optimal paths.

4 Characterizations

We let π^* denote a shortest k-link path from s to t, and we let d^* denote the (Euclidean) length of π^*. Our goal now is to give a characterization of the structure of π^*; most of the proofs are complex, and are omitted in this extended abstract.

Let the inflection edges of $\pi_G(s,t)$ be denoted $e_1, \ldots, e_I$; let e_0 (e_{I+1}) denote the first (last) link of $\pi_G(s,t)$. The edges e_j partition $\pi_G(s,t)$ into subchains that are purely left-turning or purely right-turning. We call these subchains *convex chains*, although it should be understood that they can spiral, etc. See Figure 3.

Lemma 4.1 *Let π^* be a shortest k-link path in a simple polygon P. Each inflection edge e_j in the geodesic path $\pi_G(s,t)$ must be a subset of an edge of π^*, and each inflection edge of π^* must contain an inflection edge of $\pi_G(s,t)$.*

Remark. The above lemma holds for polygons with holes, provided that we define $\pi_G(s,t)$ to be the shortest path homotopically equivalent to π^*.

For paths within a simple polygon P, we say that an edge in a polygonal s–t path is *flush* if it contains a non-inflection edge of $\pi_G(s,t)$. (A similar definition applies to polygons with holes, provided we use a homotopically equivalent geodesic path.) The following uniqueness result will be a consequence of our various results on local optimality:

Lemma 4.2 *Let a and b be consecutive flush edges along a shortest k-link path, π^*, and let i denote the number of links along π^* between a and b. Then, the subpath of π^* joining a and b is the unique shortest i-link path from a to b.*

Remark. It is not the case that shortest k-link s–t paths in a simple polygon are unique; indeed, in the full paper we give a construction to show that there can be an exponential number of such paths.

An edge of π^* that is not inflection nor flush is called *rocking* if it is in contact with a (single) vertex of P (a *rocking vertex*).

The bend points of path π^* are either *interior* bend points (interior to P) or *boundary* ("bash") bend points (lying on some boundary edge of P). We call an edge of P that contains a bash point a *bash wall* of P.

Let π be a polygonal s–t path and let π' be a subpath of π joining two consecutive interior bend points, p and q, of π. (Thus, the bend points of π', if any, are all bash points.) Let p' be the predecessor of p along π and let q' be the successor of q along π. Assume that all edges of π' are rocking. Refer to Figure 4. We say that π' is a *balanced chain with respect to* π if the path from p' to q' via π' is shortest among paths with the same number of links. In the special case that π' is a balanced chain consisting of the single edge $\overline{pq}$, we say that $\overline{pq}$ is a *balanced edge*.

We can characterize balanced chains as follows: The first link of π' rests on a rocking point r; if we perturb it by a small rotation about r, while adjusting all of the other links of π' accordingly (so that π' remains connected, with all of its bend points being bash points), then the resulting perturbed path from p' to q' must be longer than the original. By somewhat involved calculus, we can quantify this statement and derive a precise characterization of balanced chains:

Lemma 4.3 (Balanced Chains) *In order for a chain π' be to balanced with respect to a polygonal path π, the angle of turn ϕ at its endpoint q must be in a unique relationship with its angle of turn γ at p: $\phi = F(\gamma)$, where the function F depends on p', q', the rocking points of π', and the edges of P containing the bash points of π'. For the case of balanced edges, this relationship is expressed by the relationship*

$$x \cot \frac{\gamma}{2} = y \cot \frac{\phi}{2},$$

where x and y are defined in Figure 5. More generally, the expression

$$\sum_{i=1}^{k-2} \left[\left[y_i \cot \frac{\phi_i}{2} - x_i \cot \frac{\gamma_i}{2} \right] \prod_{j=2}^{i} \frac{h_j \csc^2(\gamma_{j-1} - A_j)}{H_j \csc^2 \gamma_j} \right]$$

must equal zero, where the various constants are defined in Figure 6.

Lemma 4.4 (Local Optimality) *If one perturbs any single edge e of a shortest k-link path, π^*, the result is either to disconnect π^* or to increase its length. In particular, e must be in contact with at least one vertex of P and e must fall into one of the following cases:*

- *e is an inflection edge of π^*, containing an inflection edge of $\pi_G(s,t)$; or*
- *e is a flush edge, containing $\overline{uv} \subset \pi_G(s,t)$, and the balanced position of e with respect to rocking point u is clockwise from e, while the balanced position of e with respect to rocking point v is counterclockwise from e; or*
- *e is a rocking edge with both of its endpoints being bash points; or*

e is a rocking edge with both of its endpoints being interior bends, such that e is balanced; or

e is a rocking edge with exactly one of its endpoints being a bash point — the balanced position of e with respect to its rocking point is either clockwise or counterclockwise from e depending on whether the bash endpoint is on e's left or right end, respectively.

Based on the above lemmas, we can now outline the general structure of an optimal path π^*. Path π^* is partitioned by its inflection edges into pieces, $\pi_0^*, \pi_1^*, \ldots, \pi_{I+1}^*$, with piece π_j^* joining inflection edge e_j to e_{j+1}. Path π_j^* is further partitioned according to the flush edges of π^* into *elementary paths* joining pairs of consecutive flush or inflection edges. Each elementary path joining flush/inflection edge a to flush/inflection edge b has the following structure: From a, π^* is "greedy" (following the bash points of $\pi_L(s,t)$) for some portion, until a *first interior bend point* p_1 (which may, in fact, occur on the first link of the elementary path — i.e., the greedy path may be empty). π^* then consists alternately of chains of interior bend points (i.e., chains of balanced rocking edges) and balanced chains of bash points. See Figure 8 for an example of the structure of an optimal path.

The first interior bend point, p_1, will play a special role in our search algorithm, since we perform a binary search to identify p_1 (approximately) such that the resulting path that can be traced by local optimality hits our desired target in the required number of links. Not all points along $\pi_L(s,t)$ are possible first bend points for π^*. A first bend point $p_1 \in \pi_L(s,t)$ is said to be *valid* if there exists a shortest i-link path from s to some t' that uses p_1 as first bend point. We characterize the valid first bend points as follows: Let $e = \overline{qz}$ be an edge of $\pi_L(s,t)$, with rocking point r. Let p_e be the point on $\overline{rz}$ (if it exists) such that $\overline{qp_e}$ is balanced with respect to the three-link path: predecessor of e, $\overline{qp_e}$, and the ray from p_e through its (left) tangency point, $r_2 \in \pi_G(s,t)$. Refer to Figure 7. One can show

Lemma 4.5 *The valid first bend points for $e \in \pi_L(s,t)$ are precisely the points on the (possibly empty) segment $\overline{p_e z}$.*

If interior turns before p_e were allowed, the path could be locally improved by rocking edge e. By disallowing invalid turns we know that we will be tracing only locally optimal paths.

5 Computing Shortest k-Link Paths in Simple Polygons

Overview of Method. The inflection edges of the (unique) geodesic path $\pi_G(s,t)$ permit us to decompose the full problem into a sequence of "raceway" problems, where we must find (nearly) shortest i-link paths (for many values of i) between two consecutive inflection edges, while staying within a relevant subset of P. Within a raceway, though, there still may be an exponential number of shortest i-link paths; thus, we further decompose the problem into "elementary" problems of finding shortest i-link paths between pairs of flush edges (edges that contain an edge of $\pi_G(s,t)$). Each of these problems is solved by a binary search for the first bend point in an optimal path: each test of the search involves tracing a path forward through the raceway, applying the local optimality conditions of Section 3 at each step (several lemmas are needed to justify this). The justification of the search itself is based on a key "Monotonicity Lemma" which shows that paths traced forwards in this way behave "nicely" with respect to changes in the first bend point. The search stops when every edge of the traced path is known to lie within a very tiny range of angles, of size at most $\delta(\epsilon)$. This property is guaranteed if we make the interval of first bend angles small enough — less than $\delta(\epsilon)/D^k$, where D is a "dilation" factor that measures the maximum amount by which a small interval of directions trapping link i can get larger for link $i+1$. We obtain a bound on the dilation D by bounding the change in the ith turn angle with respect to the change of the first angle (the ith angle is determined by the first angle using the local optimality condition). Our bounds and analysis assume that the vertices of P are on an integer grid of size at most N-by-N; this allows us to write lower bounds on angles between triples of vertices, etc.

Finally, we assemble all of the data from the binary searches, combining it via dynamic programming recurrences to obtain the final result: an ϵ-optimal k-link path from s to t.

5.1 Decomposing the Problem

Using Lemma 4.1, we can decompose our problem into a sequence of "raceways" between extensions of inflection edges. Raceway R_j is the portion of P that lies between inflection edges e_j and e_{j+1}. Refer to Figure 9. We further trim from R_j all of the pockets of P that are on the convex side of the subpath $\pi_G(s_j, t_j)$. (A simple lemma justifies that π^* will never enter such pockets.)

We can also replace the portion of the boundary of P between s_j and t_j (going clockwise) by the *complete visibility chain*, C_j, which is the boundary of all points p such that p sees both of its tangent points with π_j. (C_j can be found in linear time.) We show that π^* must lie within the raceway R_j, which is bounded by C_j, the inflection edges e_j and e_{j+1}, and the path π_j.

Thus, we can decompose our problem into finding shortest k_j-link paths between s_j and t_j in a raceway R_j, where k_j ranges from $d_L(s_j, t_j)$ up to $|\pi_G(s_j, t_j)|$.

5.2 Shortest k-link Path in a Raceway

Let us fix our attention on one raceway, R. We desire shortest i-link paths within R, for a variety of values i (at most k such values). By results of Section 3, a shortest i-link path may have many flush edges along it, but between each pair of consecutive flush edges, the path is an alternating sequence of chains of bash points (greedy paths) and interior-bend paths.

We introduce $O(n)$ additional special edges that further decompose the raceway problem. We call these edges *leaning* edges, and they are defined to be edges $\overline{uv}$ of $VG(P)$ such that one endpoint u is a vertex of $\pi_G(s,t)$, while v is a vertex of P such that $\overline{uv}$ is an edge of *right tangency* from v, with respect to the chain $\pi_G(s,t)$ within R. Effectively, the leaning edges can "split" our "wedge" of traced paths, causing the angular ranges of each link to amplify in an unbounded fashion (preventing us from obtaining a bounded "dilation" factor). Thus, we further subdivide the raceway problem according to the $O(n)$ leaning edges, and we are able to show that the resulting elementary problems from a to b (where a and b are now either inflection, flush, or leaning edges) permit a provably good approximation to the optimal path.

We define the *combinatorial type* of a path to be the sequence of labels, one per bend point, listing the bash wall for each bashing bend point, or noting that a bend point is interior. (Note that we do *not* include the set of rocking points in this definition of combinatorial type.) Leaning edges correspond, then, to edges of $VG(P)$ that can account for a change in the combinatorial type of our traced paths.

5.3 The Main Search Algorithm

Let a and b each be a flush, leaning, or inflection edge, where b follows a along $\pi_G(s,t)$. Let s_a be the first vertex of a on $\pi_G(s,t)$ and r_a the succeeding one. Let r_b be the first vertex of b on $\pi_G(s,t)$ and t_b the succeeding one. We now describe the main algorithm *Path* (a, b, i) to find an ϵ-optimal approximation to the shortest i-link path from a and b that does not use an intermediate flush edge.

We begin with the subprocedure that traces paths according to the local optimality conditions.

Tracing Paths. By the local optimality criteria for balanced chains, once we know a *valid* first bend point, p_1, when going from flush edge a to flush edge b, we can trace out uniquely a shortest path consistent with that first bend point. We let $\pi(\gamma, i)$ denote the resulting path, where γ is the turn angle associated with point p_1.

The crucial lemma in being able to do tracing is the following, whose very technical proof is omitted here:

Lemma 5.1 (Tracing Lemma) *Given a first bend point p_1, the next link of $\pi(\gamma, i)$ is uniquely determined (it is simply obtained by "leaning" an edge through p_1 against path $\pi_G(s,t)$). Given a subpath of $\pi(\gamma, i)$, traced some number of links beyond p_1, the next link of $\pi(\gamma, i)$* is uniquely *determined by the local optimality conditions and the subpath so far. The next rocking point can therefore be determined by advancing along $\pi_G(s,t)$, one vertex at a time, starting from the last rocking point of the current subpath.*

Remark. We advance along $\pi_G(s,t)$ to find the next rocking point, *assuming that the next bend point is an interior turn.* If, once we discover the unique next "interior" bend point, we find that it is *not* reachable while staying interior to P, then the traced path should have a bash point on the end of the current link, so we "bash" and continue. At any stage, we may have a long sequence of bash points as the last several turns in the current subpath. Preceding the sequence of bash points is an interior bend point (e.g., the first such point p_1); thus, we are able to use the balanced-chain condition to determine where the next interior bend should be (if it is feasible), etc.

The Binary Search. Let Γ_0 be the set $\bigcup_{e \in \pi_L} \Gamma_e$, where Γ_e is the subinterval $[\gamma_e, \gamma_e']$ of valid angles γ that correspond to valid first interior bend points $p_1 \in e$. Let $\pi(\gamma, i)$ for $\gamma \in \Gamma_0$ be the resulting traced path that goes at most i links, or until the first rocking point that is beyond r_b on $\pi_G(s,t)$.

A point p_1 of Γ_0 is identified with the angle γ between $\pi_L(a,b)$ and the ray from p_1 that is tangent to $\pi_G(s,t)$. Note that the total length of Γ_0, $|\Gamma_0|$, is bounded by $\sum_{e \in \pi_L} |\Gamma_e| = \sum_e (\gamma_e' - \gamma_e) \leq \pi \cdot d_L(a,b)$.

During this procedure we tabulate $g_i(a,b)$, an ϵ-optimal approximation to the shortest i-link elementary path from a and b (where a and b are flush or leaning edges in the same raceway).

Path(a, b, i):

0. $\Gamma \leftarrow \Gamma_0$
1. If $|\Gamma| \leq \delta_0 = \delta(\epsilon)/D^k$, go to Step 3.
   Otherwise, $\gamma \leftarrow$ midpoint of Γ and $\Pi \leftarrow \pi(\gamma, i)$.
   Let $r = i$th rocking point of Π.
2. If Π has less than i links (i.e. we overshot b), then $\Gamma \leftarrow$ left half of Γ and go to Step 1.
   Otherwise, if Π has i links, and $r = r_b$, then if p is to the left of $\overline{t_b r_b}$
   then $\Gamma \leftarrow$ right half of Γ and go to Step 1,
   else if p is to the right of $\overline{t_b r_b}$ (which can only happen if b is a leaning edge)
   then $\Gamma \leftarrow$ left half of Γ and go to Step 1.
   Otherwise, if r precedes r_b along $\pi_L(a, b)$, $\Gamma \leftarrow$ right half of Γ and go to Step 1.
3. If the combinatorial type of $\pi(\gamma, i)$ for $\gamma \in \Gamma = [\gamma_{\min}, \gamma_{\max}]$ is constant, then $g_i(a, b)$ is assigned the length of $\pi(\gamma_{\max}, i)$.
   Otherwise $g_i(a, b) \leftarrow \infty$, since the ϵ-optimal path from a to b that we will produce will pass through some leaning edge c, and so will be found as $g_{i'}(a, c) + g_{i-i'-1}(c, b)$ for some i'.

Correctness of the Search. Correctness of the above binary search procedure is based on the following key lemma, which is used to justify discarding the relevant half of the interval Γ in Step 2:

Lemma 5.2 (Monotonicity) *Consider a particular raceway problem. Let C denote the corresponding complete visibility profile, and let Γ_0 denote the set of valid first turn angles. Let $z(\gamma)$ denote the point on C obtained by extending the ith link of $\pi(\gamma, i)$ until it exits the raceway. Then, if $\gamma, \gamma' \in \Gamma_0$, with $\gamma < \gamma'$, then $z(\gamma)$ precedes $z(\gamma')$ along the chain C.*

Proof Outline. The proof is by contradiction, and is based on the fact that $\pi(\gamma, i)$ gives an (exact, unique) shortest k-link path from a to any point of $\pi(\gamma, i)$ that lies on the kth link of $\pi(\gamma, i)$, *after* the kth rocking point of the path. We consider the various cases of how the two paths, $\pi(\gamma, i)$ and $\pi(\gamma', i)$, can interleave, and obtain contradictions based on simple geometric inequalities and the preceding fact. □

Bounding the Path Length Error. We now sketch the analysis of how we bound the size $|\Gamma|$ in order to guarantee a path quality factor of $(1 + \epsilon)$.

Lemma 5.3 (Trapping Lemma) *For a given a and b, and for a given k, if $\Gamma = [\gamma_{\min}, \gamma_{\max}]$ is such that the paths $\pi(\gamma, k)$ all have common combinatorial type, for $\gamma \in \Gamma$, and the angles between the ith edge of $\pi(\gamma_1, k)$ and the ith edge of $\pi(\gamma_2, k)$ are each bounded above by δ, then the Euclidean length of $\pi(\gamma, k)$ is at most $(1+O(\delta N^2))$ times the length of a shortest k-link path joining a and b.*

Corollary 5.4 *For ϵ-optimality, it suffices to select $\delta(\epsilon) = O(\frac{\epsilon}{N^2})$.*

Based on careful analysis of the balanced-chain condition, we are able to bound the dilation factor:

Lemma 5.5 (Dilation) *Let θ_j denote the orientation of the jth link of path $\pi(\gamma, i)$, and let $\theta_j = F(\gamma)$ denote the functional dependence on the first interior bend angle, γ. Then, $|F'(\gamma)| \leq k^{O(1)} N^{O(k)}$, implying that the dilation $D = k^{O(1)} N^{O(k)}$.*

Lemma 5.6 *All of the values $g_i(a, b)$ can be computed in total time $O(n^3 k^3 \log(Nk/\epsilon^{1/k}))$, where N is the largest integer coordinate of any vertex of P.*

Proof Outline. There are $O(n^2 k)$ values of $g_i(a, b)$ to tabulate. Each requires a binary search with

$$O\left(\frac{|\Gamma_0|}{\delta_0}\right) = O\left(k \log \left(\frac{k}{\delta(\epsilon)}\right)^{1/k} D\right) = O\left(k^2 \log \frac{Nk}{\epsilon^{1/k}}\right)$$

tests, with each test requiring time $O(n)$. □

5.4 Putting the Pieces Together

We now show how the path pieces computed so far can be assembled into a global solution by means of dynamic programming. We have tabulated $g_i(a, b)$, an ϵ-optimal approximation to the shortest i-link elementary path from a and b (where a and b are flush or leaning edges in the same raceway) for all values of i.

We now find an ϵ-optimal approximation to a shortest k-link path from s to t in two stages. In the first stage we compute $f_i(j)$, the length of the ϵ-optimal approximation to the shortest i-link path in raceway j. Using these values, we compute $h_i(j)$, the ϵ-approximation to the shortest i-link path from e_j to t, where e_j is an inflection edge. This gives us an ϵ-optimal path from s to t.

For the first stage, let us fix the raceway R_j, bounded by inflection edges e_j and e_{j+1}. Define $F(a, i)$ to be the ϵ-optimal length of the i-link path from a to e_{j+1}, where a is a flush or leaning edge in raceway j. We need to tabulate a total of $O(nk)$

such values. Initialize $F(a, i)$ to be $g_i(a, e_{j+1})$. Compute $F(a,i) = \min\{\min_{m,c}\{g_m(a,c) + F(c, i-m+1)\}, F(a,i)\}$ for $a < c < e_{j+1}$ (and for c which are leaning edges with rocking points between a and e_{j+1}) and $1 < m < i$, with a advancing backwards along $\pi_G(s,t)$ from e_{j+1} to e_j. There are $O(kn)$ choices for m and c, so it takes total time $O(n^2k^2)$ to compute all the values $f_i(j) = F(e_j, i)$. Summing over all $O(k)$ possible raceways, it takes time $O(n^2k^3)$ to compute all values $f_i(j)$.

For the second stage let $h_i(j)$ be the ϵ-approximate length of a shortest i-link path from e_j to t. We can compute these recursively by using the following: $h_i(j) = \min_{i'}\{f_{i'}(j) + h_{i-i'}(j+1)\}$. Thus, we can tabulate all the $h_i(j)$'s in $O(k^3)$ time.

The time bounds for these two stages are dominated by the time to tabulate the values $g_i(a,b)$ (the elementary paths between flush edges and leaning edges).

Theorem 5.7 *One can compute an ϵ-optimal shortest k-link path in an n-sided simple polygon P in time $O(n^3k^3\log(Nk/\epsilon^{1/k}))$, where N is the largest integer coordinate of any vertex of P.*

6 Minimum Total-Turn k-Link Paths

Consider a polygon P with holes. One measure of how "kinked" a path is can be based on the "total turn" (TT), defined to be the integral of $|\Delta\theta|$ along the path, where θ denotes the orientation of the tangent vector. The TT measures the total integrated motion of the steering wheel if we drive a car along the path, always making the turn at a vertex according to the angle that is less than 180 degrees. In [2], we showed that the bicriteria path problem of minimizing (TT, Euclidean length) is (weakly) NP-hard; we also provided a pseudo-polynomial time algorithm.

We provide an exact polynomial-time algorithm for the bicriteria path problem with objectives (TT, link distance), with running time $O(E^3\log^2 n)$.

While we have no room here to give details, we sketch our method as follows. We identify all inflection edges of the visibility graph (i.e., VG edges that are locally supporting on opposite sides of the edge). We prove a structural result that a path π^* that is optimal for our two criteria must contain the inflection edges that lie along the geodesic path homotopically equivalent to π^*. Between two inflection edges, then, the path π^* should be purely left-turning or purely right-turning. The total turn along the various purely left-turning paths that may join an inflection edge a to another inflection edge b are all equal to the difference in angles of a and b, $|\theta_a - \theta_b|$, plus $360i$ degrees, for $i = 1, 2, 3, ..., I$ (where $I \leq n$). Note that there may in fact be an exponential number of homotopically distinct, locally optimal, left-turning paths from a to b. Our goal, then, is to compute a minimum-link left-turning path from a to b, for each value of i, and for each of the $O(E^2)$ pairs a and b of inflection edges. We accomplish this by a modification of the algorithm of Mitchell, Rote, and Woeginger [13], in which we perform *constrained illumination* at each step, allowing only those paths that are purely left-turning (or purely right-turning). The algorithm of [13] runs in time $O(E\log^2 n)$, as does our modification. This gives a total time of $O(E^3\log^2 n)$ for computing the connections between inflection edges. We then combine these TT costs/link lengths via a dynamic programming recursion (time $O(kE^2)$) to obtain the final result.

References

[1] A. Aggarwal, J. S. Chang, and C. K. Yap. Minimum area circumscribing polygons. *Visual Comput.*, 1:112–117, 1985.

[2] E. M. Arkin, J. S. B. Mitchell, and C. D. Piatko. Bicriteria shortest path problems in the plane. In *Proc. 3rd Canad. Conf. on Computational Geometry*, pages 153–156, 1991.

[3] Ta. Asano, Te. Asano, L. J. Guibas, J. Hershberger, and H. Imai. Visibility of disjoint polygons. *Algorithmica*, 1:49–63, 1986.

[4] J. S. Chang. Polygon optimization problems. Report 240, CS, New York Univ., New York, NY, 1986.

[5] K. L. Clarkson, S. Kapoor, and P. M. Vaidya. Rectilinear shortest paths through polygonal obstacles in $O(n(\log n)^2)$ time. In *Proc. 3rd Annu. ACM Sympos. Comput. Geom.*, pages 251–257, 1987.

[6] M. de Berg, M. van Kreveld, B. J. Nilsson, and M. H. Overmars. Finding shortest paths in the presence of orthogonal obstacles using a combined L^1 and link metric. In *Proc. 2nd SWAT*, volume 447 of *LNCS*, pages 213–224. Springer-Verlag, 1990.

[7] M. R. Garey and D. S. Johnson. *Computers and Intractability: A Guide to the Theory of NP-Completeness.* W. H. Freeman, New York, NY, 1979.

[8] S. K. Ghosh and D. M. Mount. An output-sensitive algorithm for computing visibility graphs. *SIAM J. Comput.*, 20:888–910, 1991.

[9] J. Hershberger and J. Snoeyink. Computing minimum length paths of a given homotopy class. In *Proc. 2nd WADS*, volume 519 of *LNCS*, pages 331–342. Springer-Verlag, 1991.

[10] D. T. Lee and F. P. Preparata. Euclidean shortest paths in the presence of rectilinear barriers. *Networks*, 14:393–410, 1984.

[11] J. S. B. Mitchell. A new algorithm for shortest paths among obstacles in the plane. *Annals of Math. and Artificial Intelligence*, 3:83–106, 1991.

[12] J. S. B. Mitchell. L_1 shortest paths among polygonal obstacles in the plane. *Algorithmica*, 8:55–88, 1992.

[13] J. S. B. Mitchell, G. Rote, and G. Woeginger. Minimum-link paths among obstacles in the plane. *Algorithmica*, 8, 1992.

[14] M. Sharir and A. Schorr. On shortest paths in polyhedral spaces. *SIAM J. Comput.*, 15:193–215, 1986.

[15] S. Suri. On some link distance problems in a simple polygon. *IEEE Transactions on Robotics and Automation*, 6(1):108–113, 1990.

[16] C. Yang, D. Lee, and C. Wong. Rectilinear paths among rectilinear obstacles revisited. Technical report, Dept. of EE & CS, Northwestern Univ., 1992.

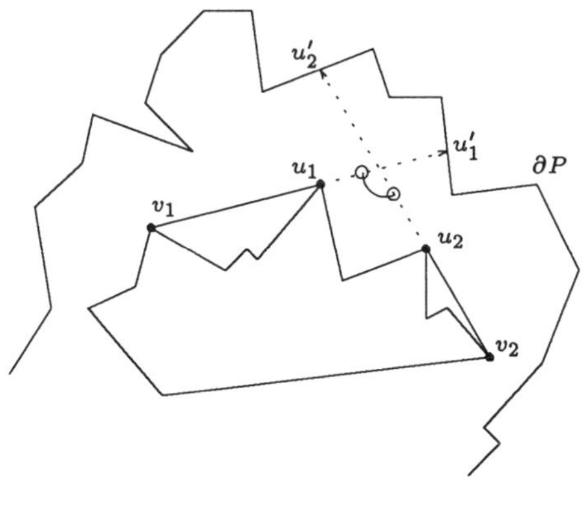

Figure 1: Definition of graph $\mathcal{G}$.

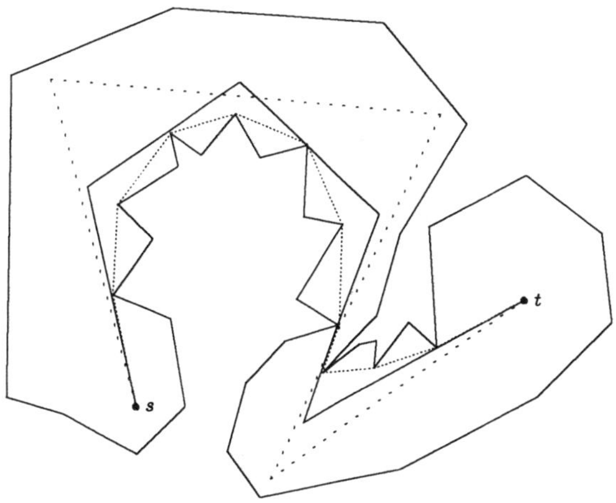

Figure 2: Example of minimum-link path, shortest path, and shortest 5-link path.

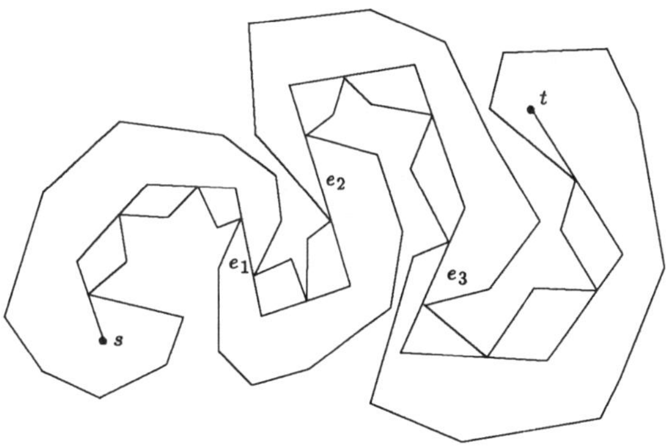

Figure 3: The inflection edges of $\pi_G(s,t)$.

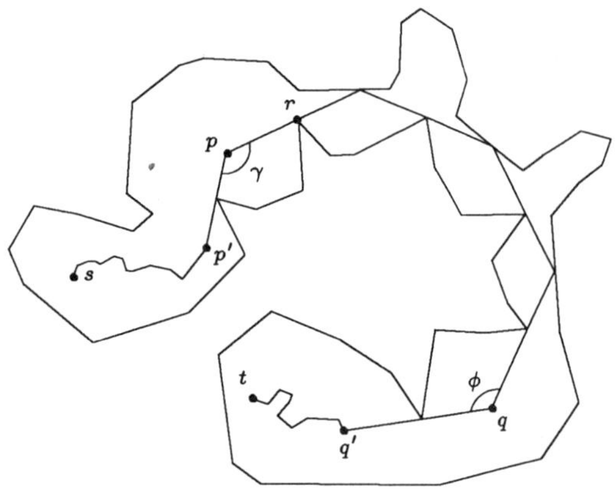

Figure 4: A balanced chain π'.

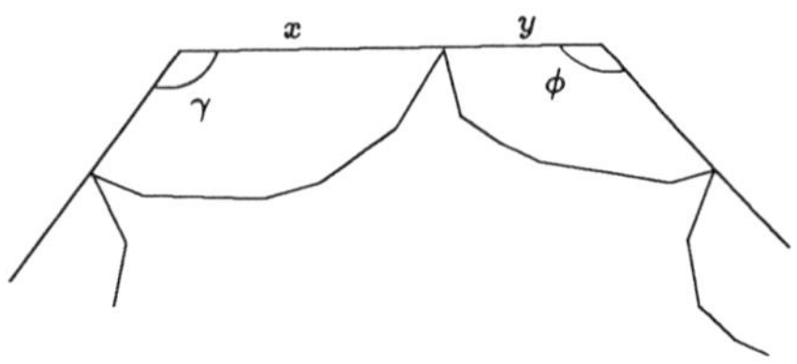

Figure 5: A balanced edge.

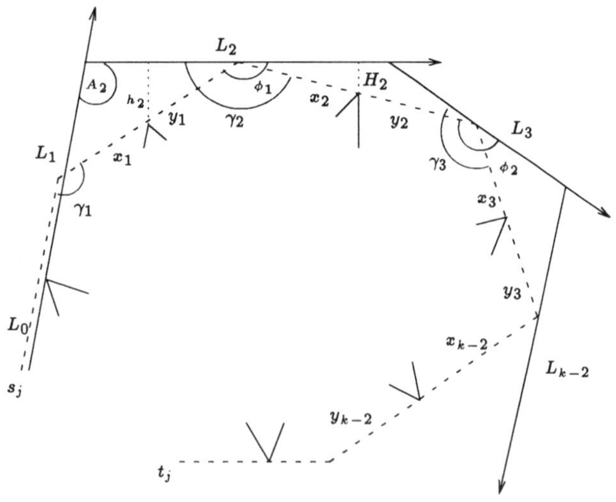

Figure 6: Balanced edges with bashes.

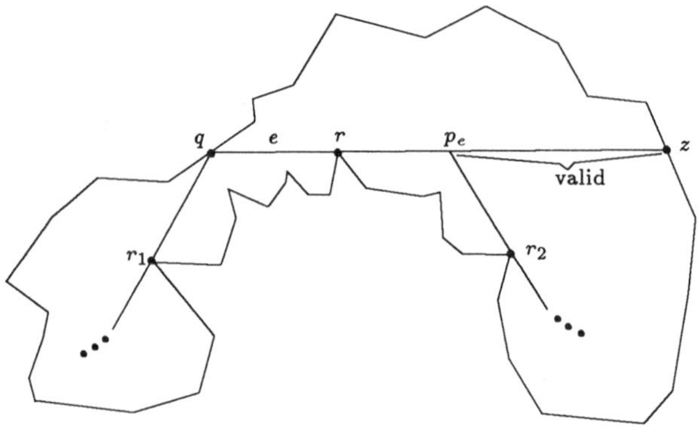

Figure 7: Valid first bend points along edge e.

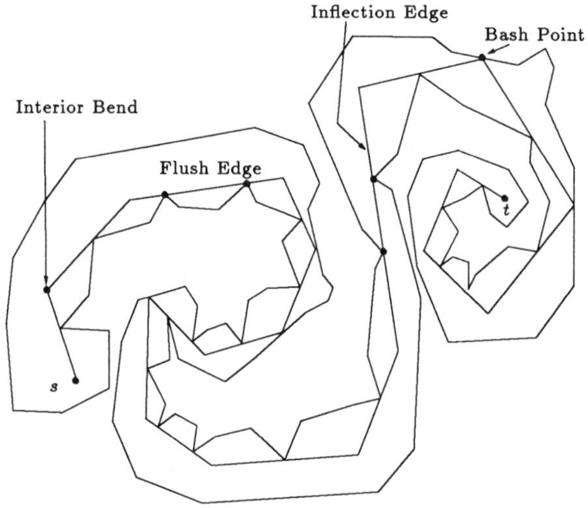

Figure 8: Structure of an optimal path.

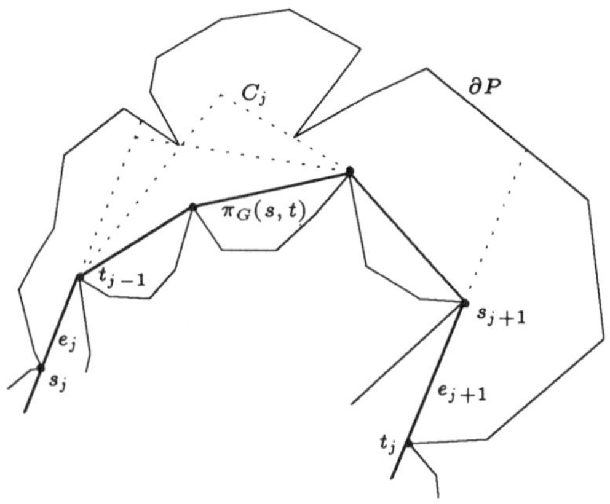

Figure 9: The raceway R_j between inflection edges e_j and e_{j+1}.

Efficient Minimum Cost Matching Using Quadrangle Inequality

Alok Aggarwal * Amotz Bar-Noy* Samir Khuller † Dina Kravets ‡
Baruch Schieber*

Abstract

We present efficient algorithms for finding a minimum cost perfect matching, and for solving the transportation problem in bipartite graphs, $G = (Red \cup Blue, Red \times Blue)$, where $|Red| = n$, $|Blue| = m$, $n \leq m$, and the cost function obeys the quadrangle inequality. Our first results assume that all the red points and all the blue points lie on a curve that is homeomorphic to either a line or a circle and the cost function is given by the Euclidean distance along the curve. We present a linear time algorithm for the matching problem that is simpler than the one in [KL75]. We generalize our method to solve the corresponding transportation problem in $O((m+n)\log(m+n))$ time, improving on the previously known algorithm in [KL75].

Our next result is an $O(n \log m)$ algorithm for minimum cost matching when the cost array is a bitonic Monge array. An example of this is when the red points lie on one straight line and the blue points lie on another straight line (that is not necessarily parallel to the first one). Finally, we provide a weakly polynomial algorithm for the transportation problem in which the associated cost array is a bitonic Monge array. Our algorithm for this problem runs in $O(m \log(\sum_{i=1}^{m} a_i))$ time, where a_i is the supply available at the ith source, b_j is the demand at the jth sink, and $\sum_{i=1}^{m} a_i \geq \sum_{j=1}^{n} b_j$.

*IBM Research Division, T. J. Watson Research Center, Yorktown Heights, NY 10598.
Email: {aggarwa,amotz,sbar}@watson.ibm.com.
†Dept. of Computer Science, University of Maryland, College Park, MD 20742.
Email: samir@cs.umd.edu. Supported in part by NSF grants CCR-8906949, CCR-9111348 and NSF-9103135. Part of this research was done while this author was visiting the IBM T. J. Watson Research Center.
‡Dept. of Computer Science, New Jersey Institute of Technology, University Heights, Newark, NJ 07102.
Email: dina@cis.njit.edu. Supported while at MIT, in part by the Air Force under Contract AFOSR-89-0271, the Defense Advanced Research Projects Agency under Contracts N00014-87-K-825 and N00014-89-J-1988.

1 Introduction

Given a complete bipartite graph $G = (Red \cup Blue, Red \times Blue)$, where $|Red| = n$, $|Blue| = m$ and $n \leq m$, a *perfect matching* on G is a subset of the edges $M \subseteq E$ such that for all red nodes p, exactly one edge of M is incident to p and for all blue nodes q, at most one edge of M is incident to q. Given a cost function defined on the edges of G, a *minimum cost perfect matching* on G is a perfect matching on G of minimum cost.

The best known algorithm for this problem for arbitrary bipartite graphs (with $m+n$ nodes and mn edges) takes $O(n(mn + m\log m))$ time. This time complexity can be achieved by using the Hungarian method [Kuh55, AMO89, GTT89]. Since this problem has a relatively high time complexity, researchers have investigated special cases. For example, Vaidya [Vai89] shows that the minimum cost perfect matching among $2n$ points in the Euclidean plane can be computed in $O(n^{5/2}\log^4 n)$ time. For the case where $n = m$, the red and blue points lie on a convex polygon (respectively, simple polygon), and the distance between two points is simply the Euclidean distance, Marcotte and Suri [MS91] show that a minimum cost matching can be computed in $O(n \log n)$ time (respectively, $O(n \log^2 n)$ time). Note that these papers assume that $n = m$, in spite of the fact that the situation $n < m$ arises in many matching problems. The only paper that considers the $n \leq m$ case is by Karp and Li [KL75]. They investigated the case where the points lie on either a line or a circle, and the cost function is given by the Euclidean distance along the corresponding curve. For this problem, they obtained a linear time algorithm for minimum weight matching, assuming that the points are given in sorted order. (See also [WPMK86].) In this paper, we continue the investigation along the lines of [KL75, WPMK86, Vai89, MS91]. As in [KL75], we do *not* assume that n equals m.

For the transportation problem we assume that each blue point i has supply a_i, and each red point j has demand b_j, where $\sum_{i=1}^{m} a_i \geq \sum_{j=1}^{n} b_j$. A *fea-*

sible transportation is an assignment of supplies from blue points to red points such that all the demands are satisfied. The cost of moving one unit of supply from a blue point to a red point is given by the cost function defined on the edges. A *minimum cost transportation* is a feasible one with minimum cost.

Hoffman [Hof63], following the French mathematician Gaspard Monge (1746–1818), considered a special case of the transportation problem in which the cost array forms an $n \times m$ *Monge* array. (The entry $a[i,j]$ of the cost array is the cost of the edge between red point i and blue point j.) An $n \times m$ array $A = \{a[i,j]\}$ is *Monge* if for all i_1, i_2, j_1, and j_2 satisfying $1 \leq i_1 < i_2 \leq n$ and $1 \leq j_1 < j_2 \leq m$,

$$a[i_1,j_1] + a[i_2,j_2] \leq a[i_1,j_2] + a[i_2,j_1] .$$

Hoffman [Hof63] shows that if the cost array associated with a transportation problem is Monge and the total supply is the *same* as the total demand, then a simple greedy algorithm solves the transportation problem in linear time. However, in reality, a more reasonable assumption is that the total supply is greater than or equal to the total demand. In this paper we consider special cases of the transportation problem in which the total supply may be greater than the total demand.

The remainder of this section lists the main results of this paper and their applications.

Our first results are for case where the red and blue points lie on a curve that is homeomorphic to either a line or a circle and the cost function is the Euclidean distance along the curve. For this case, we give a linear time algorithm for computing the minimum cost matching that is simpler than the one given by Karp and Li [KL75]. Our algorithm can be extended to the corresponding transportation problem, where each blue point has integral supply and each red point has integral demand. (We assume that the sum of the supplies exceeds the sum of the demands.) For this transportation problem we develop an algorithm with an $O((m+n)\log(m+n))$ running time. To achieve this bound, we exploit some underlying properties of the matching. This improves on the $O((m+n)^2)$ time algorithm of Karp and Li [KL75].

Our matching algorithm for the points on the circle can also be applied to the case where the red and the blue points form the vertices of a convex *unimodal* polygon [AM86]. A polygon is *unimodal* if for every vertex, the distances from it to all other vertices form a sequence that is first non-decreasing and then non-increasing when the polygon is traversed in clockwise order starting at that vertex. As an application, we note that the case when the points lie on the circle arises in pattern recognition when feature sets of different objects are compared. We refer the reader to [WPR84, WPMK86] for a detailed discussion of this application.

Our next result is for the case when the cost array forms an $n \times m$ bitonic *Monge* array. An array is bitonic if the entries in every row form a monotone non-increasing sequence that is followed by a monotone non-decreasing sequence. For the bitonic Monge array, we present an $O(n \log m)$ time algorithm for computing a minimum cost matching. Notice that the cost array for the sorted red and blue points on a line forms a bitonic Monge array[1]. As a matter of fact, this is true even for a more general case where the red points lie on one straight line and the blue points lie on another straight line (that is not necessarily parallel to the first one). Hence this result can be applied to the problem of connecting power lines (or connecting clock lines) in VLSI river routing [MC80, Won91]. In this problem, n terminals that lie on a straight line need to be connected to any n of the m power (or clock) terminals that lie on a parallel line, and the total amount of wire used should be minimized. (Another approach is to construct a Steiner tree, but then it is harder to accommodate current density limitations or the clock-skew, and therefore this approach is rarely used.)

Our results for bitonic Monge arrays can be applied to the transportation problem. We provide a weakly polynomial algorithm for the transportation problem when the associated cost array is a bitonic Monge array. Our algorithm for this problem runs in $O(m \log(\sum_{i=1}^{m} a_i))$ time where a_i is the supply available at the ith source, b_j is the demand at the jth sink, and $\sum_{i=1}^{m} a_i \geq \sum_{j=1}^{n} b_j$.

Finally, we remark that the following problem appeared in an exam for an algorithms course taught by C. E. Leiserson [Lei91]: given m pairs of skis with heights $s_1, \ldots, s_m$ and $n \leq m$ skiers with heights $t_1, \ldots, t_n$, assign skis to skiers so that the sum of the absolute differences of the heights of each skier and his/her skis is minimized. Observe that there is a fairly simply $O(nm)$ dynamic programming algorithm for this problem (which we believe was the intent of the problem in the exam). The algorithm by Karp and Li [KL75] as well as our algorithm solve this problem in $O(m \log m)$ time.

All our results use the quadrangle inequality in a crucial manner. Because of the many applications,

[1] Observe that the cost array for the points on a circle is *not* bitonic Monge.

we hope that this paper will generate more interest towards the understanding of minimum cost bipartite matching and transportation for useful special cases. For example, the three important problems that we were not able to solve are: (i) An efficient computation of the minimum cost matching when the cost array is (staircase) Monge; a special case of this is when the red and blue points form a convex polygon. (ii) An efficient computation of the minimum cost matching when the red and blue points form a simple polygon. (iii) The transportation problem when the underlying cost array is Monge and the total supply is greater than the total demand.

2 Minimum matching on a circle

In this section we present our algorithm for the minimum cost perfect matching problem for the case where the red points and the blue points lie on a circle and the cost function is the Euclidean distance along the arcs of the circle. For the sake of simplicity, we assume that all the points are distinct. The algorithm and all the proofs are analogous for points on the line. Furthermore, these results hold for points on any curve homeomorphic to a circle or a line, as long as the cost function is the distance along the curve. The results also hold for the case where all the points are vertices of a convex unimodal polygon and the cost is the Euclidean distance between points.

Consider a circle with red and blue points. Any two points p and q split the circle into two arcs (see Figure 1), one going clockwise from p to q, and one going counterclockwise from p to q. Let $cw(p,q)$ (*respectively*, $ccw(p,q)$) be the clockwise (respectively, counterclockwise) arc from p to q. Let $x(p,q)$ refer to the shorter of $cw(p,q)$ and $ccw(p,q)$. The distance between p and q, $d(p,q)$, is defined to be the length of $x(p,q)$.

We say that two edges in the matching M, $(p,q) \in M$ and $(p',q') \in M$, *cross* each other if $x(p,q) \cap x(p',q') \neq \emptyset$, $x(p,q) \not\subseteq x(p',q')$, and $x(p',q') \not\subseteq x(p,q)$. We call a matching *nested* if no two edges in the matching cross each other. In other words, a matching is nested if for any two edges in the matching: $(p,q) \in M$ and $(p',q') \in M$, $x(p,q) \cap x(p',q') \neq \emptyset$ implies that either $x(p,q) \subseteq x(p',q')$ or $x(p',q') \subseteq x(p,q)$.

Lemma 1 *There exists a nested minimum cost perfect matching for points on a circle.*

Proof: Let M be any minimum cost perfect matching. We show how to uncross any pair of crossed edges of M to get another minimum cost perfect matching with fewer edge crossings. Let $(p,q) \in M$ and $(p',q') \in M$ be some crossed pair of edges, where $p, p' \in Red$ and $q, q' \in Blue$. Consider a matching $M' = M - \{(p,q),(p',q')\} + \{(p,q'),(p',q)\}$, which is simply the matching M with (p,q) and (p',q') uncrossed. First, we show that the cost of M' is less than or equal to the cost of M.

Case 1: $q' \in x(p,q)$ and $q \in x(p',q')$ (see Figure 2 (a)). We obtain a contradiction by showing that M' costs less than M. This is because $d(p,q')+d(p',q) = [d(p,q)-d(q',q)]+[d(p',q')-d(q',q)] < d(p,q)+d(p',q')$.

Case 2: $p' \in x(p,q)$ and $q \in x(p',q')$ (see Figure 2 (b)). Here we show that the cost of M' is at most the cost of M.

$$\begin{aligned} d(p,q)+d(p',q') &= [d(p,p')+d(p',q)]+[d(p',q)+d(q,q')] \\ &= [d(p,p')+d(p',q)+d(q,q')]+[d(p',q)] \\ &\geq d(p,q')+d(p',q). \end{aligned}$$

We now argue that whenever M' costs the same as M in Case 2, then M' has fewer edge crossings than M. In particular, we show that if some edge $(s,t) \in M$ crosses either (p',q) or (p,q'), it must have crossed either (p,q) or (p',q'). This completes the proof, since we have uncrossed (p,q) and (p',q') and, hence, the number of edge crossings in M' must be at least one fewer that in M. The following case analysis proves the above claim.

Case 2.1: (s,t) crosses only (p',q), i.e. $s,t \in cw(p,q')$. W.l.o.g, assume $s \in cw(p',q)$ and $t \in ccw(p',q)$. If $t \in cw(p,p')$, then (s,t) crosses (p',q'). Otherwise, $t \in cw(q,q')$ and (s,t) crosses (p,q).

Case 2.2: (s,t) crosses only (p,q'), i.e. $s,t \notin cw(p',q)$. W.l.o.g, assume $s \in cw(p,q')$, and $t \in ccw(p,q')$. If $s \in cw(p,p')$, then (s,t) crosses (p,q). Otherwise, $s \in cw(q,q')$ and (s,t) crosses (p',q').

Case 2.3: (s,t) crosses both (p',q) and (p,q'). W.l.o.g, assume $s \in cw(p',q) \cap cw(p,q') = cw(p',q)$ and $t \in ccw(p,q') \cap ccw(p',q) = ccw(p,q')$. In this case (s,t) crosses both (p,q) and (p',q').

■

For $p \in Red$, define the *left partner* (respectively, *right partner*) of p, denoted by ℓ_p (respectively, r_p), to be the first blue point q counterclockwise (respectively, clockwise) from p, such that going counterclockwise (respectively, clockwise) from p to q on the circle, there are *as many* red points *as* blue points.

Lemma 2 *In a nested minimum cost perfect matching, every red point is matched to either its left partner or its right partner.*

Proof: (By contradiction.) W.l.o.g, suppose that $(p, q) \in M$, $x(p, q) = cw(p, q)$, and $q \neq r_p$.

Case 1: $r_p \notin x(p, q)$ (see Figure 3 (a)). From the definition of the right partner, there must be a red point $p' \in x(p, q)$ such that $(p', q') \in M$ and $q' \notin x(p, q)$. Then (p, q) crosses (p', q'), a contradiction.

Case 2: $r_p \in x(p, q)$ (see Figure 3 (b)). Since there is an equal number of red and blue points in $x(p, r_p)$, one blue point q' in $x(p, r_p)$ or r_p itself, is either not matched or matched with some p' not in $x(p, r_p)$. If q' is not in M, then $M - \{(p, q)\} + \{(p, q')\}$ costs less than M, a contradiction. If $(p', q') \in M$, then $p' \in x(r_p, q)$ since M is nested. Therefore, $M - \{(p, q), (p', q')\} + \{(p, q'), (p', q)\}$ gives a cheaper matching than M, a contradiction.

■

Define the chain $C = \langle v_0, u_1, v_1, u_2, v_2, \ldots, u_k, v_k \rangle$ to be an *alternating* chain of points if the following conditions hold:

1. $\{u_1, u_2, \ldots, u_k\} \subseteq Red$ and $\{v_0, v_1, v_2, \ldots, v_k\} \subseteq Blue$;
2. the blue point v_0 is the left partner of u_1 and the blue point v_k is the right partner of u_k;
3. the blue point v_i is the left partner of u_{i+1} and the right partner of u_i, for each $1 \leq i \leq k-1$; and
4. the chain C is maximal.

Note that since C is maximal, either v_0 is not a right partner and v_k is not a left partner of any red point, or v_0 is the same as v_k.

Observe that in the case of points on a line, a chain may not necessarily start at a blue point.

Lemma 3 *Each red point belongs to a unique alternating chain, and any two chains are disjoint.*

Proof: To see why the lemma is true, observe the following property. Consider a blue point v_i. We claim that only *one* red point can have v_i as its left partner. Suppose that two red points r_a and r_b have v_i as their left partner. Assume that we have v_i, r_a, r_b in clockwise order. Between r_a and v_i there is an equal number of red and blue points. If v_i is the left partner of r_b, then due to the presence of r_a (a red point) there must be an excess blue point between r_a and r_b. In this case, this blue point must be the left partner of r_b, yielding a contradiction. The same property is true for right partners. With this observation it is easy to see why the lemma is true. ■

The following theorem is implied by Lemma 2 and Lemma 3 and is the key for our algorithm.

Theorem 4 *Consider the points of a single chain in a nested minimum cost matching. There is one unmatched blue point in the chain. All the red points to the left of this blue point are matched to their left partners, and the red points to the right of this blue point are matched to their right partners.*

Note that the theorem holds when the chain is a cycle, i.e., $v_0 = v_k$. In this case, the unmatched blue point in the chain is either v_0 or v_k.

The algorithm

Step 1: Sort all the blue and red points (together) in some direction around the circle, say clockwise.

Step 2: Compute ℓ_p and r_p for each red point p. We show how to compute the r_p's using a stack (finding the ℓ_p's is analogous). Starting with any red point, we proceed clockwise around the circle. Any time we encounter a red point, we push it onto the stack. Any time we encounter a blue point q, we pop the last red point p from the stack and set $q = r_p$. If at any point the stack becomes empty, we push the clockwise-next red point onto it, ignoring any blue points that this action causes us to skip.

Step 3: Compute all the alternating chains. This can be done by keeping links between the red points and their partners. Starting with any red point that is not already contained in a chain, we simply trace the left and right links until we encounter the blue endpoints of the chain.

Step 4: For each alternating chain $C = \langle v_0, u_1, v_1, u_2, v_2, \ldots, u_k, v_k \rangle$, decide which blue point is free as follows. We compute M_i^C, which is the cost of the matching with the blue point v_i being unmatched. We first compute M_1^C (this is easy), and then compute M_{i+1}^C from M_i^C. This involves changing the matched edge (u_{i+1}, v_{i+1}) to (u_{i+1}, v_i). It takes $O(k)$ time to compute M_1^C (where k is the length of the chain), and $O(k)$ time to compute all the other M_i^Cs. If i^* is the index that gives the smallest value for M_i^C, the points u_i on C with $i \leq i^*$ match to their left partners, and the others match to their right partners.

The correctness of this algorithm essentially follows from Theorem 4. As for time complexity, it is not hard to verify that each step, except for sorting the points, can be done in linear time. We obtain the following theorem.

Theorem 5 (Complexity) *The algorithm runs in linear time if the points are given sorted in some direction along the circle.*

Our algorithm can be parallelized. The parallel time complexity is $O(\log m)$ time with m processors on an EREW PRAM.

3 Transportation problem on a line

We now consider the transportation problem, where the sources and sinks are on a straight line, with integer supplies and demands. The algorithm for this problem runs in $O((m+n)\log(m+n))$ steps where the number of sources (*blue* nodes) is m, and the number of sinks (*red* nodes) is n. We assume that a_i is the integer supply at the ith source node (blue node), and b_j is the integer demand at the jth sink node (red node), and that $\sum_{i=1}^{m} a_i \geq \sum_{j=1}^{n} b_j$. Due to lack of space we only outline the high-level ideas behind this algorithm. We describe the algorithm for the line, since it is simpler, and we note that the algorithm for the circle is very similar.

As in the case for the red/blue points on the line, we proceed to define *left partners* and *right partners* for the red points. We view each red node j as a cluster of b_j red points, and each blue node i as a cluster of a_i blue points. (Keep in mind the distinction between *nodes* and *points.*) Left partners and right partners of the red points are now defined exactly as before. We can assume that in each cluster the points are placed infinitesimally close to each other. Since there is a large number of red/blue points, we do not compute the partners explicitly; but these are maintained implicitly for clusters of points, and can be implicitly computed by keeping track of the supplies and demands of the nodes as they are pushed and popped from the stack. This takes time linear in the number of nodes. Each blue point p has at most one left partner and one right partner (as before). In other words, at most one red point from the left and one red point from the right may choose p as its partner.

Each blue node is now "split" into sub-nodes. Blue points p and q are in the same sub-node, if ℓ_p and ℓ_q are red points corresponding to the same red node, *and* r_p and r_q are red points corresponding to the same red node. This gives us the property that each blue sub-node can have at most one left partner and at most one right partner. The number of blue sub-nodes could exceed m (the number of blue nodes), but is $O(m+n)$. From now on we will refer to *both* nodes and sub-nodes simply as nodes. As before, we have the property that in any minimum cost solution to the transportation problem each red point is supplied by either its left partner or its right partner.

We briefly review the main steps of the algorithm. The input to this algorithm is the set of nodes, along with the location and demand/supply of each node. We also assume that the left and right partners of each blue node have been computed.

A chain C, as before, is an *alternating chain* of points. The leftmost point of a chain is called the root of the chain. We define a "bundle of chains" to be a maximal collection of chains that visit the same nodes (and also start and end at points in the same nodes). The *width* of each bundle of chains is the number of chains in that bundle. The leftmost node of the bundle of chains is called the root of the bundle.

Bundles of chains that start with a red node and end with a blue node can be handled by a scan of the nodes. Consider a red node i, with demand b_i. Suppose ℓ_i of the points in node i have left partners, and r_i of the points have right partners. Clearly, $r_i + \ell_i \geq b_i$ (since there are more supply points than demand points). The rightmost $(b_i - \ell_i)$ points in i's cluster have no left partners and must match to their right. These are chains starting at a red node, and we match these red points to the right. This will match off some of the blue points, thus leaving other red points without left partners — starting new chains. In a scan of the red points from left to right we can handle all chains that have a red left endpoint. Similarly, in a scan of the red points from right to left we can handle all the chains with a red right endpoint.

The difficult case is in handling bundles of chains that start and end with blue nodes (and processing them all simultaneously). In this situation the bundle of chains starts and ends with a blue node, and the chains could match in any direction.

We now process the blue nodes from left to right. During the execution of the algorithm, corresponding to each blue node we have a set of bundles going through the blue node. The set will be stored in a data-structure that will enable the required operations to be done efficiently. Each element in the set is a bundle that goes through that blue node with the following information:

1. The "shifting" cost of the bundle of chains — the total length of the edges from red nodes to their left partners minus the total length of the edges

from red nodes to their right partners.

2. The root node of the bundle of chains.

3. The width of the bundle (number of chains).

Bundles of chains with negative shifting costs clearly want to match to their left. Clearly, if for a chain with the least shifting cost in the set we decide to match it to the right, then we will decide the same for the rest of the chains in the set.

The algorithm scans blue nodes from left to right. In this scan, if at any time a red point decides to match to its left, it can be matched off, since it does not affect any future matches. We now describe the computation that is done when we scan over a blue node p.

Step 1: If the set of bundles of p is not empty, then remove the elements with the smallest shifting costs from the set as long as these shifting costs are negative. These bundles of chains prefer to match to their left, and can be matched off. This releases the corresponding blue points in p's cluster that are on the chains just matched to the left. These blue points are going to be roots of new chains since they have no left partners.

Step 2: If the set of bundles of p is not empty, the remaining elements in the set all have a positive shifting cost, and *so far* prefer to match to their right. The blue successor of a blue *point* q is defined to be the right (blue) partner of the right (red) partner of q. If blue successors exist, we continue to extend these chains by examining the blue successors of the blue points in the current set. We put an element in the set of each node that contains blue successors of the blue points that are in the current set. This involves locating the sets to insert elements into, and inserting them efficiently into the sets by spending time proportional to the number of nodes that contain blue successors (and not in the number of chains in the current set). Notice that for this step we also need to update the shifting costs of the chains that are inserted in the set of any particular blue node; but all these are changed by the same amount. Moreover, all the elements that are being inserted have smaller shifting costs than the elements already in the set. For the points that have no blue successors, we have reached the end of the chains, and we match the red points in these chains to the right.

Step 3: Create new elements corresponding to the points in p that have no left partners. (Some of these may be the points that were made free in Step 1.) We examine the blue successors of these blue points, and put an element in the set of each node that contains blue successors of these blue points. The shifting cost of these bundles of chains is easy to compute. Clearly, these bundles have a smaller shifting cost than bundles that were added to the blue successors in Step 2, and thus are the smallest elements in the set.

The data structure used to implement the sets is a 2-3 tree. All the required operations accessing the data structure can be implemented in $O(\log(m+n))$ time, giving us a total running time of $O((n+m)\log(n+m))$.

Theorem 6 *The transportation problem with integer supplies and demands for points on a line can be solved in $O((n+m)\log(n+m))$ time.*

4 Minimum cost matching in bitonic Monge arrays

In this section we describe an $O(n \log m)$ time algorithm for finding a minimum cost perfect matching in bitonic Monge arrays.

4.1 Preliminaries and notations

A matching in an $n \times m$ array $A = \{a[i,j]\}$ is a sequence of n entries, $a[1,j_1],\ldots,a[n,j_n]$, where $j_{i_1} \neq j_{i_2}$ for all $1 \leq i_1 < i_2 \leq n$. A minimum cost matching is a matching where $\sum_{i=1}^{n} a[i,j_i]$ is minimized. The following lemma defines the structure of one of the minimum cost matchings in a Monge array.

Lemma 7 *There exists a minimum cost matching in a Monge array A, such that the entries form a generalized diagonal; that is, for all $i_1 < i_2$, if $a[i_1,j_1]$ and $a[i_2,j_2]$ are two entries in the matching, then $j_1 < j_2$.*

Proof: Consider a minimum cost matching M for A, and suppose that M includes two entries $a[i_1,j_2]$ and $a[i_2,j_1]$ such that $i_1 < i_2$ and $j_1 < j_2$. By the Monge property, $a[i_1,j_1] + a[i_2,j_2] \leq a[i_1,j_2] + a[i_2,j_1]$. Thus, the matching M' obtained by replacing the entries $a[i_1,j_2]$ and $a[i_2,j_1]$ of M by $a[i_1,j_1]$ and $a[i_2,j_2]$ costs at most the same as M. If M' costs less than M, we have a contradiction. Otherwise, M' is a different minimum matching. We can continue in this manner until the resulting matching forms a generalized diagonal. ■

Given Lemma 7, it is easy to see that the case $n = m$ is solved by just taking the main diagonal as the solution. However, the problem is not so simple when $n < m$. The best known algorithm when $n < m$ is a dynamic programming algorithm that runs in time $O(mn)$.

Let A be an $n \times m$ bitonic Monge array. For $1 \leq j \leq m - n + 1$, define $\mathcal{D}_j$ to be the jth (full) diagonal in A; that is, $\mathcal{D}_j$ consists of the entries $a[1, j], a[2, j+1], \ldots, a[n, j+n-1]$. Define $\mathcal{D}_j(i)$ to be the ith element in this diagonal, i.e., $\mathcal{D}_j(i) = a[i, j + i - 1]$. Define $\mathcal{D}_j(t, b)$ to be elements of $\mathcal{D}_j$ between rows t and b, i.e., $\mathcal{D}_j(t, b)$ consists of entries $a[t, j+t-1], a[t+1, j+t], \ldots, a[b, j + b - 1]$.

4.2 The algorithm

Let A be a bitonic Monge array. From Lemma 7, it follows that there exists a minimum cost matching in A that only contains elements from the set $\{\mathcal{D}_1, \mathcal{D}_2, \ldots, \mathcal{D}_{m-n+1}\}$. Consequently, instead of considering the entire array, we may consider only the set of elements that belong to these diagonals.

Our algorithm uses the "divide and conquer" paradigm. The input to each step of the recursion is an array B of size $(b-t+1) \times (r-\ell+1)$ that contains elements in the set $\{\mathcal{D}_\ell(t, b), \ldots, \mathcal{D}_r(t, b)\}$. Define k to be the index of the middle diagonal of B, $k = \lfloor \frac{r+\ell}{2} \rfloor$. The output is a *separating* row s, $t \leq s \leq b$, that together with the middle diagonal of B, splits B into four quadrants such that there exists a minimum cost matching for B that is inside the top left quadrant and the bottom right quadrant (quadrants II and IV in Figure 4). In other words, there exists a minimum cost matching for B in which rows $t, \ldots, s$ are matched with entries in $B' = \{\mathcal{D}_\ell(t, s), \ldots, \mathcal{D}_k(t, s)\}$, and rows $s + 1, \ldots, b$ are matched with entries in $B'' = \{\mathcal{D}_{k+1}(s + 1, b), \ldots, \mathcal{D}_r(s + 1, b)\}$. Since quadrants II and IV do not share any columns of B it follows that the minimum cost matching for B can be found by two recursive calls: one to an array B' of size $(s - t + 1) \times (k - \ell + 1)$ and one to an array B'' of size $(b - s) \times (r - k)$.

The algorithm for finding the separating row in B has $(b - t + 1)$ stages. In stage $x \geq 1$, we process row $(t - 1 + x)$ to determine the separating row, s_x, for the subarray given by rows $t, \ldots, t - 1 + x$. Initially, $s_0 = t - 1$ and finally $s = s_{b-t+1}$. In stage $x \geq 1$, the separating row s_x is set either to $t - 1 + x$ or to s_{x-1}, according to the following criterion. Let $V(i_1, i_2) = \sum_{i=i_1}^{i_2} \mathcal{D}_k(i)$, and let $W(i_1, i_2) = \sum_{i=i_1}^{i_2} \mathcal{D}_{k+1}(i)$.

$$s_x \leftarrow \begin{cases} t - 1 + x & \text{if } V(s_{x-1} + 1, t - 1 + x) \\ & \quad < W(s_{x-1} + 1, t - 1 + x) \\ s_{x-1} & \text{otherwise} \end{cases}$$

The justification for the definition of s_x is provided in Lemma 10.

We claim that each stage takes constant time. To see this, notice that if $s_{x-1} = t - 2 + x$, then

$$\begin{aligned} V(s_{x-1} + 1, t - 1 + x) &= \mathcal{D}_k(t - 1 + x) \\ W(s_{x-1} + 1, t - 1 + x) &= \mathcal{D}_{k+1}(t - 1 + x) \end{aligned}$$

Otherwise,

$$V(s_{x-1} + 1, t - 1 + x) = V(s_{x-1} + 1, t - 2 + x) + \mathcal{D}_k(t - 1 + x)$$

$$W(s_{x-1} + 1, t - 1 + x) = W(s_{x-1} + 1, t - 2 + x) + \mathcal{D}_{k+1}(t - 1 + x).$$

Hence, it takes constant time to compute each $V(i_1, i_2)$ and $W(i_1, i_2)$, and the separating row can be found in $O(b - t)$ time.

Starting with an array B consisting of diagonals $\mathcal{D}_1, \ldots, \mathcal{D}_{m-n+1}$, we get the following recurrence relation for the running time of our algorithm. Let $T(a, b)$ denote the running time of the algorithm on a matrix with a rows and b diagonals.

$$T(n, m - n + 1) = T\left(s, \left\lfloor \tfrac{m-n}{2} \right\rfloor + 1\right) + T\left(n - s, \left\lceil \tfrac{m-n}{2} \right\rceil\right) + O(n).$$

It is not hard to see that $T(n, 1) = O(n)$ since in this case the minimum cost matching is simply the given diagonal. The solution of the recurrence implies the following theorem.

Theorem 8 (Complexity) *The time complexity of the algorithm is $O(n \log m)$.*

The algorithm can be parallelized. The parallel time complexity is $O(\log^2 m)$ time with $n/\log m$ processors on an EREW PRAM.

4.3 Correctness

The correctness proof is based on the following lemma. For $1 \leq \ell < r \leq m - n + 1$, consider the sub-array B that consists of the elements in $\{\mathcal{D}_\ell(t, b), \ldots, \mathcal{D}_r(t, b)\}$. Let $U_j = \sum_{i=t}^{b} \mathcal{D}_j(i)$.

Lemma 9 *Suppose that the minimum element in row t is to the right or on $\mathcal{D}_r$ (i.e., the column index of the minimum element in row t is at least r) and that the minimum element in row b is to the left or on $\mathcal{D}_\ell$ (i.e., the column index of the minimum element in row b is at most $\ell + b - 1$). Then, the sequence $U_\ell, \ldots, U_r$ is bitonic.*

Proof: Consider three consecutive diagonals and denote their elements by $x_1, \ldots, x_c$, $y_1, \ldots, y_c$, and $z_1, \ldots, z_c$, respectively, where $c = b - t + 1$. Let $X = \sum_{i=1}^{c} x_i$, $Y = \sum_{i=1}^{c} y_i$, and $Z = \sum_{i=1}^{c} z_i$. We claim that $Y - X \leq Z - Y$. Consequently, the sequence of the differences between the diagonals is a monotonic non-decreasing sequences and, therefore, the sequence of diagonals is bitonic.

It remains to prove the above claim. For all i, $1 \leq i \leq c-1$, the Monge property gives: $y_i + y_{i+1} \leq z_i + x_{i+1}$, or, $y_{i+1} - x_{i+1} \leq z_i - y_i$. We can write $Y - X$ and $Z - Y$ as follows:

$$Y-X = (y_1-x_1)+(y_2-x_2)+(y_3-x_3)+\cdots+(y_c-x_c)$$

$$Z-Y = (z_1-y_1)+(z_2-y_2)+\cdots+(z_{c-1}-y_{c-1})+(z_c-y_c)$$

Therefore, $(Y-X)-(Z-Y) \leq (y_1-x_1)-(z_c-y_c)$. Because of the bitonicity of the rows and since the minimum in row t is to the right or on $\mathcal{D}_r$, $y_1 - x_1$ is negative. Similarly, $z_c - y_c$ is positive. Hence, $(Y - X) - (Z - Y) \leq 0$. ■

Now, we prove the correctness of the recursive step. To simplify the notation, we consider the top level of the recursion. Let B_i be the sub-array containing the first i rows of B.

Lemma 10 *For all $1 \leq i \leq n$, row s_i of B_i is a separating row for the sub-array B_i.*

Proof: The proof is by induction on i. For the base case $i = 1$, and s_1 is either 1 or 0, depending on the values of $V(1,1)$ and $W(1,1)$. (By comparing the two values we know where the minima of row 1 is.) Now, assume that row s_i of B_i is a separating row for B_i, and we show that row s_{i+1} of B_{i+1} is a separating row for B_{i+1}.

Case 1: $s_i = i$; that is, there exists an optimal matching for B_i that lies in the first $k = \lfloor \frac{n+m}{2} \rfloor$ diagonals. Denote this matching by M_i.

Case 1.1: $V(s_i+1, i+1) = V(i+1, i+1) < W(s_i+1, i+1) = W(i+1, i+1)$, i.e., the element $\mathcal{D}_k(i+1)$ is less than the element $\mathcal{D}_{k+1}(i+1)$. In this case, the algorithm sets $s_{i+1} = i+1$. To obtain a contradiction suppose that there is no optimal matching for B_{i+1} in diagonals $\mathcal{D}_1, \ldots, \mathcal{D}_k$. Consider an optimal matching for B_{i+1}. By our assumption it must be that the match in row $i+1$ lies in diagonal $\mathcal{D}_z$ for some $z > k$. It can be shown that there exists such an optimal matching M' that contains the matching M_i. However, the matching M_i can be augmented by $\mathcal{D}_k(i+1) = a[i+1, i+k]$, since column $i+k$ does not intersect the first i rows of diagonals $\mathcal{D}_1, \ldots, \mathcal{D}_k$. Since row $i+1$ is bitonic and since $\mathcal{D}_k(i+1) < \mathcal{D}_{k+1}(i+1)$, $\mathcal{D}_k(i+1) < \mathcal{D}_z(i+1)$. Thus, the matching given by adding $\mathcal{D}_k(i+1)$ to M_i is smaller than M'. A contradiction.

Case 1.2: $V(i+1, i+1) \geq W(i+1, i+1)$, i.e., $\mathcal{D}_k(i+1) \geq \mathcal{D}_{k+1}(i+1)$. In this case the algorithm sets $s_{i+1} = i$. From the bitonicity of row $i+1$ it follows that the minimum entry in row $i+1$ lies in one of the diagonals $\mathcal{D}_{k+1}, \ldots, \mathcal{D}_{m-n+1}$. Hence, this minimum element can be added to M_i to form a matching for B_{i+1}, that costs less than any other matching containing M_i. Since it can be shown that there exists an optimal matching for B_{i+1} that contains M_i, $s_{i+1} = i$ is a separating row for B_{i+1}.

Case 2: $s_i < i$, that is, there exists an optimal matching for B_i the first s_i entries of which lie in diagonals $\mathcal{D}_1, \ldots, \mathcal{D}_k$, and the last $i - s_i$ entries of which lie in diagonals $\mathcal{D}_{k+1}, \ldots, \mathcal{D}_{m-n+1}$.

Case 2.1: $V(s_i+1, i+1) < W(s_i+1, i+1)$. In this case the algorithm sets $s_{i+1} = i+1$. Define M' to be the optimal matching for B_{i+1} for which the diagonal index of each row is minimal among all optimal matchings for B_{i+1}. We claim that such an optimal matching always exists and call it the "leftmost" matching. Consider the index of the match of row $i+1$ in M'. If this index is not greater than k, then $s_{i+1} = i+1$ is indeed a separating row.

Suppose this is not the case, and that the match of row $i+1$ lies in diagonal $\mathcal{D}_z$, for $z \geq k+1$. Let $q \leq i+1$ be the minimum index such that the match of row q in M' lies in diagonal $\mathcal{D}_z$. Notice that the minimum element in row q must be to the right or on $\mathcal{D}_z$. Otherwise, $\mathcal{D}_z(q)$ can be substituted by $\mathcal{D}_{z-1}(q)$ to obtain a valid matching that is no worse than M', a contradiction to our assumption that M' is the "leftmost" matching. Since $s_i < i$, we have $V(s_i+1, i) \geq W(s_i+1, i)$. By the assumption $V(s_i+1, i+1) < W(s_i+1, i+1)$. Consequently, the element $\mathcal{D}_k(i+1)$ must be less than the element $\mathcal{D}_{k+1}(i+1)$. This and the bitonicity of the rows imply that the minimum element in row $i+1$ must be to the left or on $\mathcal{D}_k$.

Consider the sub-array given by $\{\mathcal{D}_k(q, i+1), \ldots, \mathcal{D}_z(q, i+1)\}$. This sub-array conforms with the conditions of Lemma 9, implying that the sequence $\sum_{x=q}^{i+1} \mathcal{D}_k(x), \ldots, \sum_{x=q}^{i+1} \mathcal{D}_z(x)$ is bitonic. Since M' is the "leftmost" matching, q must be greater than s_i. Since q has not been chosen as a separating line, $V(s_i+1, q) \geq W(s_i+1, q)$. It follows that $V(q, i+1) < W(q, i+1)$. The bitonicity of the diagonals (Lemma 9) implies that $\sum_{x=q}^{i+1} \mathcal{D}_{z-1}(x) \leq \sum_{x=q}^{i+1} \mathcal{D}_z(x)$. However, in this case the matching given by substituting $\mathcal{D}_z(q), \ldots, \mathcal{D}_z(i+1)$ of M' by the corresponding elements that lie on $\mathcal{D}_{z-1}$ form a valid matching that is no worse than M', a contradiction to our assumption that M' is the "leftmost" matching.

Case 2.2: $V(s_i+1, i+1) \geq W(s_i+1, i+1)$. In this case the algorithm sets $s_{i+1} = s_i$. Let M' be an optimal matching for B_{s_i} that lies in the first k diagonals. Let M'' be the optimal "rightmost" matching for B_{i+1} that contains M'; that is, M'' is the matching that contains M', and in each row $s_i < x \leq i+1$ the diagonal index is maximal among all optimal matchings for B_{i+1}. Consider the index of the match of row s_i+1 in M''. If this index is at least $k+1$, then s_{i+1} is a separating row, and we are done.

Suppose that this is not the case, and that the match of row s_i+1 lies to the left of diagonal $\mathcal{D}_{k+1}$. Let z be the diagonal index of the match of row s_i+1. Let $s_i+1 \leq q \leq i$ be the maximum index such that the match of row q in M'' lies in diagonal $\mathcal{D}_z$. Notice that the minimum element in row q must be to the left or on $\mathcal{D}_z$. Otherwise, $\mathcal{D}_z(q)$ can be substituted by $\mathcal{D}_{z+1}(q)$ to obtain a valid matching that is no worse than M'', a contradiction to our assumption that M'' is the "rightmost" matching. On the other hand, because $V(s_i+1, s_i+1) \geq W(s_i+1, s_i+1)$, and because the rows are bitonic, it follows that the minimum element in row s_i+1 must be to the right or on $\mathcal{D}_{k+1}$.

Consider the sub-array given by $\{\mathcal{D}_z(s_i+1, q), \ldots, \mathcal{D}_{k+1}(s_i+1, q)\}$. This sub-array conforms with the conditions of Lemma 9, implying that the sequence $\sum_{x=s_i+1}^{q} \mathcal{D}_z(x), \ldots, \sum_{x=s_i+1}^{q} \mathcal{D}_{k+1}(x)$ is bitonic. Notice that $V(s_i+1, q) \geq W(s_i+1, q)$. From Lemma 9 we conclude that $\sum_{x=s_i+1}^{q} \mathcal{D}_z(x) \geq \sum_{x=s_i+1}^{q} \mathcal{D}_{z+1}(x)$. However, in this case the matching given by substituting $\mathcal{D}_z(s_i+1), \ldots, \mathcal{D}_z(q)$ of M'' by the corresponding elements that lie on $\mathcal{D}_{z+1}$ form a valid matching that is no worse from M'', a contradiction to our assumption that M'' is the "rightmost" matching.

■

The validity proof of the base recursion is trivial. The correctness of the algorithm follows from substituting $i = n$.

Theorem 11 *The algorithm described in Section 4.2 finds a minimum cost matching in a bitonic Monge array.*

4.4 The transportation problem

Suppose that we are given a transportation problem with integral supplies and demands, and a cost array A that is bitonic Monge. A simple way to transform this problem into a matching problem is by "blowing" the cost array into a $(\sum_{i=1}^{n} b_i) \times (\sum_{j=1}^{m} a_j)$ array, where the (i,j)th entry of the original array is replicated $b_i \times a_j$ times. Applying our algorithm for this array gives an $O((\sum_{i=1}^{n} b_i) \log(\sum_{j=1}^{m} a_j))$ time algorithm. However, the algorithm can be modified such that the amount of work per diagonal is $O(m+n)$, resulting in an $O(m \log(\sum_{j=1}^{m} a_j))$ time algorithm.

We outline the main modifications that are needed to the algorithm. The base case, when we have a single diagonal is quite easy: the matching is a single diagonal. The amount of time it takes to encode this matching is simply the number of *distinct* demand rows and supply columns in this diagonal. The main computational step in the divide and conquer scheme is the algorithm to compute the *separating* row. Suppose that we are computing the separating row for a matrix B (this is the "blown" up matrix) of size $(b-t+1) \times (r-\ell+1)$. If all the rows in B are identical (they correspond to the same demand row in the original cost matrix A), then the min cost matching is a single diagonal, and hence the separating row will either be $t-1$ or b (all the rows will match either to a diagonal $i \leq k$, or a diagonal $i > k$, where $k = \lfloor \frac{r+\ell}{2} \rfloor$). Recall that the diagonals form a bitonic sequence. Thus in time proportional to the number of distinct columns in B, we can figure out which side of k the cheapest diagonal is. When the rows in B are not identical, we only need to compute the value of s_x for a row that is different from its previous row. Hence the algorithm can be made to run in time proportional to the number of distinct rows and columns in B.

Acknowledgments: We would like to thank James Park for telling us about the skiers problem, and for informing us of the paper by Karp and Li [KL75]. The authors also thank Bill Pulleyblank for several useful discussions and for providing useful references.

References

[AM86] A. Aggarwal and R.C. Melville. Fast computation of the modality of polygons. *Journal of Algorithms*, 7: 369–381, 1986.

[AMO89] R.K. Ahuja, T.L. Magnanti, and J. B. Orlin. Network flows. In *Optimization, Handbooks in Operations Research and Management Science*, pages 211–370. North-Holland Publishing, 1989.

[GTT89] A.V. Goldberg, É. Tardos, and R.E. Tarjan. Network flow algorithms. Technical Report TR 860, School of Operations Research and Industrial Engineering, Cornell University, September 1989.

[Hof63] A.J. Hoffman. On simple linear programming problems. In V. Klee, editor, *Convexity: Proceedings of the Seventh Symposium in Pure Mathematics of the AMS*, volume 7, pages 317–327. American Mathematical Society, Providence, RI, 1963.

[KL75] R.M. Karp and S.Y.R. Li. Two Special Cases of the Assignment Problem. *Discrete Mathematics*, 13: 129–142, 1975.

[Kuh55] H.W. Kuhn. The hungarian method for the assignment problem. *Naval Research Logistics Quarterly*, 2(1): 83–97, 1955.

[Lei91] C.E. Leiserson, 1991. Second quiz in the Introduction to Algorithms course, problem Q-3.

[MC80] C. Mead and L. Conway. *Introduction to VLSI systems*. Addison-Wesley, Reading, MA, 1980.

[MS91] O. Marcotte and S. Suri. Fast matching algorithms for points on a polygon. *SIAM Journal on Computing* 20: 405–422, 1991.

[Vai89] P.M. Vaidya. Geometry helps in matching. *SIAM Journal on Computing* 18: 1201–1225, 1989.

[Won91] C.K. Wong, 1991. Personal Communication.

[WPMK86] M. Werman, S. Peleg, R. Melter, and T.Y. Kong. Bipartite graph matching for points on a line or a circle. *Journal of Algorithms*, 7: 277–284, 1986.

[WPR84] M. Werman, S. Peleg, and A. Rosenfeld. A distance metric for multidimensional histograms. Technical Report CAR-TR-90, Center for Automation Research, Univ. of Maryland, August 1984.

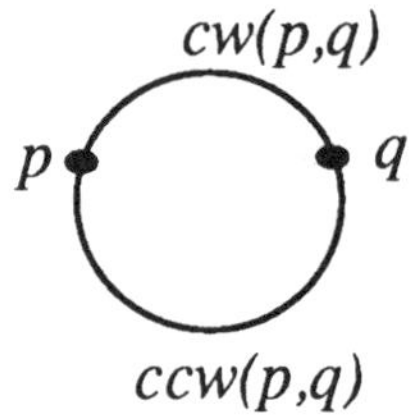

Figure 1: In this figure, $x(p,q) = cw(p,q)$.

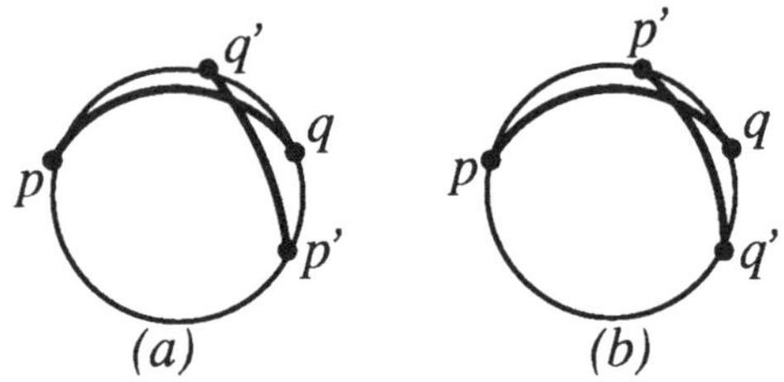

Figure 2: Thicker arcs between points represent the edges of the matching.

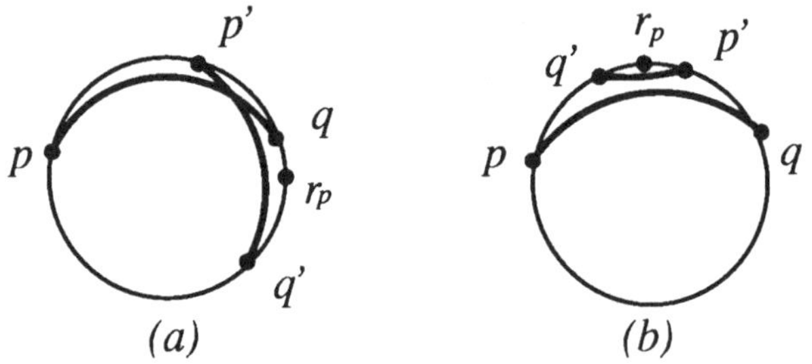

Figure 3: Thicker arcs between points represent the edges of the matching.

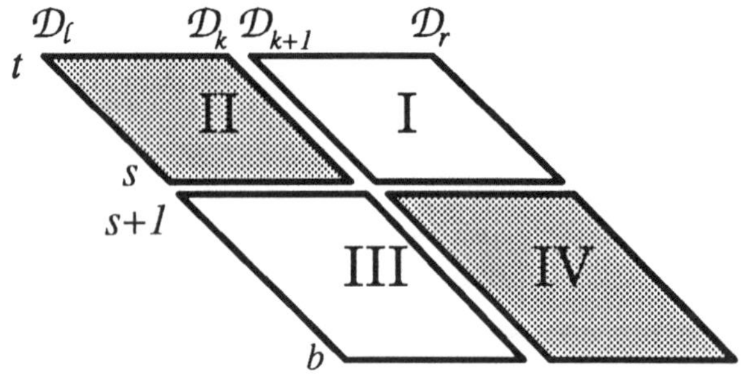

Figure 4: Quadrant *II* includes row s and diagonal k; quadrant IV includes row $s+1$ and diagonal $k+1$.

Optimal Parallel Hull Construction for Simple Polygons in $\mathcal{O}(\log\log n)$ Time

Hubert Wagener
Fachbereich Informatik
Technische Universität Berlin
W-1000 Berlin 10, Germany

Abstract

We propose an optimal parallel algorithm for computing the convex hull of a simple polygon. The algorithm achieves a runtime of $\mathcal{O}(\log\log n)$ using $\mathcal{O}(\frac{n}{\log\log n})$ processors of a CRCW-PRAM. The data structure representing the convex hull is not the standard one, i.e. an array storing the vertices of the hull in clockwise order. Indeed, a lower bound of $\Omega(\frac{\log n}{\log\log n})$ on the runtime for any algorithm employing a polynomial number of processors and computing the array-representation is known. Nevertheless, the representation we use is adequate for further parallel processing; standard queries like computing the intersection of the hull with a given line, etc., can be answered in time $\mathcal{O}(\frac{\log n}{\log p+1}+1)$ using p processors. In addition subchain hull queries are supported optimally in time $\mathcal{O}(\frac{\log k}{\log p+1}+1)$, where k is the length of the subchain.

The algorithm can easily be adapted to other hull-like structures for simple polygons; as e.g. the orthogonal hull, and the visibility region from a point under various definitions of visibility.

1 Introduction

Given a set S of points in $\mathbb{R}^2$, their convex hull is the smallest convex set enclosing S. An algorithm computing the convex hull has to produce a list of all corners of this hull in clockwise order around its perimeter.

The convex hull problem is one of the most fundamental problems in computational geometry. In the following we will consider the problem in 2-dimensional space only. It is well known that computing the convex hull for a set of n points requires serial time $\Omega(n\log n)$, and there are several algorithms achieving this time bound. If the input is not an arbitrary set of points, but a simple polygonal chain, the convex hull problem can be solved in linear time [9, 10, 11]. With respect to parallel computing it is known that the convex hull can be determined in $\mathcal{O}(\log n)$ time with an assymptotically optimal number of operations; i.e with n processors if the input is a point set [1, 3, 12], and with $\frac{n}{\log n}$ processors if a simple polygonal chain is given [12]. The model of parallel computation used for these results is the CREW-PRAM [1]. All these algorithms produce as output an array containing the required list of corners. We will refer to this as the array-representation of the convex hull. These algorithms are time-optimal in a quite strong sense with respect to the CREW-PRAM model, since the convex hull problem, even for a point set sorted by x-coordinates, is at least as hard as computing the "OR" function. Cook, Dwork, and Reischuk [6] showed that computing the "OR" of n bits on an ideal CREW-PRAM requires time $\Omega(\log n)$ regardless of the number of processors used. Thus, the complexity of the convex hull problem with respect to Exclusive Write-PRAMs is very well settled.

This contrasts with the situation for CRCW-PRAMs. It is quite trivial to give an algorithm that uses n^2 CRCW-processors and produces a linked list representation of the convex hull for an arbitrary set of n points in $\mathcal{O}(1)$ time. Such an algorithms has two severe drawbacks:

a) a list representation is inadequate for further parallel processing,

b) the algorithm is far from being work-optimal.

In this paper we give a work-optimal convex hull algorithm with a runtime of $\mathcal{O}(\log\log n)$ for simple polygonal chains. It should be mentioned that finding the maximium is at least as hard as computing the convex hull. A lower bound on the time of $\Omega(\log\log n)$

[1] The same bounds can be achieved using an EREW-PRAM (cf. [2])

0-8186-2900-2/92 $3.00 © 1992 IEEE

is known for any work–optimal, comparison–based algorithm finding the maximum. But this is only a loose argument for the time optimality of our convex hull algorithm, since shortcuts by real number arithmetic are not acknowlegded within the framework of comparison–based algorithms. The bridge tree representation produced by our convex hull algorithm is well suited for further parallel processing. Standard queries to convex hulls like point inclusion tests, supporting line queries, extreme point queries, and line intersection queries are supported as effectively as by the array–representation. All these standard operations can be performed in time $\mathcal{O}(\frac{\log n}{\log p+1}+1)$ using p processors of a CRCW–PRAM. If we would insist on an array–representation for the convex hull, then time $\Omega(\frac{\log n}{\log\log n})$ is required to solve the convex hull problem, provided the number of processors is polynomially bounded. This follows from the fact that the parity problem can be solved via the problem of computing an array–representation of the convex hull (even for point sets sorted by x–coordinates). So the lower bound for the parity problem given by Beame and Hastad [4] carries over. This shows that it is crucial for an $\mathcal{O}(\log\log n)$ time solution not to use the array–representation of the convex hull. Besides, the bridge tree supports additional interesting queries, the subchain queries. Such a query consists of a usual standard query and the specification of a consecutive subchain. The query has to be answered with respect to the convex hull of the specified subchain[2]. The query-time for subchains is bounded by $\mathcal{O}(\frac{\log k}{\log p+1}+1)$, where k is the length of the subchain. Previous solutions to the subhull query problems either have larger query times [7], or the space requirement and preprocessing time is superlinear [8].

The bridge tree data structure as well as the algorithm presented for the convex hull problem can easily be adapted to work for other hull-like structures of simple polygonal chains. This yields algorithms for computing the orthogonal hull, and the region visible from a point under various definitions of visibility with the same complexity bounds as for the convex hull.

In the following we will concentrate on the convex hull problem. In section 2 we describe bridge trees and their usage in answering the standard queries. The algorithm for computing the convex hull is given in section 3.

[2]I am indebted to Jack Snoeyink for pointing out to me, that a variant of bridge trees is used in [7] to answer subchain queries.

2 The Bridge Tree

In this section we discuss how convex hulls of simple polygonal chains are represented by bridge trees. To simplify exposition we aim not to work with convex hulls, but with *upper chains.* This is the part of the boundary of the convex hull traced by a clockwise walk from the leftmost to the rightmost vertex. It is convenient to define that the upper chain is terminated by infinite vertical rays descending from the leftmost and rightmost vertex. The lower chain is defined similarly. Note that the upper and lower chains are horizontally monotone Jordan curves. The region below (above) the upper (lower) chain containing the simple polygon chain is referred to as upper (lower) hull.

Let $\mathcal{C}=(v_1,\cdots,v_n)$ be a simple polygonal chain. With each subchain $\mathcal{C}_i=(v_b,\cdots,v_e)$ we associate the standard partition of $\mathcal{C}$ into $\mathcal{C}_i$, $\mathcal{B}_i=(v_1,\cdots,v_{b-1})$ the chain before $\mathcal{C}_i$, and $\mathcal{A}_i=(v_{e+1},\cdots,v_n)$ the chain after $\mathcal{C}_i$. Any edge of the upper chain of $\mathcal{C}$, denoted by $UC(\mathcal{C})$, that connects some vertex of $\mathcal{C}_i$ with a vertex of either $\mathcal{A}_i$ or $\mathcal{B}_i$ is called *proper bridge* of $\mathcal{C}_i$ (w.r.t. $UC(\mathcal{C})$). Any edge of $UC(\mathcal{C})$ connecting $\mathcal{A}_i$ with $\mathcal{B}_i$ is called *passing bridge* of $\mathcal{C}_i$. It immediatly follows that any consecutive subchain of $UC(\mathcal{C})$ not containing any bridge of $\mathcal{C}_i$ coincides with (a part of) the upper chain of either $\mathcal{A}_i$ or $\mathcal{B}_i$ or $\mathcal{C}_i$.

This property allows us to convert any binary search in the upper chain that is based on its x–monotonicity into a search based on the polygonal chain order of $\mathcal{C}$ in the following sense:

- Sort the endvertices of all $\mathcal{C}_i$–bridges with respect to x–coordinates.
- Determine the x–range between two consecutive endvertices in which the search has to proceed using binary search based on the x–monotonicity. Within this x–range the upper chain coincides with some bridge or with the upper chain of either $\mathcal{A}_i$ or $\mathcal{B}_i$ or $\mathcal{C}_i$.
- Continue the search with the appropriate subhull (or finish the search with the bridge).

Note that possibly there exist no $\mathcal{C}_i$–bridges, but in this case $UC(\mathcal{C})$ conincides with either $UC(\mathcal{A}_i)$ or $UC(\mathcal{B}_i)$. To find out where to proceed with the search, it suffices to check for an arbitrary vertex of $UC(\mathcal{C})$ whether it belongs to $\mathcal{A}_i$ or $\mathcal{B}_i$.

This observation leads to the following recursive definition of the bridge tree.

Definition 1 *Let $\mathcal{C} = (v_1, \cdots, v_n)$ be a simple polygonal chain. A bridge tree for $UC(\mathcal{C})$ is build up as follows:*

If $n \leq const$, use the array-representation for $UC(\mathcal{C})$.

Otherwise, partition $\mathcal{C}$ into m subchains $\mathcal{C}_1, \cdots, \mathcal{C}_m$, of roughly equal size. For our purposes it is convenient to choose $m = |\mathcal{C}|^{1/6} = n^{1/6}$.

Create a root node containing an array of m records $R_1, \cdots, R_m$, where record R_i stores a list of all $\mathcal{C}_i$-bridges and a pointer to the bridge tree for $UC(\mathcal{C}_i)$, which is build up recursively.

In addition information about the leftmost and rightmost vertex of $UC(\mathcal{C})$ is stored in the root node.

The space requirement of the bridge tree, as well as the query time that can be achieved, depend heavily on the number of bridges a subchain $\mathcal{C}_i$ may have. Fortunately, the number of bridges of $\mathcal{C}_i$ is bounded by four. This is a direct consequence of the fact that the sequence of points common to $\mathcal{C}$ and $UC(\mathcal{C})$ ordered along $UC(\mathcal{C})$ is bimodal with respect to the ordering along $\mathcal{C}$ (cf. [12, 5]). Thus the space requirement $S(n)$ of a bridge tree representing the hull of an n-vertex chain satisfies $S(n) \leq m \cdot S(n/m) + \mathcal{O}(m)$, and therefore is linear.

Let us now consider the standard queries performed on upper hulls. Recall that each of these queries can be solved by a binary search based on the x-monotonicity of the upper chain. Given some discrimination point on $UC(\mathcal{C})$ it can be decided in constant serial time whether to search to the left or to the right of this point. (In some cases the local neighborhood of the discrimination point is needed. Here we can use some point in the interior of a brigde; nevertheless the search criteria tell us on which side of the bridge to proceed). Converting this search to work on the chain order, let us determine for a given subchain $\mathcal{C}_i$ whether to proceed with $\mathcal{A}_i$ or $\mathcal{B}_i$ or $\mathcal{C}_i$ with one processor in $\mathcal{O}(1)$ time. The time bound is due to the fact that only a constant number of $\mathcal{C}_i$-bridges exist.

In order to answer a query on $UC(\mathcal{C})$, determine the subchain $UC(\mathcal{C}_i)$ to proceed with, and answer the query on this subchain recursively. To determine the subchain using $p \leq n^{1/6}$ processors, we perform a $(p+1)$-ary search on the array of records $R_1, \cdots, R_{n^{1/6}}$. This way we find the required subchain in time $\mathcal{O}(\frac{\log n}{\log p+1} + 1)$. Consequently, the query time can be bounded by the quantity $T(n)$ satisfying:

$$T(n) \leq T(n^{5/6}) + \mathcal{O}(\frac{\log n}{\log p + 1} + 1)$$

This implies a runtime of $\mathcal{O}(\frac{\log n}{\log p+1} + \log\log n)$. For large p this is not quite what we claimed. To improve this, we first observe that all standard queries can be answered without any preprocessing on $\mathcal{C}$ in constant time if enough, say n^4, processors are available. E.g. to test a point q for inclusion in the upper hull of $\mathcal{C}$, check in parallel for each pair of vertices (v_i, v_j) in $\mathcal{C}$ whether q lies below the line segment between v_i and v_j. Obviously, q is in $UC(\mathcal{C})$ iff one of these tests is positive. With n^2 processors this test requires constant time. We obtain the desired query time of $\mathcal{O}(\frac{\log n}{\log p+1} + 1)$ if we perform only $s = \frac{\log(\log n/\log p)+2}{\log(6/5)}$ recursive steps during the search. These s search-steps require $\mathcal{O}(\frac{\log n}{\log p+1} + s) = \mathcal{O}(\frac{\log n}{\log p+1} + 1)$ time, and reduce the search space to a subchain of size $n^{((5/6)^s)} = p^{(1/4)}$. Then the search can be finished by a constant time brute force method using p processors. Summarizing the above discussion we obtain:

Lemma 1 *Let $\mathcal{C} = (v_1, \cdots, v_n)$ be a simple polygonal chain. Given the upper hull of $\mathcal{C}$ as a bridge tree, the following queries can be answered in time $\mathcal{O}(\frac{\log n}{\log p+1} + 1)$ with p processors in the CRCW-PRAM model:*

- *Given a point q, test whether q lies in the upper hull.*
- *Given a point q, report the supporting (tangent) lines of the upper hull passing through q.*
- *Given a line ℓ, report the intersection of ℓ with the upper hull.*
- *Given a direction d, report the vertex (edge) extreme in direction d.*

In the rest of this section we will discuss an enhancement of the bridge tree that supports subchain queries optimally. For answering such queries we follow the paradigm of interval trees. That is, we partition the query chain into few canonical subportions, for which the upper hull is represented in the bridge tree. Then the upper hull is assembled from the subhulls of canonical subportions. In case of decomposable queries, the queries can be answered, too, by collecting the answers for the subportions and combining them. The problem with the above variant of the bridge tree is that for some query chains any partition requires too many ($\geq n^{\epsilon}$) canonical portions. The following refinement will allow us to partition each query chain into $\mathcal{O}(\log\log k)$ canonical portions, where k is the size of the query chain.

For a node w of the bridge tree, let $\mathcal{C}^w$ be the chain whose upper hull is represented by w, and let $\mathcal{C}_1^w, \cdots, \mathcal{C}_m^w$ be the chains corresponding to w's children. Instead of using w to represent $UC(\mathcal{C}^w)$ only, we will represent in w the upper hulls for all chains $\mathcal{C}^w[i,j]$, $1 \le i < j \le m$, where $\mathcal{C}^w[i,j] = \mathcal{C}_i^w \leftrightarrow \mathcal{C}_{i+1}^w \leftrightarrow \cdots \leftrightarrow \mathcal{C}_j^w$ [3]:

For each of these $\mathcal{O}(m^2)$ chains $\mathcal{C}^w[i,j]$, we introduce an array of records $R_k{}^{i,j}$, $i \le k \le j$, containing the bridges of $\mathcal{C}_k^w$ with respect to $UC(\mathcal{C}^w[i,j])$. Also, the rightmost and leftmost vertex of each $\mathcal{C}^w[i,j]$ is stored in w.

Note that the space requirement for this enhanced bridge tree remains linear, if $m \le n^{(1/3)-\epsilon}$, $\epsilon > 0$, is chosen, since $S(n) \le m \cdot S(n/m) + m^3$ provides an upper bound for the space. Recall that we use $m = n^{1/6}$.

Consider now a query chain $Q = (v_s, \cdots, v_t)$. Let $k (= t - s + 1)$ denote the size of Q. Let $l(v_s)$ and $l(v_t)$ be the leaves in the bridge tree associated with vertices v_s and v_t, respectively. Let u be the least common ancestor of $l(v_s)$ and $l(v_t)$. The partition of Q contains one canonical subchain for each node w lying on the paths from u to $l(v_s)$ and to $l(v_t)$, respectively. The canonical subchain for node w is determined as follows:

- If the ith child of w and w itself lie on the path from u to $l(v_s)$, then $\mathcal{C}_{i+1}^w \leftrightarrow \cdots \leftrightarrow \mathcal{C}_m^w$ is chosen as canonical subchain.

- If the ith child of w and w itself lie on the path from u to $l(v_t)$, then $\mathcal{C}_1^w \leftrightarrow \cdots \leftrightarrow \mathcal{C}_{i-1}^w$ is chosen as canonical subchain.

- For u the chain $\mathcal{C}_{i+1}^u \leftrightarrow \cdots \leftrightarrow \mathcal{C}_{j-1}^u$ is chosen as canonical one, if the ith and jth child of u lie on the path to $l(v_s)$ and $l(v_t)$, respectively.

Note that the height of u is bounded by $\mathcal{O}(\log\log k)$, implying the same asymptotical bound on the number of canonical subportions of Q. Note also that the size of a canonical subchain chosen for node w is bounded by $\Omega(k^{(5/6)^{d-1}})$, where d is the distance between u and w. To answer a query for such a canonical subchain using p processors requires time $\mathcal{O}((\frac{\log k^{((5/6)^{d-1})}}{\log p+1}) + 1)$ by Lemma 1.

To answer a decomposable query for Q, we first answer the query for each canonical subportion of Q, and then combine these partial answers. Assume that different queries are answered one after the other, but performing each single query in parallel. By definition of decomposable problems, the partial answers can be serially combined in time linear in the number of partial answers.

[3]Here $\leftrightarrow$ denotes the concatenation of subchains by joining the last and first vertex of two subchains by a segment.

Then the total query time is bounded by

$$\mathcal{O}(\sum_{d=0}^{c\log\log k}((5/6)^d \cdot \frac{\log k}{\log p + 1} + 1)) + \mathcal{O}(\log\log k)$$

Thus time $\mathcal{O}(\frac{\log k}{\log p+1} + \log\log k)$ is required for such a query. This can be reduced to $\mathcal{O}(\frac{\log k}{\log p+1}) + 1)$ by a trick similar to the one used in the ordinary query procedure. First from Q cut off appropriate prefix- and suffix-chains of size $\le p^{1/4}$, such that the remaining chain is partitioned into $\mathcal{O}(\frac{\log k}{\log p+1} + 1)$ canonical portions. For the prefix and suffix a constant time brute force method is used to find a partial answer. The claimed query time is now verified easily.

It is well known that supporting line queries [4] and extreme point queries are decomposable. The line intersection query is not decomposable, nevertheless, it can be answered within the same time. Indeed, even a bridge tree for Q can be computed in time $\mathcal{O}(\frac{\log k}{\log p+1} + 1)$, by assembling the subhulls of canonical portions. The details for this will appear in the final version of this paper.

Lemma 2 *Let $\mathcal{C} = (v_1, \cdots, v_n)$ be a simple polygonal chain. Let Q be any subchain of $\mathcal{C}$ having size k. Then any standard query (as listed in Lemma 1) restricted to the upper hull of Q can be answered in optimal time $\mathcal{O}(\frac{\log k}{\log p+1} + 1)$ with p processors in the CRCW-PRAM model, if $UC(\mathcal{C})$ is given by an enhanced bridge tree.*

3 The Algorithm

In this section an $n^{1/6}$-way divide-and-conquer method for constructing $UC(\mathcal{C})$ in (enhanced) bridge tree representation is given:

1. Divide the input chain $\mathcal{C} = (v_1, \cdots, v_n)$ into $n^{1/6}$ subchains $\mathcal{C}_1, \cdots, \mathcal{C}_{n^{1/6}}$ of approximately equal size.

2. For each subchain $\mathcal{C}_i$ in parallel, compute $UC(\mathcal{C}_i)$, recursively.

3. For each subchain $\mathcal{C}_i$ in parallel, calculate its bridges with respect to $UC(\mathcal{C})$ (in case of the enhanced bridge tree representation, with respect to $UC(\mathcal{C}[i,j])$, for $1 \le i, j \le n^{1/6}$).

4. Compute the leftmost and rightmost vertex of $UC(\mathcal{C})$ (in case of the enhanced bridge tree representation, of $UC(\mathcal{C}[i,j])$, for $1 \le i, j \le n^{1/6}$).

[4]Here we mean : Given a query point q, report the two supporting lines if q is outside the upper hull; otherwise report its inclusion. This also solves point inclusion queries.

5. Create a root node with the required arrays. Insert the information gathered in steps 3 and 4, and for each record R_k (R_k^{ij},resp.) create a pointer to the bridge tree for $UC(\mathcal{C}_k)$.

It is trivial to implement steps 1, 4, and 5 in $\mathcal{O}(1)$ time using $n^{2/3}$ processors. In the rest of this section we will discuss how the bridges are calculated in constant time using $n^{1-(1/36)}$ processors.

As a result the runtime of the algorithm can be bounded by $T(n)$ satisfying the recurrence $T(n) \leq T(n^{(5/6)}) + \mathcal{O}(1)$, provided n processors are available. This yields $T(n) = \mathcal{O}(\log\log n)$.

The total work performed during this algorithm is bounded by the quantity $W(n)$ satisfying: $W(n) \leq n^{1/6} \cdot W(n^{5/6}) + \mathcal{O}(n^{1-(1/36)})$. Thus a total of $\mathcal{O}(n)$ operations are performed. Applying Brent's Lemma now yields an $\mathcal{O}(\log\log n)$ time algorithm using only $\frac{n}{\log\log n}$ processors. Note that the processor distribution and scheduling necessary to apply Brent's Lemma is trivial in this case.

Now we turn to the computation of $\mathcal{C}_i$–bridges with respect to $UC(\mathcal{C})$:

1. Compute the bridges between $\mathcal{C}_i$ and $\mathcal{A}_i$ with respect to $UC(\mathcal{C}_i \leftrightarrow \mathcal{A}_i)$, and those between $\mathcal{C}_i$ and $\mathcal{B}_i$ with respect to $UC(\mathcal{B}_i \leftrightarrow \mathcal{C}_i)$. All proper $\mathcal{C}_i$–bridges with respect to $UC(\mathcal{C})$ are among the computed ones.

2. Extract the proper $\mathcal{C}_i$–bridges of $UC(\mathcal{C})$.

3. Among the proper $\mathcal{C}_j$–bridges, for $i \neq j$, find the passing $\mathcal{C}_i$–bridges and report them.

This strategy is motivated by the following facts:

Fact 1 For any two disjoint simple polygonal chains $\mathcal{C}_1$ and $\mathcal{C}_2$, there are at most two bridges between $\mathcal{C}_1$ and $\mathcal{C}_2$ in $UC(\mathcal{C}_1 \leftrightarrow \mathcal{C}_2)$. Thus between $\mathcal{A}_i$ and $\mathcal{C}_i$ there are at most two bridges. (cf. [5, 12])

Fact 2 No serial sublinear method for finding these (at most) two bridges is known, if $\mathcal{C}_1 \leftrightarrow \mathcal{C}_2$ does not form a simple chain. This clarifies why we aim to calculate the bridges between $\mathcal{A}_i$ and $\mathcal{C}_i$ directly, although $UC(\mathcal{A}_i)$ is not given explicitly, and do not compute bridges between $\mathcal{C}_i$ and $\mathcal{C}_j$, for $j > i$, and then extract the relevant ones.

It should be noted that an anologous strategy is used in [2] for merging $n^{1/4}$ visibility chains of simple polygonal paths in parallel logarithmic time.

The only nontrivial step in the bridge determination is step 1. Extracting the relevant, proper bridges (step 2) requires constant serial time. The passing bridges can be found and reported (step 3) in constant time using $n^{2/3}$ processors. This takes into account the synchronisation necessary to choose which of possibly two passing bridges has to be reported first. In the following we concentrate on the determination of bridges between $\mathcal{A}_i$ and $\mathcal{C}_i$.

Let us first sketch how extreme point queries, supporting line queries, and point inclusion tests with respect to $UC(\mathcal{A}_i)$ can be answered in constant time using $n^{1/3}$ processors. Recall that $\mathcal{A}_i$ is obtained by concatenating all subchains $\mathcal{C}_j$ with $j > i$ in appropriate order.

extreme point query: For each $UC(\mathcal{C}_j)$, $j > i$, the bridge tree is known. Perform in parallel an extreme point query for each of these upper chains with $n^{1/6}$ processors per upper chain. By Lemma 1 this requires $\mathcal{O}(1)$ time, and yields $n^{1/6}$ candidate points. By a maximum–like computation the extreme point can be extracted. This requires only constant time, if the number of processors is quadratic in the number of candidates, i.e. if $n^{1/3}$ processors are available.

supporting line query / point inclusion test: For each $UC(\mathcal{C}_j)$, $j > i$, perform a point inclusion test with the query point q. If all tests are negative, p may be above $UC(\mathcal{A}_i)$ and supporting lines may exist. In this case perform supporting line queries for each $UC(\mathcal{C}_j)$. Among the lines reported find the ones with minimal and maximal slopes. By the difference of slopes we either find that q lies below $UC(\mathcal{A}_i)$, or the two lines found are the supporting ones. By an analysis as above, a constant time bound follows, if $n^{1/3}$ processors are available.

Such queries are required in the actual calculation of bridges between $\mathcal{A}_i$ and $\mathcal{C}_i$, which starts by determining the number of such bridges. Let $X(\mathcal{C})$ denote the x–range spanned by $\mathcal{C}$, i.e. the interval between its leftmost and rightmost vertex. $UC(\mathcal{C}_i \leftrightarrow \mathcal{A}_i)$ has exactly one bridge if the x–ranges of $\mathcal{C}_i$ and $\mathcal{A}_i$ do not nest. Otherwise, there are either no bridges or two bridges. Only in case two bridges exist the chain with the inner x–range contributes vertices to $UC(\mathcal{C}_i \leftrightarrow \mathcal{A}_i)$. We will determine such a witness vertex if it exists. The knowledge of such a witness is also crucial for searching a bridge in case that two bridges exist.

The search for a witness is based on the following lemma.

Lemma 3 *Let $\mathcal{C}_1$ and $\mathcal{C}_2$ be two simple polygonal chains whose concatenation $\mathcal{C}_1 \leftrightarrow \mathcal{C}_2$ is again simple. Assume that $X(\mathcal{C}_1)$ contains $X(\mathcal{C}_2)$. (A symmetric version holds, if $X(\mathcal{C}_2)$ contains $X(\mathcal{C}_1)$).*

Let T be any set of vertices common to $\mathcal{C}_1$ and $UC(\mathcal{C}_1 \leftrightarrow \mathcal{C}_2)$ including the leftmost and rightmost vertex of $\mathcal{C}_1 \leftrightarrow \mathcal{C}_2$. Denote by v_{max} the vertex of T being maximal with respect to chain order in $\mathcal{C}_1$.

If $\mathcal{C}_1$ makes a left turn at v_{max}, then all vertices common to $\mathcal{C}_2$ and $UC(\mathcal{C}_1 \leftrightarrow \mathcal{C}_2)$ (if any) lie between v_{max} and its closest left neighbor in T. Otherwise, if $\mathcal{C}_1$ makes a right turn at v_{max}, then all witness vertices lie between v_{max} and its closest right neighbor in T.

A proof of this lemma is given in [12]. Similar statements and their proofs can be found in [8, 2].

Using Lemma 2 we can search for a point witnessing the existence of two bridges. Two cases are distinguished.

$X(\mathcal{C}_i)$ contains $X(\mathcal{A}_i)$: Test for each bridge stored in the root node of the bridge tree of $UC(\mathcal{C}_i)$, whether it is an edge in $UC(\mathcal{C}_i \leftrightarrow \mathcal{A}_i)$. This requires for each bridge an extreme point query in $UC(\mathcal{A}_i)$ with respect to the normal direction of the bridge, and a test whether this extreme point lies below the line through this bridge. If any of these bridges is no edge of $UC(\mathcal{C}_i \leftrightarrow \mathcal{A}_i)$, the corresponding extreme point in $UC(\mathcal{A}_i)$ is a witness. Otherwise, all bridge endpoints lie on $UC(\mathcal{C}_i \leftrightarrow \mathcal{A}_i)$. Using Lemma 2 the x-range, and thus the subchain of $\mathcal{C}_i$, where to continue the search, can be determined by finding maxima. During recursive calls we have to remember the x-range found so far, and perform the tests only for those bridges in this range, since for the correctness of these criteria we require that the tested bridges are indeed edges of $UC(\mathcal{C}_i)$.

Note that this search criterium can be evaluted in $\mathcal{O}(1)$ time using $n^{1/3}$ processors per tested bridge. Since $|\mathcal{C}_i| = n^{5/6}$, there are $\mathcal{O}(n^{5/36})$ bridges in the root node of $\mathcal{C}_i$. Thus $\mathcal{O}(n^{(1/2)-(1/36)})$ processors suffice to achieve constant time.

$X(\mathcal{A}_i)$ contains $X(\mathcal{C}_i)$: Since $UC(\mathcal{A}_i)$ is not given explicitly, we perform the search again on $UC(\mathcal{C}_i)$, although the search criterium given by (the symmetric version) of Lemma 2 is for $UC(\mathcal{A}_i)$: As above, test each bridge of the root node for being edge of $UC(\mathcal{C}_i \leftrightarrow \mathcal{A}_i)$. If one bridge is an edge of $UC(\mathcal{C}_i \leftrightarrow \mathcal{A}_i)$, then any endpoint can serve as witness. Otherwise, consider the vertices on $UC(\mathcal{A}_i)$ being extreme for the normal vectors of tested bridges. Using Lemma 2 determine the x-range to proceed with, and its two bounding vertices. Now we go back to $UC(\mathcal{C}_i)$ by considering the bridges corresponding to the bounding vertices. The search has to proceed between the two neighbored bridges found this way. (This is easily seen by arguing with the slope of edges in this x-range). Being neighbored, these two bridges determine a unique subchain of $\mathcal{C}_i$ for further searching. As before $n^{(1/2)-(1/36)}$ processors suffice to find this subchain in constant time.

We now use these search criteria to reduce the search space to a subchain of size $\leq n^{5/36}$. Since each recursive step reduces the size from m to $m^{5/6}$, only a constant number of recursions are required. Subsequently, the search can be finished in constant time using $n^{(1/2)-(1/36)}$ processors: In case $X(\mathcal{C}_i)$ contains $X(\mathcal{A}_i)$, first by brute force determine all edges of the upper hull of the remaining subchain. (A cubic number of processors is available). All edges that fall in the remaining x-range now can be tested in parallel. The case where $X(\mathcal{A}_i)$ contains $X(\mathcal{C}_i)$, is similar.

This shows that a witness vertex can be found in constant time using $n^{(1/2)-(1/36)}$ processors.

Having now determined the number of bridges we have to calculate them (if any). It is well known that given two upper chains and an x-range containing a unique bridge, the bridge can be found by binary search. To find the leftmost bridge we search for its endpoint in $UC(\mathcal{C}_i)$. Note that all edges of $UC(\mathcal{C}_i)$ to the left of this endpoint are also edges of $UC(\mathcal{C}_i \leftrightarrow \mathcal{A}_i)$ and all edges to the right of the endpoint, but to the left of the witness (if any), are not edges of $UC(\mathcal{C}_i \leftrightarrow \mathcal{A}_i)$, provided $UC(\mathcal{C}_i)$ contains the leftmost vertex. Otherwise, the roles of right and left are changed. This allows us to organize the search in the same way as we did for the witness vertex using extreme point queries to $UC(\mathcal{A}_i)$. This leads to an $\mathcal{O}(1)$ time search using $n^{(1/2)-(1/36)}$ processors. Now a supporting line query with the endpoint of the bridge to $UC(\mathcal{A}_i)$ suffices to complete the task. A right bridge is found similarily, in case two bridges exist.

Summarizing, we obtain that the $\mathcal{C}_i$-bridges with respect to $UC(\mathcal{C})$ can be calculated in time $\mathcal{O}(1)$ using $n^{(1/2)-(1/36)}$ processors.

To merge the $n^{1/6}$ upper chains of $\mathcal{C}_1, \cdots, \mathcal{C}_{n^{1/6}}$ in enhanced bridge tree representation, we compute in parallel the $\mathcal{C}_k$-bridges with respect to any chain $\mathcal{C}[i,j]$, for all k. Thus we have to perform $n^{1/2}$ bridge calculations in parallel in order to obtain a constant time merge procedure, which is possible with $n^{1-(1/36)}$ processors.

Theorem 1 *Given a simple polygonal chain $\mathcal{C} = (v_1, \cdots, v_n)$, in time $\mathcal{O}(\log\log n)$ using $\frac{n}{\log\log n}$ CRCW processors a representation of its convex hull can be computed that supports standard queries as well as subchain queries in optimal time $\mathcal{O}(\frac{\log n}{\log p+1} + 1)$ when performed with p CRCW processors.*

Remark A list representation of the convex hull can be obtained from the bridge tree representation in time $\mathcal{O}(\log\log n)$ with $\frac{n}{\log\log n}$ processors.

4 Conclusions

We presented a parallel algorithm for computing the convex hull of a simple n–vertex polygonal chain. The algorithms runs in time $\mathcal{O}(\log\log n)$ using $n/\log\log n$ processors in the CRCW-PRAM model. To overcome the $\Omega(\log n/\log\log n)$ lower bound for computing an array representation of the convex hull, we worked with a bridge tree representation. This representation supports standard queries to the convex hull as efficiently as the array representation does, and in addition optimally supports queries to subchain hulls. The given version of a bridge tree improves known data structures for subhull queries, namely the compact hull tree proposed in [8] and a version of bridge tree sketched in [7]. The bridge tree as well as the parallel algorithm can be adapted to other monotone hulls of simple polygonal chains, e.g. to computing the visibility region of a simple polygon from a point (under usual visibility and rectangular visibility). This complements the optimal EREW–PRAM algorithm for this problem proposed in [2]. A consequence of this algorithm is that the diameter or an area–minimal enclosing triangle of a simple polygon can be found in $\mathcal{O}(\log\log n)$ time using $n/\log\log n$ CRCW–processors (The details for this will appear in the full paper). Another quite immediate consequence is that a (useful representation) of the visibility graph of a simple polygonal chain can be computed in $\mathcal{O}(\log\log n)$ time with $n^2/\log\log n$ processors.

An interesting open question is to determine the CRCW–complexity of the convex hull problem for point sets. Is it possible to compute in time $o(\log n/\log\log n)$ a convex hull representation, that e.g. supports serial queries in logarithmic time? Does any work-optimal algorithm computing such a representation require $\Omega(\log\log n)$ time?

References

[1] A. Aggarwal, B. Chazelle, L. Guibas, C. O'Dunlaing, C. Yap. Parallel computational geometry. *Algorithmica*, vol. 3, 1988, pp. 293–328.

[2] M.J. Atallah, D.Z. Chen, H. Wagener. An optimal parallel algorithm for the visibility of a simple polygon from a point. *J. ACM*, vol. 38, 1991, pp. 516–533.

[3] M.J. Atallah, M.T. Goodrich. Efficient parallel solutions to some geometric problems. *J. Parallel and Distributed Comput.*, vol. 3, 1986, pp. 492–507.

[4] P. Beame, J. Hastad. Optimal bounds for decision problems on the CRCW PRAM. *Proc. 19th Annual ACM Symp. on Theory of Computing*, 1987, pp. 83–93.

[5] B. Chazelle, L. Guibas. Fractional cascading: II. Applications. *Algorthmica*, vol. 1, 1986, pp. 163–191.

[6] S.A. Cook, C. Dwork, R. Reischuk. Upper and lower time bounds for parallel random access machines without simultaneous writes. *SIAM J. Computing*, vol. 15, 1986, pp. 87–97.

[7] H. Edelsbrunner, L. Guibas, J. Hershberger, R. Seidel, M. Sharir, J. Snoeyink, E. Welzl. Implicitly representing arrangements of lines and segments. *Discr. Comput. Geom.*, vol. 4, 1989, pp. 433–466.

[8] L. Guibas, J. Hershberger, J. Snoeyink. Compact interval trees: a data structure for convex hulls. *Int. J. Comput. Geometry & Appl.*, vol. 1, 1991, pp. 1–22.

[9] R.L. Graham, F.F. Yao. Finding the convex hull of a simple polygon. *J. Algorith.*, vol. 4, 1983, pp. 324–331.

[10] D.T. Lee. On finding the convex hull of a simple polygon. *Int. J. Comput. Inform. Sci.*, vol. 12, 1983, pp. 87–98.

[11] D. McCallum, D. Avis. A linear algorithm for finding the convex hull of a simple polygon. *Inform. Proc. Lett.*, vol. 9, 1979, pp. 201–206.

[12] H. Wagener. Parallel Computational Geometry: Exploiting polygonal order for optimally parallel algorithms. *Ph.D. Thesis, Techn. Univ. Berlin*, 1986.

Tighter Bounds on The Exact Complexity of String Matching

Richard Cole * Ramesh Hariharan *

(Extended Abstract)

Abstract

This paper considers how many character comparisons are needed to find all occurrences of a pattern of length m in a text of length n. The main contribution is to show an upper bound of the form $n + O(n/m)$ character comparisons, following preprocessing. Specifically, we show an upper bound of $n + \frac{8}{3(m+1)}(n-m)$ character comparisons. This bound is achieved by an online algorithm which performs $O(n)$ work in total, requires $O(m)$ space and $O(m^2)$ time for preprocessing. In addition the following lower bounds are shown: for online algorithms, a bound of $n + \frac{11}{5(m+1)}(n-m)$ character comparisons for $m = 10 + 11k$, for any integer $k \geq 1$, and for general algorithms, a bound of $n + \frac{2(n-m)}{m+3}$ character comparisons, for $m = 2k + 1$, for any integer $k \geq 1$.

1 Introduction

String matching is the problem of finding all occurrences of a pattern $p[1 \ldots m]$ in a text $t[1 \ldots n]$. We assume that the characters in the text are drawn from a general (possibly infinite) alphabet unknown to the algorithm. We investigate the time complexity of string matching measuring both the exact number of comparisons and the time complexity counting all operations. As is standard, the time complexity refers to operations performed following preprocessing of the pattern; prepossessing of the text is not allowed. Our goal is to minimize the number of comparisons, while still maintaining a total linear time complexity and a polynomial in m preprocessing cost.

Note that if the algorithm is permitted to know the alphabet, then the failure function of [KMP77] yields a finite automata which performs string matching in exactly n comparisons. However, in this case the running time will depend on the alphabet size.

Perhaps the most widely known linear time algorithms for string matching are the Knuth-Morris-Pratt [KMP77] and Boyer-Moore [BM77] algorithms. We refer to them as the KMP and BM algorithms, respectively. The KMP algorithm makes at most $2n - m + 1$ comparisons and this bound is tight. The exact complexity of the BM algorithm was an open question until recently. It was shown in [KMP77] that the BM algorithm makes at most $6n$ comparisons if the pattern does not occur in the text. Guibas and Odlysko [GO80] reduced this to $4n$ under the same assumption. Cole [Co91] finally proved an essentially tight bound of $3n - \Omega(n/m)$ comparisons for the BM algorithm, whether or not the pattern occurs in the text. Apostolico and Crochemore [AC89] gave a simple variant of the KMP algorithm which makes at most $\frac{3}{2}n$ comparisons. Apostolico and Giancarlo [AG86] gave a variant of the BM algorithm which makes at most $2n - m + 1$ comparisons. Crochemore et al. [CCG92] showed recently that remembering just the most recently matched portion reduces the upper bound of BM from $3n$ to $2n$ comparisons.

Recently, Galil and Giancarlo analyzed and modified a string matching algorithm designed by Collussi [GG92]; they showed it makes at most $\frac{4}{3}n$ comparisons. This was the strongest upper bound for string matching known prior to our work. In fact, [GG92] give this bound in a sharper form as a function of the period z of the pattern; the bound becomes $n + (n-m)\min\{\frac{1}{3}, \frac{\min\{z, m-z\}+2}{2m}\}$.

[GG91] gives a lower bound of $n(1 + \frac{1}{2m})$ comparisons. For online algorithms [GG91] showed an additional lower bound of $n + \frac{2(n-m)}{m+3}$). An online algorithm is an algorithm which examines text characters only in a window of size m sliding monotonically to the right; further the window can slide to the right only when all matching pattern instances to the left of the window or aligned with the window have been discovered. Recently, Zwick and Paterson gave additional lower bounds, including a bound of $\frac{4n}{3}$ for patterns of length 3 in the general case [ZP92].

Our main contribution is a linear time online algorithm for string matching which makes at most $n(1 + \frac{8}{3(m+1)})$ character comparisons. Our algorithm requires $O(m)$ space and $O(m^2)$ preprocessing time and runs in

*Courant Institute, New York University, New York, NY 10012; this work was supported in part by NSF grants CCR-8902221 and CCR-8906949.

$O(m+n)$ time overall (exclusive of preprocessing). Independently, Breslauer and Galil discovered a similar algorithm which performs at most $n + O(\frac{n \log m}{m})$ comparisons [BG92]; this algorithm requires $O(m)$ preprocessing space and time and runs in linear time [Ga92].

In addition, we give nearly matching lower bounds: for online algorithms, a bound of $n + \frac{11}{5(m+1)}(n-m)$ character comparisons for $m = 10+11k$, for any integer $k \geq 1$, and for general algorithms a bound of $n + \frac{2(n-m)}{m+3}$ character comparisons, for $m = 2k+1$, for any integer $k \geq 1$.

Even if exponential (in m) preprocessing and exponential space are available, it is not clear that the above upper bound can be achieved (assuming a result independent of the alphabet size is sought). The difficulty is that text characters which are mismatched may need to be compared repeatedly. In order to minimize the total number of comparisons this has to be offset by other text characters not needing to be compared. The hardest patterns to handle are those which have proper suffixes which are also prefixes of the pattern. We call such substrings *presufs*. Our algorithm has two parts; a basic algorithm and a presuf handler. The basic algorithm handles patterns with no presufs and is also the core of the algorithm for the general case. The presuf handler copes with presufs; its design constituted the main challenge in this work. Understanding of the structure of the presufs was a key ingredient in its design. An understanding of this structure also led to our new lower bound constructions.

The flavor of the algorithm is as follows. Initially, the pattern is aligned with the left end of the text. Repeatedly, an attempt to match the pattern against the text is made. When a mismatch is found or the pattern is fully matched the pattern is shifted to the right. The goal is to maximize this shift without missing any possible matches. The basic algorithm has the property that the length of each shift is at least equal to the number of comparisons since the previous shift (or the start of the algorithm). This results in an algorithm that performs at most n comparisons if the pattern has no presuf (the algorithms of [GG92] and [CP89] have this property too).

The presuf handler cannot quite match the performance of the basic algorithm (which is not surprising given that the lower bounds for this problem are larger than n comparisons). Here the approach is to follow the basic algorithm until a suffix which is also a prefix is matched. The only possible matches in which a new instance of the pattern overlaps the current partially (or fully) matched instance arise with an overlap by a presuf. Ignoring, for the moment, problems introduced by periodic patterns, it is the case that at most one of these overlapping pattern instances can result in a match. An elimination is performed to determine which one, if any, of the overlapping pattern instances might result in a match. Following this elimination, a further non-trivial sequence of comparisons is made; this can lead to one of two situations: another match of a suffix which is also a prefix, or a mismatch which causes a return to the basic algorithm. The presuf handler is invoked at most once for every $\frac{m}{2}$ text characters, and performs a number of comparisons at most 2 greater than the number of characters shifted over (actually, there are two possible scenarios: an invocation after $\frac{3}{4}m$ text characters and at most 2 excess comparisons, or an invocation after $\frac{m}{2}$ text characters and at most 1 excess comparison).

Ths structure of the algorithm of Breslauer and Galil is similar; their analog of the presuf handler works in a completely different way, however.

Section 2 provides several definitions. The basic algorithm is described in Section 3. The presuf handler for non-periodic strings is presented in Section 4. The lower bounds are given in Section 5. Most proofs are omitted from this extended abstract. Full versions of the results can be found in [CH92a,CH92b].

2 Definitions and Preliminaries

A string v is a *presuf* of p if it is both a suffix and prefix of p. Let x be the length of the largest presuf of p. The *period* of a pattern p with length m is defined to be $m-x$. A string p is *periodic* if $p = wv^k$, where w is a (possibly null) proper suffix of v and $k > 1$. (A proper suffix of v is strictly shorter than v.) The smallest such v is called the *core* of p and the corresponding w is called the *head* of p. A string p is *cyclic* in string v if it is of the form v^k, $k > 1$. A string is *primitive* if it is not cyclic. Note that a core is primitive. $|v$ and $v|$ refer respectively to the leftmost and rightmost characters in string v; on occasion, we will call these characters respectively, the left end and right end of v. Two characters are said to be *distance* d apart if they are separated by $d-1$ other characters.

Let p be a pattern with length m and period l. Let the text t have length n. $p[i]$ denotes the ith character of p, reading from the left end; i is called the *index* of $p[i]$ in p. The same notation and terminology is used for string t.

The algorithm will be comparing the pattern with substrings of the text with which the pattern is aligned; as the algorithm proceeds, the pattern is shifted to the right across the text. Each possible alignment of the pattern with the text is called an *instance* of the pattern.

For each pair of overlapping instances of the pattern a location at which the two differ, if any, will be precomputed. This location is called the *difference point* of the two instances. Note, however, that for a given pair, a difference point may not exist; but this can happen only if the pattern has a non-empty presuf. Let p_1 and p_2 denote two pattern instances, where $p_1[i]$ is aligned with $p_2[1]$; then dif_i is the difference point if any; i.e., $p_1[dif_i] \neq p_2[dif_i - i + 1]$.

Let q be a pattern instance. Those pattern instances to the right of q, overlapping q, but which do not have a difference point with q are called the *presuf overlaps* of q.

3 The Basic Algorithm

If p contains only one distinct character then it is easily seen that the KMP algorithm makes at most n character comparisons. Further, if $m = 2$ and p consists of two distinct characters then the Boyer-Moore algorithm makes at most n character comparisons. Henceforth, we assume that $m > 2$ and that p has at least two distinct characters.

The algorithm proceeds by eliminating pattern instances as possible matches. It repeatedly performs the following two steps: first, it attempts to match the leftmost surviving pattern instance with the aligned text substring; then, it shifts to the next leftmost surviving pattern instance.

After a shift occurs the strategy followed depends on the nature of the shift. The order in which pattern characters are compared ensures that all the shifts satisfy one of the following two properties.

1. A shift has size greater than or equal to the number of comparisons made since the previous shift. This is called a *basic shift*.
2. When Property 1 is not true, a proper prefix x of p is completely matched with the text after the shift. Moreover, x is also a suffix of p. This is called a *presuf shift*.

Following a basic shift, the basic algorithm is continued; a presuf shift results in a transfer to the presuf handler.

The following observation is the key to the basic algorithm. Consider two overlapping instances of the pattern p. Then comparing either of the two pattern characters at their difference point with the aligned text character is sure to eliminate one of the two pattern instances from being a potential match. So long as the overlap is not a presuf of p, there will be a difference point.

More formally, let p_a and p_b be the two leftmost surviving pattern instances, where p_b is not a presuf overlap of p_a. Let d be the difference point of p_a and p_b. $p_a[d]$ is compared with the aligned text character. A match eliminates p_b; a mismatch eliminates p_a.

Next, we give the exact sequence of comparisons made by the above strategy. We precompute the following sequence S. S is the sequence of indices $dif_2, dif_3, \cdots, dif_m$ omitting repetitions and undefined indices. Henceforth, where no ambiguity will result, we will use the sequence S to refer both to the indices it contains and to the corresponding characters in p_a.

The characters in p_a are compared with their corresponding text characters in two passes, stopping if a mismatch is found. In Pass 1, those characters in p_a contained in S are compared in sequence. If all of these match then the remaining pattern characters are compared from right to left in Pass 2.

Lemma 3.1 *If a mismatch occurs at the character given by the kth index in S then the resulting shift has size at least k.*

Consequently, all shifts resulting from mismatches in Pass 1 are basic shifts. When a basic shift is made the basic algorithm is restarted. It is easy to see that if all shifts are basic shifts then the total number of comparisons made is upper bounded by n.

Next, suppose that all comparisons in Pass 1 result in matches.

Lemma 3.2 *Suppose Pass 2 results in a mismatch at $p_a[l]$. The resulting shift has length at least l.*

Consequently, all shifts resulting from Pass 2 are presuf shifts. The main challenge in minimizing the exact number of comparisons is to handle presuf shifts.

4 The Presuf Handler

In this section the presuf handler for non-semi-cyclic patterns p is described. Let x_1 be the longest presuf of p; as p is not semicyclic, $|x_1| < m/2$.

Consider the situation immediately following a presuf shift. Some prefix of p, which is also a presuf, matches the text substring it is aligned with. It is convenient for the presuf handler to assume that x_1 matches the text. Note that this will not be the case if Pass 2 in the basic algorithm mismatches before x_1 is completely matched. A simple check will prevent the declaration of any incorrect complete match that might result from the above assumption. To facilitate this check, a variable t_{last} is used. Suppose Pass 2 in the basic algorithm ends in a mismatch. Then t_{last} is set to the index of the text character where the mismatch occurred. Otherwise, if no mismatch occurs, $t_{last} \leftarrow \phi$.

As $|x_1| < \frac{m}{2}$, $p = x_1 u x_1$, for some string u. Let t_A be the substring of the text aligned with the prefix x_1 of p immediately following the presuf shift; note that x_1 matches t_A. Order all the presufs of x_1 by decreasing length and let this order be $x_1, x_2, x_3, \ldots, x_k, x_{k+1}$, where x_k is the smallest non-null presuf of x_1 and x_{k+1} is the null string and hence a trivial presuf of x_1. Let the future instances of p (i.e., potential match instances) before its left end slides beyond $t_A|$, in left to right order, be $p_1, p_2, \ldots, p_k$. Let p_{k+1} be the pattern instance whose left end is to the immediate right of $t_A|$. Then p_i, $1 \le i \le k+1$, is the pattern instance with the prefix x_i of p aligned with the suffix x_i of t_A. x_i is said to be the presuf associated with p_i. $p_1, p_2, \ldots, p_k, p_{k+1}$ are called the *presuf pattern instances.*

Lemma 4.1 *At most one of $p_1, \ldots, p_k, p_{k+1}$ can lead to a complete match.*

The presuf handler begins by eliminating all but at most one of $p_1, p_2, \ldots, p_k, p_{k+1}$. This is carried out by a procedure that performs $h \le k$ comparisons; at most two of these comparisons are unsuccessful. We seek to minimize the number of unsuccessful comparisons because while successful comparisons can be remembered, unsuccessful comparisons may lead to repeated comparison of some text characters.

The elimination procedure is described in Section 4.1. The remainder of the presuf handler procedure, for all but one special case, is given in Section 4.2 and its analysis is presented in Section 4.3. The special case and the details of the data structure are omitted from this extended abstract.

4.1 Elimination Strategy

Before describing the exact sequence of comparisons made by the elimination strategy, we need to understand some structural properties of these overlapping instances of p.

Lemma 4.2 *Suppose $x_i = uv^l$ is the ith presuf, where u is a proper suffix of v, v is primitive, and $l \ge 2$. Then $x_{i+1} = uv^{l-1}$.*

Lemma 4.3 *The presuf pattern instances can be partitioned into $g = O(\log m)$ groups $A_1, A_2, \ldots, A_g$. The groups preserve the left to right ordering of the pattern instances; i.e., the pattern instances in group A_i are all to the left of those in group A_{i+1}, for $i = 1, \ldots, g-1$. Let B_i be the set of presufs associated with the pattern instances in A_i. For $i < g$, $B_i = \{u_i v_i^{k_i}, \cdots, u_i v_i^2, u_i v_i\}$, or $B_i = \{u_i v_i^{k_i}, \cdots, u_i v_i^2\}$, where k_i is maximal, and u is a proper suffix of v; while $B_g = \{v_g^{k_g}, \cdots, v_g, \epsilon\}$, where k_g is maximal.*

Remark. The elimination strategy described below and the algorithm in Section 4.2, which uses this elimination strategy to handle presuf shifts, work for most patterns p. However, there are some patterns for which presuf shifts must be handled differently. These exception patterns are precisely those in which x_k, the smallest non-null presuf, is a single character and g, the number of groups, is one. The handling of presuf shifts for these exception patterns is omitted from this extended abstract.

Definition. A clone set is a set $Q = \{s_1, s_2, \cdots\}$ of strings, with $s_i = uv^{k_i}$, where u is a proper suffix of primitive v and $k_i \ge 0$. A set U of pattern instances is *half-done* if $|U| \le 2$ or the set of associated presufs forms a clone set.

The following lemma is the key to our elimination strategy.

Lemma 4.4 *Consider three presuf pattern instances p_a, p_b, p_c, $a < b < c$ (the order of the indices corresponds to the left-to-right order of the pattern instances). Suppose the set $\{x_a, x_b, x_c\}$ is not a clone set. Then there exists an index d in p_1 with the following properties. The characters in $p_1, p_2, \ldots, p_a$ aligned with $p_1[d]$ are all equal; however, the character aligned with $p_1[d]$ in at least one of p_b and p_c differs from $p_1[d]$. Moreover $m - |x_a| + 1 \le d \le m$, i.e., $p_1[d]$ lies in the suffix x_a of p_1.*

Lemma 4.4 implies that a comparison of $p_1[d]$ with the aligned text character has the following effect: if it is a mismatch, all of $p_1, \cdots, p_a$ are eliminated, while if it is a match, at least one of p_b and p_c is eliminated.

Lemma 4.4 enables the elimination of essentially all but one group of pattern instances with at most one mismatch. At each step, for the rightmost d yielded by Lemma 4.4, $p_1[d]$ is compared with the aligned text character. If there is a mismatch, by Lemma 4.5, the surviving set of pattern instances is half-done. While if there is no such p_a, the surviving set of pattern instances is half-done by Lemma 4.4. This procedure comprises Phase 1 of the elimination procedure.

Lemma 4.5 *If there is a mismatch in Phase 1 of the elimination procedure, the set X of surviving pattern instances is half-done.*

The elimination among the remaining half-done set of pattern instances also requires at most one mismatch.

Lemma 4.6 *Let $O = \{p_{i_1}, p_{i_2}, \ldots, p_{i_l}\}$, $l \ge 2$, be an uneliminated half-done set. Then $x_{i_j} = uv^{h-j}$, where u is a proper suffix of primitive v and $h \ge l$. Further, there exists an index d such that the characters in*

$\{p_{i_1}, p_{i_2}, \ldots, p_{i_{l-1}}\}$ *aligned with* $p_{i_l}[d]$ *are all equal, but differ from the character* $p_{i_l}[d]$. $p_{i_l}[d]$ *is aligned with or to the left of* $p_{i_1}[m]$. *In addition, if* $p_1 \neq p_{i_1}$ *then* $p_{i_l}[d]$ *is to the right of* $p_1[m]$ *and if* $p_1 = p_{i_1}$ *then* $p_{i_l}[d]$ *is to the right of* t_a.

Corollary 4.7 *To eliminate all but one of the pattern instances of a Phase 1 survivors set* $\{p_{i_1}, p_{i_2}, \ldots, p_{i_j}\}$ *it suffices to compare a sequence of characters with the property that any two consecutive characters in the sequence are distance* $|v|$ *apart, where* v *is the core of* x_{i_1}.

Let p_{i_l} be as in Lemma 4.6; the character in p_{i_1} aligned with $p_{i_l}[d]$ is compared with the aligned text character. A match eliminates p_{i_l}; a mismatch leaves only p_{i_l} surviving. Iteration of this step ends with one pattern instance surviving after at most one mismatch. This comprises Phase 2 of the elimination procedure.

The sequence of comparisons made in Phase 2 is clearly a right to left sequence. If p_1 is eliminated in Phase 1 then all comparisons in Phase 2 are made to the right of the characters compared in Phase 1. Otherwise, if p_1 is not eliminated in Phase 1, all comparisons in Phase 2 are made to the left of the characters compared in Phase 1.

We recapitulate the elimination strategy now. In Phase 1, characters in p_1 at indices given by a precomputed sequence S_1 are compared in sequence until a mismatch occurs or until the sequence is exhausted. Associated with a mismatch at the ith comparison given by S_1 is an auxiliary sequence S_{2_i} of indices. If a mismatch occurs at the ith comparison in S_1, Phase 2 begins and comparisons are now made according to the auxiliary sequence S_{2_i}. A mismatch at any index in the relevant auxiliary sequence completes the elimination process as does the exhaustion of that auxiliary sequence. In either case, only one pattern instance from the set $\{p_1, \ldots, p_k, p_{k+1}\}$ survives.

Let $|S_1| = j$. The sequences S_1 and $S_{2_1}, S_{2_2}, \ldots, S_{2_j}$ collectively form a tree ET (the *elimination tree*). ET is a binary tree. Each internal node x of ET stores an index indicating the comparison to be made. Each internal node has two children. The computation continues at the left child if the comparison at x is successful, and at the right child otherwise. The computation starts at the root of ET. Each external node stores the one pattern instance to survive the two phases of comparisons leading to that external node. The external nodes are also called terminal nodes. Note that no pattern instance p_i can be the survivor at two distinct terminal nodes of ET. This is because one of the two outcomes of the comparison at the least common ancestor of these two nodes in ET is bound to eliminate p_i. It follows that the size of ET is $O(k)$.

The total number of mismatches occurring in the elimination process is at most two because each phase terminates when a mismatch occurs.

Lemma 4.8 *All but at most one of* $p_1, \ldots, p_k, p_{k+1}$ *can be eliminated by making up to* k *comparisons using the* $O(k)$ *sized binary comparison tree* ET. *At most two of these comparisons result in mismatches. The sequence of comparisons made by the elimination strategy consists of two left to right sequences. The second sequence is either entirely to the right or entirely to the left of the first one.*

4.2 Strategy for Handling Presuf Shifts

Subsequent to the elimination due to tree ET the presuf handler proceeds in a manner reminiscent of the basic algorithm. That is, there is a current pattern instance, p_a, which is being matched, and which is the leftmost surviving pattern instance. The next leftmost surviving pattern instance, p_b, which has a difference point with p_a is a candidate for elimination. Indeed, a comparison of p_a with the text is made at the difference point.

The analysis of the presuf handler has the following flavor. Comparisons, with a few exceptions, are charged to distinct text characters. To be precise, for each suffix shift, at most 2 comparisons are charged to the shift rather than to text characters. Even more precisely, if 2 comparisons are charged to the shift, the next presuf shift is at distance at least $\frac{3(m+1)}{4}$ to the right, and otherwise it is at distance at least $\frac{m+1}{2}$ to the right. The complexity bound of the algorithm now follows readily.

Let t_a denote the text character $t_A|$.

Theorem 4.9 *The algorithm performs at most* $n + \frac{8}{3(m+1)}(n - m)$ *character comparisons.*

There are three ways in which text characters are charged:

(i) The character compared is charged.
(ii) The text character aligned with the left end of the pattern instance eliminated by the comparison is charged.
(iii) The text character to the immediate right of t_a (i.e., aligned with $|p_{k+1})$ is charged.

The three charging methods do not interact readily. To ensure that no text character is charged twice, the switching from one charging method to the other will occur only at carefully selected points in the algorithm. In addition, mismatches are not charged according to rule (i), for the text characters in question may be compared again.

Basically, charging method (i) is used if a pattern instance is successfully matched (at least up to a suffix which is a presuf). Charging method (iii) is used only for the comparison that eliminates the presuf pattern instance which survives the elimination procedure ET. Charging method (ii) is used otherwise. A partial exception arises for the characters compared by procedure ET; this is discussed further below.

Following the use of procedure ET, the aim is to perform comparisons essentially as in the basic algorithm, that is to compare the character at the difference point of the two leftmost surviving pattern instances, which are not presuf overlaps of each other. The analysis ceases to be as straightforward because of the additional $h \leq k$ comparisons performed by procedure ET; indeed, to cope with this, a modified form of the basic algorithm is needed.

There are two objectives.

1. Avoid repeating comparisons at the text characters successfully compared by procedure ET.
2. Perform essentially h fewer comparisons than in the basic algorithm.

Objective 1 is achieved by keeping a record of the successful comparisons in a bit vector of length roughly m.

The major difficulty, however, is caused by the method used for charging the h comparisons made by procedure ET. It is natural to charge these comparisons to the text characters compared. Unfortunately, this may conflict with the charging using method (ii). To avoid this difficulty, a single additional comparison, with text character t_b, is performed before using procedure ET. The following lemma can then be shown.

Lemma 4.10 *For each text character t_c compared by procedure ET, with at most $\alpha \leq 2$ exceptions, there is a distinct previously uncharged text character $t_{c'}$, $t_{c'}$ aligned with or to the left of t_c and to the right of $|p_{k+1}$, such that the pattern instance q_c whose left end is aligned with $t_{c'}$ mismatches either the text character t_b or some text character matched in procedure ET.*

Let β be the number of mismatches performed by Procedure ET. Then, in addition, $\alpha + \beta \leq 2$.

The lemma is proven by specifying a transfer function f, which associates c to c'. The form of f depends on the sequence of comparisons performed by procedure ET. The proof of the lemma is quite non-trivial; it is omitted from this extended abstract.

Lemma 4.10 is used as follows. Let q_e be the next pattern instance to match the text (or, at least, to have a suffix, which is also a presuf, matching the text). All pattern instances to the left of q_e, eliminated by comparisons made after the use of procedure ET, are charged used charging method (ii). Using the transfer function, those comparisons to the left of q_e made by procedure ET are charged to text characters which are not otherwise charged. By contrast, text characters aligned with q_e are charged using charging method (i). There will be no more than two comparisons performed by the presuf handler that are not thereby charged to a text character; these comparisons are charged to the presuf handler itself.

The algorithm requires a total of five subphases, whose details depend on exactly how q_e arises.

It is helpful to distinguish three scenarios that may ensue. To this end, let p_e denote the presuf pattern instance to survive the elimination using tree ET.

The three scenarios follow:

1. All pattern instances overlapping p_e are eliminated apart from its presuf overlaps, and p_e or at least a suffix of p_e is matched.
2. p_e is eliminated. In addition, there is some pattern instance q_c overlapping p_e, such that all pattern instances overlapping q_c are eliminated apart from its presuf overlaps; further, q_c or at least a suffix of q_c is matched.
3. p_e is eliminated as are all pattern instances overlapping p_e. Let q_d denote the leftmost surviving pattern instance in this case.

The first scenario causes no problems from the perspective of the analysis. It suffices to ensure that none of the successful comparisons made by ET are repeated. The third scenario is handled by using charging scheme (iii) for the comparison which eliminates p_e and charging scheme (ii) for the remaining comparisons in the post ET phase. Lemma 4.10 ensures that for each comparison made by ET with a text character strictly between t_a and $|q_d$, with at most two exceptions, there is a distinct pattern instance whose left end lies strictly between $|p_{k+1}$ and $|q_d$, and which is eliminated by the comparisons made by ET plus the one other comparison at text character t_b. Again, this leads to the desired complexity bound without difficulty.

The second scenario provides the greatest difficulty. In order to avoid unnecessary comparisons, the locations of successful comparisons are recorded. Then, if a difference point occurs at one of these matched text characters the present pattern instance p_b (see the first paragraph of the subsection) can be removed without further comparisons. However, following a mismatch it is not clear how to maintain this property. For, with only linear storage, it is not clear how to ensure that the current pattern instance, following the mismatch, agrees with the text on a previously matched character, at least if the total work bound is to be linear. (There is no problem if exponential in m space is available for precomputed structures.) To avoid this difficulty, only the successful comparisons since the last mismatch are recorded.

In fact, this is not quite good enough. It appears necessary to keep track of the characters compared by procedure ET regardless of how many characters are compared. This avoids subsequent comparison of these characters. Indeed, any pattern instances mismatching on one or more of these characters are eliminated immediately after the computation with procedure ET. This is done with the help of precomputed information.

With this motivation, we proceed with a precise description of the presuf handler procedure. It proceeds in five steps.

Step 1. (Before the use of tree ET). The characters in $p_1, \ldots, p_k$ aligned with $p_1[m]$, the rightmost character in p_1, are identical. If the character in p_{k+1} aligned with $p_1[m]$ is also identical to it, then $p_1[m]$ is compared with the aligned text character. A mismatch eliminates all of $p_1, \ldots, p_k, p_{k+1}$ and the basic algorithm is restarted with $|p_a$ placed immediately to the right of $|p_{k+1}$. A match is not immediately beneficial as it does not eliminate any of $p_1, \ldots, p_k, p_{k+1}$. However, it ensures the elimination of sufficiently many appropriate pattern instances for Scenarios 2 and 3 described above.

Step 2. The elimination strategy using tree ET is applied to the pattern instances $p_1, \ldots, p_k, p_{k+1}$.

Following Step 2, at most one presuf pattern instance survives. Call it p_e. Let Q denote the set of pattern instances which overlap p_1 and have their left end to the right of $|p_{k+1}$. In the elimination process, some elements of Q may also have been eliminated from being potential matches. They need not be reconsidered. Indeed, as the characters successfully matched in Step 2 must not be compared anew, it appears that these pattern instances must not be considered anew. To this end, a subset Q_x of Q is associated with each terminal node x in ET.

Let T_x denote the indices of the text characters successfully compared in Steps 1 and 2. Q_x contains those pattern instances in Q which match at all the text indices in T_x. The method for computing Q_x is omitted from this extended abstract.

Suppose that the elimination process terminates at terminal node x. Let $Q' = \{p_e\} \cup Q_x$. The elimination procedure of Step 3 is applied to the pattern instances in Q'.

Step 3. This step eliminates among the elements of Q'. q_c will denote the leftmost pattern instance to survive Step 3. Every other surviving pattern instance is a presuf overlap of q_c; actually, only if $q_c = p_e$ can there be other surviving pattern instances.

The strategy used here is similar to the one for the basic algorithm. One of two overlapping patterns instances is eliminated by comparing at the difference point of the two instances.

To prevent repeated comparisons of text characters to the right of t_a, two additional data structures are used. The first is a bit vector $BV[1\ldots 2m]$. $BV[i] = 1$ if the ith text character to the right of t_a has been successfully compared in Steps 1 and 2 or in Step 3 since the last mismatch. The second is a list LBV; it stores the indices of the bits in BV set to one in Step 3 since the last mismatch. Initially, LBV is empty.

The elimination procedure for Step 3 follows. Let q_a and q_b denote the two leftmost uneliminated pattern instances in Q'. Suppose that q_b lie i units to the right of q_a. The reader is advised to refer to Section 2 to review the definition of dif_{i+1}. If dif_{i+1} is undefined then q_b is removed from Q'. (This can happen only if $q_a = p_e$. For suppose $q_a \neq p_e$; let q be a presuf overlap of q_a; then q lies to the right of the pattern instances in Q', as Q' includes only pattern instances whose left end lies in the first $|p| - |x_1|$ characters to the right of t_a.)

If dif_{i+1} is defined then the bit in BV corresponding to the text character aligned with $q_a[dif_{i+1}]$ is read. If this bit is 1 then q_b is removed from Q' (q_b can be eliminated as it does not match an already compared text character). Otherwise, $q_a[dif_{i+1}]$ is compared with the aligned text character. If the two characters are equal, the corresponding bit in BV is set, the bit's index is added to LBV, and q_b is eliminated. If they are not equal, then the bits in BV at all indices currently in LBV are reset to 0, LBV is reset to empty, and q_a is eliminated.

The elimination procedure is iterated until only one pattern instance remains in Q'. Let q_c denote this remaining pattern instance.

Step 4. In this step, either all pattern instances overlapping q_c, apart from presuf overlaps, are eliminated, or q_c is eliminated.

Let Q'' be the set of pattern instances whose left end lies to the right of $p_1|$ but not to the right of $q_c|$. The following step is repeated until either q_c is eliminated or $Q'' = \phi$. Let q_d be the leftmost pattern instance in Q''. Suppose q_d lies i units to the right of q_c. If dif_{i+1} does not exist then q_d is removed from Q''. Otherwise, the following bit in BV is read: the bit corresponding to the text character aligned with $q_c[dif_{i+1}]$. If this bit is 1, q_d is eliminated. If it is 0, $q_c[i]$ and the aligned text character are compared. If they match then the corresponding bit in BV is set, its index is added to LBV, and q_d is eliminated. Otherwise, q_c is eliminated and Step 4 comes to an end.

If q_c is eliminated then LBV is reset to be empty, BV is reset to 0, and the basic algorithm is restarted with $p_a = q_d$. Otherwise, Step 5 is performed.

Step 5. This step seeks to complete the match of q_c. If at least a presuf of q_c is matched, the complete match, or the partial match results in a new presuf shift. Otherwise, the basic algorithm is resumed with $|p_a$ immediately to the right of $q_c|$.

Step 5 compares the characters in q_c to the right of t_a apart from those matched in Steps 1 and 2, and those matched in Steps 3 and 4 following the most recent mismatch (incidentally, there was no mismatch in Step 4, as q_c survived Step 4 if Step 5 is performed). These characters are identified with the help of bit vector BV. They are matched in right to left order until either a mismatch occurs or they are all matched.

If they all match q_c is declared a complete match if either $t_{last} = \phi$ or t_{last} lies to the left of $|q_c$. Recall that t_{last} is the index of the text character mismatched, if any, immediately prior to the most recent presuf shift (if there was no mismatch, $t_{last} = \phi$).

Next, BV is reset to zero, LBV is reset to be empty, and t_{last} is updated as follows. If the above right to left pass results in a mismatch then t_{last} is set to the index of the text character at which the mismatch occurs. Otherwise, t_{last} retains its value unless $|q_c$ is to its right. In the latter case, $t_{last} := \phi$.

The present situation is identical to that preceding a presuf shift in the basic algorithm. This resulting shift is treated in the same way; it too is called a presuf shift.

4.3 The Analysis

The comparison complexity of the algorithm of Section 4.2 is given by the following lemma.

Lemma 4.11 *The comparison complexity of the algorithm is bounded by* $n(1 + \frac{8}{3(m+1)})$.

Proof. We give a charging scheme to account for the comparisons made by the algorithm. This scheme charges almost every comparison to a distinct text character. The only exceptions are a few of the comparisons made by the presuf shift handler. For each presuf shift, depending on the distance between this presuf shift and the next one, the charging scheme fails to charge for up to two of the comparisons made by the presuf shift handler. We refer to the number of comparisons which the charging scheme fails to charge to distinct text characters as the *overhead* of the presuf shift. If a presuf shift has an overhead of two, we show that the next presuf shift must occur at least distance $\frac{3(m+1)}{4}$ to the right of the current presuf shift. The comparison complexity of our algorithm now follows from the fact that any two consecutive presuf shifts must occur at least distance $\frac{m+1}{2}$ apart.

Charging Scheme. The charging scheme charges in phases. The phases begin and end at shifts and at reversions to the basic algorithm. There are four types of phases; for each phase type a different charging scheme is used.

1. A phase beginning and ending with a basic shift.
2. A phase beginning in the basic algorithm and ending with a presuf shift.
3. A phase beginning with a presuf shift and ending with a reversion to the basic algorithm.
4. A phase beginning and ending with a presuf shift.

Consider any phase and let q_1 and q_2 refer to the leftmost surviving pattern instances at the beginning and end of the phase, respectively. Note that for Type 3 and Type 4 phases, q_1 is a presuf overlap of the pattern instance q', the leftmost uneliminated pattern instance prior to the presuf shift which initiated this phase. Specifically, the prefix x_1 of q_1 is aligned with the suffix x_1 of q' (Recall from the start of Section 4 that on a presuf shift, we assume that the suffix x_1 of q_1 matches the text).

The charging scheme obeys the following properties.

1. At the start of a Type 1 or Type 2 phase, only text characters to the left of q_1 have been charged.
2. At the start of a Type 3 or Type 4 phase, only text characters aligned with or to the left of the prefix x_1 of q_1 have been charged.

Type 1 Phase. Suppose i comparisons were made in this phase. These i comparisons are charged to text characters which are aligned with q_1 but to the left of $|q_2$. By Lemma 3.1, $|q_2$ lies at least i characters to the right of $|q_1$. Thus, each text character aligned with q_1 and to the left of $|q_2$ is charged at most once in this process. Clearly, Property 1 holds at the start of the next phase.

Type 2 Phase. In each comparison, a distinct character in q_1 is compared with the aligned text character. Each of these comparisons is charged to the text character compared. Thus, each text character aligned with q_1 is charged at most once in this process. Clearly, Property 2 holds at the start of the next phase.

The charging scheme for Type 3 and Type 4 phases is more involved. Before describing the scheme, we mention the ranges of the text characters charged in each case.

Type 3 Phase. The text characters charged lie to the right of the right end of the prefix x_1 of q_1 and to the left of $|q_2$. Each text character in this range is charged at most once. Clearly, Property 1 holds at the start of the next phase.

Type 4 Phase. The text characters charged lie to the right of the right end of the prefix x_1 of q_1 and are aligned with or to the left of the rightmost character in the prefix x_1 of q_2. Each text character in this range is charged at most once. Clearly, Property 2 holds at the start of the next phase.

Clearly, the ranges of the text characters charged for different phases are disjoint. Next, we specify the charging scheme for Type 3 and Type 4 phases and justify the claims regarding the overhead.

Consider a presuf shift which initiates a new Type 3 or Type 4 phase. Let q' be the leftmost uneliminated pattern instance immediately before the presuf shift. Recall that t_a is the text character aligned with $q'|$. Consider the comparisons made by the current use of the presuf shift handler. If a mismatch occurs in Step 1, the current phase ends immediately and the basic algorithm is resumed. The presuf shift in this case has overhead 1 and the next presuf shift occurs at least distance $m+1$ to the right. Next, suppose that the comparison in Step 1 is successful. Let p_e be the presuf pattern instance to survive the elimination using tree ET in Step 2. After the presuf shift handler finishes, one of the three scenarios mentioned Section 4.2 ensues. We consider each in turn.

1. All pattern instances overlapping p_e are eliminated apart from its presuf overlaps, and p_e or at least a suffix of p_e is matched. This is a Type 4 phase.

All comparisons made by the presuf shift handler, except the unsuccessful comparisons in Step 2, are charged to the text characters compared. The bit vector BV ensures that each of these comparisons involves a different text character. Thus each text character which lies to the right of t_a and is aligned with or to the left of $p_e|$ is charged at most once. At most two comparisons in Step 2 are unsuccessful, so this shift has overhead at most two. Note that if there are two mismatches in Step 2 then all presuf pattern instances belonging to A_1 are eliminated. So, if this presuf shift has overhead two then $p_e \notin A_1$. Let x_e be the presuf associated with p_e. Then $p = x_e w x_e z x_e w x_e$, for some non-empty strings z and w. So $|x_e| \leq \frac{m-3}{4}$. This guarantees that the next presuf shift occurs at least distance $\frac{3(m+1)}{4}$ to the right. If there is just one mismatch in Step 2 then, as $|x_1| < \frac{m}{2}$, the next presuf shift occurs at least distance $\frac{m+1}{2}$ to the right.

2. p_e is eliminated. In addition, there is some pattern instance q_c overlapping p_e, such that all pattern instances overlapping q_c are eliminated apart from its presuf overlaps; further, q_c or at least a suffix of q_c is matched. This is also a Type 4 phase.

Each comparison in Steps 1 and 2 with a text character to the left of $|q_c$ for which function f is defined is charged to the text character specified by the function f, called its f value; f values are distinct by definition. Comparisons in Step 3 fall into one of three categories (see Lemma 4.10 and the following two paragraphs):

1. Comparisons which eliminate patterns instances whose left ends lie to the right of $|p_{k+1}$ and to the left of $|q_c$.
2. Comparisons which eliminate pattern instances whose left ends are aligned with or to the right of $|q_c$.
3. The comparison which eliminates p_e.

Each comparison in the first category is charged to the text character aligned with the left end of the pattern instance eliminated. By the definition of the function f, these text characters do not occur in the range of f values. Comparisons in the second category, along with the comparisons made in Steps 4 and 5 and those successful comparisons in Steps 1 and 2 that involve text characters overlapping q_c, are charged to the text characters compared. BV ensures that each of these comparisons involves a distinct text character. Thus each text character which lies to the right of $|p_{k+1}$ and is aligned with or to the left of $q_c|$ is charged at most once. The comparison that eliminates p_e is charged to the text character aligned with $|p_{k+1}$. Since all f values lie to the right of $|p_{k+1}$ and all pattern instances eliminated by comparisons in the first category have left ends to the right of $|p_{k+1}$, this text character is charged exactly once. The two comparisons in Step 2 lacking f values constitute the overhead of this presuf shift. Since p_e is eliminated, the next presuf shift occurs at least distance $m+1$ to the right of the current presuf shift.

3. p_e is eliminated as are all pattern instances overlapping p_e. This is a Type 3 phase.

Similar to 2.

□

5 The Lower Bound

Theorem 5.1 *An online algorithm for string matching performs at least* $n+\frac{11(n-m)}{5(m+1)}$ *character comparisons* *following any pattern preprocessing, for $m = 10 + 11k$, $k \geq 1$, an integer.*

Proof Let $p = ubucubudueufububucubu$, where $u = a^k$. The pattern p allows an adversary to force two mismatches at least every $m - k$ text characters, where $m = 10 + 11k$, $k \geq 1$ an integer. The adversary forces a match at least once every $m - k$ characters; to be precise, following a match, one of the three presuf pattern instances shown below will be the next match. Note that in the three presuf pattern instances shown, at each aligned position, either all the characters are equal or they all differ; hence on any mismatch only one of these pattern instances can be eliminated. It is now easy to force two mismatches in order to eliminate two of the pattern instances.

```
u b u c u b u d u e u f u b u b u c u b u
        u b u c u b u d u e u f u b u b u ..
            u b u c u b u d u e u f u b u ..
```

□

Theorem 5.2 *An algorithm for string matching performs at least $n + \frac{2(n-m)}{(m+3)}$ character comparisons following any pattern preprocessing, for any $m = 2k + 1$, $k \geq 1$, an integer.*

Proof Let $p = a^k b a^k$. The example $k = 2$ is illustrated below. The adversary chooses the text t so that the player performs at least one mismatch every $\frac{1}{2}(m + 3)$ comparisons. $t = p(xa^{k-1})^r$, where each instance of x is chosen to be one of ba and ab, and $r \geq 0$ is an integer. x is chosen to force a mismatch on each instance of x. For each choice of x there is a separate potential match. Specifically, the matching pattern instance is either $a^k x a^{k-1}$ or $a^{k-1} x a^k$ according as x is ba or ab. Further this match is independent of the choices made for every other instance of x. This is ensured by having each potential match overlap exactly one x.

There are a few more details to handle when $k = 1$.

```
t = a a b a a ? ? a a ? ? a a ...
    a a b a a
          a a b a a
            a a b a a
                  a a b a a
                    a a b a a
```

□

Acknowledgements

We thank Dany Breslauer for a number of comments and suggestions and in particular for the observation that p_{k+1} could be viewed as a presuf pattern instance. This contributed to an improvement of our upper bound from $n + \frac{3(n-m)}{m}$ to $n + \frac{8(n-m)}{3m}$.

References

[AG86] A. Apostolico and R. Giancarlo. The Boyer-Moore-Galil string searching strategies revisited. *SIAM Journal on Computing*, Vol.15, 1(1986), 98-105.

[AC89] A. Apostolico, M. Crochemore. Optimal Canonization of all substrings of a string. Technical Report No. TR 89-75, LITP, Universite Paris 7, FRANCE, October 1989.

[BM77] R. Boyer and S. Moore. A fast string matching algorithm. *CACM*, 20(1977), 762-772.

[BG92] D. Breslauer and Z. Galil. Closing the gap in the exact complexity of string matching. Manuscript.

[Co91] R. Cole. Tight Bounds on the complexity of the Boyer-Moore algorithm. *Proceedings of the second Annual ACM-SIAM Symposium on Discrete Algorithms*, 1991, To appear, *SIAM J. Computing*.

[CH92a] R. Cole and R. Hariharan. Tighter Upper Bounds on The Exact Complexity of String Matching. In preparation.

[CH92b] R. Cole and R. Hariharan. Lower bounds on the comparison complexity of string matching. In preparation.

[CCG92] M. Crochemore, A. Czumaj, L. Gasiniec, S. Jarominek, T. Lecroq, W. Plandowski, W. Rytter. Speeding Up Two String-Matching Algorithms. STACS 1992.

[CP89] M. Crochemore and D. Perrin. Two-way pattern matching. Technical Report, Laboratoire Informatique, Théorique et Programmation, Université Paris 7, 1989.

[Ga92] Z. Galil. Private communication.

[GG91] Z. Galil and R. Giancarlo. On the Exact Complexity of String Matching: Lower Bounds. *SIAM Journal on Computing*, 6(1991), 1008-1020.

[GG92] Z. Galil and R. Giancarlo. On the Exact Complexity of String Matching: Upper Bounds. *SIAM Journal on Computing*, 3(1992), 407-437.

[GO80] L.J. Guibas and A.M. Odlyzko. A new proof of the linearity of the Boyer-Moore string searching algorithm. *SIAM Journal on Computing*, Vol.9, 4(1980), 672-682.

[KMP77] D.E. Knuth, J. Morris, V. Pratt. Fast pattern matching in strings. *SIAM Journal on Computing*, 6(1973), 323-350.

[ZP92] U. Zwick and M. Paterson. Lower bounds for string matching in the sequential comparison model. Manuscript.

Tiling a Polygon with Rectangles

Claire Kenyon*

LIP
ENS-Lyon
46, allée d'Italie
69364 Lyon Cedex 07
France

Richard Kenyon†

UFR de Mathématiques
Institut Fourier
BP 74
38402 Saint Martin d'Heres
France

Abstract

We study the problem of tiling a simple polygon of surface n with rectangles of given types (tiles). We present a linear time algorithm for deciding if a polygon can be tiled with $1 \times m$ and $k \times 1$ tiles (and giving a tiling when it exists), and a quadratic algorithm for the same problem when the tile types are $m \times k$ and $k \times m$.

1 Introduction

We present algorithms for tiling a simple region of $\mathbf{Z}^2$ (i.e. polygonal region without holes) with rectangular tiles.

In the first part, we present a linear time algorithm (in the surface area n of the region) when there are two tile types, the $1 \times m$ and $l \times 1$ rectangles. Previously the only known algorithms other than exhaustive search were for the case of dominoes ($m = 2, l = 2$), where several combinatorial methods were known (using matchings, or max-flow-min-cut algorithms). Our algorithm generalizes a domino tiling algorithm of W. P. Thurston [1] based on ideas of J. H. Conway and Lagarias which rely on geometric group theory. After the fact, one can view this problem as a flow problem as in the case of dominoes.

In the second part, we give a quadratic algorithm for tiling with $k \times l$ and $l \times k$ rectangles (i.e. when there is only one tile type, up to rotation). This case appears more complicated, but is interesting because there seems to be no natural interpretation as a flow problem.

In the last section, we define the distance between two tilings of a region in terms of the number of elementary transformations needed to go from one to the other, and study the maximum distance.

It is known from Mike Robson [2] that tiling a region with holes with $1 \times m$ and $n \times 1$ tiles is NP-complete as soon as $m \geq 2$ and $l \geq 3$. On the other hand, efficient tiling algorithms and criteria have been obtained for restricted classes of polygons [3][4]. As far as rectangles are concerned, from [5] we see that our tiling problem is NP-complete for polygonal regions with holes as soon as $k \geq 2$ and $l \geq 3$ (optimal tile salvage problem).

*Supported by CNRS URA 1398.
†supported by CNRS.

2 Tiling a polygon with $1 \times m$ and $l \times 1$ tiles

We will only present the algorithm in the case $m = l = 3$, since generalizing the algorithm is straightforward from that case. By a *polygon* we will mean a simple polygon in $\mathbf{R}^2$, having vertices in $\mathbf{Z}^2$, and vertical or horizontal edges. A polygon P is described by its perimeter ∂P, which is a sequence of directed horizontal and vertical edges of length 1.

2.1 The method of Conway and Lagarias

Let a be a symbol associated with each horizontal step (of length one) to the right and b be the symbol associated with each step upward. Let a^{-1} denote a horizontal step to the left, and b^{-1} a vertical step down; then the perimeter of a polygon, read in a counterclockwise sense from an arbitrary starting point, is a word in a, b, a^{-1}, b^{-1}.

Let $F = \langle a, b | \rangle$ denote the free group generated by a and b and in general let $\langle A|R \rangle$ denote the group generated by the elements of A with relations $r = e$ for $r \in R$. Following Thurston [1], we define the tiling group of a set of tiles to be the quotient of the free group F by the relations describing the tiles. Let $G = \langle a, b | [a^3, b], [a, b^3] \rangle$ (where the notation $[x, y]$ is shorthand for $xyx^{-1}y^{-1}$).

Let P be the polygon in Z^2 which we want to tile. Choose a point on the boundary of P arbitrarily and label it by e. Going around P from that point in counterclockwise order, we get a word w in F. The word w can also be thought as a word in G in a natural way.

Fact 1 *[1] If P can be tiled, then $w = e$ in G.*

Proof idea: First, the polygon given by a single tile gives $w = e$: a horizontal 3×1 tile corresponds to the relation $a^3ba^{-3}b^{-1} = [a^3, b] = e$, and a vertical 1×3 tile corresponds to $ab^3a^{-1}b^{-3} = [a, b^3] = e$. Starting from any region P, removing a tile from P corresponds to changing w by applying one of the relators $[a^3, b]$ or $[a, b^3]$. □

The condition $w = e$ in G is not always sufficient. For example, the polygon figure 1 admits no tiling (with 1×3 and 3×1 tiles) even though w is trivial in G:

$$w = a^2b^3aba^{-2}b^{-3}a^{-1}b^{-1} = b^3a^3bb^{-3}a^{-2}a^{-1}b^{-1} = e.$$

If $w = e$ in G, then ∂P lifts to a closed path in the Cayley graph $\Gamma(G)$ of G. From that closed path, ∂P can be recovered by projection onto $Z^2 = G/[a, b]$ (defined to be the group obtained from G by adding the relator $[a, b]$, i.e. by quotienting by the normal closure of the relator $[a, b]$).

Define a 2-complex $\Gamma^2(G)$ by glueing disks onto $\Gamma(G)$, one disk for each occurence of the relators $[a, b^3]$ and $[a^3, b]$ in $\Gamma(G)$. A tiling of P then lifts to a surface in $\Gamma^2(G)$ spanning the loop w in $\Gamma(G) \subset \Gamma^2(G)$. Define a surface area in $\Gamma^2(G)$ by giving area 3 to each disk (i.e. the area of its projection on Z^2). In general, a surface spanning w in $\Gamma^2(G)$ does not necessarily project to a tiling of P, since the projection may be self-overlapping. But we have the following key observation:

Fact 2 *[1] If P is tileable, then any minimum area surface spanning w in $\Gamma^2(G)$ projects to a tiling of P.*

The problem is now reduced to finding a surface of minimum area.

In the case of domino tilings (when the tiles are 1×2 and 2×1, $\Gamma(G)$ is naturally embeddable in $\mathbf{R}^3$, and Thurston solves the problem by first defining a "height" function in $\Gamma(G)$, secondly observing that there is a lowest tiling T spanning w, whose highest point must be on the border w,and thirdly taking the highest point of w and showing that the tile of T at that point can be determined easily from the local conditions.

To generalize Thurston's approach, the main problem is finding the correct definition of a height function.

2.2 Defining a height function

In our case, the Cayley graph $\Gamma(G)$ is a bit difficult to visualize, since it cannot be naturally embedded in $\mathbf{R}^3$. However we only need to use a quotient graph of G. Let $H = G/a^3, b^3$. Since $a^3 = b^3 = e$ implies that $ab^3 = b^3a$ and that $a^3b = ba^3$, we have $H = \langle a, b | a^3, b^3 \rangle = \mathbf{Z}_3 * \mathbf{Z}_3$, the free product of $\mathbf{Z}_3$ by $\mathbf{Z}_3$. The Cayley graph $\Gamma(H)$ of H is simply a tree of triangles (see figure 2). given $x \in G$, let x' denote its projection in H and x'' denote its projection in $\mathbf{Z}^2 = G/[a, b]$. G is a semi-direct product of H by $\mathbf{Z}^2$, which means that an element of G is determined by its projections onto H and $\mathbf{Z}^2$:

Fact 3 *The map $G \to H \times \mathbf{Z}^2$ given by $x \mapsto (x', x'')$ is bijective.*

Now, the closed path w in $\Gamma(G)$ associated to the boundary of P maps to a closed path w' in $\Gamma(H)$.

Root $\Gamma(H)$ at some arbitrary vertex r, far from w', and define the height of $x \in H$ to be the distance from x to r in the graph $\Gamma(H)$. (For example, if n is the surface area of P, we can define r as the point $(ab)^{10n}$ in H).

Lemma 1 *If P is tileable, then there is a tiling of P whose highest point is on the boundary ∂P.*

Proof: Let T be a tiling of the polygon. Every point inside P is on the boundary of a tile, and so has an associated element of G (and so a height in H). Assume that a highest point x is in the interior of P. We claim that x cannot be at the corner of a tile. For, if x is, for example, the lower left corner of some tile, then x has neighbors labelled xa and xb. In $\Gamma(H)$, it is easy to see that no matter how x is with respect to r, either xa or xb is farther from r than x, hence higher: contradiction.

Without loss of generality, we can assume then that x is on the left side of a vertical tile. Then the tile on the left side of x must also be vertical (because x is not a corner and not on the boundary). Assume for example that x is as in figure 3. Then xb^2, which labels a neighbor of x, is also highest. Since it is not a corner either, this determines the position of the tile left of x: the two tiles surrounding x must form a rectangle.

Thus $y = xbab^{-1}$ and $z = xba^{-1}b^{-1}$ are two labels of the tiling. We observe that no matter where r is, one of the two points y and z must be at the same distance as x from r, hence also of maximum height. For example, z is also a maximum in figure 4. If z is on the border of P, we are done. Otherwise, by the same argument as above, the tile left of z must be vertical and form a rectangle with the previous two tiles. We can now replace the three vertical tiles by three horizontal tiles, forming a new, lower tiling (in the sense that every point of P is lower; see figure 5). Therefore a lowest tiling must have a highest point on its boundary .□

Given P, we now consider the highest point x on the boundary ∂P of P. From the above lemma, we know that x is also the highest point of some tiling of P (if P is tileable). It is easy to see that x cannot be at a corner of ∂P. Assume that x is on a vertical side of ∂P, as in figure 6. The neighbors of x on ∂P are labelled xb and xb^{-1}. One of them must also have maximum height, for example xb. Since neither x nor xb can be at a corner of a tile, the only possibility is a vertical tile covering both x and xb.

Removing that tile, we get a region which can be tiled iff P can be tiled: iterating the process, we will obtain an algorithm for tiling P or deciding that P cannot be tiled by 1×3 and 3×1 tiles.

2.3 The algorithm

Input: a polygonal region P of $\mathbf{Z}^2$ of area n.
Initialization: Label some point of P by e. Let $r = (ab)^{10n} \in H = \langle a, b | a^3, b^3 \rangle$. Going around the boundary, label each point of ∂P by a word $w \in H$ and compute its height.
Repeat: Let x be a highest point of ∂P.
One of x's neighbors, say y, is also a highest point of

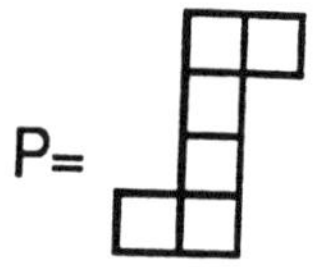

Figure 1: A necessary but not sufficient condition for tiling P

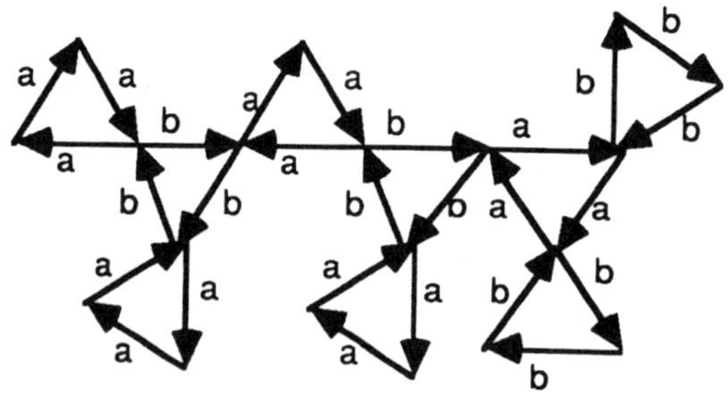

Figure 2: The Cayley graph of $H = \langle a, b | a^3 = b^3 = e \rangle$

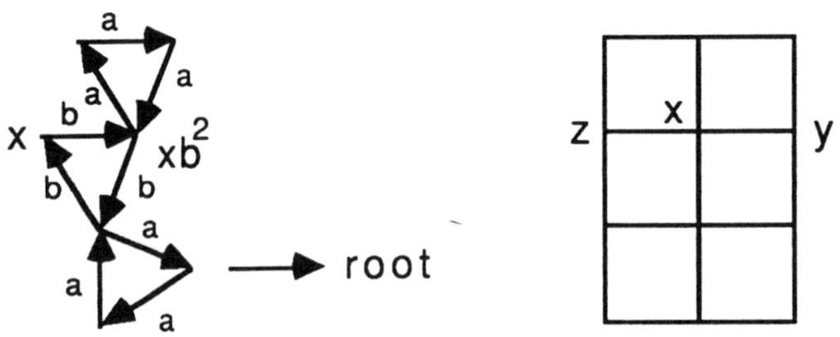

Figure 3: Proof of lemma 1: positioning the tiles surrounding the highest point

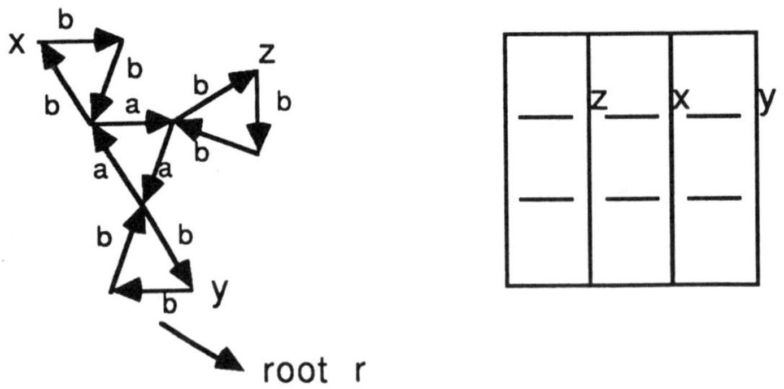

Figure 4: Proof of lemma 1: building a square with highest tiles

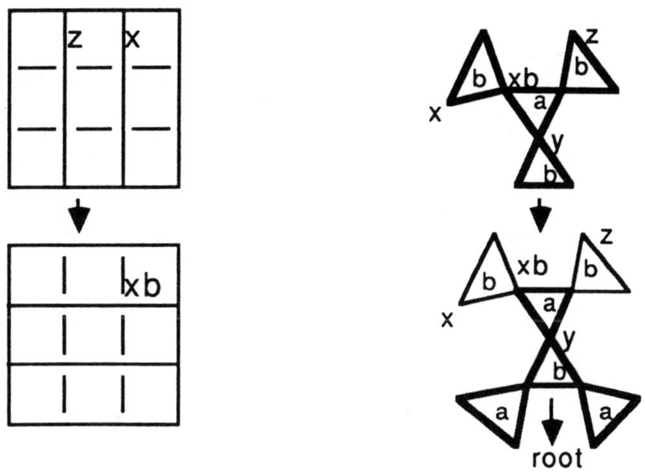

Figure 5: Proof of lemma 1: Removing interior maxima by changing the tiling of a square

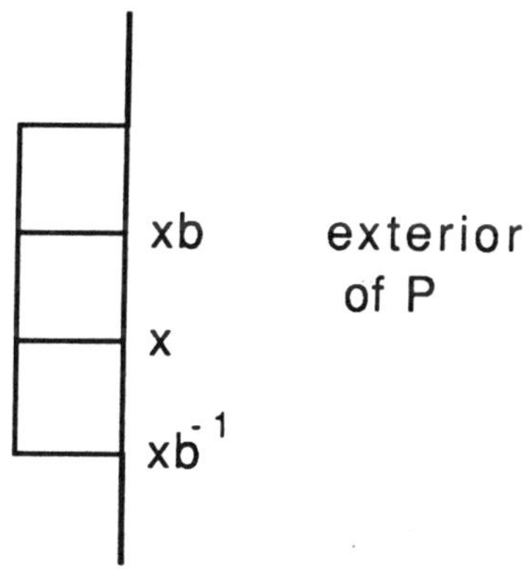

Figure 6: Tiling P: putting down the first tile

∂P. Take the tile T in P covering x and y (vertical if xy is a vertical segment, horizontal otherwise). Remove T from P.
Update ∂P, the labels and heights.
Until: P is tiled or some point of P is given two different labels (then P cannot be tiled).

It is easy to see that, since all the updates are local operations, the algorithm can be implemented so as to have linear running time.

If the tiles are $k \times 1$ and $1 \times l$ instead of 1×3 and 3×1, the algorithm can easily be generalized. The group to consider is $H = \langle a, b | a^k, b^l \rangle$, whose Cayley graph is a tree of alternating k-cycles and l-cycles. The height is similarly defined, as the distance to some arbitrary root (sufficiently far away). Given a highest boundary point, the lowest tiling must contain the tile which has x in the middle or co-middle of its long side.

Theorem 1 *A polygon of area n can be tiled by $1 \times l$ and $k \times 1$ tiles, or proved not to be tileable, in time linear in n.*

3 Tiling a polygon with $k \times l$ and $l \times k$ rectangles

We will only present the algorithm in the case $k = 2$ and $l = 3$, since generalizing the algorithm is easy from that special case.

3.1 The tiling group and its quotients

The two rectangular tiles define the relations $a^2b^3 = b^3a^2$ and $a^3b^2 = b^2a^3$, hence the tiling group is $G = \langle a, b | [a^2, b^3], [a^3, b^2] \rangle$. Let H be the quotient group $H = G/a^3, b^3 = \langle a, b | a^3, b^3 \rangle$, and K be the group $K = G/a^2, b^2 = \langle a, b | a^2, b^2 \rangle$. We have: $\mathbf{Z}^2 = G/[a, b]$. Given $w \in G$, let w', w'', w''' be the projections of w on H, K and $\mathbf{Z}^2$.

Fact 4 *The map $w \mapsto (w', w'', w''')$ is bijective.*

Defining a height function is now a more complex operation, since it apparently involves both quotient groups H and K. However, it turns out that using the labels in H already gives us "most" of the information that we need to construct a tiling.

3.2 Defining a height function

We label some arbitrary point of ∂P by e. Going around the boundary, we label each point of ∂P by an element of H. Rooting H at some point r sufficiently far away, we can define a height function as being the distance from r in the graph $\Gamma(H)$. A tiling of P extends the labellings and heights to all the points of P which are on the border of a tile (each tile has two interior points whose height is undefined).

Lemma 2 *If P is tileable, then there is a tiling of P whose maximum height h occurs either on the boundary or within distance 1 of the boundary (in which case there is a boundary point of height $h - 1$).*

Proof sketch: Let x be a highest interior point. Using the same elementary arguments as in section 2, it is easy to see that x cannot be at the corner or in the middle of the short side of a rectangle: x must be on the long side of a rectangle. Doing case-by-case analysis, we find that the tiling must contain a "block" formed by three adjacent rectangles, as in figure 7 (where x, x', y, y' are all highest points of the tiling) for vertical tiles, or a rotated version for horizontal tiles.

Definition 1 *Given a tiling of P, a* block *is a set of 3 adjacent tiles, forming a 3×6 or 6×3 rectangle, such that the points inside the block which are labelled are all highest in the tiling.*

What is there below that block? An elementary case-by-case analysis shows that there are only three cases, illustrated figure 8: either there is another block, lined up with the previous block, forming a 6×6 rectangle, or there is another block, shifted by 3, or there are two horizontal tiles, forming a 6×5 rectangle.

In the first case, we replace the 6 vertical rectangles by 6 horizontal rectangles, eliminating the highest points. In the second case, we look at what is below the second block. In the third case, we put the two horizontal tiles above the block, moving the block down by 2, which either eliminates the highest points or moves them closer to the boundary of P below the block. Iterating the process, we finally get a block which touches the boundary, and the highest point has been pushed to within distance 1 of ∂P. □.

3.3 Putting down the first tile

Let x be the highest point on the boundary ∂P. Assume that x is on a vertical part of ∂P (since x is maximum, it cannot be at a corner), and that the interior of P is to the right of x. One of its neighbors on ∂P is also highest, say y.

If the tile at x is a vertical rectangle, then it is easy to see that it has to be a rectangle covering x and y (see figure 9 – otherwise some interior point would have height 2 more than the height of x).

If it is horizontal, then the points along one of the long sides of the rectangle have height equal to 1 more than the height of x: they must therefore be highest points of P. As in the previous section, by doing case analysis to study the position of the tiles adjacent to that first tile, we see that there has to be a block, in two possible positions.

Lemma 3 *Let B be a vertical block of a tiling of P. The area to the right of B must*
1) contain some points in the exterior of P or
2) be covered by another block at the same level (figure 10a) or
3) be covered by two vertical rectangles (figure 10b) or
4) be covered by one vertical rectangle and one block shifted by 3 (figure 10c,c') or
5) be covered by two blocks shifted by 3 (figure 10d).

The proof is by inspection.

Up to rotating the 6×6 figure to change the tiling, we can assume that case a never occurs in the tiling. We will now apply the lemma repeatedly. Let B_0 be the block at x. We say that a block B is *reachable* from B_0 if there is a sequence of blocks $B_1, B_2, ..., B_m = B$ such that B_i is in the right neighborhood of B_{i-1} (as

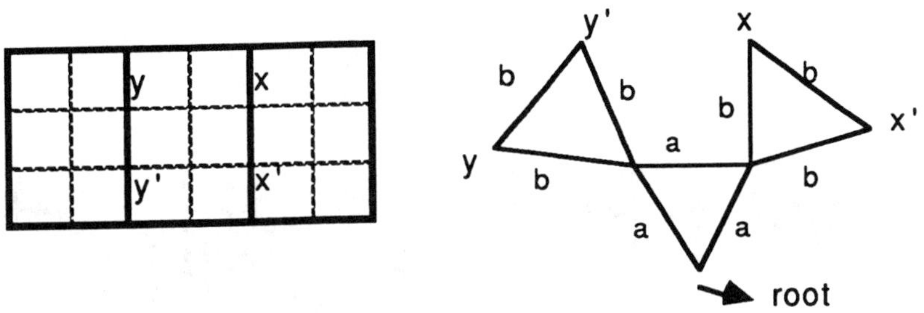

Figure 7: Interior highest points of a tiling

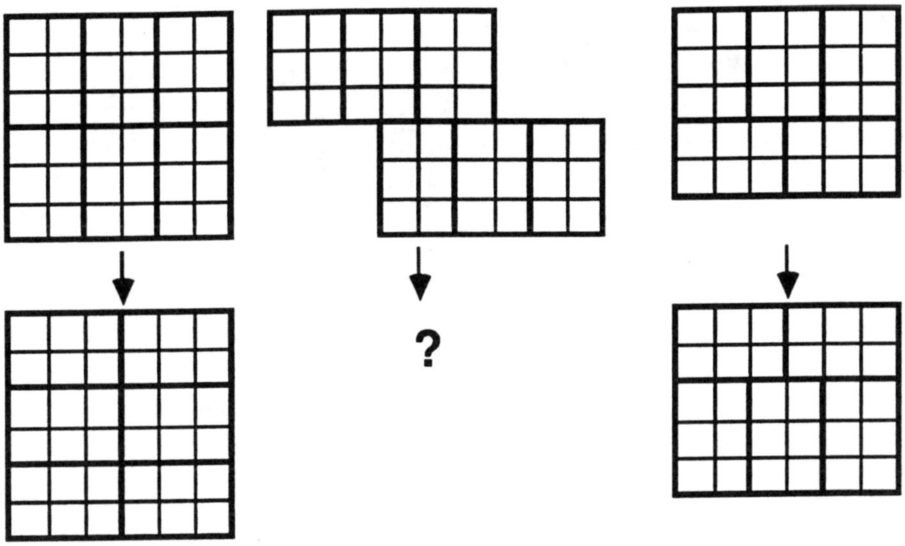

Figure 8: Pushing the highest point towards the boundary

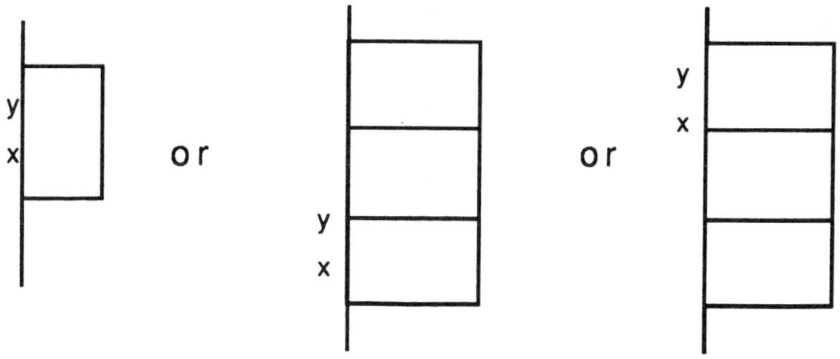

Figure 9: Putting down the first tile

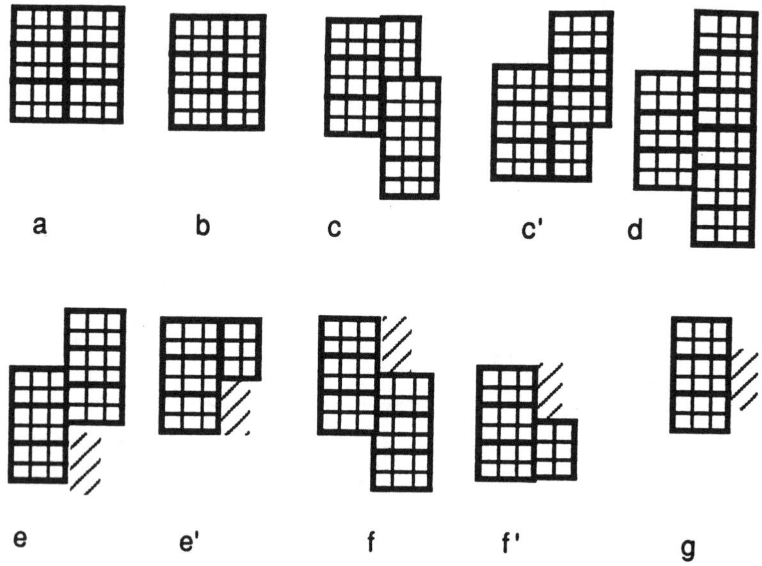

Figure 10: The right neighborhood of a block

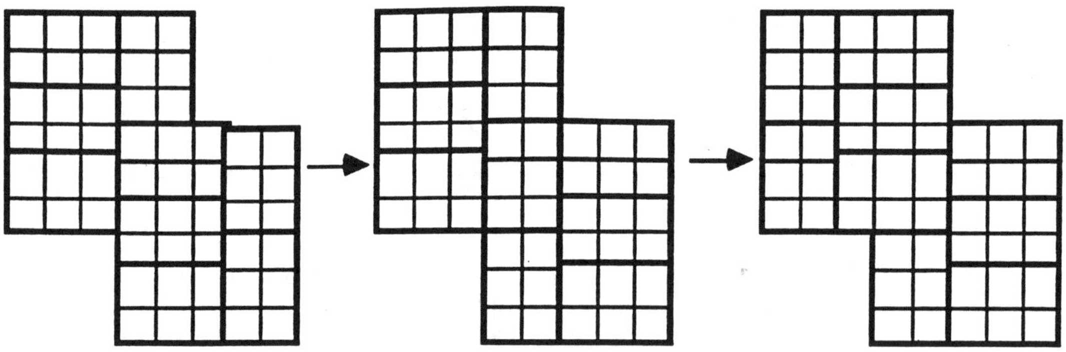

Figure 11: Pushing vertical tiles to the left

in cases c, c', e, e' and d of figure 10). We consider the set S of all blocks reachable from B_0 in the tiling.

If these blocks never touch the border ∂P outside B_0, the only cases which occur are b, c, c' and d. All the blocks farthest from B_0 have right neighborhoods as in figure 10b. Then we can "push" the vertical blocks towards the left (as in figure 11) and construct a new tiling of P such that the tile at x is vertical.

Otherwise, there must be a part S of the boundary ∂P reachable from x by a sequence of blocks, as in figure 12. We observe that in that tiling, there is a point x' of S with the same label as x in H.

Definition 2 *Given a tiling of P, a pair (x, x') of points of ∂P is* **tight** *if x and x' are both highest on ∂P, with the same label, and are linked by a sequence of blocks in the tiling.*

To have an algorithm similar to the one in the previous section, we would like to be able to say that we can always place a vertical tile at x, which would enable us to put down the first tile using local conditions only. Unfortunately tight pairs of points are a problem in this approach. However we will show that such pairs are actually independent of the tiling. In order to characterize them, we will use a different notion of height. Let $K = \langle a, b | a^2, b^2 \rangle$ be rooted at some arbitrary far away point r'. As we go around ∂P from e, points can also be labelled with a word $w \in K$. We define their K-height to be the distance from w to r' in the graph $\Gamma(K)$ (which in this case is just a line graph).

Lemma 4 *Given a tileable polygon P, a pair of points $x, x' \in \partial P$ is tight for some tiling of P iff the following 3 conditions are satisfied:*
1) x and x' are highest points of ∂P.
2) It is possible to construct a sequence of 3×6 rectangles (respectively, sequence of 6×3 rectangles) linking x to x', where every rectangle is to the right of (resp. below) the previous one and shifted by three, and all rectangles are inside P.
3)

$$|K\text{-}height(x) - K\text{-}height(x')| =$$

$$\begin{cases} 2|z - z'|/3 & \text{in case of figure 12} \\ 2|z - z'|/3 - 1 & \text{in case of figure 13} \end{cases}$$

where z and z' are the x-coordinates (resp. y-coordinates) of x and x' in $\mathbf{Z}^2$.

Proof idea: If (x, x') is tight for some tiling, then the three conditions of the lemma are clearly satisfied.

Conversely, given (x, x') which satisfy the three conditions of the lemma, and given a tiling of P, consider a shortest path from x to x' in P. One can prove that the path must only traverse horizontal rectangles of the tiling (otherwise the K-height would not have time to change by $2|z - z'|/3 - 1$). It is possible to show that those horizontal rectangles must be part of blocks, which form a sequence. Therefore (x, x') is tight □.

Consequence 1 *If (x, x') is tight for some tiling of P, then (x, x') is tight for every tiling of P.*

The three conditions of the lemma being independent of the tiling, can be checked even when a tiling of P is not known.

Finally, this gives us a criterion for putting down the first tile of the tiling: if the maximum x of ∂P is on a vertical side, then the first tile is always a vertical tile at x, except if there is x' such that (x, x') is tight: then the first tile at x must be horizontal (and its exact position is determined by whether the K-height increases or decreases when going from x to x').

3.4 A polynomial-time algorithm

The analysis of the previous subsection give a polynomial time algorithm for deciding whether a polygon can be tiled by 2×3 and 3×2 tiles, and giving a tiling if it exists. A high-level description follows.

Input: A polygon P with vertical and horizontal edges of integral lengths.
Initialization: Label the vertices of ∂P with words of H and of K; calculate their height and K-height.
Repeat: Take $x \in \partial P$ of maximum height. If there exists $y \in \partial P$ such that (x, y) is tight, then place a horizontal tile at x accordingly; else place a vertical tile at x appropriately.
Update P, ∂P, H-labels and heights, K-labels and K-heights.
Until: P is tiled or there is a conflict in the labels (in which case P is not tileable).

The exact running time of the algorithm depends on the implementation. With a little bit of work, one can see that there is an implementation for which the algorithm takes quadratic time.

For general $k \times l$ rectangles (with the two tile types $k \times l$ and $l \times k$), the algorithm can be generalized to yield a quadratic-time algorithm.

Theorem 2 *Given a polygon of area n, there is an algorithm for tiling the polygon with $k \times l$ and $l \times k$ tiles or proving that it is not tileable, with running time $O(n^2)$.*

We conjecture that the running time can be improved.

4 Properties of rectangle tilings

As a corollary of the above constructions we find:

Theorem 3 *Any two tilings of P by $m \times 1$ and $1 \times n$ tiles are obtained from one another by "rotations" of the form illustrated figure 14. That is, m vertical $1 \times n$ tiles can be replaced by n horizontal $m \times 1$ tiles and conversely.*

Any two tilings of P by 2×3 and 3×2 tiles are obtainable from one another by rotations of the form illustrated figure 15.

It is not hard to show that the distance in terms of the number of rotations between two tilings of P, in either of the above cases, is at most $O(n^{3/2})$ for area n. Furthermore, figure 16 shows two tilings of a $2k \times 3k$ square by 2×1 and 1×3 tiles having distance

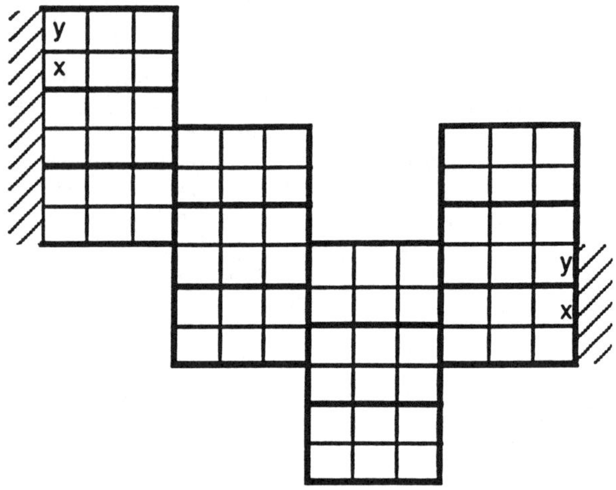

Figure 12: Reaching the boundary with a sequence of blocks

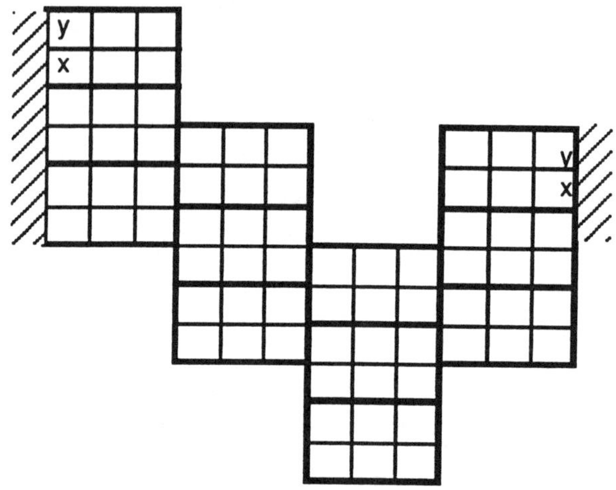

Figure 13: Chain of blocks

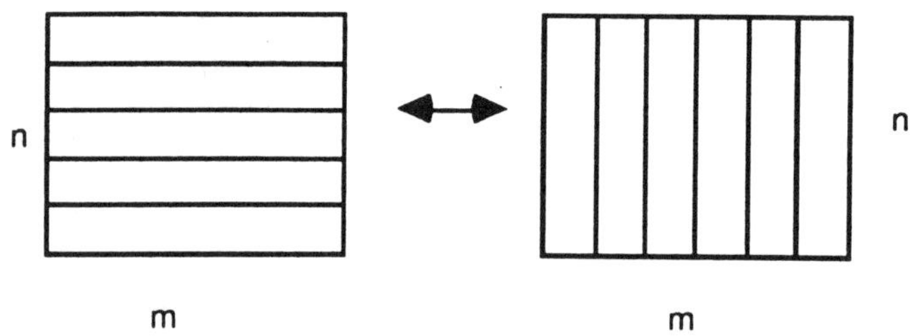

Figure 14: rotations for transforming $m \times 1$, $1 \times n$ tilings

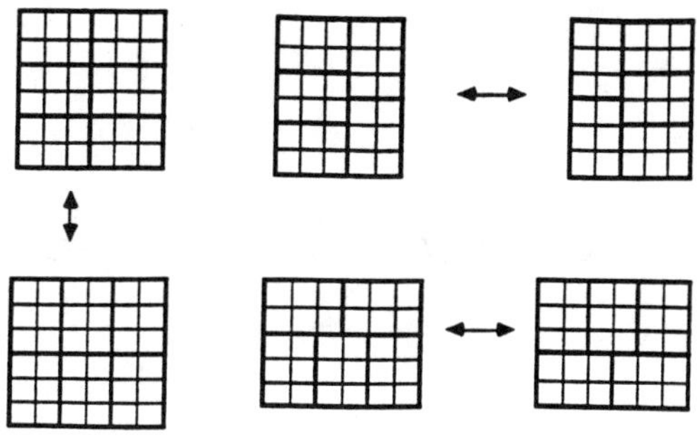

Figure 15: rotations for transforming 3 × 2 tilings

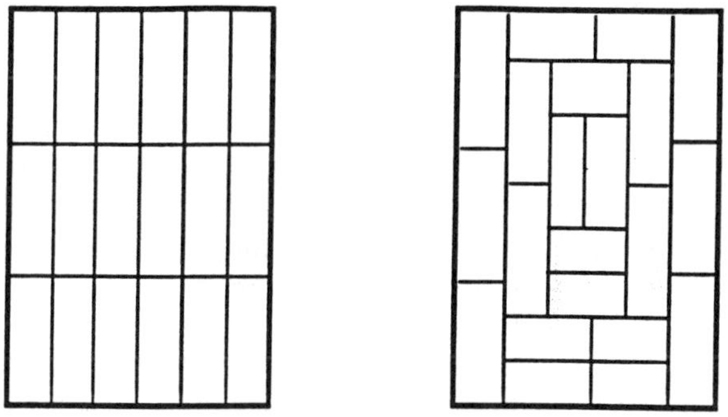

Figure 16: Two tiling which are "far apart"

$\Theta(k^3)$. This distance can be calculated by integrating the difference in height function over the tilings. Each rotation decreases the integral by a constant amount only.

References

[1] William P. Thurston, "Conway's Tiling Groups", *Am. Math. Monthly*, Oct. 1990, pp. 757-773.

[2] J.M.Robson, "Sur le pavage de figures du plan par des barres", *Actes des Journées Polyominos et Pavages*, June 1991, pp. 95-103.

[3] D.Beauquier, M.Nivat, "Pavages de pièces par h_m et v_n",*Actes des Journées Polyominos et Pavages*, June 1991, pp. 45-60.

[4] Eric Remila, "Trois algorithmes de pavages par h_m et v_n", *Actes des Journées Polyominos et Pavages*, June 1991, pp. 83-94.

[5] Fran Berman, David Johnson, Tom Leighton, Peter W. Shor, Larry Snyder, "Generalized Planar Matching", *Journal of Algorithms* 11, no 2, 1990, pp. 153-184.

Mick Gets Some (the Odds Are on His Side)

V. Chvátal

Computer Science Department
Rutgers University
New Brunswick, NJ 08903, USA

B.Reed

Forschungsinstitut f. Diskrete Mathematik
Universität Bonn
Bonn, D-5300 Germany

Abstract

Consider a randomly generated boolean formula F (in the conjunctive normal form) with m clauses of size k over n variables; k is fixed at any value greater than 1, but n tends to ininity and $m = (1 + o(1))cn$ for some c depending only on k. It is easy to see that F is unsatisfiable with probability $1 - o(1)$ whenever $c > (\ln 2)2^k$; we complement this observation by proving that F is satisfiable with probability $1 - o(1)$ whenever $c < (0.25)2^k/k$; in fact, we present a linear-time algorithm that satisfies F with probability $1 - o(1)$. (This result is a continuation of work by Chao and Franco.) In addition, we establish a threshold for 2-SAT: if $k = 2$ then F is satisfiable with probability $1 - o(1)$ whenever $c < 1$ and unsatisfiable with probability $1 - o(1)$ whenever $c > 1$.

0 Introduction

A *truth assignment* is a mapping f that assigns 0 or 1 to each variable in its domain. The *complement* $\overline{x}$ of each such variable x is defined by $f(\overline{x}) = 1 - f(x)$ for all truth assignments f; both x and $\overline{x}$ are called *literals*. A *clause* is a set of (distinct) literals and a *formula* is a family of (not necessarily distinct) clauses. A truth assignment f *satisfies* a clause C if and only if $f(w) = 1$ for at least one literal w in C; the assignment *satisfies* a formula F if and only if it satisfies every clause in F. (Thus a formula is precisely that which is often called a Boolean expression in the conjunctive normal form.) A formula is called *satisfiable* if it is satisfied by at least one truth assignment; otherwise it is called *unsatisfiable*.

Let us call a clause C *ordinary* if there is no variable x such that both x and $\overline{x}$ belong to C; let n, m, k be positive integers and let X be a set of size n. The *random formula with m clauses of size k over n variables* consists of independent random variables $C_1, C_2, \ldots, C_m$ such that each C_i is distributed uniformly over the $\binom{n}{k}2^k$ ordinary clauses of size k with variables coming from X.

Throughout, we reserve n for the number of variables, m for the number of clauses, k for the clause size, and c for any positive constant depending only on k; the asymptotic symbol $o(1)$ will always mean a quantity tending to zero as n tends to infinity.

The expected number of truth assignments that satisfy a random formula is $2^n(1 - 2^{-k})^m$; hence a random formula with $(1 + o(1))cn$ clauses of size k over n variables such that

$$c > (\ln 2) \cdot 2^k \tag{1}$$

is unsatisfiable with probability $1 - o(1)$. This observation has been made by Franco and Paull [6], by Simon et al. [8], by Chvátal and Szemerédi [3], and possibly by others; our purpose is to complement it by the following result.

THEOREM 1. If $k \geq 2$ then a random formula with $(1 + o(1))cn$ clauses of size k over n variables such that

$$c < \frac{1}{4} \cdot \frac{2^k}{k} \tag{2}$$

is satisfiable with probability $1 - o(1)$. □

(The assumption that $k \geq 2$ is crucial: it is an easy exercise to show that, with probability $1 - o(1)$, a random formula with $m(n)$ clauses of size one over n variables is unsatisfiable whenever $m(n)n^{-1/2} \to \infty$ and satisfiable whenever $m(n)n^{-1/2} \to 0$.)

In fact, we prove something better than Theorem 1: rather than merely establishing that the random formula is satisfiable with probability $1 - o(1)$, we show how to find quickly an actual truth assignment that satisfies it with probability $1 - o(1)$. Our algorithm, which we call SC, will be described in the next section;

0-8186-2900-2/92 $3.00 © 1992 IEEE

it runs in time $O(n + km)$, linear in the size of the input, and its performance guarantee goes as follows.

THEOREM 2. Let k be an integer such that $k \geq 3$ and let c be a nonnegative number such that

$$c < \frac{1}{8}\left(\frac{k-1}{k-3}\right)^{k-3} \frac{k-1}{k-2} \cdot \frac{2^k}{k}. \qquad (3)$$

(We adopt the convention that $0^0 = 1$, and so the right-hand side of (3) equals 2/3 when $k = 3$.) Then algorithm SC, given a random formula with $(1 + o(1))cn$ clauses of size k over n variables, finds a truth assignment that satisfies this formula with probability $1 - o(1)$. □

Since

$$\left(\frac{k-3}{k-1}\right)^{k-3} \frac{k-2}{k-1} < e^{-2}\frac{(k-1)(k-2)}{(k-3)^2} \leq 3e^{-2} < \frac{1}{2}$$

whenever $k \geq 5$, Theorem 2 implies Theorem 1 except when $k = 2$. We shall deal with the exceptional case separately.

THEOREM 3. A random formula with $(1+o(1))cn$ clauses of size two over n variables such that

$$c < 1$$

is satifiable with probability $1 - o(1)$. □

We do not have to worry about finding quickly an actual truth assignment that satisfies the random formula in Theorem 3 with probability $1-o(1)$: for every satisfiable formula F with $k = 2$, a truth assignment satifying F can be found in time polynomial in the size of the input. This has been pointed out by Cook [4]; later on, two linear-time algorithms were designed by Even, Itai and Shamir [5] and by Aspvall, Plass, and Tarjan [1].

Incidentally, now we may replace the proportionality constant 1/4 in (2) by 3/8 : the trick is to appeal to Theorem 2 in case $k \geq 4$ and to Theorem 3 (with one literal removed at random from each clause when $k = 3$) in case $k \leq 3$. However, we are not concerned with maximizing the proportionality constant: as we see it, the more interesting question is whether the gap between the two orders of magnitude, 2^k in (1) for unsatisfiability and $2^k/k$ in (2) for satisfiability, can be narrowed.

Perhaps this gap can be closed completely in the sense that, for every integer k greater than 1, there is a constant c_k such that a random formula with $(1 + o(1))cn$ clauses of size k over n variables is satisfiable with probability $1 - o(1)$ whenever $c < c_k$ and unsatisfiable with probability $1-o(1)$ whenever $c > c_k$. However, we can prove this only when $k = 2$.

THEOREM 4. A random formula with $(1+o(1))cn$ clauses of size two over n variables such that

$$c > 1$$

is unsatisfiable with probability $1 - o(1)$. □

After this paper was written, Valerie King informed us that our Theorems 3 and 4 were obtained independently by Goerdt [7] and by de la Vega [11].

Our work on Theorem 2 was inspired by earlier work of Chao and Franco [2]. They analyzed two algorithms, which they call UC and GUC, that attempt to satisfy a prescribed formula. (Our algorithm SC is a close relative of UC and GUC.) Two of their results pertaining to our Theorem 2 go as follows.

[2, Theorem 4]: Let k be an integer such that $k \geq 3$ and let c be a positive number such that

$$c < \frac{1}{2}\left(\frac{k-1}{k-2}\right)^{k-2} \cdot \frac{2^k}{k}.$$

Then algorithm UC, given a random formula with $(1+o(1))cn$ clauses of size k over n variables, finds a truth assignment that satisfies this formula with probability at least $\varepsilon + o(1)$ for some positive ε. □

[2, Theorem 6]: Let k be an integer such that $4 \leq k \leq 40$ and let c be a positive number such that

$$c < 0.46125\left(\frac{k-1}{k-2}\right)^{k-2} \cdot \frac{2^k}{k+1} - 1.$$

Then algorithm GUC, given a random formula with $(1 + o(1))cn$ clauses of size k over n variables, finds a truth assignment that satisfies this formula with probability $1 - o(1)$. □

(The notation that Chao and Franco use in [2] differs from ours: their r is our n and their n is our m. Our choice was motivated by the convention of graph and hypergraph theory, where n usually stands for the number of vertices and m stands for the number of edges.)

1 Algorithms

The algorithms UC, GUC, and SC follow the same scheme, where the truth assignment is constructed in n iterations with precisely one variable per iteration set at 1 or 0. Setting the value of a literal w in a formula F at 1 amounts to removing from F all the clauses that contain w and deleting $\overline{w}$ from all the clauses that contain $\overline{w}$. We shall let $F[w]$ denote the resulting formula; with this notation, the common scheme of UC, GUC, and SC can be described as follows:

> $F_0 = F$;
> **for** $t = 1$ to n **do**
> choose a literal w_t whose value has not yet been set;
> $w_t = 1; F_t = F_{t-1}[w_t]$
> **end**

The three algorithms differ only in their choice of w_t.

Trivially, the truth assignment constructed by this scheme satisfies F if an only if F_n includes no null clause (a clause of size zero); trivially, a null clause that appears in some F_t will persist in $F_{t+1}, \ldots, F_n$. These observations suggest a policy for choosing w_t: if F_{t-1} includes a clause C of size one, say $C = \{v\}$, then we must set $v = 1$ at some time in the future in order to satisfy F, and so we may just as well choose $w_t = v$ now. That is what algorithm UC (short for unit clause) does: w_t is a literal that occurs in a clause of size one in F_{t-1} if such a clause is present and w_t is chosen arbitrarily otherwise. Thus algorithm UC evades the danger of a null clause at the last moment; algorithm GUC (short for generalized UC) evades it already from far away: there, w_t is a literal that occurs in a clause of the smallest size in F_{t-1}. Our algorithm SC (short for small clause) comes between the two: we consider a clause dangerous if and only if its size is at most two and we consider clauses of size one more dangerous than clauses of size two. Thus we let w_t be a literal that occurs in a clause of size one in F_{t-1}; if no such clause is present then we let w_t be a literal that occurs in a clause of size two in F_{t-1}; if no clause of size one or two is present in F_{t-1} then we choose w_t arbitrarily.

Actually, these informal decriptions of UC, GUC, and SC are not quite correct: ties in the choice of w_t have to be broken with care in order to justify the probabilistic performance guarantees. Chao and Franco use randomization in their choice of w_t in both UC and GUC; so do we in SC, but our way is slightly different from theirs.

Let us assume that the input is represented by a matrix with m rows and k columns, whose i-th row lists the k literals that appear in the i-th clause of F. The output will be represented by an array of length n that lists the values of the n variables; to initialize this array, we fill each of its n cells with a symbol signifying that the value of the variable has not yet been set.

To keep the running time within $O(n + km)$, we first construct $2n$ linked lists that enumerate, for each of the $2n$ literals w, all the clauses that contain w; each of these clauses is represented simply by a pointer to the corresponding row of the input matrix. These linked lists will be called *incidence lists.* With each $i = 1, 2, \ldots, m$, we associate an integer *size*$[i]$ which monitors the current size of the i-th input clause (and therefore is initialized as k) and a bit *sat*$[i]$ which tells us whether the i-th input clause has been satisfied (and therefore is initialized as *false*). In addition, we make use of two stacks: STACK1 lists all the clauses whose current size is 1 (and possibly also some clauses of size 0) and STACK2 lists all the clauses whose current size is 2 (and possibly also some clauses of size at most 1). Again, each clause on these stacks is represented by a pointer to the corresponding row of the input matrix.

To choose w_t, we first attempt to find a clause of size 1 in F_{t-1} by popping STACK1 until an i with *size*$[i] = 1$ is found or the stack becomes empty; if there is no such clause, then we attempt to find a clause of size 2 in F_{t-1} by popping STACK2 until an i with *size*$[i] = 2$ is found or the stack becomes empty. If a clause of size 1 or 2 is found, then we let w_t be a randomly chosen entry (from the uniform distribution) in the corresponding row of the input matrix whose value has not yet been set; else we let w_t be the first variable in the output array whose value has not yet been set. (In the latter case, w_t can be found by moving a pointer through the output array, starting from the position where it has been left previously.)

To replace F_{t-1} by F_t, we first scan the incidence list of w and set *sat*$[i]$ = *true* for each i on this list. Then we scan the incidence list of $\overline{w}$ and, for each i on this list such that *sat*$[i]$ = *false*, we decrement *size*$[i]$ by 1; if *size*$[i]$ drops to 2, then we push i on STACK2; if *size*$[i]$ drops to 1 then we push i on STACK1. (If *size*$[i]$ drops to 0 then we might just as well return a failure message and stop. However, the analysis is smoother if we carry on even in these circumstances.)

For the proof of Theorem 2, it is crucial to note that SC maintains randomness in the following sense: if C is any clause of size s in F_{t-1} other than the small clause from which w_t is selected then $w_t \epsilon C$ with probability $s/2(n-t+1)$ and $\overline{w}_t \epsilon C$ with probability $s/2(n-t+1)$ independently of what happens between w_t and all the remaining clauses. (To see this, it may help to imagine all the entries of the input matrix concealed in the beginning and all the entries equal to w_j or $\overline{w}_j$ disclosed as soon as w_j is selected.) This invariant would be also maintained if we first preprocessed the input by permuting the k entries in each row at random and independently of all the other rows to ensure that the rows are independent identically distributed random variables with the distribution uniform over its $n(n-1)\dots(n-k+1)2^k$ possible values; then we could choose each w_t from a small clause simply as the first entry in the corresponding row of the input matrix whose value has not yet been set. The resulting implementation may be easier to see through as it resorts to randomization only in the preprocessing step and proceeds in a deterministic fashion afterwards; the implementation we chose is marginally faster.

The analysis of SC in our proof of Theorem 2 applies equally well to the implementation of GUC where k stacks of clauses are used to select w_t (and whose running time is also $O(n+km)$). Stating Theorem 2 as we do highlights the features of GUC that suffice to guarantee a high rate of success on random inputs with

$$(1+o(1))\gamma \cdot \frac{2^k}{k} n$$

clauses of size k over n variables for some positive γ independent of k. In this context, it may be interesting to note that UC has no chance of success at a comparable rate: for every choice of a positive integer k and a positive number c there is a positive ε such that UC, given a random input with $(1+o(1))cn$ claues of size k over n variables, fails with probability at least $\varepsilon + o(1)$. (The expected number of iterations in which precisely two new clauses of size one appear is at least δn for some positive δ and so their actual number a is at least $\delta n/2$ with probability greater than $\delta/2$. The probability that the two new clauses of size one clash in none of these a iterations is at most $e^{-\delta/4}$.)

2 Analysis

PROOF OF THEOREM 2. Let us begin by explaining where the right-hand side of (3) comes from: keeping c below this bound amounts to keeping the expected number of input clauses that shrink to size two after precisely t iterations below 1 for all $t = 1, 2, \dots, n$. More precisely, let p_t denote the probability that a fixed input clause shrinks to size two after precisely t iterations and let ε be any positive number such that

$$\frac{1+\varepsilon}{1-2\varepsilon} c < \frac{1}{8} \left(\frac{k-1}{k-3}\right)^{k-3} \frac{k-1}{k-2} \cdot \frac{2^k}{k}.$$

Since

$$p_t = \frac{\binom{t-1}{k-3}\binom{n-t}{2}}{\binom{n}{k}} \cdot \frac{1}{2^{k-2}} = \frac{\binom{t-1}{k-3}\binom{n-t}{2}}{\binom{n-1}{k-1}} \cdot \frac{k}{2^{k-2}n},$$

p_t is maximized when

$$\frac{k-3}{k-1} n \le t \le \frac{k-3}{k-1} n + 1,$$

and so

$$p_t \le (1+\varepsilon)\binom{k-1}{2}\left(\frac{k-3}{k-1}\right)^{k-3}\left(\frac{2}{k-1}\right)^2 \cdot \frac{k}{2^{k-2}n}$$

$$< \frac{1-\varepsilon}{m}$$

for all sufficiently large n.

The actual number a_t of input clauses that shrink to size two after precisely t iterations is likely to differ from its expected value by quite large amounts for quite a few values of t. Nevertheless, the average of the fluctuating values of a_t over every sufficiently large block of values of t is likely to stay below 1: we claim that, with probability $1 - o(1)$,

$$\sum_{t=r}^{s} a_t \le s - r \text{ whenever } s - r \ge 5\varepsilon^{-2} \ln n.$$

To justify this claim, we rely on the well-known inequality

$$\sum_{i \ge x} \binom{m}{i} p^i (1-p)^{m-i} \le \left(\frac{pm}{x}\right)^x \left(\frac{m-pm}{m-x}\right)^{m-x} \tag{4}$$

which implies that

$$\sum_{i \ge x} \binom{m}{i} p^i (1-p)^{m-i} \le \left(\frac{pm}{x}\right)^x e^{x-pm} \le \exp\left(-\frac{\varepsilon^2 x}{2}\right)$$

whenever $pm \le (1-\varepsilon)x$. In particular, if r and s are fixed so that $1 \le r \le s \le n$ then the probability of

$$\sum_{t=r}^{s} a_t \ge s - r + 1$$

is at most $\exp(-\varepsilon^2(s-r+1)/2)$, which is $o(n^{-2})$ whenever $s-r \geq 5\varepsilon^{-2}\ln n$; since there are $\binom{n+1}{2}$ choices of r and s, the desired conclusion follows.

In addition, the individual values of a_t are likely to be 0 or 1 for all t close enough to n: we claim that, with probability $1-o(1)$,

$$a_t \leq 1 \text{ whenever } n - n^{3/4} < t \leq n.$$

To justify this claim, note first that

$$p_t m = O\left(\left(\frac{n-t}{n}\right)^2\right).$$

Again, we shall rely on (4), which implies that

$$\sum_{i\geq 2}\binom{m}{i}p^i(1-p)^{m-i} \leq \left(\frac{epm}{2}\right)^2.$$

In particular, if t is fixed then the probability of $a_t \geq 2$ is $O(((n-t)/n)^4)$; since there are at most $1+n^{3/4}$ choices of t with $n-n^{3/4} < t \leq n$, the desired conclusion follows.

Now observe that the number of clauses of size one or two in F_t is at most b_t with $b_0, b_1, \ldots, b_n$ defined recursively by

$$b_0 = 0 \text{ and } b_s = \max\{b_{s-1}-1, 0\} + a_s \text{ whenever } s \geq 1.$$

An easy induction on s shows that

$$b_s \leq 1 + \max_r \sum_{t=r}^{s}(a_t - 1)$$

(we may set $r = s$ if $b_{s-1} = 0$ and let r be the maximizer for b_{s-1} otherwise). Hence, with probability $1-o(1)$,

$$b_t \leq 5\varepsilon^{-2}\ln n \text{ for all } t \tag{5}$$

and

$$b_t \leq 1 \text{ whenever } n - n^{2/3} \leq t \leq n. \tag{6}$$

We shall complete the proof by showing that, with probability $1-o(1)$, the clauses of size at most two in F_t remain distributed in a certain special way throughout the run of the algorithm. Let us say that F_t is *well-behaved* if

(i) the multigraph whose vertices are the variables in F_t and whose edges are the clauses of size two in F_t contains no cycles (including cycles of length two),

(ii) for each component Q of this multigraph (including the single-vertex components) there is at most one clause C of size one in F_t such that the variable involved in C is a vertex of Q,

(iii) there are no clauses of size zero in F_t.

We propose to prove that F_t remains well-behaved throughout the run of the algorithm with probability $1-o(1)$.

For this purpose, let G_t denote the formula consisting of all the clauses of size at most two in F_t, let V_t denote the set of variables involved in the clauses of $G_{t-1}[w_t]$, and let N_t denote the set of clauses of size two that appear in $G_t - G_{t-1}$. Now consider the following events.

C_t: the multigraph formed by N_t contains a cycle.

P_t: the multigraph formed by N_t contains a path with both endpoints in V_t.

If G_t is well-behaved then $G_{t-1}[w_t]$ is well-behaved; hence F_t ceases to be well-behaved if and only if at least one of events C_t, P_t takes place. It follows that F_j is not well-behaved with probability at most

$$\sum_{t=1}^{j}\text{Prob}(C_t) + \sum_{t=1}^{j}\text{Prob}(P_t).$$

To bound this quantity from above, consider events

B_t: $|V_t| \leq 2b$ and $|N_t| \leq b$ with $b = 5\varepsilon^{-2}\ln n$.

From (5), we have

$$\text{Prob}\,(B_1 B_2 \ldots B_n) = 1 - o(1)\,;$$

in addition,

$$\text{Prob}\,(C_t|B_t) \leq \sum_{i=2}^{n-t}(n-t)^i b^i \binom{n-t}{2}^{-i} < \frac{8b^2}{(n-t-1)^2}$$

and

$$\text{Prob}\,(P_t|B_t) \leq \sum_{i=1}^{n-t-1}(2b)^2(n-t)^{i-1}b^i\binom{n-t}{2}^{-i} < \frac{16b^3}{(n-t)(n-t-1)}$$

whenever $n-t-1 \geq 4b$. Setting $j = n - \lfloor n^{2/3} \rfloor$ we conclude that F_j is well-behaved with probability $1-o(1)$. If (6) holds then F_j includes at most one clause of size at most two and at most one new clause of size at most two appears in each subsequent iteration. Hence F_t remains well-behaved throughout $t = j+1, j+2, \ldots, n$ with probability $1-o(1)$. □

PROOF OF THEOREM 3. By a *bicycle*, we shall mean a formula with (at least two) distinct variables $x_1, x_2, \ldots, x_s$ and clauses $C_0, C_1, \ldots, C_s$ that have the following structure: there are literals $w_1, w_2 \ldots, w_s$ such that each w_r is x_r or $\overline{x}_r$, each C_r with $0 < r < s$ is $\{\overline{w}_r, w_{r+1}\}$, and $C_0 = \{u, w_1\}$, $C_s = \{\overline{w}_s, v\}$ with literals u, v chosen from $x_1, x_2, \ldots, x_s, \overline{x}_1, \overline{x}_2, \ldots, \overline{x}_s$. We propose to show that

(i) a random formula with $(1+o(1))cn$ clauses of size two over n variables such that $c < 1$ contains a bicycle with probability $o(1)$,

(ii) every unsatisfiable formula with all clauses of size two contains a bicycle.

To prove (i), let p denote the probability that a random formula with m clauses of size two over n variables contains a bicycle. Since

$$p \leq \sum_{s=2}^{n} n^s 2^s (2s)^2 m^{s+1} \left(\frac{1}{4\binom{n}{2}}\right)^{s+1} = \frac{2m}{n(n-1)} \sum_{s=2}^{n} s^2 \left(\frac{m}{n-1}\right)^s,$$

we have $p = O(n^{-1})$ whenever $m = (1+o(1))cn$ with $c < 1$.

To prove (ii), we appeal to the work of Aspvall, Plass, and Tarjan [1]. They associate a directed graph $G(F)$ with every formula F whose clauses have size two. The vertices of $G(F)$ are the $2n$ literals arising from the n variables of F; each clause$\{u, v\}$ in F gives rise to directed edges $\overline{u} \to v$ and $\overline{v} \to u$ in $G(F)$. Theorem 1 of [1] asserts that F is unsatisfiable if and only if some variable and its complement belong to the same strongly connected component of $G(F)$. In particular, if F is unsatisfiable then $G(F)$ contains a directed walk $w_0 w_1 \ldots w_i$ such that $w_0 = w_i$ and $w_t = \overline{w}_0$ for some t. Choosing a walk that minimizes t, we find that all the literals $w_1, w_2, \ldots, w_t$ are distinct and none of them is the complement of another. Let s be the largest subscript such that all the literals $w_1, w_2, \ldots, w_s$ are distinct and none of them is the complement of another. Then the clauses $C_0, C_1, \ldots, C_s$ with $C_r = \{\overline{w}_r, w_{r+1}\}$ form a bicycle. □

PROOF OF THEOREM 4. First, consider just a set of n variables; let t be an integer depending on n in such a way that

$$t/\log n \to \infty \quad \text{but} \quad t/n^{1/9} \to 0. \tag{7}$$

By a *snake*, we shall mean a sequence of distinct literals $w_1, w_2, \ldots, w_s$ with $s = 2t - 1$ such that no w_i is the complement of another. With each snake A, we shall associate the set F_A of $s+1$ clauses $\{\overline{w}_r, w_{r+1}\}$, $0 \leq r \leq s$, such that $w_0 = w_{s+1} = \overline{w}_t$. Note that F_A is unsatifiable: every truth assignment that satisfies F_A must have $w_i \leq w_j$ whenever $i \leq j$, and so it must have $\overline{w}_t = w_0 \leq w_t \leq w_{2t} = \overline{w}_t$.

Now let $p_i(n)$ denote the probability that, for a fixed snake A and a snake B chosen at random from the uniform distribution, sets F_A and F_B share precisely i clauses. A crucial part of our argument is the claim that, for all sufficiently large n,

$$p_i(n) < \frac{1300t^9}{n} \left(\frac{1}{2n}\right)^i \tag{8}$$

whenever $1 \leq i \leq t-1$ and

$$p_i(n) < 18tn \left(\frac{1}{2n}\right)^i \tag{9}$$

whenever $1 \leq i \leq 2t$.

In justifying this claim, it will be convenient to view F_A as a graph with vertices $x_1, x_2, \ldots, x_s$ (each x_r being the variable such that w_r is x_r or $\overline{x}_r$) and edges $x_r x_{r+1}$, $0 \leq r \leq s$, such that $x_0 = x_{s+1} = x_t$. When F_A and F_B are both viewed as graphs, we let F_{AB} denote their intersection with all isolated vertices removed; for a fixed snake A, we let $N(i,j)$ denote the number of snakes B such that F_{AB} has i edges and j vertices. To obtain an upper bound on $N(i,j)$, we set up a production line that manufactures all the snakes counted by $N(i,j)$: (i) choose j terms of A for membership in F_{AB}, (ii) choose j terms of B for membership in F_{AB}, (iii) assign values to the j terms in $B \cap F_{AB}$, (iv) assign values to the $s - j$ terms in $B - F_{AB}$. As for (i), members of F_{AB} can be selected from A by first deciding whether $x_0 x_1$ belongs to F_{AB} or not and then placing a marker at each x_r with $1 \leq r \leq s$ such that precisely one of $x_{r-1}x_r$ and $x_r x_{r+1}$ belongs to F_{AB}. Observing that there are at least $2(j-i)-1$ and at most $2(j-i)+2$ markers, we conclude that there are at most $2\binom{s+3}{2j-2i+2}$ choices in (i), and at most that many choices in (ii). To analyze (iii), let k denote the number of connected components in F_{AB}. Components that are paths may be mixed and matched with their counterparts in up to $k!$ ways and each of these components may flip. In addition, there may be a unique component that is not a path; this component may be mapped onto its counterpart in at most $2t$ ways. We conclude that there are at most $tk!\,2^k$ choices in (iii). Trivially, there are at most $(2n)^{s-j}$ choices in (iv).

If $1 \le i \le t-1$ then $k = j - i$; hence

$$N(i,j) \le 4\binom{2t+2}{2j-2i+2}^2 t(j-i)!\, 2^{j-i}(2n)^{s-j}$$
$$\le 4t(2t+2)^{4(j-i)+4}\, 2^{j-i}(2n)^{s-j}$$

and

$$\begin{aligned} p_i(n) &\le \frac{1}{\binom{n}{s} s! 2^s} \sum_{j \ge i+1} N(i,j) \\ &< \frac{5t(2t+2)^4}{(2n)^i} \sum_{j\ge i+1} \left(\frac{(2t+2)^4}{n}\right)^{j-i} \\ &< \frac{1300t^9}{n}\left(\frac{1}{2n}\right)^i, \end{aligned}$$

which is (8). If the upper bound on i is dropped then we can maintain only $k \le j - i + 2$; now

$$N(i,j) \le 4\binom{2t+2}{2j-2i+2}^2 t(j-i+2)!\, 2^{j-i+2}(2n)^{s-j}$$
$$\le 16t(2t+2)^{4(j-i)+4} 2^{j-i}(2n)^{s-j}$$

and

$$\begin{aligned} p_i(n) &\le \frac{1}{\binom{n}{s} s! 2^s} \sum_{j \ge i-1} N(i,j) \\ &< \frac{17t(2t+2)^4}{(2n)^i} \sum_{j\ge i-1} \left(\frac{(2t+2)^4}{n}\right)^{j-i} \\ &< 18tn\left(\frac{1}{2n}\right)^i, \end{aligned}$$

which is (9).

The rest is straightforward. We propose to show that, with probability $1 - o(1)$, a random formula F with $(1+o(1))cn$ clauses of size two over n variables such that $c > 1$ includes all the clauses of some F_A. The proof is a routine application of the second moment method: writing $X = \sum X_A$ with $X_A = 1$ if each clause of F_A appears precisely once in F and $X_A = 0$ otherwise, we shall prove that

$$E(X^2) \le (1+o(1))E(X)^2. \qquad (10)$$

The desired conclusion will follow from (10) by substituting $E(X)$ for d in the Chebyshev inequality,

$$\text{Prob}\,(|X - E(X)| \ge d) \le \frac{E(X^2) - E(X)^2}{d^2}.$$

To prove (10), consider arbitrary snakes A and B. We have $E(X_A) = E(X_B) = f(2t)$ with

$$f(x) = \binom{m}{x} x! \left(\frac{1}{4\binom{n}{2}}\right)^x \left(1 - \frac{x}{4\binom{n}{2}}\right)^{m-x};$$

if F_A and F_B share precisely i clauses then $E(X_A X_B) = f(4t-i)$. Since $m = O(n)$, we have

$$f(x) = (1+o(1))\left(\frac{m}{2n(n-1)}\right)^x$$

uniformly in every range $x = O(n^\alpha)$ with $\alpha < 1/2$; hence (7) guarantees that

$$E(X_A X_B) = (1+o(1))E(X_A)E(X_B)\left(\frac{2n(n-1)}{m}\right)^i$$

uniformly in the range $0 \le i \le 2t$. Since

$$E(X^2) = \sum_A \sum_B E(X_A X_B)$$

and

$$E(X)^2 = \sum_A \sum_B E(X_A)E(X_B),$$

it follows that

$$E(X^2) = (1+o(1))E(X)^2 \sum_{i=0}^{2t} p_i(n)\left(\frac{2n(n-1)}{m}\right)^i.$$

Finally, from (8) and (7) we have

$$\sum_{i=1}^{t-1} p_i(n)\left(\frac{2n(n-1)}{m}\right)^i < \frac{1300t^9}{n}\sum_{i=1}^{t-1}\left(\frac{n-1}{m}\right)^i = o(1);$$

from (9) and (7) we have

$$\sum_{i=t}^{2t} p_i(n)\left(\frac{2n(n-1)}{m}\right)^i < 18tn\sum_{i=t}^{2t}\left(\frac{n-1}{m}\right)^i = o(1).$$

□

Acknowledgements

Chvátal was supported by the Office of Naval Research grant N0001492J1375; Reed by the Alexander-von Humboldt Stiftung.

References

[1] B. Aspvall, M.F. Plass, and R.E. Tarjan, "A linear-time algorithm for testing the truth of certain quantified Boolean formulas," *Inform. Process. Let.*, Vol. 8, pp. 121-123, 1979.

[2] M.-T. Chao and J. Franco, "Probabilistic analysis of a generalization of the unit-clause literal section heuristic for the k-satisfiability problem," *Inform. Sci.*, Vol. 51, pp. 289-314, 1990.

[3] V.Chvátal and E. Szemerédi, "Many hard examples for resolution," *J. Assoc. Comput. Mach.*, Vol. 35, pp. 759-768, 1988.

[4] S.A. Cook, "The complexity of theorem proving procedures," *Proc. 3rd Ann. ACM Symp. Theory Comput.*, pp. 151-158, 1971.

[5] S. Even, A. Itai, and A. Shamir, "On the complexity of timetable and multicommodity flow problems," *SIAM J. Comput.*, Vol. 5, pp. 691-703, 1976.

[6] J. Franco and M. Paull, "Probabilistic analysis of the Davis-Putnam procedure for solving the satisfiability problem," *Discrete Appl. Math.*, Vol. 5, pp. 77-87, 1983.

[7] A. Goerdt, "A threshold for unsatisfiability," manuscript, 1991.

[8] J.-C. Simon, J. Carlier, O. Dubois, and O. Moulines, "Étude statistisque de l'existence de solutions de problèmes SAT, application aux systèmes-experts," *C.R. Acad. Sci. Paris. Sér. I Math.*, Vol. 302, pp. 283-286, 1986.

[9] R. Stones, *12 × 5*, PS402, London, 1964.

[10] R. Stones, *Out of our heads*, PS429, London, 1965.

[11] W. F. de la Vega, "On random 2-SAT," manuscript, 1992.

Waste Makes Haste: Tight Bounds for Loose Parallel Sorting*

TORBEN HAGERUP RAJEEV RAMAN
Max-Planck-Institut für Informatik, Im Stadtwald, W–6600 Saarbrücken, Germany
e-mail:{torben,raman}@mpi-sb.mpg.de

Abstract

Conventional parallel sorting requires the n input keys to be output in an array of size n, and is known to take $\Omega(\log n/\log\log n)$ time using any polynomial number of processors. The lower bound does not apply to the more "wasteful" convention of *padded sorting*, which requires the keys to be output in sorted order in an array of size $(1+o(1))n$. We give very fast randomized CRCW PRAM algorithms for several padded-sorting problems.

Applying only pairwise comparisons to the input and using kn processors, where $2 \le k \le n$, we can padded-sort n keys in $O(\log n/\log k)$ time with high probability (whp), which is the best possible (expected) run time for any comparison-based algorithm. We also show how to padded-sort n independent random numbers in $O(\log^* n)$ time whp with $O(n)$ work, which matches a recent lower bound, and how to padded-sort n integers in the range $1..n$ in constant time whp using n processors. If the integer sorting is required to be stable, we can still solve the problem in $O(\log\log n/\log k)$ time whp using kn processors, for any k with $2 \le k \le \log n$. The integer sorting results require the nonstandard OR PRAM. As an application of our padded-sorting algorithms, we can solve approximate prefix summation problems of size n with $O(n)$ work in constant time whp on the OR PRAM, and in $O(\log\log n)$ time whp on standard PRAM variants.

1 Introduction

Sorting is a fundamental problem that has been studied extensively in both parallel and sequential settings. The development of very fast parallel sorting algorithms has been hindered because it is sometimes harder to organize the output in the desired fashion than to actually compute the ordering of the input keys. For example, the usual output convention for sorting is that the sorted keys appear in consecutive memory locations. With this convention, sorting even a 0–1 input of size n on the powerful PRIORITY CRCW PRAM needs $\Omega(\log n/\log\log n)$ time using $n^{O(1)}$ processors [6].

*This work was supported by the ESPRIT II Basic Research Actions Program of the EC under contract No. 3075 (project ALCOM), and partly carried out while the first author was with the Departament de LSI of the Universitat Politècnica de Catalunya in Barcelona, Spain.

With the recent spate of developments in the area of almost constant-time parallel algorithms (the so-called "log-star revolution" [19]) it is clear that near-logarithmic run times cannot automatically be deemed satisfactory any more. The potential of much faster algorithms is an excellent incentive for carefully reviewing the reasons for sorting the input and, when possible, to use alternative output conventions that are not subject to the lower bound. One such convention is that of *chain-sorting*, which requires the keys to be output in a sorted linked list. Hagerup [17, 18] demonstrated that small integers can be chain-sorted much faster than they can be sorted in the usual sense. Unfortunately, a major reason for sorting is to enable fast searching, and a chain-sorted output is inadequate for this purpose.

In this paper we consider *padded sorting*, which is much closer to the usual definition of sorting. Here the n input keys are required to be output in sorted order in an array of size at most $(1+\lambda)n$, for some $\lambda \ge 0$. λ is called the *padding factor* and should be $o(1)$ and, in general, as small as possible. The empty locations in a padded array can be filled quickly with copies of the nearest preceding key, so the output of a padded sorting suffices for searching. The lower bound of [6] does not hold for padded sorting, a fact that MacKenzie and Stout [21] and Sarnath [31] exploited to give faster padded-sorting algorithms. In the sequential context, padded arrays were proposed by Itai *et al.* [20] and Willard [32] as an alternative to normal arrays because insertions into padded arrays can be processed quickly.

We show that in a variety of parallel sorting problems, a padded output can be obtained dramatically faster than a normal one; in particular, the results of [21, 31] are improved. When nothing else is stated, our model of computation is the standard ARBITRARY (CRCW) PRAM; the results also hold for the weaker TOLERANT (CRCW) PRAM. Some results use the OR (CRCW) PRAM [5], where concurrent writing of several values to the same cell results in the bitwise OR of these values being stored in the cell. The word size is limited to $O(\log(n+p))$ bits, where n is the input size and p is the number of processors of the machine under consideration. As to the computational power of the OR PRAM, note on the one hand that an n-processor OR PRAM can simulate one step of an n-processor ARBITRARY PRAM in constant time whp [5], and on the other hand that with the above limit on the word size, a standard CRCW PRAM can simulate one

0-8186-2900-2/92 $3.00 © 1992 IEEE

step of an OR PRAM in constant time with a polynomial blowup in the number of processors, so that the lower bound of [6] still holds for the OR PRAM.

We now describe our results in more detail. When stating that the run time of a randomized algorithm is $\tilde{O}(E)$, where E is some expression, what we mean is that whp the run time is $O(E)$.

1.1 Comparison-Based Sorting

Here nothing may be assumed about the keys, except that any two of them can be compared in constant time. If the desired run time is logarithmic or slower, the problem has been satisfactorily solved: For every $p \leq n$, n keys can be sorted in $O(n \log n/p)$ time on a p-processor EREW PRAM [1, 11]. The problem that we consider is therefore to sort n keys using kn processors, where $k \geq 2$, in a comparison-based setting.

It is known that in the parallel comparison-tree (PCT) model, solving this problem requires $\Omega(\log n/\log k)$ (expected) time, for $2 \leq k \leq n$ [3, 2, 9]. Lower bounds for the PCT model apply to all purely comparison-based parallel algorithms. A matching upper bound was given in [3] *for the PCT model.* Upper bounds for the PCT model do not carry over to the PRAM.

On the PRAM, no algorithm is known that matches the PCT lower bound *and* has a run time of $o(\log n/\log\log n)$. Rajasekaran and Reif [27] gave an algorithm that runs in $\tilde{O}(\log n/\log\log n)$ time using $O(n(\log n)^{\epsilon})$ processors, for arbitrary fixed $\epsilon > 0$, which matches the lower bound; their algorithm is easily modified to match the lower bound for *smaller* values of k as well. The best known deterministic solution to the problem uses $O(\lceil \log n/\log\log k \rceil)$ time for $k \geq 4$ [11] — a super-polynomial number of processors is needed to achieve fast run times. Sarnath [31] gave a deterministic padded-sorting algorithm that takes $O(\log\log n)$ time on the average to padded-sort n keys using $O(n^{1+\epsilon})$ processors, for arbitrary fixed $\epsilon > 0$, under the assumption that all permutations of the input keys are equally likely. This does not match the lower bound — with $\Theta(n^{1+\epsilon})$ processors the lower bound is $\Omega(1)$ — and the algorithm also has a padding factor of $\lambda = \Theta(n^{\epsilon})$, which may be too large for some applications. We show:

Theorem: *n keys can be padded-sorted using comparisons only in $\tilde{O}(\log n/\log k)$ time with kn processors, for any k with $2 \leq k \leq n$.*

This is the best possible run time for any comparison-based algorithm, regardless of the output convention; for example, the run time is $\tilde{O}(1)$ with $\Theta(n^{1+\epsilon})$ processors, for arbitrary fixed $\epsilon > 0$. We actually show an interesting tradeoff between run time and padding factor: the more space we allow for the output, the faster we can sort ("more waste — more haste"). At one extreme of the tradeoff — for polylogarithmic k — the padding factor drops below $1/n$, hence to zero, and we get the result of Rajasekaran and Reif.

1.2 Sorting Random Numbers

The problem of sorting n random numbers drawn independently from the uniform distribution over the unit interval $(0, 1]$ has a long history. It was first considered by McLaren [25], who gave a sequential algorithm with a linear expected run time; parallel algorithms using $\tilde{O}(\log n)$ time and $O(n)$ operations were later developed [10, 16]. MacKenzie and Stout [21] showed that a random input distributed as described can be padded-sorted in $\tilde{O}(\log\log n)$ time with $O(n)$ work. This was subsequently improved to $\tilde{O}(\log\log n/\log\log\log n)$ time and $O(n)$ work by the original authors and in [18]. MacKenzie [22] recently showed that any solution to the problem with padding factor $O(1)$ requires $\Omega(\log^* n)$ expected time on an n-processor standard PRAM. We show that this bound is tight:

Theorem: *n random numbers drawn independently from the uniform distribution over $(0, 1]$ can be padded-sorted in $\tilde{O}(\log^* n)$ time using $O(n)$ operations.*

1.3 Integer Sorting

The problem of sorting n integers in the range $1..n$ is solved in $O(n)$ time by sequential bucket sorting. Rajasekaran and Reif [27] gave a parallel algorithm that uses $\tilde{O}(\log n)$ time and $O(n)$ work. Later improvements yielded $\tilde{O}(\log n/\log\log n)$ time with $O(n)$ work [29, 17, 24].

Hagerup [18] showed that small integers can be chain-sorted in $\tilde{O}((\log^* n)^2)$ time with $O(n)$ work. This was subsequently improved to $\tilde{O}(\log^* n)$ time and $O(n)$ work [13, 19]. Note that it is not obvious how to convert a chain-sorted output to even a padded-sorted one faster than in $\Theta(\log n/\log\log n)$ time. We show:

Theorem: *n integers in the range $1..n$ can be padded-sorted in $\tilde{O}(1)$ time on an n-processor OR PRAM, and in $\tilde{O}(\log\log n)$ time with $O(n)$ work on a standard PRAM.*

A sorting algorithm is *stable* if keys with equal values appear in the same order in the output as in the input. An algorithm that sorts n keys in the range $1..n$ stably can, using the principle of radix sorting, be turned into an algorithm that sorts n keys in the range $1..n^{O(1)}$, which makes stability a very desirable property. Bucket sorting is stable and so the stable and unstable versions of integer sorting have the same sequential complexity. A different situation seems to prevail in the parallel setting: The best known time-processor product for stable integer sorting in polylogarithmic time is $\Theta(n \log\log n)$; it was achieved with $O(\log n)$ run time in [15], and with $O(\log n/\log\log n)$ run time in [8] (see also [23, 28]). We give a very fast padded-sorting algorithm for this problem:

Theorem: *n integers in the range $1..n$ can be stably padded-sorted in $\tilde{O}(\log\log n/\log k)$ time with kn processors, for any k with $2 \leq k \leq \log n$. For run times below $\Theta(\log\log n)$ the result needs the OR PRAM.*

1.4 Approximate Prefix Summation

The time complexity of exact prefix summation of n integers of $O(\log n)$ bits each on a CRCW PRAM with $n^{O(1)}$ processors is $\Theta(\log n/\log\log n)$. We consider the following *approximate prefix summation problem*: Given n nonnegative integers $x_1, \ldots, x_n$, compute n approximate prefix sums $y_1, \ldots, y_n$ such that with $y_0 = 0$, the following holds for $i = 1, \ldots, n$ and for some $\lambda \geq 0$ with $\lambda = o(1)$ called the *accuracy* of the approximation:

(1) $y_i \geq y_{i-1} + x_i$;

(2) $y_i \leq (1+\lambda)\sum_{j=1}^{i} x_j$.

Note that conditions (1) and (2) together are stronger than simply requiring each approximate prefix sum to be close to its "true value", which would allow distinct y_i's to be computed independently and could not even guarantee the monotonicity of the sequence $y_1, \ldots, y_n$. We show:

Theorem: *Approximate prefix summation problems of size n can be solved in $\tilde{O}(1)$ time on an n-processor OR PRAM, and in $\tilde{O}(\log\log n)$ time with $O(n)$ work on a standard PRAM. The constant-time result requires the input numbers to be of $O(\log n)$ bits each.*

No results whatsoever on approximate prefix summation were previously known.

2 Preliminaries

A basic fact [27, 12] is that the prefix sums of n integers of $O(\log n)$ bits each can be computed in $O(n/p + \log n/\log\log p)$ time with p processors, for all integers $n \geq 2$ and $p \geq 4$. We also make frequent use of the procedure characterized in the following lemma, which we term "Ragde compaction".

Lemma 2.1: Given an array of size n containing b objects in distinct cells (b is unknown), n processors using $O(n)$ space can in constant time move the objects to distinct cells in an array of size at most b^5.

Proof: Ragde [26] proved that the objects can be compacted to an array of size at most k^4, where k is a known upper bound on b. We use this as follows: First attempt to compact the elements to an array of size k^4, where $k = \lceil n^{1/5} \rceil$. If this succeeds, we have enough processors to try simultaneous compaction into $\Theta(n^{1/5})$ arrays of different sizes. It is easy to choose the $\Theta(n^{1/5})$ sizes such that returning the smallest array into which the objects fit satisfies the condition of the lemma. If the compaction into k^4 space fails, on the other hand, $b \geq n^{1/5}$, and the original array can be returned. ∎

Other crucial subroutines are drawn from the "log-star tool kit" that was developed in a series of papers [24, 18, 4, 13, 14, 19, 5]. One of the most frequently used algorithms is for *semisorting*, i.e., given n integers in the range $1..n$, place these in (distinct cells of) an array of size $O(n)$ such that each value in the range $1..n$ occurs only in a subarray that does not overlap the subarray of any other value (i.e., duplicates are brought together). By Lemma 2.1, we may and will assume that the subarray of a value of multiplicity b is of size at most b^5. Semisorting can be done in $\tilde{O}(\log^* n)$ time with $O(n)$ work on a standard PRAM [19]. It can also be done in $\tilde{O}(1)$ time either on a standard PRAM with $O(n \log^{(l)} n)$ processors, for arbitrary fixed $l \in \mathbb{N}$, or on an n-processor OR PRAM. Other algorithms in the log-star family exhibit the same run times on the various models. Two such algorithms are for the problem of *interval allocation*, i.e., place n intervals of total length s (s is unknown) in nonoverlapping positions in a base interval of length $O(s)$, and for the closely related *processor allocation* problem, i.e., supply each of n requesting processors with any desired number of auxiliary processors from a pool of available processors.

In the following, let U be a fixed ordered universe (i.e., a set equipped with a total order "$\leq$"). Given any finite set $B \subseteq U$, let $Pred(x, B) = \max\{y \in B \mid y \leq x\}$ and $Pred^+(x, B) = \max\{y \in B \mid y < x\}$, for all $x \in U$ for which these quantities are defined. B partitions any finite subset A of U into subsets called the *segments* induced by B in A or the segments of B in A; two elements $x, y \in A$ belong to the same segment if and only if $Pred(x, B) = Pred(y, B)$, except that we consider elements in A smaller than $\min B$ to belong to the same segment as those elements in A larger than or equal to $\max B$ (i.e., we allow "wrap-around"). If $|B| \leq 1$, there is just one segment consisting of all elements in A. To *locate* A with respect to B is to label each element of A with the segment induced by B to which it belongs (represented in the obvious way by an element of B, unless $B = \emptyset$), and to *partition* A with respect to B is to semisort the elements of A with respect to these labels. The *maximum* and *minimum gap* of B in A, $maxgap(B, A)$ and $mingap(B, A)$, are defined as the maximum and minimum cardinality, respectively, of a segment of B in A. If $A \neq \emptyset$, define the *spread* of B in A as the real number $\lambda \geq 0$ with $maxgap(B, A) = (1+\lambda) mingap(B, A)$. Note that λ is a measure of how well B splits A into segments of approximately equal sizes. Much of the present paper is concerned with computing samples of low spread of a given ground set. We now discuss two special kinds of samples. A *naive sample* B of a set A of size $m \leq |A|$ is obtained by letting each of m processors choose an element at random from the uniform distribution over A, with distinct processors acting independently. Note that the sample B may be a multiset; if we use it in a context where only totally ordered sets are meaningful, an arbitrary ordering among elements of the same value is to be assumed. If $A \neq \emptyset$ and $g \in \mathbb{N}$, define a *g-regular sample* of A as a subset B of A with $g \leq mingap(B, A) \leq maxgap(B, A) \leq g+1$ that includes the first element of A.

Lemma 2.2: For every $g \in \mathbb{N}$, every finite ordered set A of size at least g^2 has a g-regular sample. Furthermore, if each element of A is marked with its rank in A and has an associated processor, a g-regular sample of A can be computed in constant time.

By a *predecessor structure* for a set $S \subseteq U$ we mean a data structure that supports *Pred* and $Pred^+$ queries on S, i.e., is able to return $Pred(x, S)$ and $Pred^+(x, S)$ for arbitrary given $x \in U$ (with a special value "undefined" returned as appropriate).

Lemma 2.3:
(a) For all given integers n and k with $n \geq 2$ and $2 \leq k \leq n$, a predecessor structure for n keys drawn from an arbitrary ordered universe that can be queried in $O(\log n/\log k)$ time with k processors can be constructed using $O(\log n/\log k)$ time, kn processors and $O(kn)$ space with probability at least 1/2;
(b) There is a constant $\epsilon > 0$ such that for every fixed $c \in \mathbb{N}$ and for all integers $n \geq 4$, a predecessor structure for n keys drawn from $1\,..\,n^c$ that can be queried in $O(\log\log n/\log k)$ time with k processors, for any integer k with $2 \leq k \leq \log n$, can be constructed using constant time, $O(n \log n)$ processors and $O(n \log n)$ space with probability at least $1 - 2^{-n^{\epsilon}}$;
(c) For all integers $n \geq 2$, a predecessor structure for n keys drawn from $1\,..\,n$ that can be queried in constant time with one processor can be constructed in constant time either on a standard PRAM with $O(n \log n)$ processors and $O(n \log n)$ space, or on an n-processor OR PRAM with $O(n)$ space.

Proof: (a) Assume that $k \geq (\log n)^2$, since otherwise we can simply sort the keys using the algorithm of Rajasekaran and Reif [27] and execute a query by means of k-ary search. We can also assume that we have k^2 processors per key and that a query is executed with k^2 processors, since the time bounds of $O(\log n/\log k)$ are insensitive to the substitution of $\sqrt{k}$ for k.

Our approach is to construct a random search tree of degree $k+1$ over the input set. Initially the tree consists only of its root, and all keys are located at the root. In general, if m keys are present at a node u, we allow these to be stored in an array Q of size up to m^5, and the tree construction proceeds from u as follows: First we use an algorithm for interval allocation to simultaneously attempt to compact the keys in Q into arrays of sizes $1, 2, 4, \ldots, 2^{\lfloor \log |Q| \rfloor}$, where $|Q|$ denotes the size of Q, with $\Theta(\log n)$ trials for each size. Then each of k processors chooses a random location in the smallest of these arrays for which the compaction succeeded, or in Q itself if no compaction was successful. Next a multiset S is formed from the keys found in these locations, with dummy keys representing empty locations, and $k+1$ children of u are created, each of which corresponds to one of the segments of the universe induced by S. Some children will correspond to dummy keys and be useless. Except with negligible probability, however, the number of real keys in S will be $\Omega(k)$, which suffices for our purposes. Now each key located at u uses k^2 associated processors to find its predecessor in S, after which it moves to the appropriate child of u. Moving the keys to the appropriate children actually is an instance of semisorting, which can be executed in constant time with $k \geq \log n$ processors per key. Once the keys of a node u are stored in an array of size at most k, S can instead be chosen as the set of all keys, and the children of u become leaves in the search tree. It can be shown that except with negligible probability, the height of the search tree will be $O(\log n/\log k)$. Finally observe that a query can search in the tree essentially as described above.

(b) and (c) were shown by Raman [28] and by Berkman and Vishkin [7], respectively. Meeting the space bound of part (b) involves using the perfect hashing of [5]. ∎

3 Comparison-Based Sorting

We show in this section that the comparison-tree time bound of $\Theta(\log n/\log k)$ for sorting with kn processors, where $2 \leq k \leq n$, can be matched exactly on a randomized PRAM. We in fact solve the related problem of *approximate ranking*, defined as follows: Given n keys drawn from an ordered universe and $\lambda \geq 0$, label each key with a rational number such that if r_i is the label of the key of rank i (with ties broken in some way), for $i = 1, \ldots, n$, and $r_0 = 0$, then $\frac{1}{n} \leq r_i - r_{i-1} \leq \frac{1+\lambda}{n}$, for $i = 1, \ldots, n$. λ is called the *ranking accuracy*. As demonstrated in the following simple lemma, going from approximate ranking with accuracy λ to padded sorting with padding factor λ is a matter of multiplying by n and rounding.

Lemma 3.1: Let $n \in \mathbb{N}$ and let $r_0, \ldots, r_n$ be real numbers with $r_0 = 0$ and $\frac{1}{n} \leq r_i - r_{i-1} \leq \frac{1+\lambda}{n}$, for $i = 1, \ldots, n$. For $i = 0, \ldots, n$, let $y_i = \lfloor n r_i \rfloor$. Then
(a) For $i = 1, \ldots, n$, $y_i > y_{i-1}$;
(b) For $i = 1, \ldots, n$, $y_i \leq (1+\lambda)i$;
(c) For $0 \leq i \leq j \leq n$, $y_j - y_i \leq \lceil (1+\lambda)(j-i) \rceil$.

Our algorithm is best described as storing the input in an (a, b)-tree T, where a and b are large and b/a is close to 1. The n input keys are hence stored in order from left to right in the n leaves of T, all of which are at the same depth h, and the degree of each internal node in T lies in the set $\{a, \ldots, b\}$. Associate a subinterval of the unit interval $[0, 1]$ with each node of T as follows. The root of T is associated with the full interval $[0, 1]$, and the interval $[\alpha, \beta]$ associated with a nonleaf node u of degree d is partitioned into d equal-sized subintervals, the ith of which, $[\alpha + \frac{i-1}{d}(\beta - \alpha), \alpha + \frac{i}{d}(\beta - \alpha)]$, is associated with the ith child of u, for $i = 1, \ldots, d$. Since the interval associated with a leaf results from exactly h splittings into between a and b subintervals, it is clear that the length of each such leaf interval lies between b^{-h} and a^{-h}. Furthermore, $a^h \leq n \leq b^h$. Hence for any λ with $1 + \lambda/3 \geq (b/a)^h$, the length of each leaf interval lies between $\frac{1}{n(1+\lambda/3)}$ and $\frac{1+\lambda/3}{n}$. Thus if we define r_i as $1 + \lambda/3$ times the right endpoint of the interval associated with the ith leaf of T, for $1 = 1, \ldots, n$, and take $r_0 = 0$, then for $i = 1, \ldots, n$, $\frac{1}{n} \leq r_i - r_{i-1} \leq \frac{(1+\lambda/3)^2}{n} \leq \frac{1+\lambda}{n}$, provided that $\lambda \leq 1$, i.e., we have solved the approximate ranking problem with accuracy λ. Note that the above argument remains valid even if the node degrees in T do not lie between a and b, as long as the ratio between the degrees of any two internal nodes in T on the same level is bounded by b/a. We use this to allow nodes at height 1 to have more than b children.

T is constructed as follows: For an appropriate integer $g \geq 5$ we compute samples $S_0, \ldots, S_h$ of the input set X. $S_h = X$, and for $i = 0, \ldots, h-1$, $g^i \frac{1}{1+1/g} \leq |S_i| \leq g^i$, and S_i has spread at most $1/g$ in X and includes the smallest element x_1 of X. For $i = 0, \ldots, h$, we identify the nodes in T at depth i with S_i and define the parent of a node x at depth $i \geq 1$ as $Pred(x, S_{i-1})$ (because $x_1 \in S_{i-1}$ this is well-defined). It is now easy to see that the degree of every node in T at depth $i \leq h-2$ is at most

$$\left\lceil \frac{maxgap(S_i, X)}{mingap(S_{i+1}, X)} \right\rceil \leq \left\lceil \frac{n(1+1/g)^2/g^i}{n/(g^{i+1}(1+1/g))} \right\rceil \leq g+4$$

and, similarly, at least $g-4$. We have hence realized the scheme outlined above with $a = g-4$ and $b = g+4$.

We do not know how to compute $S_0, \ldots, S_h$ deterministically. Furthermore, naive random sampling falls far short of providing the required low spread. We instead use a more sophisticated sampling due to Reif and Valiant [30], the basic idea of which is very simple: to obtain a sample of size s, pick a naive sample of size $s \log n$ rather than s, then keep only every $(\log n)$th element of the sample. The resulting s keys are far more evenly spaced than if they had been chosen directly using naive sampling. Whereas Reif and Valiant keep sample elements that are exactly equally-spaced in the original larger sample, this is impossible in our setting, and we have to generalize their approach somewhat.

Lemma 3.2: Let A be a nonempty finite ordered set and let g be a positive integer with $g \geq \log|A|$. Let B be a naive sample of A and let C be an arbitrary subset of B such that the spread of C in B is at most $1/g$ and the minimum gap of C in B is at least $192g^3$. Then the spread of C in A exceeds $8/g$ with probability at most 2^{-g}.

Proof: If the spread of C in A exceeds $8/g$, then either $maxgap(C, A) \geq \frac{|A|}{|C|}\sqrt{1+8/g} \geq \frac{|A|}{|C|}(1+2/g)$ or $mingap(C, A) \leq \frac{|A|}{|C|}(1+2/g)^{-1}$. If $maxgap(C, A) \geq \frac{|A|}{|C|}(1+2/g)$, then some contiguous segment D of A (allowing "wrap-around") of size at least $\frac{|A|}{|C|}(1+2/g)-1$ contains no elements of C, and therefore fewer than $maxgap(C, B)$ elements of B. The number N of elements of B falling into D is binomially distributed with expected value

$$\begin{aligned}\frac{|B||D|}{|A|} &\geq \frac{|B|}{|A|}\left(\frac{|A|}{|C|}(1+2/g)-1\right) \geq \frac{|B|}{|C|}(1+2/g)-1 \\ &\geq \frac{maxgap(C,B)}{1+1/g}(1+2/g)-1 \geq \frac{maxgap(C,B)}{1-1/(4g)}.\end{aligned}$$

Now by the Chernoff bound $\Pr(N \leq (1-\epsilon)E(N)) \leq e^{-\epsilon^2 E(N)/2}$, used with $\epsilon = 1/(4g)$, the above event happens for each fixed set D with probability at most $e^{-192g^3/(32g^2)} \leq e^{-4g}$. Summing over the at most $|A|^2$ choices of D yields $\Pr(maxgap(C, A) \geq \frac{|A|}{|C|}(1+2/g)) \leq |A|^2 \cdot e^{-4g} \leq \frac{1}{2}|A|^2 \cdot 2^{-2g} \cdot 2^{-g} \leq \frac{1}{2} \cdot 2^{-g}$. Likewise, $\Pr(mingap(C, A) \leq \frac{|A|}{|C|}(1+2/g)^{-1}) \leq \frac{1}{2} \cdot 2^{-g}$. ∎

Our actual sampling procedure is described in the following lemma.

Lemma 3.3: Let n, k, t, s and g be given positive integers with $n, k \geq 2$, $t \geq \lceil \log n / \log k \rceil$, $\log n \leq g \leq 2^{t \log\log(kn)}$ and $sg^{64} \leq n$. Then, given an ordered set A of size n, a sample C of A with $s \cdot \frac{1}{1+1/g} \leq |C| \leq s$ that includes the first element of A and has spread at most $1/g$ in A can be computed using $O(t)$ time, kn processors and $O(kn)$ space with probability at least $1 - 2^{-g}$.

Proof: We show only a weaker statement that does not require C to contain the first element of A. Observe first that a sample C of the required form always exists, so that we can ignore values of n (and hence g) below any fixed constant. Let $g' = 192(8g)^3$ and assume (by the above observation) that $s(g')^{21} \leq n$. Let B be a naive sample of A of size sg'. We now describe the main steps of how to obtain C from B, and only afterwards worry about the actual implementation of these steps.

If $s < (g')^2$, let C be an s-element subset of B of zero spread. If $s \geq (g')^2$, instead let S be a naive sample of B of size $\lfloor s/(g')^2 \rfloor$, merge each segment of B induced by S of size less than $(g')^2$ with the segment following it by removing one element from S and let $S' \subseteq S$ be the set of elements of S that survive this process. Obviously every segment of B induced by S' is of size at least $(g')^2$. Now use Lemma 2.2 to compute a g'-regular sample of each such segment and let C be the union of these g'-regular samples. In either case we have obtained a sample C with $s \cdot \frac{1}{1+1/g} \leq |C| \leq s$ and with spread at most $1/g'$ in B; by Lemma 3.2, the spread of C in A exceeds $8/(8g) = 1/g$ with probability at most 2^{-8g}.

We now show how to carry out the procedure described above for the case $s \geq (g')^2$; it will become obvious how to handle the easier case $s < (g')^2$. It is easy to see that it suffices to describe how to execute the following steps, first with $R = S$ and afterwards with $R = S'$:

(1) Partition B according to R;

(2) Sort the elements of each segment of B induced by R (without padding); in particular, this computes the size of each segment.

We implement Step (1) using Lemma 2.3(a). By executing $2g'$ independent attempts to construct the predecessor structure of Lemma 2.3(a) and to carry out the subsequent semisorting, we can ensure that the failure probability is at most $2^{-g'}$.

In Step (2) we will assume that each segment to be sorted is of size at most $(g')^4$. If this is not the case, some $(g')^4$ successive elements of B comprise either at least $(g')^2 - 1$ elements of S (none of which are included in S'), or none at all. The expected number of elements of S among any $(g')^4$ fixed elements of B being close to g', an application of Chernoff's bounds easily shows the assumption to be violated with probability at most 2^{-8g} (say). Since we have at least $k(g')^{20}$ processors for each element of B, it is easy to sort a segment of B of size at most $(g')^4$, and therefore stored in an array of size at most $(g')^{20}$, by comparing every pair of elements in the segment and obtaining the rank of each element as one more than the number of smaller elements. The number of smaller elements is counted using prefix summation, which, given at least k processors per element, runs in time $O(\log g/\log\log(kg)) = O(t)$. Finally note that the various failure probabilities incurred add up to less than 2^{-g}. ∎

Theorem 3.4: There is a constant $\epsilon > 0$ such that for all given integers $n, k \geq 2$ and $t \geq \lceil \log n/\log k \rceil$, n elements drawn from an ordered universe can be approximately ranked with accuracy $2^{-t\log\log(kn)}$ using $O(t)$ time, kn processors and $O(kn)$ space with probability at least $1 - 2^{-n^\epsilon}$.

Proof: Obtaining the very small failure probability of 2^{-n^ϵ} requires some additional ideas not explained here. We describe a simpler algorithm with a larger (but still small) failure probability and in fact, in the interest of brevity, omit all references to actual probabilities. The algorithm furthermore achieves an accuracy of $2^{-t\log\log k}$ only, the full accuracy of $2^{-t\log\log(kn)}$ being reached via a recursive application. As in the proof of Lemma 2.3, we can assume that $k \geq \log n$ and that each input key has k^2 associated processors.

Let $g = 48 \cdot 2^{t\lceil\log\log k\rceil}$. If $g^{64} \geq n$, the input can be sorted in $O(t)$ time using the algorithm of Cole [11]. Otherwise let $h \geq 1$ be the largest integer with $g^{h-1}g^{64} \leq n$. The algorithm consists of the following steps:

(1) Construct the tree T, i.e.,

 (1.a) Compute the sets $S_0, \ldots, S_h$;

 (1.b) Determine the parent of each node in $\bigcup_{i=1}^{h} S_i$;

 (1.c) Sort each set of siblings in T;

(2) Determine the ancestors of each leaf in T;

(3) Compute the interval associated with each leaf.

The steps are implemented as follows:

Step (1.a): In order to obtain $S_0, \ldots, S_{h-1}$, simply apply Lemma 3.3 with $s = 1, g, \ldots, g^{h-1}$ (in parallel), which requires $hkn \leq k^2 n$ processors and $O(\log n/\log k) = O(t)$ time.

Step (1.b): By definition, our task is to locate S_{i+1} with respect to S_i, for $i = 0, \ldots, h-1$. We therefore use Lemma 2.3(a) to construct a predecessor structure for S_i, for $i = 0, \ldots, h-1$. Since $\sum_{i=0}^{h-1} |S_i| \leq \sum_{i=0}^{h-1} g^i \leq g^h \leq n/g^{63}$, we can attempt each construction sufficiently many times in parallel to achieve a high reliability. The construction and the subsequent search take $O(\log n/\log k)$ time.

Step (1.c): After partitioning S_{i+1} with respect to S_i using the predecessor structures constructed in Step (1.b), for $i = 0, \ldots, h-1$, we sort each set of siblings using the algorithm of Cole [11]. Since the degree of each internal node in T is $g^{O(1)}$ (note, in particular, that this holds for the nodes at level 1), the time needed is $O(\log g/\log\log k) = O(t)$.

Step (2): For each leaf v in T and for $i = 0, \ldots, h$, let $p_i(v)$ be the ancestor of v in T at depth i and note that there is a "natural candidate" for $p_i(v)$, namely $u = Pred(v, S_i)$. We may in fact have $p_i(v) \neq u$, but then $p_i(v) = Pred^+(u, S_i)$. The proof of this fact, informally, bounds how far the ancestors of v can get from v. In precise terms, let ρ_j be the rank of $p_j(v)$ in the input set X, for $j = 0, \ldots, h$. Then clearly $0 \leq \rho_{j+1} - \rho_j \leq maxgap(S_j, X)$, for $j = 0, \ldots, h-1$, and hence if $i < h$, $0 \leq \rho_h - \rho_{i+1} \leq \sum_{j=i+1}^{h-1} maxgap(S_j, X) \leq mingap(S_i, X)$, from which the claim follows.

Using the predecessor structures constructed in Step (1.b), each leaf v in T can easily determine its two candidate ancestors at each level. This leaves only 2^h candidates for the ancestor sequence $(p_h(v) = v, p_{h-1}(v), \ldots, p_0(v))$. Each candidate sequence $(u_h = v, u_{h-1}, \ldots, u_0)$ can be checked in constant time by h processors, who simply verify that u_{j-1} is indeed the parent of u_j, for $j = 1, \ldots, h$. Using $h \cdot 2^h$ processors, v can therefore check all candidate sequences in parallel and determine the correct sequence of its ancestors in constant time. Since $h = O(\log n/\log g) = O(\log k/\log\log k)$, this uses $o(k)$ processors per leaf.

Step (3): Label each node in T in the following way with a subinterval of $[0,1]$ called its *immediate interval*: The immediate interval of the root of T is $[0,1]$, and the immediate interval of the ith child of a node of degree d is $[\frac{i-1}{d}, \frac{i}{d}]$. The immediate intervals of the nodes in T should not be confused with the intervals introduced previously, which we call their *compounded intervals*. Given two subintervals I_1 and I_2 of $[0,1]$, define their *composition*, $I_1 \circ I_2$, as the interval obtained by scaling and translating I_2 in a way that would transform $[0,1]$ to I_1, i.e., $[\alpha_1, \beta_1] \circ [\alpha_2, \beta_2] = [\alpha_1 + \alpha_2(\beta_1 - \alpha_1), \alpha_1 + \beta_2(\beta_1 - \alpha_1)]$. The operation $\circ$ is associative, and it is easy to see that the compounded interval of a leaf v is $[\alpha_0, \beta_0] \circ \cdots \circ [\alpha_h, \beta_h]$, where $[\alpha_i, \beta_i]$ is the immediate interval of the ancestor of v at depth i, for $i = 0, \ldots, h$. Our task is hence to compose the immediate intervals on every root-to-leaf path in T, which we do independently for each such path.

Let us first look at the size of the objects involved. We represent an interval in the obvious way by a pair of two rational numbers, each of which is in turn represented by two integers. For every $j \in \mathbb{N}$, the endpoints of the composition of j immediate intervals can be expressed with denominators of size $g^{O(j)}$, and the naive algorithm for computing the composition (i.e., not attempting to reduce fractions) creates no larger integers. We can hence fix a constant $c \in \mathbb{N}$ such that the composition of j immediate intervals can be represented in $cj\log g$ bits, for every $j \in \mathbb{N}$. In particular, every compounded interval can be represented in $O(h\log g) = O(\log n)$ bits, which implies that all relevant operations on the intervals manipulated by the algorithm can be executed in constant time.

For $k < g^{2c}$, it is therefore easy to compute the compounded interval of a leaf v: One processor simply follows the path in T from the root to v, composing immediate intervals as it goes along, which takes $O(h) = O(t)$ time. For $k \geq g^{2c}$ let $j \in \mathbb{N}$ be maximal with $cj\log g \leq \frac{1}{2}\log k$. We compose groups of $\min\{j, h+1\}$ consecutive immediate intervals on the path in T from the root to v in constant time using table lookup. This leaves $O(\lceil h/j \rceil) = O(t)$ intervals that can be processed sequentially as before. In more detail, since the representations of j immediate intervals involves altogether at most $\frac{1}{2}\log k$ bits, these can easily be stored together in one word by $O(j\sqrt{k}) = o(k)$ processors. This word is then converted to the composition of the j intervals by lookup in a table, which, being of size $O(\sqrt{k})$, can be constructed in constant time by k processors; we omit the details. The total number of processors needed per leaf in T is $o(hk) = o(k^2)$.

As follows from calculations carried out in the beginning of this section, the algorithm achieves an accuracy of λ, where $1 + \lambda/3 = \frac{g+4}{g-4} = 1 + \frac{8}{g-4} \leq 1 + \frac{16}{g}$, i.e., $\lambda \leq 48/g \leq 2^{-t \log\log k}$. ∎

Corollary 3.5: There is a constant $\epsilon > 0$ such that for all given integers $n, k \geq 2$ and $t \geq \lceil \log n / \log k \rceil$, n elements drawn from an ordered universe can be padded-sorted with padding factor $2^{-t \log\log(kn)}$ using $O(t)$ time, kn processors and $O(kn)$ space with probability at least $1 - 2^{-n^\epsilon}$.

The corollary follows immediately from Lemma 3.1. Note the following remarkable consequence of part (c) of that lemma: Any run of $\lceil 1/\lambda \rceil$ consecutive input keys are stored in consecutive locations of the output array, except that there may be a single empty cell between the first and the last element of the run.

We finally briefly consider a generalization of padded sorting called *ordered interval allocation.* The problem here is, given n keys $x_1, \ldots, x_n$ with associated nonnegative integer demands $d_1, \ldots, d_n$ and a padding factor $\lambda \geq 0$, to allocate disjoint intervals $I_1, \ldots, I_n$ of sizes $d_1, \ldots, d_n$ from a base interval of size at most $(1 + \lambda) \sum_{j=1}^{n} d_j$ such that for all $i, j \in \{1, \ldots, n\}$, if $x_i < x_j$, then I_i is to the left of I_j. We can show that ordered interval allocation is no harder than padded sorting.

Theorem 3.6: There is a constant $\epsilon > 0$ such that for all given integers $n, k \geq 2$ and $t \geq \lceil \log n / \log k \rceil$, ordered interval allocation problems of size n with padding factor $2^{-t \log\log(kn)}$ can be solved using $O(t)$ time, kn processors and $O(kn)$ space with probability at least $1 - 2^{-n^\epsilon}$.

4 Sorting Random Numbers

Theorem 4.1: For every fixed $\gamma \in \mathbb{N}$ and for all given integers $n \geq 2$ and $t \geq \log^* n$, n random numbers drawn independently from the uniform distribution over the interval $(0, 1]$ can be padded-sorted with padding factor t^{-t} using $O(t)$ time, $O(n)$ operations and $O(n)$ space with probability at least $1 - 2^{-(\log n)^\gamma}$.

Proof sketch: Let the numbers to be sorted be $z_1, \ldots, z_n$ and conceptually assign these to n buckets by taking $x_j = \lceil n z_j \rceil$, for $j = 1, \ldots, n$. For $i = 1, \ldots, n$, let B_i be the set of those input elements z_j with $x_j = i$ and take $b_i = |B_i|$. The algorithm consists of the following steps:

(1) Semisort the input by bucket number;

(2) Sort each bucket independently (without padding). As a result, we have arrays $Q_1, \ldots, Q_n$ of sizes exactly $b_1, \ldots, b_n$ such that Q_i contains the elements of B_i in sorted order, for $i = 1, \ldots, n$;

(3) Place the arrays $Q_1, \ldots, Q_n$ in that order in an array of size at most $(1 + \lambda)n$.

Step (1) can be executed optimally in $O(\log^* n)$ time. For Step (2), we use the following facts: (a) b elements can be sorted in constant time using at most 2^{b^δ} processors, for arbitrary fixed $\delta > 0$; (b) Except with negligible probability, $\sum_{i=1}^{n} 2^{b_i^{1/(2\gamma)}} = O(n)$. For $i = 1, \ldots, n$, the semisorting in Step (1) places the elements of B_i in an array of size at most b_i^5. Hence by (b), we can allocate at least $2^{\lfloor b_i^{1/(10\gamma)} \rfloor}$ processors to B_i; by (a), these suffice to sort B_i. Step (3), which is an instance of ordered interval allocation, is more of a challenge. Our solution is yet another instance of the generic log-star algorithm of [4, 13], but several new ideas are needed. We provide an overview of the algorithm.

We start out with a set of n intervals $I_1, \ldots, I_n$, where each interval is a bucket that was created and sorted in Steps (1) and (2), and conceptually arrange these in a tree T of height $O(\log^* n)$. Define the *width* of a node u in T as the number of leaf descendants of u. Nodes in T at level 1 (directly above the leaves) have width v_1^{15}, where $v_1 = \lceil 1/\lambda \rceil$ and $\lambda = t^{-t}$, and the parent of a node of width v_l^{15} has width v_{l+1}^{15}, where $v_{l+1} = 2^{v_l}$, for $l = 1, 2, \ldots$ (i.e., the degrees increase roughly exponentially as one moves away from the leaves). We here ignore certain problems related to rounding (in particular, n may not be of the form v_l^{15}, for some $l \geq 1$). Note that each node in T is associated in a natural way with a subinterval of $(0, 1]$.

Starting from the leaves, the algorithm attempts to group the descendant leaf intervals of a node of width v^{15} in sorted order into one large interval of size at most $(1 + \lambda)v^{15}$. This may or may not succeed, depending on which we call v *good* or *bad*. We actually care only about the root and want to show that it is good with high probability.

The grouping at a node u is done using the algorithm of the previous section, and is facilitated by the fact that many descendant leaf intervals have already been grouped into larger intervals by the good children of u. A crucial observation at this point is that the intervals contributed by the good children of u are all of the same size, so that the intervals provided by a run of consecutive good children between two successive bad children can be combined into a single interval in a trivial way. This allows us to obtain enough processors per interval to make the algorithm of Theorem 3.6 run in constant time at each node.

A node u may become bad for essentially three different reasons: (1) The total length of the descendant leaf intervals of u may significantly exceed the width of u, i.e., unexpectedly many of the random input numbers fell into the subinterval of $(0, 1]$ associated with u; (2) u may have so many bad children and, as a result, so many surviving descendant intervals that enough processors to make the algorithm of Theorem 3.6 run in constant time are not available; (3) Even in the best of circumstances, the randomized algorithm executed at u may fail. The goal of the analysis is to show that a node of width v^{15} becomes bad with probability $2^{-\Omega(v^2)}$, from which it follows that the probability that the root is bad is negligible. Details of the algorithm and its analysis are omitted for lack of space. ∎

5 Integer Sorting

In this section we consider the problem of sorting a multiset of integers in the range $1..n$, both with and without the stability requirement. Note that for all $n, m \in \mathbb{N}$, sorting a multiset of n integers in the range $1..m$ stably reduces to sorting n distinct integers in the range $1..nm$.

Lemma 5.1: For all integers $m \geq 2$ and $w \geq 4$ the following problems can be solved on an m-processor OR PRAM with $O(m)$ space and a word length of w bits, using tables that can be constructed in constant time using $2^{o(w)}$ processors and $2^{o(w)}$ space:
(a) Compute the prefix sums of m integers of $O(\log m)$ bits each in $O(\log m/\log w)$ time;
(b) Sort m integers of $O(\log m)$ bits each in $O((\log m/\log w)^2)$ time.

Lemma 5.2: There is a constant $\epsilon > 0$ such that for all given integers $n \geq 2$ and $k, t \geq 1$, n distinct integers in the range $1..n^2$ can be approximately ranked as follows with probability at least $1 - 2^{-n^\epsilon}$:
(a) With accuracy $2^{-t \log\log(kn)}$ on an OR PRAM using $O(t)$ time, $O(kn(\log n)^2)$ processors and $O(kn(\log n)^2)$ space;
(b) With accuracy t^{-t} on a standard PRAM using $O(t)$ time, $O(n(\log n)^2)$ processors and $O(n(\log n)^2)$ space, provided that $t \geq \log\log n$.

Proof: We again describe an algorithm with a larger failure probability, whose top-level structure is identical to that of Theorem 3.4. We give the proof for part (a) first and outline the modifications necessary for part (b) later.

Let $g = 48 \cdot 2^{t\lceil \log\log(kn)\rceil}$. If $g^{64} \geq n$, the input can be sorted using one of the algorithms of [11, 27]. Otherwise again let $h \geq 1$ be the largest integer with $g^{h-1}g^{64} \leq n$ and execute Steps (1)–(3) of the algorithm of Theorem 3.4. For the implementation of Step (1.a), we essentially use the algorithm of Lemma 3.3 in parallel for $s = 1, g, \ldots, g^{h-1}$, which requires $O(hkn) = O(kn \log n)$ processors. Since the condition $t \geq \lceil \log n/\log k\rceil$ is not necessarily satisfied, we have to realize the steps of the algorithm slightly differently. For Step (1) we simply use part (b) of Lemma 2.3 instead of part (a); as we have $\Omega(\log n)$ processors per element, the time needed is constant. For Step (2), we use Lemma 5.1(a). Since the word length is at least $\Theta(\log(kn))$ bits we obtain a run time of $O(\log g/\log\log(kn)) = O(t)$. Step (1.b) takes constant time using predecessor structures like those constructed in Step (1.a). For Step (1.c) we first padded-sort each set of siblings using the algorithm of Corollary 3.5, run $\Theta(\log n)$ times in parallel to achieve sufficient reliability, and then compact the resulting sequence by means of Lemma 5.1(a). In Step (2) each leaf v first computes its candidate predecessors $u_i = Pred(v, S_i)$ and $u_i' = Pred^+(u_i, S_i)$ at depth i, for $i = 0, \ldots, h$, which requires $O(hn \log n) = O(n(\log n)^2)$ processors. The entire subgraph of the tree T induced by $\{u_0, u_0', \ldots, u_h, u_h'\}$ can now be represented in $O(h) = O(\log n)$ bits by noting for each of u_{i+1} and u_{i+1}', for $i = 0, \ldots, h-1$, whether its parent is u_i, u_i' or neither of these, after which the ancestors of v can be determined in constant time using table lookup. Recalling that the compounded interval of each leaf is determined by $O(\log n)$ bits, it is easy to see that Step (3) can be executed in constant time in a similar way.

This proves the lemma for the OR PRAM. For a standard PRAM we take $g = 48 \cdot t^t$, employ usual prefix summation instead of Lemma 5.1(a) and carry out Steps (2) and (3) using standard pointer-doubling techniques. ∎

Theorem 5.3: There is a constant $\epsilon > 0$ such that for all given integers $n \geq 4$, $k \geq 2$ and $t \geq \lceil \log\log n/\log k\rceil$, n integers in the range $1..n$ can be stably approximately ranked with accuracy $2^{-t\log\log(kn)}$ on an OR PRAM using $O(t)$ time, kn processors and $O(kn)$ space with probability at least $1 - 2^{-n^\epsilon}$. For $t \geq \log\log n$ the result holds for a standard PRAM with ranking accuracy t^{-t}.

Proof: We give the proof for the OR PRAM. As usual, we describe a simpler algorithm with a somewhat larger failure probability. Let X be the input set and take $g = 2^{t\lceil \log\log(kn)\rceil}$. Assume that $g \leq n$ and let $\lambda = 1/(4g)$. The algorithm consists of the following main steps:
(A) Compute a sample C of X of size $O(n/(\log n)^2)$ with $maxgap(C, X) = g^{O(1)}$ that includes the first element of X and has spread at most λ in X. For $i = 1, \ldots, |C|$, let C_i be the ith segment of C in X;
(B) Rank C approximately with accuracy λ using the algorithm of Lemma 5.2. We can assume that this marks C_i with a label q_i, for $i = 1, \ldots, |C|$, such that with $q_0 = 0$, we have $\frac{1}{|C|} \leq q_i - q_{i-1} \leq \frac{1+\lambda}{|C|}$, for $i = 1, \ldots, |C|$;
(C) For $i = 1, \ldots, |C|$, sort C_i (without padding);
(D) Output the sequence of labels of the elements of X computed as follows: If $x \in X$ is the lth element of C_j, then the label of x is $(1 + \lambda)(q_{j-1} + \frac{l}{|C_j|}(q_j - q_{j-1}))$.

We leave the proof of correctness to the reader, but discuss the implementation of the two nontrivial steps.

Step (A) is carried out using the algorithm of Lemma 3.3, modified as described for Step (1.a) in the proof of Lemma 5.2. Since we no longer have $\Omega(\log n)$ processors per element, the time bound becomes $O(\log\log n/\log k)$. In Step (C) we break each segment C_i into pieces of polylogarithmic size, each of which can be sorted in $O(\log\log n/\log k)$ time, and then concatenate the sorted pieces. In more detail, Step (C) consists of the following substeps:
(C.1) Compute a sample S of X with $|S| = O(n/(\log n)^2)$ and $maxgap(S, X) = O((\log n)^3)$;

(C.2) Padded-sort $C \cup S$ with padding factor $O(1)$ using Lemmas 5.2 and 3.1;
(C.3) Partition X according to $C \cup S$;
(C.4) Padded-sort each segment of X induced by $C \cup S$ with padding factor $O(1)$;
(C.5) For $i = 1, \ldots, |C|$, complete the sorting of C_i.

Step (C.1) is easy, since taking S as a naive sample of X of size $\Theta(n/(\log n)^2)$ will do. Steps (C.3) and (C.4) are carried out using Lemma 2.3(b) and Corollary 3.5, respectively. The task in Step (C.5) is, for $i = 1, \ldots, n$, to compact the subsegments of C_i sorted in Step (C.4) and to place them next to each other in the right order. What this involves is to use Lemma 5.1(a) to compute prefix sums, first within each segment of X induced by $C \cup S$, and afterwards within each segment of S induced by C (as computed in Step (C.2)). With high probability, this takes $O(\log g / \log\log(kn)) = O(t)$ time. ∎

Theorem 5.4: There is a constant $\epsilon > 0$ such that for all given integers $n \geq 4$ and $t \geq 1$, n integers in the range $1\,..\,n$ can be (unstably) approximately ranked with accuracy $2^{-t\log\log n}$ on an OR PRAM using $O(t)$ time, $O(n)$ operations and $O(n)$ space with probability at least $1 - 2^{-n^\epsilon}$. For $t \geq \log\log n$ the result holds for a standard PRAM with ranking accuracy t^{-t}.

Proof sketch: Again we consider only the OR PRAM. Using Lemma 2.3(c), we can construct a predecessor structure that works optimally in constant time in the context of the proof of Theorem 5.3 for input keys in the range $1\,..\,n$. If we substitute this predecessor structure for the one used in the proof of Theorem 5.3 and take $g = 2^{t\lceil\log\log n\rceil}$, only Step (C.4) needs to be modified. Recall that Step (C.4) sorts a collection of segments of polylogarithmic sizes. If subtracting an arbitrary value occurring in a segment from all keys in the segment leaves keys of absolute value bounded by $(\log n)^4$, the segment can be sorted in constant time using Lemma 5.1(b). On the other hand, the number of segments violating this condition is $O(n/(\log n)^4)$, so that we can allocate $\Theta(\log n)$ processors to each key in each such segment and padded-sort the segment in constant time using Corollary 3.5.

6 Approximate Prefix Summation

Recall that the approximate prefix summation problem with accuracy λ is, given n nonnegative integers $x_1, \ldots, x_n$, to compute n integers $y_1, \ldots, y_n$ such that with $y_0 = 0$, the following holds for $i = 1, \ldots, n$:

(1) $y_i \geq y_{i-1} + x_i$;
(2) $y_i \leq (1 + \lambda)\sum_{j=1}^{i} x_j$.

Theorem 6.1: There is a constant $\epsilon > 0$ such that for all given integers $n \geq 2$ and $t \geq 1$, approximate prefix summation problems of size n and with input numbers of size polynomial in n can be solved with accuracy $2^{-t\log\log n}$ on an OR PRAM using $O(t)$ time, $O(n)$ operations and $O(n)$ space with probability at least $1 - 2^{-n^\epsilon}$.

Proof: Let the input be $x_1, \ldots, x_n$ and take $s_i = \sum_{j=1}^{i} x_j$, for $i = 1, \ldots, n$, and $\lambda = 2^{-t\lceil\log\log n\rceil}$. Consider first the simple *unary* case where $x_i \in \{0, 1\}$, for $i = 1, \ldots, n$. Derive from the input a new sequence $z_1, \ldots, z_n$ by setting $z_i = i$ if $x_i = 1$ and $z_i = n + 1$ if $x_i = 0$, for $i = 1, \ldots, n$. Then padded-sort $z_1, \ldots, z_n$ using the algorithm of Theorem 5.4 combined with Lemma 3.1 and note that for $i = 1, \ldots, n$, if $x_i = 1$, then s_i is precisely the rank of z_i in the resulting sorted sequence. This quantity, of course, is not readily available, but it is approximated well by the position of z_i in the output array, which we therefore take to be y_i. This defines y_i for all $i \in \{1, \ldots, n\}$ with $x_i = 1$. Compute y_i for all other i by "copying the nearest value to the left", i.e., by letting $y_i = y_j$, where $j < i$ is maximal with $x_j = 1$ ($y_i = 0$ if no such j exists). Using Lemma 2.3(c), this can be done in constant time.

Condition (1) in the definition of approximate prefix summation is easily seen to be satisfied. As for condition (2), since the padded sorting of $z_1, \ldots, z_n$ places the element of rank i in position at most $(1 + \lambda)i$ of the output array, for $i = 1, \ldots, n$, we have $y_i \leq (1 + \lambda)s_i$, for $i = 1, \ldots, n$.

We now move to the general case of input numbers drawn from a set $U = \{0, \ldots, M\}$, where $M = n^{O(1)}$, and first describe a preprocessing phase that reduces the problem size by $\Theta(\log n)$. Since this is easy if $t = \Omega(\log\log n)$, we can assume that $\lambda \geq 2^{-(\log\log n)^2}$. Without loss of generality suppose that the sum of the input numbers also belongs to U. The basic idea is to use a tree of constant height and degree $\Theta((\log n)^{1/3})$ to compute prefix sums within groups of $\Theta(\log n)$ input numbers, the prefix summation at each node being performed in constant time by table lookup. The immediate difficulty with this approach is that the input numbers are of $\Theta(\log n)$ bits each, so that $\Theta((\log n)^{1/3})$ of them will not fit into one word. We therefore represent the values involved only approximately, using fewer bits. More precisely, for every fixed γ, there is a set $R \subseteq U$ of "representable" numbers such that

(1) The elements of R can be represented using $(\log\log n)^{O(1)}$ bits, and the corresponding encoding and decoding functions can be evaluated in constant time by a single processor;

(2) For every $x \in U$, there is a "rounded value" $r(x) \in R$ with $x \leq r(x) \leq (1 + \mu)x$, where $\mu = 2^{-(\log\log n)^\gamma}$. Moreover, $r(x)$ can be computed in constant time by a single processor.

Given $x, y \in R$, let $x \oplus y = r(\min\{x + y, M\})$ and note that $\oplus$ can be evaluated in constant time by a single processor. $\oplus$ serves as our approximation to addition. Every time it is applied, we incur a relative error of μ; if γ is chosen sufficiently large, however, no computed quantity will be larger than $1 + \frac{\lambda}{4}$ times its "true value". Now n processors can in constant time construct a table that "takes as input" $\Theta((\log n)^{1/3})$ numbers $x_1, x_2, x_3, \ldots$ in R and "produces as output" their approximate prefix sums $x_1, x_1 \oplus x_2, (x_1 \oplus x_2) \oplus x_3$, etc. Using this table it is easy to realize the basic idea for the preprocessing described above.

In order to compute approximate prefix sums for input numbers $x_1, \ldots, x_n$ of $O(\log n)$ bits each, we apply the algorithm for the unary case in parallel to every bit position of the input numbers (this is where we need a superlinear number of processors) with a required accuracy of $1 + \frac{\lambda}{4}$. This yields each approximate prefix sum as a collection of $\Theta(\log n)$ values, one for each bit position, that can be added with relative error $\frac{\lambda}{4}$ as in the preprocessing. Even though the input numbers $x_1, \ldots, x_n$ may also be affected by relative errors of up to $\frac{\lambda}{4}$ due to the preprocessing, the overall relative error in the output variables will be at most $(1 + \frac{\lambda}{4})^3 - 1 \leq \lambda$. ∎

It is easy to derive a result corresponding to Theorem 6.1 for the standard PRAM with a minimum execution time of $\Theta(\log \log n)$. We can do better, however. Assuming only that standard operations like addition take constant time on numbers as large as the input numbers, we can allow the latter to be any nonnegative integers whatsoever, rather than integers of $O(\log n)$ bits. We omit the details.

References

[1] M. Ajtai, J. Komlós, and E. Szemerédi, An $O(n \log n)$ sorting network, *in* Proc. 15th STOC (1983), pp. 1–9.

[2] N. Alon and Y. Azar, The average complexity of deterministic and randomized parallel comparison-sorting algorithms, *SIAM J. Comput.* **17** (1988), pp. 1178–1192.

[3] Y. Azar and U. Vishkin, Tight comparison bounds on the complexity of parallel sorting, *SIAM J. Comput.* **16** (1987), pp. 458–464.

[4] H. Bast and T. Hagerup, Fast and reliable parallel hashing (preliminary version), *in* Proc. 3rd SPAA (1991), pp. 50–61.

[5] H. Bast, M. Dietzfelbinger, and T. Hagerup, A perfect parallel dictionary, *in* Proc. 17th MFCS (1992).

[6] P. Beame and J. Håstad, Optimal bounds for decision problems on the CRCW PRAM, *J. ACM* **36** (1989), pp. 643–670.

[7] O. Berkman and U. Vishkin, Recursive *-tree parallel data-structure, *in* Proc. 30th FOCS (1989), pp. 196–202.

[8] P. C. P. Bhatt, K. Diks, T. Hagerup, V. C. Prasad, T. Radzik, and S. Saxena, Improved deterministic parallel integer sorting, *Inform. and Comp.* **94** (1991), pp. 29–47.

[9] R. B. Boppana, The average-case parallel complexity of sorting, *IPL* **33** (1989), pp. 145–146.

[10] B. S. Chlebus, Parallel iterated bucket sort, *IPL* **31** (1989), pp. 181–183.

[11] R. Cole, Parallel merge sort, *SIAM J. Comput.* **17** (1988), pp. 770–785.

[12] R. Cole and U. Vishkin, Faster optimal parallel prefix sums and list ranking, *Inform. and Comp.* **81** (1989), pp. 334-352.

[13] J. Gil, Y. Matias, and U. Vishkin, Towards a theory of nearly constant time parallel algorithms, *in* Proc. 32nd FOCS (1991), pp. 698–710.

[14] M. T. Goodrich. Using approximation algorithms to design parallel algorithms that may ignore processor allocation, *in* Proc. 32nd FOCS (1991), pp. 711–722.

[15] T. Hagerup, Towards optimal parallel bucket sorting, *Inform. and Comp.* **75** (1987), pp. 39–51.

[16] T. Hagerup, Hybridsort revisited and parallelized, *IPL* **32** (1989), pp. 35–39.

[17] T. Hagerup, Constant-time parallel integer sorting, *in* Proc. 23rd STOC (1991), pp. 299–306.

[18] T. Hagerup, Fast parallel space allocation, estimation and integer sorting, TR MPI–I–91–106, MPI für Informatik, 6600 Saarbrücken, Germany, 1991. Preliminary version *in* Proc. 23rd STOC (1991).

[19] T. Hagerup, The log-star revolution, *in* Proc. 9th STACS (1992), LNCS 577, pp. 259–278.

[20] A. Itai, A. Konheim, and M. Rodeh, A sparse table representation of sorted lists, TR RC 9146, IBM Watson Research Center, 1981.

[21] P. D. MacKenzie and Q. F. Stout, Ultra-fast expected time parallel algorithms, *in* Proc. 2nd SODA (1991), pp. 414–423.

[22] P. D. MacKenzie, Load balancing requires $\Omega(\log^* n)$ expected time, *in* Proc. 3rd SODA (1992), pp. 94–99.

[23] Y. Matias and U. Vishkin, On parallel hashing and integer sorting, *J. Algorithms* **12** (1991), pp. 573–606.

[24] Y. Matias and U. Vishkin, Converting high probability into nearly-constant time — with applications to parallel hashing, *in* Proc. 23rd STOC (1991), pp. 307–316.

[25] M. D. McLaren, Internal sorting by radix plus sifting, *J. ACM* **13** (1966), pp. 401–411.

[26] P. Ragde, The parallel simplicity of compaction and chaining, *in* Proc. 17th ICALP (1990), LNCS 443, pp. 744-751.

[27] S. Rajasekaran and J. H. Reif, Optimal and sublogarithmic time randomized parallel sorting algorithms, *SIAM J. Comput.* **18** (1989), pp. 594–607.

[28] R. Raman, The power of Collision: Randomized parallel algorithms for chaining and integer sorting, *in* Proc. 10th FST & TCS Conf. (1990), LNCS 472, pp. 161–175.

[29] R. Raman, Optimal sub-logarithmic time integer sorting on a CRCW PRAM (note), TR 370, Univ. of Rochester CS Dept., 1991.

[30] J. H. Reif and L. G. Valiant, A logarithmic time sort for linear size networks, *J. ACM* **34** (1987), pp. 60–76.

[31] R. Sarnath, Very fast parallel comparison sorting, Manuscript, 1991.

[32] D. E. Willard, A density control algorithm for doing insertions and deletions in a sequentially ordered file in good worst-case time, TR 85–14, SUNY, Albany, 1985.

The Complexity of Parallel Prefix Problems on Small Domains

Shiva Chaudhuri[*] Jaikumar Radhakrishnan[†]

Abstract

We study the complexity of some prefix problems in the CRCW PRAM model. Our main result is an $\Omega(\alpha(n))$ lower bound for chaining, matching the previous upper bound [7, 19] and solving an open problem in [5, 19, 20]. We give reductions to show an $\Omega(\alpha(n))$ lower bound on the complexity of the prefix maxima and range maxima problems even when the domain is $\{1, \ldots, n\}$. An interesting consequence is that prefix maximum is strictly harder than simple maximum. We also give a reduction to show an $\Omega(\alpha(n))$ lower bound on a parenthesis matching problem, matching the upper bound. No lower bounds were previously known for any of these problems. Our lower bounds contribute to the study of very fast parallel algorithms by introducing techniques for proving lower bounds for small domain problems.

1 Introduction

Many of the lower bounds in parallel computation depend critically on the domain size of the problem that is being solved. Typically these lower bounds use Ramsey theoretic arguments to force the algorithms to behave in a structured manner on some subset of the inputs. Then it is shown that these structured algorithms cannot solve the problem quickly. Examples of lower bounds that use this method can be found in [22, 17, 1, 2]. However, applying Ramsey theoretic arguments necessitates assuming an unrealistically large domain size, often an iterated exponential in the size of the problem. These lower bounds become invalid when considering smaller domains. Thus, a major thrust of parallel complexity is to prove lower bounds for problems defined on smaller domains.

The need for small domain lower bounds is further emphasized by the fact that in recent years, algorithms have been presented that, on small domains, actually beat the lower bounds proven for large domains. A good example is the problem of finding the maximum of n integers using a CRCW PRAM with n processors (throughout this paper, we will assume the PRIORITY model, though some results hold for weaker models as well). For a sufficiently large domain, the problem has a lower bound of $\Omega(\log\log n)$ [17]. However, if all the integers are drawn from $\{1, \ldots, n^c\}$ then it is possible to find the maximum in $O(c)$ time [12].

In this paper, we investigate the complexity of some related problems defined on small size domains. Each of the problems is to be solved on a PRIORITY CRCW PRAM with n processors.

Chaining: (Unordered) Given values $a_1, \ldots, a_n$, $a_i = 0$ or 1, $1 \leq i \leq n$, compute $b_1, \ldots, b_n$, such that there exist integers $i_1, \ldots, i_q$ such that $b_i \neq 0$ iff $i = i_j$ for some j and $b_{i_1} = 0$ and $b_{i_j} = i_{j-1}$, $1 < j \leq q$. In other words, we link the nonzeros into a chain. A stronger version requires linking the nonzeros into a chain in the order in which they appear.

Ordered Chaining: Given values $a_1, \ldots, a_n$, $a_i = 0$ or 1, $1 \leq i \leq n$, compute $b_1, \ldots, b_n$, such that $a_i = 0 \rightarrow b_i = 0$ and $b_i = \max\{j \mid a_j = 1, j < i\}$ otherwise. (Define $\max\{\} = 0$.)

Prefix-maxima: Given n integers $a_1, \ldots, a_n$ drawn from $\{1, \ldots, n^c\}$, c constant, compute $b_1, \ldots, b_n$, where, for $1 \leq i \leq n$, $b_i = \max\{a_j : 1 \leq j \leq i\}$.

Range-maxima: Given n integers $a_1, \ldots, a_n$ drawn from $\{1, \ldots, n^c\}$, c constant, preprocess the data so that one processor can quickly answer any question of the form "What is the maximum of $\{a_i, a_{i+1}, \ldots, a_j\}$?", for $1 \leq i \leq j \leq n$.

Parenthesis matching with nesting level: Given a legal sequence of matched parentheses and the nesting level of each, find the match of each parenthesis.

Our results are as follows:

Chaining: We show that the unordered chaining problem requires $\Omega(\alpha(n))$ time. ($\alpha(n)$ is the inverse of Ackerman's function, and is a very slowly growing function. See Section 1.1.) This implies the same lower bound for ordered chaining, solving an open problem in [5, 19, 20].

Prefix-maxima: We show a lower bound of $\Omega(\alpha(n)$ for the prefix-maxima problem even when the domain is

[*]Department of Computer Science, University of Waterloo, Ontario N2L 3G1, Canada.

[†]Theoretical Computer Science Group, Tata Institute of Fundamental Research, Bombay 400 005, India.

0-8186-2900-2/92 $3.00 © 1992 IEEE

just $\{1,\ldots,n\}$.
Range-maxima: We show that there exists a constant c such that any algorithm that preprocesses for range maxima over the domain $\{1,\ldots,n\}$ with n processors so that a single processor can answer a query in $c\alpha(n)$ steps requires $\Omega(\alpha(n))$ time.
Parenthesis matching: We show a lower bound of $\Omega(\alpha(n))$, even when the depth of nesting is at most 2.

All these problems appear frequently as subproblems in parallel algorithms, for example, in integer sorting, merging, lowest common ancestor and compaction (see [3, 16, 5, 21, 14, 19]). Hence considerable work has been done in developing fast algorithms for them.

Berkman and Vishkin [7] and, independently, Ragde [19] gave ingenious parallel algorithms that solve the ordered chaining problem in $O(\alpha(n))$ time, thus our lower bound is the best possible. For a restricted class of algorithms called *oblivious* algorithms, Chaudhuri [10] proved that ordered chaining requires $\Omega(\alpha(n))$ time. However, in the general case, no lower bound was previously known. Our bound is one of very few lower bounds that hold for constant size domains. In fact, the only other such bound for a CRCW PRAM that we know of is the lower bound of Beame and Hastad [4], for PARITY. In recent years, there has emerged a body of literature on very fast parallel algorithms [7, 13]. However, no lower bounds were known for any of these problems. The only other lower bound we are aware of for a problem that can be solved in $o(\log\log n)$ time is a lower bound of $\Omega(\log^* n)$ for a load balancing problem, due to Mackenzie [15].

Gil and Rudolph [14], give a prefix maxima algorithm that runs in $O(\log\log n)$ time. Berkman, Jaja, Krishnamurthy, Thurimella and Vishkin [5], give an algorithm for prefix maxima that is sensitive to the size of the domain. On the domain $\{1,\ldots,s\}$, their algorithm runs in $O(\log\log\log s)$ time with n processors. If s is small, this beats the lower bound for large domains. In [2], a preprocessing algorithm for range maxima is given that runs in $O(\log\log n)$ time. Answering a query takes constant time. Berkman and Vishkin [7], give a preprocessing algorithm that runs in $O(\alpha(n))$ time for a restricted class of inputs in which the difference between two adjacent numbers is at most a constant. This implies a prefix maxima algorithm with the same performance for this class of inputs. Recently, Berkman, Matias and Vishkin [6], gave a randomized algorithm for range maxima that runs in $O(\log^* n)$ time with high probability.

The ordered chaining problem can be reduced to the prefix maxima problem on domain $\{1,\ldots,n\}$. Thus we obtain a $\Omega(\alpha(n))$ lower bound for the prefix maxima problem even if the domain is just $\{1,\ldots,n\}$. An interesting consequence of this lower bound is that finding prefix maxima is shown to be strictly harder than just finding the maximum. This aspect is discussed further in Section 5. Prefix maxima can, in turn, be reduced to the range maxima problem which yields our lower bound for range maxima.

Berkman and Vishkin [7], give an $O(\alpha(n))$ algorithm for parenthesis matching with nesting level. Without the nesting level given, PARITY can be reduced to this problem, hence it requires $\Omega(\frac{\log n}{\log\log n})$ time. We show that with nesting level given, ordered chaining can be reduced to it, thus obtaining a matching lower bound.

Our lower bound argument for chaining is based on the work of Dolev, Dwork, Pippenger and Wigderson [11], who showed that a *weak superconcentrator* with a linear number of edges must have $\Omega(\alpha(n))$ depth. They used a clever and versatile averaging argument. Our proof uses an extension of their method.

The rest of this paper is organized as follows: Section 2 presents definitions and preliminaries for the chaining lower bound, Section 3 presents the the lower bound argument, Section 4 presents the reductions that yield the other lower bounds and Section 5 discusses some open problems.

1.1 Ackerman's Function

Ackerman's Functions are defined as follows.

$$\begin{aligned} A_1(x) &= 2x; \\ A_{i+1}(x) &= A_i^{(x)}(1). \end{aligned}$$

Here $A_i^{(x)}(1)$ is A_i applied to 1 x times. That is, $A_2(x) = 2^x$ and $A_3(x) = Tower(x)$. The k-th inverse Ackerman function, I_k, is defined by $I_k(n) = \max\{i : A_k(i) \leq n\}$. The Ackerman inverse of n, $\alpha(n)$, is given by

$$\alpha(n) = \min\{k : A_k(k) \geq n\}.$$

2 The Chaining Problem

2.1 Preliminaries

The Ackerman Tree

The tree $T_i(x)$ is defined inductively. The definition depends on a parameter d.

$T_1(x)$ is a tree of depth 2. The root has one outgoing edge with label x and the child of the root has x^d edges each with label 1. We define

$$B_i(x) = (\textit{biggest label in } T_i(x))^{2d}. \quad (1)$$

Then, $B_1(x) = x^{2d}$.

$T_{i+1}(x)$ has depth $(i+2)$. The root has one outgoing edge with label x. The child of the root is formed by collapsing the roots of the following x^d trees of depth $(i+1)$.

$$T_i(2^x),\ T_i(B_i(2^x)), \ldots, T_i(B_i^{(x^d-1)}(2^x)).$$

Then, $B_{i+1}(x) = B_i^{(x^d)}(2^x)$.

Now set $d = 2^k$. The tree $T_k^*(l)$ has depth k. It is obtained by collapsing the roots of the following l trees.

$$T_{k-1}(20),\ T_{k-1}(B_{k-1}(20)), \ldots, T_{k-1}(B_{k-1}^{(l-1)}(20)).$$

The tree $T_k^*(l)$, $k \geq 2$, may be alternatively described as follows. $T_k^*(l)$ is an ordered tree of depth k. The edges of the tree have labels. The tree satisfies the following conditions. Let $d = 2^k$.

1. The out degree of the root is l.
2. The label on the leftmost edge coming out of the root is 20.
3. The label on any edge going into a leaf is 1.
4. If the label on the edge coming into a node v is c, then the outdegree of v is c^d.
5. If $e = (v, w)$ is the leftmost edge out of a non-leaf node v, then the label on e is 2^c, where c is the label on the edge coming into v.
6. If $f = (v, w)$ is not the leftmost edge coming out of v, then its label is obtained as follows. Let e be the edge immediately to the left of f and coming out of v. Let c be the biggest label on an edge of a path starting with edge e and ending at a leaf. Then the label of f is c^{2d}.

Let H be the set of leaves of the tree $T_k^*(l)$. For $h \in H$, $c_i(h)$ is the label on the i-th edge from the root on the path connecting the root with the leaf h. Let $c_i^+(h)$ be the next bigger value of c_i after $c_i(h)$, that is

$$c_i^+(h) = \min\{c_i(h') : c_i(h') > c_i(h)\}.$$

Let $\min\{\} = \infty$. $E(h)$ will denote the product $(c_1(h)c_2(h)\ldots c_{k-1}(h))^{2^k}$.

Properties of $T_k^*(l)$. We now list the properties of $T_k^*(l)$ that we need in the proof of the lower bound.

P1. $\sum_h \frac{1}{E(h)} = l$.

P2. For all leaves h, $c_{i+1}(h) \geq 2^{c_i(h)}$, for $i = 1, \ldots, k-2$.

P3. For all leaves h, $c_i^+(h) \geq (c_{k-1}(h))^{2d}$, for $i = 1, \ldots, k-1$.

P4. The number of leaves upto h (h and the leaves to the left of h) is at most $2(c_{k-1}(h))^d$.

P5. If $l \geq 5$ and $k \geq 3$, then the number of leaves in $T_k^*(l)$ is at most $A_{3k}(l)$.

Properties P1, P2, P3 and P4 follow easily from the definition of the tree $T_k^*(l)$. A proof for P5 is given in the appendix.

2.2 Partial Inputs and the Computation Graph

In the following, A will be an algorithm solving the unordered chaining problem. For inputs of size n, let A use $P(n)$ processors and take $k(n)$ steps. (A step is defined as one round of reads followed by writes.)

A *partial input* is an element of $\{0, 1, *\}^n$. For a partial input b, we denote by $X(b)$ the set of inputs consistent with b. That is, $X(b) = \{x \in \{0,1\}^n : \textit{for } i = 1, \ldots, n,\ b_i \neq * \rightarrow b_i = x_i\}$. The positions with value 1 in b will be called the *blockers* of b and the positions with value 0 will be called the *passers* of of b. Let

$$Bl(b) = |\{j : b_j = 1\}|; \qquad Pa(b) = |\{j : b_j = 0\}|.$$

For partial inputs a and b, we say a is a refinement of b, and write $a \leq b$, if $X(a) \subseteq X(b)$.

We shall find it convenient to model the computation of A on a graph. Let b be a partial input of size n. The *computation graph* of A on b, $G(b)$, is defined as follows.

$$V(G(b)) = \{(c, i) : c \textit{ is a cell of memory and } 0 \leq i \leq k\}.$$

That is, we have $(k+1)$ levels; in each level we have one vertex for each cell in the memory. The set of vertices in level i will be called V_i. The directed edges go from vertices at one level to the vertices of the next level. Every edge is labelled by a processor. $E(G(b))$ contains the edge $((c, i), (d, i+1))$ labelled p if on some input in $X(b)$, processor p reads cell c and writes to cell d in step $(i+1)$. We use $f_v(b)$ to denote the indegree of vertex v in the graph $G(b)$. Initially, bit i of the input is assumed to be in cell i; finally, bit i of the output is assumed to be in cell i. We refer to vertex $(i, 0)$ as α_i (the *input* vertices) and vertex (i, k) as β_i (the *output* vertices).

Let $a \in \{0,1\}^n$. We shall associate with each vertex of $G(a)$ a content. The content associated with (c, i) is the content of the cell c after step i (that is, just before the write of step $(i+1)$ changes it) in the computation of A on the input a. We call this content $content(a, (c, i))$. Similarly, for a processor p and an input $a \in \{0,1\}^n$, $state(a, (p, i))$ is the state of processor p just before the write of step $(i+1)$ in the computation of A on input a. For a partial input b, let

$$\begin{aligned} contents(b, (c, i)) &= \{content(x, (c, i)) : x \in X(b)\}; \\ states(b, (p, j)) &= \{state(x, (p, i)) : x \in X(b)\}. \end{aligned}$$

We say that (c, i) is a *fixed* vertex if $|contents(b, (c, i))| = 1$; otherwise we say (c, i) is a *free* vertex. Note that the above definitions depend on the algorithm A and the size of input n. These parameters will be clear from the context where they are used.

We model the computation of the algorithm A on the computation graph as follows. We say that a processor p reads from cell (c, i) and writes to cell $(d, i+1)$ when we mean that in the step $(i+1)$ of the computation of the algorithm A, p reads cell c and writes to cell d.

The following lemma shows a lower bound on the number of different values that the output vertices may have, based on how refined the partial input is.

Lemma 2.1 *Let b be a partial input of size n. Let β_i, $i = 1, \ldots, n$, be the output vertices in the computation graph $G(b)$. Then,*

$$\sum_{i=1}^{n} |contents(b, \beta_i)| \geq \frac{(n - Pa(b))^2}{2(Bl(b) + 1)}.$$

Proof: Construct a graph G with $(n - Pa(b))$ vertices corresponding to the $(n - Pa(b))$ non-zero positions in the partial input b. Put the directed edge (i, j) in, if $b_j = *$ and on some input consistent with the partial input, the output vertex β_i can take value j. For a vertex i of G, the different edges (i, j) going out of i correspond to different contents of β_i. Note that the content of an output vertex β_j on the input obtained from b by setting all the stars to 0 does not correspond to any edge of G. Suppose G had S edges. Then, accounting for the n contents not represented by any edge of G, we get

$$\sum_{i=1}^{n} |contents(b, \beta_i)| \geq S + n. \qquad (2)$$

Suppose G has an independent set of size $Bl(b) + 2$. Consider the input formed by setting these $Bl(b) + 2$ positions to 1 and all other stars to 0. When this input is chained by the algorithm, there must be at least $Bl(b) + 1$ links in the chain. By our construction of G, these links may point only to blockers of b. But there are only $Bl(b)$ blockers. Hence G has no independent set of size $Bl(b) + 2$. By Turán's theorem we get

$$\begin{aligned} \frac{(n - Pa(b))^2}{n - Pa(b) + 2S} &\leq Bl(b) + 1 \\ \text{i.e.} \quad \frac{(n - Pa(b))^2}{Bl(b) + 1} &\leq n - Pa(b) + 2S. \end{aligned}$$

Using (2), we get

$$\sum_{i=1}^{n} |contents(b, \beta_i)| \geq \frac{(n - Pa(b))^2}{2(Bl(b) + 1)}. \quad \square$$

Overview of the Proof

The central idea of the proof is that we think of the quantity $\sum_{i=1}^{n} |contents(b, \beta_i)|$ as a measure of the difficulty of the task that the algorithm has to accomplish. Lemma 2.1 bounds this measure from below. When we refine a partial input, we potentially reduce the set of contents of cells and states of processors, thus restricting the algorithm. We will find a partial input such that the algorithm is severely restricted, however, the difficulty of the remaining task is still high. This allows us to conclude that if the algorithm runs in few steps, it must use many processors.

The partial input we seek is difficult to obtain directly, so we examine a large number of partial inputs and use an averaging argument.

3 The Lower Bound

We shall now analyze the computation graph of algorithm A. For this, we use the tree $T_k^*(l)$ defined previously. Let H denote the set of leaves of $T_k^*(l)$, and let $h \in H$. We shall associate a partial input $b(h)$ with h. The partial input $b(h)$ will be such that, in the graph $G(b(h))$, the indegree of a *free* vertex at level i will be less than $c_i(h)$, for $i = 1, 2, \ldots, k-1$. We next show how such a partial input with a small number of blockers and passers can be obtained.

The partial input $b(h)$ is produced in stages. The intermidiate partial inputs produced will be called $b^0(h), b^1(h), \ldots, b^{k-1}(h)$. In the end we shall set $b(h) = b^{k-1}(h)$. From now on we shall not mention the parameter h when referring to $b(h)$, the intermediate partial inputs, or the labels $c_i(h)$, whenever the value of h is clear from the context. Initially, we set $b^0 = *^n$. Now, in the graph $G(b^0)$, there may be free vertices in level 1 that have degree c_1 or higher. In *STAGE 1* of our procedure, we refine b^0 to obtain b^1. In $G(b^1)$ the degree of every free vertex at level 1 will be less than c_1.

When we come to *STAGE i*, we already have a partial input b^{i-1} such that, in $G(b^{i-1})$, every free vertex at level j, $j = 1, 2, \ldots, i-1$, has degree less than c_j. Our task in *STAGE i* is to ensure that this holds for level i vertices also. We obtain a refinement b^i of b^{i-1} so that, in $G(b^i)$, every free vertex at level i has degree less than c_i. Note that the degree of any vertex cannot increase upon refinement. Before describing the refinement at *STAGE i*, we show how to fix the contents of a cell, setting relatively few input bits.

Consider a partial input b such that every free vertex at level j, $j = 1, 2, \ldots, i$, has degree less than c_j. (If $i = 0$, then b can be any partial input.) Let $x \in X(b)$. Consider the state of a processor p after the read of step $(i+1)$. We wish to refine b so that this state is fixed at $state(x, (p, i))$. More precisely we wish to obtain b' so that $b' \leq b$ and

$$states(b', (p, i)) = \{state(x, (p, i))\}; \quad (3)$$

$$x \in X(b'). \quad (4)$$

Such a partial input b' is produced by the procedure $FixProc(x, b, (p, i))$ described below. Similarly, for fixing cells, the procedure $FixCell(x, b, (c, i))$ produces a b' satisfying the following conditions.

$$contents(b', (c, i)) = \{content(x, (c, i))\}; \quad (5)$$

$$x \in X(b'). \quad (6)$$

$FixProc(x, b, (p, i))$: If $i = 0$, we know that p reads the same input position in the first step no matter which input is presented to the algorithm. To fix the state of b after the first read, we fix that input bit of b (if it is not already set) consistently with x. The resulting partial input is our b'.

For $i > 0$, let b'' be the partial input produced by $FixProc(x, b, (p, i-1))$. Then, for each input in $X(b'')$, p reads the same cell, (c, i) say, in the read of step $(i+1)$. We use the $FixCell(x, b'', (c, i))$ to fix the contents of this cell and call the resulting partial input b'.

$FixCell(x, b, (c, i))$: If $i = 0$, then (c, i) is an input bit. We set this bit consistently with x and the resulting partial input is our b'.

If $i > 0$, let $p_1, p_2, \ldots, p_t$ be the processors that write to cell (c, i). We now define partial inputs $b(0), b(1), \ldots, b(t)$ inductively. Let $b(0) = b$, and for $j = 1, \ldots, t$, $b(j) =$ output of $FixProc(x, b(j-1), (p_j, i-1))$. To get the final partial input b', we invoke $FixCell(x, b(t), (c, i-1))$. *In our application, whenever* $FixCell(x, b, (c, i))$ *is invoked the indegree of* (c, i) *in* $G(b)$ *will be at most* $c_i - 1$. *Hence* $t \leq c_i - 1$.

Let $N_i(p)$ be the number of $*$'s in b that are set to 0 or 1 by $FixProc(x, b^{i-1}, (p, i))$. Let $N_i(h) = N_i = \max_p N_i(p)$. Similarly, let $M_i(c)$ be the number of $*$'s in b that are set to 0 or 1 by $FixCell(x, b^i, (c, i))$. Let $M_i(h) = M_i = \max_c M_i(c)$. It is easy to check that the following inequalities hold for $i \geq 1$.

$$M_i \leq M_{i-1} + (c_i - 1)N_{i-1};$$

$$N_i \leq N_{i-1} + M_i.$$

From these, with $N_0 = 1$ and $M_0 = 1$, the following bound for N_i, $i \geq 1$, can be deduced.

$$N_i \leq 2^i(c_1 \ldots c_i) \leq c_i^2. \quad (7)$$

Define Z_b as $x \in X(b)$, obtained by setting all the $*$'s in b to 0. We call $state(Z_b, (p, i))$ the *zero state* of p in step $(i+1)$. Note that conditions (4) and (6) ensure that only passers are created while fixing p at its zero state.

STAGE i

Consider the graph $G(b^{i-1})$. A free vertex v at level i will be called a *high degree* vertex if $c_i \leq f_v < c_i^+$; it will be called a *very high degree* vertex if $f_v \geq c_i^+$. To obtain b^i we fix high and very high degree vertices as described below.

(A) *High Degree Vertices.* For each high degree vertex v in $G(b^{i-1})$, we do the following: Fix all the processors that write to v at their zero states. Now, if one of these processors writes to v in its zero state, then v is fixed in the graph of the refined partial input. Otherwise, the indegree of v in the graph is 0. We need set at most N_{i-1} inputs for each of the processors to achieve this.

At the end of this process, all the high degree vertices in $G(b^{i-1})$ are either fixed,or no longer high degree. Note that we create only passers.

(B) *Very High Degree Vertices.* After having fixed the high degree vertices we now have a partial input, b^* say. For each very high degree vertex v we do the following: Let the highest priority processor writing to v be p. There is some input $x \in X(b^*)$ on which p writes to v. We fix the state of p to the state it has on input x using $FixProc(x, b^*, (p, i-1))$. Redefine b^* to be the new partial input. On every input in $X(b^*)$, p writes to v and, being the highest priority processor, always succeeds. To fix the state of p we need set at most N_{i-1} inputs. Note that this time we may create both passers and blockers.

At the end of this process, all the free vertices at level i have indegree less than c_i.

Let the total number of inputs set while fixing high degree vertices in *STAGE i* be $S_A^i(h)$ (all of these are passers) and the total number of inputs set while fixing very high degree vertices be $S_B^i(h)$. This completes the description of the processing at *STAGE i*.

Consider a vertex (c, i) $(i > 0)$ in the graph $G(b)$. Let the different processors that appear as labels on the edges coming into (c, i) be $p_1, \ldots, p_t$. Let the number of states in which processor p_j writes to (c, i) be S_j. Now, the content of (c, i) is determined by the state of the processor that succeeds in writing to (c, i), or, if no processor writes to (c, i), by the content of $(c, i-1)$. Thus, we have

$$|contents(b, (c, i))| \leq \sum_{j=1}^{t} S_j + |contents(b, (c, i-1))|.$$

Let $Y_i(b)$ and $Z_i(b)$ be defined as follows.

$$\begin{aligned} Y_i(b) &= \max\{|contents(b, (c, i))| : c \text{ is a cell}\}; \\ Z_i(b) &= \max\{|states(b, (p, i))| : p \text{ is a processor}\}. \end{aligned}$$

Let $b = b(h)$ be the partial input produced by the stage by stage processing described above. In $G(b)$ free vertices at level j have indegree less than c_j, for $1 \leq j \leq k-1$, and we have

Lemma 3.1 $Z_i(b) \leq 2^{2^i} \prod_{j=1}^{i} c_j^{2^{i-j}}$.

Proof: We drop the parameter b in the notation. We have that $Y_0 = 2$ and $Z_0 = 2$. Further, for $i \geq 1$,

$$\begin{aligned} Y_i &\leq (c_i - 1)Z_{i-1} + Y_{i-1}; \\ Z_i &\leq Z_{i-1}Y_i. \end{aligned}$$

Let $\Delta_i = 2^{2^i} \prod_{j=1}^{i} c_j^{2^{i-j}}$. It can then be shown by induction on i that $Z_i \leq \Delta_i$ and $Y_i \leq c_i \Delta_{i-1}$. □

In our applications, we shall always have $c_j \geq 20$ and $c_{j+1} \geq 2^{c_j}$ for $j = 1, 2, \ldots, i-1$. We may then use the following more convenient bounds for Z_i, $i \geq 1$.

$$Z_i \leq (c_i)^2; \tag{8}$$

Theorem 3.1 *Let A be an algorithm that solves the unordered chaining problem for inputs of length n in k steps using P processors. Suppose that $3 \leq k \leq \frac{\alpha(n)}{10}$. Then $P = \Omega(nI_{3k+1}(n))$.*

Proof: Consider $T_k^*(l)$ with $l = I_{3k}(n)$. Since $k \leq \frac{\alpha(n)}{10}$, $A_{10k}(10k) \leq n$. Then $A_{3k}(10k) \leq n$ and hence $I_{3k}(n) \geq 10k$. Now $l \geq 10k \geq 5$. Thus, by property P5, the number of leaves in $T_k^*(l)$ is at most $A_{3k}(l) \leq n$. For a leaf h of $T_k^*(l)$, let $b(h)$ be the associated partial input and let $Bl(h)$ and $Pa(h)$ be the number of blockers and passers. Then, $|contents(b(h), \beta_i)| \leq f_{\beta_i} Z_{k-1} + 1$ and $\sum_{i=1}^{n} f_{\beta_i} \leq PZ_{k-1}(h)$. Hence,

$$\begin{aligned} \sum_{i=1}^{n} |contents(b(h), \beta_i)| &\leq Z_{k-1} \sum_{i=1}^{n} f_{\beta_i} \\ &\leq Z_{k-1}(h)^2 P + n \\ &\leq E(h)(P + n). \end{aligned}$$

Using lemma 2.1 we get

$$E(h)(P + n) \geq \frac{(n - Pa(h))^2}{Bl(h) + 1}.$$

After simplification this yields $(P+n)(Bl(h) + \frac{2Pa(h)}{E(h)} + 1) \geq \frac{n^2}{E(h)}$. Summing over all leaves h and using properties P1 and P5, we get

$$(P + n)[\sum_h (Bl(h) + \frac{2Pa(h)}{E(h)}) + n] \geq n^2 l \geq n^2 I_{3k}(n).$$

The number of blockers is at most the number of bits set while fixing very high degree vertices. We may bound the number of passers from above by the total number of bits set.

$$\sum_h Bl(h) \leq \sum_h \sum_{i=1}^{k-1} S_B^i(h) \leq kP; \tag{9}$$

$$\sum_h \frac{Pa(h)}{E(h)} \leq \sum_h \sum_{i=1}^{k-1} \frac{S_A^i(h) + S_B^i(h)}{E(h)} \leq 3kP. \tag{10}$$

The second inequalities in (9) and (10) follow from lemma 3.2 and lemma 3.3 proved later. Thus, we have

$(P+n)(7kP+n) \geq n^2 I_{3k}(n)$. Now suppose $P \leq I_{3k+1}(n)$. Then we have

$$(nI_{3k+1}(n)+n)(n7kI_{3k+1}(n)+n) \geq n^2 I_{3k}(n).$$

Since $I_{3k+1}(n) \geq 10k$, we get $(I_{3k+1}(n))^3 \geq I_{3k}(n)$. For n large this is impossible. (See appendix for a proof.) Hence, $P = \Omega(nI_{3k+1}(n))$. □

It is now straight forward to deduce the following theorem.

Theorem 3.2 *A chaining algorithm (ordered or unordered) using n processors requires $\Omega(\alpha(n))$ steps.* □

Lemma 3.2 *For $i = 1, 2, \ldots, k-1$, $\sum_h S_B^i(h) \leq P$.*

Proof: Let $f_v(b)$ denote the indegree of v in $G(b)$. For each very high degree vertex at level i, we set at most N_{i-1} inputs. Thus,

$$\begin{aligned}\sum_h S_B^i(h) &\leq \sum_h \sum_{v\in V_i : c_i^+ \leq f_v(b^{i-1})} N_{i-1}(h) \\ &\leq \sum_{v\in V_i} \sum_{h: c_i^+ \leq f_v(b^{i-1})} N_{i-1}(h). \quad (11)\end{aligned}$$

We shall consider the case $i = 1$ later. First assume $2 \leq i \leq k-1$. Note that we then have $k \geq 3$. We group the h in the rightmost sum of (11) by the value of c_{i-1}. Then we have, using the bound for $N_{i-1}(h)$ given by (7),

$$\begin{aligned}\sum_h S_B^i(h) &\leq \sum_{v\in V_i}\sum_c \sum_{h: c_{i-1}=c \wedge c_i^+ \leq f_v(b^{i-1})} N_{i-1}(h) \\ &\leq \sum_{v\in V_i}\sum_c \sum_{h: c_{i-1}=c \wedge c_i^+ \leq f_v(b^{i-1})} c_{i-1}^2,\end{aligned}$$

where c ranges over the values taken by c_{i-1} in the tree. Now, $b^{i-1}(h)$ depends only on the values $c_1(h), \ldots, c_{i-1}(h)$ and hence it is the same for all h with the same value of c_{i-1}. Let $h' = h'(c, v)$ be the rightmost leaf satisfying the condition in the innermost sum. Then, $f_v(b^{i-1}(h')) = f_v(b^{i-1}(h))$ for all h with $c_{i-1}(h) = c$. By property P4 of the tree, the number of leaves satisfying the condition is at most $2(c_{k-1}(h'))^d$. Thus, we have that

$$\sum_h S_B^i(h) \leq \sum_{v\in V_i}\sum_c 2(c_{k-1}(h'))^d (c_{i-1}(h'))^2.$$

Now, using property P3 of the tree and the bound (8), the following holds for h'. (Since $k \geq 3$, we have $d \geq 8$.)

$$(2c_{k-1}^d c_{i-1}^2)(Z_{i-1}c_{i-1}) \leq 2c_{k-1}^d c_{k-2}^5 < c_i^+ \leq f_v(b^{i-1}).$$

Since $Z_{i-1}(h'(c,v))$ depends only on c, we have

$$\sum_h S_B^i(h) \leq \sum_c \sum_{v\in V_i} \frac{f_v(b^{i-1})}{c_{i-1}(h')Z_{i-1}(h')} \leq \sum_c \frac{PZ_{i-1}(h')}{cZ_{i-1}(h')}.$$

To see that the last inequality holds, observe that the number of edges between levels $i-1$ and i with label p can be at most $Z_{i-1}(h')$. Finally, noting that the c_{i-1} values grow very fast in the tree, we get

$$\sum_h S_B^i(h) \leq \sum_c \frac{P}{c} \leq P.$$

Next suppose $i = 1$. We use $N_{i-1}(h) = N_0(h) = 1$ and obtain from (11) that

$$\sum_h S_B^1(h) \leq \sum_{v\in V_1} |\{h : c_i^+(h) \leq f_v(b^0)\}|.$$

Let h' be the right most leaf satisfying the condition $c_i^+(h) \leq f_v(b^0)$. Then, the number of leaves satisfying this condition is at most $2(c_{k-1}(h'))^d$, by property P4. Now, $4(c_{k-1}(h'))^d < c_i^+(h') \leq f_v(b^0)$. Hence, we get

$$\sum_h S_B^1(h) \leq \sum_{v\in V_1} f_v(b^0)/2.$$

Since the number of edges between levels 0 and 1 is at most $2P$ we get that $\sum_{v\in V_1} f_v(b^0) \leq 2P$, and

$$\sum_h S_B^1(h) \leq P. \quad \square$$

Lemma 3.3 *For $i = 1, 2, \ldots, k-1$,*

$$\sum_h \frac{S_A^i(h)}{E(h)} \leq 2P.$$

Proof: Let $HDW_i(h)$ be the set of processors that write to highdegree vertices at level i. Fixing high degree vertices at *STAGE i* entails fixing each of these processors at its zero state. Thus

$$\begin{aligned}\sum_h \frac{S_A^i(h)}{E(h)} &\leq \sum_h \sum_{p\in HDW_i(h)} \frac{N_{i-1}(h)}{E(h)} \\ &\leq \sum_p \sum_{h: p\in HDW_i(h)} \frac{N_{i-1}(h)}{E(h)}. \quad (12)\end{aligned}$$

We again carry out the estimation for the case $i = 1$ separately. First assume $2 \leq i \leq k-1$. Breaking the inner sum in (12) the values of $c_{i-1}(h)$ we get

$$\sum_h \frac{S_A^i(h)}{E(h)} \leq \sum_p \sum_c \sum_{h: c_{i-1}=c\wedge p\in HDW_i(h)} \frac{N_{i-1}(h)}{E(h)},$$

where c ranges over the values taken by c_{i-1} in the tree. Now, whether or not $p \in HDW_i(h)$ is determined by the value of $c_i(h)$. Similarly, the value of $N_{i-1}(h)$ is determined by $c_1(h), c_2(h), \ldots, c_{i-1}(h)$ of h. Hence, we now break the inner sum further by the c_i values, and get

$$\sum_h \frac{S_A^i(h)}{E(h)}$$

$$\leq \sum_p \sum_c \sum_{c':p\in HDW_i(c')} \sum_{h:c_{i-1}=c\wedge c_i=c'} \frac{N_{i-1}(h)}{(c_1 \ldots c_{k-1})^{2^k}}$$

$$\leq \sum_p \sum_c \sum_{c':p\in HDW_i(c')} \frac{N_{i-1}(c)}{(c_1 \ldots c_{i-1})^{2^k}},$$

where c' ranges over the values taken by c_i in the tree. The last inequality can be explained as follows. The the values of $c_1(h), \ldots, c_{i-1}(h)$ are determined by the value of $c_i(h)$. Let the values of $c_1(h), \ldots, c_{i-1}(h)$ corresponding to $c_i = c'$ be $c_1^*, \ldots, c_{i-1}^*$. Then

$$\sum_{h:c_{i-1}=c\wedge c_i=c'} \frac{1}{(c_1 \ldots c_{k-1})^{2^k}} = \sum_{h:c_i=c'} \frac{1}{(c_1 \ldots c_{k-1})^{2^k}} = \frac{1}{(c_1^* \ldots c_{i-1}^*)^{2^k}}.$$

Fix the value of c. Now p can write to at most $Z_{i-1}(h)$ vertices at level i. Each of these vertices can be high degree for at most one value of c'. We use the bound given by (8) for Z_{i-1} and (7) for N_{i-1} Then we get

$$\sum_h \frac{S_A^i(h)}{E(h)} \leq \sum_p \sum_c \frac{Z_{i-1}N_{i-1}}{(c_1 \ldots c_{i-1})^{2^k}} \leq \sum_p \sum_c \frac{1}{c} \leq 2P.$$

The case $i = 1$ is even easier. We group the h in the right most sum of (12) by c_1 values and get

$$\sum_h \frac{S_A^1(h)}{E(h)} \leq \sum_p \sum_{c'} \sum_{h:c_1(h)=c'\wedge p\in HDW_1(h)} \frac{1}{E(h)}.$$

Now, a processor p can be $HDW_1(c')$ for at most two values of c', because after the first read p can be in at most two states. Reasoning as before we get

$$\sum_h \frac{S_A^1(h)}{E(h)} \leq \sum_p 2 \leq 2P. \quad \square$$

4 Reductions

4.1 Prefix and Range Maxima

Theorem 4.1 *An algorithm that solves prefix maxima on domain $\{1, \ldots, n\}$ with n processors requires time $\Omega(\alpha(n))$.*

Proof: We reduce the chaining problem to a prefix maxima problem on domain $\{1, \ldots, n\}$. On input $a_1, \ldots, a_n$, compute $c_1, \ldots, c_n$, $c_i = 0$ if $a_i = 0$ and $c_i = i$ if $a_i = 1$. Then solve prefix maxima for $c_1, \ldots, c_n$. Let $d_1, \ldots, d_n$ be the prefix maxima. It is easy to see that $b_1 = 0$ and $b_i = d_{i-1}$, $2 \leq i \leq n$ is the required solution to the chaining problem. □

Theorem 4.2 *There exists a constant c such that an algorithm that preprocesses for range maximum on domain $\{1, \ldots, n\}$ with n processors so that a single processor can answer a query in $c\alpha(n)$ steps requires $\Omega(\alpha(n))$ time.*

Proof: We reduce the prefix maxima problem to the range maxima problem. On input $a_1, \ldots, a_n$, first preprocess for range maxima and then assign n processors, one to find the maximum of $[1, i]$, $1 \leq i \leq n$. □

4.2 Parenthesis Matching

Theorem 4.3 *Parenthesis matching with nesting level requires $\Omega(\alpha(n))$ time, even when the depth of nesting is at most 2.*

Proof: Given an input to the chaining problem, replace each 0 with "()" and assign a nesting level of 2 to both parentheses; replace each 1 with ")(" and assign a nesting level of 1 to both parentheses. Add a "(" before and a ")" after the whole sequence, both with nesting level 1. Note that every ")" with nesting level 1 corresponds to some 1 in the original input. The "(" that matches it corresponds to the 1 preceding it in the original input. Thus, after solving the parenthesis matching problem, it is easy to recover the solution to the original problem in constant time. □

5 Conclusions and Discussion

We have presented lower bounds for chaining, prefix maxima, range maxima and parenthesis matching on small domains. The bounds are tight for the chaining problem and parenthesis matching, but we do not know about the other two problems.

The complexity of each of these problems with randomization permitted is open. Berkman et. al, [6], give randomized preprocessing algorithms that run in $O(\log^* n)$ time. Raman, [20], gives a constant time randomized chaining algorithm that works if the number of 1's in the input is not too large.

We intuitively expect prefix maxima to be harder than just finding the maximum, however, often, they turn out to have the same complexity. For example, with one processor the complexity is $\Theta(n)$ and with n processors and a sufficiently large domain, $\Theta(\log\log n)$. Our lower bound is the only instance known to us where the two are shown to have different complexities. This suggests that the difference arises because of restricting the domain size. However, if we restrict the domain size further, to a constant, then both have complexity $O(1)$. It is an interesting open question to characterize when the two problems have different complexities.

Acknowledgement: The earlier version of this paper wrongly claimed $O(\alpha(n))$ upper bounds for the prefix maxima and range maxima problems. We would like to thank Anna Lubiw for pointing out the error in the argument presented there. We are grateful to Vince Grolmusz for suggesting this problem and to Ravi Boppana for suggesting the approach.

References

[1] R. Boppana, "Optimal Separations Between Concurrent Write Parallel Machines", *Proc. of the 21st ACM STOC*, 1989.

[2] O. Berkman, D. Breslauer, Z. Galil, B. Scheiber and U. Vishkin, "Highly Parallelizable Problems", *Proc. of 21st ACM STOC*, 1989.

[3] P.C.P. Bhatt, K. Diks, T. Hagerup, V.C. Prasad, T. Radzik and S. Saxena, "Improved Deterministic Parallel Integer Sorting", Information and Computation, *to appear.*

[4] P. Beame and J. Hastad, "Optimal Bounds for Decision Problems on the CRCW PRAM", Proc. of the 19th ACM STOC, 1987.

[5] O. Berkman, J. Jaja, S. Krishnamurthy, R. Thurimella and U. Vishkin, "Some Triply-Logarithmic Parallel Algorithms",*Proc. of 31st FOCS*, 1990.

[6] O. Berkman, Y. Matias and U. Vishkin, "Randomized Range-Maxima in Nearly-Constant Parallel Time", manuscript, 1992.

[7] O. Berkman and U. Vishkin, "Recursive Star-Tree Parallel Data Structure", *Proc. of 30th FOCS*, 1989.

[8] A.K. Chandra, S. Fortune and R.J. Lipton, "Unbounded Fan-in Circuits and Associative Functions", *Proc. of the 15th ACM STOC*, 1983.

[9] A.K. Chandra, S. Fortune and R.J. Lipton, "Lower bounds for Constant Depth Circuits for Prefix Problems", *Proc. of the 10th Int. Colloquium on Automata, Languages and Programming*, Lecture Notes in Computer Science, Springer-Verlag, 1983.

[10] S. Chaudhuri, "Tight Bounds on the Chaining Problem", *Proc. of 3rd ACM SPAA*, 1991.

[11] D. Dolev, C. Dwork, N. Pippenger and A. Wigderson, "Superconcentrators, Generalizers and Generalized Connectors with Limited Depth", *Proc. of the 15th ACM STOC*, 1983.

[12] F.E. Fich, A. Wigderson and P. Ragde, "Simulations Among Concurrent-Write Models of Parallel Computation", Algorithmica 3, 1988.

[13] J. Gil, Y. Matias and U. Vishkin, "Towards a theory of nearly constant time parallel algorithms", Proc of 32nd FOCS, 1991.

[14] J. Gil and L. Rudolph, "Counting and Packing in Parallel", *International Conference on Parallel Processing*, 1986.

[15] P. D. Mackenzie, "Load Balancing requires $\Omega(\log^* n)$ expected time", Proc. of 3rd ACM-SIAM Symposium on Discrete Algorithms, 1992.

[16] Y. Matias and U. Vishkin, "On Integer Sorting and Parallel Hashing",*Proc. 17th ICALP*, 1990.

[17] F. Meyer auf der Heide and A. Wigderson, "The complexity of parallel sorting", Proc. 26th Foundations of Computer Science.

[18] I. Newman, P. Ragde and A. Wigderson, "Perfect Hashing, Graph Entropy and Circuit Complexity", Proc. Fifth Ann. Conf. on Structure in Complexity Theory (1990) 91–99.

[19] P. Ragde, "The Parallel Simplicity of Compaction and Chaining", *Proc. 17th ICALP*, 1990.

[20] R. Raman, "The Power of Collision: Randomized Parallel Algorithms for Chaining and Integer Sorting", *10th Foundations of Software Technology and Theoretical Computer Science*, 1990.

[21] L. Rudolph and W. Steiger, "Subset Selection in Parallel", *Proc. of the 1985 Int. Conference on Parallel Processing*, 1985.

[22] M. Snir, "On Parallel Searching", SIAM J. of Computing, v14, no 2, 1985.

Appendix

Proof of Property P5. It can be easily verified that

$$A_2^{(i+j)}(1) = Tower(i+j) \geq (2^i)^{2^j}. \quad (13)$$

We can verify by induction on t that

$$A_t(A_t(A_t(1))) \geq 2^t. \quad (14)$$

In the following we assume that $t > 2$. Let $d = 2^t$. If $x \geq 20$, then

$$A_t^{(x/2)}(1) \geq x^{2d}. \quad (15)$$

For, using (14) we get,

$$A_t^{(x/2)}(1) = A_t^{(x/2-3)}(A_t^{(3)}(1)) \geq A_t^{(x/2-4)} A_{t-1}^{(d)}(1).$$

Now, since $t > 2$ and $x \geq 20$, we get using (13) that

$$A_t^{(x/2-4)} A_{t-1}^{(d)}(1) \geq A_2^{(x/2-4+d)}(1) \geq (2^{x/2-4})^{2^d} \geq x^{2d}.$$

$$B_1(x) = (\textit{biggest label in } T_1(x))^{2d} = x^{2d}. \quad (16)$$

$$B_{i+1}(x) = B_i^{(x^d)}(2^x). \quad (17)$$

We shall show that $B_i(x) \leq A_{f(i)}(x)$, where $f(i) = t + 2i - 2$.

Basis. That $B_1(x) \leq A_t(x)$ follows from (15) and (16).

Step. $A_{f(i+1)}(x) = A_{f(i)+2}(x) = A_{f(i)+1}^{(x)}(1)$. Using (15) and (17) we get

$$\begin{aligned} A_{f(i)+1}^{(x)}(1) &\geq A_{f(i)+1}(x^{2d}) \geq A_{f(i)+1}(2x^d) \\ &\geq A_{f(i)}^{(x^d)}(A_{f(i)}^{(x^d)}(1)) \geq A_{f(i)}^{(x^d)}(2^x) \geq B_i^{(x^d)}(2^x) \\ &= B_{i+1}(x). \end{aligned}$$

Let y be the label on the second last edge of the right most path of $T_k^*(l)$ (also the right most path of $T_{k-1}(B_{k-1}^{(l-1)}(20))$). Then the number of leaves in $T_k^*(l)$ is at most

$$2y^d \leq B_{k-1}^{(l)}(20) \leq A_{t+2k-4}^{(l)}(20).$$

Now, we get

$$\begin{aligned} A_{t+2k}(l) \geq A_{t+2k-1}^{(l)}(1) &\geq A_{t+2k-1}^{(l-3)}(A_2(A_2(A_2(1)))) \\ &\geq A_{t+2k-1}^{(l-3)}(16) \\ &\geq A_{t+2k-1}^{(l-4)}(A_{t+2k-2}^{(16)}(1)) \\ &\geq A_{t+2k-4}^{(l)}(20). \end{aligned}$$

We take $t = k$ so that $d = 2^k$ and get that

The number of leaves in $T_k^*(l) \leq A_{(3k)}(l)$.

Proof of $(I_{3k+1}(n))^3 < I_{3k}(n)$, when $k \leq \frac{\alpha(n)}{10}$ and n is sufficiently large.
We shall first prove that $I_{3k+1}(n) \leq \log(I_{3k}(n))$, for n large. Now,

$$\begin{aligned} A_{3k+1}(\log I_{3k}(n)) &\geq A_{3k}^{\log I_{3k}(n)}(1) \\ &\geq A_{3k}(A_{3k}^{\log I_{3k}(n)-5}(64)). \end{aligned}$$

Since $A_{3k}(x) \geq 2x$,

$$\begin{aligned} A_{3k+1}(\log I_{3k}(n)) &\geq A_{3k}(\frac{64 I_{3k}(n)}{32}) \\ &\geq A_{3k}(I_{3k}(n)+1) \geq n. \end{aligned}$$

It follows that $I_{3k+1}(n) \leq \log(I_{3k}(n))$. Since $k \leq \frac{\alpha(n)}{10}$, $I_{3k}(n)$ and $I_{3k+1}(n)$ go to infinity with n. Since $I_{3k+1}(n) \leq \log(I_{3k}(n))$, $(I_{3k+1}(n))^3 < I_{3k}(n)$ for large n.

Approximate max flow on small depth networks

Edith Cohen
AT&T Bell Laboratories
Murray Hill, NJ 07974

Extended abstract

Abstract.

We consider the maximum flow problem on directed acyclic networks with m edges and *depth* r (length of the longest s-t path). Our main result is a new deterministic algorithm for solving the relaxed problem of computing an s-t flow of value at least $(1-\epsilon)$ of the maximum flow. For instances where r and ϵ^{-1} are small (i.e., $O(\text{polylog}(m))$), this algorithm is in $\mathcal{NC}$ and uses only $O(m)$ processors, which is a significant improvement over existing parallel algorithms. As one consequence, we obtain an $\mathcal{NC}$ $O(m)$ processor algorithm to find a bipartite matching of cardinality $(1-\epsilon)$ of the maximum (for $\epsilon^{-1} = O(\text{polylog}(m))$). Our parallel bounds are based on a novel approach to the blocking flow problem that produces fractional valued flow augmentations even when capacities are integral. We show that a fractional flow on any network with integral capacities can be rounded in polylogarithmic time to an integral flow of no smaller value using $O(m)$ processors. Hence, within the same resource bounds, an integral flow can be obtained when desired.

1. Introduction

A flow network is modeled by a directed acyclic graph $G = (V, E)$ with capacities $u_e \geq 0$ $(e \in E)$ associated with the edges, a designated *source* vertex $s \in V$ and a designated *sink* vertex $t \in V$. We use the parameter r to denote the *depth* of the network, which we define to be the length of the longest s-t path in G. For a vertex $v \in V$, we denote by $\text{in}(v)$ (resp., $\text{out}(v)$) the set of edges directed into (resp., out of) v. An *s-t flow* f on G is an assignment of flow values f_e $(e \in E)$ to edges such that the capacity constraints are not violated (for all $e \in E$, $0 \leq f_e \leq u_e$), and at every vertex other than the source or the sink $v \in V \setminus \{s,t\}$, flow is conserved, that is, $\sum_{e\in\text{in}(v)} f_e = \sum_{e\in\text{out}(v)} f_e$. The *value* of an s-t flow is the amount of excess flow at t (i.e., $\sum_{e\in\text{in}(t)} f_e - \sum_{e\in\text{out}(t)} f_e$). A maximum flow (max-flow) is an s-t flow of maximum value. We use M^* to denote the value of the max-flow.

Finding a maximum flow is one of the classic problems in combinatorial optimization. The fastest known sequential algorithms for the problem have time bounds close to $O(mn)$ (see [1, 11]). The known parallel algorithms for the problem are less satisfactory. The maximum flow problem with general capacities is known to be $\mathcal{P}$-complete [14] and hence not likely to have an $\mathcal{NC}$ algorithm. The fastest known deterministic parallel algorithm solves the problem (on a CRCW PRAM) in $O(n^2 \log n)$ time using $O(n)$ processors (an algorithm by Shiloach and Vishkin [22] uses $O(n^2)$ space and a later algorithm by Goldberg and Tarjan [11] uses $O(m)$ space). When the capacities are polynomial in m, the problem seems easier: It is not known to be $\mathcal{P}$-complete, and furthermore, it is in $\mathcal{RNC}$ by a standard logspace reduction to the maximum cardinality bipartite matching problem. The bipartite matching problem was first shown to be in $\mathcal{RNC}$ by Karp, Upfal, and Wigderson [17], who gave an algorithm that uses $O(n^{6.5})$ processors. Later algorithms (see [8, 20]) use fewer processors, where the best current bound is $O(nM(n))$ by Galil and Pan [8]. When capacities are in $\{0,1\}$, the maximum flow problem can be solved within the same bounds as maximum cardinality bipartite matching. If the capacities are polynomial in m, an additional factor of $O(m)$ is added to the processor bound. (When capacities are general a factor of $\log U$ is added to the running time, and hence the algorithm is not in $\mathcal{RNC}$.) To summarize, we note that max-flow with polynomial capacities can be solved sequentially using $\tilde{O}(mn)$ work, in $\tilde{O}(n^2)$ time using $\tilde{O}(n^3)$ work, and in $\mathcal{RNC}$ using expected $\tilde{O}(mnM(n))$ work.

We present a max-flow algorithm with the following bounds:

0-8186-2900-2/92 $3.00 © 1992 IEEE

Theorem 1.1 *A flow of value M such that*

$$M \geq (1-\epsilon)M^*$$

can be computed deterministically on an EREW PRAM in

i. $O(r^3\epsilon^{-3}\log^2 m\log(m\epsilon^{-1}))$ *time using* $O(m/r)$ *processors and* $O(m)$ *space, or*

ii. $O(r^2\epsilon^{-2}\log^3 m\log r\log(m\epsilon^{-1}))$ *time using* $M(n)$ *processors and* $O(M(n))$ *space.*

Observe that when the depth r and ϵ^{-1} are small (e.g., $O(\text{polylog}(m))$), the resource bounds obtained here are significantly better than known bounds given for general exact maximum flow algorithms.

Our max-flow algorithm consists of iterating calls to a subproblem of finding approximate *blocking flows*, and is based on a novel parallel blocking flow algorithm. A blocking flow is an *s*-*t* flow which can not be augmented without pushing flow "backward" through at least one edge. Dinic's algorithm [3] introduced a scheme to solve the max-flow problem by reducing it to blocking flow computations. Dinic's algorithm computes a max-flow in $O(n)$ phases, where each phase amounts to a blocking flow computation on a directed acyclic layered network. The depth of the layered network increases at each phase. The fastest known sequential blocking flow algorithm is due to Goldberg and Tarjan [13] and has an almost optimal time bound of $O(m\log(n^2/m))$. Unlike the more general max-flow problem, it is not known, even when capacities are general, whether the blocking flow problem is $\mathcal{P}$-complete. The fastest known (polynomial-work) deterministic parallel algorithm for computing blocking flows was given by Goldberg and Tarjan [12] and runs in $O(n\log n)$ time, using $O(m)$ processors. The problem, When capacities are polynomial in m, the problem is in $\mathcal{RNC}$ since this is true for the more general max-flow problem.

We give an overview of the ideas used and the structure of the paper.

In Section 2 we review commonly used terminology for network flow algorithms, sketch Dinic's maximum flow algorithm, and discuss the blocking flow problem.

In Section 3 we examine the use of Dinic's algorithm to obtain near-maximum flows. We show that in order to obtain a flow of value at least $(1-\epsilon)M^*$, it suffices to run Dinic's algorithm for at most $O(r\epsilon^{-1})$ phases (until the length of the layered networks exceeds $O(r\epsilon^{-1})$). Furthermore, we show that when only a near-maximum flow is desired, it is not necessary to find an exact blocking flow at each phase. We define a notion of an approximate blocking flow and prove that we can use a relaxed variant of Dinic's algorithm where exact blocking flow computations are replaced by approximate ones.

In Section 3 we shall see that the blocking flow instances that arise when running the approximate version of Dinic's algorithm involve networks of depth at most $O(r\epsilon^{-1})$. This fact does not benefit us when considering sequential algorithms since blocking flows can be found almost optimally regardless of the depth of the network [13]. We can gain, however, in the parallel case. The worst case behavior of the $O(n\log n)$ time Goldberg Tarjan [12] parallel blocking flow algorithm does not improve when instances are limited to networks of small depth. In Section 4 we present a novel parallel approximate blocking flow algorithm that is significantly more efficient on small depth networks than existing exact blocking flow algorithms. The algorithm uses $O(m)$ processors and is in $\mathcal{NC}$ when $r = O(\text{polylog}\, m)$. If the capacities are polynomial in m, the algorithm computes an exact blocking flow within the same resource bounds.

Our blocking flow algorithm is based on a notion of *path counts* of a network. We define the path count of an acyclic network to be the sum over all *s*-*t* paths of the product of all edge capacities along the path. The path count of an edge $e \in E$ is the same sum over paths that contain e. When the network has unit capacities, the path count reduces to the number of different *s*-*t* paths. The algorithm is fairly simple and we sketch it here. We make use of the property that path counts of edges are conserved at all vertices other than the source and the sink. That is, for each vertex $v \in V \setminus \{s,t\}$, the sum of path counts of edges entering v equals the sum of path counts of edges exiting v. Hence, an assignment of values to edges where the values are proportional (with a small enough proportion factor) to the respective path counts constitutes a legal flow. The blocking flow algorithm repeatedly computes the path counts at edges, finds the largest proportional flow augmentation that does not violate the current capacities, and updates the current flow. The following iteration is applied to the network with the new augmentation being subtracted from the capacities. The algorithm terminates when the current flow is approximately blocking. We will show that the path counts computations, and hence each iteration, can be implemented efficiently in parallel.

The blocking flow algorithm of Section 4 conceivably terminates with a fractional flow, even when capacities are integral. In Section 5 we describe an $\mathcal{NC}$ "rounding" algorithm that uses $O(m)$ processors. For a given fractional flow on a general network with integral capacities, the algorithm computes an integral flow of at least the same value. We also describe how to obtain an integral blocking flow by combining the fractional approximate-blocking flow algorithm of Section 4 with the rounding algorithm, and how to obtain, in a network with costs, an integral flow of cost no greater than the cost of a given fractional flow. Our rounding algorithm generalizes a similar algorithm for bipartite matching networks given by Goldberg, Plotkin, Shmoys, and Tardos [9].

In the full version, we discuss parallel exact maximum flow algorithms for zero-one and unit networks. Zero-one networks are networks where all capacities are in $\{0,1\}$. A unit network is a zero-one network where each vertex has either has at most one incident outgoing edge or at most one incident ingoing edge. We give algorithms that use balancing techniques similar to the ones used by Goldberg, Plotkin, and Vaidya in [10], and combine the blocking flow algorithm of Section 4 and a parallel version of the Ford-Fulkerson algorithm [6]. (The algorithm of [10] combined parallel versions of the push-relabel and the Ford-Fulkerson algorithms.) We obtain sublinear parallel running times that are comparable to the running times given in [10].

Section 6 is concerned with the maximum cardinality bipartite matching problem. By a standard reduction, an instance of the problem can be reduced to an integral max-flow problem on a zero-one network of depth $r = 3$. The corresponding max-flow instance is such that an integral flow of some value M yields a matching of cardinality M in the original problem. Hence, the results of previous sections imply an $O(\log^3 m)$ time $O(m)$ processor deterministic parallel algorithm for finding a bipartite matching of cardinality at least $(1-\epsilon)$ of the cardinality of the maximum matching when $\epsilon^{-1} = O(1)$. If $\epsilon^{-1} = O(\text{polylog}\, m)$ the algorithm remains in $\mathcal{NC}$ and has the same processor bound.

2. Preliminaries

The parallel running times and processor utilization mentioned in this paper are for the EREW PRAM model. The routines used are limited to standard ones (e.g., list rankings, BFS, shortest path computations, finding Eulerian partitions) and hence running times on other models can be deduced easily (see, e.g., the survey of Karp and Ramachandran [16]). In the context of graphs, we use the notation $\tilde{O}(f)$ to mean $O(f \,\text{polylog}\, f \,\text{polylog}\, m)$. We use $M(n)$ to denote the current record for the number of operations needed to multiply two $n \times n$ matrices. It is known (see Coppersmith and Winograd [2]) that $M(n) = o(n^{2.376})$. The quantity $M(n)$ appears in some of our processor bounds for parallel algorithms, by relying on a result of Pan and Reif [21] who had shown that two $n \times n$ matrices can be multiplied in $O(\log n)$ time using $M(n)$ processors, and the fact that the best known processor bounds for $\mathcal{NC}$ computation of transitive closure, directed s-t path, and BFS tree are obtained using matrix multiplication.

We review some standard terminology associated with maximum flow algorithm and sketch Dinic's algorithm. For further details see [24]. A flow in a network is *blocking* if every path from s to t contains a saturated edge. Consider a current flow f in G and the corresponding residual graph R. The *level* of a vertex $v \in V$ is the length of the shortest path from s to v in R. The *level graph* L for f is the subgraph of R that contains only vertices reachable from s and only edges $e = (u, v)$ such that $\text{level}(v) = \text{level}(u) + 1$. The construction of the level graph for a given flow f can be done in linear $O(m)$ time using breadth first search. In parallel, the construction can be done in $O(r \log m)$ time using $O(m/r)$ processors, where r is the level of t (using a straightforward parallel implementation of the breadth first search algorithm).

Dinic's maximum flow algorithm [3] maintains a current flow f, initialized as the zero flow, and repeats the following until t is not reachable from s in the residual graph for f.

i. Find a blocking flow f' on the level graph for the current flow f.

ii. Replace $f \leftarrow f + f'$.

Dinic showed that the level of t strictly increases in each phase and hence the algorithm terminates after at most $n-1$ phases.

3. Obtaining a near-maximum flow

We examine applying variants of Dinic's algorithm to solve the relaxed goal of obtaining a near-maximum flow, when (i) the networks have small depth or (ii) only approximately-blocking flow routines are available.

3.1. Small depth networks

Consider a network G and an s-t flow f. The following proposition states a relation between the value of f and M^* in terms of the depth r and the length of the minimum augmenting path in the residual graph induced by f.

Proposition 3.1 *Consider a network G as above, and a flow f of value M where the shortest augmenting path in the residual graph induced by f is of length $\ell \geq r+1$. Under these conditions*

$$M^* \leq (\frac{\ell + r}{\ell - r})M .$$

Proof: Without loss of generality, we assume integral flow values and capacities. Consider an integral flow f of value M. Denote by f^* a maximum integral flow with value M^*. There exists a set P of $M^* - M$ augmenting paths of capacity 1 from s to t on the residual graph that (i) augments the flow from f to f^* and (ii) does not use any edge in more than one direction. (obviously, all paths in P are of length $\geq \ell$.) Note that $M^* = M + |P|$.
For the analysis, we assign vertices to layers labeled $\{0, \ldots, r\}$ where a vertex $v \in V$ is assigned according to the length of the longest path in G from s to v. It is clear that all edges are directed from lower levels to strictly higher levels. We account for a unit flow in an arc ("weight" of the arc) as follows: if it is from layer i to layer j, account for it as $|j - i|$. The total weight of a flow on G equals r times the value of the flow.
Consider a blocking flow with no augmenting path of weight less than ℓ (note that weight ℓ suffices for the result of the proposition, length ℓ is a stronger requirement). For an augmenting path $p \in P$, denote by a_p the weight from the forward edges, and by b_p the weight from the backward edges. Obviously $a_p - b_p = r$, $a_p + b_p \geq \ell$. Note that since $\ell \geq r+1$, we have $b_p \geq 1$.
Intuitively, view a path from P as "exchanging" weight b_p out of the old flow with a larger weight a_p added toward achieving the optimal flow.
Formally: Since no two paths from P use an edge in opposite directions we have

$$\sum_{p \in P} b_p \leq rM .$$

From the inequalities $a_p - r = b_p$ and $a_p + b_p \geq \ell$ it follows that for all $p \in P$,

$$b_p \geq (\ell - r)/2 .$$

Combining the two we have

$$|P|(\ell - r)/2 \leq \sum_{p \in P} b_p \leq rM .$$

Hence,

$$|P| \leq \frac{2r}{\ell - r} M .$$

∎

Corollary 3.2 *The value of any blocking flow on G is at least $M^*/(2r)$.*

Corollary 3.3 *Consider a network G as above. An s-t flow of value at least $(1-\epsilon)M^*$ can be computed in $O(r\epsilon^{-1} m \log(n^2/m))$ time. Note that when r and ϵ are fixed this bound is almost linear.*

3.2. Using approximately-blocking flows

We introduce a notion of an approximate blocking flow, and a modified version of Dinic's algorithm which uses an approximate blocking flow in each iteration.

Definition 3.4 Consider a max flow instance as above. An *ϵ-blocking flow* is a flow for which all non saturated s-t paths contain an edge of capacity not greater than ϵ. A 0-blocking flow is a blocking flow.

Proposition 3.5 *[Modified Dinic Algorithm] Consider a modification of Dinic algorithm where in each phase we compute an ϵ-blocking flow on the current layered graph. In the following phase we construct a layered graph by treating edges of capacity no larger than ϵ as having capacity 0.*

i. At the termination of the kth phase, all augmenting paths of length at most k in the residual graph contain an edge of capacity no larger than ϵ.

ii. The depth of the layered graph strictly increases from phase to phase.

Corollary 3.6 *Consider a max flow instance as above. By running the modified Dinic algorithm until* *the depth of the layered network exceeds ℓ (this happens within ℓ phases) we can compute a flow of value M such that*

$$M + m\epsilon \geq (\frac{\ell - r}{\ell + r})M^* ,$$

where M^* is the value of the maximum flow.

In the following section we present a deterministic parallel algorithm for computing an ϵ-blocking flow. The algorithm is particularly efficient when the depth of the network is small. By combining it with Corollary 3.6 we obtain the bounds stated in Theorem 1.1.

4. Parallel ϵ-blocking flow algorithm

We consider the blocking flow problem on a directed acyclic graph $G = (V, E)$ with capacities $u_e \geq 0$ $(e \in E)$, a designated source vertex $s \in V$, and a designated sink $t \in V$. The parameter r denotes the depth of the network.

We present an algorithm for computing an ϵ-blocking flow in G. We first introduce the concept of path counts.

4.1. The path counts of a network

Definition 4.1 Suppose that G is a network as above.

i. Denote by $\mathcal{P}$ the set of all s-t paths in G. Note that $|\mathcal{P}| \leq n^r$. Denote by $\mathcal{P}_{uw}$ the set of all paths from $u \in V$ to $w \in V$.

ii. The *path count* χ of the network is

$$\chi = \sum_{p \in \mathcal{P}} \prod_{e \in p} u_e .$$

When $u_e \in \{0,1\}$ $(e \in E)$, then $\chi = |\mathcal{P}|$.

iii. The *path count of an edge* $e \in E$ is

$$\chi_e = \sum_{\{p \in \mathcal{P} | e \in p\}} \prod_{e' \in p} u_{e'} .$$

iv. The *path count from* $u \in V$ *to* $w \in V$ is

$$\chi^{uw} = \sum_{p \in \mathcal{P}_{uw}} \prod_{e \in p} u_e .$$

The algorithm we introduce here relies on the property that the path counts of edges obey "conservation constraints" at vertices, and hence, so does a flow function proportional to the edges' path counts.

Proposition 4.2 *For all $v \in V \setminus \{s,t\}$,*

$$\sum_{e \in \text{in}(v)} \chi_e = \sum_{e \in \text{out}(v)} \chi_e .$$

Complexity of computing the path counts. We suggest two algorithms to compute χ and χ_e for all $e \in E$. This is done by first computing for each vertex $u \in V$, the quantities χ^{su} and χ^{ut}. It is easy to see that the path count χ_e of an edge $e \in E$, where $e = (u,v)$, equals $\chi_e = \chi^{su}\chi^{vt}$.

Path counts can be computed as follows:

i. By using two level by level passes, where a level consists of all vertices all of whose predecessors were previously scanned. We do one forward pass starting at s to compute the quantities χ^{su} $(u \in V)$, and one pass "backward" starting at t to compute χ^{ut} $(u \in V)$. This can be done in $O(r \log m)$ time using $O(m/r)$ processors on an EREW PRAM.

ii. By using $O(\log r)$ matrix multiplications of $n \times n$ matrices. Pan and Reif [21] have shown that multiplication of two $n \times n$ matrices can be done in $O(\log n)$ time using $\max\{n^2, M(n)\}$ processors. Hence, path counts can be computed in $O(\log r \log n)$ time using $M(n)$ processors on an EREW PRAM.

4.2. The ϵ-blocking flow algorithm

We present an ϵ-blocking flow algorithm. The algorithm consists of iterations, where each iteration augments the flow. We refer to the difference between the initial capacity and the current flow value of an edge e as the *current capacity* of e. The flow on an edge e does not decrease, and hence, the current capacity of e does not increase. For the ith iteration, we denote by u_e^i $(e \in E)$ the current capacities, by χ_e^i $(e \in E)$ the respective path counts, and by $0 \leq f_e^i \leq u_e^i$ $(e \in E)$ the flow augmentation computed during the iteration. An iteration amounts to first computing the path counts χ_e $(e \in E)$, with respect to the current capacities, and then computing a valid flow augmentation which is proportional to the path counts and is of maximum possible value.

Algorithm 4.3 [Find an ϵ-blocking flow]

i. $i \leftarrow 0$

ii. Set the initial capacities:

For $e \in E$, $u_e^0 \leftarrow \begin{cases} u_e & \text{if } u_e \geq \epsilon \\ 0 & \text{if } u_e \leq \epsilon \end{cases}$

$E \leftarrow E \setminus \{e \in E | u_e^0 = 0\}$

iii. **Repeat:**

(1) Compute the path counts χ_e^i, for $e \in E$, with respect to the capacities u_e^i. Let $\mu_i = \min_{e \in E} u_e^i / \chi_e^i$.

(2) For all $e \in E$, set $f_e^i \leftarrow \mu_i \chi_e^i$, $u_e^{i+1} \leftarrow u_e^i - f_e^i$, if $u_e^{i+1} \leq \epsilon$ set $u_e^{i+1} \leftarrow 0$ ($E \leftarrow E \setminus \{e\}$).

(3) $i \leftarrow i+1$

Until: t is not reachable from s in E

iv. Output the flow f, where

$$\text{for } e \in E,\ f_e \leftarrow \sum_{j=1}^{i-1} f_e^i .$$

4.3. Correctness

For $e \in E$, the quantity $\mu_e^i \equiv u_e^i / \chi_e^i$ is the maximum flow value per path count unit we can put through the edge e without violating the capacity u_e^i. The choice of μ_i as the minimum of these quantities guarantees that for all edges $e \in E$, $f_e^i = \mu_i \chi_e^i \leq u_e^i$.

Proposition 4.2 states that the path counts χ_e obey conservation constraints at the vertices. Hence, the same holds for the quantities $f_e^i = \mu_i \chi_e$ ($e \in E$).

We showed that in each iteration, the values f_e^i ($e \in E$) obey both the conservation constraints at the vertices and the current capacity constraints at all edges, and hence, they constitute a valid flow.

It is easy to see that for $i > 0$, at the end of the ith iteration we have

$$\text{for all } e \in E, \qquad u_e^0 - \epsilon \leq u_e^{i+1} + \sum_{i=0}^{i} f_e^i \leq u_e^0 .$$

Additionally, the algorithm terminates at the ith iteration if the removal of all edges ($e \in E$) for which $u_e^0 - \sum_{j=0}^{i} f_e^j \leq \epsilon$ disconnects s and t. The correctness of the algorithm follows:

Proposition 4.4 *When the algorithm terminates, f_e ($e \in E$) computed in step iv is an ϵ-blocking flow.*

Observe that in each iteration, the current capacity of at least one edge is set to 0 (the edge e for which $\mu_i = u_e^i / \chi_e^i$). Hence, the algorithm terminates after at most m iterations. We will prove a much better bound on the number of iterations.

4.4. Bound on the number of iterations

Proposition 4.5 *For every edge $e \in E$, the quantities μ_e^i ($i \geq 0$) are a non decreasing function of i, and hence, the same is true for $\mu_i = \min_{e \in E} \mu_e^i$ ($i \geq 0$).*

Proposition 4.6

$$\mu_0^{-1} \leq \frac{(n \max_{e \in E} u_e^0)^r}{n\epsilon} .$$

Proposition 4.7 *If for some i,*

$$\mu_i^{-1} \leq \epsilon^r / \max_{e \in E} u_e^0 ,$$

then the algorithm terminates at the ith iteration.

Proposition 4.8 *If*

$$j \geq i + \lceil \log(\epsilon^{-1} \max_{e \in E} u_e^i) \rceil ,$$

then $\mu_j / \mu_i \geq 2$.

Proof: Consider the set of edges in a kth iteration

$$E_k = \{e \in E | \mu_k^{-1}/2 \leq \chi_e^k / u_e^k \leq \mu_k^{-1}\} .$$

It follows that for every edge $e \in E_k$, the current capacity, and hence, also the path count, decrease by a factor of at least 1/2 during the kth iteration (that is, for every $e \in E_k$ we have $u_e^{k+1} \leq u_e^k/2$ and $\chi_e^{k+1} \leq \chi_e^k/2$). Assume to the contrary that $\mu_j^{-1} > \mu_i^{-1}/2$. Since the μ_k's are non decreasing, there exists an edge e such that $\mu_i^{-1}/2 \leq \chi_e^k / u_e^k$ for $k = i, \ldots, j$, and hence $e \in E_k$ for $k = i, \ldots, j$. It follows that

$$u_e^j \leq \frac{u_e^i}{2^{(j-i)}} \leq \frac{u_e^i}{\epsilon^{-1} \max_{e \in E} u_e^i} \leq \epsilon .$$

Therefore, we have a contradiction, since in the jth iteration $e \notin E$. ∎

We obtain the following bound on the number of iterations.

Theorem 4.9 *The total number of iterations is at most*

$$1 + \lceil \log(\epsilon^{-1} \max_{e \in E} u_e^0) \rceil \left\lceil (r+1) \log(n\epsilon^{-1} \max_{e \in E} u_e^0) \right\rceil .$$

Proof: Suppose the algorithm terminates at iteration t. It follows from Propositions 4.6 and 4.7 that

$$\mu_{t-1}/\mu_0 \leq \frac{\max_{e \in E} u_e^0}{n\epsilon} \left(\frac{n \max_{e \in E} u_e^0}{\epsilon} \right)^r .$$

It follows from Proposition 4.8 that the total number of iterations is at most

$$t \leq \lceil \log \epsilon^{-1} \max_{e \in E} u_e^0 \rceil \lceil \log(\mu_{t-1}/\mu_0) \rceil + 1 .$$

The proof follows by combining the two inequalities. ∎

4.5. Complexity

Denote by U_f the width of the fattest s-t path, i.e.,

$$U_f = \max_{p \in \mathcal{P}} \min_{e \in p} u_e .$$

The quantity U_f is a lower bound on the maximum flow and mU_f is an upper bound. The parallel complexity of computing U_f is dominated by the complexity of computing path counts.

We may assume that $\max_{e \in E} u_e \leq mU_f$ and $\min_{e \in E} u_e \geq \epsilon$, since an ϵ-blocking flow when setting all capacities larger than mU_f to mU_f, and capacities smaller than ϵ to 0, is also ϵ-blocking with respect to the original capacities.

Proposition 4.10 *Using Algorithm 4.3, an ϵ-blocking flow can be computed in*

i. $O(r^2 \log m \log^2(\epsilon^{-1} mU_f))$ time using $O(m/r)$ processors, or

ii. $O(r \log n \log r \log^2(\epsilon^{-1} mU_f))$ time using $M(n)$ processors.

Proof: From Theorem 4.9, the number of iterations is bounded by

$$1 + \lceil \log(\epsilon^{-1} mU_f) \rceil \lceil (r+1) \log(nm\epsilon^{-1} U_f) \rceil$$
$$= O(r \log^2(\epsilon^{-1} mU_f)) .$$

The complexity of each iteration is dominated by the computation of path counts. Hence, we obtain the stated time bounds by combining the above with the complexity of computing the path counts (see Subsection 4.1). ∎

Particularly when $\epsilon = o(U_f/m^k)$, we can obtain a faster running time for finding an ϵ-blocking flow by using the following procedure:

Algorithm 4.11 [ϵ-blocking flow when $\epsilon = o(U_f/m)$]
While $U_f > \epsilon$ **Do:**

i. Compute a $\max\{U_f/m, \epsilon\}$-blocking flow (using Algorithm 4.3.)

ii. Update the capacities (subtract the flow values computed in the previous step).

It is easy to verify that when using Algorithm 4.11 we obtain the following:

Theorem 4.12 *An ϵ-blocking flow can be computed in*

i. $O(r^2 \log^2 m \log(\epsilon^{-1} mU_f))$ time using $O(m/r)$ processors, or

ii. $O(r \log r \log^3 m \log(\epsilon^{-1} mU_f))$ time using $M(n)$ processors.

We are now ready to present the proof of Theorem 1.1:
Proof of Theorem 1.1: To obtain these bounds we run the modified Dinic algorithm until the depth of the layered networks exceeds $\ell = 4r\epsilon^{-1}$. In each phase we compute an $\hat{\epsilon}$-blocking flow, where $\hat{\epsilon} = \epsilon U_f^0/2m$ (U_f^0 is the width of the fattest path in G). Denote by M the value of the flow when the modified Dinic algorithm terminates and by M^* the value of the maximum flow. We first prove that M and M^* have the desired relation. It follows from the choice of $\hat{\epsilon}$ and ℓ that

$$m\hat{\epsilon} \leq \epsilon M^*/2$$

(since $U_f^0 \leq M^*$), and that

$$(\ell - r)/(\ell + r) \geq (1 - \epsilon/2) .$$

By plugging the above in Corollary 3.6, we deduce that

$$M + \epsilon M^*/2 \geq (1 - \epsilon/2) M^* .$$

Hence, $M \geq (1-\epsilon)M^*$. We show that the computation can be performed within the desired resource bounds. It is easy to see that all layered networks obtained in the phases of the algorithm have depth at most ℓ, have at most as many nodes and edges as G, and are such that the corresponding quantity U_f is never larger than U_f^0. Hence, it follows from Theorem 4.12 that each phase can be implemented in:

i. $O(\ell^2 \log^2 m \log(\hat{\epsilon}^{-1} m U_f^0))$ time using $O(m/r)$ processors, or

ii. $O(\ell \log \ell \log^3 m \log(\hat{\epsilon}^{-1} m U_f^0))$ time using $M(n)$ processors.

To conclude note that there are at most ℓ phases. ∎

5. Rounding fractional flows

We present an $\mathcal{NC}$ algorithm that considers a network G with integral capacities u_e $(e \in E)$ and a fractional s-t flow f_e $(e \in E)$. The algorithm produces an integral flow $\hat{f}_e$ $(e \in E)$ of at least the same value such that $\hat{f}_e \in \{\lfloor f_e \rfloor, \lceil f_e \rceil\}$ for $(e \in E)$. We also discuss (i) combining the techniques of this section with the ϵ-blocking flow algorithm of Section 4 to produce an integral $\lfloor \epsilon \rfloor$-blocking flow and (ii) computing an integral flow of smaller cost, for networks where costs are associated with the edges.

It should be noted that this section generalizes an $\mathcal{NC}$ algorithm of Goldberg, Plotkin, Shmoys, and Tardos [9], for obtaining an integral minimum cost flow given a fractional nearly-minimum cost flow on bipartite matching networks (zero-one networks of depth $r = 3$). Their algorithm uses $O(m)$ processors and is based on Gabow's coloring algorithm [7].

5.1. Main iteration

We start with a subroutine for halving the smallest common denominator of the flow values, assuming it is a power of 2. Suppose $\Delta = 2^{-k}$ for some integer k, and the flow f is such that for all $e \in E$, f_e/Δ is integral. The following procedure computes a flow $\hat{f}$, of value at least as large as the value of f, such that for all $e \in E$, $\hat{f}_e/(2\Delta)$ is integral and for all $e \in E$, $|\hat{f}_e - f_e| \leq \Delta$.

Algorithm 5.1 [Double unit size]

i. Mark all edges $e \in E$ for which f_e/Δ is odd. Denote this set of edges by E'.

ii. E' is such that every vertex except for s and t has an even degree (immediate from conservation constraints).
Find an Eulerian partition of E', ignoring the directions of the edges. We obtained a collection of cycles and s-t paths.

iii. Partition the set E' into two sets E^+ (edges labeled $+$) and E^- (edges labeled $-$) as follows:

- If $e \in E'$ belongs to an s-t path in the Eulerian partition do as follows. If e is a forward edge in an s-t traversal of the path, assign $e \in E^+$, else, if e is a backward edge, assign $e \in E^-$.
- Edges that belong to cycles are labeled such that for one of the two traversals, all forward edges are in E^+ and all backward edges are in E^-.

iv. Compute a flow $\hat{f}_e$ $(e \in E)$ as follows:
If $e \in E^+$, $\hat{f}_e \leftarrow f_e + \Delta$.
If $e \in E^-$, $\hat{f}_e \leftarrow f_e - \Delta$.
If $e \in E \setminus E'$, $\hat{f}_e \leftarrow f_e$.

The computation is dominated by the construction of the Eulerian partition ($O(\log m)$ time using $O(m)$ processors), and the list ranking operations on segments of total length $|E'| = O(m)$ ($O(\log m)$ time using $O(m)$ processors). It follows that the subroutine can be implemented on an EREW PRAM to run in $O(\log m)$ time using $O(m)$ processors.

5.2. Rounding Algorithm

The following algorithm describes how to round a general flow.

Algorithm 5.2 [Obtain integral flow]

i. Round up the flow to units of $\Delta_0 = 2^{-5\lceil \log m \rceil}$. Note that this may create excesses and deficits at the vertices. The sum of the absolute values of the excesses and deficits is at most $2m\Delta_0 \leq 2m^{-4} \leq 1/4$.

ii. Iterate the following modification of Algorithm 5.1 for $k = 0, \ldots, 5\lceil \log m \rceil$ and $\Delta = 2^k \Delta_0$. Since there are excesses and deficits present, the partition computed in Step ii of Algorithm 5.1 may be such that some paths have end points at vertices other than s and t. The labels of edges along such paths are determined in the same way as cycles, where with respect to some traversal, all backward edges are labeled the same and all forward edges are labeled the same. Use the following rules to determine which of the two possibilities to choose from:

- If a path p is such that an end edge is directed into a vertex with a deficit, put the edge in E^+ (if this is true for both end edges of p, arbitrarily choose one).
- Otherwise, if p is such that an end edge is directed out of a vertex with an excess, put the edge in E^+ (if this is true for both end edges of p, arbitrarily choose one).
- Otherwise, put one of the end edges of p in E^-.

Note that (i) the rules to choose the labels guarantee that the sum of the absolute values of excesses and deficits never increases, and (ii) at each vertex, the excess or deficit is an integral number of units of the current value of Δ. Hence, when the algorithm terminates, there are no excesses or deficits at the vertices.

Proposition 5.3 *The rounding takes $O(\log^2 m)$ time using $O(m)$ processors, on an EREW PRAM.*

5.3. Computing an integral blocking flow

The rounding algorithm is such that the amount of flow on edges with integral flow is not changed. Hence, when the rounding algorithm is applied to an exact fractional blocking flow, the result is an exact integral blocking flow. If the initial fractional flow is ϵ-blocking, the resulting integral flow is $\lceil \epsilon \rceil$-blocking.

Algorithm 4.3 (ϵ-blocking flow algorithm) produces a fractional ϵ-blocking flow. To obtain an integral $\lfloor \epsilon \rfloor$-blocking flow we use Algorithm 4.3 where in each iteration i, the flow f^i is rounded to an integral flow $\hat{f}^i$ with the following property: At least a constant fraction (1/2) of the edges $e \in E$ for which $f^i_e - \lfloor f^i_e \rfloor \geq 1/2$ are such that $\hat{f}^i_e = \lceil f^i_e \rceil$. The integral flow $\hat{f}^i$ is used instead of f^i to augment the current flow. It is easy to verify that the asymptotic running time of Algorithm 4.3 is not affected by this change.

What remains is to explain how we obtain an integral flow $\hat{f}^i$ that has the additional property. We use a variant of Algorithm 5.1. Note that the choice of the Δ_0 ensures us that the sum of absolute values of excesses and deficit is less than 1/4. Hence, at the iteration where $\Delta = 1/2$, there are no excesses or deficits. Observe that Step ii of Algorithm 5.1 allows us, for each cycle, two possible choices of labels of edges. If $\Delta = 1/2$, for edges of each cycle, we choose the labels that maximize the number of edges with flow $u_e - \Delta$ which are selected to be in E^+. We argue that the rule above guarantees that the rounded flow has the additional property: Consider all edges for which initially $f^i_e - \lfloor f^i_e \rfloor \geq 1/2$. Either they are rounded up at iterations where $\Delta < 1/2$, or when $\Delta = 1/2$, they have flow value $\lfloor f^i_e \rfloor + 1/2$. The choice of labels insures that at least half of these edges are rounded up to a unit.

Using the integral version of the ϵ-blocking flow algorithm, we can compute an exact integral blocking flow when the capacities are integral and polynomial in m, in the following EREW PRAM resource bounds:

i. $O(r^2 \log^3 m)$ time using $O(m/r)$ processors, or

ii. $O(r \log r \log^4 m)$ time using $M(n)$ processors.

5.4. Computing an integral flow of smaller cost

Suppose that we are given a fractional s-t flow f_e ($e \in E$) on a network with integral capacities and integral costs c_e ($e \in E$) associated with the edges. We modify Algorithm 5.2 so that it produces an integral flow $\hat{f}_e$ with the properties $\hat{f}_e \in \{\lfloor f_e \rfloor, \lceil f_e \rceil\}$ ($e \in E$) and

$$\sum_{e \in E} c_e \hat{f}_e \leq \lfloor 2m^2 \Delta_0 \max_{e \in E} |c_e| + \sum_{e \in E} c_e f_e \rfloor ,$$

where Δ_0 is some inverse power of 2 such that $\log \Delta_0^{-1} \geq 5\lceil \log m \rceil$. The modified algorithm runs in time $O(\log m \log \Delta_0^{-1})$ and uses $O(m)$ processors. In the first step the algorithm uses the input value of Δ_0. For each cycle or s-t path p, there are two ways to assign edges to E^+ and to E^-. Make the choice such that $\sum_{e \in p \cap E^+} c_e < \sum_{e \in p \cap E^-} c_e$. This choice guarantees that the total cost does not increase as a result of changing the flow on these edges. Because of the initial rounding, there may be paths with end points at vertices with excesses or deficits. For edges on these paths, we choose the labels such that the sum of absolute values of deficits and excesses does not increase. Note, however, that the cost may increase as a result of the change. The sum of absolute values of excesses and deficits is at most $2m\Delta_0$. Hence, the total increase in cost resulting from non s-t paths is bounded by $2m^2\Delta_0 \max_{e\in E} |c_e|$.

6. Approximate bipartite matching in parallel

A matching in a graph is a set of edges such that no two edges are incident at the same vertex. The maximum cardinality bipartite matching (MCBM) problem is to find, in a bipartite graph, a matching of maximum size. The problem can be stated as an integral maximum flow problem on a unit network of depth 3. The corresponding network is such that the set of saturated edges of any integral flow turns out to be a matching of cardinality which equals the value of that flow. Hence, MCBM can be solved using Dinic's algorithm in $O(m\sqrt{n})$ time [4] (see also [15] for an algorithm stated in terms of alternating paths). A blocking flow computation on a unit network can be done in $O(m)$ time [4], and hence, it follows from Corollary 3.3, that an approximate matching can be found in $O(\epsilon^{-1}m)$ time.

As for the parallel complexity of the MCBM problem, it is still not known whether the problem is in $\mathcal{NC}$. It is known, however, to be in $\mathcal{RNC}$. The first $\mathcal{RNC}^3$ algorithm was obtained by Karp, Upfal, and Wigderson [17]. Their algorithm uses $O(n^{6.5})$ processors. A later $\mathcal{RNC}^2$ algorithm by Mulmuley, Vazirani, and Vazirani [20] uses $O(n^{3.5}m)$ processors. The best known $\mathcal{RNC}$ processor bound of $O(nM(n))$ (in $\mathcal{RNC}^3$) was achieved by Galil and Pan [8]. Pippenger, and Valiant [18] gave an $\mathcal{NC}$ algorithm for the special case of regular bipartite graphs, and Miller and Naor [19] gave an $\mathcal{NC}$ algorithm for planar bipartite graphs. An algorithm by Goldberg, Plotkin, and Vaidya [10] solves the MCBM problem in $O(n^{2/3}\log^3 m)$ time using $M(n)$ processors. An interior point based algorithm by Goldberg, Plotkin, Shmoys, and Tardos [9] solves the problem in $\tilde{O}(\sqrt{m})$ time using $O(m^3)$ processors.

In [5], Fisher, Goldberg, and Plotkin gave an $\mathcal{NC}$ algorithm which finds a matching in a graph which is at least $(1-\epsilon)$ of the maximum cardinality matching. They first showed that if a matching is such that there are no augmenting paths of length smaller than ℓ, then the matching is of cardinality at least $(1-1/\ell)$ of maximum. Their algorithm is roughly based on examining all paths of length at most ℓ, and hence uses $n^{O(\ell)}$ processors. As a corollary of Theorem 1.1, we obtain an $\mathcal{NC}$ algorithm which finds a bipartite matching of cardinality $(1-1/\operatorname{polylog} n)$ of optimal and uses only a linear $O(m)$ number of processors. A similar result was obtained very recently by Spencer [23], by using a modification of the parallel exact matching algorithm of Goldberg, Plotkin, and Vaidya [10].

Theorem 6.1 *Bipartite matching of cardinality* $(1-\epsilon)$ *of maximum can be computed in:*

i. $O(\epsilon^{-3}\log^2 m \log(m\epsilon^{-1}))$ *time using* $O(m)$ *processors, or*

ii. $O(\epsilon^{-2}\log^3 m \log\epsilon^{-1}\log(m\epsilon^{-1}))$ *time using* $O(M(n))$ *processors.*

7. Open problems

To conclude, we discuss some issues and open problems that arise from this work.

Achieving better bounds. We presented an $O(M(n))$ processors $\tilde{O}(r)$ time algorithm for approximate blocking flow (exact for polynomial capacities). We ask whether we can improve on this, that is, find an (approximate) blocking flow in $\tilde{o}(r)$ deterministic parallel time. Such an algorithm would imply that a flow with no augmenting paths shorter than r could be found in $\tilde{o}(r^2)$ deterministic parallel time. The existence of an algorithm to find such a flow with the latter bounds is an easier question which may be answered directly. A time bound of $O(r^{2-\epsilon})$ for some $\epsilon > 0$, even for the special case of unit networks, would yield a faster deterministic parallel maximum cardinality bipartite matching algorithm than the currently known ones.

Extension to minimum cost flow. We ask whether our results can be extended to finding near-minimum cost flow more efficiently on small depth networks, or more specifically, to minimum weight bipartite matching. One problem is that the augmenting path argument in the proof of Proposition 3.1 does not seem to carry over for minimum cost flows.

Weighted path counts. In this paper we introduced the notion of path counts and used path counts weighted by capacities to compute a flow augmentation in each iteration of the blocking flow algorithm. We ask whether we can benefit by considering path counts weighted by other "costs" associated with the edges, which could possibly be dependent on the capacities and other parameters. Weighted path counts keep the properties of being efficiently computable in parallel and being conserved at vertices. Consider, for simplicity, a zero-one network of depth r. Let $c = \{c_e | e \in E\}$ be nonnegative weights on the edges, and denote by χ_e $(e \in E)$ the weighted path counts (relatively to the weights c_e). Each such system of weights, corresponds to a flow $f(c)$ where

$$f_e(c) = \frac{\chi_e}{\max_{e' \in E} \chi_{e'}} \quad (e \in E) .$$

Denote the value of $f(c)$ by $M(c)$. We ask how close to the maximum flow M^* is the value of the maximum flow that has the form $f(c)$ for some nonnegative set of costs c. For unit networks we have $M^* = \max_c M(c)$. We suggest an approach for an algorithm that directly approximates the maximum flow without breaking the computation to blocking flow phases. The approach is to start with some initial costs and to keep updating them until $M(c)$ is close to M^* for the current weights c.

Acknowledgements. The author would like to thank Andrew Goldberg, David Johnson, Seffi Naor, Tomek Radzik, Peter Shor, Vijay Vazirani, and Alex Wang for relevant discussions and pointers to the literature.

References.

[1] R. K. Ahuja, J. B. Orlin, and R. E. Tarjan. Improved time bounds for the maximum flow problem. *SIAM J. Comput.*, 18:939–954, 1989.

[2] D. Coppersmith and S. Winograd. Matrix multiplication via arithmetic progressions. *J. Symb. Comput.*, 9:251–280, 1990.

[3] E. A. Dinic. Algorithm for solution of a problem of maximum flow in networks with power estimation. *Soviet Math. Dokl.*, 11:1277–1280, 1970.

[4] S. Even and R. E. Tarjan. Network flow and testing graph connectivity. *SIAM J. Comput.*, 4:507–518, 1975.

[5] T. Fisher, A. V. Goldberg, and S. A. Plotkin. Approximating matching in parallel. Manuscript, 1991.

[6] L. R. Ford Jr. and D. R. Fulkerson. *Flows in networks.* Princeton Univ. Press, Princeton, NJ, 1962.

[7] H. N. Gabow. Using Euler partitions to edge-color bipartite multi-graphs. *Int. J. Comput. Inform. Sci.*, 5:345–355, 1976.

[8] Z. Galil and V. Pan. Improved processor bounds for combinatorial problems in RNC. *Combinatorica*, 8:189–200, 1988.

[9] A. V. Goldberg, S. K. Plotkin, D. B. Shmoys, and É. Tardos. Interior point methods in parallel computation. In *Proc. 30th IEEE Annual Symposium on Foundations of Computer Science*, pages 350–355. IEEE, 1989.

[10] A. V. Goldberg, S. K. Plotkin, and P. M. Vaidya. Sublinear time parallel algorithms for matching and related problems. In *Proc. 29th IEEE Annual Symposium on Foundations of Computer Science*, pages 174–185. IEEE, 1988.

[11] A. V. Goldberg and R.E. Tarjan. A new approach to the maximum flow problem. *J. Assoc. Comput. Mach.*, 35:921–940, 1988.

[12] A. V. Goldberg and R.E. Tarjan. A parallel algorithm for finding a blocking flow in an acyclic network. *Information Processing Let.*, 31:265–271, 1989.

[13] A. V. Goldberg and R.E. Tarjan. Finding minimum cost circulations by successive approximation. *Math. of Oper. Res.*, 15:430–466, 1990.

[14] L. M. Goldschlager, R. A. Shaw, and J. Staples. The maximum flow problem is logspace complete for P. *Theor. Comp. Sci.*, 21:105–111, 1982.

[15] J. Hopcroft and R. M. Karp. An $n^{5/2}$ algorithm for maximum matching in bipartite graphs. *SIAM J. Comput.*, 2:225–231, 1973.

[16] R. M. Karp and V. Ramachandran. Parallel algorithms for shared-memory machines. In J. van Leeuwenm, editor, *Handbook of Theoretical Computer Science*, volume A, chapter 17, pages 869–941. MIT Press/Elsevier, Cambridge, MA, 1991.

[17] R. M. Karp, E. Upfal, and A. Wigderson. Constructing a perfect matching is in random NC. *Combinatorica*, 6:35–48, 1986.

[18] G. F. Lev, N. Pippenger, and L. G. Valiant. A fast parallel algorithm for routing in permutation networks. *IEEE Trans. Computers*, C-30:93–100, 1981.

[19] G. L. Miller and J. Naor. Flow in planar graphs with multiple sources and sinks. In *Proc. 30th IEEE Annual Symposium on Foundations of Computer Science*, pages 112–117. IEEE, 1989.

[20] K. Mulmuley, U. V. Vazirani, and V. V. Vazirani. Matching is as easy as matrix inversion. *Combinatorica*, 7(1):105–113, 1987.

[21] V. Pan and J. Reif. Efficient parallel solution of linear systems. In *Proc. 17th Annual ACM Symposium on Theory of Computing*, pages 143–152. ACM, 1985.

[22] Y. Shiloach and U. Vishkin. An $o(n^2 \log n)$ parallel max-flow algorithm. *J. Alg.*, 3:128–146, 1982.

[23] T. H. Spencer. Parallel approximate matching. Technical Report UNO-CS-TR-92-5, University of Nebraska at Omaha, 1992.

[24] R. E. Tarjan. *Data structures and network algorithms.* Society for Industrial and Applied Mathematics, Philadelphia, PA, 1983.

Newton's Method for Fractional Combinatorial Optimization

Tomasz Radzik *
Stanford University

Abstract

We consider Newton's method for the linear fractional combinatorial optimization. We prove a strongly polynomial bound on the number of iterations for the general case. In the second part of the paper we consider the maximum mean-weight cut problem, which is a special case of the linear fractional combinatorial optimization. This problem is closely related to the parametric flow problem and the flow problem when the maximum arc cost is being minimized. We prove that Newton's method runs in $O(m)$ iterations for the maximum mean-weight cut problem. One iteration is dominated by the maximum flow computation. This gives the best known strongly polynomial bound of $\tilde{O}(m^2 n)$ for all three problems mentioned here. The previous fastest algorithms for these problems are based on Megiddo's parametric search method and run in $\tilde{O}(n^3 m)$ time.

1 Introduction

Many problems in combinatorial optimization fit the following pattern: find a combinatorial structure with the maximum (or minimum) cost, where the cost of a structure is the sum of the costs of its elements. We call such problems *linear combinatorial optimization problems.* For example the minimum spanning tree problem and the minimum cost cycle problem are linear combinatorial optimization problems. Here the structures are the spanning trees or the cycles of a given graph, and their elements are edges. It is often the case that besides costs there are also weights associated with the individual elements, and we are asked to find a structure with the maximum (or minimum) mean-weight cost. The mean-weight cost of a structure is its cost divided by its weight, where the weight of a structure is the sum of the weights of its elements. We call such a problem a *linear fractional combinatorial optimization problem* (LFCO). For example the minimum-ratio spanning tree problem [2], the minimum-ratio cycle problem [12], and the maximum mean-weight cut problem [13] are LFCO problems (see [15] and the references there for discussion of these and other LFCO problems). We present our results in terms of maximization problems. They can be transformed to apply to minimization problems.

An LFCO problem can be stated equivalently in the following way. The cost of an element is a linear function with parameter δ. The cost of a structure is, as previously, the sum of the costs of its elements, but now this is some linear function of δ. When δ is fixed, the resulting costs of the elements are called *reduced costs.* The maximum cost over all structures is a piecewise linear convex decreasing[1] function of δ. We denote this function by $h(\delta)$. We want to compute δ^*, the minimum value of δ for which the maximum reduced cost of a structure is zero, *i.e.*, we want to compute the root of $h(\delta)$. We also want to find a structure which has this maximum cost.

We investigate the following generic algorithm for (the parametric version of) an LFCO problem. Repeatedly find a positive reduced cost structure and update the current underestimation $\bar{\delta}$ of δ^* such that the reduced cost of this structure becomes zero. When there are no positive reduced cost structures, $\bar{\delta} = \delta^*$ and the algorithm terminates. The structure found in the last iteration is an optimal one.

If during each iteration of the above algorithm we find a structure with the maximum reduced cost, then we get Newton's method for finding the root of $h(\delta)$. The main result of this paper is a proof that Newton's method solves an LFCO problem in a strongly polynomial number of iterations. It should be noted

*Research partially supported by NSF Presidential Young Investigator Grant CCR-8858097 with matching funds from AT&T and DEC, and ONR Young Investigator Award N00014-91-J-1855. E-mail: radzik@cs.stanford.edu.

[1] Monotonicity follows from the assumptions we state in the next section.

0-8186-2900-2/92 $3.00 © 1992 IEEE

that $h(\delta)$ can consist of a superpolynomial number of linear pieces [1]. Our strongly polynomial bound on the number of iterations is independent of the complexity of the underlying linear problem. In each iteration $h(\bar{\delta})$ is computed, *i.e.*, an instance of the linear problem is solved.

The other way of solving an LFCO problem is Megiddo's parametric search method [15]. In this approach the number of instances of the linear problem which have to be solved depends on the (parallel) complexity of the linear problem. Moreover, to have the whole scheme work, the algorithm for the linear problem which guides the whole computation has to be a linear algorithm: comparisons are allowed only between linear functions of the input variables. Newton's method works with any algorithm for the linear problem, since it treats this computation as a black box. On the other hand, however, the parametric search needs only an algorithm for the underlying linear problem which finds a positive cost structure, not necessarily an optimum one.

Value δ^* can be found by binary search, if a subroutine for computing $h(\delta)$ is available. Such an approach gives algorithms with a polynomial, but not a strongly polynomial, number of iterations. In section 5 we show a polynomial bound on Newton's method which is slightly better than the bound given by binary search.

Several authors investigated some LFCO problems with uniform weights [8, 9, 10, 13, 17]. These are problems of finding a combinatorial structure with the maximum mean cost (the cost divided by the cardinality). Karzanov [10] noticed that Newton's method runs in a strongly polynomial number of iterations for any LFCO problem with uniform weights. This is because function $h(\delta)$ for such a problem has at most as many linear pieces as the number of elements in the underlying set.

In the second part of the paper (Sections 6-8) we analyze Newton's method for the *maximum mean-weight cut* problem, which is an LFCO problem. We show that Newton's method for this problem runs in $O(m)$ iterations giving the overall running time $O^*(m^2n)$. The maximum mean-weight cut problem is closely related to the following two network flow problems: the minimum maximum arc cost flow problem and the parametric flow problem. In the latter problem the capacities are linear functions of one parameter and we want to find the minimum value of this parameter such that the problem is feasible. We show that using Newton's method both these problems can be solved in $O^*(m^2n)$ time.

The underlying nonfractional (nonparametric) problem for the three problems mentioned here is the standard maximum flow problem. This problem does not have an efficient parallel algorithm. Nevertheless, the previous best strongly polynomial bound for these problems, $O^*(mn^3)$, was obtained with Megiddo's parametric search [15]. In [17] we showed a $\Theta(n)$ bound on the number of iterations in Newton's method for the maximum mean cut problem, which is the uniform case of the maximum mean-weight cut problem.

2 The Class of LFCO Problems

We begin with formalizing the class of problems we investigate. A *linear fractional combinatorial optimization* problem $\mathcal{F}$ is defined as follows. An instance of $\mathcal{F}$ is a specification of a set of structures $\mathcal{X} \subseteq \{0,1\}^p$, and two vectors $\mathbf{a} = (a_1, a_2, \ldots, a_p)$, $\mathbf{b} = (b_1, b_2, \ldots, b_p) \in \mathbf{R}^p$. The task is to

$$\mathcal{F}: \quad \text{maximize} \quad \frac{\mathbf{ax}}{\mathbf{bx}}, \quad \text{subject to} \quad \mathbf{x} \in \mathcal{X}.$$

A 0-1 vector $\mathbf{x} = (x_1, x_2, \ldots, x_p) \in \mathcal{X}$ is the characteristic vector of the structure it represents. Structures are some special subsets of the underlying set of p elements. Numbers a_i and b_i are *the cost* and *the weight* of element i. $\mathbf{ax}$, $\mathbf{bx}$, and $(\mathbf{ax})/(\mathbf{bx})$ are *the cost, weight*, and *mean-weight cost* of the structure represented by vector $(x_1, x_2, \ldots, x_p)$. In this terminology problem $\mathcal{F}$ is to compute the maximum mean-weight cost of a structure in $\mathcal{X}$. We also want to find a structure which has this maximum mean-weight cost. We assume that $\mathbf{bx} > 0$ for all $\mathbf{x} \in \mathcal{X}$, and $\mathbf{ax} > 0$ for some $\mathbf{x} \in \mathcal{X}$.

Problem $\mathcal{F}$ can be equivalently formulated in the following way.

$$\mathcal{P}: \quad \text{minimize} \quad \delta, \quad \text{subject to} \quad (\mathbf{ax}) - \delta(\mathbf{bx}) \leq 0, \quad \text{for all } \mathbf{x} \in \mathcal{X}.$$

We call $\mathcal{P}$ the parametric version of $\mathcal{F}$. Let δ^* denote the optimum value of δ. Let

$$\begin{aligned} h(\delta) &\stackrel{\text{def}}{=} \max\{(\mathbf{ax}) - \delta(\mathbf{bx}) \mid \mathbf{x} \in \mathcal{X}\} \\ &= \max\{(\mathbf{a} - \delta\mathbf{b})\mathbf{x} \mid \mathbf{x} \in \mathcal{X}\}. \end{aligned}$$

For any fixed δ, vector $\mathbf{a} - \delta\mathbf{b}$ is the vector of the reduced costs. Thus $h(\delta)$ is the maximum reduced cost of a structure. Function $h(\delta)$ is convex, piecewise linear, decreasing, and δ^* is its only root. Thus we have another equivalent formulation of an LFCO problem:

$$\mathcal{R}: \quad \text{solve} \quad h(\delta) = 0.$$

The method for solving an LFCO problem we investigate in this paper is Newton's method for finding the root of $h(\delta)$.

The following are the optimization and the decision version of the underlying linear (non-parametric) combinatorial problem. Given are a specification of $\mathcal{X} \subseteq \{0,1\}^p$ and a vector $\mathbf{c} \in \mathbf{R}^p$.

$$\mathcal{L}_{\text{opt}}: \quad \text{maximize} \quad \mathbf{cx}, \quad \text{subject to} \quad \mathbf{x} \in \mathcal{X}.$$

$$\mathcal{L}_{\text{dec}}: \quad \text{is there} \quad \mathbf{x} \in \mathcal{X}, \quad \text{such that} \quad \mathbf{cx} > 0?$$

In both these problems we also want to find an appropriate $\mathbf{x}$. We assume that we know how to solve problem $\mathcal{L}_{\text{opt}}$. We will use this computation as a black box to compute for any fixed δ, $h(\delta)$, the maximum reduced cost of a structure, and a structure $\mathbf{x} \in \mathcal{X}$ which has this cost.

A *uniform* LFCO problem is

$$\mathcal{U}: \quad \text{maximize} \quad \frac{\mathbf{ax}}{\mathbf{ex}}, \quad \text{subject to} \quad \mathbf{x} \in \mathcal{X}.$$

where $\mathbf{e} \stackrel{\text{def}}{=} (1,1,\ldots,1)$. The task here is to find a structure with the maximum mean cost. The *mean cost* of a structure is its cost divided by the number of its elements.

If in problem $\mathcal{F}$, set $\mathcal{X}$ is some arbitrary[2] subset of $\mathbf{R}^p$, then we get a linear fractional program. Furthermore, if the enumerator and the denominator of the objective function are arbitrary[2] functions of $\mathbf{x} \in \mathcal{X}$, then we get a general fractional program. Both fractional programs and linear fractional programs have been extensively studied in the operations research community (see, for example, a review paper [21]). One of the main methods for solving (the parametric versions of) such problems is Newton's method, called also the Newton-Raphson method or the Dinkelbach method [7]. In such general setting, however, most often all we can hope for is an approximate solution, and a natural question to ask is how fast a given iterative method converges. Schaible [20] showed that Newton's method for a fractional program converges superlinearly.

3 Newton's Method

In this section we describe Newton's method for computing the root (δ^*) of $h(\delta)$, and present some preliminary facts.

Let $\bar{\delta} \le \delta^*$ be the current estimation to δ^*. Initially $\bar{\delta} = 0$. (Observe that our assumptions guarantee $\delta^* > 0$.) During one iteration we compute $h(\bar{\delta})$ and $\bar{\mathbf{x}} \in \mathcal{X}$ such that $h(\bar{\delta}) = (\mathbf{a} - \bar{\delta}\mathbf{b})\bar{\mathbf{x}}$, *i.e.*, we maximize linear function $(\mathbf{a} - \bar{\delta}\mathbf{b})\mathbf{x}$ over $\mathcal{X}$ (problem $\mathcal{L}_{\text{opt}}$).

[2] Additional assumptions are usually made, which reflect applications and/or allow obtaining interesting results.

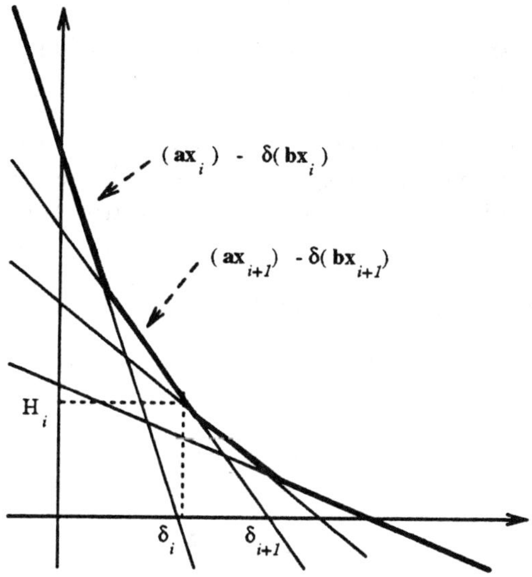

Figure 1: Newton's method for solving $h(\delta) = 0$

If $h(\bar{\delta}) = 0$, then $\delta^* = \bar{\delta}$ and the algorithm terminates. Otherwise we compute the next estimation $\bar{\delta} \leftarrow \mathbf{a}\bar{\mathbf{x}}/\mathbf{b}\bar{\mathbf{x}}$, the mean-weight cost of $\bar{\mathbf{x}}$, and go to the next iteration. The process is illustrated in Figure 1.

Let δ_i be the value of $\bar{\delta}$ at the beginning of ith iteration, and $\mathbf{x}_i$, H_i, and B_i, be $\bar{\mathbf{x}}$, $(\mathbf{a} - \delta_i\mathbf{b})\bar{\mathbf{x}}$, and $\mathbf{b}\bar{\mathbf{x}}$ from this iteration. Thus

$$\begin{aligned} H_i &= (\mathbf{a} - \delta_i\mathbf{b})\mathbf{x}_i = \max\{(\mathbf{a} - \delta_i\mathbf{b})\mathbf{x} \mid \mathbf{x} \in \mathcal{X}\}, \\ B_i &= \mathbf{b}\mathbf{x}_i, \\ \delta_{i+1} &= \frac{\mathbf{a}\mathbf{x}_i}{\mathbf{b}\mathbf{x}_i}, \end{aligned}$$

and it can be easily derived that

$$\delta_{i+1} - \delta_i = \frac{H_i}{B_i}. \tag{1}$$

The following lemma indicates fast convergence of the above algorithm.

Lemma 1

$$\frac{H_{i+1}}{H_i} + \frac{B_{i+1}}{B_i} \le 1. \tag{2}$$

Proof. Vector $\mathbf{x}_i$ maximizes $(\mathbf{a} - \delta_i\mathbf{b})\mathbf{x}$, so

$$(\mathbf{a} - \delta_i\mathbf{b})\mathbf{x}_i \ \ge \ (\mathbf{a} - \delta_i\mathbf{b})\mathbf{x}_{i+1}.$$

Therefore

$$\begin{aligned} H_i &= (\mathbf{a} - \delta_i\mathbf{b})\mathbf{x}_i \ \ge \ (\mathbf{a} - \delta_i\mathbf{b})\mathbf{x}_{i+1} \\ &= (\mathbf{a} - \delta_{i+1}\mathbf{b})\mathbf{x}_{i+1} + (\delta_{i+1} - \delta_i)\mathbf{b}\mathbf{x}_{i+1} \\ &= H_{i+1} + \frac{H_i}{B_i}B_{i+1}. \end{aligned}$$

This implies Inequality (2). ■

The above lemma gives the following polynomial bound on the number of iterations.

Theorem 1 If in an LFCO problem the coordinates of vectors **a** and **b** are integers from $[-U, U]$, then Newton's method finds the optimum in $O(\log(pU))$ iterations.

Proof (Sketch). Inequality (2) implies

$$\frac{H_{i+1}B_{i+1}}{H_i B_i} \le \frac{1}{4}. \tag{3}$$

An $O(\log(pU))$ bound follows, because for any i, if $H_i > 0$, then

$$(pU)^2 \ge H_i B_i \ge \frac{1}{pU}. \tag{4}$$

■

We will show a strongly polynomial bound on the number of iterations in Newton's method. It means that, asymptotically, Newton's method runs in a fewer number of iterations than the bisection, but to exhibit this advantage, the input numbers have to be very large. In Section 5 we present a refinement of Theorem 1. A consequence will be that even for not so large input numbers Newton's method runs in fewer iterations than the bisection method.

Another simple consequence of Lemma 1 concerns uniform LFCO problems. This fact was observed by Karzanov [10] and, in the context of the maximum mean cut problem, by McCormick and Ervolina [13].

Theorem 2 Newton's method runs in at most $p+1$ iterations for a uniform LFCO problem.

Proof. Sequence (B_i), excluding the last iteration, is decreasing. In a uniform LFCO problem B_i is a positive integer not greater than p, because B_i is the cardinality of some structure. ■

4 Strongly Polynomial Bound

In this section we prove a strongly polynomial bound on the number of iterations for the general case, when both costs and weights can be arbitrary real numbers. We first give some intuition which lies behind the analysis. Lemma 1 suggests that there are some sequences, related to the convergence of the method, which tend to zero at least geometrically fast. The elements of these sequences are obtained from only $2p$ numbers, the costs $a_1, a_2, \ldots, a_p$, and the weights $b_1, b_2 \ldots, b_p$, using only $O(p)$ additions/subtractions and at most one or two multiplications/divisions. We show that because of this limiting use of arithmetical operations, these sequences cannot be long.

To expand this intuition a little bit, let us assume that for some positive constant α, $B_{i+1}/B_i \le 1 - \alpha$, for every i. It means that sequence (B_i) tends to zero at least geometrically fast. Let us further assume that $b_1 \ge b_2 \ge \cdots \ge b_p \ge 0$. Each element of sequence (B_i) is the sum of the elements in a subset of $\{b_1, b_2, \ldots, b_p\}$. Obviously $B_1 \le pb_1$. Since sequence (B_i) decreases at least geometrically, $B_l < b_1$, for some $l = O(\log p)$. It means that b_1 is not a term in B_l, nor is it in B_i, for any $i \ge l$, so we can exclude b_1 from further consideration. Thus $B_l \le (p-1)b_2$, and after the next $O(\log p)$ iterations we can exclude b_2, then b_3, and so on. Therefore the length of sequence (B_i) can be only $O(p \log p)$.

There are two reasons why the general case is more complicated. First, we have to deal with positive and negative numbers. Even if both costs and weights are positive, negative numbers appear because subtractions are used in forming the elements of sequence (H_i). Second, if sequence (B_i) does not decrease fast enough, then we have to analyze sequence (H_i), whose elements are not just sums of elements from some small given set of numbers. The following lemma is our tool to deal with both positive and negative numbers. Here the coordinates of vector **c** are numbers which are used to form subsums, and $(\mathbf{y}_k\mathbf{c})_{k\ge1}$ is a sequence of such subsums.

Lemma 2 Let $\mathbf{c} \in \mathbf{R}^p$ and $\mathbf{y}_k \in \{0,1\}^p \backslash \{\mathbf{0}\}$, for $k = 1, 2, \ldots, q$, be such that

$$|\mathbf{y}_{k+1}\mathbf{c}| < \frac{1}{2}|\mathbf{y}_k\mathbf{c}|, \quad \text{for } k = 1, 2, \ldots, q-1. \tag{5}$$

Then $q \le 3p^2 \log p + 1$.

Proof. Let $l = \lceil 3p \log p \rceil$ and consider every l-th element of sequence $(\mathbf{y}_k)$. Let $\mathbf{w}_k = \mathbf{y}_{1+(k-1)l}$, for $1 \le k \le r = \lceil \frac{q-1}{l} \rceil$. We have for $k = 1, 2, \ldots, r-1$,

$$|\mathbf{w}_{k+1}\mathbf{c}| < \left(\frac{1}{2}\right)^l |\mathbf{w}_k\mathbf{c}| \le \frac{1}{p^{3p}}|\mathbf{w}_k\mathbf{c}|. \tag{6}$$

We prove the lemma by showing that $r \le p$. The idea is to show that if $r > p$, then there exists a linear combination of $\mathbf{w}_k\mathbf{c}$, $k = 1, 2, \ldots, r$, which is zero but the absolute values of all nonzero coefficients are in $[1/(p^p), p^p]$. This gives a contradiction because Inequality 6 implies that the nonzero terms in such a linear combination cannot cancel to zero.

Assume that $r > p$. Let $\mathbf{Y}$ denote the matrix whose rows are vectors $\mathbf{w}_1$, $\mathbf{w}_2$, ..., $\mathbf{w}_r$. Since $r > p$, there is a nonzero vector $\mathbf{z} \in \mathbf{R}^r$ such that $\mathbf{zY} = \mathbf{0}$. Moreover, $\mathbf{z}$ can be chosen in such a way that all its coordinates are rational numbers with denominators and enumerators being the determinants of submatrices of $\mathbf{Y}$. Let $\mathbf{z} = (z_1, z_2, \ldots, z_r)$ be such a vector. Thus, for $i = 1, 2, \ldots, r$, either $z_i = 0$ or

$$\frac{1}{p^p} < |z_i| < p^p. \tag{7}$$

We have

$$0 = \mathbf{zYc} = z_1(\mathbf{w}_1\mathbf{c}) + z_2(\mathbf{w}_2\mathbf{c}) + \cdots + z_r(\mathbf{w}_r\mathbf{c}). \tag{8}$$

But this is not possible, because the nonzero terms on the right side cannot cancel. Since $\mathbf{w}_r \neq \mathbf{0}$, so for some $1 \leq i \leq r-1$, $z_i \neq 0$, and $z_i\mathbf{w}_i\mathbf{c} \neq 0$. If $1 \leq i < j \leq r$ and $z_i\mathbf{w}_i\mathbf{c} \neq 0$, then (6) and (7) imply

$$|z_j(\mathbf{w}_j\mathbf{c})| < p^{2p}|z_i|\frac{1}{p^{3p}}|\mathbf{w}_i\mathbf{c}| = \frac{1}{p^p}|z_i(\mathbf{w}_i\mathbf{c})|.$$

In particular, the absolute value of the first nonzero term in (8) is bigger than the sum of the absolute values of all other terms. ■

Now we are ready to prove a strongly polynomial bound on the number of iterations. We separately consider iterations which substantially decrease B_i and those which do not.

Lemma 3 There are at most $O(p^2 \log p)$ iterations i such that $B_{i+1} \leq \frac{2}{3}B_i$.

Proof. This is immediate consequence of Lemma 2. Let $\mathbf{c} = \mathbf{b}$ and sequence $(\mathbf{y}_k)_{1\leq k\leq q}$ be the sequence of $\mathbf{x}_i$'s from every other iteration such that $B_{i+1} \leq \frac{2}{3}B_i$. We have

$$0 \leq \mathbf{y}_{k+1}\mathbf{c} \leq \frac{4}{9}\mathbf{y}_k\mathbf{c},$$

so Lemma 2 implies that $q = O(p^2 \log p)$. ■

Lemma 4 There are at most $O(p^2 \log p)$ consecutive iterations k such that $B_{k+1} \geq \frac{2}{3}B_k$.

Proof. Consider a sequence of q consecutive iterations such that for each of them

$$B_{k+1} \geq \frac{2}{3}B_k. \tag{9}$$

For convenience we renumber these iteration from 1 through q. We show that Lemma 2 can be applied to the sequence $(\mathbf{x}_k(-\mathbf{a} + \delta_{q+1}\mathbf{b}))$, where $1 \leq k \leq q$. Inequalities (9) and (2) imply that for $k = 1, 2, \ldots, q-1$,

$$H_{k+1} \leq \frac{1}{3}H_k.$$

Therefore

$$\delta_{k+2} - \delta_{k+1} = \frac{H_{k+1}}{B_{k+1}} \leq \frac{1}{2}\frac{H_k}{B_k} = \frac{1}{2}(\delta_{k+1} - \delta_k). \tag{10}$$

Using this inequality we can show

$$\delta_{q+1} - \delta_{k+1} \leq \frac{1}{2}(\delta_{q+1} - \delta_k).$$

Recall that $\delta_{i+1} = (\mathbf{ax}_i)/(\mathbf{bx}_i)$, so

$$\mathbf{x}_k(-\mathbf{a} + \delta_{q+1}\mathbf{b}) = (\delta_{q+1} - \delta_{k+1})\mathbf{bx}_k.$$

Putting

$$\begin{aligned} \mathbf{c} &= -\mathbf{a} + \delta_{q+1}\mathbf{b}, \\ \mathbf{y}_k &= \mathbf{x}_k, \quad \text{for } k = 1, 2, \ldots, q, \end{aligned}$$

we have for $k = 1, 2, \ldots, q$,

$$\begin{aligned} \mathbf{y}_{k+1}\mathbf{c} &= (\delta_{q+1} - \delta_{k+2})B_{k+1} \\ &< \frac{1}{2}(\delta_{q+1} - \delta_{k+1})B_k = \frac{1}{2}\mathbf{y}_k\mathbf{c}. \end{aligned}$$

Thus vector $\mathbf{c}$ and sequence $(\mathbf{y}_k)_{1\leq k\leq q}$ satisfy the conditions of Lemma 2, so $q = O(p^2 \log p)$. ■

Lemmas 3 and 4 immediately imply the following strongly polynomial bound on the number of iterations.

Theorem 3 Newton's method applied to an LFCO problem finds the optimum in $O(p^4 \log^2 p)$ iterations.

If the coefficients of vector $\mathbf{c}$ in Lemma 2 are nonnegative, then the simple argument outlined in the second paragraph of this section shows that the length of the sequence of sums is $O(p \log p)$. Actually, with a more balanced analysis one can show an $O(p)$ bound. This can be used to prove the following theorem.

Theorem 4 If all weights in an LFCO problem are nonnegative, then Newton's method runs in $O(p^3 \log p)$ iterations.

5 LFCO with Integral Data

In this section we consider Newton's method for LFCO problems with integral costs and weights. We present a refined version of Lemma 1. We obtain better bounds if the weights are substantially smaller than the costs. Such a case may occur, for example, in uniform LFCO problems, where all weights are equal to 1.

Let A (B) be the maximum of the absolute values of the costs (weights) of elements. We need the following technical lemma.

Lemma 5 Let μ, α, and β be positive numbers such that $\mu < 2$, $\alpha < 1$, $\beta < 1$. Let (α_i) and (β_i) be two finite positive sequences of length l such that

$$\alpha_i + \beta_i \leq \mu \text{ for } i = 1, 2, \ldots, l,$$

$$\prod_{i=1}^{l} \alpha_i \geq \alpha, \text{ and } \prod_{i=1}^{l} \beta_i \geq \beta.$$

Then $l \leq L$, where L is the solution to the equation

$$\alpha^{\frac{1}{L}} + \beta^{\frac{1}{L}} = \mu.$$

Theorem 5 Newton's method terminates after $O(\frac{\log(pAB)}{1+\log\log(pAB)-\log\log(pB)})$ iterations.

Proof (Idea). Use the above lemma with $\alpha_i = \frac{H_{i+1}}{H_i}$ and $\beta_i = \frac{B_{i+1}}{B_i}$. ∎

This theorem shows that for $A = (pB)^{\omega(1)}$ the algorithm is asymptotically faster than the binary search, and is faster by a factor of $\log\log(pA)$, if $A = \Omega((pB)^{\log^{\alpha}(pB)})$ for any positive α.

6 Maximum Mean-weight Cut

In this and the following sections we consider a specific LFCO problem: the maximum mean-weight cut problem. We show that Newton's method improves the previous best bound for this and some related network flow problems. In this section we provide definitions and preliminary facts.

A *(transshipment) network* $G = (V, E, u, d)$ is a digraph (V,E) with a capacity function $u : E \longrightarrow \mathbf{R} \cup \{+\infty\}$, and a demand function $d : V \longrightarrow \mathbf{R}$ such that $\sum_{v \in V} d(v) = 0$. We assume, for convenience in presentation but without losing generality, that E is symmetric and u is nonnegative. Negative $d(v)$ means that v is a *source* – a vertex with supply, positive $d(v)$ means that v is a *sink* – a vertex with demand. Let n and m denote the cardinality of V and the half of the cardinality of E, respectively. We assume $m \geq n$.

We adopt the convention that any function $\varphi : F \longrightarrow \mathbf{R}$ is extended additively to all finite subsets of F: $\varphi(A) = \sum_{x \in A} \varphi(x)$. Thus if $A \subseteq V$, then $d(A) = \sum_{v \in A} d(v)$, which is the net demand in A. The *total demand* in G is $\sum_{v:d(v)>0} d(v)$, which we denote by $d(G)$ (abusing a little bit our notational convention).

An *augmenting path* in G is a directed path from a source to a sink with arcs having positive upper capacities. A *pseudoflow* in G is an antisymmetric function $f : E \longrightarrow \mathbf{R}$, *i.e.*, $f(v, w) = -f(w, v)$ for each $(v, w) \in E$. A pseudoflow f creates excesses at vertices. The *excess* at vertex v is equal to the net flow into v:

$$e^f(v) \stackrel{\text{def}}{=} \sum_{w:(w,v)\in E} f(w, v).$$

If $e^f(v) = d(v)$, then we say that pseudoflow f satisfies the demand at vertex v. A pseudoflow f is a *flow* if it meets capacity constraints ($f(w, v) \leq u(w, v)$ for each $(w, v) \in E$) and does not increase demands ($e^f(v)$ is between 0 and $d(v)$ for each $v \in V$). The *value of a flow* f is the amount by which f decreases the total demand:

$$value(f) = \sum_{v:\,d(v)>0} e^f(v).$$

A *maximum flow* in G is a flow in G with the maximum value. The *maximum flow problem* is the problem of finding a maximum flow in a given network.

A *satisfying flow* is a flow which satisfies demands at all vertices. G is *feasible* if there is a satisfying flow in G. The *network feasibility* problem is the problem of verifying if a given network G is feasible. For a pseudoflow f in G, the *residual network* G^f is $(V, E, u^f = u - f, d^f = d - e^f)$. $G_{\bar{u}}$ denotes G with the capacity function changed to a new function $\bar{u}$. Thus, for example, $G^f_{\bar{u}} = (V, E, \bar{u}^f, d^f)$.

If S and T partition V, then *cut* (S, T) in G is the set of arcs (v, w) of E such that $v \in S$ and $w \in T$. The *capacity* and the *surplus* of a cut (S, T) are $u(S, T) = \sum_{e\in(S,T)} u(e)$ and $surplus(S, T) = d(T) - u(S, T)$, respectively. Our definition of $surplus(S, T)$ is the same as in [13] the definition of $V(T, S)$, the value of a cut (T, S).

It is easy to verify that the surplus of a cut is the same in G as in G^f for any flow f. A positive surplus means that the cut blocks the flow. Any flow must leave at S at least the amount $surplus(S, T)$ of the commodity, which is demanded at T. Therefore we sometimes call such a cut a *blocking cut.* A *maximum (surplus) cut* is a blocking cut with the maximum surplus. The *maximum (surplus) cut* problem is the problem of finding a maximum cut in a given network. The *mean-weight surplus* of a cut (S, T) is

$$mean\_w(S, T) \stackrel{\text{def}}{=} \frac{surplus(S, T)}{b(S, T)},$$

where $b : E \longrightarrow \mathbf{R}$ is a nonnegative weight function. A *maximum mean-weight (surplus) cut* is a blocking cut with the maximum mean-weight surplus. The *maximum mean-weight cut problem* (MWC) is the problem of finding a maximum mean-weight cut. Observe that we consider only nonnegative cuts.

The following observation will be useful in the analysis. The surplus of a maximum blocking cut is equal to the total demand left after augmenting the network with a maximum flow (*i.e.*, the total demand in G^f).

The MWC problem is an LFCO problem. Consider the notation of Section 2. In the MWC problem, $\mathcal{X}_G \subseteq \{0,1\}^{n+m}$ corresponds to the set of all cuts in a given network G. Vector $\mathbf{x} \in \mathcal{X}_G$ represents cut (S,T) such that for $1 \le i \le n$, $x_i = 1$ iff $v_i \in T$, and for $1 \le j \le m$, $x_{n+j} = 1$ iff $e_j \in (S,T)$, where v_i is the ith vertex and e_j is the jth arc. Vector $\mathbf{a}$ from the formulation of an LFCO problem is here $(\mathbf{d}, -\mathbf{u})$, where $\mathbf{d}$ and $\mathbf{u}$ are the vector representations of functions d and u. If $\mathbf{x}$ represents (S,T), then $\mathbf{ax}$ and $\mathbf{bx}$ are now $surplus(S,T)$ and $b(S,T)$.

7 Related Flow Problems

The MWC problem is related to the following two network flow problems. We assume here that cost functions and weight functions are nonnegative. The *minimum maximum arc cost flow problem* (MAC) is the problem of finding a satisfying flow in a given network which minimizes the maximum arc cost, *i.e.*, which minimizes $\max_{e\in E}\{f(e)c(e)\}$. We denote this minimum by δ^*:

$$\delta^* = \delta^*(G) = \min\{\max_{e\in E}\{f(e)c(e)\} \mid f \text{ satisfying flow in } G\}$$

In the *minimum maximum capacity violation cost flow problem* (MCVC), which is also called the *parametric flow* problem, a network G and a weight function $b : E \longrightarrow \mathbf{R}$ are given. We want to find the minimum nonnegative δ such that $G_{u+\delta b}$ is feasible. We denote this minimum again by $\delta^* = \delta^*(G)$. It will not cause confusion, because it will be always obvious from the context which problem is currently discussed. We can look at the MCVC problem in the following way. A network G is given, which might not be feasible. The objective is to obtain a feasible network by increasing the capacities. A weight function $b : E \longrightarrow \mathbf{R}$ specifies by how much the capacities of the arcs can be increased in unit cost. That is, the cost of increase of the capacity of arc e from $u(e)$ to $u(e)+\xi$ is equal to $\xi/b(e)$. Compute the minimum of the maximum cost of increasing the capacity of an arc.

Minimizing the maximum arc cost seems to be appropriate, for example, when the cost of increasing the capacities represents the time and the capacities on different arcs can be increased simultaneously. As mentioned in [15], the problem of minimizing the maximum arc cost appears, for example, when it is desirable not to use an arc at its full capacity. Each arc e has some safety level $s(e)$ and the ratio $f(e)/s(e)$ is sought to be minimized, with the general objective of getting the maximal ratio as small as possible. The MAC problem captures also the following dynamic situation. The network is in continuous activity, that is, the sources continuously keep producing commodity and sending it to the sinks. The objective is to maximize the throughput. More formally, suppose $1/c(e)$ is the amount of the commodity which can be shipped through arc e in unit time. It means that the shipment of $f(e)$ units through e takes $f(e)c(e)$ time. Further suppose that every source s generates $-d(s)$ units of the commodity every τ units of time and sends it out, and every sink t has to get $d(t)$ units of the commodity every τ units of time. Then the optimal δ^* in the formulation of the MAC problem is equal to the minimal possible τ such that no congestion arises at any vertex.

The network feasibility problem, the maximum flow problem and the maximum cut problem are the nonfractional/nonparametric underlying problems for problems MWC, MAC, and MCVC. The network feasibility problem and the maximum flow problem can be easily reduced to the standard (single-source single-sink) maximum flow problem (MF). A maximum flow in a (transshipment) network can be used to find a maximum surplus cut, in a similar way as a maximum flow in a standard maximum flow network can be used to identify a minimum capacity cut.

Let $T_{\mathrm{P}}(n,m)$ denote the time complexity of a flow problem P. The best known bound for the standard maximum flow problem is

$$T_{\mathrm{MF}}(n,m) = O(\min\{nm\log(n^2/m), nm + n^{2+\epsilon}\}),$$

which is a combination of results from [3] and [11]. The network feasibility problem, the maximum flow problem (in a transshipment network), and the maximum surplus cut problem can be solved in $T_{\mathrm{MF}}(n,m)$ time.

The following theorem shows close relation between the MAC problem and the MCVC problem.

Theorem 6

1. $T_{\mathrm{MCVC}}(n,m) \le O(m) + T_{\mathrm{MAC}}(n,2m)$.
2. $T_{\mathrm{MAC}}(n,m) \le T_{\mathrm{MF}}(n,m)O(\log m) + T_{\mathrm{MCVC}}(n,m)$.

Proof (Sketch).

1. Replace each arc e in a given instance of MCVC with two parallel arcs e_1 and e_2. Put $u'(e_1) = u(e)$, $c'(e_1) = 0$, $u'(e_2) = +\infty$, $c'(e_2) = 1/b(e)$.

2. It can be shown that the solution, δ^*, to a given instance of MAC is

$$\delta^* = \min\{\delta \geq 0 \mid G_{\min\{u,\delta/c\}} \text{ is feasible}\}.$$

Find the position of δ^* in Identify those numbers in $\{u(e)c(e) \mid e \in E\}$ which are bigger than δ^*. This can be done in $T_{\mathrm{MF}}(n,m)O(\log m)$ time. Get an instance of MCVC putting

$$(u'(e), b'(e)) = \begin{cases} (u(e), 0) & \text{if } u(e)c(e) \leq \delta^*, \\ (0, 1/c(e)) & \text{if } u(e)c(e) > \delta^*. \end{cases}$$

■

Let $mean\_w_\delta(S,T)$ denote the mean-weight surplus of (S,T) in $G_{u+\delta b}$. It can be checked that $mean\_w_\delta(S,T) = mean\_w(S,T) - \delta$, so the following lemma holds.

Lemma 6 The maximum mean-weight surplus of a blocking cut in G is equal to the minimum nonnegative δ for which $G_{u+\delta b}$ does not contain blocking cuts.

The following well know theorem gives the dual condition for feasibility of a network.

Theorem 7 [6] G is feasible iff there are no cuts in G with positive surpluses.

Theorem 7 and Lemma 6 imply that the MCVC problem and the MWC problem are equivalent, *i.e.*,

$$\min\{\delta \geq 0 \mid G_{u+\delta b} \text{ is feasible}\} = \max\{mean\_w(S,T) \mid (S,T) \text{ blocking cut in } G\}.$$

Actually, MWC and MCVC are dual to each other in the same sense as the minimum cut and the maximum flow problems are dual to each other.

Thus the complexities of MWC, MAC, and MCVC are essentially the same. For the further analysis we pick up the MCVC problem, *i.e.*, the parametric flow problem. The only previously known strongly polynomial bound for the parametric flow problem was achieved by Megiddo with his parametric search method [15]. This method gives an $O^*(n^3m)$ running time and can be faster only if a breakthrough in parallel maximum flow computation is achieved.

In the next section we analyze Newton's method for the MCVC problem. Theorem 4 gives an $O^*(m^3)$ bound on the number of iterations. Taking advantage of the flow/cut duality in network flow problems, we prove an $O(m)$ bound on the number of iterations. One iteration is dominated by the maximum flow computation. Therefore we obtain an $O(T_{\mathrm{MF}}(n,m)m) = O^*(m^2 n)$ bound on the time complexity of MCVC, MAC and MWC.

8 Newton's Method for the MCVC Problem

The input to the MCVC problem is a network G and a (nonnegative) weight function b. We assume that G is not feasible. G_δ stands for $G_{u+\delta b}$, and generally subscript δ indicates that the underlying network is $G_{u+\delta b}$. For example,

$$\begin{aligned} surplus_\delta(S,T) &\stackrel{\text{def}}{=} d(T) - (u(S,T) + \delta b(S,T)) \\ &= surplus(S,T) - \delta b(S,T). \end{aligned}$$

We want to find

$$\delta^* = \min\{\delta \mid G_\delta \text{ is feasible}\},$$

which, as stated in the previous section, is equal to

$$\max\{mean\_w(S,T) \mid (S,T) \text{ cut in } G\}.$$

The function $h(\delta)$ used in the discussion of a general LFCO problem is now

$$h(\delta) = \max\{surplus_\delta(S,T) \mid (S,T) \text{ cut in } G\}.$$

Value $h(\delta)$ is also equal to the total demand left in G^f_δ, where f is a maximum flow in G_δ.

Newton's method finds δ^*, the root of $h(\delta)$, in the following way. Let $\bar\delta \leq \delta^*$ be the current (under)estimation of δ^*. Initially $\bar\delta = 0$. During one iteration we find a maximum cut (S,T) in $G_{\bar\delta}$. This computation is done by finding a maximum flow $\bar f$ in $G_{\bar\delta}$. If the surplus of (S,T) is zero, *i.e.*, if $\bar f$ satisfies all demand, then $\delta^* = \bar\delta$ and algorithm terminates. Otherwise we compute the next estimation $\bar\delta = mean\_w(S,T)$ and go to the next iteration. Moving to the next estimation should be seen as increasing the capacities so that the surplus of (S,T) decreases to zero.

For any flow f in G, the surpluses of cuts are the same in G as in G^f. It means that in the current iteration we can perform computation on any residual network of $G_{\bar\delta}$ instead of $G_{\bar\delta}$. In the analysis we assume that the network at the beginning of the current iteration is $G^f_{\bar\delta}$, where f is the sum of the maximum flows computed in all previous iterations. It means that f is a maximum flow in $G_{\delta'}$, where δ' is $\bar\delta$ from the previous iteration.

Let δ_i be $\bar\delta$ at the beginning of iteration i, and (S_i, T_i) be the cut found in this iteration. B_i, and H_i from Section 3 have here the following meaning.

$$\begin{aligned} B_i &= b(S_i, T_i), \\ H_i &= h(\delta_i) = surplus(S_i,T_i) - \delta_i b(S_i,T_i) \\ &\qquad = surplus_{\delta_i}(S_i,T_i). \end{aligned}$$

Let f_i be the sum of the flows computed through iteration i. Flow f_i is a maximum flow in G_{δ_i}. Reexamining our algorithm, the network at the beginning of iteration i is $G_{\delta_i}^{f_{i-1}}$. Then we find a maximum flow $\hat{f}_i$ in this network and identify a maximum cut (S_i, T_i). At this point the network is $G_{\delta_i}^{f_{i-1}+\hat{f}_i} = G_{\delta_i}^{f_i}$. Now we increase the capacity function by $\hat{\delta}_i b$, where $\hat{\delta}_i = mean\_w_{\delta_i}(S_i, T_i)$. We get network $G_{\delta_i+\hat{\delta}_i}^{f_i} = G_{\delta_{i+1}}^{f_i}$, and go to the next iteration. H_i is the total demand in $G_{\delta_{i+1}}^{f_i}$, so it is the total demand left after iteration i.

Our analysis can be viewed as an instance of the following general paradigm. As computation proceeds, some constraints become unessential and can be dropped. The key part of the analysis lies in bounding the time needed for a new constraint to become unessential. Many strongly polynomial algorithms for the minimum cost circulation problem fall under this pattern (see for example [22], [16], [4], [5], [19]). In our analysis we use Inequality (2) to estimate the progress. This inequality says that if sequence (B_i) does not decrease fast, then sequence (H_i) has to. After some time, H_i, the total demand left, may be small enough in comparison with the capacities of some arcs, so these capacities are not essential any more and can be dropped. We formalize this idea.

An arc e is *unessential* in G if its capacity is greater than the total demand or its weight is greater than the weight of a maximum surplus cut. When we use expression "e is unessential" in the context of the algorithm, we mean that e is unessential in the current network. By increasing δ we increase the capacities of arcs. By augmenting with a flow we may decrease the capacity of an arc, but by not more than we decrease the total demand. It means that, if an arc is unessential in G_δ^f, for some $\delta \geq 0$ and some flow f, then it is unessential in $G_{\delta+\delta'}^{f+f'}$, for any $\delta' \geq 0$ and any flow f' in $G_{\delta+\delta'}^f$. Therefore, if at some point in the algorithm an arc is unessential, it remains unessential through the end of the computation. An unessential arc cannot belong to a maximum surplus cut. We show that few iterations are enough to make a new arc unessential.

Lemma 7 From the iteration $i+2$ on, the (current) capacity of cut (S_i, T_i) is greater than H_{i+1}.

Proof (Sketch). At the beginning of iteration $i+1$ the capacity of cut (S_i, T_i) is equal, by definition, to H_i, the remaining total demand. In iteration $i+1$ the capacity of each cut first decreases, but by at most $H_i - H_{i+1}$. Then it increases by $(H_{i+1}/B_{i+1})B$, where B is the weight of this cut. It means that in iteration $i+1$ the capacity of cut (S_i, T_i) first decreases, but does not go below H_{i+1}. Then it increases by more than H_{i+1}, because its weight is greater than B_{i+1}. Therefore at the end of iteration $i+1$ the capacity of (S_i, T_i) is greater than $2H_{i+1}$. From now on the capacity of (S_i, T_i) is always greater than H_{i+1}, because the total decrease of this capacity cannot be greater than the total demand left after iteration $i+1$, which is H_{i+1}. ∎

We first prove an $O(m \log m)$ bound to show the main idea. To prove an $O(m)$ bound, we will need a finer accounting strategy.

Theorem 8 Newton's method solves MCVC in $O(m \log m)$ iterations.

Proof. We use Inequality (3) to show that after $O(\log m)$ iterations a new arc becomes unessential. Let the current iteration be the ith one. Let $l = \lfloor \log m \rfloor + 2$. It follows from Inequality (3) that

$$H_{i+l} B_{i+l} < \frac{1}{m^2} H_{i+1} B_{i+1}. \tag{11}$$

If $B_{i+l} < \frac{1}{m} B_i$, then there exists an arc $e \in (S_i, T_i)$ such that $b(e) > B_{i+l}$. Such an arc is unessential from iteration $i+l$ on.

If $B_{i+l} \geq \frac{1}{m} B_i$, then $B_{i+l} \geq \frac{1}{m} B_{i+1}$ as well, and Inequality (11) implies that $H_{i+l} < \frac{1}{m} H_{i+1}$. Lemma 7 says that the capacity of (S_i, T_i) at the beginning of iteration $i+l+1$ is greater than H_{i+1}, which is greater than mH_{i+l}. It means that the capacity of some arc in (S_i, T_i) in network $G_{\delta_{i+l+1}}^{f_{i+l}}$ (which is the network at the beginning of iteration $i+l+1$) is greater than H_{i+l}, the total demand in $G_{\delta_{i+l+1}}^{f_{i+l}}$. Such an arc is unessential from iteration $i+l+1$ on. Observe that all arc in (S_i, T_i) are not unessential at the beginning of iteration i. ∎

Theorem 9 Newton's method solves MCVC in $O(m)$ iterations.

Proof. Lemma 1 implies that for each iteration i,

$$\frac{B_i}{B_{i-1}} \leq \frac{1}{2} \tag{12}$$

or

$$\frac{H_i}{H_{i-1}} \leq \frac{1}{2}. \tag{13}$$

We first bound the number of iterations i for which (12) holds. Let q be the number of such iterations. Let $(\mu_i)_{i=1}^q$ be the sequence of B_i's in these iterations, and $(\alpha_j)_{j=1}^p$ be the positive b_j's arranged in nonincreasing order. It is easy to see that sequences $(\alpha_j)_{j=1}^{p}$ and $(\mu_i)_{i=1}^{q}$ satisfy the conditions of Lemma 8, so $q \le p \le m$.

Now we bound the number of iterations i for which (13) holds. Here the argument is more involved, because H_i's are not just subsums of a set of m elements. They are related to the current demands and capacities, which vary from iteration to iteration.

To avoid towering subscripts, we renumber iterations taking into an account only iterations with (13). It means that now iteration i is what used to be the ith iteration with (13). From now on we consider only these iterations. All indices refer to the new numbering.

We assign subsequent iterations to arcs in such a way that at most 5 iterations are assigned to one arc. We stop the process of assigning when all but at most $q + 2 = \lceil \log m \rceil + 5$ iterations have been assigned.

Assume that there are still at least $q+3$ unassigned iterations. Let iteration i be the first among them. Consider cut (S_i, T_i). Let p be its cardinality. Let for $1 \le j \le p$ and $1 \le l \le q$, $\gamma_{l,j}$ be the capacity of the jth arc in (S_i, T_i) (assuming any order of the arcs in (S_i, T_i)) at the beginning of iteration $i + l + 2$. It follows from Lemma 7 that for each $1 \le l \le q$,

$$\sum_{j=1}^{p} \gamma_{l,j} \ge H_{i+1}. \tag{14}$$

For each arc, the difference between its capacities at the beginning of iterations $k+1$ and $k+2$ is not greater than the total demand at the beginning of iteration $k+1$, which is H_k. It means that

$$|\gamma_{l,j} - \gamma_{l+1,j}| \le H_{i+l+1} \le \frac{1}{2^l} H_{i+1}. \tag{15}$$

The definition of q, (14), and (15) imply that matrix $(\alpha_{l,j}) = (\gamma_{l,j}/H_{i+1})$ satisfies the conditions of Lemma 9. According to the definition of good elements (see Lemma 9), if $\alpha_{l,j}$ is good, then there exists $l' \le l$ such that $\alpha_{l',j} > 1/2^{l'}$. It means that $\gamma_{l',j} > 1/2^{l'} H_{i+1} \ge H_{i+l'+1}$, so arc j is unessential in iteration $i + l' + 2$ (and in all subsequent iterations). Lemma 9 says that there exists $k \ge 3$ such that at least $k-2$ elements from $\alpha_{k,1}, \alpha_{k,2}, \ldots, \alpha_{k,p}$ are good. Therefore the arcs corresponding to these $k-2$ elements are unessential in iteration $i+k+2$. We assign iterations i through $i+k+1$ to these arcs. Notice that none of these arcs was unessential at iteration i, so none of the previous iteration was assign to any of them. We assign $k+2$ iterations to $k-2$ arcs, so no more than 5 iterations are assigned to one arc.

The above process of assigning iterations to arcs implies that there are at most $5m + O(\log m)$ iterations for which (13) holds. ■

Lemma 8 Let $\alpha_1 \ge \alpha_2 \ge \cdots \ge \alpha_p > 0$ and $\mu_1 > \mu_2 > \ldots > \mu_q > 0$ be such that

1. $\mu_{i+1} \le \frac{1}{2}\mu_i$, for $i = 1, 2, \ldots, q-1$,
2. $\mu_q \ge \alpha_p$,
3. $\mu_i \le \sum\{\alpha_j \mid \alpha_j \le \mu_i\}$, for $i = 1, 2, \ldots, q$.

Then $q \le p$.

Proof. Let $\bar{\alpha}_j = \alpha_j + \alpha_{j+1} + \cdots + \alpha_p$. Condition 3 implies that $\mu_1 \le \bar{\alpha}_1$. Thus, to prove $q \le p$, it is sufficient to show that each of the intervals $(0, \bar{\alpha}_p]$, $(\bar{\alpha}_p, \bar{\alpha}_{p-1}]$, ..., $(\bar{\alpha}_3, \bar{\alpha}_2]$, $(\bar{\alpha}_2, \bar{\alpha}_1]$ contains at most one element from (μ_i). Condition 2 implies that only the last element can be in $(0, \bar{\alpha}_p]$. Let for some $1 \le j \le p-1$ and $1 \le i \le q-1$, $\mu_i \in (\bar{\alpha}_{j+1}, \bar{\alpha}_j]$. We show that $\mu_{i+1} \le \bar{\alpha}_{j+1}$.

If $\bar{\alpha}_{j+1} \ge \frac{1}{2}\bar{\alpha}_j$, then

$$\mu_{i+1} \le \frac{1}{2}\mu_i \le \frac{1}{2}\bar{\alpha}_j \le \bar{\alpha}_{j+1}.$$

If $\bar{\alpha}_{j+1} < \frac{1}{2}\bar{\alpha}_j$, then

$$\mu_{i+1} \le \frac{1}{2}\mu_i \le \frac{1}{2}\bar{\alpha}_j = (\bar{\alpha}_{j+1} - \frac{1}{2}\bar{\alpha}_j) + \alpha_j < \alpha_j.$$

This and Condition 3 imply $\mu_{i+1} \le \bar{\alpha}_{j+1}$. ■

Lemma 9 Let $(\alpha_{i,j})$ be a $q \times p$ matrix such that

1. $q \ge \log p + 3$,
2. the sum of each row is not less than 1,
3. $|\alpha_{i+1,j} - \alpha_{i,j}| \le 1/2^i$, for $1 \le i \le q$ and $1 \le j \le p$.

If $\alpha_{i,j} > 1/2^i$, then we call this and all subsequent elements in column j good elements. There is $k \ge 3$ such that row k contains at least $k-2$ good elements.

Proof. Condition 3 implies that if $1 \le i' < i'' \le q$ and $1 \le j \le p$, then

$$\begin{aligned} \alpha_{i'',j} &\le \alpha_{i',j} + \frac{1}{2^{i'}} + \frac{1}{2^{i'+1}} + \cdots + \frac{1}{2^{i''-1}} \\ &< \alpha_{i',j} + \frac{1}{2^{i'-1}}. \end{aligned} \tag{16}$$

If $\alpha_{i,j}$ is the first good element in column j and $i \ge 2$, then

$$\alpha_{i,j} \le \alpha_{i-1,j} + \frac{1}{2^{i-1}} \le \frac{1}{2^{i-1}} + \frac{1}{2^{i-1}} = \frac{1}{2^{i-2}}. \tag{17}$$

Assume that for each $k \ge 3$, row k contains at most $k-3$ good elements. (In particular, there are no good elements in rows 1, 2 and 3.) We will get contradiction by showing that the sum of the last row is less than 1. Let $j_1, j_2, \ldots, j_l$ be the indices of all columns with at least one good element. Let $\alpha_{i_1,j_1}, \alpha_{i_2,j_2}, \ldots, \alpha_{i_l,j_l}$ be the first good elements in these columns. Let $j_1, j_2, \ldots, j_l$ be ordered in such a way that $i_1 \le i_2 \le \cdots \le i_l$. Row i_k contains at least k good elements $(\alpha_{i_k,j_1}, \alpha_{i_k,j_2}, \ldots, \alpha_{i_k,j_k})$ so

$$i_k \ge k + 3. \tag{18}$$

The sum of the last row is at most

$$\frac{p-l}{2^q} + \alpha_{q,j_1} + \alpha_{q,j_2} + \cdots + \alpha_{q,j_l} \le$$

$$\le \frac{1}{8} + (\alpha_{i_1,j_1} + \frac{1}{2^{i_1-1}}) + \cdots + (\alpha_{i_l,j_l} + \frac{1}{2^{i_l-1}}) < 1.$$

The first inequality follows from Condition 1 and Inequality (16), the second one from Inequalities (17) and (18). ∎

9 Concluding Remarks

We showed a strongly polynomial bound on the number of iterations in Newton's method for LFCO problems. The main open problem is to improve our $O^*(p^4)$ bound and to show worst case constructions. We suspect that the bound in Lemma 2 is $O^*(p)$, so the number of iterations is $O^*(p^2)$. We have not been able to show an LFCO problem and a family of instances which would require more than $O(p)$ iterations.

We showed that Newton's method runs in $O(m)$ iterations for the parametric flow problem. We conjecture that the number of iterations is $\Theta(n)$. In [17] we proved this bound for the uniform case.

References

[1] P. J. Carstensen. *The Complexity of Some Problems in Parametric, Linear, and Combinatorial Programming.* PhD thesis, Department of Mathematics, Univ. of Michigan, Ann Arbor. Mich., 1983.

[2] R. Chandrasekaran. Minimum ratio spanning trees. *Networks*, 7:335–342, 1977.

[3] A. V. Goldberg and R. E. Tarjan. A New Approach to the Maximum Flow Problem. *J. Assoc. Comput. Mach.*, 35:921–940, 1988.

[4] A. V. Goldberg and R. E. Tarjan. Finding Minimum-Cost Circulations by Canceling Negative Cycles. *J. Assoc. Comput. Mach.*, 36, 1989.

[5] A. V. Goldberg and R. E. Tarjan. Finding Minimum-Cost Circulations by Successive Approximation. *Math. of Oper. Res.*, 15:430–466, 1990.

[6] A. J. Hoffman. A generalization of max flow - min cut. *Math. Prog.*, 6:352–359, 1974.

[7] T Ibaraki. Parametric approaches to fractional programs. *Math. Programming*, 26:345–362, 1983.

[8] K. Iwano, S. Misono, S. Tezuka, and S. Fujishige. A new scaling algorithm for the maximum mean cut problem. Unpublished manuscript (To appear in *Algorithmica*), 1990.

[9] R. M. Karp. A Characterization of the Minimum Cycle Mean in a Digraph. *Discrete Math.*, 23:309–311, 1978.

[10] A. V. Karzanov. On minimal mean cuts and circuits in a digraph. In *Methods for Solving Operator Equations*, pages 72–83. Yaroslavl State Univ., Yaroslavl, USSR, 1985. In Russian.

[11] V. King, S. Rao, and R. Tarjan. A Faster Deterministic Maximum Flow Algorithm. In *Proc. 3rd ACM-SIAM Symposium on Discrete Algorithms*, pages 157–164, 1992.

[12] E. L. Lawler. *Combinatorial Optimization: Networks and Matroids.* Holt, Reinhart, and Winston, New York, NY., 1976.

[13] S. T. McCormick and T. R. Ervolina. Computing Maximum Mean Cuts. UBC Faculty of Commerce Working Paper 90-MSC-011, 1990.

[14] N. Megiddo. Combinatorial optimization with rational objective functions. *Math. of Oper. Res.*, 4:414–424, 1979.

[15] N. Megiddo. Applying Parallel Computation Algorithms in the Design of Serial Algorithms. *J. Assoc. Comput. Mach.*, 30:852–865, 1983.

[16] J. B. Orlin. A Faster Strongly Polynomial Minimum Cost Flow Algorithm. In *Proc. 20th Annual ACM Symposium on Theory of Computing*, pages 377–387, 1988.

[17] T. Radzik. Minimizing capacity violations in a transshipment network. In *Proc. 3rd ACM-SIAM Symposium on Discrete Algorithms*, pages 185–194, 1992.

[18] T. Radzik. Newton's method for fractional combinatorial optimization. Technical Report STAN-CS-92-1406, Department of Computer Science, Stanford University, January 1992.

[19] T. Radzik and A. Goldberg. Tight bounds on the number of minimum-mean cycle cancellations and related results. In *Proc. 2nd ACM-SIAM Symposium on Discrete Algorithms*, pages 110–119, 1991.

[20] S. Schaible. Fractional programming 2. On Dinkelbach's Algorithm. *Management Sci.*, 22:868–873, 1976.

[21] S. Schaible and T. Ibaraki. Fractional programming. *Europ. J. of Operational Research*, 12, 1983.

[22] É. Tardos. A Strongly Polynomial Minimum Cost Circulation Algorithm. *Combinatorica*, 5(3):247–255, 1985.

A Class of Logic Problems Solvable by Linear Programming

Michele Conforti

Dipartimento di Matematica
Università di Padova
35131 Padova, Italy

Gérard Cornuéjols

GSIA
Carnegie Mellon University
Pittsburgh, PA 15213

Abstract

Several problems of propositional logic, such as satisfiability, MAXSAT and logical inference, can be formulated as integer programs. In this paper, we consider sets of clauses for which these integer programs can be solved as linear programs. We prove that balanced sets of clauses have this property.

1 Introduction

In propositional logic, *atomic propositions* $x_1, \ldots, x_j, \ldots, x_n$ can be either *true* or *false*. A *truth assignment* is an assignment of "true" or "false" to every atomic proposition. A *literal* is an atomic proposition x_j or its negation $\neg x_j$. A *clause* is a disjunction of literals and is *satisfied* by a given truth assignment if at least one of its literals is true.

This paper uses the following connection between propositional logic and integer programming, see Dantzig [9]. A survey of the area can be found in [13].

A truth assignment satisfies the set S of clauses:

$$\bigvee_{j \in P_i} x_j \vee (\bigvee_{j \in N_i} \neg x_j) \;\; for\ all\ i \in S$$

if and only if the corresponding $0,1$ vector satisfies the following system of inequalities:

$$\sum_{j \in P_i} x_j - \sum_{j \in N_i} x_j \geq 1 - |N_i| \;\; for\ all\ i \in S.$$

For a $0, \pm 1$ matrix A, denote by $n(A)$ the vector whose i^{th} component $n_i(A)$ is the number of -1's in the ith row of A. The vector of all $1's$ is denoted by $\mathbf{1}$. Hence the above system of inequalities is of the form

$$Ax \geq \mathbf{1} - n(A). \tag{1}$$

Given a set S of clauses, the *satisfiability problem* (SAT) consists in finding a truth assignment that satisfies all the clauses in S or show that none exists. Equivalently, SAT consists in finding a $0,1$ solution x to (1) or show that none exists.

Given a set S of clauses and a weight vector w whose components are indexed by the clauses in S, the *weighted maximum satisfiability problem (MAXSAT)* consists in finding a truth assignment that maximizes the total weight of the satisfied clauses. MAXSAT can be formulated as the integer program

$$\begin{array}{ll} Min & \sum_{i=1}^{m} w_i s_i \\ & Ax + s \geq 1 - n(A) \\ & x \in \{0,1\}^n, s \in \{0,1\}^m \end{array}$$

where A is a $0, \pm 1$ matrix.

Given a set S of clauses (the premises) and a clause C (the conclusion), *logical inference* in propositional logic consists in deciding whether every truth assignment that satisfies all the clauses in S also satisfies the conclusion C.

To the clause C, using transformation (1), we associate an inequality

$$cx \geq 1 - n(c),$$

where c is a $0, \pm 1$ vector. Therefore C cannot be deduced from S if and only if the integer program

$$min\ \{cx : Ax \geq \mathbf{1} - n(A),\ x \in \{0,1\}^n\} \tag{2}$$

has optimum solution value $-n(c)$.

The above three problems are NP-hard in general but SAT and logical inference can be solved efficiently for Horn clauses, clauses with at most two literals and several related classes [4],[19]. MAXSAT remains NP-hard for Horn clauses with at most two literals. In this paper, we show that the above three problems can be solved in polynomial time, as linear programs, whenever the matrix A associated with S is a balanced $0, \pm 1$ matrix as defined by Truemper [18], see also [16].

Definition 1.1 *A* $0, \pm 1$ *matrix A is* balanced *if, in every submatrix of A with exactly two nonzero entries per row and per column, the sum of the entries is a multiple of* 4.

A class of inference problems that can be solved in polynomial time occurs when the integer program (2) can be solved as a linear program. This is certainly the case when the polytope

$$Q(A) = \{x \in \mathcal{R}^n : Ax \geq \mathbf{1} - n(A),\ \mathbf{0} \leq x \leq \mathbf{1}\}$$

is either empty or all its vertices have integer coordinates. When this holds, the polytope $Q(A)$ is said to be an *integer polytope*. Then the logical inference problem can be solved as a linear program for every conclusion C. A sufficient condition for this to occur is that the determinant of every square submatrix of A be $0, \pm 1$. Such matrices are called ***totally unimodular***, see [16]. It was shown by Camion [3] that a $0, \pm 1$ matrix A is totally unimodular if and only if, in every submatrix of A with an even number of nonzero entries per row and per column, the sum of the entries is a multiple of 4. Therefore totally unimodular matrices are clearly a subclass of balanced $0, \pm 1$ matrices. Here we show that $Q(A)$ is an integer polytope when A is a balanced $0, \pm 1$ matrix.

When A is a $0, 1$ matrix, the integer program (2) is the *set covering problem* which has been extensively studied in combinatorial optimization. Balanced matrices whose entries are $0, 1$ were introduced by Berge [1] and play an important role in the study of the set covering problem, see [16]. In particular, when A is a balanced $0, 1$ matrix, Berge [2] proved that $Q(A)$ is an integer polytope and Fulkerson, Hoffman and Oppenheim [10] proved that the set covering problem has an optimum dual solution which is integer (if any), whenever the objective vector c is integer. This property, known as *total dual integrality*, is a stronger statement than the result of Berge. Lehman [14] gave a characterization of the $0, 1$ matrices such that $Q(A)$ is an integer polytope. These matrices are called *ideal* and, by Berge's theorem, they contain the class of balanced $0, 1$ matrices.

2 The main result

Theorem 2.1 *If A is a balanced* $0, \pm 1$ *matrix, then the polytope* $P(A) = \{x \in \mathcal{R}^n : Ax = \mathbf{1} - n(A),\ \mathbf{0} \leq x \leq \mathbf{1}\}$ *is an integer polytope.*

Proof: Assume A contradicts the theorem and has the smallest size (number of rows plus number of columns). Then $P(A)$ is nonempty.

Claim 1: $P(A)$ contains only one point, say $\bar{x}$, and $\mathbf{0} < \bar{x}_j < \mathbf{1}$ for all j.

Proof of Claim 1: A point $\bar{x} \in P(A)$ is a vertex if and only if there exists an nxn nonsingular system $Mx = b$ of equalities, chosen either among the rows of the system $Ax = \mathbf{1} - n(A)$ or by setting some bounds $x_j \geq 0$ or $x_j \leq 1$ at equality, such that $\bar{x}$ is the unique solution to $Mx = b$. We can assume w.l.o.g. that, if $\bar{x}_j = 0$ ($\bar{x}_j = 1$ respectively), then $Mx = b$ contains the equality $x_j = 0$ ($x_j = 1$ respectively). Let B be the square nonsingular submatrix of M whose columns correspond to the fractional components of $\bar{x}$. Clearly B is a submatrix of A. Let A' be obtained from A by removing the rows which are not in B (if any). Then $\bar{x}$ is still a fractional vertex of $P(A')$, showing that $A = A'$, by minimality of A. Since B is nonsingular,

every row of A contains an entry $a_{ij} \neq 0$ *such that* $\bar{x}_j$ *is fractional.* (3)

Let j be an index such that $\bar{x}_j = 0$ (if any). Then $a_{ij} = 0, 1$ for all i, else $\bar{x}$ does not satisfy the ith equation of $Ax = \mathbf{1} - n(A)$ as a consequence of (3). Now the polytope $P(A')$, associated with the matrix A' obtained from A by removing column j still has a fractional vertex.

Let j be an index such that $\bar{x}_j = 1$ (if any). Then $a_{ij} = 0, -1$ for all i, else, as a consequence of (3), $\bar{x}$ does not satisfy the ith equation of $Ax = \mathbf{1} - n(A)$. Again, the polytope $P(A')$, associated with the matrix A' obtained from A by removing column j has a fractional vertex.

Hence all the components of $\bar{x}$ are fractional, therefore $B = A$ and the proof of Claim 1 is complete.

Let $a^1, \ldots, a^m$ denote the row vectors of A and let A_m be the submatrix of A obtained by removing the last row. The polytope $P(A_m) = \{x \in \mathcal{R}^n : A_m x = \mathbf{1} - n(A_m),\ \mathbf{0} \leq x \leq \mathbf{1}\}$ contains the unique point $\bar{x}$ in $P(A)$ and, by the minimality of A, all the vertices of $P(A_m)$ have $0, 1$ components. This shows that $\bar{x}$ is a convex combination of $0, 1$ vectors in $P(A_m)$, but none of these vectors satisfies $a^m x = 1 - n_m(A)$. Hence there exist $0, 1$ vectors x^S, $x^T \in P(A_m)$ such that $a^m x^S < 1 - n_m(A)$ and $a^m x^T > 1 - n_m(A)$. In fact

$$a^m x^S = -n_m(A) \qquad (4)$$

Let $S = \{j : x_j^S = 1\}, T = \{j : x_j^T = 1\}, V = T \setminus S$ and $U = S \setminus T$.

Claim 2: In the submatrix of A_m with columns $U \cup V$, every nonzero row contains exactly two nonzero entries and these entries have the same sign if and only if one belongs to U and the other to V.

Proof of Claim 2: For every 0,1 vector $x \in P(A_m)$ and every row i of A_m, one of the two following properties holds:

(i) There exists a unique column k such that $x_k = 1$ and $a_{ik} = 1$, and $x_j = 1$ for all j such that $a_{ij} = -1$.

(ii) There exists a unique column k such that $x_k = 0$ and $a_{ik} = -1$, and $x_j = 0$ for all j such that $a_{ij} = 1$.

These conditions imply that there cannot exist a row i of A_m such that $a_{ij} = a_{ik} = 1$ and $x_j = x_k = 1$. Similarly, there cannot exist a row i of A_m such that $a_{ij} = a_{ik} = -1$ and $x_j = x_k = 0$. This shows that no row of A_m contains two nonzero entries of the same sign in U (in V respectively). If U contains two nonzero entries of opposite sign, then x^S satisfies (i) and x^T satisfies *(ii)*, showing that $a_{ij} = 0$ for every $j \in V$. Assume U contains a unique nonzero entry in row i. If this entry is positive, then x^S satisfies (i) and therefore $a_{ij} = 0, 1$ for all $j \notin S \cap T$. This shows that x^T satisfies (i), implying that there exists a column $k \in V$ such that $a_{ik} = 1$. If U contains a unique entry in row i which is negative, then x^T satisfies (ii) and therefore $a_{ij} = 0, -1$ for all $j \in S \cap T$. This shows that x^S satisfies (ii), implying that there exists a column $k \in V$ such that $a_{ik} = -1$. This completes the proof of Claim 2.

Let G be a graph (possibly with parallel edges) defined as follows: Its node set is $U \cup V$ and its edge set is indexed by the rows of A_m having nonzero entries in $U \cup V$. Nodes j and k are connected by edge e_i if and only if both a_{ij} and a_{ik} are nonzero.

Claim 3: $a_{mj} = 0, -1$ for all $j \in U$ and $a_{mj} = 0, 1$ for all $j \in V$.

Proof of Claim 3: Both statements follow from (4).

Since $a^m x^T > 1 - n_m(A)$, then either there exists $j \in V$ such that $a_{mj} = 1$ or else there exists $j \in U$ such that $a_{mj} = -1$. Hence there exists $j^* \in U \cup V$ such that $a_{mj^*} \neq 0$. Consider the connected component of G containing node j^*. Let C be the node set of this component.

Claim 4: $a_{mk} = 0$ for all $k \in C$, $k \neq j^*$.

Proof of Claim 4: Assume not and choose k such that the length of a shortest path P between j^* and k is as small as possible. Let B be the matrix with columns corresponding to the nodes of P and rows corresponding to the edges of P together with row m. By construction of P, B is a square matrix with two nonzero entries per row and per column. Furthermore, if both j^* and k belong to the same set U or V, then Claim 3 implies $a_{mj^*} = a_{mk}$ and Claim 2 implies that there exists an even number of rows of B, different from m, having both nonzero entries of the same sign. Hence the sum of the elements of B is equal to 2 *modulo* 4, a contradiction. Similarly, if j^* and k belong to different sets U and V, then Claim 3 implies $a_{mj^*} = -a_{mk}$ and Claim 2 implies that there exists an odd number of rows of B having both nonzero entries of the same sign. Hence the sum of the elements of B is again equal to 2 *modulo* 4 and the proof of Claim 4 is complete.

Hence the vector $x^{S \Delta C}$ where

$$x_j^{S\Delta C} = 1 \;\; if\; j \in (S \setminus C) \cup (C \setminus S), \;\; 0 \; otherwise$$

satisfies $Ax^{S\Delta C} = \mathbf{1} - n(A)$ as a consequence of (4). This contradicts Claim 1, and the proof of the theorem is complete. □

Theorem 2.2 *If A is a balanced $0, \pm 1$ matrix, then $Q(A) = \{x \in \mathcal{R}^n : Ax \geq \mathbf{1} - n(A),\ \mathbf{0} \leq x \leq \mathbf{1}\}$ is an integer polytope.*

Proof: If $\bar{x}$ is a vertex of $Q(A)$, it is a vertex of the polytope $\bar{Q}(A)$ obtained from $Q(A)$ by deleting the inequalities of $Ax \geq \mathbf{1} - n(A)$ that are not satisfied at equality by $\bar{x}$. Now $\bar{x}$ is a vertex of the face F of $\bar{Q}(A)$ obtained by setting to equality the remaining inequalities of $Ax \geq \mathbf{1} - n(A)$. By Theorem 2.1, every vertex of F has 0,1 coordinates. □

Theorem 2.3 *If A is a balanced $0, \pm 1$, then $R(A) = \{(x, s) \in \mathcal{R}^{n+m} : Ax + s \geq \mathbf{1} - n(A),\ \mathbf{0} \leq x, s \leq \mathbf{1}\}$ is an integer polytope.*

Proof: A $0, \pm 1$ matrix A is balanced if and only if (A, I) is balanced, where I denotes an identity matrix. Now $R(A) = Q(A, I)$ is an integer polytope as a consequence of Theorem 2.2. □

3 Algorithmic implications

Let S be a set of clauses and A the corresponding $0, \pm 1$ matrix as defined in (1). S is a *balanced set of clauses* if A is balanced. The following theorem is an immediate consequence of Theorems 2.2 and 2.3.

Theorem 3.1 *Let S be a balanced set of clauses. Then the satisfiability, MAXSAT and logical inference problems can be solved in polynomial time by linear programming.*

This is significant since MAXSAT is NP-hard even for 2-SAT and Horn formulae. This also has consequences for probabilistic logic as defined by Nilsson [15]. Being able to solve MAXSAT in polynomial time provides a polynomial time separation algorithm for probabilistic logic via the ellipsoid method, as observed by Georgakopoulos, Kavvadias and Papadimitriou [11]. Hence probabilistic logic is solvable in polynomial time for balanced sets of clauses.

The results of Section 2 also have the following implication. Let $w_1, \ldots, w_n$ be rational weights associated with the atomic propositions $x_1, \ldots, x_n$, let S be a set of clauses and S' be a subset of S. The *weighted exact satisfiability problem* consists in finding a truth assignment (if any) such that:

- every clause in S is satisfied and, in every clause of S', there exists exactly one literal that assumes the value true, and
- the sum of the weights of the atomic propositions that assume the value true is maximized.

Note that the weighted exact satisfiability problem contains the logical inference problem of propositional logic as a special case.

Theorem 3.2 *Let S be a balanced set of clauses. The weighted exact satifiability problem is solvable by linear programming for every subset S' of S and every vector w of rational weights.*

Proof: Let $T(A)$ be the polytope obtained from $Q(A)$ by setting at equality the inequalities of $Q(A)$ corresponding to the clauses in S'. The weighted exact satisfiability problem consists in solving the integer program:

$$max\ wx :\ x \in T(A),\ x \in \{0,1\}^n.$$

The proof of Theorem 2.2 shows that $T(A)$ is an integer polytope. Therefore the above integer program can be solved as the linear program

$$max\ wx :\ x \in T(A). \qquad \square$$

Remark 3.3 *Let S be a set of clauses such that the polytope $Q(A)$ is integer. If every clause of S contains more than one literal then, for every atomic proposition x_j, there exist at least two truth assignments satisfying S, one in which x_j is true and one in which x_j is false.*

Proof: Since the point $x_j = 1/2$, $j = 1, \ldots, n$ belongs to the polytope $Q(A)$ and $Q(A)$ is an integer polytope, then the above point can be expressed as a convex combination of $0, 1$ vectors in $Q(A)$. Clearly, for every index j, there exists in the convex combination a $0, 1$ vector with $x_j = 0$ and another with $x_j = 1$. $\square$

The above property is desirable for the set of clauses in a knowledge base. Indeed, knowledge bases arising from applications are often known to be consistent. Furthermore any atomic proposition that takes the same value in every truth assignment satisfying all the clauses, can be eliminated.

Let S be a set of clauses such that the polytope $Q(A)$ is integer. A consequence of Remark 3.3 is that SAT and logical inference can be solved more efficiently than by general linear programming. The next theorem shows that the recursive application of the following step produces a truth assignment that satisfies S whenever S is satisfiable.

Recursive Step *If $S = \emptyset$ then S is satisfiable. If S contains a clause C with a single literal (*unit clause*), set the corresponding atomic proposition x_j so that C is satisfied. Eliminate from S all clauses that become satisfied and remove x_j from all the other clauses (*unit resolution*). If a clause becomes empty, then S is not satisfiable.*

If every clause in S contains at least two literals, choose any atomic proposition x_j appearing in a clause of S and add to S an arbitrary clause x_j or $\neg x_j$.

Theorem 3.4 *Let S be a set of clauses such that the polytope $Q(A)$ is integer. Then S is satisfiable if and only if the algorithm stops with an empty set of clauses.*

Proof: If the algorithm terminates with $S = \emptyset$, then S is clearly satisfiable. We show that if the algorithm terminates with an empty clause, then S is not satisfiable.

Let $P = \{x \in \mathcal{R}^n :\ Dx \leq d\}$ be an integer polytope. Then, for every partition of the rows of D into $\begin{pmatrix} D_1 \\ D_2 \end{pmatrix}$ and corresponding partition of d into $\begin{pmatrix} d_1 \\ d_2 \end{pmatrix}$, the polytope $\{x \in \mathcal{R}^n : D_1 x = d_1,\ D_2 x \leq d_2\}$ is a face of P and therefore is also an integer polytope. Note that the two parts of the recursive step consist in setting at equality some bounds on the variables $0 \leq x_j \leq 1$ and carrying out the corresponding variable elimination. Ler S' be any set of clauses obtained from S by applying the recursive step and let

B be the corresponding 0 ± 1 matrix. Then $Q(B)$ is an integer polytope and Remark 3.3 holds. So, if there are no unit clauses in S' then S' is satisfiable and we can arbitrarily add a unit clause to S' and still obtain a satisfiable system. □.

Remark 3.5 *Let S be a set of premises with associated $0, \pm 1$ matrix A and C be a conclusion with associated $0, \pm 1$ vector c. Then C cannot be deduced from S if and only if there exists a vector $x \in Q(A)$ such that $x_j = 1$ if $c_j = -1$ and $x_j = 0$ if $c_j = 1$. Hence the logical inference problem is equivalent to determining whether the set S' of clauses obtained from S by adding the unit clauses x_j when $c_j = -1$ and $\neg x_j$ when $c_j = 1$, is satisfiable. Theorem 3.4 shows that, if $Q(A)$ is an integer polytope, then so is $Q(B)$ where B is the $0, \pm 1$ marix associated with S'. It follows that, if $Q(A)$ is integer, the above algorithm for SAT can be used to solve the logical inference problem.*

For balanced sets of clauses, an open problem is to solve the MAXSAT and weighted exact satisfiability problems in polynomial time by a direct method, without appealing to polynomial time algorithms for general linear programming.

4 Recognizing balanced matrices

In this section, we briefly discuss the question of testing whether a set of clauses (or, equivalently, a $0, \pm 1$ matrix) is balanced and we survey some related recognition problems.

Two important classes of balanced $0, \pm 1$ matrices that are well characterized are the network matrices (i.e. $0, \pm 1$ matrices that can be transformed into node-arc matrices through "pivoting") [20] and the larger class of totally unimodular matrices [17]. In both cases, the results were obtained using matroid theory. The matroids associated with network matrices are called *graphic*, those associated with totally unimodular matrices are called *regular*. Seymour [17] developped an important decomposition theory of regular matroids. Using i-sum decompositions, for $i = 1, 2, 3$, he showed that all regular matroids can be decomposed into graphic and co-graphic matroids and copies of a 10-element matroid called R_{10}. A polynomial recognition algorithm for totally unimodular matrices follows.

Our approach to recognizing balanced matrices also uses decomposition, but we do not use matroid theory. Instead we use a graph theoretic approach. To a $0, \pm 1$ matrix A we associate a weighted bipartite graph $G(A)$ as follows: the node set of $G(A)$ is partitioned into V^r and V^c which represent the row set and the column set of A. $G(A)$ has an edge connecting node i and node j if and only if $a_{ij} \neq 0$, and a_{ij} is its weight. A $0, \pm 1$ matrix is balanced if and only if, in every chordless cycle H of the associated bipartite graph, the sum of the weights of the edges in H is a multiple of 4.

If A is a balanced $0, 1$ matrix, we say that the associated bipartite graph $G(A)$ is *balanced*. Testing whether a $0, 1$ matrix A is balanced amounts to testing whether $G(A)$ contains a chordless cycle of length congruent to 2 *modulo* 4. This problem has been investigated by several authors, see [5] Part I for a survey, and has been solved for several special cases, most notably:

- Restricted balanced matrices: every cycle of $G(A)$ has length congruent to 0 *modulo* 4 [21].
- Strongly balanced: every cycle of $G(A)$ with length 2 *modulo* 4 has at least two chords [7].
- Totally balanced: every chordless cycle of $G(A)$ has length 4 [12].
- Linear balanced: no cycle of $G(A)$ has length 4 [8].

For general balanced bipartite graphs, a decomposition theorem is established in [5] Parts II-VI and used in Part VII to recognize in polynomial time whether a $0, 1$ matrix is balanced. A *2-join* in a bipartite graph G is a set of edges $E_1 \cup E_2$ such that, for $i = 1, 2$, E_i induces a complete bipartite subgraph G_i of G, the graphs G_1 and G_2 have disjoint node sets and $G \setminus (E_1 \cup E_2)$ is disconnected. A *double star cutset* in a bipartite graph G is a node set S such that $G \setminus S$ is disconnected and there exist two adjacent nodes u, v with the property that every node of S is adjacent to u or v.

Theorem 4.1 (Conforti, Cornuéjols and Rao [5]) *If a balanced bipartite graph is not restricted balanced, then it contains a 2-join or a double star cutset.*

Double star cutsets and 2-joins can be used recursively to decompose a given bipartite graph G into elementary blocks that contain neither. In [5], it is shown how to perform this decomposition so that only a polynomial number of elementary blocks are created and G is balanced if and only if all the elementary blocks are restricted balanced. A polynomial algorithm for recognizing balanced $0, 1$ matrices follows.

The decomposition theorem 4.1 has been recently extended to balanced $0, \pm 1$ matrices in [6] but a new decomposition is required as well as a new elementary block (related to R_{10}) which is not restricted balanced. The algorithmic issues are currently under investigation.

Acknowledgements: Vijay Chandru pointed out the relevance of our work to the MAXSAT problem and probabilistic logic. Klaus Truemper showed us the algorithmic implications of Remark 3.3 for logical inference.

This work was supported in part by NSF grants DDM-9001705 and DDM-9201340.

References

[1] C. Berge, Sur certains hypergraphes généralisant les graphes bipartites, in: *Combinatorial Theory and its Applications I* (P. Erdös, A. Rényi and V. Sós eds.), *Colloq. Math. Soc. János Bolyai 4*, North Holland, Amsterdam (1970) 119-133.

[2] C. Berge, Balanced matrices, *Mathematical Programming 2* (1972) 19-31.

[3] P. Camion, Characterization of totally unimodular matrices, *Proceedings of the American Mathematical Society 16* (1965) 1068-1073.

[4] V. Chandru, J.N. Hooker, Extended Horn sets in propositional logic, *Journal of the ACM 38* (1991) 205-221.

[5] M. Conforti, G. Cornuéjols, M. R. Rao, Decomposition of balanced 0,1 matrices, Parts I-VII, preprints, Carnegie Mellon University (1991).

[6] M. Conforti, G. Cornuéjols, A. Kapoor, K. Vuskovic, Decomposition of balanced $0, \pm 1$ matrices, forthcoming (1992).

[7] M. Conforti, M. R. Rao, Structural properties and recognition of restricted and strongly unimodular matrices, *Mathematical Programming 38* (1987) 17-27.

[8] M. Conforti, M. R. Rao, Structural properties and decomposition of linear balanced matrices, *Mathematical Programming 55* (1992) 129-168.

[9] G. B. Dantzig, *Linear programming and extensions*, Princeton University Press (1963).

[10] D. R. Fulkerson, A. Hoffman, R. Oppenheim, On balanced matrices, *Mathematical Programming Study 1* (1974) 120-132.

[11] G. Georgakopoulos, D. Kavvadias, C. H. Papadimitriou, Probabilistic satisfiability, *Journal of Complexity 4* (1988) 1-11.

[12] M. C. Golumbic, C. F. Goss, Perfect elimination and chordal bipartite graphs, *Journal of Graph Theory 2* (1978) 155-163.

[13] J. N. Hooker, A quantitative approach to logical inference, *Decision Support Systems 4* (1988) 45-69.

[14] A. Lehman, On the width-length inequality and degenerate projective planes, unpublished manuscript (1981), published: *Polyhedral Combinatorics* (W. Cook and P.D. Seymour eds.), *DIMACS Series in Discrete Mathematics and Theoretical Computer Science 1*, American Mathematical Society, Providence, R.I. (1990) 101-105.

[15] N. J. Nilsson, Probabilistic logic, *Artificial Intelligence 28* (1986) 71-87.

[16] A. Schrijver, *Theory of linear and integer programming*, Wiley, New York (1986).

[17] P. Seymour, Decomposition of regular matroids, *Journal of Combinatorial Theory B 28* (1980) 305-359.

[18] K. Truemper, On balanced matrices and Tutte's characterization of regular matroids, preprint (1978).

[19] K. Truemper, Polynomial theorem proving I. Central matrices, *Technical Report UTDCS 34-90* (1990).

[20] W. R. Tutte, An algorithm for determining whether a given binary matroid is graphic, *Proceedings of the American Mathematical Society 11* (1960) 905-917.

[21] M. Yannakakis, On a class of totally unimodular matrices, *Mathematics of Operations Research 10* (1985) 280-304.

Maximizing Non-Linear Concave Functions in Fixed Dimension

SIVAN TOLEDO*
Laboratory for Computer Science
Massachusetts Institute of Technology
Cambridge, Massachusetts 02139

Abstract

Consider a convex set $\mathcal{P}$ in $\mathbb{R}^d$ and a piecewise polynomial concave function $F: \mathcal{P} \to \mathbb{R}$. Let $\mathcal{A}$ be an algorithm that given a point $x \in \mathbb{R}^d$ computes $F(x)$ if $x \in \mathcal{P}$, or returns a concave polynomial p such that $p(x) < 0$ but for any $y \in \mathcal{P}$, $p(y) \geq 0$. We assume that d is fixed and that all comparisons in $\mathcal{A}$ depend on the sign of polynomial functions of the input point. We show that under these conditions, one can find $\max_{\mathcal{P}} F$ *in time which is polynomial in the number of arithmetic operations of $\mathcal{A}$. Using our method we give the first strongly polynomial algorithms for many* non-linear *parametric problems in fixed dimension, such as the parametric max flow problem, the parametric minimum s-t distance, the parametric spanning tree problem and other problems.*

In addition we show that in one dimension, the same result holds even if we only know how to approximate *the value of F. Specifically, if we can obtain an α-approximation for $F(x)$ then we can α-approximate the value of* $\max F$. *We thus obtain the first polynomial approximation algorithms for many NP-hard problems such as the parametric Euclidean Traveling Salesman Problem.*

1 Introduction

Consider a convex set $\mathcal{P}$ in $\mathbb{R}^d$ and a piecewise polynomial concave function $F: \mathcal{P} \to \mathbb{R}$. Let $\mathcal{A}$ be an algorithm that given a point $x \in \mathbb{R}^d$ computes $F(x)$ if $x \in \mathcal{P}$, or returns a *separation polynomial*, a concave polynomial p such that $p(x) < 0$ but for any $y \in \mathcal{P}$, $p(y) \geq 0$. We assume that d is fixed and that all comparisons in $\mathcal{A}$ depend on the sign of polynomial functions of the input point which are called *comparison polynomials*. Our main result is that under these conditions, one can find $\max_{\mathcal{P}} F$ and a maximizer in time which is polynomial in the number of arithmetic operations of $\mathcal{A}$. Cohen and Megiddo [3, 4] and independently Norton, Plotkin and Tardos [9] obtained a similar result for the case where F is piecewise linear and the separation and comparison polynomials are all linear.

The technique of [3, 4, 9] extends the parametric search paradigm of Megiddo [7] whose main idea is to simulate $\mathcal{A}$ symbolically on a point $x^\star$ which is a maximizer of F. Since $x^\star$ is not known, a method for resolving comparisons in the simulated algorithm must be provided. Since every comparison is assumed to depend on the sign of some polynomial p in the input point, we could decompose $\mathbb{R}^d$ into cells in which the sign of p is constant. Determining the cell which contains $x^\star$ enables us to determine the sign of $p(x^\star)$ and to resolve the comparison. When a comparison polynomial is linear, the space decomposition is into a hyperplane H and two open half spaces. We call such a hyperplane a *critical* hyperplane. The restriction of F to H is a concave function in one dimension lower. By induction, the maximum of F on H can be found. The assumption that the comparison polynomials are linear also makes it relatively easy to explore the neighborhood of H, and to determine on which side of it F is increasing, thereby resolving the comparison. Since it is assumed that F is piecewise linear, there is a maximizer of it which is a vertex of its graph which can be found using linear programming.

In this paper we show how to solve the problem without assuming that F is piecewise linear and that the comparison and separation polynomials are linear. Since in this case it is no longer true that the decomposition of the space into cells which are invariant for the sign of a comparison polynomial consists of a hyperplane and two open half spaces, we cannot use the parametric searching technique directly. Instead we use a searching technique which is based on the weighted Euclidean 1-center algorithm of Megiddo [8]. In this technique, the d dimensional algorithm

*This research was supported in part by the Defense Advanced Research Projects Agency under Grant N00014-91-J-1698. Author's e-mail address: sivan@theory.lcs.mit.edu.

0-8186-2900-2/92 $3.00 © 1992 IEEE

works by *simulating* the $d-1$ dimensional one on a hyperplane that contains a maximizer of F. Unfortunately, the parametric searching technique as described by Megiddo and others [7, 3, 4, 9] can use only a certain class of algorithms as the non-parametric algorithm. It turns out that parametric searching algorithms do not belong to this class, since they compute roots of polynomials. Using Collins' cylindrical algebraic decomposition algorithm [1], we extend the class of algorithm which can serve as non-parametric algorithms. This "closes" this class under the operation of paramertization, and enables us to apply the parametric searching technique recursively.

Another consequence of the non-linearity of the comparison polynomials is that it becomes difficult to explore the neighborhood of a critical hyperplane by exploring the behavior of the comparison polynomials in the neighborhood of a point. We therefore develop a new technique to decide on which side of a critical hyperplane F is maximized. This technique is based on the observation that we can avoid resolving some comparisons and take both sides of the associated branch simultaneously. We show that at any time during the execution of our algorithm there can be only one unresolved comparison, which is the one corresponding to the hyperplane on which the highest value of F was computed. The last problem that must be solved is that of finding a maximizer of F when there is no maximizer which is a vertex of the graph of F. This is done by computing certificates of optimality during the execution of the algorithm in lower dimensions, and using Lagrange multipliers to find a maximizer.

Using our new method we obtain the first strongly polynomial algorithms to a wide variety of non-linear parametric problems in fixed dimension. For example, given a graph in which the edges have concave polynomial weights, we can maximize the max flow in the graph, the minimum spanning tree, the minimum *s-t* distance and so on. The generality of our results does not come for free, and the cost is a double exponential dependency on the dimension in the running time of our algorithms, while in the linear case it is singly exponential.

The second result obtained in this paper is the application of Megiddo's technique to the approximation of the maximum of univariate piecewise polynomial concave functions which are NP-hard to evaluate, but for which there is an approximate evaluation algorithm. Specifically, if there is an algorithm $\mathcal{A}$ that on input $x \in [a,b]$ computes a value $F(x) \geq \mathcal{A}(x) \geq \alpha F(x)$ in time T, then we can compute in time $O(T^2)$ a value m that satisfies $\max_{[a,b]} F \geq m \geq \alpha \max_{[a,b]} F$. Since in most cases in which evaluating F is NP-hard finding $\max F$ is also NP-hard, we thus obtain the first polynomial approximation algorithm to many NP-hard problems, such as the parametric Euclidean Traveling Salesman Problem.

The model of computation we use in this paper is one in which all the solutions of a zero-dimensional polynomial ideal can be found in constant time, when the number of generators and variables is constant. It should be stressed that these assumptions are satisfied if one is using symbolic computation, and it can be verified that our algorithms are indeed polynomial both in terms of the number of arithmetic operations performed (which is our main result), and in terms of bitwise operations.

2 Maximizing One Dimensional Concave Functions

We begin with a brief review of Megiddo's parametric search technique [7] and how to use it to solve parametric maximization problems. We first define the class of algorithms we can use as evaluators of F.

Definition Let $\mathcal{A}$ be an algorithm that gets as a part of its input a point $x \in \mathbb{R}^d$, and returns a real number depending on x, denoted $F(x)$. We say that $\mathcal{A}$ is *polynomial in x with degree δ* if the only dependencies on x are:

1. $\mathcal{A}$ is allowed to evaluate the polynomials $p_1(x), \ldots, p_k(x)$ of degree at most δ, where δ does not depend on the input.
2. The only operations on variables in $\mathcal{A}$ that depend on x are addition of such variables, addition of constants, and multiplication by constants.
3. The conditional branches in $\mathcal{A}$ that depend on x depend only on signs of variables that depend on x.

Definition A point $x_0 \in \mathcal{P}$ is called a *non-singular point of F* if there is an $\epsilon > 0$ such that the restriction of F to $\mathcal{P} \cap \{x : |x - x_0| < \epsilon\}$ is a polynomial function. If x_0 is a non-singular point of F, this restriction of F is called the *piece* of F at x_0.

Corollary 1 *If $\mathcal{A}$ is polynomial in x with degree δ, then all the variables in $\mathcal{A}$ that depend on x contain polynomials of degree of at most δ, and $F(x)$ is piecewise polynomial whose pieces are polynomials of degree at most δ.*

Assume that we have an efficient algorithm $\mathcal{A}$ for evaluating $F(x)$, which is polynomial in x with some fixed degree δ, and that F is a concave function. Megiddo's main idea is to simulate $\mathcal{A}$ at a maximizer of F, denoted $x^\star$. As long as no comparisons are made, that is, no conditional branches that depend on the input point are to be executed, it is easy to simulate the algorithm, by treating the variables as polynomials and performing polynomial arithmetic. How do we resolve a conditional branch that depend on the sign of a variable? We find the roots of the polynomial stored in that variable, and locate $x^\star$ among them as follows. We evaluate F at each of the roots, and determine the location of a maximizer with respect to each of the roots. (For now we assume that if we can evaluate F at a point we can also decide the direction to $x^\star$, and in section 2.1 we justify this assumption.) In other words, for every root, we test whether it is $x^\star$, or else whether $x^\star$ is to its left or to its right. Given this information, we can easily decide which way should the branch take, since the sign of a polynomial is constant between its roots. We thus obtain a smaller and smaller interval that is known to contain $x^\star$, and finally the algorithm terminates. In section 2.1 we show how to obtain at this stage a maximizer of F and the two pieces of F to its left and right. These pieces allow us to generalize the algorithm to higher dimensions, and they provide a certificate of optimality for the maximizer.

In more abstract terms, given a comparison polynomial p, we decompose the space (here $\mathbb{R}$) into cells which are invariant for the sign of p. In the one dimensional case, the cells are points, which are the roots of p, and open intervals. Given this decomposition, we decide in which cell there is a maximizer of F, and thus resolve the comparison.

Running time analysis. Assuming that the algorithm $\mathcal{A}$ runs in T_0 time, the one dimensional maximization algorithm runs in time $T_1 = O(T_0^2)$, since whenever the algorithm makes a comparison, we evaluate the function at each of the roots. Megiddo [7] noticed that if we also have a parallel algorithm that evaluates the function, we can exploit the parallelism to obtain faster maximization algorithm. Assume that the parallel algorithm uses P processors and runs in T_p parallel time. We simulate the algorithm sequentially. In each parallel step there are at most P independent comparisons. Instead of evaluating the function at each of the roots of all the associated polynomials, we perform a binary search over the set of $O(P)$ roots to locate $x^\star$ among them. This results in $O(\log P)$ evaluations of F, and $O(P)$ overhead for performing the binary search by repeatedly finding the median of the set of unresolved roots. Having done this, we can determine the sign of each of the $O(P)$ roots at $x^\star$ and proceed to the next parallel step. The total cost of this procedure is $T_1 = O(PT_p + T_0 T_p \log P)$. Since we only require that comparisons will be made in parallel, we can use Valiant's weak model of parallel computation [10].

2.1 Where is F Maximized?

Given a point x_1, we need to determine the location of $x^\star$ relative to x_1. The techniques for doing so in one dimension and the techniques that were used by [3, 4, 9] do not seem to generalize to non-linear comparison polynomials and higher dimensions. This section describes a new technique which is easy to generalize. We evaluate $F(x_1)$. If we have previously encountered a point x_0 such that $F(x_0) \geq F(x_1)$, we can safely assume that there is a maximizer in the direction of x_0. Otherwise, we do not resolve the comparison. We duplicate the state of the simulated algorithm, and in one copy resolve the comparison as if there is a maximizer to the left of x_1, and in the other copy as if there is a maximizer to the right of x_1. We run those two copies in parallel (by interleaving their execution on a sequential machine). For each root of a comparison polynomial we obtain (from either copies; we do not know which one of them is correct), we evaluate F at that point. As long as we do not encounter a value of F larger then $F(x_1)$, we can determine which side of a given root contains a maximizer. If we run into a point x_2 where the value of F is larger than $F(x_1)$, we again will not be able to resolve the comparison. But in this case, the maximizer is on the same side of x_1 as x_2, so now we can resolve the comparison that involved x_1. In particular, we can decide which copy of the algorithm was given the correct answer and discard the other. Of course, we now must run two copies of the algorithm in which we resolve the comparison involving x_2 in different ways. There are always two copies of the algorithm executing. Eventually, both of our copies will terminate. Each one of them returns $F(x)$ as a polynomial. One of them corresponds to the piece of F to the right of the point x_k with the highest F value encountered, and the other corresponds to the piece of F to the left of this point. We maximize these polynomials over the corresponding intervals. If one of them attains a maximum higher then the other inside its interval, this is the optimum, and this polynomial is the piece of F on both sides of the maximum. Otherwise, they both attain the same maximum, and in that case the point x_k is a maximizer, and these two polynomials are the pieces of F on its two sides. Since in most cases the cost of evaluating F dominates the cost of duplicating the state of the algorithm we ignore this cost in the running time analysis.

The same idea works in any dimension. Let $F: \mathbb{R}^d \longrightarrow \mathbb{R}$ be a concave function. Suppose that we already know the value of F at some points in $\mathbb{R}^d$, and that the highest value we computed is $F(x_0)$. Given a hyperplane H, let the maximum of F on H be $F(x_1)$. If $F(x_0) \geq F(x_1)$, we can safely assume that there is a maximizer in the direction of x_0. Otherwise there is another point x on the other side of H with $F(x) > F(x_1)$. Hence at the intersection of the line segment $\overline{x x_1}$ with H the value of F must be higher then $F(x_1)$ due to the concavity of F, a contradiction.

2.2 Finding a Feasible Point

In many cases the domain $\mathcal{P}$ is either all of $\mathbb{R}^d$, or easy to compute as the intersection of a polynomial number of constraints $p_i(x) \geq 0$, where the p_i's are concave polynomials, such as in the parametric max flow problem. But there are cases in which the domain of F is defined by an exponential number of constraints, such as the parametric minimum s-t distance in a connected graph. Using ideas from [3, 4, 9], we describe how to deal with this problem in the non-linear case.

We assume that there is an algorithm $\mathcal{A}_f$ for testing whether a point x belongs to $\mathcal{P}$, which either declares that $x \in \mathcal{P}$, or declares that $x \notin \mathcal{P}$ and provides in addition a violated constraint $p(x) < 0$, where p is a concave polynomial. We use this algorithm to either find a point x_f in $\mathcal{P}$ or decide that $\mathcal{P}$ is empty. If $\mathcal{P}$ is empty we report this and halt. Otherwise, given a critical point x_0, we test whether $x_0 \in \mathcal{P}$, and if not, we know that there is a maximizer of F in the direction of x_f.

We simulate the feasibility testing algorithm $\mathcal{A}_f$ on x_f. During the simulation, we maintain an interval $[a, b]$, which is known to contain $\mathcal{P}$. In addition, for each endpoint $z \in \{a, b\}$ of the interval, if it is finite, we also maintain a constraint p_z that is violated if we pass this endpoint. (We begin with the interval $(-\infty, \infty)$.) When we must resolve a comparison, we find the roots of the comparison, and determine whether one of them is a feasible point, in which case we return this point and halt. If a given root being tested is not in $\mathcal{P}$, a violated constraint p is returned. Since for each $x \in \mathcal{P}$, $p(x) \geq 0$, we know that $\mathcal{P}$ must lie in $[a, b]$ and also in the interval $\{x : p(x) \geq 0\}$. We therefore update $[a', b'] = [a, b] \cap \{x : p(x) \geq 0\}$. If this new interval is empty, we conclude that $\mathcal{P}$ is empty. Note that this event actually carries more information, since if we assume without loss of generality that $\{x : p(x) \geq 0\}$ is to the left of $[a, b]$, then the two constraints p and p_a provide a certificate that $\mathcal{P}$ is empty. If the new interval in not empty and not equal to $[a, b]$, we replace the polynomials associated with the updated endpoints with p. It is easy to see that if we have a parallel feasibility testing algorithm, we can exploit the parallelism and obtain a faster algorithm using Megiddo's scheme.

If at no point of the simulation the feasible interval becomes empty, then our simulated algorithm terminates, and returns an answer. In addition, we have an interval $[\hat{a}, \hat{b}]$ where $\mathcal{P}$ must lie. If the algorithm returns "yes", it means that every point in $[\hat{a}, \hat{b}]$ is a feasible point. Otherwise, it returns "no" and a violated constraint p. It follows that this constraint is violated for all points of $[\hat{a}, \hat{b}]$, so this constraint together with either $p_{\hat{a}}$ or $p_{\hat{b}}$ provide proof of emptiness for $\mathcal{P}$.

3 Extending the Method to Two Dimensions

We now describe the parametric maximization algorithm in two dimensions, that is, when $F: \mathcal{P} \rightarrow \mathbb{R}$ where $\mathcal{P} \subseteq \mathbb{R}^2$. Let $(x^\star, y^\star)$ be a maximizer of F. The main idea of the algorithm is to simulate the one dimensional algorithm on F restricted to a line $x = x^\star$. Since a concave function restricted to a line (or a hyperplane in higher dimensions) is still concave, the problem of maximizing F restricted to a line is a one dimensional problem. If we can simulate the one-dimensional algorithm on such a line, we can find a maximizer $y^\star$ on the line, which is also a global maximizer, and we are done. The problem of course is how to make decisions during the simulation. Let p be a comparison polynomial in the simulated non-parametric algorithm. We compute a cylindrical decomposition of $\mathbb{R}^2$ which is invariant for the sign of p. This decomposition is constructed by computing the self intersections of the curve $p = 0$ and the points of vertical tangency of the curve. Those points are projected on the x-axis, and the plane is decomposed into vertical slabs between those points. A vertical slab (which is a generalized cylinder) may intersect the curve $p = 0$, but the roots of p do not intersect each other inside the slab (see Figure 1).

We execute the one dimensional algorithm on the vertical lines that decompose the plane into slabs, and we decide in which slab there is a maximizer (recall that in Section 2.1 we have shown that if we can max-

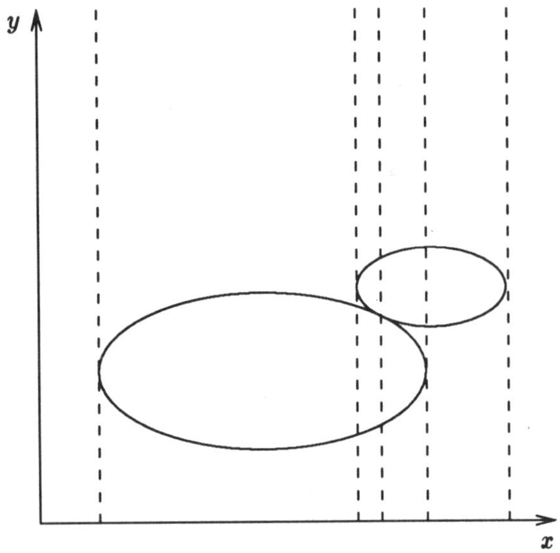

Figure 1: A cylindrical decomposition of $\mathbb{R}^2$ invariant for the sign of a polynomial. The solid curve is the root of the polynomial.

imize F on a line, we can also decide on which of its sides there is a maximizer).

The crucial point now is that in each slab there is a constant number of roots to the polynomial $p(x, y)$ as a one dimensional polynomial in y. The location of those roots depends on x, but the dependency is continuous. Hence we can simulate the one dimensional algorithm in a consistent manner. However, the one dimensional algorithm executes the non-parametric algorithm on the roots of p. We cannot perform this directly, since the location of the roots depend on x. However, we can simulate the non-parametric algorithm. When the non-parametric algorithm performs a comparison involving a polynomial q, we compute a cylindrical decomposition which is invariant for both p and q. Again, we determine the slab in this decomposition that contains a maximizer. We examine the root of p on which we simulated the non-parametric algorithm in this slab, and determine the sign of q in that cell of the decomposition, which is possible since the decomposition is invariant for the sign of q.

Once all the executions of the non-parametric algorithm terminate, we must compare the returned values, which are polynomials, to each other in order to decide which one is highest. To compare a value $r_1(x, y)$ on a root $y_1(x)$ of p with a value $r_2(x_y)$ on a root $y_2(x)$, we compute (again using cylindrical decomposition) the x-coordinates of the intersections of $\{r_1(x, y_1) = r_2(x, y_2), p(x, y_1) = p(x, y_2) = 0\}$, and decide in which slab there is a maximizer. Using this information, we can compare r_1 to r_2. Using a similar approach we can also find the maximum of a polynomial in a certain interval, which is required in the technique of Section 2.1. Finally the simulated one dimensional algorithm terminates. In fact, two copies of it terminate, one which is a simulation to the left of the vertical line l on which the highest value of F was found, and the other to its right. Each returns a curve $p_i(x, y) = 0$, $i \in \{L, R\}$ on which the maximum is obtained, and the two pieces of F above and below this curve, $p_{i,A}$ and $p_{i,B}$. We find the maximum of F to the left of the line L by solving

$$\max p_{L,A}(x, y)$$
$$p_{L,A}(x, y) = p_{L,B}(x, y)$$

using Lagrange multipliers. All the functions involved are polynomial, so this can be solved using cylindrical decomposition (since the problem reduces to finding all the solutions to a system of polynomial equations). This method establishes the global maximum, and in addition generates four pieces of F that prove that the point found is indeed a maximizer. Using Helly's theorem, it is easy to show that we can reduce the number of these pieces to three.

Running time analysis. We first note that the cost of constructing the cylindrical algebraic decomposition of a constant number of polynomials of bounded degree in fixed dimension is only a constant (in fact, the cost is polynomial in the number of polynomials, the degree, and the binary encoding of the coefficients, but not in the dimension). Denoting the running time of the non-parametric algorithm $\mathcal{A}$ by T_0 and of the d-dimensional algorithm by T_d, the running time is $T_2 = O(T_0(T_1 + T_0T_1)) = O(T_0^4)$. If there exists a parallel non-parametric algorithm that runs in T_p parallel time and uses P processors, we can again improve the running time. The total running time is $O(PT_p + T_p(\log PT_1 + \log^2 PT_1 + \log PT_p \log PT_1))$ and since $T_1 = O(PT_p + T_p \log PT_0)$, the running time is $T_2 = O(T_0(T_p \log P)^3)$. Due to lack of space we omit the details of this improvement.

3.1 Finding a Feasible Point

We now extend the technique of section 2.2 to two dimensions; the same technique works in any dimension. We use the technique we have just described for simulating the one dimensional feasibility testing algorithm on a vertical line that intersects $\mathcal{P}$. All we need to show is how to decide on what side of a given line $\mathcal{P}$

lies, since if $\mathcal{P}$ intersects the line, the one dimensional algorithm will detect this.

Suppose we are given a line in the plane, and must test on which of its sides $\mathcal{P}$ lies. Since the one dimensional algorithm determines that the line does not intersect $\mathcal{P}$, it reports two constraints that are contradictory on that line, p and q. Since we simulate the one dimensional algorithm and perform its arithmetic on polynomials, the violated constraints are polynomials in x and y. Since for any $(x, y) \in \mathcal{P}$ both $p(x, y) \geq 0$ and $q(x, y) \geq 0$, we find a point in the intersection of $p(x, y) \geq 0$ and $q(x, y) \geq 0$. If there is such a point x_0 and $\mathcal{P}$ is not empty, then $\mathcal{P}$ lies on the same side of the line as x_0, and we maintain p and q as a certificate for this fact. If $p(x, y) \geq 0 \cap q(x, y) \geq 0 = \emptyset$, then $\mathcal{P}$ is empty.

If the simulated algorithm terminates without either finding a point in $\mathcal{P}$, or deciding that $\mathcal{P}$ is empty, we have two cases. The answer it gives is valid for any line $x = x_0$ we might run it on, as long as x_0 is in the interval $[x_a, x_b]$ which is known to contain $\mathcal{P}$. When the simulated algorithm terminates, if it returns a point in $\mathcal{P}$, we are done. Otherwise it declares that the intersection of $\mathcal{P}$ with any vertical line $x = x_0$ in the vertical slab which is known to contain $\mathcal{P}$ is empty, and supplies a pair of constraints p and q as a certificate. We compute a point in $p(x, y) \geq 0 \cap q(x, y) \geq$. If there is no such point, then p and q are a proof that $\mathcal{P}$ is empty. Otherwise, if they intersect above to the left of the slab for example (i.e. to the left of x_a), then p and q together with the two constraints that assert that $\mathcal{P}$ is to the right of x_a, provide a proof that $\mathcal{P}$ is empty. Those four contradictory constraints allow us to generalize the algorithm to higher dimension, in the same way we used the one dimensional certificates of emptiness for constructing the two dimensional algorithm in this section. The number of constraints is a certificate of emptiness can be brought down to at most $d + 1$ in dimension d, by Helly's Theorem.

4 Higher Dimensions

Before we describe the algorithm and prove its correctness, we need some definitions and lemmas.

Definition A *semi-algebraic cell* of $\mathbb{R}^d$ is a set of points satisfying a finite set of polynomial equalities and inequalities.

Definition A *semi-algebraic variety* is either a semi-algebraic cell, or one of the sets $A \cap B$, $A \cup B$ and $A \setminus B$, where A and B are two semi-algebraic varieties.

Definition A *decomposition* of $\mathbb{R}^d$ is the representation of $\mathbb{R}^d$ as the union of a finite number of disjoint and connected semi-algebraic varieties.

Definition A decomposition of $\mathbb{R}^d$ is *invariant for the signs* of a family of polynomials if, over each cell of the decomposition, each polynomial is always positive, always negative, or always zero.

Definition A decomposition D_d of $\mathbb{R}^d$, that is $\mathbb{R}^d = E_1 \cup \cdots \cup E_N$ is *cylindrical* if $n = 0$ (the trivial case) or if $n > 0$ and:

1. $\mathbb{R}^{d-1}$ has a cylindrical decomposition D_{d-1} which can be written $\mathbb{R}^{d-1} = F_1 \cup \cdots \cup F_M$, and
2. For each cell E_i of D_d there is a cell F_j of D_{d-1} such that E_i can be written in one of the following forms

$$\begin{array}{lll} \{(\boldsymbol{x}, y) : \boldsymbol{x} \in F_j & \wedge & y < f_k(\boldsymbol{x})\} \quad \textit{segment} \\ \{(\boldsymbol{x}, y) : \boldsymbol{x} \in F_j & \wedge & y = f_k(\boldsymbol{x})\} \quad \textit{section} \\ \{(\boldsymbol{x}, y) : \boldsymbol{x} \in F_j & \wedge & f_k(\boldsymbol{x}) < \\ & & y < f_l(\boldsymbol{x})\} \quad \textit{segment} \\ \{(\boldsymbol{x}, y) : \boldsymbol{x} \in F_j & \wedge & y > f_k(\boldsymbol{x})\} \quad \textit{segment} \end{array}$$

where the f_k's are the solutions of polynomial equations ($\boldsymbol{x}$ denotes $x_1, \ldots, x_{d-1}$ and y denotes x_d).

Theorem 2 (Collins) *There exists an algorithm that computes a cylindrical decomposition of $\mathbb{R}^d$ invariant for the sign of a family of n polynomials. If the polynomials are all of degree δ or less, and the length of the binary encoding of their coefficients is bounded by H, the running time of this algorithm is bounded by*

$$(2\delta)^{2^{2d+8}} n^{2^{d+6}} H^3.$$

Lemma 1 *Let D_d be a cylindrical decomposition of $\mathbb{R}^d$ invariant under a family P of polynomials, and let H be a hyperplane in $\mathbb{R}^d$ specified by $x_1 = \alpha$ for some real α. Then the intersection of D_d with H is a cylindrical decomposition of $\mathbb{R}^{d-1}$ (with the natural mapping of $\mathbb{R}^{d-1}$ onto H) invariant under the restriction of the polynomials in P to H.*

Proof: The intersection of D_d with H is obviously a decomposition of $\mathbb{R}^{d-1}$ and invariant under the signs of the family of polynomials. We prove that it is also cylindrical. The proof uses induction on the recursive structure of the cylindrical decomposition. We assume that the intersection of D_{d-1} with H is cylindrical, and we prove that the intersection of D_d with H is cylindrical. The claim is obviously for $d = 1$, because D_1 is a decomposition of the x_1 axis which is invariant for the sign of some family of polynomials P_1. The intersection of H with the x_1-axis is only a point, and the decomposition of a point is always cylindrical and invariant for the signs of P_1.

We now assume that the claim is true for D_{d-1}. Let C' be a cell of the intersection of D_d with H, which is the intersection of the cell C with H. Let us assume that C is of the form

$$\{(x_1, x_2, \ldots, x_d) : \quad (x_1, x_2, \ldots, x_{d-1}) \in F \wedge \\ x_d > f_k(x_1, x_2, \ldots, x_{d-1})\}$$

where $F \in D_{d-1}$. Let F' be the intersection of F with H. Then C' can be written as

$$\{(\alpha, x_2, \ldots, x_d) : \quad (\alpha, x_2, \ldots, x_{d-1}) \in F' \wedge \\ x_d > f_k(\alpha, x_2, \ldots, x_{d-1})\}.$$

The other cases are similar. We note that the crucial point in the proof is that H is parallel to all the projection axes. ■

Lemma 2 *Using the same notation, let*

$$D_1 = \{-\infty = \alpha_0, \alpha_1, \ldots, \alpha_k, \alpha_{k+1} = \infty\}$$

(that is the α's are the points in the one dimensional decomposition). Then the intersection of D_d with H depends continuously on α as long as $\alpha_i < \alpha < \alpha_{i+1}$.

Proof: It is obvious that the intersection of H with D_1 changes continuously. Let us assume that the intersection of H with D_d changes continuously but that the intersection with D_{d+1} does not. This can only happen if for some $\alpha_i < \alpha < \alpha_{i+1}$ two sections of D_{d+1} intersect, which contradicts the previous lemma. ■

Now let us turn our attention to the d-dimensional algorithm. The algorithm has two phases. In the first phase, a series of d-dimensional cylindrical decompositions (CAD's for short) are constructed, each invariant for the signs of up to d polynomials. Once a CAD is constructed, the $(d-1)$ dimensional algorithm is executed on the hyperplanes $x_1 = \alpha_i$, where the α's are the points in D_1, which we call *critical values*. When this phase terminates, the algorithm obtains two values of F, that are the maximum of F on hyperplanes $x_1 = \alpha$; one of the values is valid for $\alpha_a < \alpha < \alpha_b$, and the other for $\alpha_b < \alpha < \alpha_c$. Each of those values, which are polynomials, is supplemented by a family of up to $d+1$ pieces of F which serve as a certificate of optimality. Let us denote those families P_L and P_R. The algorithm maintains the property that there is a maximizer of F, $(x_1^\star, \ldots, x_d^\star)$ with $\alpha_a < x_1^\star < \alpha_c$. During the second phase a global maximizer of F is found by solving

$$\max p_{L,1} \\ p_{L,1} = \cdots = p_{L,k} \quad p_{L,i} \in P_L, k \leq d+1$$

using Lagrange multipliers, and similarly for P_R. The global maximizer is the highest of the two. If one is higher than the other, the new family P that serves as a certificate for optimality is either P_L or P_R. If the two values are equal, then the new family is a subset of $P_L \cup P_R$. The $d+2$ required polynomials are found by using Helly's Theorem and examining all subsets of $P_L \cup P_R$ of size $d+2$.

The above description is true for the one dimensional algorithm and the two dimensional algorithm that we have already described, and it was already established that these are correct. It is obvious that given a $d+1$ dimensional problem, we can execute the d dimensional algorithm on any hyperplane $x_1 = \alpha$ in $\mathbb{R}^{d+1}$, and the $d-1$ dimensional algorithm on any hyperplane $\{x_1 = \alpha, x_2 = \beta\}$ and so on. Consider an execution of the d dimensional algorithm on $x_1 = \alpha$. If we carry the value α as a symbolic value, we obtain the location of the maximizer and the value of the maximum in terms of α (a value v is implicitly expressed as $p(v, \alpha) = 0$ for some polynomial p). Since the algorithm has only a finite number of execution paths, there must be discrete values of α in which the execution of the d dimensional algorithm changes. The $d+1$ dimensional algorithm simulates the d dimensional one over two adjacent open intervals, such that in each of them the execution path of the d dimensional algorithm does not change, and such that the convex hull of them contains a value $x_1^\star$ which is a projection of a maximizer of F, $(x_1^\star, \ldots, x_{d+1}^\star)$.

We use the fact that given a value α_0, it is possible to decide the relation of α_0 to $x_1^\star$ by executing the d dimensional algorithm on the hyperplane $x_1 = \alpha_0$. There is always one value with respect to which we do not know the location of $x_1^\star$. This is why we end up with two open intervals whose convex hull contains $x_1^\star$. We simulate the d dimensional algorithm. When it constructs a CAD, we construct the CAD in $\mathbb{R}^{d+1}$, and test which slab of $\mathbb{R}^{d+1}$ contains a maximizer. Within this slab, which is induced by the points in the one dimensional decomposition, the intersection of the hyperplane $x_1 = \alpha$ with the CAD is a d dimensional CAD that changes continuously, by the lemmas above. Now the d dimensional algorithm executes the $d-1$ dimensional one on the x_2 critical values of the CAD (since we associate $\mathbb{R}^d$ with the space $(\alpha, x_2, \ldots, x_{d+1})$). However, in the simulation these critical values depend on α, in the sense that they are specific roots of some polynomial $p(x_1, x_2)$. Therefore we simulate the $d-1$ dimensional algorithm, and whenever it constructs a CAD invariant for the signs of some polynomials, we construct a CAD invariant for their signs and for the sign of $p(x_1, x_2)$ in $\mathbb{R}^{d+1}$. We then test in which slab of $\mathbb{R}^{d+1}$ there is a maximizer, and in that slab the $d-1$ dimensional CAD on the root of p changes continuously.

Finally, when the two values of F are obtained, each with a family of polynomials that serve as a certificate for optimality, it is easy to find a global maximizer, by comparing the two values, finding the critical points of x_1 in which they are equal, and deciding in which slab there is a maximizer. In that slab, one of them is higher, so we use its value, and we obtain a real value by maximizing the answer (which is a function of x_1) over the interval of x_1 that is known to contain a maximizer.

Note that it is still true that this algorithm only constructs CAD's in $\mathbb{R}^{d+1}$ and executes the d dimensional algorithm on the critical values of the CAD's. This proves the correctness of the algorithm in any dimension by induction.

The running time. When the $d+1$ algorithm executes, it simulates the d dimensional one, then the $d-1$ dimensional one and so on. For each CAD constructed by one of the simulated algorithm, a CAD in $\mathbb{R}^{d+1}$ is constructed and the d dimensional algorithm is called a constant number of times. Therefore the number of CAD's that are constructed is $C_{d+1} = C_d C_{d-1} \cdots C_1$, and the running time is is $T_{d+1} = T_d C_1^{2^d-1}$. The solution of this recurrence is $C_d = C_0^{2^{d-1}}$ and $T_d = T_0 C_0^{2^d-1}$. Again, the running time can be improved when there is a parallel algorithm for evaluating F. We thus obtain the following theorem.

Theorem 3 *Let $\mathcal{A}$ be a polynomial algorithm in x with degree δ, where $x \in \mathbb{R}^d$. Let $F: \mathcal{P} \to \mathbb{R}$ be a concave function, and let $\mathcal{P} \subseteq \mathbb{R}^d$ be a convex set. Assume that for any $x \in \mathcal{P}$, $\mathcal{A}(x) = F(x)$, and for any $x \notin \mathcal{P}$, $\mathcal{A}(x) = p_x$ where p_x is a concave polynomial such that $p_x(x) < 0$, but for any $y \in \mathcal{P}$, $p_x(y) \geq 0$. Assume that $\mathcal{A}$ runs in time T, and that there is an equivalent parallel (in Valiant's model of parallel computation [10]) algorithm $\mathcal{A}_p$ that runs in time T_p and uses P processors. Then there is an algorithm $\mathcal{A}_d$ that runs in time $O(T_0(T_p \log P)^{2^d-1})$ and either decides that $\mathcal{P} = \emptyset$, or decides that F is unbounded on $\mathcal{P}$, or finds the maximum of F on $\mathcal{P}$.*

5 Approximately Maximizing NP-Hard functions

Roughly speaking, up to now we have shown that given a piecewise polynomial concave function, if we can evaluate it then we can also maximize it. However, there are many concave functions of this type that we do not know how to evaluate efficiently, but that we can approximate efficiently. For example, consider the problem of maximizing the Euclidean TSP function over an interval $[a, b]$ in which the distances in the graph satisfy the triangle inequality. The value of Δ-TSP at a point is induced by the lengths of the edges in the graph, $l_e: [a, b] \to \mathbb{R}$ for all $e \in E$. In every point of this interval, it is possible to approximately evaluate the length of the minimum TSP tour. In $O(V^3)$ time we can find a tour with a length of at most 3/2 times the length of the minimum tour, using Christofides' algorithm [2]. Since this algorithm is strongly polynomial, the natural question that arises is therefore "can one construct an algorithm for approximating the maximum of Δ-TSP?" (It is obviously NP-Hard to find the exact maximum.) The following theorem implies that the answer is yes.

Theorem 4 *Let $F: [a, b] \to \mathbb{R}$ be the minimum of some concave polynomial functions $\{p_i\}_{i \in I}$ of some fixed degree, let $M = \max_{[a,b]} F(x)$, and let $\mathcal{A}$ be an α-approximation algorithm of F. That is, $\mathcal{A}$ is an algorithm which is polynomial in x, that on input $x \in [a, b]$ returns in time T a polynomial p_j, $j \in I$, such that $F(x) \leq p_j(x) \leq \alpha F(x)$. Then a point $x^\star \in [a, b]$ can be found in time $O(T^2)$ such that $M \leq \mathcal{A}(x^\star) \leq \alpha M$.*

Proof: We employ Megiddo's technique, simulating $\mathcal{A}$, performing the arithmetic on polynomials. When we encounter a comparison in $\mathcal{A}$ involving the sign of some polynomial p, we find its roots and run $\mathcal{A}$ on the roots that fall inside $[a, b]$, and on a and b. While running $\mathcal{A}$ on the roots, we keep track of the variables as polynomials, so that we get the results as polynomials p_j. Unfortunately, there is not enough information in these polynomials to tell us between which two roots of p we can find a maximizer of F. However, given a root x_j and a concave polynomial p_j that was returned by $\mathcal{A}$ when executed on x_j, we behave as if the maximizer of F is on the side of x_j where p_j is increasing. If p_j is not increasing on either side, we halt and return $p_j(x_j)$. We keep track of the interval where we assume the maximizer is (replacing perhaps a or b with x_j), and continue to the next root. When the simulated algorithm terminates (in case we do not halt earlier), we report the highest point we have encountered, or the maximum of the polynomial that was returned by the simulated algorithm over the interval that is assumed to contain a maximizer of F, whichever is higher.

The correctness of this procedure follows from the following case analysis. If the final interval *does not* contain a maximizer of F, then we made an error somewhere. Without loss of generality assume that we decided that the maximizer is to the left of x_j, when it is on the right (see Figure 2). Since p_j is non-increasing to the right, $F(x) \leq p_j(x_j) = \mathcal{A}(x_j)$ for any x to the right of x_j. Since the maximizer is to the right, it is one of these x's, so $M \leq \mathcal{A}(x_j)$ and therefore $\mathcal{A}(x_j)$ is the required approximation for M. Otherwise, the final interval contains a maximizer of F, denoted x'. But in this case, $M = F(x') \leq \mathcal{A}(x')$, so we obtain a value which is at least M.

Finally, it is obvious that we cannot find any value $\mathcal{A}(x)$ higher than the desired approximation, otherwise $\alpha M < \mathcal{A}(x) \leq \alpha F(x) \leq \alpha M$, a contradiction. ■

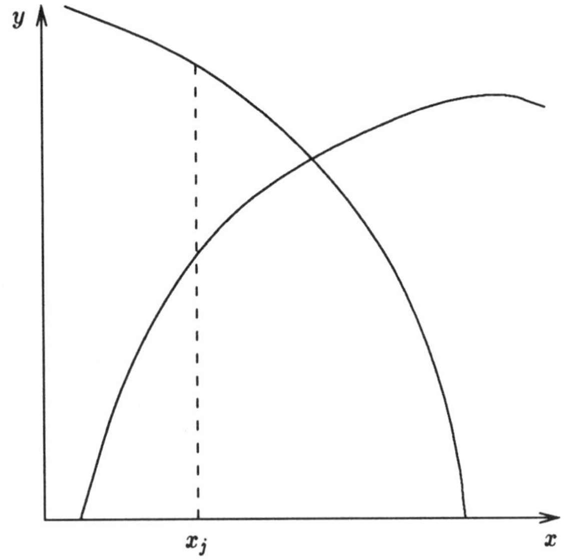

Figure 2: Making a wrong decision and searching to the left of x_j does no harm since if F is maximized to the right of x_j, then we already have an α-approximation of $\max F$.

An important point that should not be overlooked in this scheme is the problem of consistency. While in Megiddo's general framework it is not necessary to maintain the interval in which the optimum is known to be located, it is absolutely necessary to do so in our framework. The reason is that when it is possible to evaluate F exactly, we are always guaranteed to make consistent decisions with respect to where we are simulating the algorithm. But here we might make inconsistent decisions if we do not maintain this interval.

Remark. As usual, when there is also a parallel approximation algorithm, the running time can be improved. For example, using a 2-approximation algorithm for Δ-TSP which is based on minimum spanning trees, it is possible to obtain a 2-approximation for the parametric Δ-TSP in time $O(E \log V + V \log^2 V)$.

6 Applications

Let $G = (V, E)$ be a graph, let s and t be two vertices of G, and let W be a function mapping edges of G to real numbers. We use the notation W_e to denote $W(e)$. Let $S \subset 2^E$ (for example, the set of all spanning trees, all minimum s-t cuts etc.). A *minimization problem* on G is the problem of finding $\min_{s \in S} \sum_{e \in s} W_e$, and usually finding a minimizer is also desirable.

Now assume that W maps edges to concave polynomial functions over some convex set $\mathcal{P} \subseteq \mathbb{R}^d$, instead of to numbers. For every point $x \in \mathcal{P}$, we get an induced minimization problem obtained by mapping every element $e \in E$ to a real number $W_e(x)$. We define a function $F: \mathcal{P} \rightarrow \mathbb{R}$ by

$$F(x) = \min_{s \in S} \sum_{e \in s} W_e(x).$$

Lemma 3 *The function F is a concave function.*

Lemma 4 *If the edge weights W are all polynomial of degree at most δ, then F is a piecewise polynomial functions, and its pieces are of degree at most δ.*

Some examples. When S is the collection of all the edge-cuts separating s from t in G and the weights W_e are interpreted as capacities, then the associated minimization problem is the max flow problem in G, by the Max-Flow Min-Cut Theorem. The parametric max flow function is hence a concave function on $\mathcal{P} = \cap_{e \in E}\{x : W_e(x) \geq 0\}$. The definition of $\mathcal{P}$ ensures that all the edge capacities are non-negative. Since each W_e is concave, the regions $\{x : W_e(x) \geq 0\}$ are convex, and therefore their intersection $\mathcal{P}$ is convex.

When S is the collection of all paths between s and t, the minimization problem is the problem of finding the minimum s-t distance. In this case the domain of the parametric function is the convex region $\mathcal{P} = \cap_C \{x : \sum_{e \in C} W_e(x) \geq 0\}$ where the intersection is over all the simple cycles in G. The combinatorial complexity of $\mathcal{P}$ may be super-polynomial, but fortunately there is a ***separation algorithm*** for $\mathcal{P}$. The Bellman-Ford algorithm can be modified so that it either decides that the graph does not contain a negative cycle and finds the shortest path, or finds a negative cycle C (see [6]). Summing the weights of the edges of the cycle as polynomials, we find a concave violated constraint $p(x) = \sum_{e \in C} W_e(x) < 0$ which is *not* violated for any $y \in \mathcal{P}$. Therefore the conditions of Theorem 3 are satisfied, and we can find the maxi-min s-t distance in strongly polynomial time.

Many minimization problems on graphs are NP-hard. For example, when S is the set of all Hamiltonian tours in the graph, the corresponding minimization problem is the Traveling Salesman Problem. If $\mathcal{P}$ is a convex subset of $\mathbb{R}^d$ in which the weights always satisfy the triangle inequality, it is possible to approximate F up to a factor of 3/2 using Christofides' algorithm [2]. Again, it is important to observe that this approximation algorithm is strongly polynomial, and the only operations on weights in it are additions and comparisons between sums of weights. Since it always returns a tour whose length is a polynomial p_j, we can use Theorem 4 to approximate the maximum of the one dimensional parametric problem in time $O(V^6)$.

7 Conclusions and Open Problems

It is interesting to note that it is not the non-linearity of F that makes the problem hard, but the non-linearity of comparison and separation polynomials. We also note that our method of deciding on which side of a hyperplane there is a maximizer of F uses its concavity in a very strong way. We conclude the paper with some open problems that arise from our research.

- While our algorithms are indeed strongly polynomial in any fixed dimension, it is desirable to improve the running times, especially the dependency on the dimension.
- Can one obtain an approximation scheme similar to the one presented in section 5 in higher dimensions?

Acknowledgments

Thanks to Pankaj K. Agarwal for reading and commenting on a preliminary version of this paper. Thanks to Esther Jesurum, Mauricio Karchmer, Nimrod Megiddo, Boaz Patt-Shamir and Serge Plotkin for helpful discussions.

References

[1] D.S Arnon, G.E. Collins, S. McCallum, Cylindrical algebraic decomposition I: the basic algorithm, *SIAM J. Comput.* **13** (1984), 865–877.

[2] N. Christofides, Worst-case analysis of a new heuristic for the Traveling Salesman Problem, Technical Report, GSIA, Carnegie-Mellon University, 1976.

[3] E. Cohen and N. Megiddo, Strongly polynomial time and NC algorithms for detecting cycles in dynamic graphs, *Proc. 21st ACM Symp. on Theory of Computing*, 1989, 523–534.

[4] E. Cohen and N. Megiddo, Maximizing concave functions in fixed dimension, Research Report RJ 7656 (71103), IBM Almaden Research Center, San Jose, 1990.

[5] R. Cole, Parallel merge sort, *SIAM J. Comput.* **17** (1988), 770–785.

[6] T.H. Cormen, C.E. Leiserson and R.L. Rivest, *Introduction to Algorithms*, MIT Press, Cambridge, MA, 1990.

[7] N. Megiddo, Applying parallel computation in the design of serial algorithms, *J. ACM* **30** (1983), 852–865.

[8] N. Megiddo, The weighted Euclidean 1-center problem, *Math. of Operations Research*, **8** (1983), 498–504.

[9] C.H. Norton, S.A. Plotkin and É. Tardos, Using separation algorithms in fixed dimension, *J. of Algorithms*, **13** (1992), 79–98.

[10] L. Valiant, Parallelism in comparison problems, *SIAM J. Comput.* **4** (1975), 345-348.

Halvers and expanders

Miklós Ajtai — IBM San Jose
János Komlós * — Rutgers University
Endre Szemerédi — Rutgers University

Abstract

We investigate the asymptotic efficiency of certain combinatorial networks called halvers, which are basic building blocks of many parallel algorithms. We improve the efficiency of halvers in terms of their depth. The novelty is the use of combinatorial cicuits whose basic units are k-sorter switches.

1 Introduction

1.1 Comparator switches

A comparator switch in the sense of Knuth [6] is a primitive that sorts two elements. If there are n input elements in the circuit, then one can identify a comparator switch with a pair (i, j), $1 \leq i < j \leq n$. It acts – in place – by comparing the contents of registers i and j, and, by switching the contents if necessary, putting the smaller one into register i and the larger one into register j.

A comparator network is a fixed sequence of comparator switches working "in place." If a contiguous block of switches use pairwise disjoint comparisons, then their action can be performed in parallel (on a suitable machine). If the sequence of switches is split into T such blocks, then we say that the network works in parallel time (delay time) T.

We can think of comparator networks as combinatorial circuits with switches as the only (two-input two-output) primitives. Perhaps the most well-known comparator network is Batcher's sorting network [4].

1.2 Halvers

The AKS sorting network [2] [3] is based on the use of ε-halvers. These are comparator networks that split the input list into two equal halves approximately corresponding to small and large elements. More precisely, if S_m is the set of the m smallest elements in the input, where $m \leq n/2$, then at most εm of the elements of S_m will end up in the second half of the output. A similar statement holds for L_m, the set of the m largest elements of the input. That such approximate halving is possible *in constant depth*, is the cornerstone of the sorting network.

It is somewhat surprising that such imprecise halvings can be recursively continued and lead to a precise sorting network. One needs some kind of error correcting mechanism for that, and the description of the binary tree structure with elements floating up and down on the tree (but with a downward tendency) is the hard part of the construction. For a more digestible description and an improved version of the network, see Paterson [8].

In contrast, the description of the ε-halving networks is very simple. Let U and V denote the set of the first and second half of the registers (indices), and let $r = r(\varepsilon) = \frac{2}{\varepsilon} \log \frac{1}{\varepsilon}$. Then, by choosing r perfect matchings between U and V at random, we obtain, with a large probability, an ε-halving network. (A matching is a set of pairwise disjoint edges (u, v), $u \in U$, $v \in V$, and it corresponds to switches that act in parallel. A perfect matching – or one-factor – is a matching that contains all points of U and V.)

Alternatively, if a bipartite graph on (U, V) has a certain expanding property (which random graphs do have), then the edges of the graph *listed in an arbitrary order* form an ε-halving network.

Numerous parallel algorithms exist which use halvers as their basic moduls. The depth of halvers strongly influence the depth of the parallel networks using them. We devote this note to the discussion of the relation of the depth of a halver to its performance parameter ε.

1.3 Organization of the paper

In Section 2 we discuss the efficiency of classical halver circuits.

*Work supported by the NSF grant NSF-CCR 8505053

In Section 3 we introduce the new circuits, and analyze their performance.

In the Appendix we provide a sketch of proofs.

2 How efficient are halvers ?

A bipartite graph $G = (U, V, E)$, $|U| = |V| = n$ is an (α, β)-expander if

$$|N(X)| \geq \alpha|X| \text{ for all } X \subset U,\ |X| \leq \beta|U|$$

and the same holds for subsets of V.

The halvers used by the AKS networks (and several other subsequent papers) are based on the simple observation that any expander with parameters $\alpha = (1 - \varepsilon)/\varepsilon$, $\beta = \varepsilon$ is an ε-halver.

Zarankiewicz's theorem [11][5] shows that such an expander must have a depth at least $(c/\varepsilon)\log(1/\varepsilon)$. This depth is achieved by random selection as well as by some deep algebraic constructions (Lubotzky-Phillips-Sarnak [7]).

Let us introduce the function $\varepsilon(t)$ as the minimum of all ε such that there exists, for all n, an ε-halver with depth not exceeding t. Thus, the above mentioned constructions give

$$\varepsilon(t) < c(\log t)/t$$

and Zarankiewicz's theorem seems to say that this bound is best possible. Does it really ?

Since we only want to split the list into two parts, it was quite natural to work with bipartite graphs. But Zarankievicz' theorem places a strong limitation on the efficiency of halvers based on bipartite graphs. For arbitrary graphs, we only have the trivial bound

$$\varepsilon(t) \geq 2^{-t}$$

We are going to show now that using non-bipartite graphs helps dramatically, and we can actually get an exponential rate for halvers. We will use an extension of comparator-switches to construct efficient halvers.

2.1 k-comparators

In [3], we combined Knuth's comparator switches into a circuit that performed ε-halving. One can envision a more powerful primitive – let us call them k-comparators, or simply switches – with k inputs and k outputs, where the outputs are identical to the inputs in sorted order. A k-network then is a circuit with these primitives that works in place. (Parallelism for such networks is defined in the exclusive sense.)

Such (small) k-comparators may be built of hardware elements, which makes it reasonable to assume that they act swiftly compared to the software needed to organize them into a large circuit. We will thus assume that the individual k-comparators sort their k input elements in one unit of delay time.

Such a circuit can be combinatorially represented as a *sequence* of T matchings, where a matching is a family of pairwise disjoint k-sets (k-subsets of $\{1, 2, ..., n\}$) called switches. The switch $S = \{i_1, i_2, ..., i_k\}$, where $i_1 < i_2 < ... < i_k$, acts on the input $A[1], A[2], ..., A[n]$ by sorting *in place* the elements of the subsequence $A[i_1], A[i_2], ..., A[i_k]$ within each other, and the different switches within the same matching act in parallel.

This notion of k-comparators has been used earlier by Tseng and Lee [10] (for $k = 3$), and by Parberry [9].

3 The new halvers

3.1 The construction

Let us subdivide the input list into k equal size subsets. For simplicity of notation, we will assume that k divides n, and will write the input size as $n = kN$. We visualize this split as if the input elements were arranged in a $k \times N$ matrix, reading the elements into the matrix row-wise, from left to right and from top to bottom. After performing some switching operations within the matrix elements, the output is read out into a linear list as above. If the goal was to halve the list, then the output partition contains two parts, the first $k/2$ rows and the last $k/2$ rows. In general, if we want to divide the list into p parts, then the output partition is obtained by slicing the output linear list from left to right into p equal parts.

Informally, our halvers will be constructed as follows:

Split the list into k parts as above (k will be chosen exponential in t). Sort the columns of the obtained matrix. Shuffle the elements within each row, and sort the columns again.

Now the output will be well halved (if the shuffling was done appropriately). In fact, even partitioning into about $\sqrt{k}$ parts has been done quite accurately.

This was only a mathematical description. Shuffling the elements would make it an expensive algorithm. However, "shuffling and then sorting vertically" was only a graphic way to describe sorting in a diagonal fashion. More precise definitions follow.

Definitions and Notations.
We assume that the parameter k is fixed, and surpress it in most notations.

A *one-factor* is a partition of the kN elements into N disjoint k-sets such that each k-set contains exactly one element from each row. A one-factor acts on the elements as follows: within each k-set in the one-factor, the elements get sorted, in place, "light up, heavy down".

A *k-network* of depth T is a *sequence* of T one-factors. (Thus, the underlying structure is a k-partite uniform hypergraph, but, unlike in the case $k = 2$, the order of the one-factors is important.) A k-network acts on the input by performing the actions of its one-factors in the order specified.

We remark that these networks are oblivious, so the 0-1 principle of Knuth will apply. Hence we will always assume that the input is a 0-1 sequence.

Remark The *vertical* one-factor is the set of columns, and a general one-factor can be visualized as permuting the elements within each row and then selecting the vertical one-factor. We will use this comfortable way of thinking about one-factors mathematically, but, of course, the actual physical rearrangements should not be done in algorithms which work "in place." Thus, we will identify a one-factor with a permutation-vector $\Pi = (\pi_1, ..., \pi_k)$, and its (mathematical) action can be broken into two steps:

1° for every $i, 1 \leq i \leq k$, π_i permutes the elements of the i-th row

2° the matrix is sorted columnwise.

Thus, on input M, the (mathematical) output is $\mathbf{S}\Pi M$, where $\mathbf{S}$ denotes columnsorting.
This mathematical output is different from the true output but only in the order of the elements within each row. Hence, it does not change the output partition.

The actual algorithm sorts first along the vertical k-sets, then along the k-sets

$$\{(\pi_1^{-1}(j), \pi_2^{-1}(j), ..., \pi_k^{-1}(j)),\ 1 \leq j \leq N\}$$

3.2 The theorems

More Definitions and Notations.

A matrix A is *monotone* if every column of A is in a sorted order (lights up, heavy down).

Given a list of size n, and an integer $m \leq n$, S_m is the set of the m smallest elements and L_m is the set of the m largest elements of the list.

Given a $k \times N$ 0-1 matrix A, we write m for the number of ones in A, and $\mu = m/N$. Thus, $0 \leq \mu \leq k$.

A *one* in A is said to be misplaced if it is located in one of the first $k/2$ rows, and similarly, a zero in A is misplaced if it is not located in the first $k/2$ rows. The *norm* of A is defined as $1/N$ times the number of misplaced *ones* if $\mu \leq k/2$ and $1/N$ times the number of misplaced zeros if $\mu > k/2$. (Thus, $0 \leq ||A|| \leq \mu/2$.)

For simplicity, we will always assume that k is even and $\mu \leq k/2$ (we have to multiply all probabilities by 2 to make up for it).

Theorem 1 (Depth-2 Theorem) *Given $k \geq 23$, let $\varepsilon = c_0(\frac{\log k}{k})^{1/2}$*
For every $N \geq 23$, there is a k-network of depth 2 that performs ε-halving on any input of $n = kN$ elements.

We can choose $c_0 = 3$ for $k \geq 23$ and $c_0 = 2$ for $k \geq 60$.

The first one of these two one-factors will be the vertical one-factor, thus Theorem 1 will follow from the following more detailed picture.

Theorem 2 (Depth-1 Theorem) *For every N, there is a permutation-vector $\Pi = \pi_1, ..., \pi_k$ such that for any $m \leq n/2$, and any* **monotone** *$k \times N$ 0-1 input matrix M with $m = \mu N$ ones, the output matrix $M' = \mathbf{S}\Pi M$ satisfies*

$$||M'|| < \varepsilon\mu \qquad (1)$$

(ε was defined in the previous theorem). In fact, most one-factors satisfy the above inequality.

3.3 Remarks

Since simulating the columnsorts with ordinary 2-switches has a cost logarithmic in k, the above depth-2 k-network has depth $c \log k$ as an ordinary network. Hence ε, the accuracy of the network, is an exponential function of the depth. Of course, the constant involved may be large for large k, but one probably wants to use it for a small value of k.

The important property of the two one-factors used above is that they are very much different from each other (just like the larger number of one-factors in expanders). For small k, we use the vertical one-factor and a randomly chosen one-factor. Unfortunately, we do not have any combinatorial characterization that would suffice for our purposes (as we did have for $k = 2$, namely expansion).

Technically speaking, the vertical sort only served to make the input monotone. Since after shuffling a monotone matrix it won't stay monotone anymore, so what the first shuffling really achieved is to cut back on the number of input matrices from 2^{kN} (all 0-1 matrices) to $(k+1)^N$ (monotone 0-1 matrices).

For very large k, one can give simple explicit constructions, as the following example shows.

Example Andy Yao asked if there is a constant depth sorting network for sorting n elements if we can use primitives which sort $k = n^\alpha$ elements instantly (say $k = \sqrt{n}$). Note that the information theoretical lower bound is $\log n / \log k = 1/\alpha$=const.

The following simple construction has depth 4.

Let $n = kN$ where $k > N^2$. Just as above, we think about the input as a $k \times N$ 0-1 matrix. First sort the elements vertically, then sort them along the 45° lines. In other words, the second one-factor consists of the sets

$$\{ \{(i+j \ mod \ N)+1, \ 0 \le i \le k-1\}, \ 0 \le j \le N-1\}$$

It is not hard to see that not only is this an ε-halver with $\varepsilon = 2N/k < 2n^{-1/3}$ but it has the following stronger property: In the output, all elements are within $\binom{N+1}{2}$ of their proper location. Thus, the usual two finishing rounds will sort the list. (Slice the linear list to intervals of length k and sort within blocks, and then do the same with the blocks shifted by $k/2$.)

Remark In the AKS network, we constructed separators (called near-sorters) to 64 parts (say) by repeatedly halving 6 times using expanders for each halving. Since, by the theorem of Zarankiewicz, one such halving alone is already too expensive, the total cost of a near-sorter was prohibiting.

We realize now that we should have proceeded backwards, and construct halvers by splitting the list first into a larger number of parts, and then simply combining several parts into one. This way not only do we get a much more efficient halver, but could obtain near-sorters directly.

(To split into p parts would be done by splitting arbitrarily the list into $k \approx p^2$ parts first, then using two rounds of k-sorter as above, and finally combining the parts to get a good p partition.)

This remark can be used to build a shallow sorting network whose building blocks are k-sorters. This, in turn, could be used to improve drastically the constants in the AKS 2-sorter network (perhaps using a value of 16 or 32 for p). For this and further improvements on the AKS network, see [1].

References

[1] M. Ajtai, J. Komlós, M. S. Paterson, E. Szemerédi, k-sorting, in preparation

[2] M. Ajtai, J. Komlós, E. Szemerédi, Sorting in $c \log n$ parallel steps, Combinatorica 3 (1983), 1-19

[3] M. Ajtai, J. Komlós, E. Szemerédi, An $O(n \log n)$ sorting network, Proc. 15-th ACM STOC, Boston (1983), 1-9

[4] K. E. Batcher, Sorting networks and their applications, Proc. AFIPS Spring Joint Computer Conference 32 (1968), 307-314

[5] R. Guy, S. Znám, A problem of Zarankiewicz, in Recent Progress in Combinatorics, ed. W.Tutte, Academic Press (1969), 237-243

[6] D. E. Knuth, The Art of Computer Programming, Vol 3, "Sorting and Searching" (Addison-Wesley) (1968), 220-246

[7] A. Lubotzky , R. Phillips, P. Sarnak, Explicit expanders and the Ramanujan conjectures, Proc. 18th STOC (1986), 240-246

[8] M. S. Paterson, Improved Sorting Networks with $O(\log n)$ depth, Research Report 89 (1987), Dept. of Comp. Sci., Univ. of Warwick, England

[9] I. Parberry, private communication (1985)

[10] S. S. Tseng, R. C. Lee, A new parallel sorting algorithm based on min-mid-max operations, BIT 24 (1984), 187-195

[11] K. Zarankiewicz, Problem P101, Colloq. Math. 2 (1951), 301

4 Appendix: Sketch of proofs

4.1 Poisson bound on the hypergeometric distribution

Vašek Chvátal recommended the use of Hoeffding's inequality for the hypergeometric distribution, but often the following weaker inequality will do.

Lemma 1 *(Hypergeometric vs Poisson) Let the random variable X have a hypergeometric distribution, that is,*

$$P(X=i) = \binom{M}{i}\binom{N}{s-i}/\binom{M+N}{s}$$

Let us write $\lambda = sM/(M+N)$.
Then, we can estimate the probability

$$P(X \geq x) \leq (\lambda/x)^x e^{x-\lambda}$$

for all $x \geq \lambda$.

In proving the lemma, we get, as a by-product, an alternative proof for Hoeffding's inequality.

Let Y have a binomial distribution with parameters $n = M$ and $p = s/(M+N)$, and Z have a Poisson distribution with parameter $\lambda = np = sM/(M+N)$.

Writing E for expectation, we introduce the generating functions

$$HYP(u) = Eu^X, \; BIN(u) = Eu^Y = (pu + (1-p))^n$$

$$POI(u) = Eu^Z = e^{\lambda(u-1)}$$

We will prove

$$HYP(u) \;\leq\; BIN(u) \;\leq\; POI(u) \text{ for all } u \geq 1 \quad (2)$$

Then use Chernov's method to get, for any $u \geq 1$,

$$P(X \geq x) \;\leq u^{-x} HYP(u) \;\leq u^{-x} BIN(u)$$
$$\leq u^{-x} POI(u) \quad (3)$$

Choosing $u = x/\lambda$ in the inequality $P(X \geq x) \leq u^{-x}POI(u)$ we get the lemma.
Choosing $u = x(1-p)/((n-x)p)$ in the inequality $P(X \geq x) \leq u^{-x}BIN(u)$ we would get Hoeffding's inequality for one single hypergeometric variable: For any $x \geq \lambda = np$

$$P(X \geq x) \leq e^{-D(\frac{x}{n}\|p)n} \leq e^{-2(\frac{x}{n}-p)^2 n}$$

where $D(y\|p) = y\log(y/p) + (1-y)\log((1-y)/(1-p))$ is the information theoretical divergence.

It remains to prove (2).

Since all three function HYP, BIN, POI are 1 at $u = 1$, it is enough to show that for their derivatives $HYP^{(r)}(1) \leq BIN^{(r)}(1) \leq POI^{(r)}(1)$ for all r.

Now,

$$HYP(u) = \sum_{i\geq 0} u^i \binom{M}{i}\binom{N}{s-i}/\binom{M+N}{s}$$

and hence

$$HYP^{(r)}(1) = \sum_{i\geq r}\binom{i}{r} r! \binom{M}{i}\binom{N}{s-i}/\binom{M+N}{s}$$

$$= \binom{M}{r} r! \sum_{i\geq r}\binom{M-r}{i-r}\binom{N}{s-i}/\binom{M+N}{s}$$

$$= \binom{M}{r} r! \binom{M+N-r}{s-r}/\binom{M+N}{s}$$

$$= \binom{M}{r} r! \prod_{d=0}^{r-1}\frac{s-d}{M+N-d} \leq \binom{M}{r} r!\,(s/(M+N))^r$$

$$= BIN^{(r)}(1) \;\leq\; \lambda^r = POI^{(r)}(1)$$

Remark We will use Lemma 1 for a sum $X = X_1 + \ldots + X_k$ of independent hypergeometric variables. We can use the same inequality

$$P(X \geq x) \leq (\lambda/x)^x e^{x-\lambda} \text{ for all } x \geq \lambda$$

where

$$\lambda = \sum_{i=1}^{k}\lambda_i = \sum_{i=1}^{k} s_i M_i/(M_i + N_i)$$

since the sum of independent Poissons is a Poisson (multiply the generator functions). One can do the same with binomial to get the general Hoeffding inequality, by multiplying the generator functions of binomial distributions, and use

$$\prod (p_i u + q_i)^{n_i} \;\leq\; (pu+q)^n$$

where $q_i = 1-p_i$, $n = \sum n_i$, $p = \sum p_i n_i/n$, $q = 1-p$. (In the last inequality we used Jensen's inequality for the concave function $\log y$.)

Proof of Theorem 2

We start with the following simple observation.

The number of monotone 0-1 matrices with at most μN ones is $\binom{\mu N + N}{N} < [e(\mu+1)]^N$.

In general, the number of monotone 0-1 matrices M with $||M|| \leq \nu$ is less than

$$k \sum_{l=0}^{N} \binom{N}{l} \binom{\nu N}{l} \binom{\nu N + N - l}{N - l}$$

$$< k \binom{\nu N + N}{N}^3 < k[e(\nu+1)]^{3N}$$

Next we mention a trivial lemma.

Lemma 2

$$||\mathbf{S}\Pi M|| \leq ||\Pi M|| = ||M||$$

We want to estimate the probability that there exist a monotone 0-1 inputmatrix with $m = \mu N$ ones such that the output has more than εm ones in the first $k/2$ rows.

For a specific input matrix M, let A_M denote the above event. There are only $(k+1)^N$ monotone 0-1 matrices. Thus, for all M such that $P(A_M) < 0.1\,(k+1)^{-N}$, we can simply add up these probabilities and get the upper bound 0.1 in total. We will see below that this includes all matrices with at least $0.1kN$ ones.

We will write q for the number of columns in which the output matrix has more than $k/2$ ones, and $\Delta = (k/2-\mu)q+\varepsilon N$ for the number of surplus ones in these columns.

For a specific choice of these q columns, we will apply the exponential bounds for the hypergeometric random variable X, the total number of ones in these columns. Then, we will multiply by $\binom{N}{q}$, the number of choices for these columns and sum for q. Sometimes we'll simply multiply by 2^N instead. Finally, we will multiply by the number of possible input matrices.

For $\alpha k < \mu \leq k/2$ we only use $\Delta \geq \varepsilon m = \varepsilon \mu N$ to get the upper bound

$$2^N (k+1)^N \exp\{-2\Delta^2/(kq)\}$$

$$\leq \exp\{N \log(2(k+1)) - 2(\varepsilon m)^2/(kN)\}$$

$$= \exp\{N \log(2(k+1)) - 2c_0^2 N \log k\mu^2/k^2\}$$

$$< \exp\{N[\log(2(k+1)) - 2c_0^2\alpha^2 \log k]\}$$

For $\beta k < \mu \leq \alpha k$ we use the arithmetic-geometric mean inequality to get

$$\Delta^2/(kq) = [(k/2-\mu)q + \varepsilon m]^2/(kq)$$

$$\geq 2\varepsilon m(k-2\mu)/k > 2(1-2\alpha)\beta\varepsilon kN$$

giving the probability bound

$$2^N (k+1)^N \exp\{-2\Delta^2/(kq)\}$$

$$\leq \exp\{N[\log(2(k+1)) - 2(1-2\alpha)\beta\varepsilon k]\} \quad (4)$$

We assume $n \geq 23$. In the case $k \geq 60$, we choose $c_0 = 2$, $\alpha = 0.4$. This gives, for $0.4k \leq \mu \leq k/2$ the probability estimate $p_0 < \exp\{N[\log(2k+2) - 1.28 \log k]\}$.

Then, writing $\theta = 0.01$, choose $\beta_0 = \alpha$, $\beta_i = \beta_{i-1} - \theta$ until β becomes less than .1. Apply inequality (4) in the intervals (β_{i-1}, β_i). We get a probability bound $p_0 + \sum_i p_i < p_0 + \sum_i \exp\{N[\log(2(k+1)) - 2(1-2(\alpha-i\theta))(\alpha - i\theta - theta)\varepsilon k]\} < 0.3$.

(We used that the estimate is a monotone function of N and k, so we plugged in the minimal values $k = 60$, $N = 23$, and did the simple numerical work on a computer.)

Similarly, for $k \geq 23$ we choose $c_0 = 3$ and the same α and θ. This leads to the probability bound 0.2.

(For $N \geq 100$ both bounds would be less than 0.001.)

For sparser matrices, their numbers overwhelms the probability, so we have to do the analysis more carefully. We will partition them into equivalence classes, and compute the probabilities within a class more carefully, and then add up the probabilities only for different classes.

4.1.1 Equivalence classes

Set $D = (\mu + k/2)/2$, $d = k/2 - D$, and define an equivalence relation on input matrices as follows. Two input matrices M, M' are equivalent if they have the same number of ones, and are identical above the line D (in their first $k - D$ rows). The part of a matrix above the line D will be called the *top* of the matrix.

The event that *some* matrix in an equivalence class leads to an output matrix with more than Δ ones in the first $k/2$ rows, is a subset of the event that this happens to *the* matrix (not in the class) which has the same top, but it has all ones in the last D rows. This way, we can save multiplying by the very large number of matrices in the class.

First we estimate the number of equivalence classes for given $m = \mu N$.

The input is monotone, thus, writing c_i for the column-sums in the matrix ($\sum c_i = m$), t_i for the column-sums in the top, $t_i > 0$ implies $c_i \geq d+1$.

Hence, we have the following estimate.

Lemma 3 *The number of different tops of monotone matrices with m ones is at most*

$$\sum_r \binom{N}{r}\binom{m-dr-1}{r-1}$$

$$\leq \binom{N}{\frac{m}{d+1}} \sum_r \binom{m-dr-1}{r-1}$$

$$\leq (eN(d+1)/m)^{m/(d+1)}\, e^{\frac{\log d}{d} m}$$

$$\textit{for } d \geq 3,\ 0 \leq m \leq \frac{d+1}{2}N$$

Proof. We only have to show that

$$f(m) = \sum_r \binom{m-dr-1}{r-1} \leq e^{\frac{\log d}{d} m}$$

Now $f(m)$ is the number of integer solutions to the equation

$$x_1 + x_2 + \ldots = m, \quad x_i \geq d+1$$

and hence it satisfies the recurrence

$$f(m) = f(m-1) + f(m-d-1)$$

$$f(0) = 1,\ f(m) = 0 \text{ for } 1 \leq m \leq d$$

Now, the characteristic equation of this recurrence is

$$\alpha^{d+1} = \alpha^d + 1$$

and $f(m) \leq \alpha^m$. Finally, it is easy to check that $e^{\frac{\log d}{d}}$ is beyond the solution α (that is, $x^{d+1} > x^d + 1$ for $x = e^{\frac{\log d}{d}}$).

For $d \geq 4$ the following slightly better estimate holds: $\alpha < 1 + \frac{\log d}{d}$, whence $f(m) < (1 + \frac{\log d}{d})^m$.

4.1.2 Estimating the probabilities

Lemma 4 *Let $d \geq 10$ and $\varepsilon \geq \frac{2+\log d}{d}$. Then the probability of the event that for some $m \leq (d/10)N$ there is an input matrix with $m = \mu N$ ones such that the output matrix has more than εm ones above the line $\mu + d$ is less than $15dx/(1-x)$ where $x = (e/10)^d$.*

Proof (sketch). We will have the product of two geometric series as our estimate, one in q the other in m.

$$\sum_{m \leq (d/10)N} \sum_q \left(\frac{e\mu q}{dq + \varepsilon m}\right)^{dq+\varepsilon m} \left(\frac{e(d+1)}{\mu}\right)^{\frac{m}{d+1}} f(m)$$

$$\leq \frac{x}{1-x} \sum_m \left[\left(\frac{e}{10+e}\right)^{(d+1)\varepsilon - 1} e^2 \left(1 + \frac{1}{d}\right) \right]^{\frac{m}{d+1}} \left(1 + \frac{\log d}{d}\right)^m$$

$$< 15d \frac{x}{1-x}$$

Fault Tolerant Graphs, Perfect Hash Functions and Disjoint Paths

M. Ajtai * N. Alon † J. Bruck * R. Cypher * C.T. Ho * M. Naor *
E. Szemerédi ‡

Abstract

Given a graph G on n nodes we say that a graph T on n + k nodes is a k-fault tolerant version of G, if we can embed G in any n node induced subgraph of T. Thus T can sustain k faults and still emulate G without any performance degradation. We show that for a wide range of values of n, k and d, for any graph on n nodes with maximum degree d there is a k-fault tolerant graph with maximum degree O(kd). We provide lower bounds as well: there are graphs G with maximum degree d such that any k-fault tolerant version of them has maximum degree at least $\Omega(d\sqrt{k})$.

1 Introduction

Given a graph G on n nodes we say that a graph T on $n+k$ nodes is a **k-fault tolerant version** of G, if we can embed G in any n node induced subgraph of T. The embedding should be a one-to-one function, such that any two adjacent nodes in G are mapped into adjacent nodes in the subgraph of T. An equivalent way to phrase this requirement is to say that any k nodes of T can be declared faulty and the remaining graph can embed G in the above manner. Thus, if G represents some desired interconnection, then T is a network that can sustain up to k faults and still emulate G without any performance degradation.

If we take T to be the complete graph on $n+k$ nodes, then we know that T is k-fault tolerant for any G on n nodes, Our goal, however, is to minimize the maximum degree in T. Our results show that this degree can be $O(kd)$ where d is the maximum degree in G.

We present a general method of constructing such fault tolerant versions of graphs. This method depends only on n and k and not on the specific graph. It requires the construction of a directed graph M and a collection of mappings from T to M. M has k distinguished nodes called *spares*. The property that the mappings and M should have is that for any set of k faults in T there should be a mapping for which there are k disjoint paths in M connecting the mapped faulty nodes and the k spares. This method is presented in Section 2. In general, it can construct graphs T with maximum degree $O(kd)$. Sections 3 and 4 are devoted to constructing M and the mappings.

In Section 3 we consider a graph M based on the grid. We show that a good collection of mappings exists based on the existence of a certain family of perfect hash functions. Such a family exists when $k < n^{1/4}$. We provide an *explicit* construction for n and k such that n is $\Omega(k^{\log k})$. For larger k's the explicit construction yields graphs T with maximum degree larger than $O(kd)$.

In Section 4 we consider expander based graphs. We show (non-constructively) that our method works (i.e. yields T's with maximum degree $O(kd)$) for all n and k such that k is $O(n^{1-\beta})$ for some $\beta > 0$.

In Section 5 we show our lower bounds: there are graphs on n nodes with degree d such that any k-fault tolerant version of them has maximum degree at least $\Omega(d\sqrt{k})$. The relationship between n, k and d that must hold in order for the lower bound proof to work are that d be larger than $\log^2 n/\log\log n$ and k be smaller than $c_1\sqrt{d/\log d}$ and $n/2d$, where $c_1 > 0$ is some absolute constant.

1.1 History, motivation and comparison with other work

As mentioned above, the main motivation for the problem of constructing k-fault tolerant graphs is finding fault tolerant architectures. The graph G represents a desired interconnection and the graph T the actual fault tolerant network that implements it. The graph T can sustain any k node (processor) faults and still simulate the graph G with no slowdown. Note

*IBM Almaden Research Center, 650 Harry Road, San Jose, CA 95120, USA

†Department of Mathematics, Raymond and Beverly Sackler Faculty of Exact Sciences, Tel Aviv University, Tel Aviv, Israel.
Research supported in part by a United States Israel BSF Grant.
‡Department of Mathematics, Rutgers University, New Brunswick, NJ, USA

0-8186-2900-2/92 $3.00 © 1992 IEEE

that there is no assumption about the distribution of the k faults, and that the redundancy is the lowest possible, as the number of spares equals the number of faults. This approach to fault tolerance has been considered in a number of papers previously. The papers [14, 25, 21, 7, 8, 5, 6] considered the problem for some specific graphs such as cycles, arrays and trees. Rosenberg [23] has provided VLSI area lower bounds for such architectures. Dutt and Hayes [8] and Bruck, Cypher and Ho [5] have considered the problem of constructing k-fault tolerant versions for arbitrary graphs and have shown a simple $O(k^2d)$ construction outlined in Section 2.

There are different approaches for achieving fault tolerance. The approach represented by works such as [13, 15] is for the faulty network to attempt to simulate the original architecture with as little slowdown as possible. However, as there is no redundancy, some slowdown is necessary and when no assumptions are made regarding the distribution of the faults, this slowdown is often non-constant. Other approaches assume that there is some additional switching mechanism that is fault-free (see e.g. [22, 16]) or require that there be many more spare processors than faults (see e.g. [1]), or some combination of the above.

The advantages that k-fault tolerant graphs offer are clear (e.g. minimal redundancy, no slowdown, no assumptions on fault distribution, no requirement for a fault-free switching mechanism). The question is what price must be paid in terms of the degree of the network in order to obtained these advantages. Answering this question is the main goal of the paper.

Finally, we should note that some of the techniques developed in this paper might be applicable elsewhere. The results of Section 4 yield an efficient way to construct superconcentrators from expander graphs. The construction of families of perfect hash functions in Section 3 may have applications in data structures.

1.2 Notation

In the following the input graph will always be $G = (V, E)$ and the k-fault tolerant graph will be $T = (U, D)$. We will also use an intermediate directed graph $M = (W, C)$. Unless stated otherwise, $|V| = n$ and $|U| = |W| = n + k$. Given a mapping $f : U \mapsto V$ and a subset $S \subset U$, $f(S)$ is the set of all the elements of V that are the image of some element of S. For the directed graph $M = (W, C)$ and for a node $w \in W$ let $\Gamma_M(w)$ denote the set of all out-neighbors of w in M *including* w itself.

2 The General Scheme

In this section we describe our general scheme. It involves coming up with an intermediate graph M and a collection of mappings H with certain properties. These properties are a function of n and k only, and do not involve G. Given a graph M with maximum in-degree δ and a collection of mappings H of size ℓ, our scheme constructs for any input graph G with maximum degree d a k-fault tolerant graph T with maximum degree $\ell(\delta + 1)^2 d$.

Consider first the method suggested by Bruck, Cypher and Ho [5]. Let $V = \{1, \ldots, n\}$ and $U = \{1, \ldots, n+k\}$. For every edge $(i, j) \in E$ create the following edges in T: completely connect in T the nodes $\{i, \ldots, i+k\}$ to the nodes $\{j, \ldots, j+k\}$. Given the set of k faults the embedding strategy is greedy: scan the nodes of V in increasing order and embed node i in the first available (not occupied and not faulty) node in U. For any set of k or fewer faults, we know that $i \in V$ is embedded in one of $\{i, \ldots, i+k\} \subset U$. Therefore for any edge $(i, j) \in E$ we know that there is an edge between the node where i is embedded and the node where j is embedded. Every edge in E induces $(k + 1)^2$ edges in D and the maximum degree in T is $(k + 1)^2 d$.

We now discuss the limitations of such a method. Given $G = (V, E)$ and a k-fault tolerant version of it $T = (U, D)$, then for any $v \in V$ let $S(v) = \{u \in U | \exists$ set of k faults such that v is embedded in $u\}$.

In the method above $S(i) = \{i, .., i+k\}$. It is clear that for all $v \in V$ we must have $|S(v)| \geq k + 1$, otherwise all of $S(v)$ might be faulty and there will be no place to embed v. If for every $(v_1, v_2) \in E$ we must connect $S(v_1)$ to all of $S(v_2)$, we get that every edge in G induces $(k + 1)^2$ edges in T.

Our approach in reducing the degree is to partition the sets $S(v)$ in such a way that if $v_1 \in V$ is mapped to part j in $S(v_1)$, then $v_2 \in V$ is mapped to part j in $S(v_2)$. In order to implement it we choose $M = (W, C)$, a directed graph on $n+k$ nodes, and a one-to-one mapping $m : V \mapsto W$. We call the nodes $w \in W$ with no $m^{-1}(w)$ the *spare nodes*. We also choose a collection H of one-to-one mappings from U to W.

The directed graph M and the collection H now define for any input graph $G = (V, E)$ a graph $T = (V, E)$ that should be a k-fault tolerant version of G. For each edge $(v_1, v_2) \in E$ and each $h \in H$ create the following edges in T: completely connect

$h^{-1}(\Gamma_M(m(v_1))$ and $h^{-1}(\Gamma_M(m(v_2))$. Thus

$$D = \bigcup_{h \in H} \bigcup_{(v_1,v_2)\in E} \{(u_1, u_2\}| \quad h(u_1) \in \Gamma_M(m(v_1)) \text{ and } h(u_2) \in \Gamma_M(m(v_2))\}.$$

We say that a set S of k faults is *good* for a mapping $h : U \mapsto W$ if there are k node disjoint paths in M connecting $h(S)$ to the k spare nodes. Given a set S of k faults such that h is good for S we claim that the following $\varphi : V \mapsto U$ embeds G in the non faulty nodes: fix the k node disjoint paths; for all $v \in V$, if $m(v)$ is not on any of the k paths, then $\varphi(v) = h^{-1}(m(v))$. Otherwise, let $w \in W$ be the node next to $m(v)$ on the path (connecting a faulty node with a spare one) in the direction towards the spare and let $\varphi(v) = h^{-1}(w)$. Clearly:

Claim 2.1 *φ as defined above is one-to-one.*

Also:

Claim 2.2 *For all $(v_1, v_2) \in E$ there is an edge $(\varphi(v_1), \varphi(v_2)) \in D$.*

Proof: Since v_1 is embedded in $h^{-1}(\Gamma_M(m(v_1)))$ and v_2 is embedded in $h^{-1}(\Gamma_M(m(v_2)))$ by the definition (1) of D there is an edge in D between $\varphi(v_1)$ and $\varphi(v_2)$. □

Every $h \in H$ and every edge $(v_1, v_2) \in E$ induces $(deg_M(m(v_1)) + 1)(deg_M(m(v_2)) + 1)$ edges in T, where here $deg_M(w)$ denotes the out-degree of w in M. Thus we would like to choose as small H as possible so that for any set S of k faults, at least one $h \in H$ is good for S.

If the in-degree of M is bounded by δ and the size of H is ℓ, then we get that the degrees in T are bounded by $\ell(\delta + 1)^2 d$. Therefore we have the following:

Theorem 2.1 *Suppose that there exists a graph $M = (W, C)$ with maximum in-degree δ and H a family of mappings $U \mapsto W$ of size ℓ such that for any set of k faulty nodes in U there is a mapping $h \in H$ such that there are k node disjoint paths in M connecting $h(S)$ to the k spare nodes. Then for any graph $G = (V, E)$ with maximum degree d there is a k-fault tolerant graph $T = (U, D)$ with maximum degree $(\delta + 1)^2 \ell d$.*

Once we have M and H as in Theorem 2.1 the embedding strategy is straightforward: for a given set of faults S, find an $h \in H$ such that h is good for S and construct φ as above. Using a simple observation we can see the limitation of our general scheme:

Theorem 2.2 *Let M, H, δ and ℓ be as in Theorem 2.1, then $(\delta + 1)\ell > k$.*

Proof: Construct a set S as follows: pick a non-spare node $w \in W$ and make

$$S = \bigcup_{h_i \in H} h_i^{-1}(\Gamma_M(w)).$$

The size of S is at most $\ell|\Gamma_M(w)|$. No $h_i \in H$ can have node disjoint paths connecting $h_i(S)$ to the spare nodes, since w will have no non-faulty out-neighbors under any h_i. Therefore if $k \geq |\Gamma_M(w)|\ell$ then H and M do not satisfy the requirements of Theorem 2.1. Because w was an arbitrary non-spare node, it follows that $(\delta + 1)\ell > k$. □

By Theorem 2.2 it is clear that the strategy in constructing M and H should be to minimize δ as possible, since the actual degree of T will be at least $\delta k d$. In the next section we will see a construction where $\delta = 2$ and ℓ is $O(k)$ that works for $k < n^{1/4}$. A construction with $\delta = O(1/\beta)$ and $\ell k = O(k)$ that works for $k < n^{1-\beta}$ is given in section 4.

3 Grid Based Constructions

We now describe the application of the general scheme that works for k's which are smaller than $n^{\frac{1}{4}}$. It is fully constructive for k such that n is $\Omega(k^{\log k})$.

Let n and k be such that $k \mid n$ and let $M = (W, C)$ be the following graph: $W = \{(a, b)|a \in \{0, \ldots, n/k\}, b \in \{0, \ldots, k-1\}\}$. Let

$$\begin{aligned} C = \; & \{((a, b), (a-1, b))| \\ & a \in \{1, \ldots, n/k\}, b \in \{0, \ldots, k-1\}\} \\ \bigcup \; & \{((a, b), (a, b-1 \bmod k))| \\ & a \in \{1, \ldots, n/k\}, b \in \{0, \ldots, k-1\}\}. \end{aligned}$$

We refer to M as a grid and we consider all the nodes with the same a to be a row and all those with the same b to be a column. The nodes V are mapped by m arbitrarily to $\{(a, b)|a \in \{1, \ldots, n/k\}, b \in \{0, \ldots, k-1\}\}$. Therefore the bottom '0' row constitutes the set of spares.

The following claim provides a sufficient condition for the existence of k disjoint paths connecting the faults to the spares.

Claim 3.1 *Given a set $S = \{w_1 = (a_1, b_1), w_2 = (a_2, b_2) \ldots w_k = (a_k, b_k)\}$ of k nodes in W such that all the members of S are in different rows, i.e all the a_i's are different, then there exists a set of k disjoint paths connecting S to the bottom row.*

Proof: The path can be found in a greedy manner, processing the members of S bottom up. Assume that $a_1 < a_2, \ldots < a_k$. Suppose that we have arranged paths connecting the first $i-1$ nodes to the bottom row and we wish to connect w_i. We will maintain the property that the paths for the first $i-1$ nodes use at most $i-1$ different *columns*, i.e. no node from a different column is on any of the paths. Let c_i be the first column to the left of b_i that has not been used (that is, c_i is the vacant row that minimizes $b_i - c_i$ mod k). The path connecting (a_i, b_i) to the bottom row consists of the segment in row a_i connecting (a_i, b_i) to (a_i, c_i) and the segment connecting in column c_i (a_i, c_i) to $(0, c_i)$. Since a_i is the highest node processed so far, it is clear that all the nodes on $(a_i, b_i) - (a_i, c_i)$ are vacant, and since column c_i has not been used so far, the segment $(a_i, c_i) - (0, c_i)$ is vacant as well. □

Obviously, the condition that all faults are mapped to different rows is not necessary. However, in all subsequent constructions in this section we will try to fulfill it. Therefore from Claim 3.1 we have:

Theorem 3.1 *Let $M = (W, C)$ be as defined above and suppose that there exists a collection H of mappings $U \mapsto W$ of size ℓ with the property that for all $S \subset U$ where $|S| = k$ there is an $h \in H$ such that all the nodes $h(S)$ are in different rows, then M and H satisfy the properties of Theorem 2.1.*

Therefore we are left with the problem of finding the collection H. This is essentially a perfect hashing problem with the added restriction that the size of the preimages is fixed at k. For more information on perfect hashing, see [20, 11, 10, 3]. Unfortunately, no existing construction from the literature seems to fit our desired parameters.

By (simple) results in perfect hashing it follows that the minimum size of H we can hope for is $\Omega(k)$. We now present the first construction. This is not an explicit construction, but the function does have a succinct and efficient representation. It will serve as the basis for the next construction as well.

3.1 A shift based construction

Let $U = \{(x, y) | x \in \{0, \ldots, n/k\}, y \in \{0, \ldots, k-1\}\}$ and assume that $p = n/k + 1$ is a prime. The functions $h \in H$ are of the form $h((x, y)) = (ay + x \bmod p, y)$ for some $a \in \{1, \ldots, n/k\}$. In order to construct H, choose ℓ elements $a_1, a_2, \ldots a_\ell$ uniformly at random from $\{0, \ldots, n/k\}$ and let $h_i((x, y)) = (a_i y + x \bmod p, y)$. For every pair of distinct elements (x_1, y_1) and (x_2, y_2) if a_i is random, $Prob[h_i((x_1, y_1)) = h_i((x_2, y_2))] = \frac{1}{p} < \frac{k}{n}$ in case $y_1 \neq y_2$ and 0 otherwise. Therefore, we get that for any set $S = \{(x_1, y_1), (x_2, y_2), \ldots, (x_k, y_k)\}$ of k nodes in U the probability that h_i is *not* good for S is less than $\frac{k^3}{n}$. By summing up for all subset $S \subset U$ we get that the probability that there exists a set S such that none of the $h_i \in H$ is good for S is at most

$$\binom{n+k}{k} \left(\frac{k^3}{n}\right)^\ell. \tag{1}$$

If $k < n^{1/4}$ and $\ell = 4k$, then (1) is smaller than 1 and we can conclude that a good H exists. Therefore, by applying Theorem 3.1 we have:

Theorem 3.2 *For any k and n such that $k < n^{1/4}$ and any graph G with maximum degree d, there is a k-fault tolerant graph T with maximum degree which is $O(kd)$.*

Remark: In the construction above we assumed that k divides n and that $\frac{n}{k} + 1$ is a prime. However, the theorem itself can be proved without these assumptions by taking totally random functions h_i and by allowing at most one non-full row in our grid.

3.2 Explicit constructions

Let $P \geq k$ be a prime and suppose r is an integer and $P^r = (n+k)/k$. We label the nodes W (and U) with the vectors of length r over $GF[P]$ such that all the nodes on the same row receive the same label. Thus, a node $w \in W$ is $(\vec{x}, y)$ where $\vec{x} = (x_1, x_2, \ldots x_r)$ and $x_j \in GF[P]\}$ and $0 \leq y \leq k-1$.

The collection H is defined by ℓ vectors $\vec{a}_1, \vec{a}_2, \ldots \vec{a}_r$ of length r over $GF[P]$. For each $1 \leq i \leq \ell$ the function $h_i \in H$ is defined as $h_i((\vec{x}, y)) = (\vec{x} + y\vec{a}_i, y)$ where the addition is vector addition over $GF[P]$ and the multiplication is that of a vector by a scalar, and where y is treated as an element in $GF[P]$.

For such a collection to be bad means that there is a set $S = \{(\vec{x}_1, y_1), \vec{x}_2, y_2), \ldots (\vec{x}_k, y_k)\}$ such that no member of H is good for S. Therefore, for every element $h_i \in H$ there is a pair $w_{i_1} = (\vec{x}_{i_1}, y_{i_1})$ and $w_{i_2} = (\vec{x}_{i_2}, y_{i_2})$ such that $h_i(w_{i_1}) = h_i(w_{i_2})$, and

$$\vec{x}_{i_1} + y_{i_1}\vec{a}_i = \vec{x}_{i_2} + y_{i_2}\vec{a}_i.$$

Pick *one* such *colliding pair* for each $h_i \in H$ and consider the following graph: there are k nodes, each corresponding to an element of S. Connect two nodes if they were picked as a colliding pair for some h_i. Thus the number of edges is ℓ. The following fact is well-known (see [4] p. 126):

Proposition 3.1 *A graph on k nodes with ℓ edges where $\ell \geq 2k$ has a cycle of length at most*

$$g = 2\left\lceil \frac{\log k}{log\lfloor \ell/k \rfloor} \right\rceil + 1.$$

Find the cycle of length at most g whose existence the proposition ensures, and let its nodes (after relabeling) be $w_1, w_2, \ldots w_g$. Therefore we have that

$$\begin{aligned} \vec{x}_1 + y_1\vec{a}_1 &= \vec{x}_2 + y_2\vec{a}_1 \\ \vec{x}_2 + y_2\vec{a}_2 &= \vec{x_3} + y_3\vec{a}_2 \\ &\ldots \\ \vec{x}_g + y_g\vec{a}_g &= \vec{x}_1 + y_1\vec{a}_g \end{aligned}$$

by summing up we get that $\sum_{i=1}^{g}(y_{i+1} - y_i)\vec{a}_i = 0$. Since, for example, $y_1 \neq y_2$, we get that there must exist g vectors in $\vec{a}_1, \vec{a}_2, \ldots \vec{a}_\ell$ that are *linearly dependent* over $GF[P]$.

Our strategy in choosing $\vec{a}_1, \vec{a}_2, \ldots \vec{a}_\ell$ is, therefore, to make them such that no g of them are linearly dependent. This is exactly the condition required from the columns of a parity check matrix of a linear error correcting code over GF[P]. See Macwilliams and Sloane [18] for information on error correcting codes. Take, for instance, a Reed Solomon code of length ℓ, minimum distance $g + 1$ and dimension $\ell - r$. Such a code exists if $g + 1 \leq r$ and $\ell \leq P - 1$. The columns of the parity check matrix are indexed by the non-zero elements of $GF[P]$. For $i \in GF[P]$ we have $\vec{a}_i = (1, i, i^2, \ldots, i^{r-1})$ where all the computation is over $GF[P]$.

Suppose, for example, that $k \leq n^{1/20}$, $\ell = k\lceil 2^{\frac{2\log^2 k}{\log n}} \rceil$, P is a prime between ℓ and 2ℓ and $r = \frac{\log((n+k)/k)}{\log P}$ is an integer. By Proposition 3.1 we can take g to be $2\lceil \frac{\log k}{log \ell/k} \rceil + 1$ and we can verify that $g + 1 \leq r$, which implies that the appropriate code exists. Although this example required that $(n+k)/k$ be a power of P, the approach can be extended to remove this requirement, yielding:

Theorem 3.3 *For any n and k where $k \leq n^{1/20}$ and for any graph G with maximum degree d, there is an* explicit *construction for a k-fault tolerant graph T with maximum degree which is $O(\lceil 2^{\frac{2\log^2 k}{\log n}} \rceil kd)$. Note that when n is $\Omega(k^{\log k})$ this bound is $O(kd)$.*

4 Expander Based Constructions

In this section we replace the grid that appears in the constructions in Section 3 by an appropriate expander. This enables us to extend the $O(kd)$ upper bound for a wider range of the parameters n, k and d. The crucial property of an expander which is used here is the fact that some of its expansion properties remain even after deleting many of its edges. This is related to the main idea in [1], but here we need several additional ideas. Let us call an undirected graph R an (n, δ, λ)-graph if it is a δ-regular graph on n nodes, and the absolute value of each of the eigenvalues of its adjacency matrix, besides the largest, is at most λ. It is known ([12]) that random δ-regular graphs on n-nodes are almost surely (n, δ, λ)-graphs for $\lambda = O(\sqrt{\delta})$ and that for every $\delta = p + 1$ where p is a prime congruent to 1 modulo 4 there is an explicit infinite family of $(n, \delta, 2\sqrt{\delta - 1})$-graphs ([17], [19]). For more details on such graphs see [2].

Let $R = (V(R), E(R))$ denote, throughout this section, an (n, δ, λ)-graph. For a node v of R let $N(v)$ denote the set of all its neighbors. We say that two sets of nodes of equal cardinality S and S' in R can be *linked* if there are $|S|$ node disjoint paths in R connecting the nodes of S with these of S'. The main combinatorial property we need is the following result, which seems to be of independent interest. Proofs of lemmas and theorems in this section appear in the appendix.

Theorem 4.1 *Let R be as above and suppose*

$$8\frac{\lambda}{\delta} + 8(\frac{\lambda}{\delta})^2 < 1. \tag{2}$$

Then, every two sets of nodes S and S' in R, where $|S| = |S'|$ and where for every node v of R $|N(v) \cap S| \leq \delta/2$ and $|N(v) \cap S'| \leq \delta/2$, can be linked.

To prove this theorem we first need the following simple lemma, whose proof can be found in [2], page 122.

Lemma 4.1 *If $R = (V(R), E(R))$ is as above and $X \subset V(R)$ is a set of xn nodes then*

$$\sum_{v \in V(R)} (|N(v) \cap X| - x\delta)^2 \leq \lambda^2 x(1-x)n.$$

This lemma implies the following two assertions.

Lemma 4.2 *For any two sets B and B' in R each of cardinality at least $\frac{\lambda}{\delta}n$ there is at least one edge between B and B'.*

Lemma 4.3 *Let B and X be two sets of nodes of R and suppose that each node of B has at least $\delta/2$ neighbors in X. If $|X| = xn$ and $|B| = bn$ then*

$$x \geq \frac{b\delta^2}{4(b\delta^2 + \lambda^2)}. \tag{3}$$

We can now combine Theorem 4.1 and Theorem 3.1 to prove the following.

Theorem 4.2 *For any n and k and any graph G with n nodes and maximum degree d there exists a k-fault tolerant version T of G with maximum degree*

$$O\left(\frac{\log n}{\log(n/k)}kd\right).$$

Note that for $k < n^{1-\beta}$ for any fixed $\beta > 0$ this bound is $O(kd)$.

5 Lower Bounds

For a graph $G = (V, E)$ let $g(G, k)$ denote the minimum possible value of the maximum degree of a k-fault tolerant version of G. As shown in the previous section, if d is the maximum degree of G and k is not too large as a function of n (e.g., $k \leq n^{1/4}$) then $g(G, k) \leq O(dk)$. In this section we prove that for a wide range of values of k, d and n there exists a graph G on n nodes with maximum degree d so that $g(G, k) \geq \Omega(d\sqrt{k})$. It would be interesting to close the gap between these two estimates. The precise statement of our lower bound theorem is the following. Proofs of lemmas and theorems in this section appear in the appendix.

Theorem 5.1 *There is an absolute positive constants c_1 such that if d, k and n satisfy*

$$n > d \geq \frac{(\log n)^2}{\log\log n},$$

$$k \leq c_1 \frac{d^{1/2}}{(\log d)^{1/2}}$$

and

$$k < \frac{n}{2d},$$

then there exists a graph G on n nodes with maximum degree at most d so that $g(G, k) \geq \frac{1}{16}d\sqrt{k}$.

The proof employs a probabilistic construction of a suitable random graph G. Very roughly, it is based on the fact that any k-fault tolerant version T of G must contain many copies of G as subgraphs, and for an appropriate random G these copies cannot share too many common edges, due to the asymmetry of random graphs. This forces the maximum degree of any such T to be large. In what follows we omit all floor and ceiling signs whenever these are not crucial, to simplify the notation. In addition, we make no attempt to optimize the constants in the various estimates. For a graph G and for a subset W of its set of nodes let $G[W]$ denote the induced subgraph of G on the set of nodes W.

Lemma 5.1 *Let m and q be integers and let $1 > \epsilon > 1$ be a real satisfying*

$$1 > 2mqe^{-0.01\epsilon m} + 2q\binom{m}{2}e^{-0.01\epsilon^2 m} + q^2 2^{2m}(2m)!e^{-0.001\epsilon^3 m^2}.$$

Then there exists a graph $G = (V, E)$ on $n = 2mq$ nodes with the following four properties.
(i) G is the node disjoint union of q bipartite graphs $G_1, \ldots, G_q$, where the two node classes of G_i are A_i and B_i and $|A_i| = |B_i| = m$ for $1 \leq i \leq q$.
(ii) The degree of every node of G is at least $\frac{1}{2}\epsilon m$ and at most $2\epsilon m$.
(iii) No two nodes of G have more than $2\epsilon^2 m$ common neighbors.
(iv) For any $1 \leq i \leq j \leq q$ and for any two disjoint subsets $B \subset B_i$ and $B' \subset B_j$ satisfying $|B| = |B'| = \epsilon m/4$, the number of edges in any graph which is isomorphic to a subgraph of $G[B \cup A_i]$ and to a subgraph of $G[B' \cup A_j]$ does not exceed $\epsilon^3 m^2/2$.

Lemma 5.2 *Suppose m, q and ϵ satisfy (4), define $n = 2mq$ and let k, $n \geq k \geq 1$ be an integer, $\epsilon k < 1/2$. Define $d = 2\epsilon m$ and let $G = (V, E)$ be a graph satisfying the conditions (i)-(iv) in Lemma 5.1. Then $g(G, k) \geq \frac{1}{16}d\sqrt{k}$.*

Remark: A close inspection of the proof of Lemma 5.2 shows that the lower bound holds even if we allow the fault tolerant graph T to have $2n \geq n + k$ nodes. Thus, if the parameters n, d and k satisfy the assumptions in Theorem 5.1 then there is a graph G with n nodes and maximum degree d such that the following holds. If T is a graph with at most $2n$ nodes and any subgraph of T obtained by deleting k nodes of T contains a copy of G, then the maximum degree of a node of T is at least $\Omega(d\sqrt{k})$.

A Appendix: Proofs

Proof of Lemma 4.2: Suppose this is false and let B and B' be a counter-example. Put $|B| = bn$ and $|B'| = b'n$. By Lemma 4.1

$$\sum_{v \in B'} (|N(v) \cap B| - b\delta)^2 \leq \lambda^2 b(1-b)n.$$

However, by assumption there are no edges between B and B' and hence the left hand side of the last inequality is precisely $b'n(b\delta)^2$. It follows that

$$bb'\delta^2 \leq \lambda^2(1-b) < \lambda^2,$$

which is impossible, since both b and b' are at least $\frac{\lambda}{\delta}$. □

Proof of Lemma 4.3: By Lemma 4.1

$$\sum_{v\in B}(|N(v)\cap X| - x\delta)^2 \leq \lambda^2 x(1-x)n.$$

If $x \geq 1/2$ then inequality (3) follows trivially. Otherwise, the last inequality implies

$$bn(\frac{1}{2}-x)^2\delta^2 \leq \lambda^2 x(1-x)n,$$

i.e.,

$$\frac{b\delta^2}{4} \leq x(1-x)(\lambda^2+b\delta^2) \leq x(\lambda^2+b\delta^2).$$

This implies (3). □

Proof of Theorem 4.1: Suppose the theorem is false and let S and S' be a counter-example. By Menger's Theorem this implies that there exists a set C of cardinality $|C| < |S|$ $(= |S'|)$ such that in $R - C$ there is no path between a node in S and a node in S'. Let B be the set of all nodes in the connected components of $R - C$ that contain a node of S and let B' be the set of all nodes in the connected components of $R - C$ that contain a node of S'. Without loss of generality we may assume that $|B| \leq |B'|$. Put $|B| = bn$. Since obviously there is no edge between B and B', Lemma 4.2 implies that $b \leq \lambda/\delta$. Define $X = B \cup (C \setminus S)$, $|X| = xn$. We claim that $x < 2b$. Indeed, if this is false then $|X| \geq 2|B|$ and hence $|C \setminus S| \geq |B|$. Since $S \subset B \cup C$ this implies that

$$|C| = |C\cap S| + |C\setminus S| \geq |C\cap S| + |B| \geq |S|,$$

contradicting the fact that $|C| < |S|$. Hence $x < 2b$ as claimed.

Observe now that all the neighbors of every node v of B lie in $B \cup C \subset X \cup S$. Moreover, since by assumption v has at most $\delta/2$ neighbors in S it follows that it has at least $\delta/2$ neighbors in X. Therefore, by Lemma 4.3 and since $x < 2b$

$$2b > x \geq \frac{b\delta^2}{4(b\delta^2+\lambda^2)}.$$

But since $b < \lambda/\delta$ this implies that

$$8(\lambda\delta+\lambda^2) \geq 8(b\delta^2+\lambda^2) > \delta^2,$$

contradicting the assumption (2). This completes the proof. □

Proof Outline of Theorem 4.2: If n is large and k exceeds, say, $n/10$, the claimed bound is more than $n+k$ and we can simply take T to be complete. We can thus assume that $k \leq n/10$. Let R be an $(n+k, \delta, \lambda)$-graph, where $\delta = c\log n/\log(n/k)$, c is an absolute constant and inequality (2) holds. (Such graphs obviously exist, as mentioned in the beginning of the section, and can be given even constructively for some infinitely many values of n). Let M be the directed graph obtained from R by replacing each edge of R by two antiparallel directed edges. Let S' be a fixed set of k nodes in R (or M), so that no node of R has more than $\delta/2$ neighbors in S'. (A random set will have this property almost surely). This will be the set of spare nodes of M. The set of mappings H required in Theorem 3.1 is now simply chosen as a set of ℓ random bijections. For every fixed set S of k nodes, Theorem 4.1 implies that if a mapping h maps this set to a set of nodes of R that does not contain more than $\delta/2$ neighbors of any node of R, then h is good for S in the sense discussed in the previous section. It is easy to see that the probability that a random h is not good for a given fixed set S is at most $O(n2^{\delta}(k/n)^{\delta/2}) < 1/n$, where the last inequality holds if the constant c is chosen appropriately. Thus, the probability that there exists some set S for which no $h \in H$ is good is at most

$$O(\binom{n+k}{k}(n(4k/n)^{\delta/2})^{\ell}),$$

which is less than 1 for $\ell = c'k\log(n/k)/\log n$ for an appropriate c'. Combining this with the general procedure summarized in Theorem 3.1 and Theorem 2.2 the desired result follows. □

Proof of Lemma 5.1: Let $A_1,\ldots,A_q,B_1,\ldots,B_q$ be $2q$ pairwise disjoint sets of nodes, each of cardinality m. The graph G on the set of nodes

$$V = A_1\cup\ldots\cup A_q\cup B_1\cup\ldots\cup B_q$$

is the random graph obtained by choosing, for each i, $1 \leq i \leq q$ and for each $a \in A_i$ and $b \in B_i$, randomly and independently, the pair ab to be an edge with probability ϵ. The obtained graph obviously satisfies (i). To complete the proof we show that with positive probability it satisfies (ii), (iii) and (iv) as well.

The conditions (ii) and (iii) are very simple. The degree of every fixed node of G is a binomial random variable with expectation ϵm and variance $\epsilon(1-\epsilon)m$. By the well known tail estimates for binomial distributions (see, e.g., [2]), the probability that the degree of a fixed node is not between $\frac{1}{2}\epsilon m$ and $2\epsilon m$ is at most $e^{-0.01\epsilon m}$ (where the constant 0.01 can be easily improved). As there are $2mq$ nodes the probability that (ii) fails is at most

$$2mqe^{-0.01\epsilon m}. \tag{4}$$

The condition (iii) is similar. Two nodes can have common neighbors only if they both lie in the same set A_i or in the same set B_i. There are precisely $2q\binom{m}{2}$ such pairs of nodes. For a fixed pair, the number of their common neighbors is a binomial random variable with expectation $\epsilon^2 m$ and variance $\epsilon^2(1-\epsilon^2)m$. Therefore, by the known estimates for binomial distributions we conclude that the probability that (iii) fails is at most

$$2q\binom{m}{2}e^{-0.01\epsilon^2 m}. \tag{5}$$

It remains to estimate the probability that condition (iv) does not hold. Fix i and j, $1 \le i \le j \le q$ and fix two disjoint subsets $B \subset B_i$ and $B' \subset B_j$. (Since B_i and B_j are disjoint for $i < j$ the assumption that B and B' are disjoint is informative only for $i = j$.) If a copy of some graph appears in $G[B \cup A_i]$ and in $G[B' \cup A_j]$ then there is a bijection $f : B \cup A_i \mapsto B' \cup A_j$ which maps the copy in $G[B \cup A_i]$ to that in $G[B' \cup A_j]$. Fix a bijection f as above. The maximum number of edges of G in a graph that is mapped into a copy of itself by this mapping is precisely the number of edges uv in $G[B \cup A_i]$ for which $f(u)f(v)$ is an edge in $G[B' \cup A_j]$. For a fixed pair uv the probability that both uv and $f(u)f(v)$ are edges is ϵ^2, as these two pairs are distinct since $B \cap B' = \emptyset$. Moreover, the events corresponding to distinct pairs uv are mutually independent, as no edge of G is examined twice in considering all pairs

$$\{uv : u \in B, v \in A_i\} \cup \{f(u)f(v) : u \in B, v \in A_i\}.$$

It follows that the number of edges in a maximum common subgraph mapped to a copy of itself by f is a binomial random variable with expectation $\epsilon^2|B|m = \epsilon^3 m^2/4$ and variance $\epsilon^2(1-\epsilon^2)|B|m$. Therefore, the probability it exceeds $\epsilon^3 m^2/2$ is at most $e^{-0.001\epsilon^3 m^2}$. The number of choices of B and B' is less than $q^2 2^{2m}$, and the number of choices of the bijection f is less than $(2m)!$ Therefore, the probability that (iv) does not hold is at most

$$q^2 2^{2m}(2m)! e^{-0.001\epsilon^3 m^2}.$$

Combining the last inequality with inequalities (4) and (5) and with the assumption (4) we conclude that with positive probability all the conditions (i)-(iv) hold, completing the proof. □

Proof of Lemma 5.2: Let $T = (U, D)$ be a k-fault tolerant version of G. For every node $v \in V$ let $S(v)$ denote the set of all nodes u of T so that there is a copy of G in T in which u plays the role of v. Clearly $|S(v)| > k$ for all v (since $T - S(v)$ contains no copy of G). Define $A = A_1 \cup \ldots \cup A_q$, $B = B_1 \cup \ldots \cup B_q$ and consider the set of all ordered pairs $\{(v, u) : v \in A, u \in S(v)\}$. The cardinality of this set is clearly more than $|A|k$ and hence there is some $u \in U$ so that

$$|\{v \in A : u \in S(v)\}| \ge \frac{|A|k}{n+k} \ge \frac{k}{4}.$$

Put $l = k/4$ and let A' be a set of l distinct nodes in A so that $u \in S(a)$ for $a \in A'$. Since G satisfies conditions (ii) and (iii), each $a \in A'$ has at least

$$\frac{1}{2}\epsilon m - (l-1)2m\epsilon^2 > \frac{1}{4}\epsilon m$$

neighbors which are not adjacent to any other member of A'. Fix, for each $a \in A'$, a set $B(a) \subset B$ of $\epsilon m/4$ neighbors of a which are not adjacent to any other member of A'. The sets $\{B(a) : a \in A'\}$ are clearly pairwise disjoint. Let, also $A(a)$ denote the set A_i where i is the unique index for which $a \in A_i$.

Let $C \subset U$ be the set of all neighbors of u in T, and let $|C| = x$ be the degree of u in T. For each $a \in A'$, let $G(a)$ be a copy of G in T in which u plays the role of a. Also, let $G'(a)$ be the copy of $G[B(a) \cup A(a)]$ in $G(a)$. Observe that by condition (ii), the number of edges of each $G'(a)$ is at least $\frac{1}{2}\epsilon m|B(a)|$. The crucial point now is that condition (iv) implies that there are no two distinct members of the set $\{G'(a) : a \in A'\}$ that share more than $2\epsilon^2|B(a)|m$ common edges. Therefore, each $G'(a)$ has at least

$$\frac{1}{2}\epsilon m|B(a)| - (l-1)2\epsilon^2 m|B(a)| \ge \frac{\epsilon m}{4}|B(a)| = \frac{\epsilon^2 m^2}{16}$$

edges that do not belong to any other $G'(a')$. Hence, the total number of edges in the union of all the subgraphs $\{G'(a) : a \in A'\}$ of T is at least

$$l\frac{\epsilon^2 m^2}{16} = \frac{1}{64}\epsilon^2 m^2 k.$$

However, all these edges are incident with the set C of the x neighbors of u in T. It follows that the maximum degree of a node of T is at least the maximum between x and $\frac{\epsilon^2 m^2 k}{64x}$, which is at least the geometric mean of these two quantities. This shows that the maximum degree is at least

$$\frac{1}{8}\epsilon m\sqrt{k} \geq \frac{1}{16}d\sqrt{k},$$

where the last inequality follows from the fact that G satisfies condition (ii). Since T was an arbitrary k-fault tolerant version of G this shows that $g(G,k) \geq \frac{1}{8}d\sqrt{k}$ and completes the proof of the lemma. □

Proof of Theorem 5.1 Let b be a large absolute constant. If $d \geq bn^{2/3}(\log n)^{1/3}$ define $m = n/2$, $\epsilon = d/2m$ and $q = 1$, and check that these satisfy the assumptions of Lemma 5.2 (for appropriate c_1 and b). Otherwise, let m be the largest integer so that $d \geq bm^{2/3}(\log m)^{1/3}$ and define $\epsilon = d/2m$ and $q = n/2m$. Again, one can check that these satisfy the assumptions of Lemma 5.2. We omit the detailed computation. □.

References

[1] N. Alon and F. R. K. Chung, Explicit Construction of Linear Sized Tolerant Networks, Discrete Math. 72(1988), 15-19.

[2] N. Alon and J. Spencer, **The Probabilistic Method**, John Wiley and Sons Inc., New York, 1992.

[3] F. Berman, M.E. Bock, E. Dittert, M.J. O'Donnell and D. Plank, Collections of Functions for Perfect Hashing, SIAM Journal on Computing, Vol 15, No. 2, May 1986, pp. 604 - 618.

[4] B. Bollobas, **Extremal Graph Theory**, Academic Press, London, 1978.

[5] J. Bruck, R. Cypher and C.T. Ho, Fault-tolerant parallel architectures with minimal numbers of spares, IBM Research Report, RJ 8029, March 1991.

[6] J. Bruck, R. Cypher and C.T. Ho, *Fault-Tolerant Mesh and Hypercube architectures*, IBM Research Report, RJ 8566, January 1992.

[7] S. Dutt and J. P. Hayes, *On Designing and Reconfiguring k-Fault-Tolerant Tree Architectures*, IEEE Trans. on Computers, vol. C-39, no. 4, pp. 490–503, April 1990.

[8] S. Dutt and J. P. Hayes, *Designing Fault-Tolerant Systems Using Automorphisms*, Journal of Parallel and Distributed Computing, vol. 12, pp. 249–268, 1991.

[9] S. Dutt and J. P. Hayes, *Some Practical Issues in the Design of Fault-Tolerant Multiprocessors*, Proceedings of the 21st International Symposium on Fault-Tolerant Computing, pp. 292–299, June 1991.

[10] M.L. Fredman and J. Komlós, On the Size of Separating Systems and Families of Perfect Hash Functions, SIAM Journal of Algebraic and Discrete Methods, Vol 5, No. 1, March 1984, pp. 61–68.

[11] M.L. Fredman, J. Komlós and E. Szemerédi, Storing a Sparse Table with $O(1)$ Worst Case Access Time, Journal of the Association for Computing Machinery, Vol 31, No. 3, July 1984, pp. 538–544.

[12] J. Friedman, J. Kahn and E. Szemerédi, On the second eigenvalue in random regular graphs, Proc. 21st ACM STOC, ACM Press (1989), 587–598.

[13] J. Hastad, F. T. Leighton and M. Newman, *Fast Computations using Faulty Hypercubes*, Proceedings of 21st Annual ACM Symposium on Theory of Computing, pp. 251–284, 1989.

[14] J. P. Hayes, *A Graph Model for Fault-Tolerant Computing Systems*, IEEE Trans. on Computers, vol. C-25, no. 9, pp. 875–884, September 1976.

[15] C. Kaklamanis, A. R. Karlin, F. T. Leighton, V. Milenkovic, P. Raghavan, S. Rao, C. Thomborson and A. Tsantilas, *Asymptotically Tight Bounds for Computing with Faulty Arrays of Processors*, Proceedings of 31st Annual IEEE Symposium on Foundations of Computer Science, pp. 285–296, October 1990.

[16] S. Y. Kung, S. N. Jean and C. W. Chang, *Fault-Tolerant Array Processors Using Single-Track Switches*, IEEE Trans. on Computers, vol. C-38, no. 4, pp. 501–514, April 1989.

[17] A. Lubotzky, R. Phillips and P. Sarnak, Explicit expanders and the Ramanujan conjectures, Proc. 18th ACM STOC (1986), 240-246. See also: A. Lubotzky, R. Phillips and P. Sarnak, Ramanujan graphs, Combinatorica 8 (1988), 261-277.

[18] F. J. Macwilliams and N. J. A. Sloane, **The Theory of Error-Correcting Codes**, North Holland, Amsterdam, 1977.

[19] G. A. Margulis, Explicit group-theoretical constructions of combinatorial schemes and their application to the design of expanders and superconcentrators, Problemy Peredachi Informatsii 24(1988), 51-60 (in Russian). English translation in Problems of Information Transmission 24(1988), 39-46.

[20] K. Mehlhorn, **Data Structures and Algorithms 1: Sorting and Searching**, Springer-Verlag, Berlin Heidelberg, 1984.

[21] M. Paoli, W. W. Wong and C. K. Wong, *Minimum k-Hamiltonian Graphs, II,* J. of Graph Theory, Vol. 10, pp. 79–95, 1986.

[22] A. L. Rosenberg, *The Diogenes Approach to Testable Fault-Tolerant VLSI Processor Arrays*, IEEE Trans. on Computers, Vol. C-32, no. 10, pp. 902–910, October 1983.

[23] A. L. Rosenberg, *On Designing Fault-Tolerant Arrays of Processors*, Technical Report CS-1982-14, Dept. of Computer Science, Duke University, 1982.

[24] J. Spencer, **Ten Lectures on the Probabilistic Method**, SIAM (Philadelphia), 1987.

[25] W. W. Wong and C. K. Wong, *Minimum k-Hamiltonian Graphs*, J. of Graph Theory, Vol. 8, pp. 155-165, 1984.

The Power of Combining the Techniques of Algebraic and Numerical Computing: Improved Approximate Multipoint Polynomial Evaluation and Improved Multipole Algorithms

V. Y. Pan

Dept. of Mathematics & Computer Sci.
Lehman College, CUNY
Bronx, NY 10468

J. H. Reif and S. R. Tate

Computer Science Dept.
Duke University
Durham, NC 27706

Abstract

We demonstrate the power of combining the techniques of algebraic computation with ones of numerical computation. We do this by improving the known methods for polynomial evaluation on a set of real points and for simulation of n charged particles on the plane (the latter problem is equivalent to Trummer's problem). In both cases we approximate (rather than exactly compute) the solutions and do this by exploiting algebraic techniques of the algorithm design.

The previous best algorithm for approximate evaluation of a polynomial on a real set was due to Rokhlin and required the order of $mu + nu^3$ *infinite precision arithmetic operations to approximate [on a fixed bounded set* $X(m)$ *of* $m+1$ *real points] a degree* n *polynomial* $p(x) = \sum_{i=0}^{n} p_i x^i$ *within the error bound* $2^{-u} \sum_{i=0}^{n} |p_i|$. *We develop an approximation algorithm, which decreases Rokhlin's record estimate to* $O(m \log^2 u + n \min\{u, \log n\})$. *This result may also be favorably compared with the record bound* $O((m+n)\log^2 n)$ *on the complexity of the exact multipoint polynomial evaluation. Furthermore, if some values independent of the input coefficients and of the set* $X(m)$ *and depending only on* n *and* u *can be precomputed cost-free, then we decrease the computational cost estimate to* $O(m \log^2 u + u \log u)$. *All our algorithms allow NC and processor efficient parallel implementation. Because of the fundamental nature of the multipoint polynomial evaluation, our results have further applications to numerical and algebraic computational problems.*

For Trummer's problem, our algorithm approximates the output values to p *bits each, by using* $O(n \log^2 p)$ *time, thus improving the previous record time bound of* $O(np \log p)$.

1 Introduction

The techniques for algebraic computing and for numerical computing have been historically developing quite independently of each other, although the power of combining their advantages has been increasingly appreciated in recent years and has been advocated, for instance, in [31] and [3]. The present paper gives some new evidence of the advantages of such a combination: we improve the known results on the multipoint polynomial evaluation (on a real set) and on the solution of Trummer's problem, which is equivalent to the two-dimensional n-body problem of the multipole simulation of n charged particles in the electrostatic or gravitational potential fields on the plane (such a simulation is extensively used in molecular chemistry, chemistry, biochemistry, astronomy and, to a little lesser extent, in physics). In both cases we compute approximations, rather than the exact solutions (which is a typical feature of numerical computing), but we obtain such approximations by applying (some new and some old) purely algebraic techniques.

There is no apparent correlation between our two topics, and our section 9, devoted to an algorithm of [35] for Trummer's problem, can be read independently of sections 2-8, devoted to the algorithms of [32] for polynomial approximation. The technical overlaps of the solutions of both these computational problems are thus quite symptomatic.

Let us now turn to the details of our first subject, of approximate multipoint polynomial evaluation, postponing our further comments on Trummer's problem to the end of this section. The literature on efficient evaluation of a polynomial dates back to a linear time algorithm, using n additions and n multiplications, for

0-8186-2900-2/92 $3.00 © 1992 IEEE

the exact evaluation of a polynomial at a single point, usually called Horner's rule, due to the work of 1819 by Horner [17], but actually discussed by Isaac Newton [24], already in 1669. For the evaluation at a single point, this algorithm has been proved to be optimum ([26]).

We are concerned with the fundamental problem of evaluation of a polynomial of degree n, simultaneously at m points, in less than nm time (measured by the number of arithmetic operations involved). In 1971 Borodin and Munro [6] published an $O(n^{1.91})$ time algorithm for multipoint polynomial evaluation, for $m = n$, thus giving the first algorithm with the complexity below nm. The asymptotically fastest algorithm known for the multipoint exact polynomial evaluation problem is due to Moenck and Borodin [22], who reduced the problem to repeated polynomial divisions. Including here the Sieveking-Kung fast algorithm for polynomial division made this an $O((m+n)\log^2 n)$ algorithm. Strassen [39] proved the lower bound $\lceil m \log n \rceil$.

Our goal is to present efficient algorithms for multipoint *approximate* polynomial evaluation. Furthermore, in most applications, the computation needs to be done up to some limited accuracy of the machine, say, 32 or 64 bits, whereas the number of points and the degree of the polynomial may grow arbitrarily large. Thus, we desire an algorithm that achieves a fixed accuracy of the output and supports computational complexity estimates that grow linearly (with a small constant multiple) with $m + n$, or at least noticeably slower than $(m+n)\log^2 n$.

A customary requirement for numerical algorithms is numerical stability, and until 1988, the known numerically stable algorithms for the approximate evaluation of a polynomial

$$p(x) = \sum_{i=0}^{n} p_i x^i \tag{1.1}$$

on a fixed set $X(m)$ of $m+1$ points,

$$X(m) = \{x_0, x_1, \ldots, x_m\}, \tag{1.2}$$

required the order of mn arithmetic operations (hereafter referred to as to ops).

In 1988 major progress in this area was made by Rokhlin [37], who proposed the innovative idea of approximating the given polynomial only up to the amount of accuracy required, and devised an algorithm that both preserved numerical stability and decreased the computational complexity. Rokhlin's algorithm uses $O(mu + nu^3)$ (infinite precision) ops in order to compute (within the error bound $2^{-u}p$, $p \leq \sum_{i=0}^{n}|p_i|$) the set of the values

$$V(m) = \{p(x_j),\ j = 0, 1, \ldots, m\}, \tag{1.3}$$

for a positive u and for a set $X(m)$ of (1.2) lying on a real interval $\{x, 0 \leq x \leq 1\}$. The number of ops is linear in $m+n$ if u is a fixed constant. The transition to larger linear intervals can be made by means of linear transformations of the variable x and/or of applying the same algorithm on two or more than two adjacent real intervals. The algorithm of [37] is numerically stable and performs well with a finite precision. Although its computational complexity is linear in n and m, the multiplicative factor of u^3 is large even for a relatively small u, and this limits both practical application and theoritical value of the algorithm.

In the present paper we substantially modify the approach of [37] (see our Remark 3.1), making it conceptually simpler. Technically, we rely on the approximation to a given polynomial by means of its interpolation on the Chebyshev set of points by a lower degree polynomial. As in [37], we estimate the arithmetic running time assuming infinite precision computation (with no errors), even though the output values are sought within a certain fixed tolerance to the errors, and we are going to take advantage of such a combination of the powers of numerical and symbolic techniques.

Indeed, whereas the algorithm of [6] exactly computes the values $p(x_j)$, for $j = 0, 1, \ldots, m$, in $O((m + n)\log^2 n)$ ops, already our first Algorithm 3.1 of section 3 decreases this cost estimate, to $O((m + u)\log^2 u + n \min\{u, \log n\})$ ops because, instead of computing exactly, we approximate $p(x_j)$ within the error bound $2^{-u}p$, $p \leq \sum_{i=0}^{n}|p_i|$. The complexity bound of [6] (for the exact evaluation) exceeds this our bound (for approximation), by more than a constant factor, whenever $\log u = o(\log n)$. Our upper bound (on the complexity of the approximation) turns out to be strictly less than the lower bound of [39] (for the exact multipoint evaluation) already for u of the order of $\log n$. Our bound is also superior to the cited bound of [37] for the approximate evaluation problem.

Our algorithms allow NC and processor efficient parallel implementation. To specify the resulting complexity estimates, let $O(t, p)$ denote the bounds $O(t)$ on the arithmetic parallel time and, simultaneously, $O(p)$ on the number of processors used. [Note that according to a variant of Brent's scheduling principle, the bounds $O(t, ps)$ imply the bounds $O(ts, p)$ for any positive integers t, p and s; in particular, $O(t, p)$ implies the sequential bound of $O(tp)$ ops.]

Now, we may formally state our estimates, supported by Algorithm 3.1. Hereafter, $\log^{(0)} N = N$, $\log^{(h)} N = \log_2 \log^{(h-1)} N$, $h = 1, \ldots, \log^* N$, $\log^* N = \max\{h : \log^{(h)} N > 0\}$, for N standing for d, n, and u.

Theorem 1.1. *Given natural m and n, positive $g < 1$ and u, $m+1$ points $x_0, \ldots, x_m$ on a real interval $\{x: -g \leq x \leq g\}$, and the coefficients of a polynomial $p(x) = \sum_{i=0}^{n} p_i x^i$, it is possible, by using infinite precision arithmetic, to approximate the values of $p(x)$ at $x_0, \ldots, x_m$ within the error bound $E^* = 2^{-u}p, p \leq \sum_{i=0}^{n} |p_i|$, at the cost of $T = O((\log^2 u)(m+u) + n \min\{u, \log n\})$ arithmetic operations or at the parallel cost $O(t, T/t)$ where T is defined above, and $t = (\log^2 u)\log^* u + \min\{u, (\log n)\log^* n\}$.*

Remark 1.1. The factors of $\log^* N$, for $N = d, n, u$, are transfered to our parallel time estimates from the complexity bounds of [3] for polynomial division. These factors can be eliminated by using the alternate estimates of [3] if we agree to increase the processor bounds so that their products with the time bounds grow by the factor of $1 + 2^{-h}\log^{(h)} N$, for any choice of h such that $1 \leq h \leq \log^* N$.

Algorithm 3.1 first evaluates the coefficients of an auxiliary polynomial $v(x)$ (of a lower degree) approximating $p(x)$ on the set $X(m)$ and then evaluates $v(x)$ on $X(m)$. The first stage, of the evaluation of the coefficients of $v(x)$, involves irrational values of Chebyshev's real points, which deprives us of a chance of using the advantages of modular (residue) arithmetic. (Recall, in particular, that we may implement a rational algorithm applying the Chinese remainder theorem and other customary techniques of symbolic and algebraic computing [3], so as to reduce the precision of computations, by performing them modulo several fixed primes $p_1, \ldots, p_s$.)

In sections 4–7 we modify the first stage of this algorithm to ensure its *rationality*, so as to perform the computations of $v(x)$ over the field generated by the input variables $p_0, \ldots, p_n$, and we may use modular arithmetic to our advantage whenever $p_0, \ldots, p_n$ are rational. [At the last stage of the evaluation of $v(x)$ on the set $X(m)$, we have a choice between using an infinite precision rational algorithm ([22], [3]), at the cost $O((\log^2 d)\log^* d, m/\log^* d)$, or a numerically stable algorithm ([23]), at the cost $O(d, m)$.]

We achieve the rationalization of the algorithm with no increase and, surprisingly, with some decrease of its estimated computational cost [see the estimates (6.1), (6.2), (7.1) and Remark 6.1, for $d = O(u)$]. Moreover, this decrease becomes substantial [so that we reach the overall complexity bound $O(\log u, u)$, at the first stage, and $O((\log^2 u)\log^* u, ((u/\log u) + m)/\log^* u)$ for the entire algorithm], provided that we allow cost-free precomputation of some functions in n and u, which are independent of $x_0, \ldots, x_m, p_0, \ldots, p_n$ (see Theorem 6.1 in section 6).

In section 9, we study Trummer's problem. We combine numerical and algebraic approaches to improve the known solutions to this problem, which has well known applications to the solution of integral equations [36], to fluid mechanics [13], and to numerical evaluation of the Riemann zeta-function [25]. Furthermore, as we have already mentioned, Trummer's problem is equivalent to the two-dimensional n-body problem of simulation of n charged particles in the electrostatic or gravitational potential fields.

Technically, *Trummer's problem* is the problem of multiplying a structured matrix $S = (s_{i,j})$ by a vector $\vec{y}$ where

$$s_{i,j} = \begin{cases} \frac{1}{c_i - c_j} & \text{if } i \neq j, \\ 0 & \text{if } i = j. \end{cases}$$

The problem was originally posed by Golub in SIGACT News [11], as a challenge to use the structure of the problem to obtain an algorithm with running time $o(n^2)$. Indeed, Gerasoulis [10] gave an $O(n \log^2 n)$ time algebraic (and numerically unstable, for large n) algorithm that exactly solved Trummer's problem, whereas the approximation algorithms of Greengard and Rokhlin (known as the *multipole algorithms*) decreased the runnning time bound, first to $O(np^2)$ [36,14] and then to $O(np \log p)$ [15] where the output values were accurate to p bits. (We also refer the reader to [19, 5, 20, 21] for various implementations of multipole algorithms.) The factor of $p \log p$, however, is still quite large in some applications (for instance, n-body simulation typically requires about 16-bit precision in applications to molecular dynamics, and often much larger values of p are needed for the high accuracy planetary simulations).

In section 9, we will give an improved approximation algorithm that runs in time $O(n \log^2 p)$, thus saving a factor of $\Theta(p/\log p)$. In addition, our algorithm relaxes some restrictive assumptions required for the Greengard-Rokhlin algorithm.

2 Auxiliary Results for Polynomial Evaluation

For a fixed positive a, we identify the set $X(a, d)$ of the d Chebyshev points (nodes) on the real interval

$\{x\colon -a \le x \le a\}$ as follows:

$$X(a,d) = \{t_{2h+1} = a\cos\left(\tfrac{2h+1}{d}\pi\right), \quad h = 0,1,\ldots,d-1\} . \tag{2.1}$$

Evaluation of a polynomial of degree k on the set $X(a,d)$ for any $k \ge d$ and interpolation (for $k = d$) can be performed by using $T^* = O(k \min\{d, \log k\} + d\log^2 d)$ ops ([22]) or in parallel implementation, at the cost $O(d,k)$ or, alternatively, $O(\log^2 d + (\log k)\log^* k, (k/\log^* k) + d)$ (see Appendix A or [28]).

We will extend the latter algorithms to any real set $X(m)$ of (1.2), based in particular on the following

Theorem 2.1 ([9], p. 120). *For real a and b, a natural d, and a real function $f(x)$, having the d-th order bounded derivative $f^{(d)}(x)$ on the interval $\{x\colon b \le x \le a\}$, such that $a \ge b$,*

$$M = \max_{b\le x\le a} |f^{(d)}(x)| ,$$

let a polynomial $v(x) = \sum_{i=0}^{d-1} v_i x^i$ interpolate to $f(x)$ on the set of the Chebyshev points of (2.1), that is, let

$$v(t_{2h+1}) = f(t_{2h+1}) , \qquad h = 0,1,\ldots,d-1 . \tag{2.2}$$

Denote that

$$E = E(f,a,b,d) = \max_{b\le x\le a} |f(x) - s(x)|.$$

Then

$$E \le \frac{2M}{d!}\left(\frac{a-b}{4}\right)^d .$$

Since we may shift from $f(x)$ to $f(-x)$, we will hereafter assume that $a \ge |b|$, so that

$$0 \le a - b \le 2a . \tag{2.3}$$

We will apply Theorem 2.1 in the case where $a < 1$, and we will further assume that $d/(1-a)$ is an integer, so that

$$r = 1/a > 1 , \lceil\frac{d}{1-a}\rceil = \frac{d}{1-a} = \frac{dr}{r-1}, \tag{2.4}$$

and furthermore, $f(x)$ is the polynomial $p(x) = \sum_{i=0}^{n} p_i x^i$ of (1.1). In this case we will deduce that

$$E = E(f,a,b,d) \le E^* = \left(\frac{r}{de}\right)^{1/2}\sum_{i=d}^{n}|p_i|\left(\frac{1-br}{4r-4}\right)^d \tag{2.5}$$

where $e = 2.71828\ldots$, $\frac{1-br}{4r-4} \le \frac{1}{2r-2}$, due to (2.3), (2.4).

Remark 2.1. Observe that $1 - br \le 2$ for $|b| \le a$ and $1 - br = 2$ for $b = -a$. Denote that $p = \sum_{i=d}^{n}|p_i|$ and deduce from (2.5) that

$$E^* = (r/(de))^{1/2} p/(2r-2)^d,$$

for $b = -a$. In particular,

$$E^* = p(2/(de))^{1/2}2^{-d}, \text{ for } r = 2,\ a = -b = 1/2 ,$$
$$E^* = p(3/(de))^{1/2}4^{-d}, \text{ for } r = 3,\ a = -b = 1/3 ,$$
$$E^* = 2p(de)^{-1/2}6^{-d}, \text{ for } r = 4,\ a = -b = 1/4 .$$

Remark 2.2. Since the error bound E^* rapidly decreases as a and/or $a - b$ decrease, we may greatly decrease the approximation error if we partition the original interval $\{x\colon b \le x \le a\}$ into two or several smaller subintervals and approximate $p(x)$ separately on each of them.

To prove (2.5), apply Theorem 2.1, take into account (2.3), and deduce that

$$\begin{aligned} E &\le 2\left(\tfrac{a-b}{4a}\right)^d \left|\textstyle\sum_{i=d}^{n} p_i a^i \binom{i}{d}\right| \\ &\le 2m(a,d)\left(\tfrac{a-b}{4a}\right)^d \textstyle\sum_{i=d}^{n}|p_i| , \end{aligned} \tag{2.6}$$

where $\dfrac{a-b}{4a} = \dfrac{1-br}{4}$ [see (2.4)],

$$m(a,d) = \max_{d\le h\le n}\left(a^h\binom{h}{d}\right) .$$

Since $a^{h+1}\binom{h+1}{d} \le a^h\binom{h}{d}$ for $h \ge d$ if and only if $(h+1)a \le h - d$, it follows that

$$m(a,d) = a^H\binom{H}{d} = (1/r^H)\, H!/(d!(H-d)!)$$

where $r = (1/a) > 1$ [see (2.4)] and

$$H = \lfloor\frac{d}{1-a}\rfloor = \frac{dr}{r-1}.$$

Applying Stirling's formula, we obtain that

$$m(a,d) < \frac{(H/r)^H}{d^d(H-d)^{H-d}}\left(\frac{H}{d(H-d)e}\right)^{1/2}.$$

We have that

$$H - d = \frac{H}{r} = \frac{d}{r-1},$$

so that

$$m(a,d) < \frac{1}{(r-1)^d}\left(\frac{r}{de}\right)^{1/2}.$$

Combine this estimate with (2.6) and obtain (2.5).

3 The Evaluation – Interpolation – Evaluation Algorithm

We will combine the results of section 2 with those of [22] (or [28]) and [3] to arrive at a fast algorithm for real multipoint approximate polynomial evaluation.

Algorithm 3.1.
Input: a positive rational $a < 1$, natural m, n and d, real $p_0, p_1, \ldots, p_n$ and $x_0, x_1, \ldots, x_m$ [compare (1.1) and (1.2)], such that (2.4) holds and

$$|x_j| \leq a\ , \qquad j = 0, 1, \ldots, m\ .$$

Output: real values $v_0, v_1, \ldots, v_m$ such that

$$|v_j - p(x_j)| \leq E^*\ , \qquad j = 0, 1, \ldots, m\ ,$$

for $p(x)$ of (1.1) and E^* of (2.5).
Computations.

Stage 1, *evaluation on the set of the Chebyshev nodes.* Compute

$$p(t_{2h+1}) = \sum_{i=0}^{n} p_i t_{2h+1}^i\ , \qquad h = 0, 1, \ldots, d-1\ ,$$

for $t_1, t_3, \ldots, t_{2d-1}$ of (2.1).

Stage 2, *interpolation.* Compute the coefficients of the polynomial $v(x) = \sum_{i=0}^{d-1} v_i x^i$ such that $v(t_{2h+1}) = p(t_{2h+1})$, $h = 0, 1, \ldots, d-1$ [compare (2.2)].

Stage 3, *multipoint evaluation.* Compute and output the values

$$v_j = v(x_j)\ , \qquad j = 0, 1, \ldots, m\ .$$

The correctness of the algorithm immediately follows from (2.5).

At stages 1 and 2, application of the algorithms of [22], [28] yields the complexity estimates $O(d, n)$ or, alternatively, with the incorporation of a parallel polynomial division algorithm of [3], yields the estimates $O(\log^2 d + (\log n)\log^* n, (n/\log^* n) + d)$. At stage 3, we may apply the algorithm of [22], incorporating an algorithm of [3], for polynomial division, to reach the cost bound

$$O(\log^2 d \log^* d, (m+d)/\log^* d).$$

Alternatively, we may apply a slower but numerically stable algorithm having the cost bounded by $O(d, m+n+d)$. The estimates of Theorem 1.1 follow since $d = O(\log(p/E^*))$, according to (2.5) and Remark 2.1, and since we may approximate any positive $g < 1$ by a rational $a, g \leq a \leq 1$, and choose $d = d(a) \to \infty$ satisfying (2.4).

Remark 3.1. The algorithm of [37] also uses Chebyshev points, but only in order to approximate each monomial x^i as an exponential function in i. This leads to a distinct algorithm and distinct complexity estimates.

4 The Evaluation-Division Algorithm

Algorithm 3.1 still works if, instead of the coefficients $p_0, \ldots, p_n$, a black box subroutine for the evaluation of $p(x)$ on the set (1.2) of the Chebyshev nodes is available. In particular, the algorithm can be applied to the evaluation of the characteristic polynomial of a matrix without computing its coefficients. This is required, for instance, in some algorithms for matrix eigenvalues [4].

On the other hand, Algorithm 3.1 has a deficiency: generally, the values t_{2h+1} of (2.1) are not rational, and we cannot use rational arithmetic at stages 1 and 2. Thus, we should apply numerical computation with roundoff errors. To bound the resulting output errors, we may apply the known numerically stable algorithm for polynomial evaluation [23] and interpolation ([40], [12]), increasing the computational cost of stages 1, 2 and 3 to $O(d, n)$, $O(d, d)$ and $O(d, m)$, respectively. The resulting algorithm as a whole will not be numerically stable, however. Indeed, usually, the errors introduced in stage 1 are greatly magnified in stage 2 (of interpolation) because interpolation is an ill-conditioned computational problem (see Appendix B).

If, however, the coefficients of $p(x)$ are available and if they are rational, we may avoid the above difficulties by modifying Algorithm 3.1 as follows:

Algorithm 4.1.
Input, output are as in Algorithm 3.1.
Computations.

Stage 1. Evaluate the coefficients of the polynomial

$$L(x) = \prod_{h=0}^{d-1}(x - t_{2h+1}) \tag{4.1}$$

where t_{2h+1} are defined by (2.1).

Stage 2. Evaluate the coefficients of the polynomial $w(x) = p(x) \bmod L(x)$ and set $v(x) = w(x)$.

Stage 3, as in Algorithm 4.1.

Correctness of Algorithm 4.1 follows since, clearly, $p(t_{2h+1}) = w(t_{2h+1})$ for all h.

Stage 1 can be performed at the cost $O(\log^2 d, d)$ ([1] or [3]), stage 2 at the cost $O(d, n)$ or, alternatively, $O((\log n)log^* n, n/\log^* n)$ ([3]). This only leads to improving the cost bounds of stages 1 and 2 of Algorithm 3.1 by a constant factor, but we will next show how to make the computations at stages 1 and 2 of Algorithm 4.1 rational and also how to decrease their complexity further, by exploiting the following expressions (already used in [28]):

$$t_{2h+1} = (a/2)(\omega_{2d}^{2h+1} + \omega_{2d}^{-(2h+1)})\ , \ h = 0, 1, \ldots, d-1\ , \tag{4.2}$$

where $\omega_{2d} = \exp(\pi\sqrt{-1}/d)$ is a primitive $(2d)$-th root of 1.

5 Rationalization of Stage 1 of Algorithm 4.1

Let us set

$$t_h = \frac{a}{2}(\omega_{2g}^h + \omega_{2g}^{-h}),\ h = 0, 1, \ldots, 2g-1,$$

so that

$$L(x) = \prod_{h=0}^{d-1}(x - t_{2h+1}) = L_{2d}^*(x)/L_d^*(x)$$

where $L_g^*(x) = \prod_{h=0}^{g-1}(x - t_h)$, for $g = d$, $g = 2d$.

We will now compute the coefficients of $L_g^*(x)$, for $g = d$, $g = 2d$, and then will divide $L_{2d}^*(x)$ by $L_d^*(x)$, to obtain $L(x)$.

To evaluate the coefficients of the polynomial $L_g^*(x)$, for $g = d$, $g = 2d$, we will first observe the following simple expressions for the power sums of its zeros:

$$\begin{aligned}\textstyle\sum_{h=0}^{g-1} t_h^k &= \textstyle\sum_{i=0}^{g-1}(a/2)^k(\omega_g^i + \omega_g^{-i})^k \\ &= \begin{cases} 0\,, & \text{for odd } k\,, \\ g\binom{k}{k/2}(\frac{a}{2})^k\,, & \text{for even } k\,, \end{cases}\end{aligned}$$

and then will apply the rational algorithm of [38] (see also [30], appendix) to make the transition from the power sums to the coefficients, at the cost $O(\log^2 d,\ d/\log d)$, which dominates the cost of the subsequent division of $L_{2d}^*(x)$ by $L_d^*(x)$.

The latter algorithm, as well as any algorithm for the transition from the power sums to the coefficients, requires division by $2, 3, \ldots, 2d$, which cannot be performed in some fields. To compute $L(x)$ over any field (containing $a/2$), we may multiply together, modulo ω_{2d}^d+1, all the d linear factors $x-t_{2h+1}$ of (4.1), substituting the expressions (4.2) for t_{2h+1} and treating ω_{2d} as the second variable. The cost of this computation increases to $O(\log^2 d, d^2)$.

Remark 5.1. Another direction (which we leave as a chalenge to the reader) is to apply Newton's identities in order to extend the above explicit expressions for the power sums to the similar expressions for the coefficients of $L_g^*(x)$.

Remark 5.2. All our computations are ultimately reduced to polynomial multiplication for which, throughout this paper, we assume the cost bound $O(\log D, D)$, where D bounds the degree of the output polynomial. In fact, this bound turns into $O(\log D,\ D\log\log D)$ for the computation over any field of constants (see [3]), and all our estimates should be corrected respectively (we leave this slight correction to the reader).

6 Computation of the Coefficients of the Reciprocal and Stage 2 of Algorithm 4.1

In this section we will assume $L(x)$ available, and our next task will be the computation of the d trailing coefficients of the reciprocal polynomial $R(x) = (1/L(x)) \bmod x^{n-d+1}$; when this is done, the desired coefficients of $v(x)$ can be obtained as the d trailing coefficients of the polynomial $p(x) - R(x)L(x)$, at the additional cost $O(\log d,\ d)$ of a single multiplication and a single subtraction of degree d polynomials. We first observe that the polynomials $L(x)$ and $R(x)$ do not depend on the set $X(m)$ of (1.2) and on the coefficients of the polynomial $p(x)$ of (1.1) and thus, in principle, can be preprocessed.

Theorem 6.1. *If precomputation of the values depending only on degree n and the precision value u and independent of the input set $X(m)$ of the nodes of (1.2) and of the coefficients of the polynomial $p(x)$ of (1.1) is allowed cost-free, then the complexity estimates of Theorem 1.1 can be decreased to $O(u,\ m + \log u)$ (using numerically stable implementation of stage 3 of Algorithms 3.1 and 4.1) or to $O((\log^2 u)\log^* u, ((u/\log u) + m)/\log^* u)$ (using infinite precision arithmetic).*

Without cost-free preprocessing, we may rationally compute the coefficients of $R(x)$ (by using the known algorithms for polynomial reciprocal) at the cost $O(d, n)$ or, alternatively, $O((\log n)\log^* n,\ n/\log^* n)$ [3]. The overall cost of performing Algorithm 4.1 over the fields of constants allowing divisions by $2, 3, \ldots, 2d$ is thus bounded by

$$\begin{aligned}&O(t', p'),\quad t' = (\log n)\log^* n + (\log^2 d)\log^* d\,,\\ &p't' = m\log^2 d + n\min(d,\ \log n),\end{aligned} \tag{6.1}$$

whereas over any field we reach the cost bounds

$$O(t', p'')\ ; \quad p''t' = (m + d^2)\log^2 d + n\log n. \tag{6.2}$$

In all these cases, with and without preprocessing, the evaluation of the coefficients of $v(x)$ is by a rational algorithm.

Remark 6.1. Besides the reduction of the precision of the computations in the latter case, the cost of the evaluation of $p(x)$ mod $L(x)$ can be reduced to

$O(n)$ ops over the field of integers modulo p_i, for each i, provided that $d = O(\log n)$ [18].

Remark 6.2. Numerical division of $p(x)$ by $L(x)$ (with an arbitrarily high output precision) can be performed at the cost $O(\log n,\, n)$ (see [3], [33]).

7 Solution via Reduction modulo $z^d + 1$

In this section, we will develop some ideas of [28] in order to compute the coefficients of $v(x)$ at the cost $O(n, d)$ over any field of constants. This alternative to performing both stages 1 and 2 of Algorithms 3.1 and 4.1 leads to the alternate overall cost bound of

$$O(n,\, d + (m/n)\log^2 d)\ . \tag{7.1}$$

For simplicity, assume (with no loss of generality) that d divides n and that the variable x has been scaled so that $a = 1$. Substitute $x = (z + z^{-1})/2$ into (1.1) and obtain that

$$p(\,(z + z^{-1})/2) = Q(z) + Q(1/z)$$

for some unknown polynomial $Q(z) = \sum_{i=0}^{n} Q_i z^i$. It remains to compute the coefficients of the polynomial $w(x)$ (of degree at most $d-1$) such that

$$w(\,(z+z^{-1})/2) = p(\,(z+z^{-1})/2) \bmod (z^d+1) \tag{7.2}$$

and to set $v(x) = w(x)$. Indeed, due to (7.2), we have that $w(x) = p(x)$ on the set $X(1, d)$ of (2.1), because $x = (z + z^{-1})/2$ for $z = \omega_{2d}^{2h+1}$, $h = 0, 1, \ldots, d-1$, defines precisely the set (2.1).

To compute the coefficients of $w(x)$:

a) first represent $p((z + z^{-1})/2) \bmod (z^d + 1)$ as $q(z) + q(1/z)$ where $q(z)$ is a polynomial of degree at most $d-1$ and

b) then rewrite $q(z) + q(1/z)$ as $w((z + z^{-1})/2)$.

To perform stage a), recursively represent $(z + z^{-1})^i \bmod (z^d + 1)$ (for $i = 1, 2, \ldots, n$) as $q_i(z) + q_i(1/z)$ where $q_i(z)$ are polynomials of degrees at most $d-1$. Specifically, suppose that we know the coefficients of the polynomial $q_i(z) = \sum_{h=0}^{d-1} q_{i,h} z^h$. [We surely know $q_0(x)$ and $q_1(x)$.] Then let

$$q_{i+1,d-1} = q_{i,d-2}\ , \quad q_{i+1,0} = q_{i,1} - q_{i,d-1}\ ,$$

$$q_{i+1,h} = q_{i,h-1} + q_{i,h+1}\ , \quad \text{for} \quad 0 < h < d-1\ ,$$

and thus define $q_{i+1}(z)$. Knowing $q_i(z)$ for all i, we then immediately compute the coefficients of the polynomial $q(z) = \sum_{i=0}^{n} 2^{-i} p_i q_i(z) = \sum_{i=0}^{n} q_i z^i$. The overall cost of this stage is $O(n, d)$.

Remark 7.1. The reader may try to deduce some explicit expressions for $q_{i,h}$ and for all i and h in order to decrease the parallel time of performing stage a).

To perform stage b), proceed recursively, for $h = d-1, d-2, \ldots, 0$. For every h, compute $w_{h,h}$ and then $v_h = 2^h w_{h,h}$ where $w_{h,h}$ is the leading coefficient of the polynomial $w_h(z)$ of degree at most h such that

$$\begin{aligned} w(z) + w(1/z) &= q(z) + q(1/z) \\ &\quad - \textstyle\sum_{h=k+1}^{d-1} (q_h(z) + q_h(z^{-1})\,) v_h\ . \end{aligned}$$

8 Discussion

It would be interesting and desirable to improve our results on the evaluation of the coefficients of $L(x)$ (section 5), $R(x)$ and $v(x)$ (section 6) and $w(x)$ (section 7), (compare, in particular, Remarks 5.1 and 7.1).

Our algorithms can be applied recursively, to simplify the multipoint evaluation of $v(x)$ at stage 3 of Algorithms 3.1 and 4.1 if $p = \sum_{i=0}^{n} |p_i|$ substantially exceeds $v = \sum_{h=0}^{d-1} |v_h|$.

A major challenge is an extension of our results to interpolation. As a heuristic approach, we suggest replacing the input set $X(n)$ of $n+1$ nodes of interpolation (6.2) by the set $X(a, d)$ of d Chebyshev nodes (2.1). The input values of $p(x)$ at $x = x_i$, $i = 0, 1, \ldots, m$, are then used in order to approximate the values $p(t_{2h+1})$, for $h = 0, 1, \ldots, d-1$. Then interpolation to $p(x)$ is replaced by the simpler interpolation to a polynomial of degree at most $d-1$ that approximates $p(x)$ at $x = t_{2h+1}$, for $h = 0, 1, \ldots, d-1$. The approach is promising if the points of $X(m)$ closely approximate all the nodes t_{2h+1} of $X(a, d)$. Some difficulties with this heuristic may stem from the fact of ill-conditioning of the interpolation problem (see Appendix B).

Of course, it is interesting to consider approximate interpolation and multipoint evaluation with the complex input nodes, although this case is much harder to treat than the real case (compare [34]).

9 Fast Approximation Algorithm for Trummer's Problem

In this section we present our improved solution of Trummer's problem.

9.1 Quad–Tree Construction

All efficient algorithms for the n-body problem use some form of hierarchical space decomposition. The algorithms of [2] and [8] use variants of quad-trees with $O(n)$ nodes and with particles associated with the leaf nodes. (Quad-trees are also applied, in Weyl's construction, for approximating polynomial zeros [27].) We create a non-trivial modification of these trees, in which particles may be associated with *internal nodes*, as well as the leaf nodes. In addition, particles are "clustered" at nodes in sets of size s, which is a parameter of our decomposition algorithm. In doing so we guarantee that the number of nodes in our decomposition tree T is small [35].

Lemma 9.1. *The number of nodes in T is $O(\frac{n}{s})$. Moreover, building the tree T from the $O(n)$ node trees of [2, 8] can be done optimally, in sequential time $O(n)$ or by using $O(\frac{n}{\log s})$ processors and $O(\log s)$ time on a PRAM.*

9.2 A Fast Algorithm

Fast approximation algorithms for Trummer's problem operate by computing power series approximations to the desired potential function. In two dimensions this is particularly easy — since the potential function is a harmonic function, there is an analytic function in one complex variable that completely describes the potential function over the plane. It is this analytic function that we approximate with a power series. The two types of power series expansions required are a standard Taylor series (for representing the potential within a local disk, due to particles outside the disk) and a Taylor series in $1/z$, which is known as the multipole expansion (for representing the potential *outside* a disk, due to particles within the disk).

The five major components of such an approximation algorithm are

- Creating the initial multipole expansions
- Translating multipole expansions
- Converting multipole expansions to Taylor series expansions
- Translating Taylor series expansions
- Evaluating local forces

As proved by Greengard and Rokhlin [14], to perform computations with p bits of accuracy, only $O(p)$ terms of the power series expansions need to be kept. It is fairly clear from the form of the equations that translation of multipole expansions and Taylor series, as well as the conversion between these two expansions, can be done quickly via a reduction to convolution requiring $O(p \log p)$ time for each power series operation.

Let us next create the initial multipole expansions. For s particles at locations $z_1, z_2, \cdots, z_s$ with charges $q_1, q_2, \cdots, q_s$, the multipole expansion about the origin can be written (see, for example, [14]) as

$$\Lambda(z) = Q \ln z + \sum_{k=1}^{p} \frac{a_k}{z^k},$$

where

$$Q = \sum_{i=1}^{s} q_i\ , \quad a_k = \sum_{i=1}^{s} \frac{-q_i z_i^k}{k}.$$

We now consider computing only the a_k coefficients, as Q can be computed in additional $O(s)$ time.

We just need to compute the row vector $(-a_1, -2a_2, \cdots, -ka_k, \cdots, -pa_p)$, and then $O(p)$ divisions will produce exactly the multipole coefficients. Since $-ka_k = \sum_{k=1}^{s} q_i z_i^k$, it will remain to multiply the row vector $(q_1, q_2, \cdots, q_s)$ by the $s \times p$ matrix $Z = (z_{i,k} = z_i^k, i = 1, 2, \cdots, s; i = 1, 2, \cdots, p)$. We choose $s = p$, so that Z is a $p \times p$ Vandermonde matrix. Due to its special structure, we can premultiply it by a vector in time $O(p \log^2 p)$ [7,29], so that calculating all the coefficients of the multipole expansion can be done in time $O(p \log^2 p + p)$.

Finally, we need to consider the complexity of the last step of the multipole algorithm, which is the stage of calculating the local forces. This step involves two types of operations: (1) computing the force on every particle within a region of the space decomposition due to particles in another region, and (2) computing the force on every particle in a region due to the other particles in the *same* region. Clearly, each of these problem is just a smaller version of the original problem, which we solve by using Gerasoulis' algebraic algorithm [10] in time $O(s \log^2 s)$. It is shown in the full paper [35] that the total number of local calculations that need to be done is proportional to the size of the decomposition tree, which is $O(n/s)$ by Lemma 9.1, and which results in the overall $O(n \log^2 s)$ time for *all* local force calculations. We now arrive at the main result of this section.

Theorem 9.1. *Given the decomposition tree of [2,8], having $O(n)$ nodes, associated with the n-body problem in two dimensions, we can approximate (to p bits) the values of the forces acting on all the n particles in total $O(n \log^2 p)$ time.*

Proof: Each major operation in the multipole algorithm can be charged to a particular node in the tree, and no node will ever be charged by more than a constant number of these operations. In other words, there are at most $O(n/s)$ evaluations, translations, and conversions (see [35] for the details). We estimated the complexity of each of these operations above: putting all of these complexity estimates together, we can see that the entire algorithm takes time

$$O\left(\frac{n}{s}\left(p\log p + s\log^2 p + s\log^2 s\right)\right),$$

which for $s = p$, turns into $O(n\log^2 p)$.

[35] also contains a substantial improvement of the previous multipole algorithms for the *three-dimensional* n-body problem (which is the most customary means of particle simulation), but in this case the resulting time bound is still far larger than the known lower bound.

Appendix A. Special Techniques for Chebyshev's Nodes.

To simplify the evaluation of a polynomial $p_n(x)$ of (1.1) on the set $X(1,d)$ of Chebyshev's nodes and the interpolation by $p(x)$ on the set $X(1,d)$ (provided in the latter case that $n = d-1$), represent $p(x)$ as $p_0(x^2) + xp_1(x^2) = q_0(y) + xq_1(y)$ where $y = 1-2x^2$. The substitution of $y = 1-2x^2$ for x maps the Chebyshev set $X(1,d)$ of (1.2) into the half-size Chebyshev set $X(1,d/2)$. We may assume for simplicity that d and n are integer powers of 2 and recursively apply the above relations to obtain the divide-and-conquer algorithms for both evaluation and interpolation (see more details in [28]). The resulting algorithms slightly imporve the parallel complexity estimates based on the algorithm of [22], incorporating the polynomial division algorithm of [3] (compare the beginning of section 2).

Appendix B. Error Magnification in the Interpolation.

Fix a set $X(m)$ of (1.2), denote

$$L(x) = \prod_{k=0}^{m}(x - x_k),$$

$$\ell_k(x) = L(x)/(x - x_k), \quad k = 0, 1, \ldots, m,$$

assume that $m = n$, and recall Lagrange's interpolation formula,

$$p(x) = \sum_{k=0}^{m} p(x_k)\,\ell_k(x)\,/\,\ell_k(x_k).$$

Observe that an error ϵ in the value of $p(x_k)$ causes the output perturbation $\epsilon\,\ell_k(x)/\ell_k(x_k)$. This perturbation is large if $|\ell_k(x_k)|$ is small, which is frequently the case. For instance, if $x_k = -a + 2ak/m$, $k = 0, 1, \ldots, m$, then

$$\ell_m(x_m) = \max_k |\ell_k(x)| = (2a/m)^m m!,$$

so that

$$(2a/e)^m m^{1/2} e^{3/4} \le \ell_m(x_m) \le (2a/e)^m e m^{1/2}. \quad (B.1)$$

If $m = d-1$ and if $X(m) = X(a,d)$ is the Chebyshev set (2.1), then the magnificaion of the errors at $x_{d-1} = a$ (and similarly at $x_0 = -a$) is greater than (B.1) indicates, since the nodes t_{2h+1} are accumulated near $x_{d-1} = a$ and $x_0 = -a$, so that the distances from x_k to a are of the order of $(2ak/d)^2$ if $d-k = o(d)$ (and similarly for x_k near $-a$).

Acknowledgements

Pan is supported by NSF Grant CCR 9020690 and PSC CUNY Award #662478. Reif and Tate are supported by DARPA/ISTO Contracts N00014-88-K-0458, DARPA N00014-91-J-1985, N00014-91-C-0114, NASA subcontract 550-63 of prime contract NAS5-30428, US-Israel Binational NSF Grant 88-00282/2, and NSF Grant NSF-IRI-91-00681. The authors are grateful to C. Engle for her superb assistance with typing this paper.

References

[1] A. V. Aho, J. E. Hopcroft, J. D. Ullman, *The Design and Analysis of Computer Algorithms*, Addison-Wesley, Mass., 1976.

[2] J. Barnes, P. Hut, A Hierarchical $O(N\log N)$ Force-calculation Algorithm, *Nature*, 324, 446-449, 1986.

[3] D. Bini, V. Pan, *Numerical and Algebraic Computations with Matrices and Polynomials*, Birkhauser, Boston, 1992 (to appear).

[4] D. Bini, V. Pan, Practical Improvement of the Divide-and-Conquer Eigenvalue Algorithms, *Computing*, 48, 109–123, 1992.

[5] J.A. Board Jr., R.R. Batchelor, J.F. Leathrum Jr., High Performance Implementations of the

Fast Multipole Algorithm, *Symposium on Parallel and Vector Computation in Heat Transfer, Proc. 1990 AIAA/ASME Thermophysics and Heat Transfer Conference*, 1990.

[6] A. B. Borodin, I. Munro, Evaluating Polynomials at Many Points, *Information Processing Letters*, 1:2, 66–68, 1971.

[7] J. F. Canny, E. Kaltofen, Y. Lakshman, Solving System of Nonlinear Polynomial Equations Faster, *Proc. ACM-SIGSAM Intern. Symp. on Symbolic and Algebraic Comp.*, 121-128, 1989.

[8] J. Carrier, L. Greengard, V. Rokhlin, A Fast Adaptive Multipole Algorithm for Particle Simulations, *SIAM Journal of Scientific and Statistical Computing*, 9, 4, 669-686, 1988.

[9] G. Dahlquist, A. Björck, *Numerical Methods*, Prentice-Hall, Englewood Cliffs, N.J., 1974.

[10] A. Gerasoulis, A Fast Algorithm for the Multiplication of Generalized Hilbert Matrices with Vectors, *Mathematics of Computation*, 50, 181, 179-188, 1988.

[11] G. Golub, Trummer's Problem, *SIGACT News*, 17, 2, 12, 1985.

[12] G. H. Golub, C. F. van Loan, *Matrix Computations*, Johns Hopkins University Press, Baltimore, Maryland, 1989.

[13] L. Greengard, Potential Flow in Channels, *SIAM Journal on Scientific and Statistical Computing*, 11, 4, 603–620, 1990.

[14] L. Greengard, V. Rokhlin, A Fast Algorithm for Particle Simulations, *Journal of Computational Physics*, 73, 325-348, 1987.

[15] L. Greengard, V. Rokhlin, On the Efficient Implementation of the Fast Multipole Algorithm, Technical Report RR-602, *Yale University, Department of Computer Science*, 1988.

[16] R. A. Horn, C. R. Johnson, *Matrix Analysis*, Cambridge University Press, Cambridge, 1985.

[17] W. G. Horner, *Philosophical Transactions, Royal Society of London*, 109, 308-335, 1819.

[18] M. Kaminski, Linear Time Algorithm for Residue Computation and a Fast Algorithm for Division with a Sparse Divisor, *J. of ACM*, 34, 4, 968-984, 1987.

[19] J. Katzenelson, Computational Structure of the N-body Problem, *SIAM Journal of Scientific and Statistical Computing*, 10, 787-815, 1989.

[20] J.F. Leathrum Jr., J.A. Board Jr., Parallelization of the Fast Multipole Algorithm Using the b012 Transputer Network, *Transputing T91*, IOS Press, Washington, D.C., 1991.

[21] J. F. Leathrum Jr., J. A. Board Jr., Mapping the Adaptive Multipole Algorithm onto Mind Systems, *NASA/ICASE Workshop: Unstructured Parallel Scientific Computing*, MIT Press, Cambridge, MA (in press), 1992.

[22] R. Moenck, A. B. Borodin, Fast Modular Transforms via Division, *Conference Record, IEEE 13th Annual Symposium on Switching and Automata Theory*, 90–96, 1972.

[23] A. C. R. Newbery, Error Analysis for Polynomial Evaluation, *Math. Comp.*, 28, 127, 789–793, 1979.

[24] I. Newton, *Analysis per Quantitatem Series*, **10** London, 1711 (also see D. T. Whiteside, ed., *The Mathematical Papers of Isaac Newton*, 2, 222, Cambridge Univ. Press, 1968).

[25] A. M. Odlyzko, A. Schönhage, Fast Algorithm for Multiple Evaluations of the Riemann Zeta Function, *Transactions of the American Math. Soc.*, 309, 2, 1988.

[26] V. Y. Pan, Methods of Computing Values of Polynomials, *Russian Mathematical Surveys*, 21, 1, 105–136, 1966.

[27] V. Y. Pan, Sequential and Parallel Complexity of Approximate Evaluation of Polynomial Zeros, *Computers and Math. (with Applications)*, 14, 591–622, 1987.

[28] V. Y. Pan, Fast Evalulation and Interpolation at the Chebyshev Set of Points, *Applied Math. Letters*, 2, 3, 255–258, 1989.

[29] V. Y. Pan, On Computations with Dense Structured Matrices, *Mathematics of Computation*, 55, 191, 179-190, 1990.

[30] V. Y. Pan, Parallel Least-Squares Solution of General and Toeplitz-like Linear Systems, *Proc. 2nd Ann.ACM Symp. on Parallel Algorithms and Architecture*, 244-253, 1990.

[31] V. Y. Pan, Complexity of Computations with Matrices and Polynomials, *SIAM Rev.*, 34, 2, 225–262, 1992.

[32] V. Y. Pan, Approximate Evaluation of a Polynomial on a Set of Real Points, Techn. Report, *International Computer Science Institute, Berkeley, CA*, 1992.

[33] V. Pan, E. Landowne, A. Sadikou, Polynomial Division with a Remainder by Means of Evaluation and Interpolation, *Proc. of the 3rd Ann. IEEE Symp. on Parallel and Distributed Computing*, 212–217, 1991, and to appear in *Information Processing Letters.*

[34] V. Pan, A. Sadikou, E. Landowne, O. Tiga, A New Approach to Fast Polynomial Interpolation and Multipoint Evaluation, submitted to *Computers and Math. (with Applications).*

[35] J. H. Reif, S. R. Tate, N-body Simulation I: Potential Field Evaluation, Technical Report, *Duke University, Department of Computer Science*, 1992.

[36] V. Rokhlin, Rapid Solution of Integral Equations of Classical Potential Theory, *J.of Comput. Physics*, 60, 187–207, 1985.

[37] V. Rokhlin, A Fast Algorithm for the Discrete Laplace transformation, *J. of Complexity*, 4, 12–32, 1988.

[38] A. Schönhage, The Fundamental Theorem of Algebra in Terms of Computational Complexity, unpublished manuscript, 1982.

[39] V. Strassen, Die Berechnungskomplexität von elementarysymmetrischen Funktionen und von Interpolationskoeffizienten, *Numerische Math.*, 20, 3, 238–257, 1973.

[40] W. Werner, Polynomial Interpolation: Lagrange versus Newton, *Math. of Computation*, 43, 167, 205–217, 1984.

Processor-Efficient Parallel Solution of Linear Systems II The Positive Characteristic and Singular Cases*

(Extended Abstract)

Erich Kaltofen[1] and *Victor Pan*[2]

[1]Department of Computer Science, Rensselaer Polytechnic Institute
Troy, New York 12180-3590; Inter-Net: `kaltofen@cs.rpi.edu`
[2]Department of Mathematics and Computer Science
Lehman College, City University of New York
Bronx, New York 10468; Inter-Net: `vpan@lcvax.bitnet`

ABSTRACT. We show that over any field, the solution set to a system of n linear equations in n unknowns can be computed in parallel with randomization simultaneously in poly-logarithmic time in n and with only as many processors as are utilized to multiply two $n \times n$ matrices. A time unit represents an arithmetic operation in the field. For singular systems our parallel timings are asymptotically as fast as those for non-singular systems, due to our avoidance of binary search in the matrix rank problem, except when the field has small positive characteristic; in that case, binary search is avoided at a somewhat higher processor count measure.

1. Introduction

Processor-efficient parallel algorithms have been constructed in (Kaltofen and Pan 1991) for the problems of solving a non-singular linear system, computing the determinant of a matrix, and inverting a non-singular matrix; specifically, for an n-dimensional input the algorithms solve the designated problem in $O((\log n)^2)$ time using as many processors as are asymptotically required by the n-dimensional matrix multiplication problem (see Karp and Ramachandran 1990 for the notion of a processor-efficient parallel algorithm). Each processor performs addition, subtraction, multiplication, and division over the field of entries; division by zero is avoided for non-singular inputs by randomization. Our solution utilizes the Le Verrier (1840)/ Csanky (1976) algorithm (see also Preparata and Sarwate 1978 and Galil and Pan 1989) and is thus invalid for fields of small positive characteristic, in which case we have presented an n^3-processor algorithm, based on the Berkowitz (1984)/Chistov (1985) approach.

In §2 we shall show how to overcome that restriction. Specifically, if the field of entries, denoted by K, is of characteristic $1 < p \leq n$, we give processor-efficient Las Vegas randomized algorithms that compute the solution of an n-dimensional non-singular linear system, the determinant of a matrix, and the inverse of a non-singular matrix in parallel time at most $O((\log n)^3(\log\log n)/(\log p))$. Our algorithm picks for sufficiently large fields uniformly $O(n)$ random elements from a subset $S \subset \mathsf{K}$, and then reports failure with probability $O(n^2/\text{card}(S))$. In that case, the parallel time is also asymptotically reduced by a factor $\log\log n$. If K is a small finite field, we need to work in a Galois extension and therefore asymptotically require a multiple of at most $\log n$ more random elements.

A second contribution focuses on the problem of solving a singular system. In (Kaltofen and Pan 1991) we have obtained a processor-efficient Las Vegas randomized parallel algorithm in the case $p = 0$ or $p > n$. However, our solution there required asymptotically more time, namely $O((\log n)^3)$. The extra $\log(n)$ factor was introduced by performing binary search in order to determine the rank of the system, which until now seems to have been the only way to accomplish processor-efficiency. In §3 we shall show how to compute the rank of an $n \times n$ matrix directly, i.e., in random $O((\log n)^2)$ time without utilizing more processors. If binary search is to be avoided for fields of characteristic $1 < p < n$, our processor count is currently $O(n^3 \log n \, \log\log n)$.

Our solutions are facilitated by several innovations in the design of parallel linear algebra algorithms, and draw from recent developments on a diversity of topics. The key underpinnings of the results in (Kaltofen and Pan 1991) are the coordinate recurrence method for solving sparse linear systems over

*This material is based on work supported in part by the National Science Foundation under Grant No. CCR-90-06077 and under Grant No. CDA-88-05910 (first author), and under Grant No. CCR-90-20690 and by the PSC CUNY Awards #661340 and #662478 (second author).

0-8186-2900-2/92 $3.00 © 1992 IEEE

arbitrary fields by Wiedemann (1986) and parameterized Newton iteration for the inversion of the matrix associated with the characteristic polynomial of a Toeplitz matrix (Pan 1990). The latter parallel algorithm explores the well-known formula for the inverse of a Toeplitz matrix by Gohberg and Semencul (1972) (see also Trench 1964). A far-reaching generalization of the Trench/Gohberg&Semencul approach is the theory of the displacement rank of a matrix by Kailath et al. (1979) and the corresponding parallel algorithms by Pan (1990) and Bini and Pan (1992). Although both our small positive characteristic and our rank results can rely on these advances, several additional innovations come to bear on our solutions.

Our key idea in making linear system solving over a field of small positive characteristic p processor-efficient is that those Newton identities in Le Verrier's linear system for the coefficients of a characteristic polynomial that turn useless for such characteristic p can be replaced by additional linear equations obtained from the coordinate recurrences. Le Verrier's system can then be reduced to a new linear system of dimension $\lfloor n/p \rfloor$, which we may solve recursively. We call our technique "recursive parallel triangulation," since the recurring size-reduction of the intermediately arising linear systems is based on block-elimination by triangular matrices.

Our fast rank algorithm first uses the reduction by Kaltofen and Saunders (1991) of the rank determination of a general matrix to that of a certain Toeplitz matrix. The parallel solution of the latter problem is then based on Mulmuley's (1985) method. Mulmuley's algorithm, as given, multiplies the arising Toeplitz matrix by a certain diagonal matrix, which does not keep the displacement rank constant; we would have no means of computing in parallel the characteristic polynomial of a such perturbed matrix, which is needed by that algorithm, even with as many processors as are used by general matrix multiplication. We by-pass this difficulty by switching to the corresponding Hankel matrix and by modifying the perturbation such that the Hankel structure is preserved. Finally, the characteristic polynomial of the perturbed matrix can be computed in parallel with few processors by the algorithms for matrices of small displacement rank cited above.

The number of arithmetic processors used by our algorithms depends both on processor count of $n \times n$ parallel matrix multiplication and the processor count of computing in parallel the characteristic polynomial of a $n \times n$ Toeplitz or Hankel matrix. In light of the possibility that the former is asymptotically smaller than the latter, we shall introduce as our processor count measure

$$M^*(n) := \max\{M(n) \log n,\ n^2 \log n \ \mathrm{loglog}\, n\},$$

where the first of the arguments to the max-operator corresponds to the processor complexity $M(n)$ of parallel matrix multiplication; at this time we have $M(n) = n^{\omega}$ with $\omega < 2.3755$ (Coppersmith and Winograd 1990). Note that we restrict each processor to a constant number of arithmetic operations; without this restriction $M^*(n)$ can be reduced by $\log n$ factors. It should also be noted that our solutions use matrix multiplication as a black-box. Therefore, the processor count and especially the constant in the big-O estimate is directly related to the particular matrix multiplication algorithm used.

The time measures of our algorithms are for sufficiently large fields of small positive characteristic p asymptotically slower by a factor of $\log_p n$. As said above, for fields of small cardinality we work in sufficiently large Galois extensions, the purpose being the guarantee of a positive success probability of our randomizations. This introduces a further slow-down in terms of base field arithmetic but does not increase the processor count. Finally, in case $1 < p < n$ an additional $\log n$ factor is introduced by the binary search for the rank. Therefore, we shall introduce the multiplier function

$$\gamma_{\mathsf{K}}(n,p) := \begin{cases} 1 \quad \text{for } p = 0 \text{ or } p \geq n, \\ \lceil (\log n)^2/(\log p) \rceil \\ \qquad\qquad \text{for } 1 < p < n \text{ and } \mathrm{card}(\mathsf{K}) \geq n, \\ \lceil (\log n)^3/(\log p\ \log(\mathrm{card}\,\mathsf{K})) \rceil \\ \qquad\qquad\qquad\qquad \text{for } \mathrm{card}(\mathsf{K}) < n, \end{cases}$$

which becomes universal for any field. By $\mathrm{card}(\mathsf{K})$ we shall denote the cardinality of the field K; note that in the last case, by carrying out the arithmetic in the Galois extension field of algebraic degree $d_{\mathsf{K}}(n) = O(\log_{\mathrm{card}\,\mathsf{K}} n)$ in parallel, we can improve the multiplier $\gamma_{\mathsf{K}}(n,p)$ to $\lceil \log_p n\ \log d_{\mathsf{K}}(n) \rceil$, but we then need to increase the number of processors by a factor of $d_{\mathsf{K}}(n)\ \mathrm{loglog}\, d_{\mathsf{K}}(n)$. In any case, the multiplier is no more than

$$\gamma_{\mathsf{K}}(n,p) = O((\log n)^3).$$

Our main result can now be stated as follows: a Las Vegas-randomized algorithm is constructed that in parallel time $O(\gamma_{\mathsf{K}}(n,p)\,(\log n)^2)$ using $M^*(n)$ many processors finds the rank of a matrix and the solution of a linear system, which in the singular case consists of both one specific solution vector and a basis for the right null space of the coefficient matrix. For non-singular systems over fields of characteristic $1 < p < n$

our parallel time is actually a factor of $\log n$ faster.

We shall not be very specific about the parallel model of computation for which these results hold, although a suitable parallel adaptation of the probabilistic algebraic random access machine defined formally in (Kaltofen 1988) yields the stated complexity measures. In (Kaltofen and Pan 1991) we used algebraic circuits, which for the rank problem need to be amended appropriately to account for the zero-tests (cf. von zur Gathen's (1986) arithmetic networks).

2. Recursive Parallel Triangulation

We shall presume a certain familiarity of the reader with our methods in (Kaltofen and Pan 1991) for the non-singular case over fields of characteristic $p = 0$ or $p > n$. We now discuss how one can salvage the case $2 \le p \le n$ in a processor efficient manner. The key and only place where our previous methods fail is in the Le Verrier/Csanky transition from

$$s_i := \mathrm{Trace}(T^i) = \lambda_1^i + \lambda_2^i + \cdots + \lambda_n^i, \quad 1 \le i \le n-1,$$

where $\lambda_1, \ldots, \lambda_n$ are all eigenvalues of a non-singular Toeplitz matrix T, to the coefficients of the characteristic polynomial of T,

$$\mathrm{Det}(\lambda I - T) =: \lambda^n - c_1\lambda^{n-1} - c_2\lambda^{n-2} - \cdots - c_{n-1}\lambda - c_n. \quad (1)$$

The Newton identities,

$$\begin{bmatrix} 1 & & & & 0 \\ s_1 & 2 & & & \\ s_2 & s_1 & \ddots & & \\ \vdots & & & & \\ s_{n-2} & \cdots & & n-1 & \\ s_{n-1} & s_{n-2} & \cdots & s_1 & n \end{bmatrix} \begin{bmatrix} c_1 \\ c_2 \\ c_3 \\ \vdots \\ c_{n-1} \\ c_n \end{bmatrix} = \begin{bmatrix} s_1 \\ s_2 \\ s_3 \\ \vdots \\ s_{n-1} \\ s_n \end{bmatrix} \quad (2)$$

lead to a triangular non-singular system for the c_i only if in the field of entries one can divide by $n!$. For fields of small positive characteristic it is in general impossible to determine the fundamental symmetric functions from the sums of powers.

Our solution hinges on the fact that we can find other linear equations for the unknown c_i. Let us suppose for a moment that the minimum polynomial of T is equal to the characteristic polynomial (1). Then by Wiedemann's (1986) theory of coordinate recurrences we have for the column vectors $u, v \in \mathsf{K}^n$ and for the field elements $\bar{a}_i := u^{\mathrm{tr}} T^i v$ that for all $j \ge 0$

$$c_n \bar{a}_j + c_{n-1}\bar{a}_{j+1} + \cdots + c_1 \bar{a}_{j+n-1} = \bar{a}_{j+n}. \quad (3)$$

If the entries in u and v are chosen randomly and uniformly from a sufficiently large subset of K, then with a high probability the first n equations in (3) form a non-singular system (Kaltofen and Pan 1991, remarks after Theorem 1).

For simplicity, we shall continue the argument for the case that the characteristic of K is $p = 2$. We remove all even numbered rows from (2), which have 0 on their diagonal position. We also reorder the columns such that the odd numbered columns precede the even numbered ones. Thus we obtain the first $\lceil n/2 \rceil$ rows of our new system,

$$[\, L_1 \mid L_2 \,] \left[\frac{c'}{c''} \right] = [\, s' \,], \quad \text{where}$$

$$L_1 := \begin{bmatrix} 1 & & & 0 \\ s_2 & 1 & & \\ s_4 & s_2 & 1 & \\ \vdots & & & \ddots \end{bmatrix}, \quad L_2 := \begin{bmatrix} 0 & & & 0 \\ s_1 & 0 & & \\ s_3 & s_1 & 0 & \\ \vdots & & & \ddots \end{bmatrix},$$

$$\text{and } c' := \begin{bmatrix} c_1 \\ c_3 \\ c_5 \\ \vdots \end{bmatrix}, \quad c'' := \begin{bmatrix} c_2 \\ c_4 \\ c_6 \\ \vdots \end{bmatrix}, \quad s' := \begin{bmatrix} s_1 \\ s_3 \\ s_5 \\ \vdots \end{bmatrix}.$$

Finally, after rearranging the columns in the system (3) appropriately as

$$[\, \bar{A}_1 \mid \bar{A}_2 \,] \left[\frac{c'}{c''} \right] = \bar{b}, \quad (4)$$

where $\bar{A}_1 \in \mathsf{K}^{n \times \lceil n/2 \rceil}$, $\bar{A}_2 \in \mathsf{K}^{n \times \lfloor n/2 \rfloor}$, and $\bar{b} \in \mathsf{K}^n$, we compress the system (4) to $\lfloor n/2 \rfloor$ equations by multiplying both the left-hand side coefficient matrix and the right-hand side vector by a $\lfloor n/2 \rfloor \times n$ matrix C whose entries are chosen randomly from a sufficiently large subset of K. This randomization guarantees that with a high probability the system

$$\left[\frac{L_1 \mid L_2}{C\bar{A}_1 \mid C\bar{A}_2} \right] \left[\frac{c'}{c''} \right] = \left[\frac{s'}{C\bar{b}} \right] \quad (5)$$

is non-singular. The heart of argument lies in the fact that in (4) there are $\lfloor n/2 \rfloor$ rows that are linearly independent of the rows in $[\, L_1 \mid L_2 \,]$, because (3) has by our assumption full rank. Thus there exists a specific matrix C that selects those rows, and hence a matrix

$\mathcal{C}$ with indeterminate elements also has the property that the corresponding determinant is non-zero, now as polynomial in the unknown entries of $\mathcal{C}$. By a lemma of Zippel (1979)/Schwartz (1980) a matrix with random elements chosen uniformly from a sufficiently large subset of K also has with high probability that property.

We now can proceed recursively. First, we eliminate the block $C\bar{A}_1$ by pre-multiplying (5) with

$$\left[\begin{array}{c|c} I_{\lceil n/2\rceil} & 0^{\lceil n/2\rceil\times\lfloor n/2\rfloor} \\ \hline -C\bar{A}_1L_1^{-1} & I_{\lfloor n/2\rfloor}\end{array}\right].$$

Since L_1 is Toeplitz and lower triangular, its inverse can be computed easily in $O((\log n)^2)$ time with $n^2 \times \log n \operatorname{loglog} n$ processors. This leads to a $\lfloor n/2\rfloor \times \lfloor n/2\rfloor$ non-singular system for c'' which we may solve by recursive application of the entire algorithm. Finally, we determine c' by back-substituting into the first row of blocks. The algorithm clearly has depth $O((\log n)^3)$, and it uses

$$P(n) \le M^*(n) + P(\lfloor n/2\rfloor), \quad \text{i.e., } O(M^*(n))$$

many processors; constant rescaling reduces the number of processors to $M^*(n)$. For characteristic $p > 2$ the recursion is on blocks of size $\lfloor n/p\rfloor$, hence the general slow-down in time is by the factor $\gamma_{\mathsf{K}}(n,p)$.

It is possible perform the needed compression by C with fewer random elements. Suppose we first eliminate $\bar{A}_1$ in (4) using L_1^{-1}:

$$\left[\begin{array}{c|c} I_{\lceil n/2\rceil} & 0^{\lceil n/2\rceil\times n} \\ \hline -\bar{A}_1L_1^{-1} & I_n\end{array}\right]\left[\begin{array}{c|c} L_1 & L_2 \\ \hline \bar{A}_1 & \bar{A}_2\end{array}\right] = \left[\begin{array}{c|c} L_1 & L_2 \\ \hline 0^{n\times\lceil n/2\rceil} & -\bar{A}_1L_1^{-1}L_2+\bar{A}_2\end{array}\right]$$

Then by (Kaltofen and Saunders 1991, Theorem 2) it suffices to pre-multiply the $n \times \lfloor n/2\rfloor$ matrix $-\bar{A}_1 \times L_1^{-1}L_2 + \bar{A}_2$ by a random $\lfloor n/2\rfloor \times n$ unit upper triangular Toeplitz matrix C and thereby obtain with high probability a $\lfloor n/2\rfloor \times \lfloor n/2\rfloor$ compressed matrix of full rank. Applying these transformations to the right-hand side vector of our system also, we have thus established the need of only $O(n)$ many random field elements for that phase of the construction. Note that all matrices involved in the smaller system have a special structure. Therefore, our recursive triangulation approach may also be applicable to the processor-efficient solution of structured systems, such as Toeplitz and Sylvester systems.

At last, we shall consider the case where the minimum polynomial of T is a proper divisor of the characteristic polynomial, in which case the first n equations in (3) are linearly dependent. The needed sub-problem in (Kaltofen and Pan 1991), namely the determination of the coefficients $\widetilde{c}_i$ of the characteristic polynomial of the matrix $\widetilde{A}$ (ibid. p. 185, bottom of the second column), is actually the computation of $T^{-1}b$ for a known vector b, which there is solved in a processor-efficient way via the coefficients of (1). However, we may instead work with

$$\widetilde{T} := VTW \quad \text{and} \quad \widetilde{b} := Vb,$$

where

$$V := \begin{bmatrix} 1 & v_2 & v_3 & \dots & v_n \\ & 1 & v_2 & \dots & v_{n-1} \\ & & 1 & \ddots & \vdots \\ & 0 & & \ddots & v_2 \\ & & & & 1 \end{bmatrix} \tag{6}$$

and

$$W := \begin{bmatrix} w_1 & & & & 0 \\ w_2 & w_1 & & & \\ w_3 & w_2 & w_1 & & \\ \vdots & & \ddots & \ddots & \\ w_n & w_{n-1} & \dots & w_2 & w_1 \end{bmatrix}, \tag{7}$$

because then $T^{-1}b = W(\widetilde{T}^{-1}\widetilde{b})$ can still be determined efficiently. If we choose the entries v_i and w_j randomly from a sufficiently large subset of K, then with high probability the minimum polynomial of $\widetilde{T}$ agrees with its characteristic polynomial. Furthermore, we may also compute for $1 \le i < n$ all $\operatorname{Trace}(\widetilde{T}^i)$ in the same asymptotic complexity measures as those we have for the original s_i. The proofs for these two claims are, however, quite involved. The argument for minimum = characteristic polynomial can be deduced from the perturbation theory developed in Wiedemann (1986) and Kaltofen and Saunders (1991), while the argument for computing the traces of the powers of the perturbed matrix follows from the parallel algorithms by Pan (1990) associated with the theory of matrices of fixed displacement rank by Kailath et al. (1979). The matrix $\widetilde{T}$, being a product of three Toeplitz matrices, has displacement rank at most 7.

We first prove that with high probability the minimum polynomial of $\widetilde{T}$ is its characteristic polynomial.

Proposition 1. *Let $M \in \mathsf{K}^{n\times n}$ be a non-singular matrix and let the entries $v_2,\dots,v_n$ of V in (6) and $w_1,\dots,w_n$ of W in (7) be randomly and uniformly selected from a subset $S \subset \mathsf{K}$. Then the minimum polynomial of $\widetilde{M} := VMW$ is equal to the characteristic polynomial of $\widetilde{M}$ with probability no less than $1 - 4n^2/\operatorname{card}(S)$.*

Proof. We follow the proof of Wiedemann (1986, Lemma in §V) and show that with high probability the characteristic polynomial of $\widetilde{M}$ is square-free. Let $\mathcal{V}$ and $\mathcal{W}$ be Toeplitz matrices of the form V and W, respectively, but with their entries being indeterminates. We first prove the square-freeness of the characteristic polynomial of $\mathcal{M} := \mathcal{V}M\mathcal{W}$ for such generic multiplier matrices, and then consider with what probability randomly chosen values for these indeterminates will preserve this condition. In order to prove the square-freeness of the generic case, we need the additional condition that all $i \times i$ sub-matrix blocks in the right upper corner of $\mathcal{V}M$, which we denote by $(\mathcal{V}M)_{i\urcorner}$, are non-singular. This condition follows from the proof of Theorem 2 in (Kaltofen and Saunders 1991):

Let $\mathcal{V}_{I,J}$ be the determinant of the submatrix of $\mathcal{V}$ formed by including only the rows contained in the set I and only the columns contained in the set J. It is shown there that for all $i = 1, \ldots, n$ the set of all polynomials

$$\{\mathcal{V}_{\{1,\ldots,i\},J} \mid \mathrm{card}(J) = i\}$$

is linearly independent over K. Furthermore, by the Cauchy-Binet formula,

$$(\mathcal{V}M)_{\{1,\ldots,i\},\{n-i+1,\ldots,n\}} = \sum_{\substack{J=\{j_1,\ldots,j_i\}\\ 1\le j_1<\cdots<j_i\le n}} \mathcal{V}_{\{1,\ldots,i\},J}\, M_{J,\{n-i+1,\ldots,n\}}. \quad (8)$$

Since M is non-singular, there exists a set of row indices J_0 such that $M_{J_0,\{n-i+1,\ldots,n\}} \neq 0$, hence the sum (8) of linearly independent polynomials also does not vanish.

The rest of the argument is by induction on n, as in Wiedemann's lemma. Consider the characteristic polynomial $\mathrm{Det}(\lambda I - \widetilde{\mathcal{M}})$ as a polynomial in λ with coefficients being polynomials in the variable entries $v_2, \ldots, w_n$ of $\mathcal{V}$ and $\mathcal{W}$. If we set $w_1 = 0$, this polynomial is equal to

$$\lambda\, \mathrm{Det}(\lambda I - (\mathcal{V}M)_{n-1\urcorner}\, \mathcal{W}_{\llcorner\, n-1}),$$

where $\mathcal{W}_{\llcorner\, n-1}$ is the $(n-1)\times(n-1)$ sub-matrix at the lower left of $\mathcal{W}$. Since $(\mathcal{V}M)_{n-1\urcorner}$ is non-singular, as was shown above, by induction hypothesis the characteristic polynomial of $(\mathcal{V}M)_{n-1\urcorner}\mathcal{W}_{\llcorner\, n-1}$ must be square-free; it is also not divisible by λ. Therefore, the characteristic polynomial of the genericly randomized matrix $\mathcal{V}M\mathcal{W}$ is square-free even for $w_1 = 0$, hence must be square-free for an indeterminate w_1.

It remains to estimate the probability of success. We appeal to the Zippel (1979)/Schwartz (1980) lemma and must therefore estimate the total degree of the discriminant in λ of $\mathrm{Det}(\lambda I - \widetilde{\mathcal{M}})$, which is a polynomial in the entries of $\mathcal{V}$ and $\mathcal{W}$. However, that total degree is certainly less than $4n^2$. ⊠

Wiedemann chooses a random diagonal matrix in place of our W of Lemma 1. That our choice of a Toeplitz matrix can be proven to work is somewhat fortunate, since otherwise we would not know how to compute the required $\mathrm{Trace}(\widetilde{T}^i)$ efficiently. The underlying reason is the fact that a Toeplitz matrix has fixed displacement rank, while for a random diagonal matrix the displacement rank is n. A similar problem has to be overcome in §3 in regard to Mulmuley's randomization. We now shall explain the theory of Toeplitz-like matrices in some more detail.

We consider $n \times n$ matrices; define the lower-shift matrix

$$Z := \begin{bmatrix} 0 & & & & \\ 1 & 0 & & & 0 \\ & 1 & \ddots & & \\ & & \ddots & & \\ 0 & & & 1 & 0 \end{bmatrix}$$

and define the matrix shift operators

$$\downarrow\! A := ZA, \quad \Lsh\! A := AZ, \quad \text{and} \quad \Rsh\! A := AZ^{\mathrm{tr}}.$$

The matrix $\downarrow\! A$ is equal to a A after being shifted down be one row, filling the first row by zeros, and the matrices $\Lsh\! A$ and $\Rsh\! A$ are equal to A after being shifted to the left/right by one column, filling the last/first column by zeros. Following Kailath et al. (1979) we define

$$\phi_+(A) := A - \downarrow\!(\Rsh\! A) = A - Z\,A\,Z^{\mathrm{tr}}$$

and

$$\alpha_+(A) := \mathrm{rank}\,\phi_+(A),$$

the latter being the displacement rank of A. The fundamental property is that given 2α column vectors $y_1, \ldots, y_\alpha$ and $z_1, \ldots, z_\alpha$ the functional equation in the matrix X,

$$X - \downarrow\!(\Rsh X) = \sum_{j=1}^{\alpha} y_j z_j^{\mathrm{tr}} \quad (9)$$

has the unique solution

$$X = \sum_{j=1}^{\alpha} L[\![y_j]\!]\, U[\![z_j^{\mathrm{tr}}]\!], \quad (10)$$

where $L[\![y]\!]$ denotes a lower-triangular Toeplitz matrix whose first column is y and $U[\![z^{\mathrm{tr}}]\!]$ denotes an upper triangular Toeplitz matrix whose first row is z^{tr}. Therefore a matrix of displacement rank α is a sum of α

products of lower and upper triangular Toeplitz matrices. We shall call

$$Y = \sum_{j=1}^{\alpha} y_j z_j^{\mathrm{tr}} = [\, y_1 \mid y_2 \mid \dots \mid y_\alpha \,] \begin{bmatrix} z_1^{\mathrm{tr}} \\ \hline z_2^{\mathrm{tr}} \\ \hline \vdots \\ \hline z_\alpha^{\mathrm{tr}} \end{bmatrix} \qquad (11)$$

the *generators* of the resulting $n \times n$ matrix Y, which is in the above case the displaced matrix $\phi_+(X)$; the representation (10) we shall call the *Gohberg-Semencul representation* for X. That representation requires only the storage of $O(\alpha n)$ field elements. Clearly, one may derive a generator (11) for Y by choosing the vectors y_j to be the linearly independent columns of Y, and the entries in each column of the right factor matrix with the rows z_j^{tr} to be the linear combination that yields the corresponding column of Y.

We wish to argue that matrices of fixed displacement rank are closed under matirx multiplication. To show this, we introduce the alternate displacement operator (see Pan 1990)

$$\phi^+(A) := \,\upharpoonleft\! A - \downarrow\! A = AZ - ZA$$

and

$$\alpha^+(A) := \operatorname{rank} \phi^+(A).$$

We then have $\alpha_+(A) \le \alpha^+(A) + 1$, in fact we can find the generators for $\phi_+(A)$ from the generators for $\phi^+(A)$, since

$$\phi_+(A) = \phi^+(A) Z^{\mathrm{tr}} + (A e_1) e_1^{\mathrm{tr}}, \qquad (12)$$

where $e_1 := [1 \;\; 0 \;\; \dots \;\; 0]^{\mathrm{tr}}$. Note that the vectors z_j^{tr} in (11) for $\phi^+(A)$ are shifted to the right by post-multiplication by Z^{tr}. Quite similarly we can easily obtain the inequality

$$\alpha^+(AB) \le \alpha^+(A) + \alpha^+(B),$$

namely from

$$\phi^+(AB) = A\phi^+(B) + \phi^+(A)B.$$

The vectors y_j generating $\phi^+(B)$ are pre-multiplied by A, and the vectors z_j are post-multiplied by B. Note that this approach allows us to efficiently compute the Gohberg-Semencul representation (10) for $X = \widetilde{T} = VTW$. Since $\alpha^+(V) = \alpha^+(T) = \alpha^+(W) = 2$, we we will compute $6 = ((2+2)+2)$ generators (11) for $\phi^+(\widetilde{T})$ and thus 7 for $\phi_+(\widetilde{T})$.

Finally, we have the following theorem at our disposal:

Proposition 2 (Pan 1990, Proposition 3.1). *Let $\widetilde{T}$ be given in Gohberg-Semencul representation with a fixed displacement rank, i.e., with a fixed number of LU-products. Then the traces*

$$s_i = \operatorname{Trace}(\widetilde{T}^i) \quad \textit{for all } i = 2, \dots, n$$

can be computed in parallel in $O((\log n)^2)$ time using $n^2 \log n \operatorname{loglog} n$ processors.

There is a very elegant proof for this important fact, due to Dario Bini, which we shall briefly sketch. Pan's (1990) approach computes a Gohberg-Semencul representation for

$$X_i := I + \lambda\widetilde{T} + \dots + \lambda^{2^i - 1}\widetilde{T}^{2^i - 1} \equiv (I - \lambda\widetilde{T})^{-1} \pmod{\lambda^{2^i}}$$

(c.f. §3 in Kaltofen and Pan 1991). This is done by "lifting" the representation of X_i to the squared modulus using Newton iteration, namely

$$X_{i+1} = X_i(2I - (I - \lambda\widetilde{T})X_i). \qquad (13)$$

Bini's method is based on the identity

$$\begin{aligned} \phi^+(A^{-1}) &= A^{-1}Z - ZA^{-1} \\ &= -A^{-1}(AZ - ZA)A^{-1} \\ &= -A^{-1}\phi^+(A)A^{-1}. \end{aligned}$$

Then by (13)

$$\phi^+(X_{i+1}) = X_{i+1}\, \phi^+(I - \lambda\widetilde{T})\, X_{i+1} \pmod{\lambda^{2^{i+1}}}.$$

Hence the generators y_j in the representation (11) for $I - \lambda\widetilde{T}$ must be pre-multiplied by $X_i(2I - (I - \lambda\widetilde{T})X_i)$ and the generators z_j must be post-multiplied by the same matrix, all modulo $\lambda^{2^{i+1}}$. However, a Gohberg-Semencul representation for X_i makes this process as efficient as is needed when using fast polynomial multiplication for Toeplitz matrix times vector products. Finally, the Gohberg-Semencul representation (10) for X_{i+1} can be deduced from the generators (11) for $\phi^+(X_{i+1})$ and the conversion mechanism (12). In our situation there will be nine LU-products under the sum (seven for $\lambda\widetilde{T}$, one for I, and one produced by the conversion to ϕ_+).

Note that this approach does not require any generalization of the Gohberg-Semencul formula for $(I - \lambda\widetilde{T})^{-1}$, and is based solely on the solution (10) of the functional equation (9). Furthermore, the product formula for $\alpha^+(AB)$ is valid over any field, unlike Chun's et al. (1987, Lemma 3) formula for $\alpha_+(AB)$, where a division by 2 is performed.

We conclude this section by stating the main theorem.

Theorem 1. *Given a non-singular matrix* $A \in \mathsf{K}^{n\times n}$ *and a vector* $b \in \mathsf{K}^n$, *where* K *is a field of characteristic* $1 < p < n$, *a vector* $x \in \mathsf{K}^n$ *with* $Ax = b$ *can be computed (on a randomized algebraic PRAM) in*

$$O(\gamma_{\mathsf{K}}(n,p)\log n) \text{ time with } M^*(n) \text{ processors.}$$

In the case where $\operatorname{card}(\mathsf{K}) \geq n$, *the algorithm uniformly chooses* $O(n)$ *many random elements from a subset* $S \subset \mathsf{K}$ *and with probability no more than* $O(n^2/\operatorname{card}(S))$ *reports "failure." In the case where* $\operatorname{card}(\mathsf{K}) < n$, *the algorithm uniformly chooses* $O(n(\log n)/(\log \operatorname{card}\mathsf{K}))$ *many field elements and with probability no more than* $1/n^{O(1)}$ *reports "failure."*

3. Parallel Rank Computations

The results in Borodin et al. (1982) imply that a processor-efficient randomized parallel algorithm for the solution of singular linear systems can be reduced probabilistically to the problem of inverting a non-singular matrix and to the problem of determining the rank of a matrix that has the added property that all its leading principal sub-matrices of dimension no larger than its rank are non-singular. Their method picks random non-singular matrices $V, W \in \mathsf{K}^{n\times n}$ — by (Kaltofen and Saunders 1991, Theorem 2) these matrices may even be of unit upper and lower triangular Toeplitz form — and computes for the singular coefficient matrix $A \in \mathsf{K}^{n\times n}$ the product matrix $\widetilde{A} := VAW$, which can be shown to have with a certain probability non-singular $i\times i$ leading principal sub-matrices $\widetilde{A}_{\ulcorner i}$, where $i \leq r$ and $r := \operatorname{rank} A$. Then

$$\widetilde{A}E = \left[\begin{array}{c|c} \widetilde{A}_{\ulcorner r} & 0^{r\times(n-r)} \\ \hline A' & 0^{(n-r)\times(n-r)} \end{array}\right]$$

for

$$\widetilde{A} =: \left[\begin{array}{c|c} \widetilde{A}_{\ulcorner r} & B \\ \hline A' & A'' \end{array}\right] \text{ and } E := \left[\begin{array}{c|c} I_r & -\widetilde{A}_{\ulcorner r}^{-1}B \\ \hline 0^{(n-r)\times r} & I_{n-r} \end{array}\right].$$

Hence the right null space of A is spanned by the columns of

$$WE\left[\begin{array}{c} 0^{r\times(n-r)} \\ \hline I_{n-r} \end{array}\right],$$

while for a vector b such that $Ax = b$ is solvable one gets

$$AWE\left[\begin{array}{c} \widetilde{A}_{\ulcorner r}^{-1}(Vb)_{\ulcorner r \urcorner} \\ \hline 0^{n-r} \end{array}\right] = b,$$

where $(Vb)_{\ulcorner r \urcorner}$ is the vector formed by the first r enties of Vb. We mention these standard linear algebra formulas since with them the probabilistically determined rank and the solvability of $Ax = b$ can be certified. Therefore the randomized method is of the Las Vegas kind.

Using a construction by Baur and Strassen (1983) (see also Linnainmaa 1976), it is shown in (Kaltofen and Pan 1991) that the determinant and thus by (Kaltofen and Singer 1991) also the inverse of a non-singular matrix can be computed in a randomized, parallel, and processor-efficient fashion. The results of §2 extend to the determinant and inverse computation. While for non-singular matrices the recursive triangulation algorithm is Las Vegas, the method cannot produce a proof that a matrix is singular, i.e., that its determinant is equal to zero. The reason for this is that for a singular matrix, the additional linear equations (4) may never be sufficient to yield a compressed non-singular system for the coefficients of (1). An example for this is $T = 0$. Therefore, we obtain a proof for the singularity of a matrix only after having probabilistically computed its rank.

It remains to show how to determine the rank of $\widetilde{A}$. At the cost of slowing the parallel time asymptotically by a factor of $\log n$, one may perform a (Monte Carlo) binary search for the largest non-singular leading principal sub-matrix. We now give a method that avoids this slow-down without utilizing asymptotically more processors, provided the characteristic of the field K is 0 or $>n$. In (Kaltofen and Saunders 1991, Lemma 2) the problem of determining the rank of a singular $\widetilde{A}$ is probabilistically reduced to the problem of determining the rank of a Toeplitz matrix. In particular, it is shown there that if the entries in the diagonal matrix D are selected randomly from a sufficiently large set, then with a high probability the degree of the minimum polynomial $f^{\widetilde{A}D}(\lambda)$ of $\widetilde{A}D$ is equal to $\operatorname{rank}(\widetilde{A})+1$. By the Wiedemann (1986) coordinate recurrence technique, for random column vectors u and v the Toeplitz matrix

$$T := \begin{bmatrix} a_{n-1} & a_{n-2} & \cdots & a_1 & a_0 \\ a_n & a_{n-1} & \cdots & a_2 & a_1 \\ \vdots & a_n & \ddots & \vdots & a_2 \\ & \vdots & & & \vdots \\ a_{2n-3} & & & a_{n-1} & \\ a_{2n-2} & a_{2n-3} & \cdots & a_n & a_{n-1} \end{bmatrix} \qquad (14)$$

with the entries $a_i = u^{\mathrm{tr}}\widetilde{A}^i v$ has with a high probability the rank equal to $\deg(f^{\widetilde{A}D})$. We probabilistically find the rank of T by appealing to an idea of Mulmuley (1987). Consider the n-dimensional anti-diagonal unit matrix

$$J := \begin{bmatrix} 0 & & 1 \\ & 1 & \\ & \cdot^{\cdot^{\cdot}} & 0 \\ 1 & & \end{bmatrix};$$

the matrix $H := TJ$ is Hankel, i.e., on each anti-diagonal there appears a single element. In particular, a Hankel matrix is symmetric. Furthermore, for the diagonal matrix

$$X := \begin{bmatrix} 1 & & & & 0 \\ & x & & & \\ & & x^2 & & \\ & & & \ddots & \\ 0 & & & & x^{n-1} \end{bmatrix},$$

the matrix $\widetilde{H} = XHX$ is also Hankel. Note that XTX is not Toeplitz, which is the reason for switching to the Hankel form. It follows by Mulmuley's (1987) arguments that, with the possible exception of at most n^2 field elements x, the multiplicity of λ in the characteristic polynomial $\mathrm{Det}(\lambda I - \widetilde{H})$ is equal to $n - \mathrm{rank}(H)$. The key property in his proof (loc. cit., Proof of Lemma 1) is the condition that for an indeterminate x

$$\mathrm{rank}(\widetilde{H}\,\widetilde{H}) = \mathrm{rank}(\widetilde{H}).$$

It is shown there that $\mathrm{rank}(HXH) = \mathrm{rank}\,H$, hence also $\mathrm{rank}(HX^2H) = \mathrm{rank}(H)$, which by pre- and post-multiplying with the non-singular matrix X yields the needed condition. Note that the trailing coefficient of the characteristic polynomial of $\widetilde{H}$ has, as a polynomial in x, degree no more than n^2.

Therefore, we shall compute the characteristic polynomial of the Hankel matrix $\widetilde{H}$. Kailath et al. (1979, Footnote on p. 405) give a displacement operator that for fields of characteristic 0 or $>n$ leads to a $O((\log n)^2)$-time and $n^2(\log\log n)/(\log n)$-processors parallel algorithm (see also Bini 1983, Bini and Pan 1992). We shall present a direct method, which is also based on parallel algorithms for matrices with fixed displacement rank (see §2). Making some simplifying assumptions first, we shall sketch the entire method now. The key algorithm computes for a Toeplitz matrix $\widetilde{T}$ two lower triangular Toeplitz matrices $L_1(\lambda), L_2(\lambda)$ over $\mathsf{K}[\lambda]$ and two upper triangular Toeplitz matrices $U_1(\lambda), U_2(\lambda)$ such that

$$I + \lambda\widetilde{T} + \lambda^2\widetilde{T}^2 + \cdots + \lambda^{n-1}\widetilde{T}^{n-1} \equiv L_1(\lambda)U_1(\lambda) + L_2(\lambda)U_2(\lambda) \pmod{\lambda^n}. \quad (15)$$

This is the Gohberg-Semencul representation (10) of $(I - \lambda\widetilde{T})^{-1} \bmod \lambda^n$, as was explained following Proposition 2 in §2; just two LU-products are obtained by using the original Gohberg-Semencul formula (see Pan 1990 or Kaltofen and Pan (1991), §3), but this is not critical here. The trace of the right-hand-side matrix expression in (15) can now be computed in parallel with no more than $n^2 \log\log(n)/\log(n)$ processors; for instance, we have

$$\mathrm{Trace}\left(\begin{bmatrix} w_1 & & & & 0 \\ w_2 & w_1 & & & \\ w_3 & w_2 & w_1 & & \\ \vdots & & \ddots & \ddots & \\ w_n & w_{n-1} & \ldots & w_2 & w_1 \end{bmatrix} \times \begin{bmatrix} v_1 & v_2 & v_3 & \ldots & v_n \\ & v_1 & v_2 & & v_{n-1} \\ & & \ddots & \ddots & \vdots \\ & 0 & & v_1 & v_2 \\ & & & & v_1 \end{bmatrix} \right)$$
$$= nw_1v_1 + (n-1)w_2v_2 + \cdots + w_nv_n. \quad (16)$$

The coefficient of λ^i in the trace of (15) is then $s_i = \mathrm{Trace}(\widetilde{T}^i)$. Suppose for a moment that $\widetilde{T} = \widetilde{H}J$ would be also symmetric. Then $J\widetilde{T}J = \widetilde{T}$, hence for $i \geq 1$,

$$\widetilde{H}^{2i} = (\widetilde{T}J)^{2i} = \widetilde{T}^{2i}, \quad \widetilde{H}^{2i+1} = \widetilde{T}^{2i+1}J.$$

In this special case we therefore have

$$\mathrm{Trace}(\widetilde{H}^{2i}) = s_{2i}$$

and

$$\mathrm{Trace}(\widetilde{H}^{2i+1}) = \text{anti-Trace}(\widetilde{T}^{2i+1}),$$

with the anti-trace of a square matrix being the sum of all elements on the main anti-diagonal. The needed anti-traces can be computed from (15) like the traces; e.g., the anti-trace of the product-matrix in (16) is for odd n

$$\sum_{i=1}^{\lceil n/2 \rceil} w_{2i-1}(v_1 + v_3 + \cdots + v_{n+2-2i}) + \sum_{i=1}^{\lfloor n/2 \rfloor} w_{2i}(v_2 + v_4 + \cdots + v_{n+1-2i}),$$

where all the partial sums of the v_j's can be found by parallel prefix (Ladner and Fischer 1980). Thus we can compute $\mathrm{Trace}(\widetilde{H}^i)$ for all $1 \leq i < n$, from which for a field K of characteristic 0 or $>n$ we may determine the coefficients of the characteristic polynomial $\mathrm{Det}(\lambda I - \widetilde{H})$ by solving the Newton identities (13).

However, $\widetilde{H}$ is most likely not anti-symmetric. Therefore, we consider the "anti-symmetrized" block matrix

$$\underbrace{\left[\begin{array}{c|c} \widetilde{H} & 0^{n\times n} \\ \hline 0^{n\times n} & J\widetilde{H}J \end{array}\right]}_{\widetilde{H}_{\boxplus}} = \underbrace{\left[\begin{array}{c|c} 0^{n\times n} & \widetilde{H}J \\ \hline J\widetilde{H} & 0^{n\times n} \end{array}\right]}_{\widetilde{T}_{\boxplus}} \times \underbrace{\left[\begin{array}{c|c} 0^{n\times n} & J \\ \hline J & 0^{n\times n} \end{array}\right]}_{J_{2n}}$$

in place of $\widetilde{H}$ and $\widetilde{T}$. Then

$$\mathrm{Det}(\lambda I_{2n} - \widetilde{H}_{\boxplus}) = (\mathrm{Det}(\lambda I_n - \widetilde{H}))^2$$

and all $\mathrm{Trace}(\widetilde{H}^i_{\boxplus})$ can be determined from the traces and anti-traces of $\widetilde{T}_{\boxplus}$. Propostion 2 now allows the same approach for that block matrix as was discussed above. In fact $\alpha^+(\widetilde{T}_{\boxplus}) = 4$, thus one can compute five lower triangular Toeplitz matrices $L_j(\lambda)$ and five upper triangular Toeplitz matrices $U_j(\lambda)$ over $\mathsf{K}[\lambda]$ such that

$$I + \lambda\widetilde{T}_{\boxplus} + \lambda^2\widetilde{T}^2_{\boxplus} + \cdots + \lambda^{n-1}\widetilde{T}^{n-1}_{\boxplus} \equiv \sum_{j=1}^{5} L_j(\lambda)U_j(\lambda) \pmod{\lambda^n}.$$

In summary, we have the following theorem.

Theorem 2. *Given $A \in \mathsf{K}^{n\times n}$ and $b \in \mathsf{K}^n$, where K is a field of characteristic $p = 0$ or $p \geq n$, vectors $x_0, \ldots, x_{n-r} \in \mathsf{K}^n$ that determine the solution manifold*

$$A(x_0 + \mathsf{K}x_1 + \cdots + \mathsf{K}x_{n-r}) = \{b\},$$

can be computed (on a randomized algebraic PRAM) in

$$O((\log n)^2) \text{ time with } M^*(n) \text{ processors.}$$

In case the system $Ax = b$ is unsolvable the algorithm returns $\emptyset$. The algorithm uniformly chooses $O(n)$ random elements in $S \subset \mathsf{K}$, and with probability no more than $O(n^2/\mathrm{card}(S))$ reports "failure."

Finally, we comment on the case where the characteristic p of K is $1 < p < n$. For any Hankel matrix H, with

$$n^3 \log n \ \mathrm{loglog}\, n \text{ many processors}$$

we even know how to compute deterministically over any field K and in

$$O((\log n)^2) \text{ parallel time}$$

all characteristic polynomials

$$\mathrm{Det}(\lambda I_i - H_{\ulcorner i}), \quad i = 1, \ldots, n.$$

Hence, if we give ourselves slightly more processors, we can show how to determine the rank of matrices over fields of small positive characteristic in parallel time $O(\gamma_K(n,p)/(\log_p n) \log n)$, which surpasses, e.g., our current processor-efficient solution for a Galois field with 2 elements by a factor of $(\log n)^2$. We make us of an identity by Chistov (1985), namely that for any $n \times n$ matrix M

$$\frac{1}{\mathrm{Det}(I_i - \lambda M_{\ulcorner i})} \equiv \prod_{j=1}^{i} \sum_{k=0}^{n} (M^k_{\ulcorner j})[j,j]\, \lambda^k \pmod{\lambda^{n+1}}.$$

Thus, if we can find for $M = H$ the entries in row and column j of the k-th power of $H_{\ulcorner j}$, the elements $(H^k_{\ulcorner j})[j,j]$ in the above formula, we can complete the computation by parallel prefix polynomial multiplication and power series inversion. But, by the above described algorithms, we can find for any Hankle matrix $\widetilde{H}$ the Gohberg-Semencul representation for

$$I + \lambda\widetilde{T}_{\boxplus} + \cdots + \lambda^n\widetilde{T}^n_{\boxplus},$$

that in $O((\log n)^2)$ parallel time and with $n^2 \log n \times \mathrm{loglog}\, n$ many processors. By the symmetry of $\widetilde{T}_{\boxplus}$ we have

$$\widetilde{H}^{2k}_{\boxplus} = \widetilde{T}^{2k}_{\boxplus}, \quad \widetilde{H}^{2k+1}_{\boxplus} = \widetilde{T}^{2k+1}_{\boxplus} J_{2n},$$

hence we can find from the Gohberg-Semencul representation, similarly to the trace, all $(\widetilde{H}^k_{\boxplus})[n,n] = (\widetilde{H}^k)[n,n]$. The stated processor count now follows by using that approach for each of the Hankel matrices $\widetilde{H} = H_{\ulcorner i}$.

Literature Cited

Baur, W. and Strassen, V., "The complexity of partial derivatives," *Theoretical Comp. Sci.* **22**, pp. 317–330 (1983).

Berkowitz, S. J., "On computing the determinant in small parallel time using a small number of processors," *Inform. Process. Letters* **18**, pp. 147–150 (1984).

Bini, D., "On a class of matrices related to Toeplitz matrices," *Tech. Report.* **83-5**, Comput. Sci. Dept., State Univ. New York, Albany, N. Y., 1983.

Bini, D., Gemignani, L., and Pan, V., "Improved parallel computations with matrices and polynomials," in *Proc. ICALP 91*, Springer Lect. Notes Comput. Sci. **510**, edited by J. Leach Albert, B. Monien, and E. Rodríguez Artalejo; pp. 520–531, 1991.

Bini, D. and Pan, V., *Numerical and Algebraic Computations with Matrices and Polynomials*; Lecture Notes in Theor. Comput. Sci., edited by R. V. Book; Birkhäuser Boston, Inc., 1992. To appear.

Borodin, A., von zur Gathen, J., and Hopcroft, J. E., "Fast parallel matrix and GCD computations," *Inf. Control* **52**, pp. 241–256 (1982).

Chistov, A. L., "Fast parallel calculation of the rank

of matrices over a field of arbitrary characteristic," *Proc. FCT '85, Springer Lec. Notes Comp. Sci.* **199**, pp. 63–69 (1985).

Chun, J., Kailath, T., and Lev-Ari, H., "Fast parallel algorithms for QR and triangular factorizations," *SIAM J. Sci. Stat. Comput.* **8/6**, pp. 899–913 (1987).

Coppersmith, D. and Winograd, S., "Matrix multiplication via arithmetic progressions," *J. Symbolic Comput.* **9/3**, pp. 251–280 (1990).

Csanky, L., "Fast parallel matrix inversion algorithms," *SIAM J. Comput.* **5/4**, pp. 618–623 (1976).

Galil, Z. and Pan, V., "Parallel evaluation of the determinant and of the inverse of a matrix," *Inform. Process. Letters* **30**, pp. 41–45 (1989).

von zur Gathen, J., "Parallel arithmetic computation: A survey," *Proc. MFCS '86, Springer Lec. Notes Comp. Sci.* **233**, pp. 93–112 (1986).

Gohberg, I. C. and Semencul, A. A., "On the inversion of finite Toeplitz matrices and their continous analogues," *Mat. Issled.* **2**, pp. 201–233 (1972). In Russian. Math. Rev. MR 50#5524.

Kailath, T., Kung, S.-Y., and Morf, M., "Displacement ranks of matrices and linear equations," *J. Math. Analysis Applications* **68**, pp. 395–407 (1979).

Kaltofen, E., "Greatest common divisors of polynomials given by straight-line programs," *J. ACM* **35/1**, pp. 231–264 (1988).

Kaltofen, E. and Pan, V., "Processor efficient parallel solution of linear systems over an abstract field," in *Proc. 3rd Ann. ACM Symp. Parallel Algor. Architecture*; ACM Press, pp. 180–191, 1991.

Kaltofen, E. and Saunders, B. D., "On Wiedemann's method of solving sparse linear systems," in *Proc. AAECC-5*, Springer Lect. Notes Comput. Sci. **536**; pp. 29–38, 1991.

Kaltofen, E. and Singer, M. F., "Size efficient parallel algebraic circuits for partial derivatives," in *IV International Conference on Computer Algebra in Physical Research*, edited by D. V. Shirkov, V. A. Rostovtsev, and V. P. Gerdt; World Scientific Publ., Singapore, pp. 133–145, 1991.

Karp, R. M. and Ramachandran, V., "Parallel algorithms for shared-memory machines," in *Handbook of Theoretical Computer Science, Algorithms and Complexity (Volume A)*, edited by J. van Leeuwen; Elsevier Science Publ., Amsterdam, pp. 869–941, 1990.

Ladner, R. E. and Fischer, M. J., "Parallel prefix computation," *J. ACM* **27/4**, pp. 831–838 (1980).

Le Verrier, U.-J.-J., "Sur les variations séculaires des éléments elliptiques des sept planèts principales: Mercure, Vénus, la Terré, Mars, Jupiter, Saturne et Uranus," *J. Math. Pures Appl.* **5**, pp. 220–254 (1840). In French.

Linnainmaa, S., "Taylor expansion of the accumulated rounding error," *BIT* **16**, pp. 146–160 (1976).

Mulmuley, K., "A fast parallel algorithm to compute the rank of a matrix over an arbitrary field," *Combinatorica* **7**, pp. 101–104 (1987).

Pan, V., "Parameterization of Newton's iteration for computations with structured matrices and applications," *Tech. Report* **CUCS-032-90**, Comput. Sci. Dept., Columbia University, New York, N. Y., 1990. *Comput. and Math. (with Applic.)*, to appear.

Preparata, F. P. and Sarwate, D. V., "An improved parallel processor bound in fast matrix inversion," *Inform. Process. Letters* **7/3**, pp. 148–150 (1978).

Schwartz, J. T., "Fast probabilistic algorithms for verification of polynomial identities," *J. ACM* **27**, pp. 701–717 (1980).

Trench, W., "An algorithm for the inversion of finite Toeplitz matrices," *SIAM J. Appl. Math.* **12**, pp. 515–522 (1964).

Wiedemann, D., "Solving sparse linear equations over finite fields," *IEEE Trans. Inf. Theory* **IT-32**, pp. 54–62 (1986).

Zippel, R., "Probabilistic algorithms for sparse polynomials," *Proc. EUROSAM '79, Springer Lec. Notes Comp. Sci.* **72**, pp. 216–226 (1979).

Communication on Noisy Channels: A Coding Theorem for Computation

Leonard J. Schulman*
Department of Mathematics
Massachusetts Institute of Technology
Cambridge MA 02139

Abstract

Communication is critical to distributed computing, parallel computing, or any situation in which automata interact — hence its significance as a resource in computation. In view of the likelihood of errors occurring in a lengthy interaction, it is desirable to incorporate this possibility in our model of communication.

In the noisy channel model for communication complexity, two automata are to reliably solve a problem to which each has only part of the input, by communicating across a faulty channel. This contrasts with the standard model for communication complexity, introduced by A. Yao, in which the channel is noiseless (does not introduce errors).

Noisy communication channels were first considered by Shannon in his seminal work in information theory. Shannon considered the "one-way" problem of transmitting a large block of data over a noisy channel. He described the intrinsic capacity of a channel and established his coding theorem, which states that the data can be encoded for transmission in such a way that the transmission time is proportional to the quantity of data and inversely proportional to the channel capacity, while a vanishing probability of error is incurred in the decoding.

We relate the noisy channel and the standard (noiseless channel) complexities of a communication problem by establishing a "two-way" or interactive analogue of Shannon's coding theorem: every noiseless channel protocol can be simulated by a private-coin noisy channel protocol whose time bound is proportional to the original (noiseless) time bound and inversely proportional to the capacity of the channel, while the protocol errs with vanishing probability.

Our method involves simulating the original protocol while implementing a hierarchical system of progress checks which ensure that errors of any magnitude in the simulation are, with high probability, rapidly eliminated.

*Support for this research was provided by an ONR graduate fellowship, an MIT Applied Mathematics graduate fellowship, and grants NSF 8912586 CCR and AFOSR 89-0271.

1 Introduction

The study of message transmission over noisy channels was pioneered in Shannon's work of 1948 [21]. Some of his fundamental contributions may be outlined as follows: (a) Message sources are usefully modeled as continual stochastic processes; the "rate" with which such a source produces information is measured by its entropy. (b) Communication channels have an intrinsic "capacity" which measures how much information they can carry in each transmission. (c) Messages may be transmitted over the channel at rates arbitrarily close to capacity (but no more), with arbitrarily low probability of error. The fundamental technique used to approach this objective, is the joint encoding for transmission of increasingly long input blocks.

Information theory, as taken to mean the study of information sources, communication channels, and the problem of message transmission, has been studied extensively since Shannon's seminal paper. In recent years however, communication has come to be investigated from a very different perspective, within computer science. A. Yao introduced the following model [26] of communication: The argument (input) of a function is split between two processors A and B. The processors are provided with a noiseless communication channel which can transmit one bit at a time in either direction. Their goal is to compute the value of the function, by communicating with each other using some agreed-upon protocol. The protocol can terminate when both parties know the value of the function. The primary object of interest is the *communication complexity* of the function: the number of bits that must be exchanged in the protocol, in order to solve the problem. (Measured on a "worst" input; often an average is also considered).

Shannon's work focused on the *transmission* of information: and he was able to say first, what is infor-

0-8186-2900-2/92 $3.00 © 1992 IEEE

mation, and second, what is a channel. In our time the telephone or telegraph have been joined by communicating, interacting computing devices: for example in integrated circuits, distributed networks of computers, and robotic control of remote devices. Communication complexity focuses on the two-way *exchange* of information, and is an attempt to understand computation.

The distinction is not primarily in the communication apparatus — much work has focused on the potential of feedback channels for assisting in message transmission — but in the problem. A two-way or interactive problem may depend on the inputs at both processors. One-way or transmission problems are the special case when the problem depends on only one of the inputs.

The critical role of communication in distributed and parallel computing, has motivated considerable interest in the study of communication as a computational resource. (Beginning with [26, 27, 14, 23, 12]; and see [13] for a survey). In view of the likelihood of transmission errors occurring in the course of lengthy communications, it is desirable to incorporate this possibility in our study of communication complexity.

In this paper we present one step in this direction: an analogue of Shannon's coding theorem for interactive communication problems.

The correspondence between Shannon's theorem and ours is as follows. On a noiseless channel, capable of carrying one bit per transmission, processor A can, in n transmissions, send processor B a block of n bits. Now fix a channel ("binary, symmetric") of capacity C $(0 \leq C \leq 1)$. Shannon's theorem shows how the noiseless-channel procedure can be simulated on the noisy channel: i.e. how, for any small γ, A can encode the n bits into $n\frac{1}{C}(1+\gamma)$ channel transmissions, from which B can correctly decode A's data, except for an exponentially small failure probability $e^{-\theta(n)}$.

In our interactive analogue we consider *any* communication problem for which the processors have a noiseless-channel protocol π, which terminates within n transmissions on every input to the processors. We show how to simulate π on the noisy channel in $\theta(n/C)$ transmissions, except for an exponentially small failure probability $e^{-n^{1-o(1)}}$.

As in the one-way case, the computational resources of time and space available to each processor will be unrestricted. Unlike the one-way case, each processor will also have access to a private source of random coins. Our method involves simulating the original protocol while implementing a hierarchical system of progress checks, which ensure that errors of any magnitude in the simulation are, with high probability, rapidly eliminated.

2 A Coding Theorem

We begin by specifying a model of a noisy communication channel. The binary symmetric channel is a synchronous communication link which, in every unit of time, accepts at one end either a 0 or 1; and in response produces either a 0 or a 1 at the other end. With some fixed probability ϵ the output differs from the input, while with probability $1-\epsilon$ they are the same. This random event for a particular transmission, is statistically independent of the bits sent and received in all other channel transmissions. (Thus the channel is "memoryless".)

The average mutual information between two ensembles $\{P(x)\}_{x \in X}$ and $\{P(y)\}_{y \in Y}$, which have a joint distribution $\{P(xy)\}_{x \in X, y \in Y}$, is defined as $\sum_{xy} P(xy) \log \frac{P(xy)}{P(x)P(y)}$. This is a measure of how much information is provided about one ensemble by the specification of a point (chosen at random from the joint distribution) of the other ensemble.

The capacity of a channel was defined by Shannon as the maximum, ranging over probability distributions on the inputs, of the average mutual information between the input and output distributions. In the case of the binary symmetric channel the capacity (in base 2) is $C = 1 - \epsilon \lg \frac{1}{\epsilon} - (1-\epsilon) \lg \frac{1}{(1-\epsilon)}$. Observe that $0 \leq C \leq 1$; and that a noiseless channel has capacity $C = 1$. Gallager [9] provides a thorough exposition of these concepts.

In the standard (noiseless) communication complexity model, the argument (input) $z = (z_A, z_B)$ of a function $f(z)$ is split between two processors A and B, with A receiving z_A and B receiving z_B; the processors compute $f(z)$ (solve the communication problem f) by exchanging bits over a noiseless link between them. Each processor has unbounded time and space resources. Randomness may be allowed as a resource, and is typically considered at one of three levels: none (deterministic protocols); private coins (each processor has its own unbounded source of random coins, but cannot see the other processor's coins); and public coins (the processors can see a common unbounded source of random coins.) The procedure which determines the processors' actions based on their local input and transmissions received, is called a communication protocol.

In the present paper the noiseless link is replaced (in each direction) by a binary symmetric channel of capacity C.

Here is a precise statement of Shannon's coding theorem. (Not in its most general form. See [21]; [9], theorem 5.6.4).

Theorem 1 (Shannon) *Let a binary symmetric channel of capacity C be given. For every n and every $\gamma > 0$ there exists a code $\chi : \{0,1\}^n \rightarrow \{0,1\}^{n\frac{1}{C}(1+\gamma)}$ and a decoding map $\chi' : \{0,1\}^{n\frac{1}{C}(1+\gamma)} \rightarrow \{0,1\}^n$ such that every codeword transmitted across the channel is decoded correctly with probability $1 - e^{-\Omega(n)}$.*

If all one wants is to transmit one bit (or a fixed number of bits) and a very small probability of error is desired, then there is only one thing to be done: the redundancy of the transmission must be increased, in order to drive down the error probability. (By redundancy we mean the number of transmissions per bit of the message). Shannon's theorem says that this is not necessary if one may assume that the message to be transmitted is long. In that case codewords (the images of n-bit input blocks via χ, as above) can be selected in such a manner that when any one of them is transmitted over the channel, the probability that it so changed by the channel noise as to be mistaken by the receiver for another codeword, is exponentially small in n. Since the exponential error is gained from the block size, n, which may be chosen as large as desired, it is not necessary to invest extra redundancy for this purpose. It is enough just to bring the redundancy past the threshold value $1/C$.

Following is an analogue of Shannon's theorem for the more general case of two-way, or interactive, communication.

Theorem 2 *In each direction between the processors let a binary symmetric channel of capacity C be given. There is a constant σ such that for every n, every $\gamma > 0$ and every communication problem f with a noiseless channel protocol π of length n, there exists a private-coin noisy channel protocol of length $n\frac{\sigma}{C}(1+\gamma)$ which for every input pair, solves f correctly with probability $1 - e^{-n^{1-o(1)}}$.*

There is a point to be noticed here. In a general protocol π, there are *no large input blocks.* In the nature of interaction, processors generally do not know what they want to transmit more than one bit ahead. Thus the methods used for the transmission problem do not suffice for the interactive problems.

A naive simulation of the noiseless channel protocol π might involve repeating every character transmitted in π, k times. The receiving processor would decode the transmission by taking a majority vote among the k characters received. The probability of an error occurring in such a transmission is $e^{-\theta(kC)}$, where C is the capacity of the channel.

However, if any of these transmissions fails, the remainder of the protocol is wasted, as each processor will be laboring under a misunderstanding.

Thus in order to assure even a constant or polynomial probability of error, the redundancy needed is nonconstant, $k = \theta(\frac{1}{C}\log n)$. Further in order to assure an exponentially small probability of error, as we desire, this naive simulation needs polynomial redundancy $k = \frac{1}{C}n^{\theta(1)}$.

We will prove the coding theorem by using a more sophisticated simulation of π. In section 4 we describe a public-coin protocol to simulate π, and in section 5 we analyze that protocol, showing how it avoids sacrificing efficiency for reliability. In section 6 we show how to transform the public-coin protocol into one that uses only private coins.

First however we describe the notion of progress checks. They will play an important role in our solution, although as we shall see, they are not alone sufficient.

3 Progress Checks

Here is a possible general strategy: the processors alternate rounds of simulation of π, with "progress check" rounds in which they try to determine whether the simulation is proceeding correctly; and if not, they backtrack in the simulation until the checks show that they have undone the error, at which point they resume the simulation.

At time t, processor A holds a binary vector, rec_A, of length t, representing its record of the protocol to date: these are the bits transmitted from A to B (before repetition), as well as the bits A has decoded from B's transmissions. Similarly B holds such a binary vector, rec_B. Observe that the simulation to date is correct if, and only if, $\text{rec}_A = \text{rec}_B$. Thus a progress check might be implemented by having the processors compare the vectors rec_A and rec_B.

These vectors can be quite long: t ranges up to n. Even for a noiseless channel, A. Yao has shown [26] that deterministically comparing two vectors of length t requires $\Omega(t)$ transmissions. However, using randomness, a comparison can be implemented in far fewer transmissions: A *constant* number of transmissions suffice in order to compare a pair of arbitrarily long vectors, with only a small constant failure probability. Specifically, let R be a $t \times k$ matrix with entries independently and uniformly selected in $GF(2)$.

Lemma 1 *If $rec_A \neq rec_B$ then with probability* $1 - 2^{-k}$, *$rec_A R \neq rec_B R$. If $rec_A = rec_B$ then $rec_A R = rec_B R$. (Operations in $GF(2)$.)*

Proof: Standard. □

In the public-coin model, both processors can see the same random matrix R. They can implement a progress check by first using R to calculate a k-bit parity-check vector of their own record and then using a deterministic Shannon code to encode the parity-check vector into $\theta(k/C)$ channel transmissions. Except for a failure event of probability $e^{-\Omega(k)}$, each processor will correctly decode the other's parity-check vector.

There are two ways in which this procedure can fail. First, the random matrix R might map two different *rec* vectors to the same parity-check vector — resulting, in case of a successful channel transmission, in the processors mistakenly believing the simulation is correct. This is not a problem: the difference between their *rec* vectors will persist, and most likely they will soon discover it and backtrack in the simulation.

The second way in which this check might fail, is through channel errors during the checking procedure. If both processors suffer from the error, then this is no worse a problem than the first kind: in case of a "false equality" the processors lose a round before backtracking, while in the case of "false inequality", a round of the simulation is needlessly erased.

A more serious problem is that channel errors during the checking procedure will occasionally cause one processor to believe the simulation is correct, and therefore continue in the simulation; while the other believes there is an error, and backtracks a step. In this situation the processors differ in their notions of the simulation step t (i.e. in the positions of their "pointers" into the noiseless protocol), and necessarily therefore their *rec* vectors differ[1]. Henceforth in most rounds, the processors will be engaged in backtracking in order to undo the error which they detect. Unfortunately this does not help them close the gap between their pointers: in fact the only way the gap can be closed, is by further asymmetric errors which cancel the effect of the first. Since the asymmetric errors do occur with some constant frequency, the gap between the pointers will undergo an unbiased random walk. The gap starts at just one unit, and so with very high probability it will in fact vanish within a constant number of rounds; moreover the probability of it eventually vanishing is 1. However: the *expected* time until the gap vanishes is infinite. This is a classic phenomenon in gambler's ruin ([5] §XI.3, XIV). In terms of the protocol, it means that the simulation will completely unravel.

Roughly speaking, the above simulation was too homogeneous. In the next section we will describe a solution which assists in bringing the processors' pointers together by funnelling them through a hierarchy of prearranged "meeting points".

4 Public-Coin Simulation Protocol

In this section we describe a public-coin protocol for theorem 2. We defer the private-coin case to section 6.

We distinguish two notions of time. ***Step*** t will refer exclusively to the tth bit in the noiseless protocol π. ***Round*** t will refer exclusively to the tth occasion on which the noisy simulation simulates a step of π. Due to the synchronicity of the model, the processors always know and agree on what the current round is; on account of channel errors they might, however, differ as to what step they are currently simulating. We will describe each processor as having a pointer, whose value is equal to t during a certain round if the processor is then trying to simulate step t of π.

We will assume without loss of generality that in the noiseless protocol π the processors alternate single-bit transmissions; this is the "hardest" case.

If π is a protocol of complexity n, the processors will run the simulation for $N = 2^{\lceil \lg n \rceil + 1}$ simulation rounds. (Note that $2n \leq N < 4n$.) Each round will consist of one of the processors simulating a single step of π, by repeating that bit k/C times (for some constant k)[2]. In between rounds the protocol will also execute a hierarchical system of progress checks, each associated with an internal node of a complete binary tree, according to the following schedule. Checks will be labeled by their level in the tree (the root being at the highest level). The actual rounds of simulation will be associated with the leaves of the tree (level 0). The protocol is scheduled in "postorder" on this tree: that is, a level l check will be executed after first its left subtree, and then its right subtree, have been fully executed (see figure 1).

We now describe the progress checks of the protocol. Recall that errors may result in a separation between the processors' pointers, as well as in differing bits in the records. The progress checks are designed

[1] The linear test we have described will not distinguish between a vector and some extension of it with only 0's at the end. This is easily remedied, for instance by augmenting the *rec* vectors with a representation of the pointer value t.

[2] Note that due to redundancy in the implementation of the simulation rounds, and to progress checks intervening between the rounds, the elapsed simulation time will be greater than the round number. However they will be the same to within a constant factor.

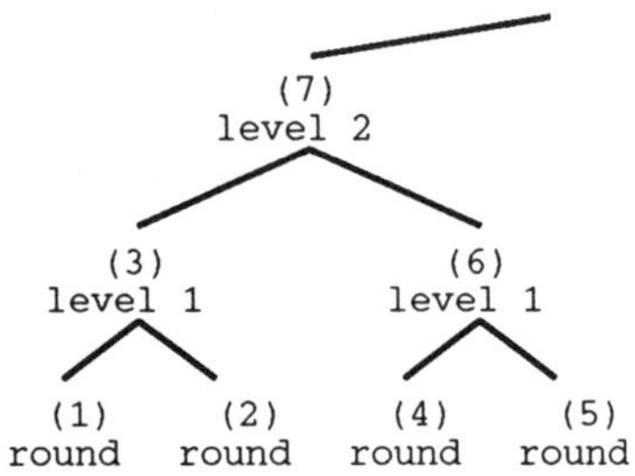

Figure 1: Simulation schedule

to deal with any combination of these events. If A's pointer is at step t_A, and B's pointer is at step t_B, then we define the current **position** of the protocol to be $\max\{t_A, t_B\}$. The current **gap** of the protocol is the difference between the position, and the end of the prefix of agreement of the two records (i.e. the greatest t such that the first t bits of rec_A agree with those of rec_B). The gap is the distance that one of the processors must backtrack, and thus a measure of the severity of the current error in the simulation. The simulation is correct after some round precisely if the gap is 0.

Performing a level-l check

A level-l check is performed as follows. Processor A writes its position t_A in the form $c_1^A 2^l + c_2^A$ (for $0 < c_2^A \leq 2^l$), and forms the three vectors of length N:

- $a_1 = \mathrm{rec}_A$ restricted to positions $\{1, ..., (c_1^A - 1)2^l\}$. (Set a_1 to 0 in $\{(c_1^A - 1)2^l + 1, ..., N\}$).
- $a_2 = \mathrm{rec}_A$ restricted to positions $\{1, ..., c_1^A 2^l\}$. (Set a_2 to 0 in $\{(c_1^A - 1)2^l + 1, ..., N\}$).
- $a_3 = \mathrm{rec}_A$. (Set a_3 to 0 in $\{(c_1^A - 1)2^l + 1, ..., N\}$).

Similarly B forms b_1, b_2, b_3 from rec_B.

Now the processors observe a common random $N \times \theta(2^l/l^2)$ matrix R. A encodes each of the parity check vectors a_1R, a_2R, a_3R into $\theta(2^l/l^2C)$ channel transmissions using a deterministic Shannon code, and sends the three codewords to B. Similarly B sends encodings of b_1R, b_2R, b_3R to A.

The construction should be understood in this way. The positions $(c_1^A - 1)2^l$ and $c_1^A 2^l$ are places at which A proposes the two processors meet, in case any recent errors have occurred in the simulation. (The comparison of a_3 with b_3 is meant to detect such errors.) B also proposes two meeting places, $(c_1^B - 1)2^l$ and $c_1^B 2^l$. The key to the processors' success is that, so long as the gap is no more than 2^l, they will always propose at least one common meeting point, and share a common history of the protocol through that point. So they can agree to shift their pointers to that point and resume the simulation from there.

This idea is implemented as follows. Each processor represents the information available to it as a bipartite graph. On one side are three vertices representing A's three vectors a_1, a_2 and a_3. On the other side are three vertices representing b_1, b_2 and b_3. In A's graph, an edge connects a_i to b_j if a_iR equals the decoding of the transmission of b_jR. Similarly in B's graph, an edge connects a_i to b_j if b_jR equals the decoding of the transmission of a_iR. Thus edges of each graph represent presumed equivalences between the a_i and b_j vectors.

Observe that in any state of the simulation, there is some underlying correct graph representing which of the pairs a_i, b_j are indeed equal. We will classify checks as "good" or "bad":

Definition *A check is* **good** *if it results in both processors drawing the correct graph. Otherwise the check is* **bad**.

A check may be bad due either to channel errors or to a poor choice of R (creating spurious equivalences between the parity check vectors).

Each processor acts, depending upon its graph, as follows (description for A; everything for B is symmetric):

Case 1 A's graph is a "parallel" matching with three edges (see figure 2).

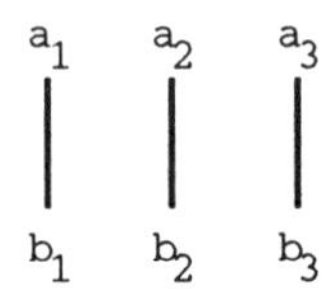

Figure 2: Graph for case 1

This suggests to A that the simulation is correct. So A continues simulating π from its current pointer position.

Case 2 A's graph is one of the "partial parallel" matchings in figure 3.

This suggests to A that, although an error exists in the simulation, the prefix of agreement nevertheless persists through a_1, a_2 or a_3 (depending on the case). So A moves its pointer back to the latest of a_1, a_2, a_3 that is incident to an edge, and

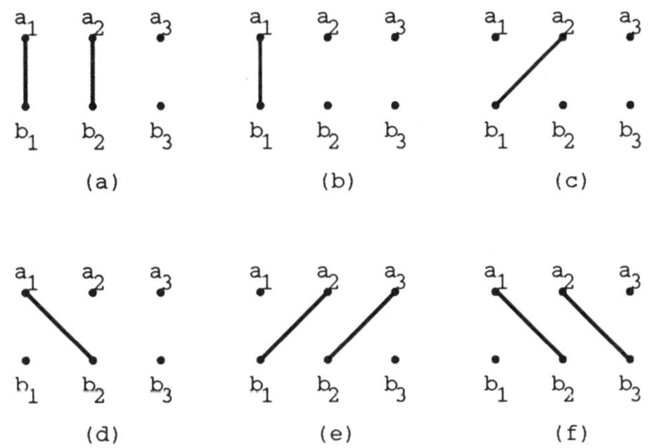

Figure 3: Graphs for case 2

continues the simulation from there. (I.e to a_2 in (a); a_1 in (b); a_2 in (c); a_1 in (d); a_3 in (e); and a_2 in (f)[3].)

Case 3 A's graph is empty. This suggests to A that there is an error in the simulation and that no a_i and b_j are equal. (Thus that the gap is greater than 2^l). So A does nothing. (Which means that it keeps its pointer fixed until a future check indicates otherwise. If there is a simulation round immediately after the check, A can send some default message, but it does not advance its pointer.)

Case 4 If A's graph is anything not described above, then the check must have been bad. So A does nothing (which means the same as in case 3).

Properties of a level-l check

Let us specify what a level-l check accomplishes.

If the check is bad, as defined above — that is if one of the processors draw a graph different from the correct one — then the check will not cause a loss in position, or an increase in gap, of more than 2^{l+1} steps.

On the other hand if the check is "good" then:

1. If the gap is 0: Both processors will know this, and will continue in the simulation.

2. If the gap is nonzero but bounded by 2^l: the check will enable the processors to eliminate the gap while incurring a loss of at most 2^{l+1} in the position.

3. If the gap is greater than 2^l: Both processors will know this, and neither will move its pointer.

[3] Cases (e) and (f) are unusual. Case (e), asserting $a_3 = b_2$, can correctly occur only if $c_2^A = 2^l$. Similarly (f) asserting $b_3 = a_2$ can correctly occur only if $c_2^B = 2^l$.

5 Analysis

Observe that if the simulation protocol is run for $N = \theta(n)$ rounds, the total transmission time will be $\theta(n/C)$, as we desire. For, each level l has $\theta(N2^{-l})$ nodes, each using $\theta(2^l/l^2C)$ transmissions. The total number of transmissions is thus $\theta(\sum_l N/l^2C) = \theta(N/C) = \theta(n/C)$.

We now restate the coding theorem for the case of public coins, and prove it. Since we will not determine the true value of σ, the θ notation will suffice in place of $\sigma(1+\gamma)\ \forall\gamma > 0$.

Theorem 3 *Let a binary symmetric channel of capacity C be given. For every n and every communication problem f with a noiseless channel protocol π of length n, there exists a public-coin noisy channel protocol of length $\theta(n/C)$ which for every input pair, solves f correctly with probability* $1-e^{-n^{1-4\log\log n/\log n}}$.

Proof: We analyze the protocol in two stages. First, we will assign a certain "bad weight" to every bad node of the simulation tree, and show that with high probability, the total bad weight of the simulation is small (bounded by a constant fraction of n). Second, we will show that a simulation with small bad weight completes π correctly.

We have already defined bad checks (internal nodes of the simulation tree) as those in which some processor draws an incorrect graph. Now we also define what it means for a round to be bad. Recall that each round of the simulation is concerned with simulating the transmission of a single bit of the noiseless protocol.

Definition *A round of the simulation (leaf of the simulation tree) is* **good** *if the character decoded equals that transmitted. Otherwise the round is* **bad**.

We will assign bad weight 2^l to a bad node at level l (e.g. a bad round has weight 1). The total bad weight of the simulation, denoted B, is the sum of the bad weights of its nodes. In view of the fact that $N \geq 2n$, the theorem is implied by the following two claims, whose proofs will be presented in the remainder of this section.

I. *With probability* $1 - e^{-\theta(N/\log^4 N)}$, $B \leq N/34$.
(With high probability the bad weight is small.)

II. *The simulation completes at least $N - 17B$ steps of π correctly.*

(A simulation with small bad weight is correct.)

□

I. With high probability the bad weight is small

Observe that, regardless of any other event in the protocol, the probability that a given node of level l is bad is $e^{-\theta(2^l/l^2)}$.

We will argue in each level of the tree separately, showing that with high probability only a small fraction of the nodes in that level are bad. Let M be any constant.

Proposition 1 *With probability $1 - e^{-\theta(N/\log^4 N)}$, at most $N/M2^l l^2$ of the $N/2^l$ nodes at level l are bad.*

Proof: Let $b_l = N/M2^l l^2$, and let $q_l = P(\text{more than } b_l \text{ nodes at level } l \text{ are bad})$.

By a union bound and by the independence in our bound on the probability of any node being bad,

$$q_l \leq \binom{N2^{-l}}{b_l} e^{-\theta(2^l/l^2)b_l}.$$

Now we apply the standard entropy bound $\binom{N}{xN} \leq e^{NH(x)}$ (valid for all $0 < x < 1$; H is the entropy function $H(x) = x \log 1/x + (1-x) \log 1/(1-x)$.) Thus

$$q_l \leq e^{N2^{-l}H(1/Ml^2) - \theta(2^l/l^2)b_l}.$$

Next we apply the inequality $H(x) \leq x\frac{\log(e/x)}{\log 2}$ (valid for all $0 < x < 1$.) Thus

$$\begin{aligned} q_l &\leq e^{N\frac{\log(eMl^2)}{2^l Ml^2 \log 2} - \theta(b_l 2^l/l^2)} \\ &= e^{N\frac{\log(eM) + 2\log l}{2^l Ml^2 \log 2} - \theta(N/l^4)} = e^{-\theta(N/l^4)}. \end{aligned}$$

Now since $l \leq \lg N$,

$$q_l \leq e^{-\theta(N/\log^4 N)}.$$

□

Now note that if every level has at most b_l bad nodes, then the total bad weight B of the simulation is at most $\sum_l 2^l b_l = \sum_l N/Ml^2$, which by a suitable choice of M we can arrange to be an arbitrarily small constant fraction of N. Thus, applying the above lemma and taking a union bound over the $\lg N$ levels of the tree (while noting that $\lg N \cdot e^{-\theta(N/\log^4 N)} = e^{-\theta(N/\log^4 N)}$) we find:

Corollary 1 *With probability $1 - e^{-\theta(N/\log^4 N)}$, $B \leq N/34$.* □

II. A simulation with small bad weight is correct

In this section we will apply an amortized analysis to relate the performance of the nodes (as measured by the total bad weight of the simulation) to the progress of the simulation.

At any point in the simulation, and in particular when it terminates, the prefix of agreement of the two processors' *rec* vectors represents the portion of π which has been correctly simulated. Recall that the length of this prefix is equal to the **position** minus the **gap**. Thus the simulation is successful if, at termination, this difference is at least n.

Proposition 2 *The simulation completes at least $N - 17B$ steps of π correctly.*

Recall that the simulation consists of running the protocol of section 4 for N rounds (with $N \geq 2n$). Thus the simulation is successful if $B \leq N/34$.

Proof: We mark every node of the simulation according to its behavior. There are three kinds of nodes:

Bad: As defined earlier: either a faulty simulation round, or a bad check.

GC: Good, correcting: These are good checks in which the processors were in case 2 of the protocol: i.e. they found that the protocol was in error, and corrected the error by bringing their pointers back to a step at which their *rec* vectors are in agreement.

GNC: Good, noncorrecting: These are good rounds; or good checks in which both processors were in either case 1 or case 3 of the protocol. This means that either they found that the simulation is correct, and continued (case 1); or they found that the protocol was in error but could not correct it (case 3).

In terms of these categories, a gap can be created or increased in only two ways in the protocol: (1) A bad node at level l can increase the gap by at most 2^{l+1}. (2) Immediately following a bad check, one or both of the processors may mistakenly advance their pointer one step (as if they were in case 1, although they are not), thus contributing 1 to the gap.

We will charge both of these effects to the bad nodes, thus saying that a bad check can increase the gap by at most $2^{l+1} + 1$, while a bad simulation round can increase the gap by at most 1. Observe that the contribution to the gap is at most 5/2 times the bad weight of the node.

A good node (of either kind) never contributes to the gap. This is true of good leaves (simulation rounds) because they can contribute gap only if they follow immediately after a bad check, to which we have charged the gap. It is true of good internal nodes (checks) because the processors agree on their assessment of the state of the protocol, and therefore either eliminate or avoid increasing the gap; furthermore if there is an error which they cannot correct (case 3), they avoid increasing the gap in the following simulation round.

Observe that after a GC node the gap is always 0 (thus the processors' pointers agree and the simulation is correct through that step).

The length of the final prefix of agreement is equal to the number of correct simulation rounds in the protocol, minus the position loss (from Bad and GC nodes) and any gap remaining at termination. Thus the proposition will follow from the two following claims, which we prove separately:

(A) At least $N-5B$ of the N simulation rounds of the protocol, are correct simulations of the steps of π.

(B) The total position loss at Bad and GC nodes, plus the gap remaining when the protocol halts, is at most $12B$.

Proof of claim (A). Observe that a simulation round is correct provided that it starts with 0 gap, and that it itself is good.

We will isolate certain subtrees of the simulation, which we will call **dismissable**, and argue that all the simulation rounds outside the dismissable subtrees are correct.

We say that the subtree rooted at a node v of level l is dismissable if:

1. The bad weight in the subtree is at most $\frac{2}{5}2^l$. (In particular v must be good.)

2. One of the subtrees rooted at a child of v, has bad weight more than $\frac{2}{5}2^{l-1}$.

3. No subtree rooted at an ancestor of v satisfies properties 1,2. (Thus dismissable subtrees are disjoint).

The definition implies that every bad node is contained within some dismissable subtree, unless $B > \frac{2}{5}N$ in which case the proposition is trivial. Now we show that all nodes outside of the dismissable subtrees, start with 0 gap. No gap is created outside of the dismissable subtrees, because all the nodes on the outside (as well as the roots of the dismissable subtrees) are good. Therefore it suffices to show that every dismissable subtree ends with 0 gap. By induction (on their order of occurrence in the simulation, namely postorder) we can assume that each dismissable subtree starts with 0 gap. Since the total bad weight inside a dismissable subtree rooted at level l is at most $\frac{2}{5}2^l$, the total gap encountered (if any) by the check node at its root is at most 2^l. Since the root is good, it can correct this, hence the subtree ends with 0 gap.

We now place an upper bound on the number of leaves within the dismissable subtrees. A dismissable subtree rooted at level l has 2^l leaves, and bad weight at least $\frac{2}{5}2^{l-1}$. Since the dismissable subtrees are disjoint, the total number of leaves in their union is at most $5B$.

We have shown that any leaf (simulation round) outside the union of the dismissable subtrees is good, and starts with 0 gap; and furthermore that there are at least $N-5B$ such leaves. Claim (A) follows.

Proof of claim (B). The only ways in which position is lost in the protocol are:

(i) A bad node at level l can decrease the position by at most 2^{l+1}.

(ii) A GC node at level l can decrease the position by at most 2^{l+1}.

Our argument now runs as follows. The difference between the number of correctly simulated steps of π (which we lower-bounded in (A)), and the length of the final prefix of agreement of the *rec* vectors, is equal to the sum of:

(a) The total position loss as in (i), (ii) above.

(b) The gap remaining at the end of the simulation.

We will amortize each of these effects against the bad weight of the simulation. We have indicated above how gap is amortized against bad weight, at a rate of 5/2 steps per unit of bad weight. Next we examine the position loss, L.

(i) The total position loss at the bad nodes is bounded by $2B$.

(ii) The amortization of position loss at the GC nodes against bad weight must be made indirectly, through an intermediate amortization against the gap being corrected at the GC nodes. The gap is due entirely to the effect of bad nodes (see (1,2) above); and as observed, the total amount of gap to be corrected is bounded by $\frac{5}{2}B$. Thus as an intermediate step, we will say that a bad node at level l creates $\frac{5}{2}2^l$ "gap coins". Next we show that the GC nodes convert gap coins into position loss, at a constant rate.

Lemma 2 *The total position loss at the GC nodes is at most four times the total gap currency.*

Proof: The gap coins created at any bad node will be used to pay for the the position loss at the next-occurring GC node (i.e. the next in postorder in the simulation tree). Thus a gap coin will be used at a unique GC node. Since a GC node at level l can reduce the position by at most 2^{l+1} steps, the lemma will follow from showing that it has at least 2^{l-1} gap coins available.

We prove this as follows. Recall that immediately after a GC node (as well as at the outset of the simulation), the gap is always 0. Therefore a GC node always receives, in the above scheme, at least as much gap currency as the size of the actual gap which it encounters.

First we consider the level-1 GC nodes. They encounter a gap of at least one step, and therefore have at least one gap coin available; furthermore they reduce the position by at most 4 steps.

Next we consider a GC node v of level $l > 1$. If v's right-hand child is bad, then at least $\frac{5}{2}2^{l-1}$ gap coins flow to v, and we are done. Otherwise the right-hand child is good; and since it left gap for v to correct, it must be a GNC node. Since it could correct any gap of up to 2^{l-1} steps, the actual gap encountered by v — and therefore the gap currency available — is at least 2^{l-1}. □

Write $B = B_1 + B_2$, where B_1 represents the total bad weight occurring before the last GC node of the protocol, and B_2 is the weight due to later bad nodes. The total position loss at Bad nodes of the protocol is at most $2B$; while the above lemma shows that the total position loss at GC nodes is at most $10B_1$. Furthermore the gap remaining at termination is at most $\frac{5}{2}B_2$. Thus the total position loss is at most $(2+10)B_1 + (2+\frac{5}{2})B_2 \leq 12B$. Part (B) of the proposition follows.

This completes the proof of the proposition, and of the public-coin coding theorem. □

6 Private Coins

The proofs of Shannon's coding theorem are via the probabilistic method. In variations, the proofs consist of describing a random coding technique, and showing that most random seeds give codes with favorable qualities; hence there exists a good code.

Our technique is similar. We have described a public-coin random protocol such that on any input pair, most random seeds give a protocol with favorable qualities. Unfortunately in the present case, due to the possibility that different input pairs favor different random seeds, it is not as easy to remove the randomness in favor of an existential statement. Nevertheless we can remove enough randomness to turn our public-coin protocol into a private-coin protocol.

The public-coin protocol used $\theta(n^2)$ random coins, i.e. a sample space of size $2^{\theta(n^2)}$. Theorem 3 showed that for any input pair, if random seeds in this space were sampled uniformly, the average conditional probability of the simulation failing was at most $e^{-n^{1-4\log\log n/\log n}}$.

We will show that there exists a relatively small subset Q of these random seeds, of size $2^{\theta(n)}$, such that for any input, if the random seeds in Q are sampled uniformly, the average conditional probability of the simulation failing is $e^{-n^{1-o(1)}}$.

The processors thus run the private-coin protocol as follows: one processor picks an element of Q uniformly. Then the seed is identified to the other processor with $O(\frac{n}{C})$ channel transmissions (using a Shannon code, and erring with probability $e^{-\theta(n)}$); following which the processors run the public-coin protocol on the selected seed.

Proposition 3 *There exists a set of random seeds Q, of size $q = 2^{\theta(n)}$, such that for every input pair, the protocol which uses a uniformly selected seed from Q, succeeds in simulating π with probability $1 - e^{-\theta(n^{1-4\log\log n/\log n})}$.*

Proof: Omitted. □

This completes the demonstration of the private-coin coding theorem (theorem 2). □

7 Discussion

Insofar as interactive protocols represent the workings of a computer whose inputs and processing power are not localized, we have presented here a coding theorem for computation. There are two questions prompted directly by this theorem. The first is, whether it can be reproduced with a deterministic (rather than randomized private-coin) protocol. The second regards the constant σ: is it 1, as for transmission?

It seems also interesting and important to ask, with regard to networks of more than two processors: to what extent might the coding theorem for interactive protocols be extended to the efficient simulation of noiseless distributed protocols, on networks with noise.

In this connection we draw attention to the work of Gallager [10], who has previously considered the problem of noise occurring in a distributed computation. He allowed for a complete network of n processors, each of which in a single transmission can broadcast one bit, which arrives at each of the other processors subject to independent noise. He studied a specific problem on this network: supposing that each processor receives a single input bit, he showed how to efficiently and reliably compute the combined parity of all the inputs.

Karchmer and Wigderson [11] observed a certain equivalence between communication complexity and circuit complexity, and thereby stimulated great recent interest in communication complexity. While noisy circuits have been studied in the literature (e.g. [24, 16, 18, 17, 1, 2, 8, 20]), the correspondence between circuits and communication protocols does not appear to extend to the noisy cases of each. Elias [3] and later Peterson and Rabin [15] investigated the possibility of encoding data for computation on noisy gates, and the extent to which these gates might be said to have a finite (nonzero) capacity for computation. (Here as for channel transmission, noiseless encoding and decoding of the data before and after the computation are allowed).

Finally, we mention two lines of research in the literature which, although they address different problems from ours, nevertheless anticipate our work in philosophy or in method. The first is work on sequential coding [25, 19, 4]: a method of implementing data transmission without the computational explosion of block codes. In this method the receiver branches on intermediate guesses regarding the message, and backtracks when inconsistencies mount. Our "progress checks" (section 3) are similarly motivated.

The second is work on the active maintenance of data stored in an unreliable medium (e.g. cellular automata subject to local noise) [22, 6, 7]: a data transmission problem from the past to the future. The use of hierarchical, rather than homogeneous, schemes was found to be important in that work [6]: a theme evident also in the present paper.

Acknowledgments

I thank Mike Sipser, whose encouragement of my work on this project, and supervision of its progress, have been invaluable. Further I thank Peter Elias for much advice and assistance. For consultations and comments thanks also to Dan Abramovich, Robert Gallager, Wayne Goddard, Mauricio Karchmer, Dan Kleitman, Mike Klugerman and Andrew Sutherland.

References

[1] R. L. Dobrushin and S. I. Ortyukov. Lower bound for the redundancy of self-correcting arrangements of unreliable functional elements. Prob. Inf. Trans., 13:59–65, 1977.

[2] R. L. Dobrushin and S. I. Ortyukov. Upper bound for the redundancy of self-correcting arrangements of unreliable functional elements. Prob. Inf. Trans., 13:203–218, 1977.

[3] P. Elias. Computation in the presence of noise. IBM Journal of Research and Development, 2(4):346–353, October 1958.

[4] R. M. Fano. A heuristic discussion of probabilistic decoding. IEEE Transactions on Information Theory, pages 64–74, 1963.

[5] W. Feller. An Introduction to Probability Theory and its Applications, volume I. Wiley, third edition, 1968.

[6] P. Gács. Reliable computation with cellular automata. J. Computer and System Sciences, 32:15–78, 1986.

[7] P. Gács and J. Reif. A simple three-dimensional real-time reliable cellular array. J. Computer and System Sciences, 36:125–147, 1988.

[8] A. Gál. Lower bounds for the complexity of reliable boolean circuits with noisy gates. In Proceedings of the 32nd Annual Symposium on Foundations of Computer Science, pages 594–601, 1991.

[9] R. G. Gallager. Information Theory and Reliable Communication. Wiley, 1968.

[10] R. G. Gallager. Finding parity in a simple broadcast network. IEEE Trans. Inform. Theory, 34(2):176–180, March 1988.

[11] M. Karchmer and A. Wigderson. Monotone circuits for connectivity require super-logarithmic depth. In Proceedings of the 20th Annual Symposium on Theory of Computing, pages 539–550, 1988.

[12] Lipton and Sedgewick. Lower bounds for VLSI. In Proceedings of the 13th Annual Symposium on Theory of Computing, pages 300–307, 1981.

[13] L. Lovász. Communication complexity: A survey. In Korde et al, editor, Algorithms and Combinatorics. Springer-Verlag, 1990.

[14] C. H. Papadimitriou and M. Sipser. Communication complexity. In Proceedings of the 14th Annual Symposium on Theory of Computing, pages 196–200, 1982.

[15] W. W. Peterson and M. O. Rabin. On codes for checking logical operations. IBM Journal of Research and Development, 3:163–168, April 1959.

[16] N. Pippenger. On networks of noisy gates. In Proceedings of the 26th Annual Symposium on Foundations of Computer Science, pages 30–36, 1985.

[17] N. Pippenger. Reliable computation by formulas in the presence of noise. IEEE Transactions on Information Theory, 34(2):194–197, March 1988.

[18] N. Pippenger. Invariance of complexity measures for networks with unreliable gates. J. ACM, 36:531–539, 1989.

[19] B. Reiffen. Sequential encoding and decoding for the discrete memoryless channel. Res. Lab. of Electronics, M.I.T. Technical Report, 374, 1960.

[20] R. Reischuk and B. Schmeltz. Reliable computation with noisy circuits and decision trees — a general $n \log n$ lower bound. In Proceedings of the 32nd Annual Symposium on Foundations of Computer Science, pages 602–611, 1991.

[21] C. E. Shannon. A mathematical theory of communication. Bell System Tech. J., 27:379–423; 623–656, 1948.

[22] M. C. Taylor. Reliable information storage in memories designed from unreliable components. Bell System Tech. J., 47(10):2299–2337, 1968.

[23] C. D. Thompson. Area-time complexity for VLSI. In Proceedings of the 11th Annual Symposium on Theory of Computing, pages 81–88, 1979.

[24] J. von Neumann. Probabilistic logics and the synthesis of reliable organisms from unreliable components. In C. E. Shannon and J. McCarthy, editors, Automata Studies. Princeton University Press, 1956.

[25] J. M. Wozencraft. Sequential decoding for reliable communications. Res. Lab. of Electronics, M.I.T. Technical Report, 325, 1957.

[26] A. C. Yao. Some complexity questions related to distributive computing. In Proceedings of the 11th Annual Symposium on Theory of Computing, pages 209–213, 1979.

[27] A. C. Yao. The entropic limitations on VLSI computations. In Proceedings of the 13th Annual Symposium on Theory of Computing, pages 308–311, 1981.

Author index

Offices of the IEEE Computer Society

Headquarters Office
1730 Massachusetts Avenue, N.W.
Washington, DC 20036-1903
Phone: (202) 371-0101 — Fax: (202) 728-9614

Publications Office
P.O. Box 3014
10662 Los Vaqueros Circle
Los Alamitos, CA 90720-1264
Membership and General Information: (714) 821-8380
Publication Orders: (800) 272-6657 — Fax: (714) 821-4010

European Office
13, avenue de l'Aquilon
B-1200 Brussels, BELGIUM
Phone: 32-2-770-21-98 — Fax: 32-3-770-85-05

Asian Office
Ooshima Building
2-19-1 Minami-Aoyama, Minato-ku
Tokyo 107, JAPAN
Phone: 81-3-408-3118 — Fax: 81-3-408-3553

IEEE Computer Society

IEEE Computer Society Press Publications

Monographs: A monograph is an authored book consisting of 100-percent original material.
Tutorials: A tutorial is a collection of original materials prepared by the editors, and reprints of the best articles published in a subject area. Tutorials must contain at least five percent of original material (although we recommend 15 to 20 percent of original material).
Reprint collections: A reprint collection contains reprints (divided into sections) with a preface, table of contents, and section introductions discussing the reprints and why they were selected. Collections contain less than five percent of original material.
Technology series: Each technology series is a brief reprint collection — approximately 126-136 pages and containing 12 to 13 papers, each paper focusing on a subset of a specific discipline, such as networks, architecture, software, or robotics.
Submission of proposals: For guidelines on preparing CS Press books, write the Editorial Director, IEEE Computer Society Press, PO Box 3014, 10662 Los Vaqueros Circle, Los Alamitos, CA 90720-1264, or telephone (714) 821-8380.

Purpose

The IEEE Computer Society advances the theory and practice of computer science and engineering, promotes the exchange of technical information among 100,000 members worldwide, and provides a wide range of services to members and nonmembers.

Membership

All members receive the acclaimed monthly magazine *Computer*, discounts, and opportunities to serve (all activities are led by volunteer members). Membership is open to all IEEE members, affiliate society members, and others seriously interested in the computer field.

Publications and Activities

***Computer* magazine:** An authoritative, easy-to-read magazine containing tutorials and in-depth articles on topics across the computer field, plus news, conference reports, book reviews, calendars, calls for papers, interviews, and new products.

Periodicals: The society publishes six magazines and five research transactions. For more details, refer to our membership application or request information as noted above.

Conference proceedings, tutorial texts, and standards documents: The IEEE Computer Society Press publishes more than 100 titles every year.

Standards working groups: Over 100 of these groups produce IEEE standards used throughout the industrial world.

Technical committees: Over 30 TCs publish newsletters, provide interaction with peers in specialty areas, and directly influence standards, conferences, and education.

Conferences/Education: The society holds about 100 conferences each year and sponsors many educational activities, including computing science accreditation.

Chapters: Regular and student chapters worldwide provide the opportunity to interact with colleagues, hear technical experts, and serve the local professional community.

Notes

Notes

Notes